D1616795

# 2019

# TAX CUTS AND JOBS ACT

*Regulatory Explanation and Analysis*

**Wolters Kluwer Editorial Staff Publication**

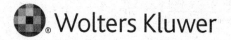 Wolters Kluwer

This publication is designed to provide accurate and authoritative information in regard to the subject matter covered. It is sold with the understanding that the publisher is not engaged in rendering legal, accounting, or other professional service. If legal advice or other expert assistance is required, the services of a competent professional person should be sought.

ISBN 978-0-8080-5199-2

2700 Lake Cook Road
Riverwoods, IL 60015
800 344 3734
CCHCPELink.com

Printed in the United States of America

# Tax Cuts and Jobs Act: Regulatory Explanation and Analysis

Over the course of a mere seven weeks in the fall of 2017, the largest and most significant piece of tax legislation in over thirty years went from being introduced on the floor of the House of Representatives to being signed into law by the President of the United States. Over that seven weeks-week period, some provisions were added, some were dropped, details were changed, but more or less, the bill that was introduced was largely still intact when it was signed on December 22, 2017. And the Tax Cuts and Jobs Act (P.L. 115-97) was now law. The landscape of the federal tax system was drastically altered in ways making it unrecognizable from the system in place on December 21, 2017. While it was the biggest piece of tax legislation since 1986, it upended tenets of the federal tax system that were more than 100 years old. But, on December 22, the Internal Revenue Code was changed, and that was that. Right?

Wrong! If you throw a pebble in the middle of a calm lake, it will make ripples that go all the way to the edges. The Tax Cuts and Jobs Act was a meteorite hitting the lake. Immediately after passage, the effects of the Act started to make enormous waves crashing throughout the federal tax system. The Internal Revenue Code is an often unwieldy and highly interconnected web, and a change over here can make ten things over there suddenly not make sense. Even something as seemingly innocuous as eliminating the personal exemption created problems that needed to be resolved. It was time for the IRS to act.

The IRS issued its first piece of guidance on December 27, 2017, five days after the bill became a law (and that included a holiday). It told taxpayers that, yes, they could deduct their prepaid 2018 property taxes in 2017, but only if they were assessed in 2017. And the IRS just kept going; 2018 was a flurry of notices, revenue procedures, proposed regulations, final regulations, form redesign, and publication revision. A large task for the IRS. An even bigger task for those who need to keep up.

The Tax Cuts and Jobs Act represented the most significant overhaul of the Internal Revenue Code in more than 30 years. But that is not the end of the road, it is only the beginning. Every U.S. taxpayer, foreign or domestic, individual or business, high-income or low-income, is impacted by the provisions of the Act.

## About This Work and Wolters Kluwer

Since 1913, Wolters Kluwer has provided tax professionals with the most comprehensive, ongoing, practical and timely analysis of the federal tax law. In the spirit of this tradition, Wolters Kluwer is providing practitioners with a single integrated explanation of the significant tax provisions of the Tax Cuts and Jobs Act (P.L. 115-97) and significant IRS guidance implementing them.

As always, Wolters Kluwer remains dedicated to responding to the needs of tax professionals in helping them quickly understand and work with these new laws and regulations as they take effect.

# Wolters Kluwer, Tax and Accounting
## EDITORIAL STAFF

# ¶1 Features of This Publication

This first-of-its-kind publication is your complete guide to the guidance issued by the Treasury and IRS in response to the Tax Cuts and Jobs Act (P.L. 115-97) (officially known as "An Act to provide for reconciliation pursuant to titles II and V of the concurrent resolution on the budget for fiscal year 2018").

The core portion of this publication contains the Explanations of this Act and, where applicable, the implementing guidance. The explanations outline the significant tax law changes and the guidance issued in the wake of those changes, providing analysis and helping you understand what it all means for you and your clients. The explanations also feature practical guidance, examples, planning opportunities and strategies, as well as pitfalls to be avoided.

## EXPLANATIONS

Explanations are designed to give you a complete, accessible understanding of the new law, as well as any new guidance issued in relation to the new law as of January 31, 2019. Explanations are arranged by subject for ease of use. There are two main finding devices you can use to locate explanations on a given topic. These are:

- A detailed table of contents at the beginning of the publication listing all of the Explanations of the provisions;
- A table of contents preceding each chapter.

Each Explanation contains special features to aid in your complete understanding of the tax law. These include:

- A summary at the beginning of each explanation providing a brief overview of the impacted provisions;
- A background or prior law discussion that puts the law and guidance changes into perspective;
- Editorial aids, including examples, cautions, planning notes, elections, comments, compliance tips, and key rates and figures, that highlight the impact of the sunset provisions;
- Charts and examples illustrating the ramifications of specific law and guidance changes; and
- Captions at the end of each explanation identifying the Code sections added, amended or repealed, as well as the Act sections containing the changes;

*The Explanations begin at ¶105.*

## REGULATORY AND OTHER GUIDANCE

Most of the significant guidance issued by the Treasury and IRS implementing the Tax Cuts and Jobs Act is contained in the sections beginning at ¶7001. It contains:

- IRS Rulings, organized first by type (IRS News Releases, Notices, Revenue Procedures, and Revenue Rulings), then organized sequentially (*see* ¶7001);
- Final Regulations, organized by Code Section (*see* ¶8001); and
- Proposed Regulations, organized by Code Section (*see* ¶9001).

# ¶2 Table of Contents

# ¶3 Detailed Table of Contents

## CHAPTER 8. EXEMPT ORGANIZATIONS, EXCISE TAXES, BONDS, AND OTHER PROVISIONS

# Individual Taxes (Income, AMT, Estate and Gift)

## TAXES AND RETURNS

## CAPITAL GAINS AND OTHER PROVISIONS

# TAXES AND RETURNS

## ¶105 Individual Income Tax Rates

### SUMMARY OF NEW LAW

The individual income tax rates and bracket amounts are modified for tax years 2018 through 2025. The temporary tax rates are 10, 12, 22, 24, 32, 35, and 37 percent. In addition, the "kiddie tax" is simplified for tax years beginning before 2026 by applying ordinary and capital gains rates applicable to trusts and estates to the net unearned income of a child. The tax treatment of capital gains and qualified dividends remains unchanged.

## BACKGROUND

Individuals generally determine their income tax liability by applying the appropriate tax rate schedule (or the tax tables) to their taxable income based on their filing status. There are seven applicable income tax rates: a 10-percent rate; a 15-percent rate; a 25-percent rate; a 28-percent rate; a 33-percent rate; a 35-percent rate; and a 39.6-percent rate (Code Sec. 1(i)). The rate schedules are divided into several ranges of income, referred to as income brackets. The bracket amounts are annually adjusted for inflation.

**Kiddie tax.** A "kiddie tax" is imposed on the net unearned income of a child meeting certain statutory requirements. (Code Sec. 1(g)). Generally, these rules apply to a child if:

- the child is required to file a tax return;
- the child does not file a joint return for the tax year;
- the child's investment income is more than $2,100 (for 2017);
- either of the child's parents is alive at the end of the year; and
- at the end of the tax year, the child is either: (a) under the age of 18; (b) under the age of 19 and does not provide more than half of his or her own support with earned income; or (c) under the age of 24, a full-time student, and does not provide more than half of his or her own support with earned income.

Under these rules, the net unearned income of a child (for 2017, over $2,100) is taxed at the parents' tax rates if the parents' tax rates are higher than those of the child. The remainder of a child's taxable income, i.e., earned income plus unearned income up to $2,100 (for 2017), less the child's standard deduction, is taxed at the child's rates, whether or not the kiddie tax applies to the child. Generally, a child is permitted to use the preferential tax rates for qualified dividends and capital gains (Code Sec. 1(h)).

The kiddie tax is calculated by computing the "allocable parental tax." The "allocable parental tax" is the amount of tax that results from subtracting the tax that would be imposed on a parent without regard to the special rules relating to a child's net unearned income from the tax that would be imposed on the parent's taxable income if such income included the net unearned income of all children of the parent (Code Sec. 1(g)(3)(A)). A child's net unearned income is the child's unearned income less the sum of (1) the minimum standard deduction allowed to dependents ($1,050 for 2017), and (2) the greater of (a) such minimum standard deduction amount or (b) the amount of allowable itemized deductions that are directly connected with the production of the unearned income (Code Sec. 1(g)(4)). A child's share of any allocable parental tax of his or her parent is equal to an amount that bears the same ratio to the total allocable parental tax as the child's net unearned income bears to the aggregate net unearned income of all children of such parent to whom the special rules on net unearned income apply (Code Sec. 1(g)(3)(B)).

A child usually must file a separate return to report his or her income (Code Sec. 1(g)(6)). In this case, items on the parents' return are not affected by the child's income, and the total tax due from the child is the greater of:

**¶105**

## BACKGROUND

- the tax on all of the child's income, calculated at the rates applicable to single individuals; or
- the sum of (a) the tax that would be imposed on a single individual if the child's taxable income were reduced by net unearned income, plus (b) the child's share of the allocable parental tax (Code Sec. 1(g)(1)).

In some instances, a parent may elect to report a child's unearned income on the parent's return (Code Sec. 1(g)(7)).

**Capital gains rates.** In the case of an individual, estate, or trust, any adjusted net capital gain that would otherwise be taxed at the 10- or 15-percent rate is taxed at zero percent. Any adjusted net capital gain that would otherwise be taxed at rates over 15-percent but below 39.6 percent is taxed at a 15-percent rate. A 20-percent rate applies to any adjusted net capital gain received by taxpayers in the top 39.6-percent income tax bracket.

Unrecaptured section 1250 gain is taxed at a maximum rate of 25 percent, and 28-percent rate gain is taxed at a maximum rate of 28 percent. Any amount of unrecaptured section 1250 gain or 28-percent rate gain otherwise taxed at a 10- or 15-percent rate is taxed at the otherwise applicable rate.

In addition, a tax is imposed on net investment income in the case of an individual, estate, or trust. In the case of an individual, the tax is 3.8 percent of the lesser of (1) net investment income, which includes gains and dividends, or (2) the excess of modified adjusted gross income over the threshold amount of $200,000 ($250,000 for married taxpayers filing jointly and surviving spouses), and $125,000 for a married taxpayer filing separately (Code Sec. 1411).

## NEW LAW EXPLAINED

**Temporary modification of income tax rates.**—The individual income tax rate structure is temporarily replaced with a new rate structure for tax years beginning after December 31, 2017, and before January 1, 2026 (Code Sec. 1(j)(1) and (2), as added by the Tax Cuts and Jobs Act (P.L. 115-97); Rev. Proc. 2018-18; Rev. Proc. 2018-57).

The tax rate schedules for 2018 are:

## NEW LAW EXPLAINED

### SINGLE TAXPAYERS
### FOR TAX YEARS BEGINNING IN 2018

| If taxable income is: | | The tax is: | of the amount |
|---|---|---|---|
| Over— | but not over— | | over— |
| $ 0 | $9,525 | 10% | $0 |
| 9,525 | 38,700 | $952.50 + 12% | 9,525 |
| 38,700 | 82,500 | 4,453.50 + 22% | 38,700 |
| 82,500 | 157,500 | 14,089.50 + 24% | 82,500 |
| 157,500 | 200,000 | 32,089.50 + 32% | 157,500 |
| 200,000 | 500,000 | 45,689.50 + 35% | 200,000 |
| 500,000 | . . . . . | 150,689.50 + 37% | 500,000 |

### MARRIED INDIVIDUALS FILING SEPARATE RETURNS
### FOR TAX YEARS BEGINNING IN 2018

| If taxable income is: | | The tax is: | of the amount |
|---|---|---|---|
| Over— | but not over— | | over— |
| $ 0 | $9,525 | 10% | $0 |
| 9,525 | 38,700 | $952.50 + 12% | 9,525 |
| 38,700 | 82,500 | 4,453.50 + 22% | 38,700 |
| 82,500 | 157,500 | 14,089.50 + 24% | 82,500 |
| 157,500 | 200,000 | 32,089.50 + 32% | 157,500 |
| 200,000 | 300,000 | 45,689.50 + 35% | 200,000 |
| 300,000 | . . . . . | 80,689.50 + 37% | 300,000 |

### MARRIED INDIVIDUALS FILING JOINT RETURNS AND SURVIVING SPOUSES
### FOR TAX YEARS BEGINNING IN 2018

| If taxable income is: | | The tax is: | of the amount |
|---|---|---|---|
| Over— | but not over— | | over— |
| $ 0 | $19,050 | 10% | $0 |
| 19,050 | 77,400 | $1,905 + 12% | 19,050 |
| 77,400 | 165,000 | 8,907 + 22% | 77,400 |
| 165,000 | 315,000 | 28,179 + 24% | 165,000 |
| 315,000 | 400,000 | 64,179 + 32% | 315,000 |
| 400,000 | 600,000 | 91,379 + 35% | 400,000 |
| 600,000 | . . . . . | 161,379 + 37% | 600,000 |

¶105

**NEW LAW EXPLAINED**

### HEADS OF HOUSEHOLD
### FOR TAX YEARS BEGINNING IN 2018

| If taxable income is: Over— | but not over— | The tax is: | of the amount over— |
|---|---|---|---|
| $0 | $13,600 | 10% | $0 |
| 13,600 | 51,800 | $1,360 + 12% | 13,600 |
| 51,800 | 82,500 | 5,944 + 22% | 51,800 |
| 82,500 | 157,500 | 12,698 + 24% | 82,500 |
| 157,500 | 200,000 | 30,698 + 32% | 157,500 |
| 200,000 | 500,000 | 44,298 + 35% | 200,000 |
| 500,000 | . . . . . | 149,298 + 37% | 500,000 |

### ESTATES AND TRUSTS
### FOR TAX YEARS BEGINNING IN 2018

| If taxable income is: Over— | but not over— | The tax is: | of the amount over— |
|---|---|---|---|
| $0 | 2,550 | 10% | $0 |
| 2,550 | 9,150 | $255 + 24% | 2,550 |
| 9,150 | 12,500 | 1,839 + 35% | 9,150 |
| 12,500 | . . . . . | 3,011.50 + 37% | 12,500 |

The tax rate schedules for 2019 are:

### SINGLE TAXPAYERS
### FOR TAX YEARS BEGINNING IN 2019

| If taxable income is: Over— | but not over— | The tax is: | of the amount over— |
|---|---|---|---|
| $0 | $9,700 | 10 % | $0 |
| 9,700 | 39,475 | $970 + 12% | 9,700 |
| 39,475 | 84,200 | 4,543 + 22% | 39,475 |
| 84,200 | 160,725 | 14,382.50 + 24% | 84,200 |
| 160,725 | 204,100 | 32,748.50 + 32% | 160,725 |
| 204,100 | 510,300 | 46,628.50 + 35% | 204,100 |
| 510,300 | . . . . . | 153,798.50 + 37% | 510,300 |

## NEW LAW EXPLAINED

### MARRIED INDIVIDUALS FILING SEPARATE RETURNS
### FOR TAX YEARS BEGINNING IN 2019

| If taxable income is: Over— | but not over— | The tax is: | of the amount over— |
|---|---|---|---|
| $0 | $9,700 | 10% | $0 |
| 9,700 | 39,475 | $970 + 12% | 9,700 |
| 39,475 | 84,200 | 4,543 + 22% | 39,475 |
| 84,200 | 160,725 | 14,382.50 + 24% | 84,200 |
| 160,725 | 204,100 | 32,748.50 + 32% | 160,725 |
| 204,100 | 306,175 | 46,628.50 + 35% | 204,100 |
| 306,175 | . . . . . | 82,354.75 + 37% | 306,175 |

### MARRIED INDIVIDUALS FILING JOINT RETURNS AND SURVIVING SPOUSES
### FOR TAX YEARS BEGINNING IN 2019

| If taxable income is: Over— | but not over— | The tax is: | of the amount over— |
|---|---|---|---|
| $0 | $19,400 | 10% | $0 |
| 19,400 | 78,950 | $1,940 + 12% | 19,400 |
| 78,950 | 168,400 | 9,086 + 22% | 78,950 |
| 168,400 | 321,450 | 28,765 + 24% | 168,400 |
| 321,450 | 408,200 | 65,497 + 32% | 321,450 |
| 408,200 | 612,350 | 93,257 + 35% | 408,200 |
| 612,350 | . . . . . | 164,709.50 + 37% | 612,350 |

### HEADS OF HOUSEHOLD
### FOR TAX YEARS BEGINNING IN 2019

| If taxable income is: Over— | but not over— | The tax is: | of the amount over— |
|---|---|---|---|
| $0 | $13,850 | 10% | $0 |
| 13,850 | 52,850 | $1,385 + 12% | 13,850 |
| 52,850 | 84,200 | 6,065 + 22% | 52,850 |
| 84,200 | 160,700 | 12,962 + 24% | 84,200 |
| 160,700 | 204,100 | 31,322 + 32% | 160,700 |
| 204,100 | 510,300 | 45,210 + 35% | 204,100 |
| 510,300 | . . . . . | 152,380 + 37% | 510,300 |

¶105

## NEW LAW EXPLAINED

ESTATES AND TRUSTS
FOR TAX YEARS BEGINNING IN 2019

| If taxable income is: | | The tax is: | |
|---|---|---|---|
| Over— | but not over— | | of the amount over— |
| $0 | 2,600 | 10% | $0 |
| 2,600 | 9,300 | $260 + 24% | 2,600 |
| 9,300 | 12,750 | 1,868 + 35% | 9,300 |
| 12,750 | . . . . . | 3,075.50 + 37% | 12,750 |

For tax years beginning after December 31, 2018, the bracket thresholds are annually adjusted for inflation using the Chained Consumer Price Index for All Urban Consumers (C-CPI-U) (see ¶ 125) (Code Sec. 1(j)(3), as added by the 2017 Tax Cuts Act).

Comment: The intent of the changes was to have uniformity in the income bracket amounts for single filers and heads of households for the 32, 35, and 37-percent rates. However, the rounding rules applicable to the brackets from the incorporation of Code Sec. 1(f)(7) into Code Sec. 1(j)(3) require the head of household brackets to be rounded to $50 increments. Thus, a technical correction is required to reflect the original intent (General Explanation of Public Law 115-97 (JCS-1-18)).

Kiddie tax. Effective for tax years beginning after December 31, 2017, and before January 1, 2026, the "kiddie tax" is simplified by effectively applying ordinary and capital gains rates applicable to trusts and estates to the net unearned income of a child (Code Sec. 1(j)(4), as added by the 2017 Tax Cuts Act). As a result, taxable income attributable to earned income is taxed according to a single individual's tax brackets and rates. Taxable income attributable to net unearned income is taxed according to the brackets applicable to trusts and estates, with respect to both ordinary income and income taxed at preferential rates.

Comment: According to the Joint Committee on Taxation, as the provision is currently enacted, a modification of brackets applicable to both single taxpayers and estates and trusts is required to ensure that the tax does not exceed that applicable to a single person who is not a child. A technical correction may be needed to reflect the intended structure (General Explanation of Public Law 115-97 (JCS-1-18)).

Comment: A child's "kiddie tax" is no longer affected by the tax situation of his or her parent or the unearned income of any siblings.

Maximum rates on capital gains. The maximum rates on net capital gain and qualified dividends are generally retained after 2017 and are 0 percent, 15 percent, and 20 percent. The breakpoints between the zero- and 15-percent rates ("15-percent breakpoint") and the 15- and 20-percent rates ("20-percent breakpoint") are the same amounts as the breakpoints under prior law, except the breakpoints are indexed using the C-CPI-U (see ¶ 125) in tax years beginning after 2018 (Code Sec. 1(j)(5)(A) and (C), as added by the 2017 Tax Cuts Act).

¶105

## NEW LAW EXPLAINED

For 2018, the 15-percent breakpoint is $77,200 for joint returns and surviving spouses (one-half of this amount ($38,600) for married taxpayers filing separately), $51,700 for heads of household, $2,600 for estates and trusts, and $38,600 for other unmarried individuals. The 20-percent breakpoint is $479,000 for joint returns and surviving spouses (one-half of this amount ($239,500) for married taxpayers filing separately), $452,400 for heads of household, $12,700 for estates and trusts, and $425,800 for other unmarried individuals (Code Sec. 1(j)(5)(B), as added by the 2017 Tax Cuts Act). For 2019, as adjusted for inflation, the 15-percent breakpoint is $78,750 for joint returns and surviving spouses (one-half of this amount ($39,375) for married taxpayers filing separately), $52,750 for heads of household, $2,650 for estates and trusts, and $39,375 for other unmarried individuals. The 20-percent breakpoint is $488,850 for joint returns and surviving spouses (one-half of this amount ($244,425) for married taxpayers filing separately), $461,700 for heads of household, $12,950 for estates and trusts, and $434,550 for other unmarried individuals (Rev. Proc. 2018-57).

> **Comment:** It is not entirely clear where the "breakpoints" for each tax range were intended to begin and end. The text of Code Sec. 1(j)(5)(B) seems to require that, for example, the 15-percent rate applies to joint filers with taxable income of at least $77,200 in 2018. However, the Schedule D Tax Worksheet in the IRS Instructions for Schedule D (2018) provides that the 15-percent rate applies to joint filers with taxable income *over* $77,200 for 2018.

As under prior law, unrecaptured section 1250 gain generally is taxed at a maximum rate of 25 percent, and 28-percent rate gain is taxed at a maximum rate of 28 percent. In addition, an individual, estate, or trust also remains subject to the 3.8 percent tax on net investment income (NII tax).

▶ **Effective date.** The amendments made by this section apply to tax years beginning after December 31, 2017 (Act Sec. 11001(c) of the Tax Cuts and Jobs Act (P.L. 115-97)).

**Other than inflation adjusted amounts for 2019, no significant guidance related to this provision has been issued.**

— Act Sec. 11001(a) of the Tax Cuts and Jobs Act (P.L. 115-97), adding Code Sec. 1(j);

— Act Sec. 11001(c), providing the effective date.

## ¶110 Alternative Minimum Tax (AMT) for Individuals

### SUMMARY OF NEW LAW

The AMT exemption amounts are temporarily increased for individuals after 2017 and before 2026. Beginning in 2018, the exemption amounts are $109,400 if married filing jointly or surviving spouse, $70,300 if single or head of household, and $54,700 if married filing separately. The phaseout thresholds are also temporarily increased after 2017 to $1 million if married filing jointly or surviving spouse and $500,000 for all other individuals. The temporary dollars amounts are indexed for inflation after 2018.

# BACKGROUND

An alternative minimum tax (AMT) is imposed on an individual, estate, or trust. A taxpayer's AMT for a tax year is the excess of the taxpayer's tentative minimum tax over regular tax liability (Code Sec. 55). For an individual, estate, or trust, the tentative minimum tax is equal to: 26 percent of the taxpayer's alternative minimum taxable income (AMTI) up to a certain threshold amount adjusted annually for inflation, plus 28 percent of any AMTI in excess of the threshold amount. For 2017, the threshold amount is $187,800 ($93,900 for married filing separately) (Rev. Proc. 2016-55).

AMTI is the taxpayer's regular taxable income increased by AMT tax preference items and modified by AMT adjustments (Code Secs. 56 and 57). A tax preference item is a deduction or exclusion not allowed in computing AMTI including the exclusion of gain from qualified small business stock, depletion deductions, and tax-exempt interest earned on private activity bonds. AMT adjustments are items of income or deductions that are computed differently in determining AMTI including certain itemized deductions, personal exemptions, the standard deduction, incentive stock options, depreciation, and net operating losses (NOLs).

A certain amount of a taxpayer's AMTI is exempt from the AMT. For individuals, the AMT exemption amount for 2017 is $84,500 for married filing jointly or surviving spouse, $54,300 for single or head of household, and $42,250 for married filing separately. For estates and trusts, the AMT exemption amount is $24,100, but is zero for the portion of an electing small business trust. The exemption amount is phased out 25 percent for each $1 that AMTI exceeds certain threshold amounts. For individuals, the threshold amount for 2017 is $160,900 for married filing jointly, $120,700 for single or head of household, and $80,450 for married filing separately. For estates or trusts, the threshold amount for 2017 is $80,450.

A noncorporate taxpayer may claim the AMT foreign tax credit in computing their tentative minimum tax. Subject to limits, AMT liability may also be reduced by nonrefundable personal credits and general business credits.

## NEW LAW EXPLAINED

**Exemption amount and phaseout thresholds for individuals temporarily increased.**—The AMT exemption amounts and phaseout thresholds are temporarily increased for individuals for tax years beginning after December 31, 2017, and before January 1, 2026 (Code Sec. 55(d)(4), as added by the Tax Cuts and Jobs Act (P.L. 115-97)). In the case of any tax year beginning after 2018, the temporary increases in the AMT exemption amounts and phaseout thresholds for individuals are adjusted annually for inflation using the Chained Consumer Price Index for All Urban Consumers (C-CPI-U) (see ¶ 125). These adjustments are temporary increases only and no additional adjustment of the temporary increases will apply.

The AMT exemption amounts for individuals for tax years beginning in 2018 are:

- $109,400 for married individuals filing jointly or surviving spouses;
- $70,300 for single or head of household filers; and

## NEW LAW EXPLAINED

- $54,700 for married individuals filing separately (Code Sec. 55(d)(4)(A)(i), as added by the 2017 Tax Cuts Act; Rev. Proc. 2018-22, superseding Rev. Proc. 2018-18).

The AMT exemption amounts for individuals for tax years beginning in 2019 are:

- $111,700 for married individuals filing jointly or surviving spouses;
- $71,700 for single or head of household filers; and
- $55,850 for married individuals filing separately (Rev. Proc. 2018-57).

The threshold amounts for phaseout or reduction of the AMT exemption amount are also temporarily increased for tax years beginning after 2017 (Code Sec. 55(d)(4)(A)(ii), as added by the 2017 Tax Cuts Act). The threshold amount for phaseout or reduction of the AMT exemption amount for tax years beginning in 2018 is $1 million for married individuals filing jointly or surviving spouses, and $500,000 for an individual filing as single, head of household, and married filing separately. The threshold amount for phaseout or reduction of the AMT exemption amount for tax years beginning in 2019 is $1,020,600 for married individuals filing jointly and surviving spouse, $510,300 for individuals filing as single, head of household, and married filing separately (Rev. Proc. 2018-57; Rev. Proc. 2018-22, superseding Rev. Proc. 2018-18).

> **Comment:** The exemption amount continues to phase out 25 percent for each $1 that AMTI exceeds certain threshold amounts. Thus, the AMT exemption amount is completely phased out for an individual for tax years beginning in 2018 when AMTI reaches $1,437,600 if married individual filing jointly or surviving spouse, $781,200 if filing as single or head of household, and $718,800 if married filing separately. The 2019 AMT exemption amount is completely phased out for individuals when AMTI reaches $1,467,400 for married individuals filing jointly and surviving spouse, $797,100 for single and head of household filers, and $733,700 for married Individuals filing separately.

> **Comment:** The AMT exemption amount and phaseout threshold for estates or trusts are not temporarily increased for tax years beginning in 2018 through 2025. For estates or trusts, the AMT exemption amount is $24,600 for 2018 and $25,000 for 2019. In the case of a portion of an electing small business trust that is treated as a separate trust, the AMT exemption amount is zero for any tax year (Code Sec. 641(c)(2)(B)). The threshold amount for phaseout or reduction of the AMT exemption amount for estates or trusts is $81,900 for 2018 and $83,500 for 2019. Thus, the AMT exemption amount is completely phased out for estates and trusts when AMTI reaches $180,300 in 2018 and $183,500 in 2019. The AMT is repealed for corporations for tax years beginning after 2017 (see ¶310).

**Net disaster losses.** An individual may claim an additional standard deduction amount for his or her net disaster loss in tax years beginning in 2016 and 2017 (Act Sec. 11028(c) of the 2017 Tax Cuts Act). The additional standard deduction is allowed in computing alternative minimum tax liability (AMT). For this purpose, a net disaster loss is the qualified disaster-related personal casualty losses, over any personal casualty gains. A qualified disaster-related personal loss means a personal casualty loss arising in a disaster area after on or after January 1, 2016, that is attributable to a federally declared disaster. See also ¶235 for a discussion of

**NEW LAW EXPLAINED**

additional relief for claiming casualty loss deductions related to net disaster losses in 2016 and 2017.

▶ **Effective date.** The amendments made by this section apply to tax years beginning after December 31, 2017 (Act Sec. 12003(b) of the Tax Cuts and Jobs Act (P.L. 115-97)). The special rules related to personal casualty losses related to net disaster losses for 2016 and 2017 are effective on December 22, 2017, the date of enactment.

**Other than inflation adjusted amounts for 2019, no significant guidance related to this provision has been issued.**

— Act Sec. 12003(a) of the Tax Cuts and Jobs Act (P.L. 115-97), adding Code Sec. 55(d)(4);

— Act Sec. 11028(a) and (c);

— Act Sec. 12003(b), providing the effective date.

# ¶115  Estate, Gift, and Generation-Skipping Transfer Tax Exclusions

## SUMMARY OF NEW LAW

The basic exclusion amount (BEA) for purposes of federal estate and gift taxes and the exemption amount for purposes of the generation-skipping transfer (GST) tax is doubled from $5 million to $10 million, before adjustment for inflation, for the estates of decedents dying and gifts and generation-skipping transfers made after 2017 and before 2026.

## BACKGROUND

The Internal Revenue Code imposes a federal estate tax, a gift tax, and a GST tax, commonly referred to as the federal "transfer taxes." The estate and gift taxes comprise a unified form of transfer taxes (i.e., a tax levied upon the transfer of a person's property at death and during life). Estate and gift taxes are progressive and are based on cumulative transfers during life and at death. As set forth in Code Sec. 2001, the unified transfer tax rates range from 18 percent on cumulative transfers of $10,000 or less to a maximum rate of 40 percent, applicable to cumulative transfers over $1,000,000. However, due to the operation of the unified credit, the effective minimum rate is also 40 percent. The unified credit, also referred to as the "applicable credit amount" (Code Sec. 2010), is a one-time credit to be used against taxable estate or gift taxes payable.

The amount of the unified credit is based on the amount of tentative tax that would be determined under Code Sec. 2001(c) using the applicable exclusion amount as the taxable estate. The applicable exclusion amount is effectively the amount of property that can be excluded from estate or gift taxes during an individual's lifetime. And, under the concept of "portability," the unused portion of a decedent's applicable exclusion amount may be utilized by the estate of the decedent's surviving spouse at

## BACKGROUND

his or her later death. To take advantage of this provision, a special election must be made by the predeceased spouse's estate on its estate tax return, Form 706. This election is often referred to as the portability, or the deceased spousal unused exclusion (DSUE), election. With the U.S. Supreme Court's decision in *E. Windsor*, SCt., 2013-2 USTC ¶60,667, the portability of a deceased spouse's unused exclusion amount is available to a surviving same-sex spouse so long as the couple was legally married.

The applicable exclusion amount for a surviving spouse who dies after December 31, 2010, is the sum of:

- the BEA ($5.49 million for 2017); and
- the aggregate DSUE amount.

Any portion of the predeceased spouse's applicable exclusion amount that was used to reduce his or her estate tax liability may not be used to reduce the surviving spouse's estate tax liability. The term "deceased spousal unused exclusion amount" (DSUE amount) is the lesser of:

- the BEA, or
- the last deceased spouse's applicable exclusion amount, minus
- the amount with respect to which the tentative tax is determined under Code Sec. 2001(b)(1) on the estate of such deceased spouse.

The third federal transfer tax, the GST tax (Code Secs. 2601 through 2663), exists primarily to keep wealthy individuals from avoiding the estate tax by using "generation-skipping transfers," that is, passing their property at death (or during lifetime) to their grandchildren (or great-grandchildren), rather than to their children. The lifetime exemption amount for purposes of the GST tax is based on the basic exclusion amount used for the estate and gift taxes. Consequently, the exemption on generation-skipping transfers occurring in 2017 is $5.49 million. Unlike the estate or gift tax, the concept of portability does not apply to the GST tax exemption.

## NEW LAW EXPLAINED

**Estate and gift tax exclusion doubled.**—The basic exclusion amount (BEA) for purposes of federal estate and gift taxes will be doubled from $5 million to $10 million, before adjustment for inflation, for the estates of decedents dying and gifts made after 2017 and before 2026 (Code Sec. 2010(c)(3)(C), as amended by the Tax Cuts and Jobs Act of 2017 (P.L. 115-97)). The $10 million amount is adjusted annually for inflation in the case of any decedent dying in a calendar year after 2017 using the Chained Consumer Price Index for All Urban Consumers (C-CPI-U) in the cost-of-living adjustment (see ¶ 125) (Code Sec. 2010(c)(3)(B)(ii), as amended by the 2017 Tax Cuts Act).

> **Caution:** The change in methodology for making inflation adjustments using chained-CPI rather than average CPI may result in smaller adjustments after 2017, particularly for higher dollar amounts, such as the estate and gift tax exclusion amount. For example, the BEA would be $11.2 million applicable to decedents dying and gifts made in 2018 ($22.4 million for married couple using portability) based on the inflation-adjusted amount of $5.6 million provided in Rev. Proc. 2017-58 using average CPI. However, the IRS issued a revised inflation adjustment for the BEA applicable for 2018 using chained CPI that

**NEW LAW EXPLAINED**

resulted in a slightly lower basic exclusion amount of $11.18 (Rev. Proc. 2018-18); for 2019, the BEA is $11.4 million (Rev. Proc. 2018-57). For decedents dying and gifts made after 2025, the BEA will revert to $5 million, as adjusted for inflation using chained CPI.

> **Example 1:** Bruce Payne, a wealthy single individual dies in 2018 leaving a taxable estate of $10 million. His estate will owe no federal estate taxes. Instead, if he had died in 2017, the estate tax payable would have been $1,804,000.

> **Example 2:** Carol Cologne, a wealthy widow dies in 2018 leaving a taxable estate of $20 million. Her late husband died earlier in 2018 having used only $2 million of his available estate tax exclusion amount. Her estate will owe no federal estate tax. However, if the couple had died under the same circumstances in 2017, the estate tax payable would have been $4,408,000.

**Comment:** Because the doubling of the estate and gift tax exclusion amount will expire for decedents dying and gifts made after December 31, 2025, the next several years present a tremendous opportunity for wealthy individuals and married couples to make large gifts, including those that leverage the amount of the available exclusion, such as those to grantor retained annuity trusts (GRATs).

**Comment:** According to the IRS Statistics of Income tables presenting data on estate tax return data for Filing Year 2016 (https://www.irs.gov/statistics/soi-tax-stats-estate-tax-filing-year-tables, see Table 1 showing data from estate tax returns filed in 2016, by tax status and size of gross estate), a total of 5,219 taxable returns were filed contrasted with 7,192 nontaxable returns. Of the taxable returns, 2,402 fell within the $5 to $10 million gross estate range, 1,293 in the $10 to $20 million range. Only 300 returns were filed with gross estates in excess of $50 million. These statistics primarily reflect data from the estates of decedents who died in 2015, when the basic exclusion amount was $5.43 million, but also include some returns for decedents who died in years prior to 2015, as well as a small number of estates with respect to deaths that occurred in 2016. The large increase in the basic exclusion amount after 2017 will no doubt lead to further decreases in the number of taxable estates.

**GST tax exemption amount.** Because the exemption from the GST tax is computed by reference to the BEA used for estate and gift tax purposes (Code Sec. 2631), the GST exemption amount for GSTs occurring in 2018 will be $10 million, before adjustment for inflation. Portability does not apply for purposes of the GST tax.

**Corresponding adjustments with respect to prior gifts.** In addition to the increase in the BEA, the 2017 Tax Cuts Act modifies the computation of gift tax payable and estate tax payable in cases where gifts have been made in prior years. (Code Sec. 2001(g), as amended by the 2017 Tax Cuts Act). With respect to the computation of gift tax payable, the tax rates in effect at the time of the decedent's death are to be used, rather than the rates that were in effect at the time the gifts were made (Code Sec. 2001(g)(1), as amended by the 2017 Tax Cuts Act).

## NEW LAW EXPLAINED

The 2017 Tax Cuts Act also directed the Secretary of the Treasury to prescribe regulations clarifying the computation of estate tax payable in situations where the BEA was different in the year of the decedent's death as opposed to the year when the prior gifts were made (Code Sec. 2001(g)(2), as amended by the 2017 Tax Cuts Act). In response, on November 23, 2018, the IRS issued proposed regulations (NPRM REG-106706-18) addressing this issue. This issue , which is commonly referred to as the "clawback" problem, was a concern of practitioners following passage of the Economic Growth and Tax Relief Reconciliation Act of 2001 (P.L. 107-16) (EGTRRA). EGTRRA included a "sunset" provision that effectively meant that the estate and GST taxes were repealed for only one year (2010) and pre-EGTRRA law would return beginning in 2011. However, this result was avoided and the estate and GST taxes were temporarily reinstated by the Tax Relief, Unemployment Insurance Reauthorization, and Job Creation Act of 2010 (P.L. 111-312) and extended "permanently" by the American Taxpayer Relief Act of 2012 (P.L. 112-240). Because many provisions of the 2017 Tax Cuts and Jobs Act, including the increase in the estate and gift tax exclusion amount, are scheduled to expire after 2025, the clawback issue was again raised by practitioners.

The preamble to the proposed regulations cites four situations involving changes in the BEA over time. The first two deal with those situations in which the BEA has *increased* between the time of a gift and the time of a subsequent gift or the decedent's death.

In the first situation, a donor makes a pre-2018 gift that exceeds the then-available BEA, incurring a gift tax liability, and subsequently makes additional gifts during the period 2018-2025 while the BEA is increased. The question posed was whether the gift tax computation would apply the increased BEA to the pre-2018 gifts, thus reducing the BEA otherwise available to apply to gifts made during the 2018-2025 period. If so, gift tax credit would be allocated to a gift on which gift tax was already paid. Instead, the IRS concluded that the existing gift tax computation reduces the increased BEA only by the amount of BEA allowable against prior period gifts. Thus, the increased BEA is not reduced by a prior gift on which gift tax was paid. This same rationale was applied to a situation involving a donor who makes a pre-2018 gift that exceeded the then-allowable BEA, and then dies during the period 2018-2025. Again, the IRS concluded that the BEA is not reduced by the portion of any prior gift on which gift tax was paid, and the full amount is available as a credit against the estate tax when the donor dies.

The last two scenarios cited in the preamble consider those situations in which the BEA has *decreased* between the time of a gift and the time of a subsequent gift or the decedent's death. In the first of these situations, a donor makes gifts during the 2018-2025 period that are sheltered from gift tax by the increased BEA and subsequently makes a post-2025 gift. The question in this case is whether the computation of the gift tax on the post-2025 gift would treat the gifts made during the increased BEA period as gifts that were not sheltered from the gift tax because the post-2025 gift tax determination is based on the BEA then in-effect rather than the increased BEA. According to the IRS, the current gift tax computation anticipates this situation and avoids it. However, no credit would be available against the tentative tax on the post-2025 gift.

¶115

## NEW LAW EXPLAINED

Finally, the IRS considered the situation where a decedent made gifts during the increased BEA period that were exempt from tax due to the increased BEA in effect during 2018-2025 and then dies after 2025. The issue is whether the estate tax computation would treat the post-1976 gifts made during the increased BEA period (2018-2025) as not being sheltered from gift tax by the amount of credit computed on the BEA because the post-2025 estate tax is computed based on the BEA in effect at the decedent's death. In this situation, the statutory requirements retroactively elimi- nate the benefit of the increased BEA that was available for the gifts made in the increased BEA period.

Proposed Reg. §20.2010-1(c) would respond to the latter problem by adjusting the amount of the credit determined in Step 4 of the estate tax calculation as described in Code Sec. 2001(b). In Step 4, the credit is equal to the tentative tax on the applicable exclusion amount as in effect on the decedent's date of death. The modification would require the credit to be equal to the tentative tax corresponding to the applicable exclusion amount as in effect on the date of the decedent's death, where the BEA included in that applicable exclusion amount is the larger of:

(1) the BEA as in effect on the date of the decedent's death under Code Sec. 2010(c)(3), or

(2) the total amount of the BEA allowable in determining the gift tax payable (Step 2) of the estate tax computation.

---

**Example 3:** Lois Graham, who was never married and was not entitled to any restored exclusion amount pursuant to Notice 2017-15, made cumulative post-1976 taxable gifts totaling $9 million. All of these gifts were sheltered from gift tax by the cumulative total of $10 million in BEA allowable when the gifts were made. Graham died after 2025 when the BEA was only $5 million. Because the total of the amounts allowable as a credit in computing the gift tax payable on Graham's post-1976 gifts (based on the $9 million BEA used to determine those credits) exceeds the credit based on the $5 million BEA applicable on the decedent's date of death, under Proposed Reg. §20.2010-1(c)(1), the credit to be applied for purposes of computing the estate tax is based on a BEA of $9 million, which was the amount used to determine the credits allowable in computing the gift tax payable on the post-1976 gifts made by Graham.

---

Proposed Reg. §20.2010-1(c) would be effective upon the publication of final regulations.

▶ **Effective date.** The amendments made by this section are effective for decedents dying and for gifts and generation-skipping transfers made after December 31, 2017 (Act Sec. 11061(c) of the Tax Cuts and Jobs Act (P.L. 115-97)).

— Act Sec. 11061(a) of the Tax Cuts and Jobs Act of 2017 (P.L. 115-97), adding Code Sec. 2010(c)(3)(C);

— Act Sec. 11061(b), amending Code Sec. 2001(g);

— Act Sec. 11061(c), providing the effective date.

## ¶120 Individual Income Tax Returns, Filing Threshold, and Tax Preparer Due Diligence

### SUMMARY OF NEW LAW

The filing thresholds for an individual to file an income tax return are modified after 2017 as a result of the increase in the standard deduction and repeal of the personal and dependency exemption. In addition, the due diligence tax return preparer penalty is expanded to apply to a taxpayer's eligibility to file as head of household.

### BACKGROUND

For each tax year, an income tax return must be filed by a U.S. citizen or a resident alien who has at least a specified minimum amount of gross income (Code Sec. 6012). The filing threshold for most individuals depends on the taxpayer's filing status and the sum of personal exemptions deduction and the standard deduction, including the additional standard deduction for the aged and/or blind, adjusted annually for inflation. A taxpayer is generally not required to file a federal income tax return for 2017 if his or her gross income is below the following thresholds (Rev. Proc. 2016-55):

| | |
|---|---:|
| Single individual | $10,400 |
| Single individual, 65 or older or blind | 11,950 |
| Single individual, 65 or older and blind | 13,500 |
| Married individual, separate return | 4,050 |
| Married couple, joint return | 20,800 |
| Married couple, joint return, one spouse 65 or older or blind | 22,050 |
| Married couple, joint return, one spouse 65 or older and blind | 23,300 |
| Married couple, joint return, both spouses 65 or older or blind | 23,300 |
| Married couple, joint return, both spouses 65 or older and blind | 25,800 |
| Head of household | 13,400 |
| Head of household, 65 or older or blind | 14,950 |
| Head of household, 65 or older and blind | 16,500 |
| Qualifying widow(er) (surviving spouse) | 16,750 |
| Qualifying widow(er) (surviving spouse), 65 or older or blind | 18,000 |
| Qualifying widow(er) (surviving spouse), 65 or older and blind | 19,250 |

**Filing status.** The tax rates applicable to an individual, as well as filing requirements and standard deduction amounts, for a tax year are determined by reference to the taxpayer's filing status. There are four tax rate schedules for individuals: married persons filing joint returns and surviving spouses; head of household; single; and married persons filing separate returns. Whether a taxpayer can file as single or either married filing separately or a joint return is generally governed by the taxpayer's marital status on the last day of the year (Code Sec. 7703(a)). Married taxpayers can either file separate returns, or elect to file a joint return (Code Sec. 6013).

## BACKGROUND

In order for a taxpayer to file a return using head of household status, a number of requirements must be satisfied. A U.S. citizen or resident alien who is unmarried or considered unmarried at the end of the tax year and who maintains as his or her home a household that is the principal place of abode for certain qualifying individuals for more than half the year may use the filing status of head of household (Code Sec. 2(b)). The taxpayer must occupy the household as his or her home for the entire tax year. However, temporary absences due to illness, education, business, vacation, or military service do not affect head of household status, as long as it is reasonable to assume that the taxpayer will return, and the taxpayer continues to maintain the household in anticipation of his or her return. The taxpayer may change the location of the household during the year without affecting his or her filing status. The taxpayer must actually occupy the home; it is not sufficient to simply pay the maintenance costs. A qualifying individual must be either a qualifying child of the taxpayer or another individual for whom the taxpayer is entitled to a dependency exemption including the taxpayer's parents (Code Sec. 2(b)).

**Due diligence requirement.** A taxpayer must also meet specific requirements to qualify for the child tax credit (Code Sec. 24), the American Opportunity and lifetime learning credits (Code Sec. 25A), and the earned income credit (Code Sec. 32). Tax return preparers are required to meet due diligence requirements in ensuring that their clients meet the qualifications for these credits on returns or refund claims on which the credits are claimed (Code Sec. 6695(g)). Tax return preparers comply with this due diligence requirement by completing a Form 8867, Paid Preparer's Due Diligence Checklist, document the calculation of the credit(s) using either the appropriate IRS worksheet or other means of calculation, retaining these items in records, and must not know, or have reason to know, that the client does not qualify for the credit(s) (Reg. § 1.6695-2; Temp. Reg. § 1.6695-2T). Each failure to exercise such due diligence results in a $500 penalty (Code Sec. 6695(g)).

### NEW LAW EXPLAINED

**Filing thresholds increased; preparer due diligence requirements added for head of household status.**—The rules for determining the filing threshold for an individual to file a federal income tax return are modified for tax years beginning after December 31, 2017, and before January 1, 2026, as a result of the temporary repeal of the personal exemption deduction (see ¶ 210) and the temporary increase in the standard deduction amount (see ¶ 205).

With respect to an individual who is not married (single or head of household), an individual is required to file a tax return if his or her gross income for the tax year exceeds the applicable standard deduction (Code Sec. 6012(f), as added by the 2017 Tax Cuts Act). A married individual reaches the filing threshold if his or her gross income, when combined with the individual's spouse's gross income for the tax year, is more than the standard deduction applicable to a joint return, and provided that:

## NEW LAW EXPLAINED

- the individual and his or her spouse, at the close of the tax year, had the same household as their home;

- the individual's spouse does not file a separate return; and

- neither the individual nor his or her spouse is a dependent of another taxpayer who has income (other than earned income) in excess of the standard deduction for dependents provided under Code Sec. 63(c)(5)(A).

> **Comment:** The standard deduction amounts are adjusted annually for inflation for tax years beginning after 2018 and before 2026 using the Chained Consumer Price Index for All Urban Consumers (C-CPI-U) in the cost-of-living adjustment (see ¶125) (Code Sec. 63(c)(7)(B), as added by the 2017 Tax Cuts Act). The standard deduction amount for a dependent, as well as the additional standard deduction amounts for the aged and/or blind are also adjusted for inflation. However, these amounts are adjusted for inflation after 2017 using chained chained-CPI rather than averaged CPI (Code Sec. 63(c)(4), as amended by the 2017 Tax Cuts Act). As a result, the IRS has issued revised inflation adjustments for 2018 for the standard deduction for a dependent, as well as the standard deduction amounts for the aged and/or blind.

The filing thresholds for 2018 are as follows:

| | |
|---|---:|
| Single individual | $12,000 |
| Single individual, 65 or older or blind | 13,600 |
| Single individual, 65 or older and blind | 15,200 |
| Married individual, separate return | 5 |
| Married couple, joint return | 24,000 |
| Married couple, joint return, one spouse 65 or older or blind | 25,300 |
| Married couple, joint return, one spouse 65 or older and blind | 26,600 |
| Married couple, joint return, both spouses 65 or older or blind | 26,600 |
| Married couple, joint return, both spouses 65 or older and blind | 29,200 |
| Head of household | 18,000 |
| Head of household, 65 or older or blind | 19,600 |
| Head of household, 65 or older and blind | 21,200 |
| Qualifying widow(er) (surviving spouse) | 24,000 |
| Qualifying widow(er) (surviving spouse), 65 or older or blind | 25,300 |
| Qualifying widow(er) (surviving spouse), 65 or older and blind | 26,600 |

The filing thresholds for 2019 are as follows:

| | |
|---|---:|
| Single individual | $12,200 |
| Single individual, 65 or older or blind | 13,850 |
| Single individual, 65 or older and blind | 15,500 |
| Married individual, separate return | 5 |
| Married couple, joint return | 24,400 |
| Married couple, joint return, one spouse 65 or older or blind | 25,700 |
| Married couple, joint return, one spouse 65 or older and blind | 27,000 |
| Married couple, joint return, both spouses 65 or older or blind | 27,000 |

**¶120**

## NEW LAW EXPLAINED

| | |
|---|---|
| Married couple, joint return, both spouses 65 or older and blind . . . . . . . . . . . . . . . . | 29,600 |
| Head of household . . . . . . . . . . . . . . . . . . . . . . . . . . . . . . . . . . . . . . . . . . . . . . . . | 18,350 |
| Head of household, 65 or older or blind . . . . . . . . . . . . . . . . . . . . . . . . . . . . . . . . | 20,000 |
| Head of household, 65 or older and blind . . . . . . . . . . . . . . . . . . . . . . . . . . . . . . . | 21,650 |
| Qualifying widow(er) (surviving spouse) . . . . . . . . . . . . . . . . . . . . . . . . . . . . . . . | 24,400 |
| Qualifying widow(er) (surviving spouse), 65 or older or blind . . . . . . . . . . . . . . . . | 25,700 |
| Qualifying widow(er) (surviving spouse), 65 or older and blind . . . . . . . . . . . . . . . | 27,000 |

**Tax return preparer due diligence.** Effective for tax years beginning after December 31, 2017, the requirement that tax return preparers must satisfy due diligence in ensuring that clients qualify for the child, American Opportunity, and earned income tax credits is extended to apply to head of household status. A penalty is imposed on a tax return preparer (whether an individual or firm) who fails to satisfy the due diligence requirements with respect to determining eligibility for head of household filing status under Code Sec. 2(b), or eligibility for, or the amount of, the child tax credit and additional child tax credit under Code Sec. 24, the American Opportunity tax credit (AOTC) under Code Sec. 25A(i), or the earned income credit (EIC) under Code Sec. 32 (Reg. §1.6695-2(a)). The due diligence requirements also apply to determining eligibility to file a return or refund claim as head of household (Reg. §1.6695-2(a), as amended by T.D. 9842).

Each failure to exercise due diligence results in a separate penalty with respect to the head of household filing status determination and to each applicable credit claimed on a return or refund claim, unless an exception to the penalty applies (Code Sec. 6695(g), as amended by the Tax Cuts and Jobs Act (P.L. 115-97); Reg. §1.6695-2(a)). The due diligence penalty for each failure is $520 in 2018 ($530 in 2019) (Rev. Proc. 2018-18;Rev. Proc. 2018-57).

**Example:** Julia Brown prepares a 2018 federal income tax return for Patrick Carlin, age 22, claiming the head of household filing status, child tax credit (CTC), and earned income tax credit (EIC). On Brown's standard intake questionnaire, Carlin stated he has never married and has two sons, ages 10 and 11. In addition, Carlin provides information that the two boys lived with him throughout 2018, thus substantiating the head of household filing status. Based on this information and the questionnaire, Brown believes Carlin may be eligible to claim each boy as a qualifying child for the CTC and EIC. However, Carlin provides no information, and Brown has no information from other sources, verifying the relationship of the boys to Carlin. Brown does not meet the due diligence requirements for the CTC or EIC and is subject to a penalty of $1,040--$520 each for failure to meet the due diligence requirements for the CTC and EIC. To meet the requirements, Brown should have made reasonable inquiries to determine that each boy is a qualifying child for purposes of the CTC and EIC, including verifying Carlin's relationship to the boys, and contemporaneously document the inquiries and responses. (Reg. §1.6695-2(b)(3)(ii), Example (A)).

**NEW LAW EXPLAINED**

▶ **Effective date.** The amendments made by this section apply to tax years beginning after December 31, 2017 (Act Secs. 11001(c) and 11041(f) of the Tax Cuts and Jobs Act (P.L. 115-97)).

— Act Sec. 11001(b) of the Tax Cuts and Jobs Act (P.L. 115-97), amending Code Sec. 6695(g);

— Act Sec. 11041(e) adding Code Sec. 6012(f);

— Act Secs. 11001(c) and 11041(f), providing the effective date.

## ¶125 Inflation Adjustments Using Chained Consumer Price Index (C-CPI-U)

### SUMMARY OF NEW LAW

Generally, for tax years beginning after December 31, 2017, the Chained Consumer Price Index for All Urban Consumers (C-CPI-U) is to be used in making annual adjustments for inflation.

### BACKGROUND

Throughout the Internal Revenue Code, there are many instances where a codified amount, whether it is a tax-bracket range, deduction amount, the amount of income at which a deduction is no longer available, retirement plan contribution limit, or even the dollar amount of a penalty, is adjusted annually for inflation. This is generally done to avoid a diminishment in the value of a tax benefit due to the relative decline in the value of the dollar over time. For example, income amounts for an individual working in the same position every year generally tend to increase annually in order to, at least in part, account for inflation through the application of cost-of-living increases. If the income ranges for a tax bracket were not also annually adjusted for inflation, those annual cost-of-living increases would eventually cause the individual to move up to a higher tax bracket, while the purchasing power of his income has remained unchanged (a phenomenon known as "bracket creep").

Inflation adjustments for any particular year for most amounts under the Internal Revenue Code are generally calculated by taking the average Consumer Price Index (CPI) for the 12-month period ending August 31 of the *previous* year, dividing that amount by the average CPI for the 12-month period ending on August 31 of the prescribed base year for that amount, then multiplying that quotient by the statutory amount, and rounding as required by the statute (Code Sec. 1(f)(3), (4), and (6)). So, for example, the statutory amount for the standard deduction for an unmarried person is $3,000, with a base year of 1987 (Code Sec. 63(c)(2)(C) and (4)(B)(i)). So, to calculate what that amount was for 2017, the IRS took the average CPI for the 12-month period ending August 31, 2016, divided by the average CPI for the 12-month period ending August 31, 1987, and multiplied by $3,000 (714.886/335.5 × $3,000 = $6,392.42). The amount is then rounded down to the next lowest multiple of

## BACKGROUND

$50 to arrive at $6,350, which is the amount of the standard deduction for an unmarried individual in 2017 (Rev. Proc. 2016-55).

The Consumer Price Index is one of several indices calculated by the Bureau of Labor Statistics (BLS) (part of the Department of Labor). The Internal Revenue Code is generally required to use the Consumer Price Index for All-Urban Consumers to determine inflation and adjustments to amounts (Code Sec. 1(f)(5)). The Consumer Price Index for All-Urban Consumers is abbreviated as CPI-U by the BLS, but, for tax purposes, the Internal Revenue Code, Treasury regulations, and the IRS all shorten this to simply "CPI." "CPI-U" and "CPI" tend to be used interchangeably.

The general methodology of calculating the CPI is to undertake a survey of monthly prices for a "basket" of goods in urban areas, which captures about 88 percent of the population of the United States, and calculate an index for the monthly change in prices from a base year (in the case of the CPI, the base year is 1967, and the base index amount is 100). Over time, this basket of goods has been adjusted to incorporate technological advances and modern consumption choices (e.g., replacing purchases of typewriters with purchases of computers). Those amounts are then normalized in order to create a consistent index (*BLS Handbook of Methods*, Chapter 17 (6/2015)).

The IRS will typically announce the inflation-adjusted amounts applicable to a particular tax year in two major releases in the prior October. A Revenue Procedure will include inflation adjustments to amounts applicable to income taxes, estate and gift taxes, and excise taxes (for example, Rev. Proc. 2016-55 for 2017 amounts). An IRS Notice will include adjustments applicable to retirement plans (for example, Notice 2017-64 for 2018 amounts), only a limited number of which use the CPI as of August 31 as a standard of adjustment; most use the same methodology used by the Social Security Administration to make annual Social Security adjustments (Reg. § 1.415(d)-1). A handful of other adjustments are made annually outside of these two major IRS releases (for example, depreciation caps for luxury vehicles in Rev. Proc. 2017-29). In total, the CPI is used to adjust more than 200 statutory amounts across more than 60 provisions of the Internal Revenue Code.

### NEW LAW EXPLAINED

**Chained consumer price index to be used in calculating annual inflation adjustments.**—For tax years beginning after December 31, 2017 (December 31, 2018, for individual tax brackets and the standard deduction), the calculation of annual inflation adjustments will be made by using the Chained Consumer Price Index for All Urban Consumers (C-CPI-U) (Code Sec. 1(f)(3) and (6), as amended by the Tax Cuts and Jobs Act (P.L. 115-97)). The C-CPI-U is calculated in much the same way as the CPI, but rather than simply accounting for the impact of inflation on the price of goods, it also accounts for consumers' diminished capacity to achieve the same standard of living due to the increase in the price of consumer goods (*BLS Handbook of Methods*, Chapter 17 (6/2015)). The effect is that adjustments for inflation will be smaller.

> **Comment:** The difference between the two methods of calculating inflation is not insignificant. Between October 2007 and October 2017, the rate of inflation using

## NEW LAW EXPLAINED

CPI has been around 18 percent, while the rate of inflation using C-CPI-U has been around 16 percent. Although this difference may appear small, it can have a much larger impact on higher amounts, such as tax bracket income thresholds or the applicable exclusion amount (unified credit) for estate and gift taxes and the exemption amount for the generation-skipping transfer tax.

Just as with CPI, the adjustment for a calendar year is based upon the average monthly C-CPI-U for the 12-month period ending on August 31 of the *prior* year. However, because the method of calculating C-CPI-U requires the additional step of making a determination of the impact of inflation on purchasing decisions, the C-CPI-U for any given month is actually the result of an iterative release by the Bureau of Labor Statistics (BLS). An initial value is calculated and announced during the month following the month at issue, which is then reassessed and re-released (with any changes) as an interim amount. Within one year, the interim amount is announced as final. However, for purposes of calculating inflation adjustments, the interim amount is to be used (Code Sec. 1(f)(6), as added by the 2017 Tax Cuts Act).

> **Comment:** The release of inflation-adjusted amounts for 2019 was nearly three weeks later than it had been in prior years. While this may have been a one-year aberration, it could also indicate that more time was needed to make calculations, or that the IRS was waiting for updated numbers from the BLS.

Many of the changes contained in the 2017 Tax Cuts Act are temporary. For example, the reduced tax rates, increased standard deduction, and elimination of the personal exemption are all temporary, applying to tax years beginning before 2026. However, the replacement of CPI-U with C-CPI-U in calculating annual inflation adjustments is *not* temporary and applies to all amounts that are adjusted for inflation, including the permanent brackets applicable after 2025, even if the temporary changes are allowed to expire (Code Sec. 1(f)(2)(A), as amended by the 2017 Tax Cuts Act and Act Sec. 11002(d) of the 2017 Tax Cuts Act). This is accomplished by adjusting the CPI-U for the base year by an amount that is adjusted to reset the index using C-CPI-U for that base year (Code Sec. 1(f)(3), as amended by the 2017 Tax Cuts Act).

> **Caution:** The amounts that apply to retirement plans that are annually adjusted using Social Security methodology per Reg. § 1.415(d)-1 are not affected by these changes. Unless the regulations are reissued and amended to mandate the use of C-CPI-U or the Social Security methodology is changed to mandate such use, these amounts will continue to be annually adjusted using CPI-U.

> **Caution:** Most of the inflation-adjusted amounts for 2018 were calculated using the CPI methodology and announced prior to the passage of the 2017 Tax Cuts Act in Rev. Proc. 2017-58. In March of 2018, the IRS released updated 2018 inflation-adjusted amounts using the C-CPI-U methodology in Rev. Proc. 2018-18, which only includes amounts that were changed due to the switch to C-CPI-U. In April 2018, the IRS corrected certain 2018 inflation amounts for alternative minimum tax and low-income housing credit in Rev. Proc. 2018-22. A taxpayer should consult with Rev. Proc. 2017-58, Rev. Proc. 2018-18, and Rev. Proc. 2018-22 attempting to find applicable inflation-adjusted amounts for 2018.

▶ **Effective date.** The amendments made by this section apply to tax years beginning after December 31, 2017 (Act Sec. 11002(e) of the Tax Cuts and Jobs Act (P.L. 115-97)).

¶125

## NEW LAW EXPLAINED

**Other than inflation adjusted amounts for 2018 and 2019, no significant guidance related to this provision has been issued.**

— Act Sec. 11002(a) of the Tax Cuts and Jobs Act (P.L. 115-97), amending Code Sec. 1(f)(3);

— Act Sec. 11002(b), striking Code Sec. 1(f)(7), redesignating Code Sec. 1(f)(6) as Code Sec. 1(f)(7) and adding new Code Sec. 1(f)(6);

— Act Sec. 11002(c)(1), amending Code Sec. 1(f)(2)(A);

— Act Sec. 11002(c)(2), amending Code Sec. 1(i);

— Act Sec. 11002(d), amending Code Secs. 23(h)(2), 25A(h)(1)(A)(ii) and (2)(A)(ii), 25B(b)(3)(B), 32(b)(2)(B)(ii)(II) and (j)(1)(B), Code Sec. 36B(f)(2)(B)(ii)(II), 41(e)(5)(C)(i) and (ii), 42(e)(3)(D)(ii), (h)(3)(H)(i)(II) and (h)(6)(G), 45R(d)(3)(B)(ii), 55(d)(4)(A)(ii), 59(j)(2)(B), 62(d)(3)(B), 63(c)(4)(B), 68(b)(2)(B), 125(i)(2)(B), 132(f)(6)(A)(ii), 135(b)(2)(B)(ii), 137(f)(2), 146(d)(2)(B), 147(c)(2)(H)(ii), 151(d)(4)(B), 162(o)(3), 179(b)(6)(A)(ii), 213(d)(10)(B), 219(b)(5)(C)(i)(II) and (g)(8)(B), 220(g)(2), 221(f)(1)(B), 223(g)(1)(B), 280F(d)(7)(B), 408A(c)(3)(D)(ii), 430(c)(7)(D)(vii)(II), 512(d)(2)(B), 513(h)(2)(C)(ii), 831(b)(2)(D)(ii), 877A(a)(3)(B)(i)(II), 911(b)(2)(D)(ii)(II), 1274A(d)(2), 2010(c)(3)(B)(ii), 2032A(a)(3)(B), 2503(b)(2)(B), 4161(b)(2)(C)(i)(II), 4261(e)(4)(A)(ii), 4980I(b)(3)(C)(v)(II), 5000A(c)(3)(D)(ii), 6039F(d), 6323(i)(4)(B), 6334(g)(1)(B), 6601(j)(3)(B), 6651(i)(1), 6652(c)(7)(A), 6695(h)(1), 6698(e)(1), 6699(e)(1), 6721(f)(1), 6722(f)(1), 7345(f)(2), 7430(c)(1), 7872(g)(5), and 9831(d)(2)(D)(ii)(II);

— Act Sec. 11002(e), providing the effective date.

# CAPITAL GAINS AND OTHER PROVISIONS

## ¶130  Self-Created Property as Capital Asset

### SUMMARY OF NEW LAW

A patent, invention, model or design (patented or not), or secret formula or process is excluded from the definition of a capital asset for dispositions after December 31, 2017, if it is held by the taxpayer who created the property or a taxpayer with a substituted or transferred basis from the taxpayer who created the property.

### BACKGROUND

Some self-created intangibles cannot be capital assets for certain taxpayers. Copyrights and literary, musical, or artistic compositions cannot be capital assets in the hands of the taxpayer who created them, or in the hands of a taxpayer whose basis is determined in whole or part by reference to the basis of the taxpayer who created them (Code Sec. 1221(a)(3)). However, a taxpayer in either of these categories may elect to treat musical compositions and copyrights in musical works as capital assets (Code Sec. 1221(b)(3); Reg. § 1.1221-3).

## BACKGROUND

Letters or memoranda and similar property cannot be capital assets in the hands of the taxpayer who created them, the taxpayer for whom they were prepared or created, or a taxpayer with substitute or carryover basis from the person who created them or for whom they were created (Code Sec. 1221(a)(3)).

## NEW LAW EXPLAINED

**Patents, inventions, designs, and secret formulas are not capital assets.**—In the case of dispositions after December 31, 2017, a patent, invention, model or design (patented or not), or secret formula or process is not a capital asset in the hands of (1) the taxpayer whose personal efforts created the property, or (2) a taxpayer with a substituted or transferred basis from the taxpayer whose personal efforts created the property (Code Sec. 1221(a)(3), as amended by the Tax Cuts and Jobs Act (P.L. 115-97)). Thus, gains or losses from the sale or exchange of a patent, invention, model or design, or a secret formula or process that is held either by the taxpayer who created the property or a taxpayer with a substituted or transferred basis from the taxpayer who created the property will not be capital gains or losses.

These types of self-created property also do not qualify for the capital gain/ordinary loss rule for dispositions after December 31, 2017 (Code Sec. 1231(b)(1)(C), as amended by the 2017 Tax Cuts Act).

> **Caution:** According to the Conference Committee Report, the exclusion of these self-created works from capital assets also applies when the taxpayer's basis is determined by reference to the basis of a person for whom the property was created (Conference Report on H.R. 1, Tax Cuts and Jobs Act (H. Rept. 115-466)). However, the amended statutory language apparently still limits this "for whom created" rule to letters, memoranda and similar property.

> **Comment:** Although patents will be excluded from the definition of capital asset after 2017, a qualified holder's gain on the disposition of a patent to an unrelated person may still be taxed at the lowest capital gain tax rate. Qualified holders include the creator of the patent and persons who provided financial backing to the creator (Code Sec. 1235).

▶ **Effective date.** The amendment made by this section applies to dispositions after December 31, 2017 (Act Sec. 13314(c) of the Tax Cuts and Jobs Act (P.L. 115-97).

**No significant guidance related to this provision has been issued.**

— Act Sec. 13314(a) of the Tax Cuts and Jobs Act (P.L. 115-97), amending Code Sec. 1221(a)(3);

— Act Sec. 13314(b), amending Code Sec. 1231(b)(1)(C);

— Act Sec. 13314(c), providing the effective date.

¶130

# ¶135  Sinai Peninsula of Egypt a Qualified Hazardous Duty Area

## SUMMARY OF NEW LAW

The Sinai Peninsula of Egypt is a qualified hazardous duty area for the applicable period and is treated the same as a combat zone for purposes of certain tax benefits for members of the U.S. Armed Forces. The applicable period is generally the portion of the first tax year beginning after June 9, 2015, and any subsequent tax year beginning before January 1, 2026.

## BACKGROUND

Members of the U.S. Armed Forces serving in a combat zone, as designated by Executive Order of the President of the United States, are entitled to numerous tax benefits. Military personnel may exclude from gross income all pay received for any month, even a part of which, was spent in a combat zone or in a hospital due to wounds, disease, or injury incurred while serving in a combat zone (Code Sec. 112). However, it does not apply to time spent in a hospital for any month beginning more than two years after the date of the end of the combatant activities that zone. Such pay is also not subject to withholding (Code Sec. 3401(a)(1)).

The gross income exclusion also applies to commissioned officers, but it is limited to the maximum enlisted amount, which is the sum of:

- the highest rate of basic pay at the highest pay grade that enlisted personnel may receive, and

- the amount of hostile fire/imminent danger pay that the officer receives (Reg. §1.112-1).

While excluded from gross income, combat pay is included in earned income for purposes of computing the earned income tax credit and calculating the refundable portion of the child tax credit (Code Secs. 24(d)(1) and 32(c)(2)(B)(vi)). Similarly, combat pay may be treated as compensation in determining the amount members of the military can contribute to their individual retirement accounts (IRAs).

The tax liability of a member of the U.S. Armed Forces is forgiven in the year the individual dies:

- while in active service in a combat zone, or

- from wounds, disease, or injury incurred while serving in a combat zone.

Any unpaid taxes that relate to tax years prior to service in a combat zone may also be abated. If the decedent filed a joint return, only the decedent's portion of joint tax liability is forgiven. This tax forgiveness rule also applies to U.S. military and civilian employees killed in terrorist or military actions, including specific domestic terrorist attacks (Code Sec. 692).

For purposes of determining surviving spouse status (and joint filing status) for a spouse of a military member who is missing in a combat zone, the military member is

## BACKGROUND

considered to have died on the date his or her status changed from missing to dead rather than the actual date of death (Code Secs. 2(a)(3) and 6013(f)(1)). The surviving spouse may use surviving spouse status for the two years following the year in which his or her spouse is deemed to have died.

An estate tax reduction is available for members of the Armed Forces who are killed while serving in a combat zone (Code Sec. 2201). The tax forgiveness discussed above extends to tax on income received by another after the decedent's death as income in respect of a decedent (Reg. § 1.692-1(a)(2)(ii)).

Administrative relief may be provided to members of the military in a combat zone or who are continuously hospitalized as a result of injuries received in a combat zone by suspending tax examination and collection actions during this time (Code Secs. 7508 and 7508A). Examination and collection actions that can be precluded or suspended include tax return audits, mailings of notices, and other actions involving the collection of overdue taxes. The collection period for taxpayers hospitalized for combat zone injuries may not be suspended by reason of any period of continuous hospitalization or the 180 days thereafter (Code Sec. 7508(e)(3)). As a result, the collection period expires 10 years after assessment, plus the actual time spent in a combat zone, regardless of the length of the postponement period available for hospitalized individuals to comply with their tax obligations.

Members of the military are also exempt from the telephone excise tax for toll telephone service that originates in a combat zone (Code Sec. 4253(d)).

## NEW LAW EXPLAINED

**Egypt's Sinai Peninsula is a qualified hazardous duty area; treated as combat zone.**—The Sinai Peninsula of Egypt is a qualified hazardous duty area and members of the U.S. Armed Forces members serving there are considered to be serving in a combat zone (Sec. 11026(b) of the Tax Cuts and Jobs Act (P.L. 115-97)). As a result, such members of the military are entitled to combat zone tax benefits.

A qualified hazardous duty area is treated in the same manner as if it were a combat zone for purposes of the following provisions of the Code:

- exclusions from income for combat zone compensation (Code Sec. 112);
- special rule for determining surviving spouse status where the deceased spouse was in missing status as a result of service in a combat zone (Code Sec. 2(a)(3));
- forgiveness of income taxes of members of the military dying in the combat zone or by reason of combat zone incurred wounds (Code Sec. 692);
- reduction in estate taxes for members of the military dying in the combat zone or by reason of combat-zone incurred wounds (Code Sec. 2201);
- exemption from income tax withholding for military pay for any month in which an employee is entitled to the exclusion from income (Code Sec. 3401(a)(1));
- exemption from the telephone excise tax for toll telephone service that originates in a combat zone (Code Sec. 4253(d));

**NEW LAW EXPLAINED**

- special rule permitting filing of a joint return where a spouse is in missing status as a result of service in a combat zone (Code Sec. 6013(f)(1));

- suspension of time provisions (Code Sec. 7508) (Sec. 11026(a) of the 2017 Tax Cuts Act).

> **Comment:** Although this designation impacts a relatively small number of members of the military (454 troops, as reported by the Multinational Force & Observers website http://mfo.org/en/contingents, visited 12/8/2017), Sen. John Cornyn, R-Texas and Sen. Amy Klobuchar, D-Minn., introduced the measure to provide combat pay and tax benefits in light of the heightened volatility in the area and increased threat to their lives from regional and Islamic State groups (https://homeland.house.gov/press/homeland-security-bipartisan-delegation-examines-spread-islamist-terror-threats-u-s-allies/, visited 12/8/2017).

Members of the military serving in the Sinai Peninsula of Egypt are granted combat zone tax benefits if, as of December 22, 2017, they are entitled to special pay under section 310 of Title 37 of the United States Code (Sec. 11026(b) of the 2017 Tax Cuts Act). Combat zone tax benefits begin June 9, 2015, and apply to every subsequent tax year through December 31, 2025 (Sec. 11026(c) of the 2017 Tax Cuts Act). The Sinai Peninsula of Egypt is considered a qualified hazardous duty zone for the same period (Sec. 11026(b) of the 2017 Tax Cuts Act).

> **Comment:** Members of the military who served in the affected area at any time from June 9, 2015 to December 31, 2017 should provide documentation of service to the applicable service finance office, and they will be issued a Form W-2c, Corrected Wage and Tax Statement. These members should then file a Form 1040X, Amended U.S. Individual Tax Return for the year at issue to reflect the retroactive exclusion. "Sinai Peninsula of Egypt" should be written at the top of page 1 of the Form 1040X.

The exemption from income tax withholding under Code Sec. 3401(a)(1) for members of the military serving in the Sinai Peninsula of Egypt is applicable from December 22, 2017, through December 31, 2025.

▶ **Effective date.** The amendments made by this section generally apply to members of the U.S. Armed Forces serving in Sinai Peninsula of Egypt beginning on June 9, 2015 (Act Sec. 11026(d)(1) of the Tax Cuts and Jobs Act (P.L. 115-97)). The amendment for wage withholding applies to remuneration paid after December 22, 2017, the date of enactment (Act Sec. 11026(d)(2) of the 2017 Tax Cuts Act).

— Act Sec. 11026(a) of the Tax Cuts and Jobs Act (P.L. 115-97), applying Code Secs. 2(a)(3), 112, 692, 2201, 3401(a)(1), 4253(d), 6013(f)(10), and 7508;

— Act Sec. 11026(b), designating qualified hazardous duty area;

— Act Sec. 11026(c), determining applicable periods;

— Act Sec. 11026(d), providing the effective date.

## ¶140   Individual Health Insurance Mandate Under the Affordable Care Act

**SUMMARY OF NEW LAW**

Effective for months beginning after December 31, 2018, the amount owed by any taxpayer under the individual health insurance mandate "shared responsibility payment" for lack of minimum essential health insurance for themselves and their dependents is zero.

**BACKGROUND**

Beginning in 2014, a penalty was imposed on applicable individuals for each month they failed to maintain "minimum essential coverage" for themselves and their dependents (Code Sec. 5000A). This penalty is also referred to as a "shared responsibility payment," and the requirement to maintain minimum essential coverage is known as the "individual mandate."

The monthly penalty amount for a taxpayer is equal to $1/12$ of the greater of:

- a flat dollar amount equal to the applicable dollar amount for each of the individuals who were not properly insured by the taxpayer, up to a maximum of 300 percent of the applicable dollar amount, or

- an applicable percentage of income (Code Sec. 5000A(c)(2)).

The flat dollar amount is the sum of the applicable dollar amounts for each individual lacking minimum essential coverage that the taxpayer is required to insure (Code Sec. 5000A(c)(2)(A)). The applicable dollar amount is: $95 for 2014, $325 for 2015, $695 for 2016, 2017, and 2018 (Code Sec. 5000A(c)(3); Rev. Proc. 2016-55; Rev. Proc. 2017-58). Due to the 300 percent limitation, the maximum penalty for purposes of the flat dollar amount is: $285 in 2014, $975 in 2015, and $2,085 in 2016, 2017, and 2018.

The applicable percentage of income is an amount equal to a percentage of the excess of the taxpayer's household income over the taxpayer's filing threshold for the tax year. The percentages are: one percent for tax years beginning in 2014, two percent for tax years beginning in 2015, and 2.5 percent for tax years beginning after 2015 (Code Sec. 5000A(c)(2)(B)). For purposes of this calculation, household income has the same meaning as used in determining the filing threshold exemption from the penalty (Code Sec. 5000A(c)(4)(B)).

The payment amount is capped at the cost of the national average premium for a bronze level health plan available through the Marketplace. For 2018, the annual national average premium for a bronze level health plan available through the Marketplace is $283 per month for an individual and $1,415 per month for a family with five or more members (Code Sec. 5000A(c)(1)(B); Rev. Proc. 2018-43).

## NEW LAW EXPLAINED

**The amount of the penalty imposed on individuals without health insurance is zero.**—For months beginning after December 31, 2018, the amount a taxpayer would otherwise owe for each month they fail to have "minimum essential coverage" for themselves and their dependents is zero (Code Sec. 5000A(c), as amended by the Tax Cuts and Jobs Act (P.L. 115-97)). No other Affordable Care Act tax or provision is affected.

**Compliance Tip:** Individuals with coverage during the year should receive a reporting form. Marketplace Exchanges are to provide Form 1095-A, Health Insurance Marketplace Statement, if the Marketplace provided coverage. An individual with employer or other health coverage ought to receive Form 1095-B, Health Coverage (indicating coverage provided), or Form 1095-C, Employer-Provided Health Insurance Offer and Coverage (indicating coverage offered or not offered, and coverage provided). These forms can be useful in applying the shared responsibility rules primarily by showing which months (if any) the individual maintained coverage during the year. Presumably, Exchanges will continue to issue Form 1095-A after 2018 since these are necessary for premium tax credit purposes.

**Compliance Tip:** Taxpayers may claim a hardship exemption from individual shared responsibility payments on their 2018 tax returns without having to obtain hardship exemption certification from the Marketplace (Notice 2019-5). With the repeal of individual shared responsibility payments starting in 2019, individuals are free to buy and insurers are free to offer inexpensive "short-term, limited duration" coverage that lasts up to nearly a year even though such coverage does not provide minimum essential coverage.

**Comment:** Though the tax imposed under Code Sec. 5000A is zeroed out, Code Sec. 5000A(f) and Reg. § 1.5000A-2 will still be relevant because they outline the key concept of minimum essential coverage (MEC). Employers that do not offer their employees MEC under an eligible employer sponsored plan may still be liable for large employer shared responsibility payments (Code Sec. 4980H). Individuals who are eligible for MEC for any month do not qualify for the premium tax credit for that month (Code Sec. 36B(c)(2)). Reimbursements under a qualified small employer health reimbursement arrangement are included in an employee's income unless the employee had MEC (Code Sec. 9831(d)(4)(B)(iii)).

▶ **Effective date.** The amendments made by this section apply to months beginning after December 31, 2018 (Act Sec. 11081(b) of the Tax Cuts and Jobs Act (P.L. 115-97)).

— Act Sec. 11081(a) of the Tax Cuts and Jobs Act (P.L. 115-97), amending Code Sec. 5000A(c);

— Act Sec. 11081(b), providing the effective date.

¶140

## ¶145  Capital Gains Reinvested in Qualified Opportunity Zones

### SUMMARY OF NEW LAW

A state may designate certain low-income communities as qualified opportunity zones. To encourage investment in qualified opportunity zones, a taxpayer may elect to temporarily exclude capital gain on the sale or exchange of property to an unrelated party if the taxpayer reinvests the gain in a qualified opportunity fund within 180 days. The taxpayer recognizes the deferred gain on the earlier of the date when the investment is disposed of or December 31, 2026. A taxpayer may also elect to exclude the post-acquisition gains on qualified opportunity fund investments that are held for at least 10 years.

### BACKGROUND

Temporary tax incentives have been used for many years to encourage economic growth and development in low-income communities and disaster areas. Empowerment and enterprise zones (Code Secs. 1391—1397F), renewal communities (Code Secs. 1400E—14000U-3), and the new markets tax credit (Code Sec. 45D), for example, were created to benefit economically disadvantaged areas. The Gulf Opportunity Zone (Code Sec. 1400N) and New York Liberty Zone (Code Sec. 1400L) were created to provide incentives to revive areas devastated by disasters. Tax incentives could include increased depreciation and expense allowances, increased credit limits, treatment of certain losses as net operating losses, and special rules for tax exempt bonds.

Taxpayers may qualify for the new markets tax credit for equity investments made in low-income communities through a qualified community development entity (CDE) (Code Sec. 45D). The equity investment must be made within five years after the CDE receives an allocation of the national credit limitation amount for the calendar year ($3.5 billion for each of the calendar years through 2019). The credit is equal to five percent of the equity investment for the first three allowance dates and six percent of the equity investment for the next four allowance dates. The total credit available is equal to 39 percent of the investment over seven years. Active involvement in the low-income communities is required, with strict penalties if the investment is terminated before seven years. The allocation of credit amounts and CDE certification is the responsibility of the U.S. Department of the Treasury's Community Development Financial Institutions Fund (CDFI).

Low-income communities, as defined for purposes of the new markets tax credit, are population census tracts that have a poverty rate of at least 20 percent, or

- if outside a metropolitan area, have a median family income of 80 percent or less of the statewide median family income; or

- if within a metropolitan area, have a median family income of 80 percent or less of the greater of statewide median family income or the metropolitan area median family income (Code Sec. 45D(e)(1)); or

## BACKGROUND

- if within a high migration rural county, have a median family income of 85 percent or less of the statewide median family income (Code Sec. 45D(e)(5)(a)).

Certain census tracts with populations of less than 2,000 that are located within a designated empowerment zone can be treated as low-income communities. The tract must be contiguous to one or more low-income communities that do not qualify as low income through this low-population provision (Code Sec. 45D(e)(4)).

The IRS may designate "targeted populations" that qualify as low-income communities, and provide rules to determine which entities are qualified active low-income community businesses with respect to such populations (Code Sec. 45D(e)(2)). A targeted population consists of individuals or an identifiable group of individuals who (1) are "low-income persons" or (2) otherwise lack adequate access to loans or equity investments (Reg. §1.45D-1(d)(9); Notice 2006-60). A targeted population is not required to be within a single census tract.

> **Comment:** The New Markets Tax Credit (NMTC) Program generates $8 of private investment for every $1 of federal funding. Since 2003, the Program has created or retained nearly 750,000 jobs, and has supported the construction of 84.6 million square feet of manufacturing space, 62.7 million square feet of office space, and 42.7 million square feet of retail space (New Markets Tax Credit Program Fact Sheet, https://www.cdfifund.gov/Documents/NMTC%20Fact%20Sheet_Jan2018.pdf).

## NEW LAW EXPLAINED

**Qualified opportunity zones created.**—A population census tract that is a low-income community, as defined for purposes of the new markets tax credit under Code Sec. 45D, may be designated as a qualified opportunity zone (Code Sec. 1400Z-1(a) and (c)(1), as added by the Tax Cuts and Jobs Act (P.L. 115-97)). A state's chief executive officer may nominate a low-income community for designation by notifying the U.S. Treasury Secretary in writing by March 22, 2018 (i.e., the end of the determination period). The Secretary must certify the nomination within 30 days of receiving the nomination (i.e., the consideration period) (Code Sec. 1400Z-1(b)(1), as added by the 2017 Tax Cuts Act). The chief executive officer may request a 30-day extension of either the determination period or the consideration period, or both (Code Sec. 1400Z-1(b)(2), as added by the 2017 Tax Cuts Act). A "state" includes any U.S. possession, and a "chief executive officer" generally refers to a state's governor, but also includes the mayor of the District of Columbia (Code Sec. 1400Z-1(c)(3), as added by the 2017 Tax Cuts Act; Conference Report on H.R. 1, Tax Cuts and Jobs Act (H. Rept. 115-466)).

Each population census tract in Puerto Rico that is a low income community is deemed to be certified and designated as a qualified opportunity zone, effective December 22, 2017 (Code Sec. 1400Z-1(b)(3), as added by the Bipartisan Budget Act of 2018 (P.L. 115-123)).

> **Compliance Note:** The IRS has provided guidance for nominating population census tracts as qualified opportunity zones (Rev. Proc. 2018-16).

> For the final list of population census tracts that were nominated and have been designated as qualified opportunity zones, see Notice 2018-48.

¶145

## NEW LAW EXPLAINED

*Number of designations.* The number of population census tracts designated as quali-fied opportunity zones in a state may not exceed 25 percent of the low-income communities in that state (Code Sec. 1400Z-1(d)(1), as added by the 2017 Tax Cuts Act, and amended by the 2018 Budget Act). However, if there are less than 100 low-income communities in a state, 25 population census tracts may be designated (Code Sec. 1400Z-1(d)(2), as added by the 2017 Tax Cuts Act).

*Contiguous tract designation.* A population census tract that is not a low-income community may still be designated as a qualified opportunity zone, if it is contiguous to a low-income community that is designated as a qualified opportunity zone, and the median family income of the tract does not exceed 125 percent of the median family income of the contiguous low-income community (Code Sec. 1400Z-1(e), as added by the 2017 Tax Cuts Act). The contiguous tract designation is limited to no more than five percent of the qualified opportunity zones in the state (Code Sec. 1400Z-1(e)(2), as added by the 2017 Tax Cuts Act).

*Period of designation.* The designation as a qualified opportunity zone remains in effect through the end of the 10th calendar year beginning on or after the date of designa-tion (Code Sec. 1400Z-1(f), as added by the 2017 Tax Cuts Act).

**Tax treatment of gain reinvested in qualified opportunity fund.** Special elective tax incentives are provided to encourage investment in qualified opportunity zones (Code Sec. 1400Z-2, as added by the 2017 Tax Cuts Act). Taxpayers can elect to:

(1) temporarily defer inclusion in gross income for certain gains to the extent that corresponding amounts are reinvested in a qualified opportunity fund (QOF); and

(2) permanently exclude from gross income the post-acquisition gains on QOF investments that are held for at least 10 years.

A taxpayer may elect to temporarily defer and exclude from gross income capital gain on the sale or exchange of any property to an unrelated party in the tax year of the sale or exchange, if the gain is reinvested in a QOF within 180 days of the sale or exchange (Code Sec. 1400Z-2(a)(1)(A), as added by the 2017 Tax Cuts Act; Proposed Reg. § 1.1400Z-2(a)-1). The amount of gain that can be excluded is equal to the amount of gain invested in the QOF (Code Sec. 1400Z-2(a)(1)(B), as added by the 2017 Tax Cuts Act). However, the election cannot be made if a previous election made with respect to the sale or exchange is in effect (Code Sec. 1400Z-2(a)(2), as added by the 2017 Tax Cuts Act). This restriction is meant to prevent artificial increases in basis that could result from multiple elections with respect to the same gain (REG-115420-18, Oct. 29, 2018).

> **Caution:** No election may be made for any sale or exchange after December 31, 2026 (Code Sec. 1400Z-2(a)(2), as added by the 2017 Tax Cuts Act).

*Eligible taxpayers.* The deferral is available to any taxpayer that may recognize capital gains. Eligible taxpayers include individuals; C corporations, including regulated investment companies (RICs) and real estate investment trusts (REITs); partnerships; S corporations; and trusts and estates (Proposed Reg. § 1.1400Z-2(a)-1(b)(1)).

# NEW LAW EXPLAINED

*Eligible interests.* A taxpayer must invest the deferred gain in an "eligible interest" in a QOF. An eligible interest is an equity interest in the QOF, including preferred stock or a partnership interest with special allocations. Debt instruments as defined by Code Sec. 1275(a)(1) and Reg. §1.1275-1(d) are not eligible interests. However, a taxpayer may use an eligible interest in a QOF as collateral for a loan, whether a purchase-money borrowing or otherwise (Proposed Reg. §1.1400Z-2(a)-1(b)(3)).

Deemed contributions of money to a partnership under Code Sec. 752(a) do not create or increase an investment in a QOF (Proposed Reg. §1.1400Z-2(e)-1(a)(2)). Therefore, a partner's increase in outside basis due to a deemed contribution is not taken into account in determining what portion of the partner's interest is or is not subject to the deferral election (REG-115420-18, Oct. 29, 2018).

> **Example 1:** Jack owns a 50 percent interest in Partnership P. Ninety percent of Jack's investment in the partnership only includes amounts to which the Code Sec. 1400Z-2(a) deferral election applies, and the remaining 10 percent is a separate investment consisting of other amounts. Partnership P borrows $8 million, and $4 million of the $8 million liability is allocated to Jack. Under Code Sec. 752(a), Jack is treated as contributing $4 million to the partnership. Jack's deemed $4 million contribution is ignored for purposes of determining the portions of Jack's investment in the partnership that are and are not subject to the deferral election. Therefore, after Jack's deemed contribution, 90 percent of his investment in Partnership P is subject to a deferral election, and 10 percent is treated as a separate investment that is not subject to a deferral election (Proposed Reg. §1.1400Z-2(e)-1(a)(3), *Example*).

*Eligible gains, generally.* Only capital gain is eligible for deferral. Eligible gains generally include capital gain from an actual or deemed sale or exchange, or any other gain that must be included in a taxpayer's capital gain computation (Proposed Reg. §1.1400Z-2(a)-1(b)(2)).

Gain from a sale or exchange with a related person does not qualify. Related persons for this purpose are defined in Code Secs. 267(b) and 707(b)(1), but by substituting "20 percent" in place of "50 percent" each place it occurs. Only gain that would be recognized before January 1, 2027 (but for a deferral election) qualifies for deferral (Code Sec. 1400Z-2(e)(2); Proposed Reg. §1.1400Z-2(a)-1(b)(2)).

> **Comment:** Code Sec. 1400Z-2(a)(1) simply provides that the provision applies to "gain" from the sale to or exchange with an unrelated person of any property held by the taxpayer. The heading of Code Sec. 1400Z-2, however, refers to special rules for "capital gain" invested in opportunity zones. The Committee Report for the Tax Cuts and Jobs Act also refers to "capital gain" (Conference Report on H.R. 1, Tax Cuts and Jobs Act (H. Rept. 115-466)). The Notice of Proposed Rulemaking notes this inconsistency, but concludes that Congress intended only for capital gains to qualify (REG-115420-18, Oct. 29, 2018).

A taxpayer that makes a deferral election with respect to some, but not all, of an eligible gain may make a separate election for the portion that was not included in

## NEW LAW EXPLAINED

the prior election (Proposed Reg. § 1.1400Z-2(a)-1(b)(2)(ii)). The elections are subject to the same 180-day limitations period, since the gain arose from the same sale or exchange.

*Eligible gains—section 1256 contracts.* For gain arising from section 1256 contracts, a taxpayer may elect to defer only capital gain net income, determined by taking into account the capital gains and losses for a tax year on all of the taxpayer's section 1256 contracts. The 180-day period for investing the capital gain net income begins on the last day of the tax year. No gain from any section 1256 contract may be deferred if at any time during the tax year, one of the taxpayer's section 1256 contracts was part of an offsetting-positions transaction (Proposed Reg. § 1.1400Z-2(a)-1(b)(2)(iii)).

*Eligible gains—offsetting-positions transaction.* Any capital gain from a position that is or has been part of an offsetting-positions transaction (other than an offsetting-positions transaction in which all of the positions are section 1256 contracts) is not eligible for deferral (Proposed Reg. § 1.1400Z-2(a)-1(b)(2)(iv)).

An offsetting-positions transaction is one in which a taxpayer has substantially diminished its risk of loss from holding one position with respect to personal property by holding one or more other positions with respect to personal property. The properties do not have to be of the same kind, and it does not matter if either position is with respect to actively traded personal property. An offsetting-positions transaction includes:

- a straddle as defined in Code Sec. 1092 and its regulations, including Code Sec. 1092(d)(4), which provides rules for positions held by related persons and certain flow-through entities (e.g., a partnership); and

- a transaction that would be a straddle but for the active trading requirement in Code Sec. 1092(d)(1) (e.g., positions in closely held stock or other non-traded personal property and substantially offsetting derivatives).

*180-day investment period.* The 180-day period for investing eligible gain in a QOF generally begins on the day the gain would be recognized for federal income tax purposes if the taxpayer did not make the deferral election (Proposed Reg. § 1.1400Z-2(a)-1(b)(4)). For example, the 180-day period for:

- gain on the sale of stock begins on the trade date;

- a capital gain dividend received by an individual RIC or REIT shareholder begins on the day on which the dividend is paid; and

- undistributed capital gain of a RIC or REIT included in a shareholder's long-term capital gains begins on the last day of the RIC's or REIT's tax year.

A taxpayer that makes a deferral election, invests in a QOF, then later sells the entire investment in the QOF can make a second deferral election by investing the gain from the sale of the original QOF in another QOF. The 180-day period for the second election begins on the date the taxpayer disposes of its entire investment in the original QOF (Proposed Reg. § 1.1400Z-2(a)-1(b)(4)(ii), *Example 4*).

A partner's election period is discussed in *"Special rules for partnerships and other passthrough entities,"* below.

**¶145**

## NEW LAW EXPLAINED

*Included gain when deferral ends.* The election allows the taxpayer to defer including the gain in gross income until the tax year that includes the earlier of:

- the date that the investment is sold or exchanged; or
- December 31, 2026 (Code Sec. 1400Z-2(b)(1), as added by the 2017 Tax Cuts Act).

When the deferred gain is included in gross income, the recognized gain increases the basis in the QOF investment (Code Sec. 1400Z-2(b)(2)(B)(ii), as added by the 2017 Tax Cuts Act).

The amount of gain the taxpayer must include in gross income is the excess of:

- the fair market value of the investment on the date the gain is included in gross income, or the amount of gain excluded, whichever is less; over
- the taxpayer's basis in the investment (Code Sec. 1400Z-2(b)(2)(A), as added by the 2017 Tax Cuts Act).

*Determining basis.* The taxpayer's basis in the investment is initially treated as zero (Code Sec. 1400Z-2(b)(2)(B)(i), as added by the 2017 Tax Cuts Act). However, basis increases the longer the taxpayer holds the investment. If the taxpayer holds the QOF investment:

- for at least five years, the zero basis is increased by 10 percent of the gain originally deferred (Code Sec. 1400Z-2(b)(2)(B)(iii), as added by the 2017 Tax Cuts Act).
- for at least seven years, basis is increased by another five percent of the gain originally deferred, in addition to the amount of basis increase for investments held for at least five years (Code Sec. 1400Z-2(b)(2)(B)(iv), as added by the 2017 Tax Cuts Act).
- for at least 10 years, the taxpayer can elect to step up basis to the fair market value of the investment on the date it is sold or exchanged (this election is discussed at *"Investment held 10 or more years,"* below) (Code Sec. 1400Z-2(c), as added by the Tax Cuts Act).

> **Comment:** If the taxpayer sells the QOF investment before holding it for five years, basis in the investment is $0 for purposes of determining the recognized deferred gain, and the entire deferred gain is recognized. If the taxpayer holds the investment for at least five years but less than seven years, the $0 dollar basis is increased by 10 percent of the deferred gain, so 90 percent of the deferred gain is recognized if the fund is sold. If the taxpayer holds the investment for at least seven years but less than 10 years, the basis is 15 percent of the deferred gain, so 85 percent of the deferred gain is recognized if the fund is sold. Some or all of the deferred gain will be recognized on December 31, 2026, if the taxpayer still holds the investment on that date.
>
> If the value of the fund investment has decreased on the date it is sold or, if earlier, on the mandatory December 31, 2026, recognition date, a taxpayer determines the amount of deferred gain that is recognized by reference to the fair market value on the date of sale or the earlier December 31, 2026, recognition

## NEW LAW EXPLAINED

date (Code Sec. 1400Z-2(b)(2)(A), as added by the 2017 Tax Cuts Act). For this purpose, basis is also considered $0 and is increased as described above if the fund investment as been held at least five years or seven years as the case may be.

---

**Example 2:** On January 2, 2018, ABC Corp. sells property to an unrelated party and has a resulting gain of $1 million. ABC Corp. reinvests the full $1 million in InvestFund, a QOF, on March 30, 2018. ABC Corp. sells its investment in InvestFund on April 2, 2021, for $1.5 million. Since ABC Corp. held its invest-ment in InvestFund for under five years, its basis in the investment is $0. In its 2021 tax year, ABC Corp. must recognize the deferred gain of $1 million as well as the $500,000 in appreciation.

---

**Example 3:** Assume same facts as Example 2 above, except that ABC Corp. sells the investment in 2025. Since ABC Corp. held the investment for more than seven years, its basis in the investment increases from $0 to $150,000 (15 percent of the deferred $1 million gain), thus reducing the amount of deferred gain it must include to $850,000 ($1,000,000 – $150,000). ABC must also recognize the additional $500,000 in appreciation.

| | |
|---|---|
| 10% of deferred gain— | $100,000 |
| 5% of deferred gain— | $50,000 |
| | $150,000 |

---

*Investment held 10 or more years.* If a taxpayer holds a QOF investment for at least 10 years, the taxpayer can elect to step up the investment's basis to its fair market value on the date it is sold or exchanged (Code Sec. 1400Z-2(c), as added by the Tax Cuts Act). Consequently, if the value of the investment has increased beyond the initial amount of invested deferred gain and the taxpayer makes this election, the taxpayer does not recognize gain on the appreciation in the investment. In the case of a mixed investment, gain is not recognized only to the extent it is attributable to the deferred gain that was invested (Proposed Reg. § 1.1400Z-2(c)-1(a); Proposed Reg. § 1.1400Z-2(e)-1(a)(1)).

The election for QOF investments held for at least 10 years may be made after the low-income community automatically loses its designation as a qualified opportunity zone, which occurs at the close of the 10th calendar year beginning on or after the date the community was designated as a QOF. However, the election cannot be made for a disposition that occurs after December 31, 2047 (Proposed Reg. § 1.1400Z-2(c)-1(b)).

**Comment:** This 2047 election deadline is intended to let taxpayers who make the latest possible deferral election (at the end of June 2027) hold their QOF invest-ment for up to 20½ years without losing the benefit of the step-up basis election. However, the IRS has requested comments on alternatives to this expiration date (REG-115420-18, Oct. 29, 2018).

¶145

## NEW LAW EXPLAINED

**Example 4:** ABC invests $1 million of deferred gain in a QOF on January 1, 2025. On December 31, 2026, ABC must recognize the entire $1 million deferred gain ($1 million deferred gain less $0 basis) even though the investment in the fund has not been sold. The $0 basis in the investment is not increased, because ABC has not owned the fund for at least five years. On January 1, 2037, ABC sells its interest in the fund for $1.5 million. Since ABC has held the investment for 10 or more years, it may elect to treat the basis as $1.5 million without recognizing any additional gain. If ABC does not make the election, its basis is considered to be $1 million (because the deferred gain that was previously recognized on December 31, 2026, increases basis). Thus, ABC must recognize $500,000 gain.

**Example 5:** Assume the same facts as in the Example 4 above, except that the value of the fund has decreased to $400,000. ABC will not make the fair market value election, and recognizes a $600,000 loss ($400,000 less $1 million previously recognized gain).

**Compliance Note:** The IRS is revising the *2019* Form 1099-B, Proceeds From Broker and Barter Exchange Transactions, to include reporting of dispositions of QOF investments. A QOF should file Form 1099-B for each person who disposed of a QOF investment, even if the QOF is not a broker or a barter exchange. Each disposition must be reported on a separate Form 1099-B. The QOF also should furnish a statement to the person who disposed of the interest in the QOF investment (2019 Instructions for Form 1099-B).

*Deferred gain tax attributes.* Any previously deferred gain included in income (e.g., upon sale of the fund, or in the tax year that includes December 31, 2026) has the same attributes in the tax year of inclusion that it would have had if tax on the gain had not been deferred. The tax attributes include those taken into account by Code Secs. 1(h), 1222, 1256, and any other applicable Code provisions (Proposed Reg. § 1.1400Z-2(a)-1(b)(5)).

**Example 6:** Taxpayer elected to defer $100 of short-term capital gain in 2019. In 2022, the taxpayer sells its interest in the fund and is required to recognize $100 of gain. The gain included in income is short-term capital gain.

**Example 7:** Taxpayer elected to defer $100 of collectibles gain (Code Sec. 1(h)(5)). When included in a later tax year in income, the gain is collectibles gain.

**Example 8:** Taxpayer deferred $100 of capital gain net income from section 1256 contracts in 2019. In 2023, taxpayer sells its interest in the fund and is required to include the $100 deferred gain in gross income. The character of the inclusion is governed by Code Sec. 1256(a)(3), which requires a 40:60 split between short-term and long-term capital gain. Accordingly, $40 of the inclusion is short-term capital gain and $60 of the inclusion is long-term capital gain.

*Fungible interests.* Separate investments providing indistinguishable property rights (such as serial purchases of common stock in a corporation that is a QOF) may be made at different times, or made at the same time with separate gains possessing different attributes (such as different holding periods). If a taxpayer disposes of less than all of its fungible interests (i.e., interests with identical rights) in a QOF, the QOF interests disposed of must be identified using a first-in, first-out (FIFO) method (Proposed Reg. § 1.1400Z-2(a)-1(b)(6)).

The FIFO method determines:

- whether a gain deferral election applies to the investment;
- the attributes of the gain that are subject to a deferral election; and
- the extent, if any, of an increase in the basis of the investment interest that is disposed of.

**Example 9:** In 2018, Taxpayer elects to defer $300 of short-term capital gain by investing in a QOF. In 2020, Taxpayer makes a second election to defer $200 of long-term capital gain by investing in the same fund. The two investments in the same fund are fungible interests, and the price of the interests was the same at the time of the two investments. Taxpayer did not purchase any additional interest in the fund or sell any of its interest in the fund until 2024, when it sold 60 percent of its interest in the fund for a gain. Using the required FIFO method, Taxpayer sold the entire 2018 initial investment in the fund ($300/$500 = 60%). The taxable gain is short-term capital gain (Proposed Reg. § 1.1400Z-2(a)-1(b)(8), Example 4).

**Example 10:** Taxpayer makes the following investments and sales with respect to Q Corporation:

- May 1, 2018—$100 cash in exchange for 100 common shares (when Q is *not* a qualified opportunity fund)
- June 1, 2018—Q becomes a qualified opportunity fund
- December 1, 2018—$500 cash (attributable to short-term capital gain) in exchange for 400 common shares
- December 10, 2018—$1,000 cash (attributable to $300 short term capital gain and $700 long term capital gain) in exchange for 800 common shares
- April 1, 2020—Taxpayer sells 100 common shares
- May 1, 2021—Taxpayer sells 400 common shares

¶145

## NEW LAW EXPLAINED

> Under the FIFO method, the 100 common shares sold on April 1, 2020 are attributable to the May 1, 2018 investment, when Q was not a qualified opportunity fund. The gain is long term capital gain because Taxpayer held the Q common stock for more than 1 year. The 400 common shares sold on May 1, 2021 are associated with the deferral of $500 of short-term capital gain. Thus, the deferred gain that must be included upon sale of the 400 Q common shares is short-term capital gain (Proposed Reg. §1.1400Z-2(a)-1(b)(8), Examples 5 and 6).

If the FIFO method does not provide a complete answer, such as where gains with different attributes are invested in indistinguishable interests at the same time, the taxpayer must use a pro-rata method to determine the character and any other attributes of the gain recognized (Proposed Reg. §1.1400Z-2(a)-1(b)(7)).

> **Example 11:** Assume that Taxpayer in Example 10 above also sold an additional 400 common shares of the fund during 2022. Taxpayer must include in income $500 of deferred gain ((400 shares sold/800 total shares purchased) × $1,000 total purchase price). Under FIFO, these shares are attributable to the December 10, 2018 purchase of 800 shares. Under the pro-rata method, $150 of the inclusion is short-term capital gain ($300 × (400/800)) and $350 is long-term capital gain ($700 × (400/800)) (Proposed Reg. §1.1400Z-2(a)-1(b)(8), Example 7).

*Mixed investment.* If a taxpayer pays more for an investment in a QOF than just the gain from a sale or exchange that it elects to defer, the investment in the QOF is treated as two separate investments. The deferral rules apply only to the portion of the investment for which the taxpayer has elected to defer gain (Code Sec. 1400Z-2(e)(1), as added by the Tax Cuts Act; Proposed Reg. §1.1400Z-2(e)-1(a)(1)).

If a QOF is treated as partnership for federal income tax purposes, deemed contributions of money under Code Sec. 752(a) do not create or increase an investment in the QOF (Proposed Reg. §1.1400Z-2(e)-1(a)(2)). Therefore, a partner's increase in outside basis due to a deemed contribution is not taken into account in determining what portion of the partner's interest is or is not subject to the deferral election (REG-115420-18, Oct. 29, 2018).

*Special rules for partnerships and other passthrough entities.* A partnership can elect to defer recognition of eligible gain by investing in a QOF. Deferred gain is not included in the distributive shares of the partners, and no basis adjustments under Code Sec. 705(a)(1) are made until the deferred gain is recognized (Proposed Reg. §1.1400Z-2(a)-1(c)(1)).

If a partnership does not elect to defer some or all of the gains for which it could make a deferral election, the partnership's treatment of these amounts is unaffected by the fact that it could have deferred the eligible gains. If a partner's distributive share includes such undeferred eligible gain, the partner can elect to defer some or all of the gain. The

## NEW LAW EXPLAINED

gain must be an eligible gain with respect to the partnership, and must not arise from a sale or exchange with a person related to the partner. The 180-day period for the partner's deferral election generally begins on the last day of the partnership tax year in which the partner's allocable share of the partnership's eligible gain is taken into account. However, the partner may elect to treat its 180-day period as the same 180-day period that would apply to the partnership if had the partnership made the deferral election (Proposed Reg. § 1.1400Z-2(a)-1(c)(2)).

---

**Example 12:** On January 17, 2019, a calendar-year partnership realizes a $1,000 capital gain that it decides not to elect to defer. Each of five partners receives a $200 allocation. One of the partners invests $200 in a qualified fund during February 2020. This investment is within the 180-day period for that partner (which begins on December 31, 2019, the last day of the partnership's tax year). Another partner invests $200 in a qualified fund during February 2019. Under the elective rule, this investment is within the 180-day period for that partner (which begins on the January 17, 2019 realization date) (Proposed Reg. § 1.1400Z-2(a)-1(c)(2)(iii)(C), Example).

---

Similar rules apply to an S corporation, a trust, or a decedent's estate that recognizes an eligible gain, or would recognize an eligible gain if it did not elect to defer recognition of the gain, as well as to the entity's shareholders or beneficiaries (Proposed Reg. § 1.1400Z-2(a)-1(c)(3)).

**Establishing and maintaining qualified opportunity funds.** A qualified opportunity fund (QOF) is a corporation or partnership organized for the purpose of investing in qualified opportunity zone property (other than another QOF) that holds at least 90 percent of its assets in such property (Code Sec. 1400Z-2(d)(1), as added by the 2017 Tax Cuts Act). Whether the 90-percent requirement is met is determined by calculating the average of the percentage of qualified zone property held by the fund as measured on the last day of the first six-month period of the fund's tax year and on the last day of the fund's tax year.

*Self-certification of QOFs.* Corporations and partnerships use Form 8996, Qualified Opportunity Fund, to self-certify as a QOF, and to annually report that the QOF meets the 90-percent asset investment standard or to calculate the penalty if it fails to meet the investment standard. The corporation or partnership attaches Form 8996 to its federal return each tax year by the due date (including extension).

The self-certification *must* identify the first tax year that the eligible entity wants to be a QOF, and *may* identify the first month of that tax year that the corporation or partnership wants to be a QOF. If the starting month is not specified, then the first month of the entity's tax year is treated as the month in which QOF status starts. Investments in the eligible entity before the entity's first month as a QOF do not qualify for deferral (Proposed Reg. § 1.1400Z-2(d)-1(a)(1)).

A pre-existing corporation or partnership may certify as a QOF, but the entity must satisfy all generally applicable Code and regulatory requirements, including the requirement that qualified opportunity zone property must be acquired after December 31, 2017 (Proposed Reg. § 1.1400Z-2(d)-1(a)(3)).

**¶145**

## NEW LAW EXPLAINED

**Compliance Note:** A corporation operating as a QOF must also complete question 25 of Form 1120, Schedule K. This question asks whether the corporation is attaching a Form 8996 and, if so, the amount reported on line 13 of Form 8996, relating to the 90-percent asset test and penalty. A partnership operating as a QOF must provide similar information on question 26 of Form 1065, Schedule B.

*Applying 90 percent investment test if QOF status begins after first month of tax year.* If a corporation's or partnership's self-certification as a QOF is first effective for a month that is not the first month of its tax year, then the fund's "first 6-month period of the tax year" in the first year of the QOF's existence means the first six months—each of which is in the tax year, and in each of which the entity is a QOF (Proposed Reg. § 1.1400Z-2(d)-1(a)(2)). Thus, if an entity becomes a QOF in the seventh or later month of a 12-month tax year, the 90-percent test takes into account only the QOF's assets on the last day of the tax year.

The penalty computation under Code Sec. 1400Z-2(f)(1) for failing to meet the 90-percent asset test does not take into account any months before the first month in which the entity is a QOF (Proposed Reg. § 1.1400Z-2(d)-1(a)(2)(ii)).

**Example 13:** Virginia, Joe, Laura, and Ishmael formed a new partnership in January 2018 to operate as a QOF, but the partnership does not receive any investments under a deferral election until July 2018. The partnership has a calendar year tax year. The QOF may choose any month from January through July 2018 to use as its first month for certification. It chooses April 2018. The first six-month period for the QOF asset test ends on September 30. January to March are not considered for purposes of the six-month period.

**Example 14:** The facts are the same as in Example 13 above, except the partnership chooses July 2018 as the certification date. The first six-month period for the QOF assets ends on December 31. The six months from January through June are not considered.

*Qualified opportunity zone property.* Qualified opportunity zone property is:

- qualified opportunity zone stock;
- qualified opportunity zone partnership interest; or
- qualified opportunity zone business property (Code Sec. 1400Z-2(d)(2), as added by the 2017 Tax Cuts Act; Proposed Reg. § 1.1400Z-2(d)-1(c)(1)).

Another QOF is not considered qualified opportunity zone property (Code Sec. 1400Z-2(d)(1)).

*Qualified opportunity zone stock.* Qualified opportunity zone stock is original issue stock in a domestic corporation acquired by the QOF directly or through an underwriter from the corporation after December 31, 2017, solely in exchange for cash (Code Sec. 1400Z-2(d)(2)(B), as added by the 2017 Tax Cuts Act; Proposed Reg. § 1.1400Z-2(d)-1(c)(2)(i)). The corporation must be a qualified opportunity zone busi-

¶145

## NEW LAW EXPLAINED

ness at the time of issue (or was being organized as such if a new corporation) and for substantially all the fund's holding period.

Rules similar to the qualified small business stock redemption rules of Code Sec. 1202(c)(3) apply to qualified opportunity zone stock (Code Sec. 1400Z-2(d)(2)(B)(ii), as added by the 2017 Tax Cuts Act; Proposed Reg. § 1.1400Z-2(d)-1(c)(2)(ii)):

(1) Stock acquired by a QOF is not qualified opportunity zone stock if, at any time during the four-year period beginning two years before the stock is issued, the issuing corporation directly or indirectly purchased any of its stock from the QOF or from a person related to the QOF. A related person is determined under Code Sec. 267(b) or Code Sec. 707(b) without any modification to the definitions provided there. The stock was never qualified opportunity zone stock even if the disqualifying purchase occurs after the issuance (Proposed Reg. § 1.1400Z-2(d)-1(c)(2)(ii)(A)).

(2) Stock is not qualified opportunity zone stock if, at any time during the two-year period beginning one year before the before the stock is issued, the issuing corporation made one or more purchases of its stock with an aggregate value exceeding five percent of the aggregate value of all of its stock as of the beginning of the two-year period. The stock was never qualified opportunity zone stock even if any of the disqualifying purchases occur after the issuance (Proposed Reg. § 1.1400Z-2(d)-1(c)(2)(ii)(B)).

(3) If any transaction is treated under Code Sec. 304(a) as a distribution in redemption of the stock of any corporation, for purposes of rule (1) or (2) above, the corporation is treated as purchasing an amount of its stock equal to the amount that is treated as a Code Sec. 304(a) distribution (Proposed Reg. § 1.1400Z-2(d)-1(c)(2)(ii)(C)).

*Qualified opportunity zone partnership interest.* A qualified opportunity zone partnership interest is any capital or profits interest in a domestic partnership acquired by the QOF after December 31, 2017, from the partnership solely in exchange for cash (Code Sec. 1400Z-2(d)(2)(C), as added by the 2017 Tax Cuts Act). The partnership must be a qualified opportunity zone business at the time of acquisition (or was being organized as such if a new partnership) and for substantially all of the fund's holding period (Proposed Reg. § 1.1400Z-2(d)-1(c)(3)).

*Qualified opportunity zone business property.* Qualified opportunity zone business property is tangible property used in a trade or business of a QOF, if:

(1) the property was purchased, as defined in Code Sec. 179(d)(2), by the QOF after December 31, 2017;

(2) the original use of the property in the qualified opportunity zone begins with the QOF, or the QOF substantially improves the property; and

(3) substantially all of the property's use is in a qualified opportunity zone during substantially all of the QOF's holding period (Code Sec. 1400Z-2(d)(2)(D)(i) and (d)(3)(A)(i), as added by the 2017 Tax Cuts Act; Proposed Reg. § 1.1400Z-2(d)-1(c)(4)).

¶145

## NEW LAW EXPLAINED

**Comment:** Only new or substantially improved property qualifies as opportunity zone business property (General Explanation of Public Law 115-97 (JCS-1-18)).

Tangible property is "substantially improved" only if, during the 30-month period beginning after its acquisition, additions to basis with respect to the property in the hands of the QOF exceed its adjusted basis at the beginning of the 30-month period in the QOF's hands (Code Sec. 1400Z-2(d)(2)(D)(ii), as added by the 2017 Tax Cuts Act). If a QOF purchases a building located on land wholly within a qualified opportunity zone, only the adjusted basis of the building is taken into account. The QOF is not required to separately substantially improve the land (Proposed Reg. §1.1400Z-2(d)-1(c)(8)).

Additional IRS guidance regarding purchases of existing buildings and land provides:

(1) If a QOF purchases an existing building on land located wholly within a qualified opportunity zone, the original use of the building is *not* considered to have commenced with the fund. Further, the requirement that the original use of tangible property in the qualified opportunity zone must commence with a QOF does not apply to the land on which the building is located.

(2) If a QOF purchases a building wholly within a qualified opportunity zone, a substantial improvement to the building is measured by the QOF's additions to the adjusted basis of the building, not by additions to the adjusted basis in the building and the land.

(3) Measuring a substantial improvement to the building by additions to the QOF's adjusted basis in the building does not require the fund to substantially improve the land on which the building is located (Rev. Rul. 2018-29).

*Qualified opportunity zone business.* A qualified opportunity zone business is a trade or business in which substantially all (70 percent or more) of the tangible property owned or leased by the trade or business is qualified opportunity zone business property (Code Sec. 1400Z-2(d)(3)(A), as added by the Tax Cuts and Jobs Act of 2017; Proposed Reg. §1.1400Z-2(d)-1(d)(1)). For this purpose, qualified opportunity zone business property is determined in the same manner as under Code Sec. 1400Z-2(d)(2)(D), except that the term "qualified opportunity zone business" is substituted for "qualified opportunity fund." The trade or business must also satisfy the requirements as an enterprise zone business under Code Sec. 1397C(b)(2), (4) and (8). In addition, the types of businesses described in Code Sec. 144(c)(6)(B) cannot qualify as qualified opportunity zone businesses (Code Sec. 1400Z-2(d)(3)(A)(ii) and (iii), as added by the 2017 Tax Cuts Act; Proposed Reg. §1.1400Z-2(d)-1(d)(1)).

**Comment:** The following trades or businesses *cannot* be a qualified opportunity zone business:

- private or commercial golf course;
- country club;
- massage parlor;

## NEW LAW EXPLAINED

- hot tub facility;
- suntan facility;
- racetrack or other gambling facility;
- liquor store (Proposed Reg. § 1.1400Z-2(d)-1(d)(6)).

Under a special rule, if tangible property ceases to be qualified opportunity zone business property, it will continue to be treated as such for the lesser of (1) five years after the date it ceases to be qualified opportunity zone business property or (2) the date it is no longer held by the qualified opportunity zone business (Code Sec. 1400Z-2(d)(3)(B), as added by the 2017 Tax Cuts Act).

*"Substantially all" requirement—valuation of assets.* The following rules apply for determining whether substantially all (70 percent or more) of the tangible property owned or leased by a trade or business is qualified opportunity zone business property (Proposed Reg. § 1.1400Z-2(d)-1(d)(3)).

If the corporation or partnership (entity) that is a qualified opportunity zone business has an applicable financial statement (AFS) as defined in Reg. § 1.475(a)-4(h), then the value of each asset reported on the entity's AFS for the relevant reporting period is used for determining whether a trade or business of the entity satisfies the 70-percent requirement (Proposed Reg. § 1.1400Z-2(d)-1(d)(3)(ii)(A)).

If the entity *does not have* an AFS, a taxpayer that holds an equity interest in the entity and has self-certified as a QOF may value the entity's assets using the same methodology that the taxpayer uses for determining its own compliance with the 90-percent asset requirement of Code Sec. 1400Z-2(d)(1) (the "compliance methodology") provided that no other equity holder in the entity is a Five-Percent Zone Taxpayer (Proposed Reg. § 1.1400Z-2(d)-1(d)(3)(ii)(B)).

If two or more taxpayers that have self-certified as QOFs hold equity interests in an entity without an AFS, and at least one of them is a Five-Percent Zone Taxpayer, then the values of the entity's assets may be calculated using the compliance methodology that both is used by a Five-Percent Zone Taxpayer and produces the highest percentage of qualified opportunity zone business property for the entity (Proposed Reg. § 1.1400Z-2(d)-1(d)(3)(ii)(B)).

A "Five-Percent Zone Taxpayer" is a taxpayer that:

(1) has self-certified as a QOF; and

(2) holds stock in the entity (if it is a corporation) representing at least five percent in voting rights and value, or holds an interest in the entity (if it is a partnership) of at least five percent in the entity's profits and capital (Proposed Reg. § 1.1400Z-2(d)-1(d)(3)(ii)(C)).

---

**Example 15:** ABC corporation conducts a trade or business. Taxpayer X holds 94% of the ABC stock, and Taxpayer Y holds the remaining 6% of that stock. Therefore, X an Y are both Five Percent Zone Taxpayers. Assuming ABC does not have an AFS, whether ABC is conducting a qualified opportunity zone

---

## NEW LAW EXPLAINED

> business may be determined by using the compliance methodology that X or Y uses for purposes of satisfying the 90-percent asset test for QOFs.

---

**Example 16:** Assume X and Y from Example 15 above use different compliance methodologies to satisfy the 90-percent asset test. Under X's compliance methodology (which is based on X's AFS), 65% of the tangible property owned or leased by ABC's trade or business is qualified opportunity zone business property. Under Y's compliance methodology (which is based on Y's cost), 73% of the tangible property owned or leased by ABC's trade or business is qualified opportunity zone business property. Because Y's compliance methodology would produce the higher percentage of qualified opportunity zone business property for ABC (73%), both X and Y may use Y's compliance methodology to value ABC's owned or leased tangible property. If ABC's trade or business satisfies all additional requirements, the trade or business is a qualified opportunity zone business, and stock in ABC is qualified opportunity zone stock in the hands of a taxpayer that has self-certified as a QOF.

---

**Comment:** The 70-percent requirement gives QOFs an incentive to invest in a qualified opportunity zone business, rather than directly owning qualified opportunity zone business property. For example, suppose a QOF with $10 million in cash plans to invest 100 percent of cash in real property. If it held the real property directly, then at least $9 million (90 percent) of the property must be located within an opportunity zone to satisfy the 90-percent asset test for the QOF. If the QOF instead invests in a subsidiary that then holds real property, only $7 million (70 percent) of the property must be located within an opportunity zone. In addition, if the QOF invested only $9 million into the subsidiary, which then held 70 percent of its property within an opportunity zone, the investors in the QOF could receive the statutory tax benefits while investing only $6.3 million (63 percent) of its assets within a qualified opportunity zone (REG-115420-18, Oct. 29, 2018).

*Qualified opportunity zone business property of a qualified opportunity zone business.* Qualified opportunity zone business property of a qualified opportunity zone business is defined in the same way as is qualified opportunity zone business property of a QOF under Code Sec. 1400Z-2(d)(2)(D), except that the term "qualified opportunity zone business" is substituted for "qualified opportunity fund" (Code Sec. 1400Z-2(d)(3)(A)(i)).

Thus, qualified opportunity zone business property of a qualified opportunity zone business is tangible property used in a trade or business of the qualified business if:

(1) the property was purchased, as defined in Code Sec. 179(d)(2), by the business after December 31, 2017;

(2) the original use of the property in the qualified opportunity zone begins with the business, or the business substantially improves the property; and

## NEW LAW EXPLAINED

(3) substantially all of the property's use is in a qualified opportunity zone during substantially all of the business's holding period for the property (Code Sec. 1400Z-2(d)(3)(A)(i), as added by the 2017 Tax Cuts Act; Proposed Reg. § 1.1400Z-2(d)-1(d)(2)).

Tangible property is "substantially improved" by a qualified opportunity zone business only if, during any 30-month period beginning after the acquisition of the property, the amount of additions to the property's basis in the hands of the business exceeds the adjusted basis of the property at the beginning of the 30-month period in the business's hands. If a business purchases a building located on land wholly within a qualified opportunity zone, only the adjusted basis of the building is taken into account. The business is not required to separately substantially improve the land (Proposed Reg. § 1.1400Z-2(d)-1(d)(4); Rev. Rul. 2018-29).

*Section 1397C requirements.* To be a qualified opportunity zone business, a trade or business must, among other things, satisfy certain requirements of an enterprise zone business under Code Sec. 1397C (Code Sec. 1400Z-2(d)(3)(A)(ii), as added by the 2017 Tax Cuts Act; Proposed Reg. § 1.1400Z-2(d)-1(d)(1)(ii)). Thus, a qualified opportunity zone business must derive at least 50 percent of its gross income from the active conduct of a trade or business in the qualified opportunity zone (Proposed Reg. § 1.1400Z-2(d)-1(d)(5)(i); Code Sec. 1397C(b)(2)). Gross income derived from amounts treated as reasonable working capital under the safe harbor discussed below is counted toward the 50-percent requirement (Proposed Reg. § 1.1400Z-2(d)-1(d)(5)(v)).

In addition, a substantial portion of intangible property of an opportunity zone business must be used in the activity conduct of a zone business (Proposed Reg. § 1.1400Z-2(d)-1(d)(5)(ii); Code Sec. 1397C(b)(4)). This requirement is met during any period that the safe harbor for working capital described below applies (Proposed Reg. § 1.1400Z-2(d)-1(d)(5)(vi)).

*Nonqualified financial property limitation, and safe harbor.* In general, less than five percent of the aggregate adjusted basis of a qualified opportunity zone business may be attributable to nonqualified financial property. Nonqualified financial property does not include reasonable amounts of working capital held in cash, cash equivalents, or debt instruments with a term of 18 months or less (Proposed Reg. § 1.1400Z-2(d)-1(d)(5)(iii); Code Sec. 1397C(b)(8)).

A working capital safe harbor allows a qualified opportunity zone business to hold cash, cash equivalents, or debt instruments for up to 31 months. The safe harbor is satisfied if:

(1) A written document designates the amounts for the acquisition, construction, or substantial improvement of tangible property in a qualified opportunity zone;

(2) A written schedule consistent with the ordinary start-up of a trade or business requires the working capital assets to be spent within 31 months of receipt by the business; and

(3) The working capital is actually spent in a manner that is substantially consistent with the acquisition, construction, or substantial improvement of tangible property (Proposed Reg. § 1.1400Z-2(d)-1(d)(5)(iv)).

**¶145**

# NEW LAW EXPLAINED

If the working capital safe harbor applies and the tangible property on which the safe-harbor working capital will be spent is expected to satisfy the definition of qualified opportunity zone business property, then the tangible property to be acquired is not treated as failing to satisfy the qualified opportunity zone property requirements solely because the scheduled expenditure of the working capital is not yet complete (Proposed Reg. § 1.1400Z-2(d)-1(d)(5)(vii)).

> **Comment:** The safe harbor is provided because developing a new business or the construction or rehabilitation of real estate may take longer than the six-month rule under the 90-percent investment test that applies to the first year of a QOF. As discussed above, the six-month rule requires that 90 percent of the QOF's assets be held in qualified opportunity zone property, determined by the average of the percentage of qualified opportunity zone property held in the fund on the last day of the first six-month period of the tax year of the fund, and on the last day of the tax year of the fund. Also, the safe harbor minimizes the distortion that may arise between purchasing and substantially rehabilitating existing property versus constructing new property, as the time frames are similar: 30 months for rehabilitation, and 31 months for new construction (REG-115420-18, Oct. 29, 2018).

**Example 17:** In 2019, John realized $10 million of capital gains, and within 180 days invested $10 million in a corporation that is a QOF. The fund immediately acquired an interest in partnership P, solely in exchange for $10 million of cash. P immediately placed the $10 million in working capital assets, where it remained until it was used.

P had written plans to acquire land in a qualified opportunity zone on which it planned to construct a commercial building. Of the $10 million, $1 million was dedicated to the land purchase, $8 million to the construction of the building, and $1 million to ancillary project costs. The written plans provided for purchase of the land within a month of receipt of the $10 million from the QOF, and for the remaining $9 million to be spent within the next 30 months on construction and ancillary expenditures. All $10 million was spent on schedule.

During P's tax years that overlap with the first 31-month period, P had no gross income other than that derived from the $10 million working capital assets. Prior to completion of the building, P's only assets were the land it purchased, the unspent amounts in the working capital assets, and its work in process as the building was constructed.

*Conclusion:* The QOF's interest in partnership P is a qualified opportunity zone partnership interest for purposes of satisfying the test that requires a qualifying fund to hold 90 percent of its assets in qualified opportunity zone property.

*Safe harbor satisfied:* The three safe harbor requirements are met because:

(1) P had a written plan to spend the $10 received from the QOF for the acquisition, construction, and/or substantial improvement of tangible property in a qualified opportunity zone;

**NEW LAW EXPLAINED**

> (2) P had a written schedule consistent with the ordinary start-up for a business for the expenditure of the working capital assets within 31 months; and
>
> (3) P's working capital assets were actually used in a manner that was substantially consistent with its written plan and the ordinary start-up of a business.
>
> *50-percent test satisfied:* Because P had no other gross income during the 31 months at issue other than the $10 million contribution and any income earned on that amount, 100 percent of P's gross income during that time is treated as derived from an active trade or business in the qualified opportunity zone for purposes of satisfying the test that requires a qualified opportunity zone business to derive at least 50 percent of its gross income from the active conduct of a trade or business in the qualified opportunity zone.
>
> *Use of substantial portion of intangible property requirement satisfied:* During the period of land acquisition and building construction, a substantial portion of P's intangible property is treated as being used in the active conduct of a trade or business in the qualified opportunity zone. Under Proposed Reg. § 1.1400Z-2(d)-1(d)(5)(vi), this requirement is met during any period that the safe harbor for working capital applies (Proposed Reg. § 1.1400Z-2(d)-1(d)(5)(viii), *Example*).

*QOF and issuing entity must be organized in U.S. or possession.* A partnership or corporation that is not organized in one of the United States, the District of Columbia, or a U.S. possession is ineligible to be a QOF. A partnership or corporation organized in a U.S. possession is eligible to be a QOF only if it is organized for the purpose of investing in qualified opportunity zone property that relates to a trade or business operated in the possession where it is organized (Proposed Reg. § 1.1400Z-2(d)-1(e)). For example, a partnership organized in Puerto Rico must invest in a qualified opportunity zone property of a business operated in Puerto Rico.

Similarly, an equity interest in a corporation or partnership organized outside of the United States, the District of Columbia, or a U.S. possession is not qualified opportunity zone stock or a qualified opportunity zone partnership interest. An equity interest in a corporation or partnership organized in a U.S. possession is qualified opportunity zone stock or a qualified opportunity zone partnership interest only if the corporation or partnership conducts a qualified opportunity zone business in the possession where it is organized; the corporation or partnership is treated as satisfying the "domestic" requirement of Code Sec. 1400Z-2(d)(2)(B)(i) or (C)(i) (Proposed Reg. § 1.1400Z-2(d)-1(e)).

*Penalty for failing 90-percent asset test.* A QOF must pay a penalty for each month it fails to hold at least 90 percent of its assets in qualified opportunity zone property (Code Sec. 1400Z-2(f)(1), as added by the 2017 Tax Cuts Act), unless the failure is due to reasonable cause (Code Sec. 1400Z-2(f)(3), as added by the 2017 Tax Cuts Act). The penalty amount is:

## NEW LAW EXPLAINED

- the excess of 90 percent of its aggregated assets over the aggregate amount of qualified opportunity property held;
- multiplied by the Code Sec. 6621(a)(2) underpayment rate for that month.

A QOF that is organized as a partnership must take the penalty into account proportionally as part of each partner's distributive share (Code Sec. 1400Z-2(f)(2), as added by the 2017 Tax Cuts Act).

> **Example 18:** Ninety percent of all assets of BuildFund Partnership, a QOF, is qualified opportunity zone property. The assets cease to be qualified opportunity zone property as of May 15, 2020. BuildFund must pay a penalty for each month that more than 10 percent of the total amount of its assets are not qualified opportunity zone property. For example, assume BuildFund had total assets worth $1 million, 80 percent of which were qualified opportunity property for a six-month period before once again meeting the 90 percent threshold. Assuming an underpayment penalty rate for those months of 4 percent, BuildFund must pay a penalty of $4,000 (($900,000 − $800,000) × 4%) each month for six months.

**Other applicable rules.** If the taxpayer is a decedent and the inclusion of the deferred gain is not properly included in his or her gross income, the amount is included in the estate's gross income as income in respect of a decedent under Code Sec. 691 (Code Sec. 1400Z-2(e)(3), as added by the 2017 Tax Cuts Act).

The IRS is authorized to issue regulations to carry out the purposes of Code Sec. 1400Z-2, including rules:

- for QOF certification;
- to ensure QOFs have reasonable time to reinvest the return of capital from investments in qualified opportunity zone stock and qualified opportunity zone partnership interests, and reinvest proceeds from the disposition of qualified opportunity zone property; and
- to prevent abuse (Code Sec. 1400Z-2(e)(4), as added by the 2017 Tax Cuts Act).

**Comment:** The IRS has issued proposed regulations, which are discussed throughout this explanation. They provide guidance under Code Sec. 1400Z-2 relating to gains that may be deferred as a result of a taxpayer's investment in a QOF, as well as specific rules that apply to QOFs. The proposed regulations would be effective on or after the publication date of final regulations. However, a taxpayer may generally rely on the proposed regulations, provided they are applied in their entirety and in a consistent manner (REG-115420-18, Oct. 29, 2018).

**Comment:** Congress intended for the QOF certification process to be done by the Community Development Financial Institutions Fund (CDFI Fund) in a manner similar to the process in place for allocating the new markets tax credit (Conference Report on H.R. 1, Tax Cuts and Jobs Act (H. Rept. 115-466)).

## NEW LAW EXPLAINED

The CDFI Fund maintains a webpage of Opportunity Zones Resources, at https://www.cdfifund.gov/Pages/Opportunity-Zones.aspx.

**Reports to Congress.** Beginning December 22, 2022, the IRS or its delegate must submit an annual report to Congress on the opportunity zone incentives. The report is to include: (a) an assessment of investments held by the QOF at both the national and state levels; (b) the number of QOFs; (c) the amount of assets held by class; (d) the percentage of designated qualified opportunity zone census tracts that received QOF investments; and (e) an assessment of the impact of the investments on economic indicators such as job creation, poverty reduction and new businesses (Conference Report on H.R. 1, Tax Cuts and Jobs Act (H. Rept. 115-466)).

▶ **Effective date.** The amendments adding Code Secs. 1400Z-1 and 1400Z-2 apply on December 22, 2017, the date of enactment of the Tax Cuts and Jobs Act (Act Sec. 13823(d) of the Tax Cuts and Jobs Act (P.L. 115-97)). The further amendments made to Code Sec. 1400Z-1(b) and (d)(1) apply on February 9, 2018, the date of enactment of the Bipartisan Budget Act of 2018 (P.L. 115-123)).

— Act Sec. 13823(a) and (c) of the Tax Cuts and Jobs Act (P.L. 115-97), adding Code Secs. 1400Z-1 and 1400Z-2;

— Act Sec. 13823(b), adding Code Sec. 1016(a)(38);

— Act Sec. 13823(d), providing the effective date;

— Act Sec. 41115(a) of the Bipartisan Budget Act of 2018 (P.L. 115-123), adding Code Sec. 1400Z-1(b)(3);

— Act Sec. 41115(b), amending Code Sec. 1400Z-1(d)(1).

# Deductions, Exclusions, and Credits for Individuals

2

# STANDARD DEDUCTION AND PERSONAL EXEMPTIONS

## ¶205  Standard Deduction for Individuals

### SUMMARY OF NEW LAW

The basic standard deduction amounts for individuals are temporarily increased for tax years 2018 through 2025. The standard deductions amounts for 2018 are: $24,000 for married individuals filing jointly (including surviving spouses), $18,000 for heads of household, and $12,000 for single individuals and married individuals filing separately. The increased amounts are adjusted annually for inflation for tax years beginning after 2018 and before 2026.

### BACKGROUND

An individual taxpayer who does not elect to itemize deductions computes taxable income by subtracting from adjusted gross income (AGI) the standard deduction, as well as the deduction for personal exemptions. Taxpayers have a choice of itemizing deductions or claiming the standard deduction, whichever will result in a higher deduction. The standard deduction amount is the sum of the basic standard deduction, plus an additional standard deduction amount for aged (at least 65) and/or blind taxpayers, if applicable (Code Sec. 63(c)).

The basic standard deduction amount varies according to the taxpayer's filing status and is adjusted annually for inflation. For 2017, the amount of the basic standard deduction is $12,700 for married individuals filing joint returns and surviving spouses, $6,350 for single individuals and married individuals filing separate returns, and $9,350 for heads of households (Rev. Proc. 2016-55). In the case of a dependent for whom a deduction for a personal exemption is allowed to another taxpayer, the standard deduction for 2017 may not exceed the greater of $1,050 or the sum of $350 plus the individual's earned income, up to the applicable standard deduction amount for single taxpayers ($6,350 for 2017).

The additional standard deduction amounts for 2017 for the aged and/or blind is $1,250 for married individuals, whether filing jointly or separately, and surviving spouses, and $1,550 for unmarried individuals, whether filing as single or as head of household. These amount increase to $1,300 and $1,600, respectively, for 2018. (Code Sec. 63(f); Rev. Procs. 2016-55 and 2017-58). The additional standard deduction amounts are also adjusted annually for inflation.

### NEW LAW EXPLAINED

**Basic standard deduction temporarily increased.**—Effective for tax years beginning after December 31, 2017, and before January 1, 2026, the basic standard deduction amounts are increased to:

## NEW LAW EXPLAINED

- $24,000 for married individuals filing jointly (including surviving spouses);
- $18,000 for heads of household;
- $12,000 for single individuals and married individuals filing separately (Code Sec. 63(c)(7)(A), as added by the Tax Cuts and Jobs Act (P.L. 115-97)).

These dollar amounts are adjusted annually for inflation for tax years beginning after 2018 and before 2026 using the Chained Consumer Price Index for All Urban Consumers (C-CPI-U) in the cost-of-living adjustment (see ¶125) (Code Sec. 63(c)(7)(B), as added by the 2017 Tax Cuts Act). The standard deduction amount for a dependent, as well as the additional standard deduction amounts for the aged and/or blind, are not affected by the law and are not temporarily increased.

**Comment:** The standard deduction amount for a dependent, as well as the additional standard deduction amounts for the aged and/or blind are adjusted for inflation. However, these amounts are adjusted for inflation after 2017 using chained chained-CPI rather than averaged CPI (Code Sec. 63(c)(4), as amended by the 2017 Tax Cuts Act). The inflation adjusted amounts for the standard deduction for a dependent and additional standard deduction for the aged and/or blind in 2018 did not change as a result of the new methodology. For tax years beginning in 2018, the additional standard deduction amount for married individuals or surviving spouses who are elderly and/or blind is $1,300 for each condition. If the taxpayer is unmarried or a head of household (but not a surviving spouse), the additional standard deduction is $1,600 for each condition. For tax years beginning in 2018, the standard deduction amount for an individual who may be claimed as a dependent by another taxpayer cannot exceed the greater of (1) $1,050, or (2) the sum of $350 and the individual's earned income (Rev. Proc. 2018-18, modifying and superseding Rev. Proc. 2017-58). For tax years beginning in 2019, the standard deduction amount is $24,400 for married filing jointly and surviving spouse; $18,350 for head of household; and $12,200 for single and married filing separately. For tax years beginning in 2019, the additional standard deduction amount for married individuals or surviving spouses who are elderly and/or blind is $1,300 for each condition. If the taxpayer is unmarried or a head of household (but not a surviving spouse), the additional standard deduction is $1,650 for each condition. For tax years beginning in 2019, the standard deduction amount for an individual who may be claimed as a dependent by another taxpayer cannot exceed the greater of (1) $1,100, or (2) the sum of $350 and the individual's earned income (Rev. Proc. 2018-57).

**Net disaster losses.** An individual may claim an additional standard deduction amount for his or her net disaster loss in tax years beginning in 2016 and 2017 (Act Sec. 11028(c) of the 2017 Tax Cuts Act). The additional standard deduction is also allowed in computing alternative minimum tax liability (AMT). For this purpose, a net disaster loss is the qualified disaster-related personal casualty losses, over any personal casualty gains. A qualified disaster-related personal loss means a personal casualty loss arising in a disaster area after on or after January 1, 2016, that is attributable to a federally declared disaster. See also ¶235 for a discussion of additional relief for claiming casualty loss deductions related to net disaster losses in 2016 and 2017.

## NEW LAW EXPLAINED

▶ **Effective date.** The amendment made by this section applies to tax years beginning after December 31, 2017 (Act Sec. 11021(b) of the Tax Cuts and Jobs Act (P.L. 115-97)). The special rules related to personal casualty losses related to net disaster losses for 2016 and 2017 are effective on December 22, 2017, the date of enactment.

**Other than inflation adjusted amounts for 2019, no significant guidance related to this provision has been issued.**

— Act Sec. 11021(a) of the Tax Cuts and Jobs Act (P.L. 115-97), adding Code Sec. 63(c)(7);

— Act Sec. 11028(a) and (c);

— Act Sec. 11021(b), providing the effective date.

## ¶210 Personal and Dependency Exemptions

### SUMMARY OF NEW LAW

The deduction for personal and dependency exemptions is temporarily repealed for tax years 2018 through 2025.

### BACKGROUND

An individual, in determining taxable income, may reduce adjusted gross income (AGI) by claiming a personal exemption deduction and an exemption deduction for each person he or she claims as a dependent on his or her tax return (Code Sec. 151). A dependent is defined as an individual who is a qualifying child or qualifying relative of the taxpayer for the year (Code Secs. 151(c) and 152; Prop. Reg. §1.152-1(a)). However, anyone claimed as a dependent by another taxpayer is barred from claiming another individual as a dependent. Thus, a married individual cannot be claimed as a dependent if he or she files a joint return with his or her spouse for the same tax year, unless the return was solely filed as a claim for refund of estimated or withheld taxes.

The amount of a personal exemption (for the taxpayer and spouse) and of a dependency exemption (for each of the taxpayer's dependents) is adjusted annually for inflation. The exemption amount is $4,050 for 2017 (originally set to increase to $4,150 for 2018) (Code Sec. 151(d); Rev. Procs. 2016-55 and 2017-58). An individual whose AGI exceeds an applicable threshold amount based on filing status must reduce the amount of their otherwise allowable exemption deduction (Code Sec. 151(d)(3)). The applicable threshold amounts for 2017 are: $313,800 for married individuals filing a joint return and surviving spouses; $287,650 for heads of households; $261,500 for single individuals and $156,900 for married individuals filing a separate return. The applicable threshold amounts for 2018 were scheduled to be: $320,000 for married individuals filing a joint return and surviving spouses; $293,350 for heads of households; $266,700 for single individuals and $160,000 for married individuals filing a separate return.

## BACKGROUND

**Estates and trusts.** In lieu of the deduction for personal exemptions, an estate is allowed a deduction of $600, and a trust is generally allowed a deduction of either $100 or, if required to distribute all its income currently, $300 (Code Sec. 642(b)(1) and (2)). An amount equal to the personal exemption of an individual is allowed in the case of a qualified disability trust (Code Sec. 642(b)(2)(C)).

**Withholding requirements.** The amount of tax required to be withheld by an employer from an employee's wages is partly based on the number of withholding exemptions or allowance the employee claims on his or her Form W-4. The amount of each withholding exemption is equal to the amount of one personal exemption prorated to the payroll period. An employee is entitled to the following withholding exemptions: (1) an exemption for the individual, unless he or she is allowed to be claimed as a dependent by another person; (2) an exemption to which the employee's spouse would be entitled, unless that spouse files a Form W-4 for that tax year claiming an exemption for his or her self; (3) an exemption for each dependent, so long as the employee's spouse does not also claim a withholding exemption for the same dependent on a Form W-4; (4) additional withholding allowances (taking into account estimated itemized deductions, estimated tax credits, and any additional deductions provided by the IRS); and (5) a standard deduction allowance (Code Sec. 3402(f)).

**Levies.** An exemption from an IRS levy is provided for the amount of an individual's wages or salary for personal services that is equal to the sum of the standard deduction and the total value of the personal exemptions allowed to the individual, divided by the number of times the taxpayer is paid, except for the first 15 percent (Code Sec. 6334(d)).

## NEW LAW EXPLAINED

**Temporary repeal of the personal and dependency exemption deduction.**—The deduction for personal and dependency exemptions by an individual taxpayer is temporarily repealed for tax years beginning after December 31, 2017, and before January 1, 2026 (Code Sec. 151(d)(5), as added by the Tax Cuts and Jobs Act (P.L. 115-97)).

> **Comment:** The rules for determining the filing threshold for an individual to file a federal income tax return are modified for tax years beginning in 2018 through 2025 as a result of the temporary repeal of the personal exemption deduction and the increase in the standard deduction (see ¶205). See ¶120 for discussion of filing thresholds for tax years beginning after 2017.

**Personal exemption amounts remain in effect for other purposes.** For certain provisions of the Code that reference the dependency deduction for other purposes, such as eligibility for head-of-household filing status, the $500 dependent credit, and the definition of "qualifying relative," the reduction of the exemption amount to zero is not taken into account (Notice 2018-70). Instead, the exemption amount remains $4,150 for 2018 (Rev. Proc. 2017-58). The inflation-adjusted exemption amount for these purposes in 2019 is $4,200 (Rev. Proc. 2018-57).

¶210

## NEW LAW EXPLAINED

**Health insurance premium assistance credit.** For purposes of the premium tax credit and the individual shared responsibility provision, a taxpayer is considered to have claimed a personal exemption deduction for himself or herself for a tax year if the taxpayer files an income tax return for the year and does not qualify as a dependent of another taxpayer for the year. A taxpayer is considered to have claimed a personal exemption deduction for an individual other than the taxpayer if the taxpayer is allowed a personal exemption deduction for the individual and lists the individual's name and taxpayer identification number on the taxpayer's return for the year (Notice 2018-84).

**Qualified disability trusts.** The annual amount a qualified disability trust is allowed to deduct for tax years beginning after December 31, 2017, and before January 1, 2026, when the personal exemption is repealed and effectively zero, is modified (Code Sec. 642(b)(2)(C)(iii), as added by the 2017 Tax Cuts Act). The amount is $4,150 for 2018 (Rev. Proc. 2017-58). The inflation-adjusted exemption amount for these purposes in 2019 is $4,200 (Rev. Proc. 2018-57).

**Withholding requirements.** The deduction for personal exemptions, as applied for withholding purposes, is temporarily repealed for tax years beginning after December 31, 2017, and before January 1, 2026 (Code Sec. 3402(a)(2), as amended by the 2017 Tax Cuts Act; Act Sec. 11041(f)(2) of the 2017 Tax Cuts Act). Release of the 2018 Form W-4 was delayed until February 28, 2018, to reflect changes made by the 2017 Tax Cuts Act. The IRS provided relief for employers and employees affected by the delayed release of the 2018 Form W-4 (Notice 2018-14). In late 2018, the IRS announced that implementation of a significantly redesigned Form W-4 would be postponed until 2020. The IRS subsequently released a 2019 Form W-4 that is substantially similar to the 2018 form. The IRS and the Treasury Department intend to update the withholding regulations to explicitly allow employees to use the IRS withholding calculator (www.irs.gov/W4App) or IRS Publication 505, Tax Withholding and Estimated Tax, to determine their Form W-4 entries, instead of having to complete certain schedules included with the Form W-4. However, the regulations are expected to provide that an employee cannot use the withholding calculator if the calculator's instructions state that it should not be used due to his or her individual tax situation. The employee will need to use Publication 505 instead (Notice 2018-92).

**Levies.** The amount exempted from an IRS levy on an individual's wages or salary for personal services for tax years beginning after December 31, 2017, and before January 1, 2026, is modified (Code Sec. 6334(d)(4), as added by the 2017 Tax Cuts Act). For those years, when the personal exemption is temporarily repealed and effectively zero, the levy exemption is equal to the sum of the standard deduction and the total of $4,150 multiplied by the number of the individual's dependents for the tax year in which the levy occurs, divided by the number of times the taxpayer is paid, except for the first 15 percent. The $4,150 amount is indexed annually for inflation after 2018 using the Chained Consumer Price Index for All Urban Consumers (C-CPI-U) in the cost-of-living adjustment (see ¶125). For 2019, the exempt amount is $4,200 (Rev. Proc. 2018-57).

¶210

## NEW LAW EXPLAINED

▶ **Effective date.** The amendments made by this section apply to tax years beginning after December 31, 2017 (Act Sec. 11041(f) of the Tax Cuts and Jobs Act (P.L. 115-97)).

— Act Sec. 11041(a) of the Tax Cuts and Jobs Act (P.L. 115-97), amending Code Sec. 151(d) and adding Code Sec. 151(d)(5);

— Act Sec. 11041(b), adding Code Sec. 642(b)(2)(C)(iii);

— Act Sec. 11041(c), striking Code Sec. 3401(e) and amending Code Sec. 3402(a), (b), (f), (g), (l), (m), (n), and 3405(a);

— Act Sec. 11041(d) adding Code Sec. 6334(d)(4);

— Act Sec. 11041(f), providing the effective dates.

# ITEMIZED DEDUCTIONS

## ¶215 Deduction of State and Local Taxes by Individuals

### SUMMARY OF NEW LAW

The itemized deduction by individuals for state, local, and foreign property taxes, and state and local income taxes and general sales taxes paid or accrued during the tax year is limited for tax years 2018 through 2025. An individual cannot deduct foreign real property taxes, but may still claim an itemized deduction of up to $10,000 ($5,000 for married taxpayer filing a separate return) for state and local property taxes, income taxes, and general sales taxes paid or accrued in the tax year. An individual may also still claim a deduction for state and local real or personal property taxes paid or accrued in carrying on a trade or business or income-producing activity.

### BACKGROUND

Taxes paid or accrued by an individual during the tax year that are not directly connected with a trade or business, or with property held for the production of income, may be deducted only as an itemized deduction on Schedule A of Form 1040 for federal income tax purposes. This includes: (1) state, local, and foreign income taxes; (2) state and local sales taxes in lieu of deducting state and local income taxes; (3) state, local, and foreign real property taxes; (4) state and local personal property taxes; and (5) federal and state generation-skipping transfer (GST) taxes imposed on income distributions (Code Sec. 164). A self-employed individual may deduct 50 percent of his or her federal self-employment taxes as an above-the-line deduction in computing adjusted gross income (AGI).

State, local, and foreign taxes directly attributable to a trade or business, or imposed on property held for the production of income are deductible either as ordinary and

## BACKGROUND

necessary business expenses or investment expenses. This includes income taxes, property taxes, sales taxes, and employment taxes, but deductions are expressly not allowed for most types of federal taxes, estate and inheritance taxes, and real estate taxes imposed on another taxpayer. Taxes that are otherwise deductible as business or income-producing expenses cannot be deducted but must be capitalized if paid or accrued in connection with the acquisition or disposition of property.

## NEW LAW EXPLAINED

**Limitation of itemized deduction for certain income, property, and sales taxes.—** The deduction for taxes paid or accrued by an individual during the tax year that are not directly connected with a trade or business, or with property held for the production of income, is limited for tax years beginning after December 31, 2017, and before January 1, 2026. Specifically, for tax years 2018 through 2025, an individual may claim an itemized deduction on Schedule A of up to only $10,000 ($5,000 for married taxpayer filing a separate return) for: (1) state and local real property taxes; (2) state and local personal property taxes; and (3) state and local income taxes, as well as state and local sales taxes deducted in lieu of state and local income taxes (Code Sec. 164(b)(6), as added by the Tax Cuts and Jobs Act (P.L. 115-97)).

For purposes of applying the dollar limit above, if an individual prepays before 2018 a state or local income tax imposed for a tax year beginning after 2017, the payment is treated as paid on the last day of the tax year for which the tax is imposed (Code Sec. 164(b)(6), as amended by the 2017 Tax Cuts Act). Thus, an individual cannot claim an itemized deduction in 2017 on a prepayment of income tax for a future tax year in order to avoid the dollar limit for tax years 2018 through 2025 (Conference Report on H.R. 1, Tax Cuts and Jobs Act (H. Rept. 115-466)).

> **Comment:** The prepayment restriction specifically applies to state or local income taxes; it does not refer to state and local property taxes. The IRS has issued guidance that a deduction for the prepayment of state and local real property taxes in 2017 depends on whether the taxes are assessed under state and local law prior to 2018 (IRS News Release IR-2017-210). If the taxes are assessed and prepaid in 2017, then the taxpayer may deduct the prepayments in 2017. On the other hand, prepayments of property taxes in 2017 that are not assessed until 2018, may not be deducted in 2017.

> **Example 1:** County A assesses property tax on July 1, 2017, for the period July 1, 2017, through June 30, 2018. On July 31, 2017, it sends notices of assessment to residents and bills the tax in two installments due September 30, 2017, and January 31, 2018. If a taxpayer elects to pay the second installment by December 31, 2017, then he or she claim a deduction for the prepayment of the taxes on his or her 2017 return.

¶215

> **Example 2:** County A intends to make the usual assessment of property taxes in July 2018 for the property tax year July 1, 2018, through June 30, 2019. The county will also accept prepayments of property taxes for the 2018-2019 property tax year. A taxpayer that prepays 2018-2019 property taxes in 2017 may not claim a deduction for prepayments on his or her 2017 income tax return because the taxes are not assessed in 2017.

After the 2017 Tax Cuts Act took effect in 2018, a number of states with high property taxes whose residents would be disproportionately affected by the new limitation on the deduction proposed legislation that would grant credits against state and local taxes in exchange for contributions to state-controlled funds that could be characterized as charitable contributions. This would effectively circumvent the limitation by transforming state and local taxes subject to a deduction limitation into charitable contributions for which there is generally less limitation. In response, the IRS issued proposed regulations providing that for taxpayers making a contribution to a charitable organization that results in a state or local tax benefit (either a credit or a deduction), the amount the charitable contribution deduction is reduced by the amount of the state or local tax credit or deduction (Prop. Reg. § 1.170A-1(h)(3)). However, the limitation does not apply in the case of an entity claiming a trade or business expense deduction (see below).

> **Comment:** While the proposed regulations may appear to be simply a reaction to the proposed legislation by some states seeking to close a loophole , it has a basis in long-standing decisions and guidance reducing charitable deductions for *quid pro quo* transactions. For example, where a $100 ticket to a charitable event includes a theater ticket with a fair market value of $30, the deduction for the contribution is limited to $70.

A taxpayer may still claim an itemized deduction for foreign income taxes subject to the $10,000/$5,000 limit. However, no deduction is available for foreign real property taxes for tax years 2018 through 2025 (Code Sec. 164(b)(6), as amended by the 2017 Tax Cuts Act).

> **Comment:** The deduction for federal and state generation-skipping transfer (GST) taxes imposed on income distributions is not affected. An individual who received a income distribution from a GST trust and paid GST taxes on the distribution may continue to claim an itemized deduction for the taxes.

In the case of state and local real property and personal property taxes, a deduction is still allowed with no dollar limit if the taxes are paid or accrued in carrying on a trade or business, or on property held for the production of income. Thus, state and local property taxes may be deducted in computing an individual's Schedule C, Schedule E, or Schedule F of Form 1040. For example, an individual may deduct property taxes if the taxes are imposed on business or income producing assets such as residential rental property.

> **Caution:** A deduction is still allowed for state and local income taxes if the taxes are paid or accrued in carrying on a trade or business, or on property held for the production of income. However, as written, the language of Code Sec. 164(b)(6) is that state and local income taxes are subject to the $10,000/$5,000

## NEW LAW EXPLAINED

limit regardless of whether or not they are paid or accrued in a business or for the production of income.

The IRS clarified that the limitation on a charitable contribution that generates a state or local tax benefit proposed in Prop. Reg. § 1.170A-1(h)(3) *does not* apply to entities claiming a deduction for similar exchanges. The IRS provided a safe harbor that allows a C corporation or a specified passthrough entity to claim a trade or business deduction for a charitable contribution if it receives, or expects to receive, a state or local tax benefit in exchange (Rev. Proc. 2019-12). The safe harbor allows for a deduction in the amount of the tax benefit received, any excess of the contribution over the tax benefit is subject to normal rules relating to trade or business deductions. A specified passthrough entity is an entity that is not a C corporation, that operates a trade or business, and is subject to state and local taxes in carrying on the trade or business that is imposed directly on the entity.

▶ **Effective date.** The amendment made by this section applies to tax years beginning after December 31, 2016 (Act Sec. 11042(b) of the Tax Cuts and Jobs Act (P.L. 115-97)).

— Act Sec. 11042(a) of the Tax Cuts and Jobs Act (P.L. 115-97), adding Code Sec. 164(b)(6);

— Act Sec. 11042(b), providing the effective date.

# ¶220 Home Mortgage Interest Deduction

## SUMMARY OF NEW LAW

The itemized deduction for home mortgage interest is limited for tax years 2018 through 2025. A taxpayer is limited to claiming the home mortgage interest deduction only for interest paid or accrued on acquisition debt during those years, or interest on home equity debt where the loan proceeds are used to buy, build, or substantially improve the home securing the debt. The maximum amount that may be treated as acquisition debt is also reduced to $750,000 ($375,000 if married filing separately) for any acquisition debt incurred after December 15, 2017.

## BACKGROUND

Personal interest generally is not deductible. However, interest paid on a home mortgage (i.e., qualified residence interest) may be claimed by an individual as an itemized deduction on Schedule A of Form 1040 (Code Sec. 163(h)(2)(D)). Qualified residence interest is interest that is paid or accrued during the tax year on either acquisition indebtedness or home equity indebtedness secured by the taxpayer's qualified residence by a mortgage, deed of trust, or land contract (Code Sec. 163(h)(3) and (4)). A qualified residence for this purpose includes the taxpayer's principal residence and one other residence such as a vacation home that is not rented out at any time during the tax year or that is used by the taxpayer for a minimum number

## BACKGROUND

of days. A qualified residence can be a house, condominium, cooperative, mobile home, house trailer, or boat.

Acquisition indebtedness is debt incurred in acquiring, constructing or substantially improving a qualified residence of the taxpayer and which secures the residence. Refinanced debt remains acquisition indebtedness to the extent that it does not exceed the principal amount of acquisition indebtedness immediately before refinancing. The maximum amount treated as acquisition indebtedness is $1 million ($500,000 if married filing separately).

Home equity indebtedness is any debt other than acquisition indebtedness that is secured by a qualified residence. Interest on such debt is deductible even if the proceeds are used for personal expenditures. The aggregate amount of home equity indebtedness may not exceed $100,000 ($50,000 if married filing separately) and may not exceed the fair market value of the qualified residence reduced by the acquisition indebtedness.

Acquisition indebtedness may constitute home equity indebtedness to the extent the debt exceeds the dollar limits for acquisition indebtedness, but subject to the dollar and fair market value limits for home equity indebtedness (Rev. Rul. 2010-25). Thus, an individual can deduct interest paid on up to $1.1 million of such debt ($550,000 if married filing separately) as qualified residence interest. Interest attributable to debt over these limits is nondeductible personal interest.

**Qualified principal residence debt.** An individual may exclude from gross income a limited amount of qualified principal residence debt discharged before January 1, 2017, or subject to an arrangement that is entered into and evidenced in writing before January 1, 2017 (Code Sec. 108(a)(1)(E) and (h)). The debt generally must be incurred in the acquisition, construction, or substantial improvement of the individual's principle residence and secured by the residence. The exclusion is limited to $2 million ($1 million for married taxpayers filing separately).

## NEW LAW EXPLAINED

**Deduction for home equity interest limited and acquisition debt limits reduced for 2018 through 2025.**—The itemized deduction for home mortgage interest (i.e., qualified residence interest) is temporarily limited to interest on acquisition debt, or interest on home equity debt where the loan proceeds are used to buy, build, or substantially improve the home securing the debt, for tax years beginning after December 31, 2017, and before January 1, 2026 (Code Sec. 163(h)(3)(F)(i)(I), as added by the Tax Cuts and Jobs Act (P.L. 115-97)).

> **Comment:** The changes made by the 2017 Tax Cuts Act seem to imply that interest on home equity indebtedness is no longer deductible. However, the IRS clarified that interest on home equity indebtedness where the proceeds from the loan are used to acquire, build or substantially improve the home securing the debt. The suspension of the deduction only applies where the proceeds from the loan are used to pay personal expenses for which interest is not deductible, such as paying credit card debt (IRS News Release IR-2018-32).

¶220

## NEW LAW EXPLAINED

**Limitation on acquisition indebtedness.** The maximum amount that may be treated as acquisition debt is also reduced to $750,000 ($375,000 if married filing separately) for tax years beginning after December 31, 2017, and before January 1, 2026 (Code Sec. 163(h)(3)(F)(i)(II), as added by the 2017 Tax Cuts Act). The reduction generally applies to any acquisition debt incurred after December 15, 2017. The maximum amount that may be treated as acquisition debt remains $1 million ($500,000 if married filing separately) for any acquisition debt incurred with respect to the taxpayer's principal residence on or before December 15, 2017 (Code Sec. 163(h)(3)(F)(i)(III), as added by the 2017 Tax Cuts Act). The acquisition debt incurred on or before December 15, 2017, reduces the $750,000/$375,000 limit to any acquisition debt incurred after December 15, 2017. The existing limits on deductible home equity interest continue to apply.

The $1 million ($500,000 if married filing separately) limit will also continue to apply to a taxpayer who enters a binding written contract before December 15, 2017, to close on the purchase of a principal residence before January 1, 2018, so long as the residence is purchased before April 1, 2018 (Code Sec. 163(h)(3)(F)(i)(IV), as added by the 2017 Tax Cuts Act). Similarly, the higher limit continues to apply to any debt incurred after December 15, 2017, to refinance existing acquisition debt on the taxpayer's principal residence to the extent the amount of the debt resulting from the refinancing does not exceed the amount of the refinanced debt (Code Sec. 163(h)(3)(F)(iii), as added by the 2017 Tax Cuts Act). Thus, the maximum dollar amount that may be treated as acquisition debt on the taxpayer's principal residence will not decrease by reason of a refinancing. The exception for refinancing existing acquisition will not apply after: (1) the expiration of the term of the original debt; or (2) the earlier of the expiration of the first refinancing of the debt or 30 years after the date of the first refinancing.

> **Comment:** A taxpayer whose adjusted gross income (AGI) exceeds a threshold normally must reduce the amount of itemize deductions claimed on his or her federal income tax return. However, the phaseout for itemized deductions is temporarily repealed for tax years beginning after 2017 and before 2026 (sees ¶250).

**Qualified principal residence debt.** The $2 million ($1 million) limit on the exclusion of discharged qualified principal residence debt is not affected by the temporary reduction the limit of acquisition debt for home mortgage interest deduction (Code Sec. 163(h)(3)(F)(iv), as added by the 2017 Tax Cuts Act).

▶ **Effective date.** The amendments made by this section apply to tax years beginning after December 31, 2017 (Act Sec. 11043(b) of the Tax Cuts and Jobs Act (P.L. 115-97)).

— Act Sec. 11043(a) of the Tax Cuts and Jobs Act (P.L. 115-97), adding Code Sec. 163(h)(3)(F);

— Act Sec. 11043(b), providing the effective date.

# ¶225 Medical Expense Deduction

## SUMMARY OF NEW LAW

The adjusted gross income (AGI) threshold to claim itemized deduction for un-reimbursed expenses paid for the medical care of the taxpayer or the taxpayer's spouse or dependents is temporarily reduced to 7.5 percent of AGI for tax years 2017 and 2018.

## BACKGROUND

An itemized deduction is allowed to an individual on Schedule A of Form 1040 for expenses paid during the tax year for the medical care of the taxpayer, the taxpayer's spouse, or the taxpayer's dependent to the extent that the expenses exceed 10 percent of the taxpayer's adjusted gross income (AGI) (Code Sec. 213). For individuals who attain age 65 before the close of the year, the threshold to claim an itemized deduction for medical expenses is 7.5 percent of AGI for tax years beginning before January 1, 2017. On a joint return, the percentage limitation is based on the total AGI of both spouses.

Expenses paid for medical care include amounts paid for the diagnosis, cure, mitigation, treatment, or prevention of disease, and for treatments affecting any part or function of the body (Code Sec. 213(d)). Only payments for legal medical services rendered by physicians, surgeons, dentists, and other medical practitioners qualify as medical expenses. Amounts paid for equipment, supplies, and diagnostic devices may be deductible if needed for medical care. Medical care expenses must be incurred primarily to alleviate or prevent a physical or mental defect or illness and do not include expenses that are merely beneficial to general health, such as vitamins or a vacation.

Medical expenses also include premiums paid for insurance that covers the expenses of medical care and amounts paid for transportation to get medical care, to the extent that the premiums have not been excluded from taxable income through the employer exclusion or self-insured deduction. Amounts paid for long-term care services and limited amounts paid for qualified long-term care insurance contract are medical expenses. The cost of medicine and drugs is deductible only for medicine and drugs that require a prescription, except for insulin.

## NEW LAW EXPLAINED

**Medical expense deduction AGI threshold temporarily reduced.**—The threshold to claim an itemized deduction for unreimbursed expenses paid for the medical care of the taxpayer or the taxpayer's spouse or dependents is reduced to 7.5 percent of adjusted gross income (AGI) for all taxpayers for tax years beginning after December 31, 2016, and before January 1, 2019 (Code Sec. 213(f) as amended by the Tax Cuts and Jobs Act (P.L. 115-97)). The reduced threshold applies for both regular tax and

**NEW LAW EXPLAINED**

alternative minimum tax purposes (Code Sec. 56(b)(1)(B) as amended by the Tax Cuts and Jobs Act).

> **Comment:** As a result of this change, the reduced AGI threshold for the medical expense deduction is available for expenses incurred in 2017 and 2018.

> **Comment:** A taxpayer whose AGI exceeds a threshold normally must reduce the amount of itemize deductions claimed on his or her federal income tax return. However, the phaseout for itemized deductions is temporarily repealed for tax years beginning after 2017 and before 2026 (sees ¶ 250).

▶  **Effective date.** The amendments made by this section applies to tax years beginning after December 31, 2016 (Act Sec. 11027(c) of the Tax Cuts and Jobs Act (P.L. 115-97)).

**No significant guidance related to this provision has been issued.**

— Act Sec. 11027(a) of the Tax Cuts and Jobs Act (P.L. 115-97), amending Code Sec. 213(f);

— Act Sec. 11027(b), amending Code Sec. 56(b)(1)(B);

— Act Sec. 11027(c), providing the effective date.

## ¶230 Charitable Contribution Deductions

### SUMMARY OF NEW LAW

The percentage limitation on the charitable deduction contribution base is increased to 60 percent of an individual's adjusted gross income for cash donations to public charities in 2018 through 2025. The deduction for amounts paid for college athletic seating rights is repealed. The exception to contemporaneous written acknowledgment requirement for contributions of $250 or more is repealed.

### BACKGROUND

Taxpayers may deduct certain charitable contributions made during the tax year to charities, governments, and other qualified organizations (Code Sec. 170). Individuals can claim an allowable charitable deduction if they elect to itemize their deductions for the tax year (Code Sec. 63(e)).

An individual's deductible charitable donations for a tax year are limited to a specified percentage of the contribution base, which is the individual's adjusted gross income (AGI) computed without regard to any net operating loss carryback (Code Sec. 170(b)(1)(G)). In general, an individual's deductible donations are limited to—

- 50 percent of the contribution base, for donations of cash or nonappreciated (ordinary income) property to public charities, private foundations other than nonoperating private foundations, and certain governmental units and other organizations (collectively, "50 percent organizations") (Code Sec. 170(b)(1)(A));

- the lesser of (i) 30 percent of the contribution base or (ii) the excess of 50 percent of the contribution base over the amount of contributions subject to the 50-percent limit, for donations of cash or nonappreciated property to nonoperating private foundations or "for the use of" 50 percent organizations (Code Sec. 170(b)(1)(B));

## BACKGROUND

- 30 percent of the contribution base (after taking into account donations other than capital gain property donations), for donations of appreciated capital gain property to 50 percent organizations; an individual may elect to bring all appreciated capital gain property donations for a tax year within the 50-percent limit (Code Sec. 170(b)(1)(C));

- the lesser of (i) 20 percent of the contribution base or (ii) the excess of 30 percent of the contribution base over the amount of contributions subject to the 30-percent limit, for donations of appreciated capital gain property to nonoperating private foundations (Code Sec. 170(b)(1)(D)); and

- 20 percent of the contribution base, for donations of capital gain property "for the use of" 50 percent organizations and nonoperating private foundations (Code Sec. 170(b)(1)(D)).

Donors can generally carry forward for five years their charitable contributions that exceed the deductible limit for the year of the donation (Code Sec. 170(d)).

**Charitable donations connected with college athletic events.** If a donor receives or expects to receive a substantial benefit in return for a payment to charity, the payment is generally not a deductible charitable contribution (see *American Bar Endowment*, SCt, 86-1 USTC ¶9482). However, the donor may be able to deduct the portion of the donation that is more than the value of the return benefit received (see Rev. Rul. 67-246). A donor who makes a charitable donation to, or for, a college or university and receives back in return the right to purchase tickets to athletic events in the institution's athletic stadium can deduct 80 percent of the payment as a charitable contribution. This special treatment does not apply if the donor receives tickets instead of the *right to purchase* tickets. Any part of the payment that is for the actual cost of tickets is not deductible (Code Sec. 170(l)).

**Substantiation for donations of $250 or more.** A donor who claims a charitable deduction must maintain reliable written records on the contribution, regardless of its value or amount (Reg. § 1.170A-13). Further, no deduction is allowed for any charitable contribution of $250 or more—for both cash and noncash donations—unless the donor substantiates the donation with a contemporaneous written acknowledgment by the donee organization (Code Sec. 170(f)(8)(A); Reg. § 1.170A-13(f)). A donor is not required to obtain the acknowledgment if the donee files a return with the IRS reporting the information required to be included in a valid acknowledgment (Code Sec. 170(f)(8)(D)). Until final regulations are issued, however, donors must obtain the required substantiation from the donee.

## NEW LAW EXPLAINED

**Percentage limit for cash charitable contributions by individuals temporarily increased.**—The income-based percentage limit is temporarily increased from 50 percent to 60 percent for an individual taxpayer's cash charitable contributions to public charities, private foundations other than nonoperating private foundations, and certain governmental units (i.e., "50 percent organizations"). The 60-percent contribution base limit applies to qualifying cash contributions made in any tax year beginning after

**NEW LAW EXPLAINED**

December 31, 2017, and before January 1, 2026. The individual may carry forward for five years any qualifying cash contributions that exceed the 60-percent ceiling for the tax year of the contribution (Code Sec. 170(b)(1)(G), as added by the Tax Cuts and Jobs Act (P.L. 115-97)).

> **Comment:** The 60-percent limit for cash contributions to public charities is intended to "encourage taxpayers to provide essential monetary support to front-line charities," because "a robust charitable sector is vital to our economy" and "charitable giving is critical to ensuring that the sector thrives" (Report of the House Ways and Means Committee on H.R. 1, Tax Cuts and Jobs Act, H. Rept. 115-409, p. 177). However, the Urban-Brookings Tax Policy Center believes that the increased standard deduction amount (see ¶205) and the scaling back of many individual itemized deductions will substantially reduce the number of taxpayers who elect to itemize, and significantly reduce the tax incentive to donate. The Tax Policy Center estimates that individual giving will decline by between $12 billion and $20 billion in 2018 (i.e., between four and five percent), with similar effects in the long run (see "The House Tax Bill Is Not Very Charitable to Nonprofits," at http://www.taxpolicycenter.org/taxvox/house-tax-bill-not-very-charitable-nonprofits).

> **Comment:** A taxpayer whose adjusted gross income (AGI) exceeds a threshold normally must reduce the amount of itemize deductions claimed on his or her federal income tax return. However, the phaseout for itemized deductions is temporarily repealed for tax years beginning after 2017 and before 2026 (sees ¶250).

Cash contributions that qualify for the 60-percent limit are not taken into account in determining contributions that are allowed under the 50-percent limit of Code Sec. 170(b)(1)(A). For each tax year beginning after December 31, 2017, and before January 1, 2026, and for each tax year to which any 60-percent cash contribution is carried over, the aggregate contribution limitation allowed under Code Sec. 170(b)(1)(A) must be reduced (but not below zero) by the total contributions allowed under the 60-percent limit provision. Further, in determining allowable contributions under Code Sec. 170(b)(1)(B) for donations of cash or nonappreciated property to nonoperating private foundations or "for the use of" 50 percent organizations, any references to the 50-percent limit determination under Code Sec. 170(b)(1)(A) must also include the 60-percent limit determination under Code Sec. 170(b)(1)(G).

> **Comment:** The temporary 60 percent limit for cash contributions is intended to be applied after the 50 percent limit for noncash contributions. However, it is possible to interpret these rules as the 50 percent limit for noncash contributions applying after the amount of cash contributions allowed under the 60 percent limit. Thus, a technical correction may be needed to clarify the coordination of the different limits (General Explanation of Public Law 115-97 (JCS-1-18)).

**Charitable deduction for college athletic seating rights payments repealed.** A charitable deduction is not allowed for any payment to a college or university in exchange for which the payer receives the right to purchase tickets or seating at an

**¶230**

## NEW LAW EXPLAINED

athletic event (Code Sec. 170(l), as amended by the 2017 Tax Cuts Act). Thus, the charitable deduction for amounts paid for college athletic seating rights has been effectively repealed.

> **Comment:** This charitable deduction has been eliminated because "taxpayers should only be permitted a charitable deduction commensurate with the value of assets given to charity" (Report of the House Ways and Means Committee on H.R. 1, Tax Cuts and Jobs Act, H. Rept. 115-409).

**Substantiation exception for donee-reported contributions repealed.** The provision relieving a donor from the requirement to obtain a contemporaneous written acknowledgment for any charitable contribution of $250 or more if the donee organization reports the required information to the IRS has been repealed (Code Sec. 170(f)(8)(D), as stricken by the 2017 Tax Cuts Act). A donor who makes a contribution of $250 or more in the 2017 tax year and later is not allowed a charitable deduction unless the donor substantiates the donation with a contemporaneous written acknowledgment by the donee (Code Sec. 170(f)(8); Reg. § 1.170A-13(f)).

▶ **Effective date.** The amendments made by this section generally apply to contributions made in tax years beginning after December 31, 2017 (Act Secs. 11023(b) and 13704(b) of the Tax Cuts and Jobs Act (P.L. 115-97)). The repeal of the exception to the contemporaneous written acknowledgment requirements applies to contributions made in tax years beginning after December 31, 2016 (Act Sec. 13705(b) of the 2017 Tax Cuts Act).

**No significant guidance related to this provision has been issued.**

— Act Sec. 11023(a) of the Tax Cuts and Jobs Act (P.L. 115-97), redesignating Code Sec. 170(b)(1)(G) as (H) and adding Code Sec. 170(b)(1)(G);

— Act Sec. 13704(a), amending Code Sec. 170(l);

— Act Sec. 13705(a), striking Code Sec. 170(f)(8)(D) and redesignating Code Sec. 170(f)(8)(E) as (D);

— Act Secs. 11023(b), 13704(b), and 13705(b), providing the effective dates.

# ¶235 Personal Casualty and Theft Loss Deduction

### SUMMARY OF NEW LAW

The itemized deduction for personal casualty losses is temporarily limited in tax years 2018 through 2025 to losses attributable to federally declared disasters. Temporary relief from the casualty loss rules is provided for 2016 net disaster losses occurring in 2016 and 2017.

### BACKGROUND

A taxpayer may generally deduct losses sustained during the tax year and not compensated for by insurance or otherwise (Code Sec. 165). For an individual, losses are deductible only if incurred in a trade or business, transaction entered into for profit, or arising from a fire, storm, shipwreck, or other casualty, or from theft (Code

## BACKGROUND

Sec. 165(c)). Personal casualty or theft losses are deductible only to the extent to which they exceed $100 per casualty or theft (Code Sec. 165(h)(1)). Further, personal casualty or theft losses for a tax year are deductible only if they exceed personal casualty gains, and only to the extent of the sum of the amount of personal casualty gains plus the amount by which the excess of personal casualty losses over gains is greater than 10 percent of the taxpayer's adjusted gross income (AGI) (Code Sec. 165(h)(2)). The deduction for casualty losses is an itemized deduction. Individuals who elect the standard deduction may not claim a deduction for casualty losses incurred during the tax year.

If a taxpayer has a casualty loss from a disaster that occurred in a federally declared disaster area, the taxpayer can elect to deduct the loss on his or her return for the tax year in which the disaster occurred or for the tax year immediately preceding the tax year in which the disaster occurred (Code Sec. 165(i)). For example, a calendar-year taxpayer who suffers a disaster loss any time during 2017 may elect to deduct it on his or her 2016 return, or the taxpayer could wait and deduct it on his or her 2017 return in the regular manner. In either case, the taxpayer is still subject to the $100 and 10 percent of AGI limits. A federally declared disaster is any disaster subsequently determined by the President of the United States to warrant assistance by the Federal Government under the Robert T. Stafford Disaster Relief and Emergency Assistance Act.

Special rules also apply to net disaster losses as a result of Hurricanes Harvey, Irma, or Maria in 2017 (Act Sec. 504 of the Disaster Tax Relief and Airport and Airway Extension Act of 2017 (P.L. 115-63)). The dollar limitation applicable to each casualty or theft is increased to $500 and the 10-percent AGI limitation is waived for net disaster losses for the tax year from the hurricanes. A net disaster loss is the excess of qualified disaster-related personal casualty losses, over any personal casualty gains.

## NEW LAW EXPLAINED

**Personal casualty and theft loss deduction limited in 2018 through 2025; special rules apply for 2016 net disaster losses in 2016 and 2017.**—The itemized deduction for personal casualty losses is limited in tax years beginning after December 31, 2017, and before January 1, 2026, to losses attributable to federally declared disasters (Code Sec. 165(h)(5)(A), as added by the Tax Cuts and Jobs Act (P.L. 115-97)). A taxpayer may still claim personal casualty losses not attributable federally declared disasters to offset any personal casualty gains during 2018 through 2025. However, any such personal casualty gains used to offset personal casualty losses attributable to a federally declared disaster are not taken into account in determining the taxpayer's 10 percent of AGI limitation (Code Sec. 165(h)(5)(B), as added by the 2017 Tax Cuts Act).

> **Comment:** A taxpayer whose adjusted gross income (AGI) exceeds a threshold normally must reduce the amount of itemize deductions claimed on his or her federal income tax return. However, the phaseout for itemized deductions is temporarily repealed for tax years beginning after 2017 and before 2026 (sees ¶250).

¶235

**NEW LAW EXPLAINED**

**Additional relief for 2016 disasters.** If an individual has a net disaster loss for tax years beginning in 2016 or 2017, the $100 limitation applicable to each casualty related to the disaster is increased to $500 and the 10 percent AGI limitation is waived (Act Sec. 11028(c) of the 2017 Tax Cuts Act). For this purpose, a net disaster loss is the qualified disaster-related personal casualty losses, over any personal casualty gains. A qualified disaster-related personal loss means a personal casualty loss arising in a disaster area after on or after January 1, 2016, that is attributable to a federally declared disaster. For an individual who does not itemize deductions, his or her standard deduction is increased by the amount of the casualty loss attributable to the disaster (see ¶205).

**Additional relief for certain California wildfires.** The net disaster loss rules have been extended to losses attributable to certain California wildfires. Thus, if an individual has a net disaster loss:

- the $100 limit applicable to each casualty related to the disaster is increased to $500;

- the 10 percent AGI limit is waived with respect to the net disaster loss; and

- the taxpayer may claim an additional standard deduction amount for the net disaster loss in computing regular income tax and alternative minimum tax (AMT) liability if he or she does not itemize deductions.

A net disaster loss for this purpose includes is the excess of the taxpayer's qualified disaster-related personal casualty losses arising in the California wildfire disaster area on or after October 8, 2017, over his or her personal casualty gains for the year. The California wildfire disaster area is the area that between January 1, 2017, and January 18, 2018, a major disaster has been declared by the President under the Robert T. Stafford Disaster Relief and Emergency Assistance Act by reason of wild-fires in California (Act Sec. 20104(b) of the Bipartisan Budget Act of 2018 (P.L. 115-123)).

▶ **Effective date.** The amendment made by this section limiting personal casualty losses to federal disaster areas declared disaster areas applies to losses incurred in tax years beginning after December 31, 2017 (Act Sec. 11044(b) of the Tax Cuts and Jobs Act (P.L. 115-97)). The special rules related to personal casualty losses related to net disaster losses for 2016 are effective on December 22, 2017, the date of enactment.

— Act Sec. 11044(a) of the Tax Cuts and Jobs Act (P.L. 115-97), adding Code Sec. 165(h)(5);

— Act Sec. 11028(a) and (c)

— Act Sec. 11044(b) providing the effective date

— Act Sec. 20104(b) of the Bipartisan Budget Act of 2018 (P.L. 115-123)

## ¶240 Gambling Losses

### SUMMARY OF NEW LAW

Losses from gambling or wagering transactions for purposes of deducting winnings is clarified to include any deduction otherwise allowed to the taxpayer for federal income tax purposes in carrying on any wagering transaction, and not just the actual costs of wagers. The change is effective for tax years 2018 through 2025.

### BACKGROUND

An individual can deduct gambling losses only to the extent of the amount of gambling winnings included in his or her gross income (Code Sec. 165(d)). This limitation applies to taxpayers who are in the trade or business of gambling as well. For most individuals, deductible gambling losses are miscellaneous itemized deductions not subject to the two-percent-of-adjusted-gross-income (AGI) floor (Code Sec. 67(b)(3)). Professional gamblers, however, can deduct losses as an adjustment to gross income (AGI) (i.e., an above-the-line deduction).

Individuals in the trade or business of gambling are also allowed to deduct reasonable business expenses (Mayo v. Commissioner, Dec. 58,524, 136 TC 81). The business expenses are not subject to the gambling loss limitation since they are not related to wagering transactions (AOD 2011-06 (Dec. 20, 2011)).

The combined losses of both spouses on a joint return are allowed to the extent of their combined gains (Reg. § 1.165-10). Furthermore, the losses need not be incurred in the same type of gambling to offset winnings. For example, lottery winnings can offset casino losses (Herman Drews v. Commissioner, Dec. 21,658, 25 TC 1354).

Documentation is required to support the deduction. A taxpayer's diary or other regularly maintained record supplemented by verifiable documentation will usually be accepted for proof of winnings or losses if it contains the date, amount, type of bet, name and address of the gambling establishment, and the names of any persons present with the taxpayer. Verifiable documentation includes wagering tickets, cancelled checks, and credit records (Rev. Proc. 77-29, 1977-2 CB 538).

### NEW LAW EXPLAINED

**Losses from wagering transactions clarified.**—The term "losses from wagering transactions" is clarified to include any deduction otherwise allowable in calculating federal income tax incurred in carrying on any wagering transaction (Code Sec. 165(d) as amended by the Tax Cuts and Jobs Act (P.L. 115-97)). The provision is effective for tax years beginning after December 31, 2017, and before January 1, 2026.

> **Comment:** The change is intended to clarify that the limitation on losses from wagering transactions applies not only to the actual costs of wagers incurred by an individual, but to other expenses incurred by the individual in connection with the conduct of that individual's gambling activities. Thus, for example,

## NEW LAW EXPLAINED

expenses incurred in travelling to and from a casino fall within the scope of the gambling loss limitation, and these expenses may only be deducted to the extent of gambling winnings (Conference Report on H.R. 1, Tax Cuts and Jobs Act (H. Rept. 115-466)).

**Comment:** A taxpayer whose adjusted gross income (AGI) exceeds a threshold normally must reduce the amount of itemize deductions claimed on his or her federal income tax return. However, the phaseout for itemized deductions is temporarily repealed for tax years beginning after 2017 and before 2026 (sees ¶250).

▶ **Effective date.** The amendment made by this section applies to tax years beginning after December 31, 2017 (Act Sec. 11050(b) of the Tax Cuts and Jobs Act (P.L. 115-97)).

**No significant guidance related to this provision has been issued.**

— Act Sec. 11050(a) of the Tax Cuts and Jobs Act (P.L. 115-97), amending Code Sec. 165(d);

— Act Sec. 11050(b), providing the effective date.

# ¶245 Miscellaneous Itemized Deductions

## SUMMARY OF NEW LAW

The deductibility of miscellaneous itemized deductions is temporarily repealed for tax years 2018 through 2025.

## BACKGROUND

Certain itemized deductions of an individual are treated as miscellaneous itemized deductions and are only allowed to the extent that their total exceeds two percent of the individual's adjusted gross income (AGI) (Code Sec. 67(a); Temp. Reg. §1.67-1T). The deductions are reported on Schedule A of Form 1040. The two-percent-of-AGI limit is applied after other deduction limits, such as the 50-percent limit on meals and entertainment, are applied.

In general, the deductions affected by the two-percent floor include, but are not limited to, the following:

- unreimbursed employee expenses (including expenses for travel, lodging, meals, entertainment, continuing education, subscriptions to professional journals, union or professional dues, professional uniforms, job hunting, and business use of an employee's home);
- expenses paid or incurred for the production or collection of income (including investment advisory fees, subscriptions to investment advisory publications, certain attorneys' fees, and safety deposit box rental), or for the determination, collection, or refund of tax (including tax counsel fees and appraisal fees) that are deductible under Code Sec. 212; and
- "hobby" expenses that are deductible under Code Sec. 183.

## BACKGROUND

Miscellaneous itemized deductions subject to the two-percent-of-AGI limit may not be claimed by an individual in calculating his or her alternative minimum tax (AMT) liability (Code Sec. 56(b)(1)(A)).

## NEW LAW EXPLAINED

**Temporary suspension of miscellaneous itemized deductions.**—All miscellaneous itemized deductions that are subject to the two-percent-of-AGI limit are temporarily repealed for tax years beginning after December 31, 2017, and before January 1, 2026 (Code Sec. 67(g), as added by the Tax Cuts and Jobs Act (P.L. 115-97)). Thus, no miscellaneous itemized deduction subject to the two-percent-of-AGI limit may be claimed by an individual on Schedule A of Form 1040 for tax years 2018 through 2025. An individual also remains unable to claim such deductions in calculating his or her AMT liability, regardless of tax year.

**Certain estate and grantor trust expenses remain deductible.** The IRS plans to issue regulations clarifying that certain estate and nongrantor trust expenses remain deductible and are not subject to the miscellaneous itemized deductions suspension (Notice 2018-61).

Under Code Sec. 67(e), the adjusted gross income of an estate or trust is computed in the same manner as that of an individual, except that the following are treated as allowable in arriving at adjusted gross income:

(1) the deductions for costs that are paid or incurred in connection with the administration of the estate or trust that would not have been incurred if the property were not held in the estate or trust; and

(2) the deductions allowable under Code Sec. 642(b) (personal exemption deduction for estate and trusts), Code Sec. 651 (deduction for trusts distributing current income only), and Code Sec. 661 (deduction for estate and trusts accumulating income or distributing corpus).

Therefore these expenses are removed from the category of itemized deductions (and thus are not miscellaneous itemized deductions) and are treated as above-the-line deductions allowable in determining adjusted gross income. As a result, the suspension of the deductibility of miscellaneous itemized deductions does not affect the deductibility of such payments.

> **Caution:** If an individual would normally incur such an expense, it is not subject to Code Sec. 67(e) and therefore may not be deducted by an estate or nongrantor trust during the suspension of miscellaneous itemized deductions.

Similarly, net operating loss carryovers and capital loss carryovers on the termination of an estate or trust are taken into account when determining adjusted gross income. Therefore, they are above-the-line deductions and thus are not miscellaneous itemized deductions on the returns of beneficiaries. However, beneficiaries must treat other deductions in excess of gross income, except for certain deductions related to the personal exemption and charitable contributions, as miscellaneous itemized deductions.

¶245

## NEW LAW EXPLAINED

> **Comment:** The IRS is studying whether deductions that would not be subject to the miscellaneous itemized deduction suspension in the hands of the trust or estate should continue to be treated as miscellaneous itemized deductions when they are excess deductions to beneficiaries.

> **Comment:** The 2018 Form 1041, U.S. Income Tax Return for Estates and Trusts, reflects the plans of the IRS to treat these expenses as above-the-line deductions on Line 15.

Additionally, Code Sec. 67(b) provides a list of itemized deductions that are not classified as miscellaneous itemized deductions. The regulations will clarify that these remain outside the definition of "miscellaneous itemized deductions" and thus are unaffected by the suspension.

**Working condition fringe benefits not affected.** The exclusion for working condition fringe benefits is not affected by the repeal of miscellaneous itemized deductions subject to the two-percent of AGI floor. A working condition fringe benefit is excluded from an employee's gross income to the extent that had the employee paid for the benefit, the payment would be deductible to the employee under Code Secs. 162 or 167 (Code Sec. 132(d)). A deduction for these items would still be allowable under Code Sec. 162, notwithstanding that the deduction may have been subsequently disallowed under Code Sec. 67 ((General Explanation of Public Law 115–97 Prepared by the Staff of the Joint Committee on Taxation (December 2018), FN 310).

> **Comment:** The result was similar in years when miscellaneous itemized deductions subject to the 2-percent floor were available. In those years, a working condition fringe benefit was excludable in its entirety, notwithstanding that a deduction under Code Sec. 162 was limited by the prior-law 2-percent-of-AGI floor on miscellaneous itemized deductions.

▶ **Effective date.** The amendment made by this section applies to tax years beginning after December 31, 2017 (Act Sec. 11045(b) of the Tax Cuts and Jobs Act (P.L. 115-97)).

— Act Sec. 11045(a) of the Tax Cuts and Jobs Act (P.L. 115-97), adding Code Sec. 67(g);

— Act Sec. 11045(b), providing the effective date.

## ¶250  Phaseout or Overall Limitation on Itemized Deductions (Pease Limitation)

### SUMMARY OF NEW LAW

The phaseout or overall limitation on itemized deductions is temporarily repealed for tax years 2018 through 2025.

### BACKGROUND

Once an individual determines adjusted gross income (AGI), he or she may claim certain itemized deductions of personal expenses specifically authorized by the Code in determining taxable income. Alternatively, he or she can simplify their deductions by claiming a standard deduction based on their filing status rather than itemizing deductions. Itemized deductions include deductions for medical and dental expenses, certain taxes, interest, charitable contributions, casualty and theft losses, and certain miscellaneous expenses. An individual whose AGI exceeds an applicable threshold amount based on filing status must reduce the total amount of otherwise allowable itemized deductions. The threshold amounts are adjusted annually for inflation (Code Sec. 68). For 2017, the AGI thresholds are: $313,800 for married individuals filing jointly or surviving spouses; $287,650 for heads of households; $261,500 for unmarried individuals filing as single; and $156,900 for married individuals filing separately (Rev. Proc. 2016-55).

If an individual's AGI exceeds the applicable threshold amount, he or she must reduce the amount of allowable itemized deductions by the lesser of: (1) three percent of the excess of the taxpayer's AGI over the applicable threshold amount, or (2) 80 percent of allowable itemized deductions, reduced by the deductions for medical expenses, investment interest, casualty and theft losses, and wagering losses. The reduction is applied after all other limitations on itemized deductions are applied, including the limit on charitable contributions, the limit on certain meal and entertainment expenses, and the two-percent-of-AGI limitation on miscellaneous itemized deductions (see ¶245).

### NEW LAW EXPLAINED

**Phaseout of itemized deductions temporarily repealed.**—The phaseout or overall limitation on itemized deductions is temporarily repealed applicable to tax years beginning after December 31, 2017, and before January 1, 2026 (Code Sec. 68(f), as added by the Tax Cuts and Jobs Act (P.L. 115-97)).

▶ **Effective date.** The amendments made by this section apply to tax years beginning after December 31, 2017 (Act Sec. 11046(b) of the Tax Cuts and Jobs Act (P.L. 115-97)).

   **No significant guidance related to this provision has been issued.**

— Act Sec. 11046(a) of the Tax Cuts and Jobs Act (P.L. 115-97), adding Code Sec. 68(f);

— Act Sec. 11046(b), providing the effective date.

# ADJUSTMENTS TO GROSS INCOME

## ¶255 Alimony and Separate Maintenance Payments

### SUMMARY OF NEW LAW

The deduction for alimony and separate maintenance payments, as well as the inclusion of the payments in gross income, are repealed. The repeal, however, is only effective for divorce or separation instruments executed or modified after 2018.

### BACKGROUND

Alimony and separate maintenance payments may be claimed as a deduction in calculating adjusted gross income (AGI) (an above-the-line deduction) of the payor (Code Secs. 62(a)(10) and 215). The payments must be included in the gross income of the payee or recipient (Code Secs. 61(a)(8) and 71). These rules apply only if the payments are made in cash under a divorce or separation agreement that does not require continuation or substitution of payments after the payee's death. The spouses must be legally separated, must not file a joint return, and must not be members of the same household. Payments that a divorce or separation instrument fixes as payable to support the payor's child or noncash property settlements are not considered qualified alimony or separate maintenance payments.

The payee spouse of an alimony trust is treated as a beneficiary of the trust and subject to the same tax treatment as the beneficiary of a regular trust, regardless of whether the trust already existed or was created at the time of divorce or separation (Code Sec. 682). As a result, the income the payee spouse is entitled to receive from the trust is taxable to him or her and excludable from the gross income of the payor spouse. However, because income from the trust is taxable to the payee spouse as a beneficiary rather than as alimony, the payor spouse may not claim a deduction for any trust distribution to the payee spouse.

### NEW LAW EXPLAINED

**Alimony deduction and exclusion repealed for instruments executed or modified after 2018.**—The deduction of qualified alimony and separate maintenance payments by a payor, the inclusion of the payments in gross income by the payee, and the special rules for alimony trusts are generally repealed after 2018 (Code Sec. 71, 215, and 682 stricken by the Tax Cuts and Jobs Act (P.L. 115-97)). However, the repeal is only effective for any divorce or separation instruments:

- executed after December 31, 2018; and
- executed before January 1, 2019, and modified after 2018 provided that the modification expressly provides that the repeal of the qualified alimony and separate maintenance rules of the Internal Revenue Code apply (Act Sec. 11051(c) of the 2017 Tax Cuts Act).

## NEW LAW EXPLAINED

> **Comment:** A taxpayer may continue to deduct qualified alimony and separate maintenance payments made, or exclude such payments received from gross income, after 2018 if his or her divorce or separation instrument is: (1) executed before 2019; or (2) is modified after 2018 so long as it does not expressly provide that the that the repeal of the qualified alimony and separate maintenance rules of the Internal Revenue Code apply. The special rules applicable to alimony trusts will also continue to apply after 2018 under the same conditions as for the deduction and the exclusion.

> **Caution:** Since the rules applicable to alimony or separate maintenance payments still apply to certain divorce or separation instruments after 2018, other rules which are amended or repealed by the 2017 Tax Cuts Act will also continue to apply. Examples include rules related to additional withholding allowances, requirements to include taxpayer identification numbers (TIN), and the definition of compensation for the purpose of IRA contributions deductions.

▶ **Effective date.** The amendments made by this section apply to: (1) any divorce or separation instrument (as defined in Code Sec. (b)(2) as in effect before December 22, 2017, the date of the enactment) and executed after December 31, 2018; (2) any divorce or separation instrument executed on or before December 31, 2018, and modified after that date if the modification expressly provides that the amendments made by this section apply to the modification (Act Sec. 11015(c) of the Tax Cuts and Jobs Act (P.L. 115-97)).

**No significant guidance related to this provision has been issued.**

— Act Sec. 11051(a) of the Tax Cuts and Jobs Act (P.L. 115-97), striking Code Sec. 215;

— Act Sec. 11051(b)(1), amending Code Sec. 61(a), striking Code Secs. 71 and 682;

— Act Sec. 11051(b)(2), (3), and (4), amending Code Secs. 121(d)(3), 152(d)(5), 219(f)(1), 220(f)(7), 223(f)(7), 382(l)(3)(B)(iii), 408(d)(6), 3402(m)(1), 6742(d)(3), 7701(a)(17), and striking Code Sec. 62(a)(10);

— Act Sec. 11051(c), providing the effective date.

## ¶260 Moving Expense Deduction

### SUMMARY OF NEW LAW

The deduction for moving expenses is temporarily repealed for tax years 2018 through 2025. However, the special rules for a member of the Armed Forces to deduct moving expenses and exclude in-kind moving expenses, and reimbursements or allowances, continues to apply during these tax years.

### BACKGROUND

An employee or self-employed individual may claim a deduction in calculating adjusted gross income (AGI) (an above-the-line deduction) for reasonable expenses of moving himself or herself, as well as family members, if the move is related to

## BACKGROUND

starting work in a new location (Code Secs. 62(a)(15) and 217). The taxpayer must satisfy certain conditions related to distance from the previous residence and minimum period of employment in the new location to deduct moving expenses. Deductible moving expenses are limited to the cost of transportation of household goods and personal effects, and travel to the new residence, including lodging but not meals.

Special rules apply to moving expenses paid or incurred by a member of the Armed Forces of the United States who is on active duty and moves pursuant to a military order and incident to a permanent change of station (Code Sec. 217(g)). First, the individual is exempt from the minimum distance and minimum period of employment conditions for claiming the moving expense deduction. Second, the individual may exclude from gross income the value of any moving and storage expenses furnished in-kind by the United States government to the individual, his or her spouse, and dependents, as well as any reimbursements or allowance for those expenses. An exclusion is also provided for moving and storage expenses incurred by the spouse or dependents of an Armed Forces member, even if they do not reside with the member either before or after the move.

## NEW LAW EXPLAINED

**Moving expense deduction temporarily repealed; special rules for Armed Forces members retained.**—The deduction for moving expenses is generally repealed for tax years beginning after December 31, 2017, and before January 1, 2026 (Code Sec. 217(k), as added by the Tax Cuts and Jobs Act (P.L. 115-97)). Thus, an employee or self-employed individual may not claim an above-the-line deduction in calculating adjusted gross income for moving expenses in 2018 through 2025.

The special rules applicable to a member of the Armed Forces of the United States will continue to apply after 2017. Thus, the Armed Forces member may still claim a deduction for moving expenses and exclude from income in-kind moving and storage expenses, as well as reimbursement or allowance for those expenses, in 2018 through 2025 if he or she is on active duty and moves pursuant to a military order and incident to a permanent change of station (Code Sec. 217(g)).

▶ **Effective date.** The amendment made by this section applies to tax years beginning after December 31, 2017 (Act Sec. 11049(b) of the Tax Cuts and Jobs Act (P.L. 115-97)).

**No significant guidance related to this provision has been issued.**

— Act Sec. 11049(a) of the Tax Cuts and Jobs Act (P.L. 115-97), adding Code Sec. 217(k);

— Act Sec. 11049(b), providing the effective date.

# EXCLUSION FROM GROSS INCOME

## ¶265  Discharge of Debt Income from Student Loans

### SUMMARY OF NEW LAW

Eligibility to exclude discharge of student loan debt from gross income is temporarily expanded to include discharges of eligible student loans before 2026 due to the student's death or total and permanent disability.

### BACKGROUND

A taxpayer's gross income generally includes discharge of debt income if a taxpayer is released from a debt for less than the full amount of the obligation (Code Sec. 108). An exception to this rules is that the discharge of a student loan does not give rise to discharge of debt income if the discharge is pursuant to a provision in the loan agreement under which all or a part of the student loan is forgiven, provided the student works for a certain period of time in certain professions for any of a broad class of employers (Code Sec. 108(f)). In addition, an individual's gross income does not include forgiveness of loans made by tax-exempt charitable organizations (e.g., educational organizations or private foundations) if the proceeds of such loans are used to pay costs of attendance at an educational institution or to refinance outstanding student loans and the student is not employed by the lender organization.

> **Caution:** This exclusion does not apply to the extent the taxpayer is insolvent or is involved in a bankruptcy case (Code Sec. 108(a)(2)).

The exclusion applies if the proceeds are used to refinance any loan made to assist an individual in attending an educational institution, not just loans made by educational organizations. The refinancing loan must be made under a program that requires the student to fulfill a public-service work requirement. A student loan is any loan to an individual to assist him or her in attending an educational organization described in Code Sec. 170(b)(1)(A)(ii), if the lender is: (1) the United States or an instrumentality or agency thereof; (2) a U.S. state, territory, or possession or the District of Columbia or any political subdivision thereof; (3) certain tax-exempt public benefit corporations that control a State, county, or municipal hospital and whose employees have been deemed to be public employees under State law; or (4) an educational organization that originally received the funds from which the loan was made from the United States, a State, or a tax-exempt public benefit corporation.

### NEW LAW EXPLAINED

**Student loan debt discharge exclusion expanded before 2025 due to death or disability.**—The exclusion of discharge of debt income for student loans is expanded to include discharges because of the student's death or total and permanent disability. The exclusion applies to discharge of debt income due to the discharge of an eligible loan

## NEW LAW EXPLAINED

after December 31, 2017, and before January 1, 2026 (Code Sec. 108(f)(5)(A), as added by the Tax Cuts and Jobs Act (P.L. 115-97)). Loans eligible for this exclusion are loans made by:

- the United States (or an instrumentality or agency of the United States);

  **Comment:** A technical correction may be needed to reflect the intent to include Parent PLUS loans (General Explanation of Public Law 115–97 Prepared by the Staff of the Joint Committee on Taxation (December 2018), FN 276).

- a state (or political subdivision of a state);

- certain tax-exempt public benefit corporations that control a state, county, or municipal hospital and whose employees have been deemed to be public employees under state law;

- an educational organization that originally received the funds from which the loan was made from the United States, a state, or a tax-exempt public benefit corporation; or

- private education loans (for this purpose, private education loan is defined in section 140(7) of the Consumer Protection Act) (Code Sec. 108(f)(5)(B), as added by the 2017 Tax Cuts Act).

> **Example:** Bridgett becomes totally and permanently disabled in 2018 as the result of an accident. She has an outstanding student loan that was made by the State of New York, which is cancelled by the state due to her disability. Because the discharge is due to Bridgett's total and permanent disability, it does not give rise to discharge of debt income in the tax year.

  **Comment:** The legislative text provides a broad catch-all exclusion for discharge of debt income of an eligible loan on account of the death or total and permanent disability of the student. It also provides specific references to provisions in the Higher Education Act of 1965 of loan forgiveness in the case of death and total and permanent disability.

▶ **Effective date.** The amendment made by this section applies to discharges of debt after December 31, 2017 (Act Sec. 11301(b) of the Tax Cuts and Jobs Act (P.L. 115-97)).

**No significant guidance related to this provision has been issued.**

— Act. Sec. 11031(a) of the Tax Cuts and Jobs Act (P.L. 115-97), adding Code Sec. 108(f)(5);

— Act Sec. 11031(b), providing the effective date.

## ¶270 Rollover of Capital Gain from Publicly Traded Securities

### SUMMARY OF NEW LAW

The election to defer recognition of capital gain realized on the sale of publicly traded securities if the taxpayer used the sale proceeds to purchase common stock or a partnership interest in a specialized small business investment company (SSBIC) is repealed for sales after 2017.

### BACKGROUND

C corporations and individuals may elect to defer recognition of capital gain realized on the sale of publicly traded securities if the taxpayer uses the sales proceeds within 60 days to purchase common stock or a partnership interest in a specialized small business investment company (SSBIC). Sales proceeds that exceed the cost of the SSBIC common stock or partnership interest must be recognized as gain. Ordinary gain cannot be deferred (Code Sec. 1044(a)). The election is not available to estates, trusts, subchapter S corporations and partnerships. The taxpayer's basis in the SSBIC stock or partnership interest is reduced, in the order acquired, by the amount of any unrecognized gain on the sale of the securities.

The amount of capital gain that an individual may elect to roll over by purchasing an interest in an SSBIC for a tax year is limited to the lesser of $50,000 or $500,000, reduced by any gain previously excluded. These limits are $25,000 and $250,000, respectively, for married individuals filing separate returns; and $250,000 and $1 million, respectively, for C corporations (Code Sec. 1044(b)).

### NEW LAW EXPLAINED

**Rollover of capital gain from publicly traded securities into specialized small business investment companies is repealed.**—The election to rollover gain from the sale of publicly traded securities if the sale proceeds are used to purchase common stock or a partnership interest in a specialized small business investment company is repealed for sales after 2017 (Code Sec. 1044, prior to being stricken by the Tax Cuts and Jobs Act (P.L. 115-97)).

▶   **Effective date.** The amendments made by this section apply to sales after December 31, 2017 (Act Sec. 13313(c) of the Tax Cuts and Jobs Act (P.L. 115-97).

   **No significant guidance related to this provision has been issued.**

— Act Sec. 13313(a) of the Tax Cuts and Jobs Act (P.L. 115-97), striking Code Sec. 1044;

— Act Sec. 13313(b), amending Code Sec. 1016(a)(23);

— Act Sec. 13313(c), providing the effective date.

# PERSONAL TAX CREDITS

## ¶280  Child Tax Credit

### SUMMARY OF NEW LAW

The child tax credit is temporarily expanded after 2017 by increasing the credit amount for each qualifying child to $2,000, increasing the phaseout threshold to $400,000 if married filing jointly ($200,000 for other taxpayers), and providing a $500 nonrefundable credit for each dependent who is not a qualifying child. The refundable portion of the credit (additional child tax credit) is limited to $1,400 per qualifying child, but is indexed for inflation and the earned income threshold is reduced to $2,500. A taxpayer must include a qualifying child's Social Security number on his or her return to receive the nonrefundable or refundable portion of the credit with respect to the child.

### BACKGROUND

An individual may claim the child tax credit of up to $1,000 for each qualifying child he or she supports during the tax year (Code Sec. 24). The definition of qualifying child for this purpose is the same as that for claiming a dependency exemption, except that the child must not have attained the age of 17 by the end of the year and must be a U.S. citizen, national, or resident. The taxpayer's return must include the name and taxpayer identification number (TIN) of each qualifying child claimed for the credit. The TIN of a qualifying child must be issued prior to the filing of the return for the tax year.

The child tax credit is $1,000 per qualifying child but phases out once the taxpayer's modified adjusted gross income (MAGI) exceeds $110,000 if married filing jointly, $75,000 if filing as single, and $55,000 if married filing separately (Code Sec. 24(b)). The credit is reduced by $50 for each $1,000, or fraction thereof, of MAGI above the threshold amount. MAGI is defined as AGI determined without regard to the exclusions from gross income for foreign earned income, foreign housing expenses, and U.S. possession income. The credit is allowed only for tax years consisting of 12 months except in cases where the tax year closes due to the death of the taxpayer.

The child tax credit is generally a nonrefundable personal credit and allowed against both the taxpayer's regular tax liability and alternative minimum tax (AMT) liability (Code Sec. 26). A portion of the credit is refundable to the extent it exceeds the taxpayer's tax liability. This is referred to as the additional child tax credit (ACTC) and is equal to the lesser of the unclaimed portion of the nonrefundable credit amount (i.e., up to $1,000 per child) or 15 percent of the taxpayer's earned income in excess of $3,000 (Code Sec. 24(d)). For a taxpayer with three or more qualifying children, the ACTC is either the unclaimed portion of the nonrefundable credit amount or the excess of the taxpayer's share of Social Security taxes, including one-half of any self-employment taxes, over his or her earned income credit for the tax year. Military families may elect to include otherwise excludable combat zone pay in

## BACKGROUND

their earned income when calculating the ACTC. Schedule 8812 is used to calculate the ACTC. The ACTC is disallowed for any taxpayer electing to exclude from gross income any foreign earned income and foreign housing expenses.

## NEW LAW EXPLAINED

**Modification of child tax credit and new credit for qualifying dependents after 2017.**—The child tax credit is temporarily expanded effective for tax years beginning after 2017 (Code Sec. 24(h)(1), as added by the Tax Cuts and Jobs Act (P.L. 115-97)). Specifically, the following modifications to the credit are effective for tax years beginning after December 31, 2017, and before January 1, 2026:

- The credit amount is increased to $2,000 per qualifying child (Code Sec. 24(h)(2), as added by the 2017 Tax Cuts Act).

- The threshold amount when the credit begins to phase out is increased to $400,000 if married filing jointly and $200,000 for any other filing status (Code Sec. 24(h)(3), as added by the 2017 Tax Cuts Act). The credit is reduced by $50 for $1,000 (or fraction thereof) that a taxpayer's modified adjusted gross income (MAGI) exceeds the threshold amount. The threshold amounts are not indexed for inflation.

- A taxpayer may claim a $500 credit for each dependent who is not a qualifying child for purposes of the child tax credit (Code Sec. 24(h)(4), as added by the 2017 Tax Cuts Act). A dependent for this purpose is a qualifying relative (and not a qualifying child) for purposes of claiming a dependency exemption under Code Sec. 152(b). In addition, the dependent must be a U.S. citizen, national, or resident of the United States. The $500 credit may not be claimed for a dependent who is resident of contiguous country to the United States (i.e., Mexico and Canada).

    **Comment:** The deduction for personal and dependency exemptions is temporarily repealed for tax years 2018 through 2025 (see ¶210), but the definition of a dependent is still applicable for the child tax credit and other tax benefits.

    **Compliance Note:** A taxpayer must file either Form 1040 or Form 1040A to claim the child tax credit. The child tax credit cannot be claimed by a taxpayer filing Form 1040-EZ.

**Refundable child tax credit.** A portion of the child tax credit remains refundable after 2017 and before 2026, referred to as the additional child tax credit (ACTC), except that the earned income threshold is temporarily decreased by $500. For tax years beginning in 2018 through 2025, a taxpayer is eligible for a refund equal to 15 percent of his or her earned income in excess of $2,500 (as opposed to $3,000) to the extent the child tax credit exceeds the taxpayer's tax liability (Code Sec. 24(h)(6), as added by the 2017 Tax Cuts Act).

The refundable amount for 2018 through 2025 is limited to $1,400 per qualifying child regardless that the credit is $2,000 per qualifying child (Code Sec. 24(h)(5), as added by the 2017 Tax Cuts Act). In addition, the $500 credit for each dependent who is not a qualifying child is disregarded in calculating the ACTC (i.e., the refundable portion is only for qualifying children claimed by the taxpayer for the credit). The $1,400

**¶280**

**NEW LAW EXPLAINED**

refund limitation per qualifying child for the ACTC is indexed annually for inflation after 2018 using the Chained Consumer Price Index for All Urban Consumers (C-CPI-U) in the cost-of-living adjustment (see ¶ 125).

> **Compliance Note:** A taxpayer claiming the ACTC must complete Schedule 8812.

**Taxpayer identification number required.** A taxpayer must include on his or her return a qualifying child's Social Security number (SSN) to receive either the refundable or nonrefundable portion of the credit with respect to that child (Code Sec. 24(h)(7), as added by the 2017 Tax Cuts Act). A SSN issued by the Social Security Administration (SSA) to the qualifying child is valid for purpose of the ACTC only if the child is a U.S. citizen or the SSN authorizes the individual to work in the United States under Section 205(c)(2)(B)(i) of the Social Security Act. In addition, the SSN must be issued to the qualifying child on or before the due date of the taxpayer's return.

> **Comment:** A Social security card labeled "not valid for employment" merely allows the holder to receive federal benefits (e.g., Medicaid) and it does not give the holder a valid SSN to work in the United States. A Social Security card that reads "Valid for work only with DHS authorization" or "Valid for work only with INS authorization" is valid for work in the United States if the authorization is still valid.

A taxpayer who cannot claim the child tax credit because a qualifying child does not have a Social Security number may nonetheless qualify for the nonrefundable $500 credit for the child (Code Sec. 24(h)(4)(C), as added by the 2017 Tax Cuts Act).

> **Comment:** A taxpayer can claim the nonrefundable $500 credit for any person claimed who could be claimed as a dependent. In order to claim a dependency exemption for any person, the taxpayer must include a taxpayer identification number (TIN) of the dependent on his or her return (Code Sec. 151(e)). This may be satisfied by including the dependent's SSN, TIN, or adoption taxpayer identification number (ATIN) (Reg. § 301.6109-1). Thus, a SSN is only required for a qualifying child in claiming the child tax credit. A SSN is not required to claim the nonrefundable $500 credit for a child or nonchild dependent. The Joint Committee on Taxation has cautioned that a technical correction may be necessary to incorporate the definition of a dependent for purposes of the $500 credit, particularly that a TIN must be provided for any dependent for which the $500 credit is to be claimed (General Explanation of Public Law 115-97 (JCS-1-18)).

The IRS has provided that, for purposes of defining a qualifying relative for the identification of a dependent, the "exemption amount" (the amount at which a taxpayer's gross income disqualifies that person to be a qualifying relative) for 2018 is $4,150. The amount is $4,200 for 2019 (Notice 2018-70; Rev. Proc. 2018-57).

▶ **Effective date.** The amendment made by this section applies to tax years beginning after December 31, 2017 (Act Sec. 11022(b) of the Tax Cuts and Jobs Act (P.L. 115-97)).

— Act Sec. 11022(a) of the Tax Cuts and Jobs Act (P.L. 115-97), adding Code Sec. 24(h);

— Act Sec. 11022(b), providing the effective date.

¶280

# Corporations and Passthrough Entities

**3**

## CORPORATIONS

## PASSTHROUGH ENTITIES

# CORPORATIONS

## ¶305  Corporate Income Tax Rate

### SUMMARY OF NEW LAW

For tax years beginning after December 31, 2017, the graduated corporate tax rate structure is eliminated and corporate taxable income is taxed at a 21-percent flat rate. No special rate is provided for qualified personal service corporations (qualified

## SUMMARY OF NEW LAW

PSCs); therefore, qualified PSCs are also taxed at a 21-percent rate. The alternative tax for net capital gains and the rules disallowing the graduated corporate tax rates or the accumulated earnings credit to transferee corporations upon certain transfers are repealed. The new law further modifies the rules limiting the use of multiple tax benefits of controlled corporate groups to leave only the limitation on the use of the accumulated earnings credit as a result of the repeal of the corporate alternative minimum tax and the elimination of the graduated corporate tax rate structure. In addition, for taxpayers subject to the normalization method of accounting (e.g., regulated public utilities), the new law provides for the normalization of excess deferred tax reserves resulting from the reduction of corporate income tax rates (with respect to prior depreciation or recovery allowances taken on assets placed in service before the corporate rate reduction takes effect).

## BACKGROUND

Corporations determine their annual income tax liability by applying a graduated rate of tax to their taxable income. The corporate income tax rates consist of four brackets. The top corporate tax rate is 35 percent on taxable income in excess of $10 million (Code Sec. 11(a) and (b)(1)). The corporate taxable income brackets and tax rates are set forth in the table below.

| Taxable Income | Tax Rate |
|---|---|
| First $50,000 | 15% |
| $50,001-$75,000 | 25% |
| $75,001-$10 million | 34% |
| over $10 million | 35% |

A corporation with taxable income over $100,000 must pay an additional tax equal to five percent of the amount in excess of $100,000, up to a maximum additional tax of $11,750. Corporations with taxable income in excess of $15 million must pay an additional tax equal to three percent of the amount in excess of $15 million, up to a maximum additional tax of $100,000 (Code Sec. 11(b)(1)). The extra five percent tax operates to phase out the benefits of graduated tax rates for corporations with taxable incomes between $100,000 and $335,000. A corporation having taxable income of $335,000 or more gets no benefit from the lower graduated tax rates and pays, in effect, a flat tax at a 34-percent rate. Similarly, the extra three-percent tax recaptures the benefits of the 34-percent rate in a manner analogous to the recapture of the 15 percent and 25-percent rates.

The benefits of the graduated corporate tax rates do not apply to the taxable income of a qualified personal service corporation (PSC). Instead, a qualified PSC is subject to a flat 35-percent tax rate (Code Sec. 11(b)(2)).

**Alternative tax for net capital gains.** If a corporation has a net capital gain for any tax year, the corporation will pay an alternative tax if it is less than the tax computed in the regular manner. Under the alternative tax, the portion of the corporation's taxable income that is net capital gain is subject to a maximum tax rate of 35 percent. The

¶305

## BACKGROUND

alternative tax rate is applied to the lesser of a corporation's net capital gain or its taxable income (Code Sec. 1201(a)).

> **Comment:** In other words, the alternative tax rate for net capital gains of corporations is 35 percent for years in which a corporation's ordinary income tax rate exceeds 35 percent. In effect, this alternative tax does not apply because the maximum corporate income tax rate is 35 percent.

An alternative maximum tax rate of 23.8 percent applies to the qualified timber gain of a C corporation for the tax year beginning in 2016. Qualified timber gain is the net gain from the sale or exchange of timber described in Code Sec. 631(a) (cutting of standing timber) and Code Sec. 631(b) (disposal of timber with a retained economic interest or outright sale). The special rate applies only to timber that had been held for more than 15 years (Code Sec. 1201(b)).

**Taxation of REITs on net capital gain.** Generally, real estate investment trusts (REITs) are subject to a tax on net capital gain. However, a REIT can pay capital gain dividends to its shareholders in order to reduce its capital gains tax liability. A REIT may elect to retain, rather than distribute, its net long-term capital gains and pay the tax on such gains, while its shareholders include their proportionate share of the undistributed long-term capital gains in income and receive a credit for their share of the tax paid by the REIT. Specifically, the REIT may designate amounts as undistributed capital gains in respect of its shareholders' shares or its holders' beneficial interests. The REIT must then pay tax on the net capital gain within 30 days after the close of its tax year (Code Sec. 857(b)(3)).

**Foreign tax credit limitation - capital gains.** Special rules apply to capital gains and losses that require certain adjustments when calculating the foreign tax credit limitation (Code Sec. 904(b)(2) and (3)). Specifically, foreign source capital gains and losses are subject to (1) a capital gain net income limitation adjustment (i.e., U.S. capital loss adjustment), and (2) a capital gain rate differential adjustment.

If there is a capital gains rate differential (e.g., capital gains are taxed at lower rates than ordinary income), adjustments must be made to capital gains and foreign source losses when calculating the numerator of the foreign tax credit limitation fraction. Capital gains, but not losses, are also adjusted in the denominator of the fraction. The adjustment is needed to take into account the difference between the maximum U.S. tax rate and the more favorable capital gains rates. For individuals, the capital gain tax rate differential exists for any tax year in which the taxpayer is subject to Code Sec. 1(h), relating to the maximum capital gains tax rate. For corporations, a differential exists if the corporate rate under Code Secs. 11, 511, 831(a) or 831(b) exceeds the alternative rate of Code Sec. 1201(a) (Code Sec. 904(b)(3)(D)). A reduction of capital gain net income is required by the rate differential portion of the income. The rate differential portion is the excess of the highest applicable rate over the alternative rate over the highest applicable rate (Code Sec. 904(b)(3)(D)).

**Disallowance of graduated corporate tax rates or accumulated earnings credit to transferee corporations.** Under Code Sec. 1551, the graduated corporate tax rates or the accumulated earnings credit may be disallowed to a transferee corporation that is controlled by the transferor or its stockholders. This provision may be utilized by the IRS when a corporation transfers all or part of its property, other than money, to a

## BACKGROUND

controlled corporation and the transferee corporation was either (i) created for the purpose of acquiring the property, or (ii) not actively engaged in business at the time of the transfer.

If the IRS utilizes the disallowance provision, it is up to the transferee corporation to prove that the major purpose of the transfer was not to secure the benefits of the graduated tax rates or the accumulated earnings credit. The IRS may disallow application of the graduated corporate tax rates or accumulated earnings credits for indirect, as well as direct transfers (Code Sec. 1551(a)).

Control means ownership of at least 80 percent of the voting power or value of the stock of each corporation. For a transfer by five or fewer persons, control means ownership of at least 80 percent of the value or voting power of each corporation's stock and more than 50 percent of the value or voting power of each corporation's stock (taking into account the ownership of each individual only to the extent their stock ownership is identical with respect to each corporation) after the transfer (Code Sec. 1551(b)). In determining whether control exists, special constructive stock ownership rules apply.

**Limitation on multiple tax benefits of controlled groups of corporations.** Corporations that are component members of controlled groups on a December 31 are required to share specific tax benefits for their tax years including that December 31 (Code Sec. 1561). These benefits include: (1) use of the Code Sec. 11(b) graduated bracket amounts; (2) use of the $250,000 ($150,000 if any component member is a personal service corporation) amount for purposes of computing the Code Sec. 535(c) accumulated earnings credit; and (3) use of the $40,000 exemption amount for purposes of computing the amount of minimum tax (Code Sec. 1561(a)).

The tax benefit amounts are generally divided equally among the group members, unless all of the members consent to an apportionment plan providing for an unequal allocation of these amounts (Reg. § 1.1561-3(b)).

A controlled group of corporation consists of corporations related through certain stock ownership. Controlled corporate groups generally include (i) a parent-subsidiary controlled group, (ii) a brother-sister controlled group, and (iii) a combined group (Code Sec. 1563(a)).

**Tax withholding on disposition of U.S. real property.** Generally, the disposition of a U.S. real property interest by a foreign person is subject to income tax withholding. The withholding obligation falls on the transferee. Generally, the transferee is required to deduct and withhold a tax equal to 15 percent of the total amount realized on the disposition (10 percent for dispositions on or before February 16, 2016) (Code Sec. 1445(a)). A higher rate of withholding applies to certain dispositions by domestic partnerships, estates and trusts, and distributions by foreign corporations, real estate investment trusts (REITs), and regulated investment companies (RICs) (generally 35 percent of the gain realized) (Code Sec. 1445(e)).

¶305

## NEW LAW EXPLAINED

**21-percent flat corporate income tax rate established; normalization requirements provided.—Reduction in corporate tax rate.** For tax years beginning after December 31, 2017, the graduated corporate tax rate structure is eliminated and corporate taxable income is taxed at a 21-percent flat rate (Code Sec. 11(b), as amended by the Tax Cuts and Jobs Act (P.L. 115-97)).

> **Comment:** The new law does not provide a special rate for qualified personal service corporations (qualified PSCs); therefore, qualified PSCs are also taxed at a 21-percent rate.

> **Comment:** The lower corporate tax rate is intended to allow domestic corporations to remain globally competitive and increase international investments in the United States. Also, it is expected that the lower corporate tax rate will lead to economic growth and jobs creation because U.S. corporations will have more money to invest. In addition, the lower corporate tax rate is supposed to provide less incentives for U.S. companies to shift operations and employees abroad and encourage investment of their foreign earnings into business expansion and employment in the United States.

The alternative tax for net capital gains is also repealed (Act Sec. 13001(b)(2) of the 2017 Tax Cuts Act, striking Code Sec. 1201).

> **Comment:** The alternative tax is obsolete in light of the new 21-percent corporate tax rate.

**Blended corporate tax rate for fiscal years including January 1, 2018.** Under IRS guidance, a corporation with a fiscal year that includes January 1, 2018, pays federal income tax using a blended tax rate determined under the Code Sec. 15 tax proration rules and not the flat 21-percent tax rate that generally applies to tax years beginning after 2017 (Notice 2018-38).

These corporations determine their federal income tax for fiscal years that include January 1, 2018, by calculating their tax for the entire tax year (i) first, using the graduated tax rates in effect before January 1, 2018, and (ii) then, using the new 21-percent rate. The corporation then apportions each of these tax amounts based on the number of days in the tax year when the different rates were in effect. The sum of these two amounts is the corporation's federal income tax for the fiscal year.

Based on the IRS guidance, corporations can figure their blended regular tax for the fiscal tax year that includes January 1, 2018, under the following steps:

(1) Determine the corporation's taxable income (Line 30, Form 1120).

(2) Compute the tax on the Line 1 amount using the graduated tax rate (or the 35-percent rate for personal service corporations (PSCs)) in effect before January 1, 2018.

(3) Compute the tax on the Line 1 amount using the 21-percent tax rate.

(4) Multiply Line 2 by the number of days in the corporation's tax year before January 1, 2018.

(5) Multiply Line 3 by the number of days in the corporation's tax year after December 31, 2017.

## NEW LAW EXPLAINED

(6) Divide Line 4 by the total number of days in the corporation's tax year.

(7) Divide Line 5 by the total number of days in the corporation's tax year.

(8) Add Lines 6 and 7. This is the corporation's total tax for the fiscal tax year.

---

**Example:** Corporation X, a subchapter C corporation, uses a June 30 tax year. For its tax year beginning July 1, 2017, and ending June 30, 2018, X's taxable income is $1,000,000. Corporation X's corporate income tax is computed by applying the Code Sec. 15 proration rules as follows:

| | | |
|---|---|---:|
| 1) | Taxable income (Line 30, Form 1120) | $ 1,000,000 |
| 2) | Tax on Line 1 amount using the rates in Code Sec. 11(b), prior to amendment by the 2017 Tax Cuts Act | 340,000 |
| 3) | Number of days in Corporation X's tax year before January, 1, 2018 | 184 |
| 4) | Multiply Line 2 by Line 3 | 62,560,000 |
| 5) | Tax on Line 1 amount using the rate in Code Sec. 11(b), as amended by the 2017 Tax Cuts Act | 210,000 |
| 6) | Number of days in the tax year after December 31, 2017 | 181 |
| 7) | Multiply Line 5 by Line 6 | 38,010,000 |
| 8) | Divide Line 4 by total number of days in the tax year | 171,397 |
| 9) | Divide Line 7 by total number of days in the tax year | 104,137 |
| 10) | Sum of Line 8 and Line 9 | $ 275,534 |

Under the tax proration rules, Corporation X's corporate tax for its tax year ending June 30, 2018, is $275,534.

---

Corporations with a fiscal tax year including January 1, 2018, that have already filed their federal income tax returns that do not reflect the blended tax rate may want to consider filing an amended return.

*Qualified personal service corporations and other taxpayers.* A qualified personal service corporation (a qualified PSC) is taxed at the 21-percent corporate tax rate for tax years beginning after 2017 and at a flat rate of 35 percent for tax years beginning before 2018. Qualified PSCs with a fiscal tax year that includes January 1, 2018, must use a blended tax rate to determine their tax for the year, as described above. Therefore, these corporations must apportion their tax using the 35-percent tax rate for the period before January 1, 2018, and the 21-percent rate for the period after December 31, 2017.

Other taxpayers, such as life insurance companies and regulated investment companies, that are taxed under other provisions that use the Code Sec. 11(b) corporate tax rates, must also apply the tax proration rules as described above to determine their tax for a fiscal year including January 1, 2018 (Notice 2018-38).

**Other law changes.** A definition of "undistributed capital gain" is provided for purposes of the rules related to the taxation of REITs on net capital gains. Specifically, undistributed capital gain is the excess of the net capital gain over the deduction for dividends

## NEW LAW EXPLAINED

paid (as defined in Code Sec. 561) determined with reference to capital gain dividends only (Code Sec. 857(b)(3)(F), as amended by the 2017 Tax Cuts Act).

The new law also clarifies that, for purposes of the capital gain rate differential adjustment in determining the foreign tax credit limitation, there is a capital gain rate differential for any year if Code Sec. 1(h) applies to the tax year. In addition, the rate differential portion of foreign source net capital gain, net capital gain, or the excess of net capital gain from sources within the United States over net capital gain, as the case may be, is the same proportion of such amount as (1) the excess of (i) the highest rate of tax set forth in Code Sec. 1(a), (b), (c), (d), or (e) (whichever applies), over (ii) the alternative rate of tax determined under Code Sec. 1(h), bears to (2) the rate referred to in item (i) (Code Sec. 904(b)(3)(D) and (E), as added by the 2017 Tax Cuts Act).

Moreover, the rules for withholding of tax on dispositions of U.S. real property are modified to replace the 35-percent tax required to be withheld on certain dispositions by domestic partnerships, estates and trusts, and distributions by foreign corporations, REITs, and RICs with the highest rate of tax in effect for the tax year under Code Sec. 11(b) (Code Sec. 1445(e), as amended by the 2017 Tax Cuts Act).

In addition, the provision disallowing the graduated corporate tax rates or the accumulated earnings credit to transferee corporations upon certain transfers is repealed (Act Sec. 13001(b)(5)(A) of the 2017 Tax Cuts Act, striking Code Sec. 1551).

The new law further modifies the former rules limiting the use of multiple tax benefits of controlled group of corporations to leave only the limitation on the use of the accumulated earnings credit. Specifically, the component members of a controlled group of corporations on a December 31 are limited, for purposes of Subtitle A of the Code, for their tax years which include that December 31, to one $250,000 ($150,000 if any component member is a personal service corporation) accumulated earnings credit under Code Sec. 535(c). This amount must be divided equally among the component members of the group on that December 31, unless an unequal allocation is allowed by regulations (Code Sec. 1561(a), as amended by the 2017 Tax Cuts Act).

> **Comment:** This change reflects the repeal of the corporate alternative minimum tax and the elimination of the graduated corporate tax rate structure by the 2017 Tax Cuts Act.

If a corporation has a short tax year that does not include a December 31 and is a component member of a controlled group of corporations with respect to that tax year, then for purposes of Subtitle A of the Code, the amount used in computing the accumulated earnings credit of the corporation for that tax year is determined by dividing $250,000 (or $150,000) by the number of corporations that are component members of the group on the last day of that tax year. For this purpose, the definition of component member in Code Sec. 1563(b) is applied as if the last day of the short tax year were substituted for December 31 (Code Sec. 1561(b), as amended by the 2017 Tax Cuts Act).

> **Comment:** The effective date provided for the amendment to Code Sec. 1561 is for transfers made after December 31, 2017 (Act Sec. 13001(c)(3) of the 2017 Tax Cuts Act). However, this effective date does not appear to be correct given the

## NEW LAW EXPLAINED

subject and application of Code Sec. 1561. More liy, the amendment to Code Sec. 1561 should apply to tax years beginning after December 31, 2017. Also, it is likely that the effective date for transfers made after December 31, 2017, is intended to apply to the repeal of Code Sec. 1551, which concerns transfers to corporations.

**Normalization requirements.** For taxpayers subject to the normalization method of accounting (e.g., regulated public utilities), the new law provides for the normalization of excess deferred tax reserves resulting from the reduction of corporate income tax rates (with respect to prior depreciation or recovery allowances taken on assets placed in service before the corporate rate reduction takes effect).

Specifically, a taxpayer is not treated as using a normalization method of accounting with respect to any public utility property for purposes of Code Secs. 167 or 168, if the taxpayer, in computing its cost of service for ratemaking purposes and reflecting operating results in its regulated books of account, reduces the excess tax reserve more rapidly or to a greater extent than such reserve would be reduced under the average rate assumption method (Act Sec. 13001(d)(1) of the 2017 Tax Cuts Act).

For this purpose, the excess tax reserve is the excess of:

(1) the reserve for deferred taxes (described in Code Sec. 168(i)(9)(A)(ii)) as of December 31, 2017 (the day before the corporate rate reductions provided in the amendments made by Act Sec. 13001 of the 2017 Tax Cuts Act take effect), over

(2) the amount that would be the balance in the reserve if the amount of the reserve were determined by assuming that the corporate rate reductions were in effect for all prior periods (Act Sec. 13001(d)(3)(A) of the 2017 Tax Cuts Act).

The average rate assumption method is the method under which the excess in the reserve for deferred taxes is reduced over the remaining lives of the property as used in the taxpayer's regulated books of account that gave rise to the reserve for deferred taxes. Under this method, during the time period in which timing differences for the property (i.e., differences between tax depreciation and regulatory depreciation with respect to the property) reverse, the amount of the adjustment to the reserve for the deferred taxes is calculated by multiplying:

(1) the ratio of the aggregate deferred taxes for the property to the aggregate timing differences for the property as of the beginning of the period in question, by

(2) the amount of the timing differences that reverse during that period (Act Sec. 13001(d)(3)(B) of the 2017 Tax Cuts Act).

**Comment:** In other words, under this method, the excess tax reserve is reduced as the timing differences reverse over the remaining life of the asset. To ensure that the deferred tax reserve, including the excess tax reserve, is reduced to zero at the end of the regulatory life of the asset that generated the reserve, the amount of the timing difference that reverses during a tax year is multiplied by the ratio of (1) the aggregate deferred taxes as of the beginning of the period in question to (2) the aggregate timing differences for the property as of the beginning of the period in question.

# NEW LAW EXPLAINED

**Comment:** The reversal of timing differences generally occurs when the amount of the tax depreciation taken with respect to an asset is less than the amount of the regulatory depreciation taken with respect to the asset.

**Example:** A calendar year regulated utility placed property costing $100 million in service in 2016. For regulatory (book) purposes, the property is depreciated over 10 years on a straight line basis with a full year's allowance in the first year. For tax purposes, the property is depreciated over 5 years using the 200 percent declining balance method and a half-year placed in service convention.

### Normalization calculation for corporate rate reduction
### (Millions of dollars)

| | 2016 | 2017 | 2018 | 2019 | 2020 | 2021 | 2022 | 2023 | 2024 | 2025 | Total |
|---|---|---|---|---|---|---|---|---|---|---|---|
| Tax expense | 20 | 32 | 19.2 | 11.52 | 11.52 | 5.76 | 0 | 0 | 0 | 0 | 100 |
| Book depreciation | 10 | 10 | 10 | 10 | 10 | 10 | 10 | 10 | 10 | 10 | 100 |
| Timing difference | 10 | 22 | 9.2 | 1.52 | 1.52 | (4.24) | (10) | (10) | (10) | (10) | 0 |
| Tax rate | 35% | 35% | 21% | 21% | 21% | 31.1% | 31.1% | 31.1% | 31.1% | 31.1% | |
| Annual adjustment to reserve | 3.5 | 7.7 | 1.9 | 0.3 | 0.3 | (1.3) | (3.1) | (3.1) | (3.1) | (3.1) | 0 |
| Cumulative deferred tax reserve | 3.5 | 11.2 | 13.1 | 13.5 | 13.8 | 12.5 | 9.3 | 6.2 | 3.1 | (0.0) | 0 |
| Annual adjustment at 21% | | | | | | (0.9) | (2.1) | (2.1) | (2.1) | (2.1) | (9.3) |
| Annual adjustment at average rate | | | | | | (1.3) | (3.1) | (3.1) | (3.1) | (3.1) | (13.8) |
| Excess tax reserve | | | | | | 0.4 | 1.0 | 1.0 | 1.0 | 1.0 | 4.5 |

The excess tax reserve as of December 31, 2017, the day before the corporate rate reduction takes effect, is $4.5 million (the cumulative deferred tax reserve as of December 31, 2017 ($11.2 million), minus the cumulative timing difference as of December 31, 2017 ($32 million), multiplied by 21 percent). The taxpayer will begin taking the excess tax reserve into account in the 2021 tax year, which is the first year in which the tax depreciation taken with respect to the property is less than the depreciation reflected in the regulated books of account. The annual adjustment to the deferred tax reserve for the 2021 through 2025 tax years is multiplied by 31.1 percent, which is the ratio of the aggregate deferred taxes as of the beginning of 2021 ($13.8 million) to the aggregate timing

## NEW LAW EXPLAINED

> differences for the property as of the beginning of 2021 ($44.2 million) (Conference Report on H.R. 1, Tax Cuts and Jobs Act (H. Rept. 115-466)).

*Alternative method for certain taxpayers.* If, as of the first day of the tax year that includes December 22, 2017:

(1) the taxpayer was required by a regulatory agency to compute depreciation for public utility property on the basis of an average life or composite rate method, and

(2) the taxpayer's books and underlying records did not contain the vintage account data necessary to apply the average rate assumption method, then

(3) the taxpayer is treated as using a normalization method of accounting if, with respect to such jurisdiction, the taxpayer uses the alternative method for public utility property that is subject to the regulatory authority of that jurisdiction (Act Sec. 13001(d)(2) of the 2017 Tax Cuts Act).

For this purpose, the alternative method is the method in which the taxpayer:

(1) computes the excess tax reserve on all public utility property included in the plant account on the basis of the weighted average life or composite rate used to compute depreciation for regulatory purposes, and

(2) reduces the excess tax reserve ratably over the remaining regulatory life of the property (Act Sec. 13001(d)(3)(C) of the 2017 Tax Cuts Act).

*Tax increase for normalization violation.* If, for any tax year ending after December 22, 2017, the taxpayer does not use a normalization method of accounting for the corporate rate reductions provided in the amendments made by Act Sec. 13001 of the 2017 Tax Cuts Act:

(1) the taxpayer's tax for the tax year is increased by the amount by which it reduces its excess tax reserve more rapidly than permitted under a normalization method of accounting, and

(2) the taxpayer is not treated as using a normalization method of accounting for purposes of Code Sec. 168(f)(2) and (i)(9)(C) (Act Sec. 13001(d)(4) of the 2017 Tax Cuts Act).

▶ **Effective date.** The amendments made by this section generally apply to tax years beginning after December 31, 2017 (Act Sec. 13001(c) of the Tax Cuts and Jobs Act (P.L. 115-97)). The amendment relating to the withholding rules on disposition of U.S. real property interests applies to distributions made after December 31, 2017. The amendment relating to the Code Sec. 1561 limitation on the use of the accumulated earnings credit by controlled corporate groups applies to transfers made after December 31, 2017 [applies to tax years beginning after December 31, 2017].

— Act Sec. 13001(a) of the Tax Cuts and Jobs Act (P.L. 115-97), amending Code Sec. 11(b);

— Act Sec. 13001(b)(1), amending Code Secs. 280C(c)(3)(B)(ii)(II), 860E(e)(2)(B), 860E(e)(6)(A)(ii), and 7874(e)(1)(B);

**NEW LAW EXPLAINED**

— Act Sec. 13001(b)(2), striking Code Sec. 1201 and Code Sec. 1374(b)(4), and amending Code Secs. 12, 453A(c)(3), 527(b), 594(a), 691(c)(4) , 801(a), 831(e), 832(c)(5), 834(b)(1)(D), 852(b)(3)(A), 857(b)(3), 882(a)(1), 904(b), 1381(b), 6425(c)(1)(A), 6655(g)(1)(A)(i), and 7518(g)(6)(A);

— Act Sec. 13001(b)(3) through (7), amending Code Secs. 535(c)(5), 852(b)(1), 1445(e), 1446(b)(2)(B), 1561, as amended by Act Sec. 12001, and 7518(g)(6)(A), and striking Code Sec. 1551;

— Act Sec. 13001(c), providing the effective date;

— Act Sec. 13001(d).

## ¶310  Alternative Minimum Tax (AMT) for Corporations

### SUMMARY OF NEW LAW

The alternative minimum tax (AMT) for corporations has been repealed, for tax years beginning after 2017. Any unused minimum tax credit of a corporation may be used to offset regular tax liability for any tax year. In addition, a portion of unused minimum tax credit is refundable in 2018 through 2021. The refundable portion is 50 percent (100 percent in 2021) of any excess minimum tax for the year over any credit allowable against regular tax for that year.

### BACKGROUND

An alternative minimum tax (AMT) is imposed on a corporation equal to the excess of the taxpayer's tentative minimum tax for the year, over regular tax liability (Code Sec. 55). For a corporation, tentative minimum tax is 20 percent of the taxpayer's alternative minimum taxable income (AMTI). A small corporation is exempt from AMT if its average annual gross receipts do not exceed $7.5 million for the previous three tax years. The dollar threshold is reduced to $5 million for a corporation in its first three years of existence.

AMTI is the taxpayer's regular taxable income increased by AMT tax preference items and modified by AMT adjustment (Code Secs. 56 and 57). Corporate tax preference items not allowed in computing AMTI include deductions for depletion and intangible drilling costs, as well the exclusion of tax-exempt interest on private activity bonds. Corporate AMT adjustments include net operating losses (NOLs), depreciation, gains and losses, as well as adjusted current earnings (ACE). A corporation generally must also reduce or cut back certain tax preference items before calculation of its AMTI. A corporation may avoid having an AMT preference or adjustment by electing to capitalize certain expenses and deduct them ratably for regular tax purposes beginning with the tax year (or month) in which the expenses were made (Code Sec. 59(e)). The amortization period is three years for circulation expenses, 60 months for intangible drilling costs (IDC), and 10 years for mineral exploration and development expenses.

## BACKGROUND

If a corporation is subject to AMT in any tax year, it may claim a tax credit against its regular income tax liability for AMT paid in previous tax years (Code Sec. 53(c)). The minimum tax credit is equal to the corporation's AMT liability for the current year, less any minimum tax credit claimed in previous years. If the taxpayer was a small corporation exempt from AMT, its minimum credit is limited to the extent the corporation's regular tax liability (reduced by other credits) exceeds 25 percent of the excess (if any) of the corporation's regular tax (reduced by other credits) over $25,000 (Code Sec. 55(e)(5)).

The minimum credit is limited to the extent that the regular tax liability, reduced by other nonrefundable credits, exceeds the taxpayer's tentative minimum tax for the tax year. Any unused minimum credit may be carried forward indefinitely as a credit against regular tax liability to the extent that the regular tax liability reduced by all other nonrefundable credits exceeds the tentative AMT liability for the tax year. The credit may not be used to offset any future AMT liability. However, a corporation may elect to claim a portion of its unused minimum tax credits outstanding, instead of claiming the bonus depreciation deduction on the property it placed in service during the tax year that qualifies for bonus depreciation (Code Sec. 168(k)(4)). In addition, any minimum tax credit carryover from a C corporation tax year may offset the built-in gains tax of a corporation in an S corporation year (Code Sec. 1374(b)(3)(B)).

## NEW LAW EXPLAINED

**Corporate AMT repealed; minimum tax credit refundable in 2018 through 2021.**—The alternative minimum tax (AMT) is repealed for corporations for tax years beginning after December 31, 2017 (Code Sec. 55(a), as amended by the Tax Cuts and Jobs Act (P.L. 115-97)). A corporation with a fiscal year that includes January 1, 2018, calculates AMT using a blended tax rate determined under Code Sec. 15 and not the zero rate that generally applies for tax years beginning after December 31, 2017 (Notice 2018-38).

> **Comment:** The AMT is only applicable to individuals, estates, and trusts for tax years beginning after 2017. The AMT exemption amounts and phaseout thresholds for individuals (but not estates and trusts) are temporarily increased beginning in 2018 (see ¶110). Partnership or S corporations are not subject to AMT, but instead a partner or S corporation shareholder computes AMT liability separately by taking into account their share of partnership or S corporation items.

A corporation's tentative minimum tax is zero ($0) for purposes of the minimum tax credit (AMT credit) beginning in 2018 (Code Sec. 53(d)(2), as amended by the 2017 Tax Cuts Act). As a result, a minimum tax credit claimed by a corporation beginning after 2017 is generally limited to the taxpayer's regular tax liability, reduced by other nonrefundable credits. The minimum tax credit is the corporation's AMT liability from tax years prior to its repeal and carried over to tax years after 2017 (Code Sec. 53(e), as added by the 2017 Tax Cuts Act). Any minimum tax credit carryover from a C corporation tax year may continue to offset the built-in gain tax of an S corporation until tax years beginning after December 31, 2021 (Code Sec. 1374(b)(3)(B), as amended by the 2017 Tax Cuts Act).

# NEW LAW EXPLAINED

Any unused minimum tax credit is refundable for tax years beginning in 2018, 2019, 2020, and 2021 (Code Sec. 53(e), as added by the 2017 Tax Cuts Act). The refundable credit amount is equal to 50 percent (100 percent for tax years beginning in 2021) of the excess of the minimum tax credit for the tax year, over the amount allowable for the year against regular tax liability. Thus, the full amount of the minimum tax credit is allowed in tax years beginning before 2022. If a corporation has a short tax year, then the refundable credit amount for that year is prorated based on the number of days in the short year compared to 365 days.

**Election to claim unused AMT credits in lieu of bonus depreciation.** The annual election provided to corporations to claim unused minimum tax credits in place of bonus depreciation on property placed in service during the tax year of the election is repealed, effective for tax years beginning after December 31, 2017 (Code Sec. 168(k)(4), stricken by the 2017 Tax Cuts Act).

**General business credit and effect on other rules.** Since corporate AMT is repealed, a corporation's tentative minimum tax is zero ($0) after 2017 for purposes of the tax liability limitation of the general business credit (Code Sec. 38(c)(6)(E), as added by the 2017 Tax Cuts Act). This means that a corporation may claim the credit to the extent it does not exceed 25 percent of its net regular tax liability above $25,000.

> **Comment:** Since the corporate AMT is repealed, a corporation may forgo the election to amortize certain expenses to avoid any AMT adjustment or preference with regard to the expenses (circulation expenses, intangible drilling costs, and mineral exploration and development expenses) (Code Sec. 59(e)).

> **Comment:** A net operating loss (NOL) deduction of a corporation from tax years beginning after 2017 is determined without regard to any AMT adjustments or preferences due to the repeal of the corporate AMT. Thus, an NOL carried back to determine the corporation's alternative minimum taxable income (AMTI) in tax years before 2018 is calculated the same as for regular tax liability.

▶ **Effective date.** The amendments made by this section generally apply to tax years beginning after December 31, 2017 (Act Secs. 12001(c) and 12002(d)(1) of the Tax Cuts and Jobs Act (P.L. 115-97)). The amendment striking the minimum tax credit carryover of an S corporation arising in a tax year in which the corporation was a C corporation to offset the built-in gains tax of the S corporation applies to tax years beginning after December 31, 2021 (Act. Sec. 12002(d)(2) of the 2017 Tax Cuts Act).

— Act Sec. 12001(a) of the Tax Cuts and Jobs Act (P.L. 115-97), amending Code Sec. 55(a);

— Act Sec. 12002(a) and (b), adding Code Sec. 53(e) and amending Code Sec. 53(d)(3);

— Act Secs. 12001(b) and 12002(c), amending Code Secs. 11(d), 38(c)(6), 53(d)(2), 55(b)(1), 55(b)(3), 55(c)(1), 55(d), 56(b)(2), 58(a), 59(a), 847(9), 882(a)(1), 897(a)(2)(A), 911(f), 962(a)(1), 1374(b)(3)(B), 1561(a), 6425(c)(1)(A), 6655(e)(2), 6655(g)(1)(A), and striking Code Secs. 12(7), 55(e), 56(c), 56(g), 59(b), 59(f), 168(k)(4), and 848(i);

— Act Secs. 12001(c) and 12002(d), providing the effective dates.

## ¶315 Dividends-Received Deduction

### SUMMARY OF NEW LAW

For tax years beginning after December 31, 2017, the 70-percent dividends-received deduction is reduced to 50 percent and the 80-percent dividends-received deduction is reduced to 65 percent.

### BACKGROUND

Generally, a corporation is allowed a deduction for dividends received from other taxable domestic corporations (Code Sec. 243(a)). The amount of the deduction is generally equal to 70 percent of the dividend received.

In the case of any dividend received from a 20-percent owned corporation, the amount of the deduction is equal to 80 percent of the dividend received (Code Sec. 243(c)). A 20-percent owned corporation is any corporation if 20 percent or more of the stock of such corporation (by vote and value) is owned by the taxpayer. For this purpose, certain preferred stock is excluded.

> **Key Rates and Figures:** Dividends subject to the 70-percent dividends-received deduction are taxed at a maximum rate of 10.5 percent (30 percent of the 35 percent top corporate tax rate). Dividends subject to the 80-percent dividends-received deduction are taxed at a maximum rate of 7 percent (20 percent of the 35 percent top corporate tax rate).

In the case of a dividend received from a corporation that is a member of the same affiliated group, the deduction is equal to 100 percent of the dividend received (Code Sec. 243(a)(3) and (b)(1)). For this purpose, an affiliated group is defined in Code Sec. 1504(a) (Code Sec. 243(b)(2)).

A domestic corporation is entitled to a 70-percent deduction for the U.S.-source portion of dividends received from a foreign corporation (other than a passive foreign investment company (PFIC)) that is at least 10-percent owned, by vote and value, by the domestic corporation (Code Sec. 245(a)(1)). The deduction is 80 percent in the case of dividends received from a 20-percent owned corporation. A 100-percent deduction is allowed for eligible dividends received from a wholly owned foreign subsidiary all of whose income is effectively connected with a U.S. business (Code Sec. 245(b)).

A U.S. corporation is allowed a 100-percent deduction for any dividends received from a corporation that are distributed from earnings and profits attributable to foreign trade income for a period during which such corporation was a foreign sales corporation (FSC) (Code Sec. 245(c)(1)). A 70-percent dividends-received deduction (80 percent in the case of dividends received from a 20-percent-owned corporation) is provided for any dividend received by a U.S. corporation from another corporation that is distributed out of earnings and profits attributable to "effectively connected income" received or accrued by such other corporation while it was an FSC (Code Sec. 245(c)(1)(B)). Effectively connected income includes all income that is actually effectively connected with a U.S. trade or business and is subject to U.S. income tax,

## BACKGROUND

and all income that is deemed to be effectively connected and is subject to U.S. tax (e.g., by the FSC rules on investment income) (Code Sec. 245(c)(4)).

The aggregate dividends-received deduction under Code Secs. 243 and 245 is limited to 70 percent of the receiving corporation's taxable income if it owns less than 20 percent of the distributing corporation, and to 80 percent of its taxable income if it owns 20 percent or more of the distributing corporation (Code Sec. 246(b)).

The 70-percent corporate dividends-received deduction (80 percent in the case of dividends received from a 20-percent owned corporation) is reduced in the case of dividends received with respect to debt-financed portfolio stock by a percentage related to the amount of debt incurred to purchase the stock (Code Sec. 246A(a)).

For purposes of the foreign tax credit limitation, dividends from a foreign corporation are treated as income from foreign sources to the extent the amount of the dividend exceeds the amount that is 100/70th (100/80th in the case of a 20-percent owned corporation) of the amount of the deduction allowable under Code Sec. 245 (Code Sec. 861(a)(2)).

## NEW LAW EXPLAINED

**Dividends-received deduction reduced.**—For tax years beginning after December 31, 2017, the 70-percent dividends-received deduction is reduced to 50 percent and the 80-percent dividends-received deduction is reduced to 65 percent (Code Sec. 243(a)(1) and (c)(1), as amended by the Tax Cuts and Jobs Act (P.L. 115-97)).

> **Comment:** The dividends-received deduction is reduced to reflect the new lower corporate tax rate of 21 percent.

> **Key Rates and Figures:** Dividends subject to the new 50-percent dividends-received deduction will be taxed at a maximum rate of 10.5 percent (50 percent of the 21 percent new corporate tax rate). Dividends subject to the new 65-percent dividends-received deduction will be taxed at a maximum rate of 7.35 percent (35 percent of the 21 percent new corporate tax rate).

A 50-percent dividends-received deduction (65 percent in the case of dividends received from a 20-percent-owned corporation) is provided for any dividend received by a U.S. corporation from another corporation that is distributed out of earnings and profits attributable to effectively connected income received or accrued by such other corporation while it was an FSC (Code Sec. 245(c)(1)(B), as amended by the 2017 Tax Cuts Act).

In addition, the aggregate amount of deductions allowed under Code Secs. 243 and 245, and Code Sec. 250, is limited to 50 percent of the receiving corporation's taxable income if it owns less than 20 percent of the distributing corporation, and to 65 percent of its taxable income if it owns 20 percent or more of the distributing corporation (Code Sec. 246(b)(3), as amended by the 2017 Tax Cuts Act). Also, the 50-percent dividends-received deduction (65 percent in the case of dividends received from a 20-percent owned corporation) is reduced in the case of dividends received with respect to debt-financed portfolio stock by a percentage related to the

## NEW LAW EXPLAINED

amount of debt incurred to purchase the stock (Code Sec. 246A(a)(1), as amended by the 2017 Tax Cuts Act).

Finally, for purposes of the foreign tax credit limitation, dividends from a foreign corporation are treated as income from foreign sources to the extent the amount of the dividend exceeds the amount that is 100/50th (100/65th in the case of a 20-percent owned corporation) of the amount of the deduction allowable under Code Sec. 245 (Code Sec. 861(a)(2), as amended by the 2017 Tax Cuts Act).

▶ **Effective date.** The amendments made by this section apply to tax years beginning after December 31, 2017 (Act Sec. 13002(f) of the Tax Cuts and Jobs Act (P.L. 115-97)).

**No significant guidance related to this provision has been issued.**

— Act Sec. 13002(a) of the Tax Cuts and Jobs Act (P.L. 115-97), amending Code Sec. 243(a)(1) and (c);

— Act Sec. 13002(b), amending Code Sec. 245(c)(1)(B);

— Act Sec. 13002(c), amending Code Sec. 246(b)(3);

— Act Sec. 13002(d), amending Code Sec. 246A(a)(1);

— Act Sec. 13002(e), amending Code Sec. 861(a)(2);

— Act Sec. 13002(f), providing the effective date.

## ¶320 Contribution of Capital to Corporations

### SUMMARY OF NEW LAW

The definition of contribution to capital is modified to exclude contributions by any governmental entity or civic group that are not made by a shareholder in its capacity as a shareholder. The special rules for contributions to water and sewage disposal utilities are eliminated.

### BACKGROUND

Contributions to the capital of a corporation are excluded from the corporation's gross income. A contribution is exempt whether it is made by shareholders or by persons other than shareholders (Code Sec. 118(a), Reg. § 1.118-1).

However, the exemption does not apply to any contribution in aid of construction or any other contribution as either a customer or potential customer. Thus, most corporate regulated utilities cannot treat contributions received in aid of construction or any other contributions by a customer or potential customer as a nontaxable contribution. Contributions that a utility receives to provide or encourage the provision of services to or for the benefit of the contributor must be reported as income by the utility (Code Sec. 118(b)).

There is an exception to this rule for water and sewage disposal utilities, under which money or property received by such utilities qualifies as a tax-free contribution to the

## BACKGROUND

capital if: (1) the amount is a contribution in aid of construction; (2) in the case of contribution of property other than water or sewerage disposal facilities, the amount meets the requirements of the expenditure rule; (3) the amount (or property acquired or constructed with such amount) is excluded from the utility's rate base for rate-making purposes. Water and sewage disposal utilities are not allowed any deductions or credits for expenditures that constitute a contribution in aid of construction. Also, the adjusted basis of any property acquired by water and sewage disposal utilities with contributions in aid of construction is zero (Code Sec. 118(c)).

An extended statute of limitations period is provided for the assessment of deficiencies attributable to a contribution of property other than water or sewage disposal facilities that is treated as a contribution to capital of a water or sewage disposal utility (Code Sec. 118(d)).

## NEW LAW EXPLAINED

**Definition of contribution to capital modified.**—For purposes of applying the general rule under Code Sec. 118(a) that excludes from a corporation's gross income any contributions to capital, contribution to capital does not include:

- any contribution in aid of construction or any other contribution as a customer or potential customer, and

- any contribution by any governmental entity or civic group (other than a contribution made by a shareholder as such) (Code Sec. 118(b), as added by the Tax Cuts and Jobs Act (P.L. 115-97)).

  **Comment:** The new law eliminates the special rules for contributions to water and sewage disposal utilities and the extended statute of limitations period for the assessment of deficiencies attributable to such contributions.

The IRS is authorized to issue regulations or other guidance as may be necessary or appropriate to carry out this provision, including regulations or other guidance for determining whether any contribution constitutes a contribution in aid of construction (Code Sec. 118(c), as added by the 2017 Tax Cuts Act).

▶ **Effective date.** The provision generally applies to contributions made after December 22, 2017, the date of the enactment (Act Sec. 13312(b)(1) of the Tax Cuts and Jobs Act (P.L. 115-97)). The provision will not apply to any contributions made after December 22, 2017, the date of enactment, by a governmental entity, which is made pursuant to a master development plan that has been approved prior to such date by a governmental entity (Act Sec. 13312(b)(2) of the Tax Cuts Act).

**No significant guidance related to this provision has been issued.**

— Act Sec. 13312(a) of the Tax Cuts and Jobs Act (P.L. 115-97), striking Code Sec. 118(b), (c), and (d), redesignating Code Sec. 118(e) as (d), and adding new Code Sec. 118(b) and (c);

— Act Sec. 13312(b), providing the effective date.

## ¶325   Alaska Native Corporations and Settlement Trusts

### SUMMARY OF NEW LAW

New rules have been enacted to establish the tax treatment of payments received by Alaska Native Corporations and transfers made to Alaska Native Settlement Trusts. Native Corporations are not required to recognize income for certain payments assigned to Settlement Trusts and can also deduct contributions to Settlement Trusts.

### BACKGROUND

In 1971 the Alaska Native Claims Settlement Act (ANCSA) was enacted to settle claims between Alaskan natives, the State of Alaska, and the federal government. Under ANCSA (43 U.S.C. § 1601 et seq.), the Alaskan native tribes gave up their territorial claims to land in exchange for title to 44 million acres of land that they had historically used, and $962.5 million. The compensation was to be transferred to 12 regional Alaska Native Corporations (Native Corporations). A thirteenth Native Corporation was later established for the benefit of Alaska natives living outside of Alaska.

Under the ANCSA, the Native Corporations could create Alaska Native Settlement Trusts (Settlement Trusts) to "promote the health, education and welfare of its beneficiaries and preserve the heritage and culture of Natives" (43 U.S.C. § 1601 et seq.; 43 U.S.C. § 1629e). A Settlement Trust generally permits the separation of portfolio assets from the business assets of a Native Corporation, and allows these portfolio assets to be invested to provide income to Alaska Natives and their future generations free of business risks of the Native Corporations.

Before enactment of Code Sec. 646, the IRS took the position that a Native Corporation's transfer of property to a Settlement Trust constituted a distribution of assets to the Settlement Trust's individual beneficiaries, who were then currently taxed on the assets to the extent of the Native Corporation's current or accumulated earnings and profits under Code Sec. 301. Thus, beneficiaries could be taxed on Native Corporation's transfer to a Settlement Trust, even though they had received only an illiquid beneficial interest in the Trust (S. Rep. No. 107-30, Restoring Earnings to Lift Individuals and Empower Families (RELIEF) Act of 2001 (S. 896)). This tax treatment of individual beneficiaries was considered to inhibit the formation of Settlement Trusts.

A Settlement Trust established by a Native Corporation may elect to have special rules apply to the trust and its beneficiaries with respect to the trust ( Code Sec. 646(c), as enacted by the Economic Growth and Tax Relief Reconciliation Act of 2001 (P.L. 2001-17)). The electing Settlement Trust will pay tax on its income at the lowest rate specified in Code Sec. 1(c) for ordinary income and capital gains of an individual ( Code Sec. 646(b)(1) and (2)). No amount will be included in the gross income of the beneficiaries by reason of a contribution to the electing Settlement Trust ( Code Sec. 646(d)(1)). The law also provides rules governing the treatment of distributions to beneficiaries by an electing Settlement Trust, the reporting requirements associated

## BACKGROUND

with the election (Code Sec. 6039H), and the consequences of the trust's disqualification due to the allowance of certain impermissible dispositions of trust interests or Native Corporation stock ( Code Sec. 646(e)). The Code Sec. 646 provisions regarding the income tax treatment of an electing Settlement Trust and its beneficiaries, and the reporting requirements under Code Sec. 6039H of a fiduciary of an electing Settlement Trust, were made permanent for tax years beginning after December 31, 2012, by the American Taxpayer Relief Act of 2012 (P.L. 112-240).

## NEW LAW EXPLAINED

**Tax treatment of payments made to Alaska Native Corporations and Alaska Native Settlement Trusts clarified.**—The tax treatment of transactions between Alaska Native Corporations (Native Corporations) and Alaska Native Settlement Trusts (Settlement Trusts) is clarified by the following new provisions:

- Native Corporations are not required to recognize income for certain payments assigned to Settlement Trusts (Code Sec. 139G, as added by the Tax Cuts and Jobs Act (P.L. 115-97)), and

- Native Corporations can deduct contributions to Settlement Trusts (other than those made pursuant to Code Sec. 139G) (Code Sec. 247, as added by the 2017 Tax Cuts Act).

Settlement Trusts may also elect to defer recognition of income for payments received from Native Corporations (Code Sec. 247(g), as added by the 2017 Tax Cuts Act).

Additionally, information reporting is required for deductible contributions made by Native Corporations to Settlement Trusts (Code Sec. 6039H(e), as added by the 2017 Tax Cuts Act).

**Native Corporations assignment of payments under ANCSA to Settlement Trusts.** The value of payments that would otherwise be made or treated as made to any one of the 13 Native Corporations under the Alaska Native Claims Settlement Act (ANCSA), (43 U.S.C. 1601 et seq.) will not be included in the gross income of the Native Corporation provided that the payments:

- are assigned in writing to a Settlement Trust, and

- were not received by the Native Corporation before it made the assignment to the Settlement Trust (Code Sec. 139G(a), as added by the 2017 Tax Cuts Act).

This nonrecognition rule also applies to payments that would otherwise have been made to a Village Corporation pursuant to 7(j) of the ANSCA (43 U.S.C. 1606(j)) (Code Sec. 139G(a), as added by the 2017 Tax Cuts Act).

A Settlement Trust that receives assigned payments from a Native Corporation must include the payments in its gross income when the payments are received pursuant to assignment. The assigned payments will have the same character as if they were received by the Native Corporation. The amount of any assignment made by a Native Corporation to a Settlement Trust must be described with reasonable particularity. It

**NEW LAW EXPLAINED**

may either be described as a percentage of one or more payments, or as a fixed dollar amount (Code Sec. 139G(b) and (c), as added by the 2017 Tax Cuts Act).

An assignment to a Settlement Trust must specify whether it is made in perpetuity or for a period of time, and whether the assignment may be revoked (Code Sec. 139G(d), as added by the 20017 Tax Cuts Act).

A Native Corporation cannot take a deduction for any amounts received under the ANCSA that were excluded from income under Code Sec. 139G(a) (Code Sec. 139G(e), as added by the 2017 Tax Cuts Act).

The terms "Native Corporation" and "Settlement Trust" are defined under Code Sec. 646(h) (Code Sec. 139G(f), as added by the 2017 Tax Cuts Act).

**Deductions for contributions by Native Corporations.** A Native Corporation may elect annually to deduct contributions made to a Settlement Trust (Code Sec. 247(a) and (e), as added by the 2017 Tax Cuts Act).

> **Comment:** No deduction will be allowed to a Native Corporation for amounts that were made nontaxable underCode Sec. 139G, as added by the Tax Cuts Act.

If otherwise allowable, the Native Corporation's deduction will be available regardless of whether or not it has made an election under Code Sec. 646 (Code Sec. 247(a), as added by the 2017 Tax Cuts Act).

The deduction will be equal to the amount of payment in the case of cash contributions, regardless of the method of payment (including currency, coins, money order, or check). In the case of all other forms of payment, the deduction will be equal to *the lesser of* the Native Corporation's adjusted basis in the property contributed, or the fair market value of the property contributed (Code Sec. 247(b), as added by the 2017 Tax Cuts Act).

A Native Corporation's deduction under Code Sec. 247(a) cannot exceed its taxable income (as determined without regard to such deduction), for the tax year in which the contribution was made. If the aggregate amount of the contributions exceeds the Native Corporation's taxable income for the tax year, the amount of the excess may be carried over in each of the 15 succeeding years (Code Sec. 247(c), as added by the 2017 Tax Cuts Act).

The terms "Native Corporation" and "Settlement Trust" are defined under Code Sec. 646(h) (Code Sec. 247(d), as added by the 2017 Tax Cuts Act).

**Election to claim deductions.** A Native Corporation may elect to claim deductions under Code Sec. 247 on its income tax return or an amendment or supplement to the return. Each election will only be effective for the tax year. The Native Corporation's election may be revoked by a timely filed amendment or supplement to its income tax return (Code Sec. 247(e), as added by the 2017 Tax Cuts Act).

If a Native Corporation claims a deduction under Code Sec. 247, the earnings and profits of the Native Corporation for the tax year will be reduced by the amount of the deduction. This rule is contrary to the rule in Code Sec. 646(d)(2), which precludes such reductions. No gain or loss will be recognized by a Native Corporation with respect to deductible contributions (Code Sec. 247(f)(1), (f)(2), as added by the 2017 Tax Cuts Act).

¶325

## NEW LAW EXPLAINED

Unless a Settlement Trust elects to defer income under Code Sec. 247(g) (discussed below), it must include in income the amount of any deduction allowed with respect to a contribution received, in the tax year in which the contribution was received (Code Sec. 247(f)(3), as added by the 2017 Tax Cuts Act).

**Holding period and basis rules.** The holding period under Code Sec. 1223 of a Settlement Trust will include the period that the property was held by the transferring Native Corporation. A Settlement Trust's basis in contributed property for which the Native Corporation claimed a deduction is the lesser of:

- the adjusted basis that the Native Corporation has in the property immediately before the contribution, or

- the fair market value of the property immediately before its contribution (Code Sec. 247(f)(5), as added by the 2017 Tax Cuts Act).

**Prohibited transfers.** No deduction under Code Sec. 247 is allowed with respect to any contribution to a Settlement Trust of subsurface property rights (estates) or timber resources (43 U.S.C. 1629(e)(a)(2) and 1629(e)(c)(2)) (Code Sec. 247(f)(6), as added by the 2017 Tax Cuts Act).

**Deferral of income recognition by Settlement Trusts.** Except for cash contributions received, a Settlement Trust may elect to defer recognition of income for contributed properties (on a property-by-property basis, if desired) until the sale or exchange of a property (Code Sec. 247(g)(1), as added by the 2017 Tax Cuts Act). In the case of such a property, income or gain realized on the sale or exchange of the property will be treated as:

- ordinary income for the income or gain realized on the sale or exchange of the property that is an amount that is less than or equal to the amount of income that would be included in income at the time of contribution under Code Sec. 247(g)(2)(A), but for the Settlement Trust's election to defer gain, and

- having the same tax character as if the deferral election did not apply for the amounts of income or gain that are in excess of the amount of income that would be included at the time of contribution under Code Sec. 247(g)(2)(B), but for the Settlement Trust's election to defer gain.

**Election procedure.** A Settlement Trust may make an yearly election to defer gain on any property (other than cash) that it received as a contribution during the tax year. Any property for which this election is made must be identified and described with reasonable particularity on the Settlement Trust's income tax return or amendment or supplement to the return. The election will be effective only for that tax year. Such an election can be revoked on a timely filed amendment or supplement to the Settlement Trust's income tax return (Code Sec. 267(g)(3)(A) and (B)).

If a Settlement Trust disposes of a property for which an income deferral election was made, within the first tax year after the property was contributed to the Settlement Trust:

## NEW LAW EXPLAINED

- the deferral election would be treated as if it had not been made;

- any income or gain that would have been included in the year of contribution under Code Sec. 247(f)(3) but for the Settlement Trust's income deferral election, is include in income for the tax year of the contribution; and

- the Settlement Trust must pay any increase in tax relating to the inclusion, plus applicable interest, as well as an additional 10 percent on the increase amount, plus interest (Code Sec. 247(g)(3)(C)(i), as added by the 2017 Tax Cuts Act).

The increase in tax applicable with respect to a disposition of property within the first tax year after contribution to a Settlement Trust may be assessed, or a court proceeding may be initiated without assessment, within four years after the date on which the return making the election for such property was filed, despite the three-year limitations period on assessment and collection in Code Sec. 6501(a) (Code Sec. 247(g)(3)(C)(ii), as added by the 2017 Tax Cuts Act).

**Information reporting of Native Corporation's deductible contributions to Settlement Trusts.** A Native Corporation that makes an election to deduct a contribution to a Settlement Trust under Code Sec. 247(e) must provide the Settlement Trust with a statement regarding the election no later than the January 31 of the calendar year after the calendar year in which the contribution was made. This statement must include:

- the total contributions to which the election under Code Sec. 247(e) applies;

- for each contribution, whether it was in cash;

- for each contribution that was not in cash, the date that the Native Corporation acquired the property, and the adjusted basis and fair market value of the property on the date it was contributed to the Settlement Trust;

- the date on which each contribution was made to the Settlement Trust; and

- such additional information that the IRS determines is needed or appropriate for identifying each contribution and to the Settlement Trust's accurate inclusion of the income relating to such contributions (Code Sec. 6039H(e), as added by the 2017 Tax Cuts Act).

▶ **Effective date.** The provisions of Code Sec. 139G, prescribing the tax treatment of assignments to Settlement Trusts, apply to tax years beginning after December 31, 2016 (Act Sec. 13821(a)(3) of the Tax Cuts and Jobs Act (P.L. 115-97)). The provisions of Code Sec. 247, allowing a deduction for contributions to Settlement Trusts, apply to tax years for which the period of limitation on refund or credit under Code Sec. 6511 has not expired (Act Sec. 13821(b)(3)(A) of the 2017 Tax Cuts Act). If the period of limitation on a credit or refund from the deduction expires before the end of the one-year period beginning on December 22, 2017, the date of enactment, the refund or credit of the overpayment may be allowed if the claim is filed before the close of the one-year period (Act Sec. 13821(b)(3)(B) of the 2017 Tax Cuts Act). The provisions of Code Sec. 6039H(e), requiring information reporting, apply to tax years beginning after December 31, 2016 (Act Sec. 13821(c)(3) of the 2017 Tax Cuts Act).

**No significant guidance related to this provision has been issued.**

¶325

**NEW LAW EXPLAINED**

— Act Sec. 13821(a) of the Tax Cuts and Jobs Act of 2017 (P.L. 115-97), adding Code Sec. 139G;

— Act Sec. 13821(b), adding Code Sec. 247;

— Act Sec. 13821(c), adding Code Sec. 6039H(e);

— Act Sec. 13821(a)(3), 13821(b)(3), and 13821(c)(3), providing the effective dates.

# PASSTHROUGH ENTITIES

## ¶330  Qualified Business Income Deduction (Passthrough Deduction)

### SUMMARY OF NEW LAW

Noncorporate taxpayers may deduct up to 20 percent of domestic qualified business income from a partnership, S corporation, or sole proprietorship. A related deduction is allowed for specified agricultural or horticultural cooperatives.

### BACKGROUND

Individuals compute their federal income tax liability for a tax year by multiplying their taxable income by the applicable tax rate, subtracting allowable credits, and adding other taxes if warranted (e.g., self-employment tax, household employment tax, etc.). There are four schedules of tax rates based on an individual's filing status: single, married filing jointly and surviving spouses, married filing separately, and head of household. The tax rates are graduated, so income is taxed at higher rates as the individual earns more. For 2017, the regular individual income tax rates are 10, 15, 25, 28, 33, 35, and 39.6 percent (Code Sec. 1).

*Passthrough business income.* An individual who·receives business income from a passthrough entity—such as a partnership, an S corporation, or a sole proprietorship—is taxed on that income at the regular individual income tax rates. A partner takes into account the partnership's items of income, gain, loss, deduction, and credit based on the partnership's accounting method, and regardless of whether the income is distributed to the partners (Code Secs. 701 and 702). Similarly, an S corporation shareholder takes into account the S corporation's items of income, gain, loss, deduction, and credit based on the S corporation's accounting method, and regardless of whether the income is distributed to the shareholders (Code Sec. 1366). An unincorporated sole proprietorship is not treated as separate from its owner for federal income tax purposes, so the owner is taxed directly on the income from the business (Reg. § 301.7701-3(b)(1)(ii)).

An individual partner or S corporation shareholder must report his or her share of partnership or S corporation income or loss on Part II of Schedule E (Form 1040), Supplemental Income and Loss. An individual who owns and operates a business as

## BACKGROUND

a sole proprietor must figure the business income or loss on Schedule C (Form 1040), Profit or Loss From Business, or Schedule C-EZ (Form 1040), Net Profit From Business. The individual reports the Schedule C, Schedule C-EZ, and Schedule E income or loss on his or her individual tax return.

*Cooperatives.* A cooperative is basically a corporation that is owned and controlled by those with or for whom it does business. The cooperative operates at cost, and its profits are shared based on patronage, not on equity ownership. A cooperative deals with or for its members (patrons) under an arrangement by which the patrons obtain patronage dividends or per-unit retain allocations measured by their dealings with the cooperative. Taxable corporations operating on a cooperative basis, and farmers' cooperatives that are otherwise exempt from federal income tax under Code Sec. 521, are taxed at regular corporate rates, but certain special deductions are allowed (Code Secs. 1381 and 1382).

*Penalty for substantial understatement of income tax.* A taxpayer may be subject to a 20-percent accuracy-related penalty for a substantial understatement of income tax for the tax year (Code Sec. 6662(a)). In general, a substantial understatement exists when the tax understatement is more than the greater of 10 percent of the tax required to be shown on the return, or $5,000 (Code Sec. 6662(d)(1)(A)).

## NEW LAW EXPLAINED

**New deduction provided for portion of passthrough business income.**—Individuals, estates and trusts may deduct up to 20 percent of certain domestic qualified business income from a partnership, S corporation, or sole proprietorship (Code Sec. 199A, as added by the Tax Cuts and Jobs Act (P.L. 115-97)). The deduction applies to tax years beginning after 2017 and before 2026.

The qualified business income (QBI) deduction is generally the lesser of (1) combined qualified business income; or (2) 20 percent of taxable income less net capital gain (Code Sec. 199A(a), as amended by the Consolidated Appropriations Act, 2018 (Division T of P.L. 115-141)). Combined qualified business income is: (1) 20 percent of qualified REIT dividends; plus (2) 20 percent of qualified income from a publicly traded partnership (PTP); plus (3) the deductible amount (up to 20 percent) of qualified business income (Code Sec. 199A(b)(1)(A), as added by the 2017 Tax Cuts Act). The deduction amount may be limited based on the taxpayer's taxable income, the type of business, the amount of wages that the business pays, and the basis of certain property held by the business.

**Combined Qualified Business Income Components.** A qualified REIT dividend is a dividend from a real estate investment trust (REIT) that is not a capital gain dividend or qualified dividend income. Qualified REIT dividends do not include dividends paid with respect to a share of REIT stock if the shareholder (1) held the share for 45 days or less during the 91-day period beginning on the date that is 45 days before the date when the share became ex-dividend; or (2) is under an obligation to make related payments with respect to positions in substantially similar or related property (Code Sec. 199A(e)(3), as added by the 2017 Tax Cuts Act; Reg. §1.199A-3(c)(2)). Taxpayers can rely on

## NEW LAW EXPLAINED

proposed regulations that may allow a regulated investment company (RIC, or mutual fund) to pass through its own REIT dividends as qualified REIT dividends (Proposed Reg. § 1.199A-3(d)).

Qualified publicly traded partnership (PTP) income is the sum of: (1) the net amount of the taxpayer's allocable share of each qualified item of income, gain, deduction, and loss from a publicly traded partnership that has passive-type income and, therefore, is not treated as a corporation; plus (2) gain or loss that the taxpayer recognizes on a disposition of the partnership interest that is attributable to its "hot assets" (that is, the partnership's unrealized receivables and inventory items) (Code Sec. 199A(e)(4), as amended by the 2018 Appropriations Act; Reg. § 1.199A-3(c)(3)).

*Qualified business income.* Qualified business income (QBI) is the net amount of qualified items of income, gain, deduction, and loss from a qualified trade or business (Code Sec. 199A(c)(1), as amended by the 2018 Appropriations Act; Reg. § 1.199A-3(b)). Items are qualified to the extent they are included or allowed in determining taxable income, and effectively connected with the conduct of a trade or business within the United States. A qualified trade or business is any trade or business carried on by the taxpayer in the United States, other than:

* the trade or business of performing services as an employee; or

* a specified service trade or business (SSTB) (Code Sec. 199A(d), as added by the 2017 Tax Cuts Act).

However, the SSTB exclusion is phased in for lower-income taxpayers, as discussed below.

There is a rebuttable presumption that a former employee who, directly or indirectly, performs substantially the same services for the former employer or a related person is still an employee for three years after the former employer stops treating him or her as an employee (Reg. § 1.199A-5(d)(3)(i)).

A qualified trade or business generally must also be a Code Sec. 162 trade or business (Reg. § 1.199A-1(b)(14)). However, some rental activities do not have to satisfy the Section 162 business test.

* A rental activity is treated as a trade or business if it rents or licenses tangible or intangible property to a commonly owned trade or business (Reg. § 1.199A-1(b)(14)). A business and a rental activity are commonly owned if the same person or group of persons directly or indirectly owns at least 50 percent of each of them (Reg. § 1.199A-4(b)(1)(i)).

* A safe harbor may treat a rental real estate enterprise as a Section 162 business if (1) separate books and records are maintained to reflect its income and expenses; (2) at least 250 hours of rental services are performed during the year; and (3) for tax years beginning after 2018, the taxpayer maintains sufficient contemporaneous records. A rental real estate enterprise is an interest in real property (or multiple properties) held for the production of rents (Notice 2019-7, January 18, 2019).

## NEW LAW EXPLAINED

Qualified business income does not include:

- reasonable compensation that the business pays to the taxpayer for services rendered;
- guaranteed payments to a partner for services rendered; or
- payments described in Code Sec. 707(a) to a partner for services rendered (Code Sec. 199A(c)(4), as added by the 2017 Tax Cuts Act; Reg. § 1.199A-3(b)(2)(ii)).

Qualified items of income, gain, deduction, or loss do not include:

(1) items of capital gain or loss (short term or long term);

(2) dividends (other than dividends from a cooperative), income equivalent to a dividend, or payments in lieu of dividends;

(3) interest income that is not properly allocable to a trade or business;

(4) the excess of gain over loss from commodities transactions, other than those entered into in the normal course of the trade or business or with respect to stock in trade or property held primarily for sale to customers in the ordinary course of the trade or business, property used in the trade or business, or supplies regularly used or consumed in the trade or business;

(5) the excess of foreign currency gains over foreign currency losses from Code Sec. 988 transactions, other than transactions directly related to the business needs of the business activity;

(6) net income from notional principal contracts, other than clearly identified hedging transactions that are treated as ordinary (that is, not capital) assets;

(7) amounts from an annuity not received in connection with the trade or business; and

(8) items of deduction or loss properly allocable to an amount described in (1)-(7) (Code Sec. 199A(c)(3)(B), as amended by the 2018 Appropriations Act; Reg. § 1.199A-3(b)(2)(ii)).

If the net amount of qualified income, gain, deduction, and loss is less than zero, the loss is carried over to the next tax year. Thus, any QBI deduction allowed in the next tax year is reduced (but not below zero) by 20 percent of the carried-over loss (Code Sec. 199A(c)(2), as added by the 2017 Tax Cuts Act). Similarly, if the combined total of qualified REIT dividends and qualified PTP income is less than zero, the negative amount is carried forward to offset combined REIT dividends and PTP income (Reg. § 1.199A-1(c)(2)(ii)).

*Aggregated businesses.* Taxpayers may aggregate qualified businesses, and treat the group as a single trade or business, if:

(1) the same person or group owns 50 percent or more of each business, directly or by attribution, for a majority of the tax year, including the last day of the tax year, in which the items attributable to each business are included in income;

(2) all items attributable to each business are reported on returns using the same tax year, not including short tax years;

(3) none of the businesses is a specified service trade or business; and

## NEW LAW EXPLAINED

(4) the businesses are actually part of a larger, integrated trade or business because they meet at least two of the following conditions:

   (i) they provide products, property or services that are the same or are customarily offered together;

   (ii) they share facilities or significant centralized business elements, such as personnel, accounting, information technology resources, etc.; or

   (iii) they are operated in coordination with or in reliance on one or more of the businesses in the aggregated group (Reg. § 1.199A-4).

An aggregated business must remain aggregated until it becomes ineligible. However, additional businesses can be added to an existing aggregation (Reg. § 1.199A-4(c)).

**Compliance Tip:** For each tax year, aggregating taxpayers must attach a statement to their returns identifying each aggregated trade or business. The statement must:

(1) describe each trade or business;

(2) provide the name and EIN of each entity in which a trade or business is operated;

(3) identify any trade or business that formed, ceased operations, or was acquired or disposed of during the tax year;

(4) identify any aggregated trade or business of a relevant passthrough entity (nonpublicly traded partnerships, S corporations, and certain other entities that are owned by at least one individual, estate, or trust) in which the taxpayer has an ownership interest; and

(5) provide any other information the IRS may require in forms, instructions, or other published guidance (Reg. § 1.199A-4(c)).

The IRS may disaggregate the trades or businesses if the taxpayer fails to attach the statement.

**Deductible Amount and Wages/Capital Limit.** The deductible amount of qualified business income (QBI) for each qualified trade or business is the lesser of:

- 20 percent of the taxpayer's QBI from the business; or
- the greater of (a) 50 percent of the taxpayer's share of the business's W-2 wages, or (b) the sum of 25 percent of the taxpayer's share of the business's W-2 wages, plus 2.5 percent of the taxpayer's share of the business's unadjusted basis in all qualified property immediately after its acquisition (Code Sec. 199A(b)(2), as added by the 2017 Tax Cuts Act; Reg. § 1.199A-1(d)(2)(iv)).

However, the wages/basis limit is phased in for lower-income taxpayers, as discussed below. The deductible amount also may be reduced for a patron who sells products to a farm cooperative, as discussed below.

*W-2 wages.* W-2 wages are wages, plus the employees' elective deferrals and deferred compensation under Code Sec. 401(k) plans, simplified employee pensions, Code Sec. 403(b) annuities, Code Sec. 457 plans, and designated Roth contributions, that are:

¶330

## NEW LAW EXPLAINED

(1) paid by the business to its employees during the calendar year that ends in the business's tax year;

(2) properly allocable to qualified business income; and

(3) properly included in a return (such as Form W-2, Wage and Tax Statement) filed with the Social Security Administration on or before the 60th day after its due date, including extensions (Code Sec. 199A(b)(4), as added by the 2017 Tax Cuts Act; Reg. § 1.199A-2(b)).

There are three methods for calculating a qualified business's W-2 wages: the unmodified box method, the Modified Box 1 method, and the tracking wages method (Rev. Proc. 2019-11, January 18, 2019).

If all of a taxpayer's qualified business income from sources within Puerto Rico is taxable under Code Sec. 1, the Puerto Rico business's wages and elective deferrals can be W-2 wages if they satisfy the other tests (Code Sec. 199A(f)(1)(C)(ii), as added by the 2017 Tax Cuts Act; Reg. § 1.199A-2(b)(2)(iv)(D)).

*Basis in qualified property.* Unadjusted basis immediately after acquisition (UBIA) in qualified property is the taxpayer's share of the business's unadjusted basis in qualified property on the date the property is placed in service. UBIA is not affected by depreciation deductions, tax credits, or expense elections. However, it is reduced to reflect non-business use of the property (Reg. § 1.199A-2(c)). UBIA may be adjusted for property acquired in non-recognition transactions (Reg. § 1.199A-2(c)(2) and (3)).

Qualified property must satisfy the following tests:

(1) it must be depreciable tangible property;

(2) it must be used during the tax year to produce qualified business income; and

(3) at the close of the tax year, (a) the property must be held by and available for use in the qualified business; and (b) the depreciable period for the property must not have ended (Code Sec. 199A(b)(6), as added by the 2017 Tax Cuts Act; Reg. § 1.199A-2(c)(1)).

The depreciable period for qualified property begins when the taxpayer first places the property in service. It ends 10 years after that date or, if later, the last day of the last full year in the applicable recovery period that would apply under the Modified Accelerated Cost Recovery System (MACRS) without regard to the alternative depreciation system (ADS) (Code Sec. 199A(b)(6)(B), as added by the 2017 Tax Cuts Act; Reg. § 1.199A-2(c)(2)).

A partner's excess Code Sec. 743(b) basis adjustments may also be qualified property (Reg. § 1.199A-2(a)(3)(iv)). Otherwise, basis adjustments under Code Sec. 734(b) and Code Sec. 743(b) are not qualified property (Reg. § 1.199A-2(c)(1)(iii)).

*Wages/capital limit phase-in.* The wages/capital limit on the deductible amount of QBI is phased in based on inflation-adjusted threshold amounts of taxable income. The phase-in is complete, so that the wages/capital limit applies in full, once taxable income exceeds the threshold amount by $50,000 ($100,000 for joint filers) (Code Sec. 199A(b)(3), as added by the 2017 Tax Cuts Act).

**¶330**

## NEW LAW EXPLAINED

**Key Rates and Figures:** For tax years beginning in 2018:

- for joint filers, the threshold amount is $315,000, so the phase-in ceiling is $415,000.
- for married taxpayers filing separate returns, the threshold amount is $157,500, so the phase-in ceiling is $207,500.
- for single and head of household returns, the threshold amount is $157,500, so the phase-in ceiling is $207,500 (Code Sec. 199A(e)(2) and (b)(3), as added by the 2017 Tax Cuts Act).

For tax years beginning in 2019:

- for joint filers, the threshold amount is $321,400, so the phase-in ceiling is $421,400.
- for married taxpayers filing separate returns, the threshold amount is $160,725, so the phase-in ceiling is $210,725.
- for single and head of household returns, the threshold amount is $160,700, so the phase-in ceiling is $210,700 (Rev. Proc. 2018-57, IRB 2018-49, 827).

When taxable income is in the phase-in range—that is, when it exceeds the applicable threshold amount but does not exceed the phase-in ceiling—the wages/capital limit for the deductible amount of QBI from each qualified business is phased in as follows:

(1) Start with 20 percent of the taxpayer's QBI from the business.

(2) Subtract the wages/capital limit amount. The result is the "excess amount."

(3) Multiply the excess amount by the ratio of (a) taxable income minus the threshold amount, over (b) $50,000, or $100,000 for joint filers.

(4) Subtract Step (3) from Step (1) to determine the amount of the phased-in limit.

(5) The deductible amount is the lesser of Step (1) or Step (4) (Code Sec. 199A(b)(3)(B), as added by the 2017 Tax Cuts Act; Reg. § 1.199A-1(d)).

**Specified Service Trade or Business.** A specified service trade or business (SSTB) is not a qualified business; thus, its income generally is not qualified business income (QBI). However, this rule is phased in for lower-income taxpayers (Code Sec. 199A(d)(2), as added by the 2017 Tax Cuts Act; Reg. § 1.199A-5).

A specified service business is a trade or business that involves the performance of:

- services in the fields of health, law, accounting, actuarial science, performing arts, consulting, athletics, financial services, brokerage services, or any trade or business whose principal asset is the reputation or skill of one or more of its employees or owners; or
- services consisting of investing and investment management, trading, or dealing in securities, partnership interests, or commodities (Code Sec. 199A(d)(2), as added by the 2017 Tax Cuts Act; Reg. § 1.199A-5(b)).

Under a de minimis safe harbor, a business is not a SSTB if the portion of its gross receipts that is attributable to the performance of services in a field listed above is less

**NEW LAW EXPLAINED**

than 10 percent of its total gross receipts (or less than five percent if its gross receipts exceed $25 million for the tax year) (Reg. § 1.199A-5(c)(1)).

If a trade or business provides services or property to an SSTB and there is at least 50-percent common ownership of the trades or businesses, the portion of the services or property provided to the SSTB is treated as a separate SSTB. Fifty percent or more common ownership includes direct or indirect ownership by related parties (Reg. § 1.199A-5(c)(2)).

> **Comment:** This rule is in response to a tax planning strategy that separates out parts of what otherwise would be an integrated SSTB (such as the administrative functions) in an attempt to qualify the separated parts for the QBI deduction. The IRS characterizes this strategy as inconsistent with the purpose of Code Sec. 199A (see NPRM REG-107892-18, August 16, 2018).

*SSTB exclusion phase-in.* The exclusion of SSTBs from qualified businesses is phased in for lower-income taxpayers, using the same inflation-adjusted thresholds that apply to the wages/capital limit on the deductible amount from a qualified business discussed above. The phase-in works as follows:

- If taxable income does not exceed the threshold amount, the SSTB exclusion does not apply. Thus, an SSTB can be a qualified trade or business if it satisfies the other requirements.
- If taxable income exceeds the threshold amount plus $50,000 ($100,000 for joint filers), the SSTB exclusion applies in full. Thus, no SSTB income can be qualified business income.
- If taxable income is in the phase-in range—that is, if it exceeds the applicable threshold amount but does not exceed the phase-in ceiling—the taxpayer takes into account an applicable percentage of the SSTB's income, wages and basis in qualified property for purposes of calculating QBI and the wages/capital limit. The applicable percentage is 100%, reduced by the ratio of (1) taxable income minus the applicable threshold amount, over (2) $50,000 ($100,000 for joint filers) (Code Sec. 199A(d)(3), as added by the 2017 Tax Cuts Act).

**Other Rules.** Several rules address the 199A deduction's coordination with other Code sections, its application to pass-through entities, and the substantial understatement penalty.

*Coordination.* The QBI deduction is not an itemized deduction, but it is available to individuals who itemize deductions and to those who claim the standard deduction (Code Sec. 63(b) and (d), as amended by the 2017 Tax Cuts Act; Conference Report on H.R. 1, Tax Cuts and Jobs Act (H. Rept. 115-466)). The QBI deduction is not allowed in determining an individual's adjusted gross income (Code Sec. 62(a), as amended by the 2017 Tax Cuts Act). For purposes of determining a tax-exempt taxpayer's unrelated business income tax (UBIT), Code Sec. 199A is applied by substituting "unrelated business taxable income" for "taxable income" (Code Sec. 199A(g)(5)(D), as amended by the 2018 Appropriations Act).

The Section 199A deduction is allowed only with respect to income tax (Code Sec. 199A(f)(3), as added by the 2017 Tax Cuts Act). In determining alternative minimum taxable income, qualified business income is determined without regard to any AMT

## NEW LAW EXPLAINED

adjustments (Code Sec. 199A(f)(2), as added by the 2017 Tax Cuts Act). The QBI deduction does not reduce net earnings from self-employment or net investment income (Reg. § 1.199A-1(e)(3)).

*Partnerships and S Corporations.* For partnerships and S corporations, the QBI deduction is applied at the partner or shareholder level. Each partner/shareholder takes into account his or her allocable/pro rata share of the partnership's/S corporation's qualified items of income, gain, deduction, and loss. The partner's/shareholder's share of the entity's W-2 wages and basis in qualified property is based on his or her share of the entity's wage expense and depreciation, respectively (Code Sec. 199A(f)(1)(A), as added by the 2017 Tax Cuts Act).

*Trusts and estates.* Most trusts and estates are eligible for the Code Sec. 199A deduction to the extent they retain items of QBI (Code Sec. 199A(f)(1)(B)). They are treated like pass-through entities to the extent they pass items of QBI through to beneficiaries (Reg. § 1.199A-6(d)(1)).

*Reporting requirements.* A nonpublicly traded partnership or S corporation that is owned, directly or indirectly by at least one individual, trust or estate (a relevant pass-through entity or RPE) must report 199A information to its owners. For any trade or business that the RPE engages in directly, including an aggregated trade or business, the owners' Schedules K-1 must:

(1) separately identify and report each owner's allocable share of QBI, W-2 wages, and UBIA attributable to each of the trades or businesses; and

(2) identify whether any of the trades or businesses is an SSTB (Reg. § 1.199A-6(b)).

**Caution:** The owner's share (and the share of any upper-tier indirect owner) of positive unreported QBI, W-2 wages, and basis in qualified property is presumed to be zero.

On an attachment to the owner's Schedule K-1, the RPE must also report: this same information that is reported to it by any RPE in which it owns a direct or indirect interest; and each owner's allocated share of any qualified REIT dividends and qualified PTP income or loss that the entity received, including through another RPE.(Reg. § 1.199A-6(b)).

*Substantial Understatement Penalty.* A taxpayer who claims the Code Sec. 199A deduction may be subject to the 20-percent accuracy-related penalty for a substantial understatement of income tax if the understatement is more than five percent (not 10 percent) of the tax required to be shown on the return or, if greater, $5,000 (Code Sec. 6662(d)(1)(C), as amended by the 2017 Tax Cuts Act).

*Proposed reliance regulations.* Taxpayers can rely on the following proposed regulations that provide additional rules for calculating and claiming the deduction:

- Proposed Reg. § 1.199A-3(b)(1)(iv) addresses the treatment of previously suspended losses that constitute QBI.

- Proposed Reg. § 1.199A-3(d) allows a regulated investment company (RIC, or mutual fund) to pass through its REIT dividends as qualified REIT dividends.

## NEW LAW EXPLAINED

- Proposed Reg. § 1.199A-6(d)(3)(iii) treats separate shares of a trust with multiple beneficiaries as a single trust for determining whether the trust's taxable income exceeds the threshold amount.

- Proposed Reg. § 1.199A-6(d)(3)(v) provides special rules for charitable remainder trusts.

**Agricultural Cooperatives and Patrons.** The 199A deduction for a specified agricultural or horticultural cooperative is calculated and passed through to patrons under rules that are similar to those that governed the domestic production activities deduction (DPAD) before the repeal of Code Sec. 199 (Code Sec. 199A(g), as amended by the 2018 Appropriations Act)

The deduction for agricultural or horticultural cooperatives is generally equal to nine percent (not 20 percent) of the lesser of the co-op's taxable income or its qualified production activities income (not qualified business income) (Code Sec. 199A(g)(1), as amended by the 2018 Appropriations Act). The Code Sec. 199A(g) deduction is limited to 50 percent of the co-op's W-2 wages that are properly allocable to domestic production gross receipts (Code Sec. 199A(g)(1)(B), as amended by the 2018 Appropriations Act). The co-op's taxable income is determined without regard to any allowable deduction under Code Sec. 1382(b) and (c) for patronage dividends, per-unit retain allocations, and nonpatronage distributions (Code Sec. 199A(g)(1)(C), as amended by the 2018 Appropriations Act). Only items that are attributable to the actual conduct of a trade or business are taken into account (Code Sec. 199A(g)(5)(C), as amended by the 2018 Appropriations Act).

The co-op may pass through some or all of its deduction to its patrons via qualified payments which, for purposes of the patron's QBI deduction, may reduce the deductible amount from the patron's qualified trade or business (Code Sec. 199A(b)(7), as amended by the 2018 Appropriations Act).

These rules apply to specified agricultural or horticultural cooperatives and their members. A specified agricultural or horticultural cooperative is an organization that:

(1) is subject to the cooperative income tax rules of Code Secs. 1381 through 1383; and

(2) either—

    (a) manufactures, produces, grows, or extracts, in whole or significant part, an agricultural or horticultural product in the United States; or

    (b) markets agricultural or horticultural products (Code Sec. 199A(g)(4), as amended by the 2018 Appropriations Act).

Under an attribution rule, a specified cooperative that markets agricultural or horticultural products produced by its members is treated as having produced those products itself (Code Sec. 199A(g)(4)(B), as amended by the 2018 Appropriations Act).

Congress intends for agricultural or horticultural products to include fertilizer, diesel fuel, and other supplies used in agricultural or horticultural production that are manufactured, produced, grown or extracted by the cooperative (Joint Committee on Taxation, Technical Explanation (JCX-6-18))

**¶330**

## NEW LAW EXPLAINED

*DPAD transition rule.* The repeal of the DPAD for tax years beginning after December 31, 2017, does not apply to a specified agricultural or horticultural cooperative's qualified payment to a member that is (1) received in a tax year beginning after December 31, 2017, and (2) attributable to qualified production activities income with respect to which the co-op can claim a DPAD for a tax year beginning before January 1, 2018. Code Sec. 199 continues to apply to the payment, and to a member's related deduction. No deduction is allowed under Code Sec. 199A for these payments (The Tax Cuts and Jobs Act, P.L. 115-97, Act § 13305(c), as amended by the Consolidated Appropriations Act, 2018, P.L. 115-141, Division T, Act § 101(c)).

▶ **Effective date.** The amendments made by the Tax Cuts and Jobs Act (P.L. 115-97) apply to tax years beginning after December 31, 2017 (Act Sec. 11011(e) of the Tax Cuts and Jobs Act (P.L. 115-97)). The amendments made by the Consolidated Appropriations Act of 2018 (Division T of P.L. 115-141) apply to tax years beginning after December 31, 2017 (Act Sec. 101(d) of the Consolidated Appropriations Act, 2018 (Division T of P.L. 115-141; Act Secs. 11011 and 13305 of the Tax Cuts and Jobs Act, 2017 (P.L. 115–97)).

The regulations discussed above generally apply to tax years ending after February 8, 2019. However, taxpayers may apply them in their entirety to earlier tax years (Preamble, T.D. 9847). The proposed regulations discussed above are generally proposed to apply to tax years ending after they are published as final. However, taxpayers may apply them, in their entirety, before that date (NPRM REG-134652-18, January 18, 2019). For tax years ending during calendar year 2018 only, taxpayers may apply an earlier set of proposed regulations in their entirety, rather than the final regulations discussed above (see NPRM REG-107892-18, August 16, 2018) (Preamble, T.D. 9847).

Rev. Proc. 2019-11 and Notice 2019-7 apply to tax years beginning after December 31, 2017.

**Expiration date.** The Code Sec. 199A deduction will not apply to tax years beginning after December 31, 2025 (Code Sec. 199A(i), as added by the 2017 Tax Cuts Act).

— Act Sec. 11011(a) of the Tax Cuts and Jobs Act (P.L. 115-97), adding new Code Sec. 199A;

— Act Sec. 11011(b), amending Code Secs. 62(a), 63(b) and (d), and 3402(m)(1);

— Act Sec. 11011(c), adding Code Sec. 6662(d)(1)(C);

— Act Sec. 11011(d), amending Code Secs. 170(b)(2)(D), 172(d), 246(b)(1), 613(a), and 613A(d)(1);

— Act Sec. 11011(e), providing the effective date.

— Act Sec. 101(a) of the Consolidated Appropriations Act of 2018 (Division T of P.L. 115-141), amending Code Secs. 62(a), 63, 172(d)(8), 199A(e)(1) and 199A(g), 613(a), and 6662(d)(1)(C);

— Act Sec. 101(b), amending Code Sec. 199A(a), 199A(b), 199A(c), and 199A(e);

— Act Sec. 101(c), amending Act Sec. 13305 of the Tax Cuts and Jobs Act (P.L. 115-97); and

— Act Sec. 101(d), providing the effective date.

## ¶335  Holding Period for Capital Gain Passed Through to Partners with Carried Interests

### SUMMARY OF NEW LAW

Capital gain passed through to fund managers via a partnership profits interest (carried interest) in exchange for investment management services must meet an extended three-year holding period to qualify for long-term capital gain treatment.

### BACKGROUND

A "carried interest" in a partnership is an interest that consists of the right to receive future partnership profits, and is given to a partner in exchange for performing services for the partnership. Carried interests are often used by partnerships in the investment management business. Such a partnership interest is not taxed when a fund-manager partner receives it. The IRS generally treats the receipt of a partnership profits interest for services as a nontaxable event (Rev. Proc. 93-27). This treatment applies only to substantially nonvested profits interests (Rev. Proc. 2001-43).

If *property*, instead of cash, is transferred in exchange for performing services, the service provider generally has to recognize income for the tax year in which the property is first substantially vested (Code Sec. 83). On the other hand, property that is subject to a substantial risk of forfeiture—including when the right to the property depends on the future performance of substantial services—is considered "nonvested" property. A service provider may elect to recognize income for the tax year of the transfer even if the property is substantially nonvested (Code Sec. 83(b)).

Under proposed regulations, a partnership interest is "property" for purposes of Code Sec. 83 (Proposed Reg. § 1.83-3(e); NPRM REG-105346-03, 5/24/2005). The transfer of a profits interest to a service provider would be included in gross income when it becomes substantially vested, or, for a substantially nonvested interest, at the time of the grant if a Code Sec. 83(b) election is in place. Further, a partnership and a partner would be allowed to elect a safe harbor that treats the fair market value of a compensatory partnership interest as being equal to the liquidation value of the interest (Proposed Reg. § 1.83-3(l)). However, the grant of a true profits interest in a partnership would result in no income inclusion under Code Sec. 83, because the fair market value of the property received by the service provider would be zero (House Committee Report for the Tax Cuts and Jobs Act (P.L. 115-97) (H.R. Rep. No. 115-409, p. 275, fn. 572)).

In recent years, the tax treatment of income from a carried interest given in exchange for asset management services—such as services for private equity funds, venture capital funds, and hedge funds—has been a hotly contested issue. Investment funds are usually partnerships, with the fund manager as the general partner and the investors as limited partners. The fund manager itself is generally a partnership whose members have investment management expertise. The fund manager receives management fees and a carried interest. Income from the carried interest, which tends to be in the range of 20 to 25 percent of profits, passes through from the fund

## BACKGROUND

manager partnership to its member partners whose professional skill generates capital income for the fund's investors. The income may be short-term or long-term capital gain realized by the underlying investment fund as it sells off investment assets. The bone of contention has been that long-term capital gain allocated to the individual partners may represent compensation for services as fund managers. Some who view this income as compensation for services have called for it to be taxed at ordinary income rates.

The holding period for a capital asset is the length of time that the taxpayer owns the property before disposing of it. The tax treatment of recognized gain or loss depends, in part, on whether the taxpayer's holding period is short-term or long-term. Long-term gain or loss arises from assets held for more than one year; anything else is short-term gain or loss (Code Secs. 1222 and 1223).

"Net capital gain" is the excess of net long-term capital gain for the tax year over net short-term capital loss for the tax year (Code Sec. 1222(11)). For an individual taxpayer, an estate, or a trust, any adjusted net capital gain that otherwise would be taxed at the ordinary 10- or 15-percent rate is not taxed. Any adjusted net capital gain that otherwise would be taxed at the ordinary rates over 15 percent and below 39.6 percent is taxed at a 15-percent rate. Any adjusted net capital gain that otherwise would be taxed at the ordinary 39.6-percent rate is taxed at a 20-percent rate (Code Sec. 1(h)(1)).

## NEW LAW EXPLAINED

**Holding period increased for long-term capital gains from "carried interest" in investment partnership.**—A three-year holding period applies to certain net long-term capital gain with respect to any applicable partnership interest held by the taxpayer. This rule applies notwithstanding Code Sec. 83 and any Code Sec. 83(b) election in effect (Code Sec. 1061(a), as added by the Tax Cuts and Jobs Act (P.L. 115-97)).

If a taxpayer holds an applicable partnership interest at any time during the tax year, this rule treats as short-term capital gain—taxed at ordinary income rates—the amount of the taxpayer's net long-term capital gain from the applicable interest that exceeds the amount of such gain calculated as if a three-year holding period applies instead of a one-year period. Long-term capital losses also are taken into account as if a three-year holding period applies (Code Sec. 1061(a), as added by the 2017 Tax Cuts Act).

An "applicable partnership interest" is any interest in a partnership that is transferred to or held by the taxpayer in connection with the performance of services by the taxpayer or a related person in any applicable trade of business, even if the taxpayer made contributions to the partnership (Code Sec. 1061(c)(1), as added by the 2017 Tax Cuts Act). A related person means a related person within the meaning of Code Sec. 267(b) or Code Sec. 707(b) (General Explanation of Public Law 115-97 (JCS-1-18), 201 fn.1003).

An applicable partnership interest does not include (1) any interest in a partnership held by a corporation, or (2) any capital interest in the partnership that provides the taxpayer with a right to share in partnership capital based on the amount of capital contributed or on the value of the interest subject to tax under Code Sec. 83 when the interest is

## NEW LAW EXPLAINED

received or vested (Code Sec. 1061(c)(4), as added by the 2017 Tax Cuts Act). The IRS plans to issue regulations to clarify that S corporations are not corporations for purposes of the first category of excluded interests. Thus, the three-year holding period applies to applicable partnership interests held by an S corporation (Notice 2018-18).

The three-year holding period applies notwithstanding the rules of Code Sec. 83 or a Code Sec. 83(b) election. As a result, the fact that an individual may have included an amount in income upon acquiring the applicable partnership interest, or may have made a Code Sec. 83(b) election with respect to the applicable partnership interest, does not change the required three-year holding period for long-term capital gain treatment (Joint Explanatory Statement of the Conference Committee, Conference Report on H.R. 1, Tax Cuts and Jobs Act (H. Rept. 115-466), p. 269).

An "applicable trade or business" is one whose regular business activity consists, in whole or in part, of (1) raising or returning capital, and (2) either investing in or disposing of specified assets, or developing specified assets (Code Sec. 1061(c)(2), as added by the 2017 Tax Cuts Act). "Specified assets" are securities, commodities, real estate held for rental or investment, cash or cash equivalents, or options or derivative contracts with respect to these assets. An interest in a partnership to the extent of the partnership's proportionate interest in these assets is also a specified asset (Code Sec. 1061(c)(3), as added by the 2017 Tax Cuts Act).

If a taxpayer transfers an applicable partnership interest to a related person, the taxpayer must include in gross income as short-term capital gain so much of the taxpayer's net long-term capital gain attributable to the sale or exchange of an asset held for not more than three years as is allocable to the interest. The amount included as short-term capital gain on the transfer is reduced by the amount treated as short-term capital gain on the transfer for the tax year under Code Sec. 1061(a) (Code Sec. 1061(d)(1), as added by the 2017 Tax Cuts Act). A "related person" is a family member under the Code Sec. 318(a)(1) attribution rules, or a colleague who performed a service within the current calendar year or the preceding three calendar years in an applicable trade or business in which or for which the taxpayer performed a service (Code Sec. 1061(d)(2), as added by the 2017 Tax Cuts Act).

To the extent provided by the Treasury Department, the short-term capital gain treatment for carried interest gain under Code Sec. 1061(a) will not apply to income or gain attributable to an asset not held for portfolio investment on behalf of third party investors (Code Sec. 1061(b) and (c)(5), as added by the 2017 Tax Cuts Act).

The Treasury Department may require reporting or issue regulations or other guidance, as is necessary to carry out the purpose of Code Sec. 1061 (Code Sec. 1061(e) and (f), as added by the 2017 Tax Cuts Act).

▶ **Effective date.** The amendments made by this section apply to tax years beginning after December 31, 2017 (Act Sec. 13309(c) of the Tax Cuts and Jobs Act (P.L. 115-97)).

— Act Sec. 13309(a) of the Tax Cuts and Jobs Act (P.L. 115-97), redesignating Code Sec. 1061 as Code Sec. 1062, and adding new Code Sec. 1061.

— Act Sec. 13309(c), providing the effective date.

# ¶340  Scope of Basis Limitation on Partner Losses

## SUMMARY OF NEW LAW

The basis limitation on partner losses applies to a partner's distributive share of charitable contributions and foreign taxes.

## BACKGROUND

A partner's distributive share of partnership loss is not allowed to the extent that it exceeds the adjusted basis of the partner's partnership interest. Disallowed loss is allowed as a deduction at the end of the next partnership tax year to the extent that the partner's adjusted basis at that point exceeds zero (Code Sec. 704(d); Reg. § 1.704-1(d)(1)).

A partner's basis in its partnership interest is increased by its distributive share of income, and decreased by distributions by the partnership. A partner's basis is also decreased by its distributive share of partnership losses and expenditures not deductible in computing partnership taxable income and not properly chargeable to capital account (Code Sec. 705).

When a partnership makes a charitable contribution of appreciated property, a partner generally can claim as a deduction his or her distributive share of the property's fair market value (Code Sec. 702(a)(4)). In turn, the partner's basis is reduced, but only by the partner's distributive share of the adjusted basis of the contributed property (and not its fair market value) (Rev. Rul. 96-11).

A partnership is not allowed to claim deductions for charitable contributions or foreign taxes (Code Sec. 703(a)(2)(B) and (C)). With respect to foreign taxes, as with charitable contributions made by the partnership, the partners take into account their distributive share of the foreign taxes paid by the partnership (Code Sec. 702(a)(6)).

Under current regulations, the basis limitation on partner losses does not take into account the partner's share of partnership charitable contributions or foreign taxes (Reg. § 1.704-1(d)(2)). Moreover, in a private letter ruling, the IRS took the position that a partner's deduction for its share of the partnership's charitable contributions is not limited by the basis limitation on partner losses (IRS Letter Ruling 8405084).

## NEW LAW EXPLAINED

**Basis limitation on partner losses takes into account charitable contributions and foreign taxes.**—The basis limitation on partner losses is modified to take into account a partner's distributive share of (1) partnership charitable contributions, and (2) taxes paid or accrued to foreign countries and U.S. possessions. For a charitable contribution by the partnership, the amount of the basis limitation on partner losses is decreased by the partner's distributive share of the adjusted basis of the contributed property. A special rule provides that if the partnership makes a charitable contribution of property whose fair market value is greater than its adjusted basis, the basis

## NEW LAW EXPLAINED

limitation on partner losses does not account for the partner's distributive share of the excess (Code Sec. 704(d), as amended by the Tax Cuts and Jobs Act (P.L. 115-97)).

▶ **Effective date.** The amendment made by this section applies to partnership tax years beginning after December 31, 2017 (Act Sec. 13503(b) of the Tax Cuts and Jobs Act (P.L. 115-97)).

   **No significant guidance related to this provision has been issued.**

— Act Sec. 13503(a) of the Tax Cuts and Jobs Act (P.L. 115-97), amending Code Sec. 704(d);

— Act Sec. 13503(b), providing the effective date.

## ¶345  Definition of Substantial Built-In Loss Upon Transfer of Partnership Interest

### SUMMARY OF NEW LAW

The Code Sec. 743 definition of a "substantial built-in loss" is modified so that a substantial built-in loss also exists *if the transferee would be allocated* a net loss in excess of $250,000 upon a hypothetical disposition at fair market value by the partnership of all partnership assets immediately after the transfer of the partnership interest.

### BACKGROUND

Upon the transfer of a partnership interest, a partnership generally does not adjust the basis of partnership property unless (1) the partnership has made a one-time Code Sec. 754 election to adjust basis, or (2) the partnership has a substantial built-in loss immediately after the transfer (Code Sec. 743(a)). If the partnership does have substantial built-in loss immediately after the transfer, adjustments are made with respect to the transferee partner.

The purpose of the adjustments is to account for differences between the transferee partner's proportionate share of the adjusted basis of the partnership property and the transferee's basis in its partnership interest (Code Sec. 743(b)). The adjustments essentially approximate the result of a direct purchase by the transferee partner of its share of the partnership property.

For example, if the basis of T's (a transferee's) interest in a partnership is substantially less than T's share of the adjusted basis to the partnership of the partnership's property, the adjusted basis of partnership property will be decreased by that difference with respect to T. That is, the adjusted basis of partnership property with respect to T will be adjusted downward to its fair market value, thereby preventing T from taking advantage of any built-in loss.

A substantial built-in loss exists if *the partnership's adjusted basis* in the property exceeds by more that $250,000 the fair market value of that property (Code Sec. 743(d)(1)).

**¶345**

## NEW LAW EXPLAINED

**Test for substantial built-in loss modified to apply at transferee partner level.**—
The definition of a "substantial built-in loss" is modified so that a substantial built-in loss
also exists *if the transferee would be allocated* a net loss in excess of $250,000 upon a
hypothetical disposition at fair market value by the partnership of all partnership assets
immediately after the transfer of the partnership interest (Code Sec. 743(d)(1), as
amended by the Tax Cuts and Jobs Act (P.L. 115-97)). In other words, even if the
partnership itself does not have an overall built-in loss, depending on allocations of gain
under the partnership agreement, a basis adjustment may be mandated with respect to
a transferee.

> **Example:** Partnership ABC has not made a Code Sec. 754 election. The partner-
> ship has two assets, X and Y. Asset X has a built-in gain of $1 million; Asset Y
> has a built-in loss of $900,000. Under the partnership agreement, any gain on
> the sale of Asset X is specially allocated to Partner A. Partners A, B and C share
> equally in all other partnership items, including the built-in loss in Asset Y.
> Each of Partner B and C has a net built-in loss of $300,000 (one third of
> $900,000) allocable to her partnership interest. But the partnership itself does
> not have an overall built-in loss. Rather, it has a net built-in gain of $100,000 ($1
> million minus $900,000). Partner C sells her partnership interest to D for
> $33,333. The test for a substantial built-in loss applies both at the partnership
> level and at the transferee partner level. If the partnership were to sell all of its
> assets for cash at their fair market value immediately after the transfer to D, D
> would be allocated a loss of $300,000 (one third of the built-in loss of $900,000 in
> Asset Y). A substantial built-in loss exists under the partner-level test, and the
> partnership adjusts the basis of its assets accordingly with respect to D (Joint
> Committee on Taxation, Description of the Chairman's Mark of the "Tax Cuts
> and Jobs Act" (JCX-51-17), November 9, 2017).

▶ **Effective date.** The amendment made by this section applies to transfers of partnership
interests after December 31, 2017 (Act Sec. 13502(b) of the Tax Cuts and Jobs Act (P.L.
115-97)).

**No significant guidance related to this provision has been issued.**

— Act Sec. 13502(a) of the Tax Cuts and Jobs Act (P.L. 115-97), amending Code Sec. 743(d);

— Act Sec. 13502(b), providing the effective date.

# ¶350  Treatment of Sale or Exchange of Partnership Interests by Foreign Persons

## SUMMARY OF NEW LAW

Gain or loss from the sale or exchange of a partnership interest is effectively connected with a U.S. trade or business to the extent that the transferor would have had effectively connected gain or loss had the partnership sold all of its assets at fair market value as of the disposition date. The transferee of a partnership interest must withhold 10 percent of the amount realized on the sale or exchange unless the transferor certifies that it is not a nonresident alien or foreign corporation.

## BACKGROUND

A foreign person that is engaged in a trade or business in the United States is taxed on income or gain that is "effectively connected" with the conduct of that trade or business (Code Secs. 871(b) and 882(a)). The effectively connected test considers (1) the extent to which income or gain is derived from assets used in the conduct of the U.S. trade or business (the "asset use" test), and (2) whether the activities of the trade or business were a material factor in realizing the income or gain (the "business activities" test) (Code Sec. 864(c)(2)).

A foreign partner in a partnership is treated as engaged in the conduct of a trade or business within the United States if the partnership is so engaged (Code Sec. 875). Even though the source of gain or loss from the sale or exchange of personal property is generally determined based on where the seller resides (Code Sec. 865(a)), a foreign partner may have effectively connected income due to the "asset use" or "business activities" of the partnership in which he is an investor.

Special rules treat gain or loss on the sale of U.S. real property interests as effectively connected with the conduct of a U.S. trade or business (Code Sec. 897(a)). If consideration received by a nonresident alien or foreign corporation for its interest in a partnership is attributable to a U.S. real property interest, that consideration is treated as received from the sale or exchange in the United States of the real property (Code Sec. 897(g)).

The IRS and the courts have clashed over the treatment of sales of partnership interests by foreign persons. A key piece of guidance is a 1991 revenue ruling that dealt with the sale of an interest in a foreign partnership (Rev. Rul. 91-32). There, the IRS said that if there is unrealized gain or loss in partnership assets that would be treated as effectively connected with the conduct of a U.S. trade or business if those assets were sold by the partnership, some or all of a foreign person's gain or loss from the sale of a partnership interest may be treated as effectively connected.

In 2017, the Tax Court rejected the IRS's reasoning and held that, in general, a foreign person's gain or loss on the sale of an interest in a partnership engaged in a U.S. trade or business is foreign-source (*Grecian Magnesite Mining*, Dec. 60,968, 149 TC No. 3 (July 13, 2017)).

¶350

## BACKGROUND

Gain from sales of U.S. real property interests may be subject to a 15-percent withholding tax on the amount realized on the transfer (Code Sec. 1445(e)(5)).

## NEW LAW EXPLAINED

**Foreign person's gain or loss on sale of partnership interest treated as effectively connected.**—Gain or loss from any sale, exchange, or other disposition of a partnership interest is effectively connected with a U.S. trade or business to the extent that the transferor would have had effectively connected (EC) gain or loss had the partnership sold all of its assets at fair market value as of the date of the sale or exchange. Any gain or loss from the hypothetical asset sale must be allocated to interests in the partnership in the same manner as nonseparately stated income and loss (Code Sec. 864(c)(8)(A), (B), and (D), as added by the Tax Cuts and Jobs Act (P.L. 115-97)).

Gain or loss treated as effectively connected income is reduced by the amount treated as effectively connected income under Code Sec. 897, which relates to gain or loss of a nonresident alien or foreign corporation from the disposition of a U.S. real property interest (Code Sec. 864(c)(8)(C), as added by the 2017 Tax Cuts Act).

In addition, the transferee of a partnership interest must withhold 10 percent of the amount realized on the sale or exchange, unless the transferor certifies that it is not a nonresident alien or foreign corporation. The amount withheld may be reduced, at the transferor's or transferee's request, if the IRS determines that the reduced withholding will not jeopardize income tax collection on the gain realized. If the transferee fails to withhold the correct amount, the partnership must deduct and withhold from distributions to the transferee partner an amount equal to the amount the transferee failed to withhold (Code Sec. 1446(f), as added by the 2017 Tax Cuts Act).

The Treasury Department is instructed to prescribe regulations and other appropriate guidance to apply these provisions and carry out the withholding requirements (Code Secs. 864(c)(8)(E) and 1446(f)(6), as added by the 2017 Tax Cuts Act). These regulations are expected to allow a broker, as agent of the transferee, to fulfill the withholding obligation (Conference Report on H.R. 1, Tax Cuts and Jobs Act (H. Rept. 115-466), p. 369).

**IRS guidance for computing effectively connected gain or loss.** Proposed regulations provide rules for computing effectively connected gain or loss under Code Sec. 864(c)(8)(A). These regulations also provide rules for the limitation under Code Sec. 864(c)(8)(B), which limits gain or loss to the portion of the foreign transferor's distributive share of gain or loss that would have been effectively connected gain or loss if the partnership had sold all of its assets at fair market value (Proposed Reg. § 1.864(c)(8)-1).

Under Code Sec. 741, a transferor generally recognizes capital gain or loss on a sale or exchange of a partnership interest. However, gain or loss is ordinary if it is attributable to the partnership's section 751 property—that is, unrealized receivables and inventory items, collectively known as "hot assets." As a result, gain or loss on the disposition of a

**NEW LAW EXPLAINED**

partnership interest can include capital gain, capital loss, ordinary income, or ordinary loss.

Under the proposed regulations, a foreign transferor must determine the portion of its effectively connected (EC) capital gain or loss, and the portion of its effectively connected ordinary income or loss from Code Sec. 751 property. The foreign partner's EC gain or loss will not exceed its outside gain or loss under Code Secs. 741 and 751 (see Proposed Reg. § 1.864(c)(8)-1(b)(3)).

In turn, the proposed regulations provide a three-step process for determining the Code Sec. 864(c)(8)(B) limitation against which a foreign partner's outside gain or loss is compared (Proposed Reg. § 1.864(c)(8)-1(c)). Specifically, the following are determined:

Step 1: For each asset held by the partnership, the amount of gain or loss that the partnership would recognize in connection with a deemed sale immediately before the partner's transfer of its partnership interest.

Step 2: The amount of that gain or loss that would be treated as effectively connected gain or loss ("deemed sale EC gain" and "deemed sale EC loss").

Step 3: The foreign transferor's distributive share of the ordinary and capital components of any deemed sale EC gain and deemed sale EC loss.

The foreign transferor would treat its outside capital gain as effectively connected gain only to the extent that it does not exceed its aggregate deemed sale EC capital gain. Further, regarding (3) above, the transferor's distributive share of gain or loss on the deemed sale would be determined in the same manner as its distributive share of the non-separately stated taxable income or loss of the partnership.

The proposed regulations also provide rules concerning the following: the application of other Code provisions treating gain or loss on the transfer of a partnership interest as effectively connected; coordination with Code Sec. 897; tiered partnerships; and the effect of tax treaties. In addition, the proposed regulations provide an anti-stuffing rule to prevent improper reductions in amounts characterized as effectively connected.

**IRS withholding guidance concerning publicly traded partnership interests.** The withholding obligation has been suspended in the case of a disposition of certain publicly traded partnership (PTP) interests, but the suspension does not apply to non-PTP interests. This suspension of withholding for dispositions of PTP interests is pending regulations or other guidance on how to withhold, deposit, and report tax withheld under Code Sec. 1446(f) with respect to a disposition of an interest in a publicly traded partnership (Notice 2018-8).

**IRS withholding guidance concerning non-publicly traded partnership interests.** The IRS intends to issue regulations under Code Sec. 1446(f) on how to qualify for exemptions from withholding, or reductions in the amount of withholding, on transfers of non-publicly traded partnership interests. Taxpayers may rely on interim guidance until regulations and other guidance have been issued (Notice 2018-29). The interim guidance, however, does not affect the transferor's tax liability under Code Sec. 864(c)(8).

**¶350**

## NEW LAW EXPLAINED

Among other things, the interim guidance provides that a transferee is not required to withhold under Code Sec. 1446(f) if:

- it receives a certification from a transferor that the disposition will not result in realized gain (Notice 2018-29, § 6.02);

- realized gain in a disposition is not recognized because of a nonrecognition provision (Notice 2018-29, § 6.05);

- a transferor certifies to a transferee that for each of the past three years the transferor's allocable share of effectively connected taxable income (ECTI) from the partnership was less than 25 percent of the transferor's total income from the partnership (Notice 2018-29, § 6.03); or

- the partnership certifies that its effectively connected gain under Code Sec. 864(c)(8) would be less than 25 percent of the total gain on the deemed sale of all its assets (Notice 2018-29, § 6.04).

*Reduction in the transferor's share of partnership liabilities.* The amount realized on the disposition of a partnership interest includes any reduction in the transferor's share of partnership liabilities. To determine the transferor's share of partnership liabilities for purposes of Code Sec. 1446(f) withholding, the transferee may generally rely on:

- a transferor's most recently issued Schedule K-1 (Form 1065) (Notice 2018-29, § 7.02); or

- a certification from the partnership (Notice 2018-29, § 7.03).

When the amount realized includes a reduction in liabilities, the amount the transferee may be required to withhold could exceed the cash or other property the transferee pays to the transferor. However, the interim rules generally limit the total amount of withholding to the total amount of cash and property transferred (Notice 2018-29, § 8).

*Gain from distribution in excess of partner's basis.* Under Code Sec. 731(a), a partner recognizes gain to the extent that any money distributed exceeds the adjusted basis of his partnership interest immediately before the distribution. This gain is considered gain or loss from the sale or exchange of the distributee partner's partnership interest. As a result, Code Sec. 1446(f) withholding may apply when a distribution of money results in gain under Code Sec. 731. Under the interim rules, the partnership may rely on its books and records, or on a certification received from the distributee partner, to determine whether the distribution exceeds the partner's basis (Notice 2018-29, § 9).

*Section 1445 rules are default rules for withholding.* Unless the interim guidance provides otherwise, transferees required to withhold under Code Sec. 1446(f) must use the rules in Code Sec. 1445 (Withholding of Tax on Dispositions of United States Real Property Interests) and the related regulations in reporting and paying over the tax until other guidance is issued under Code Sec. 1446(f).

▶ **Effective date.** The amendment made by this section treating gain or loss on the sale or exchange of a partnership interest as effectively connected with the conduct of a trade or business in the United States (as well as the related proposed regulations) applies to sales, exchanges, and dispositions on or after November 27, 2017 (Act Sec. 13501(c)(1) of the

## NEW LAW EXPLAINED

Tax Cuts and Jobs Act (P.L. 115-97)). The amendment requiring withholding on sales or exchanges of partnership interests applies to sales, exchanges, and dispositions after December 31, 2017 (Act Sec. 13501(c)(2) of the 2017 Tax Cuts Act).

— Act Sec. 13501(a) of the Tax Cuts and Jobs Act (P.L. 115-97), amending Code Sec. 864(c)(1) and adding Code Sec. 864(c)(8);

— Act Sec. 13501(b), redesignating Code Sec. 1446(f) as (g), and adding Code Sec. 1446(f);

— Act Sec. 13501(c), providing the effective date.

# ¶355  Technical Termination of Partnerships

## SUMMARY OF NEW LAW

The rule providing for technical termination of partnerships is repealed for partnership tax years beginning after December 31, 2017.

## BACKGROUND

A partnership is considered terminated if (1) no part of any business, financial operation, or venture of the partnership continues to be carried on by any of its partners, or (2) within a 12-month period, there is a sale or exchange of 50 percent of more of the total interest in partnership capital and profits (Code Sec. 708(b)). The second type of termination—sale or exchange of 50 percent of total partnership interest—is termed a "technical termination."

A technical termination causes two deemed transfers:

(1) The terminated partnership is deemed to contribute all of its assets and liabilities to a new partnership in exchange for an interest in the new partnership; and

(2) Immediately afterwards, in a liquidating distribution, the terminated partnership is deemed to distribute its interests in the new partnership to the purchasing partner and the remaining partners (Reg. § 1.708-1(b)(4)).

Neither the remaining partners nor the partnership generally recognize gain or loss on the deemed contribution to the new partnership and the subsequent deemed liquidating distribution.

A technical termination causes the following tax consequences:

• The terminated partnership's tax year closes on the date of the sale or exchange that triggers the termination. The resulting short tax year may cause a bunching of the partnership income for the remaining partners (Reg. § 1.708-1(b)(3)).

• The new partnership must file new tax elections regarding accounting methods, depreciation methods, installment sales, and amortizations and depletions.

• Generally, partnership depreciation recovery periods restart.

## BACKGROUND

- The new partnership must file a new Code Sec. 754 optional basis adjustment election (Reg. § 1.708-1(b)(5)).

Thus, a technical termination does not necessarily end the partnership's existence, but only terminates some of the "old" partnership's tax attributes.

## NEW LAW EXPLAINED

**Technical termination of partnerships repealed.**—The rule providing for the technical termination of partnerships is repealed (Code Sec. 708(b)(1), as amended by the Tax Cuts and Jobs Act (P.L. 115-97)).

▶ **Effective date.** The amendment made by this section applies to partnership tax years beginning after December 31, 2017 (Act Sec. 13504(c) of the Tax Cuts and Jobs Act (P.L. 115-97)).

   **No significant guidance related to this provision has been issued.**

— Act Sec. 13504(a) of the Tax Cuts and Jobs Act (P.L. 115-97), amending Code Sec. 708(b)(1);

— Act Sec. 13504(b), amending Code Sec. 168(i)(7)(B) and Code Sec. 743(e); and

— Act Sec. 13504(c), providing the effective date.

# ¶360 Qualified Beneficiary of Electing Small Business Trust (ESBT)

## SUMMARY OF NEW LAW

A nonresident alien individual may be a potential current beneficiary of an ESBT, effective on January 1, 2018.

## BACKGROUND

All shareholders of an S corporation must be individuals, estates, certain specified trusts or certain tax-exempt organizations (Code Sec. 1361(b)(1)(B)). An electing small business trust ("ESBT") may be a shareholder of an S corporation. Generally, the eligible beneficiaries of an ESBT include individuals, estates, and certain charitable organizations eligible to hold S corporation stock directly

Each potential current beneficiary of an ESBT is treated as a shareholder, except that for any period in which there is no potential current beneficiary of the trust, the trust itself is treated as the shareholder. A potential current beneficiary is a person who is entitled to a distribution from the trust or who may receive a distribution at the discretion of any person. Any person who may benefit from a power of appointment is not a potential current beneficiary if the power has not been exercised. A nonresident alien individual may not be a shareholder of an S corporation and may not be a

## BACKGROUND

potential current beneficiary of an ESBT without causing disqualification of the S corporation election. If the potential current beneficiaries of an ESBT would disqualify an entity from S corporation status, the ESBT has a grace period of one year to dispose of its stock in the S corporation, thereby avoiding disqualification.

The portion of an ESBT which consists of the stock of an S corporation is treated as a separate trust and generally is taxed on its share of the S corporation's income at the highest rate of tax imposed on individual taxpayers. This income is not taxed to the beneficiaries of the ESBT. This is the case whether or not the income is distributed be the ESBT (Code Sec. 641(a) and (c)).

## NEW LAW EXPLAINED

**Nonresident aliens can be potential qualifying beneficiaries of electing small business trust (ESBT) to include nonresident aliens.**—A nonresident alien individual may be a potential current beneficiary of an electing small business trust (ESBT) without causing the loss of the S corporation election (Code Sec. 1361(c)(2)(B)(v), as amended by the Tax Cuts and Jobs Act (P.L. 115-97). Thus, an ESBT's nonresident alien potential current beneficiaries are not disqualifying shareholders under Code Sec. 1361(b)(1)(C). Accordingly, the ESBT's share of S corporation income is taxed to the ESBT (whether or not distributed), not to its nonresident alien potential current beneficiaries.

> **Comment:** Although the new law permits a nonresidential alien individual to be a potential current beneficiary of an ESBT, it does not allow a nonresidential alien to be an S corporation shareholder.

No significant guidance related to this provision has been issued.

▶ **Effective date.** The amendment made by this section is effective on January 1, 2018 (Act Sec. 13541(b) of the Tax Cuts and Jobs Act (P.L. 115-97)).

**No significant guidance related to this provision has been issued.**

— Act Sec. 13541(a) of the Tax Cuts and Jobs Act (P.L. 115-97), amending Code Sec. 1361(c)(2)(B)(v);

— Act Sec. 13541(b), providing the effective date.

# ¶365 Charitable Contribution Deduction for Electing Small Business Trust (ESBT)

## SUMMARY OF NEW LAW

The charitable contribution deduction of an ESBT is generally to be determined by the rules applicable to individuals, not the rules generally applicable to trusts. This change applies to tax years beginning after December 31, 2017.

## BACKGROUND

An electing small business trust (ESBT) can be an S corporation shareholder so long as the trust does not have as a beneficiary any person other than an individual, estate, or organization eligible to accept charitable contributions under Code Sec. 170 (other than a political entity) (Code Sec. 1361(e)(1)(A)(i). The portion of an ESBT that consists of the stock of an S corporation is treated as a separate trust and generally is taxed on its share of the S corporation's income at the highest rate of tax imposed on individual taxpayers. This income is not taxed to the beneficiaries of the ESBT. This is the case whether or not the income is distributed by the ESBT.

The deduction for charitable contributions by an ESBT is determined by the rules applicable to trusts, rather than the rules applicable to individuals. Generally, a trust is allowed a charitable contribution deduction for amounts of gross income, without limitation, which pursuant to the terms of the governing instrument are paid for a charitable purpose. No carryover of excess contributions is allowed. An individual is allowed a charitable contribution deduction limited to certain percentages of adjusted gross income generally with a five-year carryforward of amounts in excess of this limitation.

## NEW LAW EXPLAINED

**Charitable deduction of ESBT determined by rules for individuals.**—The charitable contribution deduction of an electing small business trust (ESBT) is not determined by the rules generally applicable to trusts under Code Sec. 642(c) (Code Sec. 641(c)(2)(E)(i), as added by the Tax Cuts and Jobs Act (P.L. 115-97)). The deduction, instead is determined by rules applicable to individuals (Code Sec. 641(c)(2)(E)(ii), as added by the 2017 Tax Cuts Act). Thus, the percentage limitations and carryforward provisions applicable to individuals apply to charitable contributions made by the portion of an ESBT holding S corporation stock.

Specifically for purposes of the contribution base for percentage limitations under Code Sec. 170(b)(1)(G), adjusted gross income is computed in the same manner as in the case of an individual. However, the deductions for costs which are paid or incurred in connection with the administration of the trust and which would not have been incurred if the property were not held in such trust are to be treated as allowable in arriving at adjusted gross income (Code Sec. 641(c)(2)(E)(ii), as added by the 2017 Tax Cuts Act).

▶ **Effective date.** The amendment made by this section applies to tax years beginning after December 31, 2017 (Act Sec. 13542(b) of the Tax Cuts and Jobs Act (P.L. 115-97)).

**No significant guidance related to this provision has been issued.**

— Act Sec. 13542(a) of the Tax Cuts and Jobs Act (P.L. 115-97), adding Code Sec. 641(c)(2)(E);

— Act Sec. 13542(b), providing the effective date.

# ¶370  S Corporation Conversions to C Corporations

## SUMMARY OF NEW LAW

S corporations that convert to C corporations take any resulting Code Sec. 481(a) adjustments into account over a six-year period. If an eligible terminated S corporation distributes money after the post-termination transition period, the accumulated adjustments account is allocated to the distribution.

## BACKGROUND

Generally, once S corporation status ends, C corporation rules apply. There are, however, special rules for distributions during the post-termination transition period (Code Sec. 1371(e)). Distributions made by a former S corporation during its post-termination transition period are treated in the same manner as if the distributions were made by an S corporation. The post-termination transition period is:

(1) the period beginning on the day after termination of S corporation status and ending on the later of (i) the day that is one year after the termination, or (ii) the due date for filing the return for the last year as an S corporation (including extensions);

(2) the 120-day period beginning on the date of any determination pursuant to an audit following the termination of the corporation's S election and which adjusts a Subchapter S item of income, loss, or deduction of the corporation arising during the S period (as defined in Code Sec. 1368(e)(2)); and

(3) the 120-day period beginning on the date of a determination that the corporation's election under Code Sec. 1362(a) had terminated for a previous tax year (Code Sec. 1377(b)).

An S corporation's accumulated adjustment account determines the tax effect of distributions when the corporation has accumulated earnings and profits. Additionally, if the corporation's S election is terminated, the accumulated adjustment account balance will be necessary to determine the amount of money that can be distributed tax-free during the post-termination period (Code Sec. 1371(e)). Distributions from a terminated S corporation are treated as paid from its accumulated adjustment account if made during the post-termination transition period.

A taxpayer that changes its accounting method may have to make Code Sec. 481(a) adjustments to account for timing differences between the old and the new method. For the year of change, the taxpayer must take into account adjustments that are necessary to prevent items of income or expense from being duplicated or omitted (Code Sec. 481(a)(2)). The year of change is the tax year for which the taxable income of the taxpayer is computed under a different method than the prior year (Reg. § 1.481-1(a)). Net adjustments that decrease taxable income generally are taken into account entirely in the year of change, and net adjustments that increase taxable income generally are taken into account ratably during the four-tax-year period beginning with the year of change (Rev. Proc. 2015-13).

## NEW LAW EXPLAINED

**Code Sec. 481 adjustment period extended for S corporation conversion to C corporation.**—Any Code Sec. 481(a) adjustment resulting from an accounting method change that is attributable to an eligible S corporation's revocation of its S corporation election during the two-year period beginning on December 22, 2017, is taken into account ratably over a six-year period beginning with the year of change (Code Sec. 481(d), as added by the Tax Cuts and Jobs Act (P.L. 115-97)). An eligible terminated S corporation is any C corporation that:

- was an S corporation on December 21, 2017;

- revokes its S corporation election during the two-year period beginning on December 22, 2017; and

- has the same shareholders in identical proportions both on December 22, 2017, and on the date of revocation (Code Sec. 481(d)(2), as added by the 2017 Tax Cuts Act).

An eligible terminated S corporation's accumulated adjustments account (AAA) is allocated to money that the corporation distributes after the post-termination transition period. The distribution is chargeable to accumulated earnings and profits in the same ratio as the amount of the AAA bears to the amount of the earnings and profits (Code Sec. 1371(f), as added by the 2017 Tax Cuts Act). The JCT Bluebook notes that a technical correction may be needed to make this allocation of the AAA elective rather than mandatory (General Explanation of Public Law 115-97 (JCS-1-18), fn 1218).

*Accounting Method Changes.* The six-year adjustment period may also apply when an eligible terminated S corporation uses the Rev. Proc. 2018-31 automatic IRS consent procedures to change from the cash method of accounting to the accrual method of accounting for its first tax year as a C corporation.

- The six-year spread is mandatory if the eligible terminated S corporation is required to change from the cash to the accrual method.

- The six-year spread is optional if the eligible terminated S corporation could continue to use the cash method as a C corporation but instead changes to the accrual method. The corporation must specify the six-year spread period in its Form 3115, Application for Change in Accounting Method (Rev. Proc. 2018-44, modifying Rev. Proc. 2018-31).

▶ **Effective date.** No specific effective date is provided by the Act. The provision is, therefore, considered effective on December 22, 2017, the date of enactment.

— Act Sec. 13543(a) of the Tax Cuts and Jobs Act (P.L. 115-97), adding Code Sec. 481(d);

— Act Sec. 13543(b), adding Code Sec. 1371(f).

# Depreciation and Expense Deductions

**4**

## ¶405 Section 179 Expensing of Depreciable Assets

### SUMMARY OF NEW LAW

The Code Sec. 179 dollar limitation is increased to $1 million and the investment limitation is increased to $2.5 million for tax years beginning after 2017. The definition of qualified real property eligible for expensing is redefined to include improvements to the interior of any nonresidential real property ("qualified improvement property"), as well as roofs, heating, ventilation, and air-conditioning property, fire protection and alarm systems, and security systems installed on such property. The exclusion from expensing for tangible personal property used in connection with lodging facilities (such as residential rental property) is eliminated. The $25,000 Code Sec. 179 expensing limit on certain heavy vehicles is inflation-adjusted after 2018.

### BACKGROUND

Taxpayers (other than estates, trusts, and certain noncorporate lessors) may elect to treat the cost of qualifying property, called "section 179 property," as a deductible expense rather than a capital expenditure (Code Sec. 179). Section 179 property is generally defined as new or used depreciable tangible section 1245 property that is purchased for use in the active conduct of a trade or business (Code Sec. 179(d)(1)).

**Dollar limitation.** For tax years beginning in 2017, the inflation-adjusted dollar limit on the cost of section 179 property that the taxpayer can elect to deduct is $510,000 (Code Sec. 179(b)(1); Rev. Proc. 2017-58).

## BACKGROUND

**Investment limitation.** The annual dollar limit is reduced dollar for dollar by the portion of the cost of section 179 property placed in service during the tax year that exceeds an investment limitation (Code Sec. 179(b)(2)). The inflation-adjusted investment limitation is $2,030,000 for tax years beginning in 2017 (Rev. Proc. 2017-58).

**$25,000 SUV limitation.** The maximum amount of the cost of a sport utility vehicle (SUV) that may be expensed under Code Sec. 179 if the SUV is exempt from the luxury car caps (e.g., has a gross vehicle weight rating in excess of 6,000 pounds) is limited to $25,000. The $25,000 limitation also applies to exempt trucks with an interior cargo bed length of less than six feet and exempt passenger vans that seat fewer than ten persons behind the driver's seat. To qualify, the vehicle must be rated at not more than 14,000 pounds gross vehicle weight. Exempt cargo vans are generally not subject to the $25,000 limitation (Code Sec. 179(b)(5)). This limitation is not inflation-adjusted.

**Qualified real property.** A taxpayer may elect to treat qualified real property as section 179 property (Code Sec. 179(f)(1)). Qualified real property generally consists of qualified leasehold improvements as defined in Code Sec. 168(e)(6), qualified restaurant property as defined in Code Sec. 168(e)(7), and qualified retail improvement property as defined in Code Sec. 168(e)(8) (Code Sec. 179(f)(2)). These types of property are depreciable under MACRS over 15-years using the straight-line method.

**Property used in connection with lodging.** Property that is used predominantly to furnish lodging or in connection with the furnishing of lodging does not qualify for expensing (Code Sec. 179(d)(1)). The term "lodging facility" includes an apartment house (e.g., MACRS residential rental property), hotel, motel, dormitory, or (subject to certain exceptions) any other facility or part of a facility where sleeping accommodations are provided and let. However, property used by a hotel, motel, inn, or other similar establishment is not considered used in connection with the furnishing of lodging if more than half of the living quarters are used to accommodate tenants on a transient basis (rental periods of 30 days or less) (Code Sec. 50(b)(2)(B); Reg. §1.48-1(h)(1)(i) and (2)(ii)). Property used in the living quarters of a lodging facility, including beds and other furniture, refrigerators, ranges, and other equipment is used predominantly to furnish lodging (Reg. §1.48-1(h)(1)(i)). Property that is used predominantly in the operation of a lodging facility or in serving tenants is used in connection with the furnishing of lodging, whether furnished by the owner of the lodging facility or another person. Examples of property used in connection with the furnishing of lodging include lobby furniture, office equipment, and laundry and swimming pool equipment. Property used in furnishing electrical energy, water, sewage disposal services, gas, telephone service or similar services are not used in connection with the furnishing of lodging (Reg. §1.48-1(h)(1)(ii)).

## NEW LAW EXPLAINED

**Code Sec. 179 deduction limitations increased, qualified real property expensing expanded, lodging facility property made eligible, $25,000 limit on SUVs inflation-adjusted**—The overall Code Sec. 179 expensing dollar limitation is increased from $500,000 (inflation-adjusted to $510,000 for 2017) to $1 million, and the investment

## NEW LAW EXPLAINED

limitation is increased from $2 million (inflation-adjusted to $2,030,000 in 2017) to $2.5 million, effective for property placed in service in tax years beginning in 2018 (Code Sec. 179(b)(1) and (2), as amended by the Tax Cuts and Jobs Act (P.L. 115-97)).

These increases are permanent and are inflation-adjusted in tax years beginning after 2018 (Code Sec. 179(b)(6), as amended by the 2017 Tax Cuts Act). The amount of the inflation adjustment is based on the cost-of-living adjustment determined under Code Sec. 1(f)(3) for the calendar year in which the tax year begins, by substituting calendar year 2017 for calendar year 2016. When adjusting the dollar limitation or the investment limitation for inflation, the resulting amount must be rounded to the nearest multiple of $10,000.

For tax years beginning in 2019, the inflation-adjusted limitations are $1,020,000 and $2,550,000 (Rev. Proc. 2018-57).

**Qualified real property definition expanded.** The definition of qualified real property that taxpayers may elect to treat as section 179 property is significantly expanded. Effective for tax years beginning after 2017, qualified real property is defined as:

(1) Qualified improvement property; and

(2) Any of the following improvements to nonresidential real property that are placed in service after the nonresidential real property was first placed in service:

- roofs;
- heating, ventilation, and air-conditioning property (HVACs);
- fire protection and alarm systems; and
- security systems (Code Sec. 179(f), as amended by the 2017 Tax Cuts Act; Rev. Proc. 2019-8).

A central HVAC system includes all components that are in, on, or adjacent to the nonresidential real property (Rev. Proc. 2019-8; Reg. § 1.48-1(e)(2)).

Qualified improvement property is an improvement to *an interior portion* of a building that is nonresidential real property provided the improvement is placed in service after the date that the building was first placed in service. However, improvements related to the enlargement of the building, an elevator or escalator, or the internal structural framework of the building are not qualified improvement property (Code Sec. 168(e)(6), as amended by the 2017 Tax Cuts Act).

> **Comment:** A technical correction may be needed to clarify that qualified improvement property and the preceding enumerated improvements must be made and placed in service by the taxpayer claiming the expense deduction (General Explanation of Public Law 115-97 (JCS-1-18), footnotes 421 and 633).

> **Comment:** As under prior law, a taxpayer must elect to treat qualified real property as section 179 property (Code Sec. 179(d)(1)(B)(ii), as amended by the 2017 Tax Cuts Act). If the election is made and the total cost of all section 179 property, including qualified real property, exceeds the investment limitation ($2.5 million in 2018), the dollar limitation ($1 million in 2018) is subject to reduction.

## NEW LAW EXPLAINED

A taxpayer may elect to expense the entire cost, or a portion of the cost, of qualified real property placed in service by the taxpayer during any tax year beginning after 2017 by filing an original or amended Federal tax return for that taxable year in accordance with procedures similar to those Reg. § 1.179-5(c)(2) and section 3.02 of Rev. Proc. 2017-33. If a taxpayer elects or elected to expense a portion of the cost of qualified real property placed in service by the taxpayer during any tax year beginning after 2017, the taxpayer is permitted to increase the portion of the cost of such property expensed by filing an amended Federal tax return for that tax year. Any increase in the amount expensed is not deemed to be a revocation of the prior election for that tax year (Rev. Proc. 2019-8, Sec. 3.02).

> **Comment:** In tax years beginning before 2018, qualified real property eligible for expensing consisted of qualified leasehold improvement property, qualified retail improvement property, and qualified restaurant improvements and buildings that are eligible for an MACRS 15-year recovery period. Qualified leasehold improvement property is any improvement to the interior portion of a building that is not residential rental property and is made under or pursuant to the terms of a lease by the lessor or lessee. Qualified retail improvement property is any improvement to the interior portion of a building that is not residential rental property, which is open to the general public, and is used in the retail trade or business of selling tangible personal property to the general public. The improvement to leasehold or retail improvement property must be placed in service more than three years after the date the building was first placed in service by any person, and improvements related to the enlargement of the building, any elevator or escalator, any structural component benefitting a common area, or the internal structural framework of the building do not qualify. Qualified restaurant property is a restaurant building or any improvement to a restaurant building. No additional restrictions apply to restaurant property.

> **Comment:** Qualified improvement property became a category of property eligible for bonus depreciation for property placed in service after 2015 and before 2018 (Code Sec. 168(k)(3), as added by Division Q of P.L. 114-113 (PATH Act), December 18, 2015). See ¶410. The new law does not change the definition of qualified improvement property but now includes it as a category of property eligible for expensing under Code Sec. 179 as "qualified real property." Under the new law, qualified real property also includes roofs, HVAC property, fire protection or alarm systems, and security systems placed in service in or on a commercial building after the building is placed in service. Under prior law, qualified real property included only 15-year leasehold improvement property, 15-year retail improvement, and 15-year restaurant improvements and buildings.

> **Comment:** A separate provision eliminates the 15-year recovery period for 15-year leasehold improvement property, 15-year retail improvement, and 15-year restaurant improvements and buildings effective for property placed in service after 2017 (Code Sec. 168(e)(3)(E), as amended by the 2017 Tax Cuts Act). In its place, Congress intended to assign a 15-year recovery period for qualified

**NEW LAW EXPLAINED**

improvement property (Conference Report on H.R. 1, Tax Cuts and Jobs Act (H. Rept. 115-466)). However, the final bill text, while eliminating the 15-year classifications for leasehold improvement property, etc., inadvertently failed to assign a 15-year recovery period to qualified improvement property. A technical correction is necessary to assign the intended 15-year recovery period, which in turn will make qualified improvement property once again eligible for bonus depreciation (General Explanation of Public Law 115-97 (JCS-1-18), footnote 632). However, even without the technical correction, qualified improvement property placed in service in tax years beginning after 2017 may be expensed as a category of section "qualified real property." See ¶425 for a detailed discussion of qualified improvement property.

**Comment:** The new definition of qualified real property is especially unfavorable to restaurant owners. Previously, restaurant buildings and improvements to the exterior as well as the interior of a restaurant building qualified for expensing under the qualified real property category. Under the new law, a restaurant improvement (or improvement to any other type of building) must meet the definition of "qualified improvement property." This means that only internal improvements to a restaurant building (and also roofs, HVAC property, fire protection and alarm systems, and security systems) will qualify for expensing. Furthermore, because restaurant buildings are not "qualified improvement property," they cannot be depreciated over the intended 15-year recovery period for qualified improvement property or expensed under Code Sec. 179 as qualified improvement property.

**Exclusion for property used in connection with lodging repealed.** Effective for property placed in service in tax years beginning after December 31, 2017, property that is used predominantly to furnish lodging or in connection with the furnishing of lodging qualifies for Code Sec. 179 expensing (Code Sec. 179(d)(1), as amended by the 2017 Tax Cuts Act).

**Comment:** The primary impact of this provision is to allow expensing of section 1245 property purchased for use in connection with a residential rental building. See "*Background*" section above for examples of types of property that are used in connection with the furnishing of lodging and are now eligible for expensing.

**Property acquired by purchase—Code Sec. 336(e) election.** A proposed regulation provides that property deemed acquired by a new target corporation as a result of a section 336(e) election is considered acquired by purchase for purposes of section 179 (Proposed Reg. §1.179-4(c)(2)). The IRS indicates in the preamble to the proposals (REG-104397-18) that this proposed regulation merely clarifies existing law.

**Comment:** Only property that is acquired by "purchase" qualifies for expensing. In addition, used property acquired after September 27, 2017 qualifies for bonus depreciation only if it is acquired by purchase.

**$25,000 limit on certain vehicles adjusted for inflation.** The $25,000 maximum Code Sec. 179 deduction that may be claimed on specified vehicles that are exempt from the luxury car caps is adjusted for inflation in tax years beginning after 2018 (Code Sec. 179(b)(6), as amended by the 2017 Tax Cuts Act). For tax years beginning in 2019, the inflation-adjusted limitation is $25,500 (Rev. Proc. 2018-57).

## NEW LAW EXPLAINED

> **Comment:** The $25,000 limit applies to a sport utility vehicle, a truck with an interior cargo bed length less than six feet, or a van that seats fewer than 10 persons behind the driver's seat, if the vehicle is exempt from the Code Sec. 280F annual depreciation caps because it has a gross vehicle weight rating in excess of 6,000 pounds or is otherwise exempt, and is rated at not more than 14,000 pounds gross vehicle weight (Code Sec. 179(b)(5)).

The amount of the inflation adjustment is based on the cost-of-living adjustment determined under Code Sec. 1(f)(3) for the calendar year in which the tax year begins, but substituting calendar year 2017 for calendar year 2016. When adjusting the $25,000 limit for inflation, the resulting amount must be rounded to the nearest multiple of $100.

▶ **Effective date.** The provisions apply to property placed in service in tax years beginning after December 31, 2017 (Act Sec. 13101(d) of the Tax Cuts and Jobs Act (P.L. 115-97)).

— Act Sec. 13101(a) of the Tax Cuts and Jobs Act (P.L. 115-97), amending Code Sec. 179(b);

— Act Sec. 13101(b)(1), amending Code Sec. 179(d)(1)(B);

— Act Sec. 13101(b)(2), amending Code Sec. 179(f);

— Act Sec. 13101(c), amending last sentence of Code Sec. 179(d)(1);

— Act Sec. 13101(d), providing the effective date.

# ¶410  Additional Depreciation Allowance (Bonus Depreciation)

## SUMMARY OF NEW LAW

The bonus depreciation rate is increased to 100 percent for property acquired and placed in service after September 27, 2017, and before January 1, 2023. The rate phases down thereafter. Used property, films, television shows, and theatrical productions are eligible for bonus depreciation. Property used by rate-regulated utilities, and property of certain motor vehicle, boat, and farm machinery retail and lease businesses that use floor financing indebtedness, is excluded from bonus depreciation.

## BACKGROUND

A 50-percent bonus depreciation deduction is allowed for the first tax year qualifying MACRS property is placed in service. The property's original use must begin with the taxpayer (so the property must be new) and it must be placed in service after December 31, 2007, and before January 1, 2020 (or before January 1, 2021, for longer production period property (LPP) and certain noncommercial aircraft (NCA)) (Code Sec. 168(k)). The bonus depreciation allowance rate was temporarily increased from 50 percent to 100 percent for qualified property acquired after September 8, 2010, and before January 1, 2012, and placed in service before January 1, 2012 (before January 1, 2013, for LPP and NCA).

# BACKGROUND

The bonus depreciation rate is 50 percent for qualified property placed in service in 2017. It drops to 40 percent for 2018, and to 30 percent for 2019. These deadlines are extended for one year for NCA and LPP (so the rate is 50 percent for property placed in service in 2017 or 2018, 40 percent for 2019, and 30 percent for 2020 (Code Sec. 168(k)(6)).

There is no limit on the total amount of bonus depreciation that may be claimed in any given tax year. The amount of the bonus depreciation deduction is not affected by a short tax year. The bonus depreciation deduction is allowed in full for alternative minimum tax (AMT) purposes. In addition, the regular depreciation deductions claimed on property that qualifies for bonus depreciation are also allowed in full for AMT purposes even if an election out of bonus depreciation is made (Code Sec. 168(k)(2)(G)).

**Qualifying property.** The bonus depreciation allowance is available only for new property (i.e., property the original use of which begins with the taxpayer after December 31, 2007) that is:

- depreciable under MACRS and has a recovery period of 20 years or less;

- MACRS water utility property;

- computer software depreciable over three years under Code Sec. 167(f); or

- qualified improvement property (Code Sec. 168(k)(2)(A)).

Qualified improvement property is any improvement to an interior portion of a building that is nonresidential real property if the improvement is placed in service after the date the building was first placed in service by any person. Qualified improvement property, however, does not include improvements attributable to the enlargement of a building, any elevator or escalator, or the internal structural framework of the building (Code Sec. 168(k)(3)). No specific MACRS recovery period is assigned to qualified improvement property. Unless qualified improvement property meets the separate definitions for 15-year qualified leasehold improvement property, 15-year retail improvement property, or 15-year restaurant property, it is depreciated as MACRS 39-year nonresidential real property.

**Longer production period property and noncommercial aircraft.** In the case of LPP and NCA:

- The original use of the property must begin with the taxpayer;

- The property must be acquired by the taxpayer before 2020 or acquired pursuant to a binding contract entered into before 2020; and

- The property must be placed in service before 2021 (Code Sec. 168(k)(2)(B)(i) and (k)(2)(C)(i)).

If the NCA or LPP is constructed, the acquisition deadline is satisfied if the taxpayer begins manufacturing, constructing, or producing the NCA or LPP before January 1, 2020 (Code Sec. 168(k)(2)(E)(i)). Progress expenditures in 2020 can qualify for bonus depreciation only for NCA, but not for LPP (Code Sec. 168(k)(2)(B)(ii) and (iv)).

## BACKGROUND

LPP is property that:

- meets the general requirements for qualifying property;
- is subject to the Code Sec. 263A uniform capitalization rules;
- has a production period greater than one year and a cost exceeding $1 million; and
- has a MACRS recovery period of at least 10 years or is used in the trade or business of transporting persons or property for hire, such as commercial aircraft (i.e., "transportation property") (Code Sec. 168(k)(2)(B)(i)).

**Election out.** A taxpayer may elect out of the bonus depreciation allowance for any class of property for the tax year (Code Sec. 168(k)(7)).

**Luxury car depreciation caps.** Unless the taxpayer elects out of bonus depreciation, the first-year Code Sec. 280F depreciation cap for passenger automobiles that qualify for bonus depreciation is increased by $8,000 for vehicles placed in service during 2017, $6,400 for 2018, and $4,800 for 2019 (Code Sec. 168(k)(2)(F)).

**Coordination with long-term contract method of accounting.** Solely for purposes of determining the percentage of completion under the Code Sec. 460(b)(1)(A) long-term contract accounting method, the cost of property with a MACRS recovery period of seven years or less that qualifies for bonus depreciation is taken into account as a cost allocated to the contract as if bonus depreciation had not been enacted. This rule applies to property placed in service in 2010 (2010 or 2011 for LPP), and property placed in service after December 31, 2012, and before January 1, 2020 (before January 1, 2021, for LPP) (Code Sec. 460(c)(6)(B)).

### NEW LAW EXPLAINED

**Bonus depreciation extended and increased to 100 percent; additional modifications made.**—The 50-percent bonus depreciation rate is increased to 100 percent for qualified property acquired and placed in service after September 27, 2017, and before January 1, 2023 (Code Sec. 168(k)(1)(A) and (6)(A), as amended by the Tax Cuts and Jobs Act (P.L. 115-97); Proposed Reg. § 1.168(k)-2; NPRM REG-104397-18 (Aug. 8, 2018)). After 2022, the 100-percent rate is phased down by 20 percent per year as follows:

- 100 percent for property placed in service after September 27, 2017, and before January 1, 2023;
- 80 percent for property placed in service after December 31, 2022, and before January 1, 2024;
- 60 percent for property placed in service after December 31, 2023, and before January 1, 2025;
- 40 percent for property placed in service after December 31, 2024, and before January 1, 2026;
- 20 percent for property placed in service after December 31, 2025, and before January 1, 2027;
- 0 percent (bonus expires) for property placed in service after December 31, 2026 (Code Sec. 168(k)(6)(A), as amended by the 2017 Tax Cuts Act).

## NEW LAW EXPLAINED

**Comment:** The IRS released proposed regulations on the bonus depreciation allowance for qualified property acquired and placed in service after September 27, 2017 and before 2027 on August 3, 2018 (REG-104397-18; Proposed Reg. § 1.168(k)-2). The proposed regulations are comprehensive. In many respects they are similar to or identical to the current final regulations in Reg. § 1.168(k)-1. However, they incorporate detailed guidance on changes made by the 2017 Tax Cuts Act. For most taxpayers the most important change (other than the rate increase to 100 percent) allows bonus depreciation on used property acquired after September 27, 2017.

When the proposals are adopted as final regulations, the final regulations will apply to property placed in service during or after the tax year in which final regulations are published. The proposals are "reliance regulations." Accordingly, a taxpayer may apply the proposals to property placed in service after September 27, 2017, in tax years ending on or after September 28, 2017, and before the date of publication of the final regulations (Proposed Reg. § 1.168(k)-2(g)).

*Property acquired before September 28, 2017.* Property acquired before September 28, 2017, is subject to the 50-percent rate if placed in service in 2017, a 40-percent rate if placed in service in 2018, and a 30-percent rate if placed in service in 2019. Property acquired before September 28, 2017, and placed in service after 2019 is not eligible for bonus depreciation. However, in the case of longer production property (LPP) and noncommercial aircraft (NCA), each of these placed-in-service dates is extended one year. Thus, a 50 percent rate applies to LPP and NCA acquired before September 28, 2017, and placed in service in 2017 or 2018, a 40 percent rate applies if such property is placed in service in 2019, and a 30 percent rate applies if such property is placed in service in 2020 (Code Sec. 168(k)(8), as added by the 2017 Tax Cuts Act)). If LPP is placed in service in 2020, 2020 progress expenditures do not qualify for bonus depreciation. Earlier expenditures are eligible for the 30 percent rate (General Explanation of Public Law 115-97 (JCS-1-18)). These are the phase-down rates that applied before enactment of the 2017 Tax Cuts Act. They continue to apply to property acquired before the September 28, 2017 cut-off date set by Congress.

**Caution:** A technical correction to the effective date of the Tax Cuts Act may be needed to clarify that the rates for property acquired before September 28, 2017, and placed in service after September 27, 2017, are effective for property acquired before September 28, 2017. The current effective date provides that the provision is effective for property acquired after September 27, 2017 (General Explanation of Public Law 115-97 (JCS-1-18), FNs 538, 558).

**Binding contracts.** Property acquired pursuant to a written binding contract entered into before September 28, 2017, does not qualify for the 100 percent bonus rate (Act Sec. 13201(h)(1) of the 2017 Tax Cuts Act). The acquisition date is the date that the contract was entered into (Proposed Reg. § 1.168(k)-2(b)(5)(ii)).

The proposed regulations retain the rules in Reg. § 1.168(k)-1(b)(4)(ii) defining a binding contract and provide additionally that a letter of intent for an acquisition is not a binding contract (Proposed Reg. § 1.168(k)-2(b)(5)(iii)(D)).

## NEW LAW EXPLAINED

Property manufactured, constructed, or produced for a taxpayer by another person under a written binding contract entered into prior to manufacture, construction, or production is considered acquired pursuant to a written binding contract. Consequently, if a taxpayer enters such a contract before September 28, 2017, the property does not qualify for the 100 percent rate (Proposed Reg. § 1.168(k)-2(b)(5)(iv)).

A binding contract to acquire one or more components of a larger property is not considered a contract to acquire the larger property. If a taxpayer entered into a written binding contract to acquire the components before September 27, 2017, the components do not qualify for the 100 percent rate regardless of whether the larger property is constructed by or for the taxpayer (Proposed Reg. § 1.168(k)-2(b)(5)(iii)(F); Proposed Reg. § 1.168(k)-2(b)(5)(iv)(C)).

**Specified plants.** The applicable 100 percent and phase-down rates above also apply to specified plants acquired after September 27, 2017, except that the date the specified plant was planted or grafted replaces the placed in service date (Code Sec. 168(k)(5)(A) and (6)(C), as amended by the 2017 Tax Cuts Act). In general, a specified plant is any tree or vine which bears fruits or nuts, and any other plant which will have more than one yield of fruits or nuts and which generally has a pre-productive period of more than two years from the time of planting or grafting to the time at which such plant begins bearing fruits or nuts (Code Sec. 168(k)(5)).

A taxpayer must make an election to claim bonus depreciation on specified plants in the year of planting or grafting by the due date (including extensions) of the return for the year of the planting or grafting. The election may be made for one or more specified plants by the person owning the plant. The taxpayer, therefore, may make the election on a selective basis (Proposed Reg. § 1.168(k)-2(e)(2)).

An election may be made to claim the 50 percent bonus rate on specified plants that are planted or grafting during the tax year that includes September 28, 2017. The election applies to all specified plants other than those for which an election out of bonus depreciation is made (Proposed Reg. § 1.168(k)-2(e)(3)).

**Self-constructed property.** In order for self-constructed property to be considered acquired after September 27, 2017, the taxpayer must begin manufacturing, constructing, or producing the property for use in its trade or business after that date. In cases where another person manufactures, constructs, or produces property for the taxpayer under a written binding agreement, the property is not self-constructed property if taxpayer enters into the agreement prior to the beginning of manufacture, construction, or production (Proposed Reg. § 1.168(k)-2(b)(5)(iv)(B)).

If the manufacture, construction, or production of self-constructed property begins before September 28, 2017, the self constructed property and any components of that property, whether or not self-constructed, do not qualify for the 100 percent rate (Proposed Reg. § 168(k)-2(b)(5)(iv)(C)(2); Proposed Reg. § 1.168(k)-2(b)(5)(vii), Example 8). However, if the manufacture of self-constructed components begins before September 28, 2017, the self-constructed property may qualify for the 100 percent rate if its manufacture begins after September 27, 2017.

Manufacture, construction, or production begins when physical work of a significant nature begins or, under an elective safe harbor, when the taxpayer pays or incurs 10

## NEW LAW EXPLAINED

percent or more of the cost of the property (excluding the cost of land and preliminary activities) (Proposed Reg. § 1.168(k)-2(b)(5)(iv)(B)). Preliminary work does not constitute the beginning of construction. These are the same standards that apply under the final regulations.

**Property with longer production period and noncommercial aircraft.** In the case of property with a longer production period (LPP) and noncommercial aircraft (NCA), the placed-in-service deadlines for property acquired after September 27, 2017, and before January 1, 2027, are extended for one year. The applicable rates are as follows:

- 100 percent for property placed in service after September 27, 2017, and before January 1, 2024;

- 80 percent for property placed in service after December 31, 2023, and before January 1, 2025;

- 60 percent for property placed in service after December 31, 2024, and before January 1, 2026;

- 40 percent for property placed in service after December 31, 2025, and before January 1, 2027;

- 20 percent for property placed in service after December 31, 2026, and before January 1, 2028;

- 0 percent (bonus expires) for property placed in service after December 31, 2027 (Code Sec. 168(k)(6)(B), as amended by the 2017 Tax Cuts Act).

2027 production expenditures for LPP do not qualify for bonus depreciation (Code Sec. 168(k)(2)(B)(ii), as amended by the 2017 Tax Cuts Act; Proposed Reg. § 1.168(k)-2(d)(1)(iii)). This rule does not apply to noncommercial aircraft (NCA).

Solely for purposes of determining whether LPP or NCA are acquired before January 1, 2027, property that is constructed for the taxpayer under a written binding contract that is entered into prior to the beginning of construction is considered constructed by the taxpayer (Proposed Reg. § 1.168(k)-2(c)(3)(i)).

Construction begins when work of a significant nature begins or when the taxpayer pays or incurs more than 10 percent of the total cost of the property (excluding the cost of land and any preliminary activities).

When LPP or NCA is constructed for the taxpayer by another person, the taxpayer must satisfy the 10 percent safe harbor test (Proposed Reg. § 1.168(k)-2(c)(3)(ii)(B)).

*Acquired components of LPP or NCA.* Components of a LPP or NCA that are acquired pursuant to a written binding contract entered into after 2026 do not qualify for the extended placed-in-service deadline. However, bonus depreciation may apply to the LPP or NCA without regard to the cost of those components. If a binding contract for a component is entered into before January 1, 2027 but construction of the LPP or NCA does not begin before January 1, 2027, the component qualifies for bonus depreciation, assuming all other requirements are met (Proposed Reg. § 1.168(k)-2(c)(3)(iii)(A)).

*Self-constructed components of LPP or NCA.* If construction of a component does not begin before January 1, 2027, the component does not qualify for bonus depreciation.

## NEW LAW EXPLAINED

The LPP or NCA, however, will qualify for bonus depreciation if the construction of the LPP or NCA begins before January 1, 2027. A self-constructed component may qualify for bonus depreciation if its construction begins before January 1, 2027, even though construction of the LPP or NCA does not begin before January 1, 2027 (Proposed Reg. § 1.168(k)-2(c)(3)(iii)(B)).

**Election to apply 50-percent rate.** A taxpayer may elect to claim 50 percent bonus depreciation in place of 100 percent bonus depreciation for qualified property acquired after September 27, 2017, and placed in service during the tax year that includes September 28, 2017. The proposed regulations clarify that the election applies to all qualified property placed in service during this period for which an election out of bonus depreciation is not made. The 50 percent election is not made at the property class level (Code Sec. 168(k)(10), as added by the 2017 Tax Cuts Act; Proposed Reg. § 1.168(k)-2(e)(3)). For example, a calendar year taxpayer making this election applies the 50-percent rate to all qualified property placed in service in 2017 and ignores the 100-percent rate that would otherwise apply to qualified property acquired and placed in service after September 27, 2017, and before January 1, 2018.

> **Comment:** The election is made by attaching a statement to a timely filed return (including extensions) for the tax year that includes September 2017 indicating that the taxpayer is "electing to claim a 50 percent special depreciation allowance on all qualified property."
>
> The election must be made separately by each person owning qualified property (for example, by the partnership, by the S corporation, or for each member of a consolidated group by the common parent of the group. See Instructions to 2017 Form 4562 and IRS Pub. 946 (2017).
>
> The election is revocable only with IRS consent obtained by filing a letter ruling. However, a taxpayer may file an amended return within 6 months of the due date (excluding extensions) of the original return to change the election. Taxpayers who are affected by the election change (e.g., partners) are also required to file amended returns (Proposed Reg. § 1.168(k)-2(e)(5)).

**Qualified improvement property.** Qualified improvement property is removed as a separate category of property eligible for bonus depreciation, effective for property placed in service after December 31, 2017 (this provision applies without regard to the acquisition date) (Code Sec. 168(k)(2)(A)(i)(IV) and (k)(3), stricken by the 2017 Tax Cuts Act). Qualified improvement property placed in service after 2017 is only eligible for bonus depreciation if a technical correction assigning a 15-year recovery period to qualified improvement property is enacted (General Explanation of Public Law 115-97 (JCS-1-18), FN 632). The IRS does not believe it has the authority to assign a 15-year recovery period even though the legislative history makes it clear that Congress intended to assign a 15-year recovery period. The assignment of a 15-year recovery period will make qualified improvement property eligible for bonus depreciation by reason of the general rule that tangible MACRS property with a recovery period of 20 years or less qualifies for bonus depreciation.

The new law does not change the definition of qualified improvement property. Qualified improvement property is defined as an improvement to the interior of nonresidential real property, but does not include improvements for expenditures

## NEW LAW EXPLAINED

attributable to the enlargement of a building, any elevator or escalator, or the internal structural framework of a building (Code Sec. 168(e)(6), as added by the 2017 Tax Cuts Act). The new law eliminates the categories of 15-year qualified leasehold improvement property, 15-year qualified retail improvement property, and 15-year restaurant property, effective for property placed in service after December 31, 2017. 15-year qualified leasehold improvement property and 15-year retail improvement property qualify for bonus depreciation as qualified improvement property if placed in service after 2015 and before 2018. 15-year qualified restaurant improvements placed in service after 2015 and before 2018 qualifies for bonus depreciation if it meets the definition of qualified improvement property (Proposed Reg. § 168(k)-2(b)(2)). See ¶ 425 for a detailed discussion of qualified improvement property.

> **Example:** A calendar-year taxpayer makes an improvement to the interior of an office building in June 2016. Assume the improvement is depreciable over 39 years as nonresidential real property because it does not satisfy the definition of 15-year qualified leasehold improvement, 15-year retail improvement, or 15-year restaurant property. Even though the improvement has a 39-year recovery period, it may qualify for bonus depreciation because, for property placed in service after 2015 and before 2018, qualified improvement property is listed as a separate category of property eligible for bonus depreciation. If the same improvement is made in 2018, it does not qualify for bonus depreciation unless a technical correction assigning a 15-year recovery period to qualified improvement property is enacted.

**Exclusion for property of rate-regulated utility.** Under a new provision, rate-regulated utilities are prevented from claiming bonus depreciation, effective for property placed in service in tax years beginning after 2017 (Code Secs. 168(k)(9) and 163(j)(7)(A)(iv), as added by the 2017 Tax Cuts Act; Proposed Reg. § 1.168(k)-2(b)(2)(ii)(F) providing the effective date; General Explanation of Public Law 115-97 (JCS-1-18), FN 549 indicating a technical correction may be necessary to clarify the effective date). Specifically, property does not qualify for bonus depreciation if it is primarily used in a trade or business of furnishing or selling for regulated rates:

- electrical energy or water;
- sewage disposal services;
- gas or steam through a local distribution system; or
- transportation of gas or steam by pipeline.

Rates are regulated if established or approved by a state or political subdivision thereof, by any agency or instrumentality of the United States, by a public service or public utility commission or other similar body of any state or political subdivision thereof, or by the governing or ratemaking body of an electric cooperative.

**Exclusion for property used by certain motor vehicle, boat, farm machinery businesses that used floor financing indebtedness.** Property used in a trade or business that has had floor plan financing indebtedness does not qualify for bonus

## NEW LAW EXPLAINED

depreciation if the floor plan financing interest on the indebtedness was taken into account under the new rules that limit the business interest deduction to 30 percent of adjusted taxable income plus floor plan financing interest and interest income in the case of taxpayers with average annual gross receipts in excess of $25 million (Code Secs. 168(k)(9) and 163(j)(9), as added by the 2017 Tax Cuts Act). This provision applies to property placed in service in tax years beginning after 2017 (Proposed Reg. § 1.168(k)-2(b)(2)(ii)(G)).

Floor plan financing indebtedness means indebtedness:

- used to finance the acquisition of motor vehicles held for sale or lease; and

- secured by the inventory acquired (Code Sec. 163(j)(9), as added by the 2017 Tax Cuts Act).

A motor vehicle means:

- any self-propelled vehicle designed for transporting persons or property on a public street, highway, or road;

- a boat; or

- farm machinery or equipment.

> **Comment:** The interest deduction limitation does not apply in any tax year that a taxpayer meets the gross receipts test of Code Sec. 448(c) by having average annual gross receipts for the three-tax-year period ending with the prior tax year that do not exceed $25 million (Code Sec. 163(j)(3), as added by the 2017 Tax Cuts Act). However, if a taxpayer has had floor financing interest in any tax year that it is not exempt from the 30-percent deduction limitation by reason of the gross receipts test or otherwise, the exclusion from bonus depreciation continues to apply in tax years that it is exempt.

> The 30 percent of taxable business limitation on deductible interest is discussed at ¶510.

**Used property qualifies for bonus depreciation.** Effective for property acquired and placed in service after September 27, 2017, property previously used by an unrelated person may qualify for bonus depreciation if it meets "acquisition requirements" (Code Sec. 168(k)(2)(A)(ii), as amended by the 2017 Tax Cuts Act). The acquisition requirements are met if:

- the taxpayer did not use the property at any time before acquiring it; and

- the taxpayer acquired the property by "purchase" within the meaning of Code Sec. 179(d)(2) (Code Sec. 168(k)(2)(E)(ii), as amended by the 2017 Tax Cuts Act; Proposed Reg. § 1.168(k)-2(b)(3)(iii)(A)).

Under Code Sec. 179(d)(2), any acquisition is considered a purchase unless the property:

- is acquired from a person whose relationship to the taxpayer would bar recognition of a loss in any transaction between them under Code Sec. 267 (with the taxpayer's family limited to spouse, ancestors and lineal descendants) or Code Sec. 707(b);

## NEW LAW EXPLAINED

- is acquired by one member of a controlled group of corporations from another member (substituting 50 percent for the 80 percent that would otherwise apply with respect to stock ownership requirements);

- has a basis in the hands of the acquiring taxpayer determined in whole or in part by reference to the adjusted basis of the person from who the property was acquired (e.g., a gift or section 1022 basis property); or

- has a basis determined under Code Sec. 1014(a) relating to inherited or bequested property (Reg. § 1.179-4(c)).

> **Comment:** Property deemed acquired by a new target corporation as a result of a Code Sec. 336(e) election is considered acquired by purchase for purposes of Code Sec. 179 (Proposed Reg. § 1.179-4(c)(2)). Although this rule is only provided in proposed regulations, the IRS noted that it considers the proposal a reaffirmation of present law (REG-104397-18).

*Like-kind exchanges and involuntary conversions.* The proposed regulations retain the rule that the exchanged basis and excess basis of the replacement property in a tax-free like-kind exchange or involuntary conversion is eligible for bonus depreciation if the replacement property is new. However, if the replacement property is used, bonus depreciation only applies to the excess basis, if any, of the replacement property (Proposed Reg. § 1.168(k)-2(f)(5)).

The tax-free like-kind exchange rules of Code Sec. 1031 only apply to real property, generally effective for exchanges completed after 2017 (Code Sec. 1031(a)). See ¶505.

*Property previously used by taxpayer.* Property used by a taxpayer or predecessor at any time prior to its acquisition does not qualify for bonus depreciation (Code Sec. 168(k)(2)(E)(ii)(I)). Property was previously used by the taxpayer, however, only if the taxpayer or predecessor had a depreciable interest in the property any time prior to its acquisition (Proposed Reg. § 1.168(k)-2(b)(3)(iii)(B)(1)). Thus, a lessee may purchase leased property (e.g., a machine) and qualify for bonus depreciation since the lessee did not have a depreciable interest.

If a taxpayer has a depreciable interest in a portion of a property and later acquires an additional interest, the additional interest is not tainted and may qualify for bonus depreciation. For example, if a lessee with a depreciable interest in an improvement to leased property acquires the entire leased property, the improvement does not qualify for bonus depreciation. However, the remainder of the property may qualify (Proposed Reg. § 1.168(k)-2(b)(3)(iii)(B)(1)).

If a taxpayer sells a portion of an interest in property and then later reacquires another portion of the same property, bonus depreciation only applies to the extent the newly acquired interest is greater than the original interest (Proposed Reg. § 1.168(k)-2(b)(3)(iii)(B)(2)).

*Used property converted from personal to business use.* Used property acquired by a taxpayer for personal use and then converted to business use is eligible for bonus depreciation. However, the 100 percent rate only applies if the used personal use property is acquired after September 27, 2017, and converted to business use before 2023. Used personal use property acquired before September 28, 2017, does not qualify for bonus depreciation upon later conversion to business use. Property

## NEW LAW EXPLAINED

converted from business use to personal use in the same tax year does not qualify for bonus depreciation (Proposed Reg. § 1.168(k)-2(f)(6)).

*Property acquired from related parties.* Used property acquired from a related party does not qualify for bonus depreciation (Proposed Reg. § 1.168(k)-2(b)(3)(iii)(A)). Related parties are defined in Code Sec. 267 and Code Sec. 707(b) which disallow losses created in transfers between related parties (Code Sec. 179(d)(2)(A)).

*Series of related transactions.* In any series of related transactions, property is considered transferred directly from the original transferor to the ultimate transferee. For example, a taxpayer may not circumvent the related party rule by first selling the property to an unrelated person (Proposed Reg. § 1.168(k)-2(b)(3)(iii)(C)).

> **Example:** Father sells machinery to an unrelated party and the father's daughter purchases the equipment. The daughter is treated as purchasing the equipment directly from her father. Since her father is a related party the property does not qualify for bonus depreciation. Moreover, the transfer of the machine to the daughter is treated as a direct transfer from the father to the daughter. Therefore, the unrelated party may not claim bonus depreciation (Proposed Reg. § 1.168(k)-2(b)(3)(vi), Example 18).

*Property transferred within consolidated groups.* Property acquired by a member of a consolidated group does not qualify for bonus depreciation if any prior or current member of the group had a depreciable interest in the property while a member of the group (Proposed Reg. § 1.168(k)-2(b)(3)(iii)(B)(3)).

> **Example:** ABC and BCD are members of the same consolidated group. ABC sells machinery to BCD. BCD may not claim bonus depreciation because ABC is a current group member that held a depreciable interest in the property. Furthermore ABC and BCD are related parties (Proposed Reg. § 1.168(k)-2(b)(3)(vi), Example 19).

> **Example:** ABC and BCD are members of the same consolidated group. ABC sells equipment to U, an unrelated party. In a later tax year, BCD purchases the equipment from U. The equipment does not qualify for bonus depreciation because ABC previously had a depreciable interest in the machinery. The equipment does not qualify even if ABC left the consolidated group prior to BCD's purchase (Proposed Reg. § 1.168(k)-2(b)(3)(vi), Example 20).

Property acquired by a member of a consolidated group does not qualify if it was previously owned by a corporation that is acquired by any member of the consolidated group and the acquisition of the corporation and the property are part of a series of related transactions.

**¶410**

**NEW LAW EXPLAINED**

> **Example:** ABC corporation sells machinery to Jane. XYZ, a member of a consolidated group, purchases the machinery from Jane. WXY, another member of the group, in a related transaction, purchases ABC. The machinery does not qualify for bonus depreciation (Proposed Reg. § 1.168(k)-2(b)(3)(vi), Example. 22)

*Used property received in carryover basis transactions.* The acquisition is also subject to the cost requirements of Code Sec. 179(d)(3) (Code Sec. 168(k)(2)(E)(ii)(II), as added by the 2017 Tax Cuts Act). Code Sec. 179(d)(3) (see also Reg. § 1.179-4(d)) provides that the cost of property eligible for Code Sec. 179 expensing does not include the portion of the basis of property that is determined by reference to the basis of other property held at any time by the person acquiring the property (e.g., the carryover basis in a like-kind exchange does not qualify for expensing but any additional cash paid does) (Conference Report on H.R. 1, Tax Cuts and Jobs Act (H. Rept. 115-466)).

> **Comment:** The reference to Code Sec. 179(d)(3) means that in the case of like-kind exchanges or involuntary conversions, bonus depreciation only applies to any money paid in addition to the trade-in property or in excess of the adjusted basis of the replaced property (Proposed Reg. § 1.168(k)-2(b)(3)(iii)(B)(1)). This limitation only applies when the replacement property is used property. Bonus depreciation regulations currently in effect and the preceding proposed regulation provide that bonus depreciation may be claimed on the carryover and excess basis of property acquired in a like-kind exchange if the property received in the exchange meets all other qualification requirements, including the original use requirement (Reg. § 1.168(k)-1(f)(5)). After 2017, the like-kind exchange rules only apply to exchanges of real property (Code Sec. 1031(a), as amended by the 2017 Tax Cuts Act). See ¶ 505.

*Rule for sale-leasebacks eliminated.* Since the original use requirement is now supplemented with the rule above allowing used property to qualify for bonus depreciation, a special rule for sale-leasebacks in Code Sec. 168(k)(2)(E)(ii), prior to amendment by the 2017 Tax Cuts Act, has been stricken.

> **Comment:** The eliminated rule provides an exception to the requirement that original use must begin with the taxpayer in a sale-leaseback. The rule applies to new property that was originally placed in service after December 31, 2007, by a person who sells it to the taxpayer and then leases it from the taxpayer within three months after the date that the property was originally placed in service. In this situation, the property is treated as originally placed in service by the taxpayer-lessor, and the taxpayer-lessor's placed-in-service date is deemed to occur no earlier than the date that the property is used by the lessee under the leaseback.

**Used property partnership transactions**. Bonus depreciation has not been claimed in most transactions involving transfers of property to or from partnerships or transfers

## NEW LAW EXPLAINED

of interests in partnership property in connection with the transfer of a partnership interest. The requirement that the original use of the property must begin with the taxpayer claiming bonus depreciation is not satisfied. Now that used property can qualify for bonus depreciation the IRS proposals reconsider whether bonus depreciation can be claimed in some partnership transactions.

*Code Sec. 754 elections.* Any increase in the basis of partnership property under Code Sec. 734(b) as the result of the distribution of property to a partner with respect to which a Code Sec. 754 election is in effect does not qualify for bonus depreciation (Proposed Reg. § 1.168(k)-2(b)(3)(iv)(C)).

However, an increase to the inside basis of a new partner's interest in partnership property under Code Sec. 743(b) pursuant to a partnership's Code Sec. 754 election may qualify for bonus depreciation (Proposed Reg. § 1.168(k)-2(b)(3)(iv)(D); Proposed Reg. § 1.168(k)-2(b)(3)(vi), Example 13). A new partner includes an existing partner who acquires an additional partnership interest. The basis increase is generally equal to the difference between the cost of the partnership interest and partnership's inside basis in the new partner's share of partnership property to which the new partnership interest relates.

*Limitations.* The transferor partner and new partner may not be part of the same controlled group. The new partner's basis in the partnership property may not be determined in whole or in part by reference to the transferor's adjusted basis or under Code Sec. 1014. For example, a basis increases on account of a transfer at death does not qualify if the transferee takes a fair market value basis under Code Sec. 1014 (Proposed Reg. § 1.168(k)-2(b)(3)(vi), Example 15). No bonus may be claimed if the new partner or any predecessor previously had a depreciable interest in portion of the property deemed transferred (Proposed Reg. § 1.168(k)-2(b)(3)(vi), Example 16). It does not matter that the partnership previously used the property. In addition, the transferor and new partner may not be related (Proposed Reg. § 1.168(k)-2(b)(3)(iv); Proposed Reg. § 1.168(k)-2(b)(3)(vi), Example 14).

*Contributions to partnerships.* Contributions of property to a partnership do not qualify for bonus depreciation because the basis of the property in the hands of the partnership is determined by reference to the basis in the hands of the contributor (Code Sec. 723; Proposed Reg. § 1.168(k)-2(b)(3)(vi), Example 12).

> **Example:** O and P form an equal partnership, OP, in 2018. O contributes cash to OP, and P contributes equipment to OP. OP's basis in the equipment contributed by P is determined under section 723. Because OP's basis in such equipment is determined in whole or in part by reference to P's adjusted basis in such equipment, OP's acquisition does not satisfy the used property acquisition requirements.

*Remedial allocations.* Remedial allocations under Code Sec. 704(c) for contributions of property with an adjusted tax basis less than book basis do not qualify for bonus depreciation because the partnership's basis in the property is determined by reference to the contributing partner's basis in the property. In addition, the partnership has a

## NEW LAW EXPLAINED

depreciable interest in the contributed property at the time the remedial allocation is made (Proposed Reg. § 1.168(k)-2(b)93)(iv)(A); Proposed Reg. § 1.704-3(d)(2)).

*Distributions other than in liquidation.* No portion of the basis of distributed partnership property as determined under Code Sec. 732 qualifies for bonus depreciation (Proposed Reg. § 1.168(k)-2(b)(3)(iv)(B)). Because the partnership used the property prior to the distribution the original use requirement is not satisfied. The requirements for used property are not met because the basis is determined by reference to the distributee partner's basis in the partnership interest and the partnership's basis in the property.

*Book depreciation on contributed property.* Bonus depreciation does not apply for purposes of determining book depreciation on property contributed to a partnership with a zero adjusted tax basis (Proposed Reg. § 1.704-1(b)(2)(iv)(g)(3)).

**Bonus allowed for film and television productions and live theatrical productions.** Bonus depreciation is allowed for a qualified film, television show, or theatrical production acquired and placed in service after September 27, 2017, if it would have qualified for the Code Sec. 181 expense election without regard to the $15 million expensing limit or the December 31, 2016, expiration date (Code Sec. 168(k)(2)(A)(i), as amended by the 2017 Tax Cuts Act). A qualified film or television production is placed in service at the time of its initial release or broadcast. A qualified live theatrical production is placed in service at the time of its initial live staged performance (Code Sec. 168(k)(2)(H), as added by the 2017 Tax Cuts Act).

A qualified film or television production is acquired on the date principal photography begins and placed in service on the date of initial release or broadcast (Proposed Reg. § 1.168(k)-2(b)(4)(iii) and (5)(v)).

A qualified live theatrical production is acquired on the date all necessary elements for producing the production are secured and is placed in service on the date of the first commercial performance before a live audience. A performances primarily for publicity, the raising of funds to finish production, or to determine the need for further production activity is not the first commercial performance. (Proposed Reg. § 1.168(k)-2(b)(4)(iii)(B) and (5)(v)).

Film, television, and theatrical productions acquired before September 28, 2017 under these rules do no qualify for bonus depreciation.

> **Comment:** The Code Sec. 181 deduction expired effective for productions commencing after December 31, 2017 (Code Sec. 181(g)) and was not extended by the new law. In the case of a film or television show, a production commences on the date of first principal photography. A theatrical production commences on the date of the first public performance before a paying audience. If a Code Sec. 181 election is made, production costs are expensed in the tax year paid or incurred. If the production does not commence until after the December 31, 2017, expiration date, costs expensed under Code Sec. 181 are subject to recapture. Under the bonus depreciation rule, production costs will now be expensed in the tax year the production is placed in service and without regard to the $15 million limit.

## NEW LAW EXPLAINED

> **Comment:** A taxpayer generally makes an election under Code Sec. 181 on the income tax return for the tax year in which production costs are first paid or incurred (Reg. §1.181-2(b)) and not at the later time when the production is placed in service, as defined above for bonus depreciation purposes. A taxpayer that made a Code Sec. 181 election at the time a production commenced is prohibited from claiming bonus depreciation unless the IRS grants permission to revoke the election (Code Sec. 181(b) and (c)). Automatic consent, however, will be granted without filing a letter ruling request if the taxpayer recaptures previously claimed deductions under Code Sec. 181 (Reg. § 181-2(d)(2)).

**Coordination with passenger automobile depreciation caps.** The first-year depreciation cap on a passenger vehicle that is subject to the annual depreciation limitations of Code Sec. 280F because its gross vehicle rate rating does not exceed 6,000 pounds is increased by $8,000 if 100-percent bonus depreciation is claimed. This is the same increase that applies when bonus depreciation is claimed at a 50-percent rate. The scheduled decrease in the $8,000 bump-up to $6,400 in 2018 and $4,800 in 2019 to reflect the formerly-scheduled decreases in the bonus rate from 50 percent to 40 percent in 2018 and to 30 percent in 2019 will only apply to vehicles acquired before September 28, 2017, and placed in service after September 27, 2017 (Code Sec. 168(k)(2)(F)(iii), as amended by the 2017 Tax Cuts Act).

> **Comment:** The annual depreciation caps are substantially increased by the new law (Code Sec. 280F(a), as amended by the 2017 Tax Cuts Act; Rev. Proc. 2018-25). In addition, for taxpayers that claim 100-percent bonus depreciation on a vehicle subject to the caps, the IRS has issued a safe harbor for calculating annual depreciation deductions (Rev. Proc. 2019-13). See ¶415.

**Long-term accounting method relief.** In determining the percentage of completion under Code Sec. 460(b)(1)(A) for purposes of the long-term contract method of accounting, the cost of property with a MACRS recovery period of 7 years or less that qualifies for bonus depreciation is taken into account as a cost allocated to the contract as if the bonus depreciation had not been enacted. The provision applies only to property placed in service (1) after December 31, 2009, and before January 1, 2011 (before January 1, 2012, in the case of property with a longer production period) and (2) after December 31, 2012, and before January 1, 2027 (before January 1, 2028, in the case of long production property) (Code Sec. 460(c)(6)(B), as amended by the 2017 Tax Cuts Act).

> **Comment:** With the exception of transportation property, property with a longer production period must have a recovery period of 10 years or greater. Thus, longer production property that is not transportation property does not qualify for the special treatment provided by this provision. Transportation property is tangible personal property used in the trade or business of transporting persons or property, such as an airliner, and is not subject to the rule that requires a MACRS depreciation period of 10 years or greater in order to constitute long-production property (Code Sec. 168(k)(2)(B)(iii)).

**Corporate election to claim unused AMT credits in lieu of bonus depreciation.** The annual election provided to corporations to claim unused alternative minimum tax (AMT) credits in place of bonus depreciation on property placed in service during the

## NEW LAW EXPLAINED

tax year of the election is stricken effective for tax years beginning after December 31, 2017 (Code Sec. 168(k)(4), stricken by the 2017 Tax Cuts Act).

> **Comment:** The corporate AMT is repealed, effective for tax years beginning after December 31, 2017. See ¶310.

▶ **Effective date.** The amendments generally apply to property which is acquired after September 27, 2017, and is placed in service after September 27, 2017. For this purpose, property shall not be treated as acquired after the date on which a written binding contract is entered into for such acquisition (Act Sec. 13201(h)(1) of the Tax Cuts and Jobs Act (P.L. 115-97)). The amendments related to specified plants apply to specified plants planted or grafted after September 27, 2017 (Act. Sec. 13201(h)(2) of the 2017 Tax Cuts Act).

Proposed Reg. § 1.168(k)-2(b)(2)(ii)(G) provides that the new Code Sec. 168(k)(9), preventing bonus depreciation for rate-regulated utilities and also certain businesses with floor-plan indebtedness applies to property placed in service in tax years beginning after 2017.

— Act Sec. 13201(a) of the Tax Cuts and Jobs Act (P.L. 115-97), amending Code Sec. 168(k)(1), (5), and (6), and adding Code Sec. 168(k)(8);

— Act Sec. 13201(b), amending Code Sec. 168(k)(2) and (5), and Code Sec. 460(c)(6)(B);

— Act Sec. 13201(c), amending Code Sec. 168(k)(2);

— Act Sec. 13201(d), adding Code Sec. 168(k)(9);

— Act Sec. 13201(e), adding Code Sec. 168(k)(10);

— Act Sec. 13201(f), amending Code Sec. 168(k)(2)(F);

— Act Sec. 13201(g), amending Code Sec. 168(k)(2)(A), and adding Code Sec. 168(k)(2)(A)(i)(IV) and (V), and 168(k)(2)(H);

— Act Sec. 13201(h), providing the effective dates.

# ¶415 Depreciation Caps on Luxury Cars

## SUMMARY OF NEW LAW

The annual limits on depreciation deductions for "luxury cars" are nearly quadrupled for property placed in service after 2017. The IRS has issued a safe harbor (Rev. Proc. 2019-13) in order to allow taxpayers to claim depreciation after the first year a vehicle is placed in service if the 100-percent bonus depreciation deduction is claimed.

## BACKGROUND

Annual depreciation deductions that may be claimed for "passenger automobiles" are limited to specific dollar amounts (Code Sec. 280F(a)). These caps are often referred to as the "luxury car caps" even though they generally affect vehicles in the $18,000 purchase price range and above. The caps are adjusted each year for inflation (Code Sec. 280F(d)(7)); however, the caps in effect for the year the vehicle is placed in

## BACKGROUND

service continue to apply throughout its recovery period (Rev. Proc. 2003-75). The limits are reduced to reflect any personal (as opposed to business) use of the vehicle (Code Sec. 280F(a)(2)).

If bonus depreciation is claimed on a vehicle, the first-year depreciation cap that is otherwise applicable is increased by $8,000. The $8,000 bump-up is scheduled to decrease to $6,400 in 2018 and to $4,800 in 2019 (Code Sec. 168(k)(2)(F)(iii)).

The Code Sec. 179 expense deduction and the bonus depreciation allowance are treated as a depreciation deduction for the tax year in which a car is placed in service (Code Sec. 280F(a)(1)(B) and (d)(1)). Thus, the combined Code Sec. 179 deduction, bonus deduction, and regular first-year depreciation deduction is limited to the applicable first-year depreciation cap. Depreciation deductions in subsequent years of the vehicle's recovery period are limited to the applicable cap for the applicable year in the recovery period.

Separate caps apply to (a) passenger automobiles other than trucks (including SUVs) and vans, and to (b) trucks (including SUVs) and vans.

Deductions that are disallowed by the depreciation cap are deferred until after the end of the vehicle's recovery period, when the taxpayer may begin to deduct the unrecovered basis of the vehicle at a specified annual rate.

| For Cars Placed in Service After | Before | Year 1 | Year 2 | Year 3 | Year 4, etc. | Authority |
|---|---|---|---|---|---|---|
| 12/31/10 | 1/01/12 | $11,060 * $3,060 | $4,900 | $2,950 | $1,775 | Rev. Proc. 2011-21 |
| 12/31/11 | 1/01/13 | $11,160 * $3,160 | $5,100 | $3,050 | $1,875 | Rev. Proc. 2012-23 |
| 12/31/12 | 1/01/14 | $11,160 * $3,160 | $5,100 | $3,050 | $1,875 | Rev. Proc. 2013-21 |
| 12/31/13 | 1/01/15 | $11,160 * $3,160 | $5,100 | $3,050 | $1,875 | Rev. Proc. 2014-21, modified by Rev. Proc. 2015-19 |
| 12/31/14 | 1/01/16 | $11,160 * $3,160 | $5,100 | $3,050 | $1,875 | Rev. Proc. 2015-19, modified by Rev. Proc. 2016-23 |
| 12/31/15 | 1/01/17 | $11,160 * $3,160 | $5,100 | $3,050 | $1,875 | Rev. Proc. 2016-23 |
| 12/31/16 | 1/01/18 | $11,160 * $3,160 | $5,100 | $3,050 | $1,875 | Rev. Proc. 2017-29 |

*Depreciation Allowable in—*

* The higher first-year limit applies if the vehicle qualifies for, and the taxpayer does not elect out of, bonus depreciation.

Assuming that the 200-percent declining balance method and half-year convention apply, a car placed in service in 2017 on which bonus depreciation is claimed at the 50-percent rate is subject to the first-year cap if the cost of the vehicle exceeds $18,600 ($9,300 bonus + (9,300 remaining basis × 20 percent first-year table percentage) = $11,160).

Trucks (including SUVs treated as trucks) and vans are subject to their own set of depreciation caps that reflect the higher costs associated with such vehicles. How-

¶415

## BACKGROUND

ever, the caps do not apply to trucks and vans that have a gross vehicle weight rating (GVWR) greater than 6,000 pounds, or to certain trucks and vans that, because of their design, are not likely to be used for personal purposes. Although the depreciation caps do not apply, the cost that can be taken into account for purposes of the Code Sec. 179 expense election cannot exceed $25,000 for an SUV with a GVWR in excess of 6,000 pounds, a pickup truck with a GVWR in excess of 6,000 pounds and a bed length of less than six feet, or a passenger van that seats fewer than 10 persons behind the driver's seat (Code Sec. 179(b)(5)).

| For Trucks and Vans Placed in Service | | Depreciation Allowable in— | | | | |
|---|---|---|---|---|---|---|
| After | Before | Year 1 | Year 2 | Year 3 | Year 4, etc. | Authority |
| 12/31/10 | 1/01/12 | $11,260 * $3,260 | $5,200 | $3,150 | $1,875 | Rev. Proc. 2011-21 |
| 12/31/11 | 1/01/13 | $11,360 * $3,360 | $5,300 | $3,150 | $1,875 | Rev. Proc. 2012-23 |
| 12/31/12 | 1/01/14 | $11,360 * $3,360 | $5,400 | $3,250 | $1,975 | Rev. Proc. 2013-21 |
| 12/31/13 | 1/01/15 | $11,460 * $3,460 | $5,500 | $3,350 | $1,975 | Rev. Proc. 2014-21, modified by Rev. Proc. 2015-19 |
| 12/31/14 | 1/01/16 | $11,460 * $3,460 | $5,600 | $3,350 | $1,975 | Rev. Proc. 2015-19 modified by Rev. Proc. 2016-23 |
| 12/31/15 | 1/01/17 | $11,560 * $3,560 | $5,700 | $3,350 | $2,075 | Rev. Proc. 2016-23 |
| 12/31/16 | 1/01/18 | $11,560 * $3,560 | $5,700 | $3,450 | $2,075 | Rev. Proc. 2017-29 |

* The higher first-year limit applies if the vehicle qualifies for bonus depreciation and no election out is made.

Assuming that the 200-percent declining balance method and half-year convention apply and that 50-percent bonus depreciation is claimed, a truck or van placed in service in 2017 is subject to the first-year cap if the cost of the vehicle exceeds $19,266 ($9,633 bonus + ($9,633 remaining basis × 20 percent) = $11,560).

## NEW LAW EXPLAINED

**Depreciation caps for passenger automobiles increased.**—The annual depreciation caps are increased, effective for vehicles placed in service after December 31, 2017 (Code Sec. 280F(a)(1)(A), as amended by the Tax Cuts and Jobs Act (P.L. 115-97)). The increased caps that apply to vehicles placed in service in 2018 are (Rev. Proc. 2018-25):

- Tax Year 1...............$10,000 ($18,000 if bonus depreciation claimed)
- Tax Year 2...............$16,000
- Tax Year 3...............$ 9,600
- Tax Years 4-6...........$ 5,760

## NEW LAW EXPLAINED

Any unrecovered basis remaining at the end of the regular recovery period of a vehicle is recovered at the rate of $5,760 per tax year (Code Sec. 280F(a)(1)(B), as amended by the 2017 Tax Cuts Act).

> **Comment:** The recovery period of a vehicle is five years. However, the 5-year recovery period covers six tax years because, under the MACRS half-year or mid-quarter convention, a full year's depreciation is not allowed in the tax year that the vehicle is placed in service.

These caps are adjusted annually for inflation effective for vehicles placed in service after 2018 (Code Sec. 280F(d)(7), as amended by the 2017 Tax Cuts Act). The $8,000 bump-up to the first-year cap if bonus depreciation is claimed is not adjusted for inflation.

> **Comment:** For vehicles placed in service in 2018, the preceding caps will apply to all types of vehicles. However, the IRS figures inflation adjustments differently for (1) trucks (including SUVs treated as trucks) and vans and (2) regular passenger cars. Thus, beginning in 2019 when these figures are first adjusted for inflation, separate inflation adjusted caps will be provided for trucks (including SUVs) and vans, and for regular passenger cars.

**$8,000 increase in first-year cap if bonus depreciation claimed.** The first-year depreciation cap on a passenger vehicle that is subject to the annual depreciation limitations of Code Sec. 280F is increased by $8,000 if 100-percent bonus depreciation is claimed. This is the same increase that applies when bonus depreciation is claimed at a 50-percent rate. However, the scheduled decrease in the $8,000 bump-up to $6,400 in 2018 and $4,800 in 2019 will continue to apply in the rare situation where a vehicle is acquired before September 28, 2017, and placed in service in 2018 or 2019 (Code Sec. 168(k)(2)(F)(iii), as amended by the 2017 Tax Cuts Act; Proposed Reg. § 1.168(k)-2(f)(8)).

> **Comment:** No bump up would apply if a vehicle acquired before September 28, 2017 is placed in service after 2019. These vehicles are not eligible for bonus depreciation.

**Safe harbor allows depreciation deductions after first recovery year if 100-percent bonus claimed.** When Congress last enacted a 100-percent bonus rate in the Tax Relief, Unemployment Insurance Reauthorization, and Job Creation Act of 2010 (P.L. 111-312), for property acquired after September 8, 2010, and placed in service before January 1, 2012, an unforeseen consequence was that taxpayers claiming the 100-percent bonus deduction on a vehicle were limited to a deduction equal to the first-year cap amount and could not claim any further depreciation deductions until after the end of the vehicle's regular recovery period. This is because (1) the basis of qualified property is reduced by the full amount of depreciation, including the bonus and Code Sec. 179 allowance, without regard to the caps, and (2) depreciation deductions that are disallowed by the depreciation caps (including bonus depreciation) are deferred until after the end of the vehicle's recovery period (Code Sec. 280F(a)(1)(B)).

The IRS, however, provided a safe harbor method that allowed a taxpayer to claim depreciation deductions during the entire recovery period of the vehicle (Rev. Proc. 2011-26, § 3.03(5)(c)).

**¶415**

## NEW LAW EXPLAINED

The IRS has provided a somewhat similar safe harbor for taxpayers claiming 100 percent bonus depreciation on vehicles acquired after September 27, 2017 and placed in service before 2023 (Rev. Proc. 2019-13).

The following example illustrates why the safe harbor is needed.

---

**Example:** A car (5-year MACRS property) costing $60,000 that is subject to the luxury car limitations is placed in service in January 2018 by a calendar-year taxpayer. The taxpayer claims 100-percent bonus depreciation on its 5-year property, including the vehicle. The 100-percent rate applies to property acquired and placed in service after September 27, 2017 (see ¶410). However, because the first-year depreciation cap for a vehicle placed in service in $18,000, the bonus deduction that may be deducted is limited to $18,000. If the safe harbor is not elected the taxpayer may only recover the $42,000 excess ($60,000 – $42,000) at the rate of $5,760 per year beginning in 2024, which is the first year after the end of the vehicle's recovery period. No regular depreciation deductions are allowed after the first year of the vehicle's regular recovery period because the vehicle's basis for computing depreciation deductions is reduced to $0 by the entire amount of the bonus depreciation allowable without regard to the first-year depreciation cap. The table percentages when applied to a depreciable basis of $0 are equal to $0 in each year of the vehicle's regular 5-year recovery period.

| Year | Regular Deduction | Luxury Car Cap | Allowable Depreciation |
|---|---|---|---|
| 2018 | $60,000 | $18,000 | $18,000 |
| 2019 | $0 | $16,000 | $0 |
| 2020 | $0 | $9,600 | $0 |
| 2021 | $0 | $5,760 | $0 |
| 2022 | $0 | $5,760 | $0 |
| 2023 | $0 | $5,760 | $0 |
| | | TOTAL | $18,000 |

---

If a taxpayer elects to use the safe harbor provided in Rev. Proc. 2019-13, the taxpayer claims a first year bonus deduction equal to the $18,000 first-year cap. In each subsequent year of the vehicle's recovery period the taxpayer may deduct the lesser of: (1) the depreciation cap for the recovery period or (2) the depreciation deduction for the recovery period computed by applying the applicable table percentage to $42,000 (the $60,000 cost of the vehicle as reduced by $18,000).

The following example shows how depreciation is computed under the safe harbor based on the same facts as the preceding example.

## NEW LAW EXPLAINED

**Example:**

| Year | Regular Deduction | Luxury Car Cap | Allowable Depreciation |
|------|-------------------|----------------|------------------------|
| 2018 | $60,000 | $18,000 | $18,000 |
| 2019 | $13,440 | $16,000 | $13,440 |
| 2020 | $8,064 | $9,600 | $8,064 |
| 2021 | $4,838 | $5,760 | $4,838 |
| 2022 | $4,838 | $5,760 | $4,838 |
| 2023 | $2,419 | $5,760 | $2,419 |
| | | TOTAL | $51,599 |

The unrecovered basis is $8,401 ($60,000 – $51,599). This amount is recovered at the rate of $5,760 per year beginning in 2024. The 2024 deduction is $5,760 and the 2025 deduction is $2,641 ($5,760 + $2,641 = $8,401).

*Electing the safe harbor.* A taxpayer elects the safe harbor by making the safe harbor computation beginning in the first tax year following the tax year in which the vehicle is placed in service. It is not necessary to file an election statement. The election doesn't need to be made for all of a taxpayer's vehicles.

The election may only be made if:

- 100 percent bonus depreciation is claimed on the vehicle
- The vehicle costs at least $18,000
- No portion of the vehicle's cost is expensed under section 179
- The taxpayer uses the optional depreciable table percentages to compute the depreciation

    **Comment:** If the taxpayer previously filed a return claiming the section 179 allowance on a vehicle that qualified for 100 percent bonus, an amended return to revoke the election may be filed within the three-year limitations period. The taxpayer should then be able to use the safe harbor assuming no election out of bonus depreciation was made. Generally, revocation of an election out of bonus depreciation may be made on an amended return filed within six months after the due date of the original return (excluding extensions). If this deadline is not met, a letter ruling request for permission to revoke must be filed.

The election does not apply if the vehicle is used 50 percent or less for business in the placed-in-service year. Under the listed property rules a vehicle used 50 percent or less for business is not eligible for bonus depreciation and the vehicle must be depreciated using the MACRS alternative depreciation system (ADS).

If business use declines to 50 percent or less after the placed-in-service year, the taxpayer must cease using the safe harbor method. As required by the listed property rules, prior depreciation deductions are recaptured in an amount equal to the difference between the depreciation claimed and the depreciation that would have

**NEW LAW EXPLAINED**

been claimed if ADS has originally applied an no bonus deduction was claimed. ADS is used to depreciate the vehicle for the remaining years of the vehicle's recovery period.

> **Comment:** A taxpayer may elect to apply the 50-percent rate instead of the 100-percent rate for property placed in service during the taxpayer's first tax year ending after September 27, 2017 (Code Sec. 168(k)(8), as added by the 2017 Tax Cuts Act). See ¶410. Thus, for the 2017 tax year only, the taxpayer in the preceding example could avoid the adverse result in the first example by electing the 50-percent rate. The safe harbor, however, produces a somewhat more accelerated write-off. The 50 percent election also applies to all 5-year property placed in service during the 2017 tax year and not just vehicles with a 5-year recovery period. Taxpayers may revoke this election by filing an amended return within 6 months of the original due date (excluding extensions). Thereafter, a letter ruling request is required.

**$25,000 limit on certain vehicles adjusted for inflation.** The $25,000 maximum Code Sec. 179 deduction that may be claimed on specified vehicles that are exempt from the luxury car caps will be adjusted for inflation in tax years beginning after 2018 (Code Sec. 179(b)(6), as amended by the 2017 Tax Cuts Act). The inflation-adjusted limitation for tax years beginning in 2019 is $25,500 (Rev. Proc. 2018-57).

> **Comment:** The $25,000 limit applies to a sport utility vehicle, truck with an interior cargo bed length less than six feet, and a van that seats fewer than 10 persons behind the driver's seat if the vehicle is exempt from the annual depreciation caps because it has a gross vehicle weight rating in excess of 6,000 pounds, or if it is otherwise exempt, and is rated at not more than 14,000 pounds gross vehicle weight (Code Sec. 179(b)(5)).

The amount of the inflation adjustment is based on the cost-of-living adjustment determined under Code Sec. 1(f)(3) for the calendar year in which the tax year begins, by substituting calendar year 2017 for calendar year 2016. When adjusting the $25,000 limit for inflation, the resulting amount must be rounded to the nearest multiple of $100.

▶ **Effective date.** The provisions apply to property placed in service after December 31, 2017, in tax years ending after such date (Act Sec. 13202(c) of the Tax Cuts and Jobs Act (P.L. 115-97)).

— Act Sec. 13202(a) of the Tax Cuts and Jobs Act (P.L. 115-97), amending Code Sec. 280F(a)(1) and (d)(7);

— Act Sec. 13202(c), providing the effective date.

**¶415**

# ¶420 Computers as Listed Property

## SUMMARY OF NEW LAW

Computers and related peripheral equipment are no longer "listed property" subject to strict substantiation and depreciation requirements, effective for property placed in service after December 31, 2017.

## BACKGROUND

To deduct an expense for "listed property," a high level of substantiation is required. No deduction (or credit) is allowed for listed property unless the taxpayer can substantiate each expenditure or use by adequate records or sufficient evidence corroborating the taxpayer's own statement, and the *Cohan* rule (2 USTC ¶489) cannot be applied (Code Sec. 274(d)(4); Temporary Reg. §1.274-5T(a)(4) and (c)). Listed property is defined as:

- passenger automobiles and other property used as a means of transportation;
- entertainment, recreational, and amusement property;
- computers and peripheral equipment; and
- any other property specified by regulation (Code Sec. 280F(d)(4)(A)).

The elements of each expenditure or use for listed property that must be substantiated are—

(1) the amount of each separate expenditure;

(2) the amount of each business/investment use based on the appropriate measure (i.e., mileage for vehicles, time for other listed property) and the total use of the listed property for the tax year;

(3) the date of the expenditure or use; and

(4) the business purpose of the expenditure or use (Code Sec. 274(d); Temporary Reg. §1.274-5T(b)(6)).

**Fringe benefits.** Generally, an employee can exclude from gross income a working condition fringe benefit, which is any property or service provided to an employee, to the extent the employee would have been allowed a business expense deduction under Code Sec. 162 or a depreciation deduction under Code Sec. 167 had the employee paid for the property or services without reimbursement (Code Sec. 132(a) and (d)). However, an employee cannot exclude the value of the use of listed property as a working condition fringe unless the employee substantiates the exclusion amount as required by Code Sec. 274(d) (Reg. §1.132-5(c)(1); Temporary Reg. §1.274-5T(e)(1)(i)).

**Depreciation of listed property.** If listed property, such as a computer, is not used more than 50 percent for business in the tax year that it is placed in service, depreciation must be computed using the straight-line method under the MACRS alternative depreciation system (ADS), and no first-year bonus depreciation deduction or Code Sec. 179 expense allowance may be claimed (Code Sec. 280F(b)(1), (b)(3)

## BACKGROUND

and (d)(1); Reg. § 1.280F-6(d)). If the listed property satisfies the more-than-50-percent business use requirement in the tax year that it is placed in service but fails to meet that test in a later tax year that occurs during any year of the property's ADS recovery period, previous depreciation deductions (including any bonus depreciation deduction and any amount expensed under Code Sec. 179) claimed in tax years before business use drops to 50 percent or less are subject to recapture in such later year (Code Secs. 280F(b)(2) and 168(k)(2)(D)(ii); Temporary Reg. § 1.280F-3T(c) and (d)).

> **Comment:** Computers and peripheral equipment are 5-year MACRS property (Code Sec. 168(e)(3)(B)(iv) and (i)(2)). A 5-year recovery period also applies under the ADS system (Code Sec. 168(g)(3)(C)).

Under a generally applicable rule, any amount expensed under Code Sec. 179 is recaptured if business use of the expensed asset falls to 50 percent or less during any year of the expensed asset's recovery period (Code Sec. 179(d)(10); Reg. § 1.179-1(e)). If a property is not a listed property and business use falls to 50 percent or less, the Code Sec. 179 deduction is subject to recapture but bonus depreciation and regular depreciation deductions are not recaptured.

For purposes of determining the depreciation deduction allowed to an employee (including first-year bonus depreciation allowance and Code Sec. 179 expense allowance), or the amount of any deduction allowable to the employee for rentals or other payments under a lease of listed property, employee use of listed property can be treated as use in a trade or business only if the use is for the convenience of the employer and required as a condition of employment (Code Sec. 280F(d)(1) and (3)).

> **Comment:** An employee may not depreciate or expense under Code Sec. 179 the cost of a computer or other listed property unless its use is for the convenience of the employer and required as a condition of employment. If these two requirements are not satisfied, none of the use of the computer is considered business use (Rev. Rul. 86-129).

## NEW LAW EXPLAINED

**Computers and peripheral equipment removed from listed property treatment.**—Effective for property placed in service after December 31, 2017, computers and peripheral equipment are removed from the definition of listed property (Code Sec. 280F(d)(4)(A), as amended by the Tax Cuts and Jobs Act (P.L. 115-97)). As a result, the cost of computers and peripheral equipment can be deducted or depreciated like other business property and are no longer subject to the strict substantiation requirements of Code Sec. 274(d).

> **Comment:** The removal of computers from listed property status will allow more employees to depreciate or expense the cost of computers because the convenience of the employer and condition of employment requirements of Code Sec. 280F(d)(3) will no longer apply.

A conforming amendment strikes a provision which excludes a computer or peripheral equipment from the definition of listed property if it is used exclusively at a

## NEW LAW EXPLAINED

regular business establishment and owned or leased by the person operating the establishment (Code Sec. 280F(d)(4)(B), stricken by the 2017 Tax Cuts Act).

**Impact on depreciation.** The declassification of computers as listed property means that a computer used 50 percent or less for business purposes in the year that it is placed in service is no longer required to be depreciated under the MACRS alternative depreciation system (ADS) using the straight-line method and a five-year ADS recovery period. Instead, the five-year recovery period and the 200-percent declining balance method under the MACRS general depreciation system (GDS) will apply. Furthermore, if the computer is placed in service after 2017, bonus depreciation may be claimed even if business use is 50 percent or less, because the rule under Code Sec. 168(k)(2)(D)(ii) that bonus depreciation may not be claimed on a listed property used 50 percent or less for business in the year it is placed in service will no longer apply.

Removal of computers from listed property status also means that if business use drops to 50 percent or less in a tax year after the computer is placed in service, the listed property recapture rules will not apply. Consequently, regular depreciation deductions (including any bonus deduction) will not be recaptured upon such a business use decline. However, as explained below, Code Sec. 179 recapture is still required.

**Impact on section 179 expensing.** Under current law, property may not be expensed under Code Sec. 179 if it is not used more than 50 percent for trade or business purposes in the tax year that it is placed in service (Code Sec. 179(d)(10); Reg. § 1.179-1(d)(1)). This rule applies to listed and nonlisted property (Temporary Reg. § 1.280F-3T(c)(1)). Thus, although computers are no longer considered listed property if placed in service after December 31, 2017, the failure to use the computer more than 50 percent in a trade or business in the tax year that the computer is placed in service will continue to prevent a taxpayer from expensing the portion of the cost of the computer that is not attributable to business use.

The amount expensed under Code Sec. 179 is recaptured if business use falls to 50 percent or less during any year of the expensed asset's recovery period (Code Sec. 179(d)(10); Reg. § 1.179-1(e)). However, if the Code Sec. 179 deduction is claimed on a listed property, the amount recaptured is determined by applying the listed property recapture rules when business use drops to 50 percent or less (Code Sec. 280F(d)(1)). That is, the listed property recapture rules take precedence in determining the recapture amount. As a result of the removal of computers from listed property classification, the Code Sec. 179 recapture rules will now be used to determined the amount of Code Sec. 179 allowance that is recaptured. The recapture amount included in ordinary income under these recapture rules is the difference between the Code Sec. 179 expense allowance claimed and the depreciation (including bonus depreciation, if applicable) that would have been allowed on the amount expensed for prior tax years and the tax year of recapture (Reg. § 1.179-1(e)(1)).

**Caution:** Since the provision declassifying computers as listed property applies to property placed in service after December 31, 2017, the listed property recapture rules continue to apply to computers placed in service before January 1, 2018.

**¶420**

## NEW LAW EXPLAINED

**Impact on fringe benefits.** The declassification of computers as listed property means that employees no longer must meet the substantiation requirements under Code Sec. 274(d) in order to exclude the value of the availability of the computer from income as a working condition fringe benefit (Temporary Reg. § 1.274-5T(e)). The new law does not affect the IRS's authority to determine the appropriate characterization of computers as a working condition fringe benefit under Code Sec. 132(d), or that the personal use of computers that are provided primarily for business purposes may constitute a *de minimis* fringe benefit under Code Sec. 132(e), the value of which is so small as to make accounting for it administratively impracticable.

▶ **Effective date.** The provisions apply to property placed in service after December 31, 2017, in tax years ending after such date (Act Sec. 13202(c) of the Tax Cuts and Jobs Act (P.L. 115-97).

   **No significant guidance related to this provision has been issued.**

— Act Sec. 13202(b) of the Tax Cuts and Jobs Act (P.L. 115-97), amending Code Sec. 280F(d)(4);

— Act Sec. 13202(c), providing the effective date.

# ¶425  Recovery Periods for MACRS Real Property

## SUMMARY OF NEW LAW

Assuming a technical correction is enacted, qualified improvement property is assigned a 15-year recovery period as intended by Congress. The property classes for 15-year leasehold improvement property, retail improvement property, and restaurant property are eliminated. The MACRS alternative depreciation system (ADS) must be used for certain property by a real property trade or business or farming business if an election out of the interest deduction limits is made. The ADS recovery period for residential rental property is reduced from 40 years to 30 years.

## BACKGROUND

"Qualified improvement property" is a category of property which is eligible for the 50-percent MACRS bonus depreciation deduction (Code Sec. 168(k)(2)(A)(i)(IV)). In general, qualified improvement property is defined as an improvement to the interior of a nonresidential building but does not include improvements related to the enlargement of the building or to the internal structural framework of the building. In addition, improvements related to elevators and escalators are not qualified improvement property (Code Sec. 168(k)(3)).

The depreciation period for qualified improvement property is either 15 years or 39 years. A 15-year recovery period applies if the qualified improvement property meets the definitions provided for 15-year qualified leasehold improvement property, 15-year qualified restaurant property, or 15-year qualified retail improvement prop-

## BACKGROUND

erty (Code Sec. 168(e)(3)(E)(iv), (v), and (ix)). In all other cases, the default recovery period for qualified improvement property is 39 years under the rule that treats an addition or improvement to nonresidential real property (whether or not depreciated under MACRS) as MACRS 39-year nonresidential real property (Code Sec. 168(i)(6)).

15-year qualified leasehold improvement property and 15-year qualified retail improvement property are defined similarly to qualified improvement property, except that 15-year qualified leasehold improvements must be made to the interior of the building pursuant to a lease more than three years after the leased building was first placed in service (Code Sec. 168(e)(6)), and 15-year retail improvements must be made to the interior of a building open to the general public and used in the retail trade or business of selling tangible personal property to the general public more than three years after the building was first placed in service (Code Sec. 168(e)(8)). 15-year restaurant property is broadly defined to mean any improvement to a restaurant building (interior or exterior) regardless of when the building was placed in service. Moreover, 15-year restaurant property also includes a restaurant building (Code Sec. 168(e)(7)).

Certain categories of property, such as property used predominantly outside of the United States, must be depreciated using the MACRS alternative depreciation system (ADS) (Code Sec. 168(g)). Under ADS, property is depreciated using the straight-line method over recovery periods generally equal to the class life of the property. Usually, the ADS recovery period is longer than the regular recovery period that would otherwise apply under MACRS. For example, the ADS recovery period for 39-year nonresidential real property and 27.5-year residential rental property is 40 years (Code Sec. 168(g)(2)(C)).

### NEW LAW EXPLAINED

**Depreciation of real property.**—The Tax Cuts and Jobs Act (P.L. 115-97) makes the following changes related to MACRS recovery periods for real property, effective for property placed in service after December 31, 2017:

- qualified improvement property is assigned a 15-year recovery period if a technical correction is enacted (see *"Caution,"* below);
- the property classes for 15-year leasehold improvement property, retail improvement property, and restaurant improvements and buildings are eliminated;
- the MACRS alternative depreciation system (ADS) must be used by a real property trade or business that elects out of the interest deduction limits to depreciate residential rental property, nonresidential real property, and qualified improvement property (effective for tax years beginning after December 31, 2017 and regardless of when the property was placed in service);
- the MACRS alternative depreciation system (ADS) must be used by a farming business that elects out of the interest deduction limits to depreciate MACRS property with a recovery period of ten years or greater (effective for tax years beginning after December 31, 2017 and regardless of when the property was placed in service); and

¶425

## NEW LAW EXPLAINED

- the ADS recovery period for residential rental property is reduced from 40 years to 30 years.

   **Caution:** Qualified improvement property placed in service after December 31, 2017, was intended by Congress to have a 15-year recovery period. However, a technical correction is required to achieve this result (General Explanation of Public Law 115-97 (JCS-1-18), footnote 632). Without a technical correction, qualified improvement property placed in service after 2017 has a 39-year recovery period and is depreciated using the straight-line method and mid-month convention. Furthermore, without a 15-year recovery period, qualified improvement property placed in service after 2017 is not eligible for bonus depreciation (Proposed Reg. §1.168(k)-2(b)(2)(D); Proposed Reg. §1.168(b)-1(a)(5)(i)(B) and (C)).

   The original Senate bill would have provided a 10-year recovery period for qualified improvement property. The House bill contained no provision. The final bill, according to the Conference Report on H.R. 1, Tax Cuts and Jobs Act (H. Rept. 115-466) set a 15-year recovery period for qualified improvement property effective for property placed in service after December 31, 2017. However, the text of the final bill inadvertently omitted the provision, which would have given a 15-year recovery period for qualified improvement property.

   An unintended consequence of failing to provide a 15-year recovery period for qualified improvement property placed in service after December 31, 2017, is that such property will not qualify for bonus depreciation. As explained at ¶410, qualified improvement property was removed as a specific category of bonus depreciation property, effective for property placed in service after December 31, 2017 (Code Sec. 168(k)(3), as stricken by the 2017 Tax Cuts Act) on the assumption that all qualified improvement property would have a 15-year recovery period and, therefore, qualify for bonus depreciation under the general rule that allows MACRS property with a recovery period of 20 years or less to qualify for bonus depreciation.

**Qualified improvement property.** Assuming a technical correction is enacted, qualified improvement property is assigned a recovery period of 15 years, effective for property placed in service after December 31, 2017. 15-year qualified improvement property would be depreciated using the straight-line method and half-year convention or, if applicable, the mid-quarter convention (Code Sec. 168(b)(3)(G), as added by the 2017 Tax Cuts Act)). The alternative depreciation system (ADS) recovery period for qualified improvement property would be 20 years assuming a technical correction is made (Code Sec. 168(g)(3)(B), as amended by the 2017 Tax Cuts Act; General Explanation of Public Law 115-97 (JCS-1-18), footnote 634).

   **Comment:** The amended table in Code Sec. 168(g)(3)(B), makes an erroneous reference to subparagraph (D)(iv) of Code Sec. 168(e)(3) in establishing the intended 20-year ADS period for qualified improvement property. In the original Senate Bill, subparagraph (D)(iv) of Code Sec. 168(e)(3) added qualified improvement property to the list of property with a 10-year recovery period. Subparagraph (D)(iv) was not included in the text of the final bill because the

## NEW LAW EXPLAINED

final bill intended to change the recovery period of qualified improvement property to 15-years instead. See "*Caution*," above.

The definition of qualified improvement property for purposes of the new 15-year recovery period is the same as the definition that has applied for bonus depreciation purposes. Specifically, qualified improvement property is defined as any improvement to an interior portion of a building which is nonresidential real property if the improvement is placed in service after the date the building was first placed in service by any taxpayer (Code Sec. 168(e)(6)(A), as added by the 2017 Tax Cuts Act). However, qualified improvement property does not include expenditures attributable to:

- the enlargement of a building;

- any elevator or escalator; or

- the internal structural framework of a building (Code Sec. 168(e)(6)(B), as added by the 2017 Tax Cuts Act).

> **Comment:** A technical correction may be needed to clarify that qualified improvement property must be made (i.e., constructed) by the taxpayer (General Explanation of Public Law 115-97 (JCS-1-18), footnote 633).

> **Comment:** Qualified improvement property has been a category of property eligible for bonus depreciation since the enactment of the Protecting Americans from Tax Hikes Act of 2015 (December 18, 2015) (P.L. 114-113) (PATH Act), effective for property placed in service after December 31, 2015. However, the depreciation period for property which met the definition of qualified improvement property for bonus depreciation purposes was 15 years if the improvement also met the definition of a qualified leasehold improvement, a qualified retail improvement, or a qualified restaurant improvement. If the 15-year recovery period did not apply, then the qualified improvement property was depreciated over 39 years as MACRS nonresidential real property. With a technical correction, all qualified improvement property would be assigned a 15-year recovery period. The 15-year recovery periods previously provided for a qualified leasehold, retail, and restaurant improvements are repealed effective for property placed in service after 2017 whether or not a technical correction is enacted.

> **Comment:** The definition of qualified improvement property for bonus depreciation purposes was formerly located in Code Sec. 168(k)(3), relating to bonus depreciation. The new law moves the definition of qualified improvement property to Code Sec. 168(e)(6).

*Section 179 deduction on qualified improvement property.* Effective for tax years beginning after 2017, the definition of qualified real property eligible for expensing under Code Sec. 179 is changed to include qualified improvement property (Code Sec. 179(f), as amended by the 2017 Tax Cuts Act). No technical correction is needed for qualified improvement property to qualify for expensing. See ¶405.

**¶425**

## NEW LAW EXPLAINED

**15-year qualified leasehold, retail, and restaurant improvement property classes eliminated.** The property classifications for 15-year qualified leasehold improvement property, qualified retail improvement property, and qualified restaurant property are removed, effective for property placed in service after 2017 (Code Sec. 168(e)(3)(E), as amended by the 2017 Tax Cuts Act; Code Sec. 168(e)(6), (7), and (8), stricken by the 2017 Tax Cuts Act). See *"Background"* section, above, for the definition of these categories of property. All improvements which previously qualified for a 15-year recovery period as qualified leasehold improvement property or qualified retail improvement property fall within the definition of qualified improvement property and will have a 15-year recovery period, effective for property placed in service after December 31, 2017 if a technical correction is made; see *"Caution,"* above). Improvements to a restaurant would only qualify for the 15-year recovery period as qualified improvement property if the improvement to is to the interior of the restaurant and does not relate to an enlargement or the internal structural framework of the building, or to an elevator or escalator. External improvements to a restaurant and restaurant buildings which currently qualify as 15-year qualified restaurant property do not meet the definitional requirements of qualified improvement property and are not eligible for the 15-year recovery period even with a technical correction. Such property is depreciated over 39 years, effective for property placed in service after December 31, 2017.

> **Comment:** If any property meets the definition of 15-year qualified leasehold improvement property or 15-year qualified retail property, it will necessarily meet the definitional requirements of qualified improvement property and be eligible for the 15-year recovery period that would apply to qualified improvement property if a technical correction is enacted. Consequently, the elimination of these two property classifications would have no negative impact. Not all 15-year restaurant property, however, meets the definitional requirements of qualified improvement property. Most significantly, 15-year qualified restaurant property is defined to include restaurant buildings. Qualified improvement property only includes internal improvements to a building. This means that a restaurant building will not qualify for a 15-year recovery period as qualified improvement property. Instead, effective for restaurants placed in service after December 31, 2017, restaurant buildings will once again be treated as nonresidential real property and the 39-year recovery period for nonresidential real property applies. 15-year restaurant property is also defined to include external as well as internal improvements. Since external improvements to a building are excluded from the definition of qualified improvement property, external improvements to a restaurant are also treated as 39-year nonresidential real property, effective for improvements placed in service after December 31, 2017, whether or not a technical correction assigns a 15-year recovery period to qualified improvement property.

**Real property trade or business electing out of interest deduction limits must use ADS for residential rental property, nonresidential real property, and qualified improvement property.** A real property trade or business that elects out of the business interest deduction limitations (Code Sec. 163(j), see ¶510) must use the MACRS alternative depreciation system (ADS) to depreciate any nonresidential real

## NEW LAW EXPLAINED

property, residential rental property, or qualified improvement property it holds (Code Sec. 168(g)(1), as amended by the 2017 Tax Cuts Act; Code Sec. 168(g)(8), as added by the 2017 Tax Cuts Act). The provision is effective for tax years beginning after December 31, 2017 (Act Sec. 13204(b)(2) of the 2017 Tax Cuts Act).

> **Comment:** A technical correction is necessary to clarify that 15-year leasehold improvement property, 15-year retail improvement property, and 15-year restaurant property placed in service before 2018 by an electing real property trade or business must be depreciated using ADS beginning in the election year if the taxpayer still owns the property (General Explanation of Public Law 115-97 (JCS-1-18), footnote 636). These categories of property are eliminated after 2017 and replaced with the qualified improvement property category.

If the election is made, ADS must be used for covered property placed in service before, during, and after the election year. The IRS has issued guidance which clarifies that in the case of property placed in service before the election year, switching to ADS is not a change in accounting method provided the switch is made in the election year (Rev. Proc. 2019-8). A timely switch to ADS is made by applying the change-in-use rules of Reg. § 1.168(i)-4(d). In general, these rules allow a taxpayer to begin depreciating the property previously placed in service property by using the remaining ADS recovery period as of the election year. Previously claimed depreciation, including bonus depreciation is not recaptured.

> **Example:** ABC, a calendar-year real property trade or business, placed 27.5 year residential rental property costing $100,000 in service in January 2010 and makes an irrevocable election out of the business interest deduction limitation in 2018. The ADS recovery period for residential rental property placed in service before 2018 is 40 years. As of December 31, 2017, the property has been depreciated for seven years and eleven and one-half months. Only eleven and one-half month's depreciation was allowed in 2010 under the mid-month convention. Depreciation claimed through December 31, 2017 is $28,937. Under the change in use regulations, ABC will depreciate the remaining $71,063 basis using the straight-line method over the remaining ADS recovery period of 32 years and one-half month beginning on January 1, 2018.

In this example, no switch to ADS is required if the residential rental property is fully depreciated before 2018. There is no undepreciated basis to recover using ADS even though the 40 year ADS recovery period has not expired.

If a taxpayer files two or more returns without making the required switch to ADS in the election year, an improper accounting method is adopted. In this situation, the taxpayer is required to file a change in accounting method using Form 3115, Application for Change in Accounting Method. The taxpayer must report a Code Sec. 481(a) adjustment. The adjustment is equal to the difference between (1) the depreciation claimed in the election year and all following years prior to the year for which the accounting method change is filed and (2) the amounts of ADS depreciation that should have been claimed during those years (Rev. Proc. 2019-8).

**¶425**

## NEW LAW EXPLAINED

An electing real property trade or business is a real property trade or business that elects out of new rules which disallow deduction for net interest expense in excess of 30 percent of a business' adjusted taxable income (Code Sec. 163(j)(7)(B), as added by the 2017 Tax Cuts Act). "Real property trade or business" means any real property development, redevelopment, construction, reconstruction, acquisition, conversion, rental, operation, management, leasing, or brokerage trade or business (Code Sec. 469(c)(7)(C)). See ¶ 510 for a discussion of the net interest deduction limitation and the election out for a real property trade or business.

> **Comment:** The ADS period for nonresidential real property is 40 years. The ADS period for residential rental property is reduced from 40 years to 30 years, effective for property placed in service after December 31, 2017 (Code Sec. 168(g)(2)(C), as amended by the 2017 Tax Cuts Act; Rev. Proc. 2019-8). The ADS period for qualified improvement property is intended to be 20 years, although a technical correction is necessary to create the intended 15-year regular depreciation period and 20-year ADS period for such property. Without the technical correction, the regular depreciation period and ADS period for qualified improvement property is 40 years. See *"Caution,"* above.

**Farming business electing out of interest limitations must use ADS to depreciate property with a recovery period of 10 years or greater.** If a farming business elects out of the interest limitations of Code Sec. 163(j), a more restrictive rules applies. The farming business must use ADS to depreciate any property with a recovery period of ten years or greater which is placed in service before, during, or after the election year (Code Sec. 168(g)(1)(G), as added by the 2017 Tax Cuts Act). As in the case of an electing real property trade or business, the ADS switch for property placed in service before the election year is made by applying the change in use rules of Reg. §1.168(i)-4(d). If two or more erroneous returns are filed an accounting method change is required (Rev. Proc. 2019-8).

**Regular and ADS recovery periods for MACRS residential rental and MACRS nonresidential real property.** The MACRS alternative depreciation system (ADS) recovery period for residential rental property is reduced from 40 years to 30 years (Code Sec. 168(g)(2)(C), as amended by the 2017 Tax Cuts Act).

> **Comment:** A provision in the original Senate bill would have reduced the recovery period for MACRS residential rental property from 27.5 years to 25 years, and would have reduced the recovery period for nonresidential real property from 39 years to 25 years, effective for property placed in service after December 31, 2017. This provision was dropped from the final bill. Consequently, the recovery period remains 27.5 years for residential rental property and 39 years for nonresidential real property. The ADS recovery period for nonresidential real property remains 40 years.

The IRS has released the following new depreciation table that reflects the 30 years ADS period for residential rental property (Rev. Proc. 2019-8).

## NEW LAW EXPLAINED

TABLE 12A (Rev. Proc. 2019-8)
Alternative Depreciation System
Applicable Depreciation Method: Straight Line
Applicable Recovery Period: 30 years
Applicable Convention: Mid-month

| If the Recovery Year is: | and the Month in the First Recovery Year the Property is Placed in Service is: | | | | | | | | | | | |
|---|---|---|---|---|---|---|---|---|---|---|---|---|
| | 1 | 2 | 3 | 4 | 5 | 6 | 7 | 8 | 9 | 10 | 11 | 12 |
| | the Depreciation Rate is: | | | | | | | | | | | |
| 1 | 3.204 | 2.926 | 2.649 | 2.371 | 2.093 | 1.815 | 1.528 | 1.250 | 0.972 | 0.694 | 0.417 | 0.139 |
| 2-30 | 3.333 | 3.333 | 3.333 | 3.333 | 3.333 | 3.333 | 3.333 | 3.333 | 3.333 | 3.333 | 3.333 | 3.333 |
| 31 | 0.139 | 0.417 | 0.694 | 0.972 | 1.250 | 1.528 | 1.815 | 2.093 | 2.371 | 2.649 | 2.926 | 3.204 |

▶ **Effective date.** The amendments in this section apply to property placed in service after December 31, 2017 (Act Sec. 13204(b)(1) of the Tax Cuts and Jobs Act (P.L. 115-97). The amendment requiring an electing real property trade or business to use ADS to depreciate its real property is effective for tax years beginning after December 31, 2017 (Act Sec. 13204(b)(2) of the 2017 Tax Cuts Act). The amendment requiring an electing farming business to use ADS to depreciate property with a recovery period of 10 years or greater is effective for tax years beginning after December 31, 2017 (Act Sec. 13205(b) of the 2017 Tax Cuts Act).

— Act Sec. 13204(a)(1)(A), of the Tax Cuts and Jobs Act (P.L. 115-97) amending Code Sec. 168(e)(3)(E);

— Act Sec. 13204(a)(1)(B), striking Code Secs. 168(e)(6), (7), and (8);

— Act Sec. 13204(a)(2), adding Code Sec. 168(b)(3)(G);

— Act Sec. 13204(a)(3)(A), adding Code Secs. 168(g)(1)(F) and Code Sec. 168(g)(8);

— Act Sec. 13204(a)(3)(B), amending Code Sec. 168(g)(3)(B);

— Act Sec. 13204(a)(3)(C), amending Code Sec. 168(g)(2)(C);

— Act Sec. 13204(a)(4), adding Code Sec. 168(e)(6) and striking Code Sec. 168(k)(2)(A)(iv) and (k)(3);

— Act Sec. 13204(b), providing the effective date.

## ¶435 Depreciation of Farm Property

### SUMMARY OF NEW LAW

New farming machinery and equipment placed in service after December 31, 2017, are classified as 5-year MACRS property rather than 7-year MACRS property. The 7-year property classification, however, continues to apply to grain bins, cotton ginning assets, fences, and other land improvements. The 150-percent declining balance method is not mandatory for farming property placed in service after

## SUMMARY OF NEW LAW

December 31, 2017. A farming business that elects out of the interest deduction limits must depreciate property with a recovery period of 10 years or greater using the alternative depreciation system.

## BACKGROUND

Machinery and equipment, grain bins, and fences used in agriculture are classified as 7-year MACRS property (Rev. Proc. 87-56, Asset Class 01.1). Agriculture is defined as the production of crops or plants, vines, and trees; livestock; the operation of farm dairies, nurseries, greenhouses, sod farms, mushroom cellars, cranberry bogs, apiaries (i.e., bee production activities), and fur farms; and the performance of agricultural, animal husbandry, and horticultural services (Asset Class 01.1). A 10-year alternative depreciation system (ADS) recovery period applies.

Under an expired provision, a five-year recovery period applies to any machinery or equipment (other than a grain bin, cotton ginning asset, fence, or other land improvement) if the original use began with the taxpayer after 2008, and the property was used by the taxpayer in a farming business and placed in service in 2009 (Code Sec. 168(e)(3)(B)(vii), as added by the Emergency Economic Stabilization Act of 2008 (P.L. 110-343)). Such property has a recovery period of 10 years under ADS (Code Sec. 168(g)(3)(B), as amended by P.L. 110-343). This provision was not extended.

3-, 5-, 7-, and 10-year MACRS property placed in service after 1988 and used in a farming business may not be depreciated using the 200-percent declining balance (DB) method which normally applies to these property classes (the 150-percent DB method has always applied to 15- and 20-year property whether or not used in farming). Instead, farming property in these classes is depreciated using the 150-percent DB method (unless the ADS or straight-line method is required or elected) (Code Sec. 168(b)(2)(B)).

## NEW LAW EXPLAINED

**Farming machinery depreciated over five years; 200-percent DB method allowed; ADS required if farming business elects out of interest deduction limits.**—Modifications to the treatment of certain farm equipment include:

- a decrease in the 7-year recovery period for new farming machinery and equipment to a 5-year recovery period,

- elimination of the rule requiring use of the 150-percent declining balance method on 3-, 5-, 7-, and 10-year property used in a farming business, and

- ADS required on farm property with a recovery period of ten years or greater if farming business elects out of the interest deduction limits of Code Sec. 163(j).

**Five-year recovery period for new farming machinery and equipment.** Effective for property placed in service after December 31, 2017, a 5-year recovery period applies to any machinery or equipment (other than any grain bin, cotton ginning asset, fence, or other land improvement) used in a farming business if the original use commences with

¶435

**NEW LAW EXPLAINED**

the taxpayer after December 31, 2017 (Code Sec. 168(e)(3)(B)(vii), as amended by the Tax Cuts and Jobs Act (P.L. 115-97). Generally, a 7-year recovery period previously applied to this property (Rev. Proc. 87-56, Asset Class 01.1).

A 10-year alternative depreciation system (ADS) recovery period applies to farming machinery and equipment with a 5-or 7-year recovery period. Code Sec. 168(g)(3)(B), referencing Code Sec. 168(e)(3)(B)(vii) and Asset Class 01.1 of Rev. Proc. 87-56, both provide a 10-year ADS period.

> **Caution:** The provision only applies to new machinery and equipment used in a farming business. A 7-year recovery period continues to apply to used farming machinery and equipment.

**200-percent declining method allowed for farming property.** The provision that requires MACRS 3-, 5-, 7-, and 10-year property placed in service after 1988 and used in a farming business to be depreciated using the 150-percent declining balance (DB) method instead of the normally applicable 200-percent DB method is repealed, effective for property placed in service after December 31, 2017 (Code Sec. 168(b)(2)(B), as stricken by the 2017 Tax Cuts Act).

> **Comment:** A taxpayer may now elect to depreciate any class of 3-, 5-, 7-, or 10-year farming property using the 150-percent declining balance method (Code Sec. 168(b)(2)(C), as redesignated by the 2017 Tax Cuts Act). The election was not previously available because such property had to be depreciated using the 150-percent declining balance method unless an election to use the MACRS straight-line method or the MACRS alternative depreciation system (ADS) was made.

*Farming business defined.* As defined in Code Sec. 263A(e)(4) and Reg. § 1.263A-4(a)(4), the term "farming business" means a trade or business involving the cultivation of land or the raising or harvesting of any agricultural or horticultural commodity (e.g., the trade or business of operating a nursery or sod farm; the raising or harvesting of trees bearing fruit, nuts, or other crops; the raising of ornamental trees (other than evergreen trees that are more than six years old at the time they are severed from their roots); and the raising, shearing, feeding, caring for, training, and management of animals). A farming business includes processing activities that are normally incident to the growing, raising, or harvesting of agricultural or horticultural products. A farming business does not include contract harvesting of an agricultural or horticultural commodity grown or raised by another taxpayer, or merely buying and reselling plants or animals grown or raised by another taxpayer.

**Farming business electing out of interest deduction limitation must use ADS for property with recovery period of 10 years or greater.** Any property with a recovery period of 10 years or greater which is held by an "electing farming business" that makes an election out of the new rules which disallow the deduction for net interest expense in excess of 30 percent of the business' adjusted taxable income must be depreciated using the MACRS alternative depreciation system (ADS) (Code Sec. 168(g)(1)(G), as added by the 2017 Tax Cuts Act). See ¶510 for discussion of 30-percent limitation on business interest expense deductions under Code Sec. 163(j).

The provision is effective for tax years beginning after 2017 and not to *property placed in service* in tax years beginning after 2017. Therefore, if the election is made, ADS applies to property placed in service before, during, and after the election year. The

**NEW LAW EXPLAINED**

ADS switch for property placed in service before the election year is made by applying the change in use rules of Reg. §1.168(i)-4(d). However, if two or more returns are filed before making the required switch, an impermissible accounting method has been adopted. It is then necessary to file an accounting method change and compute a Code Sec. 481(a) adjustment (Rev. Proc. 2019-8). See ¶425 discussion of electing real property trades or businesses for additional details.

> **Comment:** Under ADS, the straight-line method applies using a recovery period that is usually longer than the regular recovery period. The ADS recovery period is the asset's class life, usually as shown in Rev. Proc. 87-56.

An electing farming business is a farming business (as defined above) that elects out of the interest deduction limitation, or any trade or business of a "specified agricultural or horticultural cooperative" (as defined in new Code Sec. 199A(g)(2)) with respect to which the cooperative makes an election out of the interest deduction limitation (Code Sec. 163(j)(7)(C), as added by the 2017 Tax Cuts Act).

A specified agricultural or horticultural cooperative is an organization to which part I of subchapter T applies, and which is engaged in—

(1) the manufacturing, production, growth, or extraction in whole or significant part of any agricultural or horticultural product;

(2) the marketing of agricultural or horticultural products which its patrons have so manufactured, produced, grown, or extracted; or

(3) the provision of supplies, equipment, or services to farmers or to organizations in items (1) or (2) (Code Sec. 199A(g), as added by the 2017 Tax Cuts Act).

▶ **Effective date.** The amendments reducing the recovery period of farm machinery and allowing use of the 200-percent declining method apply to property placed in service after December 31, 2017, in tax years ending after such date (Act Sec. 13203(c) of the Tax Cuts and Jobs Act (P.L. 115-97)). The amendment requiring an electing farming business to use ADS to depreciate property with a recovery period of 10 years or greater applies to tax years beginning after December 31, 2017 (Act Sec. 13205(b) of the 2017 Tax Cuts Act).

— Act Sec. 13203(a) of the Tax Cuts and Jobs Act (P.L. 115-97), amending Code Sec. 168(e)(3)(B);

— Act Sec. 13203(b), striking Code Sec. 168(b)(2)(B), and redesignating Code Sec. 168(b)(2)(C) and (D) as Code Sec. 168(b)(2)(B) and (C);

— Act Sec. 13205(a), adding Code Sec. 168(g)(1)(G);

— Act Secs. 13203(c) and 13205(b), providing the effective dates.

## ¶440 Expensing of Certain Costs of Replanting Citrus Plants

**SUMMARY OF NEW LAW**

The special rule for deducting the costs incurred in connection with replanting citrus plants lost by reason of casualty is modified. The modified rule allows for a deduction in certain instances when the cost is incurred by a person other than the taxpayer.

## BACKGROUND

A taxpayer that is subject to the uniform capitalization (UNICAP) rules must capitalize all direct costs and an allocable portion of most indirect costs that are associated with certain production or resale activities. The UNICAP rules generally apply to: (1) real or tangible personal property produced by the taxpayer for use in a trade or business or in an activity engaged in for profit; (2) real or tangible personal property produced by the taxpayer for sale to customers; and (3) real or personal property, both tangible and intangible, acquired by the taxpayer for resale (Code Sec. 263A).

The UNICAP rules apply to plants and animals produced by certain farming businesses (corporations, partnerships, and tax shelters) that are required to use the accrual method of accounting. For other farming businesses, the UNICAP rules apply only to plants produced in the farming business that have a preproductive period of more than two years (Code Sec. 263A(d)(1)).

The UNICAP rules do not apply to costs that are attributable to the replanting, cultivation, maintenance, and development of any plants (of the same type of crop) bearing an edible crop for human consumption (normally eaten or drunk by humans) that were lost or damaged while in the hands of the taxpayer as the result of freezing temperatures, disease, drought, pests, or casualty. Replanting or maintenance costs may be incurred on domestic property other than the damaged property if the acreage does not exceed that of the damaged property (Code Sec. 263A(d)(2)(A)).

This casualty exception can also apply to amounts paid by a person other than the taxpayer holding the crops if:

- the taxpayer has an equity interest of more than 50 percent in the damaged plants at all times during the tax year in which the replanting costs were paid or incurred; and

- the other person holds any part of the remaining equity interest and materially participates in the planting, maintenance, cultivation, or development of the damaged plants during the tax year in which these amounts were paid or incurred (Code Sec. 263A(d)(2)(B)).

Whether an individual materially participates is determined in a manner similar to that for determining whether there is material participation for net earnings from self-employment income purposes (Code Sec. 263A(d)(2)(B); see Code Secs. 2032A(e)(6) and 1402(a)(1)).

### NEW LAW EXPLAINED

**Certain costs of replanting citrus plants lost to casualty deductible by a person other than the taxpayer.**—A temporary exception to the UNICAP rules applies to certain costs incurred by persons other than the taxpayer in connection with replanting citrus plants following loss or damage while in the taxpayer's hands due to freezing temperatures, disease, drought, pests, or casualty (Code Sec. 263A(d)(2)(C)(i), as added by the Tax Cuts and Jobs Act (P.L. 115-97)). A person other than the taxpayer may deduct the replanting costs if:

¶440

## NEW LAW EXPLAINED

- the taxpayer has an equity interest of at least 50 percent in the replanted citrus plants at all times during tax year that the replanting costs were paid or incurred, and the person who incurred the costs holds any part of the remaining equity interest; or

- the person who incurred the replanting costs acquires all of the taxpayer's equity interest in the land on which the lost or damaged citrus plants were located at the time of the loss or damage, and the replanting is on that land.

This rule does not apply to costs paid or incurred after December 22, 2027 (i.e., 10 years after the date of enactment) (Code Sec. 263A(d)(2)(C)(ii), as added by the 2017 Tax Cuts Act).

**Automatic accounting method change procedure.** The person who incurred the planting costs must follow certain procedures to obtain automatic consent from the IRS to change its accounting method from applying to not applying the UNICAP rules to citrus plant replanting costs under Code Sec. 263A(d)(2)(C) (Rev. Proc. 2018-35, modifying Rev. Proc. 2018-31).

▶ **Effective date.** The amendment made by this section applies to costs paid or incurred after December 22, 2017, the date of enactment (Act Sec. 13207(b) of the Tax Cuts and Jobs Act (P.L. 115-97)).

— Act Sec. 13207(a) of the Tax Cuts and Jobs Act (P.L. 115-97), adding new Code Sec. 263A(d)(2)(C);

— Act Sec. 13207(b), providing the effective date.

# Business Income, Deductions and Credits

**5**

## INCOME EXCLUSION, ETC.

## BUSINESS TAX CREDITS

¶585    Employer Credit for Paid Family and Medical Leave

¶590    Rehabilitation Credit

¶595    Orphan Drug Credit

# INCOME EXCLUSIONS, ETC.

## ¶505  Like-Kind Exchanges of Real Property

### SUMMARY OF NEW LAW

Like-kind exchanges are allowed only for real property after 2017. Thus, as under current law, no gain or loss is recognized on the exchange of real property held for productive use in a trade or business or for investment if that real property is exchanged solely for real property of like kind that will be held either for productive use in a trade or business or for investment. Like-kind exchanges are not allowed for depreciable tangible personal property, and intangible and nondepreciable personal property after 2017.

### BACKGROUND

Gain or loss on the disposition of property can be deferred if the taxpayer receives like-kind property in exchange (Code Sec. 1031). Specifically, no gain or loss is recognized on a transfer of property held for productive use in a trade or business or for investment, to the extent the property is exchanged for property of like kind that will be held for productive use in a trade or business or for investment (Code Sec. 1031(a)(1)). Like-kind property is property of the same nature or character. There are three categories of like-kind property: (1) depreciable tangible personal property, (2) intangible and nondepreciable personal property, and (3) real property (Reg. §§ 1.1031(a)-1 and 1.1031(a)-2).

Virtually any real property is like-kind to other real property, regardless of how dissimilar the properties are. For instance, improved real estate is like-kind to unimproved real estate, urban lots are like-kind to rural tracts, commercial property is like-kind to residential rental or investment property, etc. A leasehold or similar property interest with at least 30 years left to run is like-kind to a fee title (Reg. § 1.1031(a)-1(c)). However, real property in the United States is not like-kind to real property outside the United States (Code Sec. 1031(h)(1)).

*Ineligible property.* Property that is not eligible for a like-kind exchange includes: (1) stock in trade or inventory property held primarily for sale; (2) stocks, bonds or notes, other than stock in a mutual ditch, reservoir or irrigation company described in Code Sec. 501(c)(12)(A) that is treated as real property under applicable state law; (3) other securities or evidences of indebtedness or interest; (4) partnership interests; (5) certificates of trust or beneficial interests; and (6) choses in action (Code Sec. 1031(a)(2) and (j)). Thus, for instance, real property held primarily for sale is not

¶505

## BACKGROUND

eligible for a like-kind exchange. Although partnership interests are not eligible, if the partnership has elected out of subchapter K (that is, if it has elected to not be treated as a partnership for tax purposes), an interest in the partnership is treated as an interest in each of the partnership's assets, rather than a partnership interest (Code Sec. 1031(a)(2)).

*Timing.* Dispositions in a like-kind exchange do not have to be simultaneous. In a deferred exchange, a taxpayer may relinquish property before receiving the replacement property. Conversely, in a reverse-Starker exchange, the taxpayer may receive the replacement property before relinquishing the surrendered property. In a deferred exchange, once one property has been transferred, the taxpayer must identify the property for the second transfer within 45 days; and the second transfer must actually occur within 180 days or, if earlier, before the due date (including extensions) for the taxpayer's return for the tax year the property is relinquished (Code Sec. 1031(a)(3)). The IRS has provided a safe harbor for reverse-Starker exchanges (also known as parking transactions) that incorporates similar deadlines (Rev. Proc. 2000-37).

## NEW LAW EXPLAINED

**Like-kind exchanges limited to real property.**—Like-kind exchanges are allowed only for real property after 2017. Thus, as under current law, no gain or loss is recognized on the exchange of real property held for productive use in a trade or business or for investment if that real property is exchanged solely for real property of like kind that will be held either for productive use in a trade or business or for investment. Like-kind exchanges are not allowed for depreciable tangible personal property, and intangible and nondepreciable personal property after 2017 (Code Sec. 1031(a)(1), as amended by the Tax Cuts and Jobs Act (P.L. 115-97)).

> **Comment:** Although most real property is like-kind to other real property, disputes as to whether properties are genuinely like-kind are still likely to arise when an exchange involves limited or partial property interests, such as life estates, remainder interests, and tenancies-in-common.

As under current law: (1) real property is not eligible for a like-kind exchange if it is held primarily for sale (Code Sec. 1031(a)(2), as amended by the 2017 Tax Cuts Act); (2) real property in the United States and foreign real property are not like-kind (Code Sec. 1031(h), as amended by the 2017 Tax Cuts Act); and (3) an interest in a partnership that has elected out of subchapter K is treated as an interest in each of the partnership's assets, rather than a partnership interest (Code Sec. 1031(e), as amended by the 2017 Tax Cuts Act). Stock in a mutual ditch, reservoir or irrigation company described in Code Sec. 501(c)(12)(A) is still eligible for a like-kind exchange if it is treated as real property under applicable state law (IRS News Release IR-2018-227, November 19, 2018).

**Transition rule.** The restriction of like-kind exchanges to real property does not apply to an exchange if the relinquished property is disposed of or the replacement property is received on or before December 31, 2017 (Act Sec. 13303(c)(2) of the 2017 Tax Cuts Act).

## NEW LAW EXPLAINED

> **Comment:** This transition rule allows taxpayers to complete a deferred or reverse-Starker exchange that involves depreciable tangible personal property or intangible and nondepreciable personal property. However, the 45-day identification deadline and the 180-day exchange deadline still apply.

▶ **Effective date.** The amendments made by this section generally apply to exchanges completed after December 31, 2017 (Act Sec. 13303(c)(1) of the Tax Cuts and Jobs Act (P.L. 115-97). However, the amendments do not apply to an exchange if (1) the property disposed of by the taxpayer in the exchange is disposed of on or before December 31, 2017; or (2) the property received by the taxpayer in the exchange is received on or before December 31, 2017 (Act Sec. 13303(c)(2) of the 2017 Tax Cuts Act).

— Act Sec. 13303(a) of the Tax Cuts and Jobs Act (P.L. 115-97), amending Code Sec. 1031(a)(1);

— Act Sec. 13303(b), amending Code Sec. 1031(a)(2), (e) and (h), and striking Code Sec. 1031(i);

— Act Sec. 13303(c), providing the effective date.

# BUSINESS DEDUCTIONS

## ¶510  Limitation on Deduction of Business Interest

### SUMMARY OF NEW LAW

The deduction of business interest is limited for any tax year beginning after 2017 to the sum of the taxpayer's business interest income, floor plan financing, and 30 percent of adjusted taxable income. The limitation generally applies to all taxpayers, but does not apply for small businesses with average gross receipts of $25 million or less (adjusted for inflation). Any disallowed interest generally may be carried forward indefinitely. In the case of a partnership or S corporation, the deduction limitation applies at the entity level, except that disallowed interest of the entity is allocated to each partner or shareholder as excess business interest.

### BACKGROUND

Interest and other borrowing expenses incurred in a trade or business are generally deductible from gross income in the year paid or accrued depending on the taxpayer's method of accounting (Code Sec. 163). If a debt instrument is issued with original issue discount (OID), the OID is deducted as interest by the issuer of the debt over the life of the obligation on a yield to maturity basis. There are several limitations on the deduction of interest including tax-exempt interest, interest from obligations not in registered form, interest paid in connection with insurance contracts, and interest paid on original issue discount (OID) high-yield obligation. Interest may also be required to be capitalized if allocable to the production of certain property.

## BACKGROUND

In the case of a taxpayer other than a corporation, the amount of investment interest they may deduct in a given tax year may not exceed net investment income (Code Sec. 163(d)). Any excess investment interest expense is carried forward indefinitely until net investment income is recognized. Investment interest is interest paid or accrued by the taxpayer on debt allocable to property held for investment that is otherwise deductible. However, investment expenses are determined after application of the two-percent-over adjusted gross income (AGI) limitation on miscellaneous itemized deductions. Investment income is the gross income derived from property held for investment or from its disposition including interest received, annuities, dividends, royalties, and short-term gain on the disposition of property. However, investment income includes capital gain and qualified dividend income only to the extent that the taxpayer elects to treat it as investment income.

A corporation is not allowed to deduct disqualified interest paid or accrued during the tax year if: (1) the debt-to-equity ratio of the corporation exceeds 1.5 to 1.0 as of the close of the tax year; and (2) the corporation has net interest expenses for the tax year that exceed 50 percent of its adjusted taxable income (Code Sec. 163(j)). Interest disallowed may be carried forward and treated as disqualified interest in succeeding tax years. In addition, any excess limitation (i.e., the excess of 50 percent of the adjusted taxable income of the payor over the payor's net interest expense) can be carried forward three years. Disqualified interest is generally interest paid or accrued by the taxpayer: (1) to a related person not subject to U.S. income tax on the interest; (2) on debt held by an unrelated person in which there is a disqualified guarantee by a related person; and (3) to a taxable real estate investment trust (REIT) by a subsidiary of the trust. This limitation is often referred to as the "earnings stripping" rule.

## NEW LAW EXPLAINED

**Limitation on deduction of business interest.**—A taxpayer's deduction of business interest expenses paid or incurred for tax years beginning after December 31, 2017, is limited to the sum of:

- the taxpayer's business interest income for the tax year for which the taxpayer is claiming the deduction (not including investment income);

- 30 percent of the taxpayer's adjusted taxable income (ATI), but not less than zero; and

- the taxpayer's floor plan financing interest (Code Sec. 163(j), as amended by the Tax Cuts and Jobs Act (P.L. 115-97).

  **Comment:** The practical effect of the rule is to limit the deduction of net interest expenses to 30 percent of the taxpayer's ATI. The deduction for business interest and floor plan financing interest is permitted to the full extent of business interest income and floor plan financing interest. If the taxpayer has any interest expenses that exceed these amounts, then the deduction is limited to 30 percent of ATI.

## NEW LAW EXPLAINED

Any business interest not deductible generally may be carried forward indefinitely to succeeding tax years. The limit applies to all taxpayers except a small business with average annual gross receipts for the three prior tax years of $25 million or less ($26 million for 2019). It also does not apply to certain excepted businesses including a trade or business of providing services as an employee, an electing real property business, an electing farming business, and certain regulated utility businesses.

> **Compliance Note:** Form 8990 is used to calculate a taxpayer's business interest deduction and the amount carried forward to the next year.

> **Comment:** The limitation on the deduction of business interest, along with the reduction of income tax rates for corporation (¶305) and the business income deduction for passthrough entities (¶330), helps to reduce the differences in marginal tax rates based on different sources of financing and in the choice of business entities.

In the case of a partnership or S corporation, the limitation on the deduction of business interest is applied at the entity level with respect to the entity's indebtedness. Any deduction for business interest is taken into account in determining the non-separately stated taxable income or loss of the partnership or S corporation. However, in the case of a partnership any disallowed business interest of a partnership is allocated to each partner as excess business interest.

The Treasury and IRS have issued proposed regulations on the Code Sec. 163(j) interest expense deduction limitation. The proposed regulations may be applied by taxpayers and their related parties to a tax year beginning after December 31, 2017, so long as the taxpayers and their related parties consistently apply them (REG-106089-18; Proposed Reg. §1.163(j)-2). The proposed regulations provide that the limit on the deduction for business interest applies to the total amount of business interest of the taxpayer in the tax year, including disallowed business interest carried forward from prior tax years. It does not trace interest to any particular debt obligation of the taxpayer. The deduction limit applies regardless of how the taxpayer's business is organized (i.e., corporation, partnership, sole proprietorship, etc.). The limit generally applies after application of other interest limits other than the at-risk and passive loss limits.

**Adjusted taxable income (ATI).** The ATI of a taxpayer for purposes of the limitation is the taxpayer's regular taxable income for the tax year without regard to any:

- income, gain, deduction, or loss that is not properly allocable to a trade or business;

- business interest income or business interest expense (including floor plan financing interest expense);

- net operating loss (NOL) deduction (including NOLs arising in tax years before 2018 and carried forward to the current tax year);

- qualified business income (QBI) deduction allowed under Code Sec. 199A (see ¶330);

- for tax years beginning before January 1, 2022, deductions for depreciations, amortization, or depletion attributable to a trade or business (including bonus depreciation);

## NEW LAW EXPLAINED

- capital loss carryback or carryover deductions; and
- deductions or losses allocable to a non-excepted trade or business (Code Sec. 163(j)(8), as added by the 2017 Tax Cuts Act; Proposed Reg. § 1.163(j)-1(b)(1)).

Depreciation, amortization, or depletion expense that is capitalized to inventory under the UNICAP rules of Code Sec. 263A is not a depreciation, amortization, or depletion deduction for purposes of the Code Sec. 163(j) limit. Thus, for tax years beginning before January 1, 2022, ATI is similar to EBITDA of the taxpayer (earnings before interest, taxes, depreciation, and amortization). Beginning in 2022, ATI is similar to EBIT (earnings before interest and taxes). Additional adjustments to ATI are provided under proposed regulations to prevent double counting if a taxpayer sells or otherwise disposes of property subject to depreciation, amortization, or depletion.

The ATI of a beneficiary of a trust or estate is reduced by any income (including any distributable net income) received from the trust or estate by the beneficiary (Proposed Reg. § 1.163(j)-2(f)). The reduction applies to the extent such income supported a deduction for business interest expense in computing the trust or estate's taxable income. Additional rules relating to the ATI apply to partnerships, S corporations, C corporations, and foreign persons with effectively connected income.

**Carryfoward of disallowed business interest.** Any business interest expense not allowed as a deduction for any tax year generally may be carried forward and treated as business interest expense paid or accrued in the succeeding tax year. Disallowed business interest for this purpose includes any business interest properly allocable to a non-excepted trade or business (services as employee, electing real property business, electing farm business, regulated utilities) (Code Sec. 163(j)(2), as added by the 2017 Tax Cuts Act; Proposed Reg. § 1.163(j)-2(c)). The disallowed business interest may be carried forward indefinitely, subject to certain restrictions. If it is carried forward to a tax year that the small business exemption applies to the taxpayer, then the limitation does not apply to the disallowed business interest expense carryforward in that tax year.

Disallowed business interest of a partnership is not carried forward to the succeeding tax year. Instead, the disallowed interest of the partnership is treated as excess business interest that is allocated to each partner in the same manner as any non-separately stated taxable income or loss (discussed below). Disallowed business interest of an C or S corporation is carried forward in the succeeding tax year. However, current-year business interest expense is deducted before any disallowed business interest carryforward from a prior tax year is deducted. Carryforwards of corporations are generally deducted in the order of the tax year that they arose, beginning with the earliest tax year, subject to certain limitations (Reg. § 1.163(j)-5; Proposed Reg. § 1.163(j)-6(l)(5)).

**Small business exemption.** The Code Sec. 163(j) limit generally does not apply to any taxpayer for the tax year if it meets the gross receipts test under Code Sec. 448(c) to use the cash method of accounting (see ¶ 570). A taxpayer meets the small business test for the tax year if its average annual gross receipts for the three prior tax years do not exceed $25 million for 2018 ($26 million for 2019) (Code Sec. 163(j)(3), as added by the 2017 Tax Cuts Act; Proposed Reg. § 1.163(j)-2(d); Rev. Proc. 2018-57). The gross

## NEW LAW EXPLAINED

receipts test is an annual determination. Thus, a taxpayer's status as an exempt small business under Code Sec. 163(j) may change from year to year.

An individual's gross receipts for this purpose include all items specified as gross receipts under Code Sec. 448(c), whether or not derived in the ordinary course of the taxpayer's trade or business. An individual taxpayer's gross receipts do not include inherently personal amounts (e.g., W-2 wages received as an employee, Social Security benefits, disability benefits, and personal injury awards or settlements with respect to an injury of the taxpayer).

Each partner in a partnership generally includes a share of partnership gross receipts in proportion to his or her distributive share of partnership gross income unless the aggregation rules of Code Sec. 448(c) apply. Each shareholder in an S corporation also includes a pro rata share of S corporation gross receipts. The gross receipts of a charitable organization subject to the tax on it unrelated business income includes only gross receipts taken into account in determining its unrelated business taxable income.

**Business interest expense and income.** Business interest expense for purpose of the Code Sec. 163(j) limit is any interest that is properly allocable to a trade or business of the taxpayer or that is floor plan financing interest (Code Sec. 163(j)(5), as added by the 2017 Tax Cuts Act; Proposed Reg. § 1.163(j)-1(b)(2)). It also includes any disallowed business interest carryforward. Similarly, business interest income is any interest income includible in the taxpayer's gross income that is properly allocable to a trade or business of the taxpayer (Code Sec. 163(j)(6), as added by the Tax Cuts and Jobs Act; Proposed Reg. § 1.163(j)-1(b)(3)).

Interest for this purpose is an amount paid, received, or accrued as compensation for the use or forbearance of money under the terms of a contract or instrument, including a series of transactions, that is treated as debt and not as stock. Thus, interest is associated with conventional debt instruments, as well as transactions that are debt in substance although not in form (Proposed Reg. § 1.163(j)-1(b)(20)). Any amount treated as interest under any other provision of the Code is considered interest for the deduction limit.

All floor plan financing interest is business interest expense for purposes of Code Sec. 163(j) regardless whether it would be properly allocable to a non-excepted trade or business. Floor plan financing interest expense is interest paid or accrued on floor plan financing indebtedness. Floor plan financing indebtednessis means indebtedness used to finance the acquisition of motor vehicles held for sale or lease, and secured by the inventory (Code Sec. 163(j)(9), as added by the 2017 Tax Cuts Act; Proposed Reg. § 1.163(j)-1(b)(16); Proposed Reg. § 1.163(j)-1(b)(17); Proposed Reg. § 1.163(j)-1(b)(25)).

*Excepted trades and businesses.* Business interest expense and income does not include interest allocable to certain excepted business including a trade or business of providing services as an employee, an electing real property business, an electing farming business, and certain regulated utility businesses. Business interest expense and income also do not include any investment interest as defined under Code Sec. 163(d). In the case of a C corporation, all interest expense and interest income is treated as business interest expense and business interest income.

¶510

## NEW LAW EXPLAINED

> **Comment:** Investment interest is interest allocable to property that produces interest, dividends, annuities, royalties, gains, or losses not derived in the ordinary course of a trade or business. It also includes interest in a trade or business activity that is not a passive activity and in which the taxpayer does not materially participate. Investment income is the gross income derived from property held for investment purposes or from its disposition (Code Sec. 163(d)).

> **Compliance Note:** A taxpayer must make an election out of the Code Sec. 163(j) limit for a real property trade or business, or farming business, with respect to each eligible trade business. The election is made by attaching a statement to the taxpayer's timely filed original tax return (including extensions) (Proposed Reg. §1.163(j)-9). A taxpayer may make elections for multiple trades or businesses on a single election statement. In the case of a partnership, the election is made on the partnership return. The election applies to the current tax year and all subsequent tax years. Once made, the election is irrevocable but may be automatically terminated in certain circumstances. A taxpayer may not elect to be an electing real property trade or business or electing farm business if the taxpayer is already meets the small business exemption. A real property trade or business or farming business that elects out of the business interest deduction limitations must depreciate certain property using alternative depreciation system (ADS). The IRS has clarified that the MACRS change-in-use rules will apply in switching the depreciation of existing property to the ADS method (Code Sec. 163(j)(10), as added by the 2017 Tax Cuts Act; Rev. Proc. 2019-8). See ¶405.

*Electing real property trade or business.* A real property trade or business that may elect out of the Code Sec. 163(j) limitation is any real property development, redevelopment, construction, reconstruction, acquisition, conversion, rental, operation, management, leasing, or brokerage trade or business (Code Sec. 163(j)(7)(B), as added by the 2017 Tax Cuts Act; Proposed Reg. §1.163(j)-1(b)(12)). However, if at least 80 percent of the business's real property (determined by fair market value) is leased to a trade or business under common control (50 percent threshold), the trade or business is not eligible for the election.

> **Comment:** Under the passive activity rules, the way in which a taxpayer otherwise groups activities does not control the determination of the taxpayer's real property trades or businesses (Reg. §1.469-9(d)).

An exception is provided to a real estate investment trust (REIT) that leases qualified lodging facilities or qualified healthcare properties to taxable REIT subsidiary (Proposed Reg. §1.163(j)-9(h)). Under a safe harbor, a REIT is also eligible to make an election to be an electing real property trade or business for all or part of its assets Proposed Reg. §1.163(j)-9(g)). An additional safe harbor is provided that allows taxpayers to treat certain infrastructure trades or businesses as electing real property trades or businesses. If a taxpayer makes this election, the taxpayer must use the alternative depreciation system (ADS) to depreciate property (Rev. Proc. 2018-59.

*Electing farm business.* A farming business and specified agricultural and horticultural cooperatives may elect out of the Code Sec. 163(j) limitation. A farming business is defined under Code Sec. 263A(e)(4) as a trade or business that includes livestock, dairy, poultry, fish, fruit, nuts, and truck farms. It also includes plantations, ranches,

## NEW LAW EXPLAINED

ranges, and orchards. A fish farm is an area where fish and other marine animals are grown or raised and artificially fed, protected, etc., but it does not include an area where they are merely caught or harvested. A plant nursery is a farm for purposes of deducting soil and water conservation expenses (Code Sec. 163(j)(7)(C), as added by the 2017 Tax Cuts Act; Proposed Reg. § 1.163(j)-1(b)(11)).

A specified agricultural or horticultural cooperative is defined under Code Sec. 199A(g)(4) as an organization that is engaged that is subject to the federal income tax rules for cooperatives, and engaged in (1) manufacturing, producing, growing, or extracting, in whole or significant part, an agricultural or horticultural product; or (2) marketing agricultural or horticultural products. A specified cooperative that markets agricultural or horticultural products produced by its patrons is treated as having produced those products itself.

*Utility business.* The Code Sec. 163(j) limit does not apply to a utility's trade or business of furnishing or sale of: electrical energy, water, or sewage disposal services; gas or steam through a local distribution system; or transportation of gas or steam by pipeline (Proposed Reg. § 1.163(j)-1(b)(13)). The rates for furnishing or sale must be established or approved by a (1) state or political subdivision thereof, (2) agency or instrumentality of the United States, (3) public service or public utility commission or similar body of any state or political subdivision thereof, or (4) governing or rate-making body of an electric cooperative. No election is required for an excepted utility trade or business.

> **Comment:** Any property primarily used the trade or business of a regulated utility and electric cooperative as described above is not qualified property (¶ 410) eligible for the additional first-year depreciation deduction (bonus depreciation) (Code Sec. 168(k)(9), as added the 2017 Tax Cuts Act).

*Allocation of interest, income, etc.* If a taxpayer is engaged in both excepted and non-excepted trades or businesses it must allocate and apportion interest expense, interest income, and other tax items between the trades or businesses. Allocation occurs only after the taxpayer has determined whether its tax items are properly allocable to a trade or business (e.g., interest tracing rules) (Proposed Reg. § 1.163(j)-10).

Interest expense and interest income are generally allocated between excepted and non-excepted trades or businesses based on the taxpayer's adjusted basis in the assets used in the trades or businesses. The taxpayer must attach a statement to its timely filed tax return, providing information related to the asset basis and allocation determination. If the taxpayer fails to file a statement, the IRS may treat all of the taxpayer's interest expense allocated to a non-excepted trade or business unless there is reasonable cause (Proposed Reg. § 1.163(j)-10(c)).

Under a *de minimis* rule, if at least 90 percent of the taxpayer's basis in its assets for the tax year is allocable to either excepted or non-excepted trades or businesses, then all of the taxpayer's interest expense and interest income for that year is properly allocable to that trade or business. If an asset is used in more than one trade or business, the taxpayer's basis should be allocated using a permissible methodology that most reasonably reflects the use of the asset in each trade or business.

A number of special rules apply in determining basis of depreciable and nondepreciable property, land, cash, customer receivables, and deemed asset sales of corporate

## NEW LAW EXPLAINED

stock or partnership interests. Look-through rules are required if the taxpayer owns at least 80 percent of a partnership or corporation unless the entity is exempted from the Code Sec. 163(j) deduction limit because it meets the gross receipts test as a small business. A direct allocation (rather than basis allocation) is also required for interest expenses from qualified nonrecourse indebtedness, as well as interest of a taxpayer engaged banking, insurance, financing, or a similar trade or business (Proposed Reg. §1.163(j)-10(d)).

For purposes of calculating adjusted taxable income (ATI), gross income other than dividends and interest income is allocated to the trade or business that generated the gross income. Expenses, losses, and deductions other than interest that are definitely related to a trade or business are allocable to that trade or business. All other expenses are ratably apportioned to gross income (Proposed Reg. §1.163(j)-10(b)).

Dividend income from a C corporation and controlled foreign corporation (CFC) is allocated based on the adjusted basis of the assets of the corporation if the taxpayer owns 80 percent or more its stock. A shareholder in an S corporation is required to look through to the corporation's assets to allocate dividends received if the look-through rule applies to allocated interest expense and income.

If at least 90 percent of the corporation's adjusted basis is allocable to either excepted or non-excepted trades or businesses, than all dividend income is allocated accordingly. If a taxpayer receives a dividend that is not investment income and if the dividend look-through rule does not apply, then the dividend income as allocable to a non-excepted trade or business.

**Business interest limit for partnerships.** In the case of a partnership, the Code Sec. 163(j) limit on the deduction of business interest is applied at the entity level (Code Sec. 163(j)(4)(A), as added by the 2017 Tax Cuts Act; Proposed Reg. §1.163(j)-6). If a partnership has deductible business interest expense, it is not subject to any additional application of Code Sec. 163(j) at the partner level because it is taken into account in determining the non-separately stated taxable income or loss of the partnership.

> **Comment:** The Joint Committee on Taxation's General Explanation of Public Law 115-97 (JCS-1-18) (i.e., Blue Book) states that technical corrections may be necessary to achieve the provision's application to pass-through entities including partnerships.

Deductible business interest expense and excess business interest expense retain their character as business interest expense at the partner-level for all other purposes of the Code. For example, deductible business interest expense retains its character as either passive or non-passive in the hands of a partner for purpose of the passive activity rules of Code Sec 469. Similarly, deductible business interest expense from a partnership remains interest derived from a trade or business in the hands of a partner even if the partner does not materially participate in the partnership's trade or business activity (Proposed Reg. §1.163(j)-6(c)). The Code Sec. 163(j) limit applies before the application of the at-risk rules, passive activity loss rules, and the limitation on excess business losses of noncorporate taxpayers (Proposed Reg. §1.163(j)-3).

*Carryfoward of excess business interest.* Any disallowed interest of a partnership is not carried forward by the partnership to the succeeding tax year. Instead, the disallowed

## NEW LAW EXPLAINED

interest of the partnership is treated as "excess business interest" that is allocated to each partner in the same manner as any non-separately stated taxable income or loss (Code Sec. 163(j)(4)(B), as added by the 2017 Tax Cuts Act; Proposed Reg. § 163(j)-6(g)). The allocated excess business interest of a partnership for the current tax year is treated by the partner as business interest paid or accrued by the partner in the next succeeding year. In other words, the allocated excess business interest is carried forward to the next succeeding tax year by the partner, but only to the extent the partner is allocated excess taxable income or excess business interest income from the partnership in the succeeding year.

Excess taxable income allocated to a partner for any tax year must be used against excess business interest from the partnership from all tax years before it may be used against any other business interest. If the partner does not have enough excess taxable income from the partnership to offset the carried forward excess business interest, then the excess business interest must continue to be carried forward to succeeding tax years. In all subsequent tax years, the excess business interest carried forward by the partner is treated as paid or accrued in the next subsequent tax year that may only be used against excess taxable income allocated by the partnership to the partner for that tax year.

*ATI of partnerships and partners.* The ATI of a partnership is determined under the general Code Sec. 163(j) rules. A partnership also takes into account partnership-level adjustments to the basis of its property under Code Sec. 734(b). Partner-level adjustments (partner basis items and remedial items) are taken into account at the partner level, rather than partnership level, when determining the partner's ATI. A partnership's taxable income for purposes of calculating ATI is the same as determined under Code Sec. 703(a) and includes both separately and non-separately stated items of income, loss, deduction, or credit that could affect a partner's tax liability (Proposed Reg. § 1.163(j)-6(d)).

The ATI of a partner is determined without regard to the partner's distributive share of any items of income, gain, deduction, or loss of such partnership. It is also is increased by the partner's distributive share of such partnership's excess taxable income which is determined in the same manner as the partner's distributive share of non-separately stated taxable income or loss of the partnership (Code Sec. 163(j)(4)(A)(ii), as added by the 2017 Tax Cuts Act; Proposed Reg. § 1.163(j)-6(e)).

If a partner is allocated partner-based items or remedial items, the partner's ATI is increased or decreased accordingly. Also, if a partner recognizes gain or loss upon the disposition of interests in a partnership, and the partnership owns only non-excepted trade or business assets, the gain or loss is included in the partner's ATI. In calculating a partner's Code Sec. 163(j) limit, the partner does not include its allocable share of:

- business interest income from a partnership that is subject to the Code Sec. 163(j) limit except to the extent it is allocated excess business interest income from that partnership, and
- floor plan financing interest expense from the partnership.

*Allocations of partnership items.* Allocations and determinations of excess business interest expense and Code Sec. 163(j) excess items by a partnership are made in the

# NEW LAW EXPLAINED

same manner as the non-separately stated taxable income or loss of the partnership. The phrase "non-separately stated taxable income or loss of the partnership" is not defined in Code Sec. 163(j) but proposed regulations have provided an provided an 11-step process to allocate items (1.163(j)-6(f)).

**Compliance Note:** Worksheets in the Instructions to Form 8990 can be used to determine the amount of each item allocable to each partner.

The allocation rules do prohibit a partnership from making an allocation to a partner of partnership income, gain, loss, or deduction that is otherwise permitted under Code Sec. 704. The 11-step process is solely for purposes of determining each partner's deductible business interest expense and Code Sec. 163(j) excess items. Also, floor plan financing interest expense of a partnership is not allocated in accordance with 11-step process because it is allocated to its partners under Code Sec. 704(b) and is taken into account as a non-separately stated item of loss.

*Basis adjustments in partnership items.* A partner's adjusted basis in his or her partnership interest generally is reduced under Code Sec. 704(d) by allocated items of partnership loss or deduction. Deductible business interest expense and excess business interest expense under Code Sec. 163(j) are subject to this rule and the same Code Sec. 704(d) loss class will include:

- any deductible business interest expense (whether allocated to the partner in the current tax year or suspended under Code Sec. 704(d) in a prior tax year),

- any excess business interest expense allocated to the partner in the current tax year, and

- any excess business interest expense from a prior tax year that was suspended under Code Sec. 704(d) ("negative section 163(j) expense") (Code Sec. 163(j)(4)(B)(iii)(I), as added by the 2017 Tax Cuts Act; Proposed Reg. § 1.163(j)-6(h)).

Once the partner determines the amount of limitation on losses apportioned to this Code Sec. 704(d) loss class, any deductible business interest expense is taken into account before any excess business interest expense or negative section 163(j) expense. The adjusted basis of a partner in a partnership interest is reduced (but not below zero) by the amount of excess business interest expense allocated to the partner. Negative section 163(j) expense is not treated as excess business interest expense in any subsequent year until such negative section 163(j) expense is no longer suspended under Code Sec. 704(d). Therefore, negative section 163(j) expense does not affect, and is not affected by, any allocation of excess taxable income to the partner.

Any excess taxable income allocated to a partner from a partnership while the partner still has negative section 163(j) expense is included in the partner's ATI. However, once the negative section 163(j) expense is no longer suspended under Code Sec. 704(d), it becomes excess business interest expense subject to the carryover rules.

*Disposition of partnership interest.* If a partner sells or otherwise disposes of all or substantially all of a partnership interest, the adjusted basis of the partnership interest is increased before the disposition before the disposition by the amount of the excess (if any) of:

## NEW LAW EXPLAINED

- the amount of the basis reduction for any excess business interest expense allocated to a partner, over

- any portion of any excess business interest expense allocated to the partner that has previously been treated under the carryover rules as business interest expense paid or accrued by the partner, regardless of whether the disposition was a result of a taxable or nontaxable transaction (Code Sec. 163(j)(4)(B)(iii)(II), as added by the 2017 Tax Cuts Act; Proposed Reg. § 1.163(j)-6(h)(3)).

The adjusted basis of a partner in a partnership interest is therefore not increased by any negative section 163(j) expense upon the disposition of a partnership interest. No deduction under Code Sec. 163(j) is allowed to the transferor or transferee for federal income tax purposes for any excess business interest expense resulting in a basis increase under these rules or any negative section 163(j) expense.

If a partner disposes of less than substantially all of its interest in a partnership, the partner may not increase its basis in its partnership by the amount of any excess business interest expense that has not yet been treated as paid or accrued by the partner. Any such excess business interest expense would remain excess business interest expense in the hands of the transferor partner until the partner is either:

- allocated an appropriate amount of excess taxable income or excess business interest income from the partnership, or

- added to the basis of its partnership interest when the partner fully disposes of the partnership interest.

Also, any negative section 163(j) expense remains negative section 163(j) expense of the transferor partner until it is no longer suspended Code Sec. 704(d). These rules are similar to the rules under Code Sec. 469 relating to suspended passive activity loss deductions.

**Business interest limit for S corporations.** In the case of an S corporation, the Code Sec. 163(j) limit on the deduction of business interest is applied at the entity level (Code Sec. 163(j)(4)(D), as added by the 2017 Tax Cuts Act; Proposed Reg. § 1.163(j)-6(l)). Any deduction for business interest is taken into account in determining the non-separately stated taxable income or loss of the S corporation.

> **Comment:** The Joint Committee on Taxation's General Explanation of Public Law 115-97 (JCS-1-18) (i.e., Blue Book) states that technical corrections may be necessary to achieve the provision's application to pass-through entities including S corporations.

The ATI of the S corporation is determined under the general Code Sec. 163(j) rules without any additional modifications. In computing the S corporation's ATI, its taxable income is the same as under Code Sec. 1363(b) and includes separately stated items of income, loss, deduction, or credit that could affect a shareholder's tax liability and any other item with S corporation rules. Allocations of excess taxable income and excess business interest income are made in accordance with the shareholders' respective pro rata interests in the S corporation. As a result, if an S corporation has deductible business interest expense, it is not subject to any additional Code Sec. 163(j) limit at the shareholder-level.

## NEW LAW EXPLAINED

Deductible business interest expense retains its character as business interest expense at the S shareholder-level for all other purposes of the Code, other than the Code Sec. 163(j) limit. For example, deductible business interest expense retains its character as either passive or non-passive in the hands of the shareholder for purpose of the passive activity rules of Code Sec. 469. Similarly, deductible business interest expense from an S corporation remains interest derived from a trade or business in the hands of a shareholder even if the shareholder does not materially participate in the S corporation's trade or business activity.

*Carryforward of disallowed business interest.* Disallowed business interest of an S corporation is carried forward in the succeeding tax year (whether it is an S corporation or C corporation tax year). An S corporation is subject to the same ordering rules a C corporation (discussed below) and the Code Sec. 382 limitation (Proposed Reg. § 1.163(j)-6(l)(5)). Carryforwards of a corporation are generally deducted in the order of the tax year that they arose, beginning with the earliest tax year, subject to certain limitations and current-year business interest expense is deducted before any disallowed business interest carryforward from a prior tax year are deducted.

An S corporation shareholder's adjusted basis in its S corporation stock is reduced, but not below zero, when a disallowed business interest expense carryforward becomes deductible under Code Sec. 163(j) (Proposed Reg. § 1.163(j)-6(l)(6)). Similarly, the accumulated adjustment account of an S corporation is adjusted to take into account business interest expense in the year in which the S corporation treats such business interest expense as deductible under Code Sec. 163(j) (Proposed Reg. § 1.163(j)-6(l)(7)). If the election for a qualified subsidiary of an S corporation (QSub) terminates, any disallowed business interest expense carryforward attributable to the activities of the QSub remain with the parent S corporation. No portion is allocable to the former QSub (Proposed Reg. § 1.163(j)-6(l)(8)).

*ATI of S corporation shareholder.* The ATI of an S corporation shareholder is determined without regard to the shareholder's distributive share of any items of income, gain, deduction, or loss of such S corporation. It is increased by the shareholder's distributive share of such S corporation's excess taxable income. Any item of an S corporation's income, gain, deduction, or loss that is investment interest income or expense is also allocated to each shareholder in accordance with the shareholders' pro rata interests in the S corporation (Proposed Reg. § 1.163(j)-6(l)(4); Proposed Reg. § 1.163(j)-6(l)(9)).

If a shareholder of an S corporation recognizes gain or loss upon the disposition of stock in the S corporation, the gain or loss is included in the shareholder's ATI if the corporation only owns non-excepted trade or business assets. The gain or loss must be allocated if the S corporation owns non-excepted assets and excepted assets, investment assets, or both. In calculating an S corporation shareholder's Code Sec. 163(j) limit, the shareholder does not include the shareholder's share of:

- business interest income from an S corporation that is subject to the Code Sec. 163(j) limit except to the extent it is allocated excess business interest income from that S corporation;

- floor plan financing interest expense from the S corporation.

## NEW LAW EXPLAINED

**Business interest limit for C corporations.** All of the C corporation's interest expense and interest income is subject to the Code Sec. 163(j) limit except to the extent the interest is allocable to an excepted trade or business (Proposed Reg. § 1.163(j)-4). Thus, a C corporation does not have investment expense or investment income for purposes of the limit. All other items of income, gain, deduction, or loss of a C corporation are also properly allocable to a trade or business for purposes of the limit. Such tax items are factored into a C corporation's calculation of ATI except to the extent such items are properly allocable to an excepted trade or business.

*Carryforward of disallowed business interest.* Disallowed business interest of a C corporation is carried forward to the succeeding tax year. However, current-year business interest expense is deducted before any disallowed business interest carryforward from a prior tax year are deducted (Code Sec. 163(j)(2), as added by the 2017 Tax Cuts Act; Proposed Reg. § 1.163(j)-5).

Carryforwards of a C corporation are generally deducted in the order of the tax year that they arose, beginning with the earliest tax year, subject to certain limitations. A C corporation with disqualified interest under the earnings stripping rules for the last tax year beginning before 2018 may carry it forward as business interest to the first tax year beginning after 2017, but subject to the post-2017 interest deduction limitation and the base erosion tax under Code Sec. 59A in the same manner as interest paid or accrued after 2017 (Proposed Reg. § 1.163(j)-11(b)).

In the case of a nontaxable corporation acquisition or liquidation, the acquiring corporation generally succeeds to any carryover of disallowed business interest to tax years ending after the date of distribution or transfer (Code Sec. 381(c)(20), as added by the 2017 Tax Cuts Act). Similarly, the amount of any pre-change loss of a loss corporation (i.e., target corporation) that may be used to offset post-change taxable income of an acquiring corporation includes the carryover of disallowed business interest to the tax year ending with the ownership change or in which the change date occurs (Code Sec. 382(d)(3), as added by the 2017 Tax Cuts Act). A loss corporation for this purpose includes any corporation with carryforwards of disallowed business interest deductions (Code Sec. 382(k)(1), as amended by the 2017 Tax Cuts Act).

*C corporation partner.* Although a C corporation cannot have investment interest or expenses for purposes of the Code Sec. 163(j) limit, a partnership in which a C corporation is a partner may allocate such tax items to the C corporation (Proposed Reg. § 1.163(j)-4(b)(3)). In such cases, investment interest expenses and income allocated to the C corporation partner are recharacterized as properly allocable to a trade or business of the C corporation. The only exception is if the C corporation partner is allocated a share of a domestic partnership's gross income inclusion under Code Sec. 951(a) or Code Sec. 951A(a) that are treated as investment income at the partnership level.

The recharacterization of investment items at the C corporation partner level does not affect the character of these items at the partnership level. It also does not affect the character of the investment interest, investment income, and investment expenses allocated to other (non-C corporation) partners. Investment interest expense of a partnership that is treated as business interest expense by a C corporation partner is

# NEW LAW EXPLAINED

not treated as excess business interest expense. Similarly, investment interest income of a partnership that is treated as business interest income by a C corporation partner is not treated as excess taxable income.

*Other rules affecting C corporations.* The disallowance and carryforward of a deduction for a C corporation business interest expense generally does not affect whether or when such expenses reduce the earnings and profits (E&P) of the corporation Proposed Reg. § 1.163(j)-4(c); Proposed Reg. § 1.163(j)-11(b)). The Code Sec. 163(j) limit applies to all C corporations, including regulated investment companies (RICs), real estate investment trusts (REITs), and tax-exempt organizations Proposed Reg. § 1.163(j)-4(b)(4); Proposed Reg. § 1.163(j)-4(b)(5). Special rules are provided for the calculation of the limit for members of a consolidated group Proposed Reg. § 1.163(j)-4(d); Proposed Reg. § 1.163(j)-5(b)(3)).

**Controlled foreign corporations (CFCs).** The business interest deduction limit applies to the business interest of a controlled foreign corporation (CFC) in the same manner as it applies to a domestic C corporation (Proposed Reg. § 1.163(j)-7(b)). Also, if a CFC is a partner in a partnership, the limitation applies to the partnership in the same manner as if the CFC is a domestic C corporation.

The limit applies to a foreign corporation that is a CFC within the meaning of Code Sec. 957 if the foreign corporation has at least one U.S. shareholder that owns, directly or indirectly, stock of the foreign corporation under Code Sec. 958(a) (i.e., an applicable CFC). Thus, a CFC with business interest expense applies the limit to subpart F income under Code Sec. 952 and tested income under the Code Sec. 951A(c)(2)(A) global intangible low-taxed income (GILTI) rules. The disallowance and carryforward of a deduction of a foreign corporation's business interest expense does not affect whether and when the business interest expense reduces the corporation's earnings and profits (Proposed Reg. § 1.163(j)-1(e)).

Instead of determining the Code Sec. 163(j) limit for each CFC on a CFC-by-CFC basis, an election may be made to apply an alternative method that treats related CFCs as a group. The alternative method limits the business interest expense of a CFC group member to the amount of the CFC group member's allocable share of the CFC group's applicable net business interest expense (Proposed Reg. § 1.163(j)-7(b)(3)).

**Effectively connected income.** The business interest deduction limit of Code Sec. 163(j) applies to a nonresident alien or foreign corporation that is *not* an applicable CFC that has income effectively connected with a U.S. trade or business. However, the Code Sec. 163(j) rules are modified since these foreign persons are only taxed on their effectively connected income (ECI) (Proposed Reg. § 1.163(j)-8).

▶ **Effective date.** The amendments made by this section apply to tax years beginning after December 31, 2017 (Act Sec. 13301(c) of the Tax Cuts and Jobs Act (P.L. 115-97)).

— Act Sec. 13301(a) of the Tax Cuts and Jobs Act (P.L. 115-97), amending Code Sec. 163(j);

— Act Sec. 13301(b), adding Code Sec. 381(c)(20), adding Code Sec. 382(d)(3), and amending Code Sec. 382(k)(1);

— Act Sec. 13301(c), providing the effective date.

# ¶515  Net Operating Losses (NOLs)

## SUMMARY OF NEW LAW

Net operating losses (NOLs) arising in a tax year ending after 2017 are generally not allowed to be carried back but may only be carried forward indefinitely. However, the five-year carryback period for farming losses is reduced to two years and a two-year carryback and 20-year carryforward period is retained for insurance companies other than life insurance companies. An NOL arising in a tax year beginning after 2017 may only reduce 80 percent of taxable income in a carryback or carryforward tax year. The taxable income limitation does not apply to non-life insurance companies.

## BACKGROUND

A net operating loss ("NOL") generally means the amount by which a taxpayer's business deductions exceed its gross income. In general, an NOL is carried back two years and then carried forward 20 years to offset taxable income in the carryback and carryforward years. Extended carryback periods apply to the following types of losses:

- three years for an NOL of an individual arising from a fire, storm, shipwreck, other casualty, or theft (Code Sec. 172(b)(1)(E)(ii)(I));

- three years for an NOL of a small business or taxpayer engaged in farming if the loss is attributable to a federally declared disaster (Code Sec. 172(b)(1)(E)(ii)(II) and (III));

- five years in the case of a farming loss (Code Sec. 172(b)(1)(F) and (h)); and

- 10-years in the case of a specified liability loss (Code Sec. 172(b)(1)(C) and (f)).

**Farming loss.** A farming loss is the smaller of (1) the amount that would be the NOL for the tax year if only income and deductions attributable to farming businesses were taken into account, or (2) the NOL for the tax year. A taxpayer may elect to waive the five-year carryback for a farming loss. In this case, the two-year carryback period generally applies. For ordering purposes, the farming loss is treated as a separate NOL to be taken into account after the remaining portion of the NOL for the tax year (Code Sec. 172(h)(1).

**Specified liability loss.** A specified liability loss is the portion of an NOL that is attributable to product liability or arises out of satisfaction of a liability under federal or state law requiring land reclamation, nuclear power plant decommissioning, drilling platform dismantling, environmental remediation, or a payment under any workers' compensation act (Code Sec. 172(f)(1)(B)(i)).

**REITS.** Real estate investment trust NOLs may not be carried back but may be carried forward 20 years (Code Sec. 172(b)(1)(B)).

**Corporate equity reduction interest loss (CERT).** A C corporation may not carry back a portion of its NOL if $1 million or more of interest expense is incurred in a "major stock acquisition" of another corporation or in an "excess distribution" by the corporation (Code Sec. 172(b)(1)(D) and (g)). The amount subject to the limitation is

## BACKGROUND

the lesser of: (1) the corporation's deductible interest expense allocable to the CERT, or (2) the amount by which the corporation's interest expense for the current tax year exceeds the average interest expense for the three tax years preceding the tax year in which the CERT occurs.

**Computation of NOL.** Code Sec. 172(d) lists various modifications that corporate and non-corporate taxpayers must make in computing taxable income for purposes of determining the NOL for a tax year. For this purpose, the domestic production activities deduction is not allowed (Code Sec. 172(d)(7)).

## NEW LAW EXPLAINED

**NOL deduction limited; carryback eliminated and unlimited carryforwward period provided.**—Net operating losses (NOLs) arising in tax years beginning after 2017 may only reduce 80 percent of a taxpayer's taxable income in carryback and carryforward years. The generally applicable two-year carryback period, as well as the longer carryback periods for special types of losses, are eliminated, effective for NOLs arising in tax years ending after 2017. NOLs, however, may be carried forward indefinitely. Exceptions described below apply to farming losses and losses of casualty and property insurance companies (Code Sec. 172, as amended by the Tax Cuts and Jobs Act (P.L. 115-97).

> **Caution:** The effective date provides that the provision limiting an NOL deduction to 80 percent of taxable income is effective for NOLs arising in tax years *beginning* after 2017 (Act Sec. 13302(e)(1) of P.L. 115-97). On the other hand, the provision eliminating the two-year carryback period is effective for NOLs arising in tax years *ending* after 2017 (Act Sec. 13302(e)(2) of P.L. 115-97). The difference is important to a 2017/2018 fiscal year filer. An NOL arising in the 2017/2018 fiscal-year may not be carried back two years since it arose in a tax year ending after 2017. However, the same NOL is not subject to the 80 percent of taxable income limitation because the NOL did not arise in a tax year beginning after 2017.

> The committee report to the 2017 Tax Cuts Act states that the effective date for both the 80 percent taxable income limitation and the elimination of the two-year carryback and twenty-year carryforward period is for NOLs arising in tax years beginning after 2017 (Conference Report on H.R. 1, Tax Cuts and Jobs Act (H. Rept. 115-466)).

> According to the Joint Committee on Taxation's report to the 2017 Tax Cuts Act (commonly referred to as the Bluebook), a technical correction may be necessary to reflect that the changes to NOL carryovers and carrybacks apply to losses arising in tax years beginning after December 31, 2017. The intent is that NOLs arising in tax years beginning before January 1, 2018, remain subject to prior law. Accordingly, such NOLs are not subject to the 80-percent limitation, and remain subject to the 20-year carryover limitation and to the prior-law carryback rules (General Explanation of Public Law 115-97 (JCS-1-18)).

> The 2018 instructions to Form 1045, Application for Tentative Refund (Individuals) and instructions to Form 1139, Corporate Application for Tentative Refund,

## NEW LAW EXPLAINED

both indicate in the "What's New" section that the termination of the two-year carryback and 20-year carryforward applies to NOLS arising in tax years ending after 2017. Thus, the instructions are in accordance with the law as enacted.

**NOL deduction limited to 80 percent of taxable income.** Effective for net operating losses that arise in tax years beginning after December 31, 2017, the NOL deduction for a tax year is limited to the lesser of:

- the aggregate of net operating loss carryovers (i.e., carryforwards) to the tax year, plus NOL carrybacks to the tax year; or
- 80 percent of taxable income computed for the tax year without regard to the NOL deduction allowed for the tax year (Code Sec. 172(a), as amended by the 2017 Tax Cuts Act (P.L. 115-97)).

> **Comment:** Since the 80-percent taxable income limit applies to losses arising in tax years beginning after December 31, 2017, NOL carrybacks and carryforwards attributable to losses that arose in tax years beginning before January 1, 2018, are not subject to the 80-percent limitation (Act Sec. 13302(e)(1) of the 2017 Tax Cuts Act).

> **Caution:** The Joint Committee on Taxation's report to the 2017 Tax Cuts Act (the Bluebook) explains how a taxpayer with NOL carryovers to a tax year from both tax years beginning before 2018 ("pre-2018 NOL carryovers' ') and tax years beginning after 2017 ("post-2017 NOL carryovers' ') computes its tax liability and provides an example (below) illustrating the rules for carryovers of pre-2018 NOLs and post-2017 NOLs. First, the taxpayer is entitled to an NOL deduction in the amount of its pre-2018 NOL carryovers without limitation. Second, the taxpayer is entitled to an additional NOL deduction equal to the lesser of (i) its post-2017 NOL carryovers, or (ii) 80 percent of the excess (if any) of the taxpayer's taxable income (before any NOL deduction attributable to post- 2017 NOL carryovers) over the NOL deduction attributable to pre- 2018 NOL carryovers. A technical correction may be necessary to reflect this intent (General Explanation of Public Law 115-97 (JCS-1-18)).

> **Example:** A taxpayer (a calendar-year corporation) has $120 of pre-2018 NOL carryovers and $70 of post-2017 NOL carryovers to 2019. In 2019, the taxpayer has $100 of taxable income (before any NOL deduction). The taxpayer is entitled to an NOL deduction equal to the sum of (i) its pre-2018 NOL carryovers, and (ii) the lesser of its post-2017 carryovers or 80 percent of its taxable income in 2019 (determined without regard to the NOL deduction attributable to post-2017 NOL carryovers). In this case, the taxpayer's pre-2018 NOL carryovers ($120) exceed its pre-NOL taxable income ($100), so the taxpayer is entitled to an NOL deduction fully offsetting its taxable income. The taxpayer will have $20 of pre-2018 NOL carryovers and $70 of post-2017 NOL carryovers to 2020.
>
> If, in 2020, the taxpayer again has $100 of taxable income (before any NOL deduction), the taxpayer is entitled to an NOL deduction equal to the sum of (i) its pre-2018 NOL carryovers, and (ii) the lesser of its post-2017 carryovers or 80

# NEW LAW EXPLAINED

percent of its taxable income in 2020 (determined without regard to the NOL deduction attributable to post-2017 NOL carryovers). In this case, the taxpayer's NOL deduction is $20 plus the lesser of $70 or 80 percent of the taxpayer's taxable income (before any NOL deduction attributable to post-2017 NOL carryovers). 80 percent of taxable income computed without regard to post-2017 NOL carryovers is $64 (80 percent of $80 ($100 taxable income less the NOL deduction of $20 attributable to pre-2018 NOL carryovers)). Thus, for 2020, the taxpayer is entitled to an NOL deduction of $84 ($20 plus $64). The taxpayer will have $6 ($70 less $64) of post- 2017 NOL carryovers to 2021 (General Explanation of Public Law 115-97 (JCS-1-18)).

In determining the amount of a NOL that remains available for carryback or carryforward, the taxable income for any prior tax year to which the NOL was carried is not treated as exceeding 80 percent (Code Sec. 172(b)(2), as amended by the 2017 Tax Cuts Act).

*Taxable income of REIT.* In the case of a real estate investment trust (REIT), the 80 percent taxable income limitation is determined by reference to "real estate investment trust taxable income" as defined in Code Sec. 857(b)(2) but without regard to the dividends paid deduction (Code Sec. 172(d)(6)(C), as added by 2017 Tax Cuts Act).

**NOL carrybacks generally eliminated and carryforwards allowed indefinitely.** The carryback of NOLs is generally eliminated, except for NOLs attributable to farm losses and certain insurance companies as described below. The 20-year limitation on carryforwards is also eliminated and NOLs may be carried forward indefinitely (Code Sec. 172(b)(1)(A), as amended by 2017 Tax Cuts Act). This change is effective for NOLs arising in tax years ending after December 31, 2017 (Act Sec. 13302(e)(2) of the 2017 Tax Cuts Act).

> **Caution:** A technical correction may be necessary to reflect that the changes to NOL carryovers and carrybacks apply to losses arising in tax years beginning after December 31, 2017. The intent is that NOLs arising in tax years beginning before January 1, 2018, remain subject to prior law. Accordingly, such NOLs remain subject to the 20-year carryover limitation and to the prior-law carryback rules (General Explanation of Public Law 115-97 (JCS-1-18)).

As a result of the elimination of NOL carrybacks except for NOLs attributable to farm losses and certain insurance companies, the special carryback rules that apply to the following have also been eliminated:

- real estate investment trusts (Code Sec. 172(b)(1)(B), stricken by the 2017 Tax Cuts Act);
- specified liability losses (Code Sec. 172(b)(1)(C), stricken by the 2017 Tax Cuts Act);
- limitation on carryback of excess interest loss in a corporate equity reduction transaction (CERT) (Code Sec. 179(b)(1)(D), stricken by the 2017 Tax Cuts Act);
- certain casualty and disaster losses of individuals, small businesses, and farmers (Code Sec. 172(b)(1)(E), stricken by the 2017 Tax Cuts Act);
- farming losses (Code Sec. 172(b)(1)(F), stricken by the 2017 Tax Cuts Act).

## NEW LAW EXPLAINED

**Two-year carryback for farming losses.** The five-year carryback period for farming losses is replaced with a two-year carryback period (Code Sec. 172(b)(1)(B), as added by the 2017 Tax Cuts Act). This provision is effective for NOLs arising in tax years ending after December 31, 2017 (Act Sec. 13302(e)(2) of the 2017 Tax Cuts Act).

> **Caution:** A technical correction may be necessary to reflect that the changes to NOL carryovers and carrybacks apply to losses arising in tax years beginning after December 31, 2017 (General Explanation of Public Law 115-97 (JCS-1-18)). See "Caution Note", above.

The example, below, illustrates the interaction of the 80-percent limitation and the two-year carryback of farming losses.

> **Example:** In 2018, a calendar-year taxpayer has a $300 farming loss. The taxpayer has no other NOLs and is not limited by Code Sec. 461(l). Because the new law allows a special two-year carryback in the case of certain farming losses, the taxpayer may carry back the farming loss to 2016 or 2017. However, the NOL deduction for such carryback year will be limited to 80 percent of taxable income (determined without regard to the NOL deduction) for such tax year. If the taxpayer had $100 of taxable income in 2016 and $200 of taxable income in 2017 (both without regard to any NOL deduction), the taxpayer is entitled to an $80 NOL deduction in 2016 (80 percent of $100) and a $160 NOL deduction in 2017 (80 percent of $200). The taxpayer will have $60 of post-2017 NOL carryovers to 2019 (i.e., the $300 2018 NOL less (i) the $80 2016 NOL carryback and (ii) the $160 2017 NOL carryback (General Explanation of Public Law 115-97 (JCS-1-18)).

> **Comment:** The definition of a farming loss remains unchanged and taxpayers may continue to waive the carryback period (Code Sec. 172(b)(1)(B)(ii) and (iv), as added by the 2017 Tax Cuts Act). Also, as under prior law, where a NOL for a tax year consists of both a farming loss and a non-farming loss, the two losses are treated separately and the farming loss is taken into account in carryback and carryforward years after the non-farming loss (Code Sec. 172(b)(1)(B)(iii), as added by the 2017 Tax Cuts Act). This rule was previously provided by a cross-reference to a similar rule for specified liability losses (Code Sec. 172(f)(5), stricken by the 2017 Tax Cuts Act).

**Two-year carryback and 20-year carryforward for casualty and property insurance company losses.** The NOL of an insurance company other than a life insurance company (e.g., a property and casualty insurance company) may continue to be carried back two years and forward twenty years (Code Sec. 172(b)(1)(C), as added by the 2017 Tax Cuts Act). In addition, the 80 percent taxable income limitation does not apply to a non-life insurance company. Thus, the deductible amount of a non-life insurance company's NOL for a tax year is the sum of the NOL carryovers to the tax year, plus the NOL carrybacks to the tax year (Code Sec. 172(f), as added by the 2017 Tax Cuts Act).

**¶515**

## NEW LAW EXPLAINED

**Comment:** The two-carryback and 20-year carryforward period are retained for insurance companies other then life insurance companies. In addition, the 80 percent of taxable income limitation does not apply to these companies. The operations loss deduction for life insurance companies is repealed and life insurance companies will claim NOLs in a manner similar to other corporations under Code Sec. 172 (i.e., no carryback, indefinite carryforward, and 80 percent taxable income limitation on deduction). The NOL deduction of a life insurance company is determined by treating the NOL for any tax year generally as the excess of the life insurance deductions for such tax year, over the life insurance gross income for such tax year.

**Determination of remaining carryback or carryforward.** In determining the portion of a NOL that arose in a tax year beginning after 2017 that remains for carryback or carryforward, the new 80 percent taxable income limitation applies. Consequently, the portion of such a NOL that remains available for carryback or carryforward to another tax year is the excess, if any, of the amount of the loss over the sum of 80 percent of the taxable income (computed with certain of the modifications described in Code Sec. 172(d)) for each of the tax years to which the loss was previously carried (Code Sec. 172(b)(2), as amended by 2017 Tax Cuts Act).

**Modifications to taxable income in computing NOL for loss year.** A taxpayer's NOL for the tax year is computed in the same manner as taxable income or loss with certain modifications. Effective for tax years beginning after December 31, 2017, the 20-percent deduction for qualified business income of a passthrough entity under Code Sec. 199A (see ¶330) and the deduction for foreign-derived intangible income (FDII) under Code Sec. 250 (¶735) are not taken into account for this purpose (Code Sec. 172(d)(8) and (d)(9), as added by the 2017 Tax Cuts Act). The domestic production activities deduction under Code Sec. 199 is removed from the list of deductions that may not be claimed in computing the NOL for a loss year as the deduction has been repealed effective for tax years beginning after 2017 (see ¶530) (Code Sec. 172(d)(7), stricken by the 2017 Tax Cuts Act).

▶ **Effective date.** The amendments made by this section limiting net operating losses (NOLs) to 80 percent of taxable income, determining the amount of remaining carryback or carryforward, and exempting life insurance companies from the 80 percent of taxable income limitation apply to losses arising in tax years beginning after December 31, 2017 (Act Sec. 13302(e)(1) of the Tax Cuts and Jobs Act (P.L. 115-97)).

The amendments removing the Code Sec. 199 manufacturing deduction from and adding the 20 percent deduction for qualified business income (Code Sec. 199A) and the deduction for foreign-derived intangible Income (Code Sec. 250) to the list of deductions not taken into account in computing an NOL are effective for tax years beginning after 2017.

The amendments eliminating the carryback periods, making the carryforward period indefinite, reducing the farming loss carryback period from five years to two years, and allowing a two-year carryback and twenty-year carryforward for the NOL of an insurance company apply to NOLs arising in tax years ending after December 31, 2017 (Act Sec. 13302(e)(2) of the 2017 Tax Cuts Act).

**Caution:** A technical correction may be required to reflect the intent that the amendments allowing indefinite carryovers and modifying carrybacks apply to

## NEW LAW EXPLAINED

losses arising in tax years beginning after December 31, 2017 (General Explanation of Public Law 115-97 (JCS-1-18)). See "Caution Notes" above.

**No significant guidance related to this provision has been issued.**

— Act Sec. 13302(a) of the Tax Cuts and Jobs Act (P.L. 115-97), amending Code Sec. 172(a), (b)(2), and (d)(6);

— Act Sec. 13302(b), amending Code Sec. 172(b)(1)(A) and striking Code Sec. 172(b)(1)(B) through (F)

— Act Sec. 13302(c), adding Code Sec. 172(b)(1)(B) and striking Code Sec. 172(f), (g), and (h);

— Act Sec. 13302(d), adding Code Sec. 172(b)(1)(C) and (f);

— Act Sec. 13302(e), providing the effective date for the preceding provisions;

— Act Sec. 13305(b)(3), striking Code Sec. 172(d)(7);

— Act 13305(c), providing the effective date for the preceding provision;

— Act Sec. 11011(d)(1) adding Code Sec. 172(d)(8)

— Act Sec. 11011(e), providing the effective date of the preceding provision.

— Act Sec. 14202(b)(1), adding Code Sec. 172(d)(9)

— Act Sec. 14202(c), providing the effective date of the preceding provision.

# ¶520 Excess Business Losses for Noncorporate Taxpayers

## SUMMARY OF NEW LAW

Excess business losses of noncorporate taxpayers are not allowed for tax years beginning in 2018 through 2025. Any disallowed excess business loss is treated as a net operating loss (NOL) carryover to the following tax year. However, the passive activity loss rules apply before application of the excess business loss rules.

## BACKGROUND

A taxpayer's method of accounting determines when deductions and credits can be taken (Code Sec. 461(a)). Ordinarily, taxpayers on the cash method take deductions and credits in the year in which they are paid. Accrual-method taxpayers take deductions or credits in the year in which the items are accrued or incurred. Items accrue when: (1) all events have occurred that fix the fact of liability and the liability can be determined with reasonable accuracy (the "all-events test"), and (2) economic performance has occurred (Code Sec. 461(h)). A number of special timing rules and exceptions may also apply to taxes for accrual-method taxpayers, contested liabilities, prepaid interest for cash-method taxpayers, amounts accrued by reason of death of an accrual-method taxpayer, tax shelters, excess farm losses, and dividends or interest paid by mutual savings banks.

## BACKGROUND

**Passive activity losses (PALs).** Under the passive activity rules, losses and expenses attributable to passive activities may be deducted only from income attributable to passive activities (Code Sec. 469). The effect of this treatment is to prohibit the use of passive losses to offset nonpassive income. A passive activity is any trade or business activity in which the taxpayer owns an interest but does not materially participate. Passive activities generally include rental activities, regardless of whether the taxpayer materially participates in the activity. The passive activity rules apply to individuals, trusts, estates, closely held C corporations, and personal service corporations. The passive activity rules do not apply to S corporations and partnerships, but do apply to losses and credits that these entities pass through to their respective shareholders and partners.

A passive activity loss is the amount by which passive activity deductions from all passive activities exceed passive activity gross income from all passive activities for the tax year (Code Sec. 469(d)(1)). A taxpayer's passive activity loss for the tax year is disallowed and may not be deducted against other income. The disallowed passive activity loss is carried forward until the taxpayer has available passive activity income to offset (Code Sec. 469(b)).

**Excess farm losses.** Taxpayers other than C corporations that receive applicable subsidies, such as Commodity Credit Corporation (CCC) loans and agricultural program payments, cannot deduct their excess farm losses (Code Sec. 461(j)). Disallowed losses can be carried forward to the next tax year. The disallowance of excess farm losses is applied before the rules that limit passive activity losses.

An "excess farm loss" is the excess of the taxpayer's aggregate deductions for the tax year that are attributable to farming businesses, over the applicable threshold amount for the tax year in which the farming business receives applicable subsidies. The threshold amount is the greater of: $300,000 ($150,000 for a married taxpayer filing a separate return) or the taxpayer's aggregate net farm income for the five preceding tax years.

**Net operating losses.** A net operating loss (NOL) for the tax year is the excess of allowable deductions over gross income, with certain modifications (Code Sec. 172). If a taxpayer has an NOL for the current tax year, no deduction is allowed in the year the loss is incurred. Instead, the taxpayer carries the NOL to other tax years as a deduction against taxable income in those years. The NOL deduction amount may not exceed the amount of taxable income for the year of the deduction.

### NEW LAW EXPLAINED

**Excess business losses of noncorporate taxpayers disallowed.**—Excess business losses of noncorporate taxpayers are not allowed for tax years beginning after December 31, 2017, and before January 1, 2026 (Code Sec. 461(l)(1)(B), as added by the Tax Cuts and Jobs Act (P.L. 115-97)). Any excess business loss that is disallowed is treated as a net operating loss (NOL) carryover to the following tax year (Code Sec. 461(l)(2), as added by the 2017 Tax Cuts Act). However, noncorporate taxpayers must apply the passive activity loss rules before application of the rules for excess business losses (Code Sec. 461(l)(6), as added by the 2017 Tax Cuts Act).

## NEW LAW EXPLAINED

> **Comment:** For losses arising in tax years beginning after December 31, 2017, an NOL may only reduce 80 percent of taxable income in a carryback or carryforward tax year. See ¶ 515 for further details on the modified NOL rules.

An "excess business loss" is the excess, if any, of:

- the taxpayer's aggregate deductions for the tax year from the taxpayer's trades or businesses, determined without regard to whether or not such deductions are disallowed for such tax year under the excess business loss limitation; over

- the sum of:

  — the taxpayer's aggregate gross income or gain for the tax year from such trades or businesses, plus

  — $250,000, adjusted annually for inflation ($255,000 in 2019) (200 percent of the $250,000 amount in the case of a joint return) ($510,000 in 2019) (Code Sec. 461(l)(3)(A), as added by the 2017 Tax Cuts Act).

The $250,000 amount above is adjusted annually for inflation for tax years beginning after December 31, 2018, using the Chained Consumer Price Index for All Urban Consumers (C-CPI-U) in the cost-of-living adjustment (see ¶ 125) (Code Sec. 461(l)(3)(B), as added by the 2017 Tax Cuts Act).

> **Comment:** A technical correction may be needed to clarify that excess business losses are determined without taking into consideration deductions from Code Secs. 172 or 199A. In addition, a technical correction may be needed to reflect that the calculation does not include any income or deductions attributable to the taxpayer's work as an employee (General Explanation of Public Law 115–97 Prepared by the Staff of the Joint Committee on Taxation (December 2018), FN 208 and 209).

> **Example:** For 2018, Ned Brown has $1 million of gross income and $1.4 million of deductions from a retail business that is not a passive activity. His excess business loss is $150,000 ($1,400,000 – ($1,000,000 + $250,000)). Brown must treat his excess business loss of $150,000 as an NOL carryover to 2019.

> **Comment:** During the period that excess business losses are disallowed (tax years beginning after December 31, 2017, and before January 1, 2026), the limit on excess farm losses of noncorporate taxpayers will not apply (Code Sec. 461(l)(1)(A), as added by the 2017 Tax Cuts Act).

**Partnerships and S corporations.** For partnerships and S corporations, the limit on excess business losses is applied at the partner or shareholder level (Code Sec. 461(l)(4), as added by the 2017 Tax Cuts Act; Conference Report on H.R. 1, Tax Cuts and Jobs Act (H. Rept. 115-466)). Each partner's distributive share or each S corporation shareholder's pro rata share of items of income, gain, deduction, or loss of the partnership or S corporation is taken into account by the partner or shareholder in applying the excess business loss rules to the partner's or shareholder's tax year with or within which the partnership's or S corporation's tax year ends.

**¶520**

## NEW LAW EXPLAINED

**Reporting requirements.** The IRS is authorized to issue additional reporting requirements that it determines are necessary to carry out the purposes of the excess business loss rules (Code Sec. 461(l)(5), as added by the 2017 Tax Cuts Act)).

▶ **Effective date.** The amendments made by this section apply to tax years beginning after December 31, 2017 (Act Sec. 11012(b) of the Tax Cuts and Jobs Act (P.L. 115-97)).

**Other than inflation adjusted amounts for 2019, no significant guidance related to this provision has been issued.**

— Act Sec. 11012(a) of the Tax Cuts and Jobs Act (P.L. 115-97), adding Code Sec. 461(l);

— Act Sec. 11012(b), providing the effective date.

# ¶525 Research and Experimental Expenditures

## SUMMARY OF NEW LAW

Research and experimental expenditures paid or incurred in tax year beginning after 2021 generally must be amortized ratably over five years. Any amount paid or incurred in connection with the development of any software is treated as a research or experimental expenditure for this purposes of this amortization provision. A 15-year amortization period applies to research or experimental expenditures attributable to foreign research.

## BACKGROUND

A taxpayer may use one of three alternative methods to account for research and experimental expenditures: (1) currently deduct the expenditures in the year in which they are paid or incurred; (2) elect to treat the expenditures as deferred expenses, amortizable over a period of at least 60 months beginning in the month that benefits are first realized from the expenditures; or (3) elect to amortize the expenditures over 10 years beginning in the tax year in which they are paid or incurred (Code Secs. 174 and 59(e)). A taxpayer that fails to account for its research and experimental expenditures using one of these three methods is generally required to capitalize the expenditures (Reg. § 1.174-1).

If the 10-year amortization election is made by a taxpayer other than a corporation, the amortization deduction is claimed in full for alternative minimum tax (AMT) purposes and is not subject to adjustment (Code Sec. 59(e)). In the case of a taxpayer other than a corporation, the Code Sec. 174 deduction is allowed in full for AMT purposes if a taxpayer materially participates in the activity (Code Sec. 56(b)(2)(D)). In the case of a corporation, the research deduction is allowed in full for AMT purposes even if the 10-year amortization election is not made.

## BACKGROUND

No deduction is generally allowable for expenditures for the acquisition or improvement of land or of depreciable or depletable property used in connection with any research or experimentation (Code Sec. 174(f)). In addition, no deduction is allowed for research expenses incurred for the purpose of ascertaining the existence, location, extent, or quality of any deposit of ore or other mineral, including oil and gas (Code Sec. 174(d)).

A credit is also allowed for increased research and experimental expenses (Code Sec. 41).

## NEW LAW EXPLAINED

**Five-year amortization of research expenditures; 15-years for foreign research expenditures.**—Amounts paid or incurred for specified research or experimental expenditures in tax years beginning after December 31, 2021, generally must be amortized ratably over five years (Code Sec. 174(a), as amended by Tax Cuts and Jobs Act (P.L. 115-97)). The amortization period begins at the mid-point of the tax year in which the expenditures are paid or incurred.

> **Comment:** The rule that allows taxpayers to currently deduct research and experimental expenditures is eliminated after 2021. Similarly, the rule that taxpayers may elect an amortization period 60 months or greater beginning when benefits are first realized is eliminated after 2021. The rule in Code Sec. 59(e) which allows a taxpayer to elect 10-year amortization of research and experimental expenditures beginning in the year the expenditures are paid or incurred remains available after 2021, but the specific reference in Code Sec. 174 has been removed.

> **Planning Note:** Taxpayers with significant losses have often elected 10-year amortization to reduce amounts that could be subject to expiration under the 20-year net operating loss (NOL) carryfoward limitation even if they had no alternative minimum tax (AMT) liability. However, NOLs arising in tax years ending after December 31, 2017, may be carried forward indefinitely (see ¶515). Thus, taxpayers are less likely to elect 10-year amortization.

Amounts paid or incurred for specified research or experimental expenditures after December 31, 2021, attributable to foreign research must be amortized ratably over 15 years (Code Sec. 174(a)(2), as amended by the 2017 Tax Cuts Act). Foreign research for this purpose is defined by reference to Code Sec. 41(d)(4)(F) to mean any research conducted outside the United States, the Commonwealth of Puerto Rico, or any possession of the United States. Similar to the general five-year amortization period, the 15-year amortization period for foreign research begins at the mid-point of the tax year in which the expenditures are paid or incurred.

> **Comment:** There is no restriction on the deduction of research or experimental expenditures attributable to foreign research if paid or accrued before 2022.

**Specified research or experimental expenditures.** The five-year amortization period (15-year period for foreign research) applies to specified research or experimental expenditures which are simply research or experimental expenditures paid or in-

## NEW LAW EXPLAINED

curred by the taxpayer during a tax year in connection with the taxpayer's trade or business (Code Sec. 174(b), as amended by the 2017 Tax Cuts Act).

> **Comment:** Research and experimental expenditures are defined in Reg. § 1.174-2.

Any amount paid or incurred in connection with the development of any software is treated as a research or experimental expenditure for purposes of this amortization provision (Code Sec. 174(c)(3), as added by the 2017 Tax Cuts Act).

> **Comment:** Under current law, the IRS allows a taxpayer to treat all software development expenses as currently deductible even if such expenses do not otherwise meet the requirements of Code Sec. 174 (Rev. Proc. 2000-50). However, no portion of software development costs paid or incurred in tax years beginning after 2021 are currently deductible and all such expenses must be amortized as research expenditures over five years (15-years for foreign research).

Expenditures for acquiring land, acquiring or improving depreciable property, or acquiring property subject to a depletion allowance continue to not be treated as research expenditures for this purpose even if used in connection with research and experimentation and depreciation and depletion allowances on such property are considered research expenditures (Code Sec. 174(c)(1), as amended by the 2017 Tax Cuts Act). Also, amounts paid or incurred for the purpose of determining the existence, location, extent, or quality of an ore, mineral, or oil and gas deposit continue to not be treated as research expenditures (Code Sec. 174(c)(2), as amended the 2017 Tax Cuts Act).

**Amortization after disposition.** Taxpayers must continue to amortize research or experimental expenditures under these rules even if the property with respect to which the expenditures were paid or incurred is disposed, retired, or abandoned during the five-year amortization period (15-year period for foreign research) (Code Sec. 174(d), as amended by the 2017 Tax Cuts Act).

> **Comment:** Under current law, taxpayers may claim a deduction for the unamortized basis upon a disposition, retirement, or abandonment.

**Change in method of accounting.** The switch to a five-year amortization period (15-year period for foreign research) is a change in accounting method (Act Sec. 13206(b) of the 2017 Tax Cuts Act). However, it is not be necessary for taxpayers to file an accounting method change and no Code Sec. 481(a) adjustment is required or allowed. Instead, the changes only apply on a cut-off basis to research or experimental expenditures paid or incurred in tax years beginning after December 31, 2021. The change is treated as initiated by taxpayers and as made with the consent with the IRS.

**Coordination with research credit.** Effective for expenditures paid or incurred in tax years beginning after 2021, the amount chargeable to capital account for the taxable year for qualified research expenses or basic research expenses is reduced by the excess (if any) the excess (if any) of the research credit allowed for the tax year over the amount allowable as an amortization deduction for the tax year as qualified research expenses or basic research expenses (Code Sec. 280C(d)(1), as amended by the 2017 Tax Cuts Act)). A similar rule applies under current law.

In a conforming amendment, the definition of qualified research for purposes of the research credit (Code Sec. 41) is adjusted to mean research with respect to which

## NEW LAW EXPLAINED

expenditures paid or incurred in tax years beginning after 2021 are treated as specified research or experimental expenditures under Code Sec. 174. In other words, qualified research relates to research costs which must be amortized over five-years (15-years for foreign research (Code Sec. 41(d)(1)(A), as amended by the 2017 Tax Cuts Act). For amounts paid or incurred before 2022, qualified research is defined by reference to expenditures which may be currently deducted under Code Sec. 174. No change is made to the additional requirements for the research credit, such as the requirement that the research be undertaken for the purpose of discovering information which technological in nature and intended to be useful in the development of a new or improved business component of the taxpayer.

▶ **Effective date.** The amendments made by this section apply to amounts paid or incurred in tax years beginning after December 31, 2021 (Act Sec. 13206(e) of the Tax Cuts and Jobs Act (P.L. 115-97)).

   **No significant guidance related to this provision has been issued.**

— Act Sec. 13206(a) of the Tax Cuts and Jobs Act (P.L. 115-97), amending Code Sec. 174;

— Act Sec. 13206(b) providing change of accounting method rules;

— Act Sec. 13206(d) amending Code Sec. 41(d)(1)(A) and Code Sec. 280C(c);

— Act Sec. 13206(e), providing the effective date.

# ¶530  Domestic Production Activities Deduction (DPAD)

## SUMMARY OF NEW LAW

The domestic production activities deduction (DPAD) under Code Sec. 199 is repealed for tax years beginning after 2017.

## BACKGROUND

The domestic production activities deduction (DPAD) is generally equal to nine percent of the lesser of qualified production activities income or taxable income (adjusted gross income for individuals, estates, and trusts) (Code Sec. 199). A taxpayer's qualified production activities income (QPAI) is its domestic production gross receipts (DPGR), reduced by allocable cost of goods sold and other deductions, expenses, and losses.

DPGR are generally gross receipts of the taxpayer that are derived from: (1) any sale, exchange, or other disposition, or any lease, rental, or license, of qualifying production property that was manufactured, produced, grown or extracted by the taxpayer in whole or in significant part within the United States; (2) any sale, exchange, or other disposition, or any lease, rental, or license, of qualified film produced by the taxpayer; (3) any sale, exchange, or other disposition, or any lease, rental, or license, of electricity, natural gas, or potable water produced by the taxpayer in the United

## BACKGROUND

States; (4) construction of real property performed in the United States by a taxpayer in the ordinary course of a construction trade or business; or (5) engineering or architectural services performed in the United States for the construction of real property located in the United States.

The DPAD for a tax year is limited to 50 percent of the W-2 wages paid by the taxpayer to its employees for the calendar year ending during the tax year that are properly allocable to the taxpayer's DPGR (the wages that the taxpayer deducts in calculating its QPAI).

## NEW LAW EXPLAINED

**Domestic production activities deduction repealed.**—The domestic production activities deduction (DPAD) is repealed for tax years beginning after December 31, 2017 (Code Sec. 199, as stricken by the Tax Cuts and Jobs Act (P.L. 115-97)).

▶ **Effective date.** The amendment made by this section applies to tax years beginning after December 31, 2017 (Act 13305(c) of the Tax Cuts and Jobs Act (P.L. 115-97)).

**No significant guidance related to this provision has been issued.**

— Act Sec. 13305(a) of the Tax Cuts and Jobs Act (P.L. 115-97), striking Code Sec. 199;

— Act Sec. 13305(b), amending Code Secs. 74(d)(2)(B), 86(b)(2)(A), 135(c)(4)(A), 137(b)(3)(A), 170(b)(2)(D), 219(g)(3)(A)(ii), 221(b)(2)(C), 222(b)(2)(C), 246(b)(1), 469(i)(3)(F)(iii), 613(a), and 613A(d)(1), and striking Code Sec. 172(d)(7);

— Act Sec. 13305(c), providing the effective date.

# ORDINARY AND NECESSARY EXPENSES

## ¶535 Employer's Deduction for Entertainment, Commuting Benefits, and Meals

### SUMMARY OF NEW LAW

Business expense deductions are eliminated for most entertainment costs and commuting benefits after 2017, as well as certain employer-provided meal expenses after 2025.

### BACKGROUND

Employers and other taxpayers generally may deduct ordinary and necessary business expenses, including cash and noncash compensation (fringe benefits) paid for services rendered (Code Sec. 162(a)(1)). Special requirements and limits apply to several types of business expense deductions, including entertainment expenses,

## BACKGROUND

traveling and commuting benefits, and expenses for employer-provided meals for employees (Code 274).

**Entertainment expenses.** Expenses for entertainment, or for a facility used in connection with entertainment, are generally deductible only to the extent: (1) they are directly related to the active conduct of the taxpayer's trade or business, or (2) they are associated with the active conduct of the taxpayer's trade or business, and the expense item directly precedes or follows a substantial and bone fide business discussion (Code Sec. 274(a)(1)).

Entertainment includes any activity of a type that is generally considered to constitute entertainment, amusement, or recreation, such as entertaining at night clubs, cocktail lounges, theaters, country clubs, golf and athletic clubs and sporting events, and on hunting, fishing, vacation, and similar trips. Entertainment may include expenses that satisfy personal or family needs, such as food and beverages, a hotel room, or a car (Reg. § 1.274-2(b)). When entertainment expense deductions are disallowed for any portion of a facility, that portion is treated as used for personal, living and family purposes rather than as an asset used in a trade or business (Code Sec. 274(g)). A club is an entertainment facility unless it is used primarily to further the taxpayer's trade or business and the expense item is directly related to the active conduct of that trade or business (Code Sec. 274(a)(2)(C)). Club dues are not deductible (Code Sec. 274(a)(3)).

Deductions for tickets to entertainment and sporting events are subject to two additional rules. First, an expense for seats in a skybox or other luxury box that is leased for more than one event is limited to the sum of the face value of non-luxury box seat tickets for the events. Second, the expense that is taken into account for a ticket to an entertainment event or facility cannot exceed the face value of the ticket (so, for instance, additional payments to scalpers or other resellers are not taken into account). However, this limit does not apply to tickets to a charitable sporting event. A charitable sporting event is one that benefits a Section 501(c)(3) tax-exempt organization, and for which volunteers perform substantially all of the work (Code Sec. 274(l)).

The deduction for entertainment is generally limited to 50 percent of the expense, but there are several exceptions, including: (a) certain entertainment expenses for goods, services, and facilities that are treated as compensation to an employee-recipient; (b) expenses for recreational, social, or similar activities and related facilities primarily for the benefit of employees who are not highly compensated employees; (c) expenses for entertainment available to the general publicers; and (d) entertainment expenses for goods, services, and facilities that are includible in the gross income of a non-employee recipient as compensation for services rendered or as a prize or award (Code Sec. 274(e) and (n)).

Entertainment expense deductions must satisfy strict substantiation requirements. The taxpayer must show (a) the amount of the expense; (b) the time and place of the entertainment; (c) the business purpose of the expense, and (d) the business relationship with the persons entertained (Code Sec. 274(d)).

**Transportation and commuting benefits.** The cost of traveling between an individual's residence and work location is almost always a nondeductible personal com-

¶535

## BACKGROUND

muting expense rather than a deductible business expense (Reg. §§ 1.162-2(e) and 1.262-1(b)(5)). However, an employer may deduct qualified transportation fringe benefits that are excludable from the employee's income (Code Sec. 132(a)(5)).

A qualified transportation fringe is (a) transportation in a commuter highway vehicle (most commonly a van pool) between the employee's residence and workplace; (b) a transit pass; (c) qualified parking; or (d) a qualified bicycle commuting reimbursement. For 2017, the employee's exclusion is limited to $255 per month for aggregated highway vehicle transport and transit passes, or for qualified parking benefits ($260 per month for 2018) (Rev. Proc. 2016-55 and Rev. Proc. 2017-58). The maximum exclusion for bicycle commuting reimbursements is $20 per month (Code Sec. 132(f)). Thus, these transportation fringes can defray a significant amount of an employee's commuting expenses and increase the employer's deductible business expenses, all without increasing the employee's income.

**Employer-provided meals.** In certain situations, an employer may deduct expenses for meals it provides to employees, and the employees may exclude the value of the meals from gross income. For instance, if an employer provides meals to employees and their spouses and dependents for the employer's convenience and on the employer's business premises, the value of the meals is excludable from the employee's income (Code Sec. 119(a)). The employer can claim a business expense deduction, but it is subject to the general rule that limits deductions for food and beverages to 50 percent of the expense (Code Sec. 274(n); IRS Chief Counsel Advice 201151020).

In contrast, employer-provided meals are fully deductible if they are de minimis fringe benefits. De minimis fringes are benefits that are so small as to make accounting for them unreasonable or impractical. An employer's operation of an eating facility for employees is a de minimis fringe benefit if (a) the facility is located at or near the employer's business premises, and (b) revenue derived from the facility normally equals or exceeds its direct operating costs. De minimis fringe benefits are excludable from the employee's income (Code Sec. 132(e)). The employer may deduct the full cost of de minimis fringe meals because they are exempt from the 50-percent limit that applies to most meal expenses (Code Sec. 274(n)(2)(B)).

## NEW LAW EXPLAINED

**Deductions eliminated for some entertainment, meal and transportation expenses.**—Business expense deductions are eliminated or reduced as follows:

- deductions are eliminated for most entertainment expenses after 2017 (Code Sec. 274(a)(1), as amended by the Tax Cuts and Jobs Act (P.L. 115-97));

- deductions are eliminated for transportation and commuting benefits after 2017 (Code Sec. 274(a)(4), as added by the 2017 Tax Cuts Act, and Code Sec. 274(l), as amended by the 2017 Tax Cuts Act); and

- deductions are eliminated after 2025 for employer-provided meals that are excludable from an employee's income or are *de minimis* fringes (Code Sec. 274(o), as added by the 2017 Tax Cuts Act).

## NEW LAW EXPLAINED

**Entertainment expenses.** Entertainment expenses, including expenses for a facility used in connection with entertainment, that are paid or incurred after 2017 generally are not deductible. The exception that allowed deductions for entertainment expenses that were directly related to, or associated with, the active conduct of the taxpayer's trade or business is eliminated (Code Sec. 274(a)(1), as amended by the 2017 Tax Cuts Act).

Since directly-related and associated-with entertainment expenses are not deductible, the following related provisions are also removed: (1) the rules that treated a club as an entertainment facility unless it was used primarily to further, and was directly related to the active conduct of, the taxpayer's trade or business (Code Sec. 274(a)(2)(C), prior to being stricken by the 2017 Tax Cuts Act); (2) the limit on deductions for tickets to entertainment and sporting events, including the special rules for seats in skyboxes and the special exception for charitable sporting events (Code Sec. 274(l)(1)(B), prior to being stricken by the 2017 Tax Cuts Act); and (3) the 50-percent limit on entertainment expense deductions (Code Sec. 274(n)(1)(B), prior to being stricken by the 2017 Tax Cuts Act).

> **Comment:** Some entertainment-related rules do not change. As under current law, club dues and membership costs are not deductible (Code Sec. 274(a)(3)) and when entertainment deductions are disallowed with respect to any portion of a facility, that portion is treated as a personal, rather than a business asset (Code Sec. 274(g)).

> Some entertainment expenses also remain fully deductible, including: (1) certain entertainment expenses for goods, services, and facilities that are treated as compensation to an employee-recipient; (2) expenses for recreational, social, or similar activities and related facilities primarily for the benefit of employees who are not highly compensated employees; (3) expenses for entertainment sold to customers; and (4) entertainment expenses for goods, services, and facilities that are includible in the gross income of a non-employee recipient as compensation for services rendered or as a prize or award (Code Sec. 274(e) and (n)(2)(A)). As under current law, these deductions must satisfy strict substantiation requirements; however, the taxpayer will not have to substantiate the time and place of the entertainment (Code Sec. 274(d), as amended by the 2017 Tax Cuts Act).

> **Comment:** A technical correction may be necessary to clarify that entertainment, amusement, or recreation expenses are not deductible for business meetings described in Code Sec. 274(e)(5) and meeting for organizations described in (Code Sec. 274(e)(6) (General Explanation of Public Law 115–97 (JCS-1-18)), FN 957).

**Meal expenses.** The amendments to Code Sec. 274 do not affect the general rule that 50 percent of food and beverage expenses associated with operating a trade or business are deductible. Such expenses continue to be deductible at a 50 percent rate if: (1) the expense is ordinary and necessary and paid in carrying on a trade or business; (2) the expense is not lavish or extravagant; (3) the taxpayer or an employee is present when the food or beverages are furnished; and (4) the food and beverages are provided to a current or potential business customer, client, consultant, or similar business contact (Notice 2018-76).

¶535

## NEW LAW EXPLAINED

A taxpayer may deduct food and beverages served during an entertainment activity if they are invoiced separately (Notice 2018-76).

> **Example:** A taxpayer invites a business contact to a baseball game. The cost of the tickets is a nondeductible entertainment expense. However, 50 percent of the cost of hot dogs and beverages purchased separately are deductible as meal expenses. If the cost of the tickets includes meals and beverages and the tickets do not separately state the value of the meal and beverages, the entire cost of the tickets is a nondeductible entertainment expense. If the invoice for the game tickets separately states the cost of the food and beverages, 50 percent of the separately stated cost is a deductible meal expense.

**Transportation and commuting benefits.** An employer cannot deduct expenses paid or incurred after December 31, 2017, for any qualified transportation fringe as defined under Code Sec. 132(f) (van pools, transit passes, qualified parking, and bicycle commuting) (Code Sec. 274(a)(4), as added by the 2017 Tax Cuts Act).

> **Comment:** A technical correction may also be necessary to reflect that the determination of costs associated with providing qualified transportation fringes includes pretax salary amounts attributable to any qualified transportation fringe benefit, costs for parking facilities used in connection with qualified parking defined by Code Sec. 132(f)(5)(C), and appropriate allocations of depreciation and other costs for such facilities (General Explanation of Public Law 115–97 (JCS-1-18), FN 962).

An employer also cannot deduct expenses paid or incurred after 2017 for providing any transportation, or any payment or reimbursement, to an employee in connection with travel between the employee's residence and place of employment, except as necessary to ensure the employee's safety. This prohibition does not apply to a qualified bicycle commuting reimbursement (as described in Code Sec. 132(f)(5)(F)) that is paid or incurred after December 31, 2017, and before January 1, 2026 (Code Sec. 274(l), as added by the 2017 Tax Cuts Act).

> **Comment:** Qualified bicycle commuting benefits are includible in the employee's income for tax years beginning after 2017 and before 2026 (see ¶615).

> **Caution:** It is not clear how this exception for qualified bicycle commuting benefits will coordinate with the blanket prohibition on deductions for qualified transportation fringes.

**Qualified parking.** As stated above, employers are prohibited from deducting qualified parking expenses paid or incurred after December 31, 2017 (Code Sec. 274(a)(4), as added by the 2017 Tax Cuts Act). When an employer contracts with a third party for the use of the parking lot, the disallowance under Code Sec. 274(a)(4) is generally the amount that the employer pays to the third party. However, if that monthly amount exceeds the inflation-adjusted limit on the employee's exclusion for parking benefits under Code Sec. 132(f)(2), the employer must treat the excess as additional compensation. Thus, for 2018 the monthly amount in excess of $260 is excluded from the disallowance amount (Notice 2018-99).

## NEW LAW EXPLAINED

**Key Rates and Figures:** An employee's maximum excludable parking benefit is $260 per month for 2018 (Notice 2018-99); and $265 per month for 2019 (Rev. Proc. 2018-57).

---

**Example:** During 2018, an employer pays $285 per month for each of its ten employees to park. Code Sec. 274(a)(4) prohibits a deduction for, $31,200 (($260 x 10) x 12). The remaining $1,800 (($15 x 10) x 12) is not subject to Code Sec. 274(a)(4) because it exceeds the $260 monthly limit on an employee's excludable benefit. The employer may deduct this $1,800 as additional compensation to the employees.

---

When an employer owns or leases the parking lot, it may use any reasonable method to calculate the Code Sec. 274(a)(4) disallowance. In Notice 2018-99, the IRS provided a four-step reasonable method:

(1) calculate the disallowance for reserved employee spots;

(2) determine the primary use of the remaining spots (for the general public (over 50 percent) or for employees);

(3) calculate the allowance for reserved non-employee spots; and

(4) determine the remaining use and allocable expenses.

**Gray Area:** Notice 2018-99 states that the taxpayer should disregard the amount of depreciation claimed on a parking lot when determining the parking lot expenses. However, the Joint Committee Report says that the amount of depreciation is taken into account in determining the value of the parking benefit (General Explanation of Public Law 115–97 (JCS-1-18), FN 962).

---

**Example:** Employer E owns a surface parking lot adjacent to its plant. E incurs $10,000 of total parking expenses. E's parking lot has 500 spots that are used by its visitors and employees. E has 50 spots reserved for management and has approximately 400 employees parking in the lot in non-reserved spots during normal business hours on a typical business day. Additionally, E has 10 reserved nonemployee spots for visitors.

(1) Step 1: because E has 50 reserved spots for management, $1,000 of its parking expenses ((50/500) x $10,000) is subject to the Code Sec. 274(a)(4) disallowance.

(2) Step 2: the primary use of the remainder of E's parking lot is not to provide parking to the general public because 89% (400/450 = 89 percent) of the remaining parking spots in the lot are used by its employees. Therefore, expenses allocable to these spots are not excluded from the Code Sec. 274(a)(4) disallowance.

(3) Step 3: two percent (10/450 = 2.2%) of E's remaining parking lot spots are reserved non-employee spots. Thus, the $200 allocable to those spots ($10,000 x 2 percent) is not subject to the Code Sec. 274(a)(4) disallowance.

---

## NEW LAW EXPLAINED

> (4) Step 4: E must reasonably determine the employee use of the remaining parking spots during normal business hours on a typical business day and the expenses allocable to employee parking spots. Because 89 percent of the parking spots are used by E's employees during normal business hours on a typical business day, E reasonably determines that $8,010 (($10,000 – 1,000) × 89%) of its $10,000 total parking expenses is subject to the §274(a)(4) disallowance.
>
> Thus, Code Sec. 274(a)(4) disallows deductions for $9,010 ($1,000 + 8,010) of E's $10,000 parking expense.

For more information on disallowed fringe benefits, including qualified parking, see ¶807.

**Employer-provided meals.** No deduction is allowed for amounts that an employer pays or incurs after December 31, 2025, for:

- meals that are excludable from an employee's income under Code Sec. 119(a) because they are provided to employees and their spouses and dependents for the employer's convenience and on the employer's business premises; or

- food, beverage, and facility expenses for meals that are *de minimis* fringe benefit under Code Sec. 132(e) (Code Sec. 274(o), as added by the 2017 Tax Cuts Act).

    **Comment:** The employer's deduction for meal expenses is eliminated only for expenses described in Code Secs. 119(a) or 132(e). Thus, an employer may continue to deduct 50 percent of its expenses for food, beverages, and related facilities that are furnished on its business premises primarily for its employees, such as in a typical company cafeteria or executive dining room (Code Sec. 274(e)(1); Reg. §1.274-2(f)(2)(ii)).

▶ **Effective date.** The amendments made by this section generally apply to amounts incurred or paid after December 31, 2017 (Act Sec. 13304(e)(1) of the Tax Cuts and Jobs Act (P.L. 115-97)). The amendment related to the elimination of the deduction for employer-provided meals that are excludable by employees or are *de minimis* fringe benefits applies to amounts incurred or paid after December 31, 2025 (Act Sec. 13304(e)(2) of the 2017 Tax Cuts Act).

— Act Sec. 13304(a) of the Tax Cuts and Jobs Act (P.L. 115-97), amending Code Secs. 274(a), (d), (n), and 7701(b)(5)(A)(iv), and striking Code Sec. 274(l);

— Act Sec. 13304(b), amending Code Sec. 274(n);

— Act Sec. 13304(c), amending Code Sec. 274(a), and adding Code Sec. 274(a)(4) and (l);

— Act Sec. 13304(d), redesignating Code Sec. 274(o) as 274(p) and adding new Code Sec. 274(o);

— Act Sec. 13304(e), providing the effective date.

## ¶537  Prohibition on Non-Tangible Personal Property as Employee Achievement Awards

### SUMMARY OF NEW LAW

For purposes of employee achievement awards, employers are prohibited from deducting awards that are given in cash, cash equivalents, gift cards, gift coupons, gift certificates, vacations, meals, lodging, tickets to theater or sporting events, stocks, bonds, other securities or similar items.

### BACKGROUND

In general, employers may deduct under Code Sec. 162 or 212 the cost of achievement awards given to employees for length of service or for safety achievement, subject to certain limitations (Code Sec. 274(j)). A maximum $400 deduction limit applies on the amount an employer may deduct with respect to all nonqualified employee achievement plan awards (safety and length of service) provided to the same employee. In the case of one or more qualified plan awards (safety and length of service) made to a single employee, the employer's deduction limitation for all such qualified plan awards may not exceed $1,600. All qualified and nonqualified employee achievement awards must meet the following requirements:

- the award must be an item of tangible personal property, other than gift certificates, entitling an employee to choose between receiving merchandise, cash, or a reduction in the balance on an account with the issuer of a gift certificate; and

- the award must be by reason of an employee's length of service achievement or safety achievement.

Work-related prizes and awards are excludable from the recipient's gross income only if they qualify as employee achievement awards (Code Sec. 74(c)(1)). An employee achievement award is an item of tangible personal property that is transferred by an employer to an employee for length of service achievement or safety achievement, awarded as part of a meaningful presentation, and awarded under conditions and circumstances that indicate the payment is not disguised compensation. The exclusion does not apply to awards of cash, gift certificates, or equivalent items (Senate Committee Report for the Tax Reform Act of 1986 (P.L. 99-514)).

### NEW LAW EXPLAINED

**Non-tangible personal property prohibited as employee achievement award.—** The definition of "tangible personal property," for purposes of what is a deductible as an employee achievement award is amended to exclude cash, cash equivalents, gift cards, gift coupons, and gift certificates (except an arrangement giving an employee the limited right to select and receive tangible personal property from a limited number of pre-selected or pre-approved items) (Code Sec. 274(j)(3)(A)(ii), as added by the Tax Cuts and Jobs Act (P.L. 115-97)). The term also excludes vacations, meal, lodging,

## NEW LAW EXPLAINED

tickets to theater or sporting events, stocks, bonds, other securities, and other similar items. This amendment is not intended to be an inference that present law and guidance is changed (Conference Report on H.R. 1, Tax Cuts and Jobs Act (H. Rept. 115-466)).

▶ **Effective date.** The amendments made by this section apply to amounts paid or incurred after December 31, 2017 (Act Sec. 13310(b) of the Tax Cuts and Jobs Act (P.L. 115-97)).

   **No significant guidance related to this provision has been issued.**

— Act Sec. 13310(a) of the Tax Cuts and Jobs Act (P.L. 115-97), amending Code Sec. 274(j)(3)(A)(i) and adding Code Sec. 274(j)(3)(A)(ii);

— Act Sec. 13310(b), providing the effective date.

# ¶540  Limitation on Excessive Employee Compensation

## SUMMARY OF NEW LAW

For purposes of the limitation on the deduction for employee compensation paid by publicly held corporations, the definition of covered employee is expanded to include both the principal executive officer and the principal financial officer, as well as the other three most highly compensated employees. Employees who are covered employees after December 31, 2016, remain as covered employees for all future tax years. The exclusions from the limitation for commission-based and performance based compensation have been repealed.

## BACKGROUND

A publicly held corporation may not deduct applicable employee compensation (remuneration) in excess of $1 million paid to any covered employee for a tax year (Code Sec. 162(m)(1)). The $1 million cap is reduced by excess parachute payments that are not deductible by the corporation (Code Sec. 162(m)(4)(F)).

Generally, "covered employees" include the chief operating officer (CEO) of the corporation and the four most highly compensated employees of the corporation other than the CEO, whose compensation is required to be reported to the shareholders by the Securities and Exchange Commission (SEC) under the Securities Exchange Act of 1934 (Code Sec. 162(m)(3); Notice 2007-49). This includes the principal executive officer (PEO), the principal financial officer (PFO), and the three most highly compensated officers other than the PEO or PFO must disclose their compensation.

Compensation subject to the deduction limit generally includes the taxable wages paid to the employee for services performed (Code Sec. 162(m)(4); Reg. § 1.162-27). Types of compensation that are not taken into account in determining whether compensation exceeds the $1 million limit include: specified commissions, compensation based on performance goals, income payable under a written binding contract that was in effect on February 17, 1993, and compensation paid before a corporation

## BACKGROUND

became publicly held. Payments excluded from the definition of compensation include: (1) payments to a tax-favored retirement plan (including salary reduction contributions), and (2) amounts that are excludable from the executive's gross income (such as employer-provided health benefits and miscellaneous fringe benefits).

## NEW LAW EXPLAINED

**Requirements for the limitations on employee remuneration amended.**—Effective for tax years beginning after December 31, 2017, the definitions of "covered employee," "compensation," and "publicly held corporation" have been modified for purposes of the limitation on the deduction for excessive employee compensation paid by publicly held corporations.

**Covered employee.** A covered employee is any employee of the corporation who:

- is the principal executive officer (PEO) of the corporation (or an individual acting in such capacity) at any time during the tax year;
- is the principal financial officer (PFO) of the corporation (or an individual acting in such capacity) at any time during the tax year;
- has total compensation for the tax year that must be reported to shareholders under the Securities Exchange Act of 1934 because the employee is among the three highest compensated officers for the tax year (other than the PEO or the PFO);
- would be described as being among the three highest compensated officers for the tax year if reporting to shareholders under the Securities Exchange Act of 1934 were required (for a corporation that is not otherwise required to so report); or
- was a covered employee of the corporation (or any predecessor) for any prior tax year beginning on or after January 1, 2017 (Code Sec. 162(m)(3), as amended by the Tax Cuts and Jobs Act (P.L. 115-97)).

    **Comment:** Amendments to Code Sec. 162(m) reflect changes made by to the definition of covered employees made by Notice 2007-49.

For an employee who is among the three highest compensated officers for the tax year, there is no requirement that the employee must still work for the publicly held company at the end of the tax year to be considered a covered employee. Furthermore, the employee is a covered employee even if he or she is no longer serving as an officer at the end of the company's tax year. In addition, the definition applies regardless of whether the officer's compensation is subject to disclosure for the last completed fiscal year under the applicable SEC rules (Notice 2018-68).

> **Example:** Smith Co. is a publicly held corporation with a calendar year tax year. In 2018, Employee A, served as the sole PEO and Employees B and C both served as the PFO at different times during the year. Employees D, E, and F were, respectively, the first, second, and third most highly compensated executive officers for 2018 other than the PEO and PFO, and all three retired before the end of 2018. Employees G, H, and I were, respectively, the fourth, fifth, and

**NEW LAW EXPLAINED**

sixth highest compensated executive officers other than the PEO and PFO for 2018, and all three were serving at the end of 2018.

On March 1, 2019, Smith Co. filed its Annual Report with the SEC. Smith Co. disclosed the compensation of Employee A for serving as the PEO, and of Employees B and C for serving as the PFO. Smith Co. also disclosed the compensation of Employees D, E, F, G, H, and I in accordance with SEC rules.

Employees A, B, and C are covered employees because they served as either the PEO or PFO during 2018. Employees D, E, and F also are covered employees, because they are the three highest compensated executive officers other than the PEO and PFO for 2018. This is the case even though the SEC rules require Smith Co. to disclose the compensation of Employees D, E, F, G, H, and I for 2018.

---

**Example:** Assume the same facts as in the Example above, except that Smith Co. is a "smaller reporting company" or "emerging growth company" under the SEC rules. In accordance with SEC rules for these types of companies, Smith Co. disclosed the compensation of Employee A for serving as the PEO, and the compensation of Employees D, E, G, and H. Under the SEC rules, Smith Co. was not required to report the compensation of Employees C, F, and I.

Here, Employees A, B, C, D, E, and F are covered employees just as they are in Example 1. For purposes of identifying a corporation's covered employees, it is not relevant whether the SEC rules for smaller reporting companies and emerging growth companies apply, or whether the specific executive officers' compensation must be disclosed under the applicable SEC rules.

---

**Compensation.** The exceptions for commissions and performance-based compensation are repealed (Code Sec. 162(m)(4), as amended by the 2017 Tax Cuts Act). Applicable employee compensation (remuneration) for tax years beginning after 2017, includes any cash and noncash benefits paid for services, including commissions and performance-based compensation, but does not include:

- income from specified employee trusts, annuity plans, or pensions;
- any benefit that is reasonably anticipated to be tax free under the Code;
- income payable under a written binding contract which was in effect on February 17, 1993; and
- compensation paid before a corporation became publicly held (Code Sec. 162(m)(4), as amended by the 2017 Tax Cuts Act).

A covered employee's compensation is still subject to the deduction limit even if it is paid to or includible in the income of another person. This includes compensation paid to a covered employee's estate, a beneficiary of the employee's estate, or to a former spouse (Code Sec. 162(m)(4)(F), as added by the 2017 Tax Cuts Act; Conference Report on H.R. 1, Tax Cuts and Jobs Act (H. Rept. 115-466)).

## NEW LAW EXPLAINED

**Transition rule.** A transition rule provides that the Code Sec. 162(m) amendments discussed above do not apply to compensation payable under a written binding contract which was in effect on November 2, 2017, and was not modified in any material respect on or after such date (Act Sec. 13601(e)(2) of the 2017 Tax Cuts Act). Compensation is payable under such a written binding contract only to the extent the corporation is required by applicable law (for example, state contract law) to pay the compensation under the contract if the employee performs services or satisfies the vesting conditions that apply. Thus, the amendments apply to compensation that exceeds the amount required by applicable law (Notice 2018-68). In addition, the amendments apply to any contract that is renewed, canceled or terminated after November 2, 2017.

Compensation paid pursuant to a plan qualifies for this exception provided that the right to participate in the plan is part of a written binding contract with the covered employee in effect on November 2, 2017. The fact that a plan was in existence on November 2, 2017 is not by itself sufficient to qualify the plan for the exception for binding written contracts (Conference Report on H.R. 1, Tax Cuts and Jobs Act (H. Rept. 115-466); Notice 2018-68).

> **Example:** A covered employee is hired by XYZ Corporation on October 2, 2017. One of the terms of her written employment contract is that she is eligible to participate in the company's deferred compensation plan. The written plan provides for participation after six months of employment, amounts payable under the plan are not subject to discretion, and the corporation does not have the right to amend materially the plan or terminate the plan except on a prospective basis. Payments to the executive under the plan meet the binding contract exception even though she was not actually a participant in the plan on November 2, 2017.

The binding written contract exception ceases to apply to amounts paid after there has been a material modification to the terms of the contract. The exception also does not apply to new contracts entered into or renewed after November 2, 2017. For this purpose, any contract entered into on or before November 2, 2017, that is renewed after such date is treated as a new contract. A contract that may be terminated or cancelled unconditionally by either party to the contract is treated as a new contract. However, a contract that can be terminated or cancelled only by terminating the employment relationship of the covered employee is not covered by this rule (Conference Report on H.R. 1, Tax Cuts and Jobs Act (H. Rept. 115-466); Notice 2018-68).

A contract is materially modified when it is amended to:

- increase the amount of compensation payable to the employee;
- accelerate the payment of compensation, but not if the amount of compensation paid is discounted to reasonably reflect the time value of money; or
- defer payment of compensation, but not if any additional compensation paid or to be paid in excess of the amount originally payable under the contract is based on a reasonable rate of interest, or on a predetermined actual investment such that the

## NEW LAW EXPLAINED

amount payable at the later date will be based on the actual rate of return on the predetermined actual investment (including any decrease or increase in the value of the investment).

Supplemental contracts or agreements may also materially modify the existing contract (Notice 2018-68).

---

**Example:** On October 2, 2017, W Co. executed a 3-year employment agreement with Employee V for an annual salary of $2 million beginning on January 1, 2018. V serves as the PFO for the 2017, 2018, 2019, and 2020 tax years. The agreement provides for automatic extensions after the 3-year term for additional 1-year terms, unless the corporation exercises its option to terminate the agreement within 30 days before the end of the term. Termination of the employment agreement does not require the termination of V's employment.

V is considered a covered employee for W Co.'s 2018, 2019, and 2020 tax years. However, the employment agreement executed on October 2, 2017, is a written binding contract under applicable law. Thus, the amendments to Code Sec. 162(m) do not apply to V's annual salary. Accordingly, V's annual salary is not subject to the $1 million deduction limitation for the 2018, 2019, and 2020 tax years. Under the employment agreement's automatic extension provision, however, the agreement is treated as renewed on January 1, 2021. If the employment agreement is not previously terminated, the amendments to Code Sec. 162(m) will apply to any payments made under the agreement on or after that date.

---

**Publicly held corporations.** The $1 million deduction cap for covered employees only applies to publicly held corporations. Effective for tax years beginning after 2017, publicly held corporations include all domestic publicly traded corporations and all foreign companies publicly traded through American depository receipts (ADRs) (Code Sec. 162(m)(2) as amended by the 2017 Tax Cuts Act). According to the Conference Committee Report, publicly held corporations may also include large private C corporations and S corporations that are not publicly traded (Conference Report on H.R. 1, Tax Cuts and Jobs Act (H. Rept. 115-466)).

▶ **Effective date.** The amendments made by this section generally apply to tax years beginning after December 31, 2017 (Act Sec. 13601(e) of the Tax Cuts and Jobs Act (P.L. 115-97)). The amendments do not apply to remuneration which is provided pursuant to a written binding contract which was in effect on November 2, 2017, and which was not modified in any material respect on or after November 2, 2017.

— Act Sec. 13601(a) of the 2017 Tax Cuts Act (P.L. 115-97), amending Code Sec. 162(m)(4), (m)(5), and (m)(6);

— Act Sec. 13601(b), amending Code Sec. 162(m)(3)(A) and (3)(B) and adding Code Sec. 162(m)(3)(C);

— Act Sec. 13601(c) amending Code Sec. 162(m)(2) and (m)(3);

— Act Sec. 13601(d), adding Code Sec. 162(m)(4)(F);

— Act Sec. 13601(e), providing the effective date.

# ¶545  Deduction for Fines, Penalties, and Other Amounts

## SUMMARY OF NEW LAW

Businesses generally may not deduct fines and penalties paid or incurred after December 21, 2017, due to the violation of a law (or the investigation of a violation) if a government (or similar entity) is a complainant or investigator. Exceptions to this rule are available in certain cases where the payment was compensation for damages, compliance with the law, paid to satisfy a court order where the government is not a party, or paid for taxes due.

## BACKGROUND

Fines and penalties paid to a government entity for the violation of any law (including settlement payments) are not deductible business expenses (Code Sec. 162(f)). This includes fines and penalties imposed by federal, state, local, and foreign governments (Reg. § 1.162-21(a)).

The amount of a fine or penalty does not include (1) legal fees and related expenses paid or incurred in the defense of an action in which the nondeductible fine or penalty may be imposed, or (2) court costs assessed against the taxpayer (Reg. § 1.162-21(b)(2)). Compensatory damages, including damages under Section 4A of the Clayton Antitrust Act, which are intended to return the parties to the status quo, do not constitute fines or penalties. Where the payments serve both purposes, the court will decide what purpose the payment is designated to serve (Reg. § 1.162-21(b)).

## NEW LAW EXPLAINED

**Prohibition of deduction for fines and penalties amended; reporting requirement added.**—Fines and penalties paid or incurred after December 21, 2017, except under any binding order agreement entered into before December 22, 2017, are not deductible as business expenses if paid or incurred to, or at the direction of, any federal, state or foreign government or governmental entity due to the violation of a law (or the investigation or inquiry into the potential violation of a law) (Code Sec. 162(f)(1), as amended by the Tax Cuts and Jobs Act (P.L. 115-97). There are certain exceptions to this rule, including:

• amounts paid that constitute restitution (including the remediation of property) for damages due or may be due to the violation (or potential violation) of a law (Code Sec. 162(f)(2)(A)(i)(I), as amended by the 2017 Tax Cuts Act);

• amounts paid to come into compliance with a violated law, or the investigation or inquiry into the violation or potential violation of a law (Code Sec. 162(f)(2)(A)(i)(II), as amended by the 2017 Tax Cuts Act);

• amounts paid to satisfy a court order where the government is not a party (Code Sec. 162(f)(3), as amended by the 2017 Tax Cuts Act); and

• amounts paid for taxes due (Code Sec. 162(f)(4), as amended by the 2017 Tax Cuts Act).

## NEW LAW EXPLAINED

In order for the restitution or compliance exceptions to apply, the payment must be identified as restitution or compliance in a court order or settlement agreement. In addition, restitution for the failure to pay a tax imposed under the Internal Revenue Code, would be deductible only to the extent that deduction for the tax would have been allowable if it had been timely paid (Code Sec. 162(f)(2)(A)(ii) and (iii), as amended by the 2017 Tax Cuts Act).

Under transitional guidance, the identification requirement is treated as satisfied if the settlement agreement or court order specifically states on its face that the amount is restitution, remediation, or for coming into compliance with the law, until proposed regulations are issued (Notice 2018-23). Note that taxpayers must still meet the restitution or compliance exceptions in order to claim the deduction (Code Sec. 162(f)(2)(A)(ii), as amended by the 2017 Tax Cuts Act).

**Nongovernment entities.** The following nongovernment entities are treated as governmental entities for purposes of Code Sec. 162(f):

- any nongovernmental entity which exercises self-regulatory powers (including the authority to impose sanctions) in connection with a qualified board or exchange , defined in Code Sec. 1256(g)(7) (Code Sec. 162(f)(5)(A), as amended by the 2017 Tax Cuts Act), and

- any nongovernmental entity with self-regulatory powers (including the authority to impose sanctions) that was established by governmental regulations in order to perform an essential governmental function (Code Sec. 162(f)(5)(B), as amended by the 2017 Tax Cuts Act.

**Reporting requirements.** The officer or employee that has control over the suit or agreement, or the individual designated by the government or entity must file a return with the IRS (Code Sec. 6050X(a) and (c), as amended by the 2017 Tax Cuts Act. This return must state:

- the total amount to be paid as a result of the suit or agreement,

- any amount to be paid for restitution or remediation of property, and

- any amount to be paid for compliance (Code Sec. 6050X(a)(1), as added by the 2017 Tax Cuts Act).

The return must be filed at the time the agreement is entered into Code Sec. 6050X(a)(3), as added by the 2017 Tax Cuts Act)

In addition, the individual filing the return must also simultaneously provide a statement to each person or entity that is a party to the suit or agreement. The statement must provide: the name of the government or entity, and the information included in the return that the individual filed with the IRS (Code Sec. 6050X(b), as added by the 2017 Tax Cuts Act).

For the purposes of the reporting requirements, a suit or agreement is defined as:

- a suit that results in a court order in which a government or entity has authority or

- an agreement that is entered into with respect to a violation or potential violation of the law, over which a government or entity has authority.

## NEW LAW EXPLAINED

The amount of the suit or agreement must exceed $600. The IRS may change that amount as necessary to ensure efficient administration (Code Sec. 6050X(a)(2), as added by the 2017 Tax Cuts Act)

**Transitional guidance.** According to transitional guidance, the IRS will not require governmental and nongovernmental regulatory entities to report amounts obligated to be paid or incurred under a binding court order or agreement that is entered into before a date to be provided in proposed regulations that the IRS has not yet issued (Notice 2018-23).

The IRS intends to release additional transitional guidance to clarify the reporting requirements and provide governmental and nongovernmental regulatory entities additional time to develop their systems for collecting and reporting the required information (Notice 2018-23).

▶ **Effective date.** The amendments by this section generally apply to amounts paid or incurred on or after December 22, 2017, the date of enactment, except that they will not apply to amounts paid or incurred under any binding order or agreement entered into before December 22, 2017 (Act Sec. 13306(a)(2) and Act Sec. 13306(b)(3) of the Tax Cuts and Jobs Act (P.L. 115-97)). The exception will not apply to an order or agreement requiring court approval unless the approval was obtained before December 22, 2017.

— Act Sec. 13306(a) of the 2017 Tax Cuts Act (P.L. 115-97), amending Code Sec. 162(f);

— Act Sec. 13306(b)(1), adding Code Sec. 6050X;

— Act Sec. 13306(a)(2) and (b)(3), providing the effective date.

## ¶550 Deduction for Settlements Paid for Sexual Harassment or Abuse Subject to Nondisclosure Agreements

### SUMMARY OF NEW LAW

A taxpayer may not claim a deduction as an ordinary and necessary business expense any settlement or payment made after December 22, 2017, for sexual harassment or sexual abuse if subject to a nondisclosure agreement.

### BACKGROUND

Settlement payments made to avoid litigation, including any related attorneys's fees and court costs, are generally deductible as ordinary and necessary business expenses provided the origin and character of the litigation indicates that the cause of action arose from a business activity under the origin of the claim doctrine (*D. Gilmore, SCt.*, 63-1 USTC ¶9285). Accordingly, if the acts that gave rise to the litigation were performed in the ordinary conduct of the taxpayer's business, payments made in settlement of lawsuits are deductible.

## NEW LAW EXPLAINED

**Elimination of deduction for settlements paid for sexual harassment or abuse subject to nondisclosure agreements.**—No deduction may be claimed for any settlement or payment paid or incurred after December 22, 2017, related to sexual harassment or sexual abuse if the settlement is subject to a nondisclosure agreement. Attorney's fees related to such payments or agreements are also not deductible (Code Sec. 162(q), as added by the Tax Cuts and Jobs Act (P.L. 115-97)).

▶ **Effective date.** The amendments made by this section apply to amounts paid or incurred after December 22, 2017 (Act Sec. 13307(b) of the Tax Cuts and Jobs Act (P.L. 115-97)).

**No significant guidance related to this provision has been issued.**

— Act Sec. 13307(a) of the 2017 Tax Cuts Act (P.L. 115-97), redesignating subsection Code Sec. 162(q) as subsection (r) and inserting the new subsection (q);

— Act Sec. 13307(b), providing the effective date.

# ¶555 Deduction of Local Lobbying Expenses

## SUMMARY OF NEW LAW

The deduction for local lobbying expenses by a taxpayer as an ordinary and necessary business is repealed for expenses paid after December 22, 2017.

## BACKGROUND

A taxpayer may claim business deductions for certain types of expenses incurred with respect to legislation of any local council or similar governing body (local legislation) (Code Sec. 162(e)(2)). The deductible expenses relate to:

(1) appearances before, submission of statements to, or sending of communications to, committees or individual members of local legislative bodies with respect to legislation or proposed legislation of direct interest to the taxpayer;

(2) communication of information between the taxpayer and an organization of which he is a member with respect to legislation or proposed legislation of direct interest to the taxpayer or to such organization; and

(3) the portion of membership dues in such an organization which is attributable to the activities described in (1) and (2).

Legislation or proposed legislation is of direct interest to a taxpayer if it is of such a nature that it will, or may reasonably be expected to, affect the taxpayer's trade or business, whether the effect be beneficial or detrimental or immediate. It is not of

## BACKGROUND

direct interest to the taxpayer merely because it may affect business in general; however, if it affects the taxpayer's trade or business, it is of direct interest to him even though it also affects other taxpayers or business in general. Not all of the provisions of the legislation or proposed legislation need affect the taxpayer's business; one provision will suffice. Examples of legislation or proposed legislation which meet the direct interest test are those which would increase or decrease the taxes applicable to the trade or business, increase or decrease the operating costs or earnings of the trade or business, or increase or decrease the administrative burdens connected with the trade or business.

## NEW LAW EXPLAINED

**Deductions for local lobbying expenses repealed.**—The deduction for lobbying for local legislation is repealed for amounts paid or incurred after December 21, 2017 (Code Sec. 162(e)(2), as stricken by the Tax Cuts and Jobs Act (P.L. 115-97)). In addition to the elimination of the deduction for local lobbying expenses, the deduction for lobbying for Indian tribal government is also repealed, as an Indian tribal government is treated in the same manner as a local council or similar governing body (Code Sec. 162(e)(7), as stricken by the 2017 Tax Cuts Act).

▶ **Effective date.** The amendments made by this section apply to amounts paid or incurred on or after December 22, 2017, the date of the enactment (Act Sec. 13308(c) of the Tax Cuts and Jobs Act (P.L. 115-97)).

**No significant guidance related to this provision has been issued.**

— Act Sec. 13308(a) of the Tax Cuts and Jobs Act (P.L. 115-97), striking Code Sec. 162(e)(2) and (7), and redesignating (e)(3), (e)(4), (e)(5), (e)(6), and (e)(8) as Code Sec. 162(e)(2), Code Sec. 162(e)(3), (e)(4), (e)(5), and (e)(6), respectively;

— Act Sec. 13308(b), amending Code Sec. 6033(e)(1)(B)(ii);

— Act Sec. 13308(c), providing the effective date.

## ¶560 Deduction for Living Expenses Incurred by Congressional Members

### SUMMARY OF NEW LAW

The special provision allowing Members of Congress a deduction of up to $3,000 per year of living expenses incurred while on official business in the District of Columbia is repealed.

### BACKGROUND

The tax home of a member of the United States Congress is the location of his home within the District from which he or she is elected. Thus, a legislator is allowed to

## BACKGROUND

deduct meals and lodging expenses incurred while on official business in the District of Columbia, up to a maximum amount of $3,000 per year (Code Sec. 162(a)). This deduction is in addition to deductible moving expenses.

### NEW LAW EXPLAINED

**Deduction for living expenses incurred by members of Congress repealed.—** Members of Congress may no longer claim the deduction for up to $3,000 per year of living expenses incurred while on official business in the District of Columbia (Code Sec. 162(a), as amended by the Tax Cuts and Jobs Act (P.L. 115-97)).

▶ **Effective date.** The amendment made by this section applies to tax years beginning after December 22, 2017, the date of the enactment (Act Sec. 13311(b) of the Tax Cuts and Jobs Act (P.L. 115-97)).

**No significant guidance related to this provision has been issued.**

— Act Sec. 13311(a) of the 2017 Tax Cuts Act (P.L. 115-97), amending Code Sec. 162(a);

— Act Sec. 13311(b), providing the effective date.

# ¶565 Deduction of FDIC Premiums

### SUMMARY OF NEW LAW

The deduction for the applicable percentage of Federal Deposit Insurance Corporation (FDIC) premiums paid by banks and other financial institutions with consolidated assets of over $10 billion is limited after 2017. Banks and other financial institutions with more than $50 billion in assets may not deduct the applicable percentage of any FDIC premium paid.

### BACKGROUND

In order for a bank and other lending institutions to maintain their status as insured depository institutions, it must make semi annual payments into the deposit insurance fund provided by the FDIC. These assessments are deductible as ordinary and necessary business expenses if the all events test has been satisfied (Rev. Rul. 80-230). For federal income tax purposes, banks are generally taxed as and treated as a C corporation (Reg. § 1.581-1).

### NEW LAW EXPLAINED

**Limitation of deductions of FDIC premiums.—**The deduction of the applicable percentage of FDIC premiums for banks and other financial institutions with over $10 billion in consolidated assets is generally limited (Code Sec. 162(r), as added by the Tax Cuts and Jobs Act (P.L. 115-97)). Banks and other financial institutions with more than $50 billion in assets may not deduct the applicable percentage of any FDIC premium paid.

## NEW LAW EXPLAINED

**Applicable percentage.** The applicable percentage is determined by subtracting $10 billion from the total amount of consolidated assets in a tax year, and the dividing that amount by $40 billion.

---

**Example:** Bank X ended the tax year with $26 billion in consolidated assets. No deduction is allowed for 40 percent of FDIC premiums ($26 billion – $10 billion) / $40 billion.

---

**Example:** Bank Y ended the tax year with $46 billion in consolidated assets. No deduction is allowed for 90 percent of FDIC premiums ($46 billion – $10 billion) / $40 billion.

---

Banks with $50 billion or more in consolidated assets may not deduct the entire FDIC premiums. Such institutions have an applicable percentage of 100 percent (Code Sec. 162(r)(3), as added by the 2017 Tax Cuts Act). This provision does not apply to banks and other financial institutions with $10 billion or less in consolidated assets at the end of the tax year (Code Sec. 162(r)(2), as added by the 2017 Tax Cuts Act).

FDIC premiums for this purpose refers to assessments imposed under section 7(b) of the Federal Deposit Insurance Act (12 U.S.C. sec. 1817(b)) (Code Sec. 162(r)(4), as added by the 2017 Tax Cuts Act). The term total consolidated assets in this provision has the same meaning as the term in section 165 of the Dodd-Frank Wall Street Reform and Consumer Protection Act (P.L. 111-203) (Code Sec. 162(r)(5), as added by the 2017 Tax Cuts Act).

**Expanded affiliated groups.** When determining the amount of consolidated assets held in a bank or financial institution, members of an expanded affiliated group are treated as a single taxpayer (Code Sec. 162(r)(6), as added by the 2017 Tax Cuts Act). An expanded affiliated group is defined under Code Sec. 1504(a), except that the phrase "more than 50 percent" is substituted for "at least 80 percent" in Code Sec. 1504(a)(2). Thus, under Code Sec. 162(r), an expanded affiliated group is one or more chains of includible corporations connected through stock ownership with a common parent that meets the following requirements:

- the common parent must directly own stock possessing more than 50 percent of the total voting power of at least one of the other includible corporations and having a value equal to at more than 50 percent of the total value of the stock of that corporation; and

- stock meeting the 50-percent test in each includible corporation other than the common parent must be owned directly by one or more of the other includible corporations.

¶565

## NEW LAW EXPLAINED

Insurance companies and foreign corporations are exempt from the definition (Code Sec. 162(r)(6)(B)(i)(II), as added by the 2017 Tax Cuts Act). Partnerships or entities other than corporations are considered members of an expanded affiliated group if such entity is controlled by a corporation in the group.

▶ **Effective date.** The amendments made by this section apply to tax years beginning after December 31, 2017 (Act Sec. 13531(b) of the Tax Cuts and Job Act (P.L. 115-97)).

**No significant guidance related to this provision has been issued.**

— Act Sec. 13531(a) of the 2017 Tax Cuts Act (P.L. 115-97), redesignating subsection Code Sec. 162(r) as subsection (s) and adding (r);

— Act Sec. 13531(b), providing the effective date.

# ACCOUNTING FOR BUSINESSES

## ¶570 Cash Method of Accounting for Small Businesses, Including Exceptions for Inventories, UNICAP, and Small Construction Contracts

### SUMMARY OF NEW LAW

The cash method of accounting and other simpler accounting methods have been made available to more taxpayers. Most taxpayers who meet a $25 million average annual gross receipts test will be able to use the cash method, will not be required to apply the inventory or uniform capitalization (UNICAP) rules, and will not be required to use the percentage of completion method for small construction contracts.

### BACKGROUND

An accounting method includes both an overall system of accounting and the accounting treatment of any individual item. The accounting method used for tax purposes must clearly reflect income and must be consistently applied (Code Sec. 446(b)). Taxpayers can compute taxable income using the cash receipts and disbursements method or cash method, the accrual method, any other special method allowed under the income tax rules, such as a long-term contract method, or a hybrid method that combines any of the above methods (Code Sec. 446(c)).

**Cash method of accounting.** The cash method is the simplest of the overall accounting methods (Code Sec. 446(c)(1)). Under the cash method, taxpayers report income in the year in which it is received in the form of cash, property, or services with a determinable value. Cash-method taxpayers take deductions and credits in the year in which the expenses are actually paid, unless a special rule requires the expenses to be taken in a different year to clearly reflect income (Reg. §1.446-1(c)(1)(i)).

## BACKGROUND

Certain taxpayers cannot use the cash method for tax purposes and must adopt the accrual method. Under the general rule, entities that cannot use the cash method are: (1) C corporations, (2) partnerships that have one or more C corporations as a partner or partners, (3) tax shelters, and (4) certain trusts subject to tax on unrelated business income (Code Sec. 448(a)). However, despite the general rule, C corporations and partnerships that have one or more C corporations as a partner or partners can use the cash method if they meet a $5 million gross receipts test, are farming businesses, or are qualified personal service corporations.

In addition, the cash method cannot be used by a taxpayer if the purchase, production, or sale of merchandise is an income-producing factor. In that case, the taxpayer must keep inventories and use the accrual method for the inventory items (Reg. §§ 1.446-1(c)(2) and 1.471-1).

**Large farming corporations.** Large C corporations and partnerships with a C corporation partner that are engaged in the trade or business of farming are generally required to use the accrual method (Code Sec. 447(a)). Farming C corporations and farming partnerships with a C corporation partner that meet a $1 million gross receipts test and family farming C corporations that meet a $25 million gross receipts test are not required to use the accrual method and can use the cash method instead (Code Sec. 447(d)). Exceptions to the required use of the accrual method also apply for certain types of farming businesses.

A family farming C corporation that is required to change its method of accounting because it does not meet the $25 million gross receipts test must compute a Code Sec. 481 adjustment and include the amount in income over a period of 10 years, beginning with the year of the accounting method change (Code Sec. 447(f) and (i)). Prior to the Taxpayer Relief Act of 1997 (P.L. 105-34), a family farming corporation could avoid the 10-year recognition period by creating a suspense account that deferred recognition of the Code Sec. 481 adjustment indefinitely, pending the termination of the corporation or the happening of certain other events. For tax years ending after June 8, 1997, new suspense accounts could not be established, and existing suspense accounts were gradually being phased out over a period of 20 years (Code Sec. 447(i)(5)).

**Businesses with inventory.** Businesses must take inventories at the beginning and end of each tax year in which the production, purchase or sale of merchandise is an income-producing factor (Code Sec. 471(a); Reg. § 1.471-1). Although businesses with inventories generally must use the accrual method, certain small businesses do not need to account for inventories and can use the cash method. Small businesses qualify for this exception if they have average annual gross receipts of $1 million or less, or are engaged in certain trades or businesses and have average annual gross receipts of $10 million or less (Rev. Proc. 2001-10 and Rev. Proc. 2002-28).

**UNICAP rules.** Businesses that produce real or tangible personal property or acquire property for resale must use the uniform capitalization (UNICAP) rules and include the direct costs and a portion of the allocable indirect costs of producing or acquiring property in their inventory costs (Code Sec. 263A). However, businesses may qualify for an exception to the UNICAP rules for personal property purchased for resale if the business has average annual gross receipts of $10 million or less for the preceding

**¶570**

## BACKGROUND

three tax years (Code Sec. 263A(b)(2)). This exception does not apply to real property acquired for resale (Reg. § 1.263A-3(b)(1)).

Other exceptions to the required use of the UNICAP rules also apply, including exceptions for costs of raising, harvesting or growing trees, costs of producing animals or producing plants with a preproductive period of two years or less (unless the taxpayer is required to use the accrual method), and qualified creative expenses of freelance authors, photographers and artists (Code Sec. 263A(c)(5), (d)(1) and (h)).

**Long-term construction contracts.** Taxpayers generally must account for their long-term contracts using the percentage of completion method of accounting (Code Sec. 460(a)). Under the percentage of completion method, taxpayers recognize income from the contract as the contract is completed. The income for the year is equal to the percentage of the contract that was completed multiplied by the gross contract price. The percentage of the contract completed during the tax year is determined by comparing costs allocated to the contract and incurred before the end of the tax year with the estimated total contract costs (Code Sec. 460(b)).

The required use of the percentage of completion method and most of the cost allocation rules for long-term contracts do not apply to small construction contracts, home construction contracts, and residential construction contracts. A small construction contract is any contract for the construction or improvement of real property that: (1) is expected to be completed within the two-year period beginning on the commencement date of the contract, and (2) is performed by a taxpayer whose average annual gross receipts for the three tax years preceding the tax year in which the contract is entered into do not exceed $10 million (Code Sec. 460(e)(1)). In addition to the percentage of completion method, taxpayers can report income from small construction contracts under the completed contract method, the exempt-contract percentage of completion method, or any other permissible method (Reg. § 1.460-4(c)(1)).

**Changes of accounting method.** Taxpayers cannot change from an established accounting method to a different method unless they first obtain the IRS's consent for the change (Code Sec. 446(e)). The IRS has issued procedures that taxpayers must follow in order to receive the IRS's consent for an accounting method change (Rev. Proc. 2015-13). The IRS will grant automatic consent for certain changes in accounting method that are in the IRS's "List of Automatic Changes" (Rev. Proc. 2017-30). Code Sec. 481 adjustments are generally required in order to prevent duplication or omission of income items resulting from the accounting method change.

## NEW LAW EXPLAINED

**Single gross receipts test added for cash method, inventory, UNICAP, construction contract rules.**—A single $25 million gross receipts test has been put in place for determining whether certain taxpayers qualify as small taxpayers that can use the cash method of accounting, are not required to use inventories, are not required to apply the UNICAP rules, and are not required to use the percentage of completion method for a small construction contract (Act Sec. 13102 of the Tax Cuts and Jobs Act (P.L. 115-97)).

## NEW LAW EXPLAINED

> **Comment:** The combined effect of the statutory changes is to replace a number of different gross receipts tests for determining what is a small taxpayer with a single gross receipts test with a $25 million threshold. In nearly all cases, the $25 million threshold is a significant increase from the prior thresholds which ranged from $1 million to $25 million. The changes not only increase the number of businesses that will qualify as small taxpayers but also greatly simplify the gross receipts determinations.

**Gross receipts test expanded.** The exception to the general limit on the use of the cash method for small businesses is expanded for tax years beginning after December 31, 2017. Under the exception, a C corporation or a partnership with a C corporation partner that meets a gross receipts test can qualify to use the cash method of accounting (Code Sec. 448(b)(3), as amended by the 2017 Tax Cuts Act). A C corporation or a partnership with a C corporation partner meets the gross receipts test for a tax year if its average annual gross receipts for the three-tax-year period that ends with the tax year preceding such tax year do not exceed $25 million (Code Sec. 448(c)(1), as amended by the 2017 Tax Cuts Act). The average annual gross receipts amount of $25 million is adjusted for inflation for tax years beginning after December 31, 2018, using the Chained Consumer Price Index for All Urban Consumers (C-CPI-U) in the cost-of-living adjustment (see ¶125) (Code Sec. 448(c)(4), as added by the 2017 Tax Cuts Act). The adjusted amount for 2019 is $26 million (Rev. Proc. 2018-57).

> **Caution:** Tax shelters are not allowed to use the cash method even if they meet the gross receipts test (Code Sec. 448(a)(3)).

The steps for the gross receipts test are:

- determine gross receipts for each year in the three-tax-year period;
- compute the average annual gross receipts for the three-tax-year period; and
- determine if the average annual gross receipts for the three-tax-year period are less than or equal to the $25 million amount (as adjusted after 2018).

> **Example:** A C corporation wants to determine if it can use the cash method under the expanded gross receipts test for the 2018 tax year. For the three tax years ending with the 2017 tax year, the corporation has gross receipts of $21 million, $26 million and $25 million (tax years 2015, 2016 and 2017, respectively). Its average annual gross receipts for the three-tax-year period are $24 million (($21 million + $26 million + $25 million) ÷ 3). The corporation meets the gross receipts test for 2018.

> **Comment:** Many additional C corporations and partnerships with a corporate partner will be able to use the cash method under the $25 million gross receipts test since the prior test capped the amount of qualifying annual gross receipts at only $5 million.

> **Comment:** The other exceptions to the general limitation on the use of the cash method continue to apply for qualified personal service corporations and taxpayers other than C corporations. Thus, qualified personal service corporations, partnerships without C corporation partners, S corporations, and other passth-

## NEW LAW EXPLAINED

rough entities are allowed to use the cash method without regard to whether they meet the $25 million gross receipts test if the cash method clearly reflects income and the entity is not a tax shelter (Conference Report on H.R. 1, Tax Cuts and Jobs Act (H. Rept. 115-466)).

A taxpayer making a change in accounting method under the Code Sec. 448 rules limiting the use of the cash method should treat the change as initiated by the taxpayer and made with the IRS's consent for purposes of any Code Sec. 481 adjustment (Code Sec. 448(d)(7), as amended by the 2017 Tax Cuts Act). The IRS has provided procedures for making this change under the automatic consent procedure, as discussed below. The special Code Sec. 481 adjustment periods for Code Sec. 448 accounting method changes of up to four years and up to 10 years for a hospital have been eliminated for tax years beginning after December 31, 2017 (Code Sec. 448(d)(7), prior to amendment by the 2017 Tax Cuts Act).

**Use of cash method by large farming corporations expanded.** The exception to the required use of the accrual method by large farming C corporations and farming partnerships with a C corporation partner has been expanded. For tax years beginning after December 31, 2017, a farming C corporation or a farming partnership in which a C corporation is a partner can use the cash method if it meets the $25 million gross receipts test of Code Sec. 448(c) (discussed above) (Code Sec. 447(c), as amended by the 2017 Tax Cuts Act).

> **Comment:** Many additional farming corporations and farming partnerships with a corporate partner will be able to use the cash method under the $25 million gross receipts test since the prior test capped the amount of qualifying annual gross receipts at only $1 million.

> **Comment:** Since the test for *family* farming corporations was already set at average annual gross receipts of $25 million, the rules in Code Sec. 447 that applied to *family* farming corporations are no longer needed and have been removed (Code Sec. 447(d), (e), (h) and (i), prior to being stricken by the 2017 Tax Cuts Act). However, the rules under former Code Sec. 447(i) for establishing suspense accounts for Code Sec. 481 adjustments from accounting method changes will continue to apply to any suspense accounts established before the date of enactment (Act Sec. 13102(e)(2) of the 2017 Tax Cuts Act).

A farming corporation or farming partnership with a corporate partner making a change in accounting method under the Code Sec. 447 accounting method rules should treat the change as initiated by the taxpayer and made with the IRS's consent for purposes of any Code Sec. 481 adjustment (Code Sec. 447(d), as amended by the 2017 Tax Cuts Act). The IRS has provided procedures for making this change under the automatic change procedure, as discussed below.

**Exception to required use of inventories expanded for small businesses.** The exception to the required use of inventories for taxpayers that qualify as a small business has been expanded. For tax years beginning after December 31, 2017, a business is not required to use inventories if it meets the $25 million gross receipts test of Code Sec. 448(c) (discussed above) (Code Sec. 471(c)(1), as added by the 2017 Tax Cuts Act).

## NEW LAW EXPLAINED

> **Comment:** The exceptions previously provided in Rev. Proc. 2001-10 and Rev. Proc. 2002-28 no longer apply (Rev. Proc. 2018-40).

Any taxpayer that is not a corporation or partnership should apply the gross receipts test as if each trade or business of the taxpayer were a corporation or a partnership (Code Sec. 471(c)(3), as added by the 2017 Tax Cuts Act). Thus, in the case of a sole proprietorship, the $25 million gross receipts test is applied as if the sole proprietorship were a corporation or partnership (Conference Report on H.R. 1, Tax Cuts and Jobs Act (H. Rept. 115-466)).

> **Caution:** Tax shelters that are not allowed to use the cash method do not qualify as small businesses that can avoid using inventories (Code Sec. 448(a)(3); Code Sec. 471(c)(1), as added by the 2017 Tax Cuts Act).

A business that meets the $25 million gross receipts test can use a method of accounting for inventory that:

- treats inventory as non-incidental materials and supplies; or
- conforms to the business's financial accounting treatment of inventories (Code Sec. 471(c)(1)(B), as added by the 2017 Tax Cuts Act; Conference Report on H.R. 1, Tax Cuts and Jobs Act (H. Rept. 115-466)).

A business's financial accounting treatment of inventories is the method of accounting reflected in an applicable financial statement or, if the business does not have an applicable financial statement, in the business's books and records as prepared in accordance with its accounting procedures (Code Sec. 471(c)(1)(B), as added by the 2017 Tax Cuts Act). An "applicable financial statement" is defined in Code Sec. 451(b)(3) (see ¶580) (Code Sec. 471(c)(2), as added by the 2017 Tax Cuts Act).

A taxpayer making a change in accounting method under the exception to the required use of inventories for small businesses should treat the change as initiated by the taxpayer and made with the IRS's consent for purposes of any Code Sec. 481 adjustment (Code Sec. 471(c)(4), as added by the 2017 Tax Cuts Act). The IRS has provided procedures for making this change under the automatic consent procedure, as explained below.

**Exception to required use of UNICAP rules expanded for small taxpayers.** The exception to the UNICAP rules for small taxpayers that purchase personal property for resale has been expanded. For tax years beginning after December 31, 2017, a taxpayer is not required to apply the UNICAP rules for the tax year if it meets the $25 million gross receipts test of Code Sec. 448(c) (discussed above) (Code Sec. 263A(i)(1), as added by the 2017 Tax Cuts Act). The expanded exception to the UNICAP rules applies to any producer or reseller, other than a tax shelter, that meets the $25 million gross receipts test (Conference Report on H.R. 1, Tax Cuts and Jobs Act (H. Rept. 115-466)).

A taxpayer that is not a corporation or partnership should apply the gross receipts test as if each trade or business of the taxpayer were a corporation or a partnership (Code Sec. 263A(i)(2), as added by the 2017 Tax Cuts Act). Thus, in the case of a sole proprietorship, the $25 million gross receipts test is applied as if the sole proprietorship were a corporation or partnership (Conference Report on H.R. 1, Tax Cuts and Jobs Act (H. Rept. 115-466)).

**¶570**

## NEW LAW EXPLAINED

**Caution:** Tax shelters that are not allowed to use the cash method do not qualify as small businesses that can avoid the UNICAP rules (Code Sec. 448(a)(3); Code Sec. 263A(i)(1), as added by the 2017 Tax Cuts Act).

**Comment:** The prior exception to the UNICAP rules only applied to small taxpayers that purchase personal property for resale while the expanded exception to the UNICAP rules applies to any *producer or reseller*, other than a tax shelter, that meets the $25 million gross receipts test (Conference Report on H.R. 1, Tax Cuts and Jobs Act (H. Rept. 115-466)). It also appears that the exception will apply to *real property* acquired for resale.

A taxpayer making a change in accounting method under the exception to the UNICAP rules for small businesses meeting the $25 million gross receipts test should treat the change as initiated by the taxpayer and made with the IRS's consent for purposes of any Code Sec. 481 adjustment (Code Sec. 263A(i)(3), as added by the 2017 Tax Cuts Act). The IRS has provided procedures for making this change under the automatic change procedures, as discussed below.

**Small construction contract exception expanded.** The small construction contract exception to the required use of the percentage of completion method for long-term contracts has been expanded. For contracts entered into after December 31, 2017, in tax years ending after such date, the exception applies to a construction contract entered into by a taxpayer:

- who estimates at the time the contract is entered into that the contract will be completed within the two-year period beginning on the contract commencement date; and

- who meets the $25 million gross receipts test of Code Sec. 448(c) (discussed above) for the tax year in which the contract is entered into (Code Sec. 460(e)(1)(B), as amended by the 2017 Tax Cuts Act).

A taxpayer that is not a corporation or partnership should apply the gross receipts test as if each trade or business of the taxpayer were a corporation or a partnership (Code Sec. 460(e)(2)(A), as added by the 2017 Tax Cuts Act). Thus, in the case of a sole proprietorship, the $25 million gross receipts test is applied as if the sole proprietorship were a corporation or partnership (Conference Report on H.R. 1, Tax Cuts and Jobs Act (H. Rept. 115-466)).

**Caution:** The expanded exception for small contraction contracts cannot be applied by a tax shelter that is not allowed to use the cash method of accounting under Code Sec. 448(a)(3) (Code Sec. 460(e)(1)(B), as amended by the 2017 Tax Cuts Act).

If a taxpayer changes its method of accounting based on the small construction contract exception, then:

- the change is treated as initiated by the taxpayer and made with the IRS's consent; and

- the change is made on a cut-off basis for all similarly classified contracts entered into on or after the year of change (Code Sec. 460(e)(2)(B), as added by the 2017 Tax Cuts Act).

## NEW LAW EXPLAINED

**Changes of accounting method.** The IRS has provided procedures allowing small business taxpayers to obtain automatic consent to change their methods of accounting to conform with these provisions (Rev. Proc. 2018-40). Taxpayers that can use the automatic change procedures include:

- taxpayers newly eligible to use the cash method under the $25 million gross receipts test;

- small business taxpayers that capitalize costs under the uniform capitalization rules that want to change to a method that no longer does so, including to self-constructed assets;

- small business taxpayers that want to change their method of accounting for inventory from an inventory method to treating inventory as non-incidental material and supplies, or conforming to the method of accounting reflected in applicable financial statements with respect to the tax year, or if the taxpayer does not have an applicable financial statement for the tax year, the taxpayer's books and records prepared in accordance with the taxpayer's accounting procedures; and

- small business taxpayers that want to change their method of accounting for exempt long-term construction contracts from the percentage-of-completion method of accounting to an exempt contract method of accounting or choose to stop capitalizing costs under the uniform capitalization method for home construction contracts.

▶ **Effective date.** The amendments made by this section generally apply to tax years beginning after December 31, 2017 (Act Sec. 13102(e)(1) of the Tax Cuts and Jobs Act (P.L. 115-97)). The amendments made by this provision for small construction contracts apply to contracts entered into after December 31, 2017, in tax years ending after such date (Act Sec. 13102(e)(3) of the 2017 Tax Cuts Act).

## ¶580 Accrual Method of Accounting for Deferral of Advance Payments and Income Based on Financial Accounting Treatment

### SUMMARY OF NEW LAW

The income recognition rules for accrual-method taxpayers have been modified. First, amounts are generally included in income no later than when the amounts are included for financial accounting purposes. Second, accrual-method taxpayers can elect to defer including certain advance payments in income until the tax year after the tax year in which the payments were received, subject to limitations.

### BACKGROUND

Taxpayers include gains, profits, and other income items in gross income in the tax year received, unless their accounting method requires the items to be accounted for

## BACKGROUND

in a different year (Code Sec. 451(a)). Under the cash method, taxpayers report income in the year in which it is actually or constructively received in the form of cash, property, or services with a determinable value (Code Sec. 446(c)(1); Reg. §1.446-1(c)(1)(i)).

Under the accrual method, taxpayers include items in income when all events have occurred that fix the taxpayer's right to receive the income and the amount can be determined with reasonable accuracy (Code Sec. 446(c)(2); Reg. §1.446-1(c)(1)(ii)). This means that an item of income is included in gross income on the earliest of when payment is received, when the income amount is due, when the income is earned, or when title has passed. Thus, accrual-method taxpayers who are paid in advance for goods or services that they will provide in the future normally include the advance payments in income when received. Instead of reporting advance payments when they are received, accrual-method taxpayers can use one of two deferral methods to postpone reporting the advance payments to a later time. The methods apply to sales of goods and sales of services and certain goods.

**Deferral of advance payments received for sales of goods.** Under the deferral method for goods, accrual-method taxpayers can include advance payments for future sales of goods in income when the payments accrue (Reg. §1.451-5). The method applies to advance payments from: (1) sales of goods held primarily for sale to customers in the ordinary course of the taxpayer's business, and (2) long-term contracts for building, installing, constructing, or manufacturing items uncompleted during the tax year. An accrual-method seller using the deferral method for goods can postpone including advance payments in income until the earlier of:

(1) the tax year in which the payments are properly accruable under the accounting method used for tax purposes; or

(2) the tax year in which the payments are included in gross receipts under the accounting method used for financial reports (Reg. §1.451-5(b)).

**Deferral of advance payments received for services and certain goods.** Accrual-method taxpayers who receive advance payments for services to be performed in a later tax year normally include all of the payments in income in the year received. However, a taxpayer can choose to defer including qualifying advance payments in income. A taxpayer using the deferral method for services and certain goods must:

(1) include the advance payment in income in the tax year received to the extent the payment is recognized in revenue in the taxpayer's applicable financial statement or, if the taxpayer does not have an applicable financial statement, to the extent the payment is earned in that year; and

(2) include the remaining amount of the advance payment in income in the following tax year (Rev. Proc. 2004-34).

Under the deferral method, no advance payment can be deferred past the year following the year the payment is received. Thus, all of the advance payment must be included in income by the year following the year received regardless of whether all of the remaining services are provided in that year.

An advance payment for the deferral method for services and certain goods is a payment that: (1) is allowed to be included in gross income for tax purposes in the

## BACKGROUND

year it is received; and (2) in whole or in part, is earned in a later tax year or is recognized as revenue on the taxpayer's applicable financial statement in a later tax year (Rev. Proc. 2004-34).

An advance payment must be made for one of the following items:

(1) services;

(2) the sale of goods (for which the taxpayer does not use the deferral method for advance payments for sales of goods (Reg. § 1.451-5(b)(1)(ii)));

(3) the use of intellectual property;

(4) the occupancy or use of property, if the occupancy or use is ancillary to providing services to the property user;

(5) the sale, lease, or license of computer software;

(6) a guaranty or warranty contract related to one of the items listed above;

(7) subscriptions (other than prepaid subscriptions for which an election is made to include them in income over the years that the liability exists under Code Sec. 455);

(8) memberships in organizations (other than prepaid membership dues for which an election is made to include them in income over the years that the liability exists under Code Sec. 456);

(9) an eligible gift card sale; or

(10) any combination of the items listed above.

Advance payments do *not* include rents not listed above, insurance premiums whose recognition is governed by the insurance company rules, payments with respect to financial instruments, payments accounted for under the rules for service warranty contracts (Rev. Proc. 97-38), payments with respect to warranty and guaranty contracts under which a third party is the primary obligor, payments subject to the withholding rules for nonresident aliens or foreign corporations (Code Secs. 1441 and 1442), and payments of property transferred in connection with performance of services (Code Sec. 83).

A taxpayer's applicable financial statement is the first that it has of the following:

(1) a financial statement to be filed with the Securities and Exchange Commission (the 10-K or the Annual Statement to Shareholders);

(2) a certified audited financial statement accompanied by the report of an independent CPA that is used for credit purposes, reporting to shareholders, or any other substantial non-tax purpose; or

(3) another financial statement (other than a tax return) required to be provided to the federal or a state government or agency other than the IRS or SEC.

If the taxpayer does not have an applicable financial statement, the amount earned in the year of receipt must be included in taxable income in that year. The remainder of the advance payment is included in taxable income in the next tax year.

**Original issue discount.** Code Sec. 1271 is the first of a group of Code sections dealing with how to account for debt instruments with original issue discount (OID).

## BACKGROUND

A debt instrument has been issued at a discount if the instrument's stated redemption price at maturity is greater than its issue price. For most purposes, OID will be treated as interest. The holder of a debt instrument with OID will accrue and include the OID in income over the term of the instrument, regardless of when the stated interest, if any, is paid (Conference Report on H.R. 1, Tax Cuts and Jobs Act (H. Rept. 115-466)). Special rules also apply for determining the amount of OID for debt instruments that may be subject to prepayment and to pools of debt instruments where payments on the debt instruments may be accelerated by prepayments.

## NEW LAW EXPLAINED

**Special rules added on time for including amounts in income.**—Two special rules have been added on the proper time for including amounts in income by accrual-method taxpayers. Under the first rule, amounts are generally included in income no later than when the amounts are included for financial accounting purposes (Code Sec. 451(b), as added by the Tax Cuts and Jobs Act (P.L. 115-97)). The second rule allows taxpayers to elect to defer including certain advance payments in income until the tax year after the tax year in which the payments were received, subject to limitations (Code Sec. 451(c), as added by the 2017 Tax Cuts Act). These income recognition rules generally apply to tax years beginning after December 31, 2017 (Act Sec. 13221(c) of the 2017 Tax Cuts Act). However, in the case of income from a debt instrument having original issue discount (OID), the rules apply to tax years beginning after December 31, 2018 (Act Sec. 13221(e)(1) of the 2017 Tax Cuts Act).

**Amounts included in income based on financial accounting treatment.** For an accrual-method taxpayer, the all-events test is met with respect to any item of gross income if all the events have occurred which fix the right to receive such income and the amount of such income can be determined with reasonable accuracy (Code Sec. 451(b)(1)(C), as added by the 2017 Tax Cuts Act). However, the all-events test with respect to any item of gross income or portion of such item cannot be treated as met any later than when the item of gross income or portion of such item is taken into account in revenue in the taxpayer's applicable financial statement or other financial statement specified by the IRS (Code Sec. 451(b)(1)(A), as added by the 2017 Tax Cuts Act).

*Applicable financial statement.* A taxpayer's applicable financial statement is:

(1) a financial statement that is certified as being prepared according to generally accepted accounting principles and is:

    (a) a 10-K or Annual Statement to Shareholders that is required to be filed with the U.S. Securities and Exchange Commission (SEC),

    (b) if there is no statement described in (a), an audited financial statement that is used for credit purposes, reporting to shareholders, partners, or other proprietors, or to beneficiaries, or any other substantial non-tax purpose, or

    (c) if there is no statement described in (a) or (b), a financial statement filed with any federal agency for purposes other than federal tax purposes;

## NEW LAW EXPLAINED

(2) if there is no statement described in (1), above, a financial statement that is made on the basis of international financial reporting standards and is filed with a foreign government agency that is equivalent to the SEC and which has reporting standards that are not less stringent than the SEC standards; or

(3) if there is no statement described in (1) or (2), above, a financial statement filed with any other regulatory or governmental body specified by the IRS (Code Sec. 451(b)(3), as added by the 2017 Tax Cuts Act).

If the financial results of a taxpayer are reported on the applicable financial statement for a group of entities, the statement is treated as the applicable financial statement of the taxpayer (Code Sec. 451(b)(5), as added by the 2017 Tax Cuts Act).

*Allocation of transaction price.* In the case of a contract that contains multiple performance obligations, the allocation of the transaction price to each performance obligation is equal to the amount allocated to each performance obligation for purposes of including such item in revenue in the taxpayer's applicable financial statement (Code Sec. 451(b)(4), as added by the 2017 Tax Cuts Act).

The IRS is expected to provide guidance regarding whether and how to allocate the transaction price:

(1) to performance obligations that are not contractually based (e.g., the provision of free goods or services to a customer or the provision of a customary amount of training or support);

(2) for arrangements that include both income subject to Code Sec. 451 and long-term contracts subject to Code Sec. 460; and

(3) when the income realization event for federal income tax purposes differs from the income realization event for financial statement purposes (General Explanation of Public Law 115–97 Prepared by the Staff of the Joint Committee on Taxation (December 2018), FN 806).

*Exceptions to financial statement rule.* The rule for including amounts in income no later than they are included for financial accounting purposes does not apply to a taxpayer that does not have an applicable financial statement or other financial statement specified by the IRS. In addition, the rule does not apply to any item of gross income in connection with a mortgage servicing contract (Code Sec. 451(b)(1)(B), as added by the 2017 Tax Cuts Act). Income from mortgage servicing rights should continue to be recognized under the current rules where: (1) "normal" mortgage servicing rights are included in income upon the earlier of earned or received under the all-events test and not averaged over the life of the mortgage, and (2) "excess" mortgage servicing rights are treated as stripped coupons and subject to the original issue discount (OID) rules (Conference Report on H.R. 1, Tax Cuts and Jobs Act (H. Rept. 115-466)).

The rule for including amounts in income no later than they are included for financial accounting purposes also does not apply with respect to any item of gross income for which the taxpayer uses a special method of accounting provided under the income tax provisions of the Internal Revenue Code, other than the rules for bonds and debt instruments in Code Secs. 1271—1288 (Code Sec. 451(b)(2), as added by the 2017 Tax

## NEW LAW EXPLAINED

Cuts Act). Thus, accrual-method taxpayers apply the applicable financial statement rule before applying the special rules in Code Secs. 1271—1288, which cover the original issue discount (OID) rules and also rules on the treatment of market discount on bonds, discounts on short-term obligations, OID on tax-exempt bonds, and stripped bonds and stripped coupons (Conference Report on H.R. 1, Tax Cuts and Jobs Act (H. Rept. 115-466)).

*Accrued market discount.* Accrued market discount is not includible in income under Code Sec. 451(b). The IRS plans to issue proposed regulations providing guidance on this treatment. Under the all events test, an accrual method taxpayer recognizes income when:

- all the events have occurred that fix the right to receive the income and;
- the amount of income can be determined with reasonable accuracy. As noted above, the general rule under Code Sec. 451(b) does not apply to an item of gross income for which the taxpayer uses a special method of accounting, other than items accounted for under Code Secs. 1271 through 1288.

Under Code Sec. 1276, (1) gain on the disposition of a market discount bond is ordinary income to the extent that the gain does not exceed the bond's accrued market discount, and (2) a partial principal payment on a market discount bond is includible in gross income to the extent the payment does not exceed accrued market discount on the bond (Notice 2018-80).

**Accrual-method taxpayers allowed to defer including advance payments in income.** Generally, for tax years beginning after December 31, 2017, an accrual-method taxpayer who receives an advance payment during the tax year must either:

(1)  include the advance payment in gross income for the tax year of receipt; or

(2)  make an election to defer the inclusion of the advance payment in gross income with respect to the category of advance payments to which the advance payment belongs (Code Sec. 451(c)(1), as added by the 2017 Tax Cuts Act).

Under the deferral election, any portion of the advance payment that is required to be included in gross income under the financial statement rule described above would be included in gross income in the tax year in which it is received and the remaining portion of the advance payment would be included in gross income in the tax year following the tax year in which it is received (Code Sec. 451(c)(1)(B), as added by the 2017 Tax Cuts Act). An item of gross income is received by the taxpayer if it is actually or constructively received, or if it is due and payable to the taxpayer (Code Sec. 451(c)(4)(C), as added by the 2017 Tax Cuts Act).

> **Comment:** The new rule for deferring advance payments from income essentially codifies IRS guidance in Rev. Proc. 2004-34 on deferral of advance payments with some modifications.

*Advance payment defined.* An advance payment is any payment:

(1)  the full inclusion of which in the taxpayer's gross income for the tax year of receipt is a permissible method of accounting without regard to this advance payment rule;

## NEW LAW EXPLAINED

(2) any portion of which is included in revenue by the taxpayer in a 10-K or Annual Statement to Shareholders that is required to be filed with the U.S. Securities and Exchange Commission (SEC) or an audited financial statement that is used for credit purposes, reporting to shareholders, partners, or other proprietors, or to beneficiaries, or any other substantial non-tax purpose, for a subsequent tax year; and

(3) which is for goods, services, or such items as may be identified by the IRS (Code Sec. 451(c)(4)(A), as added by the 2017 Tax Cuts Act).

An advance payment does not include:

(1) rent;

(2) insurance premiums governed by subchapter L (Insurance Companies);

(3) payments with respect to financial instruments;

(4) payments with respect to warranty or guarantee contracts under which a third party is the primary obligor;

(5) payments subject to Code Sec. 871(a) or Code Sec. 881 (tax on certain amounts received from U.S sources by a nonresident alien or foreign corporation) or Code Sec. 1441 or Code Sec. 1442 (payments subject to the withholding rules for nonresident aliens or foreign corporations);

(6) payments to which Code Sec. 83 applies (property transferred in connection with the performance of services); and

(7) any other payment identified by the IRS for this purpose (Code Sec. 451(c)(4)(B), as added by the 2017 Tax Cuts Act).

For purposes of the advance payment rules, rules similar to the allocation of transaction price rules of Code Sec. 451(b)(4), above, apply (Code Sec. 451(c)(4)(D), as added by the 2017 Tax Cuts Act). Thus, if advance payments are received for a combination of services, goods, or other specified items, the taxpayer should allocate the transaction price according to the allocation made in the taxpayer's applicable financial statement (Conference Report on H.R. 1, Tax Cuts and Jobs Act (H. Rept. 115-466)).

Unless otherwise provided by the IRS, the deferral election for advance payments will not apply to advance payments received by a taxpayer during a tax year if the taxpayer ceases to exist during or with the close of such tax year (Code Sec. 451(c)(3), as added by the 2017 Tax Cuts Act). Thus, any deferred advance payment must be included in gross income if the taxpayer ceases to exist (Conference Report on H.R. 1, Tax Cuts and Jobs Act (H. Rept. 115-466)).

The IRS is expected to provide guidance regarding whether and how to allocate the transaction price:

(1) to performance obligations that are not contractually based (e.g., the provision of free goods or services to a customer or the provision of a customary amount of training or support);

(2) for arrangements that include both income subject to Code Sec. 451 and long-term contracts subject to Code Sec. 460; and

## NEW LAW EXPLAINED

(3) when the income realization event for federal income tax purposes differs from the income realization event for financial statement purposes (General Explanation of Public Law 115–97 Prepared by the Staff of the Joint Committee on Taxation (December 2018), FN 842).

*How to elect to defer inclusion of advance payments in income.* The IRS is instructed to provide details on making the election to defer the inclusion of advance payments in income. This includes the time, form and manner, and the categories of advance payments. The election will be effective for the tax year with respect to which it is first made and for all subsequent tax years, unless the taxpayer obtains the IRS's consent to revoke the election (Code Sec. 451(c)(2), as added by the 2017 Tax Cuts Act).

*Transitional guidance.* Until further guidance for the treatment of advance payments applies, taxpayers may continue to rely on Rev. Proc. 2004-34 for the treatment of advance payments. During this time, the IRS will not challenge a taxpayer's use of Rev. Proc. 2004-34 to satisfy the requirements of Code Sec. 451 (Notice 2018-35).

*Regulations to be removed.* Code Sec. 451(c) and its election to defer advance payments override the deferral method provided by Reg. § 1.451-5. Accordingly, the IRS plans to remove Reg. § 1.451-5 and its cross references. Taxpayers changing a method of accounting for advance payments from a method described in Reg. § 1.451-5 to another method should apply the rules of Code Sec. 446 regarding changes in methods of accounting (NPRM REG-104872-18).

**Change of accounting method.** The computation of taxable income under the deferral election for advance payments is treated as a method of accounting (Code Sec. 451(c)(2)(B), as added by the 2017 Tax Cuts Act). In the case of any qualified change of accounting method for the taxpayer's first tax year beginning after December 31, 2017, the change is treated as initiated by the taxpayer and made with the IRS's consent. A qualified change of accounting method is any change of accounting method that is required by the new income recognition rules or was prohibited and is now permitted under the new rules (Act Sec. 13221(d) of the 2017 Tax Cuts Act). For a qualified change of accounting method involving income from a debt instrument with original issue discount (OID), taxpayers should use a six-year period for taking into account any required Code Sec. 481 adjustments (Act Sec. 13221(e)(2) of the 2017 Tax Cuts Act).

The IRS will grant automatic consent to accounting method changes to comply with new Code Sec. 451(b), as added by the 2017 Tax Cuts Act (Rev. Proc. 2018-60). In addition, some taxpayers may make the accounting method change on their tax returns, without filing a Form 3115, Application for Change in Accounting Method. The automatic consent procedures apply to a taxpayer with an applicable financial statement that:

- wants to change to a method of accounting that complies with Code Sec. 451(b); and/or

- for the year of the change, is not adopting Financial Accounting Standards Board (FASB) and International Accounting Standards Board (IASB) financial accounting standards for revenue recognition, titled "Revenue from Contracts with Customers (Topic 606)" that were announced on May 28, 2014.

## NEW LAW EXPLAINED

For income from a debt instrument having OID, the Code Sec. 481(a) adjustment period for the change is six tax years (year of change plus the next five tax years). However, this applies only for the taxpayer's first tax year beginning after December 31, 2018.

The automatic consent procedures do not apply to a taxpayer that wants to make a change to a method that adopts the FASB/IASB standard, or to a special accounting method as described in Code Sec. 451(b)(2).

For its first tax year beginning after December 31, 2017, a qualified taxpayer can change its accounting method to comply with Code Sec. 451(b) without filing a Form 3115. An eligible taxpayer must either:

(1) meet the Code Sec. 448(c) gross receipts test for a small business taxpayers (so the taxpayer's average annual gross receipts for the three prior tax years cannot exceed $25 million); or

(2) be making the change to comply with Code Sec. 451(b)(1)(A) and/or (b)(4), and the Code Sec. 481(a) adjustment for each of the changes is zero.

These streamlined procedures do not apply to a taxpayer that wants to make a change to a method that adopts the FASB/IASB standard, or to a special accounting method as described in Code Sec. 451(b)(2), or certain other concurrent accounting method changes. Tax shelters also are not eligible.

▶ **Effective date.** The amendments made by this section generally apply to tax years beginning after December 31, 2017 (Act Sec. 13221(c) of the Tax Cuts and Jobs Act (P.L. 115-97)). In the case of income from a debt instrument having original issue discount (OID), the amendments made by this section apply to tax years beginning after December 31, 2018 (Act Sec. 13221(e)(1) of the 2017 Tax Cuts Act).

— Act Sec. 13221(a) of the Tax Cuts and Jobs Act (P.L. 115-97), redesignating Code Sec. 451(b) through (i) as (c) through (j), respectively, and adding new (b);

— Act Sec. 13221(b), redesignating Code Sec. 451(c) through (j) (as redesignated by Act Sec. 13221(a)), as (d) through (k), respectively, and adding new (c);

— Act Sec. 13221(d).

— Act Sec. 13221(c) and (e)(1), providing the effective dates.

# BUSINESS TAX CREDITS

## ¶585  Employer Credit for Paid Family and Medical Leave

### SUMMARY OF NEW LAW

Eligible employers are entitled to claim a credit for paid family and medical leave equal to 12.5 percent of wages paid to qualifying employees during any period in which such employees are on leave under the Family and Medical Leave Act (FMLA)

## SUMMARY

provided that the rate of payment is 50 percent of the wages normally paid to the employee. The credit is part of the general business credit and only available for wages paid in tax years beginning after December 31, 2017, and before January 1, 2020.

## BACKGROUND

The Family and Medical Leave Act of 1993 (P.L. 103-3) requires an employer with 50 or more employees (within a 75 mile radius) to give eligible employees 12 weeks of unpaid leave for births, adoptions, and family illnesses. An employer is required to provide coverage for: (a) the birth of a child; (b) the placement of a child with the employee for adoption or foster care; (c) the employee to care for a seriously ill child, spouse or parent; and (d) an employee's own serious illness. An employer may require that a request for leave be supported by certification issued by the health care provider for the applicable party. Spouses who are employed by the same employer may be limited to an aggregate of 12 weeks if leave is sought for a birth, adoption, or to care for an ill parent.

In order to be eligible, an employee must have worked at least one year for the employer providing coverage. During that period, the employee must have worked at least 1,250 hours. Generally, an employer is entitled to 30 days' notice of an employee's intent to take leave if the leave is "foreseeable," such as for the birth or adoption of a child. However, the 30-day requirement is relaxed for unforeseen circumstances (e.g., a premature birth or a sudden change in medical condition).

An employer who provides health care coverage to employees is required to continue that coverage during the leave period. Health care coverage must be maintained at the level and under the conditions coverage would have been provided if the employee had continued being employed. If the employee fails to return to work at the end of 12 weeks for reasons other than the continued serious illness of the employee or another family member that necessitated the leave initially, the employer may recover the premium paid for maintenance of coverage during the leave period.

An employer is required to guarantee that employees will be allowed to return to the same, or an equivalent, job upon their return to work. Eligible employees retain all accrued benefits while on leave; however, they are not entitled to the accrual of any seniority or employment benefits during the period of leave. An employer does not receive a tax credit for compensation paid to employees while on leave.

## NEW LAW EXPLAINED

**Employer credit for paid family and medical leave provided.**—A tax credit is available for employers for paid leave provided under the Family and Medical Leave Act (FMLA) after 2017. An eligible employer is allowed the FMLA credit in an amount equal to the applicable percentage of the wages paid to qualifying employees during the period in which such employees are on leave (Code Sec. 45S(a)(1), as added by the Tax Cuts and Jobs Act (P.L. 115-97)). Applicable percentage means 12.5 percent increased (but not above 25 percent) by 0.25 percentage points for each percentage point by

## NEW LAW EXPLAINED

which the rate of payment exceeds 50 percent (Code Sec. 45S(a)(2), as added by the 2017 Tax Cuts Act). The IRS issued guidance on the paid family and medical leave credit in the form of questions and answers. The guidance is effective September 24, 2018, and applies to wages paid in tax years beginning after December 31, 2017, and before January 1, 2020 (Notice 2018-71).

> **Caution:** The FMLA credit is only available with respect to wages paid in tax years beginning in 2018. Wages incurred but unpaid in a tax year beginning in 2018 do not qualify for the credit (Act Sec. 13403(e) of the 2017 Tax Cuts Act). In addition, the credit terminates after 2019 and therefore may not be claimed to wages paid in tax years beginning after 2019 Code Sec. 45S(i), as added by the 2017 Tax Cuts Act).

The FMLA credit allowed with respect to any employee for any tax year shall not exceed an amount equal to the product of:

- the normal hourly wage rate of the employee for each hour (or fraction thereof) of actual services performed for the employer; and
- the number of hours (or fraction thereof for which the leave under FMLA is taken) (Code Sec. 45S(b)(1), as added by the 2017 Tax Cuts Act).

If an employee is not paid an hourly wage rate, the wages of such an employee should be prorated to an hourly wage rate in accordance with regulations established by the IRS (Code Sec. 45S(b)(2), as added by the 2017 Tax Cuts Act). The maximum amount of leave subject to the credit for any employee for any tax year may not exceed 12 weeks (Code Sec. 45S(b)(3), as added by the 2017 Tax Cuts Act).

**Eligible employer.** An eligible employer for purposes of the FMLA credit is an employer that has a written policy in place that meets the following requirements:

- The policy provides: (a) in the case of a qualifying employee who is not a part-time employee, not less than 2 weeks of annual paid FMLA leave, and (b) in the case of a qualifying employee who is a part-time employee, annual paid FMLA leave that is not less than an amount which bears the same ratio to the amount of annual paid FML that is provided to a qualified employee who is not part-time as (i) the number of hours the employee is expected to work during any week, over (ii) the number of hours an equivalent qualifying employee who is not part-time is expected to work during the week.
- The policy requires that the rate of payment under the program is not less than 50 percent of the wages normally paid to the employee for services performed for the employer (Code Sec. 45S(c)(1), as added by the 2017 Tax Cuts Act).

The written policy may be contained in one or more documents. For example, an employer may maintain different documents to cover different classifications of employees or different types of leave, and those documents collectively constitute the employer's written policy. The written policy may be included in the same document that governs the employer's other leave policies. However, if an employer's written policy provides paid leave for FMLA purposes and additional paid leave for other reasons (such as vacation or personal leave), only the leave specifically designated for FMLA purposes is treated as family and medical leave eligible for the credit (Notice 2018-71).

**¶585**

# NEW LAW EXPLAINED

An employer's written policy for family and medical leave must be in place before the leave is taken to which the credit relates. The written policy is considered in place on the later of the policy's adoption date or the policy's effective date. However, an eligible employer may establish a qualifying paid family leave program or amend an existing program by December 31, 2018, in order to retroactively claim the credit for qualifying leave previously provided during 2018 (Notice 2018-71).

An "added employer" is not treated as an eligible employer unless the employer provides FMLA leave that conforms with a written policy that ensures that the employer (i) will not interfere with, restrain, or deny the exercise of or the attempt to exercise, any right provided under the policy, and (ii) will not discharge or in any other manner discriminate against any individual for opposing any practice prohibited by the policy (Code Sec. 45S(c)(2)(A), as added by the 2017 Tax Cuts Act). An "added employee" is defined as a qualifying employee who is not covered by Title I of the FMLA (P.L. 103-3) (Code Sec. 45S(c)(2)(B)(i), as added by the 2017 Tax Cuts Act). An "added employer" is defined to mean an eligible employer whether or not covered by Title I of the FMLA, who offers paid family and medical leave to added employees (Code Sec. 45S(c)(2)(B)(ii), as added by the 2017 Tax Cuts Act).

All members of an aggregate group that are treated as a single employer under Code Secs. 52(a) and (b) are treated as a single taxpayer for purposes of the FMLA credit (Code Sec. 45S(c)(3), as added by the 2017 Tax Cuts Act). One exception is that each member of an aggregate group is treated separately for purposes of the requirement for an employer to have in place a written policy, but a technical correction may be needed to reflect this intent (General Explanation of Public Law 115-97 (JCS-1-18), footnote 1037). In addition, any leave that is paid by a state or local government or is required by state or local law is not considered in determining the amount of paid FMLA leave that is provided by the employer (Code Sec. 45S(c)(4), as added by the 2017 Tax Cuts Act). Failure to provide paid family and medical leave by an employer will not subject an employer to any penalty, liability, or other consequence, except that the employer is not eligible to take the FMLA credit (Code Sec. 45S(c)(5), as added by the 2017 Tax Cuts Act).

The leave paid under the policy must provide a rate of payment equal to at least 50 percent of the wages normally paid to the employee. In determining the rate of payment under the policy, leave paid by a State or local government or required under State or local law is not taken into account. If family leave is required under state law but there is no requirement that the leave be paid, amounts that an employer chooses to pay count toward the 50 percent rate of payment requirement. Overtime (other than regularly-scheduled overtime) and discretionary bonuses are excluded from wages normally paid. Wages normally paid to employees who are not salaried or not paid an hourly rate should be determined using the rules for determining regular rate of pay set forth in regulations issued under the Fair Labor Standards Act of 1938 (Notice 2018-71).

**Qualifying employee.** A qualifying employee for purpose of the FMLA credit is any employee, which is defined in section 3(e) of the Fair Labor Standard Act of 1938, who has been employed by the employer for at least one year. In addition, the employee must have received in the preceding year compensation not in excess of an amount equal to 60 percent of the amount applicable for a highly-compensated

## NEW LAW EXPLAINED

employee under the nondiscrimination requirements rules for qualified retirement plans (Code Sec. 45S(d), as added by the 2017 Tax Cuts Act).

An employer may use any reasonable method to determine whether an employee has been employed for one year or more until further guidance is issued (Notice 2018-71). It is reasonable to treating employees as employed for one year or more if they have been employed for 12 months. However, any requirement that an employee work 12 consecutive months to be a qualifying employee is not reasonable. Any requirement that an employee work a minimum number of hours to be a qualifying employee is not reasonable. The FMLA rules that require an employee to work a minimum of 1,250 hours of service to be an eligible employee under the FMLA do not apply for the credit. An employer's written policy may not exclude any classification of employees, such as unionized employees, if they are qualifying employees.

> **Comment:** The nondiscrimination requirements for qualified retirement plans provide that an employee is generally considered highly compensated if he or she: (1) was a five-percent owner at any time during the current or preceding year, or (2) had compensation from the employer for the preceding year in excess of $120,000 for 2018 (Code Sec. 414(q)(1)(B)(i); Notice 2017-64). Thus, a qualifying employee for purposes of the FMLA credit must not have received more than $72,000 in compensation in 2018 (60 percent × $120,000).

**FMLA leave.** Family and medical leave is defined as leave for any one or more purposes described in Sections 102(a)(1)(A)-(E) or (3) of the FMLA, whether that leave is provided under the Act or due to an employer's policy (Code Sec. 45S(e)(1), as added by the 2017 Tax Cuts Act). An eligible employee is entitled to FMLA leave under the following circumstances:

- the birth of a child of the employee and in order to care for such child;
- the placement of a child for adoption or foster care;
- a serious health condition of a spouse, child, or parent requiring the employee to care for such person;
- the employee's serious health condition that makes the employee unable to perform the functions of the employee's position;
- any "qualifying exigency" arising out of the fact that the employee's spouse, child, or parent is a military member on covered active duty or call to covered active duty status; or
- to care for a covered service member with a serious injury or illness.

An employer's policy may allow leave to be used to care for additional persons not specified in the FMLA (e.g., a grandparent). However, this paid leave will not qualify for the credit (Notice 2018-71).

If the employer provides paid leave as vacation leave, personal leave, or medical or sick leave (other than leave specifically for one or more of the purposes referred to above), that paid leave is not considered FMLA leave (Code Sec. 45S(e)(2), as added by the 2017 Tax Cuts Act).

¶585

## NEW LAW EXPLAINED

**IRS determinations.** Determinations as to whether an employer or employee meets the requirements to be an "eligible employer" or "qualifying employee" for the FMLA credit are made by the IRS (Code Sec. 45S(f), as added by the 2017 Tax Cuts Act).

**Wages.** The term wages for purposes of the FMLA credit has the same meaning as that given in Code Sec. 3306(b) for FUTA (federal unemployment taxes) without regard to the $7,000 FUTA limitation. Wages do not include any amount taken into account for purposes of determining any other business related tax credit (Code Sec. 45S(g), as added by the 2017 Tax Cuts Act).

FUTA wages generally includes all remuneration paid for employment, including the cash value of all remuneration, including benefits, paid in any medium other than cash. Wages paid by a tax-exempt Code Sec. 501(c)(3) organization are excluded from the definition of FUTA wages and, therefore, do not qualify for the credit even if the organization is subject to the unrelated business income tax during the tax year. A technical correction may be necessary to reflect that the wages with respect to the credit are limited to the employee's normal hourly wage rate and do not include additional amounts, such as a bonus, that could be paid during the leave period (General Explanation of Public Law 115-97 (JCS-1-18)). An employer's deduction for wages is reduced by the amount of the credit claimed (Notice 2018-71).

An employer takes wages paid by a third-party payer (including an insurance company, a professional employer organization, or a Certified Professional Employer Organization) to qualifying employees for services performed for an eligible employer into account in computing the credit. Wages paid through an employer's short-term disability program for family and medical leave are taken into account in determining the credit provided that the program (in combination with any other employer-paid leave arrangement) meets the minimum paid leave requirements. Wages paid to an employee for family and medical leave taken before an employee becomes a qualifying employee are excluded in determining the employer's credit (Notice 2018-71).

**Notice requirement.** Although Code Sec. 45S does not impose a notice requirement on employers with respect to its written policy. However, if an employer chooses to provide notice of the written policy to qualifying employees, the credit may not be claimed unless availability of paid leave is communicated to employees in a manner reasonably designed to reach each qualifying employee. This may include, for example, email communication, use of internal websites, employee handbooks, or posted displays in employee work areas (Notice 2018-71).

**Election to not claim credit.** An employer may elect not to claim the FMLA credit (Code Sec. 45S(h), as added by the 2017 Tax Cuts Act). The election can be made at any time before the expiration of the three-year period beginning on the last day for filing the tax return for the year of the election (without regard to extensions). The election is simply made by not claiming the credit. The election to claim or not claim the credit is made separately by each member of a controlled group and each member

## NEW LAW EXPLAINED

of a group of businesses under common control. However, in the case of a consolidated group, the election is made by the group's agent (Notice 2018-71).

The FMLA credit is calculated on Form 8994 and claimed as a component of the general business credit on Form 3800 (Code Sec. 38(b), as amended by the 2017 Tax Cuts Act). The credit is allowed as a credit against the alternative minimum tax (AMT) (Code Sec. 38(c)(4)(B), as amended by the 2017 Tax Cuts Act).

▶ **Effective date.** The amendments made by this section apply to wages paid in tax years beginning after December 31, 2017 (Act Secs. 13403(e) of the Tax Cuts and Jobs Act (P.L. 115-97)).

— Act Sec. 13403(a) of the Tax Cuts and Jobs Act (P.L. 115-97), adding Code Sec. 45S;

— Act Sec. 13403(b), adding Code Sec. 38(b)(37);

— Act Sec. 13403(c), redesignating clauses Code Sec. 38(c)(4)(ix), (x), and (xi) as Code Sec. 38(c)(4)(x), (xi), and (xii) and adding Code Sec. 38(c)(4)(ix);

— Act Sec. 13403(d), amending Code Sec. 280C(a) and Code Sec. 6501(m);

— Act Sec. 13403(e), providing the effective date.

# ¶590 Rehabilitation Credit

## SUMMARY OF NEW LAW

The 20 percent credit for qualified rehabilitation expenditures with respect to certified historic structures is now claimed ratably over a five-year period. In addition, the 10 percent credit for qualified rehabilitation expenditures with respect to non-historic structures first placed in service before 1936 is eliminated.

## BACKGROUND

A rehabilitation credit is available to a taxpayer to encourage the preservation and rehabilitation of older and historic buildings. The credit is equal to the sum of:

• 10 percent of qualified rehabilitation expenditures (QREs) of the taxpayer for qualified rehabilitated buildings that are not certified historic structures; and

• 20 percent of the QREs of the taxpayer for certified historic structures (Code Sec. 47(a)).

Generally, the credit is claimed in the tax year in which the qualified rehabilitated building is placed in service (Code Sec. 47(b)). However, a taxpayer may elect to claim an advance credit for progress expenditures on certain rehabilitated buildings before the property is actually placed in service (Code Sec. 47(d)).

A "qualified rehabilitated building" is a building and its structural components for which depreciation is allowable and that has been substantially rehabilitated and placed in service before the beginning of the rehabilitation. A building is treated as substantially rehabilitated only if the QREs during a 24-month period (60 months for

## BACKGROUND

projects completed in phases) selected by the taxpayer and ending within the tax year for which the credit is claimed exceed the greater of the adjusted basis of the building (and its structural components) or $5,000. If the building is not a certified historic structure, it must have been placed in service before 1936. It also must satisfy a wall retention test, under which 50 percent or more of the existing external walls must be kept in place as external walls, 75 percent or more of the existing external walls must be kept in place as external or internal walls, and 75 percent or more of the existing internal structural framework must be kept in place (Code Sec. 47(c)(1)).

A "certified historic structure" is any building (and its structural components) that is (1) listed in the National Register of Historic Places, or (2) located in a registered historic district and certified by the Secretary of the Interior as being of historic significance (Code Sec. 47(c)(3)(A)). Only "certified rehabilitations" on certified historic structures or buildings in a registered historic district qualify for the credit. However, certification is not required to claim the credit for expenditures on buildings in registered historic districts if:

— the building is not a certified historic structure;

— the Secretary of the Interior has certified to the IRS that the building is not of historic significance to the district; and

— if certification that the building is not historically significant occurs after the rehabilitation begins, the taxpayer certifies to the IRS it was not aware of the certification requirement at the beginning of the rehabilitation (Code Sec. 47(c)(2)(B)(iv)).

## NEW LAW EXPLAINED

**Rehabilitation credit limited to certified historic structures; claimed ratably over five years.**—The rehabilitation credit is limited to 20 percent of qualified rehabilitation expenditures (QREs) of the taxpayer for qualified rehabilitated buildings and is claimed ratably over a five-year period beginning in the tax year in which the rehabilitated building is placed in service (Code Sec. 47(a), as amended by the Tax Cuts and Jobs Act (P.L. 115-97)). The definition of a "qualified rehabilitated building" remains a building and its structural components for which depreciation is allowable and that has been substantially rehabilitated and placed in service before the beginning of the rehabilitation (Code Sec. 47(c)(1), as amended by the 2017 Tax Cuts Act). However, the building must be a certified historic structure, but any expenditure attributable to rehabilitation of the structure is not a QRE unless it is a certified rehabilitation (Code Sec. 47(c)(2)(B)(iv), as amended by the 2017 Tax Cuts Act). The 10 percent rehabilitation credit for QREs with respect to qualified rehabilitated buildings placed in service before 1936 that are not certified historic structures is eliminated.

**Coordination of rehabilitation credit with bonus depreciation.** Proposed regulations (NPRM REG-104397-18) issued with respect to bonus depreciation (¶ 410), note that a taxpayer may claim bonus depreciation on qualified rehabilitation expenditures (as defined in Code Sec. 47(c)(2)) that qualify for bonus depreciation. However, assuming no election out of bonus depreciation is made, the rehabilitation credit may

## NEW LAW EXPLAINED

only be claimed on the cost (or other applicable basis) of the rehabilitation expenditures, less the amount claimed or allowable as bonus depreciation. And, the credit only applies if the taxpayer depreciates the remaining basis of the rehabilitation expenditures using an MACRS straight-line method (Proposed Reg. § 1.168(k)-2(f)(9)). The proposed regulations will generally be effective upon publication as final regulations, however, taxpayers may choose to rely on them for qualified property acquired and placed in service after September 27, 2017 for tax years ending on or after September 28, 2017.

> **Compliance Tip:** The rehabilitation credit is part of the investment credit that a taxpayer claims on Form 3468, Investment Credit.

> **State Tax Consequences:** States with historic building rehabilitation credits that incorporate federal law for purposes of determining eligibility and/or credit amounts will be affected by the changes to Code Sec. 47. For example, Maine allows a credit for QREs incurred for a certified historic structure in the state that is equal to the taxpayer's federal rehabilitation credit (limited to $100,000 annually per taxpayer). Therefore, any change in a taxpayer's federal rehabilitation credit resulting from the Code Sec. 47 amendments will also have a corresponding effect on the taxpayer's Maine credit. In addition, taxpayers in Wisconsin, which adopts the federal definitions of qualified rehabilitated buildings and qualified rehabilitation expenditures for its historic rehabilitation credit, may gain or lose eligibility for the state credit because of changes to Code Sec. 47.

▶ **Effective date.** The amendments made by this provision generally apply to amounts paid or incurred after December 31, 2017 (Act Sec. 13402(c)(1) of the Tax Cuts and Jobs Act (P.L. 115-97)). Under a transition rule, in case of qualified rehabilitation expenditures (for either a certified historic structure or a pre-1936 building), with respect to any building owned or leased by the taxpayer at all times after December 31, 2017, the 24-month period selected by the taxpayer, or the 60-month period selected by the taxpayer under the rule for phased rehabilitation, begins no later than the end of the 180-day period beginning on the date of the enactment, and the amendments made by the provision apply to such expenditures paid or incurred after the end of the tax year in which such 24-month or 60-month period ends (Act Sec. 13402(c)(2) of the Tax Cuts Act).

— Act Sec. 13402(a) of the Tax Cuts and Jobs Act (P.L. 115-97), amending Code Sec. 47(a);

— Act Sec. 13402(b), amending Code Secs. 47(c)(1), (c)(2)(B), and 145(d)(4);

— Act Sec. 13402(c), providing the effective date.

# ¶595 Orphan Drug Credit

## SUMMARY OF NEW LAW

The amount of the elective tax credit for qualified clinical testing expenses that are paid or incurred with respect to low or unprofitable drugs for rare diseases and conditions (i.e., the orphan drug credit) is reduced to 25 percent. In addition, taxpayers may elect a reduced credit in lieu of reducing otherwise allowable deductions.

## BACKGROUND

A taxpayer that invests in the development of drugs to diagnose, treat, or prevent qualified rare diseases (i.e., those that affect fewer than 200,000 persons in the United States) and conditions can claim a nonrefundable tax credit equal to 50 percent of qualified clinical testing expenses incurred or paid during the development process under Sec. 526 of the Federal Food, Drug, and Cosmetic Act (Code Sec. 45C). The credit is part of the general business credit, and is subject to the limitations, as well as the carryback and carryforward rules, that apply to the general credit (Code Sec. 38(b)(12)).

Other tax credits and deductions claimed by a taxpayer claiming the orphan drug credit are restricted to prevent a double tax benefit for the same expenditure. For example, expenses used to claim the orphan drug tax credit cannot also be used to claim the research and development tax credit. Similarly, a taxpayer that is entitled to the credit may not also claim a deduction for the portion of the qualified clinical testing expenses that exceed the amount of allowable credit (Code Sec. 280C(b)). if the credit exceeds the amount of otherwise deductible clinical testing expenses, the excess may not be charged to the capital account.

## NEW LAW EXPLAINED

**Orphan drug credit amount reduced to 25 percent; election of reduced credit.—** The amount of the orphan drug credit is reduced to 25 percent of qualified clinical testing expenses paid or incurred by a taxpayer for tax years beginning after December 31, 2017 (Code Sec. 45C(a), as amended by the Tax Cuts and Jobs Act (P.L. 115-97)). A taxpayer also may elect a reduced credit amount in lieu of reducing otherwise allowable deductions. In the case of any tax year for which a reduced credit election is made, the amount of the credit will be the amount equal to the excess of: (1) the amount of credit otherwise determined without regard to the reduction, over (2) the product of the credit amount determined and the maximum income tax for a corporation. An election of reduced credit for any tax year must be made no later than the time for filing the taxpayer's return for the year (including extensions). Once made, the election is irrevocable.

▶ **Effective date.** The amendments made by this section apply to tax years beginning after December 31, 2017 (Act Sec. 13401(c) of the Tax Cuts and Jobs Act (P.L. 115-97).

**No significant guidance related to this provision has been issued.**

— Act Sec. 13401(a) of the Tax Cuts and Jobs Act (P.L. 115-97), amending Code Sec. 45C(a);

— Act Sec. 13401(b), amending Code Sec. 280C(b);

— Act Sec. 13401(c), providing the effective date.

# Compensation, Retirement, Education and Disability Benefits

## COMPENSATION

### RETIREMENT PLANS AND BENEFITS

### EDUCATION AND DISABILITY BENEFITS

# COMPENSATION

## ¶605 Qualified Equity Grants

**SUMMARY OF NEW LAW**

Employees who are granted stock options are able to elect to defer recognition of income for up to five years. The election is not available to certain executives, highly compensated officers, and "one-percent owners" of the corporation. The corporation must maintain a written plan under which at least 80 percent of all employees providing services to the corporation are granted stock options with the same rights and privileges.

## BACKGROUND

Specific income tax rules apply to property, including employer stock, that is transferred to an employee in connection with the performance of services (Code Sec. 83). These rules control the timing and the amount of the compensation that is recognized by the employee and deducted by the employer. Property includes real and personal property, other than money or an unfunded and unsecured promise to pay money in the future (Reg. § 1.83-3(e)).

If property is transferred in connection with the performance of services, the person who performed the services must include the excess of the fair market value of the property over any amount paid for the property in his or her gross income in the first tax year in which the property becomes substantially vested (Code Sec. 83(a)). Property is substantially vested if the rights of the person having the beneficial interest in the property are not subject to a substantial risk of forfeiture, or are freely transferable, whichever is applicable (Reg. § 1.83-3(b)). In general, an employee's right to stock or other property is subject to a substantial risk of forfeiture if the employee's right to full enjoyment of the property is subject to a condition, such as the future performance of substantial services. An employee's right to stock or other property is transferable if the employee can transfer an interest in the property to any person other than the transferor of the property (Code Sec 83(c)(1); Reg. § 1.83-3(c)).

> **Comment:** Under this rule, if the employee's right to the stock is substantially vested when the stock is transferred to the employee, the employee recognizes income in the tax year of the transfer, equal to the fair market value of the stock as of the transfer date (less any amount paid for the stock). If the employee's right to the stock is not substantially vested (i.e., is "nonvested") at the time of transfer, the employee does not recognize income attributable to the stock transfer until the tax year in which his or her right becomes substantially vested. In this case, the amount includible in the employee's income is the fair market value of the stock as of the date that the employee's right to the stock is substantially vested, less any amount paid for the stock.

A person who receives property (including employer stock) in connection with the performance of services can elect to have the excess of the fair market value of the restricted property over his or her cost included in gross income and taxed in the year the property is received, even though the property remains substantially nonvested (Code Sec. 83(b)). The election must be made no later than 30 days after the property is transferred (Reg. § 1.83-2(b)). If a proper and timely election under Code Sec. 83(b) is made, the amount of compensatory income is capped at the fair market value of the property as of the transfer date (less any amount paid for the property). Once made, the restricted property election cannot be revoked without IRS consent.

In the case of employer stock transferred to an employee, the employer is allowed a deduction (to the extent a deduction for a business expense is otherwise allowable) equal to the amount included in the employee's income as a result of transfer of the stock (Code Sec 83(h)). The employer deduction generally is permitted in the employer's tax year in which or with which ends the employee's tax year when the amount is included and properly reported in the employee's income (Reg. § 1.83-6).

**¶605**

## BACKGROUND

The Code Sec. 83 rules—including the Code Sec. 83(b) election—are available for grants of "restricted stock" (nonvested stock), but do not generally apply to the grant of options on employer stock unless the option has a readily ascertainable fair market value (Code Sec. 83(e)(3); Reg. § 1.83-7).

**Employment taxes and reporting.** Unless an exception applies under the applicable rules, compensation provided to an employee constitutes wages subject to employment taxes: namely, the Federal Insurance Contributions Act (FICA) tax (i.e., Social Security tax), the Federal Unemployment Tax Act (FUTA) tax (i.e., unemployment tax), and income taxes required to be withheld from wages by employers. "Wages" generally means all remuneration for services performed by an employee for his or her employer, including the cash value of all remuneration (including benefits) paid in any medium other than cash (including employer stock) (see Code Sec. 3401).

An employer must furnish a statement of compensation information to each employee for a calendar year, including taxable compensation, FICA wages, and withheld income and FICA taxes (Code Sec. 6051). Information relating to certain nontaxable items must also be reported, such as certain retirement and health plan contributions. The employer makes the statement on Form W-2, Wage and Tax Statement, which the employer must furnish to the employee, and file with the Social Security Administration, by January 31 of the succeeding year.

**Statutory options.** Two types of statutory options apply with respect to employer stock: incentive stock options (ISOs) and options provided under an employee stock purchase plan (ESPP) (Code Secs. 421—424). Stock received by a statutory option is subject to special rules, rather than the rules for nonqualified options. No amount is includible in an employee's income on the grant, vesting, or exercise of a statutory option. In addition, generally no deduction is allowed to the employer regarding the option or the stock transferred to an employee.

Employment taxes do not apply to the grant or vesting of a statutory option, the transfer of stock pursuant to the option, or a disposition of the stock. However, certain special reporting requirements apply (Code Secs. 421(b), 3121(a)(22), and 3306(b)(19)).

**Nonqualified deferred compensation.** Compensation is generally includible in an employee's income when paid to the employee. However, in the case of a nonqualified deferred compensation plan, the amount of deferred compensation is first includible in income for the tax year when it is not subject to a substantial risk of forfeiture (unless the arrangement either is exempt from or meets the requirements of Code Sec. 409A) (Reg. § 1.409A-1(d)). This is so even if payment will not occur until a later year. In general, to meet the requirements of Code Sec. 409A, the time when nonqualified deferred compensation will be paid, and the amount paid must be specified at the time of deferral, with limits on further deferral after the time for payment. Various other requirements apply, including that payment can only occur on specific defined events.

Various exemptions from Code Sec. 409A apply, including transfers of property subject to Code Sec. 83. Nonqualified options may be structured so as not to be considered nonqualified deferred compensation (Reg. § 1.409A-1(b)(5)). A restricted stock unit (RSU) is an arrangement under which an employee has the right to receive

## BACKGROUND

at a specified time in the future an amount determined by reference to the value of one or more shares of employer stock. An employee's right to receive the future amount may be subject to a condition, such as continued employment for a certain period or the attainment of certain performance goals. An arrangement providing RSUs is generally considered a nonqualified deferred compensation plan and is subject to the rules and limits of Code Sec. 409A. The employer deduction generally is allowed in the employer's tax year in which or with which ends the employee's tax year when the amount is included and properly reported in the employee's income (Code Sec. 404(a)(5)).

## NEW LAW EXPLAINED

**Treatment of qualified equity grants.**—A qualified employee of a privately held company may elect to defer including in his or her gross income the amount of income attributable to qualified stock transferred to the employee by the employer (Code Sec. 83(i), as added by the Tax Cuts and Jobs Act (P.L. 115-97)). This election is an alternative to being taxed in the year in which the property vests under Code Sec. 83(a) or in the year it is received under Code Sec. 83(b). The election to defer income inclusion for qualified stock must be made no later than 30 days after the first date the employee's right to the stock is substantially vested or is transferable, whichever occurs earlier (Code Sec. 83(i)(4), as added by the 2017 Tax Cuts Act).

If a qualified employee elects to defer income inclusion, the employee must include the income in his or her gross income for the tax year that includes the earliest of:

- the first date the qualified stock becomes transferable, including transferable to the employer;

- the date the employee first becomes an excluded employee;

- the first date on which any stock of the employer becomes readily tradable on an established securities market;

- the date five years after the earlier of the first date the employee's right to the stock is transferable or is not subject to a substantial risk of forfeiture; or

- the date on which the employee revokes his or her inclusion deferral election (Code Sec. 83(i)(1), as added by the 2017 Tax Cuts Act).

The inclusion deferral election is made in a manner similar to that for a Code Sec. 83(b) election. The election is not allowed for income with respect to nonvested stock that is includible in gross income as a result of a Code Sec. 83(b) election (Code Sec. 83(i)(4)(B), as added by the 2017 Tax Cuts Act).

An employee may not make an inclusion deferral election for a year with respect to qualified stock if the corporation purchased any of its outstanding stock in the preceding calendar year, unless (1) at least 25 percent of the total dollar amount of the stock so purchased is stock with respect to which an inclusion deferral election is in effect ("deferral stock") and (2) the determination of which individuals from whom deferral stock is purchased is made on a reasonable basis (Code Sec. 83(i)(4)(B) and (C), as

## NEW LAW EXPLAINED

added by the 2017 Tax Cuts Act). These two requirements are met if the corporation purchases all of its deferral stock (Code Sec. 83(i)(4)(C)(iii), as added by the 2017 Tax Cuts Act).

Stock that the corporation purchased from an individual is not treated as deferral stock (and the purchase is not treated as a purchase of deferral stock) if, immediately after the purchase, the individual holds any deferral stock for which a deferral election has been in effect for a longer period than the election regarding the purchased stock (Code Sec. 83(i)(4)(C)(ii), as added by the 2017 Tax Cuts Act).

Deferred income inclusion applies also for purposes of the employer's deduction of the amount of income attributable to the qualified stock. If an employee makes an inclusion deferral election, the employer's deduction is deferred until the employer's tax year in which or with which ends the tax year of the employee for which the amount is included in the employee's income as described above (Conference Report on H.R. 1, Tax Cuts and Jobs Act (H. Rept. 115-466); see Code Sec. 83(h)).

**Qualified stock.** Qualified stock is any stock in a corporation that is the employer of the qualified employee if (1) the stock is received in connection with the exercise of an option or in settlement of a restricted stock unit (RSU) and (2) the option or RSU was granted by the corporation in connection with the performance of services as an employee and during a calendar year in which such corporation was an eligible corporation (Code Sec. 83(i)(2)(A), as added by the 2017 Tax Cuts Act).

Qualified stock does not include any stock if, at the time the employee's right to the stock becomes substantially vested, the employee may sell the stock to, or otherwise receive cash in lieu of stock from, the corporation (Code Sec. 83(i)(2)(B), as added by the 2017 Tax Cuts Act). Qualified stock can only be such if it relates to stock received in connection with options or RSUs, and does not include stock received in connection with other forms of equity compensation, including stock appreciation rights or restricted stock (Conference Report on H.R. 1, Tax Cuts and Jobs Act (H. Rept. 115-466)).

A corporation is responsible for creating the conditions that would allow an employee to make the Code Sec. 83(i) election. If a corporation does not intend to create the conditions that would allow an employee to make the election, the terms of a stock option or RSU may provide that no election under Code Sec. 83(i) will be available with respect to stock received upon the exercise of the stock option or settlement of the RSU. This designation would inform employees that no Code Sec. 83(i) election may be made with respect to stock received upon exercise of the option or settlement of the RSU even if the stock is qualified stock (Notice 2018-97).

A corporation is an eligible corporation for a calendar year if:

- no stock of the employer corporation (or any predecessor) is readily tradable on an established securities market during any preceding calendar year; and

- the corporation has a written plan under which, in the calendar year, not less than 80 percent of all employees who provide services to the corporation in the United States (or any U.S. possession) are granted stock options, or RSUs, with the same rights and privileges to receive qualified stock ("80-percent requirement") (Code Sec. 83(i)(2)(C), as added by the 2017 Tax Cuts Act).

## NEW LAW EXPLAINED

> **Comment:** Under a transition rule, until the Treasury issues regulations or other implementing guidance, a corporation will be treated as being in compliance with the 80-percent requirement if it complies with a reasonable good-faith interpretation of the requirement (Act Sec. 13603(g) of the 2017 Tax Cuts Act).

In general, the determination of rights and privileges with respect to stock is determined in a manner similar to that under the Code Sec. 423(b)(5) employee stock purchase plan rules. Employees will not fail to be treated as having the same rights and privileges to receive qualified stock solely because the number of shares available to all employees is not equal in amount, provided that the number of shares available to each employee is more than a *de minimis* amount. Further, rights and privileges with respect to the exercise of an option cannot be treated as the same as rights and privileges with respect to the settlement of an RSU (Code Sec. 83(i)(2)(C)(ii), as added by the 2017 Tax Cuts Act). The requirement that 80 percent of all applicable employees be granted stock options or RSUs with the same rights and privileges cannot be satisfied in a tax year by granting a combination of stock options and RSUs, and instead all such employees must either be granted stock options or be granted restricted stock units for that year (Conference Report on H.R. 1, Tax Cuts and Jobs Act (H. Rept. 115-466)).

The IRS has clarified that the determination of whether a corporation qualifies as an eligible corporation is made "with respect to any calendar year." To meet the 80-percent requirement, the corporation must have granted "in such calendar year" stock options to 80 percent of its employees or RSUs to 80 percent of its employees. So the determination that the corporation is an eligible corporation must be made on a calendar year basis, and whether the corporation has satisfied the 80-percent requirement is based solely on the stock options or the RSUs granted in that calendar year to employees who provide services to the corporation in the United States. In calculating whether the 80 percent requirement is satisfied, the corporation must take into account the total number of individuals employed at any time during the year in question as well as the total number of employees receiving grants during the year (Notice 2018-97).

All persons treated as a single employer under the Code Sec. 414(b) controlled group rules are treated as one corporation (Code Sec. 83(i)(5), as added by the 2017 Tax Cuts Act).

**Qualified employees and excluded employees.** A qualified employee is an individual who is not an "excluded employee," and who agrees, in the inclusion deferral election, to meet the requirements the IRS deems necessary to ensure that the employer corporation's income tax withholding requirements regarding the qualified stock are met (Code Sec. 83(i)(3)(A), as added by the 2017 Tax Cuts Act).

The deferral election is not available to "excluded employees" of the employer corporation. This is any employee:

(1) who is a one-percent owner of the corporation at any time during the calendar year, or was at any time during the 10 preceding calendar years;

(2) who is, or has been at any prior time, the chief executive officer or chief financial officer of the corporation, or an individual acting in either capacity;

(3) who is a family member of an individual described in (1) or (2); or

**¶605**

## NEW LAW EXPLAINED

(4) who has been one of the four highest compensated officers of the corporation for the tax year or for any of the 10 preceding tax years (Code Sec. 83(i)(3)(B), as added by the 2017 Tax Cuts Act).

**Notice, withholding, and reporting requirements.** An election to defer income inclusion with respect to qualified stock must be made no later than 30 days after the first time the employee's right to the stock is substantially vested or is transferable, whichever occurs earlier (Code Sec. 83(i)(4), as added by the 2017 Tax Cuts Act).

Employers are required to provide notice to their employees that they are eligible for this election at the time (or a reasonable period before) the employee's right to the qualified stock is substantially vested (and income attributable to the stock would first be includible absent an inclusion deferral election) (Code Sec. 83(i)(6), as added by the 2017 Tax Cuts Act). The notice to the employee must:

- certify that the stock is qualified stock;
- notify the employee that he or she may be eligible to elect to defer income inclusion with respect to the stock; and
- notify the employee that, if he or she makes the election, the amount of income required to be included at the end of the deferral period will be

  — based on the value of the stock at the time the employee's right to the stock first becomes substantially vested, notwithstanding that the stock's value may have declined during the deferral period (and even if the stock's value has declined below the employee's tax liability with respect to such stock), and

  — subject to withholding as provided under the provision, as well as of the employee's required withholding responsibilities.

After December 31, 2017, an employer's failure to provide this notice can result in a fine of $100 for each failure, not to exceed $50,000 (Code Sec. 6652(p), as added by the 2017 Tax Cuts Act).

> **Comment:** Under a transition rule, until the Treasury issues regulations or other implementing guidance, a corporation will be treated as being in compliance with the employee notice requirement under Code Sec. 83(i)(6) if it complies with a reasonable good-faith interpretation of the requirement (Act Sec. 13603(g) of the 2017 Tax Cuts Act).

For withholding purposes, qualified stock with respect to which a Code Sec. 83(i) election is made, will be treated as wages received on the earliest date possible under Code Sec. 83(i)(1)(B) and in the amount included as income (Code Sec. 3401(i), as added by the 2017 Tax Cuts Act). For the tax year for which income subject to an inclusion deferral election is required to be included in income by the employee (as described above), the amount required to be included in income is treated as wages with respect to which the employer is required to withhold income tax at a rate not less than the highest income tax rate applicable to individual taxpayers (Code Sec. 3402(t), as added by the 2017 Tax Cuts Act). By January 31 of the following year, the employer must determine the actual value of the deferral stock on the date it is includible in the employee's income and report that amount and the withholding on Form W-2 and Form 941. With respect to income tax withholding for the deferral stock that the employer pays from its own funds, the employer may recover that income tax withholding from the employee until April 1 of the year following the

**NEW LAW EXPLAINED**

calendar year in which the wages were paid. An employer that fails to deduct and withhold federal income tax is liable for the payment of the tax whether or not the employer collects it from the employee (Notice 2018-97).

▶ **Effective date.** The amendments made by this section generally apply to stock attributable to options exercised, or restricted stock units settled, after December 31, 2017 (Act Sec. 13603(f)(1) of the Tax Cuts and Jobs Act (P.L. 115-97)). The penalty for the failure of an employer to provide notice of tax consequences to a qualified employee applies to failures after December 31, 2017 (Act Sec. 13603(f)(2) of the 2017 Tax Cuts Act).

— Act Sec. 13603(a) of the Tax Cuts and Jobs Act (P.L. 115-97), adding Code Sec. 83(i);

— Act Sec. 13603(b), adding Code Sec. 3401(i) and Code Sec. 3402(t);

— Act Sec. 13603(c), amending Code Sec. 422(b) and Code Sec. 423(b)(5), and adding Code Sec. 423(d) and Code Sec. 409A(d)(7);

— Act Sec. 13603(d), adding Code Sec. 6051(a)(16) and (17);

— Act Sec. 13603(e), adding Code Sec. 6652(p);

— Act Sec. 13603(g), providing a transition rule;

— Act Sec. 13603(f), providing the effective date.

## ¶610  Qualified Moving Expense Reimbursement

**SUMMARY OF NEW LAW**

The exclusion for qualified moving expense reimbursements is suspended for tax years 2018 through 2025.

**BACKGROUND**

Qualified moving expense reimbursements are excluded from an employee's gross income. Qualified moving expense reimbursements are amounts received (directly or indirectly) from an employer as payment for (or reimbursement of) expenses that would be deductible as moving expenses under Code Sec. 217 if directly paid or incurred by the employee (Code Sec. 132(g)).

Qualified moving expense reimbursements do not include amounts actually deducted by the individual in a prior year. Amounts excludable from gross income for income tax purposes as qualified moving expense reimbursements are also excluded from wages for employment tax purposes. Only reimbursements made under an accountable plan may be excluded from income. An accountable plan requires the employee to make an adequate accounting to the employer of the moving expenses and to return any excess reimbursements.

> **Comment:** Reimbursements that meet the definition of moving expenses, but are not made under an accountable plan are included in Box 1 of the employee's Form W-2. If the employee is claiming a moving expense deduction because he or she was not fully reimbursed, this amount must be carried to Form 3903, Moving Expenses, to reduce the otherwise allowable expenses.

**¶610**

## NEW LAW EXPLAINED

**Exclusion for qualified moving expenses reimbursement suspended.**—The exclusion for qualified moving expense reimbursements is suspended for tax years 2018 through 2025 (Code Sec. 132(g), as amended by the Tax Cuts and Jobs Act (P.L. 115-97)). However, members of the U.S. Armed Forces on active duty who move pursuant to a military order and incident to a permanent change of station are still permitted to exclude qualified moving expense reimbursements from their income (Code Sec. 132(g)(2), as amended by the 2017 Tax Cuts Act). This suspension does not apply to amounts received in 2018 from an employer for expenses incurred in connection with a move occurring prior to January 1, 2018, if the amounts would have been considered excludable qualified moving expense reimbursements at the time they were incurred (Notice 2018-75).

▶ **Effective date.** The amendment made by this section applies to tax years beginning after December 31, 2017 (Act Sec. 11048(b) of the Tax Cuts and Jobs Act (P.L. 115-97)).

— Act Sec. 11048(a) of the Tax Cuts and Jobs Act (P.L. 115-97), amending Code Sec. 132(g);

— Act Sec. 11048(b) providing the effective date.

## ¶615  Qualified Bicycle Commuting Reimbursements

### SUMMARY OF NEW LAW

After December 31, 2017, and before January 1, 2026, taxpayers are not permitted to exclude qualified bicycle commuting reimbursements from their income.

### BACKGROUND

Employees are permitted to exclude up to $20 per month in qualified bicycle commuting reimbursements (Code Sec. 132(f)(1)(D)). A qualifying bicycle commuting month is any month during which the employee regularly uses the bicycle for a substantial portion of travel to a place of employment and during which the employee does not receive transportation in a commuter highway vehicle, a transit pass, or qualified parking from an employer.

Qualified reimbursements are any amount received from an employer during a 15-month period beginning with the first day of the calendar year as payment for reasonable expenses during that calendar year for the purchase of a bicycle and bicycle improvements, bicycle repair, and bicycle storage, provided that the employee uses the bicycle regularly for travel between the employee's residence and place of employment.

## BACKGROUND

Amounts that are excludable from gross income for income tax purposes are also excluded from wages for employment tax purposes. Qualified bicycle commuting reimbursements cannot be funded by elective salary reduction contributions.

## NEW LAW EXPLAINED

**Exclusion for qualified bicycle commuting reimbursement suspended.**—The exclusion from gross income and wages for qualified bicycle commuting reimbursements is suspended for tax years beginning after December 31, 2017, and before January 1, 2026 (Code Sec. 132(f)(8), as added by the Tax Cuts and Jobs Act (P.L. 115-97)).

▶ **Effective date.** The amendment made by this section applies to tax years beginning after December 31, 2017 (Act Sec. 11047(b)) of the Tax Cuts and Jobs Act (P.L. 115-97)).

**No significant guidance related to this provision has been issued.**

— Act Sec. 11047(a) of the Tax Cuts and Jobs Act (P.L. 115-97), adding Code Sec. 132(f)(8);

— Act Sec. 11047(b), providing the effective date.

# RETIREMENT PLANS AND BENEFITS

## ¶620  Recharacterization of IRA Contributions

### SUMMARY OF NEW LAW

The special rule that allows a contribution to one type of an IRA to be recharacterized as a contribution to the other type of IRA will no longer apply to a conversion contribution to a Roth IRA after 2017. Recharacterization is still permitted with respect to other contributions. For example, an individual may make a contribution for a year to a Roth IRA and, before the due date for the individual's income tax return for that year, recharacterize it as a contribution to a traditional IRA.

### BACKGROUND

There are two basic types of individual retirement arrangements (IRAs): traditional IRAs, to which both deductible and nondeductible contributions may be made, and Roth IRAs, to which only nondeductible contributions may be made. The principal difference between these two types of IRAs is the timing of income tax inclusion.

Contributions to traditional IRAs and to Roth IRAs must be segregated into separate IRAs, meaning arrangements with separate trusts, accounts, or contracts, and separate IRA documents. Except in the case of a conversion or recharacterization, amounts cannot be transferred or rolled over between the two types of IRAs. A recharacterization election effectively reverses the contribution from one type of IRA to another (e.g., Roth to traditional or traditional to Roth). The contribution being

## BACKGROUND

recharacterized is treated as having been originally contributed to the second IRA on the same date and for the same tax year as that in which the contribution was made to the first IRA (Reg. § 1.408A-5).

If on or before the due date for any tax year, a taxpayer transfers in a trustee-to-trustee transfer any contribution to an IRA made during the tax year from that IRA to any other IRA, the contribution is treated as having been made to the transferee plan and not the transferor plan (Code Sec. 408A(d)(6)(A)). This rule is not available unless the amount transferred in a recharacterization is accompanied by any net income allocable to the contribution (Code Sec. 408A(d)(6)(B)(i)). Furthermore, it applies only to the extent no deduction was allowed with respect to the contribution to the transferor plan (Code Sec. 408A(d)(6)(B)(ii))

The election to recharacterize and the transfer of the assets must both take place on or before the due date (including extensions) of the tax return for the year for which the contribution was made for the first IRA. Once a recharacterization election has been made, it cannot be revoked. However, in some situations, the amount may be reconverted at a later date (Reg. § 1.408A-5).

## NEW LAW EXPLAINED

**Recharacterization of Roth IRA conversions are no longer permitted.**—For tax years beginning after December 31, 2017, the special rule that allows a contribution to one type of IRA to be recharacterized as a contribution to the other type of IRA does not apply to a conversion contribution to a Roth IRA. Thus, recharacterization cannot be used to unwind a Roth IRA conversion (Code Sec. 408A(d)(6)(B)(iii), as amended by the Tax Cuts and Jobs Act (P.L. 115-97)).

> **Comment:** Earlier versions of the Tax Cuts and Jobs Act enacted by both the House and Senate eliminated recharacterization entirely. The provision was narrowed considerably in the reconciled version to target only conversions to Roth IRAs. Thus, for example, an individual may still make a contribution for a year to a Roth IRA and, before the due date for the individual's income tax return for that year, recharacterize it as a contribution to a traditional IRA. In addition, an individual may still make a contribution to a traditional IRA and convert the traditional IRA to a Roth IRA, but the individual is precluded from later unwinding the conversion through a recharacterization.

> **Comment:** The strategy behind recharacterizing a conversion hinged on changes in the market price of the IRA assets during the course of the year. The owner pays tax in a conversion based on the value of the assets on the conversion date, so the tax liability is locked in on that date. If the value of the assets goes up significantly, the conversion looks like a shrewd move because the tax bill would have been higher if the taxpayer had waited. If instead the value goes down (e.g., through a market correction or recession), the conversion looks like a foolish mistake because the tax bill is much higher than if the owner had waited until the asset prices fell. The option to recharacterize reduced the risk.

## NEW LAW EXPLAINED

▶ **Effective date.** The amendments made by this section apply to tax years beginning after December 31, 2017 (Act Sec. 13611(b) of the Tax Cuts and Jobs Act (P.L. 115-97)).

**No significant guidance related to this provision has been issued.**

— Act Sec. 13611(a) of the Tax Cuts and Jobs Act (P.L. 115-97), amending Code Sec. 408A(d)(6);

— Act Sec. 13611(b), providing the effective date.

# ¶625  Rollovers of Plan Loan Offset Amounts

## SUMMARY OF NEW LAW

For plan loan offset amounts that are treated as distributed after 2017, a participant whose plan terminates or who is severed from employment while having a plan loan outstanding will have until the due date for filing their tax return for that year to contribute the loan balance to an IRA in order to avoid the loan being taxed as a distribution.

## BACKGROUND

Defined contribution plans are permitted, but not required, to allow plan loans. Loans are treated as distributions, unless the balance of all outstanding loans does not exceed the lesser of:

- $50,000, reduced by the excess, if any, of the participant's highest outstanding loan balance during the preceding one-year period ending on the day before the date of the new loan, over the outstanding balance on the date of the new loan; or

- the greater of $10,000 or half of the participant's vested accrued benefit under the plan (Code Sec. 72(p)(2)).

Only qualified employer plans can use this exception to distribution treatment, and for these purposes such plans include:

- qualified pension, profit-sharing, or stock bonus plans;

- qualified annuity plans;

- plans under which amounts are contributed for the purchase of employees' annuity contracts by employers that are charitable organizations or public schools; and

- government plans (Code Sec. 72(p)(4)).

## BACKGROUND

If an employee fails to abide by the applicable rules, the loan is treated as a taxable distribution of the accrued benefit, and may be subject to the 10-percent penalty for early withdrawals (Code Sec. 72(p); Reg. § 1.72(p)-1, Q&A 11).

Loan distributions can also occur through a reduction (or offset) of the account balance. Typically, these distributions occur when the plan terminates or the employee terminates employment. If the employee does not repay the outstanding balance, it will be deducted from the account and is treated as a distribution. The offset loan balance must be included in the employee's gross income and may be subject to the 10-percent additional tax on early distributions. The distribution is reported on Form 1099-R (Reg. § 1.402(c)-2, Q&A 9).

An amount equal to the plan loan offset amount can be rolled over by the employee (or spousal distributee) to an eligible retirement plan within the 60-day period (Reg. § 1.402(c)-2, Q&A 9(a)).

## NEW LAW EXPLAINED

**Employees whose plans terminate or who are severed from employment have extra time to roll over plan loan offsets.**—An employee can exclude from income a transfer of a qualified plan loan offset amount as long as it is made by the due date (including extensions) for filing the tax return for the tax year in which the amount is treated as distributed from a qualified employer plan (Code Sec. 402(c)(3)(C)(i), as added by the Tax Cuts and Jobs Act (P.L. 115-97)). A qualified plan loan offset amount is a plan loan offset amount that is distributed solely by reason of:

- the termination of the qualified employer plan, or
- a severance from employment (Code Sec. 402(c)(3)(C)(ii), as added by the 2017 Tax Cuts Act).

A "plan loan offset amount" is the amount by which the participant's accrued benefit under the plan is reduced in order to repay a loan from the plan (Code Sec. 402(c)(3)(C)(iii), as added by the 2017 Tax Cuts Act).

This treatment of plan loan offset amounts is available only if the loan qualifies under Code Sec. 72(p)(2) (Code Sec. 402(c)(3)(C)(iv), as added by the 2017 Tax Cuts Act) and only if the plan qualifies as a qualified employer plan under Code Sec. 72(p)(4) (Code Sec. 402(c)(3)(C)(v), as added by the 2017 Tax Cuts Act).

> **Comment:** Code Sec. 402(f) requires plan administrators to provide a written notice to recipients of an eligible rollover distribution explaining their rights and obligations. The IRS has model safe harbor language administrators may use for these "402(f) notices." Note that the IRS recently updated its safe harbor language to reflect the new offset rules as well as other changes in the law (Notice 2018-74).

▶ **Effective date.** The amendment made by this section applies to plan loan offset amounts that are treated as distributed in tax years beginning after December 31, 2017 (Act Sec. 13613(c) of the Tax Cuts and Jobs Act (P.L. 115-97)).

## NEW LAW EXPLAINED

— Act Sec. 13613(a) and (b) of the Tax Cuts and Jobs Act (P.L. 115-97), amending Code Sec. 402(c)(3);

— Act Sec. 13613(c), providing the effective date.

# ¶635  Length-of-Service Award Exclusion for Bona Fide Public Safety Volunteers

## SUMMARY OF NEW LAW

The dollar limit on the length-of-service award exclusion for bona fide public safety volunteers is doubled from $3,000 to $6,000, effective for tax years beginning after December 31, 2017.

## BACKGROUND

Under Code Sec. 457, employees of a state or local government or a tax-exempt organization are not currently taxed on compensation deferred under an eligible deferred compensation plan. An eligible plan must meet participation, deferral, payout, trust, and other requirements. There are a number of plans to which the Code Sec. 457 rules do not apply (Code Sec. 457(e)(11)).

Plans that pay length-of-service awards to bona fide safety volunteers or to their beneficiaries on account of firefighting and prevention services, emergency medical services, or ambulance services performed by the volunteers are not subject to the Code Sec. 457 requirements for unfunded deferred compensation plans with respect to awards accrued after 1996 (Code Sec. 457(e)(11)(A)(ii) and (C); Reg. § 1.457-2(k)). A bona fide volunteer is an individual who does not receive any compensation for performing the qualified services other than (1) reimbursements or reasonable allowances for expenses incurred in performing the services or (2) benefits and nominal fees for performing the services that are reasonable and customarily paid by tax-exempt and governmental employers for such services (Code Sec. 457(e)(11)(B)(i)). A length-of-service award plan will not qualify for this treatment if the total amount of awards accrued for any year of service of any volunteer exceeds $3,000 (Code Sec. 457(e)(11)(B)(ii)).

## NEW LAW EXPLAINED

**$3,000 accrued benefit limit for bona fide public safety volunteers increased to $6,000.**—The maximum deferral amount for length-of-service award exclusion is increased from $3,000 to $6,000, with inflation adjustments for years beginning after December 31, 2017 (Code Sec. 457(e)(11)(B), as amended by the Tax Cuts and Jobs Act (P.L. 115-97)).

**¶635**

## NEW LAW EXPLAINED

In the case of a defined benefits plan paying solely length-of-service awards to bona fide volunteers on account of qualified services performed by such volunteers, the $6,000 limitation applies to the actuarial present value of the aggregate amount of length-of-service awards accruing with respect to any year of service. The actuarial present value with respect to any year is calculated using reasonable actuarial assumptions and methods, assuming payment will be made under the most valuable form of payment under the plan with payment commencing at the later of the earliest age at which unreduced benefits are payable under the plan or the participant's age at the time of the calculation (Code Sec. 457(e)(11)(B)(iv), as amended by the 2017 Tax Cuts Act).

▶ **Effective date.** The amendments made by this section apply to tax years beginning after December 31, 2017 (Act Sec. 13612(d) of the Tax Cuts and Jobs Act (P.L. 115-97)).

   **No significant guidance related to this provision has been issued.**

— Act Sec. 13612(a), (b), and (c) of the Tax Cuts and Jobs Act (P.L. 115-97), amending Code Sec. 457(e)(11);

— Act Sec. 13612(d), providing the effective date.

# EDUCATION AND DISABILITY BENEFITS

## ¶640 Distributions and Rollovers from Qualified Tuition Programs

### SUMMARY OF NEW LAW

For distributions made from qualified tuition programs (QTPs), qualified education expenses may include up to $10,000 paid for elementary or secondary school tuition incurred after 2017. Amounts in a 529 account can also be rolled over to an ABLE account without penalty before 2026 if the ABLE account is owned by the same designated beneficiary or a member of his or her family.

### BACKGROUND

An individual may open an account in a qualified tuition program (QTP or 529 plan) to help pay for the qualified higher education expenses of a designated beneficiary either through a prepaid tuition or college savings program (Code Sec. 529). A QTP can be established and maintained by a state, state agency, or by an eligible educational institution (i.e., virtually any accredited public, nonprofit, or private college or university).

Contributions to a QTP on behalf of a designated beneficiary must be made in cash and are limited to the necessary amount of qualified higher education expenses for the beneficiary as determined under the program. The contributions are not deductible but are not subject to any modified adjusted gross income phaseout limits.

## BACKGROUND

Distributions from a QTP account are excludable from gross income to the extent that they are used to pay the designated beneficiary's qualified higher education expenses. Distributions that exceed the beneficiary's qualified expenses are generally includible in the designated beneficiary's gross income as an annuity and subject to a 10-percent addition to tax or penalty.

Qualified higher education expenses for a QTP include tuition, fees, books, supplies, and equipment required by an educational institution for enrollment or attendance. They also include amounts paid for computers and peripheral equipment, software, and internet access and related services if the items are to be used primarily by the beneficiary during any of the years the beneficiary is enrolled at an eligible educational institution. Qualified expenses also include the reasonable cost of room and board if the beneficiary is enrolled at least half-time. Certain expenses of special needs beneficiaries may also be considered qualified expenses.

Distributions from a QTP may be excluded from gross income if rolled over or transferred to another 529 tuition account of the same designated beneficiary or family member of the designated beneficiary within 60 days and no other rollover has been made in the previous 12 months. Similarly, a change of the designated beneficiary of a 529 tuition account during the tax year is not considered a distribution required to be included in gross income if the new beneficiary is an eligible individual for the tax year and a member of the family of the former designated beneficiary.

## NEW LAW EXPLAINED

**Distributions from qualified tuition programs expanded.**—For any distribution from a QTP made after December 31, 2017, qualified education expense includes up to $10,000 of expenses for tuition in connection with the designated beneficiary's enrollment or attendance at an elementary or secondary school during the tax year, whether public, private, or religious school (Code Secs. 529(c)(7) and 529(e)(3)(A), as added by the Tax Cuts and Jobs Act (P.L. 115-97)). Elementary or secondary school for this purposes means kindergarten through grade 12 as determined under State law, the same as for Coverdell education savings accounts (Notice 2018-58).

The $10,000 limit applies on a per-student, not per-account basis. As a result, if an individual is a designated beneficiary of multiple accounts, a maximum of $10,000 in distributions is excluded from gross income, regardless of whether the funds are distributed from multiple accounts. Any distribution in excess of $10,000 is subject to tax under the rules of Code Sec. 529 (Conference Report on H.R. 1, the Tax Cuts and Jobs Act (H.R. Rept. 115-466)).

**Rollovers to ABLE accounts.** For tax years beginning after December 22, 2017, and before January 1, 2026, distributions from a QTP can be excluded from a designated beneficiary's gross income if it is rolled over or transferred to an ABLE account of the designated beneficiary or a member of his or her family. A member of the designated beneficiary's family for this purpose is defined as for QTPs and not for ABLE accounts (Code Sec. 529(c)(3)(C)(i), as amended by the 2017 Tax Cuts Act; Notice 2018-58).

**¶640**

## NEW LAW EXPLAINED

> **Comment:** A family member for a 529 account includes the designated benefici-
> ary's spouse, child (including the child's spouse and descendents), parent (in-
> cluding parent's spouse, ancestors and siblings), step-parents (including spouse),
> and in-laws (including son or daugher-in-law, mother or father-in-law, and
> sister or brother-in law and their spouses), and first cousin. A family member for
> an ABLE account is limited to siblings only, whether by blood or by adoption,
> and includes a brother, sister, stepbrother, stepsister, half-brother, and half-
> sister.

The exclusion for rollovers applies only if the distribution is contributed to the ABLE
account within 60 days after withdrawal from the QTP. Also, the rollover distribution
and all other contributions to the ABLE account for the tax year may not exceed the
contribution limit to the ABLE account (i.e., annual gift tax exclusion amount). Any
excess contributions will be includible in the designated beneficiary's gross income
and subject to a 10 percent penalty.

> **Comment:** The ABLE contribution limit for this purpose does not include
> additional contributions of the designated beneficiary's compensation for tax
> years beginning after December 22, 2017, and before January 1, 2026 (see ¶645).

The rollover rule applies regardless of whether a QTP distribution is contributed by
the beneficiary or completed through a direct transfer to an ABLE account. However,
the IRS intends to issue regulations that a QTP must prohibit any direct transfer to an
ABLE account that exceeds the ABLE contribution limit. Similarly, an ABLE account
must be prohibited from accepting any excess contributions.

The IRS encourages the designated beneficiary and QTP to contact the ABLE account
before contributing any rollover distribution to ensure the contribution limit will not
be exceeded. In the case of a direct transfer, any excess contributions that are rejected
by the ABLE account and returned to the QTP will not be deemed a new contribution
for purposes of the QTP contribution limits.

▶ **Effective date.** The amendments made by this section regarding rollover distributions to
ABLE account apply to tax years beginning after December 22, 2017, the date of enactment
(Act Sec. 11025(b) of the Tax Cuts and Jobs Act (P.L. 115-97)). The amendments regarding
distributions for elementary or secondary school tuition apply to distributions made after
December 31, 2017 (Act Sec. 11032(b) of the 2017 Tax Cuts Act).

— Act Sec. 11025(a), of the Tax Cuts and Jobs Act of 2017 (P.L. 115-97), amending Code Sec.
529(c)(3)(C)(i);

— Act Sec. 11032(a)(1), adding Code Sec. 529(c)(7);

— Act Sec. 11032(a)(2), amending Code Sec. 529(e)(3)(A);

— Act Secs. 11025(b) and 11032(b), providing the effective date.

**¶640**

## ¶645 Contributions and Rollovers to ABLE Accounts

### SUMMARY OF NEW LAW

An employed ABLE account beneficiary may make additional contributions to the account before 2026 of up to the lesser of (1) his or her taxable compensation for the tax year, or (2) the poverty line for a one-person household for the year. Also, distributions from a beneficiary's qualified tuition plan (QTP or 529 plan) may be rolled over to an ABLE account of the beneficiary or family member.

### BACKGROUND

Achieving a Better Life Experience (ABLE) programs can be established by a state, or agency or instrumentality of a state, to encourage individuals and families in saving funds to assist a disabled individual in paying qualified disability expenses through a tax-favored savings account (Code Sec. 529A(b)(1)). The structure and tax treatment of an ABLE account under the program are similar to qualified tuition programs under Code Sec. 529.

Contributions to an ABLE account may only be made in cash in the form of a check, money order, credit card, electronic transfer, or similar method. Except for rollover contributions, the aggregate annual contributions to a single ABLE account cannot exceed the inflation-adjusted annual gift tax exclusion amount ($15,000 in 2018 and 2019) (Code Sec. 529A(b)(2); Rev. Proc. 2017-58; Rev. Proc. 2018-57). If amounts contributed to an ABLE account exceed the annual contribution limit, the excess contributions and the earnings on those contributions must be returned to the contributors. The excess contributions and earnings must be returned by the due date of the designated beneficiary's income tax return (including extension) or the designated beneficiary is subject to a six percent excise tax.

A rollover distribution from one ABLE account to another, whether in the same ABLE program or a different ABLE program, that meets certain conditions is not includible in the distributee's gross income. In order to be excluded from income, the distribution must be paid into another ABLE account in a qualified ABLE program not later than the 60th day after the date of payment or distribution (Code Sec 529A(c)(1)(C)(i)).

To encourage low- and middle-income taxpayers to establish or maintain private savings accounts to ensure adequate savings for retirement, a nonrefundable credit for contributions or deferrals to retirement savings plans was established (Code Sec. 25B). As a nonrefundable personal credit, the qualified retirement savings contribution credit, commonly referred as the saver's credit, may not exceed income tax liability.

## NEW LAW EXPLAINED

**Contribution amount to ABLE accounts increased and rollovers from qualified tuition plans allowed.**—For tax years beginning after December 22, 2017, and before January 1, 2026, a designated beneficiary may make additional contributions to his or her own ABLE account in excess of the general dollar limit (i.e., annual gift tax exclusion amount). A designated beneficiary may make additional contributions up to the lesser of:

- his or her taxable compensation includible in gross income for the tax year; or
- the federal poverty line for a one-person household for the year (Code Sec. 529A(b)(2)(B), as added by the Tax Cuts and Jobs Act (P.L. 115-97)).

A designated beneficiary eligible to make the additional contribution must be an employee, including a self-employed individual or owner-employee, for whom *no contribution* was made for the tax year to: (1) a defined contribution plan (including a 401(k) plan); (2) a 403(b) tax-sheltered annuity plan; and (3) an eligible 457(b) deferred compensation plan (Code Sec. 529A(b)(7)(A), as added by the 2017 Tax Cuts Act).

The poverty line for the additional contribution limit is the poverty guidelines updated periodically by the Department of Health and Human Services (HHS) (Code Sec. 529A(b)(7)(B), as added by the 2017 Tax Cuts Act). The additional contribution limit will be determined using the guideline for the state of the designated beneficiary's residence, not the state where the ABLE account is established (Notice 2018-62). The poverty line amount for 2018 is $12,140 in the continental United States, $13,960 in Hawaii, and $15,180 in Alaska (IRS Pub. 907).

> **Comment:** "Poverty line" is defined in Section 673 of the Community Services Block Grant Act as the official poverty line set forth by the Office of Management and Budget based on the most recent census data. Annual adjustments are made to the poverty line by multiplying the official poverty line by the percentage change in the Consumer Price Index for All Urban Consumers.

The employed designated beneficiary (or person acting on his or her behalf) is solely responsible for ensuring that the additional contribution limit is met. The ABLE account will use the normal rules to return any excess contribution and earnings. As a result, for any excess contributions of the designated beneficiary's compensation income:

- the designated beneficiary is solely responsible (or a person acting on the designated beneficiary's behalf) to identify and request the return of any excess contribution and earnings; and
- the ABLE program may rely on self-certifications made under penalties of perjury of the designated beneficiary or person acting on his or her behalf (Notice 2018-62).

The retirement savings contribution credit can be claimed by a designated beneficiary of an ABLE account for contributions made to the designated beneficiary's ABLE account before January 1, 2026 (Code Sec. 25B(d)(1)(D), as added by the 2017 Tax Cuts Act).

## NEW LAW EXPLAINED

**Rollovers to ABLE accounts.** For tax years beginning after December 22, 2017, and before January 1, 2026, distributions from a QTP may be excluded from a designated beneficiary's gross income if it is rolled over or transferred to an ABLE account of the designated beneficiary or a member of his or her family (Code Sec. 529(c)(3)(C)(i), as amended by the 2017 Tax Cuts Act; Notice 2018-58). The rollover contribution and all other contributions to the ABLE account for the tax year may not exceed the contribution limit to the ABLE account (i.e., annual gift tax exclusion amount).

> **Comment:** The ABLE contribution limit for this purpose does not include additional contributions of the designated beneficiary's compensation.

The rollover rule applies regardless of whether a QTP distribution is contributed by the beneficiary or completed through a direct transfer to the ABLE account. However, the IRS intends to issues regulations that a QTP and ABLE account must prohibit any direct transfer that exceeds the ABLE contribution limit. See ¶640 for further information on the rollover of QTP distributions to an ABLE account.

▶ **Effective date.** The amendments made by these sections apply to tax years beginning after December 22, 2017, the date of enactment of this Act (Act Secs. 11024(c) and 11025(b) of the Tax Cuts and Jobs Act (P.L. 115-97)).

— Act Sec. 11024(a) of the Tax Cuts and Job Act (P.L. 115-97) amending Code Sec. 529A(b)(2) and adding Code Sec. 529A(b)(7);

— Act Sec. 11024(b), amending Code Sec. 25B(d)(1);

— Act Sec. 11025(a), amending Code Sec. 529(c)(3)(C)(i);

— Act Secs. 11024(c) and 11025(b), providing the effective date.

# International Tax Provisions

# 7

## TAXATION OF FOREIGN INCOME

## FOREIGN TAX CREDIT

## CFCs AND SUBPART F INCOME

## BASE EROSION PREVENTION

# TAXATION OF FOREIGN INCOME

## ¶705 Participation Exemption Deduction for Foreign-Source Portion of Dividends

### SUMMARY OF NEW LAW

Effective generally for distributions after December 31, 2017, a 100-percent participation exemption deduction is allowed for the foreign-source portion of dividends received from specified 10-percent owned foreign corporations by U.S. corporate shareholders, subject to a one-year holding period (a participation dividends-received deduction (DRD)). No foreign tax credit or deduction is allowed for any taxes paid or accrued with respect to a dividend that qualifies for the deduction. The participation DRD is not available for hybrid dividends received from CFCs.

### BACKGROUND

A U.S. person is subject to U.S. tax on its worldwide income. Generally, a U.S. person is currently taxed on directly earned foreign income (such as income earned directly from the conduct of a foreign business). However, a U.S. person that earns foreign-source income indirectly as a shareholder in a foreign corporation generally is not subject to U.S. tax until the foreign income is distributed to the U.S. person as a dividend.

> **Comment:** The United States is one of the few industrialized countries with a worldwide system of taxation and has the highest statutory corporate tax rates among countries that are members of the Organisation for Economic Co-operation and Development (OECD). The worldwide system of taxation and the high tax rates provide incentives for U.S. companies to keep foreign earnings offshore because such earnings are not taxed until repatriated to the United States.

Certain anti-deferral rules may currently tax a U.S. person on certain categories of passive or highly mobile foreign-source income, regardless of whether the income has been distributed to the U.S. person.

**Subpart F and CFC rules.** The main category of anti-deferral rules are the subpart F rules (Code Secs. 951—965). Under the subpart F rules, U.S. shareholders of a controlled foreign corporation (CFC) are currently taxed on their pro rata shares of

## BACKGROUND

the CFC's subpart F income without regard to whether the income is distributed to the shareholders (Code Sec. 951(a)). A CFC generally is any foreign corporation in which U.S. shareholders own more than 50 percent of the corporation's stock (measured by vote or value) (Code Sec. 957). For this purpose, a U.S. shareholder is a U.S. person who owns at least 10 percent of the voting stock of the foreign corporation (Code Sec. 951(b)).

With certain exceptions, subpart F income generally includes passive income and other income that is readily movable from one taxing jurisdiction to another (Code Sec. 952). A U.S. shareholder of a CFC may exclude from its income actual distributions of the CFC's earnings and profits that were previously included in the shareholder's income under subpart F (Code Sec. 959).

**PFIC regime.** Another set of anti-deferral rules are the passive foreign investment company (PFIC) rules (Code Secs. 1291-1298). A PFIC is generally any foreign corporation if 75 percent or more of its gross income for the tax year consists of passive income, or 50 percent or more of its assets consists of assets that produce, or are held for the production of, passive income (Code Sec. 1297). Different sets of income inclusion rules apply to U.S. persons that are shareholders in a PFIC, regardless of their percentage ownership in the company.

A shareholder of a PFIC generally may make an election to treat the PFIC as a qualified electing fund (QEF) and depending on when the election is effective, the company may be either a "pedigreed" or an "unpedigreed" QEF with respect to that shareholder. When a PFIC carries the unpedigreed QEF designation, the shareholder is taxed under both Code Secs. 1291 and 1293. If the unpedigreed QEF is also a CFC for the tax year of the QEF election, the shareholder may make a deemed dividend election to limit taxation to one set of rules. In this case, the shareholder is treated as receiving a dividend on the qualification date, which is the first day of the PFIC's first tax year as a QEF, and the deemed dividend is taxed under Code Sec. 1291 as an excess distribution.

**Foreign tax credit.** To prevent double taxation of foreign-source income, a foreign tax credit is generally available to offset, in whole or in part, the U.S. tax owed on foreign-source income, regardless of whether the income is earned directly by the U.S. taxpayer, repatriated as an actual dividend, or included in the taxpayer's income under one of the anti-deferral regimes (Code Secs. 901 and 960). The credit is allowed for any income, war profits, and excess profits taxes paid or accrued during the tax year to a foreign country or U.S. possession. The foreign tax credit cannot be used to offset U.S. tax on U.S.-source income, so it is generally limited to a taxpayer's U.S. tax liability on its foreign source taxable income (Code Sec. 904).

**Holding period requirement.** A corporation may claim a dividends-received deduction under Code Secs. 243 and 245 for certain dividends received with respect to stock that has been held for 46 days during the 91-day period beginning 45 days before the ex-dividend date. For preferred stock, the stock must be held for 91 days during the 181-day period beginning 90 days before the date on which the stock becomes ex-dividend. The holding period is reduced for any period during which the taxpayer's risk of loss with respect to the stock is diminished. No dividends-received deduction is allowed to the extent that the taxpayer is under an obligation (pursuant to a short

## BACKGROUND

sale or otherwise) to make related payments with respect to positions in substantially similar or related property (Code Sec. 246(c)).

**Extraordinary dividends.** A corporate shareholder that receives an "extraordinary dividend" must reduce the basis of the stock with respect to which the dividend was received by the non-taxed portion of the dividend. There is an exception if the corporation has held the stock for more than two years before the earliest date on which either the amount or the payment of the dividend is declared, agreed to, or announced. The non-taxed portion of the extraordinary dividend is the excess, if any, of the amount of the dividend over the taxable portion of such dividend. The taxable portion of the dividend is the amount of the dividend includible in income, reduced by any allowable deduction with respect to the dividend under Code Secs. 243 and 245 (Code Sec. 1059).

## NEW LAW EXPLAINED

**100-percent participation exemption deduction allowed for foreign-source portion of dividends.**—A 100-percent deduction is allowed for the foreign-source portion of dividends received from a specified 10-percent owned foreign corporation by a domestic corporation that is a U.S. shareholder of the foreign corporation (a participation dividends-received deduction (DRD)) (Code Sec. 245A(a), as added by the Tax Cuts and Jobs Act (P.L. 115-97)).

> **Comment:** The 2017 Tax Cuts Act generally establishes a participation exemption (territorial) system for the taxation of foreign income that replaces the prior-law system of taxing U.S. corporations on the foreign earnings of their foreign subsidiaries when the earnings are distributed. The exemption, which is provided in the form of a participation DRD, is intended to encourage U.S. companies to repatriate their accumulated foreign earnings and invest them in the United States.

> **Caution:** Dividends from foreign companies that are less than 10 percent owned by domestic corporations are not eligible for the participation DRD and will continue to be treated the same as under prior law (i.e., such dividends generally will be taxed when distributed, subject to any applicable anti-deferral rules). Also, dividends received by non-corporate U.S. shareholders are not eligible for the participation DRD.

> **Comment:** According to the Conference Committee Report, it is intended that the term "dividend received" be interpreted broadly, consistently with the meaning of "amount received as dividends" and "dividends received" used in Code Secs. 243 and 245, respectively. Thus, for example, gain included in gross income as a dividend under Code Sec. 1248(a) or 964(e) would constitute a dividend for which the participation DRD may be available. Regulations or other guidance issued pursuant to the regulatory authority granted under Code Sec. 245A(g) (discussed below) may clarify the intended broad scope of the term "dividend received." For example, if a domestic corporation indirectly owns stock of a foreign corporation through a partnership and the domestic corporation would qualify for the participation DRD with respect to dividends from the

## NEW LAW EXPLAINED

foreign corporation if the domestic corporation owned the stock directly, the domestic corporation would be allowed a participation DRD with respect to its distributive share of the partnership's dividend from the foreign corporation (Conference Report on H.R. 1, Tax Cuts and Jobs Act (H. Rept. 115-466)).

**Caution:** According to the Joint Committee on Taxation's report on the 2017 Tax Cuts Act (i.e., Bluebook), a technical correction may be necessary to reflect that a corporate U.S. shareholder of a CFC receiving a dividend from a 10-percent owned foreign corporation will be allowed a participation DRD with respect to the subpart F inclusion attributable to such dividend in the same manner as a dividend would be allowable under Code Sec. 245A. However, certain dividends that qualify for the participation DRD may result in an inclusion under Code Sec. 951(a) (subpart F) or Code Sec. 951A (GILTI) in cases in which any such inclusion is reduced under Code Sec. 951(a)(2)(B) by reason of a dividend or in certain cases in which the CFC ceases to have a U.S. shareholder with Code Sec. 958(a) ownership. In addition, a technical correction may be required to reflect the intent that the participation DRD be excluded from adjusted current earnings (ACE) adjustments for purposes of the corporate alternative minimum tax (AMT) as applicable to certain fiscal-year taxpayers for their 2017 tax year (General Explanation of Public Law 115-97 (JCS-1-18)). The corporate AMT is repealed for tax years beginning after 2017.

A specified 10-percent owned foreign corporation is any foreign corporation (other than a PFIC that is not also a CFC) with respect to which any domestic corporation is a U.S. shareholder (Code Sec. 245A(b), as added by the 2017 Tax Cuts Act).

**Comment:** The subpart F definitions of a U.S. shareholder and CFC are expanded so that they are used for purposes of Title 26 (including the participation DRD), and not just the subpart F provisions (Code Secs. 951(b) and 957(a), as amended by the 2017 Tax Cuts Act). The U.S. shareholder definition is further expanded so that a U.S. shareholder includes a U.S. person that owns at least 10 percent of the total combined voting power of all classes of stock entitled to vote or at least 10 percent of the total value of all classes of stock of the foreign corporation (Act Sec. 14214(a) of the 2017 Tax Cuts Act, amending Code Sec. 951(b); see ¶745).

**Comment:** Taxation of income earned by PFICs remains subject to the anti-deferral PFIC regime and dividends received from non-CFC PFICs are ineligible for the participation DRD.

**Comment:** A domestic corporation includes a CFC treated as a domestic corporation for purposes of computing its taxable income (Reg. § 1.952-2(b)(1)). Therefore, a CFC receiving a dividend from a 10-percent owned foreign corporation that constitutes subpart F income may be eligible for the DRD with respect to that income. In addition, the participation DRD is available only to C corporations that are not RICs or REITs (Conference Report on H.R. 1, Tax Cuts and Jobs Act (H. Rept. 115-466)).

**Foreign-source portion of a dividend.** The foreign-source portion of any dividend from a specified 10-percent owned foreign corporation is the amount that bears the same ratio to the dividend as (1) the undistributed foreign earnings of the specified

## NEW LAW EXPLAINED

10-percent owned foreign corporation, bears to (2) the total undistributed earnings of that corporation (Code Sec. 245A(c)(1), as added by the 2017 Tax Cuts Act).

Undistributed earnings are the earnings and profits of a specified 10-percent owned foreign corporation (computed in accordance with Code Secs. 964(a) and 986) as of the close of the tax year of the specified 10-percent owned foreign corporation in which the dividend is distributed that are not reduced by dividends distributed during that tax year (Code Sec. 245A(c)(2), as added by the 2017 Tax Cuts Act).

> **Comment:** Under Code Sec. 959(d), a distribution of previously taxed income does not constitute a dividend, even if it reduces earnings and profits.

Undistributed foreign earnings of a specified 10-percent owned foreign corporation are the portion of the undistributed earnings of that corporation that is not attributable to (1) the corporation's income that is effectively connected with the conduct of a trade or business within the United States, and subject to tax under Chapter 1 of the Code, or (2) any dividend received (directly or through a wholly owned foreign corporation) from an 80-percent owned (by vote or value) domestic corporation (Code Sec. 245A(c)(3), as added by the 2017 Tax Cuts Act).

**Foreign tax credit disallowance.** No foreign tax credit or deduction is allowed for any taxes paid or accrued (or treated as paid or accrued) with respect to a dividend that qualifies for the participation DRD (Code Sec. 245A(d), as added by the 2017 Tax Cuts Act). For purposes of computing the Code Sec. 904(a) foreign tax credit limitation, a domestic corporation that is a U.S. shareholder of a specified 10-percent owned foreign corporation must compute its foreign-source taxable income (and entire taxable income) by disregarding

- the foreign-source portion of any dividend received from that foreign corporation for which a participation DRD is allowed, and
- any deductions properly allocable or apportioned to that foreign source portion or the stock with respect to which it is paid.

For this purpose, any term that is used in this rule and in Code Sec. 245A has the meaning used in Code Sec. 245A (Code Sec. 904(b)(5), as added by the 2017 Tax Cuts Act).

**Hybrid dividends.** The participation DRD is not available for any dividend received by a U.S. shareholder from a CFC if the dividend is a hybrid dividend (Code Sec. 245A(e)(1), as added by the 2017 Tax Cuts Act).

A hybrid dividend is an amount received from a CFC for which a participation DRD would otherwise be allowed and for which the CFC received a deduction (or other tax benefit) with respect to any income, war profits, or excess profits taxes imposed by any foreign country or U.S. possession (Code Sec. 245A(e)(4), as added by the 2017 Tax Cuts Act).

If a CFC with respect to which a domestic corporation is a U.S. shareholder receives a hybrid dividend from any other CFC with respect to which the domestic corporation is also a U.S. shareholder, then:

- the hybrid dividend is treated as subpart F income of the recipient CFC for the tax year of the CFC in which the dividend was received, and

¶705

## NEW LAW EXPLAINED

- the U.S. shareholder must include an amount equal to the shareholder's pro rata share of such subpart F income in gross income (Code Sec. 245A(e)(2), as added by the 2017 Tax Cuts Act).

    **Caution:** A technical correction may be required to reflect that this tiered hybrid dividend rule applies to an amount treated as a dividend in the hands of the recipient CFC (as opposed to amounts for which the participation DRD is allowed) and for which the distributing CFC received a deduction or other tax benefit (General Explanation of Public Law 115-97 (JCS-1-18)).

No foreign tax credit or deduction is allowed for any taxes paid or accrued (or treated as paid or accrued) with respect to any hybrid dividend received by a U.S. shareholder or included in the U.S. shareholder's income under the rules, discussed above (Code Sec. 245A(e)(3), as added by the 2017 Tax Cuts Act).

    **Comment:** Proposed regulations under Code Sec. 245A(e) address certain dividends involving hybrid arrangements (Proposed Reg. §1.245A(e)-1; NPRM REG-104352-18, December 28, 2018; see a discussion of the proposed regulations further below).

**Special rule for purging distributions of PFICs.** Any amount that is treated as a dividend pursuant to the deemed dividend election under Code Sec. 1291(d)(2)(B) is not treated as a dividend for purposes of the participation DRD (Code Sec. 245A(f), as added by the 2017 Tax Cuts Act).

**Regulatory authority.** The Secretary of the Treasury is authorized to issue regulations or other guidance that is necessary or appropriate to carry out these provisions, including regulations for the treatment of U.S. shareholders owning stock of a specified 10-percent owned foreign corporation through a partnership (Code Sec. 245A(g), as added by the 2017 Tax Cuts Act).

**One-year holding period requirement.** A domestic corporation is not permitted a participation DRD for any dividend on any share of stock that is held by the domestic corporation for 365 days or less during the 731-day period beginning on the date that is 365 days before the date on which the share becomes ex-dividend with respect to the dividend (Code Sec. 246(c)(5)(A), as added by the 2017 Tax Cuts Act).

    **Comment:** The special holding period rule for preference dividends in Code Sec. 246(c)(2) does not apply in this case.

The holding period requirement is treated as met only if the foreign corporation is a specified 10-percent owned foreign corporation and the taxpayer is a U.S. shareholder with respect to that specified 10-percent owned foreign corporation at *all* times during the required period (Code Sec. 246(c)(5)(B), as added by the 2017 Tax Cuts Act).

    **Comment:** Under Code Sec. 246, the participation DRD is not permitted for any dividend on any share of stock to the extent the domestic corporation that owns the share is under an obligation (under a short sale or otherwise) to make related payments with respect to positions in substantially similar or related property. In addition, the required holding periods must be reduced for any period during which the domestic corporation has diminished its risk of loss in respect of stock on which a dividend is paid.

## NEW LAW EXPLAINED

**Application of other rules.** The participation DRD does not apply to dividends received from Code Sec. 501 tax-exempt organizations and farmers' cooperative associations exempt from tax under Code Sec. 521 (Code Sec. 246(a)(1), as amended by the 2017 Tax Cuts Act).

In addition, the participation DRD reduces the amount of the dividend includible in gross income for purposes of computing the nontaxed portion of an extraordinary dividend (Code Sec. 1059(b)(2)(B), as amended by the 2017 Tax Cuts Act).

**Proposed regulations on hybrid dividends.** Proposed regulations under Code Sec. 245A(e) address certain dividends involving hybrid arrangements (Proposed Reg. §1.245A(e)-1; NPRM REG-104352-18, December 28, 2018). The proposed regulations neutralize the double non-taxation effects of these dividends by either denying the participation DRD or requiring an inclusion under Code Sec. 951(a), depending on whether the dividend is received by a domestic corporation or a CFC.

*Hybrid dividend definition.* A dividend generally is a hybrid dividend if it satisfies two conditions:

- but for Code Sec. 245A(e), the participation DRD would be allowed; and
- the dividend is one for which the CFC (or a related person) is or was allowed a deduction or other tax benefit under a relevant foreign tax law (a hybrid deduction) (Proposed Reg. § 1.245A(e)-1(b) and (d)).

    **Comment:** The proposed regulations take into account certain deductions or other tax benefits allowed to a person related to a CFC (such as a shareholder) because, for example, certain tax benefits allowed to a shareholder of a CFC are economically equivalent to the CFC having been allowed a deduction.

*Relevant foreign tax law.* A relevant foreign tax law, with respect to a CFC, is any regime of any foreign country or possession of the United States that imposes an income, war profits, or excess profits tax on the CFC's income, other than a foreign anti-deferral regime under which an owner of the CFC is liable to tax (Proposed Reg. § 1.245A(e)-1(f)).

    **Comment:** For example, a relevant foreign tax law includes the tax law of a foreign country of which the CFC is a tax resident, as well as the tax law applicable to a foreign branch of the CFC.

*Deduction or other tax benefit (hybrid deduction).* Only deductions or other tax benefits that are allowed under the relevant foreign tax law may constitute a hybrid deduction (Proposed Reg. § 1.245A(e)-1(d)).

    **Comment:** For example, if the relevant foreign tax law contains hybrid mismatch rules under which a CFC is denied a deduction for interest paid with respect to a hybrid instrument to prevent a deduction/no-inclusion (D/NI) outcome, the payment of the interest does not give rise to a hybrid deduction because the deduction is not allowed. This prevents double-taxation that could arise if a hybrid dividend were subject to both Code Sec. 245A(e) and a hybrid mismatch rule under a relevant foreign tax law (NPRM REG-104352-18).

For a deduction or other tax benefit to be a hybrid deduction, it must relate to or result from an amount paid, accrued, or distributed with respect to an instrument of

## NEW LAW EXPLAINED

the CFC that is treated as stock for U.S. tax purposes. That is, there must be a connection between the deduction or other tax benefit under the relevant foreign tax law and the instrument that is stock for U.S. tax purposes.

> **Comment:** For example, a hybrid deduction includes an interest deduction under a relevant foreign tax law with respect to a hybrid instrument (stock for U.S. tax purposes, debt for foreign tax purposes). However, it does not include an exemption provided to a CFC under its tax law for certain types of income (such as income attributable to a foreign branch), because there is not a connection between the tax benefit and the instrument that is stock for U.S. tax purposes (NPRM REG-104352-18).

Deductions or other tax benefits allowed pursuant to certain integration or imputation systems do not constitute hybrid deductions (Proposed Reg. §1.245A(e)-1(d)(2)(i)(B)). However, a system that has the effect of exempting earnings that fund a distribution from foreign tax at both the CFC and shareholder level gives rise to a hybrid deduction (Proposed Reg. §1.245A(e)-1(g)(2), Example 2). The proposed regulations also take into account foreign currency gain or loss recognized with respect to a deduction or other tax benefit in determining hybrid deductions (Proposed Reg. §1.245A(e)-1(d)(6)).

*Tiered hybrid dividends.* The proposed regulations provide rules related to hybrid dividends of tiered corporations (tiered hybrid dividends) (Proposed Reg. §1.245A(e)-1(c)). A tiered hybrid dividend is an amount received by a CFC from another CFC to the extent that the amount would be a hybrid dividend if the receiving CFC were a domestic corporation.

> **Comment:** The amount must be treated as a dividend under U.S. tax law in order to be treated as a tiered hybrid dividend. The treatment of the amount under the tax law in which the receiving CFC is a tax resident (or under any other foreign tax law) is irrelevant for this purpose.

If a CFC receives a tiered hybrid dividend from another CFC, and a domestic corporation is a U.S. shareholder of both CFCs, then:

- the tiered hybrid dividend is treated as subpart F income of the receiving CFC;

- the U.S. shareholder must include in gross income its pro rata share of the subpart F income; and

- Code Sec. 245A(d) applies to the amount included in the U.S. shareholder's gross income (Proposed Reg. §1.245A(e)-1(c)(1)).

This treatment applies regardless of the application of any other provisions.

*Interaction with Code Sec. 959.* A tiered hybrid dividend does not include amounts described in Code Sec. 959(b) (distributions of previously taxed earnings and profits (PTEP) from a CFC to an upper-tier CFC that are excluded from the gross income of the upper-tier CFC under Code Sec. 959(b)) (Proposed Reg. §1.245A(e)-1(c)(2)).

*Interaction with Code Sec. 964(e).* The proposed regulations coordinate the tiered hybrid dividend rules and the Code Sec. 964(e) rules by providing that, to the extent a dividend arising under Code Sec. 964(e)(1) is a tiered hybrid dividend, the tiered

## NEW LAW EXPLAINED

hybrid dividend rules, rather than the Code Sec. 964(e)(4) rules, apply (Proposed Reg. §1.245A(e)-1(c)(1) and (4)).

> **Comment:** Accordingly, in such a case, a U.S. shareholder that includes in income an amount under the tiered hybrid dividend rule is not allowed the participation DRD, or foreign tax credits or deductions, for this amount.

*Hybrid deduction accounts.* The proposed regulations define a hybrid dividend (or tiered hybrid dividend) based, in part, on the extent of the balance of the hybrid deduction accounts of the domestic corporation (or CFC) receiving the dividend (Proposed Reg. §1.245A(e)-1(b) and (d)). This ensures that dividends are subject to Code Sec. 245A(e) regardless of whether the same payment gives rise to the dividend and the hybrid deduction.

> **Comment:** In some cases, the actual payment by a CFC of an amount that is treated as a dividend for U.S. tax purposes will result in a corresponding hybrid deduction. In many cases, however, the dividend and the hybrid deduction may not arise pursuant to the same payment and may be recognized in different tax years. This may occur in the case of a hybrid instrument for which under a relevant foreign tax law the CFC is allowed deductions for accrued (but not yet paid) interest. In such a case, to the extent that an actual payment has not yet been made on the instrument, there generally would not be a dividend for U.S. tax purposes. However, because the earnings and profits of the CFC would not be reduced by the accrued interest deduction, the earnings and profits may give rise to a dividend when subsequently distributed to the U.S. shareholder (NPRM REG-104352-18).

A hybrid deduction account must be maintained with respect to each share of stock of a CFC held by a person that, given its ownership of the CFC and the share, could be subject to the participation DRD rules upon a dividend paid by the CFC on the share (Proposed Reg. §1.245A(e)-1(d) and (f)). The account, which is maintained in the functional currency of the CFC, reflects the amount of hybrid deductions of the CFC (allowed in tax years beginning after 2017) that have been allocated to the share.

A dividend paid by a CFC to a shareholder that has a hybrid deduction account with respect to the CFC is generally treated as a hybrid dividend or tiered hybrid dividend to the extent of the shareholder's balance in all of its hybrid deduction accounts with respect to the CFC, even if the dividend is paid on a share that has not had any hybrid deductions allocated to it.

> **Comment:** Absent such an approach, the purposes of Code Sec. 245A(e) might be avoided by, for example, structuring dividend payments so that they are generally made on shares of stock to which a hybrid deduction has not been allocated (rather than on shares of stock to which a hybrid deduction has been allocated, such as a share that is a hybrid instrument) (NPRM REG-104352-18).

Once an amount in a hybrid deduction account gives rise to a hybrid dividend or a tiered hybrid dividend, the account is correspondingly reduced (Proposed Reg. §1.245A(e)-1(d)).

## NEW LAW EXPLAINED

*Hybrid deduction accounts and transfers of stock.* Because hybrid deduction accounts are with respect to stock of a CFC, the proposed regulations include rules that take into account transfers of the stock (Proposed Reg. § 1.245A(e)-1(d)(4)(ii)(A)).

> **Comment:** These rules, which are similar to the Code Sec. 959 successor PTEP rules, ensure that Code Sec. 245A(e) properly applies to dividends that give rise to a D/NI outcome in cases where the shareholder that receives the dividend is not the same shareholder that held the stock when the hybrid deduction was incurred (NPRM REG-104352-18).

These rules only apply when the stock is transferred among persons that are required to keep hybrid deduction accounts. Thus, if the stock is transferred to a person that is not required to keep a hybrid deduction account - such as an individual or a foreign corporation that is not a CFC - the account terminates (subject to the anti-avoidance rule, discussed below).

The proposed regulations also take into account certain non-recognition exchanges of the stock, and transfers and exchanges that occur mid-way through a CFC's tax year (Proposed Reg. § 1.245A(e)-1(d)(4)(ii)(B) and (5)).

*Hybrid deduction accounts and dividends from lower-tier CFCs.* A special rule addresses earnings and profits of a lower-tier CFC that are included in a domestic corporation's income as a dividend under Code Sec. 1248(c)(2). In these cases, the domestic corporation is treated as having certain hybrid deduction accounts with respect to the lower-tier CFC that are held and maintained by other CFCs (Proposed Reg. § 1.245A(e)-1(b)(3)).

This ensures that, to the extent the earnings and profits of the lower-tier CFC give rise to the dividend, hybrid deduction accounts with respect to the lower-tier CFC are taken into account for purposes of the determinations under Code Sec. 245A(e), even though the accounts are held indirectly by the domestic corporation. A similar rule applies with respect to gains on stock sales treated as dividends under Code Sec. 964(e)(1) (Proposed Reg. § 1.245A(e)-1(c)(3)).

*Anti-avoidance rule.* An anti-avoidance rule provides that appropriate adjustments are made, including adjustments that would disregard a transaction or arrangement, if a transaction or arrangement is engaged in with a principal purpose of avoiding the purposes of the proposed regulations (Proposed Reg. § 1.245A(e)-1(e)).

*Applicability date.* The proposed regulations are proposed to apply to distributions made after December 31, 2017 (Proposed Reg. § 1.245A(e)-1(h)). The IRS expects to finalize these regulations by June 22, 2019. However if the regulations are finalized after June 22, 2019, then the IRS expects that the regulations will apply only to tax years ending on or after December 28, 2018 (NPRM REG-104352-18).

▶ **Effective date.** The amendments made by this section apply to distributions made (and for purposes of determining a taxpayer's foreign tax credit limitation under Code Sec. 904, deductions with respect to tax years ending) after December 31, 2017 (Act Sec. 14101(f) of the Tax Cuts and Jobs Act (P.L. 115-97)).

— Act Sec. 14101(a) of the Tax Cuts and Jobs Act (P.L. 115-97), adding Code Sec. 245A;

— Act Sec. 14101(b), amending Code Sec. 246(c);

— Act Sec. 14101(c), amending Code Sec. 246(a)(1) and Code Sec. 1059(b)(2)(B);

## NEW LAW EXPLAINED

— Act Sec. 14101(d), adding Code Sec. 904(b)(5);

— Act Sec. 14101(e)(1), amending Code Sec. 951(b);

— Act Sec. 14101(e)(2), amending Code Sec. 957(a);

— Act Sec. 14101(f), providing the effective date.

## ¶707 Sales or Transfers Involving Specified 10-Percent Owned Foreign Corporations

### SUMMARY OF NEW LAW

Amounts received by a domestic corporation upon the sale or exchange of stock in a foreign corporation held for at least one year that are treated as Section 1248 dividends are also treated as dividends for purposes of the participation dividends-received deduction (DRD). In addition, solely for purposes of determining a loss, a domestic corporation's basis in the stock of a specified 10-percent owned foreign corporation is reduced by the amount of the participation DRD allowable to the domestic corporation for dividends received with respect to that stock, effective for distributions made after December 31, 2017. In the case of a sale by a CFC of a lower-tier CFC, the foreign-source portion of the amount treated as a dividend under Code Sec. 964(e)(1) is treated as subpart F income. A U.S shareholder of the selling CFC includes in income a pro rata share of that amount and is allowed a participation DRD. Also, a loss recapture rule requires a domestic corporation that transfers, after December 31, 2017, substantially all of the assets of a foreign branch to a specified 10-percent owned foreign corporation in which it is a U.S. shareholder after the transfer to include in income the amount of transferred losses, subject to certain limitations. Finally, the active trade or business exception to the Code Sec. 367(a) outbound transfer rules is repealed, effective for transfers after December 31, 2017.

### BACKGROUND

Generally, a U.S. person that earns foreign-source income indirectly as a shareholder in a foreign corporation is not subject to U.S. tax until the foreign income is distributed to the U.S. person as a dividend. Certain anti-deferral rules may currently tax a U.S. person on certain categories of passive or highly mobile foreign-source income, regardless of whether the income has been distributed to the U.S. person.

The main category of anti-deferral rules are the subpart F rules (Code Secs. 951-965). Under the subpart F rules, U.S. shareholders of a controlled foreign corporation (CFC) are currently taxed on their pro rata shares of the CFC's subpart F income without regard to whether the income is distributed to the shareholders (Code Sec. 951(a)). A CFC generally is any foreign corporation in which U.S. shareholders own more than 50 percent of the corporation's stock (measured by vote or value) (Code Sec. 957). For this purpose, a U.S. shareholder is a U.S. person that owns at least 10 percent of the voting stock of the foreign corporation (Code Sec. 951(b)).

## BACKGROUND

With certain exceptions, subpart F income generally includes passive income and other income that is readily movable from one taxing jurisdiction to another (Code Sec. 952). A U.S. shareholder of a CFC may exclude from its income actual distributions of the CFC's earnings and profits that were previously included in the shareholder's income under subpart F (Code Sec. 959).

In general, a 10-percent U.S. shareholder of a CFC increases its basis in the CFC stock with the amount of the CFC's earnings that are included in the shareholder's income under subpart F. Similarly, a 10-percent U.S. shareholder generally reduces its basis in the CFC stock in an amount equal to any distributions received from the CFC that are excluded from the shareholder's income as previously taxed under subpart F (Code Sec. 961).

Gain on a U.S. person's disposition of CFC stock that would otherwise be treated as capital gain, is included in the taxpayer's gross income as dividend income to the extent of the CFC's earnings and profits (E&P) attributable to the stock while the taxpayer held the shares. For this treatment to apply, the foreign corporation must be a CFC at any time during the five-year period ending on the date of the disposition, and the U.S. person must own 10 percent or more of the total combined voting power of the foreign corporation at any time during that five-year period. Any income previously taxed as subpart F income is not included in determining the CFC's E&P attributable to the stock sold, unless the income was distributed before the disposition. Any gain in excess of the CFC's E&P is treated as capital gain. In determining the gain from the disposition of the CFC stock, a shareholder's basis in the stock is increased by the CFC's subpart F income and decreased by any distribution (Code Sec. 1248).

Gain on the sale or exchange of stock in a foreign corporation by a CFC is included in the CFC's gross income as a dividend to the same extent that it would have been included under Code Sec. 1248(a) if the CFC were a U.S. person. A CFC is treated as having sold or exchanged stock if it is treated as having gain from the sale or exchange of the stock under the income tax provisions of the Code (Code Sec. 964(e)).

**Active trade or business exception for Code Sec. 367 outbound transfers.** Generally, if a U.S. person transfers property to a foreign corporation in connection with a corporate organization, reorganization, and liquidation, the foreign corporation is not treated as a corporation and the otherwise tax-free transfer is treated as a taxable exchange (Code Sec. 367(a)). There are a number of exceptions to the general gain recognition rule on the outbound transfers of property, including a transfer of property to be used in an active trade or business outside of the United States (the active trade or business exception).

For the active trade or business exception to apply (i) the property must be eligible property (e.g., tangible property, financial assets, stock in trade, accounts receivables, etc.), (ii) the property must be transferred for use by the foreign corporation in the active conduct of a trade or business outside of the United States, and (iii) the U.S. transferor must comply with the reporting requirements of Code Sec. 6038B (Code Sec. 367(a)(3); Reg. § 1.367(a)-2(a)). In addition, four factual determinations must be made to determine whether the transferred property qualifies for the active trade or business exception (Reg. § 1.367(a)-2(d)(1)).

## BACKGROUND

The active conduct of a trade or business exception does not apply in the case where a U.S. person transfers assets of a foreign branch with previously deducted losses to a foreign corporation. The U.S. person is required to recognize gain on the transfer equal to the sum of the previously deducted ordinary and capital losses of the branch (Code Sec. 367(a)(3)(C); Temp. Reg. § 1.367(a)-6T).

## NEW LAW EXPLAINED

**Special rules provided for sales or transfers involving specified 10-percent owned foreign corporations.—Sale of stock by U.S. persons.** If a domestic corporation sells or exchanges stock in a foreign corporation held for one year or more, any amount received by the domestic corporation that is treated as a dividend under Code Sec. 1248 is treated as a dividend for purposes of the 100-percent participation exemption deduction for the foreign-source portion of dividends under Code Sec. 245A (the participation dividends-received deduction (DRD)) (Code Sec. 1248(j), as added by the Tax Cuts and Jobs Act (P.L. 115-97)).

> **Comment:** This rule allows gain on the disposition of the foreign corporation stock to be reduced or eliminated as a result of the recharacterization of the gain as a dividend for which a 100-percent participation DRD is allowed.

> **Comment:** The 2017 Tax Cuts Act generally establishes a participation exemption (territorial) system for the taxation of foreign income that replaces the prior-law system of taxing U.S. corporations on the foreign earnings of their foreign subsidiaries when the earnings are distributed. The exemption, which is provided in the form of a participation DRD, is intended to encourage U.S. companies to repatriate their accumulated foreign earnings and invest them in the United States. See ¶ 705 for a discussion of the participation DRD.

**Reduction in the basis of certain foreign stock.** If a domestic corporation receives a dividend from a specified 10-percent owned foreign corporation in any tax year, solely for the purpose of determining a loss on the disposition of the stock of that foreign corporation in that tax year or any subsequent tax year, the domestic corporation's basis in that stock is reduced (but not below zero) by the amount of the participation DRD allowable to the domestic corporation with respect to that stock. The basis in the specified 10-percent owned foreign corporation stock is not reduced under this rule to the extent the basis was reduced under Code Sec. 1059 by reason of a dividend for which the participation DRD was allowable (Code Sec. 961(d), as added by the 2017 Tax Cuts Act). Thus, the reduction in basis is for the portion of the dividend received from the foreign corporation that was exempt from tax by reason of the participation DRD in any tax year of the domestic corporation.

> **Comment:** The reduction in basis addresses the concern that taxpayers may obtain inappropriate double benefit that would otherwise be created as a result of the participation DRD. In particular, a distribution from a foreign corporation that is eligible for a participation DRD would reduce the value of the foreign corporation, thus reducing any built-in gain or increasing any built-in loss in the shareholder's stock of the foreign corporation. While reducing gain in this way is consistent with the application of Code Sec. 1248 to recharacterize such gain as a

## NEW LAW EXPLAINED

dividend for which a participation DRD is allowed (see above), increasing any loss in the stock will create an inappropriate double U.S. tax benefit - first, a tax-free distribution from the foreign corporation and second, a tax loss on the disposition of the foreign corporation's stock.

A specified 10-percent owned foreign corporation is any foreign corporation (other than a passive foreign investment company (PFIC) that is not also a CFC) with respect to which any domestic corporation is a U.S. shareholder (Code Sec. 245A(b), as added by the 2017 Tax Cuts Act; see ¶705).

> **Comment:** The subpart F definitions of a U.S. shareholder and CFC are expanded so that they are used for purposes of the Internal Revenue Code (including the participation DRD), and not just the subpart F provisions (Code Secs. 951(b) and 957(a), as amended by the 2017 Tax Cuts Act, see ¶705). The U.S. shareholder definition is further expanded so that a U.S. shareholder includes a U.S. person that owns at least 10 percent of the total combined voting power of all classes of stock entitled to vote or at least 10 percent of the total value of all classes of stock of the foreign corporation (see ¶745).

**Sale by a CFC of a lower-tier CFC.** If for any tax year of a CFC beginning after December 31, 2017, an amount is treated as a dividend under Code Sec. 964(e)(1) because of a sale or exchange by the CFC of stock in another foreign corporation held for one year or more, then:

(1) the foreign-source portion of the dividend is treated as subpart F income of the selling CFC for that tax year for purposes of the subpart F income inclusion rules;

(2) a U.S. shareholder with respect to the selling CFC includes in income for the tax year of the shareholder with or within which the tax year of the CFC ends, an amount equal to the shareholder's pro rata share of the amount treated as subpart F income under item (1), above; and

(3) a participation DRD is allowable to the U.S. shareholder with respect to the included subpart F income under item (2), above, in the same manner as if the subpart F income were a dividend received by the shareholder from the selling CFC (Code Sec. 964(e)(4)(A), as added by the 2017 Tax Cuts Act).

> **Comment:** The foreign-source portion of any amount treated as a dividend under this rule is determined in the same manner as the foreign-source portion of a dividend eligible for the participation DRD (see ¶705) (Code Sec. 964(e)(4)(C), as added by the 2017 Tax Cuts Act).

If a CFC sells or exchanges stock in another foreign corporation in a tax year of the selling CFC beginning after December 31, 2017, stock basis adjustment rules similar to the rules of Code Sec. 961(d) apply (Code Sec. 964(e)(4)(B), as added by the 2017 Tax Cuts Act).

**Treatment of foreign branch losses transferred to specified 10-percent owned foreign corporations.** If a domestic corporation transfers substantially all of the assets of a foreign branch (within the meaning of Code Sec. 367(a)(3)(C), as in effect before December 22, 2017) to a specified 10-percent owned foreign corporation with respect to which it is a U.S. shareholder after the transfer, the domestic corporation includes

## NEW LAW EXPLAINED

in income, for the tax year of the transfer, an amount equal to the transferred loss amount, subject to certain limitations (Code Sec. 91(a), as added by the 2017 Tax Cuts Act).

The transferred loss amount, with respect to any transfer of substantially all of the assets of a foreign branch, is the excess (if any) of:

- the losses incurred by the foreign branch after December 31, 2017, and before the transfer, for which a deduction was allowed to the domestic corporation, over

- the sum of (i) any taxable income earned by the foreign branch in tax years after the tax year in which the loss is incurred and through the close of the tax year of the transfer, and (ii) gain recognized by reason of a Code Sec. 904(f)(3) overall foreign loss recapture arising out of disposition of assets on account of the underlying transfer (Code Sec. 91(b), as added by the 2017 Tax Cuts Act).

> **Comment:** According to the Conference Committee Report, this loss recapture rule addresses the concern that taxpayers may wish to arbitrarily apply the participation exemption system to foreign subsidiaries but not foreign branches. Specifically, a taxpayer may deduct losses from a foreign branch operation against U.S. taxable income and then incorporate that branch once it becomes profitable. Even though there are other loss recapture rules, such as Code Sec. 367(a)(3)(C), these rules generally rely on the worldwide system of taxation to recapture losses in excess of built-in gains by taxing future earnings when the earnings are repatriated to the United States. Instead of only recapturing such losses upon later repatriation of earnings, the 2017 Tax Cuts Act intends to recapture the U.S. tax benefits of these losses immediately upon the incorporation of a foreign branch that has generated losses. This way, the repatriation of foreign earnings will not carry negative tax consequences, thus discouraging repatriation, which is one of the reasons to transition to a participation exemption system of taxation (Conference Report on H.R. 1, Tax Cuts and Jobs Act (H. Rept. 115-466)).

The transferred loss amount is reduced (but not below zero) by the amount of gain recognized by the taxpayer (other than gain recognized by reason of an overall foreign loss recapture) on account of the transfer (Code Sec. 91(c), as added by the 2017 Tax Cuts Act).

Amounts included in gross income under the above foreign branch loss recapture rules are treated as derived from sources within the United States (Code Sec. 91(d), as added by the 2017 Tax Cuts Act).

Consistent with regulations or other guidance as the Secretary of the Treasury may prescribe, proper adjustments are made in the adjusted basis of the taxpayer's stock in the specified 10-percent owned foreign corporation to which the transfer is made, and in the transferee's adjusted basis in the property transferred, to reflect amounts included in gross income under the foreign branch loss recapture rules, discussed above (Code Sec. 91(e), as added by the 2017 Tax Cuts Act).

¶707

## NEW LAW EXPLAINED

Under a transition rule, the amount of gain taken into account under Code Sec. 91(c) is reduced by the amount of gain that would be recognized under Code Sec. 367(a)(3)(C) (determined without regard to the repeal of the Code Sec. 367(a)(3) active trade or business requirement by the 2017 Tax Cuts Act, discussed below) with respect to losses incurred before January 1, 2018 (Act Sec. 14102(d)(4) of the 2017 Tax Cuts Act).

**Repeal of the active trade or business exception under Code Sec. 367.** The active trade or business exception to the Code Sec. 367(a) rule requiring recognition of gain on the outbound transfer of property by a U.S. transferor to a foreign corporation is repealed (Act Sec. 14102(e)(1) of the 2017 Tax Cuts Act, striking Code Sec. 367(a)(3)).

> **Comment:** As a result of the repeal, transfers of property used in the active conduct of a trade or business from a U.S. corporation to a foreign corporation in an otherwise tax-free transaction will be treated as taxable exchanges since the foreign corporation will not be considered a corporation.

▶ **Effective date.** The amendments made by this section relating to sales or exchanges of foreign corporation stock by a domestic corporation and sales or exchanges of a lower-tier CFC stock by a CFC apply to sales or exchanges after December 31, 2017 (Act Secs. 14102(a)(2) and (c)(2) of Tax Cuts and Jobs Act (P.L. 115-97)). The amendment relating to the reduction of basis in stock of a specified 10-percent owned foreign corporation for purposes of determining loss applies to distributions made after December 31, 2017 (Act Sec. 14102(b)(2) of the 2017 Tax Cuts Act). The amendments relating to the transfer of loss amounts from foreign branches to certain foreign corporations and to the repeal of the active trade or business exception under Code Sec. 367 apply to transfers after December 31, 2017 (Act Secs. 14102(d)(3) and (e)(3) of the 2017 Tax Cuts Act). No specific effective dates are provided for the other provisions; therefore, such provisions are considered effective on December 22, 2017, the date of enactment.

**No significant guidance related to this provision has been issued**.

— Act Sec. 14102(a)(1) of the Tax Cuts and Jobs Act (P.L. 115-97), redesignating Code Sec. 1248(j) as Code Sec. 1248(k) and adding Code Sec. 1248(j);

— Act Sec. 14102(b)(1), adding Code Sec. 961(d);

— Act Sec. 14102(c)(1), adding Code Sec. 964(e)(4);

— Act Sec. 14102(d)(1), adding Code Sec. 91;

— Act Sec. 14102(d)(4);

— Act Sec. 14102(e)(1) and (2), amending Code Sec. 367(a);

— Act Sec. 14102(a)(2), (b)(2), (c)(2), (d)(3) and (e)(3), providing the effective date.

## ¶710 Treatment of Deferred Foreign Income Upon Transition to Participation Exemption System of Taxation

### SUMMARY OF NEW LAW

A transition tax is generally imposed on accumulated foreign earnings, without requiring an actual distribution, upon the transition to the new participation exemption system. Under the transition rule, for the last tax year beginning before January 1, 2018, any U.S. shareholder of any CFC or other foreign corporation (other than a PFIC that is not a CFC) that is at least 10-percent owned by a domestic corporation must include in income its pro rata share of the accumulated post-1986 foreign earnings of the corporation as of November 2, 2017, or December 31, 2017, whichever amount is greater (mandatory inclusion). A portion of the mandatory income inclusion is deductible depending on whether the deferred earnings are held in cash or other assets. The deduction results in a reduced rate of tax of 15.5 percent for the included deferred foreign income held in liquid form and eight percent for the remaining deferred foreign income. A corresponding portion of the foreign tax credit is disallowed. The transition tax can be paid in installments over an eight-year period. Special rules are provided for U.S. shareholders that are S corporations or REITs, or that become expatriated entities after December 22, 2017.

### BACKGROUND

A U.S. person is subject to U.S. tax on its worldwide income. Generally, a U.S. person is currently taxed on any directly earned foreign income (such as income earned directly from the conduct of a foreign business). However, a U.S. person that earns foreign-source income indirectly as a shareholder in a foreign corporation generally is not subject to U.S. tax until the foreign income is distributed to the U.S. person as a dividend.

> **Comment:** The United States is one of the few industrialized countries with a worldwide system of taxation and has the highest statutory corporate tax rates among OECD member countries. The worldwide system of taxation and the high tax rates provide incentives for U.S. companies to keep foreign earnings offshore because such earnings are not taxed until repatriated to the United States. As a result, many U.S. companies have accumulated significant untaxed and undistributed foreign earnings.

Certain anti-deferral rules may currently tax a U.S. person on certain categories of passive or highly mobile foreign-source income, regardless of whether the income has been distributed to the U.S. person.

**Subpart F and CFC rules.** The main category of anti-deferral rules are the subpart F rules (Code Secs. 951-965). Under the subpart F rules, U.S. shareholders of a controlled foreign corporation (CFC) are currently taxed on their pro rata shares of the CFC's subpart F income without regard to whether the income is distributed to the

# BACKGROUND

shareholders (Code Sec. 951(a)). A CFC generally is any foreign corporation in which U.S. shareholders own more than 50 percent of the corporation's stock (measured by vote or value) (Code Sec. 957). For this purpose, a U.S. shareholder is a U.S. person who owns at least 10 percent of the voting stock of the foreign corporation (Code Sec. 951(b)).

Subpart F income generally includes passive income and other income that is readily movable from one taxing jurisdiction to another (Code Sec. 952). A U.S. shareholder of a CFC may exclude from its income actual distributions of the CFC's earnings and profits (E&P) that were previously included in the shareholder's income under subpart F (Code Sec. 959).

The subpart F amount included in the gross income of any U.S. shareholder for any tax year and attributable to a qualified activity is reduced by the amount of the shareholder's pro rata share of any qualified deficit. The term "qualified deficit" means any deficit in E&P of the CFC for any prior tax year that began after December 31, 1986, and for which the CFC was a CFC, but only to the extent the deficit (i) is attributable to the same qualified activity as the activity giving rise to the income being offset, and (ii) has not previously been taken into account (Code Sec. 952(c)(1)(B)).

**PFIC regime.** Another set of anti-deferral rules are the passive foreign investment company (PFIC) rules (Code Secs. 1291-1298). A PFIC is generally any foreign corporation if 75 percent or more of its gross income for the tax year consists of passive income, or 50 percent or more of its assets consists of assets that produce, or are held for the production of, passive income (Code Sec. 1297). Different sets of income inclusion rules apply to U.S. persons that are shareholders in a PFIC, regardless of their percentage ownership in the company.

**Foreign tax credit.** To prevent double taxation of foreign-source income, a foreign tax credit is generally available to offset, in whole or in part, the U.S. tax owed on foreign-source income, regardless of whether the income is earned directly by the U.S. taxpayer, repatriated as an actual dividend, or included in the taxpayer's income under one of the anti-deferral regimes (Code Secs. 901 and 960). The credit is allowed for any income, war profits and excess profits taxes paid or accrued during the tax year to a foreign country or U.S. possession. The foreign tax credit cannot be used to offset U.S. tax on U.S.-source income, so it is generally limited to a taxpayer's U.S. tax liability on its foreign source taxable income (Code Sec. 904).

**Temporary dividends-received deduction for repatriated foreign earnings.** Code Sec. 965 to provide a temporary 85-percent dividends-received deduction (DRD) for certain cash dividends received by U.S. corporate shareholders from CFCs during one tax year that an election under Code Sec. 965 was in effect. The deduction provided temporary relief and was intended to reduce the U.S. tax on repatriated dividends, and thus, encourage U.S. companies to repatriate their accumulated foreign earnings and invest them in the United States. At the taxpayer's election, the deduction was available for dividends received either during the taxpayer's first tax year beginning on or after October 22, 2004, or during the taxpayer's last tax year beginning before such date.

¶710

## BACKGROUND

The temporary deduction was subject to a number of general limitations. It applied only to cash repatriations generally in excess of the taxpayer's average repatriation level calculated for a three-year base period preceding the year of the deduction. The amount of dividends eligible for the deduction was generally limited to the amount of earnings shown as permanently invested outside the United States on the tax-payer's recent audited financial statements. In addition, to qualify for the deduction, dividends were required to be invested in the United States according to a domestic reinvestment plan approved by the taxpayer's senior management and board of directors.

No foreign tax credit or deduction was allowed for foreign taxes attributable to the deductible portion of any dividend. For this purpose, the taxpayer was permitted to specifically identify which dividends were treated as carrying the deduction and which dividends were not. Deductions were also disallowed for expenses that were directly allocable to the deductible portion of any dividend.

**Expatriated entities.** In a corporate inversion transaction (1) a U.S. corporation or partnership (the expatriated entity) becomes a subsidiary of a foreign corporation (a surrogate foreign corporation) or otherwise transfers substantially all of its properties to it, (2) the former shareholders or partners of the expatriated entity hold 60 percent or more (by vote or value) of the stock of the surrogate foreign corporation after the transaction, and (3) the surrogate foreign corporation's expanded affiliated group (EAG) does not conduct substantial business activities in the foreign corporation's country of incorporation (Code Sec. 7874(a)(2)). In this case, a corporate inversion "tax" is imposed on the inversion gain of expatriated entities during the 10-year period after the inversion. If after the inversion transaction, former shareholders or partners of the expatriated entity hold 80 percent or more (by vote or value) of the stock of the surrogate foreign corporation after the transaction, the surrogate foreign corporation is treated as a domestic corporation for U.S. tax purposes (Code Sec. 7874(b)).

**Real estate investment trusts.** To qualify as a real estate investment trust (REIT), an entity must meet certain income requirements. A REIT is restricted to earning certain types of generally passive income. Among other requirements, at least 75 percent of the gross income of a REIT in each tax year must consist of real estate-related income (Code Sec. 856). In addition, a REIT is required to distribute at least 90 percent of REIT income (other than net capital gain) annually (Code Sec. 857). Unlike a regular subchapter C corporation, a REIT is able to deduct the portion of its income that is distributed to its shareholders as a dividend or qualifying liquidating distribution each year. The distributed income of the REIT is not taxed at the entity level, but at the investor level.

## NEW LAW EXPLAINED

**Transition tax imposed on accumulated foreign earnings upon transition to participation exemption system.**—A transition tax is imposed on accumulated post-1986 foreign earnings determined as of a certain measurement date, without requiring an actual distribution, upon the transition to the new participation exemption

## NEW LAW EXPLAINED

system. The transition rule requires mandatory inclusion of such deferred foreign income as subpart F income by U.S. shareholders of deferred foreign income corporations (DFICs), including domestic pass-through owners of a domestic pass-through U.S. shareholder. The included amount is taxed at a reduced rate that depends on whether the deferred earnings are held in cash or other assets (Code Sec. 965, as amended by the Tax Cuts and Jobs Act (P.L. 115-97)).

> **Comment:** In transitioning to the new participation exemption (territorial) system of taxation, many U.S. corporations with undistributed accumulated foreign earnings will be eligible for the 100-percent participation exemption deduction for foreign-source dividends under new Code Sec. 245A (a participation dividends-received deduction (DRD)). To avoid a potential windfall for such corporations, and to ensure that all distributions from foreign corporations are treated in the same manner under the participation exemption system, a transition rule is provided under which accumulated foreign earnings are taxed as if they had been distributed under prior law, but at a reduced rate of tax. Generally, the new participation exemption system for taxation of foreign income replaces the prior-law system of taxing U.S. corporations on the foreign earnings of their foreign subsidiaries when the earnings are distributed. The exemption is provided in the form of a participation DRD, which is intended to encourage U.S. companies to repatriate their accumulated foreign earnings and invest them in the United States. See ¶705 for a discussion of the participation DRD.

> **Comment:** The Treasury and IRS have issued final regulations on the application of the Code Sec. 965 transition tax (T.D. 9846, February 4, 2019). The final regulations generally apply beginning the last tax year of the foreign corporation that begins before January 1, 2018, and with respect to a U.S. person, beginning the tax year in which or with which such tax year of the foreign corporation ends (Reg. § 1.965-9).

**Subpart F income inclusion of deferred foreign income.** The mechanism for the mandatory inclusion of accumulated foreign earnings is subpart F. For the last tax year beginning before January 1, 2018, the subpart F income of a DFIC (as otherwise determined for that tax year under Code Sec. 952) is increased by the greater of (i) the accumulated post-1986 deferred foreign income of the corporation determined as of November 2, 2017, or (ii) the accumulated post-1986 deferred foreign income of the corporation determined as of December 31, 2017 (Code Sec. 965(a), as amended by the 2017 Tax Cuts Act; Reg. § 1.965-1(b)). The increase in the foreign corporation's subpart F income is referred to as the "section 956(a) earnings amount " (Reg. § 1.965-1(f)(36)).

> **Comment:** Foreign corporations no longer in existence and for which there is no tax year beginning or ending in 2017 are not within the scope of this transition rule.

For this purpose, a DFIC with respect to any U.S. shareholder is any specified foreign corporation of the U.S. shareholder that has accumulated post-1986 deferred foreign income as of November 2, 2017, or December 31, 2017, greater than zero (Code Sec. 965(d)(1), as amended by the 2017 Tax Cuts Act; Reg. § 1.965-1(f)(17)).

## NEW LAW EXPLAINED

A specified foreign corporation is (1) a controlled foreign corporation (CFC), or (2) any foreign corporation in which a domestic corporation is a U.S. shareholder, other than a passive foreign investment company (PFIC) that is not a CFC. For purposes of the Code Sec. 951 subpart F inclusion rules and the Code Sec. 961 rules requiring adjustments to the basis of the CFC stock, a foreign corporation described in item (2), above, is treated as a CFC solely for purposes of taking into account the subpart F income of the corporation under the transition rule and determining the U.S. shareholder pro rata share of that income (Code Sec. 965(e), as amended by the 2017 Tax Cuts Act; Reg. § 1.965-1(f)(45)).

The regulations address the application of the constructive ownership rules providing for the downward attribution of stock from a partner to a partnership (Code Sec. 958(b)). Because the rules can make it difficult to determine if a foreign corporation is a specified foreign corporation, for purposes of making this determination, stock owned, directly or indirectly by or for a partner (tested partner), will not be considered owned by the partnership if the partner owns less than 10 percent of the interests in the partnership's capital and profits. The rules also apply to a beneficiary (tested beneficiary) if the value of the tested beneficiary is less than 10 percent of the value of the trust property.

> **Comment:** A non-CFC foreign corporation must have at least one U.S. shareholder that is a domestic corporation in order for the foreign corporation to be a specified foreign corporation. In addition, unlike the participation DRD that is available only to domestic corporations that are U.S. shareholders under subpart F, the transition rule applies to all U.S. shareholders of a specified foreign corporation. The subpart F definitions of a U.S. shareholder and CFC are expanded so that they are used for purposes of the Internal Revenue Code, and not just the subpart F provisions (Code Secs. 951(b) and 957(a), as amended by the 2017 Tax Cuts Act; see ¶705). The U.S. shareholder definition is further expanded so that a U.S. shareholder includes a U.S. person that owns at least 10 percent of the total combined voting power of all classes of stock entitled to vote or at least 10 percent of the total value of all classes of stock of the foreign corporation. The expanded definition of U.S. shareholder does not apply to the transition tax because the transition tax applies to the last tax year of a foreign corporation, beginning before January 1, 2018. A U.S. shareholder must own 10 percent or more of the voting stock of the foreign corporation (Code Sec. 951(b), as amended by the 2017 Tax Cuts Act; see ¶745).

> **Comment:** For purposes of taking into account its subpart F income under the transition rule, a noncontrolled 10/50 corporation is treated as a CFC (Conference Report on H.R. 1, Tax Cuts and Jobs Act (H. Rept. 115-466)).

The accumulated post-1986 deferred foreign income includes the post-1986 earning and profits that (i) are not attributable to income that is effectively connected with the conduct of a trade or business in the United States and subject to tax under Chapter 1 of the Code, or (ii) if distributed, in the case of a CFC, would be excluded from the gross income of a U.S. shareholder as previously taxed income under Code Sec. 959 (Code Sec. 965(d)(2), as amended by the 2017 Tax Cuts Act; Reg. § 1.965-1(f)(7)). Additionally, if a CFC has non-U.S. shareholders on an E&P measurement date, the

## NEW LAW EXPLAINED

accumulated post-1986 deferred foreign income on that date is reduced by amounts that would be PTI, if the shareholders were U.S. shareholders. The E&P of the specified foreign corporation as of a measurement date is described as PTI under Code Sec. 959(c)(2) only to the extent the income is accrued by the specified foreign corporation as of the E&P measurement date

Post-1986 earnings and profits include the E&P of the foreign corporation accumulated in tax years beginning after December 31, 1986, and determined (i) as of November 2, 2017, or December 31, 2017, whichever measurement date applies to the foreign corporation, and (ii) without decrease for dividends distributed during the last tax year beginning before January 1, 2018, other than dividends distributed to another specified foreign corporation. Post-1986 earnings and profits are computed under the rules of Code Secs. 964(a) and 986 for determining E&P of a CFC, but only taking into account periods when the foreign corporation was a specified foreign corporation (Code Sec. 965(d)(3), as amended by the 2017 Tax Cuts Act; Reg. § 1.965-1(f)(29)).

> **Comment:** Post-1986 earnings and profits that are subject to the transition tax do not include E&P that were accumulated by a foreign corporation prior to attaining its status as a specified foreign corporation. However, post-1986 earnings and profits are taken into account even if arising from periods during which the U.S. shareholder did not own stock of the foreign corporation.

An alternative method for determining post-1986 earnings and profits is provided in the regulations because it may be difficult to gather the data for a date that is not an the end of the month (i.e., November 2, 2017) (Reg. § 1.965-7(f)). If the alternative method is elected, the amount of the post-1986 earnings and profits (including a deficit) of a specified foreign corporation (other than a specified foreign corporation with a 52-53-week tax year) as of November 2, 2017, is the sum of: (1) the corporation's post-1986 earnings and profits as of October 31, 2017, and (2) the corporation's annualized E&P amount (i.e., the product of 2 and the daily earnings amount for the specified foreign corporation).

> **Compliance Note:** The election is made on behalf of the specified foreign corporation by a controlling domestic shareholder, no later than the due date, taking into account extensions, for the person's return for the tax year in which the person has a section 965(a) inclusion amount with respect to the specified foreign corporation or in which the person takes into account specified E&P deficit. Once made, the election is irrevocable.

**Reduction of amounts included in the U.S. shareholder's income.** Consistent with the general operation of subpart F, each U.S. shareholder of a DFIC must include in income its pro rata share of the foreign corporation's subpart F income attributable to its accumulated post-1986 deferred foreign income. If the taxpayer is a U.S. shareholder of at least one DFIC and at least one E&P deficit foreign corporation, the mandatory inclusion amount of the U.S. shareholder that otherwise would be taken into account as the U.S. shareholder's pro rata share of the subpart F income of each DFIC is reduced by the amount of the U.S. shareholder's aggregate foreign E&P deficit that is allocated to that DFIC (Code Sec. 965(b)(1), as amended by the 2017 Tax Cuts Act; Reg. § 1.965-1(b)(1), (f)(36), and (f)(38)). In other words, the mandatory

## NEW LAW EXPLAINED

inclusion amount under the transition rule is reduced by the portion of the aggregate foreign E&P deficit allocated to the U.S. shareholder by reason of the shareholder's interest in one or more E&P deficit foreign corporations.

> **Comment:** For purposes of the mandatory inclusion rule, the determination of the U.S. shareholder's pro rata share of any amount with respect to any specified foreign corporation is determined under the subpart F inclusion rules by treating that amount in the same manner as subpart F income, and by treating the specified foreign corporation as a CFC. The portion of the U.S. shareholder's mandatory inclusion amount that is equal to the deduction allowed under Code Sec. 965(c) (discussed further below) is treated as tax-exempt income for purposes of Code Sec. 705(a)(1)(B) (which requires an increase in a partner's basis in a partnership by the partner's distributive share of the partnership's tax-exempt income) and Code Sec. 1367(a)(1)(A) (which requires an increase in an S shareholder's basis in stock for tax-exempt income). However, that amount is not treated as tax-exempt income for purposes of determining whether an adjustment is made to an accumulated adjustment account under Code Sec. 1368(e)(1)(A) (Code Sec. 965(f), as amended by the 2017 Tax Cuts Act).

The regulations provide rules for determining the status of a specified foreign corporation as a DFIC or an E&P deficit foreign corporation (Reg. § 1.965-1(f)(22)). An E&P deficit foreign corporation is any specified foreign corporation with respect to which the taxpayer is a U.S. shareholder, if as of November 2, 2017 (i) the specified foreign corporation has a deficit in post-1986 earnings and profits, (ii) the corporation was a specified foreign corporation, and (iii) the taxpayer was a U.S. shareholder of the corporation.

The specified E&P deficit with respect to any E&P deficit foreign corporation is the amount of the deficit in its post-1986 earnings and profits, described in the previous sentence (Code Sec. 965(b)(3)(B), as amended by the 2017 Tax Cuts Act). Thus, the deficits of a foreign subsidiary that accumulated prior to its acquisition by the U.S. shareholder may be taken into account in determining the aggregate foreign E&P deficit of the U.S. shareholder. Deficits related to post-1986 earnings and profits, including hovering deficits defined in Reg. § 1.367(b)-7(d)(2), of a specified foreign corporation are taken into account in determining post-1986 earnings and profits, including deficits (Reg. § 1.965-1(f)(29)(iii)).

> **Comment:** For example, if a foreign corporation organized after December 31, 1986, has $100 of accumulated E&P as of November 2, 2017, and December 31, 2017 (determined without reduction for dividends distributed during the tax year and after any increase for qualified deficits), which consist of $120 general limitation E&P and a $20 passive limitation deficit, the foreign corporation's post-1986 earnings and profits would be $100, even if the $20 passive limitation deficit was a hovering deficit. Foreign income taxes related to the hovering deficit, however, would not generally be deemed paid by the U.S. shareholder recognizing an incremental income inclusion (Conference Report on H.R. 1, Tax Cuts and Jobs Act (H. Rept. 115-466)).

**¶710**

## NEW LAW EXPLAINED

The U.S. shareholder allocates the aggregate foreign E&P deficit among the deferred foreign income corporations in which the shareholder is a U.S. shareholder. The aggregate foreign E&P deficit is allocable to a specified foreign corporation in the same ratio as (i) the U.S. shareholder's pro rata share of post-1986 deferred income in that corporation bears to (ii) the aggregate of the U.S. shareholder's pro rata share of accumulated post-1986 deferred foreign income from all deferred income companies of the shareholder (Code Sec. 965(b)(2), as amended by the 2017 Tax Cuts Act; Reg. §1.965-1(f)(11), (33), and (36)).

The aggregate foreign E&P deficit is the lesser of (i) the aggregate of the U.S. shareholder's pro rata shares of the specified E&P deficits of the E&P deficit foreign corporations of the shareholder, or (ii) the aggregate of the U.S. shareholder's pro rata share of the accumulated post-1986 deferred foreign income of all deferred foreign income corporations (Code Sec. 965(b)(3)(A)(i), as added by the 2017 Tax Cuts Act; Reg. §1.965-1(f)(9), (22), (33), and (36)). If the amount described in (ii), above, is less than the amount described in (i), above, then the shareholder must designate (in the form and manner determined by the Secretary of the Treasury):

- the amount of the specified E&P deficit that is to be taken into account for each E&P deficit corporation with respect to the taxpayer; and

- in the case of an E&P deficit corporation that has a qualified deficit (as defined in Code Sec. 952), the portion (if any) of the deficit taken into account under item (1), above, that is attributable to a qualified deficit, including the qualified activities to which such portion is attributable (Code Sec. 965(b)(3)(A)(ii), as added by the 2017 Tax Cuts Act).

*Adjustments to E&P.* To prevent double taxation, E&P of a foreign corporation that are attributable to subpart F inclusions are excluded from gross income when actually distributed (Code Sec. 959). The amounts and categories of current and accumulated E&P must be determined in order to apply the rules. Reg. §1.965-2 provides rules relating to adjustments to E&P and basis to account for application of Code Sec. 965 transition tax, and the treatment of distributions under Code Sec. 959. Rules also are provided for gain recognition under Code Sec. 961(b)(2) upon the distribution of previously taxed income.

A five-step ordering rule apply to determine the interaction between the previously taxed income rules of Code Secs. 965 and 959 for the last tax year of the specified foreign corporation that begins before January 1, 2018, and the tax year of the U.S. shareholder of the specified foreign corporation in which or with which such year ends:

(1) Subpart F income of a specified foreign corporation and amounts required to be included under Code Sec. 1248 are determined;

(2) the treatment of a distribution made by the specified foreign corporation to another specified foreign corporation made before January 1, 2018 is determined under Code Sec. 959;

(3) the specified foreign corporation's inclusion amount under Code Sec. 965(a) is determined;

## NEW LAW EXPLAINED

(4) the treatment of distributions in Step (2) that are disregarded under Reg. § 1.965-4 are redetermined and the treatment of all distributions from the specified foreign corporation other than those described in Step (2) is determined under Code Sec. 959; and

(5) an amount is determined under Code Sec. 956 with respect to the specified foreign corporation and the Code Sec. 958(a) U.S. shareholder (Reg. § 1.965-2(b)).

After Reg. § 1.965-2(b) adjustments to E&P have been made, deemed paid taxes under Code Secs. 902 and 960 are determined in accordance with the ordering rule provided under Reg. § 1.906-1(i)(2) (Reg. § 1.965-2(b)). However, for any pre-2018 distributions between specified foreign corporations that are not disregarded under Reg. § 1.965-4, Code Sec. 902 is applied before Code Sec. 960 with respect to a distribution or inclusion described in Reg. § 1.965-2(b)(3) through Reg. § 1.965-2(b)(5) (Reg. § 1.965-2(b)).

*Treatment of earnings and profits in future years.* For purposes of excluding previously taxed earnings from the U.S. shareholder's income in any tax year beginning with the last tax year beginning before January 1, 2018, an amount equal to the reduction for the U.S. shareholder's aggregate foreign E&P deficit allocated to the deferred foreign income corporation is treated as an amount included in the U.S. shareholder's gross income under the subpart F inclusion rules (Code Sec. 965(b)(4)(B), as amended by the 2017 Tax Cuts Act). Thus, the reduced earnings and profits are treated as previously taxed income when distributed.

In addition, the U.S. shareholder's pro rata share of the earnings and profits of any specified E&P deficit foreign corporation is increased by the amount of the corporation's specified E&P deficit taken into account in computing the mandatory inclusion. For purposes of determining subpart F income, this increase is attributable to the same activity to which the deficit taken into account was attributable (Code Sec. 965(b)(4)(A), as amended by the 2017 Tax Cuts Act).

> **Caution:** According to the Joint Committee on Taxation's report on the 2017 Tax Cuts Act (commonly referred to as the Bluebook), a technical correction may be necessary to reflect that while the earnings and profits of the E&P deficit foreign corporation that are taken into account by a U.S. shareholder are increased at the foreign corporation level by the amount of the specified E&P deficit of such corporation that was used, it is not intended that such increase apply for purposes of determining post-1986 undistributed earnings under Code Sec. 902 (General Explanation of Public Law 115-97 (JCS-1-18)).

*Adjustments to basis.* Under Code Sec. 961, a U.S. shareholder's basis in the stock of a DFIC (or basis on applicable property) is increased by the U.S. shareholder's Code Sec. 965 inclusion amount. If an individual U.S. shareholder elects to be taxed as a corporation under Code Sec. 962, the increase in the basis of the stock or applicable property cannot exceed an amount equal to the amount of tax paid under chapter 1 of the Code with respect to the U.S. shareholder's inclusion amount with respect to the DFIC, taking into account any election to pay the tax in installments (Reg. § 1.965-2(e)).

In general, there is no adjustment to the basis of stock or property under Code Sec. 961 to take into account the reduction to a U.S. shareholder's pro rata share of the

## NEW LAW EXPLAINED

section 965(a) earnings amount of the DFIC under the Code Sec. 965(b) reduction rules. The earnings of a DFIC are treated under Code Sec. 965(b)(4)(A) as previously taxed E&P (section 965(b) previously taxed E&P) if a deficit is used to offset those earnings for purposes of a taxpayer's inclusion (Reg. § 1.965-1(f)(36) and (40)).

A taxpayer may, however, elect, to make relevant basis adjustments. The basis adjustments include (1) an increase in the section 958(a) U.S. shareholder's basis in the section 958(a) stock of a DFIC or applicable property with respect to the DFIC by an amount equal to the section 965(b) previously taxed E&P of the DFIC with respect to the section 958(a) U.S. shareholder, and (2) a reduction in the section 958(a) U.S. shareholder's basis in the section 958(a) stock of an E&P deficit corporation or applicable property with respect to an E&P deficit foreign corporation by an amount equal to the portion of the section 958(a) U.S. shareholder's pro rata share of the specified E&P deficit of the E&P deficit foreign corporation taken into account under the reduction rules (Reg. §§ 1.965-1(f)(33), (40), 1.965-2(f)(2)(ii)(A)(1) and (B)(1)). Gain is recognized to the extent the reduction exceeds the taxpayer's basis in the stock or property. An individual taxpayer electing to be taxed as a corporation under Code Sec. 962 cannot make the basis adjustments (Reg. § 1.965-2(h)).

> **Compliance Note:** The basis adjustment election must be made with a U.S. shareholder's first return that includes a Code Sec. 965(a). Consistent with Notice 2018-78, an extended time period is provided for taxpayers under the transition rule to make the election. Elections made before the final Regulations are issued are revocable for up to 90-days after the Final Regulations publication date (Reg. § 1.965-2(f)(2)(iii)(B)(1)).

In lieu of the rules above, a taxpayer may limit the downward adjustments to stock or applicable property with respect to an E&P deficit foreign corporation to the available basis, so that gain is not recognized (referred to as the "to-the-extent rule"). If the to-the-extent rule is applied, the corresponding upward basis adjustment is limited. The taxpayer can with certain limitations designate the stock or applicable property, with respect to the DFIC, to which the upward adjustments are made (Reg. § 1.965-2(f)(2)(ii)(B)(2) and (A)(2)).

An individual taxpayer electing to be taxed as a corporation under Code Sec. 962 cannot make the basis adjustments (Reg. § 1.965-1(f)(2)(ii)(C)).

*Intragroup netting among U.S. shareholders in an affiliated group.* The transition rule permits intragroup netting among U.S. shareholders in an affiliated group in which there is at least one U.S. shareholder with a net E&P surplus (i.e., the shareholder's mandatory inclusion amount is greater than zero) and another with a net E&P deficit (i.e., the aggregate foreign E&P deficit of the shareholder exceeds the shareholder's mandatory inclusion amount). The net E&P surplus shareholder may reduce its net surplus by the shareholder's applicable share of the group's aggregate unused E&P deficit, based on the group ownership percentage of the members (Code Sec. 965(b)(5), as amended by the 2017 Tax Cuts Act).

> **Comment:** As a result, deferred earnings of a U.S. shareholder are reduced by the shareholder's share of deficits as of November 2, 2017, from a specified foreign corporation that is not a deferred foreign income corporation, including the pro rata share of deficits of another U.S. shareholder in a different U.S. ownership chain within the same U.S. affiliated group.

## NEW LAW EXPLAINED

> **Comment:** A consolidated group is treated as a single-shareholder and for purposes of calculating the Code Sec. 965(c) deduction, the consolidated group aggregate foreign cash position is calculated as though all Section 958(a) U.S. shareholders of an specified foreign corporation are a single U.S. shareholder (Reg. § 1.965-8).

The applicable share with respect to any E&P net surplus shareholder in the group is the amount that bears the same proportion to the group's aggregate unused E&P deficit as (i) the product of the shareholder's group ownership percentage, multiplied by the mandatory inclusion amount that would otherwise be taken into account by the shareholder, bears to (ii) the aggregate amount in item (i) determined with respect to all E&P net surplus shareholders in the group (Code Sec. 965(b)(5)(E), as amended by the 2017 Tax Cuts Act).

The group's aggregate unused E&P deficit is the lesser of the sum of the net E&P deficit of each E&P net deficit shareholder in the group (or a percentage of that amount based on the group ownership percentage of each shareholder), or the amount determined in item (ii), above (Code Sec. 965(b)(5)(D), as amended by the 2017 Tax Cuts Act).

The group ownership percentage with respect to a U.S. shareholder in the group is the percentage of the value of the U.S. shareholder stock that is held by other includible corporations in the group. However, the group ownership percentage of the common parent of the affiliated group is 100 percent (Code Sec. 965(b)(5)(F), as amended by the 2017 Tax Cuts Act).

> **Example:** A U.S. corporation has two domestic subsidiaries, X and Y, each of which it owns 100 percent and 80 percent, respectively. If X has a $1,000 net E&P surplus, and Y has $1,000 net E&P deficit, X is an E&P net surplus shareholder, and Y is an E&P net deficit shareholder. The net E&P surplus of X is reduced by the net E&P deficit of Y to the extent of the group's ownership percentage in Y, which is 80 percent. The remaining net E&P deficit of Y is unused. If the U.S. shareholder Z is also a wholly owned subsidiary of the same U.S. parent as X and Y, the group ownership percentage of Y is unchanged, and the surpluses of X and Z are reduced ratably by 800 of the net E&P deficit of Y.

> **Comment:** The Conference Committee Report states that it expects that the Secretary of the Treasury will exercise his authority under the consolidated return provisions to appropriately limit the netting across chains of ownership within a group of related parties in the application of the mandatory inclusion rules. However, nothing in these rules is intended to be interpreted as limiting the Secretary's authority to use such regulatory authority to prescribe regulations on proper application of the mandatory inclusion rules on a consolidated basis for affiliated groups filing a consolidated return (Conference Report on H.R. 1, Tax Cuts and Jobs Act (H. Rept. 115-466)).

**Deduction from mandatory inclusion.** A U.S. shareholder of a specified foreign corporation is allowed a deduction of a portion of the increased subpart F income

¶710

## NEW LAW EXPLAINED

attributable to the mandatory inclusion of deferred foreign income. The amount of the deduction is the sum of (i) the 15.5-percent rate equivalent percentage of the inclusion amount that is the shareholder's aggregate foreign cash position, and (ii) the eight percent rate equivalent percentage of the portion of the inclusion amount that exceeds the shareholder's aggregate foreign cash position (Code Sec. 965(c)(1), as added by the 2017 Tax Cuts Act; Reg. § 1.965-1(f)(1) through (4), (41), and (42)).

> **Comment:** The calculation is based on the highest rate of tax applicable to corporations in the tax year of inclusion, even if the U.S. shareholder is an individual.

The eight-percent rate equivalent percentage (or the 15.5-percent rate equivalent percentage) with respect to any U.S. shareholder for any tax year is the percentage that would result in the amount to which that percentage applies being subject to an eight-percent rate of tax (or a 15.5-percent rate of tax, respectively) determined by only taking into account a deduction equal to the percentage of that amount and the highest rate of tax under Code Sec. 11 for the tax year. In the case of any tax year of a U.S. shareholder to which Code Sec. 15 applies, the highest rate of tax under Code Sec. 11 before the effective date of the change in rates and the highest rate of tax under that section after the effective date of that change is each taken into account under this rule in the same proportions as the portion of the year that is before and after that effective date, respectively (Code Sec. 965(c)(2), as added by the 2017 Tax Cuts Act).

> **Comment:** The use of rate equivalent percentages is intended to ensure that the rates of tax imposed on the deferred foreign income is similar for all U.S. shareholders, regardless of the year of the mandatory inclusion. By stating the permitted deduction in the form of a tax rate equivalent percentage, the transition rule ensures that the accumulated post-1986 deferred foreign income is subject to either an eight-percent or 15.5-percent rate of tax, depending on the underlying assets as of the measurement date, without regard to the corporate tax rate that may be in effect at the time of the inclusion. For example, fiscal-year corporate taxpayers may report the increased subpart F income in a tax year for which a reduced corporate tax rate would otherwise apply (on a prorated basis under Code Sec. 15), but the allowable deduction would be reduced so that the rate of U.S. tax on the income inclusion would be eight or 15.5 percent.

*Aggregate foreign cash position.* With respect to any U.S. shareholder, the aggregate foreign cash position is the greater of:

(1) the aggregate of the U.S. shareholder's pro rata share of the cash position of each specified foreign corporation of the U.S. shareholder determined as of the close of the last tax year of the specified foreign corporation that begins before January 1, 2018; or

(2) one half of the sum of:

    (a) the aggregate described in item (1), above, determined as of the close of the last tax year of each specified foreign corporation that ends before November 2, 2017, plus

## NEW LAW EXPLAINED

    (b)  the aggregate described in item (1), above, determined as of the close of the tax year of each specified foreign corporation that precedes the tax year referred to in item (a), above (Code Sec. 965(c)(3)(A), as amended by the 2017 Tax Cuts Act).

**Comment:** In other words, the aggregate foreign cash position is the greater of the aggregate cash position as of the last day of the last tax year beginning before January 1, 2018, and the average aggregate cash position as of the last day of each of the last two years ending before the date of introduction (November 2, 2017).

The cash position of any specified foreign corporation is the sum of:

- cash held by the foreign corporation;
- the net accounts receivable of the foreign corporation (the excess (if any) of the corporation's accounts receivable over its accounts payable, determined under Code Sec. 461), plus
- the fair market value of the following assets held by the corporation:
  — actively traded personal property for which there is an established financial market,
  — commercial paper, certificates of deposit, the securities of the Federal government and of any State or foreign government,
  — any foreign currency,
  — any obligation with a term of less than one year, and
  — any asset that the Secretary identifies as being economically equivalent to the assets described above (Code Sec. 965(c)(3)(B) and (C), as amended by the 2017 Tax Cuts Act; Reg. § 1.965-1(f)(13) and (16)).

**Comment:** A cash equivalent asset includes personal property that is the type to be actively traded on an established financial market, not including specified commodities (Reg. § 1.965-1(f)(13)). A specified commodity means a commodity held by an specified foreign corporation that in the hand of the specified foreign corporation is property described in Code Sec. 1221(a)(1) and Code Sec. 1221(a)(8). For dealers and traders in commodities the exception does not apply (Reg. § 1.965-1(f)(13)(ii)). Additionally, forward contracts and short positions with respect to specified commodities are excluded from the definition of derivative financial instrument, and excluded from the cash position of an specified foreign corporation (Reg. § 1.965-1(f)(18)(iii) and (v)).

To avoid double counting, cash assets described in receivables, actively traded personal property and cash holdings are not taken into account in determining the aggregate foreign cash position to the extent that the U.S. shareholder demonstrates to the satisfaction of the Secretary that the amount is taken into account by the shareholder with respect to another specified foreign corporation (Code Sec. 965(c)(3)(D), as added by the 2017 Tax Cuts Act). Thus, cash holdings of a specified foreign corporation in the form of publicly traded stock may be excluded to the extent that a U.S. shareholder can demonstrate that the value of the stock was taken into account as cash or cash equivalent by another specified foreign corporation of the U.S. shareholder.

## NEW LAW EXPLAINED

**Compliance Tip:** To demonstrate double-counting of cash amounts to the extent that such amounts have been taken into account in determining the Code Sec. 958 U.S. shareholder's pro rata share of the cash position of another specified foreign corporation on the same cash measurement date, a shareholder must attach a statement to its timely filed return (taking into account extensions, if any) for the Code Sec. 958(a) U.S. shareholder inclusion year, or, if the Code Sec. 958(a) U.S. shareholder has multiple Code Sec. 958(a) U.S. shareholder inclusion years, the later of such years. The statement must contain the following information with respect to each specified foreign corporation for which the cash position is reduced (Reg. § 1.965-3(b)(2)):

- a description of the asset that would be taken into account with respect to both specified foreign corporations;

- a statement of the amount by which its pro rata share of the cash position of one specified foreign corporation is reduced;

- a detailed explanation of why there would otherwise be double-counting, including the computation of the amount taken into account with respect to the other specified foreign corporation; and

- an explanation of why Reg. § 1.965-3(b)(1) does not apply to disregard such amount.

Relief is not available under Reg. § 301.9100-2 or Reg. § 301.9100-3 to allow late filing of the statement (Reg. § 1.965-3(b)(2)).

*Cash positions of certain noncorporate entities.* A noncorporate entity is treated as a specified foreign corporation of a U.S. shareholder for purposes of determining the shareholder's aggregate foreign cash position if (i) any interest in the entity is held by a specified foreign corporation of the U.S. shareholder (determined after application of this rule), and (ii) the entity would be a specified foreign corporation of the shareholder if the entity were a foreign corporation (Code Sec. 965(c)(3)(E), as added by the 2017 Tax Cuts Act; Reg. § § 1.965-1(f)(33) and 1.965-3(b)(3)).

**Comment:** As stated in the Conference Committee Report, the cash position of a U.S. shareholder does not generally include the cash attributable to a direct ownership interest in a partnership, but cash positions of certain noncorporate foreign entities owned by a specified foreign corporation are taken into account if such entities would be specified foreign corporations if the entity were a foreign corporation. For example, if a U.S. shareholder owns a five-percent interest in a partnership, the balance of which is held by specified foreign corporations of the U.S. shareholder, the partnership is treated as a specified foreign corporation with respect to the U.S. shareholder, and the cash or cash equivalents held by the partnership are includible in the aggregate cash position of the U.S. shareholder on a look-through basis (Conference Report on H.R. 1, Tax Cuts and Jobs Act (H. Rept. 115-466)).

**Caution:** A technical correction may be required for situations where an individual U.S. shareholder of a DFIC does not make an election under Code Sec. 962 (i.e., does not elect application of corporate tax rates for the year of inclusion),

## NEW LAW EXPLAINED

that the partial participation exemption deduction may still be claimed for computing adjusted gross income, without regard to applicable limitations on itemized deductions, to reflect the intention that the Code Sec. 965(c) deduction is not treated as an itemized deduction for any purpose. (General Explanation of Public Law 115-97 (JCS-1-18)).

*Anti-abuse rule.* The Secretary is authorized to disregard transactions that are determined to have the principal purpose of reducing the aggregate foreign cash position (Code Sec. 965(c)(2)(F), as added by the 2017 Tax Cuts Act).

**Disallowance of foreign tax credit and deduction for taxes.** No foreign tax credit or deduction is allowed for a portion (referred to as an applicable percentage) of any foreign income taxes paid or accrued (or deemed paid or accrued) with respect to any mandatory inclusion amount for which a deduction is allowed under the above rules (Code Sec. 965(g)(1) and (3), as added by the 2017 Tax Cuts Act; Reg. § 1.965-5). As a result of this foreign tax credit disallowance rule, the foreign tax credit is limited to the taxable portion of the mandatory inclusion amount. Other foreign tax credits used by a taxpayer against tax liability resulting from the deemed inclusion apply in full.

The disallowed portion of the foreign tax credit is 55.7 percent of foreign taxes paid attributable to the portion of the inclusion amount attributable to the U.S. shareholder's aggregate foreign cash position, plus 77.1 percent of foreign taxes paid attributable to the remaining portion of the mandatory inclusion amount (Code Sec. 965(g)(2), as added by the 2017 Tax Cuts Act; Reg. §§ 1.965-1(f)(10), (33), (34), and 1.965-5(d)). As a result of this foreign tax credit disallowance rule, the foreign tax credit is limited to the taxable portion of the mandatory inclusion amount.

> **Caution:** A technical correction may be required to reflect that it is intended that no deduction or credit is allowed for taxes associated with earnings and profits that, by reason of Code Sec. 965(b), are not included in income (General Explanation of Public Law 115-97 (JCS-1-18)).

A special rule coordinates the disallowance of foreign tax credits described above with the Code Sec. 78 requirement that a domestic corporate shareholder is deemed to receive a dividend in an amount equal to foreign taxes it is deemed to have paid and for which it claimed a credit. Under the coordination rule, the foreign taxes treated as paid or accrued by a domestic corporation as a result of the mandatory inclusion are limited to those taxes in proportion to the taxable portion of the mandatory inclusion. The gross-up amount equals the total foreign income taxes multiplied by a fraction, the numerator of which is the taxable portion of the increased subpart F income inclusion under the transition rule and the denominator of which is the total increase in subpart F income under the transition rule (Code Sec. 965(g)(4), as added by the 2017 Tax Cuts Act; Reg. § 1.965-5(c)(3)).

**Installment payments.** A U.S. shareholder of a deferred foreign income corporation may elect to pay the net tax liability resulting from the mandatory inclusion of deferred foreign income in eight installments. If installment payment is elected, the payments for each of the first five years equals eight percent of the net tax liability. The amount of the sixth installment is 15 percent of the net tax liability, increasing to 20 percent for the seventh installment and 25 percent for the eighth installment (Code

¶710

## NEW LAW EXPLAINED

Sec. 965(h)(1), as added by the 2017 Tax Cuts Act; Reg. § 1.965-7(b)). The election may be revoked only by paying the full amount of the unpaid net tax liability.

The first installment must be paid on the due date (determined without regard to extensions) of the tax return for the last tax year that begins before January 1, 2018 (the tax year of the mandatory inclusion). Succeeding installments must be paid annually no later than the due dates (without extensions) for the income tax return of each succeeding tax year (Code Sec. 965(h)(2), as added by the 2017 Tax Cuts Act). Thus, a U.S. shareholder can elect to pay the transition tax arising from the mandatory inclusion over a period of eight years.

*Making the election.* An election to pay the net tax liability from the mandatory inclusion in installments must be made by the due date of the tax return for the last tax year that begins before January 1, 2018 (the tax year in which the pre-effective-date undistributed earnings are included in income under the transition rule). The Treasury Secretary has authority to prescribe the manner of making the election (Code Sec. 965(h)(5), as added by the 2017 Tax Cuts Act). The regulations provide an extended period to make the election. The election must be made by the return due date, taking into account extensions, if any, or any additional time that would have been granted if the person had made an extension request. Relief is not available under Reg. § 301.9100-2 or Reg. § 301.9100-3 to file a late election. To make the election, a statement with the required information, signed under penalties of perjury must be attached to the return (Reg. § 1.965-7(b)(2)).

*Net tax liability.* The net tax liability that may be paid in installments is the excess of (i) the U.S. shareholder's net income tax for the tax year in which an amount is included in income under the mandatory inclusion rules, over (ii) the taxpayer's net income tax for that year determined without regard to the mandatory inclusion and any income or deduction properly attributable to a dividend received by the U.S. shareholder from any deferred foreign income corporation. The net income tax is the regular tax liability reduced by the general business credit (Code Sec. 965(h)(6), as added by the 2017 Tax Cuts Act).

> **Caution:** A technical correction may be required to reflect the intent that regular tax liability means regular tax as defined in Code Sec. 26, which includes neither the minimum tax under Code Sec. 59 nor the base erosion and anti-abuse tax of Code Sec. 59A. As a result, neither the alternative minimum tax (if applicable in computing the tax liability without regard to the Code Sec. 965 inclusions) nor the base erosion and anti-abuse tax is considered in determining the portion of the tax liability that is eligible to be paid over eight installments.(General Explanation of Public Law 115-97 (JCS-1-18)).

The regulations introduce the term "total net tax liability". Under the regulations, the term "section 965(h) net tax liability" means, with respect to person who has made the "section 965(h) election" the total net tax liability, reduced by the aggregate of the person's net section 965(i) tax liabilities (Reg. § 1.965-7(g)(4)). Total net tax liability is the excess of:

- the person's net income tax (i.e., regular tax liability, reduced by credits), for the tax year of the Code Sec. 965(a) inclusion, over

## NEW LAW EXPLAINED

- the person's net income tax for the tax year, determined without regard to Code Sec. 965 and any income, deduction or credit attributable to a dividend received (directly or through a chain of ownership described in Code Sec. 958(a)) by the person (or, in the case of a domestic pass-through owner, by the person's domestic pass-through entity) from, or an inclusion under Code Sec. 951(a)(1)(B) and Code Sec. 956 with respect to, a deferred foreign income corporation and paid during, or included with respect to, the deferred foreign income corporation's inclusion year (Reg. § 1.965-7(g)(10)).

  **Compliance Note:** An individual or an entity taxed as an individual who has a section 965(h) net tax liability under Reg. § 1.965-7(g)(4) for any tax year or a liability remaining unpaid at any time during a tax year must file Form 965-A. The form is intended to be a cumulative report of a taxpayer's net 965 tax liabilities through payment in full. Any corporate taxpayer who has a net 965 tax liability for any tax year or has any net 965 tax liability remaining unpaid at any time during a tax year, or an electing REIT with any section 965 amount taken into account in accordance with Code Sec. 965(m) or not taken into account at any time during a tax year must file Form 965-B. The form is intended to be a cumulative report of a taxpayer's net 965 tax liabilities through payment in full, and for an electing REIT, a report of section 965 amounts taken into account over time until such amounts are fully taken into account.

*Acceleration rule.* The unpaid remaining installment payments will become due upon the date of the following acceleration events (Code Sec. 965(h)(3), as added by the 2017 Tax Cuts Act):

- there is an addition to tax for failure to pay timely any required installment of the transition tax;

- there is a liquidation or sale of substantially all of the U.S. shareholder's assets (including in a bankruptcy case);

- the U.S. shareholder ceases business; or

- another similar circumstance arises, the unpaid portion of all remaining installments is due on the date of the event (or, in a bankruptcy proceeding or similar case, the day before the petition is filed).

The regulations provide the following additional acceleration events, including: any exchange or other disposition of substantially all of the assets of the taxpayer; a person no longer being a U.S. person; a person becoming a member of a consolidated group; or a consolidated group ceasing to exist or no longer filing a consolidated return (Reg. § 1.965-7(b)(iii)).

This acceleration rule does not apply to the sale of substantially all the assets of the U.S. shareholder to a buyer if the buyer enters into a transfer agreement with the Secretary under which the buyer is liable for the remaining installments due in the same manner as if the buyer were the U.S. shareholder. The regulations provide details for entering into the transfer agreement (Reg. § 1.965-7(b)(3)(iii)(B)). The transfer agreement must be filed within 30 days of the date the acceleration event occurs.

**¶710**

# NEW LAW EXPLAINED

> **Compliance Note:** Under a transition rule, if an acceleration event occurs on or before December 31, 2018, the transfer agreement must be filed by January 31, 2019, to be considered timely filed. Relief is not available under Reg. § 301.9100-2 and Reg. § 301.9100-3, to file a transfer agreement late.

*Proration of deficiency to installments.* If an election is made to pay the net tax liability from the mandatory inclusion in installments and a deficiency is later determined with respect to that net tax liability, the additional tax due is prorated among the installment payments. The portions of the deficiency prorated to an installment that was due before the deficiency was assessed must be paid upon notice and demand. The portion prorated to any remaining installment is payable with the timely payment of that installment payment. However, these rules do not apply if the deficiency is attributable to negligence, intentional disregard of rules or regulations, or fraud with intent to evade tax (Code Sec. 965(h)(4), as added by the 2017 Tax Cuts Act; Reg. § 1.965-7(b)(1)(ii)). If the deficiency is attributable to negligence, intentional disregard of rules or regulations, or fraud with intent to evade tax, the entire deficiency is payable upon notice and demand.

> **Comment:** The timely payment of an installment does not incur interest. If a deficiency is determined that is attributable to an understatement of the net tax liability due under the transition rule, the deficiency is payable with underpayment interest for the period beginning on the date on which the net tax liability would have been due, without regard to an election to pay in installments, and ending with the payment of the deficiency. Furthermore, any amount of deficiency prorated to a remaining installment also bears interest on the deficiency, but not on the original installment amount (Conference Report on H.R. 1, Tax Cuts and Jobs Act (H. Rept. 115-466)).

**Special rules for S corporations.** A special rule permits deferral of the transition net tax liability for shareholders of a U.S. shareholder that is an S corporation. Under this rule, any shareholder of the S corporation may elect to defer the payment of his portion of the net tax liability resulting from the mandatory inclusion until the shareholder's tax year in which a triggering event occurs. The deferred transition tax is assessed as an addition to tax on the shareholder's return for the tax year of the triggering event (Code Sec. 965(i)(1), as added by the 2017 Tax Cuts Act; Reg. § 1.965-7(c) and (g)(6)).

Any shareholder (including a person listed in Reg. § 1.1362-6(b)(2), with respect to a trust or estate, other than a domestic pass-through entity) of an S corporation that is a U.S. shareholder of a DFIC can make the election, regardless of whether it owns Code Sec. 958(a) stock of the DFIC. If, however, the S corporation is not a U.S. shareholder with respect to the DFIC, the S corporation shareholders may not make the election for their shares of the Code Sec. 965(a) inclusion and the Code Sec. 965(c) deduction ( Reg. § 1.965-7(c)(1)).

For purposes of this rule, the shareholder's net tax liability is the net tax liability that would be determined under the transition rule if the only subpart F income taken into account by the shareholder under the mandatory inclusion were allocations from the S corporation (Code Sec. 965(i)(3), as added by the 2017 Tax Cuts Act). The

## NEW LAW EXPLAINED

regulations provide that section 965(i) net tax liability is determined, with respect to an S corporation and an S corporation shareholder, as the excess of:

- the person's net income tax (i.e., regular tax liability, reduced by credits), for the tax year of the Code Sec. 965(a) inclusion, determined as if the only Code Sec. 965(a) inclusions included in income by the person are domestic pass-through entity shares of Code Sec. 965(a) inclusions by the S corporation with respect to DFICs of which the S corporation is a U.S. shareholder, over

- the person's net income tax for the tax year, determined without regard to Code Sec. 965(a) and any income, deduction or credit attributable to a dividend received (directly or through a chain of ownership described in Code Sec. 958(a)) by the person (or, in the case of a domestic pass-through owner, by the person's domestic pass-through entity) from, or an inclusion under Code Sec. 951(a)(1)(B) and Code Sec. 956 with respect to, a deferred foreign income corporation and paid during, or included with respect to, the deferred foreign income corporation's inclusion year (Reg. § 1.965-7(g)(6)).

The S corporation shareholder must make the election to defer the transition tax not later than the due date (taking into account extensions) for the shareholder's return for each tax year that includes the last day of the S corporation's tax year in which the S corporation has a Code Sec. 965(a) inclusion to which the shareholder's section 965(i) net tax liability is attributable. The election is made in the manner provided by the Secretary of the Treasury. The regulations require that a statement with the required information be signed under penalties of perjury and attached to the return (Code Sec. 965(i)(8), as added by the 2017 Tax Cuts Act; Reg. § 1.965-7(c)(2)). No relief will be granted under Reg. § 301.9100-2 or Reg. § 301.9100-3 for late elections.

*Triggering events.* The following three types of events may trigger an end to deferral of the net tax liability of an S corporation shareholder:

- the corporation ceases to be an S corporation (determined as of the first day of the first tax year that the corporation is not an S corporation);

- a liquidation, a sale of substantially all of the S corporation's assets (including in a bankruptcy or similar case), a termination of the S corporation, a cessation of its business, or a similar event; and

- a transfer of shares of stock in the S corporation by the electing taxpayer, whether by sale, death or otherwise, unless the transferee of the stock agrees with the Secretary to be liable for net tax liability in the same manner as the transferor (Code Sec. 965(i)(2), as added by the 2017 Tax Cuts Act; Reg. § 1.965-7(c)(3)).

Partial transfers of the S corporation stock trigger the end of deferral only with respect to the portion of tax properly allocable to the portion of stock sold (Code Sec. 965(i)(2)(B), as added by the 2017 Tax Cuts Act).

*Election to pay deferred liability in installments.* After a triggering event occurs, an S corporation shareholder that has elected to defer the net tax liability may elect to pay the net tax liability in eight installments, subject to rules similar to those generally applicable absent deferral. However, if the triggering event is a liquidation, sale of substantially all corporate assets, termination of the S corporation or end of its

## NEW LAW EXPLAINED

business, or similar event, the installment payment election can be made only with the consent of the Secretary. The installment election must be made by the due date (taking into account extensions) of the return for the tax year in which the triggering event occurs, and the first installment payment is required by that due date, determined without regard to extensions of time to file. No relief will be granted under Reg. § 301.9100-2 or Reg. § 301.9100-3 for late elections (Code Sec. 965(i)(4), as added by the 2017 Tax Cuts Act; Reg. § 1.965-7(c)(3)(v)).

*Joint and several liability; extension of limitation on collection.* If a shareholder of an S corporation has elected deferral and a triggering event occurs, the S corporation and the electing shareholder are jointly and severally liable for any net tax liability and related interest or penalties (Code Sec. 965(i)(5), as added by the 2017 Tax Cuts Act). The period within which the IRS may collect a deferred liability does not begin before the date of the triggering event (Code Sec. 965(i)(6), as added by the 2017 Tax Cuts Act).

*Annual reporting of net tax liability.* If an election to defer payment of the net tax liability is in effect for an S corporation shareholder, the shareholder must report the amount of the deferred net tax liability on its return for the tax year for which the election is made and on each subsequent tax year return until the deferred amount has been fully assessed on the returns. Failure to include that information with each income tax return during the period that the election is in effect will result in a penalty equal to five-percent of the amount that should have been reported. For this purpose, a deferred net tax liability is the amount of the net tax liability the payment of which has been deferred under these rules and which has not been assessed on a return of tax for any prior tax year (Code Sec. 965(i)(7), as added by the 2017 Tax Cuts Act; Reg. § 1.965-7(c)(6)).

*Reporting by S corporations.* An S corporation that is a U.S. shareholder of a specified foreign corporation is required to report on its income tax return the amount includible in gross income under the mandatory inclusion rules, as well as the amount of deduction from mandatory inclusion that would be allowable under the transition rule. In addition, the corporation must furnish a copy of that information to its shareholders. The information provided to shareholders also must include a statement of the shareholder's pro rata share of these amounts (Code Sec. 965(j), as added by the 2017 Tax Cuts Act).

**Limitations on assessment extended.** Under an exception to the otherwise generally applicable limitations period for assessment of tax, the period for the assessment of the transition net tax liability arising from the mandatory inclusion does not expire prior to six years from the date on which the tax return initially reflecting the mandatory inclusion was filed (Code Sec. 965(k), as added by the 2017 Tax Cuts Act).

> **Caution:** A technical correction may be required to reflect that to the extent that such return was filed by a U.S. shareholder that is a domestic partnership, a commensurate extension of the period for making adjustments to a partnership return is intended (General Explanation of Public Law 115-97 (JCS-1-18)).

**Recapture for expatriated entities.** A special recapture rule applies if a U.S. shareholder is allowed a deduction from mandatory inclusion under the transition rule and first becomes an expatriated entity at any time during the 10-year period

## NEW LAW EXPLAINED

beginning on December 22, 2017, with respect to a surrogate foreign corporation that first becomes a surrogate foreign corporation during that period (i.e., post-enactment). In this case, the tax imposed by Chapter 1 of the Code is increased for the first tax year in which the taxpayer becomes an expatriated entity by an amount equal to 35 percent of the amount of the allowed deduction from mandatory inclusion. In addition, no tax credits are allowed against the additional tax due as a result of the recapture rule (Code Sec. 965(l)(1), as added by the 2017 Tax Cuts Act; Reg. § 1.965-3(d)).

> **Comment:** Although the amount due is computed by reference to the year in which the deemed subpart F income was originally reported, the additional tax arises and is assessed for the tax year in which the U.S. shareholder becomes an expatriated entity.

For purposes of this rule, an expatriated entity is a domestic corporation or partnership acquired in an inversion transaction and the surrogate foreign corporation is the foreign corporation acquiring the expatriated entity in the inversion transaction (Code Sec. 7874(a)(2)). However, an entity is not treated as an expatriated entity, and is not within the scope of this recapture rule, if the surrogate foreign corporation is treated as a domestic corporation under Code Sec. 7874(b) because former shareholders or partners of the acquired entity hold 80 percent or more (by vote or value) of the stock of the surrogate foreign corporation after the transaction (Code Sec. 965(l)(2) and (3), as added by the 2017 Tax Cuts Act; Reg. § 1.965-3(d)(2)).

**Special rules for U.S. shareholders that are REITs.** Special rules are provided if a U.S. shareholder is a REIT in order to reduce the burden of compliance with the transition rule by REITs. First, if a real estate investment trust (REIT) is a U.S. shareholder in one or more deferred foreign income corporations, any amount required to be included as mandatory subpart F inclusion is not taken into account as gross income of the REIT for purposes of determining the qualified REIT's income in applying the Code Sec. 856(c)(2) and (3) income tests to any tax year for which the amount is taken into account under the subpart F inclusion (Code Sec. 965(m)(1)(A), as added by the 2017 Tax Cuts Act; Reg. § 1.965-7(d)(6)).

In addition, although a REIT generally must take into account the mandatory inclusion in determining its taxable income under Code Sec. 857(b), the REIT is allowed to make an election to defer the mandatory inclusion and take it into income over the period of eight years as follows:

- Eight percent of the amount in the case of each of the tax years in the five-tax year period beginning with the tax year in which the amount would otherwise be included.
- 15 percent of the amount in the case of the first tax year following that period.
- 20 percent of the amount in the case of the second tax year following that period.
- 25 percent of the amount in the case of the third tax year following that period (Code Sec. 965(m)(1)(B), as added by the 2017 Tax Cuts Act; Reg. § 1.965-7(d)(2)).

A REIT that makes the election, may not make a Code Sec. 965(h) election for any year that the Code Sec. 965(m) election is in effect (Reg. § 1.965-7(d)(4)). The election may be revoked only by including in gross income when computing the REIT's

**NEW LAW EXPLAINED**

taxable income under Code Sec. 857(b), the full amount of the REIT Code Sec. 965 amounts (Reg. § 1.965-7(d)(1)).

> **Comment:** A REIT is required to distribute at least 90 percent of the REIT income (other than net capital gain) annually under Code Sec. 857. A required inclusion under the transition rule may trigger a requirement that the REIT distribute an amount equal to 90 percent of that inclusion despite the fact that it did not receive distribution from the deferred foreign income corporation. To avoid the requirement that any distribution requirement be satisfied in one year, an election to defer the mandatory inclusion is permitted.

The election for deferred inclusion must be made not later than the due date (including extensions) for the return for the first tax year in the five-tax year period during which eight percent of the inclusion is taken into account. No relief will be granted under Reg. § 1.301.9100-2 or Reg. § 301.9100-3 for late elections (Code Sec. 965(m)(2)(A), as added by the 2017 Tax Cuts Act; Reg. § 1.965-7(d)(3)(ii)).

> **Compliance Note:** The election is made by attaching a statement, signed under penalties of perjury and with the required information, to the return for the tax year, in which it would otherwise be required to include the REIT Code Sec. 965 amounts in gross income.

Special rules apply if the deferral election is in effect. Thus, in each of those years, the REIT may claim a partial deduction from mandatory inclusion under Code Sec. 965(c)(1) in the applicable percentages in proportion to the amount included in each of the eight years. The REIT also cannot elect to use the installment payment for any tax year from the eight-year period, discussed above (Code Sec. 965(m)(2)(B)(i), as added by the 2017 Tax Cuts Act).

> **Caution:** A technical correction may be required to reflect the correct cross reference under Code Sec. 965(m)(2)(B)(i)(III), a rule barring an electing trust from making an election to pay in installments refers to subsection (g), which deals with foreign tax credits, rather than subsection (h), which deals with the installment payment election. (General Explanation of Public Law 115-97 (JCS-1-18)).

In addition, if there is a liquidation or sale of substantially all the assets of the REIT (including in a bankruptcy or similar case), a cessation of business by the REIT, or any similar circumstance, any portion of the required inclusion not yet taken into income is accelerated and required to be included as gross income as of the day before the event and the unpaid portion of any tax liability with respect to such inclusion will be due on the date of the event (or in the case of a bankruptcy or similar case, the day before the petition is filed) (Code Sec. 965(m)(2)(B)(ii), as added by the 2017 Tax Cuts Act; Reg. § 1.965-7(d)(5)).

> **Compliance Note:** An electing REIT with any Code Sec. 965 amount taken into account under Code Sec. 965(m), or not taken into account at any time during a tax year, must file Form 965-B.

**Election not to apply the NOL deduction.** A U.S. shareholder of a deferred foreign income corporation can make an election for the last tax year beginning before January 1, 2018 (the tax year of the mandatory subpart F inclusion) not to take into

## NEW LAW EXPLAINED

account the mandatory inclusion and certain other amounts (described below) in determining (i) the net operating loss (NOL) deduction under Code Sec. 172 for that tax year, or (ii) the amount of taxable income for that tax year which may be reduced by NOL carryovers or carrybacks to that tax year (Code Sec. 965(n)(1), as added by the 2017 Tax Cuts Act ; Reg. § 1.965-7(e)). The regulations clarify that the election applies to NOLs for the tax year for which the election is made, as well as NOL carryovers or carrybacks to the tax year. The regulation also provides that the election must be made for the entire NOL and the election may be made by a consolidated group. The election is irrevocable.

> **Caution:** A technical correction may be required to reflect that deductions, whether taken for current year expenses or a net operating loss carry-over, when taken into account in the election year, may not exceed gross income determined regardless of the transition inclusion and related Code Sec. 78 gross-up (General Explanation of Public Law 115-97 (JCS-1-18)).

> The reference in Code Sec. 965(n)(1)(A) to "a net operating loss deduction under Code Sec. 172" may be read as limiting the election to carryover or carryback of a taxpayer's net operating loss, but not allow losses in the year of the election. However, any deductions that are deferred to preserve a NOL for the year may not also be deducted in the election year, in order that the taxpayer's taxable income for the tax year cannot be less than the amount as described in Code Sec. 965(n) (General Explanation of Public Law 115-97 (JCS-1-18)).

The amount not taken into account includes the mandatory inclusion and, in the case of a domestic corporation that chooses to have the benefits of subpart A of part III of subchapter N for the tax year, the taxes deemed to be paid by the corporation under the deemed-paid credit rules of Code Sec. 960(a) and (b) for the tax year with respect to the mandatory inclusion that are treated as dividends under Code Sec. 78 (Code Sec. 965(n)(2), as added by the 2017 Tax Cuts Act; Reg. § 1.965-7(e)(1)(ii)).

> **Compliance Note:** The election is made not later than the due date (including extensions) for filing the return for the tax year in the manner prescribed by the Secretary (Code Sec. 965(n)(3), as added by the 2017 Tax Cuts Act; Reg. § 1.965-7(e)(1)(ii)). A person makes the election by attaching a statement, with the required information, signed under the penalties for perjury, to the return for the tax year (taking into account extensions) to which the election applies. Relief is not available under Reg. § 301.9100-2 and Reg. § 301.9100-3 for late elections (Reg. § 1.965-7(e)(2)).

**Regulations.** The Secretary is authorized to issue regulations or other guidance as may be necessary or appropriate to carry out the mandatory inclusion provisions or to prevent the avoidance of the purposes of these rules, including through a reduction in earnings and profits through changes in entity classification, changes in accounting methods, or otherwise (Code Sec. 965(o), as added by the 2017 Tax Cuts Act).

> **Comment:** The anti-avoidance rules provide that certain transactions will be disregarded for purposes of applying Code Sec. 965 to a U.S. shareholder (Reg. § 1.965-4(a)).

**¶710**

**NEW LAW EXPLAINED**

Generally, transactions undertaken with a principal purpose of changing the amount of a Code Sec. 965 element of a U.S. shareholder are disregarded if the transaction occurs on or after November 2, 2017, the transaction is undertaken with a principal purpose of changing the amount of a Code Sec. 965 element of a U.S. shareholder, and the transaction would change the amount of the Code Sec. 965 element of the U.S. shareholder (Reg. § 1.965-4(b)(1)(i), (ii), and (iii)).

The term "section 965 element" means:

- The U.S. shareholder's Code Sec. 965(a) inclusion amount with respect to a specified foreign corporation (Reg. § 1.965-4(d)(1));

- The aggregate foreign cash position of the U.S. shareholder (Reg. § 1.965-4(d)(2)); or,

- The amount of foreign income taxes of a specified foreign corporation deemed paid by the U.S. shareholder under Code Sec. 960 as a result of a Code Sec. 965 inclusion (Reg. § 1.965-4(d)(3)).

Under the general rule, certain transactions are presumed to be undertaken for the principal purpose of changing the amount of a Code Sec. 965 element of a U.S. shareholder, and the presumption may only be rebutted if facts and circumstances clearly establish the principal purpose of the transaction was not to change the amount of a Code Sec. 965 element of a U.S. shareholder (Reg. § 1.965-4(b)(2)(i)). The transactions presumed to be undertaken with the principal purpose of changing the amount of a Code Sec. 965 element of a U.S. shareholder include cash reduction transactions, E&P reduction transactions, and pro rata share transactions (Reg. § 1.965-4(b)(2)(iii), (iv), and (v)). In addition, certain changes in method of accounting and entity classification elections will be disregarded for purposes of determining the amounts of all Code Sec. 965 elements of a U.S. shareholder (Reg. § 1.965-4(c)(1) and (2)).

Under the anti-avoidance rules, for purposes of determining the Code Sec. 965 elements of a United States shareholder on the liquidation of a disregarded specified foreign corporation, the date of the liquidation generally is treated as the close of the specified foreign corporation's tax year (Reg. § 1.965-4(e)(4)). Also, a cash reduction transaction is not considered to be an intentional plan to transfer cash or cash equivalent assets of any specified foreign corporation of a U.S. shareholder if the transfer is made by the U.S. shareholder based on a legal obligation entered into before November 2, 2017 (Reg. § 1.965-4(b)(2)(iii)(B)).

*Applicability Date.* Generally Reg. § 1.965-1 through Reg. § 1.965-8 apply beginning the last taxable year of a foreign corporation that begins before January 1, 2018, and with respect to a United States person, beginning the taxable year in which or with which such taxable year of the foreign corporation ends (Reg. § 1.965-9(a)).

For rules disregarding certain transactions, Reg. § 1.965-4 applies regardless of whether, with respect to a foreign corporation, the transaction, effective date of a change in method of accounting, effective date of an entity classification election, or specified payment described in Reg. § 1.965-4 occurred before the first day of the foreign corporation's last taxable year that begins before January 1, 2018, or, with respect to a United States person, the transaction, effective date of a change in

## NEW LAW EXPLAINED

method of accounting, effective date of an entity classification election, or specified payment described in Reg. § 1.965-4 occurred before the first day of the taxable year of the United States person in which or with which the taxable year of the foreign corporation ends (Reg. § 1.965-9(b)).

▶ **Effective date.** No specific effective date is provided. The amendment is, therefore, considered effective on December 22, 2017, the date of enactment.

— Act Sec. 14103(a) of the Tax Cuts and Jobs Act (P.L. 115-97), amending Code Sec. 965.

# FOREIGN TAX CREDIT

## ¶715 Recapture of Overall Domestic Losses

### SUMMARY OF NEW LAW

A taxpayer may elect to recapture pre-2018 unused overall domestic losses (ODLs) by recharacterizing up to 100 percent of the taxpayer's U.S. source taxable income as foreign source taxable income, from 2018 through 2027.

### BACKGROUND

U.S. taxpayers are taxed on their worldwide income, but are allowed a foreign tax credit for foreign income taxes paid or accrued, in order to prevent the double taxation of foreign source income (Code Sec. 901). The foreign tax credit limitation provides that when the foreign income tax is higher than U.S. income tax, the foreign tax credit is limited to the U.S. tax that would be due on foreign income (Code Sec. 904). The purpose of the limitation is to protect the U.S. tax base and to prevent the reduction of U.S. tax on U.S. source income. The limitation is determined by multiplying a taxpayer's total U.S. tax liability (before the foreign tax credit) for the tax year by the ratio of the taxpayer's foreign source taxable income to worldwide taxable income (Code Sec. 904(a)).

The foreign tax credit limitation requires that the foreign tax credit limitation be calculated separately for certain categories of income or "baskets". There are generally two foreign separate limitation categories or baskets-a "passive category income" basket and a "general category income" basket (Reg. § 1.904-4). Foreign source taxable income for each category is gross income for the category, less expenses, losses and other deductions (referred to as deductions). The allocation and apportionment of deductions for purposes of determining the foreign tax credit limitation generally requires that the expense is first allocated to a specific class of income, and then apportioned, between the statutory groupings (i.e., foreign general and passive limitation income) and the residual grouping (i.e., U.S. source income) (Reg. § 1.861-8). The foreign tax credit limitation can be increased by increasing the portion of worldwide taxable income that is foreign source taxable income. Minimizing the expenses that are allocated or apportioned to foreign source income will increase foreign source taxable income.

## BACKGROUND

Foreign and domestic losses can impact the foreign tax credit limitation. To the extent that the allocation and apportionment of the deductions results in a loss in a separate limitation income category, the loss is first used to reduce income in the other separate limitation income categories and then to reduce income of a different source. When this occurs, the loss recapture rules come in to play. For example, if an overall foreign loss (OFL) reduces U.S. source income or an overall domestic loss (ODL) reduces foreign source income, the loss is recaptured by recharacterizing a portion of the foreign source income or U.S. source income that is subsequently earned, as U.S. source income or foreign source income, respectively (Code Sec. 904(f) and (g)).

A domestic loss is the amount by which the U.S. source income is exceeded by the sum of properly allocated and apportioned deductions to that gross income, taking into account net operating carryforwards (Code Sec. 904(g)(2)(B); Reg. § 1.904(g)-2(c)(2)). An ODL is a loss that offsets or reduces foreign source taxable income, in a qualifying tax year, or any qualifying preceding year by reason of a loss carryback. A qualified tax year is a year in which the taxpayer elects the foreign tax credit. If there is a domestic loss in a year in which taxes are deducted, it may only be used in a preceding year in which the foreign tax credit is claimed (Code Sec. 904(g)(2); Reg. § 1.904(g)-1(c)).

A domestic loss that does not exceed the separate limitation income (SLI) is allocated and reduces the SLI amounts on a proportionate basis. SLI is the foreign source taxable income for each separate limitation income category. A separate limitation loss (SLL) for each category is the amount by which the foreign source gross income in the category is exceeded by the sum of the deductions are properly allocated and apportion to the category. SLLs are allocated proportionately among the separate categories that have SLI. The allocation of the domestic loss occurs after the allocation of the SLLs to SLI amounts (Reg. § 1.904(g)-3(e)).

ODL accounts are established for each separate category in which the SLI is offset by domestic loss. The balance in the accounts are ODLs, subject to recapture in a given year. If a domestic loss is carried back or carried forward as part of a net operating loss that reduces foreign source taxable income, the ODL is treated as sustained in the later of the year in which the domestic loss was incurred or the year to which the loss was carried. (Reg. § § 1.904(f)-7(b)(1) and 1.904(g)-1(b)).

ODLs are recaptured by treating a portion of a taxpayer's U.S. source taxable income as foreign source taxable income (Reg. § 1.904(g)-2). If the taxpayer has ODL accounts attributable to more than one separate category, the recharacterized income is allocated among the categories on a pro rata basis. The amount of U.S. source taxable income subject to recapture is the lesser of the aggregate balance in the ODL accounts, to the extent not recaptured in prior years, or 50 percent of the taxpayer's U.S. taxable income for the year. The taxpayer who elects the foreign tax credit will have foreign source taxable income increased by the amount of the recapture, for purposes of the foreign tax credit limitation, increasing the amount of the foreign tax credit for the year. Once an amount is recaptured, the account is reduced by the amount of the recapture and recapture occurs each year until the account balance is zero.

¶715

## BACKGROUND

> **Example:** In Year 1, the taxpayer has a domestic loss of $200 that it allocates proportionately to $1,000 of foreign source taxable income, $600 of foreign source taxable income or 60% in the general category ($120) and to $400 foreign source taxable income or 40% in the passive category ($80). The taxpayer has a $120 ODL account in the general category and a $80 ODL account in the passive category. In Year 2, U.S. taxable income is $100. The taxpayer may recapture $50, the lesser of 50% of the U.S. taxable income of $100 or the $200 aggregate balance in the ODL accounts. The $50 of U.S, taxable income is recharacterized proportionately, 60% or $30 to general category income and 40% or $20 to passive category income. The ODL accounts are reduced to $90 in the general category ODL account and $60 in the passive category ODL account.

## NEW LAW EXPLAINED

**Recapture of ODLs accelerated.**—A taxpayer who claims the foreign tax credit and has an overall domestic loss (ODL) may elect to recapture the ODL by recharacterizing up to 100 percent of U.S. source taxable income earned in subsequent years as foreign source taxable income. The amount that is recharacterized each year is limited to the lesser of the aggregate amount in the ODL account or up to 100 percent of the taxpayer's U.S. source taxable income for the year (Code Sec. 904(g)(5)(A), as added by the Tax Cuts and Jobs Act (P.L. 115-97)).

The increased recapture amount applies to the pre-2018 unused ODL, meaning a loss that arises in a qualified tax year beginning before January 1, 2018, and that has not been used for any tax year before that date (Code Sec. 904(g)(5)(B), as added by the 2017 Tax Cuts Act). A qualified tax year is a year for which the taxpayer elects the foreign tax credit (Code Sec. 904(g)(2)(C)). The pre-2018 unused ODL must be taken into account for tax years of the taxpayer beginning after December 31, 2017, and before January 1, 2028 (Code Sec. 904(g)(5)(C), as added by the Tax Cuts Act).

▶ **Effective date.** The amendments made by this section apply to tax years beginning after December 31, 2017 (Act Sec. 14304(b) of the Tax Cuts and Jobs Act (P.L. 115-97)).

**No significant guidance related to this provision has been issued**.

— Act Sec. 14304(a) of the Tax Cuts and Jobs Act (P.L. 115-97), adding Code Sec. 904(g)(5);

— Act Sec. 14304(b), providing the effective date.

¶715

# ¶720  Deemed-Paid Foreign Tax Credit

## SUMMARY OF NEW LAW

The Code Sec. 902 deemed-paid foreign tax credit is repealed and the Code Sec. 960 deemed-paid foreign tax credit is modified so that it is determined on a current year basis.

## BACKGROUND

A foreign tax credit is allowed to a domestic corporation that owns at least 10 percent of the voting stock in a foreign corporation from which it receives a dividend (Code Sec. 902). The credit is determined by reference to the portion of the foreign corporation's post-1986 foreign income taxes that the dividend received by the foreign corporation bears to the foreign corporation's post-1986 undistributed earnings. The credit is referred to as the "deemed-paid" or "indirect" credit (Code Sec. 902(a)).

The deemed-paid credit is allowed for foreign income taxes of the first-tier foreign corporation and lower-tier foreign corporations (second- through sixth-tier corporations). The lower-tier foreign corporation must be in a chain of corporations that includes the first-tier corporation. Each corporation in the chain must own at least 10 percent of the voting stock of the lower-tier corporation and the domestic shareholder must own at least five percent of the voting stock of the foreign corporation indirectly in the chain. A foreign corporation below the third-level must be a controlled foreign corporation (CFC) and the domestic corporation must be a U.S. shareholder (Code Sec. 902(b)).

A domestic corporation that has a subpart F inclusion under Code Sec. 951(a) can obtain an indirect or deemed-paid foreign tax credit for foreign income taxes paid or deemed paid by the foreign corporation. The principles of Code Sec. 902 are used to determine the portion of the CFC's post-1986 foreign taxes that are deemed-paid by the shareholder in connection with the subpart F inclusion (Code Sec. 960). The Code Sec. 960 credit is limited with respect to taxes deemed paid on amounts included in a domestic corporate U.S. shareholder's gross income under Code Sec. 956. Under Code Sec. 956, U.S. shareholders are taxed under subpart F on their pro rata share of the CFC's investment in U.S. property (the "Code Sec. 956 amount"). Under the limitation, the credit may not exceed the amount of taxes that would be deemed paid if the corporation had made an actual distribution of cash through a chain of ownership to the U.S. shareholder (Code Sec. 960(c)).

A change in a taxpayer's foreign tax liability may affect the taxpayer's foreign tax credit, including the deemed-paid credits under Code Sec. 902 and Code Sec. 960. If a taxpayer does not pay accrued taxes within two years of the close of the tax year to which the taxes relate, there is a foreign tax redetermination that affects the taxpayer's foreign tax credit because no credit is allowed for accrued taxes not paid before that date. Taxes subsequently paid are taken into account in the year to which the taxes relate (Code Sec. 905(c)(2)(B)). In the case of the deemed-paid credit, regulations provide that, in lieu of a redetermination, adjustments to the foreign

## BACKGROUND

corporation's pools of post-1986 undistributed earnings and post-1986 foreign income taxes are made. Accrued taxes that are subsequently paid after the two year period are taken into account in the pools for the year of payment (Code Sec. 905(c)(2)(B)(i)(I); Temp. Reg. § 1.905-3T(d)(2)).

A domestic corporation must include foreign taxes deemed paid in gross income under Code Sec. 78 (referred to as the "Code Sec. 78 gross-up").

Under a matching rule, taxpayers are prevented from claiming the foreign tax credit for foreign taxes that are paid or accrued, before the tax year in which the related income is taken into account (referred to as a foreign tax credit splitting event). Special rules apply to foreign taxes paid or accrued by Code Sec. 902 corporations (Code Sec. 909(b)).

A passive foreign investment company (PFIC) is a foreign corporation that meets either an income or asset test (Code Sec. 1297(a)). Under these tests, 75 percent or more of the corporation's gross income must be passive income or 50 percent or more of its average percentage of assets must produce passive income. A U.S. shareholder of a PFIC can make a qualified electing fund (QEF) election to include in gross income currently its pro rata share of the PFIC's ordinary earnings and net capital gain (Code Sec. 1293).

A domestic corporate shareholder of a PFIC that owns at least 10 percent of the QEF's voting stock can claim a Code Sec. 960 deemed-paid credit for foreign income taxes paid by the QEF. The credit is computed in the same manner as if there were a current inclusion under subpart F. If the shareholder is later entitled to exclude a distribution as earnings that were previously taxed, the rules of Code Sec. 959 apply and there is generally no foreign tax credits available for the later distribution. The amounts included in income are generally treated as income in the passive basket for purposes of the foreign tax credit limitation (Code Sec. 904(d)(2)(B)(ii)). If the PFIC is a Code Sec. 902 noncontrolled foreign corporation, the inclusion is treated as a dividend from the corporation and is subject to the look-through rule. Dividends paid by a Code Sec. 902 noncontrolled foreign corporation (a so-called "10/50" corporation) are subject to a look-through rule when calculating the foreign tax credit limitation for the dividends paid (Code Sec. 904(d)(4); Reg. § 1.904-5(c)(4)(iii)). If the PFIC is a CFC and the U.S. shareholder is a domestic corporation owning at least 10 percent of the voting stock, the look-through rules for CFCs apply (Code Sec. 904(d)(3)(H)).

## NEW LAW EXPLAINED

**Code Sec. 902 deemed-paid credit repealed.**—The Code Sec. 902 deemed-paid foreign tax credit is repealed for tax years of foreign corporations beginning after December 31, 2017, and to tax years of U.S. shareholders in which or with which such tax years of foreign corporations end (Code Sec. 902, stricken by the Tax Cuts and Jobs Act (P.L. 115-97)). The deemed-paid credit is repealed as a result of the implementation of the participation exemption system under which a a specified 10-percent owned foreign corporation is provided a 100-percent deduction for the foreign-source portion of

## NEW LAW EXPLAINED

the dividends received from the foreign corporation (Code Sec. 245A, as added by the 2017 Tax Cuts Act). This deduction is referred to as the "participation DRD". No foreign tax credit or deduction is allowed for any foreign taxes paid or accrued with respect to the deductible portion of the dividend (see ¶ 705).

> **Comment:** The House Committee Report states that to continue to provide a Code Sec. 902 deemed-paid credit in light of the participation DRD would provide a double tax benefit, by allowing the dividend exemption and then reducing U.S. tax with a credit for taxes paid on the foreign source income (House Committee Report for Tax Cuts and Jobs Act (P.L. 115-97) (H. R. Rep. No. 115-409)).

**Code Sec. 960 deemed-paid credit for subpart F inclusions.** The Code Sec. 960 deemed-paid foreign tax credit for subpart F inclusions is retained, but modified as a result of the repeal of Code Sec. 902. The deemed-paid credit for subpart F inclusions is no longer computed under the principles of Code Sec. 902. Rather, the credit is determined on a current year basis. If income is included in the gross income of a domestic corporation that is a U.S. shareholder of a controlled foreign corporation (CFC), the deemed-paid credit is the amount of the foreign corporation's foreign income taxes properly attributable to the subpart F income inclusion (Code Sec. 960(a), as added by the 2017 Tax Cuts Act).

> **Comment:** The provision changes the method for computing the deemed-paid taxes, which required the domestic corporation to multiply the foreign subsidiary's post-1986 foreign income tax payments by the ratio of: (1) the Code Sec. 951(a)(1) inclusion, to (2) the foreign subsidiary's post-1986 undistributed earnings pool. The provision eliminates the need for tracking cumulative tax pools.

The look-through rule that applied for purposes of determining the foreign tax credit limitation for dividends received from a Code Sec. 902 noncontrolled foreign corporation now applies to dividends received from a noncontrolled 10-percent owned foreign corporation. A noncontrolled 10-percent owned foreign corporation is a specified foreign corporation, defined in Code Sec. 245A(b). The term also includes a PFIC with respect to which the taxpayer meets the stock ownership requirements of Code Sec. 902(a) or (b), as in effect before repeal by the 2017 Tax Cuts Act. A CFC will not be treated as a noncontrolled 10-percent owned foreign corporation with respect to any distribution out of its earnings and profits for periods during which it was a CFC (Code Sec. 904(d)(2)(E)(i) and (d)(4), as amended by the 2017 Tax Cuts Act).

> **Comment:** The limitation on the Code Sec. 960 deemed-paid credit with respect to Code Sec. 956 inclusions of domestic corporate shareholders is eliminated (Code Sec. 960(c), stricken by the 2017 Tax Cuts Act). Proposed regulations under Code Sec. 960(a) provide that no foreign income tax is deemed paid with regard to inclusion under Code Sec. 956 (Proposed Reg. § 1.960-2(b)(1); NPRM REG-105600, November 28, 2018). Note that provisions in the House-passed bill would have made the Code Sec. 956 amount zero with respect to a domestic corporation, while the Senate-passed bill excepted domestic corporations from Code Sec. 956. However, Code Sec. 956 was not modified in the final version of the 2017 Tax Cuts Act.

## NEW LAW EXPLAINED

**Code Sec. 960 deemed-paid credit and distributions from previously taxed earnings and profits.** The amount of foreign taxes deemed paid upon a distribution of previously taxed income is also no longer determined under the principles of Code Sec. 902. If a domestic corporation that is a U.S. shareholder receives a distribution from a CFC, any part of which is excluded from gross income as previously taxed income under Code Sec. 959(a), the domestic corporation is deemed to pay the foreign corporation's foreign income taxes as: (1) are properly attributable to the previously taxed income, and (2) that were not deemed paid by the domestic corporation under Code Sec. 960, for the tax year or any prior tax year (Code Sec. 960(b)(1), as added by the 2017 Tax Cuts Act).

If a CFC receives a distribution from another CFC, any portion of which was excluded from gross income of the CFC because the amounts were attributable to previously taxed income under Code Sec. 959(b), the CFC receiving the distribution will be deemed to have paid so much of the other CFC's taxes as: (1) are attributable to such portion, and (2) have not been deemed to have been paid by a domestic corporation under Code Sec. 960, for the tax year or any prior tax year (Code Sec. 960(b)(2), as added by the 2017 Tax Cuts Act).

> **Caution:** According to the Joint Committee on Taxation's report on the 2017 Tax Cuts Act, a technical correction may be required to reflect that the credit under Code Sec. 901 is for only 80 percent of the foreign income tax imposed as it relates to previously taxed earnings and profits that are attributed to global intangible low-taxed income (GILTI), and with respect to distributions of previously taxed amounts under Code Sec. 965(b)(4)(A) no credit is allowed (General Explanation of Public Law 115-97 (JCS-1-18)).

> **Caution:** A technical correction also may be required to reflect that the provision does not allow a credit for taxes not attributable to actual distributions of previously taxed earnings and profits, such as the portion of taxes disallowed as a deemed paid credit for taxes properly attributable to tested income by reason of the inclusion percentage or 80 percent multiplicand of Code Sec. 960(d)(1) (General Explanation of Public Law 115-97 (JCS-1-18).

**Adjustments to the Code Sec. 960 deemed-paid credit.** Accrued foreign income taxes that were not paid within two years from the close of the tax year to which they relate and so reduce the foreign tax credit, but that are subsequently paid, are taken into account for the tax year to which the taxes relate. The same rule applies for both taxes deemed paid under Code Sec. 960 and foreign income taxes directly paid (Code Sec. 905(c)(2)(B)(i), as amended by the 2017 Tax Cuts Act).

> **Comment:** Temp. Reg. § 1.905-3T(d)(2), which requires adjustments to the earnings and tax pools, in lieu of a foreign tax redetermination, is inconsistent with the determination of the Code Sec. 960 deemed-paid credit on a current basis.

**Other provisions related to the Code Sec. 960 deemed-paid credit.** For purposes of the Code Sec. 960 deemed-paid credit, the term foreign income taxes means income, war profits, or excess profits taxes paid or accrued to any foreign country or possession of the United States (Code Sec. 960(e), as added by the 2017 Tax Cuts Act). The IRS may provide regulations or other guidance necessary to carry out the provisions of Code Sec. 960 (Code Sec. 960(f), as added by the 2017 Tax Cuts Act).

## NEW LAW EXPLAINED

> **Comment:** According to the House Committee Report, the regulations could provide rules similar to those in Reg. §1.904-6(a) for allocating taxes to specific foreign tax credit baskets. Under these rules, taxes are not attributable to an item of subpart F income if the base upon which the tax was imposed does not include the item of subpart F income. For example, if foreign law exempts from tax certain income from its tax base, no deemed credit can result from the subpart F inclusion. Tax that is not imposed on subpart F income is not attributable to subpart F income (House Committee Report for Tax Cuts and Jobs Act (P.L. 115-97) (H. R. Rep. No. 115-409)).

A domestic corporation that owns or is treated as owning under the attribution of ownership rules of Code Sec. 1298(a), the stock of a qualified electing fund (QEF) can claim the Code Sec. 960 deemed-paid credit for the inclusion of income of the QEF. The domestic corporation must meet the stock ownership requirements in Code Sec. 902(a) and (b), prior to repeal by the 2017 Tax Cuts Act (Code Sec. 1293(f)(3), as added by the 2017 Tax Cuts Act).

**Code Sec. 78 gross-up.** The Code Sec. 78 gross-up for foreign taxes deemed paid under Code Sec. 902 no longer applies as a result of the repeal of Code Sec. 902. The gross-up applies to taxes deemed paid under Code Sec. 960(a) and (b).

For tax years beginning after 2017, the Code Sec. 78 gross-up also applies to foreign income taxes deemed paid with respect to amounts of global intangible low-taxed income (GILTI) included in the gross income of a domestic corporation under Code Sec. 951A (see ¶735). A domestic corporation's deemed-paid credit for GILTI is 80 percent of the product of the corporation's inclusion percentage and the aggregate tested foreign income taxes paid or accrued, with respect to tested income, by each CFC with respect to which the domestic corporation is a U.S. shareholder. The Code Sec. 78 gross-up, however, takes into account 100 percent of the product of the inclusion percentage and aggregate tested foreign taxes.

> **Caution:** A technical correction may be necessary to reflect the intent that the Code Sec. 78 gross-up amount attributable to a GILTI inclusion is considered GILTI for foreign tax credit limitation purposes (General Explanation of Public Law 115-97 (JCS-1-18).

The Code Sec. 78 gross-up applies for all purposes, except for the deductions for dividends received under Code Secs. 245 and 245A. The amounts are treated as a dividend received by a domestic corporation from a foreign corporation (Code Sec. 78, as amended by the 2017 Tax Cuts Act and Code Sec. 960(d), as added by the 2017 Tax Cuts Act). Additionally, Code Sec. 78 dividends received after 2017 that relate to tax years of foreign corporations that begin before 2018 are not treated as dividends for purposes of Code Sec. 245A (Proposed Reg. §1.78-1).

> **Caution:** A technical correction to the effective date of the Code Sec. 78 changes may be required to reflect the intent that fiscal-year taxpayers are not eligible the benefit of the participation exemption for Code Sec. 78 gross-ups made in tax years beginning before December 21, 2017. Also, a technical correction to Code Sec. 78 may be necessary to reflect the intent to allow previously taxed income from lower-tier CFCs giving rise to deemed paid credits under Code Sec. 960(b) to be distributed without additional U.S. tax. Further, it may be necessary to

## NEW LAW EXPLAINED

issue a technical correction to reflect the intent that the Code Sec. 78 gross-up amount that is attributable to a GILTI inclusion should be assigned to the basket that the corresponding taxes relate for foreign tax credit limitation purposes (General Explanation of Public Law 115-97 (JCS-1-18).

**Code Sec. 909 matching rule.** The special matching rule that applied to Code Sec. 902 corporations is replaced with a rule that applies to specified 10-percent owned foreign corporations. Under the rule, if there is a foreign tax credit splitting event, a foreign income tax paid or accrued by a specified 10-percent owned foreign corporation will not be taken into account, for purposes of Code Sec. 960 or determining earnings and profits under Code Sec. 964(a), before the tax year in which the related income is taken into account by the corporation or a domestic corporation which is a U.S. shareholder of the corporation (Code Sec. 909(b), as amended by the 2017 Tax Cuts Act).

A specified 10-percent owned foreign corporation is any corporation with respect to which a domestic corporation is a U.S. shareholder. The definition is modified for this purpose to include PFICs that are not CFCs (Code Sec. 245A(b), as added by the 2017 Tax Cuts Act) (see ¶705). A U.S. shareholder is a U.S. person who owns, either directly, indirectly, or constructively: (1) 10 percent or more of the total combined voting power of all classes of stock of the foreign corporation, or (2) 10 percent or more of the total value of shares of all classes of stock of the foreign corporation (see ¶745) (Code Sec. 951(b), as amended by the 2017 Tax Cuts Act).

**Foreign tax credit limitation look-through rule.** The look-through rule that applied for purposes of determining the foreign tax credit limitation for dividends received from a Code Sec. 902 noncontrolled foreign corporation now applies to dividends received from a noncontrolled 10-percent owned foreign corporation. A noncontrolled 10-percent owned foreign corporation is a specified 10-percent owned foreign corporation, defined in Code Sec. 245A(b) (see ¶705). The term also refers to a PFIC with respect to which the taxpayer meets the stock ownership requirements of Code Sec. 902(a) or (b), as in effect before repeal by the 2017 Tax Cuts Act. A CFC will not be treated as a noncontrolled 10-percent owned foreign corporation with respect to any distribution out of its earnings and profits for periods during which it was a CFC (Code Sec. 904(d)(2)(E)(i) and (d)(4), as amended by the 2017 Tax Cuts Act).

**Dividends received deduction.** The U.S. source portion of a dividend received from a 10-percent foreign corporation that may be deducted under Code Sec. 245 is the amount of the dividend multiplied by the ratio of post-1986 undistributed U.S. earnings to the post-1986 undistributed earnings. Post-1986 undistributed earnings were defined by reference to Code Sec. 902(c)(1). The definition of post-1986 undistributed earnings from Code Sec. 902(c)(1) is now included in Code Sec. 245 (Code Sec. 245(a)(4), as amended by the 2017 Tax Cuts Act).

**Proposed regulations for determining foreign income taxes deemed paid.** Proposed regulations under Code Sec. 960 provide definitions, computational rules, and grouping rules for determining the foreign income taxes paid by a domestic corporation that is a U.S. shareholder (NPRM REG-105600-18, November 28, 2018). Under the proposed regulations, only foreign income taxes of a CFC that are associated with a Subpart F or GILTI inclusion amount of a domestic corporation that is a U.S.

## NEW LAW EXPLAINED

shareholder of the CFC, or with previously taxed earnings and profits are eligible to be deemed paid (Proposed Reg. § 1.960-1(a)).

For purposes of computing deemed paid foreign taxes under Code Sec. 960, the proposed regulations provide six rules, to be followed in order, beginning with the lowest-tier CFC in a chain with respect to which the domestic corporation is a U.S. shareholder (Proposed Reg. § 1.960-1(c)(1)):

(1) *Assignment of current year gross income to Code Sec. 904 categories and income groups.* Income categories under Code Sec. 904 include passive, general, foreign branch, GILTI, and specified separate categories as provided for in the Code Sec. 904 regulations (Proposed Reg. § 1.960-1(d)(2)). After assignment to a category, income must be assigned to an income group within the respective category. The income groups include Subpart F income groups, tested income groups, and the residual income group.

(2) *Allocation and Apportionment of Deductions.* The current year gross income of the CFC that has been assigned to Code Sec. 904 categories and income groups is now reduced by the allocation and apportionment of deductions (Proposed Reg. § 1.960-1(d)(3)). First, the rules in Code Secs. 861 through 865, and 904(d) are applied to each Code Sec. 904 category and income group, followed by the allocation and apportionment of related party interest expense among the Subpart F income groups within the passive income category, and finally any remaining deductions are allocated and apportioned.

Second, the proposed regulations provide for the allocation and apportionment of current year taxes to further reduce the CFCs gross income in each Code Sec. 904 category and income group. If a current year tax is imposed on a previously taxed earnings and profits (PTEP) group solely by reason of the receipt of a Code Sec. 959(b) distribution, then the PTEP group is treated as an income group within the Code Sec. 904 category for purposes of allocating and apportioning the current year tax. Current year taxes attributable to timing differences are treated as related to the appropriate Code Sec. 904 category and income group to which it would be assigned if the income on which the tax was imposed was recognized under federal income tax principles in the same year the tax was imposed. For purposes of computing foreign deemed taxes paid, current year taxes allocated and apportioned to income groups and PTEP groups in Code Sec. 904 categories are converted to U.S. dollars under Code Sec. 986(a) (Proposed Reg. § § 1 960-1(c)(1)(ii) and (c)(3)).

(3) *Determination of foreign taxes deemed paid.* The proposed regulations provide rules for determining taxes deemed paid by a domestic corporation with respect to income of a CFC under Code Sec. 960(a) (Subpart F income), Code Sec. 960(d) (tested income), and Code Sec. 960(b)(2) (distribution of previously taxed earnings and profits) (Proposed Reg. § § 1.960-2(a) and 3(b)).

For purposes of Code Sec. 960(a), the domestic corporation is generally deemed to have paid the amount of the CFC's foreign income taxes that are properly attributable to the items of income in a subpart F group of the CFC that give rise to the subpart F inclusion of the domestic corporation that is attributable to the

## NEW LAW EXPLAINED

subpart F income group (Proposed Reg. § 1.960-2(b)). The domestic corporation's proportionate share is equal to the total U.S. dollar amount of current year taxes allocated and apportioned to the subpart F income group multiplied by a fraction (not to exceed one), the numerator of which is the portion of the domestic corporation's subpart F inclusion attributable to the subpart F income group, and the denominator, which is the total net income of the subpart F income group. No foreign income tax is deemed paid with regard to inclusion under Code Sec. 956.

For purposes of Code Sec. 960(d), the proposed regulations provide similar rules to determine the domestic corporation's proportionate share of foreign taxes for the current year that are properly attributable to tested income, the numerator of which is the portion of the tested income of the CFC in the tested income group within the Code Sec. 904 category that is included in computing the domestic corporation's tested income, and the denominator is the income in the tested income group within the Code Sec. 904 category (Proposed Reg. § 1.960-2(c)).

For the distribution of previously taxed earnings and profits under Code Sec. 960(b)(2), a CFC is deemed to have paid the foreign income taxes of another CFC not previously deemed paid by a U.S. shareholder and that are properly attributable to a distribution from the other CFC to which the Code Sec. 959(b) applies (Proposed Reg. § 1.960-3(b)). The recipient CFC's proportionate share of the PTEP group taxes with respect to a PTEP group within the Code Sec. 904 category is equal to the total amount of the PTEP group taxes with respect to the PTEP group, multiplied by a fraction (not to exceed one), the numerator of which is the amount of the Code Sec. 959(b) distribution from the PTEP group, and the denominator consisting of the total amount of previously taxed earnings and profits in the PTEP group, both determined in the functional currency of the CFC (Proposed Reg. § 1.960-3(b)(2)).

(4) *Separation of certain previously taxed earnings and profits to be added to an annual PTEP account.* Previously taxed earnings and profits of the CFC are separated out resulting in subpart F and GILTI inclusion amounts with respect to the CFC's current tax year from other earnings and profits of the CFC. The previously taxed earnings and profits of the CFC are added to an established annual PTEP account for tracking purposes. The account must correspond with the inclusion year of the previously taxed earnings and profits and to the Code Sec. 904 category to which the subpart F and GILTI inclusions amounts were assigned at the level of the U.S. shareholders. Amounts in the annual PTEP account are further assigned to one or more of ten PTEP groups of previously taxed earnings and profits in the account (Proposed Reg. § 1.960-3(c); NPRM REG-105600-18).

(5) *Repeat Steps 1-4.* For each next higher-tier CFC in the chain, the rules in steps 1 through 4 are repeated (Proposed Reg. § 1.960-1(c)(1)(v)).

(6) *Taxes deemed paid under Code Sec. 960(b)(1).* If the highest tier CFC in a chain is directly owned by a domestic corporation, then the foreign taxes deemed paid under Code Sec. 960(b)(1) in connection with the receipt of a Code Sec. 959(a) distribution are determined using the rules provided under Proposed Reg.

## NEW LAW EXPLAINED

§ 1.960-3(b) and as described in step 3. The CFC's portion of foreign taxes properly attributable to the distribution to the PTI group not previously deemed paid would be deemed paid by the U.S. shareholder.

*Applicability date.* The proposed regulations are proposed to apply to the taxable year of a foreign corporation beginning after December 31, 2017, and the taxable year of a domestic corporation that is a United States shareholder of the foreign corporation in which or with which such taxable year of such foreign corporation ends (Proposed Reg. § 1.960-7).

▶ **Effective date.** The amendments made by this section apply to tax years of foreign corporations beginning after December 31, 2017, and to tax years of U.S. shareholders in which or with which such tax years of foreign corporations end (Act Sec. 14301(d) of the Tax Cuts and Jobs Act (P.L. 115-97)).

— Act Sec. 14301(a) of the Tax Cuts and Jobs Act (P.L. 115-97), striking Code Sec. 902;

— Act Sec. 14301(b) amending Code Sec. 960, as amended by Act Sec. 14201 of the 2017 Tax Cuts Act;

— Act Sec. 14301(c), amending Code Secs. 78, 245(a)(4), 245(a)(10)(C), 535(b)(1), 545(b)(1), 814(f)(1), 865(h)(1)(B), 901(a), 901(e)(2), 901(f), 901(j)(1)(A), 901(j)(1)(B),901(k)(2),901(k)(6), 901(m)(1)(B), 904(d)(2)(E), 904(d)(4), 904(d)(6)(A), 904(h)(10)(A), 904(k), 905(c)(1), 905(c)(2)(B)(i), 906(a), 906(b), 907(b)(2)(B), 907(c)(3)(A), 907(c)(5), 907(f)(2)(B)(i), 908(a); 909(b), 909(d)(5); 958(a)(1), 959(d), 959(e), 1291(g)(2)(A), 6038(c)(1)(B), 6038(c)(4), and adding Code Sec. 1293(f);

— Act Sec. 14301(d), providing the effective date.

## ¶725 Foreign Tax Credit Limitation Baskets

### SUMMARY OF NEW LAW

A new foreign tax credit limitation basket is added for foreign branch income.

### BACKGROUND

U.S. taxpayers are taxed on their worldwide income, but are allowed a foreign tax credit for foreign income taxes paid or accrued, in order to prevent the double taxation of foreign source income (Code Sec. 901). The foreign tax credit limitation provides that when foreign income tax is higher than U.S. income tax, the foreign tax credit is limited to the U.S. tax that would be due on the foreign income (Code Sec. 904). The purpose of the limitation is to protect the U.S. tax base and to prevent the reduction of U.S. tax on U.S. source income. The limitation is determined by multiplying a taxpayer's total U.S. tax liability (before the foreign tax credit) for the tax year by the ratio of the taxpayer's foreign source taxable income to worldwide taxable income (Code Sec. 904(a)). If foreign taxes exceed the U.S. tax that would be

## BACKGROUND

due, the excess foreign taxes cannot be credited. Excess credits, however may be carried back one year and forward 10 years (Code Sec. 904(c)).

The foreign tax credit is determined on an overall basis, meaning that income and credits from all countries are combined. Determining the foreign tax credit on an overall basis can result in cross-crediting, which allows excess credits for taxes paid in high foreign tax countries to offset credits paid in lower foreign tax countries. The foreign tax credit limitation requires that the foreign tax credit limitation be calculated separately for certain categories of income or "baskets" to limit cross-crediting. There are generally two foreign limitation categories or baskets-a "passive category income" basket and a "general category income" basket (Reg. § 1.904-4). The separate foreign tax credit limitations prevent the averaging of high foreign income taxes on income such as active business with low-taxed income such as that in the passive category. Cross-crediting is permitted with respect to the separate income categories-the overall combined tax rate on the basket may not be higher than the U.S. tax rate.

Taxpayers must determine their foreign tax credit carrybacks and carryforward separately for each category of income (Code Sec. 904(d)(1)). The carryback or carryforward can be claimed to the extent of the excess limit in the category (i.e., the amount by which the limit is more than the qualified taxes paid or accrued for that category).

Passive income is generally any type of income that would qualify as subpart F income foreign personal holding company income under Code Sec. 954(c) if the recipient was a controlled foreign corporation (CFC) (e.g., dividends, interest, rents, royalties, and annuities) (Code Sec. 904(d)(2)). Specified passive category income includes dividends from a domestic international sales corporation (DISC) or former DISC and distributions from a former foreign sales corporation (FSC) (Reg. § 1.904-4(b)(3)). General category income includes income other than passive category income. Income that would otherwise be treated as passive category income is treated as general category income if it is earned by a qualifying financial services entity. Additionally, high-taxed income (i.e., income that is subject to foreign tax at rates exceeding the rates in Code Sec. 1 and Code Sec. 11) is treated as general category income.

## NEW LAW EXPLAINED

**Foreign tax credit limitation basket added.**—A new separate foreign tax credit limitation basket is added for foreign branch income (Code Sec. 904(d)(1)(B), as added by the Tax Cuts and Jobs Act (P.L. 115-97)). Foreign branch income means the business profits of a U.S. person that are attributable to one or more qualified business units (QBUs) in one or more foreign countries. A QBU is defined as any separate and clearly identified unit of a trade or business of a taxpayer that maintains separate books and records (Code Sec. 989(b)). The rules for determining the amount of business profits attributable to a QBU will be set forth in regulations (discussed below) (Code Sec. 904(d)(2)(J)(i), as added by the 2017 Tax Cuts Act).

## NEW LAW EXPLAINED

> **Comment:** The income of a foreign branch is subject to U.S. tax and a foreign tax credit may be claimed. If the foreign branch is located in a high-tax country, absent the new foreign tax credit limitation basket, those taxes could offset taxes paid in low-tax countries in the general category basket. The addition of the new basket also means that carrybacks and carryforwards of excess foreign tax credits in the foreign branch company basket will be allowed only to the extent of the excess limitation in the basket.

The additional foreign tax credit limitation basket does not apply to income of the foreign branch that is passive category income (Code Sec. 904(d)(2)(J)(ii)).

> **Caution:** According to the Joint Committee on Taxation's report on the 2017 Tax Cuts Act, a technical correction may be required to reflect the intent that although business profits of a QBU do not include passive category income, financial services income attributable to a QBU shall not be treated as passive category income (General Explanation of Public Law 115-97 (JCS-1-18)).

Passive category income includes passive income and specified passive income (Code Sec. 904(d)(2)(A)(i);Reg. §1.904-4(b)(1)). Passive income is generally any type of income that would qualify as subpart F income foreign personal holding company income under Code Sec. 954(c) if the recipient was a controlled foreign corporation (CFC) (e.g., dividends, interest, rents, royalties, and annuities). Specified passive category income includes dividends from a domestic international sales corporation (DISC) or former DISC and distributions from a former foreign sales corporation (FSC) (Code Sec. 904(d)(2)(v); Reg. §1.904-4(b)(3)).

> **Comment:** Passive category income is typically low-taxed income that would not be subject to cross-crediting.

> A new separate foreign tax credit limitation basket was also added for global intangible low-taxed income (see ¶735).

**Proposed regulations on foreign branch category income.** Proposed regulations address several revisions to Code Sec. 904 related to the additional foreign branch category of income, such as transition rules for carryover and carryback of unused taxes and recapture of SLLs (separate limitation losses, OFLs (Overall Foreign Losses), and ODLs (Overall Domestic Losses); foreign branch category income defined and attributable gross income; and, disregarded transactions and reallocation of gross income (Proposed Reg. §§1.904-2, 1.904-4, 1.904-5, and 1.904-6; NPRM REG-105600, November 28, 2018).

*Carryovers of unused foreign taxes.* Because the Tax Cuts and Jobs Act (P.L. 115-97) does not provide transition rules for carryover of unused taxes, the proposed regulations generally preserve pre-2018 categories under Code Sec. 904 that are carried forward into post-2017 tax years. However, the proposed regulations allow for taxpayers to allocate foreign tax credit carryforwards in the general income category to the post-2017 foreign branch income category to the extent the taxes would have been assigned to the foreign branch income category had the taxes been paid or accrued in a post-2017 tax year (Proposed Reg. §1.904-2(j)(1)(ii)). Conversely, unused foreign taxes in the foreign branch and general income category incurred in a post-2017 tax

## NEW LAW EXPLAINED

year and carried back to a pre-2018 tax year are to be allocated to the pre-2018 general income category (Proposed Reg. § 1.904-2(j)(1)(iii)).

*Separate Limitation Losses, Overall Foreign Losses, and Overall Domestic Losses.* Similar to the transition rules for carryforward and carryback of unused foreign taxes, the proposed regulations also provide rules for recapture of pre-2018 separate limitation loss (SLL), overall foreign loss (OFL), and overall domestic loss (ODL). Pre-2018 SLL or OFL accounts in the passive income category remain in the passive income category post-2017. Pre-2018 SLL or OFL accounts in the general income category are allocated to the post-2017 foreign branch and general income category in the same proportion used to allocate pre-2018 unused taxes between post-2017 categories. As such, for taxpayers that do not apply the exception in Proposed Reg. § 1.904-2(j)(1)(iii), all pre-2018 SLL or OFL accounts for general category income will remain in the general category. Similar rules are provided for the recapture of pre-2018 SLLs or ODLs and the foreign loss portion of a pre-2018 net operating loss (Proposed Reg. § 1.904(f)-12(j)).

*Gross income in the category.* Foreign branch category income is defined as the business profits of a United States person attributable to a QBU in a foreign country, excluding passive category income (Code Sec. 904(d)(2)(J)). Because the definition limits foreign branch income to the income of a United States person, foreign taxpayers cannot have foreign branch income. Accordingly, a domestic partnership with distributable income attributable to a foreign branch cannot be foreign branch income to foreign partners. To avoid potential conflict, the proposed regulations provide for that foreign branch category income be defined as the gross income of a United States person (other than a pass-through entity) that is attributable to foreign branches held directly or indirectly through disregarded entities by the United States person (Proposed Reg. § 1.904-4(f)(1)(i)).

Generally gross income is attributable to a foreign branch to the extent it is reflected on the foreign branch's separate set of books and records. These items of gross income must then be adjusted to conform with federal income tax principles. Several additional rules are provided for adjusting gross income attributable to a foreign branch from what is reflected on the foreign branch's separate set of books and records, including:

- gross income attributable to a foreign branch does not include items arising from activities carried out in the United States (Proposed Reg. § 1.904-4(f)(2));

- gross income attributable to a foreign branch does not include income from stock, including dividends and gain on disposition of stock, and income included under Code Sec. 951(a), Code Sec. 951A(a), or Code Sec. 1293(a) (Proposed Reg. § 1.904-(f)(2)(iii)(A));

- exclusion of gain realized by a foreign branch owner on disposition of an interest in a disregarded entity, a partnership, or other pass-through entity (Proposed Reg. § 1.904-4(f)(2)(iv)(B));

**¶725**

## NEW LAW EXPLAINED

- addition of an anti-abuse rule providing for reattribution of gross income if a principal purpose of recording, or failing to record, an item on the books and records of the foreign branch is avoidance of federal income tax (Proposed Reg. § (1.904-4(f)(v)(2)); and,

- adjustment of gross income attributable to a foreign branch that is not passive category income to reflect certain transactions that are disregarded for federal income tax purposes, such as transactions between a foreign branch and its foreign branch owner, and transactions between or among foreign branches involving payments that would otherwise be deductible or capitalized (Proposed Reg. § 1.904-4(f)(2)(vi)).

*Look through rules.* The Code Sec. 904(d)(3) look-through rules apply solely for payments allocable to the passive category and that any other payment described in Code Sec. 904(d)(3) be assigned to a separate non-passive category under Reg. § 1.904-4 (Proposed Reg. § 1.960-5).

*Allocation and Apportionment of Foreign Taxes.* Clarification is provided that base differences are generally a limited occurrence, as in the case of categories of items such as life insurance proceeds or gifts, which are excluded from income for federal income tax purposes, but may be taxed under foreign tax laws (Proposed Reg. § 1.904-6(a)(1)(iv)). Also, foreign taxes are generally allocated and apportioned to separate categories by reference to the separate category of the income to which the foreign tax relates, however, the proposed regulations include special rules to coordinate existing regulations under Reg. § 1.904-6(a)(1) with the computation of foreign branch income in Proposed Reg. § 1.904-4(f) (Proposed Reg. § 1.904-(6)(a)(2)).

▶ **Effective date.** The amendments made by this section apply tax years beginning after December 31, 2017 (Act Sec. 14302(c) of the Tax Cuts and Jobs Act (P.L. 115-97)).

— Act Sec. 14302(a), of the Tax Cuts and Jobs Act (P.L. 115-97), amending Code Sec. 904(d)(1), as amended by Act Sec. 14201, by redesignating Code Sec. 904(d)(1)(B) and (C), as (C) and (D), respectively, and adding newCode Sec. 904(d)(1)(B);

— Act Sec. 14302(b)(1), adding Code Sec. 904(d)(2)(J);

— Act Sec. 14302(b)(2), amending Code Sec. 904(d)(2)(J), as amended by Act Sec. 14201.

— Act Sec. 14302(c), providing the effective date.

# ¶730 Source of Income Rules for Cross-Border Inventory Sales

## SUMMARY OF NEW LAW

Income from cross-border sales of inventory is sourced on the basis of the production activities.

## BACKGROUND

Income from the sale of inventory property that is produced by the taxpayer (in whole or in part) in the United States and sold outside of the United States (or vice versa) is sourced in part to the United States (U.S. source income) and in part outside of the United State (foreign source income). (Code Sec. 863(b)(2)). Income from the sales of inventory is first allocated between production activities and sales activities, using one of the following three methods: (1) 50-50 method (50 percent of the inventory sales income is sourced to the location of production and 50 percent of the inventory sales income is sourced to the location of sales), (2) independent factory price (IFP) method (taxpayer may establish an IFP to determine income from production), and (3) books and records method (with IRS permission, taxpayer may use books of account to make the allocation) (Reg. § 1.863-3(b)).

After the allocation is made, the source of the gross income attributable to the production activity is determined based on the location of the production assets. If production assets are located both in the United States and a foreign country, income is apportioned using a property fraction that takes into account the production assets at their adjusted tax basis (Reg. § 1.863-3(c)(1)).

The source of the gross income attributable to the sales activity is the place of sale, which is generally where the title passes (title passage rule) (Reg. § § 1.863-3(c)(2) and 1.861-7(c)). Under a special rule, property that is produced in the United States, but destined for a U.S. market, may be U.S.-source income even if title passes in a foreign country. The rule is intended to prevent taxpayers from producing goods in the United States, passing title to the goods in a foreign country and then selling the goods to U.S. customers. For the rule to apply, the property must be wholly produced in the United States, and must be for use, consumption or disposition within the United States (T.D. 8687; Reg. § 1.863-3(c)(2)).

## NEW LAW EXPLAINED

**Cross-border inventory sales sourced based on production activities.**—Gains, profits, and income from the sale or exchange of inventory property that is produced in whole or in part within the United States and sold outside of the United States (or vice versa) is allocated and apportioned between U.S. and foreign sources solely on the basis of the production activities with respect to the property (Code Sec. 863(b), as amended by the Tax Cuts and Jobs Act (P.L. 115-97)). Under the rule, if income is produced entirely in the United States, it is U.S. source income and income produced entirely in a foreign country is foreign source income. Inventory produced in both the United States and a foreign country is mixed-source income.

> **Comment:** Cross-border inventory sales will now be sourced without regard to the title passage rule. The title passage rule is seen as a means by which taxpayers can manipulate the source of income rules.

The current regulations, which provide rules for sourcing income attributable to production activity, should continue to apply with respect to determining where production activities are located and allocating and apportioning mixed-source income. The regulations provide rules for sourcing income attributable to production activity.

¶730

## NEW LAW EXPLAINED

Under the regulations, production activity means activity that creates, fabricates, manufactures, extracts, processes, cures or ages inventory. With some exceptions, the only production activities that are taken into account are those carried on by the taxpayer. The income attributable to production activities is sourced according to the location of the production assets, where the production activity is solely in the United States (Reg. § 1.863-3(c)(1)(i)(A)). Production assets include only tangible and intangible assets that are directly used by the taxpayer to produce inventory. Production assets do not include assets that are not directly used to produce inventory, such as accounts receivable, marketing intangibles, and customer lists (Reg. § 1.863-3(c)(1)(i)(B)).

If there is production both inside and outside of the United States, the regulations provide that the source of the income is determined by multiplying the income attributable to the production activities by the ratio of the average adjusted basis of the production assets located outside of the United States to the total adjusted basis of all production assets. The remaining income is U.S. source income (Reg. § 1.863-3(c)(1)(ii)).

▶ **Effective date.** The amendment made by this section applies to tax years beginning after December 31, 2017 (Act Sec. 14303(b) of the Tax Cuts and Jobs Act (P.L. 115-97)).

**No significant guidance related to this provision has been issued.**

— Act Sec. 14303(a) of the Tax Cuts and Jobs Act (P.L. 115-97), amending Code Sec. 863(b);

— Act Sec. 14303(b), providing the effective date.

# CFCs AND SUBPART F INCOME

## ¶735 Global Intangible Low-Taxed Income (GILTI) of U.S. Shareholders and Foreign Derived Intangible Income (FDII) Deduction

### SUMMARY OF NEW LAW

A current year inclusion of global intangible low-taxed income (GILTI) by a person who is a U.S. shareholder of a controlled foreign corporation (CFC) is required. Domestic corporations are provided with reduced rates of U.S. tax on their foreign-derived intangible income (FDII) and GILTI.

### BACKGROUND

In general, foreign income earned by a foreign subsidiary of a U.S. corporation is not subject to U.S. tax until it has been distributed to its U.S. parent in the form of a dividend. These dividends less credits obtained for foreign income taxes paid are regarded as taxable income of the U.S. corporation. The primary exception to the deferral of U.S. tax is the subpart F rules (Code Secs. 951-965).

## BACKGROUND

A U.S. parent corporation is typically subject to current U.S. tax on subpart F income earned by its foreign subsidiaries and earnings invested by the subsidiaries in U.S. property, minus any foreign income taxes paid on that income. The federal corporate tax rates apply to the U.S. corporation's taxable income irrespective of whether the income is from tangible or intangible property.

For the subpart F rules to apply, the corporation must be a controlled foreign corporation (CFC), with substantial U.S. shareholders, meaning generally, those who own 10 percent or more of the voting stock of the foreign corporation (Code Sec. 951). However, the amount included in gross income under subpart F for any given year is limited to the current earnings and profits. The amount of the subpart F inclusions are reduced, in certain circumstances, by deficits in earnings and profits (Code Sec. 952(c)). This treatment differs from the normal rules for domestic corporations which treat any distribution for the year as a dividend to the extent of current earnings and profits, regardless of offsetting deficits in prior years.

A U.S. corporation owning at least 10 percent of the voting stock of a foreign corporation from which it receives dividends is treated as if it had paid a share of the foreign taxes paid by the foreign corporation in the year in which that corporation's earnings and profits become subject to U.S. tax as dividend income of the U.S. corporation. This is called the deemed-paid or indirect foreign tax credit (Code Sec. 902; Reg. §1.78-1(a)). A U.S. corporation also gets a deemed credit with respect to amounts included in gross income that are attributable to deemed inclusions of a CFC's earnings and profits (Code Sec. 960).

A 10 percent-or-more U.S. shareholder of a CFC must report as a dividend the shareholder's pro rata share of the corporation's earnings and profits accumulated in tax years (beginning after 1962) in which the stock was held. The report must also be made upon disposition of the U.S. shareholder's stock, and the dividend cannot be greater than the gain on disposition (Code Sec. 1248). The earnings and profits of the foreign corporation function as a limitation on the amount treated as a dividend.

### NEW LAW EXPLAINED

**Global intangible low-taxed income and foreign-derived intangible income.**—A person who is a U.S. shareholder of any controlled foreign corporation (CFC) is required to include its global intangible low-taxed income (GILTI) in gross income for the tax year in a manner generally similar to that for subpart F inclusions (Code Sec. 951A(a) and (f), as added by the Tax Cuts and Jobs Act (P.L. 115-97)). Specifically, GILTI that is included in gross income is treated in the same manner as amounts included under Code Sec. 951(a)(1)(A) when applying:

- Code Sec. 168(h)(2)(B) (exception from ACRS for certain property subject to U.S. tax that is used by a foreign person or entity);
- Code Sec. 535(b)(10) (adjustments to taxable income for CFCs);
- Code Sec. 851(b) (limitations on definition of a regulated investment company);
- Code Sec. 904(h)(1) (source rules for U.S. owned foreign corporations for purposes of the limitation on the foreign tax credit);

## NEW LAW EXPLAINED

- Code Sec. 959 (exclusion from gross income of previously taxed earnings and profits);

- Code Sec. 961 (adjustments to the basis of stock held in a CFC by a U.S. shareholder);

- Code Sec. 962 (election by individuals to be taxed at corporate rates);

- Code Sec. 993(a)(1)(E) (treatment of dividends with respect to the stock of a related foreign export corporation as qualified export receipts);

- Code Sec. 996(f)(1) (allocation rules for DISC income);

- Code Sec. 1248(b)(1) (limitation on the tax applicable to individuals on the pro rata share of taxes paid by a foreign corporation);

- Code Sec. 1248(d)(1) (exclusion from earnings and profits of a foreign corporation);

- Code Sec. 6501(e)(1)(C) (substantial omission of constructive dividends);

- Code Sec. 6654(d)(2)(D) (treatment of subpart F and possession credit income for the purposes of a failure by an individual to pay estimated income tax);

- Code Sec. 6655(e)(4) (treatment of subpart F and possession credit income for the purposes of a failure by a corporation to pay estimated income tax) (Code Sec. 951A(f)(1)(A), as added by the 2017 Tax Cuts Act).

Determining the GILTI inclusion amount begins with the calculation of certain items of the CFC, including tested income (i.e., the CFC's gross income with certain exclusions), tested loss, qualified business asset investment (QBAI) (i.e., average adjusted basis, determined quarterly, in tangible depreciable property, used in the trade or business and to produce tested income), net deemed tangible income return, and specified interest expense (Code Sec. 951A(b), as added by the 2017 Tax Cuts Act).

The U.S. shareholder determines its pro rata share of each of the CFC-level items under the rules that apply to subpart F income. The amounts are taken into account by the shareholder in determining the GILTI included in the shareholder's gross income. The shareholder will then compute a single GILTI inclusion amount by reference to all of its CFCs (Code Sec. 951A(e), as added by the 2017 Tax Cuts Act).

Specifically, the U.S. shareholder aggregates (and then nets or multiplies) its pro rata share of each item into a single shareholder-level item. For example, aggregated tested income is reduced by aggregated tested loss, and results in net CFC tested income (Code Sec. 951A(c), as added by the 2017 Tax Cuts Act). Aggregate QBAI multiplied by 10 percent becomes deemed tangible income return (Code Sec. 951A(b)(2)(A), as added by the 2017 Tax Cuts Act)).

A U.S. shareholder's GILTI inclusion amount for the tax year is determined by subtracting one aggregate U.S. shareholder-level amount from another. The shareholder's net deemed tangible income return (net DTIR) is the excess of the deemed tangible

## NEW LAW EXPLAINED

income return over certain interest expense. The GILTI inclusion amount is the excess of net CFC tested income over net DTIR (Code Sec. 951A(b) and (b)(2), as added by the 2017 Tax Cuts Act)).

> **Comment:** In comparison to the GILTI computation, subpart F income is determined at the CFC level and then included in the gross income of the U.S. shareholder according to the U.S. shareholder's pro rata share of the income. Computation of the U.S. shareholder's pro rata share of the CFC's subpart F income is generally the last step in the process. The amounts are taken into account on a CFC-by-CFC basis. Determining the GILTI inclusion amount on the basis of all of the U.S. shareholder's CFCs ensures that the U.S. shareholder is taxed on GILTI, wherever it is derived.

The total amount of GILTI included by a U.S. shareholder is allocated across all CFCs with respect to which it is a U.S. shareholder. The allocation is required in order to coordinate with the other provisions of subpart F. The portion of the GILTI treated as being allocable to a CFC is zero for a CFC with no tested income. For CFCs with tested income, the portion of GILTI allocated to a CFC is determined by multiplying the GILTI by the U.S. shareholder's pro rata share of the CFC's tested income divided by the aggregate amount of the U.S. shareholder's pro rata share of tested income of each CFC (Code Sec. 951A(f)(2), as added by the 2017 Tax Cuts Act; Proposed Reg. § 1.951A-6(b)(2)). The GILTI that is allocated to a CFC is treated as an amount included in the gross income of a U.S. shareholder under Code Sec. 951(a)(1)(A) for purposes of the previously taxed earnings and profits rules of Code Sec. 959. The IRS has previewed regulations it intends to issue on previously taxed earnings and profits (Notice 2019-1).

The Treasury may issue rules and other guidance to assist in coordinating the GILTI inclusion with provisions that require the determination of subpart F income at the CFC level (Code Sec. 951A(f)(1)(B), as added by the 2017 Tax Cuts Act). Proposed regulations provide general rules for computing the GILTI inclusion and associated definitions. The proposed regulations generally are proposed to apply to tax years of foreign corporations beginning after December 31, 2017, and to tax years of U.S. shareholders in which or with which such tax years of foreign corporations end (NPRM REG-104390-18, October 10, 2018). The proposed regulations also cover:

- anti-abuse rules;
- consolidated groups;
- domestic partners and partnerships; and
- basis adjustments for tested loss.

Separate proposed regulations issued on the foreign tax credit and related rules for allocating and apportioning expenses for purposes of the foreign tax credit limitation take into account the GILTI provisions and the deduction for FDII. The proposed regulations that relate to the Tax Cuts and Jobs Act generally are proposed to apply to tax years beginning after December 22, 2017 (NPRM REG-105600-18, December 7, 2018).

¶735

## NEW LAW EXPLAINED

The IRS has also previewed regulations it intends to issue on the previously taxed earnings and profits rules of Code Sec. 959, required in part due to the new inclusion under Code Sec. 951A (Notice 2019-1).

**GILTI defined.** The term "global intangible low-taxed income" is defined as the excess (if any) of:

- the U.S. shareholder's net CFC tested income for that tax year, over
- the U.S. shareholder's net deemed tangible income return for that tax year (Code Sec. 951A(b)(1), as added by the 2017 Tax Cuts Act; Proposed Reg. §1.951A-1(c)(1)).

*Net deemed tangible income return.* The term "net deemed tangible income return" means with respect to any U.S. shareholder for the tax year, the excess (if any) of:

- 10 percent of the aggregate of its pro rata share of the qualified business asset investment (QBAI) of each CFC in which it is a U.S. shareholder for the tax year, over
- the amount of interest expense taken into account in determining its net CFC tested income for the tax year to the extent that the interest expense exceeds the interest income properly allocable to the interest expense that is taken into account in determining its net CFC tested income (Code Sec. 951A(b)(2), as added by the 2017 Tax Cuts Act; Proposed Reg. §1.951A-1(c)(3)).

  **Comment:** The formula for calculating GILTI is: GILTI = Net CFC Tested Income − [(10% × QBAI) − Interest Expense]. If the amount of interest expense exceeds 10% × QBAI, then the quantity in brackets in the formula equals zero in the GILTI determination (Conference Report on H.R. 1, Tax Cuts and Jobs Act (H. Rept. 115-466)).

*Net CFC tested income and loss.* A CFC's tested income for any tax year is the gross income of the corporation in excess of the properly allocated deductions (including taxes) (Code Sec. 951A(c)(2)(A), as added by the 2017 Tax Cuts Act; Proposed Reg. §1.951A-2). The corporation's gross income is determined without regard to the following:

- effectively connected income of the CFC, defined in Code Sec. 952(b);
- gross income taken into account in determining subpart F income;
- gross income excluded from foreign base company income and insurance income as high-taxed income under Code Sec. 954(b)(4);
- dividends received from related persons, defined in Code Sec. 954(d)(3); and
- foreign oil and gas extraction income, as defined in Code Sec. 907(c)(1).

A CFC with tested income for a CFC inclusion year is referred to as "a tested income CFC" (Proposed Reg. §1.951A-2(b)(1)).

A CFC's tested loss for any tax year is the excess of the properly allocated deductions over the CFC's tested income (Code Sec. 951A(c)(2)(B), as added by the 2017 Tax Cuts Act). A CFC without tested income for a CFC inclusion year is referred to as "a tested loss CFC" (Proposed Reg. §1.951A-2(b)(2)).

## NEW LAW EXPLAINED

A U.S. shareholder's income inclusion under Code Sec. 951A is not subject to limitation based on the earnings and profits (E&P) of its CFCs for the tax year in Code Sec. 952(c)(1)(A). A CFC's E&P may be increased, however, by the amount of a tested loss for purposes of applying the limitation in Code Sec. 952(c)(1)(A) in order to deny a double benefit of losses (Code Sec. 951A(c)(2)(B)(ii); Proposed Reg. §1.951A-6(d)).

The term "net CFC tested income" means with respect to a U.S. shareholder for any tax year of the shareholder, the excess (if any) of (1) the aggregate of the shareholder's pro rata share of the tested income of each CFC with respect to which the shareholder is a U.S. shareholder for the tax year of the U.S. shareholder, over (2) the aggregate of the shareholder's pro rata share of the tested loss of each CFC with respect to which the shareholder is a U.S. shareholder for the tax year of the U.S. shareholder. The amounts are determined for each tax year of the CFC which ends in or with such tax year of the U.S. shareholder (Code Sec. 951A(c)(1), as added by the 2017 Tax Cuts Act; Proposed Reg. §1.951A-1(c)(2)).

> **Comment:** The definition of a U.S. shareholder was expanded by the 2017 Tax Cuts Act to include a U.S. person that owns at least 10 percent of the total value of all classes of stock of the foreign corporation, in addition to a U.S. person that owns at least 10 percent of the voting stock of the foreign corporation. The definition applies for purposes of the entire Internal Revenue Code, not just subpart F (Code Secs. 951(b) and 957(a), as amended by the 2017 Tax Cuts Act).

**Qualified business asset investment (QBAI).** The term "qualified business asset investment" is defined by reference to specified tangible property that is used in a trade or business and is depreciable under Code Sec. 167. Specified tangible property is property used in the production of tested income, unless the rule for dual use property applies. Specifically, QBAI is the CFC's average aggregate adjusted bases in the property as of the close of each quarter of the tax year (Code Sec. 951A(d)(1), as added by the 2017 Tax Cuts Act; Proposed Reg. §1.951A-3(b) and (c)). Dual-use property is property used both in the production of gross tested income and income that is not gross tested income. The percentage of a domestic corporation's adjusted basis in dual-use property that is included in QBAI equals the gross tested income produced with respect to the property divided by the total gross income produced with respect to the property (Code Sec. 951A(d)(2)(B), as added by the 2017 Tax Cuts Act; Proposed Reg. §1.951A-3(d)).

The adjusted basis of the property is determined using the alternative depreciation system (ADS) under Code Sec. 168(g) and allocating depreciation deductions for the property ratably to each day during the period in the tax year to which the depreciation relates (Code Sec. 951A(d)(3), as added by the 2017 Tax Cuts Act; Proposed Reg. §1.951A-3(e)(1)).

Under the proposed regulations, the adjusted basis of property placed in service before December 22, 2017 (the date of enactment), is determined using ADS, as if this system had applied from the date the property was placed in service (Proposed Reg. §1.951A-3(e)(3)).

## NEW LAW EXPLAINED

The proposed regulations provide a methodology to reduce the QBAI of a CFC with a short tax year to an amount that, if annualized, would produce an amount of QBAI equal to the QBAI for a 12-month tax year (Proposed Reg. § 1.951A-3(f)).

Further, if a CFC holds an interest in a partnership at the end of the CFC's tax year, the CFC takes into account its distributive share of the aggregate of the partnership's adjusted basis in tangible property held by the partnership to the extent that the property is used in the trade or business of the partnership, is of a type to which a deduction is allowed under Code Sec. 167, and is used in the production of tested income. The CFC's distributive share of the adjusted basis of any property is the CFC's distributive share of income with respect to the property (Code Sec. 951A(d)(3)[sic], as added by the 2017 Tax Cuts Act; Conference Report on H.R. 1, Tax Cuts and Jobs Act (H. Rept. 115-466); Proposed Reg. § 1.951A-3(g)).

The proposed regulations clarify that the CFC partner's share of the partnership's adjusted basis in the specified tangible property is determined by reference to the partnership's average adjusted basis in the property, as of the close of each quarter of the partnership's tax year that ends with or within the CFC's tax year (Proposed Reg. § 1.951A-3(g)(3)). Additionally, a CFC partner determines its share of the partnership's average adjusted basis in the property based on the amount of its distributive share of the gross income produced by the property that is included in the CFC partner's gross tested income relative to the total amount of gross income produced by the property (Proposed Reg. § 1.951A-3(g)(2)).

Under an anti-abuse rule in the proposed regulations, specified tangible property of a tested income CFC is disregarded for purposes of determining the tested income CFC's average aggregate basis in specified tangible property if the tested income CFC:

- acquires the property with a principal purpose of reducing the GILTI inclusion; and

- holds the property temporarily, but over at least the close of one quarter (Proposed Reg. § 1.951A-3(h)(1)).

Property that is held for less than a 12 month period that includes at least the close of one quarter during the tax year of a tested income CFC is treated as temporarily held and acquired for a principal purpose of reducing the GILTI inclusion.

An additional anti-abuse rule disallows the benefit of stepped-up basis in specified tangible property transferred between related CFCs during the period before the transferor CFC's first inclusion year for purposes of calculating the transferee CFC's QBAI (Proposed Reg. § 1.951A-3(h)(2)).

**Interest expense.** Specified interest expense reduces 10 percent of the aggregate of the U.S. shareholder's pro rata share of the QBAI of each CFC in calculating the U.S. shareholder's net deemed tangible income return (DTIR), to the extent the interest income attributable to the expense is not taken into account in determining the U.S. shareholder's net CFC tested income (Code Sec. 951A(b)(2)(B), as added by the 2017 Tax Cuts Act; Proposed Reg. § 1.951A-1(c)(3)(i)). Specified interest expense is the excess, if any, of:

## NEW LAW EXPLAINED

- the aggregate of the shareholder's pro rata share of the tested interest expense of each CFC, for the year, over

- the aggregate of the shareholder's pro rata share of the tested interest income of each CFC for the year (Proposed Reg. §1.951A-1(c)(3)(iii)).

Tested interest expense and tested interest income are generally defined by reference to all interest expense and interest income that is taken into account in determining a CFC's tested income or loss (Proposed Reg. §1.951A-4(b)(1) and (2)).

**Pro rata share.** A shareholder's pro rata share for purposes of determining GILTI and net CFC tested income is determined under the rules of Code Sec. 951(a)(2) with respect to subpart F income. The pro rata shares are taken into account in the U.S. shareholder's tax year in which or with which the CFC's tax year ends (Code Sec. 951A(e)(1), as added by the 2017 Tax Cuts Act; Proposed Reg. §1.951A-1(d)).

A person is treated as a U.S. shareholder of a CFC only if the person owns, within the meaning of Code Sec. 958(a) (direct or indirect ownership) stock in the foreign corporation on the last day of the foreign corporation's tax year on which the foreign corporation is a CFC (Code Sec. 951A(e)(2), as added by the 2017 Tax Cuts Act). A foreign corporation is treated as a CFC for any tax year if the foreign corporation is a CFC at any time during the tax year (Code Sec. 951A(e)(3), as added by the 2017 Tax Cuts Act).

The proposed regulations modify the rules for determining pro rata share under Code Sec. 951(a)(2) (Proposed Reg. §1.951-1(e)). In determining pro rata share, earnings and profits of the tax year are first hypothetically distributed among the classes of stock and then to each share in the class, based on a hypothetical distribution date (i.e., the last day of the CFC's tax year on which it was a CFC). Transactions or arrangements are disregarded if they are part of a plan, a principal purpose of which is to reduce a U.S. shareholder's pro rata share of the subpart F income of a CFC (Proposed Reg. §1.951-1(e)(6)).

In applying the rules to determine a U.S. shareholder's pro rata share of the CFC's tested income, the same rules generally apply (Proposed Reg. §1.951A-1(d)(2)(i)). Because tested income is not limited to the earnings and profits of the CFC, and because a CFC's tested loss increases its earnings and profits for purposes of determining the subpart F income limitation in Code Sec. 952(c)(1), the earnings and profits allocated in the hypothetical distribution may exceed the earnings and profits of the CFC computed under Code Sec. 964. Accordingly, the hypothetical distribution in the proposed regulations is based on the greater of the Code Sec. 964 earnings and profits or the sum of the subpart F income (increased by reason of any tested loss add-back under Code Sec. 951A(c)(2)(B)(ii); Proposed Reg. §1.951A-6(d)) and tested income of the CFC.

In determining a U.S. shareholder's pro rata share of the CFC's QBAI, the amount of the QBAI distributed in the hypothetical distribution is generally proportionate to the amount of the CFC tested income distributed in the hypothetical distribution. There is a cap on QBAI allocated to preferred stock (10 times tested income). The excess is allocated to common stock (Proposed Reg. §1.951A-1(d)(3), Examples 1 and 2; Proposed Reg. §1.951-1(e)(7), Example 6).

¶735

# NEW LAW EXPLAINED

In determining a U.S. shareholder's pro rata share of the CFC's tested loss, the amount distributed in the hypothetical distribution is the amount of tested loss, rather than the CFC's current earnings and profits, and the tested loss is distributed solely with respect to the CFC's common stock, with a limited exception (Proposed Reg. § 1.951A-1(d)(4)).

A U.S. shareholder's pro rata share of tested interest expense of a CFC for the U.S. shareholder's inclusion year is equal to the amount by which the tested interest expense reduces the shareholder's pro rata share of tested income of the CFC for the U.S. shareholder's inclusion year, increases the shareholder's pro rata share of the tested loss of the CFC for the U.S. shareholder's inclusion year, or both (Proposed Reg. § 1.951A-1(d)(5)).

A U.S. shareholder's pro rata share of tested interest income of a CFC for the U.S. shareholder's inclusion year is equal to the amount by which the tested interest income increases the shareholder's pro rata share of tested income of the CFC for the U.S. shareholder's inclusion year, reduces the shareholder's pro rata share of the tested loss of the CFC for the U.S. shareholder's inclusion year, or both (Proposed Reg. § 1.951A-1(d)(6)).

**Basis adjustments for tested losses.** New basis adjustment rules are provided when a tested loss of a CFC is used (Proposed Reg. § 1.951A-6(e)). A corporate U.S. shareholder (excluding REITs and RICs) generally must reduce the basis of the stock of a CFC by the amount of tested loss that has been used to offset tested income in calculating the shareholder's net CFC tested income, when determining gain, loss or income on the direct or indirect disposition of CFC stock. The basis adjustment applies only to the extent that a net tested loss of the CFC has been used. Additionally:

- basis adjustments may also apply to a tested loss CFC treated as owned by the U.S. shareholder through certain intervening foreign entities by reason of Code Sec. 958(a)(2);

- ordering rules apply for making adjustments when a direct disposition of CFC stock results in the indirect disposition of stock in lower-tier CFCs;

- rules prevent the elimination or avoidance of basis adjustments through nonrecognition transactions involving CFCs; and

- rules address dispositions of CFC stock by another CFC that is not wholly owned by a single domestic corporation.

The basis adjustment rules were added to prevent the inappropriate results that can occur when a U.S. shareholder's pro rata share of the tested loss of one CFC offsets the shareholder's pro rata share of the tested income of another CFC in determining the shareholder's GILTI inclusion amount and the stock of the tested loss CFC is disposed of. Absent basis adjustments to the stock, the U.S. shareholder could recognize a second, duplicative benefit from the loss, either through the recognition of a loss or a reduction in gain.

**Rules for consolidated groups.** New rules are added on the computation of GILTI by a consolidated group. A consolidated group member's GILTI amount is determined by reference to the relevant items of each CFC owned by members of the same

## NEW LAW EXPLAINED

consolidated group. The GILTI inclusion amount of a member for a U.S. shareholder inclusion year is the excess (if any) of the member's net CFC tested income for the U.S. shareholder inclusion year, over the member's net deemed tangible income return for the U.S. shareholder inclusion year (Proposed Reg. § 1.1502-51(b) and (e)). Specifically, to determine a member's GILTI inclusion amount:

- the pro rata shares of tested loss, QBAI, tested interest expense, and tested interest income of each member are aggregated; and

- a portion of each aggregate amount is allocated to each member of the group that is a U.S. shareholder of a tested income CFC based on the proportion of (i) the member's aggregate pro rata share of tested income to (ii) the total tested income of the consolidated group.

Special rules are provided for adjusting the basis of the stock of a CFC owned by a member immediately before its disposition (Proposed Reg. § 1.1502-51(c)). The proposed rules also provide for adjustments to the basis of the stock of a member (Proposed Reg. § 1.1502-32(b)(3)(ii)(E), (b)(3)(ii)(F), and (b)(3)(iii)(C)). For this purpose, a portion of a member's offset tested income amount is treated as tax-exempt income, and all of a member's used tested loss amount is treated as a noncapital, nondeductible expense.

In addition, a special rule treats a member as receiving tax-exempt income immediately before another member recognizes income, gain, deduction, or loss with respect to a share of the first member's stock (Proposed Reg. § 1.1502-32(b)(3)(ii)(F)). The amount of this additional tax-exempt income is:

- the net offset tested income amount allocable to the shares of any CFC owned by the first member, to the extent that

- a distribution of this amount would have been treated as a dividend eligible for the Code Sec. 245A participation exemption deduction.

This special rule reduces the incentives for a sale of the stock of a CFC over a sale of stock of a member, since gain recognized on the disposition of CFC stock attributable to offset tested income would, in most cases, be eliminated to the extent the gain is eligible for the participation exemption deduction.

**New rules for domestic partnerships and partners.** The statute does not contain specific rules on domestic partnerships and their partners that directly or indirectly own the stock of CFCs. However, the IRS has issued proposed regulations on how a domestic partnership and its partners compute the GILTI inclusion amounts (Proposed Reg. § 1.951A-5). The guidance also applies to S corporations and their shareholders, that are treated as partnerships and partners for purposes of the subpart F rules (Code Sec. 1373).

In applying the rules, neither a pure aggregate or pure entity approach is taken. A domestic partnership is treated as an entity with respect to partners that are not U.S. shareholders of any CFC owned by the partnership. The partnership is treated as an aggregate for purposes of partners that are themselves U.S. shareholders with respect to one or more CFCs owned by the partnership.

¶735

## NEW LAW EXPLAINED

The approach ensures that each non-U.S. shareholder partner takes into income its distributive share of the domestic partnership's GILTI inclusion amount, while permitting a partner that is itself a U.S. shareholder to determine a single GILTI inclusion amount by reference to all of its CFCs. Additionally, a corporate U.S. shareholder partner will be able to calculate a foreign tax credit under Code Sec. 960(d) with respect to each CFC, and compute a Code Sec. 250 deduction with respect to its GILTI inclusion amount by reference to each CFC.

In general, a domestic partnership that is a U.S. shareholder of one or more CFCs ("a U.S. shareholder partnership") computes its own GILTI inclusion amount in the same manner as any other U.S. shareholder, and each partner takes into account its distributive share of the partnership's GILTI inclusion amount under Code Sec. 702 and Reg. § 1.702-1(a)(8)(ii) (Proposed Reg. § 1.951A-5(b)).

A partner that is itself a U.S. shareholder of a CFC owned by a domestic partnership computes its GILTI inclusion amount for the tax year by taking into account its proportionate share of the partnership's pro rata share of each of the relevant items of the CFC (e.g., tested income, tested loss, QBAI, tested interest income, and tested interest expense) (Proposed Reg. § 1.951A-5(c)).

**Foreign tax credit.** Foreign tax credits are allowed for foreign income taxes paid on GILTI included in the gross income of a domestic corporation. The foreign income taxes paid are restricted to 80 percent of the product of the domestic corporation's inclusion percentage multiplied by the aggregate tested foreign income taxes paid or accrued by CFCs. The inclusion percentage is the ratio (which is expressed as a percentage) of the corporation's GILTI divided by the aggregate amounts of the shareholder's pro rata share of the tested income of each CFC with respect to which the shareholder is a U.S. shareholder for the shareholder's tax year (Code Sec. 960(d), as added by the 2017 Tax Cuts Act; Proposed Reg. § § 1.960-1, 1.960-2, and 1.960-3).

Under the provision, these are considered deemed-paid credits for taxes properly attributed to tested income, and a separate foreign tax credit basket is created for GILTI (see ¶725) (Code Sec. 904(d)(1)(A), as added by the 2017 Tax Cuts Act). No carryforward or carryback of excess taxes paid or accrued is permitted (Code Sec. 904(c), as amended by the 2017 Tax Cuts Act; Proposed Reg. § 1.904-2(a)).

Look-through payments (e.g. dividends, interest, rents and royalties) paid to a U.S. shareholder by its CFC are generally allocated to general category income to the extent not treated as passive category income (Code Sec. 904(d)(3)(A)). A GILTI inclusion that is allocable to passive category income under the look-through rules is excluded from GILTI category income (Proposed Reg. § 1. 904-5(c)(6)).

> **Comment:** A passive category GILTI inclusion could arise from a CFC's distribution of partnership income in which the CFC owns less than 10 percent of the value in the partnership.

The proposed regulations apply the existing approach of expense allocation to determine taxable income in the Code Sec. 951A separate foreign tax credit limitation category (GILTI category income). However, gross income that is offset by the FDII deduction under Code Sec. 250 (see below) is treated as exempt income, and stock or other assets giving rise to the income is treated as a partially exempt asset (Proposed Reg. 1.861-8(d)(2)(ii)(C)).

## NEW LAW EXPLAINED

> **Comment:** This provision has the effect of reducing the amount of expenses apportioned to the GILTI category income, because expenses are not allocated and apportioned to tax-exempt assets (Code Sec. 864(e)(3)). Fewer expenses allocated to the category results in higher foreign source taxable income in the category and a higher foreign tax credit limitation.

The proposed regulations also include rules for allocating and apportioning the Code Sec. 250 deduction. The portion of the Code Sec. 250 deduction is treated as definitely related and allocable to a specific class of gross income that is included in the taxpayer's foreign-derived deduction eligible income, defined in Code Sec. 250(b)(4) (Proposed Reg. 1.861-8(e)(13)). A similar rule applies for the portion of the deduction allowed for the GILTI inclusion and Code Sec. 78 gross up (Proposed Reg. §1.861-8(e)(14)).

**Reporting requirements.** U.S. shareholders must file Schedule I-1 (Form 5471) and Form 8992 to provide the information needed to determine the U.S. shareholder's GILTI inclusion amount for a tax year. Schedule I-1 is used to report information determined at the CFC level with respect to amounts used to determine the income inclusions of the U.S. shareholder under Code Sec. 951A.

The U.S. shareholder will use the information on the schedule to complete and file Form 8992. A U.S. shareholder files Form 8992, Schedule A, to report its pro rata share of amounts for each CFC from each CFC's Schedule I-1, to determine the U.S. shareholder's GILTI, if any, and to determine the amount of the U.S. shareholder's GILTI, if any, allocated to each CFC (Instructions for Form 5471 and Instructions for Form 8992). The information may also be used to compute foreign tax credits on Form 1118 and Form 1116. Failure to file Form 8992 will result in penalties. The penalties will increase if the failure to file continues for more than 90 days after the notice of failure is mailed ($10,000) and additional penalties are imposed for each 30-day period, up to $50,000 (Code Sec. 6038; Proposed Reg. §1.6038-5(c)).

A U.S. shareholder partnership must include on its Schedule K-1 (Form 1065) information to determine a partner's distributive share of the partnership's GILTI inclusion amount, or a U.S. shareholder partner's own GILTI inclusion amount (Proposed Reg. §1.951A-5(f)).

**Deduction for FDII and GILTI.** Domestic corporations are provided with reduced rates of U.S. tax on foreign-derived intangible income (FDII) and global intangible low-taxed income (GILTI). For tax years beginning after December 31, 2017, and before January 1, 2026, a deduction is generally allowed in an amount equal to the sum of: (1) 37.5 percent of its FDII, plus (2) 50 percent of its GILTI, if any, and the amount treated as a dividend received by the corporation under Code Sec. 78 and attributable to its GILTI (Code Sec. 250(a)(1), as added by the 2017 Tax Cuts Act). For tax years beginning after December 31, 2025, the deduction for FDII is 21.875 and 37.5 percent for GILTI (Code Sec. 250(a)(3), as added by the 2017 Tax Cuts Act).

The amount of the deduction is limited based on taxable income. If the sum of a domestic corporation's FDII and GILTI amounts exceeds its taxable income, then the amount of the FDII and GILTI deduction is similarly reduced by an amount determined by the excess. The reduction in the amount of the FDII for which a deduction

## NEW LAW EXPLAINED

is allowed equals the excess multiplied by a percentage equal to the FDII divided by the sum of the FDII and GILTI. The reduction in the GILTI for which a deduction is allowed equals the remainder of the excess (Code Sec. 250(a)(2), as added by the 2017 Tax Cuts Act).

> **Comment:** According to the Joint Committee on Taxation, the taxable income limitation is determined by also including the GILTI-attributable Code Sec. 78 gross-up amount. A technical correction may be needed. For example, assume a domestic corporation has $1,250 of FDII, $650 of GILTI, $100 of GILTI-attributable Code Sec. 78 gross-up, and taxable income (determined without regard to Code Sec. 250) of $1,500. The sum of the corporation's FDII, GILTI, and GILTI-attributable Code Sec. 78 gross-up is $2,000, which exceeds $1,500 taxable income by $500. The amount of FDII for which a deduction is allowed is reduced by $500 multiplied by $1,250/$2,000, or $312.50. The sum of the amount of GILTI and GILTI-attributable Code Sec. 78 gross-up amounts for which a deduction is allowed is reduced by the remainder of the excess, or $187.50 ($500 × $750/$2,000) (General Explanation of Public Law 115-97 (JCS-1-18)). See ¶720 for general discussion of the Code Sec. 78 gross-up.

**FDII defined.** A domestic corporation's foreign-derived intangible income (FDII) is the portion of its intangible income, determined according to a codified formula, that is derived from serving foreign markets. This means income derived in connection with property that is sold by the taxpayer to any person who is not a U.S. person and that such property is for foreign use, consumption or disposition that is not within the United States (Code Sec. 250(b), as added by the 2017 Tax Cuts Act).

A domestic corporation's FDII is generally its deemed intangible income multiplied by the percentage of its deduction-eligible income that is foreign derived: FDII = Deemed Intangible Income × [Foreign-Derived Deduction Eligible Income divided by Deduction Eligible Income]. Deduction eligible income means the excess of the gross income of the domestic corporation over deductions (including taxes) properly allocated to gross income (Code Sec. 250(b)(3), as added by the 2017 Tax Cuts Act). The corporation's gross income is determined without taking into account certain types of income. These exceptions include:

- Subpart F income of the corporation determined under Code Sec. 951;
- GILTI of the corporation;
- Financial services income of the corporation;
- Dividends received from a CFC with respect to which the corporation is a U.S. shareholder;
- Domestic oil and gas extraction income of the corporation; and
- Foreign branch income of the corporation.

> **Comment:** According to the Joint Committee on Taxation, a technical correction may be needed to add exceptions for (1) income received or accrued that is personal holding company income under Code Sec. 954(c), and (2) amounts included in the corporation's gross income under Code Sec. 1293 with respect to a qualified electing fund (General Explanation of Public Law 115-97 (JCS-1-18)).

## NEW LAW EXPLAINED

Deemed intangible income is the excess of the deduction eligible income over the deemed tangible income return of the corporation. Deemed tangible income return is 10 percent of the corporation's QBAI under Code Sec. 951A(d) (discussed above), but determined by substituting "deduction eligible income" for "tested income" and without regard to whether the corporation is a CFC (Code Sec. 250(b)(2), as added by the 2017 Tax Cuts Act).

Foreign-derived deduction eligible income means deduction eligible income derived in connection with: (1) property sold by the taxpayer to any person who is not a U.S. person if the taxpayer satisfies the IRS that the property was for foreign use, or (2) services provided by the taxpayer if the taxpayer satisfies the IRS that the services are provided to any person, or with respect to any property, not located in the United States (Code Sec. 250(b)(4), as added by the 2017 Tax Cuts Act).

Special rules apply for determining foreign use, including rules for related parties. Foreign use is any use, disposition or consumption that is not within the United States (Code Sec. 250(b)(5)(A), as added by the 2017 Tax Cuts Act). Property that is sold to domestic intermediaries (but not related parties) for further manufacture or modification in the United States is not treated as sold for foreign use even if it is subsequently used for foreign use (Code Sec. 250(b)(5)(B)(i), as added by the 2017 Tax Cuts Act). Services that are provided to another person (not a related party) located in the United States are not treated as services for foreign use even if the other person uses the services in providing services for foreign use (Code Sec. 250(b)(5)(B)(ii), as added by the 2017 Tax Cuts Act).

If property is sold to a related party who is not a U.S. person, that sale will not be treated as a sale for foreign use unless:

- the property is ultimately sold by a related party (or used by a related party in connection with property that is sold or services provided) to another unrelated party who is not a U.S. person; and

- the taxpayer establishes that the property is for foreign use (Code Sec. 250(b)(5)(C), as added by the 2017 Tax Cuts Act).

Income derived in connection with services provided to a related party who is not located in the United States is not treated as foreign-derived deduction eligible income unless the taxpayer establishes that the service is not substantially similar to services provided by the related party to persons located in the United States (Code Sec. 250(b)(5)(C)(ii), as added by the 2017 Tax Cuts Act).

A related party is any member of an affiliated group, as defined in Code Sec. 1504(a), where corporations are connected through the ownership of a common parent, except that, for purposes of this provision, ownership is determined by owning more than 50 percent of the vote or value of the stock of one or more of the corporations included in the affiliated group (Code Sec. 250(b)(5)(D), as added by the 2017 Tax Cuts Act). Any person (except for a corporation) is treated as a member of the affiliated group if the person is controlled by members of the group or if the person controls a member of the group. Control is determined under Code Sec. 954(d)(3).

¶735

## NEW LAW EXPLAINED

The Treasury may issue regulations or other guidance as necessary (Code Sec. 250(c), as added by the 2017 Tax Cuts Act). (At the time this publication went to press, no significant guidance related to this provision had been issued.) Proposed regulations have been issued on the allocation of the deduction for purposes of the foreign tax credit limitation (discussed above).

> **Comment:** According to clarifications and modifications provided in the Conference Agreement, the deduction for FDII and GILTI is only available to C corporations that are not RICs or REITs. Further, the deduction for GILTI applies to the amount treated as a dividend received by a domestic corporation under Code Sec. 78 that is attributable to the corporation's GILTI amount under new Code Sec. 951A (Conference Report on H.R. 1, Tax Cuts and Jobs Act (H. Rept. 115-466)).

**FDII deduction illustrated.** The Joint Committee on Taxation has provided an example of the FDII calculation.

---

**Example:** A domestic corporation USCo has only $5,000 of gross deduction eligible income and $2,000 of deductions allocable to that gross income. USCo's deduction eligible income is its gross deduction eligible income less deductions allocable to that income, or $5,000 − $2,000 = $3,000. Assume that USCo establishes that $1,200 of its deduction eligible income is foreign-derived, and that USCo has $10,000 of QBAI.

USCo's deemed intangible income equals its deduction eligible income minus a 10 percent return on its QBAI, or $3,000 − (10 percent × $10,000) = $2,000.

USCo's FDII is its deemed intangible income multiplied by the percentage of its deduction eligible income that is foreign-derived, or $2,000 × ($1,200/$3,000) = $800. USCo is allowed a deduction of 37.5 percent on its FDII of $800, or $300.

USCo's taxable income, less the deduction for FDII, is $3,000 - $300 = $2,700. Under a 21-percent corporate tax rate (see ¶305), USCo's tax liability is $567 (21 percent × $2,700). Therefore, the deduction for FDII has reduced the effective tax rate on USCo's pre-deduction taxable income of $3,000 from 21 percent to 18.9 percent ($567/ $3,000) (General Explanation of Public Law 115-97 (JCS-1-18)).

---

**Reporting requirements.** Form 8993, is used to figure the amount of the eligible deduction for FDII and GILTI under Code Sec. 250. The form is attached to the income tax return and must be filed by the due date of the return (including extensions) (Instructions for Form 8993).

Form 5472, requires that transactions that qualify for foreign-derived deduction eligible income (FDDEI) for a domestic corporation be identified (Instructions for Form 5472). The penalty for failure to furnish information or maintain records is increased from $10,000 to $25,000 after 2017 (Code Sec. 6038A(d)).

▶ **Effective date.** The GILTI provisions apply to tax years of foreign corporations beginning after December 31, 2017, and to tax years of U.S. shareholders in which or with which such

## NEW LAW EXPLAINED

tax years of foreign corporations end (Act Sec. 14201(d) of the Tax Cuts and Jobs Act (P.L. 115-97)). The deduction for foreign-derived intangible income and GILTI provisions apply to tax years beginning after December 31, 2017 (Act Sec. 14202(c) of the 2017 Tax Cuts Act).

— Act Sec. 14201(a) of the Tax Cuts and Jobs Act (P.L. 115-97), adding new Code Sec. 951A;

— Act Sec. 14201(b), adding new Code Sec. 960(d), redesignating Code Sec. 904(d)(1)(A) and (B) as (B) and (C), respectively, and adding new (A), and amending Code Sec. 904(c) and (d)(2)(A)(ii);

— Act Sec. 14202(a), adding new Code Sec. 250;

— Act Sec. 14202(b), amending Code Secs. 172(d), 246(b)(1), and 469(i)(3)(F)(iii);

— Act Sec. 14201(d) and Act Sec. 14202(c), providing the effective dates.

# ¶737  Foreign Base Company Oil Related Income

## SUMMARY OF NEW LAW

Foreign base company oil related income is eliminated as a category of foreign base company income and so is no longer subpart F income.

## BACKGROUND

Under the subpart F rules, certain income earned by a foreign corporation that is a controlled foreign corporation (CFC) may be currently taxed to U.S. shareholders, even though the earnings are not distributed to the shareholder (Code Secs. 951-965). In general, a CFC is any foreign corporation with respect to which U.S. shareholders own more than 50 percent of the total combined voting power of all classes of stock entitled to vote or the total value of the stock of the corporation (Code Sec. 957). The foreign corporation must be a CFC for an uninterrupted period of 30 days or more during the tax year (Code Sec. 951(a)). A U.S. shareholder is any U.S. person who owns 10 percent or more of the total combined voting power of all classes of stock of the foreign corporation (Code Sec. 951(b)).

Subpart F income is one of the categories of income currently taxed (Code Sec. 951(a)(1)(A)). One of the main categories of subpart F income is foreign base company income (Code Sec. 952). Foreign base company income is made up of several subcategories of income, one of which is foreign base company oil related income (Code Sec. 954(g)).

Foreign base company oil related income is foreign oil related income (FORI) or taxable income derived outside of the United States and its possessions from:

• the processing of minerals extracted from oil and gas wells into their primary products;

• the transportation of the minerals or primary products;

• the distribution or sale of the minerals or primary products;

## BACKGROUND

- the disposition of assets used by the taxpayer in its trade or business, described above; or

- the performance of any related service (Code Sec. 907(c)(2)).

Foreign oil related income also includes dividends and interest from a foreign corporation for which taxes are deemed paid under Code Sec. 902 or Code Sec. 960 and a taxpayer's distributable share of partnership income, to the extent the amounts are attributable to FORI (Code Sec. 907(c)(3)).

Foreign base company oil related income does not include oil related income of a CFC from sources within a foreign country where the oil or gas was extracted (extraction exception) or within the foreign country where the oil or gas is used or consumed (or is loaded in the foreign country on a vessel or aircraft as fuel for the vessel or aircraft) (use or consumption exception) (Code Sec. 954(g)(1)). Foreign base company oil related income does not include any income of a foreign corporation that is not a large oil producer (i.e., produces 1,000 barrels a day or more) (Code Sec. 954(g)(2)).

## NEW LAW EXPLAINED

**Foreign base company oil related income eliminated from foreign base company income.**—Foreign oil related income is eliminated as a category of foreign base company income. Thus, U.S. shareholders of controlled foreign corporations (CFCs) are no longer required to include this type of income in gross income as subpart F income (Code Sec. 954(a), as amended by the Tax Cuts and Jobs Act (P.L. 115-97)). Foreign base company oil related income was defined as income of a foreign corporation and large oil producer (i.e., producer of 1,000 barrels a day or more) that is foreign oil related income (FORI), defined in Code Sec. 907(c)(2) and (c)(3).

Foreign base company oil related income did not include oil related income of a CFC from sources within a foreign country where the oil or gas was extracted (extraction exception) or within the foreign country where the oil or gas is used or consumed (or is loaded in the foreign country on a vessel or aircraft as fuel for the vessel or aircraft) (use or consumption exception) (Code Sec. 954(g), prior to being stricken by the 2017 Tax Cuts Act).

> **Comment:** According to the House Committee Report, the foreign base company oil related income rules were not necessary in the context of the other international tax reforms. Moving to the participation exemption system could put U.S. oil and gas companies at a competitive disadvantage because of the loss of the Code Sec. 902 credit (see ¶705). Additionally, separate anti-base erosion rules under the bill (see ¶750 et seq.) make the separate anti-base erosion rules for oil and gas operations unnecessary (House Committee Report for the Tax Cuts and Jobs Act (P.L. 115-97) (H. R. Rep. No. 115-409)).

> **Comment:** Worksheet A, Summary of U.S. Shareholder's Pro Rata Share of Subpart F Income of a CFC, found in the Form 5471 Instructions (Rev. December 2018), has been modified to reflect this change.

## NEW LAW EXPLAINED

▶ **Effective date.** The amendments made by this section apply to tax years of foreign corporations beginning after December 31, 2017, and to tax years of U.S. shareholders with or within which such tax years of foreign corporations end (Act Sec. 14211(c) of the Tax Cuts and Jobs Act (P.L. 115-97)).

**No significant guidance related to this provision has been issued.**

— Act Sec. 14211(a) of the Tax Cuts and Jobs Act (P.L. 115-97), amending Code Sec. 954(a)(2) and (3), and striking Code Sec. 954(a)(5);

— Act Sec. 14211(b), amending Code Sec. 952(c)(1)(B)(iii) and Code Sec. 954(b)(4) and (5), and striking Code Sec. 954(b)(6) and (g); and

— Act Sec. 14211(c), providing the effective date.

# ¶741  Subpart F Inclusions for Withdrawal of Qualified Investments

## SUMMARY OF NEW LAW

The subpart F inclusion for a CFC's previously excluded subpart F income withdrawn from foreign base company shipping operations is repealed. Also repealed is the subpart F inclusion for amounts withdrawn from qualified investment in less developed countries and decreases in export trade assets.

## BACKGROUND

Prior to 1987, the subpart F rules partially favored shipping income. Code Sec. 954(b)(2), prior to repeal by the Tax Reform Act of 1986 (P.L. 99-514), provided a deferral from tax for foreign base company shipping income that was reinvested in foreign base company shipping operations. The exclusion applied only with respect to "qualified investments". After the repeal of the provision, taxpayers could not exclude foreign base company shipping income by making qualified investments. However, while total excluded income could not be increased, previously excluded income was not subject to tax until income was withdrawn from foreign base company shipping operations.

A U.S. shareholder of a controlled foreign corporation (CFC) must include in its gross income its pro rata share of amounts of the corporation's subpart F income previously excluded that are withdrawn from foreign base company shipping operations (Code Sec. 951(a)(1)(A)(iii)). The amount of previously excluded subpart F income withdrawn from qualified investments in foreign base company shipping operations is generally equal to the decrease in investments in foreign base company shipping operations for the tax year (Code Sec. 955).

The foreign base company income category for foreign base company shipping income was eliminated after December 31, 2004, by the American Jobs Creation Act of 2004 (P.L. 108-357). Parallel rules applied to qualified investments in less devel-

## BACKGROUND

oped countries for the years 1962 through 1975 (i.e., generally stock and long-term debt obligations of less developed country corporations) (Code Secs. 955, as in effect prior to the Tax Reduction Act of 1975 (P.L. 94-12), and 951(a)(1)(A)(ii); Reg. § 1.955-1).

An export trade corporation is a CFC that sells abroad products that it produces, manufactures, grows or extracts abroad. These corporations are allowed to reduce foreign base company income by the portion of their income that is export trade income (i.e., income derived from export trade activities). The provision was partially repealed in that any corporation that qualified as an export trade corporation for any year beginning before November 1, 1971, can continue to be treated as a export trade corporation if it does not fail to qualify as an export trade corporation for three consecutive tax years (Code Secs. 970 and 971). If export trade income is deferred, it must be included in a U.S. shareholder's gross income under Code Sec. 951(a)(1)(A)(ii) if there is a decrease in export trade assets.

## NEW LAW EXPLAINED

**Subpart F inclusions for withdrawal of qualified investments repealed.**—The rules for determining a U.S. shareholder's pro rata share of the controlled foreign corporation's previously excluded subpart F income withdrawn from qualified investment in foreign base shipping operations are repealed (Act Sec. 14212(a) of the Tax Cuts and Jobs Act (P.L. 115-97), striking Code Sec. 955). The U.S. shareholder's corresponding subpart F inclusion for the decrease in investment in foreign base company shipping operations is repealed. Also repealed are the provisions requiring a subpart F inclusion for:

- a U.S. shareholder's pro rata share of the corporation's previously excluded subpart F income withdrawn from investment in less developed countries, and

- a decrease in export trade assets, with respect to deferred export trade income (Code Sec. 951(a)(1)(A), as amended by the 2017 Tax Cuts Act and Act Sec. 14213(b)(5), striking Code Sec. 970(b)).

  **Comment:** The House Committee Report states that because foreign base company shipping income is no longer taxed under subpart F, a corresponding decrease in the CFC's investment should not result in an income inclusion for a U.S. shareholder of the CFC (House Committee Report for the Tax Cuts and Jobs Act (P.L. 115-97) (H.R. Rep. No. 115-409)).

  **Comment:** Modifications to Form 5471 have been made to reflect this change. Old Line 3 of Schedule I, Summary of Shareholder's Income From Foreign Corporation, is deleted. Old Worksheet C, U.S. Shareholder's Pro Rata Share of Previously Excluded Subpart F Income of a CFC Withdrawn From Qualified Investments in Less Developed Countries and From Qualified Investments in Foreign Base Company Shipping Operations, is deleted. Old Worksheet D is now Worksheet C, U.S. Shareholder's Pro Rata Share of Previously Excluded Export Trade Income of a CFC Withdrawn From Investment in Export Trade Assets.

¶741

## NEW LAW EXPLAINED

▶ **Effective date.** The amendments made by this section apply to tax years of foreign corporations beginning after December 31, 2017, and to tax years of U.S. shareholders in which or with which such tax years of foreign corporations end (Act Sec. 14212(c) of the Tax Cuts and Jobs Act (P.L. 115-97)).

**No significant guidance related to this provision has been issued**.

— Act Sec. 14212(a) of the Tax Cuts and Jobs Act (P.L. 115-97), striking Code Sec. 955;

— Act Sec. 14212(b), amending Code Secs. 951(a)(1)(A), 851(b), 952(c)(1)(B)(i), 953(c)(1)(C), 953(d)(4)(B)(iv)(II), and 964(b), and striking Code Secs. 951(a)(3) and 970(b);

— Act Sec. 14212(c), providing the effective date.

## ¶743  CFC Stock Attribution Rules

### SUMMARY OF NEW LAW

Stock ownership may be attributed downward from a foreign person to a related U.S. person for purposes of determining whether a U.S. person is a U.S. shareholder of a corporation, such that the foreign corporation is a CFC.

### BACKGROUND

Direct, indirect and constructive ownership is used to determine whether a U.S. person is a U.S. shareholder with respect to a foreign corporation, such that the foreign corporation is a controlled foreign corporation (CFC), and for other provisions of subpart F (Code Sec. 958). Only the direct and indirect ownership rules, however, are used to determine the percentage of stock owned by a U.S. shareholders in computing the amount of the subpart F inclusion. Under the indirect stock ownership rules, stock that is owned directly by a foreign entity, such as a foreign corporation, foreign partnership or foreign estate, is considered to be owned indirectly by the shareholders, partners or beneficiaries, in proportion to their ownership in the entity. Attribution stops with the first U.S. person in the chain of ownership (Code Sec. 958(a)).

Constructive ownership takes into account stock actually owned by related persons. The rules of constructive ownership in Code Sec. 318(a) apply, with certain modifications (Code Sec. 958(b)).

The general constructive ownership rules provide rules for attributing stock ownership to an entity ("to attribution" rules of Code Sec. 318(a)(3)). Under these rules, stock owned, by or for, a partner or beneficiary of an estate is treated as owned by the partnership or estate. Stock owned, directly or indirectly, by or for a beneficiary of a trust is treated as owned by the trust, with special rules for contingent interest and grantor trusts. A corporation is considered as owning all of the stock owned directly or indirectly, by or for any person holding 50 percent or more in value of the corporation's stock, directly or indirectly. These rules are modified so that they

## BACKGROUND

cannot be applied to treat a U.S. person as owning stock owned by a person who is not a U.S. person (Code Sec. 958(b)(4); Reg. § 1.958-2(d)(2)).

> **Example:** Foreign Corporation A owns 100 percent of one class of stock of Domestic Corporation B and 100 percent of one class of stock of another Foreign Corporation C. Under the modified rule, Domestic Corporation B is not considered as owning the stock owned by its sole shareholder Foreign Corporation A, in Foreign Corporation C (Reg. § 1.958-2(g), Example 4).

## NEW LAW EXPLAINED

**CFC constructive stock ownership attribution rule modified.**—The modified constructive ownership rule of Code Sec. 958(b)(4), which precludes the attribution rules of Code Sec. 318(a)(3) from applying when stock of a foreign person would be treated as owned by a U.S. person, is eliminated. Elimination of this provision allows for the downward attribution of stock ownership from a foreign person to a related U.S. person (Code Sec. 958(b), as amended by the Tax Cuts and Jobs Act (P.L. 115-97)).

> **Example:** Foreign Corporation A owns 100 percent of one class of stock of Domestic Corporation B and 100 percent of one class of stock of another Foreign Corporation C. Under the constructive ownership rule, Domestic Corporation B is considered as owning the stock owned by its sole shareholder Foreign Corporation A, in Foreign Corporation C.

**Comment:** According to the Conference Committee Report, the reason for modifying the constructive stock ownership rule is to prevent the avoidance of the subpart F rules by turning off the constructive stock ownership rules that would otherwise treat a U.S. person as owning the stock of a foreign person. This type of avoidance transaction converts former CFCs to non-CFCs despite continuous ownership by U.S. shareholders (Conference Report on H.R. 1, Tax Cuts and Jobs Act (H. Rept. 115-466)). The subpart F inclusion amount continues to be determined based on direct or indirect ownership of the CFC, without application of the new downward attribution rule.

**Comment:** Form 5471 requires U.S. shareholders of a controlled foreign corporation (CFC) to file an information return with respect to its CFC ownership (Code Sec. 6038(a)). A U.S. shareholder is defined in Code Sec. 951(b) and the U.S. shareholder's ownership is determined based on direct and indirect ownership in Code Sec. 958(a) and constructive ownership under Code Sec. 958(b). The inclusion of income under the subpart F rules is based on the direct and indirect ownership rules of Code Sec. 958(a) and without application of the downward attribution rules.

## NEW LAW EXPLAINED

The Form 5471 Instructions provide an exception from filing for Category 1 and Category 5 filers when ownership is based on the downward attribution rules. The exception applies if no U.S. shareholder (including the U.S. person) owns, within the meaning of Code Sec. 958(a) stock in the foreign corporation, and the foreign corporation is a specified foreign corporation or CFC solely because one or more U.S. persons is considered to own stock of the foreign corporation owned by a foreign person under the downward attribution rules of Code Sec. 318(a)(3).

▶ **Effective date.** The amendments made by this section apply to: (1) the last tax year of foreign corporation, beginning before January 1, 2018, and each subsequent tax year of such foreign corporations, and (2) tax years of U.S. shareholders in which or with which such tax years of foreign corporations end (Act Sec. 14213(b) of the Tax Cuts and Jobs Act (P.L. 115-97)).

**No significant guidance related to this provision has been issued..**

— Act Sec. 14213(a) of the Tax Cuts and Jobs Act (P.L. 115-97), amending Code Sec. 958(b) and striking Code Sec. 958(b)(4);

— Act Sec. 14213(b), providing the effective date.

# ¶745  Definition of U.S. Shareholder

## SUMMARY OF NEW LAW

The definition of a U.S. shareholder is expanded to include a shareholder who owns 10 percent or more of a foreign corporation's stock by value. The definition of a U.S. shareholder now applies for purposes of the Internal Revenue Code.

## BACKGROUND

Under the subpart F rules, certain income earned by a foreign corporation that is a controlled foreign corporation (CFC) may be currently taxed to U.S. shareholders, even though the earnings are not distributed (Code Secs. 951-965). In general, a CFC is any foreign corporation with respect to which U.S. shareholders own more than 50 percent of the total combined voting power of all classes of stock entitled to vote or the total value of the stock of the corporation (Code Sec. 957). The foreign corporation must be a CFC for an uninterrupted period of 30 days or more during the tax year (Code Sec. 951(a)). A U.S. shareholder is any U.S. person who owns directly, indirectly, or constructively, 10 percent or more of the total combined voting power of all classes of stock of the foreign corporation (Code Sec. 951(b)).

## NEW LAW EXPLAINED

**Definition of U.S. shareholder expanded.**—The definition of a U.S. shareholder is expanded to include a U.S. shareholder who owns 10 percent or more of the foreign corporation's stock by value. A U.S. shareholder is defined as any U.S. person who owns directly, indirectly, or constructively:

- 10 percent or more of the total combined voting power of all classes of stock of the foreign corporation, or

- 10 percent or more of the total value of shares of all classes of stock of the foreign corporation (Code Sec. 951(b), as amended by the Tax Cuts and Jobs Act (P.L. 115-97)).

The definition of a U.S. shareholder also applies for purposes of the Internal Revenue Code, and not just the subpart F provisions. Proposed Reg. § 1.951-1(g)(1) reflects the modifications to the definition of U.S. shareholder, for purposes of Code Sec. 951 through Code Sec. 964. The proposed regulation applies to tax years beginning after December 31, 2017, and to tax years of U.S. shareholders with or within which such tax years of foreign corporations end (Proposed Reg. § 1.951-1(i)).

The Joint Committee on Taxation notes that a technical correction may be needed in order for the expanded definition to apply to dispositions of controlled foreign corporation (CFC) stock by U.S. shareholders under Code Sec. 1248. The provision currently states that it applies to U.S. shareholders that own 10 percent or more of the foreign corporation's voting stock (Code Sec. 1248(a); General Explanation of Public Law 115-97 (JCS-1-18)).

> **Comment:** Expanding the definition of a U.S. shareholder also expands the number of shareholders who will be subject to the subpart F rules. The definition of a U.S. shareholder now corresponds to the definition of a CFC in Code Sec. 957(a), which looks to vote or value.

> **Compliance Note:** The Instructions for Form 5471 have been updated as of December 2018 to reflect the revised definition of a U.S. shareholder for purposes of defining categories of filers.

See ¶747 for a discussion of the elimination of the 30-day required period of CFC status.

▶ **Effective date.** The amendment made by this section applies to tax years of foreign corporations beginning after December 31, 2017, and to tax years of U.S. shareholders with or within which such tax years of foreign corporations end (Act Sec. 14214(b) of the Tax Cuts and Jobs Act (P.L. 115-97)).

— Act Sec. 14214(a) of the Tax Cuts and Jobs Act (P.L. 115-97), amending Code Sec. 951(b);

— Act Sec. 14214(b), providing the effective date.

# ¶747   Required Period of CFC Status

## SUMMARY OF NEW LAW

The requirement that a foreign corporation must be a CFC for an uninterrupted period of 30 days or more before a U.S. shareholder is required to include amounts in gross income under subpart F is eliminated.

## BACKGROUND

If a foreign corporation is a controlled foreign corporation (CFC) for an uninterrupted period of at least 30 days during the tax year, U.S. shareholders of the CFC are subject to current taxation on the CFC's subpart F income, certain amounts of subpart F income withdrawn from investment and amounts determined under Code Sec. 956. In general, a CFC is any foreign corporation with respect to which U.S. shareholders own more than 50 percent of the total combined voting power of all classes of the stock entitled to vote or the total value of the stock of the corporation at any time during the tax year of the foreign corporation (Code Sec. 957). A U.S. shareholder is any U.S. person who owns directly, indirectly, or constructively, 10 percent or more of the total combined voting power of all classes of stock of the foreign corporation (Code Sec. 951(b)).

## NEW LAW EXPLAINED

**Required period of CFC status eliminated.**—In determining whether a U.S. shareholder is required to include amounts in income under subpart F, the required period that the controlled foreign corporation (CFC) must be controlled by U.S. shareholders is eliminated (Code Sec. 951(a)(1), as amended by the Tax Cuts and Jobs Act (P.L. 115-97)). The foreign corporation is no longer required to be a CFC for an uninterrupted period of 30 days or more during the tax year. Instead, if the foreign corporation is a CFC at any time during the tax year, U.S. shareholders must include amounts in income under subpart F.

> **Comment:** The provision now corresponds to the definition of a CFC in Code Sec. 957, which only requires that the stock ownership requirements be met on any day during the tax year. The House Committee Report states that the original purpose of the provision to facilitate tax administration is no longer necessary in light of technology that tracks owner and corporate tax attributes on a daily basis. It also states that the rule presents opportunities for taxpayers to structure transactions to avoid tax (House Committee Report for the Tax Cuts and Jobs Act (P.L. 115-97) (H. Rept. 115-409)).

See ¶745 for a discussion of the expanded definition of a U.S. shareholder.

**Effect on U.S. shareholder reporting.** The IRS has proposed amendments to the Code Sec. 951 regulations to eliminate the 30-day requirement (Proposed Reg. §1.951-1(a)). Under related information reporting rules, every U.S. person that is a U.S. shareholder of a CFC must complete Form 5471 and file it with their income tax

**NEW LAW EXPLAINED**

return (Code Sec. 6038; Reg. § 1.6038-2). The current rules require annual reporting by a U.S. shareholder who owns stock in a foreign corporation that is a CFC for an uninterrupted period of at least 30 days during the corporation's tax year.

The IRS has proposed regulations that would eliminate the 30-day CFC status requirement from the reporting rules. Under the proposed regulations, a U.S. person that controls a foreign corporation at any time during the foreign corporation's annual accounting period ending with or within the U.S. person's tax year must file Form 5471 (Proposed Reg. § 1.6038-2(a); Instructions for Form 5471).

Proposed Reg. § 1.951-1(a) is proposed to apply to tax years of foreign corporations beginning after December 31, 2017, and to tax years of U.S. shareholders with or within which such tax years of foreign corporations end (Proposed Reg. § 1.951-1(i)). Proposed Reg. § 1.6038-2(a) is proposed to apply to tax years of foreign corporations beginning on or after October 3, 2018 (Proposed Reg. § 1.6038-2(m)).

▶ **Effective date.** The amendment made by this section applies to tax years of foreign corporations beginning after December 31, 2017, and to tax years of U.S. shareholders with or within which such tax years of foreign corporations end (Act Sec. 14215(b) of the Tax Cuts and Jobs Act (P.L. 115-97)).

— Act Sec. 14215(a) of the Tax Cuts and Jobs Act (P.L. 115-97), amending Code Sec. 951(a)(1);

— Act Sec. 14215(b), providing the effective date.

# BASE EROSION PREVENTION

## ¶750  Base Erosion and Anti-Abuse Tax

**SUMMARY OF NEW LAW**

Applicable taxpayers with average gross receipts of at least $500 million over the past three years are required to pay tax equal to the base erosion minimum tax amount for the tax year. The base erosion minimum tax amount is generally derived by comparing 10 percent (five percent for tax years beginning in calendar year 2018) of the taxpayer's modified taxable income (determined by disregarding certain deductions with respect to base erosion payments made to foreign related persons) to the taxpayer's regular tax liability (reduced for certain credit amounts). For tax years beginning after December 31, 2025, the 10-percent rate is increased to 12.5 percent and the taxpayer's regular tax liability is reduced by the aggregate amount of allowable credits. An 11-percent rate and two percent base erosion percentage apply to taxpayers that are members of an affiliated group that includes a bank or registered securities dealer. In addition, new reporting requirements will require the collection of information regarding a taxpayer's base erosion payments, and the applicable penalty for failure to report is increased.

## BACKGROUND

Foreign corporations are subject to tax in the United States on their U.S.-source income. There are two systems in place to tax this income. Regular tax rates apply to income that is effectively connected with a U.S. trade or business (effectively connected income or "ECI"), and a 30-percent tax rate applies to non-effectively connected income (fixed or determinable annual or periodical gains, profits and income or "FDAP income") (Code Secs. 864 and 871). FDAP income is subject to withholding at the source and the 30-percent tax rate may be reduced by an applicable income tax treaty (Code Secs. 871 and 881). ECI is subject to similar rules that apply to the business income of U.S. persons. Deductions are available to reduce the amount of ECI that is subject to tax in the United States (Reg. § 1.874-1). As a result, foreign owned U.S. subsidiaries are able to reduce their U.S. tax liability through deductible payments of interest, royalties, management fees and reinsurance to related foreign parties (Code Secs. 871 and 881). These payments are thought to erode the U.S. tax base if they are subject to reduced or zero rates of tax withholding in the United States.

A domestic corporation that is 25-percent foreign owned must provide certain required information to the IRS on Form 5472 (Code Sec. 6038A). A corporation required to file Form 5472 must also maintain records (or cause another party to maintain records) necessary to determine the correct treatment of transactions with related parties (Code Sec. 6038A(a)). A corporation is 25-percent foreign owned if 25 percent or more of the total voting power or value of its stock is owned by at least one foreign person at any time during the tax year (Code Sec. 6038A(c)(1)).

A related party is: (1) any 25-percent foreign shareholder of the domestic "reporting corporation," (2) any person related (within the meaning of Code Sec. 267(b) and Code Sec. 707(b)(1)) to the reporting corporation or to a 25-percent foreign shareholder of the reporting corporation, or (3) any other person related to the reporting corporation within the meaning of Code Sec. 482 (Code Sec. 6038A(c)(2)). In addition, any foreign related party must agree to authorize the domestic reporting corporation to act as its agent for purposes of an IRS examination of books and records or for the service and enforcement of a summons with respect to any transaction that it has with the reporting corporation (Code Sec. 6038A(e)(1)). If the related party does not make the requisite agency authorization or substantially comply with a summons for records or testimony, a noncompliance penalty may apply.

## NEW LAW EXPLAINED

**Tax imposed on base erosion payments of taxpayers with substantial gross receipts.**—Applicable taxpayers are required to pay, for any tax year, a tax equal to the base erosion minimum tax amount for the year. The tax is paid in addition to any other income taxes imposed under Subtitle A of the Code (Code Sec. 59A(a), as added by the Tax Cuts and Jobs Act (P.L. 115-97)).

The base erosion minimum tax amount for any tax year is the excess, if any, of:

- 10 percent (five percent for tax years beginning in calendar year 2018) of the modified taxable income of the taxpayer for the tax year, over

## NEW LAW EXPLAINED

- the regular tax liability for the tax year reduced (but not below zero) by the excess, if any, of:

  — the credits allowed against regular tax liability under Chapter 1 of the Code, over

  — the sum of (i) the credit allowed under Code Sec. 38 (the general business credit) that is allocable to the research credit determined under Code Sec. 41(a), plus (ii) the portion of the applicable Code Sec. 38 credits that do not exceed 80 percent of the lesser of the amount of those credits or the base erosion minimum tax amount (Code Sec. 59A(b)(1), as added by the 2017 Tax Cuts Act).

For tax years beginning after December 31, 2025, for purposes of determining the base erosion minimum tax amount, the 10-percent rate is increased to 12.5 percent of the taxpayer's modified taxable income and the regular tax liability is reduced (but not below zero) by the aggregate amount of allowable credits, rather than the excess described in item (2), above, (Code Sec. 59A(b)(2), as added by the 2017 Tax Cuts Act).

Applicable taxpayers that are members of an affiliated group that includes a bank or registered securities dealer under section 15(a) of the Securities Exchange Act of 1934 are subject to an additional increase of one percentage point in the tax rates, discussed above (i.e., 11 percent for tax years beginning on or before December 31, 2025, and 13.5 percent for tax years beginning after December 31, 2025) (Code Sec. 59A(b)(3), as added by the 2017 Tax Cuts Act).

For purposes of the above computation, the applicable Code Sec. 38 credits are the credits allowed under Code Sec. 38 for the tax year that are properly allocable to:

- the low-income housing credit under Code Sec. 42(a);
- the renewable electricity production credit under Code Sec. 45(a);
- the investment credit under Code Sec. 46, but only to the extent it is properly allocable to the Code Sec. 48 energy credit (Code Sec. 59A(b)(4), as added by the 2017 Tax Cuts Act).

An applicable taxpayer's modified taxable income is determined by computing the taxpayer's taxable income under Chapter 1 for the tax year without regard to (i) any base erosion tax benefit with respect to any base erosion payment, or (ii) the base erosion percentage of any net operating loss deduction allowed under Code Sec. 172 for the tax year (Code Sec. 59A(c)(1), as added by the 2017 Tax Cuts Act).

> **Comment:** Proposed regulations (discussed below) provide guidance for determining whether a taxpayer is an applicable taxpayer for BEAT purposes and for computing the taxpayer's BEAT liability (NPRM REG-104259-18, December 21, 2018). The regulations are proposed to apply to tax years beginning after December 31, 2017, but taxpayers may rely on them until final regulations are issued.

**Base erosion payment.** A base erosion payment is any amount paid or accrued by a taxpayer to a foreign person that is a related party of the taxpayer and with respect to which a deduction is allowable under Chapter 1 of the Code (Code Sec. 59A(d)(1), as added by the 2017 Tax Cuts Act). These payments include any amount paid or accrued by the taxpayer to the related party in connection with the acquisition by the

## NEW LAW EXPLAINED

taxpayer from the related party of property of a character subject to the allowance of depreciation (or amortization in lieu of depreciation) (Code Sec. 59A(d)(2), as added by the 2017 Tax Cuts Act). A base erosion payment also includes any premium or other consideration paid or accrued by the taxpayer to a foreign person that is a related party of the taxpayer for any reinsurance payments taken into account under Code Secs. 803(a)(1)(B) or 832(b)(4)(A) (Code Sec. 59A(d)(3), as added by the 2017 Tax Cuts Act).

> **Comment:** Base erosion payments generally do not include any amount that constitutes reductions in gross receipts including payments for costs of goods sold (COGS). However, an exception applies for certain payments to expatriated entities, described below.

Base erosion payments include any amount that results in a reduction of gross receipts of the taxpayer that is paid or accrued by the taxpayer with respect to: (1) a surrogate foreign corporation that is a related party of the taxpayer, but only if such corporation first became a surrogate foreign corporation after November 9, 2017, or (2) a foreign person that is a member of the surrogate foreign corporation's expanded affiliated group (EAG) (Code Sec. 59A(d)(4), as added by the 2017 Tax Cuts Act).

> **Comment:** For this purpose, a surrogate foreign corporation is a foreign corporation that: (1) acquires (after March 4, 2003) substantially all of the properties held by a U.S. corporation, or substantially all of the properties constituting a trade or business of a domestic partnership, (2) after the acquisition, the U.S. corporation's former shareholders or the domestic partnership's former partners, own at least 60 percent of the stock (by vote or value) of the foreign acquiring corporation, and (3) the surrogate foreign corporation's EAG does not have substantial business activities in the country where that corporation is organized or created compared to the total business activities of the EAG (Code Sec. 7874(a)(2)(B)). A surrogate foreign corporation does not include a foreign corporation treated as a domestic corporation under Code Sec. 7874(b) (where the former shareholders of the U.S. corporation or the former partners of the domestic partnership hold 80 percent or more (by vote or value) of the stock of the foreign acquiring corporation after the transaction). The EAG includes the foreign acquiring corporation and all companies connected to it by a chain of greater than 50-percent ownership (Code Sec. 7874(c)(1)).

A base erosion payment does not include any amount paid or accrued by a taxpayer for services, if such services meet the requirements for eligibility for use of the services cost method described in Reg. §1.482-9, determined without regard to the requirement that the services not contribute significantly to fundamental risks of business success or failure, and if the payments for services have no markup component (Code Sec. 59A(d)(5), as added by the 2017 Tax Cuts Act).

**Exception for certain payments in the ordinary course of trade or business.** There is an exception provided for some types of payments made in the ordinary course of a trade or business. Under this exception, qualified derivative payments are generally not treated as base erosion payments (Code Sec. 59A(h)(1), as added by the 2017 Tax Cuts Act).

**¶750**

## NEW LAW EXPLAINED

A qualified derivative payment is any payment made by a taxpayer pursuant to a derivative where the taxpayer:

- recognizes gain or loss as if the derivative were sold for its fair market value (FMV) on the last business day of the tax year (and at additional times that are required by Title 26 or the taxpayer's method of accounting),
- treats any gain or loss recognized as ordinary, and
- treats the character of all items of income, deduction, gain or loss regarding a payment pursuant to the derivative as ordinary (Code Sec. 59A(h)(2)(A), as added by the 2017 Tax Cuts Act).

Payments are not treated as qualified derivative payments unless the taxpayer includes in the information required to be reported under Code Sec. 6038B(b)(2), information that is necessary to identify which payments are to be treated as qualified derivative payments and such other information as the Secretary of the Treasury determines necessary (Code Sec. 59A(h)(2)(B), as added by the 2017 Tax Cuts Act).

The rule for qualified derivative payments does not apply if the payment would be treated as a base erosion payment if it was not made pursuant to a derivative (including royalty, interest or service payments), or where a contract has derivative and nonderivative component and the payment is allocable to the nonderivative component (Code Sec. 59A(h)(3), as added by the 2017 Tax Cuts Act).

For these purposes, a derivative is any contract (including any option, forward contract, futures contract, short position, swap, or similar contract) whose value, or any payment or other transfer with respect to said contract, is (directly or indirectly) determined by reference to one or more of the following:

- any share of stock of a corporation,
- any evidence of indebtedness,
- any commodity which is actively traded,
- any currency,
- any rate, price, amount, index, formula, or algorithm (Code Sec. 59A(h)(4)(A), as added by the 2017 Tax Cuts Act).

A erivative does not include any items described above.

Except as otherwise provided by the Secretary, American depository receipts (and similar instruments), with respect to shares of stock in foreign corporations, are treated as shares of stock in such foreign corporations for purposes of Part VII, Subchapter A of Chapter 1 (Code Sec. 59A(h)(4)(B), as added by the 2017 Tax Cuts Act).

In addition, a derivative does not include any insurance, annuity, or endowment contract issued by an insurance company (to which subchapter L applies) or issued by any foreign corporation where subchapter L would apply if such foreign corporation were a domestic corporation (Code Sec. 59A(h)(4)(C), as added by the 2017 Tax Cuts Act).

## NEW LAW EXPLAINED

**Base erosion tax benefit.** A base erosion tax benefit includes:

- any deduction allowed under Chapter 1 for the tax year with respect to any base erosion payment;

- for base erosion payments made to purchase property subject to depreciation (or amortization in lieu of depreciation), any deduction allowed in Chapter 1 for depreciation (or amortization in lieu of depreciation) for the tax year with respect to the property acquired with the payment;

- in the case of reinsurance payments, any reduction under Code Sec. 803(a)(1)(B) in the gross amounts of premiums or other consideration on insurance, annuity contracts or indemnity insurance, and any deduction under Code Sec. 832(b)(4)(A) from the amount of gross premiums written on insurance contracts during the tax year for the premiums paid for reinsurance; and

- in the case of a payment with respect to a surrogate foreign corporation or a foreign member of that corporation's expanded affiliated group, any reduction in gross receipts with respect to that payment in computing the taxpayer's gross income for the tax year (Code Sec. 59A(c)(2)(A), as added by the 2017 Tax Cuts Act).

The base erosion tax benefit attributable to any base erosion payment on which tax is imposed by Code Secs. 871 and 881, and with respect to which tax has been deducted and withheld under Code Secs. 1441 and 1442, is not taken into account in computing modified taxable income or the base erosion percentage. However, the amount not taken into account in computing modified taxable income is reduced under rules similar to the rules under Code Sec. 163(j)(5)(B), as in effect before December 22, 2017, the date of the enactment of the 2017 Tax Cuts Act (which determines whether interest is treated as tax-exempt to the extent of a treaty reduction) (Code Sec. 59A(c)(2)(B), as added by the 2017 Tax Cuts Act).

For purposes of determining an applicable taxpayer's modified taxable income, in the case of a taxpayer to which Code Sec. 163(j) applies for the tax year, the reduction in the amount of interest for which a deduction is allowed by reason of that provision is treated as allocable first to interest paid or accrued to persons who are not related parties with respect to the taxpayer and then to related parties (Code Sec. 59A(c)(3), as added by the 2017 Tax Cuts Act).

**Base erosion percentage.** The base erosion percentage is the percentage, for any tax year, that is determined by dividing:

- the aggregate amount of base erosion tax benefits of the taxpayer for the tax year, by

- the aggregate amount of the deductions allowable to the taxpayer for the tax year, taking into account the base erosion tax benefits and disregarding: (i) any deduction allowed under Code Secs. 172, 245A or 250 for the tax year, (ii) any deduction for amounts paid or accrued for services to which the exception for the services cost method (described in Reg. §1.482-9) applies, and (iii) any deduction for qualified derivative payments that are not treated as a base erosion payment (Code Sec. 59A(c)(4), as added by the 2017 Tax Cuts Act).

**Applicable taxpayer.** The base erosion tax applies to applicable taxpayers. Applicable taxpayers include corporations, other than a regulated investment company (RIC), a

## NEW LAW EXPLAINED

real estate investment trust (REIT), or an S corporation, that have average annual gross receipts of at least $500 million over the past three tax years and a base erosion percentage of three percent or higher for the tax year (two percent for taxpayers that are members of an affiliated group that includes a bank or registered securities dealer) (Code Sec. 59A(e)(1), as added by the 2017 Tax Cuts Act).

In the case of a foreign person (that is, any person who is not a U.S. person) the gross receipts test generally only takes into account gross receipts that are taken into account in determining ECI. This rule does not apply to the gross receipts of any U.S. person that are aggregated with the gross receipts of a foreign person under the aggregation rules, discussed below. In determining gross receipts, rules similar to the rules of Code Sec. 448(c)(3)(B), (C), and (D) apply (Code Sec. 59A(e)(2), and (f), as added by the 2017 Tax Cuts Act).

Under the aggregation rules, persons treated as a single employer under Code Sec. 52(a) are treated as one person for purposes of determining the average annual gross receipts and the base erosion percentage, except that the exception for foreign corporations under Code Sec. 1563(b)(2)(C) is disregarded (Code Sec. 59A(e)(3), as added by the 2017 Tax Cuts Act).

> **Comment:** Accordingly, if a foreign person's gross receipts are aggregated with a U.S. person's gross receipts, the gross receipts of the U.S. person that are aggregated with the foreign person's gross receipts are not limited to the gross receipts taken into account in determining ECI.

**Related party.** For purposes of the base erosion tax rules, a related party is: (i) any 25-percent owner (of the vote or value) of the taxpayer, (ii) any person who is related to the taxpayer, or to any 25-percent owner (of the vote or value) of the taxpayer, within the meaning of Code Secs. 267(b) or 707(b)(1), and (iii) any other person related to the taxpayer within the meaning of Code Sec. 482 (Code Sec. 59A(g)(1), as added by the 2017 Tax Cuts Act).

A 25-percent owner with respect to any corporation is any person who owns at least 25 percent of: (i) the total voting power of all classes of stock of a corporation entitled to vote, or (ii) the total value of all classes of stock of the corporation (Code Sec. 59A(g)(2), as added by the 2017 Tax Cuts Act).

For purposes of determining a related party, the Code Sec. 318 constructive stock ownership rules apply to these related party rules except that "10-percent" is substituted for "50-percent" in Code Sec. 318(a)(2)(C), and Code Sec. 318(a)(3)(A), (B) and (C) do not apply to cause a U.S. person to own stock owned by a person who is not a U.S. person (Code Sec. 59A(g)(3), as added by the 2017 Tax Cuts Act).

**Regulatory authority.** The Secretary of the Treasury is authorized to prescribe such regulations or other guidance as may be necessary or appropriate to carry out this provision, including regulations providing for such adjustments to the application of this provision necessary to prevent avoidance of the provision, including through: (1) the use of unrelated persons, conduit transactions, or other intermediaries, or (2) transactions or arrangements designed in whole or in part: (a) to characterize payments otherwise subject to this provision as payments not subject to this provision, or (b) to substitute payments not subject to this provision for payments otherwise

**NEW LAW EXPLAINED**

subject to this provision. The regulations or other guidance may also include regulations for the application of the related party rules, including rules to prevent the avoidance of the exceptions to the application of Code Sec. 318 (Code Sec. 59A(i), as added by the 2017 Tax Cuts Act).

**Reporting requirements and penalties.** The Secretary of the Treasury is authorized to prescribe additional reporting requirements under Code Sec. 6038A relating to: (i) the name, principal place of business, and country or countries in which organized or resident, of each person that is a related party to the reporting corporation, and that had any transaction with the reporting corporation during its tax year, (ii) the manner of relation between the reporting corporation and each person referred to in (i), and (iii) the transactions between the reporting corporation and each related foreign person (Code Sec. 6038A(b)(1), as amended by the 2017 Tax Cuts Act).

Additional information is required regarding base erosion payments. Specifically, for purposes of information reporting under Code Secs. 6038A and 6038C, if the reporting corporation or the foreign corporation to which Code Sec. 6038C applies is an applicable taxpayer, the information that is required includes: (i) information that the Secretary determines necessary to determine the base erosion minimum tax amount, base erosion payments, and base erosion tax benefits of the taxpayer for purposes of Code Sec. 59A for the tax year, and (ii) such other information as the Secretary of the Treasury determines is necessary. For these purposes, any term used in this provision and Code Sec. 59A has the meaning as when used in Code Sec. 59A (Code Sec. 6038A(b)(2), as amended by the 2017 Tax Cuts Act).

The $10,000 penalties for failure to furnish information or maintain records provided in Code Sec. 6038A(d)(1) and (2) are both increased to $25,000 (Code Sec. 6038A(d)(1) and (2), as amended by the 2017 Tax Cuts Act).

> **Comment:** Proposed regulations (discussed below) identify information that must be reported by corporations that are subject to Code Secs. 6038A and 6038C reporting requirements and that are also applicable taxpayers for BEAT purposes (Proposed Reg. § 1.6038A-2).

**Other changes.** The base erosion and anti-abuse tax of Code Sec. 59A is excluded from regular tax liability for purposes of the limitation on nonrefundable personal credits (Code Sec. 26(b)(2)(B), as added by the 2017 Tax Cuts Act). Also, a foreign corporation engaged in a trade or business within the United States during the tax year is subject to tax under Code Secs. 11 and 59A on its taxable income that is effectively connected with the conduct of a U.S. trade or business (Code Sec. 882(a)(1), as amended by the 2017 Tax Cuts Act). In addition, for purposes of the rules allowing a corporation to apply for a quick refund of an overpayment of estimated tax and the rules for estimated tax payments by corporations, income tax liability also includes the Code Sec. 59A base erosion tax (Code Sec. 6425(c)(1)(A) and Code Sec. 6655(g)(1)(A), (e)(2)(A) and (e)(2)(B), as amended by the 2017 Tax Cuts Act).

**Proposed BEAT regulations.** Proposed regulations provide guidance for determining whether a taxpayer is an applicable taxpayer for BEAT purposes and for computing the taxpayer's BEAT liability (NPRM REG-104259-18, December 21, 2018). The regulations are proposed to apply to tax years beginning after December 31, 2017, but taxpayers may rely on them until final regulations are issued.

**¶750**

## NEW LAW EXPLAINED

*Applicable taxpayer.* Generally, an applicable taxpayer is a corporation (other than a regulated investment company (RIC), a real estate investment trust (REIT), or an S corporation) that satisfies the gross receipts test and the base erosion percentage test (Proposed Reg. § 1.59A-2(b)). The taxpayer and certain other corporations that are related to the taxpayer are treated as one person for purposes of determining whether a taxpayer satisfies these tests.

> **Comment:** In the case of consolidated groups, the BEAT is determined at the consolidated group level, rather than separately for each member of the group. Thus, all members of a consolidated group are treated as a single taxpayer, and the consolidated group is treated as a single member of an aggregate group (Proposed Reg. § 1.1502-59A). The proposed regulations provide special rules for the application of the BEAT to partnerships. Generally, the BEAT rules are applied at the partner level (Proposed Reg. § 1.59A-7).

*Aggregate group.* A taxpayer that is a member of an aggregate group determines its gross receipts and its base erosion percentage on the basis of the aggregate group as of the end of the taxpayer's tax year. An aggregate group is the same controlled group of corporations for purposes of Code Sec. 52(a); that is, a controlled group of corporations defined in Code Sec. 1563(a), except that (i) the "more than 50 percent" test is substituted for "at least 80 percent" test, and (ii) certain rules related to insurance companies and providing for an exception from attribution for stock owned by a tax exempt employees' trust do not apply. In addition, members of the aggregate group for this purpose are:

- domestic corporations, and
- foreign corporations with regard to income that is effectively connected with the conduct of a trade or business in the United States and subject to tax under Code Sec. 882(a) (Proposed Reg. § § 1.59A-1(b)(1) and 1.59A-2(c)).

> **Comment:** The proposed regulations limit the aggregate group to corporations that benefit from deductions, and accordingly may have base erosion tax benefits, while excluding foreign corporations that are not subject to U.S. income tax (except on a gross basis under Code Sec. 881, with respect to income that is not effectively connected with a trade or business in the United States) and do not benefit from deductions.

Generally, payments between members of the aggregate group are not included in the gross receipts of the aggregate group, consistent with the single entity concept in Code Sec. 59A(e)(3). Similarly, payments between members of the aggregate group are also not taken into account for purposes of the numerator or the denominator in the base erosion percentage calculation.

Payments between the aggregate group and any foreign corporation that is not within the aggregate group with respect to the payment are taken into account in applying both the gross receipts test and the base erosion percentage test. However, payments to a foreign corporation from within the aggregate group that are subject to net income tax in the United States are eliminated and not taken into account in applying the gross receipts test and the base erosion percentage test (Proposed Reg. § 1.59A-2(c) and (d)(3)).

## NEW LAW EXPLAINED

*Gross receipts test.* A taxpayer satisfies the gross receipts test if the taxpayer, or the aggregate group of which the taxpayer is a member, has $500 million or more of average annual gross receipts during the three prior tax years (Proposed Reg. §1.59A-2(d)(1)). In the case of a foreign corporation, the gross receipts test only takes into account gross receipts that are taken into account in determining:

- income that is subject to net income tax as income effectively connected with the conduct of a trade or business within the United States, or

- net taxable income under an applicable U.S. income tax treaty (Proposed Reg. §1.59A-2(d)(3)).

In the case of an aggregate group, a taxpayer's gross receipts are measured by reference to the taxpayer's aggregate group determined as of the end of the taxpayer's tax year for which the BEAT liability is being computed. Gross receipts of those aggregate group members are taken into account during the three-year period preceding that tax year. The proposed regulations also clarify how a taxpayer computes gross receipts, including in cases where (i) corporations have short tax years, (ii) members of the aggregate group have different tax years, (iii) members of an aggregate group own an interest in a partnership, or (iv) insurance companies are involved (Proposed Reg. §1.59A-2(d)).

*Base erosion percentage test.* The base erosion percentage test is satisfied with respect to a taxpayer if the taxpayer (or the aggregate group of which the taxpayer is a member) has a base erosion percentage of three percent or more (Proposed Reg. §1.59A-2(e)(1)). Generally, a lower threshold of two percent applies, subject to a de minimis exception, if the taxpayer, or a member of the taxpayer's aggregate group, is a member of an affiliated group that includes a domestic bank or registered securities dealer (Proposed Reg. §1.59A-2(e)(2)).

*Computation of base erosion percentage.* The base erosion percentage for a tax year is computed by dividing:

- the aggregate amount of base erosion tax benefits (the numerator), by

- the sum of the aggregate amount of deductions plus certain other base erosion tax benefits (the denominator) (Proposed Reg. §1.59A-2(e)(3)(i)).

In the case of a taxpayer that is a member of an aggregate group, the base erosion percentage is measured by reference to the deductions or certain reductions in gross income of the taxpayer and members of the taxpayer's aggregate group as of the end of the taxpayer's tax year. Base erosion tax benefits are generally the deductions or reductions in gross income that result from base erosion payments.

Generally, the following deductions are excluded from the numerator and denominator of the base erosion percentage:

- amounts paid or accrued to foreign related parties for services qualifying for the services cost method (SCM) exception (discussed below);

- payments covered by the qualified derivatives payments (QDP) exception (discussed below);

**¶750**

## NEW LAW EXPLAINED

- amounts excluded pursuant to the total loss-absorbing capacity (TLAC) exception (discussed below); and

- exchange losses from a Code Sec. 988 transaction (Proposed Reg. § 1.59A-2(e)(3)(ii)).

> **Comment:** An applicable taxpayer may make a payment to a foreign related party that is not a member of the aggregate group, if, for example, the recipient of the payment is a 25-percent owner who does not own more than 50 percent of the applicable taxpayer, and that payment may qualify for the ECI exception. If so, and if that payment also qualifies for either the SCM exception, the QDP exception, or the TLAC exception, the payment is included in the denominator of the base erosion percentage. However, if the applicable taxpayer makes a deductible payment to a foreign related person and that payment is a QDP, but not otherwise subject to federal income taxation, that deductible payment is excluded from the denominator of the base erosion percentage (NPRM REG-104259-18).

The numerator of the base erosion percentage only takes into account base erosion tax benefits, which generally are base erosion payments for which a deduction is allowed under the Code for a tax year. Similarly, the denominator of the base erosion percentage only takes into account deductions allowed under the Code. However, a Code Sec. 172 NOL deduction, Code Sec. 245A participation exemption deduction, or deduction for foreign-derived intangible income (FDII) and global intangible low-taxed income (GILTI) under Code Sec. 250 allowed for the tax year is excluded from the denominator (Proposed Reg. § 1.59A-2(e)(3)(ii)). In addition, a base erosion tax benefit is not included in the numerator when the payment was subject to tax under Code Sec. 871 or 881 and that tax has been deducted and withheld under Code Sec. 1441 or 1442 (discussed below).

*Base erosion percentage computation - aggregate group members with different tax years.* Since each member must compute the aggregate group amount of gross receipts and base erosion payments based on its own tax year and based on those corporations that are members of the aggregate group at the end of the year, members with different tax years may have different base erosion percentages. However, each corporation that is an applicable taxpayer computes its modified taxable income and base erosion minimum tax amount on a separate taxpayer basis, except for consolidated groups that compute these amounts on a consolidated group basis. Thus, each taxpayer determines its gross receipts and base erosion percentage by reference to its own tax year, taking into account the results of other members of its aggregate group during that year (Proposed Reg. § 1.59A-2(e)(3)(vii)).

*Mark-to-market deductions.* The proposed regulations provide rules for determining the amount of base erosion tax benefits in the case of transactions that are marked to market. Rules are also provided for computing the total amount of the deductions that are included in the denominator of the base erosion percentage. To ensure that only a single deduction is claimed with respect to each transaction, all income, deduction, gain, or loss on each transaction for the year are combined to determine the amount of the deduction that is used for purposes of the base erosion percentage test (Proposed Reg. § 1.59A-2(e)(3)(vi)).

## NEW LAW EXPLAINED

*Base erosion payments.* The proposed regulations define a base erosion payment as a payment or accrual by the taxpayer to a foreign related party that is described in one of four categories:

- a payment with respect to which a deduction is allowable;
- a payment made in connection with the acquisition of depreciable or amortizable property;
- premiums or other consideration paid or accrued for reinsurance that is taken into account under Code Sec. 803(a)(1)(B) or Code Sec. 832(b)(4)(A); or
- a payment resulting in a reduction of the gross receipts of the taxpayer that is with respect to certain surrogate foreign corporations or related foreign persons (Proposed Reg. § 1.59A-3(b)(1)).

   **Comment:** A payment or accrual that is not within one of the categories may be a base erosion payment described in one of the other categories. For example, a deductible payment related to reinsurance that does not meet the requirements for the third category of base erosion payments may still be a base erosion payment under the first category because the payment is deductible. Nonetheless, to the extent all or a portion of a payment or accrual is described in more than one of these categories, the amount is only taken into account once as a base erosion payment. Generally, the determination of whether a payment or accrual by the taxpayer to a foreign related party is described in one of these four categories is made under general U.S. federal income tax law (NPRM REG-104259-18).

The proposed regulations provide operating rules for certain specific types of base erosion payments, including:

- payments or accruals that consist of non-cash consideration;
- interest expense allocable to a foreign corporation's effectively connected income;
- other deductions allowed with respect to effectively connected income;
- certain deductions from internal dealings based on tax treaty positions; and
- certain payments to domestic passthrough entities with foreign owners or to another aggregate group member (Proposed Reg. § § 1.59A-3(b)(2) and (b)(4)).

*Exceptions to base erosion payments.* The proposed regulations provide the following exceptions to the definition of base erosion payments.

**The services cost method (SCM) exception.** An exception from the definition of base erosion payment is allowed for certain payments made to foreign related persons for services that meet the eligibility requirements for use of the services cost method (SCM) under Code Sec. 482. Under the proposed regulations, the exception is allowed for the total cost of services, even if there is a profit markup. The portion of the payment that exceeds the total cost of services, however, is not eligible for the exception and is a base eroding payment. To be eligible for the SCM exception, all of the requirements of Reg. § 1.482-9(b), as modified by the proposed regulations, must be satisfied (Proposed Reg. § 1.59A-3(b)(3)(i)).

# NEW LAW EXPLAINED

Taxpayers are required to maintain books and records adequate to permit verification of, among other things, the amount paid for services, the total services cost incurred by the renderer, and the allocation and apportionment of costs to services in accordance with Reg. § 1.482-9(k).

*Qualified derivative payments (QDPs).* A qualified derivative payment (QDP) is any payment made by a taxpayer to a foreign related party pursuant to a derivative for which (i) the taxpayer recognizes gain or loss on the derivative on a mark-to-market basis (treats the derivative as sold on the last business day of the tax year), (ii) the gain or loss is ordinary, and (iii) any gain, loss, income or deduction on a payment made pursuant to the derivative is also treated as ordinary (Proposed Reg. §§ 1.59A-3(b)(3)(ii) and 1.59A-6).

The QDP exception applies only if the taxpayer satisfies the reporting requirements in Proposed Reg. § 1.6038A-2(b)(7)(ix). If a taxpayer satisfies the reporting requirements for some QDPs, but not all, then only the payments for which the taxpayer fails to satisfy the reporting requirements will be ineligible for the QDP exception (Proposed Reg. § 1.59A-6).

> **Compliance Note:** These reporting requirements will first apply to tax years beginning after final regulations are published, which provides taxpayers additional time to meet the reporting requirements. Before final regulations are published, taxpayers satisfy the reporting requirements for QDPs by reporting the aggregate amount of QDPs for the tax year on Form 8991, Tax on Base Erosion Payments of Taxpayers With Substantial Gross Receipts.

*Effectively connected income.* An exception from the definition of base erosion payment is provided for amounts that are subject to tax as income effectively connected with the conduct of a U.S. trade or business. In the case of a foreign recipient that determines its net taxable income under an applicable income tax treaty, the exception applies to payments taken into account in determining net taxable income under the treaty (Proposed Reg. § 1.59A-3(b)(3)(iii)).

*Exchange losses from Code Sec. 988 transactions.* Code Sec. 988 exchange losses that are allowable deductions and that result from payments or accruals by the taxpayer to a foreign related party are not base erosion payments. As mentioned above, such losses are excluded from the numerator and the denominator of the base erosion percentage (Proposed Reg. § 1.59A-3(b)(3)(iv)).

*Amounts paid or accrued with respect to TLAC securities.* An exception to base erosion payment status is provided for interest paid or accrued on TLAC securities that are (i) are issued by certain global systemically important banking organizations (GSIBs) as part of a global system to address bank solvency, and (ii) required by the Federal Reserve (Proposed Reg. § 1.59A-3(b)(3)(v)).

*Amounts paid or accrued in tax years beginning before 2018.* Any amount paid or accrued in tax years beginning before January 1, 2018, is not considered a base erosion payment (Proposed Reg. § 1.59A-3(b)(3)(vi)).

> **Comment:** Since the definition of a base erosion tax benefit is based upon the definition of a base erosion payment and the BEAT applies to base erosion payments paid or accrued in tax years beginning after December 31, 2017, the

## NEW LAW EXPLAINED

proposed regulations exclude a deduction described in Code Sec. 59A(c)(2)(A)(i) (deduction allowed under Chapter 1 with respect to any base erosion payment) or Code Sec. 59A(c)(2)(A)(ii) (deduction allowed under Chapter 1 for depreciation or amortization with respect to any property acquired with such payment) that is allowed in a tax year beginning after December 31, 2017, if it relates to a base erosion payment that occurred in a tax year beginning before January 1, 2018.

***Business interest carried forward from tax years beginning before 2018.*** Any disallowed business interest described in Code Sec. 163(j)(2) that is carried forward from a tax year beginning before January 1, 2018, is not treated as a base erosion payment (Proposed Reg. §1.59A-3(b)(3)(vii)).

> **Comment:** This treatment of disallowed disqualified interest under Code Sec. 163(j) that resulted from a payment or accrual to a foreign related party and that is carried forward from a tax year beginning before 2018 is contrary to the approach described in Notice 2018-28. However, any disallowed business interest expense described in Code Sec. 163(j) that resulted from a payment or accrual to a foreign related party that first arose in a tax year beginning after December 31, 2017, is treated as a base erosion payment in the year that the business interest expense initially arose (Proposed Reg. §1.59A-3(b)(4)(vi)).

*Base erosion tax benefits.* The amount of base erosion tax benefits is important for the computation of (i) the base erosion percentage test, and (ii) the modified taxable income. Generally, a base erosion tax benefit is the amount of any deduction relating to a base erosion payment that is allowed under the Code for the tax year (Proposed Reg. §1.59A-3(c)(1)).

However, if tax is imposed by Code Sec. 871 or 881 and is deducted and withheld under Code Sec. 1441 or 1442, the base erosion payment is treated as having a base erosion tax benefit of zero for purposes of calculating a taxpayer's modified taxable income (Proposed Reg. §1.59A-3(c)(2)). If an income tax treaty reduces the amount of withholding imposed on the base erosion payment, the base erosion payment is treated as a base erosion tax benefit to the extent of the reduction in withholding (Proposed Reg. §1.59A-3(c)(3)).

In the case where Code Sec. 163(j) limits the amount of a taxpayer's business interest expense that is deductible in the tax year, the taxpayer is required to treat all disallowed business interest first as interest paid or accrued to persons who are not related parties, and then as interest paid or accrued to related parties for purposes of the BEAT (Proposed Reg. §1.59A-3(c)(4)).

*Modified taxable income.* The proposed regulations clarify that the computation of modified taxable income and the computation of the base erosion minimum tax amount are made on a taxpayer-by-taxpayer basis. In addition, the modified taxable income is computed on an add-back basis. The computation starts with a taxpayer's taxable income (or taxable loss) as computed for regular tax purposes, and adds to that amount (i) the gross amount of base erosion tax benefits for the tax year, and (ii) the base erosion percentage of any NOL deduction for the tax year (Proposed Reg. §1.59A-4(b)).

¶750

## NEW LAW EXPLAINED

In determining modified taxable income, the allowed NOL deduction may not exceed taxable income before taking into account the NOL deduction. Also, the base erosion percentage for the tax year that the NOL arose is used to determine the addition in (ii), above. For an NOL that arose in a tax year beginning before January 1, 2018, the base erosion percentage for the tax year is zero.

*Base erosion minimum tax amount.* Generally, the taxpayer's base erosion minimum tax amount (BEMTA) for the tax year equals the excess of:

- the applicable tax rate for the tax year (the BEAT rate) multiplied by the taxpayer's modified taxable income for the tax year, over

- the taxpayer's adjusted regular tax liability for that year (Proposed Reg. § 1.59A-5(b)).

In determining the taxpayer's adjusted regular tax liability, credits are generally subtracted from the regular tax liability amount. However, credits for overpayment of taxes and for taxes withheld at source are not subtracted from the taxpayer's regular tax liability. In addition, for tax years beginning on or before December 31, 2025, the regular tax liability is not reduced by (i) the Code Sec. 41(a) research credit, and (ii) the portion of the applicable Code Sec. 38 credits not in excess of 80 percent of the lesser of (a) the amount of those credits, or (b) the BEMTA (determined without regard to this rule).

For purposes of calculating the BEMTA, the BEAT rate is as follows:

- five percent for tax years beginning in calendar year 2018;

- 10 percent for tax years beginning after December 31, 2018, and before January 1, 2026; and

- 12.5 percent for tax years beginning after December 31, 2025 (Proposed Reg. § 1.59A-5(c)).

In the case of a taxpayer that is a member of an affiliated group that includes a bank or a registered securities dealer, the BEAT rate percentage is increased by one percentage point. The Code Sec. 15 tax rate proration rules do not apply to any tax year that includes January 1, 2018. For a taxpayer using a tax year other than the calendar year, the tax rate proration rules apply to any tax year beginning after January 1, 2018.

*Anti-abuse and recharacterization rules.* Under the proposed regulations, certain transactions that have a principal purpose of avoiding the BEAT are disregarded or deemed to result in a base erosion payment (Proposed Reg. § 1.59A-9(b)).

*Reporting requirements under Code Sec. 6038A.* The proposed regulations identify information that must be reported by corporations that are subject to the reporting requirements of Code Secs. 6038A and 6038C and that are also applicable taxpayers for BEAT purposes. The information is required to be reported on Form 5472 and Form 8991. The proposed regulations also provide the time and manner for reporting. While an applicable taxpayer that is not a reporting corporation would not be subject to monetary penalties and collateral provisions specific to Code Secs. 6038A and 6038C, the taxpayer remains subject to BEAT-related reporting obligations, including

## NEW LAW EXPLAINED

Form 8991, and applicable consequences for noncompliance (Proposed Reg. § 1.6038A-2).

Since the status of a foreign shareholder as a surrogate foreign corporation can affect the treatment of payments from a taxpayer to that corporation under Code Sec. 59A(d), all reporting corporations must state whether a foreign shareholder required to be listed on Form 5472 is a surrogate foreign corporation. The form may provide for reporting of whether the shareholder is a member of an expanded affiliated group including the surrogate foreign corporation.

In addition, the IRS may require by form or by form instructions the following information: (1) reporting of particular details of the reporting corporation's relationships with related parties in regard to which it is required to file a Form 5472, (2) reporting of transactions within certain categories on a more detailed basis, (3) reporting of the manner (such as type of transfer pricing method used) in which the reporting corporation determined the amount of particular reportable transactions and items, and (4) summarization of a reporting corporation's reportable transactions and items with all foreign related parties on a schedule to its annual Form 5472 filing.

*Applicability date.* The BEAT regulations are proposed to apply to tax years beginning after December 31, 2017 (Proposed Reg. § 1.59A-10). However, taxpayers may rely on these proposed regulations for tax years beginning after 2017, until final regulations are published, provided the taxpayer and all related parties consistently apply the proposed regulations for all those tax years that end before the finalization date (NPRM REG-104259-18).

The proposed reporting requirements for qualified derivative payments (QDPs) apply to tax years beginning one year after the final regulations are published. However, the simplified QDP reporting requirements are proposed to apply to tax years beginning after December 31, 2017 (Proposed Reg. § 1.6038A-2(g)).

Any provision that is finalized after June 22, 2019, will apply only to tax years ending on or after December 17, 2018.

▶ **Effective date.** The amendments made by this section apply to base erosion payments (as defined in Code Sec. 59A(d), as added by the Tax Cuts and Jobs Act of 2017 (P.L. 115-97)) paid or accrued in tax years beginning after December 31, 2017 (Act Sec. 14401(e) of the 2017 Tax Cuts Act).

— Act Sec. 14401(a) of the Tax Cuts and Jobs Act (P.L. 115-97), adding new Code Sec. 59A;

— Act Sec. 14401(b), amending Code Sec. 6038A(b), (d)(1) and (d)(2);

— Act Sec. 14401(c), adding Code Sec. 26(b)(2)(B);

— Act Sec. 14401(d), amending Code Secs. 882(a)(1), 6425(c)(1)(A), 6655(g)(1)(A), and 6655(e)(2)(A) and (B);

— Act Sec. 14401(e), providing the effective date.

# ¶755  Limits on Income Shifting Through Intangible Property Transfers

## SUMMARY OF NEW LAW

The Code Sec. 936(h)(3)(B) definition of intangible property is modified to include goodwill, going concern value, and workforce in place as well as any other item the value of which is not attributable to tangible property or services of any individual. The Secretary of the Treasury is authorized to require the use of certain valuation methods in determining the value of intangible property in the context of Code Sec. 367(d) transfers and Code Sec. 482 intercompany pricing allocations.

## BACKGROUND

Under the definition of intangible property in Code Sec. 936(h)(3)(B), intangible property includes the following:

- patent, invention, formula, process, design, pattern, or know-how;
- copyright or literary, musical, or artistic composition;
- trademark, trade name, or brand name;
- franchise, license, or contract;
- method, program, system, procedure, campaign, survey, study, forecast, estimate, customer list, or technical data; and
- any similar item.

Each of the above items must have substantial value independent of the services of any individual (Code Sec. 936(h)(3)(B)).

The above statutory definition of intangible property is used for purposes of the Code Sec. 367(d) rules for transfers of intangibles and the transfer pricing rules under Code Sec. 482. Generally, Code Sec. 367(d) requires income recognition by U.S. transferors on outbound transfers of intangibles described in Code Sec. 936(h)(3)(B), if the transfer occurs in a Code Sec. 351 or 361 exchange. For such transfers, the U.S. transferor is generally treated as having sold the intangible property in exchange for annual payments that are contingent upon the productivity or use of the property. The U.S. transferor must annually include in gross income, over the useful life of the property, an amount that is commensurate with the income attributable to the intangible and that represents an appropriate arms-length charge for the use of the property. The appropriate charge is determined under the transfer pricing rules of Code Sec. 482.

Code Sec. 482 authorizes the IRS to allocate income, deductions, and other tax items among related taxpayers in order to prevent the evasion of tax or to more clearly reflect income. Code Sec. 482 permits reallocation in any common control situation, including between two U.S. entities. However, Code Sec. 482 is largely employed in the international tax area where there is incentive for multinational operations to use transfer pricing to take advantage of different tax systems and effective tax rates.

## BACKGROUND

Generally, the transfer pricing price is subject to reallocation by the IRS if an arm's-length pricing standard is not maintained (Code Sec. 482).

> **Comment:** The statutory definition of intangible property has proved problematic especially in the transfer pricing context. Intangible assets and the income attributable to them are considered highly mobile. Countries are becoming increasingly aware of the need to improve their regulation as one means of retaining the tax base, preventing base erosion shifting of income across national borders and deterring tax evasion.

Even though both Code Sec. 367(d) and Code Sec. 482 rely on the statutory definition of intangible property in Code Sec. 936(h)(3)(B), this definition is regarded as unclear. Recurring definitional and methodological issues with respect to transfers of intangibles under these provisions have arisen in recent Tax Court cases (*Veritas Software Corp. v. Commissioner*, Dec. 58,016, 133 T.C. 297, (nonacq., Action on Decision Memorandum, AOD-2010-5; *Amazon v. Commissioner*, Dec. 60,857, 148 T.C. No. 8 (2017)).

Further, conventional valuation methodologies, which have been highly effective in reflecting an arm's-length price with respect to transfers of certain assets, have been less so with respect to the transfer of intangibles. This is particularly the case with Code Sec. 367(d) transfers of multiple intangible properties in one or more related transactions in the context of outbound restructurings of U.S. operations and of intercompany pricing allocations.

## NEW LAW EXPLAINED

**Intangible property definition modified and allowable valuation methods clarified.**—The scope of the statutory definition of intangible property is revised to include goodwill, going concern value, and workforce in place as well as a residual category that includes any other item the value or potential value of which is not attributable to tangible property or services of any individual. In addition, the requirement that each specific type of intangible property have substantial value independent of the services of any individual is removed so that the source or amount of value is no longer relevant in determining whether that property is within the scope of the definition (Code Sec. 936(h)(3)(B), as amended by the Tax Cuts and Jobs Act (P.L. 115-97)).

In addition, the IRS has the authority of the Secretary of the Treasury to specify the method to be used to determine the value of intangible property in the context of both Code Sec. 367(d) transfers as part of outbound restructurings of U.S. operations and Code Sec. 482 intercompany pricing allocations. Specifically, the Secretary will require: (i) the valuation of transfers of intangible property, including intangible property transferred with other property or services, on an aggregate basis, or (ii) the valuation of such a transfer on the basis of the realistic alternatives to such a transfer, if the Secretary determines that such basis is the most reliable means of valuation of such transfers (Code Sec. 367(d)(2)(D), as added by the 2017 Tax Cuts Act; Code Sec. 482, as amended by the 2017 Tax Cuts Act). In the Code Sec. 367(d)(2) context, the use of

## NEW LAW EXPLAINED

these valuation methods is required for purposes of determining if the annual amounts taken into account are commensurate with the income attributable to the intangible.

> **Comment:** Accordingly, the use of the aggregate basis valuation method is required in the case of transfers of multiple intangible properties in one or more related transactions if the Secretary determines that an aggregate basis achieves a more reliable result than an asset-by-asset approach. This is consistent with the position that the additional value resulting from the interrelation of intangible assets can be properly attributed to the underlying intangible assets in the aggregate, if doing so produces a more reliable result. This approach is also consistent with the cost-sharing regulations in Reg. § 1.482-7(g)(2)(iv).

> **Comment:.** The provision codifies the realistic alternative principle, which is based on the concept that a taxpayer would only enter into a transaction if none of its realistic alternatives were economically preferable to the transaction undertaken.

> **Comment:** Due to the repeal of Code Sec. 936, by P.L. 115-141, effective March 23, 2018, the definition of intangible property is included in the Code Sec. 367(d) rules that require income recognition by U.S. transferors on outbound transfers of intangibles. The definition also applies for purposes of the transfer pricing rules under Code Sec. 482.

▶ **Effective date.** The amendments made by this section apply to transfers in tax years beginning after December 31, 2017. Nothing in the amendment to the Code Sec. 936(h)(3)(B) definition of intangible property will be construed to create any inference with respect to the application of Code Sec. 936(h)(3) or the authority of the Secretary of the Treasury to provide regulations for such application, with respect to tax years beginning before January 1, 2018 (Act Sec. 14221(c) of the Tax Cuts and Jobs Act (P.L. 115-97)).

**No significant guidance related to this provision has been issued**.

— Act Sec.14221(a) of the Tax Cuts and Jobs Act (P.L. 115-97), amending Code Sec. 936(h)(3)(B);

— Act Sec. 14221(b), adding Code Sec. 367(d)(2)(D) and amending Code Sec. 482;

— Act Sec. 14221(c), providing the effective date.

## ¶760 Related Party Payments Involving Hybrid Entities or Hybrid Transactions

### SUMMARY OF NEW LAW

A deduction is not allowed for related party payments of interest or royalties involving hybrid transactions or entities.

## BACKGROUND

The choice of entity type has a significant impact on the legal and tax treatment of a business. In general, a business may elect to be taxed as a partnership, corporation, or disregarded entity (Reg. § 301.7701-3(a)). Of these three types of entities, the corporation pays tax on taxable income at the entity level, whereas liability for income tax is the responsibility of the owner(s) of a disregarded entity and partnership. Because the tax attributes of these entities flow through to the owners, the entities are known as pass-through entities or fiscally transparent entities. When an entity has not made a tax election (i.e., "check-the-box" election), a default tax classification is provided (Reg. § 301.7701-3(b)). Typically corporations are not fiscally transparent entities. Limited liability companies and miscellaneous foreign entities may or may not be fiscally transparent, and should be reviewed on an entity-by-entity basis.

Under Reg. § 1.894-1(d)(3)(ii) and (iii), an entity that is "fiscally transparent" for U.S. tax purposes, but not fiscally transparent for foreign tax purposes is considered to be a hybrid entity. Generally, to be fiscally transparent, an entity's current year profits must be currently taxable to the entity owners. An entity is treated as a reverse hybrid entity when it is fiscally transparent for foreign tax purposes, but not fiscally transparent for U.S. tax purposes. Where entities are treated the same for both foreign and U.S. tax purposes they are not considered to be hybrids.

---

**Example:** Company A is taxed as a partnership in the United States, but taxed as a corporation in Foreign Country. For U.S. tax purposes, Company A is a hybrid entity that pays its own tax in Foreign Country, whereas income and deductions pass through to the owners in the United States.

---

The use of hybrid transactions and entities can create potential tax mismatches and exploit gaps in the domestic tax laws of multiple jurisdictions. These gaps and mismatches may result in a variety of tax advantages for cross-border arrangements and activity, such as:

- double nontaxation of income;

- multiple deductions for a single expense;

- deductions in one jurisdiction without corresponding taxable income in another jurisdiction;

- long-term deferral of income; and

- imported mismatches allowing for offset of includible income in the payee's jurisdiction.

As part of its Base Erosion and Profit Shifting (BEPS) framework, the multinational intergovernmental Organisation for Economic Cooperation and Development (OECD) has focused on combatting hybrid and branch mismatch arrangements. Recommendations designed to eliminate advantageous hybrid tax planning opportunities and deter companies from their use are set forth in OECD/G20, Neutralising the Effects of Hybrid Mismatch Arrangements, Action 2: 2015 Final Report (October 2015). Recommendations neutralizing the tax effects of certain arrangements involving branches that

## BACKGROUND

result in mismatches similar to hybrid mismatches are set forth in OECD/G20, Neutralising the Effect of Branch Mismatch Arrangements, Action 2: Inclusive Framework on BEPS (July 2017). These reports may be found at the OECD Library (https://www.oecd-ilibrary.org).

## NEW LAW EXPLAINED

**Deduction for related party payments involving hybrid transactions or hybrid entities disallowed.**—A deduction is disallowed for a disqualified related party amount paid or accrued pursuant to a hybrid transaction. A deduction is also disallowed for a disqualified related party amount paid or accrued by, or to, a hybrid entity (Code Sec. 267A(a), as added by the Tax Cuts and Jobs Act (P.L. 115-97)).

Any interest or royalty paid or accrued to a related party is a "disqualified related party amount" to the extent that under the tax law of the country where the related party is a resident for tax purposes or is subject to tax:

- the amount is not included in the income of the related party; or
- the related party is allowed a deduction for the amount (Code Sec. 267A(b)(1), as added the 2017 Tax Cuts Act).

  **Comment:** Code Sec. 267A addresses cases where the taxpayer gets a deduction under U.S. tax law, but the payee does not have a corresponding income inclusion, referred to as "deduction/no-inclusion" (D/NI) outcome.

Proposed regulations provide specificity with respect to the terms and other calculations that taxpayers are required to apply under Code Sec. 267A, and clarity as to the type of structures subject to the rules (NPRM REG-104352-18, December 28, 2018). The proposed regulations include the following:

- Proposed Reg. § 1.267A-1, providing the general disallowance rule;
- Proposed Reg. § 1.267A-2, describing hybrid and branch arrangements;
- Proposed Reg. § 1.267A-3, providing rules for determining income inclusions and amounts not treated as disqualified;
- Proposed Reg. § 1.267A-4, providing an imported mismatch rule;
- Proposed Reg. § 1.267A-5, providing definitions and special rules;
- Proposed Reg. § 1.267A-6, providing examples; and
- Proposed Reg. § 1.267A-7, providing the applicability dates.

The proposed regulations generally apply to specified payments made in tax years beginning after December 31, 2017. However, certain rules—including the disregarded payment rule, the deemed branch payment rule, and the imported mismatch rule—apply to specified payments made in tax years beginning on or after December 28, 2018 (Proposed Reg. § 1.267A-7). The proposed regulations deny the deduction for specified payments (interest or royalties) only if the payment is:

- a "disqualified hybrid amount";
- an "imported mismatch amount"; or

## NEW LAW EXPLAINED

- made pursuant to a transaction that has the principal purpose of avoiding the purposes of the regulations under Code Sec. 267A (discussed below) (Proposed Reg. § 1.267A-1(b)).

The terms interest and royalty are defined in the proposed regulations. Interest is defined broadly to include interest associated with conventional debt instruments, other amounts treated as interest under the Code, and transactions that are indebtedness in substance but not form (Proposed Reg. § 1.267A-5(a)(12)). The term royalty is defined as amounts paid or accrued as consideration for the use of or right to use copyrights, patents, or similar property or information concerning industrial, commercial or scientific experience (Proposed Reg. § 1.267A-5(a)(16)).

The proposed regulations deny a deduction under Code Sec. 267A only to the extent that the D/NI outcome is a result of a hybrid arrangement, and not just a feature of the jurisdiction's tax system. Absent the proposed regulations, the statute would deny a deduction if a D/NI outcome occurs and a hybrid arrangement exists, without there being a link between the arrangement and hybridity (Proposed Reg. § 1.267A-2(a)(1)(ii)).

The proposed regulations narrow the scope of Code Sec. 267A so that the disallowance rule applies only to specified parties, defined as:

- a tax resident of the United States;

- a controlled foreign corporation (CFC) that has U.S. shareholders that own directly or indirectly at least 10 percent of the CFC's stock; and

- a U.S. taxable branch (Proposed Reg. § 1.267A-5(a)(17)).

The specified recipient of the specified payments is defined as any tax resident or taxable branch (i.e., any party that may be subject to tax on the specified payment under its tax law) (Proposed Reg. § 1.267A-5(a)(19)). Whether the amount of the specified payment is or is not included (no-inclusion) depends on whether, under the foreign tax law, the payment is included in income or the tax base at the full marginal rate imposed on ordinary income and the payment is not reduced or offset by certain items. Only the tax law of a specific recipient related to the specified party is taken into account in determining whether the specified payment is made pursuant to a hybrid transaction (Proposed Reg. §§ 1.267A-2(f) and 1.267A-3(a)). Related status is defined under Code Sec. 954(d)(3) (involving ownership of more than 50 percent of interests), but without regard to downward attribution. Tax residents and taxable branches that are disregarded entities are treated as corporations when applying the relatedness test (Code Sec. 267A(b)(2), as added by the 2017 Tax Cuts Act; Proposed Reg. § 1.267A-5(a)(14)).

The proposed regulations provide a de minimis rule that excepts small taxpayers from the disallowance rules of Code Sec. 267A. The de minimis exception applies to any tax year in which the sum of the taxpayer's interest and royalty deductions is below $50,000. The rule looks to the overall amount of interest and royalty payments, whether or not the payments involve hybrid arrangements (Proposed Reg. § 1.267A-1(c)).

**¶760**

## NEW LAW EXPLAINED

The disallowance rule also does not apply to any payment that is included in the gross income of a U.S. shareholder under subpart F and Code Sec. 951(a) (Code Sec. 267(b)(1), as added by the 2017 Tax Cuts Act). Code Sec. 267(b)(1) does not state whether the exception applies to payments that are made directly to U.S. shareholders or U.S. branches or that are included as global intangible low-taxed income (GILTI). The proposed regulations extend the exception from the disallowance rule to payments directly included in the U.S. tax base or that are included as GILTI because these payments do not present a risk of erosion of the U.S. tax base (Code Sec. 267A(e)(7)(B), as added by the 2017 Tax Cuts Act; Proposed Reg. §§1.267A-3(b), 1.267A-6(c)(7)).

> **Example:** Foreign Corporation wholly owns a U.S. subsidiary, C Corporation. Foreign Corporation holds an instrument issued by C Corporation that is treated as equity in the foreign country where Foreign Corporation was established, and is treated as debt for U.S. tax purposes. C Corporation pays $50x to Foreign Corporation pursuant to the instrument. The amount is treated as interest for U.S. tax purposes and as an excludable dividend under a participation exemption by the foreign country. C Corporation is a specified party, so a deduction for the $50x specified payment is disallowed under Code Sec. 267A.
>
> The payment is a disqualified hybrid amount under the hybrid transaction rule of Proposed Reg. §1.267A-2(a) for the following reasons. First, the payment is treated as interest for U.S. tax purposes, but not for purposes of the foreign country's tax law (i.e., the tax law of Foreign Corporation, which is a specified recipient that is related to C Corporation). Further, there is a no-inclusion with respect to Foreign Corporation, because the $50x is not included in income due to the foreign country's participation exemption. Finally, Foreign Corporation's $50x no-inclusion is a result of the payment being made pursuant to the hybrid transaction, because if the payment were treated as interest for the foreign country's tax purposes, Foreign Corporation would include $50x in income and the no-inclusion would not occur (Proposed Reg. §1.267A-6(c)(1)).

**Hybrid and branch arrangements.** A hybrid transaction means any transaction, series of transactions, agreement, or instrument, if one or more payments are treated as interest or royalties for federal income tax purposes, but are not treated as such for purposes of the tax law of the foreign country where the recipient of the payment is resident for tax purposes or is subject to tax (Code Sec. 267A(c), as added by the 2017 Tax Cuts Act; Proposed Reg. §1.267A-2(a)(2)). There must be a mismatch in the character of the instrument or arrangement, such that the payment is not treated as interest or a royalty under the tax law of the specified recipient. Such a payment exists when, for example, an instrument has a payment that is treated as interest for U.S. purposes, but is treated as a distribution with respect to equity or a return of principal for purposes of the specified recipient's tax law (NPRM REG-104352-18, December 28, 2018; Proposed Reg. §1.267A-6(c)(8)).

## NEW LAW EXPLAINED

Additionally, to address timing differences, there must be a long mismatch between when the deduction is allowed and the income is included. The proposed regulations allow short-term deferral. An inclusion during a tax year that ends no more than 36 months after the end of the specified party's tax year does not give rise to a D/NI outcome. Inclusions outside of the 36-month time frame, however, are treated as giving rise to a D/NI outcome (Proposed Reg. §§ 1.267A-3(a)(1) and 1.267A-6(c)(8); NPRM REG-104352-18, December 28, 2018).

Special rules address securities lending transactions, sale-repurchase transactions, and similar transactions. In these cases, the specified payment (i.e., the interest consistent with the substance of the transaction) might not be regarded under foreign law and there might not be a specified recipient of the payment. The proposed regulations provide that the identity of the specified recipient under the foreign tax law is made with respect to the amount connected to the specified payment and regarded under the foreign tax law (Proposed Reg. §§ 1.267A-2(a)(3) and 1.267A-6(c)(2)).

Disregarded payments are treated separately from hybrid transactions because they are more likely to offset dual inclusion income. Disregarded payments are payments that are regarded under the payer's tax law, but not the payee's tax law. This could include, for example, a payment in a disregarded transaction involving a single taxpayer or between consolidated group members. A disregarded payment is a disqualified hybrid payment only to the extent the amount exceeds dual inclusion income. In general, this is the net of the items of gross income and deductible expense used to determine the specified party's income for U.S. tax purposes, and the tax resident's or taxable branch's income for foreign tax purposes (Proposed Reg. §§ 1.267A-2(b) and 1.267A-6(c)(3)).

The proposed regulations expand the application of the disallowance rule to the following:

- *Deemed branch payments.* These payments result in a D/NI outcome when, under an income tax treaty, a deductible payment is deemed to be made by a permanent establishment to its home office and offsets income not taxed to the home office, but the payment is not taken into account under the home office's tax law (Proposed Reg. §§ 1.267A-2(c) and 1.267A-6(c)(4));

- *Reverse hybrid payments.* These payments may result in a D/NI outcome because the entity is fiscally transparent in the country in which it is established, but not for purposes of the tax law of its owner (Proposed Reg. §§ 1.267A-2(d) and 1.267A-6(c)(5));

- *Branch mismatch payments.* These payments result in a D/NI outcome due to differences between the home office's tax law and the branch's tax law regarding the allocation of items of income or the treatment of the branch (Proposed Reg. §§ 1.267A-2(e) and 1.267A-6(c)(6)); and

- *Imported mismatch payments.* An indirect D/NI outcome is produced as a result of the effects of an offshore hybrid or branch arrangement being imported into the U.S. tax system (Proposed Reg. §§ 1.267A-4, 1.267A-6(c)(8), 1.267A-6(c)(9), and 1.267A-6(c)(10)).

## NEW LAW EXPLAINED

**Hybrid entity.** A hybrid entity is any entity that is either:

- treated as fiscally transparent for federal income tax purposes, but not under the tax law of the foreign country where the entity is resident for tax purposes or is subject to tax; or

- treated as fiscally transparent under the tax law of the foreign country where the entity is resident for tax purposes or is subject to tax, but not for federal income tax purposes (Code Sec. 267A(d), as added by the 2017 Tax Cuts Act).

The proposed regulations define the term entity as any person defined in Code Sec. 7701(a)(1) (other than an individual), including disregarded entities under Reg. § 301.7701-1 through Reg. § 301.7701-3 (Proposed Reg. § 1.267A-5(a)(7)). The proposed regulations define the term fiscally transparent with respect to an entity to mean fiscally transparent with respect to an item of income, applying the rules of Reg. § 1.894-1(d)(3)(ii) and (iii), without regard to whether the tax resident is a resident of a country with a tax treaty with the United States (Proposed Reg. § 1.267A-5(a)(8)).

**Regulations.** The Treasury Secretary is authorized under Code Sec. 267A to issue regulations or other guidance as necessary and appropriate to carry out this provision (Code Sec. 276A(e), as added by the 2017 Tax Cuts Act). The following is a list of the guidance areas for which rules are authorized to be issued and the corresponding proposed regulations:

- denying deductions for conduit arrangements involving a hybrid transaction or hybrid entity (see Proposed Reg. § 1.267A-4);

- the application of Code Sec. 267A to foreign branches or domestic entities (see Proposed Reg. § 1.267A-2(c), 1.267A-2(d), and 1.267A-2(e);

- applying Code Sec. 267A to certain structured transactions (see Proposed Reg. §§ 1.267A-1(b) and 1.267A-5(b)(5);

- denying all or a portion of a deduction claimed for an interest or a royalty payment that, as a result of the hybrid transaction or entity, is included in the recipient's income under a preferential tax regime of the country of residence of the recipient and has the effect of reducing the country's generally applicable statutory tax rate by at least 25 percent (Proposed Reg. § 1.267A-3(a)(1), 1.267A-6(c)(1), (2), and (7));

- denying all of a deduction claimed for an interest or a royalty payment if the amount is subject to a participation exemption system or other system providing for the exclusion or deduction of a substantial portion of the amount (see Proposed Reg. § 1.267A-3(a)(1)(ii));

- rules for determining the tax residence of a foreign entity if the foreign entity is otherwise considered a resident of more than one country or of no country (see Proposed Reg. § 1.267A-5(a)(23));

- exceptions to the general rules of Code Sec. 267A (see Proposed Reg. § 1.267A-3(b)); and

- requirements for record keeping and information in addition to any requirements imposed by Code Sec. 6038A (see Proposed Reg. §§ 1.6038-2(f)(13), 1.6038-3(g)(3), and 1.6038A-2(b)(5)(iii)).

## NEW LAW EXPLAINED

**Additional rules.** Under a coordination provision, the rules of Code Sec. 267A will apply, except as otherwise provided, after other applicable provisions of the Code and regulations (Proposed Reg. § 1.267A-5(b)(1)).

Foreign currency gain or loss recognized under Code Sec. 988 is not separately taken into account under Code Sec. 267A. Foreign currency gain or loss recognized with respect to a specified payment is taken into account under Code Sec. 267A only to the extent that the specified payment is in respect of accrued interest or an accrued royalty for which a deduction is disallowed under Code Sec. 267A (Proposed Reg. § 1.267A-5(b)(2)).

Expenses of a nonresident alien or foreign corporation may be deducted in determining effectively connected income under Code Sec. 873(a) and Code Sec. 882(c). If the deductions arise from transactions involving certain hybrid or branch arrangements, the rules of Code Sec. 267A can apply. The proposed regulations treat a U.S. taxable branch as a specified person, and interest or royalties considered paid or accrued by the U.S. taxable branch are specified payments subject to the rules (Proposed Reg. §§ 1.267A-5(b)(3) and 1.267A-6(c)(4)).

The disallowance of a deduction under Code Sec. 267A does not affect whether a corporation's earnings and profits are reduced (Proposed Reg. § 1.267A-5(b)(4)).

Under an anti-avoidance rule, a specified party's deduction for a specified payment is disallowed if (1) the payment is not included in the income of the tax resident or taxable branch, but without regard to the de minimis and full inclusion rules of Proposed Reg. § 1.267A-3(a), and (2) a principal purpose of the plan or arrangement is to avoid the purposes of the regulations (Proposed Reg. § 1.267A-5(b)(6)).

The proposed regulations make changes to both the dual consolidated loss rules and the entity classification rules to prevent domestic reverse hybrid entities from claiming the same deduction under both the tax laws of the foreign corporation and the United States. A domestic reverse hybrid generally is a domestic business entity that elects to be treated as a corporation for U.S. tax purposes, but is treated as fiscally transparent under the tax laws of its investors (Proposed Reg. §§ 1.1503(d)-1(b)(2)(iii), (c), 1.1503(d)-3(e)(3), 1.1503(d)-6, 1.1503(d)-7(c)(41), 301.7701-3(a), and (c)). These rules apply to tax years ending, transfers occurring, or elections filed, as applicable, on or after December 20, 2018 (Proposed Reg. §§ 1.1503(d)-8(b)(6), (7), and 301.7701-3(c)(3)(iii)).

**Reporting requirements.** If a corporation is disallowed a deduction under Code Sec. 267A during an annual accounting period, information about the disallowance must be reported on Schedule G, Form 5471 (Proposed Reg. § 1.6038-2(f)(13); Form 5471 Instructions).

A controlled foreign partnership that is disallowed a deduction under Code Sec. 267A during the tax year must provide information about the disallowance on Form 8865 (Proposed Reg. § 1.6038-3(g)(3); Form 8865 Instructions).

## NEW LAW EXPLAINED

A reporting corporation that is disallowed a deduction under Code Sec. 267A during the tax year must provide information about the disallowance on Form 5472 (Proposed Reg. § 1.6038A-2; Form 5472 Instructions).

The reporting requirements apply to information for annual accounting periods or tax years, as applicable, beginning on or after December 20, 2018 (Proposed Reg. § § 1.6038-2(m), 1.6038-3(l), and 1.6038A-2(g)).

▶ **Effective date.** The amendment made by this section applies to tax years beginning after December 31, 2017 (Act Sec. 14222(c) of the Tax Cuts and Jobs Act (P.L. 115-97)).

— Act Sec. 14222(a) of the Tax Cuts and Jobs Act (P.L. 115-97)), adding new Code Sec. 267A;

— Act Sec. 14222(b);

— Act Sec. 14222(c), providing the effective date.

# ¶765  Surrogate Foreign Corporation Dividends

## SUMMARY OF NEW LAW

Dividends received from surrogate foreign corporations are not eligible for lower tax rate treatment as qualified dividend income.

## BACKGROUND

Reduced tax rates on dividends are intended to encourage certain types of equity investments. Accordingly, dividends paid by certain qualified foreign corporations to an individual shareholder are treated as qualified dividend income and are taxed at long-term capital gains rates (Code Sec. 1(h)(11)(C)).

> **Comment:** The tax rate for long-term capital gains is: 0 percent for taxpayers in the 10 or 15 percent brackets; 15 percent for taxpayers in the 25, 28, 33 or 35 percent brackets; and 20 percent for taxpayers in the 39.6 percent bracket (Code Sec. 1(h)).

A qualified foreign corporation is a corporation that is incorporated in a possession of the United States or a corporation that is eligible for benefits of a comprehensive income tax treaty with the United States that includes an exchange of information program (Code Sec. 1(h)(11)(C)(i)). Foreign corporations may also be treated as qualified foreign corporations if they pay dividends on stock that is readily tradable in an established U.S. securities market (Code Sec. 1(h)(11)(C)(ii)). If a foreign corporation is a passive foreign investment company (PFIC), as defined in Code Sec. 1297, during the year the dividend was paid or during the preceding tax year, then the corporation is not considered to be a qualified foreign corporation (Code Sec. 1(h)(11)C)(iii)).

NEW LAW EXPLAINED

**Dividends from surrogate foreign corporations excluded from reduced rate.—** Surrogate foreign corporations that are not treated as domestic corporations under Code Sec. 7874(b) are excluded from the meaning of qualified foreign corporation (Code Sec. 1(h)(11)(C)(iii), as amended by the Tax Cuts and Jobs Act (P.L. 115-97)). Generally, a surrogate foreign corporation is a foreign corporation that:

- acquires (after March 4, 2003) substantially all of the properties held by a U.S. corporation,

- after the acquisition, the U.S. corporation's former shareholders own at least 60 percent of the stock (by vote or value) of the foreign acquiring corporation, and

- the expanded affiliated group does not have substantial business activities in the country where the entity is organized or created compared to the total business activities of the expanded affiliated group (Code Sec. 7874(a)(2)(B)).

Dividends paid after December 22, 2017, by surrogate foreign corporations that are not treated as domestic corporations under Code Sec. 7874(b), do not qualify as qualified dividend income under Code Sec. 1(h)(11)(B)(i) (Code Sec. 1(h)(11)(C)(iii), as amended by the 2017 Tax Cuts Act). As such, dividends paid to shareholders after December 22, 2017, by surrogate foreign corporations that are not treated as domestic corporations under Code Sec. 7874(b) are ineligible for the reduced tax rate applicable to qualified dividends.

> **Comment:** The Senate Budget Committee's explanation of the tax reform bill states that while reduced tax rates on dividends are meant to encourage equity investments, the Committee does not believe that investments in surrogate foreign corporations fits within this parameter (JCX-56R-17)

▶ **Effective date.** The amendments made by this section apply to dividends paid after December 22, 2017, the date of enactment (Act Sec. 14223(b) of the Tax Cuts and Jobs Act of 2017 (P.L. 115-97)).

**No significant guidance related to this provision has been issued.**

— Act Sec. 14223(a) of the Tax Cuts and Jobs Act (P.L. 115-97)), amending Code Sec. 1(h)(11)(C)(iii) and adding (h)(11)(C)(iii)(II);

— Act Sec. 14223(b), providing the effective date.

# ¶770 Stock Compensation Excise Tax on Insiders in Expatriated Corporations

## SUMMARY OF NEW LAW

The excise tax rate on stock compensation received by insiders in an expatriated corporation increases from 15 percent to 20 percent.

## BACKGROUND

An excise tax is imposed on and payable by an individual who is a disqualified individual with respect to any expatriated corporation (Code Sec. 4985). The excise tax applies only if any of the expatriated corporation's shareholders recognize gains on any stock in the corporation by reason of the corporate inversion transaction that caused the expatriation.

Disqualified individuals generally include individuals who are officers, directors, and 10-percent-or-greater owners (including both private and publicly held corporations) with respect to the corporation during the 12-month period beginning on the date that precedes the expatriation by six months.

An inversion is a transaction in which, pursuant to a plan or a series of related transactions:

- a U.S. corporation or partnership becomes a subsidiary of a foreign-incorporated entity or otherwise transfers substantially all of its properties to such an entity after March 4, 2003;

- the former shareholders of the U.S. corporation hold (by reason of holding stock in the U.S. corporation) 60 percent or more (by vote or value) of the stock of the foreign incorporated entity after the transaction; and

- the foreign incorporated entity, considered together with all companies connected to it by a chain of greater than 50-percent ownership (i.e., the "expanded affiliated group") does not conduct substantial business activities in the entity's country of incorporation compared to the total worldwide business activities of the expanded affiliated group (Code Sec. 7874(a)(2)(B)).

## NEW LAW EXPLAINED

The excise tax does not apply to a stock option which is exercised on the expatriation date or during the six-month period before that date and to the stock acquired in such exercise, if income is recognized under the usual restricted property transfer compensation rules of Code Sec. 83 on or before the expatriation date (Code Sec. 4985(d)(1)). Also, the excise tax does not apply to any other specified stock compensation which is exercised, sold, exchanged, distributed, cashed-out, or otherwise paid during such period in a transaction in which income, gain, or loss is recognized in full (Code Sec. 4985(d)(2)).

**Excise tax on stock compensation of insiders in expatriated corporations increased.**—The excise tax rate on stock compensation received by insiders in an expatriated corporation is increased from 15 percent to 20 percent, effective on the date of enactment for corporations that first become expatriated after that date. (Code Sec. 4985(a)(1), as amended by the Tax Cuts and Jobs Act (P.L. 115-97); Code Sec. 1(h)(1)(D)).

▶ **Effective date.** The amendment made by this section applies to corporations first becoming expatriated corporations after December 22, 2017, the date of enactment of this Act (Act Sec. 13604(b) of the Tax Cuts and Jobs Act (P.L. 115-97)).

## NEW LAW EXPLAINED

**No significant guidance related to this provision has been issued.**

— Act Sec. 13604(a) of the Tax Cuts and Jobs Act (P.L. 115-97), amending Code Sec. 4985(a)(1);

— Act Sec. 13604(b), providing the effective date.

# OTHER INTERNATIONAL REFORMS

## ¶775 Insurance Business Exception to the Passive Foreign Investment Company Rules

### SUMMARY OF NEW LAW

The rule for determining what is not considered passive income for a passive foreign investment company (PFIC) has been modified. The test for nonpassive income that is based on whether a corporation is predominantly engaged in an insurance business has been replaced with a test based on the amount of the corporation's insurance liabilities.

### BACKGROUND

The passive foreign investment company (PFIC) rules apply to U.S. shareholders of foreign corporations that derive a significant amount of their income from investments in passive assets (Code Secs. 1291 and 1297). The PFIC rules attempt to eliminate the tax deferral that PFIC shareholders could otherwise receive because a foreign corporation is generally exempt from U.S. tax on foreign source income and its U.S. shareholders are generally not taxed until they dispose of their stock or receive a distribution (Senate Finance Committee Report and Conference Committee Report, Tax Reform Act of 1986 (P.L. 99-514)). The benefit of the tax deferral is eliminated by requiring a U.S. shareholder of a PFIC to pay a special tax plus an interest charge on gain recognized from the disposition or pledge of stock in the PFIC or upon the receipt of an excess distribution from the PFIC (Code Sec. 1291(a)).

When determining whether a foreign corporation is a PFIC under the income and asset tests (Code Sec. 1291(a)), passive income is income that would be considered foreign personal holding company income as defined in Code Sec. 954(c). However, passive income does not include any income that is: (1) derived in the active conduct of a banking business by certain foreign corporations; (2) derived in the active conduct of an insurance business by a corporation that is predominantly engaged in an insurance business that would be subject to tax under subchapter L (Insurance Companies) if it were a domestic corporation; (3) interest, a dividend, rent, or a

## BACKGROUND

royalty that is received or accrued from a related person to the extent such amount is allocable to income of such related person that is not passive income; or (4) export trade income of an export trade corporation (ETC) under Code Sec. 971 (Code Sec. 1297(b)(2)).

## NEW LAW EXPLAINED

**Insurance business exception to PFIC rules modified.**—The insurance business exception to the definition of passive income for the passive foreign investment company (PFIC) rules is modified for tax years beginning after December 31, 2017 (Code Sec. 1297(b)(2)(B), as amended by the Tax Cuts and Jobs Act (P.L. 115-97)). The test based on whether a corporation is predominantly engaged in an insurance business is replaced with a test based on the amount of the corporation's insurance liabilities (Code Sec. 1297(f)(1), as added by the 2017 Tax Cuts Act; Conference Report on H.R. 1, Tax Cuts and Jobs Act (H. Rept. 115-466)).

Except as provided in regulations, the term "passive income" does not include any income derived in the active conduct of an insurance business by a qualifying insurance corporation (Code Sec. 1297(b)(2)(B), as amended by the 2017 Tax Cuts Act). With respect to any tax year, a "qualifying insurance corporation" is a foreign corporation that:

- would be subject to tax under subchapter L of the Internal Revenue Code if the corporation were a domestic corporation; and

- has applicable insurance liabilities that are more than 25 percent of its total assets, determined on the basis of the insurance liabilities and total assets reported on the corporation's applicable financial statement for the last year ending with or within the tax year (Code Sec. 1297(f)(1), as added by the 2017 Tax Cuts Act).

A foreign corporation that fails to qualify as an insurance corporation because it does not have applicable insurance liabilities that are more than 25 percent of its total assets can apply an alternative facts and circumstances test (see "Alternative facts and circumstances test", below).

> **Comment:** The modification provides a more limited exception to PFIC status. The exception for corporations predominately engaged in an insurance business is replaced with a more stringent test based generally on a comparison of the corporation's insurance liabilities and total assets. The more stringent test is expected to mitigate the need for reporting on U.S. owners of these companies under FATCA. Under proposed regulations, premiums for insurance contracts that do not have cash value, are excludable nonfinancial payments, and therefore, are not withholdable payments. The proposed regulations may be relied upon until final regulations are issued (Proposed Reg. § 1.1473-1(a)(4)(iii); NPRM REG-132881-17, December 18, 2018).

**Insurance liabilities, financial statement, insurance regulatory body defined.** For purposes of the insurance business test, the "applicable insurance liabilities" of any life insurance or property and casualty insurance business are its:

## NEW LAW EXPLAINED

- loss and loss adjustment expenses; and

- reserves, other than deficiency, contingency, or unearned premium reserves, for both life and health insurance risks and life and health insurance claims with respect to contracts providing coverage for mortality or morbidity risks (Code Sec. 1297(f)(3), as added by the 2017 Tax Cuts Act).

The amount of any applicable insurance liability cannot exceed the lesser of such amount: (1) as reported to the applicable insurance regulatory body in the applicable financial statement (or, if less, the amount required by applicable law or regulation), or (2) as determined under regulations (Code Sec. 1297(f)(3)(B), as added by the 2017 Tax Cuts Act).

> **Comment:** In determining an insurance company's applicable insurance liabilities, its reserves include loss reserves for property and casualty, life, and health insurance contracts and annuity contracts. However, unearned premium reserves with respect to any type of risk are not treated as applicable insurance liabilities (Conference Report on H.R. 1, Tax Cuts and Jobs Act (H. Rept. 115-466)).

A corporation's "applicable financial statement" is a statement for financial reporting purposes that:

- is made on the basis of generally accepted accounting principles;

- is made on the basis of international financial reporting standards, if there is no statement that is made on the basis of generally accepted accounting principles; or

- unless otherwise provided in regulations, is the annual statement that must be filed with the applicable insurance regulatory body, if there is no statement that is made on the basis of generally accepted accounting principles or international financial reporting standards (Code Sec. 1297(f)(4)(A), as added by the 2017 Tax Cuts Act).

An "applicable insurance regulatory body" is the entity established by law to license, authorize or regulate an insurance business and to which the business files its applicable financial statement (Code Sec. 1297(f)(4)(B), as added by the 2017 Tax Cuts Act).

**Alternative facts and circumstances test.** If a corporation fails to qualify as a qualified insurance corporation solely because the percentage of its applicable insurance liabilities is 25 percent or less of its total assets, a U.S. person that owns stock in the corporation can elect to apply an alternative facts and circumstances test. Under the alternative facts and circumstances test, the U.S. person can elect to treat the stock as stock of a qualifying insurance corporation if:

(1) the percentage of the corporation's applicable insurance liabilities is at least 10 percent of its total assets; and

(2) based on the applicable facts and circumstances, the corporation is predominantly engaged in an insurance business and its failure to meet the more-than-25-percent threshold is due solely to run-off related or rating-related circumstances involving such insurance business (Code Sec. 1297(f)(2), as added by the 2017 Tax Cuts Act).

## NEW LAW EXPLAINED

The applicable facts and circumstances for (2), above, would be determined under regulations to be provided by the IRS. Some of the facts and circumstances that tend to show that a corporation may not be predominantly engaged in an insurance business include a small number of insured risks with low likelihood but large potential costs; workers focused to a greater degree on investment activities than underwriting activities; and low loss exposure (Conference Report on H.R. 1, Tax Cuts and Jobs Act (H. Rept. 115-466)).

A company is in "runoff" if it is not taking on new insurance business (and consequently has little or no premium income), and is using its remaining assets to pay off claims with respect to pre-existing insurance risks on its books (Conference Report on H.R. 1, Tax Cuts and Jobs Act (H. Rept. 115-466)).

▶ **Effective date.** The amendments made by this section apply to tax years beginning after December 31, 2017 (Act Sec. 14501(c) of the Tax Cuts and Jobs Act (P.L. 115-97)).

**No significant guidance related to this provision has been issued**.

— Act Sec. 14501(a) of the Tax Cuts and Jobs Act (P.L. 115-97), amending Code Sec. 1297(b)(2)(B);

— Act Sec. 14501(b), adding new Code Sec. 1297(f);

— Act Sec. 14501(c), providing the effective date.

## ¶780 Interest Expense Allocation and Apportionment

### SUMMARY OF NEW LAW

The fair market value method for allocating and apportioning interest expense may no longer be used.

### BACKGROUND

U.S. taxpayers are taxed on their worldwide income, but are allowed a foreign tax credit for foreign income taxes paid or accrued, in order to prevent the double taxation of foreign source income (Code Sec. 901). The foreign tax credit limitation provides that when foreign income tax is higher than U.S. income tax, the foreign tax credit is limited to the U.S. tax that would be due on the foreign income (Code Sec. 904). The purpose of the limitation is to protect the U.S. tax base and to prevent the reduction of U.S. tax on U.S. source income. The limitation is determined by multiplying a taxpayer's total U.S. tax liability (before the foreign tax credit) for the tax year by the ratio of the taxpayer's foreign source taxable income to worldwide taxable income (Code Sec. 904(a)).

The foreign tax credit limitation requires that the foreign tax credit limitation be calculated separately for certain categories of income or "baskets". There are generally two foreign separate limitation categories or baskets—a "passive category income" basket and a "general category income" basket (Reg. § 1.904-4). Foreign source

## BACKGROUND

taxable income for each category is gross income for the category, less expenses, losses and other deductions. The allocation and apportionment of deductions for purposes of determining the foreign tax credit limitation generally requires that the expense is first allocated to a specific class of income, and then apportioned between the statutory groupings (i.e., foreign source general and passive limitation income) and the residual grouping (i.e., U.S. source income) (Reg. § 1.861-8). The foreign tax credit limitation can be increased by maximizing the portion of worldwide taxable income that is foreign source taxable income. Minimizing the amount of interest expense that is allocated and apportioned to foreign source income is one way to increase foreign source taxable income. The term interest expense refers to amounts deductible under Code Sec. 163.

The method for allocating and apportioning interest expense to U.S. or foreign source income recognizes that money is a fungible asset and, accordingly, interest expense is attributable to all activities and property without regard to the specific reason for incurring debt. Deductions for interest expense are considered related to all income-producing activities and assets of the taxpayer and are allocated to all gross income that the assets of the taxpayer generate (Code Sec. 864(e)(2); Temp. Reg. § 1.861-9T(a)).

Allocation and apportionment of interest expense must be made on the basis of the assets and not gross income. Under the asset method, taxpayers apportion interest expense to the various statutory groupings based on the average total value of the assets within the grouping for the tax year, according to the asset valuation rules and asset characterization rules of Temp. Reg. §§ 1.861-9T(g) and 1.861-12T. Taxpayers may choose to value their assets on the basis of either the tax book value (TBV) (i.e., adjusted basis), the alternative tax book value method or the fair market value method (Temp. Reg. § 1.861-9T(g)(1)(ii) and (h); Reg. § 1.861-9(i)).

### NEW LAW EXPLAINED

**Fair market value method of interest expense allocation and apportionment eliminated.**—Taxpayers may no longer use the fair market value method to allocate and apportion interest expense. All allocations and apportionments of interest expense must be determined using the adjusted basis of the assets. The use of gross income to allocate and apportion interest expense continues to be disallowed (Code Sec. 864(e)(2), as amended by the Tax Cuts and Jobs Act (P.L. 115-97)).

Proposed regulations reflect the repeal of the fair market value method of valuing assets (Proposed Reg. § 1.861-9(g)(1)(ii); REG NPRM 105600-18, December 7, 2018). A taxpayer must switch to the tax book or alternative tax book value, for purposes of apportioning interest expense, for the taxpayer's first tax year beginning after December 31, 2017. The IRS is not required to consent to the change (Proposed Reg. §§ 1.861-8(c)(2) and 1.861-9(i)(2)).

Transitional relief is provided to taxpayers that previously used the fair market value method (Proposed Reg. § 1.861-9(g)(2)(i)). For the first tax year beginning after December 31, 2017, a taxpayer that has been using the fair market value method may choose to determine asset values using an average of the end of the first quarter and the year-

## NEW LAW EXPLAINED

end values of its assets, provided that all members of an affiliated group make the same choice and no substantial distortion would result. The fair market value method was repealed for purposes of allocating and apportioning interest expenses, however, the fair market value method and the rules in Reg. § 1.861-9(h) remain applicable for non-interest expenses that are properly allocated and apportioned on the basis of relative fair market value of assets (Proposed Reg. § 1.861-9(h)).

> **Comment:** Use of the fair market value method required that certain documentation and information requirements be met (Rev. Proc. 2003-37). Use of this method was also more likely to result in disputes with the IRS. Electing the fair market value method, however, could result in an increase in foreign source taxable income, and therefore, foreign tax credit limitation, particularly if U.S. based assets have higher appreciated values than foreign assets. Use of the adjusted tax basis method, requires that assets located outside of the United States be depreciated using the alternative depreciation system (ADS) under Code Sec. 168(g). This method results in slower depreciation than that allowed under the Modified Accelerated Recovery System (MACRS), the method used for assets located in the United States. As a result, more interest expense is allocated to foreign source income, which can reduce foreign source taxable income and the taxpayer's foreign tax credit limitation. An election to use the alternative tax book value method under Reg. § 1.861-9(i) allows a taxpayer to use the straight-line method, conventions and recovery periods for tangible property.

▶ **Effective date.** The amendment made by this section applies to tax years beginning after December 31, 2017 (Act Sec. 14502(b) of the Tax Cuts and Jobs Act (P.L. 115-97)).

— Act Sec. 14502(a) of the Tax Cuts and Jobs Act (P.L. 115-97), amending Code Sec. 864(e)(2);

— Act Sec. 14502(b), providing the effective date.

# Exempt Organizations, Bonds, and Other Provisions

**8**

## TAX-EXEMPT ORGANIZATIONS

## BONDS

## TAX PRACTICE AND PROCEDURE

# TAX-EXEMPT ORGANIZATIONS

## ¶805 Unrelated Business Taxable Income Separately Computed for Each Trade or Business Activity

### SUMMARY OF NEW LAW

Exempt organizations with more than one unrelated business will be required to calculate unrelated business taxable income separately for each unrelated trade or business.

¶805

## BACKGROUND

The income of an exempt organization is subject to the tax on unrelated business income imposed by Code Sec. 511 only if the income is from a trade or business that is regularly carried on by the organization and the trade or business is not substantially related—aside from the need of the organization for funds or the use it makes of the profits—to the organization's exercise or performance of the purposes or functions on which its exemption is based.

The unrelated business taxable income of an organization regularly carrying on two or more unrelated businesses is the aggregate of its gross income from all unrelated businesses, less the aggregate of the deductions allowed with respect to all such unrelated businesses (Reg. § 1.512(a)-1). As a result, an organization may use a deduction from one unrelated trade or business to offset income from another, thereby reducing total unrelated business taxable income.

The net operating loss deduction is allowed in determining unrelated business taxable income, but must reflect only taxable "business" income (Code Sec. 512(b)(6)). A net operating loss is allowable in a year where unrelated business income occurs. Losses can be carried back two years and forward 20 years (Code Sec. 172(b)(1)(A)). Years during which there is no unrelated business income do not count toward expiration of the carryforward period (Reg. § 1.512(b)-1(e)).

## NEW LAW EXPLAINED

**Unrelated business taxable income must be separately calculated for each unrelated business.**—A special rule has been added for exempt organizations that have unrelated business taxable income from operating more than one unrelated business. For all purposes, including the calculating of any net operating loss deduction, the unrelated business taxable income of each trade or business will be determined separately and without regard to Code Sec. 512(b)(12), which generally permits a specific deduction of $1,000 (Code Sec. 512(a)(6)(A), as added by the Tax Cuts and Jobs Act (P.L. 115-97)).

The unrelated business taxable income of the exempt organization having more than one unrelated trade or business will be the sum of the unrelated business taxable income of those unrelated businesses, less the specific deduction permitted by Code Sec. 512(b)(12) (Code Sec. 512(a)(6)(B), as added by the 2017 Tax Cuts Act). However, the unrelated business taxable income of any particular trade or business cannot be less than zero (Code Sec. 512(a)(6)(C), as added by the 2017 Tax Cuts Act).

The effects of the new rule are to prevent a deduction from one unrelated trade or business from offsetting income from another unrelated business in the same tax year, and to prevent the specific $1,000 deduction from being claimed more than once in a tax year regardless of how many unrelated businesses an exempt organization may have (Conference Report on H.R. 1, Tax Cuts and Jobs Act (H. Rept. 115-466). It does not, however, prevent the carryover of unused deductions to subsequent tax years if they were previously permitted and so long as they are utilized by the same unrelated business that generated such deduction.

¶805

## NEW LAW EXPLAINED

A transition rule provides that net operating losses arising in tax years beginning before January 1, 2018, that are carried over to tax years beginning on or after January 1, 2018, are not subject to the rule requiring unrelated business taxable income to be computed separately for each trade or business for purposes of determining the amount of the NOL. The NOL will reduce unrelated business taxable income of the organization computed as the sum of the unrelated business taxable income from each of its trades or businesses, less the specific deduction of $1,000 (Act Sec. 13702(b)(2) of the 2017 Tax Cuts Act).

*Interim guidance.* Until proposed regulations are issued, Notice 2018-67 provides interim guidance, portions of which may be relied upon by taxpayers. Organizations should rely on reasonable, good-faith interpretations of Code Secs. 511 through 514 when determining whether an exempt organization has more than one unrelated business for purposes of Code Sec. 512(a)(6), including whether to separate:

- debt-financed income described in Code Secs. 512(b)(4) and 514;

- income from a controlled entity described in Code Sec. 512(b)(13); or

- insurance income earned through a controlled foreign corporation as described in Code Sec. 512(b)(17).

Reliance on the use of NAICS 6-digit codes will be considered a reasonable, good-faith interpretation until proposed regulations are published.

*Aggregating income from partnership interests.* Exempt organizations, other than social clubs exempt under Code Sec. 501(c)(7), may rely on the rules provided for aggregating income from partnerships, including any unrelated debt-financed income that is earned through a partnership that meets certain requirements. An exempt organization may aggregate its unrelated business taxable income from its interest in a single partnership with multiple trades or businesses as long as the directly-held interest in the partnership meets the requirements of either a de minimis or a control test.

The de minimus test is met if the exempt organization holds directly no more than two percent of the profits interest and no more than two percent of the capital interest. The organization may rely on the information it receives on its Schedule K-1 in making this determination.

The control test is met if the organization's partnership interest is:

- not more than 20 percent of the capital interest, and

- the organization has control or influence over the partnership, as determined by all of the facts and circumstances.

Reliance on the information on its Schedule K-1 is permitted. A transition rule is provided allowing for aggregating income within each direct partnership interest acquired before August 21, 2018.

## NEW LAW EXPLAINED

*Other points of reliance.* Other items of guidance on which taxpayers may rely include:

- The nondeductible amount of certain fringe benefit expenses paid or incurred by an exempt organization, as described in Code Sec. 512(a)(7), is not income from a trade or business for purposes of Code Sec. 512(a)(6).

- When calculating unrelated business taxable income, any global intangible low-taxed income is included under Code Sec. 951A(a) in the same manner as Subpart F income is included under Code Sec. 951(a)(1)(A). It is therefore treated as a dividend, and treated in the same manner as other dividends are treated for purposes of Code Sec. 511 under Code Secs. 512(b)(1) and (b)(4).

▶ **Effective date.** The amendment made by this section generally applies to tax years beginning after December 31, 2017 (Act Sec. 13702(b)(1) of the Tax Cuts and Jobs Act (P.L. 115-97)). However, if any net operating loss (NOL) arising in a tax year beginning before January 1, 2018, is carried over to any succeeding tax year, then Code Sec. 512(a)(6)(A) will not apply to the NOL and the unrelated business taxable income of the exempt organization (after application of Code Sec. 512(a)(6)(B)) will be reduced by the amount of the NOL (Act Sec. 13702(b)(2) of the 2017 Tax Cuts Act).

— Act Sec. 13702(a) of the Tax Cuts and Jobs Act (P.L. 115-97), adding Code Sec. 512(a)(6);

— Act Sec. 13702(b), providing the effective date.

## ¶807  Unrelated Business Taxable Income Increased by Certain Fringe Benefit Expenses

### SUMMARY OF NEW LAW

Unrelated business taxable income will be increased by the nondeductible amount of certain fringe benefit expenses paid or incurred by an exempt organization after December 31, 2017.

### BACKGROUND

The income of an exempt organization is subject to the tax on unrelated business income if two conditions are present: (1) the income must be from a trade or business regularly carried on by the organization, and (2) the trade or business must not be substantially related—aside from the need of the organization for funds or the use it makes of the profits—to the organization's exercise or performance of the purposes or functions on which its exemption is based (Code Secs. 511 and 512).

Unrelated business taxable income (UBTI), which is subject to the tax under Code Sec. 511, is the gross income derived by any organization from any unrelated trade or business regularly carried on by it, less the regular deductions allowed for income tax purposes which are directly connected with the carrying on of such trade or business (Code Sec. 512(a)).

## BACKGROUND

Ordinary and necessary business expenses are generally tax deductible, while expenses incurred for personal reasons or pleasure are not deductible (Code Secs. 162 and 262). This distinction can be difficult to make when expenses have both personal and business components, such as entertainment, gift and travel expenses incurred to promote business. Code Sec. 274 addresses this problem by imposing additional limits on expenses that are otherwise deductible under other Internal Revenue Code provisions.

Fringe benefits are a form of compensation and, as such, must be included in income and are subject to withholding unless explicitly excluded under the Internal Revenue Code. Eight basic types of fringe benefits are excluded from an employee's gross income, including a no-additional-cost service, a qualified employee discount, a working condition fringe, a de minimis fringe, a qualified transportation fringe, a qualified moving expense reimbursement, qualified retirement planning services, and qualified military base realignment and closure fringe benefit payments (Code Sec. 132). Special rules also exclude eating and athletic facilities, and the use of certain demonstrator automobiles.

## NEW LAW EXPLAINED

**Disallowed fringe benefits treated as additions to unrelated income.**—The unrelated business taxable income (UBTI) of an exempt organization will be increased by the nondeductible amount of certain fringe benefit expenses incurred by the organization in that tax year, effective for amounts paid or incurred after December 31, 2017 (Code Sec. 512(a)(7), as added by the Tax Cuts and Jobs Act (P.L. 115-97)). These fringe benefits are expenses for which a deduction is not available due to Code Sec. 274, and specifically include:

- any qualified transportation fringe, as defined in Code Sec. 132(f);

- any parking facility used in connection with qualified parking, as defined in Code Sec. 132(f)(5)(C); and

- any on-premises athletic facility, as defined in Code Sec. 132(j)(4)(B).

   **Comment:** The calculation of UBTI associated with providing qualified transportation fringes, including parking facilities used in connection with qualified parking, is intended to be determined in a manner consistent with the deduction disallowance under Code Sec. 274. However, a technical correction may be required to properly reflect this intent (General Explanation of Public Law 115-97 (JCS-1-18)).

To the extent the amount paid or incurred is directly connected with an unrelated trade or business that is regularly carried on by the organization, such amounts will *not* increase an organization's UBTI (Code Sec. 512(a)(7), as added by the 2017 Tax Cuts Act). Thus, the increases to UBTI for disallowed fringe benefits are for expenses paid or incurred by the organization that are not associated with any unrelated business of the organization.

## NEW LAW EXPLAINED

> **Comment:** The increase in UBTI for certain fringe benefits is an *addition to* UBTI, rather than a change in the normal calculation of UBTI.

**Regulations and other guidance.** The IRS is directed to issue regulations or other guidance that may be necessary or appropriate to carry out the purposes of the rule on fringe benefit expenses, such as guidance on the appropriate allocation of depreciation and other costs of facilities used for parking or for on-premises athletic facilities (Code Sec. 512(a)(7), as added by the 2017 Tax Cuts Act).

*Interim guidance.* Notice 2018-99 provides interim guidance on which a taxpayer may rely, until the IRS releases further guidance, providing that a tax-exempt organization with only one unrelated trade or business can reduce the increase to UBTI under Code Sec. 512(a)(7) to the extent that the deductions directly connected with the carrying on of that unrelated trade or business exceed the gross income derived from such unrelated trade or business. Examples are provided.

▶ **Effective date.** The amendment made by this section applies to amounts paid or incurred after December 31, 2017 (Act Sec. 13703(b) of the Tax Cuts and Jobs Act (P.L. 115-97)).

— Act Sec. 13703(a) of the Tax Cuts and Jobs Act (P.L. 115-97), adding Code Sec. 512(a)(7);

— Act Sec. 13703(b), providing the effective date.

## ¶810 Excise Tax on Excess Tax-Exempt Organization Executive Compensation

### SUMMARY OF NEW LAW

A new excise tax has been established, payable by exempt organizations on remuneration in excess of $1 million and any excess parachute payments made to certain highly-compensated current and former employees in the tax year.

### BACKGROUND

Generally, for-profit employers are allowed a deduction for reasonable compensation expenses under Code Sec. 162(a). In some cases, however, compensation in excess of specific levels is not deductible. A publicly held corporation cannot deduct compensation to a covered employee to the extent the compensation exceeds $1 million per tax year (Code Sec. 162(m)). The $1 million threshold is reduced (but not below zero) by excess parachute payments that are not deductible under the golden parachute provisions of Code Sec. 280G. These deduction limits generally do not affect tax-exempt organizations.

A payment in the nature of compensation made to or for the benefit of a disqualified individual is a parachute payment if:

## BACKGROUND

- it is contingent on a change in the ownership or effective control of the corporation or the ownership of a substantial portion of the assets of a corporation, and its present value equals or exceeds 300 percent of the individual's average annual compensation for the last five years (a "change-in-control parachute payment"), or

- it is made under an agreement that violates securities laws (a "securities violation parachute payment").

Certain amounts are not considered parachute payments, including payments under a qualified retirement plan, a simplified employee pension plan, or a simple retirement account.

For this purpose, disqualified individuals (also called "covered employees") are employees, independent contractors, and other persons who perform personal services for a corporation *and* who are officers, shareholders or highly compensated individuals are subject to the golden parachute provisions. Disqualified individuals also include personal service corporations and similar entities (Code Sec. 280G(c)).

Negative tax consequences are imposed only on excess parachute payments. An excess parachute payment is the portion of any parachute payment that exceeds the base amount, which is the recipient's average annual compensation over the five years before the change in ownership, reduced, in the case of a change-in-control parachute payment, by the excess of the amount of the payment determined to be reasonable compensation for services performed before the date of the change over average compensation. The excess amount is determined separately for each parachute payment received.

## NEW LAW EXPLAINED

**Excise tax applies to remuneration of highly-compensated exempt organization executives.**—A tax-exempt organization will be liable within a tax year for a 21 percent excise tax (equal to the maximum corporate tax rate on income) on the sum of:

- "remuneration" paid to a "covered employee" in excess of $1 million (not including any excess parachute payment) by an "applicable tax-exempt organization", and

- any excess parachute payments paid to a covered employee by that tax-exempt organization (Code Sec. 4960, as added by the Tax Cuts and Jobs Act of 2017 (P.L. 115-97)).

It should be noted that an exempt organization can be liable for this tax even when a covered employee's remuneration is less than $1 million if there is an excess parachute payment.

It is intended that the liability for the excise tax on an excess parachute payment will be treated the same as the liability for the excise tax on remuneration. However, a technical correction may be necessary to reflect this intent (General Explanation of Public Law 115-97 (JCS-1-18)).

> **Comment:** The IRS has issued interim guidance on the applicability and implementation of the excise tax in Notice 2019-9.

## NEW LAW EXPLAINED

For purposes of this excise tax, there is a new definition for parachute payments that is limited to the payment of compensation to a covered employee when such payment is contingent on:

- the employee's separation from employment with the tax-exempt employer, and
- the aggregate present value of the compensation payments being equal or in excess of an amount equal to three times the base amount (Code Sec. 4960(c)(5)(B), as added by the 2017 Tax Cuts Act).

The base amount is determined under Code Sec. 280G(b)(3). However, certain payments are excluded from calculating the aggregate present value, including:

- payments under qualified plans, as described in Code Sec. 280G(b)(6));
- payments made to or under a tax-deferred annuity contract as described in Code Sec. 403(b), or the deferred compensation plan of a government employer as described in Code Sec. 457(b);
- payments to a doctor, nurse, or veterinarian for the performance of medical or veterinarian professional services; and
- payments to an individual who is not a highly compensated employee as defined in Code Sec. 414(q) (Code Sec. 4960(c)(5)(C), as added by the 2017 Tax Cuts Act).

In addition, compensation will be considered to be paid when no substantial risk of forfeiture (as defined in Code Sec. 457(f)(3)(B)) exists (Code Sec. 4960(a), as added by the 2017 Tax Cuts Act). Therefore, such compensation may be considered paid when fully vested even if not yet actually paid.

An "applicable tax-exempt organization" (ATEO) is one that is exempt from taxation under Code Sec. 501(a), a farmers' cooperative under Code Sec. 521(b)(1), a political organization described in Code Sec. 527(e)(1), or an organization that has income excluded from taxation under Code Sec. 115(1) (Code Sec. 4960(c)(1), as added by the 2017 Tax Cuts Act). ATEO is intended to include state colleges and universities, but a technical correction may be required before this intent is realized (General Explanation of Public Law 115-97 (JCS-1-18)).

For purposes of this provision, a "covered employee" includes any current or former employee of the ATEO who is one of the five highest compensated employees for the current tax year, or a covered employee of the organization (or any predecessor organization) for any preceding tax year that began after December 31, 2016 (Code Sec. 4960(c)(2), as added by the 2017 Tax Cuts Act). In calculating remuneration for purposes of determining the five highest compensated employees, remuneration from all organizations related to the ATEO, is included (other than remuneration for medical or veterinary services). Remuneration from the ATEO or related organization is not included in this determination if the ATEO paid less that ten percent of the employee's total remuneration, unless no ATEO paid at least ten percent of the employees total remuneration (Notice 2019-9).

"Remuneration" generally means wages, as defined in Code Sec. 3401(a). Remuneration, for purposes of this section, specifically includes amounts required to be included in income by Code Sec. 457(f), but does not include:

**NEW LAW EXPLAINED**

- any designated Roth contribution under Code Sec. 402A(c); or

- any remuneration paid to a licensed medical professional (doctor, nurse, or veterinarian) for the performance of medical or veterinary services (Code Sec. 4960(c)(3), as added by the 2017 Tax Cuts Act).

The remuneration of a covered employee includes not only compensation paid by an ATEO in a tax year, but also any compensation paid to that employee for employment by any related organization of the ATEO in that same tax year. Related organizations include any person or government agency that, during the tax year:

- controls, or is controlled by, the organization;

- is controlled by one or more persons that control the organization;

- is a supported organization, as defined in Code Sec. 509(f)(3), of the organization;

- is a supporting organization, as defined in Code Sec. 509(a)(3), of the organization; or

- establishes, maintains, or makes contributions to an ATEO that is a voluntary employees' beneficiary association (VEBA), as defined in Code Sec. 501(c)(9) (Code Sec. 4960(c)(4), as added by the 2017 Tax Cuts Act).

A technical correction may be necessary to reflect that the related organization rules also apply to excess parachute payments and for purposes of determining covered employees (General Explanation of Public Law 115-97 (JCS-1-18)).

Any remuneration that is not deductible due to the $1 million limit on deductible compensation under Code Sec. 162(m) is not included in determining the total remuneration of a covered employee (Code Sec. 4960(c)(6), as added by the 2017 Tax Cuts Act). When remuneration from more than one employer is included in determining the tax imposed by Code Sec. 4960(a), each employer will be liable for its respective percentage of the total tax debt according to the percentage of income it paid into the employee's aggregate remuneration from all employers (Code Sec. 4960(c)(4), as added by the 2017 Tax Cuts Act).

▶ **Effective date.** The amendment made by this section applies to tax years beginning after December 31, 2017 (Act Sec. 13602(c) of the Tax Cuts and Jobs Act of 2017 (P.L. 115-97)).

— Act Sec. 13602(a) of the Tax Cuts and Jobs Act of 2017 (P.L. 115-97), adding Code Sec. 4960;

— Act Sec. 13602(c), providing the effective date.

## ¶815　Excise Tax Based on Investment Income of Private Colleges and Universities

**SUMMARY OF NEW LAW**

A new Code section imposes a 1.4 percent excise tax on the net investment income of certain private colleges and universities.

## BACKGROUND

Private foundations (other than exempt operating foundations) are generally subject to a two-percent excise tax on their net investment income under Code Sec. 4940(a). Net investment income is gross investment income and net capital gain, less expenses paid or incurred in earning the gross investment income. Tax-exempt interest on governmental obligations and related expenses are excluded. Gross investment income means the gross amount of income from interest, dividends, rents, and royalties received by a private foundation from all sources, unless the income is taxable as unrelated business income under Code Sec. 511.

The two-percent excise tax is reduced to one percent on the net investment income of a private foundation if the amount of the qualifying charitable distributions made by the foundation during the tax year equals or exceeds the average historic level of its charitable distributions, determined by calculating the sum of: (1) an amount equal to the foundation's assets for the tax year multiplied by the average percentage payout for the base period, *plus* (2) one percent of the foundation's net investment income for the year (Code Sec. 4940(e)). In addition, the foundation must not have been subject to the excise tax under Code Sec. 4942 for failure to make minimum qualifying distributions during the "base period"—five tax years preceding the current tax year.

Private colleges and universities are generally considered 501(c)(3) educational organizations and thus public charities rather than private foundations. They are therefore not subject to the private foundation excise tax on net investment income.

## NEW LAW EXPLAINED

**Net investment income of private colleges and universities taxed.**—A new Internal Revenue Code section imposes a 1.4 percent tax on the net investment income of certain private colleges and universities in each tax year beginning after December 31, 2017 (Code Sec. 4968, as added by the Tax Cuts and Jobs Act of 2017 (P.L. 115-97)). For this purpose, net investment income is defined by reference to Code Sec. 4940(c), which defines it for purposes of the excise tax applicable to private foundations.

The tax is imposed on "applicable educational institutions," defined as eligible educational institutions (as described in Code Sec. 25A(f)(2)) that:

- have at least 500 students during the preceding tax year, of which more than 50 percent are located in the United States,

- are private educational institutions and not state colleges and universities described in Code Sec. 511(a)(2)(B), and

- have assets with an aggregate fair market value of at least $500,000 per student (not including assets used directly in carrying out the institution's exempt purpose) as measured at the end of the preceding tax year.

For these purposes, the number of students of an institution is based on the daily average number of full-time students attending the institution, with part-time students being taken into account on a full-time student equivalent basis.

¶815

## NEW LAW EXPLAINED

The assets and net investment income of any related organization are treated as assets and net investment income of the applicable educational institution. Related organizations include any organization that:

- controls, or is controlled by, an applicable education institution;

- is controlled by one or more persons who also control that educational institution; or

- is either a supported organization (as defined in Code Sec. 509(f)(3)) or a organization described in Code Sec. 509(a)(3) in regards to the educational institution during the tax year.

*Interim guidance.* Notice 2018-55 provides guidance on which applicable educational institutions (as described in Code Sec. 4968(b)(1)) may rely for determining gain or loss until proposed regulations are issued that clarify the calculation of net investment income for purposes of Code Sec. 4968.

For any educational institution to which Code Sec. 4968 applies, in the case of any property held on December 31, 2017, and continuously thereafter to the date of its disposition, the basis of such property for the purpose of determining gain will be deemed to be not less than the fair market value of such property on December 31, 2017, plus (or minus) all adjustments after that date and before the date of disposition. For purposes of determining loss, basis rules consistent with those in Code Sec. 4940(c) will apply.

The Notice also states that proposed regulations will be issued that provide that losses from sales or other dispositions of property will generally be allowed only to the extent of gains from such sales or other dispositions. No capital loss carryovers or carrybacks will be permitted.

▶ **Effective date.** The amendment made by this section applies to tax years beginning after December 31, 2017 (Act Sec. 13701(c) of the Tax Cuts and Jobs Act of 2017 (P.L. 115-97)).

— Act Sec. 13701(a) of the Tax Cut and Jobs Act of 2017 (P.L. 115-97), adding Code Sec. 4968;

— Act Sec. 13701(c), providing the effective date.

# BONDS

## ¶870  Advance Refunding Bonds

### SUMMARY OF NEW LAW

Interest paid on advance refunding bonds issued after 2017 is not excludable from gross income as interest paid on state and local government bonds.

## BACKGROUND

Interest received on exempt state and local bonds is generally excludable from income (Code Sec. 103). There are two types of exempt state and local bonds: governmental bonds that finance governmental facilities, and qualified private activity bonds in which a state or local government acts as a conduit to provide financing to private business or individuals (Code Secs. 103 and 141).

The exclusion may also apply to interest on bonds that are issued to retire an outstanding exempt bond (refunding bonds). There are two types of refunding bonds. A current refunding bond must be redeemed within 90 days of issuance of the refunding bonds. An advance refunding bond is issued more than 90 days before the redemption of the refunded bond. Interest on advance refunding bonds may be exempt only when several requirements are satisfied; for instance, most exempt bonds may be advance refunded only once, exempt advance refunding bonds generally must be called at the earliest redemption date, and the only private activity bonds that may be advance refunded with interest-exempt bonds are qualified 501(c)(3) bonds (Code Sec. 149(d)).

## NEW LAW EXPLAINED

**Exclusion eliminated for interest on advance refunding bonds.**—Interest paid on advance refunding bonds issued after December 31, 2017, is not excludable from gross income (Code Sec. 149(d), as amended by the Tax Cuts and Jobs Act (P.L. 115-97)).

▶ **Effective date.** The amendments apply to advance refunding bonds issued after December 31, 2017 (Act Sec. 13532(c) of the Tax Cuts and Jobs Act (P.L. 115-97)).

**No significant guidance related to this provision has been issued.**

— Act Sec. 13532(a) of the Tax Cuts and Jobs Act (P.L. 115-97), amending Code Sec. 149(d)(1);

— Act Sec. 13532(b), amending Code Secs. 148(f)(4)(C) and 149(d);

— Act Sec. 13532(c), providing the effective date.

## ¶875  Tax Credit Bonds

### SUMMARY OF NEW LAW

New tax credit bonds cannot be issued after December 31, 2017.

### BACKGROUND

State and local governments and other entities may issue various kinds of tax credit bonds to finance specific types of projects. Each kind of tax credit bond has its own set of rules regarding volume cap and allocation. The authority to issue some types of tax credit bonds has expired, and the volume cap to issue some of these bonds has been fully used.

## BACKGROUND

A tax credit bond produces a tax credit for a taxpayer who holds the bond on the credit allowance date (Code Sec. 54A). Qualified tax credit bonds include:

- Qualified forestry conservation bonds which governments, local governments, and charitable organizations exempt from tax under Code Sec. 501(c)(3) may be authorized by the IRS to issue, the proceeds of which must be used to acquire certain land adjacent to U.S. Forest Service Land with restrictions to ensure conservation (Code Sec. 54B);

- Clean renewable energy bonds (Code Sec. 54) and new clean renewable energy bonds (Code Sec. 54C) which public power providers, cooperative electric companies, governmental bodies, clean renewable energy bond lenders, and certain not-for-profit electric utilities may issue, the proceeds of which must be used as capital expenditures incurred for qualified renewable energy facilities;

- Qualified energy conservation bonds which state governments and local governments may issue, the proceeds of which must be used for qualified conservation purposes (Code Sec. 54D);

- Qualified zone academy bonds which certain state and local governments are authorized to issue, the proceeds of which must be used to improve public schools (Code Sec. 54E for bonds issued on or after October 3, 2008, and Code Sec. 1397E for prior bonds);

- Qualified school construction bonds which state and local governments may issue if the proceeds are used to build, rehabilitate, or repair public schools or to purchase land on which to build a school (Code Sec. 54F), and

- Build America bonds which pay interest to the bondholders and also provide a tax credit (Code Sec. 54AA).

During 2009 and 2010, an issuer could elect to issue certain tax credit bonds as "direct-pay bonds." Instead of a credit to the holder, the federal government pays the issuer a percentage of the interest on the bonds. Tax credit bonds for which an issuer could make a direct-pay election include new clean renewable energy bonds, qualified energy conservation bonds, and qualified school construction bonds (Code Sec. 6431).

## NEW LAW EXPLAINED

**New tax credit bonds cannot be issued after 2017.**—Tax credit bond provisions are repealed and new tax credit bonds cannot be issued after December 31, 2017 (Code Secs. 54, 54A, 54B, Code Sec. 54C, 54D, 54E, 54F, 54AA and 6431, stricken by the Tax Cut and Jobs Act of 2017 (P.L. 115-97)).

> **Comment:** Holders and issuers will continue receiving tax credits and payments for tax credit bonds already issued (House Committee Report for the Tax Cuts and Jobs Act of 2017 (P.L. 115-97) (H.R. Rep. No. 115-409)).

## NEW LAW EXPLAINED

▶ **Effective date.** The amendments made by this section apply to bonds issued after December 31, 2017 (Act Sec. 13404(d) of the Tax Cut and Jobs Act of 2017 (P.L. 115-97)).

**No significant guidance related to this provision has been issued.**

— Act Sec. 13404(a) and (b) of the Tax Cut and Jobs Act of 2017 (P.L. 115-97), striking Code Secs. 54, 54A, 54B, 54C, 54D, 54E, 54F, 54AA and 6431;

— Act Sec. 13404(c), providing conforming amendments to Code Secs. 54, 1397E, 6211, and 6401;

— Act Sec. 13404(d), providing the effective date.

# TAX PRACTICE AND PROCEDURE

## ¶880  Time Limits to File Suit and Return Property for Wrongful Levies

### SUMMARY OF NEW LAW

The time limit that the IRS has to return monetary proceeds from a wrongfully levied sale of property has been extended to two years from the date of levy. Additionally, the time limit for a taxpayer to bring a civil action for wrongful levy has been extended to two years from the date of the notice of seizure.

### BACKGROUND

If a taxpayer fails to pay an assessed tax after notice and demand for payment, the IRS may seek collection of the taxes, including interest and penalties, by levy against all the taxpayer's property (real, personal, tangible, and intangible), including after-acquired property and rights to property (Code Sec. 6321; Reg. § 301.6321-1). Whether the taxpayer owns or has an interest in property is determined under the appropriate state law. Although a tax lien attaches to all of the debtor's property, some property is exempt from levy. Once a tax lien arises, it continues until the tax liability is paid or the lien becomes unenforceable due to a lapse of time (Code Sec. 6322).

A wrongful levy civil suit may be brought in district court by a person other than the taxpayer who owes the taxes, for the return of property believed to be wrongfully levied. This is generally done when the person making the request believes that the levy is wrongful because the property belongs to them, or that they have a security interest with priority over the IRS. The suit must be filed before the expiration of nine months from the date of the notice of seizure or notice of levy is delivered (Code Sec. 6532(c)).

> **Comment:** The IRC distinguishes between a "wrongful levy" and an "erroneous levy." A levy is considered "wrongful" when the IRS improperly attaches a levy to property belonging to a third-party in which the taxpayer has no rights. A

## BACKGROUND

levy is considered "erroneous" when the IRS attempts to levy the taxpayer's property (rather than a third-party's property), but violates an administrative procedure or law in the process.

**Comment:** The nine-month period of time in which to initiate a wrongful levy suit has been held to be a jurisdictional prerequisite and cannot be equitably tolled (*Becton Dickinson and Co. v. Wolckenhauer*, CA-3, 2000-2 USTC ¶ 50,542, 215 F3d 340, cert. denied, 531 US 1071). However, one court has held that the statute of limitations should not be enforced when it deprives the taxpayer of due process (*Carter v. United States*, CA-6, 110 FAppx 591, aff'g W.D. Tenn., 2002-2 USTC ¶ 50,493, 216 FSupp 2d 700).

Once it is determined that property has been wrongfully levied, the IRS may return:

- the specific property that was wrongfully levied;

- if money was levied, then the exact amount of money levied; or

- if the property was sold, an amount not exceeding the greater of (1) the proceeds from the sale of the property; or (2) the fair market value of the property immediately before the levy (Code Sec. 6343(b)).

The return of the money or property by the IRS must occur within nine months from the date of levy (Code Sec. 6343(b)).

## NEW LAW EXPLAINED

**Time limits for wrongful levy civil suits and the return of property increased.—** The time period for bringing a civil action in district court for wrongfully levied property is extended to two years from the date of levy (Code Sec. 6532(c), as amended by the Tax Cuts and Jobs Act (P.L. 115-97)). Additionally, the time period that the IRS has to return monetary proceeds from the sale of wrongfully levied property is also extended to two years (Code Sec. 6343(b), as amended by the 2017 Tax Cuts Act).

▶ **Effective date.** The amendments made by this section apply to levies made after December 22, 2017, the date of enactment, and levies made on or before December 22, 2017, if the nine-month period has not expired under Code Secs. 6343(b) (without regard to this section) as of such date (Act Sec. 11071(c) of the Tax Cuts and Jobs Act (P.L. 115-97)).

**No significant guidance related to this provision has been issued.**

— Act Sec. 11071(a) of the Tax Cuts and Jobs Act (P.L. 115-97), amending Code Sec. 6343(b);

— Act Sec. 11071(b), amending Code Sec. 6532(c);

— Act Sec. 11071(c), providing the effective date.

# IRS Rulings

## ¶7001 Introduction

Reproduced below are selected pieces of guidance, including IRS News Releases, Notices, Revenue Procedures and a Revenue Ruling, issued by the IRS in response to the Tax Cuts and Jobs Act (P.L. 115-97) becoming law. The guidance covers all manner of issues, from critical guidance issued just after the Act became law on the ability to deduct under Code Sec. 164 prepaid 2018 property tax, to guidance on important elections and safe harbors related to the qualified business income deduction under Code Sec. 199A. NOTE: Rev. Proc. 2018-31, and all revenue procedures modifying and/or superseding Rev. Proc. 2018-31 (including Rev. Procs. 2018-35, 2018-40, 2018-49, 2018-56, 2018-60, 2019-8, and 2019-10) are not reproduced below. Also not reproduced are revenue procedures providing inflation adjusted amounts. Use CCH® AnswerConnect and CCH Axcess™ iQ to view that guidance and to keep up-to-date with all of the recently issued guidance.

### IR-2017-210, December 27, 2017

**IRS Advisory: Prepaid Real Property Taxes May Be Deductible in 2017 if Assessed and Paid in 2017**

IR-2017-210,

WASHINGTON - The Internal Revenue Service advised tax professionals and taxpayers today that pre-paying 2018 state and local real property taxes in 2017 may be tax deductible under certain circumstances.

The IRS has received a number of questions from the tax community concerning the deductibility of prepaid real property taxes. In general, whether a taxpayer is allowed a deduction for the prepayment of state or local real property taxes in 2017 depends on whether the taxpayer makes the payment in 2017 and the real property taxes are assessed prior to 2018. A prepayment of anticipated real property taxes that have not been assessed prior to 2018 are not deductible in 2017. State or local law determines whether and when a property tax is assessed, which is generally when the taxpayer becomes liable for the property tax imposed.

The following examples illustrate these points.

*Example 1*: Assume County A assesses property tax on July 1, 2017 for the period July 1, 2017 - June 30, 2018. On July 31, 2017, County A sends notices to residents notifying them of the assessment and billing the property tax in two installments with the first installment due Sept. 30, 2017 and the second installment due Jan. 31, 2018. Assuming taxpayer has paid the first installment in 2017, the taxpayer may choose to pay the second installment on Dec. 31, 2017, and may claim a deduction for this prepayment on the taxpayer's 2017 return.

*Example 2*: County B also assesses and bills its residents for property taxes on July 1, 2017, for the period July 1, 2017 - June 30, 2018. County B intends to make the usual assessment in July 2018 for the period July 1, 2018 - June 30, 2019. However, because county residents wish to prepay their 2018-2019 property taxes in 2017, County B has revised its computer systems to accept prepayment of property taxes for the 2018-2019 property tax year. Taxpayers who prepay their 2018-2019 property taxes in 2017 will not be allowed to deduct the prepayment on their federal tax returns because the county will not assess the property tax for the 2018-2019 tax year until July 1, 2018.

The IRS reminds taxpayers that a number of provisions remain available this week that could affect 2017 tax bills. Time remains to make charitable donations. See *IR-17-191* for more information. The deadline to make contributions for individual retirement accounts - which can be used by some taxpayers on 2017 tax returns - is the April 2018 tax deadline.

IRS.gov has more information on these and other provisions to help taxpayers prepare for the upcoming filing season.

# IR-2018-32, February 22, 2018

### Interest on Home Equity Loans Often Still Deductible Under New Law

IR-2018-32

WASHINGTON - The Internal Revenue Service today advised taxpayers that in many cases they can continue to deduct interest paid on home equity loans.

Responding to many questions received from taxpayers and tax professionals, the IRS said that despite newly-enacted restrictions on home mortgages, taxpayers can often still deduct interest on a home equity loan, home equity line of credit (HELOC) or second mortgage, regardless of how the loan is labelled. The Tax Cuts and Jobs Act of 2017, enacted Dec. 22, suspends from 2018 until 2026 the deduction for interest paid on home equity loans and lines of credit, unless they are used to buy, build or substantially improve the taxpayer's home that secures the loan.

Under the new law, for example, interest on a home equity loan used to build an addition to an existing home is typically deductible, while interest on the same loan used to pay personal living expenses, such as credit card debts, is not. As under prior law, the loan must be secured by the taxpayer's main home or second home (known as a qualified residence), not exceed the cost of the home and meet other requirements.

### New dollar limit on total qualified residence loan balance

For anyone considering taking out a mortgage, the new law imposes a lower dollar limit on mortgages qualifying for the home mortgage interest deduction. Beginning in 2018, taxpayers may only deduct interest on $750,000 of qualified residence loans. The limit is $375,000 for a married taxpayer filing a separate return. These are down from the prior limits of $1 million, or $500,000 for a married taxpayer filing a separate return. The limits apply to the combined amount of loans used to buy, build or substantially im-

prove the taxpayer's main home and second home.

The following examples illustrate these points.

**Example 1**: In January 2018, a taxpayer takes out a $500,000 mortgage to purchase a main home with a fair market value of $800,000. In February 2018, the taxpayer takes out a $250,000 home equity loan to put an addition on the main home. Both loans are secured by the main home and the total does not exceed the cost of the home. Because the total amount of both loans does not exceed $750,000, all of the interest paid on the loans is deductible. However, if the taxpayer used the home equity loan proceeds for personal expenses, such as paying off student loans and credit cards, then the interest on the home equity loan would not be deductible.

**Example 2**: In January 2018, a taxpayer takes out a $500,000 mortgage to purchase a main home. The loan is secured by the main home. In February 2018, the taxpayer takes out a $250,000 loan to purchase a vacation home. The loan is secured by the vacation home. Because the total amount of both mortgages does not exceed $750,000, all of the interest paid on both mortgages is deductible. However, if the taxpayer took out a $250,000 home equity loan on the main home to purchase the vacation home, then the interest on the home equity loan would not be deductible.

**Example 3**: In January 2018, a taxpayer takes out a $500,000 mortgage to purchase a main home. The loan is secured by the main home. In February 2018, the taxpayer takes out a $500,000 loan to purchase a vacation home. The loan is secured by the vacation home. Because the total amount of both mortgages exceeds $750,000, not all of the interest paid on the mortgages is deductible. A percentage of the total interest paid is deductible (see Publication 936).

For more information about the new tax law, visit the *Tax Reform* page on IRS.gov.

---

# IR-2018-227, November 20, 2018

### Like-kind exchanges now limited to real property

IR-2018-227

WASHINGTON — The Internal Revenue Service today reminded taxpayers that like-kind exchange tax treatment is now generally limited to exchanges of real property. The Tax Cuts and Jobs Act, passed in December 2017, made tax law

changes that will affect virtually every business and individual in 2018 and the years ahead.

Effective Jan. 1, 2018, exchanges of personal or intangible property such as machinery, equipment, vehicles, artwork, collectibles, patents, and other intellectual property generally do not qualify for nonrecognition of gain or loss as like-kind exchanges. However, certain exchanges of mutual ditch, reservoir or irrigation stock are still eligible.

Like-kind exchange treatment now applies only to exchanges of real property that is held for use in a trade or business or for investment. Real property, also called real estate, includes land and generally anything built on or attached to it. An exchange of real property held primarily for sale still does not qualify as a like-kind exchange.

A transition rule in the new law allows like-kind treatment for some exchanges of personal or intangible property. If the taxpayer disposed of the personal or intangible property on or before Dec. 31, 2017, or received replacement property on or before that date, the exchange may qualify for like-kind exchange treatment.

Properties are of like-kind if they're of the same nature or character, even if they differ in grade or quality. Improved real property is generally of like-kind to unimproved real property. For example, an apartment building would generally be of like-kind to unimproved land. However, real property in the United States is not of like-kind to real property outside the U.S.

To report a like-kind exchange, taxpayers must file *Form 8824*, Like-Kind Exchanges, with their tax return for the year the taxpayer transfers property as part of a like-kind exchange. This form helps a taxpayer figure the amount of gain deferred as a result of the like-kind exchange, as well as the basis of the like-kind property received, if cash or property that isn't of like kind is involved in the exchange. Form 8824 helps compute the amount of gain the taxpayer must report.

For more information about this and other tax reform changes, visit irs.gov/taxreform.

---

## Notice 2018-8, I.R.B. 2018-4, December 29, 2017

**Revised Timeline and Other Guidance Regarding the Implementation of New Section 1446(f)**

SECTION 1. OVERVIEW

This notice announces that the Department of the Treasury ("Treasury Department") and the Internal Revenue Service ("IRS") are suspending the application of new section 1446(f) of the Internal Revenue Code ("Code") in the case of a disposition of certain publicly traded partnership interests. New section 1446(f) was added by section 13501 of "An Act to provide for reconciliation pursuant to titles II and V of the concurrent resolution on the budget for fiscal year 2018," P.L. 115-97 (the "Act"), which was enacted on December 22, 2017. Section 13501 of the Act also added new section 864(c)(8). Section 2 of this notice provides background on new sections 864(c)(8) and section 1446(f). Section 3 of this notice describes the revised timeline for the application of new section 1446(f) to a disposition of certain interests in publicly traded partnerships. Section 4 of this notice requests comments and provides contact information.

SECTION 2. BACKGROUND

In general, new section 864(c)(8) provides that a nonresident alien individual's or foreign corporation's gain or loss from the sale, exchange, or other disposition of a partnership interest is effectively connected with the conduct of a trade or business in the United States to the extent that the person would have had effectively connected gain or loss had the partnership sold all of its assets at fair market value. New section 864(c)(8) applies to sales, exchanges, or other dispositions occurring on or after November 27, 2017. See Revenue Ruling 91-32, 1991-1 C.B. 107, for the IRS's position with respect to sales, exchanges, or other dispositions of an interest in a partnership occurring before November 27, 2017.

In general, new section 1446(f)(1) provides that if any portion of the gain on any disposition of an interest in a partnership would be treated under new section 864(c)(8) as effectively connected with the conduct of a trade or business within the United States ("effectively connected gain"), then the transferee must withhold a tax equal to 10 percent of the amount realized on the disposition. Under an exception in new section 1446(f)(2), however, withholding is generally not required if the transferor furnishes an affidavit to the transferee stating, among other things, that the transferor is not a foreign person.

New section 1446(f)(6) authorizes the Secretary to issue such regulations or other guidance as may be necessary to carry out the purposes of new section 1446(f), including regulations providing for exceptions from the provisions of new section 1446(f). Furthermore, new section 1446(g) authorizes regulations that are necessary to carry out the purposes of new section 1446 generally, including regulations providing for the application of new section 1446 in the case of publicly traded partnerships. New section 1446(f) applies to sales, exchanges, or other dispositions occurring after December 31, 2017.

## SECTION 3. TIMING OF APPLICATION OF NEW SECTION 1446(f) TO DISPOSITIONS OF CERTAIN PUBLICLY TRADED PARTNERSHIP INTERESTS

Stakeholders have indicated that, in the case of a disposition of a publicly traded partnership interest, applying new section 1446(f) without guidance presents significant practical problems. For example, stakeholders stated that a transferee of an interest in a publicly traded partnership typically will not be able to determine whether the transferor partner is foreign or domestic or whether any portion of a transferor partner's gain would be treated under new section 864(c)(8) as effectively connected gain. This may be the case because publicly traded partnership interests are generally held in street name by a broker and transferred through a clearinghouse. Moreover, a particular sale may be aggregated with other sales and purchases of partnership interests by other customers of the same broker. As a result, it may be difficult for a transferee to determine whether it must withhold under new section 1446(f). Furthermore, although the Conference Report suggests the Treasury Department and the IRS provide guidance providing that in the case of a publicly traded partnership interest sold by a foreign partner through a broker, the broker may deduct and withhold on behalf of the transferee, H.R. Rep. No. 115-466, at 511 (2017), until guidance is provided and new withholding and reporting systems are developed, it would not be possible for brokers to perform any such withholding.

In consideration of these concerns and others raised by stakeholders, and to allow for an orderly implementation of the requirements of new section 1446(f), the Treasury Department and the IRS have determined that withholding under new section 1446(f) should not be required with respect to any disposition of an interest in a publicly traded partnership (within the meaning of section 7704(b)) until regulations or other guidance have been issued under new section 1446(f). This temporary suspension is limited to dispositions of interests that are publicly traded and does not extend to non-publicly traded interests. The Treasury Department and the IRS intend to issue future regulations or other guidance on how to withhold, deposit, and report the tax withheld under new section 1446(f) with respect to a disposition of an interest in a publicly traded partnership. Future guidance under new section 1446(f) with respect to a disposition of an interest in a publicly traded partnership will be prospective and will include transition rules to allow sufficient time to prepare systems and processes for compliance.

The rules described in this notice suspending withholding under new section 1446(f) do not extend to new section 864(c)(8), which remains applicable.

## SECTION 4. REQUEST FOR COMMENTS AND CONTACT INFORMATION

The Treasury Department and the IRS request comments on the rules to be issued under new section 1446(f). Comments are specifically requested regarding: (i) the application of new section 1446(f) to interests in publicly traded partnerships, including the role of brokers in collecting the tax; (ii) rules for determining the amount realized taking into account section 752(d); and (iii) procedures for requesting a reduced amount required to be withheld, including how to determine an appropriate reduced amount and whether such procedures should be automatic or require approval by the IRS. The Treasury Department and the IRS also request comments on whether a temporary suspension of new section 1446(f) for partnership interests that are not publicly traded partnership interests is needed and what additional guidance, or forms and instructions, may be needed to assist taxpayers in applying new sections 864(c)(8) and section 1446(f).

Written comments may be submitted to the Office of Associate Chief Counsel (International), Attention: Ronald M. Gootzeit, Internal Revenue Service, IR-4569B, 1111 Constitution Avenue, NW, Washington, DC 20224. Alternatively, taxpayers may submit comments electronically to Notice.comments@irscounsel.treas.gov. Comments will be available for public inspection and copying.

The principal author of this notice is Mr. Gootzeit of the Office of Associate Chief Counsel (International). For further information regarding this notice, contact Mr. Gootzeit at (202) 317-6937 (not a toll free call).

---

# Notice 2018-14, I.R.B. 2018-7, January 29, 2018

## I. PURPOSE

This notice: (1) extends the effective period of Forms W-4, Employee's Withholding Allowance Certificate, furnished to claim exemption from income tax withholding under section 3402(n) of the Internal Revenue Code (Code) for 2017 until February 28, 2018, and permits employees to claim exemption from withholding for 2018 by temporarily using the 2017 Form W-4; (2) temporarily suspends the requirement under section 3402(f)(2)(B)[1] that employees must furnish their employers new Forms W-4 within 10 days of changes in status that reduce the withholding allowances they are entitled to claim; (3) provides that the optional withholding rate on supplemental wage payments under Treas. Reg. § 31.3402(g)-1 is 22 percent for 2018 through 2025; and (4) provides that, for 2018, withholding under section 3405(a)(4) on periodic payments when no withholding certificate is in effect is based on treating the payee as a married individual claiming three withholding allowances.

Sections 11001 and 11041 of "An Act to provide for reconciliation pursuant to titles II and V of the concurrent resolution on the budget for fiscal year 2018," P.L. 115-97 (the "Act"), which was enacted on December 22, 2017, made significant changes to income tax rates, income tax deductions and credits, and federal income tax withholding. The Internal Revenue Service (IRS) is currently working on revising Form W-4 to reflect the changes made by the Act, such as changes in available itemized deductions, increases in the child tax credit, the new dependent credit, and the repeal of dependent exemptions. As a result, the 2018 Form W-4 may not be released until after February 15, 2018.

The Act does not mandate that employees furnish new Forms W-4 for 2018 and expressly permits the IRS to administer income tax withholding under section 3402 for 2018 without regard to the changes in the withholding rules and the suspension of personal exemptions. Accordingly, and in order to minimize burden on employees and employers, the IRS and the Department of the Treasury (Treasury Department) designed the 2018 withholding tables to work with the Forms W-4 that employees have already furnished their employers. *See* Notice 1036, Early Release Copies of the 2018 Percentage Method Tables for Income Tax Withholding, and Publication 15 (Circular E), Employer's Tax Guide, for use in 2018. For employees with simpler tax situations, the new tables are designed to produce the correct amount of tax withholding. The revisions are also aimed at avoiding over- and under-withholding of tax as much as possible. The IRS is also working on revising the withholding calculator on *www.irs.gov* to reflect the changes made by the Act. When released, the modified calculator and 2018 Form W-4 can be used by employees who wish to update their withholding in response to the Act or changes in their personal circumstances in 2018. Until a new Form W-4 is issued, employees and employers should continue to use the 2017 Form W-4.

Section II of this notice extends the effective period of Forms W-4 furnished to claim exemption from income tax withholding for 2017 to February 28, 2018, and describes the procedures by which employees may claim exemption from withholding for 2018 under section 3402(n) using the 2017 Form W-4. These procedures expire 30 days after the 2018 Form W-4 is released. They may be relied upon for actions taken in 2017 with respect to the 2018 tax year. Section III of this notice temporarily suspends the requirement that employees must furnish employers new Forms W-4 within 10 days after a change in status that results in reduced withholding allowances under section 3402(f)(2)(B) and Treas. Reg. § 31.3402(f)(2)-1. Section IV of this notice clarifies that the optional withholding rate for supplemental wages is 22 percent for taxable years beginning after December 31, 2017 and before January 1, 2026. Section V of this notice provides that, for 2018, the rules for default withholding under section 3405(a)(4) parallel the rules for prior years and treat the payee as a married individual claiming three withholding allowances.

## II. GUIDANCE FOR EMPLOYEES EXEMPT FROM WITHHOLDING

Under section 3402(n), an employee may claim exemption from income tax withholding if the employee certifies on Form W-4 that (1) the employee incurred no liability for income tax for the preceding taxable year; and (2) the employee anticipates that he or she will incur no liability for income tax for the current taxable year. *See also* Treas. Reg. §§ 31.3402(f)(4)-2 and 31.3402(n)-1. Under Treas. Reg. § 31.3402(f)(4)-2(c), Forms W-4 furnished to the employer claiming exemption from withholding for a taxable year are effective up to and including February 15 of the following year, and an employer may continue to rely on employees' Forms W-4 claiming exemption from withholding until February 16 of the following year. Thus, the effective period of Forms W-4 furnished to claim exemption from withholding under section 3402(n) for 2017 is scheduled to expire on February 15, 2018. As noted above, due to changes in the Code made by the Act, the IRS may not release the 2018 Form W-4 until after February 15, 2018.

---

[1] All references to sections in this document are to Code sections unless specifically provided otherwise.

To provide additional time for employers and employees to implement the procedures in this notice, the Treasury Department and the IRS have determined that 2017 Forms W-4 claiming exemption from withholding under section 3402(n) for 2017 may be treated as effective through February 28, 2018. The 2017 Forms W-4 claiming exemption from withholding for 2017 are not effective for wage payments made after February 28, 2018.

With respect to any claim for exemption from withholding for 2018 (whether renewing a claim from 2017 or making a new claim), the IRS will allow employees to claim exemption using the 2017 Form W-4 until 30 days after the 2018 Form W-4 is released in one of the following ways: (1) modifying the 2017 Form W-4 by striking "2017" in the text on Line 7 of the Form W-4 and entering "2018" in its place and signing the form in 2018; (2) modifying the 2017 Form W-4 by entering "Exempt 2018" on Line 7 of the 2017 Form W-4 and signing the form in 2018; (3) using the 2017 Form W-4 without modification and signing the form in 2018, provided that the employer establishes and communicates to employees a procedure under which an employee signs and furnishes the 2017 Form W-4 in 2018 to certify both that the employee incurred no income tax liability for 2017 and that the employee anticipates that he or she will incur no income tax liability for 2018 and thus claims exemption from withholding for 2018; or (4) any method substantially similar to (1)-(3) that clearly conveys in writing an employee's intent to certify his or her exemption from withholding for 2018.

Employers that have established electronic systems for furnishing withholding allowance certificates under Treas. Reg. § 31.3402(f)(5)-1(c) may make alterations to their electronic systems to substantially conform with options (1)-(4) above. An employer must keep records of all Forms W-4 furnished to the employer by its employees. *See* Treas. Reg. § 31.6001-5(a)(13). If an employer uses options (3) or (4) above, the employer must clearly identify 2017 Forms W-4 furnished by employees to claim exemption from withholding in 2017 and those furnished to claim exemption from withholding in 2018. Employees and employers may also rely on these procedures for 2017 Forms W-4 that employees signed and furnished in 2017 to claim exemption from withholding for 2018.

Employees are reminded to furnish employers Forms W-4 in good faith and claim exemption from withholding for 2018 only if they did not have tax liability in 2017 and do not anticipate any tax liability in 2018. Any alteration or unauthorized addition to a 2017 Form W-4, other than the ones described in this notice to indicate the certificate is for exemption in 2018, will cause the altered 2017 Form W-4 to be invalid. *See* Treas. Reg. § 31.3402(f)(2)-1(e). Moreover, any oral or written statement clearly indicating that an employee's Form W-4 is false that is made by the employee to the employer on or before the date on which the employee furnishes the Form W-4 also will cause the employee's Form W-4 to be invalid. *See* Treas. Reg. § 31.3402(f)(2)-1(e). Employees who claimed exemption from withholding for 2017 and are renewing claims for exemption from withholding for 2018 need to furnish their Forms W-4 claiming exemption from withholding for 2018 by February 28, 2018, under the revised rule of this notice. Employees who claim exemption from withholding for 2018 using the 2017 Form W-4 as permitted by this notice do not need to furnish a 2018 Form W-4 after the 2018 Form W-4 is released.

## III. TEMPORARY SUSPENSION OF 10-DAY REQUIREMENT TO FURNISH NEW FORMS W-4 TO EMPLOYERS

Section 3402(f)(2)(B) and Treas. Reg. § 31.3402(f)(2)-1(b) provide that if a change in status occurs that reduces the number of withholding allowances to which employees are entitled, employees must, within 10 days, furnish the employer with a new Form W-4 claiming the proper number of withholding allowances.

The Treasury Department and the IRS have determined that employees experiencing a change in status that causes a reduction in the number of withholding allowances are not required to furnish employers new withholding allowance certificates until 30 days after the 2018 Form W-4 is released. Moreover, because the 2018 withholding tables are designed to work with the Forms W-4 that employees have already furnished their employers, employees who have a reduction in the number of withholding allowances solely due to the changes made by the Act are not required to furnish employers new withholding allowance certificates during 2018. However, employees may update their withholding at any time in response to the Act. Employees who choose to update their withholding may use the 2017 Form W-4 instead of the 2018 Form W-4 to report changes in withholding allowances until 30 days after the 2018 Form W-4 is released. Likewise, new hires may continue to claim allowances by using the 2017 Form W-4 until 30 days after the 2018 Form W-4 is released. Employees who furnish new Forms W-4 using a 2017 Form W-4 do not need to furnish a 2018 Form W-4 after the 2018 Form W-4 is released.

## IV. OPTIONAL FLAT RATE FOR WITHHOLDING ON SUPPLEMENTAL WAGES

Under certain circumstances, employers may withhold income tax from supplemental wage payments at an optional flat rate. *See* Treas. Reg. § 31.3402(g)-1. Section 904(a) of the American Jobs Creation Act of 2004 (AJCA, P.L. 108-357), which is not included in the Code, provides that for purposes of optional flat rate withholding, the "rate to be used in determining the amount to be so deducted and withheld shall not be less than 28 percent (or the corresponding rate in effect under section 1(i)(2) of the Internal Revenue Code of 1986 for taxable years beginning in the calendar year in which the payment is made)." Accordingly, Treas. Reg. § 31.3402(g)-1(a)(7)(iii)(F) provides that employers using the optional flat rate withhold "[f]rom supplemental wages paid after December 31, 2004, by using a flat percentage rate of 28 percent (or the corresponding rate in effect under section 1(i)(2) for taxable years beginning in the calendar year in which the payment is made)." Under Treas. Reg. § 31.3402(g)-1(a)(7)(iii)(F), the optional withholding rate for supplemental wage payments made in 2005 through 2017 was 25 percent because that was "the corresponding rate in effect under section 1(i)(2)."[2]

The Act changed the income tax rate tables effective under section 1 by adding section 1(j) to the Code. Section 1(j)(1) provides that "[i]n the case of a taxable year beginning after December 31, 2017, and before January 1, 2026—(A) subsection (i) shall not apply, and (B) this section (other than subsection (i)) shall be applied as provided in paragraphs (2) through (6)." Section 1(j)(2) provides the income tax rate tables that are to be applied for taxable years beginning after December 31, 2017, and before January 1, 2026. Based on the change in the rate tables under added section 1(j), the optional flat rate changed from 25 percent to 22 percent for wages paid during 2018 and the remainder of the period to which section 1(j) of the Code applies. *See* Notice 1036.

Employers and other entities paying supplemental wages should implement the 22 percent optional flat rate for withholding on supplemental wages as soon as possible, but not later than February 15, 2018. Employers using optional flat rate withholding that withheld at a higher rate than 22 percent (for example, employers that

withheld at the 2017 optional flat rate of 25 percent) may, but are not required to, correct such withholding on supplemental wages paid on or after January 1, 2018, and before February 15, 2018, under the rules applicable to corrections of overcollections of federal income tax. *See* Treas. Reg. §§ 31.6413(a)-1(b) and 31.6413(a)-2(c).

## V. WITHHOLDING UNDER SECTION 3405 FOR PERIODIC PAYMENTS IF NO WITHHOLDING CERTIFICATE IS IN EFFECT

Under section 3405, the payor of certain periodic payments for pensions, annuities, and other deferred income generally is required to withhold from the payments as if they were wages unless an individual elects not to have withholding apply to the periodic payment. (The election is unavailable with respect to certain payments to be made outside of the United States or its possessions. *See* section 3405(e)(13).) The withholding election generally is made using Form W-4P, Withholding Certificate for Pension or Annuity Payments.

Under the law in effect before 2018, section 3405(a)(4) provided that, in the case of a payee entitled to periodic payments with respect to which a withholding certificate has not been furnished, the amount to be withheld from each such payment "shall be determined by treating the payee as a married individual claiming 3 withholding exemptions." The Act amended section 3405(a)(4) to provide that the withholding rate when no withholding certificate is furnished "shall be determined under rules prescribed by the Secretary." *See* section 11041(c)(2)(G) of the Act. For 2018, the rules for withholding when no withholding certificate is furnished with respect to periodic payments under section 3405(a) will parallel the rules for prior years and be based on treating the payee as a married individual claiming three withholding allowances.

## DRAFTING INFORMATION

The principal authors of this notice are A.G. Kelley and Mikhail Zhidkov of the Office of Associate Chief Counsel (Tax Exempt and Government Entities). However, other personnel from the Treasury Department and the IRS participated in its development. For further information regarding this notice, contact Mikhail Zhidkov at (202) 317-4774 (not a toll-free call).

---

[2] Section 1(i)(2)(A) provides that the rate tables under sections 1(a), 1(b), 1(c), 1(d), and 1(e) shall be applied "by substituting '25%' for '28%' each place it appears ...."

# Notice 2018-18, I.R.B. 2018-12, March 1, 2018

## SECTION 1. OVERVIEW

This notice announces that the Department of the Treasury (Treasury Department) and the Internal Revenue Service (IRS) intend to issue regulations providing guidance on the application of section 1061 of the Internal Revenue Code as enacted by "An Act to provide for reconciliation pursuant to titles II and V of the concurrent resolution on the budget for fiscal year 2018," Public Law 115-97 on December 22, 2017. This notice further announces that the Treasury Department and the IRS intend that those regulations will provide that the term "corporation" for purposes of section 1061(c)(4)(A) does not include an S corporation.

## SECTION 2. APPLICABLE LAW

Section 1061(a) provides in general that if one or more applicable partnership interests are held by a taxpayer at any time during the taxable year, the excess (if any) of (1) the taxpayer's net long-term capital gain with respect to such interests for such taxable year, over (2) the taxpayer's net long-term capital gain with respect to such interests for such taxable year computed by applying paragraphs (3) and (4) of section 1222 by substituting "3 years" for "1 year," shall be treated as short-term capital gain, notwithstanding section 83 or any election in effect under section 83(b).

Section 1061(c)(1) generally defines the term "applicable partnership interest" as meaning any interest in a partnership which, directly or indirectly, is transferred to (or is held by) the taxpayer in connection with the performance of substantial services by the taxpayer, or any other related person, in any applicable trade or business.

Section 1061(c)(4)(A) provides that the term "applicable partnership interest" shall not include any interest in a partnership directly or indirectly held by a corporation.

Section 1361(a)(1) provides in general that the term "S corporation" means, with respect to any

taxable year, a small business corporation for which an election under § 1362(a) is in effect for such year.

Section 1361(a)(2) provides in general that the term "C corporation" means, with respect to any taxable year, a corporation which is not an S corporation for such year.

Section 1361(b)(1) defines a "small business corporation" as a domestic corporation which is not an ineligible corporation and which does not — (A) have more than 100 shareholders, (B) have as a shareholder a person (other than an estate, a trust described in section 1361(c)(2), or an organization described in section 1361(c)(6)) who is not an individual, (C) have a nonresident alien as a shareholder, and (D) have more than 1 class of stock.

## SECTION 3. THE EXCEPTION IN SECTION 1061(c)(4)(A) DOES NOT APPLY TO PARTNERSHIP INTERESTS HELD BY S CORPORATIONS.

The regulations will provide that the term "corporation" in section 1061(c)(4)(A) does not include an S corporation.

## SECTION 4. EFFECTIVE DATE

Section 1061 is effective for taxable years beginning after December 31, 2017. The Treasury Department and the IRS intend to provide that regulations implementing section 3 of this notice will be effective for taxable years beginning after December 31, 2017.

## SECTION 5. CONTACT INFORMATION

The principal authors of this notice are Faith P. Colson and Wendy L. Kribell of the Office of the Associate Chief Counsel (Passthroughs & Special Industries). For further information regarding this notice contact Faith P. Colson or Wendy L. Kribell on 202-317-6850 (not a toll-free call).

---

# Notice 2018-23, I.R.B. 2018-15, March 27, 2018

Transitional Guidance Under § § 162(f) and 6050X with Respect to Certain Fines, Penalties, and Other Amounts

## SECTION 1. PURPOSE

Section 13306 of "An Act to provide for reconciliation pursuant to titles II and V of the concurrent resolution on the budget for fiscal year

2018," Pub. L. 115-97 (the "Act"), which was signed into law on December 22, 2017, amended § 162(f) of the Internal Revenue Code ("Code") and added new § 6050X to the Code. The Department of the Treasury ("Treasury Department") and the Internal Revenue Service ("IRS") intend to publish proposed regulations under § § 162(f) and 6050X. This notice provides transitional guidance under §§162(f) and 6050X. Specifically, as provided in section 3.01 of this notice, to ensure efficient administration of this new provision, reporting will not be required under §6050X until the date specified in the proposed regulations. The specified date will not be earlier than January 1, 2019, and will not be earlier than the date of publication of the proposed regulations. Reporting will not be required with respect to amounts required to be paid or incurred under a binding court order or agreement entered into before the specified date. Further, section 3.02 of this notice provides transitional guidance for purposes of satisfying the identification requirement in §162(f)(2)(A)(ii). Finally, section 4 of this notice requests comments regarding issues to be addressed in the proposed regulations.

SECTION 2. LAW

Section 162(f)(1), as amended by the Act, disallows a deduction for amounts paid or incurred (whether by suit, agreement, or otherwise) to, or at the direction of, a government or governmental entity in relation to the violation of any law or the investigation or inquiry by such government or entity into the potential violation of any law. Section 162(f)(2) provides an exception to the general rule under §162(f)(1). Under the exception, an amount described in §162(f)(1) that is otherwise deductible under the Code is not disallowed if the taxpayer satisfies all of the requirements in §162(f)(2)(A)(i), (ii), and (iii).

Section 162(f)(2)(A)(i) requires that the taxpayer establish that the amount paid or incurred (1) constitutes restitution (including remediation of property) for damage or harm that was or may be caused by violation of any law or the potential violation of any law, or (2) is paid to come into compliance with any law that was violated or otherwise involved in the investigation or inquiry into the potential violation of any law (the "establishment requirement"). Section 162(f)(2)(A)(ii) further requires that the amount paid or incurred be identified as restitution or as an amount paid to come into compliance with such law in the court order or settlement agreement (the "identification requirement"). Finally, §162(f)(2)(A)(iii) provides that in the case of any amount of restitution for failure to pay any tax imposed under the Code, the amount is treated as if such amount were such tax if it would have been allowed as a deduction had it been timely paid. Section 162(f)(2)(A) further provides that meeting the identification requirement alone is not sufficient to meet the establishment requirement under §162(f)(2)(A)(i).

Section 6050X(a)(1) requires the appropriate official of any government or nongovernmental entity described in §162(f)(5) that is involved in suits or agreements described in §6050X(a)(2) to make a return in such form as determined by the Secretary setting forth (1) the amount required to be paid as a result of the suit or agreement to which §162(f)(1) applies; (2) any amount required to be paid as a result of the suit or agreement that constitutes restitution or remediation of property; and (3) any amount required to be paid as a result of the suit or agreement for the purpose of coming into compliance with any law that was violated or involved in the investigation or inquiry.

Under §6050X(a)(2), amounts required to be paid as a result of a suit or agreement are required to be reported under §6050X(a)(1) if the suit or agreement is a type described in §6050X(a)(2)(A)(i) and the dollar threshold in §6050X(a)(2)(A)(ii) is met. A suit or agreement is described in §6050X(a)(2)(A)(i) if it is (1) a suit with respect to a violation of any law over which the government or entity has authority and with respect to which there has been a court order, or (2) an agreement that is entered into with respect to a violation of any law over which the government or entity has authority or with respect to an investigation or inquiry by the government or entity into the potential violation of any law over which the government or entity has authority.

Under §6050X(a)(2)(A)(ii), the dollar threshold for reporting is met if the aggregate amount involved in all court orders and agreements with respect to the violation, investigation, or inquiry is $600 or more. However, §6050X(a)(2)(B) requires the Secretary to adjust the $600 amount as necessary to ensure the efficient administration of the internal revenue laws.

Section 6050X(a)(3) requires the return to be filed at the time the agreement is entered into, as determined by the Secretary.

Section 6050X(b) requires every person required to make a return under §6050X(a) to furnish to each person who is a party to the suit or agreement a written statement showing (1) the name of the government or entity, and (2) the information supplied to the Secretary under §6050X(a)(1). This information must be furnished at the same time it is provided to the Secretary.

Section 6050X(c) defines "appropriate official" as the officer or employee having control of the suit, investigation, or inquiry or the person appropriately designated for purposes of §6050X.

Under §13306(a)(2) and (b)(3) of the Act, §162(f) as amended and new §6050X generally apply to amounts paid or incurred on or after

December 22, 2017, except that they do not apply to amounts paid or incurred under any binding order or agreement entered into before that date. If the order or agreement required court approval and the approval was not obtained before that date, §162(f) as amended and new §6050X will apply.

## SECTION 3. TRANSITIONAL GUIDANCE

Section 162(f) as amended and new §6050X were effective on December 22, 2017, the date of the enactment of the Act. Parties to suits and agreements covered by these sections have an immediate need for guidance and have contacted the Treasury Department and the IRS with questions regarding the reporting requirement of §6050X and the identification requirement of §162(f)(2)(A)(ii). This section provides transitional guidance regarding those requirements.

### .01 SECTION 6050X REPORTING

Following the enactment of the Act, officials of a number of governments and governmental entities contacted the Treasury Department and the IRS requesting additional time to make the necessary changes to their systems to comply with their new reporting responsibilities under §6050X. In addition, the IRS needs additional time to make necessary programming and form changes to implement §6050X. Accordingly, the Treasury Department and the IRS are providing transitional guidance with respect to reporting obligations under §6050X. Under this transitional guidance, to ensure efficient administration of this new provision, reporting will not be required under §6050X until the date specified in the proposed regulations. The specified date will not be earlier than January 1, 2019, and will not be earlier than the date of publication of the proposed regulations. Reporting will not be required with respect to any amounts required to be paid or incurred under a binding court order or settlement agreement entered into before the specified date. For purposes of this notice, an agreement that requires court approval is binding when court approval is obtained. This transitional guidance will provide additional time for dialogue with stakeholders in an effort to clarify the reporting requirements consistent with effective implementation of the law. Transitional guidance will also provide governmental and nongovernmental regulatory entities additional time to develop their systems for collecting and reporting the required information.

### .02 SECTION 162(f)(2)(A)(ii) IDENTIFICATION

The transitional guidance provided in section 3.01 of this notice does not affect or delay the applicability of §162(f). Accordingly, the identification requirement in §162(f)(2)(A)(ii) applies to amounts paid or incurred on or after December 22, 2017, unless the amounts were paid or incurred under any binding order or agreement entered into before that date. Taxpayers and officials of governments and governmental entities have asked for immediate guidance regarding the identification requirement.

Until proposed regulations under §162(f) are issued, the identification requirement in §162(f)(2)(A)(ii) is treated as satisfied for an amount if the settlement agreement or court order specifically states on its face that the amount is restitution, remediation, or for coming into compliance with the law. Even if the identification requirement under this section 3.02 is treated as satisfied, taxpayers must also meet the establishment requirement in order to qualify for the §162(f)(2) exception.

## SECTION 4. COMMENTS

The Treasury Department and the IRS intend to issue proposed regulations amending and adding sections to the Income Tax Regulations with respect to §§162(f) and 6050X. To assist in the development of the proposed regulations, this notice requests comments from the public and affected governments and nongovernmental entities, on any and all issues related to the application and implementation of §§162(f) and 6050X that the proposed regulations should address. In particular, the Treasury Department and the IRS request comments on:

1. The timing of the reporting required under §6050X;

2. The threshold amount for reporting under §6050X(a)(2);

3. Any anticipated administrative difficulties in securing information needed to report under §6050X, including situations involving multiple payors or payees;

4. How to define key terms in §162(f); and

5. What entities are nongovernmental entities under §162(f)(5).

## WHERE TO SEND COMMENTS

Comments may be submitted by May 18, 2018, using one of the following methods:

• By Mail:

Internal Revenue Service

Attn: CC:PA:LPD:PR (Notice 2018-23)

Room 5203

P.O. Box 7602

Ben Franklin Station

Washington, D.C. 20444

• By Hand or Courier Delivery: Submissions may be hand-delivered Monday through Friday between the hours of 8 a.m. and 4 p.m. to:

Courier's Desk

Internal Revenue Service

Attn: CC:PA:LPD:PR (Notice 2018-23)

1111 Constitution Avenue, N.W.

Washington, D.C. 20224

• Electronic: Alternatively, persons may submit comments electronically to No-

tice.Comments@irscounsel.treas.gov. Please include "Notice 2018-23" in the subject line of any electronic communications. All submissions will be available for public inspection and copying in room 1621, 1111 Constitution Avenue, N.W., Washington, D.C., from 9 a.m. to 4 p.m.

## SECTION 5. CONTACT INFORMATION

The principal author of this notice is Christopher Wrobel of the Office of the Associate Chief Counsel (Income Tax and Accounting). For further information regarding this notice, contact Mr. Wrobel at (202) 317-7011 (not a toll-free number).

---

# Notice 2018-29, I.R.B. 2018-16, April 2, 2018

Guidance Regarding the Implementation of New Section 1446(f) for Partnership Interests That Are Not Publicly Traded

## SECTION 1. OVERVIEW

This notice announces that the Department of the Treasury ("Treasury Department") and the Internal Revenue Service ("IRS") intend to issue regulations under new section 1446(f) of the Internal Revenue Code ("Code") regarding the disposition of a partnership interest that is not publicly traded. This notice also provides interim guidance that taxpayers may rely on pending the issuance of regulations. New section 1446(f) was added by section 13501 of "An Act to provide for reconciliation pursuant to titles II and V of the concurrent resolution on the budget for fiscal year 2018," P.L. 115-97 (the "Act"), which was enacted on December 22, 2017. Section 13501 of the Act also added new section 864(c)(8).

## SECTION 2. BACKGROUND AND SUMMARY OF COMMENTS

In general, section 864(c)(8) provides that gain or loss from the sale, exchange, or other disposition of a partnership interest by a nonresident alien or foreign corporation is effectively connected with the conduct of a trade or business in the United States to the extent that the person would have had effectively connected gain or loss had the partnership sold all of its assets at fair market value. Section 864(c)(8) applies to sales, exchanges, or other dispositions occurring on or after November 27, 2017. *See* Rev. Rul. 91-32, 1991-1 C.B. 107, for the IRS's position with respect to sales, exchanges, or other dispositions of an interest in a partnership by a nonresident alien individual or foreign corporation occurring before November 27, 2017.

In general, section 1446(f)(1) provides that if any portion of the gain on any disposition of an interest in a partnership would be treated under section 864(c)(8) as effectively connected with the conduct of a trade or business within the United States, then the transferee must deduct and withhold a tax equal to 10 percent of the amount realized on the disposition. Under an exception in section 1446(f)(2), however, withholding is generally not required if the transferor furnishes an affidavit to the transferee stating, among other things, that the transferor is not a foreign person.

Section 1446(f)(4) provides that if a transferee fails to withhold any amount required to be withheld under section 1446(f)(1), the partnership shall be required to deduct and withhold from distributions to the transferee a tax in an amount equal to the amount the transferee failed to withhold (plus interest under the Code on such amount).

Section 1446(f)(6) authorizes the Secretary to prescribe such regulations or other guidance as may be necessary to carry out the purposes of section 1446(f), including regulations providing for exceptions from the provisions of section 1446(f). Furthermore, section 1446(g) authorizes the Secretary to prescribe such regulations as may be necessary to carry out the purposes of section 1446 generally. Section 1446(f) applies to sales, exchanges, or other dispositions occurring after December 31, 2017.

On December 29, 2017, the Treasury Department and IRS advance released Notice 2018-08, 2018-7 I.R.B. 352 ("PTP Notice"). The PTP Notice suspended the requirement to withhold on dispositions of certain interests in publicly traded partnerships ("PTPs") in response to stakeholder concerns that applying section 1446(f) to PTPs without guidance presented significant practical problems. The PTP Notice also requested comments on the implementation of section 1446(f), including whether a temporary suspension of section 1446(f) for partnership interests that are not publicly traded ("non-PTP interests") was needed. Several comments were received.

Comments in response to the PTP Notice requested guidance minimizing the application of section 1446(f) until further guidance was issued, including suspension of section 1446(f) for non-PTP interests. This notice does not suspend the application of section 1446(f) for non-PTP interests in all cases, but does include guidance under section 1446(f) designed to allow for an effective and orderly implementation, including minimizing occasions of overwithholding. The rules in this notice (including section 6) that modify or suspend withholding under section 1446(f) do not affect the transferor's tax liability under section 864(c)(8). *See* section 4.06 of this notice.

Comments stated that applying section 1446(f) to dispositions of non-PTP interests presents significant practical problems. Comments stated that a transferee is obligated to withhold with respect to dispositions occurring after December 31, 2017, but without forms, instructions or other guidance, it is unclear when or how to deposit the withheld amounts. To address this concern, section 5 of this notice provides interim guidance on reporting and paying over the amount required to be withheld under section 1446(f)(1). This guidance generally adopts the forms and procedures relating to withholding on dispositions of U.S. real property interests under section 1445 and the regulations thereunder.

Comments requested guidance on the procedures for the transferor to furnish an affidavit of non-foreign status to the transferee as described in section 1446(f)(2) to be relieved from withholding. Section 6.01 of this notice provides this guidance by generally adopting the rules in the section 1445 regulations for similar situations.

Section 1446(f) applies only when there is gain on a disposition of an interest in a partnership. To prevent withholding when no gain occurs on a disposition, section 6.02 of this notice provides that if a transferee receives a certification from a transferor that the disposition will not result in gain, then the transferee generally is not required to withhold under section 1446(f).

Comments requested relief from withholding obligations when the amount of effectively connected gain under section 864(c)(8) is zero or a small amount. One comment recommended a rule providing relief based on the value of the assets producing effectively connected income,

modeled on § 1.1445-11T. Section 1.1445-11T provides an exception from the requirement that a transferee withhold on the transfer of an interest in a partnership that holds U.S. real property interests. The transferee is relieved from withholding under this exception if the partnership provides the transferee a statement certifying that fifty percent or more of the value of the gross assets does not consist of U.S. real property interests, or that ninety percent or more of the value of the gross assets of the partnership does not consist of U.S. real property interests plus cash or cash equivalents. Instead of adopting a rule based on the test in § 1.1445-11T, sections 6.03 and 6.04 of this notice provide two rules that relieve the transferee from withholding in circumstances similar to those described by the comments.

Section 6.03 of this notice provides generally that, if a transferor certifies to a transferee that for each of the past three years the transferor's effectively connected taxable income from the partnership was less than 25 percent of the transferor's total income from the partnership, the transferee is not required to withhold. This rule is designed to provide a simple approach, obviating the need for the partnership to make the computation required by section 864(c)(8) or to otherwise provide information to the transferor or transferee at the time of the transaction. However, in certain cases transferees may not be able to obtain this certification, so section 6.04 of this notice provides a separate rule relieving a transferee of its withholding obligation under section 1446(f)(1) when the transferee receives a certification from the partnership that the partnership's effectively connected gain under section 864(c)(8) would be less than 25 percent of the total gain on the deemed sale of all its assets. The Treasury Department and the IRS intend to provide future guidance that will reduce the threshold for withholding below 25 percent for both of these rules. Other limitations are also under consideration. The Treasury Department and the IRS expect that any such reduction in the threshold for withholding would be effective at the same time as guidance providing for withholding certificates or otherwise providing for withholding determined by reference to gain recognized under section 1446(f)(3).

A comment recommended guidance providing that no gain or loss be recognized under section 864(c)(8) in certain dispositions that would otherwise be considered nonrecognition transactions, provided that gain or loss is preserved. Specifically, the comment suggested alternative rules, one considering whether the gain or loss is preserved in the U.S. tax base, and the other considering whether the gain or loss is preserved in the hands of the transferee. The Treasury Department and the IRS are studying the appropriate treatment of nonrecognition transactions under section 864(c)(8), and comments are requested on this issue, including the relationship between nonrecognition transactions under sections 864(c)(8) and 897. *See* § 1.897-6T. Until this guidance is provided, section 6.05 of this notice provides that no withholding is required under section 1446(f) in a transaction in which no gain is recognized.

Section 1446(f)(1) applies to the amount realized on the disposition of a partnership interest. The amount realized includes a reduction in the transferor's share of partnership liabilities and other liabilities to which the partnership interest is subject. *See* §§ 1.752-1(h) and 1.1001-2. Section 7 of this notice provides two rules for determining the amount of partnership liabilities that are included in the amount realized. Section 7.02 of this notice provides that a transferee may generally rely on a transferor's most recently issued Schedule K-1 (Form 1065), *Partner's Share of Income, Deductions, Credits, etc.*, for purposes of determining the transferor's share of partnership liabilities included in the amount realized for purposes of section 1446(f). Alternatively, section 7.03 provides that a transferee may generally rely on a certification from the partnership providing the amount of the transferor's share of partnership liabilities.

Comments stated that when the amount realized includes a reduction in liabilities, the amount the transferee may be required to withhold could exceed the cash or other property the transferee pays to the transferor. Further, in some situations, a transferor may not provide any information to the transferee about its share of partnership liabilities, making a determination of the total amount realized difficult. To address these issues, section 8 of this notice provides that in certain cases, the total amount of withholding is generally limited to the total amount of cash and property to be transferred. The Treasury Department and the IRS expect that the exception in section 8 will not apply after guidance is issued providing for withholding certificates or otherwise providing for withholding determined by reference to gain recognized under section 1446(f)(3).

The comments also raised an issue relating to the determination of a transferor's basis in its partnership interest. Section 731(a) provides that in the case of a distribution by a partnership to a partner, gain shall not be recognized to such partner, except to the extent that any money distributed exceeds the adjusted basis of such partner's interest in the partnership immediately before the distribution. Any gain recognized under section 731(a) is considered gain from the sale or exchange of the partnership interest of the distributee partner. Thus, section 1446(f) applies in certain cases when a distribution of money (including marketable securities) results in gain under section 731. According to a comment, when a partnership distributes money, it may not know the distributee partner's basis in its interest and, thus, may not know whether the distribution will cause the distributee partner to recognize gain. In response to this comment, section 9 of this notice provides that the partnership may generally rely on its books and records, or on a certification received from the distributee partner, to determine whether the distribution exceeds the partner's basis.

Section 10 of this notice responds to requests for guidance on the interaction of section 1445 with section 1446(f).

The Treasury Department and the IRS are considering rules that would relieve a partnership of its obligation under section 1446(f)(4) if it provides the information required by a transferor and transferee to comply with the requirements under sections 864(c)(8) and 1446(f), including the certification described in section 6.04 of this notice, information on the calculation of the tax liability under section 864(c)(8) to the transferor, and information necessary to calculate the amount realized (including calculations relating to section 752) by the transferor. Section 11 of this notice provides that the withholding requirements described in section 1446(f)(4) will not apply until regulations or other guidance have been issued under that section.

## SECTION 3. DEFINITIONS

.01 *Effectively connected gain.* The term "effectively connected gain" means the amount of net gain (if any) that would have been effectively connected with the conduct of a trade or business within the United States if the partnership had sold all of its assets at their fair market value as of the date of the transfer described in section 864(c)(8)(A).

.02 *Transfer.* The term "transfer" means any sale, exchange or other disposition.

.03 *Transferor.* The term "transferor" means any person that transfers a partnership interest, and includes a person that receives a distribution from a partnership.

.04 *Transferee.* The term "transferee" means any person that acquires a partnership interest by transfer, and includes a partnership that makes a distribution.

**.05** *Related person.* The term "related person" is a person that is related within the meaning of section 267(b) or section 707(b)(1).

## SECTION 4. RULES OF GENERAL APPLICABILITY

**.01** *U.S. taxpayer identification numbers ("U.S. TINs").* A certificate described in sections 6.02, 6.03, and 7.02 of this notice must include the transferor's U.S. TIN to the extent that the transferor is required to have, or does have, a U.S. TIN. A transferee may rely on an otherwise valid certificate that does not include a U.S. TIN for the transferor unless the transferee knows that the transferor is required to have a U.S. TIN or that the transferor does in fact have a U.S. TIN. An affidavit of non-foreign status or Form W-9, *Request for Taxpayer Identification Number and Certification*, provided for purposes of section 6.01 of this notice must include a U.S. TIN in all cases.

**.02** *Penalties of perjury.* For purposes of this notice, a certification signed under "penalties of perjury" must provide the following: "Under penalties of perjury I declare that I have examined the information on this document, and to the best of my knowledge and belief, it is true, correct, and complete." Such a certification by an entity must further provide the following: "I further declare that I have authority to sign this document on behalf of [name of entity]."

**.03** *Authority to sign certifications.* For purposes of this notice, a certification described in section 6, 7, or 9 of this notice from an entity must be signed by an individual who is an officer, director, general partner, or managing member of the entity, or, if the general partner or managing member of the entity is itself an entity, an individual who is an officer, director, general partner, or managing member of the entity that is the general partner or managing member.

**.04** *Retention period.* A transferee that obtains and relies upon an affidavit or certification provided for in this notice must retain that document with its books and records for a period of five calendar years following the close of the last calendar year in which the entity relied upon the certification or as long as it may be relevant to the determination of the transferee's withholding obligation under section 1446(f), whichever period is longer.

**.05** *Publicly traded partnerships.* The rules in this notice do not apply to the transfer of a publicly traded interest in a publicly traded partnership (within the meaning of section 7704(b)).

**.06** *Applicability of Section 864(c)(8).* The rules in this notice that modify or suspend withholding under section 1446(f) do not affect the transferor's tax liability under section 864(c)(8).

## SECTION 5. USE OF SECTION 1445 PRINCIPLES FOR REPORTING AND PAYING OVER SECTION 1446(f) WITHHOLDING FOR DISPOSITIONS OF NON-PUBLICLY TRADED PARTNERSHIP INTERESTS

The Treasury Department and the IRS have determined that, until regulations, other guidance, or forms and instructions have been issued under section 1446(f), transferees required to withhold under section 1446(f)(1) must use the rules in section 1445 and the regulations thereunder for purposes of reporting and paying over the tax, except as otherwise provided in this notice. *See, e.g.,* § 1.1445-1(c). The forms specified in those rules include Form 8288, *U.S. Withholding Tax Return for Dispositions by Foreign Persons of U.S. Real Property Interests*, and Form 8288-A, *Statement of Withholding on Dispositions by Foreign Persons of U.S. Real Property Interests*. The transferee must include the statement "Section 1446(f)(1) withholding" at the top of both the relevant Form 8288 and the relevant Form 8288-A. Except as provided in section 8 of this notice, the transferee must also enter the amount subject to withholding under section 1446(f)(1) on line 5b of Part I of the Form 8288 and on line 3 of Form 8288-A and enter the amount withheld on line 6 of Part I of Form 8288 and on line 2 of Form 8288-A. At this time, the IRS will not issue withholding certificates under section 1446(f)(3), such as those provided on Form 8288-B, *Application for Withholding Certificate for Dispositions by Foreign Persons of U.S. Real Property Interests.*

The rules for reporting and paying over amounts withheld and the rules regarding the contents of Form 8288 and Form 8288-A contained in § 1.1445-1(c) and (d) (such as the requirement to report and pay over withholding within 20 days of a transfer) apply to the submission of section 1446(f)(1) withholding. A transferee that is required to pay over a withholding tax under section 1446(f) is made liable for that tax under section 1461 (including any applicable penalties and interest). A person that is required, but fails, to pay over the withholding tax required by section 1446(f) may also be subject to civil and criminal penalties. Officers or other responsible persons of either an entity that is required to pay over the withholding tax or any other withholding agent may be subject to a civil penalty under section 6672. The Treasury Department and the IRS intend to issue regulations providing that with respect to any forms that were required to be filed, or amounts that were due, under section 1446(f) on or before May 31, 2018, no penalties or interest will be asserted if these forms are filed with, and such amounts are paid over to, the IRS on or before May 31, 2018.

## SECTION 6. EXCEPTIONS TO SECTION 1446(f) WITHHOLDING ON DISPOSITIONS OF NON-PUBLICLY TRADED PARTNERSHIP INTERESTS

### .01 *Certifying Non-Foreign Status*

Section 1446(f)(2) provides that no person shall be required to deduct and withhold any amount under section 1446(f)(1) with respect to any disposition of an interest in a partnership if the transferor furnishes to the transferee an affidavit by the transferor stating, under penalty of perjury, the transferor's U.S. TIN and that the transferor is not a foreign person. Thus, unless the transferee receives the required affidavit, it must presume that the transferor is foreign for purposes of withholding under section 1446(f)(1).

The Treasury Department and the IRS intend to issue regulations applying rules substantially similar to § 1.1445-2(b), except § 1.1445-2(b)(2)(ii), for making a certification of non-foreign status for purposes of applying section 1446(f)(2). Section 1.1445-2(b) provides rules pursuant to which a transferor of a U.S. real property interest can provide a certification of non-foreign status to inform the transferee that withholding is not required. Until regulations on certifications of non-foreign status under section 1446(f) are issued, a transferor may furnish the certification described in § 1.1445-2(b), as modified to take into account section 1446(f) to satisfy the requirements of section 1446(f)(2). Further, a transferor may submit a Form W-9 for this purpose if: (i) it includes the name and U.S. TIN of the transferor; (ii) it is signed and dated by the transferor; and (iii) the jurat has not been deleted. A transferee may generally rely on a Form W-9 that it has previously received from the transferor if it meets these requirements. Until further notice, the certification of non-foreign status or Form W-9 the transferor provides to the transferee should not be furnished to the IRS. *See* section 1446(f)(2)(B)(ii). If the transferee has actual knowledge that the certification or Form W-9 is false, or the transferee receives a notice (as described in section 1445(d)) from a transferor's agent or transferee's agent that it is false, it may not be relied upon. *See* section 1446(f)(2)(B)(i).

### .02 *Transferee Receives a Certification of No Realized Gain*

The Treasury Department and the IRS intend to issue regulations providing that, if the transferee receives a certification, issued by the transferor (signed under penalties of perjury and including a U.S. TIN, to the extent required under section 4.01 of this notice), stating that the transfer of its partnership interest will not result in realized gain, a transferee may generally rely on the certification and be relieved from liability for withholding under section 1446(f). The transferee may not rely on the certification and is not relieved from withholding if it has knowledge that the certification is false under the principles of § 1.1445-2(b)(4). Pending the issuance of other guidance, the transferor should not submit to the IRS Form 8288-B for this purpose. If gain is realized in a transfer but not recognized as a result of a nonrecognition provision, the transferee cannot apply this section 6.02. In this circumstance, see section 6.05 of this notice.

### .03 *Transferee Receives a Certification that Transferor Had Less than 25 Percent Effectively Connected Taxable Income in Three Prior Taxable Years*

The Treasury Department and the IRS intend to issue regulations providing that no withholding is required under section 1446(f)(1) upon the transfer of a partnership interest if no earlier than 30 days before the transfer the transferee receives from the transferor a certification (signed under penalties of perjury and including a U.S. TIN, to the extent required under section 4.01 of this notice) that for the transferor's immediately prior taxable year and the two taxable years that precede it the transferor was a partner in the partnership for the entirety of each of those years, and that the transferor's allocable share of effectively connected taxable income (ECTI) (as determined under § 1.1446-2) for each of those taxable years was less than 25 percent of the transferor's total distributive share of income for that year. For this purpose, the transferor's immediately prior taxable year is the most recent taxable year of the transferor that includes the partnership taxable year that ends with or within the transferor's taxable year and for which both a Form 8805, *Foreign Partner's Information Statement of Section 1446 Withholding Tax*, and a Schedule K-1 (Form 1065) were due (including extensions) or filed (if earlier) by the time of the transfer. In no event may a transferee rely on a certification provided prior to the transferor's receipt of the relevant Forms 8805 and Schedules K-1 (Form 1065). For purposes of this rule, a transferor that had a distributive share of deductions and expenses attributable to the partnership's U.S. trade or business but no ECTI allocated to it in a year must treat its allocable share of ECTI for that year as zero. A transferor that did not have a distributive share of income in any of its three immediately prior taxable years during which the partnership had effectively connected income cannot provide this certification. A transferee may not rely on the certification and is not relieved from withholding if it has actual knowledge that the certification is false. When a partnership is a transferee by reason of making a distribution, this section 6.03 does not apply.

### .04 Transferee Receives a Certification from Partnership of Less than 25 Percent Effectively Connected Gain Under Section 864(c)(8)

The Treasury Department and the IRS intend to issue regulations providing that no withholding is required under section 1446(f)(1) upon the transfer of a partnership interest if the transferee is provided a certification, issued by the partnership and signed under penalties of perjury no earlier than 30 days before the transfer, certifying that if the partnership had sold all of its assets at their fair market value, the amount of gain that would have been effectively connected with the conduct of a trade or business within the United States would be less than 25 percent of the total gain. For purposes of this section 6.04, effectively connected gain includes gain treated as effectively connected with a trade or business in the United States under section 897. Principles similar to the rules of § 1.1445-11T(d)(2)(ii) and (iii) apply to certifications furnished pursuant to this section 6.04. When a partnership is a transferee by reason of making a distribution, the transferee partnership must retain a record of the documentation relied upon to determine the amount of gain (if any), and the portion of the gain that would have been effectively connected with the conduct of a trade or business in the United States (if any). This documentation must be retained for the period described in section 4.04 of this notice.

### .05 Nonrecognition Transactions

The Treasury Department and the IRS intend to issue regulations providing that no withholding is required under section 1446(f)(1) upon the transfer of a partnership interest if the transferee receives from the transferor a notice that satisfies the requirements of § 1.1445-2(d)(2), treating references to section 1445(a) as references to section 1446(f), and references to "U.S. real property interest" as "partnership interest", except as pro-

vided in this section 6.05. A transferee should not mail a copy of the transferor's notice to the IRS as described in § 1.1445-2(d)(2)(i)(B). The Treasury Department and the IRS are studying the appropriate treatment of nonrecognition transactions under section 864(c)(8). Until guidance providing for the treatment of nonrecognition transactions under section 864(c)(8) is issued, a transfer in which the transferor is not required to recognize any gain or loss by reason of a nonrecognition provision of the Code (without regard to section 864(c)(8)) will be eligible for the exception from withholding provided in this section 6.05. When a partnership is a transferee by reason of making a distribution in which no gain is recognized, the transferee partnership is not required to withhold and the transferor is not required to provide a notice to the transferee partnership.

### .06 Rules for Agents

Section 1446(f)(2)(C) provides that the rules of section 1445(d) shall apply to a transferor's agent or transferee's agent with respect to any affidavit of nonforeign status in the same manner as such rules apply with respect to the disposition of a United States real property interest under such section. The Treasury Department and the IRS intend to issue regulations providing that the principles of § 1.1445-4 apply for agents to fulfill their responsibilities with respect to any certification provided for purposes of section 1446(f).

### SECTION 7. DETERMINING THE AMOUNT OF PARTNERSHIP LIABILITIES INCLUDED IN AMOUNT REALIZED

### .01 In General

The Treasury Department and the IRS intend to issue regulations providing that a transferee may rely upon a certification described in section 7.02 or section 7.03 of this notice to determine the amount of liabilities of the partnership that are included in the amount realized on a transfer for purposes of section 1446(f), unless the transferee has actual knowledge that the certification is incorrect or unreliable.

### .02 Transferor Certification

A transferor that is not a controlling partner (as defined below) may provide to the transferee a certification (signed under penalties of perjury and including a U.S. TIN, to the extent required under section 4.01 of this notice) that provides (i) the amount of the transferor's share of partnership liabilities reported on the most recently received Schedule K-1 (Form 1065) from the partnership, for a partnership taxable year that closed no more than 10 months before the date of

ringng

rion

transfer, and (ii) that the transferor does not have actual knowledge of events occurring after the Schedule K-1 (Form 1065) was issued that would cause the amount of the transferor's share of partnership liabilities at the time of the transfer to be significantly different than the amount shown on the Schedule K-1 (Form 1065). A difference in the amount of the transferor's share of partnership liabilities of 25 percent or less is not a significant difference. A transferor is a controlling partner for purposes of this section 7.02 if the transferor (and related persons) owned a 50 percent or greater interest in capital, profits, deductions or losses in the 12 months before the transfer.

*.03 Partnership Certification*

The partnership may issue a certification, signed under penalties of perjury, no earlier than 30 days before the transfer, that provides (i) the amount of the transferor's share of partnership liabilities, which may be the amount reported on the most recently prepared Schedule K-1 (Form 1065), and (ii) that the partnership does not have actual knowledge of events occurring after its determination of the amount of the transferor's share of partnership liabilities that would cause the amount of the transferor's share of partnership liabilities at the time of the transfer to be significantly different than the amount shown on the certification provided to the transferee. A difference in the amount of the transferor's share of partnership liabilities of 25 percent or less is not a significant difference.

## SECTION 8. WITHHOLDING LIMITATION IN CERTAIN CASES RELATING TO THE TRANFEROR'S SHARE OF PARTNERSHIP LIABILITIES

The Treasury Department and the IRS intend to issue regulations providing that if the amount otherwise required to be withheld under section 1446(f) exceeds the amount realized less the decrease in the transferor partner's share of partnership liabilities, then the amount of withholding required by section 1446(f)(1) is the amount realized less the decrease in the transferor partner's share of partnership liabilities. In addition, if a transferee is unable to determine the amount realized because it does not have knowledge of the transferor partner's share of partnership liabilities (and does not receive a certification described in section 7.02 or section 7.03 of this notice on which it can rely), then the amount of withholding required is the entire amount realized, determined without regard to

the decrease in the transferor partner's share of partnership liabilities. In both cases, the amount of withholding under section 1446(f) is generally the amount that the transferor would, but for the transferee remitting it as withholding under section 1446(f), receive from the transferee. A transferee may rely on this rule only if the transferee (1) is not the partnership in which the transferor is a partner, and (2) is not a related person to the transferor. A transferee applying this section 8 must check the box on line 5c of Part I of Form 8288 and include the amount withheld in the total reported on line 6, Part I of Form 8288 and line 2 of Form 8288-A.

## SECTION 9. DETERMINATION OF APPLICABILITY OF SECTION 1446(f)(1) TO DISTRIBUTIONS BY PARTNERSHIPS

The Treasury Department and the IRS intend to issue regulations providing that for purposes of section 1446(f)(1), if a partnership makes a distribution to a partner, the partnership may rely on its books and records, or on a certification received from the distributee partner, to determine whether the distribution exceeds the partner's basis in its partnership interest, provided that the partnership does not know or have reason to know that its books and records, or the distributee partner's certification, is incorrect and the partnership retains a record of the documentation relied upon to establish the partner's basis for the period described in section 4.04 of this notice.

## SECTION 10. COORDINATION WITH SECTION 1445 WITHHOLDING

The Treasury Department and the IRS intend to issue regulations providing that a transferee that is otherwise required to withhold under section 1445(e)(5) or § 1.1445-11T(d)(1) with respect to the amount realized, as well as under section 1446(f)(1), will be subject to the payment and reporting requirements of section 1445 only, and not section 1446(f)(1), with respect to such amount. However, this rule applies only if the transferor has not obtained a withholding certificate that is provided for in the last sentence of § 1.1445-11T(d)(1). If the transferor has obtained such a withholding certificate, the transferee must withhold the greater of the amounts required under section 1445(e)(5) or section 1446(f)(1). Under these circumstances, a transferee that has complied with the withholding requirements under either section 1445(e)(5) or section 1446(f)(1), as applicable, will be deemed to satisfy the other withholding requirement.

## SECTION 11. TIMING OF THE WITHHOLDING REQUIREMENT OF SECTION 1446(f)(4)

The Treasury Department and the IRS intend to issue regulations providing that the withholding requirements in section 1446(f)(4) will not apply until regulations or other guidance have been issued under that section.

## SECTION 12. TIERED PARTNERSHIPS

The Treasury Department and the IRS intend to issue regulations clarifying that if a transferor transfers an interest in a partnership (upper-tier partnership) that owns an interest (directly or indirectly) in another partnership (lower-tier partnership), and the lower-tier partnership would have effectively connected gain upon the deemed transaction described in section 864(c)(8)(B)(i)(I) that would be taken into account by the transferor at the time of the transfer of the interest in the upper-tier partnership, a portion of the gain recognized by the transferor is characterized as effectively connected gain. These regulations will require lower-tier partnerships to furnish information to their partners in order for their indirect partners to be able to comply with sections 864(c)(8) and 1446(f). *See* section 6031(b); § 1.6031(b)-1T.

## SECTION 13. REQUEST FOR COMMENTS AND CONTACT INFORMATION

The Treasury Department and the IRS request comments on the rules to be issued under section 1446(f). In addition to requests for comments identified in the PTP Notice (which may also be applicable to non-PTP interests) and in section 2 of this notice, comments are requested concerning the following:

(i) rules for determining the amount realized, including when the amount of required withholding may exceed the proceeds of a sale of a partnership interest;

(ii) procedures for reducing the amount required to be withheld, such as (a) limiting the withholding to the tax on the gain recognized (if determinable) and (b) relieving identifiable historically compliant taxpayers from withholding;

(iii) credit and refund forms and processes, such as (a) forms of standardized documentation that could be used by transferors when claiming refunds or credits for the withholding to facilitate IRS's evaluation of such claims, or (b) providing for an expedited refund procedure if a taxpayer can demonstrate substantial overwithholding;

(iv) rules implementing the requirement for a partnership to withhold under section 1446(f)(4) on distributions to a transferee that fails to withhold under section 1446(f)(1);

(v) rules that should apply under sections 864(c)(8), 897, 1445, and 1446(f) when a partner disposes of an interest in a partnership that holds both U.S. real property interests and other property used in the conduct of a trade or business in the United States; and

(vi) the calculation of the amount of gain or loss from the sale, exchange, or other disposition of a partnership interest that is effectively connected with the conduct of a trade or business in the United States by operation of section 864(c)(8).

Comments must be submitted by **[INSERT DATE 60 DAYS AFTER DATE NOTICE IS RELEASED]**. All comments received will be available for public inspection and copying.

Written comments responding to this notice should be mailed to:

Internal Revenue Service

CC:PA:LPD:PR (Notice 2018-29)

Room 5203

P.O. Box 7604

Ben Franklin Station

Washington, DC 20044

Please include "Notice 2018-29" on the cover page.

Submissions may be hand delivered Monday through Friday between the hours of 8 a.m. and 4 p.m. to:

Internal Revenue Service

Courier's Desk

1111 Constitution Ave., N.W.

Washington, DC 20224

Attn: CC:PA:LPD:PR

(Notice 2018-29)

Alternatively, taxpayers may submit comments electronically to the following email address: Notice.comments@irscounsel.treas.gov. Please include "Notice 2018-29" in the subject line of any electronic submission.

The principal authors of this notice are Ronald M. Gootzeit of the Office of Associate Chief Counsel (International) and Kevin I. Babitz of the Office of Associate Chief Counsel (Passthroughs and Special Industries). However, other personnel from the Treasury Department and the IRS also participated in its development. For further information regarding this notice contact Mr. Gootzeit at 202.317.4953 (not a toll-free call).

**Notice 2018-29**

# Notice 2018-35, I.R.B. 2018-18, April 12, 2018

## SECTION 1. PURPOSE

This notice provides transitional guidance relating to advance payments under Rev. Proc. 2004-34, 2004-1 C.B. 991, as modified and clarified by Rev. Proc. 2011-18, 2011-5 I.R.B. 443, and Rev. Proc. 2013-29, 2013-33 I.R.B. 141, and as modified by Rev. Proc. 2011-14, 2011-4 I.R.B. 330. Section 13221 of "An Act to provide for reconciliation pursuant to titles II and V of the concurrent resolution on the budget for fiscal year 2018," Pub. L. No. 115-97 (December 22, 2017) (the "Act") amended § 451 of the Internal Revenue Code. The amendments included a new section 451(c), which allows accrual method taxpayers to elect a limited deferral of the inclusion of income associated with certain advance payments. The rules in new § 451(c) largely track the approach in Rev. Proc. 2004-34. The Department of the Treasury (Treasury Department) and the Internal Revenue Service (the Service) expect to issue future guidance regarding the treatment of advance payments to implement this legislative change. Taxpayers, with or without applicable financial statements, receiving advance payments may continue to rely on Rev. Proc. 2004-34 until future guidance is effective.

## SECTION 2. BACKGROUND

Section 451(a) provides that the amount of any item of gross income is included in gross income for the taxable year in which received by the taxpayer, unless, under the method of accounting used in computing taxable income, the amount is to be properly accounted for as of a different period.

Section 1.451-1(a) of the Income Tax Regulations provides that, under an accrual method of accounting, income is includible in gross income when all the events have occurred that fix the right to receive the income and the amount can be determined with reasonable accuracy. All the events that fix the right to receive income generally occur when: (1) the payment is earned through performance, (2) payment is due to the taxpayer, or (3) payment is received by the taxpayer, whichever happens earliest. *See* Rev. Rul. 2003-10, 2003-1 C.B. 288.

Rev. Proc. 2004-34 provides a full inclusion method (the Full Inclusion Method) and a deferral method (the Deferral Method) of accounting

for the treatment of advance payments for goods, services, and other items. Under the Full Inclusion Method, advance payments are included in income in the year of receipt. Under the Deferral Method, an advance payment is included in gross income for the taxable year of receipt to the extent recognized in revenue in a taxpayer's applicable financial statement for that taxable year or earned (for taxpayers without an applicable financial statement) in that taxable year, and the remaining amount of the advance payment is included in the next succeeding taxable year after the taxable year in which the payment is received.

Section 13221 of the Act amends § 451 by redesignating subsections (b) through (i) as (d) through (k), respectively, and by inserting new subsections (b) and (c), effective generally for taxable years beginning after December 31, 2017. Section 451(b)(1)(A)(i) provides that for an accrual method taxpayer, the all events test for any item of gross income shall not be treated as met any later than when the item is taken into account as revenue in an applicable financial statement of the taxpayer. Section 451(c)(1)(A) generally provides that an accrual method taxpayer shall include an advance payment in gross income in the taxable year of receipt. Alternatively, under § 451(c)(1)(B), an accrual method taxpayer may elect to defer the recognition of all or a portion of an advance payment to the taxable year following the taxable year in which the payment is received, except any portion of such advance payment that is required under § 451(b) to be included in gross income in the taxable year in which the payment is received.

Section 451(c)(4)(A) defines an advance payment as any payment: (1) the full inclusion of which in the gross income of the taxpayer for the taxable year of receipt is a permissible method of accounting, (2) any portion of which is included in revenue by the taxpayer in an applicable financial statement, or such other financial statement as the Secretary may specify, for a subsequent taxable year, and (3) which is for goods, services, or such other items as may be identified by the Secretary. Section 451(c) generally contains rules similar to Rev. Proc. 2004-34. *See* H.R. Rep. No. 115-466, at 429 (2017) (Conf. Rep.).

## SECTION 3. INTERIM GUIDANCE FOR REV. PROC. 2004-34

The Treasury Department and the Service expect to issue guidance for the treatment of advance payments to implement the changes made to § 451 by the Act. Until further guidance for the treatment of advance payments is applicable, taxpayers may continue to rely on Rev. Proc. 2004-34 for the treatment of advance payments. During this time, the Service will not challenge a taxpayer's use of Rev. Proc. 2004-34 to satisfy the requirements of § 451, although the Service will continue to verify on examination that taxpayers are properly applying Rev. Proc. 2004-34. In addition, the Service intends to modify section 16.07 of Rev. Proc. 2017-30, 2017-18 I.R.B. 1131, to provide a waiver of the eligibility rule in section 5.01(1)(f) of Rev. Proc. 2015-13, 2015-5 I.R.B. 419, to enable taxpayers to make a change to a method of accounting that is permitted under Rev. Proc. 2004-34.

## SECTION 4. REQUEST FOR COMMENTS ON ADVANCE PAYMENTS

The Treasury and Service invite comments containing suggestions for future guidance under § 451(b) and (c). In particular, comments are requested concerning the following issues under § 451(c): (1) whether taxpayers without an applicable financial statement may continue to use the Deferral Method, as provided in Rev. Proc. 2004-34; (2) whether clarity is needed for the definition of an applicable financial statement under § 451(b)(3); (3) whether the definition of applicable financial statement under § 451(b) and (c) should be the same as the definition in section 4.06 of Rev. Proc. 2004-34; (4) whether other items in addition to those listed in section 4.01(3) of Rev. Proc. 2004-34 should be included in the definition of an advance payment; (5) whether certain payments other than those listed in section 4.02 of Rev. Proc. 2004-34 should be excluded from the definition of an advance payment; (6) whether any new procedural rules for changing a method of accounting for advance payments would be appropriate and helpful; and (7) the extent, if any, to which the Service may provide procedures expanding the rules of § 451(c) to apply to additional taxpayers and types of income.

## WHERE TO SEND COMMENTS

Comments must be submitted by May 14, 2018. Comments, identified by Notice 2018-35, may be sent by one of the following methods:

- By Mail:

Internal Revenue Service

Attn: CC:PA:LPD:PR (Notice 2018-35)

Room 5203

P.O. Box 7604

Ben Franklin Station

Washington, DC 20044

- By Hand or Courier Delivery: Submissions may be hand-delivered Monday through Friday between the hours of 8 a.m. and 4 p.m. to:

Courier's Desk

Internal Revenue Service

Attn: CC:PA:LPD:PR

(Notice 2018-35)

1111 Constitution Avenue, NW

Washington, DC 20224

- Electronic: Alternatively, persons may submit comments electronically to Notice.Comments@irscounsel.treas.gov. Please include "Notice 2018-35)" in the subject line of any electronic communications.

All submissions will be available for public inspection and copying in room 1621, 1111 Constitution Avenue, NW, Washington, DC, from 9 a.m. to 4 p.m.

## SECTION 5. DRAFTING INFORMATION

The principal author of this notice is Peter E. Ford of the Office of Associate Chief Counsel (Income Tax & Accounting). For further information regarding this notice, contact Peter E. Ford, at (202) 317-7011 (not a toll-free call).

---

# Notice 2018-38, I.R.B. 2018-18, April 16, 2018

2018 Fiscal-year Blended Tax Rates for Corporations

PURPOSE

This notice provides guidance on the changes made by "An Act to provide for reconciliation pursuant to titles II and V of the concurrent resolution on the budget for fiscal year 2018," P.L. 115-97 (the Act), to federal income tax rates for corporations under § 11(b) of the Internal Revenue Code (Code) and to the alternative minimum tax for corporations under § 55 and on the application of § 15 in determining the federal income tax (including the alternative minimum tax) of a corporation for a taxable year that begins before January 1, 2018, and ends after December 31, 2017.

BACKGROUND

Section 11(a) of the Code imposes a tax on the taxable income of every corporation (corporate tax). Prior to changes made by the Act, § 11(b) provided that the amount of tax imposed was based on a graduated rate structure starting at 15 percent of the corporation's taxable income and increasing to 35 percent of taxable income. In addition, § 55(a) imposed a tax (the "alternative minimum tax" or AMT) equal to the excess, if any, of the tentative minimum tax (TMT) for the taxable year, over the corporate tax for the taxable year. Section 55(b)(1)(B) provided that in the case of a corporation, the TMT for the taxable year is 20 percent of so much of the alternative minimum taxable income (AMTI) for the taxable year as exceeds the exemption amount, reduced by the alternative minimum tax foreign tax credit for the taxable year.

Section 13001(a) of the Act amended § 11(b) of the Code to provide that the amount of tax imposed by § 11(a) shall be 21 percent of a corporation's taxable income. Section 13001(c)(1) provides generally that this change in the tax rate for corporations is effective for taxable years beginning after December 31, 2017.

Section 12001(a) of the Act amended § 55(a) of the Code by limiting the application of the AMT to non-corporate taxpayers, thereby repealing the AMT for corporations. Section 12001(c) of the Act provides that the changes made by § 12001 apply to taxable years beginning after December 31, 2017.

Section 15(a) of the Code provides that if any rate of tax imposed by chapter 1 of the Code changes, and if the taxable year includes the effective date of the change (unless that date is the first day of the taxable year), then -

(1) tentative taxes shall be computed by applying the rate for the period before the effective date of the change, and the rate for the period on and after such date, to the taxable income for the entire taxable year; and

(2) the tax for such taxable year shall be the sum of that proportion of each tentative tax which the number of days in each period bears to the number of days in the entire taxable year.

Section 15(b) of the Code provides that for purposes of § 15(a), if a tax is repealed, the repeal shall be considered a change of rate, and the rate for the period after the repeal shall be zero. Section 15(c) provides in part that for purposes of § 15(a) and (b), if the rate changes for taxable years "beginning after" or "ending after" a certain date, the following day shall be considered the effective date of the change.

APPLICATION

*Corporate Tax under § 11*

The changes made by § 13001 of the Act to the federal income tax rates imposed on corporations under § 11(b) of the Code are effective for taxable years beginning after December 31, 2017. Under § 15(c), for purposes of § 15(a) and (b), the effective date of the change made by § 13001 of the Act is January 1, 2018. The computation of tax provided under § 15(a) applies to a change in any rate of tax imposed by chapter 1 of the Code if the taxable year includes the effective date of the change, unless that date is the first day of the taxable year. The tax under § 11 is a tax imposed by chapter 1 of the Code. Consequently, a corporation with a taxable year that includes January 1, 2018, but does not start on that day, must apply § 15(a) to determine the amount of federal income tax imposed under § 11 for that taxable year. Pursuant to § 15(a), a tentative tax of a corporation for the taxable year that includes January 1, 2018, shall be computed by applying the rates of tax imposed under § 11(b) prior to the change of the tax rate under § 13001 of the Act, and a tentative tax for a corporation shall be computed by applying the 21 percent rate of tax imposed under § 11(b) as amended by § 13001 of the Act. The tax imposed under § 11 for the taxable year that includes January 1, 2018, is the sum of that proportion of each tentative tax which the number of days in each period bears to the number of days in the entire taxable year.

*Other Applications using § 11(b) Rates*

Certain taxpayers, such as life insurance companies and regulated investment companies, are not subject to the tax imposed under § 11(a), but are nonetheless taxed under other Code provisions that use the rates of tax set forth in § 11(b). The application of § 15 will apply in determining the chapter 1 tax for these taxpayers in the same manner as described above for corporations subject to the tax imposed by § 11(a).

*Alternative Minimum Tax under § 55*

Section 12001 of the Act repealed the application of the AMT imposed under § 55 to corporations effective for taxable years beginning after December 31, 2017. Under § 15(b), the repeal of a tax shall be considered a change of tax rate, and the rate for the period after the repeal is zero for purposes of § 15(a). As a result, the repeal of the

AMT for corporations is a change in the TMT rate from 20 percent to zero. Further, under § 15(c), the effective date of this change of rate is January 1, 2018. The computation of tax provided under § 15(a) applies to a change in any rate of tax imposed by chapter 1 of the Code if the taxable year includes the effective date of the change, unless that date is the first day of the taxable year. The tax under § 55 is a tax imposed by chapter 1 of the Code. Consequently, a corporation with a taxable year that includes January 1, 2018, but does not start on that day, must apply § 15(a) to determine the amount of its TMT for that taxable year. Pursuant to § 15(a), a tentative TMT for the corporation shall be computed by applying the 20 percent TMT rate provided under § 55(b)(1)(B) prior to the change under § 12001 of the Act, and a tentative TMT shall be computed by applying the zero percent TMT rate resulting from the repeal under § 12001 of the Act of the AMT for corporations. The corporation's TMT for the taxable year that includes January 1, 2018, is the sum of that proportion of each tentative TMT which the number of days in each period bears to the number of days in the entire taxable year.

EXAMPLE

The following example illustrates the application of § 15(a) of the Code in determining the tax under §§ 11 and 55 of a corporation using a fiscal year as its taxable year for the taxable year that includes January 1, 2018.

*Example.* Corporation X, a subchapter C corporation, uses a June 30 taxable year. For its taxable year beginning July 1, 2017, and ending June 30, 2018, X's taxable income is $1,000,000, and its AMTI in excess of its AMT exemption amount is $2,000,000.

*Computation under § 11*

Corporation X's corporate tax under § 11 of the Code is computed by applying § 15(a) as follows:

| | | |
|---|---|---:|
| 1) | Taxable income (Line 30, Form 1120) | $ 1,000,000 |
| 2) | Tax on Line 1 amount using § 11(b) rates before the Act | 340,000 |
| 3) | Number of days in Corporation X's taxable year before January, 1, 2018 | 184 |
| 4) | Multiply Line 2 by Line 3 | 62,560,000 |
| 5) | Tax on Line 1 amount using § 11(b) rate after the Act | 210,000 |
| 6) | Number of days in the taxable year after December 31, 2017 | 181 |
| 7) | Multiply Line 5 by Line 6 | 38,010,000 |
| 8) | Divide Line 4 by total number of days in the taxable year | 171,397 |
| 9) | Divide Line 7 by total number of days in the taxable year | 104,137 |
| 10) | Sum of Line 8 and Line 9 | $ 275,534 |

Under § 15(a), Corporation X's corporate tax for its taxable year ending June 30, 2018 is $275,534.

*Computation under § 55*

Corporation X's TMT and resulting AMT under § 55 of the Code is computed by applying § 15(a) as follows:

| | | |
|---|---|---:|
| 1) | AMTI in excess of AMT exemption amount (Line 9, Form 4626) | $ 2,000,000 |
| 2) | TMT on Line 1 amount using § 55(b)(1)(B) rate before the Act | 400,000 |
| 3) | Number of days in Corporation X's taxable year before January, 1, 2018 | 184 |
| 4) | Multiply Line 2 by Line 3 | 73,600,000 |
| 5) | Divide Line 4 by total number of days in the taxable year | $ 201,644 |

It is unnecessary to compute a TMT for the portion of the taxable year beginning on and after the effective date of § 12001 of the Act because the TMT is repealed as of the effective date for purposes of applying § 15(a). Corporation X's TMT for its taxable year ending June 30, 2018 is $201,644. Because this TMT amount for the taxable year does not exceed Corporation X's corporate tax amount of $275,534, Corporation X does not have an AMT liability for its taxable year ending June 30, 2018.

## APPLICABILITY DATE

This notice applies to taxable years of corporations that begin before January 1, 2018, and end after December 31, 2017.

## CONTACT INFORMATION

For further information regarding this notice, contact Bill Jackson at (202) 317-4731 or Forest Boone at (202) 317-4904 (not a toll-free call).

---

## Notice 2018-55, I.R.B. 2018-26, June 8, 2018

Guidance on the Calculation of Net Investment Income for Purposes of the Section 4968 Excise Tax Applicable to Certain Private Colleges and Universities

### SECTION 1. PURPOSE

This notice announces that the Department of the Treasury (the Treasury Department) and the Internal Revenue Service (the IRS) intend to issue proposed regulations providing clarification regarding the calculation of net investment income for purposes of section 4968(c) of the Internal Revenue Code (Code). Taxpayers may rely on section 3 of this notice until further guidance is issued.

### SECTION 2. BACKGROUND

Section 13701 of Pub. L. No. 115-97, an Act to Provide for Reconciliation Pursuant to Titles II and V of the Concurrent Resolution on the Budget for Fiscal Year 2018, imposes on each applicable educational institution, as defined in section 4968(b)(1), an excise tax equal to 1.4% of the institution's net investment income for the taxable year. Section 4968(c) provides that net investment income is to be determined under rules similar to the rules of section 4940(c). Section 4968(d)(1) provides that certain assets and net investment income of related organizations described in section 4968(d)(2) are treated as assets and net investment income of the educational institution. Section 4968 applies to taxable years beginning after December 31, 2017.

Section 4940(c)(1) provides that net investment income is the amount by which the sum of the gross investment income and the capital gain income exceeds allowable deductions. Except to the extent inconsistent with the provisions of section 4940, net investment income is determined under the principles of subtitle A of the Code.

Section 4940(c)(2) provides that, for purposes of section 4940(c)(1), gross investment income means the gross amount of income from interest, dividends, rents, payments with respect to securities loans (as defined in section 512(a)(5)), and royalties, but not including any such income to the extent included in computing the tax imposed by section 511. Investment income also includes income from sources similar to those specifically listed in the preceding sentence.

Section 4940(c)(3) provides that, for purposes of section 4940(c)(1), there is allowed as a deduction all the ordinary and necessary expenses paid or incurred for the production or collection of gross investment income or for the management, conservation, or maintenance of property held for the production of such income, determined with the following modifications: (i) the deduction provided by section 167 is allowed, but only on the basis of the straight line method of depreciation; and (ii) the deduction for depletion provided by section 611 is allowed, but such deduction shall be determined without regard to section 613 (relating to percentage depletion).

Section 4940(c)(4) provides that, for purposes of section 4940(c)(1): (A) no gain or loss from the sale or other disposition of property is taken into account to the extent that any such gain or loss is taken into account for purposes of computing the tax imposed by section 511; (B) in the case of property held by a private foundation on December 31, 1969, and continuously thereafter to the date of its disposition, the basis for determining gain shall be deemed to be not less than the fair market value of such property on December 31, 1969; (C) losses from sales or other dispositions of property are allowed only to the extent of gains from such sales or other dispositions, and there shall be no capital loss carryovers or carrybacks; and (D) except to the extent provided by regulation, under rules similar to the rules of section 1031 (including the exception under subsection (a)(2) thereof), no gain or loss is taken into account with respect to any portion of property used for a period of not less than 1 year for a purpose or function constituting the basis of the private foundation's exemption if the entire property is exchanged immediately following such period solely for property of like kind which is to be used primarily for a purpose or function constituting the basis for such foundation's exemption.

Treasury Regulations § 53.4940-1(f)(2)(i) provides that basis for purposes of determining gain from the sale or other disposition of property shall be the greater of: (A) fair market value on December 31, 1969, plus or minus all adjustments after December 31, 1969, and before the date of disposition under the rules of Part II of Subchapter O of Chapter 1, provided that the property was held by the private foundation on December 31, 1969, and continuously thereafter to the date of disposition, or (B) basis as determined under the rules of Part II of Subchapter O of Chapter 1, subject to the provisions of section 4940(c)(3)(B) (and without regard to section 362(c)). Treas. Reg. §53.4940-1(f)(2)(ii) provides that for purposes of determining loss from the sale or other disposition of property, basis shall be determined under the rules of Part II of Subchapter O of Chapter 1, subject to the provisions of section 4940(c)(3)(B) (and without regard to section 362(c)).

Section 4940(c)(5) provides that, for purposes of section 4940, net investment income is determined by applying section 103 (relating to State and local bonds) and section 265 (relating to expenses and interest relating to tax-exempt income).

## SECTION 3. BASIS FOR DETERMINING GAIN OR LOSS ON DISPOSITION OF PROPERTY

Similar to the rules found in section 4940(c), the Treasury Department and the IRS intend to propose regulations stating that, in the case of property held by an applicable educational institution on December 31, 2017, and continuously thereafter to the date of its disposition, basis of such property for determining gain shall be deemed to be not less than the fair market value of such property on December 31, 2017, plus or minus all adjustments after December 31, 2017, and before the date of disposition consistent with the regulations under section 4940(c). In addition, for purposes of determining loss, basis rules that are consistent with the regulations under section 4940(c) will apply.

## SECTION 4. NETTING CAPITAL GAINS AND LOSSES

Similar to the rules found in section 4940(c)(4)(C), the Treasury Department and the IRS intend to propose regulations stating that losses from sales or other dispositions of property generally shall be allowed only to the extent of gains from such sales or other dispositions,

and there shall be no capital loss carryovers or carrybacks. The Treasury Department and the IRS also expect that with respect to related organizations described in section 4968(d)(2), overall net losses from sales or other dispositions of property in one related organization (or from the applicable educational institution) will be allowed to offset overall net gains from such sales or other dispositions from other related organizations (or from the applicable educational institution), but request comments on this issue.

## SECTION 5. RELIANCE

Before the issuance of the proposed regulations described in this notice, applicable educational institutions described in section 4968(b)(1) may rely on the rules described in section 3 of this notice.

## SECTION 6. REQUEST FOR PUBLIC COMMENTS

The Treasury Department and the IRS request comments on the issues addressed in this notice, including comments on what other guidance under section 4968(c) is needed and whether, and what type of, transitional relief may be necessary.

Written comments may be submitted by September 6, 2018, to Internal Revenue Service, CC:PA:LPD:PR (Notice 2018-55), Room 5203, P.O. Box 7604, Ben Franklin Station, Washington, DC 20044, or electronically to Notice.Comments@irscounsel.treas.gov (please include "Notice 2018-55" in the subject line). Alternatively, comments may be hand delivered between the hours of 8:00 a.m. and 4:00 p.m. Monday to Friday to CC:PA:LPD:PR (Notice 2018-55), Courier's Desk, Internal Revenue Service, 1111 Constitution Avenue NW, Washington, D.C. Comments will be available for public inspection and copying.

## SECTION 7. DRAFTING INFORMATION

The principal author of this notice is Amber Mackenzie of the Office of Associate Chief Counsel (Tax Exempt and Government Entities). For further information regarding this notice, contact Amber Mackenzie or Melinda Williams at (202) 317-5800 (not a toll-free number).

# Notice 2018-58, I.R.B. 2018-33, July 30, 2018

**Guidance on Recontributions, Rollovers and Qualified Higher Education Expenses under Section 529**

## I. PURPOSE AND OVERVIEW

This notice announces that the Department of the Treasury (the Treasury Department) and the Internal Revenue Service (the IRS) intend to issue regulations providing clarification regarding (1) the special rules for contributions of refunded qualified higher education expenses to a qualified tuition program under §529(c)(3)(D) of the Internal Revenue Code (Code); (2) the new rules under §529(c)(3)(C)(i)(III) permitting a rollover from a qualified tuition program to an ABLE account under §529A; and (3) the new rules under §529(c)(7) treating certain elementary or secondary school expenses as qualified higher education expenses.

## II. BACKGROUND

Under §529, a State or its agency or instrumentality may establish or maintain a program that permits a person to prepay or contribute to an account for a designated beneficiary's qualified higher education expenses (QHEEs). In addition, an eligible educational institution may establish or maintain a program that permits a person to prepay a designated beneficiary's QHEEs. These programs are collectively referred to as section 529 qualified tuition programs (QTPs). Section 529(c)(3) provides that distributions (including any attributable earnings) from a QTP are not included in gross income if such distributions do not exceed the designated beneficiary's QHEEs. To the extent distributions exceed the designated beneficiary's QHEEs, a portion of the distribution is included in gross income.

Prior to its amendment by "An Act to provide for reconciliation pursuant to titles II and V of the concurrent resolution on the budget for fiscal year 2018", Pub.L. 115-97 (the "2017 Act"), signed into law on December 22, 2017, §529(e)(3)(A) defined QHEEs to include tuition, fees, books, supplies, and equipment required for the enrollment or attendance of a designated beneficiary at an eligible educational institution,[1] including certain computer equipment and software used primarily by the beneficiary during any years the beneficiary is enrolled at an eligible educational institution. In the case of a special needs beneficiary, QHEEs include expenses for special needs services that are incurred in connection with such enrollment or attendance. QHEEs also include reasonable costs for room and board for eligible students as defined in §25A(b)(3) (generally, those who are enrolled at least half-time).

Sections 529(c)(3)(C)(i)(I) and (II) permit a tax-free rollover of a distribution from a QTP, made within 60 days of the distribution, to another QTP for the benefit of either the same designated beneficiary or another designated beneficiary who is a member of the family of the original designated beneficiary. However, Notice 2001-81, 2001-52 I.R.B. 617, provides that the distributing QTP must provide a breakdown of the earnings portion of the rollover amount to the recipient QTP and, until the recipient QTP receives appropriate documentation showing the earnings portion, the entire rollover amount is treated as earnings. Notice 2001-81 applies the same rule to a direct transfer (i.e., a trustee-to-trustee transfer) from a QTP to another QTP.

Section 529(c)(3)(D), added to the Code by the Protecting Americans from Tax Hikes Act of 2015 (PATH Act), part of the Consolidated Appropriations Act, 2016 (Pub. L. 114-113), addresses situations in which QTP funds are distributed for a beneficiary's QHEEs, but some portion of those expenses is refunded to the beneficiary by the eligible educational institution. This could occur, for example, if the beneficiary were to drop a class mid-semester. Section 529(c)(3)(D) provides that the portion of such a distribution refunded to an individual who is the beneficiary of a QTP by an eligible educational institution is not subject to income tax to the extent that the refund is recontributed to a QTP of which that individual is the beneficiary not later than 60 days after the date of such refund and does not exceed the refunded amount. Section 529(c)(3)(D) applies to refunds received after December 31, 2014. The PATH Act also included a transition rule with regard to the deadline for recontributing a refund received after 2014 but before the date of enactment (December 18, 2015). Specifically, those refunded distributions are exempt from income tax if they were recontributed to the beneficiary's QTP not later than February 16, 2016 (60 days after the date of enactment of the PATH Act).

---

[1] Section 529(e)(5) defines f an "eligible educational institution" as an institution (A) which is described in §481 of the Higher Education Act of 1965 (20 U.S.C. 1088), as in effect on the date of the enactment of this paragraph, and (B) which is eligible to participate in a program under title IV of such Act.

The 2017 Act added § 529(c)(3)(C)(i)(III) which provides that a distribution from a QTP made after December 22, 2017, and before January 1, 2026, is not subject to income tax if, within 60 days of the distribution, it is transferred to an ABLE account (as defined in § 529A(e)(6))[2] of the designated beneficiary or a member of the family of the designated beneficiary. Under § 529(c)(3)(C)(i), the amount of any rollover to an ABLE account is limited to the amount that, when added to all other contributions made to the ABLE account for the taxable year, does not exceed the contribution limit for the ABLE account under § 529A(b)(2)(B)(i), i.e., the annual gift tax exclusion amount under § 2503(b).

In addition, the 2017 Act expanded the definition of QHEEs to include tuition in connection with the designated beneficiary's enrollment or attendance at an elementary or secondary public, private, or religious school. See § 529(c)(7). The 2017 Act also amended § 529(e)(3)(A) to limit the total amount of these tuition distributions for each designated beneficiary to $10,000 per year from all QTPs of the designated beneficiary. Both amendments apply to distributions made after December 31, 2017.

## III. RECONTRIBUTION OF REFUNDED QHEEs

The Treasury Department and the IRS are aware of concerns expressed by QTP administrators regarding the administrative burdens that would arise if a recontribution of a refunded QHEE is treated in the same manner as a rollover under Notice 2001-81 requiring a breakdown of the earnings portion of the recontribution. Because the amount is refunded by the eligible educational institution, which will have no information regarding the income portion of each tuition payment (whether made from a single or multiple QTPs), QTP administrators generally would be unable to determine the earnings portion of the recontribution. Accordingly, the Treasury Department and the IRS intend to issue regulations providing that the entire recontributed amount will be treated as principal. This rule of administrative convenience will eliminate the burdens associated with determining the earnings portion. Furthermore, because the recontributed amount previously was taken into account in applying the overall contribution limit under § 529(b)(6), the Treasury Department and the IRS anticipate that

the regulations will provide that the recontributed amount does not count against the limit on contributions on behalf of the designated beneficiary under § 529(b)(6). In addition, consistent with § 529(c)(3)(D), the Treasury Department and the IRS anticipate that the regulations will confirm that the recontribution must be to a QTP for the benefit of the designated beneficiary who received the refund of QHEEs, although the recontribution need not be to the QTP from which the distributions for the QHEEs were made.

## IV. ROLLOVER FROM A QTP TO AN ABLE ACCOUNT

In accordance with new § 529(c)(3)(C)(i)(III), the Treasury Department and the IRS intend to issue regulations providing that a distribution from a QTP made after December 22, 2017, and before January 1, 2026, to the ABLE account of the designated beneficiary of that QTP, or of a member of the family of that designated beneficiary, is not subject to income tax if two requirements are satisfied. First, the distributed funds must be contributed to the ABLE account within 60 days after their withdrawal from the QTP. Second, the distribution, when added to all other contributions made to the ABLE account for the taxable year that are subject to the limitation under § 529A(b)(2)(B)(i) (the annual gift tax exclusion under § 2503(b)), must not exceed that limitation. Specifically, the regulations are expected to provide that the sum of the distribution and all other contributions to the ABLE account for the taxable year, other than contributions of the designated beneficiary's compensation as described in § 529A(b)(2)(B)(ii), must not exceed the annual gift tax exclusion for that taxable year. Consistent with the longstanding approach of treating direct transfers similarly to rollovers in Notice 2001-81, the Treasury Department and the IRS also anticipate that the regulations will provide that the same rules will apply regardless of whether such a QTP distribution is rolled over to an ABLE account or instead is transferred by a direct transfer from a QTP to an ABLE account.

To the extent that a direct transfer (or, in the case of a rollover, a contribution of the distributed amount) would cause the contribution limit under § 529A(b)(2)(B)(i) to be exceeded, it would be subject to income tax and a 10% additional tax under § 529(c)(6), if applicable.[3] Therefore, the

---

[2] Generally, an ABLE account is established under a § 529A qualified ABLE program to pay the qualified disability expenses of an eligible individual who is blind or has a disability.

[3] Section 529(c)(6) provides that the additional 10% tax imposed by § 530(d)(4) applies to any payment or distribu-

tion from a QTP in the same manner as it applies to a payment or distribution from a Coverdell education savings account.

Treasury Department and the IRS anticipate that the regulations will require a QTP to prohibit the direct transfer of any amount that would cause the limit under § 529A(b)(2)(B)(i) to be exceeded. Furthermore, a qualified ABLE program is prohibited from accepting certain contributions in excess of the limitations applicable to ABLE accounts, and any violation of those rules could cause the designated beneficiary to incur tax, and could adversely affect the ABLE beneficiary's eligibility for certain public benefits.[4]

The Treasury Department and the IRS encourage the QTP designated beneficiary, in the case of a rollover, or the QTP, in the case of a direct transfer, to contact the qualified ABLE program before contributing any funds to the ABLE account to ensure that the § 529A(b)(2)(B)(i) limit will not be exceeded. However, the Treasury Department and the IRS anticipate that the regulations will provide that, in the case of a direct transfer, any excess contribution that is rejected by the qualified ABLE program and returned to the QTP will not be deemed to be a new contribution to the QTP for purposes of the § 529(b)(6) contribution limit.

Further, the Treasury Department and the IRS anticipate that the regulations will specify that, for purposes of identifying the ABLE accounts permitted to receive such a rollover from a designated beneficiary's QTP, a member of the family of the designated beneficiary means a member of the family as defined in § 529(e)(2), rather than the more limited definition in § 529A(e)(4) that applies for purposes of qualified ABLE programs.

## V. SECTION 529 EXPANSION OF QHEES TO INCLUDE ELEMENTARY AND SECONDARY EDUCATION TUITION EXPENSES

Consistent with new § 529(c)(7) and (e)(3)(A), respectively, the Treasury Department and the IRS anticipate that the regulations will provide

that QHEEs include tuition in connection with the designated beneficiary's enrollment or attendance at an elementary or secondary public, private, or religious school, but that such QHEEs are limited to a total of $10,000 per year per designated beneficiary, regardless of the number of QTPs making such distributions for that same designated beneficiary. The Treasury Department and IRS intend to issue regulations defining the term "elementary or secondary" to mean kindergarten through grade 12 as determined under State law, consistent with the definition applicable for Coverdell education savings accounts in § 530(b)(3)(B). Coverdell education savings accounts are another type of tax-favored savings account governed under § 530 and also may be established to pay for tuition and other expenses in connection with enrollment or attendance at an elementary or secondary public, private, or religious school. Applying the same definition to both a QTP and a Coverdell education savings account will facilitate the allocation of expenses between those two accounts as is required by § 530(d)(2)(C)(ii) if a designated beneficiary receives distributions from both a QTP and a Coverdell education savings account and those total distributions exceed the designated beneficiary's qualified expenses.

## VI. RELIANCE

Before the issuance of the proposed regulations described in this notice, taxpayers, beneficiaries, and administrators of 529 and ABLE programs may rely on the rules described in sections III, IV, and V of this notice.

## VII. DRAFTING INFORMATION

The principal author of this notice is Peter A. Holiat of the Office of the Associate Chief Counsel (TEGE). For further information regarding this notice contact Mr. Holiat at 202-317-4541 (not a toll-free number).

---

## Notice 2018-61, I.R.B. 2018-31, July 13, 2018

### SECTION 1. PURPOSE

This notice announces that the Department of the Treasury (Treasury Department) and the Internal Revenue Service (IRS) intend to issue regulations providing clarification of the effect of newly enacted section 67(g) of the Internal Revenue Code (Code) on the deductibility of certain expenses described in section 67(b) and (e) and § 1.67-4 of the Income Tax Regulations that are

incurred by estates and non-grantor trusts. Section 67(g) was added by "An Act to provide for reconciliation pursuant to titles II and V of the concurrent resolution on the budget for fiscal year 2018," P.L. 115-97 (Act), which was enacted December 22, 2017. This notice also requests comments on issues relating to section 642(h)(2) and § 1.642(h)-2(a) in light of new section 67(g).

---

[4] For more information on the effect of ABLE accounts on the beneficiary's eligibility for public benefits, see the preamble of the Notice of Proposed Rulemaking (80 FR 35602) published in the *Federal Register* on 6/22/2015.

## SECTION 2. BACKGROUND

Section 11045 of the Act added section 67(g) to the Code, which generally provides that, notwithstanding section 67(a), no miscellaneous itemized deductions shall be allowed for any taxable year beginning after December 31, 2017, and before January 1, 2026.

Section 61(a) defines gross income as all income from whatever source derived, including (but not limited to) the items listed in sections 61(a)(1) through (15), except as otherwise provided in subtitle A.

Section 62(a) defines the term "adjusted gross income" for purposes of subtitle A as, in the case of an individual, gross income minus the deductions listed in sections 62(a)(1) through (21).

Section 63(a) defines "taxable income" for individuals who itemize their deductions, for purposes of subtitle A, as gross income minus the deductions allowed by chapter 1 (other than the standard deduction).

Section 63(d) defines the term "itemized deductions" for purposes of subtitle A as the deductions allowable under chapter 1 other than (1) the deductions allowable in arriving at adjusted gross income, (2) the deduction for personal exemptions provided by section 151, and (3) the deduction provided in section 199A.

Section 67(a) provides generally that, in the case of an individual, the miscellaneous itemized deductions for any taxable year shall be allowed only to the extent that the aggregate of such deductions exceeds 2 percent of adjusted gross income.

Section 67(b) defines the term "miscellaneous itemized deductions" for purposes of section 67 as meaning the itemized deductions other than those listed in sections 67(b)(1) through (12).

Section 67(e) provides that, for purposes of section 67, the adjusted gross income of an estate or trust shall be computed in the same manner as that of an individual, except that (1) the deductions for costs which are paid or incurred in connection with the administration of the estate or trust and which would not have been incurred if the property were not held in such estate or trust, and (2) the deductions allowable under sections 642(b), 651, and 661 shall be treated as allowable in arriving at adjusted gross income.

Section 1.67-4(a) states that section 67(e) provides an exception to the 2-percent floor on miscellaneous itemized deductions for costs that are paid or incurred in the administration of an estate or a trust not described in § 1.67-2T(g)(1)(i) (a non-grantor trust) and that would not have been incurred if the property were not held in such estate or trust. A cost is subject to the 2-percent floor to the extent that it is included in the definition of miscellaneous itemized deductions under section 67(b), is incurred by an estate or non-grantor trust, and commonly or customarily would be incurred by a hypothetical individual holding the same property.

Section 1.67-4(b) provides generally that, in analyzing a cost to determine whether it commonly or customarily would be incurred by a hypothetical individual owning the same property, it is the type of product or service rendered to the estate or non-grantor trust in exchange for the cost, rather than the description of the cost of that product or service, that is determinative. It further provides specific examples of costs that will be considered commonly or customarily incurred by individuals and those that will not.

Section 1.67-4(c) provides that, subject to certain exceptions, if an estate or non-grantor trust pays a single fee, commission, or other expense for both costs that are subject to the 2-percent floor and costs (in a more than de minimis amount) that are not, then, except to the extent provided otherwise by guidance published in the Internal Revenue Bulletin, the single fee, commission, or other expense (bundled fee) must be allocated, for purposes of computing the adjusted gross income of the estate or non-grantor trust in compliance with section 67(e), between the costs that are subject to the 2-percent floor and those that are not.

## SECTION 3. REGULATIONS TO BE ISSUED ADDRESSING THE EFFECT OF SECTION 67(g) ON CERTAIN ESTATE AND NON-GRANTOR TRUST EXPENSES

Commentators have suggested that new section 67(g) might be read to eliminate the ability of estates and non-grantor trusts to deduct any expenses described in section 67(e)(1) and § 1.67-4 for the taxable years during which the application of section 67(a) is suspended. The Treasury Department and the IRS do not believe that this is a correct reading of section 67(g). For the taxable years during which it is effective, section 67(g) denies a deduction for miscellaneous itemized deductions. Section 67(b) defines miscellaneous itemized deductions as itemized deductions other than those listed therein. Section 63(d) defines itemized deductions by excluding personal exemptions, section 199A deductions, and deductions used to arrive at adjusted gross income. Therefore, neither the above-the-line deductions used to arrive at adjusted gross income nor the expenses listed in section 67(b)(1) - (12) are miscellaneous itemized deductions. Section 62(a) defines adjusted gross income of an individual, and section 67(e) provides that the adjusted gross income of a trust or estate is determined in the same way as for an individual, except that expenses described in section 67(e)(1) and deductions pursuant to sections 642(b), 651, and 661 are allowable as deductions in arriving at adjusted gross income. Thus, section 67(e) removes the expenses described in section 67(e)(1) from the category of itemized deductions (and thus necessarily also from the subset of miscellaneous itemized deductions) and instead treats them as above-the-line deductions allowable in determining adjusted gross income under section 62(a). Therefore, the suspension of the deductibility of miscellaneous itemized deductions under section 67(a) does not affect the deductibility of payments described in section 67(e)(1). However, an expense that commonly or customarily would be incurred by an individual (including the appropriate portion of a bundled fee) is affected by section 67(g) and thus is not deductible to the estate or non-grantor trust during the suspension of section 67(a). Nothing in section 67(g) impacts the determination of what expenses are described in section 67(e)(1).

Additionally, nothing in section 67(g) affects the ability of the estate or trust to take a deduction listed under section 67(b). These deductions remain outside of the definition of "miscellaneous itemized deduction." For example, section 691(c) deductions (relating to the deduction for estate tax on income in respect of the decedent), which are identified in section 67(b)(7), remain unaffected by the enactment of section 67(g)).

The Treasury Department and the IRS intend to issue regulations clarifying that estates and non-grantor trusts may continue to deduct expenses described in section 67(e)(1) and amounts allowable as deductions under section 642(b), 651 or 661, including the appropriate portion of a bundled fee, in determining the estate or non-grantor trust's adjusted gross income during taxable years, for which the application of section 67(a) is suspended pursuant to section 67(g). Additionally, the regulations will clarify that deductions enumerated in section 67(b) and (e) continue to remain outside the definition of "miscellaneous itemized deductions" and thus are unaffected by section 67(g).

SECTION 4. REQUEST FOR COMMENTS CONCERNING A BENEFICIARY'S ABILITY TO CLAIM EXCESS DEDUCTIONS PURSUANT TO SECTION 642(h)

The Treasury Department and the IRS are aware of some concerns that the enactment of section 67(g) will affect a beneficiary's ability to

deduct section 67(e) expenses upon the termination of the trust or estate as provided in section 642(h).

Section 642(h) provides that if, on the termination of an estate or trust, the trust or estate has: (1) a net operating loss carryover under section 172 or a capital loss carryover under section 1212, or (2) for the last taxable year of the estate or trust, deductions (other than the deductions allowed under section 642(b) (relating to personal exemption) or section 642(c) (relating to charitable contributions)) in excess of gross income for such year, then such carryover or such excess shall be allowed as a deduction, in accordance with the regulations prescribed by the Secretary, to the beneficiaries succeeding to the property of the estate or trust.

Section 1.642(h)-1(b) provides, in part, that net operating loss carryovers and capital loss carryovers are taken into account when determining adjusted gross income. Therefore, they are above-the-line deductions and thus are not miscellaneous itemized deductions on the returns of beneficiaries. Conversely, § 1.642(h)-2(a) provides that if, on the termination of an estate or trust, the estate or trust has for its last taxable year deductions (other than the deductions allowed under section 642(b) (relating to personal exemption) or section 642(c) (relating to charitable contributions)) in excess of gross income, the excess is allowed under section 642(h)(2) as a deduction (section 642(h)(2) excess deduction) to the beneficiaries. However, the section 642(h)(2) excess deduction is allowed only in computing the taxable income of the beneficiaries and must be taken into account in computing the items of tax preference of the beneficiaries. Therefore, a section 642(h)(2) excess deduction is not used in computing the beneficiaries' adjusted gross income and is treated as a miscellaneous itemized deduction of the beneficiaries. *See* sections 63(d) and 67(b).

The section 642(h)(2) excess deduction may include expenses described in section 67(e). As previously discussed, prior to enactment of section 67(g), miscellaneous itemized deductions were allowed subject to the restrictions contained in section 67(a). For the years in which section 67(g) is effective, miscellaneous itemized deductions are not permitted, and that appears to include the section 642(h)(2) excess deduction. The Treasury Department and the IRS are studying whether section 67(e) deductions, as well as other deductions that would not be subject to the limitations imposed by sections 67(a) and (g) in the hands of the trust or estate, should continue to be treated as miscellaneous itemized deductions when they are included as a section

642(h)(2) excess deduction. Taxpayers should note that section 67(e) provides that appropriate adjustments shall be made in the application of part I of subchapter J of chapter 1 of the Code to take into account the provisions of section 67.

The Treasury Department and the IRS intend to issue regulations in this area and request comments regarding the effect of section 67(g) on the ability of the beneficiary to deduct amounts comprising the section 642(h)(2) excess deduction upon the termination of a trust or estate in light of sections 642(h) and 1.642(h)-2(a). In particular, the Treasury Department and the IRS request comments concerning whether the separate amounts comprising the section 642(h)(2) excess deduction, such as any amounts that are section 67(e) deductions, should be separately analyzed when applying section 67. Written comments may be submitted by U.S. Postal Service to Internal Revenue Service, CC:PA:LPD:RU (Notice 2018-61), Room 5203, P.O. Box 7604, Ben Franklin Station, Washington, D.C. 20044, or by hand delivery (between the hours of 8:00 am to 4:00 pm) to CC:PA:LPD:RU (Notice 2018-61), Courier's Desk, Internal Revenue Service, 1111 Constitution Ave., N.W., Washington, D.C. 20224. Comments may also be submitted by email to *Notice.Comments@irscounsel.treas.gov*. Comments submitted by email should include Notice 2018-61 in the subject line as well as in the body of the email. Comments will be available for public inspection and copying.

SECTION 5. EFFECTIVE DATE

This notice is effective July 13, 2018. Estates and non-grantor trusts may rely on this notice for taxable years beginning after December 31, 2017.

SECTION 6. DRAFTING INFORMATION

The principal author of this notice is Meghan M. Howard of the Office of Associate Chief Counsel (Passthroughs & Special Industries). For further information regarding this notice contact Ms. Howard at (202) 317-5279 (not a toll-free number).

---

# Notice 2018-62, I.R.B. 2018-34, August 3, 2018

**Guidance on the Contribution Limits Applicable to ABLE Accounts**

SECTION 1. PURPOSE

This notice announces that the Department of the Treasury (the Treasury Department) and the Internal Revenue Service (the IRS) intend to issue proposed regulations providing clarification regarding the contribution limits provided in § 529A(b)(2) of the Internal Revenue Code (Code).

SECTION 2. BACKGROUND

The Stephen Beck, Jr., Achieving a Better Life Experience Act of 2014 (the "ABLE Act") was enacted on December 19, 2014, as part of The Tax Increase Prevention Amendments (P.L. 113-295). The ABLE Act added § 529A to the Code. Section 529A allows a State (or its agency or instrumentality) to establish and maintain a tax-advantaged savings program under which contributions may be made to an ABLE account for the purpose of paying for the qualified disability expenses of the designated beneficiary of the account. Section 529A was amended by "An Act to provide for reconciliation pursuant to titles II and V of the concurrent resolution on the budget for fiscal year 2018," P.L. 115-97 (2017 Act), signed into law on December 22, 2017.

Prior to amendment by the 2017 Act, § 529A(b)(2) stated that a program shall not be treated as a qualified ABLE program unless it provides that no contribution will be accepted unless it is in cash and if the contribution (other than a rollover contribution described in § 529A(c)(1)(C)) would not result in aggregate contributions from all contributors in excess of the amount of the § 2503(b) gift tax exclusion for the calendar year in which the designated beneficiary's taxable year begins. Under § 529A(b)(2), rules similar to the rules of § 408(d)(4) apply to permit the return of excess contributions (with any attributable net income) on or before the due date (including extensions) of the designated beneficiary's income tax return. In addition, under § 529A(b)(6), a qualified ABLE program must provide adequate safeguards to ensure that total contributions do not exceed the State's limit for aggregate contributions under its qualified tuition program as described in § 529(b)(6). A qualified tuition program under § 529 is a program established by a State or its agency or instrumentality that permits a person to prepay or contribute to a tax-favored savings account for a designated beneficiary's qualified higher education expenses (QHEEs) or a program established by an eligible educational institution that permits a person to prepay a designated beneficiary's QHEEs.

The Treasury Department and the IRS issued proposed regulations concerning qualified ABLE programs. These proposed regulations were released on June 19, 2015 and published in the Federal Register on June 22, 2015 (80 Fed. Reg. 35602). The proposed regulations provide rules by which states or state agencies or instrumentalities may establish and maintain a qualified ABLE program. Prop. Treas. Reg. § 1.529A-2(g)(4) would require a qualified ABLE program to return any excess contribution or excess aggregate contribution, including all net income attributable to that excess contribution or excess aggregate contribution, to the person or persons who made that contribution. The qualified ABLE program must use the rules set forth in § 1.408-11 for this purpose, treating an ABLE account the same way that an IRA is treated, and must return excess contributions or excess aggregate contributions in accordance with § 408(d)(4). To facilitate the proper tax treatment of returned excess contributions, Prop. Treas. Reg. § 1.529A-6(d) would require ABLE programs to collect the taxpayer identification number (TIN) of all contributors to an ABLE account.

The Treasury Department and the IRS issued Notice 2015-81, 2015-49 IRB 784 (Dec. 7, 2015), which, in response to comments on the proposed regulations, describes how the Treasury Department and the IRS intend to revise certain provisions of the proposed regulations under § 529A when those regulations are finalized. One of the provisions is the requirement under Prop. Treas. Reg. § 1.529A-6(d) to collect the TIN of each contributor to the ABLE account (if the program does not already have a record of the person's correct TIN). Notice 2015-81 states that it is anticipated that the final regulations will not require ABLE programs to request the TIN of ABLE contributors if the program has a system in place to identify and reject contributions that exceed the annual or cumulative limits. However, if an excess contribution is deposited into a designated beneficiary's ABLE account, the program must request the TIN of the contributor that made the excess contribution. Final regulations under § 529A are included on the 2017-2018 Priority Guidance Plan.

The contribution limits and other provisions of section 529A were modified by the 2017 Act. Specifically, the 2017 Act amended § 529A(b)(2)(B) to allow a designated beneficiary described in § 529A(b)(7) to contribute, prior to January 1, 2026, an additional amount in excess of the limit in § 529A(b)(2)(B)(i) (the annual gift tax exclusion amount in § 2503(b), formerly set forth in § 529A(b)(2)(B)). This additional amount is set forth in § 529A(b)(2)(B)(ii) and is equal to the lesser of (I) the designated beneficiary's compensation as defined by § 219(f)(1) for the taxable year, or (II) an amount equal to the poverty line

for a one-person household for the calendar year preceding the calendar year in which the taxable year begins. The 2017 Act also amended the § 529A(b)(2) flush language by adding that the designated beneficiary, or a person acting on behalf of the designated beneficiary, is required to maintain adequate records to ensure, and is responsible for ensuring, that the requirements of § 529A(b)(2)(B)(ii) are met.

The 2017 Act added § 529A(b)(7)(A) to identify a designated beneficiary eligible to make such an additional contribution as one who is an employee (including a self-employed individual) with respect to whom there has been no contribution made for the taxable year to the following: a defined contribution plan meeting the requirements of §§ 401(a) or 403(a); an annuity contract described in § 403(b); or an eligible deferred contribution plan under § 457(b). The 2017 Act also added § 529A(b)(7)(B) to the Code, which states that the term poverty line has the meaning given in section 673 of the Community Services Block Grant Act (42 U.S.C. 9902).

Finally, the 2017 Act amended § 529A(c)(3)(C)(i)(III) (related to qualified tuition programs) to permit, before January 1, 2026, a limited rollover from a qualified tuition program to an ABLE account. Notice 2018-58, 2018-33 I.R.B. 305, addresses, among other things, the new rule under § 529A(c)(3)(C)(i)(III).

## SECTION 3. ADDITIONAL CONTRIBUTIONS BY AN EMPLOYED DESIGNATED BENEFICIARY

As amended by the 2017 Act, § 529A(b)(2) generally provides that a program is not treated as a qualified ABLE program unless it provides that contributions will not be accepted in excess of the sum of the contribution limits set forth in § 529A(b)(2)(B)(i) and (ii). Section 529A(b)(2)(B)(ii) allows an employed or self-employed designated beneficiary described in § 529A(b)(7) to contribute the lesser of his or her compensation for the taxable year or an amount equal to the poverty line for a one-person household for the calendar year preceding the calendar year in which the taxable year begins. Consistent with § 529A(b)(2), as amended by the 2017 Act, the Treasury Department and the IRS intend to issue proposed regulations that confirm that the employed designated beneficiary, or the person acting on his or her behalf, is solely responsible for ensuring that the requirements in § 529A(b)(2)(B)(ii) are met and for maintaining adequate records for that purpose. In addition, to minimize burdens for the designated beneficiary and the qualified ABLE program, the proposed regulations are expected to provide that ABLE programs may allow a designated beneficiary to certify under penalties of perjury that he or she is a designated beneficiary described in §529A(b)(7) and that his or her contributions do not exceed the limit set forth in §529A(b)(2)(B)(ii).

## SECTION 4. APPLICABLE POVERTY LINE

Section 529A(b)(2)(B)(ii) bases the employed designated beneficiary's contribution limit, in part, on an amount equal to the poverty line for a one-person household for the preceding calendar year. Section 529A(b)(7)(B) provides that the term poverty line has the same meaning given such term by section 673 of the Community Services Block Grant Act (42 U.S.C. 9902). The Treasury Department and the IRS intend to issue proposed regulations to clarify that this reference to the poverty line means the poverty guidelines updated periodically in the *Federal Register* by the U.S. Department of Health and Human Services under the authority of 42 U.S.C. 9902(2). In addition, the poverty guidelines differ by geography; there are separate guidelines for (1) the 48 contiguous states and the District of Columbia, (2) Alaska, and (3) Hawaii. Because the poverty guideline that most closely relates to the designated beneficiary's cost of living appears to be the most relevant for the purpose of determining the contribution limit, the Treasury Department and the IRS anticipate that the proposed regulations will provide that a designated beneficiary's contribution limit should be determined using the poverty guideline applicable in the state of the designated beneficiary's residence, rather than the guideline applicable in the state in which the designated beneficiary's ABLE account is established, or elsewhere.

## SECTION 5. EXCESS CONTRIBUTIONS FROM THE DESIGNATED BENEFICIARY

Section 529A(b)(2) provides that a program will not be treated as a qualified ABLE program if it accepts contributions that are not in cash or that exceed the contribution limits in §529A(b)(2)(B). Because §529A(b)(2) also provides that rules similar to §408(d)(4) will apply to excess contributions to ABLE accounts, Prop. Treas. Reg. §1.529A-2(g)(4) includes a requirement that a qualified ABLE program must return any excess contribution, including all net income attributable to that excess contribution, to the person or persons who made that contribution.

With the addition by the 2017 Act to allow certain contributions of the designated benefici-

ary's compensation income, the Treasury Department and the IRS intend to issue proposed regulations to also apply the proposed required return of excess contributions to any excess contributions of the designated beneficiary's compensation income. Specifically, the proposed regulations are expected to provide that the qualified ABLE program should use the rules set forth in §1.408-11 to return any excess contribution, including any contributions in excess of the limit in §529A(b)(2)(B)(ii). However, because §529A(b)(2), as amended by the Act, imposes on the designated beneficiary (rather than on the qualified ABLE program) the responsibility for ensuring compliance with the limitation on the amount of the designated beneficiary's contributions of compensation income under §529A(b)(2)(B)(ii), the proposed regulations are expected to provide that: (i) it will be the sole responsibility of the designated beneficiary (or the person acting on the designated beneficiary's behalf) to identify and request the return of any excess contribution of such compensation income; and (ii) for purposes of determining the limit on contributions made under §529A(b)(2)(B)(ii), the qualified ABLE program may rely on self-certifications, made under penalties of perjury, of the designated beneficiary or the person acting on his or her behalf.

## SECTION 6. TRANSITION RELIEF

The Treasury Department and the IRS are aware that, once final regulations are issued, qualified ABLE programs may need to adjust their systems and account documents to be in compliance with regulatory requirements. The Treasury Department and the IRS also are aware that, in some cases, a necessary change may require state legislative action. Therefore, the regulations are expected to provide transition relief with respect to any necessary changes to ensure that the state programs and accounts meet the requirements in the regulations, including providing sufficient time after issuance of the final regulations in order for changes to be implemented.

## SECTION 7. RELIANCE

Before the issuance of the proposed regulations described in this notice, taxpayers, beneficiaries, and administrators of ABLE programs may rely on the rules described in sections 3, 4, and 5 of this notice.

**Notice 2018-62**

## SECTION 8. REQUEST FOR PUBLIC COMMENTS

The Treasury Department and the IRS request comments on the issues addressed in this notice, including any necessary transition relief.

Written comments may be submitted by November 1, 2018 to Internal Revenue Service, CC:PA:LPD:PR (Notice 2018-62), Room 5203, P.O. Box 7604, Ben Franklin Station, Washington, DC 20044, or electronically to Notice.Comments@irscounsel.treas.gov (please include "Notice 2018-62" in the subject line). Alternatively, comments may be hand delivered between the hours of 8:00 a.m. and 4:00 p.m.

Monday to Friday to CC:PA:LPD:PR (Notice 2018-62), Courier's Desk, Internal Revenue Service, 1111 Constitution Avenue NW, Washington, D.C. Comments will be available for public inspection and copying.

## SECTION 9. DRAFTING INFORMATION

The principal author of this notice is Julia E. Parnell of the Office of Associate Chief Counsel (Tax Exempt and Government Entities). For further information regarding this notice, contact Ms. Parnell at (202) 317-5800 (not a toll-free number).

## Notice 2018-67, I.R.B. 2018-36, August 21, 2018

### SECTION 1. PURPOSE

Section 13702 of "An Act to provide for reconciliation pursuant to titles II and IV of the concurrent resolution on the budget for fiscal year 2018," Public Law 115-97 (131 Stat. 2054 (2017)) (the Act), enacted December 22, 2017, added new §512(a)(6) to the Internal Revenue Code (Code). Section 512(a)(6) requires an organization subject to the unrelated business income tax under §511, with more than one unrelated trade or business, to calculate unrelated business taxable income (UBTI) separately with respect to each trade or business. This notice discusses, and solicits comments regarding, various issues arising under §512(a)(6) and sets forth interim guidance and transition rules relating to that section. This notice also provides guidance on the treatment of global intangible low-taxed income (GILTI) under §951A for purposes of the unrelated business income tax under §511.

The contents of this notice are as follows. Section 2 provides a general background of the law on UBTI and §512(a)(6). Section 3 outlines general concepts for identifying separate trades or businesses for purposes of §512(a)(6) and provides interim reliance on a reasonable, good-faith standard for making such a determination. Section 4 discusses the possible treatment of income described in §512(b)(4), (13), and (17). Section 5 discusses general principles surrounding income from partnerships. Section 6 sets forth interim and transition rules under §512(a)(6) for aggregating income from partnerships and debt-financed income from partnerships. Section 7 discusses the application of §512(a)(6) to certain

organizations subject to the UBTI rules of §512(a)(3). Section 8 discusses the effect of §512(a)(6) on income described in §512(a)(7) (fringe benefits). Section 9 provides information on how to calculate net operating losses (NOLs) within the framework of §512(a)(6). Section 10 concludes that, for purposes of calculating UBTI, an inclusion of GILTI is treated as a dividend and follows the treatment of dividends under §512(b)(1) and 512(b)(4). Section 11 summarizes reliance on rules provided in this notice. Section 12 requests comments and provides information for submitting comments.

### SECTION 2. BACKGROUND

Under §501(a), organizations described in §§401(a) and 501(c) generally are exempt from federal income taxation. However, §511(a)(1) imposes a tax (computed as provided in §11) on the UBTI of organizations described in §511(a)(2), which includes organizations described in §§401(a) and 501(c) (other than a trust described in §511(b) or an instrumentality of the United States described in §501(c)(1)) as well as state colleges and universities. Additionally, §511(b)(1) imposes a tax (computed as provided in §1(e)) on the UBTI of certain trusts described in §511(b)(2).[1] Organizations described in §511(a)(2) and trusts described in §511(b)(2) are collectively called "exempt organizations" throughout this notice, unless otherwise stated.

Section 512(a)(1) defines UBTI as the gross income derived by any exempt organization from an unrelated trade or business regularly carried on by it, less the deductions allowed by

[1] Section 408(e) states that an individual retirement account (IRA) is subject to the taxes imposed by §511. Accordingly, any reference to an exempt organization in this notice includes an IRA, without regard to whether it is a tradi-

tional IRA, Roth IRA, simplified employee pension (SEP-IRA), or savings incentive match plans for employees (SIMPLE IRA).

Chapter 1 that are directly connected with the carrying on of such trade or business, both computed with the modifications described in §512(b). An exempt organization determines whether it has income from an unrelated trade or business under the general principles of §§511 through 514 and the Treasury regulations thereunder.

Section 513(a) defines "unrelated trade or business" as any trade or business the conduct of which is not substantially related (aside from the need of such organization for income or funds or the use it makes of the profits derived) to the exercise or performance by such exempt organization, other than trusts described in §513(b)(2), of its charitable, educational, or other purpose or function constituting the basis for its exemption under §501 (or, in the case of a state college or university, to the exercise or performance of any purpose or function described in §501(c)(3)). In the case of a trust that is exempt from tax under §501(a) and described in §401(a) (qualified retirement plans) or §501(c)(17) (supplemental unemployment compensation benefits trusts (SUBs)), however, §513(b) defines "unrelated trade or business," as any trade or business regularly carried on by such trust or by a partnership of which it is a member.

An exempt organization may conduct an unrelated trade or business directly or indirectly through another entity, such as a partnership (including any entity treated as a partnership for federal tax purposes). Section 512(c) provides that, if a trade or business regularly carried on by a partnership of which an exempt organization is a partner is an unrelated trade or business with respect to such organization, the exempt organization includes in UBTI - subject to the exceptions, additions, and limitations of §512(b) - its distributive share of partnership gross income (whether or not distributed) and partnership deductions directly connected with such gross income. See §1.512(c)-1 (describing how UBTI is calculated in a situation in which an exempt organization's distributive share of partnership income consists of both UBTI and income that is excluded from the calculation of UBTI). In determining whether a partnership conducts one or more trades or businesses that are unrelated trades or businesses with respect to

an exempt organization partner, the exempt organization would use the applicable definition of "unrelated trade or business" in §513(a) or (b).[2] Section 512(c) applies regardless of whether an exempt organization is a general or limited partner. Rev. Rul. 79-222, 1979-2 C.B. 236.

Except as described in §512(a)(3) (discussed in section 7 of this notice), exempt organizations exclude from the calculation of UBTI gross income from dividends, interest, annuities, etc.; royalties; rents; and gains and losses from the sale, exchange, or other disposition of property. See §512(b)(1), (2), (3), & (5). The reason that these and "similar items" are excluded from UBTI is because Congress indicated that such items "are not likely to result in serious competition for taxable businesses having similar income." S. Rep. No. 81-2375, at 30-31 (1950). Additionally, Congress stated that "investment-producing incomes of these types have long been recognized as a proper source of revenue for [exempt] organizations and trusts." Id. However, gross income from other sources in the nature of investments are not specifically excluded by §512(b) and are generally included in the calculation of UBTI. Such gross income could include an exempt organization's share (whether or not distributed) of the gross income of a partnership when the exempt organization is a partner and the partnership is engaged in one or more trades or businesses that are unrelated trades or businesses with respect to the exempt organization partner.[3]

An exempt organization may engage in more than one unrelated trade or business. Prior to the enactment of §512(a)(6), §1.512(a)-1(a) provided that, with respect to an exempt organization that derives gross income from the regular conduct of two or more unrelated trades or businesses, UBTI was the aggregate gross income from all such unrelated trades or businesses less the aggregate deductions allowed with respect to all such unrelated trades or businesses. However, §512(a)(6) changes this calculation for exempt organizations with more than one unrelated trade or business. Congress intended "that a deduction from one trade or business for a taxable year may not be used to offset income from a different unrelated trade or business for the same taxable year." H.R. Rep. No. 115-466, at 548

---

[2] Because IRAs described in §408 are subject to the tax imposed by §511, under §408(e), and IRAs are most similar to §401(a) trusts, it is reasonable to apply the definition of "unrelated trade or business" described in §513(b) to IRAs. The Treasury Department and the IRS intend to provide that the §513(b) definition of unrelated trades or businesses should be used in application of §511 for accounts subject to the tax in §511 pursuant to §408(e).

[3] In the case of a trust that is exempt from tax under §501(a) that is described in §401(a) or §501(c)(17), §513(b) defines "unrelated trade or business" as any trade or business regularly carried on a partnership of which it is a member.

**Notice 2018-67**

(2017). Specifically, §512(a)(6) provides that, in the case of any exempt organization with more than one unrelated trade or business:

(A) UBTI, including for purposes of determining any net operating loss (NOL) deduction, shall be computed separately with respect to each trade or business and without regard to §512(b)(12) (allowing a specific deduction of $1,000),

(B) The UBTI of such organization shall be the sum of the UBTI so computed with respect to each trade or business, less a specific deduction under §512(b)(12), and

(C) For purposes of §512(a)(6)(B), UBTI with respect to any such trade or business shall not be less than zero.

Thus, §512(a)(6) no longer allows aggregation of income and deductions from all unrelated trades or businesses. Section 512(a)(6) applies to taxable years beginning after December 31, 2017, but, as discussed in more detail in section 9 of this notice, not to NOLs arising before January 1, 2018, that are carried over to taxable years beginning on or after such date.

Separately, section 14201 of the Act added new §951A of the Code. Section 951A(a) provides that "each person who is a United States shareholder of any controlled foreign corporation for any taxable year of such United States shareholder shall include in gross income such shareholder's global intangible low-taxed income for such taxable year."

SECTION 3. SEPARATE TRADE OR BUSINESS

.01 *In General*

In the case of any exempt organization with more than one unrelated trade or business, §512(a)(6)(A) requires the organization to calculate UBTI, including for purposes of determining any NOL deduction (discussed in section 9 of this notice), separately with respect to each trade or business. In enacting §512(a)(6), Congress did not provide criteria for determining whether an exempt organization has more than one unrelated trade or business or how to identify separate unrelated trades or businesses for purposes of calculating UBTI. The Treasury Department and the IRS intend to propose regulations for determining whether an exempt organization has more than one unrelated trade or business for purposes of §512(a)(6) and how to identify separate trades or businesses for purposes of calculating UBTI under §512(a)(6)(A).

.02 *Reasonable, Good-Faith Interpretation of §§511 through 514*

Pending issuance of proposed regulations, and pursuant to additional interim guidance provided in section 6 of this notice, exempt organizations may rely on a reasonable, good-faith interpretation of §§511 through 514, considering all the facts and circumstances, when determining whether an exempt organization has more than one unrelated trade or business for purposes of §512(a)(6). A reasonable, good-faith interpretation includes using the North American Industry Classification System 6-digit codes described in section 3.03.

The Treasury Department and the IRS note that the fragmentation principle in §513(c) and §1.513-1(b), and related guidance, may also provide helpful guidance. Prior to the passage of §512(a)(6), the fragmentation principle was primarily used to separate unrelated trades or businesses from exempt activities, but it might also have utility in identifying separate trades or businesses for purposes of §512(a)(6)(A). The fragmentation principle provides that an activity does not lose its identity as a trade or business merely because it is carried on within a larger aggregate of similar activities or within a larger complex of other endeavors which may, or may not, be related to the exempt purposes of an organization. For example, the regular sale of pharmaceutical supplies to the general public by a hospital pharmacy does not lose its status as a trade or business merely because the pharmacy also furnishes supplies to the hospital and patients of the hospital in accordance with its exempt purposes or in compliance with the terms of §513(a)(2) (stating, in part, that the term "trade or business" does not include any trade or business that is carried on by an organization described in §501(c)(3) or a state college or university primarily for the convenience of its members, students, patients, officers, or employees). *See* §1.513-1(b). Similarly, activities of soliciting, selling, and publishing commercial advertising do not lose their statuses as trades or businesses even though the advertising is published in an exempt organization periodical that contains editorial matter related to the exempt purposes of the organization. *Id.* Additionally, several revenue rulings provide examples of how the fragmentation principle has been applied. *See, e.g.,* Rev. Rul. 78-145, 1978-1 C.B. 169 (regarding the sale of blood products by a blood bank).

**.03** *Possible Methods for Identifying Separate Trades or Businesses*

There is no general statutory or regulatory definition defining what constitutes a "trade or business" for purposes of the Internal Revenue Code. Whether an activity constitutes a trade or business may vary depending on which Code section is involved. *See generally Commissioner v. Groetzinger*, 480 U.S. 23, 27 (1987). The Treasury Department and the IRS request comments regarding rules to identify separate trades or businesses that achieve the intent of Congress in enacting § 512(a)(6) and are administrable for exempt organizations and the IRS.

Several Code sections describe factors for determining whether an organization is engaged in a trade or business or a line of business, including §§ 132, 162, 183, 414, and 469 (see also section 5.02 of this notice), and the regulations thereunder. The Treasury Department and the IRS have considered these Code sections and are concerned that they do not provide useful models for identifying separate trades or businesses for purposes of § 512(a)(6). Nonetheless, the Treasury Department and the IRS request comments describing whether and how these and other Code sections (and the regulations thereunder) may aid in determining how to identify an exempt organization's separate trades or businesses for purposes of § 512(a)(6)(A).

Although some commenters have suggested the creation of a facts and circumstances test to identify separate trades or businesses for purposes of § 512(a)(6), the Treasury Department and the IRS would like to set forth a more administrable method than a facts and circumstances test alone for identifying separate trades or businesses for purposes of § 512(a)(6). A facts and circumstances test would increase the administrative burden on exempt organizations in complying with § 512(a)(6) because such organizations would have to perform a fact-intensive analysis with respect to each of their trades or businesses, document the analysis, and then track and keep records consistent with such analysis. Additionally, such a test would likely result in inconsistency across the exempt organization sector in light of differing approaches in budgeting and staffing and thus create unequal burdens and cause exempt organizations to make business decisions such as budgeting and staffing solely to avoid the requirements of § 512(a)(6). Finally, such a test would also increase the administrative burden on the IRS in implementing and enforcing § 512(a)(6) because verifying whether an exempt organization calculated its UBTI correctly would require a fact-intensive analysis of the organization's trades or businesses and the determinations made with respect to identifying separate trades or businesses for purposes of calculating UBTI under § 512(a)(6)(A).

To provide additional guidance in proposed regulations for determining whether an exempt organization has more than one unrelated trade or business for purposes of § 512(a)(6) and how to identify separate trades or businesses for purposes of calculating UBTI under § 512(a)(6)(A), the Treasury Department and the IRS are considering the use of North American Industry Classification System (NAICS) codes. Prior to proposed regulations, the Treasury Department and the IRS will consider the use of NAICS 6-digit codes to be a reasonable, good-faith interpretation under section 3.02 of this notice.

The NAICS is an industry classification system for purposes of collecting, analyzing, and publishing statistical data related to the United States business economy. *See* Executive Office of the President, Office of Management and Budget, North American Industry Classification System (2017), *available at https://www.census.gov/eos/www/na-ics/2017NAICS/2017_NAICS_Manual.pdf*. For example, under a NAICS 6-digit code, all of an exempt organization's advertising activities and related services (NAICS code 541800) might be considered one unrelated trade or business activity, regardless of the source of the advertising income. Use of all 6 digits of the NAICS codes would result in more specific categories of trades or businesses whereas use of fewer than 6 digits of the NAICS codes would result in broader categories of trades or businesses. Exempt organizations filing Form 990-T, "Exempt Organization Business Income Tax Return," already are required to use the 6-digit NAICS codes when describing the organization's unrelated trades or businesses in Block E. The Treasury Department and the IRS request comments regarding whether using less than 6 digits of the NAICS codes, or combining NAICS codes with other criteria, would appropriately identify separate trades or businesses for purposes of achieving the objective of § 512(a)(6). The Treasury Department and the IRS also request comments on the utility of this method, other methods, or a combination of methods that could be used for making this determination.

**.04** *Allocation of Directly Connected Deductions*

Section 512(a)(1) permits an exempt organization with an unrelated trade or business to reduce the income from that trade or business by the deductions allowed by Chapter 1 of the Code that are directly connected with the carrying on of such trade or business. To be "directly connected" with a trade or business, an item of deduction must have a proximate and primary relationship to the carrying on of the unrelated trade or business generating the gross income. *See* §1.512(a)-1(a). Expenses, depreciation, and similar items attributable solely to the conduct of an unrelated trade or business are proximately and primarily related to that trade or business and qualify to reduce income from such trade or business under §512(a)(1) to the extent such items meet the requirements of §§162 (trade or business expenses), 167 (depreciation), and other relevant provisions.

To the extent that an exempt organization may have items of deduction that are shared between an exempt activity and an unrelated trade or business, the Treasury regulations at §1.512(a)-1(c) and (d) provide special rules for allocating such expenses. For example, if facilities are used both to carry on exempt activities and to conduct unrelated trade or business activities, then expenses, depreciation, and similar items attributable to such facilities must be allocated between the two uses on a reasonable basis. *See* §1.512(a)-1(c).

The Treasury Department and the IRS currently have an item on the Priority Guidance Plan regarding methods of allocating expenses relating to dual use facilities. The allocation issues under §512(a)(1) also are relevant under §512(a)(6) because an exempt organization with more than one unrelated trade or business must not only allocate indirect expenses among exempt and taxable activities as described in §1.512(a)-1(c) and (d) but also among separate unrelated trades or businesses. The Treasury Department and the IRS therefore are considering modifying the underlying reasonable allocation method in §1.512(a)-1(c) and providing specific standards for allocating expenses relating to dual use facilities and the rules under §512(a)(6). The Treasury Department and the IRS are requesting comments regarding possible rules or defined standards for the allocation of indirect expenses between separate unrelated trades or businesses for purposes of calculating UBTI under §512(a)(6)(A), and, in particular, regarding what allocation methods should be considered "reasonable."

## SECTION 4. INCOME TREATED AS AN ITEM OF GROSS INCOME FROM AN UNRELATED TRADE OR BUSINESS

Sections 512(b)(4), (13), and (17) treat unrelated debt financed income, specified payments received from controlled entities, and certain insurance income (as defined in §953) as items of

gross income derived from an unrelated trade or business and therefore includable in the calculation of UBTI under §512(a) even though such amounts ordinarily would be excluded from the calculation of UBTI under §512(b)(1), (2), (3), or (5). At least one commenter has questioned how income that is included in UBTI under §512(b)(4), (13), and (17) is treated for purposes of §512(a)(6) because that commenter states that amounts included in UBTI under these provisions do not have a nexus to an unrelated trade or business.

The Treasury Department and the IRS note that, in the absence of §512(b)(1), (2), (3), and (5), interest, royalties, rents, and gains (or losses) from the sale, exchange, or other disposition of property would be included in the calculation of UBTI to the extent that such amounts are "gross income derived by any organization from any unrelated trade or business . . . regularly carried on by it" under §512(a)(1). Accordingly, the Treasury Department and the IRS see no distinction between "gross income derived by any organization from any unrelated trade or business . . . regularly carried on by it" within the meaning of §512(a)(1) and amounts included in UBTI "as an item of gross income derived from an unrelated trade or business" under §512(b)(4), (13), and (17).

However, the Treasury Department and the IRS recognize that one interpretation of §512(a)(6) might impose a significant burden on organizations required to include amounts in UBTI under §512(b)(4), (13), or (17). For example, one interpretation of §512(a)(6) might require treating each debt-financed property owned by an exempt organization as a separate trade or business for purposes of §512(a)(6)(A), because the debt/basis percentage used to calculate the portion of income that is unrelated debt-financed income included in the calculation of UBTI under §512(b)(4) is specific to each property. Similarly, an exempt organization might be required to report income from each controlled entity as income from a separate trade or business for purposes of §512(a)(6)(A). The exempt organization would have to track and report each debt-financed property owned directly by an exempt organization or income from each controlled entity separately, which imposes a burden both on the exempt organization and on the IRS. Accordingly, aggregating income included in UBTI under §512(b)(4), (13), or (17) may be appropriate in certain circumstances. The Treasury Department and the IRS therefore request comments regarding the treatment under §512(a)(6) of income that is not from a partnership, but is included in UBTI under §512(b)(4), (13), and (17).

## SECTION 5. ACTIVITIES IN THE NATURE OF INVESTMENTS

### .01 *Partnership Interests*

In general, for exempt organizations, the activities of a partnership are considered the activities of the partners.[4] Section 512(c) requires an exempt organization that is a partner in a partnership that conducts a trade or business that is an unrelated trade or business with respect to the exempt organization to include in UBTI its distributive share of gross partnership income (and directly connected partnership deductions) from such unrelated trade or business. Whether a trade or business engaged in by the partnership is an unrelated trade or business with respect to the exempt organization is determined under §§511 through 514, and the regulations thereunder. Based on §512(c) and the fragmentation principle, as discussed in section 3.02 of this notice, one interpretation of §512(a)(6) might require an exempt organization to calculate UBTI separately with respect to each unrelated trade or business regularly carried on by the partnership in which the exempt organization is a direct or indirect partner. For example, if an exempt organization is a partner in a holding partnership that is a partner in multiple partnerships, many of which engage in one or more unrelated trades or businesses with respect to the exempt organization partner, the exempt organization may be engaged in multiple separate unrelated trades or businesses through its interest in the partnership.

### .02 *Permitting the Aggregation of Gross Income and Directly Connected Deductions from Certain "Investment Activities"*

The Treasury Department and the IRS have received comments regarding the potential significant reporting and administrative burden imposed by §512(a)(6) on exempt organizations with various activities in the nature of an investment including ownership interests in multi-tier partnership structures that generate UBTI if the Treasury Department and the IRS adopt the interpretation of §512(a)(6) discussed in section 5.01 of this notice. The administrative burden related to owning partnership interests would be heightened by the difficulty of obtaining sufficient information regarding the trade or business activities of lower-tier partnerships. Accordingly, as a matter of administrative convenience, the Treasury Department and the IRS intend to propose regulations treating certain activities in the nature of an investment ("investment activities") of an exempt organization as one trade or business for purposes of §512(a)(6)(A) in order to permit exempt organizations to aggregate gross income and directly connected deductions from such "investment activities." The Treasury Department and the IRS expect that treating these "investment activities" as one trade or business for this purpose will reduce the reporting and administrative burden on organizations required to comply with §512(a)(6) and will also reduce the burden the IRS may experience in implementing and enforcing §512(a)(6).

The Treasury Department and the IRS request comments regarding the scope of the activities, both investment partnership interests or other activities in the nature of an investment that may generate unrelated business income, that should be included in the category of "investment activities" for purposes of §512(a)(6). The Treasury Department and the IRS have received some comments suggesting the definition of material participation in §469 could serve as a basis for separating investment activities from more active involvement in an unrelated trade or business. The Treasury Department and the IRS are concerned that the criteria for finding material participation under §469 are more extensive than appropriate. With respect to partnership interests that could be included in the category of "investment activities" for purposes of §512(a)(6), the Treasury Department and the IRS note that "investment activities" as discussed in section 6 of this notice should capture only partnership interests in which the exempt organization does not significantly participate in any partnership trade or business.

## SECTION 6. INTERIM AND TRANSITION RULES FOR PARTNERSHIP INVESTMENTS

### .01 *Aggregation of Income and Directly Connected Deductions*

(1) *In General.* Except as provided in section 6.01(2) through (4) of this notice, exempt organizations with partnership investments should use a reasonable, good-faith interpretation of §§511 and 514, considering all the facts and circumstances, when identifying separate trades or businesses for purposes of §512(a)(6)(A) until

---

[4] See IRC §§512(c), 513(a); Treas. Reg. §1.513-1(d)(1) and (2); *Plumstead Theatre Society, Inc. v. Commissioner*, 74 T.C. 1324 (1980); 675 F.2d 244 (9th Cir. 1995); *Service Bolt & Nut Co. Profit Sharing Trust v. Commissioner*, 724 F.2d 519 (6th Cir.1983), *aff'g*, 78 T.C. 812 (1982); Rev. Rul. 98-15, 1998-1 C.B. 718.

the issuance of proposed regulations (see section 3.02 of this notice).

(2) *Interim Rule for Aggregation of Qualifying Partnership Interests under the De Minimis and Control Tests.* Pending publication of proposed regulations, an exempt organization may aggregate its UBTI from its interest in a single partnership with multiple trades or businesses, including trades or businesses conducted by lower-tier partnerships, as long as the directly-held interest in the partnership meets the requirements of either the *de minimis* test (described in section 6.02 of this notice) or the control test (described in section 6.03 of this notice) ("qualifying partnership interest"). Additionally, under this interim rule, an exempt organization may aggregate all qualifying partnership interests and treat the aggregate group of qualifying partnership interests as comprising a single trade or business for purposes of §512(a)(6)(A).

(3) *Transition Rule.* Pending publication of proposed regulations, an exempt organization may follow the transition rule (described in section 6.04 of this notice) for partnership interests with respect to which it is not applying the interim rule described in section 6.01(2) of this notice.

(4) *Limitations.* The interim rule and the transition rule do not apply to exempt organizations described in §501(c)(7) that are subject to §512(a)(3). See section 7 of this notice. Furthermore, these rules do not otherwise impact the application of §512(c) and the fragmentation principle under §513(c).

*.02 De minimis test*

(1) *In general.* A partnership interest is a qualifying partnership interest that meets the requirements of the *de minimis* test if the exempt organization holds directly no more than 2 percent of the profits interest and no more than 2 percent of the capital interest. But see section 6.02(2)(b) of this notice for rules requiring the combining of related interests in certain circumstances.

(2) *Percentage Interest.* (a) *Reliance on Schedule K-1.* In determining the exempt organization's percentage interest in a partnership, the exempt organization may rely on the Schedule K-1 it receives from the partnership. In Part II, line J, a partnership enters the partner's share of profit, loss, and capital interests at the beginning and the ending of the partnership's taxable year. An organization will be considered to have no more than 2 percent of the profits or capital interests in the case of a partnership, if the average of the organization's percentage interest at the beginning and the end of the partnership's taxable

year, or, in the case of a partnership interest held for less than a year, the percentage interest held at the beginning and end of the period of ownership within the partnership's taxable year, entered in Part II, line J, of Schedule K-1 is no more than 2 percent (without regard to the number of days each such percentage is held during the taxable year). For example, if an exempt organization acquires an interest in a partnership that files on a calendar year basis in May and the partnership reports in Part II, Line J, of Schedule K-1 that the partner held a 3 percent profits interest at the date of acquisition but held a 1 percent profits interest at the end of the calendar year, the exempt organization will be considered to have held 2 percent of the profits interest in that partnership for that year ((3 percent + 1 percent)/2 = 2 percent). To the extent that a specific profits interest is not identified in Part II, Line J, of Schedule K-1, an organization does not meet the *de minimis* test.

(b) *Combining Related Interests.* (i) *In General.* When determining an exempt organization's percentage partnership interest, the interest of a disqualified person, a supporting organization, or a controlled entity in the same partnership will be taken into account. For example, if an exempt organization owns 1.5 percent of the profits interests in a partnership and a disqualified person with respect to the exempt organization owns an additional 1 percent profits interest in that partnership, the exempt organization would not meet the requirements of the *de minimis* test because its aggregate percentage interest exceeds 2 percent. However, the exempt organization may still be able to aggregate the income (and directly connected deductions) from that partnership interest with other qualifying partnership interests if the partnership interest meets the requirements of the control test (described in section 6.03 of this notice).

(ii) *Disqualified Person.* For purposes of section 6.02(2)(b)(i) of this notice, the term "disqualified person" has the same meaning as in §4958(f).

(iii) *Supporting Organization.* For purposes of section 6.02(2)(b)(i) of this notice, the term "supporting organization" has the same meaning as in §509(a)(3).

(iv) *Controlled Entity.* For purposes of section 6.02(2)(b)(i) of this notice, the term "controlled entity" has the same meaning as in §512(b)(13)(D).

*.03 Control Test*

(1) *In General.* A partnership interest is a qualifying partnership interest that meets the requirements of the control test if the exempt

organization (i) directly holds no more than 20 percent of the capital interest; and (ii) does not have control or influence over the partnership. The rules in section 6.02(2)(b) of this notice requiring the combination of related interests also apply for purposes of the control test.

(2) *Reliance on Schedule K-1.* When determining the exempt organization's percentage interest in a partnership the exempt organization may rely on the Schedule K-1 it receives from the partnership. An organization will be considered to have no more than 20 percent of the capital interest, if the average of the organization's percentage interest at the beginning and the end of the partnership's taxable year, or, in the case of a partnership interest held for less than a year, the percentage interest held at the beginning and end of the period of ownership within the partnership's taxable year, entered in Part II, line J, of Schedule K-1 is no more than 20 percent (without regard to the number of days each such percentage is held during the taxable year).

(3) *Control or Influence.* All facts and circumstances are relevant for determining whether an exempt organization has control or influence over a partnership. An exempt organization has control or influence if the exempt organization may require the partnership to perform, or may prevent the partnership from performing, any act that significantly affects the operations of the partnership. An exempt organization also has control or influence over a partnership if any of the exempt organization's officers, directors, trustees, or employees have rights to participate in the management of the partnership or conduct the partnership's business at any time, or if the exempt organization has the power to appoint or remove any of the partnership's officers, directors, trustees, or employees.

.04 *Transition rule*

A previously acquired partnership interest may be difficult to modify to meet the *de minimis* test (as described in section 6.02 of this notice) or control test (as described in section 6.03 of this notice) under the interim rule and the exempt organization may have to incur significant transactions costs to do so. Thus, an organization may choose to apply the following transition rule, if applicable, for a partnership interest acquired prior to August 21, 2018: an exempt organization may treat each such partnership interest as comprising a single trade or business for purposes of § 512(a)(6) whether or not there is more than one trade or business directly or indirectly conducted by the partnership or lower-tier partnerships. For example, if an organization has a thirty-five percent interest in a partnership prior to August

21, 2019, it can treat the partnership as being in a single unrelated trade or business even if the partnership's investments generated UBTI from various lower-tier partnerships that were engaged in multiple types of trades or businesses.

.05 *Unrelated Debt-Financed Income.*

The income from qualifying partnership interests permitted to be aggregated under the interim rule includes any unrelated debt-financed income (within the meaning of § 514) that arises in connection with the qualifying partnership interest that meets the requirements of either the *de minimis* test or the control test. *See* § § 512(b)(4) and 514. For example, assume an exempt organization has an interest in a hedge fund that is treated as a partnership for federal income tax purposes, the interest is a qualifying partnership interest that meets the requirements of the *de minimis* test, and the hedge fund regularly trades stock on margin. Ordinarily, the dividends from such stock and any income (or loss) from the sale, exchange, or other disposition of such stock would be excluded from UBTI under § 512(b)(1) and (5). However, because all or a portion of the stock's purchase is debt-financed, § 512(b)(4) requires that all of or a portion (depending on the debt-basis percentage applied) of the dividend income (if any) and any income (or loss) from the sale of the stock be included in UBTI. For the purpose of the interim rule, the exempt organization may aggregate unrelated debt-financed income generated by the hedge fund with any other UBTI generated by any of the hedge fund's trades or businesses that are unrelated trades or businesses with respect to the exempt organization.

Similarly, any unrelated debt-financed income that arises in connection with a partnership interest that meets the requirements of the transition rule may be aggregated with the other UBTI that arises in connection with that partnership interest.

SECTION 7. SOCIAL CLUBS, VOLUNTARY EMPLOYEES' BENEFICIARY ASSOCIATIONS, AND SUPPLEMENTAL UNEMPLOYMENT COMPENSATION BENEFITS TRUSTS

Section 512(a)(3) provides special rules applicable to exempt organizations described in § 501(c)(7) (social clubs), (9) (voluntary employees' beneficiary associations (VEBAs)), and (17) (supplemental unemployment compensation benefits trusts (SUBs)). For these exempt organizations, § 512(a)(3)(A) provides that UBTI means the gross income (excluding any exempt function income), less the deductions allowed by Chapter 1 of the Code that are directly connected with the production of the gross income (excluding exempt function income), both computed with the modifications provided in §512(b)(6) (the NOL deduction), (10) (charitable contribution deduction by exempt organizations), (11) (charitable contribution deduction by certain trusts), and (12) (specific deduction). Thus, social clubs, VEBAs, and SUBs are taxed under §511 on their non-exempt function income, which generally includes investment income and income derived from an unrelated trade or business.

In particular, §512(a)(3)(B) defines "exempt function income" as the gross income from dues, fees, charges, or similar amounts paid by members of the organization as consideration for providing such members or their dependents or guests goods, facilities, or services in furtherance of the purposes constituting the basis for the organization's tax-exempt status. However, §512(a)(3)(B) specifically excludes from the definition of "exempt function income" gross income derived from any unrelated trade or business regularly carried on by such organization (computed as if the organization were subject to §512(a)(1)).[5] For example, a social club's nonmember income is treated as gross income from an unrelated trade or business under §512(a)(3). *See* Rev. Rul. 2003-64, 2003-1 C.B. 1036. Accordingly, even though §512(a)(3) uses terminology different from §512(a)(1), §512(a)(6) applies to an organization subject to §512(a)(3) if such organization has more than one unrelated trade or business. For example, a social club that receives non-member income from multiple sources, such as from a dining facility and from a retail store, would have more than one unrelated trade or business and therefore be subject to the requirements of §512(a)(6).

The Treasury Department and the IRS anticipate that any rules issued regarding how an exempt organization identifies separate trades or businesses for purposes of §512(a)(6)(A) will apply equally under §512(a)(1) and (3).[6] Nonetheless, because social clubs, VEBAs, and SUBs are taxed differently than other exempt organizations under §511, the Treasury Department and the IRS request comments regarding any additional considerations that should be given to how §512(a)(6) applies within the context of §512(a)(3). In particular, the Treasury Department and the IRS request comments regarding how these exempt organizations' investment in-

come should be treated for purposes of §512(a)(6).

## SECTION 8. TOTAL UBTI

### .01 *In General*

To determine total UBTI under §512(a)(6)(B), an exempt organization takes the sum of the UBTI computed with respect to each separate trade or business under §512(a)(6)(A), less a specific deduction under §512(b)(12). However, in calculating total UBTI under §512(a)(6)(B), §512(a)(6)(C) provides that UBTI with respect to any trade or business cannot be less than zero.

### .02 *Fringe Benefits*

Section 512(a)(7) increases UBTI by any amount for which a deduction is not allowable under this chapter by reason of §274 and which is paid or incurred by such exempt organization for any qualified transportation fringe (as defined in §132(f)), any parking facility used in connection with qualified parking (as defined in §132(f)(5)(C)), or any on-premises athletic facility (as defined in §132(j)(4)(B)). However, §512(a)(7) does not apply to the extent the amount paid or incurred is directly connected with an unrelated trade or business that is regularly carried on by the organization. Unlike other paragraphs of §512, §512(a)(7) does not treat amounts included in UBTI as a result of that section as an item of gross income derived from an unrelated trade or business (see section 4 of this notice). Furthermore, the Treasury Department and the IRS do not believe that the provision of the fringe benefits described in §512(a)(7) is an unrelated trade or business. Accordingly, any amount included in UBTI under §512(a)(7) is not subject to §512(a)(6).

## SECTION 9. NOLS AND UBTI

Prior to the Act, §172 allowed an NOL deduction equal to the sum of NOLs permitted to be carried back to the taxable year from succeeding taxable years and the NOLs permitted to be carried forward from preceding taxable years. An NOL generally could be carried back two years and carried forward twenty years. See §172(b) (prior to the Act). Section 512(b)(6), which was not changed by the Act, generally permits exempt organizations subject to the unrelated business income tax under §511, including exempt

---

[5] However, VEBAs and SUBs are taxed on income to the extent that the amount of assets in the VEBA or SUB at the close of the taxable year exceed the account limit described in §512(a)(3)(E) and §1.512(a)-5T. *See also* Prop. Reg. §1.512(a)-5.

[6] However, the rules in section 6 of this notice for aggregating UBTI from partnership interests do not apply to social clubs described in §501(c)(7).

organizations with more than one unrelated trade or business, to take the NOL deduction provided in §172. In particular, §512(b)(6)(A) states that the NOL for any taxable year, the amount of the NOL carryback or carryover to any taxable year, and the NOL deduction for any taxable year shall be determined under §172 without taking into account any amount of income or deduction that is excluded under §512(b) in computing UBTI. For example, a loss attributable to an unrelated trade or business is not to be reduced by reason of the receipt of dividend income. *See* §1.512(b)-1(e)(1). An NOL carryover is allowed only from a taxable year for which the taxpayer is subject to the provisions of §511, or a corresponding provision of prior law. *See* §512(b)(6)(B); §1.512(b)-1(e)(3).

However, §512(a)(6) changes how an exempt organization with more than one unrelated trade or business calculates and takes NOLs into account with respect to a particular trade or business. In particular, §512(a)(6)(A) requires such an organization to calculate UBTI, including for purposes of determining any NOL deduction, separately with respect to each trade or business for taxable years beginning after December 31, 2017 (post-2017 NOLs). The Congressional intent behind this change is to allow an NOL deduction "only with respect to a trade or business from which the loss arose." H.R. Rep. No. 115-466, at 547-48. In the first taxable year beginning after December 31, 2017, no exempt organization with more than one unrelated trade or business will have an NOL deduction to take against the UBTI of a particular trade or business calculated under §512(a)(6)(A).

Additionally, in order to preserve NOLs from tax years prior to the effective date of the Act, Congress created a special transition rule to permit the carryover of any NOL arising in a taxable year beginning before January 1, 2018 (pre-2018 NOLs). In particular, section 13702(b)(2) of the Act provides that §512(a)(6)(A) does not apply to pre-2018 NOLs; rather, pre-2018 NOLs are taken against total UBTI calculated under §512(a)(6)(B). Accordingly, even though an exempt organization with more than one unrelated trade or business will not have any NOL deductions when calculating UBTI with respect to a separate trade or business under §512(a)(6)(A) for the first taxable year beginning after December 31, 2017, such an organization may be able to take an NOL deduction against total UBTI calculated for such year under §512(a)(6)(B) if the organization has pre-2018 NOLs.

In the second taxable year beginning after December 31, 2017, an exempt organization with more than one unrelated trade or business may

have both pre-2018 NOLs and post-2017 NOLs. Section 512(a)(6) may have changed the order in which an organization would ordinarily take losses because §512(a)(6)(A) requires an organization with more than one unrelated trade or business to calculate UBTI separately (including for purposes of determining any NOL deduction) with respect to each such trade or business before calculating total UBTI under §512(a)(6)(B). If §512(a)(6) is read as an ordering rule for purposes of calculating and taking the NOL deduction, post-2017 NOLs will be calculated and taken before pre-2018 NOLs because the UBTI with respect to each separate trade or business is calculated under §512(a)(6)(A) before calculating total UBTI under §512(a)(6)(B).

Furthermore, section 13302 of the Act made extensive changes to §172, including limiting post-2017 NOLs to the lesser of (1) the aggregate NOL carryovers to such year, plus the NOL carrybacks to such year, or (2) 80 percent of taxable income computed without regard to the deduction generally allowable under §172. The limitation in §172(a) applies only to post-2017 NOLs, but a question exists regarding how the §172(a) 80 percent income limitation applies when both pre-2018 and post-2017 NOLs exist. The Treasury Department and the IRS intend to issue guidance regarding how §172 generally applies. However, because §512(a)(6) provides a more specific rule than the one found in §172 regarding how the NOL deduction is calculated and taken in the context of calculating UBTI, the Treasury Department and the IRS are requesting comments regarding how the NOL deduction should be taken under §512(a)(6) by exempt organizations with more than one unrelated trade or business and, in particular, by such organizations with both pre-2018 and post-2017 NOLs. The Treasury Department and the IRS also request comments on the ordering of pre-2018 and post-2017 NOLs and the potential treatment of pre-2018 NOLs that may expire in a given tax year if not taken before post-2017 NOLs.

## SECTION 10. TREATMENT OF GLOBAL INTANGIBLE LOW-TAXED INCOME

Commenters have asked whether an exempt organization must include GILTI (included in gross income under §951A) in the calculation of UBTI. In particular, these commenters have questioned whether GILTI is treated in the same manner as an inclusion of subpart F income under §951(a)(1)(A) for purposes of the unrelated business income tax under §511.

The IRS treats an inclusion of subpart F income as a dividend for purposes of §512(b)(1). Accordingly, subpart F income generally is excluded from the calculation of UBTI. Congress approved of the IRS's long-standing position when it enacted § 512(b)(17) as part of the Small Business Job Protection Act of 1996, Public Law 104-188 (110 Stat. 1755 (1996)). See H.R. Rep. No. 105-586, at 136 (1996) (stating that "income inclusions under subpart F have been characterized as dividends for unrelated business income tax purposes" and citing several private letter rulings issued by the IRS taking this position). Although an inclusion of subpart F income under § 951(a)(1)(A) is generally excluded from the calculation of UBTI as a dividend under § 512(b)(1), § 512(b)(17) requires any amount included in gross income under § 951(a)(1)(A) that is attributable to insurance income (as defined in § 953) which, if derived directly by the organization, would be treated as gross income from an unrelated trade or business to be included in the calculation of UBTI.

GILTI is not an inclusion of subpart F income under § 951(a)(1)(A), but instead is a separate inclusion under § 951A(a). Nonetheless, an inclusion of GILTI is generally treated in a manner similar to an inclusion of subpart F income for other purposes of the Code. See H.R. Rep. No. 115-446, at 641 (stating that, "[u]nder the provision, a U.S. shareholder of any [controlled foreign corporation] must include in gross income for a taxable year its [GILTI] in a manner generally similar to inclusions of subpart F income"). The Treasury Department and the IRS have determined that an inclusion of GILTI under § 951A(a) should be treated in the same manner as an inclusion of subpart F income under § 951(a)(1)(A) for purposes of § 512(b)(1) and (4). Accordingly, an inclusion of GILTI will be treated as a dividend which is generally excluded from UBTI under § 512(b)(1).

Commenters have also questioned whether § 512(b)(17) will apply to treat as UBTI an inclusion of GILTI to the extent attributable to insurance income (as defined in § 953) that does not constitute subpart F income. The Treasury Department and the IRS note that Congress made no changes to § 512(b) when enacting § 951A, and has not otherwise specifically required the inclusion of such insurance income in UBTI. Accordingly, unless provided otherwise in proposed regulations, the Treasury Department and the IRS will not treat GILTI included in gross income under § 951A(a) that is attributable to insurance income as includible in the UBTI of a tax-exempt organization.

SECTION 11. RELIANCE

For taxable years beginning after December 31, 2017, organizations described in § 511(a)(2)

and trusts described in § 511(b)(2), collectively called "exempt organizations" throughout this notice, may rely on methods of aggregating or identifying separate trades or businesses under § 512(a)(6) provided in this notice until proposed regulations are published. All such organizations may rely on a reasonable, good-faith interpretation of § § 511 through 514 taking into account all the facts and circumstances when determining whether an exempt organization has more than one unrelated trade or business for purposes of § 512(a)(6). For an exempt organization this also includes using a reasonable, good-faith interpretation when determining:

- Whether to separate debt-financed income described in § § 512(b)(4) and 514;

- Whether to separate income from a controlled entity described in § 512(b)(13); and

- Whether to separate insurance income earned through a controlled foreign corporation as described in § 512(b)(17).

The use of NAICS 6-digit codes will be considered a reasonable, good-faith interpretation until regulations are proposed.

For taxable years beginning after December 31, 2017, exempt organizations, other than organizations described in § 501(c)(7) (social clubs), may also rely on the rules provided for aggregating income from partnerships in section 6 of this notice until proposed regulations are published. These aggregation rules include any unrelated debt-financed income that is earned through a partnership that meets the requirements of the rules described in section 6 of this notice. The rules described in section 6 of this notice include:

- The interim rule that permits the aggregation of qualifying partnership interests that meet either the de minimis test or control test into a single trade or business; and

- The transition rule, which allows for aggregating income within each direct partnership interest acquired before August 21, 2018.

Finally, exempt organizations may rely on sections 8.02 and 10 of this notice. These sections provide that:

- Income under § 512(a)(7) is not income from a trade or business for purposes of § 512(a)(6); and

- For purposes of calculating UBTI, an inclusion of GILTI under § 951A(a) is treated as a dividend and follows the treatment of dividends under § 512(b)(1) and (b)(4).

## SECTION 12. REQUEST FOR COMMENTS

The Treasury Department and the IRS request comments regarding the application of §512(a)(6) to exempt organizations with more than one unrelated trade or business. Specifically, the Treasury Department and the IRS seek comments on the general interim rule for distinguishing between trades and businesses under §512(a)(6) (section 3 of this notice); whether other Code sections (and the regulations thereunder) may provide an administrable model for identifying an exempt organization's separate trades or businesses (section 3.03 of this notice); whether NAICS 6-digit (or less) codes might be the basis of a method for identifying separate trades or businesses (section 3.03 of this notice); the general rules for allocating deductions between trades or businesses (section 3.04 of this notice); the treatment of income treated as an item of gross income from an unrelated trade or business, including the treatment of debt-financed income ((13), and (17)) (section 4 of this notice); the scope of the activities that should be included in the category of "investment activities" (section 5.02 of this notice); the treatment of income derived from activities in the nature of an investment through partnerships (sections 5 and 6 of this notice); any additional considerations that should be given to how §512(a)(6) applies within the context of §512(a)(3) (section 7 of this notice); and the calculation and ordering of pre-2018 and post-2017 NOLs and the treatment of pre-2018 NOLs that will expire in a given tax year if not taken before post-2017 NOLs (section 9 of this notice). Comments should be submitted on or before **December 3, 2018**. Please include Notice 2018-67 on the cover page. Comments should be sent to the following address:

Internal Revenue Service

CC:PA:LPD:PR (Notice 2018-67), Room 5203

P.O. Box 7604

Ben Franklin Station

Washington, DC 20044

Submissions may be hand delivered Monday through Friday between the hours of 8 a.m. and 4 p.m. to:

Internal Revenue Service

Courier's Desk

1111 Constitution Ave., N.W.

Washington, DC 20224

Attn: CC:PA:LPD:PR (Notice 2018-67)

Submissions may also be sent electronically to the following e-mail address:

Notice.Comments@irscounsel.treas.gov.

Please include "Notice 2018-67" in the subject line.

All comments will be available for public inspection and copying.

## SECTION 13. PAPERWORK REDUCTION ACT

The collection of information in this notice is the requirement under §512(a)(6) that an exempt organization with more than one unrelated trade or business calculate UBTI separately with respect to each such trade or business. The collection of information contained in this notice is reflected in the collection of information for Form 990-T that has been reviewed and approved by the Office of Management and Budget in accordance with the Paperwork Reduction Act (44 U.S.C. 3507(c)) under control number 1545-0687.

An agency may not conduct or sponsor, and a person is not required to respond to, a collection of information unless the collection of information displays a valid OMB control number.

Books or records relating to a collection of information must be retained as long as their contents may become material in the administration of any internal revenue law. Generally, tax returns and tax return information are confidential, as required by §6103.

## SECTION 14. DRAFTING INFORMATION

The principal authors of this notice are Stephanie N. Robbins and Jonathan A. Carter of the Office of Associate Chief Counsel (TEGE). For further information regarding this notice contact Mr. Carter at (202) 317-5800 (not a toll-free call).

---

# Notice 2018-68, I.R.B. 2018-36, August 21, 2018

Guidance on the Application of Section 162(m)

## I. PURPOSE

This notice provides initial guidance on the application of section 162(m) of the Internal Revenue Code (Code), as amended by section 13601 of "An Act to provide for reconciliation pursuant to titles II and V of the concurrent resolution on the budget for fiscal year 2018," Public Law 115-97 (2017) (the Act). Section 162(m)(1) generally limits the allowable deduction for a taxable year for remuneration paid by any publicly held corporation with respect to a covered employee. Section 13601 of the Act made significant amendments to section 162(m) and provided a transition rule applicable to certain outstanding arrangements (commonly referred to as the grandfather rule).

Stakeholders have submitted comments indicating that they would benefit from initial guidance on certain aspects of the amendments made by section 13601 of the Act, in particular on the amended rules for identifying covered employees and the operation of the grandfather rule, including when a contract will be considered materially modified so that it is no longer grandfathered. This notice addresses these limited issues. The Department of the Treasury (Treasury Department) and the Internal Revenue Service (IRS) anticipate that further guidance on the amendments made by section 13601 of the Act will be issued in the form of proposed regulations, which will incorporate the guidance provided in this notice.

## II. BACKGROUND

Section 162(m)(1) disallows the deduction by any publicly held corporation for applicable employee remuneration paid to any covered employee to the extent that such remuneration for the taxable year exceeds $1,000,000.

### A. Amendments to the Definition of Publicly Held Corporation

Section 162(m)(2) defines the term "publicly held corporation" for purposes of identifying the entities subject to the deduction limitation of section 162(m)(1). Before the amendments made by section 13601(c) of the Act, section 162(m)(2) defined the term "publicly held corporation" as any corporation issuing any class of common equity securities required to be registered under section 12 of the Securities Exchange Act of 1934. Section 13601(c) of the Act amended the definition of "publicly held corporation" in section 162(m)(2) to mean any corporation which is an issuer (as defined in section 3 of the Securities Exchange Act of 1934) (A) the securities of which are required to be registered under section 12 of the Securities Exchange Act of 1934, or (B) that is required to file reports under section 15(d) of the Securities Exchange Act of 1934.

### B. Amendments to the Definition of Covered Employee

Section 162(m)(3) defines the term "covered employee" for purposes of identifying employees whose remuneration may be subject to the deduction limitation under section 162(m)(1). Before the amendments made by section 13601(b) of the Act, section 162(m)(3) defined the term "covered employee" as any employee of the taxpayer if (A) as of the close of the taxable year, such employee is the chief executive officer of the taxpayer or is an individual acting in such capacity, or (B) the total compensation of such employee for the taxable year is required to be reported to shareholders under the Securities Exchange Act of 1934 by reason of such employee being among the four highest compensated officers for the taxable year (other than the chief executive officer). Section 13601(b) of the Act amended the definition of "covered employee" in section 162(m)(3) to mean any employee of the taxpayer if (A) such employee is the principal executive officer (PEO) or principal financial officer (PFO) of the taxpayer at any time during the taxable year, or was an individual acting in such a capacity, (B) the total compensation of such employee for the taxable year is required to be reported to shareholders under the Securities Exchange Act of 1934 by reason of such employee being among the three highest compensated officers for the taxable year (other than any individual described in subparagraph (A)), or (C) such employee was a covered employee of the taxpayer (or any predecessor) for any preceding taxable year beginning after December 31, 2016.

Section 13601(c) of the Act also added flush language to section 162(m)(3) providing that the term "covered employee" includes any employee who would be described in section 162(m)(3)(B) if the reporting described in such subparagraph were required as so described. The legislative history to section 13601 of the Act explains that the term "covered employee" includes "officers of a corporation not required to file a proxy statement but which otherwise falls within the revised definition of a publicly held corporation." House Conf. Rpt. 115-466, 489. Furthermore, the legislative history provides that the term "covered employee" includes "officers of a publicly traded corporation that would otherwise have been required to file a proxy statement for the year (for example, but for the fact that the corporation delisted its securities or underwent a transaction that resulted in the nonapplication of the proxy statement requirement)." *Id.*

### C. Amendments to the Definition of Applicable Employee Remuneration

Section 162(m)(4) defines the term "applicable employee remuneration" for purposes of identifying the remuneration of a covered employee that may be subject to the deduction limitation under section 162(m)(1). Section 162(m)(4) generally provides that the term "applicable employee remuneration" means, with respect to any covered employee for any taxable year, the aggregate amount allowable as a deduction for such taxable year (determined without regard to section 162(m)) for remuneration for services performed by such employee (whether or not during the taxable year). Before the amendments made by section 13601(a) of the Act, the term "applicable employee remuneration" did not include remuneration payable on a commission basis (as defined in section 162(m)(4)(B)) or qualified performance-based compensation (as described in section 162(m)(4)(C)). Section 13601(a) of the Act amended the definition of "applicable employee remuneration" in section 162(m)(4) to remove these two exclusions. Section 13601(d) of the Act also amended the definition of "applicable employee remuneration" by adding a special rule for remuneration paid to beneficiaries. As amended, section 162(m)(4)(F) provides that remuneration shall not fail to be applicable employee remuneration merely because it is includible in the income of, or paid to, a person other than the covered employee, including after the death of the covered employee.

## D. Grandfather Rule

Section 13601(e) of the Act generally provides that the amendments made to section 162(m) shall apply to taxable years beginning after December 31, 2017. However, section 13601(e) of the Act further provides that the amendments to section 162(m) shall not apply to remuneration which is provided pursuant to a written binding contract which was in effect on November 2, 2017, and which was not modified in any material respect on or after such date. The text of section 13601(e) of the Act is almost identical to the text of pre-amendment section 162(m)(4)(D), which provides a grandfather rule addressing the initial addition of section 162(m) to the Code and grandfathers remuneration payable under a written binding contract which was in effect on February 17, 1993, and which was not modified thereafter in any material respect before such remuneration was paid. Section 1.162-27(h) of the Income Tax Regulations (Regulations) provides guidance under pre-amendment section 162(m)(4)(D) on the definitions of "written binding contract" and "material modification" for purposes of applying that original grandfather provision.

## III. GUIDANCE

### A. Application of Amended Definition of Covered Employee

Section 162(m)(3)(A)[1] provides that the term "covered employee" includes any employee who is the PEO or PFO of the publicly held corporation at any time during the taxable year, or was an individual acting in such a capacity.

Section 162(m)(3)(B) provides that a "covered employee" also includes any employee whose total compensation for the taxable year is required to be reported to shareholders under the Securities Exchange Act of 1934 by reason of such employee being among the three highest compensated officers for the taxable year (other than the PEO or PFO, or an individual acting in such capacity). Stakeholders have asked whether an employee must have served as an executive officer at the end of the taxable year to be a covered employee under section 162(m)(3)(B). The statutory provisions do not impose an end-of-year requirement, and nothing in the legislative history indicates that Congress intended such a requirement to apply. Accordingly, the Treasury Department and the IRS have determined that there is no end-of-year requirement under section 162(m)(3)(B).

Some commenters have asserted that an end-of-year requirement should apply under section 162(m)(3)(B) because the Securities and Exchange Commission (SEC) rules relating to executive compensation disclosure under the Securities Exchange Act of 1934 require disclosure of the compensation of the registrant's three most highly compensated executive officers other than the PEO and the PFO who were serving as executive officers at the end of the last completed fiscal year. See Item 402 of Regulation S-K, 17 CFR § 229.402(a)(3)(iii).[2] The SEC rules, however, do not limit the disclosure of compensation by reason of an executive officer being among the highest compensated executive officers solely to executive officers who serve at the end of the last completed fiscal year. For example, in addition to requiring the disclosure of the three most highly compensated executive officers (other than the PEO and PFO) who were serving as executive officers at the end of the last completed fiscal year, the SEC rules also require disclosure of the compensation of up to two additional individuals for whom disclosure

---

[1] References to section 162(m) in sections III, IV and V of this notice refer to section 162(m) as amended by section 13601 of the Act, except as otherwise explicitly provided herein.

[2] References to Item 402 in this Notice refer to Item 402 of Regulation S-K, 17 CFR § 229.402, which contains the SEC rules regarding the executive compensation disclosure requirements.

would have been required pursuant to 17 CFR § 229.402(a)(3)(iii) but for the fact that the individual was not serving as an executive officer of the registrant at the end of the last completed fiscal year. See Item 402 of Regulation S-K, 17 CFR § 229.402(a)(3)(iv).[3] Moreover, as previously noted, the section 162(m)(3)(B) statutory language and legislative history do not impose an end-of-year requirement. While certain aspects of section 162(m) are interpreted consistent with the SEC rules, the SEC rules do not serve as the sole basis for interpreting section 162(m).

Stakeholders have also questioned whether an employee whose compensation is not required to be disclosed under the SEC rules could nevertheless be a covered employee under section 162(m)(3)(B). The flush language at the end of section 162(m)(3) provides that the term "covered employee" includes any employee who would be described in section 162(m)(3)(B) if the reporting described there were required. Although this flush language was added by a conforming amendment under section 13601(c) of the Act, which expanded the definition of publicly held corporation to include issuers required to file reports under section 15(d) of the Securities Exchange Act of 1934, the legislative history clarifies that the flush language was intended to apply more broadly, explaining that this language applies, for example, to a corporation that does not file a proxy statement for the year because it delists its securities. See House Conf. Rpt. 115-466, 489. Thus, executive officers of publicly held corporations can be covered employees under section 162(m)(3)(B) even when disclosure of their compensation is not required under the SEC rules.

Accordingly, the term "covered employee" for any taxable year means any employee who is among the three highest compensated executive officers for the taxable year (other than the PEO or PFO, or an individual acting in such capacity), regardless of whether the executive officer is serving at the end of the publicly held corporation's taxable year, and regardless of whether the executive officer's compensation is subject to disclosure for the last completed fiscal year under the applicable SEC rules. The determination of the amount of compensation used to identify the three most highly compensated executive officers for purposes of section 162(m)(3)(B) is

made consistent with the Instructions to Item 402(a)(3) and the Instructions to Item 402(m)(2), 17 CFR § 229.402(a)(3), § 229.402(m)(2). In cases in which a publicly held corporation's last completed fiscal year and the taxable year do not end on the same date (for example, due to a short taxable year as a result of a corporate transaction), the publicly held corporation will have three most highly compensated executive officers under section 162(m)(3)(B) for the taxable year. The Treasury Department and IRS request comments on the application of the SEC executive compensation disclosure rules to determine the three most highly compensated executive officers for a taxable year that does not end on the same date as the last completed fiscal year. Until additional guidance is issued, to determine the three most highly compensated employees for purposes of section 162(m)(3)(B), taxpayers should base their determination upon a reasonable good faith interpretation of the statute, taking into account the guidance provided under this notice.

Pursuant to section 162(m)(3)(C), the term "covered employee" also includes any individual who was a covered employee of the publicly held corporation (or any predecessor) for any taxable year beginning after December 31, 2016. For taxable years beginning prior to January 1, 2018, "covered employees" are identified pursuant to section 162(m)(3) as in effect before the amendments made by section 13601(b) of the Act. Accordingly, covered employees identified for the taxable year beginning during 2017 (in accordance with the pre-amendment rules for identifying covered employees) will continue to be covered employees for taxable years beginning in 2018 and beyond.

The following examples illustrate how these rules apply under certain circumstances, including how their application may differ from the application of the SEC's executive compensation disclosure requirements. For each example, assume that none of the employees were covered employees for the 2017 taxable year (since being a covered employee for the 2017 taxable year would provide a separate and independent basis for classifying that employee as a covered employee for the 2018 taxable year). For each example, assume that the corporation has a fiscal year ending December 31 for SEC reporting purposes.

---

[3] *See also* Item 402(m)(2) of Regulation S-K, 17 CFR § 229.402(m)(2) (SEC rules for executive compensation disclosure requirements for smaller reporting companies and emerging growth companies). These rules require disclosure of compensation with respect to (i) all individuals serving as the PEO or acting in a similar capacity during the last completed fiscal year, regardless of compensation level; (ii)

the two most highly compensated executive officers other than the PEO who were serving as executive officers at the end of the last completed fiscal year; and (iii) up to two additional individuals for whom disclosure would have been provided based on compensation level but for the fact that the individual was not serving as an executive officer at the end of the last completed fiscal year.

*Example 1.* (i) *Facts.* Corporation Z is a calendar year taxpayer and a publicly held corporation within the meaning of section 162(m)(2). Corporation Z is not a smaller reporting company or emerging growth company under the SEC rules. For 2018, Employee A served as the sole PEO of Corporation Z and Employees B and C both served as the PFO of Corporation Z at different times during the year. Employees D, E, and F were, respectively, the first, second, and third most highly compensated executive officers of Corporation Z for 2018 other than the PEO and PFO, and all three retired before the end of 2018. Employees G, H, and I were, respectively, Corporation Z's fourth, fifth, and sixth highest compensated executive officers other than the PEO and PFO for 2018, and all three were serving at the end of 2018. On March 1, 2019, Corporation Z filed its Form 10-K, Annual Report Pursuant to Section 13 or 15(d) of the Securities Exchange Act of 1934 with the SEC. With respect to Item 11, Executive Compensation (as required by Part III of Form 10-K), Corporation Z disclosed the compensation of Employee A for serving as the PEO, Employees B and C for serving as the PFO, and Employees G, H, and I pursuant to Item 402 of Regulation S-K, 17 CFR § 229.402(a)(3)(iii). Corporation Z also disclosed the compensation of Employees D and E pursuant to Item 402 of Regulation S-K, 17 CFR § 229.402(a)(3)(iv).

*(ii) Conclusion: PEO.* Because Employee A served as the PEO during 2018, Employee A is a covered employee under section 162(m)(3)(A) for 2018.

*(iii) Conclusion: PFO.* Because Employees B and C served as the PFO during 2018, Employees B and C are covered employees under section 162(m)(3)(A) for 2018.

*(iv) Conclusion: Three Highest Compensated Executive Officers.* Even though the SEC rules require Corporation Z to disclose the compensation of Employees D, E, G, H, and I for 2018, Corporation Z's covered employees for 2018 under section 162(m)(3)(B) are Employees D, E, and F, because these are the three highest compensated executive officers other than the PEO and PFO for 2018.

*Example 2.* (i) *Facts.* Assume the same facts as in *Example 1,* except that Corporation Z is a smaller reporting company or emerging growth company under the SEC rules. Accordingly, with respect to Item 11, Executive Compensation (as required by Part III of Form 10-K), Corporation Z disclosed the compensation of Employee A for serving as the PEO, Employees G and H pursuant to Item 402(m) of Regulation S-K, 17 CFR § 229.402(m)(2)(ii), and Employees D and E pur-

suant to Item 402(m) of Regulation S-K, 17 CFR § 229.402(m)(2)(iii).

*(ii) Conclusion.* The results are the same as in *Example 1.* For purposes of identifying a corporation's covered employees under section 162(m)(3), it is not relevant whether the SEC rules for smaller reporting companies and emerging growth companies apply to the corporation, nor is it relevant whether the specific executive officers' compensation must be disclosed under the SEC rules applicable to the corporation.

*Example 3.* (i) *Facts.* Corporation Y is a domestic publicly held corporation within the meaning of section 162(m)(2) for its 2018 taxable year and a calendar year taxpayer. Corporation X is a domestic corporation and a calendar year taxpayer; however, Corporation X is not a publicly held corporation within the meaning of section 162(m)(2) for its 2018 and 2019 taxable years. On July 31, 2019, Corporation X acquires for cash 80% of the only class of outstanding stock of Corporation Y. The group (comprised of Corporations X and Y) elects to file a consolidated income tax return. As a result of this election, Corporation Y has a short taxable year ending on July 31, 2019. Corporation Y does not change its fiscal year for SEC reporting purposes to correspond to the short taxable year. Corporation Y remains a domestic publicly held corporation within the meaning of section 162(m)(2) for its short taxable year ending on July 31, 2019 and its subsequent taxable year ending on December 31, 2019, for which it files a consolidated income tax return with Corporation X.

For Corporation Y's taxable year ending July 31, 2019, Employee N serves as the only PEO, and Employee O serves as the only PFO. Employees J, K, and L are the three most highly compensated executive officers of Corporation Y for the taxable year ending July 31, 2019, other than the PEO and PFO. As a result of the acquisition, effective July 31, 2019, Employee N ceases to serve as the PEO of Corporation Y. Instead, Employee M begins serving as the PEO of Corporation Y on August 1, 2019. Employee N continues to provide services for Corporation Y and never serves as PEO again (or as an individual acting in such capacity). For Corporation Y's taxable year ending December 31, 2019, Employee M serves as the only PEO, and Employee O serves as the only PFO. Employees J, K, and L continued to be the three most highly compensated executive officers of Corporation Y, other than the PEO and PFO, for the taxable year ending December 31, 2019.

*(ii) Conclusion: Employee N.* Because Employee N served as the PEO during Corporation Y's taxable year ending July 31, 2019, Employee N is a covered employee for Corporation Y's taxable year ending July 31, 2019. Furthermore, Employee N is a covered employee for Corporation Y's taxable year ending July 31, 2019, even though Employee N's compensation is required to be disclosed pursuant to the SEC executive compensation disclosure rules only for the fiscal year ending December 31, 2019. Because Employee N was a covered employee for Corporation Y's taxable year ending July 31, 2019, Employee N is also a covered employee for Corporation Y's taxable year ending December 31, 2019.

*(iii) Conclusion: Employee O.* Because Employee O served as the PFO during Corporation Y's taxable years ending July 31, 2019, and December 31, 2019, Employee O is a covered employee for these taxable years. Furthermore, Employee O is a covered employee for Corporation Y's taxable year ending July 31, 2019, even though Employee O's compensation is required to be disclosed pursuant to the SEC executive compensation disclosure rules only for the fiscal year ending December 31, 2019. Employee O would be a covered employee for Corporation Y's taxable year ending December 31, 2019 even if Employee O did not serve as the PFO during this taxable year because Employee O was a covered employee for Corporation Y's taxable year ending July 31, 2019.

*(iv) Conclusion: Employees J, K, and L.* Employees J, K, and L are covered employees for Corporation Y's taxable years ending July 31, 2019, and December 31, 2019, because these employees are the three highest compensated executive officers for these taxable years. Employees J, K, and L would be covered employees for Corporation Y's taxable year ending December 31, 2019, even if Employees J, K, and L were not the three highest compensated executive officers during this taxable year because Employees J, K, and L were covered employees for Corporation Y's taxable year ending July 31, 2019. Accordingly, Employees J, K, and L would be covered employees for Corporation Y's taxable years ending July 31, 2019 and December 31, 2019, even if their compensation would not be required to be disclosed pursuant to the SEC executive compensation disclosure rules.

*(v) Conclusion: Employee M.* Because Employee M served as the PEO during Corporation Y's taxable year ending December 31, 2019, Employee M is a covered employee for Corporation Y's taxable year ending December 31, 2019.

**B. Remuneration Provided pursuant to a Written Binding Contract**

**1. Written Binding Contract**

The amendments to section 162(m) made by the Act do not apply to remuneration payable under a written binding contract which was in effect on November 2, 2017, and which is not modified in any material respect on or after such date. Remuneration is payable under a written binding contract that was in effect on November 2, 2017, only to the extent that the corporation is obligated under applicable law (for example, state contract law) to pay the remuneration under such contract if the employee performs services or satisfies the applicable vesting conditions. Accordingly, the amendments to section 162(m) made by the Act apply to any amount of remuneration that exceeds the amount of remuneration that applicable law obligates the corporation to pay under a written binding contract that was in effect on November 2, 2017, if the employee performs services or satisfies the applicable vesting conditions.

The Act's amendments to section 162(m) also apply to a written binding contract that is renewed after November 2, 2017. A written binding contract that is terminable or cancelable by the corporation without the employee's consent after November 2, 2017, is treated as renewed as of the date that any such termination or cancellation, if made, would be effective. Thus, for example, if the terms of a contract provide that it will be automatically renewed or extended as of a certain date unless either the corporation or the employee provides notice of termination of the contract at least 30 days before that date, the contract is treated as renewed as of the date that termination would be effective if that notice were given. Similarly, for example, if the terms of a contract provide that the contract will be terminated or canceled as of a certain date unless either the corporation or the employee elects to renew within 30 days of that date, the contract is treated as renewed by the corporation as of that date (unless the contract is renewed before that date, in which case, it is treated as renewed on that earlier date). Alternatively, if the corporation will remain legally obligated by the terms of a contract beyond a certain date at the sole discretion of the employee, the contract will not be treated as renewed as of that date if the employee exercises the discretion to keep the corporation bound to the contract. A contract is not treated as terminable or cancelable if it can be terminated or canceled only by terminating the employment relationship of the employee. A contract is not treated as renewed if upon termination or cancelation of the contract the employment relationship continues but would no longer be covered by the contract. However, if the employment continues after such termination or cancellation, payments with respect to such employment are not made pursuant to the contract (and, therefore, are not grandfathered).

If a compensation plan or arrangement is binding, the amount that is required to be paid as of November 2, 2017, to an employee pursuant to the plan or arrangement will not be subject to the Act's amendments to section 162(m) even though the employee was not eligible to participate in the plan or arrangement as of November 2, 2017. However, the Act's amendments to section 162(m) will apply to such compensation plan or arrangement unless the employee was employed on November 2, 2017, by the corporation that maintained the plan or arrangement, or the employee had the right to participate in the plan or arrangement under a written binding contract as of that date.

**2. Material Modification**

The Act's amendments to section 162(m) will apply to any written binding contract that is materially modified after November 2, 2017. A material modification occurs when the contract is amended to increase the amount of compensation payable to the employee. If a written binding contract is materially modified, it is treated as a new contract entered into as of the date of the material modification. Thus, amounts received by an employee under the contract before a material modification are not affected, but amounts received subsequent to the material modification are treated as paid pursuant to a new contract, rather than as paid pursuant to a written binding contract in effect on November 2, 2017. A modification of the contract that accelerates the payment of compensation is a material modification unless the amount of compensation paid is discounted to reasonably reflect the time value of money. If the contract is modified to defer the payment of compensation, any compensation paid or to be paid that is in excess of the amount that was originally payable to the employee under the contract will not be treated as resulting in a material modification if the additional amount is based on either a reasonable rate of interest or a predetermined actual investment (whether or not assets associated with the amount originally owed are actually invested therein) such that the amount payable by the employer at the later date will be based on the actual rate of return on the predetermined actual investment (including any decrease, as well as any increase, in the value of the investment).

The adoption of a supplemental contract or agreement that provides for increased compensation, or the payment of additional compensation, is a material modification of a written binding contract if the facts and circumstances demonstrate that the additional compensation is paid on the basis of substantially the same elements or conditions as the compensation that is otherwise paid pursuant to the written binding contract. However, a material modification of a written binding contract does not include a supplemental payment that is equal to or less than a reasonable cost-of-living increase over the payment made in the preceding year under that written binding contract. In addition, the failure, in whole or in part, to exercise negative discretion under a contract does not result in the material modification of that contract.

The following examples illustrate the rules in this section III.B of this notice. For each example, assume for all relevant years that the corporation is a publicly held corporation within the meaning of section 162(m)(2) and is a calendar year taxpayer.

*Example 1.* (i) *Facts.* On October 2, 2017, Corporation W executed a 3-year employment agreement with Employee V for an annual salary of $2,000,000 beginning on January 1, 2018. Employee V serves as the PFO of Corporation W for the 2017, 2018, 2019, and 2020 taxable years. The terms of the agreement provide for automatic extensions after the 3-year term for additional 1-year periods, unless the corporation exercises its option to terminate the agreement within 30 days before the end of the 3-year term or, thereafter, within 30 days before each anniversary date. Termination of the employment agreement does not require the termination of Employee V's employment relationship with Corporation W. Under applicable law, the agreement constitutes a written binding contract in effect on November 2, 2017, to pay $2,000,000 of annual salary to Employee V for three years through December 31, 2020.

(ii) *Conclusion.* Employee V is a covered employee for Corporation W's 2018, 2019, and 2020 taxable years. Before the Act's amendments to section 162(m)(3), an individual serving as a PFO was not considered a covered employee. Thus, Employee V is a covered employee solely as a result of the Act's amendment to section 162(m)(3). Because the employment agreement executed on October 2, 2017, is a written binding contract under applicable law to pay Employee V an annual salary of $2,000,000, the Act's amendments to section 162(m) do not apply to Employee V's annual salary. Accordingly, Employee V's annual salary of $2,000,000 for the

2018, 2019, and 2020 taxable years is not subject to the deduction limitation under section 162(m). However, the employment agreement is treated as renewed on January 1, 2021, unless it is previously terminated, and the Act's amendments to section 162(m) apply to any payments made under the employment agreement on or after that date.

*Example 2.* (i) *Facts.* On December 31, 2015, Employee U, an employee of Corporation V, makes an election to defer the entire amount that would otherwise be paid to Employee U under Corporation V's 2016 annual bonus plan. Pursuant to the deferral election, the bonus, plus earnings based on a predetermined actual investment, is to be paid in a lump sum at Employee U's separation from service. Employee U earns a $200,000 bonus for the 2016 taxable year. Under applicable law, the deferred compensation agreement into which Corporation V and Employee U entered on December 31, 2015 constitutes a written binding contract. On January 1, 2018, Employee U is promoted to serve as PEO of Corporation V. Prior to January 1, 2018, Employee U was never a covered employee as defined in section 162(m)(3). On December 15, 2020, Employee U separates from service and, on that date, Corporation V pays $225,000 (the deferred $200,000 bonus plus $25,000 in earnings) to Employee U.

(ii) *Conclusion.* Employee U is a covered employee for Corporation V's 2020 taxable year because Employee U served as the PEO of Corporation V during the taxable year. Moreover, Employee U is a covered employee for Corporation V's 2020 taxable because Employee U was a covered employee of Corporation V for a prior taxable year beginning after December 31, 2016. Before the Act's amendment to section 162(m)(3), a PEO qualified as a covered employee under section 162(m)(3)(A) only if that employee served as the PEO as of the close of the taxable year, and the rule in section 162(m)(3)(C) did not apply. Thus, Employee U is a covered employee for the 2020 taxable year solely as a result of the Act's amendment to section 162(m)(3). Because, under applicable law, the deferred compensation agreement into which Corporation V and Employee U entered on December 31, 2015, constitutes a written binding contract to pay the bonus plus earnings based on a predetermined actual investment, the Act's amendments to section 162(m) do not apply to the $225,000 payment Corporation V is obligated to pay Employee U at Employee U's separation from service. Accordingly, the $225,000 payment is not subject to the deduction limitation under section 162(m).

*Example 3.* (i) *Facts.* Employee P serves as the PEO of Corporation U for the 2017 and 2018 taxable years. On February 1, 2017, Corporation U establishes a bonus plan, under which Employee P will receive a cash bonus of $1,500,000 if a specified performance goal is satisfied; the outcome of the performance goal is uncertain on February 1, 2017. The compensation committee retains the right, if the performance goal is met, to reduce the bonus payment to no less than $400,000 if, in its judgment, other subjective factors warrant a reduction. On November 2, 2017, under applicable law, which takes into account the employer's ability to exercise negative discretion, the bonus plan established on February 1, 2017 constitutes a written binding contract to pay $400,000. On March 1, 2018, the compensation committee certifies that the performance goal was satisfied. However, the compensation committee reduces the award to $500,000 due to the sale of certain corporate assets that resulted in the lowering of the fair market value of Corporation U's goodwill. On April 1, 2018, Corporation U pays $500,000 to Employee P. The payment satisfies the requirements of §1.162-27(e) as qualified performance-based compensation.

(ii) *Conclusion.* Employee P is a covered employee for Corporation U's 2018 taxable year. Prior to the Act's amendment to section 162(m)(4), section 162(m) did not apply to qualified performance-based compensation because such compensation was excluded from the definition of applicable employee remuneration. Thus, the $500,000 payment constitutes applicable employee remuneration solely as a result of the amendment to section 162(m)(4). Because, under applicable law, as of November 2, 2017, the bonus plan established on February 1, 2017, constitutes a written binding contract to pay $400,000, the Act's amendments to section 162(m) do not apply to $400,000 of the $500,000 payment to Employee P. Furthermore, the failure of the compensation committee to exercise negative discretion to reduce the award to $400,000, instead of $500,000, does not result in a material modification of the contract. Accordingly, the $400,000 is not subject to the deduction limitation under section 162(m). The remaining $100,000 of the $500,000 payment is subject to the deduction limitation under section 162(m) regardless of whether the payment satisfies the requirements of §1.162-27(e) as qualified performance-based compensation.

*Example 4.* (i) *Facts.* Employee Q serves as the PFO of Corporation T for the 2016, 2017, and 2018 taxable years. On January 4, 2016, Corporation T and Employee Q enter into a nonqualified deferred compensation arrangement that is an account balance plan. Under the terms of the plan, Corporation T will pay Employee Q's account balance on April 1, 2019, but only if Employee Q continues to serve as the PFO through December 31, 2018. Pursuant to the terms of the plan, Corporation T credits $100,000 to Employee Q's account annually for three years on December 31 of each year beginning on December 31, 2016, and credits earnings on each principal amount on each subsequent December 31. The plan also provides that Corporation T may, at any time, amend the plan to either stop or reduce the amount of future credits to the account balance in its discretion; however, Corporation T may not deprive Employee Q of any benefit accrued before the date of any such amendment. Under applicable law, the plan constitutes a written binding contract in effect on November 2, 2017, to pay $100,000 of remuneration that Corporation T credited to the account balance on December 31, 2016. On April 1, 2019, Corporation T pays Employee Q $350,000 (including earnings).

(ii) *Conclusion.* Employee Q is a covered employee for Corporation T's 2019 taxable year. Prior to the Act's amendment to section 162(m)(3), an individual serving as a PFO was not considered a covered employee. Thus, Employee Q is a covered employee solely as a result of the amendment to section 162(m)(3). Because, as of November 2, 2017, the nonqualified deferred compensation arrangement between Corporation T and Employee Q is a written binding contract under applicable law only with respect to the $100,000 credited as of that date, the Act's amendments to section 162(m) do not apply to $100,000 of the payment. Accordingly, $250,000 of the $350,000 payment (the difference between the $350,000 payment on April 1, 2019 and the $100,000 credited to the account balance on December 31, 2016) is subject to the deduction limitation under section 162(m).

*Example 5.* (i) *Facts.* Assume the same facts as in *Example 4*, except that under the plan earnings are credited quarterly; thus, under applicable law, the plan constitutes a written binding contract in effect on November 2, 2017, to pay the account balance as of November 2, 2017, to Employee Q on April 1, 2019. On November 2, 2017, the account balance under the plan is $110,000 (the $100,000 credited on December 31, 2016, plus earnings).

(ii) *Conclusion.* Employee Q is a covered employee for Corporation T's 2019 taxable year. Prior to the Act's amendment to section 162(m)(3), an individual serving as a PFO was not considered a covered employee. Thus, Employee Q is a covered employee solely as a result of the Act's amendment to section 162(m)(3). Because the nonqualified deferred compensation arrangement between Corporation T and Employee Q is a written binding contract under applicable law to pay only the $110,000 account balance as of November 2, 2017, to Employee Q on April 1, 2019, the Act's amendments to section 162(m) do not apply to $110,000 of the $350,000 payment. Accordingly, $240,000 of the $350,000 payment (the difference between the $350,000 payment on April 1, 2019 and the $110,000 account balance on November 2, 2017) is subject to the deduction limitation under section 162(m).

*Example 6.* (i) *Facts.* Assume the same facts as in *Example 4*, except that, Employee Q serves as PEO (rather than PFO) of Corporation T for the 2016, 2017, and 2018 taxable years, and continues to serve as the PEO through December 31, 2019.

(ii) *Conclusion.* Employee Q is a covered employee for Corporation T's 2019 taxable year because Employee Q served as the PEO of Corporation T during the taxable year. Moreover, Employee Q is a covered employee for Corporation T's 2019 taxable year because Employee Q was a covered employee of Corporation T for a prior taxable year beginning after December 31, 2016. Prior to the Act's amendments to section 162(m)(3)(A), a PEO was a covered employee if such employee served as the PEO as of the close of the taxable year. Because Employee Q continues to serve as the PEO through December 31, 2019, Employee Q is a covered employee not solely as a result of the amendments to section 162(m)(3). Accordingly, the entire $350,000 payment is subject to the deduction limitation under section 162(m).

*Example 7.* (i) *Facts.* On January 2, 2017, Corporation S executed a 4-year employment agreement with Employee R to serve as its PEO. Employee R serves as the PEO of Corporation S for four years and receives an annual salary of $1,000,000. Pursuant to the employment agreement, on January 2, 2017, Corporation S granted to Employee R nonstatutory stock options to purchase 1,000 shares of Corporation S stock, stock appreciation rights (SARs) on 1,000 shares, and 1,000 shares of Corporation S restricted stock. On the date of grant, the stock options had no readily ascertainable fair market value as defined in § 1.83-7(b) and neither the stock options nor the SARs provided for a deferral of compensation under section 409A and § 1.409A-1(b)(5)(i)(A). The stock options and SARs vest and become exercisable on January 2, 2019. Employee R can exercise the stock options and the SARs at any time from January 2, 2019, through January 2, 2022. On January 2, 2019, Employee R exercises the stock options and the SARs, and the 1,000 shares of restricted stock become substantially vested (as defined in § 1.83-3(b)). The grants of the stock options, SARs, and shares of restricted stock constitute a written binding contract under applicable law. The compensation attributable to the stock options and the SARs satisfy the requirements of § 1.162-27(e) as qualified performance-based compensation.

(ii) *Conclusion.* Employee R is a covered employee for Corporation S's 2019 taxable year. Because the January 2, 2017, grants of the stock options, SARs, and shares of restricted stock constitute a written binding contract in effect on November 2, 2017, under applicable law, the Act's amendments to section 162(m) do not apply to compensation received pursuant to the exercise of the stock options and the SARs, or the restricted stock becoming substantially vested (as defined in § 1.83-3(b)). Section 162(m) does not disallow Corporation S's deduction for compensation attributable to the stock options or the SARs, because the compensation satisfies the requirements of § 1.162-27(e) as qualified performance-based compensation, and the Act's elimination of the exception for qualified performance-based compensation does not apply. However, Corporation S's deduction for the compensation attributable to the restricted stock is disallowed by section 162(m) even though the Act's amendments do not apply to this compensation.

*Example 8.* (i) *Facts.* Assume the same facts as in *Example 7,* except that the employment agreement provides that the stock options, SARs, and restricted stock will be granted on January 2, 2018, subject to the approval of the board of directors of Corporation S. As of November 2, 2017, under applicable law, the potential grants of stock options, SARs, and restricted stock do not constitute a written binding contract.

(ii) *Conclusion.* Because, under applicable law, as of November 2, 2017, the potential grants of the stock options, SARs, and shares of restricted stock do not constitute a written binding contract, the Act's amendments to section 162(m) apply to compensation paid pursuant to the exercise of the stock options and SARs, and the restricted stock becoming substantially vested (as defined in § 1.83-3(b)). Accordingly, section 162(m) disallows Corporation S's deduction with respect to compensation attributable to the stock options, SARs, and restricted stock.

*Example 9.* (i) *Facts.* On January 2, 2015, Corporation R executes a deferred compensation agreement with Employee T providing for a payment of $3,000,000 if Employee T continues to provide services through December 31, 2017. On October 2, 2017, Employee T terminates employment with Corporation R, executes an employment agreement with Corporation Q to serve as its PFO, and commences employment with Corporation Q. The employment agreement, which is a written binding contract under applicable law, provides that, on April 1, 2018, Employee T will participate in the nonqualified deferred compensation plan available to all executive officers of Corporation Q and that Employee T's benefit accrued on that date will be $3,000,000. On April 1, 2021, Employee T receives a payment of $4,500,000, which is the entire benefit accrued under the plan.

(ii) *Conclusion.* Employee T is a covered employee for Corporation Q's 2021 taxable year. Before the Act's amendment to section 162(m)(3), an individual serving as a PFO was not considered a covered employee. Thus, Employee T is a covered employee solely as a result of the Act's amendment to section 162(m)(3). Even though Employee T was not eligible to participate in the nonqualified deferred compensation plan on November 2, 2017, Employee T was employed on November 2, 2017 and had the right to participate in the plan under a written binding contract as of that date. Because, as of November 2, 2017, the amount that is required to be paid pursuant to the written binding contract is $3,000,000, the Act's amendments to section 162(m) do not apply to $3,000,000 of the $4,500,000 payment made on April 1, 2021. Accordingly, $1,500,000 of the $4,500,000 payment (the difference between the $4,500,000 payment and the $3,000,000 grandfathered amount) is subject to the deduction limitation under section 162(m).

*Example 10.* (i) *Facts.* Corporation P executed a 5-year employment agreement with Employee S on January 1, 2017, providing for a salary of $1,800,000 per year to serve as Corporation P's PFO. The agreement constitutes a written binding contract under applicable law. In 2017 and 2018, Employee S receives the salary of $1,800,000 per year. In 2019, Corporation P increases Employee S's compensation with a supplemental payment of $40,000. On January 1, 2020, Corporation P increases Employee S's salary to $2,400,000.

(ii) *Conclusion: $40,000 Payment in 2019.* Employee S is a covered employee for Corporation P's 2018, 2019, and 2020 taxable years. Before the

Act's amendment to section 162(m)(3), an individual serving as a PFO was not considered a covered employee. Thus, Employee S is a covered employee solely as a result of the Act's amendment to section 162(m)(3). Accordingly, the salary of $1,800,000 per year payable to Employee S under the employment agreement, which is a written binding contract under applicable law, is grandfathered unless the change in Employee S's compensation in either 2019 or 2020 is a material modification. The $40,000 supplemental payment does not constitute a material modification of the written binding contract because the $40,000 payment is less than or equal to a reasonable cost-of-living increase from 2017. However, the $40,000 supplemental payment is subject to the Act's amendments to section 162(m). Therefore, section 162(m) disallows Corporation P's deduction for the $40,000 supplemental payment, but does not disallow any portion of Corporation P's deduction for the $1,800,000 salary.

(iii) *Conclusion: Salary Increase to $2,400,000 in 2020*. The $560,000 increase in salary in 2020 is a material modification of the written binding contract because the additional compensation is paid on the basis of substantially the same elements or conditions as the compensation that is otherwise paid pursuant to the written binding contract and it is greater than a reasonable, annual cost-of-living increase. Because the written binding contract is materially modified as of January 1, 2020, all compensation paid to Employee S in 2020 and thereafter is subject to the Act's amendments to section 162(m). Therefore, section 162(m) disallows Corporation P's deduction for Employee S's compensation in excess of $1,000,000.

*Example 11.* (i) *Facts.* Assume the same facts as in *Example 10*, except that instead of an increase in salary, Employee S receives a restricted stock grant subject to Employee S's continued employment for the balance of the contract.

(ii) *Conclusion.* The restricted stock grant is not a material modification of the written binding contract because any additional compensation paid to Employee S under the grant is not paid on the basis of substantially the same elements and conditions as Employee S's salary because it is based both on the stock price and Employee S's continued service. However, compensation attributable to the restricted stock grant is subject to the Act's amendments to section 162(m). Therefore, section 162(m) disallows Corporation P's deduction for the restricted stock, but does not disallow any portion of Corporation P's deduction for the $1,800,000 salary.

## IV. EFFECTIVE DATE

The Act's amendments to section 162(m) apply to taxable years beginning on or after January 1, 2018. The Treasury Department and the IRS anticipate that the guidance in this notice will be incorporated in future regulations that, with respect to the issues addressed in this notice, will apply to any taxable year ending on or after September 10, 2018. Any future guidance, including regulations, addressing the issues covered by this notice in a manner that would broaden the definition of "covered employee" as described under section III.A, or restrict the application of the definition of "written binding contract" as described in section III.B, will apply prospectively only.

## V. REQUEST FOR COMMENTS

The Treasury Department and the IRS anticipate issuing further guidance on other aspects of section 162(m), including the Act's amendments to section 162(m). Accordingly, comments are requested on additional issues under section 162(m) that future guidance, including regulations, should address. Specifically, comments are requested on (1) the application of the definition of "publicly held corporation" to foreign private issuers, including the reference to issuers that are required to file reports under section 15(d) of the Securities Exchange Act of 1934, (2) the application of the definition of "covered employee" to an employee who was a covered employee of a predecessor of the publicly held corporation, (3) the application of section 162(m) to corporations immediately after they become publicly held either through an initial public offering or a similar business transaction, and (4) the application of the SEC executive compensation disclosure rules for determining the three most highly compensated executive officers for a taxable year that does not end on the same date as the last completed fiscal year.

Written comments may be submitted through November 9, 2018. Comments should include a reference to Notice 2018-68. Send submissions to CC:PA:LPD:PR (Notice 2018-68), Room 5203, Internal Revenue Service, P.O. Box 7604, Ben Franklin Station, Washington, DC 20044. Submissions may be hand delivered Monday through Friday between the hours of 8 a.m. and 4 p.m. to CC:PA:LPD:PR (Notice 2018-68), Courier's Desk, Internal Revenue Service, 1111 Constitution Avenue, NW, Washington, DC 20224, or sent electronically, via the following e-mail address: Notice.comments@irscounsel.treas.gov. Please include "Notice 2018-68" in the subject line of any electronic communication. All material submitted will be available for public inspection and copying.

## VI. DRAFTING INFORMATION

The principal author of this notice is Ilya Enkishev of the Associate Chief Counsel (Tax Exempt and Government Entities), although other Treasury and IRS officials participated in its development. For further information on the provisions of this notice, contact Ilya Enkishev at (202) 317-5600 (not a toll-free number).

---

## Notice 2018-70, I.R.B. 2018-38, August 28, 2018

Guidance on Qualifying Relative and the Exemption Amount

### SECTION 1. PURPOSE

The Department of the Treasury (Treasury Department) and the Internal Revenue Service (IRS) intend to issue proposed regulations clarifying the definition of "qualifying relative" in § 152(d) for purposes of various provisions of the Internal Revenue Code (Code), including the new $500 credit for other dependents under § 24(h)(4) and head of household filing status under § 2(b), for taxable years in which the § 151(d) exemption amount is zero.

### SECTION 2. BACKGROUND

In general, § 151(a) of the Code allows a taxpayer to claim deductions for exemptions for the taxpayer and his or her spouse (§ 151(b)), and for any dependents (§ 151(c)). Before amendment by "An Act to provide for reconciliation pursuant to titles II and V of the concurrent resolution on the budget for fiscal year 2018," Pub. L. No. 115-97 (Act), § 151(d) provided for an exemption amount of a base dollar amount that was adjusted for inflation. Before the Act, the exemption amount for 2018 was calculated to be $4,150. See Rev. Proc. 2017-58, 2017-45 I.R.B. 489, modified and superseded by Rev. Proc. 2018-18, 2018-10 I.R.B. 392.

Section 152(a) of the Code generally defines a "dependent" to mean a "qualifying child" or a "qualifying relative." Section 152(d)(1) defines a qualifying relative to mean an individual (A) who bears a specific relationship to the taxpayer, (B) whose gross income for the calendar year in which the taxpayer's taxable year begins is less than the exemption amount (as defined in § 151(d)), (C) who receives over one-half of his or her support from the taxpayer for the calendar year in which the taxpayer's taxable year begins, and (D) who is not a qualifying child of the taxpayer or any other taxpayer for any taxable year beginning in the calendar year in which the taxpayer's taxable year begins.

Section 11041(a)(2) of the Act added § 151(d)(5) to provide special rules for taxable years 2018 through 2025 for the exemption amount in § 151(d). Specifically, § 151(d)(5)(A) provides that, for a taxable year beginning after December 31, 2017, and before January 1, 2026, the term "exemption amount" means zero, thereby suspending the deduction for personal exemptions. See H.R. Rep. No. 115-466 at 204 (2017) (Conf. Rep.). However, § 151(d)(5)(B) provides that, for purposes of any other provision of the Code, the reduction of the exemption amount to zero will not be taken into account in determining whether a deduction is allowed or allowable, or whether a taxpayer is entitled to a deduction, under § 151. The Conference Report states that this provision clarifies that the reduction of the personal exemption to zero "should not alter the operation of those provisions of the Code which refer to a taxpayer allowed a deduction . . . under section 151," including the child tax credit in § 24(a). Id. at 203 n.16.

Section 11022(a) of the Act amended § 24 of the Code to create a $500 credit for certain dependents of a taxpayer other than a qualifying child described in § 24(c), for whom the child tax credit is allowed. The $500 credit applies to two categories of dependents: (1) qualifying children for whom a child tax credit is not allowed and (2) qualifying relatives as defined in § 152(d). See § 24(h)(4)(A). Like the amendment to § 151(d) reducing the exemption amount to zero, this new credit applies for taxable years 2018 through 2025. The Conference Report explains the intended scope of this credit: "The credit is further modified to temporarily provide for a $500 nonrefundable credit for qualifying dependents other than qualifying children. The provision generally *retains the present-law definition of dependent*." See H.R. Rep. No. 115-466 at 227 (emphasis added).

Separately, Code § 2(b)(1)(A) defines a head of household to include an individual who is not married at the close of the taxable year, who is not a surviving spouse (as defined in § 2(a)), and who maintains as his or her home a household for a qualifying individual for the required period of time. A qualifying individual under § 2(b)(1)(A)(ii) includes a qualifying relative if the taxpayer is entitled to a deduction under § 151 for the person for the taxable year. Under

§ 151(c), a deduction is allowed for individuals who are dependents as defined in § 152, including qualifying relatives described in § 152(d).

## SECTION 3. GUIDANCE UNDER CONSIDERATION

The Treasury Department and the IRS intend to issue proposed regulations providing that the reduction of the exemption amount to zero under § 151(d)(5)(A) for taxable years 2018-2025 will not be taken into account in determining whether a person is a qualifying relative under § 152(d)(1)(B). Accordingly, in defining a qualifying relative for purposes of various provisions of the Code that refer to the definition of dependent in § 152, including, without limitation, for purposes of the new credit under § 24(h)(4) and head of household filing status under § 2(b), the § 151(d) exemption amount referenced in § 152(d)(1)(B) will be treated as $4,150 (adjusted for inflation), for taxable years in which the § 151(d)(5)(A) exemption amount is zero.

Section 151(d) provides for two different exemption amounts for taxable years 2018 through 2025. For purposes of determining whether a deduction is allowed for personal exemptions, § 151(d)(5)(A) requires that the exemption amount be zero—thereby suspending this deduction. But for other provisions of the Code that reference the deduction for other purposes, Congress indicated in § 151(d)(5)(B) that the reduction of the exemption amount to zero is not to be taken into account. Instead, the exemption amount should remain $4,150 for 2018 (adjusted for inflation in future years).

Construing § 152 in light of the structure of the statute, the Treasury Department and the IRS believe that the exemption amount referenced in that section must be $4,150 (adjusted for inflation), rather than zero, for purposes of determining who is a qualifying relative. This interpretation accords with § 151(d)(5), which aims to suspend the deduction for personal exemptions without substantively changing other Code provisions that directly or indirectly reference the § 151(d) exemption amount.

This interpretation is also confirmed by the structure of several Code provisions that necessitate a non-zero exemption amount in § 152(d)(1)(B). For example, to be a qualifying relative under § 152(d)(1)(B), an individual must have gross income that is "less than the exemption amount." But if the exemption amount were

zero, an individual's gross income would have to be less than zero—a near impossibility. And because it would be highly unusual for an individual to have gross income less than zero,[1] virtually no individuals would be eligible as qualifying relatives. A zero exemption amount would thus effectively render § 152(d)(1)(B) inoperable and eliminate an entire category of dependents. The Treasury Department and IRS do not believe Congress intended to make such a significant change in such an indirect manner.

In addition, the new $500 credit that Congress enacted at the same time, and in the same Act, as it reduced the § 151(d) exemption amount likewise depends on a non-zero exemption amount in § 152(d)(1)(B). Section 24(h)(4)(A), as amended, creates a $500 credit available for each dependent of the taxpayer other than a qualifying child for whom the child tax credit is allowed. This provision references the definition of dependent in section 152, which includes both qualifying relatives and qualifying children, and it was understood at the time of enactment that this provision "generally retain[ed] the present-law definition of dependent." H.R. Rep. No. 115-466 at 227. But if the exemption amount referenced in § 152(d)(1)(B) were zero, the entire category of qualifying relatives would be effectively excised from the definition of dependent. As a consequence, the $500 credit generally would not be available for qualifying relatives, and the availability of this credit would shrink to only a limited category of qualifying children for whom the child tax credit is not allowed. This does not appear to be what Congress intended when it enacted the new $500 credit.

Further, head of household filing status also depends on a non-zero exemption amount in § 152(d)(1)(B). Under § 2(b)(1)(A), an individual is considered a head of household if, *inter alia*, he or she maintains as his or her home a household for either (i) a qualifying child or (ii) "any other person who is a dependent of the taxpayer." Because the only dependents other than qualifying children are qualifying relatives, a zero exemption amount in § 152(d)(1)(B), and the resulting near elimination of qualifying relatives, would render the express provision for other dependents in § 2(b)(1)(A)(ii) superfluous. It also would deny head of household filing status to many individuals who previously qualified for that filing status and otherwise would continue to qualify. There is no reason to believe that

---

[1] This could occur if an individual engaged in a business involving the sale of goods incurs inventory costs that exceed gross sales revenue. See § 1.61-3(a).

Congress intended its alteration of the § 151(d) exemption amount to have this effect.

Accordingly, the Treasury Department and IRS intend to propose regulations to clarify that the reduction of the exemption amount to zero in § 151(d)(5)(A) for taxable years 2018-2025 does not apply to the gross income limitation in the definition of qualifying relative in § 152(d)(1)(B).

## SECTION 4. RELIANCE

Before the issuance of the proposed regulations described in this notice, taxpayers may rely on the rules described in section 3 of this notice.

## SECTION 5. REQUEST FOR COMMENTS

The Treasury Department and the IRS request comments on all aspects of the proposed guidance under consideration as described in this notice.

Written comments may be submitted by November 16, 2018, to Internal Revenue Service, CC:PA:LPD:PR (Notice 2018-70), Room 5203, P.O. Box 7604, Ben Franklin Station, Washington, D.C. 20044, or electronically to Notice.Comments@irscounsel.treas.gov (please include "Notice 2018-70" in the subject line). Alternatively, comments may be hand-delivered between the hours of 8:00 a.m. and 4:00 p.m. Monday to Friday to CC:PA:LPD:PR (Notice 2018-70), Courier's Desk, Internal Revenue Service, 1111 Constitution Avenue NW, Washington, D.C. 20224. Comments will be available for public inspection and copying.

## SECTION 6. DRAFTING INFORMATION

The principal author of this notice is Victoria J. Driscoll of the Office of Associate Chief Counsel (Income tax & Accounting). For further information regarding this notice contact Victoria J. Driscoll at (202) 317-4718 (not a toll-free call).

---

# Notice 2018-71, I.R.B. 2018-41, September 24, 2018

## PURPOSE

This notice provides guidance on the employer credit for paid family and medical leave under section 45S of the Internal Revenue Code (Code). This notice also announces that the Department of the Treasury (Treasury Department) and the Internal Revenue Service (IRS) intend to publish proposed regulations under section 45S.

## BACKGROUND

Section 45S was added to the Code by "An Act to Provide for Reconciliation Pursuant to Titles II and V of the Concurrent Resolution on the Budget for Fiscal Year 2018" (the Act), Pub. L. 115-97, 131 Stat. 2504, enacted December 22, 2017. For purposes of section 38, regarding the general business credit, section 45S establishes a business credit for employers that provide paid family and medical leave (the credit). The credit is equal to a percentage of wages paid to qualifying employees while they are on family and medical leave. As explained below, the purposes for which an employee may take family and medical leave under section 45S are the same purposes for which an employee may take family and medical leave under title I of the Family and Medical Leave Act of 1993, as amended (FMLA), Pub. L. 103-3; 29 U.S.C. sec. 2601.

The questions and answers in this notice provide further details regarding the requirements of section 45S, but a brief summary follows. To be eligible to claim the credit, an employer must have a written policy that satisfies certain requirements. First, the policy must cover all qualifying employees; that is, all employees who have been employed for a year or more and were paid not more than a specified amount during the preceding year. In general, in determining whether an employee is a qualifying employee in 2018, the employee must not have had compensation from the employer of more than $72,000 in 2017. Second, the policy must provide at least two weeks of annual paid family and medical leave for each full-time qualifying employee and at least a proportionate amount of leave for each part-time qualifying employee. Third, the policy must provide for payment of at least 50 percent of the qualifying employee's wages while the employee is on leave. Fourth, if an employer employs qualifying employees who are not covered by title I of the FMLA, the employer's written policy must include language providing "non-interference" protections, as described in Section A of this notice. Thus, the written policy must incorporate the substantive rules that must be met in order for an employer to be eligible for the credit.

Any leave paid by a State or local government or required by State or local law is not taken into account for any purpose in determining the amount of paid family and medical leave provided by the employer. Thus, any such leave is not taken into account in determining the amount of paid family and medical leave provided by the employer, the rate of payment under the employer's written policy, or the determination of the credit.

For purposes of the credit, an employer is any person for whom an individual performs services as an employee under the usual common law rules applicable in determining the employer-employee relationship. Similarly, wages qualifying for the credit generally have the same meaning as wages subject to the Federal Unemployment Tax Act (FUTA) pursuant to section 3306(b), determined without regard to the $7,000 FUTA wage limitation.

GUIDANCE

This notice includes sections on the following topics:

A. Eligible Employer

B. Family and Medical Leave

C. Minimum Paid Leave Requirements

D. Calculating and Claiming the Credit

E. Effective Date

A. ELIGIBLE EMPLOYER

The credit is available only to eligible employers. Under section 45S(c)(1), an eligible employer is an employer that has a written policy in place that satisfies the requirements set forth in Q&A-2 below.

*Question 1:* Must an employer be subject to title I of the FMLA to be an eligible employer under section 45S?[1]

*Answer 1:* No. Any employer will be an eligible employer under section 45S if it has a written policy in place that provides paid family and medical leave, as described in Section B of this notice, satisfies the minimum paid leave requirements set forth in Section C of this notice, and, if applicable, includes the "non-interference" language described in Q&A-3.

*Question 2:* What must an eligible employer's written policy provide?

*Answer 2:* An eligible employer's written policy must provide paid family and medical leave, as described in Section B of this notice (Q&A-8 through Q&A-11) and must satisfy the minimum paid leave requirements set forth in Section C of

this notice (Q&A-12 through Q&A-21). In summary, an eligible employer's written policy must provide all qualifying employees with at least two weeks of paid family and medical leave (prorated for part-time employees), at a rate of at least 50 percent of the employee's normal wages, as these terms are defined and described in more detail in Sections B and C of this notice. In addition, if the employer employs any qualifying employees, as defined in Q&A-12, who are not covered by title I of the FMLA, the employer's written policy must include "non-interference" language, as set forth in Q&A-3.

*Question 3:* If an employer employs any qualifying employees who are not covered by title I of the FMLA, do additional requirements apply in determining whether the employer is an eligible employer?[2]

*Answer 3:* Yes. If an employer employs at least one qualifying employee who is not covered by title I of the FMLA (including any employee who is not covered by title I of the FMLA because he or she works less than 1,250 hours per year), in accordance with section 45S(c)(2), the employer must include "non-interference" language in its written policy and comply with this language to be an eligible employer. This requirement applies to: (a) an employer subject to title I of the FMLA that has at least one qualifying employee who is not covered by title I of the FMLA, and (b) an employer not subject to title I of the FMLA (that, thus, has no employees covered by title I of the FMLA). The "non-interference" language must ensure that the employer will not interfere with, restrain, or deny the exercise of, or the attempt to exercise, any right provided under the policy, and will not discharge, or in any other manner discriminate against, any individual for opposing any practice prohibited by the policy. The following "non-interference" language is an example of a written provision that would satisfy section 45S:

*[Employer] will not interfere with, restrain, or deny the exercise of, or the attempt to exercise, any right provided under this policy. [Employer] will not discharge, or in any other manner discriminate against, any individual for opposing any practice prohibited by this policy.*

*Question 4:* Must an eligible employer's written policy under section 45S be set forth in a single,

---

[1] Section 101(4) of the FMLA defines "employer" as any person engaged in commerce or in any industry or activity affecting commerce who employs 50 or more employees for each working day during each of 20 or more calendar workweeks in the current or preceding calendar year, which includes (a) any person who acts, directly or indirectly, in the interest of an employer to any of the employees of such

employer; and (b) any successor in interest of an employer; and includes any "public agency," as defined in section 3(x) of the Fair Labor Standards Act of 1938 (29 U.S.C. 203(x)).

[2] An employer that employs any qualifying employees who are not covered by title I of the FMLA is an "added employer" under section 45S(c)(2)(B)(ii)).

separate document or meet other documentary requirements?

**Answer 4:** An eligible employer's written policy under section 45S may be set forth in a single document or in multiple documents. For example, an employer may maintain different documents to cover different classifications of employees or different types of leave, and those documents collectively will constitute the employer's written policy under section 45S. An eligible employer's written policy under section 45S also may be included in the same document that governs the employer's other leave policies. However, if an employer's written policy provides paid leave for FMLA purposes and additional paid leave for other reasons (such as vacation or personal leave), only the leave specifically designated for FMLA purposes is considered to be family and medical leave under section 45S. *See* Q&A-9.

**Question 5:** What is the general rule for determining when an employer's written policy must be in place?

**Answer 5:** Except as provided in the transition rule in Q&A-6 for the first taxable year of an employer beginning after December 31, 2017, the employer's written policy must be in place before the paid family and medical leave for which the employer claims the credit is taken. The written policy is considered to be in place on the later of the policy's adoption date or the policy's effective date.

*Example. Facts*: Employer adopts a written policy that satisfies all of the requirements of section 45S on June 15, 2019, with an effective date of July 1, 2019.

*Conclusion*: Assuming all other requirements for the credit are met, Employer may claim the credit with respect to family and medical leave paid in accordance with that policy to qualifying employees for leave taken on or after July 1, 2019.

**Question 6:** For the first taxable year of an employer beginning after December 31, 2017, what is the transition rule for determining when the employer's written policy must be in place?

**Answer 6:** For an employer's first taxable year beginning after December 31, 2017, a written leave policy or an amendment to a policy (whether it is a new policy for the taxable year or an existing policy) will be considered to be in place as of the effective date of the policy (or amendment), rather than a later adoption date, if (a) the policy (or amendment) is adopted on or before December 31, 2018, and (b) the employer brings its leave practices into compliance with

the terms of the retroactive policy (or retroactive amendment) for the entire period covered by the policy (or amendment), including making any retroactive leave payments no later than the last day of the taxable year.

*Example 1. Facts*: Employer's taxable year is the calendar year. Employee takes two weeks of unpaid family and medical leave beginning January 15, 2018. Employer adopts a written policy that satisfies the requirements of section 45S on October 1, 2018, and chooses to make the policy effective retroactive to January 1, 2018. At the time the policy is adopted, Employer pays Employee (at a rate of payment provided by the policy) for the two weeks of unpaid leave taken in January 2018.

*Conclusion*: Assuming all other requirements for the credit are met, Employer may claim the credit with respect to the family and medical leave paid to Employee for the leave taken in January 2018.

*Example 2. Facts*: Employer's taxable year is the calendar year. Employer amends its FMLA policy in writing on April 15, 2018, effective for leave taken on or after April 15, 2018, to provide that four weeks of FMLA leave will be paid leave. Employer's FMLA policy does not provide for leave for qualifying employees who are not covered by title I of the FMLA or include "non-interference" language. Employee, who is a qualifying employee, but who is not covered by title I of the FMLA, takes three weeks of unpaid family and medical leave beginning June 18, 2018. On October 1, 2018, Employer amends its written policy to include "non-interference" language and to provide paid leave effective April 15, 2018, for qualifying employees who are not covered by title I of the FMLA. On October 15, 2018, Employer pays Employee for the three weeks of family and medical leave Employee took beginning June 18, 2018.

*Conclusion*: Assuming all other requirements for the credit are met, Employer may claim the credit with respect to the family and medical leave paid to Employee for the leave taken beginning in June 2018.

**Question 7:** Is an eligible employer required to provide notice to employees that it has a written policy in place providing for paid family and medical leave under section 45S?

**Answer 7:** No. Section 45S does not impose a notice requirement with respect to the written policy on employers. However, if an employer chooses to provide notice of the written policy to qualifying employees, the policy will not be considered to provide for paid leave to all qualifying employees as required under section 45S, unless the availability of paid leave is communicated to employees in a manner reasonably designed to reach each qualifying employee. This may include, for example, email communication, use of internal websites, employee handbooks, or posted displays in employee work areas.

B. FAMILY AND MEDICAL LEAVE

An eligible employer may claim the credit under section 45S only with respect to paid family and medical leave. Under section 45S(e)(1), family and medical leave means leave for any one or more of the purposes described under subparagraph (A), (B), (C), (D), or (E) of paragraph (1), or paragraph (3), of section 102(a) of the FMLA ("FMLA purposes"), whether the leave is provided under the FMLA or by a policy of the employer. Under section 45S(e)(2), if an employer provides paid leave as vacation leave, personal leave, or medical or sick leave (other than leave specifically for one or more of the FMLA purposes), that paid leave is not considered family and medical leave under section 45S.

**Question 8:** What are the FMLA purposes for which paid family and medical leave under section 45S may be provided to a qualifying employee?

**Answer 8:** The FMLA purposes for which paid family and medical leave under section 45S may be provided are:

(a) The birth of a son or daughter of the employee and in order to care for the son or daughter.

(b) The placement of a son or daughter with the employee for adoption or foster care.

(c) Caring for the spouse, or a son, daughter, or parent, of the employee, if the spouse, son, daughter, or parent has a serious health condition.

(d) A serious health condition that makes the employee unable to perform the functions of the employee's position.

(e) Any qualifying exigency (as the Secretary of Labor shall, by regulation, determine) arising out of the fact that the spouse, or a son, daughter, or parent of the employee is a member of the Armed Forces (including the National Guard and Reserves) who is on covered active duty (or has been notified of an impending call or order to covered active duty).

(f) Caring for a covered service member with a serious injury or illness if the employee is the spouse, son, daughter, parent, or next of kin of the service member. The FMLA purposes are the

purposes for which an employee may take leave under the FMLA. The terms used in this Q&A-8 have the same meaning as defined in section 825.102 of the FMLA regulations, 29 CFR §825.102.

**Question 9:** Under what circumstances is paid leave considered family and medical leave under section 45S?

**Answer 9:** Other than the narrow exception described in Q&A-10, paid leave made available to an employee is considered family and medical leave under section 45S only if the leave is specifically designated for one or more FMLA purposes, may not be used for any other reason, and is not paid by a State or local government or required by State or local law. *See also* Q&A-21.

**Example 1.** *Facts*: Employer's written policy provides six weeks of annual paid leave for the birth of an employee's child, and to care for that child (an FMLA purpose). The leave may not be used for any other reason. No paid leave is provided by a State or local government or required by State or local law.

*Conclusion*: Employer's policy provides six weeks of family and medical leave under section 45S.

**Example 2.** *Facts*: Employer's written policy provides three weeks of annual paid leave that is specifically designated for any FMLA purpose and may not be used for any other reason. No paid leave is provided by a State or local government or required by State or local law.

*Conclusion*: Employer's policy provides three weeks of family and medical leave under section 45S.

**Example 3.** *Facts*: Employer's written policy provides three weeks of annual paid leave for any of the following reasons: FMLA purposes, minor illness, vacation, or specified personal reasons. No paid leave is provided by a State or local government or required by State or local law.

*Conclusion*: Employer's policy does not provide family and medical leave under section 45S because the leave is not specifically designated for one or more FMLA purposes and can be used for reasons other than FMLA purposes. This is true even if an employee uses the leave for an FMLA purpose.

**Question 10:** What is the consequence under section 45S if an employer's written policy provides paid leave that otherwise would be specifically designated for an FMLA purpose (for example, to care for a spouse, child, or parent who has a serious medical condition), except for the fact that the leave is available to care for additional individuals not specified in the FMLA (for example, a grandchild, or grandparent who has a serious medical condition)?

*Answer 10*: In this limited circumstance, the fact that the leave could also be used to care for additional individuals for whom care under the FMLA purpose is not required does not prevent the leave from being considered specifically designated for an FMLA purpose. However, the employer may not claim the credit for any leave taken to care for an individual other than a qualifying employee's spouse, parent, or child. *See also* Q&A-28.

*Example*. *Facts*: Employer's written policy provides four weeks of annual paid leave to care for family members with a serious health condition. The policy's definition of "family members" includes the individuals specified in the FMLA (spouse, children, and parents), and also includes grandparents, grandchildren, and domestic partners. Employee uses one week of annual paid leave to care for her grandmother, and at a later time, uses one week of annual paid leave to care for her son.

*Conclusion*: Employer's policy provides paid leave specifically designated for an FMLA purpose. Although the paid leave taken by Employee to care for her grandmother is not family and medical leave under section 45S, and Employer may not claim the credit for this leave, the paid leave taken by Employee to care for her son is family and medical leave under section 45S for which Employer may claim the credit, assuming all other requirements for the credit are met.

*Question 11*: May paid leave provided pursuant to an employer's short-term disability program be characterized as family and medical leave under section 45S?

*Answer 11*: Yes. Paid leave provided under an employer's short-term disability program, whether self-insured by an employer or provided through a short-term disability insurance policy, may be characterized as family and medical leave under section 45S if it otherwise meets the requirements to be family and medical leave under section 45S. *See* Q&A-9 and Q&A-15.

## C. MINIMUM PAID LEAVE REQUIREMENTS

For an employer to be eligible to claim the credit, an employer's written policy must meet certain minimum requirements with respect to paid family and medical leave, as described in section 45S(c)(1) and (c)(2). These requirements are:

(1) the policy must provide at least two weeks of annual paid family and medical leave to all qualifying employees who are not part-time employees, and at least a proportionate amount of paid family and medical leave to qualifying employees who are part-time employees,

(2) the policy must require a rate of payment that is not less than 50 percent of the wages normally paid to the qualifying employee for services performed for the employer, and

(3) if the employer employs one or more qualifying employees who are not covered by title I of the FMLA, the employer's written policy also must include the "non-interference" language described in Q&A-3.

Under section 45S(c)(4), any leave that is paid by a State or local government or required by State or local law is not taken into account for any purpose in determining the amount of paid family and medical leave provided by the employer.

*Question 12*: Who is a qualifying employee?

*Answer 12*: A qualifying employee is an employee (as defined in section 3(e) of the Fair Labor Standards Act of 1938, as amended (FLSA)) who has been employed by the employer for one year or more, and whose compensation for the preceding year does not exceed an amount equal to 60 percent of the amount applicable for that year under section 414(q)(1)(B)(i).[3] For 2017, the applicable amount of compensation under section 414(q)(1)(B)(i) is $120,000.[4] Accordingly, to be a qualifying employee in 2018, an employee must have earned no more than $72,000 (60 percent of $120,000) in compensation in 2017 (or if applicable, in the employer's fiscal year beginning in 2017). Section 414(q)(4) provides that an employee's compensation is determined under section 415(c)(3).

---

[3] While the "preceding year" used for this purpose is generally the preceding calendar year, an employer whose fiscal year is not the calendar year may choose to use as the "preceding year" either (a) the employer's immediately preceding fiscal year, or (b) the calendar year ending in the employer's immediately preceding fiscal year.

[4] *See* Notice 2016-62, 2016-46 IRB 725. Each year, the IRS adjusts the applicable amount under section 414(q)(1)(B)(i) (and amounts under other Code sections) and publishes the adjusted amounts in a notice. The applicable amount under section 414(q)(1)(B)(i) for 2018 is $120,000. *See* Notice 2017-64, 2017-45 IRB 486.

**Question 13:** How does an employer determine whether an employee has been employed for one year or more?

**Answer 13:** Until further guidance is issued, an employer may use any reasonable method to determine whether an employee has been employed for one year or more. Treating employees as employed for one year or more if they have been employed for 12 months, as set forth in section 825.110(b) of the FMLA regulations, 29 CFR §825.110(b), is an example of a reasonable method. However, any requirement that an employee work 12 consecutive months to be a qualifying employee would not be viewed as a reasonable method for determining whether an employee has been employed for one year.

**Question 14:** Must an employee work a minimum number of hours per year to be a qualifying employee?

**Answer 14:** No. Section 45S does not require an employee to work a minimum number of hours per year to be a qualifying employee. Until further guidance is issued, any requirement that an employee work a minimum number of hours to be a qualifying employee would not be viewed as a reasonable method for determining whether an employee has been employed for one year. The rules under section 101(2)(A)(ii) of title I of the FMLA, which require an employee to work a minimum of 1,250 hours of service to be an eligible employee under the FMLA, do not apply to section 45S.

**Question 15:** May the employer's written policy exclude any classification of employees from eligibility for paid family and medical leave?

**Answer 15:** No. An employer's written policy must provide at least two weeks of annual paid family and medical leave to all qualifying employees who are not part-time employees, and at least a proportionate amount of annual paid family and medical leave to all qualifying employees who are part-time employees. The policy may not exclude any classification of employees (for example, collectively bargained employees) if they are qualifying employees.

*Example 1. Facts:* Employer has an insured short-term disability plan that provides disability benefits to any employee who becomes disabled after having completed six months of continuous service. Under the plan, a disability caused by, or resulting from, a pre-existing condition is not covered if the disability begins in the first 12 months after the effective date of coverage. For purposes of the plan, a pre-existing condition is one for which an employee consulted a physician, received medical treatment, or took prescribed drugs in the three

months immediately prior to the effective date of coverage. The exclusion from coverage for pre-existing conditions applies to all employees of the employer during the applicable 12-month period.

*Conclusion:* Employees subject to the pre-existing condition exclusion are effectively not covered under the plan when they first become qualifying employees. In addition, in some cases, the requirement that an employee complete six months of continuous service might exclude some qualifying employees. Therefore, the plan will not in all cases cover all qualifying employees, and Employer may not claim the credit under section 45S for paid family and medical leave provided under the written policy with respect to any employees.

*Example 2. Facts:* Same facts as in *Example 1*, except that Employer adopts a written policy that provides for paid leave to any qualifying employee who is not covered under the short-term disability plan as a result of the six months of service requirement or the pre-existing condition exclusion. This leave is paid from Employer's general assets and the length of the paid leave is the same as the leave that would have been available under the short-term disability plan if neither the six months of service requirement nor the pre-existing condition exclusion applied to a qualifying employee.

*Conclusion:* Taking into account the leave available under Employer's insured short-term disability plan and Employer's supplemental self-insured paid leave arrangement as permitted under Q&A-4, Employer's written policy does not exclude any classification of qualifying employees and, assuming all other requirements for the credit are met, Employer may claim the credit under section 45S for paid family and medical leave provided under the written policy.

**Question 16:** How many weeks of annual paid family and medical leave must an employer provide to qualifying employees to claim the credit under section 45S?

**Answer 16:** An employer's written policy must provide qualifying employees who are not part-time employees with at least two weeks of annual paid family and medical leave and must provide at least a proportionate amount of annual paid family and medical leave to qualifying employees who are part-time employees. For part-time employees, the paid leave ratio must be at least equal to the ratio of the expected weekly hours worked by a qualifying employee who is a part-time employee to the expected weekly hours worked by an equivalent qualifying employee who is not a part-time employee, as described in section 45S(c)(1)(A)(ii). In determining the amount of paid family and medical leave provided by the employer for purposes of section 45S, any leave paid by a State or local government or required by State or local law is not taken into account.

*Example*. *Facts*: Employer's written policy provides four weeks of annual paid family and medical leave to any qualifying employee expected to work 40 hours per week, and two weeks of paid family and medical leave to any equivalent qualifying employee who is a part-time employee and is expected to work 20 hours per week. All of Employer's employees work either 20 or 40 hours per week.

*Conclusion*: Employer's policy meets the minimum paid leave requirements because each employee who is not a part-time employee may take at least the minimum two weeks of annual paid leave and each part-time employee may take at least a proportionate number of weeks of leave. Specifically, with respect to the proportionate amount, the ratio of expected weekly hours worked by a qualifying employee who is a part-time employee (20 hours) to the expected weekly hours worked by an equivalent qualifying employee who is not a part-time employee (40 hours) is 1:2, and the policy provides two weeks of paid leave to qualifying employees who are part-time employees and four weeks of paid leave to equivalent qualifying employees who are not part-time employees, satisfying the 1:2 ratio.

*Question 17*: How does an employer determine who is a part-time employee?

*Answer 17*: A part-time employee is an employee who is customarily employed for fewer than 30 hours per week.[5] Until further guidance is issued, an employer may use any reasonable method to determine how many hours an employee customarily works per week for the employer. Reasonable methods include the methods set forth in 29 CFR § 2530.200b-2 for calculating hours of service in connection with certain plans, such as qualified pension plans, subject to the Employee Retirement Income Security Act of 1974, as amended.

*Question 18*: What rate of payment must an employer's written policy provide?

*Answer 18*: The employer's written policy must provide that each qualifying employee who is on paid family and medical leave will be paid at least 50 percent of the wages normally paid to

the employee for services performed for the employer. In determining the rate of payment under the policy, leave paid by a State or local government or required under State or local law is not taken into account. *See* Q&A-21.

*Question 19*: For this purpose, how does an employer determine the wages normally paid to an employee?

*Answer 19*: Wages normally paid to an employee means the wages normally paid to the employee for services performed for the employer. Overtime (other than regularly-scheduled overtime) and discretionary bonuses are excluded from wages normally paid. Until further guidance is issued, for employees who are paid (in whole or in part) on a basis other than a salaried or hourly rate, an employer must determine wages normally paid to the employee using the rules for determining regular rate of pay set forth in regulations issued under the FLSA. *See* 29 CFR § 778.109.

*Question 20*: Must the rate of payment or period of paid family and medical leave provided under an employer's written policy be uniform with respect to all qualifying employees and for all FMLA purposes?

*Answer 20*: No. Section 45S does not require an employer's rate of payment or period of paid family and medical leave to be uniform with respect to all qualifying employees and for all FMLA purposes. However, to the extent an employer's policy provides different rates of payment or periods of paid family and medical leave for different FMLA purposes, the minimum paid leave requirements must be satisfied with respect to each FMLA purpose for which the employer intends to claim the credit. Conversely, if an employer's policy provides a uniform rate of payment and period of paid family and medical leave for all qualifying employees and for all FMLA purposes (or a uniform rate of payment and period for several specified FMLA purposes), the policy as a whole must satisfy the minimum paid leave requirements, and it is not necessary for the minimum paid leave requirements to be satisfied separately with respect to each FMLA purpose.

*Example 1*. *Facts*: Employer's written policy provides each qualifying employee with six weeks of annual paid leave for the birth or adoption of the employee's child, or to care for that child (an FMLA purpose) at a rate of payment of 100 percent of wages normally paid to the em-

---

[5] Section 45S(c)(1)(A)(i) uses the definition of part-time employee set forth in section 4980E(d)(4)(B), which states that a part-time time employee is any employee who is customarily employed for fewer than 30 hours per week.

ployee for services performed for Employer. For all other FMLA purposes, the policy provides each qualifying employee with two weeks of annual paid leave at a rate of payment of 75 percent of wages normally paid to the employee.

*Conclusion*: Employer's written policy satisfies the minimum paid leave requirements.

*Example 2. Facts*: Employer's written policy provides each qualifying employee with two weeks of annual paid leave for the birth or adoption of the employee's child, or to care for that child (an FMLA purpose) at a rate of payment of 100 percent of wages normally paid to the employee, and also provides each qualifying employee who is not covered by a collective bargaining agreement with two weeks of annual paid leave for a serious health condition that makes the employee unable to perform the duties of his or her position (also an FMLA purpose) at a rate of payment of 100 percent of wages normally paid to the employee.

*Conclusion*: The portion of Employer's policy that provides paid leave to each qualifying employee for the birth or adoption of the employee's child, or to care for that child, satisfies the minimum paid leave requirements. However, the portion of the policy providing only certain qualifying employees (those who are not covered by a collective bargaining agreement) with paid leave for a serious health condition that makes the employee unable to perform the duties of his or her position does not satisfy the minimum paid leave requirements, and Employer may not claim the credit for any leave taken under that portion of the policy.

*Example 3. Facts*: Employer's written policy provides each qualifying employee with two weeks of annual paid leave for any FMLA purpose at a rate of payment of 100 percent of the wages normally paid to the employee, and each qualifying employee who has 10 years of service with an additional two weeks of annual paid leave for any FMLA purpose at a rate of payment of 100 percent of wages normally paid to the employee.

*Conclusion*: Employer's policy satisfies the minimum paid leave requirements.

*Question 21*: In determining the rate of payment under the employer's written policy, is leave paid by a State or local government or required by State or local law taken into account?

*Answer 21*: No. Leave paid by a State or local government or required by State or local law is not taken into account in determining whether an employer's written policy provides a rate of payment of at least 50 percent of the wages normally paid to an employee for services per-

formed for the employer. To be eligible to claim the credit, an employer must independently satisfy the minimum paid leave requirements, including providing a rate of payment of at least 50 percent of wages normally paid to an employee. *See also* Q&A-9.

*Example 1. Facts*: Under State law, an employee on family and medical leave is eligible to receive six weeks of benefits paid by a State insurance fund at a rate of 50 percent of the employee's normal wages. Additionally, Employer's written policy concurrently provides each qualifying employee with six weeks of annual paid family and medical leave at a rate of payment of 30 percent of the wages normally paid to the employee for services performed for Employer. Consequently, in the aggregate, a qualifying employee can receive six weeks of annual paid family and medical leave at a rate of payment of 80 percent of the wages normally paid to the employee.

*Conclusion*: Employer's policy does not independently satisfy the requirement that the rate of payment be at least 50 percent of the wages normally paid to an employee.

*Example 2. Facts*: Same facts as *Example 1*, except that Employer's written policy provides each qualifying employee with six weeks of annual paid family and medical leave at a rate of payment of 50 percent of the wages normally paid to the employee that runs concurrently with the State leave. Consequently, in the aggregate, a qualifying employee can receive six weeks of annual paid family and medical leave at a rate of payment of 100 percent of the wages normally paid to the employee.

*Conclusion*: Employer's policy independently satisfies the requirement that the rate of payment be at least 50 percent of the wages normally paid to an employee. Only wages paid under Employer's written policy (50 percent of wages normally paid to the employee) may be used in calculating the credit. Wages paid pursuant to State law are not used in calculating the credit. *See* Q&A-26.

*Example 3. Facts*: Under State law, employers are required to provide employees six weeks of family and medical leave, and the State law permits this leave to be either paid or unpaid. Employer's written policy provides each qualifying employee with six weeks of annual paid family and medical leave at a rate of payment of 50 percent of the wages normally paid to the employee.

*Conclusion*: Employer's policy independently satisfies the requirement that the rate of payment

**Notice 2018-71**

be at least 50 percent of the wages normally paid to an employee.

## D. CALCULATING AND CLAIMING THE CREDIT

Section 45S(a)(1) provides that, in the case of an eligible employer, the credit is an amount equal to the applicable percentage of the amount of wages paid to qualifying employees during any period in which the employees are on family and medical leave. Under section 45S(a)(2), the term "applicable percentage" means 12.5 percent increased (but not above 25 percent) by 0.25 percentage points for each percentage point by which the rate of payment exceeds 50 percent.

Under section 45S(b)(3), the amount of family and medical leave that may be taken into account with respect to any qualifying employee for any taxable year may not exceed 12 weeks. Section 45S(b)(1) provides that the credit with respect to any qualifying employee for any taxable year cannot exceed an amount equal to the product of the employee's normal hourly wage rate for each hour (or fraction thereof) of actual services performed for the employer and the number of hours (or fraction thereof) for which family and medical leave is taken.

Applicable Percentage

**Example 2.** *Facts*: Same facts as *Example 1*, except that Employer's written policy provides each qualifying employee who has at least 10 years of service a rate of payment of 100 percent of the wages normally paid to the employee for services performed by the employer, rather than 75 percent.

*Conclusion*: Because the rate of payment for a qualifying employee who has at least 10 years of service is 100 percent (which is 50 percentage points greater than 50) the base applicable per-

Applicable Percentage

**Question 23:** How is the credit calculated?

**Answer 23:** The credit is equal to the applicable percentage of the amount of wages normally paid to a qualifying employee during any period (up to 12 weeks) that the employee is on family and medical leave.

**Example 1.** *Facts*: Employer's written policy provides each qualifying employee with four weeks of annual paid family and medical leave at a rate of payment of 75 percent of wages normally paid to the employee. During 2018,

**Question 22:** How is the applicable percentage calculated?

**Answer 22:** The applicable percentage is based on the rate of payment for the leave under the employer's policy. The base applicable percentage of 12.5 percent applies if the rate of payment is 50 percent. If the rate of payment under the policy is greater than 50 percent, the applicable percentage is increased by 0.25 percentage points for each percentage point by which the rate of payment exceeds 50 percent, up to a maximum applicable percentage of 25 percent.

**Example 1.** *Facts*: Employer's written policy provides each qualifying employee with four weeks of annual paid family and medical leave at a rate of payment of 75 percent of the wages normally paid to the employee.

*Conclusion*: Because the rate of payment under the policy exceeds 50 percent by 25 percentage points, the base applicable percentage of 12.5 percent is increased by 6.25 percent (.25 percent multiplied by 25), for an applicable percentage of 18.75 percent.

| = | 12.5 percent + (0.25 percent x 25) |
| = | 12.5 percent + 6.25 percent |
| = | 18.75 percent |

centage for these employees is increased by 12.5 percent (0.25 percent multiplied by the 50). The applicable percentage with respect to such an employee is therefore 25 percent (the base percentage of 12.5 percent, plus 12.5 percent). For a qualifying employee who has less than 10 years of service, the applicable percentage is the same as determined in *Example 1*.

*Calculation for employee who has at least 10 years of service*:

| = | 12.5 percent + (0.25 percent x 50) |
| = | 12.5 percent + 12.5 percent |
| = | 25 percent |

Employee takes four weeks of leave under the policy. Employee is normally paid $1,000 per week. Employer pays Employee a total of $3,000 ($750 per week for four weeks) for family and medical leave under section 45S.

*Conclusion*: Assuming all the requirements for the credit are met, Employer may claim a credit of $562.50 with respect to Employee (18.75 percent of $3,000).

**Example 2.** *Facts*: Same facts as *Example 1*, except that Employer's written policy provides each qualifying employee who has at least 10 years of service with a rate of payment of 100 percent of the wages normally paid to the employee. During 2018, Employee A, who has been employed for 12 years, takes leave under the policy for four weeks, and Employee B, who has been employed for five years, takes leave under the policy for two weeks. Both Employee A and Employee B are normally paid $1,000 per week. Employer pays Employee A a total of $4,000, and Employee B a total of $1,500, for family and medical leave under section 45S.

*Conclusion*: Assuming all the requirements for the credit are met, Employer may claim a total credit of $1,281.25 with respect to Employee A and Employee B. The credit for Employee A is $1,000 (25 percent of $4,000), and the credit for Employee B is $281.25 (18.75 percent of $1,500).

*Question 24*: What are wages for purposes of section 45S?

*Answer 24*: For purposes of section 45S, pursuant to section 45S(g), the term "wages" has the same meaning given to that term by section 3306(b) (regarding FUTA wages), determined without regard to the $7,000 FUTA wage limitation. Section 3306(b) generally defines wages as all remuneration for employment, as defined by section 3306(c), subject to certain limitations. However, for purposes of section 45S, the term "wages" does not include any amount taken into account for purposes of determining any other credit allowed under section 38, which provides for several separate business-related credits.

*Example 1. Facts*: Employer pays wages to Employee that qualify as a research expense for purposes of determining the amount of Employer's research credit under section 41(a). The research credit under section 41(a) is a general business credit allowed under section 38. Some of the wages paid to Employee for the performance of qualified services under section 41(b) were paid while Employee was on family and medical leave.

*Conclusion*: For purposes of determining the amount of Employer's credit under section 45S, Employer must exclude from the wages paid while Employee was on family and medical leave any wages treated as a qualified research expense for purposes of determining the amount of Employer's research credit under section 41(a).

*Example 2. Facts*: Employer is tax-exempt under section 501(a) as an educational organization described in section 501(c)(3). Employment with Employer is not employment for purposes of FUTA tax pursuant to section 3306(c)(8); thus,

compensation paid by Employer is not FUTA wages within the meaning of section 3306(b). Although Employer is exempt from federal income tax under section 501(a), it earns unrelated business taxable income from a trade or business that is not substantially related to the performance of Employer's exempt purpose. Employer maintains a written paid leave policy that provides at least two weeks of paid family and medical leave to all qualifying employees, including those performing services for the unrelated trade or business. Employer would like to claim the credit against its unrelated business income tax liability.

*Conclusion*: Because Employer does not pay FUTA wages within the meaning of section 3306(b), compensation paid by Employer does not constitute wages for purposes of section 45S(g). Consequently, amounts paid by Employer to its employees while on paid family and medical leave are not eligible for the credit.

*Question 25*: Are wages paid by a third-party payer (including an insurance company, a professional employer organization, or a Certified Professional Employer Organization) to qualifying employees for services performed for an eligible employer considered wages for purposes of section 45S?

*Answer 25*: Yes. However, only the eligible employer, and not the third-party payer, may take into account wages paid to qualifying employees for services performed for the eligible employer in determining the credit under section 45S.

*Question 26*: Is leave paid by a State or local government or required by a State or local law taken into account in determining the credit?

*Answer 26*: No. Leave paid by a State or local government or required by a State or local law is not taken into account in determining the credit.

*Question 27*: Are wages paid through an employer's short-term disability program for family and medical leave taken into account in determining the credit?

*Answer 27*: Yes. Wages paid through an employer's short-term disability program for family and medical leave are taken into account in determining the credit provided that the program (in combination with any other employer-paid leave arrangement) meets the minimum paid leave requirements. *See* Q&A-11.

*Question 28*: May an employer claim the credit with respect to an employee who is not a qualifying employee when the paid family and medical leave is taken, but who becomes a qualifying employee at a later time during the taxable year?

**Notice 2018-71**

*Answer 28*: No. An eligible employer may claim the credit only with respect to wages paid to an employee who is a qualifying employee at the time family and medical leave is taken. Wages paid to an employee for family and medical leave taken before an employee becomes a qualifying employee are excluded in determining the employer's credit. However, if an employer's written policy provides that employees may take paid family and medical leave before they become qualifying employees and does not provide a dedicated amount of leave meeting the minimum paid leave requirements that may only be taken after an employee becomes a qualifying employee, the leave will not fail to (a) be specifically designated for an FMLA purpose, or (b) meet the minimum paid leave requirements, solely because an employee may take paid leave before becoming a qualifying employee.

*Example*. *Facts*: Employer's written policy provides all employees who have completed at least six months of employment with four weeks of annual paid family and medical leave at a rate of payment of 100 percent of wages normally paid to the employee for services performed by the employer. Employee completes six months of employment with employer as of January 1, 2019, and one year of employment (becoming a qualifying employee) as of July 1, 2019. On June 15, 2019, Employee begins a four week period of paid family and medical leave under the policy.

*Conclusion*: Assuming all the requirements to claim the credit are met, Employer may use wages paid to Employee for family and medical leave on or after July 1, 2019, the date that Employee becomes a qualifying employee, in the calculation of the credit. Wages paid for family and medical leave taken before Employee becomes a qualifying employee are not eligible for the credit.

*Question 29*: Who may claim the credit?

*Answer 29*: Only an eligible employer for whom qualifying employees perform services may claim the credit with respect to wages paid. *See also* Q&A-25.

*Question 30*: Does claiming the credit affect an employer's deduction for wages or salaries paid for the taxable year?

*Answer 30*: Yes. Section 280C denies a deduction for wages or salaries paid for the taxable year equal to the amount of the credit. Under section 280C(a), an employer's deduction for wages paid is reduced by an amount equal to the amount of the credit.

*Question 31*: How does an eligible employer claim the credit?

*Answer 31*: An eligible employer must file IRS Form 8994, Employer Credit for Paid Family and Medical Leave, and IRS Form 3800, General Business Credit, with its tax return to claim the credit.

*Question 32*: For purposes of the limitation described in section 45S(b)(1), how does an employer determine the normal hourly wage rate of an employee who is not paid an hourly wage rate?

*Answer 32*: Until further guidance is issued, an employer may use any reasonable method to convert the normal wages paid to an employee who is not paid an hourly wage rate to an hourly rate.

*Question 33*: Are employers aggregated under section 45S for purposes of calculating the credit?

*Answer 33*: No. Section 45S(c)(3) provides that all persons who are treated as a single employer under section 52(a) and (b) are treated as a single taxpayer. In accordance with this aggregation rule, employers are aggregated for purposes of section 45S(h)(1), which provides that a taxpayer may elect to have section 45S not apply for any taxable year. This is the only purpose for which employers are aggregated under section 45S. Consequently, employers are not aggregated for any other purpose under section 45S, including calculating the credit as set forth in this Section D.

*Question 34*: Does each member of a controlled group of corporations (as defined in section 52(a)) and each member of a group of businesses under common control (as defined in section 52(b)) generally make a separate election to claim or not to claim the credit under section 45S(h)?

*Answer 34*: Yes. Each member of a controlled group of corporations and each member of a group of businesses under common control generally makes a separate election to claim or not to claim the credit in accordance with rules set forth under section 51(j)(2) and (3). However, in the case of a consolidated group (as defined in §1.1502-1(h)), the election is made by the agent (as defined in §1.1502-77) of the group. An election to claim or not to claim the credit is made for the taxable year in which the credit is available by claiming or not claiming the credit on either an original return or an amended return filed for that taxable year. *See* Q&A 31.

E. EFFECTIVE DATE

This notice is effective as of September 24, 2018, and applies to wages paid in taxable years beginning after December 31, 2017, and before January 1, 2020.

## PUBLIC COMMENTS

This notice generally provides guidance that the Treasury Department and the IRS intend to incorporate into proposed regulations. The proposed regulations will provide interested parties an opportunity to comment on the issues addressed in the proposed regulations. However, to assist in development of the proposed regulations, the Treasury Department and the IRS request comments on the guidance provided in this notice. Public comments should be submitted no later than November 23, 2018. Comments should include a reference to Notice 2018-71. Send submissions to CC:PA:LPD:PR (Notice 2018-71), Room 5203, Internal Revenue Service, P.O. Box 7604, Ben Franklin Station, Washington, DC 20044. Submissions may be hand-delivered Monday through Friday between the hours of 8 a.m. and 4 p.m. to CC:PA:LPD:PR (Notice 2018-71), Courier's Desk, Internal Revenue Service, 1111 Constitution Avenue, NW, Washington, DC 20044, or sent electronically, via the following e-mail address: *Notice.comments@irscounsel.treas.gov*. Please include "Notice 2018-71" in the subject line of any electronic communication. All material submitted will be available for public inspection and copying.

## PAPERWORK REDUCTION ACT

The collection of information contained in this notice will be submitted through IRS Form 8944 to the Office of Management and Budget (OMB) in accordance with the Paperwork Reduction Act of 1995 (44 U.S.C. 3507(d)). An agency may not conduct or sponsor, and a person is not required to respond to, a collection of information unless the collection of information displays a valid OMB control number. The collection of information is required to obtain a general business credit for employers that provide paid family and medical leave. The likely respondents are individuals, households, businesses, and other for-profit or not-for-profit institutions. Books or records relating to a collection of information must be retained as long as their contents may become material in the administration of any internal revenue law. Generally, tax returns and tax return information are confidential, as required by section 6103.

## DRAFTING INFORMATION

The principal author of this notice is Dara Alderman of the Office of Associate Chief Counsel (Tax Exempt and Government Entities). For further information regarding this notice contact Dara Alderman at (202) 317-5500 (not a toll-free call).

---

# Notice 2018-74, I.R.B. 2018-40, September 18, 2018

**Safe Harbor Explanations – Eligible Rollover Distributions**

## I. PURPOSE

This notice modifies the two safe harbor explanations in Notice 2014-74, 2014-50 I.R.B. 937, that may be used to satisfy the requirement under § 402(f) of the Internal Revenue Code ("Code") that certain information be provided to recipients of eligible rollover distributions. The safe harbor explanations as modified by this notice take into consideration certain legislative changes and recent guidance, including changes related to qualified plan loan offsets (as defined in section 13613 of the Tax Cuts and Jobs Act of 2017 ("TCJA"), P.L. 115-97) and guidance issued on self-certification of eligibility for a waiver of the deadline for completing a rollover (described in Rev. Proc. 2016-47, 2016-37 I.R.B. 346), and include other clarifying changes.

To assist with the implementation of the modified safe harbor explanations, this notice contains two appendices. Appendix A contains two model safe harbor explanations: one for distributions that are not from a designated Roth account, and a second for distributions from a designated Roth account. Appendix B provides instructions on how to amend the safe harbor explanations contained in Notice 2014-74 to reflect the revisions included in the modified safe harbor explanations in Appendix A.

## II. BACKGROUND

### A. Section 402(f)

Section 402(f) requires the plan administrator of a plan qualified under § 401(a) to provide the written explanation described in § 402(f)(1) to any recipient of an eligible rollover distribution, as defined in § 402(c)(4). In addition, §§ 403(a)(4)(B) and 457(e)(16)(B) require the plan administrator of a § 402(f)§ 403(a) plan, or an eligible § 457(b) plan maintained by a governmental employer described in § 457(e)(1)(A), to provide the written explanation to any recipient of an eligible rollover distribution. Further, § 403(b)(8)(B) requires a payor under a § 403(b) plan to provide the written explanation to any recipient of an eligible rollover distribution.

Section 1.402(f)-1, Q&A-1(a), provides that the *plan* administrator of a *qualified plan* is required, within a reasonable period of time before making an eligible rollover distribution, to provide the distributee with the written explanation described in § 402(f) ("§ 402(f) notice").

Notice 2014-74 contains two safe harbor explanations that reflect relevant law as of December 8, 2014: one safe harbor explanation is for payments not from a designated Roth account and the other safe harbor explanation is for payments from a designated Roth account. Notice 2014-74 provides that the safe harbor explanations may be used by plan administrators and payors to satisfy § 402(f) to the extent that the explanations accurately reflect current law.

**B. Recent Statutory Changes Related to Qualified Plan Loan Offsets**

Section 1.402(c)-2, Q&A-3(a), provides that, unless specifically excluded, an eligible rollover distribution means any distribution to an *employee* (or to a spousal distributee described in § 1.402(c)-2, Q&A-12(a)) of all or any portion of the balance to the credit of the *employee* in a *qualified plan*. Section 1.402(c)-2, Q&A-3(b), provides that certain distributions (for example, required minimum distributions under § 401(a)(9)) are not eligible rollover distributions.

Section 1.402(c)-2, Q&A-9(a), provides that a distribution of a plan loan offset amount (as defined in § 1.402(c)-2, Q&A-9(b)) is an eligible rollover distribution if it satisfies § 1.402(c)-2, Q&A-3. Thus, an amount up to the plan loan offset amount may be rolled over by the employee (or spousal distributee) to an eligible retirement plan within the 60-day period described in § 402(c)(3), unless the plan loan offset amount fails to be an eligible rollover distribution for another reason.

Section 1.402(c)-2, Q&A-9(b), provides that a distribution of a plan loan offset amount is a distribution that occurs when, under the plan terms governing a plan loan, the participant's accrued benefit is reduced (offset) in order to repay the loan. This can occur when, for example, the terms governing a plan loan require that, in the event of an employee's termination of

employment or request for a distribution, the loan is to be repaid immediately or treated as in default. A plan loan offset can also occur when, under the terms of the plan loan, the loan is canceled, accelerated, or treated as if it were in default (for example, when the plan treats a loan as in default upon an employee's termination of employment or within a specified period thereafter). See also § 1.72(p)-1, Q&A-13(a)(2). Because a plan loan offset is an actual distribution for purposes of the Code, not a deemed distribution under § 72(p), a plan loan offset cannot occur prior to a distributable event. See generally § 1.72(p)-1, Q&A-13(b).

Section 13613 of the TCJA amended § 402(c)(3) of the Code to provide an extended rollover deadline for qualified plan loan offset amounts (as defined in § 402(c)(3)(C)(ii)). Any portion of a qualified plan loan offset amount (up to the entire qualified plan loan offset amount) may be rolled over into an eligible retirement plan by the individual's tax filing due date (including extensions) for the taxable year in which the offset occurs.

A qualified plan loan offset amount is defined in § 402(c)(3)(C)(ii) as a plan loan offset amount that is distributed from a qualified employer plan to a participant or beneficiary solely by reason of: (1) the termination of the qualified employer plan, or (2) the failure to meet the repayment terms of the loan from such plan because of the severance from employment of the participant. Additionally, under § 402(c)(3)(C)(iv), a qualified plan loan offset may occur only if the relevant plan loan meets the requirements of § 72(p)(2).

**C. Other Recent Statutory Changes[1]**

Section 100121 of the Moving Ahead for Progress in the 21st Century Act ("MAP-21"), P.L. 112-141, amended chapters 83 and 84 of title 5 of the United States Code ("U.S.C."), to permit certain federal retirees to participate in phased retirement. MAP-21 amended the Code to add § 72(t)(2)(A)(viii), which provides that if an employee participates in phased retirement, any payments made under a phased retirement annuity under § 8336a(a)(5) or 8412a(a)(5) of title 5 of the U.S.C., or a composite retirement annuity under § 8336a(a)(1) or 8412a(a)(1) of title 5 of the

---

[1] Although not requiring modifications to the safe harbor explanations, section 41104 of the Bipartisan Budget Act of 2018, P.L. 115-123, amended § 6343 of the Code to provide that certain retirement plan benefits distributed from a plan as a result of an improper levy may, when they are returned to an individual, be eligible to be rolled over into the plan or an IRA. These amounts may be rolled over by the tax filing due date (not including extensions) for the tax year during which the Internal Revenue Service ("IRS") returns the improperly levied funds to the individual. As amended, § 6343 provides that, when the IRS returns improperly levied funds, the Secretary of the Treasury will notify the individual that the returned amount may be eligible to be rolled over.

U.S.C., are excepted from the 10% additional tax under § 72(t).

Section 2 of the Defending Public Safety Employees' Retirement Act ("DPSERA"), P.L. 114-26, amended § 72(t)(10)(B) with respect to the exception to the 10% additional tax under § 72(t) on early distributions from a governmental retirement plan for qualified public safety employees who have reached age 50 by expanding the exception to include specified federal law enforcement officers, customs and border protection officers, federal firefighters, and air traffic controllers who have reached age 50, and eliminating the requirement that the distributions be from a defined benefit plan. Section 306 of the Protecting Americans from Tax Hikes Act of 2015, P.L. 114-113, includes a list of federal governmental employees added to the definition of qualified public safety employee in § 72(t)(10)(B).

**D. Other Extensions of 60-Day Rollover Deadline**

Rev. Proc. 2016-47 provides guidance concerning waivers of the 60-day rollover deadline contained in § § 402(c)(3) and 408(d)(3). Specifically, it provides for a self-certification procedure (subject to verification on audit) that may be used by a taxpayer claiming, in specified circumstances, eligibility for a waiver under § 402(c)(3)(B) or 408(d)(3)(I) with respect to a rollover into a qualified plan or individual retirement arrangement ("IRA"). A plan administrator or an IRA trustee generally may rely on a taxpayer's self-certification in determining whether a taxpayer has satisfied the conditions for a waiver of the 60-day rollover deadline.

Rev. Proc. 2007-56, 2007-2 C.B. 388, provides a list of time-sensitive acts, the performance of which may be postponed under § § 7508 (relating to service in combat zones or contingency operations) and 7508A (relating to taxpayers affected by a federally declared disaster or a terrorist or military action). Rev. Proc. 2007-56 includes on the list of acts that may be postponed under § § 7508 and 7508A the 60-day deadline for rolling over an eligible rollover distribution to an eligible retirement plan (which includes an IRA). Rev. Proc. 2007-56 does not, by itself, provide any postponements under § 7508A. Rather, for taxpayers to be entitled to a postponement

under § 7508A of any act listed in the revenue procedure, the IRS must publish a notice or issue other guidance (including an IRS News Release) providing relief with respect to a federally declared disaster or a terrorist or military action. For example, News Release TX-2018-05, July 9, 2018, provides tax relief relating to severe storms and flooding in Texas.[2]

**III. MODIFICATIONS TO THE SAFE HARBOR EXPLANATIONS**

There are two updated safe harbor explanations appended to this notice (see Appendix A). The safe harbor explanations modify the safe harbor explanations in Notice 2014-74 to reflect certain legislative changes and guidance issued after December 8, 2014, including: (1) the extended rollover deadline for qualified plan loan offset amounts under TCJA, (2) the exception to the 10% additional tax under § 72(t) for phased retirement distributions to certain federal retirees under MAP-21, (3) the expanded exception to the 10% additional tax under § 72(t) for specified federal employees who have reached age 50 under DPSERA, and (4) the self-certification procedures under Rev. Proc. 2016-47 for claiming eligibility for a waiver of the deadline for making rollovers. The safe harbor explanations also include other clarifying modifications, such as modifications clarifying that the 10% additional tax under § 72(t) for early distributions applies only to amounts includable in income, explaining how the rollover rules apply to governmental § 457(b) plans that include designated Roth accounts, clarifying that the general exception to the 10% additional tax under § 72(t) for payments from a governmental plan made after a qualified public safety employee separates from service (if the employee will be at least age 50 in the year of the separation) is not available for payments from IRAs, and recognizing the possibility that taxpayers affected by federally declared disasters and other events may have an extended deadline for making rollovers. For instructions on how to amend the safe harbor explanations in Notice 2014-74 to reflect these modifications, see Appendix B. The updated safe harbor explanations provided in this notice may be used by plan administrators and payors to satisfy § 402(f). However, the updated safe harbor explanations will not satisfy § 402(f) to the

---

[2] For certain disasters, Congress has enacted legislation providing special rules for distributions made on account of the disaster. For information on rules applicable to distributions (and the ability to repay those distributions) made on account of Hurricane Harvey or Tropical Storm Harvey, Hurricane Irma, Hurricane Maria, the 2017 California wild-fires, and certain 2016 disasters, see Publication 976, *Disaster Relief*. Distributions made on account of these disasters (assuming certain requirements are met) are not treated as eligible rollover distributions for purposes of § 402(f). See, for example, section 502(a)(6)(A) of the Disaster Tax Relief and Airport and Airway Extension Act of 2017, P.L. 115-63.

extent the explanations are no longer accurate because of a change in the relevant law occurring after September 18, 2018.

The first safe harbor explanation reflects the rules relating to distributions not from a designated Roth account. Thus, the first safe harbor explanation should only be used for a distribution that is not from a designated Roth account. The second safe harbor explanation reflects the rules relating to distributions from a designated Roth account. Thus, the second safe harbor explanation should only be used for a distribution from a designated Roth account. Both explanations should be provided to a participant if the participant is eligible to receive eligible rollover distributions both from a designated Roth account and from an account other than a designated Roth account.

The safe harbor explanation in this notice for distributions not from a designated Roth account meets the requirements of § 402(f) for an eligible rollover distribution that is not from a designated Roth account if provided to the recipient of the eligible rollover distribution within a reasonable period of time before the distribution is made. Similarly, the safe harbor explanation in this notice for distributions from a designated Roth account meets the requirements of § 402(f) for an eligible rollover distribution from a designated Roth account if provided to the recipient of the eligible rollover distribution within a reasonable period of time before the distribution is made.

Section 1.402(f)-1, Q&A-2, provides, in general, that a reasonable period of time for providing an explanation is no less than 30 days (subject to waiver) and no more than 90 days before the date on which the distribution is made. However, § 1.402(f)-1, Q&A-2(a), of the Proposed Income Tax Regulations, pursuant to section 1102(a)(1)(B) of the Pension Protection Act of 2006, P.L. 109-280, provides that a notice required to be provided under § 402(f) may be provided to a participant as much as 180 days before the date on which the distribution is made (or the annuity starting date). These proposed regulations further provide that, with respect to the extended period for notices, plans may rely on the proposed regulations for notices provided during the period beginning on the first day of the first plan year beginning on or after January 1, 2007 and ending on the effective date of final regulations. Thus, the § 402(f) notice may be provided as much as 180 days before the date on which the distribution is made (or the annuity starting date).

A plan administrator or payor may customize a safe harbor explanation by omitting any information that does not apply to the plan. For example, if the plan does not hold after-tax employee contributions, it would be appropriate to eliminate the section "If your payment includes after-tax contributions" in the explanation for payments not from a designated Roth account. Similarly, if the plan does not provide for distributions of employer stock or other employer securities, it would be appropriate to eliminate the section "If your payment includes employer stock that you do not roll over." Other information that may not be relevant to a particular plan includes, for example, the sections "If your payment is from a governmental section 457(b) plan" and "If you are an eligible retired public safety officer and your payment is used to pay for health coverage or qualified long-term care insurance." In addition, the plan administrator or payor may provide additional information with a safe harbor explanation if the information is not inconsistent with § 402(f).

Alternatively, a plan administrator or payor may satisfy § 402(f) by providing an explanation that is different from a safe harbor explanation. Any explanation must contain the information required by § 402(f) and must be written in a manner designed to be easily understood.

## IV. EFFECT ON OTHER DOCUMENTS

Notice 2014-74 is modified.

## DRAFTING INFORMATION

The principal author of this notice is Naomi Lehr of the Office of Associate Chief Counsel (Tax Exempt and Government Entities). For further information regarding this notice, contact Ms. Lehr at (202) 317-4102 (not a toll-free number).

\* \* \*

### Appendix A

For Payments Not From a Designated Roth Account

#### YOUR ROLLOVER OPTIONS

You are receiving this notice because all or a portion of a payment you are receiving from the [INSERT NAME OF PLAN] (the "Plan") is eligible to be rolled over to an IRA or an employer plan. This notice is intended to help you decide whether to do such a rollover.

This notice describes the rollover rules that apply to payments from the Plan that are *not* from a designated Roth account (a type of account with special tax rules in some employer plans). If you also receive a payment from a designated Roth account in the Plan, you will be provided a different notice for that payment, and the Plan administrator or the payor will tell you the amount that is being paid from each account.

Rules that apply to most payments from a plan are described in the "General Information About Rollovers" section. Special rules that only apply in certain circumstances are described in the "Special Rules and Options" section.

## GENERAL INFORMATION ABOUT ROLLOVERS

### How can a rollover affect my taxes?

You will be taxed on a payment from the Plan if you do not roll it over. If you are under age 59½ and do not do a rollover, you will also have to pay a 10% additional income tax on early distributions (generally, distributions made before age 59½), unless an exception applies. However, if you do a rollover, you will not have to pay tax until you receive payments later and the 10% additional income tax will not apply if those payments are made after you are age 59½ (or if an exception applies).

### What types of retirement accounts and plans may accept my rollover?

You may roll over the payment to either an IRA (an individual retirement account or individual retirement annuity) or an employer plan (a tax-qualified plan, section 403(b) plan, or governmental section 457(b) plan) that will accept the rollover. The rules of the IRA or employer plan that holds the rollover will determine your investment options, fees, and rights to payment from the IRA or employer plan (for example, no spousal consent rules apply to IRAs and IRAs may not provide loans). Further, the amount rolled over will become subject to the tax rules that apply to the IRA or employer plan.

### How do I do a rollover?

There are two ways to do a rollover. You can do either a direct rollover or a 60-day rollover.

*If you do a direct rollover*, the Plan will make the payment directly to your IRA or an employer plan. You should contact the IRA sponsor or the administrator of the employer plan for information on how to do a direct rollover.

*If you do not do a direct rollover*, you may still do a rollover by making a deposit into an IRA or eligible employer plan that will accept it. Generally, you will have 60 days after you receive the

payment to make the deposit. If you do not do a direct rollover, the Plan is required to withhold 20% of the payment for federal income taxes (up to the amount of cash and property received other than employer stock). This means that, in order to roll over the entire payment in a 60-day rollover, you must use other funds to make up for the 20% withheld. If you do not roll over the entire amount of the payment, the portion not rolled over will be taxed and will be subject to the 10% additional income tax on early distributions if you are under age 59½ (unless an exception applies).

### How much may I roll over?

If you wish to do a rollover, you may roll over all or part of the amount eligible for rollover. Any payment from the Plan is eligible for rollover, except:

- Certain payments spread over a period of at least 10 years or over your life or life expectancy (or the lives or joint life expectancy of you and your beneficiary);
- Required minimum distributions after age 70½ (or after death);
- Hardship distributions;
- ESOP dividends;
- Corrective distributions of contributions that exceed tax law limitations;
- Loans treated as deemed distributions (for example, loans in default due to missed payments before your employment ends);
- Cost of life insurance paid by the Plan;
- Payments of certain automatic enrollment contributions requested to be withdrawn within 90 days of the first contribution; and
- Amounts treated as distributed because of a prohibited allocation of S corporation stock under an ESOP (also, there will generally be adverse tax consequences if you roll over a distribution of S corporation stock to an IRA).

The Plan administrator or the payor can tell you what portion of a payment is eligible for rollover.

### If I don't do a rollover, will I have to pay the 10% additional income tax on early distributions?

If you are under age 59½, you will have to pay the 10% additional income tax on early distributions for any payment from the Plan (including amounts withheld for income tax) that you do not roll over, unless one of the exceptions listed below applies. This tax applies to the part of the distribution that you must include in income and is in addition to the regular income tax on the payment not rolled over.

The 10% additional income tax does not apply to the following payments from the Plan:

- Payments made after you separate from service if you will be at least age 55 in the year of the separation;

- Payments that start after you separate from service if paid at least annually in equal or close to equal amounts over your life or life expectancy (or the lives or joint life expectancy of you and your beneficiary);

- Payments from a governmental plan made after you separate from service if you are a qualified public safety employee and you will be at least age 50 in the year of the separation;

- Payments made due to disability;

- Payments after your death;

- Payments of ESOP dividends;

- Corrective distributions of contributions that exceed tax law limitations;

- Cost of life insurance paid by the Plan;

- Payments made directly to the government to satisfy a federal tax levy;

- Payments made under a qualified domestic relations order (QDRO);

- Payments up to the amount of your deductible medical expenses (without regard to whether you itemize deductions for the taxable year);

- Certain payments made while you are on active duty if you were a member of a reserve component called to duty after September 11, 2001 for more than 179 days;

- Payments of certain automatic enrollment contributions requested to be withdrawn within 90 days of the first contribution;

- Payments for certain distributions relating to certain federally declared disasters; and

- Phased retirement payments made to federal employees.

### If I do a rollover to an IRA, will the 10% additional income tax apply to early distributions from the IRA?

If you receive a payment from an IRA when you are under age 59½, you will have to pay the 10% additional income tax on early distributions on the part of the distribution that you must include in income, unless an exception applies. In general, the exceptions to the 10% additional income tax for early distributions from an IRA are the same as the exceptions listed above for early distributions from a plan. However, there are a few differences for payments from an IRA, including:

- The exception for payments made after you separate from service if you will be at least age 55 in the year of the separation (or age 50 for qualified public safety employees) does not apply.

- The exception for qualified domestic relations orders (QDROs) does not apply (although a special rule applies under which, as part of a divorce or separation agreement, a tax-free transfer may be made directly to an IRA of a spouse or former spouse).

- The exception for payments made at least annually in equal or close to equal amounts over a specified period applies without regard to whether you have had a separation from service.

- There are additional exceptions for (1) payments for qualified higher education expenses, (2) payments up to $10,000 used in a qualified first-time home purchase, and (3) payments for health insurance premiums after you have received unemployment compensation for 12 consecutive weeks (or would have been eligible to receive unemployment compensation but for self-employed status).

### Will I owe State income taxes?

This notice does not describe any State or local income tax rules (including withholding rules).

### SPECIAL RULES AND OPTIONS

### If your payment includes after-tax contributions

After-tax contributions included in a payment are not taxed. If a payment is only part of your benefit, an allocable portion of your after-tax contributions is included in the payment, so you cannot take a payment of only after-tax contributions. However, if you have pre-1987 after-tax contributions maintained in a separate account, a special rule may apply to determine whether the after-tax contributions are included in a payment. In addition, special rules apply when you do a rollover, as described below.

You may roll over to an IRA a payment that includes after-tax contributions through either a direct rollover or a 60-day rollover. You must keep track of the aggregate amount of the after-tax contributions in all of your IRAs (in order to determine your taxable income for later payments from the IRAs). If you do a direct rollover of only a portion of the amount paid from the Plan and at the same time the rest is paid to you, the portion directly rolled over consists first of the amount that would be taxable if not rolled over. For example, assume you are receiving a distribution of $12,000, of which $2,000 is after-tax contributions. In this case, if you directly roll over $10,000 to an IRA that is not a Roth IRA, no amount is taxable because the $2,000 amount not directly rolled over is treated as being after-tax contributions. If you do a direct rollover of the entire amount paid from the Plan to two or more destinations at the same time, you can choose which destination receives the after-tax contributions.

If you do a 60-day rollover to an IRA of only a portion of a payment made to you, the after-tax contributions are treated as rolled over last. For example, assume you are receiving a distribution of $12,000, of which $2,000 is after-tax contributions, and no part of the distribution is directly rolled over. In this case, if you roll over $10,000 to an IRA that is not a Roth IRA in a 60-day rollover, no amount is taxable because the $2,000 amount not rolled over is treated as being after-tax contributions.

You may roll over to an employer plan all of a payment that includes after-tax contributions, but only through a direct rollover (and only if the receiving plan separately accounts for after-tax contributions and is not a governmental section 457(b) plan). You can do a 60-day rollover to an employer plan of part of a payment that includes after-tax contributions, but only up to the amount of the payment that would be taxable if not rolled over.

### If you miss the 60-day rollover deadline

Generally, the 60-day rollover deadline cannot be extended. However, the IRS has the limited authority to waive the deadline under certain extraordinary circumstances, such as when external events prevented you from completing the rollover by the 60-day rollover deadline. Under certain circumstances, you may claim eligibility for a waiver of the 60-day rollover deadline by making a written self-certification. Otherwise, to apply for a waiver from the IRS, you must file a private letter ruling request with the IRS. Private letter ruling requests require the payment of a nonrefundable user fee. For more information, see IRS Publication 590-A, *Contributions to Individual Retirement Arrangements (IRAs)*.

### If your payment includes employer stock that you do not roll over

If you do not do a rollover, you can apply a special rule to payments of employer stock (or other employer securities) that are either attributable to after-tax contributions or paid in a lump sum after separation from service (or after age 59½, disability, or the participant's death). Under the special rule, the net unrealized appreciation on the stock will not be taxed when distributed from the Plan and will be taxed at capital gain rates when you sell the stock. Net unrealized appreciation is generally the increase in the value of employer stock after it was acquired by the Plan. If you do a rollover for a payment that includes employer stock (for example, by selling the stock and rolling over the proceeds within 60 days of the payment), the special rule relating to the distributed employer stock will not apply to any subsequent payments from the IRA or employer plan. The Plan administrator can tell you the amount of any net unrealized appreciation.

### If you have an outstanding loan that is being offset

If you have an outstanding loan from the Plan, your Plan benefit may be offset by the outstanding amount of the loan, typically when your employment ends. The offset amount is treated as a distribution to you at the time of the offset. Generally, you may roll over all or any portion of the offset amount. Any offset amount that is not rolled over will be taxed (including the 10% additional income tax on early distributions, unless an exception applies). You may roll over offset amounts to an IRA or an employer plan (if the terms of the employer plan permit the plan to receive plan loan offset rollovers).

How long you have to complete the rollover depends on what kind of plan loan offset you have. If you have a qualified plan loan offset, you will have until your tax return due date (including extensions) for the tax year during which the offset occurs to complete your rollover. A qualified plan loan offset occurs when a plan loan in good standing is offset because your employer plan terminates, or because you sever from employment. If your plan loan offset occurs for any other reason, then you have 60 days from the date the offset occurs to complete your rollover.

### If you were born on or before January 1, 1936

If you were born on or before January 1, 1936 and receive a lump sum distribution that you do not roll over, special rules for calculating the amount of the tax on the payment might apply to you. For more information, see IRS Publication 575, *Pension and Annuity Income*.

### If your payment is from a governmental section 457(b) plan

If the Plan is a governmental section 457(b) plan, the same rules described elsewhere in this notice generally apply, allowing you to roll over the payment to an IRA or an employer plan that accepts rollovers. One difference is that, if you do not do a rollover, you will not have to pay the 10% additional income tax on early distributions from the Plan even if you are under age 59½ (unless the payment is from a separate account holding rollover contributions that were made to the Plan from a tax-qualified plan, a section 403(b) plan, or an IRA). However, if you do a rollover to an IRA or to an employer plan that is not a governmental section 457(b) plan, a later distribution made before age 59½ will be subject to the 10% additional income tax on early distributions (unless an exception applies). Other differences include that you cannot do a rollover if the payment is due to an "unforeseeable emergency" and the special rules under "If your payment includes employer stock that you do not roll over" and "If you were born on or before January 1, 1936" do not apply.

### If you are an eligible retired public safety officer and your payment is used to pay for health coverage or qualified long-term care insurance

If the Plan is a governmental plan, you retired as a public safety officer, and your retirement was by reason of disability or was after normal retirement age, you can exclude from your taxable income Plan payments paid directly as premiums to an accident or health plan (or a qualified long-term care insurance contract) that your employer maintains for you, your spouse, or your dependents, up to a maximum of $3,000 annually. For this purpose, a public safety officer is a law enforcement officer, firefighter, chaplain, or member of a rescue squad or ambulance crew.

### If you roll over your payment to a Roth IRA

If you roll over a payment from the Plan to a Roth IRA, a special rule applies under which the amount of the payment rolled over (reduced by any after-tax amounts) will be taxed. However, the 10% additional income tax on early distributions will not apply (unless you take the amount rolled over out of the Roth IRA within 5 years, counting from January 1 of the year of the rollover).

If you roll over the payment to a Roth IRA, later payments from the Roth IRA that are qualified distributions will not be taxed (including earnings after the rollover). A qualified distribution from a Roth IRA is a payment made after you are age 59½ (or after your death or disability, or as a qualified first-time homebuyer distribution of up to $10,000) and after you have had a Roth IRA for at least 5 years. In applying this 5-year rule, you count from January 1 of the year for which your first contribution was made to a Roth IRA. Payments from the Roth IRA that are not qualified distributions will be taxed to the extent of earnings after the rollover, including the 10% additional income tax on early distributions (unless an exception applies). You do not have to take required minimum distributions from a Roth IRA during your lifetime. For more information, see IRS Publication 590-A, *Contributions to Individual Retirement Arrangements (IRAs)*, and IRS Publication 590-B, *Distributions from Individual Retirement Arrangements (IRAs)*.

### If you do a rollover to a designated Roth account in the Plan

You cannot roll over a distribution to a designated Roth account in another employer's plan. However, you can roll the distribution over into a designated Roth account in the distributing Plan. If you roll over a payment from the Plan to a designated Roth account in the Plan, the amount of the payment rolled over (reduced by any after-tax amounts directly rolled over) will be taxed. However, the 10% additional tax on early distributions will not apply (unless you take the amount rolled over out of the designated Roth account within the 5-year period that begins on January 1 of the year of the rollover).

If you roll over the payment to a designated Roth account in the Plan, later payments from the designated Roth account that are qualified distributions will not be taxed (including earnings after the rollover). A qualified distribution from a designated Roth account is a payment made both after you are age 59½ (or after your death or disability) and after you have had a designated Roth account in the Plan for at least 5 years. In applying this 5-year rule, you count from January 1 of the year your first contribution was made to the designated Roth account. However, if you made a direct rollover to a designated Roth account in the Plan from a designated Roth account in a plan of another employer, the 5-year period begins on January 1 of the year you made the first contribution to the designated Roth account in the Plan or, if earlier, to the designated Roth account in the plan of the other employer. Payments from the designated Roth account that are not qualified distributions will be taxed to the extent of earnings after the rollover, including the 10% additional income tax on early distributions (unless an exception applies).

### If you are not a Plan participant

*Payments after death of the participant.* If you receive a distribution after the participant's death that you do not roll over, the distribution will generally be taxed in the same manner described elsewhere in this notice. However, the 10% additional income tax on early distributions and the special rules for public safety officers do not apply, and the special rule described under the section "If you were born on or before January 1, 1936" applies only if the participant was born on or before January 1, 1936.

**If you are a surviving spouse.** If you receive a payment from the Plan as the surviving spouse of a deceased participant, you have the same rollover options that the participant would have had, as described elsewhere in this notice. In addition, if you choose to do a rollover to an IRA, you may treat the IRA as your own or as an inherited IRA.

An IRA you treat as your own is treated like any other IRA of yours, so that payments made to you before you are age 59½ will be subject to the 10% additional income tax on early distributions (unless an exception applies) and required minimum distributions from your IRA do not have to start until after you are age 70½.

If you treat the IRA as an inherited IRA, payments from the IRA will not be subject to the 10% additional income tax on early distributions. However, if the participant had started taking required minimum distributions, you will have to receive required minimum distributions from the inherited IRA. If the participant had not started taking required minimum distributions from the Plan, you will not have to start receiving required minimum distributions from the inherited IRA until the year the participant would have been age 70½.

**If you are a surviving beneficiary other than a spouse**. If you receive a payment from the Plan because of the participant's death and you are a designated beneficiary other than a surviving spouse, the only rollover option you have is to do a direct rollover to an inherited IRA. Payments from the inherited IRA will not be subject to the 10% additional income tax on

early distributions. You will have to receive required minimum distributions from the inherited IRA.

*Payments under a qualified domestic relations order.* If you are the spouse or former spouse of the participant who receives a payment from the Plan under a qualified domestic relations order (QDRO), you generally have the same options and the same tax treatment that the participant would have (for example, you may roll over the payment to your own IRA or an eligible employer plan that will accept it). However, payments under the QDRO will not be subject to the 10% additional income tax on early distributions.

### If you are a nonresident alien

If you are a nonresident alien and you do not do a direct rollover to a U.S. IRA or U.S. employer plan, instead of withholding 20%, the Plan is generally required to withhold 30% of the payment for federal income taxes. If the amount withheld exceeds the amount of tax you owe (as may happen if you do a 60-day rollover), you may request an income tax refund by filing Form 1040NR and attaching your Form 1042-S. See Form W-8BEN for claiming that you are entitled to a reduced rate of withholding under an income tax treaty. For more information, see also IRS Publication 519, *U.S. Tax Guide for Aliens*, and IRS Publication 515, *Withholding of Tax on Nonresident Aliens and Foreign Entities*.

### Other special rules

If a payment is one in a series of payments for less than 10 years, your choice whether to make a direct rollover will apply to all later payments in the series (unless you make a different choice for later payments).

If your payments for the year are less than $200 (not including payments from a designated Roth account in the Plan), the Plan is not required to allow you to do a direct rollover and is not required to withhold federal income taxes. However, you may do a 60-day rollover.

Unless you elect otherwise, a mandatory cashout of more than $1,000 (not including payments from a designated Roth account in the Plan) will be directly rolled over to an IRA chosen by the Plan administrator or the payor. A mandatory cashout is a payment from a plan to a participant made before age 62 (or normal retirement age, if later) and without consent, where the participant's benefit does not exceed $5,000 (not including any amounts held under the plan as a result of a prior rollover made to the plan).

You may have special rollover rights if you recently served in the U.S. Armed Forces. For more information on special rollover rights related to the U.S. Armed Forces, see IRS Publication 3, *Armed Forces' Tax Guide*. You also may have special rollover rights if you were affected by a federally declared disaster (or similar event), or if you received a distribution on account of a disaster. For more information on special rollover rights related to disaster relief, see the IRS website at *www.irs.gov*.

### FOR MORE INFORMATION

You may wish to consult with the Plan administrator or payor, or a professional tax advisor, before taking a payment from the Plan. Also, you can find more detailed information on the federal tax treatment of payments from employer plans in: IRS Publication 575, *Pension and Annuity Income*; IRS Publication 590-A, *Contributions to Individual Retirement Arrangements (IRAs)*; IRS Publication 590-B, *Distributions from Individual Retirement Arrangements (IRAs)*; and IRS Publication 571, *Tax-Sheltered Annuity Plans (403(b) Plans)*. These publications are available from a local IRS office, on the web at *www.irs.gov*, or by calling 1-800-TAX-FORM.

For Payments From a Designated Roth Account

### *YOUR ROLLOVER OPTIONS*

You are receiving this notice because all or a portion of a payment you are receiving from the [INSERT NAME OF PLAN] (the "Plan") is eligible to be rolled over to a Roth IRA or designated Roth account in an employer plan. This notice is intended to help you decide whether to do a rollover.

*This notice describes the rollover rules that apply to payments from the Plan that are from a designated Roth account*. If you also receive a payment from the Plan that is not from a designated Roth account, you will be provided a different notice for that payment, and the Plan administrator or payor will tell you the amount that is being paid from each account.

Rules that apply to most payments from a designated Roth account are described in the "General Information About Rollovers" section. Special rules that only apply in certain circumstances are described in the "Special Rules and Options" section.

### GENERAL INFORMATION ABOUT ROLLOVERS

#### How can a rollover affect my taxes?

After-tax contributions included in a payment from a designated Roth account are not taxed, but earnings might be taxed. The tax treatment of earnings included in the payment depends on whether the payment is a qualified distribution. If a payment is only part of your designated Roth account, the payment will include an allocable portion of the earnings in your designated Roth account.

If the payment from the Plan is not a qualified distribution and you do not do a rollover to a Roth IRA or a designated Roth account in an employer plan, you will be taxed on the earnings in the payment. If you are under age 59½, a 10% additional income tax on early distributions (generally, distributions made before age 59½) will also apply to the earnings (unless an exception applies). However, if you do a rollover, you will not have to pay taxes currently on the earnings and you will not have to pay taxes later on payments that are qualified distributions.

If the payment from the Plan is a qualified distribution, you will not be taxed on any part of the payment even if you do not do a rollover. If you do a rollover, you will not be taxed on the amount you roll over and any earnings on the amount you roll over will not be taxed if paid later in a qualified distribution.

A qualified distribution from a designated Roth account in the Plan is a payment made after you are age 59½ (or after your death or disability) and after you have had a designated Roth account in the Plan for at least 5 years. In applying the 5-year rule, you count from January 1 of the year your first contribution was made to the designated Roth account. However, if you did a direct rollover to a designated Roth account in the Plan from a designated Roth account in another employer plan, your participation will count from January 1 of the year your first contribution was made to the designated Roth account in the Plan or, if earlier, to the designated Roth account in the other employer plan.

#### What types of retirement accounts and plans may accept my rollover?

You may roll over the payment to either a Roth IRA (a Roth individual retirement account or

Roth individual retirement annuity) or a designated Roth account in an employer plan (a tax-qualified plan, section 403(b) plan, or governmental section 457 plan) that will accept the rollover. The rules of the Roth IRA or employer plan that holds the rollover will determine your investment options, fees, and rights to payment from the Roth IRA or employer plan (for example, no spousal consent rules apply to Roth IRAs and Roth IRAs may not provide loans). Further, the amount rolled over will become subject to the tax rules that apply to the Roth IRA or the designated Roth account in the employer plan. In general, these tax rules are similar to those described elsewhere in this notice, but differences include:

- If you do a rollover to a Roth IRA, all of your Roth IRAs will be considered for purposes of determining whether you have satisfied the 5-year rule (counting from January 1 of the year for which your first contribution was made to any of your Roth IRAs).

- If you do a rollover to a Roth IRA, you will not be required to take a distribution from the Roth IRA during your lifetime and you must keep track of the aggregate amount of the after-tax contributions in all of your Roth IRAs (in order to determine your taxable income for later Roth IRA payments that are not qualified distributions).

- Eligible rollover distributions from a Roth IRA can only be rolled over to another Roth IRA.

**How do I do a rollover?**

There are two ways to do a rollover. You can either do a direct rollover or a 60-day rollover.

*If you do a direct rollover*, the Plan will make the payment directly to your Roth IRA or designated Roth account in an employer plan. You should contact the Roth IRA sponsor or the administrator of the employer plan for information on how to do a direct rollover.

*If you do not do a direct rollover*, you may still do a rollover by making a deposit (generally within 60 days) into a Roth IRA, whether the payment is a qualified or nonqualified distribution. In addition, you can do a rollover by making a deposit within 60 days into a designated Roth account in an employer plan if the payment is a nonqualified distribution and the rollover does not exceed the amount of the earnings in the payment. You cannot do a 60-day rollover to an employer plan of any part of a qualified distribution. If you receive a distribution that is a non-qualified distribution and you do not roll over an amount at least equal to the earnings allocable to the distribution, you will be taxed on the amount of those earnings not rolled over, including the 10% additional income tax on early distributions if you are under age 59$\frac{1}{2}$ (unless an exception applies).

If you do a direct rollover of only a portion of the amount paid from the Plan and a portion is paid to you at the same time, the portion directly rolled over consists first of earnings.

If you do not do a direct rollover and the payment is not a qualified distribution, the Plan is required to withhold 20% of the earnings for federal income taxes (up to the amount of cash and property received other than employer stock). This means that, in order to roll over the entire payment in a 60-day rollover to a Roth IRA, you must use other funds to make up for the 20% withheld.

**How much may I roll over?**

If you wish to do a rollover, you may roll over all or part of the amount eligible for rollover. Any payment from the Plan is eligible for rollover, except:

- Certain payments spread over a period of at least 10 years or over your life or life expectancy (or the lives or joint life expectancy of you and your beneficiary);

- Required minimum distributions after age 70$\frac{1}{2}$ (or after death);

- Hardship distributions;

- ESOP dividends;

- Corrective distributions of contributions that exceed tax law limitations;

- Loans treated as deemed distributions (for example, loans in default due to missed payments before your employment ends);

- Cost of life insurance paid by the Plan;

- Payments of certain automatic enrollment contributions requested to be withdrawn within 90 days of the first contribution; and

- Amounts treated as distributed because of a prohibited allocation of S corporation stock under an ESOP (also, there will generally be adverse tax consequences if S corporation stock is held by an IRA).

The Plan administrator or the payor can tell you what portion of a payment is eligible for rollover.

**If I don't do a rollover, will I have to pay the 10% additional income tax on early distributions?**

If a payment is not a qualified distribution and you are under age 59½, you will have to pay the 10% additional income tax on early distributions with respect to the earnings allocated to the payment that you do not roll over (including amounts withheld for income tax), unless one of the exceptions listed below applies. This tax is in addition to the regular income tax on the earnings not rolled over.

The 10% additional income tax does not apply to the following payments from the Plan:

- Payments made after you separate from service if you will be at least age 55 in the year of the separation;

- Payments that start after you separate from service if paid at least annually in equal or close to equal amounts over your life or life expectancy (or the lives or joint life expectancy of you and your beneficiary);

- Payments from a governmental plan made after you separate from service if you are a qualified public safety employee and you will be at least age 50 in the year of the separation;

- Payments made due to disability;

- Payments after your death;

- Payments of ESOP dividends;

- Corrective distributions of contributions that exceed tax law limitations;

- Cost of life insurance paid by the Plan;

- Payments made directly to the government to satisfy a federal tax levy;

- Payments made under a qualified domestic relations order (QDRO);

- Payments up to the amount of your deductible medical expenses (without regard to whether you itemize deductions for the taxable year);

- Certain payments made while you are on active duty if you were a member of a reserve component called to duty after September 11, 2001 for more than 179 days;

- Payments of certain automatic enrollment contributions requested to be withdrawn within 90 days of the first contribution; and

- Payments for certain distributions relating to certain federally declared disasters.

**If I do a rollover to a Roth IRA, will the 10% additional income tax apply to early distributions from the IRA?**

If you receive a payment from a Roth IRA when you are under age 59½, you will have to pay the 10% additional income tax on early distributions on the earnings paid from the Roth IRA, unless an exception applies or the payment is a qualified distribution. In general, the exceptions to the 10% additional income tax for early distributions from a Roth IRA listed above are the same as the exceptions for early distributions from a plan. However, there are a few differences for payments from a Roth IRA, including:

- The exception for payments made after you separate from service if you will be at least age 55 in the year of the separation (or age 50 for qualified public safety employees) does not apply.

- The exception for qualified domestic relations orders (QDROs) does not apply (although a special rule applies under which, as part of a divorce or separation agreement, a tax-free transfer may be made directly to a Roth IRA of a spouse or former spouse).

- The exception for payments made at least annually in equal or close to equal amounts over a specified period applies without regard to whether you have had a separation from service.

- There are additional exceptions for (1) payments for qualified higher education expenses, (2) payments up to $10,000 used in a qualified first-time home purchase, and (3) payments for health insurance premiums after you have received unemployment compensation for 12 consecutive weeks (or would have been eligible to receive unemployment compensation but for self-employed status).

**Will I owe State income taxes?**

This notice does not describe any State or local income tax rules (including withholding rules).

**SPECIAL RULES AND OPTIONS**

**If you miss the 60-day rollover deadline**

Generally, the 60-day rollover deadline cannot be extended. However, the IRS has the limited authority to waive the deadline under certain extraordinary circumstances, such as when external events prevented you from completing the rollover by the 60-day rollover deadline. Under

**Notice 2018-74**

certain circumstances, you may claim eligibility for a waiver of the 60-day rollover deadline by making a written self-certification. Otherwise, to apply for a waiver from the IRS, you must file a private letter ruling request with the IRS. Private letter ruling requests require the payment of a nonrefundable user fee. For more information, see IRS Publication 590-A, *Contributions to Individual Retirement Arrangements (IRAs)*.

**If your payment includes employer stock that you do not roll over**

If you receive a payment that is not a qualified distribution and you do not roll it over, you can apply a special rule to payments of employer stock (or other employer securities) that are paid in a lump sum after separation from service (or after age 59½, disability, or the participant's death). Under the special rule, the net unrealized appreciation on the stock included in the earnings in the payment will not be taxed when distributed to you from the Plan and will be taxed at capital gain rates when you sell the stock. If you do a rollover to a Roth IRA for a nonqualified distribution that includes employer stock (for example, by selling the stock and rolling over the proceeds within 60 days of the distribution), you will not have any taxable income and the special rule relating to the distributed employer stock will not apply to any subsequent payments from the Roth IRA or employer plan. Net unrealized appreciation is generally the increase in the value of the employer stock after it was acquired by the Plan. The Plan administrator can tell you the amount of any net unrealized appreciation.

If you receive a payment that is a qualified distribution that includes employer stock and you do not roll it over, your basis in the stock (used to determine gain or loss when you later sell the stock) will equal the fair market value of the stock at the time of the payment from the Plan.

**If you have an outstanding loan that is being offset**

If you have an outstanding loan from the Plan, your Plan benefit may be offset by the outstanding amount of the loan, typically when your employment ends. The offset amount is treated as a distribution to you at the time of the offset. Generally, you may roll over all or any portion of the offset amount. If the distribution attributable to the offset is not a qualified distribution and you do not roll over the offset amount, you will be taxed on any earnings included in the distribution (including the 10% additional income tax on early distributions, unless an exception applies). You may roll over the earnings

included in the loan offset to a Roth IRA or designated Roth account in an employer plan (if the terms of the employer plan permit the plan to receive plan loan offset rollovers). You may also roll over the full amount of the offset to a Roth IRA.

How long you have to complete the rollover depends on what kind of plan loan offset you have. If you have a qualified plan loan offset, you will have until your tax return due date (including extensions) for the tax year during which the offset occurs to complete your rollover. A qualified plan loan offset occurs when a plan loan in good standing is offset because your employer plan terminates, or because you sever from employment. If your plan loan offset occurs for any other reason, then you have 60 days from the date the offset occurs to complete your rollover.

**If you receive a nonqualified distribution and you were born on or before January 1, 1936**

If you were born on or before January 1, 1936, and receive a lump sum distribution that is not a qualified distribution and that you do not roll over, special rules for calculating the amount of the tax on the earnings in the payment might apply to you. For more information, see IRS Publication 575, *Pension and Annuity Income*.

**If your payment is from a governmental section 457(b) plan**

If the Plan is a governmental section 457(b) plan, the same rules described elsewhere in this notice generally apply, allowing you to roll over the payment to an IRA or an employer plan that accepts rollovers. One difference is that, if you receive a payment that is not a qualified distribution and you do not roll it over, you will not have to pay the 10% additional income tax on early distributions with respect to the earnings allocated to the payment that you do not roll over, even if you are under age 59½ (unless the payment is from a separate account holding rollover contributions that were made to the Plan from a tax-qualified plan, a section 403(b) plan, or an IRA). However, if you do a rollover to an IRA or to an employer plan that is not a governmental section 457(b) plan, a later distribution that is not a qualified distribution made before age 59½ will be subject to the 10% additional income tax on earnings allocated to the payment (unless an exception applies). Other differences include that you cannot do a rollover if the payment is due to an "unforeseeable emergency" and the special rules under "If your payment includes employer stock that you do not roll over" and "If you were born on or before January 1, 1936" do not apply.

**If you receive a nonqualified distribution, are an eligible retired public safety officer, and your payment is used to pay for health coverage or qualified long-term care insurance**

If the Plan is a governmental plan, you retired as a public safety officer, and your retirement was by reason of disability or was after normal retirement age, you can exclude from your taxable income nonqualified distributions paid directly as premiums to an accident or health plan (or a qualified long-term care insurance contract) that your employer maintains for you, your spouse, or your dependents, up to a maximum of $3,000 annually. For this purpose, a public safety officer is a law enforcement officer, firefighter, chaplain, or member of a rescue squad or ambulance crew.

**If you are not a Plan participant**

*Payments after death of the participant.* If you receive a distribution after the participant's death that you do not roll over, the distribution will generally be taxed in the same manner described elsewhere in this notice. However, whether the payment is a qualified distribution generally depends on when the participant first made a contribution to the designated Roth account in the Plan. Also, the 10% additional income tax on early distributions and the special rules for public safety officers do not apply, and the special rule described under the section "If you receive a nonqualified distribution and you were born on or before January 1, 1936" applies only if the participant was born on or before January 1, 1936.

**If you are a surviving spouse.** If you receive a payment from the Plan as the surviving spouse of a deceased participant, you have the same rollover options that the participant would have had, as described elsewhere in this notice. In addition, if you choose to do a rollover to a Roth IRA, you may treat the Roth IRA as your own or as an inherited Roth IRA.

A Roth IRA you treat as your own is treated like any other Roth IRA of yours, so that you will not have to receive any required minimum distributions during your lifetime and earnings paid to you in a nonqualified distribution before you are age 59½ will be subject to the 10% additional income tax on early distributions (unless an exception applies).

If you treat the Roth IRA as an inherited Roth IRA, payments from the Roth IRA will not be subject to the 10% additional income tax on early distributions. An inherited Roth IRA is

subject to required minimum distributions. If the participant had started taking required minimum distributions from the Plan, you will have to receive required minimum distributions from the inherited Roth IRA. If the participant had not started taking required minimum distributions, you will not have to start receiving required minimum distributions from the inherited Roth IRA until the year the participant would have been age 70½.

**If you are a surviving beneficiary other than a spouse.** If you receive a payment from the Plan because of the participant's death and you are a designated beneficiary other than a surviving spouse, the only rollover option you have is to do a direct rollover to an inherited Roth IRA. Payments from the inherited Roth IRA, even if made in a nonqualified distribution, will not be subject to the 10% additional income tax on early distributions. You will have to receive required minimum distributions from the inherited Roth IRA.

*Payments under a qualified domestic relations order.* If you are the spouse or a former spouse of the participant who receives a payment from the Plan under a qualified domestic relations order (QDRO), you generally have the same options and the same tax treatment that the participant would have (for example, you may roll over the payment as described in this notice).

**If you are a nonresident alien**

If you are a nonresident alien and you do not do a direct rollover to a U.S. IRA or U.S. employer plan, instead of withholding 20%, the Plan is generally required to withhold 30% of the payment for federal income taxes. If the amount withheld exceeds the amount of tax you owe (as may happen if you do a 60-day rollover), you may request an income tax refund by filing Form 1040NR and attaching your Form 1042-S. See Form W-8BEN for claiming that you are entitled to a reduced rate of withholding under an income tax treaty. For more information, see also IRS Publication 519, *U.S. Tax Guide for Aliens*, and IRS Publication 515, *Withholding of Tax on Nonresident Aliens and Foreign Entities*.

**Other special rules**

If a payment is one in a series of payments for less than 10 years, your choice whether to make a direct rollover will apply to all later payments in the series (unless you make a different choice for later payments).

If your payments for the year (only including payments from the designated Roth account in the Plan) are less than $200, the Plan is not required to allow you to do a direct rollover and is not required to withhold federal income taxes. However, you can do a 60-day rollover.

Unless you elect otherwise, a mandatory cashout from the designated Roth account in the Plan of more than $1,000 will be directly rolled over to a Roth IRA chosen by the Plan administrator or the payor. A mandatory cashout is a payment from a plan to a participant made before age 62 (or normal retirement age, if later) and without consent, where the participant's benefit does not exceed $5,000 (not including any amounts held under the plan as a result of a prior rollover made to the plan).

You may have special rollover rights if you recently served in the U.S. Armed Forces. For more information on special rollover rights related to the U.S. Armed Forces, see IRS Publication 3, *Armed Forces' Tax Guide*. You also may have special rollover rights if you were affected by a federally declared disaster (or similar event), or if you received a distribution on account of a disaster. For more information on special rollover rights related to disaster relief, see the IRS website at *www.irs.gov*.

### FOR MORE INFORMATION

You may wish to consult with the Plan administrator or payor, or a professional tax advisor, before taking a payment from the Plan. Also, you can find more detailed information on the federal tax treatment of payments from employer plans in: IRS Publication 575, *Pension and Annuity Income*; IRS Publication 590-A, *Contributions to Individual Retirement Arrangements (IRAs)*; IRS Publication 590-B, *Distributions from Individual Retirement Arrangements (IRAs)*; and IRS Publication 571, *Tax-Sheltered Annuity Plans* (403(b) Plans). These publications are available from a local IRS office, on the web at *www.irs.gov*, or by calling 1-800-TAX-FORM.

### Appendix B

Some plan administrators that have been using the safe harbor explanations in Notice 2014-74 may wish to update those explanations by making amendments to them (rather than by simply replacing them with the revised safe harbor explanations in Appendix A). This appendix provides instructions on how to amend the safe harbor explanations in Notice 2014-74 to reflect the modifications made in the revised safe harbor explanations in Appendix A. Part 1 contains amendments to the safe harbor explanation for payments not from a designated Roth account and Part 2 contains amendments to the safe har-

bor explanation for payments from a designated Roth account.

*Part 1 – Amendments to the Safe Harbor Explanation for Payments not from a Designated Roth Account*

1. Under the heading "**How can a rollover affect my taxes?**," replace the second sentence with the following:

If you are under age 59½ and do not do a rollover, you will also have to pay a 10% additional income tax on early distributions (generally, distributions made before age 59½), unless an exception applies.

2. Replace the heading "**Where may I roll over the payment?**" with the following:

**What types of retirement accounts and plans may accept my rollover?**

3. Under the heading "**How do I do a rollover?**," replace the second sentence of the third paragraph beginning "*If you do not do a direct rollover*" with the following:

Generally, you will have 60 days after you receive the payment to make the deposit.

4. Under the heading "**How much may I roll over?**," add semicolons at the end of the first 8 bullets, and the word "and" after the semicolon in the eighth bullet.

5. Under the heading "**If I don't do a rollover, will I have to pay the 10% additional income tax on early distributions?**," replace the second sentence of the first paragraph with the following:

This tax applies to the part of the distribution that you must include in income and is in addition to the regular income tax on the payment not rolled over.

6. Under the heading "**If I don't do a rollover, will I have to pay the 10% additional income tax on early distributions?**," replace the bullet list with the following:

• Payments made after you separate from service if you will be at least age 55 in the year of the separation;

• Payments that start after you separate from service if paid at least annually in equal or close to equal amounts over your life or life expectancy (or the lives or joint life expectancy of you and your beneficiary);

• Payments from a governmental plan made after you separate from service if you are a qualified public safety employee and you will be at least age 50 in the year of the separation;

- Payments made due to disability;
- Payments after your death;
- Payments of ESOP dividends;
- Corrective distributions of contributions that exceed tax law limitations;
- Cost of life insurance paid by the Plan;
- Payments made directly to the government to satisfy a federal tax levy;
- Payments made under a qualified domestic relations order (QDRO);
- Payments up to the amount of your deductible medical expenses (without regard to whether you itemize deductions for the taxable year);
- Certain payments made while you are on active duty if you were a member of a reserve component called to duty after September 11, 2001 for more than 179 days;
- Payments of certain automatic enrollment contributions requested to be withdrawn within 90 days of the first contribution;
- Payments for certain distributions relating to certain federally declared disasters; and
- Phased retirement payments made to federal employees.

7. Under the heading "**If I do a rollover to an IRA, will the 10% additional income tax apply to early distributions from the IRA?**," replace the first sentence of the first paragraph with the following:

If you receive a payment from an IRA when you are under age 59½, you will have to pay the 10% additional income tax on early distributions on the part of the distribution that you must include in income, unless an exception applies.

8. Under the heading "**If I do a rollover to an IRA, will the 10% additional income tax apply to early distributions from the IRA?**," replace the first bullet with the following:

The exception for payments made after you separate from service if you will be at least age 55 in the year of the separation (or age 50 for qualified public safety employees) does not apply.

9. Under the heading, "**If you miss the 60-day rollover deadline**," replace the paragraph with the following:

Generally, the 60-day rollover deadline cannot be extended. However, the IRS has the limited authority to waive the deadline under certain extraordinary circumstances, such as when external events prevented you from completing the rollover by the 60-day rollover deadline. Under certain circumstances, you may claim eligibility for a waiver of the 60-day rollover deadline by making a written self-certification. Otherwise, to apply for a waiver from the IRS, you must file a private letter ruling request with the IRS. Private letter ruling requests require the payment of a nonrefundable user fee. For more information, see IRS Publication 590-A, *Contributions to Individual Retirement Arrangements (IRAs)*.

10. Under the heading, "**If you have an outstanding loan that is being offset**," replace the paragraph with the following two paragraphs:

If you have an outstanding loan from the Plan, your Plan benefit may be offset by the outstanding amount of the loan, typically when your employment ends. The offset amount is treated as a distribution to you at the time of the offset. Generally, you may roll over all or any portion of the offset amount. Any offset amount that is not rolled over will be taxed (including the 10% additional income tax on early distributions, unless an exception applies). You may roll over offset amounts to an IRA or an employer plan (if the terms of the employer plan permit the plan to receive plan loan offset rollovers).

How long you have to complete the rollover depends on what kind of plan loan offset you have. If you have a qualified plan loan offset, you will have until your tax return due date (including extensions) for the tax year during which the offset occurs to complete your rollover. A qualified plan loan offset occurs when a plan loan in good standing is offset because your employer plan terminates, or because you sever from employment. If your plan loan offset occurs for any other reason, then you have 60 days from the date the offset occurs to complete your rollover.

11. Under the heading "**If your payment is from a governmental section 457(b) plan**," replace the last sentence with the following:

Other differences include that you cannot do a rollover if the payment is due to an "unforeseeable emergency" and the special rules under "If your payment includes employer stock that you do not roll over" and "If you were born on or before January 1, 1936" do not apply.

12. Replace the heading "**If you are an eligible retired public safety officer and your pension payment is used to pay for health coverage or qualified long-term care insurance**" with the following:

**If you are an eligible retired public safety officer and your payment is used to pay for health coverage or qualified long-term care insurance**

13. Under the heading "**If you are an eligible retired public safety officer and your payment is used to pay for health coverage or qualified long-term care insurance**," replace the first sentence with the following:

If the Plan is a governmental plan, you retired as a public safety officer, and your retirement was by reason of disability or was after normal retirement age, you can exclude from your taxable income Plan payments paid directly as premiums to an accident or health plan (or a qualified long-term care insurance contract) that your employer maintains for you, your spouse, or your dependents, up to a maximum of $3,000 annually.

14. Replace the heading "**If you are not a plan participant**" with the following:

**If you are not a Plan participant**

15. Replace the paragraph under the heading "*Payments under a qualified domestic relations order*" with the following:

If you are the spouse or former spouse of the participant who receives a payment from the Plan under a qualified domestic relations order (QDRO), you generally have the same options and the same tax treatment that the participant would have (for example, you may roll over the payment to your own IRA or an eligible employer plan that will accept it). However, payments under the QDRO will not be subject to the 10% additional income tax on early distributions.

16. Under the heading "**Other special rules**," replace the first sentence of the second paragraph with the following:

If your payments for the year are less than $200 (not including payments from a designated Roth account in the Plan), the Plan is not required to allow you to do a direct rollover

and is not required to withhold federal income taxes.

17. Under the heading "**Other special rules**," replace the fourth paragraph with the following:

You may have special rollover rights if you recently served in the U.S. Armed Forces. For more information on special rollover rights related to the U.S. Armed Forces, see IRS Publication 3, *Armed Forces' Tax Guide*. You also may have special rollover rights if you were affected by a federally declared disaster (or similar event), or if you received a distribution on account of a disaster. For more information on special rollover rights related to disaster relief, see the IRS website at *www.irs.gov*.

*Part 2 – Amendments to the Safe Harbor Explanation for Payments from a Designated Roth Account*

1. Under the heading "**How can a rollover affect my taxes?**," replace the second sentence of the second paragraph with the following:

If you are under age 59½, a 10% additional income tax on early distributions (generally, distributions made before age 59½) will also apply to the earnings (unless an exception applies).

2. Replace the heading "**Where may I roll over the payment?**" with the following:

**What types of retirement accounts and plans may accept my rollover?**

3. Under the heading "**What types of retirement accounts and plans may accept my rollover?**," replace the second parenthetical in the first sentence with the following:

(a tax-qualified plan, section 403(b) plan, or governmental section 457 plan)

4. Under the heading "**How do I do a rollover?**," replace the first sentence of the third paragraph beginning "*If you do not do a direct rollover*" with the following:

*If you do not do a direct rollover*, you may still do a rollover by making a deposit (generally within 60 days) into a Roth IRA, whether the payment is a qualified or nonqualified distribution.

5. Under the heading "**How much may I roll over?**," add semicolons at the end of the first eight bullets, and the word "and" after the semicolon in the eighth bullet.

6. Under the heading "**If I don't do a rollover, will I have to pay the 10% addi-**

tional income tax on early distributions?," replace the bullet list with the following:

- Payments made after you separate from service if you will be at least age 55 in the year of the separation;

- Payments that start after you separate from service if paid at least annually in equal or close to equal amounts over your life or life expectancy (or the lives or joint life expectancy of you and your beneficiary);

- Payments from a governmental plan made after you separate from service if you are a qualified public safety employee and you will be at least age 50 in the year of the separation;

- Payments made due to disability;

- Payments after your death;

- Payments of ESOP dividends;

- Corrective distributions of contributions that exceed tax law limitations;

- Cost of life insurance paid by the Plan;

- Payments made directly to the government to satisfy a federal tax levy;

- Payments made under a qualified domestic relations order (QDRO);

- Payments up to the amount of your deductible medical expenses (without regard to whether you itemize deductions for the taxable year);

- Certain payments made while you are on active duty if you were a member of a reserve component called to duty after September 11, 2001 for more than 179 days;

- Payments of certain automatic enrollment contributions requested to be withdrawn within 90 days of the first contribution; and

- Payments for certain distributions relating to certain federally declared disasters.

7. Under the heading "**If I do a rollover to a Roth IRA, will the 10% additional income tax apply to early distributions from the IRA?,**" replace the first bullet with the following:

The exception for payments made after you separate from service if you will be at least age 55 in the year of the separation (or age 50 for qualified public safety employees) does not apply.

8. Under the heading "**If you miss the 60-day rollover deadline,**" replace the paragraph with the following:

Generally, the 60-day rollover deadline cannot be extended. However, the IRS has the limited authority to waive the deadline under certain extraordinary circumstances, such as when external events prevented you from completing the rollover by the 60-day rollover deadline. Under certain circumstances, you may claim eligibility for a waiver of the 60-day rollover deadline by making a written self-certification. Otherwise, to apply for a waiver from the IRS, you must file a private letter ruling request with the IRS. Private letter rulings require the payment of a nonrefundable user fee. For more information, see IRS Publication 590-A, *Contributions to Individual Retirement Arrangements (IRAs)*.

9. Under the heading "**If you have an outstanding loan that is being offset,**" replace the paragraph with the following two paragraphs:

If you have an outstanding loan from the Plan, your Plan benefit may be offset by the outstanding amount of the loan, typically when your employment ends. The offset amount is treated as a distribution to you at the time of the offset. Generally, you may roll over all or any portion of the offset amount. If the distribution attributable to the offset is not a qualified distribution and you do not roll over the offset amount, you will be taxed on any earnings included in the distribution (including the 10% additional income tax on early distributions, unless an exception applies). You may roll over the earnings included in the loan offset to a Roth IRA or designated Roth account in an employer plan (if the terms of the employer plan permit the plan to receive plan loan offset rollovers). You may also roll over the full amount of the offset to a Roth IRA.

How long you have to complete the rollover depends on what kind of plan loan offset you have. If you have a qualified plan loan offset, you will have until your tax return due date (including extensions) for the tax year during which the offset occurs to complete your rollover. A qualified plan loan offset occurs when a plan loan in good standing is offset because your employer plan terminates, or because you sever from employment. If your plan loan offset occurs for any other reason, then you have 60 days from the date the offset occurs to complete your rollover.

10. Before the heading "**If you receive a non-qualified distribution, are an eligible retired public safety officer, and your pension payment is used to pay for health coverage or qualified long-term care insurance**," add the following new heading and paragraph:

**If your payment is from a governmental section 457(b) plan**

If the Plan is a governmental section 457(b) plan, the same rules described elsewhere in this notice generally apply, allowing you to roll over the payment to an IRA or an employer plan that accepts rollovers. One difference is that, if you receive a payment that is not a qualified distribution and you do not roll it over, you will not have to pay the 10% additional income tax on early distributions with respect to the earnings allocated to the payment that you do not roll over, even if you are under age 59½ (unless the payment is from a separate account holding rollover contributions that were made to the Plan from a tax-qualified plan, a section 403(b) plan, or an IRA). However, if you do a rollover to an IRA or to an employer plan that is not a governmental section 457(b) plan, a later distribution that is not a qualified distribution made before age 59½ will be subject to the 10% additional income tax on earnings allocated to the payment (unless an exception applies). Other differences include that you cannot do a rollover if the payment is due to an "unforeseeable emergency" and the special rules under "If your payment includes employer stock that you do not roll over" and "If you were born on or before January 1, 1936" do not apply.

11. Replace the heading "**If you receive a non-qualified distribution, are an eligible retired public safety officer, and your pension payment is used to pay for health coverage or qualified long-term care insurance**" with the following:

**If you receive a nonqualified distribution, are an eligible retired public safety officer,** and your payment is used to pay for health coverage or qualified long-term care insurance

12. Replace the heading "**If you are not a plan participant**" with the following:

**If you are not a Plan participant**

13. Replace the paragraph under the heading "*Payments under a qualified domestic relations order*" with the following:

If you are the spouse or former spouse of the participant who receives a payment from the Plan under a qualified domestic relations order (QDRO), you generally have the same options and the same tax treatment that the participant would have (for example, you may roll over the payment as described in this notice).

14. Under the heading "**Other special rules**," replace the first sentence of the second paragraph with the following:

If your payments for the year (only including payments from the designated Roth account in the Plan) are less than $200, the Plan is not required to allow you to do a direct rollover and is not required to withhold federal income taxes.

15. Under the heading "**Other special rules**," replace the fourth paragraph with the following:

You may have special rollover rights if you recently served in the U.S. Armed Forces. For more information on special rollover rights related to the U.S. Armed Forces, see IRS Publication 3, *Armed Forces' Tax Guide*. You also may have special rollover rights if you were affected by a federally declared disaster (or similar event), or if you received a distribution on account of a disaster. For more information on special rollover rights related to disaster relief, see the IRS website at *www.irs.gov*.

---

# Notice 2018-75, I.R.B. 2018-41, September 21, 2018

Guidance under Section 132(g) for the Exclusion from Income of Qualified Moving Expense Reimbursements

PURPOSE

This notice provides guidance on the application of section 132(g)(2) of the Internal Revenue Code (Code) to employer reimbursements in a taxable year beginning after December 31, 2017, for qualified moving expenses incurred in connection with a move that occurred prior to January 1, 2018. Specifically, this notice provides that the suspension of the exclusion from income provided by section 132(a)(6) under section 132(g)(2) does not apply to amounts received directly or indirectly by an individual in 2018 from an employer for expenses incurred in connection with a move occurring prior to January 1, 2018, that would have been deductible as moving expenses under section 217 of the Code if they had been paid directly by the individual prior to January 1, 2018, and that otherwise satisfy the requirements under section 132(g)(1). Such amounts will be qualified moving expense reimbursements under section 132(g)(1) that are excludable under section 132(a)(6).

BACKGROUND

Section 132(a)(6) provides that gross income does not include qualified moving expense reimbursements. Section 132(g)(1) defines a "qualified moving expense reimbursement" as any amount directly or indirectly received by an individual from an employer as payment for (or a reimbursement of) expenses which would be deductible as moving expenses under section 217 if such expenses were directly paid or incurred by the individual. The term qualified moving expense reimbursement does not include any payment for (or reimbursement of) an expense that was actually deducted by the individual in a prior taxable year. Qualified moving expense reimbursements are also excludable from wages and compensation for employment tax purposes. *See* sections 3121(a)(20), 3231(e)(5), 3306(b)(16), and 3401(a)(19).

Section 11048(a) of the Tax Cuts and Jobs Act, Pub. L. No. 115-97, 131 Stat. 2054, 2088 (2017) (the "Act"), amended section 132(g) by adding paragraph 132(g)(2). Section 132(g)(2) provides that section 132(a)(6) does not apply to taxable years beginning after December 31, 2017, and before January 1, 2026, except in the case of a member of the Armed Forces of the United States on active duty who moves pursuant to a military order and incident to a permanent change of station. Section 11048(b) of the Act provides that this amendment applies to taxable years beginning after December 31, 2017.[1]

The Internal Revenue Service (IRS) and the Department of the Treasury (Treasury Department) have received questions concerning the applicability of section 132(a)(6) to payments or reimbursements received after December 31, 2017, for expenses resulting from moves that occurred prior to January 1, 2018.[2] Specifically, the questions concern the following two situations:

(1) An employer pays a third party moving service provider after December 31, 2017, for moving services provided to an individual prior to January 1, 2018; or

(2) An employer reimburses an individual after December 31, 2017, for expenses incurred in connection with a move by the individual prior to January 1, 2018.

In inquiring whether, with respect to employment-related moves occurring in 2017, the change made by section 132(g)(2) prohibits an exclusion from income for payments for moving services made to third parties or reimbursements for moving services made to individuals on or after January 1, 2018, stakeholders noted that given the time of the year when the TCJA was passed, individuals who relocated in 2017 but who did not receive payment or reimbursement until 2018 would not have anticipated that the expected payment or reimbursement could become taxable if received in 2018 rather than 2017.

DISCUSSION

The exclusion from income provided in section 132(g)(1) applies if, among other things, the expenses being paid or reimbursed (1) would be deductible under section 217 if directly paid or incurred by the individual, and (2) the expenses were not deducted by the individual. Section 11048(b) of the Act, providing the effective date for the suspension of the exclusion from income for qualified moving expense reimbursements, does not specify whether the suspension applies to all payments or reimbursements received after December 31, 2017, irrespective of when the move occurred, or, alternatively, only to payments or reimbursements for expenses incurred for moves that occurred after December 31, 2017.

This notice provides that the suspension of the exclusion in section 132(a)(6) applies only to payments or reimbursements for expenses incurred in connection with moves that occurred after December 31, 2017. Thus, if an individual moved in 2017 and the expenses for the move would have been deductible by the individual under section 217 as in effect prior to the amendments made by the Act if they had been paid directly by the individual in 2017, and the individual did not deduct the moving expenses, then the

---

[1] Similarly, section 11049(a) of the Act enacted section 217(k), which suspended the deduction for certain moving expenses provided by section 217 of the Code for any taxable year beginning after December 31, 2017, and before January 1, 2026, except for individuals who are members of the Armed Forces of the United States on active duty and meet the requirements of section 217(g).

[2] Since individual taxpayers generally have the calendar year as their taxable year and employers report income and wages to employees on a calendar year basis, as a practical matter, section 132(g)(2) is generally effective on January 1, 2018. Accordingly, this notice generally refers to moving expenses paid or incurred in 2017 and payments or reimbursements received in 2018.

amount received (directly or indirectly) in 2018 by the individual from an employer as payment for or reimbursement of the expenses will be a qualified moving expense reimbursement under section 132(g)(1). As such, the payment or reimbursement of the expenses is excludable from income as a qualified moving expense reimbursement under section 132(a)(6), and the amount is both excludable from wages under sections 3121(a)(20), 3306(b)(16), and 3401(a)(19) and excludable from compensation under section 3231(e)(5).[3]

Employers that have included such amounts in individuals' wages or compensation for purposes of federal employment taxes and have withheld and paid federal employment taxes on these amounts may use the adjustment process under section 6413 or the refund claim process under section 6402 to correct the overpayment of federal employment taxes on these amounts (for information on these adjustment and refund claim processes see the regulations under these sections, Rev. Rul. 2009-39, 2009-52 I.R.B. 951 (2009), Publication 15 (Circular E), Employer's Tax Guide, and the Instructions for Form 941-X, Adjusted Employer's QUARTERLY Federal Tax Return or Claim for Refund).

DRAFTING INFORMATION

The principal author of this notice is Andrew K. Holubeck, Office of Associate Chief Counsel (Tax Exempt and Government Entities). However, other personnel from the Treasury Department and the IRS participated in its development. For further information regarding this notice, contact Mr. Holubeck at (202) 317-4774 (not a toll-free number).

## Notice 2018-76, I.R.B. 2018-42, October 3, 2018

Expenses for Business Meals Under § 274 of the Internal Revenue Code

PURPOSE

This notice provides transitional guidance on the deductibility of expenses for certain business meals under § 274 of the Internal Revenue Code. Section 274 was amended by the Tax Cuts and Jobs Act, Pub. L. No. 115-97, § 13304, 131 Stat. 2054, 2123 (2017) (the Act). As amended by the Act, § 274 generally disallows a deduction for expenses with respect to entertainment, amusement, or recreation. However, the Act does not specifically address the deductibility of expenses for business meals.

This notice also announces that the Department of the Treasury (Treasury Department) and the Internal Revenue Service (IRS) intend to publish proposed regulations under § 274, which will include guidance on the deductibility of expenses for certain business meals. Until the proposed regulations are effective, taxpayers may rely on the guidance in this notice for the treatment under § 274 of expenses for certain business meals.

BACKGROUND

Section 162(a) allows a deduction for ordinary and necessary expenses paid or incurred during the taxable year in carrying on any trade or business. However, § 274(a)(1), as revised by the Act, generally disallows a deduction for any item with respect to an activity that is of a type generally considered to constitute entertainment, amusement, or recreation.

Section 274(k) generally provides that no deduction is allowed for the expense of any food or beverages unless (A) such expense is not lavish or extravagant under the circumstances, and (B) the taxpayer (or an employee of the taxpayer) is present at the furnishing of such food or beverages. Section 274(n)(1) generally provides that the amount allowable as a deduction for any expense for food or beverages shall not exceed 50 percent of the amount of the expense that otherwise would be allowable.

Prior to amendment by the Act, § 274(a)(1)(A) generally prohibited a deduction with respect to an activity of a type considered to constitute entertainment, amusement, or recreation ("entertainment expenses"). However, § 274(a)(1)(A) provided exceptions to that prohibition if the taxpayer established that: (1) the item was directly related to the active conduct of the taxpayer's trade or business (the "directly related" exception), or (2) in the case of an item directly preceding or following a substantial and bona fide business discussion (including business meetings at a convention or otherwise), that the item was associated with the active conduct of the taxpayer's trade or business (the "business discussion" exception).

---

[3] Some of the employer payments covered by this Notice may also be excludable from the general definition of "compensation" under section 3231(e).

Prior to amendment by the Act, §274(n)(1) generally limited the deduction of food and beverage (meal) expenses and entertainment expenses to 50 percent of the amount that otherwise would have been allowable. Thus, under prior law, taxpayers could deduct 50 percent of meal expenses and could deduct 50 percent of entertainment expenses that met the directly related or business discussion exceptions.

The Act repealed the directly related and business discussion exceptions to the general prohibition on deducting entertainment expenses in §274(a)(1)(A). Thus, entertainment expenses are no longer deductible. The Act also amended the 50 percent limitation in §274(n)(1) to remove the reference to entertainment expenses. Otherwise allowable meal expenses remain deductible, subject to the 50 percent limitation in §274(n)(1).

Section 1.274-2(b)(1)(i) of the Income Tax Regulations provides that the term "entertainment" means any activity which is of a type generally considered to constitute entertainment, amusement, or recreation, such as entertaining at night clubs, cocktail lounges, theaters, country clubs, golf and athletic clubs, sporting events, and on hunting, fishing, vacation, and similar trips, including such activity relating solely to the taxpayer or the taxpayer's family. The term "entertainment" may include an activity, the cost of which is claimed as a business expense by the taxpayer, which satisfies the personal, living, or family needs of any individual, such as providing food and beverages, a hotel suite, or an automobile to a business customer or the customer's family. The term "entertainment" does not include activities which, although satisfying personal, living, or family needs of an individual, are clearly not regarded as constituting entertainment, such as (a) supper money provided by an employer to an employee working overtime, (b) a hotel room maintained by an employer for lodging of employees while in business travel status, or (c) an automobile used in the active conduct of trade or business even though also used for routine personal purposes such as commuting to and from work. On the other hand, the providing of a hotel room or an automobile by an employer to an employee who is on vacation would constitute entertainment of the employee.

Section 1.274-2(b)(1)(ii) provides that an objective test shall be used to determine whether an activity is of a type generally considered to constitute entertainment. Thus, if an activity is generally considered to be entertainment, it will constitute entertainment for purposes of §274(a)

and §1.274-2 regardless of whether the expenditure for the activity can also be described otherwise, and even though the expenditure relates to the taxpayer alone. This objective test precludes arguments such as that "entertainment" means only entertainment of others or that an expenditure for entertainment should be characterized as an expenditure for advertising or public relations. However, in applying this test the taxpayer's trade or business shall be considered. Thus, although attending a theatrical performance would generally be considered entertainment, it would not be considered entertainment for a professional theater critic attending in a professional capacity. Similarly, if a manufacturer of dresses conducts a fashion show to introduce its products to a group of store buyers, the show generally would not be considered to constitute entertainment. In contrast, if an appliance distributor conducts a fashion show for its retailers, the fashion show generally would be considered to constitute entertainment.

Section 274(e) enumerates nine specific exceptions to §274(a). Expenses that are within one of the exceptions in §274(e), which may include certain meal expenses, are not disallowed under §274(a). However, those expenses may be subject to the 50 percent limit on deductibility under §274(n). The Treasury Department and the IRS intend to issue separate guidance addressing the treatment under §274(e)(1) and 274(n) of expenses for food and beverages furnished primarily to employees on the employer's business premises.

INTERIM GUIDANCE FOR BUSINESS MEALS

The Act did not change the definition of entertainment under §274(a)(1); therefore, the regulations under §274(a)(1) that define entertainment continue to apply. The Act did not address the circumstances in which the provision of food and beverages might constitute entertainment. However, the legislative history of the Act clarifies that taxpayers generally may continue to deduct 50 percent of the food and beverage expenses associated with operating their trade or business. See H.R. Rep. No. 115-466, at 407 (2017) (Conf. Rep.).

The Treasury Department and the IRS intend to publish proposed regulations under §274 clarifying when business meal expenses are nondeductible entertainment expenses and when they are 50 percent deductible expenses. Until the proposed regulations are effective, taxpayers may rely on the guidance in this notice for the treatment under §274 of expenses for certain business meals.

Under this notice, taxpayers may deduct 50 percent of an otherwise allowable business meal expense if:

1. The expense is an ordinary and necessary expense under § 162(a) paid or incurred during the taxable year in carrying on any trade or business;

2. The expense is not lavish or extravagant under the circumstances;

3. The taxpayer, or an employee of the taxpayer, is present at the furnishing of the food or beverages;

4. The food and beverages are provided to a current or potential business customer, client, consultant, or similar business contact; and

5. In the case of food and beverages provided during or at an entertainment activity, the food and beverages are purchased separately from the entertainment, or the cost of the food and beverages is stated separately from the cost of the entertainment on one or more bills, invoices, or receipts. The entertainment disallowance rule may not be circumvented through inflating the amount charged for food and beverages.

## EXAMPLES

For each example, assume that the food and beverage expenses are ordinary and necessary expenses under § 162(a) paid or incurred during the taxable year in carrying on a trade or business and are not lavish or extravagant under the circumstances. Also assume that the taxpayer and the business contact are not engaged in a trade or business that has any relation to the entertainment activity.

*Example 1.* (i) Taxpayer A invites B, a business contact, to a baseball game. A purchases tickets for A and B to attend the game. While at the game, A buys hot dogs and drinks for A and B.

(ii) The baseball game is entertainment as defined in § 1.274-2(b)(1)(i) and, thus, the cost of the game tickets is an entertainment expense and is not deductible by A. The cost of the hot dogs and drinks, which are purchased separately from the game tickets, is not an entertainment expense and is not subject to the § 274(a)(1) disallowance. Therefore, A may deduct 50 percent of the expenses associated with the hot dogs and drinks purchased at the game.

*Example 2.* (i) Taxpayer C invites D, a business contact, to a basketball game. C purchases tickets for C and D to attend the game in a suite, where they have access to food and beverages. The cost of the basketball game tickets, as stated on the invoice, includes the food and beverages.

(ii) The basketball game is entertainment as defined in § 1.274-2(b)(1)(i) and, thus, the cost of the game tickets is an entertainment expense and is not deductible by C. The cost of the food and beverages, which are not purchased separately from the game tickets, is not stated separately on the invoice. Thus, the cost of the food and beverages also is an entertainment expense that is subject to the § 274(a)(1) disallowance. Therefore, C may not deduct any of the expenses associated with the basketball game.

*Example 3.* (i) Assume the same facts as in *Example 2*, except that the invoice for the basketball game tickets separately states the cost of the food and beverages.

(ii) As in *Example 2*, the basketball game is entertainment as defined in § 1.274-2(b)(1)(i) and, thus, the cost of the game tickets, other than the cost of the food and beverages, is an entertainment expense and is not deductible by C. However, the cost of the food and beverages, which is stated separately on the invoice for the game tickets, is not an entertainment expense and is not subject to the § 274(a)(1) disallowance. Therefore, C may deduct 50 percent of the expenses associated with the food and beverages provided at the game.

## REQUEST FOR COMMENTS

The Treasury Department and the IRS request comments for future guidance to further clarify the treatment of business meal expenses and entertainment expenses under § 274. In particular, comments are requested concerning the following issues: (1) whether and what further guidance is needed to clarify the treatment of (a) entertainment expenses under § 274(a)(1)(A) and (b) business meal expenses; (2) whether the definition of entertainment in § 1.274-2(b)(1)(i) should be retained and, if so, whether and how it should be revised; (3) whether the objective test in § 1.274-2(b)(1)(ii) should be retained and, if so, whether and how it should be revised; and (4) whether and what additional examples should be addressed in guidance.

## WHERE TO SEND COMMENTS

Comments must be submitted by December 2, 2018. Comments, identified by Notice 2018-76, may be sent by one of the following methods to the applicable address listed below:

- By Mail:

Internal Revenue Service

Attn: CC:PA:LPD:PR (Notice 2018-76)

Room 5203

P.O. Box 7604

Ben Franklin Station

Washington, DC 20044

- By Hand or Courier Delivery: Submissions may be hand-delivered Monday through Friday between the hours of 8 a.m. and 4 p.m. to:

Courier's Desk

Internal Revenue Service

Attn: CC:PA:LPD:PR (Notice 2018-76)

1111 Constitution Avenue, NW

Washington, DC 20224

- Electronically: Submissions may be made electronically to *Notice.Comments@irscounsel.treas.gov*, with "Notice 2018-76" in the subject line.

All submissions will be available for public inspection and copying in room 1621, 1111 Constitution Avenue, NW, Washington, DC, from 9 a.m. to 4 p.m.

DRAFTING INFORMATION

The principal author of this notice is Patrick M. Clinton of the Office of Associate Chief Counsel (Income Tax & Accounting). For further information regarding this notice, contact Patrick M. Clinton at (202) 317-7005 (not a toll-free call).

---

# Notice 2018-78, I.R.B. 2018-42, October 1, 2018

Additional Guidance Under Section 965

## SECTION 1. OVERVIEW

On August 9, 2018, the Department of the Treasury ("Treasury Department") and the Internal Revenue Service ("IRS") published in the Federal Register (83 FR 39514) a notice of proposed rulemaking (REG-104226-18), which contained proposed §§ 1.962-1 and 1.962-2, 1.965-1 through 1.965-9, and 1.986(c)-1 (the "proposed regulations"). The proposed regulations relate to section 965 of the Internal Revenue Code.

## SECTION 2. BASIS ELECTION UNDER PROPOSED § 1.965-2(f)(2)

Proposed § 1.965-2(f)(2) allows a section 958(a) U.S. shareholder (as defined in proposed § 1.965-1(f)(33)) to elect to make certain basis adjustments with respect to each deferred foreign income corporation (as defined in proposed § 1.965-1(f)(17)) and each E&P deficit foreign corporation (as defined in proposed § 1.965-1(f)(22)) (such election, the "basis election"). Proposed § 1.965-2(f)(2)(iii)(B)(1)(i) provides the general rule that the basis election must be made no later than the due date (taking into account extensions, if any) for the section 958(a) U.S. shareholder's return for the first taxable year that includes the last day of the last taxable year of a deferred foreign income corporation or E&P deficit foreign corporation of the section 958(a) U.S. shareholder that begins before January 1, 2018. If the due date referred to in proposed § 1.965-2(f)(2)(iii)(B)(1)(i) occurred before September 10, 2018, proposed § 1.965-2(f)(2)(iii)(B)(1)(ii) (the "transition rule") provides that the basis election must be made by October 9, 2018.

The Treasury Department and the IRS have determined that requiring taxpayers to make a binding basis election before the proposed regulations are finalized would be too onerous for taxpayers. Accordingly, the Treasury Department and the IRS intend that when final regulations under section 965 are published in the Federal Register (the "final regulations"), the final regulations will provide that the transition rule will apply with respect to returns due (determined with regard to any extension) before the date that is 90 days after the date that the final regulations are published and that in such cases the basis election must be made no later than 90 days after the publication of the final regulations in the Federal Register. In addition, the final regulations will provide that if a basis election was made on or before the date the final regulations are published, the basis election may be revoked no later than 90 days after the publication of the final regulations in the Federal Register. Relevant tax returns must be filed consistently with an election that has been made and not revoked.

## SECTION 3. APPLICATION OF PROPOSED § 1.965-3(b) TO CONSOLIDATED GROUPS

Proposed § 1.965-3(b) provides rules allowing a section 958(a) U.S. shareholder to disregard certain assets for purposes of determining its aggregate foreign cash position (as defined in proposed § 1.965-1(f)(8)). Proposed § 1.965-8(e) provides that all members of a consolidated group that are section 958(a) U.S. shareholders of a specified foreign corporation (as defined in proposed § 1.965-1(f)(45)) are treated as a single section 958(a) U.S. shareholder for certain enumerated purposes that do not include proposed

§1.965-3(b). To prevent the overstatement of the aggregate foreign cash position, the final regulations will provide that all members of a consolidated group that are section 958(a) U.S. shareholders of a specified foreign corporation are also treated as a single section 958(a) U.S. shareholder for purposes of proposed §1.965-3(b).

## SECTION 4. RELIEF IN CONNECTION WITH HURRICANE FLORENCE

On September 15, 2018, and September 24, 2018, in response to Hurricane Florence, the IRS announced (IR-2018-187, NC-2018-03, SC-2018-01) that certain individual and business taxpayers would have until January 31, 2019, to file certain tax returns and make certain tax payments. Questions have arisen as to whether that announcement applies to elections with respect to section 965 and transfer agreements required to be filed under the proposed regulations. This notice provides a postponement for affected taxpayers to make elections with respect to section 965 and file transfer agreements required to be filed under the proposed regulations. Affected taxpayers for whom elections with respect to section 965 or transfer agreements are due on or after September 7, 2018, and before January 31, 2019, are granted additional time to file such elections or transfer agreements until January 31, 2019.

An affected taxpayer is any taxpayer whose principal residence or principal place of business was located in a Hurricane Florence covered disaster area, as defined in §301.7508A-1(d)(2), or whose records necessary to meet its obligation were maintained in such a covered disaster area, or in the case of a transfer agreement, a taxpayer who intends to enter into a transfer agreement with such a taxpayer.

Taxpayers who believe they are entitled to this relief should mark "Hurricane Florence" on the top of the relevant section 965 election statement or transfer agreement, and, in the case of a transfer agreement, a notation of which party to the agreement is an affected taxpayer whose principal residence or principal place of business was located in a Hurricane Florence covered disaster area, as defined in §301.7508A-1(d)(2), or whose records necessary to meet its filing obligation were maintained in such a covered disaster area.

## SECTION 5. SUBMISSION OF COMMENTS

The Treasury Department and the IRS requested comments in the proposed regulations on all aspects of the proposed regulations, with a deadline of October 9, 2018, for comments to be submitted. The Treasury Department and the IRS are still considering all of the comments that have been submitted as of the date of this notice with respect to the proposed regulations in the course of developing final regulations under section 965. The Treasury Department and the IRS continue to welcome the submission of additional comments with respect to the proposed regulations by the October 9, 2018, deadline. This notice is being issued in advance of final regulations under section 965 due to the imminent filing deadlines that could otherwise apply to the forms and elections described herein.

## SECTION 6. DRAFTING INFORMATION

The principal author of this notice is Leni Perkins of the Office of Associate Chief Counsel (International). However, other personnel from the Treasury Department and the IRS participated in its development. For further information regarding this notice, contact Ms. Perkins at (202) 317-6934 (not a toll free call).

---

# Notice 2018-80, I.R.B. 2018-42, September 27, 2018

Guidance Under Section 451(b) Relating to Market Discount

## SECTION 1. PURPOSE

This notice announces that the Department of the Treasury (Treasury Department) and the Internal Revenue Service (IRS) intend to issue proposed regulations under section 451(b) of the Internal Revenue Code that will address the applicability of section 451(b) to market discount as defined in section 1278(a)(2). Section 451(b) was added on December 22, 2017, by section 13221 of An Act to provide for reconciliation pursuant to titles II and V of the concurrent resolution on the

budget for fiscal year 2018, Pub. L. No. 115-97, 131 Stat. 2054, 2116 (2017).

## SECTION 2. TREATMENT OF MARKET DISCOUNT UNDER SECTION 451(b)

For an accrual method taxpayer, income is includible in gross income when all the events have occurred which fix the right to receive such income and the amount thereof can be determined with reasonable accuracy (all events test). See §451(b)(1)(C); §1.451-1(a) of the Income Tax Regulations. Section 451(b)(1)(A) provides that the all events test is met with respect to an item of gross income no later than when the taxpayer takes that item of gross income into account as revenue for financial accounting purposes in an "applicable financial statement" as defined in section 451(b)(3). Section 451(b)(2) provides that the general rule in section 451(b)(1) does not apply to any item of gross income for which the taxpayer uses a special method of accounting, other than items accounted for under a provision of part V of subchapter P, which contains sections 1271 through 1288.

Section 1276(a)(1) treats gain (if any) on the disposition of a market discount bond as ordinary income to the extent that the gain does not exceed the accrued market discount on the bond. Section 1276(a)(3) provides that any partial principal payment on a market discount bond is includible in gross income to the extent the payment does not exceed accrued market discount on the bond.

Taxpayers have requested guidance as to whether market discount is includible in income under section 451(b). The Treasury Department and the IRS intend to issue proposed regulations providing that accrued market discount is not includible in income under section 451(b). The guidance described in this notice will be applicable as of January 1, 2018.

## SECTION 3. DRAFTING AND GENERAL CONTACT INFORMATION

The principal author of this notice is Alexa T. Dubert of the Office of the Associate Chief Counsel (Financial Institutions and Products). Other personnel from the Treasury Department and the IRS participated in its development. For further information regarding this notice, contact Charles W. Culmer of the Office of the Associate Chief Counsel (Financial Institutions and Products) at (202) 317-4528 (not a toll-free number).

---

# Notice 2018-84, I.R.B. 2018-45, October 18, 2018

## PURPOSE

Section 11041 of the Tax Cuts and Jobs Act, Pub. L. No. 115-97, 131 Stat. 2054, 2082 (the Act), added § 151(d)(5) to the Internal Revenue Code (Code). Section 151(d)(5) reduces the amount of the personal exemption deduction to zero for taxable years beginning after December 31, 2017, and before January 1, 2026. This notice provides interim guidance clarifying how the reduction of the personal exemption deduction to zero in § 151(d)(5) applies for purposes of certain rules under §§ 36B and 6011 relating to the premium tax credit and under § 5000A relating to the individual shared responsibility provision. This notice also announces that the Department of the Treasury (Treasury Department) and the Internal Revenue Service (IRS) intend to amend the regulations under §§ 36B and 6011 to clarify the application of § 151(d)(5). Until further guidance is issued, the interim guidance described in this notice applies for purposes of the regulations under §§ 36B and 5000A and for purposes of § 1.6011-8(a).

## BACKGROUND

Section 151 generally allows a taxpayer to claim a personal exemption deduction for the taxpayer, the taxpayer's spouse, and any dependents, based on the exemption amount defined in § 151(d). For tax years prior to 2018, a taxpayer claimed a personal exemption deduction for an individual by putting the individual's name and taxpayer identification number (TIN) on the taxpayer's income tax return, multiplying the number of allowed exemptions by the exemption amount, and entering that amount on the tax return.

Section 11041 of the Act added § 151(d)(5) to the Code. Section 151(d)(5)(A) provides that, for taxable years beginning after December 31, 2017, and before January 1, 2026, the term "exemption amount" means zero. Section 151(d)(5)(B) provides that the reduction of the exemption amount to zero "shall not be taken into account in determining whether a [personal exemption] deduction is allowed or allowable, or whether a taxpayer is entitled to a deduction under this section." Thus, even though the amount of the personal exemption deduction is reduced to zero, taxpayers are still allowed personal exemption deductions under § 151 for purposes of other provisions of the Code. See H.R. Rep. No. 115-466 at 203 n.16 (Conf. Rep.) (2017) ("The provision [amendments to § 151] also clarifies that, for purposes of taxable years in which the personal exemption is reduced to zero, this should not alter the operation of those provisions of the Code which refer to a taxpayer allowed a deduction (or an individual with respect to whom a taxpayer is allowed a deduction) under section 151.").

Section 36B allows a premium tax credit to eligible individuals who enroll themselves, their spouse, or any dependent (as defined in § 152) in a qualified health plan through an Exchange, and §6011 provides general rules related to income tax return filing requirements. The regulations under §§36B and 6011 include rules that apply based on whether a taxpayer claims or claimed a personal exemption deduction under §151 for an individual. These rules affect eligibility for the premium tax credit, computation of the premium tax credit, reconciliation of advance payments of the premium tax credit, and income tax return filing requirements related to the premium tax credit. Specifically, references such as "claim a personal exemption deduction," "claims a personal exemption deduction," or "claimed as a personal exemption deduction," are included in §§1.36B-1(d); 1.36B-2(c)(4); 1.36B-4(a)(1)(ii)(B)(1), (a)(1)(ii)(B)(2), (a)(1)(ii)(C), and (a)(4); and §1.6011-8(a). The Treasury Department and the IRS intend to amend the regulations under §§36B and 6011 to clarify the meaning of claiming a personal exemption deduction for the taxable years for which the exemption amount is reduced to zero.

Section 5000A provides that if a taxpayer, or dependent of the taxpayer who is an applicable individual for whom the taxpayer is liable, is without minimum essential coverage or a coverage exemption for one or more months in a taxable year, the taxpayer must include an individual shared responsibility payment when filing his or her federal income tax return. The regulations under §5000A include rules that apply based on whether a taxpayer claims or claimed a personal exemption deduction under §151 for an individual. Specifically, §1.5000A-1(d)(4) refers to a taxpayer who "claims a deduction for a personal exemption," and §1.5000A-3(e)(3)(ii)(B) refers to "an individual for whom a personal exemption deduction . . . is claimed."

Section 11081 of the Act reduced the amount of the shared responsibility payment to zero for months beginning after December 31, 2018. Accordingly, although this notice provides interim guidance related to §5000A, the Treasury Department and the IRS do not intend to propose regulations under §5000A.

## INTERIM GUIDANCE

Because the Act reduces the exemption amount to zero, taxpayers will no longer claim a personal exemption deduction on their individual income tax returns by listing an individual's name and TIN, multiplying the number of allowed exemptions by the exemption amount, and entering that amount on their tax return. Accordingly, taxpayers may have questions about what it means to claim a personal exemption deduction for purposes of the premium tax credit and the individual shared responsibility provision. Until further guidance is issued, the following rules apply for purposes of the regulations under §§36B and 5000A and for purposes of §1.6011-8(a):

(1) A taxpayer is considered to have claimed a personal exemption deduction for himself or herself for a taxable year if the taxpayer files an income tax return for the year and does not qualify as a dependent of another taxpayer under §152 for the year;

(2) A taxpayer is considered to have claimed a personal exemption deduction for an individual other than the taxpayer if the taxpayer is allowed a personal exemption deduction for the individual (taking into account §151(d)(5)(B)) and lists the individual's name and TIN on the Form 1040, U.S. Individual Income Tax Return, or Form 1040NR, U.S. Nonresident Alien Income Tax Return, the taxpayer files for the year.

## INFERENCE

No inference should be drawn from any provision of this notice concerning any other provision of the Act or any other section of the Code.

## EFFECTIVE/APPLICABILITY DATE

This notice applies to taxable years beginning in 2018.

## DRAFTING INFORMATION

The principal author of this notice is Lisa Mojiri-Azad of the Office of Chief Counsel (Income Tax and Accounting). For further information regarding this notice, contact Ms. Mojiri-Azad or Steve Toomey at 202-317-4718 (not a toll-free number)

---

# Notice 2018-97, I.R.B. 2018-52, December 7, 2018

## I. PURPOSE

This notice provides initial guidance on the application of section 83(i) of the Internal Revenue Code (Code), as enacted by section 13603 of the Tax Cuts and Jobs Act, Pub. Law 115-97, 131 Stat. 2054, 2155 (2017) (Act). Section 83 generally provides for the federal income tax treatment of property transferred in connection with the performance of services. Section 13603 of the Act amended section 83 by adding section 83(i) to allow certain employees to defer recognition of income attributable to the receipt or vesting of qualified stock.

Stakeholders have indicated that they would benefit from initial guidance on certain aspects of section 83(i), in particular on (1) the application of the requirement in section 83(i)(2)(C)(i)(II) that grants be made to not less than 80% of all employees who provide services to the corporation in the United States, (2) the application of federal income tax withholding to the deferred income related to the qualified stock, and (3) the ability of an employer to opt out of permitting employees to elect the deferred tax treatment even if the requirements under section 83(i) are otherwise met. In response, this notice addresses these three issues. The Department of the Treasury (Treasury Department) and the Internal Revenue Service (IRS) anticipate that further guidance on section 83(i) will be issued in the form of proposed regulations, which are expected to incorporate the guidance provided in this notice.

## II. BACKGROUND

Section 83(i) allows certain employees to elect to defer inclusion in income of the amount that would otherwise be included under section 83(a) upon the transfer of stock pursuant to the exercise of a stock option or the settlement of a restricted stock unit (RSU). Inclusion of that income may be deferred for up to 5 years as the result of a section 83(i) election, subject to certain limitations described in this Background section.

### A. Effect of a Section 83(i) Election

Section 83(i)(1)(A) provides that if qualified stock is transferred to a qualified employee who makes an election under section 83(i) with respect to such stock, the amount determined under section 83(a) with respect to such stock will be included in income in the taxable year determined under section 83(i)(1)(B). Accordingly, such income shall be included in the taxable year of the employee which includes the earliest of:

(i) the first date such qualified stock becomes transferable (including, solely for purposes of this clause, transferable to the employer);

(ii) the date the employee first becomes an excluded employee;

(iii) the first date on which any stock of the issuing corporation becomes readily tradable on an established securities market;

(iv) the date that is 5 years after the first date the rights of the employee in such stock are transferable or not subject to a substantial risk of forfeiture, whichever occurs earlier; or

(v) the date on which the employee revokes the election (at such time and in such manner as the Secretary of the Treasury (Secretary) provides).

### B. Definition of "Qualified Employee"

Section 83(i)(3)(A) defines a "qualified employee" as any individual who is not an "excluded employee" and who agrees to meet such requirements as are determined by the Secretary to be necessary to ensure that the withholding requirements of the corporation under chapter 24 (Collection of Income Tax at Source on Wages) with respect to the qualified stock are met.

An "excluded employee" is defined under section 83(i)(3)(B) as, with respect to any corporation, any individual:

(i) who is a 1 percent owner at any time during the calendar year or who was a 1 percent owner at any time during the 10 preceding calendar years;

(ii) who is or has been at any prior time (I) the chief executive officer (or an individual acting in such capacity) or (II) the chief financial officer (or an individual acting in such capacity);

(iii) who bears a relationship described in section 318(a)(1) to any individual described in subclause (I) or (II) of clause (ii); or

(iv) who is one of the 4 highest compensated officers of the corporation for the taxable year, or was one of the 4 highest compensated officers of such corporation for any of the 10 preceding taxable years, determined on the basis of the shareholder disclosure rules for compensation under the Securities Exchange Act of 1934 (as if such rules applied to such corporation).

### C. Definition of "Qualified Stock"

Section 83(i)(2)(A) defines "qualified stock" as any stock in a corporation that is the employer of a qualified employee, if such stock is received (i) in connection with the exercise of a stock option or in settlement of an RSU, and (ii) such stock option or RSU was granted in connection with the performance of services as an employee and during a calendar year that the employer corporation was an eligible corporation. Section 83(i)(5) provides that, for purposes of this subsection, all persons treated as a single employer under section 414(b) shall be treated as one corporation. Section 83(i)(2)(B) provides that qualified stock does not include any stock if the employee may sell the stock to, or otherwise receive cash in lieu of stock from, the corporation at the time that the employee's rights to the stock first become transferable or not subject to a substantial risk of forfeiture.

### D. Definition of "Eligible Corporation"

Section 83(i)(2)(C)(i) defines an "eligible corporation" as any corporation that, with respect to any calendar year, (i) has none of its (or any predecessor's) stock readily tradable on an established securities market during any preceding calendar year, and (ii) has a written plan under which, in such calendar year, not less than 80% of all employees who provide services to the corporation in the United States (or any possession of the United States) are granted stock options, or are granted RSUs, with the same rights and privileges to receive qualified stock. As provided in section 83(i)(2)(C)(iii), for purposes of section 83(i)(2)(C)(i)(II), the term "employee" does not include any excluded employee or any employee described in section 4980E(d)(4) (certain part-time employees).

Section 83(i)(2)(C)(ii)(I) provides that the determination of rights and privileges shall be made in a manner similar to the determination under section 423(b)(5). However, in accordance with section 83(i)(2)(C)(ii)(II), employees shall not fail to be treated as having the same rights and privileges to receive qualified stock solely because the number of shares available to all employees is not equal in amount, so long as the number of shares available to each employee is more than a de minimis amount. In addition, section 83(i)(2)(C)(ii)(III) provides that rights and privileges with respect to the exercise of an option shall not be treated as the same as rights and privileges with respect to the settlement of an RSU. Finally, in the case of any calendar year beginning before January 1, 2018, section 83(i)(2)(C)(iv) provides that neither stock options nor RSUs are required to have been granted with the same rights and privileges for the stock received to be treated as qualified stock.

### E. Manner of Making Election

Section 83(i)(4)(A) provides that an election with respect to qualified stock shall be made no later than 30 days after the first date the rights of the employee in such stock are transferable or are not subject to a substantial risk of forfeiture, whichever occurs earlier, and shall be made in a manner similar to the manner in which an elec-

tion is made under section 83(b). Section 83(i)(4)(C) provides that the term "deferral stock" is used to refer to stock with respect to which a section 83(i) election has been made.

Section 83(i)(4)(B) provides that no election may be made under section 83(i) if the qualified employee has made an election under section 83(b) with respect to such qualified stock, or if any stock of the corporation which issued the qualified stock is readily tradable on an established securities market at any time before the election is made. In addition, no election may be made under section 83(i) with respect to any qualified stock if the corporation that issued the stock purchased any of its outstanding stock in the calendar year preceding the calendar year which includes the first date the rights of the employee are transferable or are not subject to a substantial risk of forfeiture, unless (i) not less than 25% of the total dollar amount of the stock so purchased is deferral stock, and (ii) the determination of which individuals from whom deferral stock is purchased is made on a reasonable basis.

### F. Notice Requirement

Section 83(i)(6) provides that any corporation which transfers qualified stock to a qualified employee shall, at the time an amount attributable to such stock would first be includible in the gross income of such employee (or a reasonable time before), certify to the employee that such stock is qualified stock, and notify the employee that the employee may be eligible under section 83(i) to defer income on such stock. Section 83(i)(6) provides that the corporation must also notify the employee that if the employee makes such an election:

(i) the amount of income recognized at the end of the deferral period will be based on the value of the stock at the time at which the rights of the employee first become transferable or not subject to a risk of forfeiture, notwithstanding whether the value of the stock has declined during the deferral period;

(ii) the amount of such income recognized at the end of the deferral period will be subject to withholding under section 3401(i) at the rate determined under section 3402(t); and

(iii) the responsibilities of the employee, as determined by the Secretary under section 83(i)(3)(A)(ii), with respect to such withholding.

Section 6652 was amended by the Act to include a new subsection (p) which imposes a $100 penalty for each failure to provide a notice as required by section 83(i)(6) (up to a maximum of $50,000 per calendar year), unless it is shown that such failure is due to reasonable cause and not to willful neglect. The penalty applies to failures after December 31, 2017.

### G. Transition Rule

Section 13603(g) of the Act provides that until the Secretary (or the Secretary's delegate) issues regulations or other guidance for purposes of implementing the 80% requirement of section 83(i)(2)(C)(i)(II) or the notice requirements of section 83(i)(6), a corporation shall be treated as in compliance with those requirements if the corporation complies with a reasonable good faith interpretation of such requirements.

### III. GUIDANCE

### A. Application of the 80% Requirement

As described above, section 83(i)(2)(C) defines an "eligible corporation," in relevant part, as, with respect to any calendar year, any corporation that has a written plan under which, in such calendar year, not less than 80% of all employees who provide services to the corporation in the United States (or any possession of the United States) are granted stock options, or are granted RSUs, with the same rights and privileges to receive qualified stock. Stakeholders have asked whether the 80% requirement of section 83(i)(2)(C)(i)(II) with respect to a calendar year is applied on a cumulative basis that takes into account stock options or RSUs granted in prior calendar years.

The determination of whether a corporation qualifies as an eligible corporation is made "with respect to any calendar year." Furthermore, to meet the 80% requirement, the corporation must have granted "in such calendar year" stock options to 80% of its employees or RSUs to 80% of its employees. Therefore, the determination that the corporation is an eligible corporation must be made on a calendar year basis, and whether the corporation has satisfied the 80% requirement is based solely on the stock options or the RSUs granted in that calendar year to employees who provide services to the corporation in the United States (or any possession of the United States). In calculating whether the 80% requirement is satisfied, the corporation must take into account the total number of individuals em-

ployed at any time during the year in question as well as the total number of employees receiving grants during the year (in each case, without regard to excluded employees or part-time employees described in section 4980E(d)(4)), regardless of whether the employees were employed by the corporation at the beginning of the calendar year or the end of the calendar year.

The Treasury Department and the IRS have determined that interpreting the 80% requirement of section 83(i)(2)(C)(i)(II) with respect to a calendar year on a cumulative basis that takes into account stock options or RSUs granted in prior calendar years is contrary to the language of the statute and is not a reasonable good faith interpretation of the 80% requirement. Accordingly, the transition rule in section 13603(g) of the Act does not apply to such an interpretation.

### B. Employment Taxes (including Income Tax Withholding)

### 1. General

Employment taxes under Subtitle C of the Code include Federal Insurance Contributions Act (FICA) taxes, Federal Unemployment Tax Act (FUTA) tax, and federal income tax withholding. The Act made no amendments to FICA and FUTA taxation with respect to deferral stock. Thus, the FICA and FUTA taxation of deferral stock is unaffected by the Act. See H.R. Rep. No. 115-466, at 501 (2017).[1]

The Act did amend the income tax withholding provisions in the Code with respect to deferral stock. Specifically, section 13603(b) of the Act amended the income tax withholding provisions, as described below, to conform the income tax withholding provisions in section 3401 and section 3402 to the income taxation of deferral stock. The remainder of the discussion of employment taxes concerns only federal income tax withholding.

Section 3402(a) provides that, except as otherwise provided in section 3402, every employer making payment of wages shall deduct and withhold upon such wages a tax determined in accordance with tables or computational procedures prescribed by the Secretary. The term "wages" is defined in section 3401(a) for income tax withholding purposes as including all remuneration for services performed by an employee for his or her employer including the cash value of all remuneration (including benefits) paid in any medium other than cash, with certain spe-

[1] See H.R. Rep. No. 115-466, pages 496-497 for a discussion of FICA and FUTA taxation.

cific exceptions. Section 3401(i), as added by section 13603(b)(1) of the Act, provides that for purposes of section 3401(a), qualified stock (as defined in section 83(i)) with respect to which an election is made under section 83(i) is treated as wages (1) received on the earliest date described in section 83(i)(1)(B), and (2) in an amount equal to the amount included in income under section 83 for the taxable year which includes such date. Thus, under section 3401(i), the amount of the deferral stock included in gross income is treated as wages subject to federal income tax withholding on the earliest date described in section 83(i)(1)(B), which sets forth the end date of the applicable deferral period.

Section 3402(t), which was added by section 13603(b)(2) of the Act, provides that, in the case of any qualified stock with respect to which an election is made under section 83(i), (1) the rate of tax under section 3402(a) must not be less than the maximum rate in effect under section 1 (37% in 2018), and (2) such stock is treated for purposes of section 3501(b) in the same manner as a noncash fringe benefit. Section 3501(b) provides that the taxes imposed by Subtitle C with respect to noncash fringe benefits must be collected (or paid) by the employer at the time and in the manner prescribed by the Secretary by regulations. Questions and Answers 5 and 6 of §31.3501(a)-1T provide that the employer is liable for the payment of the tax with respect to a noncash fringe benefit regardless of whether the benefit is paid by another entity.

Noncash fringe benefits that fall within section 3501(b) generally are subject to the provisions of Announcement 85-113, 1985-31 I.R.B. 31, which provides guidelines for withholding, paying, and reporting employment tax on taxable noncash fringe benefits. Announcement 85-113 provides generally that taxpayers may rely on the guidelines in the announcement until the issuance of regulations that supersede the temporary and proposed regulations under section 3501(b). No regulations have been issued under section 3501(b) that supersede the announcement. Thus, Announcement 85-113 generally is applicable to current payments of noncash fringe benefits, and until further regulatory guidance is issued, it applies to deferral stock, except as limited by the specific rules of section 3401 (i) and the terms of the announcement itself, as discussed further below.

Section 2 of Announcement 85-113 sets out the general income tax and accounting rule, which

provides, in relevant part, that employers must withhold the applicable income tax on the date the benefits are paid and must deposit the withheld taxes under the regular rules for tax deposits. The employer may make a reasonable estimate of the value of the fringe benefit on the date the fringe benefit is paid for purposes of meeting the timely deposit requirements. The actual value of the fringe benefit must be determined by January 31 of the following year and reported on Form W-2, Wage and Tax Statement, and Form 941, Employer's Quarterly Federal Tax Return (or Form 944, Employer's Annual Federal Tax Return, if applicable instead of Form 941).

Announcement 85-113 states that if the employer underestimates the value of the fringe benefit and as a result deposits less than the amount required to be deposited (that is, the amount the employer would be required to deposit if the employer had correctly withheld the applicable taxes), the employer may be subject to the failure to deposit penalty under section 6656. Under Announcement 85-113, if the employer overestimates the value and deposits more than the amount required, the employer may claim a refund or elect to have the overpayment applied to the employer's next Form 941 (or other employment tax return).

Generally, under §31.6205-1(d)(2), if an employer collects less than the correct amount of income tax required to be withheld from wages during a calendar year, the employer must collect the amount of the undercollection *on or before the last day of the year* by deducting the amount from remuneration of the employee. Under §31.6205-1(d)(2),[2] if such a deduction is not made, the obligation of the employee to the employer with respect to the undercollection is a matter for settlement between the employee and the employer *within the calendar year*. However, in the case of noncash fringe benefits, Announcement 85-113 permits the employer to recover the undercollection of income tax withholding from the employee after the end of the calendar year during which the wage payment is made, as long as the recovery occurs prior to April 1 of the year following the year in which the benefits are paid. This rule in Announcement 85-113 applies to the amount included in wages under section 3401(i). Thus, with regard to any income tax withholding that the employer deposits for deferral stock included in wages under section 3401(i) that has not been collected from the employee, the employer may recover the income tax

---

[2] The reference in Announcement 85-113 is to the section of the regulations (§31.6205-1(c)(4)) setting forth the same principle in the section 6205 regulations before amendments to the regulations after 1985. See T.D. 9405, 72 FR 37376 (July 1, 2008).

from the employee prior to April 1 of the year following the year in which the inclusion in wages under section 3401(i) occurs.

Section 3401(i) provides the specific date on which deferral stock must be treated as wages for income tax withholding purposes and the special rules for timing of inclusion in income under Announcement 85-113 available with respect to certain noncash fringe benefits do not apply.[3] The withholding rates described in section 2 of Announcement 85-113 also do not apply to deferral stock because, under section 3402(t)(1), the income tax withholding rate under section 3402(a) "shall not be less than the maximum rate of tax in effect under section 1." The Treasury Department and the IRS expect that proposed regulations providing further guidance on section 83(i) will provide that the rate of withholding under section 3402(t)(1) on deferral stock is the maximum rate of tax in effect under section 1 and will provide that withholding is applied (1) without reference to any payment of regular wages, (2) without allowance for the number of allowances or other dollar amounts claimed by the employee on Form W-4, Employee's Withholding Allowance Certificate, (3) without regard to whether the employee has requested additional withholding, and (4) without regard to the withholding method used by the employer. Thus, under the anticipated proposed regulations, only one rate, the maximum rate of tax under section 1, would be used in withholding on deferral stock under section 3402(t), and employers would not be able to increase or decrease the rate at the request of the employee. Under Code section 3402(t) and this notice and unless and until superseding guidance is issued, with respect to wages resulting from deferral stock under section 3402(t), employers must withhold taxes at the maximum rate of income tax under section 1 without regard to whether the employee has requested additional withholding and without regard to any withholding allowances or dollar amounts entered on the employee's Form W-4.

In summary, deferral stock constitutes wages under section 3401(i) and is treated as received on the earliest date described in section 83(i)(1)(B) in an amount equal to the amount included in income under section 83 for the taxable year that includes such date. When the wages are treated as paid under section 3401(i), the employer must make a reasonable estimate of the value of the stock and make deposits of the amount of income tax withholding liability based on that estimate. The wages included under section 3401 (i) are subject to withholding at the maximum rate of tax in effect under section 1, and withholding is determined without regard to the employee's Form W-4. By January 31 of the following year, the employer must determine the actual value of the deferral stock on the date it is includible in the employee's income and report that amount and the withholding on Form W-2 and Form 941. With respect to income tax withholding for the deferral stock that the employer pays from its own funds, the employer may recover that income tax withholding from the employee until April 1 of the year following the calendar year in which the wages were paid.

An employer that fails to deduct and withhold federal income tax under section 3402 is liable for the payment of the tax whether or not the employer collects it from the employee, unless section 3402(d) applies.[4] Section 3402(d) provides that if the employer fails to deduct and withhold the correct amount of income tax withholding, and thereafter the income tax against which the tax under section 3402 may be credited is paid, the tax imposed under section 3402(a) shall not be collected from the employer. Section 3402(d) does not relieve the employer from liability for any penalties in respect of the failure to deduct and withhold.

## 2. Escrow Arrangement

Section 83(i)(3)(A)(ii) provides the Secretary with authority to impose any requirements as the Secretary determines to be necessary to ensure that the withholding requirements of the corporation under chapter 24 with respect to the qualified stock are met. In order to be a qualified employee, an employee making an election under section 83(i) must agree in the election to these requirements.

---

[3] Announcement 85-113 provides two rules applicable to the date of payment of some noncash fringe benefits that do not apply to deferral stock. The first rule allows payors of certain noncash fringe benefits to treat the benefits as paid on any day(s) during the year so long as they treat benefits provided in a calendar year as paid not later than December 31 of the calendar year. The second rule allows employers to treat certain benefits paid during the last two months of the year (or any shorter period) as paid during the subsequent calendar year. However, Announcement 85-113 provides that neither of these two rules applies when the fringe benefit is the transfer of personal property (either tangible or intangible) of a kind normally held for investment or the transfer of real property. Because deferral stock is personal property of a kind normally held for investment, neither of these rules may be used with respect to deferral stock.

[4] Section 3403, Section 31.3403-1.

Pursuant to the authority provided to the Secretary under section 83(i)(3)(A)(ii), in order to be a qualified employee an employee making a section 83(i) election with respect to qualified stock must agree in the election that all deferral stock will be held in an escrow arrangement, the terms of which are consistent with the following requirements:

(i) The deferral stock must be deposited into escrow before the end of the calendar year during which the section 83(i) election is made and must remain in escrow until removed in accordance with clause (ii) or the corporation has otherwise recovered from the employee an amount equal to the corresponding income tax withholding obligation under section 3401(i) for the taxable year determined in accordance with section 83(i)(1)(B).

(ii) At any time between the date of income inclusion under section 83(i)(1)(B) and March 31 of the following calendar year, the corporation may remove from escrow and retain the number of shares of deferral stock with a fair market value equal to the income tax withholding obligation that has not been recovered from the employee by other means. The fair market value of the shares must be determined pursuant to the rules in §1.409A-1(b)(5)(iv). The fair market value used for purposes of this calculation is the fair market value of the shares at the time the corporation retains shares held in escrow to satisfy the income tax withholding obligation.

(iii) Any remaining shares held in escrow after the corporation's income tax withholding obligation has been met, whether by retention of shares in accordance with clause (ii) or otherwise, must be delivered to the employee as soon as reasonably practicable thereafter.

The Treasury Department and the IRS have concluded that the escrow arrangement described above adequately ensures the statutory income tax withholding requirements of the corporation will be met and that this approach is less burdensome than alternatives that would require a cash outlay by the corporation or the employee before the due date for the relevant withholding, and thus allow less flexibility with respect to resource allocation. If the corporation and the employee do not agree to deposit the deferral stock into an escrow arrangement consistent with the terms outlined above, the employee is not a "qualified employee" within the meaning of section 83(i)(3). The Treasury Department and the IRS are aware that this has the effect of allowing a corporation to preclude its employees from making section 83(i) elections by declining to establish an escrow arrangement consistent with the terms outlined above.

Future guidance on section 83(i)(3)(A)(ii) may establish alternative or substitute mechanisms to ensure a corporation's income tax withholding requirements are satisfied. Such mechanisms may be more restrictive than the above described escrow arrangement.

## C. Designation of Stock as Not Eligible for Section 83(i) Election

As described above, section 83(i) imposes a number of requirements and limitations that must be met for a section 83(i) election to be allowed. Although the election, if allowed, may be made by an employee, the corporation is responsible for creating the conditions that would allow an employee to make the election. Stakeholders have indicated that a corporation may wish to compensate its employees with equity-based compensation for which no section 83(i) election may be made. As noted above, a corporation can preclude its employees from making section 83(i) elections by declining to establish an escrow arrangement as described in Section III.B.2 of this notice. As a result, a corporation need not be concerned that it would inadvertently create the requisite conditions for its employees to make section 83(i) elections or be required to comply with the notice requirement of section 83(i)(6). If a corporation does not intend to deposit qualified stock into an escrow arrangement (as described in Section III.B.2 of this notice) or otherwise create the conditions that would allow an employee to make the section 83(i) election, the terms of a stock option or RSU may provide that no election under section 83(i) will be available with respect to stock received upon the exercise of the stock option or settlement of the RSU. This designation would inform employees that no section 83(i) election may be made with respect to stock received upon exercise of the option or settlement of the RSU even if the stock is qualified stock.

## IV. EFFECTIVE DATE

Section 83(i) applies to stock attributable to stock options exercised, or RSUs settled, after December 31, 2017. The Treasury Department and the IRS anticipate that the guidance in this notice will be incorporated into future regulations that, with respect to issues addressed in this notice, will apply to any taxable year ending on or after December 7, 2018. Any future guidance, including regulations, addressing the issues covered by this notice, such as the establishment of more restrictive mechanisms to ensure a corporation's income tax withholding requirements are satisfied, will apply prospectively only.

## V. REQUEST FOR COMMENTS

The Treasury Department and the IRS anticipate issuing further guidance on section 83(i). Accordingly, comments are requested on additional issues under section 83(i) that future guidance should address, as well as any clarifications or further guidance that may be helpful on the issues addressed in this notice. Comments specifically are requested on additional or alternative mechanisms that could be established to ensure the collection of the required income tax withholding in accordance with section 83(i)(3)(A)(ii).

Written comments may be submitted through February 5, 2019. Comments should include a reference to Notice 2018-97. Comments may be submitted electronically via the Federal eRulemaking Portal at *www.regulations.gov* (type IRS-2018-0039 in the search field on the *regulations.gov* homepage to find this notice and submit comments). Alternatively, submissions may be sent to CC:PA:LPD:PR (Notice 2018-97), Room 5203, Internal Revenue Service, P.O. Box 7604, Ben Franklin Station, Washington, DC 20044. Submissions also may be hand delivered Monday through Friday between the hours of 8 a.m. and 4 p.m. to CC:PA:LPD:PR (Notice 2018-97), Courier's Desk, Internal Revenue Service, 1111 Constitution Avenue, NW, Washington, DC 20044. All recommendations for guidance submitted by the public in response to this notice will be available for public inspection and copying in their entirety.

## VI. DRAFTING INFORMATION

The principal author of this notice is Michael Hughes of the Office of Associate Chief Counsel (Tax Exempt and Government Entities), although other Treasury and IRS officials participated in its development. For further information on the provisions of this notice, contact Michael Hughes at (202) 317-5600 (not a toll-free number). For further information regarding issues with respect to income tax withholding, contact A.G. Kelley at (202) 317-4774 (not a toll-free number).

---

# Notice 2018-99, I.R.B. 2018-52, December 10, 2018

Parking Expenses for Qualified Transportation Fringes Under § 274(a)(4) and § 512(a)(7) of the Internal Revenue Code.

## PURPOSE

This notice provides interim guidance for taxpayers to determine the amount of parking expenses for qualified transportation fringes (QTFs) that is nondeductible under § 274(a)(4) of the Internal Revenue Code (Code) and for tax-exempt organizations to determine the corresponding increase in the amount of unrelated business taxable income (UBTI) under § 512(a)(7) attributable to the nondeductible parking expenses. Sections 274 and 512 were amended by the Tax Cuts and Jobs Act, Pub. L. No. 115-97, §§ 13304 and 13703, 131 Stat. 2054, 2123, 2169 (2017) (the Act), effective for amounts paid or incurred after December 31, 2017. As amended by the Act, § 274(a)(4) generally disallows a deduction for expenses with respect to QTFs provided by taxpayers to their employees, and § 512(a)(7) generally provides that a tax-exempt organization's UBTI is increased by the amount of the QTF expense that is nondeductible under § 274. However, the Act does not address how to determine the amount of the QTF expense that is nondeductible or treated as an increase in UBTI.

This notice also announces that the Department of the Treasury (Treasury Department) and the Internal Revenue Service (IRS) intend to publish proposed regulations under §§ 274 and 512 (and under § 6012 with regard to the exempt organization's related filing requirement). The proposed regulations will include guidance on the determination of nondeductible parking expenses and other expenses for QTFs and the calculation of increased UBTI attributable to QTFs. Until such guidance is issued, taxpayers and tax-exempt organizations that own or lease parking facilities where their employees park may use any reasonable method, as provided in section B of the Interim Guidance on QTF Parking section of this notice, to determine the amount of nondeductible expenses under § 274(a)(4) or the amount of the increase in UBTI under § 512(a)(7). Furthermore, until further guidance is issued, taxpayers may rely on the guidance in this notice to determine the amount of nondeductible parking expenses for QTFs under § 274(a)(4), and tax-exempt organizations may rely on the guidance in this notice to determine the amount of the increase in UBTI under § 512(a)(7).

**Notice 2018-99**

BACKGROUND AND ANALYSIS

Section 274(a)(4), as added by the Act, provides that no deduction is allowed under Chapter 1 of the Code for the expense of any QTF (as defined in section 132(f)) provided by taxpayers to their employees. Section 132 generally excludes from employees' gross income the value of certain fringe benefits, including QTFs under § 132(f). Although the value of a QTF is relevant in determining the exclusion under § 132(f) and whether the § 274(e)(2) exception (discussed below) applies, the deduction disallowed under § 274(a)(4) relates to the expense of providing a QTF, not its value.

QTFs are defined in § 132(f)(1) to include: (1) transportation in a commuter highway vehicle between the employee's residence and place of employment, (2) any transit pass, and (3) qualified parking.[1] Qualified parking is defined in § 132(f)(5)(C) as parking provided to an employee on or near the business premises of the employer or on or near a location from which the employee commutes to work. The term does not include any parking on or near property used by the employee for residential purposes. The term "employee" for these purposes is defined in §§ 1.132-1(b)(2)(i) and 1.132-9(b) of the Income Tax Regulations, Q/A-5, as any individual who is currently employed by the employer; the term includes common law employees and other statutory employees, such as officers of corporations. Section 1.132-9(b), Q/A-24, explains that partners, 2-percent shareholders of S Corporations, sole proprietors, and independent contractors are not employees for purposes of § 132(f).

Section 132(a)(5) generally provides that gross income does not include any fringe benefit that qualifies as a QTF. Section 132(f)(2) provides that the amount of QTFs provided by an employer to any employee that can be excluded from gross income under § 132(a)(5) cannot exceed a maximum monthly dollar amount, adjusted for inflation. The adjusted maximum monthly excludable amount for 2018 is $260.

An employer may provide QTFs as a supplement to an employee's compensation, either in kind or through a bona fide cash reimbursement arrangement. In addition, § 132(f)(4) provides that QTFs may be provided via compensation reduction agreements. See also § 1.132-9(b), Q/A-11 through 15. Section 274(a)(4) disallows a deduction for expenses incurred for QTFs regardless of whether the benefit is provided by

the employer in-kind, through a bona fide cash reimbursement arrangement, or through a compensation reduction agreement. Additional guidance regarding qualified parking and other QTFs is provided in § 1.132-9.

Section 274(e) enumerates nine specific exceptions to § 274(a), two of which are discussed in more detail below as applied to parking expenses. Deductions for expenses that are within one of the exceptions in § 274(e) are not disallowed under § 274(a).

Section 274(e)(2) provides an exception for expenses for goods, services, and facilities, to the extent that the expenses are treated by the taxpayer, with respect to the recipient of the entertainment, amusement, or recreation, as compensation to its employees under Chapter 1 and as wages to its employees under chapter 24. Although the language in § 274(e)(2) refers to a recipient of entertainment, amusement, or recreation, it applies as a specific exception to the application of § 274(a), which, as amended by the Act includes the QTF expense disallowance in § 274(a)(4). Thus, the Treasury Department and the IRS have determined that QTF expenses are included in this exception to the extent that the fair market value of the QTF exceeds the § 132(f)(2) limitation on exclusion and such excess amount is included in an employee's compensation under Chapter 1 and wages under chapter 24. See § 1.132-9(b), Q/A-8. This interpretation is consistent with Congressional intent. See H.R. Rep. No.115-409, at 266 (2017) ("As part of its broader tax reform effort, the Committee believes that certain nontaxable fringe benefits should not be deductible by employers if not includible in income of employees.").

Section 274(e)(7) provides an exception for expenses for goods, services, and facilities made available by the taxpayer to the general public. When enacting § 274(n) in 1986 (limiting the deduction for meal and entertainment expenses), Congress acknowledged that a taxpayer's customers and potential customers are members of the general public for purposes of § 274(e)(7):

The reduction rule [in § 274(n)] does not apply in the case of items, such as samples and promotional activities, that are made available to the general public. For example, if the owner of a hardware store advertises that tickets to a baseball game will be provided to the first 50 people who visit the store on a particular date, or who purchase an item from the store during

---

[1] Although § 132(f)(1)(D) lists qualified bicycle commuting reimbursements as a QTF, § 132(f)(8) suspends the reference in § 132(f)(1)(D) for taxable years beginning after

December 31, 2017, and before January 1, 2026. Thus, for 2018–2025, QTFs do not include bicycle commuting reimbursements.

a sale, then the full amount of the face value of the tickets is deductible by the owner.

H.R. Rep. No. 99-426 (1986), reprinted in 1986-3 (Vol. 2) C.B. 1, 124, and S. Rep. No. 99-313(1986), reprinted in 1986-3 (Vol. 3) C.B. 1, 72. Thus, the Treasury Department and the IRS have determined that expenses for parking made available to the general public are within this exception. The regulations under §274(e)(7) further explain the general public exception:

> Expenditures for entertainment of the general public by means of television, radio, newspapers and the like, will come within this exception, as will expenditures for distributing samples to the general public. Similarly, expenditures for maintaining private parks, golf courses and similar facilities, to the extent that they are available for public use, will come within this exception. For example, if a corporation maintains a swimming pool which it makes available for a period of time each week to children participating in a local public recreational program, the portion of the expense relating to such public use of the pool will come within this exception.

Section 1.274-2(f)(2)(viii). However, goods, services, and facilities are not made available to the general public if they are made available only to an exclusive list of guests. *See Churchill Downs, Inc. v. Commissioner*, 307 F.3d 423 (6th Cir. 2002).

Generally, §274 is not applicable to tax-exempt organizations except with regard to determining their deductions connected with unrelated trades or businesses. However, under §512(a)(7), as added by the Act, the UBTI of organizations described in §511(a)(2) ("tax-exempt organizations") is increased by any amount for which a deduction is not allowable by reason of §274 and which is paid or incurred by such organization for (1) any QTF as defined in §132(f), (2) any parking facility used in connection with qualified parking as defined in §132(f)(5)(C), or (3) any on-premises athletic facility as defined in §132(j)(4)(B).

## INTERIM GUIDANCE ON QTF PARKING ISSUES

The Treasury Department and the IRS have received questions about how to determine the amount of parking expenses that is nondeductible or treated as an increase in UBTI. This notice provides guidance to determine the nondeductible amount of parking expenses, as well as the amount treated as increasing UBTI. The method of determining the nondeductible amount depends on whether the taxpayer pays a third party to provide parking for its employees or the

taxpayer owns or leases a parking facility where its employees park.

A. *Taxpayer Pays a Third Party for Employee Parking Spots*

If a taxpayer pays a third party an amount so that its employees may park at the third party's parking lot or garage, the §274(a)(4) disallowance generally is calculated as the taxpayer's total annual cost of employee parking paid to the third party. However, if the amount the taxpayer pays to a third party for an employee's parking exceeds the §132(f)(2) monthly limitation on exclusion, which for 2018 is $260 per employee, that excess amount must be treated by the taxpayer as compensation and wages to the employee. As a result, the total of the monthly amount in excess of $260 that is treated as compensation and wages is excepted from the taxpayer's §274(a) disallowance amount by §274(e)(2).

B. *Taxpayer Owns or Leases All or a Portion of a Parking Facility*

Until further guidance is issued, if a taxpayer owns or leases all or a portion of one or more parking facilities where its employees park, the §274(a)(4) disallowance may be calculated using any reasonable method. The methodology described in Steps 1-4 of this section B is deemed to be a reasonable method. Using the value of employee parking to determine expenses allocable to employee parking in a parking facility owned or leased by the taxpayer is not a reasonable method because §274(a)(4) disallows a deduction for the expense of providing a QTF, regardless of its value. Furthermore, for taxable years beginning on or after January 1, 2019, a method that fails to allocate expenses to reserved employee spots (within the meaning of step 1 in this section B) cannot be a reasonable method; however, see the rule later in this notice providing that changes in employee reserved spot designations made by March 31, 2019, may be treated as applying retroactively for purposes of this notice.

For purposes of this notice, a "parking facility" includes indoor and outdoor garages and other structures, as well as parking lots and other areas, where employees may park on or near the business premises of the employer or on or near a location from which the employee commutes to work. The term does not include any parking on or near property used by the employee for residential purposes. If a taxpayer owns or leases more than one parking facility in a single geographic location, the taxpayer may aggregate the number of spots in those parking facilities when using the methodology in this section B. However, if a taxpayer owns or leases parking facilities in more than one geographic location, the taxpayer may not aggregate the spots in parking facilities that are in different geographic locations. See example 8 below.

For purposes of this notice, "total parking expenses" include, but are not limited to, repairs, maintenance, utility costs, insurance, property taxes, interest, snow and ice removal, leaf removal, trash removal, cleaning, landscape costs, parking lot attendant expenses, security, and rent or lease payments or a portion of a rent or lease payment (if not broken out separately). A deduction for an allowance for depreciation on a parking structure owned by a taxpayer and used for parking by the taxpayer's employees is an allowance for the exhaustion, wear and tear, and obsolescence of property, and not a parking expense for purposes of this notice. *Compare* § 274(a)(1) (disallowing deductions for any "item" with respect to entertainment activities or facilities) to § 274(a)(4) (disallowing deductions for the "expense" of any QTF). *See also W.L. Schautz v. United* States, 567 F.2d 373, 376 (Ct. Cl. 1977) (noting that § 274(a)(1) applies to deductions broadly, not to expenses), and *Gordon v. Commissioner*, 37 T.C. 986, 987 (1962) ("Any allowance for depreciation is not an 'expense paid' or 'amount paid.'"). Expenses paid for items not located on or in the parking facility, including items related to property next to the parking facility, such as landscaping or lighting, also are not included.

Step 1. Calculate the disallowance for reserved employee spots

A taxpayer that owns or leases all or a portion of one or more parking facilities must identify the number of spots in the parking facility, or the taxpayer's portion thereof, exclusively reserved for the taxpayer's employees ("reserved employee spots"). Employee spots in the parking facility, or portion thereof, may be exclusively reserved for employees by a variety of methods, including, but not limited to, specific signage (for example, "Employee Parking Only") or a separate facility or portion of a facility segregated by a barrier to entry or limited by terms of access.

The taxpayer must then determine the percentage of reserved employee spots in relation to total parking spots and multiply that percentage by the taxpayer's total parking expenses for the parking facility. The product is the amount of the deduction for total parking expenses that is disallowed under § 274(a)(4) for reserved employee spots. Until March 31, 2019, taxpayers that have

reserved employee spots as defined in this notice may change their parking arrangements (changing signage, access, etc.) to decrease or eliminate their reserved employee spots and treat those parking spots as not reserved employee spots for purposes of this notice retroactively to January 1, 2018.

Step 2. Determine the primary use of remaining spots (the "primary use test")

The taxpayer may identify the remaining parking spots in the parking facility and determine whether their primary use is to provide parking to the general public. If the primary use of the remaining parking spots in the parking facility is to provide parking to the general public, then the remaining total parking expenses for the parking facility are excepted from the § 274(a) disallowance by the general public exception under § 274(e)(7). For purposes of § 274(a)(4) and this notice, "primary use" means greater than 50 percent of actual or estimated usage of the parking spots in the parking facility. Primary use of the parking spots is tested during normal business hours on a typical business day, or in the case of an exempt organization during the normal hours of the exempt organization's activities on a typical day. Non-reserved parking spots that are available to the general public but empty during normal business hours on a typical business day, or in the case of an exempt organization, during the normal hours of the exempt organization's activities on a typical day, are treated as provided to the general public. In addition, if the actual or estimated usage of the parking spots varies significantly between days of the week or times of the year, the taxpayer may use any reasonable method to determine the average actual or estimated usage.

For purposes of § 274(a)(4) and this notice, the "general public" includes, but is not limited to, customers, clients, visitors, individuals delivering goods or services to the taxpayer, patients of a health care facility, students of an educational institution, and congregants of a religious organization. The general public does not include employees, partners or independent contractors of the taxpayer.

Step 3. Calculate the allowance for reserved nonemployee spots

If the primary use of a taxpayer's remaining parking spots is not to provide parking to the general public, the taxpayer may identify the number of spots in the parking facility, or the taxpayer's portion thereof, exclusively reserved for nonemployees ("reserved nonemployee spots"). For example, reserved nonemployee

**Notice 2018-99**

spots include spots reserved for visitors and customers, as well as spots reserved for partners, sole proprietors, and 2-percent shareholders of S Corporations.

The number of reserved nonemployee spots in the parking facility, or portion thereof, may be exclusively reserved for nonemployees by a variety of methods, including, but not limited to, specific signage (for example, "Customer Parking Only") or a separate facility or portion of a facility segregated by a barrier to entry or limited by terms of access. A taxpayer that has no reserved nonemployee spots may go to Step 4.

If the taxpayer has reserved nonemployee spots, it may determine the percentage of reserved nonemployee spots in relation to the remaining total parking spots and multiply that percentage by the taxpayer's remaining total parking expenses. The product is the amount of the deduction for remaining total parking expenses that is not disallowed under § 274(a)(4).

Step 4. Determine remaining use and allocable expenses

If the taxpayer completes Steps 1-3 in the methodology above and has any remaining parking expenses not specifically categorized as deductible or nondeductible, the taxpayer must reasonably determine the employee use of the remaining parking spots during normal business hours on a typical business day (or, in the case of an exempt organization, during the normal hours of the exempt organization's activities on a typical day) and the related expenses allocable to employee parking spots. Methods to determine employee use of the remaining parking spots may include specifically identifying the number of employee spots based on actual or estimated usage. Actual or estimated usage may be based on the number of spots, the number of employees, the hours of use, or other measures. *See* examples 7 and 8 below.

EXAMPLES

For each example, assume that the parking expenses are otherwise deductible expenses; that all or some portion of the expenses relate to a QTF under § 132(f); and that the § 132(f)(2) limitation on an employee's exclusion is $260 per month. For examples 3-10, also assume that the taxpayer or tax-exempt organization uses the methodology described in Steps 1-4 in Section B of this notice,, as applicable.

*Example 1.* Taxpayer A pays B, a third party who owns a parking garage across the street from A, $100 per month for each of A's 10 employees to park in B's garage, or $12,000 per year

(($100 × 10) × 12 = $12,000). The $100 per month paid for each employee for parking is excludible under § 132(a)(5), and none of the § 274(e) exceptions apply. Thus, the entire $12,000 is subject to the § 274(a)(4) disallowance.

*Example 2.* Assume the same facts as *Example 1*, except A pays B $300 per month for each employee, or $36,000 per year (($300 × 10) × 12 = $36,000). Of the $300 per month paid for parking for each employee, $260 is excludible under § 132(a)(5) and none of the § 274(e) exceptions apply to this amount. Thus, $31,200 (($260 × 10) × 12 = $31,200) is subject to the § 274(a)(4) disallowance.

The excess amount of $40 per employee per month is not excludible under § 132(a)(5) and is treated as compensation and wages. As a result, the § 274(e)(2) exception applies to this amount. Thus, $4,800 ($36,000 - $31,200 = $4,800) is not subject to the § 274(a)(4) disallowance and remains deductible.

*Example 3.* Taxpayer C, a big box retailer, owns a surface parking lot adjacent to its store. C incurs $10,000 of total parking expenses. C's parking lot has 500 spots that are used by its customers and employees. C usually has approximately 50 employees parking in the lot in non-reserved spots during normal business hours on a typical business day. C usually has approximately 300 non-reserved parking spots that are empty during normal business hours on a typical business day.

Step 1. Because none of C's parking spots are exclusively reserved for employees, there is no amount to be specifically allocated to reserved employee spots.

Step 2. The primary use of C's parking lot is to provide parking to the general public because 90% (450/500 = 90%) of the lot is used by the public. The 300 empty non-reserved parking spots are treated as provided to the general public. Thus, expenses allocable to these spots are excepted from the § 274(a) disallowance by § 274(e)(7). Because the primary use of the parking lot is to provide parking to the general public, none of the $10,000 is subject to the § 274(a)(4) disallowance.

*Example 4.* Taxpayer D, a manufacturer, owns a surface parking lot adjacent to its plant. D incurs $10,000 of total parking expenses. D's parking lot has 500 spots that are used by its visitors and employees. D usually has approximately 400 employees parking in the lot in non-reserved spots during normal business hours on a typical business day. Additionally, D has 25 spots reserved for nonemployee visitors.

Step 1. Because none of D's parking spots are exclusively reserved for employees, there is no amount to be specifically allocated to reserved employee spots.

Step 2. The primary use of D's parking lot is not to provide parking to the general public because 80% (400/500 = 80%) of the lot is used by its employees. Thus, expenses allocable to those spots are not excepted from the §274(a) disallowance by §274(e)(7) under the primary use test.

Step 3. Because 5% (25/500 = 5%) of D's parking lot spots are reserved nonemployee spots, up to $9,500 ($10,000 × 95% = $9,500) of D's total parking expenses are subject to the §274(a)(4) disallowance under this step.

Step 4. D must reasonably determine the employee use of the remaining parking spots during normal business hours on a typical business day and the expenses allocable to employee parking spots.

*Example 5.* Taxpayer E, a manufacturer, owns a surface parking lot adjacent to its plant. E incurs $10,000 of total parking expenses. E's parking lot has 500 spots that are used by its visitors and employees. E has 50 spots reserved for management and has approximately 400 employees parking in the lot in non-reserved spots during normal business hours on a typical business day. Additionally, E has 10 reserved nonemployee spots for visitors.

Step 1. Because E has 50 reserved spots for management, $1,000 ((50/500) × $10,000 = $1,000) is the amount of total parking expenses that is nondeductible for reserved employee spots under §274(a)(4).

Step 2. The primary use of the remainder of E's parking lot is not to provide parking to the general public because 89% (400/450 = 89%) of the remaining parking spots in the lot are used by its employees. Thus, expenses allocable to these spots are not excepted from the §274(a) disallowance by §274(e)(7) under the primary use test.

Step 3. Because 2% (10/450 = 2.22%) of E's remaining parking lot spots are reserved nonemployee spots, the $200 allocable to those spots ($10,000 × 2%)) is not subject to the §274(a)(4) disallowance and continues to be deductible.

Step 4. E must reasonably determine the employee use of the remaining parking spots during normal business hours on a typical business day and the expenses allocable to employee parking spots.

*Example 6.* Taxpayer F, a financial services institution, owns a multi-level parking garage adjacent to its office building. F incurs $10,000 of total parking expenses. F's parking garage has 1,000 spots that are used by its visitors and employees. However, one floor of the parking garage is segregated by an electronic barrier and can be entered only with an access card provided by F to its employees. The segregated floor of the parking garage contains 100 spots. The other floors of the parking garage are not used by employees for parking during normal business hours on a typical business day.

Step 1. Because F has 100 reserved spots for employees, $1,000 ((100/1,000) × $10,000 = $1,000) is the amount of total parking expenses that is nondeductible for reserved employee spots under §274(a)(4).

Step 2. The primary use of the remainder of F's parking lot is to provide parking to the general public because 100% (900/900 = 100%) of the remaining parking spots are used by the public. Thus, expenses allocable to those spots are excepted from the §274(a) disallowance by §274(e)(7) under the primary use test, and only $1,000 is subject to the §274(a)(4) disallowance.

*Example 7.* Taxpayer G, an accounting firm, leases a parking lot adjacent to its office building. G incurs $10,000 of total parking expenses related to the lease payments. G's leased parking lot has 100 spots that are used by its clients and employees. G usually has approximately 60 employees parking in the leased parking lot in non-reserved spots during normal business hours on a typical business day.

Step 1. Because none of G's leased parking spots are exclusively reserved for employees, there is no amount to be specifically allocated to reserved employee spots.

Step 2. The primary use of G's leased parking lot is not to provide parking to the general public because 60% (60/100 = 60%) of the lot is used by its employees. Thus, G may not utilize the general public exception from the §274(a) disallowance provided by §274(e)(7).

Step 3. Because none of G's parking spots are exclusively reserved for nonemployees, there is no amount to be specifically allocated to reserved nonemployee spots.

Step 4. G must reasonably determine the use of the parking spots and the related expenses allocable to employee parking. Because 60% (60/100 = 60%) of G's parking spots are used by G's employees during normal business hours on a typical business day, G reasonably determines that $6,000 ($10,000 × 60% = $6,000) of G's total parking expenses is subject to the §274(a)(4) disallowance.

*Example 8.* Taxpayer H, a large manufacturer, owns multiple parking lots and garages adjacent to its manufacturing plant, warehouse, and office building at its complex in the city of X. H owns parking lots and garages in other cities as well. For purposes of applying the methodology in this notice, H chooses to aggregate the parking spots in the lots and garages at its complex in city X. However, H may not aggregate the spots in parking lots and garages in other cities with its parking spots in city X. H incurs $50,000 of total parking expenses related to the parking lots and garages at its complex in city X. H's parking lots and garages at its complex in city X have 10,000 spots in total that are used by its visitors and employees. H has 500 spots reserved for management and has approximately 8,000 employees parking in the garages and lots in non-reserved spots during normal business hours on a typical business day at H's complex in city X.

Step 1. Because H has 500 reserved spots for management, $2,500 ((500/10,000) × $50,000 = $2,500) is the amount of total parking expenses that is nondeductible for reserved employee spots under §274(a)(4).

Step 2. The primary use of the remainder of H's parking facility is not to provide parking to general public because 84% (8,000/9,500 = 84%) of the remaining parking spots in the facility are used by its employees. Thus, expenses allocable to these spots are not excepted from the §274(a) disallowance by §274(e)(7) under the primary use test.

Step 3. Because none of H's parking spots are exclusively reserved for nonemployees, there is no amount to be specifically allocated to reserved nonemployee spots.

Step 4. H must reasonably determine the employee use of the remaining parking spots during normal business hours on a typical business day and the expenses allocable to employee parking spots at its complex in city X. Because 84% (8,000/9,500 = 84%) of the remaining parking spots in the lot are used by its employees during normal business hours on a typical business day, H reasonably determines that $39,900 (($50,000-$2,500) × 84% = $39,900) of H's total parking expenses is subject to the §274(a)(4) disallowance.

INTERIM GUIDANCE ON SECTION 512(a)(7) ISSUES

As noted above, under the Act, tax-exempt organizations that have employees are required

by §512(a)(7) to increase their UBTI by any amount for which a deduction is not allowable by reason of §274 for any QTF (as defined by §132(f)), any parking facility used in connection with qualified parking (as defined in §132(f)(5)(C)), or any on-premises athletic facility (as defined in §132(j)(4)(B)). Because §512(a)(7) increases UBTI for any QTF amount for which a deduction is disallowed by reason of §274, the rules governing tax-exempt organizations necessarily mirror the rules for taxpayers under §274. *See* H.R. Rep. No. 115-409, at 266 (2017) ("The Committee believes that aligning the tax treatment between for-profit and tax-exempt employers with respect to nontaxable transportation and gym benefits provided to employees will make the tax system simpler and fairer for all businesses."). However, §512(a)(7) does not apply to the extent the amount paid or incurred is directly connected with an unrelated trade or business that is regularly carried on by the organization. In such case, the amount of the QTF expenses directly connected with the unrelated trade or business is subject to the disallowance under §274(a)(4) and, thus, is disallowed as a deduction in calculating the UBTI attributable to such unrelated trade or business under the general rule of §512(a)(1).

Section 512(a)(7) specifically requires UBTI to be increased by any amount for which a deduction is not allowable under §274 for any parking facility used in connection with qualified parking (as defined in §132(f)(5)(C)). Although parking facilities are not separately listed in §274(a)(4), §274(a)(4) disallows a deduction for QTFs (as defined in §132(f)), and §132(f)(1)(C) provides that QTFs include qualified parking. Under §132(f)(5)(C) and §1.132-9(b), Q/A-4, qualified parking means parking provided to an employee by an employer on or near the employer's business premises or at a location from which the employee commutes to work (other than property used by the employee for residential purposes) and may be provided on property that the employer owns or leases. Thus, the expenses for a parking facility referenced in §512(a)(7) are those expenses related to the property an employer owns or leases, at or near the employer's business or at a location from which the employee commutes to work. Expenses for these parking facilities used in connection with qualified parking and as part of the provision of qualified parking are nondeductible under §274(a)(4) as expenses for QTFs and result in an increase in UBTI under §512(a)(7).

Section 512(a)(7) mentions on-premises athletic facilities. However, the Act did not include a corresponding change to §274 disallowing deductions generally for on-premises athletic facilities. Accordingly, a deduction for expenses paid or incurred for on-premises athletic facilities is not disallowed under §274 if the athletic facility is primarily for the benefit of the tax-exempt organization's employees and does not discriminate in favor of highly compensated employees. *See* §274(e)(4); §1.274-2(f)(2)(v).

The provision of QTFs that results in an increase in UBTI under §512(a)(7) is not an unrelated trade or business. See Notice 2018-67, 2018-36 I.R.B. 409, which discusses and solicits comments regarding the calculation of UBTI under §512(a)(6) for exempt organizations with more than one unrelated trade or business. Therefore, any increase in UBTI under §512(a)(7) is not subject to §512(a)(6), meaning that an exempt organization with only one unrelated trade or business and an increase in UBTI under §512(a)(7) does not become an exempt organization with more than one unrelated trade or business subject to §512(a)(6). Accordingly, for taxable years beginning after December 31, 2017, until further guidance is issued, a tax-exempt organization with only one unrelated trade or business can reduce the increase to UBTI under §512(a)(7) to the extent that the deductions directly connected with the carrying on of that unrelated trade or business exceed the gross income derived from such unrelated trade or business.

Section 512(b)(12) generally provides a specific deduction of $1,000 as a modification to the UBTI otherwise determined under §512(a), which, after the Act, includes the increase in UBTI determined under §512(a)(7). Furthermore, tax-exempt organizations are required to file a return on Form 990-T, *Exempt Organization Business Income Tax Return*, if they have gross income, included in computing UBTI, of $1,000 or more. *See* §1.6012-2(e). This threshold amount for filing Form 990-T also applies to UBTI calculated with respect to §512(a)(7). Therefore, organizations for which the sum of (1) gross income from unrelated trades or businesses and (2) the increase of UBTI under §512(a)(7) is less than $1,000 need not file a Form 990-T. Organizations for which this amount is $1,000 or more must file a Form 990-T. The Treasury Department and the IRS intend to revise the regulations under §6012 to clarify that amounts which increase UBTI under §512(a)(7) are included in applying the $1,000 threshold for filing the Form 990-T.

## EXAMPLES FOR TAX-EXEMPT ORGANIZATIONS

The principles illustrated in examples 1 through 8 above apply to tax-exempt organizations. Accordingly, the amount of the deduction disallowed under §274(a)(4) for each entity

would, in the case of a tax-exempt organization with the same relevant facts, be the increase in UBTI under §512(a)(7). These principles are further illustrated by the following examples:

*Example 9.* Tax-Exempt Organization J, a religious organization that operates a church and a school, owns a surface parking lot adjacent to its buildings. J incurs $10,000 of total parking expenses. J's parking lot has 500 spots that are used by its congregants, students, visitors, and employees, and 10 spots that are reserved for certain employees. During the normal hours of J's activities on weekdays, J usually has approximately 50 employees parking in the lot in non-reserved spots and approximately 440 non-reserved parking spots that are empty. During the normal hours of J's activities on weekends, J usually has approximately 400 congregants parking in the lot in non-reserved spots and 20 employees parking in the lot in non-reserved spots.

Step 1. Because J has 10 reserved spots for certain employees, $200 ((10/500) × $10,000 = $200) is the amount of total parking expenses that is nondeductible for reserved employee spots under §274(a)(4). Thus, under §512(a)(7), J must increase its UBTI by $200, the amount of the deduction disallowed under §274(a)(4).

Step 2. Because usage of the parking spots varies significantly between days of the week, J uses a reasonable method to determine that the primary use of the remainder of J's parking lot is to provide parking to the general public because 90% (440/490 = 90%) of the spots are used by the public during the weekdays and 95% (470/490) of the spots are used by the public on the weekends. The empty, non-reserved parking spots are treated as provided to the general public. Thus, expenses allocable to these spots are excepted from the §274(a) disallowance by §274(e)(7) under the primary use test, and only $200 of the $10,000 is subject to the §274(a)(4) disallowance. Therefore, only $200 of the expenses for the provision of the QTF will result in an increase to UBTI under §512(a)(7).

If J does not have gross income from any unrelated trades or businesses of $800 or more included in computing its UBTI (to reach the $1,000 filing threshold), J is not required to file a Form 990-T for that year.

*Example 10.* Tax-Exempt Organization K is a hospital and owns a surface parking lot adjacent to its building. K incurs $10,000 of total parking expenses. K's parking lot has 500 spots that are used by its patients, visitors, and employees. K has 50 spots reserved for management and has approximately 100 employees parking in the lot in non-reserved spots during the normal operating hours of the hospital.

Step 1. Because K has 50 reserved spots for employees, $1,000 ((50/500) × $10,000 = $1,000) is the amount of total parking expenses that is nondeductible for reserved employee spots under § 274(a)(4). Thus, under § 512(a)(7), K must increase its UBTI by $1,000, the amount of the deduction disallowed under § 274(a)(4).

Step 2. The primary use of the remainder of K's parking lot is to provide parking to the general public because 78% (350/450 = 78%) of the remaining spots in the lot are open to the public. Thus, expenses allocable to these spots are excepted from the § 274(a) disallowance by § 274(e)(7) under the primary use test, and only $1,000 is subject to the § 274(a)(4) disallowance. Therefore, only $1,000 of the expenses for the provision of the QTF will result in an increase in UBTI under § 512(a)(7).

K will need to add the $1,000 increase of UBTI under § 512(a)(7) to its gross income from unrelated trades or businesses. K is required to file a Form 990-T because the $1,000 increase to UBTI under § 512(a)(7) meets the filing threshold.

## RELIANCE

Until further guidance is issued, taxpayers may rely on the guidance provided in this notice to determine the amount of expenses for QTFs that is nondeductible under § 274(a)(4) or treated as an increase in UBTI under § 512(a)(7).

## REQUEST FOR COMMENTS

The Treasury Department and the IRS request comments for future guidance to further clarify the treatment of QTFs under §§ 274 and 512. In particular, the Treasury Department and the IRS request comments about the definitions of "primary use" and "general public" and whether primary use should be used to determine the extent to which parking is made available to the general public under § 274(e)(7). The Treasury Department and the IRS request comments on other methods for determining the use of the parking spots and the related expenses allocable to employee parking. The Treasury Department and the IRS also request comments on the applicability of § 274(e)(8) to expenses for any goods or services that constitute a QTF sold by the taxpayer to an employee in a bona fide transaction for an adequate and full consideration in money or money's worth and the circumstances under which such a transaction should be excluded from the term QTF for purposes of § 274(a)(4).

## WHERE TO SEND COMMENTS

Public comments should be submitted by February 22, 2019 and should include a reference to Notice 2018-99. Comments may be submitted electronically via the Federal eRulemaking Portal at *www.regulations.gov* (type IRS-2018-0038 in the search field on the *regulations.gov* homepage to find this notice and submit comments). Alternatively, submissions may be sent by one of the following methods:

- By Mail:

  Internal Revenue Service

  Attn: CC:PA:LPD:PR (Notice 2018-99)

  Room 5203

  P.O. Box 7604

  Ben Franklin Station

  Washington, DC 20044

- By Hand or Courier Delivery: Submissions may be hand-delivered Monday through Friday between the hours of 8 a.m. and 4 p.m. to:

  Courier's Desk

  Internal Revenue Service

  Attn: CC:PA:LPD:PR

  (Notice 2018-99)

  1111 Constitution Avenue, NW

  Washington, DC 20224

All recommendations for guidance submitted by the public in response to this notice will be available for public inspection and copying in their entirety.

## DRAFTING INFORMATION

The principal author of this notice is Patrick M. Clinton of the Office of Associate Chief Counsel (Income Tax & Accounting). However, other personnel from the Treasury Department and the IRS participated in its development. For further information about income tax issues addressed in this notice, please contact Patrick M. Clinton at (202) 317-7005; for further information about qualification as a QTF, please contact Mikhail Zhidkov at (202) 317-4774; and for further information about exempt organization issues addressed in this notice, please contact La Vonne Fischer at (202) 317-5800. These are not toll-free calls.

**Notice 2018-99**

# Notice 2019-1, I.R.B. 2019-2, December 14, 2018

Previously Taxed Earnings and Profits Accounts

## SECTION 1. OVERVIEW

This notice announces that the Department of the Treasury ("Treasury Department") and the Internal Revenue Service ("IRS") intend to issue regulations addressing certain issues arising from the enactment of the Tax Cuts and Jobs Act, Pub. L. 115-97 (2017) (the "Act"), on December 22, 2017, with respect to foreign corporations with previously taxed earnings and profits ("PTEP"). Section 2 of this notice provides background on section 959 of the Internal Revenue Code ("Code") and other relevant Code provisions. Section 3 of this notice describes proposed regulations that the Treasury Department and the IRS intend to issue concerning PTEP arising under provisions of the Act (the "forthcoming regulations"). Section 4 of this notice describes the proposed applicability date of the forthcoming regulations. Section 5 of this notice requests comments and provides contact information; as explained in that section, the Treasury Department and the IRS intend to address additional PTEP issues in separate guidance.

## SECTION 2. BACKGROUND

The term PTEP refers to earnings and profits ("E&P") of a foreign corporation attributable to amounts which are, or have been, included in the gross income of a United States shareholder (as defined under section 951(b)) ("U.S. shareholder") under section 951(a) or under section 1248(a). See sections 959(a) and (e). Under section 959(a)(1), distributions of PTEP are excluded from the U.S. shareholder's gross income, or the gross income of any other U.S. person who acquires the U.S. shareholder's interest (or a portion thereof) in the foreign corporation (such U.S. person, a "successor in interest"). Section 959(a)(2) further excludes PTEP from a U.S. shareholder's gross income if such E&P would be included in the gross income of the U.S. shareholder or successor in interest under section 951(a)(1)(B) as an amount determined under section 956. Distributions of PTEP to a U.S. shareholder or successor in interest generally are not treated as dividends except that such distributions immediately reduce the E&P of the foreign corporation. Section 959(d).

Section 959(c) ensures that distributions from a foreign corporation are first attributable to PTEP described in section 959(c)(1) ("section 959(c)(1) PTEP") and then to PTEP described in section 959(c)(2) ("section 959(c)(2) PTEP"), and finally to non-previously taxed E&P ("section 959(c)(3) E&P"). In addition, section 959(f) ensures that, in determining the amount of any inclusion under sections 951(a)(1)(B) and 956 with respect to a foreign corporation, PTEP attributable to section 951(a)(1)(A) inclusions remaining after any distributions during the year are taken into account before non-previously taxed E&P described in section 959(c)(3).

On August 29, 2006, a notice of proposed rulemaking (REG-121509-00) was published in the Federal Register (71 FR 51155) relating to the exclusion from gross income of PTEP and associated basis adjustments, corrections to which were published in the Federal Register on December 8, 2006 (71 FR 71116) (together, the "2006 proposed regulations"). The 2006 proposed regulations were intended to address some of the complexities and open issues regarding the application of sections 959 and 961 that are not specifically addressed in the current final regulations, which were originally published in 1965 and were amended in 1974, 1978, and 1983. See TD 6795 (1965-1 CB 287); TD 7334 (1975-1 CB 246); TD 7545 (1978-1 CB 245); TD 7893 (1983-1 CB 132). The 2006 proposed regulations have not been finalized. The Treasury Department and the IRS intend to withdraw the 2006 proposed regulations and to issue new proposed regulations under sections 959 and 961.

Under proposed § 1.959-3(b), shareholders must account for PTEP with respect to their stock in a foreign corporation, and foreign corporations must account for the aggregate amount of PTEP of all shareholders, as well as section 959(c)(3) E&P. Before the Act, annual accounts generally were maintained for each separate category of income described in section 904(d)(1) and segregated between section 959(c)(1) PTEP and section 959(c)(2) PTEP. See Notice 88-71, 1988-2 C.B. 374. Section 959(c)(1) PTEP consisted of E&P previously included in gross income under sections 951(a)(1)(B) and (C), and section 959(c)(2) PTEP consisted of E&P previously included in gross income under section 951(a)(1)(A) or amounts included in gross income as a dividend under section 1248. See § 1.959-3(b)(1) and (2); see also proposed § 1.959-3(e)(2). Section 959(c)(1) PTEP also included E&P that had been originally classified as section 959(c)(2) PTEP and was reclassified as section 959(c)(1) PTEP because it reduced the amount of an income inclusion under section 951(a)(1)(B) or section 951(a)(1)(C) (before its repeal) pursuant to section 959(a)(2) or section 959(a)(3) (before its repeal). *See* § 1.959-3(b).

Under the provisions of the Act, the portion of a U.S. shareholder's global intangible low-taxed income ("GILTI") included in gross income under section 951A(a) that is allocated to a controlled foreign corporation (as defined in section 957) ("CFC") under section 951A(f)(2) and proposed § 1.951A-6(b)(2) is treated as an amount included in the gross income of a U.S. shareholder under section 951(a)(1)(A) for purposes of section 959. Section 951A(f)(1). Likewise, amounts determined under section 965(a), as amended by the Act, with respect to certain foreign corporations are treated as increases to subpart F income, and a U.S. shareholder with respect to such a foreign corporation generally includes in gross income under section 951(a)(1)(A) its pro rata share of such amounts, subject to reduction under section 965(b) for certain deficits attributable to stock in another foreign corporation owned by the U.S. shareholder. Amounts of a U.S. shareholder's inclusions under section 965(a) that are reduced by deficits attributable to stock of another foreign corporation under section 965(b) are treated as amounts included in the shareholder's gross income under section 951(a) for purposes of section 959. Section 965(b)(4)(A). Additionally, section 245A(e)(2) treats certain hybrid dividends received by a CFC as subpart F income for purposes of section 951(a)(1)(A). Finally, section 964(e)(4) treats a certain portion of gain on the disposition of CFC stock as subpart F income of the selling CFC for purposes of section 951(a)(1)(A). Accordingly, after the Act, section 959(c)(2) PTEP may arise from income inclusions under section 951(a)(1)(A) (including by reason of section 245A(e)(2), 951A(f)(1), 959(e), 964(e)(4), or 965(a)) or by reason of the application of section 965(b)(4)(A).

Section 965 and proposed regulations under that section provide special foreign tax credit and deduction rules, and proposed regulations under section 986 provide special foreign currency gain or loss rules, for distributions of PTEP attributable to income inclusions arising from the application of section 965(a) and PTEP attributable to the application of section 965(b)(4)(A) (collectively, "section 965 PTEP"). *See* proposed §§ 1.965-5 and 1.986(c)-1. Section 245A(e)(3) applies the disallowance of foreign tax credits in section 245A(d) with respect to any amount included in the income of a U.S. shareholder pursuant to section 245A(e)(2).

In addition, proposed regulations under section 960 establish, for purposes of determining the amount of foreign income taxes deemed paid, a system of accounting for PTEP in annual accounts for each separate category of income as defined in proposed § 1.904-5(a)(4)(v) ("section 904 category") and further segregate each annual account among ten PTEP groups. Proposed § 1.960-3(c). The groups correspond to various types of income inclusions under section 951(a) (including amounts treated as giving rise to an income inclusion under section 951(a) for purposes of section 959) and PTEP reclassifications that can arise after the Act.

Finally, certain provisions of the Act provide for a deduction with respect to certain amounts that are included in the income of a domestic corporation and treated as section 951(a)(1)(A) inclusions for purposes of section 959. Sections 245A and 1248(j) generally allow a deduction with respect to gain on the sale of stock of a foreign corporation treated as a dividend under section 1248. In the case of gain treated as a dividend under section 964(e)(1) upon the sale or exchange by a CFC of stock of a lower tier foreign corporation and included in the CFC's subpart F income under section 964(e)(4), section 964(e)(4) generally allows a deduction under section 245A with respect to a domestic corporation's pro rata share of the subpart F income that it includes in gross income as a dividend pursuant to section 964(e)(4).

## SECTION 3. REGULATIONS TO BE ISSUED ADDRESSING PREVIOUSLY TAXED EARNINGS AND PROFITS

*.01 Annual Accounts and Groups of Previously Taxed Earnings and Profits*

The Act created the need to account for new groups of PTEP because section 959(c)(2) PTEP may arise by reason of income inclusions under section 951(a)(1)(A), 245A(e)(2), 951A(f)(1), 959(e), 964(e)(4), or 965(a) or by reason of the application of section 965(b)(4)(A), and those different groups of PTEP may be subject to different rules under sections 960, 965(g), 245A(e)(3), and 986(c). Additionally, because section 959(c)(2) PTEP may be reclassified as section 959(c)(1) PTEP as a result of sections 956 and 959(a)(2), similar groups for section 959(c)(1) PTEP must be maintained in order to properly apply sections 960, 965(g), 245A(e)(3), and 986(c) when earnings are reclassified. Groups of section 959(c)(1) PTEP must also be maintained with respect to inclusions under section 951(a)(1)(B) and section 951(a)(1)(C) (before its repeal) (in such cases, not by reason of the application of section 959(a)(2) or section 959(a)(3) (before its repeal)).

The Treasury Department and the IRS expect that the forthcoming regulations will provide that an annual account (each an "annual PTEP account") must be maintained and each annual PTEP account must be segregated into the 16 groups described below in each section 904 category (individually, a "PTEP group" and collectively, "PTEP groups"). For rules regarding the year and section 904 category to which an account corresponds, see proposed § 1.960-3(c)(1). These 16 groups include the ten groups identified in proposed § 1.960-3(c)(2), which is discussed in section 2 of this notice, and six additional groups.

1. E&P described in section 959(c)(1)(A) that were initially described in section 959(c)(2) by reason of section 965(a) ("reclassified section 965(a) PTEP");

2. E&P described in section 959(c)(1)(A) that were initially described in section 959(c)(2) by reason of section 965(b)(4)(A) ("reclassified section 965(b) PTEP");

3. E&P described in section 959(c)(1)(A) by reason of section 951(a)(1)(B) and not by reason of section 959(a)(2) ("section 951(a)(1)(B) PTEP");

4. E&P described in section 959(c)(1)(A) that were initially described in section 959(c)(2) by reason of section 951A(f)(2) ("reclassified section 951A PTEP");

5. E&P described in section 959(c)(1)(A) that were initially described in section 959(c)(2) by reason of section 245A(e)(2) ("reclassified section 245A(e)(2) PTEP");

6. E&P described in section 959(c)(1)(A) that were initially described in section 959(c)(2) by reason of section 959(e) ("reclassified section 959(e) PTEP");

7. E&P described in section 959(c)(1)(A) that were initially described in section 959(c)(2) by reason of section 964(e)(4) ("reclassified section 964(e)(4) PTEP");

8. E&P described in section 959(c)(1)(A) that were initially described in section 959(c)(2) by reason of section 951(a)(1)(A) (other than E&P that were initially described in (10) through (15) of this list) ("reclassified section 951(a)(1)(A) PTEP");

9. E&P described in section 959(c)(1)(B), including by reason of section 959(a)(3) (before its repeal) ("section 956A PTEP");

10. E&P described in section 959(c)(2) by reason of section 965(a) ("section 965(a) PTEP");

11. E&P described in section 959(c)(2) by reason of section 965(b)(4)(A) ("section 965(b) PTEP");

12. E&P described in section 959(c)(2) by reason of section 951A(f)(2) ("section 951A PTEP");

13. E&P described in section 959(c)(2) by reason of section 245A(e)(2) ("section 245A(e)(2) PTEP");

14. E&P described in section 959(c)(2) by reason of section 959(e) ("section 959(e) PTEP");

15. E&P described in section 959(c)(2) by reason of section 964(e)(4) ("section 964(e) PTEP"); and

16. E&P described in section 959(c)(2) by reason of section 951(a)(1)(A) not otherwise described in (10) through (15) of this list ("section 951(a)(1)(A) PTEP").

Accordingly, after the Act, section 959(c)(1) PTEP will be comprised of PTEP groups described in (1) through (9) of the preceding paragraph, and section 959(c)(2) PTEP will be comprised of PTEP groups described in (10) through (16) of the preceding paragraph. The forthcoming regulations will provide that once PTEP is assigned to a PTEP group within an annual PTEP account for the year of the income inclusion under section 951(a)(1) (including by reason of section 245A(e)(2), 951A(f)(1), 959(e), 964(e)(4), or 965(a)) or the year of application of section 965(b)(4)(A), the PTEP will be maintained in an annual PTEP account with a year that corresponds to the year of the account from which the PTEP originated if PTEP is distributed or reclassified in a subsequent taxable year. *See also* proposed § § 1.960-3(c)(3) and 1.960-3(c)(4) (providing similar rules for purposes of determining the amount of foreign income taxes deemed paid under section 960(b)).

As discussed in section 2 of this notice, proposed § 1.960-3(c) provides that, for purposes of determining the amount of foreign income taxes deemed paid under section 960(b), with respect to a CFC, a separate annual PTEP account is maintained in each relevant section 904 category and the PTEP in each such account is assigned to one or more of the PTEP groups. However, the Treasury Department and the IRS recognize that for purposes of applying the ordering rules described in section 3.02 of this notice, it may be necessary to aggregate amounts across section 904 categories. The Treasury Department and the IRS expect that the forthcoming regulations will provide that, to the extent a CFC has E&P in a PTEP group that is in more than one section 904 category, any distribution out of that PTEP group is made pro rata out of the earnings and profits in each section 904 category. Additionally, the rules in proposed §§ 1.960-1 and 1.960-3 addressing the types of PTEP groups and their treatment for purposes of applying section 960(b) will be coordinated, as appropriate, with the forthcoming regulations when finalized.

It is expected that forthcoming regulations will provide that dollar basis must be tracked for each annual PTEP account, and, to the extent provided in the forthcoming regulations, separately for each PTEP group within an annual account. The forthcoming regulations will confirm that distributions from any PTEP group reduce the shareholder's stock basis under section 961(b)(1) without regard to how that basis was originally created, including if the basis was created under section 961(a) due to an inclusion unrelated to the PTEP group being distributed.

It is expected that the forthcoming regulations will provide transition rules for annual PTEP accounts maintained before the applicability date of the regulations. Annual PTEP accounts established for taxable years before the applicability date of the forthcoming regulations will only need to be segregated between the section 951(a)(1)(B) PTEP group, the section 956A PTEP group, and the section 951(a)(1)(A) PTEP group, except for the taxable year to which section 965 applies. For the taxable year to which section 965 applies, annual PTEP accounts must also be segregated between the reclassified section 965(a) PTEP group, the reclassified section 965(b) PTEP group, the section 965(a) PTEP group, and the section 965(b) PTEP group (the "section 965 PTEP groups"). A shareholder that has maintained a multi-year pool instead of annual PTEP accounts for its section 951(a)(1)(B) PTEP, section 956A PTEP, or its section 951(a)(1)(A) PTEP will be permitted to treat the respective pool as a PTEP group in a single annual PTEP account with an average dollar basis, and that annual PTEP account will be considered the annual PTEP account for the last taxable year ending before the applicability date of the proposed regulations. Additionally, a shareholder that has maintained aggregate dollar basis pools to reflect the dollar basis of its total section 959(c)(1) PTEP or its total section 959(c)(2) PTEP (or both) for taxable years before the applicability date of the regulations will be permitted to assign an average dollar basis to the PTEP in each annual account (other than the section 965 PTEP groups), if it maintained annual accounts for section 959(c)(1) PTEP and section 959(c)(2) PTEP.

The forthcoming regulations described herein are intended to allow for the most flexibility in applying the limitations on the creditability of certain foreign income taxes, and the rules under section 986(c) regarding the recognition of foreign currency gain or loss, to the different types of PTEP. Implementing all of the operative provisions relating to PTEP following the Act with complete precision requires maintaining PTEP in 16 PTEP groups across the section 904 categories in annual accounts. The Treasury Department and the IRS recognize the complexity and both the administrative and compliance challenges associated with maintaining such a large number of PTEP groups and are weighing those considerations against the need for precision in applying the related foreign tax credit and foreign currency rules. Some of the proposed PTEP groups, such as reclassified 245A(e) PTEP, reclassified section 959(e) PTEP, reclassified section 964(e)(4) PTEP, section 956A PTEP, section 245A(e) PTEP, section 959(e) PTEP, and section 964(e)(4) PTEP are unlikely to arise on a routine basis. Additionally, because of the one-time nature of section 965, once all of the PTEP in the section 965 PTEP groups are distributed, those groups will be completely eliminated. See section 3.02 of this notice. Furthermore, the Treasury Department and the IRS are considering ways to simplify the rules associated with PTEP by consolidating PTEP groups or grouping accounts into multi-year accounts, or by other methods, and request comments in this regard.

*.02 Ordering of Earnings and Profits upon Distribution and Reclassification*

Section 959(c) provides that, for purposes of sections 959(a) and (b), section 316(a)(2) (relating to E&P of the taxable year) ("current E&P") and then section 316(a)(1) (relating to E&P accumulated after February 28, 1913) ("accumulated E&P") apply first to section 959(c)(1) PTEP, then to section 959(c)(2) PTEP, and finally to section 959(c)(3) E&P. The reference to section 316 in section 959 indicates that a distribution of PTEP is dependent upon the existence of E&P otherwise sufficient to support a dividend under section 316. The forthcoming regulations will clarify that a distribution will be a distribution of PTEP only to the extent it would have otherwise been a dividend under section 316. For example, if a foreign corporation has no current E&P or accumulated E&P at the end of a taxable year, a distribution from the corporation to a shareholder during the taxable year will be a return of basis or treated as gain from the sale or exchange of property under section 301(c)(2) or (3), respectively, regardless of whether the shareholder has one or more annual PTEP accounts with respect to its stock in the foreign corporation.

Under section 316, distributions are considered first as distributions from current E&P, to the extent thereof, and then as distributions from the most recently accumulated E&P, to the extent thereof. As noted above, PTEP will be maintained in annual PTEP accounts. To facilitate the rule in section 959(c), which incorporates the ordering rule of section 316, the forthcoming regulations will require a "last in, first out" approach to the sourcing of distributions from annual PTEP accounts, subject to the special priority rule for PTEP arising by reason of the application of section 965, as discussed in the following paragraph. Thus, in general, section 959(c)(1) PTEP in the most recent annual PTEP account will be distributed first (with an exception for section 965 PTEP), followed by the next most recent annual PTEP account, and so on, after which the same approach will apply to section 959(c)(2) PTEP. Within each annual PTEP account, the PTEP attributable to each group of PTEP earned in that year will be distributed in the order prescribed in the following paragraphs in this section 3.02.

The forthcoming regulations will provide, under the grants of regulatory authority in sections 965(o) and 7805(a), that PTEP attributable to income inclusions under section 965(a) or by reason of section 965(b)(4)(A) receive priority when determining the group of PTEP from which a distribution is made. This priority will be integrated into the general ordering rule of section 959(c) that sources PTEP first from section 959(c)(1) PTEP and then from section 959(c)(2) PTEP. Thus, starting with section 959(c)(1) PTEP, under the forthcoming regulations, as an exception to the last-in, first-out approach, distributions will be sourced first from the reclassified section 965(a) PTEP and then from the reclassified section 965(b) PTEP. Once those PTEP groups are exhausted, under the last-in, first-out approach, distributions will be sourced pro rata from the remaining section 959(c)(1) PTEP groups in each annual PTEP account, starting from the most recent annual account.

Once the PTEP groups relating to section 959(c)(1) PTEP are exhausted, distributions will be sourced from section 959(c)(2) PTEP. As described in the preceding paragraph, the forthcoming regulations will provide that, as an exception to the last-in, first-out approach, distributions will be sourced first from section 965(a) PTEP and then section 965(b) PTEP. Once those two PTEP groups are exhausted, under the last-in, first-out approach, distributions will be sourced pro rata from the remaining section 959(c)(2) PTEP groups in each annual PTEP account, starting from the most recent annual PTEP account. Finally, once all the PTEP groups have been exhausted, the remaining amount of any distributions will be sourced from section 959(c)(3) E&P, to the extent thereof.

The forthcoming regulations will also provide that reclassifications of PTEP pursuant to the application of section 959(a)(2) will be sourced first from section 965(a) PTEP, then section 965(b) PTEP, and then, under a last-in, first-out approach, pro rata from the remaining section 959(c)(2) PTEP groups in each annual PTEP account, starting from the most recent annual PTEP account.

These ordering rules are expected to simplify PTEP recordkeeping in the future because, once a foreign corporation distributes all of its section 965 PTEP, the foreign corporation and its U.S. shareholder(s) will have reduced the number of PTEP groups that need to be tracked. Absent the ordering rules described in the preceding paragraphs of this section 3.02, the last in, first out approach to PTEP distributions would trap annual PTEP accounts with section 965 PTEP behind subsequent annual PTEP accounts, requiring the section 965 PTEP to be tracked indefinitely. The ordering rules to be provided in forthcoming regulations are illustrated by an example in section 3.04 of this notice.

*.03 Adjustments Due to an Income Inclusion in Excess of Current Earnings and Profits*

A U.S. shareholder's income inclusion under section 951A is not subject to a limitation based on the E&P of its CFCs for the taxable year. Consequently, in a year in which the portion of a U.S. shareholder's GILTI inclusion amount allocated to a CFC under section 951A(f)(2) and proposed § 1.951A-6(b)(2) exceeds the CFC's current E&P, the PTEP resulting by reason of section 951A(f)(1) and proposed § 1.951A-6(b)(1) will exceed the CFC's current E&P and, in some cases, may exceed the CFC's accumulated E&P as well. Similarly, an income inclusion under section 951(a)(1)(A) by reason of section 965 is not subject to an E&P limitation. Further, while an inclusion under section 951(a)(1)(A) (other than by reason of section 965) with respect to a CFC is generally subject to an E&P limitation under section 952(c)(1)(A), a U.S. shareholder's inclusion under section 951(a)(1)(A) with respect to the

CFC can exceed its E&P if such CFC has a tested loss. *See* section 951A(c)(2)(B)(ii) and proposed §1.951A-6(d) (increasing a CFC's E&P by the amount of a tested loss solely for purposes of applying the E&P limitation of section 952(c)(1)(A)).

As noted in section 3.02 of this notice, the aggregate of the amounts of section 959(c)(1) PTEP, section 959(c)(2) PTEP, and section 959(c)(3) E&P of a foreign corporation must equal the amount of E&P of the foreign corporation. The forthcoming regulations under section 959 will provide that current E&P are first classified as section 959(c)(3) E&P and then section 959(c)(3) E&P are reclassified as section 959(c)(1) PTEP or section 959(c)(2) PTEP, as appropriate, in full, which may have the effect of creating or increasing a deficit in section 959(c)(3) E&P. For example, in a case in which the portion of a U.S. shareholder's GILTI inclusion amount allocated to a CFC under section 951A(f)(2) and proposed §1.951A-6(b)(2) exceeds the current E&P of the CFC, section 959(c)(3) E&P will first be increased by the CFC's current E&P and then decreased by the entire amount of the portion of the GILTI inclusion amount allocated to the CFC, possibly below zero, and section 959(c)(2) PTEP will be increased by the same amount. For a similar rule in the case in which a U.S. shareholder's inclusion under section 951(a) by reason of section 965(a) exceeds E&P, see proposed §1.965-2(d)(1).

Finally, in a case where a foreign corporation has a current-year deficit in E&P, that deficit will solely reduce the foreign corporation's section 959(c)(3) E&P without affecting the amount of its section 959(c)(1) PTEP or section 959(c)(2) PTEP.

## .04 Examples

The rules described in sections 3.02 and 3.03 of this notice are illustrated in the following examples:

*Example 1*–(i) *Facts.* USP, a domestic corporation, wholly owns FC, a foreign corporation that has the U.S. dollar as its functional currency. Both USP and FC use the calendar year as their taxable year. Before 2018, the PTEP of FC was maintained in annual accounts. As of December 31, 2018, FC's $300x of E&P (before taking into account distributions made or inclusions under section 951(a)(1)(B) in 2018) applicable to USP's interest in FC are classified under section 3.01 of this notice as follows:

| Year | Section 959(c)(1) | | | Section 959(c)(2) | | | | Section 959(c)(3) |
| | Reclassified Section 965(a) PTEP | Reclassified Section 965(b) PTEP | Section 951(a)(1)(B) PTEP | Section 965(a) PTEP | Section 965(b) PTEP | Section 951A PTEP | Section 951(a)(1)(A) PTEP | |
| --- | --- | --- | --- | --- | --- | --- | --- | --- |
| 2018 | | | | | | 50x | 30x | |
| 2017 | | | 100x | 50x | | | | 20x |
| 2016 | | 25x | | | | 25x | | |
| Total | | 25x | | | | 255x | | 20x |

In 2018, FC has an amount described in section 956(a) ("section 956(a) amount") of $125x, without considering the application of section 959(a)(2). In 2019, FC earns $25x of current E&P, and the amount of USP's income inclusion under section 951A(a) that is allocated to FC under section 951A(f)(2) and proposed §1.951A-6(b)(2) is $20x. FC also makes a distribution of $195x in 2019. In 2020, FC earns no current E&P, but FC makes a distribution of $60x. For all years, the PTEP of FC in each PTEP group is described in a single section 904 category, and all section 959(c)(3) E&P of FC are described in a single section 904 category.

(ii) *Analysis*–(A) *2018.* As of December 31, 2018, before considering FC's section 956(a) amount, FC has total section 959(c)(2) PTEP of $255x. Under section 959(a)(2) and (f)(1), because FC's section 959(c)(2) PTEP exceeds its section 956(a) amount, USP does not include any amount in income under section 951(a)(1)(B). However, under section 959(c)(1)(A), $125x of FC's section 959(c)(2) earnings must be reclassified as section 959(c)(1) PTEP. Under the rules described in section 3.02 of this notice, the reclassification is sourced first from section 965(a) PTEP and then from section 965(b) PTEP. Under the rules in section 3.01 of this notice, the reclassified PTEP remains in the 2017 annual PTEP account. Thus, in FC's 2017 annual PTEP account, FC's reclassified section 965(a) PTEP is increased by $100x and its section 965(a) PTEP is decreased by $100x. Additionally, FC's reclassified section 965(b) PTEP is increased by $25x and its section 965(b) PTEP is decreased by $25x. Accordingly, as of December 31, 2018, FC's E&P

applicable to USP's interest in FC are classified under section 3.01 of this notice as follows:

| Year | Section 959(c)(1) | | | Section 959(c)(2) | | | | Section 959(c)(3) |
|---|---|---|---|---|---|---|---|---|
| | Reclassified Section 965(a) PTEP | Reclassified Section 965(b) PTEP | Section 951(a)(1)(B) PTEP | Section 965(a) PTEP | Section 965(b) PTEP | Section 951A PTEP | Section 951(a)(1)(A) PTEP | |
| 2018 | | | | | | 50x | 30x | |
| 2017 | 100x | 25x | | 25x | | | | 20x |
| 2016 | | | 25x | | | | 25x | |
| Total | | 150x | | | 130x | | | 20x |

(B) *2019–(1) Current year adjustments.* During 2019, FC earns $25x of current E&P, and the amount of USP's income inclusion under section 951A(a) that is allocated to FC under section 951A(f)(2) and proposed § 1.951A-6(b)(2) is $20x. Thus, before taking into account USP's income inclusions with respect to FC and any distributions by FC, FC's section 959(c)(3) E&P is initially increased by $25x. As a result of USP's income inclusion under section 951A, FC's section 951A PTEP increases by $20x and FC's section 959(c)(3) E&P is decreased by $20x. Accordingly, as of December 31, 2019, FC's E&P (before taking into account distributions made in 2019) applicable to USP's interest in FC are classified under section 3.01 of this notice as follows:

| Year | Section 959(c)(1) | | | Section 959(c)(2) | | | | Section 959(c)(3) |
|---|---|---|---|---|---|---|---|---|
| | Reclassified Section 965(a) PTEP | Reclassified Section 965(b) PTEP | Section 951(a)(1)(B) PTEP | Section 965(a) PTEP | Section 965(b) PTEP | Section 951A PTEP | Section 951(a)(1)(A) PTEP | |
| 2019 | | | | | | 20x | | |
| 2018 | | | | | | 50x | 30x | |
| 2017 | 100x | 25x | | 25x | | | | 25x |
| 2016 | | | 25x | | | | 25x | |
| Total | | 150x | | | 150x | | | 25x |

(2) *Distribution.* FC's distribution of $195x is from PTEP because the entire distribution would be a dividend under section 316(a) without regard to section 959 (that is, for purposes of section 316, at the end of 2019, FC has $325x of E&P (without regard to the distribution), $25x of which is current E&P). Under section 959(c), the distribution is first treated as attributable to section 959(c)(1) PTEP.

(i) *Section 959(c)(1) PTEP.* Under the rules described in section 3.02 of this notice, the distribution is first sourced from reclassified section 965(a) PTEP and then from reclassified section 965(b) PTEP, and then pro rata from the remaining PTEP groups that contain section 959(c)(1) PTEP under a last-in, first-out ("LIFO") approach. Thus, in FC's 2017 annual PTEP account, FC's reclassified section 965(a) PTEP is decreased by $100x and its reclassified section 965(b) PTEP is decreased by $25x. In FC's 2016 annual PTEP

account, FC's section 951(a)(1)(B) PTEP is reduced by $25x. Thus, of the distribution of $195x, $150x is treated as attributable to section 959(c)(1) PTEP ($100x + $25x + $25x).

(ii) *Section 959(c)(2) PTEP.* After the section 959(c)(1) PTEP is exhausted, the remaining portion of the distribution ($45x) is treated as attributable to section 959(c)(2) PTEP, to the extent thereof. Under the rules described in section 3.02 of this notice, distributions are first sourced from section 965(a) PTEP and then from section 965(b) PTEP, and then pro rata from the remaining PTEP groups that contain section 959(c)(2) PTEP under a LIFO approach. Thus, in FC's 2017 annual PTEP account, FC's section 965(b) PTEP is decreased by $25x. In FC's 2019 annual PTEP account, FC's section 951A PTEP is decreased by $20x. Because the entire distribution has been accounted for, the remaining PTEP groups that contain section 959(c)(2) PTEP and FC's section

959(c)(3) E&P are not affected. Accordingly, as of December 31, 2019, FC's E&P applicable to USP's interest in FC are classified under section 3.01 of this notice as follows:

| | Section 959(c)(1) | | | Section 959(c)(2) | | | | Section 959(c)(3) |
|---|---|---|---|---|---|---|---|---|
| Year | Reclassified Section 965(a) PTEP | Reclassified Section 965(b) PTEP | Section 951(a)(1)(B) PTEP | Section 965(a) PTEP | Section 965(b) PTEP | Section 951A PTEP | Section 951(a)(1)(A) PTEP | |
| 2019 | | | | | | | | |
| 2018 | | | | | | 50x | 30x | |
| 2017 | | | | | | | | 25x |
| 2016 | | | | | | | 25x | |
| Total | | | | | | 105x | | 25x |

(C) *2020.* FC's distribution of $60x is from PTEP because the entire distribution would be a dividend under section 316(a) without regard to section 959 (that is, for purposes of section 316, at the end of 2020, FC has $130x of E&P (without regard to the distribution), all which is accumulated E&P). Under section 959(c), the distribution is first treated as attributable to section 959(c)(1) PTEP; however, FC has no section 959(c)(1) PTEP. Additionally, FC has no section 965(a) PTEP or section 965(b) PTEP. Under the rules described in section 3.02 of this notice, the distribution is sourced pro rata from the remaining PTEP groups that contain section 959(c)(2) PTEP under a LIFO approach. Thus, in FC's 2018 annual PTEP account, FC's section 951A PTEP is decreased by $37.5x ($60x x $50x/$80x) and its section 951(a)(1)(A) PTEP is decreased by $22.5x ($60x x $30x/$80x). Because the entire distribution has been accounted for, the remaining PTEP groups that contain section 959(c)(2) PTEP and FC's section 959(c)(3) E&P are not affected. Accordingly, as of December 31, 2020, FC's E&P applicable to USP's interest in FC are classified under section 3.01 of this notice as follows:

| | Section 959(c)(1) | | | Section 959(c)(2) | | | | Section 959(c)(3) |
|---|---|---|---|---|---|---|---|---|
| Year | Reclassified Section 965(a) PTEP | Reclassified Section 965(b) PTEP | Section 951(a)(1)(B) PTEP | Section 965(a) PTEP | Section 965(b) PTEP | Section 951A PTEP | Section 951(a)(1)(A) PTEP | |
| 2019 | | | | | | | | |
| 2018 | | | | | | 12.5x | 7.5x | |
| 2017 | | | | | | | | 25x |
| 2016 | | | | | | | 25x | |
| Total | | | | | | 45x | | 25x |

*Example 2.* (i) *Facts.* USP, a domestic corporation, wholly owns FC, a foreign corporation that has the U.S. dollar as its functional currency. Both USP and FC use the calendar year as their taxable year. At the beginning of Year 1, FC has accumulated E&P of $50x, all of which is section 959(c)(3) E&P. In Year 1, FC has $25x of current E&P and FC makes no distributions. Furthermore, in Year 1, USP's income inclusion under section 951A(a) that is allocated to FC under section 951A(f)(2) and proposed § 1.951A-6(b)(2) is $100x.

(ii) *Analysis.* Before taking into account USP's income inclusions with respect to FC in Year 1, FC's current E&P for Year 1 increase FC's section 959(c)(3) E&P by $25x to $75x ($50x + $25x). The $100x of USP's income inclusion under section 951A(a) allocated to FC results in an increase of $100x to FC's section 951A PTEP (resulting in a balance of $100x) and a reduction of $100x to FC's section 959(c)(3) E&P resulting in a deficit of $25x ($75x - $100x). The sum of the amounts of FC's section 959(c)(1) PTEP ($0x), section 959(c)(2) PTEP ($100x), and section 959(c)(3) E&P

**Notice 2019-1**

(deficit of $25x) equals the amount of FC's E&P ($75x).

## SECTION 4. APPLICABILITY DATE

It is expected that the forthcoming regulations will apply to taxable years of United States shareholders (and successors in interest) ending after December 14, 2018 and to taxable years of foreign corporations ending with or within such taxable years of United States shareholders. *See* section 7805(b)(1)(C). Before the issuance of the forthcoming regulations, a shareholder may rely on the rules described in section 3 of this notice if the shareholder and each person related to the shareholder under section 267(b) or 707(b) (each such person, a "related shareholder") apply the rules consistently with respect to PTEP of all foreign corporations in which the shareholder or related shareholder, as the case may be, owns stock for all taxable years beginning with the shareholder's or the related shareholder's taxable year that includes the taxable year end of any such foreign corporation to which section 965 applies.

## SECTION 5. REQUEST FOR COMMENTS AND CONTACT INFORMATION

The Treasury Department and the IRS request comments on the rules described in this notice, including potential simplification of the rules described in section 3.02 of this notice through the establishment of multi-year PTEP accounts. The Treasury Department and the IRS also request comments concerning the following topics:

1. The extent to which basis created under section 961(c) should be treated as basis for purposes of determining tested income in applying section 951A;

2. The extent to which gain or loss, including foreign currency gain or loss, should be recognized by reason of distributions of PTEP. Additionally, the Treasury Department and the IRS request comments regarding a potential election pursuant to which the shareholder would agree to establish and maintain a multi-year section 951A PTEP group and not apply section 250(a)(2) to the extent such provision would otherwise be relevant in calculating its foreign currency gain or loss on a distribution of section 951A PTEP;

3. The application of sections 959 and 961 to domestic and foreign partnerships; and

4. Other guidance that should be issued under sections 959 and 961, including comments on the 2006 proposed regulations and the extent to which guidance in the 2006 proposed regulations should be incorporated into new proposed regulations.

Comments should be submitted by February 12, 2019. Comments may be submitted electronically via the Federal eRulemaking Portal at **www.regulations.gov** (type IRS-2018-0041 in the search field on the *regulations.gov* homepage to find this notice and submit comments). Written comments may be submitted to the Office of Associate Chief Counsel (International), Attention: Melinda E. Harvey, Internal Revenue Service, IR-4579, 1111 Constitution Avenue, NW, Washington, DC 20224.

Comments will be available for public inspection and copying.

The principal author of this notice is Melinda E. Harvey of the Office of Associate Chief Counsel (International). For further information regarding this notice, contact Ms. Harvey at (202) 317-6934 (not a toll-free number).

---

# Notice 2019-5, I.R.B. 2019-2, December 21, 2018

Individual Shared Responsibility Payment Hardship Exemptions that May Be Claimed on a Federal Income Tax Return Without Obtaining a Hardship Exemption Certification from the Marketplace for the 2018 Tax Year

## PURPOSE

This notice supplements Notice 2014-76, 2014-50 I.R.B. 946, as supplemented by Notice 2017-14, 2017-6 I.R.B. 783, by identifying additional hardship exemptions from the individual shared responsibility payment under § 5000A of the Internal Revenue Code (Code) that a taxpayer may claim on a Federal income tax return for the 2018 tax year without obtaining a hardship exemption certification from the Health Insurance Marketplace (Marketplace).

## BACKGROUND

For each month beginning after December 31, 2013, § 5000A of the Code requires taxpayers to have minimum essential coverage for themselves and any nonexempt family member whom the taxpayer may claim as a dependent, to qualify for an exemption, or to include an individual shared responsibility payment with their Federal income tax return. Section 11081 of the Tax Cuts and Jobs Act, Pub. L. No. 115-97, 131

Stat. 2054, 2082, amended §5000A(c) to reduce the amount of the individual shared responsibility payment to zero for taxable years beginning after December 31, 2018.

Section 5000A(e)(5) of the Code and §1.5000A-3(h) of the Income Tax Regulations provide that, in general, an individual is exempt from the requirement to have minimum essential coverage for a month if he or she has in effect a hardship exemption certification issued by the Marketplace certifying that the individual has suffered a hardship (as that term is defined in 45 CFR 155.605(d)) affecting the individual's capability to obtain minimum essential coverage in that month. Section 1.5000A-3(h)(3) provides that a taxpayer may claim a hardship exemption for the taxpayer and any dependent of the taxpayer on a Federal income tax return without obtaining a hardship exemption certification from the Marketplace if (i) the taxpayer or his or her dependent is eligible for a hardship exemption described in guidance released by the Department of Health and Human Services (HHS) and (ii) the exemption is allowed to be claimed on the taxpayer's Federal income tax return without obtaining a hardship exemption certification from the Marketplace pursuant to guidance published by the Treasury Department and the Internal Revenue Service.

Notice 2014-76 provides a list of hardship exemptions that may be claimed on a Federal income tax return without obtaining a hardship exemption certification. *See also* 45 CFR 155.605(e) (providing a partial list of hardship exemptions that may be claimed on a tax return without obtaining an exemption certification). Notice 2017-14 supplements that list by providing an additional hardship exemption that may be claimed on a Federal income tax return for the 2016 tax year without obtaining a hardship exemption certification.[1]

## GUIDANCE

To provide additional flexibility for the 2018 tax year, HHS announced in guidance released on September 12, 2018, that all hardship exemptions available under 45 CFR 155.605(d)(1) may be claimed by a qualifying individual (or the taxpayer who may claim a qualifying individual as a dependent) on a Federal income tax return for the 2018 tax year without obtaining a hardship exemption certification from the Marketplace.[2] Under 45 CFR 155.605(d)(1), a person is eligible for a hardship exemption for at least the month before, the month(s) during, and the month after the specific event or circumstance that creates the hardship, if the Marketplace determines that:

(i) He or she experienced financial or domestic circumstances, including an unexpected natural or human-caused event, such that he or she had a significant, unexpected increase in essential expenses that prevented him or her from obtaining coverage under a qualified health plan;

(ii) The expense of purchasing a qualified health plan would have caused him or her to experience serious deprivation of food, shelter, clothing, or other necessities; or

(iii) He or she has experienced other circumstances that prevented him or her from obtaining coverage under a qualified health plan.

The option to claim an exemption on a Federal income tax return for the 2018 tax year applies in addition to the existing procedures for applying for hardship exemptions using the Marketplace exemption determination process.

## EFFECT ON OTHER DOCUMENTS

Notice 2014-76, 2014-50 I.R.B. 946, as supplemented by Notice 2017-14, 2017-6 I.R.B. 783, is supplemented.

## EFFECTIVE DATE

This notice applies to taxable years beginning after December 31, 2017 and before January 1, 2019.

## DRAFTING INFORMATION

The principal author of this notice is Lisa Mojiri-Azad of the Office of Associate Chief Counsel (Income Tax & Accounting). For further information regarding this notice contact Ms. Mojiri-Azad (202) 317-4649 (not a toll-free call).

---

[1] *See also* HHS Centers for Medicare & Medicaid Services, Guidance on Health Coverage Tax Credit Hardship Exemption (Aug. 12, 2016) (available at *https://www.cms.gov/CCIIO/Resources/Regulations-and-Guidance/Downloads/Final-Guidance-for-5000A-HCTC.pdf*).

[2] *See* HHS Centers for Medicare & Medicaid Services, Guidance on Claiming a Hardship Exemption through the Internal Revenue Service (IRS) (Sept. 12, 2018) (available at *https://www.cms.gov/CCIIO/Resources/Regulations-and-Guidance/Downloads/Authority-to-Grant-HS-Exemptions-2018-Final-91218.pdf*).

# Notice 2019-9, December 31, 2018

Contents

tain future event or condition, how is the present value of the payment determined?

Q–29: What is the base amount for purposes of section 4960(c)(5)(D)?

Q–30: What is the base period?

Q–31: How is the base amount determined in the case of a covered employee who did not perform services for the applicable tax-exempt organization (or a predecessor entity or a related organization), prior to the calendar year in which the separation from employment with the applicable tax-exempt organization occurred?

H. Computation of Excess Parachute Payments

Q–32: How is the amount of an excess parachute payment computed?

I. Reporting Liability Under Section 4960

Q–33: How do applicable tax-exempt organizations or related organizations report and pay the excise tax imposed under section 4960?

Q–34: When is the excise tax imposed under section 4960 due?

Q–35: Are applicable tax-exempt organizations or related organizations required to pay estimated taxes for the excise tax imposed under section 4960?

J. Miscellaneous Issues

Q–36: Does the payment of remuneration subject to excise tax under section 4960 automatically constitute an excess benefit transaction under section 4958?

Q–37: Does the payment of remuneration subject to excise tax under section 4960 necessarily constitute an act of self-dealing described in section 4941?

Q–38: Does section 4960 apply to amounts to which section 162(m) applies?

K. Effective Date

Q–39: What is the effective date of section 4960?

III. REQUEST FOR COMMENTS

IV. RELIANCE

V. PAPERWORK REDUCTION ACT

VI. DRAFTING INFORMATION

I. PURPOSE AND OVERVIEW

This notice provides interim guidance regarding section 4960 of the Internal Revenue Code (Code), enacted on December 22, 2017, pursuant to section 13602 of Tax Cuts and Jobs Act, Pub. L.

No. 115-97 (the Act). Section 4960(a) imposes an excise tax equal to the rate of tax under section 11 (currently 21 percent) on the amount of remuneration in excess of $1 million and any excess parachute payment paid by an applicable tax-exempt organization to a covered employee.

The interim guidance is intended to assist taxpayers in applying section 4960 while the Department of the Treasury (Treasury Department) and the Internal Revenue Service (IRS) develop further guidance on the application of section 4960, and addresses certain issues under section 4960 on which stakeholders have indicated that they would benefit from interim guidance. Specifically, the Treasury Department and the IRS intend to issue proposed regulations on the amendments made by section 13602 of the Act that will incorporate the guidance provided in this notice. However, as provided in Section IV of this notice, any future guidance under section 4960 will be prospective and will not apply to taxable years beginning before the issuance of that guidance. Until further guidance is issued, to comply with the requirements of section 4960, taxpayers may base their positions upon a good faith, reasonable interpretation of the statute, including consideration of the legislative history, if appropriate. The positions reflected in this notice constitute a good faith, reasonable interpretation of the statute. Whether a taxpayer's position that is inconsistent with this notice constitutes a good faith, reasonable interpretation of the statute generally will be determined based upon all of the relevant facts and circumstances, including whether the taxpayer has applied the position consistently and the extent to which the taxpayer has resolved interpretive issues based on consistent principles and in a consistent manner. Notwithstanding the previous sentence, this preamble describes certain positions that the Treasury Department and the IRS have concluded are not consistent with a good faith, reasonable interpretation of the statutory language. The Treasury Department and the IRS intend to embody these positions as part of the forthcoming proposed regulations.

Comments are requested on all aspects of this notice. See Section III of this notice regarding requests for comments on specific aspects of this notice and for information on how to submit comments.

A. *Section 4960 — In General*

Section 4960(a) of the Code generally provides that an applicable tax-exempt organization (ATEO), or a related organization, that pays remuneration in excess of $1 million or any excess parachute payment to a covered employee is subject to an excise tax on the amount of the excess remuneration and excess parachute payments at a rate equal to the rate of tax imposed on corporations under section 11 (currently 21 percent).

Section 4960(a)(1) refers to remuneration paid "for the taxable year," but does not specify which taxpayer's taxable year is used, what it means for remuneration to be paid "for" a taxable year, or how to measure remuneration if an ATEO and a related organization have different taxable years. Q/A–2 provides that the excise tax imposed on excess remuneration and excess parachute payments is determined based on remuneration paid and excess parachute payments made in the calendar year ending with or within the taxable year of the employer. This measurement period, as commenters suggested, will reduce the administrative burdens that would arise if taxpayers were required to allocate remuneration paid during a single calendar year to multiple non-calendar taxable years. Moreover, this approach will reduce administrative burdens by aligning more closely with the calendar year reporting of compensation on Form W-2, Wage and Tax Statement, and Form 990, Return of Organization Exempt From Income Tax.

Some commenters recommended that ATEOs and related organizations be allowed, but not required, to treat remuneration paid during the calendar year ending with or within the taxable year of the employer as remuneration paid "for the taxable year" under section 4960(a)(1). Commenters recommended this rule be elective in order for non-calendar year taxpayers to avoid the potential inclusion of remuneration for a period prior to the effective date of section 4960 (the first taxable year beginning after December 31, 2017). Q/A–13 and Q/A–39 avoid that result by treating remuneration in which the covered employee vested before the effective date of section 4960 as paid before that effective date. Because these Q/As address the issue raised by the commenters, the Treasury Department and the IRS have concluded that an election for the remuneration measurement period is unnecessary.

The guidance in this notice provides rules regarding the entity that is liable for the excise tax under section 4960, and how that excise tax is calculated. Q/A–3 provides that the common-law employer, as determined generally for federal tax purposes, is liable for the excise tax imposed under section 4960. A common-law employer may not avoid treating a payment as remuneration under section 4960 by reason of a third party payor arrangement. A payment to the employer's employee from a third party payor (including a payroll agent, common paymaster, statutory employer under section 3401(d)(1), or certified professional employer organization) or from an unrelated management company, is considered a payment to the employee from the common-law employer. Similarly, a payment to the employee from a related entity, including a related entity that is an ATEO, for services rendered to the common-law employer, is considered a payment to the employee from the common-law employer for purposes of calculating remuneration and determining liability for the excise tax. Q/A–3 also clarifies that calculation of the excise tax is separate from any arrangement that an ATEO and any related organization may have for bearing the cost of the excise tax under section 4960.

One commenter requested guidance providing that remuneration paid by a separate employer that is a related for-profit or governmental entity (other than an ATEO) is taken into account in determining whether a covered employee has remuneration in excess of $1 million, but that the related entity is not liable for its share of the excise tax under section 4960. There is no statutory support for creating such an exception for for-profit and governmental entities. Section 4960(c)(4)(B), which defines related organizations, applies to any "person or governmental entity" that meets any of the relationship tests in section 4960(c)(4)(B)(i)-(v). Unlike the definition of an ATEO under section 4960(c)(1)(C), which applies only to a governmental entity that excludes income from taxation under section 115(1),[1] section 4960(c)(4)(B) applies to any "governmental entity" that is related to an ATEO. Similarly, a for-profit entity is a "person" under generally applicable tax principles. In addition, excepting for-profit entities from liability as related organizations would be inconsistent with section 4960(c)(6), which coordinates the tax on excess parachute payments with the section 162(m) deduction limitation (which only applies to for-profit entities). Further, section 4960(c)(4)(C), which describes the liability for the excise tax, refers to any case in which remuneration from more than one employer is taken into account, stating that "each such employer" shall be liable, without qualification as to the em-

---

[1] Section 4960(c)(1)(C) refers to an entity that "has income excluded from taxation under section 115(1)." However, section 115(1) refers to income that is excluded from gross income. For consistency with the language in section 115(1), this notice refers to an entity that "has income excluded from gross income under section 115(1)," except where directly quoting section 4960(c)(1)(C).

ployer's status as an ATEO. For these reasons, the Treasury Department and the IRS have concluded that the position that a for-profit or governmental entity that is a related organization with regard to an ATEO is not liable for its share of the excise tax under section 4960 is not consistent with a good faith, reasonable interpretation of the statute.

Some ATEOs will not be impacted by section 4960 because they do not pay an employee enough remuneration to trigger the tax. There can be no excess remuneration under section 4960(a)(1) if an ATEO (together with any related organization) pays remuneration of less than $1 million to each of its employees for a taxable year, and there can be no excess parachute payment under section 4960(a)(2) if the employer does not have any "highly compensated employees" under section 414(q)[2] for the taxable year. In that case, no excise tax under section 4960 is owed. For example, an ATEO that does not pay compensation (within the meaning of section 414(q)) of $125,000 or more to any employee in 2018 and 2019 is not subject to excise tax under section 4960 for 2019.

However, there is no minimum dollar threshold for an employee to be a covered employee. Even if an ATEO has no liability under section 4960 for one year, the ATEO may later need to determine its five highest-compensated employees for that taxable year, as those employees continue be covered employees in all future years and may be paid excess remuneration or excess parachute payments in a future year.

## B. *Applicable Tax-Exempt Organizations and Related Organizations*

Section 4960(c)(1) provides that an "applicable tax-exempt organization" is any organization that for the taxable year—(A) is exempt from taxation under section 501(a), (B) is a farmers' cooperative organization described in section 521(b)(1), (C) has income excluded from taxation under section 115(1), or (D) is a political organization described in section 527(e)(1).

One commenter requested clarification on the application of section 4960 to governmental entities. Q/A–5 clarifies that certain governmental entities are not ATEOs within the meaning of section 4960(c)(1). A governmental entity (including a state college or university) that is not recognized as exempt from taxation under section 501(a) and does not exclude income from gross income under section 115(1) is not an

ATEO described in section 4960(c)(1). Conversely, a governmental entity that excludes income from gross income under section 115(1) (even if the entity has other income that is not excluded from gross income under section 115(1)), or is recognized as exempt from taxation under section 501(a), is an ATEO described in section 4960(c)(1).

Q/A–6 clarifies that a governmental entity that sought and received a determination letter recognizing its tax-exempt status under section 501(c)(3) may relinquish this status pursuant to the procedures described in section 3.01(12) of Rev. Proc. 2018-5, 2018-1 I.R.B. 233, 239. However, an entity that excludes income from gross income under section 115(1) is an ATEO regardless of whether it has a private letter ruling to that effect.

Section 4960(c)(4)(A) provides that remuneration paid to a covered employee by an ATEO includes any remuneration paid with respect to employment of the employee by any related person or governmental entity. The Treasury Department and the IRS interpret the phrase "any related person or governmental entity" to include not only related ATEOs but also related taxable organizations and related governmental units or other governmental entities. Section 4960(c)(4)(B) provides that a person or governmental entity is related to an ATEO if such person or governmental entity— (i) controls, or is controlled by, the organization; (ii) is controlled by one or more persons which control the organization; (iii) is a supported organization (as defined in section 509(f)(3)) during the taxable year with respect to the organization; (iv) is a supporting organization described in section 509(a)(3) during the taxable year with respect to the organization; or (v) in the case of an organization which is a voluntary employees' beneficiary association described in section 501(c)(9), establishes, maintains, or makes contributions to such voluntary employees' beneficiary association.

For purposes of defining "control" within the meaning of section 4960(c)(4)(B)(i)-(ii), Q/A–8 provides rules based on the definition of control under section 512(b)(13)(D). Thus, the definition of related organization for purposes of section 4960 generally aligns with the definition of related organization for purposes of the annual reporting requirements on Form 990, reducing the burden on organizations in identifying related organizations, calculating compensation

---

[2] The limitation used in the definition of highly compensated employee under section 414(q)(1)(B) is adjusted for inflation. For 2019, the limitation is $125,000. Notice 2018-83, 2018-47 I.R.B. 774.

from related organizations, and determining liability under section 4960.

Q/A–8 does not adopt the test for control under section 414(b) and (c), which generally uses the same test for control of a nonprofit organization as section 512(b)(13)(D) except that it replaces the 50 percent threshold with an 80 percent threshold. Instead, Q/A–8 adopts the control test under section 512(b)(13)(D) for the administrative convenience of taxpayers, to align more closely with other exempt organization control tests, and to prevent abuse that may occur in the section 4960 context under the higher 80 percent control threshold that was established for qualified plans.

### C. *Covered Employees*

Section 4960(c)(2) defines a covered employee as any employee who is one of an ATEO's five highest-compensated employees for the current taxable year or who was a covered employee of the ATEO (or any predecessor) for any preceding taxable year beginning after December 31, 2016. Therefore, once an employee is a covered employee, he or she continues to be a covered employee for all subsequent taxable years. There is no minimum dollar threshold for an employee to be a covered employee; thus, an employee need not be paid excess remuneration or an excess parachute payment nor be a highly compensated employee within the meaning of section 414(q) to be a covered employee for a taxable year and all future years.

Commenters requested that the Treasury Department and the IRS provide a rule of administrative convenience under which a covered employee is no longer considered a covered employee of an ATEO after a certain period of time. The guidance in this notice does not adopt that suggestion because it is inconsistent with the statute. For this reason, the Treasury Department and the IRS have concluded that the position that a covered employee ceases to be a covered employee after a certain period of time is not consistent with a good faith, reasonable interpretation of the statute.

Section 4960 does not provide rules for identifying an ATEO's five highest-compensated employees for a taxable year. Q/A–10 provides that whether an employee is one of an ATEO's five highest-compensated employees is based on remuneration paid in the calendar year ending with or within the employer's taxable year. The Treasury Department and the IRS considered using certain existing reporting standards for determining the amount of compensation paid, such as the Securities and Exchange Commission standards that are used for section 162(m) purposes or the standards that are used for Form 990 reporting purposes. However, Q/A–10 uses remuneration paid for purposes of identifying an ATEO's five highest-compensated employee because, as defined in Q/A–12, remuneration is a fair representation of compensation earned by an employee and it is more administrable to use a single standard for both identifying covered employees and computing the tax, if any, imposed by section 4960(a)(1). In addition, having the calendar year ending with or within the ATEO's or related organization's taxable year as the measurement period for identifying the ATEO's five highest-compensated employees is consistent with the measurement period for purposes of determining remuneration paid for a taxable year.

Q/A–10 provides that remuneration paid for medical services is not taken into account for purposes of identifying the five highest-compensated employees. One commenter requested that remuneration paid for medical services be taken into account for purposes of determining the five highest-compensated employees. An interpretation that remuneration for medical services is taken into account for purposes of identifying the five-highest compensated employees would be inconsistent with the statutory structure and the legislative intent, and therefore the Treasury Department and the IRS have concluded that this interpretation is not consistent with a good faith, reasonable interpretation of section 4960. As the Conference Report to accompany H.R. 1 (Conference Report) states, "[f]or purposes of determining a covered employee, remuneration paid to a licensed medical professional which is directly related to the performance of medical or veterinary services by such professional is not taken into account, whereas remuneration paid to such a professional in any other capacity is taken into account." H.R. Rep. No. 115-466, at 494 (2017) (Conf. Rep.).

As set forth in Q/A–9, only an ATEO's common law employees (including officers) can be one of an ATEO's five highest-compensated employees. To identify its five highest-compensated employees, the ATEO must include remuneration paid for the taxable year by any related organization, including remuneration paid by a related for-profit organization or governmental entity, for services performed as an employee of such related organization. Q/A–12(c) also provides that remuneration paid by a separate organization on behalf of the ATEO, whether related to the ATEO or not, for services performed as an employee of the ATEO is treated as remuneration paid by the ATEO for purposes of section 4960. To prevent circumstances in which an employee to whom the ATEO paid minimal remuneration displaces an employee who would otherwise be a covered employee of the ATEO, Q/A–10(b) provides a limited services exception under which, unless an ATEO pays at least 10 percent of the total remuneration paid by the ATEO and all related organizations to an employee during the calendar year, the employee is not treated as one of the ATEO's five highest-compensated employees. However, if no ATEO pays at least 10 percent of an employee's total remuneration during a calendar year, this exception does not apply to the ATEO that paid the most remuneration to the employee during the calendar year.

Whether an employee is one of the five highest-compensated employees is determined separately for each ATEO, and not for the entire group of related organizations; thus, each ATEO has its five highest-compensated employees. As a result, in many cases, a group of related organizations will have more than five covered employees. Some commenters suggested that a group of related ATEOs should have only five highest-compensated employees among all of the related ATEOs, noting that this is the case for purposes of section 162(m)(1)-(4), as Treas. Reg. § 1.162-27(c)(1)(ii) treats a publicly held corporation and all nonpublic corporations related to the publicly held corporation as a single corporation. Section 4960 does not provide for such treatment. Further, under Treas. Reg. § 1.162-27(c)(1)(ii), each related subsidiary within an affiliated group of corporations that is itself a publicly held corporation is separately subject to the deduction limitation, just as each ATEO within a group of related organizations is separately subject to section 4960. Accordingly, this notice does not adopt the commenter's suggestion, and the Treasury Department and the IRS have concluded that the position that a group of related organizations with more than one ATEO has a single set of five highest-compensated employees is not consistent with a good faith, reasonable interpretation of section 4960.

### D. Excess Remuneration

In general, the excise tax imposed under section 4960(a)(1) is based on the remuneration paid (other than any excess parachute payment) by an ATEO for the taxable year with respect to employment of any covered employee in excess of $1 million. Q/A–11 provides that this amount is referred to as "excess remuneration." Consistent

with the statute, the $1 million threshold is not adjusted for inflation.

Section 4960(c)(3)(A) generally defines "remuneration" as wages under section 3401(a) (wages subject to federal income tax withholding), but excluding designated Roth contributions under section 402A(c) and including amounts required to be included in gross income under section 457(f). Q/A–12 clarifies that remuneration includes a parachute payment that is not an excess parachute payment, but remuneration does not include certain retirement benefits (*see* section 3401(a)(12)) or certain directors' fees (*see* Rev. Rul. 57-246, 1957-1 C.B. 338).

The flush language at the end of section 4960(a) provides that, for purposes of section 4960(a), remuneration is treated as paid when there is no substantial risk of forfeiture of the rights to the remuneration. The term "substantial risk of forfeiture" is defined by cross-reference to section 457(f)(3)(B). Proposed regulations under section 457(f) were published in 2016 (81 FR 40548 (Jun. 22, 2016)). The preamble to the proposed regulations states that taxpayers may rely on them before they are finalized. Q/A–13 provides that the definition of substantial risk of forfeiture under Prop. Treas. Reg. § 1.457-12(e)(1) is the definition of substantial risk of forfeiture within the meaning of section 457(f)(3)(B) for purposes of section 4960(a).[3] Under Prop. Treas. Reg. § 1.457-12(e)(1), an amount of compensation is subject to a substantial risk of forfeiture only if entitlement to the amount is conditioned on the future performance of substantial services, or upon the occurrence of a condition that is related to a purpose of the compensation if the possibility of forfeiture is substantial. Consistent with common usage, Q/A–13 refers to an amount the right to which is not subject to a substantial risk of forfeiture as being "vested" and the lapsing of a substantial risk of forfeiture as "vesting."

Q/A–13 clarifies that although section 4960(a) cross-references the definition of substantial risk of forfeiture in section 457(f)(3)(B), the rule under section 4960(a) providing that remuneration is treated as paid upon vesting is not limited to remuneration that is otherwise subject to section 457(f), nor is it limited to nonqualified deferred compensation under section 457(f) or section 409A. Rather, this timing rule for determining when remuneration is treated as paid applies to all forms of remuneration.

[3] Any changes to the proposed regulations under section 457(f) when finalized will be taken into account for purposes of section 4960, and further guidance may be issued if appropriate.

Some commenters argued that section 4960(c)(3), which defines remuneration largely by cross-reference to the definition of wages under section 3401(a), should be interpreted as a timing rule. Section 3401(a) primarily focuses on whether, not when, amounts are includible in wages; the basic timing rule for wage inclusion appears in regulations under section 3402(a), not section 3401(a). Specifically, Treas. Reg. § 31.3402(a)-1(b) provides that wages are paid when actually or constructively paid and explains what it means for an amount to be constructively paid. Thus, the Treasury Department and the IRS conclude that the cross-reference to section 3401(a) (and not section 3402(a)) in section 4960(c)(3) establishes the scope of the term "remuneration" without regard to timing, and that the flush language in section 4960(a) establishes the timing rule that applies to all forms of remuneration. Accordingly, Q/A-13 provides that, for purposes of determining when remuneration is treated as paid, the timing rule in section 4960(a) applies and the timing rule for wage inclusion under Treas. Reg. § 31.3402(a)-1(b) is not relevant.

Under Q/A-13, the amount of remuneration treated as paid at vesting is the present value of the remuneration in which the covered employee vests. The employer must determine the present value using reasonable actuarial assumptions regarding the time and likelihood of actual or constructive payment. The employer may use the rules set forth in Prop. Treas. Reg. § 1.457-12(c)(1) to determine the present value. In addition, for purposes of determining the present value of remuneration that is scheduled to be paid within 90 days of vesting, the employer may elect to treat the amount that is to be paid as the present value of the amount on the date of vesting. Until actually or constructively paid, the amount treated as paid at vesting is referred to as "previously paid remuneration."

Q/A-13 provides specific rules for timing of inclusion for earnings and losses on previously paid remuneration. Net earnings on previously paid remuneration are treated as paid at the close of the calendar year in which they accrue. For example, the present value of vested remuneration credited to an employee's account under an account balance plan described in Treas. Reg. § 1.409A-1(c)(2)(i)(A) (under which the earnings and losses attributed to the account are based solely on a predetermined actual investment or a reasonable market interest rate) is treated as paid on the date credited to the employee's account and, until subsequently actually or constructively paid, is treated as previously paid remuneration. However, at the

close of each calendar year in which there is previously paid remuneration allocable to a covered employee, the present value of any net earnings accrued on that previously paid remuneration (the increase in present value due to the predetermined actual investment or a reasonable market interest rate) is treated as remuneration paid (and subsequently is treated as previously paid remuneration until actually or constructively paid). Similarly, the present value of a vested, fixed amount of remuneration under a nonaccount balance plan described in Treas. Reg. § 1.409A-1(c)(2)(i)(C) is treated as paid on the date of vesting and subsequently as previously paid remuneration until actually or constructively paid. But, at the close of each calendar year in which there is previously paid remuneration allocable to a covered employee, the net increase in the present value of that amount during the year constitutes earnings and is treated as remuneration paid (and subsequently is also treated as previously paid remuneration until actually or constructively paid). For this purpose, earnings and losses from one arrangement may be aggregated with earnings and losses from any other arrangement provided by the same employer in which the employee participates, resulting in a single amount of remuneration and one amount, if any, of carryover losses (but no carryover gains, since any net gain would be treated as remuneration for the taxable year). For purposes of determining earnings and losses, previously paid remuneration is reduced by the amount actually or constructively paid under the plan or arrangement granting the rights to such remuneration. Q/A-13 further illustrates the operation of these rules through examples.

One commenter requested a "grandfather" rule like the transition rule under section 13601 of the Act that amended section 162(m). Because section 13602 of the Act, which added section 4960 to the Code, does not provide a transition rule (in contrast to section 13601 of the Act), and there is no indication in the legislative history that Congress intended there to be a transition rule for section 4960, the Treasury Department and the IRS have concluded that it is inappropriate to provide an effective date exception similar to the one provided for purposes of section 13601 of the Act. However, Q/A-13 clarifies and demonstrates the grandfathering effect of the remuneration payment timing rule. Specifically, Q/A-13 clarifies that any vested remuneration, including vested but unpaid earnings on deferred amounts, that is treated as paid before section 4960 is applicable (January 1, 2018, in the case of a calendar year employer) is not subject to the excise tax imposed under section 4960(a)(1), although earnings after the effective date on those amounts are treated as remuneration paid for purposes of section 4960(a)(1). Similarly, Q/A–13 clarifies that vested amounts that would have been treated as remuneration paid (including vested but unpaid earnings) before the year in which an employee first becomes a covered employee are not remuneration for the first year the employee becomes a covered employee or any subsequent year and, therefore, are not subject to the excise tax imposed under section 4960(a)(1). However, subsequent earnings on that vested remuneration may be subject to excise tax under section 4960(a)(1).

To reduce administrative burdens, some commenters recommended that remuneration be determined solely by reference to the amount reportable in Form W-2, box 1. For the following reasons, the Treasury Department and the IRS have concluded it is inappropriate to adopt that recommendation. In defining remuneration, section 4960(c)(3) explicitly cross-references and modifies the definition of wages under section 3401(a). Although the amount reportable in Form W-2, box 1 includes wages as defined under section 3401(a), it may also include amounts that are includible in the employee's gross income but are not wages under section 3401(a). In addition, as explained previously, the timing rule for when remuneration is paid under section 4960(a) differs from the timing rule for when wages are paid under section 3401(a). Therefore, the amount reported in Form W-2, box 1 in many cases will not be the same as the employee's remuneration for purposes of section 4960.

As an alternative to using the amount reported in Form W-2, box 1, some commenters recommended that remuneration be defined solely by reference to the amount reportable in Form W-2, box 5, which reports the amount of wages (as defined in section 3121(a)) subject to the Hospital Insurance tax under sections 3101(b) and 3111(b). However, there are differences between the definitions of wages under sections 3401(a) and 3121(a), and there is no indication in the statute or legislative history that Congress intended that the definition of wages in section 3121(a) be used to determine remuneration under section 4960(a). In addition, the payment timing differences discussed previously apply so that the amounts reported in Form W-2, box 5 may not accurately reflect the remuneration paid for the applicable period for purposes of section 4960. For these reasons, the Treasury Department and the IRS have concluded it is not appropriate to adopt this recommendation.

An individual may perform services as a common-law employee for two different related organizations during the calendar year, one or both of which is an ATEO, in which case remuneration paid for the taxable year is aggregated for purposes of determining whether excess remuneration has been paid. To address these cases, Q/A–14 provides rules for allocating liability for the excise tax among the employers. As provided in section 4960(c)(4)(C), in any case in which an ATEO includes remuneration from one or more related organizations as separate employers of the individual in determining the excise tax imposed by section 4960(a), each employer is liable for its proportionate share of the excise tax.

The guidance in this notice provides specific instructions for calculating the excise tax on excess remuneration under section 4960(a)(1), including rules for allocating the excise tax among related employers and rules regarding a change in related status during the calendar year. As described further in Q/A–14, an employee may be a covered employee of more than one ATEO and each ATEO employer calculates its liability under section 4960(a)(1) taking into account the organizations to which it is related. In that case, Q/A–14 provides that, rather than owing tax as both an ATEO and a related organization for the same remuneration paid to a covered employee, an employer is liable only for the greater of the excise tax it would owe as an ATEO or the excise tax it would owe as a related organization with respect to that covered employee.

### E. *Medical and Veterinary Services*

Section 4960(c)(3)(B) and (c)(5)(C)(iii) exclude from remuneration and parachute payments, respectively, the portion of any compensation that is for the performance of medical or veterinary services by a licensed medical professional (including a veterinarian). The Conference Report states that "[f]or purposes of determining a covered employee, remuneration paid to a licensed medical professional which is *directly* related to the performance of medical or veterinary services by such professional is not taken into account, whereas remuneration paid to such a professional in any other capacity is taken into account." Conf. Rep. at 494 (emphasis added).

Sections 4960(c)(3)(B) and (c)(5)(C)(iii) both use the phrase "medical or veterinary services." Consistent with the legislative history quoted previously, Q/A–15 provides that remuneration for the direct performance of medical or veterinary services is excluded for purposes of section 4960. Commenters requested guidance as to the meaning of "licensed medical professional," which is not defined in the statute. The Conference Report states that "[a] medical professional for this purpose includes a doctor, nurse, or veterinarian." Conf. Rep. at 494. Q/A-15 provides that a licensed medical professional is an individual who is licensed under state or local law to perform medical or veterinary services. In addition to those professionals listed, this generally includes dentists and nurse practitioners and may include other medical professionals depending on state or local law.

Commenters also requested guidance on the definition of medical services for purposes of section 4960. Q/A-15 adopts the definition of medical care under section 213(d) for purposes of determining whether services are medical services. This standard is consistent with the legislative intent that the exception apply only to remuneration for the direct performance of medical services and is a familiar standard for taxpayers. Section 213(d) provides that medical care consists of services for the diagnosis, cure, mitigation, treatment, or prevention of disease, including services for the purpose of affecting any structure or function of the body. For a veterinarian or other licensed veterinary professional, section 213(d)(1)(A) applies by analogy to determine whether the activity constitutes veterinary services.

In addition, commenters requested guidance on whether activities related to medical services, such as administrative, teaching, and research services, are medical services. Q/A-15 provides that these activities generally are not medical services. However, to the extent a licensed medical professional provides direct medical care to a patient in the course of these activities, he or she performs medical services, and remuneration allocable to those services is not taken into account for purposes of section 4960.

When a covered employee is compensated for both medical services and other services, the employer must allocate remuneration paid to such employee between medical services and such other services. Q/A-15 permits taxpayers to use any reasonable, good faith method to allocate remuneration between medical services and other services. For this purpose, taxpayers may rely on a reasonable allocation set forth in an employment agreement that explicitly allocates a portion of the remuneration as for medical services or other services. If some or all of the remuneration is not reasonably allocated in an employment agreement, taxpayers must use a reasonable method of allocation. As an example of a reasonable method, a taxpayer may use records such as patient, insurance, and Medicare/Medicaid billing records or internal time reporting mechanisms to determine the time spent providing medical services, and then allocate remuneration to medical services in the proportion such time bears to the total hours the covered employee worked for the employer. The same rules apply with respect to veterinary services.

### F. Excess Parachute Payments

Section 4960(a)(2) imposes an excise tax on "any excess parachute payment." Section 4960(c)(5)(A) provides that the term "excess parachute payment" means an amount equal to the excess of any parachute payment over the portion of the base amount allocated to such payment. Section 4960(c)(5)(B) provides that the term "parachute payment" means any payment in the nature of compensation to (or for the benefit of) a covered employee if (i) such payment is contingent on such employee's separation from employment with the employer, and (ii) the aggregate present value of the payments in the nature of compensation to (or for the benefit of) such individual which are contingent on such separation equals or exceeds an amount equal to three times the base amount. Section 4960(c)(5)(C) provides exceptions for certain retirement plans, certain payments to licensed medical professionals, and payments to individuals who are not highly compensated employees as defined in section 414(q).[4]

The excess parachute payment rules under section 4960 are modeled after section 280G. Section 280G disallows a deduction for any excess parachute payment. Although sections 280G and 4960 both use the term "parachute payment," they define it differently. Whereas the section 4960 definition refers to payments contingent on an employee's separation from employment, the section 280G definition refers to payments contingent on a change in the ownership or effective control of a corporation (or in the ownership of a substantial portion of the assets of the corpora-

---

[4] Under section 414(q), a highly compensated employee generally is defined as any employee who was a five-percent owner at any time during the year or the preceding year or who had compensation from the employer in the preceding year in excess of an inflation-adjusted amount. Notice 2017-64, 2017-45 I.R.B. 486, and Notice 2018-83, provide that the inflation-adjusted amounts for 2018 and 2019 are $120,000 and $125,000, respectively. See section 414(q) and the regulations thereunder for additional details, including the availability of an election to treat no more than the top 20 percent of an employer's employees as highly compensated employees by reason of their compensation.

**Notice 2019-9**

tion). There are also other differences between sections 280G and 4960. For example, section 280G does not include exceptions for payments to licensed medical professionals or non-highly compensated employees. The guidance in this notice incorporates many of the questions and answers (Q/As) under Treas. Reg. § 1.280G-1, with modifications to reflect the statutory differences between sections 280G and 4960. However, certain Q/As under Treas. Reg. § 1.280G-1 are not incorporated into this notice because they address issues that do not arise under section 4960. Conversely, certain Q/As in this notice do not have parallel Q/As under Treas. Reg. § 1.280G-1 because they address issues that arise under section 4960 but not under section 280G.

The discussion of Q/A-16 through Q/A-34 that follows provides an overview of the guidance in this notice for purposes of calculating the excise tax under section 4960(a)(2), noting certain similarities and differences between those Q/As and the Q/As under Treas. Reg. § 1.280G-1. As a preliminary matter, however, the following summarizes the basic steps used to determine the amount of excise tax (if any) under section 4960(a)(2):

Step 1: Determine if a covered employee is entitled to receive payments in the nature of compensation that are contingent on an involuntary separation from employment and are not subject to an exclusion.

Step 2: Calculate the total aggregate present value of the contingent payments, taking into account the special valuation rules that apply when an involuntary separation from employment accelerates payment or vesting of a right to a payment.

Step 3: Calculate the covered employee's base amount with respect to the base period.

Step 4: Determine if the contingent payments are parachute payments. The contingent payments are parachute payments if their total aggregate present value equals or exceeds an amount equal to three times the covered employee's base amount.

Step 5: Calculate the amount of excess parachute payments. A parachute payment is an excess parachute payment to the extent the payment exceeds the base amount allocated to the payment. (Note that this is the excess over 1 times the base amount, and not the excess over 3 times the base amount.)

Step 6: Calculate the amount of excise tax under section 4960(a)(2). The excise tax is the amount equal to the product of the rate of tax under section 11 and the sum of any excess

parachute payments paid by an ATEO or related organization to the covered employee.

Q/A-16 defines the term "excess parachute payment," and Q/A-17 defines the term "parachute payment." Q/A-18, which defines a "payment in the nature of compensation," is based on Treas. Reg. § 1.280G-1, Q/A-11. Q/A-19, which describes when a payment is considered made for purposes of section 4960(a)(2), including the treatment of section 83 property, stock options, and stock appreciation rights and the treatment of consideration paid by an employee, is based on Treas. Reg. § 1.280G-1, Q/A-12 through Q/A-14.

Q/A-20 describes when a payment is contingent on an employee's separation from employment. Commenters requested that the Treasury Department and the IRS clarify what it means for a payment to be contingent on a separation from employment, noting that the statute does not provide a definition. One commenter suggested that the Treasury Department and the IRS issue guidance treating a payment as contingent on an employee's separation from employment only if the payment is subject to a substantial risk of forfeiture (defined in a manner consistent with section 457(f) or section 409A) at the time of a separation from employment and the separation causes the risk of forfeiture to lapse. The guidance in this notice is generally consistent with that suggestion, with certain exceptions discussed in the next several paragraphs.

Separation from employment (whether voluntary or involuntary) is often used in compensation arrangements as the trigger to pay vested amounts. For example, it is typical for a nonqualified deferred compensation plan to provide that payments will be made or begin upon a separation from employment, including separation from employment resulting from death or disability. In contrast, Treas. Reg. § 1.280G-1, Q/A-22 generally treats a payment as contingent on a change in ownership or control if the payment would not have been made had no change in ownership or control occurred, taking into consideration whether vesting or payment is accelerated by reason of the change in ownership or control. Similarly, in defining when a payment is contingent on separation from employment, this notice does not focus solely on whether the payment would not have been made but for a separation from employment, but instead also takes into consideration whether the separation from employment results in the employee becoming vested or otherwise accelerates the right to payment.

The guidance in this notice limits the payments treated as contingent on a separation from employment to payments contingent on an involuntary separation from employment because payments that vest upon a separation from employment typically vest only upon an involuntary separation from employment. If an employee may voluntarily separate from service and still be entitled to a payment, then the payment either is not subject to a substantial risk of forfeiture or the forfeiture condition is not related to the separation from employment. If, however, there are other types of separation from employment conditions that may result in the lapse of a substantial risk of forfeiture applicable to a payment, the standard in this notice may be expanded in future guidance to ensure that those payments are also treated as contingent on a separation from employment.

Specifically, Q/A–20 provides that a payment is contingent on a separation from employment if the payment would not have been made in the absence of an involuntary separation from employment. It further provides that if the right to a payment vests as a result of an involuntary separation from employment, the payment is treated as a payment that is contingent on a separation from employment. For example, a right to a severance payment provided in an employment agreement that vests upon an involuntary separation from employment is a payment contingent on a separation from employment.

However, not all payments that are made after an involuntary separation from employment are contingent on a separation from employment. For example, a payment of deferred compensation after an involuntary separation from employment that vested based on years of service completed before the involuntary separation from employment generally is not a payment that is contingent on a separation from employment because the payment would be paid at some point, and the separation from employment may impact the time of, but not the right to, the payment. Similarly, medical benefits that vested based on years of service completed before an involuntary separation from employment but that are provided after the involuntary separation from employment generally are not treated as payments that are contingent on a separation from employment.

Q/A–20 also provides that an amount that was included in gross income in a previous year and excess remuneration that was treated as paid under Q/A–13 before the separation from employment are not contingent on the separation from employment. Therefore, while these amounts may be included in the employee's base amount, payments of these amounts are not parachute payments.

Q/A–24 provides that if a payment is accelerated or a substantial risk of forfeiture lapses as a result of an involuntary separation from employment, the additional value due to the acceleration is treated as a payment contingent on a separation from employment. Q/A–24 is based on the rules of Treas. Reg. § 1.280G-1, Q/A–24(b) and (c) for purposes of determining the value of these accelerations.

Notwithstanding the foregoing, if the facts and circumstances demonstrate that either vesting or payment of an amount (whether before or after the involuntary separation from employment) would not have occurred but for the involuntary nature of the separation from employment, the amount will be treated as contingent on a separation from employment. For example, an employer's exercise of discretion to accelerate vesting of an amount shortly before an involuntary separation from employment may indicate that the acceleration of vesting was due to the involuntary nature of the separation from employment and, thus, was contingent on the employee's separation from employment. Similarly, payment of an amount in excess of an amount otherwise payable (for example, increased salary) shortly before or after an involuntary separation from employment may indicate that the amount was paid because the separation was involuntary and, thus, was contingent on the employee's separation from employment.

Q/A–21 provides that payments pursuant to certain window programs are treated as payments contingent on a separation from employment and is based on Treas. Reg. § 1.409A-1(b)(9).

Q/A–23 generally adopts the standards of the regulations under section 409A for purposes of determining whether there has been a separation from employment, except that a bona fide change from employee to independent contractor status is treated as a separation from employment. However, the IRS may assert based on all the facts and circumstances that there was not a bona fide change from employee to independent contractor status. Specifically, Q/A–23 adopts the standards of Treas. Reg. § 1.409A-1(h)(1)(ii), providing that an anticipated reduction in the level of services of more than 80 percent is treated as a separation from employment and an anticipated reduction in the level of services of less than 50 percent is not treated as a separation from employment, with the treatment of an anticipated reduction between these two levels depending on the facts and circumstances. The guidance in this notice does not adopt the rule of Treas. Reg. § 1.409A-1(h)(1)(ii) under which an employer may modify the level of the anticipated reduction in future services that will be considered to result in a separation from employment. Instead, the default 80 percent and 50 percent levels provided under Treas. Reg. § 1.409A-1(h)(1)(ii) apply for purposes of section 4960.

Unlike Q/A–25 and Q/A–26 of Treas. Reg. § 1.280G-1, the guidance in this notice does not provide a presumption that a payment made pursuant to an agreement entered into or modified within twelve months of a separation from employment is a payment that is contingent on a separation from employment. However, as noted previously, if the facts and circumstances demonstrate that either the vesting or the payment of an amount would not have occurred but for the involuntary nature of the separation from employment, the amount will be treated as a payment contingent on a separation from employment.

In addition, the guidance in this notice does not incorporate Treas. Reg. § 1.280G-1, Q/A–9, excluding reasonable compensation for services from the definition of parachute payment. In many cases, whether payments after a separation from employment are reasonable compensation for services will not be an issue because the employee will not provide services after the separation from employment. However, if the employee continues to provide services (including as a bona fide independent contractor) after a separation from employment, payments for those services are not contingent on the involuntary separation from employment to the extent those payments are reasonable and are not made due to the involuntary nature of the separation from employment.

Finally, the guidance in this notice does not include a rule similar to Treas. Reg. § 1.280G-1, Q/A–16, under which a personal service corporation (PSC) is treated as an employee. Q/A–3 provides that section 4960 applies to amounts paid to common law employees who are covered employees of an ATEO. Although a PSC that performs services for an ATEO is not treated as an employee, the IRS may assert that the individual owner of a PSC is in fact a common law employee of an ATEO based on all the facts and circumstances.

### G. *Three-Times-Base-Amount Test for Parachute Payments*

Section 4960(c)(5)(B) provides that a payment is a parachute payment only if the aggregate present value of the payments in the nature of

compensation to (or for the benefit of) an individual that are contingent on a separation from employment equals or exceeds an amount equal to three times the base amount.

Section 4960(c)(5)(D) provides that rules similar to the rules of section 280G(b)(3) apply for purposes of determining the base amount, and section 4960(c)(5)(E) provides that rules similar to the rules of paragraphs (3) and (4) of section 280G(d) apply for purposes of present value determinations. Section 280G(b)(3) provides that the term "base amount" means an individual's annualized includible compensation for a base period. Section 280G(d)(2) defines "base period" as the period consisting of the five most recent taxable years of the service provider ending before the date on which the change in ownership or control occurs or the portion of such period during which the individual performed personal services for the corporation. Section 280G(d)(3) provides that any transfer of property is treated as a payment and is taken into account at its fair market value. Section 280G(d)(4) provides that present value is determined using a discount rate equal to 120 percent of the applicable Federal rate determined under section 1274(d), compounded semiannually.

Q/A–25 through Q/A–31 are based on the rules under Treas. Reg. § 1.280G-1, Q/A–30 through Q/A–35 (substituting an involuntary separation from employment for a change in control) for determining whether a payment is an excess parachute payment, including the rules for applying the three-times-base-amount test, determining the base amount and base period, and determining present value, including determining the present value of payments that are contingent on uncertain future events.

### H. *Computation of Excess Parachute Payments*

Section 4960(c)(5)(A) provides that an "excess parachute payment" is an amount equal to the excess of any parachute payment over the portion of the base amount allocated to such payment. Q/A–32(a) is based on Treas. Reg. § 1.280G-1, Q/A–38, regarding allocating the base amount to a parachute payment (that is, determining the portion that is not a parachute payment because it does not exceed the base amount). Q/A–2 provides that the excise tax on excess parachute payments for a taxable year is based on any excess parachute payments made in the calendar year ending with or within the taxable year of the ATEO.

### I. *Reporting Liability Under Section 4960*

As requested by some commenters, Q/A–34 provides guidance as to the reporting and due date for paying the section 4960 excise tax. On November 7, 2018, the Treasury Department and the IRS issued proposed regulations under sections 6011 and 6071 (Prop. Treas. Reg. §§ 53.6011-1 and 53.6071-1, 83 F.R. 55653) to address reporting and the due date for paying the tax. The proposed regulations provide that the excise tax under section 4960 is reported on Form 4720, Return of Certain Excise Taxes Under Chapters 41 and 42 of the Internal Revenue Code, which is the form generally used for reporting and paying chapter 42 taxes. Each employer liable for section 4960 tax, whether an ATEO or a related organization described in section 4960(c)(4)(B), is responsible for separately reporting and paying its share of the tax. The proposed regulations provide that Form 4720 and payment are due when chapter 42 taxes ordinarily are due (the 15th day of the 5th month after the end of the taxpayer's taxable year— May 15 for a calendar year employer), subject to an extension of time for filing that generally applies. This rule is also reflected in Q/A-34(a).

Q/A-34(b) provides that an employer may elect to prepay the excise tax imposed under section 4960(a)(2) in the year of separation from employment (or any taxable year prior to the year in which the parachute payment is actually paid). This rule is similar to the rule in Treas. Reg. § 1.280G-1, Q/A-11(c), under which a disqualified employee may elect to prepay the excise tax under section 4999 based on the present value of the excise tax that would be owed by the employee when the parachute payments are actually made.

Some commenters requested clarification as to whether section 4960 excise tax is subject to quarterly payments of estimated tax under section 6655. Since section 6655 was not amended to include section 4960, no quarterly payments of estimated section 4960 tax are required under section 6655. See Q/A-35.

**J.** *Miscellaneous Issues*

Q/A-36 through Q/A-38 address coordination of section 4960 with other Code provisions. Commenters requested clarification of the relationship between the section 4960 excise tax and excise taxes for unreasonable or excessive compensation under section 4958 or, in the case of compensation to disqualified persons for personal services, section 4941. Q/A-36 and Q/A-37 confirm that there is no particular relationship between liability for excise tax under section 4960 and liability under these other provisions. In cases involving excessive compensation for purposes of section 4958 or section 4941, there may or may not be concurrent excise tax liability

under section 4960, and in cases involving section 4960 excise tax liability, there may or may not be concurrent liability under section 4958 or section 4941.

Q/A-38 addresses the rule under section 4960(c)(6) that remuneration for which a deduction is disallowed under section 162(m) is not taken into account under section 4960. For example, an ATEO's covered employee may also be a covered employee of a publicly held corporation (as those terms are defined in section 162(m)(2) and (3)) if the publicly held corporation is related to the ATEO under section 4960(c)(4)(B). In that case, any portion of remuneration disallowed as a deduction by reason of section 162(m) is not taken into account under section 4960.

**K.** *Effective Date*

Section 4960 is effective for the first taxable year beginning after December 31, 2017. Q/A-39 provides that amounts paid before the beginning of that taxable year are not subject to the excise tax under section 4960. As described previously in the discussion of remuneration for purposes of section 4960(a)(1), remuneration that was vested before the effective date of section 4960 is not subject to excise tax under section 4960 because it is treated as having been paid at vesting. For example, amounts includible in gross income under section 457(f)(1)(A) and any vested earnings that accrued before the effective date of section 4960 are not subject to the excise tax under section 4960. However, earnings accrued on those amounts in taxable years beginning after December 31, 2017, may be subject to excise tax under section 4960(a)(1).

II. INTERIM GUIDANCE ON APPLICATION OF SECTION 4960

**A.** *Section 4960 — In General*

**Q-1: What is the effect of section 4960?**

A-1: An ATEO or related organization that pays excess remuneration or an excess parachute payment to a covered employee is subject to an excise tax on that amount at a rate equal to the rate of tax under section 11. For taxable years beginning after December 31, 2017, the rate of tax under section 11 is 21 percent. *See* section 13001 of the Act.

**Q-2: What year is used in calculating the section 4960 excise tax?**

A-2: Excess remuneration paid and excess parachute payments made in the calendar year ending with or within the taxable year of an ATEO or a related organization, whichever is the applicable employer, are treated as paid for that taxable year. Thus, the excise tax on excess remuneration and excess parachute payments is calculated based on excess remuneration paid and excess parachute payments made during the calendar year ending with or within the employer's taxable year.

### Q–3: Who is liable for the section 4960 excise tax?

A–3: (a) *In general*. The common-law employer, as generally determined for federal tax purposes, is liable for the excise tax imposed under section 4960. Only an ATEO has covered employees, but a covered employee may also be an employee of a related organization. When an employer that is an ATEO or a related organization pays a covered employee either excess remuneration or an excess parachute payment, each employer is liable for the excise tax under section 4960. See Q/A–14 for rules that apply when more than one employer is liable for the excise tax on excess remuneration.

Whether a person or entity is the common-law employer generally depends on the facts and circumstances. A common-law employer may not avoid liability under section 4960 by reason of a third party payor arrangement, such as an arrangement with a payroll agent, common paymaster, statutory employer under section 3401(d)(1), or certified professional employer organization, or any similar arrangement. For purposes of section 4960, a payment to an employee by a third-party payor is considered paid by the common-law employer with respect to the services for which the payment is made. Similarly, a payment to an employee on behalf of the common-law employer (such as a payment from a related organization for which the individual is not providing services as an employee or a payment from an unrelated management company), is considered paid by the common-law employer for purposes of section 4960.

(b) *Disregarded entities*. In the case of employment by a disregarded entity described in Treas. Reg. §301.7701-3, the sole owner of the disregarded entity is treated as the common-law employer for purposes of section 4960.

(c) *Arrangements between an ATEO and a related organization*. Calculation of, and liability for, the excise tax based on excess remuneration or an excess parachute payment in accordance with this Q/A–3 is separate from and unaffected by any arrangement that the ATEO and any related organization may have for bearing the cost of any excise tax liability under section 4960.

### B. *Applicable Tax-Exempt Organizations and Related Organizations*

### Q–4: What is an applicable tax-exempt organization within the meaning of section 4960(c)(1)?

A–4: As provided in section 4960(c)(1), an ATEO is any organization which for its taxable year–

(A) is exempt from taxation under section 501(a),

(B) is a farmers' cooperative organization described in section 521(b)(1),

(C) has income excluded from taxation under section 115(1), or

(D) is a political organization described in section 527(e)(1).

### Q–5: When is a governmental entity an applicable tax-exempt organization within the meaning of section 4960(c)(1)?

A–5: Governmental entities specifically described in section 4960(c)(1), that is, organizations that have income excluded from taxation under section 115(1) and organizations that are exempt from taxation under section 501(a), are ATEOs. For example, federal instrumentalities exempt from tax under section 501(c)(1) and public universities with IRS determination letters recognizing their tax-exempt status under section 501(c)(3) are governmental entities exempt from tax under section 501(a), and thus are ATEOs.

A governmental entity that is separately organized from a state or political subdivision of a state may meet the requirements to exclude income from gross income (and thereby have income excluded from taxation) under section 115(1). See Rev. Rul. 77-261, 1977-2 C.B.45. However, a state, political subdivision of a state, or integral part of a state or political subdivision, often referred to as a "governmental unit," does not meet the requirements to exclude income from gross income under section 115(1) because section 115(1) does not apply to income from an activity that the state conducts directly, rather than through a separate entity. See Rev. Rul. 77-261; see also Rev. Rul. 71-131, 1971-1 C.B. 28 (superseding and restating the position stated in G.C.M. 14407, C.B. XIV-1 103).

Instead, under the doctrine of implied statutory immunity, the income of a governmental unit generally is not taxable in the absence of specific statutory authorization for taxing that income. See Rev. Rul. 87-2, 1987-1 C.B. 18; Rev.

Rul. 71-131; Rev. Rul. 71-132, 1971-1 C.B. 29; and G.C.M. 14407. Section 511(a)(2)(B), which imposes tax on the unrelated business taxable income of state colleges and universities, is an example of a specific statutory authorization for taxing income earned by a state, a political subdivision of a state, or an integral part of a state or political subdivision of a state.

Thus, a governmental unit (including a state college or university) that does not have a determination letter recognizing its exemption from taxation under section 501(a) and does not exclude income from gross income under section 115(1) is not an ATEO described in section 4960(c)(1). However, such a governmental unit may be liable for excise tax under section 4960 if it is a related organization under section 4960(c)(4)(B) with respect to an ATEO.

**Q–6: May a governmental entity with a determination letter recognizing its tax exemption relinquish its section 501(c)(3) status?**

A–6: Yes, a governmental entity may voluntarily relinquish its section 501(c)(3) tax-exempt status pursuant to section 3.01(12) of Rev. Proc. 2018-5, 2018-1 I.R.B. 233, 239 (or the analogous section in any successor revenue procedure), under the procedures described in that revenue procedure.

**Q–7: What is a related organization for purposes of section 4960?**

A–7: As provided in section 4960(c)(4)(B), a person or governmental entity is related to an ATEO if such person or governmental entity–

(i) controls, or is controlled by, the ATEO;

(ii) is controlled by one or more persons which control the ATEO;

(iii) is a supported organization (as defined in section 509(f)(3)) with respect to the ATEO;

(iv) is a supporting organization described in section 509(a)(3) with respect to the ATEO; or

(v) in the case of an ATEO which is a voluntary employees' beneficiary association described in section 501(c)(9), establishes, maintains, or makes contributions to such voluntary employees' beneficiary association.

See Q/A–14(c) for rules regarding a change in related status during the year.

**Q–8: What is the meaning of "control" for purposes of section 4960(c)(4)(B)(i)-(ii) and Q/A–7 of this notice?**

A–8: (a) *In general*. For purposes of section 4960(c)(4)(B)(i)-(ii) and Q/A–7 of this notice, the term "control" is defined as follows:

(1) *Stock corporation*. In the case of a stock corporation, control means ownership (by vote or value) of more than 50 percent of the stock in such corporation.

(2) *Partnership*. In the case of a partnership, control means ownership of more than 50 percent of the profits interest or capital interest in such partnership.

(3) *Trust*. In the case of a trust with beneficial interests, control means ownership of more than 50 percent of the beneficial interests in the trust.

(4) *Nonstock organization*. In the case of a nonprofit organization or other organization without owners or persons having beneficial interests (nonstock organization), including a governmental entity, control means that (i) more than 50 percent of the directors or trustees of the ATEO or nonstock organization are either representatives of, or are directly or indirectly controlled by, the other entity; or (ii) more than 50 percent of the directors or trustees of the nonstock organization are either representatives of, or are directly or indirectly controlled by, one or more persons that control the ATEO. For purposes of this paragraph, a "representative" means a trustee, director, agent, or employee, and control includes the power to remove a trustee or director and designate a new trustee or director.

(5) *Constructive ownership*. For purposes of Q/A–7 and this Q/A–8, section 318 (relating to constructive ownership of stock) applies for purposes of determining control of stock in a corporation. For purposes of determining control of any other entity, including a nonstock organization, under this Q/A–8, the principles of section 318 apply.

(b) *Examples*. The following examples illustrate how the rules of Q/A–7 and this Q/A–8 apply:

**Example 1.** A, B, and C are nonstock organizations and are ATEOs within the meaning of section 4960(c)(1). C owns 80 percent of the stock of corporation D. Eighty percent of B's directors are representatives of A. In addition, 80 percent of

C's directors are representatives of A. A is a related organization with respect to B (and vice versa) because more than 50 percent of B's directors are representatives of A; thus, A controls B. Based on the same analysis, A is also a related organization with respect to C (and vice versa). D is a related organization with respect to C because, as the owner of more than 50 percent of D's stock, C controls D. Applying the principles of section 318, A is deemed to own 64 percent of the stock of D (80 percent of C's stock in D). Thus, D is a related organization with respect to A because A controls D. B is a related organization with respect to C, C is a related organization with respect to B, and D is a related organization with respect to B because B, C, and D are all controlled by the same person (A).

**Example 2.** X, Y, and Z are nonstock organizations and are ATEOs within the meaning of section 4960(c)(1). Sixty percent of Y's directors are representatives of X. In addition, 60 percent of Z's directors are representatives of Y. X is a related organization with respect to Y (and vice versa) because more than 50 percent of Y's directors are representatives of X; thus, X controls Y. Based on the same analysis, Z is a related organization with respect to Y (and vice versa). Applying the principles of section 318, X is deemed to control 36 percent of Z's directors (60 percent of Y's 60 percent control over Z). Because less than 50 percent of Z's directors are representatives of or controlled by X, and absent any facts suggesting that X directly or indirectly controls Z, X is not a related organization with respect to Z.

### C. Covered Employees

**Q–9: Who is a covered employee within the meaning of section 4960(c)(2)?**

A–9: The term "covered employee" means any employee (including any former employee) of an ATEO, if the employee–

(A) is one of the five highest-compensated employees of the organization for the taxable year of the ATEO, or

(B) was a covered employee of the ATEO (or any predecessor) for any of the ATEO's preceding taxable years beginning after December 31, 2016.

**Q–10: How are the five highest-compensated employees determined?**

A–10: (a) *In general.* Except as provided in Q/A–10(b), the determination of whether an employee is one of the five highest-compensated employees of an ATEO is made on the basis of his or her remuneration for services performed as an employee of the ATEO, including remuneration for services performed as an employee of a related organization with respect to the ATEO. The remuneration used for purposes of identifying the five highest-compensated employees is the remuneration paid to an employee during the calendar year ending with or within the ATEO's or related organization's taxable year. Remuneration paid for medical services (or veterinary services) is not taken into account for purposes of identifying the five highest-compensated employees.

(b) *Limited services exception.* An employee is not one of an ATEO's five highest-compensated employees for a taxable year if, during the calendar year ending with or within the taxable year, as described in Q/A–2, the ATEO paid less than 10 percent of the employee's total remuneration for services performed as an employee of the ATEO and all related organizations. However, if an employee would not be treated as one of the five highest-compensated employees of any ATEO in an ATEO's group of related organizations because no ATEO in the group paid at least 10 percent of the total remuneration paid by the group during the calendar year, then this exception does not apply to the ATEO that paid the employee the most remuneration during that year.

(c) *Examples.* The following examples illustrate the rules of this Q/A–10:

**Example 1.** X and Y are both calendar year taxpayers and ATEOs that are related organizations with respect to each other, and both employ E during calendar year 2020. Of the total remuneration paid to E for services performed as an employee of X and Y, 50 percent was for services for X and 50 percent was for services for Y. Based on the aggregate remuneration from X and Y, E is one of the five highest-compensated employees of both X and Y. E is a covered employee of both X and Y for 2020 and all future taxable years.

**Example 2.** Assume the same facts as **Example 1**, except that of the total remuneration paid to E for services performed as an employee of X and Y, 95 percent was for services for X and 5 percent was for services for Y. E is a covered employee of X for 2020 and all future taxable years, but is not a covered employee of Y for 2020 because Y did not pay at least 10 percent of the total remuneration paid to E by Y and all related organizations and at least one other related ATEO paid at least 10 percent of that remuneration.

## D. *Excess Remuneration*

**Q–11: What is excess remuneration paid by an applicable tax-exempt organization under section 4960(a)(1)?**

A–11: For each covered employee, excess remuneration is the excess (if any) for a taxable year of the remuneration that is paid (other than any excess parachute payment) by an ATEO, including remuneration paid by a related organization, over $1 million for the taxable year.

**Q–12: What is remuneration under section 4960(c)(3)?**

A–12: (a) *General rule.* The term "remuneration" has the same meaning as the term "wages," as defined in section 3401(a), except that it excludes any designated Roth contribution (as defined in section 402A(c)) and includes amounts required to be included in gross income under section 457(f). Remuneration includes an amount that is a parachute payment; however, a parachute payment is not subject to tax as excess remuneration if it is also subject to tax as an excess parachute payment. Further, remuneration does not include the portion of any remuneration paid to a licensed medical professional (including a veterinarian) that is directly related to the performance of medical or veterinary services by such professional.

(b) *Section 3401(a) wages.* Section 3401(a) provides that the term "wages" generally means all remuneration for services performed by an employee for his employer (with certain exceptions provided under section 3401(a)(1) through (a)(23)), including the cash value of all remuneration (including benefits) paid in any medium other than cash. Among the more broadly applicable exclusions, section 3401(a)(12) provides that wages do not include remuneration paid to, or on behalf of, an employee or his beneficiary–

(1) from or to a trust described in section 401(a) which is exempt from tax under section 501(a) at the time of such payment unless such payment is made to an employee of the trust as remuneration for services rendered as such employee and not as a beneficiary of the trust;

(2) under or to an annuity plan which, at the time of such payment, is a plan described in section 403(a);

(3) for a payment described in section 402(h)(1) and (2) if, at the time of such payment, it is reasonable to believe that the employee will be entitled to an exclusion under such section for payment;

(4) under an arrangement to which section 408(p) applies; or

(5) under or to an eligible deferred compensation plan which, at the time of such payment, is a plan described in section 457(b) that is maintained by an eligible employer described in section 457(e)(1)(A) (governmental employer).

(c) *Remuneration paid by related organizations.* Remuneration includes remuneration paid to a covered employee by any related organization with respect to the employee's employment by that related organization. (See Q/A–14(b) for rules on allocating the liability for the excise tax when remuneration from more than one employer is taken into account in determining the liability for the excise tax under section 4960(a)(1).) In contrast, remuneration paid by another organization, whether or not a related organization, with respect to an employee's employment by an ATEO, is treated as remuneration paid by that ATEO for purposes of section 4960.

(d) *Directors.* Compensation paid by an organization to a member of its board of directors (or an individual holding a substantially similar position) for serving in that capacity is not remuneration because the fees received by the director for performing those services constitute self-employment income, rather than wages under section 3401(a). *See* Rev. Rul. 57-246, 1957-1 C.B. 338. If the individual also performs services for the organization as an employee, then the compensation paid for the services as an employee is remuneration. Moreover, for purposes of section 4960, compensation that an employer pays to an employee to serve as a director of another organization is remuneration.

**Q–13: When is remuneration treated as paid for purposes of section 4960(a)(1)?**

A–13: (a) *General rule.* For purposes of section 4960(a)(1), remuneration is paid for a taxable year if it is paid during the calendar year ending with or within the employer's taxable year. Remuneration is treated as paid on the first date that the right to the remuneration is not subject to a substantial risk of forfeiture within the meaning of section 457(f)(3)(B) (regardless of whether the arrangement under which the amount is or will be paid is subject to section 457(f) or section 409A). An amount of remuneration is subject to a substantial risk of forfeiture if the right to the remuneration would be treated as subject to a substantial risk of forfeiture under Prop. Treas. Reg. § 1.457-12(e)(1). In general, this means that the amount is subject to a substantial risk of forfeiture only if entitlement to the amount is conditioned on the future performance of substantial services, or upon the occurrence of a condition that is related to a purpose of the remuneration if the possibility of forfeiture is substantial. *See* Prop. Treas. Reg. § 1.457-12(e)(1) for further guidance on the application of this standard.[5] For purposes of this notice, remuneration that is no longer subject to a substantial risk of forfeiture is referred to as "vested" remuneration and the lapsing of a substantial risk of forfeiture is referred to as "vesting."

(b) *Amount of remuneration treated as paid* –(1) *In general.* The amount of remuneration treated as paid upon vesting is the present value (on the vesting date) of the future payments to which the participant has a legally binding right. The present value of the right to future payments as of the vesting date includes any earnings that have accrued as of the vesting date. The present value must be determined using reasonable actuarial assumptions. Present value determined in accordance with the rules set forth in Prop. Treas. Reg. § 1.457-12(c)(1), including the assumptions regarding payment timing set forth in those proposed regulations, will be deemed to have been determined using reasonable actuarial assumptions. For purposes of determining the present value of remuneration under a nonaccount balance plan described in Treas. Reg. § 1.409A-1(c)(2)(i)(C) that is scheduled to be actually or constructively paid within 90 days of vesting, the employer may elect to treat the nominal amount that is to be paid as the present value of the amount on the date of vesting.

Net earnings, as defined in paragraph (b)(2)(C), on previously paid remuneration, as defined in paragraph (b)(2)(D)(i), are treated as paid at the close of the calendar year in which they accrue. For example, the present value of vested remuneration credited to an employee's account under an account balance plan described in Treas. Reg. § 1.409A-1(c)(2)(i)(A) (under which the earnings and losses attributed to the account are based solely on a predetermined actual investment or a reasonable market interest rate) is treated as paid on the date credited to the employee's account, but the present value of any net earnings accrued on that amount (the increase in value due to the predetermined actual investment or a reasonable market interest rate) is treated as paid at the close of the calendar year in which they accrue. Similarly, the present value of a vested, fixed amount of remuneration under a nonaccount balance plan described in Treas. Reg. § 1.409A-1(c)(2)(i)(C) is treated as paid on the date of vesting, but the present value of the net earnings on that amount (the increase

in the present value) is treated as paid at the close of the calendar year in which they accrue.

(2) *Earnings and losses.* (A) *Earnings.* Earnings generally refer to any increase in the vested present value of any previously paid remuneration as of the close of a calendar year, regardless of whether the plan or arrangement denominates such increase as earnings, to the extent the employee's right to payment of the increase is vested. For example, an increase in the vested account balance of a nonqualified deferred compensation plan based solely on the investment return of a predetermined actual investment (and disregarding any additional contributions) constitutes earnings. Similarly, an increase in the vested present value of a benefit under a nonqualified nonaccount balance plan described in Treas. Reg. § 1.409A-1(c)(2)(i)(C) due solely to the passage of time (and disregarding any additional benefit accruals) constitutes earnings. However, an increase in an account balance of a nonqualified deferred compensation plan due to a salary reduction contribution or an employer contribution does not constitute earnings. Likewise, an increase in the benefit under a nonaccount balance plan described in Treas. Reg. § 1.409A-1(c)(2)(i)(C) due to an additional year of service or an increase in compensation that is reflected in a benefit formula does not constitute earnings.

(B) *Losses.* Losses generally refer to any decrease in the vested present value of any previously paid remuneration as of the close of the calendar year, regardless of whether the plan denominates that decrease as losses.

(C) *Net earnings and losses.* Net earnings and losses for each covered employee are determined on a net aggregate basis for each taxable year based on the previously paid remuneration paid by the employer. For example, losses under an account balance plan described in Treas. Reg. § 1.409A-1(c)(2)(i)(A) may offset earnings under a nonaccount balance plan described in Treas. Reg. § 1.409A-1(c)(2)(i)(C) maintained by the same employer for the same employee, but earnings and losses from a plan maintained by another employer are disregarded.

Net earnings refer to the amount (if any) by which the earnings accrued during a calendar year ending with or within the taxable year (as described in Q/A–2) on any previously paid remuneration exceeds the sum of the losses accrued on those amounts during that calendar year and any net losses carried forward from a

---

[5] When the proposed regulations under section 457(f) are finalized, the Treasury Department and the IRS anticipate providing further guidance on how and when those final regulations apply for purposes of section 4960.

previous taxable year. Net losses refer to the amount (if any) by which the sum of the losses accrued during a calendar year ending with or within the taxable year (as described in Q/A–2) on any previously paid remuneration and the net losses carried forward from a previous taxable year exceeds the earnings accrued on those amounts during that calendar year. Losses do not reduce the remuneration treated as paid in a calendar year except to the extent of the earnings for that calendar year. Thus, if an employee vests in an amount of earnings under a nonaccount balance plan within the meaning of Treas. Reg. §1.409A-1(c)(2)(i)(C), and also has losses under an account balance plan within the meaning of Treas. Reg. §1.409A-1(c)(2)(i)(A) that exceed the vested earnings treated as remuneration under the nonaccount balance plan, those excess losses are carried forward to the next following taxable year and offset vested earnings for purposes of determining net earnings or losses for that taxable year. If, for the next following year, there are not sufficient earnings to offset the entire amount of losses carried forward from the previous year (and any additional losses), the offset process repeats for each later year until there are earnings for the calendar year in excess of the losses carried forward.

(D) *Previously paid remuneration -(i) In general.* Remuneration is treated as previously paid remuneration for a taxable year to the extent that, by the close of the calendar year ending with or within such taxable year (as described in Q/A–2), it is treated as paid under Q/A–13(b)(1) but is not actually or constructively paid.

(ii) *Employee who becomes a covered employee.* Any remuneration that is vested but is not actually or constructively paid as of the close of the calendar year preceding the calendar year ending with or within the taxable year of the employer for which an employee first becomes a covered employee of an ATEO is treated as paid for the employer's preceding taxable year. For example, if an employee first becomes a covered employee of an employer for the employer's taxable year ending June 30, 2022, any remuneration that was vested but was not actually or constructively paid as of December 31, 2020, is treated as paid for the taxable year ending June 30, 2021, and thus is not subject to the excise tax. Net losses from the preceding taxable year do not carry forward to the taxable year an employee becomes a covered employee.

(iii) *Pre-effective date remuneration.* Any remuneration that was vested but was not actually or constructively paid as of the close of the taxable year preceding the first taxable year in which section 4960 is effective for the employer is

treated as paid for the preceding taxable year and is not subject to the excise tax. Thus, for an employer that uses a calendar year taxable year, the present value of any remuneration that was vested but was not actually or constructively paid as of December 31, 2017, is treated as paid for taxable year 2017. For an employer that uses a non-calendar year taxable year, the present value of any remuneration that was vested but was not actually or constructively paid as of the close of the taxable year that includes December 31, 2017 (for example, June 30, 2018 in the case of an employer with a taxable year beginning July 1 and ending June 30) is treated as paid for that taxable year. Regardless of the employer's taxable year, there is no carryover of net losses from the preceding taxable year to the first taxable year for which section 4960 is effective.

(f) *Examples.* The following examples illustrate the rules described in this Q/A–13.

**Example 1**. E is a covered employee of R, an ATEO that uses a calendar year taxable year. E participates in a nonqualified deferred compensation plan in which the account balance is adjusted based on the investment returns on predetermined actual investments chosen by the employee. On January 1, 2019, R credits $100,000 to E's account under the plan, subject to the requirement that E remain employed through June 30, 2021. On June 30, 2021, the vested account balance is $110,000. Due to earnings or losses on the account balance, the closing account balance on each of the following dates is: (i) $115,000 on December 31, 2021, (ii) $120,000 on December 31, 2022, (iii) $100,000 on December 31, 2023, and (iv) $110,000 on December 31, 2024. During 2025, E defers an additional $10,000 under the plan, which is vested at the time of deferral. On December 31, 2025, the closing account balance is $125,000. In 2026, R distributes $10,000 to E under the plan. On December 31, 2026, the closing account balance is $135,000 due to earnings on the account balance.

*2019 and 2020 (nonvested amounts).* For 2019 and 2020, R pays no remuneration to E under the plan. The substantial future services condition is not met; thus, any amount deferred under the plan, including unvested earnings, remains subject to a substantial risk of forfeiture within the meaning of section 457(f)(3)(B) as of December 31, 2019, and December 31, 2020.

*2021 (amounts in year of vesting).* For 2021, R pays E $115,000 of remuneration, including (i) $110,000 of remuneration on June 30, 2021, when the substantial future services condition is met and the amount is no longer subject to a substantial risk of forfeiture within the meaning of section 457(f)(3)(B), and (ii) an additional $5,000 of earnings on the previously paid remuneration ($110,000) on December 31, 2021.

*2022 (earnings).* For 2022, R pays E $5,000 of remuneration, the additional earnings on the previously paid remuneration ($115,000) as of December 31, 2022.

*2023 (losses).* For 2023, R pays no remuneration to E since the vested present value of the previously paid remuneration ($120,000) declines to $100,000 as of December 31, 2023. The $20,000 loss for 2023 does not reduce any amount previously treated as remuneration but is available for carry over to future taxable years.

*2024 (recovery of losses through earnings).* For 2024, R pays no remuneration to E, since the vested present value of the previously paid remuneration ($120,000) was $110,000 as of December 31, 2024. Due to earnings on the account balance, R recovers $10,000 of the $20,000 of losses carried over from 2023. The net losses as of December 31, 2024, are $10,000, and none of the $10,000 in earnings during 2024 is remuneration paid in 2024.

*2025 (no recovery of losses against additional deferrals of compensation).* For 2025, R pays E $10,000 of remuneration to E. The additional $10,000 deferral is not subject to a substantial risk of forfeiture within the meaning of section 457(f)(3)(B), and thus is remuneration paid on the date deferred. This deferral increases the amount previously treated as remuneration from $120,000 to $130,000. Additionally, due to earnings on the account balance, R recovers $5,000 of losses of the $10,000 of losses carried over from 2024, none of which was remuneration for 2025, so that the net losses as of December 31, 2025 is $5,000.

*2026 (distributions, recovery of remainder of losses through earnings and additional earnings).* For 2026, R pays E $15,000 in remuneration. The vested present value of the account balance increases by $20,000 to $135,000 as of December 31, 2026. Therefore, due to earnings on the account balance, R recovers the remaining $5,000 of losses carried over from 2025 and pays E an additional $15,000 of remuneration as earnings. The $10,000 distribution reduces the amount of previously paid remuneration ($130,000) to $120,000, and the additional remuneration paid in 2026 increases the amount of previously paid remuneration by $15,000 to $135,000.

**Example 2**. F is a covered employee of S, an ATEO, and is also employed by corporation C, a related organization. S and C are calendar year taxpayers. On January 1, 2018, C and F enter into an agreement under which C will pay F $100,000 on December 31, 2021, if F remains employed by C through January 1, 2020. F remains employed by C through January 1, 2020. On January 1, 2020, the present value based on reasonable actuarial assumptions of the $100,000 to be paid on December 31, 2021 is $75,000. On December 31, 2020, the vested present value increases to $85,000 due solely to the passage of time. On December 31, 2021, C pays F $100,000.

*2018 and 2019.* For 2018 and 2019, C pays F no remuneration because the amount deferred under the plan remains subject to a substantial risk of forfeiture within the meaning of section 457(f)(3)(B).

*2020.* For 2020, C pays F $75,000 in remuneration on January 1, 2020, which is the vested present value of $100,000 payable on December 31, 2021. In addition C pays F an additional $10,000 in remuneration on December 31, 2020 as earnings based on the increase in the vested present value of the previously paid remuneration ($75,000) to $85,000 as of December 31, 2020.

*2021.* For 2021, C pays R $15,000 in additional remuneration and distributes $100,000 of previously paid remuneration. The $100,000 distribution is treated as reducing the amount of previously paid remuneration ($85,000) to zero, and the remaining $15,000 is a payment of earnings.

**Example 3**. G is a covered employee of T, an ATEO that uses a calendar year taxable year. G participates in a nonqualified deferred compensation plan in which the account balance is adjusted based on the investment returns on predetermined actual investments chosen by the employee. All amounts credited under the plan are vested when credited. On December 31, 2017, T credits $100,000 to G's account and the closing account balance is $100,000. On June 30, 2018, T credits $50,000 to G's account. On December 31, 2018, T credits $50,000 to G's account and the closing account balance is $210,000.

*2017.* T is a calendar year taxpayer, so the present value of all remuneration in which G was vested but that was not actually or constructively paid to G as of December 31, 2017, ($100,000) is treated as paid for 2017 and is not subject to excise tax under section 4960.

*2018.* For 2018, T pays G $110,000 of remuneration, including $50,000 credited to G's account on June 30 and $50,000 credited on December 31 (totaling $100,000), plus $10,000 in remuneration as earnings, as the vested present value of the $200,000 of previously paid remuneration ($100,000 as of December 31, 2017 + $100,000 in 2018) increases to $210,000 as of December 31 2018.

**Example 4**. Assume the same facts as **Example 3**, except that T uses a non-calendar year taxable year that begins on July 1 and ends on June 30. The closing account balance on June 30, 2018 is $155,000.

*Amounts paid through June 30, 2018*. T is a non-calendar year taxpayer, so the present value of all remuneration in which G is vested but that is not actually or constructively paid as of the close of the first taxable year ending after December 31, 2017 (June 30, 2018) ($155,000) is treated as paid for that year and is not subject to excise tax under section 4960.

*Amounts paid from July 1 through December 31, 2018*. For the taxable year ending June 30, 2019, T pays G $55,000 in remuneration, including $50,000 credited to G's account on December 31, 2018, plus $5,000 in remuneration as earnings, as the previously paid remuneration ($155,000 as of June 30, 2018 + $50,000 credited on December 31, 2018) increases to $210,000 as of December 31, 2018.

**Example 5**. H is an employee of U, an ATEO that uses a calendar year taxable year. H participates in a nonqualified deferred compensation plan in which the account balance is adjusted based on the investment returns on predetermined actual investments chosen by the employee. All amounts credited under the plan are vested when credited. On January 1, 2018, U credits $100,000 to H's account under the plan. On December 31, 2018, the closing account balance is $105,000. On January 1, 2019, U credits $100,000 to H's account. On December 31, 2019, the closing account balance is $210,000. H becomes a covered employee of U for U's taxable year ending December 31, 2019.

*2018 (remuneration paid before becoming a covered employee)*. Remuneration that is vested as of the last day of the calendar year preceding the calendar year for which the employee becomes a covered employee is not subject to excise tax under section 4960. Thus, H's vested account balance on December 31, 2018 ($105,000) is not subject to excise tax under section 4960.

*2019 (remuneration in the year an employee becomes a covered employee)*. For the taxable year ending December 31, 2019, U pays H $105,000 of remuneration, including the $100,000 credited to H's account on January 1, 2019, plus $5,000 in net earnings in 2019, the amount by which the vested account balance at the close of the calendar year ($210,000) exceeds the amount of previously paid remuneration ($205,000, consisting of $105,000 as of December 31, 2018 + $100,000 paid on January 1, 2019).

**Example 6**. J is a covered employee of T, an ATEO that uses a calendar year taxable year. J participates in a nonqualified deferred compensation plan under which T agrees to pay J $100,000 two months after the date a specified performance goal that is a substantial risk of forfeiture within the meaning of section 457(f)(3)(B) is satisfied. J satisfies the performance goal on November 30, 2019. T elects to treat the amount to be paid as the present value of the amount at vesting.

*Election to treat amount payable within 90 days treated as paid at vesting*. For taxable year 2019, T pays J $100,000 of remuneration. J vests in the $100,000 amount in 2019 upon meeting the performance goal. Under the general rule, T would be required to treat the present value as of November 30, 2019 of $100,000 payable in 2020 (two months after the performance goal was met) as paid in 2019, the difference between that amount and the present value as of December 31, 2019 as earnings for 2019, and any difference between the sum of the two present values and $100,000 as earnings for 2020. However, because T elected to treat the amount of remuneration payable within 90 days of vesting as paid at vesting in 2019, the $100,000 payable to J in 2020 is treated as remuneration paid in 2019 for purposes of section 4960(a)(1).

**Q–14: How is liability for the section 4960(a)(1) excise tax determined if remuneration is paid to a covered employee by both an applicable tax-exempt organization and a related organization?**

A–14: (a) *In general*. As provided in section 4960(c)(4)(C), in any case in which an ATEO includes remuneration from one or more other employers of a covered employee that are related organizations in determining the excise tax imposed by section 4960(a)(1), each employer is liable for the excise tax in an amount that bears the same ratio to the total excise tax determined with respect to the remuneration as–

(1) the amount of remuneration paid by the employer with respect to that employee, bears to

(2) the amount of remuneration paid by all the employers to that employee.

(b) *Calculation of excise tax involving multiple related organizations*. Each ATEO calculates liability for the excise tax under section 4960(a)(1) with respect to a covered employee by including remuneration paid by the ATEO and any related organization that employs the covered employee and then allocating that excise tax liability among each of the employers. However, the

ATEO may also be liable for the excise tax under section 4960(a)(1) as a related organization with respect to another ATEO that calculates the excise tax for its own covered employees. If an employer is liable for the excise tax under section 4960(a)(1) as an ATEO and as a related organization for the same remuneration to a covered employee, the employer is not liable for the excise tax in both capacities; rather it is liable for the greater of the excise tax it would owe as an ATEO or the excise tax it would owe as a related organization with respect to that covered employee.

In order to calculate liability under this provision, an ATEO should take the following steps:

(1) calculate remuneration paid (other than any excess parachute payment) for each of its covered employees, including remuneration from any related organization (if remuneration for any covered employee calculated in this step (1) is more than $1 million, then the remuneration over $1 million is subject to the excise tax under section 4960(a)(1) at the rate of tax under section 11);

(2) calculate the share of liability for each employer that employs the covered employee that was included in step (1) as a fraction of the total excise tax liability that bears the same ratio to the total excise tax as the amount of remuneration paid by the employer bears to the total remuneration calculated in step (1);

(3) inform any related organization of its share of liability calculated in step (2);

(4) obtain information on the ATEO's share of liability as a related organization for any covered employee of another ATEO. If the ATEO is a related organization to more than one other ATEO, treat the ATEO's highest share of liability as a related organization as its liability as a related organization for the covered employee; and

(5) compare the ATEO's liability as an ATEO in step (2) to its share of liability as a related organization under step (4) for each of the ATEO's covered employees. The ATEO reports the greater of the share calculated under step (4) or the share calculated under step (2) (or the share calculated under step (2) if they are the same) as the ATEO's share of liability for remuneration paid to the covered employee.

(c) *Change in related status during the year.* If an employer becomes or ceases to be a related organization with respect to an ATEO during the calendar year ending with or within the ATEO's taxable year, then only the remuneration paid by the related organization to a covered employee with respect to services performed during that portion of the calendar year that the employer is a related organization is included for purposes of calculating liability for the excise tax under section 4960(a)(1). Thus, only remuneration that vests while the employer is a related organization with regard to the ATEO is taken into account for purposes of section 4960.

(d) *Examples.* The following examples illustrate the rules of this Q/A–14. Assume for purposes of these examples that the rate of excise tax under section 4960 is 21 percent.

**Example 1.** F and G are each ATEOs; G is a related organization with respect to F. E is a covered employee of both F and G. F pays E $1.2 million of remuneration, and G pays E $800,000 of remuneration for a total of $2 million of remuneration, and $1 million of excess remuneration. The total excise tax is $210,000 (21 percent of the $1 million excess remuneration). F paid 3/5 of E's total remuneration ($1.2 million / $2 million); thus, F is liable for 3/5 of the excise tax, which is $126,000. G is liable for 2/5 of the excise tax, which is $84,000.

**Example 2.** H, I, and J are each ATEOs. J owns 60 percent of the stock of Corporation K. Sixty percent of I's directors are representatives of H. In addition, 60 percent of J's directors are representatives of I. Employee L is a covered employee of H, I, and J. H, I, J, and K each pay Employee L $1.2 million per year. Under the rules described in Q/A–7 and Q/A–8, I determines that its related organizations are H and J. H determines that its related organization is I. J determines that its related organizations are I and K.

*ATEO I.* Under I's calculation as an ATEO, Employee L receives a total of $3.6 million in remuneration from H, I, and J (3 x $1.2 million). The total excise tax is $546,000 (21 percent of the $2.6 million excess remuneration). H, I, and J each paid 1/3 of the total remuneration to Employee L ($1.2 million / $3.6 million); thus, H, I, and J are each liable for 1/3 of the excise tax, which is $182,000.

*ATEO H.* Under H's calculation as an ATEO, Employee L receives a total of $2.4 million in remuneration from H and I (2 x $1.2 million). The total excise tax is $294,000 (21 percent of the $1,400,000 excess remuneration). H and I each paid 1/2 of the total remuneration to Employee L ($1.2 million / $2.4 million); thus, H and I are each liable for 1/2 of the excise tax, which is $147,000.

*ATEO J.* Under J's calculation as an ATEO, L receives a total of $3.6 million in remuneration from I, J, and K (3 x $1.2 million). The total excise tax is $546,000 (21 percent of the $2.6 million

**Notice 2019-9**

excess remuneration). I, J, and K each paid 1/3 of the total remuneration to Employee L ($1.2 million / $3.6 million); thus, I, J, and K are each liable for 1/3 of the excise tax, which is $182,000.

*Liability of H, I, J, and K.* I is liable as a related organization for $147,000 of excise tax according to H's calculation and $182,000 according to J's calculation, but under I's calculation, I is liable for $182,000 of excise tax. Thus, I's excise tax liability is $182,000. H is liable for $182,000 of excise tax under I's calculation, which is greater than the $147,000 of excise tax H calculated under H's calculation. Thus, H's excise tax liability is $182,000. J is liable as a related organization for $182,000 of excise tax under I's calculation, but is liable for $182,000 of excise tax under J's calculation. Thus, J's excise tax liability is $182,000. K is liable as a related organization for $182,000 of excise tax according to J's calculation.

### E. *Medical and Veterinary Services*

**Q–15: How is remuneration for medical services treated under section 4960?**

A–15: (a) *In general.* Remuneration paid to a licensed medical professional for the direct performance of medical services (including nursing services) or veterinary services by the professional is not remuneration for purposes of calculating the excess remuneration (if any) subject to the excise tax. However, remuneration paid to the professional for any other services, including administrative and management services associated with the performance of medical or veterinary services, is remuneration for purposes of calculating the excess remuneration (if any) subject to the excise tax. Remuneration for medical services is also disregarded for purposes of determining whether an individual is a covered employee and for purposes of determining whether a payment is a parachute payment.

(b) *Licensed medical professional.* A licensed medical professional is an individual who is licensed under state or local law to perform medical services (including nursing services) or veterinary services.

(c) *Medical and veterinary services.* A licensed medical professional directly performs medical services to the extent that the services constitute "medical care" as defined in section 213(d)(1)(A) and the regulations thereunder. Thus, medical services are services for the diagnosis, cure, mitigation, treatment, or prevention of disease, including services for the purpose of affecting any structure or function of the body. For example, teaching or research services are not medical services to the extent the services performed do not relate directly to the diagnosis, cure, mitiga-

tion, treatment, or prevention of disease or affect a structure or function of the body. For purposes of section 4960, documenting the care and condition of a patient is part of the direct performance of medical services, as is accompanying another licensed professional as a supervisor while that medical professional performs medical services. But managing an organization's operations, including scheduling, staffing, appraisal, and other similar functions that may relate to a particular medical professional or professionals who perform medical services, is not the performance of medical services. With respect to veterinary services, the rules in this paragraph apply by analogy to determine whether services performed with respect to an animal are veterinary services.

(d) *Allocation.* If during a calendar year an employer pays a covered employee remuneration for both medical services and other services, the employer must make a reasonable, good faith allocation between remuneration for medical services and other services. For example, if a medical doctor receives remuneration for both medical services and for administrative or management services, the employer must make a reasonable allocation between remuneration for the medical services and remuneration for the administrative or management services. For this purpose, if an employment agreement or similar written arrangement sets forth the remuneration to be paid for particular services, that allocation of remuneration must be applied unless the facts and circumstances demonstrate that the amount allocated for medical services is unreasonable for those services or that the allocation was established for purposes of avoiding application of the excise tax under section 4960. If some or all of the remuneration is not reasonably allocated in an employment or other agreement, an employer may use any reasonable allocation method. For example, an employer may use a representative sample of records, such as patient, insurance, and Medicare/Medicaid billing records or internal time reporting mechanisms to determine the time spent providing medical services, and then allocate remuneration to medical services in the proportion such time bears to the total hours the covered employee worked for the employer for purposes of making a reasonable allocation of remuneration. Similarly, if some or all of the remuneration is not reasonably allocated in an employment or other agreement, an employer may use salaries or other remuneration for duties comparable to those the employee performs (for example, hospital administrator and physician) for purposes of making a reasonable allocation between remuneration for medical services and nonmedical services. These same

**Notice 2019-9**

allocation rules also apply with respect to veterinary services.

(e) *Examples*. The following examples illustrate the rules of this Q/A–15. Assume for purposes of these examples that there is no employment agreement or similar written arrangement allocating remuneration to any particular services.

**Example 1.** H is a hospital and is an ATEO. A is a covered employee of H. A provides patient care services to H and also provides management and administrative services to H as the head of a medical practice group within H. Based on a representative sample of insurance and Medicare billing records, as well as time reports that A submits to H, H determines that A spends half of her time providing medical care to patients and half of her time performing administrative and management services in her capacity as head of the practice group. H allocates half of A's remuneration to medical services. H's allocation of A's remuneration is a reasonable, good faith allocation. Accordingly, only the portion of A's remuneration allocated to the other, non-medical services is remuneration for purposes of the excise tax.

**Example 2.** R is a medical research organization and is an ATEO. B is a covered employee of R. B is employed to work on a research trial. B provides an experimental treatment to patients afflicted by a disease. B tracks the patients' individual conditions in a manner that occurs ordinarily in a medical practice. As part of the research trial, B also compiles the patients' records on their individual conditions and prepares reports detailing both individual and overall results. These reports are not ordinarily prepared for patients or provided to patients in a medical practice. Although the primary purpose of B's activities is research, B is treating a patient's disease within the meaning of section 213(d) when B performs services that are ordinarily performed in a medical practice, and, thus, these services are medical services for purposes of section 4960. Accordingly, any remuneration allocable to the medical services is not remuneration for purposes of the excise tax. However, B does not directly perform medical services to the extent B performs research services that are not ordinarily performed in a medical practice; accordingly, any remuneration allocable to those services is remuneration for purposes of section 4960.

**Example 3.** C is a medical doctor who is employed by a university hospital that is an ATEO. C's duties include overseeing and teaching a group of resident physicians who have a restricted license to practice medicine. C's duties include supervising and instructing the resident physicians while they treat patients. C's other duties include instructing the resident physicians in a classroom setting. To the extent that C, in conjunction with the resident physicians, performs services directly related to the diagnosis, cure, mitigation, treatment or prevention of a patient's disease, or affecting a structure or function of the patient's body, those services constitute "medical care" for purposes of section 213(d), and, thus, C directly performs medical services. Accordingly, any remuneration allocable to those medical services is not remuneration for purposes of the excise tax. However, because classroom instruction does not involve actual patient treatment, those activities are not medical care for purposes of section 213(d), and, thus, do not constitute the direct performance of medical services. Accordingly, any remuneration allocable to those services is remuneration for purposes of section 4960.

**F. Excess Parachute Payments**

**Q–16: What is an excess parachute payment under section 4960(c)(5)(A)?**

A–16: The term "excess parachute payment" means an amount equal to the excess (if any) of the total amount of any parachute payment over the portion of the base amount allocated to such payment.

**Q–17: What is a parachute payment under section 4960(c)(5)(B)?**

A–17: (a) *In general*. The term "parachute payment" means any payment in the nature of compensation made by an ATEO (or a predecessor organization of the ATEO) or a related organization to (or for the benefit of) a covered employee if–

(1) the payment is contingent on the employee's separation from employment with the employer; and

(2) the aggregate present value of the payments in the nature of compensation to (or for the benefit of) the individual that are contingent on the separation equals or exceeds an amount equal to three times the base amount.

(b) *Exclusions*. The term "parachute payment" does not include any payment: (1) to or from a plan described in section 401(a) that includes a trust exempt from tax under section 501(a), an annuity plan described in section 403(a), a simplified employee pension (as defined in section 408(k)), or a simple retirement account described in section 408(p);

(2) made under or to an annuity contract described in section 403(b) or a plan described in section 457(b);

(3) made to a licensed medical professional (including a veterinarian) for the performance of medical or veterinary services performed by such professional; or

(4) made to an individual who is not a highly compensated employee as defined in section 414(q). *See generally* Treas. Reg. § 1.414(q)-1T. Under Treas. Reg. § 1.414(q)-1T, Q/A–14(a)(1), for purposes of determining the group of highly compensated employees for a determination year, the determination year calculation is made on the basis of the applicable year of the plan or other entity for which a determination is made and the look-back year calculation is made on the basis of the twelve month period immediately preceding that year. An ATEO that maintains a qualified retirement plan should have already identified the employees who are HCEs for purposes of the plan and the same individuals as HCEs for purposes of section 4960. For an ATEO that does not maintain a qualified retirement plan, the rules are applied by analogy, substituting the calendar year for the plan year. Accordingly, in 2019, for an ATEO that does not maintain a qualified retirement plan, the ATEO would use the employees' 2018 annual compensation (as defined in Treas. Reg. § 1.414(q)-1T Q/A–13, including any of the safe harbor definitions if applied consistently to all employees) to determine whether and which employees were HCEs for 2019 for purposes of section 4960. If an employee is an HCE at the time of the separation from employment, then any parachute payment made as a consequence of the separation from employment is treated as paid to an HCE, even if the payments occur during one or more later taxable years (that is, taxable years after the taxable year during which the employee separated from employment).

**Q–18: What is a payment in the nature of compensation?**

A–18: For purposes of section 4960(a)(2), any payment—in whatever form—is a payment in the nature of compensation if the payment arises out of an employment relationship, including holding oneself out as available to perform services and refraining from performing services. Thus, for example, payments made under a covenant not to compete or a similar arrangement are payments in the nature of compensation. A payment in the nature of compensation includes (but is not limited to) wages and salary, bonuses, severance pay, fringe benefits, life insurance, pension benefits, and other deferred compensa-

tion (including any amount characterized by the parties as interest or earnings thereon). A payment in the nature of compensation also includes cash when paid, the value of the right to receive cash, including the value of accelerated vesting, or a transfer of property. However, a payment in the nature of compensation does not include attorney's fees or court costs paid or incurred in connection with the payment of any parachute payment or a reasonable rate of interest accrued on any amount during the period the parties contest whether a payment will be made.

**Q–19: When is a payment in the nature of compensation considered to be made?**

A–19: (a) *In general.* A payment in the nature of compensation is considered made in the taxable year in which it is includible in the covered employee's gross income (in the case of taxable non-cash fringe benefits, consistent with Announcement 85-113, 1985-31 I.R.B. 31) or, in the case of fringe benefits and other benefits that are excludible from income, in the taxable year the benefits are received.

(b) *Transfers of section 83 property.* A transfer of property in connection with the performance of services that is subject to section 83 is considered a payment made in the taxable year in which the property is transferred or would be includible in the gross income of the covered employee under section 83 and the regulations thereunder, disregarding any election made by the employee under section 83(b) or 83(i). Thus, in general, such a payment is considered made at the later of the date the property is transferred (as defined in Treas. Reg. § 1.83-3(a)) to the covered employee or the date the property becomes substantially vested (as defined in Treas. Reg. § 1.83-3(b) and (j)). The amount of the payment is the compensation income as determined under section 83 and the regulations thereunder, disregarding any amount includible in income pursuant to an election made by an employee under section 83(b).

(c) *Stock options and stock appreciation rights.* For purposes of this Q/A–19, an option (including an option to which section 421 applies) is treated as property that is transferred when the option becomes vested (regardless of whether the option has a readily ascertainable fair market value as defined in Treas. Reg. § 1.83-7(b)). For purposes of determining the timing and amount of any payment related to the option, the principles of Treas. Reg. § 1.280G-1, Q/A–13 and Rev. Proc. 2003-68, 2003-2 C.B. 398, apply. Thus, the vesting of an option as a result of a covered employee's separation from employment is a payment in the nature of compensation.

(d) *Consideration paid by covered employee.* Any payment in the nature of compensation is reduced by the amount of any money or the fair market value of any property (owned by the covered employee without restriction) that is (or will be) transferred by the covered employee in exchange for the payment.

### Q–20: What is a payment that is contingent on an employee's separation from employment?

A-20: (a) *In general.* A payment is contingent on an employee's separation from employment if the facts and circumstances indicate that the employer would not make the payment in the absence of an involuntary separation from employment. A payment, the right to which is not subject to a substantial risk of forfeiture within the meaning of section 457(f)(3)(B) at the time of an involuntary separation from employment, generally is a payment that would have been made in the absence of a separation from employment (and, thus, is not contingent on a separation from employment), except that the increased value of an accelerated payment of a vested amount described in Q/A–24(b) resulting from an involuntary separation from employment is not treated as a payment that would have been made in the absence of a separation from employment. A payment the right to which is no longer subject to a substantial risk of forfeiture within the meaning of section 457(f)(3)(B) as a result of an involuntary separation from employment, including a payment the vesting of which would have occurred had the employee remained employed for a subsequent period of time but that is accelerated due to the separation from employment as described in Q/A–24(c), is not treated as a payment that would have been made in the absence of an involuntary separation from employment (and thus is contingent on a separation from employment). A payment would be made in the absence of a separation from employment if it is substantially certain at the time of the separation from employment that the payment would be made whether or not the separation occurred. A payment does not fail to be contingent on a separation from employment merely because the payment is conditioned upon the execution of a release of claims, noncompetition or nondisclosure provisions, or other similar requirements. If an employee separates from service and continues to provide services (including as a bona fide independent contractor), payments for those services are not payments that are contingent on a separation from employment to the extent those payments are reasonable and are not made because of the involuntary separation from employment.

(b) *Employment agreements.* (1) If a covered employee involuntarily separates from employment before the end of a contract term and is paid damages for breach of contract pursuant to an employment agreement, those damages are treated as a payment that is contingent on a separation from employment. For purposes of this paragraph (b), an employment agreement means an agreement between an employee and employer that describes, among other things, the amount of compensation or remuneration payable to the employee for services performed during the term of the agreement.

(2) The following example illustrates the rules of this Q/A–20(b):

**Example.** A, a covered employee, has a three-year employment agreement with X, an ATEO. Under the agreement, A will receive a salary of $200,000 for the first year of the agreement, and for each succeeding year, an annual salary that is $100,000 higher than the previous year. The agreement provides that, in the event of A's involuntary separation from employment without cause, A will receive the remaining salary due under the agreement. At the beginning of the second year of the agreement, X involuntarily terminates A's employment without cause and pays A $700,000 representing the remaining salary due under the employment agreement ($300,000 for the second year of the agreement + $400,000 for the third year of the agreement). The $700,000 payment is treated as a payment that is contingent on a separation from employment.

(c) *Noncompetition agreements.* A payment under an agreement requiring a covered employee to refrain from performing services (for example, a covenant not to compete) is a payment that is contingent on a separation from employment for purposes of this Q/A–20 if the payment would not have been made in the absence of an involuntary separation from employment. For example, if a covenant not to compete including one or more payments contingent on compliance in whole or in part with the covenant not to compete is negotiated as part of a severance arrangement arising from an involuntary separation from employment, generally the payment(s) will be treated as contingent on a separation from employment.

(d) *Payment of amounts previously included in income or excess remuneration.* Actual or constructive payment of an amount that was previously includible in gross income is not a payment contingent on a separation from employment. For example, payment of an amount includible in income under section 457(f)(1)(A) due to the lapsing of a substantial risk of forfeiture on a date before the separation from employment is not a payment that is contingent on a separation from employment, even if the amount is paid in cash or otherwise to the employee because of the separation from employment. In addition, actual or constructive payment of an amount treated as excess remuneration is not a payment that is contingent on a separation from employment (and thus is not a parachute payment), even if the amount is paid to the employee because of the separation from employment.

(e) *Window programs.* A payment under a window program is contingent on a separation from employment.

(f) *Anti-abuse provision.* Notwithstanding the foregoing paragraphs (a) through (e) of this Q/A-20, if the facts and circumstances demonstrate that either vesting or the payment of an amount (whether before or after the involuntary separation from employment) would not have occurred but for the involuntary nature of the separation from employment, the payment of the amount will be treated as contingent on a separation from employment. For example, an employer's exercise of discretion to accelerate vesting of an amount shortly before an involuntary separation from employment may indicate that the acceleration of vesting was due to the involuntary nature of the separation from employment and, thus, was contingent on the employee's separation from employment. Similarly, payment of amount in excess of an amount otherwise payable (for example, increased salary), shortly before or after an involuntary separation from employment, may indicate that the amount was paid because the separation was involuntary and, thus, was contingent on the employee's separation from employment.

**Q-21: What is a payment made under a window program?**

A-21: A window program is a program established by an employer in connection with an impending separation from employment to provide separation pay, where the program is made available by the employer for a limited period of time (no longer than 12 months) to employees who separate from employment during that period or to employees who separate from service during that period under specified circumstances. A payment made under a window program is treated as a payment that is contingent on an employee's separation from employment notwithstanding that the employee may not have had an involuntary separation from employment.

**Q-22: What is an involuntary separation from employment?**

A-22: An involuntary separation from employment means a separation from employment due to the independent exercise of the employer's unilateral authority to terminate the employee's services, other than due to the employee's implicit or explicit request, if the employee was willing and able to continue performing services. An involuntary separation from employment may include an employer's failure to renew a contract at the time the contract expires, provided that the employee was willing and able to execute a new contract providing terms and conditions substantially similar to those in the expiring contract and to continue providing services. The determination of whether a separation from employment is involuntary is based on all the facts and circumstances. An employee's voluntary separation from employment for good reason (as defined in Prop. Treas. Reg. §1.457-11(d)(2)(ii), 81 FR 40548, 40560) is treated as an involuntary separation from employment

**Q-23: What is a separation from employment?**

A-23: For purposes of section 4960, separation from employment generally has the same meaning as separation from service as defined in Treas. Reg. §1.409A-1(h), without regard to Treas. Reg. §1.409A-1(h)(2) and (5) (application to independent contractors), since generally only an employee may have a separation from employment and a change from employee status to bona fide independent contractor status would also be a separation from employment. See Q/A-12(d) regarding the treatment of an employee who also serves as a director (or in a substantially similar position). In addition, the definition of termination of employment in Treas. Reg. §1.409A-1(h)(1)(ii) is modified such that an employer may not set the level of the anticipated reduction in future services that will give rise to a separation from employment and that the defaults set forth in the regulations apply. Thus, an anticipated reduction of the level of service of less than 50 percent is not treated as a separation from employment, an anticipated reduction of more than 80 percent is treated as a termination of employment, and the treatment of an anticipated reduction between those two levels is determined based on the facts and circumstances. Pursuant to Treas. Reg. §1.409A-1(h), an employee generally separates from employment with the employer if the employee dies, retires, or otherwise has a termination of employment with the employer. Treas. Reg. §1.409A-1(h) provides additional rules addressing leaves of absence, including military leaves of absence (Treas. Reg. § 1.409A-1(h)(1)(i)), asset purchase transactions (Treas. Reg. § 1.409A-1(h)(4)), and employees participating in collectively bargained plans covering multiple employers (Treas. Reg. § 1.409A-1(h)(6)). This notice adopts the rules provided in Treas. Reg. § 1.409A-1(h)(3), under which an employee separates from employment only if the employee has a separation from employment with the employer and all employers that would be considered a single employer under section 414(b) and (c), except that for purposes of section 4960, this notice uses the "at least 80 percent" rule under section 414(b) and (c) rather than replacing it with "at least 50 percent." However, for purposes of determining whether there has been a separation from employment, a purported ongoing employment relationship between a covered employee and an ATEO or a related organization will be disregarded if the facts and circumstances demonstrate that the purported employment relationship is not bona fide or the primary purpose of the establishment or continuation of the relationship is avoidance of the application of section 4960.

## Q–24: How is an accelerated payment or accelerated vesting resulting from an involuntary separation from employment treated?

A–24: (a) *In general.* As described in Q/A–24(b) and (c), if a payment is accelerated or a substantial risk of forfeiture lapses as a result of an involuntary separation from employment, only the value due to the acceleration is treated as contingent on a separation from employment. For purposes of this Q/A–24, the terms "vested" and "substantial risk of forfeiture" have the same meaning as provided in Q/A–13(a).

(b) *Vested payments.* If an involuntary separation from employment accelerates actual or constructive payment of an amount that vested without regard to the separation, the portion of the payment, if any, that is contingent on the separation from employment is the amount by which the present value of the accelerated payment exceeds the present value of the payment absent the acceleration. For this purpose, the payment of an amount otherwise due upon a separation from employment (whether voluntary or involuntary) is not treated as an acceleration of the payment because the payment timing was not accelerated due to the involuntary nature of the separation from employment. If the value of the payment absent the acceleration is not reasonably ascertainable, and the acceleration of the payment does not significantly increase the present value of the payment absent

the acceleration, the present value of the payment absent the acceleration is the amount of the accelerated payment (so the amount contingent on the separation from employment is zero). If the present value of the payment absent the acceleration is not reasonably ascertainable, but the acceleration significantly increases the present value of the payment, the future value of the payment contingent on the separation from employment is treated as equal to the amount of the accelerated payment. For this purpose, the acceleration of a payment by 90 days or less is not treated as significantly increasing the present value of the payment. For rules on determining present value, see Q/A–24(f) and Q/A–26 through Q/A–28.

(c) *Nonvested payments subject to a vesting service condition*—(1) If–

(A) a payment vests as a result of an involuntary separation from employment;

(B) disregarding the separation from employment, the payment was contingent only on the continued performance of services for the employer for a specified period of time; and

(C) the payment is attributable, at least in part, to the performance of services before the date the payment is made or becomes certain to be made; then the portion that is contingent on the separation from employment is the amount described in Q/A–24(b), plus the value of the lapse of the obligation to continue to perform services described in paragraph (c)(3). The portion of the payment that is contingent on the separation from employment under this Q/A–24(c) cannot exceed the amount of the accelerated payment, or, if the payment is not accelerated, the present value of the payment.

(2) For purposes of paragraph Q/A–24(b), the acceleration of the vesting of a stock option or the lapse of a restriction on restricted stock is considered to significantly increase the value of a payment.

(3) The value of the lapse of the obligation to continue to perform services (described in Q/A–24(c)(1)) is one percent of the amount of the accelerated payment multiplied by the number of full months between the date that the employee's right to receive the payment is vested and the date that, absent the acceleration, the payment would have been vested. This paragraph (c)(3) applies to the accelerated vesting of a payment in the nature of compensation even if the time when the payment is made is not accelerated. In that case, the amount reflecting the lapse of the obligation to continue to perform services is one percent of the present value of the future payment multiplied by the number of full

months between the date that the individual's right to receive the payment is vested and the date that, absent the acceleration, the payment would have been vested.

(d) *Nonvested payments subject to a vesting condition other than a service condition.* Neither Q/A–24(b) nor (c) applies to a payment if (without regard to the separation from employment) vesting of the payment depends on an event other than the performance of services, such as the attainment of a performance goal, and the vesting event does not occur prior to the separation from employment. For example, neither Q/A–24(b) nor (c) apply if the payment not only vests due to the involuntary separation from employment (despite not having met a separate alternative vesting condition other than the continued performance of services) but the payment also is accelerated due to the involuntary separation from employment. In these circumstances, the full amount of the accelerated payment is treated as contingent on the separation from employment under this Q/A–24(d).

(e) *Application to benefits under a nonqualified deferred compensation plan.* In the case of a payment of benefits under a nonqualified deferred compensation plan, Q/A–24(b) applies to the extent benefits under the plan are vested without regard to the separation from employment but the payment of benefits is accelerated due to the involuntary separation from employment. Q/A–24(c) applies to the extent benefits under the plan become vested as a result of the separation from employment and are attributable, at least in part, to the performance of services prior to vesting. For any other payment of benefits under a nonqualified deferred compensation plan (such as a contribution made due to the employee's involuntary separation from employment) the full amount of the payment is contingent on the employee's separation from employment.

(f) *Present value.* For purposes of this Q/A–24, if an accelerated payment is made, the increase in the present value of the payment due under the original payment schedule is determined based on the date on which the accelerated payment is made. The amount that is treated as contingent on the separation from employment is the amount by which the present value of the accelerated payment exceeds the present value of the payment absent the acceleration.

(g) *Examples. See* Treas. Reg. §1.280G, Q/A–24(f) for examples that may be applied by analogy to illustrate the rules of this Q/A–24.

### G. *Three-Times-Base-Amount Test for Parachute Payments*

**Q–25: Are all payments that are in the nature of compensation, made to a covered employee, and contingent on a separation from employment, parachute payments?**

A–25: (a) *In general.* To determine whether payments in the nature of compensation made to a covered employee that are contingent on the covered employee separating from employment with the ATEO are parachute payments, they must be compared to the individual's base amount. To do this, the aggregate present value of all payments in the nature of compensation that are made or to be made to (or for the benefit of) the same covered employee by an ATEO (or any predecessor of the ATEO) or related organization and that are contingent on the separation from employment must be determined. If this aggregate present value equals or exceeds the amount equal to three times the individual's base amount, the payments are parachute payments. If this aggregate present value is less than the amount equal to three times the individual's base amount, no portion of the payments is a parachute payment. See Q/A–26 and Q/A–27 for rules on determining present value.

(b) *Examples.* The following examples illustrate the rules of this Q/A–25:

**Example 1**. A is a covered employee with respect to M, an ATEO. A's base amount is $200,000. Payments in the nature of compensation that are contingent on a separation from employment totaling $800,000 are made to A on the date of the separation from employment. The payments are parachute payments because they have an aggregate present value at least equal to three times A's base amount of $200,000 (3 x $200,000 = $600,000).

**Example 2**. Assume the same facts as in **Example 1**, except that the payments contingent on the separation from employment total $580,000. Because the payments do not have an aggregate present value at least equal to three times A's base amount, no portion of the payments is a parachute payment.

**Q–26: As of what date is the present value of a payment determined?**

A–26: (a) *In general.* Except as otherwise provided in this Q/A–26, for purposes of determining if a parachute payment exceeds three times the base amount, the present value of a payment is determined as of the date of the separation from employment, or, if the payment is made prior to that date, the date on which the payment is made.

(b) *Deferred payments.* For purposes of determining whether a payment is a parachute payment, if a payment in the nature of compensation is the right to receive payments in a year (or years) subsequent to the year of the separation from employment, the value of the payment is the present value of the payment (or payments) calculated on the basis of reasonable actuarial assumptions and using the applicable discount rate for the present value calculation that is determined in accordance with Q/A–27.

(c) *Health care.* If the payment in the nature of compensation is an obligation to provide health care (including an obligation to purchase or provide health insurance), then for purposes of this Q/A–26 and for applying the three-times-base-amount test under Q/A–25, the present value of the obligation should be calculated in accordance with generally accepted accounting principles. For purposes of Q/A–25 and this Q/A–26, the obligation to provide health care is permitted to be measured by projecting the cost of premiums for health care insurance, even if no health care insurance is actually purchased. If the obligation to provide health care is made in coordination with a health care plan that the employer makes available to a group, then the premiums used for this purpose may be the allocable portion of group premiums.

**Q–27: What discount rate is used to determine present value?**

A–27: For purposes of computing the excise tax under section 4960(a)(2), present value generally is determined by using a discount rate equal to 120 percent of the applicable Federal rate (determined under section 1274(d) and the regulations thereunder) compounded semiannually. The applicable Federal rate to be used is the Federal rate that is in effect on the date as of which the present value is determined, using the period until the payment is expected to be made as the term of the debt instrument under section 1274(d). See Q/A–26. However, for any payment, the employer and the covered employee may elect to use the applicable Federal rate that is in effect on the date that the contract that provides for the payment is entered into, if that election is made in the contract.

**Q–28: If the present value of a payment to be made in the future is contingent on an uncertain future event or condition, how is the present value of the payment determined?**

A–28: (a) *Treatment based on the estimated probability of payment.* In certain cases, it may be

necessary to apply the three-times-base-amount test or to allocate a portion of the base amount to a payment that is contingent on separation from employment at a time when the aggregate present value of all the payments is uncertain because the time, amount, or right to receive one or more of the payments is also contingent on the occurrence of an uncertain future event or condition. In that case, the employer must reasonably estimate whether it will make the payment. If the employer reasonably estimates there is a 50-percent or greater probability that it will make the payment, the full amount of the payment is considered for purposes of the three-times-base-amount test and the allocation of the base amount. If the employer reasonably estimates there is a less than 50-percent probability that the payment will be made, the payment is not considered for either purpose.

(b) *Correction of incorrect estimates.* If the ATEO later determines that the estimate made under Q/A–28(a) was incorrect, it must reapply the three-times-base-amount test described in Q/A–25 (and, if necessary, reallocate the portion of the base allocated to previous paymeqnts in accordance with Q/A–32) to reflect the actual time and amount of the payment. In reapplying the three-times-base-amount test (and, if necessary, reallocating the base amount), the ATEO must determine the aggregate present value of payments paid or to be paid as of the date described in Q/A–26, using the discount rate described in Q/A–27. This redetermination may affect the amount of any excess parachute payment for a prior taxable year. However, if, based on the application of the three-times-base-amount test without regard to the payment described in this Q/A–28, an ATEO has determined it will pay an employee an excess parachute payment or payments, then the three-times-base-amount test does not have to be reapplied when a payment described in this Q/A–28 is made (or becomes certain to be made) if no base amount is allocated to such payment.

(c) *Initial option value estimate.* To the extent provided in published guidance of general applicability under § 601.601(d)(2) of this Chapter, an initial estimate of the value of an option subject to Q/A–19(c) is permitted to be made, with the valuation subsequently redetermined, and the three-times-base-amount test reapplied. Until such guidance is published, the guidance under section 280G applies by analogy.

(d) *Examples. See* Treas. Reg. § 1.280G–1, Q/A–33(d), for examples that may be applied by analogy to illustrate the rules of this Q/A–28.

**Q–29: What is the base amount for purposes of section 4960(c)(5)(D)?**

A–29: (a) *In general.* A covered employee's base amount is the average annual compensation for services performed as an employee of the ATEO (including compensation for services performed for a predecessor entity of the ATEO), or a related organization with respect to which there has been a separation from employment, if the compensation was includible in the gross income of the individual for taxable years in the base period (including amounts that were excluded under section 911), or would have been includible in the individual's gross income if the individual had been a United States citizen or resident. See Q/A–30 for the definition of base period and for examples of base amount computations.

(b) *Short or incomplete taxable years.* If the base period of a covered employee includes a short taxable year or less than all of a taxable year of the employee, compensation for the short or incomplete taxable year must be annualized before determining the average annual compensation for the base period. In annualizing compensation, the frequency with which payments are expected to be made over an annual period must be taken into account. Thus, any amount of compensation for a short or incomplete taxable year that represents a payment that will not be made more often than once per year is not annualized.

(c) *Excludable fringe benefits.* Because the base amount includes only compensation that is includible in gross income, the base amount does not include certain items that constitute parachute payments. For example, payments in the form of excludible fringe benefits or excludible health care benefits are not included in the base amount but may be treated as parachute payments.

(d) *Section 83(b) income.* The base amount includes the amount of compensation included in income under section 83(b) during the base period.

**Q–30: What is the base period?**

A–30: (a) *In general.* The base period of a covered employee is the covered employee's five most recent taxable years ending before the date on which the separation from employment occurs. However, if the covered employee was not an employee of the ATEO for this entire five-year period, the individual's base period is the portion of the five-year period during which the covered employee performed services for the

ATEO, a predecessor entity, or a related organization.

(b) *Examples.* The following examples illustrate the rules of Q/A–29 and this Q/A–30:

**Example 1.** C, a covered employee, receives an annual salary of $500,000 per year during the base period. C defers $100,000 of salary each year under a nonqualified deferred compensation plan (none of which is includible in C's income until paid). C's base amount is $400,000 (($400,000 x 5) / 5).

**Example 2.** D, a covered employee, was employed by an ATEO for two years and four months preceding the year in which D separates from employment. D's compensation includible in gross income was $100,000 for the four-month period, $420,000 for the first full year, and $450,000 for the second full year. D's base amount is $390,000 ((3 x $100,000) + $420,000 + $450,000) / 3).

**Example 3.** Assume the same facts as in **Example 2**, except that D also received a $60,000 signing bonus when D's employment with the ATEO commenced at the beginning of the four-month period. D's base amount is $410,000 ((($60,000 + (3 x $100,000)) + $420,000 + $450,000) / 3). Since the bonus is a payment that will not be paid more often than once per year, the bonus is not taken into account in annualizing D's compensation for the four-month period.

**Example 4.** E, a covered employee with respect to ATEO X, was not an employee of X for the full five-year base period. In 2024 and 2025, E is a director of X and receives $30,000 per year for E's services. On January 1, 2026, E becomes an officer and covered employee of X. E's includible compensation for services as an officer of X is $250,000 for each of 2026 and 2027, and $300,000 for 2028. In 2028, E separates from employment. E's base amount is $250,000 ((2 x $250,000) / 2). The $300,000 salary paid in 2028 does not affect the base amount because it was paid in the year of separation.

**Q–31: How is the base amount determined in the case of a covered employee who did not perform services for the applicable tax-exempt organization (or a predecessor entity or a related organization), prior to the calendar year in which the separation from employment with the applicable tax-exempt organization occurred?**

A–31: (a) *In general.* In that case, the covered employee's base amount is the annualized compensation for services performed for the ATEO (or a predecessor entity or related organization) that—

(1) was includible in the employee's gross income for that portion of the employee's taxable year prior to the employee's separation from employment (including amounts that were excluded under section 911), or would have been includible in the employee's gross income if the employee had been a United States citizen or resident; and

(2) was not contingent on the separation from employment. (b) *Examples*. The following examples illustrate the rules of this Q/A–31:

**Example 1**. On January 1, 2026, A, a covered employee, enters into a four–year employment contract with ATEO M as an officer of the organization. A did not previously perform services for M (or any predecessor entity or related organization). Under the employment contract, A is to receive an annual salary of $420,000 for each of the four years that A remains employed by M, with any remaining unpaid balance to be paid immediately in the event that A's employment is terminated without cause. On July 1, 2026, after A has worked six months and received compensation of $210,000, A's employment is involuntarily terminated without cause, and A receives a payment of $1,470,000. The payment of $1,470,000 is contingent on A's separation from employment from M. In this case, A's base amount is $420,000 (2 x $210,000). Since the present value of the payment that is contingent on A's separation from employment with M ($1,470,000) is more than three times A's base amount of $420,000 (3 x $420,000 = $1,260,000), the payment is a parachute payment.

**Example 2**. Assume the same facts as in **Example 1**, except that A also receives a signing bonus of $500,000 from M on January 1, 2026. The bonus is not contingent on A's separation from employment with M. When A's separation occurs on July 1, 2026, A has received compensation of $710,000 (the $500,000 bonus + $210,000 in salary). A's base amount is $940,000 ($500,000 + (2 x $210,000)). Because the $500,000 bonus will not be paid more than once per year, the amount of the bonus is not taken into account in annualizing A's compensation. The present value of the potential parachute payment ($1,470,000) is less than three times A's base amount of $940,000 (3 x $940,000 = $2,820,000), and therefore no portion of the payment is a parachute payment.

### H. *Computation of Excess Parachute Payments*

#### Q–32: How is the amount of an excess parachute payment computed?

A–32: (a) *Calculation*. The amount of an excess parachute payment is the excess of the amount of any parachute payment made by an ATEO (or related organization or predecessor organization) over the portion of the covered employee's base amount that is allocated to the payment. For this purpose, the portion of the base amount allocated to any parachute payment is the amount that bears the same ratio to the base amount as the present value of the parachute payment bears to the aggregate present value of all parachute payments made or to be made to (or for the benefit of) the same covered employee. Thus, the portion of the base amount allocated to any parachute payment is determined by multiplying the base amount by a fraction, the numerator of which is the present value of the parachute payment and the denominator of which is the aggregate present value of all parachute payments.

(b) *Examples*. The following examples illustrate the rules of this Q/A–32:

**Example 1**. E is a covered employee of ATEO X and an employee of related organization Y. E's base amount is $200,000 with respect to X and $400,000 with respect to Y. E receives $1 million from X and $1 million from Y contingent upon E's involuntary separation from employment from X and Y. For purposes of determining the excise tax under section 4960(a)(2), E has a base amount of $600,000 ($200,000 + $400,000). The two $1 million payments are parachute payments because their aggregate present value is at least three times E's base amount (3 x $600,000 = $1.8 million). The portion of the base amount allocated to each parachute payment is $300,000 (($1 million / $2 million) x $600,000). Thus, the amount of each excess parachute payment is $700,000 ($1 million - $300,000).

**Example 2**. A covered employee with a base amount of $200,000 is entitled to receive two parachute payments, one of $200,000 and the other of $900,000. The $200,000 payment is made upon separation from employment, and the $900,000 payment is to be made on a date in a future taxable year. The present value of the $900,000 payment is $800,000 as of the date of the separation from employment. The portions of the base amount allocated to these payments are $40,000 (($200,000 / $1 million) x $200,000) and $160,000 (($800,000 / $1 million) x $200,000), respectively. Thus, the amount of the first excess parachute payment is $160,000 ($200,000 − $40,000) and that of the second is $740,000 ($900,000 − $160,000).

### I. Reporting Liability Under Section 4960

**Q–33: How do applicable tax-exempt organizations or related organizations report and pay the excise tax imposed under section 4960?**

A–33: (a) *In general*. Taxes imposed under section 4960 are reported and paid using Form 4720, Return of Certain Excise Taxes Under Chapters 41 and 42 of the Internal Revenue Code. *See also* Prop. Treas. Reg. §§ 53.6011-1 and 54.6071-1, 83 F.R. 55653. In any case in which remuneration from a related organization is included to determine the excise tax imposed by section 4960, each ATEO and related organization (including a related taxable organization) must file a separate Form 4720 to report its share of liability. ATEOs and related organizations that are not liable for excise tax under section 4960 for the taxable year need not a file Form 4720 for the taxable year unless filing is required under other provisions of the Code or regulations.

(b) *Examples*. The following examples illustrate the rules of this Q/A–33:

**Example 1**. P, an ATEO, pays $250,000 of remuneration to Employee A for the taxable year for services performed as a common-law employee of P. A is a covered employee of P and is a highly-compensated employee within the meaning of section 414(q) for the taxable year. P also pays A an excess parachute payment of $550,000 for the taxable year. Q is a for-profit entity that is a related organization with respect to P. P and Q both use a calendar year taxable year. Q pays A $1 million of remuneration for the taxable year for services rendered as a common-law employee of Q, and pays no other remuneration to or parachute payment to any covered employee of P.

P and Q must report their respective liabilities for the excise tax for the taxable year on separate Forms 4720. P must report liability for the $50,000 of excess remuneration it paid to A (($250,000 / $1.25 million) x $250,000) and the $550,000 excess parachute payment it paid to A. Even though Q has no covered employees because it is not an ATEO, Q must report liability for the $200,000 of excess remuneration it paid to A (($1 million / $1.25 million) x $250,000) as a related organization of P.

**Example 2**. R, an ATEO, pays $25,000 of remuneration each to five employees (the highest-compensated group) for each of the taxable year and the preceding taxable year for services performed as common-law employees of R and pays less than $10,000 of remuneration each to all other employees for each of the taxable year and the preceding taxable year. The amount described in section 414(q)(1)(A), adjusted for inflation for the taxable year, is $125,000. In addition, for the taxable year, R pays B, a member of the highest-compensated group, an $80,000 payment in the nature of compensation that was contingent on B involuntarily separating from employment and that exceeds three times B's base amount.

R is not liable for tax under section 4960 and therefore does not need to file a Form 4720 for the taxable year (assuming R is not liable for excise tax under a provision other than section 4960). R paid no excess remuneration for the taxable year because it did not pay any employee remuneration in excess of $1 million. R paid no excess parachute payment for the taxable year, even though B received a parachute payment that was more than three times the base amount, because B (who received $105,000 of remuneration in the year of the separation from employment) is not a highly-compensated employee within the meaning of section 414(q).

**Q–34: When is the excise tax imposed under section 4960 due?**

A–34: (a) *In general*. The section 4960 excise tax must be paid and reported by filing Form 4720 by the 15th day of the 5th month after the end of the employer's taxable year. An employer may file Form 8868, Application for Automatic Extension of Time to File an Exempt Organization Return, to request an automatic extension of time to file Form 4720. The automatic extension will be granted if Form 8868 is properly completed, and timely filed. Form 8868 does not extend the time to pay tax. To avoid interest and penalties, an employer must pay the tax due by the original due date of Form 4720.

(b) *Election to prepay tax*. Notwithstanding the general rule described in Q/A–2 and Q/A–34(a), an employer may prepay the excise tax under section 4960(a)(2) for the taxable year of the separation from employment or any later taxable year before the taxable year for which the parachute payment is actually or constructively paid (see Q/A–2). (However, an employer may not prepay the excise tax on a payment to be made in cash if the present value of the payment is not reasonably ascertainable under section 3121(v)(2) and Treas. Reg. § 31.3121(v)(2)-1(e)(4) or on a payment related to health coverage.) Any prepayment must be based on the present value of the excise tax that would be due for the taxable year for which the employer will pay the excess parachute payment, and be calculated using the discount rate equal to 120 percent of the applicable Federal rate (determined under section 1274(d) and regulations thereunder; see Q/A–27) and the tax rate in effect under section 11 for the year in which the excise tax is paid. For purposes of projecting the future value of a payment that provides for interest to be credited at a variable interest rate, the employer may make a reasonable assumption regarding the variable rate. An employer is not required to adjust the excise tax paid under this Q/A–34(b) merely because the actual future interest rates are not the same as the rate used for purposes of projecting the future value of the payment.

(c) *Example*. The following example illustrates the rules of this Q/A–34:

**Example 1**. A covered employee with a base amount of $200,000 is entitled to receive two parachute payments, one of $200,000 and the other of $900,000. The $200,000 payment is made upon separation from employment, and the $900,000 payment is to be made on a date in a future taxable year. The present value of the $900,000 payment is $800,000 as of the date of the separation from employment. The employer elects to prepay the excise tax on the $900,000 future parachute payment (of which $740,000 is an excess parachute payment). The tax rate under section 11 is 21 percent for the taxable year the excise tax is paid and, using a discount rate determined under Q/A–27, the present value of the $155,400 ($740,000 x 21 percent) excise tax on the $740,000 future excess parachute payment is $140,000. To prepay the excise tax on the $740,000 future excess parachute payment, the employer must satisfy its $140,000 obligation under section 4960 with respect to the future payment, in addition to the $33,600 excise tax ($160,000 x 21 percent) on the $160,000 excess parachute payment made upon separation from employment. For purposes of determining the amount of excess remuneration (if any) under Q/A–11, the amount of remuneration paid by the employer to the covered employee for the taxable year of the separation from employment is reduced by the $900,000 of total excess parachute payments ($160,000 + $740,000).

**Q–35: Are applicable tax-exempt organizations or related organizations required to pay estimated taxes for the excise tax imposed under section 4960?**

A–35: No. There is no requirement under section 6655 for ATEOs or related organizations to pay estimated taxes on excise taxes imposed under

section 4960. Instead, the excise tax is reported and paid annually on Form 4720.

**J.** *Miscellaneous Issues*

**Q–36: Does the payment of remuneration subject to excise tax under section 4960 automatically constitute an excess benefit transaction under section 4958?**

A–36: No, the imposition of excise tax under section 4960 is not determinative as to whether the remuneration paid to the covered employee is excessive or unreasonable compensation for purposes of section 4958. Similarly, there is no presumption, inference, or basis for concluding that remuneration paid to a covered employee that is not subject to excise tax under section 4960 is reasonable compensation for purposes of determining liability for excise tax under section 4958.

**Q–37: Does the payment of remuneration subject to excise tax under section 4960 necessarily constitute an act of self-dealing described in section 4941?**

A–37: No, if the covered employee is a disqualified person described in section 4946, the imposition of excise tax under section 4960 is not determinative as to whether the remuneration paid to the covered employee is excessive or unreasonable compensation for purposes of section 4941. Similarly, there is no presumption, inference, or basis for concluding that remuneration paid to a covered employee that is not subject to excise tax under section 4960 is reasonable compensation for purposes of determining excise tax under section 4941.

**Q–38: Does section 4960 apply to amounts to which section 162(m) applies?**

A–38: (a) *In general*. Remuneration paid by a publicly held corporation within the meaning of section 162(m)(2) to a covered employee within the meaning of section 162(m)(3) generally is taken into account for purposes of section 4960. Similarly, remuneration paid by a covered health insurance provider within the meaning of section 162(m)(6)(C) to an applicable individual within the meaning of section 162(m)(6)(F) generally is taken into account for purposes of section 4960. However, any amount of remuneration for which a deduction is not allowed by reason of section 162(m) is not taken into account for purposes of section 4960.

(b) *Example*. The following example illustrates the rules of this Q/A–38:

**Example**. Employee A is an officer of Corporation X. Corporation X is a related organization as described in Q/A–7 with respect to an ATEO. A is also a covered employee of the ATEO. A receives compensation of $1.5 million from X, of which $500,000 is nondeductible by reason of section 162(m)(1). The amount of deduction disallowed under section 162(m) ($500,000) is not treated as remuneration for purposes of section 4960. However, the remuneration paid by X that is not disallowed by reason of section 162(m)(1) ($1 million) is treated as remuneration for section 4960 purposes.

**K.** *Effective Date*

**Q–39: What is the effective date of section 4960?**

A–39: (a) *In general*. Section 4960 applies to taxable years of an employer beginning after December 31, 2017. Remuneration paid before the beginning of the first taxable year that begins after December 31, 2017, is not subject to the excise tax under section 4960.

(b) *Example*. The following examples illustrate the rules of this Q/A–39:

**Example 1**. ATEO X uses a calendar year taxable year. ATEO Y is a related organization with respect to X and uses a taxable year beginning July 1 and ending June 30. X and Y each pay covered employee L $1.2 million of remuneration in calendar year 2018 ($2.4 million total) in equal monthly amounts.

X and Y's liability under section 4960(a)(1) is determined by taking into account only remuneration paid during their respective taxable years beginning after December 31, 2017. X pays L a total of $1.2 million in remuneration during X's first taxable year beginning after December 31, 2017 (January 1, 2018 through December 31, 2018). Y pays L $600,000 during the portion of the calendar year ending with or within Y's first taxable year beginning after December 31, 2017 (July 1, 2018 through December 31, 2018), resulting in $800,000 ($1.2 million + $600,000 - $1 million) of excess remuneration paid in calendar year 2018.

**Example 2**. ATEO Z uses a calendar year taxable year. On January 1, 2017, Z credits $1 million of remuneration to an account under a nonqualified account balance plan on behalf of covered employee M. Under the plan, M will not vest in the amount unless M performs substantial services through December 31, 2018. On December 31, 2017, the account balance is $1.1 million. On December 31, 2018, the account balance is $1.2 million. Although M's account balance as of December 31, 2017 was $1.1 million, the entire $1.2

million is treated as remuneration paid in calendar year 2018, because vesting did not occur until December 31, 2018. If instead the $1.1 million had vested during 2017, only the $100,000 increase in the account balance during 2018 would have been treated as remuneration paid in 2018 potentially subject to the excise tax under section 4960(a)(1).

III. REQUEST FOR COMMENTS

The Treasury Department and the IRS intend to issue proposed regulations with respect to section 4960. The Treasury Department and the IRS request comments on the topics addressed in this notice and any other issues arising under section 4960. The Treasury Department and the IRS specifically request comments regarding the following topics:

(1) Whether, for purposes of determining whether an employee is a covered employee, calculating remuneration, and calculating excess parachute payments, an employer should be permitted to rely on the employee's written representation that the employee did not perform services for any other employer during the calendar year ending with or within the ATEO's taxable year (or did not perform services for one or more specified employers). If so, whether there are circumstances (for example, an employer has reason to know that the written representation was incorrect) under which an employer should not be permitted to rely on such a representation, and in what manner such a written representation must be documented in order to be relied upon.

(2) Whether, for purposes of calculating remuneration from a related organization with a change in status as a related organization during the year, there should be an alternative to calculating the actual amount paid while the employer was a related organization with respect to the ATEO and, if so, what alternative(s) should be available that would continue to provide a useful calculation with respect to both the ATEO and the related organizations without creating opportunities for abusive reallocations of remuneration among the related organizations.

(3) How remuneration based on the appreciation and depreciation of the fair market value of the stock underlying stock options and stock appreciation rights (or other similar equity rights) should be taken into account.

(4) How a related organization should treat remuneration on which it was subject to excise tax under section 4960 in a prior taxable year and

for which it is denied a deduction under section 162(m) in the current taxable year.

(5) How the term "predecessor" should be defined for purposes of defining covered employees.

(6) How remuneration paid to medical service providers should be reasonably allocated between medical services and other services, including how reasonable allocations can be made taking into account comparable salaries, time spent performing medical services and other services, and any applicable employment agreements.

All materials submitted will be available for public inspection and copying. Public comments should be submitted no later than April 2, 2019. Comments should include a reference to Notice 2018-XX. Comments may be submitted electronically via the Federal eRulemaking Portal at *www.regulations.gov* (type IRS-2018-XX in the search field on the *regulations.gov* homepage to find this notice and submit comments). Alternatively, submissions may be sent to CC:PA:LPD:PR (Notice 2018-XX), Room 5203, Internal Revenue Service, P.O. Box 7604, Ben Franklin Station, Washington, DC 20044. Submissions also may be hand delivered Monday through Friday between the hours of 8 a.m. and 4 p.m. to CC:PA:LPD:PR (Notice 2018-88), Courier's Desk, Internal Revenue Service, 1111 Constitution Avenue, NW, Washington, DC 20044. All recommendations for guidance submitted by the public in response to this notice will be available for public inspection and copying in their entirety.

## IV. RELIANCE

The Treasury Department and the IRS intend to issue further guidance regarding section 4960 in the form of proposed regulations. Until further guidance is issued, taxpayers may rely on the rules in this notice for purposes of section 4960 effective from December 22, 2017 (the date of enactment). Further guidance will be prospective and will not apply to taxable years beginning before the issuance of such guidance.

## V. PAPERWORK REDUCTION ACT

The collection of information in this notice is the requirement under section 4960 that an ATEO determine and keep records of its covered employees, related organizations, and excess remuneration and excess parachute payments paid to covered employees by the ATEO and related organizations, disclose this information to each related organization, and that each ATEO and related organization report excise tax liability to the IRS. The collection of information contained in this notice is reflected in the collection of information for Form 4720 that has been reviewed and approved by the Office of Management and Budget in accordance with the Paperwork Reduction Act (44 U.S.C. 3507(c)) under control number 1545-0052.

An agency may not conduct or sponsor, and a person is not required to respond to, a collection of information unless the collection of information displays a valid OMB control number.

Books or records relating to a collection of information must be retained as long as their contents may become material in the administration of any internal revenue law. Generally, tax returns and tax return information are confidential, as required by § 6103.

## VI. DRAFTING INFORMATION

The principal authors of this notice are William McNally and Chelsea Rubin of the Office of Associate Chief Counsel (Tax Exempt and Government Entities). For Executive Compensation questions, contact Mr. McNally at (202) 317-5600 (not a toll-free number). For Exempt Organizations questions, contact Ms. Rubin at (202) 317-5800 (not a toll-free number).

---

# Rev. Proc. 2018-16, I.R.B. 2018-9, February 8, 2018

## SECTION 1. PURPOSE

This revenue procedure provides guidance to the Chief Executive Officers of any State, any possession of the United States, and the District of Columbia regarding the procedure for designating population census tracts as Qualified Opportunity Zones for purposes of §§ 1400Z-1 and 1400Z-2 of the Internal Revenue Code (Code).

## SECTION 2. BACKGROUND

.01 *Enactment.* Section 13823 of "An Act to provide for reconciliation pursuant to titles II and V of the concurrent resolution on the budget for fiscal year 2018," P.L. 115-97, which was enacted on December 22, 2017, amended the Code by adding §§ 1400Z-1 and 1400Z-2 to the Code.

.02 *Tax incentives.* Section 1400Z-2 of the Code allows the temporary deferral of inclusion in gross income for certain realized gains to the extent that corresponding amounts are timely invested in a qualified opportunity fund. Investments in a qualified opportunity fund may also be eligible for additional tax benefits.

.03 *Qualified Opportunity Fund.* Section 1400Z-2(d)(1) of the Code provides that a qualified opportunity fund is an investment vehicle that is organized as a partnership or a corporation for the purpose of investing in Qualified Opportunity Zone property.

.04 *Designations, in general.* Section 1400Z-1 of the Code allows the Chief Executive Officer (CEO) of each State to nominate a limited number of population census tracts to be designated as Qualified Opportunity Zones (QOZs). For purposes of §§ 1400Z-1 and 1400Z-2 and this revenue procedure, the term "State" means any State, any possession of the United States, and the District of Columbia. *See* §§ 1400Z-1(c)(3) and 7701(a)(10) of the Code. Under § 1400Z-1(c)(1), a population census tract is eligible for designation as a QOZ if it satisfies the definition of "low-income community" (LIC) in § 45D(e) of the Code.

.05 *Tracts Contiguous with LICs.* In addition, under § 1400Z-1(e) of the Code, a tract that is not an LIC is eligible for designation if both of the following conditions are met:

(1) The non-LIC tract is contiguous with an LIC that is designated as a QOZ (the contiguous LIC QOZ need not be in the same State.); and

(2) The median family income of the non-LIC tract does not exceed 125 percent of the median family income of that contiguous LIC QOZ.

.06 *Determination Period and Extension.* Pursuant to § 1400Z-1(b)(1)(A) and (c)(2)(B) of the Code, the CEO of the State in which a tract is located may nominate the tract to be a QOZ, and any such nomination must be made no later than March 21, 2018. Under § 1400Z-1(b)(2), however, the State CEO may request, and receive, a 30-day extension of this deadline.

.07 *Consideration Period and Extension.* In general, not later than the end of a 30-day period beginning on the date that the Secretary of the Treasury (Secretary) receives notice of a nomination, the Secretary may certify the nomination and designate the nominated tract as a QOZ. Under § 1400Z-1(b)(2) of the Code, however, the State CEO may request, and receive, a 30-day extension of the Secretary's deadline.

.08 *Qualified Opportunity Zone.* Section 1400Z-1 of the Code defines a QOZ as any population census tract (either a nominated LIC or a nominated non-LIC, contiguous census tract) that is designated as a QOZ.

.09 *Number of Designations.*

(1) In general, § 1400Z-1(d)(1) of the Code provides that the number of population census tracts in a State that may be designated as QOZs may not exceed 25 percent of the number of population census tracts in the State that are LICs. If the number of LICs in a State is not evenly divisible by 4, the 25 percent limitation is determined by rounding the fractional quotient up to the next whole number. For example, if a State contains 197 LICs, the maximum number of designations is 50, even though 25 percent of 197 is 49.25.

(2) Section 1400Z-1(d)(2) of the Code further provides that, notwithstanding the 25 percent limitation, if a State contains fewer than 100 LICs, then a total of 25 tracts may be designated.

(3) Section 1400Z-1(e)(2) of the Code provides that not more than 5 percent of the tracts designated in a State may be non-LIC, contiguous tracts designated under § 1400Z-1(e)(1). Thus, designations under § 1400Z-1(d)(1) and (d)(2) may include a limited number of non-LIC contiguous tracts. If the number of designated QOZs in a State is not evenly divisible by 20, the 5 percent limitation is determined by rounding the fractional quotient up to the next whole number. For example, suppose that State B has 80 LICs. Under § 1400Z-1(d)(2), State B is allowed to nominate 25 tracts for QOZ designation because State B has fewer than 100 LICs. If State B nominates all 25 of the QOZs allowed, then of the 25 nominated tracts, only 2 (5 percent of 25 or 1.25, rounded up to 2) nominated tracts may be non-LIC contiguous tracts. But if State B nominated only 18 LICs, then it could nominate only 1 (5 percent of 19 or 0.95, rounded up to 1) additional non-LIC contiguous tract.

SECTION 3. IDENTITY OF LICs AND OF THE CONTIGUOUS TRACTS THAT ARE ALSO ELIGIBLE FOR DESIGNATION AS QOZs

.01 Based on the 2011-2015 American Community Survey (ACS) 5-Year data from the Census Bureau, a public, on-line resource (Information Resource) identifies over 41,000 population census tracts that are eligible for designation as a QOZ:

(1) 31,680 population census tracts that are LICs eligible for designation as QOZs; and

(2) 9,453 non-LIC population census tracts that are eligible for designation if a particular LIC contiguous to the non-LIC tract is designated as a QOZ.

.02 This Information Resource includes detailed mapping, which makes it possible to see the exact location of every tract and to view a variety of demographic information for each eligible tract.

.03 In the case of each tract described in section 3.01(2) of this revenue procedure, the Information Resource includes one or more LIC tracts on whose designation as a QOZ the non-LIC tract's eligibility depends.

.04 The Information Resource can be accessed at *https://www.cdfifund.gov/Pages/Opportunity-Zones.aspx*.

.05 In the fall of 2017, the Census Bureau released the 2012-2016 ACS 5-Year data. Because of the March 21, 2018, deadline for State CEOs to nominate tracts for designation as QOZs, the maximum aggregate number of designations in a State is determined on the basis of the 2011-2015 ACS, as reflected in the Information Resource described above.

.06 In addition, the Information Resource is a "safe harbor." That is, if the Information Resource identifies a census tract as being either an eligible LIC or an eligible non-LIC contiguous tract, a State CEO's nomination of that tract will not fail to be certified on the grounds that the tract is no longer eligible under more recent census data.

.07 On the other hand, in many cases, if a tract is eligible under the most recent available ACS 5-Year data, the tract is eligible to be nominated for designation. If the Information Resource, however, does not identify the tract as eligible,

the nomination must be accompanied by an analysis demonstrating that eligibility, including appropriate supporting data from that ACS.

## SECTION 4. SCOPE

This revenue procedure applies to the CEO of any State that desires to nominate for designation as QOZs population census tracts that are either LICs that qualify under § 1400Z-1(c)(1) of the Code or non-LIC contiguous tracts that qualify under § 1400Z-1(e)(1) of the Code.

## SECTION 5. PROCEDURE

.01 A Nomination Tool, which can be accessed online, has been developed for the benefit of State CEOs that are making nominations of census tracts for designation as QOZs.

.02 Further information on the nomination process under § 1400Z-1 of the Code, including how to access the on-line Nomination Tool and how to request an extension of the determination period, will be sent individually to all State CEOs.

## SECTION 6. EFFECTIVE DATE

This revenue procedure is effective on February 8, 2018.

## SECTION 7. DRAFTING INFORMATION

The principal author of this revenue procedure is Erika Reigle of the Office of Associate Chief Counsel (Income Tax and Accounting). For further information regarding this revenue procedure contact Erika Reigle at (202) 317-7006 (not a toll free call). For further information regarding the Information Resource, contact the CDFI Fund Help Desk at (202) 653-0421 (not a toll-free call).

---

# Rev. Proc. 2018-59, I.R.B. 2018-50, November 26, 2018

## SECTION 1. PURPOSE

This revenue procedure provides a safe harbor that allows taxpayers to treat certain infrastructure trades or businesses as real property trades or businesses solely for purposes of qualifying as an electing real property trade or business under section 163(j)(7)(B) of the Internal Revenue Code.

## SECTION 2. BACKGROUND

.01 On December 22, 2017, section 163(j) was amended by the Tax Cuts and Jobs Act, Pub. L. 115-97 (TCJA). Section 163(j), as amended by the TCJA, provides new rules limiting the amount of

business interest expense that can be deducted for taxable years beginning after December 31, 2017. *See* TCJA § 13301(a).

.02 Under section 163(j)(1), the amount allowed as a deduction for business interest expense is limited to the sum of: (1) the taxpayer's business interest income (as defined in section 163(j)(6)) for the taxable year; (2) 30 percent of the taxpayer's adjusted taxable income (as defined in section 163(j)(8)) for such taxable year; and (3) the taxpayer's floor plan financing interest (as defined in section 163(j)(9)) for such taxable year.

.03 The limitation under section 163(j) on the deductibility of business interest expense applies to all taxpayers with business interest (as defined in section 163(j)(5)), except for certain taxpayers (other than tax shelters under section 448(a)(3)) that meet the gross receipts test in section 448(c).

.04 Section 163(j)(5) generally provides that the term "business interest" means any interest properly allocable to a trade or business. Section 163(j)(7)(A)(ii) provides that, for purposes of the limitation on the deduction for business interest, the term "trade or business" does not include an "electing real property trade or business." Thus, for purposes of section 163(j), interest expense that is properly allocable to an electing real property trade or business is not properly allocable to a trade or business, and is not business interest expense that is subject to section 163(j)(1).

.05 The term "electing real property trade or business" under section 163(j)(7)(B) means any trade or business that is described in section 469(c)(7)(C) that makes an election to be an electing real property trade or business.

.06 Section 168(g)(1)(F) provides that an electing real property trade or business (within the meaning of section 163(j)(7)(B)) must use the alternative depreciation system for property described in section 168(g)(8). *See* section 163(j)(10)(A).

.07 Section 469(c)(7)(C) defines a real property trade or business as any real property development, redevelopment, construction, reconstruction, acquisition, conversion, rental, operation, management, leasing, or brokerage trade or business.

.08 The Department of the Treasury (Treasury Department) and the Internal Revenue Service (IRS) are aware that there may be uncertainty as to whether certain infrastructure arrangements between private persons and governmental entities under which private persons maintain or provide other services with respect to core infrastructure property such as roads, bridges, or other similar property are included in the definition of a real property trade or business under section 469(c)(7)(C).

.09 In light of the concerns relating to certain infrastructure arrangements in the context of section 163(j), this revenue procedure provides a safe harbor that allows taxpayers to treat certain trades or businesses that are conducted in connection with the designing, building, managing, operating, or maintaining of certain core infrastructure projects as real property trades or businesses for purposes of qualifying as an electing real property trade or business under section 163(j)(7)(B) (infrastructure safe harbor).

.10 The infrastructure safe harbor in this revenue procedure is based on the proposed eligibility parameters for public infrastructure projects for purposes of the private activity bond financing proposals described in the "Legislative Outline for Rebuilding Infrastructure in America," which the White House released publicly and transmitted to Congress on February 12, 2018. *See* https://www.whitehouse.gov/wp-content/uploads/2018/02/INFRASTRUCTURE-211.pdf (last visited Oct. 17, 2018).

## SECTION 3. SCOPE AND INFRASTRUCTURE SAFE HARBOR

.01 *Scope.* This revenue procedure applies to a taxpayer with a trade or business that—

(1) Is conducted by a party contractually obligated to fulfill the terms of a specified infrastructure arrangement, as defined in section 4.11 of this revenue procedure;

(2) Is conducted in connection with fulfilling the terms of a specified infrastructure arrangement; and

(3) Would not otherwise be treated as a real property trade or business under section 163(j)(7)(B) or 469(c)(7)(C).

.02 *Safe harbor for certain infrastructure trades or businesses.* Taxpayers described in section 3.01 of this revenue procedure are eligible to make an election to be an electing real property trade or business for purposes of sections 163(j)(7)(B) and 168(g)(1)(F). If a taxpayer makes this election, the taxpayer must use the alternative depreciation system of section 168(g) to depreciate the property described in section 168(g)(8). The taxpayer makes the election in accordance with the time and in such form and manner as prescribed by the Commissioner in regulations, guidance published in the Internal Revenue Bulletin, or in IRS forms, instructions, or publications.

.03 *Treatment as real property.* For purposes of applying section 163(j) and this revenue procedure, a "specified infrastructure arrangement," as defined in section 4.11 of this revenue procedure, is treated as real property.

.04 *Special rule for certain assets.* For purposes of applying section 163(j) and this revenue procedure, "qualified public infrastructure property," as defined in section 4.08 of this revenue procedure, is treated as used in a trade or business described in section 3.01 of this revenue procedure even if such property is being designed, built, constructed, reconstructed, developed, or redeveloped.

.05 *No inference.* No inference should be drawn from this revenue procedure regarding the definition of a real property trade or business for purposes of section 469.

## SECTION 4. DEFINITIONS FOR THE INFRASTRUCTURE SAFE HARBOR

The following definitions apply for purposes of this revenue procedure:

.01 The term "Brownfield site" means any real property the use of which may be complicated by the presence of or potential presence of a hazardous substance, pollutant, or contaminant.

.02 The term "environmental remediation costs" means costs chargeable to a capital account that are paid or incurred to control or abate hazardous substances.

.03 The term "flood control and stormwater facilities" means any capital assets used to control floodwater or to contain stormwater.

.04 The term "government" means—

(1) The United States or any agency or instrumentality of the United States;

(2) A State or any political subdivision thereof, including the District of Columbia and any possession or territory of the United States, within the meaning of section 103 and § 1.103-1; or

(3) Any foreign government.

.05 The term "foreign government" means any foreign government, any political subdivision of a foreign government, or any wholly owned agency or instrumentality of any one of the foregoing within the meaning of § 1.1471-6(b).

.06 The term "hydroelectric generating facilities" means facilities used to generate electricity from water, including water impounded through a dam or diverted from a river, or pumped storage, and structures for housing generating equipment, up to, but not including, the stage of electrical transmission.

.07 The term "infrastructure property" means—

(1) Airports, within the meaning of section 142;

(2) Docks, and wharves, within the meaning of section 142;

(3) Maritime and inland waterway ports, and waterway infrastructure, including dredging and navigation improvements;

(4) Mass commuting facilities, within the meaning of section 142;

(5) Facilities for the furnishing of water, within the meaning of section 142;

(6) Sewage facilities, within the meaning of section 142;

(7) Solid waste disposal facilities, within the meaning of section 142;

(8) Facilities for the local furnishing of electrical energy or gas, within the meaning of section 142;

(9) Local district heating or cooling facilities, within the meaning of section 142;

(10) Qualified hazardous waste facilities, within the meaning of section 142;

(11) High-speed intercity rail facilities, within the meaning of section 142;

(12) Hydroelectric generating facilities, together with environmental enhancements of hydroelectric generating facilities, within the meaning of section 142;

(13) Qualified public educational facilities, within the meaning of section 142;

(14) Flood control and stormwater facilities;

(15) Surface transportation facilities;

(16) Rural broadband service facilities; and

(17) Environmental remediation costs on Brownfield and Superfund sites.

.08 The term "qualified public infrastructure property" means infrastructure property if—

(1) The infrastructure property either—

(a) Is owned by a government; or

(b) Is not property of a trade or business described in section 163(j)(7)(A)(iv) and is owned by a private trade or business that operates under an arrangement in which rates charged for the use or services provided by the infrastructure property are subject to regulatory or contractual control by a government, or government approval; and

(2) The infrastructure property is, or will be once operational, available for use by the general public or the services provided by the infrastructure property are made available to members of the general public, including electric utility, industrial, agricultural, or commercial users on the same basis as individual members of the general public.

.09 The term "rural area" means, as confirmed by the latest decennial census of the U.S. Census Bureau, (a) any area that is not located within a city, town, or incorporated area that has a population of greater than 20,000 inhabitants or (b) an urbanized area contiguous and adjacent to a city or town that has a population of greater than 50,000 inhabitants. For purposes of the definition of rural area, an urbanized area means a densely populated territory as defined in the latest decennial census of the U.S. Census Bureau.

.10 The term "rural broadband service facilities" means broadband telecommunications assets that provide high-speed internet access for data transmission through wired or wireless networks and that primarily serve any rural area.

.11 The term "specified infrastructure arrangement" means a contract or contracts with a term in excess of 5 years between a government and a private trade or business under which a private trade or business has contractual responsibility to provide one or more of the functions of designing, building, constructing, reconstructing, developing, redeveloping, managing, operating, or maintaining qualified public infrastructure property.

.12 The term "Superfund site" means any site designated by the Environmental Protection Agency as a Superfund site on its national priorities list under the Comprehensive Environmen-

tal Response, Compensation, and Liability Act of 1980, Public Law 96-510 (94 Stat. 2767 (1980)), as amended.

.13 The term "surface transportation facilities" includes any road, bridge, tunnel, passenger railroad, surface freight transfer facility, and any other facility that facilitates surface transportation.

## SECTION 5. EFFECTIVE DATE

This revenue procedure is effective on December 10, 2018. Taxpayers may apply the safe harbor set forth in this revenue procedure to taxable years beginning after December 31, 2017.

## SECTION 6. DRAFTING INFORMATION

The principal authors of this revenue procedure are Charles Gorham, Joanna Trebat, and Zachary King of the Office of Associate Chief Counsel (Income Tax & Accounting). For further information regarding this revenue procedure, contact Mr. Gorham at (202) 317-5091, Ms. Trebat at (202) 317-7003, or Mr. King at (202) 317-7003 (not toll-free calls).

---

# Rev. Proc. 2019-8, I.R.B. 2019-3, December 21, 2018

## SECTION 1. PURPOSE

This revenue procedure provides guidance under §§ 13101(b), 13204(a)(3), and 13205 of the Tax Cuts and Jobs Act, Pub. L. No. 115-97, 131 Stat. 2054 (Dec. 22, 2017) (the "TCJA"). Section 13101(b) of the TCJA amended § 179 of the Internal Revenue Code by modifying the definition of qualified real property that may be eligible as § 179 property under § 179(d)(1). Section 13204(a)(3) of the TCJA amended § 168 by (i) requiring certain property held by an electing real property trade or business, as defined in § 163(j)(7)(B), to be depreciated under the alternative depreciation system in § 168(g), and (ii) changing the recovery period under the alternative depreciation system from 40 to 30 years for residential rental property. Section 13205 of the TCJA amended § 168 by requiring certain property held by an electing farming business, as defined in § 163(j)(7)(C), to be depreciated under the alternative depreciation system. This revenue procedure also modifies Rev. Proc. 87-57, 1987-2 C.B. 687, to provide an optional depreciation table for residential rental property depreciated under the alternative depreciation system with a 30-year recovery period, and Rev. Proc. 2018-31, 2018-22 I.R.B. 637, to provide guidance for calculating a § 481(a) adjustment for a change in method of accounting due to a change in the use of depreciable tangible property.

## SECTION 2. BACKGROUND

.01 *Modifications to § 179.*

(1) Section 179(a) allows a taxpayer to elect to treat the cost (or a portion of the cost) of any § 179 property as an expense for the taxable year in which the taxpayer places the property in service. Sections 179(b)(1) and (2) prescribe a dollar limitation on the aggregate cost of § 179 property that can be treated as an expense under § 179(a). The dollar limitation is the amount under § 179(b)(1) (the § 179(b)(1) limitation), reduced (but not below zero) by the amount by which the cost of § 179 property placed in service during the taxable year exceeds the amount under § 179(b)(2) (the § 179(b)(2) limitation). For taxable years beginning after 2017, the § 179(b)(1) limitation is $1,000,000 and the § 179(b)(2) limitation is $2,500,000. Pursuant to § 179(b)(6), these limitation amounts are adjusted for inflation for taxable years beginning after 2018. For taxable years beginning in 2019, section 3.26 of Rev. Proc. 2018-57, 2018-49 I.R.B. 827, provides that the § 179(b)(1) limitation is $1,020,000 and the § 179(b)(2) limitation is $2,550,000.

(2) Section 179(b)(3)(A) provides that a taxpayer's § 179 deduction for any taxable year, after application of the § 179(b)(1) and (2) limitations, is limited to the taxpayer's taxable income for that taxable year that is derived from the

taxpayer's active conduct of any trade or business during that taxable year (taxable income limitation). Section 179(b)(3)(B) provides that the amount of any cost of § 179 property elected to be expensed in a taxable year that is disallowed as a § 179 deduction under the taxable income limitation may be carried forward for an unlimited number of years and may be deducted under § 179(a) in a future year, subject to the same limitations.

(3) Section 179(c) provides the rules for making and revoking elections under § 179 ("§ 179 election"). Pursuant to § 179(c)(1), a § 179 election is made in the manner prescribed by regulations. Section 1.179-5(c)(1) of the Income Tax Regulations provides the manner for making or revoking a § 179 election for any taxable year beginning after 2002 and before 2008. Section 1.179-5(c) was promulgated in 2005 and has not been amended to reflect subsequent amendments to § 179(c). However, in 2017, the Treasury Department and the IRS issued Rev. Proc. 2017-33, 2017-19 I.R.B. 1236. Section 3.02 of Rev. Proc. 2017-33 provides that for a taxable year beginning after 2014, the taxpayer will be permitted to make a § 179 election for any § 179 property without the Commissioner's consent on an amended federal tax return for the taxable year in which the taxpayer places in service the § 179 property. Section 3.02 of Rev. Proc. 2017-33 further provides that until § 1.179-5(c) is amended to incorporate this guidance, taxpayers may rely on such guidance.

(4) Section 179(d) defines the term "§ 179 property." Prior to amendment by the TCJA, § 179(d)(1) defined § 179 property as property that is: (A)(i) tangible property to which § 168 applies, or (ii) computer software, as defined in § 197(e)(3)(B), that is described in § 197(e)(3)(A)(i) and to which § 167 applies; (B) § 1245 property as defined in § 1245(a)(3); and (C) acquired by purchase for use in the active conduct of a trade or business. Prior to amendment by the TCJA, § 179(d)(1) further provided that § 179 property does not include any property described in § 50(b).

Section 13101(b)(1) of the TCJA amended § 179(d)(1)(B) to provide that if the taxpayer elects, § 179 property may include qualified real property as defined in § 179(f). Section 13101(c) of the TCJA also amended the flush language in § 179(d)(1) to allow property used predominantly to furnish lodging or in connection with the furnishing of lodging as described in § 50(b)(2) to be § 179 property. These amendments apply to property placed in service in taxable years beginning after December 31, 2017.

(5) Prior to amendment by the TCJA, § 179(f)(1) provided that § 179 property included qualified real property if the taxpayer elected the application of § 179(f) for the taxable year, and § 179(f)(2) defined "qualified real property" as meaning qualified leasehold improvement property, qualified restaurant property, and qualified retail improvement property described in § 168(e)(6), (7), and (8), respectively, as in effect on the day before the date of the enactment of the TCJA. Section 13101(b)(2) of the TCJA amended § 179(f) by defining qualified real property as (1) any qualified improvement property described in § 168(e)(6) and (2) any of the following improvements to nonresidential real property placed in service after the date such property was first placed in service: roofs; heating, ventilation, and air-conditioning property; fire protection and alarm systems; and security systems. These amendments apply to property placed in service in taxable years beginning after December 31, 2017.

Some taxpayers have inquired as to whether the election to treat qualified real property as § 179 property is made in accordance with the § 179 election procedures in § 1.179-5(c) or the procedures in Notice 2013-59, 2013-40 I.R.B. 297, for electing the application of former § 179(f)(1). Section 3 of this revenue procedure addresses this issue.

(6) Section 401(b)(15)(A) of the Consolidated Appropriations Act, 2018, Pub. L. No. 115-141, Div. U, Title IV, 132 Stat. 348 (Mar. 23, 2018) (the "2018 Act"), removed § 179(e), which provided special rules for qualified disaster assistance property, and redesignated § 179(f) as § 179(e).

*.02 Modifications to § 168(g).*

(1) Prior to amendment by the TCJA, § 168(g)(1) provided that the depreciation deduction provided by § 167(a) is determined under the alternative depreciation system for: (A) any tangible property that during the taxable year is used predominantly outside the United States; (B) any tax-exempt use property; (C) any tax-exempt bond financed property; (D) any imported property covered by an Executive order under § 168(g)(6); and (E) any property to which an election under § 168(g)(7) applies. Sections 13204(a)(3)(A)(i) and 13205(a) of the TCJA amended § 168(g)(1) by requiring the depreciation deduction provided by § 167(a) to be determined under the alternative depreciation system for the following additional property: nonresidential real property, residential rental property, and qualified improvement property held by an electing real property trade or business as de-

fined in § 163(j)(7)(B); and any property with a recovery period of 10 years or more that is held by an electing farming business as defined in § 163(j)(7)(C). These amendments apply to taxable years beginning after December 31, 2017, without regard to when the property is or was placed in service.

Some taxpayers that are electing real property trades or businesses or electing farming businesses have inquired about how depreciation is changed from the general depreciation system under § 168(a) to the alternative depreciation system under § 168(g) for property placed in service in taxable years beginning before 2018. Section 4 of this revenue procedure addresses this issue.

(2) Prior to amendment by the TCJA, the table of recovery periods under § 168(g)(2)(C) provided that the recovery period was 40 years for residential rental property. Section 13204(a)(3)(C) of the TCJA amended that table by providing that the recovery period is 30 years for residential rental property. This amendment applies to property placed in service after December 31, 2017.

Some taxpayers have inquired whether residential rental property placed in service before 2018 has a recovery period of 30 or 40 years under the alternative depreciation system. Section 4 of this revenue procedure addresses this issue.

.03 *Optional depreciation table under the alternative depreciation system for residential rental property placed in service after 2017.* Rev. Proc. 87-57 provides guidance for computing depreciation deductions for tangible property under § 168. Sections 2-7 of Rev. Proc. 87-57 prescribe the manner of computing such depreciation deductions. Section 8 of Rev. Proc. 87-57 contains optional depreciation tables that may be used by certain taxpayers in lieu of computing depreciation deductions in the manner described in sections 2-7 of Rev. Proc. 87-57.

Section 8.01 of Rev. Proc. 87-57 provides that the optional depreciation tables may be used for any item of property placed in service in a taxable year. For all items of property placed in service in a taxable year for which the optional depreciation tables are not used, depreciation deductions must be computed in the manner prescribed in sections 2-7 of Rev. Proc. 87-57.

Section 8.02 of Rev. Proc. 87-57 provides that the optional depreciation tables specify schedules of annual depreciation rates to be applied to the unadjusted basis of the property in each taxable year. If a taxpayer uses an optional depreciation table to compute the annual depreciation deduction for any item of property, the taxpayer must use the table to compute the annual depreciation deductions for the entire recovery period of such property. However, a taxpayer may not continue to use the table if there are any adjustments to the basis of such item of property for reasons other than (1) depreciation allowed or allowable, or (2) an addition or an improvement to such property that is subject to depreciation as a separate item of property. Use of the optional depreciation tables to compute depreciation deductions does not require the filing of any notice with the Internal Revenue Service (IRS).

The IRS has not previously published an optional table for property depreciated under the alternative depreciation system with a recovery period of 30 years and the mid-month convention. Some taxpayers have requested the IRS to provide an optional depreciation table for residential rental property that is placed in service after December 31, 2017, and depreciated under the alternative depreciation system of § 168(g) using the straight-line method, the new 30-year recovery period required by the TCJA, and the mid-month convention. This table is provided in section 4 of this revenue procedure.

.04 *Subsequent References.* Unless otherwise specifically stated, all references in the subsequent sections of this revenue procedure to § 168(g) are to § 168(g) as in effect after the enactment of the TCJA and to § 179 are to § 179 as in effect after the enactment of the 2018 Act.

## SECTION 3. QUALIFIED REAL PROPERTY UNDER § 179

.01 *Definition.*

(1) *Taxable year beginning after 2017.* For property placed in service by the taxpayer in any taxable year beginning after 2017, the following types of property are qualified real property that may be eligible as § 179 property under § 179(d)(1):

(a) Qualified improvement property, as described in § 168(e)(6), that is placed in service by the taxpayer. The definition of qualified improvement property in § 168(e)(6) is the same definition of that term in § 168(k)(3) as in effect on the day before the date of enactment of the TCJA. Accordingly, see section 4.02 of Rev. Proc. 2017-33 for further guidance on the definition of qualified improvement property; and

(b) An improvement to nonresidential real property, as defined in § 168(e)(2)(B), if the improvement:

(i) Is placed in service by the taxpayer after the date such nonresidential real property was first placed in service by any person;

(ii) Is § 1250 property; and

(iii) Is:

(A) A roof;

(B) Heating, ventilation, and air-conditioning property (HVAC). A central HVAC system includes all components that are in, on, or adjacent to the nonresidential real property. *See* § 1.48-1(e)(2);

(C) A fire protection and alarm system; or

(D) A security system.

(2) *Taxable year beginning in 2017 and ending in 2018.* For property placed in service by the taxpayer in a taxable year beginning in 2017 and ending in 2018, qualified real property is qualified leasehold improvement property, qualified restaurant property, or qualified retail improvement property as described in § 179(f)(1) and (2) as in effect on the day before the date of enactment of the TCJA. Qualified leasehold improvement property, qualified restaurant property, and qualified retail improvement property are defined in § 168(e)(6), (e)(7), and (e)(8), respectively, as in effect on the day before the date of the enactment of the TCJA.

.02 *Election to Treat Qualified Real Property as § 179 Property.* A taxpayer may elect to expense under § 179(a) the cost, or a portion of the cost, of qualified real property placed in service by the taxpayer during any taxable year beginning after 2017 by filing an original or amended Federal tax return for that taxable year in accordance with procedures similar to those in § 1.179-5(c)(2) and section 3.02 of Rev. Proc. 2017-33. If a taxpayer elects or elected to expense under § 179(a) a portion of the cost of qualified real property placed in service by the taxpayer during any taxable year beginning after 2017, the taxpayer is permitted to increase the portion of the cost of such property expensed under § 179(a) by filing an amended Federal tax return for that taxable year. Any such increase in the amount expensed under § 179 is not deemed to be a revocation of the prior election for that taxable year.

## SECTION 4. ALTERNATIVE DEPRECIATION SYSTEM UNDER § 168(g)

.01 *Recovery period of residential rental property.*

(1) *In general.* The recovery period under the table in § 168(g)(2)(C) is 30 years for residential rental property placed in service by the taxpayer after December 31, 2017, and is 40 years for residential rental property placed in service by the taxpayer before January 1, 2018.

(2) *Optional depreciation table.* Below is the optional depreciation table for residential rental property placed in service by the taxpayer after December 31, 2017, and depreciated by the taxpayer under the alternative depreciation system of § 168(g) using the straight-line method, a 30-year recovery period, and the mid-month convention.

| | 1 | 2 | 3 | 4 | 5 | 6 | 7 | 8 | 9 | 10 | 11 | 12 |
|---|---|---|---|---|---|---|---|---|---|---|---|---|
| Year | | | | | | | | | | | | |
| 1 | 3.204% | 2.926% | 2.649% | 2.371% | 2.093% | 1.815% | 1.528% | 1.250% | 0.972% | 0.694% | 0.417% | 0.139% |
| 2-30 | 3.333% | 3.333% | 3.333% | 3.333% | 3.333% | 3.333% | 3.333% | 3.333% | 3.333% | 3.333% | 3.333% | 3.333% |
| 31 | 0.139% | 0.417% | 0.694% | 0.972% | 1.250% | 1.528% | 1.815% | 2.093% | 2.371% | 2.649% | 2.926% | 3.204% |

Table—Alternative Depreciation System

Method: Straight line

Convention: Mid-month

Recovery period: 30 years

Month in the 1st recovery year the property is placed in service

.02 *Electing real property trade or business or electing farming business.*

(1) *In general.* Section 168(g)(1)(F) and (G) provide that the depreciation deduction provided by § 167(a) must be determined in accordance with the alternative depreciation system in § 168(g) for the following types of MACRS property (as defined in § 1.168(b)-1(a)(2)):

(a) Any nonresidential real property (as defined in § 168(e)(2)(B)), residential rental property (as defined in § 168(e)(2)(A)), and qualified improvement property (as defined in § 168(e)(6)) held by an electing real property trade or business (as defined in § 163(j)(7)(B) and the regulations thereunder); and

(b) Any property with a recovery period of 10 years or more that is held by an electing farming business (as defined in § 163(j)(7)(C) and the regulations thereunder). For determining what

MACRS property has a recovery period of 10 years or more, the recovery period is determined in accordance with § 168(c).

(2) *Changing depreciation of property to the alternative depreciation system.*

(a) *In general.* For the first taxable year for which an electing real property trade or business or an electing farming business makes an election under § 163(j)(7)(B) or (C), respectively, and the regulations thereunder (the "election year"), that trade or business must begin depreciating the properties described in section 4.02(1) of this revenue procedure, as applicable, in accordance with the alternative depreciation system in § 168(g). The preceding sentence applies to such property placed in service by the trade or business in taxable years beginning before the election year ("existing property") and such property placed in service by the trade or business in the election year and subsequent taxable years ("newly-acquired property").

(b) *Existing property.* For existing property described in section 4.02(1) of this revenue procedure, as applicable, a change in use occurs under § 168(i)(5) and § 1.168(i)-4(d) for the election year as a result of the election under § 163(j)(7)(B) or (C), as applicable. Accordingly, depreciation for such property beginning for the election year is determined in accordance with § 1.168(i)-4(d). Pursuant to § 1.168(i)-4(f), a change in computing depreciation for the election year for such existing property is not a change in method of accounting under § 446(e). If any such existing property was qualified property under § 168(k) in the taxable year in which the trade or business placed the property in service, the additional first year depreciation deduction allowable for that property is not redetermined. *See* § 1.168(k)-1(f)(6)(iv)(A).

(c) *Newly-acquired property.* For newly-acquired property described in section 4.02(1) of this revenue procedure, as applicable, the taxpayer determines the depreciation in accordance with the alternative depreciation system for such property for its placed-in-service year and the subsequent taxable years. Because such newly-acquired property is required to be depreciated under the alternative depreciation system, the property is not qualified property for purposes of the additional first year depreciation deduction under § 168(k). See § 168(k)(2)(D).

(3) *Failure to change to alternative depreciation system.*

(a) *Existing property.* If an electing real property trade or business or an electing farming business does not depreciate any existing property that is described in section 4.02(1) of this

revenue procedure, as applicable, under the alternative depreciation system for the election year and the subsequent taxable year then that trade or business has adopted an impermissible method of accounting for that item of MACRS property. As a result, a change from that impermissible method of accounting to the straight-line method, the applicable recovery period, and/or the applicable convention under the alternative depreciation system for the item of MACRS property is a change in method of accounting under § 446(e). *See* § 1.446-1(e)(2)(ii)(*d*)(2)(*i*). The taxpayer requests to make such a method change by filing Form 3115, *Application for Change in Accounting Method*, in accordance with the automatic change procedures or non-automatic change procedures, as applicable, in Rev. Proc. 2015-13, 2015-5 I.R.B. 419 (or any successor). If the taxpayer is eligible to make this method change under the automatic change procedures, the method change is described in section 6.05 of Rev. Proc. 2018-31 (or any successor). The § 481(a) adjustment as of the first day of the year of change is calculated as though the change in use occurred for the item of MACRS property in the election year.

(b) *Newly-acquired property.* If an electing real property trade or business or an electing farming business does not determine its depreciation under the alternative depreciation system for any newly-acquired property that is described in section 4.02(1) of this revenue procedure, as applicable, for its placed-in-service year and the subsequent taxable year then that trade or business has adopted an impermissible method of accounting for that item of MACRS property. As a result, a change from that impermissible method of accounting to the straight-line method, the applicable recovery period, and/or the applicable convention under the alternative depreciation system for the item of MACRS property is a change in method of accounting under § 446(e). *See* § 1.446-1(e)(2)(ii)(d)(2)(i)). The taxpayer requests to make such a method change by filing Form 3115 in accordance with the automatic change procedures or non-automatic change procedures, as applicable, in Rev. Proc. 2015-13 (or any successor). If the taxpayer is eligible to make this method change under the automatic change procedures, the method change is described in section 6.01 of Rev. Proc. 2018-31 (or any successor), provided none of the inapplicability provisions in section 6.01(1)(c) of Rev. Proc. 2018-31 (or any successor) apply. The § 481(a) adjustment as of the first day of the year of change is calculated as though the taxpayer determined depreciation under the alternative depreciation system for the item of MACRS property beginning for its placed-in-service year.

## SECTION 5. MODIFICATION TO REV. PROC. 2018-31

Section 6.05 of Rev. Proc. 2018-31 provides the procedures for obtaining automatic consent to change the method of accounting for depreciation due to a change in the use of MACRS property. Section 6.05 of Rev. Proc. 2018-31 is modified as follows:

.01 Section 6.05(3), (4), and (5) are redesignated as section 6.05(4), (5), and (6), respectively; and

.02 New section 6.05(3) is added to read as follows:

(3) *Section 481(a) adjustment.* A taxpayer changing its method of accounting under this section 6.05 is required to calculate a § 481(a) adjustment as of the first day of the year of change as if the proposed method of accounting had always been used by the taxpayer beginning with the taxable year in which the change in the use of the MACRS property occurred by the taxpayer.

## SECTION 6. EFFECTIVE DATE

This revenue procedure is effective December 21, 2018.

## SECTION 7. EFFECT ON OTHER DOCUMENTS

Rev. Proc. 87-57 and Rev. Proc. 2018-31 are modified.

## SECTION 8. DRAFTING INFORMATION

The principal author of this revenue procedure is Charles Magee of the Office of Associate Chief Counsel (Income Tax & Accounting). For further information regarding this revenue procedure, contact Mr. Magee at (202) 317-7005 (not a toll-free call).

---

# Rev. Proc. 2019-11, January 18, 2019

## SECTION 1. PURPOSE

This revenue procedure provides methods for calculating W-2 wages, as defined in section 199A(b)(4) and § 1.199A-2 of the Income Tax Regulations, (1) for purposes of section 199A(b)(2) of the Internal Revenue Code (Code) which, for certain taxpayers, provides a limitation based on W-2 wages to the amount of the deduction for qualified business income (QBI); and (2) for purposes of section 199A(b)(7), which, for certain specified agricultural and horticultural cooperative patrons, provides a reduction to the section 199A deduction based on W-2 wages.

## SECTION 2. BACKGROUND

For taxpayers above a certain amount of taxable income, section 199A(b)(2) limits the amount of a taxpayer's section 199A deduction for each qualified trade or business to the lesser of (1) 20 percent of the taxpayer's QBI with respect to the qualified trade or business, or (2) the greater of (A) 50 percent of the W-2 wages with respect to the qualified trade or business, or (B) the sum of 25 percent of the W-2 wages with respect to the qualified trade or business plus 2.5 percent of the unadjusted basis immediately after acquisition of all qualified property. Section 199A(b)(7) provides that in the case of any qualified trade or business of a patron of a specified agricultural or horticultural cooperative, the amount determined under section 199A(b)(2) with respect to such trade or business shall be reduced by the lesser of (A) 9 percent of so much of the qualified business income with respect to such trade or business as is properly allocable to qualified payments received from such cooperative, or (B) 50 percent of so much of the W-2 wages with respect to such trade or business as are so allocable.

Section 199A(b)(4)(A) defines the term "W-2 wages" to mean, with respect to any person for any taxable year of such person, the amounts described in section 6051(a)(3) and (8) paid by such person with respect to employment of employees by such person during the calendar year ending during such taxable year. Section 199A(b)(4)(B) provides that W-2 wages does not include any amount which is not properly allocable to qualified business income for purposes of section 199A(c)(1). Section 199A(b)(4)(C) provides that W-2 wages shall not include any amount that is not properly included in a return filed with the Social Security Administration (SSA) on or before the 60th day after the due date (including extensions) for such return.

Section 1.199A-2(b)(2)(iv)(A) of the regulations provides the Internal Revenue Service with authority to issue guidance providing the methods that may be used to calculate W-2 wages.

This revenue procedure provides three methods for calculating W-2 wages, as defined in section 199A(b)(4) and § 1.199A-2, for purposes of section 199A(b) and the regulations thereunder. The first method (the unmodified Box method) allows for a simplified calculation while the second and third methods (the modified Box 1 method and the tracking wages method) provide greater accuracy.

W-2 wages calculated under this revenue procedure are not necessarily the W-2 wages that are properly allocable to QBI and eligible for use in computing the section 199A limitations. As mentioned above, only W-2 wages that are properly allocable to QBI may be taken into account in computing the section 199A(b)(2) W-2 wage limitations. Thus, after computing W-2 wages under this revenue procedure, under §1.199A-2(b)(3), the taxpayer must determine the extent to which the W-2 wages are properly allocable to QBI. Then, the properly allocable W-2 wages amount is used in determining the W-2 wages limitation under section 199A(b)(2) for that trade or business as well as any reduction for income received from cooperatives under section 199A(b)(7).

SECTION 3. RULES FOR APPLICATION

.01 *In general.* In calculating W-2 wages for a taxable year under the methods described in this revenue procedure, include only wages properly reported on Forms W-2 that meet the applicable rules of §1.199A-2(b). Specifically, §1.199A-2(b)(2)(i) provides that, except as provided in §1.199A-2(b)(2)(iv)(C)(2) (concerning short taxable years that do not include December 31) and §1.199A-2(b)(2)(iv)(D) (concerning remuneration for services performed in the Commonwealth of Puerto Rico), the Forms W-2, "Wage and Tax Statement," or any subsequent form or document used in determining the amount of W-2 wages are those that are issued for the calendar year ending during the person's taxable year for wages paid to employees (or former employees) of the person for employment by the person. Section 1.199A-2(b)(2)(i) also provides that, for purposes of §1.199A-2, employees of the person are limited to employees of the person as defined in section 3121(d)(1) and (2) (that is, officers of a corporation and employees of the person under the common law rules). Therefore, Forms W-2 provided to statutory employees described in section 3121(d)(3) (that is, Forms W-2 in which the "Statutory Employee" box in Box 13 is checked) should not be included in calculating W-2 wages under any of the methods described in this revenue procedure.

.02 *No application in determining whether amounts are wages for employment tax purposes.* The discussions of "wages" in this revenue procedure and in the regulations under section 199A are for purposes of section 199A only and have no application in determining whether amounts are wages under section 3121(a) for purposes of the Federal Insurance Contributions Act, under section 3306(b) for purposes of the Federal Unemployment Tax Act, or under section 3401(a) for purposes of the Collection of Income Tax at Source on Wages (federal income tax withholding), or any other wage-related determination. See §1.199A-2 of the regulations.

SECTION 4. DEFINITION OF W-2 WAGES AND CORRELATION WITH BOXES ON FORM W-2

.01 *Definition of W-2 wages.* Section 199A(b)(4)(A) provides that W-2 wages means, with respect to any person for any taxable year of such person, the sum of the amounts described in section 6051(a)(3) and (8) paid by such person with respect to employment of employees by such person during the calendar year ending during such taxable year. Thus, W-2 wages include: (i) the total amount of wages as defined in section 3401(a); (ii) the total amount of elective deferrals (within the meaning of section 402(g)(3)); (iii) the compensation deferred under section 457; and (iv) the amount of designated Roth contributions (as defined in section 402A).

.02 *Correlation with Form W-2.* Under the 2018 Forms W-2, the elective deferrals under section 402(g)(3) and the amounts deferred under section 457 directly correlate to coded items reported in Box 12 on Form W-2. Box 12, Code D is for elective deferrals to a section 401(k) cash or deferred arrangement plan (including a SIMPLE 401(k) arrangement); Box 12, Code E is for elective deferrals under a section 403(b) salary reduction agreement; Box 12, Code F is for elective deferrals under a section 408(k)(6) salary reduction Simplified Employee Pension (SEP); Box 12, Code G is for elective deferrals and employer contributions (including nonelective deferrals) to any governmental or nongovernmental section 457(b) deferred compensation plan; Box 12, Code S is for employee salary reduction contributions under a section 408(p) SIMPLE (simple retirement account); Box 12, Code AA is for designated Roth contributions (as defined in section 402A) under a section 401(k) plan; and Box 12, Code BB is for designated Roth contributions (as defined in section 402A) under a section 403(b) salary reduction agreement. However, designated Roth contributions are also reported in Box 1, Wages, tips, other compensation and are subject to income tax withholding.

SECTION 5. METHODS FOR CALCULATING W-2 WAGES

For any taxable year, a taxpayer must calculate W-2 wages for purposes of section 199A(b)(2) using one of the three methods described in sections 5.01, 5.02, and 5.03 of this revenue procedure. For a taxpayer with a short taxable year, see section 6 of this revenue procedure. In calculating W-2 wages for a taxable year under the methods below, the taxpayer includes only those Forms W-2 that are for the calendar year ending with or within the taxable year of the taxpayer and that meet the rules of application described in section 3 of this revenue procedure.

.01 *Unmodified box method.* Under the unmodified box method, W-2 wages are calculated by taking, without modification, the lesser of—

(A) The total entries in Box 1 of all Forms W-2 filed with SSA by the taxpayer with respect to employees of the taxpayer for employment by the taxpayer; or

(B) The total entries in Box 5 of all Forms W-2 filed with SSA by the taxpayer with respect to employees of the taxpayer for employment by the taxpayer.

.02 *Modified Box 1 method.* Under the Modified Box 1 method, the taxpayer makes modifications to the total entries in Box 1 of Forms W-2 filed with respect to employees of the taxpayer. W-2 wages under this method are calculated as follows—

(A) Total the amounts in Box 1 of all Forms W-2 filed with SSA by the taxpayer with respect to employees of the taxpayer for employment by the taxpayer;

(B) Subtract from the total in paragraph .02(A) of this section amounts included in Box 1 of Forms W-2 that are not wages for Federal income tax withholding purposes, including amounts that are treated as wages for purposes of income tax withholding under section 3402(o) (for example, supplemental unemployment compensation benefits within the meaning of Rev. Rul. 90-72); and

(C) Add to the amount obtained after paragraph .02(B) of this section the total of the amounts that are reported in Box 12 of Forms W-2 with respect to employees of the taxpayer for employment by the taxpayer and that are properly coded D, E, F, G, and S.

.03 *Tracking wages method.* Under the tracking wages method, the taxpayer actually tracks total wages subject to federal income tax withholding and makes appropriate modifications. W-2 wages under this method are calculated as follows—

(A) Total the amounts of wages subject to federal income tax withholding that are paid to employees of the taxpayer for employment by the taxpayer and that are reported on Forms W-2 filed with SSA by the taxpayer for the calendar year; plus

(B) The total of the amounts that are reported in Box 12 of Forms W-2 with respect to employees of the taxpayer for employment by the taxpayer and that are properly coded D, E, F, G, and S.

## SECTION 6. APPLICATION IN CASE OF SHORT TAXABLE YEAR

.01 *Special rule for taxpayers with a short taxable year.* In the case of a taxpayer with a short taxable year, subject to the rules of application described in section 3 of this revenue procedure, the W-2 wages of the taxpayer for the short taxable year shall include only those wages paid during the short taxable year to employees of the taxpayer, only those elective deferrals (within the meaning of section 402(g)(3)) made during the short taxable year by employees of the taxpayer, and only compensation actually deferred under section 457 during the short taxable year with respect to employees of the taxpayer. See § 1.199A-2(b)(2)(iv)(C) of the regulations.

.02 *Method required for a short taxable year and modifications required in application of method.* The W-2 wages of a taxpayer with a short taxable year shall be determined under the tracking wages method described in section 5.03 of this revenue procedure. In applying the tracking wages method in the case of a short taxable year, the taxpayer must apply the method as follows—

(A) For purposes of section 5.03(A), the total amount of wages subject to federal income tax withholding and reported on Form W-2 must include only those wages subject to federal income tax withholding that are actually or constructively paid to employees during the short taxable year and reported on Form W-2 for the calendar year ending with or within that short taxable year (or, for a short taxable year that does not contain a calendar year ending with or within such short taxable year, wages subject to federal income tax withholding that are actually or constructively paid to employees during the short taxable year and reported on Form W-2 for the calendar year containing such short taxable year); and

(B) For purposes of section 5.03(B), only the portion of the total amounts reported in Box 12, Codes D, E, F, G, and S on Forms W-2, that are actually deferred or contributed during the short taxable year are included in W-2 wages.

## SECTION 7. EFFECTIVE DATE

This revenue procedure applies to taxable years ending after December 31, 2017.

**Rev. Proc. 2019-11**

## SECTION 8. DRAFTING INFORMATION

The principal authors of this revenue procedure are Andrew Holubeck and Mikhail Zhidkov of the Office of Associate Chief Counsel (Employee Benefits, Exempt Organizations, and Employment Taxes) and Margaret Burow and Frank J. Fisher of the Office of Associate Chief Counsel (Passthroughs & Special Industries).

However, other personnel from the Treasury Department and the IRS participated in its development. For further information regarding this revenue procedure contact Andrew Holubeck or Mikhail Zhidkov at (202) 317-4774, or Margaret Burow or Frank J. Fisher at (202) 317-6850 (not toll free calls).

---

# Rev. Proc. 2019-12, December 28, 2018

## SECTION 1. PURPOSE

This revenue procedure provides safe harbors under section 162 of the Internal Revenue Code (Code) for certain payments made by a C corporation or a specified pass-through entity to or for the use of an organization described in section 170(c) if the C corporation or specified pass-through entity receives or expects to receive a state or local tax credit in return for such payment.

## SECTION 2. BACKGROUND

Section 162(a) allows a deduction for all the ordinary and necessary expenses paid or incurred during the taxable year in carrying on any trade or business. Section 162(b) provides that no deduction shall be allowed under subsection (a) for any contribution or gift that would be allowed as a deduction under section 170 were it not for the percentage limitations, the dollar limitations, or the requirements as to the time of payments set forth in that section.

Section 170(a)(1) generally allows an itemized deduction for any "charitable contribution" paid within the taxable year. Section 170(c) defines "charitable contribution" as a "contribution or gift to or for the use of" any organization described in that section. Under section 170(c)(1), such an organization includes a State, a possession of the United States, or any political subdivision of the foregoing, including the District of Columbia. Section 170(c)(2) includes certain corporations, trusts, or community chests, funds, or foundations, organized and operated exclusively for religious, charitable, scientific, literary, or educational purposes, or to foster national or international amateur sports competition, or for the prevention of cruelty to children or animals.

Section 1.170A-1(c)(5) provides that transfers of property to an organization described in section 170(c) that bear a direct relationship to the taxpayer's trade or business and that are made with a reasonable expectation of financial return commensurate with the amount of the transfer may constitute allowable deductions as trade or business expenses rather than as charitable contributions.

Section 164(a) allows a deduction for the payment of certain taxes, including: (1) state and local, and foreign, real property taxes; (2) state and local personal property taxes; and (3) state and local, and foreign, income, war profits, and excess profits taxes. In addition, section 164 permits a deduction for taxes not described in the preceding sentence that are paid or accrued within the taxable year in carrying on a trade or business or an activity described in section 212. Moreover, section 164(a)(5) provides taxpayers an annual election to allow a deduction under section 164(a) for the payment of state and local general sales taxes in lieu of state and local income taxes.

Section 164(b)(6), as added by section 11042(a) of "An Act to provide for reconciliation pursuant to titles II and V of the concurrent resolution on the budget for fiscal year 2018", Pub. L. 115-97, provides that deductions for foreign real property taxes are not allowable under section 164(a)(1) and limits an individual's deduction to $10,000 ($5,000 in the case of a married individual filing a separate return) for the aggregate amount of the following state and local taxes paid during the calendar year: (1) real property taxes; (2) personal property taxes; (3) income, war profits, and excess profits taxes, and (4) general sales taxes. This limitation applies to taxable years beginning after December 31, 2017, and does not apply to foreign taxes described in section 164(a)(3) or to any taxes described in section 164(a)(1) and (2) that are paid and incurred in carrying on a trade or business or an activity described in section 212.

Since the enactment of section 164(b)(6), some taxpayers have looked for ways to avoid the new limitation on the deductibility of their state and local taxes. In response to these efforts, the Department of the Treasury (Treasury Department) and the Internal Revenue Service (IRS) have issued guidance on whether certain approaches correctly apply the Code and Treasury regulations. On June 11, 2018, the Treasury Department and the IRS issued Notice 2018-54, 2018-24 I.R.B. 750, announcing the intention to propose regulations addressing the federal income tax treatment of transfers to certain transferees pursuant to state and local tax credit programs. On August 27, 2018, proposed regulations under sections 170 and 642(c) were published in the Federal Register (83 FR 43563). The proposed regulations generally state that if a taxpayer makes a payment or transfers property to or for the use of an entity listed in section 170(c), and the taxpayer receives or expects to receive a state or local tax credit in return for such payment, the tax credit constitutes a return benefit, or *quid pro quo*, to the taxpayer and reduces the taxpayer's charitable contribution deduction under section 170(a).

After the publication of the proposed regulations, the Treasury Department and the IRS received questions from taxpayers and other stakeholders regarding the application of the proposed regulations to business entities that make payments to charitable organizations described in section 170(c) pursuant to state and local tax credit programs. These questions related to the application of section 162 to these payments, that is, whether a business entity may deduct these payments under section 162 as ordinary and necessary business expenses incurred in carrying on a trade or business.

On September 5, 2018, the IRS released an FAQ addressing these concerns. The FAQ states that the proposed regulations do not affect the availability of an ordinary and necessary business expense deduction under section 162. Specifically, the FAQ states that a business taxpayer making a payment to a charitable or government entity described in section 170(c) is generally permitted to deduct the payment as an ordinary and necessary business expense under section 162 if the payment is made with a business purpose. The FAQ also notes that the rules permitting an ordinary and necessary business expense deduction under section 162 apply to a taxpayer engaged in carrying on a trade or business regardless of the form of the business.

Since the release of the FAQ, the Treasury Department and the IRS have continued to receive questions regarding the application of the proposed regulations and sections 162 and 164 to taxpayers engaged in trades or businesses. These questions include whether payments by these taxpayers to organizations described in section 170 in return for state income, property, and other business tax credits would bear a direct relationship to the taxpayer's trade or business, such that these payments would be considered ordinary and necessary business expenses of car-

rying on such trade or business under section 162(a) to the extent of the credit received or expected.

To the extent a C corporation receives or expects to receive a state or local tax credit in return for a payment to an organization described in section 170(c), it is reasonable to conclude that there is a direct benefit to the C corporation's business in the form of a reduction in the state or local taxes the C corporation would otherwise have to pay and, therefore, to the extent of the amount of the credit received or expected to be received, there is a reasonable expectation of financial return to the C corporation commensurate with the amount of the transfer.

Similarly, in the case of a business entity other than a C corporation that is regarded as separate from its owner for all federal tax purposes under section 301.7701-3 of the Procedure and Administration Regulations (pass-through entity) and that is operating a trade or business within the meaning of section 162, to the extent the credit received in return for such a payment can reduce the pass-through entity's tax liability, it is reasonable to conclude that there is a direct benefit to the pass-through entity in the form of a reduction in the state or local taxes the entity would otherwise have to pay. However, under the principles of sections 702 and 1366, the deductibility of the payment must be determined at the level of the individual owners of the entity if the credit received or expected to be received will reduce a state or local income tax subject to the limitations in section 164(b)(6).

Accordingly, section 3 of this revenue procedure provides a safe harbor for C corporations, and section 4 of this revenue procedure provides a separate safe harbor for specified pass-through entities described in section 4.02 this revenue procedure.

## SECTION 3. SAFE HARBOR FOR C CORPORATIONS

.01 *Scope*. The safe harbor provided by this section 3 applies to a C corporation that makes payments described in section 3.02 of this revenue procedure in carrying on its trade or business.

.02 *Safe harbor*. If a C corporation makes a payment to or for the use of an organization described in section 170(c) and receives or expects to receive a tax credit that reduces a state or local tax imposed on the C corporation in return for such payment, the C corporation may treat such payment as meeting the requirements of an ordinary and necessary business expense for purposes of section 162(a) to the extent of the credit received or expected to be received.

*.03 Examples.*

(1) *Example 1.* A, a C corporation engaged in a trade or business, makes a payment of $1,000 to an organization described in section 170(c). In return for the payment, A receives or expects to receive a dollar-for-dollar state tax credit to be applied to A's state corporate income tax liability. Under section 3 of this revenue procedure, A may treat the $1,000 payment as meeting the requirements of an ordinary and necessary business expense under section 162.

(2) *Example 2.* B, a C corporation engaged in a trade or business, makes a payment of $1,000 to an organization described in section 170(c). In return for the payment, B receives or expects to receive a tax credit equal to 80 percent of the amount of this payment ($800) to be applied to B's local real property tax liability. Under section 3 of this revenue procedure, B may treat $800 as meeting the requirements of an ordinary and necessary business expense under section 162. The treatment of the remaining $200 will depend upon the facts and circumstances and is not affected by this revenue procedure.

## SECTION 4. SAFE HARBOR FOR SPECIFIED PASS-THROUGH ENTITIES

*.01 Scope.* The safe harbor provided by this section 4 applies to a specified pass-through entity described in section 4.02 of this revenue procedure that makes payments described in section 4.03 of this revenue procedure in carrying on its trade or business.

*.02 Specified pass-through entity.* An entity will be considered a *specified pass-through entity* described in this section 4.02 only if each of the requirements set forth in section 4.02(1) through (4) is satisfied.

(1) The entity is a business entity other than a C corporation that is regarded for all federal income tax purposes as separate from its owners under section 301.7701-3;

(2) The entity operates a trade or business within the meaning of section 162;

(3) The entity is subject to a state or local tax incurred in carrying on its trade or business that is imposed directly on the entity; and

(4) In return for a payment to an organization described in section 170(c), the entity receives or expects to receive a state or local tax credit that the entity applies or expects to apply to offset a

state or local tax described in section 4.02(3) of this revenue procedure other than a state or local income tax.

*.03 Safe harbor.* If a specified pass-through entity described in section 4.02 of this revenue procedure makes a payment to or for the use of an organization described in section 170(c) and receives or expects to receive a tax credit described in section 4.02(4) of this revenue procedure that the entity applies or expects to apply to offset a state or local tax described in section 4.02(3) of this revenue procedure other than a state or local income tax, the specified pass-through entity may treat such payment as meeting the requirements of an ordinary and necessary business expense for purposes of section 162(a) to the extent of the credit received or expected to be received.

*.04 Examples.*

(1) *Example 1.* P is a limited liability company (LLC) classified as a partnership for federal income tax purposes under section 301.7701-3 and is owned by individuals A and B. P is engaged in a trade or business within the meaning of section 162 and makes a payment of $1,000 to an organization described in section 170(c). In return for the payment, P receives or expects to receive a dollar-for-dollar state tax credit to be applied to P's state excise tax liability incurred by P in carrying on its trade or business. Under applicable state law, the state's excise tax is imposed at the entity level (not the owner level). Under section 4 of this revenue procedure, P may treat the $1,000 payment as meeting the requirements of an ordinary and necessary business expense under section 162.

(2) *Example 2.* S is an S corporation engaged in a trade or business and is owned by individuals C and D. S makes a payment of $1,000 to an organization described in section 170(c). In return for the payment, S receives or expects to receive a state tax credit equal to 80 percent of the amount of this payment ($800) to be applied to S's local real property tax liability incurred by S in carrying on its trade or business. Under applicable state and local law, the real property tax is imposed at the entity level (not the owner level). Under section 4 of this revenue procedure, S may treat $800 of the payment as meeting the requirements of an ordinary and necessary business expense under section 162. The treatment of the remaining $200 will depend upon the facts and circumstances and is not affected by this revenue procedure.

**Rev. Proc. 2019-12**

## SECTION 5. APPLICABILITY OF SAFE HARBORS

*.01 Applicability date.* This revenue procedure applies to amounts described in section 3.02 of this revenue procedure that are paid on or after January 1, 2018, by a C corporation described in section 3.01 of this revenue procedure. In addition, this revenue procedure applies to amounts described in section 4.03 of this revenue procedure that are paid on or after January 1, 2018, by a specified pass-through entity described in section 4.02 of this revenue procedure.

*.02 No multiple deductions.* Nothing in this revenue procedure may be construed as permitting a C corporation that applies the safe harbor in section 3.02 of this revenue procedure or a speci-

fied pass-through entity that applies the safe harbor in section 4.03 of this revenue procedure to treat the amount of any payment as deductible under more than one provision of the Code or Treasury regulations.

## SECTION 6. DRAFTING INFORMATION

The principal authors of this revenue procedure are personnel from the Office of the Associate Chief Counsel (Income Tax and Accounting). However, other personnel from the Treasury Department and the IRS participated in its development. For further information regarding this revenue procedure, contact Robin Tuczak (202) 317-4059 (not a toll-free call).

---

# Rev. Proc. 2019-13, I.R.B. 2019-9, February 13, 2019

This revenue procedure provides a safe harbor method of accounting for determining depreciation deductions for passenger automobiles that qualify for the 100-percent additional first year depreciation deduction under § 168(k) of the Internal Revenue Code, as amended by § 13201 of the Tax Cuts and Jobs Act, Public Law 115-97, 131 Stat. 2054 (December 22, 2017) (the "Act"), and that are subject to the depreciation limitations under § 280F(a), as amended by § 13202(a)(1) of the Act.

## SECTION 2. BACKGROUND

.01 Section 13201 of the Act amended § 168(k) to extend and modify the additional first year depreciation deduction for qualified property acquired and placed in service by the taxpayer after September 27, 2017, and generally placed in service by the taxpayer before January 1, 2027. Section 168(k)(1) provides that, in the case of qualified property, the depreciation deduction allowed under § 167(a) for the taxable year in which the property is placed in service includes an allowance equal to the applicable percentage of the property's adjusted basis. Pursuant to § 168(k)(6)(A), the applicable percentage is 100-percent for qualified property acquired and placed in service after September 27, 2017, and placed in service before January 1, 2023 (hereinafter, referred to as "100-percent additional first year depreciation deduction"). The applicable percentage is phased down by 20 percentage points each year for qualified property placed in service after December 31, 2022, through December 31, 2026.

.02 Section 168(k)(7) provides that a taxpayer may elect out of the additional first year deprecia-

ation deduction with respect to any class of property that is qualified property placed in service during the taxable year.

.03 Section 168(k)(10) allows a taxpayer to elect to deduct 50-percent, instead of 100-percent, additional first year depreciation for all qualified property acquired after September 27, 2017, by the taxpayer and placed in service by the taxpayer during its first taxable year that includes September 28, 2017.

.04 For owners of passenger automobiles, § 280F(a), as modified by § 13202(a) of the Act, imposes dollar limitations on the depreciation deduction for the year the taxpayer places the passenger automobile in service and for each succeeding year. For a passenger automobile that is qualified property under § 168(k) and for which the 100-percent additional first year depreciation deduction is allowable, § 168(k)(2)(F)(i) increases the first year limitation amount under § 280F(a)(1)(A)(i) by $8,000. On April 30, 2018, the Treasury Department and the Internal Revenue Service (IRS) published Rev. Proc. 2018-25, 2018-18 I.R.B. 543, which provides the dollar limitation amounts provided in § 280F(a)(1)(A)(i) that apply to passenger automobiles first placed in service by the taxpayer during calendar year 2018.

.05 Under § 280F(a)(1)(B), the unrecovered basis of any passenger automobile is treated as an expense for the first taxable year after the recovery period, subject to the limitation under § 280F(a)(1)(B)(ii). Under that section, the unrecovered basis that may be treated as an expense in any succeeding taxable year may not exceed $5,760.

.06 Section 280F(d)(1) provides that any deduction allowable under § 179 for a passenger automobile is subject to the limitations of § 280F(a) in the same manner as if it were a depreciation deduction allowable under § 168.

.07 Section 280F(d)(7) provides that the limitations of § 280F(a) will be adjusted for inflation for any passenger automobile placed in service by the taxpayer after 2018.

## SECTION 3. SCOPE AND DEFINITIONS

.01 *Scope.* This revenue procedure applies to a passenger automobile (other than a leased passenger automobile):

(1) That is acquired and placed in service by the taxpayer after September 27, 2017;

(2) That is qualified property under § 168(k) for which the 100-percent additional first year depreciation deduction is allowable;

(3) That has an unadjusted depreciable basis, as defined in section 3.02(5) of this revenue procedure, exceeding the first year limitation amount under § 280F(a)(1)(A)(i); and

(4) For which the taxpayer did not elect to treat the cost or a portion of the cost as an expense under § 179.

.02 *Definitions.* Solely for purposes of this revenue procedure, the following definitions apply:

(1) *Adjusted depreciable basis* is the unadjusted depreciable basis, as defined in section 3.02(5) of this revenue procedure, of the passenger automobile reduced by the depreciation deductions allowable under the safe harbor method of accounting provided in section 4.03 of this revenue procedure.

(2) *Applicable optional depreciation table* is based on the depreciation system, depreciation method, recovery period, and convention applicable to the passenger automobile for its placed-in-service year, as provided in section 8 of Rev. Proc. 87-57, 1987-2 C.B. 687, 693. See Appendix A in IRS Publication 946 for the applicable optional depreciation tables.

(3) *Passenger automobile* is defined in § 280F(d)(5).

(4) *Remaining adjusted depreciable basis* is the unadjusted depreciable basis, as defined in section 3.02(5) of this revenue procedure, of the passenger automobile reduced by the first year limitation amount allowable under section 4.03(2) of this revenue procedure.

(5) *Unadjusted depreciable basis* is defined in § 1.168(b)-1(a)(3) of the Income Tax Regulations, except that there is no reduction by reason of an election to expense any portion of the basis under § 179.

(6) *Unrecovered basis* is defined in § 280F(d)(8).

## SECTION 4. SAFE HARBOR FOR SECTION 280F(a) LIMITATIONS ON PASSENGER AUTOMOBILES

.01 *In general.* If the unadjusted depreciable basis of a passenger automobile for which the 100-percent additional first year depreciation deduction is allowable exceeds the first year limitation amount under § 280F(a)(1)(A)(i), the excess amount is the unrecovered basis of the passenger automobile for purposes of § 280F(a)(1)(B)(i) and, therefore, is treated as a deductible expense in the first taxable year succeeding the end of the recovery period subject to the limitation under § 280F(a)(1)(B)(ii). For example, if a calendar-year taxpayer places in service in December 2018 a passenger automobile that costs $50,000 and is qualified property for which the 100-percent additional first year depreciation deduction is allowable, the 100-percent additional first year depreciation deduction and any § 179 deduction for this property is limited to $18,000 under § 280F(a)(1)(A)(i) (see Table 2 of Rev. Proc. 2018-25) and the excess amount of $32,000 is recovered by the taxpayer beginning in 2024, subject to the annual limitation of $5,760 under § 280F(a)(1)(B)(ii).

.02 *Safe harbor method of accounting.* To mitigate the anomalous result that occurs in the taxable years subsequent to the placed-in-service year and before the first taxable year succeeding the end of the recovery period for a passenger automobile within the scope of this revenue procedure, the Treasury Department and the IRS provide a safe harbor method of accounting under section 4.03 of this revenue procedure. A taxpayer adopts this safe harbor method of accounting by applying it to deduct depreciation of its passenger automobile on its federal tax return for the first taxable year succeeding the placed-in-service year of the passenger automobile. To use the safe harbor method of accounting, the taxpayer must comply with section 4.03 of this revenue procedure. If a taxpayer's taxable year is less than 12 months, the depreciation deductions determined under section 4.03 of this revenue procedure must be adjusted for a short taxable year (for further guidance, see Rev. Proc. 89-15, 1989-1 C.B. 816).

.03 *Operation of the safe harbor.* For a taxpayer with a passenger automobile within the scope of this revenue procedure, the safe harbor method of accounting operates as follows:

(1) The taxpayer must use the applicable optional depreciation table for computing the depreciation deductions for the passenger automobile;

(2) For the placed-in-service year of the passenger automobile, the taxpayer deducts the first year limitation amount under § 280F(a)(1)(A)(i). See Table 2 of Rev. Proc. 2018-25 for the first year limitation amount under § 280F(a)(1)(A)(i) for a passenger automobile placed in service in calendar year 2018 for which the 100-percent additional first year depreciation deduction is allowable. For a passenger automobile placed in service after 2018, further guidance will be issued to provide the limitation amounts under § 280F(a)(1) for the applicable placed-in-service year;

(3) For the 12-month taxable year subsequent to the placed-in-service year and for each succeeding 12-month taxable year in the recovery period, the taxpayer determines the depreciation deduction for the passenger automobile by multiplying the remaining adjusted depreciable basis of the passenger automobile by the annual depreciation rate for each taxable year subsequent to the placed-in-service year specified in the applicable optional depreciation table, subject to the limitation amounts under § 280F(a)(1)(A);

(4) The adjusted depreciable basis of the passenger automobile as of the beginning of the first taxable year succeeding the end of the recovery period is treated as a deductible depreciation expense for the first taxable year succeeding the end of the recovery period, subject to the limitation under § 280F(a)(1)(B)(ii). Any excess is treated as a deductible depreciation expense for the succeeding taxable years, subject to the limitation under § 280F(a)(1)(B)(ii); and

(5) If § 280F(b) applies to the passenger automobile in a taxable year subsequent to the placed-in-service year, the safe harbor method of accounting ceases to apply beginning for the first year in which § 280F(b) applies. Any passenger automobile that is not predominantly used in a qualified business use, as defined in § 280F(d)(6)(B) and (C), for any taxable year is subject to § 280F(b) for such taxable year and any subsequent taxable year.

.04 *Examples.* The following examples illustrate the application of the safe harbor method of accounting.

(1) *Example 1 - Application of § 280F(a) safe harbor method of accounting.* In 2018, X, a calendar-year taxpayer, purchased and placed in service for use in its business a new passenger automobile that costs $60,000. The passenger automobile

is 5-year property under § 168(e), is qualified property under § 168(k) for which the 100-percent additional first year depreciation deduction is allowable, and is used 100 percent in X's trade or business. X does not claim a § 179 deduction for the passenger automobile and does not make an election under § 168(b), (g)(7), or (k). X depreciates the passenger automobile under the general depreciation system by using the 200-percent declining balance method, a 5-year recovery period, and the half-year convention. X adopts the safe harbor method of accounting provided in section 4.03 of this revenue procedure. As a result:

(a) X must use the applicable optional depreciation table that corresponds with the 200-percent declining balance method of depreciation, a 5-year recovery period, and the half-year convention, for determining the depreciation deductions for the passenger automobile (see Table A-1 in Appendix A of IRS Publication 946);

(b) For 2018, X deducts depreciation of $18,000 for the passenger automobile, which is the depreciation limitation for 2018 under § 280F(a)(1)(A)(i) (see Table 2 in Rev. Proc. 2018-25). As a result, the remaining adjusted depreciable basis of the passenger automobile as of January 1, 2019, is $42,000 ($60,000 unadjusted depreciable basis less $18,000 depreciation deduction claimed for 2018);

(c) For 2019 through 2023, the total depreciation allowable for the passenger automobile for each taxable year is determined by multiplying the annual depreciation rate in the applicable optional depreciation table by the remaining adjusted depreciable basis of $42,000, subject to the limitation under § 280F(a)(1)(A) for that year. Accordingly, for 2019, the total depreciation allowable for the passenger automobile is $13,440 (32 percent multiplied by the remaining adjusted depreciable basis of $42,000). Because this amount is less than the depreciation limitation of $16,000 for 2019 (see Table 2 in Rev. Proc. 2018-25), X deducts $13,440 as depreciation on its federal income tax return for the 2019 taxable year. For 2020, the total depreciation allowable for the passenger automobile is $8,064 (19.20 percent multiplied by $42,000). Because this amount is less than the depreciation limitation of $9,600 for 2020 (see Table 2 in Rev. Proc. 2018-25), X deducts $8,064 as depreciation on its federal income tax return for the 2020 taxable year. Below is a table showing the depreciation allowable for the passenger automobile under the safe harbor method of accounting for the 2018 through 2023 taxable years. X deducts these amounts.

| Taxable year | Depreciation limitations under Table 2 of Rev. Proc. 2018-25 | Depreciation deduction under the safe harbor |
|---|---|---|
| 2018 | $18,000 | $18,000 |
| 2019 | $16,000 | $13,440 ($42,000 x .32) |
| 2020 | $ 9,600 | $ 8,064 ($42,000 x .1920) |
| 2021 | $ 5,760 | $ 4,838 ($42,000 x .1152) |
| 2022 | $ 5,760 | $ 4,838 ($42,000 x .1152) |
| 2023 | $ 5,760 | $ 2,419 ($42,000 x .0576) |
| TOTAL | | $51,599 |

(d) As of January 1, 2024 (the beginning of the first taxable year succeeding the end of the recovery period), the adjusted depreciable basis of the passenger automobile is $8,401 ($60,000 unadjusted depreciable basis less the total depreciation allowable of $51,599 for 2018-2023 (see above table)). Accordingly, for the 2024 taxable year, X deducts depreciation of $5,760 for the passenger automobile (the lesser of the adjusted depreciable basis of $8,401 as of January 1, 2024, or the § 280F(a)(1)(B)(ii) limitation of $5,760).

(e) As of January 1, 2025, the adjusted depreciable basis of the passenger automobile is $2,641 ($8,401 adjusted depreciable basis as of January 1, 2024, less the depreciation claimed of $5,760 for 2024). Accordingly, for the 2025 taxable year, X deducts depreciation of $2,641 for the passenger automobile (the lesser of the adjusted depreciable basis of $2,641 as of January 1, 2025, or the § 280F(a)(1)(B)(ii) limitation of $5,760).

(2) *Example 2 - Section 179 deduction claimed.* The facts are the same as in *Example 1*, except X elects to treat $18,000 of the cost of the passenger automobile as an expense under § 179. As a result, this passenger automobile is not within the scope of this revenue procedure pursuant to section 3.01(4) of this revenue procedure. Accordingly, the safe harbor method of accounting in section 4.03 of this revenue procedure does not apply to the passenger automobile. For 2018, the 100-percent additional first year depreciation deduction and the § 179 deduction for this passenger automobile is limited to $18,000 under § 280F(a)(1)(A)(i) (see Table 2 of Rev. Proc. 2018-25). Therefore, for 2018, X deducts $18,000 for the passenger automobile under § 179, and X deducts the excess amount of $42,000 beginning in 2024, subject to the annual limitation of $5,760 under § 280F(a)(1)(B)(ii).

(3) *Example 3 - Section 168(k)(7) election made.* The facts are the same as in *Example 1*, except X makes an election under § 168(k)(7) to not claim the 100-percent additional first year depreciation deduction for 5-year property placed in service during 2018. As a result, the 100-percent additional first year depreciation deduction is not allowable for the passenger automobile. Accordingly, the passenger automobile is not within the scope of this revenue procedure pursuant to section 3.01(2) of this revenue procedure, and the safe harbor method of accounting in section 4.03 of this revenue procedure does not apply to the passenger automobile. For 2018 and subsequent taxable years, X determines the depreciation deductions for the passenger automobile in accordance with the general depreciation system of § 168(a), subject to the § 280F(a) limitations.

SECTION 5. EFFECT ON OTHER DOCUMENTS

Rev. Proc. 2018-25 is amplified as provided in section 4.03 of this revenue procedure.

SECTION 6. EFFECTIVE DATE

This revenue procedure is effective on February 13, 2019.

SECTION 7. DRAFTING INFORMATION

The principal author of this revenue procedure is Jaime C. Park of the Office of Associate Chief Counsel (Income Tax & Accounting). For further information regarding this revenue procedure contact Ms. Park on (202) 317-7005 (not a toll free call).

**Rev. Proc. 2019-13**

# Rev. Rul. 2018-29, I.R.B. 2018-45, October 19, 2018

ISSUES

(1) If a qualified opportunity fund (QOF), as defined in § 1400Z-2(d)(1) of the Internal Revenue Code (Code), purchases an existing building located on land that is wholly within a qualified opportunity zone (QOZ), as defined in § 1400Z-1, can the original use of the building or the land in the QOZ be considered to have commenced with the QOF?

(2) If a QOF purchases an existing building in a QOZ and the land upon which the building is located in a QOZ, is a substantial improvement to the building measured by additions to the adjusted basis in the building or is it measured by additions to the adjusted basis in the building and the land?

(3) If a substantial improvement to the building is measured by additions to the QOF's adjusted basis in the building, does § 1400Z-2(d) require the QOF to separately substantially improve the land?

FACTS

In September 2018, QOF A purchases for $800x Property X, which is located wholly within the boundaries of a QOZ. Property X consists of a building previously used as a factory erected prior to 2018 and land on which the factory building is located. QOF A intends to convert the factory building to residential rental property. Sixty percent ($480x) of the $800x purchase price for Property X is attributable to the value of the land and forty percent ($320x) is attributable to the value of the building. Within 24 months after the date of QOF A's acquisition of Property X, QOF A invests an additional $400x in converting the building to residential rental property.

LAW AND ANALYSIS

Pursuant to § 1400Z-1(b)(1)(A) of the Code, the Chief Executive Officer of each State nominated a limited number of population census tracts to be designated as QOZs for purposes of §§ 1400Z-1 and 1400Z-2.

Under § 1400Z-2(d)(1), the term "qualified opportunity fund" (QOF) means any investment vehicle organized as a corporation or a partnership for the purpose of investing in qualified opportunity zone property (Zone Property) (other than another QOF) that holds at least 90 percent of its assets in Zone Property.

Under § 1400Z-2(d)(2)(A), Zone Property means property that is either qualified opportunity zone stock (Zone Stock), qualified opportunity zone partnership interest (Zone Partnership Interest), or qualified opportunity zone business property (Zone Business Property).

Zone Business Property is defined in § 1400Z-2(d)(2)(D). Section 1400Z-2(d)(2)(D)(i) provides that Zone Business Property is tangible property used in a trade or business of the QOF if (a) such tangible property is purchased by the QOF after December 31, 2017, (b) the original use of such tangible property commences with the QOF or the QOF substantially improves the tangible property, and (c) during substantially all of the QOF's holding period for such tangible property, substantially all of the use of such tangible property is in a QOZ.

Under § 1400Z-2(d)(2)(D)(ii), tangible property used in a QOF's trade or business is treated as substantially improved by the QOF only if, during any 30-month period beginning after the date of acquisition of such tangible property, additions to basis with respect to such tangible property in the hands of the QOF exceed an amount equal to the adjusted basis of such tangible property at the beginning of such 30-month period in the hands of the QOF.

Questions have arisen as to whether for purposes of § 1400Z-2(d)(2)(D)(i) the original use of land in the QOZ can be considered to have commenced with a QOF and, therefore, constitute Zone Business Property. In addition, if the original use of land in the QOZ cannot commence with a QOF and if land is treated as property separate from a building for purposes of § 1400Z-2(d), must land be substantially improved in order to qualify as Zone Business Property?

Given the permanence of land, land can never have its original use in a QOZ commencing with a QOF. Section 1400Z-2 seeks to encourage economic growth and investment in the designated QOZs by providing Federal income tax benefits to taxpayers who newly invest in businesses located within these economically distressed communities. Consistent with this intent, a building located on land within a QOZ is treated as substantially improved within the meaning of § 1400Z-2(d)(2)(D)(ii) if, during any 30-month period beginning after the date of acquisition of the building, additions to the taxpayer's basis in the building exceed an amount equal to the taxpayer's adjusted basis of the building at the beginning of such 30-month period. Further, the fact that the cost of the land within the QOZ upon which the building is located is not included in the taxpayer's adjusted basis in the building does not mean that the taxpayer is required to separately substantially improve such land for it to qualify as Zone Business Property.

Under the facts of this revenue ruling, QOF A purchased Property X, a factory building and the land on which was located (both wholly within a QOZ), for $800x with the intent to convert the building into residential rental property. Sixty percent ($480x) of the purchase price for Property X was attributable to the value of the land and forty percent ($320x) was attributable to the value of the building. Section 1400Z-2(d)(2)(D)(ii) does not apply to the land on which the factory building is located, but does apply to the building. Because the factory building existed on land within the QOZ prior to QOF A's purchase of Property X, the building's original use within the QOZ did not commence with QOF A. However, under § 1400Z-2(d)(2)(D)(ii) QOF A substantially improved Property X because during the 30-month period beginning after the date of QOF A's acquisition of Property X QOF A's additions to the basis of the factory building ($400x) exceed an amount equal to QOF A's adjusted basis of the building at the beginning of the 30-month period ($320x). The fact that the cost of the land on which the building is located is not included in QOF A's adjusted basis of the building does not mean that QOF A is required to separately substantially improve the land.

## HOLDING

(1) If a QOF purchases an existing building located on land that is wholly within a QOZ, the original use of the building in the QOZ is not considered to have commenced with the QOF for purposes of § 1400Z-2(d)(2)(D)(i), and the requirement under § 1400Z-2(d)(2)(D)(i) that the original use of tangible property in the QOZ commence with a QOF is not applicable to the land on which the building is located.

(2) If a QOF purchases a building wholly within a QOZ, under § 1400Z-2(d)(2)(D)(ii) a substantial improvement to the building is measured by the QOF's additions to the adjusted basis of the building.

(3) Under § 1400Z-2(d), measuring a substantial improvement to the building by additions to the QOF's adjusted basis of the building does not require the QOF to separately substantially improve the land upon which the building is located.

## DRAFTING INFORMATION

The principal author of this revenue ruling is Erika C. Reigle of the Office of Associate Chief Counsel Income Tax & Accounting. For further information regarding this revenue ruling, contact Erika C. Reigle at (202) 317-7006 (not a toll-free call).

# IRS Final Regulations

## ¶8001 Introduction

Reproduced below are all final regulations issued by the Treasury and IRS in the wake of the Tax Cuts and Jobs Act (P.L. 115-97) becoming law. The list of final regulations is relatively short, but that should not minimize the impact of the guidance. These final regulations cover the qualified business income deduction under Code Sec. 199A, the transition tax under Code Sec. 965, and the less flashy, but no less significant, tax return preparer due diligence requirements under Code Sec. 6695. Use CCH® AnswerConnect and CCH Axcess™ iQ to keep up-to-date with all of the recently issued guidance.

**[Reg. §1.199A-0]**

(3) UBIA of qualified property.

(i) In general.

(ii) UBIA of qualified property held by a partnership.

(iii) UBIA of qualified property held by an S corporation.

(iv) UBIA and section 743(b) basis adjustments.

(A) In general.

(B) Excess section 743(b) basis adjustments.

(C) Computation of partner's share of UBIA with excess section 734(b) basis adjustments.

(D) Examples.

(b) W-2 wages.

(1) In general.

(2) Definition of W-2 wages.

(i) In general.

(ii) Wages paid by a person other than a common law employer.

(iii) Requirement that wages must be reported on return filed with the Social Security Administration.

(A) In general.

(B) Corrected return filed to correct a return that was filed within 60 days of the due date.

(C) Corrected return filed to correct a return that was filed later than 60 days after the due date.

(iv) Methods for calculating W-2 Wages.

(A) In general.

(B) Acquisition or disposition of a trade or business.

(1) In general.

(2) Acquisition or disposition.

(C) Application in the case of a person with a short taxable year.

(1) In general.

(2) Short taxable year that does not include December 31.

(D) Remuneration paid for services performed in the Commonwealth of Puerto Rico.

(3) Allocation of wages to trades or businesses.

(4) Allocation of wages to QBI.

(5) Non-duplication rule.

(c) UBIA of qualified property.

(1) Qualified property.

(i) In general.

(ii) Improvements to qualified property.

(iii) Adjustments under sections 734(b) and 743(b).

(iv) Property acquired at end of year.

(2) Depreciable period.

(i) In general.

(ii) Additional first-year depreciation under section 168.

(iii) Qualified property acquired in transactions subject to section 1031 or section 1033.

(A) Replacement property received in a section 1031 or 1033 transaction.

(B) Other property received in a section 1031 or 1033 transaction.

(iv) Qualified property acquired in transactions subject to section 168(i)(7)(B).

(v) Excess section 743(b) basis adjustment.

(3) Unadjusted basis immediately after acquisition.

(i) In general.

(ii) Qualified property acquired in a like-kind exchange.

(A) In general.

(B) Excess boot.

(iii) Qualified property acquired pursuant to an involuntary conversion.

(A) In general.

(B) Excess boot.

(iv) Qualified property acquired in transactions described in section 168(i)(7)(B).

(v) Qualified property acquired from a decedent.

(vi) Property acquired in a nonrecognition transaction with principal purpose of increasing UBIA.

(4) Examples.

(d) Applicability date.

(1) General rule.

(2) Exceptions.

(i) Anti-abuse rules.

(ii) Non-calendar year RPE.

§1.199A-3 *Qualified business income, qualified REIT dividends, and qualified PTP income.*

(a) In general.

(b) Definition of qualified business income.

(1) In general.

(i) Section 751 gain.

(ii) Guaranteed payments for the use of capital.

(iii) Section 481 adjustments.

(iv) Previously disallowed losses.

(v) Net operating losses.

(vi) Other deductions.

(2) Qualified items of income, gain, deduction, and loss.

(i) In general.

(ii) Items not taken into account.

(3) Commonwealth of Puerto Rico.

(4) Wages.

(5) Allocation of items among directly-conducted trades or businesses.

(c) Qualified REIT dividends and qualified PTP income.

(1) In general.

(2) Qualified REIT dividend.

(3) Qualified PTP income.

(i) In general.

(ii) Special rules.

(d) [Reserved]

(e) Applicability date.
  (1) General rule.
  (2) Exceptions.
    (i) Anti-abuse rules.
    (ii) Non-calendar year RPE.
§1.199A-4 *Aggregation.*
  (a) Scope and purpose.
  (b) Aggregation rules.
    (1) General rule.
    (2) Operating rules.
      (i) Individuals.
      (ii) RPEs.
  (c) Reporting and consistency.
    (1) For individual.
    (2) Individual disclosure.
      (i) Required annual disclosure.
      (ii) Failure to disclose.
    (3) For RPEs.
      (i) Required annual disclosure.
      (ii) Failure to disclose.
  (d) Examples.
  (e) Applicability date.
    (1) General rule.
    (2) Exception for non-calendar year RPE.
§1.199A-5 *Specified service trades or businesses and the trade or business of performing services as an employee.*
  (a) Scope and effect.
    (1) Scope.
    (2) Effect of being an SSTB.
    (3) Trade or business of performing services as an employee.
  (b) Definition of specified service trade or business.
    (1) Listed SSTBs.
    (2) Additional rules for applying section 199A(d)(2) and paragraph (b) of this section.
      (i) In general.
        (A) No effect on other tax rules.
        (B) Hedging transactions.
      (ii) Meaning of services performed in the field of health.
      (iii) Meaning of services performed in the field of law.
      (iv) Meaning of services performed in the field of accounting.
      (v) Meaning of services performed in the field of actuarial science.
      (vi) Meaning of services performed in the field of performing arts.
      (vii) Meaning of services performed in the field of consulting.
      (viii) Meaning of services performed in the field of athletics.
      (ix) Meaning of services performed in the field of financial services.
      (x) Meaning of services performed in the field of brokerage services.
      (xi) Meaning of the provision of services in investing and investment management.
      (xii) Meaning of the provision of services in trading.
      (xiii) Meaning of the provision of services in dealing.
        (A) Dealing in securities.
        (B) Dealing in commodities.
          (*1*) Qualified active sale.
          (*2*) Active conduct of a commodities business.
          (*3*) Directly holds commodities as inventory or similar property.
          (*4*) Directly incurs substantial expenses in the ordinary course.
          (*5*) Significant activities for purposes of paragraph (b)(2)(xiii)(B)(4)(*iii*) of this section.
        (C) Dealing in partnership interests.
      (xiv) Meaning of trade or business where the principal asset of such trade or business is the reputation or skill of one or more of its employees or owners.
    (3) Examples.
  (c) Special rules.
    (1) De minimis rule.
      (i) Gross receipts of $25 million or less.
      (ii) Gross receipts of greater than $25 million.
    (2) Services or property provided to an SSTB.
      (i) In general.
      (ii) 50 percent or more common ownership.
      (iii) Examples.
  (d) Trade or business of performing services as an employee.
    (1) In general.
    (2) Employer's Federal employment tax classification of employee immaterial.
    (3) Presumption that former employees are still employees.
      (i) Presumption.
      (ii) Rebuttal of presumption.
      (iii) Examples.
  (e) Applicability date.
    (1) General rule.
    (2) Exceptions.
      (i) Anti-abuse rules.
      (ii) Non calendar year RPE.
§1.199A-6 *Relevant passthrough entities (RPEs), publicly traded partnerships (PTPs), trusts, and estates.*
  (a) Overview.
  (b) Computational and reporting rules for RPEs.
    (1) In general.
    (2) Computational rules.
    (3) Reporting rules for RPEs.
      (i) Trade or business directly engaged in.
      (ii) Other items.
      (iii) Failure to report information.

(c) Computational and reporting rules for PTPs.

(1) Computational rules.

(2) Reporting rules.

(d) Application to trusts, estates, and beneficiaries.

(1) In general.

(2) Grantor trusts.

(3) Non-grantor trusts and estates.

(i) Calculation at entity level.

(ii) Allocation among trust or estate and beneficiaries.

(iii) [Reserved]

(iv) Threshold amount.

(v) [Reserved]

(vi) Electing small business trusts.

(vii) Anti-abuse rule for creation of a trust to avoid exceeding the threshold amount.

(viii) Example.

(e) Applicability date.

(1) General rule.

(2) Exceptions.

(i) Anti-abuse rules.

(ii) Non-calendar year RPE.

[Reg. § 1.199A-0.]

☐ [T.D. 9847, 2-4-2019.]

### [Reg. § 1.199A-1]

**§ 1.199A-1. Operational rules.—**
(a) *Overview.*—(1) *In general.*—This section provides operational rules for calculating the section 199A(a) qualified business income deduction (section 199A deduction) under section 199A of the Internal Revenue Code (Code). This section refers to the rules in §§ 1.199A-2 through 1.199A-6. This paragraph (a) provides an overview of this section. Paragraph (b) of this section provides definitions that apply for purposes of section 199A and §§ 1.199A-1 through 1.199A-6. Paragraph (c) of this section provides computational rules and examples for individuals whose taxable income does not exceed the threshold amount. Paragraph (d) of this section provides computational rules and examples for individuals whose taxable income exceeds the threshold amount. Paragraph (e) of this section provides special rules for purposes of section 199A and §§ 1.199A-1 through 1.199A-6. This section and §§ 1.199A-2 through 1.199A-6 do not apply for purposes of calculating the deduction in section 199A(g) for specified agricultural and horticultural cooperatives.

(2) *Usage of term individual.*—For purposes of applying the rules of §§ 1.199A-1 through 1.199A-6, a reference to an individual includes a reference to a trust (other than a grantor trust) or an estate to the extent that the section 199A deduction is determined by the trust or estate under the rules of § 1.199A-6.

(b) *Definitions.*—For purposes of section 199A and §§ 1.199A-1 through 1.199A-6, the following definitions apply:

(1) *Aggregated trade or business* means two or more trades or businesses that have been aggregated pursuant to § 1.199A-4.

(2) *Applicable percentage* means, with respect to any taxable year, 100 percent reduced (not below zero) by the percentage equal to the ratio that the taxable income of the individual for the taxable year in excess of the threshold amount, bears to $50,000 (or $100,000 in the case of a joint return).

(3) *Net capital gain* means *net capital gain* as defined in section 1222(11) plus any *qualified dividend income* (as defined in section 1(h)(11)(B)) for the taxable year.

(4) *Phase-in range* means a range of taxable income between the threshold amount and the threshold amount plus $50,000 (or $100,000 in the case of a joint return).

(5) *Qualified business income (QBI)* means the net amount of qualified items of income, gain, deduction, and loss with respect to any trade or business (or aggregated trade or business) as determined under the rules of § 1.199A-3(b).

(6) *QBI component* means the amount determined under paragraph (d)(2) of this section.

(7) *Qualified PTP income* is defined in § 1.199A-3(c)(3).

(8) *Qualified REIT dividends* are defined in § 1.199A-3(c)(2).

(9) *Reduction amount* means, with respect to any taxable year, the excess amount multiplied by the ratio that the taxable income of the individual for the taxable year in excess of the threshold amount, bears to $50,000 (or $100,000 in the case of a joint return). For purposes of this paragraph (b)(9), the *excess amount* is the amount by which 20 percent of QBI exceeds the greater of 50 percent of W-2 wages or the sum of 25 percent of W-2 wages plus 2.5 percent of the UBIA of qualified property.

(10) *Relevant passthrough entity (RPE)* means a partnership (other than a PTP) or an S corporation that is owned, directly or indirectly, by at least one individual, estate, or trust. Other passthrough entities including common trust funds as described in § 1.6032-T and religious or apostolic organizations described in section 501(d) are also treated as RPEs if the entity files a Form 1065, *U.S. Return of Partnership Income,* and is owned, directly or indirectly, by at least one individual, estate, or trust. A trust or estate is treated as an RPE to the extent it passes through QBI, W-2 wages, UBIA of qualified property, qualified REIT dividends, or qualified PTP income.

(11) *Specified service trade or business (SSTB)* means a specified service trade or business as defined in § 1.199A-5(b).

(12) *Threshold amount* means, for any taxable year beginning before 2019, $157,500 (or $315,000 in the case of a taxpayer filing a joint return). In the case of any taxable year beginning after 2018, the threshold amount is the dollar amount in the preceding sentence increased by an amount equal to such dollar amount, multiplied by the cost-of-living adjustment determined under section 1(f)(3) of the Code for the calendar year in which the taxable year begins, determined by substituting "calendar year 2017" for "calendar year 2016" in section 1(f)(3)(A)(ii). The amount of any increase under the preceding sentence is rounded as provided in section 1(f)(7) of the Code.

(13) *Total QBI amount* means the net total QBI from all trades or businesses (including the individual's share of QBI from trades or business conducted by RPEs).

(14) *Trade or business* means a trade or business that is a trade or business under section 162 (a section 162 trade or business) other than the trade or business of performing services as an employee. In addition, rental or licensing of tangible or intangible property (rental activity) that does not rise to the level of a section 162 trade or business is nevertheless treated as a trade or business for purposes of section 199A, if the property is rented or licensed to a trade or business conducted by the individual or an RPE which is commonly controlled under §1.199A-4(b)(1)(i) (regardless of whether the rental activity and the trade or business are otherwise eligible to be aggregated under §1.199A-4(b)(1)).

(15) *Unadjusted basis immediately after acquisition of qualified property* (*UBIA of qualified property*) is defined in §1.199A-2(c).

(16) *W-2 wages* means W-2 wages of a trade or business (or aggregated trade or business) properly allocable to QBI as determined under §1.199A-2(b).

(c) *Computation of the section 199A deduction for individuals with taxable income not exceeding threshold amount.*—(1) *In general.*—The section 199A deduction is determined for individuals with taxable income for the taxable year that does not exceed the threshold amount by adding 20 percent of the total QBI amount (including the individual's share of QBI from an RPE and QBI attributable to an SSTB) and 20 percent of the combined amount of qualified REIT dividends and qualified PTP income (including the individual's share of qualified REIT dividends and qualified PTP income from RPEs and qualified PTP income attributable to an SSTB). That sum is then compared to 20 percent of the amount by which the individual's taxable income exceeds net capital gain. The lesser of these two amounts is the individual's section 199A deduction.

(2) *Carryover rules.*—(i) *Negative total QBI amount.*—If the total QBI amount is less than zero, the portion of the individual's section 199A deduction related to QBI is zero for the taxable

year. The negative total QBI amount is treated as negative QBI from a separate trade or business in the succeeding taxable years of the individual for purposes of section 199A and this section. This carryover rule does not affect the deductibility of the loss for purposes of other provisions of the Code.

(ii) *Negative combined qualified REIT dividends/qualified PTP income.*—If the combined amount of REIT dividends and qualified PTP income is less than zero, the portion of the individual's section 199A deduction related to qualified REIT dividends and qualified PTP income is zero for the taxable year. The negative combined amount must be carried forward and used to offset the combined amount of REIT dividends and qualified PTP income in the succeeding taxable years of the individual for purposes of section 199A and this section. This carryover rule does not affect the deductibility of the loss for purposes of other provisions of the Code.

(3) *Examples.*—The following examples illustrate the provisions of this paragraph (c). For purposes of these examples, unless indicated otherwise, assume that all of the trades or businesses are trades or businesses as defined in paragraph (b)(14) of this section and all of the tax items are effectively connected to a trade or business within the United States within the meaning of section 864(c). Total taxable income does not include the section 199A deduction.

(i) *Example 1.* A, an unmarried individual, owns and operates a computer repair shop as a sole proprietorship. The business generates $100,000 in net taxable income from operations in 2018. A has no capital gains or losses. After allowable deductions not relating to the business, A's total taxable income for 2018 is $81,000. The business's QBI is $100,000, the net amount of its qualified items of income, gain, deduction, and loss. A's section 199A deduction for 2018 is equal to $16,200, the lesser of 20% of A's QBI from the business ($100,000 x 20% = $20,000) and 20% of A's total taxable income for the taxable year ($81,000 x 20% = $16,200).

(ii) *Example 2.* Assume the same facts as in *Example 1* of paragraph (c)(3)(i) of this section, except that A also has $7,000 in net capital gain for 2018 and that, after allowable deductions not relating to the business, A's taxable income for 2018 is $74,000. A's taxable income minus net capital gain is $67,000 ($74,000 - $7,000). A's section 199A deduction is equal to $13,400, the lesser of 20% of A's QBI from the business ($100,000 x 20% = $20,000) and 20% of A's total taxable income minus net capital gain for the taxable year ($67,000 x 20% = $13,400).

(iii) *Example 3.* B and C are married and file a joint individual income tax return. B earns $50,000 in wages as an employee of an unrelated company in 2018. C owns 100% of the shares of X, an S corporation that provides landscaping services. X generates $100,000 in net income from operations in 2018. X pays C $150,000 in wages in 2018. B and C have no capital gains or losses. After allowable deductions not related to X, B and C's total taxable income for 2018 is $270,000. B's and C's wages are not considered to be income from a trade or business for purposes of the section 199A deduction. Because X is an S corporation, its QBI is determined at the S corporation level. X's QBI is $100,000, the net amount of its qualified items of income, gain, deduction, and loss. The wages paid by X to C are considered to be a qualified item of deduction for purposes of determining X's QBI. The section 199A deduction with respect to X's QBI is then determined by C, X's sole shareholder, and is claimed on the joint return filed by B and C. B and C's section 199A deduction is equal to $20,000, the lesser of 20% of C's QBI from the business ($100,000 x 20% = $20,000) and 20% of B and C's total taxable income for the taxable year ($270,000 x 20% = $54,000).

(iv) *Example 4.* Assume the same facts as in *Example 3* of paragraph (c)(3)(iii) of this section except that B also earns $1,000 in qualified REIT dividends and $500 in qualified PTP income in 2018, increasing taxable income to $271,500. B and C's section 199A deduction is equal to $20,300, the lesser of:

(A) 20% of C's QBI from the business ($100,000 x 20% = $20,000) plus 20% of B's combined qualified REIT dividends and qualified PTP income ($1500 x 20% = $300); and

(B) 20% of B and C's total taxable for the taxable year ($271,500 x 20% = $54,300).

(d) *Computation of the section 199A deduction for individuals with taxable income above threshold amount.*—(1) *In general.*—The section 199A deduction is determined for individuals with taxable income for the taxable year that exceeds the threshold amount by adding the QBI component described in paragraph (d)(2) of this section and the qualified REIT dividends/qualified PTP income component described in paragraph (d)(3) of this section (including the individual's share of qualified REIT dividends and qualified PTP income from RPEs). That sum is then compared to 20 percent of the amount by which the individual's taxable income exceeds net capital gain. The lesser of these two amounts is the individual's section 199A deduction.

(2) *QBI component.*—An individual with taxable income for the taxable year that exceeds the threshold amount determines the QBI component using the following computational rules, which are to be applied in the order they appear.

(i) *SSTB exclusion.*—If the individual's taxable income is within the phase-in range, then only the applicable percentage of QBI, W-2 wages, and UBIA of qualified property for each SSTB is taken into account for all purposes of determining the individual's section 199A deduction, including the application of the netting and carryover rules described in paragraph (d)(2)(iii) of this section. If the individual's taxa-

ble income exceeds the phase-in range, then none of the individual's share of QBI, W-2 wages, or UBIA of qualified property attributable to an SSTB may be taken into account for purposes of determining the individual's section 199A deduction.

(ii) *Aggregated trade or business.*—If an individual chooses to aggregate trades or businesses under the rules of §1.199A-4, the individual must combine the QBI, W-2 wages, and UBIA of qualified property of each trade or business within an aggregated trade or business prior to applying the netting and carryover rules described in paragraph (d)(2)(iii) of this section and the W-2 wage and UBIA of qualified property limitations described in paragraph (d)(2)(iv) of this section.

(iii) *Netting and carryover.*—(A) *Netting.*—If an individual's QBI from at least one trade or business (including an aggregated trade or business) is less than zero, the individual must offset the QBI attributable to each trade or business (or aggregated trade or business) that produced net positive QBI with the QBI from each trade or business (or aggregated trade or business) that produced net negative QBI in proportion to the relative amounts of net QBI in the trades or businesses (or aggregated trades or businesses) with positive QBI. The adjusted QBI is then used in paragraph (d)(2)(iv) of this section. The W-2 wages and UBIA of qualified property from the trades or businesses (including aggregated trades or businesses) that produced net negative QBI are not taken into account for purposes of this paragraph (d) and are not carried over to the subsequent year.

(B) *Carryover of negative total QBI amount.*—If an individual's QBI from all trades or businesses (including aggregated trades or businesses) combined is less than zero, the QBI component is zero for the taxable year. This negative amount is treated as negative QBI from a separate trade or business in the succeeding taxable years of the individual for purposes of section 199A and this section. This carryover rule does not affect the deductibility of the loss for purposes of other provisions of the Code. The W-2 wages and UBIA of qualified property from the trades or businesses (including aggregated trades or businesses) that produced net negative QBI are not taken into account for purposes of this paragraph (d) and are not carried over to the subsequent year.

(iv) *QBI component calculation.*—(A) *General rule.*—Except as provided in paragraph (d)(2)(iv)(B) of this section, the QBI component is the sum of the amounts determined under this paragraph (d)(2)(iv)(A) for each trade or business (or aggregated trade or business). For each trade or business (or aggregated trade or business) (including trades or businesses operated through RPEs) the individual must determine the lesser of—

(1) 20 percent of the QBI for that trade or business (or aggregated trade or business); or

(2) The greater of—

(i) 50 percent of W-2 wages with respect to that trade or business (or aggregated trade or business); or

(ii) The sum of 25 percent of W-2 wages with respect to that trade or business (or aggregated trade or business) plus 2.5 percent of the UBIA of qualified property with respect to that trade or business (or aggregated trade or business).

(B) *Taxpayers with taxable income within phase-in range.*—If the individual's taxable income is within the phase-in range and the amount determined under paragraph (d)(2)(iv)(A)(2) of this section for a trade or business (or aggregated trade or business) is less than the amount determined under paragraph (d)(2)(iv)(A)(1) of this section for that trade or business (or aggregated trade or business), the amount determined under paragraph (d)(2)(iv)(A) of this section for such trade or business (or aggregated trade or business) is modified. Instead of the amount determined under paragraph (d)(2)(iv)(A)(2) of this section, the QBI component for the trade or business (or aggregated trade or business) is the amount determined under paragraph (d)(2)(iv)(A)(1) of this section reduced by the reduction amount as defined in paragraph (b)(9) of this section. This reduction amount does not apply if the amount determined in paragraph (d)(2)(iv)(A)(2) of this section is greater than the amount determined under paragraph (d)(2)(iv)(A)(1) of this section (in which circumstance the QBI component for the trade or business (or aggregated trade or business) will be the unreduced amount determined in paragraph (d)(2)(iv)(A)(1) of this section).

(3) *Qualified REIT dividends/qualified PTP income component.*—(i) *In general.*—The qualified REIT dividend/qualified PTP income component is 20 percent of the combined amount of qualified REIT dividends and qualified PTP income received by the individual (including the individual's share of qualified REIT dividends and qualified PTP income from RPEs).

(ii) *SSTB exclusion.*—If the individual's taxable income is within the phase-in range, then only the applicable percentage of qualified PTP income generated by an SSTB is taken into account for purposes of determining the individual's section 199A deduction, including the determination of the combined amount of qualified REIT dividends and qualified PTP income described in paragraph (d)(1) of this section. If the individual's taxable income exceeds the phase-in range, then none of the individual's share of qualified PTP income generated by an

SSTB may be taken into account for purposes of determining the individual's section 199A deduction.

(iii) *Negative combined qualified REIT dividends/qualified PTP income.*—If the combined amount of REIT dividends and qualified PTP income is less than zero, the portion of the individual's section 199A deduction related to qualified REIT dividends and qualified PTP income is zero for the taxable year. The negative combined amount must be carried forward and used to offset the combined amount of REIT dividends/qualified PTP income in the succeeding taxable years of the individual for purposes of section 199A and this section. This carryover rule does not affect the deductibility of the loss for purposes of other provisions of the Code.

(4) *Examples.*—The following examples illustrate the provisions of this paragraph (d). For purposes of these examples, unless indicated otherwise, assume that all of the trades or businesses are trades or businesses as defined in paragraph (b)(14) of this section, none of the trades or businesses are SSTBs as defined in paragraph (b)(11) of this section and §1.199A-5(b); and all of the tax items associated with the trades or businesses are effectively connected to a trade or business within the United States within the meaning of section 864(c). Also assume that the taxpayers report no capital gains or losses or other tax items not specified in the examples. Total taxable income does not include the section 199A deduction.

(i) *Example 1.* D, an unmarried individual, operates a business as a sole proprietorship. The business generates $1,000,000 of QBI in 2018. Solely for purposes of this example, assume that the business paid no wages and holds no qualified property for use in the business. After allowable deductions unrelated to the business, D's total taxable income for 2018 is $980,000. Because D's taxable income exceeds the applicable threshold amount, D's section 199A deduction is subject to the W-2 wage and UBIA of qualified property limitations. D's section 199A deduction is limited to zero because the business paid no wages and held no qualified property.

(ii) *Example 2.* Assume the same facts as in *Example 1* of paragraph (d)(4)(i) of this section, except that D holds qualified property with a UBIA of $10,000,000 for use in the trade or business. D reports $4,000,000 of QBI for 2020. After allowable deductions unrelated to the business, D's total taxable income for 2020 is $3,980,000. Because D's taxable income is above the threshold amount, the QBI component of D's section 199A deduction is subject to the W-2 wage and UBIA of qualified property limitations. Because the business has no W-2 wages, the QBI component of D's section 199A deduction is limited to the lesser of 20% of the business's QBI or 2.5% of its UBIA of qualified property. Twenty percent of the $4,000,000 of QBI is $800,000. Two and one-half percent of the $10,000,000 UBIA of qualified property is $250,000. The QBI component of D's section 199A deduction is thus limited to $250,000. D's section 199A deduction is equal to the lesser of:

(A) 20% of the QBI from the business as limited ($250,000); or

(B) 20% of D's taxable income ($3,980,000 x 20% = $796,000). Therefore, D's section 199A deduction for 2020 is $250,000.

(iii) *Example 3.* E, an unmarried individual, is a 30% owner of LLC, which is classified as a partnership for Federal income tax purposes. In 2018, the LLC has a single trade or business and reports QBI of $3,000,000. The LLC pays total W-2 wages of $1,000,000, and its total UBIA of qualified property is $100,000. E is allocated 30% of all items of the partnership. For the 2018 taxable year, E reports $900,000 of QBI from the LLC. After allowable deductions unrelated to LLC, E's taxable income is $880,000. Because E's taxable income is above the threshold amount, the QBI component of E's section 199A deduction will be limited to the lesser of 20% of E's share of LLC's QBI or the greater of the W-2 wage or UBIA of qualified property limitations. Twenty percent of E's share of QBI of $900,000 is $180,000. The W-2 wage limitation equals 50% of E's share of the LLC's wages ($300,000) or $150,000. The UBIA of qualified property limitation equals $75,750, the sum of 25% of E's share of LLC's wages ($300,000) or $75,000 plus 2.5% of E's share of UBIA of qualified property ($30,000) or $750. The greater of the limitation amounts ($150,000 and $75,750) is $150,000. The QBI component of E's section 199A deduction is thus limited to $150,000, the lesser of 20% of QBI ($180,000) and the greater of the limitations amounts ($150,000). E's section 199A deduction is equal to the lesser of 20% of the QBI from the business as limited ($150,000) or 20% of E's taxable income ($880,000 x 20% = $176,000). Therefore, E's section 199A deduction is $150,000 for 2018.

(iv) *Example 4.* F, an unmarried individual, owns a 50% interest in Z, an S corporation for Federal income tax purposes that conducts a single trade or business. In 2018, Z reports QBI of $6,000,000. Z pays total W-2 wages of $2,000,000, and its total UBIA of qualified property is $200,000. For the 2018 taxable year, F reports $3,000,000 of QBI from Z. F is not an employee of Z and receives no wages or reasonable compensation from Z. After allowable deductions unrelated to Z and a deductible qualified net loss from a PTP of ($10,000), F's taxable income is $1,880,000. Because F's taxable income is above the threshold amount, the QBI component of F's section 199A deduction will be limited to the lesser of 20% of F's share of Z's QBI or the greater of the W-2 wage and UBIA of qualified property limitations. Twenty percent of F's share of Z's QBI ($3,000,000) is $600,000. The W-2 wage limitation equals 50% of F's share of Z's W-2 wages ($1,000,000) or $500,000. The UBIA of qualified property limitation equals $252,500, the

sum of 25% of F's share of Z's W-2 wages ($1,000,000) or $250,000 plus 2.5% of E's share of UBIA of qualified property ($100,000) or $2,500. The greater of the limitation amounts ($500,000 and $252,500) is $500,000. The QBI component of F's section 199A deduction is thus limited to $500,000, the lesser of 20% of QBI ($600,000) and the greater of the limitations amounts ($500,000). F reports a qualified loss from a PTP and has no qualified REIT dividend. F does not net the ($10,000) loss from the PTP against QBI. Instead, the portion of F's section 199A deduction related to qualified REIT dividends and qualified PTP income is zero for 2018. F's section is 199A deduction is equal to the lesser of 20% of the QBI from the business as limited ($500,000) or 20% of F's taxable income over net capital gain ($1,880,000 x 20% = $376,000). Therefore, F's section 199A deduction is $376,000 for 2018. F must also carry forward the ($10,000) qualified loss from a PTP to be netted against F's qualified REIT dividends and qualified PTP income in the succeeding taxable year.

(v) *Example 5*: *Phase-in range.* (A) B and C are married and file a joint individual income tax return. B is a shareholder in M, an entity taxed as an S corporation for Federal income tax purposes that conducts a single trade or business. M holds no qualified property. B's share of the M's QBI is $300,000 in 2018. B's share of the W-2 wages from M in 2018 is $40,000. C earns wage income from employment by an unrelated company. After allowable deductions unrelated to M, B and C's taxable income for 2018 is $375,000. B and C are within the phase-in range because their taxable income exceeds the applicable threshold amount, $315,000, but does not exceed the threshold amount plus $100,000, or $415,000. Consequently, the QBI component of B and C's section 199A deduction may be limited by the W-2 wage and UBIA of qualified property limitations but the limitations will be phased in.

(B) Because M does not hold qualified property, only the W-2 wage limitation must be calculated. In order to apply the W-2 wage limitation, B and C must first determine 20% of B's share of M's QBI. Twenty percent of B's share of M's QBI of $300,000 is $60,000. Next, B and C must determine 50% of B's share of M's W-2 wages. Fifty percent of B's share of M's W-2 wages of $40,000 is $20,000. Because 50% of B's share of M's W-2 wages ($20,000) is less than 20% of B's share of M's QBI ($60,000), B and C must determine the QBI component of their section 199A deduction by reducing 20% of B's share of M's QBI by the reduction amount.

(C) B and C are 60% through the phase-in range (that is, their taxable income exceeds the threshold amount by $60,000 and their phase-in range is $100,000). B and C must determine the excess amount, which is the excess of 20% of B's share of M's QBI, or $60,000, over 50% of B's share of M's W-2 wages, or $20,000. Thus, the excess amount is $40,000. The reduction amount is equal to 60% of the excess amount, or $24,000.

Thus, the QBI component of B and C's section 199A deduction is equal to $36,000, 20% of B's $300,000 share M's QBI (that is, $60,000), reduced by $24,000. B and C's section 199A deduction is equal to the lesser of 20% of the QBI from the business as limited ($36,000) or 20% of B and C's taxable income ($375,000 x 20% = $75,000). Therefore, B and C's section 199A deduction is $36,000 for 2018.

(vi) *Example 6*. (A) Assume the same facts as in *Example 5* of paragraph (d)(4)(v) of this section, except that M is engaged in an SSTB. Because B and C are within the phase-in range, B must reduce the QBI and W-2 wages allocable to B from M to the applicable percentage of those items. B and C's applicable percentage is 100% reduced by the percentage equal to the ratio that their taxable income for the taxable year ($375,000) exceeds their threshold amount ($315,000), or $60,000, bears to $100,000. Their applicable percentage is 40%. The applicable percentage of B's QBI is ($300,000 x 40% =) $120,000, and the applicable percentage of B's share of W-2 wages is ($40,000 x 40% =) $16,000. These reduced numbers must then be used to determine how B's section 199A deduction is limited.

(B) B and C must apply the W-2 wage limitation by first determining 20% of B's share of M's QBI as limited by paragraph (d)(4)(vi)(A) of this section. Twenty percent of B's share of M's QBI of $120,000 is $24,000. Next, B and C must determine 50% of B's share of M's W-2 wages. Fifty percent of B's share of M's W-2 wages of $16,000 is $8,000. Because 50% of B's share of M's W-2 wages ($8,000) is less than 20% of B's share of M's QBI ($24,000), B and C's must determine the QBI component of their section 199A deduction by reducing 20% of B's share of M's QBI by the reduction amount.

(C) B and C are 60% through the phase-in range (that is, their taxable income exceeds the threshold amount by $60,000 and their phase-in range is $100,000). B and C must determine the excess amount, which is the excess of 20% of B's share of M's QBI, as adjusted in paragraph (d)(4)(vi)(A) of this section or $24,000, over 50% of B's share of M's W-2 wages, as adjusted in paragraph (d)(4)(vi)(A) of this section, or $8,000. Thus, the excess amount is $16,000. The reduction amount is equal to 60% of the excess amount or $9,600. Thus, the QBI component of B and C's section 199A deduction is equal to $14,400, 20% of B's share M's QBI of $24,000, reduced by $9,600. B and C's section 199A deduction is equal to the lesser of 20% of the QBI from the business as limited ($14,400) or 20% of B's and C's taxable income ($375,000 x 20% = $75,000). Therefore, B and C's section 199A deduction is $14,400 for 2018.

(vii) *Example 7*. (A) F, an unmarried individual, owns as a sole proprietor 100 percent of three trades or businesses, Business X, Business Y, and Business Z. None of the businesses hold qualified property. F does not aggregate the trades or businesses under §1.199A-4. For taxable year 2018, Business X generates $1 million of QBI and pays $500,000 of W-2 wages with respect to the business. Business Y also generates $1 million of QBI but pays no wages. Business Z generates $2,000 of QBI and pays $500,000 of W-2 wages with respect to the business. F also has $750,000 of wage income from employment with an unrelated company. After allowable deductions unrelated to the businesses, F's taxable income is $2,722,000.

(B) Because F's taxable income is above the threshold amount, the QBI component of F's section 199A deduction is subject to the W-2 wage and UBIA of qualified property limitations. These limitations must be applied on a business-by-business basis. None of the businesses hold qualified property, therefore only the 50% of W-2 wage limitation must be calculated. Because QBI from each business is positive, F applies the limitation by determining the lesser of 20% of QBI and 50% of W-2 wages for each business. For Business X, the lesser of 20% of QBI ($1,000,000 x 20 percent = $200,000) and 50% of Business X's W-2 wages ($500,000 x 50% = $250,000) is $200,000. Business Y pays no W-2 wages. The lesser of 20% of Business Y's QBI ($1,000,000 x 20% = $200,000) and 50% of its W-2 wages (zero) is zero. For Business Z, the lesser of 20% of QBI ($2,000 x 20% = $400) and 50% of W-2 wages ($500,000 x 50% = $250,000) is $400.

(C) Next, F must then combine the amounts determined in paragraph (d)(4)(vii)(B) of this section and compare that sum to 20% of F's taxable income. The lesser of these two amounts equals F's section 199A deduction. The total of the combined amounts in paragraph (d)(4)(vii)(B) of this section is $200,400 ($200,000 + zero + 400). Twenty percent of F's taxable income is $544,400 ($2,722,000 x 20%). Thus, F's section 199A deduction for 2018 is $200,400.

(viii) *Example 8*. (A) Assume the same facts as in *Example 7* of paragraph (d)(4)(vii) of this section, except that F aggregates Business X, Business Y, and Business Z under the rules of §1.199A-4.

(B) Because F's taxable income is above the threshold amount, the QBI component of F's section 199A deduction is subject to the W-2 wage and UBIA of qualified property limitations. Because the businesses are aggregated, these limitations are applied on an aggregated basis. None of the businesses holds qualified property, therefore only the W-2 wage limitation must be calculated. F applies the limitation by determining the lesser of 20% of the QBI from the aggregated businesses, which is $400,400 ($2,002,000 x 20%) and 50% of W-2 wages from the aggregated businesses, which is $500,000 ($1,000,000 x 50%). F's section 199A deduction is equal to the lesser of $400,400 and 20% of F's taxable income ($2,722,000 x 20% = $544,400). Thus, F's section 199A deduction for 2018 is $400,400.

(ix) *Example 9.* (A) Assume the same facts as in *Example 7* of paragraph (d)(4)(vii) of this section, except that for taxable year 2018, Business Z generates a loss that results in ($600,000) of negative QBI and pays $500,000 of W-2 wages. After allowable deductions unrelated to the businesses, F's taxable income is $2,120,000. Because Business Z had negative QBI, F must offset the positive QBI from Business X and Business Y with the negative QBI from Business Z in proportion to the relative amounts of positive QBI from Business X and Business Y. Because Business X and Business Y produced the same amount of positive QBI, the negative QBI from Business Z is apportioned equally among Business X and Business Y. Therefore, the adjusted QBI for each of Business X and Business Y is $700,000 ($1 million plus 50% of the negative QBI of $600,000). The adjusted QBI in Business Z is $0, because its negative QBI has been fully apportioned to Business X and Business Y.

(B) Because F's taxable income is above the threshold amount, the QBI component of F's section 199A deduction is subject to the W-2 wage and UBIA of qualified property limitations. These limitations must be applied on a business-by-business basis. None of the businesses hold qualified property, therefore only the 50% of W-2 wage limitation must be calculated. For Business X, the lesser of 20% of QBI ($700,000 x 20% = $140,000) and 50% of W-2 wages ($500,000 x 50% = $250,000) is $140,000. Business Y pays no W-2 wages. The lesser of 20% of Business Y's QBI ($700,000 x 20% = $140,000) and 50% of its W-2 wages (zero) is zero.

(C) F must combine the amounts determined in paragraph (d)(4)(ix)(B) of this section and compare the sum to 20% of taxable income. F's section 199A deduction equals the lesser of these two amounts. The combined amount from paragraph (d)(4)(ix)(B) of this section is $140,000 ($140,000 + zero) and 20% of F's taxable income is $424,000 ($2,120,000 x 20%). Thus, F's section 199A deduction for 2018 is $140,000. There is no carryover of any loss into the following taxable year for purposes of section 199A.

(x) *Example 10.* (A) Assume the same facts as in *Example 9* of paragraph (d)(4)(ix) of this section, except that F aggregates Business X, Business Y, and Business Z under the rules of §1.199A-4.

(B) Because F's taxable income is above the threshold amount, the QBI component of F's section 199A deduction is subject to the W-2 wage and UBIA of qualified property limitations. Because the businesses are aggregated, these limitations are applied on an aggregated basis. None of the businesses holds qualified property, therefore only the W-2 wage limitation must be calculated. F applies the limitation by determining the lesser of 20% of the QBI from the aggregated businesses ($1,400,000 x 20% = $280,000) and 50% of W-2 wages from the aggregated businesses ($1,000,000 x 50% = $500,000), or $280,000. F's section 199A deduction is equal

to the lesser of $280,000 and 20% of F's taxable income ($2,120,000 x 20% = $424,000). Thus, F's section 199A deduction for 2018 is $280,000. There is no carryover of any loss into the following taxable year for purposes of section 199A.

(xi) *Example 11.* (A) Assume the same facts as in *Example 7* of paragraph (d)(4)(vii) of this section, except that Business Z generates a loss that results in ($2,150,000) of negative QBI and pays $500,000 of W-2 wages with respect to the business in 2018. Thus, F has a negative combined QBI of ($150,000) when the QBI from all of the businesses are added together ($1 million plus $1 million minus the loss of ($2,150,000)). Because F has a negative combined QBI for 2018, F has no section 199A deduction with respect to any trade or business for 2018. Instead, the negative combined QBI of ($150,000) carries forward and will be treated as negative QBI from a separate trade or business for purposes of computing the section 199A deduction in the next taxable year. None of the W-2 wages carry forward. However, for income tax purposes, the $150,000 loss may offset F's $750,000 of wage income (assuming the loss is otherwise allowable under the Code).

(B) In taxable year 2019, Business X generates $200,000 of net QBI and pays $100,000 of W-2 wages with respect to the business. Business Y generates $150,000 of net QBI but pays no wages. Business Z generates a loss that results in ($120,000) of negative QBI and pays $500 of W-2 wages with respect to the business. F also has $750,000 of wage income from employment with an unrelated company. After allowable deductions unrelated to the businesses, F's taxable income is $960,000. Pursuant to paragraph (d)(2)(iii)(B) of this section, the ($150,000) of negative QBI from 2018 is treated as arising in 2019 from a separate trade or business. Thus, F has overall net QBI of $80,000 when all trades or businesses are taken together ($200,000) plus $150,000 minus $120,000 minus the carryover loss of $150,000). Because Business Z had negative QBI and F also has a negative QBI carryover amount, F must offset the positive QBI from Business X and Business Y with the negative QBI from Business Z and the carryover amount in proportion to the relative amounts of positive QBI from Business X and Business Y. Because Business X produced 57.14% of the total QBI from Business X and Business Y, 57.14% of the negative QBI from Business Z and the negative QBI carryforward must be apportioned to Business X, and the remaining 42.86% allocated to Business Y. Therefore, the adjusted QBI in Business X is $45,722 ($200,000 minus 57.14% of the loss from Business Z ($68,568), minus 57.14% of the carryover loss ($85,710). The adjusted QBI in Business Y is $34,278 ($150,000, minus 42.86% of the loss from Business Z ($51,432) minus 42.86% of the carryover loss ($64,290)). The adjusted QBI in Business Z is $0, because its negative QBI has been apportioned to Business X and Business Y.

**Reg. §1.199A-1(d)(4)**

(C) Because F's taxable income is above the threshold amount, the QBI component of F's section 199A deduction is subject to the W-2 wage and UBIA of qualified property limitations. These limitations must be applied on a business-by-business basis. None of the businesses hold qualified property, therefore only the 50% of W-2 wage limitation must be calculated. For Business X, 20% of QBI is $9,144 ($45,722 x 20%) and 50% of W-2 wages is $50,000 ($100,000 x 50%), so the lesser amount is $9,144. Business Y pays no W-2 wages. Twenty percent of Business Y's QBI is $6,856 ($34,278 x 20%) and 50% of its W-2 wages (zero) is zero, so the lesser amount is zero.

(D) F must then compare the combined amounts determined in paragraph (d)(4)(xi)(C) of this section to 20% of F's taxable income. The section 199A deduction equals the lesser of these amounts. F's combined amount from paragraph (d)(4)(xi)(C) of this section is $9,144 ($9,144 plus zero) and 20% of F's taxable income is $192,000 ($960,000 x 20%) Thus, F's section 199A deduction for 2019 is $9,144. There is no carryover of any negative QBI into the following taxable year for purposes of section 199A.

(xii) *Example 12.* (A) Assume the same facts as in *Example 11* of paragraph (d)(4)(xi) of this section, except that F aggregates Business X, Business Y, and Business Z under the rules of § 1.199A-4. For 2018, F's QBI from the aggregated trade or business is ($150,000). Because F has a combined negative QBI for 2018, F has no section 199A deduction with respect to any trade or business for 2018. Instead, the negative combined QBI of ($150,000) carries forward and will be treated as negative QBI from a separate trade or business for purposes of computing the section 199A deduction in the next taxable year. However, for income tax purposes, the $150,000 loss may offset taxpayer's $750,000 of wage income (assuming the loss is otherwise allowable under the Code).

(B) In taxable year 2019, F will have QBI of $230,000 and W-2 wages of $100,500 from the aggregated trade or business. F also has $750,000 of wage income from employment with an unrelated company. After allowable deductions unrelated to the businesses, F's taxable income is $960,000. F must treat the negative QBI carryover loss ($150,000) from 2018 as a loss from a separate trade or business for purposes of section 199A. This loss will offset the positive QBI from the aggregated trade or business, resulting in an adjusted QBI of $80,000 ($230,000 - $150,000).

(C) Because F's taxable income is above the threshold amount, the QBI component of F's section 199A deduction is subject to the W-2 wage and UBIA of qualified property limitations. These limitations must be applied on a business-by-business basis. None of the businesses hold qualified property, therefore only the 50% of W-2 wage limitation must be calculated. For the aggregated trade or business, the lesser of 20% of QBI ($80,000 x 20% = $16,000)

and 50% of W-2 wages ($100,500 x 50% = $50,250) is $16,000. F's section 199A deduction equals the lesser of that amount ($16,000) and 20% of F's taxable income ($960,000 x 20% = $192,000). Thus, F's section 199A deduction for 2019 is $16,000. There is no carryover of any negative QBI into the following taxable year for purposes of section 199A.

(e) *Special rules.*—(1) *Effect of deduction.*—In the case of a partnership or S corporation, section 199A is applied at the partner or shareholder level. The rules of subchapter K and subchapter S of the Code apply in their entirety for purposes of determining each partner's or shareholder's share of QBI, W-2 wages, UBIA of qualified property, qualified REIT dividends, and qualified PTP income or loss. The section 199A deduction has no effect on the adjusted basis of a partner's interest in the partnership, the adjusted basis of a shareholder's stock in an S corporation, or an S corporation's accumulated adjustments account.

(2) *Disregarded entities.*—An entity with a single owner that is treated as disregarded as an entity separate from its owner under any provision of the Code is disregarded for purposes of section 199A and § § 1.199A-1 through 1.199A-6.

(3) *Self-employment tax and net investment income tax.*—The deduction allowed under section 199A does not reduce net earnings from self-employment under section 1402 or net investment income under section 1411.

(4) *Commonwealth of Puerto Rico.*—If all of an individual's QBI from sources within the Commonwealth of Puerto Rico is taxable under section 1 of the Code for a taxable year, then for purposes of determining the QBI of such individual for such taxable year, the term "United States" includes the Commonwealth of Puerto Rico.

(5) *Coordination with alternative minimum tax.*—For purposes of determining alternative minimum taxable income under section 55, the deduction allowed under section 199A(a) for a taxable year is equal in amount to the deduction allowed under section 199A(a) in determining taxable income for that taxable year (that is, without regard to any adjustments under sections 56 through 59).

(6) *Imposition of accuracy-related penalty on underpayments.*—For rules related to the imposition of the accuracy-related penalty on underpayments for taxpayers who claim the deduction allowed under section 199A, see section 6662(d)(1)(C).

(7) *Reduction for income received from cooperatives.*—In the case of any trade or business of a patron of a *specified agricultural or horticultural cooperative*, as defined in section 199A(g)(4), the amount of section 199A deduction determined

under paragraph (c) or (d) of this section with respect to such trade or business must be reduced by the lesser of:

(i) Nine percent of the QBI with respect to such trade or business as is properly allocable to qualified payments received from such cooperative; or

(ii) 50 percent of the W-2 wages with respect to such trade or business as are so allocable as determined under § 1.199A-2.

(f) *Applicability date.*—(1) *General rule.*—Except as provided in paragraph (f)(2) of this section, the provisions of this section apply to taxable years ending after February 8, 2019.

(2) *Exception for non-calendar year RPE.*—For purposes of determining QBI, W-2 wages, UBIA of qualified property, and the aggregate amount of qualified REIT dividends and qualified PTP income, if an individual receives any of these items from an RPE with a taxable year that begins before January 1, 2018, and ends after December 31, 2017, such items are treated as having been incurred by the individual during the individual's taxable year in which or with which such RPE taxable year ends. [Reg. § 1.199A-1.]

☐ [T.D. 9847, 2-4-2019.]

**[Reg. § 1.199A-2]**

**§ 1.199A-2. Determination of W-2 wages and unadjusted basis immediately after acquisition of qualified property.**—(a) *Scope.*—(1) *In general.*—This section provides guidance on calculating a trade or business's W-2 wages properly allocable to QBI (W-2 wages) and the trade or business's unadjusted basis immediately after acquisition of all qualified property (UBIA of qualified property). The provisions of this section apply solely for purposes of section 199A of the Internal Revenue Code (Code).

(2) *W-2 wages.*—Paragraph (b) of this section provides guidance on the determination of W-2 wages. The determination of W-2 wages must be made for each trade or business by the individual or RPE that directly conducts the trade or business (or aggregated trade or business). In the case of W-2 wages paid by an RPE, the RPE must determine and report W-2 wages for each trade or business (or aggregated trade or business) conducted by the RPE. W-2 wages are presumed to be zero if not determined and reported for each trade or business (or aggregated trade or business).

(3) *UBIA of qualified property.*—(i) *In general.*—Paragraph (c) of this section provides guidance on the determination of the UBIA of qualified property. The determination of the UBIA of qualified property must be made for each trade or business (or aggregated trade or business) by the individual or RPE that directly conducts the trade or business (or aggregated trade or business). The UBIA of qualified property is presumed to be zero if not determined

and reported for each trade or business (or aggregated trade or business).

(ii) *UBIA of qualified property held by a partnership.*—In the case of qualified property held by a partnership, each partner's share of the UBIA of qualified property is determined in accordance with how the partnership would allocate depreciation under § 1.704-1(b)(2)(iv)(g) on the last day of the taxable year.

(iii) *UBIA of qualified property held by an S corporation.*—In the case of qualified property held by an S corporation, each shareholder's share of the UBIA of qualified property is the share of the unadjusted basis proportionate to the ratio of shares in the S corporation held by the shareholder on the last day of the taxable year over the total issued and outstanding shares of the S corporation.

(iv) *UBIA and section 743(b) basis adjustments.*—(A) *In general.*—A partner will be allowed to take into account UBIA with respect to an item of qualified property in addition to the amount of UBIA with respect to such qualified property determined under paragraphs (a)(3)(i) and (c) of this section and allocated to such partner under paragraph (a)(3)(ii) of this section to the extent of the partner's excess section 743(b) basis adjustment with respect to such item of qualified property.

(B) *Excess section 743(b) basis adjustment.*—A partner's *excess section 743(b) basis adjustment* is an amount that is determined with respect to each item of qualified property and is equal to an amount that would represent the partner's section 743(b) basis adjustment with respect to the same item of qualified property, as determined under §§ 1.743-1(b) and 1.755-1, but calculated as if the adjusted basis of all of the partnership's property was equal to the UBIA of such property. The absolute value of the excess section 743(b) basis adjustment cannot exceed the absolute value of the total section 743(b) basis adjustment with respect to qualified property.

(C) *Computation of partner's share of UBIA with excess section 743(b) basis adjustments.*—The partnership first computes its UBIA with respect to qualified property under paragraphs (a)(3)(i) and (c) of this section and allocates such UBIA under paragraph (a)(3)(ii) of this section. If the sum of the excess section 743(b) basis adjustment for all of the items of qualified property is a negative number, that amount will be subtracted from the partner's UBIA of qualified property determined under paragraphs (a)(3)(i) and (c) of this section and allocated under paragraph (a)(3)(ii) of this section. A partner's UBIA of qualified property may not be below $0. Excess section 743(b) basis adjustments are computed with respect to all section 743(b) adjustments, including adjustments made as a result of a substantial built-in loss under section 743(d).

(D) *Examples.*—The provisions of this paragraph (a)(3)(iv) are illustrated by the following examples:

(1) *Example 1*—(i) *Facts.* A, B, and C are equal partners in partnership, PRS. PRS has a single trade or business that generates QBI. PRS has no liabilities and only one asset, a single item of qualified property with a UBIA equal to $900,000. Each partner's share of the UBIA is $300,000. A sells its one-third interest in PRS to T for $350,000 when a section 754 election is in effect. At the time of the sale, the tax basis of the qualified property held by PRS is $750,000. The amount of gain that would be allocated to T from a hypothetical transaction under § 1.743-1(d)(2) is $100,000. Thus, T's interest in PRS's previously taxed capital is equal to $250,000 ($350,000, the amount of cash T would receive if PRS liquidated immediately after the hypothetical transaction, decreased by $100,000, T's share of gain from the hypothetical transaction). The amount of T's section 743(b) basis adjustment to PRS's qualified property is $100,000 (the excess of $350,000, T's cost basis for its interest, over $250,000, T's share of the adjusted basis to PRS of the partnership's property).

(iii) *Analysis.* In order for T to determine its UBIA, T must calculate its excess section 743(b) basis adjustment. T's excess section 743(b) basis adjustment is equal to an amount that would represent T's section 743(b) basis adjustment with respect to the same item of qualified property, as determined under § § 1.743-1(b) and 1.755-1, but calculated as if the adjusted basis of all of PRS's property was equal to the UBIA of such property. T's section 743(b) basis adjustment calculated as if adjusted basis of the qualified property were equal to its UBIA is $50,000 (the excess of $350,000, T's cost basis for its interest, over $300,000, T's share of the adjusted basis to PRS of the partnership's property). Thus, T's excess section 743(b) basis adjustment is equal to $50,000. For purposes of applying the UBIA limitation to T's share of QBI from PRS's trade or business, T's UBIA is equal to $350,000 ($300,000, T's one-third share of the qualified property's UBIA, plus $50,000, T's excess section 743(b) basis adjustment).

(2) *Example 2*—(i) *Facts.* Assume the same facts as in *Example 1* of paragraph (a)(3)(iv)(D)(1) of this section, except that A sells its one-third interest in PRS to T for $200,000 when a section 754 election is in effect. At the time of the sale, the tax basis of the qualified property held by PRS is $750,000, and the amount of loss that would be allocated to T from a hypothetical transaction under § 1.743-1(d)(2) is $50,000. Thus, T's interest in PRS's previously taxed capital is equal to $250,000 ($200,000, the amount of cash T would receive if PRS liquidated immediately after the hypothetical transaction, increased by $50,000, T's share of loss

from the hypothetical transaction). The amount of T's section 743(b) basis adjustment to PRS's qualified property is negative $50,000 (the excess of $250,000, T's share of the adjusted basis to PRS of the partnership's property, over $200,000, T's cost basis for its interest).

(ii) *Analysis.* In order for T to determine its UBIA, T must calculate its excess section 743(b) basis adjustment. T's excess section 743(b) basis adjustment is equal to an amount that would represent T's section 743(b) basis adjustment with respect to the same item of qualified property, as determined under § § 1.743-1(b) and 1.755-1, but calculated as if the adjusted basis of all of PRS's property was equal to the UBIA of such property T's section 743(b) basis adjustment calculated as if adjusted basis of the qualified property were equal to its UBIA is negative $100,000 (the excess of $300,000, T's share of the adjusted basis to PRS of the partnership's property, over $200,000, T's cost basis for its interest). T's excess section 743(b) basis adjustment to the qualified property is limited to the amount of T's section 743(b) basis adjustment of negative $50,000. Thus, T's excess section 743(b) basis adjustment is equal to negative $50,000. For purposes of applying the UBIA limitation to T's share of QBI from PRS's trade or business, T's UBIA is equal to $250,000 ($300,000, T's one-third share of the qualified property's UBIA, reduced by T's negative $50,000 excess section 743(b) basis adjustment).

(b) *W-2 wages.*—(1) *In general.*—Section 199A(b)(2)(B) provides limitations on the section 199A deduction based on the W-2 wages paid with respect to each trade or business (or aggregated trade or business). Section 199A(b)(4)(B) provides that W-2 wages do not include any amount which is not properly allocable to QBI for purposes of section 199A(c)(1). This section provides a three step process for determining the W-2 wages paid with respect to a trade or business that are properly allocable to QBI. First, each individual or RPE must determine its total W-2 wages paid for the taxable year under the rules in paragraph (b)(2) of this section. Second, each individual or RPE must allocate its W-2 wages between or among one or more trades or businesses under the rules in paragraph (b)(3) of this section. Third, each individual or RPE must determine the amount of such wages with respect to each trade or business, which are allocable to the QBI of the trade or business (or aggregated trade or business) under the rules in paragraph (b)(4) of this section.

(2) *Definition of W-2 wages.*—(i) *In general.*—Section 199A(b)(4)(A) provides that the term W-2 wages means with respect to any person for any taxable year of such person, the amounts described in section 6051(a)(3) and (8) paid by such person with respect to employment of employees by such person during the calendar year ending during such taxable year. Thus, the term W-2 wages includes the total amount of wages

**Reg. § 1.199A-2(b)(2)(i)**

as defined in section 3401(a) plus the total amount of elective deferrals (within the meaning of section 402(g)(3)), the compensation deferred under section 457, and the amount of designated Roth contributions (as defined in section 402A). For this purpose, except as provided in paragraphs (b)(2)(iv)(C)(2) and (b)(2)(iv)(D) of this section, the Forms W-2, "Wage and Tax Statement," or any subsequent form or document used in determining the amount of W-2 wages, are those issued for the calendar year ending during the individual's or RPE's taxable year for wages paid to employees (or former employees) of the individual or RPE for employment by the individual or RPE. For purposes of this section, employees of the individual or RPE are limited to employees of the individual or RPE as defined in section 3121(d)(1) and (2). (For purposes of section 199A, this includes officers of an S corporation and employees of an individual or RPE under common law.)

(ii) *Wages paid by a person other than a common law employer.*—In determining W-2 wages, an individual or RPE may take into account any W-2 wages paid by another person and reported by the other person on Forms W-2 with the other person as the employer listed in Box c of the Forms W-2, provided that the W-2 wages were paid to common law employees or officers of the individual or RPE for employment by the individual or RPE. In such cases, the person paying the W-2 wages and reporting the W-2 wages on Forms W-2 is precluded from taking into account such wages for purposes of determining W-2 wages with respect to that person. For purposes of this paragraph (b)(2)(ii), persons that pay and report W-2 wages on behalf of or with respect to others can include, but are not limited to, certified professional employer organizations under section 7705, statutory employers under section 3401(d)(1), and agents under section 3504.

(iii) *Requirement that wages must be reported on return filed with the Social Security Administration (SSA).*—(A) *In general.*—Pursuant to section 199A(b)(4)(C), the term W-2 wages does not include any amount that is not properly included in a return filed with SSA on or before the 60th day after the due date (including extensions) for such return. Under § 31.6051-2 of this chapter, each Form W-2 and the transmittal Form W-3, "Transmittal of Wage and Tax Statements," together constitute an information return to be filed with SSA. Similarly, each Form W-2c, "Corrected Wage and Tax Statement," and the transmittal Form W-3 or W-3c, "Transmittal of Corrected Wage and Tax Statements," together constitute an information return to be filed with SSA. In determining whether any amount has been properly included in a return filed with SSA on or before the 60th day after the due date (including extensions) for such return, each Form W-2 together with its accompanying Form W-3 will be considered a separate information return and each Form W-2c together with its

accompanying Form W-3 or Form W-3c will be considered a separate information return. Section 6071(c) provides that Forms W-2 and W-3 must be filed on or before January 31 of the year following the calendar year to which such returns relate (but see the special rule in § 31.6071(a)-1T(a)(3)(1) of this chapter for monthly returns filed under § 31.6011(a)-5(a) of this chapter). Corrected Forms W-2 are required to be filed with SSA on or before January 31 of the year following the year in which the correction is made.

(B) *Corrected return filed to correct a return that was filed within 60 days of the due date.*—If a corrected information return (Return B) is filed with SSA on or before the 60th day after the due date (including extensions) of Return B to correct an information return (Return A) that was filed with SSA on or before the 60th day after the due date (including extensions) of the information return (Return A) and paragraph (b)(2)(iii)(C) of this section does not apply, then the wage information on Return B must be included in determining W-2 wages. If a corrected information return (Return D) is filed with SSA later than the 60th day after the due date (including extensions) of Return D to correct an information return (Return C) that was filed with SSA on or before the 60th day after the due date (including extensions) of the information return (Return C), and if Return D reports an increase (or increases) in wages included in determining W-2 wages from the wage amounts reported on Return C, then such increase (or increases) on Return D will be disregarded in determining W-2 wages (and only the wage amounts on Return C may be included in determining W-2 wages). If Return D reports a decrease (or decreases) in wages included in determining W-2 wages from the amounts reported on Return C, then, in determining W-2 wages, the wages reported on Return C must be reduced by the decrease (or decreases) reflected on Return D.

(C) *Corrected return filed to correct a return that was filed later than 60 days after the due date.*—If an information return (Return F) is filed to correct an information return (Return E) that was not filed with SSA on or before the 60th day after the due date (including extensions) of Return E, then Return F (and any subsequent information returns filed with respect to Return E) will not be considered filed on or before the 60th day after the due date (including extensions) of Return F (or the subsequent corrected information return). Thus, if a Form W-2c is filed to correct a Form W-2 that was not filed with SSA on or before the 60th day after the due date (including extensions) of the Form W-2 (or to correct a Form W-2c relating to Form W-2 that had not been filed with SSA on or before the 60th day after the due date (including extensions) of the Form W-2), then this Form W-2c will not be considered to have been filed with SSA on or before the 60th day after the due date (including extensions) for this Form W-2c (or corrected Form W-2), regardless of when the Form W-2c is filed.

(iv) *Methods for calculating W-2 wages.*— (A) *In general.*—The Secretary may provide for methods to be used in calculating W-2 wages, including W-2 wages for short taxable years by publication in the Internal Revenue Bulletin (see § 601.601(d)(2)(ii)(*b*) of this chapter).

(B) *Acquisition or disposition of a trade or business.*—(*1*) *In general.*—In the case of an acquisition or disposition of a trade or business, the major portion of a trade or business, or the major portion of a separate unit of a trade or business that causes more than one individual or entity to be an employer of the employees of the acquired or disposed of trade or business during the calendar year, the W-2 wages of the individual or entity for the calendar year of the acquisition or disposition are allocated between each individual or entity based on the period during which the employees of the acquired or disposed of trade or business were employed by the individual or entity, regardless of which permissible method is used for reporting predecessor and successor wages on Form W-2, "Wage and Tax Statement." For this purpose, the period of employment is determined consistently with the principles for determining whether an individual is an employee described in paragraph (b) of this section.

(*2*) *Acquisition or disposition.*—For purposes of this paragraph (b)(2)(iv)(B), the term *acquisition or disposition* includes an incorporation, a formation, a liquidation, a reorganization, or a purchase or sale of assets.

(C) *Application in the case of a person with a short taxable year.*—(*1*) *In general.*—In the case of an individual or RPE with a short taxable year, subject to the rules of paragraph (b)(2) of this section, the W-2 wages of the individual or RPE for the short taxable year include only those wages paid during the short taxable year to employees of the individuals or RPE, only those elective deferrals (within the meaning of section 402(g)(3)) made during the short taxable year by employees of the individual or RPE and only compensation actually deferred under section 457 during the short taxable year with respect to employees of the individual or RPE.

(*2*) *Short taxable year that does not include December 31.*—If an individual or RPE has a short taxable year that does not contain a calendar year ending during such short taxable year, wages paid to employees for employment by such individual or RPE during the short taxable year are treated as W-2 wages for such short taxable year for purposes of paragraph (b) of this section (if the wages would otherwise meet the requirements to be W-2 wages under this section but for the requirement that a calendar year must end during the short taxable year).

(D) *Remuneration paid for services performed in the Commonwealth of Puerto Rico.*—In the case of an individual or RPE that conducts a trade or business in the Commonwealth of Puerto Rico, the determination of W-2 wages of such individual or RPE will be made without regard to any exclusion under section 3401(a)(8) for remuneration paid for services performed in the Commonwealth of Puerto Rico. The individual or RPE must maintain sufficient documentation (for example, Forms 499R-2/W-2PR) to substantiate the amount of remuneration paid for services performed in the Commonwealth of Puerto Rico that is used in determining the W-2 wages of such individual or RPE with respect to any trade or business conducted in the Commonwealth of Puerto Rico.

(3) *Allocation of wages to trades or businesses.*—After calculating total W-2 wages for a taxable year, each individual or RPE that directly conducts more than one trade or business must allocate those wages among its various trades or businesses. W-2 wages must be allocated to the trade or business that generated those wages. In the case of W-2 wages that are allocable to more than one trade or business, the portion of the W-2 wages allocable to each trade or business is determined in the same manner as the expenses associated with those wages are allocated among the trades or businesses under § 1.199A-3(b)(5).

(4) *Allocation of wages to QBI.*—Once W-2 wages for each trade or business have been determined, each individual or RPE must identify the amount of W-2 wages properly allocable to QBI for each trade or business (or aggregated trade or business). W-2 wages are properly allocable to QBI if the associated wage expense is taken into account in computing QBI under § 1.199A-3. In the case of an RPE, the wage expense must be allocated and reported to the partners or shareholders of the RPE as required by the Code, including subchapters K and S of chapter 1 of subtitle A of the Code. The RPE must also identify and report the associated W-2 wages to its partners or shareholders.

(5) *Non-duplication rule.*—Amounts that are treated as W-2 wages for a taxable year under any method cannot be treated as W-2 wages of any other taxable year. Also, an amount cannot be treated as W-2 wages by more than one trade or business (or aggregated trade or business).

(c) *UBIA of qualified property.*—(1) *Qualified property.*—(i) *In general.*—The term *qualified property* means, with respect to any trade or business (or aggregated trade or business) of an individual or RPE for a taxable year, tangible property of a character subject to the allowance for depreciation under section 167(a)—

(A) Which is held by, and available for use in, the trade or business (or aggregated trade or business) at the close of the taxable year;

**Reg. § 1.199A-2(c)(1)(i)(A)**

(B) Which is used at any point during the taxable year in the trade or business's (or aggregated trade or business's) production of QBI; and

(C) The depreciable period for which has not ended before the close of the individual's or RPE's taxable year.

(ii) *Improvements to qualified property.*—In the case of any addition to, or improvement of, qualified property that has already been placed in service by the individual or RPE, such addition or improvement is treated as separate qualified property first placed in service on the date such addition or improvement is placed in service for purposes of paragraph (c)(2) of this section.

(iii) *Adjustments under sections 734(b) and 743(b).*—Excess section 743(b) basis adjustments as defined in paragraph (a)(3)(iv)(B) of this section are treated as qualified property. Otherwise, basis adjustments under sections 734(b) and 743(b) are not treated as qualified property.

(iv) *Property acquired at end of year.*—Property is not qualified property if the property is acquired within 60 days of the end of the taxable year and disposed of within 120 days of acquisition without having been used in a trade or business for at least 45 days prior to disposition, unless the taxpayer demonstrates that the principal purpose of the acquisition and disposition was a purpose other than increasing the section 199A deduction.

(2) *Depreciable period.*—(i) *In general.*—The term *depreciable period* means, with respect to qualified property of a trade or business, the period beginning on the date the property was first placed in service by the individual or RPE and ending on the later of—

(A) The date that is 10 years after such date; or

(B) The last day of the last full year in the applicable recovery period that would apply to the property under section 168(c), regardless of any application of section 168(g).

(ii) *Additional first-year depreciation under section 168.*—The additional first-year depreciation deduction allowable under section 168 (for example, under section 168(k) or (m)) does not affect the applicable recovery period under this paragraph for the qualified property.

(iii) *Qualified property acquired in transactions subject to section 1031 or section 1033.*—Solely for purposes of paragraph (c)(2)(i) of this section, the following rules apply to qualified property acquired in a like-kind exchange or in an involuntary conversion (replacement property).

(A) *Replacement property received in a section 1031 or 1033 transaction.*—The date on which replacement property that is of like-kind to relinquished property or is similar or related

in service or use to involuntarily converted property was first placed in service by the individual or RPE is determined as follows—

(1) For the portion of the individual's or RPE's UBIA, as defined in paragraph (c)(3) of this section, in such replacement property that does not exceed the individual's or RPE's UBIA in the relinquished property or involuntarily converted property, the date such portion in the replacement property was first placed in service by the individual or RPE is the date on which the relinquished property or involuntarily converted property was first placed in service by the individual or RPE; and

(2) For the portion of the individual's or RPE's UBIA, as defined in paragraph (c)(3) of this section, in such replacement property that exceeds the individual's or RPE's UBIA in the relinquished property or involuntarily converted property, such portion in the replacement property is treated as separate qualified property that the individual or RPE first placed in service on the date on which the replacement property was first placed in service by the individual or RPE.

(B) *Other property received in a section 1031 or 1033 transaction.*—Other property, as defined in paragraph (c)(3)(ii) or (iii) of this section, that is qualified property is treated as separate qualified property that the individual or RPE first placed in service on the date on which such other property was first placed in service by the individual or RPE.

(iv) *Qualified property acquired in transactions described in section 168(i)(7)(B).*—If an individual or RPE acquires qualified property in a transaction described in section 168(i)(7)(B) (pertaining to treatment of transferees in certain nonrecognition transactions), the individual or RPE must determine the date on which the qualified property was first placed in service solely for purposes of paragraph (c)(2)(i) of this section as follows—

(A) For the portion of the transferee's UBIA in the qualified property that does not exceed the transferor's UBIA in such property, the date such portion was first placed in service by the transferee is the date on which the transferor first placed the qualified property in service; and

(B) For the portion of the transferee's UBIA in the qualified property that exceeds the transferor's UBIA in such property, such portion is treated as separate qualified property that the transferee first placed in service on the date of the transfer.

(v) *Excess section 743(b) basis adjustment.*—Solely for purposes of paragraph (c)(2)(i) of this section, an excess section 743(b) basis adjustment with respect to an item of partnership property that is qualified property is treated as being placed in service when the transfer of the partnership interest occurs, and the recovery period for such property is determined under § 1.743-1(j)(4)(i)(B) with respect to positive basis adjustments and § 1.743-1(j)(4)(ii)(B) with respect to negative basis adjustments.

(3) *Unadjusted basis immediately after acquisition.*—(i) *In general.*—Except as provided in paragraphs (c)(3)(ii) through (v) of this section, the term *unadjusted basis immediately after acquisition* (UBIA) means the basis on the placed in service date of the property as determined under section 1012 or other applicable sections of chapter 1 of the Code, including the provisions of subchapters O (relating to gain or loss on dispositions of property), C (relating to corporate distributions and adjustments), K (relating to partners and partnerships), and P (relating to capital gains and losses). UBIA is determined without regard to any adjustments described in section 1016(a)(2) or (3), to any adjustments for tax credits claimed by the individual or RPE (for example, under section 50(c)), or to any adjustments for any portion of the basis which the individual or RPE has elected to treat as an expense (for example, under sections 179, 179B, or 179C). However, UBIA does reflect the reduction in basis for the percentage of the individual's or RPE's use of property for the taxable year other than in the trade or business.

(ii) *Qualified property acquired in a like-kind exchange.*—(A) *In general.*—Solely for purposes of this section, if property that is qualified property (replacement property) is acquired in a like-kind exchange that qualifies for deferral of gain or loss under section 1031, then the UBIA of such property is the same as the UBIA of the qualified property exchanged (relinquished property), decreased by excess boot or increased by the amount of money paid or the fair market value of property not of a like kind to the relinquished property (other property) transferred by the taxpayer to acquire the replacement property. If the taxpayer acquires more than one piece of qualified property as replacement property that is of a like kind to the relinquished property in an exchange described in section 1031, UBIA is apportioned between or among the qualified replacement properties in proportion to their relative fair market values. Other property received by the taxpayer in a section 1031 transaction that is qualified property has a UBIA equal to the fair market value of such other property.

(B) *Excess boot.*—For purposes of paragraph (c)(3)(ii)(A) of this section, *excess boot* is the amount of any money or the fair market value of other property received by the taxpayer in the exchange over the amount of appreciation in the relinquished property. Appreciation for this purpose is the excess of the fair market value of the relinquished property on the date of the exchange over the fair market value of the relinquished property on the date of the acquisition by the taxpayer.

(iii) *Qualified property acquired pursuant to an involuntary conversion.*—(A) *In general.*—Solely for purposes of this section, if qualified property is compulsorily or involuntarily converted (converted property) within the meaning of section 1033 and qualified replacement property is acquired in a transaction that qualifies for deferral of gain under section 1033, then the UBIA of the replacement property is the same as the UBIA of the converted property, decreased by excess boot or increased by the amount of money paid or the fair market value of property not similar or related in service or use to the converted property (other property) transferred by the taxpayer to acquire the replacement property. If the taxpayer acquires more than one piece of qualified replacement property that meets the similar or related in service or use requirements in section 1033, UBIA is apportioned between the qualified replacement properties in proportion to their relative fair market values. Other property acquired by the taxpayer with the proceeds of an involuntary conversion that is qualified property has a UBIA equal to the fair market value of such other property.

(B) *Excess boot.*—For purposes of paragraph (c)(3)(iii)(A) of this section, *excess boot* is the amount of any money or the fair market value of other property received by the taxpayer in the conversion over the amount of appreciation in the converted property. Appreciation for this purpose is the excess of the fair market value of the converted property on the date of the conversion over the fair market value of the converted property on the date of the acquisition by the taxpayer.

(iv) *Qualified property acquired in transactions described in section 168(i)(7)(B).*—Solely for purposes of this section, if qualified property is acquired in a transaction described in section 168(i)(7)(B) (pertaining to treatment of transferees in certain nonrecognition transactions), the transferee's UBIA in the qualified property shall be the same as the transferor's UBIA in the property, decreased by the amount of money received by the transferor in the transaction or increased by the amount of money paid by the transferee to acquire the property in the transaction.

(v) *Qualified property acquired from a decedent.*—In the case of qualified property acquired from a decedent and immediately placed in service, the UBIA of the property will generally be the fair market value at the date of the decedent's death under section 1014. See section 1014 and the regulations thereunder. Solely for purposes of paragraph (c)(2)(i) of this section, a new depreciable period for the property commences as of the date of the decedent's death.

(vi) *Property acquired in a nonrecognition transaction with principal purpose of increasing*

*UBIA.*—If qualified property is acquired in a transaction described in section 1031, 1033, or 168(i)(7) with the principal purpose of increasing the UBIA of the qualified property, the UBIA of the acquired qualified property is its basis as determined under relevant Code sections and not under the rules described in paragraphs (c)(3)(i) through (iv) of this section. For example, in a section 1031 transaction undertaken with the principal purpose of increasing the UBIA of the replacement property, the UBIA of the replacement property is its basis as determined under section 1031(d).

(4) *Examples.*—The provisions of this paragraph (c) are illustrated by the following examples:

(i) *Example 1.* (A) On January 5, 2012, A purchases Real Property X for $1 million and places it in service in A's trade or business. A's trade or business is not an SSTB. A's basis in Real Property X under section 1012 is $1 million. Real Property X is qualified property within the meaning of section 199A(b)(6). As of December 31, 2018, A's basis in Real Property X, as adjusted under section 1016(a)(2) for depreciation deductions under section 168(a), is $821,550.

(B) For purposes of section 199A(b)(2)(B)(ii) and this section, A's UBIA of Real Property X is its $1 million cost basis under section 1012, regardless of any later depreciation deductions under section 168(a) and resulting basis adjustments under section 1016(a)(2).

(ii) *Example 2.* (A) The facts are the same as in *Example 1* of paragraph (c)(4)(i) of this section, except that on January 15, 2019, A enters into a like-kind exchange under section 1031 in which A exchanges Real Property X for Real Property Y. Real Property Y has a value of $1 million. No cash or other property is involved in the exchange. As of January 15, 2019, A's basis in Real Property X, as adjusted under section 1016(a)(2) for depreciation deductions under section 168(a), is $820,482.

(B) A's UBIA in Real Property Y is $1 million as determined under paragraph (c)(3)(ii) of this section. Pursuant to paragraph (c)(2)(iii)(A) of this section, Real Property Y is first placed in service by A on January 5, 2012, which is the date on which Real Property X was first placed in service by A.

(iii) *Example 3.* (A) The facts are the same as in *Example 1* of paragraph (c)(4)(i) of this section, except that on January 15, 2019, A enters into a like-kind exchange under section 1031, in which A exchanges Real Property X for Real Property Y. Real Property X has appreciated in value to $1.3 million, and Real Property Y also has a value of $1.3 million. No cash or other property is involved in the exchange. As of January 15, 2019, A's basis in Real Property X, as adjusted under section 1016(a)(2), is $820,482.

(B) A's UBIA in Real Property Y is $1 million as determined under paragraph (c)(3)(ii) of this section. Pursuant to paragraph (c)(2)(iii)(A)

of this section, Real Property Y is first placed in service by A on January 5, 2012, which is the date on which Real Property X was first placed in service by A.

(iv) *Example 4.* (A) The facts are the same as in *Example 1* of paragraph (c)(4)(i) of this section, except that on January 15, 2019, A enters into a like-kind exchange under section 1031, in which A exchanges Real Property X for Real Property Y. Real Property X has appreciated in value to $1.3 million, but Real Property Y has a value of $1.5 million. A therefore adds $200,000 in cash to the exchange of Real Property X for Real Property Y. On January 15, 2019, A places Real Property Y in service. As of January 15, 2019, A's basis in Real Property X, as adjusted under section 1016(a)(2), is $820,482.

(B) A's UBIA in Real Property Y is $1.2 million as determined under paragraph (c)(3)(ii) of this section ($1 million in UBIA from Real Property X plus $200,000 cash paid by A to acquire Real Property Y). Because the UBIA of Real Property Y exceeds the UBIA of Real Property X, Real Property Y is treated as being two separate qualified properties for purposes of applying paragraph (c)(2)(iii)(A) of this section. One property has a UBIA of $1 million (the portion of A's UBIA of $1.2 million in Real Property Y that does not exceed A's UBIA of $1 million in Real Property X) and it is first placed in service by A on January 5, 2012, which is the date on which Real Property X was first placed in service by A. The other property has a UBIA of $200,000 (the portion of A's UBIA of $1.2 million in Real Property Y that exceeds A's UBIA of $1 million in Real Property X) and it is first placed in service by A on January 15, 2019, which is the date on which Real Property Y was first placed in service by A.

(v) *Example 5.* (A) The facts are the same as in *Example 1* of paragraph (c)(4)(i) of this section, except that on January 15, 2019, A enters into a like-kind exchange under section 1031, in which A exchanges Real Property X for Real Property Y. Real Property X has appreciated in value to $1.3 million. Real Property Y has a fair market value of $1 million. As of January 15, 2019, A's basis in Real Property X, as adjusted under section 1016(a)(2), is $820,482. Pursuant to the exchange, A receives Real Property Y and $300,000 in cash.

(B) A's UBIA in Real Property Y is $1 million as determined under paragraph (c)(3)(ii) of this section ($1 million in UBIA from Real Property X, less $0 excess boot ($300,000 cash received in the exchange over $300,000 in appreciation in Property X, which is equal to the excess of the $1.3 million fair market value of Property X on the date of the exchange over $1 million fair market value of Property X on the date of acquisition by the taxpayer)). Pursuant to paragraph (c)(2)(iii)(A) of this section, Real Property Y is first placed in service by A on January 5, 2012, which is the date on which Real Property X was first placed in service by A.

(vi) *Example 6.* (A) The facts are the same as in *Example 1* of paragraph (c)(4)(i) of this section, except that on January 15, 2019, A enters into a like-kind exchange under section 1031, in which A exchanges Real Property X for Real Property Y. Real Property X has appreciated in value to $1.3 million. Real Property Y has a fair market value of $900,000. Pursuant to the exchange, A receives Real Property Y and $400,000 in cash. As of January 15, 2019, A's basis in Real Property X, as adjusted under section 1016(a)(2), is $820,482.

(B) A's UBIA in Real Property Y is $900,000 as determined under paragraph (c)(3)(ii) of this section ($1 million in UBIA from Real Property X less $100,000 excess boot ($400,000 in cash received in the exchange over $300,000 in appreciation in Property X, which is equal to the excess of the $1.3 million fair market value of Property X on the date of the exchange over the $1 million fair market value of Property X on the date of acquisition by the taxpayer)). Pursuant to paragraph (c)(2)(iii)(A) of this section, Real Property Y is first placed in service by A on January 5, 2012, which is the date on which Real Property X was first placed in service by A.

(vii) *Example 7.* (A) The facts are the same as in *Example 1* of paragraph (c)(4)(i) of this section, except that on January 15, 2019, A enters into a like-kind exchange under section 1031, in which A exchanges Real Property X for Real Property Y. Real Property X has declined in value to $900,000, and Real Property Y also has a value of $900,000. No cash or other property is involved in the exchange. As of January 15, 2019, A's basis in Real Property X, as adjusted under section 1016(a)(2), is $820,482.

(B) Even though Real Property Y is worth only $900,000, A's UBIA in Real Property Y is $1 million as determined under paragraph (c)(3)(ii) of this section because no cash or other property was involved in the exchange. Pursuant to paragraph (c)(2)(iii)(A) of this section, Real Property Y is first placed in service by A on January 5, 2012, which is the date on which Real Property X was first placed in service by A.

(viii) *Example 8.* (A) C operates a trade or business that is not an SSTB as a sole proprietorship. On January 5, 2011, C purchases Machinery Y for $10,000 and places it in service in C's trade or business. C's basis in Machinery Y under section 1012 is $10,000. Machinery Y is qualified property within the meaning of section 199A(b)(6). Assume that Machinery Y's recovery period under section 168(c) is 10 years, and C depreciates Machinery Y under the general depreciation system by using the straight-line depreciation method, a 10-year recovery period, and the half-year convention. As of December 31, 2018, C's basis in Machinery Y, as adjusted under section 1016(a)(2) for depreciation deductions under section 168(a), is $2,500. On January 1, 2019, C incorporates the sole proprietorship and elects to treat the newly formed entity as an S corporation for Federal income tax purposes. C contributes Machinery Y and all other assets of the trade or business to the S corporation in a nonrecognition transaction under section 351. The S corporation immediately places all the assets in service.

(B) For purposes of section 199A(b)(2)(B)(ii) and this section, C's UBIA of Machinery Y from 2011 through 2018 is its $10,000 cost basis under section 1012, regardless of any later depreciation deductions under section 168(a) and resulting basis adjustments under section 1016(a)(2). The S corporation's basis of Machinery Y is $2,500, the basis of the property under section 362 at the time the S corporation places the property in service. Pursuant to paragraph (c)(3)(iv) of this section, S corporation's UBIA of Machinery Y is $10,000, which is C's UBIA of Machinery Y. Pursuant to paragraph (c)(2)(iv)(A) of this section, for purposes of determining the depreciable period of Machinery Y, the S corporation's placed in service date of Machinery Y will be January 5, 2011, which is the date C originally placed the property in service in 2011. Therefore, Machinery Y may be qualified property of the S corporation (assuming it continues to be used in the business) for 2019 and 2020 and will not be qualified property of the S corporation after 2020, because its depreciable period will have expired.

(ix) *Example 9.* (A) LLC, a partnership, operates a trade or business that is not an SSTB. On January 5, 2011, LLC purchases Machinery Z for $30,000 and places it in service in LLC's trade or business. LLC's basis in Machinery Z under section 1012 is $30,000. Machinery Z is qualified property within the meaning of section 199A(b)(6). Assume that Machinery Z's recovery period under section 168(c) is 10 years, and LLC depreciates Machinery Z under the general depreciation system by using the straight-line depreciation method, a 10-year recovery period, and the half-year convention. As of December 31, 2018, LLC's basis in Machinery Z, as adjusted under section 1016(a)(2) for depreciation deductions under section 168(a), is $7,500. On January 1, 2019, LLC distributes Machinery Z to Partner A in full liquidation of Partner A's interest in LLC. Partner A's outside basis in LLC is $35,000.

(B) For purposes of section 199A(b)(2)(B)(ii) and this section, LLC's UBIA of Machinery Z from 2011 through 2018 is its $30,000 cost basis under section 1012, regardless of any later depreciation deductions under section 168(a) and resulting basis adjustments under section 1016(a)(2). Prior to the distribution to Partner A, LLC's basis of Machinery Z is $7,500. Under section 732(b), Partner A's basis in Machinery Z is $35,000. Pursuant to paragraph (c)(3)(iv) of this section, upon distribution of Machinery Z, Partner A's UBIA of Machinery Z is $30,000, which was LLC's UBIA of Machinery Z.

(d) *Applicability date.*—(1) *General rule.*—Except as provided in paragraph (d)(2) of this section, the provisions of this section apply to taxable years ending after February 8, 2019.

**Reg. § 1.199A-2(d)(1)**

(2) *Exceptions.*—(i) *Anti-abuse rules.*—The provisions of paragraph (c)(1)(iv) of this section apply to taxable years ending after December 22, 2017.

(ii) *Non-calendar year RPE.*—For purposes of determining QBI, W-2 wages, UBIA of qualified property, and the aggregate amount of qualified REIT dividends and qualified PTP income if an individual receives any of these items from an RPE with a taxable year that begins before January 1, 2018, and ends after December 31, 2017, such items are treated as having been incurred by the individual during the individual's taxable year in which or with which such RPE taxable year ends. [Reg. § 1.199A-2.]

☐ [T.D. 9847, 2-4-2019.]

[Reg. § 1.199A-3]

§1.199A-3. Qualified business income, qualified REIT dividends, and qualified PTP income.—(a) *In general.*—This section provides rules on the determination of a trade or business's qualified business income (QBI), as well as the determination of qualified real estate investment trust (REIT) dividends and qualified publicly traded partnership (PTP) income. The provisions of this section apply solely for purposes of section 199A of the Internal Revenue Code (Code). Paragraph (b) of this section provides rules for the determination of QBI. Paragraph (c) of this section provides rules for the determination of qualified REIT dividends and qualified PTP income. QBI must be determined and reported for each trade or business by the individual or relevant passthrough entity (RPE) that directly conducts the trade or business before applying the aggregation rules of § 1.199A-4.

(b) *Definition of qualified business income.*—(1) *In general.*—For purposes of this section, the term *qualified business income* or *QBI* means, for any taxable year, the net amount of qualified items of income, gain, deduction, and loss with respect to any trade or business of the taxpayer as described in paragraph (b)(2) of this section, provided the other requirements of this section and section 199A are satisfied (including, for example, the exclusion of income not effectively connected with a United States trade or business).

(i) *Section 751 gain.*—With respect to a partnership, if section 751(a) or (b) applies, then gain or loss attributable to assets of the partnership giving rise to ordinary income under section 751(a) or (b) is considered attributable to the trades or businesses conducted by the partnership, and is taken into account for purposes of computing QBI.

(ii) *Guaranteed payments for the use of capital.*—Income attributable to a guaranteed payment for the use of capital is not considered to be attributable to a trade or business, and thus is not taken into account for purposes of computing QBI except to the extent properly allocable to a trade or business of the recipient. The partnership's deduction associated with the guaranteed payment will be taken into account for purposes of computing QBI if such deduction is properly allocable to the trade or business and is otherwise deductible for Federal income tax purposes.

(iii) *Section 481 adjustments.*—Section 481 adjustments (whether positive or negative) are taken into account for purposes of computing QBI to the extent that the requirements of this section and section 199A are otherwise satisfied, but only if the adjustment arises in taxable years ending after December 31, 2017.

(iv) *Previously disallowed losses.*—Generally, previously disallowed losses or deductions (including under sections 465, 469, 704(d), and 1366(d)) allowed in the taxable year are taken into account for purposes of computing QBI. These losses shall be used, for purposes of section 199A and these regulations, in order from the oldest to the most recent on a first-in, first-out (FIFO) basis. However, losses or deductions that were disallowed, suspended, limited, or carried over from taxable years ending before January 1, 2018 (including under sections 465, 469, 704(d), and 1366(d)), are not taken into account in a later taxable year for purposes of computing QBI.

(v) *Net operating losses.*—Generally, a net operating loss deduction under section 172 is not considered with respect to a trade or business and therefore, is not taken into account in computing QBI. However, an excess business loss under section 461(l) is treated as a net operating loss carryover to the following taxable year and is taken into account for purposes of computing QBI in the subsequent taxable year in which it is deducted.

(vi) *Other deductions.*—Generally, deductions attributable to a trade or business are taken into account for purposes of computing QBI to the extent that the requirements of section 199A and this section are otherwise satisfied. For purposes of section 199A only, deductions such as the deductible portion of the tax on self-employment income under section 164(f), the self-employed health insurance deduction under section 162(l), and the deduction for contributions to qualified retirement plans under section 404 are considered attributable to a trade or business to the extent that the individual's gross income from the trade or business is taken into account in calculating the allowable deduction, on a proportionate basis to the gross income received from the trade or business.

(2) *Qualified items of income, gain, deduction, and loss.*—(i) *In general.*—The term *qualified items of income, gain, deduction, and loss* means items of gross income, gain, deduction, and loss to the extent such items are—

(A) Effectively connected with the conduct of a trade or business within the United States (within the meaning of section 864(c), determined by substituting "trade or business (within the meaning of section 199A)" for "nonresident alien individual or a foreign corporation" or for "a foreign corporation" each place it appears); and

(B) Included or allowed in determining taxable income for the taxable year.

(ii) *Items not taken into account.*—Notwithstanding paragraph (b)(2)(i) of this section and in accordance with section 199A(c)(3)(B) and (c)(4), the following items are not taken into account as qualified items of income, gain, deduction, or loss and thus are not included in determining QBI:

(A) Any item of short-term capital gain, short-term capital loss, long-term capital gain, or long-term capital loss, including any item treated as one of such items under any other provision of the Code. This provision does not apply to the extent an item is treated as anything other than short-term capital gain, short-term capital loss, long-term capital gain, or long-term capital loss.

(B) Any dividend, income equivalent to a dividend, or payment in lieu of dividends described in section 954(c)(1)(G). Any amount described in section 1385(a)(1) is not treated as described in this clause.

(C) Any interest income other than interest income which is properly allocable to a trade or business. For purposes of section 199A and this section, interest income attributable to an investment of working capital, reserves, or similar accounts is not properly allocable to a trade or business.

(D) Any item of gain or loss described in section 954(c)(1)(C) (transactions in commodities) or section 954(c)(1)(D) (excess foreign currency gains) applied in each case by substituting "trade or business (within the meaning of section 199A)" for "controlled foreign corporation."

(E) Any item of income, gain, deduction, or loss described in section 954(c)(1)(F) (income from notional principal contracts) determined without regard to section 954(c)(1)(F)(ii) and other than items attributable to notional principal contracts entered into in transactions qualifying under section 1221(a)(7).

(F) Any amount received from an annuity which is not received in connection with the trade or business.

(G) Any qualified REIT dividends as defined in paragraph (c)(2) of this section or qualified PTP income as defined in paragraph (c)(3) of this section.

(H) Reasonable compensation received by a shareholder from an S corporation. However, the S corporation's deduction for such reasonable compensation will reduce QBI if such deduction is properly allocable to the trade or business and is otherwise deductible for Federal income tax purposes.

(I) Any guaranteed payment described in section 707(c) received by a partner for services rendered with respect to the trade or business, regardless of whether the partner is an individual or an RPE. However, the partnership's deduction for such guaranteed payment will reduce QBI if such deduction is properly allocable to the trade or business and is otherwise deductible for Federal income tax purposes.

(J) Any payment described in section 707(a) received by a partner for services rendered with respect to the trade or business, regardless of whether the partner is an individual or an RPE. However, the partnership's deduction for such payment will reduce QBI if such deduction is properly allocable to the trade or business and is otherwise deductible for Federal income tax purposes.

(3) *Commonwealth of Puerto Rico.*—For the purposes of determining QBI, the term *United States* includes the Commonwealth of Puerto Rico in the case of any taxpayer with QBI for any taxable year from sources within the Commonwealth of Puerto Rico, if all of such receipts are taxable under section 1 for such taxable year. This paragraph (b)(3) only applies as provided in section 199A(f)(1)(C).

(4) *Wages.*—Expenses for all wages paid (or incurred in the case of an accrual method taxpayer) must be taken into account in computing QBI (if the requirements of this section and section 199A are satisfied) regardless of the application of the W-2 wage limitation described in § 1.199A-1(d)(2)(iv).

(5) *Allocation of items among directly-conducted trades or businesses.*—If an individual or an RPE directly conducts multiple trades or businesses, and has items of QBI that are properly attributable to more than one trade or business, the individual or RPE must allocate those items among the several trades or businesses to which they are attributable using a reasonable method based on all the facts and circumstances. The individual or RPE may use a different reasonable method with respect to different items of income, gain, deduction, and loss. The chosen reasonable method for each item must be consistently applied from one taxable year to another and must clearly reflect the income and expenses of each trade or business. The overall combination of methods must also be reasonable based on all facts and circumstances. The books and records maintained for a trade or business must be consistent with any allocations under this paragraph (b)(5).

(c) *Qualified REIT Dividends and Qualified PTP Income.*—(1) *In general.*—Qualified REIT dividends and qualified PTP income are the sum of qualified REIT dividends as defined in paragraph (c)(2) of this section earned directly or through an RPE and the net amount of qualified PTP income as defined in paragraph (c)(3) of this section earned directly or through an RPE.

(2) *Qualified REIT dividend.*—(i) The term *qualified REIT dividend* means any dividend from a REIT received during the taxable year which—

(A) Is not a capital gain dividend, as defined in section 857(b)(3); and

(B) Is not qualified dividend income, as defined in section 1(h)(11).

(ii) The term qualified REIT dividend does not include any REIT dividend received with respect to any share of REIT stock—

(A) That is held by the shareholder for 45 days or less (taking into account the principles of section 246(c)(3) and (4)) during the 91-day period beginning on the date which is 45 days before the date on which such share becomes ex-dividend with respect to such dividend; or

(B) To the extent that the shareholder is under an obligation (whether pursuant to a short sale or otherwise) to make related payments with respect to positions in substantially similar or related property.

(3) *Qualified PTP income.*—(i) *In general.*— The term *qualified PTP income* means the sum of—

(A) The net amount of such taxpayer's allocable share of income, gain, deduction, and loss from a PTP as defined in section 7704(b) that is not taxed as a corporation under section 7704(a); plus

(B) Any gain or loss attributable to assets of the PTP giving rise to ordinary income under section 751(a) or (b) that is considered attributable to the trades or businesses conducted by the partnership.

(ii) *Special rules.*—The rules applicable to the determination of QBI described in paragraph (b) of this section also apply to the determination of a taxpayer's allocable share of income, gain, deduction, and loss from a PTP. An individual's allocable share of income from a PTP, and any section 751 gain or loss is qualified PTP income only to the extent the items meet the qualifications of section 199A and this section, including the requirement that the item is included or allowed in determining taxable income for the taxable year, and the requirement that the item be effectively connected with the conduct of a trade or business within the United States. For example, if an individual owns an interest in a PTP, and for the taxable year is allocated a distributive share of net loss which is disallowed under the passive activity rules of section 469, such loss is not taken into account for purposes of section 199A. The specified service trade or business limitations described in §§1.199A-1(d)(3) and 1.199A-5 also apply to income earned from a PTP. Furthermore, each PTP is required to determine its qualified PTP income

for each trade or business and report that information to its owners as described in §1.199A-6(b)(3).

(d) *Reserved.*

(e) *Applicability date.*—(1) *General rule.*—Except as provided in paragraph (e)(2) of this section, the provisions of this section apply to taxable years ending after February 8, 2019.

(2) *Exceptions.*—(i) *Anti-abuse rules.*—The provisions of paragraph (c)(2)(ii) of this section apply to taxable years ending after December 22, 2017.

(ii) *Non-calendar year RPE.*—For purposes of determining QBI, W-2 wages, UBIA of qualified property, and the aggregate amount of qualified REIT dividends and qualified PTP income if an individual receives any of these items from an RPE with a taxable year that begins before January 1, 2018, and ends after December 31, 2017, such items are treated as having been incurred by the individual during the individual's taxable year in which or with which such RPE taxable year ends. [Reg. §1.199A-3.]

☐ [T.D. 9847, 2-4-2019.]

### [Reg. §1.199A-4]

**§1.199A-4. Aggregation.**—(a) *Scope and purpose.*—An individual or RPE may be engaged in more than one trade or business. Except as provided in this section, each trade or business is a separate trade or business for purposes of applying the limitations described in §1.199A-1(d)(2)(iv). This section sets forth rules to allow individuals and RPEs to aggregate trades or businesses, treating the aggregate as a single trade or business for purposes of applying the limitations described in §1.199A-1(d)(2)(iv). Trades or businesses may be aggregated only to the extent provided in this section, but aggregation by taxpayers is not required.

(b) *Aggregation rules.*—(1) *General rule.*— Trades or businesses may be aggregated only if an individual or RPE can demonstrate that—

(i) The same person or group of persons, directly or by attribution under sections 267(b) or 707(b), owns 50 percent or more of each trade or business to be aggregated, meaning in the case of such trades or businesses owned by an S corporation, 50 percent or more of the issued and outstanding shares of the corporation, or, in the case of such trades or businesses owned by a partnership, 50 percent or more of the capital or profits in the partnership;

(ii) The ownership described in paragraph (b)(1)(i) of this section exists for a majority of the taxable year, including the last day of the taxable year, in which the items attributable to each trade or business to be aggregated are included in income;

(iii) All of the items attributable to each trade or business to be aggregated are reported on returns with the same taxable year, not taking into account short taxable years;

(iv) None of the trades or businesses to be aggregated is a *specified service trade or business* (SSTB) as defined in § 1.199A-5; and

(v) The trades or businesses to be aggregated satisfy at least two of the following factors (based on all of the facts and circumstances):

(A) The trades or businesses provide products, property, or services that are the same or customarily offered together.

(B) The trades or businesses share facilities or share significant centralized business elements, such as personnel, accounting, legal, manufacturing, purchasing, human resources, or information technology resources.

(C) The trades or businesses are operated in coordination with, or reliance upon, one or more of the businesses in the aggregated group (for example, supply chain interdependencies).

(2) *Operating rules.*—(i) *Individuals.*—An individual may aggregate trades or businesses operated directly or through an RPE to the extent an aggregation is not inconsistent with the aggregation of an RPE. If an individual aggregates multiple trades or businesses under paragraph (b)(1) of this section, QBI, W-2 wages, and UBIA of qualified property must be combined for the aggregated trades or businesses for purposes of applying the W-2 wage and UBIA of qualified property limitations described in § 1.199A-1(d)(2)(iv). An individual may not subtract from the trades or businesses aggregated by an RPE but may aggregate additional trades or businesses with the RPE's aggregation if the rules of this section are otherwise satisfied.

(ii) *RPEs.*—An RPE may aggregate trades or businesses operated directly or through a lower-tier RPE to the extent an aggregation is not inconsistent with the aggregation of a lower-tier RPE. If an RPE itself does not aggregate, multiple owners of an RPE need not aggregate in the same manner. If an RPE aggregates multiple trades or businesses under paragraph (b)(1) of this section, the RPE must compute and report QBI, W-2 wages, and UBIA of qualified property for the aggregated trade or business under the rules described in § 1.199A-6(b). An RPE may not subtract from the trades or businesses aggregated by a lower-tier RPE but may aggregate additional trades or businesses with a lower-tier RPE's aggregation if the rules of this section are otherwise satisfied.

(c) *Reporting and consistency requirements.*—(1) *Individuals.*—Once an individual chooses to aggregate two or more trades or businesses, the individual must consistently report the aggregated trades or businesses in all subsequent taxable years. A failure to aggregate will not be considered to be an aggregation for purposes of this rule. An individual that fails to aggregate may not aggregate trades or businesses on an

amended return (other than an amended return for the 2018 taxable year). However, an individual may add a newly created or newly acquired (including through nonrecognition transfers) trade or business to an existing aggregated trade or business (including the aggregated trade or business of an RPE) if the requirements of paragraph (b)(1) of this section are satisfied. In a subsequent year, if there is a significant change in facts and circumstances such that an individual's prior aggregation of trades or businesses no longer qualifies for aggregation under the rules of this section, then the trades or businesses will no longer be aggregated within the meaning of this section, and the individual must reapply the rules in paragraph (b)(1) of this section to determine a new permissible aggregation (if any). An individual also must report aggregated trades or businesses of an RPE in which the individual holds a direct or indirect interest.

(2) *Individual disclosure.*—(i) *Required annual disclosure.*—For each taxable year, individuals must attach a statement to their returns identifying each trade or business aggregated under paragraph (b)(1) of this section. The statement must contain —

(A) A description of each trade or business;

(B) The name and EIN of each entity in which a trade or business is operated;

(C) Information identifying any trade or business that was formed, ceased operations, was acquired, or was disposed of during the taxable year;

(D) Information identifying any aggregated trade or business of an RPE in which the individual holds an ownership interest; and

(E) Such other information as the Commissioner may require in forms, instructions, or other published guidance.

(ii) *Failure to disclose.*—If an individual fails to attach the statement required in paragraph (c)(2)(i) of this section, the Commissioner may disaggregate the individual's trades or businesses that are disaggregated by the Commissioner for the subsequent three taxable years.

(3) *RPEs.*—Once an RPE chooses to aggregate two or more trades or businesses, the RPE must consistently report the aggregated trades or businesses in all subsequent taxable years. A failure to aggregate will not be considered to be an aggregation for purposes of this rule. An RPE that fails to aggregate may not aggregate trades or businesses on an amended return (other than an amended return for the 2018 taxable year). However, an RPE may add a newly created or newly acquired (including through non-recognition transfers) trade or business to an existing aggregated trade or business (other than the aggregated trade or business of a lower-tier RPE) if the requirements of paragraph (b)(1) of this section are satisfied. In a subsequent year, if there is

a significant change in facts and circumstances such that an RPE's prior aggregation of trades or businesses no longer qualifies for aggregation under the rules of this section, then the trades or businesses will no longer be aggregated within the meaning of this section, and the RPE must reapply the rules in paragraph (b)(1) of this section to determine a new permissible aggregation (if any). An RPE also must report aggregated trades or businesses of a lower-tier RPE in which the RPE holds a direct or indirect interest.

(4) *RPE disclosure.*—(i) *Required annual disclosure.*—For each taxable year, RPEs (including each RPE in a tiered structure) must attach a statement to each owner's Schedule K-1 identifying each trade or business aggregated under paragraph (b)(1) of this section. The statement must contain —

(A) A description of each trade or business;

(B) The name and EIN of each entity in which a trade or business is operated;

(C) Information identifying any trade or business that was formed, ceased operations, was acquired, or was disposed of during the taxable year;

(D) Information identifying any aggregated trade or business of an RPE in which the RPE holds an ownership interest; and

(E) Such other information as the Commissioner may require in forms, instructions, or other published guidance.

(ii) *Failure to disclose.*—If an RPE fails to attach the statement required in paragraph (c)(2)(i) of this section, the Commissioner may disaggregate the RPE's trades or businesses. The RPE may not aggregate trades or businesses that are disaggregated by the Commissioner for the subsequent three taxable years.

(d) *Examples.*—The following examples illustrate the principles of this section. For purposes of these examples, assume the taxpayer is a United States citizen, all individuals and RPEs use a calendar taxable year, there are no ownership changes during the taxable year, all trades or businesses satisfy the requirements under section 162, all tax items are effectively connected to a trade or business within the United States within the meaning of section 864(c), and none of the trades or businesses is an SSTB within the meaning of §1.199A-5. Except as otherwise specified, a single capital letter denotes an individual taxpayer.

(1) *Example 1*—(i) *Facts.* A wholly owns and operates a catering business and a restaurant through separate disregarded entities. The catering business and the restaurant share centralized purchasing to obtain volume discounts and a centralized accounting office that performs all of the bookkeeping, tracks and issues statements on all of the receivables, and prepares the payroll for each business. A maintains a website and print advertising materials that reference both

the catering business and the restaurant. A uses the restaurant kitchen to prepare food for the catering business. The catering business employs its own staff and owns equipment and trucks that are not used or associated with the restaurant.

(ii) *Analysis.* Because the restaurant and catering business are held in disregarded entities, A will be treated as operating each of these businesses directly and thereby satisfies paragraph (b)(1)(i) of this section. Under paragraph (b)(1)(v) of this section, A satisfies the following factors: paragraph (b)(1)(v)(A) of this section is met as both businesses offer prepared food to customers; and paragraph (b)(1)(v)(B) of this section is met because the two businesses share the same kitchen facilities in addition to centralized purchasing, marketing, and accounting. Having satisfied paragraphs (b)(1)(i) through (v) of this section, A may treat the catering business and the restaurant as a single trade or business for purposes of applying §1.199A-1(d).

(2) *Example 2*—(i) *Facts.* Assume the same facts as in *Example 1* of paragraph (d)(1) of this section, but the catering and restaurant businesses are owned in separate partnerships and A, B, C, and D each own a 25% interest in each of the two partnerships. A, B, C, and D are unrelated.

(ii) *Analysis.* Because under paragraph (b)(1)(i) of this section A, B, C, and D together own more than 50% of each of the two partnerships, they may each treat the catering business and the restaurant as a single trade or business for purposes of applying §1.199A-1(d).

(3) *Example 3*—(i) *Facts.* W owns a 75% interest in S1, an S corporation, and a 75% interest in PRS, a partnership. S1 manufactures clothing and PRS is a retail pet food store. W manages S1 and PRS.

(ii) *Analysis.* W owns more than 50% of the stock of S1 and more than 50% of PRS thereby satisfying paragraph (b)(1)(i) of this section. Although W manages both S1 and PRS, W is not able to satisfy the requirements of paragraph (b)(1)(v) of this section as the two businesses do not provide goods or services that are the same or customarily offered together; there are no significant centralized business elements; and no facts indicate that the businesses are operated in coordination with, or reliance upon, one another. W must treat S1 and PRS as separate trades or businesses for purposes of applying §1.199A-1(d).

(4) *Example 4*—(i) *Facts.* E owns a 60% interest in each of four partnerships (PRS1, PRS2, PRS3, and PRS4). Each partnership operates a hardware store. A team of executives oversees the operations of all four of the businesses and controls the policy decisions involving the business as a whole. Human resources and accounting are centralized for the four businesses. E reports PRS1, PRS3, and PRS4 as an aggregated trade or business under paragraph (b)(1) of this section and reports PRS2 as a separate trade or business. Only PRS2 generates a net taxable loss.

(ii) *Analysis*. E owns more than 50% of each partnership thereby satisfying paragraph (b)(1)(i) of this section. Under paragraph (b)(1)(v) of this section, the following factors are satisfied: paragraph (b)(1)(v)(A) of this section because each partnership operates a hardware store; and paragraph (b)(1)(v)(B) of this section because the businesses share accounting and human resource functions. E's decision to aggregate only PRS1, PRS3, and PRS4 into a single trade or business for purposes of applying § 1.199A-1(d) is permissible. The loss from PRS2 will be netted against the aggregate profits of PRS1, PRS3, and PRS4 pursuant to § 1.199A-1(d)(2)(iii).

(5) *Example 5*—(i) *Facts*. Assume the same facts as *Example 4* of paragraph (d)(4) of this section, and that F owns a 10% interest in PRS1, PRS2, PRS3, and PRS4.

(ii) *Analysis*. Because under paragraph (b)(1)(i) of this section E owns more than 50% of the four partnerships, F may aggregate PRS 1, PRS2, PRS3, and PRS4 as a single trade or business for purposes of applying § 1.199A-1(d), provided that F can demonstrate that the ownership test is met by E.

(6) *Example 6*—(i) *Facts*. D owns 75% of the stock of S1, S2, and S3, each of which is an S corporation. Each S corporation operates a grocery store in a separate state. S1 and S2 share centralized purchasing functions to obtain volume discounts and a centralized accounting office that performs all of the bookkeeping, tracks and issues statements on all of the receivables, and prepares the payroll for each business. S3 is operated independently from the other businesses.

(ii) *Analysis*. D owns more than 50% of the stock of each S corporation thereby satisfying paragraph (b)(1)(i) of this section. Under paragraph (b)(1)(v) of this section, the grocery stores satisfy paragraph (b)(1)(v)(A) of this section because they are in the same trade or business. Only S1 and S2 satisfy paragraph (b)(1)(v)(B) of this section because of their centralized purchasing and accounting offices. D is only able to show that the requirements of paragraph (b)(1)(v)(B) of this section are satisfied for S1 and S2; therefore, D only may aggregate S1 and S2 into a single trade or business for purposes of § 1.199A-1(d). D must report S3 as a separate trade or business for purposes of applying § 1.199A-1(d).

(7) *Example 7*—(i) *Facts*. Assume the same facts as *Example 6* of paragraph (d)(6) of this section except each store is independently operated and S1 and S2 do not have centralized purchasing or accounting functions.

(ii) *Analysis*. Although the stores provide the same products and services within the meaning of paragraph (b)(1)(v)(A) of this section, D cannot show that another factor under paragraph (b)(1)(v) of this section is present. Therefore, D must report S1, S2, and S3 as separate trades or

businesses for purposes of applying § 1.199A-1(d).

(8) *Example 8*—(i) *Facts*. G owns 80% of the stock in S1, an S corporation and 80% of LLC1 and LLC2, each of which is a partnership for Federal tax purposes. LLC1 manufactures and supplies all of the widgets sold by LLC2. LLC2 operates a retail store that sells LLC1's widgets. S1 owns the real property leased to LLC1 and LLC2 for use by the factory and retail store. The entities share common advertising and management.

(ii) *Analysis*. G owns more than 50% of the stock of S1 and more than 50% of LLC1 and LLC2 thus satisfying paragraph (b)(1)(i) of this section. LLC1, LLC2, and S1 share significant centralized business elements and are operated in coordination with, or in reliance upon, one or more of the businesses in the aggregated group. G can treat the business operations of LLC1 and LLC2 as a single trade or business for purposes of applying § 1.199A-1(d). S1 is eligible to be included in the aggregated group because it leases property to a trade or business within the aggregated trade or business as described in § 1.199A-1(b)(14) and meets the requirements of paragraph (b)(1) of this section.

(9) *Example 9*—(i) *Facts*. Same facts as *Example 8* of paragraph (d)(8) of this section, except G owns 80% of the stock in S1 and 20% of each of LLC1 and LLC2. B, G's son, owns a majority interest in LLC2, and M, G's mother, owns a majority interest in LLC1. B does not own an interest in S1 or LLC1, and M does not own an interest in S1 or LLC2.

(ii) *Analysis*. Under the rules in paragraph (b)(1) of this section, B and M's interest in LLC2 and LLC1, respectively, are attributable to G and G is treated as owning a majority interest in LLC2 and LLC1; G thus satisfies paragraph (b)(1)(i) of this section. G may aggregate his interests in LLC1, LLC2, and S1 as a single trade or business for purposes of applying § 1.199A-1(d). Under paragraph (b)(1) of this section, S1 is eligible to be included in the aggregated group because it leases property to a trade or business within the aggregated trade or business as described in § 1.199A-1(b)(14) and meets the requirements of paragraph (b)(1) of this section.

(10) *Example 10*—(i) *Facts*. F owns a 75% interest and G owns a 5% interest in five partnerships (PRS1-PRS5). H owns a 10% interest in PRS1 and PRS2. Each partnership operates a restaurant and each restaurant separately constitutes a trade or business for purposes of section 162. G is the executive chef of all of the restaurants and as such he creates the menus and orders the food supplies.

(ii) *Analysis*. F owns more than 50% of the partnerships thereby satisfying paragraph (b)(1)(i) of this section. Under paragraph (b)(1)(v) of this section, the restaurants satisfy paragraph (b)(1)(v)(A) of this section because they are in the same trade or business, and para-

**Reg. § 1.199A-4(d)**

graph (b)(1)(v)(B) of this section is satisfied as G is the executive chef of all of the restaurants and the businesses share a centralized function for ordering food and supplies. F can show the requirements under paragraph (b)(1) of this section are satisfied as to all of the restaurants. Because F owns a majority interest in each of the partnerships, G can demonstrate that paragraph (b)(1)(i) of this section is satisfied. G can also aggregate all five restaurants into a single trade or business for purposes of applying § 1.199A-1(d). H, however, only owns an interest in PRS1 and PRS2. Like G, H satisfies paragraph (b)(1)(i) of this section because F owns a majority interest. H can, therefore, aggregate PRS1 and PRS2 into a single trade or business for purposes of applying § 1.199A-1(d).

(11) *Example 11*—(i) *Facts.* H, J, K, and L own interests in PRS1 and PRS2, each a partnership, and S1 and S2, each an S corporation. H, J, K, and L also own interests in C, an entity taxable as a C corporation. H owns 30%, J owns 20%, K owns 5%, and L owns 45% of each of the five entities. All of the entities satisfy 2 of the 3 factors under paragraph (b)(1)(v) of this section. For purposes of section 199A the taxpayers report the following aggregated trades or businesses: H aggregates PRS1 and S1 together and aggregates PRS2 and S2 together; J aggregates PRS1, S1 and S2 together and reports PRS2 separately; K aggregates PRS1 and PRS2 together and aggregates S1 and S2 together; and L aggregates S1, S2, and PRS2 together and reports PRS1 separately. C cannot be aggregated.

(ii) *Analysis.* Under paragraph (b)(1)(i) of this section, because H, J, and K together own a majority interest in PRS1, PRS2, S1, and S2, H, J, K, and L are permitted to aggregate under paragraph (b)(1) of this section. Further, the aggregations reported by the taxpayers are permitted, but not required for each of H, J, K, and L. C's income is not eligible for the section 199A deduction and it cannot be aggregated for purposes of applying § 1.199A-1(d).

(12) *Example 12*—(i) *Facts.* L owns 60% of PRS1, a partnership, a business that sells non-food items to grocery stores. L also owns 55% of PRS2, a partnership, which owns and operates a distribution trucking business. The predominant portion of PRS2's business is transporting goods for PRS1.

(ii) *Analysis.* L is able to meet paragraph (b)(1)(i) of this section as the majority owner of PRS1 and PRS2. Under paragraph (b)(1)(v) of this section, L is only able to show the operations of PRS1 and PRS2 are operated in reliance of one another under paragraph (b)(1)(v)(C) of this section. For purposes of applying § 1.199A-1(d), L must treat PRS1 and PRS2 as separate trades or businesses.

(13) *Example 13*—(i) *Facts.* C owns a majority interest in a sailboat racing team and also owns an interest in PRS1 which operates a marina.

PRS1 is a trade or business under section 162, but the sailboat racing team is not a trade or business within the meaning of section 162.

(ii) *Analysis.* C has only one trade or business for purposes of section 199A and, therefore, cannot aggregate the interest in the racing team with PRS1 under paragraph (b)(1) of this section.

(14) *Example 14*—(i) *Facts.* Trust wholly owns LLC1, LLC2, and LLC3. LLC1 operates a trucking company that delivers lumber and other supplies sold by LLC2. LLC2 operates a lumber yard and supplies LLC3 with building materials. LLC3 operates a construction business. LLC1, LLC2, and LLC3 have a centralized human resources department, payroll, and accounting department.

(ii) *Analysis.* Because Trust owns 100% of the interests in LLC1, LLC2, and LLC3, Trust satisfies paragraph (b)(1)(i) of this section. Trust can also show that it satisfies paragraph (b)(1)(v)(B) of this section as the trades or businesses have a centralized human resources department, payroll, and accounting department. Trust also can show it meets paragraph (b)(1)(v)(C) of this section as the trades or businesses are operated in coordination, or reliance upon, one or more in the aggregated group. Trust can aggregate LLC1, LLC2, and LLC3 for purposes of applying § 1.199A-1(d).

(15) *Example 15*—(i) *Facts.* PRS1, a partnership, directly operates a food service trade or business and owns 60% of PRS2, which directly operates a movie theater trade or business and a food service trade or business. PRS2's movie theater and food service businesses operate in coordination with, or reliance upon, one another and share a centralized human resources department, payroll, and accounting department. PRS1's and PRS2's food service businesses provide products and services that are the same and share centralized purchasing and shipping to obtain volume discounts.

(ii) *Analysis.* PRS2 may aggregate its movie theater and food service businesses. Paragraph (b)(1)(v) of this section is satisfied because the businesses operate in coordination with one another and share centralized business elements. If PRS does aggregate the two businesses, PRS1 may not aggregate its food service business with PRS2's aggregated trades or businesses. Because PRS1 owns more than 50% of PRS2, thereby satisfying paragraph (b)(1)(i) of this section, PRS1 may aggregate its food service businesses with PRS2's food service business if PRS2 has not aggregated its movie theater and food service businesses. Paragraph (b)(1)(v) of this section is satisfied because the businesses provide the same products and services and share centralized business elements. Under either alternative, PRS1's food service business and PRS2's movie theater cannot be aggregated because there are no factors in paragraph (b)(1)(v) of this section present between the businesses.

(16) *Example 16*—(i) *Facts.* PRS1, a partnership, owns 60% of a commercial rental office building in state A, and 80% of a commercial rental office building in state B. Both commercial rental office building operations share centralized accounting, legal, and human resource functions. PRS1 treats the two commercial rental office buildings as an aggregated trade or business under paragraph (b)(1) of this section.

(ii) *Analysis.* PRS1 owns more than 50% of each trade or business thereby satisfying paragraph (b)(1)(i) of this section. Under paragraph (b)(1)(v) of this section, PRS1 may aggregate its commercial rental office buildings because the businesses provide the same type of property and share accounting, legal, and human resource functions.

(17) *Example 17*—(i) *Facts.* S, an S corporation owns 100% of the interests in a residential condominium building and 100% of the interests in a commercial rental office building. Both building operations share centralized accounting, legal, and human resource functions.

(ii) *Analysis.* S owns more than 50% of each trade or business thereby satisfying paragraph (b)(1)(i) of this section. Although both businesses share significant centralized business elements, S cannot show that another factor under paragraph (b)(1)(v) of this section is present because the two building operations are not of the same type of property. S must treat the residential condominium building and the commercial rental office building as separate trades or businesses for purposes of applying § 1.199A-1(d).

(18) *Example 18*—(i) *Facts.* M owns 75% of a residential apartment building. M also owns 80% of PRS2. PRS2 owns 80% of the interests in a residential condominium building and 80% of the interests in a residential apartment building. PRS2's residential condominium building and residential apartment building operations share centralized back office functions and management. M's residential apartment building and PRS2's residential condominium and apartment building operate in coordination with each other in renting apartments to tenants.

(ii) *Analysis.* PRS2 may aggregate its residential condominium and residential apartment building operations. PRS2 owns more than 50% of each trade or business thereby satisfying paragraph (b)(1)(i) of this section. Paragraph (b)(1)(v) of this section is satisfied because the businesses are of the same type of property and share centralized back office functions and management. M may also add its residential apartment building operations to PRS2's aggregated residential condominium and apartment building operations. M owns more than 50% of each trade or business thereby satisfying paragraph (b)(1)(i) of this section. Paragraph (b)(1)(v) of this section is also satisfied because the businesses operate in coordination with each other.

(e) *Applicability date.*—(1) *General rule.*—Except as provided in paragraph (e)(2) of this sec-

tion, the provisions of this section apply to taxable years ending after February 8, 2019.

(2) *Exception for non-calendar year RPE.*—For purposes of determining QBI, W-2 wages, and UBIA of qualified property, and the aggregate amount of qualified REIT dividends and qualified PTP income, if an individual receives any of these items from an RPE with a taxable year that begins before January 1, 2018, and ends after December 31, 2017, such items are treated as having been incurred by the individual during the individual's taxable year in which or with which such RPE taxable year ends. [Reg. § 1.199A-4.]

☐ [T.D. 9847, 2-4-2019.]

### [Reg. § 1.199A-5]

**§ 1.199A-5. Specified service trades or businesses and the trade or business of performing services as an employee.**—(a) *Scope and effect.*—(1) *Scope.*—This section provides guidance on specified service trades or businesses (SSTBs) and the trade or business of performing services as an employee. This paragraph (a) describes the effect of a trade or business being an SSTB and the trade or business of performing services as an employee. Paragraph (b) of this section provides definitional guidance on SSTBs. Paragraph (c) of this section provides special rules related to SSTBs. Paragraph (d) of this section provides guidance on the trade or business of performing services as an employee. The provisions of this section apply solely for purposes of section 199A of the Internal Revenue Code (Code).

(2) *Effect of being an SSTB.*—If a trade or business is an SSTB, no qualified business income (QBI), W-2 wages, or unadjusted basis immediately after acquisition (UBIA) of qualified property from the SSTB may be taken into account by any individual whose taxable income exceeds the phase-in range as defined in § 1.199A-1(b)(4), even if the item is derived from an activity that is not itself a specified service activity. The SSTB limitation also applies to income earned from a publicly traded partnership (PTP). If a trade or business conducted by a relevant passthrough entity (RPE) or PTP is an SSTB, this limitation applies to any direct or indirect individual owners of the business, regardless of whether the owner is passive or participated in any specified service activity. However, the SSTB limitation does not apply to individuals with taxable income below the threshold amount as defined in § 1.199A-1(b)(12). A phase-in rule, provided in § 1.199A-1(d)(2), applies to individuals with taxable income within the phase-in range, allowing them to take into account a certain "applicable percentage" of QBI, W-2 wages, and UBIA of qualified property from an SSTB. The phase-in rule also applies to income earned from a PTP. A direct or indirect owner of a trade or business engaged in the performance of a specified ser-

vice is engaged in the performance of the specified service for purposes of section 199A and this section, regardless of whether the owner is passive or participated in the specified service activity.

(3) *Trade or business of performing services as an employee.*—The trade or business of performing services as an employee is not a trade or business for purposes of section 199A and the regulations thereunder. Therefore, no items of income, gain, deduction, or loss from the trade or business of performing services as an employee constitute QBI within the meaning of section 199A and §1.199A-3. No taxpayer may claim a section 199A deduction for wage income, regardless of the amount of taxable income.

(b) *Definition of specified service trade or business.*—Except as provided in paragraph (c)(1) of this section, the term *specified service trade or business (SSTB)* means any of the following:

(1) *Listed SSTBs.*—Any trade or business involving the performance of services in one or more of the following fields:

(i) *Health* as described in paragraph (b)(2)(ii) of this section;

(ii) *Law* as described in paragraph (b)(2)(iii) of this section;

(iii) *Accounting* as described in paragraph (b)(2)(iv) of this section;

(iv) *Actuarial science* as described in paragraph (b)(2)(v) of this section;

(v) *Performing arts* as described in paragraph (b)(2)(vi) of this section;

(vi) *Consulting* as described in paragraph (b)(2)(vii) of this section;

(vii) *Athletics* as described in paragraph (b)(2)(viii) of this section;

(viii) *Financial services* as described in paragraph (b)(2)(ix) of this section;

(ix) *Brokerage services* as described in paragraph (b)(2)(x) of this section;

(x) *Investing and investment management* as described in paragraph (b)(2)(xi) of this section;

(xi) *Trading* as described in paragraph (b)(2)(xii) of this section;

(xii) *Dealing in securities (as defined in section 475(c)(2)), partnership interests, or commodities (as defined in section 475(e)(2))* as described in paragraph (b)(2)(xiii) of this section; or

(xiii) *Any trade or business where the principal asset of such trade or business is the reputation or skill of one or more of its employees or owners* as defined in paragraph (b)(2)(xiv) of this section.

(2) *Additional rules for applying section 199A(d)(2) and paragraph (b) of this section.*—(i) *In general.*—(A) *No effect on other tax rules.*—This paragraph (b)(2) provides additional rules for determining whether a business is an SSTB within the meaning of section 199A(d)(2) and paragraph (b) of this section only. The rules of this paragraph (b)(2) apply solely for purposes of

section 199A and therefore may not be taken into account for purposes of applying any provision of law or regulation other than section 199A and the regulations thereunder, except to the extent such provision expressly refers to section 199A(d) or this section.

(B) *Hedging transactions.*—Income, deduction, gain or loss from a *hedging transaction* (as defined in §1.1221-2(b)) entered into by an individual or RPE in the normal course of the individual's or RPE's trade or business is treated as income, deduction, gain, or loss from that trade or business for purposes of this paragraph (b)(2). See also §1.446-4.

(ii) *Meaning of services performed in the field of health.*—For purposes of section 199A(d)(2) and paragraph (b)(1)(i) of this section only, the *performance of services in the field of health* means the provision of medical services by individuals such as physicians, pharmacists, nurses, dentists, veterinarians, physical therapists, psychologists, and other similar healthcare professionals performing services in their capacity as such. The performance of services in the field of health does not include the provision of services not directly related to a medical services field, even though the services provided may purportedly relate to the health of the service recipient. For example, the performance of services in the field of health does not include the operation of health clubs or health spas that provide physical exercise or conditioning to their customers, payment processing, or the research, testing, and manufacture and/or sales of pharmaceuticals or medical devices.

(iii) *Meaning of services performed in the field of law.*—For purposes of section 199A(d)(2) and paragraph (b)(1)(ii) of this section only, the *performance of services in the field of law* means the performance of legal services by individuals such as lawyers, paralegals, legal arbitrators, mediators, and similar professionals performing services in their capacity as such. The performance of services in the field of law does not include the provision of services that do not require skills unique to the field of law; for example, the provision of services in the field of law does not include the provision of services by printers, delivery services, or stenography services.

(iv) *Meaning of services performed in the field of accounting.*—For purposes of section 199A(d)(2) and paragraph (b)(1)(iii) of this section only, the *performance of services in the field of accounting* means the provision of services by individuals such as accountants, enrolled agents, return preparers, financial auditors, and similar professionals performing services in their capacity as such.

(v) *Meaning of services performed in the field of actuarial science.*—For purposes of section

199A(d)(2) and paragraph (b)(1)(iv) of this section only, the *performance of services in the field of actuarial science* means the provision of services by individuals such as actuaries and similar professionals performing services in their capacity as such.

(vi) *Meaning of services performed in the field of performing arts.*—For purposes of section 199A(d)(2) and paragraph (b)(1)(v) of this section only, the *performance of services in the field of the performing arts* means the performance of services by individuals who participate in the creation of performing arts, such as actors, singers, musicians, entertainers, directors, and similar professionals performing services in their capacity as such. The performance of services in the field of performing arts does not include the provision of services that do not require skills unique to the creation of performing arts, such as the maintenance and operation of equipment or facilities for use in the performing arts. Similarly, the performance of services in the field of the performing arts does not include the provision of services by persons who broadcast or otherwise disseminate video or audio of performing arts to the public.

(vii) *Meaning of services performed in the field of consulting.*—For purposes of section 199A(d)(2) and paragraph (b)(1)(vi) of this section only, the *performance of services in the field of consulting* means the provision of professional advice and counsel to clients to assist the client in achieving goals and solving problems. Consulting includes providing advice and counsel regarding advocacy with the intention of influencing decisions made by a government or governmental agency and all attempts to influence legislators and other government officials on behalf of a client by lobbyists and other similar professionals performing services in their capacity as such. The performance of services in the field of consulting does not include the performance of services other than advice and counsel, such as sales (or economically similar services) or the provision of training and educational courses. For purposes of the preceding sentence, the determination of whether a person's services are sales or economically similar services will be based on all the facts and circumstances of that person's business. Such facts and circumstances include, for example, the manner in which the taxpayer is compensated for the services provided. Performance of services in the field of consulting does not include the performance of consulting services embedded in, or ancillary to, the sale of goods or performance of services on behalf of a trade or business that is otherwise not an SSTB (such as typical services provided by a building contractor) if there is no separate payment for the consulting services. Services within the fields of architecture and engineering are not treated as consulting services.

(viii) *Meaning of services performed in the field of athletics.*—For purposes of section 199A(d)(2) and paragraph (b)(1)(vii) of this section only, the *performance of services in the field of athletics* means the performance of services by individuals who participate in athletic competition such as athletes, coaches, and team managers in sports such as baseball, basketball, football, soccer, hockey, martial arts, boxing, bowling, tennis, golf, skiing, snowboarding, track and field, billiards, and racing. The performance of services in the field of athletics does not include the provision of services that do not require skills unique to athletic competition, such as the maintenance and operation of equipment or facilities for use in athletic events. Similarly, the performance of services in the field of athletics does not include the provision of services by persons who broadcast or otherwise disseminate video or audio of athletic events to the public.

(ix) *Meaning of services performed in the field of financial services.*—For purposes of section 199A(d)(2) and paragraph (b)(1)(viii) of this section only, the *performance of services in the field of financial services* means the provision of financial services to clients including managing wealth, advising clients with respect to finances, developing retirement plans, developing wealth transition plans, the provision of advisory and other similar services regarding valuations, mergers, acquisitions, dispositions, restructurings (including in title 11 of the Code or similar cases), and raising financial capital by underwriting, or acting as a client's agent in the issuance of securities and similar services. This includes services provided by financial advisors, investment bankers, wealth planners, retirement advisors, and other similar professionals performing services in their capacity as such. Solely for purposes of section 199A, the performance of services in the field of financial services does not include taking deposits or making loans, but does include arranging lending transactions between a lender and borrower.

(x) *Meaning of services performed in the field of brokerage services.*—For purposes of section 199A(d)(2) and paragraph (b)(1)(ix) of this section only, the *performance of services in the field of brokerage services* includes services in which a person arranges transactions between a buyer and a seller with respect to securities (as defined in section 475(c)(2)) for a commission or fee. This includes services provided by stock brokers and other similar professionals, but does not include services provided by real estate agents and brokers, or insurance agents and brokers.

(xi) *Meaning of the provision of services in investing and investment management.*—For purposes of section 199A(d)(2) and paragraph (b)(1)(x) of this section only, the *performance of services that consist of investing and investment management* refers to a trade or business involving the receipt of fees for providing investing, asset management, or investment management services, including providing advice with respect to buying and selling investments. The performance of services of investing and investment management does not include directly managing real property.

(xii) *Meaning of the provision of services in trading.*—For purposes of section 199A(d)(2) and paragraph (b)(1)(xi) of this section only, the *performance of services that consist of trading* means a trade or business of trading in securities (as defined in section 475(c)(2)), commodities (as defined in section 475(e)(2)), or partnership interests. Whether a person is a trader in securities, commodities, or partnership interests is determined by taking into account all relevant facts and circumstances, including the source and type of profit that is associated with engaging in the activity regardless of whether that person trades for the person's own account, for the account of others, or any combination thereof.

(xiii) *Meaning of the provision of services in dealing.*—(A) *Dealing in securities.*—For purposes of section 199A(d)(2) and paragraph (b)(1)(xii) of this section only, the *performance of services that consist of dealing in securities (as defined in section 475(c)(2))* means regularly purchasing securities from and selling securities to customers in the ordinary course of a trade or business or regularly offering to enter into, assume, offset, assign, or otherwise terminate positions in securities with customers in the ordinary course of a trade or business. Solely for purposes of the preceding sentence, the performance of services to originate a loan is not treated as the purchase of a security from the borrower in determining whether the lender is dealing in securities.

(B) *Dealing in commodities.*—For purposes of section 199A(d)(2) and paragraph (b)(1)(xii) of this section only, the *performance of services that consist of dealing in commodities (as defined in section 475(e)(2))* means regularly purchasing commodities from and selling commodities to customers in the ordinary course of a trade or business or regularly offering to enter into, assume, offset, assign, or otherwise terminate positions in commodities with customers in the ordinary course of a trade or business. Solely for purposes of the preceding sentence, gains and losses from qualified active sales as defined in paragraph (b)(2)(xiii)(B)(1) of this section are not taken into account in determining whether a person is engaged in the trade or business of dealing in commodities.

(1) *Qualified active sale.*—The term *qualified active sale* means the sale of commodities in the active conduct of a commodities business as a producer, processor, merchant, or handler of commodities if the trade or business is as an active producer, processor, merchant or handler of commodities. A hedging transaction described in paragraph (b)(2)(i)(B) of this section is treated as a qualified active sale. The sale of commodities held by a trade or business other than in its capacity as an active producer, processor,

merchant, or handler of commodities is not a qualified active sale. For example, the sale by a trade or business of commodities that were held for investment or speculation would not be a qualified active sale.

(2) *Active conduct of a commodities business.*—For purposes of paragraph (b)(2)(xiii)(B)(1) of this section, a trade or business is engaged in the active conduct of a commodities business as a producer, processor, merchant, or handler of commodities only with respect to commodities for which each of the conditions described in paragraphs (b)(2)(xiii)(B)(3) through (5) of this section are satisfied.

(3) *Directly holds commodities as inventory or similar property.*—The commodities trade or business holds the commodities directly, and not through an agent or independent contractor, as inventory or similar property. The term inventory or similar property means property that is stock in trade of the trade or business or other property of a kind that would properly be included in the inventory of the trade or business if on hand at the close of the taxable year, or property held by the trade or business primarily for sale to customers in the ordinary course of its trade or business.

(4) *Directly incurs substantial expenses in the ordinary course.*—The commodities trade or business incurs substantial expenses in the ordinary course of the commodities trade or business from engaging in one or more of the following activities directly, and not through an agent or independent contractor—

(i) Substantial activities in the production of the commodities, including planting, tending or harvesting crops, raising or slaughtering livestock, or extracting minerals;

(ii) Substantial processing activities prior to the sale of the commodities, including the blending and drying of agricultural commodities, or the concentrating, refining, mixing, crushing, aerating or milling of commodities; or

(iii) Significant activities as described in paragraph (b)(2)(xiii)(B)(5) of this section.

(5) *Significant activities for purposes of paragraph (b)(2)(xiii)(B)(4)(iii) of this section.*—The commodities trade or business performs significant activities with respect to the commodities that consists of—

(i) The physical movement, handling and storage of the commodities, including preparation of contracts and invoices, arranging transportation, insurance and credit, arranging for receipt, transfer or negotiation of shipping documents, arranging storage or warehousing, and dealing with quality claims;

(ii) Owning and operating facilities for storage or warehousing; or *(iii)* Owning, chartering, or leasing vessels or vehicles for the transportation of the commodities.

(C) *Dealing in partnership interests.*—For purposes of section 199A(d)(2) and paragraph (b)(1)(xii) of this section only, *the performance of services that consist of dealing in partnership interests* means regularly purchasing partnership interests from and selling partnership interests to customers in the ordinary course of a trade or business or regularly offering to enter into, assume, offset, assign, or otherwise terminate positions in partnership interests with customers in the ordinary course of a trade or business.

(xiv) *Meaning of trade or business where the principal asset of such trade or business is the reputation or skill of one or more employees or owners.*— For purposes of section 199A(d)(2) and paragraph (b)(1)(xiii) of this section only, the term *any trade or business where the principal asset of such trade or business is the reputation or skill of one or more of its employees or owners* means any trade or business that consists of any of the following (or any combination thereof):

(A) A trade or business in which a person receives fees, compensation, or other income for endorsing products or services;

(B) A trade or business in which a person licenses or receives fees, compensation, or other income for the use of an individual's image, likeness, name, signature, voice, trademark, or any other symbols associated with the individual's identity; or

(C) Receiving fees, compensation, or other income for appearing at an event or on radio, television, or another media format.

(D) For purposes of paragraphs (b)(2)(xiv)(A) through (C) of this section, the term *fees, compensation, or other income* includes the receipt of a partnership interest and the corresponding distributive share of income, deduction, gain, or loss from the partnership, or the receipt of stock of an S corporation and the corresponding income, deduction, gain, or loss from the S corporation stock.

(3) *Examples.*—The following examples illustrate the rules in paragraphs (a) and (b) of this section. The examples do not address all types of services that may or may not qualify as specified services. Unless otherwise provided, the individual in each example has taxable income in excess of the threshold amount.

(i) *Example 1.* B is a board-certified pharmacist who contracts as an independent contractor with X, a small medical facility in a rural area. X employs one full time pharmacist, but contracts with B when X's needs exceed the capacity of its full-time staff. When engaged by X, B is responsible for receiving and reviewing orders from physicians providing medical care at the facility; making recommendations on dosing and alternatives to the ordering physician; performing inoculations, checking for drug interactions, and filling pharmaceutical orders for patients receiving care at X. B is engaged in the performance of services in the field of health within the meaning of section 199A(d)(2) and paragraphs (b)(1)(i) and (b)(2)(ii) of this section.

(ii) *Example 2.* X is the operator of a residential facility that provides a variety of services to senior citizens who reside on campus. For residents, X offers standard domestic services including housing management and maintenance, meals, laundry, entertainment, and other similar services. In addition, X contracts with local professional healthcare organizations to offer residents a range of medical and health services provided at the facility, including skilled nursing care, physical and occupational therapy, speech-language pathology services, medical social services, medications, medical supplies and equipment used in the facility, ambulance transportation to the nearest supplier of needed services, and dietary counseling. X receives all of its income from residents for the costs associated with residing at the facility. Any health and medical services are billed directly by the healthcare providers to the senior citizens for those professional healthcare services even though those services are provided at the facility. X does not perform services in the field of health within the meaning of section 199A(d)(2) and paragraphs (b)(1)(i) and (b)(2)(ii) of this section.

(iii) *Example 3.* Y operates specialty surgical centers that provide outpatient medical procedures that do not require the patient to remain overnight for recovery or observation following the procedure. Y is a private organization that owns a number of facilities throughout the country. For each facility, Y ensures compliance with state and Federal laws for medical facilities and manages the facility's operations and performs all administrative functions. Y does not employ physicians, nurses, and medical assistants, but enters into agreements with other professional medical organizations or directly with the medical professionals to perform the procedures and provide all medical care. Patients are billed by Y for the facility costs relating to their procedure and by the healthcare professional or their affiliated organization for the actual costs of the procedure conducted by the physician and medical support team. Y does not perform services in the field of health within the meaning of section 199A(d)(2) and paragraphs (b)(1)(i) and (b)(2)(ii) of this section.

(iv) *Example 4.* Z is the developer and the only provider of a patented test used to detect a particular medical condition. Z accepts test orders only from health care professionals (Z's clients), does not have contact with patients, and Z's employees do not diagnose, treat, or manage any aspect of patient care. A, who manages Z's testing operations, is the only employee with an advanced medical degree. All other employees are technical support staff and not healthcare professionals. Z's workers are highly educated, but the skills the workers bring to the job are not often useful for Z's testing methods. In order to perform the duties required by Z, employees receive more than a year of specialized training for working with Z's test, which is of no use to other employers. Upon completion of an ordered test, Z analyses the results and provides its clients a report summarizing the findings. Z does not discuss the report's results, or the patient's diagnosis or treatment with any health care provider or the patient. Z is not informed by the healthcare provider as to the healthcare provider's diagnosis or treatment. Z is not providing services in the field of health within the meaning of section 199A(d)(2) and paragraphs (b)(1)(i) and (b)(2)(ii) of this section or where the principal asset of the trade or business is the reputation or skill of one or more of its employees within the meaning of paragraphs (b)(1)(xiii) and (b)(2)(xiv) of this section.

(v) *Example 5.* A, a singer and songwriter, writes and records a song. A is paid a mechanical royalty when the song is licensed or streamed. A is also paid a performance royalty when the recorded song is played publicly. A is engaged in the performance of services in an SSTB in the field of performing arts within the meaning of section 199A(d)(2) or paragraphs (b)(1)(v) and (b)(2)(vi) of this section. The royalties that A receives for the song are not eligible for a deduction under section 199A.

(vi) *Example 6.* B is a partner in Movie LLC, a partnership. Movie LLC is a film production company. Movie LLC plans and coordinates film production. Movie LLC shares in the profits of the films that it produces. Therefore, Movie LLC is engaged in the performance of services in an SSTB in the field of performing arts within the meaning of section 199A(d)(2) or paragraphs (b)(1)(v) and (b)(2)(vi) of this section. B is a passive owner in Movie LLC and does not provide any services with respect to Movie LLC. However, because Movie LLC is engaged in an SSTB in the field of performing arts, B's distributive share of the income, gain, deduction, and loss with respect to Movie LLC is not eligible for a deduction under section 199A.

(vii) *Example 7.* C is a partner in Partnership, which solely owns and operates a professional sports team. Partnership employs athletes and sells tickets and broadcast rights for games in which the sports team competes. Partnership sells the broadcast rights to Broadcast LLC, a separate trade or business. Broadcast LLC solely broadcasts the games. Partnership is engaged in the performance of services in an SSTB in the field of athletics within the meaning of section 199A(d)(2) or paragraphs (b)(1)(vii) and (b)(2)(viii) of this section. The tickets sales and the sale of the broadcast rights are both the performance of services in the field of athletics. C is a passive owner in Partnership and C does not provide any services with respect to Partnership or the sports team. However, because Partnership is engaged in an SSTB in the field of athlet-

ics, C's distributive share of the income, gain, deduction, and loss with respect to Partnership is not eligible for a deduction under section 199A. Broadcast LLC is not engaged in the performance of services in an SSTB in the field of athletics.

(viii) *Example 8.* D is in the business of providing services that assist unrelated entities in making their personnel structures more efficient. D studies its client's organization and structure and compares it to peers in its industry. D then makes recommendations and provides advice to its client regarding possible changes in the client's personnel structure, including the use of temporary workers. D does not provide any temporary workers to its clients and D's compensation and fees are not affected by whether D's clients used temporary workers. D is engaged in the performance of services in an SSTB in the field of consulting within the meaning of section 199A(d)(2) or paragraphs (b)(1)(vi) and (b)(2)(vii) of this section.

(ix) *Example 9.* E is an individual who owns and operates a temporary worker staffing firm primarily focused on the software consulting industry. Business clients hire E to provide temporary workers that have the necessary technical skills and experience with a variety of business software to provide consulting and advice regarding the proper selection and operation of software most appropriate for the business they are advising. E does not have a technical software engineering background and does not provide software consulting advice herself. E reviews resumes and refers candidates to the client when the client indicates a need for temporary workers. E does not evaluate her clients' needs about whether the client needs workers and does not evaluate the clients' consulting contracts to determine the type of expertise needed. Rather, the client provides E with a job description indicating the required skills for the upcoming consulting project. E is paid a fixed fee for each temporary worker actually hired by the client and receives a bonus if that worker is hired permanently within a year of referral. E's fee is not contingent on the profits of its clients. E is not considered to be engaged in the performance of services in the field of consulting within the meaning of section 199A(d)(2) or (b)(1)(vi) and (b)(2)(vii) of this section.

(x) *Example 10.* F is in the business of licensing software to customers. F discusses and evaluates the customer's software needs with the customer. The taxpayer advises the customer on the particular software products it licenses. F is paid a flat price for the software license. After the customer licenses the software, F helps to implement the software. F is engaged in the trade or business of licensing software and not engaged in an SSTB in the field of consulting within the meaning of section 199A(d)(2) or paragraphs (b)(1)(vi) and (b)(2)(vii) of this section.

**Reg. §1.199A-5(b)(3)**

(xi) *Example 11*. G is in the business of providing services to assist clients with their finances. G will study a particular client's financial situation, including, the client's present income, savings, and investments, and anticipated future economic and financial needs. Based on this study, G will then assist the client in making decisions and plans regarding the client's financial activities. Such financial planning includes the design of a personal budget to assist the client in monitoring the client's financial situation, the adoption of investment strategies tailored to the client's needs, and other similar services. G is engaged in the performance of services in an SSTB in the field of financial services within the meaning of section 199A(d)(2) or paragraphs (b)(1)(viii) and (b)(2)(ix) of this section.

(xii) *Example 12*. H is in the business of franchising a brand of personal financial planning offices, which generally provide personal wealth management, retirement planning, and other financial advice services to customers for a fee. H does not provide financial planning services itself. H licenses the right to use the business tradename, other branding intellectual property, and a marketing plan to third-party financial planner franchisees that operate the franchised locations and provide all services to customers. In exchange, the franchisees compensate H based on a fee structure, which includes a one-time fee to acquire the franchise. H is not engaged in the performance of services in the field of financial services within the meaning of section 199A(d)(2) or paragraphs (b)(1)(viii) and (b)(2)(ix) of this section.

(xiii) *Example 13*. J is in the business of executing transactions for customers involving various types of securities or commodities generally traded through organized exchanges or other similar networks. Customers place orders with J to trade securities or commodities based on the taxpayer's recommendations. J's compensation for its services typically is based on completion of the trade orders. J is engaged in an SSTB in the field of brokerage services within the meaning of section 199A(d)(2) or paragraphs (b)(1)(ix) and (b)(2)(x) of this section.

(xiv) *Example 14*. K owns 100% of Corp, an S corporation, which operates a bicycle sales and repair business. Corp has 8 employees, including K. Half of Corp's net income is generated from sales of new and used bicycles and related goods, such as helmets, and bicycle-related equipment. The other half of Corp's net income is generated from bicycle repair services performed by K and Corp's other employees. Corp's assets consist of inventory, fixtures, bicycle repair equipment, and a leasehold on its retail location. Several of the employees and G have worked in the bicycle business for many years, and have acquired substantial skill and reputation in the field. Customers often consult with the employees on the best bicycle for purchase. K is in the business of sales and repairs of bicycles

and is not engaged in an SSTB within the meaning of section 199A(d)(2) or paragraphs (b)(1)(xiii) and (b)(2)(xiv) of this section.

(xv) *Example 15*. L is a well-known chef and the sole owner of multiple restaurants each of which is owned in a disregarded entity. Due to L's skill and reputation as a chef, L receives an endorsement fee of $500,000 for the use of L's name on a line of cooking utensils and cookware. L is in the trade or business of being a chef and owning restaurants and such trade or business is not an SSTB. However, L is also in the trade or business of receiving endorsement income. L's trade or business consisting of the receipt of the endorsement fee for L's skill and/or reputation is an SSTB within the meaning of section 199A(d)(2) or paragraphs (b)(1)(xiii) and (b)(2)(xiv) of this section.

(xvi) *Example 16*. M is a well-known actor. M entered into a partnership with Shoe Company, in which M contributed her likeness and the use of her name to the partnership in exchange for a 50% interest in the partnership and a guaranteed payment. M's trade or business consisting of the receipt of the partnership interest and the corresponding distributive share with respect to the partnership interest for M's likeness and the use of her name is an SSTB within the meaning of section 199A(d)(2) or paragraphs (b)(1)(xiii) and (b)(2)(xiv) of this section.

(c) *Special rules.*—(1) *De minimis rule.*—(i) *Gross receipts of $25 million or less.*—For a trade or business with gross receipts of $25 million or less for the taxable year, a trade or business is not an SSTB if less than 10 percent of the gross receipts of the trade or business are attributable to the performance of services in a field described in paragraph (b) of this section. For purposes of determining whether this 10 percent test is satisfied, the performance of any activity incident to the actual performance of services in the field is considered the performance of services in that field.

(ii) *Gross receipts of greater than $25 million.*—For a trade or business with gross receipts of greater than $25 million for the taxable year, the rules of paragraph (c)(1)(i) of this section are applied by substituting "5 percent" for "10 percent" each place it appears.

(iii) *Examples.*—The following examples illustrate the provisions of paragraph (c)(1) of this section.

(A) *Example 1*. Landscape LLC sells lawn care and landscaping equipment and also provides advice and counsel on landscape design for large office parks and residential buildings. The landscape design services include advice on the selection and placement of trees, shrubs, and flowers and are considered to be the performance of services in the field of consulting under paragraphs (b)(1)(vi) and (b)(2)(vii) of this section. Landscape LLC separately invoices for its landscape design services and does not sell the trees, shrubs, or flowers it recommends for use in the landscape design. Landscape LLC maintains one set of books and records and treats the equipment sales and design services as a single trade or business for purposes of sections 162 and 199A. Landscape LLC has gross receipts of $2 million. $250,000 of the gross receipts is attributable to the landscape design services, an SSTB. Because the gross receipts from the consulting services exceed 10 percent of Landscape LLC's total gross receipts, the entirety of Landscape LLC's trade or business is considered an SSTB.

(B) *Example 2.* Animal Care LLC provides veterinarian services performed by licensed staff and also develops and sells its own line of organic dog food at its veterinarian clinic and online. The veterinarian services are considered to be the performance of services in the field of health under paragraphs (b)(1)(i) and (b)(2)(ii) of this section. Animal Care LLC separately invoices for its veterinarian services and the sale of its organic dog food. Animal Care LLC maintains separate books and records for its veterinarian clinic and its development and sale of its dog food. Animal Care LLC also has separate employees who are unaffiliated with the veterinary clinic and who only work on the formulation, marketing, sales, and distribution of the organic dog food products. Animal Care LLC treats its veterinary practice and the dog food development and sales as separate trades or businesses for purposes of section 162 and 199A. Animal Care LLC has gross receipts of $3,000,000. $1,000,000 of the gross receipts is attributable to the veterinary services, an SSTB. Although the gross receipts from the services in the field of health exceed 10 percent of Animal Care LLC's total gross receipts, the dog food development and sales business is not considered an SSTB due to the fact that the veterinary practice and the dog food development and sales are separate trades or businesses under section 162.

(2) *Services or property provided to an SSTB.*— (i) *In general.*—If a trade or business provides property or services to an SSTB within the meaning of this section and there is 50 percent or more common ownership of the trades or businesses, that portion of the trade or business of providing property or services to the 50 percent or more commonly-owned SSTB will be treated as a separate SSTB with respect to the related parties.

(ii) *50 percent or more common ownership.*— For purposes of paragraph (c)(2)(i) and (ii) of this section, 50 percent or more common ownership includes direct or indirect ownership by related parties within the meaning of sections 267(b) or 707(b).

(iii) *Examples.*—The following examples illustrate the provisions of paragraph (c)(2) of this section.

(A) *Example 1.* Law Firm is a partnership that provides legal services to clients, owns its own office building and employs its own administrative staff. Law Firm divides into three partnerships. Partnership 1 performs legal services to clients. Partnership 2 owns the office building and rents the entire building to Partnership 1. Partnership 3 employs the administrative staff and through a contract with Partnership 1 provides administrative services to Partnership 1 in exchange for fees. All three of the partnerships are owned by the same people (the original owners of Law Firm). Because Partnership 2 provides all of its property to Partnership 1, and Partnership 3 provides all of its services to Partnership 1, Partnerships 2 and 3 will each be treated as an SSTB under paragraph (c)(2) of this section.

(B) *Example 2.* Assume the same facts as in Example 1 of this paragraph (c)(2), except that Partnership 2, which owns the office building, rents 50 percent of the building to Partnership 1, which provides legal services, and the other 50 percent to various unrelated third party tenants. Because Partnership 2 is owned by the same people as Partnership 1, the portion of Partnership 2's leasing activity related to the lease of the building to Partnership 1 will be treated as a separate SSTB. The remaining 50 percent of Partnership 2's leasing activity will not be treated as an SSTB.

(d) *Trade or business of performing services as an employee.*—(1) *In general.*—The trade or business of performing services as an employee is not a trade or business for purposes of section 199A and the regulations thereunder. Therefore, no items of income, gain, deduction, and loss from the trade or business of performing services as an employee constitute QBI within the meaning of section 199A and § 1.199A-3. Except as provided in paragraph (d)(3) of this section, income from the trade or business of performing services as an employee refers to all wages (within the meaning of section 3401(a)) and other income earned in a capacity as an employee, including payments described in § 1.6041-2(a)(1) (other than payments to individuals described in section 3121(d)(3)) and § 1.6041-2(b)(1).

(2) *Employer's Federal employment tax classification of employee immaterial.*—For purposes of determining whether wages are earned in a capacity as an employee as provided in paragraph (d)(1) of this section, the treatment of an employee by an employer as anything other than an employee for Federal employment tax purposes is immaterial. Thus, if a worker should be properly classified as an employee, it is of no consequence that the employee is treated as a nonemployee by the employer for Federal employment tax purposes.

(3) *Presumption that former employees are still employees.*—(i) *Presumption.*—Solely for purposes of section 199A(d)(1)(B) and paragraph (d)(1) of

**Reg. § 1.199A-5(c)(2)**

this section, an individual that was properly treated as an employee for Federal employment tax purposes by the person to which he or she provided services and who is subsequently treated as other than an employee by such person with regard to the provision of substantially the same services directly or indirectly to the person (or a related person), is presumed, for three years after ceasing to be treated as an employee for Federal employment tax purposes, to be in the trade or business of performing services as an employee with regard to such services. As provided in paragraph (d)(3)(ii) of this section, this presumption may be rebutted upon a showing by the individual that, under Federal tax law, regulations, and principles (including common-law employee classification rules), the individual is performing services in a capacity other than as an employee. This presumption applies regardless of whether the individual provides services directly or indirectly through an entity or entities.

(ii) *Rebuttal of presumption.*—Upon notice from the IRS, an individual rebuts the presumption in paragraph (d)(3)(i) of this section by providing records, such as contracts or partnership agreements, that provide sufficient evidence to corroborate the individual's status as a non-employee.

(iii) *Examples.*—The following examples illustrate the provision of paragraph (d)(3) of this section. Unless otherwise provided, the individual in each example has taxable income in excess of the threshold amount.

(A) *Example 1.* A is employed by PRS, a partnership for Federal tax purposes, as a full-time employee and is treated as such for Federal employment tax purposes. A quits his job for PRS and enters into a contract with PRS under which A provides substantially the same services that A previously provided to PRS in A's capacity as an employee. Because A was treated as an employee for services he provided to PRS, and now is no longer treated as an employee with regard to such services, A is presumed (solely for purposes of section 199A(d)(1)(B) and paragraphs (a)(3) and (d) of this section) to be in the trade or business of performing services as an employee with regard to his services performed for PRS. Unless the presumption is rebutted with a showing that, under Federal tax law, regulations, and principles (including the common-law employee classification rules), A is not an employee, any amounts paid by PRS to A with respect to such services will not be QBI for purposes of section 199A. The presumption would apply even if, instead of contracting directly with PRS, A formed a disregarded entity, or a passthrough entity, and the entity entered into the contract with PRS.

(B) *Example 2.* C is an attorney employed as an associate in a law firm (Law Firm 1) and was treated as such for Federal employment tax purposes. C and the other associates in Law Firm 1 have taxable income below the threshold amount. Law Firm 1 terminates its employment relationship with C and its other associates. C and the other former associates form a new partnership, Law Firm 2, which contracts to perform legal services for Law Firm 1. Therefore, in form, C is now a partner in Law Firm 2 which earns income from providing legal services to Law Firm 1. C continues to provide substantially the same legal services to Law Firm 1 and its clients. Because C was previously treated as an employee for services she provided to Law Firm 1, and now is no longer treated as an employee with regard to such services, C is presumed (solely for purposes of section 199A(d)(1)(B) and paragraphs (a)(3) and (d) of this section) to be in the trade or business of performing services as an employee with respect to the services C provides to Law Firm 1 indirectly through Law Firm 2. Unless the presumption is rebutted with a showing that, under Federal tax law, regulations, and principles (including common-law employee classification rules), C's distributive share of Law Firm 2 income (including any guaranteed payments) will not be QBI for purposes of section 199A. The results in this example would not change if, instead of contracting with Law Firm 1, Law Firm 2 was instead admitted as a partner in Law Firm 1.

(C) *Example 3.* E is an engineer employed as a senior project engineer in an engineering firm, Engineering Firm. Engineering Firm is a partnership for Federal tax purposes and structured such that after 10 years, senior project engineers are considered for partner if certain career milestones are met. After 10 years, E meets those career milestones and is admitted as a partner in Engineering Firm. As a partner in Engineering Firm, E shares in the net profits of Engineering Firm, and also otherwise satisfies the requirements under Federal tax law, regulations, and principles (including common-law employee classification rules) to be respected as a partner. E is presumed (solely for purposes of section 199A(d)(1)(B) and paragraphs (a)(3) and (d) of this section) to be in the trade or business of performing services as an employee with respect to the services E provides to Engineering Firm. However, E is able to rebut the presumption by showing that E became a partner in Engineering Firm as a career milestone, shares in the overall net profits in Engineering Firm, and otherwise satisfies the requirements under Federal tax law, regulations, and principles (including common-law employee classification rules) to be respected as a partner.

(D) *Example 4.* F is a financial advisor employed by a financial advisory firm, Advisory Firm, a partnership for Federal tax purposes, as a fulltime employee and is treated as such for Federal employment tax purposes. F has taxable income below the threshold amount. Advisory Firm is a partnership and offers F the opportunity to be admitted as a partner. F elects to be admitted as a partner to Advisory Firm and is

**Reg. §1.199A-5(d)(3)(iii)**

admitted as a partner to Advisory Firm. As a partner in Advisory Firm, F shares in the net profits of Advisory Firm, is obligated to Advisory Firm in ways that F was not previously obligated as an employee, is no longer entitled to certain benefits available only to employees of Advisory Firm, and has materially modified his relationship with Advisory Firm. F's share of net profits is not subject to a floor or capped at a dollar amount. F is presumed (solely for purposes of section 199A(d)(1)(B) and paragraphs (a)(3) and (d) of this section) to be in the trade or business of performing services as an employee with respect to the services F provides to Advisory Firm. However, F is able to rebut the presumption by showing that F became a partner in Advisory Firm by sharing in the profits of Advisory Firm, materially modifying F's relationship with Advisory Firm, and otherwise satisfying the requirements under Federal tax law, regulations, and principles (including common-law employee classification rules) to be respected as a partner.

(e) *Applicability date.*—(1) *General rule.*—Except as provided in paragraph (e)(2) of this section, the provisions of this section apply to taxable years ending after February 8, 2019.

(2) *Exceptions.*—(i) *Anti-abuse rules.*—The provisions of paragraphs (c)(2) and (d)(3) of this section apply to taxable years ending after December 22, 2017.

(ii) *Non-calendar year RPE.*—For purposes of determining QBI, W-2 wages, UBIA of qualified property, and the aggregate amount of qualified REIT dividends and qualified PTP income, if an individual receives any of these items from an RPE with a taxable year that begins before January 1, 2018, and ends after December 31, 2017, such items are treated as having been incurred by the individual during the individual's taxable year in which or with which such RPE taxable year ends. [Reg. § 1.199A-5.]

☐ [T.D. 9847, 2-4-2019.]

[Reg. § 1.199A-6]

**§ 1.199A-6. Relevant passthrough entities (RPEs), publicly traded partnerships (PTPs), trusts, and estates.**—(a) *Overview.*—This section provides special rules for RPEs, PTPs, trusts, and estates necessary for the computation of the section 199A deduction of their owners or beneficiaries. Paragraph (b) of this section provides computational and reporting rules for RPEs necessary for individuals who own interests in RPEs to calculate their section 199A deduction. Paragraph (c) of this section provides computational and reporting rules for PTPs necessary for individuals who own interests in PTPs to calculate their section 199A deduction. Paragraph (d) of this section provides computational and reporting rules for trusts (other than grantor trusts) and estates necessary for their beneficiaries to calculate their section 199A deduction.

(b) *Computational and reporting rules for RPEs.*—(1) *In general.*—An RPE must determine and report information attributable to any trades or businesses it is engaged in necessary for its owners to determine their section 199A deduction.

(2) *Computational rules.*—Using the following four rules, an RPE must determine the items necessary for individuals who own interests in the RPE to calculate their section 199A deduction under § 1.199A-1(c) or (d). An RPE that chooses to aggregate trades or businesses under the rules of § 1.199A-4 may determine these items for the aggregated trade or business.

(i) First, the RPE must determine if it is engaged in one or more trades or businesses. The RPE must also determine whether any of its trades or businesses is an SSTB under the rules of § 1.199A-5.

(ii) Second, the RPE must apply the rules in § 1.199A-3 to determine the QBI for each trade or business engaged in directly.

(iii) Third, the RPE must apply the rules in § 1.199A-2 to determine the W-2 wages and UBIA of qualified property for each trade or business engaged in directly.

(iv) Fourth, the RPE must determine whether it has any qualified REIT dividends as defined in § 1.199A-3(c)(1) earned directly or through another RPE. The RPE must also determine the amount of qualified PTP income as defined in § 1.199A-3(c)(2) earned directly or indirectly through investments in PTPs.

(3) *Reporting rules for RPEs.*—(i) *Trade or business directly engaged in.*—An RPE must separately identify and report on the Schedule K-1 issued to its owners for any trade or business (including an aggregated trade or business) engaged in directly by the RPE—

(A) Each owner's allocable share of QBI, W-2 wages, and UBIA of qualified property attributable to each such trade or business; and

(B) Whether any of the trades or businesses described in paragraph (b)(3)(i) of this section is an SSTB.

(ii) *Other items.*—An RPE must also report on an attachment to the Schedule K-1, any QBI, W-2 wages, UBIA of qualified property, or SSTB determinations, reported to it by any RPE in which the RPE owns a direct or indirect interest. The RPE must also report each owner's allocated share of any qualified REIT dividends received by the RPE (including through another RPE) as well as any qualified PTP income or loss received by the RPE for each PTP in which the RPE holds an interest (including through another RPE). Such information can be reported on an amended or late filed return to the extent that the period of limitations remains open.

(iii) *Failure to report information.*—If an RPE fails to separately identify or report on the Schedule K-1 (or any attachments thereto) issued to an owner an item described in paragraph (b)(3)(i) of this section, the owner's share (and the share of any upper-tier indirect owner) of each unreported item of positive QBI, W-2 wages, or UBIA of qualified property attributable to trades or businesses engaged in by that RPE will be presumed to be zero.

(c) *Computational and reporting rules for PTPs.*—(1) *Computational rules.*—Each PTP must determine its QBI under the rules of § 1.199A-3 for each trade or business in which the PTP is engaged in directly. The PTP must also determine whether any of the trades or businesses it is engaged in directly is an SSTB.

(2) *Reporting rules.*—Each PTP is required to separately identify and report the information described in paragraph (c)(1) of this section on Schedules K-1 issued to its partners. Each PTP must also determine and report any qualified REIT dividends or qualified PTP income or loss received by the PTP including through an RPE, a REIT, or another PTP. A PTP is not required to determine or report W-2 wages or the UBIA of qualified property attributable to trades or businesses it is engaged in directly.

(d) *Application to trusts, estates, and beneficiaries.*—(1) *In general.*—A trust or estate computes its section 199A deduction based on the QBI, W-2 wages, UBIA of qualified property, qualified REIT dividends, and qualified PTP income that are allocated to the trust or estate. An individual beneficiary of a trust or estate takes into account any QBI, W-2 wages, UBIA of qualified property, qualified REIT dividends, and qualified PTP income allocated from a trust or estate in calculating the beneficiary's section 199A deduction, in the same manner as though the items had been allocated from an RPE. For purposes of this section and §§ 1.199A-1 through 1.199A-5, a trust or estate is treated as an RPE to the extent it allocates QBI and other items to its beneficiaries, and is treated as an individual to the extent it retains the QBI and other items.

(2) *Grantor trusts.*—To the extent that the grantor or another person is treated as owning all or part of a trust under sections 671 through 679, such person computes its section 199A deduction as if that person directly conducted the activities of the trust with respect to the portion of the trust treated as owned by the grantor or other person.

(3) *Non-grantor trusts and estates.*—(i) *Calculation at entity level.*—A trust or estate must calculate its QBI, W-2 wages, UBIA of qualified property, qualified REIT dividends, and qualified PTP income. The QBI of a trust or estate must be computed by allocating qualified items of deduction described in section 199A(c)(3) in accordance with the classification of those deductions under § 1.652(b)-3(a), and deductions not directly attributable within the meaning of § 1.652(b)-3(b) (other deductions) are

allocated in a manner consistent with the rules in § 1.652(b)-3(b). Any depletion and depreciation deductions described in section 642(e) and any amortization deductions described in section 642(f) that otherwise are properly included in the computation of QBI are included in the computation of QBI of the trust or estate, regardless of how those deductions may otherwise be allocated between the trust or estate and its beneficiaries for other purposes of the Code.

(ii) *Allocation among trust or estate and beneficiaries.*—The QBI (including any amounts that may be less than zero as calculated at the trust or estate level), W-2 wages, UBIA of qualified property, qualified REIT dividends, and qualified PTP income of a trust or estate are allocated to each beneficiary and to the trust or estate based on the relative proportion of the trust's or estate's *distributable net income (DNI)*, as defined by section 643(a), for the taxable year that is distributed or required to be distributed to the beneficiary or is retained by the trust or estate. For this purpose, the trust's or estate's DNI is determined with regard to the separate share rule of section 663(c), but without regard to section 199A. If the trust or estate has no DNI for the taxable year, any QBI, W-2 wages, UBIA of qualified property, qualified REIT dividends, and qualified PTP income are allocated entirely to the trust or estate.

(iii) [Reserved]

(iv) *Threshold amount.*—The threshold amount applicable to a trust or estate is $157,500 for any taxable year beginning before 2019. For taxable years beginning after 2018, the threshold amount shall be $157,500 increased by the cost-of-living adjustment as outlined in § 1.199A-1(b)(12). For purposes of determining whether a trust or estate has taxable income in excess of the threshold amount, the taxable income of the trust or estate is determined after taking into account any distribution deduction under sections 651 or 661.

(v) [Reserved]

(vi) *Electing small business trusts.*—An electing small business trust (ESBT) is entitled to the deduction under section 199A. Any section 199A deduction attributable to the assets in the S portion of the ESBT is to be taken into account by the S portion. The S portion of the ESBT must take into account the QBI and other items from any S corporation owned by the ESBT, the grantor portion of the ESBT must take into account the QBI and other items from any assets treated as owned by a grantor or another person (owned portion) of a trust under sections 671 through 679, and the non-S portion of the ESBT must take into account any QBI and other items from any other entities or assets owned by the ESBT. For purposes of determining whether the taxable income of an ESBT exceeds the threshold amount, the S portion and the non-S portion of an ESBT are treated as a single trust. *See* § 1.641(c)-1.

(vii) *Anti-abuse rule for creation of a trust to avoid exceeding the threshold amount.*—A trust formed or funded with a principal purpose of avoiding, or of using more than one, threshold amount for purposes of calculating the deduction under section 199A will not be respected as a separate trust entity for purposes of determining the threshold amount for purposes of section 199A. *See also* § 1.643(f)-1 of the regulations.

(viii) *Example.*—The following example illustrates the application of paragraph (d) of this section.

(A) *Example*—(1) *Computation of DNI and inclusion and deduction amounts*—(i) *Trust's distributive share of partnership items.* Trust, an irrevocable testamentary complex trust, is a 25% partner in PRS, a family partnership that operates a restaurant that generates QBI and W-2 wages. A and B, Trust's beneficiaries, own the remaining 75% of PRS directly. In 2018, PRS properly allocates gross income from the restaurant of $55,000, and expenses directly allocable to the restaurant of $45,000 (including W-2 wages of $25,000, and miscellaneous expenses of $20,000) to Trust. These items are properly included in

Trust's DNI. PRS distributes $10,000 of cash to Trust in 2018.

(ii) *Trust's activities.* In addition to its interest in PRS, Trust also operates a family bakery conducted through an LLC wholly-owned by the Trust that is treated as a disregarded entity. In 2018, the bakery produces $100,000 of gross income and $155,000 of expenses directly allocable to operation of the bakery (including W-2 wages of $50,000, rental expense of $75,000, miscellaneous expenses of $25,000, and depreciation deductions of $5,000). (The net loss from the bakery operations is not subject to any loss disallowance provisions outside of section 199A.) Trust maintains a reserve of $5,000 for depreciation. Trust also has $125,000 of UBIA of qualified property in the bakery. For purposes of computing its section 199A deduction, Trust and its beneficiaries have properly chosen to aggregate the family restaurant conducted through PRS with the bakery conducted directly by Trust under § 1.199A-4. Trust also owns various investment assets that produce portfolio-type income consisting of dividends ($25,000), interest ($15,000), and tax-exempt interest ($15,000). Accordingly, Trust has the following items which are properly included in Trust's DNI:

Table 1 to Paragraph (d)(3)(viii)(A)(1)(ii)

| | |
|---|---|
| Interest Income | 15,000 |
| Dividends | 25,000 |
| Tax-exempt interest | 15,000 |
| Net business loss from PRS and bakery | (45,000) |
| Trustee commissions | 3,000 |
| State and local taxes | 5,000 |

(iii) *Allocation of deductions under § 1.652(b)-3 (Directly attributable expenses).* In computing Trust's DNI for the taxable year, the distributive share of expenses of PRS are directly attributable under § 1.652(b)-3(a) to the distributive share of income of PRS. Accordingly, Trust has gross business income of $155,000 ($55,000 from PRS and $100,000 from the bakery) and direct business expenses of $200,000 ($45,000 from PRS and $155,000 from the bakery). In addition, $1,000 of the trustee commissions and $1,000 of state and local taxes are directly attributable under § 1.652(b)-3(a) to Trust's business income. Accordingly, Trust has excess business deductions of $47,000. Pursuant to its authority recognized under § 1.652(b)-3(d), Trust allocates the $47,000 excess business deductions as follows: $15,000 to the interest income, resulting in $0 interest income, $25,000 to the dividends, resulting in $0 dividend income, and $7,000 to the tax exempt interest.

(iv) *Allocation of deductions under § 1.652(b)-3 (Non-directly attributable expenses).* The trustee must allocate the sum of the balance of the trustee commissions ($2,000) and state and

local taxes ($4,000) to Trust's remaining tax-exempt interest income, resulting in $2,000 of tax exempt interest.

(v) *Amounts included in taxable income.* For 2018, Trust has DNI of $2,000. Pursuant to Trust's governing instrument, Trustee distributes 50%, or $1,000, of that DNI to A, an individual who is a discretionary beneficiary of Trust. In addition, Trustee is required to distribute 25%, or $500, of that DNI to B, a current income beneficiary of Trust. Trust retains the remaining 25% of DNI. Consequently, with respect to the $1,000 distribution A receives from Trust, A properly excludes $1,000 of tax-exempt interest income under section 662(b). With respect to the $500 distribution B receives from Trust, B properly excludes $500 of tax exempt interest income under section 662(b). Because the DNI consists entirely of tax-exempt income, Trust deducts $0 under section 661 with respect to the distributions to A and B.

(2) *Section 199A deduction*—(i) *Trust's W-2 wages and QBI.* For the 2018 taxable year, prior to allocating the beneficiaries' shares of the section

199A items, Trust has $75,000 ($25,000 from PRS + $50,000 of Trust) of W-2 wages. Trust also has $125,000 of UBIA of qualified property. Trust has negative QBI of ($47,000) ($155,000 gross income from aggregated businesses less the sum of $200,000 direct expenses from aggregated businesses and $2,000 directly attributable business expenses from Trust under the rules of § 1.652(b)-3(a)).

(*ii*) *A's Section 199A deduction computation.* Because the $1,000 Trust distribution to A equals one-half of Trust's DNI, A has W-2 wages from Trust of $37,500. A also has W-2 wages of $2,500 from a trade or business outside of Trust (computed without regard to A's interest in Trust), which A has properly aggregated under § 1.199A-4 with the Trust's trade or businesses (the family's restaurant and bakery), for a total of $40,000 of W-2 wages from the aggregate trade or businesses. A also has $62,500 of UBIA from Trust and $25,000 of UBIA of qualified property from the trade or business outside of Trust for $87,500 of total UBIA of qualified property. A has $100,000 of QBI from the non-Trust trade or businesses in which A owns an interest. Because the $1,000 Trust distribution to A equals one-half of Trust's DNI, A has (negative) QBI from Trust of ($23,500). A's total QBI is determined by combining the $100,000 QBI from non-Trust sources with the ($23,500) QBI from Trust for a total of $76,500 of QBI. Assume that A's taxable income is $357,500, which exceeds A's applicable threshold amount for 2018 by $200,000. A's tentative deductible amount is $15,300 (20% x $76,500 of QBI), limited to the greater of (i) $20,000 (50% x $40,000 of W-2 wages), or (ii) $12,187.50 ($10,000, 25% x $40,000 of W-2 wages, plus $2,187.50, 2.5% x $87,500 of UBIA of qualified property). A's section 199A deduction is equal to the lesser of $15,300, or $71,500 (20% x $357,500 of taxable income). Accordingly, A's section 199A deduction for 2018 is $15,300.

(*iii*) *B's Section 199A deduction computation.* For 2018, B's taxable income is below the threshold amount so B is not subject to the W-2 wage limitation. Because the $500 Trust distribution to B equals one-quarter of Trust's DNI, B has a total of ($11,750) of QBI. B also has no QBI from non-Trust trades or businesses, so B has a total of ($11,750) of QBI. Accordingly, B's section 199A deduction for 2018 is zero. The ($11,750) of QBI is carried over to 2019 as a loss from a qualified business in the hands of B pursuant to section 199A(c)(2).

(*iv*) *Trust's Section 199A deduction computation.* For 2018, Trust's taxable income is below the threshold amount so it is not subject to the W-2 wage limitation. Because Trust retained 25% of Trust's DNI, Trust is allocated 25% of its QBI, which is ($11,750). Trust's section 199A deduction for 2018 is zero. The ($11,750) of QBI is carried over to 2019 as a loss from a qualified business in the hands of Trust pursuant to section 199A(c)(2).

(B) [Reserved]

(e) *Applicability date.*—(1) *General rule.*—Except as provided in paragraph (e)(2) of this section, the provisions of this section apply to taxable years ending after February 8, 2019.

(2) *Exceptions.*—(i) *Anti-abuse rules.*—The provisions of paragraph (d)(3)(vii) of this section apply to taxable years ending after December 22, 2017.

(ii) *Non-calendar year RPE.*—For purposes of determining QBI, W-2 wages, UBIA of qualified property, and the aggregate amount of qualified REIT dividends and qualified PTP income, if an individual receives any of these items from an RPE with a taxable year that begins before January 1, 2018, and ends after December 31, 2017, such items are treated as having been incurred by the individual during the individual's taxable year in which or with which such RPE taxable year ends. [Reg. § 1.199A-6.]

☐ [T.D. 9847, 2-4-2019.]

### [Reg. § 1.643(f)-1]

§ 1.643(f)-1. Treatment of multiple trusts.— (a) *General rule.*—For purposes of subchapter J of chapter 1 of subtitle A of Title 26 of the United States Code, two or more trusts will be aggregated and treated as a single trust if such trusts have substantially the same grantor or grantors and substantially the same primary beneficiary or beneficiaries, and if a principal purpose for establishing one or more of such trusts or for contributing additional cash or other property to such trusts is the avoidance of Federal income tax. For purposes of applying this rule, spouses will be treated as one person.

(b) *Applicability date.*—The provisions of this section apply to taxable years ending after August 16, 2018. [Reg. § 1.643(f)-1.]

☐ [T.D. 9847, 2-4-2019.]

### [Reg. § 1.962-1]

§ 1.962-1. Limitation of tax for individuals on amounts included in gross income under section 951(a).—(a) *In general.*—An individual United States shareholder may, in accordance with § 1.962-2, elect to have the provisions of section 962 apply for his taxable year. In such case—

(1) The tax imposed under chapter 1 of the Internal Revenue Code on all amounts which are included in his gross income for such taxable year under section 951(a) shall (in lieu of the tax determined under section 1) be an amount equal to the tax which would be imposed under section 11 if such amounts were received by a domestic corporation (determined in accordance with paragraph (b)(1) of this section), and

(2) For purposes of applying section 960(a)(1) (relating to foreign tax credit) such

amounts shall be treated as if received by a domestic corporation (as provided in paragraph (b)(2) of this section).

Thus, an individual United States shareholder may elect to be subject to tax at corporate rates on amounts included in his gross income under section 951(a) and to have the benefit of a credit for certain foreign tax paid with respect to the earnings and profits attributable to such amounts. Section 962 also provides rules for the treatment of an actual distribution of earnings and profits previously taxed in accordance with an election of the benefits of this section. See § 1.962-3. For transitional rules for certain taxable years, see § 1.962-4.

(b) *Rules of application.*—For purposes of this section—

(1) *Application of section 11.*—For purposes of applying section 11 for a taxable year as provided in paragraph (a)(1) of this section in the case of an electing United States shareholder—

(i) *Determination of taxable income.*—The term *taxable income* means the excess of—

(A) The sum of—

(1) All amounts required to be included in his gross income under section 951(a) for the taxable year with respect to a foreign corporation of which he is a United States shareholder, including—

(i) His section 965(a) inclusion amounts (as defined in § 1.965-1(f)(38)); and

(ii) His domestic pass-through owner shares (as defined in § 1.965-1(f)(21)) of section 965(a) inclusion amounts with respect to deferred foreign income corporations (as defined in § 1.965-1(f)(17)) of which he is a United States shareholder; plus

(2) [Reserved]

(3) All amounts which would be required to be included in his gross income under section 78 for the taxable year with respect to the amounts referred to in paragraph (b)(1)(i)(A)(1) and (2) of this section if the shareholder were a domestic corporation; over

(B) The sum of the following deductions, but no other deductions or amounts—

(1) His section 965(c) deduction amount (as defined in § 1.965-1(f)(42)) for the taxable year;

(2) His domestic pass-through owner shares of section 965(c) deduction amounts corresponding to the amounts referred to in paragraph (b)(1)(i)(A)(1)(ii) of this section; and

(3) [Reserved]

(ii) *Limitation on surtax exemption.*—The surtax exemption provided by section 11(c) shall not exceed an amount which bears the same ratio to $25,000 ($50,000 in the case of a taxable year ending after December 31, 1974, and before January 1, 1976) as the amounts included in his gross income under section 951(a) for the taxable year bear to his pro rata share of the earnings

and profits for the taxable year of all controlled foreign corporations with respect to which such United States shareholder includes any amount in his gross income under section 951(a) for the taxable year.

(2) *Allowance of foreign tax credit.*—(i) *In general.*—Subject to the applicable limitation of section 904 and to the provisions of this subparagraph, there shall be allowed as a credit against the United States tax on the amounts described in subparagraph (1)(i) of this paragraph the foreign income, war profits, and excess profits taxes deemed paid under section 960(a)(1) by the electing United States shareholder with respect to such amounts.

(ii) *Application of section 960(a)(1).*—In applying section 960 (a)(1) for purposes of this subparagraph in the case of an electing United States shareholder, the term "domestic corporation" as used in sections 960(a)(1) and 78, and the term "corporation" as used in section 901, shall be treated as referring to such shareholder with respect to the amounts described in subparagraph (1)(i) of this paragraph.

(iii) *Carryback and carryover of excess tax deemed paid.*—For purposes of this subparagraph, any amount by which the foreign income, war profits, and excess profits taxes deemed paid by the electing United States shareholder for any taxable year under section 960(a)(1) exceed the limitation determined under subdivision (iv)(a) of this subparagraph shall be treated as a carryback and carryover of excess tax paid under section 904(d), except that in no case shall excess tax paid be deemed paid in a taxable year if an election under section 962 by such shareholders does not apply for such taxable year. Such carrybacks and carryovers shall be applied only against the United States tax on amounts described in subparagraph (1)(i) of this paragraph.

(iv) *Limitation on credit.*—For purposes of determining the limitation under section 904 on the amount of the credit for foreign income, war profits, and excess profit taxes—

(A) Deemed paid with respect to amounts described in subparagraph (1)(i) of this paragraph, the electing United States shareholder's taxable income shall be considered to consist only of the amounts described in such subparagraph (1)(i), and

(B) Paid with respect to amounts other than amounts described in subparagraph (1)(i) of this paragraph, the electing United States shareholder's taxable income shall be considered to consist only of amounts other than the amounts described in such subparagraph (1)(i).

(v) *Effect of choosing benefits of sections 901 to 905.*—The provisions of this subparagraph shall apply for a taxable year whether or not the electing United States shareholder chooses the benefits of subpart A of part III of subchapter N of chapter 1 (sections 901 to 905) of the Internal Revenue Code for such year.

(c) *Illustration.*—The application of this section may be illustrated by the following example:

*Example.* Throughout his taxable year ending December 31, 1964, A, an unmarried individual who is not the head of a household, owns 60 of the 100 shares of the one class of stock in foreign corporation M and 80 of the 100 shares of the one class of stock in foreign corporation N. A and corporations M and N use the calendar year as a taxable year, corporations M and N are controlled foreign corporations throughout the period here involved, and neither corporation is a less developed country corporation. The earnings and profits and subpart F income of, and the foreign income taxes paid by, such corporations for 1964 are as follows:

| | M | N |
|---|---|---|
| Pretax earnings and profits | $500,000 | $1,200,000 |
| Foreign income taxes | 200,000 | 400,000 |
| Earnings and profits | 300,000 | 800,000 |
| Subpart F income | 150,000 | 750,000 |

Apart from his section 951(a) income, A has gross income of $200,600 and $100,000 of deductions attributable to such income. He is required to include $90,000 (.60 × $150,000) in gross income under section 951(a) with respect to M Corporation and $600,000 (.80 × $750,000) with respect to N Corporation. A elects to have the provisions of section 962 apply for 1964 and computes his tax as follows:

| | | | |
|---|---|---|---|
| Tax on amounts included under sec. 951(a): | | | |
| Income under sec. 951(a) from M Corporation | $90,000 | | |
| Gross-up under secs. 960(a)(1) and 78 ($90,000/$300,000 × $200,000) | 60,000 | | |
| Income under sec. 951(a) from N Corporation | $600,000 | | |
| Gross-up under secs. 960(a)(1) and 78 ($600,000/$800,000 × $400,000) | 300,000 | | |
| Taxable income under sec. 11 | $1,050,000 | | |
| Normal tax (.22 × $1,050,000) | | $231,000 | |
| Surtax exemption ([$90,000+$600,000]/[.60 × $300,000 + (.80 × $800,000)] × $25,000) | 21,036 | | |
| Subject to surtax under sec. 11 ($1,050,000 − $21,036) | 1,028,964 | | |
| Surtax (.28 × $1,028,964) | | 288,110 | |
| Tentative U.S. tax | | $519,110 | |
| Foreign tax credit ($60,000 + $300,000) | | 360,000 | |
| Total U.S. tax payable on amounts included under sec. 951(a) | | | $159,110 |
| Tax with respect to other income: | | | |
| Gross income | | 200,600 | |
| Less: | | | |
| Personal exemption | $600 | | |
| Deductions | 100,000 | 100,600 | |
| Taxable income | | $100,000 | |
| Tax with respect to such other taxable income | | | 59,340 |
| Total tax ($159,110 + $59,340) | | | $218,450 |

(d) *Applicability dates.*—Paragraph (b)(1)(i) of this section applies beginning the last taxable year of a foreign corporation that begins before January 1, 2018, and with respect to a United States person, for the taxable year in which or with which such taxable year of the foreign corporation ends. [Reg. § 1.962-1.]

☐ [T.D. 6858, 10-27-65. *Amended by T.D. 7413, 3-25-76 and T.D. 9846, 2-4-2019.*]

**[Reg. § 1.962-2]**

**§ 1.962-2. Election of limitation of tax for individuals.**—(a) *Who may elect.*—The election under section 962 may be made only by an individual (including a trust or estate) who is a United States shareholder (including an individual who is a United States shareholder because, by reason of section 958(b), he is considered to own stock of a foreign corporation owned (within the meaning of section 958(a)) by a domestic pass-through entity (as defined in § 1.965-1(f)(19))).

(b) *Time and manner of making election.*—Except as provided in § 1.962-4, a United States shareholder shall make an election under this section by filing a statement to such effect with his return for the taxable year with respect to which the election is made. The statement shall include the following information:

(1) The name, address, and taxable year of each controlled foreign corporation with respect to which the electing shareholder is a United States shareholder and of all other corporations, partnerships, trusts, or estates in any applicable chain of ownership described in section 958(a);

(2) The amounts, on a corporation-by-corporation basis, which are included in such shareholder's gross income for his taxable year under section 951(a);

(3) Such shareholder's pro rata share of the earnings and profits (determined under § 1.964-1) of each such controlled foreign corporation with respect to which such shareholder includes any amount in gross income for his taxable year under section 951(a) and the foreign income, war profits, excess profits, and similar taxes paid on or with respect to such earnings and profits;

(4) The amount of distributions received by such shareholder during his taxable year from each controlled foreign corporation referred to in subparagraph (1) of this paragraph from excludable section 962 earnings and profits (as defined in paragraph (b)(1)(i) of § 1.962-3), from taxable section 962 earnings and profits (as defined in paragraph (b)(1)(ii) of § 1.962-3), and from earnings and profits other than section 962 earnings and profits, showing the source of such amounts by taxable year; and

(5) Such further information as the Commissioner may prescribe by forms and accompanying instructions relating to such election.

(c) *Effect of election.*—(1) *In general.*—Except as provided in subparagraph (2) of this paragraph and § 1.962-4, an election under this section by a United States shareholder for a taxable year shall be applicable to all controlled foreign corporations with respect to which such shareholder includes any amount in gross income for his taxable year under section 951(a) and shall be binding for the taxable year for which such election is made.

(2) *Revocation.*—Upon application by the United States shareholder, an election made under this election may, subject to the approval of the Commissioner, be revoked. Approval will not be granted unless a material and substantial change in circumstances occurs which could not have been anticipated when the election was made. The application for consent to revocation shall be made by the United States shareholder's

mailing a letter for such purpose to Commissioner of Internal Revenue, Attention: T.R., Washington, D.C. 20224 containing a statement of the facts upon which such shareholder relies in requesting such consent.

(d) *Applicability dates.*—Paragraph (a) of this section applies beginning the last taxable year of a foreign corporation that begins before January 1, 2018, and with respect to a United States person, for the taxable year in which or with which such taxable year of the foreign corporation ends. [Reg. § 1.962-2.]

☐ [T.D. 6858, 10-27-65. *Amended by* T.D. 9846, 2-4-2019.]

## [Reg. § 1.965-0]

**§ 1.965-0. Outline of section 965 regulations.**—This section lists the headings for §§ 1.965-1 through 1.965-9.

*§ 1.965-1 Overview, general rules, and definitions.*

(a) Overview.

(1) In general.

(2) Scope.

(b) Section 965(a) inclusion amounts.

(1) Inclusion of the pro rata share of the section 965(a) earnings amount.

(2) Reduction by the allocable share of the aggregate foreign E&P deficit.

(c) Section 965(c) deduction amounts.

(d) Treatment of specified foreign corporation as a controlled foreign corporation.

(e) Special rule for certain controlled domestic partnerships.

(1) In general.

(2) Definition of a controlled domestic partnership.

(f) Definitions.

(1) 8 percent rate amount.

(2) 8 percent rate equivalent percentage.

(3) 15.5 percent rate amount.

(4) 15.5 percent rate equivalent percentage.

(5) Accounts payable.

(6) Accounts receivable.

(7) Accumulated post-1986 deferred foreign income.

(8) Aggregate foreign cash position.

(9) Aggregate foreign E&P deficit.

(10) Aggregate section 965(a) inclusion amount.

(11) Allocable share.

(12) Bona fide hedging transaction.

(13) Cash-equivalent asset.

(i) In general.

(ii) Specified commodity.

(14) Cash-equivalent asset hedging transaction.

(i) In general.

(ii) Aggregate hedging transactions.

(15) Cash measurement dates.

(16) Cash position.

(2) Election to make adjustments to basis to account for the application of section 965(b).

  (i) In general.

  (ii) Basis adjustments.

    (A) Increase in basis with respect to a deferred foreign income corporation.

      *(1)* In general.

      *(2)* Limited basis adjustment.

    (B) Reduction in basis with respect to an E&P deficit foreign corporation.

      *(1)* In general.

      *(2)* Limited basis adjustment.

    (C) Section 962 election.

  (iii) Rules regarding the election.

    (A) Consistency requirement.

    (B) Manner of making election.

      *(1)* Timing.

        *(i)* In general.

        *(ii)* Transition rule.

      *(2)* Election statement.

(g) Gain reduction rule.

  (1) Reduction in gain recognized under section 961(b)(2) by reason of distributions attributable to section 965 previously taxed earnings and profits in the inclusion year.

    (i) In general.

    (ii) Definition of section 965 previously taxed earnings and profits.

  (2) Reduction in basis by an amount equal to the gain reduction amount.

(h) Rules of application for specified basis adjustments.

  (1) Timing of basis adjustments.

  (2) Netting of basis adjustments.

  (3) Gain recognition for reduction in excess of basis.

  (4) Adjustments with respect to each share.

    (i) Section 958(a) stock.

    (ii) Applicable property.

  (5) Stock or property for which adjustments are made.

    (i) In general.

    (ii) Special rule for an interest in a foreign pass-through entity.

(i) Definitions.

  (1) Applicable property.

  (2) Foreign pass-through entity.

  (3) Property.

(j) Examples.

  (1) Example 1.

    (i) Facts.

    (ii) Analysis.

      (A) Adjustments to section 959(c) classification of earnings and profits for inclusion under section 951(a)(1)(A) without regard to section 965.

      (B) Distributions between specified foreign corporations before January 1, 2018.

      (C) Section 965(a) inclusion amount.

        *(1)* CFC1 section 965(a) earnings amount.

        *(2)* CFC2 section 965(a) earnings amount.

        *(3)* Effect on earnings and profits described in section 959(c)(2) and (3).

      (D) Distribution to United States shareholder.

      (E) Section 902 and section 960 consequences.

        *(1)* Distribution by and inclusions with respect to CFC2.

        *(2)* Inclusions with respect to CFC1.

  (2) Example 2.

    (i) Facts.

    (ii) Analysis.

      (A) Adjustments to section 959(c) classification of earnings and profits for inclusion under section 951(a)(1)(A) without regard to section 965.

      (B) Distributions between specified foreign corporations before January 1, 2018.

      (C) Section 965(a) inclusion amount.

        *(1)* CFC1 section 965(a) earnings amount.

        *(2)* CFC2 section 965(a) earnings amount.

        *(3)* Effect on earnings and profits described in section 959(c)(2) and (3).

      (D) Distribution to United States shareholder.

  (3) Example 3.

    (i) Facts.

    (ii) Analysis.

      (A) Adjustments to section 959(c) classification of earnings and profits for inclusion under section 951(a)(1)(A) without regard to section 965.

      (B) Distributions between specified foreign corporations before January 1, 2018.

      (C) Section 965(a) inclusion amount.

        *(1)* CFC1 section 965(a) earnings amount.

        *(2)* CFC2 section 965(a) earnings amount.

        *(3)* Effect on earnings and profits described in section 959(c)(2) and (3).

      (D) Distribution to United States shareholder.

  (4) Example 4.

    (i) Facts.

    (ii) Analysis.

      (A) Adjustments to section 959(c) classification of earnings and profits for inclusion under section 951(a)(1)(A) without regard to section 965.

      (B) Distributions between specified foreign corporations before January 1, 2018.

      (C) Section 965(a) inclusion amount.

        *(1)* CFC1 section 965(a) earnings amount.

        *(2)* CFC2 section 965(a) earnings amount.

*(3)* Effect on earnings and profits described in section 959(c)(2) and (3).

(D) Distribution to United States shareholder.

*(1)* Distribution that is a specified payment.

*(2)* Distribution to United States shareholder.

(E) Section 902 and section 960 consequences.

(5) Example 5.

(A) Section 965(a) inclusion amount.

*(1)* CFC section 965(a) earnings amount.

*(2)* Effect on earnings and profits described in section 959(c)(2) and (3).

(6) Example 6.

(i) Facts.

(ii) Analysis.

(A) Adjustments to section 959(c) classification of earnings and profits for section 1248 inclusion.

(B) Section 965(a) inclusion amount.

(C) Distributions to United States shareholders.

(7) Example 7.

(i) Facts.

(ii) Analysis.

(8) Example 8.

(i) Facts.

(ii) Analysis.

(A) Application of the gain reduction rule.

(B) Adjustments to the basis of CFC1.

(9) Example 9.

(i) Facts.

(ii) Analysis.

(A) Application of the gain reduction rule.

(B) Adjustments to the basis of CFC1 and CFC2.

*§1.965-3 Section 965(c) deductions.*

(a) Scope.

(b) Rules for disregarding certain assets for determining aggregate foreign cash position.

(1) Disregard of certain obligations between related specified foreign corporations.

(2) Disregard of other assets upon demonstration of double-counting.

(3) Disregard of portion of cash position of noncorporate entities treated as specified foreign corporations.

(4) Examples.

(i) Example 1.

(A) Facts.

(B) Analysis.

*(1)* Loan from CFC1 to CFC2.

*(2)* Account receivable of CFC1 held by CFC2.

*(3)* Loan from CFC1 to CFC3.

(ii) Example 2.

(A) Facts.

(B) Analysis.

(iii) Example 3.

(A) Facts.

(B) Analysis.

(iv) Example 4.

(A) Facts.

(B) Analysis.

(v) Example 5.

(A) Facts.

(B) Analysis.

*(1)* Treatment of PS1.

*(2)* Treatment of PS2.

(c) Determination of aggregate foreign cash position for a section 958(a) U.S. shareholder inclusion year.

(1) Single section 958(a) U.S. shareholder inclusion year.

(2) Multiple section 958(a) U.S. shareholder inclusion years.

(i) Allocation to first section 958(a) U.S. shareholder inclusion year.

(ii) Allocation to succeeding section 958(a) U.S. shareholder inclusion years.

(3) Estimation of aggregate foreign cash position.

(4) Examples.

(i) Example 1.

(A) Facts.

(B) Analysis.

(ii) Example 2.

(A) Facts.

(B) Analysis.

(d) Increase of income by section 965(c) deduction of an expatriated entity.

(1) In general.

(2) Definition of expatriated entity.

(3) Definition of surrogate foreign corporation.

(e) Section 962 election.

(1) In general.

(2) Example.

(i) Facts.

(ii) Analysis.

(f) Treatment of section 965(c) deduction under certain provisions of the Internal Revenue Code.

(1) Section 63(d).

(2) Sections 705, 1367, and 1368.

(i) Adjustments to basis

(ii) S corporation accumulated adjustments account.

(iii) Example.

(A) Facts.

(B) Analysis.

(3) Section 1411.

(4) Section 4940.

(g) Domestic pass-through entities.

*§1.965-4 Disregard of certain transactions.*

(a) Scope.

(b) Transactions undertaken with a principal purpose of changing the amount of a section 965 element.

  (1) General rule.

  (2) Presumptions and exceptions for the application of the general rule.

    (ii) Definitions.

      (A) Relatedness.

      (B) Transfer.

        *(1)* In general.

        *(2)* Indirect transfer.

    (iii) Cash reduction transactions.

      (A) General rule.

      (B) Per se rules for certain distributions.

    (iv) E&P reduction transactions.

      (A) General rule.

        *(1)* Definition of pro rata share reduction transaction.

        *(2)* Definition of E&P deficit transaction.

      (B) Per se rule for internal group transactions.

      (C) Example.

        *(1)* Facts.

        *(2)* Analysis.

(c) Disregard of certain changes in method of accounting and entity classification elections.

  (1) Changes in method of accounting.

  (2) Entity classification elections.

(d) Definition of a section 965 element.

(e) Rules for applying paragraphs (b) and (c) of this section.

  (1) Determination of whether there is a change in the amount of a section 965 element.

  (2) Treatment of domestic pass-through owners as United States shareholders.

  (3) Exception for certain incorporation transactions.

    (i) In general.

    (ii) Aggregate foreign cash position.

  (4) Consequences of liquidation.

    (i) In general.

    (ii) Specified liquidation date.

(f) Disregard of certain transactions occurring between E&P measurement dates.

  (1) Disregard of specified payments.

  (2) Definition of specified payment.

  (3) Non-application of disregard rule.

  (4) Examples.

    (i) Example 1.

      (A) Facts.

      (B) Analysis.

    (ii) Example 2.

      (A) Facts.

      (B) Analysis.

    (iii) Example 3.

      (A) Facts.

      (B) Analysis.

    (iv) Example 4.

      (A) Facts.

      (B) Analysis.

    (v) Example 5.

      (A) Facts.

      (B) Analysis.

    (vi) Example 6.

      (A) Facts.

      (B) Analysis.

*§ 1.965-5 Allowance of credit or deduction for foreign income taxes.*

(a) Scope.

(b) Rules for foreign income taxes paid or accrued.

(c) Rules for foreign income taxes treated as paid or accrued.

  (1) Disallowed credit.

    (i) In general.

    (ii) Foreign income taxes deemed paid under section 960(a)(3) (as in effect on December 21, 2017).

    (iii) [Reserved]

  (2) Disallowed deduction.

  (3) Coordination with section 78.

    (i) In general.

    (ii) Domestic corporation that is a domestic pass-through owner.

(d) Applicable percentage.

  (1) In general.

  (2) No section 965(a) inclusion amount.

  (3) Applicable percentage for domestic pass-through owners.

  (4) Applicable percentage with respect to certain distributions of previously taxed earnings and profits.

*§ 1.965-6 Computation of foreign income taxes deemed paid and allocation and apportionment of deductions.*

(a) Scope.

(b) Computation of foreign income taxes deemed paid.

  (1) In general.

  (2) Dividend or inclusion in excess of post-1986 undistributed earnings.

  (3) Treatment of adjustment under section 965(b)(4)(B).

  (4) Section 902 fraction.

(c) Allocation and apportionment of deductions.

(d) Hovering deficits.

*§ 1.965-7 Elections, payment, and other special rules.*

(a) Scope.

(b) Section 965(h) election.

  (1) In general.

    (i) Amount of installments.

    (ii) Increased installments due to a deficiency or a timely filed or amended return.

      (A) In general.

      (B) Timing.

      (C) Exception for negligence, intentional disregard, or fraud.

(iv) [Reserved]

(2) Manner of making election.

(i) Eligibility.

(ii) Timing.

(iii) Election statement.

(f) Election to use alternative method for calculating post-1986 earnings and profits.

(1) Effect of election for specified foreign corporations that do not have a 52-53-week taxable year.

(2) Effect of election for specified foreign corporations that have a 52-53-week taxable year.

(3) Computation of post-1986 earnings and profits using alternative method.

(4) Definitions.

(i) 52-53-week taxable year.

(ii) Annualized earnings and profits amount.

(iii) Daily earnings amount.

(iv) Notional measurement date.

(5) Manner of making election.

(i) Eligibility.

(ii) Timing.

(iii) Election statement.

(6) Examples.

(i) Example 1.

(A) Facts.

(B) Analysis.

(ii) Example 2.

(A) Facts.

(B) Analysis.

(g) Definitions.

(1) Deferred net tax liability.

(2) REIT section 965 amounts.

(3) Section 965(h) election.

(4) Section 965(h) net tax liability.

(5) Section 965(i) election.

(6) Section 965(i) net tax liability.

(7) Section 965(m) election.

(8) Section 965(n) election.

(9) Specified individual.

(10) Total net tax liability under section 965.

(i) General rule.

(ii) Net income tax.

(iii) Foreign tax credits.

§1.965-8 *Affiliated groups (including consolidated groups).*

(a) Scope.

(b) Reduction of E&P net surplus shareholder's pro rata share of the section 965(a) earnings amount of a deferred foreign income corporation by the allocable share of the applicable share of the aggregate unused E&P deficit.

(1) In general.

(2) Consolidated group as part of an affiliated group.

(c) Designation of portion of excess aggregate foreign E&P deficit taken into account.

(1) In general.

(2) Consolidated group as part of an affiliated group.

(d) [Reserved]

(1) [Reserved]

(2) Consolidated groups.

(e) Treatment of a consolidated group as a single section 958(a) U.S. shareholder or a single person.

(1) In general.

(2) Limitation.

(3) Determination of section 965(c) deduction amount.

(f) Definitions.

(1) Aggregate unused E&P deficit.

(i) In general.

(ii) Reduction with respect to E&P net deficit shareholders that are not wholly owned by the affiliated group.

(2) Allocable share.

(3) Applicable share.

(4) Consolidated group aggregate foreign cash position.

(5) E&P net deficit shareholder.

(6) E&P net surplus shareholder.

(7) Excess aggregate foreign E&P deficit.

(8) Group cash ratio.

(9) Group ownership percentage.

(g) Examples.

(1) Example 1.

(i) Facts.

(A) In general.

(B) Facts relating to section 965.

(ii) Analysis.

(A) Section 965(a) inclusion amounts before application of section 965(b)(5).

(B) Application of section 965(b)(5).

*(1)* Determination of E&P net surplus shareholders and E&P net deficit shareholders.

*(2)* Determining section 965(a) inclusion amounts under section 965(b)(5).

(C) Aggregate foreign cash position.

(D) Section 965(c) deduction amount.

(2) Example 2.

(i) Facts.

(ii) Analysis.

(A) Section 965(a) inclusion amount.

*(1)* Single section 958(a) U.S. shareholder treatment.

*(2)* Determination of inclusion amount.

(B) Consolidated group aggregate foreign cash position.

(C) Section 965(a) deduction amount.

§1.965-9 *Applicability dates.*

(a) In general.

(b) Applicability dates for rules disregarding certain transactions.

[Reg. §1.965-0.]

☐ [*T.D.* 9846, 2-4-2019.]

[Reg. § 1.965-1]

## § 1.965-1. Overview, general rules, and definitions.—(a) *Overview.*—(1) *In general.*—
This section provides general rules and definitions under section 965. Section 1.965-2 provides rules relating to adjustments to earnings and profits and basis to determine and account for the application of section 965 and a rule that limits the amount of gain recognized under section 961(b)(2) by reason of distributions attributable to section 965 previously taxed earnings and profits (as defined in § 1.965-2(g)(1)(ii)) in the inclusion year. Section 1.965-3 provides rules regarding the determination of section 965(c) deductions. Section 1.965-4 sets forth rules that disregard certain transactions for purposes of section 965. Sections 1.965-5 and 1.965-6 provide rules with respect to foreign tax credits. Section 1.965-7 provides rules regarding elections and payments. Section 1.965-8 provides rules regarding affiliated groups, including consolidated groups. Section 1.965-9 provides dates of applicability. *See also* §§ 1.962-1 and 1.962-2 (providing rules regarding the application of section 962) and 1.986(c)-1 (providing rules regarding the application of section 986(c)).

(2) *Scope.*—Paragraph (b) of this section provides the general rules concerning section 965(a) inclusion amounts. Paragraph (c) of this section provides the general rule concerning section 965(c) deduction amounts. Paragraph (d) of this section provides a rule for specified foreign corporations that are not controlled foreign corporations. Paragraph (e) of this section treats certain controlled domestic partnerships as foreign partnerships for purposes of section 965. Paragraph (f) of this section provides definitions applicable for the section 965 regulations and §§ 1.962-1, 1.962-2, and 1.986(c)-1. Paragraph (g) of this section contains examples illustrating the general rules and definitions set forth in this section.

(b) *Section 965(a) inclusion amounts.*—(1) *Inclusion of the pro rata share of the section 965(a) earnings amount.*—For an inclusion year of a deferred foreign income corporation, the subpart F income of the deferred foreign income corporation (as otherwise determined for the inclusion year under section 952 and § 1.952-1) is increased by the section 965(a) earnings amount of the deferred foreign income corporation. *See* section 965(a). Accordingly, a section 958(a) U.S. shareholder with respect to a deferred foreign income corporation generally includes in gross income under section 951(a)(1) for the section 958(a) U.S. shareholder inclusion year its pro rata share of the section 965(a) earnings amount of the deferred foreign income corporation, translated (if necessary) into U.S. dollars using the spot rate on December 31, 2017, and subject to reduction under section 965(b), paragraph (b)(2) of this section, and § 1.965-8(b). The amount of the section 958(a) U.S. shareholder's inclusion with respect to a deferred foreign income corporation as re-

a result of section 965(a) and this paragraph (b)(1), as reduced under section 965(b), paragraph (b)(2) of this section, and § 1.965-8(b), as applicable, is referred to as the *section 965(a) inclusion amount*. Neither the section 965(a) earnings amount nor the section 965(a) inclusion amount is subject to the rules or limitations in section 952 or limited by the accumulated earnings and profits of the deferred foreign income corporation on the date of the inclusion.

(2) *Reduction by the allocable share of the aggregate foreign E&P deficit.*—For purposes of determining a section 958(a) U.S. shareholder's section 965(a) inclusion amount with respect to a deferred foreign income corporation, the U.S. dollar amount of the section 958(a) U.S. shareholder's pro rata share of the section 965(a) earnings amount of the deferred foreign income corporation, translated (if necessary) into U.S. dollars using the spot rate on December 31, 2017, is reduced by the deferred foreign income corporation's allocable share of the section 958(a) U.S. shareholder's aggregate foreign E&P deficit. *See* section 965(b). If the section 958(a) U.S. shareholder is a member of a consolidated group, under § 1.965-8(e), all section 958(a) U.S. shareholders that are members of the consolidated group are treated as a single section 958(a) U.S. shareholder for purposes of this paragraph (b)(2).

(c) *Section 965(c) deduction amounts.*—For a section 958(a) U.S. shareholder inclusion year, a section 958(a) U.S. shareholder is generally allowed a deduction in an amount equal to the section 965(c) deduction amount.

(d) *Treatment of specified foreign corporation as a controlled foreign corporation.*—A specified foreign corporation described in section 965(e)(1)(B) and paragraph (f)(45)(i)(B) of this section that is not otherwise a controlled foreign corporation is treated as a controlled foreign corporation solely for purposes of paragraph (b) of this section and sections 951, 961, and § 1.1411-10. *See* 965(e)(2).

(e) *Special rule for certain controlled domestic partnerships.*—(1) *In general.*—For purposes of the section 965 regulations, a controlled domestic partnership is treated as a foreign partnership for purposes of determining the section 958(a) U.S. shareholder of a specified foreign corporation and the section 958(a) stock of the specified foreign corporation owned by the section 958(a) U.S. shareholder if the following conditions are satisfied—

(i) Without regard to this paragraph (e), the controlled domestic partnership is a section 958(a) U.S. shareholder of the specified foreign corporation and thus owns section 958(a) stock of the specified foreign corporation (*tested section 958(a) stock*);

(ii) If the controlled domestic partnership (and all other controlled domestic partnerships in the chain of ownership of the specified foreign corporation) were treated as foreign—

(A) The specified foreign corporation would continue to be a specified foreign corporation; and

(B) At least one United States shareholder of the specified foreign corporation—

(1) Would be treated as a section 958(a) U.S. shareholder of the specified foreign corporation; and

(2) Would be treated as owning (within the meaning of section 958(a)) tested section 958(a) stock of the specified foreign corporation through another foreign corporation that is a direct or indirect partner in the controlled domestic partnership.

(2) *Definition of a controlled domestic partnership.*—For purposes of paragraph (e)(1) of this section, the term *controlled domestic partnership* means a domestic partnership that is controlled by a United States shareholder described in paragraph (e)(1)(ii)(B) of this section and persons related to the United States shareholder. For purposes of this paragraph (e)(2), control is determined based on all the facts and circumstances, except that a partnership will be deemed to be controlled by a United States shareholder and related persons if those persons, in the aggregate, own (directly or indirectly through one or more partnerships) more than 50 percent of the interests in the partnership capital or profits. For purposes of this paragraph (e)(2), a related person is, with respect to a United States shareholder, a person that is related (within the meaning of section 267(b) or 707(b)(1)) to the United States shareholder.

(f) *Definitions.*—This paragraph (f) provides definitions that apply for purposes of the section 965 regulations and §§1.962-1, 1.962-2, and 1.986(c)-1. Unless otherwise indicated, all amounts are expressed as positive numbers.

(1) *8 percent rate amount.*—The term *8 percent rate amount* means, with respect to a section 958(a) U.S. shareholder and a section 958(a) U.S. shareholder inclusion year, the excess, if any, of the section 958(a) U.S. shareholder's aggregate section 965(a) inclusion amount for the section 958(a) U.S. shareholder inclusion year over the amount of the section 958(a) U.S. shareholder's aggregate foreign cash position for the section 958(a) U.S. shareholder inclusion year as determined under §1.965-3(c).

(2) *8 percent rate equivalent percentage.*—The term *8 percent rate equivalent percentage* means, with respect to a section 958(a) U.S. shareholder and a section 958(a) U.S. shareholder inclusion year, the percentage that would result in the 8 percent rate amount being subject to an 8 percent rate of tax determined by only taking into account a deduction equal to such percentage of such amount and the highest rate of tax specified in section 11 for the section 958(a) U.S. shareholder inclusion year. In the case of a section 958(a) U.S. shareholder inclusion year of a sec-

tion 958(a) U.S. shareholder to which section 15 applies, the highest rate of tax under section 11 before the effective date of the change in rates and the highest rate of tax under section 11 after the effective date of such change will each be taken into account under the preceding sentence in the same proportions as the portion of the section 958(a) U.S. shareholder inclusion year that is before and after such effective date, respectively.

(3) *15.5 percent rate amount.*—The term *15.5 percent rate amount* means, with respect to a section 958(a) U.S. shareholder and a section 958(a) U.S. shareholder inclusion year, the amount of the section 958(a) U.S. shareholder's aggregate foreign cash position for the section 958(a) U.S. shareholder inclusion year as determined under §1.965-3(c) to the extent it does not exceed the section 958(a) U.S. shareholder's aggregate section 965(a) inclusion amount for the section 958(a) U.S. shareholder inclusion year.

(4) *15.5 percent rate equivalent percentage.*—The term *15.5 percent rate equivalent percentage*, with respect to a section 958(a) U.S. shareholder and a section 958(a) U.S. shareholder inclusion year, has the meaning provided for the term "8 percent rate equivalent percentage" applied by substituting "15.5 percent rate amount" for "8 percent rate amount" and "15.5 percent rate of tax" for "8 percent rate of tax."

(5) *Accounts payable.*—The term *accounts payable* means payables arising from the purchase of property described in section 1221(a)(1) or section 1221(a)(8) or the receipt of services from vendors or suppliers, provided the payables have a term upon issuance of less than one year.

(6) *Accounts receivable.*—The term *accounts receivable* means receivables described in section 1221(a)(4) that have a term upon issuance of less than one year.

(7) *Accumulated post-1986 deferred foreign income.*—(i) *In general.*—The term *accumulated post-1986 deferred foreign income* means, with respect to a specified foreign corporation, the post-1986 earnings and profits of the specified foreign corporation except to the extent such earnings and profits—

(A) Are attributable to income of the specified foreign corporation that is effectively connected with the conduct of a trade or business within the United States and subject to tax under chapter 1;

(B) If distributed, would, in the case of a controlled foreign corporation, be excluded from the gross income of a United States shareholder under section 959; or

(C) If distributed, would, in the case of a controlled foreign corporation that has shareholders that are not United States shareholders on an E&P measurement date, be excluded from the gross income of such shareholders under section 959 if such shareholders were United States shareholders, determined by applying the principles of Revenue Ruling 82-16, 1982-1 C.B. 106.

(ii) *Earnings and profits attributable to sub-part F income in the same taxable year as an E&P measurement date.*—For purposes of determining the accumulated post-1986 deferred foreign income of a specified foreign corporation as of an E&P measurement date, earnings and profits of the specified foreign corporation that are or would be, applying the principles of Revenue Ruling 82-16, 1982-1 C.B. 106, described in section 959(c)(2) by reason of subpart F income (as defined in section 952 without regard to section 965(a)) are described in section 965(d)(2)(B) and paragraph (f)(7)(i)(B) or (f)(7)(i)(C) of this section only to the extent that such income has been accrued by the specified foreign corporation as of the E&P measurement date. For rules regarding the interaction of sections 951, 956, 959, and 965 generally, see § 1.965-2(b).

(8) *Aggregate foreign cash position.*—(i) *In general.*—The term *aggregate foreign cash position* means, with respect to a section 958(a) U.S. shareholder that is not a member of a consolidated group, the greater of—

(A) The aggregate of the section 958(a) U.S. shareholder's pro rata share of the cash position of each specified foreign corporation determined as of the final cash measurement date of the specified foreign corporation; or

(B) One half of the sum of—

*(1)* The aggregate described in paragraph (f)(8)(i)(A) of this section determined as of the second cash measurement date of each specified foreign corporation, plus

*(2)* The aggregate described in paragraph (f)(8)(i)(A) of this section determined as of the first cash measurement date of each specified foreign corporation.

(ii) *Other rules.*—For rules for determining the aggregate foreign cash position for a section 958(a) U.S. shareholder inclusion year of the section 958(a) U.S. shareholder, see § 1.965-3(c). For the rule for determining the aggregate foreign cash position of a section 958(a) U.S. shareholder that is a member of a consolidated group, see § 1.965-8(e)(3). For rules disregarding certain assets for purposes of determining the aggregate foreign cash position of a section 958(a) U.S. shareholder, see § 1.965-3(b).

(9) *Aggregate foreign E&P deficit.*—The term *aggregate foreign E&P deficit* means, with respect to a section 958(a) U.S. shareholder, the lesser of—

(i) The aggregate of the section 958(a) U.S. shareholder's pro rata share of the specified E&P deficit of each E&P deficit foreign corpora-

tion, translated (if necessary) into U.S. dollars using the spot rate on December 31, 2017, or

(ii) The aggregate of the section 958(a) U.S. shareholder's pro rata share of the section 965(a) earnings amount of each deferred foreign income corporation, translated (if necessary) into U.S. dollars using the spot rate on December 31, 2017.

(10) *Aggregate section 965(a) inclusion amount.*—The term *aggregate section 965(a) inclusion amount* means, with respect to a section 958(a) U.S. shareholder, the sum of all of the section 958(a) U.S. shareholder's section 965(a) inclusion amounts.

(11) *Allocable share.*—The term *allocable share* means, with respect to a deferred foreign income corporation and an aggregate foreign E&P deficit of a section 958(a) U.S. shareholder, the product of the aggregate foreign E&P deficit and the ratio determined by dividing—

(i) The section 958(a) U.S. shareholder's pro rata share of the section 965(a) earnings amount of the deferred foreign income corporation, translated (if necessary) into U.S. dollars using the spot rate on December 31, 2017, by

(ii) The amount described in paragraph (f)(9)(ii) of this section with respect to the section 958(a) U.S. shareholder.

(12) *Bona fide hedging transaction.*—The term *bona fide hedging transaction* means a hedging transaction that meets (or that would meet if the specified foreign corporation were a controlled foreign corporation) the requirements of a bona fide hedging transaction described in § 1.954-2(a)(4)(ii), except that in the case of a specified foreign corporation that is not a controlled foreign corporation, the identification requirements of § 1.954-2(a)(4)(ii)(B) do not apply.

(13) *Cash-equivalent asset.*—(i) *In general.*—The term *cash-equivalent asset* means any of the following assets—

(A) Personal property which is of a type that is actively traded and for which there is an established financial market, other than a specified commodity;

(B) Commercial paper, certificates of deposit, the securities of the Federal government and of any State or foreign government;

(C) Any foreign currency;

(D) A short-term obligation; or

(E) Derivative financial instruments, other than bona fide hedging transactions.

(ii) *Specified commodity.*—The term *specified commodity* means a commodity held by a specified foreign corporation that, in the hands of the specified foreign corporation, is property described in section 1221(a)(1) or 1221(a)(8). This paragraph (f)(13)(ii) does not apply with respect to a specified foreign corporation that is a dealer or trader in commodities.

(14) *Cash-equivalent asset hedging transaction.*—(i) *In general.*—The term *cash-equivalent asset hedging transaction* means a bona fide hedging transaction identified on a specified foreign corporation's books and records as hedging a cash-equivalent asset.

(ii) *Aggregate hedging transactions.*—For purposes of paragraph (f)(14)(i) of this section, the amount of a bona fide hedging transaction described in § 1.1221-2(c)(3) (an *aggregate hedging transaction)* that is treated as a cash-equivalent asset hedging transaction is the amount that bears the same proportion to the fair market value of the aggregate hedging transaction as the value of the cash-equivalent assets being hedged by the aggregate hedging transaction bears to the value of all assets being hedged by the aggregate hedging transaction.

(15) *Cash measurement dates.*—The term *cash measurement dates* means, with respect to a specified foreign corporation, the first cash measurement date, the second cash measurement date, and the final cash measurement date, collectively, and each a *cash measurement date.*

(16) *Cash position.*—(i) *General rule.*—The term *cash position* means, with respect to a specified foreign corporation, the sum of—

(A) Cash held by the corporation;

(B) The net accounts receivable of the corporation; and

(C) The fair market value of the cash-equivalent assets held by the corporation.

(ii) *Fair market value of cash-equivalent assets.*—For purposes of determining the fair market value of a cash-equivalent asset of a specified foreign corporation, the value of the cash-equivalent asset must be adjusted by the fair market value of any cash-equivalent asset hedging transaction with respect to the cash-equivalent asset, but only to the extent that the cash-equivalent asset hedging transaction does not reduce the fair market value of the cash-equivalent asset below zero.

(iii) *Measurement of derivative financial instruments.*—The amount of derivative financial instruments taken into account in determining the cash position of a specified foreign corporation is the aggregate fair market value of its derivative financial instruments that constitute cash-equivalent assets, provided such amount is not less than zero.

(iv) *Translation of cash position amounts.*—The cash position of a specified foreign corporation with respect to a cash measurement date must be expressed in U.S. dollars. For this purpose, the amounts described in paragraph (f)(16)(i) of this section must be translated (if

necessary) into U.S. dollars using the spot rate on the relevant cash measurement date.

(17) *Deferred foreign income corporation.*—(i) *In general.*—The term *deferred foreign income corporation* means a specified foreign corporation that has accumulated post-1986 deferred foreign income greater than zero as of an E&P measurement date.

(ii) *Priority rule.*—If a specified foreign corporation satisfies the definition of a deferred foreign income corporation under section 965(d)(1) and paragraph (f)(17)(i) of this section, it is classified solely as a deferred foreign income corporation and not also as an E&P deficit foreign corporation even if it otherwise satisfies the requirements of section 965(b)(3)(B) and paragraph (f)(22) of this section.

(18) *Derivative financial instrument.*—The term *derivative financial instrument* includes a financial instrument that is one of the following—

(i) A notional principal contract,

(ii) An option contract,

(iii) A forward contract, other than a forward contract with respect to a specified commodity (as defined in paragraph (f)(13)(ii) of this section), but solely to the extent that the specified foreign corporation identified, or could have identified, the forward contract as a hedging transaction (within the meaning of § 1.1221-2(b)) with respect to one or more specified commodities held by the specified foreign corporation,

(iv) A futures contract,

(v) A short position in securities or commodities, other than a forward contract with respect to a specified commodity, but solely to the extent that the specified foreign corporation identified, or could have identified, the forward contract as a hedging transaction (within the meaning of § 1.1221-2(b)) with respect to one or more specified commodities held by the specified foreign corporation, or

(vi) Any financial instrument similar to one described in paragraphs (f)(18)(i) through (v) of this section.

(19) *Domestic pass-through entity.*—The term *domestic pass-through entity* means a pass-through entity that is a United States person (as defined in section 7701(a)(30)).

(20) *Domestic pass-through owner.*—The term *domestic pass-through owner* means, with respect to a domestic pass-through entity, a United States person (as defined in section 7701(a)(30)) that is a partner, shareholder, beneficiary, grantor, or owner, as the case may be, in the domestic pass-through entity. Notwithstanding the preceding sentence, the term does not include a partner, shareholder, beneficiary, grantor, or owner of the domestic pass-through entity that is itself a domestic pass-through entity but does include any other United States person that is an

indirect partner, shareholder, beneficiary, grantor, or owner of the domestic pass-through entity through one or more other pass-through entities.

(21) *Domestic pass-through owner share.*—The term *domestic pass-through owner share* means, with respect to a domestic pass-through owner and a domestic pass-through entity, the domestic pass-through owner's share of the aggregate section 965(a) inclusion amount and the section 965(c) deduction amount, as applicable, of the domestic pass-through entity, including the domestic pass-through owner's share of the aggregate section 965(a) inclusion amount and section 965(c) deduction amount, as applicable, of a domestic pass-through entity owned indirectly by the domestic pass-through owner through one or more other pass-through entities.

(22) *E&P deficit foreign corporation.*—(i) *In general.*—The term *E&P deficit foreign corporation* means, with respect to a section 958(a) U.S. shareholder, a specified foreign corporation, other than a deferred foreign income corporation, if, as of November 2, 2017—

(A) The specified foreign corporation had a deficit in post-1986 earnings and profits,

(B) The corporation was a specified foreign corporation, and

(C) The shareholder was a United States shareholder of the corporation.

(ii) *Determination of deficit in post-1986 earnings and profits.*—In the case of a specified foreign corporation that has post-1986 earnings and profits that include earnings and profits described in section 959(c)(1) or 959(c)(2) (or both) and a deficit in earnings and profits (including hovering deficits, as defined in § 1.367(b)-7(d)(2)(i)), the specified foreign corporation has a deficit in post-1986 earnings and profits described in paragraph (f)(22)(i)(A) of this section only to the extent the deficit in post-1986 earnings and profits exceeds the aggregate of its post-1986 earnings and profits described in section 959(c)(1) and 959(c)(2).

(23) *E&P measurement dates.*—The term *E&P measurement dates* means November 2, 2017, and December 31, 2017, collectively, and each an *E&P measurement date*.

(24) *Final cash measurement date.*—The term *final cash measurement date* means, with respect to a specified foreign corporation, the close of the last taxable year of the specified foreign corporation that begins before January 1, 2018, and ends on or after November 2, 2017, if any.

(25) *First cash measurement date.*—The term *first cash measurement date* means, with respect to a specified foreign corporation, the close of the last taxable year of the specified foreign corporation that ends after November 1, 2015, and before November 2, 2016, if any.

(26) *Inclusion year.*—The term *inclusion year* means, with respect to a deferred foreign income corporation, the last taxable year of the deferred foreign income corporation that begins before January 1, 2018.

(27) *Net accounts receivable.*—The term *net accounts receivable* means, with respect to a specified foreign corporation, the excess (if any) of—

(i) The corporation's accounts receivable, over

(ii) The corporation's accounts payable (determined consistent with the rules of section 461).

(28) *Pass-through entity.*—The term *pass-through entity* means a partnership, S corporation, or any other person (whether domestic or foreign) other than a corporation to the extent that the income or deductions of the person are included in the income of one or more direct or indirect owners or beneficiaries of the person. For example, if a domestic trust is subject to federal income tax on a portion of its section 965(a) inclusion amount and its domestic pass-through owners are subject to tax on the remaining portion, the domestic trust is treated as a domestic pass-through entity with respect to such remaining portion.

(29) *Post-1986 earnings and profits.*—(i) *General rule.*—The term *post-1986 earnings and profits* means, with respect to a specified foreign corporation and an E&P measurement date, the earnings and profits (including earnings and profits described in section 959(c)(1) and 959(c)(2)) of the specified foreign corporation (computed in accordance with sections 964(a) and 986, subject to § 1.965-4(f), and by taking into account only periods when the foreign corporation was a specified foreign corporation) accumulated in taxable years beginning after December 31, 1986, and determined—

(A) As of the E&P measurement date, except as provided in paragraph (f)(29)(ii) of this section, and

(B) Without diminution by reason of dividends distributed during the last taxable year of the foreign corporation that begins before January 1, 2018, other than dividends distributed to another specified foreign corporation to the extent the dividends increase the post-1986 earnings and profits of the distributee specified foreign corporation.

(ii) *Foreign income taxes.*—For purposes of determining a specified foreign corporation's post-1986 earnings and profits as of the E&P measurement date on November 2, 2017, in the case in which foreign income taxes (as defined in section 901(m)(5)) of the specified foreign corporation accrue after November 2, 2017, but on or before December 31, 2017, and during the specified foreign corporation's U.S. taxable year that

Tax Cuts and Jobs Act: Regulatory Explanation and Analysis

includes November 2, 2017, the specified foreign corporation's post-1986 earnings and profits as of November 2, 2017, are reduced by the applicable portion of such foreign income taxes. For purposes of the preceding sentence, the applicable portion of the foreign income taxes is the amount of the taxes that are attributable to the portion of the taxable income (as determined under foreign law) that accrues on or before November 2, 2017.

(iii) *Deficits in earnings and profits.*—Any deficit related to post-1986 earnings and profits, including a hovering deficit (as defined in § 1.367(b)-7(d)(2)(i)), of a specified foreign corporation is taken into account for purposes of determining the post-1986 earnings and profits (including a deficit) of the specified foreign corporation.

(30) *Pro rata share.*—The term *pro rata share* means, with respect to a section 958(a) U.S. shareholder of a specified foreign corporation, a deferred foreign income corporation, or an E&P deficit foreign corporation, as applicable—

(i) With respect to the section 965(a) earnings amount of a deferred foreign income corporation, the portion of the section 965(a) earnings amount that would be treated as distributed to the section 958(a) U.S. shareholder under § 1.951-1(e), determined as of the last day of the inclusion year of the deferred foreign income corporation on which it is a specified foreign corporation;

(ii) With respect to the specified E&P deficit of an E&P deficit foreign corporation, the portion of the specified E&P deficit allocated to the section 958(a) U.S. shareholder, determined by allocating the specified E&P deficit among the shareholders of the corporation's common stock in proportion to the liquidation value of the common stock held by the shareholders, determined as of the last day of the last taxable year of the E&P deficit foreign corporation that begins before January 1, 2018, provided that—

(A) If the corporation's common stock has a liquidation value of zero and there is at least one other class of equity with a liquidation preference relative to the common stock, then the specified E&P deficit is allocated as if it were distributed in a hypothetical distribution described in § 1.951-1(e)(1)(i) with respect to the most junior class of equity with a positive liquidation value to the extent of such liquidation value, and then to the next most junior class of equity to the extent of its liquidation value, and so on, applying § 1.951-1(e) by substituting "specified E&P deficit" for "subpart F income" each place it appears and treating the amount of current earnings and profits of the corporation for the year as being equal to the specified E&P deficit of the corporation for the year; and

(B) If the corporation's common stock has a liquidation value of zero and there is no other class of equity with a liquidation preference relative to the common stock, the specified E&P deficit is allocated among the common stock using any reasonable method consistently applied; and

(iii) With respect to the cash position of a specified foreign corporation on a cash measurement date, the portion of the cash position that would be treated as distributed to the section 958(a) U.S. shareholder under § 1.951-1(e) if the cash position were subpart F income, determined as of the close of the cash measurement date and without regard to whether the section 958(a) U.S. shareholder is a section 958(a) U.S. shareholder of the specified foreign corporation as of any other cash measurement date of the specified foreign corporation, including the final cash measurement date of the specified foreign corporation.

(31) *Second cash measurement date.*—The term *second cash measurement date* means, with respect to a specified foreign corporation, the close of the last taxable year of the specified foreign corporation that ends after November 1, 2016, and before November 2, 2017, if any.

(32) *Section 958(a) stock.*—The term *section 958(a) stock* means, with respect to a specified foreign corporation, a deferred foreign income corporation, or an E&P deficit foreign corporation, as applicable, stock of the corporation owned (directly or indirectly) by a United States shareholder within the meaning of section 958(a).

(33) *Section 958(a) U.S. shareholder.*—The term *section 958(a) U.S. shareholder* means, with respect to a specified foreign corporation, a deferred foreign income corporation, or an E&P deficit foreign corporation, as applicable, a United States shareholder of such corporation that owns section 958(a) stock of the corporation.

(34) *Section 958(a) U.S. shareholder inclusion year.*—The term *section 958(a) U.S. shareholder inclusion year* means the taxable year of a section 958(a) U.S. shareholder in which or with which the last day of the inclusion year of a deferred foreign income corporation on which it is a specified foreign corporation occurs.

(35) *Section 965 regulations.*—The term *section 965 regulations* means the regulations under § § 1.965-1 through 1.965-9, collectively.

(36) *Section 965(a) earnings amount.*—The term *section 965(a) earnings amount* means, with respect to a deferred foreign income corporation, the greater of the accumulated post-1986 deferred foreign income of the deferred foreign income corporation as of the E&P measurement date on November 2, 2017, or the accumulated post-1986 deferred foreign income of the deferred foreign income corporation as of the E&P measurement date on December 31, 2017, determined in each case in the functional currency of the specified foreign corporation. If the functional currency of a specified foreign corporation

Reg. § 1.965-1(f)(29)(iii)

changes between the two E&P measurement dates, the comparison must be made in the functional currency of the specified foreign corporation as of December 31, 2017, by translating the specified foreign corporation's accumulated post-1986 deferred foreign income as of November 2, 2017, into the new functional currency using the spot rate on November 2, 2017.

(37) *Section 965(a) inclusion.*—The term *section 965(a) inclusion* means, with respect to a person and a deferred foreign income corporation, an amount included in income by the person by reason of section 965 with respect to the deferred foreign income corporation, whether because the person is a section 958(a) U.S. shareholder of the deferred foreign income corporation with a section 965(a) inclusion amount with respect to the deferred foreign income corporation or because the person is a domestic pass-through owner with respect to a domestic pass-through entity that is a section 958(a) U.S. shareholder of the deferred foreign income corporation and the person includes in income its domestic pass-through owner share of the section 965(a) inclusion amount of the domestic pass-through entity with respect to the deferred foreign income corporation.

(38) *Section 965(a) inclusion amount.*—The term *section 965(a) inclusion amount* has the meaning provided in paragraph (b)(1) of this section.

(39) *Section 965(a) previously taxed earnings and profits.*—The term *section 965(a) previously taxed earnings and profits* has the meaning provided in §1.965-2(c).

(40) *Section 965(b) previously taxed earnings and profits.*—The term *section 965(b) previously taxed earnings and profits* has the meaning provided in §1.965-2(d).

(41) *Section 965(c) deduction.*—The term *section 965(c) deduction* means, with respect to a person, an amount allowed as a deduction to the person by reason of section 965(c), whether because the person is a section 958(a) U.S. shareholder with a section 965(c) deduction amount or because the person is a domestic pass-through owner with respect to a domestic pass-through entity that is a section 958(a) U.S. shareholder and the person takes into account its domestic pass-through owner share of the section 965(c) deduction amount of the domestic pass-through entity.

(42) *Section 965(c) deduction amount.*—The term *section 965(c) deduction amount* means an amount equal to the sum of—

(i) A section 958(a) U.S. shareholder's 8 percent rate equivalent percentage of the section 958(a) U.S. shareholder's 8 percent rate amount for the section 958(a) U.S. shareholder inclusion year, plus

(ii) The section 958(a) U.S. shareholder's 15.5 percent rate equivalent percentage of the section 958(a) U.S. shareholder's 15.5 percent rate amount for the section 958(a) U.S. shareholder inclusion year.

(43) *Short-term obligation.*—The term *short-term obligation* means any obligation with a term upon issuance that is less than one year and any loan that must be repaid at the demand of the lender (or that must be repaid within one year of such demand), but does not include any accounts receivable.

(44) *Specified E&P deficit.*—The term *specified E&P deficit* means, with respect to an E&P deficit foreign corporation, the amount of the deficit described in paragraph (f)(22)(i)(A) of this section.

(45) *Specified foreign corporation.*—(i) *General rule.*—Except as provided in paragraph (f)(45)(iii) of this section, the term *specified foreign corporation* means—

(A) A controlled foreign corporation, or

(B) A foreign corporation of which one or more domestic corporations is a United States shareholder.

(ii) *Special attribution rule.*—(A) *In general.*—Solely for purposes of determining whether a foreign corporation is a specified foreign corporation within the meaning of section 965(e)(1)(B) and paragraph (f)(45)(i)(B) of this section, stock owned, directly or indirectly, by or for—

(1) A partner (*tested partner*) will not be considered as being owned by a partnership under sections 958(b) and 318(a)(3)(A) and §1.958-2(d)(1)(i) if the tested partner owns less than ten percent of the interests in the partnership's capital and profits; and

(2) A beneficiary (*tested beneficiary*) will not be considered as being owned by a trust under sections 958(b) and 318(a)(3)(B) and §1.958-2(d)(1)(ii) if the value of the interest of the tested beneficiary, computed actuarially, whether vested or contingent, current or remainder, is less than ten percent of the value of the trust property, assuming the maximum exercise of discretion in favor of the beneficiary.

(B) *Attribution for purposes of the ten percent standard.*—For purposes of paragraph (f)(45)(ii)(A) of this section, an interest in a partnership or trust owned by a partner or beneficiary other than the tested partner or tested beneficiary will be considered as being owned by the tested partner or tested beneficiary under the principles of sections 958(b) and 318, as modified by this paragraph (f)(45)(ii), as if interests in a partnership or trust were stock.

(iii) *Passive foreign investment companies.*— A foreign corporation that is a passive foreign investment company (as defined in section 1297) with respect to a United States shareholder and that is not a controlled foreign corporation is not a specified foreign corporation of the United States shareholder.

(46) *Spot rate.*—The term *spot rate* has the meaning provided in § 1.988-1(d).

(47) *United States shareholder.*—The term *United States shareholder* has the meaning provided in section 951(b).

(g) *Examples.*—The following examples illustrate the definitions and general rules set forth in this section.

(1) *Example 1. Definition of specified foreign corporation.* (i) *Facts.* A, an individual, owns 1% of the interests in a partnership, PS, and 10% by vote and value of the stock of a foreign corporation, FC. PS owns 100% of the stock of a domestic corporation, DC. A United States citizen, USI, owns an additional 10% by vote and value of the stock of FC. The remaining 80% by vote and value of the stock of FC is owned by non-United States persons that are unrelated to A, USI, DC, and PS.

(ii) *Analysis.* (A) Absent the application of sections 958(b), 318(a)(3)(A), and 318(a)(3)(C), and § 1.958-2(d)(1)(i) and (iii), FC would not be a specified foreign corporation because FC is not a controlled foreign corporation and there would be no domestic corporation that is a United States shareholder of FC. However, under sections 958(b) and 318(a)(3)(A) and § 1.958-2(d)(1)(i), absent the special attribution rule in paragraph (f)(45)(ii) of this section, PS would be treated as owning 10% of the stock of FC. As a result, under sections 958(b), 318(a)(5)(A), and 318(a)(3)(C), and § 1.958-2(f)(1)(i) and (d)(1)(iii), DC would be treated as owning the stock of FC treated as owned by PS, and thus DC would be a United States shareholder with respect to FC, causing FC to be a specified foreign corporation within the meaning of section 965(e)(1)(B) and paragraph (f)(45)(i)(B) of this section. The results would be the same whether A or PS or both are domestic or foreign persons.

(B) Under the special attribution rule in paragraph (f)(45)(ii) of this section, solely for purposes of determining whether a foreign corporation is a specified foreign corporation within the meaning of section 965(e)(1)(B) and paragraph (f)(45)(i)(B) of this section, the stock of FC owned by A is not considered as being owned by PS under sections 958(b) and 318(a)(3)(A) and § 1.958-2(d)(1)(i) because A owns less than 10% of the interests in PS's capital and profits. Accordingly, FC is not a specified foreign corporation within the meaning of section 965(e)(1)(B) and paragraph (f)(45)(i)(B) of this section.

(2) *Example 2. Definition of specified foreign corporation.* (i) *Facts.* The facts are the same as in paragraph(g)(1)(i) of this section (the facts in

*Example* 1), except that A is a foreign corporation wholly owned by B, a foreign corporation, and B directly owns 9% of the interests in PS.

(ii) *Analysis.* Applying the principles of sections 958(b) and 318, as modified by paragraph (f)(45)(ii) of this section, as if the interest in PS were stock, A is treated as owning the interests in PS owned by B (in addition to the 1% interest in PS that A owns directly), and thus A is not treated as owning less than 10% of the interests in PS's capital and profits. Accordingly, the special attribution rule in paragraph (f)(45)(ii) of this section does not apply, and PS is treated as owning A's stock of FC for purposes of determining whether FC is a specified foreign corporation within the meaning of section 965(e)(1)(B) and paragraph (f)(45)(i)(B) of this section. Accordingly, under the analysis described in paragraph (ii)(A) of *Example 1* of paragraph (g)(1) of this section, FC is a specified foreign corporation within the meaning of section 965(e)(1)(B) and paragraph (f)(45)(i)(B) of this section.

(3) *Example 3. Determination of accumulated post-1986 deferred foreign income.* (i) *Facts.* USP, a domestic corporation, and FP, a foreign corporation unrelated to USP, have owned 70% and 30% respectively, by vote and value, of the only class of stock of FS, a foreign corporation, from January 1, 2016, until December 31, 2017. USP and FS both have a calendar year taxable year. FS had no income until its taxable year ending December 31, 2016, in which it had 100u of income, all of which constituted subpart F income, and USP included 70u in income with respect to FS under section 951(a)(1) for such year. FS earned no income in 2017. Therefore, FS's post-1986 earnings and profits are 100u as of both E&P measurement dates.

(ii) *Analysis.* Because USP included 70u in income with respect to FS under section 951(a)(1), 70u of such post-1986 earnings and profits would, if distributed, be excluded from the gross income of USP under section 959. Thus, FS's accumulated post-1986 deferred foreign income would be reduced by 70u pursuant to section 965(d)(2)(B) and paragraph (f)(7)(i)(B) of this section. Furthermore, under paragraph (f)(7)(i)(C) of this section, the accumulated post-1986 deferred foreign income of FS is reduced by amounts that would be excluded from the gross income of FP if FP were a United States shareholder, consistent with the principles of Revenue Ruling 82-16. Accordingly, FS's accumulated post-1986 deferred foreign income is reduced by the remaining 30u of the 100u of post-1986 earnings and profits to which USP's 70u of section 951(a)(1) income inclusions were attributable. As a result, FS's accumulated post-1986 deferred foreign income is 0u (100u minus 70u minus 30u).

(4) *Example 4. Determination of status as a deferred foreign income corporation or an E&P deficit foreign corporation; specified foreign corporation is solely a deferred foreign income corporation.* (i) *Facts.* USP, a domestic corporation, owns all of the

stock of FS, a foreign corporation. As of November 2, 2017, FS has a deficit in post-1986 earnings and profits of 150u. As of December 31, 2017, FS has 200u of post-1986 earnings and profits. FS does not have earnings and profits that are attributable to income of the specified foreign corporation that is effectively connected with the conduct of a trade or business within the United States and subject to tax under chapter 1, or that, if distributed, would be excluded from the gross income of a United States shareholder under section 959 or from the gross income of another shareholder if such shareholder were a United States shareholder.

(ii) *Analysis.* FS's accumulated post-1986 deferred foreign income is equal to its post-1986 earnings and profits because no adjustment to post-1986 earnings and profits is made under section 965(d)(2) or § 1.965-1(f)(7). Under paragraph (f)(17)(i) of this section, FS is a deferred foreign income corporation because FS has accumulated post-1986 deferred foreign income greater than zero as of the E&P measurement date on December 31, 2017. In addition, under paragraph (f)(17)(ii) of this section, because FS is a deferred foreign income corporation, FS is not also an E&P deficit foreign corporation, notwithstanding that FS has a deficit in post-1986 earnings and profits as of the E&P measurement date on November 2, 2017.

(5) *Example 5. Determination of status as a deferred foreign income corporation or an E&P deficit foreign corporation; specified foreign corporation is neither a deferred foreign income corporation nor an E&P deficit foreign corporation.* (i) *Facts.* USP, a domestic corporation, owns all of the stock of FS, a foreign corporation. As of both November 2, 2017, and December 31, 2017, FS has 100u of earnings and profits described in section 959(c)(2) and a deficit of 90u in earnings and profits described in section 959(c)(3), all of which were accumulated in taxable years beginning after December 31, 1986, while FS was a specified foreign corporation. Accordingly, as of both November 2, 2017, and December 31, 2017, FS has 10u of post-1986 earnings and profits.

(ii) *Analysis.* (A) *Determination of status as a deferred foreign income corporation.* Under paragraph (f)(17) of this section, for purposes of determining whether FS is a deferred foreign income corporation, a determination must be made whether FS has accumulated post-1986 deferred foreign income greater than zero as of either the E&P measurement date on November 2, 2017, or the E&P measurement date on December 31, 2017. Under section 965(d)(2) and paragraph (f)(7) of this section, FS's accumulated post-1986 deferred foreign income is its post-1986 earnings and profits, except to the extent such earnings and profits are attributable to income of the specified foreign corporation that is effectively connected with the conduct of a trade or business within the United States and subject to tax under chapter 1, or that, if distributed, would be excluded from the gross income

of a United States shareholder under section 959 or from the gross income of another shareholder if such shareholder were a United States shareholder. Disregarding FS's 100u of post-1986 earnings and profits described in paragraph (f)(7)(i)(B) of this section, FS has a 90u deficit in accumulated post-1986 deferred foreign income as of both E&P measurement dates. Accordingly, FS does not have accumulated post-1986 deferred foreign income greater than zero as of either E&P measurement date, and, therefore, FS is not a deferred foreign income corporation.

(B) *Determination of status as an E&P deficit foreign corporation.* Under paragraph (f)(22)(i) of this section, for purposes of determining whether FS is an E&P deficit foreign corporation, a determination must be made whether FS has a deficit in post-1986 earnings and profits as of the E&P measurement date on November 2, 2017. Under paragraph (f)(22)(ii) of this section, because the deficit in the earnings and profits of FS described in section 959(c)(3) of 90u does not exceed the earnings and profits of FS described in section 959(c)(2) of 100u, FS does not have a deficit in post-1986 earnings and profits as of the E&P measurement date on November 2, 2017, and, therefore, FS is not an E&P deficit foreign corporation. Accordingly, FS is neither a deferred foreign income corporation nor an E&P deficit foreign corporation.

(6) *Example 6. Application of currency translation rules.* (i) *Facts.* As of November 2, 2017, and December 31, 2017, USP, a domestic corporation, owns all of the stock of CFC1, an E&P deficit foreign corporation with the "u" as its functional currency; CFC2, an E&P deficit foreign corporation with the "v" as its functional currency; CFC3, a deferred foreign income corporation with the "y" as its functional currency; and CFC4, a deferred foreign income corporation with the "z" as its functional currency. USP, CFC1, CFC2, CFC3, and CFC4 each have a calendar year taxable year. As of December 31, 2017, 1u=$1, .75v=$1, .50y=$1, and .25z=$1. CFC1 has a specified E&P deficit of 100u, CFC2 has a specified E&P deficit of 120v, CFC3 has a section 965(a) earnings amount of 50y, and CFC4 has a section 965(a) earnings amount of 75z.

(ii) *Analysis.* (A) Under paragraph (f)(38) of this section, for purposes of determining USP's section 965(a) inclusion amounts with respect to CFC3 and CFC4, the section 965(a) earnings amount of each of CFC3 and CFC4 is translated into U.S. dollars at the spot rate on December 31, 2017, which equals $100 (50y at .50y=$1) and $300 (75z at .25z=$1), respectively. Furthermore, USP's pro rata share of the section 965(a) earnings amounts, as translated, is $100 and $300, respectively, or 100% of each section 965(a) earnings amount.

(B) Under paragraph (f)(9) of this section, for purposes of determining USP's aggregate foreign E&P deficit, the specified E&P deficit of each of CFC1 and CFC2 is translated into U.S.

dollars at the spot rate on December 31, 2017, which equals $100 (100u at 1u=$1) and $160 (120v at .75v=$1), respectively. Furthermore USP's pro rata share of each specified E&P deficit, as translated, is $100 and $160, respectively, or 100% of each specified E&P deficit. Therefore, USP's aggregate foreign E&P deficit is $260.

(C) Under section 965(b)(1) and paragraph (b)(2) of this section, for purposes of determining USP's inclusion amount with respect to each of CFC3 and CFC4, the U.S. dollar amount of USP's pro rata share of the section 965(a) earnings amount of each of CFC3 and CFC4 is reduced by each of CFC3 and CFC4's allocable share of USP's aggregate foreign E&P deficit. Under section 965(b)(2) and paragraph (f)(11) of this section, CFC3's allocable share of USP's aggregate foreign E&P deficit of $260 is $65 ($260 x ($100/$400)) and CFC4's allocable share of USP's aggregate foreign E&P deficit is $195 ($260 x ($300/400)). After reduction under section 965(b)(1) and paragraph (b)(2) of this section, the section 965(a) inclusion amount of USP with respect to CFC3 is $35 ($100-$65) and the section 965(a) inclusion amount of USP with respect to CFC4 is $105 ($300-$195). Under §1.965-2(c), the section 965(a) previously taxed earnings and profits of each of CFC3 and CFC4, translated into the respective functional currencies of CFC3 and CFC4 at the spot rate on December 31, 2017, are 17.5y ($35 at .50y=$1) and 26.25z ($105 at .25z=$1), respectively. Under §1.965-6(b)(1), for purposes of applying section 960(a)(1), the amounts treated as a dividend paid by each of CFC3 and CFC4, translated into the respective functional currencies of CFC3 and CFC4 at the spot rate on December 31, 2017, are 17.5y ($35 at .50y=$1) and 26.25z ($105 at .25z=$1).

(D) For purposes of determining the section 965(b) previously taxed earnings and profits of each of CFC3 and CFC4 under section 965(b)(4)(A) and §1.965-2(d)(1) as a result of the reduction to USP's section 965(a) inclusion

amounts with respect to CFC3 and CFC4, the amount of the aggregate foreign E&P deficit of USP allocated to each of CFC3 and CFC4 under section 965(b)(2) and paragraph (f)(11) of this section, translated into the respective functional currencies of CFC3 and CFC4 at the spot rate on December 31, 2017, is 32.5y ($65 at .50y=$1) and 48.75z ($195 at .25z=$1), respectively.

(7) *Example 7. Determination of cash measurement dates and pro rata shares of cash positions.* (i) *Facts.* Except as otherwise provided, for all relevant periods, USP, a domestic corporation, has owned directly at least 10% of the stock of CFC1, CFC2, CFC3, and CFC4, each a foreign corporation. CFC1 and CFC2 have calendar year taxable years. CFC3 and CFC4 have taxable years that end on November 30. No entity has a short taxable year, except as a result of the transactions described below.

(A) USP transferred all of its stock of CFC2 to an unrelated person on June 30, 2016, at which point USP ceased to be a United States shareholder with respect to CFC2.

(B) CFC4 dissolved on December 30, 2010, and, as a result, its final taxable year ended on December 30, 2010.

(ii) *Analysis.* Each of CFC1, CFC2, CFC3, and CFC4 is a specified foreign corporation of USP, subject to the sale of CFC2 on June 30, 2016, and the dissolution of CFC4 on December 30, 2010. Under the definition of aggregate foreign cash position in paragraph (f)(8)(i) of this section, the definition of pro rata share of a cash position in paragraph (f)(30)(iii) of this section, and the definitions of the final cash measurement date, second cash measurement date, and first cash measurement date in paragraphs (f)(24), (25), and (31) of this section, the cash measurement dates of the specified foreign corporations to be taken into account by USP in determining its aggregate foreign cash position are summarized in the following table:

|  | Final | Cash Measurement Dates | |
|---|---|---|---|
|  |  | Second | First |
| CFC1 | December 31, 2017 | December 31, 2016 | December 31, 2015 |
| CFC2 | N/A | N/A | December 31, 2015 |
| CFC3 | November 30, 2018 | November 30, 2016 | November 30, 2015 |
| CFC4 | N/A | N/A | N/A |

(8) *Example 8. Determination of section 958(a) U.S. shareholder in case of a controlled domestic partnership.* (i) *Facts.* USP, a domestic corporation, owns all of the stock of CFC1 and CFC2. CFC1 and CFC2 own 60% and 40%, respectively, of the interests in the capital and profits of DPS, a domestic partnership. DPS owns all of the stock of CFC3 and CFC4. This ownership structure has existed since the date of formation of CFC1, CFC2, CFC3, and CFC4. CFC1, CFC2,

CFC3, and CFC4 are each a foreign corporation. USP, DPS, CFC1, CFC2, CFC3, and CFC4 have calendar year taxable years. On both E&P measurement dates, CFC3 has 50u of accumulated post-1986 deferred foreign income. On both E&P measurement dates, CFC4 has a deficit in post-1986 earnings and profits of 30u. On all cash measurement dates, CFC1, CFC2, and CFC3 each have a cash position of 0u, and CFC4 has a cash position of 200u.

(ii) *Analysis.* DPS is a controlled domestic partnership with respect to USP within the meaning of paragraph (e)(2) of this section because more than 50% of the interests in its capital and profits are owned by persons related to USP within the meaning of section 267(b), CFC1 and CFC2, and thus DPS is controlled by USP and related persons. Without regard to paragraph (e) of this section, DPS is a section 958(a) U.S. shareholder of CFC3 and CFC4, each of which is a controlled foreign corporation. If DPS were treated as foreign, CFC3 and CFC4 would each continue to be a controlled foreign corporation, and USP would be treated as a section 958(a) U.S. shareholder of each of CFC3 and CFC4, and would be treated as owning (within the meaning of section 958(a)) tested section 958(a) stock of each of CFC3 and CFC4 through CFC1 and CFC2, which are both partners in DPS. Thus, under paragraph (e)(1) of this section, DPS is treated as a foreign partnership for purposes of determining the section 958(a) U.S. shareholder of both CFC3 and CFC4 and the section 958(a) stock of both CFC3 and CFC4 owned by the section 958(a) U.S. shareholder. Thus, USP's pro rata share of CFC3's section 965(a) earnings amount is 50u, and its pro rata share of CFC4's specified E&P deficit is 30u. USP's aggregate foreign cash position is 200u. DPS is not a section 958(a) U.S. shareholder with respect to either CFC3 or CFC4. [Reg. § 1.965-1.]

☐ [*T.D. 9846, 2-4-2019.*]

**[Reg. § 1.965-2]**

**§ 1.965-2. Adjustments to earnings and profits and basis.**—(a) *Scope.*—This section provides rules relating to adjustments to earnings and profits and basis to determine and account for the application of section 965(a) and (b) and § 1.965-1(b) and a rule that limits the amount of gain recognized under section 961(b)(2) by reason of distributions attributable to section 965 previously taxed earnings and profits (as defined in paragraph (g)(1)(ii) of this section) in the inclusion year. Paragraph (b) of this section provides rules relating to adjustments to earnings and profits of a specified foreign corporation for purposes of applying sections 902, 959, 960, and 965. Paragraph (c) of this section provides rules regarding adjustments to earnings and profits by reason of section 965(a). Paragraph (d) of this section provides rules regarding adjustments to earnings and profits by reason of section 965(b). Paragraph (e) provides rules regarding adjustments to basis by reason of section 965(a). Paragraph (f) of this section provides an election to make certain adjustments to basis corresponding to adjustments to earnings and profits by reason of section 965(b). Paragraph (g) of this section provides rules that limit the amount of gain recognized in connection with the application of section 961(b)(2) and that require related reductions in basis. Paragraph (h) of this section provides rules regarding basis adjustments. Paragraph (i) of this section provides definitions

that apply for purposes of this section. Paragraph (j) of this section provides examples illustrating the application of this section.

(b) *Determination of and adjustments to earnings and profits of a specified foreign corporation for purposes of applying sections 902, 959, 960, and 965.*—For the taxable year of a specified foreign corporation in which an E&P measurement date occurs, and the last taxable year of a specified foreign corporation that begins before January 1, 2018, and the taxable year of a section 958(a) U.S. shareholder in which or with which any such year ends, the adjustments to earnings and profits described in paragraphs (b)(1) through (b)(5) of this section apply in sequence. For purposes of determining the consequences under sections 902 and 960 of a distribution or an inclusion under section 951(a)(1), after the application of those paragraphs, the ordering rule in § 1.960-1(i)(2) applies except that section 902 is applied with respect to any distributions from the specified foreign corporation described in paragraph (b)(2) of this section that are not disregarded under § 1.965-4 before section 960 is applied with respect to an inclusion or distribution described in paragraph (b)(3), (b)(4), or (b)(5) of this section.

(1) Each of the subpart F income of the specified foreign corporation and the amount required to be included in income under section 1248, if any, are determined without regard to section 965(a), but taking into account any relevant distributions, and earnings and profits of the specified foreign corporation that are described in section 959(c)(2) with respect to the section 958(a) U.S. shareholder are increased to the extent of the section 958(a) U.S. shareholder's inclusion under section 951(a)(1)(A) without regard to section 965(a) (including to the extent provided in section 959(e)).

(2) The treatment of a distribution by the specified foreign corporation to another specified foreign corporation that is made before January 1, 2018, is determined under section 959.

(3) Each of the post-1986 earnings and profits (including a deficit) of the specified foreign corporation, the accumulated post-1986 deferred foreign income of the specified foreign corporation, the section 965(a) earnings amount of the specified foreign corporation, and the section 965(a) inclusion amount with respect to the specified foreign corporation, if any, is determined, taking into account the rules of § 1.965-4, and the earnings and profits (including a deficit) of the specified foreign corporation are adjusted as provided in paragraphs (c) and (d) of this section. For a rule disregarding subpart F income earned after an E&P measurement date for purposes of calculating accumulated post-1986 deferred foreign income as of the E&P measurement date, see § 1.965-1(f)(7)(ii).

(4) The treatment of distributions described in paragraph (b)(2) of this section that are disregarded under § 1.965-4 is redetermined and the

**Reg. § 1.965-2(b)(4)**

treatment of all distributions from the specified foreign corporation other than those described in paragraph (b)(2) of this section is determined under section 959.

(5) An amount is determined under section 956 with respect to the specified foreign corporation and the section 958(a) U.S. shareholder; earnings and profits of the specified foreign corporation described in section 959(c)(2) with respect to the section 958(a) U.S. shareholder are reclassified as earnings and profits described in section 959(c)(1) with respect to the section 958(a) U.S. shareholder to the extent the amount determined under section 956 would, but for section 959(a)(2), be included by the section 958(a) U.S. shareholder under section 951(a)(1)(B); and earnings and profits described in section 959(c)(1) with respect to the section 958(a) U.S. shareholder are further increased to the extent of the section 958(a) U.S. shareholder's inclusion under section 951(a)(1)(B).

(c) *Adjustments to earnings and profits by reason of section 965(a)*.—The earnings and profits of a deferred foreign income corporation described in section 959(c)(2) with respect to a section 958(a) U.S. shareholder are increased by an amount equal to the section 965(a) inclusion amount of the section 958(a) U.S. shareholder with respect to the deferred foreign income corporation, if any, translated (if necessary) into the functional currency of the deferred foreign income corporation using the spot rate on December 31, 2017, provided the section 965(a) inclusion amount is included in income by the section 958(a) U.S. shareholder. For purposes of the section 965 regulations, the earnings and profits described in section 959(c)(2) by reason of this paragraph (c) and the earnings and profits initially described in section 959(c)(2) by reason of this paragraph (c) but subsequently reclassified as earnings and profits described in section 959(c)(1), if any, are referred to as *section 965(a) previously taxed earnings and profits*. Furthermore, the earnings and profits (including a deficit) of the deferred foreign income corporation that are described in section 959(c)(3) (or that would be described in section 959(c)(3) but for the application of section 965(a) and the section 965 regulations) are reduced (or, in the case of a deficit, increased) by an amount equal to the section 965(a) previously taxed earnings and profits.

(d) *Adjustments to earnings and profits by reason of section 965(b)*.—(1) *Adjustments to earnings and profits described in section 959(c)(2) and (c)(3) of deferred foreign income corporations*.—The earnings and profits of a deferred foreign income corporation described in section 959(c)(2) with respect to a section 958(a) U.S. shareholder are increased by an amount equal to the reduction to the section 958(a) U.S. shareholder's pro rata share of the section 965(a) earnings amount of the deferred foreign income corporation under section 965(b), §1.965-1(b)(2), and §1.965-8(b), as applicable, translated (if necessary) into the functional cur-

rency of the deferred foreign income corporation using the spot rate on December 31, 2017, provided the section 958(a) U.S. shareholder includes the section 965(a) inclusion amount (if any) with respect to the deferred foreign income corporation in income. For purposes of the section 965 regulations, the earnings and profits described in section 959(c)(2) by reason of this paragraph (d) and the earnings and profits initially described in section 959(c)(2) by reason of this paragraph (d) but subsequently reclassified as earnings and profits described in section 959(c)(1) are referred to as *section 965(b) previously taxed earnings and profits*, and are treated as having been previously included in the gross income of the section 958(a) U.S. shareholder under section 951 for purposes of section 1248(d)(1). Furthermore, the earnings and profits (including a deficit) described in section 959(c)(3) of the deferred foreign income corporation (or that would be described in section 959(c)(3) but for the application of section 965(b) and the section 965 regulations) are reduced (or, in the case of a deficit, increased) by an amount equal to the section 965(b) previously taxed earnings and profits.

(2) *Adjustments to earnings and profits described in section 959(c)(3) of E&P deficit foreign corporations*.—(i) *Increase in earnings and profits by an amount equal to the portion of the section 958(a) U.S. shareholder's pro rata share of the specified E&P deficit taken into account*.—(A) *In general*.—For an E&P deficit foreign corporation's last taxable year that begins before January 1, 2018, the earnings and profits of the E&P deficit foreign corporation described in section 959(c)(3) are increased by an amount equal to the portion of a section 958(a) U.S. shareholder's pro rata share of the specified E&P deficit of the E&P deficit foreign corporation taken into account under section 965(b), §1.965-1(b)(2), and §1.965-8(b), as determined under paragraph (d)(2)(ii) of this section, translated (if necessary) into the functional currency of the E&P deficit foreign corporation using the spot rate on December 31, 2017. For purposes of section 316, the earnings and profits of the E&P deficit foreign corporation attributable to the increase described in the preceding sentence are not treated as earnings and profits of the taxable year described in section 316(a)(2). See also §1.965-6(b)(3) for the timing of this adjustment for purposes of determining foreign taxes deemed paid under sections 902 and 960.

(B) *Reduction of a qualified deficit*.—For purposes of section 952, a section 958(a) U.S. shareholder's pro rata share of the earnings and profits of an E&P deficit foreign corporation is increased by an amount equal to the portion of the section 958(a) U.S. shareholder's pro rata share of the specified E&P deficit of the E&P deficit foreign corporation taken into account under section 965(b), §1.965-1(b)(2), or §1.965-8(b), as applicable, as determined under paragraph (d)(2)(ii) of this section, translated (if necessary) into the functional currency of the E&P deficit foreign corporation using the spot rate on December 31, 2017, and such increase is attributable to the same activity to which the deficit so taken into account was attributable.

(ii) *Determination of portion of a section 958(a) U.S. shareholder's pro rata share of a specified E&P deficit taken into account.*—(A) *In general.*— The portion of a section 958(a) U.S. shareholder's pro rata share of a specified E&P deficit of an E&P deficit foreign corporation taken into account under section 965(b), §1.965-1(b)(2), or §1.965-8(b), as applicable, is 100 percent of the section 958(a) U.S. shareholder's pro rata share of the specified E&P deficit if either of the following conditions is satisfied:

(1) The section 958(a) U.S. shareholder (including a consolidated group of which the section 958(a) U.S. shareholder is a member) does not have an excess aggregate foreign E&P deficit (as defined in §1.965-8(f)(7)(i)), or

(2) If the section 958(a) U.S. shareholder is a member of an affiliated group in which not all members are members of the same consolidated group, the amount described in §1.965-8(f)(1)(i)(B) with respect to the affiliated group is equal to or greater than the amount described §1.965-8(f)(1)(i)(A).

(B) *Designation of portion of a section 958(a) U.S. shareholder's pro rata share of a specified E&P deficit taken into account.*—If neither the condition in paragraph (d)(2)(ii)(A)(1) nor the condition in paragraph (d)(2)(ii)(A)(2) is satisfied with respect to a section 958(a) U.S. shareholder, then the section 958(a) U.S. shareholder must designate the portion taken into account by reporting to each E&P deficit foreign corporation of the section 958(a) U.S. shareholder, and maintaining, in its books and records, a statement setting forth the following information—

(1) The portion of the section 958(a) U.S. shareholder's pro rata share of the specified E&P deficit of the E&P deficit foreign corporation taken into account under section 965(b), §1.965-1(b)(2), or §1.965-8(b), as designated under §1.965-8(c), as applicable, and

(2) In the case of an E&P deficit foreign corporation that has a qualified deficit (as determined under section 952 and §1.952-1), the portion (if any) of the section 958(a) shareholder's pro rata share of the specified E&P deficit of the E&P deficit foreign corporation taken into account under paragraph (d)(2)(ii)(B)(1) of this section that is attributable to a qualified deficit, including the qualified activities to which such portion is attributable.

(e) *Adjustments to basis by reason of section 965(a).*—(1) *General rule.*—Except as provided in paragraph (e)(2) of this section, a section 958(a) U.S. shareholder's basis in section 958(a) stock of a deferred foreign income corporation, or a section 958(a) U.S. shareholder's basis in applicable property with respect to a deferred foreign in-

come corporation, is increased by the section 958(a) U.S. shareholder's section 965(a) inclusion amount with respect to the deferred foreign income corporation included in income by the section 958(a) U.S. shareholder. *See* section 961(a).

(2) *Section 962 election.*—In the case of a section 958(a) U.S. shareholder who has made an election under section 962 for a section 958(a) U.S. shareholder's inclusion year, the increase in basis in the section 958(a) U.S. shareholder's section 958(a) stock of, or applicable property with respect to, a deferred foreign income corporation cannot exceed an amount equal to the amount of tax paid under chapter 1 of the Code with respect to the section 958(a) U.S. shareholder's section 965(a) inclusion amount with respect to the deferred foreign income corporation, taking into account any section 965(h) election made by the section 958(a) U.S. shareholder.

(f) *Adjustments to basis by reason of section 965(b).*—(1) *In general.*—Except as provided in paragraph (f)(2) of this section, no adjustments to basis of stock or property are made under section 961 (or any other provision of the Code) to take into account the reduction to a section 958(a) U.S. shareholder's pro rata share of the section 965(a) earnings amount of a deferred foreign income corporation under section 965(b), §1.965-1(b)(2), or §1.965-8(b), as applicable.

(2) *Election to make adjustments to basis to account for the application of section 965(b).*—(i) *In general.*—If a section 958(a) U.S. shareholder makes the election as provided in this paragraph (f)(2), the adjustments to basis described in paragraph (f)(2)(ii) of this section are made with respect to each deferred foreign income corporation and each E&P deficit foreign corporation in which the section 958(a) U.S. shareholder owns section 958(a) stock.

(ii) *Basis adjustments.*—(A) *Increase in basis with respect to a deferred foreign income corporation.*—(1) *In general.*—Except as provided in paragraphs (f)(2)(ii)(A)(2) and (C) of this section, a section 958(a) U.S. shareholder's basis in section 958(a) stock of a deferred foreign income corporation, or a section 958(a) U.S. shareholder's basis in applicable property with respect to a deferred foreign income corporation, is increased by an amount equal to the section 965(b) previously taxed earnings and profits of the deferred foreign income corporation with respect to the section 958(a) U.S. shareholder, translated (if necessary) into U.S. dollars using the spot rate on December 31, 2017.

(2) *Limited basis adjustment.*—A section 958(a) U.S. shareholder may, in lieu of applying paragraph (f)(2)(ii)(A)(1) of this section, designate the amount by which it increases its basis in section 958(a) stock of, or applicable property with respect to, a deferred foreign income corporation, provided that—

**Reg. §1.965-2(f)(2)(ii)(A)(2)**

*(i)* The increase does not exceed the section 965(b) previously taxed earnings and profits of the deferred foreign income corporation with respect to the section 958(a) U.S. shareholder, translated (if necessary) into U.S. dollars using the spot rate on December 31, 2017; and

*(ii)* The aggregate amount of a section 958(a) U.S. shareholder's increases in basis with respect to stock or applicable property pursuant to paragraph (f)(2)(ii)(A)(2) of this section does not exceed the aggregate amount of the section 958(a) U.S. shareholder's reductions in basis pursuant to paragraph (f)(2)(ii)(B) of this section subject to the limitation under paragraph (f)(2)(ii)(B)(2) of this section.

(B) *Reduction in basis with respect to an E&P deficit foreign corporation.—(1) In general.* Except as provided in paragraphs (f)(2)(ii)(B)(2) and (f)(2)(ii)(C) of this section, a section 958(a) U.S. shareholder's basis in section 958(a) stock of an E&P deficit foreign corporation, or a section 958(a) U.S. shareholder's basis in applicable property with respect to an E&P deficit foreign corporation, is reduced by an amount equal to the portion of the section 958(a) U.S. shareholder's pro rata share of the specified E&P deficit of the E&P deficit foreign corporation taken into account under section 965(b), § 1.965-1(b)(2), and § 1.965-8(b), as applicable, as determined under paragraph (d)(2)(ii) of this section, translated (if necessary) into U.S. dollars using the spot rate on December 31, 2017. For rules requiring gain recognition, see paragraph (h)(3) of this section.

*(2) Limited basis adjustment.—*If a section 958(a) U.S. shareholder adjusts its basis in section 958(a) stock of, or applicable property with respect to, one or more deferred foreign income corporations under paragraph (f)(2)(ii)(A)(2) of this section, the section 958(a) U.S. shareholder's aggregate reductions in basis in section 958(a) stock of, or applicable property with respect to, an E&P deficit foreign corporation pursuant to paragraph (f)(2)(ii)(B)(1) of this section on a day may not exceed the amount of the section 958(a) U.S. shareholder's basis in the section 958(a) stock of, or applicable property with respect to, such E&P deficit foreign corporation, determined without taking into account specified basis adjustments to the section 958(a) stock of, or applicable property with respect to, such E&P deficit foreign corporation.

(C) *Section 962 election.—*In the case of a section 958(a) U.S. shareholder who has made an election under section 962 for a section 958(a) U.S. shareholder's inclusion year, the adjustments provided in paragraphs (f)(2)(ii)(A) and (B) of this section do not apply.

*(iii) Rules regarding the election.—*(A) *Consistency requirement.—*In order for the election described in this paragraph (f)(2) to be effective, a section 958(a) U.S. shareholder and each section 958(a) U.S. shareholder of an E&P

deficit foreign corporation or of a deferred foreign income corporation with respect to which the second section 958(a) U.S. shareholder's pro rata share of the section 965(a) earnings amount is reduced under section 965(b), § 1.965-1(b)(2), or § 1.965-8(b) that is related to the first section 958(a) U.S. shareholder must make the election described in this paragraph (f)(2). For purposes of this paragraph (f)(2)(iii)(A), a person is treated as related to a section 958(a) U.S. shareholder if the person bears a relationship to the section 958(a) U.S. shareholder described in section 267(b) or 707(b).

(B) *Manner of making election.—(1) Timing.—(i) In general.—*Except as provided in paragraph (f)(2)(iii)(B)(1)(ii) of this section, the election provided in this paragraph (f)(2) must be made no later than the due date (taking into account extensions, if any) for the section 958(a) U.S. shareholder's return for the first taxable year that includes the last day of the last taxable year of a deferred foreign income corporation or E&P deficit foreign corporation of the shareholder that begins before January 1, 2018. Relief is not available under § 301.9100-2 or 301.9100-3 to file a late election. Except as provided in paragraph (f)(2)(iii)(B)(1)(ii) of this section, the election provided in this paragraph (f)(2) is irrevocable.

*(ii) Transition rule.—*If the due date referred to in paragraph (f)(2)(iii)(B)(1)(i) of this section occurs before May 6, 2019, the election must be made by May 6, 2019. In the case of an election made before February 5, 2019, the election may be revoked by attaching a statement, signed under penalties of perjury, to an amended return filed by May 6, 2019. The statement must contain the section 958(a) U.S. shareholder's name and taxpayer identification number and a statement that the section 958(a) U.S. shareholder and all related persons, as defined in paragraph (f)(2)(iii)(A) of this section, that are section 958(a) U.S. shareholders of E&P deficit foreign corporations or of deferred foreign income corporations with respect to which the section 958(a) U.S. shareholder's pro rata share of the section 965(a) earnings amount is reduced under section 965(b), § 1.965-1(b)(2), or § 1.965-8(b) revoke the election provided in this paragraph (f)(2).

*(2) Election statement.—*Except as otherwise provided in publications, forms, instructions, or other guidance, to make the election provided in this paragraph (f)(2), a section 958(a) U.S. shareholder must attach a statement, signed under penalties of perjury consistent with the rules for signatures applicable to the section 958(a) U.S. shareholders return, to its return for the first taxable year that includes the last day of the last taxable year of a deferred foreign income corporation or E&P deficit foreign corporation of the shareholder that begins before January 1, 2018. The statement must include the section

958(a) U.S. shareholder's name, taxpayer identification number, and a statement that the section 958(a) U.S. shareholder and all related persons, as defined in paragraph (f)(2)(iii)(A) of this section, that are section 958(a) U.S. shareholders of E&P deficit foreign corporations or of deferred foreign income corporations with respect to which the section 958(a) U.S. shareholder's pro rata share of the section 965(a) earnings amount is reduced under section 965(b), § 1.965-1(b)(2), or § 1.965-8(b) make the election provided in this paragraph (f)(2). If the section 958(a) U.S. shareholder increases its basis in stock or applicable property under paragraph (f)(2)(ii)(A)(2) of this section and decreases its basis in stock or applicable property pursuant to paragraph (f)(2)(ii)(B) of this section subject to the limitation under paragraph (f)(2)(ii)(B)(2) of this section, the election statement must so indicate. The attachment of an unsigned copy of the election statement to the timely-filed return for the relevant taxable year satisfies the signature requirement of this paragraph (f)(2)(iii)(B)(2) if the section 958(a) U.S. shareholder retains the original signed election statement in the manner specified by § 1.6001-1(e).

(g) *Gain reduction rule.*—(1) *Reduction in gain recognized under section 961(b)(2) by reason of distributions attributable to section 965 previously taxed earnings and profits in the inclusion year.*—(i) *In general.*—If a section 958(a) U.S. shareholder receives a distribution from a deferred foreign income corporation (including through a chain of ownership described under section 958(a)) during the inclusion year of the deferred foreign income corporation that is attributable to section 965 previously taxed earnings and profits of the deferred foreign income corporation, then the amount of gain that otherwise would be recognized under section 961(b)(2) by the section 958(a) U.S. shareholder with respect to the section 958(a) U.S. shareholder's section 958(a) stock of the deferred foreign income corporation or interest in applicable property with respect to the deferred foreign income corporation is reduced (but not below zero) by an amount equal to the section 965 previously taxed earnings and profits of the deferred foreign income corporation with respect to the section 958(a) U.S. shareholder, translated (if necessary) into U.S. dollars at the spot rate on December 31, 2017.

(ii) *Definition of section 965 previously taxed earnings and profits.*—For purposes of paragraph (g)(1)(i) of this section, the term *section 965 previously taxed earnings and profits* means, with respect to a deferred foreign income corporation and a section 958(a) U.S. shareholder, the sum of the section 965(a) previously taxed earnings and profits of the deferred foreign income corporation with respect to the section 958(a) U.S. shareholder, and, if the section 958(a) U.S. shareholder has made the election described in paragraph (f)(2) of this section, the section 965(b) previously taxed earnings and profits of the deferred for-

eign income corporation with respect to the section 958(a) U.S. shareholder.

(2) *Reduction in basis by an amount equal to the gain reduction amount.*—If a section 958(a) U.S. shareholder does not recognize gain under section 961(b)(2) by reason of paragraph (g)(1) of this section with respect to a distribution from a deferred foreign income corporation (including through a chain of ownership described under section 958(a)), the section 958(a) U.S. shareholder's basis in the section 958(a) stock of the deferred foreign income corporation, or the section 958(a) U.S. shareholder's basis in the applicable property with respect to the deferred foreign income corporation, is reduced by the amount of gain that would otherwise be recognized by the section 958(a) U.S. shareholder without regard to paragraph (g)(1) of this section.

(h) *Rules of application for specified basis adjustments.*—This paragraph (h) applies for purposes of making any adjustment to the basis of section 958(a) stock or applicable property with respect to a specified foreign corporation described in paragraph (e), (f)(2), or (g)(2) of this section (collectively, *specified basis adjustments*, and each a *specified basis adjustment*).

(1) *Timing of basis adjustments.*—Except as provided in paragraph (e)(2) of this section, a specified basis adjustment to section 958(a) stock or applicable property with respect to a specified foreign corporation is made as of the last day of the last taxable year of the specified foreign corporation that begins before January 1, 2018, on which it is a specified foreign corporation.

(2) *Netting of basis adjustments.*—If one or more specified basis adjustments occur on the same day with respect to the same section 958(a) stock or applicable property, a single basis adjustment is made as of the close of such day with respect to such stock or applicable property in an amount equal to the net amount, if any, of the increase or reduction, as applicable.

(3) *Gain recognition for reduction in excess of basis.*—The excess (if any) of a net reduction in basis with respect to section 958(a) stock or applicable property of a section 958(a) U.S. shareholder by reason of one or more specified basis adjustments over the section 958(a) U.S. shareholder's basis in such stock or applicable property without regard to the specified basis adjustments is treated as gain from the sale or exchange of property.

(4) *Adjustments with respect to each share.*—(i) *Section 958(a) stock.*—If a specified basis adjustment is made with respect to section 958(a) stock, the specified basis adjustment is made with respect to each share of the section 958(a) stock in a manner consistent with the section 958(a) U.S. shareholder's pro rata share of the

**Reg. § 1.965-2(h)(4)(i)**

section 965(a) earnings amount or specified E&P deficit, as applicable, by reason of such share.

(ii) *Applicable property.*—If a specified basis adjustment is made with respect to applicable property, the adjustment is made with respect to the applicable property in a manner consistent with the application of paragraph (h)(4)(i) of this section.

(5) *Stock or property for which adjustments are made.*—(i) *In general.*—Except as provided in paragraph (h)(5)(ii) of this section, a specified basis adjustment is made solely with respect to section 958(a) stock owned by the section 958(a) U.S. shareholder within the meaning of section 958(a)(1)(A) or applicable property owned directly by the section 958(a) U.S. shareholder.

(ii) *Special rule for an interest in a foreign pass-through entity.*—If the applicable property of the section 958(a) U.S. shareholder described in paragraph (h)(5)(i) of this section is an interest in a foreign pass-through entity, then, for purposes of determining the foreign pass-through entity's basis in section 958(a) stock or applicable property, as applicable, with respect to the section 958(a) U.S. shareholder, a specified basis adjustment is made with respect to section 958(a) stock or applicable property of the section 958(a) U.S. shareholder owned through the foreign pass-through entity in the same manner as if the section 958(a) stock or applicable property were owned directly by the section 958(a) U.S. shareholder. In the case of tiered foreign pass-through entities, this paragraph (h)(5)(ii) applies with respect to each foreign pass-through entity.

(i) *Definitions.*—This paragraph (i) provides definitions that apply for purposes of this section.

(1) *Applicable property.*—The term *applicable property* means, with respect to a section 958(a) U.S. shareholder and a specified foreign corporation, property owned by the section 958(a) U.S. shareholder (including through one or more foreign pass-through entities) by reason of which the section 958(a) U.S. shareholder is considered under section 958(a)(2) as owning section 958(a) stock of the specified foreign corporation.

(2) *Foreign pass-through entity.*—The term *foreign pass-through entity* means a foreign partnership or a foreign estate or trust (as defined in section 7701(a)(31)) (including a controlled domestic partnership treated as a foreign partnership pursuant to § 1.965-1(e)).

(3) *Property.*—The term *property* has the meaning provided in § 1.961-1(b)(1).

(j) *Examples.*—The following examples illustrate the application of this section.

(1) *Example 1. Determination of accumulated post-1986 deferred foreign income with subpart F income earned before E&P measurement date on November 2, 2017.* (i) *Facts.* USP, a domestic corpora-

tion, owns all of the stock of CFC1, a foreign corporation, which owns all of the stock of CFC2, also a foreign corporation. USP, CFC1, and CFC2 all have taxable years ending December 31, 2017. As of January 1, 2017, CFC1 has no earnings and profits, and CFC2 has 100u of earnings and profits described in section 959(c)(3) that were accumulated in taxable years beginning after December 31, 1986, while CFC2 was a specified foreign corporation, and $21x of post-1986 foreign income taxes. None of CFC2's earnings and profits are attributable to income treated as effectively connected with the conduct of a trade or business within the United States. On March 1, 2017, CFC1 earns 30u of subpart F income (as defined in section 952), and CFC2 earns 20u of subpart F income. No foreign income tax is imposed on CFC1's or CFC2's subpart F income. For purposes of section 904, the post-1986 undistributed earnings, subpart F income, and post-1986 foreign income taxes are in the general category. On July 1, 2017, CFC2 distributes 40u to CFC1. On November 1, 2017, CFC1 distributes 60u to USP. USP does not have an aggregate foreign E&P deficit. USP includes in gross income all amounts that it is required to include under section 951. No foreign income tax is imposed or withheld on the distribution by CFC2 to CFC1 or the distribution by CFC1 to USP.

(ii) *Analysis.* (A) *Adjustments to section 959(c) classification of earnings and profits for inclusion under section 951(a)(1)(A) without regard to section 965.* The distribution from CFC2 to CFC1 does not give rise to subpart F income to CFC1 due to the application of section 954(c)(6). Accordingly, USP's inclusion under section 951(a)(1)(A) without regard to section 965(a) is 30u with respect to CFC1 and 20u with respect to CFC2 for their taxable years ending December 31, 2017. As a result of the inclusions under section 951(a)(1)(A), CFC1 and CFC2 increase their earnings and profits described in section 959(c)(2) by 30u and 20u, respectively.

(B) *Distributions between specified foreign corporations before January 1, 2018.* The distribution of 40u from CFC2 to CFC1 is treated as a distribution of 20u out of earnings and profits described in section 959(c)(2) (attributable to inclusions under section 951(a)(1)(A) without regard to section 965(a)) and 20u out of earnings and profits described in section 959(c)(3).

(C) *Section 965(a) inclusion amount.* USP determines whether CFC1 and CFC2 are deferred foreign income corporations and, if so, determines its section 965(a) inclusion amounts with respect to CFC1 and CFC2. CFC1 and CFC2 are specified foreign corporations, and CFC1 and CFC2 each have accumulated post-1986 deferred foreign income greater than zero as of an E&P measurement date. Accordingly, CFC1 and CFC2 are deferred foreign income corporations. USP's section 965(a) inclusion amount with respect to each of CFC1 and CFC2, respectively, equals the section 965(a) earnings amount of CFC1 and CFC2, respectively.

*(1) CFC1 section 965(a) earnings amount.* The section 965(a) earnings amount with respect to CFC1 is 20u, the amount of its accumulated post-1986 deferred foreign income as of both November 2, 2017, and December 31, 2017, which is equal to 70u of post-1986 earnings and profits (30u earned and 40u attributable to the CFC2 distribution) reduced by 50u of such post-1986 earnings and profits described in section 959(c)(2) (30u earned and 20u attributable to the CFC2 distribution) under section 965(d)(2)(B) and § 1.965-1(f)(7)(i)(B). Under section 965(d)(3)(B) and § 1.965-1(f)(29)(i)(B), the post-1986 earnings and profits of CFC1 are not reduced by the 60u distribution to USP.

*(2) CFC2 section 965(a) earnings amount.* The section 965(a) earnings amount with respect to CFC2 is 80u, the amount of its accumulated post-1986 deferred foreign income as of both November 2, 2017, and December 31, 2017, which is equal to the amount of CFC2's post-1986 earnings and profits of 80u. CFC2's accumulated post-1986 deferred foreign income is equal to its post-1986 earnings and profits because CFC2 does not have earnings and profits that are attributable to income of the specified foreign corporation that is effectively connected with the conduct of a trade or business within the United States and subject to tax under chapter 1, or that, if distributed, would be excluded from the gross income of a United States shareholder under section 959 or from the gross income of another shareholder if such shareholder were a United States shareholder, and, therefore, no adjustment is made under section 965(d)(2) or § 1.965-1(f)(7). CFC2's 80u of post-1986 earnings and profits consists of 120u of earnings and profits that it earned, reduced by the 40u distribution to CFC1 under section 965(d)(3)(B) and § 1.965-1(f)(29)(i)(B). The amount of the reduction to the post-1986 earnings and profits of CFC2 for the 40u distribution is not limited by § 1.965-1(f)(29)(i)(B) because CFC1's post-1986 earnings and profits are increased by 40u as a result of the distribution. Furthermore, because the 40u distribution was made on July 1, 2017, which is before the E&P measurement date on November 2, 2017, § 1.965-4(f) is not relevant.

*(3) Effect on earnings and profits described in section 959(c)(2) and (3).* CFC1 and CFC2 increase their earnings and profits described in section 959(c)(2) by USP's section 965(a) inclusion amounts with respect to CFC1 and CFC2, 20u and 80u, respectively, and reduce their earnings and profits described in section 959(c)(3) by an equivalent amount.

*(D) Distribution to United States shareholder.* The distribution from CFC1 to USP is treated as a distribution of 60u out of the earnings and profits of CFC1 described in section 959(c)(2), which include earnings and profits attributable to the section 965(a) inclusion amount taken into account by USP.

*(E) Section 902 and section 960 consequences. (1) Distribution by and inclusions with respect to CFC2.* Under section 960, USP is deemed to pay $3.50x ($21x x (20u/120u)) of CFC2's post-1986 foreign income taxes as a result of its inclusion under section 951(a)(1)(A) without regard to section 965(a) with respect to CFC2. As a result of the distribution from CFC2 to CFC1, CFC2's post-1986 foreign income taxes are reduced, and CFC1's post-1986 foreign income taxes are increased, by the foreign income taxes deemed paid by CFC1 under section 902 of $3.50x (($21x-$3.50x) x (20u/120u-20u)). Under section 960, USP is deemed to pay $14x (($21x-$3.50x-$3.50x) x 80u/(120u-40u)) of CFC2's post-1986 foreign income taxes as a result of its section 965(a) inclusion with respect to CFC2. The taxes deemed paid by USP as a result of its section 965(a) inclusion with respect to CFC2 are subject to the applicable percentage disallowance under section 965(g).

*(2) Inclusions with respect to CFC1.* As determined in paragraph (j)(1)(ii)(E)(1) of this *section (paragraph (E)(1) in the analysis in this Example 1),* as a result of the distribution from CFC2 to CFC1, CFC1 is deemed under section 902 to pay $3.50x of CFC2's post-1986 foreign income taxes. Under section 960, USP is deemed to pay $2.10x ($3.50x x (30u/(30u+20u))) of CFC1's post-1986 foreign income taxes as a result of its inclusion under section 951(a)(1)(A) without regard to section 965(a) with respect to CFC1. Under section 960, USP is deemed to pay $1.40x (($3.50x-$2.10x) x 20u/(30u+20u-30u)) of CFC1's post-1986 foreign income taxes as a result of its section 965(a) inclusion with respect to CFC1. The taxes deemed paid by USP as a result of its section 965(a) inclusion with respect to CFC1 are subject to the applicable percentage disallowance under section 965(g).

*(2) Example 2. Determination of accumulated post-1986 deferred foreign income with subpart F income earned after E&P measurement date on November 2, 2017. (i) Facts.* The facts are the same as in paragraph (j)(1)(i) of this section (the facts in *Example 1),* except that on December 1, 2017, CFC1 earns an additional 50u of subpart F income (as defined in section 952), and neither CFC1 nor CFC2 has any post-1986 foreign income taxes.

*(ii) Analysis. (A) Adjustments to section 959(c) classification of earnings and profits for inclusion under section 951(a)(1)(A) without regard to section 965.* USP determines its inclusion under section 951(a)(1)(A) without regard to section 965(a), which is 80u with respect to CFC1 and 20u with respect to CFC2 for their taxable years ending December 31, 2017. As a result of the inclusions under section 951(a)(1)(A), CFC1 and CFC2 increase their earnings and profits described in section 959(c)(2) by 80u and 20u, respectively.

*(B) Distributions between specified foreign corporations before January 1, 2018.* The analysis is the same as in paragraph (j)(1)(ii)(B) of this section (paragraph (B) in the analysis in *Example 1).*

Tax Cuts and Jobs Act: Regulatory Explanation and Analysis

(C) *Section 965(a) inclusion amount.* USP determines whether CFC1 and CFC2 are deferred foreign income corporations and, if so, determines its section 965(a) inclusion amounts with respect to CFC1 and CFC2. CFC1 and CFC2 are specified foreign corporations, and CFC1 and CFC2 each have accumulated post-1986 deferred foreign income greater than zero as of an E&P measurement date. Accordingly, CFC1 and CFC2 are deferred foreign income corporations. USP's section 965(a) inclusion amount with respect to each of CFC1 and CFC2, respectively, equals the section 965(a) earnings amount of CFC1 and CFC2, respectively.

*(1) CFC1 section 965(a) earnings amount.* The section 965(a) earnings amount with respect to CFC1 is 20u, the greater of—

*(i)* The amount of its accumulated post-1986 deferred foreign income as of November 2, 2017, 20u, which is equal to 70u of post-1986 earnings and profits (30u earned and 40u attributable to the CFC2 distribution) reduced by 50u of such post-1986 earnings and profits described in section 959(c)(2) without regard to the subpart F income earned after November 2, 2017 (30u earned and 20u attributable to the CFC2 distribution) under section 965(d)(2)(B) and §1.965-1(f)(7)(i)(B) and (ii), and

*(ii)* The amount of its accumulated post-1986 deferred foreign income as of December 31, 2017, 20u, which is equal to 120u of post-1986 earnings and profits (80u earned and 40u attributable to the CFC2 distribution) reduced by 100u of such post-1986 earnings and profits described in section 959(c)(2) with regard to the subpart F income earned on or before December 31, 2017 (80u earned and 20u attributable to the CFC2 distribution) under section 965(d)(2)(B) and §1.965-1(f)(7)(i)(B) and (ii).

*(2) CFC2 section 965(a) earnings amount.* The analysis is the same as in paragraph (j)(1)(ii)(C)(2) of this section (paragraph (C)(2) in the analysis in *Example 1*).

*(3) Effect on earnings and profits described in section 959(c)(2) and (3).* The analysis is the same as in paragraph (j)(1)(ii)(C)(3) of this section (paragraph (C)(3) in the analysis in *Example 1*).

(D) *Distribution to United States shareholder.* The analysis is the same as in paragraph (j)(1)(ii)(D) of this section (paragraph (D) in the analysis in *Example 1*).

*(3) Example 3.* Determination of accumulated post-1986 deferred foreign income with subpart F income earned after E&P measurement date on November 2, 2017, but previously taxed earnings and profits attributable to the subpart F income distributed before E&P measurement date on November 2, 2017. (i) *Facts.* The facts are the same as in paragraph (j)(1)(i) of this section (the facts in *Example 1*), except that on December 1, 2017, CFC2 earns an additional 50u of subpart F income (as defined in section 952), and neither CFC1 nor CFC2 has any post-1986 foreign income taxes.

(ii) *Analysis.* (A) *Adjustments to section 959(c) classification of earnings and profits for inclusion*

under section 951(a)(1)(A) without regard to section 965. USP determines its inclusion under section 951(a)(1)(A) without regard to section 965(a), which is 30u with respect to CFC1 and 70u with respect to CFC2 for their taxable years ending December 31, 2017. As a result of the inclusions under section 951(a)(1)(A), CFC1 and CFC2 increase their earnings and profits described in section 959(c)(2) by 30u and 70u, respectively.

(B) *Distributions between specified foreign corporations before January 1, 2018.* The distribution of 40u from CFC2 to CFC1 is treated as a distribution of 40u out of earnings and profits described in section 959(c)(2) (attributable to inclusions under section 951(a)(1)(A) without regard to section 965(a)).

(C) *Section 965(a) inclusion amount.* USP determines whether CFC1 and CFC2 are deferred foreign income corporations, and, if so, determines its section 965(a) inclusion amounts with respect to CFC1 and CFC2. Because USP wholly owns CFC1 and CFC2 under section 958(a) and USP does not have an aggregate foreign E&P deficit, USP's section 965(a) inclusion amount with respect to each of CFC1 and CFC2, respectively, equals the section 965(a) earnings amount, if any, of CFC1 and CFC2, respectively.

*(1) CFC1 section 965(a) earnings amount.* CFC1 is not a deferred foreign income corporation and does not have a section 965(a) earnings amount because the amount of its accumulated post-1986 deferred foreign income as of both November 2, 2017, and December 31, 2017, is 0u, which is equal to 70u of post-1986 earnings and profits (30u earned and 40u attributable to the CFC2 distribution) reduced by 70u of such post-1986 earnings and profits described in section 959(c)(2) (30u earned and 40u attributable to the CFC2 distribution) under section 965(d)(2)(B) and §1.965-1(f)(7)(i)(B).

*(2) CFC2 section 965(a) earnings amount.* The section 965(a) earnings amount with respect to CFC2 is 100u, the greater of the amounts in paragraph (j)(3)(ii)(C)(2)(i) and (ii) of this section (paragraph (C)(2)(i) and (ii) in the analysis in this *Example 3*)—

*(i)* The amount of its accumulated post-1986 deferred foreign income as of November 2, 2017, 80u. CFC2's 80u of accumulated post-1986 deferred foreign income as of November 2, 2017, is equal to its 80u of post-1986 earnings and profits because no adjustment is made under section 965(d)(2) or §1.965-1(f)(7), as CFC2 does not have earnings and profits that are attributable to income of the specified foreign corporation that is effectively connected with the conduct of a trade or business within the United States and subject to tax under chapter 1, or that, if distributed, would be excluded from the gross income of a United States shareholder under section 959 or from the gross income of another shareholder if such shareholder were a United States shareholder, without regard to the subpart F income earned after November 2, 2017. CFC2's 80u of post-1986 earnings and profits consists of 120u of

earnings and profits that it earned, reduced by the 40u distribution to CFC1 under section 965(d)(3)(B) and § 1.965-1(f)(29)(i)(B). The amount of the reduction to the post-1986 earnings and profits of CFC2 for the 40u distribution is not limited by § 1.965-1(f)(29)(i)(B) because CFC1's post-1986 earnings and profits are increased by 40u as a result of the distribution. Furthermore, because the 40u distribution was made on July 1, 2017, which is before any E&P measurement date, § 1.965-4(f) is not relevant.

(*ii*) The amount of its accumulated post-1986 deferred foreign income as of December 31, 2017, 100u, which is equal to 130u of post-1986 earnings and profits reduced by 30u of such post-1986 earnings and profits described in section 959(c)(2) with regard to the subpart F income earned before December 31, 2017, under section 965(d)(2)(B) and § 1.965-1(f)(7)(i)(B) and (ii). CFC2's 130u of post-1986 earnings and profits consists of 170u of earnings and profits that it earned, reduced by the 40u distribution to CFC1 under section 965(d)(3)(B) and § 1.965-1(f)(29)(i)(B).

(*3*) *Effect on earnings and profits described in section 959(c)(2) and (3).* CFC2 increases its earnings and profits described in section 959(c)(2) by USP's section 965(a) inclusion amount with respect to CFC2, 100u, and reduces its earnings and profits described in section 959(c)(3) by an equivalent amount.

(*D*) *Distribution to United States shareholder.* The analysis is the same as in paragraph (j)(1)(ii)(D) of this section (paragraph (D) in the analysis in *Example 1*.

(*4*) *Example 4. Determination of accumulated post-1986 deferred foreign income with distribution made after E&P measurement date on November 2, 2017.* (i) *Facts.* USP, a domestic corporation, owns all of the stock of CFC1, a foreign corporation, which owns all of the stock of CFC2, also a foreign corporation. USP, CFC1, and CFC2 all have taxable years ending December 31, 2017. As of January 1, 2017, CFC1 has 10u of earnings and profits described in section 959(c)(3) that were accumulated in taxable years beginning after December 31, 1986, while CFC1 was a specified foreign corporation, and $2x of post-1986 foreign income taxes; and CFC2 has 100u of earnings and profits described in section 959(c)(3) that were accumulated in taxable years beginning after December 31, 1986, while CFC2 was a specified foreign corporation and $10x of post-1986 foreign income taxes. For purposes of section 904, the post-1986 undistributed earnings and post-1986 foreign income taxes are in the general category. None of CFC1's or CFC2's earnings and profits are attributable to income treated as effectively connected with the conduct of a trade or business within the United States. On December 1, 2017, CFC2 distributes 100u to CFC1, and CFC1 distributes 10u to USP. USP does not have an aggregate foreign E&P deficit. USP includes in gross income all amounts that it is required to include under section 951. No foreign income tax

is imposed or withheld on the distribution by CFC2 to CFC1 or the distribution by CFC1 to USP. USP does not apply § 1.965-4(f)(3) to determine the post-1986 earnings and profits of CFC1 and CFC2.

(ii) *Analysis.* (A) *Adjustments to section 959(c) classification of earnings and profits for inclusion under section 951(a)(1)(A) without regard to section 965.* The distribution from CFC2 to CFC1 does not give rise to subpart F income to CFC1 due to the application of section 954(c)(6). Accordingly, USP does not have an inclusion under section 951(a)(1)(A) without regard to section 965(a) with respect to CFC1 or CFC2 for their taxable years ending December 31, 2017. As a result, neither CFC1 nor CFC2 has earnings and profits described in section 959(c)(2).

(B) *Distributions between specified foreign corporations before January 1, 2018.* The distribution of 100u from CFC2 to CFC1 is initially treated as a distribution out of earnings and profits described in section 959(c)(3).

(C) *Section 965(a) inclusion amount.* USP determines whether CFC1 and CFC2 are deferred foreign income corporations, and, if so, determines its section 965(a) inclusion amounts with respect to CFC1 and CFC2. CFC1 and CFC2 are specified foreign corporations, and CFC1 and CFC2 each have accumulated post-1986 deferred foreign income greater than zero as of an E&P measurement date. Accordingly, CFC1 and CFC2 are deferred foreign income corporations. USP's section 965(a) inclusion amount with respect to each of CFC1 and CFC2, respectively, equals the section 965(a) earnings amount of CFC1 and CFC2, respectively.

(1) *CFC1 section 965(a) earnings amount.* The section 965(a) earnings amount with respect to CFC1 is 10u, the amount of its accumulated post-1986 deferred foreign income as of both November 2, 2017, and December 31, 2017, which is equal to the amount of CFC1's post-1986 earnings and profits of 10u. CFC1's accumulated post-1986 deferred foreign income is equal to its post-1986 earnings and profits because CFC1 does not have earnings and profits that are attributable to income of the specified foreign corporation that is effectively connected with the conduct of a trade or business within the United States and subject to tax under chapter 1, or that, if distributed, would be excluded from the gross income of a United States shareholder under section 959 or from the gross income of another shareholder if such shareholder were a United States shareholder, and therefore no adjustment is made under section 965(d)(2) or § 1.965-1(f)(7). But for § 1.965-4(f), CFC1's post-1986 earnings and profits as of December 31, 2017, would be 110u, but because the distribution from CFC2 is a specified payment, it is disregarded in determining CFC1's post-1986 earnings and profits as of December 31, 2017, under § 1.965-4(f). Under section 965(d)(3)(B) and § 1.965-1(f)(29)(i)(B), the post-1986 earnings

and profits of CFC1 are not reduced by the 10u distribution to USP.

(2) *CFC2 section 965(a) earnings amount.* The section 965(a) earnings amount with respect to CFC2 is 100u, the amount of its accumulated post-1986 deferred foreign income as of both November 2, 2017, and December 31, 2017, which is equal to the amount of CFC2's post-1986 earnings and profits of 100u. CFC2's accumulated post-1986 deferred foreign income is equal to its post-1986 earnings and profits because CFC2 does not have earnings and profits that are attributable to income of the specified foreign corporation that is effectively connected with the conduct of a trade or business within the United States and subject to tax under chapter 1, or that, if distributed, would be excluded from the gross income of a United States shareholder under section 959 or from the gross income of another shareholder if such shareholder were a United States shareholder, and therefore no adjustment is made under section 965(d)(2) or § 1.965-1(f)(7). But for § 1.965-4(f), CFC2's post-1986 earnings and profits as of December 31, 2017, would be 0u, but because the distribution to CFC1 is a specified payment, it is disregarded in determining CFC2's post-1986 earnings and profits as of December 31, 2017, under § 1.965-4(f).

(3) *Effect on earnings and profits described in section 959(c)(2) and (3).* CFC1 and CFC2 increase their earnings and profits described in section 959(c)(2) by USP's section 965(a) inclusion amounts with respect to CFC1 and CFC2, 10u and 100u, respectively, and reduce their earnings and profits described in section 959(c)(3) by an equivalent amount.

(D) *Distributions—(1) Distribution that is a specified payment.* The distribution from CFC2 to CFC1 is recharacterized as a distribution of 100u out of the earnings and profits of CFC2 described in section 959(c)(2), which include earnings and profits attributable to the section 965(a) inclusion amount taken into account by USP.

(2) *Distribution to United States shareholder.* The distribution from CFC1 to USP is treated as a distribution of 10u out of the earnings and profits of CFC1 described in section 959(c)(2), which include earnings and profits attributable to the section 965(a) inclusion amount taken into account by USP.

(E) *Section 902 and section 960 consequences.* Under section 960, USP is deemed to pay $10x ($10x x (100u/100u)) of CFC2's post-1986 foreign income taxes as a result of its section 965(a) inclusion with respect to CFC2 and $2x ($2x x (10u/10u) of CFC1's post-1986 foreign income taxes as a result of its section 965(a) inclusion with respect to CFC1. Such taxes are subject to the applicable percentage disallowance under section 965(g).

(5) *Example 5. Determination of accumulated post-1986 deferred foreign income with section 951(a)(1)(B) inclusion after E&P measurement date on November 2, 2017.* (i) *Facts.* USP, a domestic corporation, owns all of the stock of CFC, a foreign corporation. USP has a taxable year ending December 31, 2017, and CFC has a taxable year ending November 30, 2017. As of December 1, 2016, CFC has 110u of earnings and profits described in section 959(c)(3) that were accumulated in taxable years beginning after December 31, 1986, while CFC was a specified foreign corporation. CFC holds 150u of United States property throughout its taxable year ending November 30, 2017, but disposes of it on December 1, 2017, recognizing no gain or loss on the property. Between December 1, 2017, and December 31, 2017, CFC earns an additional 10u of income that does not constitute subpart F income or income treated as effectively connected with the conduct of a trade or business within the United States that gives rise to 10u of earnings and profits. USP includes in income all amounts that it is required to include under section 951.

(ii) *Analysis.* (A) *Section 965(a) inclusion amount.* USP determines whether CFC is a deferred foreign income corporation, and, if so, determines its section 965(a) inclusion amount with respect to CFC. CFC is a specified foreign corporation, and CFC has accumulated post-1986 deferred foreign income greater than zero as of an E&P measurement date. Accordingly, CFC is a deferred foreign income corporation. USP's section 965(a) inclusion amount with respect to CFC equals the section 965(a) earnings amount of CFC.

(1) *CFC section 965(a) earnings amount.* The section 965(a) earnings amount with respect to CFC is 110u, the greater of the amount of its accumulated post-1986 deferred foreign income as of November 2, 2017, which is 110u, and the amount of its accumulated post-1986 deferred foreign income as of December 31, 2017, which is 10u. CFC's accumulated post-1986 deferred foreign income as of November 2, 2017, is equal to its 110u of post-1986 earnings and profits, which are not reduced by the 110u of earnings and profits described in section 959(c)(1) as a result of USP's section 951(a)(1)(B) inclusion with respect to CFC as of December 31, 2017, because such amounts would not be excluded from the gross income of a United States shareholder under section 959 under section 965(d)(2) or § 1.965-1(f)(7) if distributed on November 2, 2017. CFC's accumulated post-1986 deferred foreign income as of December 31, 2017, is equal to its 120u of post-1986 earnings and profits reduced by the 110u of earnings and profits described in section 959(c)(1) as a result of USP's section 951(a)(1)(B) inclusion with respect to CFC as of December 31, 2017, which would be excluded from the gross income of a United States shareholder under section 959 under section 965(d)(2) or § 1.965-1(f)(7) if distributed on December 31, 2017.

(2) *Effect on earnings and profits described in section 959(c)(2) and (3).* In USP's taxable year ending December 31, 2018, CFC increases its

earnings and profits described in section 959(c)(2) by USP's section 965(a) inclusion amount with respect to CFC, 110u, and reduces its earnings and profits described in section 959(c)(3) by an equivalent amount.

(B) *Section 956 inclusion.* In USP's taxable year ending December 31, 2017, USP increases its earnings and profits described in section 959(c)(1) by USP's amount included under sections 951(a)(1)(B) and 956 with respect to CFC, 110u, and reduces its earnings and profits described in section 959(c)(3) by an equivalent amount.

(6) *Example 6. Section 1248 inclusion.* (i) *Facts.* USP1, a domestic corporation, owns all of the stock of CFC, a foreign corporation, until it sells all of such stock to USP2, a domestic corporation, on December 1, 2017, in a sale on which USP1 recognizes $100x of gain. Throughout 2017, 1u=$1x. USP1, USP2, and CFC all have taxable years ending December 31, 2017. As of January 1, 2017, CFC has 100u of earnings and profits described in section 959(c)(3) that were accumulated in taxable years beginning after December 31, 1986, while CFC was wholly owned by USP1. On March 1, 2017, CFC distributes 20u to USP1. None of CFC's earnings and profits are attributable to income treated as effectively connected with the conduct of a trade or business within the United States. USP2 does not have an aggregate foreign E&P deficit. USP1 and USP2 include in income all amounts that they are required to include under sections 951 and 1248.

(ii) *Analysis.* (A) *Adjustments to section 959(c) classification of earnings and profits for section 1248 inclusion.* USP1's inclusion under section 1248 with respect to CFC is $80x ($100x-$20x). As a result of the inclusion under section 1248, under section 959(e), CFC increases its earnings and profits described in section 959(c)(2) by 80u.

(B) *Section 965(a) inclusion amount.* USP2 determines whether CFC is a deferred foreign income corporation and, if so, determines its section 965(a) inclusion amount with respect to CFC. CFC is a specified foreign corporation, and CFC has accumulated post-1986 deferred foreign income greater than zero as of an E&P measurement date. Accordingly, CFC is a deferred foreign income corporation. USP2's section 965(a) inclusion amount with respect to CFC equals the section 965(a) earnings amount of CFC. The section 965(a) earnings amount with respect to CFC is 20u, the amount of its accumulated post-1986 deferred foreign income as of both November 2, 2017, and December 31, 2017, which is equal to 100u of post-1986 earnings and profits reduced by 80u of such post-1986 earnings and profits described in section 959(c)(2) under section 965(d)(2)(B) and § 1.965-1(f)(7)(i)(B). CFC increases its earnings and profits described in section 959(c)(2) by USP2's section 965(a) inclusion amount with respect to CFC, 20u, and reduces its earnings and profits that would be described in section

959(c)(3) but for the application of section 965(a) by an equivalent amount.

(C) *Distributions to United States shareholders.* The distributions from CFC to USP1 (including the deemed dividend under section 1248) are treated as distributions out of the earnings and profits of CFC described in section 959(c)(3).

(7) *Example 7. Distribution attributable to section 965(a) previously taxed earnings and profits.* (i) *Facts.* USP, a domestic corporation, owns all of the stock of CFC1, a specified foreign corporation that has no post-1986 earnings and profits (or deficit in post-1986 earnings and profits), and CFC1 owns all the stock of CFC2, a deferred foreign income corporation. USP is a calendar year taxpayer. CFC1's last taxable year beginning before January 1, 2018, ends on November 30, 2018; CFC2 has an inclusion year that ends on November 30, 2018. The functional currency of CFC1 and CFC2 is the U.S. dollar. USP's adjusted basis in the stock of CFC1 is zero. On January 1, 2018, CFC2 distributes $100x to CFC1, and CFC1 distributes $100x to USP. USP has a section 965(a) inclusion amount of $100x with respect to CFC2 that is taken into account for USP's taxable year ending December 31, 2018. CFC2 has no earnings and profits described in section 959(c)(1) or (2) other than section 965(a) previously taxed earnings and profits.

(ii) *Analysis.* Under paragraph (c) of this section, CFC2 has $100x of section 965(a) previously taxed earnings and profits with respect to USP. USP receives a distribution from CFC2 through a chain of ownership described in section 958(a) during the inclusion year of CFC2 that is attributable to the $100x of section 965(a) previously taxed earnings and profits of CFC2. Under paragraph (g)(1) of this section, the amount of gain that USP otherwise would recognize with respect to the stock of CFC1 under section 961(b)(2) is reduced (but not below zero) by $100x, the amount of CFC2's section 965(a) previously taxed earnings and profits with respect to USP. As of the close of November 30, 2018, USP's basis in CFC1 is increased under paragraph (e) of this section by USP's section 965(a) inclusion amount with respect to CFC2 ($100x), and is reduced under paragraph (g)(2) of this section by the amount of gain that would have been recognized by USP under section 961(b)(?) but for the application of paragraph (g)(1) of this section ($100x).

(8) *Example 8. Distribution attributable to section 965(b) previously taxed earnings and profits; parent-subsidiary.* (i) *Facts.* The facts are the same as in paragraph (j)(7)(i) of this section (the facts in *Example 7*), except that CFC1 has a specified E&P deficit of $100x. Because of the specified E&P deficit of CFC1, USP's section 965(a) inclusion amount with respect to CFC2 is reduced to zero pursuant to section 965(b)(1) and § 1.965-1(b)(2). USP makes the election described in paragraph (f)(2) of this section.

(ii) *Analysis.* (A) *Application of the gain reduction rule.* Under paragraph (d)(1) of this section, CFC2 has $100x of section 965(b) previously taxed earnings and profits with respect to USP, and, under paragraph (d)(2) of this section, CFC1's earnings and profits described in section 959(c)(3) are increased by $100x to $0. USP receives a distribution from CFC2 through a chain of ownership described in section 958(a) during the inclusion year of CFC2 that is attributable to the $100x of section 965(b) previously taxed earnings and profits of CFC2. Under paragraph (g)(1) of this section, the amount of gain that USP otherwise would recognize with respect to the stock of CFC1 under section 961(b)(2) is reduced (but not below zero) by $100x, the amount of CFC2's section 965(b) previously taxed earnings and profits with respect to USP under paragraph (d)(1) of this section.

(B) *Adjustments to the basis of CFC1.* Because USP makes the election described in paragraph (f)(2) of this section, as of the close of November 30, 2018, USP's basis in CFC1 is increased under paragraph (f)(2)(ii)(A) of this section by an amount equal to CFC2's section 965(b) previously taxed earnings and profits with respect to USP under paragraph (d)(1) of this section ($100x), reduced under paragraph (f)(2)(ii)(B) of this section by an amount equal to the portion of the specified E&P deficit of CFC1 taken into account in determining USP's section 965(a) inclusion amount with respect to CFC2 ($100x), and reduced under paragraph (g)(2) of this section by the amount of gain that would have been recognized by USP with respect to the stock of CFC1 under section 961(b)(2) but for the application of paragraph (g)(1) of this section ($100x). Under paragraph (h)(2) and (3) of this section, the excess of the net reduction from the adjustments under paragraphs (f) and (g) of this section over USP's basis in the stock of CFC1 (in this case, $100x) is treated as gain recognized by USP from the sale or exchange of property.

(9) *Example 9. Distribution attributable to section 965(b) previously taxed earnings and profits; brother-sister.* (i) *Facts.* The facts are the same as in paragraph (j)(8)(i) of this section (the facts in *Example 8*), except that USP owns all the stock of CFC2, USP's adjusted basis in the stock of CFC2 is zero, CFC1 made no distributions, and on January 1, 2018, CFC2 distributes $100x to USP.

(ii) *Analysis.* (A) *Application of the gain reduction rule.* Under paragraph (d)(1) of this section, CFC2 has $100x of section 965(b) previously taxed earnings and profits with respect to USP, and, under paragraph (d)(2) of this section, CFC1's earnings and profits described in section 959(c)(3) (deficit of $100x) are increased by $100x to $0. USP receives a distribution from CFC2 during the inclusion year of CFC2 that is attributable to the $100x of section 965(b) previously taxed earnings and profits of CFC2. Under paragraph (g)(1) of this section, the amount of gain that USP otherwise would recognize with respect to the stock of CFC2 under section

961(b)(2) is reduced (but not below zero) by $100x, the amount of CFC2's section 965(b) previously taxed earnings and profits with respect to USP under paragraph (d)(1) of this section.

(B) *Adjustments to the basis of CFC1 and CFC2.* Because USP makes the election described in paragraph (f)(2) of this section, as of the close of November 30, 2018, USP's basis in the stock of CFC2 is increased under paragraph (f)(2)(ii)(A) of this section by the amount of CFC2's section 965(b) previously taxed earnings and profits with respect to USP under paragraph (d)(1) of this section ($100x) and reduced under paragraph (g)(2) of this section by the amount of gain that would have been recognized by USP with respect to the stock of CFC2 under section 961(b)(2) but for the application of paragraph (g)(1) of this section ($100x). As of the close of November 30, 2018, USP's basis in CFC1 is reduced under paragraph (f)(2)(ii)(B) of this section by an amount equal to the portion of USP's pro rata share of the specified E&P deficit of CFC1 taken into account in determining USP's section 965(a) inclusion amount with respect to CFC2 ($100x). Under paragraph (h)(3) of this section, the excess of the reduction under paragraph (f) of this section over USP's basis in the stock of CFC1 (in this case, $100x) is treated as gain recognized by USP from the sale or exchange of property. [Reg. § 1.965-2.]

☐ [*T.D.* 9846, 2-4-2019.]

**[Reg. § 1.965-3]**

**§ 1.965-3. Section 965(c) deductions.—** (a) *Scope.*—This section provides rules regarding section 965(c) deductions and section 965(c) deduction amounts. Paragraph (b) of this section provides rules for disregarding certain assets for purposes of determining the aggregate foreign cash position of a section 958(a) U.S. shareholder. Paragraph (c) of this section provides rules for determining the aggregate foreign cash position for a section 958(a) U.S. shareholder inclusion year. Paragraph (d) of this section provides a rule regarding certain expatriated entities. Paragraph (e) of this section provides a rule for the treatment of section 965(c) deductions in connection with an election under section 962. Paragraph (f) of this section provides rules regarding the treatment of a section 965(c) deduction under certain provisions of the Internal Revenue Code. Paragraph (g) of this section provides a rule for domestic pass-through entities.

(b) *Rules for disregarding certain assets for determining aggregate foreign cash position.*—(1) *Disregard of certain obligations between related specified foreign corporations.*—In determining the aggregate foreign cash position of a section 958(a) U.S. shareholder, any account receivable, account payable, short-term obligation, or derivative financial instrument between a specified foreign corporation with respect to which the section 958(a) U.S. shareholder owns section 958(a) stock and a related specified foreign corporation on corresponding cash measurement dates is disregarded to the extent of the smallest of the product of the amount of the item on such corresponding cash measurement dates of each specified foreign corporation and the section 958(a) U.S. shareholder's ownership percentage of section 958(a) stock of the specified foreign corporation owned by the section 958(a) U.S. shareholder on such dates. For purposes of this paragraph (b)(1)(i), a specified foreign corporation is treated as a related specified foreign corporation with respect to another specified foreign corporation if, as of the cash measurement date referred to in the preceding sentence of each specified foreign corporation, the specified foreign corporations are related persons within the meaning of section 954(d)(3), substituting the term "specified foreign corporation" for "controlled foreign corporation" in each place that it appears.

(2) *Disregard of other assets upon demonstration of double-counting.*—For purposes of determining the aggregate foreign cash position of a section 958(a) U.S. shareholder, the section 958(a) U.S. shareholder's pro rata share of the cash position of a specified foreign corporation on a cash measurement date is reduced by amounts of net accounts receivable, actively traded property, and short-term obligations to the extent such amounts are attributable to amounts taken into account in determining the section 958(a) U.S. shareholder's pro rata share of the cash position of another specified foreign corporation on the corresponding cash measurement date of such other specified foreign corporation and to the extent not disregarded pursuant to paragraph (b)(1) of this section. However, the preceding sentence applies only if the section 958(a) U.S. shareholder attaches a statement containing the information outlined in paragraphs (b)(2)(i) through (v) of this section to its timely filed return (taking into account extensions, if any) for the section 958(a) U.S. shareholder inclusion year, or, if the section 958(a) U.S. shareholder has multiple section 958(a) U.S. shareholder inclusion years, the later of such years. Relief is not available under § 301.9100-2 or 301.9100-3 to allow late filing of the statement. The statement must contain the following information with respect to each specified foreign corporation for which the cash position is reduced under this paragraph (b)(2)—

(i) A description of the asset that would be taken into account with respect to both specified foreign corporations,

(ii) A statement of the amount by which its pro rata share of the cash position of one specified foreign corporation is reduced,

(iii) A detailed explanation of why there would otherwise be double-counting, including the computation of the amount taken into account with respect to the other specified foreign corporation, and

(iv) An explanation of why paragraph (b)(1) of this section does not apply to disregard such amount.

(3) *Disregard of portion of cash position of noncorporate entities treated as specified foreign corporations.*—If an entity is treated as a specified foreign corporation of a section 958(a) U.S. shareholder pursuant to section 965(c)(3)(E), for purposes of determining the aggregate foreign cash position of the section 958(a) U.S. shareholder, the section 958(a) U.S. shareholder's pro rata share of the cash position of the entity (determined taking into account paragraphs (b)(1) and (b)(2) of this section) is reduced by the amount of the pro rata share attributable to deemed stock of the entity not owned (within the meaning of section 958(a), applied by treating domestic pass-through entities as foreign) by a specified foreign corporation of the section 958(a) U.S. shareholder (determined without taking into account section 965(c)(3)(E)).

(4) *Examples.*—The following examples illustrate the application of this paragraph (b).

(i) *Example 1.* (A) *Facts.* USP, a domestic corporation, owns all of the stock of CFC1, a foreign corporation. CFC1 owns 95% of the only class of stock of CFC2, also a foreign corporation, and 40% of the only class of stock of CFC3, also a foreign corporation. The remaining 5% of the only class of stock of CFC2 is owned by a person unrelated to USP, CFC1, and CFC2; and the remaining 60% of the only class of stock of CFC3 is owned by a person unrelated to USP and CFC1. USP, CFC1, and CFC3 have calendar year taxable years. CFC2 has a taxable year ending on November 30. On November 15, 2015, CFC1 makes a loan of $100x to CFC2, which is required to be and is, in fact, repaid on January 1, 2016. On November 15, 2016, CFC2 sells inventory to CFC1 in exchange for an account receivable of $200x, which is required to be and is, in fact, repaid on December 15, 2016. On August 1, 2017, CFC1 makes a loan of $300x to CFC3, which is required to be and is, in fact, repaid on January 31, 2018.

(B) *Analysis*—(1) *Loan from CFC1 to CFC2.* For purposes of determining the aggregate foreign cash position of USP, a section 958(a) U.S. shareholder of CFC1, under paragraph (b)(1) of this section, because CFC1 and CFC2 are related within the meaning of paragraph (b)(1) of this section, the short-term obligation of CFC2 held by CFC1 outstanding on the first cash measurement date of each specified foreign corporation, November 30, 2015, and December 31, 2015, respectively, is disregarded to the extent of 95%, the smallest ownership percentage of section 958(a) stock of CFC1 and CFC2 owned by USP on such first cash measurement dates. Accordingly, USP only takes into account $5 ($100 - 95% of $100) of the short-term obligation in determining CFC1's cash position for purposes of determining its aggregate foreign cash position.

**Reg. §1.965-3(b)(4)**

(2) *Account receivable of CFC1 held by CFC2.* Because the account receivable of CFC1 held by CFC2 on its second cash measurement date, November 30, 2016, is not outstanding on CFC1's second cash measurement date, December 31, 2016, paragraph (b)(1) of this section does not apply to disregard any portion of such account receivable.

(3) *Loan from CFC1 to CFC3.* Because CFC3 is not related to CFC1 within the meaning of paragraph (b)(1) of this section, paragraph (b)(1) of this section does not apply to disregard any portion of such short-term obligation.

(ii) *Example 2.* (A) *Facts.* The facts are the same as in paragraph (b)(4)(i)(A) of this section (the facts in *Example 1*), except that on December 1, 2015, CFC1 sells 5% of the stock of CFC2 to an unrelated person.

(B) *Analysis.* The analysis is the same as in paragraph (b)(4)(i)(B) of this section (the analysis in *Example 1*), except that the short-term obligation of CFC2 held by CFC1 outstanding on both of their first cash measurement dates, November 30, 2015, and December 31, 2015, respectively, is disregarded under paragraph (b)(1) of this section to the extent of 90%, the smallest ownership percentage of section 958(a) stock of CFC1 and CFC2 by USP on such first cash measurement dates. Accordingly, USP takes into account $10 ($100 - 90% of $100) of the short-term obligation in determining CFC1's cash position for purposes of determining its aggregate foreign cash position.

(iii) *Example 3.* (A) *Facts.* USP, a domestic corporation, owns all of the stock of CFC1, a foreign corporation, which owns 45% of the only class of stock of CFC2, also a foreign corporation. The remainder of the CFC2 stock is actively traded on an established financial market but is not owned by any person related to USP or CFC1. USP, CFC1, and CFC2 have calendar year taxable years. The value of the CFC2 stock owned by CFC1 is $500x on each of the cash measurement dates. Also on each of the cash measurement dates, CFC2 has $300x of assets described in section 965(c)(3)(B) and § 1.965-1(f)(16) that are taken into account in determining its cash position.

(B) *Analysis.* For purposes of determining USP's aggregate foreign cash position, USP's pro rata share of the cash position of CFC1 on each cash measurement date may be reduced by the amount of the stock of CFC2 to the extent attributable to amounts taken into account in determining USP's pro rata share of the cash position of CFC2 on such cash measurement date (that is, to the extent of the $135x taken into account with respect to CFC2), provided USP attaches a statement to its timely filed return (taking into account extensions, if any) containing the following: a description of the CFC2 stock and the assets of CFC2 taken into account in determining its cash position; a statement that USP's pro rata share of the cash position of CFC1 is being reduced by $135x; the computation of the

$135x taken into account with respect to CFC2; and an explanation of why paragraph (b)(1) of this section does not apply to disregard such amount.

(iv) *Example 4.* (A) *Facts.* USP, a domestic corporation, owns all of the stock of CFC1 and CFC2, each a foreign corporation. USP, CFC1, and CFC2 have calendar year taxable years. CFC1 buys goods on credit from a third party for $100x and thus has an account payable of $100x. CFC1 modifies the goods and sells to CFC2 for $105x in exchange for an account receivable of $105x. CFC2 modifies the goods and sells to another third party for $110x in exchange for an account receivable of $110x. All of the accounts payable and accounts receivable are outstanding on the final cash measurement date.

(B) *Analysis.* For purposes of determining USP's aggregate foreign cash position, on the final cash measurement date, CFC1 has net accounts receivable of $0 because, pursuant to paragraph (b)(1) of this section, CFC1's account receivable from CFC2 is disregarded, and CFC2 has net accounts receivable of $110x because, pursuant to paragraph (b)(1) of this section, CFC2's account payable to CFC1 is disregarded. USP cannot rely on the rule in paragraph (b)(2) of this section because no amounts attributable to CFC2's net accounts receivable are taken into account with respect to another specified foreign corporation.

(v) *Example 5.* (A) *Facts.* USP, a domestic corporation, owns all of the stock of CFC1 and CFC2, each a foreign corporation. USP and CFC1 own 60% and 40%, respectively, of the interests in the capital and profits of PS1, a partnership. PS1 and CFC2 own 70% and 30%, respectively, of the interests in the capital and profits of PS2, a partnership. On each cash measurement date, PS1's cash position of $100x consists entirely of cash, and PS2's cash position of $200x includes a $50x short-term obligation of CFC2.

(B) *Analysis.* (1) *Treatment of PS1.* Because an interest in PS1 is held by CFC1, a specified foreign corporation of USP, and PS1 would be a specified foreign corporation of USP if it were a foreign corporation, PS1 is treated as a specified foreign corporation of USP for purposes of determining USP's aggregate foreign cash position. Without regard to paragraph (b)(3) of this section, USP must take into account $100x, its pro rata share of PS1's cash position, for purposes of determining its aggregate foreign cash position. However, 60% of that amount is attributable to deemed stock of PS1 that is not owned (within the meaning of section 958(a)) by a specified foreign corporation of USP. Accordingly, pursuant to paragraph (b)(3) of this section, the amount of PS1's cash position that USP must take into account for purposes of determining its aggregate foreign cash position is reduced by $60x (60% of $100x) to $40x ($100x - $60x).

(2) *Treatment of PS2.* Because an interest in PS2 is held by CFC2, a specified foreign corporation of USP, and PS2 would be a specified for-

eign corporation of USP if it were a foreign corporation, PS2 is treated as a specified foreign corporation of USP for purposes of determining USP's aggregate foreign cash position. USP, CFC1, CFC2, PS1, and PS2 all have calendar year taxable years. For purposes of determining the aggregate foreign cash position of USP, a section 958(a) U.S. shareholder of PS2, under paragraph (b)(1) of this section, the short-term obligation of CFC2 held by PS2 outstanding on each cash measurement date of each specified foreign corporation is disregarded on such cash measurement dates. Accordingly, without regard to paragraph (b)(3) of this section, USP must take into account $150x ($200x - $50x) of PS2's cash position for purposes of determining its aggregate foreign cash position. However, 42% (60% x 70%) of that amount is attributable to deemed stock of PS2 that is not owned (within the meaning of section 958(a), applied by treating PS1 as foreign if it is a domestic pass-through entity) by a specified foreign corporation of USP (determined without taking into account section 965(c)(3)(E)). Accordingly, pursuant to paragraph (b)(3) of this section, the amount of PS2's cash position that USP must take into account for purposes of determining its aggregate foreign cash position is reduced by $63x (42% of $150x) to $87x ($150x - $63x).

(c) *Determination of aggregate foreign cash position for a section 958(a) U.S. shareholder inclusion year.*—(1) *Single section 958(a) U.S. shareholder inclusion year.*—If a section 958(a) U.S. shareholder has a single section 958(a) U.S. shareholder inclusion year, then the section 958(a) U.S. shareholder's aggregate foreign cash position for the section 958(a) U.S. shareholder inclusion year is equal to the aggregate foreign cash position of the section 958(a) U.S. shareholder.

(2) *Multiple section 958(a) U.S. shareholder inclusion years.*—If a section 958(a) U.S. shareholder has multiple section 958(a) U.S. shareholder inclusion years, then the section 958(a) U.S. shareholder's aggregate foreign cash position for each section 958(a) U.S. shareholder inclusion year is determined by allocating the aggregate foreign cash position to a section 958(a) U.S. shareholder inclusion year under paragraphs (c)(2)(i) and (c)(2)(ii) of this section.

(i) *Allocation to first section 958(a) U.S. shareholder inclusion year.*—A portion of the aggregate foreign cash position of the section 958(a) U.S. shareholder is allocated to the first section 958(a) U.S. shareholder inclusion year in an amount equal to the lesser of the section 958(a) U.S. shareholder's aggregate foreign cash position or the section 958(a) U.S. shareholder's aggregate section 965(a) inclusion amount for the section 958(a) U.S. shareholder inclusion year.

(ii) *Allocation to succeeding section 958(a) U.S. shareholder inclusion years.*—The amount of the section 958(a) U.S. shareholder's aggregate foreign cash position allocated to any succeeding

section 958(a) U.S. shareholder inclusion year equals the lesser of the excess, if any, of the section 958(a) U.S. shareholder's aggregate foreign cash position over the aggregate amount of its aggregate foreign cash position allocated to preceding section 958(a) U.S. shareholder inclusion years under paragraph (c)(2)(i) of this section and this paragraph (c)(2)(ii) or the section 958(a) U.S. shareholder's aggregate section 965(a) inclusion amount for such succeeding section 958(a) U.S. shareholder inclusion year.

(3) *Estimation of aggregate foreign cash position.*—For purposes of determining the aggregate foreign cash position of a section 958(a) U.S. shareholder, the section 958(a) U.S. shareholder may assume that its pro rata share of the cash position of any specified foreign corporation whose last taxable year beginning before January 1, 2018, ends after the date the return for such section 958(a) U.S. shareholder inclusion year (the *estimated section 958(a) U.S. shareholder inclusion year*) is timely filed (taking into account extensions, if any) is zero as of the cash measurement date with which the taxable year of such specified foreign corporation ends. If a section 958(a) U.S. shareholder's pro rata share of the cash position of a specified foreign corporation is treated as zero pursuant to the preceding sentence, the amount described in § 1.965-1(f)(8)(i)(A) with respect to such section 958(a) U.S. shareholder in fact exceeds the amount described in § 1.965-1(f)(8)(i)(B) with respect to such section 958(a) U.S. shareholder, and the aggregate section 965(a) inclusion amount for the estimated section 958(a) U.S. shareholder inclusion year exceeds the amount described in § 1.965-1(f)(8)(i)(B) with respect to such section 958(a) U.S. shareholder, interest and penalties will not be imposed if such section 958(a) U.S. shareholder amends the return for the estimated section 958(a) U.S. shareholder inclusion year to account for the correct aggregate foreign cash position for the year. The amended return must be filed by the due date (taking into account extensions, if any) for the return for the year after the estimated section 958(a) U.S. shareholder inclusion year.

(4) *Examples.*—The following examples illustrate the application of this paragraph (c).

(i) *Example 1. Estimation of aggregate foreign cash position for a section 958(a) U.S. shareholder inclusion year*—(A) *Facts.* USP, a domestic corporation, owns all of the stock of CFC1, a foreign corporation, which owns all of the stock of CFC2, also a foreign corporation. USP is a calendar year taxpayer. CFC1 has a taxable year ending on December 31, and CFC2 has a taxable year ending on November 30. The cash position of CFC1 on each of December 31, 2015, December 31, 2016, and December 31, 2017, is $100x. The cash position of CFC2 on each of November 30, 2015, and November 30, 2016, is $200x. USP has a section 965(a) inclusion amount of $300x with respect to CFC1.

Reg. § 1.965-3(c)(4)

(B) *Analysis.* In determining its aggregate foreign cash position for its 2017 taxable year, USP may assume that its pro rata share of the cash position of CFC2 will be zero as of November 30, 2018, for purposes of filing its return due on April 18, 2018 (or due on October 15, 2018, with extension). Therefore, USP's aggregate foreign cash position is treated as $300x, which is the greater of (a) $300x, 50% of the sum of USP's pro rata shares of the cash position of CFC1 as of December 31, 2015, and December 31, 2016, and of the cash position of CFC2 as of November 30, 2015, and November 30, 2016, and (b) $100x, USP's pro rata share of the cash position of CFC1 as of December 31, 2017. If USP's pro rata share of the cash position of CFC2 as of November 30, 2018, in fact exceeds $200x, USP must amend its return for its 2017 taxable year to reflect the correct aggregate foreign cash position by the due date for its return for its 2018 taxable year, April 15, 2019 (or October 15, 2019, with extension).

(ii) *Example 2. Allocation of aggregate foreign cash position among section 958(a) U.S. shareholder inclusion years*—(A) *Facts.* The facts are the same as in paragraph (c)(4)(i)(A) of this section (the facts in *Example 1*), except that the cash position of each of CFC1 and CFC2 on all relevant cash measurement dates is $200x, with the result that USP has an aggregate foreign cash position determined under § 1.965-1(f)(8)(i) of $400x. For its 2017 taxable year, USP has a section 965(a) inclusion amount with respect to CFC1 of $300x, and for its 2018 taxable year, USP has a section 965(a) inclusion amount with respect to CFC2 of $300x.

(B) *Analysis.* Under paragraph (c)(2)(i) of this section, USP's aggregate foreign cash position for 2017 is $300x, which is the lesser of USP's aggregate foreign cash position determined under § 1.965-1(f)(8)(i) ($400x) or the section 965(a) inclusion amount ($300x) that USP takes into account in 2017. Under paragraph (c)(2)(ii) of this section, the amount of USP's aggregate foreign cash position for 2018 is $100x, USP's aggregate foreign cash position determined under § 1.965-1(f)(8)(i) ($400x) reduced by the amount of its aggregate foreign cash position for 2017 ($300x) under paragraph (c)(2)(i) of this section.

(d) *Increase of income by section 965(c) deduction of an expatriated entity.*—(1) *In general.*—If a person is allowed a section 965(c) deduction and the person (or a successor) first becomes an expatriated entity, with respect to a surrogate foreign corporation, at any time during the 10-year period beginning on December 22, 2017, then the tax imposed by chapter 1 of the Internal Revenue Code is increased for the first taxable year in which such person becomes an expatriated entity by an amount equal to 35 percent of the person's section 965(c) deductions, and no credits are allowed against such increase in tax. The preceding sentence applies only if the surrogate foreign corporation first becomes a surrogate foreign corporation on or after December 22, 2017.

(2) *Definition of expatriated entity.*—For purposes of paragraph (d)(1) of this section, the term *expatriated entity* has the same meaning given such term under section 7874(a)(2), except that such term does not include an expatriated entity if the surrogate foreign corporation with respect to the expatriated entity is treated as a domestic corporation under section 7874(b).

(3) *Definition of surrogate foreign corporation.*—For purposes of paragraph (d)(1) of this section, the term *surrogate foreign corporation* has the meaning given such term in section 7874(a)(2)(B).

(e) *Section 962 election.*—(1) *In general.*—In the case of an individual (including a trust or estate) that makes an election under section 962, any section 965(c) deduction taken into account under § 1.962-1(b)(1)(i)(B) in determining taxable income as used in section 11 is not taken into account for purposes of determining the individual's taxable income under section 1.

(2) *Example.*—The following example illustrates the application of the rule in this paragraph (e).

(i) *Facts.* USI, a United States citizen, owns 10% of the capital and profits of USPRS, a domestic partnership that has a calendar year taxable year, the remainder of which is owned by foreign persons unrelated to USI or USPRS. USPRS owns all of the stock of FS, a foreign corporation that is a controlled foreign corporation with a calendar year taxable year. USPRS has a section 965(a) inclusion amount with respect to FS of $1,000x and has a section 965(c) deduction amount of $700x. FS has no post-1986 foreign income taxes. USI makes a valid election under section 962 for 2017.

(ii) *Analysis.* USI's "taxable income" described in § 1.962-1(b)(1)(i) equals $100x (USI's domestic pass-through owner share of USPRS's section 965(a) inclusion amount) minus $70x (USI's domestic pass-through owner share of USPRS's section 965(c) deduction amount), or $30x. No other deductions are allowed in determining this amount. USI's tax on the $30x section 965(a) inclusion will be equal to the tax that would be imposed on such amount under section 11 if USI were a domestic corporation. Under paragraph (e)(1) of this section, USI cannot deduct $70x for purposes of determining USI's taxable income that is subject to tax under section 1.

(f) *Treatment of section 965(c) deduction under certain provisions of the Internal Revenue Code.*—(1) *Sections 62(a) and 63(d).*—A section 965(c) deduction is treated as a deduction described in section 62(a) and is not treated as an itemized deduction for any purpose of the Internal Revenue Code.

(2) *Sections 705, 1367, and 1368.*—(i) *Adjustments to basis.*—In the case of a domestic partnership or S corporation—

(A) The aggregate amount of its section 965(a) inclusions net of the aggregate amount of its section 965(c) deductions is treated as a separately stated item of net income solely for purposes of calculating basis under section 705(a) and § 1.705-1(a) and section 1367(a)(1) and § 1.1367-1(f), and

(B) The aggregate amount of its section 965(a) inclusions equal to the aggregate amount of its section 965(c) deductions is treated as income exempt from tax solely for purposes of calculating basis under sections 705(a)(1)(B), 1367(a)(1)(A), and § 1.1367-1(f).

(ii) *S corporation accumulated adjustments account.*—In the case of an S corporation, the aggregate amount of its section 965(a) inclusions equal to the aggregate amount of its section 965(c) deductions is treated as income not exempt from tax solely for purposes of determining whether an adjustment is made to an accumulated adjustments account under section 1368(e)(1)(A) and § 1.1368-2(a)(2).

(iii) *Example.*—The following example illustrates the application of this paragraph (f)(2).

(A) *Facts.* USI, a United States citizen, owns all of the stock of S Corp, an S corporation, which owns all of the stock of FS, a foreign corporation. S Corp has a section 965(a) inclusion of $1,000x with respect to FS and has a $700x section 965(c) deduction.

(B) *Analysis.* As a result of the application of paragraph (f)(2)(i)(A) of this section, solely for purposes of calculating basis under section 1367(a)(1) and § 1.1367-1(f), USI treats as a separately stated item of net income $300x (its pro rata share of the net of S Corp's $1,000x aggregate section 965(a) inclusion and S Corp's $700x aggregate section 965(c) deduction). Accordingly, USI's basis in S Corp is increased under section 1367(a)(1) by $300x. As a result of the application of paragraph (f)(2)(i)(B) of this section, an amount of S Corp's aggregate section 965(a) inclusion equal to its aggregate section 965(c) deduction, $700x, is treated as tax exempt income solely for purposes of calculating basis under section 1367(a)(1)(A) and § 1.1367-1(f), and accordingly, USI's basis in S Corp is further increased by its pro rata share of such amount, $700x. S Corp's accumulated adjustments account ("AAA") is increased under section 1368(e)(1)(A) by the $1,000x section 965(a) inclusion taken into account and reduced by the $700x section 965(c) deduction taken into account. In addition, as a result of the application of paragraph (f)(2)(ii) of this section, S Corp's AAA is further increased by an amount of S Corp's aggregate section 965(a) inclusion equal to its aggregate section 965(c) deduction, $700x, which is not treated as tax-exempt income for purposes of § 1.1368-2(a)(2).

(3) *Section 1411.*—For purposes of section 1411 and § 1.1411-4(f)(6), a section 965(c) deduc-

tion is not treated as being properly allocable to any section 965(a) inclusion.

(4) *Section 4940.*—For purposes of section 4940(c)(3)(A), a section 965(c) deduction is not treated as an ordinary and necessary expense paid or incurred for the production or collection of gross investment income.

(g) *Domestic pass-through entities.*—For purposes of determining a domestic pass-through owner share, a section 965(c) deduction amount of a domestic pass-through entity must be allocated to a domestic pass-through owner in the same proportion as an aggregate section 965(a) inclusion amount of the domestic pass-through entity for a section 958(a) U.S. shareholder inclusion year is allocated to the domestic pass-through owner. [Reg. § 1.965-3.]

☐ [*T.D.* 9846, 2-4-2019.]

**[Reg. § 1.965-4]**

**§ 1.965-4. Disregard of certain transactions.**—(a) *Scope.*—This section provides rules that disregard certain transactions for purposes of applying section 965 to a United States shareholder. Paragraph (b) of this section provides rules that disregard transactions undertaken with a principal purpose of changing the amount of a section 965 element of a United States shareholder. Paragraph (c) of this section provides rules that disregard certain changes in method of accounting and entity classification elections that would otherwise change the amount of a section 965 element. Paragraph (d) of this section defines the term section 965 element. Paragraph (e) of this section provides rules of application concerning paragraphs (b) and (c) of this section. Paragraph (f) of this section provides rules that disregard certain transactions occurring between E&P measurement dates. Paragraph (g) of this section provides examples illustrating the application of this section.

(b) *Transactions undertaken with a principal purpose of changing the amount of a section 965 element.*—(1) *General rule.*—Except as otherwise provided in paragraph (e)(3) of this section, a transaction is disregarded for purposes of determining the amounts of all section 965 elements of a United States shareholder if each of the following conditions is satisfied with respect to any section 965 element of the United States shareholder—

(i) The transaction occurs, in whole or in part, on or after November 2, 2017 (the *specified date*);

(ii) The transaction is undertaken with a principal purpose of changing the amount of a section 965 element of the United States shareholder; and

(iii) The transaction would, without regard to this paragraph (b)(1), change the amount of the section 965 element of the United States shareholder.

(2) *Presumptions and exceptions for the application of the general rule.*—(i) *Overview.*—Under paragraphs (b)(2)(iii) through (v) of this section, certain transactions are presumed to be undertaken with a principal purpose of changing the amount of a section 965 element of a United States shareholder for purposes of paragraph (b)(1) of this section. The presumptions described in paragraphs (b)(2)(iii) through (v) of this section may be rebutted only if facts and circumstances clearly establish that the transaction was not undertaken with a principal purpose of changing the amount of a section 965 element of a United States shareholder. A taxpayer that takes the position that the presumption is rebutted must attach a statement to its return for its taxable year in which or with which the relevant taxable year of the relevant specified foreign corporation ends disclosing that it has rebutted the presumption. In the case of a transaction described in paragraph (b)(2)(iii) or (iv) of this section, if the presumption does not apply because the transaction occurs in the ordinary course of business, whether the transaction was undertaken with a principal purpose of changing the amount of a section 965 element of a United States shareholder must be determined under all the facts and circumstances. Under paragraphs (b)(2)(iii) through (v) of this section, certain transactions are treated per se as being undertaken with a principal purpose of changing the amount of a section 965 element of a United States shareholder, and, therefore, such transactions are disregarded under paragraph (b)(1) of this section if the conditions of paragraphs (b)(1)(i) and (iii) of this section are satisfied. Further, under paragraph (b)(2)(iii) of this section, certain distributions are treated per se as not being undertaken with a principal purpose of changing the amount of a section 965 element of a United States shareholder and therefore are not disregarded under paragraph (b)(1) of this section.

(ii) *Definitions.*—(A) *Relatedness.*—For purposes of paragraphs (b)(2)(iii) through (v) of this section, a person is treated as related to a United States shareholder if, either immediately before or immediately after the transaction (or series of related transactions), the person bears a relationship to the United States shareholder described in section 267(b) or section 707(b).

(B) *Transfer.*—(1) *In general.*—For purposes of paragraphs (b)(2)(iii) and (v) of this section, the term *transfer* includes any disposition of stock or property, including a sale or exchange, contribution, distribution, issuance, redemption, recapitalization, or loan of stock or property, and includes an indirect transfer of stock or property.

(2) *Indirect transfer.*—For purposes of paragraph (b)(2)(ii)(B)(1) of this section, the term *indirect transfer* includes a transfer of property or stock owned by an entity through a transfer of an interest in such entity (or an interest in an entity that has a direct or indirect interest in such entity), and a transfer of property or stock to a person through a transfer of property or stock to a pass-through entity of which such person is a direct or indirect owner.

(iii) *Cash reduction transactions.*— (A) *General rule.*—For purposes of paragraph (b)(1) of this section, a cash reduction transaction is presumed to be undertaken with a principal purpose of changing the amount of a section 965 element of a United States shareholder. For this purpose, the term *cash reduction transaction* means a transfer of cash, accounts receivable, or cash-equivalent assets by a specified foreign corporation to a United States shareholder of the specified foreign corporation or a person related to a United States shareholder of the specified foreign corporation, or an assumption by a specified foreign corporation of an account payable of a United States shareholder of the specified foreign corporation or a person related to a United States shareholder of the specified foreign corporation, if such transfer or assumption would, without regard to paragraph (b)(1) of this section, reduce the aggregate foreign cash position of the United States shareholder. The presumption described in this paragraph (b)(2)(iii) does not apply to a cash reduction transaction that occurs in the ordinary course of business.

(B) *Per se rules for certain distributions.*— Notwithstanding the presumption described in paragraph (b)(2)(iii)(A) of this section, except in the case of a specified distribution, a cash reduction transaction that is a distribution by a specified foreign corporation to a United States shareholder of the specified foreign corporation is treated per se as not being undertaken with a principal purpose of changing the amount of a section 965 element of the United States shareholder for purposes of paragraph (b)(1) of this section. A specified distribution is treated per se as being undertaken with a principal purpose of changing the amount of a section 965 element of a United States shareholder for purposes of paragraph (b)(1) of this section. For purposes of this paragraph (b)(2)(iii)(B), the term *specified distribution* means a cash reduction transaction that is a distribution by a specified foreign corporation of a United States shareholder if and to the extent that, at the time of the distribution, there was a plan or intention for the distributee to transfer cash, accounts receivable, or cash-equivalent assets to any specified foreign corporation of the United States shareholder or a distribution that is a non pro rata distribution to a foreign person that is related to the United States shareholder. For purposes of the preceding sentence, there is no plan or intention for the distributee to transfer cash, accounts receivable, or cash-equivalent assets to any specified foreign corporation of the United States shareholder if the transfer is pursuant to a legal obligation entered into before November 2, 2017. A taxpayer that takes the position that a cash reduction transaction is not a specified distribution because a transfer of cash, accounts receivable, or cash-equivalent asset is pursuant to a legal obligation entered into before November 2, 2017, must attach a statement to its return for its taxable year in which or with which the relevant taxable year of the relevant specified foreign corporation ends disclosing the position.

(iv) *E&P reduction transactions.*— (A) *General rule.*—For purposes of paragraph (b)(1) of this section, an E&P reduction transaction is presumed to be undertaken with a principal purpose of changing the amount of a section 965 element of a United States shareholder. For purposes of this paragraph (b)(2)(iv), the term *E&P reduction transaction* means a transaction between a specified foreign corporation and any of a United States shareholder of the specified foreign corporation, another specified foreign corporation of a United States shareholder of the specified foreign corporation, or any person related to a United States shareholder of the specified foreign corporation, if the transaction would, without regard to paragraph (b)(1) of this section, reduce either the accumulated post-1986 deferred foreign income or the post-1986 undistributed earnings (as defined in section 902(c)(1)) of the specified foreign corporation or another specified foreign corporation of any United States shareholder of such specified foreign corporation. The presumption described in this paragraph (b)(2)(iv)(A) does not apply to an E&P reduction transaction that occurs in the ordinary course of business.

(B) *Per se rule for specified transactions.*— A specified transaction is treated per se as being undertaken with a principal purpose of changing the amount of a section 965 element of a United States shareholder for purposes of paragraph (b)(1) of this section. For purposes of the preceding sentence, the term *specified transaction* means an E&P reduction transaction that involves one or more of the following: a complete liquidation of a specified foreign corporation to which section 331 applies; a sale or other disposition of stock by a specified foreign corporation; or a distribution by a specified foreign corporation that reduces the earnings and profits of the specified foreign corporation pursuant to section 312(a)(3).

(v) *Pro rata share transactions.*— (A) *General rule.*—For purposes of paragraph (b)(1) of this section, a pro rata share transaction is presumed to be undertaken with a principal purpose of changing the amount of a section 965 element of a United States shareholder. For this purpose, the term *pro rata share transaction* means either a pro rata share reduction transaction or an E&P deficit transaction.

(1) *Definition of pro rata share reduction transaction.*—For purposes of this paragraph

(b)(2)(v)(A), the term *pro rata share reduction transaction* means a transfer of the stock of a specified foreign corporation by either a United States shareholder of the specified foreign corporation or a person related to a United States shareholder of the specified foreign corporation (including by the specified foreign corporation itself) to a person related to the United States shareholder if the transfer would, without regard to paragraph (b)(1) of this section, reduce the United States shareholder's pro rata share of the section 965(a) earnings amount of the specified foreign corporation, reduce the United States shareholder's pro rata share of the cash position of the specified foreign corporation, or both.

(2) *Definition of E&P deficit transaction.*—For purposes of this paragraph (b)(2)(v)(A), the term *E&P deficit transaction* means a transfer to either a United States shareholder or a person related to the United States shareholder of the stock of an E&P deficit foreign corporation by a person related to the United States shareholder (including by the E&P deficit foreign corporation itself) if the transfer would, without regard to paragraph (b)(1) of this section, increase the United States shareholder's pro rata share of the specified E&P deficit of the E&P deficit foreign corporation.

(B) *Per se rule for internal group transactions.*—An internal group transaction is treated per se as being undertaken with a principal purpose of changing the amount of a section 965 element of a United States shareholder for purposes of paragraph (b)(1) of this section. For purposes of the preceding sentence, the term *internal group transaction* means a pro rata share transaction if, immediately before or after the transfer, the transferor of the stock of the specified foreign corporation and the transferee of such stock are members of an affiliated group in which the United States shareholder is a member. For this purpose, the term *affiliated group* has the meaning set forth in section 1504(a), determined without regard to paragraphs (1) through (8) of section 1504(b), and the term *members of an affiliated group* means entities included in the same affiliated group. For purposes of identifying an affiliated group and the members of such group, each partner in a partnership, as determined without regard to this sentence, is treated as holding its proportionate share of the stock held by the partnership, as determined under the rules and principles of sections 701 through 777, and if one or more members of an affiliated group own, in the aggregate, at least 80 percent of the interests in a partnership's capital or profits, the partnership will be treated as a corporation that is a member of the affiliated group.

(C) *Example.*—The following example illustrates the application of the rules in this paragraph (b)(2)(v).

(1) *Facts.* FP, a foreign corporation, owns all of the stock of USP, a domestic corpora-

tion. USP owns all of the stock of FS, a foreign corporation. USP has a calendar year taxable year; FS's taxable year ends November 30. On January 2, 2018, USP transfers all of the stock of FS to FP in exchange for cash. On January 3, 2018, FS makes a distribution with respect to the stock transferred to FP. USP treats the transaction as a taxable sale of the FS stock and claims a dividends received deduction under section 245A with respect to its deemed dividend under section 1248(j) as a result of the sale. FS has post-1986 earnings and profits as of December 31, 2017, and no post-1986 earnings and profits that are attributable to income effectively connected with the conduct of a trade or business within the United States and subject to tax under chapter 1 or that, if distributed, would be excluded from the gross income of a United States shareholder under section 959.

(2) *Analysis.* The transfer of the stock of FS is a pro rata share reduction transaction and thus a pro rata share transaction because such transfer is by USP, a United States shareholder, to FP, a person related to USP, and the transfer would, without regard to the rule in paragraph (b)(1) of this section, reduce USP's pro rata share of the section 965(a) earnings amount of FS. Because USP and FP are also members of an affiliated group within the meaning of paragraph (b)(2)(v)(B) of this section, the transfer of the stock of FS is also an internal group transaction and is treated per se as being undertaken with a principal purpose of changing the amount of a section 965 element of USP. Accordingly, because the transfer occurs after the specified date and reduces USP's section 965(a) inclusion amount with respect to FS, the transfer is disregarded for purposes of determining any section 965 element of USP with the result that, among other things, USP's pro rata share of FS's section 965(a) earnings amount is determined as if USP owned (within the meaning of section 958(a)) 100% of the stock of FS on the last day of FS's inclusion year and no other person received a distribution with respect to such stock during such year. *See* section 951(a)(2)(A) and (B).

(c) *Disregard of certain changes in method of accounting and entity classification elections.*— (1) *Changes in method of accounting.*—Any change in method of accounting made for a taxable year of a specified foreign corporation that ends in 2017 or 2018 is disregarded for purposes of determining the amounts of all section 965 elements with respect to a United States shareholder if the change in method of accounting would, without regard to this paragraph (c)(1), change the amount of any section 965 element described in paragraph (d)(1) or (2) of this section with respect to the United States shareholder, or change the amount of the section 965 element described in paragraph (d)(3) of this section other than by reason of an increase in a section 965(a) inclusion amount with respect to the specified foreign corporation, regardless of whether the change in method of accounting is

made with a principal purpose of changing the amount of a section 965 element with respect to the United States shareholder. The rule described in the preceding sentence applies regardless of whether the change in method of accounting was made in accordance with the procedures described in Rev. Proc. 2015-13, 2015-5 I.R.B. 419 (or successor), and regardless of whether the change in method of accounting was properly made, but it does not apply to a change in method of accounting for which the original and/or duplicate copy of any Form 3115, "Application for Change in Accounting Method," requesting the change was filed before the specified date (as defined in paragraph (b)(1) of this section).

(2) *Entity classification elections.*—Except as otherwise provided in paragraph (e)(3) of this section, an election under § 301.7701-3 to change the classification of an entity that is filed on or after the specified date (as defined in paragraph (b)(1) of this section) is disregarded for purposes of determining the amounts of all section 965 elements of a United States shareholder if the election would, without regard to this paragraph (c)(2), change the amount of any section 965 element of the United States shareholder, regardless of whether the election is made with a principal purpose of changing the amount of a section 965 element of the United States shareholder. An election filed on or after the specified date is subject to the preceding sentence even if the election was filed with an effective date that is before the specified date.

(d) *Definition of a section 965 element.*—For purposes of paragraphs (b) and (c) of this section, the term *section 965 element* means, with respect to a United States shareholder, any of the following amounts (collectively, *section 965 elements*)—

(1) The United States shareholder's section 965(a) inclusion amount with respect to a specified foreign corporation;

(2) The aggregate foreign cash position of the United States shareholder; or

(3) The amount of foreign income taxes of a specified foreign corporation deemed paid by the United States shareholder under section 960 as a result of a section 965(a) inclusion.

(e) *Rules for applying paragraphs (b) and (c) of this section.*—(1) *Determination of whether there is a change in the amount of a section 965 element.*—For purposes of paragraphs (b) and (c) of this section, there is a change in the amount of a section 965 element of a United States shareholder as a result of a transaction, change in accounting method, or election to change an entity's classification, if, without regard to paragraph (b)(1), (c)(1), or (c)(2) of this section, the transaction, change in accounting method, or change in entity classification would—

(i) Reduce the amount described in paragraph (d)(1) of this section,

(ii) Reduce the amount described in paragraph (d)(2) of this section, but only if such amount is less than the United States shareholder's aggregate section 965(a) inclusion amount, or

(iii) Increase the amount described in paragraph (d)(3) of this section.

(2) *Treatment of domestic pass-through owners as United States shareholders.*—For purposes of paragraphs (b) and (c) of this section, if a domestic pass-through entity is a United States shareholder, then a domestic pass-through owner with respect to the domestic pass-through entity that is not otherwise a United States shareholder is treated as a United States shareholder.

(3) *Exception for certain incorporation transactions.*—(i) *In general.*—Paragraphs (b) and (c)(2) of this section do not apply to disregard a transfer of stock of a specified foreign corporation by a United States shareholder to a domestic corporation (for this purpose, including an S corporation), provided that—

(A) The transferee's section 965(a) inclusion amount with respect to the transferred stock of the specified foreign corporation is no lower than the transferor's section 965(a) inclusion amount with respect to the transferred stock of the specified foreign corporation, determined without regard to the transfer; and

(B) The transferee and the transferor determine their aggregate foreign cash position under paragraph (e)(3)(ii) of this section.

(ii) *Aggregate foreign cash position.*—In the case of a transfer described in paragraph (e)(3)(i) of this section, in order to rely on the exception in paragraph (e)(3)(i) of this section—

(A) The transferee must treat its pro rata share of the cash position of a specified foreign corporation as of a cash measurement date as of which it did not own the transferred stock of the specified foreign corporation as including the transferor's pro rata share of the cash position of the specified foreign corporation with respect to the transferred stock of the specified foreign corporation as of such cash measurement date for purposes of determining its aggregate foreign cash position; and

(B) The transferor must treat its pro rata share of the cash position of a specified foreign corporation as of a cash measurement date as of which it did not own the transferred stock of the specified foreign corporation as including the transferee's pro rata share of the cash position of the specified foreign corporation with respect to the transferred stock of the specified foreign corporation as of such cash measurement date for purposes of determining its aggregate foreign cash position.

(4) *Consequences of liquidation.*—(i) *In general.*—In the case of a liquidation of a specified foreign corporation that is disregarded for purposes of determining the section 965 elements of

a United States shareholder pursuant to paragraph (b) or (c)(2) of this section, for purposes of determining the amounts of the section 965 elements of the United States shareholder, the date that is treated as the last day of the taxable year of the specified foreign corporation is the later of—

(A) The date of the liquidation; and

(B) The specified liquidation date, if any.

(ii) *Specified liquidation date.*—The term *specified liquidation date* means, in the case of a liquidation of a specified foreign corporation pursuant to an entity classification election that is disregarded for purposes of determining the section 965 elements of a United States shareholder—

(A) November 30, 2017, with respect to a United States shareholder that must include in income under § 1.367(b)-3 as a deemed dividend the all earnings and profits amount with respect to the United States shareholder's stock of the liquidating specified foreign corporation; or

(B) The date of filing of the entity classification election, with respect to all other United States shareholders.

(f) *Disregard of certain transactions occurring between E&P measurement dates.*—(1) *Disregard of specified payments.*—Except as provided in paragraph (f)(3) of this section, a specified payment made by a specified foreign corporation (*payor specified foreign corporation*) to another specified foreign corporation (*payee specified foreign corporation*) is disregarded for purposes of determining the post-1986 earnings and profits of each of the payor specified foreign corporation and the payee specified foreign corporation as of the E&P measurement date on December 31, 2017.

(2) *Definition of specified payment.*—For purposes of paragraph (f)(1) of this section, the term *specified payment* means any amount paid or accrued by the payor specified foreign corporation, including a distribution by the payor specified foreign corporation with respect to its stock, if each of the following conditions are satisfied:

(i) Immediately before or immediately after the payment or accrual of the amount, the payor specified foreign corporation and the payee specified foreign corporation are related within the meaning of section 954(d)(3), substituting the term "specified foreign corporation" for "controlled foreign corporation" in each place that it appears;

(ii) The payment or accrual of the amount occurs after November 2, 2017, and on or before December 31, 2017; and

(iii) The payment or accrual of the amount would, without regard to the application of paragraph (f)(1) of this section, reduce the post-1986 earnings and profits of the payor specified foreign corporation as of the E&P measurement date on December 31, 2017.

**Reg. § 1.965-4(f)(2)(iii)**

(3) *Non-application of disregard rule.*—A section 958(a) U.S. shareholder may determine the post-1986 earnings and profits of a specified foreign corporation without regard to paragraph (f)(1) of this section, provided that it and every section 958(a) U.S. shareholder related to the first section 958(a) U.S. shareholder determines the post-1986 earnings and profits of each of its specified foreign corporations without regard to paragraph (f)(1) of this section. For purposes of this paragraph (f)(3), a person is treated as related to a section 958(a) U.S. shareholder if the person bears a relationship to the section 958(a) U.S. shareholder described in section 267(b) or 707(b).

(4) *Examples.*—The following examples illustrate the application of the rules in this paragraph (f).

(i) *Example 1. Deductible payment between wholly owned specified foreign corporations is a specified payment.* (A) *Facts.* USP, a domestic corporation, owns all of the stock of CFC1, a foreign corporation, which owns all of the stock of CFC2, also a foreign corporation. USP, CFC1, and CFC2 have calendar year taxable years. On November 2, 2017, each of CFC1 and CFC2 has post-1986 earnings and profits of 100u. Neither CFC1 nor CFC2 has post-1986 earnings and profits that are attributable to income of the specified foreign corporation that is effectively connected with the conduct of a trade or business within the United States and subject to tax under chapter 1 or that, if distributed, would be excluded from the gross income of a United States shareholder under section 959 or from the gross income of another shareholder if such shareholder were a United States shareholder; therefore, no adjustment is made under section 965(d)(2) or §1.965-1(f)(7), and each of CFC1's and CFC2's accumulated post-1986 deferred foreign income is equal to such corporation's post-1986 earnings and profits. On November 3, 2017, CFC2 makes a deductible payment of 10u to CFC1. The payment does not constitute subpart F income. CFC1 and CFC2 have no other items of income or deduction.

(B) *Analysis.* The payment from CFC2 to CFC1 is a specified payment because (*1*) CFC1 and CFC2 are related specified foreign corporations; (*2*) the payment occurs after November 2, 2017, and on or before December 31, 2017; and (*3*) the payment would, without regard to the application of the rule in paragraph (f)(1) of this section, reduce the post-1986 earnings and profits of CFC2 as of the E&P measurement date on December 31, 2017. Under paragraph (f)(1) of this section, the payment is disregarded, and CFC1 and CFC2 each have post-1986 earnings and profits of 100u as of December 31, 2017. Accordingly, the section 965(a) earnings amount of each of CFC1 and CFC2 is 100u.

(ii) *Example 2. Distribution is a specified payment.* (A) *Facts.* The facts are the same as in paragraph (f)(4)(i)(A) of this section (the facts in *Example 1*), except instead of a deductible payment to CFC1, CFC2 makes a 10u distribution on November 3, 2017, that, without regard to paragraph (f)(1) of this section would reduce the post-1986 earnings and profits of CFC2 as of the E&P measurement date on December 31, 2017, and increase the post-1986 earnings and profits of CFC1 as of the E&P measurement date on December 31, 2017, by 10u.

(B) *Analysis.* The distribution is a specified payment because (*1*) CFC1 and CFC2 are related specified foreign corporations; (*2*) the distribution occurs after November 2, 2017, and on or before December 31, 2017; and (*3*) the distribution would, without regard to the application of the rule in paragraph (f)(1) of this section, reduce the post-1986 earnings and profits of CFC2 as of the E&P measurement date on December 31, 2017. Under paragraph (f)(1) of this section, the distribution is disregarded with the result that CFC1 and CFC2 each have post-1986 earnings and profits of 100u as of the E&P measurement date on December 31, 2017, and a section 965(a) earnings amount of 100u.

(iii) *Example 3. Deductible payment between related (but not wholly owned) specified foreign corporations is a specified payment.* (A) *Facts.* The facts are the same as in paragraph (f)(4)(i)(A) of this section (the facts in *Example 1*), except that CFC1 owns only 51% of the only class of stock of CFC2, the remainder of which is owned by USI, a United States citizen unrelated to USP, CFC1, and CFC2.

(B) *Analysis.* The analysis is the same as in paragraph (f)(4)(i)(B) of this section (the analysis in *Example 1*); thus, the payment is disregarded with the result that CFC1 and CFC2 each have post-1986 earnings and profits of 100u as of the E&P measurement date on December 31, 2017, and a section 965(a) earnings amount of 100u.

(iv) *Example 4. Deductible payment between unrelated specified foreign corporations is not a specified payment.* (A) *Facts.* The facts are the same as in paragraph (f)(4)(i)(A) of this section (the facts in *Example 1*), except that CFC1 owns only 50% of the only class of stock of CFC2, the remainder of which is owned by USI, a United States citizen unrelated to USP, CFC1, and CFC2.

(B) *Analysis.* Paragraph (f)(1) of this section does not apply because CFC1 and CFC2 are not related. Thus, the payment is taken into account with the result that CFC1 has post-1986 earnings and profits of 110u as of the E&P measurement date on December 31, 2017, and a section 965(a) earnings amount of 110u.

(v) *Example 5. Deductible payment and income accrued from unrelated persons are not specified payments.* (A) *Facts.* The facts are the same as in paragraph (f)(4)(i)(A) of this section (the facts in *Example 1*), except that CFC2 does not make a deductible payment to CFC1, and, between E&P measurement dates, CFC2 accrues gross income of 20u from a person that is not related to CFC2, and CFC1 incurs a deductible expense of 20u to a person that is not related to CFC1.

(B) *Analysis.* Paragraph (f)(1) of this section does not apply because neither the deductible expense of CFC1 nor the income accrual by CFC2 are attributable to a specified payment.

(vi) *Example 6. Deductible payment and income accrued with respect to unrelated persons are not specified payments; deductible payment between wholly specified foreign corporations is a specified payment.* (A) *Facts.* The facts are the same as in paragraph (f)(4)(v)(A) of this section (the facts in *Example 5*), except that CFC2 also makes a deductible payment of 10u to CFC1 on November 3, 2017.

(B) *Analysis.* The deductible payment is a specified payment because (1) CFC1 and CFC2 are related specified foreign corporations; (2) the payment occurs after November 2, 2017, and on or before December 31, 2017; and (3) the deductible payment would, without regard to the application of the rule in paragraph (f)(1) of this section, reduce the post-1986 earnings and profits of CFC2 as of the E&P measurement date on December 31, 2017. Accordingly, under paragraph (f)(1) of this section, the deductible payment is disregarded with the result that CFC1 and CFC2 have 80u and 120u of post-1986 earnings and profits as of the E&P measurement date on December 31, 2017, respectively. Accordingly, CFC1 and CFC2 have section 965(a) earnings amounts of 100u and 120u, respectively. [Reg. § 1.965-4.]

☐ [*T.D.* 9846, 2-4-2019.]

**[Reg. § 1.965-5]**

**§ 1.965-5. Allowance of a credit or deduction for foreign income taxes.**—(a) *Scope.*—This section provides rules for the allowance of a credit or deduction for foreign income taxes in connection with the application of section 965. Paragraph (b) of this section provides rules under section 965(g) for the allowance of a credit or deduction for foreign income taxes paid or accrued. Paragraph (c) of this section provides rules for the allowance of a credit or deduction for foreign income taxes treated as paid or accrued in connection with the application of section 965. Paragraph (d) of this section defines the term applicable percentage.

(b) *Rules for foreign income taxes paid or accrued.*—Neither a deduction (including under section 164) nor a credit under section 901 is allowed for the applicable percentage of any foreign income taxes paid or accrued with respect to any amount for which a section 965(c) deduction is allowed for a section 958(a) U.S. shareholder inclusion year. Neither a deduction (including under section 164) nor a credit under section 901 is allowed for the applicable percentage of any foreign income taxes attributable to a distribution of section 965(a) previously taxed earnings and profits or section 965(b) previously taxed earnings and profits. Accordingly, for example, no deduction or credit is allowed for the applicable percentage of any withholding taxes imposed on a United States shareholder by the jurisdiction of residence of the distributing for-

eign corporation with respect to a distribution of section 965(a) previously taxed earnings and profits or section 965(b) previously taxed earnings and profits. Similarly, for example, no deduction or credit is allowed for the applicable percentage of foreign income taxes imposed on a United States citizen by the citizen's jurisdiction of residence upon receipt of a distribution of section 965(a) previously taxed earnings and profits or section 965(b) previously taxed earnings and profits.

(c) *Rules for foreign income taxes treated as paid or accrued.*—(1) *Disallowed credit.*—(i) *In general.*—A credit under section 901 is not allowed for the applicable percentage of any foreign income taxes treated as paid or accrued with respect to any amount for which a section 965(c) deduction is allowed for a section 958(a) U.S. shareholder inclusion year. For purposes of the preceding sentence, taxes treated as paid or accrued include foreign income taxes deemed paid under section 960(a)(1) with respect to a section 965(a) inclusion, foreign income taxes deemed paid under section 960(a)(3) (as in effect on December 21, 2017) or section 960(b) (as applicable to taxable years of controlled foreign corporations beginning after December 31, 2017) with respect to distributions of section 965(a) previously taxed earnings and profits or section 965(b) previously taxed earnings and profits, foreign income taxes allocated to an entity under § 1.901-2(f)(4), and a distributive share of foreign income taxes paid or accrued by a partnership.

(ii) *Foreign income taxes deemed paid under section 960(a)(3) (as in effect on December 21, 2017).*—Foreign income taxes deemed paid by a domestic corporation under section 960(a)(3) with respect to a distribution of section 965(a) previously taxed earnings and profits or section 965(b) previously taxed earnings and profits include only the foreign income taxes paid or accrued by an upper-tier foreign corporation with respect to a distribution of section 965(a) previously taxed earnings and profits or section 965(b) previously taxed earnings and profits from a lower-tier foreign corporation. No credit is allowed under section 960(a)(3) or any other section for foreign income taxes that would have been deemed paid under section 960(a)(1) with respect to the portion of a section 965(a) earnings amount that is reduced under § 1.965-1(b)(2) or § 1.965-8(b).

(iii) [Reserved]

(2) *Disallowed deduction.*—No deduction (including under section 164) is allowed for the applicable percentage of any foreign income taxes treated as paid or accrued with respect to any amount for which a section 965(c) deduction is allowed. Such taxes include foreign income taxes allocated to an entity under § 1.901-2(f)(4) and a distributive share of foreign income taxes paid or accrued by a partnership.

**Reg. § 1.965-5(c)(2)**

(3) *Coordination with section 78.*—(i) *In general.*—With respect to foreign income taxes deemed paid by a domestic corporation with respect to its section 965(a) inclusion amount for a section 958(a) U.S. shareholder inclusion year, section 78 applies only to so much of such taxes as bears the same proportion to the amount of such taxes as—

    (A) The excess of—

        (1) The section 965(a) inclusion amount for a section 958(a) U.S. shareholder inclusion year, over

        (2) The section 965(c) deduction amount allowable with respect to such section 965(a) inclusion amount, bears to

    (B) Such section 965(a) inclusion amount.

    (ii) *Domestic corporation that is a domestic pass-through owner.*—With respect to foreign income taxes deemed paid by a domestic corporation attributable to such corporation's domestic pass-through owner share of a section 965(a) inclusion amount of a domestic pass-through entity, section 78 applies only to so much of such taxes as bears the same proportion to the amount of such taxes as the proportion determined under paragraph (c)(3)(i) of this section as applied to the domestic pass-through entity's section 965(a) inclusion amount for a section 958(a) U.S. shareholder inclusion year.

(d) *Applicable percentage.*—(1) *In general.*—For purposes of this section, except as provided in paragraph (d)(2) and (d)(3) of this section, the term *applicable percentage* means, with respect to a section 958(a) U.S. shareholder and a section 958(a) U.S. shareholder inclusion year, the amount (expressed as a percentage) equal to the sum of—

    (i) 0.771 multiplied by the ratio of—

        (A) The section 958(a) U.S. shareholder's 8 percent rate amount for the section 958(a) U.S. shareholder inclusion year, divided by

        (B) The sum of the section 958(a) U.S. shareholder's 8 percent rate amount for the section 958(a) U.S. shareholder inclusion year plus the section 958(a) U.S. shareholder's 15.5 percent rate amount for the section 958(a) U.S. shareholder inclusion year; plus

    (ii) 0.557 multiplied by the ratio of—

        (A) The section 958(a) U.S. shareholder's 15.5 percent rate amount for the section 958(a) U.S. shareholder inclusion year, divided by

        (B) The amount described in paragraph (d)(1)(i)(B) of this section.

(2) *No section 965(a) inclusion amount.*—If a section 958(a) U.S. shareholder does not have an aggregate section 965(a) inclusion amount, the section 958(a) U.S. shareholder's applicable percentage is 55.7 percent.

(3) *Applicable percentage for domestic pass-through owners.*—In the case of a domestic pass-through owner with respect to a domestic pass-through entity, the domestic pass-through owner's applicable percentage that is applied to foreign income taxes attributable to the domestic pass-through owner share of the section 965(a) inclusion amount or of distributions of section 965(a) previously taxed earnings and profits or section 965(b) previously taxed earnings and profits is equal to the applicable percentage determined under paragraph (d)(1) or (2) of this section, as applicable, with respect to the domestic pass-through entity.

(4) *Applicable percentage with respect to certain distributions of previously taxed earnings and profits.*—In the case of a distribution of section 965(a) previously taxed earnings and profits or section 965(b) previously taxed earnings and profits (other than with respect to a section 958(a) U.S. shareholder described in paragraph (d)(2) of this section), the applicable percentage that is applied to foreign income taxes attributable to the distribution is the applicable percentage that applied with respect to the section 958(a) U.S. shareholder and the section 958(a) U.S. inclusion year in which, or with which, the inclusion year of the relevant deferred foreign income corporation ends. For this purpose, the relevant deferred foreign income corporation is the deferred foreign income corporation with respect to which the section 958(a) U.S. shareholder had the section 965(a) inclusion as a result of which the section 965(a) previously taxed earnings and profits first arose (as described in § 1.965-2(c)) or the section 965(b) previously taxed earnings and profits first arose (as described in § 1.965-2(d)). [Reg. § 1.965-5.]

  ☐ [*T.D.* 9846, 2-4-2019.]

### [Reg. § 1.965-6]

**§ 1.965-6. Computation of foreign income taxes deemed paid and allocation and apportionment of deductions.**—(a) *Scope.*—This section provides rules for the computation of foreign income taxes deemed paid and the allocation and apportionment of deductions. Paragraph (b) of this section provides the general rules for the computation of foreign income taxes deemed paid under sections 902 and 960. Paragraph (c) of this section provides rules for allocation and apportionment of expenses. Paragraph (d) of this section provides rules for foreign income taxes associated with hovering deficits.

(b) *Computation of foreign incomes taxes deemed paid.*—(1) *In general.*—For purposes of determining foreign income taxes deemed paid under section 960(a)(1) with respect to a section 965(a) inclusion attributable to a deferred foreign income corporation that is a member of a qualified group (as defined in section 902(b)(2)), section 902 applies as if the section 965(a) inclusion, translated (if necessary) into the functional currency of the deferred foreign income corporation using the spot rate on December 31, 2017, were a dividend paid by the deferred foreign income corporation. For purposes of computing the amount of foreign income taxes deemed paid under section 960(a)(1), §§1.965-2(b), 1.965-5, sections 902 and 960, the regulations under those sections, and this section apply.

(2) *Dividend or inclusion in excess of post-1986 undistributed earnings.*—When the denominator of the section 902 fraction is positive but less than the numerator of such fraction, the section 902 fraction is one. When the denominator of the section 902 fraction is zero or less than zero, the section 902 fraction is zero, and no foreign taxes are deemed paid.

(3) *Treatment of adjustment under section 965(b)(4)(B).*—For purposes of section 902(c)(1), the post-1986 undistributed earnings of an E&P deficit foreign corporation are increased under section 965(b)(4)(B) and §1.965-2(d)(2)(i)(A) as of the first day of the foreign corporation's first taxable year following the E&P deficit foreign corporation's last taxable year that begins before January 1, 2018.

(4) *Section 902 fraction.*—The term *section 902 fraction* means, with respect to either a deferred foreign income corporation or an E&P deficit foreign corporation, the fraction that is—

(i) The dividends paid by, or the inclusion under section 951(a)(1) (including a section 965(a) inclusion) with respect to, the foreign corporation, as applicable (the *numerator*), divided by

(ii) The foreign corporation's post-1986 undistributed earnings or pre-1987 accumulated profits, as applicable (the *denominator*).

(c) *Allocation and apportionment of deductions.*— For purposes of allocating and apportioning expenses, a section 965(c) deduction does not result in any gross income, including a section 965(a) inclusion, being treated as exempt, excluded, or eliminated income within the meaning of section 864(e)(3) or §1.861-8T(d). Similarly, a section 965(c) deduction does not result in the treatment of stock as an exempt asset within the meaning of section 864(e)(3) or §1.861-8T(d). In addition, consistent with the general inapplicability of §1.861-8T(d)(2) to earnings and profits described in section 959(c)(1) or 959(c)(2), neither section 965(a) previously taxed earnings and profits nor section 965(b) previously taxed earnings and profits are treated as giving rise to gross income that is exempt, excluded, or eliminated income. Similarly, the asset that gives rise to a section 965(a) inclusion, section 965(a) previously taxed earnings and profits, or section 965(b) previously taxed earnings and profits is not treated as a tax-exempt asset.

(d) *Hovering deficits.*—In the last taxable year that begins before January 1, 2018, of a deferred

foreign income corporation that is also a foreign surviving corporation, as defined in §1.367(b)-7(a), solely for purposes of determining the amount of related taxes that are included in post-1986 foreign income taxes under §1.367(b)-7(d)(2)(iii)—

(1) The post-transaction earnings described in §1.367(b)-7(d)(2)(ii) that can be offset by a hovering deficit include any post-transaction earnings earned in that year that were not considered accumulated because they were included in income under section 965 and §1.965-1(b)(1) by a section 958(a) U.S. shareholder; and

(2) Any offset for purposes of §1.367(b)-7(d)(2)(ii) is treated as occurring on the last day of the foreign surviving corporation's inclusion year. [Reg. §1.965-6.]

☐ [*T.D.* 9846, 2-4-2019.]

## [Reg. §1.965-7]

**§1.965-7. Elections, payment, and other special rules.**—(a) *Scope.*—This section provides rules regarding certain elections and payments. Paragraph (b) of this section provides rules regarding the section 965(h) election. Paragraph (c) of this section provides rules regarding the section 965(i) election. Paragraph (d) of this section provides rules regarding the section 965(m) election and a special rule for real estate investment trusts. Paragraph (e) of this section provides rules regarding the section 965(n) election. Paragraph (f) of this section provides rules regarding the election to use the alternative method for calculating post-1986 earnings and profits. Paragraph (g) of this section provides definitions that apply for purposes of this section.

(b) *Section 965(h) election.*—(1) *In general.*— Any person with a section 965(h) net tax liability (that is, a section 958(a) U.S. shareholder or a domestic pass-through owner with respect to a domestic pass-through entity that is a section 958(a) U.S. shareholder, but not a domestic pass-through entity itself) may elect under section 965(h) and this paragraph (b) to pay its section 965(h) net tax liability in eight installments. This election may be revoked only by paying the full amount of the remaining unpaid section 965(h) net tax liability.

(i) *Amount of installments.*—Except as provided in paragraph (b)(3) of this section, if a person makes a section 965(h) election, the amounts of the installments are—

(A) Eight percent of the section 965(h) net tax liability in the case of each of the first five installments;

(B) Fifteen percent of the section 965(h) net tax liability in the case of the sixth installment;

(C) Twenty percent of the section 965(h) net tax liability in the case of the seventh installment; and

(D) Twenty-five percent of the section 965(h) net tax liability in the case of the eighth installment.

(ii) *Increased installments due to a deficiency or a timely filed or amended return.*—(A) *In general.*—If a person makes a section 965(h) election, except as provided in paragraph (b)(1)(ii)(C) of this section, any deficiency or additional liability will be prorated to the installments described under paragraph (b)(1)(i) of this section if any of the following occur:

(1) A deficiency is assessed with respect to the person's section 965(h) net tax liability;

(2) The person files a return by the due date of the return (taking into account extensions, if any) increasing the amount of its section 965(h) net tax liability beyond that taken into account in paying the first installment described under paragraph (b)(1)(i) of this section; or

(3) The person files an amended return that reflects an increase in the amount of its section 965(h) net tax liability.

(B) *Timing.*—If the due date for the payment of an installment to which the deficiency is prorated has passed, the amount prorated to such installment must be paid on notice and demand by the Secretary, or, in the case of an additional liability reported on a return increasing the amount of the section 965(h) net tax liability after payment of the first installment or on an amended return, with the filing of the return. If the due date for the payment of an installment to which the deficiency or additional liability is prorated has not passed, then such amount will be due at the same time as, and as part of, the relevant installment.

(C) *Exception for negligence, intentional disregard, or fraud.*—If a deficiency or additional liability is due to negligence, intentional disregard of rules and regulations, or fraud with intent to evade tax, the proration rule of this paragraph (b)(1)(ii) will not apply, and the deficiency or additional liability (as well as any applicable interest and penalties) must be paid on notice and demand by the Secretary or, in the case of an additional liability reported on a return increasing the amount of the section 965(h) net tax liability after payment of the first installment or on an amended return, with the filing of the return.

(iii) *Due date of installments.*—(A) *In general.*—If a person makes a section 965(h) election, the first installment payment is due on the due date (without regard to extensions) for the return for the relevant taxable year. For purposes of this paragraph (b), the term *relevant taxable year* means, in the case in which the person is a section 958(a) U.S. shareholder, the section 958(a) U.S. shareholder inclusion year, or, in the case in which the person is a domestic pass-through owner, the taxable year in which the person has

the section 965(a) inclusion to which the section 965(h) net tax liability is attributable. Each succeeding installment payment is due on the due date (without regard to extensions) for the return for the taxable year following the taxable year with respect to which the previous installment payment was made.

(B) *Extension for specified individuals.*—If a person is a specified individual with respect to a taxable year within which an installment payment is due pursuant to paragraph (b)(1)(iii)(A) of this section, then, for purposes of determining the due date of an installment payment under paragraph (b)(1)(iii)(A) of this section, the due date of the return (without regard to extensions) due within the taxable year will be treated as the fifteenth day of the sixth month following the close of the prior taxable year. This paragraph (b)(1)(iii)(B) is applicable regardless of whether the person is a specified individual with respect to the relevant taxable year.

(2) *Manner of making election.*—(i) *Eligibility.*—Any person with a section 965(h) net tax liability may make the section 965(h) election, provided that, with respect to the person, none of the acceleration events described in paragraph (b)(3)(ii) of this section has occurred before the election is made. Notwithstanding the preceding sentence, a person that would be eligible to make the section 965(h) election but for the occurrence of an event described in paragraph (b)(3)(ii) of this section may make the section 965(h) election if the exception described in paragraph (b)(3)(iii)(A) of this section applies.

(ii) *Timing.*—A section 965(h) election must be made no later than the due date (taking into account extensions, if any, or any additional time that would have been granted if the person had made an extension request) for the return for the relevant taxable year. Relief is not available under § 301.9100-2 or § 301.9100-3 to file a late election.

(iii) *Election statement.*—Except as otherwise provided in publications, forms, instructions, or other guidance, to make a section 965(h) election, a person must attach a statement, signed under penalties of perjury consistent with the rules for signatures applicable to the person's return, to its return for the relevant taxable year. The statement must include the person's name, taxpayer identification number, total net tax liability under section 965, section 965(h) net tax liability, section 965(i) net tax liability with respect to which a section 965(i) election is effective (if applicable), and the anticipated amounts of each installment described under paragraph (b)(1)(i) of this section. The statement must be filed in the manner prescribed in publications, forms, instructions, or other guidance. The attachment of an unsigned copy of the election statement to the timely-filed return for the relevant taxable year satisfies the signature requirement of this paragraph (b)(2)(iii) if the person making the election retains the original signed election statement in the manner specified by § 1.6001-1(e).

(3) *Acceleration of payment.—* (i) *Acceleration.*—Notwithstanding paragraph (b)(1)(i) of this section, if a person makes a section 965(h) election and an acceleration event described in paragraph (b)(3)(ii) of this section subsequently occurs, then, except as provided in paragraph (b)(3)(iii) of this section, the unpaid portion of the remaining installments will be due on the date of the acceleration event (or in the case of a title 11 or similar case, the day before the petition is filed).

(ii) *Acceleration events.*—The following events are acceleration events for purposes of paragraph (b)(3)(i) of this section with respect to a person that has made a section 965(h) election—

(A) An addition to tax is assessed for the failure to timely pay an installment described in paragraph (b)(1)(i) of this section;

(B) A liquidation, sale, exchange, or other disposition of substantially all of the assets of the person (including in a title 11 or similar case, or, in the case of an individual, by reason of death);

(C) In the case of a person that is not an individual, a cessation of business by the person;

(D) Any event that results in the person no longer being a United States person, including a resident alien (as defined in section 7701(b)(1)(A)) becoming a nonresident alien (as defined in section 7701(b)(1)(B));

(E) In the case of a person that was not a member of any consolidated group, the person becoming a member of a consolidated group;

(F) In the case of a consolidated group, the group ceasing to exist (including by reason of the acquisition of a consolidated group within the meaning of § 1.1502-13(j)(5)) or the group otherwise discontinuing in the filing of a consolidated return; or

(G) A determination by the Commissioner described in the second sentence of paragraph (b)(3)(iii)(C)(2) of this section.

(iii) *Eligible section 965(h) transferee exception.*—(A) *In general.*—Paragraph (b)(3)(i) of this section does not apply (such that the unpaid portion of all remaining installments will not be due as of the date of the acceleration event) to a person with respect to which an acceleration event occurs if the requirements described in paragraphs (b)(3)(iii)(A)(1) and (2) of this section are satisfied. A person with respect to which an acceleration event described in this paragraph (b)(3)(iii)(A) occurs is referred to as an *eligible section 965(h) transferor.*

(1) *Requirement to have a covered acceleration event.*—The acceleration event satisfies

the requirements of this paragraph (b)(3)(iii)(A)(1) if it is described in—

(i) Paragraph (b)(3)(ii)(B) of this section, and the acceleration event is a qualifying consolidated group member transaction within the meaning of paragraph (b)(3)(iii)(E) of this section;

(ii) Paragraph (b)(3)(ii)(B) of this section (other than, in the case of an individual, an acceleration event caused by reason of death) in a transaction that is not a qualifying consolidated group member transaction;

(iii) Paragraph (b)(3)(ii)(E) of this section;

(iv) Paragraph (b)(3)(ii)(F) of this section, and the acceleration event results from the acquisition of a consolidated group within the meaning of § 1.1502-13(j)(5), and the acquired consolidated group members join a different consolidated group as of the day following the acquisition;

(v) Paragraph (b)(3)(ii)(F) of this section, and the group ceases to exist as a result of the transfer of all of the assets of one or more members of the consolidated group to other members with only one entity remaining (the *successor entity*); or

(vi) Paragraph (b)(3)(ii)(F) of this section, and the group ceases to exist as a result of the termination of the subchapter S election pursuant to section 1362(d) of a shareholder of the common parent of the consolidated group and, for the shareholder's taxable year immediately following the termination, the shareholder joins in the filing of a consolidated return as a consolidated group that includes all of the former members of the former consolidated group.

(2) *Requirement to enter into a transfer agreement.*—An eligible section 965(h) transferor and an eligible section 965(h) transferee (as defined in paragraph (b)(3)(iii)(B)(1) of this section) must enter into an agreement with the Commissioner that satisfies the requirements of paragraph (b)(3)(iii)(B) of this section.

(B) *Transfer agreement.*—(1) *Eligibility.*—A transfer agreement that satisfies the requirements of this paragraph (b)(3)(iii)(B) must be entered into by an eligible section 965(h) transferor and an eligible section 965(h) transferee. For this purpose, the term *eligible section 965(h) transferee* refers to a single United States person that is not a domestic pass-through entity and that—

(i) With respect to an acceleration event described in paragraph (b)(3)(iii)(A)(1)(i) of this section, is a departing member (as defined in paragraph (b)(3)(iii)(E)(1)(i) of this section) or its qualified successor (as defined in paragraph (b)(3)(iii)(E)(2) of this section);

(ii) With respect to an acceleration event described in paragraph (b)(3)(iii)(A)(1)(ii) of this section, acquires substantially all of the assets of an eligible section 965(h) transferor;

(*iii*) With respect to an acceleration event described in paragraph (b)(3)(iii)(A)(*1*)(*iii*) of this section, is the agent (within the meaning of § 1.1502-77) of the consolidated group that the eligible section 965(h) transferor joins;

(*iv*) With respect to an acceleration event described in paragraph (b)(3)(iii)(A)(*1*)(*iv*) of this section, is the agent (within the meaning of § 1.1502-77) of the surviving consolidated group;

(*v*) With respect to an acceleration event described in paragraph (b)(3)(iii)(A)(*1*)(*v*) of this section, is the successor entity (within the meaning of paragraph (b)(3)(iii)(A)(*1*)(*v*) of this section); or

(*vi*) With respect an acceleration event described in paragraph (b)(3)(iii)(A)(*1*)(*vi*) of this section, is the agent (within the meaning of § 1.1502-77) of the consolidated group that includes the shareholder whose subchapter S election was terminated and all of the former members of the former consolidated group.

(*2*) *Filing requirements.*—(*i*) *In general.*—A transfer agreement must be timely filed. Except as provided in paragraph (b)(3)(iii)(B)(*2*)(*ii*) of this section, a transfer agreement is considered timely filed only if the transfer agreement is filed within 30 days of the date that the acceleration event occurs. The transfer agreement must be filed in accordance with the rules provided in publications forms, instructions, or other guidance. In addition, a duplicate copy of the transfer agreement must be attached to the returns of both the eligible section 965(h) transferee and the eligible section 965(h) transferor for the taxable year during which the acceleration event occurs filed by the due date for such returns (taking into account extensions, if any). Relief is not available under § 301.9100-2 or 301.9100-3 to file a transfer agreement late.

(*ii*) *Transition rule.*—If an acceleration event occurs on or before February 5, 2019, the transfer agreement must be filed by March 5, 2019, to be considered timely filed.

(*3*) *Signature requirement.*—The transfer agreement that is filed within 30 days of the acceleration event or by the due date specified in paragraph (b)(3)(iii)(B)(*2*)(*ii*) of this section must be signed under penalties of perjury by a person who is authorized to sign a return on behalf of the eligible section 965(h) transferor and a person who is authorized to sign a return on behalf of the eligible section 965(h) transferee.

(*4*) *Terms of agreement.*—A transfer agreement under this paragraph (b)(3)(iii)(B) must be entitled "Transfer Agreement Under Section 965(h)(3)" and must contain the following information and representations—

(*i*) A statement that the document constitutes an agreement by the eligible section 965(h) transferee to assume the liability of the eligible section 965(h) transferor for any unpaid installment payments of the eligible section 965(h) transferor under section 965(h);

(*ii*) A statement that the eligible section 965(h) transferee (and, if the eligible section 965(h) transferor continues in existence immediately after the acceleration event, the eligible section 965(h) transferor) agrees to comply with all of the conditions and requirements of section 965(h) and paragraph (b) of this section, as well as any other applicable requirements in the section 965 regulations;

(*iii*) The name, address, and taxpayer identification number of the eligible section 965(h) transferor and the eligible section 965(h) transferee;

(*iv*) The amount of the eligible section 965(h) transferor's section 965(h) net tax liability remaining unpaid, as determined by the eligible section 965(h) transferor, which amount is subject to adjustment by the Commissioner;

(*v*) A copy of the eligible section 965(h) transferor's most recent Form 965-A or Form 965-B, as applicable, if the eligible section 965(h) transferor has been required to file a Form 965-A or Form 965-B;

(*vi*) A detailed description of the acceleration event that led to the transfer agreement;

(*vii*) A representation that the eligible section 965(h) transferee is able to make the remaining payments required under section 965(h) and paragraph (b) of this section with respect to the section 965(h) net tax liability being assumed;

(*viii*) If the eligible section 965(h) transferor continues to exist immediately after the acceleration event, an acknowledgement that the eligible section 965(h) transferor and any successor to the eligible section 965(h) transferor will remain jointly and severally liable for any unpaid installment payments of the eligible section 965(h) transferor under section 965(h), including, if applicable, under § 1.1502-6;

(*ix*) A statement as to whether the leverage ratio of the eligible section 965(h) transferee and all subsidiary members of its affiliated group immediately after the acceleration event exceeds three to one, which ratio may be modified as provided in publications, forms, instructions, or other guidance;

(*x*) A certification by the eligible section 965(h) transferee stating that the eligible section 965(h) transferee waives the right to a notice of liability and consents to the immediate assessment of the portion of the section 965(h) net tax liability remaining unpaid; and

(*xi*) Any additional information, representation, or certification required by the Commissioner in publications, forms, instructions, or other guidance.

*(5) Consolidated groups.*—For purposes of this paragraph (b)(3)(iii)(B), in the case of a consolidated group, the terms "eligible section 965(h) transferor" and "eligible section 965(h) transferee" each refer to a consolidated group that is a party to a covered acceleration event described in paragraph (b)(3)(iii)(A)(*1*) of this section. In such a case, any transfer agreement under this paragraph (b)(3)(iii)(B) must be entered into by the agent (as defined in § 1.1502-77) of the relevant consolidated group.

*(6) Leverage ratio.*—For purposes of paragraph (b)(3)(iii)(B)(*4*)(*ix*) of this section, and except as otherwise provided in publications, forms, instructions, or other guidance, the term *leverage ratio* means the ratio that the total indebtedness of the eligible section 965(h) transferee bears to the sum of its money and all other assets reduced (but not below zero) by such total indebtedness. For this purpose, the amount taken into account with respect to any asset is the adjusted basis thereof for purposes of determining gain, and the amount taken into account with respect to any indebtedness with original issue discount is its issue price plus the portion of the original issue discount previously accrued as determined under the rules of section 1272 (determined without regard to subsection (a)(7) or (b)(4) thereof).

*(C) Consent of Commissioner.*—(1) In *general.*—Except as otherwise provided in publications, forms, instructions, or other guidance, if an eligible section 965(h) transferor and an eligible section 965(h) transferee file a transfer agreement in accordance with the provisions of paragraph (b)(3)(iii)(B) of this section, the eligible section 965(h) transferor and the eligible section 965(h) transferee will be considered to have entered into an agreement described in paragraph (b)(3)(iii)(A)(*2*) of this section with the Commissioner for purposes of section 965(h)(3) and paragraph (b)(3)(iii) of this section. If the Commissioner determines that additional information is necessary (for example, additional information regarding the ability of the eligible section 965(h) transferee to fully pay the remaining section 965(h) net tax liability), the eligible section 965(h) transferee must provide such information upon request.

*(2) Material misrepresentations and omissions.*—If the Commissioner determines that an agreement filed by an eligible section 965(h) transferor and an eligible section 965(h) transferee contains a material misrepresentation or material omission, or if the eligible section 965(h) transferee does not provide the additional information requested under paragraph (b)(3)(iii)(C)(*1*) of this section within a reasonable timeframe communicated by the Commissioner to the eligible section 965(h) transferee, then the Commissioner may reject the transfer agreement (effective as of the date of the related acceleration event). In the alternative, on the date that the Commissioner determines that the transfer

agreement includes a material misrepresentation or material omission, the Commissioner may determine that an acceleration event has occurred with respect to the eligible section 965(h) transferee as of the date of the determination, such that any unpaid installment payments of the eligible section 965(h) transferor that were assumed by the eligible section 965(h) transferee become due on the date of the determination.

*(D) Effect of assumption.*—(1) In *general.*—If the exception in this paragraph (b)(3)(iii) applies with respect to an eligible section 965(h) transferor and an eligible section 965(h) transferee, the eligible section 965(h) transferee assumes all of the outstanding obligations and responsibilities of the eligible section 965(h) transferor with respect to the section 965(h) net tax liability as though the eligible section 965(h) transferee had included the section 965(a) inclusion in income. Accordingly, the eligible section 965(h) transferee is responsible for making payments and reporting with respect to any unpaid installment payments. In addition, for example, if an acceleration event described in paragraph (b)(3)(ii) of this section occurs with respect to an eligible section 965(h) transferee, any unpaid installment payments of the eligible section 965(h) transferor that were assumed by the eligible section 965(h) transferee will become due on the date of such event, subject to any applicable exception in paragraph (b)(3)(iii) of this section.

*(2) Eligible section 965(h) transferor liability.*—An eligible section 965(h) transferor (or a successor) remains jointly and severally liable for any unpaid installment payments of the eligible section 965(h) transferor that were assumed by the eligible section 965(h) transferee, as well as any penalties, additions to tax, or other additional amounts attributable to such net tax liability.

*(E) Qualifying consolidated group member transaction.*—(1) Definition of qualifying consolidated group member transaction.*—For purposes of this paragraph (b)(3), the term *qualifying consolidated group member transaction* means a transaction in which—

*(i)* A member of a consolidated group (the *departing member*) ceases to be a member of the consolidated group (including by reason of the distribution, sale, or exchange of the departing member's stock);

*(ii)* The transaction results in the consolidated group (which is treated as a single person for this purpose under § 1.965-8(e)(1)) being treated as transferring substantially all of its assets for purposes of paragraph (b)(3)(ii)(B) of this section; and

*(iii)* The departing member either continues to exist immediately after the transaction or has a qualified successor.

*(2) Definition of qualified successor.*—For purposes of this paragraph (b)(3), the term

*qualified successor* means, with respect to a departing member described in this paragraph (b)(3)(iii)(E), another domestic corporation (or consolidated group) that acquires substantially all of the assets of the departing member (including in a transaction described in section 381(a)(2)).

*(3) Departure of multiple members of a consolidated group.*—Multiple members that deconsolidate from the same consolidated group as a result of a single transaction are treated as a single departing member to the extent that, immediately after the transaction, they become members of the same (second) consolidated group, which would be treated as a single person under § 1.965-8(e)(1).

*(c) Section 965(i) election.*—(1) *In general.*— Each shareholder of an S corporation (including a person listed in § 1.1362-6(b)(2) with respect to a trust or estate, but not a domestic pass-through entity itself) that is a United States shareholder of a deferred foreign income corporation may elect under section 965(i) and this paragraph (c) to defer the payment of the shareholder's section 965(i) net tax liability with respect to the S corporation until the shareholder's taxable year that includes a triggering event described in paragraph (c)(3) of this section. This election may be revoked only by paying the full amount of the unpaid section 965(i) net tax liability.

*(2) Manner of making election.*— (i) *Eligibility.*—Each shareholder with a section 965(i) net tax liability with respect to an S corporation may make the section 965(i) election with respect to such S corporation, provided that, with respect to the shareholder, none of the triggering events described in paragraph (c)(3)(ii) of this section have occurred before the election is made. Notwithstanding the preceding sentence, a shareholder that would be eligible to make the section 965(i) election but for the occurrence of an event described in paragraph (c)(3)(ii) of this section may make the section 965(i) election if an exception described in paragraph (c)(3)(iv) of this section applies.

*(ii) Timing.*—A section 965(i) election must be made no later than the due date (taking into account extensions, if any) for the shareholder's return for each taxable year that includes the last day of the taxable year of the S corporation in which the S corporation has a section 965(a) inclusion to which the shareholder's section 965(i) net tax liability is attributable. Relief is not available under § 301.9100-2 or 301.9100-3 to make a late election.

*(iii) Election statement.*—Except as otherwise provided in publications, forms, instructions, or other guidance, to make a section 965(i) election, a shareholder must attach a statement, signed under penalties of perjury consistent with the rules for signatures applicable to the person's

return, to its return for the taxable year that includes the last day of a taxable year of the S corporation in which the S corporation has a section 965(a) inclusion to which the shareholder's section 965(i) net tax liability is attributable. The statement must include the shareholder's name, taxpayer identification number, the name and taxpayer identification number of the S corporation with respect to which the election is made, the amount described in paragraph (g)(10)(i)(A) of this section as modified by paragraph (g)(6) of this section for purposes of determining the section 965(i) net tax liability with respect to the S corporation, the amount described in paragraph (g)(10)(i)(B) of this section, and the section 965(i) net tax liability with respect to the S corporation. The statement must be filed in the manner prescribed in publications, forms, instructions, or other guidance. The attachment of an unsigned copy of the election statement to the timely-filed return for the relevant taxable year satisfies the signature requirement of this paragraph (c)(2)(iii) if the shareholder retains the original signed election statement in the manner specified by § 1.6001-1(e).

*(3) Triggering events.*—(i) *In general.*—If a shareholder makes a section 965(i) election with respect to an S corporation, the shareholder defers payment of its section 965(i) net tax liability with respect to the S corporation until the shareholder's taxable year that includes the occurrence of a triggering event described in paragraph (c)(3)(ii) of this section with respect to the section 965(i) net tax liability with respect to the S corporation. If a triggering event described in paragraph (c)(3)(ii) of this section with respect to an S corporation occurs, except as provided in paragraph (c)(3)(iv) of this section, the shareholder's section 965(i) net tax liability with respect to the S corporation will be assessed as an addition to tax for the shareholder's taxable year that includes the triggering event.

*(ii) Triggering events.*—The following events are considered triggering events for purposes of paragraph (c)(3)(i) of this section with respect to a shareholder's section 965(i) net tax liability with respect to an S corporation—

(A) The corporation ceases to be an S corporation (determined as of the first day of the first taxable year that the corporation is not an S corporation);

(B) A liquidation, sale, exchange, or other disposition of substantially all of the assets of the S corporation (including in a title 11 or similar case), a cessation of business by the S corporation, or the S corporation ceasing to exist;

(C) The transfer of any share of stock of the S corporation by the shareholder (including by reason of death or otherwise) that results in a change of ownership for federal income tax purposes; or

(D) A determination by the Commissioner described in the second sentence of paragraph (c)(3)(iv)(C)(2) of this section.

(iii) *Partial transfers.*—If an S corporation shareholder transfers less than all of its shares of stock of the S corporation, the transfer will be a triggering event only with respect to the portion of a shareholder's section 965(i) net tax liability that is properly allocable to the transferred shares.

(iv) *Eligible section 965(i) transferee exception.*—(A) *In general.*—Paragraph (c)(3)(i) of this section will not apply (such that a shareholder's section 965(i) net tax liability with respect to an S corporation will not be assessed as an addition to tax for the shareholder's taxable year that includes the triggering event) if the requirements described in paragraphs (c)(3)(iv)(A)(1) and (2) of this section are satisfied. A shareholder with respect to which a triggering event described in this paragraph (c)(3)(iv)(A) occurs is referred to as an *eligible section 965(i) transferor.*

(1) *Requirement to have a covered triggering event.*—The triggering event satisfies the requirements of this paragraph (c)(3)(iv)(A)(1) if it is described in paragraph (c)(3)(ii)(C) of this section.

(2) *Requirement to enter into a transfer agreement.*—The shareholder with respect to which a triggering event occurs and an eligible section 965(i) transferee (as defined in paragraph (c)(3)(v)(B)(1) of this section) must enter into an agreement with the Commissioner that satisfies the requirements of paragraph (c)(3)(iv)(B) of this section.

(B) *Transfer agreement.*—(1) *Eligibility.*— A transfer agreement that satisfies the requirements of this paragraph (c)(3)(iv)(B) may be entered into by an eligible section 965(i) transferor and an eligible section 965(i) transferee. For this purpose, the term *eligible section 965(i) transferee* refers to a single United States person that becomes a shareholder of the S corporation (including a person listed in §1.1362-6(b)(2) with respect to a trust or estate, but not a domestic pass-through entity itself). In the case of a transfer that consists of multiple partial transfers (as described in paragraph (c)(3)(iii) of this section), a transfer agreement that satisfies the requirements of this paragraph (c)(3)(iv)(B) may be entered into by an eligible section 965(i) transferor and an eligible section 965(i) transferee for each partial transfer.

(2) *Filing requirements.*—(i) *In general.*—A transfer agreement must be timely filed. Except as provided in paragraphs (c)(3)(iv)(B)(2)(ii) and (iii) of this section, a transfer agreement is considered timely filed only if the transfer agreement is filed within 30 days of the date that the triggering event occurs. The transfer agreement must be filed in accordance with the rules provided in publications, forms, instructions, or other guidance. In addition, a duplicate copy of the transfer agreement must be attached to the returns of both the eligible section 965(i) transferee and the eligible section 965(i) transferor for the taxable year during which the triggering event occurs filed by the due date (taking into account extensions, if any) for such returns. Relief is not available under § 301.9100-2 or 301.9100-3 to file a transfer agreement late.

(ii) *Transition rule.*—If a triggering event occurs on or before February 5, 2019, the transfer agreement must be filed by March 5, 2019, to be considered timely filed.

(iii) *Death of eligible section 965(i) transferor.*—If the triggering event is the death of the eligible section 965(i) transferor, the transfer agreement must be filed by the later of the unextended due date for the eligible section 965(i) transferor's final income tax return or March 5, 2019.

(3) *Signature requirement.*—The transfer agreement that is filed within 30 days of the triggering event or by the due date specified in paragraph (c)(3)(iv)(B)(2)(ii) or (iii) of this section must be signed under penalties of perjury by a person who is authorized to sign a return on behalf of the eligible section 965(i) transferor and a person who is authorized to sign a return on behalf of the eligible section 965(i) transferee.

(4) *Terms of agreement.*—A transfer agreement under this paragraph (c)(3)(iv)(B) must be entitled "Transfer Agreement Under Section 965(i)(2)" and must contain the following information and representations:

(i) A statement that the document constitutes an agreement by the eligible section 965(i) transferee to assume the liability of the eligible section 965(i) transferor for the unpaid portion of the section 965(i) net tax liability, or, in the case of a partial transfer, for the unpaid portion of the section 965(i) net tax liability attributable to the transferred stock;

(ii) A statement that the eligible section 965(i) transferee agrees to comply with all of the conditions and requirements of section 965(i) and paragraph (c) of this section, including the annual reporting requirement, as well as any other applicable requirements in the section 965 regulations;

(iii) The name, address, and taxpayer identification number of the eligible section 965(i) transferor and the eligible section 965(i) transferee;

(iv) The amount of the eligible section 965(i) transferor's unpaid section 965(i) net tax liability or, in the case of a partial transfer, the unpaid portion of the section 965(i) net tax liability attributable to the transferred stock, each as determined by the eligible section 965(i) transferor, which amount is subject to adjustment by the Commissioner;

*(v)* A copy of the eligible section 965(i) transferor's most recent Form 965-A, if the eligible section 965(i) transferor has been required to file a Form 965-A;

*(vi)* A detailed description of the triggering event that led to the transfer agreement, including the name and taxpayer identification number of the S corporation with respect to which the section 965(i) election was effective;

*(vii)* A representation that the eligible section 965(i) transferee is able to pay the section 965(i) net tax liability being assumed;

*(viii)* An acknowledgement that the eligible section 965(i) transferor and any successor to the eligible section 965(i) transferor will remain jointly and severally liable for the section 965(i) net tax liability being assumed by the eligible section 965(i) transferee

*(ix)* A statement as to whether the leverage ratio of the eligible section 965(i) transferee immediately after the triggering event exceeds three to one, which ratio may be modified as provided in publications, forms, instructions, or other guidance;

*(x)* Any additional information, representation, or certification required by the Commissioner in publications, forms, instructions, or other guidance.

*(5) Special rule in the case of death of eligible section 965(i) transferor.*—Except in the case of transfers to trusts, if the triggering event is the death of the eligible section 965(i) transferor, and the identity of the beneficiary or beneficiaries (in the case of multiple partial transfers) is determined as of the due date for the transfer agreement described in paragraph (c)(3)(iv)(B)(2)(*iii*) of this section, then the transfer may be treated as a transfer directly between the eligible 965(i) transferor and the beneficiary or beneficiaries. If, however, the identity of the beneficiary or beneficiaries is not determined as of the due date for the transfer agreement described in paragraph (c)(3)(iv)(B)(2)(*iii*) of this section, then the transfer must be treated first as a transfer between the eligible section 965(i) transferor and his or her estate at the time of death and second as a transfer between the estate and the beneficiary or beneficiaries when the shares are actually transferred to the beneficiary or beneficiaries. Separate transfer agreements must be filed for each transfer. The transfer from the eligible section 965(i) transferor to his or her estate is a transfer resulting from a triggering event that is the death of the eligible section 965(i) transferor, and the transfer agreement is subject to the timing rules in paragraph (c)(3)(iv)(B)(2)(*iii*) of this section. The transfer from the estate to the beneficiary or beneficiaries is not a transfer resulting from a triggering event that is the death of the eligible section 965(i) transferor, and the transfer agreement is subject

to the timing rules in paragraph (c)(3)(iv)(B)(2)(*i*) and (*ii*) of this section.

*(6) Leverage ratio.*—For purposes of paragraph (c)(3)(iv)(B)(4)(*ix*) of this section, and except as otherwise provided in publications, forms, instructions, or other guidance, the term *leverage ratio* means the ratio that the total indebtedness of the eligible section 965(i) transferee bears to the sum of its money and all other assets reduced (but not below zero) by such total indebtedness. For this purpose, the amount taken into account with respect to any asset is the adjusted basis thereof for purposes of determining gain, and the amount taken into account with respect to any indebtedness with original issue discount is its issue price plus the portion of the original issue discount previously accrued as determined under the rules of section 1272 (determined without regard to subsection (a)(7) or (b)(4) thereof).

*(C) Consent of Commissioner.—(1) In general.*—Except as otherwise provided in publications, forms, instructions, or other guidance, if an eligible section 965(i) transferor and an eligible section 965(i) transferee file a transfer agreement in accordance with the provisions of paragraph (c)(3)(iv)(B) of this section, the eligible section 965(i) transferor and the eligible section 965(i) transferee will be considered to have entered into an agreement with the Commissioner for purposes of section 965(i)(2) and paragraph (c)(3)(iv) of this section. If the Commissioner determines that additional information is necessary (for example, additional information regarding the ability of the eligible section 965(i) transferee to pay the eligible section 965(i) transferor's unpaid section 965(i) net tax liability), the eligible section 965(i) transferee must provide such information upon request.

*(2) Material misrepresentations and omissions.*—If the Commissioner determines that an agreement filed by an eligible section 965(i) transferor and an eligible section 965(i) transferee contains a material misrepresentation or material omission, or if the eligible section 965(i) transferee does not provide the additional information requested under paragraph (c)(3)(iv)(C)(*1*) of this section within a reasonable timeframe communicated by the Commissioner to the eligible section 965(i) transferee, then the Commissioner may reject the transfer agreement (effective as of the date of the related triggering event). In the alternative, on the date that the Commissioner determines that the transfer agreement includes a material misrepresentation or material omission, the Commissioner may determine that a triggering event has occurred with respect to the eligible section 965(i) transferee as of the date of the determination, such that the unpaid section 965(i) net tax liability of the eligible section 965(i) transferor that was assumed by

the eligible section 965(i) transferee becomes due on the date of the determination.

(D) *Effect of assumption.*—*(1) In general.*—When the exception in this paragraph (c)(3)(iv) applies with respect to an eligible section 965(i) transferor and an eligible section 965(i) transferee, the eligible section 965(i) transferee assumes all of the outstanding obligations and responsibilities of the eligible section 965(i) transferor with respect to the section 965(i) net tax liability with respect to the S corporation as though the eligible section 965(i) transferee had included the section 965(a) inclusion in income. Accordingly, the eligible section 965(i) transferee is responsible for making payments and reporting with respect to any unpaid section 965(i) net tax liability with respect to the S corporation. In addition, for example, if a triggering event described in paragraph (c)(3)(ii) of this section occurs with respect to an eligible section 965(i) transferee, any unpaid portion of the section 965(i) net tax liability of the eligible section 965(i) transferor that was assumed by the eligible section 965(i) transferee becomes due on the date of such event, subject to any applicable exception in paragraph (c)(3)(iv) or (v) of this section.

(2) *Eligible section 965(i) transferor liability.*—An eligible section 965(i) transferor remains jointly and severally liable for any unpaid installment payments of the eligible section 965(i) transferor that were assumed by the eligible section 965(i) transferee, as well as any penalties, additions to tax, or other additional amounts attributable to such net tax liability.

(v) *Coordination with section 965(h) election.*—(A) *In general.*—Subject to the limitation described in paragraph (c)(3)(v)(D) of this section, a shareholder that has made a section 965(i) election with respect to an S corporation, upon the occurrence of a triggering event with respect to such S corporation, may make a section 965(h) election with respect to the portion of the shareholder's section 965(i) net tax liability with respect to such S corporation that is assessed as an addition to tax for the shareholder's taxable year that includes the triggering event pursuant to paragraph (c)(3)(i) of this section as if such portion were a section 965(h) net tax liability.

(B) *Timing for election.*—A section 965(h) election made pursuant to section 965(i)(4) and paragraph (c)(3)(v)(A) of this section must be made no later than the due date (taking into account extensions, if any) for the shareholder's return for the taxable year in which the triggering event with respect to the S corporation occurs. Relief is not available under § 301.9100-2 or § 301.9100-3 to make a late election.

(C) *Due date for installment.*—If a shareholder makes a section 965(h) election pursuant to section 965(i)(4) and paragraph (c)(3)(v)(A) of this section, the payment of the first installment

(as described in paragraph (b)(1)(i) of this section) must be made no later than the due date (without regard to extensions) for the shareholder's return of tax for the taxable year in which the triggering event with respect to the S corporation occurs.

(D) *Limitation.*—(1) *In general.*—Notwithstanding paragraph (c)(3)(v)(A) of this section, if the triggering event with respect to an S corporation is a triggering event described in paragraph (c)(3)(ii)(B) of this section, then the section 965(h) election may only be made with the consent of the Commissioner.

(2) *Manner of obtaining consent.*—(i) *In general.*—In order to obtain the consent of the Commissioner as required by paragraph (c)(3)(v)(D)(1) of this section, the shareholder intending to make the section 965(h) election must file the agreement described in paragraph (c)(3)(v)(D)(4) of this section within 30 days of the occurrence of the triggering event, except as described in paragraph (c)(3)(v)(D)(2)(ii) of this section. The agreement must be filed in accordance with the rules provided in publications, forms, instructions, or other guidance. In addition, a duplicate copy of the agreement must be filed, with the shareholder's timely-filed return for the taxable year during which the triggering event occurs (taking into account extensions, if any), along with the election statement described in paragraph (b)(2)(iii) of this section. Relief is not available under § 301.9100-2 or § 301.9100-3 to file an agreement late.

(ii) *Transition rule.*—If a triggering event occurs on or before February 5, 2019, the agreement must be filed by March 5, 2019, in order to be considered timely filed.

(3) *Signature requirement.*—The agreement that is filed within 30 days of the triggering event or by the due date specified in paragraph (c)(3)(v)(D)(2)(ii) of this section must be signed under penalties of perjury by the shareholder.

(4) *Terms of agreement.*—The agreement under this paragraph (c)(3)(v)(D) must be entitled "Consent Agreement Under Section 965(i)(4)(D)" and must contain the following information and representations—

(i) A statement that the shareholder agrees to comply with all of the conditions and requirements of section 965(h) and paragraph (b) of this section, as well as any other applicable requirements in the section 965 regulations;

(ii) The name, address, and taxpayer identification number of the shareholder;

(iii) The amount of the section 965(i) net tax liability under section 965 remaining unpaid with respect to which the section 965(h) election is made pursuant to section 965(i)(4)(D) and paragraph (c)(3)(v)(A) of this section, as determined by the shareholder, which amount is subject to adjustment by the Commissioner; and

(iv) A representation that the shareholder is able to make the payments required under section 965(h) and paragraph (b) of this section with respect to the portion of the total net tax liability under section 965 remaining unpaid described in paragraph (c)(3)(v)(D)(4)(iii) of this section.

(v) A statement as to whether the leverage ratio of the shareholder and all subsidiary members of its affiliated group immediately following the triggering event exceeds three to one; and

(vi) Any additional information, representation, or certification required by the Commissioner in publications, forms, instructions, or other guidance.

(5) Consent of Commissioner.—(i) In general.—If a shareholder files an agreement in accordance with the provisions of paragraph (c)(3)(v)(D) of this section, the shareholder will be considered to have obtained the consent of the Commissioner for purposes of section 965(i)(4)(D) and paragraph (c)(3)(v)(D)(1) of this section. However, if the Commissioner reviews the agreement and determines that additional information is necessary, the shareholder must provide such information upon request.

(ii) Material misrepresentations and omissions.—If the Commissioner determines that an agreement filed by a shareholder in accordance with the provisions of this paragraph (c)(3)(v)(D) contains a material misrepresentation or material omission, or if the shareholder does not provide the additional information requested under paragraph (c)(3)(v)(D)(5)(i) of this section within a reasonable timeframe communicated by the Commissioner to the shareholder, then the Commissioner may reject the agreement (effective as of the date of the related triggering event).

(6) Leverage ratio.—For purposes of paragraph (c)(3)(v)(D)(4)(v) of this section, and except as otherwise provided in publications, forms, instructions, or other guidance, the term leverage ratio means the ratio that the total indebtedness of the shareholder bears to the sum of its money and all other assets reduced (but not below zero) by such total indebtedness. For this purpose, the amount taken into account with respect to any asset is the adjusted basis thereof for purposes of determining gain, and the amount taken into account with respect to any indebtedness with original issue discount is its issue price plus the portion of the original issue discount previously accrued as determined under the rules of section 1272 (determined without regard to subsection (a)(7) or (b)(4) thereof).

(4) Joint and several liability.—If any shareholder of an S corporation makes a section 965(i)

election, the S corporation is jointly and severally liable for the payment of the shareholder's section 965(i) net tax liability with respect to the S corporation, as well as any penalties, additions to tax, or other additional amounts attributable to such net tax liability.

(5) Extension of limitation on collection.—If an S corporation shareholder makes a section 965(i) election with respect to its section 965(i) net tax liability with respect to an S corporation, any limitation on the time period for the collection of the net tax liability shall not begin before the date of the triggering event with respect to the section 965(i) net tax liability.

(6) Annual reporting requirement.—(i) In general.—A shareholder that makes a section 965(i) election with respect to its section 965(i) net tax liability with respect to an S corporation is required to report the amount of its deferred net tax liability on its return of tax for the taxable year in which the election is made and on the return of tax for each subsequent taxable year until such net tax liability has been fully assessed.

(ii) Failure to report.—If a shareholder fails to report the amount of its deferred net tax liability as required with respect to any taxable year by the due date (taking into account extensions, if any) for the return of tax for that taxable year, five percent of such deferred net tax liability will be assessed as an addition to tax for such taxable year.

(d) Section 965(m) election and special rule for real estate investment trusts.—(1) In general.—A real estate investment trust may elect under section 965(m) and this paragraph (d) to defer the inclusion in gross income (for purposes of the computation of real estate investment trust taxable income under section 857(b)) of its REIT section 965 amounts and include them in income according to the schedule described in paragraph (d)(2) of this section. This election is revocable only by including in gross income (for purposes of the computation of real estate investment trust taxable income under section 857(b)) the full amount of the REIT section 965 amounts.

(2) Inclusion schedule for section 965(m) election.—If a real estate investment trust makes the section 965(m) election, the REIT section 965 amounts will be included in the real estate investment trust's gross income as follows—

(i) Eight percent of the REIT section 965 amounts in each taxable year in the five-taxable year period beginning with the taxable year the amount would otherwise be included;

(ii) Fifteen percent of the REIT section 965 amounts in the first year following the five year period described in paragraph (d)(2)(i) of this section;

(iii) Twenty percent of the REIT section 965 amounts in the second year following the five year period described in paragraph (d)(2)(i) of this section; and

(iv) Twenty-five percent of the REIT section 965 amounts in the third year following the five year period described in paragraph (d)(2)(i) of this section.

(3) *Manner of making election.*— (i) *Eligibility.*—A real estate investment trust with section 965(a) inclusions may make the section 965(m) election.

(ii) *Timing.*—A section 965(m) election must be made no later than the due date (taking into account extensions, if any) for the return for the first year of the five year period described in paragraph (d)(2)(i) of this section. Relief is not available under § 301.9100-2 or § 301.9100-3 to make a late election.

(iii) *Election statement.*—Except as otherwise provided in publications, forms, instructions, or other guidance, to make a section 965(m) election, a real estate investment trust must attach a statement, signed under penalties of perjury consistent with the rules for signatures applicable to the person's return, to its return for the taxable year in which it would otherwise be required to include the REIT section 965 amounts in gross income. The statement must include the real estate investment trust's name, taxpayer identification number, REIT section 965 amounts, and the anticipated amounts of each portion of the REIT section 965 amounts described under paragraph (d)(2) of this section, and the statement must be filed in the manner prescribed in publications, forms, instructions, or other guidance. The attachment of an unsigned copy of the election statement to the timely-filed return for the relevant taxable year satisfies the signature requirement of this paragraph (d)(3)(iii) if the real estate investment trust retains the original signed election statement in the manner specified by § 1.6001-1(e).

(4) *Coordination with section 965(h).*—A real estate investment trust that makes the section 965(m) election may not also make a section 965(h) election for any year with respect to which a section 965(m) election is in effect.

(5) *Acceleration of inclusion.*—If a real estate investment trust makes a section 965(m) election and subsequently there is a liquidation, sale, exchange, or other disposition of substantially all of the assets of the real estate investment trust (including in a title 11 or similar case), or a cessation of business by the real estate investment trust, any amount not yet included in gross income (for purposes of the computation of real estate investment trust taxable income under section 857(b)) as a result of the section 965(m) election will be so included as of the day before the date of the event. The unpaid portion of any tax liability with respect to such inclusion will be due on the date of the event (or in the case of a title 11 or similar case, the day before the petition is filed).

(6) *Treatment of section 965(a) inclusions of a real estate investment trust.*—Regardless of whether a real estate investment trust has made a section 965(m) election, and regardless of whether it is a United States shareholder of a deferred foreign income corporation, any section 965(a) inclusions of the real estate investment trust are not taken into account as gross income of the real estate investment trust for purposes of applying paragraphs (2) and (3) of section 856(c) for any taxable year for which the real estate investment trust takes into account a section 965(a) inclusion, including pursuant to paragraph (d)(2) of this section.

(e) *Section 965(n) election.*—(1) *In general.*— (i) *General rule.*—A person may elect to not take into account the amount described in paragraph (e)(1)(ii) of this section in determining its net operating loss under section 172 for the taxable year or in determining the amount of taxable income for such taxable year (computed without regard to the deduction allowable under section 172) that may be reduced by net operating loss carryovers or carrybacks to such taxable year under section 172. The election for each taxable year is irrevocable.

(ii) *Applicable amount for section 965(n) election.*—If a person makes a section 965(n) election, the amount referred to in paragraph (e)(1)(i) of this section is the sum of—

(A) The person's section 965(a) inclusions for the taxable year reduced by the person's section 965(c) deductions for the taxable year, and

(B) In the case of a domestic corporation, the taxes deemed paid under section 960(a)(1) for the taxable year with respect to the person's section 965(a) inclusions that are treated as dividends under section 78.

(iii) *Scope of section 965(n) election.*—If a person makes a section 965(n) election, the election applies to both net operating losses for the taxable year for which the election is made and the net operating loss carryovers or carrybacks to such taxable year, each in their entirety. Any section 965(n) election made by the agent (within the meaning of § 1.1502-77) of a consolidated group applies to all net operating losses available to the consolidated group, including all components of the consolidated net operating loss deduction (as defined in § 1.1502-21(a)).

(iv) [Reserved]

(2) *Manner of making election.*— (i) *Eligibility.*—A person with a section 965(a) inclusion may make the section 965(n) election.

(ii) *Timing.*—A section 965(n) election must be made no later than the due date (taking into account extensions, if any) for the person's return for the taxable year to which the election applies. Relief is not available under § 301.9100-2 or § 301.9100-3 to make a late election.

(iii) *Election statement.*—Except as otherwise provided in publications, forms, instructions, or other guidance, to make a section 965(n) election, a person must attach a statement, signed under penalties of perjury consistent with the rules for signatures applicable to the person's return, to its return for the taxable year to which the election applies. The statement must include the person's name, taxpayer identification number, the amounts described in section 965(n)(2)(A) and paragraph (e)(1)(ii)(A) of this section and section 965(n)(2)(B) and paragraph (e)(1)(ii)(B) of this section, and the sum thereof, and the statement must be filed in the manner prescribed in publications, forms, instructions, or other guidance. The attachment of an unsigned copy of the election statement to the timely-filed return for the relevant taxable year satisfies the signature requirement of this paragraph (e)(2)(iii) if the person making the election retains the original signed election statement in the manner specified by § 1.6001-1(e).

(f) *Election to use alternative method for calculating post-1986 earnings and profits.*—(1) *Effect of election for specified foreign corporations that do not have a 52-53-week taxable year.*—If an election is made under this paragraph (f) with respect to a specified foreign corporation that does not have a 52-53-week taxable year, the amount of the post-1986 earnings and profits (including a deficit) as of the E&P measurement date on November 2, 2017, is determined under paragraph (f)(3) of this section. The election described in this paragraph (f) is irrevocable. A specified foreign corporation that does not have a 52-53-week taxable year may not use the alternative method of determination in paragraph (f)(3) of this section for purposes of determining its post-1986 earnings and profits on the E&P measurement date on December 31, 2017.

(2) *Effect of election for specified foreign corporations that have a 52-53-week taxable year.*—If an election is made under this paragraph (f) with respect to a specified foreign corporation that has a 52-53-week taxable year, the amount of the post-1986 earnings and profits (including a deficit) as of both E&P measurement dates is determined under paragraph (f)(3) of this section. The election described in this paragraph (f) is irrevocable.

(3) *Computation of post-1986 earnings and profits using alternative method.*—With respect to an E&P measurement date, the post-1986 earnings and profits of a specified foreign corporation for which an election is properly made equals the sum of—

(i) The specified foreign corporation's post-1986 earnings and profits (including a deficit) determined as of the notional measurement

date, as if it were an E&P measurement date, plus

(ii) The specified foreign corporation's annualized earnings and profits amount with respect to the notional measurement date.

(4) *Definitions.*—(i) *52-53-week taxable year.*—The term *52-53-week taxable year* means a taxable year described in § 1.441-2(a)(1).

(ii) *Annualized earnings and profits amount.*—The term *annualized earnings and profits amount* means, with respect to a specified foreign corporation, an E&P measurement date, and a notional measurement date, the amount equal to the product of the number of days between the notional measurement date and the E&P measurement date (not including the former, but including the latter) multiplied by the daily earnings amount of the specified foreign corporation. The annualized earnings and profits amount is expressed as a negative number if the E&P measurement date precedes the notional measurement date.

(iii) *Daily earnings amount.*—The term *daily earnings amount* means, with respect to a specified foreign corporation and a notional measurement date, the post-1986 earnings and profits (including a deficit) of the specified foreign corporation determined as of the close of the notional measurement date that were earned (or incurred) during the specified foreign corporation's taxable year that includes the notional measurement date, divided by the number of days that have elapsed in such taxable year as of the close of the notional measurement date.

(iv) *Notional measurement date.*—The term *notional measurement date* means—

(A) With respect to an E&P measurement date of a specified foreign corporation with a 52-53-week taxable year, the closest end of a fiscal month to such E&P measurement date, and

(B) With respect to the E&P measurement date on November 2, 2017, of all specified foreign corporations not described in paragraph (f)(4)(iv)(A) of this section, October 31, 2017.

(5) *Manner of making election.*—(i) *Eligibility.*—An election with respect to a specified foreign corporation to use the alternative method of calculating post-1986 earnings and profits as of an E&P measurement date pursuant to this paragraph (f) must be made on behalf of the specified foreign corporation by a controlling domestic shareholder (as defined in § 1.964-1(c)(5)) pursuant to the rules of § 1.964-1(c)(3), except that the controlling domestic shareholder is not required to file the statement described in § 1.964-1(c)(3)(ii).

(ii) *Timing.*—An election under this paragraph (f) must be made no later than the due date (taking into account extensions, if any) for the person's return for the first taxable year in which the person has a section 965(a) inclusion amount with respect to the specified foreign corporation or in which the person takes into account a specified E&P deficit with respect to the specified corporation for purposes of computing a section 965(a) inclusion amount with respect to another specified foreign corporation. Relief is not available under § 301.9100-2 or § 301.9100-3 to make a late election.

(iii) *Election statement.*—Except as otherwise provided in publications, forms, instructions, or other guidance, to make an election under this paragraph (f), a person must attach a statement, signed under penalties of perjury consistent with the rules for signatures applicable to the person's return, to the person's return for the taxable year described in paragraph (f)(5)(ii) of this section. The statement must include the person's name, taxpayer identification number, and the name and taxpayer identification number, if any, of each of the specified foreign corporations with respect to which the election is made, and the statement must be filed in the manner prescribed in instructions or other guidance. The attachment of an unsigned copy of the election statement to the timely-filed return for the relevant taxable year satisfies the signature requirement of this paragraph (f)(5)(iii) if the person making the election retains the original signed election statement in the manner specified by § 1.6001-1(e).

(6) *Examples.*—The following examples illustrate the application of this paragraph (f).

(i) *Example 1.* (A) *Facts.* FS, a foreign corporation, has a calendar year taxable year, and as of October 31, 2017, FS has post-1986 earnings and profits of 10,000u, 3,040u of which were earned during the taxable year that includes October 31, 2017. An election is properly made under paragraph (f)(5) of this section with respect to FS, allowing FS to determine its post-1986 earnings and profits under the alternative method with respect to its E&P measurement date on November 2, 2017.

(B) *Analysis.* As of the close of October 31, 2017, the notional measurement date with respect to the E&P measurement date on November 2, 2017, 304 days have elapsed in the taxable year of FS that includes October 31, 2017. Therefore, FS's daily earnings amount is 10u (3,040u divided by 304), and FS's annualized earnings and profits amount is 20u (10u multiplied by 2 (the number of days between the notional measurement date on October 31, 2017, and the E&P measurement date on November 2, 2017)). Accordingly, FS's post-1986 earnings and profits as of November 2, 2017, are 10,020u (its post-1986 earnings and profits as of October 31, 2017 (10,000u), plus its annualized earnings and profits amount (20u)).

(ii) *Example 2.* (A) *Facts.* The facts are the same as in paragraph (f)(6)(i)(A) of this section (the facts in *Example 1*), except that a deficit of 3,040u was incurred during the taxable year that includes October 31, 2017.

(B) *Analysis.* The analysis is the same as in paragraph (f)(6)(i)(B) of this section (the analysis in *Example 1*), except that FS's daily earnings amount is (10u) ((3,040u) divided by 304), and FS's annualized earnings and profits amount is (20u) ((10u) multiplied by 2 (the number of days between the notional measurement date on October 31, 2017, and the E&P measurement date on November 2, 2017)). Accordingly, FS's post-1986 earnings and profits as of November 2, 2017, are 9,980u (its post-1986 earnings and profits as of October 31, 2017 (10,000u), plus its annualized earnings and profits amount ((20u))).

(g) *Definitions.*—This paragraph (g) provides definitions that apply for purposes of this section.

(1) *Deferred net tax liability.*—The term *deferred net tax liability* means, with respect to any taxable year of a person, the amount of the section 965(i) net tax liability the payment of which has been deferred under section 965(i) and paragraph (c) of this section.

(2) *REIT section 965 amounts.*—The term *REIT section 965 amounts* means, with respect to a real estate investment trust and a taxable year of the real estate investment trust, the aggregate amount of section 965(a) inclusions and section 965(c) deductions that would (but for section 965(m)(1)(B) and paragraph (d) of this section) be taken into account in determining the real estate investment trust's income for the taxable year.

(3) *Section 965(h) election.*—The term *section 965(h) election* means the election described in section 965(h)(1) and paragraph (b)(1) of this section.

(4) *Section 965(h) net tax liability.*—The term *section 965(h) net tax liability* means, with respect to a person that has made a section 965(h) election, the total net tax liability under section 965 reduced by the aggregate amount of the person's section 965(i) net tax liabilities, if any, with respect to which section 965(i) elections are effective.

(5) *Section 965(i) election.*—The term *section 965(i) election* means the election described in section 965(i)(1) and paragraph (c)(1) of this section.

(6) *Section 965(i) net tax liability.*—The term *section 965(i) net tax liability* means, with respect to an S corporation and a shareholder of the S corporation, in the case in which a section 965(i) election is made, the amount determined pursuant to paragraph (g)(10)(i) of this section by adding before the word "over" in (g)(10)(i)(A) of this section "determined as if the only section 965(a) inclusions included in income by the person are domestic pass-through entity shares of section 965(a) inclusions by the S corporation with respect to deferred foreign income corpora-

tions of which the S corporation is a United States shareholder."

(7) *Section 965(m) election.*—The term *section 965(m) election* means the election described in section 965(m)(1)(B) and paragraph (d)(1) of this section.

(8) *Section 965(n) election.*—The term *section 965(n) election* means the election described in section 965(n)(1) and paragraph (e)(1)(i) of this section.

(9) *Specified individual.*—The term *specified individual* means, with respect to a taxable year, a person described in §1.6081-5(a)(5) or (6) who receives an extension of time to file and pay under §1.6081-5(a) for the taxable year.

(10) *Total net tax liability under section 965.*—(i) *General rule.*—The term *total net tax liability under section 965* means, with respect to a person, the excess (if any) of—

(A) The person's net income tax for the taxable year in which the person includes a section 965(a) inclusion in income, over—

(B) The person's net income tax for the taxable year determined—

(1) Without regard to section 965, and

(2) Without regard to any income, deduction, or credit properly attributable to a dividend received (directly or through a chain of ownership described in section 958(a)) by the person (or, in the case of a domestic pass-through owner, by the person's domestic pass-through entity) from, or an inclusion under sections 951(a)(1)(B) and 956 with respect to, a deferred foreign income corporation and paid during, or included with respect to, the deferred foreign income corporation's inclusion year.

(ii) *Net income tax.*—For purposes of this paragraph (g)(10), the term *net income tax* means the regular tax liability (as defined in section 26(b)) reduced by the credits allowed under subparts A, B, and D of part IV of subchapter A of chapter 1 of subtitle A of the Internal Revenue Code.

(iii) *Foreign tax credits.*—The foreign tax credit disregarded in determining net income tax determined under paragraph (g)(10)(i)(B) of this section includes the credit for foreign income taxes deemed paid with respect to section 965(a) inclusions or foreign income taxes deemed paid with respect to a dividend, including a distribution that would have been treated as a dividend in the absence of section 965. The foreign tax credit disregarded under paragraph (g)(10)(i)(B) of this section also includes the credit for foreign income taxes imposed on distributions of section 965(a) previously taxed earnings and profits or 965(b) previously taxed earnings and profits made in the taxable year in which the person includes a section 965(a) inclusion in income. [Reg. §1.965-7.]

☐ [*T.D.* 9846, 2-4-2019.]

**[Reg. §1.965-8]**

**§1.965-8. Affiliated groups (including consolidated groups).**—(a) *Scope.*—This section provides rules for applying section 965 and the section 965 regulations to members of an affiliated group (as defined in section 1504(a)), including members of a consolidated group (as defined in §1.1502-1(h)). Paragraph (b) of this section provides guidance regarding the application of section 965(b)(5) to determine the section 965(a) inclusion amounts of a member of an affiliated group. Paragraph (c) of this section provides guidance for designating the source of aggregate unused E&P deficits. Paragraph (d) provides rules regarding earning and profits and stock basis adjustments. Paragraph (e) of this section provides rules that treat members of a consolidated group as a single person for certain purposes. Paragraph (f) of this section provides definitions that apply for purposes of this section. Paragraph (g) of this section provides examples illustrating the application of this section.

(b) *Reduction of E&P net surplus shareholder's pro rata share of the section 965(a) earnings amount of a deferred foreign income corporation by the allocable share of the applicable share of the aggregate unused E&P deficit.*—(1) *In general.*—This paragraph (b) applies after the application of §1.965-1(b)(2) for purposes of determining the section 965(a) inclusion amount with respect to a deferred foreign income corporation of a section 958(a) U.S. shareholder that is both an E&P net surplus shareholder and a member of an affiliated group in which not all members are members of the same consolidated group. If this paragraph (b) applies, the U.S. dollar amount of the section 958(a) U.S. shareholder's pro rata share of the section 965(a) earnings amount of the deferred foreign income corporation is further reduced (but not below zero) by the deferred foreign income corporation's allocable share of the section 958(a) U.S. shareholder's applicable share of the affiliated group's aggregate unused E&P deficit.

(2) *Consolidated group as part of an affiliated group.*—If some, but not all, members of an affiliated group are members of a consolidated group, then the consolidated group is treated as a single member of the affiliated group for purposes of §1.965-1(b)(2) and paragraph (b)(1) of this section.

(c) *Designation of portion of excess aggregate foreign E&P deficit taken into account.*—(1) *In general.*—This paragraph (c) provides rules for designating the source of an aggregate unused E&P deficit of an affiliated group that is not also a consolidated group taken into account under section 965(b)(5) and paragraph (b) of this section if the amount described in paragraph (f)(1)(i)(A) of this section with respect to the affiliated group exceeds the amount described in paragraph (f)(1)(i)(B) of this section with respect to the affiliated group. If this paragraph (c)(1) applies, each member of the affiliated group that is an E&P net deficit shareholder must designate by maintaining in its books and records a statement (identical to the statement maintained by all other such members) setting forth the portion of the excess aggregate foreign E&P deficit of the E&P net deficit shareholder taken into account under section 965(b)(5) and paragraph (b) of this section. See § 1.965-2(d)(2)(ii)(B) for a rule for designating the portion of a section 958(a) U.S. shareholder's pro rata share of a specified E&P deficit of an E&P deficit foreign corporation taken into account under section 965(b), § 1.965-1(b)(2), and paragraph (b) of this section, as applicable.

(2) *Consolidated group as part of an affiliated group.*—If some, but not all, members of an affiliated group are properly treated as members of a consolidated group, then the consolidated group is treated as a single member of the affiliated group for purposes of applying paragraph (c)(1) of this section.

(d) *Adjustments to earning and profits and stock basis.*—(1) [Reserved]

(2) *Consolidated groups.*—See § 1.1502-33(d)(1) for adjustments to members' earnings and profits and § 1.1502-32(b)(3) for adjustments to members' basis.

(e) *Treatment of a consolidated group as a single section 958(a) U.S. shareholder or a single person.*— (1) *In general.*—All members of a consolidated group that are section 958(a) U.S. shareholders of a specified foreign corporation are treated as a single section 958(a) U.S. shareholder for purposes of section 965(b), § 1.965-1(b)(2), and § 1.965-3. Furthermore, all members of a consolidated group are treated as a single person for purposes of paragraphs (h), (k), and (n) of section 965 and § 1.965-7. Thus, for example, any election governed by section 965(h) and § 1.965-7(b) must be made by the agent (within the meaning of § 1.1502-77) of the group as a single election on behalf of all members of the consolidated group. Similarly, the determination of whether the transfer of assets by one member to a non-member of the consolidated group would constitute an acceleration event under section § 1.965-7(b)(3)(ii)(B) takes into account all of the assets of the consolidated group, which for purposes of this determination, includes all of the assets of each consolidated group member. In analyzing issues relating to the transfer of assets of a consolidated group, appropriate adjustments are made to prevent the duplication of assets or asset value.

(2) *Limitation.*—Paragraph (e)(1) of this section does not apply to treat all members of a consolidated group as a single section 958(a) U.S. shareholder or a single person, as applicable, for purposes of determining the amount of any member's inclusion under section 951 (including a section 965(a) inclusion), the foreign income taxes deemed paid with respect to a section 965(a) inclusion (see sections 960 and 902), or any purpose other than those specifically listed in paragraph (e)(1) of this section or another provision of the section 965 regulations.

(3) *Determination of section 965(c) deduction amount.*—For purposes of determining the section 965(c) deduction amount of any section 958(a) U.S. shareholder that is a member of a consolidated group, the aggregate foreign cash position of the section 958(a) U.S. shareholder is equal to the aggregate section 965(a) inclusion amount of the section 958(a) U.S. shareholder multiplied by the group cash ratio of the consolidated group.

(f) *Definitions.*—This paragraph (f) provides definitions that apply for purposes of applying the section 965 regulations to members of an affiliated group, including members of a consolidated group.

(1) *Aggregate unused E&P deficit.*— (i) *General rule.*—The term *aggregate unused E&P deficit* means, with respect to an affiliated group, the lesser of—

(A) The sum of the excess aggregate foreign E&P deficit with respect to each E&P net deficit shareholder that is a member of the affiliated group, or

(B) The amount determined under paragraph (f)(3)(ii) of this section.

(ii) *Reduction with respect to E&P net deficit shareholders that are not wholly owned by the affiliated group.*—If the group ownership percentage of an E&P net deficit shareholder is less than 100 percent, the amount of the excess aggregate foreign E&P deficit with respect to the E&P net deficit shareholder that is taken into account under paragraph (f)(1)(i) of this section is the product of the group ownership percentage multiplied by the excess aggregate foreign E&P deficit.

(2) *Allocable share.*—The term *allocable share* means, with respect to a deferred foreign income corporation and an E&P net surplus shareholder's applicable share of an aggregate unused E&P deficit of an affiliated group, the product of the E&P net surplus shareholder's applicable share of the affiliated group's aggregate unused E&P deficit and the ratio described in § 1.965-1(f)(11) with respect to the deferred foreign income corporation.

(3) *Applicable share.*—The term *applicable share* means, with respect to an E&P net surplus shareholder and an aggregate unused E&P deficit of an affiliated group, the amount that bears the same proportion to the affiliated group's aggregate unused E&P deficit as—

(i) The product of—

(A) The E&P net surplus shareholder's group ownership percentage, multiplied by

(B) The amount that would (but for section 965(b)(5) and paragraph (b) of this section) constitute the E&P net surplus shareholder's aggregate section 965(a) inclusion amount, bears to

(ii) The aggregate amount determined under paragraph (f)(3)(i) of this section with respect to all E&P net surplus shareholders that are members of the group.

(4) *Consolidated group aggregate foreign cash position.*—The term *consolidated group aggregate foreign cash position* means, with respect to a consolidated group, the aggregate foreign cash position (as defined in §1.965-1(f)(8)(i)) determined by treating each member of the consolidated group that is a section 958(a) U.S. shareholder as a single section 958(a) U.S. shareholder pursuant to paragraph (e)(1) of this section.

(5) *E&P net deficit shareholder.*—The term *E&P net deficit shareholder* means a section 958(a) U.S. shareholder that has an excess aggregate foreign E&P deficit.

(6) *E&P net surplus shareholder.*—The term *E&P net surplus shareholder* means a section 958(a) U.S. shareholder that would (but for section 965(b)(5) and paragraph (b) of this section) have an aggregate section 965(a) inclusion amount greater than zero.

(7) *Excess aggregate foreign E&P deficit.*—The term *excess aggregate foreign E&P deficit* means, with respect to a section 958(a) U.S. shareholder, the amount, if any, by which the amount described in §1.965-1(f)(9)(i) with respect to the section 958(a) U.S. shareholder exceeds the amount described in §1.965-1(f)(9)(ii) with respect to the section 958(a) U.S. shareholder.

(8) *Group cash ratio.*—The term *group cash ratio* means, with respect to a consolidated group, the ratio of—

(i) The consolidated group aggregate foreign cash position, to

(ii) The sum of the aggregate section 965(a) inclusion amounts of all members of the consolidated group.

(9) *Group ownership percentage.*—The term *group ownership percentage* means, with respect to a section 958(a) U.S. shareholder that is a member of an affiliated group, the percentage of the value of the stock of the United States shareholder which is held by other includible corporations in the affiliated group. Notwithstanding the preceding sentence, the group ownership percentage of the common parent of the affiliated group is 100 percent. Any term used in this paragraph (f)(9) that is also used in section 1504 has the same meaning as when used in such section. Additionally, if the term is used in the context of a rule for which all members of a

consolidated group are treated as a single section 958(a) U.S. shareholder under paragraph (e)(1) of this section, then the group ownership percentage is determined solely with respect to the value of the stock of the common parent of the consolidated group held by other includible corporations that are not members of the consolidated group.

(g) *Examples.*—The following examples illustrate the application of this section.

(1) *Example 1. Application of affiliated group rule.* (i) *Facts.* (A) *In general.* USP owns all of the stock of USS1, USS2, and USS3. Each of USP, USS1, USS2, and USS3 is a domestic corporation and is a member of an affiliated group of which USP is the common parent (the "USP Group"). The USP Group has not elected to file a consolidated federal income tax return. USS1 owns all of the stock of CFC1 and CFC2, USS2 owns all of the stock of CFC3, and USS3 owns all of the stock of CFC4. Each of CFC1, CFC2, CFC3, and CFC4 is a controlled foreign corporation within the meaning of section 957(a), and, therefore, each is a specified foreign corporation under section 965(e) and §1.965-1(f)(45). Each of USP, USS1, USS2, USS3, CFC1, CFC2, CFC3, and CFC4 has the calendar year as its taxable year.

(B) *Facts relating to section 965.* CFC1 and CFC3 are deferred foreign income corporations with section 965(a) earnings amounts of $600x and $300x, respectively. CFC1 and CFC3 have cash positions of $0x and $50x, respectively, on each of their cash measurement dates. CFC2 and CFC4 are E&P deficit foreign corporations with specified E&P deficits of $400x and $100x, respectively. CFC2 and CFC4 have cash positions of $100x and $50x, respectively, on each of their cash measurement dates. The cash positions all consist solely of cash. CFC1, CFC2, CFC3, and CFC4 all use the U.S. dollar as their functional currency.

(ii) *Analysis.* (A) *Section 965(a) inclusion amounts before application of section 965(b)(5).* USS1 is a section 958(a) U.S. shareholder with respect to CFC1 and CFC2; USS2 is a section 958(a) U.S. shareholder with respect to CFC3; and USS3 is a section 958(a) U.S. shareholder with respect to CFC4. USS1's pro rata share of CFC1's section 965(a) earnings amount is $600x. Under section 965(b)(3)(A) and §1.965-1(f)(9), USS1's aggregate foreign E&P deficit is $400x, the lesser of the aggregate of USS1's pro rata share of the specified E&P deficit of each E&P deficit foreign corporation ($400x) and the amount described in §1.965-1(f)(9)(ii) with respect to USS1 ($600x). Under section 965(b) and §1.965-1(b)(2), in determining its section 965(a) inclusion amount with respect to CFC1, USS1 reduces its pro rata share of the U.S. dollar amount of section 965(a) earnings amount of CFC1 by CFC1's allocable share of USS1's aggregate foreign E&P deficit. CFC1's allocable share of USS1's aggregate foreign E&P deficit is $400x, which is the product of USS1's aggregate foreign E&P deficit ($400x) and 1, which is the ratio determined by dividing USS1's pro rata share of the section 965(a) earnings amount of CFC1 ($600x), by the amount described in §1.965-1(f)(9)(ii) with respect to USS1 ($600x). Accordingly, under section 965(b) and §1.965-1(b)(2) (before applying section 965(b)(5) and paragraph (b) of this section), USS1's section 965(a) inclusion amount with respect to CFC1 would be $200x (USS1's pro rata share of the section 965(a) earnings amount of CFC1 of $600x reduced by CFC1's allocable share of USS1's aggregate foreign E&P deficit of $400x). Under section 965(b) and §1.965-1(b)(2) (before applying section 965(b)(5) and paragraph (b) of this section), USS2's section 965(a) inclusion amount with respect to CFC3 would be $300x (USS2's pro rata share of the section 965(a) earnings amount of CFC3).

(B) *Application of section 965(b)(5)—(1) Determination of E&P net surplus shareholders and E&P net deficit shareholders.* USS1 is an E&P net surplus shareholder because it would have an aggregate section 965(a) inclusion amount of $200x but for the application of section 965(b)(5) and paragraph (b) of this section. USS2 is also an E&P net surplus shareholder because it would have an aggregate section 965(a) inclusion amount of $300x but for the application of section 965(b)(5) and paragraph (b) of this section. USS3 is an E&P net deficit shareholder because it has an excess aggregate foreign E&P deficit of $100x.

(2) *Determining section 965(a) inclusion amounts under section 965(b)(5).* Under section 965(b) and paragraph (b) of this section, for purposes of determining the section 965(a) inclusion amount of a section 958(a) U.S. shareholder with respect to a deferred foreign income corporation, if, after applying §1.965-1(b)(2), the section 958(a) U.S. shareholder is an E&P net surplus shareholder, then the U.S. dollar amount of the section 958(a) U.S. shareholder's pro rata share of the section 965(a) earnings amount of the deferred foreign income corporation is further reduced (but not below zero) by the deferred foreign income corporation's allocable share of the section 958(a) U.S. shareholder's applicable share of the affiliated group's aggregate unused E&P deficit. USS3 is the only E&P net deficit shareholder in the USP Group, and, therefore, the aggregate unused E&P deficit of the USP Group is equal to USS3's excess aggregate foreign E&P deficit ($100x). The applicable share of the USP Group's aggregate unused E&P deficit of each of USS1 and USS2, respectively, is an amount that bears the same proportion to the USP Group's aggregate unused E&P deficit as the product of the group ownership percentage of USS1 and USS2, respectively, multiplied by the amount that would (but for section 965(b)(5) and paragraph (b) of this section) constitute the aggregate section 965(a) inclusion amount of USS1 and USS2, respectively, bears to the aggregate of such amounts with respect to both USS1 and USS2. Therefore, USS1's applicable share of the USP Group's aggregate unused E&P deficit is $40

($100x x ($200x/($200x + $300x))) and USS2's applicable share of the USP Group's aggregate unused E&P deficit is $60x ($100x x ($300x/ ($200x + $300x))). Because USS1 is a section 958(a) U.S. shareholder with respect to only one deferred foreign income corporation, the entire $60x of USS1's applicable share of the USP Group's aggregate unused E&P deficit is treated as CFC1's allocable share of USS1's applicable share of the USP Group's aggregate unused E&P deficit, and thus USS1's section 965(a) inclusion amount with respect to CFC1 is reduced to $160x ($200x - $40x). Because USS2 is a section 958(a) U.S. shareholder with respect to only one deferred foreign income corporation, the entire $60x of USS2's applicable share of the USP Group's aggregate unused E&P deficit is treated as CFC3's allocable share of USS2's applicable share of the USP Group's aggregate unused E&P deficit, and thus USS2's section 965(a) inclusion amount with respect to CFC3 is reduced to $240x ($300x - $60x).

(C) *Aggregate foreign cash position.* Under section 965(c) and §1.965-1(c), a section 958(a) U.S. shareholder that includes a section 965(a) inclusion amount in income is allowed a deduction equal to the section 965(c) deduction amount. The section 965(c) deduction amount is computed by taking into account the aggregate foreign cash position of the section 958(a) U.S. shareholder. Under §1.965-1(f)(8)(i), the aggregate foreign cash position of USS1 is $100x, and the aggregate foreign cash position of USS2 is $50x.

(D) *Section 965(c) deduction amount.* The section 965(c) deduction amount of USS1 is $102x, which is equal to (i) USS1's 8 percent rate equivalent percentage (77.1428571%) of its 8 percent rate amount for USS1's 2017 year ($60x ($160x - $100x)), plus USS1's 15.5 percent rate equivalent percentage (55.7142857%) of its 15.5 percent rate amount for USS1's 2017 year ($100x). The section 965(c) deduction amount of USS2 is $174.43x, which is equal to (i) USS2's 8 percent rate equivalent percentage (77.1428571%) of its 8 percent rate amount for USS2's 2017 year ($190x ($240x - $50x)), plus USS2's 15.5 percent rate equivalent percentage (55.7142857%) of its 15.5 percent rate amount for USS2's 2017 year ($50x). Because USS3 has no section 965(a) inclusion amount, it has no section 965(c) deduction amount and therefore is not allowed a section 965(c) deduction.

(2) *Example 2. Application to members of a consolidated group.* (i) *Facts.* The facts are the same as in paragraph (g)(1)(i) of this section (the facts in *Example 1*), except that the USP Group has elected to file a consolidated return.

(ii) *Analysis—(A) Section 965(a) inclusion amount—(1) Single section 958(a) U.S. shareholder treatment.* Because each of USS1, USS2, and USS3 is a section 958(a) U.S. shareholder of a specified foreign corporation and is a member of a consolidated group, paragraph (e)(1) of this section applies to treat USS1, USS2, and USS3 as a single section 958(a) U.S. shareholder for purposes of section 965(b) and § 1.965-1(b)(2).

*(2) Determination of inclusion amount.* The single section 958(a) U.S. shareholder composed of USS1, USS2, and USS3 is a section 958(a) U.S. shareholder with respect to CFC1, CFC2, CFC3, and CFC4. Under § 1.965-1(b)(2), in determining USS1's section 965(a) inclusion amount, the single section 958(a) U.S. shareholder decreases its pro rata share of the U.S. dollar amount of the section 965(a) earnings amount of CFC1 by CFC1's allocable share of the aggregate foreign E&P deficit of the single section 958(a) U.S. shareholder. CFC1's allocable share of the aggregate foreign E&P deficit is $333.33x, which is the product of the aggregate foreign E&P deficit of the single section 958(a) U.S. shareholder ($500x ($400x + $100x)) and .67, which is the ratio determined by dividing its pro rata share of the section 965(a) earnings amount of CFC1 ($600x) by the amount described in § 1.965-1(f)(9)(ii) with respect to the single section 958(a) U.S. shareholder ($900x ($600x + $300x)). Therefore, USS1's section 965(a) inclusion amount with respect to CFC1 is $266.67 (its pro rata share of the section 965(a) earnings amount of CFC1 ($600) less CFC1's allocable share of the aggregate foreign E&P deficit of the single section 958(a) U.S. shareholder ($333.33x)). Similarly, under § 1.965-1(b)(2), in determining the section 965(a) inclusion amount of USS2, the single section 958(a) U.S. shareholder decreases its pro rata share of the U.S. dollar amount of the section 965(a) earnings amount of CFC3 by CFC3's allocable share of the aggregate foreign E&P deficit of the single section 958(a) U.S. shareholder. CFC3's allocable share of the aggregate foreign E&P deficit is $166.67x, which is the product of the aggregate foreign E&P deficit of the single section 958(a) U.S. shareholder ($500x) and .33, which is the ratio determined by dividing its pro rata share of the section 965(a) earnings amount of CFC3 ($300x) by the amount described in § 1.965-1(f)(9)(ii) with respect to the single section 958(a) U.S. shareholder ($900x ($600x + $300x)). Therefore, USS2's section 965(a) inclusion amount with respect to CFC3 is $133.33x (its pro rata share of the section 965(a) earnings amount of CFC3 ($300x) less CFC3's allocable share of the aggregate foreign E&P deficit of the single section 958(a) U.S. shareholder ($166.67x)).

*(B) Consolidated group aggregate foreign cash position.* Because USS1 and USS2 are members of a consolidated group, the aggregate foreign cash position of each of USS1 and USS2 is determined under paragraph (e)(3) of this section. Under paragraph (e)(3) of this section, the aggregate foreign cash position of each of USS1 and USS2 is equal to the aggregate section 965(a) inclusion amount of USS1 and USS2, respectively, multiplied by the group cash ratio of the USP Group, as determined pursuant to paragraph (f)(8) of this section. The group cash ratio of the USP Group is .50, which is the ratio of the USP

Group's consolidated group aggregate foreign cash position ($200x ($50x + $100x + $50x)) and the sum of the aggregate section 965(a) inclusion amounts of all members of the USP Group ($400x ($266.67x + $133.33x)). Therefore, under paragraph (e)(3) of this section, the aggregate foreign cash positions of USS1 and USS2 are, respectively, $133.34x ($266.67x x ($200x/$400x)) and $66.67 ($133.33x x ($200x/400x)).

*(C) Section 965(c) deduction amount.* The section 965(c) deduction amount of USS1 is $177.14x, which is equal to (i) USS1's 8 percent rate equivalent percentage (77.1428571%) of its 8 percent rate amount for USS1's 2017 year ($133.33x ($266.67x - $133.34x)), plus USS1's 15.5 percent rate equivalent percentage (55.7142857%) of its 15.5 percent rate amount for USS1's 2017 year ($133.34x). The section 965(c) deduction amount of USS2 is $88.56x, which is equal to (i) USS2's 8 percent rate equivalent percentage (77.1428571%) of its 8 percent rate amount for USS2's 2017 year ($66.66x ($133.33x - $66.67x)), plus USS2's 15.5 percent rate equivalent percentage (55.7142857%) of its 15.5 percent rate amount for USS2's 2017 year ($66.67x). Because USS3 has no section 965(a) inclusion amount, it has no section 965(c) deduction amount and therefore is not allowed a section 965(c) deduction. [Reg. § 1.965-8.]

☐ [*T.D.* 9846, 2-4-2019.]

**[Reg. § 1.965-9]**

**§ 1.965-9. Applicability dates.**—(a) *In general.*—Sections 1.965-1 through 1.965-8 apply beginning the last taxable year of a foreign corporation that begins before January 1, 2018, and with respect to a United States person, beginning the taxable year in which or with which such taxable year of the foreign corporation ends.

(b) *Applicability dates for rules disregarding certain transactions.*—Section 1.965-4 applies regardless of whether, with respect to a foreign corporation, the transaction, effective date of a change in method of accounting, effective date of an entity classification election, or specified payment described in § 1.965-4 occurred before the first day of the foreign corporation's last taxable year that begins before January 1, 2018, or, with respect to a United States person, the transaction, effective date of a change in method of accounting, effective date of an entity classification election, or specified payment described in § 1.965-4 occurred before the first day of the taxable year of the United States person in which or with which the taxable year of the foreign corporation ends. [Reg. § 1.965-9.]

☐ [*T.D.* 9846, 2-4-2019.]

**[Reg. § 1.986(c)-1]**

**§ 1.986(c)-1. Coordination with section 965.**— (a) *Amount of foreign currency gain or loss.*—Foreign currency gain or loss with respect to distributions of section 965(a) previously taxed earnings and profits (as defined in § 1.965-1(f)(39)) is determined based on movements in the exchange rate between December 31, 2017, and the time such distributions are made.

(b) *Section 965(a) previously taxed earnings and profits.*—Any gain or loss recognized under section 986(c) with respect to distributions of section 965(a) previously taxed earnings and profits is reduced in the same proportion as the reduction by a section 965(c) deduction amount (as defined in § 1.965-1(f)(42)) of the section 965(a) inclusion amount (as defined in § 1.965-1(f)(38)) that gave rise to such section 965(a) previously taxed earnings and profits.

(c) *Section 965(b) previously taxed earnings and profits.*—Section 986(c) does not apply with respect to distributions of section 965(b) previously taxed earnings and profits (as defined in § 1.965-1(f)(40)).

(d) *Applicability dates.*—The section applies beginning the last taxable year of a foreign corporation that begins before January 1, 2018, and with respect to a United States person, for the taxable year in which or with which such taxable year of the foreign corporation ends. [Reg. § 1.986(c)-1.]

☐ [*T.D. 9846, 2-4-2019.*]

### [Reg. § 1.6695-2]

**§ 1.6695-2. Tax return preparer due diligence requirements for certain credits.**—(a) *Penalty for failure to meet due diligence requirements.*—(1) *In general.*—A person who is a tax return preparer (as defined in section 7701(a)(36)) of a tax return or claim for refund under the Internal Revenue Code who determines the taxpayer's eligibility to file as head of household under section 2(b), or who determines the taxpayer's eligibility for, or the amount of, the child tax credit (CTC)/additional child tax credit (ACTC) under section 24, the American opportunity tax credit (AOTC) under section 25A(i), or the earned income credit (EIC) under section 32, and who fails to satisfy the due diligence requirements of paragraph (b) of this section will be subject to a penalty as prescribed in section 6695(g) (indexed for inflation under section 6695(h)) for each failure. A separate penalty applies to a tax return preparer with respect to the head of household filing status determination and to each applicable credit claimed on a return or claim for refund for which the due diligence requirements of this section are not satisfied and for which the exception to penalty provided by paragraph (d) of this section does not apply.

(2) *Examples.*—The provisions of paragraph (a)(1) of this section are illustrated by the following examples:

(i) *Example 1.* Preparer A prepares a federal income tax return for a taxpayer claiming the CTC and the AOTC. Preparer A did not meet the due diligence requirements under this section with respect to the CTC or the AOTC claimed on the taxpayer's return. Unless the exception to penalty provided by paragraph (d) of this section applies, Preparer A is subject to two penalties under section 6695(g): one for failure to meet the due diligence requirements for the CTC and a second penalty for failure to meet the due diligence requirements for the AOTC.

(ii) *Example 2.* Preparer B prepares a federal income tax return for a taxpayer claiming the CTC and the AOTC. Preparer B did not meet the due diligence requirements under this section with respect to the CTC claimed on the taxpayer's return, but Preparer B did meet the due diligence requirements under this section with respect to the AOTC claimed on the taxpayer's return. Unless the exception to penalty provided by paragraph (d) of this section applies, Preparer B is subject to one penalty under section 6695(g) for the failure to meet the due diligence requirements for the CTC. Preparer B is not subject to a penalty under section 6695(g) for failure to meet the due diligence requirements for the AOTC.

(iii) *Example 3.* Preparer C prepares a federal income tax return for a taxpayer using the head of household filing status and claiming the CTC and the AOTC. Preparer C did not meet the due diligence requirements under this section with respect to the head of household filing status and the CTC claimed on the taxpayer's return. Preparer C did meet the due diligence requirements under this section with respect to the AOTC claimed on the taxpayer's return. Unless the exception to penalty provided by paragraph (d) of this section applies, Preparer C is subject to two penalties under section 6695(g) for the failure to meet the due diligence requirements: one for the head of household filing status and one for the CTC. Preparer C is not subject to a penalty under section 6695(g) for failure to meet the due diligence requirements for the AOTC.

(b) *Due diligence requirements.*—A preparer must satisfy the following due diligence requirements:

(1) *Completion and submission of Form 8867.*—(i) The tax return preparer must complete Form 8867, "Paid Preparer's Due Diligence Checklist," or complete such other form and provide such other information as may be prescribed by the Internal Revenue Service (IRS), and—

(A) In the case of a signing tax return preparer electronically filing the tax return or claim for refund, must electronically file the completed Form 8867 (or successor form) with the tax return or claim for refund;

(B) In the case of a signing tax return preparer not electronically filing the tax return or claim for refund, must provide the taxpayer with the completed Form 8867 (or successor form) for inclusion with the filed tax return or claim for refund; or

(C) In the case of a nonsigning tax return preparer, must provide the signing tax return preparer with the completed Form 8867 (or successor form), in either electronic or non-electronic format, for inclusion with the filed tax return or claim for refund.

(ii) The tax return preparer's completion of Form 8867 must be based on information provided by the taxpayer to the tax return preparer or otherwise reasonably obtained or known by the tax return preparer.

(2) *Computation of credit or credits.*—(i) When computing the amount of a credit or credits described in paragraph (a) of this section to be claimed on a return or claim for refund, the tax return preparer must either—

(A) Complete the worksheet in the Form 1040, 1040A, 1040EZ, and/or Form 8863 instructions or such other form including such other information as may be prescribed by the IRS applicable to each credit described in paragraph (a) of this section claimed on the return or claim for refund; or

(B) Otherwise record in one or more documents in the tax return preparer's paper or electronic files the tax return preparer's computation of the credit or credits claimed on the return or claim for refund, including the method and information used to make the computations.

(ii) The tax return preparer's completion of an applicable worksheet described in paragraph (b)(2)(i)(A) of this section (or other record of the tax return preparer's computation of the credit or credits permitted under paragraph (b)(2)(i)(B) of this section) must be based on information provided by the taxpayer to the tax return preparer or otherwise reasonably obtained or known by the tax return preparer.

(3) *Knowledge.*—(i) *In general.*—The tax return preparer must not know, or have reason to know, that any information used by the tax return preparer in determining the taxpayer's eligibility to file as head of household or in determining the taxpayer's eligibility for, or the amount of, any credit described in paragraph (a) of this section and claimed on the return or claim for refund is incorrect. The tax return preparer may not ignore the implications of information furnished to, or known by, the tax return preparer, and must make reasonable inquiries if a reasonable and well-informed tax return preparer knowledgeable in the law would conclude that the information furnished to the tax return preparer appears to be incorrect, inconsistent, or incomplete. The tax return preparer must also contemporaneously document in the preparer's paper or electronic files any inquiries made and the responses to those inquiries.

(ii) *Examples.*—The provisions of paragraph (b)(3)(i) of this section are illustrated by the following examples:

(A) *Example 1.* In 2018, Q, a 22-year-old taxpayer, engages Preparer C to prepare Q's 2017 federal income tax return. Q completes Preparer C's standard intake questionnaire and states that Q has never been married and has two sons, ages 10 and 11. Based on the intake sheet and other information that Q provides, including information that shows that the boys lived with Q throughout 2017, Preparer C believes that Q may be eligible to claim each boy as a qualifying child for purposes of the EIC and the CTC. However, Q provides no information to Preparer C, and Preparer C does not have any information from other sources, to verify the relationship between Q and the boys. To meet the knowledge requirement in paragraph (b)(3) of this section, Preparer C must make reasonable inquiries to determine whether each boy is a qualifying child of Q for purposes of the EIC and the CTC, including reasonable inquiries to verify Q's relationship to the boys, and Preparer C must contemporaneously document these inquiries and the responses.

(B) *Example 2.* Assume the same facts as in *Example 1* of paragraph (b)(3)(ii)(A) of this section. In addition, as part of preparing Q's 2017 federal income tax return, Preparer C made sufficient reasonable inquiries to verify that the boys were Q's legally adopted children. In 2019, Q engages Preparer C to prepare Q's 2018 federal income tax return. When preparing Q's 2018 federal income tax return, Preparer C is not required to make additional inquiries to determine each boy's relationship to Q for purposes of the knowledge requirement in paragraph (b)(3) of this section.

(C) *Example 3.* In 2018, R, an 18-year-old taxpayer, engages Preparer D to prepare R's 2017 federal income tax return. R completes Preparer D's standard intake questionnaire and states that R has never been married, has one child, an infant, and that R and R's infant lived with R's parents during part of the 2017 tax year. R also provides Preparer D with a Form W-2 showing that R earned $10,000 during 2017. R provides no other documents or information showing that R earned any other income during the tax year. Based on the intake sheet and other information that R provides, Preparer D believes that R may be eligible to claim the infant as a qualifying child for the EIC and the CTC. To meet the knowledge requirement in paragraph (b)(3) of this section, Preparer D must make reasonable inquiries to determine whether R is eligible to claim these credits, including reasonable inquiries to verify that R is not a qualifying child of R's parents (which would make R ineligible to claim the EIC) or a dependent of R's parents (which would make R ineligible to claim the CTC), and Preparer D must contemporaneously document these inquiries and the responses.

(D) *Example 4.* Assume the same facts as the facts in *Example 3* of paragraph (b)(3)(ii)(C) of this section. In addition, Preparer D previously prepared the 2017 joint federal income tax return for R's parents. Based on information provided by R's parents, Preparer D has determined that R is not eligible to be claimed as a dependent or as a qualifying child for purposes of the EIC or the CTC on R's parents' return. Therefore, for purposes of the knowledge requirement in paragraph (b)(3) of this section, Preparer D is not required to make additional inquiries to determine that R is not R's parents' qualifying child or dependent.

(E) *Example 5.* In 2019, S engages Preparer E to prepare S's 2018 federal income tax return. During Preparer E's standard intake interview, S states that S has never been married and that S's niece and nephew lived with S for part of the 2018 tax year. Preparer E believes S may be eligible to file as head of household and claim each of these children as a qualifying child for purposes of the EIC and the CTC, but the information furnished to Preparer E is incomplete. To meet the knowledge requirement in paragraph (b)(3) of this section, Preparer E must make reasonable inquiries to determine whether S is eligible to file as head of household and whether each child is a qualifying child for purposes of the EIC and the CTC, including reasonable inquiries about the children's residency, S's relationship to the children, the children's income, the sources of support for the children, and S's contribution to the payment of costs related to operating the household, and Preparer E must contemporaneously document these inquiries and the responses.

(F) *Example 6.* Assume the same facts as the facts in *Example 5* of paragraph (b)(3)(ii)(E) of this section. In addition, Preparer E knows from prior social interactions with S that the children resided with S for more than one-half of the 2018 tax year and that the children did not provide over one-half of their own support for the 2018 tax year. To meet the knowledge requirement in paragraph (b)(3) of this section, Preparer E must make the same reasonable inquiries to determine whether S is eligible to file as head of household and whether each child is a qualifying child for purposes of the EIC and the CTC as discussed in *Example 5* of this section, and Preparer E must contemporaneously document these inquiries and the responses.

(G) *Example 7.* W engages Preparer F to prepare W's federal income tax return. During Preparer F's standard intake interview, W states that W is 50 years old, has never been married, and has no children. W further states to Preparer F that during the tax year W was self-employed, earned $10,000 from W's business, and had no business expenses or other income. Preparer F believes W may be eligible for the EIC. To meet the knowledge requirement in paragraph (b)(3) of this section, Preparer F must make reasonable inquiries to determine whether W is eligible for the EIC, including reasonable inquiries to determine whether W's business income and expenses are correct, and Preparer F must contemporaneously document these inquiries and the responses.

(H) *Example 8.* Y, who is 32 years old, engages Preparer G to prepare Y's federal income tax return. Y completes Preparer G's standard intake questionnaire and states that Y has never been married. As part of Preparer G's client intake process, Y provides Preparer G with a copy of the Form 1098-T Y received showing that University M billed $4,000 of qualified tuition and related expenses for Y's enrollment or attendance at the university and that Y was at least a half-time undergraduate student. Preparer G believes that Y may be eligible for the AOTC. To meet the knowledge requirement in paragraph (b)(3) of this section, Preparer G must make reasonable inquiries to determine whether Y is eligible for the AOTC, as Form 1098-T does not contain all the information needed to determine eligibility for the AOTC or to calculate the amount of the credit if Y is eligible, and contemporaneously document these inquiries and the responses.

(4) *Retention of records.*—(i) The tax return preparer must retain—

(A) A copy of the completed Form 8867 (or successor form);

(B) A copy of each completed worksheet required under paragraph (b)(2)(i)(A) of this section (or other record of the tax return preparer's computation permitted under paragraph (b)(2)(i)(B) of this section); and

(C) A record of how and when the information used to complete Form 8867 and the applicable worksheets required under paragraph (b)(2)(i)(A) of this section (or other record of the tax return preparer's computation permitted under paragraph (b)(2)(i)(B) of this section) was obtained by the tax return preparer, including the identity of any person furnishing the information, as well as a copy of any document that was provided by the taxpayer and on which the tax return preparer relied to complete Form 8867 and/or an applicable worksheet required under paragraph (b)(2)(i)(A) of this section (or other record of the tax return preparer's computation permitted under paragraph (b)(2)(i)(B) of this section).

(ii) The items in paragraph (b)(4)(i) of this section must be retained for three years from the latest of the following dates, as applicable:

(A) The due date of the tax return (determined without regard to any extension of time for filing);

(B) In the case of a signing tax return preparer electronically filing the tax return or claim for refund, the date the tax return or claim for refund was filed;

(C) In the case of a signing tax return preparer not electronically filing the tax return or claim for refund, the date the tax return or claim for refund was presented to the taxpayer for signature; or

**Reg. §1.6695-2(b)(4)(ii)(C)**

(D) In the case of a nonsigning tax return preparer, the date the nonsigning tax return preparer submitted to the signing tax return preparer that portion of the tax return or claim for refund for which the nonsigning tax return preparer was responsible.

(iii) The items in paragraph (b)(4)(i) of this section may be retained on paper or electronically in the manner prescribed in applicable regulations, revenue rulings, revenue procedures, or other appropriate guidance (see § 601.601(d)(2) of this chapter).

(c) *Special rule for firms.*—A firm that employs a tax return preparer subject to a penalty under section 6695(g) is also subject to penalty if, and only if—

(1) One or more members of the principal management (or principal officers) of the firm or a branch office participated in or, prior to the time the return was filed, knew of the failure to comply with the due diligence requirements of this section;

(2) The firm failed to establish reasonable and appropriate procedures to ensure compliance with the due diligence requirements of this section; or

(3) The firm disregarded its reasonable and appropriate compliance procedures through willfulness, recklessness, or gross indifference (including ignoring facts that would lead a person of reasonable prudence and competence to investigate) in the preparation of the tax return or claim for refund with respect to which the penalty is imposed.

(d) *Exception to penalty.*—The section 6695(g) penalty will not be applied with respect to a particular tax return or claim for refund if the tax return preparer can demonstrate to the satisfaction of the IRS that, considering all the facts and circumstances, the tax return preparer's normal office procedures are reasonably designed and routinely followed to ensure compliance with the due diligence requirements of paragraph (b) of this section, and the failure to meet the due diligence requirements of paragraph (b) of this section with respect to the particular tax return or claim for refund was isolated and inadvertent. The preceding sentence does not apply to a firm that is subject to the penalty as a result of paragraph (c) of this section.

(e) *Applicability date.*—The rules of this section apply to tax returns and claims for refund for tax years beginning after December 31, 2015, that are prepared on or after December 5, 2016. However, the rules relating to the determination of a taxpayer's eligibility to file as head of household under section 2(b) apply to tax returns and claims for refund for tax years beginning after December 31, 2017, that are prepared on or after November 7, 2018.

☐ [*T.D.* 8905, 10-16-2000. *Amended by T.D.* 9436, 12-15-2008, *T.D.* 9570, 12-19-2011, *T.D.* 9799, 12-2-2016 *and T.D.* 9842, 11-5-2018 (*corrected* 12-14-2018).]

# IRS Proposed Regulations

## ¶9001 Introduction

Reproduced below are all proposed regulations issued by the Treasury and IRS in the wake of the Tax Cuts and Jobs Act (P.L. 115-97) becoming law. The majority of guidance that has been issued in the wake of the landmark tax reform act has been in the form of proposed regulations. As of the date of publication, only the proposed regulations on the qualified business income deduction under Code Sec. 199A and the transition tax under Code Sec. 965 have been finalized by the IRS, so the proposed regulations are in many cases the only guidance available on a number of critical areas. This includes bonus depreciation under Code Sec. 168, the BEAT tax under Code Sec. 59A, and the limitation on the deduction of business interest under Code Sec. 163(j). Use CCH® AnswerConnect and CCH Axcess™ iQ to keep up-to-date with all of the recently issued guidance.

**[Prop. Reg. §1.59A-1]**

**§1.59A-1. Base erosion and anti-abuse tax.**—(a) *Purpose.*—This section and §§1.59A-2 through 1.59A-10 (collectively, the "section 59A regulations") provide rules under section 59A to determine the amount of the base erosion and anti-abuse tax. Paragraph (b) of this section provides definitions applicable to the section 59A regulations. Section 1.59A-2 provides rules regarding how to determine whether a taxpayer is an applicable taxpayer. Section 1.59A-3 provides rules regarding base erosion payments and base erosion tax benefits. Section 1.59A-4 provides rules for calculating modified taxable income. Section 1.59A-5 provides rules for calculating the base erosion minimum tax amount. Section 1.59A-6 provides rules relating to qualified derivative payments. Section 1.59A-7 provides rules regarding application of section 59A to partnerships. Section 1.59A-8 is reserved for rules regarding the application of section 59A to certain expatriated entities. Section 1.59A-9 provides an anti-abuse rule to prevent avoidance of section 59A. Finally, §1.59A-10 provides the applicability date for the section 59A regulations.

(b) *Definitions.*—For purposes of this section and §§1.59A-2 through 1.59A-10, the following terms have the meanings described in this paragraph (b).

(1) *Aggregate group.*—The term *aggregate group* means the group of corporations determined by—

(i) Identifying a controlled group of corporations as defined in section 1563(a), except that the phrase "more than 50 percent" is substituted for "at least 80 percent" each place it appears in section 1563(a)(1) and the determination is made without regard to sections 1563(a)(4) and (e)(3)(C), and

(ii) Once the controlled group of corporations is determined, excluding foreign corporations except with regard to income that is, or is treated as, effectively connected with the conduct of a trade or business in the United States under an applicable provision of the Internal Revenue Code or regulations published under 26 CFR chapter I. Notwithstanding the foregoing, if a foreign corporation determines its net taxable income under an applicable income tax treaty of the United States, it is excluded from the controlled group of corporations except with regard to income taken into account in determining its net taxable income.

(2) *Applicable section 38 credits.*—The term *applicable section 38 credits* means the credits allowed under section 38 for the taxable year that are properly allocable to—

(i) The low-income housing credit determined under section 42(a),

(ii) The renewable electricity production credit determined under section 45(a), and

(iii) The investment credit determined under section 46, but only to the extent properly allocable to the energy credit determined under section 48.

(3) *Applicable taxpayer.*—The term *applicable taxpayer* means a taxpayer that meets the requirements set forth in §1.59A-2(b).

(4) *Bank.*—The term *bank* means an entity defined in section 581.

(5) *Base erosion and anti-abuse tax rate.*—The term *base erosion and anti-abuse tax rate* means the percentage that the taxpayer applies to its modified taxable income for the taxable year to calculate its base erosion minimum tax amount. See §1.59A-5(c) for the base erosion and anti-abuse tax rate applicable to the relevant taxable year.

**Prop. Reg. §1.59A-1(b)(5)**

(6) *Business interest expense.*—The term *business interest expense*, with respect to a taxpayer and a taxable year, has the meaning provided in §1.163(j)-1(b)(2).

(7) *Deduction.*—The term *deduction* means any deduction allowable under chapter 1 of subtitle A of the Internal Revenue Code.

(8) *Disallowed business interest expense carryforward.*—The term *disallowed business interest expense carryforward* has the meaning provided in §1.163(j)-1(b)(9).

(9) *Domestic related business interest expense.*—The term *domestic related business interest expense* for any taxable year is the taxpayer's business interest expense paid or accrued to a related party that is not a foreign related party.

(10) *Foreign person.*—The term *foreign person* means any person who is not a United States person. For purposes of the preceding sentence, a United States person has the meaning provided in section 7701(a)(30), except that any individual who is a citizen of any possession of the United States (but not otherwise a citizen of the United States) and who is not a resident of the United States is not a United States person. See §1.59A-7(b) for rules applicable to partnerships.

(11) *Foreign related business interest expense.*—The term *foreign related business interest expense* for any taxable year is the taxpayer's business interest expense paid or accrued to a foreign related party.

(12) *Foreign related party.*—The term *foreign related party* means a foreign person, as defined in paragraph (b)(10) of this section, that is a related party, as defined in paragraph (b)(17) of this section, with respect to the taxpayer. In addition, for purposes of §1.59A-3(b)(4)(v)(B), a foreign related party also includes the foreign corporation's home office or a foreign branch of the foreign corporation. See §1.59A-7(c) for rules applicable to partnerships.

(13) *Gross receipts.*—The term *gross receipts* has the meaning provided in §1.448-1T(f)(2)(iv).

(14) *Member of an aggregate group.*—The term *member of an aggregate group* means a corporation that is included in an aggregate group, as defined in paragraph (b)(1) of this section.

(15) *Registered securities dealer.*—The term *registered securities dealer* means any dealer as defined in section 3(a)(5) of the Securities Exchange Act of 1934 that is registered, or required to be registered, under section 15 of the Securities Exchange Act of 1934.

(16) *Regular tax liability.*—The term *regular tax liability* has the meaning provided in section 26(b).

(17) *Related party.*—(i) *In general.*—A *related party*, with respect to an applicable taxpayer, is—

(A) Any 25-percent owner of the taxpayer;

(B) Any person who is related (within the meaning of section 267(b) or 707(b)(1)) to the taxpayer or any 25-percent owner of the taxpayer; or

(C) A controlled taxpayer within the meaning of §1.482-1(i)(5) together with, or with respect to, the taxpayer.

(ii) *25-percent owner.*—With respect to any corporation, a *25-percent owner* means any person who owns at least 25 percent of—

(A) The total voting power of all classes of stock of the corporation entitled to vote; or

(B) The total value of all classes of stock of the corporation.

(iii) *Application of Section 318.*—section 318 applies for purposes of paragraphs (b)(17)(i) and (ii) of this section, except that—

(A) "10 percent" is substituted for "50 percent" in section 318(a)(2)(C); and

(B) Section 318(a)(3)(A) through (C) are not applied so as to consider a United States person as owning stock that is owned by a person who is not a United States person.

(18) *TLAC long-term debt required amount.*—The term *TLAC long-term debt required amount* means the specified minimum amount of debt that is required pursuant to 12 CFR 252.162(a).

(19) *TLAC securities amount.*—The term *TLAC securities amount* is the sum of the adjusted issue prices (as determined for purposes of §1.1275-1(b)) of all TLAC securities issued and outstanding by the taxpayer.

(20) *TLAC security.*—The term *TLAC security* means an eligible internal debt security, as defined in 12 CFR 252.161.

(21) *Unrelated business interest expense.*—The term *unrelated business interest expense* for any taxable year is the taxpayer's business interest expense paid or accrued to a party that is not a related party. [Reg. §1.59A-1.]

[Proposed 12-21-2018.]

**[Prop. Reg. §1.59A-2]**

**§1.59A-2. Applicable taxpayer.**—(a) *Scope.*—This section provides rules for determining whether a taxpayer is an applicable taxpayer. Paragraph (b) of this section defines an applicable taxpayer. Paragraph (c) of this section provides rules for determining whether a taxpayer is an applicable taxpayer by reference to the aggregate group of which the taxpayer is a member. Paragraph (d) of this section provides rules regarding the gross receipts test. Paragraph (e) of this section provides rules regarding the base erosion percentage calculation. Paragraph (f) of this section provides examples illustrating the rules of this section.

(b) *Applicable taxpayer.*—For purposes of section 59A, a taxpayer is an applicable taxpayer with respect to any taxable year if the taxpayer—

(1) Is a corporation, but not a regulated investment company, a real estate investment trust, or an S corporation;

(2) Satisfies the gross receipts test of paragraph (d) of this section; and

(3) Satisfies the base erosion percentage test of paragraph (e) of this section.

(c) *Aggregation rules.*—A taxpayer that is a member of an aggregate group determines its gross receipts and its base erosion percentage on the basis of the aggregate group as of the end of the taxpayer's taxable year. For these purposes, transactions that occur between members of the taxpayer's aggregate group that were members of the aggregate group as of the time of the transaction are not taken into account. In the case of a foreign corporation that is a member of an aggregate group, only transactions that relate to income effectively connected with, or treated as effectively connected with, the conduct of a trade or business in the United States are disregarded for this purpose. In the case of a foreign corporation that is a member of an aggregate group and that determines its net taxable income under an applicable income tax treaty of the United States, only transactions that are taken into account in determining its net taxable income are disregarded for this purpose.

(d) *Gross receipts test.*—(1) *Amount of gross receipts.*—A taxpayer, or the aggregate group of which the taxpayer is a member, satisfies the gross receipts test if it has average annual gross receipts of at least $500,000,000 for the three-taxable-year period ending with the preceding taxable year.

(2) *Period for measuring gross receipts for an aggregate group.*—(i) *Calendar year taxpayers that are members of an aggregate group.*—In the case of a corporation that has a calendar year and that is a member of an aggregate group, the corporation applies the gross receipts test in paragraph (d)(1) of this section on the basis of the gross receipts of the aggregate group for the three-calendar-year period ending with the preceding calendar year, without regard to the taxable year of any other member of the aggregate group.

(ii) *Fiscal year taxpayers that are members of an aggregate group.*—In the case of a corporation that has a fiscal year and that is a member of an aggregate group, the corporation applies the gross receipts test in paragraph (d)(1) of this section on the basis of the gross receipts of the aggregate group for the three-fiscal-year period ending with the preceding fiscal year of the corporation, without regard to the taxable year of any other member of the aggregate group.

(3) *Gross receipts of foreign corporations.*—With respect to any foreign corporation, only gross receipts that are taken into account in determining income that is effectively connected with the conduct of a trade or business within the United States are taken into account for purposes of paragraph (d)(1) of this section. In the case of a foreign corporation that is a member of an aggregate group and that determines its net taxable income under an applicable income tax treaty of the United States, the foreign corporation includes only gross receipts that are attributable to transactions taken into account in determining its net taxable income.

(4) *Gross receipts of an insurance company.*—For any corporation that is subject to tax under subchapter L or any corporation that would be subject to tax under subchapter L if that corporation were a domestic corporation, gross receipts are reduced by return premiums, but are not reduced by any reinsurance premiums paid or accrued.

(5) *Gross receipts from partnerships.*—See § 1.59A-7(b)(5)(ii).

(6) *Taxpayer not in existence for entire three-year period.*—If a taxpayer was not in existence for the entire three-year period referred to in paragraph (d)(1) of this section, the taxpayer determines a gross receipts average for the period that it was in existence, taking into account paragraph (d)(7) of this section.

(7) *Treatment of short taxable year.*—If a taxpayer has a taxable year of fewer than 12 months (a short period), gross receipts are annualized by multiplying the gross receipts for the short period by 365 and dividing the result by the number of days in the short period.

(8) *Treatment of predecessors.*—For purposes of determining gross receipts under this paragraph (d), any reference to a taxpayer includes a reference to any predecessor of the taxpayer. For this purpose, a predecessor includes the distributor or transferor corporation in a transaction described in section 381(a) in which the taxpayer is the acquiring corporation.

(9) *Reductions in gross receipts.*—Gross receipts for any taxable year are reduced by returns and allowances made during that taxable year.

(10) *Gross receipts of consolidated groups.*—For purposes of section 59A, the gross receipts of a consolidated group are determined by aggregating the gross receipts of all of the members of the consolidated group. See § 1.1502-59A(b).

(e) *Base erosion percentage test.*—(1) *In general.*—A taxpayer, or the aggregate group of which the taxpayer is a member, satisfies the base erosion percentage test if its base erosion percentage is three percent or higher.

(2) *Base erosion percentage test for banks and registered securities dealers.*—(i) *In general.*—A taxpayer that is a member of an affiliated group (as defined in section 1504(a)(1)) that includes a bank (as defined in § 1.59A-1(b)(4)) or a regis-

tered securities dealer (as defined in section §1.59A-1(b)(15)) satisfies the base erosion percentage test if its base erosion percentage is two percent or higher.

(ii) *Aggregate groups.*—An aggregate group of which a taxpayer is a member and that includes a bank or a registered securities dealer that is a member of an affiliated group (as defined in section 1504(a)(1)) will be subject to the base erosion percentage threshold described in paragraph (e)(2)(i) of this section.

(iii) *De minimis exception for banking and registered securities dealer activities.*—An aggregate group that includes a bank or a registered securities dealer that is a member of an affiliated group (as defined in section 1504(a)(1)) is not treated as including a bank or registered securities dealer for purposes of paragraph (e)(2)(i) of this section for a taxable year, if, in that taxable year, the total gross receipts of the aggregate group attributable to the bank or the registered securities dealer represent less than two percent of the total gross receipts of the aggregate group, as determined under paragraph (d) of this section. When there is no aggregate group, a consolidated group that includes a bank or a registered securities dealer is not treated as including a bank or registered securities dealer for purposes of paragraph (e)(2)(i) of this section for a taxable year, if, in that taxable year, the total gross receipts of the consolidated group attributable to the bank or the registered securities dealer represent less than two percent of the total gross receipts of the consolidated group, as determined under paragraph (d) of this section.

(3) *Computation of base erosion percentage.*—(i) *In general.*—The taxpayer's base erosion percentage for any taxable year is determined by dividing—

(A) The aggregate amount of the taxpayer's (or in the case of a taxpayer that is a member of an aggregate group, the aggregate group's) base erosion tax benefits (as defined in §1.59A-3(c)(1)) for the taxable year, by

(B) The sum of—

(1) The aggregate amount of the deductions (including deductions for base erosion tax benefits described in §1.59A-3(c)(1)(i) and base erosion tax benefits described in §1.59A-3(c)(1)(ii)) allowable to the taxpayer (or in the case of a taxpayer that is a member of an aggregate group, any member of the aggregate group) under chapter 1 of Subtitle A for the taxable year;

(2) The base erosion tax benefits described in §1.59A-3(c)(1)(iii) with respect to any premiums or other consideration paid or accrued by the taxpayer (or in the case of a taxpayer that is a member of an aggregate group, any member of the aggregate group) to a foreign related party for any reinsurance payment taken into account under sections 803(a)(1)(B) or 832(b)(4)(A) for the taxable year; and

(3) Any amount paid or accrued by the taxpayer (or in the case of a taxpayer that is a member of an aggregate group, any member of the aggregate group) resulting in a reduction of gross receipts described in §1.59A-3(c)(1)(iv) for the taxable year.

(ii) *Certain items not taken into account in denominator.*—Except as provided in paragraph (e)(3)(viii) of this section, the amount under paragraph (e)(3)(i)(B) of this section is determined by not taking into account—

(A) Any deduction allowed under section 172, 245A, or 250 for the taxable year;

(B) Any deduction for amounts paid or accrued for services to which the exception described in §1.59A-3(b)(3)(i) applies;

(C) Any deduction for qualified derivative payments that are not treated as base erosion payments by reason of §1.59A-3(b)(3)(ii);

(D) Any exchange loss within the meaning of §1.988-2 from a section 988 transaction as described in §1.988-1(a)(1);

(E) Any deduction for amounts paid or accrued to foreign related parties with respect to TLAC securities that are not treated as base erosion payments by reason of §1.59A-3(b)(3)(v); and

(F) Any deduction not allowed in determining taxable income from the taxable year.

(iii) *Effect of treaties on base erosion percentage determination.*—In computing the base erosion percentage, the amount of the base erosion tax benefit with respect to a base erosion payment on which tax is imposed by section 871 or 881 and with respect to which tax has been deducted and withheld under section 1441 or 1442 is equal to the gross amount of the base erosion tax benefit before the application of the applicable treaty multiplied by a fraction equal to—

(A) The rate of tax imposed without regard to the treaty, reduced by the rate of tax imposed under the treaty; over

(B) The rate of tax imposed without regard to the treaty.

(iv) *Amounts paid or accrued between members of a consolidated group.*—See §1.1502-59A(b).

(v) *Deductions and base erosion tax benefits from partnerships.*—See §1.59A-7(b).

(vi) *Mark-to-market positions.*—For any position with respect to which the taxpayer (or in the case of a taxpayer that is a member of an aggregate group, a member of the aggregate group) applies a mark-to-market method of accounting for federal income tax purposes, the taxpayer must determine its gain or loss with respect to that position for any taxable year by combining all items of income, gain, loss, or deduction arising with respect to the position during the taxable year, regardless of how each item arises (including from a payment, accrual, or mark) for purposes of paragraph (e)(3) of this

**Prop. Reg. §1.59A-2(e)(2)(ii)**

section. See paragraph (f)(1) of this section (*Example 1*) for an illustration of this rule. For purposes of section 59A, a taxpayer computes its losses resulting from positions subject to a mark-to-market regime under the Internal Revenue Code based on a single mark for the taxable year on the earlier of the last business day of the taxpayer's taxable year and the disposition (whether by sale, offset, exercise, termination, expiration, maturity, or other means) of the position, regardless of how frequently a taxpayer marks to market for other purposes. See § 1.59A-3(b)(2)(iii) for the application of this rule for purposes of determining the amount of base erosion payments.

(vii) *Computing the base erosion percentage when members of an aggregate group have different taxable years.*—(A) *Calendar year taxpayers that are members of an aggregate group.*—In the case of a taxpayer that has a calendar year and that is a member of an aggregate group, the taxpayer applies the base erosion percentage in paragraph (e)(1) or (2) of this section (and determines the base erosion percentage used in § 1.59A-4(b)(2)(ii)) on the basis of the base erosion percentage for the calendar year in the manner set forth in paragraph (e)(3) of this section, without regard to the taxable year of any other member of the aggregate group. See paragraph (f)(2) of this section (*Example 2*) for an illustration of this rule. For purposes of applying paragraph (e)(3)(vi) of this section, all members of the aggregate group are treated as having a calendar year.

(B) *Fiscal year taxpayers that are members of an aggregate group.*—In the case of a taxpayer that has a fiscal year and that is a member of an aggregate group, the taxpayer applies the base erosion percentage test in paragraph (e)(1) or (2) of this section (and determines the base erosion percentage used in § 1.59A-4(b)(2)(ii)) on the basis of the base erosion percentage for its fiscal year in the manner set forth in paragraph (e)(3) of this section, without regard to the taxable year of any other member of the aggregate group. See paragraph (f)(2) of this section (*Example 2*) for an illustration of this rule. For purposes of applying paragraph (e)(3)(vi) of this section, all members of the aggregate group are treated as having the taxpayer's fiscal year.

(C) *Transition rule for aggregate group members with different taxable years.*—For purposes of this paragraph (e)(3)(vii), if the taxpayer has a different taxable year than another member of the taxpayer's aggregate group, each taxpayer that is a member of the aggregate group determines the availability of the exception in § 1.59A-3(b)(3)(vi) (amounts paid or accrued in taxable years beginning before January 1, 2018) by using the taxpayer's taxable year for all members of the taxpayer's aggregate group.

(viii) *Certain payments that qualify for the effectively connected income exception and another base erosion payment exception.*—Subject to paragraph (c) of this section (transactions that occur between members of the taxpayer's aggregate group), a payment that qualifies for the effectively connected income exception described in § 1.59A-3(b)(3)(iii) and either the service cost method exception described in § 1.59A-3(b)(3)(i), the qualified derivative payment exception described in § 1.59A-3(b)(3)(ii), or the TLAC exception described in § 1.59A-3(b)(3)(v) is not subject to paragraph (e)(3)(ii)(B), (C), or (E) of this section and those amounts are included in the denominator of the base erosion percentage if the foreign related party who received the payment is not a member of the aggregate group.

(f) *Examples.*—The following examples illustrate the rules of this section.

(1) *Example 1: Mark-to-market.* (i) *Facts.* (A) Foreign Parent (FP) is a foreign corporation that owns all of the stock of domestic corporation (DC) and foreign corporation (FC). FP and FC are foreign related parties of DC under § 1.59A-1(b)(12) but not members of the aggregate group. DC is a registered securities dealer that does not hold any securities for investment. On January 1 of year 1, DC enters into two interest rate swaps for a term of two years, one with unrelated Customer A as the counterparty (position A) and one with unrelated Customer B as the counterparty (position B). Each of the swaps provides for semiannual periodic payments to be made or received on June 30 and December 31. No party makes any payment to any other party upon initiation of either of the swaps (that is, they are entered into at-the-money). DC is required to mark-to-market positions A and B for federal income tax purposes. DC is a calendar year taxpayer.

(B) For position A in year 1, DC makes a payment of $150 on June 30, and receives a payment of $50 on December 31. There are no other payments in year 1. On December 31, position A has a value to DC of $110 (that is, position A is in-the-money by $110).

(C) For position B in year 1, DC receives a payment of $120 on June 30, and makes a payment of $30 on December 31. There are no other payments in year 1. On December 31, position B has a value to DC of ($130) (that is, position B is out-of-the-money by $130).

(ii) *Analysis.* (A) With respect to position A, based on the total amount of payments made and received in year 1, DC has a net deduction of $100. In addition, DC has a mark-to-market gain of $110. As described in paragraph (e)(3)(vi) of this section, the mark-to-market gain of $110 is combined with the net deduction of $100 resulting from the payments. Therefore, with respect to position A, DC has a gain of $10, and thus has no deduction in year 1 for purposes of section 59A.

(B) With respect to position B, based on the total amount of payments made and received in year 1, DC has net income of $90. In addition, DC has a mark-to-market loss of $130. As described in paragraph (e)(3)(vi) of this section, the

**Prop. Reg. § 1.59A-2(f)**

mark-to-market loss of $130 is combined with the net income of $90 resulting from the payments. Therefore, with respect to position B, DC has a loss of $40, and thus has a $40 deduction in year 1 for purposes of section 59A.

(2) *Example 2: Determining gross receipts test and base erosion percentage when aggregate group members have different taxable years.* (i) *Facts.* Foreign Parent (FP) is a foreign corporation that owns all of the stock of a domestic corporation that uses a calendar year (DC1) and a domestic corporation that uses a fiscal year ending on January 31 (DC2). FP does not have income effectively connected with the conduct of a trade or business within the United States. DC2 is a member of DC1's aggregate group, and DC1 is a member of DC2's aggregate group.

(ii) *Analysis.* (A) For DC1's tax return filed for the calendar year ending December 31, 2026, DC1 determines its gross receipts based on gross receipts of DC1 and DC2 for the calendar years ending December 31, 2023, December 31, 2024, and December 31, 2025. Further, DC1 determines its base erosion percentage for the calendar year ending December 31, 2026, on the basis of transactions of DC1 and DC2 for the calendar year ending December 31, 2026.

(B) For DC2's tax return filed for the fiscal year ending January 31, 2027, DC2 determines its gross receipts based on gross receipts of DC2 and DC1 for the fiscal years ending January 31, 2024, January 31, 2025, and January 31, 2026. Further, DC2 determines its base erosion percentage for the fiscal year ending January 31, 2027, on the basis of transactions of DC2 and DC1 for the fiscal year ending January 31, 2027. [Reg. §1.59A-2.]

[Proposed 12-21-2018.]

### [Prop. Reg. §1.59A-3]

**§1.59A-3. Base erosion payments and base erosion tax benefits.**—(a) *Scope.*—This section provides definitions and related rules regarding base erosion payments and base erosion tax benefits. Paragraph (b) of this section provides definitions and rules regarding base erosion payments. Paragraph (c) of this section provides rules for determining the amount of base erosion tax benefits. Paragraph (d) of this section provides examples illustrating the rules described in this section.

(b) *Base erosion payments.*—(1) *In general.*—Except as provided in paragraph (b)(3) of this section, a *base erosion payment* means—

(i) Any amount paid or accrued by the taxpayer to a foreign related party of the taxpayer and with respect to which a deduction is allowable under chapter 1 of subtitle A of the Internal Revenue Code;

(ii) Any amount paid or accrued by the taxpayer to a foreign related party of the taxpayer in connection with the acquisition of property by the taxpayer from the foreign related party if the character of the property is subject to

the allowance for depreciation (or amortization in lieu of depreciation);

(iii) Any premium or other consideration paid or accrued by the taxpayer to a foreign related party of the taxpayer for any reinsurance payments that are taken into account under section 803(a)(1)(B) or 832(b)(4)(A); or

(iv) Any amount paid or accrued by the taxpayer that results in a reduction of the gross receipts of the taxpayer if the amount paid or accrued is with respect to—

(A) A surrogate foreign corporation, as defined in section 59A(d)(4)(C)(i), that is a related party of the taxpayer (but only if the corporation first became a surrogate foreign corporation after November 9, 2017); or

(B) A foreign person that is a member of the same expanded affiliated group, as defined in section 59A(d)(4)(C)(ii), as the surrogate foreign corporation.

(2) *Operating rules.*—(i) *Amounts paid or accrued in cash and other consideration.*—For purposes of paragraph (b)(1) of this section, an amount paid or accrued includes an amount paid or accrued using any form of consideration, including cash, property, stock, or the assumption of a liability.

(ii) *Transactions providing for net payments.*—Except as otherwise provided in paragraph (b)(2)(iii) of this section or as permitted by the Internal Revenue Code or the regulations, the amount of any base erosion payment is determined on a gross basis, regardless of any contractual or legal right to make or receive payments on a net basis. For this purpose, a right to make or receive payments on a net basis permits the parties to a transaction or series of transactions to settle obligations by offsetting any amounts to be paid by one party against amounts owed by that party to the other party. For example, any premium or other consideration paid or accrued by a taxpayer to a foreign related party for any reinsurance payments is not reduced by or netted against other amounts owed to the taxpayer from the foreign related party or by reserve adjustments or other returns.

(iii) *Amounts paid or accrued with respect to mark-to-market position.*—For any transaction with respect to which the taxpayer applies the mark-to-market method of accounting for federal income tax purposes, the rules set forth in §1.59A-2(e)(3)(vi) apply to determine the amount of base erosion payment.

(iv) *Coordination among categories of base erosion payments.*—A payment that does not satisfy the criteria of one category of base erosion payment may be a base erosion payment described in one of the other categories.

(v) *Certain domestic passthrough entities.*—(A) *In general.*—If an applicable taxpayer pays or accrues an amount that would be a base erosion payment except for the fact that the payment is made to a specified domestic passthrough, then the applicable taxpayer will be treated as making a base erosion payment to each specified foreign related party for purposes of section 59A and §§1.59A-2 through 1.59A-10. This rule has no effect on the taxation of the specified domestic passthrough under subchapter J or subchapter M of the Code (as applicable).

(B) *Amount of base erosion payment.*— The amount of the base erosion payment is equal to the lesser of the amount paid or accrued by the applicable taxpayer to or for the benefit of the specified domestic passthrough and the amount of the deduction allowed under section 561, 651 or 661 to the specified domestic passthrough with respect to amounts paid, credited, distributed, deemed distributed or required to be distributed to a specified foreign related party.

(C) *Specified domestic passthrough.*—For purposes of this paragraph (b)(2)(v), specified domestic passthrough means:

(1) A domestic trust that is not a grantor trust under subpart E of subchapter J of Chapter 1 of the Code ("domestic trust") and which domestic trust is allowed a deduction under section 651 or section 661 with respect to amounts paid, credited, or required to be distributed to a specified foreign related party;

(2) A real estate investment trust (as defined in §1.856-1(a)) that pays, or is deemed to pay, a dividend to a specified foreign related party for which a deduction is allowed under section 561; or

(3) A regulated investment company (as defined in §1.851-1(a)) that pays, or is deemed to pay, a dividend to a specified foreign related party for which a deduction is allowed under section 561.

(D) *Specified foreign related party.*—For purposes of this paragraph (b)(2)(v), specified foreign related party means, with respect to a specified domestic passthrough, any foreign related party of an applicable taxpayer that is a direct or indirect beneficiary or shareholder of the specified domestic passthrough.

(vi) *Transfers of property to related taxpayers.*—If a taxpayer owns property of a character subject to the allowance for depreciation (or amortization in lieu of depreciation) with respect to which paragraph (c)(1)(ii) of this section applies, and the taxpayer sells, exchanges, or otherwise transfers the property to another taxpayer that is a member of an aggregate group that includes the taxpayer, any deduction for depreciation (or amortization in lieu of depreciation) by the transferee taxpayer remains subject to paragraph (c)(1)(ii) of this section to the same extent the amounts would have been so subject in the hands of the transferor. See paragraph (d)(7) of this section (*Example 7*) for an illustration of this rule.

(3) *Exceptions to base erosion payment.*—Paragraph (b)(1) of this section does not apply to the types of payments or accruals described in paragraphs (b)(3)(i) through (vii) of this section.

(i) *Certain services cost method amounts.*— (A) *In general.*—Amounts paid or accrued by a taxpayer to a foreign related party for services that meet the requirements in paragraph (b)(3)(i)(B) of this section, but only to the extent of the total services cost of those services. Thus, any amount paid or accrued to a foreign related party in excess of the total services cost of services eligible for the services cost method exception (the mark-up component) remains a base erosion payment. For this purpose, services are an activity as defined in §1.482-9(l)(2) performed by a foreign related party (the renderer) that provides a benefit as defined in §1.482-9(l)(3) to the taxpayer (the recipient).

(B) *Eligibility for the services cost method exception.*—To be eligible for the services cost method exception, all of the requirements of §1.482-9(b) must be satisfied, except that:

(1) The requirements of §1.482-9(b)(5) do not apply for purposes of determining eligibility for the service cost method exception in this section; and

(2) Adequate books and records must be maintained as described in paragraph (b)(3)(i)(C) of this section, instead of as described in §1.482-9(b)(6).

(C) *Adequate books and records.*—Permanent books of account and records must be maintained for as long as the costs with respect to the services are incurred by the renderer. The books and records must be adequate to permit verification by the Commissioner of the amount charged for the services and the total services costs incurred by the renderer, including a description of the services in question, identification of the renderer and the recipient of the services, calculation of the amount of profit mark-up (if any) paid for the services, and sufficient documentation to allow verification of the methods used to allocate and apportion the costs to the services in question in accordance with §1.482-9(k).

(D) *Total services cost.*—For purposes of this section, total services cost has the same meaning as total services costs in §1.482-9(j).

(ii) *Qualified derivative payments.*—Any qualified derivative payment as described in §1.59A-6.

(iii) *Effectively connected income.*—(A) *In general.*—Amounts paid or accrued to a foreign related party that are subject to federal income taxation as income that is, or is treated as, effectively connected with the conduct of a trade or business in the United States under an applicable provision of the Internal Revenue Code or regulations. This paragraph (b)(3)(iii) applies only if

**Prop. Reg. §1.59A-3(b)(3)(iii)(A)**

the taxpayer receives a withholding certificate on which the foreign related party claims an exemption from withholding under section 1441 or 1442 because the amounts are effectively connected income.

(B) *Application to certain treaty residents.*—Notwithstanding paragraph (b)(3)(iii)(A) of this section, if a foreign related party determines its net taxable income under an applicable income tax treaty, amounts paid or accrued to the foreign related party taken into account in determining its net taxable income.

(iv) *Exchange loss on a section 988 transaction.*—Any exchange loss within the meaning of § 1.988-2 from a section 988 transaction described in § 1.988-1a(a)(1) that is an allowable deduction and that results from a payment or accrual by the taxpayer to a foreign related party of the taxpayer.

(v) *Amounts paid or accrued with respect to TLAC securities.*—(A) *In general.*—Except as provided in paragraph (b)(3)(v)(B) of this section, amounts paid or accrued to foreign related parties with respect to TLAC securities.

(B) *Limitation on exclusion for TLAC securities.*—The amount excluded under paragraph (b)(3)(v)(A) of this section is no greater than the product of the scaling ratio and amounts paid or accrued to foreign related parties with respect to TLAC securities for which a deduction is allowed.

(C) *Scaling ratio.*—For purposes of this paragraph (b)(3)(v), the scaling ratio for a taxable year of a taxpayer is a fraction the numerator of which is the average TLAC long-term debt required amount and the denominator of which is the average TLAC securities amount. The scaling ratio may in no event be greater than one.

(D) *Average TLAC securities amount.*—The average TLAC securities amount for a taxable year is the average of the TLAC securities amounts for the year, computed at regular time intervals in accordance with this paragraph. The TLAC securities amounts used in calculating the average TLAC securities amount is computed on a monthly basis.

(E) *Average TLAC long-term debt required amount.*—The average TLAC long-term debt required amount for a taxable year is the average of the TLAC long-term debt required amounts, computed on a monthly basis.

(vi) *Amounts paid or accrued in taxable years beginning before January 1, 2018.*—Any amount paid or accrued in taxable years beginning before January 1, 2018.

(vii) *Business interest carried forward from taxable years beginning before January 1, 2018.*—Any disallowed business interest described in section 163(j)(2) that is carried forward from a taxable year beginning before January 1, 2018.

(4) *Rules for determining the amount of certain base erosion payments.*—The following rules apply in determining the deductible amount that is a base erosion payment.

(i) *Interest expense allocable to a foreign corporation's effectively connected income.*—(A) *Method described in § 1.882-5(b) through (d).*—A foreign corporation that has interest expense allocable under section 882(c) to income that is, or is treated as, effectively connected with the conduct of a trade or business within the United States applying the method described in § 1.882-5(b) through (d) has base erosion payments under paragraph (b)(1)(i) of this section for the taxable year equal to the sum of—

(1) The interest expense on a liability described in § 1.882-5(a)(1)(ii)(A) or (B) (direct allocations) or interest expense on U.S.-booked liabilities, as described in § 1.882-5(d)(2), that is paid or accrued by the foreign corporation to a foreign related party; and

(2) The interest expense on U.S.-connected liabilities in excess of U.S.-booked liabilities (hereafter, excess U.S.-connected liabilities), as described in § 1.882-5(d)(5), multiplied by a fraction, the numerator of which is the foreign corporation's average worldwide liabilities due to a foreign related party, and the denominator of which is the foreign corporation's average total worldwide liabilities. For purposes of this fraction, any liability that is a U.S.-booked liability or is subject to a direct allocation is excluded from both the numerator and the denominator of the fraction.

(B) *Separate currency pools method.*—A foreign corporation that has interest expense allocable under section 882(c) to income that is, or is treated as, effectively connected with the conduct of a trade or business within the United States applying the separate currency pools method described in § 1.882-5(e) has a base erosion payment under paragraph (b)(1)(i) of this section for the taxable year equal to the sum of—

(1) The interest expense on a liability described in § 1.882-5(a)(1)(ii)(A) or (B) (direct allocations) that is paid or accrued by the foreign corporation to a foreign related party; and

(2) The interest expense attributable to each currency pool, as described in § 1.882-5(e)(1)(iii), multiplied by a fraction equal to the foreign corporation's average worldwide liabilities denominated in that currency and that is due to a foreign related party over the foreign corporation's average total worldwide liabilities denominated in that currency. For purposes of this fraction, any liability that has a direct allocation is excluded from both the numerator and the denominator.

(C) *U.S.-booked liabilities in excess of U.S.-connected liabilities.*—A foreign corporation that is computing its interest expense under the method described in § 1.882-5(b) through (d) and that has U.S.-booked liabilities in excess of U.S.-

connected liabilities must apply the scaling ratio pro-rata to all interest expense consistent with §1.882-5(d)(4) for purposes of determining the amount of allocable interest expense that is a base erosion payment.

(D) *Liability reduction election.*—A foreign corporation that elects to reduce its liabilities under §1.884-1(e)(3) must reduce its liabilities on a pro-rata basis, consistent with the requirements under §1.884-1(e)(3)(iii), for purposes of determining the amount of allocable interest expense that is a base erosion payment.

(ii) *Other deductions allowed with respect to effectively connected income.*—A deduction allowed under §1.882-4 for an amount paid or accrued by the foreign corporation to a foreign related party (including a deduction for an amount apportioned in part to effectively connected income and in part to income that is not effectively connected income) is treated as a base erosion payment under paragraph (b)(1) of this section.

(iii) *Depreciable property.*—Any amount paid or accrued by the foreign corporation to a foreign related party of the taxpayer in connection with the acquisition of property by the foreign corporation from the foreign related party if the character of the property is subject to the allowance for depreciation (or amortization in lieu of depreciation) is a base erosion payment to the extent the property so acquired is used, or held for use, in the conduct of a trade or business within the United States.

(iv) *Coordination with ECI exception.*—For purposes of this paragraph (b)(4), amounts paid or accrued to a foreign related party treated as effectively connected income (or, in the case of foreign related party that determines net taxable income under an applicable income tax treaty, such amounts that are taken into account in determining net taxable income) are not treated as paid to a foreign related party. Additionally, for purposes of paragraph (b)(4)(i)(A)(2) or (b)(4)(i)(B)(2) of this section, a liability with interest paid or accrued to a foreign related party that is treated as effectively connected income (or, in the case of foreign related party that determines net taxable income under an applicable income tax treaty, interest taken into account in determining net taxable income) is treated as a liability not due to a foreign related party.

(v) *Coordination with certain tax treaties.*—(A) *Allocable expenses.*—If a foreign corporation elects to determine its taxable income pursuant to business profits provisions of an income tax treaty rather than provisions of the Internal Revenue Code, or the regulations published under 26 CFR chapter I, for determining effectively connected income, and the foreign corporation does not apply §§1.882-5 and 1.861-8 to allocate interest and other deductions, then in applying paragraphs (b)(4)(i) and (ii) of this section, the foreign corporation must determine whether each allowable deduction attributed to the permanent establishment in its determination of business profits is a base erosion payment under paragraph (b)(1) of this section.

(B) *Internal dealings under certain income tax treaties.*—If, pursuant to the terms of an applicable income tax treaty, a foreign corporation determines the profits attributable to a permanent establishment based on the assets used, risks assumed, and functions performed by the permanent establishment, then any deduction attributable to any amount paid or accrued (or treated as paid or accrued) by the permanent establishment to the foreign corporation's home office or to another branch of the foreign corporation (an "internal dealing") is a base erosion payment to the extent such payment or accrual is described under paragraph (b)(1) of this section.

(vi) *Business interest expense arising in taxable years beginning after December 31, 2017.*—Any disallowed business interest expense described in section 163(j)(2) that resulted from a payment or accrual to a foreign related party that first arose in a taxable year beginning after December 31, 2017, is treated as a base erosion payment under paragraph (b)(1)(i) of this section in the year that the business interest expense initially arose. See paragraph (c)(4) of this section for rules that apply when business interest expense is limited under section 163(j)(1) in order to determine whether the disallowed business interest expense is attributed to business interest expense paid to a person that is not a related party, a foreign related party, or a domestic related party.

(c) *Base erosion tax benefit.*—(1) *In general.*—Except as provided in paragraph (c)(2) of this section, a base erosion tax benefit means:

(i) In the case of a base erosion payment described in paragraph (b)(1)(i) of this section, any deduction that is allowed under chapter 1 of subtitle A of the Internal Revenue Code for the taxable year with respect to that base erosion payment;

(ii) In the case of a base erosion payment described in paragraph (b)(1)(ii) of this section, any deduction allowed under chapter 1 of subtitle A of the Internal Revenue Code for the taxable year for depreciation (or amortization in lieu of depreciation) with respect to the property acquired with that payment;

(iii) In the case of a base erosion payment described in paragraph (b)(1)(iii) of this section, any reduction under section 803(a)(1)(B) in the gross amount of premiums and other consideration on insurance and annuity contracts for premiums and other consideration arising out of indemnity insurance, or any deduction under section 832(b)(4)(A) from the amount of gross premiums written on insurance contracts during the taxable year for premiums paid for reinsurance; or

(iv) In the case of a base erosion payment described in paragraph (b)(1)(iv) of this section,

714      Tax Cuts and Jobs Act: Regulatory Explanation and Analysis

any reduction in gross receipts with respect to the payment in computing gross income of the taxpayer for the taxable year for purposes of chapter 1 of subtitle A of the Internal Revenue Code.

(2) *Withholding tax exception to base erosion tax benefit.*—Except as provided in paragraph (c)(3) of this section, any base erosion tax benefit attributable to any base erosion payment is not taken into account as a base erosion tax benefit if tax is imposed on that payment under section 871 or 881, and the tax has been deducted and withheld under section 1441 or 1442.

(3) *Effect of treaty on base erosion tax benefit.*— If any treaty between the United States and any foreign country reduces the rate of tax imposed by section 871 or 881, the amount of base erosion tax benefit that is not taken into account under paragraph (c)(2) of this section is equal to the amount of the base erosion tax benefit before the application of paragraph (c)(2) of this section multiplied by a fraction of—

(i) The rate of tax imposed without regard to the treaty, reduced by the rate of tax imposed under the treaty; over

(ii) The rate of tax imposed without regard to the treaty.

(4) *Application of section 163(j) to base erosion payments.*—(i) *Classification of payments or accruals of business interest expense based on the payee.*— The following rules apply for corporations and partnerships:

(A) *Classification of payments or accruals of business interest expense of a corporation.*—For purposes of this section, in the year that business interest expense of a corporation is paid or accrued the business interest expense is classified as foreign related business interest expense, domestic related business interest expense, or unrelated business interest expense.

(B) *Classification of payments or accruals of business interest expense by a partnership.*—For purposes of this section, in the year that business interest expense of a partnership is paid or accrued, the business interest expense that is allocated to a partner is classified separately with respect to each partner in the partnership as foreign related business interest expense, domestic related business interest expense, or unrelated business interest expense.

(C) *Classification of payments or accruals of business interest expense that is subject to the exception for effectively connected income.*—For purposes of paragraph (c)(4)(i)(A) and (B) of this section, business interest expense paid or accrued to a foreign related party to which the exception in paragraph (b)(3)(iii) of this section (effectively connected income) applies is classified as domestic related business interest expense.

(ii) *Ordering rules for business interest expense that is limited under section 163(j)(1) to deter-*

*mine which classifications of business interest expense are deducted and which classifications of business interest expense are carried forward.*—(A) *In general.*—Section 163(j) and the regulations published under 26 CFR chapter I provide a limitation on the amount of business interest expense allowed as a deduction in a taxable year by a corporation or a partner in a partnership. In the case of a corporation with a disallowed business interest expense carryforward, the regulations under section 163(j) determine the ordering of the business interest expense deduction that is allowed on a year-by-year basis by reference first to business interest expense incurred in the current taxable year and then to disallowed business interest expense carryforwards from prior years. To determine the amount of base erosion tax benefit under paragraph (c)(1) of this section, this paragraph (c)(4)(ii) sets forth ordering rules that determine the amount of the deduction of business interest expense allowed under section 163(j) that is classified as paid or accrued to a foreign related party for purposes of paragraph (c)(1)(i) of this section. This paragraph (c)(4)(ii) also sets forth similar ordering rules that apply to disallowed business interest expense carryforwards for which a deduction is permitted under section 163(j) in a later year.

(B) *Ordering rules for treating business interest expense deduction and disallowed business interest expense carryforwards as foreign related business interest expense, domestic related business interest expense, and unrelated business interest expense.*—(1) *General ordering rule for allocating business interest expense deduction between classifications.*—For purposes of paragraph (c)(1) of this section, if a deduction for business interest expense is not subject to the limitation under section 163(j)(1) in a taxable year, the deduction is treated first as foreign related business interest expense and domestic related business interest expense (on a pro-rata basis), and second as unrelated business interest expense. The same principle applies to business interest expense of a partnership that is deductible at the partner level under § 1.163(j)-6(f).

(2) *Ordering of business interest expense incurred by a corporation.*—If a corporation's business interest expense deduction allowed for any taxable year is attributable to business interest expense paid or accrued in that taxable year and to disallowed business interest expense carryforwards from prior taxable years, the ordering of business interest expense deduction provided in paragraph (c)(4)(ii)(B)(1) of this section among the classifications described therein applies separately for the carryforward amount from each taxable year, following the ordering set forth in § 1.163(j)-5(b)(2). Corresponding adjustments to the classification of disallowed business interest expense carryforwards are made consistent with this year-by-year approach. For purposes of section 59A and this section, an acquiring corporation in a transaction described in section 381(a) will succeed to and take into account the classifi-

cation of any disallowed business interest expense carryforward. See § 1.381(c)(20)-1.

(3) *Ordering of business interest expense incurred by a partnership and allocated to a corporate partner.*—For a corporate partner in a partnership that is allocated a business interest expense deduction under § 1.163(j)-6(f), the ordering rule provided in paragraph (c)(4)(ii)(B)(*1*) of this section applies separately to the corporate partner's allocated business interest expense deduction from the partnership; that deduction is not comingled with the business interest expense deduction addressed in paragraph (c)(4)(ii)(B)(*1*) or (2) of this section or the corporate partner's items from any other partnership. Similarly, when a corporate partner in a partnership is allocated excess business interest expense from a partnership under the rules set forth in § 1.163(j)-6(f) and the excess interest expense becomes deductible to the corporate partner, that partner applies the ordering rule provided in paragraph (c)(4)(ii)(B)(*1*) of this section separately to that excess interest expense on a year-by-year basis. Corresponding adjustments to the classification of disallowed business interest expense carryforwards are made consistent with this year-by-year and partnership-by-partnership approach.

(d) *Examples.*—The following examples illustrate the application of this section. For purposes of all the examples, assume that the taxpayer is an applicable taxpayer and all payments apply to a taxable year beginning after December 31, 2017.

(1) *Example 1: Determining a base erosion payment.* (i) *Facts.* FP is a foreign corporation that owns all of the stock of FC, a foreign corporation, and DC, a domestic corporation. FP has a trade or business in the United States with effectively connected income (USTB). DC owns FDE, a foreign disregarded entity. DC pays interest to FDE and FC. FDE pays interest to USTB. All interest paid by DC to FC and by FDE to USTB is deductible by DC in the current year for regular income tax purposes. FDE also acquires depreciable property from FP during the taxable year. FP's income from the sale of the depreciable property is not effectively connected with the conduct of FP's trade or business in the United States. DC and FP (based only on the activities of USTB) are applicable taxpayers under § 1.59A-2(b).

(ii) *Analysis.* The payment of interest by DC to FC is a base erosion payment under paragraph (b)(1)(i) of this section because the payment is made to a foreign related party and the interest payment is deductible. The payment of interest by DC to FDE is not a base erosion payment because the transaction is not a payment to a foreign person and the transaction is not a deductible payment. With respect to the payment of interest by FDE to USTB, if FP's USTB treats the payment of interest by FDE to USTB as income that is effectively connected with the conduct of a trade or business in the United States pursuant to section 864 or as profits attributable

to a U.S. permanent establishment of a tax treaty resident, and if DC receives a withholding certificate from FP with respect to the payment, then the exception in paragraph (b)(3)(iii) of this section applies. Accordingly, the payment from DC, through FDE, to USTB is not a base erosion payment even though the payment is to the USTB of FP, a foreign related party. The acquisition of depreciable property by DC, through FDE, is a base erosion payment under paragraph (b)(1)(ii) of this section because there is a payment to a foreign related party in connection with the acquisition by the taxpayer of property of a character subject to the allowance for depreciation and the exception in paragraph (b)(3)(iii) of this section does not apply because FP's income from the sale of the depreciable property is not effectively connected with the conduct of FP's trade or business in the United States. See § 1.59A-2 for the application of the aggregation rule with respect to DC and FP's USTB.

(2) *Example 2: Interest allocable under § 1.882-5.* (i) *Facts.* FC, a foreign corporation, has income that is effectively connected with the conduct of a trade or business within the United States. FC determines its interest expense under the three-step process described in § § 1.882-5(b) through (d) with a total interest expense of $125x. The total interest expense is comprised of interest expense of $100x on U.S.-booked liabilities ($60x paid to a foreign related party and $40x paid to unrelated persons) and $25x of interest on excess U.S.-connected liabilities. FC has average total liabilities (that are not U.S.-booked liabilities) of $10,000x and of that number $2000x are liabilities held by a foreign related party. FC is an applicable taxpayer with respect to its effectively connected income. Assume all of the interest expense is deductible in the current taxable year and that none of the interest is subject to the effectively connected income exception in paragraph (b)(3)(iii) of this section.

(ii) *Analysis.* Under paragraph (b)(4)(i) of this section, the total amount of interest expense determined under § 1.882-5 that is a base erosion payment is $65x ($60x + 5x). FC has $60x of interest on U.S.-booked liabilities that is paid to a foreign related party and that is treated as a base erosion payment under paragraph (b)(4)(i)(A)(*1*) of this section. Additionally, $5x of the $25x of interest on excess U.S.-connected liabilities is treated as a base erosion payment under paragraph (b)(4)(i)(A)(*2*) of this section ($25x * ($2000x / $10,000x)).

(3) *Example 3: Interaction with section 163(j).* (i) *Facts.* Foreign Parent (FP) is a foreign corporation that owns all of the stock of DC, a domestic corporation that is an applicable taxpayer. In Year 1, DC has adjusted taxable income, as defined in section 163(j)(8), of $1000x and pays the following amounts of business interest expense: $420x that is paid to unrelated Bank, and $360x that is paid to FP. DC does not earn any business interest income or incur any floor plan financing interest expense in Year 1. None of the excep-

**Prop. Reg. § 1.59A-3(d)**

tions in paragraph (b)(3) of this section apply, and the interest is not subject to withholding.

(ii) *Analysis*— (A) *Classification of business interest.* In Year 1, DC is only permitted to deduct $300x of business interest expense under section 163(j)(1) ($1000x x 30%). Paragraph (c)(4)(ii)(B) of this section provides that for purposes of paragraph (c)(1) of this section the deduction is treated first as foreign related business interest expense and domestic related business interest expense (here, only FP); and second as unrelated business interest expense (Bank). As a result, the $300x of business interest expense that is permitted under section 163(j)(1) is treated entirely as the business interest paid to the related foreign party, FP. All of DC's $300x deductible interest is treated as an add-back to modified taxable income in the Year 1 taxable year for purposes of § 1.59A-4(b)(2)(i).

(B) *Ordering rules for business interest expense carryforward.* Under section 163(j)(2), the $480x of disallowed business interest ($420x + $360x - $300x) is carried forward to the subsequent year. Under paragraph (c)(4)(ii)(B)(1) and (2) of this section, the interest carryforward is correspondingly treated first as unrelated business interest expense, and second pro-rata as foreign related business interest expense and domestic related business interest expense. As a result, $420x of the $480x business interest expense carryforward is treated first as business interest expense paid to Bank and the remaining $60x of the $480x business interest expense carryforward is treated as interest paid to FP and as an add-back to modified taxable income.

(4) *Example 4: Interaction with section 163(j); carryforward.* (i) *Facts.* The facts are the same as in paragraph (d)(3) of this section (the facts in *Example 3*), except that in addition, in Year 2, DC has adjusted taxable income of $250x, and pays the following amounts of business interest expense: $50x that is paid to unrelated Bank, and $45x that is paid to FP. DC does not earn any business interest income or incur any floor plan financing interest expense in Year 2. None of the exceptions in paragraph (b)(3) of this section apply.

(ii) *Analysis*— (A) *Classification of business interest.* In Year 2, for purposes of section 163(j)(1), DC is treated as having paid or accrued total business interest of $575x, consisting of $95x business interest expense actually paid in Year 2 and $480x of business interest expense that is carried forward from Year 1. DC is permitted to deduct $75x of business interest expense in Year 2 under the limitation in section 163(j)(1) ($250x x 30%). Section 1.163(j)-5(b)(2) provides that, for purposes of section 163(j), the allowable business interest expense is first attributed to amounts paid or accrued in the current year, and then attributed to amounts carried over from earlier years on a first-in-first-out basis from the earliest year. Accordingly, the $75x of deductible business interest expense is deducted entirely from the $95x business interest expense incurred in Year 2 for section 163(j) purposes. Because DC's

business interest expense deduction is limited under section 163(j)(1) and because DC's total business interest expense is attributable to more than one taxable year, paragraph (c)(4)(ii)(B)(2) of this section provides that the ordering rule in paragraph (c)(4)(ii)(B)(1) of this section is applied separately to each annual amount of section 163(j) disallowed business interest carryforward. With respect to the Year 2 layer, which is deducted first, paragraph (c)(4)(ii)(B) of this section provides that, for purposes of paragraph (c)(1) of this section, the Year 2 $75x deduction is treated first as foreign related business interest expense and domestic related business interest expense (here, only FP, $45x); and second as unrelated business interest expense (Bank, $30x). Consequentially, all of the $45x deduction of business interest expense that was paid to FP in Year 2 is treated as a base erosion tax benefit and an add-back to modified taxable income for the Year 2 taxable year for purposes of § 1.59A-4(b)(2)(i).

(B) *Ordering rules for business interest expense carryforward.* The disallowed business interest expense carryforward of $20x from Year 2 is correspondingly treated first as interest paid to Bank under paragraph (c)(4)(i) of this section. The disallowed business interest expense carryforward of $480x from the Year 1 layer that is also not allowed as a deduction in Year 2 remains treated as $420x paid to Bank and $60 paid to FP.

(5) *Example 5: Interaction with section 163(j); carryforward.* (i) *Facts.* The facts are the same as in paragraph (d)(4) of this section (the facts in *Example 4*), except that in addition, in Year 3, DC has adjusted taxable income of $4000x and pays no business interest expense. DC does not earn any business interest income or incur any floor plan financing interest expense in Year 3.

(ii) *Analysis.* In Year 3, DC is treated as having paid or accrued total business interest expense of $500x, consisting of $480x of business interest expense that is carried forward from Year 1 and $20x of business interest expense that is carried forward from Year 2 for purposes of section 163(j)(1). DC is permitted to deduct $1200x of business interest expense in Year 3 under the limitation in section 163(j)(1) ($4000x x 30%). For purposes of section 163(j), DC is treated as first deducting the business interest expense from Year 1 then the business interest expense from Year 2. See § 1.163(j)-5(b)(2). Because none of DC's $500x business interest expense is limited under section 163(j), the stacking rule in paragraph (c)(4)(ii) of this section for allowed and disallowed business interest expense does not apply. For purposes of § 1.59A-4(b)(2)(i), DC's add-back to modified taxable income is $60x determined by the classifications in paragraph (c)(4)(i)(A) of this section ($60x treated as paid to FP from Year 1).

(6) *Example 6: Interaction with section 163(j); partnership.* (i) *Facts.* The facts are the same as in paragraph (d)(4) of this section (the facts in *Example 4*), except that in addition, in Year 2, DC forms a domestic partnership (PRS) with Y, a

domestic corporation that is not related to DC within the meaning of §1.59A-1(b)(17). DC and Y are equal partners in partnership PRS. In Year 2, PRS has ATI of $100x and $48x of business interest expense. $12x of PRS's business interest expense is paid to Bank, and $36x of PRS's business interest expense is paid to FP. PRS allocates the items comprising its $100x of ATI $50x to DC and $50x to Y. PRS allocates its $48x of business interest expense $24x to DC and $24x to Y. DC classifies its $24x of business interest expense as $6x unrelated business interest expense (Bank) and $18x as foreign related business interest expense (FP) under paragraph (c)(4)(i)(B) of this section. Y classifies its $24x of business interest expense as entirely unrelated business interest expense of Y (Bank and FP) under paragraph (c)(4)(i)(B) of this section. None of the exceptions in paragraph (b)(3) of this section apply.

(ii) *Partnership level analysis.* In Year 2, PRS's section 163(j) limit is 30 percent of its ATI, or $30x ($100x x 30 percent). Thus, PRS has $30x of deductible business interest expense and $18x of excess business interest expense ($48x - $30x). The $30x of deductible business interest expense is includible in PRS's non-separately stated income or loss, and is not subject to further limitation under section 163(j) at the partners' level.

(iii) *Partner level allocations analysis.* Pursuant to §1.163(j)-6(f)(2), DC and Y are each allocated $15x of deductible business interest expense and $9x of excess business interest expense. At the end of Year 2, DC and Y each have $9x of excess business interest expense from PRS, which under §1.163(j)-6 is not treated as paid or accrued by the partner until such partner is allocated excess taxable income or excess business interest income from PRS in a succeeding year. Pursuant to §1.163(j)-6(e), DC and Y, in computing their limit under section 163(j), do not increase any of their section 163(j) items by any of PRS's section 163(j) items.

(iv) *Partner level allocations for determining base erosion tax benefits.* The $15x of deductible business interest expense allocated to DC is treated first as foreign related business interest expense (FP) under paragraph (c)(4)(ii)(B) of this section. DC's excess business interest expense from PRS of $9x is classified first as the unrelated business interest expense with respect to Bank ($6x) and then as the remaining portion of the business interest expense paid to FP ($3x, or $18x - $15x). Under paragraph (c)(4)(ii)(B)(3) of this section, these classifications of the PRS items apply irrespective of the classifications of DC's own interest expense as set forth in paragraph (d)(4) of this section (*Example 4*).

(v) *Computation of modified taxable income.* For Year 2, DC is treated as having incurred base erosion tax benefits of $60x, consisting of the $15x base erosion tax benefit with respect to its interest in PRS that is computed in paragraph (d)(6)(iii) of this section (*Example 6*) and $45x that is computed in paragraph (d)(4) of this section (*Example 4*).

(7) *Example 7: Transfers of property to related taxpayers.* (i) *Facts.* FP is a foreign corporation that owns all of the stock of DC1 and DC2, both domestic corporations. DC1 and DC2 are both members of the same aggregate group but are not members of the same consolidated tax group under section 1502. In Year 1, FP sells depreciable property to DC1. On the first day of the Year 2 tax year, DC1 sells the depreciable property to DC2.

(ii) *Analysis*— (A) *Year 1.* The acquisition of depreciable property by DC1 from FP is a base erosion payment under paragraph (b)(1)(ii) of this section because there is a payment to a foreign related party in connection with the acquisition by the taxpayer of property of a character subject to the allowance for depreciation.

(B) *Year 2.* The acquisition of the depreciable property in Year 2 by DC2 is not itself a base erosion payment because DC2 did not acquire the property from a foreign related party. However, under paragraph (b)(2)(vi) of this section any depreciation expense taken by DC2 on the property acquired from DC1 is a base erosion payment and a base erosion tax benefit under paragraph (c)(1)(ii) of this section because the acquisition of the depreciable property was a base erosion payment by DC1 and the property was sold to a member of the aggregate group; therefore, the depreciation expense continues as a base erosion tax benefit to DC2 as it would have been to DC1 if it continued to own the property. [Reg. §1.59A-3.]

[Proposed 12-21-2018.]

### [Prop. Reg. §1.59A-4]

**§1.59A-4. Modified taxable income.**— (a) *Scope.*—Paragraph (b)(1) of this section provides rules for computing modified taxable income. Paragraph (b)(2) of this section provides rules addressing how base erosion tax benefits and net operating losses affect modified taxable income. Paragraph (b)(3) of this section provides a rule for a holder of a residual interest in a REMIC. Paragraph (c) of this section provides examples illustrating the rules described in this section.

(b) *Computation of modified taxable income.*— (1) *In general.*—The term *modified taxable income* means a taxpayer's taxable income, as defined in section 63(a), determined with the additions described in paragraph (b)(2) of this section. Notwithstanding the foregoing, the taxpayer's taxable income may not be reduced to an amount less than zero as a result of a net operating loss deduction allowed under section 172. See paragraphs (c)(1) and (2) of this section (*Examples 1* and 2).

(2) *Modifications to taxable income.*—The amounts described in this paragraph (b)(2) are added back to a taxpayer's taxable income to determine its modified taxable income.

**(i)** *Base erosion tax benefits.*—The amount of any base erosion tax benefit as defined in §1.59A-3(c)(1).

**(ii)** *Certain net operating loss deductions.*—The base erosion percentage, as described in §1.59A-2(e)(3), of any net operating loss deduction allowed to the taxpayer under section 172 for the taxable year. For purposes of determining modified taxable income, the net operating loss deduction allowed does not exceed taxable income before taking into account the net operating loss deduction. See paragraph (c)(1) and (2) of this section (*Examples 1 and 2*). The base erosion percentage for the taxable year that the net operating loss arose is used to determine the addition under this paragraph (b)(2)(ii). For a net operating loss that arose in a taxable year beginning before January 1, 2018, the base erosion percentage for the taxable year is zero.

**(3)** *Rule for holders of a residual interest in a REMIC.*—For purposes of paragraph (b)(1) of this section, the limitation in section 860E(a)(1) is not taken into account for determining the taxable income amount that is used to compute modified taxable income for the taxable year.

**(c)** *Examples.*—The following examples illustrate the rules of paragraph (b) of this section.

**(1)** *Example 1: Current year loss.* (i) *Facts.* A domestic corporation (DC) is an applicable taxpayer that has a calendar taxable year. In 2020, DC has gross income of $100x, a deduction of $80x that is not a base erosion tax benefit, and a deduction of $70x that is a base erosion tax benefit. In addition, DC has a net operating loss carryforward to 2020 of $400x that arose in 2016.

**(ii)** *Analysis.* DC's starting point for computing modified taxable income is $(50x), computed as gross income of $100x, less a deduction of $80x (non-base erosion tax benefit) and a deduction of $70x (base erosion tax benefit). Under paragraph (b)(2)(ii) of this section, DC's starting point for computing modified taxable income does not take into account the $400x net operating loss carryforward because the allowable deductions for 2020, not counting the NOL deduction, exceed the gross income for 2020. DC's modified taxable income for 2020 is $20x, computed as $(50x) + $70x base erosion tax benefit.

**(2)** *Example 2: Net operating loss deduction.* (i) *Facts.* The facts are the same as in paragraph (c)(1)(i) of this section (the facts in *Example 1*), except that DC's gross income in 2020 is $500x.

**(ii)** *Analysis.* DC's starting point for computing modified taxable income is $0x, computed as gross income of $500x, less: a deduction of $80x (non-base erosion tax benefit), a deduction of $70x (base erosion tax benefit), and a net operating loss deduction of $350x (which is the amount of taxable income before taking into account the net operating loss deduction, as provided in paragraph (b)(2)(ii) of this section ($500x - $150x)). DC's modified taxable income for 2020 is $70x, computed as $0x + $70x base erosion tax benefit. DC's modified taxable income is not increased as

a result of the $350x net operating loss deduction in 2020 because the base erosion percentage of the net operating loss that arose in 2016 is zero under paragraph (b)(2)(ii) of this section. [Reg. §1.59A-4.]

[Proposed 12-21-2018.]

**[Prop. Reg. §1.59A-5]**

**§1.59A-5. Base erosion minimum tax amount.**—**(a)** *Scope.*—Paragraph (b) of this section provides rules regarding the calculation of the base erosion minimum tax amount. Paragraph (c) of this section describes the base erosion and anti-abuse tax rate applicable to the taxable year.

**(b)** *In general.*—With respect to any applicable taxpayer, the base erosion minimum tax amount for any taxable year is, the excess (if any) of—

**(1)** An amount equal to the base erosion and anti-abuse tax rate multiplied by the modified taxable income of the taxpayer for the taxable year, over

**(2)** An amount equal to the regular tax liability as defined in §1.59A-1(b)(16) of the taxpayer for the taxable year, reduced (but not below zero) by the excess (if any) of-

**(i)** The credits allowed under chapter 1 of subtitle A of the Code against regular tax liability over

**(ii)** The sum of the credits described in paragraph (b)(3) of this section.

**(3)** *Credits that do not reduce regular tax liability.*—The sum of the following credits are used in paragraph (b)(2)(ii) of this section to limit the amount by which the credits allowed under chapter 1 of subtitle A of the Internal Revenue Code reduce regular tax liability—

**(i)** *Taxable years beginning on or before December 31, 2025.*—For any taxable year beginning on or before December 31, 2025—

**(A)** The credit allowed under section 38 for the taxable year that is properly allocable to the research credit determined under section 41(a);

**(B)** The portion of the applicable section 38 credits not in excess of 80 percent of the lesser of the amount of those applicable section 38 credits or the base erosion minimum tax amount (determined without regard to this paragraph (b)(3)(i)(B)); and

**(C)** Any credits allowed under sections 33 and 37.

**(ii)** *Taxable years beginning after December 31, 2025.*—For any taxable year beginning after December 31, 2025, any credits allowed under sections 33 and 37.

**(c)** *Base erosion and anti-abuse tax rate.*—**(1)** *In general.*—For purposes of calculating the base erosion minimum tax amount, the base erosion minimum tax amount, the base erosion and anti-abuse tax rate is—

(i) *Calendar year 2018.*—For taxable years beginning in calendar year 2018, five percent.

(ii) *Calendar years 2019 through 2025.*—For taxable years beginning after December 31, 2018, through taxable years beginning before January 1, 2026, 10 percent.

(iii) *Calendar years after 2025.*—For taxable years beginning after December 31, 2025, 12.5 percent.

(2) *Increased rate for banks and registered securities dealers.*—In the case of a taxpayer that is a member of an affiliated group (as defined in section 1504(a)(1)) that includes a bank or a registered securities dealer, the percentage otherwise in effect under paragraph (c)(1) of this section is increased by one percentage point.

(3) *Application of section 15.*—Section 15 does not apply to any taxable year that includes January 1, 2018. See § 1.15-1(d). For a taxpayer using a taxable year other than the calendar year, section 15 applies to any taxable year beginning after January 1, 2018. [Reg. § 1.59A-5.]

[Proposed 12-21-2018.]

### [Prop. Reg. § 1.59A-6]

**§ 1.59A-6. Qualified derivative payment.**—(a) *Scope.*—This section provides additional guidance regarding qualified derivative payments. Paragraph (b) of this section defines the term qualified derivative payment. Paragraph (c) of this section provides guidance on certain payments that are not treated as qualified derivative payments. Paragraph (d) defines the term derivative for purposes of section 59A. Paragraph (e) of this section provides an example illustrating the rules of this section.

(b) *Qualified derivative payment.*—(1) *In general.*—A *qualified derivative payment* means any payment made by a taxpayer to a foreign related party pursuant to a derivative with respect to which the taxpayer—

(i) Recognizes gain or loss as if the derivative were sold for its fair market value on the last business day of the taxable year (and any additional times as required by the Internal Revenue Code or the taxpayer's method of accounting);

(ii) Treats any gain or loss so recognized as ordinary; and

(iii) Treats the character of all items of income, deduction, gain, or loss with respect to a payment pursuant to the derivative as ordinary.

(2) *Reporting requirements.*—(i) *In general.*—No payment is a qualified derivative payment under paragraph (b)(1) of this section for any taxable year unless the taxpayer reports the information required in § 1.6038A-2(b)(7)(ix) for the taxable year.

(ii) *Failure to satisfy the reporting requirement.*—If a taxpayer fails to satisfy the reporting requirement described in paragraph (b)(2)(i) of this section with respect to any payments, those payments will not be eligible for the qualified derivative payment exception described in § 1.59A-3(b)(3)(ii). A taxpayer's failure to report a payment as a qualified derivative payment does not impact the eligibility of any other payment which the taxpayer properly reported under paragraph (b)(2)(i) of this section from being a qualified derivative payment.

(3) *Amount of any qualified derivative payment.*—The amount of any qualified derivative payment excluded from the denominator of the base erosion percentage as provided in § 1.59A-2(e)(3)(ii)(C) is determined as provided in § 1.59A-2(e)(3)(vi).

(c) *Exceptions for payments otherwise treated as base erosion payments.*—A payment does not constitute a qualified derivative payment if—

(1) The payment would be treated as a base erosion payment if it were not made pursuant to a derivative, including any interest, royalty, or service payment; or

(2) In the case of a contract that has derivative and nonderivative components, the payment is properly allocable to the nonderivative component.

(d) *Derivative defined.*—(1) *In general.*—For purposes of this section, the term *derivative* means any contract (including any option, forward contract, futures contract, short position, swap, or similar contract) the value of which, or any payment or other transfer with respect to which, is (directly or indirectly) determined by reference to one or more of the following:

(i) Any share of stock in a corporation;

(ii) Any evidence of indebtedness;

(iii) Any commodity that is actively traded;

(iv) Any currency; or

(v) Any rate, price, amount, index, formula, or algorithm.

(2) *Exceptions.*—The following contracts are not treated as derivatives for purposes of section 59A.

(i) *Direct interest.*—A derivative contract does not include a direct interest in any item described in paragraph (d)(1)(i) through (v) of this section.

(ii) *Insurance contracts.*—A derivative contract does not include any insurance, annuity, or endowment contract issued by an insurance company to which subchapter L applies (or issued by any foreign corporation to which the subchapter would apply if the foreign corporation were a domestic corporation).

(iii) *Securities lending and sale-repurchase transactions.*—A derivative contract does not include any securities lending transaction, sale-repurchase transaction, or substantially similar transaction. Securities lending transaction and sale-repurchase transaction have the same meaning as provided in § 1.861-2(a)(7).

(3) *American depository receipts.*—For purposes of section 59A, American depository receipts (or any similar instruments) with respect to shares of stock in a foreign corporation are treated as shares of stock in that foreign corporation.

(e) *Example.*—The following example illustrates the rules of this section.

(1) *Facts.* Domestic Corporation (DC) is a dealer in securities within the meaning of section 475. On February 1, 2019, DC enters into a contract (Interest Rate Swap) with Foreign Parent (FP), a foreign related party, for a term of five years. Under the Interest Rate Swap, DC is obligated to make a payment to FP each month, beginning March 1, 2019, in an amount equal to a variable rate determined by reference to the prime rate, as determined on the first business day of the immediately preceding month, multiplied by a notional principal amount of $50 million. Under the Interest Rate Swap, FP is obligated to make a payment to DC each month, beginning March 1, 2019, in an amount equal to 5% multiplied by the same notional principal amount. The Interest Rate Swap satisfies the definition of a notional principal contract under § 1.446-3(c). DC recognizes gain or loss on the Interest Rate Swap pursuant to section 475. DC reports the information required to be reported for the taxable year under § 1.6038A-2(b)(7)(ix).

(2) *Analysis.* The Interest Rate Swap is a derivative as described in paragraph (d) of this section because it is a contract that references the prime rate and a fixed rate for determining the amount of payments. The exceptions described in paragraph (c) of this section do not apply to the Interest Rate Swap. Because DC recognizes ordinary gain or loss on the Interest Rate Swap pursuant to section 475(d)(3), it satisfies the condition in paragraph (b)(1)(ii) of this section. Because DC satisfies the requirement relating to the information required to be reported under paragraph (b)(2) of this section, any payment to FP with respect to the Interest Rate Swap will be a qualified derivative payment. Therefore, under § 1.59A-3(b)(3)(ii), the payments to FP are not base erosion payments. [Reg. § 1.59A-6.]

[Proposed 12-21-2018.]

### [Prop. Reg. § 1.59A-7]

**§ 1.59A-7. Application of base erosion and anti-abuse tax to partnerships.**—(a) *Scope.*— This section provides rules regarding how partnerships and their partners are treated for purposes of section 59A. Paragraph (b) of this section provides the general application of an aggregate approach to partnerships for purposes of section 59A, including specific rules addressing the application of section 59A to amounts paid or accrued by a partnership to a related party, rules addressing the application of section 59A to amounts paid or accrued to a partnership

from a related party, and other operating rules. Paragraph (c) of this section provides rules for determining whether a party is a foreign related party.

(b) *Application of section 59A to a partnership.*— (1) *In general.*—Except as otherwise provided in this section, section 59A is applied at the partner level in the manner described in this section. The provisions of section 59A must be interpreted in a manner consistent with this approach.

(2) *Payment made by a partnership.*—Except as provided in paragraph (b)(4) of this section, for purposes of determining whether a payment or accrual by a partnership is a base erosion payment, any amount paid or accrued by a partnership is treated as paid or accrued by each partner based on the partner's distributive share of items of deduction (or other amounts that could be base erosion tax benefits) with respect to that amount (as determined under section 704).

(3) *Payment received by a partnership.*—For purposes of determining whether a payment or accrual to a partnership is a base erosion payment of the payor, any amount paid or accrued to a partnership is treated as paid or accrued to each partner based on the partner's distributive share of the income or gain with respect to that amount (as determined under section 704).

(4) *Exception for base erosion tax benefits of certain partners.*—(i) *In general.*—For purposes of determining a partner's amount of base erosion tax benefits, a partner does not take into account its distributive share of any partnership amount of base erosion tax benefits for the taxable year if —

(A) The partner's interest in the partnership represents less than ten percent of the capital and profits of the partnership at all times during the taxable year;

(B) The partner is allocated less than ten percent of each partnership item of income, gain, loss, deduction, and credit for the taxable year; and

(C) The partner's interest in the partnership has a fair market value of less than $25 million on the last day of the partner's taxable year, determined using a reasonable method.

(ii) *Attribution.*—For purposes of paragraph (b)(4)(i) of this section, a partner's interest in a partnership or partnership item is determined by adding the interests of the partner and any related party of the partner (as determined under section 59A), taking into account any interest owned directly, indirectly, or through constructive ownership (applying the section 318 rules as modified by section 59A (except section 318(a)(3)(A) through (C) will also apply so as to consider a United States person as owning stock that is owned by a person who is not a United States person), but excluding any interest to the extent already taken into account).

(5) *Other relevant items.*—(i) *In general.*—For purposes of section 59A, subject to paragraph (b)(4) of this section, each partner is treated as owning its share of the partnership items determined under section 704, including the assets of the partnership, using a reasonable method with respect to the assets. For items that are allocated to the partners, the partner is treated as owning its distributive share (including of deductions and base erosion tax benefits). For items that are not allocated to the partners, the partner is treated as owning an interest proportionate with the partner's distributive share of partnership income.

(ii) *Gross receipts.*—(A) *In general.*—For purposes of section 59A, each partner in the partnership includes a share of partnership gross receipts in proportion to the partner's distributive share (as determined under section 704) of items of gross income that were taken into account by the partnership under section 703.

(B) *Foreign corporation.*—A foreign corporation takes into account a share of gross receipts only with regard to receipts that produce income that is effectively connected with the conduct of a trade or business within the United States. In the case of a foreign corporation that determines its net taxable income under an applicable income tax treaty, the foreign corporation takes into account its share of gross receipts only with regard to such gross receipts that are taken into account in determining its net taxable income.

(iii) *Registered securities dealers.*—If a partnership, or a branch of the partnership, is a registered securities dealer, each partner is treated as a registered securities dealer unless the partner's interest in the registered securities dealer would satisfy the criteria for the exception in paragraph (b)(4) of this section. For purposes of applying the de minimis exception in § 1.59A-2(e)(2)(iii), the partner takes into account its distributive share of the relevant partnership items.

(iv) *Application of sections 163(j) and 59A(c)(3) to partners of partnerships.*—See § 1.59A-3(c)(4).

(6) *Tiered partnerships.*—If the partner of a partnership is a partnership, then paragraphs (b) and (c) of this section are applied again at the level of the partner, applying this paragraph successively until the partner is not a partnership. Paragraph (b)(4) of this section is only applied at the level where the partner is not itself a partnership.

(c) *Foreign related party.*—With respect to any person that owns an interest in a partnership, the related party determination in section 59A(g) applies at the partner level. [Reg. § 1.59A-7.]

[Proposed 12-21-2018.]

**[Prop. Reg. § 1.59A-8]**

**§ 1.59A-8. Application of base erosion and anti-abuse tax to certain expatriated entities.**—[Reserved]

[Reg. § 1.59A-8.]

[Proposed 12-21-2018.]

**[Prop. Reg. § 1.59A-9]**

**§ 1.59A-9. Anti-abuse and recharacterization rules.**—(a) *Scope.*—This section provides rules for recharacterizing certain transactions according to their substance for purposes of applying section 59A and the section 59A regulations. Paragraph (b) of this section provides specific anti-abuse rules. Paragraph (c) of this section provides examples illustrating the rules of paragraph (b) of this section.

(b) *Anti-abuse rules.*—(1) *Transactions involving unrelated persons, conduits, or intermediaries.*—If a taxpayer pays or accrues an amount to one or more intermediaries (including an intermediary unrelated to the taxpayer) that would have been a base erosion payment if paid or accrued to a foreign related party, and one or more of the intermediaries makes (directly or indirectly) corresponding payments to or for the benefit of a foreign related party as part of a transaction (or series of transactions), plan or arrangement that has as a principal purpose avoiding a base erosion payment (or reducing the amount of a base erosion payment), the role of the intermediary or intermediaries is disregarded as a conduit, or the amount paid or accrued to the intermediary is treated as a base erosion payment, as appropriate.

(2) *Transactions to increase the amount of deductions taken into account in the denominator of the base erosion percentage computation.*—A transaction (or component of a transaction or series of transactions), plan or arrangement that has a principal purpose of increasing the deductions taken into account for purposes of § 1.59A-2(e)(3)(i)(B) (the denominator of the base erosion percentage computation) is disregarded for purposes of § 1.59A-2(e)(3).

(3) *Transactions to avoid the application of rules applicable to banks and registered securities dealers.*—A transaction (or series of transactions), plan or arrangement that occurs among related parties that has a principal purpose of avoiding the rules applicable to certain banks and registered securities dealers in § 1.59A-2(e)(2) (base erosion percentage test for banks and registered securities dealers) or § 1.59A-5(c)(2) (increased base erosion and anti-abuse tax rate for banks and registered securities dealers) is not taken into account for purposes of § 1.59A-2(e)(2) or § 1.59A-5(c)(2).

(c) *Examples.*—The following examples illustrate the application of paragraph (b) of this section. For purposes of all of the examples, assume that FP, a foreign corporation, owns all the stock of DC, a domestic corporation and an applicable taxpayer and that none of the foreign corporations are subject to federal income taxation with respect to income that is, or is treated as, effectively connected with the conduct of a trade or business in the United States under an applicable provision of the Internal Revenue Code or regulations thereunder. Also assume that all payments occur in a taxable year beginning after December 31, 2017.

(1) *Example 1: Substitution of payments that are not base erosion payments for payments that otherwise would be base erosion payments through a conduit or intermediary.* (i) *Facts.* FP owns Property 1 with a fair market value of $95x, which FP intends to transfer to DC. A payment from DC to FP for Property 1 would be a base erosion payment. Corp A is a domestic corporation that is not a related party with respect to DC. As part of a plan with a principal purpose of avoiding a base erosion payment, FP enters into an arrangement with Corp A to transfer Property 1 to Corp A in exchange for $95x. Pursuant to the same plan, Corp A transfers Property 1 to DC in exchange for $100x. Property 1 is subject to the allowance for depreciation (or amortization in lieu of depreciation) in the hands of DC.

(ii) *Analysis.* The arrangement between FP, DC, and Corp A is deemed to result in a $95x base erosion payment under paragraph (b)(1) of this section because DC's payment to Corp A would have been a base erosion payment if paid to a foreign related person, and Corp A makes a corresponding payment to FP as part of the series of transactions that has as a principal purpose avoiding a base erosion payment.

(2) *Example 2: Alternative transaction to base erosion payment.* (i) *Facts.* The facts are the same as in paragraph (c)(1)(i) of this section (the facts in *Example 1*), except that DC does not purchase Property 1 from FP or Corp A. Instead, DC purchases Property 2 from Corp B, a domestic corporation that is not a related party with respect to DC and that originally produced or acquired Property 2 for Corp B's own account. Property 2 is substantially similar to Property 1, and DC uses Property 2 in substantially the same manner that DC would have used Property 1.

(ii) *Analysis.* Paragraph (b)(1) of this section does not apply to the transaction between DC and Corp B because Corp B does not make a corresponding payment to or for the benefit of FP as part of a transaction, plan or arrangement.

(3) *Example 3: Alternative financing source.* (i) *Facts.* On Date 1, FP loaned $200x to DC in exchange for Note A. DC pays or accrues interest annually on Note A, and the payment or accrual is a base erosion payment within the meaning of § 1.59A-3(b)(1)(i). On Date 2, DC borrows $200x from Bank, a corporation that is not a related party with respect to DC, in exchange for Note B. The terms of Note B are substantially similar to the terms of Note A. DC uses the proceeds from Note B to repay Note A.

(ii) *Analysis.* Paragraph (b)(1) of this section does not apply to the transaction between DC and Bank because Bank does not make a corresponding payment to or for the benefit of FP as part of the series of transactions.

(4) *Example 4: Alternative financing source that is a conduit.* (i) *Facts.* The facts are the same as in paragraph (c)(3)(i) of this section (the facts in *Example 3*) except that in addition, with a principal purpose of avoiding a base erosion payment, and as part of the same plan or arrangement as the Note B transaction, FP deposits $250x with Bank. The difference between the interest rate paid by Bank to FP on FP's deposit and the interest rate paid by DC to Bank is less than one percentage point. The interest rate charged by Bank to DC would have differed absent the deposit by FP.

(ii) *Analysis.* The transactions between FP, DC, and Bank are deemed to result in a base erosion payment under paragraph (b)(1) of this section because DC's payment to Bank would have been a base erosion payment if paid to a foreign related person, and Bank makes a corresponding payment to FP as part of the series of transactions that has a principal purpose avoiding a base erosion payment. See Rev. Rul. 87-89, 1987-2 C.B. 195, Situation 3.

(5) *Example 5: Transactions to increase the amount of deductions taken into account in the denominator of the base erosion percentage computation.* (i) *Facts.* With a principal purpose of increasing the deductions taken into account by DC for purposes of § 1.59A-2(e)(3)(i)(B), DC enters into a long position with respect to Asset with Financial Institution 1 and simultaneously enters into a short position with respect to Asset with Financial Institution 2. Financial Institution 1 and Financial Institution 2 are not related to DC and are not related to each other.

(ii) *Analysis.* Paragraph (b)(2) of this section applies and the transactions between DC and Financial Institution 1 and DC and Financial Institution 2. These transactions are not taken into account for purposes of § 1.59A-2(e)(3)(i)(B) because the transactions have a principal purpose of increasing the deductions taken into account for purposes of § 1.59A-2(e)(3)(i)(B). [Reg. § 1.59A-9.]

[Proposed 12-21-2018.]

### [Prop. Reg. § 1.59A-10]

**§ 1.59A-10. Applicability date.**—Sections 1.59A-1 through 1.59A-9 apply to taxable years beginning after December 31, 2017. [Reg. § 1.59A-10.]

[Proposed 12-21-2018.]

### [Prop. Reg. § 1.78-1]

**§ 1.78-1. Gross up for deemed paid foreign tax credit.**—(a) *Taxes deemed paid by certain domestic corporations treated as a dividend.*—If a domestic corporation chooses to have the benefits of the foreign tax credit under section 901 for any taxable year, an amount that is equal to the foreign income taxes deemed to be paid by the corporation for the year under section 960 (in the case of section 960(d), determined without regard to the phrase "80 percent of" in section 960(d)(1)) is, to the extent provided by this section, treated as a dividend (a *section 78 dividend*) received by the domestic corporation from the foreign corporation. A section 78 dividend is treated as a dividend for all purposes of the Code, except that it is not treated as a dividend for purposes of section 245 or 245A, and does not increase the earnings and profits of the domestic corporation or decrease the earnings and profits of the foreign corporation. Any reduction under section 907(a) of the foreign income taxes deemed paid with respect to combined foreign oil and gas income does not affect the amount treated as a section 78 dividend. *See* § 1.907(a)-1(e)(3). Similarly, any reduction under section 901(e) of the foreign income taxes deemed paid with respect to foreign mineral income does not affect the amount treated as a section 78 dividend. *See* § 1.901-3(a)(2)(i), (b)(2)(i)(b), and (d), *Example 8.* Any reduction under section 6038(c)(1)(B) in the foreign taxes paid or accrued by a foreign corporation is taken into account in determining foreign taxes deemed paid and the amount treated as a section 78 dividend. See, for example, § 1.6038-2(k)(5), *Example 1.* To the extent provided in the Code, section 78 does not apply to any tax not allowed as a credit. See, for example, sections 901(j)(3), 901(k)(7), 901(l)(4), 901(m)(6), and 908(b). For rules on determining the source of a section 78 dividend in computing the limitation on the foreign tax credit under section 904, see § § 1.861-3(a)(3), 1.862-1(a)(1)(ii), and 1.904-5(m)(6). For rules on assigning a section 78 dividend to a separate category, see § 1.904-4(o).

(b) *Date on which section 78 dividend is received.*—A section 78 dividend is considered received by a domestic corporation on the date on which—

(1) The corporation includes in gross income under section 951(a)(1)(A) the amounts by reason of which there are deemed paid under section 960(a) the foreign income taxes that give rise to that section 78 dividend, notwithstanding that the foreign income taxes may be carried back or carried over to another taxable year and deemed to be paid or accrued in such other taxable year under section 904(c); or

(2) The corporation includes in gross income under section 951A(a) the amounts by reason of which there are deemed paid under section 960(d) the foreign income taxes that give rise to that section 78 dividend.

(c) *Applicability date.*—This section applies to taxable years of foreign corporations that begin after December 31, 2017, and to taxable years of United States shareholders in which or with which such taxable years of foreign corporations end. The second sentence of paragraph (a) of this section also applies to section 78 dividends that are received after December 31, 2017, by reason

of taxes deemed paid under section 960(a) with respect to a taxable year of a foreign corporation beginning before January 1, 2018.

[Proposed 12-7-2018.]

**[Prop. Reg. § 1.163(j)-1]**

**§ 1.163(j)-1. Definitions.**—(a) *In general.*— This section defines terms used in the section 163(j) regulations. For purposes of the rules sets forth in § § 1.163(j)-2 through 1.163(j)-11, additional definitions for certain terms are provided in those sections.

(b) *Definitions.*—(1) *Adjusted taxable income.*— The term *adjusted taxable income* (ATI) means the taxable income of the taxpayer for the taxable year, with the adjustments in this paragraph (b).

(i) *Additions.*—The amounts of the following items (if any) are added to taxable income to determine ATI —

(A) Any business interest expense;

(B) Any net operating loss deduction under section 172;

(C) Any deduction under section 199A;

(D) For taxable years beginning before January 1, 2022, any deduction for depreciation under section 167, section 168, or section 168 of the Internal Revenue Code of 1954 (former section 168);

(E) For taxable years beginning before January 1, 2022, any deduction for the amortization of intangibles (for example, under section 167 or 197) and other amortized expenditures (for example, under section 195(b)(1)(B), 248, or 1245(a)(2)(C));

(F) For taxable years beginning before January 1, 2022, any deduction for depletion under section 611;

(G) Any deduction for a capital loss carryback or carryover; and

(H) Any deduction or loss that is not properly allocable to a non-excepted trade or business (for rules governing the allocation of items to an excepted trade or business, see § § 1.163(j)-1(b)(38) and 1.163(j)-10).

(ii) *Subtractions.*—The amounts of the following items (if any) are subtracted from taxable income to determine ATI—

(A) Any business interest income;

(B) Any floor plan financing interest expense for the taxable year;

(C) With respect to the sale or other disposition of property, the lesser of:

*(1)* Any gain recognized on the sale or other disposition of such property; and

*(2)* Any depreciation, amortization, or depletion deductions for the taxable years beginning after December 31, 2017, and before January 1, 2022, with respect to such property;

(D) With respect to the sale or other disposition of stock of a member of a consolidated group that includes the selling member, the investment adjustments, as defined under

**Prop. Reg. § 1.163(j)-1(b)(1)(ii)(D)**

§1.1502-32, with respect to such stock that are attributable to deductions described in paragraph (b)(1)(ii)(C) of this section;

(E) With respect to the sale or other disposition of an interest in a partnership, the taxpayer's distributive share of deductions described in paragraph (b)(1)(ii)(C) of this section with respect to property held by the partnership at the time of such sale or other disposition to the extent such deductions were allowable under section 704(d); and

(F) Any income or gain that is not properly allocable to a non-excepted trade or business (for rules governing the allocation of items to an excepted trade or business, see §§1.163(j)-1(b)(38) and 1.163(j)-10)).

(iii) *Depreciation, amortization, or depletion expenses capitalized to inventory under section 263A.*—Depreciation, amortization, or depletion expense that is capitalized to inventory under section 263A is not a depreciation, amortization, or depletion deduction for purposes of this paragraph (b)(1).

(iv) *Other adjustments.*—ATI is computed with the other adjustments provided in §§1.163(j)-2 through 1.163(j)-11.

(v) *Additional rules relating to adjusted taxable income in other sections.*—(A) For rules governing the ATI of C corporations, see §§1.163(j)-4(b)(2) and (3) and 1.163(j)-10(a)(2)(ii).

(B) For rules governing the ATI of RICs and REITs, see §1.163(j)-4(b)(4).

(C) For rules governing the ATI of tax-exempt corporations, see §1.163(j)-4(b)(5).

(D) For rules governing the ATI of consolidated groups, see §1.163(j)-4(d)(2)(iv) and (v).

(E) For rules governing the ATI of partnerships, see §1.163(j)-6(d).

(F) For rules governing the ATI of partners, see §1.163(j)-6(e).

(G) For rules governing partnership basis adjustments impacting ATI, see §1.163(j)-6(h)(2).

(H) For rules governing the ATI of S corporations, see §1.163(j)-6(l)(3).

(I) For rules governing the ATI of S corporation shareholders, see §1.163(j)-6(l)(4).

(J) For rules governing the ATI of applicable CFCs and certain CFC group members, as defined in §1.163(j)-7(f), see §1.163(j)-7(c).

(K) For rules governing the ATI of United States shareholders of applicable CFCs, including the treatment of inclusions under sections 78, 951(a), and 951A(a), see §1.163(j)-7(d).

(L) For rules governing the ATI of specified foreign persons, as defined in §1.163(j)-8(g)(7), with effectively connected income, see §1.163(j)-8(b)(2).

(M) For rules governing the ATI of specified foreign partners, as defined in §1.163(j)-8(g)(6), other than applicable CFCs, as defined in §1.163(j)-8(g)(1), see §1.163(j)-8(c)(1).

(N) For rules governing the ATI of certain beneficiaries of trusts and estates, see §1.163(j)-2(f).

(2) *Business interest expense.*—(i) *In general.*—The term *business interest expense* means interest expense that is properly allocable to a non-excepted trade or business or that is floor plan financing interest expense. Business interest expense also includes disallowed business interest expense carryforwards (as defined in paragraph (b)(9) of this section). For the treatment of investment interest, see section 163(d); and for the treatment of personal interest, see section 163(h).

(ii) *Special rules.*—For special rules for defining business interest expense in certain circumstances, see §§1.163(j)-3(b)(2) (regarding disallowed interest expense), 1.163(j)-4(b) (regarding C corporations) and (d)(2)(iii) (regarding consolidated groups), and 1.163(j)-8(b)(3) (regarding foreign persons engaged in a U.S. trade or business).

(3) *Business interest income.*—(i) *In general.*—The term *business interest income* means interest income which is properly allocable to a non-excepted trade or business. For the treatment of investment income, see section 163(d).

(ii) *Special rules.*—For special rules defining business interest income in certain circumstances, see §§1.163(j)-4(b) (regarding C corporations) and (d)(2)(iii) (regarding consolidated groups) and 1.163(j)-8(b)(4) (regarding foreign persons engaged in a U.S. trade or business).

(4) *C corporation.*—The term *C corporation* has the meaning provided in section 1361(a)(2).

(5) *Cleared swap.*—The term *cleared swap* means a swap that is cleared by a derivatives clearing organization, as such term is defined in section 1a of the Commodity Exchange Act (7 U.S.C. 1a), or by a clearing agency, as such term is defined in section 3 of the Securities Exchange Act of 1934 (15 U.S.C. 78c), that is registered as a derivatives clearing organization under the Commodity Exchange Act or as a clearing agency under the Securities Exchange Act of 1934, respectively, if the derivatives clearing organization or clearing agency requires the parties to the swap to post and collect margin or collateral.

(6) *Consolidated group.*—The term *consolidated group* has the meaning provided in §1.1502-1(h).

(7) *Consolidated return year.*—The term *consolidated return year* has the meaning provided in §1.1502-1(d).

(8) *Disallowed business interest expense.*—The term *disallowed business interest expense* means the amount of business interest expense for a taxable year in excess of the amount allowed as a deduc-

tion for the taxable year under section 163(j)(1) and § 1.163(j)-2(b).

(9) *Disallowed business interest expense carryforward.*—The term *disallowed business interest expense carryforward* means any business interest expense described in § 1.163(j)-2(c).

(10) *Disallowed disqualified interest.*—The term *disallowed disqualified interest* means interest expense, including carryforwards, for which a deduction was disallowed under old section 163(j) (as defined in paragraph (b)(26) of this section) in the taxpayer's last taxable year beginning before January 1, 2018, and that was carried forward pursuant to old section 163(j).

(11) *Electing farming business.*—The term *electing farming business* means a trade or business that makes an election as provided in § 1.163(j)-9 or other published guidance and that is—

(i) A farming business, as defined in section 263A(e)(4) or § 1.263A-4(a)(4); or

(ii) Any trade or business of a specified agricultural or horticultural cooperative, as defined in section 199A(g)(4).

(12) *Electing real property trade or business.*—The term *electing real property trade or business* means a trade or business that makes an election as provided in § 1.163(j)-9 or other published guidance and that is described in—

(i) Section 469(c)(7)(C) and § 1.469-9(b)(2); or

(ii) Section 1.163(j)-9(g).

(13) *Excepted regulated utility trade or business.*—(i) *In general.*—The term *excepted regulated utility trade or business* means a trade or business—

(A) That furnishes or sells:

(1) Electrical energy, water, or sewage disposal services;

(2) Gas or steam through a local distribution system; or

(3) Transportation of gas or steam by pipeline; and

(B) To the extent that the rates for the furnishing or sale of the items in paragraph (b)(13)(i)(A) of this section—

(1) Have been established or approved by a State or political subdivision thereof, by any agency or instrumentality of the United States, or by a public service or public utility commission or other similar body of any State or political subdivision thereof and are determined on a cost of service and rate of return basis; or

(2) Have been established or approved by the governing or ratemaking body of an electric cooperative.

(ii) *Excepted and non-excepted utility trades or businesses.*—If a taxpayer is engaged in both an excepted trade or business and a non-excepted trade or business described in this paragraph (b)(13), the taxpayer must allocate items between the trades or businesses. See §§ 1.163(j)-1(b)(38) and 1.163(j)-10(c)(3)(iii)(C). Some trades or businesses with de minimis furnishing or sales of items described in paragraph (b)(13)(i)(A) of this section that are not sold pursuant to rates determined on a cost of service and rate of return basis as required in paragraph (b)(13)(i)(B)(1) of this section, or by the governing or ratemaking body of an electric cooperative as required in paragraph (b)(13)(i)(B)(2) of this section are treated as excepted trades or businesses. See § 1.163(j)-10(c)(3)(iii)(C)(3).

(14) *Excess business interest expense.*—The term *excess business interest expense* means, with respect to a partnership, the amount of disallowed business interest expense of the partnership for a taxable year under section § 1.163(j)-2(b), except as provided in § 1.163(j)-6(h)(2).

(15) *Excess taxable income.*—With respect to any partnership or S corporation, the term *excess taxable income* means the amount which bears the same ratio to the partnership's ATI as—

(i) The excess (if any) of—

(A) The amount determined for the partnership or S corporation under section 163(j)(1)(B); over

(B) The amount (if any) by which the business interest expense of the partnership, reduced by the floor plan financing interest expense, exceeds the business interest income of the partnership or S corporation; bears to

(ii) The amount determined for the partnership or S corporation under section 163(j)(1)(B).

(16) *Floor plan financing indebtedness.*—The term floor plan financing indebtedness means indebtedness—

(i) Used to finance the acquisition of motor vehicles held for sale or lease; and

(ii) Secured by the inventory so acquired.

(17) *Floor plan financing interest expense.*—The term *floor plan financing interest expense* means interest paid or accrued on floor plan financing indebtedness. For purposes of the section 163(j) regulations, all floor plan financing interest expense is treated as business interest expense. See paragraph (b)(2) of this section.

(18) *Group.*—The term *group* has the meaning provided in § 1.1502-1(a).

(19) *Intercompany transaction.*—The term *intercompany transaction* has the meaning provided in § 1.1502-13(b)(1)(i).

(20) *Interest.*—The term *interest* means any amount described in paragraph (b)(20)(i), (ii), (iii), or (iv) of this section.

(i) *In general.*—Interest is an amount paid, received, or accrued as compensation for the use or forbearance of money under the terms of an instrument or contractual arrangement, including a series of transactions, that is treated as a debt instrument for purposes of section 1275(a) and § 1.1275-1(d), and not treated as stock under § 1.385-3, or an amount that is treated as interest under other provisions of the Internal Revenue Code (Code) or the regulations thereunder. Thus, for example, interest includes—

(A) Original issue discount (OID), as adjusted by the holder for any acquisition premium or amortizable bond premium;

(B) Qualified stated interest, as adjusted by the holder for any amortizable bond premium or by the issuer for any bond issuance premium;

(C) Acquisition discount;

(D) Amounts treated as taxable OID under section 1286 (relating to stripped bonds and stripped coupons);

(E) Accrued market discount on a market discount bond to the extent includible in income by the holder under either section 1276(a) or 1278(b);

(F) OID includible in income by a holder that has made an election under § 1.1272-3 to treat all interest on a debt instrument as OID;

(G) OID on a synthetic debt instrument arising from an integrated transaction under § 1.1275-6;

(H) Repurchase premium to the extent deductible by the issuer under § 1.163-7(c);

(I) Deferred payments treated as interest under section 483;

(J) Amounts treated as interest under a section 467 rental agreement;

(K) Amounts treated as interest under section 988;

(L) Forgone interest under section 7872;

(M) De minimis OID taken into account by the issuer;

(N) Amounts paid or received in connection with a sale-repurchase agreement treated as indebtedness under Federal tax principles; in the case of a sale-repurchase agreement relating to tax-exempt bonds, however, the amount is not tax-exempt interest;

(O) Redeemable ground rent treated as interest under section 163(c); and

(P) Amounts treated as interest under section 636.

(ii) *Swaps with significant nonperiodic payments.*—(A) *Non-cleared swaps.*—A swap other than a cleared swap with significant nonperiodic payments is treated as two separate transactions consisting of an on-market, level payment swap and a loan. The loan must be accounted for by the parties to the contract independently of the swap. The time value component associated with the loan, determined in accordance with § 1.446-3(f)(2)(iii)(A), is recognized as interest expense to the payor and interest income to the recipient.

(B) [Reserved]

(iii) *Other amounts treated as interest.*—(A) *Treatment of premium.*—(1) *Issuer.*—If a debt instrument is issued at a premium within the meaning of § 1.163-13, any ordinary income under § 1.163-13(d)(4) is treated as interest income of the issuer.

(2) *Holder.*—If a taxable debt instrument is acquired at a premium within the meaning of § 1.171-1 and the holder elects to amortize the premium, any amount otherwise deductible under section 171(a)(1) as a bond premium deduction under § 1.171-2(a)(4)(i)(A) or (C) is treated as interest expense of the holder.

(B) *Treatment of ordinary income or loss on certain debt instruments.*—If an issuer of a contingent payment debt instrument subject to § 1.1275-4(b), a nonfunctional currency contingent payment debt instrument subject to § 1.988-6, or an inflation-indexed debt instrument subject to § 1.1275-7 recognizes ordinary income on the debt instrument in accordance with the rules in § 1.1275-4(b), § 1.988-6(b)(2), or § 1.1275-7(f), whichever is applicable, the ordinary income is treated as interest income of the issuer. If a holder of a contingent payment debt instrument subject to § 1.1275-4(b), a nonfunctional currency contingent payment debt instrument subject to § 1.988-6, or an inflation-indexed debt instrument subject to § 1.1275-7 recognizes an ordinary loss on the debt instrument in accordance with the rules in § 1.1275-4(b), § 1.988-6(b)(2), or § 1.1275-7(f), whichever is applicable, the ordinary loss is treated as interest expense of the holder.

(C) *Substitute interest payments.*—A substitute interest payment described in § 1.861-2(a)(7) is treated as interest expense to the payor or interest income to the recipient; in the case of a sale-repurchase agreement or a securities lending transaction relating to tax-exempt bonds, however, the recipient of a substitute payment does not receive tax-exempt interest income.

(D) *Section 1258 gain.*—Any gain treated as ordinary gain under section 1258 is treated as interest income.

(E) *Amounts affecting a taxpayer's effective cost of borrowing.*—Income, deduction, gain, or loss from a derivative, as defined in section 59A(h)(4)(A), that alters a taxpayer's effective cost of borrowing with respect to a liability of the taxpayer is treated as an adjustment to interest expense of the taxpayer. For example, a taxpayer that is obligated to pay interest at a floating rate on a note and enters into an interest rate swap that entitles the taxpayer to receive an amount that is equal to or that closely approximates the interest rate on the note in exchange for a fixed amount is, in effect, paying interest expense at a fixed rate by entering into the interest rate swap. Income, deduction, gain, or loss from the swap is treated as an adjustment to interest expense. Similarly, any gain or loss resulting from a termi-

**Prop. Reg. § 1.163(j)-1(b)(20)(i)(A)**

nation or other disposition of the swap is an adjustment to interest expense, with the timing of gain or loss subject to the rules of § 1.446-4.

(F) *Yield adjustments.*—Income, deduction, gain, or loss from a derivative, as defined in section 59A(h)(4)(A), that alters a taxpayer's effective yield with respect to a debt instrument held by the taxpayer is treated as an adjustment to interest income by the taxpayer.

(G) *Certain amounts labeled as fees.—* (1) *Commitment fees.*—Any fees in respect of a lender commitment to provide financing are treated as interest if any portion of such financing is actually provided.

(2) [Reserved]

(H) *Debt issuance costs.*—Any debt issuance costs subject to § 1.446-5 are treated as interest expense of the issuer.

(I) *Guaranteed payments.*—Any guaranteed payments for the use of capital under section 707(c) are treated as interest.

(J) *Factoring income.*—The excess of the amount that a taxpayer collects on a factored receivable (or realizes upon the sale or other disposition of the factored receivable) over the amount paid for the factored receivable by the taxpayer is treated as interest income. For purposes of this paragraph (b)(20)(iii)(J), the term *factored receivable* includes any account receivable or other evidence of indebtedness, whether or not issued at a discount and whether or not bearing stated interest, arising out of the disposition of property or the performance of services by any person, if such account receivable or evidence of indebtedness is acquired by a person other than the person who disposed of the property or provided the services that gave rise to the account receivable or evidence of indebtedness.

(iv) *Anti-avoidance rule for amounts predominantly associated with the time value of money.*—Any expense or loss, to the extent deductible, incurred by a taxpayer in a transaction or series of integrated or related transactions in which the taxpayer secures the use of funds for a period of time is treated as interest expense of the taxpayer if such expense or loss is predominantly incurred in consideration of the time value of money.

(v) *Examples.*—The examples in this paragraph (b)(20)(v) illustrate the application of paragraphs (b)(20)(i) through (iv) of this section. Unless otherwise indicated, assume the following: A, B, C, D, and Bank are domestic C corporations that are publicly traded; the exemption for certain small businesses in § 1.163(j)-2(d) does not apply; A is not engaged in an excepted trade or business; and all amounts of interest expense are deductible except for the potential application of section 163(j).

(A) *Example 1*—(1) *Facts.* (i) A is a calendar year taxpayer that is engaged in a manufacturing business. In January 2019, A, which has an in-

vestment-grade credit rating, enters into the following transactions (the transactions): Bank transfers a portfolio of U.S. Treasury bonds (the Treasury portfolio) to A; A agrees to pay Bank an amount equivalent to any interest paid on the Treasury portfolio during the transactions and a fee for lending the Treasury portfolio to A; A agrees to return to Bank securities that are substantially identical to the Treasury portfolio upon request, regardless of any value increases or decreases in the market value of the Treasury portfolio; A rehypothecates the Treasury portfolio in exchange for cash, which A uses to purchase a portfolio of corporate bonds (the debt portfolio); and the transactions remain in place for the duration of the 2019 calendar year until Bank delivers a notice to A recalling the Treasury portfolio 5 business days before December 31, 2019.

(ii) The obligations undertaken with respect to the transactions are not collateralized. Assume that the transactions do not result in a sale-repurchase agreement treated as indebtedness under Federal tax principles. During the course of the transactions, the debt portfolio generates $70x of interest income. The Treasury portfolio generates $60x of interest income during the course of the transactions and A pays $60x to Bank under its obligation to pay amounts equivalent to the interest paid on the Treasury portfolio.

(2) *Analysis.* The transactions involving Bank and A are transactions described in paragraph (b)(20)(iii)(C) of this section. Consequently, the $60x of substitute interest payments that A paid to Bank in 2019 is treated as interest expense for purposes of section 163(j). In addition, the $70x of interest income generated by the debt portfolio is interest income to A.

(B) *Example 2*—(1) *Facts.* A is a calendar year taxpayer that is engaged in a manufacturing business. In early 2019, A enters into the following transactions:

(i) A enters into a loan obligation in which A borrows Japanese yen from Bank in an amount equivalent to $2000x with an interest rate of 1 percent (at the time of the loan, the U.S. dollar equivalent interest rate on a loan of $2,000x is 5 percent); and

(ii) A enters into a foreign currency swap transaction (FX Swap) with Bank with a notional principal amount of $2000x under which A receives Japanese yen at 1 percent multiplied by the amount of Japanese yen borrowed from Bank (which for 2019 equals $20x) and pays U.S. dollars at 5 percent multiplied by a notional amount of $2000x ($100x per year). The FX Swap is not integrated with the loan obligation under § 1.988-5.

(2) *Analysis.* The FX Swap alters A's cost of borrowing within the meaning of paragraph (b)(20)(iii)(E) of this section. As a result, for purposes of section 163(j), the $100x paid by A to Bank on the FX Swap is treated by A as interest expense and the $20x paid by Bank to A on the FX Swap is treated by A as a reduction of interest expense.

**Prop. Reg. § 1.163(j)-1(b)(20)(v)**

(C) *Example 3*—(1) *Facts.* A borrows from B two ounces of gold at a time when the spot price for gold is $500x per ounce. A agrees to return the two ounces of gold in six months. A sells the two ounces of gold to C for $1,000x. A then enters into a contract with D to purchase two ounces of gold six months in the future for $1,013x. In exchange for the use of $1,000x in cash, A has sustained a loss of $13x on related transactions.

(2) *Analysis.* A has obtained the use of $1,000x and, in a series of related transactions, created a loss of $13x predominantly associated with the time value of money. As a result, for purposes of section 163(j), the loss of $13x is treated as interest expense under paragraph (b)(20)(iv) of this section.

(21) *Interest expense.*—The term *interest expense* means interest that is paid or accrued, or treated as paid or accrued, for the taxable year.

(22) *Interest income.*—The term *interest income* means interest that is included in gross income for the taxable year.

(23) *Inventory.*—The term *inventory* means property held for sale or for lease, or both, by a taxpayer in the ordinary course of its trade or business.

(24) *Member.*—The term *member* has the meaning provided in § 1.1502-1(b).

(25) *Motor vehicle.*—The term *motor vehicle* means a motor vehicle as defined in section 163(j)(9)(C).

(26) *Old section 163(j).*—The term *old section 163(j)* means section 163(j) immediately prior to its amendment by Public Law 115-97, 131 Stat. 2054 (2017).

(27) *Real estate investment trust.*—The term *real estate investment trust* (REIT) has the meaning provided in section 856.

(28) *Real property.*—The term *real property* includes—

(i) Real property as defined in § 1.469-9(b)(2); and

(ii) Any direct or indirect right, including a license or other contractual right, to share in the appreciation in value of, or the gross or net proceeds or profits generated by, an interest in real property, including net proceeds or profits associated with tolls, rents or other similar fees.

(29) *Regulated investment company.*—The term *regulated investment company* (RIC) has the meaning provided in section 851.

(30) *S corporation.*—The term *S corporation* has the meaning provided in section 1361(a)(1).

(31) *Section 163(j) limitation.*—The term *section 163(j) limitation* means the limit on the amount of business interest expense that a taxpayer may deduct in a taxable year under section 163(j) and § 1.163(j)-2(b).

(32) *Section 163(j) regulations.*—The term *section 163(j) regulations* means this section and §§ 1.163(j)-2 through 1.163(j)-11.

(33) *Separate return limitation year.*—The term *separate return limitation year* (SRLY) has the meaning provided in § 1.1502-1(f).

(34) *Separate return year.*—The term *separate return year* has the meaning provided in § 1.1502-1(e).

(35) *Separate taxable income.*—The term *separate taxable income* has the meaning provided in § 1.1502-12.

(36) *Tax-exempt corporation.*—The term *tax-exempt corporation* means any corporation subject to tax under section 511.

(37) *Taxable income.*—(i) *In general.*—The term *taxable income*, with respect to a taxpayer and a taxable year, has the meaning provided in section 63, but for this purpose computed without regard to the application of section 163(j) and the section 163(j) regulations.

(ii) *General rules to coordinate the application of sections 163(j) and 250.*—If for a taxable year a taxpayer is allowed a deduction under section 250(a)(1) that is properly allocable to a non-excepted trade or business, then taxable income for the taxable year is determined without regard to the limitation in section 250(a)(2). For this purpose, the amount of the deduction allowed under section 250(a)(1), without regard to the limitation in section 250(a)(2), is determined without regard to the application of section 163(j) and the section 163(j) regulations.

(iii) [Reserved]

(iv) *Special rules for defining taxable income.*—(A) For special rules defining the taxable income of a RIC or REIT, see § 1.163(j)-4(b)(4)(ii).

(B) For special rules defining the taxable income of consolidated groups, see § 1.163(j)-4(d)(2)(iv).

(C) For special rules defining the taxable income of a partnership, see § 1.163(j)-6(d)(1).

(D) For special rules defining the taxable income of an S corporation, see § 1.163(j)-6(l)(3).

(E) For special rules defining the taxable income of certain controlled foreign corporations, see § 1.163(j)-7(c)(1).

(38) *Trade or business.*—(i) *In general.*—The term *trade or business* means a trade or business within the meaning of section 162.

(ii) *Excepted trade or business.*—The term *excepted trade or business* means a trade or business that is described in paragraphs (b)(38)(ii)(A) through (D) of this section. For additional rules related to excepted trades or businesses, including elections made under section 163(j)(7)(B) and (C), see § 1.163(j)-9.

(A) The trade or business of performing services as an employee.

(B) Any electing real property trade or business.

(C) Any electing farming business.

(D) Any excepted regulated utility trade or business.

(iii) *Non-excepted trade or business.*—The term *non-excepted trade or business* means any trade or business that is not an excepted trade or business.

(39) *Unadjusted basis.*—The term *unadjusted basis* means the basis as determined under section 1012 or other applicable sections of chapter 1 of subtitle A of the Code, including subchapters O (relating to gain or loss on dispositions of property), C (relating to corporate distributions and adjustments), K (relating to partners and partnerships), and P (relating to capital gains and losses) of the Code. Unadjusted basis is determined without regard to any adjustments described in section 1016(a)(2) or (3), to any adjustments for tax credits claimed by the taxpayer (for example, under section 50(c)), or to any adjustments for any portion of the basis for which the taxpayer has elected to treat as an expense (for example, under section 179, 179B, or 179C).

(c) *Applicability date.*—This section applies to taxable years ending after the date the Treasury decision adopting these regulations as final regulations is published in the **Federal Register**. However, taxpayers and their related parties, within the meaning of sections 267(b) and 707(b)(1), may apply the rules of this section to a taxable year beginning after December 31, 2017, so long as the taxpayers and their related parties consistently apply the rules of the section 163(j) regulations, and if applicable, §§ 1.263A-9, 1.381(c)(20)-1, 1.382-6, 1.383-1, 1.469-9, 1.882-5, 1.1502-13, 1.1502-21, 1.1502-36, 1.1502-79, 1.1502-91 through 1.1502-99, (to the extent they effectuate the rules of §§ 1.382-6 and 1.383-1), and 1.1504-4 to those taxable years. [Reg. § 1.163(j)-1.]

[Proposed 12-28-2018.]

### [Prop. Reg. § 1.163(j)-2]

**§ 1.163(j)-2. Deduction for business interest expense limited.**—(a) *Overview.*—This section provides general rules regarding the section 163(j) limitation. Paragraph (b) of this section provides rules regarding the basic computation of the section 163(j) limitation. Paragraph (c) of this section provides rules for disallowed business interest expense carryforwards. Paragraph (d) of this section provides rules regarding the small business exemption from the section 163(j) limitation. Paragraph (e) of this section provides rules regarding real estate mortgage investment conduits (REMICs). Paragraph (f) of this section provides examples illustrating the application of this section. Paragraph (g) of this section provides an anti-avoidance rule.

(b) *General rule.*—Except as otherwise provided in this section or in §§ 1.163(j)-3 through 1.163(j)-11, the amount allowed as a deduction for business interest expense for the taxable year cannot exceed the sum of—

(1) The taxpayer's business interest income for the taxable year;

(2) 30 percent of the taxpayer's ATI for the taxable year, or zero if the taxpayer's ATI for the taxable year is less than zero; and

(3) The taxpayer's floor plan financing interest expense for the taxable year.

(c) *Disallowed business interest expense carryforward.*—(1) *In general.*—Under section 163(j)(2), any business interest expense disallowed under paragraph (b) of this section, or any disallowed disqualified interest that is properly allocable to a non-excepted trade or business under § 1.163(j)-10, is carried forward to the succeeding taxable year as business interest expense that is subject to paragraph (b) of this section in such succeeding taxable year (a disallowed business interest expense carryforward).

(2) *Coordination with small business exemption.*—If disallowed business interest expense is carried forward under the rules of paragraph (c)(1) of this section to a taxable year in which the small business exemption in paragraph (d) of this section applies to the taxpayer, then the general rule in paragraph (b) of this section does not apply to limit the deduction of the disallowed business interest expense carryforward in that taxable year.

(3) *Cross-references.*—(i) For special rules regarding disallowed business interest expense carryforwards for taxpayers that are C corporations, including members of a consolidated group, see § 1.163(j)-5.

(ii) For special rules regarding disallowed business interest expense carryforwards of S corporations, see §§ 1.163(j)-5(b)(2) and 1.163(j)-6(l)(5).

(iii) For special rules regarding disallowed business interest expense carryforwards from partnerships, see § 1.163(j)-6.

(iv) For special rules regarding disallowed business interest expense carryforwards from partnerships engaged in a U.S. trade or business, see § 1.163(j)-8(c)(2).

(d) *Small business exemption.*—(1) *Exemption.*—The general rule in paragraph (b) of this section does not apply to any taxpayer, other than a tax shelter as defined in section 448(d)(3), in any taxable year if the taxpayer meets the gross receipts test of section 448(c) and the regulations thereunder for the taxable year.

(2) *Application of the gross receipts test.*—(i) *In general.*—In the case of any taxpayer that is not a corporation or a partnership, and except as provided in paragraphs (d)(2)(ii), (iii), and (iv) of

this section, the gross receipts test and aggregation rules of section 448(c) and the regulations thereunder are applied in the same manner as if such taxpayer were a corporation or partnership.

(ii) *Gross receipts of individuals.*—Except as provided in paragraph (d)(2)(iii) of this section regarding partnership and S corporation interests and when the aggregation rules of section 448(c) apply, an individual taxpayer's gross receipts include all items specified as gross receipts in regulations under section 448(c), whether or not derived in the ordinary course of the taxpayer's trade or business. For purposes of section 163(j), an individual taxpayer's gross receipts do not include inherently personal amounts, including, but not limited to, personal injury awards or settlements with respect to an injury of the individual taxpayer, disability benefits, Social Security benefits received by the taxpayer during the taxable year, and wages received as an employee that are reported on Form W-2.

(iii) *Partners and S corporation shareholders.*—Except when the aggregation rules of section 448(c) apply, each partner in a partnership includes a share of partnership gross receipts in proportion to such partner's distributive share (as determined under section 704) of items of gross income that were taken into account by the partnership under section 703. Additionally, each shareholder in an S corporation includes a pro rata share of S corporation gross receipts.

(iv) *Tax-exempt organizations.*—For purposes of section 163(j), the gross receipts of an organization subject to tax under section 511 includes only gross receipts taken into account in determining its unrelated business taxable income.

(e) *REMICs.*—For the treatment of interest expense by a REMIC as defined in section 860D, see § 1.860C-2(b)(2)(ii).

(f) *Calculation of ATI with respect to certain beneficiaries.*—The ATI of a trust or estate beneficiary is reduced by any income (including any distributable net income) received from the trust or estate by the beneficiary to the extent such income supported a deduction for business interest expense under section 163(j)(1)(B) or § 1.163(j)-2(b)(2) in computing the trust or estate's taxable income.

(g) *Examples.*—The examples of this paragraph (g) illustrate the application of section 163(j) and the provisions of this section. Unless otherwise indicated, assume the following: X and Y are domestic C corporations; C and D are U.S. resident individuals not subject to any foreign income tax; PRS is a domestic partnership with partners who are all individuals; all taxpayers use a calendar taxable year; the exemption for certain small businesses in section 163(j)(3) and paragraph (d) of this section does not apply; and the interest expense would be deductible but for section 163(j).

(1) *Example 1: Limitation on business interest expense deduction*—(i) *Facts.* During its taxable year ending December 31, 2019, X has ATI of $100x. X has business interest expense of $50x, which includes $10x of floor plan financing interest expense, and business interest income of $20x.

(ii) *Analysis.* X's section 163(j) limitation is $60x, which is the sum of its business interest income ($20x), plus 30 percent of its ATI ($100x x 30 percent = $30x), plus its floor plan financing interest expense ($10x). See § 1.163(j)-2(b). Because X's business interest expense ($50x) does not exceed X's section 163(j) limitation ($60x), X can deduct all $50x of its business interest expense for the 2019 taxable year.

(2) *Example 2: Carryforward of business interest expense*—(i) *Facts.* The facts are the same as in *Example 1* in paragraph (g)(1)(i) of this section, except that X has $80x of business interest expense, which includes $10x of floor plan financing interest expense.

(ii) *Analysis.* As in *Example 1* in paragraph (g)(1)(ii) of this section, X's section 163(j) limitation is $60x. Because X's business interest expense ($80x) exceeds X's section 163(j) limitation ($60x), X may only deduct $60x of its business interest expense for the 2019 taxable year, and the remaining $20x of its business interest expense will be carried forward to the succeeding taxable year as a disallowed business interest expense carryforward. See § 1.163(j)-2(c).

(3) *Example 3: ATI computation*—(i) *Facts.* During the 2019 taxable year, Y has taxable income of $30x (without regard to the application of section 163(j)), which includes the following: $20x of business interest income; $50x of business interest expense, which includes $10x of floor plan financing interest expense; $25x of net operating loss deduction under section 172; and $15x of depreciation deduction under section 167.

(ii) *Analysis.* (A) For purposes of determining the section 163(j) limitation, Y's ATI is $90x, calculated as follows:

Table 1 to paragraph (g)(3)(ii)(A)

| | |
|---|---|
| Taxable income: | $30x |
| Less: | |
| Floor plan financing interest | 10x |
| Business interest income | 20x |
| | 0x |

(B) Plus:

Table 1 to paragraph (g)(3)(ii)(B)

| | |
|---|---|
| Business interest expense | $50x |
| Net operating loss deduction | 25x |
| Depreciation deduction | 15x |
| ATI | $90x |

(4) *Example 4: Floor plan financing interest expense*—(i) *Facts.* C is the sole proprietor of an

automobile dealership that uses a cash method of accounting. In the 2019 taxable year, C paid $30x of interest on a loan that was obtained to purchase sedans for sale by the dealership. The indebtedness is secured by the sedans purchased with the loan proceeds. In addition, C paid $20x of interest on a loan, secured by the dealership's office equipment, which C obtained to purchase convertibles for sale by the dealership.

(ii) *Analysis.* For the purpose of calculating C's section 163(j) limitation, only the $30x of interest paid on the loan to purchase the sedans is floor plan financing interest expense. The $20x paid on the loan to purchase the convertibles is not floor plan financing interest expense for purposes of section 163(j) because the indebtedness was not secured by the inventory of convertibles. However, because under § 1.163(j)-10 the interest paid on the loan to purchase the convertibles is properly allocable to C's dealership trade or business, and because floor plan financing interest expense is also business interest expense, C has $50x of business interest expense for the 2019 taxable year.

(5) *Example 5: Interest not properly allocable to non-excepted trade or business*—(i) *Facts.* The facts are the same as in *Example 4* in paragraph (g)(4)(i) of this section, except that the $20x of interest C pays is on acquisition indebtedness obtained to purchase C's personal residence and not to purchase convertibles for C's dealership trade or business.

(ii) *Analysis.* Because the $20x of interest expense is not properly allocable to a non-excepted trade or business, and therefore is not business interest expense as defined in § 1.163(j)-1(b)(2), C's only business interest expense is the $30x that C pays on the loan used to purchase sedans for sale in C's dealership trade or business. C deducts the $20x of interest related to his residence under the rules of section 163(h), without regard to section 163(j).

(6) *Example 6: Small business exemption*—(i) *Facts.* During the 2019 taxable year, D, the sole proprietor of a trade or business reported on Schedule C, has interest expense properly allocable to that trade or business. D also earns gross income from providing services as an employee that is reported on a Form W-2. Under section 448(c) and the regulations thereunder, D has average annual gross receipts of $21 million, including $1 million of wages in each of the three prior taxable years and $2 million of income from investments not related to a trade or business in each of the three prior taxable years. Also, in each of the three prior taxable years, D received $5 million in periodic payments of compensatory damages awarded in a personal injury lawsuit.

(ii) *Analysis.* Section 163(j) does not apply to D for the taxable year, because D qualifies for the small business exemption under § 1.163(j)-2(d). The wages that D receives as an employee and the compensatory damages that D received from

D's personal injury lawsuit are not gross receipts, as provided in § 1.163(j)-2(d)(2)(ii). D may deduct all of its business interest expense for the 2019 taxable year without regard to section 163(j).

(7) *Example 7: Aggregation of gross receipts*—(i) *Facts.* X and Y are domestic C corporations under common control, within the meaning of section 52(a) and § 1.52-1(b). X's only trade or business is a farming business described in § 1.263A-4(a)(4). During the taxable year ending December 31, 2019, X has average annual gross receipts under section 448(c) of $6 million. During the same taxable year, Y has average annual gross receipts under section 448(c) of $21 million.

(ii) *Analysis.* Because X and Y are under common control, they must aggregate gross receipts for purposes of section 448(c) and the small business exemption in § 1.163(j)-2(d). See section 448(c)(2). Therefore, X and Y are both considered to have $27 million in average annual gross receipts for 2019. X and Y must separately apply section 163(j) to determine any limitation on the deduction for business interest expense. Assuming X otherwise meets the requirements in § 1.163(j)-9 in 2019, X may elect for its farming business to be an excepted trade or business.

(h) *Anti-avoidance rule.*—Arrangements entered into with a principal purpose of avoiding the rules of section 163(j) or the section 163(j) regulations, including the use of multiple entities to avoid the gross receipts test of section 448(c), may be disregarded or recharacterized by the Commissioner of the IRS to the extent necessary to carry out the purposes of section 163(j).

(i) *Applicability date.*—This section applies to taxable years ending after the date the Treasury decision adopting these regulations as final regulations is published in the **Federal Register**. However, taxpayers and their related parties, within the meaning of sections 267(b) and 707(b)(1), may apply the rules of this section to a taxable year beginning after December 31, 2017, so long as the taxpayers and their related parties consistently apply the rules of the section 163(j) regulations, and if applicable, §§ 1.263A-9, 1.381(c)(20)-1, 1.382-6, 1.383-1, 1.469-9, 1.882-5, 1.1502-13, 1.1502-21, 1.1502-36, 1.1502-79, 1.1502-91 through 1.1502-99, (to the extent they effectuate the rules of §§ 1.382-6 and 1.383-1), and 1.1504-4 to those taxable years. [Reg. § 1.163(j)-2.]

[Proposed 12-28-2018.]

### [Prop. Reg. § 1.163(j)-3]

**§ 1.163(j)-3. Relationship of business interest deduction limitation to other provisions affecting interest.**—(a) *Overview.*—This section contains rules regarding the relationship between section 163(j) and certain other provisions of the Code. Paragraph (b) of this section provides the general rules concerning the relationship between section 163(j) and certain other provisions

**Prop. Reg. § 1.163(j)-3(a)**

of the Code. Paragraph (c) of this section provides examples illustrating the application of this section. For rules regarding the relationship between sections 163(j) and 704(d), see § 1.163(j)-6(h)(1) and (2).

(b) *Coordination of section 163(j) with certain other provisions.*—(1) *In general.*—Section 163(j) and the section 163(j) regulations generally apply only to business interest expense that would be deductible in the current taxable year without regard to section 163(j). Except as otherwise provided in this section, section 163(j) applies after the application of provisions that subject interest expense to disallowance, deferral, capitalization, or other limitation. For the rules that must be applied in determining whether excess business interest is paid or accrued by a partner, see section 163(j)(4)(B)(ii) and § 1.163(j)-6.

(2) *Disallowed interest provisions.*—For purposes of section 163(j), business interest expense does not include interest expense that is permanently disallowed as a deduction under another provision of the Code, such as in section 163(e)(5)(A)(i), (f), (l), or (m), or section 264(a), 265, 267A, or 279.

(3) *Deferred interest provisions.*—Other than sections 461(l), 465, and 469, Code provisions that defer the deductibility of interest expense, such as section 163(e)(3) and (e)(5)(A)(ii), 267(a)(2) and (3), 1277, or 1282, apply before the application of section 163(j). For purposes other than sections 465 and 469, interest expense is taken into account for section 163(j) purposes in the taxable year when it is no longer deferred under another section of the Code.

(4) *At risk rules, passive activity loss provisions, and limitation on excess business losses of noncorporate taxpayers.*—Section 163(j) applies before the application of sections 461(l), 465, and 469.

(5) *Capitalized interest expenses under sections 263A and 263(g).*—Sections 263A and 263(g) apply before the application of section 163(j). Capitalized interest expense under those sections is not treated as business interest expense for purposes of section 163(j). For ordering rules that determine whether interest expense is capitalized under section 263A(f), see the regulations under section 263A(f), including § 1.263A-9(g).

(6) *Reductions under section 246A.*—Section 246A applies before section 163(j). Any reduction in the dividends received deduction under section 246A reduces the amount of business interest expense taken into account under section 163(j).

(7) *Section 381.*—Disallowed business interest expense carryforwards are items to which an acquiring corporation succeeds under section

381(a). See section 381(c)(20), and § § 1.163(j)-5(c) and 1.381(c)(20)-1.

(8) *Section 382.*—For rules governing the interaction of sections 163(j) and 382, see section 382(d)(3) and (k)(1), § § 1.163(j)-5(e) and 1.163(j)-11(b), the regulations under sections 382 and 383, and § § 1.1502-91 through 1.1502-99.

(9) *Other types of interest provisions.*—Except as otherwise provided in the section 163(j) regulations, provisions that characterize interest expense as something other than business interest expense under section 163(j), such as section 163(d), govern the treatment of that interest expense, and such interest expense will not be treated as business interest expense for any purpose under section 163(j).

(10) [Reserved]

(c) *Examples.*—The examples of this paragraph (c) illustrate the application of section 163(j) and the provisions of this section. Unless otherwise indicated, assume the following: X and Y are domestic C corporations with a calendar taxable year; D is a U.S. resident individual not subject to any foreign income tax; none of the taxpayers have floor plan financing interest expense; and the exemption for small businesses in § 1.163(j)-2(d) does not apply.

(1) *Example 1: Disallowed interest expense*—(i) *Facts.* In 2019, X has $30x of interest expense. Of X's interest expense, $10x is permanently disallowed under section 265. X's business interest income is $3x and X's ATI is $90x.

(ii) *Analysis.* Under paragraph (b)(2) of this section, the $10x interest expense that is permanently disallowed under section 265 cannot be taken into consideration for purposes of section 163(j) in the 2019 taxable year. X's section 163(j) limitation, or the amount of business interest expense that X may deduct is limited to $30x under § 1.163(j)-2(b), determined by adding X's business interest income ($3x) and 30 percent of X's 2018 ATI ($27x). Therefore, in the 2019 taxable year, none of the $20x of X's deduction for its business interest expense is disallowed under section 163(j).

(2) *Example 2: Deferred interest expense*—(i) *Facts.* In 2019, Y has no business interest income, $120x of ATI, and $70x of interest expense. Of Y's interest expense, $30x is not currently deductible under section 267(a)(2). Assume that the $30x expense will be allowed as a deduction under section 267(a)(2) in 2020.

(ii) *Analysis.* Under paragraph (b)(3) of this section, section 267(a)(2) is applied before section 163(j). Accordingly, $30x of Y's interest expense cannot be taken into consideration for purposes of section 163(j) in 2019 because it is not currently deductible under section 267(a)(2). Accordingly, in 2019, if the interest expense is properly allocable to a non-excepted trade or business, Y will have $4x of disallowed business interest expense because the $40x of business interest expense in 2019 ($70x - $30x) exceeds 30 percent of its ATI for the taxable year ($36x). The $30x of interest expense not allowed as a deduction in the 2019 taxable year under section 267(a)(2) will be taken into account in determining the business interest expense deduction under section 163(j) in 2020, the taxable year in which it is allowed as a deduction under section 267(a)(2), if it is allocable to a trade or business. Additionally, the $4x of disallowed business interest expense in 2019 will be carried forward to 2020 as a disallowed business interest expense carryforward. See § 1.163(j)-2(c).

(3) *Example 3: Passive activity loss*—(i) *Facts.* D is engaged in a rental activity treated as a passive activity within the meaning of section 469. For tax year 2019, D receives $200x of rental income and incurs $300x of expenses all properly allocable to the rental activity, consisting of $150x of interest expense, $60x of maintenance expenses, and $90x of depreciation expense. D's ATI is $400x.

(ii) *Analysis.* Under paragraph (b)(4) of this section, section 163(j) is applied before the section 469 passive activity loss rules apply. D's section 163(j) limitation is $120x, determined by adding to D's business interest income ($0), floor plan financing ($0), and 30 percent of D's ATI ($120x). See § 1.163(j)-2(b). Because D's business interest expense of $150x exceeds D's section 163(j) limitation for 2019, $30x of D's business interest expense is disallowed under section 163(j) and will be carried forward as a disallowed business interest expense carryforward. See § 1.163(j)-2(c). Because the section 163(j) limitation is applied before the limitation under section 469, only $120x of the business interest expense allowable under section 163(j) is included in determining D's passive activity loss limitation for the 2019 tax year under section 469. The $30x of disallowed business interest expense is not an allowable deduction under section 163(j) and, therefore, is not a deduction under section 469 in the current taxable year. See § 1.469-2(d)(8).

(4) *Example 4: Passive activity loss by taxpayer that also participates in a non-passive activity*—(i) *Facts.* For 2019, D has no business interest income and ATI of $1,000x, entirely attributable to a passive activity within the meaning of section 469. D has business interest expense of $1,000x, $900x of which is properly allocable to a passive activity and $100x of which is properly allocable to a non-passive activity in which D materially participates. D has other business deductions that are not subject to section 469 of $600x, and a section 469 passive loss from the previous year of $250x.

(ii) *Analysis.* Under paragraph (b)(4) of this section, section 163(j) is applied before the section 469 passive loss rules apply. D's section 163(j) limitation is $300x, determined by adding D's business interest income ($0), floor plan financing ($0), and 30 percent of D's ATI ($300x).

Next, applying the limitation under section 469 to the $300x business interest expense deduction allowable under sections 163(a) and (j), $270x (a proportionate amount of the $300x (0.90 x $300x)) is business interest expense included in determining D's passive activity loss limitation under section 469, and $30x (a proportionate amount of the $300x (0.10 x $300)) is business interest expense not included in determining D's passive activity loss limitation under section 469. Because D's interest expense of $1,000x exceeds 30 percent of its ATI for 2019, $700x of D's interest expense is disallowed under section 163(j) and will be carried forward as a disallowed business interest expense carryforward. Section 469 does not apply to any portion of the $700x disallowed business interest expense because that business interest expense is not an allowable deduction under section 163(j) and, therefore, is not an allowable deduction under section 469 in the current taxable year. See § 1.469-2(d)(8).

(d) *Applicability date.*—The provisions of this section apply to taxable years ending after the date the Treasury decision adopting these regulations as final regulations is published in the **Federal Register**. However, taxpayers and their related parties, within the meaning of sections 267(b) and 707(b)(1), may apply the rules of this section to a taxable year beginning after December 31, 2017, so long as the taxpayers and their related parties consistently apply the rules of the section 163(j) regulations, and if applicable, §§ 1.263A-9, 1.381(c)(20)-1, 1.382-6, 1.383-1, 1.469-9, 1.882-5, 1.1502-13, 1.1502-21, 1.1502-36, 1.1502-79, 1.1502-91 through 1.1502-99 (to the extent they effectuate the rules of §§ 1.382-6 and 1.383-1), and 1.1504-4 to those taxable years. [Reg. § 1.163(j)-3.]

[Proposed 12-28-2018.]

**[Prop. Reg. § 1.163(j)-4]**

**§ 1.163(j)-4. General rules applicable to C corporations (including REITs, RICs, and members of consolidated groups) and tax-exempt corporations.**—(a) *Scope.*—This section provides certain rules regarding the computation of items of income and expense under section 163(j) for taxpayers that are C corporations (including members of a consolidated group, REITs, and RICs) and tax-exempt corporations. Paragraph (b) of this section provides rules regarding the characterization of items of income, gain, deduction, or loss. Paragraph (c) of this section provides rules regarding adjustments to earnings and profits. Paragraph (d) of this section provides special rules applicable to members of a consolidated group. Paragraph (e) of this section provides cross-references to other rules within the 163(j) regulations that may be applicable to C corporations.

(b) *Characterization of items of income, gain, deduction, or loss.*—(1) *Interest expense and interest income.*—Solely for purposes of section 163(j), all interest expense of a taxpayer that is a C corporation is treated as properly allocable to a trade or business. Similarly, solely for purposes of section 163(j), all interest income of a taxpayer that is a C corporation is treated as properly allocable to a trade or business. For rules governing the allocation of interest expense and interest income between excepted and non-excepted trades or businesses, see § 1.163(j)-10.

(2) *Adjusted taxable income.*—Solely for purposes of section 163(j), all items of income, gain, deduction, or loss of a taxpayer that is a C corporation are treated as properly allocable to a trade or business. For rules governing the allocation of tax items between excepted and non-excepted trades or businesses, see § 1.163(j)-10.

(3) *Investment interest, investment income, and investment expenses of a partnership with a C corporation partner.*—(i) *Characterization as expense or income properly allocable to a trade or business.*—For purposes of section 163(j), any investment interest, within the meaning of section 163(d), that a partnership pays or accrues and that is allocated to a C corporation partner is treated by the C corporation as interest expense that is properly allocable to a trade or business of that partner. Similarly, for purposes of section 163(j), except as provided in § 1.163(j)-7(d)(1)(ii), any investment income or investment expenses, within the meaning of section 163(d), that a partnership receives, pays, or accrues and that is allocated to a C corporation partner is treated by the C corporation as properly allocable to a trade or business of that partner.

(ii) *Impact of characterization on partnership.*—The characterization of a partner's investment interest, investment income, or investment expenses pursuant to paragraph (b)(3)(i) of this section will not affect the characterization of these items as investment interest, investment income, or investment expenses at the partnership level.

(iii) *Investment interest expense and investment interest income of a partnership not treated as excess business interest expense or excess taxable income of a C corporation partner.*—Investment interest expense of a partnership that is treated as business interest expense by a C corporation partner is not treated as excess business interest expense. Investment interest income of a partnership that is treated as business interest income by a C corporation partner is not treated as excess taxable income. For rules governing excess business interest expense and excess taxable income, see § 1.163(j)-6.

(4) *Application to RICs and REITs.*—(i) *In general.*—Except as otherwise provided in paragraphs (b)(4)(ii) and (iii) of this section, the rules in this paragraph (b) apply to RICs and REITs.

(ii) *Taxable income for purposes of calculating the adjusted taxable income of RICs and REITs.*—The taxable income of a RIC or REIT for pur-

poses of calculating adjusted taxable income (ATI) is the taxable income of the corporation, without any adjustment that would be made under section 852(b)(2) or 857(b)(2) to compute investment company taxable income or real estate investment trust taxable income, respectively. For example, the taxable income of a RIC or REIT is not reduced by the deduction for dividends paid, but is reduced by the dividends received deduction (DRD) and the other deductions described in sections 852(b)(2)(C) and 857(b)(2)(A), taking into account § 1.163(j)-1(b)(37)(ii). See paragraph (b)(4)(iii) of this section for an adjustment to adjusted taxable income in respect of these items.

(iii) *Other adjustments to adjusted taxable income for RICs and REITs.*—In the case of a taxpayer that, for a taxable year, is a RIC to which section 852(b) applies or a REIT to which section 857(b) applies, the taxpayer's ATI for the taxable year is increased by the amounts of any deductions described in section 852(b)(2)(C) or 857(b)(2)(A), taking into account § 1.163(j)-1(b)(37)(ii).

(5) *Application to tax-exempt corporations.*—The rules in this paragraph (b) apply to a corporation that is subject to the unrelated business income tax under section 511 only with respect to that corporation's items of income, gain, deduction, or loss that are taken into account in computing the corporation's unrelated business taxable income, as defined in section 512.

(6) *Examples.*—The principles of this paragraph (b) are illustrated by the following examples. For purposes of the examples in this paragraph (b)(6), T is a taxable domestic C corporation whose taxable year ends on December 31; T is neither a consolidated group member nor a RIC or a REIT; neither T nor PS1, a domestic partnership, owns at least 80 percent of the stock of any corporation; neither T nor PS1 qualifies for the small business exemption in § 1.163(j)-2(d) or is engaged in an excepted trade or business; T has no floor plan financing expense; all interest expense is deductible except for the potential application of section 163(j); and the facts set forth the only corporate or partnership activity.

(i) *Example 1: C corporation items properly allocable to a trade or business*—(A) *Facts.* In taxable year 2019, T's taxable income (without regard to the application of section 163(j)) is $320x. This amount is comprised of the following tax items: $1,000x of revenue from inventory sales; $500x of ordinary and necessary business expenses (excluding interest and depreciation); $200x of interest expense; $50x of interest income; $50x of depreciation deductions under section 168; and a $20x gain on the sale of stock.

(B) *Analysis.* For purposes of section 163(j), each of T's tax items is treated as properly allocable to a trade or business. Thus, T's ATI for the 2019 taxable year is $520x ($320x of taxable income + $200x business interest expense - $50x business interest income + $50x depreciation deductions = $520x), and its section 163(j) limitation for the 2019 taxable year is $206x ($50x of business interest income + 30 percent of its ATI (30 percent x $520x) = $206x). As a result, all $200x of T's interest expense is deductible in the 2019 taxable year under section 163(j).

(C) *Taxable year beginning in 2022.* The facts are the same as in *Example 1* in paragraph (b)(6)(i)(A) of this section, except that the taxable year is 2022 and therefore depreciation deductions are not added back to ATI under §1.163(j)-1(b)(1)(i)(E). As a result, T's ATI for 2022 is $470x ($320x of taxable income + $200x business interest expense - $50x business interest income = $470x), and its section 163(j) limitation for the 2022 taxable year is $191x ($50x of business interest income + 30 percent of its ATI (30 percent x $470x) = $191x). As a result, T may only deduct $191x of its business interest expense for the taxable year, and the remaining $9x will be carried forward to the 2023 taxable year as a disallowed business interest expense carryforward. See §1.163(j)-2(c).

(ii) *Example 2: C corporation partner*—(A) *Facts.* T and individual A each own a 50 percent interest in PS1, a general partnership. PS1 borrows funds from a third party (Loan 1) and uses those funds to buy stock in publicly-traded corporation X. PS1's only activities are holding X stock (and receiving dividends) and making payments on Loan 1. In the 2019 taxable year, PS1 receives $150x in dividends and pays $100x in interest on Loan 1.

(B) *Analysis.* For purposes of section 163(d) and (j), PS1 has investment interest expense of $100x and investment income of $150x, and PS1 has no interest expense or interest income that is properly allocable to a trade or business. PS1 allocates its investment interest expense and investment income to its two partners pursuant to §1.163(j)-6(j). Pursuant to paragraph (b)(3) of this section, T's allocable share of PS1's investment interest expense is treated as a business interest expense of T, and T's allocable share of PS1's investment income is treated as properly allocable to a trade or business of T. This business interest expense is not treated as excess business interest expense, and this income is not treated as excess taxable income. See paragraph (h)(3)(iii) of this section. T's treatment of its allocable share of PS1's investment interest expense and investment income as business interest expense and income properly allocable to a trade or business, respectively, does not affect the character of these items at the PS1 level and does not affect the character of A's allocable share of PS1's investment interest and investment income.

(C) *Partnership engaged in a trade or business.* The facts are the same as in *Example 2* in paragraph (b)(6)(ii)(A) of this section, except that PS1 also is engaged in Business 1, and PS1 borrows funds from a third party to finance Business 1 (Loan 2). In 2019, Business 1 earns $150x of net income (excluding interest expense and depreciation), and PS1 pays $100x of interest on Loan 2. For purposes of §1.163-8T, the interest paid on Loan 2 is allocated to a trade or business (and is therefore not treated as investment interest expense under section 163(d)). As a result, PS1 has investment interest expense of $100x (attributable to Loan 1), business interest expense of $100x (attributable to Loan 2), $150x of investment income, and $150x of income from Business 1. PS1's ATI is $150x (its net income from Business 1 excluding interest and depreciation), and its section 163(j) limitation is $45x (30 percent x $150x). Pursuant to §1.163(j)-6, PS1 has $55x of excess business interest expense ($100x - $45x), half of which ($27.5x) is allocable to T. Additionally, pursuant to paragraph (b)(3)(i) of this section, T's allocable share of PS1's investment interest expense ($50x) is treated as a business interest expense of T for purposes of section 163(j), and T's allocable share of PS1's investment income ($75x) is treated as properly allocable to a trade or business of T. Therefore, with respect to T's interest in PS1, T is treated as having $50x of business interest expense that is not treated as excess business interest expense, $75x of income that is properly allocable to a trade or business, and $27.5x of excess business interest expense.

(c) *Effect on earnings and profits.*—(1) *In general.*—In the case of a taxpayer that is a C corporation, except as otherwise provided in paragraph (c)(2) of this section, the disallowance and carryforward of a deduction for the taxpayer's business interest expense under §1.163(j)-2 will not affect whether or when the business interest expense reduces the taxpayer's earnings and profits.

(2) *Special rule for RICs and REITs.*—In the case of a taxpayer that is a RIC or a REIT for the taxable year in which a deduction for the taxpayer's business interest expense is disallowed under §1.163(j)-2(b), or in which the RIC or REIT is allocated any excess business interest expense from a partnership under section 163(j)(4)(B)(i) and §1.163(j)-6, the taxpayer's earnings and profits are adjusted in the taxable year or years in which the business interest expense is deductible or, if earlier, in the first taxable year for which the taxpayer no longer is a RIC or a REIT.

(3) *Special rule for partners that are C corporations.*—If a taxpayer that is a C corporation is allocated any excess business interest expense from a partnership under section 163(j)(4)(B)(i) and §1.163(j)-6, and if any amount of the excess business interest expense has not yet been treated as business interest expense by the taxpayer at the time of the taxpayer's disposition of all or substantially all of its interest in the partnership, then the taxpayer must increase its earnings and profits by that amount immediately prior to its disposition of the partnership interest.

**Prop. Reg. §1.163(j)-4(c)(3)**

(4) *Examples.*—The principles of this paragraph (c) are illustrated by the following examples. For purposes of the examples in this paragraph (c)(4), except as otherwise provided in the examples, X is a taxable domestic C corporation whose taxable year ends on December 31; X is not a member of a consolidated group; X does not qualify for the small business exemption under § 1.163(j)-2(d); X is not engaged in an excepted trade or business; X has no floor plan financing indebtedness; all interest expense is deductible except for the potential application of section 163(j); X has no accumulated earnings and profits at the beginning of the 2019 taxable year; and the facts set forth the only corporate activity.

(i) *Example 1: Earnings and profits of a taxable domestic C corporation other than a RIC or a REIT*—(A) *Facts.* X is a corporation that does not intend to qualify as a RIC or a REIT for its 2019 taxable year. In that year, X has taxable income (without regard to the application of section 163(j)) of $0, which includes $100x of gross income and $100x of interest expense on a loan from an unrelated third party. X also makes a $100x distribution to its shareholders that year.

(B) *Analysis.* The $100x of interest expense is business interest expense for purposes of section 163(j) (see paragraph (b)(1) of this section). X's ATI in the 2019 taxable year is $100x ($0 of taxable income computed without regard to $100x of business interest expense). Thus, X may deduct $30x of its $100x of business interest expense in the 2019 taxable year under § 1.163(j)-2(b) (30 percent x $100x), and X may carry forward the remainder ($70x) to X's 2020 taxable year as a disallowed business interest expense carryforward under § 1.163(j)-2(c). Although X may not currently deduct all $100x of its business interest expense in the 2019 taxable year, X must reduce its earnings and profits in that taxable year by the full amount of its business interest expense ($100x) in that taxable year. As a result, no portion of X's distribution of $100x to its shareholders in the 2019 taxable year is a dividend within the meaning of section 316(a).

(ii) *Example 2: RIC adjusted taxable income and earnings and profits*—(A) *Facts.* X is a corporation that intends to qualify as a RIC for its 2019 taxable year. In that taxable year, X's only items are $100x of interest income, $50x of dividend income from C corporations that only issue common stock and in which X has less than a twenty percent interest (by vote and value), $10x of net capital gain, and $125x of interest expense. None of the dividends are received on debt financed portfolio stock under section 246A. The DRD determined under section 243(a) with respect to X's $50x of dividend income is $25x. X pays $42x in dividends to its shareholders, meeting the requirements of section 562 during X's 2019 taxable year, including $10x that X reports as capital gain dividends in written statements furnished to X's shareholders.

(B) *Analysis.* (1) Under paragraph (b) of this section, all of X's interest expense is considered business interest expense, all of X's interest income is considered business interest income, and all of X's other income is considered to be properly allocable to a trade or business. Under paragraph (b)(4)(ii) of this section, prior to the application of section 163(j), X's taxable income is $10x ($100x business interest income + $50x dividend income + $10x net capital gain - $125x business interest expense - $25x DRD = $10x). Under paragraph (b)(4)(iii) of this section, X's ATI is increased by the DRD. As such, X's ATI for the 2019 taxable year is $60x ($10x taxable income + $125x business interest expense - $100x business interest income + $25x DRD = $60x).

(2) X may deduct $118x of its $125x of business interest expense in the 2019 taxable year under section 163(j)(1) ($100x business interest income + (30 percent x $60x of ATI) = $118x), and X may carry forward the remainder ($7x) to X's taxable year ending December 31, 2020. See § 1.163(j)-2(b) and (c).

(3) After the application of section 163(j), X has taxable income of $17x ($100x interest income + $50x dividend income + $10x capital gain - $25x DRD - $118x allowable interest expense = $17x) for the 2019 taxable year. X will have investment company taxable income (ICTI) in the amount of $0 ($17x taxable income - $10x capital gain + $25x DRD - $32x dividends paid deduction for ordinary dividends = 0). The excess of X's net capital gain ($10x) over X's dividends paid deduction determined with reference to capital gain dividends ($10x) is also $0.

(4) Under paragraph (c)(2) of this section, X will not reduce its earnings and profits by the amount of interest expense disallowed as a deduction in the 2019 taxable year under section 163(j). Thus, X has current earnings and profits in the amount of $42x ($100x interest income + $50x dividend income + $10x capital gain - $118x allowable business interest expense = $42x) before giving effect to dividends paid during the 2019 taxable year.

(iii) *Example 3: Carryforward of disallowed interest expense*—(A) *Facts.* The facts are the same as the facts in *Example 2* in paragraph (c)(4)(ii)(A) of this section for the 2019 taxable year. In addition, X has $50x of interest income and $20x of interest expense for the 2020 taxable year.

(B) *Analysis.* Under paragraph (b) of this section, all of X's interest expense is considered business interest expense, all of X's interest income is considered business interest income, and all of X's other income is considered to be properly allocable to a trade or business. Because X's $50x of business interest income exceeds the $20x of business interest expense from the 2020 taxable year and the $7x of disallowed business interest expense carryforward from the 2019 taxable year, X may deduct $27x of business interest expense in the 2020 taxable year. Under paragraph (c)(2) of this section, X must reduce its current earnings and profits for the 2020 taxable year by the full amount of the deductible business interest expense ($27x).

(iv) *Example 4: REIT adjusted taxable income and earnings and profits*—(A) *Facts.* X is a corporation that intends to qualify as a REIT for its 2019 taxable year. X is not engaged in an excepted trade or business and is not engaged in a trade or business that is eligible to make any election under section 163(j)(7). In that year, X's only items are $100x of mortgage interest income, $30x of dividend income from C corporations that only issue common stock and in which X has less than a ten percent interest (by vote and value) in each C corporation, $10x of net capital gain from the sale of mortgages on real property that is not property described in section 1221(a)(1), and $125x of interest expense. None of the dividends are received on debt financed portfolio stock under section 246A. The DRD determined under section 243(a) with respect to X's $30x of dividend income is $15x. X pays $28x in dividends meeting the requirements of section 562 during X's 2019 taxable year, including $10x that X properly designates as capital gain dividends under section 857(b)(3)(B).

(B) *Analysis.* (1) Under paragraph (b) of this section, all of X's interest expense is considered business interest expense, all of X's interest income is considered business interest income, and all of X's other income is considered to be properly allocable to a trade or business. Under paragraph (b)(4)(ii) of this section, prior to the application of section 163(j), X's taxable income is $0 ($100x business interest income + $30x dividend income + $10x net capital gain - $125x business interest expense - $15x DRD = $0). Under paragraph (b)(4)(iii) of this section, X's ATI is increased by the DRD. As such, X's ATI for the 2019 taxable year is $40x ($0 taxable income + $125x business interest expense - $100x business interest income + $15x DRD = $40x).

(2) X may deduct $112x of its $125x of business interest expense in the 2019 taxable year under section 163(j)(1) ($100x business interest income + (30 percent x $40x of ATI) = $112x), and X may carry forward the remainder of its business interest expense ($13x) to X's 2020 taxable year.

(3) After the application of section 163(j), X has taxable income of $13x ($100x business interest income + $30x dividend income + $10x capital gain - $15x DRD - $112x allowable business interest expense = $13x) for the 2019 taxable year. X will have real estate investment trust taxable income (REITTI) in the amount of $0 ($13x taxable income + $15x of DRD - $28x dividends paid deduction = $0).

(4) Under paragraph (c)(2) of this section, X will not reduce earnings and profits by the amount of business interest expense disallowed as a deduction in the 2019 taxable year. Thus, X has current earnings and profits in the amount of $28x ($100x business interest income + $30x dividend income + $10x capital gain - $112x allowable business interest expense = $28x) before

giving effect to dividends paid during X's 2019 taxable year.

(v) *Example 5: Carryforward of disallowed interest expense*—(A) *Facts.* The facts are the same as in *Example 4* in paragraph (c)(4)(iv)(A) of this section for the 2019 taxable year. In addition, X has $50x of mortgage interest income and $20x of interest expense for the 2020 taxable year. X has no other tax items for the 2020 taxable year.

(B) *Analysis.* Because X's $50x of business interest income exceeds the $20x of business interest expense from the 2020 taxable year and the $13x of disallowed business interest expense carryforwards from the 2019 taxable year, X may deduct $33x of business interest expense in 2020. Under paragraph (c)(2) of this section, X must reduce its current earnings and profits for 2020 by the full amount of the deductible interest expense ($33x).

(d) *Special rules for consolidated groups.*— (1) *Scope.*—This paragraph (d) provides certain rules applicable to members of a consolidated group. For all members of a consolidated group for a consolidated return year, the computations required by section 163(j) and the section 163(j) regulations are made in accordance with the rules of this paragraph (d) unless otherwise provided elsewhere in the section 163(j) regulations. For rules governing the carryforward of disallowed business interest expense, including rules governing the treatment of disallowed business interest expense carryforwards when members enter or leave a group, see § 1.163(j)-5.

(2) *Calculation of the section 163(j) limitation for members of a consolidated group.*—(i) *In general.*—A consolidated group has a single section 163(j) limitation, the absorption of which is governed by § 1.163(j)-5(b)(3)(ii).

(ii) *Interest.*—For purposes of determining whether amounts, other than amounts in respect of intercompany obligations, as defined in § 1.1502-13(g)(2)(ii), intercompany items, as defined in § 1.1502-13(b)(2), or corresponding items, as defined in § 1.1502-13(b)(3), are treated as interest within the meaning of § 1.163(j)-1(b)(20), all members of a consolidated group are treated as a single taxpayer.

(iii) *Calculation of business interest expense and business interest income for a consolidated group.*—For purposes of calculating the section 163(j) limitation for a consolidated group, the consolidated group's current-year business interest expense (as defined in § 1.163(j)-5(a)(2)(i)) and business interest income, respectively, are the sum of each member's current-year business interest expense and business interest income, including amounts treated as business interest expense and business interest income under paragraph (b)(3) of this section.

(iv) *Calculation of adjusted taxable income.*—For purposes of calculating the ATI for a consolidated group, the relevant taxable income is the consolidated group's consolidated taxable income, determined under § 1.1502-11 without regard to any carryforwards or disallowances under section 163(j). Additionally, if for a taxable year a member of a consolidated group is allowed a deduction under section 250(a)(1) that is properly allocable to a non-excepted trade or business, then, for purposes of calculating ATI, consolidated taxable income for the taxable year is determined as if the deduction were not subject to the limitation in section 250(a)(2). For this purpose, the amount of the deduction allowed under section 250(a)(1) is determined without regard to the application of section 163(j) and the section 163(j) regulations. Further, for purposes of calculating the ATI of the group, intercompany items and corresponding items are disregarded to the extent that they offset in amount. Thus, for example, certain portions of the intercompany items and corresponding items of a group member engaged in a non-excepted trade or business will not be included in ATI to the extent that the counterparties to the relevant intercompany transactions are engaged in one or more excepted trades or businesses.

(v) *Treatment of intercompany obligations.*— For purposes of determining a member's business interest expense and business interest income, and for purposes of calculating the consolidated group's ATI, all intercompany obligations, as defined in § 1.1502-13(g)(2)(ii), are disregarded. Therefore, interest expense and interest income from intercompany obligations are not treated as business interest expense and business interest income.

(3) *Investment adjustments.*—For rules governing investment adjustments within a consolidated group, see § 1.1502-32(b).

(4) *Ownership of partnership interests by members of a consolidated group.*—(i) *Dispositions of partnership interests.*—The transfer of a partnership interest in an intercompany transaction that does not result in the termination of the partnership is treated as a disposition for purposes of the basis adjustment rule in section 163(j)(4)(B)(iii)(II), regardless of whether the transfer is one in which gain or loss is recognized. See § 1.1502-13 for rules applicable to the redetermination of attributes of group members. A change in status of a member (becoming or ceasing to be a member) is not treated as a disposition for purposes of section 163(j)(4)(B)(iii)(II).

(ii) *Basis adjustments under § 1.1502-32.*— A member's allocation of excess business interest expense from a partnership and the resulting decrease in basis in the partnership interest under section 163(j)(4)(B) is not a noncapital, nondeductible expense for purposes of § 1.1502-32(b)(3)(iii). Additionally, an increase in a member's basis in a partnership interest under section 163(j)(4)(B)(iii)(II) to reflect excess business interest expense not deducted by the consolidated group is not tax-exempt income for

purposes of § 1.1502-32(b)(3)(ii). Investment adjustments are made under § 1.1502-32(b)(3)(i) when the excess business interest expense from the partnership is absorbed by the consolidated group. See § 1.1502-32(b).

(iii) [Reserved]

(5) *Examples.*—The principles of this paragraph (d) are illustrated by the following examples (see also § 1.1502-13(c)(7)(ii)(R) and (S)). For purposes of the examples in this paragraph (d)(5), S is a member of the calendar-year consolidated group of which P is the common parent; the P group does not qualify for the small business exemption in § 1.163(j)-2(d); no member of the P group is engaged in an excepted trade or business; all interest expense is deductible except for the potential application of section 163(j); and the facts set forth the only corporate activity.

(i) *Example 1: Calculation of the section 163(j) limitation*—(A) *Facts.* In the 2019 taxable year, P has $50x of separate taxable income after taking into account $65x of interest paid on a loan from a third party (without regard to any disallowance under section 163(j)) and $35x of depreciation deductions under section 168. In turn, S has $40x of separate taxable income in the 2019 taxable year after taking into account $10x of depreciation deductions under section 168. S has no interest expense in the 2019 taxable year. The P group's consolidated taxable income for the 2019 taxable year is $90x, determined under § 1.1502-11 without regard to any disallowance under section 163(j).

(B) *Analysis.* As provided in paragraph (b)(1) of this section, P's interest expense is treated as business interest expense for purposes of section 163(j). If P and S were to apply the section 163(j) limitation on a separate-entity basis, then P's ATI would be $150x ($50x + $65x + $35x = $150x), its section 163(j) limitation would be $45x (30 percent x $150x = $45x), and a deduction for $20x of its $65x of business interest expense would be disallowed in the 2019 taxable year under section 163(j). However, as provided in paragraph (d)(2) of this section, the P group computes a single section 163(j) limitation, and that computation begins with the P group's consolidated taxable income (as determined prior to the application of section 163(j)), or $90x. The P group's ATI is $200x ($50x + $40x + $65x + $35x + $10x = $200x). Thus, the P group's section 163(j) limitation for the 2019 taxable year is $60x (30 percent x $200x = $60x). As a result, all but $5x of the P group's business interest expense is deductible in the 2019 taxable year. P carries over the $5x of disallowed business interest expense to the succeeding taxable year.

(ii) *Example 2: Intercompany obligations*—(A) *Facts.* On January 1, 2019, G, a corporation unrelated to P and S, lends P $100x in exchange for a note that accrues interest at a 10 percent annual rate. A month later, P lends $100x to S in exchange for a note that accrues interest at a 12 percent annual rate. In 2019, P accrues and pays $10x of interest to G on P's note, and S accrues

**Prop. Reg. § 1.163(j)-4(d)(2)(v)**

and pays $12x of interest to P on S's note. For that year, the P group's only other items of income, gain, deduction, and loss are $40x of income earned by S from the sale of inventory, and a $30x deductible expense arising from P's payment of tort liability claims.

(B) *Analysis.* As provided in paragraph (d)(2)(v) of this section, the intercompany obligation between P and S is disregarded in determining P and S's business interest expense and business interest income and in determining the P group's ATI. For purposes of section 163(j), P has $10x of business interest expense and a $30x deduction for the payment of tort liability claims, and S has $40x of income. The P group's ATI is $10x ($40x - $30x = $10x), and its section 163(j) limitation is $3x (30 percent x $10x = $3x). The P group may deduct $3x of its business interest expense in the 2019 taxable year. A deduction for P's remaining $7x of business interest expense is disallowed in the 2019 taxable year, and this amount is carried forward to the 2020 taxable year.

(e) *Cross-references.*—For rules governing the treatment of disallowed business interest expense carryforwards for C corporations, see § 1.163(j)-5. For rules governing the application of section 163(j) to a C corporation or a consolidated group engaged in both excepted and nonexcepted trades or businesses, see § 1.163(j)-10.

(f) *Applicability date.*—The provisions of this section apply to taxable years ending after the date the Treasury decision adopting these regulations as final regulations is published in the **Federal Register**. However, taxpayers and their related parties, within the meaning of sections 267(b) and 707(b)(1), may apply the rules of this section to a taxable year beginning after December 31, 2017, so long as the taxpayers and their related parties consistently apply the rules of the section 163(j) regulations, and if applicable, § § 1.263A-9, 1.381(c)(20)-1, 1.382-6, 1.383-1, 1.469-9, 1.882-5, 1.1502-13, 1.1502-21, 1.1502-36, 1.1502-79, 1.1502-91 through 1.1502-99 (to the extent they effectuate the rules of § § 1.382-6 and 1.383-1), and 1.1504-4 to those taxable years. [Reg. § 1.163(j)-4.]

[Proposed 12-28-2018.]

### [Prop. Reg. § 1.163(j)-5]

**§ 1.163(j)-5. General rules governing disallowed business interest expense carryforwards for C corporations.**—(a) *Scope and definitions.*—(1) *Scope.*—This section provides certain rules regarding disallowed business interest expense carryforwards for taxpayers that are C corporations, including members of a consolidated group. Paragraph (b) of this section provides rules regarding the treatment of disallowed business interest expense carryforwards. Paragraph (c) of this section provides cross-references to other rules regarding disallowed business interest expense carryforwards in transactions to which section 381(a) applies. Paragraph (d) of this section provides rules regarding limitations

on disallowed business interest expense carryforwards from separate return limitation years (SRLYs). Paragraph (e) of this section provides cross-references to other rules regarding the application of section 382 to disallowed business interest expense carryforwards. Paragraph (f) of this section provides rules regarding the overlap of the SRLY limitation with section 382.

(2) *Definitions.*—(i) *Current-year business interest expense.*—The term *current-year business interest expense* means business interest expense (as defined in § 1.163(j)-1(b)(2)) that would be deductible in the current taxable year without regard to section 163(j) and that is not a disallowed business interest expense carryforward (as defined in § 1.163(j)-1(b)(9)) from a prior taxable year.

(ii) *Allocable share of the consolidated group's remaining section 163(j) limitation.*—The term *allocable share of the consolidated group's remaining section 163(j) limitation* means, with respect to any member of a consolidated group, the product of the consolidated group's remaining section 163(j) limitation and the member's remaining current-year interest ratio.

(iii) *Consolidated group's remaining section 163(j) limitation.*—The term *consolidated group's remaining section 163(j) limitation* means the amount of the consolidated group's section 163(j) limitation calculated pursuant to § 1.163(j)-4(d)(2), reduced by the amount of interest deducted by members of the consolidated group pursuant to paragraph (b)(3)(ii)(C)(2) of this section.

(iv) *Remaining current-year interest ratio.*—The term *remaining current-year interest ratio* means, with respect to any member of a consolidated group for a particular taxable year, the ratio of the remaining current-year business interest expense of the member after applying the rule in paragraph (b)(3)(ii)(C)(2) of this section, to the sum of the amounts of remaining current-year business interest expense for all members of the consolidated group after applying the rule in paragraph (b)(3)(ii)(C)(2) of this section.

(b) *Treatment of disallowed business interest expense carryforwards.*—(1) *In general.*—The amount of any business interest expense of a C corporation not allowed as a deduction for any taxable year as a result of the limitation under section 163(j)(1) and § 1.163(j)-2(b) is carried forward to the succeeding taxable year as a disallowed business interest expense carryforward under section 163(j)(2) and § 1.163(j)-2(c).

(2) *Deduction of business interest expense.*—For a taxpayer that is a C corporation, current-year business interest expense is deducted in the current taxable year before any disallowed business interest expense carryforwards from a prior taxable year are deducted in that year. Disallowed business interest expense carryforwards are deducted in the order of the taxable years in

which they arose, beginning with the earliest taxable year, subject to certain limitations (for example, the limitation under section 382). For purposes of section 163(j), disallowed disqualified interest is treated as carried forward from the taxable year in which a deduction was disallowed under old section 163(j).

(3) *Consolidated groups.*—(i) *In general.*—A consolidated group's disallowed business interest expense carryforwards for the current consolidated return year (the current year) are the carryforwards from the group's prior consolidated return years plus any carryforwards from separate return years.

(ii) *Deduction of business interest expense.*— (A) *General rule.*—All current-year business interest expense of members of a consolidated group is deducted in the current year before any disallowed business interest expense carryforwards from prior taxable years are deducted in the current year. Disallowed business interest expense carryforwards from prior taxable years are deducted in the order of the taxable years in which they arose, beginning with the earliest taxable year, subject to the limitations described in this section.

(B) *Section 163(j) limitation is equal to or exceeds the current-year business interest expense and disallowed business interest expense carryforwards from prior taxable years.*—If a consolidated group's section 163(j) limitation for the current year is equal to or exceeds the aggregate amount of its members' current-year business interest expense and disallowed business interest expense carryforwards from prior taxable years that are available for deduction, then none of the current-year business interest expense or disallowed business interest expense carryforwards will be subject to disallowance in the current year under section 163(j). However, a deduction for the members' business interest expense may be subject to limitation under other provisions of the Code or the regulations promulgated thereunder (see, for example, paragraphs (c), (d), (e), and (f) of this section).

(C) *Current-year business interest expense and disallowed business interest expense carryforwards exceed section 163(j) limitation.*—If the aggregate amount of members' current-year business interest expense and disallowed business interest expense carryforwards from prior taxable years exceeds the consolidated group's section 163(j) limitation for the current year, then the following rules apply in the order provided.

(1) The group first determines whether its section 163(j) limitation for the current year equals or exceeds the aggregate amount of the members' current-year business interest expense.

(i) If the group's section 163(j) limitation for the current year equals or exceeds the aggregate amount of the members' current-year business interest expense, then no amount of the group's current-year business interest expense

will be subject to disallowance in the current year under section 163(j). Once the group has taken into account its members' current-year business interest expense, the group applies the rules of paragraph (b)(3)(ii)(C)(4) of this section.

(ii) If the aggregate amount of members' current-year business interest expense exceeds the group's section 163(j) limitation for the current year, then the group applies the rule in paragraph (b)(3)(ii)(C)(2) of this section.

(2) If this paragraph (b)(3)(ii)(C)(2) applies (see paragraph (b)(3)(ii)(C)(1)(ii) of this section), then each member with current-year business interest expense and with current-year business interest income or floor plan financing interest deducts current-year business interest expense in an amount that does not exceed the sum of the member's business interest income and floor plan financing interest expense for the current year.

(3) After applying the rule in paragraph (b)(3)(ii)(C)(2) of this section, if the group has any section 163(j) limitation remaining for the current year, then each member with remaining current-year business interest expense deducts a portion of its expense based on its allocable share of the consolidated group's remaining section 163(j) limitation.

(4) If this paragraph (b)(3)(ii)(C)(4) applies (see paragraph (b)(3)(ii)(C)(1)(i) of this section), and if the group has any section 163(j) limitation remaining for the current year after applying the rules in paragraph (b)(3)(ii)(C)(1) of this section, then disallowed business interest expense carryforwards permitted to be deducted in the current year will be deducted in the order of the taxable years in which they arose, beginning with the earliest taxable year. Disallowed business interest expense carryforwards from taxable years ending on the same date that are available to offset consolidated taxable income for the current year generally will be deducted on a pro rata basis, under the principles of paragraph (b)(3)(ii)(C)(3) of this section. For example, assume that P and S are the only members of a consolidated group with a section 163(j) limitation for the current year (Year 2) of $200x; the amount of current-year business interest expense deducted in Year 2 is $100x; and P and S, respectively, have $140x and $60x of disallowed business interest expense carryforwards from Year 1 that are not subject to limitation under paragraph (c), (d), or (e) of this section. Under these facts, P would be allowed to deduct $70x of its carryforwards from Year 1 ($100x x ($140x / ($60x + $140x)) = $70x), and S would be allowed to deduct $30x of its carryforwards from Year 1 ($100x x ($60x / ($60x + $140x)) = $30x). But see § 1.383-1(d)(1)(ii), providing that, if losses subject to and not subject to the section 382 limitation are carried from the same taxable year, losses subject to the limitation are deducted before losses not subject to the limitation.

(5) Each member with remaining business interest expense after applying the rules of this paragraph (b)(3)(ii), taking into account

the limitations in paragraphs (c), (d), (e), and (f) of this section, will carry the expense forward to the succeeding taxable year as a disallowed business interest expense carryforward under section 163(j)(2) and § 1.163(j)-2(c).

(iii) *Departure from group.*—If a corporation ceases to be a member during a consolidated return year, the corporation's current-year business interest expense from the taxable period ending on the day of the corporation's change in status as a member, as well as the corporation's disallowed business interest expense carryforwards from prior taxable years that are available to offset consolidated taxable income in the consolidated return year, are first made available for deduction during that consolidated return year.

See § 1.1502-76(b)(1)(i); see also § 1.1502-36(d) (regarding reductions of deferred deductions on the transfer of loss shares of subsidiary stock). Only the amount that is neither deducted by the group in that consolidated return year nor otherwise reduced under the Code or regulations may be carried to the corporation's first separate return year after its change in status.

(iv) *Example: Deduction of interest expense*— (A) *Facts.* (1) P wholly owns A, which is a member of the consolidated group of which P is the common parent. P and A each borrow money from Z, an unrelated third party. The business interest expense of P and A in Years 1, 2, and 3, and the P group's section 163(j) limitation for those years, are as follows:

Table 1 to paragraph (b)(3)(iv)(A)(1)

| Year | P's business interest expense | A's business interest expense | P group's section 163(j) limitation |
|---|---|---|---|
| 1 | $150x | $50x | $100x |
| 2 | 60x | 90x | 120x |
| 3 | 25x | 50x | 185x |

(2) P and A have neither business interest income nor floor plan financing interest expense in Years 1, 2, and 3. Additionally, the P group is neither eligible for the small business exemption in § 1.163(j)-2(d) nor engaged in an excepted trade or business within the meaning of § 1.163(j)-1(b)(38)(ii).

(B) *Analysis*—(1) *Year 1.* In Year 1, the aggregate amount of the P group members' current-year business interest expense ($150x + $50x) exceeds the P group's section 163(j) limitation ($100x). As a result, the rules of paragraph (b)(3)(ii)(C) of this section apply. Because the P group members' current-year business interest expense exceeds the group's section 163(j) limitation for Year 1, P and A must apply the rule in paragraph (b)(3)(ii)(C)(2) of this section. Pursuant to paragraph (b)(3)(ii)(C)(2) of this section, each of P and A must deduct its current-year business interest expense to the extent of its business interest income and floor plan financing interest expense. Neither P nor A has business interest income or floor plan financing interest expense in Year 1. Next, pursuant to paragraph (b)(3)(ii)(C)(3) of this section, each of P and A must deduct a portion of its current-year business interest expense based on its allocable share of the consolidated group's remaining section 163(j) limitation ($100x). P's allocable share is $75x ($100x x ($150x / $200x) = $75x), and A's allocable share is $25x ($100x x ($50x / $200x) = $25x). Accordingly, in Year 1, P deducts $75x of its current-year business interest expense, and A deducts $25x of its current-year business interest expense. P has a disallowed business interest expense carryforward from Year 1 of $75x ($150x - $75x = $75x), and A has a disallowed business interest expense carryforward from Year 1 of $25x ($50x - $25x = $25x).

(2) *Year 2.* In Year 2, the aggregate amount of the P group members' current-year business interest expense ($60x + $90x) and disallowed business interest expense carryforwards ($75x + $25x) exceeds the P group's section 163(j) limitation ($120x). As a result, the rules of paragraph (b)(3)(ii)(C) of this section apply. Because the P group members' current-year business interest expense exceeds the group's section 163(j) limitation for Year 2, P and A must apply the rule in paragraph (b)(3)(ii)(C)(2) of this section. Pursuant to paragraph (b)(3)(ii)(C)(2) of this section, each of P and A must deduct its current-year business interest expense to the extent of its business interest income and floor plan financing interest expense. Neither P nor A has business interest income or floor plan financing interest expense in Year 2. Next, pursuant to paragraph (b)(3)(ii)(C)(3) of this section, each of P and A must deduct a portion of its current-year business interest expense based on its allocable share of the consolidated group's remaining section 163(j) limitation ($120x). P's allocable share is $48x (($120x x ($60x / $150x)) = $48x), and A's allocable share is $72x (($120x x ($90x / $150x)) = $72x). Accordingly, in Year 2, P deducts $48x of current-year business interest expense, and A deducts $72x of current-year business interest expense. P has a disallowed business interest expense carryforward from Year 2 of $12x ($60x - $48x = $12x), and A has a disallowed business interest expense carryforward from Year 2 of $18x ($90x - $72x = $18x). Additionally, because the P group has no section 163(j) limitation remaining after deducting current-year business interest expense in Year 2, the full amount of P and A's disallowed business interest expense carryforwards from Year 1 ($75x and $25x, respectively) also are carried forward to Year 3. As

a result, at the beginning of Year 3, P and A's respective disallowed business interest expense carryforwards are as follows:

Table 1 to paragraph (b)(3)(iv)(B)(2)

|  | Year 1 disallowed business interest expense carryforwards | Year 2 disallowed business interest expense carryforwards | Total disallowed business interest expense carryforwards |
|---|---|---|---|
| P | $75x | $12x | $87x |
| A | 25x | 18x | 43x |
| Total | 100x | 30x | 130x |

(3) *Year 3.* In Year 3, the aggregate amount of the P group members' current-year business interest expense ($25x + $50x = $75x) and disallowed business interest expense carryforwards ($130x) exceeds the P group's section 163(j) limitation ($185x). As a result, the rules of paragraph (b)(3)(ii)(C) of this section apply. Because the P group's section 163(j) limitation for Year 3 equals or exceeds the P group members' current-year business interest expense, no amount of the members' current-year business interest expense will be subject to disallowance under section 163(j) (see paragraph (b)(3)(ii)(C)(*1*) of this section). After each of P and A deducts its current-year business interest expense, the P group has $110x of section 163(j) limitation remaining for Year 3 ($185x - $25x - $50x = $110x). Next, pursuant to paragraph (b)(3)(ii)(C)(*4*) of this section, $110x of disallowed business interest expense carryforwards are deducted on a pro rata basis, beginning with carryforwards from Year 1. Because the total amount of carryforwards from Year 1 ($100x) is less than the section 163(j) limitation remaining after the deduction of Year 3 business interest expense ($110x), all of the Year 1 carryforwards are deducted in Year 3. After current-year business interest expense and Year 1 carryforwards are deducted, the P group's remaining section 163(j) limitation in Year 3 is $10x. Because the Year 2 carryforwards ($30x) exceed the remaining section 163(j) limitation ($10x), under paragraph (b)(3)(ii)(C)(*4*) of this section, each of P and A will deduct a portion of its Year 2 carryforwards based on its allocable share of the consolidated group's remaining section 163(j) limitation. P's allocable share is $4x (($10x x ($12x / $30x)) = $4x), and A's allocable share is $6x (($10x x ($18x / $30x)) = $6x). Accordingly, P and A may deduct $4x and $6x, respectively, of their Year 2 carryforwards. For Year 4, P and A have $8x and $12x of disallowed business interest expense carryforwards from Year 2, respectively.

(c) *Disallowed business interest expense carryforwards in transactions to which section 381(a) applies.*—For rules governing the application of section 381(c)(20) to disallowed business interest expense carryforwards, including limitations on an acquiring corporation's use of the disallowed business interest expense carryforwards of the transferor or distributor corporation in the acquiring corporation's first taxable year ending

after the date of distribution or transfer, see § 1.381(c)(20)-1.

(d) *Limitations on disallowed business interest expense carryforwards from separate return limitation years.*—(1) *General rule.*—Except as provided in paragraph (f) of this section (relating to an overlap with section 382), the disallowed business interest expense carryforwards of a member arising in a separate return limitation year (or SRLY (see § 1.1502-1(f))) that are included in the consolidated group's business interest expense deduction for any taxable year under paragraph (b) of this section may not exceed the group's section 163(j) limitation for that year, determined by reference only to the member's items of income, gain, deduction, and loss for that year (section 163(j) SRLY limitation). For purposes of this paragraph (d), the SRLY subgroup principles of § 1.1502-21(c)(2) apply with appropriate adjustments.

(2) *Deduction of disallowed business interest expense carryforwards arising in a SRLY.*—Notwithstanding paragraph (d)(1) of this section, disallowed business interest expense carryforwards of a member arising in a SRLY are available for deduction by the consolidated group in the current year only to the extent the group has any remaining section 163(j) limitation for the current year after the deduction of current-year business interest expense and disallowed business interest expense carryforwards from earlier taxable years that are permitted to be deducted in the current year (see paragraph (b)(3)(ii)(A) of this section), and only to the extent the section 163(j) SRLY limitation for the current year exceeds the amount of the member's business interest expense already deducted by the group in that year under paragraph (b)(3)(ii) of this section. SRLY-limited disallowed business interest expense carryforwards are deducted on a pro rata basis (under the principles of paragraph (b)(3)(ii)(C)(3) of this section) with non-SRLY limited disallowed business interest expense carryforwards from taxable years ending on the same date.

(3) *Examples.*—The principles of this paragraph (d) are illustrated by the following examples. For purposes of the examples in this paragraph (d)(3), unless otherwise stated, P, R, S, and T are taxable domestic C corporations that

are not regulated investment companies (RICs) or real estate investment trusts (REITs) and that file their tax returns on a calendar-year basis; none of P, R, S, or T qualifies for the small business exemption under section 163(j)(3) or is engaged in an excepted trade or business; all interest expense is deductible except for the potential application of section 163(j); and the facts set forth the only corporate activity.

(i) *Example 1: Determination of SRLY limitation*—(A) *Facts.* Individual A owns P. In 2019, A forms T, which pays or accrues a $100x business interest expense for which a deduction is disallowed under section 163(j) and that is carried forward to 2020. P does not pay or accrue business interest expense in 2019, and P has no disallowed business interest expense carryforwards from prior taxable years. At the close of 2019, P acquires all of the stock of T, which joins with P in filing a consolidated return beginning in 2020. Neither P nor T pays or accrues business interest expense in 2020, and the P group has a section 163(j) limitation of $300x in that year. This limitation would be $70x if determined by reference solely to T's items for 2020.

(B) *Analysis.* T's $100x of disallowed business interest expense carryforwards from 2019 arose in a SRLY. P's acquisition of T was not an ownership change as defined by section 382(g); thus, T's disallowed business interest expense carryforwards are subject to the SRLY limitation in paragraph (d)(1) of this section. The section 163(j) SRLY limitation for 2020 is the P group's section 163(j) limitation, determined by reference solely to T's items for 2020 ($70x). See paragraph (d)(1) of this section. Thus, $70x of T's disallowed business interest expense carryforwards are available to be deducted by the P group in 2020, and the remaining $30x of T's disallowed business interest expense carryforwards are carried forward to 2021.

(C) *Section 163(j) limitation of $0.* The facts are the same as in paragraph (A) of this *Example 1*, except that the section 163(j) SRLY limitation for 2020 (computed by reference solely to T's items for that year) is $0. Because the amount of T's disallowed business interest expense carryforwards that may be deducted by the P group in 2020 may not exceed the section 163(j) SRLY limitation for that year, none of T's carryforwards from 2019 may be deducted by the P group in 2020.

(ii) *Example 2: Deduction of disallowed business interest expense carryforwards arising in a SRLY*—(A) *Facts.* P and S are the only members of a consolidated group. P has neither current-year business interest expense nor disallowed business interest expense carryforwards. S has $100x of disallowed business interest expense carryforwards that arose in a SRLY and $150x of current-year business interest. The section 163(j) SRLY limitation for the current year (computed by reference solely to S's items for that year) is $200x. Assume that the P group's section 163(j) limitation for the current year would permit all of S's current-year business interest expense and disal-

lowed business interest expense carryforwards to be deducted in the current year but for the rules of this paragraph (d).

(B) *Analysis.* Under paragraph (d)(1) of this section, the section 163(j) SRLY limitation for the current year of $200x (computed by reference solely to S's items for that year) exceeds the amount of S's business interest expense taken into account by the P group in the current year under paragraph (b)(3)(ii) of this section ($150x) by $50x. Thus, $50x of S's disallowed business interest expense carryforwards that arose in a SRLY may be taken into account by the P group in the current year.

(e) *Application of section 382.*—(1) *Pre-change loss.*—For rules governing the treatment of a disallowed business interest expense as a pre-change loss for purposes of section 382, see §§ 1.382-2(a) and 1.382-6. For rules governing the application of section 382 to disallowed disqualified interest carryforwards, see § 1.163(j)-11(b)(4).

(2) *Loss corporation.*—For rules governing when a disallowed business interest expense causes a corporation to be a loss corporation within the meaning of section 382(k)(1), see § 1.382-2(a). For the application of section 382 to disallowed disqualified interest carryforwards, see § 1.163(j)-11(b)(4).

(3) *Ordering rules for utilization of pre-change losses and for absorption of the section 382 limitation.*—For ordering rules for the utilization of disallowed business interest expense, net operating losses, and other pre-change losses, and for the absorption of the section 382 limitation, see § 1.383-1(d).

(4) *Disallowed business interest expense from the pre-change period in the year of a testing date.*—For rules governing the treatment of disallowed business interest expense from the pre-change period (within the meaning of § 1.382-6(g)(2)) in the year of a testing date, see § 1.382-2.

(f) *Overlap of SRLY limitation with section 382.*—The limitation provided in paragraph (d) of this section does not apply to disallowed business interest expense carryforwards when the application of paragraph (d) of this section results in an overlap with the application of section 382. For purposes of applying this paragraph (f), the principles of § 1.1502-21(g) apply with appropriate adjustments.

(g) *Additional limitations.*—Additional rules provided under the Code or regulations also apply to limit the use of disallowed business interest expense carryforwards. For rules governing the relationship between section 163(j) and other provisions affecting the deductibility of interest, see § 1.163(j)-3.

(h) *Applicability date.*—This section applies to taxable years ending after the date the Treasury decision adopting these regulations as final regulations is published in the **Federal Register**.

**Prop. Reg. § 1.163(j)-5(h)**

However, taxpayers and their related parties, within the meaning of sections 267(b) and 707(b)(1), may apply the rules of this section to a taxable year beginning after December 31, 2017, so long as the taxpayers and their related parties consistently apply the rules of the section 163(j) regulations, and if applicable, §§ 1.263A-9, 1.381(c)(20)-1, 1.382-6, 1.383-1, 1.469-9, 1.882-5, 1.1502-13, 1.1502-21, 1.1502-36, 1.1502-79, 1.1502-91 through 1.1502-99 (to the extent they effectuate the rules of §§ 1.382-6 and 1.383-1), and 1.1504-4 to those taxable years. [Reg. § 1.163(j)-5.]

[Proposed 12-28-2018.]

**[Prop. Reg. § 1.163(j)-6]**

**§ 1.163(j)-6. Application of the business interest deduction limitation to partnerships and subchapter S corporations.**—(a) *Overview.*—If a deduction for business interest expense of a partnership or S corporation is subject to limitation under section 163(j), section 163(j)(4) provides that the section 163(j) limitation applies at the partnership or S corporation level and any deduction for business interest expense within the meaning of section 163(j) is taken into account in determining the nonseparately stated taxable income or loss of the partnership or S corporation. Once a partnership or S corporation determines its business interest expense, business interest income, ATI, and floor plan financing interest expense, the partnership or S corporation calculates its section 163(j) limitation by applying the rules of § 1.163(j)-2(b) and this section. Paragraph (b) of this section provides definitions used in this section. Paragraph (c) of this section provides rules regarding the character of a partnership's deductible business interest expense and excess business interest expense. Paragraph (d) of this section provides rules regarding the calculation of a partnership's ATI and floor plan financing interest expense. Paragraph (e) of this section provides rules regarding a partner's ATI and business interest income. Paragraph (f) of this section provides an eleven-step computation necessary for properly allocating a partnership's deductible business interest expense and section 163(j) excess items to its partners. Paragraph (g) of this section applies carryforward rules at the partner level if a partnership has excess business interest expense, as defined in § 1.163(j)-1(b)(14). Paragraph (h) of this section provides basis adjustment rules and paragraph (j) of this section provides rules regarding investment items of a partnership. Paragraph (l) of this section provides rules regarding S corporations. Paragraph (m) of this section provides rules for partnerships and S corporations not subject to section 163(j). Paragraph (o) of this section provides examples illustrating the rules of this section. Paragraph (p) provides the applicability date of the rules in this section.

(b) *Definitions.*—In addition to the definitions contained in § 1.163(j)-1, the following definitions apply for purposes of this section.

(1) *Section 163(j) items.*—The term *section 163(j) items* means the partnership or S corporation's business interest expense, business interest income, and items comprising ATI, as defined in § 1.163(j)-1(b)(1).

(2) *Partner basis items.*—The term *partner basis items* means any items of income, gain, loss, or deduction resulting from either an adjustment to the basis of partnership property used in a non-excepted trade or business made pursuant to section 743(b) or the operation of section 704(c)(1)(C)(i) with respect to such property. Partner basis items also include section 743(b) basis adjustments used to increase or decrease a partner's share of partnership gain or loss on the sale of partnership property used in a non-excepted trade or business (as described in § 1.743-1(j)(3)(i)) and amounts resulting from the operation of section 704(c)(1)(C)(i) used to decrease a partner's share of partnership gain or increase a partner's share of partnership loss on the sale of such property.

(3) *Remedial items.*—The term *remedial items* means any allocation to a partner of remedial items of income, gain, loss, or deduction pursuant to section 704(c) and § 1.704-3(d).

(4) *Excess business interest income.*—The term *excess business interest income* means the amount by which a partnership's or S corporation's business interest income exceeds its business interest expense in a taxable year.

(5) *Deductible business interest expense.*—The term *deductible business interest expense* means the amount of a partnership's or S corporation's business interest expense that is deductible under section 163(j) in the current taxable year following the application of the limitation contained in § 1.163(j)-2(b).

(6) *Section 163(j) excess items.*—The term *section 163(j) excess items* means the partnership's excess business interest expense, excess taxable income, and excess business interest income.

(7) *Non-excepted assets.*—The term *non-excepted assets* means assets from a trade or business other than assets from an excepted regulated utility trade or business, electing farming business, or electing real property trade or business, as such terms are defined in § 1.163(j)-1.

(8) *Excepted assets.*—The term *excepted assets* means assets from an excepted regulated utility trade or business, electing farming business, or electing real property trade or business, as such terms are defined in § 1.163(j)-1.

(c) *Character of business interest expense.*—If a partnership has deductible business interest expense, such deductible business interest expense is not subject to any additional application of section 163(j) at the partner-level because it is taken into account in determining the non-separately stated taxable income or loss of the partnership. For all other purposes of the Code, however, deductible business interest expense and excess business interest expense retain their character as business interest expense at the partner-level. For example, for purposes of section 469, such business interest expense retains its character as either passive or non-passive in the hands of the partner. Additionally, for purposes of section 469, deductible business interest expense and excess business interest expense from a partnership remain interest derived from a trade or business in the hands of a partner even if the partner does not materially participate in the partnership's trade or business activity. For additional rules regarding the interaction between sections 465, 469, and 163(j), see § 1.163(j)-3.

(d) *Adjusted taxable income of the partnership.*— (1) *Modification of adjusted taxable income for partnerships.*—The ATI of the partnership generally is determined in accordance with § 1.163(j)-1(b)(1). For purposes of computing the partnership's ATI, the taxable income of the partnership is determined under section 703(a) and includes any items described in section 703(a)(1) to the extent such items are otherwise included under § 1.163(j)-1(b)(1).

(2) *Section 734(b), partner basis items, and remedial items.*—A partnership takes into account items resulting from adjustments made to the basis of its property pursuant to section 734(b) for purposes of calculating its ATI pursuant to § 1.163(j)-1(b)(1). However, partner basis items and remedial items are not taken into account in determining a partnership's ATI under § 1.163(j)-1(b)(1). Instead, partner basis items and remedial items are taken into account by the partner in determining the partner's ATI pursuant to § 1.163(j)-1(b)(1). See *Example 8* in paragraph (o)(8) of this section.

(e) *Adjusted taxable income and business interest income of partners.*—(1) *Modification of adjusted taxable income for partners.*—The ATI of a partner in a partnership generally is determined in accordance with § 1.163(j)-1(b)(1) without regard to such partner's distributive share of any items of income, gain, deduction, or loss of such partnership, and is increased by such partner's distributive share of such partnership's excess taxable income determined under paragraph (f) of this section. For rules regarding corporate partners, see § 1.163(j)-4(b)(3).

(2) *Partner basis items and remedial items.*— Partner basis items and remedial items are taken into account as items derived directly by the partner in determining the partner's ATI for purposes of the partner's section 163(j) limitation. If a partner is allocated remedial items, such partner's ATI is increased or decreased by the amount of such items. Additionally, to the extent a partner is allocated partner basis items, such partner's ATI is increased or decreased by the

amount of such item. See *Example 8* in paragraph (o)(8) of this section.

(3) *Disposition of partnership interests.*—If a partner recognizes gain or loss upon the disposition of interests in a partnership, and the partnership in which the interest is being disposed owns only non-excepted trade or business assets, the gain or loss on the disposition of the partnership interest is included in the partner's ATI. For dispositions of interests in partnerships that own:

(i) Non-excepted assets and excepted assets; or

(ii) Investment assets; or

(iii) Both. See § 1.163(j)-10(b)(4)(ii).

(4) *Double counting of business interest income and floor plan financing interest expense prohibited.*—For purposes of calculating a partner's section 163(j) limitation, the partner does not include—

(i) Business interest income from a partnership that is subject to section 163(j) except to the extent it is allocated excess business interest income from that partnership pursuant to paragraph (f)(2) of this section; and

(ii) The partner's allocable share of the partnership's floor plan financing interest expense because such floor plan financing interest expense has already been taken into account by the partnership in determining its nonseparately stated taxable income or loss for purposes of section 163(j).

(f) *Allocation and determination of section 163(j) excess items made in the same manner as nonseparately stated taxable income or loss of the partnership.*—(1) *Overview.*—(i) *In general.*—The purpose of this section is to provide guidance regarding how a partnership must allocate its deductible business interest expense and section 163(j) excess items, if any, among its partners. For purposes of section 163(j)(4) and this section, allocations and determinations of deductible business interest expense and section 163(j) excess items are considered made in the same manner as the nonseparately stated taxable income or loss of the partnership if, and only if, such allocations and determinations are made in accordance with the eleven-step computation set forth in paragraphs (f)(2)(i) through (xi) of this section. A partnership first determines its section 163(j) limitation, total amount of deductible business interest expense, and section 163(j) excess items under paragraph (f)(2)(i) of this section. The partnership then applies paragraphs (f)(2)(ii) through (xi) of this section, in that order, to determine how those items of the partnership are allocated among its partners. At the conclusion of the eleven-step computation set forth in paragraphs (f)(2)(i) through (xi) of this section, the total amount of deductible business interest expense and section 163(j) excess items allocated to each partner will equal the partnership's total amount of deductible business interest expense and section 163(j) excess items.

(ii) *Relevance solely for purposes of section 163(j).*—No rule set forth in paragraph (f)(2) of this section prohibits a partnership from making an allocation to a partner of any item of partnership income, gain, loss, or deduction that is otherwise permitted under section 704 and the regulations thereunder. Accordingly, any calculations in paragraphs (f)(2)(i) through (xi) of this section are solely for the purpose of determining each partner's deductible business interest expense and section 163(j) excess items, and do not otherwise affect any other provision under the Code, such as section 704(b). Additionally, floor plan financing interest expense is not allocated in accordance with paragraph (f)(2) of this section. Instead, floor plan financing interest expense of a partnership is allocated to its partners under section 704(b) and is taken into account as a nonseparately stated item of loss for purposes of section 163(j).

(2) *Steps for allocating deductible business interest expense and section 163(j) excess items.*— (i) *Partnership-level calculation required by section 163(j)(4)(A).*—First, a partnership must determine its section 163(j) limitation pursuant to § 1.163(j)-2(b). This calculation determines a partnership's total amounts of excess business interest income, excess taxable income, excess business interest expense (that is, the partnership's section 163(j) excess items), and deductible business interest expense under section 163(j) for a taxable year.

(ii) *Determination of each partner's relevant section 163(j) items.*—Second, a partnership must determine each partner's allocable share of each section 163(j) item under section 704(b) and the regulations thereunder including any allocations under section 704(c), other than remedial items as defined in paragraph (b)(3) of this section. Only section 163(j) items that were actually taken into account in the partnership's section 163(j) calculation under paragraph (f)(2)(i) of this section are taken into account for purposes of this paragraph (f)(2)(ii). Partner basis items, allocations of investment income and expense, remedial items, and amounts determined for the partner under § 1.163(j)-8T are not taken into account for purposes of this paragraph (f)(2)(ii). For purposes of paragraphs (f)(2)(ii) through (xi) of this section, the term *allocable ATI* means a partner's distributive share of the partnership's ATI (i.e., a partner's distributive share of gross income and gain items comprising ATI less such partner's distributive share of gross loss and deduction items comprising ATI), the term *allocable business interest income* means a partner's distributive share of the partnership's business interest income, and the term *allocable business interest expense* means a partner's distributive share of the partnership's business interest expense that is not floor plan financing interest expense.

(iii) *Partner-level comparison of business interest income and business interest expense.*—Third, a partnership must compare each partner's allocable business interest income to such partner's allocable business interest expense. Paragraphs (f)(2)(iii) through (v) of this section determine how a partnership must allocate its excess business interest income among its partners, as well as the amount of each partner's allocable business interest expense that is not deductible business interest expense after taking the partnership's business interest income into account. To the extent a partner's allocable business interest income exceeds its allocable business interest expense, the partner has an *allocable business interest income excess*. The aggregate of all the partners' allocable business interest income excess amounts is the *total allocable business interest income excess*. To the extent a partner's allocable business interest expense exceeds its allocable business interest income, the partner has an *allocable business interest income deficit*. The aggregate of all the partners' allocable business interest income deficit amounts is the *total allocable business interest income deficit*. These amounts are required to perform calculations in paragraphs (f)(2)(iv) and (v) of this section, which appropriately reallocate allocable business interest income excess to partners with allocable business interest income deficits in order to reconcile the partner-level calculation under paragraph (f)(2)(iii) of this section with the partnership-level result under paragraph (f)(2)(i) of this section.

(iv) *Matching partnership and aggregate partner excess business interest income.*—Fourth, a partnership must determine each partner's final allocable business interest income excess. A partner's *final allocable business interest income excess* is determined by reducing, but not below zero, such partner's allocable business interest income excess (if any) by the partner's step four adjustment amount. A partner's *step four adjustment amount* is the product of the total allocable business interest income deficit and the ratio of such partner's allocable business interest income excess to the total allocable business interest income excess. The rules of this paragraph (f)(2)(iv) ensure that, following the application of paragraph (f)(2)(xi) of this section, the aggregate of all the partners' allocations of excess business interest income equals the total amount of the partnership's excess business interest income as determined in paragraph (f)(2)(i) of this section.

(v) *Remaining business interest expense determination.*—Fifth, a partnership must determine each partner's remaining business interest expense. A partner's *remaining business interest expense* is calculated by reducing, but not below zero, such partner's allocable business interest income deficit (if any) by such partner's step five adjustment amount. A partner's *step five adjustment amount* is the product of the total allocable

**Prop. Reg. § 1.163(j)-6(f)(1)(ii)**

business interest income excess and the ratio of such partner's allocable business interest income deficit to the total allocable business interest income deficit. Generally, a partner's remaining business interest expense is a partner's allocable business interest income deficit adjusted to reflect a reallocation of allocable business interest income excess from other partners. Determining a partner's remaining business interest expense is necessary to perform an ATI calculation that begins in paragraph (f)(2)(vii) of this section.

(vi) *Determination of final allocable ATI.*— Sixth, a partnership must determine each partner's final allocable ATI. Paragraphs (f)(2)(vi) through (x) of this section determine how a partnership must allocate its excess taxable income and excess business interest expense among its partners.

(A) *Positive allocable ATI.*—To the extent a partner's income and gain items comprising its allocable ATI exceed its deduction and loss items comprising its allocable ATI, the partner has *positive allocable ATI*. The aggregate of all the partners' positive allocable ATI amounts is the *total positive allocable ATI.*

(B) *Negative allocable ATI.*—To the extent a partner's deduction and loss items comprising its allocable ATI exceed its income and gain items comprising its allocable ATI, the partner has negative allocable ATI. The aggregate of all the partners' negative allocable ATI amounts is the *total negative allocable ATI.*

(C) *Final allocable ATI.*—Any partner with a negative allocable ATI, or an allocable ATI of $0, has a positive allocable ATI of $0. Any partner with a positive allocable ATI of $0 has a final allocable ATI of $0. The final allocable ATI of any partner with a positive allocable ATI greater than $0 is such partner's positive allocable ATI reduced, but not below zero, by the partner's step six adjustment amount. A partner's *step six adjustment amount* is the product of the total negative allocable ATI and the ratio of such partner's positive allocable ATI to the total positive allocable ATI. The total of the partners' final allocable ATI amounts must equal the partnership's ATI amount used to compute its section 163(j) limitation pursuant to § 1.163(j)-2(b).

(vii) *Partner level comparison of thirty percent of adjusted taxable income and remaining business interest expense.*—Seventh, a partnership must compare each partner's ATI capacity to such partner's remaining business interest expense as determined under paragraph (f)(2)(v) of this section. A partner's *ATI capacity* is the amount that is thirty percent of such partner's final allocable ATI as determined under paragraph (f)(2)(vi) of this section. A partner's final allocable ATI is grossed down to thirty percent prior to being compared to its remaining business interest expense in this calculation to parallel the partnership's adjustment to its ATI under section 163(j)(1)(B). To the extent a partner's ATI

capacity exceeds its remaining business interest expense, the partner has an *ATI capacity excess.* The aggregate of all the partners' ATI capacity excess amounts is the *total ATI capacity excess.* To the extent a partner's remaining business interest expense exceeds its ATI capacity, the partner has an *ATI capacity deficit.* The aggregate of all the partners' ATI capacity deficit amounts is the *total ATI capacity deficit.* These amounts (which may be subject to adjustment under paragraph (f)(2)(viii) of this section) are required to perform calculations in paragraphs (f)(2)(ix) and (x) of this section, which appropriately reallocate ATI capacity excess to partners with ATI capacity deficits in order to reconcile the partner-level calculation under paragraph (f)(2)(vii) of this section with the partnership-level result under paragraph (f)(2)(i) of this section.

(viii) *Partner priority right to ATI capacity excess determination.*—(A) Eighth, the partnership must determine whether it is required to make any adjustments described in this paragraph (f)(2)(viii) and, if it is, make such adjustments. The rules of this paragraph (f)(2)(viii) are necessary to account for adjustments made to a partner's allocable ATI in paragraph (f)(2)(vi) of this section to ensure that the partners who had a negative allocable ATI do not inappropriately benefit under the rules of paragraphs (f)(2)(ix) through (xi) of this section to the detriment of the partners who had positive allocable ATI. The partnership must perform the calculations and make the necessary adjustments described under paragraphs (f)(2)(viii)(B) and (C) or paragraph (f)(2)(viii)(D) of this section if, and only if, there is—

(1) An excess business interest expense amount greater than $0 under paragraph (f)(2)(i) of this section;

(2) A total negative allocable ATI amount greater than $0 under paragraph (f)(2)(vi) of this section; and

(3) A total ATI capacity excess amount greater than $0 under paragraph (f)(2)(vii) of this section.

(B) A partnership must determine each partner's priority amount and usable priority amount. A partner's *priority amount* is thirty percent of the amount by which a partner's positive allocable ATI under paragraph (f)(2)(vi)(A) of this section exceeds such partner's final allocable ATI under paragraph (f)(2)(vi)(C) of this section. However, only partners with an ATI capacity deficit as determined under paragraph (f)(2)(vii) of this section can have a priority amount greater than $0. The aggregate of all the partners' priority amounts is the *total priority amount.* A partner's *usable priority amount* is the lesser of such partner's priority amount and such partner's ATI capacity deficit as determined under paragraph (f)(2)(vii) of this section. The aggregate of all the partners' usable priority amounts is the *total usable priority amount.* If the total ATI capacity excess amount, as determined under paragraph (f)(2)(vii) of this section, is greater than or equal

**Prop. Reg. § 1.163(j)-6(f)(2)(viii)(B)**

to the total usable priority amount, then the partnership must perform the adjustments described in paragraph (f)(2)(viii)(C) of this section. If the total usable priority amount is greater than the total ATI capacity excess, as determined under paragraph (f)(2)(vii) of this section, then the partnership must perform the adjustments described in paragraph (f)(2)(viii)(D) of this section.

(C) For purposes of paragraph (f)(2)(ix) of this section, each partner's final ATI capacity excess is $0. For purposes of paragraph (f)(2)(x) of this section, the following terms have the following meanings for each partner:

*(1)* Each partner's *ATI capacity deficit* is such partner's ATI capacity deficit as determined under paragraph (f)(2)(vii) of this section reduced by such partner's usable priority amount.

*(2)* The *total ATI capacity deficit* is the total ATI capacity deficit as determined under paragraph (f)(2)(vii) of this section reduced by the total usable priority amount.

*(3)* The *total ATI capacity excess* is the total ATI capacity excess as determined under paragraph (f)(2)(vii) of this section reduced by the total usable priority amount.

(D) Any partner with a priority amount greater than $0 is a *priority partner.* Any partner that is not a priority partner is a *non-priority partner.* For purposes of paragraph (f)(2)(ix) of this section, each partner's final ATI capacity excess amount is $0. For purposes of paragraph (f)(2)(x) of this section, each non-priority partner's final ATI capacity deficit amount is such partner's ATI capacity deficit as determined under paragraph (f)(2)(vii) of this section. For purposes of paragraph (f)(2)(x) of this section, the following terms have the following meanings for priority partners.

*(1)* Each priority partner must determine its step eight excess share. A partner's *step eight excess share* is the product of the total ATI capacity excess as determined under paragraph (f)(2)(vii) of this section and the ratio of the partner's priority amount to the total priority amount.

*(2)* To the extent a priority partner's step eight excess share exceeds its ATI capacity deficit as determined under paragraph (f)(2)(vii) of this section, such excess amount is the priority partner's *ATI capacity excess* for purposes of paragraph (f)(2)(x) of this section. The *total ATI capacity excess* is the aggregate of the priority partners' ATI capacity excess amounts as determined under this paragraph (f)(2)(viii)(D)(2).

*(3)* To the extent a priority partner's ATI capacity deficit as determined under paragraph (f)(2)(vii) of this section exceeds its step eight excess share, such excess amount is the priority partner's *ATI capacity deficit* for purposes of paragraph (f)(2)(x) of this section. The *total ATI capacity deficit* is the aggregate of the priority partners' ATI capacity deficit amounts as determined under this paragraph (f)(2)(viii)(D)(3).

(ix) *Matching partnership and aggregate partner excess taxable income.*—Ninth, a partnership must determine each partner's final ATI capacity excess. A partner's *final ATI capacity excess* amount is determined by reducing, but not below zero, such partner's ATI capacity excess (if any) by the partner's step nine adjustment amount. A partner's *step nine adjustment amount* is the product of the total ATI capacity deficit and the ratio of such partner's ATI capacity excess to the total ATI capacity excess. The rules of this paragraph (f)(2)(ix) ensure that, following the application of paragraph (f)(2)(xi) of this section, the aggregate of all the partners' allocations of excess taxable income equals the total amount of the partnership's excess taxable income as determined in paragraph (f)(2)(i) of this section.

(x) *Matching partnership and aggregate partner excess business interest expense.*—Tenth, a partnership must determine each partner's final ATI capacity deficit. A partner's *final ATI capacity deficit* amount is determined by reducing, but not below zero, such partner's ATI capacity deficit (if any) by the partner's step ten adjustment amount. A partner's *step ten adjustment amount* is the product of the total ATI capacity excess and the ratio of such partner's ATI capacity deficit to the total ATI capacity deficit. Generally, a partner's final ATI capacity deficit is a partner's ATI capacity deficit adjusted to reflect a reallocation of ATI capacity excess from other partners. The rules of this paragraph (f)(2)(x) ensure that, following the application of paragraph (f)(2)(xi) of this section, the aggregate of all the partners' allocations of excess business interest expense equals the total amount of the partnership's excess business interest expense as determined in paragraph (f)(2)(i) of this section.

(xi) *Final section 163(j) excess item and deductible business interest expense allocation.*—Eleventh, a partnership must allocate section 163(j) excess items and deductible business interest expense to its partners. Excess business interest income calculated under paragraph (f)(2)(i) of this section, if any, is allocated dollar for dollar by the partnership to its partners with final allocable business interest income excess amounts. Excess business interest expense calculated under paragraph (f)(2)(i) of this section, if any, is allocated dollar for dollar to partners with final ATI capacity deficit amounts. After grossing up each partner's final ATI capacity excess amount by ten-thirds, excess taxable income calculated under paragraph (f)(2)(i) of this section, if any, is allocated dollar for dollar to partners with final ATI capacity excess amounts. A partner's allocable business interest expense is deductible business interest expense to the extent it exceeds such partner's share of excess business interest expense. See paragraphs (o)(11) through (15) of this section.

(g) *Carryforwards.*—(1) *In general.*—The amount of any business interest expense not allowed as a deduction to a partnership by reason of § 1.163(j)-2(b) and paragraph (f)(2) of this section for any taxable year is—

(i) Not treated as business interest expense of the partnership in the succeeding taxable year; and

(ii) Subject to paragraph (g)(2) of this section, treated as excess business interest expense which is allocated to each partner pursuant to paragraph (f)(2) of this section.

(2) *Treatment of excess business interest expense allocated to partners.*—If a partner is allocated excess business interest expense from a partnership under paragraph (f)(2) of this section for any taxable year —

(i) Solely for purposes of section 163(j), such excess business interest expense is treated as business interest expense paid or accrued by the partner in the next succeeding taxable year in which the partner is allocated excess taxable income or excess business interest income from such partnership, but only to the extent of such excess taxable income or excess business interest income; and

(ii) Any portion of such excess business interest expense remaining after the application of paragraph (g)(2)(i) of this section is excess business interest expense that is subject to the limitations of paragraph (g)(2)(i) of this section in succeeding years, unless paragraph (m)(3) of this section applies. See paragraphs (o)(1) through (10) of this section.

(3) *Excess taxable income and excess business interest income ordering rule.*—In the event a partner has excess business interest expense from a prior taxable year and is allocated excess taxable income or excess business interest income from the same partnership in a succeeding taxable year, the partner must treat, for purposes of section 163(j), the excess business interest expense as business interest expense paid or accrued by the partner in an amount equal to the partner's share of the partnership's excess taxable income or excess business interest income in such succeeding taxable year. See paragraphs (o)(2) through (10) of this section.

(h) *Basis adjustments.*—(1) *Section 704(d) ordering.*—Deductible business interest expense and excess business interest expense are subject to section 704(d). If a partner is subject to a limitation on loss under section 704(d) and a partner is allocated losses from a partnership in a taxable year, § 1.704-1(d)(2) requires that the limitation on losses under section 704(d) be apportioned amongst these losses based on the character of each loss (each grouping of loses based on character being a "section 704(d) loss class"). If there are multiple section 704(d) loss classes in a given year, § 1.704-1(d)(2) requires the partner to apportion the limitation on losses under section 704(d) to each section 704(d) loss class proportionately. For purposes of applying this proportionate rule, any deductible business interest expense (whether allocated to the partner in the current taxable year or suspended under section 704(d) in a prior taxable year), any excess business interest expense allocated to the partner in the current taxable year, and any excess business interest expense from a prior taxable year that was suspended under section 704(d) ("negative section 163(j) expense") shall comprise the same section 704(d) loss class. Once the partner determines the amount of limitation on losses apportioned to this section 704(d) loss class, any deductible business interest expense is taken into account before any excess business interest expense or negative section 163(j) expense. See paragraph (o)(9) of this section.

(2) *Excess business interest expense basis adjustments.*—The adjusted basis of a partner in a partnership interest is reduced, but not below zero, by the amount of excess business interest expense allocated to the partner pursuant to paragraph (f)(2) of this section. Negative section 163(j) expense is not treated as excess business interest expense in any subsequent year until such negative section 163(j) expense is no longer suspended under section 704(d). Therefore, negative section 163(j) expense does not affect, and is not affected by, any allocation of excess taxable income to the partner. Accordingly, any excess taxable income allocated to a partner from a partnership while the partner still has negative section 163(j) expense will be included in the partner's ATI. However, once the negative section 163(j) expense is no longer suspended under section 704(d), it becomes excess business interest expense, which is subject to the general rules in paragraph (g) of this section. See paragraph (o)(10) of this section.

(3) *Basis adjustments upon disposition of partnership interest.*—(i) *Complete disposition of partnership interest.*—If a partner disposes of all or substantially all of a partnership interest (whether by sale, exchange, or redemption), the adjusted basis of the partnership interest is increased immediately before the disposition by the amount of the excess (if any) of the amount of the basis reduction under paragraph (h)(2) of this section over the portion of any excess business interest expense allocated to the partner under paragraph (f)(2) of this section which has previously been treated under paragraph (g) of this section as business interest expense pair or accrued by the partner, regardless of whether the disposition was a result of a taxable or nontaxable transaction. Therefore, the adjusted basis of a partner in a partnership interest is not increased by any negative section 163(j) expense upon the disposition of a partnership interest. No deduction under section 163(j) is allowed to the transferor or transferee under chapter 1 of subtitle A of the Code for any excess business interest expense resulting in a basis increase under this section or any negative section 163(j) expense.

(ii) *Partial disposition of partnership interest.*—If a partner disposes of less than substan-

**Prop. Reg. § 1.163(j)-6(h)(3)(ii)**

tially all of its interest in a partnership (whether by sale, exchange, or redemption), a partner shall not increase its basis in its partnership interest by the amount of any excess business interest expense that has not yet been treated as business interest expense paid or accrued by the partner in accordance with paragraph (g) of this section. Any such excess business interest expense shall remain excess business interest expense of the transferor partner until such time as the transferor partner is allocated an appropriate amount of excess taxable income or excess business interest income from the partnership or the partner disposes of its partnership interest in accordance with paragraph (h)(2)(i) of this section. Additionally, any negative section 163(j) expense shall remain negative section 163(j) expense of the transferor partner until such negative section 163(j) expense is no longer suspended under section 704(d).

(i) [Reserved]

(j) *Investment items.*—Any item of a partnership's income, gain, deduction, or loss that is investment interest income or expense pursuant to § 1.163-8T is allocated to each partner in accordance with section 704(b) and the regulations thereunder and the effect of such allocation for purposes of section 163 is determined at the partner-level. See § 1.163(j)-4(b)(3), section 163(d), and § 1.163-8T.

(k) [Reserved]

(l) *S corporations.*—(1) *In general.*—In the case of any S corporation, the section 163(j) limitation is applied at the S corporation level, and any deduction allowed for business interest expense is taken into account in determining the nonseparately stated taxable income or loss of the S corporation. An S corporation determines its section 163(j) limitation in the same manner as set forth in § 1.163(j)-2(b). Allocations of excess taxable income and excess business interest income are made in accordance with the shareholders' respective pro rata interests in the S corporation pursuant to section 1366(a)(1) after determining the S corporation's section 163(j) limitation pursuant to § 1.163(j)-2(b).

(2) *Character of deductible business interest expense.*—If an S corporation has deductible business interest expense, such deductible business interest expense is not subject to any additional application of section 163(j) at the shareholder-level because such deductible business interest expense is taken into account in determining the nonseparately stated taxable income or loss of the S corporation. For all other purposes of the Code, however, deductible business interest expense retains its character as business interest expense at the shareholder-level. For example, for purposes of section 469, such deductible business interest expense retains its character as either passive or non-passive in the hands of the shareholder. Additionally, for purposes of section 469, deductible business interest expense from an S corporation remains interest derived

from a trade or business in the hands of a shareholder even if the shareholder does not materially participate in the S corporation's trade or business activity. For additional rules regarding the interaction between sections 465, 469, and 163(j), see § 1.163(j)-3.

(3) *Adjusted taxable income of an S corporation.*—The ATI of an S corporation generally is determined in accordance with § 1.163(j)-1(b)(1). For purposes of computing the S corporation's ATI, the taxable income of the S corporation is determined under section 1363(b) and includes—

(i) Any item described in section 1363(b)(1); and

(ii) Any item described in § 1.163(j)-1(b)(1), to the extent such item is consistent with subchapter S of the Code.

(4) *Adjusted taxable income and business interest income of S corporation shareholders.*—(i) *Adjusted taxable income of S corporation shareholders.*—The ATI of an S corporation shareholder is determined in accordance with § 1.163(j)-1(b)(1) without regard to such shareholder's distributive share of any items of income, gain, deduction, or loss of such S corporation, and is increased by such shareholder's distributive share of such S corporation's excess taxable income, as defined in § 1.163(j)-1(b)(15).

(ii) *Disposition of S corporation stock.*—If a shareholder of an S corporation recognizes gain or loss upon the disposition of stock of the S corporation, and the corporation in which the stock is being disposed only owns non-excepted trade or business assets, the gain or loss on the disposition of the stock is included in the shareholder's ATI. For dispositions of stock of S corporations that own:

(A) Non-excepted assets and excepted assets; or

(B) Investment assets; or

(C) Both. See § 1.163(j)-10(b)(4)(ii).

(iii) *Double counting of business interest income and floor plan financing interest expense prohibited.*—For purposes of calculating an S corporation shareholder's section 163(j) limitation, the shareholder does not include—

(A) Business interest income from an S corporation that is subject to section 163(j) except to the extent it is allocated excess business interest income from that S corporation pursuant to paragraph (l)(1) of this section; and

(B) The shareholder's share of the S corporation's floor plan financing interest expense because such floor plan financing interest expense has already been taken into account by the S corporation in determining its nonseparately stated taxable income or loss for purposes of section 163(j).

(5) *Carryforwards.*—The amount of any business interest expense not allowed as a deduction

for any taxable year by reason of the limitation contained in § 1.163(j)-2(b) is carried forward in the succeeding taxable year as a disallowed business interest expense carryforward under the rules set forth in § 1.163(j)-2(c) (whether to an S corporation or C corporation taxable year). S corporations are subject to:

(i) The same ordering rules as a C corporation that is not a member of a consolidated group; and

(ii) The limitation under section 382. See § 1.163(j)-5(b)(2) and (e).

(6) *Basis adjustments and disallowed business interest expense carryforwards.*—An S corporation shareholder's adjusted basis in its S corporation stock is reduced, but not below zero, when a disallowed business interest expense carryforward becomes deductible under section 163(j).

(7) *Accumulated adjustment accounts.*—The accumulated adjustment account of an S corporation is adjusted to take into account business interest expense in the year in which the S corporation treats such business interest expense as deductible under the section 163(j) limitation. See section 1368(e)(1).

(8) *Termination of qualified subchapter S subsidiary election.*—If a corporation's qualified subchapter S subsidiary election terminates and any disallowed business interest expense carryforward is attributable to the activities of the qualified subchapter S subsidiary at the time of termination, such disallowed business interest expense carryforward remains with the parent S corporation and no portion of these items is allocable to the former qualified subchapter S subsidiary.

(9) *Investment items.*—Any item of an S corporation's income, gain, deduction, or loss that is investment interest income or expense pursuant to § 1.163-8T is allocated to each shareholder in accordance with the shareholders' pro rata interests in the S corporation pursuant to section 1366(a)(1). See section 163(d), § 1.163-8T.

(m) *Partnerships and S corporations not subject to section 163(j).*—(1) *Partnerships and S corporations not subject to section 163(j) by reason of the small business exemption.*—If a partnership or S corporation is not subject to section 163(j) by reason of § 1.163(j)-2(d) (exempt entity), the exempt entity does not calculate the section 163(j) limitation under § 1.163(j)-2 and these regulations. Because an exempt entity is not subject to section 163(j)(4), it does not take its deduction for business interest expense into account in determining its non-separately stated taxable income or loss within the meaning of section 163(j)(4)(A)(i) and retains its character as business interest expense. See § 1.163(j)-6(c). Thus, if a partner or S corporation shareholder is allocated business interest expense from an exempt entity, that allocated business interest expense will be subject to the partner's or S corporation shareholder's section 163(j) limitations. Additionally, contrary to

the general rule in § 1.163(j)-6(e)(1), a partner or S corporation shareholder includes items of income, gain, loss, or deduction of such exempt entity when calculating its ATI. Finally, business interest income of such exempt entity is included in the partner's or S corporation shareholder's section 163(j) limitation regardless of the exempt entity's business interest expense amount.

(2) *Partnerships and S corporations not subject to section 163(j) by reason of an excepted trade or business.*—To the extent a partnership or S corporation is not subject to section 163(j) because it has an excepted trade or business as defined in § 1.163(j)-1(b)(38)(ii) (excepted entity), the entity does not apply its section 163(j) limitation under § 1.163(j)-2 and this section with respect to the business interest expense that is allocable to such excepted trade or business. If a partner or S corporation shareholder is allocated any section 163(j) item that is allocable to the partnership's or S corporation's excepted trade or business (excepted 163(j) items), such excepted 163(j) items are excluded from the partner or shareholder's section 163(j) deduction calculation. See § 1.163(j)-10(c) (regarding the allocation of items between excepted and non-excepted trades or businesses).

(3) *Partnerships that allocated excess business interest expense prior to becoming not subject to section 163(j).*—If a partnership allocates excess business interest expense to one or more of its partners, and in a succeeding taxable year becomes not subject to the requirements of section 163(j), the excess business interest expense from the prior taxable years is treated as paid or accrued by the partner in such succeeding taxable year. See paragraphs (o)(6) and (7) of this section.

(4) *S corporations with disallowed business interest expense carryforwards prior to becoming not subject to section 163(j).*—If an S corporation has a disallowed business interest expense carryforward for a taxable year, and in the succeeding taxable year becomes not subject to the requirements of section 163(j), then such disallowed business interest expense carryforward—

(i) Continues to be carried forward at the S corporation level;

(ii) Is no longer subject to the section 163(j) limitation; and

(iii) Is taken into account in determining the nonseparately stated taxable income or loss of the S corporation.

(n) [Reserved]

(o) *Examples.*—The examples in this paragraph illustrate the provisions of section 163(j) as applied to partnerships and subchapter S corporations. For purposes of these examples, each partnership is subject to the provisions of section 163(j), was created or organized in the United States, and is a calendar year taxpayer. Unless stated otherwise, all partners are subject to the provisions of section 163(j), are not subject to a

**Prop. Reg. § 1.163(j)-6(o)**

limitation under section 704(d) or 1366(d), have no tax items other than those listed in the example, are U.S. citizens, and are calendar year taxpayers. The phrase "section 163(j) limit" shall equal the maximum potential deduction allowed under section 163(j)(1). Unless stated otherwise, business interest expense means business interest expense that is not floor plan financing interest expense. With respect to partnerships, all allocations are in accordance with section 704(b) and the regulations thereunder.

(1) *Example 1*—(i) *Facts.* X and Y are equal partners in partnership PRS. In Year 1, PRS has $100 of ATI and $40 of business interest expense. PRS allocates the items comprising its $100 of ATI $50 to X and $50 to Y. PRS allocates its $40 of business interest expense $20 to X and $20 to Y. X has $100 of ATI and $20 of business interest expense from its sole proprietorship. Y has $0 of ATI and $20 of business interest expense from its sole proprietorship.

(ii) *Partnership-level.* In Year 1, PRS's section 163(j) limit is 30 percent of its ATI, or $30 ($100 x 30 percent). Thus, PRS has $30 of deductible business interest expense and $10 of excess business interest expense. Such $30 of deductible business interest expense is includable in PRS's non-separately stated income or loss, and is not subject to further limitation under section 163(j) at the partners' level.

(iii) *Partner-level allocations.* Pursuant to §1.163(j)-6(f)(2), X and Y are each allocated $15 of deductible business interest expense and $5 of excess business interest expense. At the end of Year 1, X and Y each have $5 of excess business interest expense from PRS, which is not treated as paid or accrued by the partner until such partner is allocated excess taxable income or excess business interest income from PRS in a succeeding taxable year. Pursuant to §1.163(j)-6(e)(1), X and Y, in computing their limit under section 163(j), do not increase any of their section 163(j) items by any of PRS's section 163(j) items. X and Y each increase their outside basis in PRS by $30 ($50 - $20).

(iv) *Partner-level computations.* X, in computing its limit under section 163(j), has $100 of ATI and $20 of business interest expense from its sole proprietorship. X's section 163(j) limit is $30 ($100 x 30 percent). Thus, X's $20 of business interest expense is deductible business interest expense. Y, in computing its limit under section 163(j), has $20 of business interest expense from its sole proprietorship. Y's section 163(j) limit is $0 ($0 x 30 percent). Thus, Y's $20 of business interest expense is not allowed as a deduction and is treated as business interest expense paid or accrued by Y in Year 2.

(2) *Example 2*—(i) *Facts.* The facts are the same as in *Example 1* in paragraph (o)(1)(i) of this section. In Year 2, PRS has $200 of ATI, $0 of business interest income, and $30 of business interest expense. PRS allocates the items comprising its $200 of ATI $100 to X and $100 to Y. PRS allocates its $30 of business interest expense $15 to X and $15 to Y. X has $100 of ATI and $20

of business interest expense from its sole proprietorship. Y has $0 of ATI and $20 of business interest expense from its sole proprietorship.

(ii) *Partnership-level.* In Year 2, PRS's section 163(j) limit is 30 percent of its ATI plus its business interest income, or $60 ($200 x 30 percent). Thus, PRS has $100 of excess taxable income, $30 of deductible business interest expense, and $0 of excess business interest expense. Such $30 of deductible business interest expense is includable in PRS's non-separately stated income or loss, and is not subject to further limitation under section 163(j) at the partners' level.

(iii) *Partner-level allocations.* Pursuant to §1.163(j)-6(f)(2), X and Y are each allocated $50 of excess taxable income, $15 of deductible business interest expense, and $0 of excess business interest expense. As a result, X and Y each increase their ATI by $50. Because X and Y are each allocated $50 of excess taxable income from PRS, and excess business interest expense from a partnership is treated as paid or accrued by a partner to the extent excess taxable income and excess business interest income are allocated from such partnership to a partner, X and Y each treat $5 of excess business interest expense (the carryforward from Year 1) as paid or accrued in Year 2. X and Y each increase their outside basis in PRS by $85 ($100 - $15).

(iv) *Partner-level computations.* X, in computing its limit under section 163(j), has $150 of ATI ($100 from its sole proprietorship, plus $50 excess taxable income) and $25 of business interest expense ($20 from its sole proprietorship, plus $5 excess business interest expense treated as paid or accrued in Year 2). X's section 163(j) limit is $45 ($150 x 30 percent). Thus, X's $25 of business interest expense is deductible business interest expense. At the end of Year 2, X has $0 of excess business interest expense from PRS ($5 from Year 1, less $5 treated as paid or accrued in Year 2). Y, in computing its limit under section 163(j), has $50 of ATI ($0 from its sole proprietorship, plus $50 excess taxable income) and $45 of business interest expense ($20 from its sole proprietorship, plus $20 disallowed business interest expense from Year 1, plus $5 excess business interest expense treated as paid or accrued in Year 2). Y's section 163(j) limit is $15 ($50 x 30 percent). Thus, $15 of Y's business interest expense is deductible business interest expense. The $30 of Y's business interest expense not allowed as a deduction ($45 business interest expense, less $15 section 163(j) limit) is treated as business interest expense paid or accrued by Y in Year 3. At the end of Year 2, Y has $0 of excess business interest expense from PRS ($5 from Year 1, less $5 treated as paid or accrued in Year 2).

(3) *Example 3*—(i) *Facts.* The facts are the same as in *Example 1* in paragraph (o)(1)(i) of this section. In Year 2, PRS has $0 of ATI, $60 of business interest income, and $40 of business interest expense. PRS allocates its $60 of business interest income $30 to X and $30 to Y. PRS allocates its $40 of business interest expense $20 to X and $20 to Y. X has $100 of ATI and $20 of

business interest expense from its sole proprietorship. Y has $0 of ATI and $20 of business interest expense from its sole proprietorship.

(ii) *Partnership-level.* In Year 2, PRS's section 163(j) limit is 30 percent of its ATI plus its business interest income, or $60 (($0 x 30 percent) + $60). Thus, PRS has $20 of excess business interest income, $0 of excess taxable income, $40 of deductible business interest expense, and $0 of excess business interest expense. Such $40 of deductible business interest expense is includable in PRS's non-separately stated income or loss, and is not subject to further limitation under section 163(j) at the partners' level.

(iii) *Partner-level allocations.* Pursuant to § 1.163(j)-6(f)(2), X and Y are each allocated $10 of excess business interest income, and $20 of deductible business interest expense. As a result, X and Y each increase their business interest income by $10. Because X and Y are each allocated $10 of excess business interest income from PRS, and excess business interest expense from a partnership is treated as paid or accrued by a partner to the extent excess taxable income and excess business interest income are allocated from such partnership to a partner, X and Y each treat $5 of excess business interest expense (the carryforward from Year 1) as paid or accrued in Year 2. X and Y each increase their outside basis in PRS by $10 ($30 - $20).

(iv) *Partner-level computations.* X, in computing its limit under section 163(j), has $100 of ATI (from its sole proprietorship), $10 of business interest income (from the allocation of $10 of excess business interest income from PRS), and $25 of business interest expense ($20 from its sole proprietorship, plus $5 excess business interest expense treated as paid or accrued in Year 2). X's section 163(j) limit is $40 (($100 x 30 percent) + $10). Thus, X's $25 of business interest expense is deductible business interest expense. At the end of Year 2, X has $0 of excess business interest expense from PRS ($5 from Year 1, less $5 treated as paid or accrued in Year 2). Y, in computing its limit under section 163(j), has $0 of ATI (from its sole proprietorship), $10 of business interest income, and $45 of business interest expense ($20 from its sole proprietorship, plus $20 disallowed business interest expense from Year 1, plus $5 excess business interest expense treated as paid or accrued in Year 2). Y's section 163(j) limit is $10 (($0 x 30 percent) + $10). Thus, $10 of Y's business interest expense is deductible business interest expense. The $35 of Y's business interest expense not allowed as a deduction ($45 business interest expense, less $10 section 163(j) limit) is treated as business interest expense paid or accrued by Y in Year 3. At the end of Year 2, Y has $0 of excess business interest expense from PRS ($5 from Year 1, less $5 treated as paid or accrued in Year 2).

(4) *Example 4*—(i) *Facts.* The facts are the same as in *Example 1* in paragraph (o)(1)(i) of this section. In Year 2, PRS has $100 of ATI, $60 of business interest income, and $40 of business interest expense. PRS allocates the items comprising its $100 of ATI $50 to X and $50 to Y. PRS allocates its $60 of business interest income $30 to X and $30 to Y. PRS allocates its $40 of business interest expense $20 to X and $20 to Y. X has $100 of ATI and $20 of business interest expense from its sole proprietorship. Y has $0 of ATI and $20 of business interest expense from its sole proprietorship.

(ii) *Partnership-level.* In Year 2, PRS's section 163(j) limit is 30 percent of its ATI plus its business interest income, or $90 (($100 x 30 percent)) + $60). Thus, PRS has $20 of excess business interest income, $100 of excess taxable income, $40 of deductible business interest expense, and $0 of excess business interest expense. Such $40 of deductible business interest expense is includable in PRS's non-separately stated income or loss, and is not subject to further limitation under section 163(j) at the partners' level.

(iii) *Partner-level allocations.* Pursuant to § 1.163(j)-6(f)(2), X and Y are each allocated $10 of excess business interest income, $50 of excess taxable income, and $20 of deductible business interest expense. As a result, X and Y each increase their business interest income by $10 and ATI by $50. Because X and Y are each allocated $10 of excess business interest income and $50 of excess taxable income from PRS, and excess business interest expense from a partnership is treated as paid or accrued by a partner to the extent excess taxable income and excess business interest income are allocated from such partnership to a partner, X and Y each treat $5 of excess business interest expense (the carryforward from Year 1) as paid or accrued in Year 2. X and Y each increase their outside basis in PRS by $60 ($80 - $20).

(iv) *Partner-level computations.* X, in computing its limit under section 163(j), has $150 of ATI ($100 from its sole proprietorship, plus $50 excess taxable income), $10 of business interest income, and $25 of business interest expense ($20 from its sole proprietorship, plus $5 excess business interest expense treated as paid or accrued in Year 2). X's section 163(j) limit is $55 (($150 x 30 percent) + $10). Thus, $25 of X's business interest expense is deductible business interest expense. At the end of Year 2, X has $0 of excess business interest expense from PRS ($5 from Year 1, less $5 treated as paid or accrued in Year 2). Y, in computing its limit under section 163(j), has $50 of ATI ($0 from its sole proprietorship, plus $50 excess taxable income), $10 of business interest income, and $45 of business interest expense ($20 from its sole proprietorship, plus $20 disallowed business interest expense from Year 1, plus $5 excess business interest expense treated as paid or accrued in Year 2). Y's section 163(j) limit is $25 (($50 x 30 percent) + $10). Thus, $25 of Y's business interest expense is deductible business interest expense. Y's $20 of business interest expense not allowed as a deduction ($45 business interest expense, less $25 section 163(j) limit) is treated as business interest expense paid or accrued by Y in Year 3. At the end of Year 2, Y has $0 of excess business interest expense from

PRS ($5 from Year 1, less $5 treated as paid or accrued in Year 2).

(5) *Example 5*—(i) *Facts.* The facts are the same as in *Example 1* in paragraph (o)(1)(i) of this section. In Year 2, PRS has $100 of ATI, $11.20 of business interest income, and $40 of business interest expense. PRS allocates the items comprising its $100 of ATI $50 to X and $50 to Y. PRS allocates its $11.20 of business interest income $5.60 to X and $5.60 to Y. PRS allocates its $40 of business interest expense $20 to X and $20 to Y. X has $100 of ATI and $20 of business interest expense from its sole proprietorship. Y has $0 of ATI and $20 of business interest expense from its sole proprietorship.

(ii) *Partnership-level.* In Year 2, PRS's section 163(j) limit is 30 percent of its ATI plus its business interest income, or $41.20 (($100 x 30 percent) + $11.20). Thus, PRS has $0 of excess business interest income, $4 of excess taxable income, and $40 of deductible business interest expense. Such $40 of deductible business interest expense is includable in PRS's non-separately stated income or loss, and is not subject to further limitation under section 163(j) at the partners' level.

(iii) *Partner-level allocations.* Pursuant to § 1.163(j)-6(f)(2), X and Y are each allocated $2 of excess taxable income, $20 of deductible business interest expense, and $0 of excess business interest expense. As a result, X and Y each increase their ATI by $2. Because X and Y are each allocated $2 of excess taxable income from PRS, and excess business interest expense from a partnership is treated as paid or accrued by a partner to the extent excess taxable income and excess business interest income are allocated from such partnership to a partner, X and Y each treat $2 of excess business interest expense (a portion of the carryforward from Year 1) as paid or accrued in Year 2. X and Y each increase their outside basis in PRS by $35.60 ($55.60 - $20).

(iv) *Partner-level computations.* X, in computing its limit under section 163(j), has $102 of ATI ($100 from its sole proprietorship, plus $2 excess taxable income), $0 of business interest income, and $22 of business interest expense ($20 from its sole proprietorship, plus $2 excess business interest expense treated as paid or accrued). X's section 163(j) limit is $30.60 ($102 x 30 percent). Thus, X's $22 of business interest expense is deductible business interest expense. At the end of Year 2, X has $3 of excess business interest expense from PRS ($5 from Year 1, less $2 treated as paid or accrued in Year 2). Y, in computing its limit under section 163(j), has $2 of ATI ($0 from its sole proprietorship, plus $2 excess taxable income), $0 of business interest income, and $42 of business interest expense ($20 from its sole proprietorship, plus $20 disallowed business interest expense from Year 1, plus $2 excess business interest expense treated as paid or accrued in Year 2). Y's section 163(j) limit is $0.60 ($2 x 30 percent). Thus, $0.60 of Y's business interest expense is deductible business interest expense. Y's $41.40 of business interest expense not allowed

as a deduction ($42 business interest expense, less $0.60 section 163(j) limit) is treated as business interest expense paid or accrued by Y in Year 3. At the end of Year 2, Y has $3 of excess business interest expense from PRS ($5 from Year 1, less $2 treated as paid or accrued in Year 2).

(6) *Example 6*—(i) *Facts.* The facts are the same as in *Example 5* in paragraph (o)(5)(i) of this section, except in Year 2 Y becomes not subject to section 163(j) under section 163(j)(3).

(ii) *Partnership-level.* Same analysis as *Example 5* in paragraph (o)(5)(ii) of this section.

(iii) *Partner-level allocations.* Same analysis as *Example 5* in paragraph (o)(5)(iii) of this section.

(iv) *Partner-level computations.* For X, same analysis as *Example 5* in paragraph (o)(5)(iv) of this section. Y is not subject to section 163(j) under section 163(j)(3). Thus, all $42 of business interest expense ($20 from its sole proprietorship, plus $20 disallowed business interest expense from Year 1, plus $2 excess business interest expense treated as paid or accrued in Year 2) is not subject to limitation under § 1.163(j)-2(d). At the end of Year 2, Y has $3 of excess business interest expense from PRS ($5 from Year 1, less $2 treated as paid or accrued in Year 2).

(7) *Example 7*—(i) *Facts.* The facts are the same as in *Example 5* in paragraph (o)(5)(i) of this section, except in Year 2 PRS and Y become not subject to section 163(j) under section 163(j)(3).

(ii) *Partnership-level.* In Year 2, PRS becomes not subject to section 163(j)(4) by reason of section 163(j)(3). As a result, none of PRS's $30 of business interest expense is subject to limitation at the partnership level.

(iii) *Partner-level allocations.* Because section 163(j) does not apply, PRS's $30 of business interest expense is not taken into account in determining its non-separately stated taxable income or loss. Thus, PRS's $30 of business interest expense retains its character as business interest expense for purposes of section 163(j), and is potentially subject to limitation at the partners' level. As a result, X and Y each increase their business interest expense by $15. Further, because PRS is not subject to section 163(j)(4) by reason of section 163(j)(3), the provision requiring each partner of the partnership to determine their ATI without regard to such partner's distributive share of any items of income, gain, deduction, or loss of such partnership (section 163(j)(4)(ii)(I)) is no longer applicable under § 1.163(j)-6(m)(1). As a result, X and Y each increase their ATI by $100. Further, because PRS is not subject to section 163(j)(4) by reason of section 163(j)(3), the excess business interest expense from Year 1 is treated as paid or accrued by the partners pursuant to § 1.163(j)-6(m)(3). As a result, X and Y each treat their $5 of excess business interest expense from Year 1 as paid or accrued in Year 2, and increase their business interest expense by $5.

(iv) *Partner-level computations.* X, in computing its limit under section 163(j), has $200 of ATI

($100 from its sole proprietorship, plus $100 ATI from PRS) and $40 of business interest expense ($20 from its sole proprietorship, plus $15 from PRS, plus $5 of excess business interest expense treated as paid or accrued in Year 2). X's section 163(j) limit is $60 ($200 x 30 percent). Thus, $40 of X's business interest expense is deductible business interest expense. Y is not subject to section 163(j) under section 163(j)(3). As a result, Y's business interest expense is not subject to limitation under section 163(j). Thus, all $60 of Y's business interest expense ($20 from its sole proprietorship, plus $20 disallowed from year 1, plus $15 from PRS from year 2, plus $5 of excess business interest expense treated as paid or accrued in Year 2) is not subject to limitation under section 163(j).

(8) *Example 8*—(i) *Facts.* In Year 1, X, Y, and Z formed partnership PRS. Upon formation, X and Y each contributed $100, and Z contributed non-excepted and non-depreciable trade or business property with a basis of $0 and fair market value of $100 (Blackacre). PRS allocates all items pro rata between its partners. Immediately after the formation of PRS, Z sold all of its interest in PRS to A for $100 (assume the interest sale is respected for U.S. federal income tax purposes). In connection with the interest transfer, PRS made a valid election under section 754. Therefore, after the interest sale, A had a $100 positive section 743(b) adjustment in Blackacre. In Year 1, PRS had $0 of ATI, $15 of business interest expense, and $0 of business interest income. Pursuant to § 1.163(j)-6(f)(2), PRS allocated each of the partners $5 of excess business interest expense. In Year 2, PRS sells Blackacre for $100 which generated $100 of ATI. The sale of Blackacre was PRS's only item of income in Year 2. In accordance with section 704(c), PRS allocates all $100 of gain resulting from the sale of Blackacre to A. Additionally, PRS has $15 of business interest expense, all of which it allocates to X. A has $50 of ATI and $20 of business interest expense from its sole proprietorship.

(ii) *Partnership-level.* In Year 2, PRS's section 163(j) limit is 30 percent of its ATI, or $30 ($100 x 30 percent). Thus, PRS has $15 of deductible business interest expense and $50 of excess taxable income. Such $15 of deductible business interest expense is includable in PRS's non-separately stated income or loss, and is not subject to further limitation under section 163(j) at X's level.

(iii) *Partner-level allocations.* Pursuant to § 1.163(j)-6(f)(2), X is allocated $15 of deductible business interest expense and X's outside basis in PRS is reduced by $15. A is allocated $50 of excess taxable income and, as a result, A increases its ATI by $50. Because A is allocated $50 of excess taxable income, and excess business interest expense from a partnership is treated as paid or accrued by a partner to the extent excess taxable income and excess business interest income are allocated from such partnership to a partner, A treats $5 of excess business interest expense (the carryforward from Year 1) as paid

or accrued in Year 2. PRS's $100 of gain allocated to A in Year 2 is fully reduced by A's $100 section 743(b) adjustment. Therefore, at the end of Year 2, there is no change to A's outside basis in PRS.

(iv) *Partner-level.* A, in computing its limit under section 163(j), has $0 of ATI ($50 from its sole proprietorship, plus $50 excess taxable income, less $100 ATI reduction as a result of A's section 743(b) adjustment under § 1.163(j)-6(e)(2)) and $25 of business interest expense ($20 from its sole proprietorship, plus $5 excess business interest expense treated as paid or accrued in Year 2). A's section 163(j) limit is $0 ($0 x 30 percent). Thus, all $25 of A's business interest expense is not allowed as a deduction and is treated as business interest expense paid or accrued by A in Year 3.

(9) *Example 9*—(i) *Facts.* X and Y are equal partners in partnership PRS. At the beginning of Year 1, X and Y each have an outside basis in PRS of $5. In Year 1, PRS has $0 of ATI, $20 of business interest income, and $40 of business interest expense. PRS allocates its $20 of business interest income $10 to X and $10 to Y. PRS allocates $40 of business interest expense $20 to X and $20 to Y. X has $100 of ATI and $20 of business interest expense from its sole proprietorship. Y has $0 of ATI and $20 of business interest expense from its sole proprietorship.

(ii) *Partnership-level.* In Year 1, PRS's section 163(j) limit is 30 percent of its ATI plus its business interest income, or $20 (($0 x 30 percent) + $20). Thus, PRS has $0 of excess business interest income, $0 of excess taxable income, $20 of deductible business interest expense, and $20 of excess business interest expense. Such $20 of deductible business interest expense is includable in non-separately stated income or loss of PRS, and not subject to further limitation under section 163(j) by the partners.

(iii) *Partner-level allocations.* Pursuant to § 1.163(j)-6(f)(2), X and Y are each allocated $10 of deductible business interest expense and $10 of excess business interest expense. After adjusting each partners respective basis for business interest income under section 705(a)(1)(A), pursuant to § 1.163(j)-6(h)(1), X and Y each take their $10 of deductible business interest expense into account when reducing their outside basis in PRS before taking the $10 of excess business interest expense into account. Following each partner's reduction in outside basis due to the $10 of deductible business interest expense, each partner has $5 of outside basis remaining in PRS. Pursuant to § 1.163(j)-6(h)(2), each partner has $5 of excess business interest expense and $5 of negative section 163(j) expense. In sum, at the end of Year 1, X and Y each have $5 of excess business interest expense from PRS which reduces each partner's outside basis to $0 (and is not treated as paid or accrued by the partners until such partner is allocated excess taxable income or excess business interest income from PRS in a succeeding taxable year), and $5 of

**Prop. Reg. § 1.163(j)-6(o)**

negative section 163(j) expense (which is suspended under section 704(d) and not treated as excess business interest expense of the partners until such time as the negative section 163(j) expense is no longer subject to a limitation under section 704(d)).

(iv) *Partner-level computations.* X, in computing its limit under section 163(j), has $100 of ATI (from its sole proprietorship) and $20 of business interest expense (from its sole proprietorship). X's section 163(j) limit is $30 ($100 x 30 percent). Thus, $20 of X's business interest expense is deductible business interest expense. Y, in computing its limit under section 163(j), has $20 of business interest expense (from its sole proprietorship). Y's section 163(j) limit is $0 ($0 x 30 percent). Thus, $20 of Y's business interest expense is not allowed as a deduction in Year 1, and is treated as business interest expense paid or accrued by Y in Year 2.

(10) *Example 10*—(i) *Facts.* The facts are the same as in *Example 9* in paragraph (o)(9)(i) of this section. In Year 2, PRS has $20 of gross income that is taken into account in determining PRS's ATI (i.e., properly allocable to a trade or business), $30 of gross deductions from an investment activity, and $0 of business interest expense. PRS allocates the items comprising its $20 of ATI $10 to X and $10 to Y. PRS allocates the items comprising its $30 of gross deductions $15 to X and $15 to Y. X has $100 of ATI and $20 of business interest expense from its sole proprietorship. Y has $0 of ATI and $20 of business interest expense from its sole proprietorship.

(ii) *Partnership-level.* In Year 2, PRS's section 163(j) limit is 30 percent of its ATI plus its business interest income, or $6 ($20 x 30 percent). Because PRS has no business interest expense, all $20 of its ATI is excess taxable income.

(iii) *Partner-level allocations.* Pursuant to § 1.163(j)-6(f)(2), X and Y are each allocated $10 of excess taxable income. Because X and Y are each allocated $10 of excess taxable income from PRS, X and Y each increase their ATI by $10. Pursuant to § 1.704-(1)(d)(2), each partner's limitation on losses under section 704(d) must be allocated to its distributive share of each such loss. Thus, each partner reduces its adjusted basis of $10 (attributable to the allocation of items comprising PRS's ATI in Year 2) by $7.50 of gross deductions from Year 2 ($10 x ($15 of total gross deductions from Year 2 / $20 of total losses disallowed)), and $2.50 of excess business interest expense that was carried over as negative section 163(j) expense from Year 1 ($10 x ($5 of negative section 163(j) expense treated as excess business interest expense solely for the purposes of section 704(d) / $20 of total losses disallowed)). Following the application of section 704(d), each partner has $7.50 of excess business interest expense from PRS ($5 excess business interest expense from Year 1, plus $2.50 of excess business interest expense that was formerly negative section 163(j) expense carried over from Year 1). Excess business interest expense from a partnership is treated as paid or accrued by a

partner to the extent excess taxable income and excess business interest income are allocated from such partnership to the partner. As a result, X and Y each treat $7.50 of excess business interest expense as paid or accrued in Year 2.

(iv) *Partner-level computations.* X, in computing its limit under section 163(j), has $110 of ATI ($100 from its sole proprietorship, plus $10 excess taxable income) and $27.50 of business interest expense ($20 from its sole proprietorship, plus $7.50 excess business interest expense treated as paid or accrued in Year 2). X's section 163(j) limit is $33 ($110 x 30 percent). Thus, $27.50 of X's business interest expense is deductible business interest expense. At the end of Year 2, X has $0 of excess business interest expense from PRS ($5 from Year 1, plus $2.50 treated as excess business interest expense in Year 2, less $7.50 treated as paid or accrued in Year 2), and $2.50 of negative section 163(j) expense from PRS. Y, in computing its limit under section 163(j), has $10 of ATI ($0 from its sole proprietorship, plus $10 excess taxable income) and $47.50 of business interest expense ($20 from its sole proprietorship, plus $20 disallowed business interest expense from Year 1, plus $7.50 excess business interest expense treated as paid or accrued in Year 2). Y's section 163(j) limit is $3 ($10 x 30 percent). Thus, $3 of Y's business interest expense is deductible business interest expense. The $44.50 of Y's business interest expense not allowed as a deduction ($47.50 business interest expense, less $3 section 163(j) limit) is treated as business interest expense paid or accrued by Y in Year 3. At the end of Year 2, Y has $0 of excess business interest expense from PRS ($5 from Year 1, plus $2.50 treated as excess business interest expense in Year 2, less $7.50 treated as paid or accrued in Year 2), and $2.50 of negative section 163(j) expense from PRS.

(11) *Example 11: Facts.* A (an individual) and B (a corporation) own all of the interests in partnership PRS. In Year 1, PRS has $100 of ATI, $10 of investment interest income, $20 of business interest income (BII), $60 of business interest expense (BIE), and $10 of floor plan financing interest expense. PRS's ATI consists of $100 of gross income and $0 of gross deductions. PRS allocates its items comprising ATI $100 to A and $0 to B. PRS allocates its business interest income $10 to A and $10 to B. PRS allocates its business interest expense $30 to A and $30 to B. PRS allocates all $10 of its investment interest income and all $10 of its floor plan financing interest expense to B. A has ATI from a sole proprietorship, unrelated to PRS, in the amount of $300.

(i) First, PRS determines its limitation pursuant to § 1.163(j)-2. PRS's section 163(j) limit is 30 percent of its ATI plus its business interest income, or $50 (($100 x 30 percent) + $20). Thus, PRS has $0 of excess business interest income (EBII), $0 of excess taxable income, $50 of deductible business interest expense, and $10 of excess business interest expense. PRS takes its $10 of floor plan financing into account in determining its nonseparately stated taxable income or loss.

(ii) Second, PRS determines each partner's allocable share of section 163(j) items used in its own section 163(j) calculation. B's $10 of investment interest income is not included in B's allocable business interest income amount because the $10 of investment interest income was not taken into account in PRS's section 163(j) calculation. B's $10 of floor plan financing interest expense is not included in B's allocable business interest expense. The $300 of ATI from A's sole proprietorship is not included in A's allocable ATI amount because the $300 was not taken into account in PRS's section 163(j) calculation.

| Table 1 to paragraph (o)(11)(ii) | | | |
|---|---|---|---|
| | A | B | Total |
| Allocable ATI | $100 | $0 | $100 |
| Allocable BII | $10 | $10 | $20 |
| Allocable BIE | $30 | $30 | $60 |

(iii) Third, PRS compares each partner's allocable business interest income to such partner's allocable business interest expense. Because each partner's allocable business interest expense exceeds its allocable business interest income by $20 ($30 - $10), each partner has an allocable business interest income deficit of $20. Thus, the total allocable business interest income deficit is $40 ($20 + $20). No partner has allocable business interest income excess because no partner has allocable business interest income in excess of its allocable business interest expense. Thus, the total allocable business interest income excess is $0.

| Table 1 to paragraph (o)(11)(iii) | | | |
|---|---|---|---|
| | A | B | Total |
| Allocable BII | $10 | $10 | N/A |
| Allocable BIE | $30 | $30 | N/A |
| If allocable BII exceeds allocable BIE, then such amount = Allocable BII excess | $0 | $0 | $0 |
| If allocable BIE exceeds allocable BII, then such amount = Allocable BII deficit | $20 | $20 | $40 |

(iv) Fourth, PRS determines each partner's final allocable business interest income excess. Because no partner had any allocable business interest income excess, each partner has final allocable business interest income excess of $0.

(v) Fifth, PRS determines each partner's remaining business interest expense. PRS determines A's remaining business interest expense by reducing, but not below $0, A's allocable business interest income deficit ($20) by the product of the total allocable business interest income excess ($0) and the ratio of A's allocable business interest income deficit to the total business interest income deficit ($20/$40). Therefore, A's allocable business interest income deficit of $20 is reduced by $0 ($0 x 50 percent). As a result, A's remaining business interest expense is $20. PRS determines B's remaining business interest expense by reducing, but not below $0, B's allocable business interest income deficit ($20) by the product of the total allocable business interest income excess ($0) and the ratio of B's allocable business interest income deficit to the total business interest income deficit ($20/$40). Therefore, B's allocable business interest income deficit of $20 is reduced by $0 ($0 x 50 percent). As a result, B's remaining business interest expense is $20.

| Table 1 to paragraph (o)(11)(v) | | | |
|---|---|---|---|
| | A | B | Total |
| Allocable BII deficit | $20 | $20 | $40 |
| Less: (Total allocable BII excess) x (Allocable BII deficit / Total allocable BII deficit) | $0 | $0 | N/A |
| = Remaining BIE | $20 | $20 | $40 |

(vi) Sixth, PRS determines each partner's final allocable ATI. Any partner with a negative allocable ATI, or an allocable ATI of $0, has a positive allocable ATI of $0. Therefore, B has a positive allocable ATI of $0. Because A's allocable ATI is comprised of $100 of income and gain and $0 of deduction and loss, A has positive allocable ATI of $100. Thus, the total positive allocable ATI is $100 ($100 + $0). PRS determines A's final allocable ATI by reducing, but not below $0, A's positive allocable ATI ($100) by the product of total negative allocable ATI ($0) and the ratio of A's positive allocable ATI to the total positive allocable ATI ($100/$100). Therefore,

**Prop. Reg. §1.163(j)-6(o)**

A's positive allocable ATI is reduced by $0 ($0 x 100 percent). As a result, A's final allocable ATI is $100. Because B has a positive allocable ATI of $0, B's final allocable ATI is $0.

| Table 1 to paragraph (o)(11)(vi) | | | |
|---|---|---|---|
| | A | B | Total |
| Allocable ATI | $100 | $0 | $100 |
| If deduction and loss items comprising allocable ATI exceed income and gain items comprising allocable ATI, then such excess amount = Negative allocable ATI | $0 | $0 | $0 |
| If income and gain items comprising allocable ATI equal or exceed deduction and loss items comprising allocable ATI, then such amount = Positive allocable ATI | $100 | $0 | $100 |

| Table 2 to paragraph (o)(11)(vi) | | | |
|---|---|---|---|
| | A | B | Total |
| Positive allocable ATI | $100 | $0 | $100 |
| Less: (Total negative allocable ATI) x (Positive allocable ATI / Total positive allocable ATI) | $0 | $0 | N/A |
| = Final allocable ATI | $100 | $0 | $100 |

(vii) Seventh, PRS compares each partner's ATI capacity (ATIC) amount to such partner's remaining business interest expense. A's ATIC amount is $30 ($100 x 30 percent) and B's ATIC amount is $0 ($0 x 30 percent). Because A's ATIC amount exceeds its remaining business interest expense by $10 ($30 - $20), A has an ATIC excess of $10. B does not have any ATIC excess. Thus, the total ATIC excess is $10 ($10 + $0). A does not have any ATIC deficit. Because B's remaining business interest expense exceeds its ATIC amount by $20 ($20 - $0), B has an ATIC deficit of $20. Thus, the total ATIC deficit is $20 ($0 + $20).

| Table 1 to paragraph (o)(11)(vii) | | | |
|---|---|---|---|
| | A | B | Total |
| ATIC (Final allocable ATI x 30 percent) | $30 | $0 | N/A |
| Remaining BIE | $20 | $20 | N/A |
| If ATIC exceeds remaining BIE, then such excess = ATIC excess | $10 | $0 | $10 |
| If remaining BIE exceeds ATIC, then such excess = ATIC deficit | $0 | $20 | $20 |

(viii)(A) Eighth, PRS must perform the calculations and make the necessary adjustments described under paragraph (f)(2)(viii) of this section if, and only if, PRS has:

(1) An excess business interest expense greater than $0 under paragraph (f)(2)(i) of this section;

(2) A total negative allocable ATI greater than $0 under paragraph (f)(2)(vi) of this section; and

(3) A total ATIC excess amount greater than $0 under paragraph (f)(2)(vii) of this section.

(B) Because PRS does not meet all three requirements in paragraph (o)(11)(viii)(A) of this section, PRS does not perform the calculations or adjustments described in paragraph (f)(2)(viii) of this section. In sum, the correct amounts to be used in paragraphs (o)(11)(ix) and (x) of this section are as follows.

| Table 1 to paragraph (o)(11)(viii)(B) | | | |
|---|---|---|---|
| | A | B | Total |
| ATIC excess | $10 | $0 | $10 |
| ATIC deficit | $0 | $20 | $20 |

(ix) Ninth, PRS determines each partner's final ATIC excess amount. Because A has an ATIC excess, PRS must determine A's final ATIC excess amount. A's final ATIC excess amount is A's ATIC excess ($10), reduced, but not below $0, by the product of the total ATIC deficit ($20) and

**Prop. Reg. §1.163(j)-6(o)**

the ratio of A's ATIC excess to the total ATIC excess ($10/$10). Therefore, A has $0 of final ATIC excess ($10 — ($20 x 100 percent)).

| Table 1 to paragraph (o)(11)(ix) | | | |
|---|---|---|---|
|  | A | B | Total |
| ATIC excess | $10 | $0 | N/A |
| Less: (Total ATIC deficit) x (ATIC excess / Total ATIC excess) | $20 | $0 | N/A |
| = Final ATIC excess | $0 | $0 | $0 |

(x) Tenth, PRS determines each partner's final ATIC deficit amount. Because B has an ATIC deficit, PRS must determine B's final ATIC deficit amount. B's final ATIC deficit amount is B's ATIC deficit ($20), reduced, but not below $0, by the product of the total ATIC excess ($10) and the ratio of B's ATIC deficit to the total ATIC deficit ($20/$20). Therefore, B has $10 of final ATIC deficit ($20 — ($10 x 100 percent)).

| Table 1 to paragraph (o)(11)(x) | | | |
|---|---|---|---|
|  | A | B | Total |
| ATIC deficit | $0 | $20 | N/A |
| Less: (Total ATIC excess) x (ATIC deficit / Total ATIC deficit) | $0 | $10 | N/A |
| = Final ATIC deficit | $0 | $10 | $10 |

(xi) Eleventh, PRS allocates deductible business interest expense and section 163(j) excess items to the partners. Pursuant to paragraph (f)(2)(i) of this section, PRS has $10 of excess business interest expense. PRS allocates the excess business interest expense dollar for dollar to the partners with final ATIC deficits amounts. Thus, PRS allocates all $10 of its excess business interest expense to B. A partner's allocable business interest expense is deductible business interest expense to the extent it exceeds such partner's share of excess business interest expense. Therefore, A has deductible business interest expense of $30 ($30 - $0) and B has deductible business interest expense of $20 ($30 - $10).

| Table 1 to paragraph (o)(11)(xi) | | | |
|---|---|---|---|
|  | A | B | Total |
| Deductible BIE | $30 | $20 | $50 |
| EBIE allocated | $0 | $10 | $10 |
| ETI allocated | $0 | $0 | $0 |
| EBII allocated | $0 | $0 | $0 |

(12) *Example 12: Facts.* A, B, and C own all of the interests in partnership PRS. In Year 1, PRS has $150 of ATI, $10 of business interest income, and $40 of business interest expense. PRS's ATI consists of $200 of gross income and $50 of gross deductions. PRS allocates its items comprising ATI ($50) to A, $200 to B, and $0 to C. PRS allocates its business interest income $0 to A, $0 to B, and $10 to C. PRS allocates its business interest expense $30 to A, $10 to B, and $0 to C.

(i) First, PRS determines its limitation pursuant to § 1.163(j)-2. PRS's section 163(j) limit is 30 percent of its ATI plus its business interest income, or $55 (($150 x 30 percent) + $10). Thus, PRS has $0 of excess business interest income, $50 of excess taxable income, $40 of deductible business interest expense, and $0 of excess business interest expense.

(ii) Second, PRS determines each partner's allocable share of section 163(j) items used in its own section 163(j) calculation.

| Table 1 to paragraph (o)(12)(ii) | | | | |
|---|---|---|---|---|
|  | A | B | C | Total |
| Allocable ATI | ($50) | $200 | $0 | $150 |
| Allocable BII | $0 | $0 | $10 | $10 |
| Allocable BIE | $30 | $10 | $0 | $40 |

(iii) Third, PRS compares each partner's allocable business interest income to such partner's allocable business interest expense. Because A's allocable business interest expense exceeds its allocable business interest income by $30 ($30 - $0), A has an allocable business interest income deficit of $30. Because B's allocable business interest expense exceeds its allocable business interest income by $10 ($10 - $0), B has an allocable business interest income deficit of $10. C does

not have any allocable business interest income deficit. Thus, the total allocable business interest income deficit is $40 ($30 + $10 + $0). A and B do not have any allocable business interest income excess. Because C's allocable business interest income exceeds its allocable business interest expense by $10 ($10 - $0), C has an allocable business interest income excess of $10. Thus, the total allocable business interest income excess is $10 ($0 + $0 + $10).

| Table 1 to paragraph (o)(12)(iii) | | | | |
|---|---|---|---|---|
| | A | B | C | Total |
| Allocable BII | $0 | $0 | $10 | N/A |
| Allocable BIE | $30 | $10 | $0 | N/A |
| If allocable BII exceeds allocable BIE, then such amount = Allocable BII excess | $0 | $0 | $10 | $10 |
| If allocable BIE exceeds allocable BII, then such amount = Allocable BII deficit | $30 | $10 | $0 | $40 |

(iv) Fourth, PRS determines each partner's final allocable business interest income excess. Because A and B do not have any allocable business interest income excess, each partner has final allocable business interest income excess of $0. PRS determines C's final allocable business interest income excess by reducing, but not below $0, C's allocable business interest income

excess ($10) by the product of the total allocable business interest income deficit ($40) and the ratio of C's allocable business interest income excess to the total allocable business interest income excess ($10/$10). Therefore, C's allocable business interest income excess of $10 is reduced by $10 ($40 x 100 percent). As a result, C's allocable business interest income excess is $0.

| Table 1 to paragraph (o)(12)(iv) | | | | |
|---|---|---|---|---|
| | A | B | C | Total |
| Allocable BII excess | $0 | $0 | $10 | N/A |
| Less: (Total allocable BII deficit) x (Allocable BII excess / Total allocable BII excess) | $0 | $0 | $40 | N/A |
| = Final Allocable BII Excess | $0 | $0 | $0 | $10 |

(v) Fifth, PRS determines each partner's remaining business interest expense. PRS determines A's remaining business interest expense by reducing, but not below $0, A's allocable business interest income deficit ($30) by the product of the total allocable business interest income excess ($10) and the ratio of A's allocable business interest income deficit to the total business interest income deficit ($30/$40). Therefore, A's allocable business interest income deficit of $30 is reduced by $7.50 ($10 x 75 percent). As a result, A's remaining business interest expense is $22.50. PRS determines B's remaining business

interest expense by reducing, but not below $0, B's allocable business interest income deficit ($10) by the product of the total allocable business interest income excess ($10) and the ratio of B's allocable business interest income deficit to the total business interest income deficit ($10/$40). Therefore, B's allocable business interest income deficit of $10 is reduced by $2.50 ($10 x 25 percent). As a result, B's remaining business interest expense is $7.50. Because C does not have any allocable business interest income deficit, C's remaining business interest expense is $0.

| Table 1 to paragraph (o)(12)(v) | | | | |
|---|---|---|---|---|
| | A | B | C | Total |
| Allocable BII deficit | $30 | $10 | $0 | $40 |
| Less: (Total allocable BII excess) x (Allocable BII deficit / Total allocable BII deficit) | $7.50 | $2.50 | $0 | N/A |
| = Remaining BIE | $22.50 | $7.50 | $0 | N/A |

(vi) Sixth, PRS determines each partner's final allocable ATI. Because A's allocable ATI is comprised of $50 of items of deduction and loss and $0 of income and gain, A has negative allocable ATI of $50. A is the only partner with negative

allocable ATI. Thus, the total negative allocable ATI amount is $50. Any partner with a negative allocable ATI, or an allocable ATI of $0, has a positive allocable ATI of $0. Therefore, A and C have a positive allocable ATI of $0. Because B's allocable ATI is comprised of $200 of items of income and gain and $0 of deduction and loss, B has positive allocable ATI of $200. Thus, the total positive allocable ATI is $200 ($0 + $200 + $0). PRS determines B's final allocable ATI by reducing, but not below $0, B's positive allocable ATI

($200) by the product of total negative allocable ATI ($50) and the ratio of B's positive allocable ATI to the total positive allocable ATI ($200/$200). Therefore, B's positive allocable ATI is reduced by $50 ($50 x 100 percent). As a result, B's final allocable ATI is $150.

| Table 1 to paragraph (o)(12)(vi) | | | | |
|---|---|---|---|---|
| | A | B | C | Total |
| Allocable ATI | ($50) | $200 | $0 | $150 |
| If deduction and loss items comprising allocable ATI exceed income and gain items comprising allocable ATI, then such excess amount = Negative allocable ATI | $50 | $0 | $0 | $50 |
| If income and gain items comprising allocable ATI equal or exceed deduction and loss items comprising allocable ATI, then such amount = Positive allocable ATI | $0 | $200 | $0 | $200 |

| Table 2 to paragraph (o)(12)(vi) | | | | |
|---|---|---|---|---|
| | A | B | C | Total |
| Positive allocable ATI | $0 | $200 | $0 | $200 |
| Less: (Total negative allocable ATI) x (Positive allocable ATI / Total positive allocable ATI) | $0 | $50 | $0 | N/A |
| = Final allocable ATI | $0 | $150 | $0 | $150 |

(vii) Seventh, PRS compares each partner's ATI capacity (ATIC) amount to such partner's remaining business interest expense. A's ATIC amount is $0 ($0 x 30 percent), B's ATIC amount is $45 ($150 x 30 percent), and C's ATIC amount is $0 ($0 x 30 percent). A does not have any ATIC excess. Because B's ATIC amount exceeds its remaining business interest expense by $37.50 ($45

- $7.50), B has an ATIC excess amount of $37.50. C does not have any ATIC excess. Thus, the total ATIC excess amount is $37.50 ($0 + $37.50 + $0). Because A's remaining business interest expense exceeds its ATIC amount by $22.50 ($22.50 - $0), A has an ATIC deficit of $22.50. B and C do not have any ATIC deficit. Thus, the total ATIC deficit is $22.50 ($22.50 + $0 + $0).

| Table 1 to paragraph (o)(12)(vii) | | | | |
|---|---|---|---|---|
| | A | B | C | Total |
| ATIC (Final allocable ATI x 30 percent) | $0 | $45 | $0 | N/A |
| Remaining BIE | $22.50 | $7.50 | $0 | N/A |
| If ATIC exceeds remaining BIE, then such excess = ATIC excess | $0 | $37.50 | $0 | $37.50 |
| If remaining BIE exceeds ATIC, then such excess = ATIC deficit | $22.50 | $0 | $0 | $22.50 |

(viii)(A) Eighth, PRS must perform the calculations and make the necessary adjustments described under paragraph (f)(2)(viii) of this section if, and only if, PRS has:

(1) An excess business interest expense greater than $0 under paragraph (f)(2)(i) of this section;

(2) A total negative allocable ATI greater than $0 under paragraph (f)(2)(vi) of this section; and

(3) A total ATIC excess amount greater than $0 under paragraph (f)(2)(vii) of this section.

(B) Because PRS does not meet all three requirements in paragraph (o)(12)(viii)(A) of this section, PRS does not perform the calculations or adjustments described in paragraph (f)(2)(viii) of this section. In sum, the correct amounts to be used in paragraphs (o)(12)(ix) and (x) of this section are as follows.

| Table 1 to paragraph (o)(12)(viii)(B) | | | | |
|---|---|---|---|---|
| | A | B | C | Total |
| ATIC excess | $0 | $37.50 | $0 | $37.50 |
| ATIC deficit | $22.50 | $0 | $0 | $22.50 |

(ix) Ninth, PRS determines each partner's final ATIC excess amount. Because B has ATIC excess, PRS must determine B's final ATIC excess amount. B's final ATIC excess amount is B's ATIC excess ($37.50), reduced, but not below $0, by the product of the total ATIC deficit ($22.50) and the ratio of B's ATIC excess to the total ATIC excess ($37.50/$37.50). Therefore, B has $15 of final ATIC excess ($37.50 — ($22.50 x 100 percent)).

| Table 1 to paragraph (o)(12)(ix) | | | | |
|---|---|---|---|---|
| | A | B | C | Total |
| ATIC excess | $0 | $37.50 | $0 | N/A |
| Less: (Total ATIC deficit) x (ATIC excess / Total ATIC excess) | $0 | $22.50 | $0 | N/A |
| = Final ATIC excess | $0 | $15 | $0 | $15 |

(x) Tenth, PRS determines each partner's final ATIC deficit amount. Because A has an ATIC deficit, PRS must determine A's final ATIC deficit amount. A's final ATIC deficit amount is A's ATIC deficit ($22.50), reduced, but not below $0, by the product of the total ATIC excess ($37.50) and the ratio of A's ATIC deficit to the total ATIC deficit ($22.50/$22.50). Therefore, A has $0 of final ATIC deficit ($22.50 — ($37.50 x 100 percent)).

| Table 1 to paragraph (o)(12)(x) | | | | |
|---|---|---|---|---|
| | A | B | C | Total |
| ATIC deficit | $22.50 | $0 | $0 | N/A |
| Less: (Total ATIC excess) x (ATIC deficit / Total ATIC deficit) | $37.50 | $0 | $0 | N/A |
| = Final ATIC deficit | $0 | $0 | $0 | $0 |

(xi) Eleventh, PRS allocates deductible business interest expense and section 163(j) excess items to the partners. Pursuant to paragraph (f)(2)(i) of this section, PRS has $50 of excess taxable income and $40 of deductible business interest expense. After grossing up each partner's final ATIC excess amounts by ten-thirds, excess taxable income is allocated dollar for dollar to partners with final ATIC excess amounts. Thus, PRS allocates its excess taxable income (ETI) $50 to B. A partner's allocable business interest expense is deductible business interest expense to the extent it exceeds such partner's share of excess business interest expense (EBIE). Therefore, A has deductible business interest expense of $30 ($30 - $0), B has deductible business interest expense of $10 ($10 - $0), and C has deductible business interest expense of $0 ($0 - $0).

| Table 1 to paragraph (o)(12)(xi) | | | | |
|---|---|---|---|---|
| | A | B | C | Total |
| Deductible BIE | $30 | $10 | $0 | $40 |
| EBIE allocated | $0 | $0 | $0 | $0 |
| ETI allocated | $0 | $50 | $0 | $50 |
| EBII allocated | $0 | $0 | $0 | $0 |

(13) *Example 13: Facts.* A, B, and C own all of the interests in partnership PRS. In Year 1, PRS has $100 of ATI, $0 of business interest income, and $50 of business interest expense. PRS's ATI consists of $200 of gross income and $100 of gross deductions. PRS allocates its items comprising ATI $100 to A, $100 to B, and ($100) to C. PRS allocates its business interest expense $0 to A, $25 to B, and $25 to C.

(i) First, PRS determines its limitation pursuant to § 1.163(j)-2. PRS's section 163(j) limit is 30 percent of its ATI plus its business interest income, or $30 ($100 x 30 percent). Thus, PRS has $30 of deductible business interest expense and $20 of excess business interest expense.

**Prop. Reg. § 1.163(j)-6(o)**

(ii) Second, PRS determines each partner's allocable share of section 163(j) items used in its own section 163(j) calculation.

| Table 1 to paragraph (o)(13)(ii) | A | B | C | Total |
|---|---|---|---|---|
| Allocable ATI | $100 | $100 | ($100) | $100 |
| Allocable BII | $0 | $0 | $0 | $0 |
| Allocable BIE | $0 | $25 | $25 | $50 |

(iii) Third, PRS compares each partner's allocable business interest income to such partner's allocable business interest expense. No partner has allocable business interest income. Consequently, each partner's allocable business interest income deficit is equal to such partner's allocable business interest income deficit is $0, B's allocable business interest income deficit is $25, and C's allocable business interest income deficit is $25. The total allocable business interest income deficit is $50 ($0 + $25 + $25). No partner has allocable business interest income excess because no partner has allocable business interest income in excess of its allocable business interest expense. Thus, the total allocable business interest income excess is $0.

| Table 1 to paragraph (o)(13)(iii) | A | B | C | Total |
|---|---|---|---|---|
| Allocable BII | $0 | $0 | $0 | N/A |
| Allocable BIE | $0 | $25 | $25 | N/A |
| If allocable BII exceeds allocable BIE, then such amount = Allocable BII excess | $0 | $0 | $0 | $0 |
| If allocable BIE exceeds allocable BII, then such amount = Allocable BII deficit | $0 | $25 | $25 | $50 |

(iv) Fourth, PRS determines each partner's final allocable business interest income excess. Because no partner had any allocable business interest income excess, each partner has final allocable business interest income excess of $0.

(v) Fifth, PRS determines each partner's remaining business interest expense. Because no partner has any allocable business interest income excess, each partner's remaining business interest expense equals its allocable business interest income deficit. Thus, A's remaining business interest expense is $0, B's remaining business interest expense is $25, and C's remaining business interest expense is $25.

| Table 1 to paragraph (o)(13)(v) | A | B | C | Total |
|---|---|---|---|---|
| Allocable BII deficit | $0 | $25 | $25 | $50 |
| Less: (Total allocable BII excess) x (Allocable BII deficit / Total allocable BII deficit) | $0 | $0 | $0 | N/A |
| = Remaining BIE | $0 | $25 | $25 | N/A |

(vi) Sixth, PRS determines each partner's final allocable ATI. Because C's allocable ATI is comprised of $100 of items of deduction and loss and $0 of income and gain, C has negative allocable ATI of $100. C is the only partner with negative allocable ATI. Thus, the total negative allocable ATI amount is $100. Any partner with a negative allocable ATI, or an allocable ATI of $0, has a positive allocable ATI of $0. Therefore, C has a positive allocable ATI of $0. Because A's allocable ATI is comprised of $100 of items of income and gain and $0 of deduction and loss, A has positive allocable ATI of $100. Because B's allocable ATI is comprised of $100 of items of income and gain and $0 of deduction and loss, B has positive allocable ATI of $100. Thus, the total positive allocable ATI is $200 ($100 + $100 + $0).

PRS determines A's final allocable ATI by reducing, but not below $0, A's positive allocable ATI ($100) by the product of total negative allocable ATI ($100) and the ratio of A's positive allocable ATI to the total positive allocable ATI ($100/$200). Therefore, A's positive allocable ATI is reduced by $50 ($100 x 50 percent). As a result, A's final allocable ATI is $50. PRS determines B's final allocable ATI by reducing, but not below $0, B's positive allocable ATI ($100) by the product of total negative allocable ATI ($100) and the ratio of B's positive allocable ATI to the total positive allocable ATI ($100/$200). Therefore, B's positive allocable ATI is reduced by $50 ($100 x 50 percent). As a result, B's final allocable ATI is $50. Because C has a positive allocable ATI of $0, C's final allocable ATI is $0.

**Prop. Reg. §1.163(j)-6(o)**

| Table 1 to paragraph (o)(13)(vi) | | | | |
|---|---|---|---|---|
| | A | B | C | Total |
| Allocable ATI | $100 | $100 | ($100) | $100 |
| If deduction and loss items comprising allocable ATI exceed income and gain items comprising allocable ATI, then such excess amount = Negative allocable ATI | $0 | $0 | $100 | $100 |
| If income and gain items comprising allocable ATI equal or exceed deduction and loss items comprising allocable ATI, then such amount = Positive allocable ATI | $100 | $100 | $0 | $200 |

| Table 2 to paragraph (o)(13)(vi) | | | | |
|---|---|---|---|---|
| | A | B | C | Total |
| Positive allocable ATI | $100 | $100 | $0 | $200 |
| Less: (Total negative allocable ATI) x (Positive allocable ATI / Total positive allocable ATI) | $50 | $50 | $0 | N/A |
| = Final allocable ATI | $50 | $50 | $0 | $100 |

(vii) Seventh, PRS compares each partner's ATI capacity (ATIC) amount to such partner's remaining business interest expense. A's ATIC amount is $15 ($50 x 30 percent), B's ATIC amount is $15 ($50 x 30 percent), and C's ATIC amount is $0 ($0 x 30 percent). Because A's ATIC amount exceeds its remaining business interest expense by $15 ($15 - $0), A has an ATIC excess of $15. B and C do not have any ATIC excess.

Thus, the total ATIC excess is $15 ($15 + $0 + $0). A does not have any ATIC deficit. Because B's remaining business interest expense exceeds its ATIC amount by $10 ($25 - $15), B has an ATIC deficit of $10. Because C's remaining business interest expense exceeds its ATIC amount by $25 ($25 - $0), C has an ATIC deficit of $25. Thus, the total ATIC deficit is $35 ($0 + $10 + $25).

| Table 1 to paragraph (o)(13)(vii) | | | | |
|---|---|---|---|---|
| | A | B | C | Total |
| ATIC (Final allocable ATI x 30 percent) | $15 | $15 | $0 | N/A |
| Remaining BIE | $0 | $25 | $25 | N/A |
| If ATIC exceeds remaining BIE, then such excess = ATIC excess | $15 | $0 | $0 | $15 |
| If remaining BIE exceeds ATIC, then such excess = ATIC deficit | $0 | $10 | $25 | $35 |

(viii)(A) Eighth, PRS must perform the calculations and make the necessary adjustments described under paragraph (f)(2)(viii) of this section if, and only if, PRS has:

(1) An excess business interest expense greater than $0 under paragraph (f)(2)(i) of this section;

(2) A total negative allocable ATI greater than $0 under paragraph (f)(2)(vi) of this section; and

(3) A total ATIC excess greater than $0 under paragraph (f)(2)(vii) of this section. Because PRS satisfies each of these three requirements, PRS must perform the calculations and make the necessary adjustments described under paragraph (f)(2)(viii)(B) and (C) or (D) of this section.

(B) PRS must determine each partner's priority amount and usable priority amount. Only partners with an ATIC deficit under paragraph (f)(2)(vii) of this section can have a priority

amount greater than $0. Thus, only partners B and C can have a priority amount greater than $0. PRS determines a partner's priority amount as thirty percent of the amount by which such partner's allocable positive ATI exceeds its final allocable ATI. Therefore, A's priority amount is $0, B's priority amount is $15 (($100 - $50) x 30 percent), and C's priority amount is $0 (($0 - $0) x 30 percent). Thus, the total priority amount is $15 ($0 + $15 + $0). Next, PRS must determine each partner's usable priority amount. Each partner's usable priority amount is the lesser of such partner's priority amount or ATIC deficit. Thus, A has a usable priority amount of $0, B has a usable priority amount of $10, and C has a usable priority amount of $0. As a result, the total usable priority amount is $10 ($0 + $10 + $0). Because the total ATIC excess under paragraph (f)(2)(vii) of this section ($15) is greater than the total usable priority amount ($10), PRS must perform the adjustments described in paragraph (f)(2)(viii)(C) of this section.

| Table 1 to paragraph (o)(13)(viii)(B) | | | | |
|---|---|---|---|---|
| | A | B | C | Total |
| (Positive allocable ATI - Final allocable ATI) | $0 | $50 | $0 | N/A |
| Multiplied by 30 percent | 30 percent | 30 percent | 30 percent | N/A |
| = Priority amount | $0 | $15 | $0 | $15 |

| Table 2 to paragraph (o)(13)(viii)(B) | | | | |
|---|---|---|---|---|
| | A | B | C | Total |
| Priority amount | $0 | $15 | $0 | N/A |
| ATIC deficit | $0 | $10 | $25 | N/A |
| Lesser of priority amount or ATIC deficit = Usable priority amount | $0 | $10 | $0 | $10 |

(C) For purposes of paragraph (f)(2)(ix) of this section, each partner's ATIC deficit is $0. For purposes of paragraph (f)(2)(x) of this section, the following terms shall have the following meanings. Each partner's ATIC deficit is such partner's ATIC deficit as determined pursuant to paragraph (f)(2)(vii) of this section reduced by such partner's usable priority amount. Thus, A's ATIC deficit is $0 ($0 - $0), B's ATIC deficit is $0 ($10 - $10), and C's ATIC deficit is $25 ($25 - $0). The total ATIC deficit is the total ATIC deficit determined pursuant to paragraph (f)(2)(vii) ($35) reduced by the total usable priority amount ($10). Thus, the total ATIC deficit is $25 ($35 - $10). The total ATIC excess is the total ATIC excess determined pursuant to paragraph (f)(2)(vii) of this section ($15) reduced by the total usable priority amount ($10). Thus, the total ATIC excess is $5 ($15 - $5).

| Table 1 to paragraph (o)(13)(viii)(C) | | | | |
|---|---|---|---|---|
| | A | B | C | Total |
| ATIC deficit | $0 | $10 | $25 | N/A |
| Less: Usable priority amount | $0 | $10 | $0 | N/A |
| = ATIC deficit for purposes of paragraph (f)(2)(x) of this section | $0 | $0 | $25 | $25 |

(D) In light of the fact that the total ATIC excess was greater than the total usable priority amount under paragraph (f)(2)(viii)(B) of this section, paragraph (f)(2)(viii)(D) of this section does not apply. In sum, the correct amounts to be used in paragraph (f)(2)(x) of this section are as follows.

| Table 1 to paragraph (o)(13)(viii)(C) | | | | |
|---|---|---|---|---|
| | A | B | C | Total |
| ATIC excess | $5 | $0 | $0 | $5 |
| ATIC deficit | $0 | $0 | $25 | $25 |

(ix) Ninth, PRS determines each partner's final ATIC excess amount. Pursuant to paragraph (f)(2)(viii)(C) of this section, each partner's final ATIC excess amount is $0.

(x) Tenth, PRS determines each partner's final ATIC deficit amount. Because C has an ATIC deficit, PRS must determine C's final ATIC defi-cit amount. C's final ATIC deficit amount is C's ATIC deficit ($25), reduced, but not below $0, by the product of the total ATIC excess ($5) and the ratio of C's ATIC deficit to the total ATIC deficit ($25/$25). Therefore, C has $20 of final ATIC deficit ($25 — ($5 x 100 percent)).

| Table 1 to paragraph (o)(13)(x) | | | | |
|---|---|---|---|---|
| | A | B | C | Total |
| ATIC deficit | $0 | $0 | $25 | N/A |
| Less: (Total ATIC excess) x (ATIC deficit / Total ATIC deficit) | $0 | $0 | $5 | N/A |
| = Final ATIC deficit | $0 | $0 | $20 | $20 |

(xi) Eleventh, PRS allocates deductible business interest expense and section 163(j) excess items to the partners. Pursuant to paragraph (f)(2)(i) of this section, PRS has $20 of excess business interest expense. PRS allocates the excess business interest expense dollar for dollar to the partners with final ATIC deficits. Thus, PRS allocates its excess business interest expense $20 to C. A partner's allocable business interest expense is deductible business interest expense to the extent it exceeds such partner's share of excess business interest expense. Therefore, A has deductible business interest expense of $0 ($0 - $0), B has deductible business interest expense of $25 ($25 - $0), and C has deductible business interest expense of $5 ($25 - $20).

| Table 1 to paragraph (o)(13)(xi) | | | | |
|---|---|---|---|---|
| | A | B | C | Total |
| Deductible BIE | $0 | $25 | $5 | $30 |
| EBIE allocated | $0 | $0 | $20 | $20 |
| ETI allocated | $0 | $0 | $0 | $0 |
| EBII allocated | $0 | $0 | $0 | $0 |

(14) *Example 14: Facts.* A, B, C, and D own all of the interests in partnership PRS. In Year 1, PRS has $200 of ATI, $0 of business interest income, and $140 of business interest expense. PRS's ATI consists of $600 of gross income and $400 of gross deductions. PRS allocates its items comprising ATI $100 to A, $100 to B, $400 to C, and ($400) to D. PRS allocates its business interest expense $0 to A, $40 to B, $60 to C, and $40 to D.

(i) First, PRS determines its limitation pursuant to § 1.163(j)-2. PRS's section 163(j) limit is 30 percent of its ATI plus its business interest income, or $60 ($200 x 30 percent). Thus, PRS has $60 of deductible business interest expense and $80 of excess business interest expense.

(ii) Second, PRS determines each partner's allocable share of section 163(j) items used in its own section 163(j) calculation.

| Table 1 to paragraph (o)(14)(ii) | | | | | |
|---|---|---|---|---|---|
| | A | B | C | D | Total |
| Allocable ATI | $100 | $100 | $400 | ($400) | $200 |
| Allocable BII | $0 | $0 | $0 | $0 | $0 |
| Allocable BIE | $0 | $40 | $60 | $40 | $140 |

(iii) Third, PRS compares each partner's allocable business interest income to such partner's allocable business interest expense. No partner has allocable business interest income. Consequently, each partner's allocable business interest income deficit is equal to such partner's allocable business interest expense. Thus, A's allocable business interest income deficit is $0, B's allocable business interest income deficit is $40, C's allocable business interest income deficit is $60, and D's allocable business interest income deficit is $40. The total allocable business interest income deficit is $140 ($0 + $40 + $60 + $40). No partner has allocable business interest income excess because no partner has allocable business interest income in excess of its allocable business interest expense. Thus, the total allocable business interest income excess is $0.

| Table 1 to paragraph (o)(14)(iii) | | | | | |
|---|---|---|---|---|---|
| | A | B | C | D | Total |
| Allocable BII | $0 | $0 | $0 | $0 | N/A |
| Allocable BIE | $0 | $40 | $60 | $40 | N/A |
| If allocable BII exceeds allocable BIE, then such amount = Allocable BII excess | $0 | $0 | $0 | $0 | $0 |
| If allocable BIE exceeds allocable BII, then such amount = Allocable BII deficit | $0 | $40 | $60 | $40 | $140 |

(iv) Fourth, PRS determines each partner's final allocable business interest income excess. Because no partner has any allocable business interest income excess, each partner has final allocable business interest income excess of $0.

(v) Fifth, PRS determines each partner's remaining business interest expense. Because no partner has any allocable business interest income excess, each partner's remaining business interest expense equals its allocable business interest income deficit. Thus, A's remaining business interest expense is $0, B's remaining business interest expense is $40, C's remaining business interest expense is $60, and D's remaining business interest expense is $40.

| Table 1 to paragraph (o)(14)(v) | | | | | |
|---|---|---|---|---|---|
| | A | B | C | D | Total |
| Allocable BII deficit | $0 | $40 | $60 | $40 | $140 |
| Less: (Total allocable BII excess) x (Allocable BII deficit / Total allocable BII deficit) | $0 | $0 | $0 | $0 | N/A |
| = Remaining BIE | $0 | $40 | $60 | $40 | N/A |

(vi) Sixth, PRS determines each partner's final allocable ATI. Because D's allocable ATI is comprised of $400 of items of deduction and loss and $0 of income and gain, D has negative allocable ATI of $400. D is the only partner with negative allocable ATI. Thus, the total negative allocable ATI amount is $400. Any partner with a negative allocable ATI, or an allocable ATI of $0, has a positive allocable ATI of $0. Therefore, D has a positive allocable ATI of $0. PRS determines A's final allocable ATI by reducing, but not below $0, A's positive allocable ATI ($100) by the product of total negative allocable ATI ($400) and the ratio of A's positive allocable ATI to the total positive allocable ATI ($100/$600). Therefore, A's positive allocable ATI is reduced by $66.67 ($400 x 16.67 percent). As a result, A's final allocable ATI is $33.33. PRS determines B's final allocable ATI by reducing, but not below $0, B's positive allocable ATI ($100) by the product of total negative allocable ATI ($400) and the ratio of B's positive allocable ATI to the total positive allocable ATI ($100/$600). Therefore, B's positive allocable ATI is reduced by $66.67 ($400 x 16.67 percent). As a result, B's final allocable ATI is $33.33. PRS determines C's final allocable ATI by reducing, but not below $0, C's positive allocable ATI ($400) by the product of total negative allocable ATI ($400) and the ratio of C's positive allocable ATI to the total positive allocable ATI ($400/$600). Therefore, C's positive allocable ATI is reduced by $266.67 ($400 x 66.67 percent). As a result, C's final allocable ATI is $133.33. Because D has a positive allocable ATI of $0, D's final allocable ATI is $0.

| Table 1 to paragraph (o)(14)(vi) | | | | | |
|---|---|---|---|---|---|
| | A | B | C | D | Total |
| Allocable ATI | $100 | $100 | $400 | ($400) | $200 |
| If deduction and loss items comprising allocable ATI exceed income and gain items comprising allocable ATI, then such excess amount = Negative allocable ATI | $0 | $0 | $0 | $400 | $400 |
| If income and gain items comprising allocable ATI equal or exceed deduction and loss items comprising allocable ATI, then such amount = Positive allocable ATI | $100 | $100 | $400 | $0 | $600 |

| Table 2 to paragraph (o)(14)(vi) | | | | | |
|---|---|---|---|---|---|
| | A | B | C | D | Total |
| Positive allocable ATI | $100 | $100 | $400 | $0 | $600 |
| Less: (Total negative allocable ATI) x (Positive allocable ATI / Total positive allocable ATI) | $66.67 | $66.67 | $266.67 | $0 | N/A |
| = Final allocable ATI | $33.33 | $33.33 | $133.33 | $0 | $200 |

(vii) Seventh, PRS compares each partner's ATI capacity (ATIC) amount to such partner's remaining business interest expense. A's ATIC amount is $10 ($33.33 x 30 percent), B's ATIC amount is $10 ($33.33 x 30 percent), B's ATIC amount is $10 ($33.33 x 30 percent), C's ATIC amount is $40 ($133.33 x 30 percent), and D's ATIC amount is $0 ($0 x 30 percent). Because A's ATIC amount exceeds its remaining business interest expense by $10 ($10 - $0), A has an ATIC excess of $10. B, C, and D do not have any ATIC excess. Thus, the total ATIC excess is $10 ($10 + $0 + $0 + $0). A does not have any ATIC deficit. Because B's remaining business interest expense exceeds its ATIC amount by $30 ($40 - $10), B has an ATIC deficit of $30. Because C's remaining business interest expense exceeds its ATIC amount by $20 ($60 - $40), C has an ATIC deficit of $20. Because D's remaining business interest expense exceeds its ATIC amount by $40 ($40 - $0), D has an ATIC deficit of $40. Thus, the total ATIC deficit is $90 ($0 + $30 + $20 + $40).

| Table 1 to paragraph (o)(14)(vii) | | | | | |
|---|---|---|---|---|---|
| | A | B | C | D | Total |
| ATIC (Final allocable ATI x 30 percent) | $10 | $10 | $40 | $0 | N/A |
| Remaining BIE | $0 | $40 | $60 | $40 | N/A |
| If ATIC exceeds remaining BIE, then such excess = ATIC excess | $10 | $0 | $0 | $0 | $10 |
| If remaining BIE exceeds ATIC, then such excess = ATIC deficit | $0 | $30 | $20 | $40 | $90 |

(viii)(A) Eighth, PRS must perform the calculations and make the necessary adjustments described under paragraph (f)(2)(viii) of this section if, and only if, PRS has (1) an excess business interest expense greater than $0 under paragraph (f)(2)(i) of this section, (2) a total negative allocable ATI greater than $0 under paragraph (f)(2)(vi) of this section, and (3) a total ATIC excess amount greater than $0 under paragraph (f)(2)(vii) of this section. Because PRS satisfies each of these three requirements, PRS must perform the calculations and make the necessary adjustments described under paragraphs (f)(2)(viii)(B) and (C) or paragraph (f)(2)(viii)(D) of this section.

(B) PRS must determine each partner's priority amount and usable priority amount. Only partners with an ATIC deficit under paragraph (f)(2)(vii) of this section can have a priority amount greater than $0. Thus, only partners B, C, and D can have a priority amount greater than $0. PRS determines a partner's priority amount as thirty percent of the amount by which such partner's allocable positive ATI exceeds its final allocable ATI. Therefore, B's priority amount is $20 (($100 - $33.33) x 30 percent), C's priority amount is $80 (($400 - $133.33) x 30 percent), and D's priority amount is $0 (($0 - $0) x 30 percent). Thus, the total priority amount is $100 ($0 + $20 + $80 + $0). Next, PRS must determine each partner's usable priority amount. Each partner's usable priority amount is the lesser of such partner's priority amount or ATIC deficit. Thus, A has a usable priority amount of $0, B has a usable priority amount of $20, C has a usable priority amount of $20, and D has a usable priority amount of $0. As a result, the total usable priority amount is $40 ($0 + $20 + $20 + $0). Because the total usable priority amount ($40) is greater than the total ATIC excess under paragraph (f)(2)(vii) ($10), PRS must perform the adjustments described in paragraph (f)(2)(viii)(D) of this section.

| Table 1 to paragraph (o)(14)(viii)(B) | | | | | |
|---|---|---|---|---|---|
| | A | B | C | D | Total |
| (Positive allocable ATI - Final allocable ATI) | $0 | $66.67 | $266.67 | $0 | N/A |
| Multiplied by 30 percent | 30 percent | 30 percent | 30 percent | 30 percent | N/A |
| = Priority amount | $0 | $20 | $80 | $0 | $100 |

| Table 2 to paragraph (o)(14)(viii)(B) | | | | | |
|---|---|---|---|---|---|
| | A | B | C | D | Total |
| Priority amount | $0 | $20 | $80 | $0 | N/A |
| ATIC deficit | $0 | $30 | $20 | $40 | N/A |
| Lesser of priority amount or ATIC deficit = Usable priority amount | $0 | $20 | $20 | $0 | $40 |

(C) In light of the fact that the total usable priority amount is greater than the total ATIC excess under paragraph (f)(2)(viii)(B) of this section, paragraph (f)(2)(viii)(C) of this section does not apply.

**Prop. Reg. §1.163(j)-6(o)**

(D)(*1*) Because B and C are the only partners with priority amounts greater than $0, B and C are priority partners, while A and D are non-priority partners. For purposes of paragraph (f)(2)(ix) of this section, each partner's final ATIC excess amount is $0. For purposes of paragraph (f)(2)(x) of this section, each non-priority partner's final ATIC deficit amount is such partner's ATIC deficit determined pursuant to paragraph (f)(2)(vii) of this section. Therefore, A has a final ATIC deficit of $0 and D has a final ATIC deficit of $40. Additionally, for purposes of paragraph (f)(2)(x) of this section, PRS must determine each priority partner's step eight excess share. A priority partner's step eight excess share is the product of the total ATIC excess and the ratio of the partner's priority amount to the total priority amount. Thus, B's step eight excess share is $2 ($10 x ($20/$100)) and C's step eight excess share is $8 ($10 x ($80/$100)). To the extent a priority partner's step eight excess share exceeds its ATIC deficit, the excess shall be the partner's ATIC excess for purposes of paragraph (f)(2)(x) of this section. Thus, B and C each have an ATIC excess of $0, resulting in a total ATIC excess is $0. To the extent a priority partner's ATIC deficit exceeds its step eight excess share, the excess shall be the partner's ATIC deficit for purposes of paragraph (f)(2)(x) of this section. Because B's ATIC deficit ($30) exceeds its step eight excess share ($2), B's ATIC deficit for purposes of paragraph (f)(2)(x) of this section is $28 ($30 - $2). Because C's ATIC deficit ($20) exceeds its step eight excess share ($8), C's ATIC deficit for purposes of paragraph (f)(2)(x) of this section is $12 ($20 - $8). Thus, the total ATIC deficit is $40 ($28 + $12).

| Table 1 to paragraph (o)(14)(viii)(D)(*1*) | | | | | |
|---|---|---|---|---|---|
| | A | B | C | D | Total |
| Non-priority partners ATIC deficit in paragraph (f)(2)(vii) = Final ATIC deficit for purposes of paragraph (f)(2)(x) of this section | $0 | N/A | N/A | $40 | N/A |

| Table 2 to paragraph (o)(14)(viii)(D)(*1*) | | | | | |
|---|---|---|---|---|---|
| | A | B | C | D | Total |
| Priority partners step eight excess share = (Total ATIC excess) x (Priority / Total priority) | N/A | $2 | $8 | N/A | N/A |
| ATIC deficit | N/A | $30 | $20 | N/A | N/A |
| If step eight excess share exceeds ATIC deficit, then such excess = ATIC excess for purposes of paragraph (f)(2)(x) of this section | N/A | $0 | $0 | N/A | $0 |
| If ATIC deficit exceeds step eight excess share, then such excess = ATIC deficit for purposes of paragraph (f)(2)(x) of this section | N/A | $28 | $12 | N/A | $40 |

(2) In sum, the correct amounts to be used in paragraph (f)(2)(x) of this section are as follows:

| Table 1 to paragraph (o)(14)(viii)(D)(2) | | | | | |
|---|---|---|---|---|---|
| | A | B | C | D | Total |
| ATIC excess | $0 | $0 | $0 | $0 | $0 |
| ATIC deficit | $0 | $28 | $12 | $0 | $40 |
| Non-priority partner final ATIC deficit | $0 | $0 | $0 | $40 | N/A |

(ix) Ninth, PRS determines each partner's final ATIC excess amount. Pursuant to paragraph (f)(2)(viii)(D) of this section, each priority and non-priority partner's final ATIC excess amount is $0.

(x) Tenth, PRS determines each partner's final ATIC deficit amount. Because B has an ATIC deficit, PRS must determine B's final ATIC deficit amount. B's final ATIC deficit amount is B's ATIC deficit ($28), reduced, but not below $0, by the product of the total ATIC excess ($0) and the ratio of B's ATIC deficit to the total ATIC deficit ($28/$40). Therefore, B has $28 of final ATIC deficit ($28 — ($0 x 70 percent)). Because C has an ATIC deficit, PRS must determine C's final ATIC deficit amount. C's final ATIC deficit amount is C's ATIC deficit ($12), reduced, but not below $0, by the product of the total ATIC excess ($0) and the ratio of C's ATIC deficit to the total ATIC deficit ($12/$40). Therefore, C has

12 of final ATIC deficit ($12 — ($0 x 30 percent)). Pursuant to paragraph (f)(2)(viii)(D) of this section, D's final ATIC deficit amount is $40.

| Table 2 to paragraph (o)(14)(x) | | | | | |
| --- | --- | --- | --- | --- | --- |
| | A | B | C | D | Total |
| ATIC deficit | N/A | $28 | $12 | N/A | N/A |
| Less: (Total ATIC excess) x (ATIC deficit / Total ATIC deficit) | N/A | $0 | $0 | N/A | N/A |
| = Final ATIC deficit | $0 | $28 | $12 | $40 | $80 |

(xi) Eleventh, PRS allocates deductible business interest expense and section 163(j) excess items to the partners. Pursuant to paragraph (f)(2)(i) of this section, PRS has $80 of excess business interest expense. PRS allocates the excess business interest expense dollar for dollar to the partners with final ATIC deficits. Thus, PRS allocates its excess business interest expense $28 to B, $12 to C, and $40 to D. A partner's allocable business interest expense is deductible business interest expense to the extent it exceeds such partner's share of excess business interest expense. Therefore, A has deductible business interest expense of $0 ($0 - $0), B has deductible business interest expense of $12 ($40 - $28), C has deductible business interest expense of $48 ($60 - $12), and D has deductible business interest expense of $0 ($40 - $40).

| Table 1 to paragraph (o)(14)(xi) | | | | | |
| --- | --- | --- | --- | --- | --- |
| | A | B | C | D | Total |
| Deductible BIE | $0 | $12 | $48 | $0 | $60 |
| EBIE allocated | $0 | $28 | $12 | $40 | $80 |
| ETI allocated | $0 | $0 | $0 | $0 | $0 |
| EBII allocated | $0 | $0 | $0 | $0 | $0 |

(15) *Example 15: Facts.* A, B, C, and D own all of the interests in partnership PRS. In Year 1, PRS has $200 of ATI, $0 of business interest income, and $150 of business interest expense. PRS's ATI consists of $500 of gross income and $300 of gross deductions. PRS allocates its items comprising ATI $50 to A, $50 to B, $400 to C, and ($300) to D. PRS allocates its business interest expense $0 to A, $50 to B, $50 to C, and $50 to D.

(i) First, PRS determines its limitation pursuant to § 1.163(j)-2. PRS's section 163(j) limit is 30 percent of its ATI plus its business interest income, or $60 ($200 x 30 percent). Thus, PRS has $60 of deductible business interest expense, and $90 of excess business interest expense.

(ii) Second, PRS determines each partner's allocable share of section 163(j) items used in its own section 163(j) calculation.

| Table 1 to paragraph (o)(15)(ii) | | | | | |
| --- | --- | --- | --- | --- | --- |
| | A | B | C | D | Total |
| Allocable ATI | $50 | $50 | $400 | ($300) | $200 |
| Allocable BII | $0 | $0 | $0 | $0 | $0 |
| Allocable BIE | $0 | $50 | $50 | $50 | $150 |

(iii) Third, PRS compares each partner's allocable business interest income to such partner's allocable business interest expense. No partner has allocable business interest income. Consequently, each partner's allocable business interest income deficit is equal to such partner's allocable business interest expense. Thus, A's allocable business interest income deficit is $0, B's allocable business interest income deficit is $50, C's allocable business interest income deficit is $50, and D's allocable business interest income deficit is $50. The total allocable business interest income deficit is $150 ($0 + $50 + $50 + $50). No partner has allocable business interest income excess because no partner has allocable business interest income in excess of its allocable business interest expense. Thus, the total allocable business interest income excess is $0.

| Table 1 to paragraph (o)(15)(iii) | A | B | C | D | Total |
|---|---|---|---|---|---|
| Allocable BII | $0 | $0 | $0 | $0 | N/A |
| Allocable BIE | $0 | $50 | $50 | $50 | N/A |
| If allocable BII exceeds allocable BIE, then such amount = Allocable BII excess | $0 | $0 | $0 | $0 | $0 |
| If allocable BIE exceeds allocable BII, then such amount = Allocable BII deficit | $0 | $50 | $50 | $50 | $150 |

(iv) Fourth, PRS determines each partner's final allocable business interest income excess. Because no partner has any allocable business interest income excess, each partner has final allocable business interest income excess of $0.

(v) Fifth, PRS determines each partner's remaining business interest expense. Because no partner has any allocable business interest income excess, each partner's remaining business interest expense equals its allocable business interest income deficit. Thus, A's remaining business interest expense is $0, B's remaining business interest expense is $50, C's remaining business interest expense is $50, and D's remaining business interest expense is $50.

| Table 1 to paragraph (o)(15)(v) | A | B | C | D | Total |
|---|---|---|---|---|---|
| Allocable BII deficit | $0 | $50 | $50 | $50 | $150 |
| Less: (Total allocable BII excess) x (Allocable BII deficit / Total allocable BII deficit) | $0 | $0 | $0 | $0 | N/A |
| = Remaining BIE | $0 | $50 | $50 | $50 | N/A |

(vi) Sixth, PRS determines each partner's final allocable ATI. Because D's allocable ATI is comprised of $300 of items of deduction and loss and $0 of income and gain, D has negative allocable ATI of $300. D is the only partner with negative allocable ATI. Thus, the total negative allocable ATI amount is $300. Any partner with a negative allocable ATI, or an allocable ATI of $0, has a positive allocable ATI of $0. Therefore, D has a positive allocable ATI of $0. PRS determines A's final allocable ATI by reducing, but not below $0, A's positive allocable ATI ($50) by the product of total negative allocable ATI ($300) and the ratio of A's positive allocable ATI to the total positive allocable ATI ($50/$500). Therefore, A's positive allocable ATI is reduced by $30 ($300 x 10 percent). As a result, A's final allocable ATI is $20. PRS determines B's final allocable ATI by reducing, but not below $0, B's positive allocable ATI ($50) by the product of total negative allocable ATI ($300) and the ratio of B's positive allocable ATI to the total positive allocable ATI ($50/$500). Therefore, B's positive allocable ATI is reduced by $30 ($300 x 10 percent). As a result, B's final allocable ATI is $20. PRS determines C's final allocable ATI by reducing, but not below $0, C's positive allocable ATI ($400) by the product of total negative allocable ATI ($300) and the ratio of C's positive allocable ATI to the total positive allocable ATI ($400/$500). Therefore, C's positive allocable ATI is reduced by $240 ($300 x 80 percent). As a result, C's final allocable ATI is $160. Because D has a positive allocable ATI of $0, D's final allocable ATI is $0.

| Table 1 to paragraph (o)(15)(vi) | A | B | C | D | Total |
|---|---|---|---|---|---|
| Allocable ATI | $50 | $50 | $400 | ($300) | $200 |
| If deduction and loss items comprising allocable ATI exceed income and gain items comprising allocable ATI, then such excess amount = Negative allocable ATI | $0 | $0 | $0 | $300 | $300 |
| If income and gain items comprising allocable ATI equal or exceed deduction and loss items comprising allocable ATI, then such amount = Positive allocable ATI | $50 | $50 | $400 | $0 | $500 |

| Table 2 to paragraph (o)(15)(vi) | | | | | |
| --- | --- | --- | --- | --- | --- |
| | A | B | C | D | Total |
| Positive allocable ATI | $50 | $50 | $400 | $0 | $500 |
| Less: (Total negative allocable ATI) x (Positive allocable ATI / Total positive allocable ATI) | $30 | $30 | $240 | $0 | N/A |
| = Final allocable ATI | $20 | $20 | $160 | $0 | $200 |

(vii) Seventh, PRS compares each partner's ATI capacity (ATIC) amount to such partner's remaining business interest expense. A's ATIC amount is $6 ($20 x 30 percent), B's ATIC amount is $6 ($20 x 30 percent), C's ATIC amount is $48 ($160 x 30 percent), and D's ATIC amount is $0 ($0 x 30 percent). Because A's ATIC amount exceeds its remaining business interest expense by $6 ($6 - $0), A has an ATIC excess of $6. B, C, and D do not have any ATIC excess. Thus, the total ATIC excess amount is $6 ($6 + $0 + $0 + $0). A does not have any ATIC deficit. Because B's remaining business interest expense exceeds its ATIC amount by $44 ($50 - $6), B has an ATIC deficit of $44. Because C's remaining business interest expense exceeds its ATIC amount by $2 ($50 - $48), C has an ATIC deficit of $2. Because D's remaining business interest expense exceeds its ATIC amount by $50 ($50 - $0), D has an ATIC deficit of $50. Thus, the total ATIC deficit is $96 ($0 + $44 + $2 + $50).

| Table 1 to paragraph (o)(15)(vii) | | | | | |
| --- | --- | --- | --- | --- | --- |
| | A | B | C | D | Total |
| ATIC (Final allocable ATI x 30 percent) | $6 | $6 | $48 | $0 | N/A |
| Remaining BIE | $0 | $50 | $50 | $50 | N/A |
| If ATIC exceeds remaining BIE, then such excess = ATIC excess | $6 | $0 | $0 | $0 | $6 |
| If remaining BIE exceeds ATIC, then such excess = ATIC deficit | $0 | $44 | $2 | $50 | $96 |

(viii)(A) Eighth, PRS must perform the calculations and make the necessary adjustments described under paragraph (f)(2)(viii) of this section if, and only if, PRS has:

(1) An excess business interest expense greater than $0 under paragraph (f)(2)(i) of this section;

(2) A total negative allocable ATI greater than $0 under paragraph (f)(2)(vi) of this section; and

(3) A total ATIC excess amount greater than $0 under paragraph (f)(2)(vii) of this section. Because PRS satisfies each of these three requirements, PRS must perform the calculations and make the necessary adjustments described under paragraph (f)(2)(viii) of this section.

(B) PRS must determine each partner's priority amount and usable priority amount. Only partners with an ATIC deficit under paragraph (f)(2)(vii) of this section of this section can have a priority amount greater than $0. Thus, only partners B, C, and D can have a priority amount greater than $0. PRS determines a partner's priority amount as thirty percent of the amount by which such partner's allocable positive ATI exceeds its final allocable ATI. Therefore, B's priority amount is $9 (($50 - $20) x 30 percent), C's priority amount is $72 (($400 - $160) x 30 percent), and D's priority amount is $0 (($0 - $0) x 30 percent). Thus, the total priority amount is $81 ($0 + $9 + $72 + $0). Next, PRS must determine each partner's usable priority amount. Each partner's usable priority amount is the lesser of such partner's priority amount or ATIC deficit. Thus, B has a usable priority amount of $9, C has a usable priority amount of $2, and D has a usable priority amount of $0. As a result, the total usable priority amount is $11 ($0 + $9 + $2 + $0). Because the total usable priority amount ($11) is greater than the total ATIC excess ($6) under paragraph (f)(2)(vii) of this section, PRS must perform the adjustments described in paragraph (f)(2)(viii)(D) of this section.

| Table 1 to paragraph (o)(15)(viii)(B) | | | | | |
| --- | --- | --- | --- | --- | --- |
| | A | B | C | D | Total |
| (Positive allocable ATI - Final allocable ATI) | $0 | $30 | $240 | $0 | N/A |
| Multiplied by 30 percent | | 30 percent | 30 percent | 30 percent | 30 percent | N/A |
| = Priority amount | $0 | $9 | $72 | $0 | $81 |

| Table 2 to paragraph (o)(15)(viii)(B) | A | B | C | D | Total |
|---|---|---|---|---|---|
| Priority amount | $0 | $9 | $72 | $0 | N/A |
| ATIC deficit | $0 | $44 | $2 | $50 | N/A |
| Lesser of priority amount or ATIC deficit = Usable priority amount | $0 | $9 | $2 | $0 | $11 |

(C) In light of the fact that the total usable priority amount is greater than the total ATIC excess under paragraph (f)(2)(viii)(B) of this section, paragraph (f)(2)(viii)(C) of this section does not apply.

(D)(1) Because B and C are the only partners with priority amounts greater than $0, B and C are priority partners, while A and D are non-priority partners. For purposes of paragraph (f)(2)(ix) of this section, each partner's final ATIC excess amount is $0. For purposes of paragraph (f)(2)(x) of this section, each non-priority partner's final ATIC deficit amount is such partner's ATIC deficit determined pursuant to paragraph (f)(2)(vii) of this section. Therefore, A has a final ATIC deficit of $0 and D has a final ATIC deficit of $50. Additionally, for purposes of paragraph (f)(2)(x) of this section, PRS must determine each priority partner's step eight excess share. A priority partner's step eight excess share is the product of the total ATIC excess and the ratio of the partner's priority amount to the total priority amount. Thus, B's step eight excess share is $0.67

($6 x ($9/$81)) and C's step eight excess share is $5.33 ($6 x ($72/$81)). To the extent a priority partner's step eight excess share exceeds its ATIC deficit, the excess shall be the partner's ATIC excess for purposes of paragraph (f)(2)(x) of this section. B's step eight excess share does not exceed its ATIC deficit. Because C's step eight excess share ($5.33) exceeds its ATIC deficit ($2), C's ATIC excess for purposes of paragraph (f)(2)(x) of this section is $3.33 ($5.33 - $2). Thus, the total ATIC excess for purposes of paragraph (f)(2)(x) of this section is $3.33 ($0 + $3.33). To the extent a priority partner's ATIC deficit exceeds its step eight excess share, the excess shall be the partner's ATIC deficit for purposes of paragraph (f)(2)(x) of this section. Because B's ATIC deficit ($44) exceeds its step eight excess share ($0.67), B's ATIC deficit for purposes of paragraph (f)(2)(x) of this section is $43.33 ($44 - $0.67). C's ATIC deficit does not exceed its step eight excess share. Thus, the total ATIC deficit for purposes of paragraph (f)(2)(x) of this section is $43.33 ($43.33 + $0).

| Table 1 to paragraph (o)(15)(viii)(D)(1) | A | B | C | D | Total |
|---|---|---|---|---|---|
| Non-priority partners ATIC deficit in paragraph (f)(2)(vii) = Final ATIC deficit for purposes of paragraph (f)(2)(x) of this section | $0 | N/A | N/A | $50 | N/A |

| Table 2 to paragraph (o)(15)(viii)(D)(1) | A | B | C | D | Total |
|---|---|---|---|---|---|
| Priority partners step eight excess share = (Total ATIC excess) x (Priority / Total priority) | N/A | $0.67 | $5.33 | N/A | N/A |
| ATIC deficit | N/A | $44 | $2 | N/A | N/A |
| If step eight excess share exceeds ATIC deficit, then such excess = ATIC excess for purposes of paragraph (f)(2)(x) of this section | N/A | $0 | $3.33 | N/A | $3.33 |
| If ATIC deficit exceeds step eight excess share, then such excess = ATIC deficit for purposes of paragraph (f)(2)(x) of this section | N/A | $43.33 | $0 | N/A | $43.33 |

(2) In sum, the correct amounts to be used in paragraph (f)(2)(x) of this section are as follows.

| Table 1 to paragraph (o)(15)(viii)(D)(2) | | | | | |
| --- | --- | --- | --- | --- | --- |
| | A | B | C | D | Total |
| ATIC excess | $0 | $0 | $3.33 | $0 | $3.33 |
| ATIC deficit | $0 | $43.33 | $0 | $0 | $43.33 |
| Non-priority partner final ATIC deficit | $0 | $0 | $0 | $50 | N/A |

(ix) Ninth, PRS determines each partner's final ATIC excess amount. Pursuant to paragraph (f)(2)(viii)(D) of this section, each priority and non-priority partner's final ATIC excess amount is $0.

(x) Tenth, PRS determines each partner's final ATIC deficit amount. Because B has an ATIC deficit, PRS must determine B's final ATIC defi-

cit amount. B's final ATIC deficit amount is B's ATIC deficit ($43.33), reduced, but not below $0, by the product of the total ATIC excess ($3.33) and the ratio of B's ATIC deficit to the total ATIC deficit ($43.33/$43.33). Therefore, B has $40 of final ATIC deficit ($43.33 — ($3.33 x 100 percent)). Pursuant to paragraph (f)(2)(viii)(D) of this section, D's final ATIC deficit amount is $40.

| Table 1 to paragraph (o)(15)(x) | | | | | |
| --- | --- | --- | --- | --- | --- |
| | A | B | C | D | Total |
| ATIC deficit | $0 | $43.33 | $0 | N/A | N/A |
| Less: (Total ATIC excess) x (ATIC deficit / Total ATIC deficit) | $0 | $3.33 | $0 | N/A | N/A |
| = Final ATIC deficit | $0 | $40 | $0 | $50 | $90 |

(xi) Eleventh, PRS allocates deductible business interest expense and section 163(j) excess items to the partners. Pursuant to paragraph (f)(2)(i) of this section, PRS has $90 of excess business interest expense. PRS allocates the excess business interest expense dollar for dollar to the partners with final ATIC deficits. Thus, PRS allocates its excess business interest expense $40 to B and $50 to D. A partner's allocable business

interest expense is deductible business interest expense to the extent it exceeds such partner's share of excess business interest expense. Therefore, A has deductible business interest expense of $0 ($0 - $0), B has deductible business interest expense of $10 ($50 - $40), C has deductible business interest expense of $50 ($50 - $0), and D has deductible business interest expense of $0 ($50 - $50).

| Table 1 to paragraph (o)(15)(xi) | | | | | |
| --- | --- | --- | --- | --- | --- |
| | A | B | C | D | Total |
| Deductible BIE | $0 | $10 | $50 | $0 | $60 |
| EBIE allocated | $0 | $40 | $0 | $50 | $90 |
| ETI allocated | $0 | $0 | $0 | $0 | $0 |
| EBII allocated | $0 | $0 | $0 | $0 | $0 |

(16) *Example 16*—(i) *Facts.* A and B are equal shareholders in X, a subchapter S corporation. In Year 1, X has $100 of ATI and $40 of business interest expense. A has $100 of ATI and $20 of business interest expense from its sole proprietorship. B has $0 of ATI and $20 of business interest expense from its sole proprietorship.

(ii) *S corporation-level.* In Year 1, X's section 163(j) limit is 30 percent of its ATI, or $30 ($100 x 30 percent). Thus, X has $30 of deductible business interest expense and $10 of disallowed business interest expense. Such $30 of deductible business interest expense is includable in X's non-separately stated income or loss, and is not subject to further limitation under section 163(j). X carries forward the $10 of disallowed business interest expense to Year 2 as a disallowed business interest expense carryforward under §1.163(j)-2(c). X may not currently deduct all $40 of its business interest expense in Year 1. X only reduces its accumulated adjustments account in

Year 1 by the $30 of deductible business interest expense in Year 1 under §1.163(j)-6(l)(7).

(iii) *Shareholder allocations.* A and B are each allocated $35 of nonseparately stated taxable income ($50 items of income or gain, less $15 of deductible business interest expense) from X. A and B do not reduce their basis in X by the $10 of disallowed business interest expense.

(iv) *Shareholder-level computations.* A, in computing its limit under section 163(j), has $100 of ATI and $20 of business interest expense from its sole proprietorship. A's section 163(j) limit is $30 ($100 x 30 percent). Thus, A's $20 of business interest expense is deductible business interest expense. B, in computing its limit under section 163(j), has $20 of business interest expense from its sole proprietorship. B's section 163(j) limit is $0 ($0 x 30 percent). Thus, B's $20 of business interest expense is not allowed as a deduction and is treated as business interest expense paid or accrued by B in Year 2.

(17) *Example 17*—(i) *Facts.* The facts are the same as in *Example 16* in paragraph (o)(16) of this section. In Year 2, X has $233.33 of ATI, $0 of business interest income, and $30 of business interest expense. A has $100 of ATI and $20 of business interest expense from its sole proprietorship. B has $0 of ATI and $20 of business interest expense from its sole proprietorship.

(ii) *S corporation-level.* In Year 2, X's section 163(j) limit is 30 percent of its ATI plus its business interest income, or $70 ($233.33 x 30 percent). Because X's section 163(j) limit exceeds X's $40 of business interest expense ($30 from Year 2, plus the $10 disallowed business interest expense carryforwards from Year 1), X may deduct all $40 of business interest expense in Year 2. Such $40 of deductible business interest expense is includable in X's non-separately stated income or loss, and is not subject to further limitation under section 163(j). Pursuant to § 1.163(j)-6(l)(7), X must reduce its accumulated adjustments account by $40. Additionally, X has $100 of excess taxable income under § 1.163(j)-1(b)(15).

(iii) *Shareholder allocations.* A and B are each allocated $96.67 of nonseparately stated taxable income ($116.67 items of income or gain, less $20 of deductible business interest expense) from X. Additionally, A and B are each allocated $50 of excess taxable income under § 1.163(j)-6(l)(4). As a result, A and B each increase their ATI by $50.

(iv) *Shareholder-level computations.* A, in computing its limit under section 163(j), has $150 of ATI ($100 from its sole proprietorship, plus $50 excess taxable income) and $20 of business interest expense (from its sole proprietorship). A's section 163(j) limit is $45 ($150 x 30 percent). Thus, A's $20 of business interest expense is deductible business interest expense. B, in computing its limit under section 163(j), has $50 of ATI ($0 from its sole proprietorship, plus $50 excess taxable income) and $40 of business interest expense ($20 from its sole proprietorship, plus $20 disallowed business interest expense from its sole proprietorship in Year 1). B's section 163(j) limit is $15 ($50 x 30 percent). Thus, $15 of B's business interest expense is deductible business interest expense. The $25 of B's business interest expense not allowed as a deduction ($40 business interest expense, less $15 section 163(j) limit) is treated as business interest expense paid or accrued by B in Year 3.

(p) *Applicability date.*—This section applies to taxable years ending after the date the Treasury decision adopting these regulations as final regulations is published in the **Federal Register**. However, taxpayers and their related parties, within the meaning of sections 267(b) and 707(b)(1), may apply the rules of this section to a taxable year beginning after December 31, 2017, so long as the taxpayers and their related parties consistently apply the rules of the section 163(j) regulations, and if applicable, §§ 1.263A-9,

1.381(c)(20)-1, 1.382-6, 1.383-1, 1.469-9, 1.882-5, 1.1502-13, 1.1502-21, 1.1502-36, 1.1502-79, 1.1502-91 through 1.1502-99 (to the extent they effectuate the rules of §§ 1.382-6 and 1.383-1), and 1.1504-4 to those taxable years. [Reg. § 1.163(j)-6.]

[Proposed 12-28-2018.]

### [Prop. Reg. § 1.163(j)-7]

**§ 1.163(j)-7. Application of the business interest deduction limitation to foreign corporations and United States shareholders.**— (a) *Overview.*—This section provides rules for the application of section 163(j) to foreign corporations with shareholders that are United States persons. Paragraph (b) of this section provides rules regarding the application of section 163(j) to certain controlled foreign corporations. Paragraph (c) of this section provides rules concerning the computation of adjusted taxable income (ATI) of certain controlled foreign corporations. Paragraph (d) of this section provides rules concerning the computation of ATI of a United States shareholder of certain controlled foreign corporations (CFC). Paragraph (e) of this section provides a rule regarding the effect of section 163(j) on the earnings and profits of foreign corporations. Paragraph (f) of this section provides definitions that apply for purposes of this section. Paragraph (g) of this section provides examples illustrating the application of this section. Paragraph (h) of this section provides dates of applicability.

(b) *Application of section 163(j) to an applicable CFC and certain partnerships.*—(1) *Scope.*—This paragraph (b) provides rules regarding the application of section 163(j) to an applicable CFC and certain partnerships. Paragraph (b)(2) of this section describes the general application of section 163(j) to an applicable CFC and certain partnerships in which an applicable CFC is a partner. Paragraph (b)(3) of this section provides an election to use an alternative method for computing the deduction for business interest expense of a member of a CFC group. Paragraph (b)(4) of this section treats certain partnerships as members of a CFC group for purposes of this paragraph (b). Paragraph (b)(5) of this section provides the rules regarding an election to apply paragraph (b)(3) of this section.

(2) *General application of section 163(j) to an applicable CFC and a partnership with at least one partner that is an applicable CFC.*—Except as otherwise provided in this paragraph (b) or in the section 163(j) regulations, section 163(j) and the section 163(j) regulations apply to determine the deductibility of an applicable CFC's business interest expense for purposes of computing its taxable income in the same manner as those provisions apply to determine the deductibility of a domestic C corporation's business interest expense for purposes of computing its taxable income. Furthermore, if an applicable CFC is a partner in a partnership, except as otherwise

**Prop. Reg. § 1.163(j)-7(b)(2)**

provided in this paragraph (b) or in the section 163(j) regulations, section 163(j) and the section 163(j) regulations apply to the partnership in the same manner as those provisions would apply if the applicable CFC were a domestic C corporation. If an applicable CFC has income that is, or is treated as, effectively connected with the conduct of a trade or business in the United States or if a partnership is engaged in a trade or business conducted in the United States, see also §§ 1.163(j)-8(d) and 1.882-5 for additional rules concerning the deduction for interest.

(3) *Alternative approach for computing the deduction for business interest expense.*—If a CFC group election is properly made and in effect with respect to a specified taxable year of a CFC group member of a CFC group, then—

(i) The portion of the CFC group member's business interest expense that is subject to the general rule under § 1.163(j)-2(b) is the amount equal to the CFC group member's allocable share of the CFC group's applicable net business interest expense, or, in the case in which the CFC group member is also a member of a financial services subgroup, the allocable share of the applicable subgroup net business interest expense; and

(ii) The limitation provided in § 1.163(j)-2(b) is applied without regard to § 1.163(j)-2(b)(1) and (3).

(4) *Treatment of certain partnerships as a CFC group member.*—(i) *General rule.*—If one or more CFC group members of the same CFC group, in the aggregate, own more than 80 percent of the interests in the capital or profits in a partnership, then, except as provided in paragraph (b)(4)(ii) of this section, the partnership is treated as a CFC group member. If there is a financial services subgroup with respect to the CFC group, this paragraph (b)(4) will apply only if all of the CFC group members described in the preceding sentence are financial services subgroup members or none of them are financial services subgroup members. If a partnership is treated as a CFC group member, then an interest in the partnership is treated as stock for purposes of applying this section.

(ii) *Exception for certain partnerships engaged in a United States trade or business.*—Notwithstanding paragraph (b)(4)(i) of this section, a partnership is not treated as a CFC group member if the partnership is engaged in a trade or business in the United States, directly or indirectly through another passthrough entity, and one or more partners has income that is effectively connected with the conduct of a trade or business in the United States, including any income that is treated as effectively connected income under an applicable provision of the Code or regulations, and at least one of the partners is not exempt from U.S. tax by reason of a U.S. income tax treaty. Notwithstanding the preceding sentence, a partnership that, without regard to this paragraph (b)(4)(ii), would be treated as a

CFC group member under paragraph (b)(4)(i) of this section, is treated as a CFC group member solely for purposes of determining if another entity is a CFC group member with respect to the CFC group.

(5) *CFC group election.*—(i) *Manner of making a CFC group election.*—Subject to paragraph (b)(5)(ii) of this section, a CFC group election is made by applying paragraph (b)(3) of this section for purposes of computing the amount of a CFC group member's deduction for business interest expense. Except as otherwise provided in publications, forms, instructions, or other guidance, a separate statement or form evidencing the election need not be filed.

(ii) *Consistency requirement.*—An election under paragraph (b)(5)(i) of this section is not effective unless all CFC group members of the CFC group make the election. If an entity becomes a CFC group member of a CFC group for which a CFC group election is in effect, the entity must make the CFC group election.

(iii) *Duration of a CFC group election.*—A CFC group election is irrevocable. If an entity ceases to be a CFC group member of a CFC group for which a CFC group election is in effect, the election terminates solely with respect to such entity. If a CFC group ceases to exist, a CFC group election terminates with respect to all CFC group members of the CFC group.

(c) *Rules concerning the computation of adjusted taxable income of an applicable CFC and certain CFC group members.*—(1) *Computation of taxable income.*—For purposes of computing taxable income of an applicable CFC for a taxable year, the applicable CFC's gross income and allowable deductions are determined under the principles of § 1.952-2 or the rules of section 882 for determining taxable income that is effectively connected with the conduct of a trade or business in the United States, as applicable.

(2) *Treatment of certain dividends.*—For purposes of computing the ATI of an applicable CFC for a taxable year, any dividend included in gross income that is received from a related person, within the meaning of section 954(d)(3), with respect to the distributee is subtracted from taxable income.

(3) *Treatment of CFC excess taxable income.*—(i) *In general.*—If a CFC group election is in effect for a specified taxable year of a CFC group member and if the CFC group member (*upper-tier member*) directly owns stock in one or more other CFC group members (*lower-tier member*), then, for purposes of computing ATI of the upper-tier member for the specified taxable year, there is added to taxable income the sum of the products of the following amounts with respect to each lower-tier member—

(A) The CFC excess taxable income (if any) of the lower-tier member for the lower-tier member's specified taxable year; and

(B) The percentage (by value) of the stock of the lower-tier member that is directly owned by the upper-tier member on the last day of the lower-tier member's specified taxable year.

(ii) *Ordering rules.*—For purposes of applying paragraph (c)(3)(i) of this section, if a CFC group member is an upper-tier member with respect to a CFC group member and a lower-tier member with respect to another CFC group member, paragraph (c)(3)(i) of this section is applied starting with the lowest-tier CFC group member in the chain of ownership. If an upper-tier member is a partner in a lower-tier member that is a partnership, which is an entity that does not have CFC excess taxable income but that may have excess taxable income (as defined in § 1.163(j)-1(b)(15)), see § 1.163(j)-6(f) for determining the upper-tier member's share of the lower-tier member's excess taxable income (if any).

(d) *Rules concerning the computation of adjusted taxable income of a United States shareholder.*— (1) *In general.*—(i) *Treatment of gross income inclusions that are properly allocable to a non-excepted trade or business.*—If for a taxable year a United States shareholder with respect to one or more applicable CFCs includes amounts in gross income under section 78, 951(a), or 951A(a) that are properly allocable to a non-excepted trade or business (each amount, a *specified deemed inclusion* and such amounts, collectively *specified deemed inclusions*), then, for purposes of computing ATI of the United States shareholder, there is subtracted from taxable income an amount equal to the specified deemed inclusions, reduced by the portion of the deduction allowed under section 250(a)(1), without regard to the taxable income limitation of section 250(a)(2), by reason of the specified deemed inclusions (such a deduction, a *specified section 250 deduction*). For rules concerning inclusions under sections 78, 951(a), and 951A(a) and deductions allowable under section 250 that are not properly allocable to a non-excepted trade or business, see § 1.163(j)-1(b)(1)(ii)(F) and (b)(1)(i)(H), respectively.

(ii) *Treatment of deemed inclusions of a domestic partnership that are not allocable to any trade or business.*—If a United States shareholder that is a domestic partnership includes amounts in gross income under section 951(a) or 951A(a) that are not properly allocable to trade or business of the domestic partnership, then, notwithstanding § 1.163(j)-4(b)(3), to the extent a C corporation partner, including an indirect partner in the case of tiered partnerships, takes such amounts into account as a distributive share in accordance with section 702 and § 1.702-1(a)(8)(ii), the C corporation partner may not treat such amounts as properly allocable to a trade or business of the C corporation partner.

(2) *Additional rule after application of paragraph (d)(1) of this section for a United States shareholder of a CFC group member with a CFC group election in effect.*—(i) *In general.*—Subject to paragraph (d)(3) of this section, if for a taxable year, a United States shareholder owns directly, or indirectly through one or more foreign pass-through entities, stock of one or more CFC group members of a CFC group for which a CFC group election is in effect for the specified taxable year of each CFC group member that ends with or within the taxable year of the United States shareholder, then, for purposes of computing ATI of the United States shareholder, in addition to the subtraction described in paragraph (d)(1) of this section, there is added to taxable income the amount equal to the sum of the amounts of eligible CFC group ETI, as defined in paragraph (d)(2)(ii) of this section, with respect to each specified highest-tier member of the United States shareholder, but not in excess of the amount of the CFC group inclusions, as defined in paragraph (d)(2)(iii) of this section, of the United States shareholder for the taxable year. For purposes of this paragraph (d)(2)(i), members of a consolidated group are treated as a single United States shareholder.

(ii) *Eligible CFC group ETI.*—The term *eligible CFC group ETI* means, with respect to a specified highest-tier member and a specified taxable year, the amount equal to the product of the following three amounts—

(A) The specified highest-tier member's CFC excess taxable income for the specified taxable year, taking into account the application of paragraph (c)(3) of this section;

(B) The specified highest-tier member's specified ETI ratio for the specified taxable year; and

(C) The percentage, by value, of the stock of the specified highest-tier member that is owned directly, or indirectly through one or more foreign passthrough entities, by the United States shareholder on the last day of the specified taxable year.

(iii) *CFC group inclusions.*—The term *CFC group inclusions* means, with respect to a United States shareholder and a taxable year, the amounts of the specified deemed inclusions subtracted from taxable income under paragraph (d)(1)(i) of this section that are with respect to CFC group members, other than amounts included in gross income by reason of section 78, reduced by the portion of any specified section 250 deduction described in paragraph (d)(1)(i) of this section that is allowable by reason of such specified deemed inclusions.

(3) *Special rules if a domestic partnership is a United States shareholder of a CFC group member with a CFC group election in effect.*—Paragraph (d)(2) of this section does not apply with respect to a United States shareholder described in paragraph (d)(2) of this section that is a domestic partnership (such a partnership, a *U.S. shareholder partnership*). If a U.S. shareholder partnership has a domestic C corporation partner,

**Prop. Reg. § 1.163(j)-7(d)(3)**

including an indirect partner in the case of tiered partnerships, (such a partner, a *U.S. corporate partner*), then, for purposes of computing ATI of the U.S. corporate partner, paragraph (d)(2) of this section is applied by treating the U.S. shareholder partnership, and in case of tiered partnerships, any tiered partnership that is a domestic partnership, as if it were a foreign partnership and by making the following modifications—

(i) The term "U.S. corporate partner" is substituted for the term "United States shareholder" each place it appears in paragraph (d)(2) of this section; and

(ii) If a U.S. shareholder partnership includes an amount in gross income under section 951(a) or 951(A) with respect to a CFC group member, then to the extent the amount is taken into account by a U.S. corporate partner as a distributive share in accordance with section 702 and § 1.702-1(a)(8)(ii), such amount is treated as a specified deemed inclusion of the U.S. corporate partner with respect to the CFC group member for purposes of applying paragraph (d)(2)(iii) of this section.

(4) *Inclusions under section 951A(a).*—For purposes of applying paragraph (d) of this section, the portion of a United States shareholder's inclusion under section 951A(a) treated as being with respect to a CFC group member is determined under section 951A(f)(2) and § 1.951A-6(b)(2).

(e) *Effect on earnings and profits.*—In the case of a foreign corporation, the disallowance and carryforward of a deduction for the corporation's business interest expense under § 1.163(j)-2 will not affect whether and when such business interest expense reduces the corporation's earnings and profits. Thus, for example, if a United States person has elected under section 1295 to treat a passive foreign investment company (as defined in section 1297) (PFIC) as a qualified electing fund, then the disallowance and carryforward of a deduction for the PFIC's business interest expense under § 1.163(j)-2 will not affect whether or when such business interest expense reduces the PFIC's earnings and profits. Similarly, the disallowance and carryforward of a deduction for an applicable CFC's business interest expense will not affect the earnings and profits limitation for subpart F income under section 952(c). See also § 1.163(j)-4(c).

(f) *Definitions.*—The following definitions apply for purposes of this section.

(1) *Allocable share.*—(i) *General rule.*—The term *allocable share* means, with respect to a CFC group member of a CFC group and a specified taxable year, the amount equal to the product of the CFC group's applicable net business interest expense (multiplicand), if any, and a fraction, the numerator of which is equal to the amount of the CFC group member's net business interest expense, and the denominator of which is equal to the sum of the amounts of the net business interest expense of each CFC group member.

(ii) *Special rule if there is a financial services subgroup.*—If there is a financial services subgroup with respect to a CFC group, then paragraph (f)(1)(i) of this section is applied with the following modifications—

(A) With respect to a CFC group member that is also a financial services subgroup member—

(1) The multiplicand is equal to the amount of the applicable subgroup net business interest expense; and

(2) The denominator of the fraction is determined by replacing the term "CFC group member" with the term "financial services subgroup member."

(B) With respect to a CFC group member this is not a financial services subgroup member—

(1) The multiplicand is reduced by the amount of the applicable subgroup net business interest expense; and

(2) The denominator of the fraction is reduced by the sum of the amounts of the net business interest expense of each financial services subgroup member.

(2) *Applicable CFC.*—The term *applicable CFC* means a controlled foreign corporation described in section 957, but only if the foreign corporation has at least one United States shareholder that owns, within the meaning of section 958(a), stock of the foreign corporation.

(3) *Applicable net business interest expense.*—The term *applicable net business interest expense* means, with respect to a CFC group and a majority U.S. shareholder taxable year, the excess, if any, of the sum of the amounts of the business interest expense of each CFC group member for the specified taxable year, over the sum of the amounts of the business interest income of each CFC group member for the specified taxable year.

(4) *Applicable subgroup net business interest expense.*—The term *applicable subgroup net business interest expense* means, with respect to a financial services subgroup of a CFC group and a majority U.S. shareholder taxable year, the excess, if any, of the sum of the amounts of the business interest expense of each financial services subgroup member for the specified taxable year, over the sum of the amounts of the business interest income of each financial services subgroup member for the specified taxable year.

(5) *CFC excess taxable income.*—(i) *In general.*—The term *CFC excess taxable income* means, with respect to a CFC group member, other than a partnership described in paragraph (b)(4)(i) of this section, and a specified taxable year, the amount which bears the same ratio to the CFC group member's ATI, as—

(A) The excess (if any) of—

(1) The amount determined for the CFC group member under § 1.163(j)-2(b)(2); over

*(2)* The CFC group member's allocable share of either the applicable net business interest expense or the applicable subgroup net business interest expense, as applicable; bears to

(B) The amount determined for the CFC group member under § 1.163(j)-2(b)(2).

(ii) *CFC group member is a partnership.*—If a CFC group member is a partnership, see § 1.163(j)-1(b)(15) for determining the extent to which the partnership has excess taxable income. For rules concerning a partner's share of a partnership's excess taxable income, see § 1.163(j)-6(f).

(6) *CFC group.*—(i) *In general.*—The term *CFC group* means two or more applicable CFCs if 80 percent or more of the total value of shares of all classes of stock of each applicable CFC is owned, within the meaning of section 958(a), either by a single United States shareholder or by multiple U.S. shareholders that are related persons, within the meaning of section 267(b) or 707(b)(1), (each a *related United States shareholder* and collectively *related United States shareholders*), provided the stock of each applicable CFC is owned in the same proportion by each related United States shareholder.

(ii) *Aggregation rules.*—The following rules apply for the purpose of applying paragraph (f)(6)(i) of this section—

(A) Members of a consolidated group and individuals described in section 318(a)(1)(A)(i) who file a joint tax return are treated as a single person; and

(B) If a single United States person, as defined in section 957(c), taking into account the application of paragraph (f)(6)(ii)(A) of this section, owns, directly or indirectly through one or more passthrough entities, more than 80 percent of the interests in a pass-through entity that is a United States shareholder that owns, within the meaning of section 958(a), stock in an applicable CFC, then that United States person is treated as owning the stock of the applicable CFC that is owned by the passthrough entity. For purposes of applying the 80-percent threshold described in the preceding sentence, if the pass-through entity is a partnership, then the 80-percent threshold is satisfied if the United States person owns at least 80 percent of the interests in the capital or the profits of the partnership, and if the pass-through entity is not a partnership, then the 80-percent threshold is satisfied if the United States person owns at least 80 percent of the value of all interests of the passthrough entity.

(7) *CFC group election.*—The term *CFC group election* means an election to apply paragraph (b)(3) of this section.

(8) *CFC group member.*—The term *CFC group member* means, with respect to a CFC group, an entity included in the CFC group. An entity that has, including through ownership of an interest in a passthrough entity, income which is effectively connected with a trade or business conducted in the United States, including any income that is treated as effectively connected income under an applicable provision of the Code or regulations, and not exempt from U.S. tax by reason of a U.S. income tax treaty is not treated as a member of a CFC group, other than solely for purposes of determining if another entity is a CFC group member with respect to the CFC group.

(9) *Financial services subgroup.*—The term *financial services subgroup* means, with respect to a CFC group, a group comprised of each CFC group member of the CFC group that is an eligible controlled foreign corporation (as defined in section 954(h)(2)(A)), a qualified insurance company (as defined in section 953(e)(3)), or eligible for the dealer exception in computing foreign personal holding company income (as described in section 954(c)(2)(C)).

(10) *Financial services subgroup member.*—The term *financial services subgroup member* means, with respect to a financial services subgroup of a CFC group, a CFC group member that is also a member of the financial services subgroup.

(11) *Majority U.S. shareholder taxable year.*—The term *majority U.S. shareholder taxable year* means, with respect to a CFC group, one of the following taxable years, applied sequentially—

(i) If there is a single United States shareholder of the CFC group for purposes of paragraph (f)(6)(i) of this section, then the taxable year of the United States shareholder;

(ii) If paragraph (f)(11)(i) of this section does not apply and a related United States shareholder owns, within the meaning of section 958(a), more stock of the members of the CFC group, by value, than is owned, within the meaning of section 958(a), by any other related United States shareholder, then the taxable year of the first-mentioned related United States shareholder;

(iii) If paragraphs (f)(11)(i) and (ii) of this section do not apply and if one or more related United States shareholders with the same taxable year, in aggregate, own, within the meaning of section 958(a), more stock of the members of the CFC group (by value) than is, in aggregate, owned, within the meaning of section 958(a), by other related United States shareholders with the same taxable year, then the taxable year of the first-mentioned related United States shareholders; and

(iv) If paragraphs (f)(11)(i), (ii), and (iii) of this section do not apply, then the calendar year.

(12) *Net business interest expense.*—The term *net business interest expense* means, with respect to a CFC group member of a CFC group and a specified taxable year, the excess, if any, of the amount of the CFC group member's business interest expense over the amount of the CFC group member's business interest income, in each case determined without regard to section 163(j) and the section 163(j) regulations.

**Prop. Reg. § 1.163(j)-7(f)(12)**

(13) *Passthrough entity.*—The term *passthrough entity* means a partnership, S corporation, or any other entity (domestic or foreign) that is not a corporation if all items of income and deduction of the entity are included in the income of its owners or beneficiaries. An *interest in a passthrough entity* means an interest in the capital or profits of the entity or stock of an S corporation, as applicable.

(14) *Specified ETI ratio.*—(i) *In general.*—The term *specified ETI ratio* means, with respect to a specified highest-tier member of a CFC group and a specified taxable year, the ratio computed as a fraction (expressed as a percentage), the numerator of which is the sum of the amounts described in paragraph (f)(14)(iii) of this section with respect to each CFC group member described in paragraph (f)(14)(ii) of this section, and the denominator of which is the sum of the amounts described in paragraph (f)(14)(iv) of this section with respect to each CFC group member described in paragraph (f)(14)(ii) of this section that has amounts included in the numerator. The specified ETI ratio may not exceed 100 percent. If the numerator and the denominator of the fraction are not both greater than zero, the specified ETI ratio is treated as being equal to zero.

(ii) *Includable CFC group members.*—For purposes of applying paragraph (f)(14)(i) of this section, a CFC group member is described in this paragraph (f)(14)(ii) if—

(A) The CFC group member is the specified highest-tier member or a specified lower-tier member with respect to the specified highest-tier member; and

(B) The CFC group member has CFC excess taxable income without regard to paragraph (c)(3) of this section.

(iii) *Numerator.*—For purposes of applying (f)(14)(i) of this section, the amount described in this paragraph (f)(14)(iii) is, with respect to a CFC group member and a specified taxable year, the sum of the amounts included in gross income under sections 951(a) and 951A(a) of each United States shareholder with respect to the CFC group member for the taxable years of the United States shareholders in which or with which the specified taxable year of the CFC group member ends. For purposes of this paragraph (f)(14)(iii), the portion of a United States shareholder's inclusion under section 951A(a) treated as being with respect to a CFC group member is determined under section 951A(f)(2) and § 1.951A-6(b)(2).

(iv) *Denominator.*—For purposes of applying (f)(14)(i) of this section, the amount described in this paragraph (f)(14)(iv) is, with respect to a CFC group member and a specified taxable year, the taxable income of the CFC group member for the specified taxable year.

(15) *Specified highest-tier member.*—The term *specified highest-tier member* means, with respect to a CFC group, a CFC group member in which a United States shareholder owns directly, or indirectly through one or more foreign passthrough entities, stock of the CFC group member.

(16) *Specified lower-tier member.*—The term *specified lower-tier member* means, with respect to a specified highest-tier member of a CFC group, a CFC group member in which the specified highest-tier member owns stock directly or indirectly through a chain of ownership.

(17) *Specified taxable year.*—The term *specified taxable year* means, with respect to a CFC group member of a CFC group, the taxable year that ends with or within a majority U.S. shareholder year.

(18) *United States shareholder.*—The term *United States shareholder* has the meaning provided in section 951(b).

(g) *Examples.*—The following examples illustrate the application of this section. For each example, unless otherwise stated, the referenced business interest expense is deductible but for the application of section 163(j), no exemptions from the application of section 163(j) are available, none of the business interest expense is floor plan financing interest expense, and no foreign corporation has income that is effectively connected with a trade or business conducted in the United States or is an entity described in paragraph (f)(9) of this section (regarding entities that provide certain types of financial services).

(1) *Example 1: Computation of section 163(j) limitation of CFC group members*—(i) *Facts.* USP, a domestic C corporation, wholly owns US1 and US2, each of which is a domestic C corporation. USP, US1, and US2 are members of a consolidated group of which USP is the common parent (USP group). US1 wholly owns CFC1, a foreign corporation, and US2 wholly owns CFC2 and CFC3, each of which is a foreign corporation. The USP group has a calendar year taxable year. For U.S. tax purposes, CFC1, CFC2, and CFC3 each have a fiscal taxable year ending on November 30. CFC1 has an outstanding loan of $1,000x from a third-party (CFC1 note). CFC1 has a receivable of $500x from each of CFC2 and CFC3 (CFC2 note and CFC3 note, respectively). Interest on all debt is paid and accrued annually on November 30. During the taxable year ending November 30, 2019, CFC1 has business interest expense of $90x attributable to CFC1 note and business interest income of $100x attributable to CFC2 note and CFC3 note, and CFC2 and CFC3 each have $50x of business interest expense attributable to CFC2 note and CFC3 note, respectively. Assume that each of CFC1, CFC2, and CFC3 has ATI of $100x computed on a separate company basis for the taxable year ending November 30, 2019. The USP group has no business interest expense.

(ii) *Analysis*—(A) *Determination of CFC group.* US1 owns (within the meaning of section 958(a)) all of the stock of CFC1, and US2 owns (within the meaning of section 958(a)) all of the stock of each of CFC2 and CFC3. Under paragraph (f)(2) of this section, each of CFC1, CFC2, and CFC3 is an applicable CFC. Under paragraph (f)(6)(ii)(A) of this section, because US1 and US2 are members of a consolidated group, US1 and US2 are treated as a single person for purposes determining a CFC group under paragraph (f)(6)(i) of this section. Therefore, because 80 percent or more of the stock of each of CFC1, CFC2, and CFC3 is owned (within the meaning of section 958(a)) by a single United States shareholder, under paragraph (f)(6)(i) of this section, CFC1, CFC2, and CFC3 are members of a CFC group (USP CFC group).

(B) *CFC group election is made.* Assume a CFC group election is properly made. Under paragraph (f)(11)(i) of this section, because there is a single United States shareholder of the USP CFC group with a calendar taxable year, the majority U.S. shareholder taxable year with respect to the USP CFC group ends on December 31, 2019. Under paragraph (f)(17) of this section, the specified taxable year of each of CFC1, CFC2, and CFC3 is November 30, 2019, which is the taxable year that ends with or within the majority U.S. shareholder taxable year ending on December 31, 2019. Under paragraph (f)(3) of this section, the applicable net business interest expense of the USP CFC group is $90x. The $90x is the excess of $190x, which is the sum of the amounts of the business interest expense of each of CFC1, CFC2, and CFC3 ($90x, $50x, and $50x, respectively), over $100x, which is the sum of the amounts of the business interest income of each of CFC1, CFC2, and CFC3 ($100x, $0, and $0, respectively). Under paragraph (f)(12) of this section, CFC1 has $0 of net business interest expense ($90x business interest expense does not exceed $100x of business interest income), and CFC2 and CFC3 each have $50x of net business interest expense (each has $50x business interest expense and $0 business interest income). Because CFC2 and CFC3 each has net business interest expense, under paragraph (f)(1) of this section, each has an allocable share of the applicable net business interest expense of the USP CFC group. The allocable share of each of CFC2 and CFC3 is $45x, computed as $90x (the applicable net business interest expense) multiplied by the fraction equal to $50x / $100x (the net business interest expense of the member and the sum of the amounts of net business interest expense of all members, respectively). Under paragraph (b)(3)(i) of this section, none of CFC1's $90x of business interest expense and $45x of each of CFC2's and CFC3's $50x of business interest expense is subject to the general rule under § 1.163(j)-2(b) (and $5x of each of CFC2's and CFC3's business interest expense is not subject to limitation under § 1.163(j)-2(b)), and, under paragraph (b)(3)(ii) of this section, the general rule under § 1.163(j)-2(b), as applied to CFC2 and CFC3, is computed without regard to § 1.163(j)-2(b)(1) and (3). Thus, under § 1.163(j)-2(b), CFC2's limitation is $30x ($100x

ATI computed on a separate company basis x 30 percent). The amount of CFC2's business interest expense subject to limitation under paragraph (b)(3) of this section, $45x, exceeds CFC2's limitation under § 1.163(j)-2(b), $30x. Accordingly, $35x ($5x not subject to limitation + $30x) of CFC2's business interest expense is deductible, and under § 1.163(j)-2(c), the remaining $15x of business interest expense is not deductible and will be carried forward as a disallowed business interest expense carryforward. The analysis for CFC3 is the same as for CFC2. Because the USP group has no business interest expense, the application of paragraph (d) of this section is not relevant.

(C) *CFC group election is not made.* Instead, assume a CFC group election is not made. In this case, each of CFC1, CFC2, and CFC3 must compute its interest deduction limitation under § 1.163(j)-2(b), without regard to paragraph (b)(3) of this section. CFC1's business interest expense of $90x is deductible because it has business interest income of $100x. CFC2's business interest expense limitation is $30x ($100x ATI computed on a separate company basis x 30 percent). Accordingly, $30x of CFC2's business interest expense is deductible, and under § 1.163(j)-2(c), the remaining $20x of business interest expense is disallowed business interest expense and will be carried forward as a disallowed business interest expense carryforward. The analysis for CFC3 is the same as for CFC2.

(2) *Example 2: Computation and allocation of CFC excess taxable income*—(i) *Facts.* USP, a domestic C corporation, wholly owns CFC1, a foreign corporation. CFC1 wholly owns CFC2, a foreign corporation, and CFC2 wholly owns each of CFC3 and CFC4, both of which are foreign corporations (CFC1, CFC2, CFC3, and CFC4, collectively, the USP CFC group). All entities have a calendar year for U.S. tax purposes. For Year 1, assume the following additional facts: Prior to the application of section 163(j), CFC1 has no items of income, gain, deduction, or loss; CFC2 has a taxable loss of $5x (including $5x of business interest expense); CFC3 has taxable income of $85x (including $15x of business interest expense); CFC4 has $60x of taxable income (including $40x of business interest expense); a CFC group election is in effect for the CFC group; there is no intercompany debt between any CFC group member; 50 percent of CFC3's items of income and gain are subpart F income (as defined in section 952), and 50 percent of CFC3's items of deduction and loss are properly allocable to subpart F income, and with respect to the remaining portion of CFC3's items of income, gain, deduction, and loss, no portion is taken into account in computing tested income (as defined in section 951A(c)(2)(A)) or tested loss (as defined in section 951A(c)(2)(B)) of CFC3; CFC4's items of income and gain are all tested income, and CFC4's items of deduction are all properly allocable to such income; no portion of CFC2's items of income, gain, deduction, or loss

**Prop. Reg. § 1.163(j)-7(g)**

is taken into account in computing tested income or tested loss; no CFC group member has qualified business asset investment (as defined in section 951A(d)); for purposes of computing ATI, there are no subtractions or additions to taxable income described in §1.163(j)-1(b)(1) with respect to any CFC group member of the USP CFC group other than for business interest expense; for simplicity, no foreign income taxes are paid by any CFC group member of the USP CFC group; in addition to the inclusions in gross income under sections 951(a)(1) and 951A(a) with respect to the CFC group members of the USP CFC group, USP has business interest expense of $20x.

(ii) *Analysis*—(A) *Application of section 163(j) to CFC group members of the USP CFC group; computation of USP CFC group's applicable net business interest expense.* Under paragraph (f)(3) of this section, the USP CFC group's applicable net business interest expense is $60x ($0 + $5x + $15x + $40x with respect to CFC1, CFC2, CFC3, and CFC4, respectively). Because there is no debt between the CFC group members of the USP CFC group, under paragraph (b)(3) of this section, each of the CFC group members allocable share of the $60x is equal to its separate company business interest expense. In particular, CFC1's allocable share of the USP CFC group's applicable net interest expense is zero, CFC2's allocable share is $5x, CFC3's allocable share is $15x, and CFC4's allocable share is $40x.

(B) *Application of section 163(j) to CFC4.* Under §1.163(j)-1(b)(1), CFC4's ATI is $100x ($60x taxable income + $40x business interest expense). Under §1.163(j)-2(b), CFC4's limitation is $30x ($100x ATI computed on a separate company basis x 30 percent). The amount of CFC4's business interest expense subject to limitation, $40x, exceeds CFC4's limitation, $30x. Accordingly, under §1.163(j)-2(c), $10x of business interest expense is not deductible and will be carried forward as a disallowed business interest expense carryforward. Because $10x of business interest expense is not currently deductible, CFC4's tested income is $70x ($60x taxable income prior to application of section 163(j), increased by $10x of disallowed business interest expense).

(C) *Application of section 163(j) to CFC3.* Under §1.163(j)-1(b)(1), CFC3's ATI is $100x ($85x taxable income + 15x business interest expense). Under §1.163(j)-2(b), CFC3's limitation is $30x ($100x ATI computed on a separate company basis x 30 percent). Because the amount of CFC3's business interest expense subject to limitation, $15x, does not exceed CFC3's limitation, $30x, all of CFC3's business interest expense is currently deductible. Accordingly, CFC3's subpart F income is $42.50x ($85x taxable income x 50 percent). Furthermore, CFC3 has CFC excess taxable income of $50x ($100x x ($15x / $30x)).

(D) *Application of section 163(j) to CFC2.* Under §1.163(j)-1(b)(1), taking into account the application of paragraph (c)(3) of this section, CFC2's ATI is $50x (($5x) taxable loss + $5x business interest expense + $50x (100 percent x $50x of CFC3's excess taxable income)). Under §1.163(j)-2(b), CFC2's limitation is $15x ($50x ATI x 30 percent. Because the amount of CFC2's business interest expense subject to limitation, $5x, does not exceed CFC2's limitation, $15x, all of CFC2's business interest expense is currently deductible. Furthermore, CFC2 has CFC excess taxable income of $33.33x ($50x x ($10x / $15x)).

(E) *Application of section 163(j) to CFC1.* Under §1.163(j)-1(b)(1), taking into account the application of paragraph (c)(3) of this section, CFC1's ATI is $33.33x ($0 taxable income + $33.33x (100 percent x $33.33x of CFC2's excess taxable income)). CFC1 has no business interest expense subject to limitation and therefore CFC1 has CFC excess taxable income of $33.33x.

(F) *Application of section 163(j) to USP.* Under section 951(a)(1), USP includes $42.50x in gross income with respect to CFC3. Under section 951A(a), USP includes $70x in gross income, all of which is allocable to CFC4 under section 951A(f)(2), and under section 250(a)(1)(B), USP is allowed a deduction of $35x. Thus, the amount of USP's CFC group inclusions is $77.50x ($42.50 + $70x - $35x), and USP's taxable income prior to the application of section 163(j) is $57.50x ($77.50x - $20x business interest expense). Under §1.163(j)-1(b)(1), taking into account the application of paragraph (d)(2) of this section, USP's ATI is $16.67x. USP's ATI, $16.67x, is equal to $57.50x of taxable income + $20x of business interest expense - $77.50x of CFC group inclusions + $16.67x of eligible CFC group ETI. The eligible CFC group ETI, $16.67x, is determined as $33.33x (CFC1's excess taxable income) x 50 percent (CFC1's specified ETI ratio) x 100 percent (percentage of stock of CFC1 owned directly by USP)). Under paragraph (f)(14) of this section, the specified ETI ratio of CFC1 is 50 percent ($42.50x / $85x). The numerator of the fraction, $42.50x, is equal to the amount of USP's gross income inclusion under section 951(a) with respect to CFC3. The denominator of the fraction, $85x, is equal to the amount of the taxable income of CFC3. The numerator and the denominator of the fraction do not include amounts with respect to CFC1, CFC2, and CFC4, because none of them has CFC excess taxable income without regard to the application of paragraph (c)(3) of this section. Furthermore, USP includes no amounts in gross income under section 951(a) or 951A(a) with respect to CFC1 or CFC2. Under §1.163(j)-2(b), USP's section 163(j) limitation is $5x ($16.67x ATI x 30 percent). The amount of USP's business interest expense, $20x, exceeds USP's section 163(j) limitation, $5x. Accordingly, under §1.163(j)-2(c), $15x of business interest expense is not deductible and is carried forward as a disallowed business interest expense carryforward.

(h) *Applicability date.*—This section applies to a taxable year of a foreign corporation ending after the date the Treasury decision adopting these regulations as final regulations is published in the **Federal Register** and to a taxable year of a shareholder of the foreign corporation ending with or within the taxable year of the foreign corporation. However, a foreign corporation and its shareholders and their related parties, within the meaning of sections 267(b) and 707(b)(1), may apply this section to a taxable year of the foreign corporation beginning after December 31, 2017, and to a taxable year of a shareholder of the foreign corporation ending with or within the taxable year of the foreign corporation, if the foreign corporation and its shareholders and their related parties consistently apply all of the section 163(j) regulations, and if applicable, §§ 1.263A-9, 1.381(c)(20)-1, 1.382-6, 1.383-1, 1.469-9, 1.882-5, 1.1502-13, 1.1502-21, 1.1502-36, 1.1502-79, 1.1502-91 through 1.1502-99 (to the extent they effectuate the rules of §§ 1.382-6 and 1.383-1), and 1.1504-4 to those taxable years. [Reg. § 1.163(j)-7.]

[Proposed 12-28-2018.]

### [Prop. Reg. § 1.163(j)-8]

**§ 1.163(j)-8. Application of the business interest deduction limitation to foreign persons with effectively connected income.—** (a) *Overview.*—This section provides rules concerning the application of section 163(j) to foreign persons engaged in a trade or business in the United States. Paragraph (b) of this section modifies the application of section 163(j) for specified foreign persons with effectively connected taxable income. Paragraph (c) of this section modifies the application of section 163(j) for specified foreign partners in a partnership engaged in a trade or business in the United States. Paragraph (d) of this section provides rules for certain controlled foreign corporations with effectively connected taxable income. Paragraph (e) of this section coordinates the application of section 163(j) and § 1.882-5. Paragraph (f) of this section provides a coordination rule for determining effectively connected earnings and profits for purposes of the branch profits tax under section 884. Paragraph (g) of this section provides definitions that apply for purposes of this section. Paragraph (h) of this section provides examples that illustrate the application of this section. Paragraph (i) of this section provides dates of applicability.

(b) *Application of section 163(j) and the section 163(j) regulations to specified foreign persons with effectively connected taxable income.*—(1) *In general.*—If a taxpayer is a specified foreign person, then the modifications described in this paragraph (b) are made to the application of section 163(j) and the section 163(j) regulations. If a specified foreign person is also a specified foreign partner, then the modifications described in this paragraph (b) are subject to the partner-level modifications described in paragraph (c) of this section.

(2) *Modification of adjusted taxable income.*— ATI for a specified foreign person for a taxable year means the specified foreign person's effectively connected taxable income for the taxable

year, adjusted for the items described in § 1.163(j)-1(b)(1)(i) through (iv) that are taken into account in determining effectively connected taxable income.

(3) *Modification of business interest expense.*— (i) *General rule.*—Business interest expense for a specified foreign person means interest described in § 1.163(j)-1(b)(2) that is determined under § 1.882-5, in the case of a foreign corporation, or under § 1.861-9T(d)(2), in the case of a non-resident alien individual, and allocable to income which is effectively connected taxable income.

(ii) *Exclusion of certain business interest expense of a specified foreign partner.*—If a foreign corporation is a specified foreign partner in a partnership engaged in a trade or business in the United States, then, for purposes of paragraph (b)(3)(i) of this section, business interest expense excludes the portion of interest expense determined under § 1.882-5 that is attributable to interest on U.S. booked liabilities of the partnership determined under § 1.882-5(d)(2)(vii).

(4) *Modification of business interest income.*— The business interest income of a specified foreign person means interest described in § 1.163(j)-1(b)(3) that is effectively connected taxable income.

(5) *Modification of floor plan financing interest expense.*—The floor plan financing interest expense of a specified foreign person means interest described § 1.163(j)-1(b)(17) that is allocable to income which is effectively connected taxable income.

(6) *Modification of allocation of interest expense and interest income that is properly allocable to a trade or business.*—For purposes of § 1.163(j)-10(c), a specified foreign person's interest expense and interest income that is properly allocable to a trade or business is only allocated to the specified foreign person's excepted or non-excepted trades or business that have effectively connected taxable income. If the specified foreign person is also a specified foreign partner, this rule only applies to the trades or business not in the partnership.

(c) *Partner-level modifications to § 1.163(j)-6 for partnerships engaged in a U.S. trade or business.*— (1) *Modification related to a partnership's excess taxable income.*—If for a taxable year a specified foreign partner, other than an applicable CFC, has allocable excess taxable income with respect to a partnership, then, for purposes of computing the specified foreign partner's ATI for the taxable year, the excess, if any, of the amount of the allocable excess taxable income over the amount of the specified excess taxable income is subtracted from ATI.

(2) *Modification related to a partnership's excess business interest expense.*—If for a taxable year a specified foreign partner, other than an appli-

**Prop. Reg. § 1.163(j)-8(c)(2)**

cable CFC, has allocable excess business interest expense with respect to a partnership, then, for purposes of determining the specified foreign partner's business interest expense for a succeeding taxable year, the amount of the allocable excess business interest expense treated as disallowed business interest expense carryforward under § 1.163(j)-6(f) is determined by taking into account only the portion of allocable excess business interest expense that is specified excess business interest expense and such excess business interest expense is limited to the portion of allocable excess taxable income for the succeeding taxable year that is specified excess taxable income.

(3) *Modification related to a partnership's excess business interest income.*—If for a taxable year a specified foreign partner, other than an applicable CFC, has allocable excess business interest income (as defined in § 1.163(j)-6(b)(4)) with respect to a partnership, then, for purposes of determining the specified foreign partner's section 163(j) limitation, the amount of allocable excess business interest income that can be used by the specified foreign partner cannot exceed the amount of ECI excess business interest income.

(d) *An applicable CFC with effectively connected taxable income.*—If an applicable CFC has effectively connected taxable income for a taxable year in which the applicable CFC has disallowed business interest expense, then a portion of the disallowed business interest expense is treated as being with respect to the applicable CFC's interest expense determined under § 1.882-5. That portion is equal to the amount of the applicable CFC's disallowed business interest expense multiplied by a fraction, the numerator of which is the applicable CFC's effectively connected taxable income for the taxable year, adjusted for the items described in § 1.163(j)-1(b)(1)(i) through (iv) that are taken into account in determining effectively connected taxable income, and the denominator of which is the applicable CFC's ATI for the taxable year. However, in no case will such portion exceed the amount of interest expense determined under § 1.882-5. See also § 1.163(j)-7(b)(2) (concerning the general application of section 163(j) to an applicable CFC).

(e) *Coordination of section 163(j) and § 1.882-5.*— (1) *General rules.*—(i) *Ordering rule.*—A foreign corporation first determines its interest expense under § 1.882-5 and then determines the amount of disallowed business interest expense.

(ii) *Treatment of disallowed business interest expense carryforward.*—If a foreign corporation has a disallowed business interest expense carryforward from a taxable year, then such carryforward is not taken into account for purposes of determining interest expense under § 1.882-5 in the succeeding taxable year.

(iii) *Treatment of allocable excess business interest expense.*—If a foreign corporation has allocable excess business interest expense from a

taxable year that is treated under § 1.163(j)-6(g)(2) as disallowed business interest expense carryforward, such interest is not taken into account for purposes of determining interest expense under § 1.882-5 in the succeeding taxable year.

(iv) *Scaling ratio.*—If a foreign corporation determines its interest expense under the method described in § 1.882-5(b) through (d) and has U.S. booked liabilities in excess of U.S. connected liabilities, the foreign corporation must apply the scaling ratio (as defined in § 1.882-5(d)(4)(ii)) pro rata to all interest expense paid or accrued by the foreign corporation consistent with § 1.882-5(d)(4)(i), including for purposes of paragraph (b)(3)(ii) of this section.

(2) *Amount of interest determined under § 1.882-5 that is disallowed business interest expense.*—(i) *Foreign corporation is not a specified foreign partner.*—If a foreign corporation is not a specified foreign partner for a taxable year, then the amount of the foreign corporation's interest expense determined under § 1.882-5 for which a deduction is disallowed for the taxable year is either—

(A) The amount of disallowed business interest expense computed under § 1.163(j)-2(b) with respect to business interest expense described in paragraph (b)(3)(i) of this section, in the case of a foreign corporation that is not an applicable CFC; or

(B) The amount of disallowed business interest expense determined under paragraph (d) of this section, in the case of an applicable CFC.

(ii) *Foreign corporation is a specified foreign partner.*—If a foreign corporation is a specified foreign partner with respect to one or more partnerships engaged in a trade or business in the United States for a taxable year, then the portion of the foreign corporation's business interest expense determined under § 1.882-5 for which a deduction is disallowed for the taxable year is equal to the sum of the following amounts—

(A) Either—

(1) The amount described in paragraph (e)(2)(i)(A) of this section, in the case of a foreign corporation that is not an applicable CFC; or

(2) The amount described in paragraph (e)(2)(i)(B) of this section, in the case of an applicable CFC; and

(B) With respect to each partnership that has excess business interest expense for the taxable year that ends with or within the foreign corporation's taxable year, the amount of the foreign corporation's specified excess business interest expense.

(f) *Coordination with branch profits tax.*—(1) *Effect on effectively connected earnings and profits.*—The disallowance and carryforward of business interest expense under § 1.163(j)-2(b) and (c) will not affect when such business interest expense reduces the effectively connected earnings and profits of a foreign corporation, as defined in § 1.884-1(f).

(2) *Effect on U.S. net equity.*—The disallowance and carryforward of business interest expense under § 1.163(j)-2(b) and (c) will not affect the computation of the U.S. net equity of a foreign corporation, as defined in § 1.884-1(c).

(g) *Definitions.*—The following definitions apply for purposes of this section.

(1) *Applicable CFC.*—The term *applicable CFC* means a foreign corporation described in section 957, but only if the foreign corporation has at least one United States shareholder that owns, within the meaning of section 958(a), stock of the foreign corporation.

(2) *ECI excess business interest income.*—The term *ECI excess business interest income* means, with respect to a specified foreign partner and a partnership, the excess, if any, of the specified foreign partner's allocable business interest income (as defined in § 1.163(j)-6(f)(2)(ii)) over its allocable business interest expense (as defined in § 1.163(j)-6(f)(2)(ii)), but, for purposes of determining a specified foreign partner's allocable business interest income and allocable business interest expense, taking into account only the portion of the partnership's business interest income determined under paragraph (b)(4) of this section as if the partnership were a specified foreign person, over the business interest expense on the U.S. booked liabilities of the partnership as determined under § 1.882-5(d)(2)(vii).

(3) *Effectively connected taxable income.*—The term *effectively connected taxable income* means taxable income of a person that is, or is treated as. effectively connected with the conduct of a trade business in the United States under an applicable provision of the Code or regulations or, if an income tax treaty applies, business profits attributable to a U.S. permanent establishment of a tax treaty resident eligible for benefits under an income tax treaty between the United States and the treaty country.

(4) *Specified excess business interest expense.*— The term *specified excess business interest expense* means, with respect to a specified foreign partner and a partnership, the amount determined by multiplying the specified foreign partner's allocable excess business interest expense (as determined under § 1.163(j)-6(f)) by the partnership's specified ratio for the taxable year.

(5) *Specified excess taxable income.*—The term *specified excess taxable income* means, with respect to a specified foreign partner and a partnership, the amount determined by multiplying the amount of the specified foreign partner's allocable excess taxable income (as determined under § 1.163(j)-6(f)) by the amount of the partnership's specified ratio for the taxable year.

(6) *Specified foreign partner.*—The term *specified foreign partner* means, with respect to a partnership that is engaged in a U.S. trade or business, a partner that is a specified foreign person or an applicable CFC.

(7) *Specified foreign person.*—The term *specified foreign person* means a nonresident alien individual, as defined in section 7701(b) and the regulations thereunder, or a foreign corporation other than an applicable CFC.

(8) *Specified ratio.*—The term *specified ratio* means, with respect to a partnership, a fraction (expressed as a percentage), the numerator of which is the ATI for the partnership determined under paragraph (b)(2) of this section as if the partnership were a specified foreign person, and the denominator of which is the ATI for the partnership determined under § 1.163(j)-6(d).

(h) *Examples.*—The following examples illustrate the application of this section. For all examples, assume that all referenced interest expense is deductible but for the application of section 163(j), the small business exemption under § 1.163(j)-2(d) is not available, no party is engaged in an excepted trade or business, and no business interest expense is floor plan financing interest expense.

(1) *Example 1: Limitation on business interest deduction of a foreign corporation*—(i) *Facts.* FC, a foreign corporation that is not an applicable CFC, has $100x of gross income that is effectively connected income. FC has $60x of other income which is not effectively connected income. FC has total expenses of $100x. Assume that under § 1.882-5, FC has $30x of interest expense allocable to income which is effectively connected income. Under section 882(c) and the regulations thereunder, FC has $40x of other expenses properly allocated and apportioned to income which is effectively connected taxable income. FC does not have any business interest income.

(ii) *Analysis.* FC is a specified foreign person under paragraph (g)(7) of this section. Under paragraph (e)(2) of this section, the amount of FC's interest expense determined under § 1.882-5 that is disallowed is the disallowed business interest expense computed under § 1.163(j)-2(b) with respect to interest expense described in paragraph (b)(3) of this section. Under § 1.163(j)-4(b)(1), all interest paid or accrued by FC is properly allocable to a trade or business and therefore under paragraph (b)(3) of this section, FC has business interest expense of $30x. FC has $30x of effectively connected taxable income described in paragraph (g)(3) of this section ($100x - $30x - $40x). Under paragraph (b)(2) of this section, FC has ATI of $60x, determined as $30x of effectively connected taxable income, increased by $30x of business interest expense. Accordingly, FC's section 163(j) limitation is $18x ($60x x 30 percent). Because FC's business interest expense ($30x) exceeds the section 163(j) limi-

**Prop. Reg. § 1.163(j)-8(h)**

tation ($18x), FC may only deduct $18x of business interest expense. Under § 1.163(j)-2(c), the remaining $12x is disallowed business interest expense carryforward and under paragraph (e)(1)(ii) of this section, the $12x is not taken into account for purposes of applying § 1.882-5 in the succeeding taxable year.

(2) *Example 2: Use of a disallowed business interest expense carryforward*—(i) *Facts.* The facts are the same as in *Example 1* in paragraph (h)(1)(i) of this section except that FC has $300x of gross income which is all effectively connected income. Furthermore assume that FC has a disallowed business interest expense carryforward of $25x from the prior taxable year.

(ii) *Analysis.* Under paragraph (e)(1)(ii) of this section, FC's $25x of disallowed business interest expense carryforward is not taken into account for purposes of determining FC's interest under § 1.882-5. Therefore, FC has $30x of business interest expense determined under § 1.882-5. Under paragraph (g)(3) of this section, FC has effectively connected taxable income of $205x ($300x gross income - $55x interest expense ($30x + $25x) - $40x other expenses). Under paragraph (b)(2) of this section, FC has ATI of $260x, determined as $205x of effectively connected taxable income, increased by $55x of business interest expense. Accordingly, FC's section 163(j) limitation is $78x ($260x x 30 percent). Under paragraph (b)(3) of this section, FC has business interest expense of $55x ($30x + $25x disallowed interest carryforward) for the taxable year. Because FC's business interest expense ($55x) does not exceed the section 163(j) limitation ($78x), FC may deduct all $55x of business interest expense.

(3) *Example 3: Foreign corporation is engaged in a U.S. trade or business and a specified foreign partner in a partnership engaged in a U.S. trade or business*—(i) *Facts.* FC, a foreign corporation that is not an applicable CFC, owns a 50-percent interest in ABC, a foreign partnership that is engaged in a trade or business in the United States. ABC has two lines of businesses, Business A and Business B. Business A produces $120x of taxable income (including interest expense) and Business B produces $80x of taxable income. FC is allocated 50 percent of all items of income and expense of Business A and Business B. Business A has business interest expense of $20x on $400x of liabilities but has no business interest income. Business B does not have any business interest expense or business interest income. With respect to FC, only Business A produces effectively connected income. FC has an outside basis of $500x in the ABC partnership for purposes of § 1.882-5(b), step 1. All of the liabilities of Business A are U.S. booked liabilities for purposes of § 1.882-5(d). In addition to owning a 50-percent interest in ABC, FC conducts a separate business that is engaged in a trade or business in the United States (Business X). Business X has effectively connected taxable income of $50x, U.S. assets with an adjusted basis of $300x, U.S. booked liabilities of $160x, and interest on U.S. booked liabilities of $15x. FC computes its inter-

est expense under the three-step method described in § 1.882-5(b) through (d) and uses the fixed ratio of 50 percent for purposes of § 1.882-5(c), step 2. Assume the interest rate on excess U.S. connected liabilities is 5 percent. For the taxable year, FC has total interest expense of 500x for purposes of § 1.882-5(a)(3).

(ii) *Analysis*—(A) *Application of section 163(j) to ABC.* Under § 1.163(j)-6(a), ABC computes a section 163(j) limitation at the partnership level. Under § 1.163(j)-6(d), ABC has ATI of $220x, determined as $200x of taxable income ($120x from Business A + $80x from Business B), increased by $20x of business interest expense of Business A. Under § 1.163(j)-2(b), ABC's section 163(j) limitation is $66x ($220x x 30 percent). Because ABC's business interest expense ($20x) does not exceed the section 163(j) limitation ($66x), ABC can deduct all of its business interest expense for the taxable year. Under § 1.163(j)-1(b)(15), ABC has excess taxable income of $153.33x ($220x x ($46x/$66x)). Under § 1.163(j)-6(f), FC is allocated 50 percent of the $153.33x of ABC's excess taxable income, or $76.67x of allocable excess taxable income, but, under paragraph (c)(1) of this section, the amount by which the allocable excess taxable income exceeds FC's specified excess taxable income (as defined in paragraph (g)(5) of this section) is a subtraction from FC's ATI. Under paragraph (g)(5) of this section, FC's specified excess taxable income is $48.79x, which is equal to the product of $76.67x and ABC's specified ratio of 63.64 percent. Under paragraph (g)(8) of this section, ABC's specified ratio of 63.64 percent is determined as $140x / $220x (where the numerator of $140x is the ATI of ABC determined under paragraph (b)(2) of this section as if ABC were a specified foreign person ($120x taxable income of Business A, increased by $20x of business interest expense), and the denominator of $220x is the ATI of ABC under § 1.163(j)-6(d)). FC's allocable excess taxable income ($76.67x) exceeds its specified excess taxable income ($48.79x) by $27.88x.

(B) *Application of § 1.882-5 to FC.* FC is a specified foreign partner under paragraph (g)(6) of this section. Under paragraph (e)(1) of this section, FC first determines its interest expense under § 1.882-5 and then determines its disallowed business interest expense. Under § 1.882-5(b), step 1, FC has U.S. assets of $800x ($500x (FC's basis in its interest in ABC) + $300x (FC's assets in Business X assets). Under § 1.882-5(c), step 2, applying the 50-percent safe harbor in § 1.882-5 for a non-banking business, FC has U.S. connected liabilities of $400x ($800x x 50 percent). Under § 1.882-5(d), step 3, FC has U.S. booked liabilities of $360x ($200x (50-percent share of Business A liabilities of ABC of $400x) + $160x (Business X liabilities) and interest on U.S. booked liabilities of $25x ($10x (50-percent share of $20x interest expense of Business A) + $15x (interest expense of Business X)). FC has excess U.S. connected liabilities of $40x ($400x – $360x) and interest on such excess liabilities of $2x ($40x x 5 percent). FC's interest expense determined under § 1.882-5 is $27x ($25x + $2x).

(C) *Application of section 163(j) to FC.* Under paragraph (e)(2)(ii) of this section, the amount of business interest expense that is disallowed for FC is equal to only the amount of interest described in paragraph (b)(3) of this section that is disallowed because there is no specified excess business interest expense with respect to ABC. Under paragraph (b)(3) of this section, FC's business interest expense (at the corporate level) is $17x, the amount determined under § 1.882-5 ($27x) less the amount of interest on U.S. booked liabilities from ABC determined under § 1.882-5(d)(2)(vii) ($10x), which was subject to the section 163(j) limitation at the ABC partnership level. Under § 1.163(j)-6(e)(1), FC's ATI is determined under § 1.163(j)-1(b)(1) without regard to FC's distributive share of any items of income, gain, deduction, or loss of ABC. Under paragraph (b)(2) of this section, taking into account the application of paragraph (c)(1) of this section, FC's ATI is $115.77x ($50x effectively connected taxable income with respect to Business X, + $17x (business interest expense under § 1.882-5 of 27x less the amount of interest on U.S. booked liabilities from ABC determined under § 1.882-5(d)(2)(vii) of $10x) + $76.65x (excess taxable income from ABC) - $27.88x (amount excess taxable income exceeds specified excess taxable income)). FC's section 163(j) limitation is $34.73x ($115.77x x 30 percent). Because FC's business interest expense ($17x) is less than FC's section 163(j) limitation ($34.73x) and all of its share of ABC's interest is deductible, FC may deduct all $27x of interest determined under § 1.882-5.

(4) *Example 4: Scaleback of interest expense under § 1.882-5*—(i) *Facts.* Assume the same facts in *Example 3* in paragraph (h)(3)(i) of this section except that Business X has U.S. booked liabilities of $300x and interest on U.S. booked liabilities of $20x.

(ii) *Analysis*—(A) *Application of section 163(j) to ABC.* The analysis is the same as *Example 3* in paragraph (h)(3)(ii)(A) of this section.

(B) *Application of § 1.882-5 to FC.* Under § 1.882-5(b), step 1, FC has U.S. assets of $800x ($500x (FC's basis in its interest in ABC) + $300x (FC's basis in Business X assets)). Under § 1.882-5(c), step 2, applying the 50-percent safe harbor in § 1.882-5 for a non-banking business, FC has U.S. connected liabilities of $400x ($800x x 50 percent). Under § 1.882-5(d), step 3, FC has U.S. booked liabilities of $500x ($200x (50-percent share of Business A liabilities of ABC of $400x) + $300x (Business X liabilities) and interest on U.S. booked liabilities of $30x ($10x (50-percent share of $20x interest expense of Business A) + $20x (interest expense of Business X)). FC has excess U.S. booked liabilities of $100x ($500x – $400x) and the interest expense on U.S. booked liabilities must be reduced by the scaling ratio as provided in § 1.882-5(d)(4). FC's interest expense determined under § 1.882-5 is $24x ($30x x (400/500 scaling ratio)).

(C) *Application of section 163(j) to FC.* Under paragraph (b)(3) of this section, FC's business interest expense is $16x, the amount determined under § 1.882-5 ($24x) less the amount of interest on U.S. booked liabilities from ABC determined under § 1.882-5(d)(2)(vii) after applying the scaling ratio ($8x, determined as interest expense of Business A of $10x x scaling ratio of 400/500), which was subject to the section 163(j) limitation at the ABC partnership level. Under § 1.163(j)-6(e)(1), FC's ATI is determined under § 1.163(j)-1(b)(1) without regard to FC's distributive share of any items of income, gain, deduction, or loss of ABC. Under paragraph (b)(2) of this section, taking into account the application of paragraph (c)(1) of this section, FC's ATI is $114.79x ($50x effectively connected taxable income with respect to Business X + $16x (business interest expense under § 1.882-5 of 24x less the amount of interest on U.S. booked liabilities from ABC determined under § 1.882-5(d)(2)(vii), after applying the scaleback, of $8x) + $76.67x (excess taxable income from ABC) - $27.88x (amount excess taxable income exceeds specified excess taxable income)). FC's section 163(j) limitation is $34.44x ($114.79x x 30 percent). Because FC's business interest expense ($16x) is less than FC's section 163(j) limitation ($34.44x) and all of ABC's interest is deductible, FC may deduct all $24x of interest determined under § 1.882-5.

(5) *Example 5: Separate currency pools method*—(i) *Facts.* Assume the same facts in *Example 3* in paragraph (h)(3)(i) of this section except that FC does not conduct Business X; the value of FC's interest in ABC for purposes of § 1.882-5(e)(i), step 1, is $1,000x; and FC computes its interest expense under the separate currency pools method in § 1.882-5(e) and for purposes of applying such method, the prescribed interest rate is 5 percent.

(ii) *Analysis*—(A) *Application of section 163(j) to ABC.* The analysis is the same as in *Example 3* in paragraph (h)(1)(ii)(A) of this section.

(B) *Application of § 1.882-5 to FC.* Under § 1.882-5(e)(i), step 1, FC has U.S. assets of $1,000x (FC's basis in its partnership interest in ABC). Under § 1.882-5(e)(1)(ii), step 2, FC has U.S. connected liabilities of $500x ($1,000x x 50 percent) applying the 50 percent safe harbor for non-banking business. Under § 1.882-5(e)(1)(iii), step 3, the interest expense under § 1.882-5 is $25x ($500x x 5 percent).

(C) *Application of section 163(j) to FC.* Under paragraph (b)(3) of this section, FC's business interest expense is $15x, the amount determined under § 1.882-5 ($25x) less the amount of interest on U.S. booked liabilities from ABC determined under § 1.882-5(d)(2)(vii) of $10x, which was subject to the section 163(j) limitation at the ABC partnership level. Under § 1.163(j)-6(e)(1), FC's ATI is determined under § 1.163(j)-1(b)(1) without regard to FC's distributive share of any items of income, gain, deduction, or loss of ABC. Under paragraph (b)(2) of this section, taking into account the application of paragraph (c)(1) of this section, FC's ATI is $48.79x ($76.67x (ex-

**Prop. Reg. § 1.163(j)-8(h)**

cess taxable income from ABC) — $27.88x (amount excess taxable income exceeds specified excess taxable income)). FC's section 163(j) limitation is $14.64x ($48.79x x 30 percent). Because FC's business interest expense ($15x) exceeds the 163(j) limitation ($14.64x), FC may only deduct $14.64x of its business interest expense. Under § 1.163(j)-2(c), the remaining $0.36x is disallowed business interest expense carryforward and under paragraph (e)(1)(ii) of this section, the $0.36x is not taken into account for purposes of applying § 1.882-5 in the succeeding taxable year. Accordingly, FC may deduct 24.64x of the $25x interest determined under § 1.882-5.

(6) *Example 6: Specified foreign partner with excess business interest expense*—(i) *Facts - Year 1.* FC, a foreign corporation that is not an applicable CFC, owns a 50-percent interest in XYZ, a foreign partnership that is engaged in a trade or business in the United States. XYZ has two lines of businesses, Business S and Business T. Business S produces $50x of taxable income (including interest expense), and Business T produces $40x of taxable income (including interest expense). FC is allocated 50 percent of all items of income and expenses of Business S and Business T. Business S has business interest expense of $30x on $500x of liabilities but has no business interest income. Business T has business interest expense of $50x on $500x of liabilities but has no business interest income. With respect to FC, only Business S produces effectively connected income. FC has an adjusted basis of $500x in XYZ for purposes of § 1.882-5(b), step 1. All of the liabilities of Business S are U.S. booked liabilities for purposes of § 1.882-5(d). FC computes its interest expense under the three-step method described in § 1.882-5(b) through (d) and uses the fixed ratio of 50 percent for purposes of § 1.882-5(c), step 2.

(ii) *Analysis with respect to Year 1*—(A) *Application of section 163(j) to XYZ.* Under § 1.163(j)-6(a), XYZ computes a section 163(j) limitation at the partnership-level. Under § 1.163(j)-6(d), XYZ has ATI of $170x, determined as $90x of taxable income ($50x from Business S + $40x from Business T), increased by $80x of business interest expense ($30x from Business S + $50x from Business T). Under § 1.163(j)-2(b), XYZ's section 163(j) limitation is $51x ($170x x 30 percent). Because XYZ's business interest expense ($80x) exceeds the section 163(j) limitation ($51x), XYZ may only deduct $51x of business interest expense and $29x is disallowed under section 163(j). Under § 1.163(j)-6(f), FC is allocated $14.5x of excess business interest expense (50 percent x $29x). Under paragraph (c)(2) of this section, the amount of allocable business interest expense that can be used by FC is equal to the amount of specified excess business interest, and the amount of such interest that is treated as paid or accrued by FC in the succeeding taxable year is limited to the amount of FC's specified excess taxable income allocated to FC in the succeeding taxable year.

(B) *Application of § 1.882-5 to FC.* FC is a specified foreign partner under paragraph (g)(6) of this section. Under paragraph (e)(1) of this section, FC first determines its interest expense under § 1.882-5 and then determines its disallowed business interest expense. Under § 1.882-5(b), step 1, FC has U.S. assets of $500x (FC's adjusted basis in its interest in XYZ). Under § 1.882-5(c), step 2, applying the 50-percent fixed ratio in § 1.882-5 for a non-banking business, FC has U.S. connected liabilities of $250x ($500x x 50 percent). Under § 1.882-5(d), step 3, FC has U.S. booked liabilities of $250x ($500x x 50-percent share of Business S liabilities of XYZ) and interest on U.S. booked liabilities of $15x (50 percent share of $30x interest expense of Business S). Because FC has U.S. connected liabilities equal to its U.S. booked liabilities, its interest expense under § 1.882-5 is $15x (the amount of interest expense on its U.S. booked liabilities).

(C) *Application of section 163(j) to FC.* Under paragraph (e)(2)(ii) of this section, the amount of business interest expense that is disallowed for FC is equal to the sum of the amount of interest described in paragraph (b)(3) of this section that is disallowed plus the amount of FC's specified excess business interest expense. FC's business interest expense (at the corporate level) under paragraph (b)(3) of this section is $0, the amount determined under § 1.882-5 ($15x) less the amount of interest on U.S. booked liabilities from XYZ determined under § 1.882-5(d)(2)(vii) ($15x), which was subject to the section 163(j) limitation at the XYZ partnership level. Because FC (at the corporate level) has no business interest expense, there is no business interest expense subject to the section 163(j) limitation. However, because FC has excess business interest expense with respect to XYZ, a deduction for a portion of the $15x of interest on U.S. booked liabilities from XYZ determined under § 1.882-5(d)(2)(vii) will be disallowed for the taxable year. The amount of such interest that is limited is equal to the amount of the FC's specified excess business interest expense determined under paragraph (g)(4) of this section. The specified excess business interest expense is $6.82x, determined by multiplying FC's distributive share of excess business interest expense ($14.5x) by XYZ's specified ratio of 47.06 percent, determined under paragraph (g)(8) of this section. The specified ratio of 47.06 percent is determined by dividing $80x ATI determined under paragraph (b)(2) of the section as if XYZ were a specified foreign person (determined as $50x taxable income from Business S + $30x business interest expense from Business S) by $170x of XYZ ATI. FC may only deduct $8.18x ($15x - $6.82x) of business interest expense. Under § 1.163(j)-2(c), the remaining $6.82x is disallowed business interest expense carryforward and under paragraph (e)(1)(ii) of this section, the $6.82x is not taken into account for purposes of applying § 1.882-5 in the succeeding taxable year.

(iii) *Facts - Year 2.* During Year 2, Business S produces $170x of taxable income (including interest expense) and Business T produces $150x (including interest expense) of taxable income. Business S has business interest expense of $30x on $500x of liabilities but has no business interest income. Business T has business interest expense of $50x on $500x of liabilities but no business interest income. With respect to FC, only Business S produces effectively connected taxable income. FC has an adjusted basis of $600x in XYZ for purposes of § 1.882-5(b), step 1. All of the liabilities of Business S are U.S. booked liabilities for purposes of § 1.882-5(d). FC computes its interest expense under the three-step method described in § 1.882-5(b) through (d) and uses the fixed ratio of 50 percent for purposes of § 1.882-5(c), step 2. The interest rate on excess U.S. connected liabilities is 5 percent. For the taxable year, FC has total interest expense of $1,000x for purposes of § 1.882-5(a)(3).

(iv) *Analysis with respect to Year 2*—(A) *Application of section 163(j) to XYZ.* Under § 1.163(j)-6(a), XYZ computes a section 163(j) limitation at the partnership-level. Under § 1.163(j)-6(d), XYZ has ATI of $400x, determined as $320x of taxable income ($170x from Business S + $150x from Business T), increased by $80x of business interest expense ($30x from Business S + $50x from Business T). Under § 1.163(j)-2(b), XYZ's section 163(j) limitation is $120x ($400x x 30 percent). Because XYZ's business interest expense ($80x) does not exceed the section 163(j) limitation ($120x), XYZ can deduct all of its business interest expense for the taxable year. Under § 1.163(j)-1(b)(15), XYZ has excess taxable income of $133.30x ($400x x ($40x/$120x)). Under § 1.163(j)-6(f), FC is allocated 50 percent of the $133.33x of XYZ's excess taxable income, or $66.66x of allocable excess taxable income, but, under paragraph (c)(1) of this section, the amount by which the allocable excess taxable income exceeds FC's specified excess taxable income (as defined in paragraph (g)(5) of this section) is a subtraction from FC's ATI. Under paragraph (g)(5) of this section, FC's specified excess taxable income is $33.33x, which is equal to the product of FC's allocable excess taxable income of $66.66x and XYZ's specified ratio of 50 percent. Under paragraph (g)(8) of this section, XYZ's specified ratio of 50 percent is determined as $200x / $400x (where the numerator of $200x is the ATI of XYZ determined under paragraph (b)(2) of this section as if XYZ were a specified foreign person ($170x taxable income of Business S, increased by $30x of business interest expense), and the denominator of $400x is the ATI of XYZ under § 1.163(j)-6(d)). FC's allocable excess taxable income ($66.66x) exceeds its specified excess taxable income ($33.33x) by $33.33x.

(B) *Treatment of excess business interest expense from Year 1.* In Year 1, XYZ had disallowed business interest expense of $29x and under § 1.163(j)-6(f), FC's allocable excess business interest expense was $14.50x. Under paragraph (c)(2) of this section, FC may use its allocable excess business interest expense in a succeeding taxable year only to the extent of its specified excess business interest expense, which, in this case, was determined to be $6.82x, and, with respect to Year 2, the amount of specified excess business interest expense treated as paid or accrued by FC is limited to FC's specified excess taxable income ($33.33x). Thus, FC can treat the entire $6.82x as business interest expense paid or accrued in Year 2.

(C) *Application of § 1.882-5 to FC.* Under § 1.882-5(b), step 1, FC has U.S. assets of $600x (FC's adjusted basis in its interest in XYZ). Under § 1.882-5(c), step 2, applying the 50 percent fixed ratio in § 1.882-5 for a non-banking business, FC has U.S. connected liabilities of $300x ($600x x 50 percent). Under § 1.882-5(d), step 3, FC has U.S. booked liabilities of $250x ($500x x 50-percent share of Business S liabilities of XYZ) and interest on U.S. booked liabilities of $15x (50 percent share of $30x interest expense of Business S). FC has excess U.S. connected liabilities of $50x ($300x − $250x) and interest on such excess liabilities of $2.5x ($50x x 5 percent). FC's interest expense determined under § 1.882-5 is $17.5x ($15x + $2.5x).

(D) *Application of section 163(j) to FC.* Under paragraph (e)(2)(ii) of this section, the amount of business interest expense that is disallowed for FC is equal to only the amount of interest described in paragraph (b)(3) of this section that is disallowed because there is no excess business interest expense with respect to XYZ. FC's business interest expense (at the corporate level) under paragraphs (b)(3) and (e)(1) of this section is $9.32x, determined as the sum of $2.50x (the amount determined under § 1.882-5 ($17.50x) less the amount of interest on U.S. booked liabilities from XYZ determined under § 1.882-5(d)(2)(vii) ($15x) that is excluded under paragraph (b)(3)(ii) of this section) + $6.82x (allocable business interest expense from Year 1 treated as paid or accrued in Year 2). Under § 1.163(j)-6(e)(1), FC's ATI is determined under § 1.163(j)-1(b)(1) without regard to FC's distributive share of any items of income, gain, deduction, or loss of XYZ. Under paragraph (b)(2) of this section, taking into account the application of paragraph (c)(1) of this section, FC's ATI is $33.33x, determined as $66.66x (excess taxable income from XYZ) — $33.33x (amount excess taxable income exceeds specified excess taxable income). FC's section 163(j) limitation is $10x ($33.33x x 30 percent). Because FC's business interest expense (at the corporate level) of $9.32x is less than FC's section 163(j) limitation of $10x, FC may deduct all $9.32x of business interest expense ($2.50x from Year 2 and $6.82x from Year 1). Because all of XYZ's business interest expense is deductible, FC may also deduct the $15x of business interest expense on U.S. booked liabilities of XYZ for Year 2.

(7) *Example 7: Coordination of section 163(j) and branch profits tax*—(i) *Facts.* FC, a foreign corporation that is not an applicable CFC, uses cash that

**Prop. Reg. § 1.163(j)-8(h)**

is treated as a U.S. asset under §1.884-1(d) in order to pay interest described in paragraph (b)(3) of this section for which a deduction for such interest is disallowed under §1.163(j)-2(b).

(ii) *Analysis.* Assuming that FC's U.S. assets otherwise remain constant during the year, the U.S. assets of FC will have decreased by the amount of cash used to pay the interest expense, and the U.S. net equity of FC will be computed accordingly.

(i) *Applicability date.*—This section applies to taxable years ending after the date the Treasury decision adopting these regulations as final regulations is published in the **Federal Register.** However, taxpayers and their related parties, within the meaning of sections 267(b) and 707(b)(1), may apply this section to a taxable year beginning after December 31, 2017, if the taxpayers and their related parties consistently apply all of the section 163(j) regulations, and if applicable, §§1.263A-9, 1.381(c)(20)-1, 1.382-6, 1.383-1, 1.469-9, 1.882-5, 1.1502-13, 1.1502-21, 1.1502-36, 1.1502-79, 1.1502-91 through 1.1502-99 (to the extent they effectuate the rules of §§1.382-6 and 1.383-1), and 1.1504-4 to those taxable years. [Reg. §1.163(j)-8.]

[Proposed 12-28-2018.]

**[Prop. Reg. §1.163(j)-9]**

**§1.163(j)-9. Elections for excepted trades or businesses; safe harbor for certain REITs.**— (a) *Overview.*—This section provides rules and procedures for making an election under section 163(j)(7)(B) to be an electing real property trade or business, as defined in §1.163(j)-1(b)(12), and an election under section 163(j)(7)(C) to be an electing farming business, as defined in §1.163(j)-1(b)(11).

(b) *Scope and effect of election.*—(1) *In general.*— An election under this section is made with respect to each eligible trade or business of the taxpayer and applies only to such trade or business for which the election is made. An election under this section applies to the taxable year in which the election is made and to all subsequent taxable years, except as otherwise provided in this section.

(2) *Irrevocability.*—An election under this section is irrevocable.

(c) *Time and manner of making election.*—(1) *In general.*—Subject to paragraph (e) of this section, a taxpayer makes an election under this section by attaching an election statement to the taxpayer's timely filed original Federal income tax return, including extensions. A taxpayer may make elections for multiple trades or businesses on a single election statement.

(2) *Election statement contents.*—The election statement should be titled "Section 1.163(j)-9 Election" and must contain the following information for each trade or business:

(i) The taxpayer's name;

(ii) The taxpayer's address;

(iii) The taxpayer's social security number (SSN) or employer identification number (EIN);

(iv) A description of the taxpayer's electing trade or business, including the principal business activity code; and

(v) A statement that the taxpayer is making an election under section 163(j)(7)(B) or (C), as applicable.

(3) *Consolidated group's trade or business.*— For a consolidated group's trade or business, the election under this section is made by the agent for the group, as defined in §1.1502-77, on behalf of itself and members of the consolidated group. Only the name and taxpayer identification number (TIN) of the agent for the group, as defined in §1.1502-77, must be provided on the election statement.

(4) *Partnership's trade or business.*—An election for a partnership must be made on the partnership's return with respect to any trade or business that the partnership conducts. An election by a partnership does not apply to a trade or business conducted by a partner outside the partnership.

(d) *Termination of election.*—(1) *In general.*—An election under this section automatically terminates if a taxpayer ceases to engage in the electing trade or business. A taxpayer is considered to cease to engage in an electing trade or business if the taxpayer sells or transfers substantially all of the assets of the electing trade or business to an acquirer that is not a related party in a taxable asset transfer. A taxpayer is also considered to cease to engage in an electing trade or business if the taxpayer terminates its existence for Federal income tax purposes or ceases operation of the electing trade or business, except to the extent that such termination or cessation results in the sale or transfer of substantially all of the assets of the electing trade or business to an acquirer that is a related party, or in a transaction that is not a taxable asset transfer.

(2) *Taxable asset transfer defined.*—For purposes of this paragraph (d), the term taxable asset transfer means a transfer in which the acquirer's basis or adjusted basis in the assets is not determined, directly or indirectly, in whole or in part, by reference to the transferor's basis in the assets.

(3) *Related party defined.*—For purposes of this paragraph (d), the term *related party* means any person who bears a relationship to the taxpayer which is described section 267(b) or 707(b)(1).

(4) *Anti-abuse rule.*—If, within 60 months of a sale or transfer of assets described in paragraph (d)(1) of this section, the taxpayer or a related party reacquires substantially all of the

assets that were used in the taxpayer's prior electing trade or business, or substantially similar assets, and resumes conducting such prior electing trade or business, the taxpayer's previously terminated election under this section is reinstated and is effective on the date the prior electing trade or business is reacquired.

(e) *Additional guidance.*—The rules and procedures regarding the time and manner of making an election under this section and the election statement contents in paragraph (c) of this section may be modified through other guidance (see §§601.601(d) and 601.602 of this chapter). Additional situations in which an election may terminate under paragraph (d) of this section may be provided through guidance published in the **Federal Register** or in the Internal Revenue Bulletin (see §601.601(d) of this chapter).

(f) *Examples.*—The examples of this paragraph (f) illustrate the application of this section. Unless otherwise indicated, assume the following: X and Y are domestic C corporations; D and E are U.S. resident individuals not subject to any foreign income tax; and the exemption for certain small businesses in §1.163(j)-2(d) does not apply.

(1) *Example 1: Scope of election*—(i) *Facts.* During her taxable year ending December 31, 2019, D, a sole proprietor, owned and operated a dairy farm and a tree farm as separate farming businesses described in section 263A(e)(4). D filed its original Federal income tax return for the 2019 taxable year on August 1, 2020, and included with the return an election statement meeting the requirements of paragraph (c)(2) of this section. The election statement identified D's dairy farm business as an electing trade or business under this section. On March 1, 2021, D sold some but not all or substantially all of the assets from her dairy farm business to her neighbor, E, who is unrelated to D. After the sale, D continued to operate the dairy farm trade or business.

(ii) *Analysis.* D's election under this section was properly made and is effective for the 2019 taxable year and subsequent years. D's dairy farm business is an excepted trade or business because D made the election with her timely filed Federal income tax return. D's tree farm business is a non-excepted trade or business. The sale of some but not all or substantially all of the assets from D's dairy farm business has no impact on D's election under this section.

(2) *Example 2: Cessation of entire trade or business*—(i) *Facts.* X has a real property trade or business for which X made an election under this section by attaching an election statement to A's 2019 Federal income tax return. On March 1, 2020, X sold all of the assets used in its real property trade or business to Y, an unrelated party, and ceased to engage in the electing trade or business. On June 1, 2027, X started a new real property trade or business that was substantially similar to X's prior electing trade or business.

(ii) *Analysis.* X's election under this section terminated on March 1, 2020, under paragraph

(d)(1) of this section. X may choose whether to make an election under this section for X's new real property trade or business that A started in 2027.

(3) *Example 3: Anti-abuse rule*—(i) *Facts.* The same facts are the same as in *Example 2* in paragraph (f)(2)(i) of this section, except that X restarted her previous real property trade or business on February 1, 2021, when X reacquired substantially all of the assets that X had sold on March 1, 2020.

(ii) *Analysis.* X's election under this section terminated on March, 1, 2020, under paragraph (d)(1) of this section. On February 1, 2021, X's election was reinstated under paragraph (d)(4) of this section. X's new real property trade or business is treated as a resumption of X's prior electing trade or business and is therefore treated as an electing real property trade or business.

(4) *Example 4: Trade or business continuing after acquisition*—(i) *Facts.* X has a farming business for which X made an election under this section by attaching an election statement to X's timely filed 2019 Federal income tax return. Y, unrelated to X, also has a farming business, but Y has not made an election under this section. On July 1, 2020, X transferred all of its assets to Y in a transaction described in section 368(a)(1)(D) (a "D reorganization"). After the transfer, Y continues to operate the farming trade or business acquired from X.

(ii) *Analysis.* Under paragraph (d)(1) of this section, Y is subject to X's election under this section for the trade or business that uses X's assets because the sale or transfer was not in a taxable transaction. Y cannot revoke X's election, but X's election has no effect on Y's existing farming business for which Y has not made an election under this section.

(5) *Example 5: Trade or business merged after acquisition*—(i) *Facts.* The facts are the same as in *Example 4* in paragraph (f)(4)(i) of this section, except that Y uses the assets acquired from X in a trade or business that is neither a farming business (as defined in section 263A(e)(4) or §1.263A-4(a)(4)) nor a trade or business of a specified agricultural or horticultural cooperative (as defined in section 199A(g)(4)).

(ii) *Analysis.* Y is not subject to X's election for Y's farming business because the farming trade or business ceased to exist after the acquisition.

(g) *Safe harbor for REITs.*—(1) *In general.*—If a REIT holds real property, as defined in §1.856-10, interests in partnerships holding real property, as defined in §1.856-10, or shares in other REITs holding real property, as defined in §1.856-10, the REIT is eligible to make the election described in paragraph (b)(1) of this section to be an electing real property trade or business for purposes of sections 163(j)(7)(B) and 168(g)(1)(F) for all or part of its assets. The portion of the REIT's assets eligible for this election is determined under paragraph (g)(2) or (3) of this section.

(2) *REITs that do not significantly invest in real property financing assets.*—If a REIT makes an election described in paragraph (g)(1) of this section and the value of the REIT's real property financing assets, as defined in paragraphs (g)(5) and (6) of this section, at the close of the taxable year is 10 percent or less of the value of the REIT's total assets at the close of the taxable year, as determined under section 856(c)(4)(A), then all of the REIT's assets are treated as assets of an excepted trade or business.

(3) *REITs that significantly invest in real property financing assets.*—If a REIT makes an election described in paragraph (g)(1) of this section and the value of the REIT's real property financing assets, as defined in paragraphs (g)(5) and (6) of this section, at the close of the taxable year is more than 10 percent of the value of the REIT's total assets at the close of the taxable year, as determined under section 856(c)(4)(A), then for allocation of interest expense, interest income, and other items of expense and gross income to excepted and non-excepted trades or businesses, the REIT must apply the rules set forth in § 1.163(j)-10 as modified by paragraph (g)(4) of this section.

(4) *REIT real property assets, interests in partnerships, and shares in other REITs.*—(i) *Real property assets.*—Assets held by a REIT described in paragraph (g)(3) of this section that meet the definition of real property under § 1.856-10 are treated as assets of an excepted trade or business.

(ii) *Partnership interests.*—If a REIT described in paragraph (g)(3) of this section holds an interest in a partnership, in applying the partnership look-through rule described in § 1.163(j)-10(c)(5)(ii)(A)(2), the REIT treats assets of the partnership that meet the definition of real property under § 1.856-10 as assets of an excepted trade or business. This application of the definition of real property under § 1.856-10 does not affect the characterization of the partnership's assets at the partnership level or for any non-REIT partner.

(iii) *Shares in other REITs.*—If a REIT (shareholder REIT) described in paragraph (g)(3) of this section holds an interest in another REIT, then for purposes of applying the allocation rules in § 1.163(j)-10, the partnership look-through rule described in § 1.163(j)-10(c)(5)(ii)(A)(2) applies to the assets of the other REIT (as if the other REIT were a partnership) in determining the extent to which shareholder REIT's adjusted basis in the shares of the other REIT is allocable to an excepted or non-excepted trade or business of shareholder REIT. However, no portion of the adjusted basis of shareholder REIT's shares in the other REIT is allocated to a non-excepted trade or business if all of the other REIT's assets are treated as assets of an excepted trade or business under paragraph (g)(2) of this section. If shareholder REIT does not receive from the other REIT the infor-

mation necessary to determine whether and the extent that the assets of the other REIT are investments in real property financing assets, then shareholder REIT's shares in the other REIT are treated as assets of a non-excepted trade or business under § 1.163(j)-10(c).

(5) *Value of shares in other REITs.*—If a REIT (shareholder REIT) holds shares in another REIT, then for purposes of applying the value tests under paragraphs (g)(2) and (3) of this section, the value of shareholder REIT's real property financing assets includes the portion of the value of shareholder REIT's shares in the other REIT that is attributable to the other REIT's investments in real property financing assets. However, no portion of the value of shareholder REIT's shares in the other REIT is included in the value of shareholder REIT's real property financing assets if all of the other REIT's assets are treated as assets of an excepted trade or business under paragraph (g)(2) of this section. If shareholder REIT does not receive from the other REIT the information necessary to determine whether and the extent that the assets of the other REIT are investments in real property financing assets, then shareholder REIT's shares in the other REIT are treated as real property financing assets for purposes of paragraphs (g)(2) and (3) of this section.

(6) *Real property financing assets.*—For purposes of this paragraph (g), *real property financing assets* include interests, including participation interests, in the following: mortgages, deeds of trust, and installment land contracts; mortgage pass-thru certificates guaranteed by Government National Mortgage Association (GNMA), Federal National Mortgage Association (FNMA), Federal Home Loan Mortgage Corporation (FHLMC), or Canada Mortgage and Housing Corporation (CMHC); REMIC regular interests; other interests in investment trusts classified as trusts under § 301.7701-4(c) of this chapter that represent undivided beneficial ownership in a pool of obligations principally secured by interests in real property and related assets that would be permitted investments if the investment trust were a REMIC; obligations secured by manufactured housing treated as single family residences under section 25(e)(10), without regard to the treatment of the obligations or the properties under state law; and debt instruments issued by publicly offered REITs.

(h) *Special anti-abuse rule for certain real property trades or businesses.*—(1) In *general.* Except as provided in paragraph (h)(2) of this section, a real property trade or business does not constitute a trade or business eligible for an election described in paragraph (b)(1) of this section to be an electing real property trade or business if at least 80 percent, determined by fair market value, of the business's real property is leased, whether or not the arrangement is pursuant to a written lease or pursuant to a service contract or another agreement that is not denominated as a lease, to a trade or business under common control with the real property trade or business. For purposes of this paragraph (h), two trades or businesses are under common control if 50 percent of the direct and indirect ownership of both businesses are held by related parties within the meaning of sections 267(b) and 707(b).

(2) *Exception for certain REITs.*—The special anti-abuse rule in paragraph (h)(1) does not apply to REITs that lease qualified lodging facilities, as defined in section 856(d)(9)(D), and qualified health care properties, as defined in section 856(e)(6)(D).

(i) *Applicability date.*—This section applies to taxable years ending after the date the Treasury decision adopting these regulations as final regulations is published in the **Federal Register**. However, taxpayers and their related parties, within the meaning of sections 267(b) and 707(b)(1), may apply the rules of this section to a taxable year beginning after December 31, 2017, so long as the taxpayers and their related parties consistently apply the rules of the section 163(j) regulations, and if applicable, §§1.263A-9, 1.381(c)(20)-1, 1.382-6, 1.383-1, 1.469-9, 1.882-5, 1.1502-13, 1.1502-21, 1.1502-36, 1.1502-79, 1.1502-91 through 1.1502-99 (to the extent they effectuate the rules of §§1.382-6 and 1.383-1), and 1.1504-4 to those taxable years. [Reg. §1.163(j)-9.]

[Proposed 12-28-2018.]

**[Prop. Reg. §1.163(j)-10]**

**§1.163(j)-10. Allocation of interest expense, interest income, and other items of expense and gross income to an excepted trade or business.**—(a) *Overview.*—(1) *In general.*—(i) *Purposes.*—This section provides the exclusive rules for allocating tax items that are properly allocable to a trade or business between excepted trades or businesses and non-excepted trades or businesses for purposes of section 163(j). The amount of a taxpayer's interest expense that is properly allocable to excepted trades or businesses is not subject to limitation under section 163(j). The amount of a taxpayer's other items of income, gain, deduction, or loss, including interest income, that is properly allocable to excepted trades or businesses is excluded from the calculation of the taxpayer's section 163(j) limitation. See section 163(j)(6) and (j)(8)(A)(i); see also §1.163(j)-1(b)(1)(i)(H), (b)(1)(ii)(F), and (b)(3). The general method of allocation set forth in paragraph (c) of this section is based on the approach that money is fungible and that interest expense is attributable to all activities and property, regardless of any specific purpose for incurring an obligation on which interest is paid. In no event may the amount of interest expense allocated under this section exceed the amount of interest paid or accrued, or treated as paid or accrued, by the taxpayer within the taxable year.

(ii) *Application of section.*—The amount of a taxpayer's tax items properly allocable to a trade or business, other than interest expense and interest income, that is properly allocable to excepted trades or businesses for purposes of section 163(j) is determined as set forth in paragraph (b) of this section. The amount of a taxpayer's interest expense and interest income that is properly allocable to excepted trades or businesses for purposes of section 163(j) generally is determined as set forth in paragraph (c) of this section, except as otherwise provided in paragraph (d) of this section. For purposes of this section, a taxpayer's activities are not treated as a trade or business if those activities do not involve the provision of services or products to a person other than the taxpayer. For example, if a taxpayer engaged in a manufacturing trade or business has in-house legal personnel that provide legal services solely to the taxpayer, the taxpayer is not treated as also engaged in the trade or business of providing legal services.

(2) *Coordination with other rules.*—(i) *In general.*—The rules of this section apply after a taxpayer has determined whether any interest expense or interest income paid, received, or accrued is properly allocable to a trade or business. Similarly, the rules of this section apply to other tax items after a taxpayer has determined whether those items are properly allocable to a trade or business. For instance, a taxpayer must apply §1.163-8T to determine which items of interest expense are investment interest under section 163(d) before applying the rules in paragraph (c) of this section to allocate interest expense between excepted and non-excepted trades or businesses. After determining whether its tax items are properly allocable to a trade or business, a taxpayer that is engaged in both excepted and non-excepted trades or businesses must apply the rules of this section to determine the amount of interest expense that is business interest expense subject to limitation under section 163(j) and to determine which items are included or excluded in computing its section 163(j) limitation.

(ii) *Treatment of investment interest, investment income, and investment expenses of a partnership with a C corporation or tax-exempt corporation as a partner.*—For rules governing the treatment of investment interest, investment income, and investment expenses of a partnership with a C corporation or tax-exempt corporation as a partner, see §§1.163(j)-4(b)(3) and 1.163(j)-6(j).

(3) *Application of allocation rules to foreign corporations and foreign partnerships.*—The rules of this section apply to foreign corporations and foreign partnerships. See §§1.163(j)-7 and 1.163(j)-8.

(4) *Application of allocation rules to members of a consolidated group.*—(i) *In general.*—As provided in §1.163(j)-4(d), the computations required by section 163(j) and the section 163(j) regulations generally are made for a consolidated group on a consolidated basis. In this re-

**Prop. Reg. §1.163(j)-10(a)(4)(i)**

gard, for purposes of applying the allocation rules of this section, all members of a consolidated group are treated as one corporation. Therefore, the rules of this section apply to the activities conducted by the group as if those activities were conducted by a single corporation. For example, the group (rather than a particular member) is treated as engaged in excepted or non-excepted trades or businesses. In the case of intercompany obligations, within the meaning of § 1.1502-13(g)(2)(ii), for purposes of allocating asset basis between excepted and non-excepted trades or businesses, the obligation of the member borrower is not considered an asset of the creditor member. Similarly, intercompany transactions, within the meaning of § 1.1502-13(b)(1)(i), are disregarded for purposes of this section, as are the resulting offsetting items, and property is not treated as used in a trade or business to the extent the use of such property in that trade or business derives from an intercompany transaction. Further, stock of a group member that is owned by another member of the same group is not treated as an asset for purposes of this section, and the transfer of any amount of member stock to a non-member is treated by the group as a transfer of the member's assets proportionate to the amount of member stock transferred. Additionally, stock of a corporation that is not a group member is treated as owned by the group.

(ii) *Application of excepted business percentage to members of a consolidated group.*—After a consolidated group has determined the percentage of the group's interest expense allocable to excepted trades or businesses for the taxable year (and thus not subject to limitation under section 163(j)), this exempt percentage is applied to the interest paid or accrued by each member during the taxable year to any lender that is not a group member. Therefore, except to the extent paragraph (d) of this section (providing rules for certain qualified nonrecourse indebtedness) applies, an identical percentage of the interest paid or accrued by each member of the group to any lender that is not a group member will be treated as allocable to excepted trades or businesses, regardless of whether any particular member actually engaged in an excepted trade or business.

(iii) *Basis in assets transferred in an intercompany transaction.*—For purposes of allocating interest expense and interest income under paragraph (c) of this section, the basis of property does not include any gain or loss realized with respect to the property by another member in an intercompany transaction, as defined in § 1.1502-13(b), whether or not the gain or loss is deferred.

(5) *Tax-exempt organizations.*—For organizations subject to tax under section 511, section 512 and the regulations thereunder determine the rules for allocating all income and expenses among multiple trades or businesses.

(6) [Reserved]

(7) *Examples.*—The following examples illustrate the principles of this paragraph (a).

(i) *Example 1: Items properly allocable to a trade or business*—(A) *Facts.* Individual T operates Business X, a non-excepted trade or business, as a sole proprietor. In Year 1, T pays or accrues $40x of interest expense and receives $100x of gross income with respect to Business X that is not eligible for a section 199A deduction. T borrows money to buy a car for personal use, and T pays or accrues $20x of interest expense with respect to the car loan. T also invests in corporate bonds, and, in Year 1, T receives $50x of interest income on those bonds.

(B) *Analysis.* Under paragraphs (a)(1) and (2) of this section, T must determine which items of income and expense, including items of interest income and interest expense, are properly allocable to a trade or business. T's $100x of gross income and T's $40x of interest expense with respect to Business X are properly allocable to a trade or business. However, the interest expense on T's car loan is personal interest within the meaning of section 163(h)(2) rather than interest properly allocable to a trade or business. Similarly, T's interest income from corporate bonds is not properly allocable to a trade or business because it is interest from investment activity. See section 163(d)(4)(B).

(ii) *Example 2: Intercompany transaction*—(A) *Facts.* S is a member of a consolidated group of which P is the common parent. P conducts an electing real property trade or business (Business X), and S conducts a non-excepted trade or business (Business Y). P leases Building V (which P owns) to S for use in Business Y.

(B) *Analysis.* Under paragraph (a)(4)(i) of this section, a consolidated group is treated as a single corporation for purposes of applying the allocation rules of this section, and the consolidated group (rather than a particular member of the group) is treated as engaged in excepted and non-excepted trades or businesses. Thus, intercompany transactions are disregarded for purposes of this section. As a result, the lease of Building V by P to S is disregarded. Moreover, because Building V is used in Business Y, basis in this asset is allocated to Business Y rather than Business X for purposes of these allocation rules, regardless of which member (P or S) owns the building.

(b) *Allocation of tax items other than interest expense and interest income.*—(1) *In general.*—For purposes of calculating ATI, tax items other than interest expense and interest income are allocated to a particular trade or business in the manner described in this paragraph (b). It is not necessary to allocate items under this paragraph (b) for purposes of calculating ATI if all of the taxpayer's items subject to allocation under this paragraph (b) are allocable to excepted trades or businesses, or if all of those items are allocable to non-excepted trades or businesses.

**Prop. Reg. § 1.163(j)-10(a)(4)(ii)**

(2) *Gross income other than dividends and interest income.*—A taxpayer's gross income other than dividends and interest income is allocated to the trade or business that generated the gross income.

(3) *Dividends.*—(i) *Look-through rule.*—If a taxpayer receives a dividend, within the meaning of section 316, that is not investment income, within the meaning of section 163(d), and if the taxpayer looks through to the assets of the payor corporation under paragraph (c)(5)(ii) of this section for the taxable year, then, solely for purposes of allocating amounts received as a dividend during the taxable year to excepted or non-excepted trades or businesses under this paragraph (b), the dividend income is treated as allocable to excepted or non-excepted trades or businesses based upon the relative amounts of the payor corporation's adjusted basis in the assets used in its trades or businesses, determined pursuant to paragraph (c) of this section. If at least 90 percent of the payor corporation's adjusted basis in its assets during the taxable year, determined pursuant to paragraph (c) of this section, is allocable to either excepted trades or businesses or to non-excepted trades or businesses, all of the taxpayer's dividend income from the payor corporation for the taxable year is treated as allocable to either excepted or non-excepted trades or businesses, respectively.

(ii) *Inapplicability of the look-through rule.*—If a taxpayer receives a dividend that is not investment income, within the meaning of section 163(d), and if the taxpayer does not look through to the assets of the payor corporation under paragraph (c)(5)(ii) of this section for the taxable year, then the taxpayer must treat the dividend as allocable to a non-excepted trade or business.

(4) *Gain or loss from the disposition of non-consolidated C corporation stock, partnership interests, or S corporation stock.*—(i) *Non-consolidated C corporations.*—If a taxpayer recognizes gain or loss upon the disposition of stock in a non-consolidated C corporation that is not property held for investment, within the meaning of section 163(d)(5), and if the taxpayer looks through to the assets of the C corporation under paragraph (c)(5)(ii) of this section for the taxable year, then the taxpayer must allocate gain or loss from the disposition of stock to excepted or non-excepted trades or businesses based upon the relative amounts of the corporation's adjusted basis in the assets used in its trades or businesses, determined pursuant to paragraph (c) of this section. However, if a taxpayer recognizes gain or loss upon the disposition of stock in a non-consolidated C corporation that is not property held for investment, within the meaning of section 163(d)(5), and if the taxpayer does not look through to the assets of the C corporation under paragraph (c)(5)(ii) of this section for the taxable year, then the taxpayer must treat the gain or loss from the disposition of stock as allocable to

a non-excepted trade or business. For rules governing the transfer of stock of a member of a consolidated group, see paragraph (a)(4)(i) of this section.

(ii) *Partnerships and S corporations.*—(A) If a taxpayer recognizes gain or loss upon the disposition of interests in a partnership or stock in an S corporation that owns:

(1) Non-excepted assets and excepted assets;

(2) Investment assets; or

(3) Both;

(B) The taxpayer determines a proportionate share of the amount properly allocable to a non-excepted trade or business in accordance with the allocation rules set forth in paragraph (c)(5)(ii)(A) or (c)(5)(ii)(B)(3) of this section, as appropriate, and includes such proportionate share of gain or loss in the taxpayer's ATI. This rule also applies to tiered passthrough entities, as defined in § 1.163(j)-7(f)(13), by looking through each passthrough entity tier (for example, an S corporation that is the partner of the highest-tier partnership would look through each lower-tier partnership), subject to paragraph (c)(5)(ii)(D) of this section. With respect to a partner that is a C corporation or tax-exempt corporation, a partnership's investment assets are taken into account and treated as non-excepted trade or business assets.

(5) *Expenses, losses, and other deductions.*—(i) *Expenses, losses, and other deductions that are definitely related to a trade or business.*—Expenses (other than interest expense), losses, and other deductions (collectively, *deductions* for purposes of this paragraph (b)(5)) that are definitely related to a trade or business are allocable to the trade or business to which they relate. A deduction is considered definitely related to a trade or business if the item giving rise to the deduction is incurred as a result of, or incident to, an activity of the trade or business or in connection with property used in the trade or business (see § 1.861-8(b)(2)). If a deduction is definitely related to one or more excepted trades or businesses and one or more non-excepted trades or businesses, the deduction is apportioned between the excepted and non-excepted trades or businesses based upon the relative amounts of the taxpayer's adjusted basis in the assets used in those trades or businesses, as determined under paragraph (c) of this section.

(ii) *Other deductions.*—Deductions that are not described in paragraph (b)(5)(i) of this section are ratably apportioned to all gross income.

(6) *Treatment of certain investment items of a partnership with a C corporation partner.*—Any investment income or investment expenses that a partnership receives, pays, or accrues and that is treated as properly allocable to a trade or business of a C corporation partner under § 1.163(j)-4(b)(3)(i) is treated as properly allocable

**Prop. Reg. § 1.163(j)-10(b)(6)**

to a non-excepted trade or business of the C corporation partner.

(7) *Example: Allocation of income and expense.*—The following example illustrates the principles of this paragraph (b):

(i) *Facts.* T conducts an electing real property trade or business (Business Y), which is an excepted trade or business. T also operates a lumber yard (Business Z), which is a non-excepted trade or business. In Year 1, T receives $100x of gross rental income from real property leasing activities. T also pays or accrues $60x of expenses in connection with its real property leasing activities and $20x of legal services performed on behalf of both Business Y and Business Z. T receives $60x of gross income from lumber yard customers and pays or accrues $50x of expenses related to the lumber yard business. For purposes of expense allocations under paragraphs (b) and (c) of this section, T has $240x of adjusted basis in its Business Y assets and $80x of adjusted basis in its Business Z assets.

(ii) *Analysis.* Under paragraph (b)(2) of this section, for Year 1, $100x of rental income is allocated to Business Y, and $60x of income from lumber yard customers is allocated to Business Z. Under paragraph (b)(5)(i) of this section, $60x of expenses paid or accrued in connection with real property leasing activities are allocated to Business Y, and $50x of expenses related to the lumber yard are allocated to Business Z. The $20x of remaining expenses for legal services performed on behalf of both Business Y and Business Z are allocated according to the relative amounts of T's basis in the assets used in each business. The total amount of T's basis in the assets used in Businesses Y and Z is $320x, of which 75 percent ($240x / $320x) is used in Business Y and 25 percent ($80x / $320x) is used in Business Z. Accordingly, $15x of the expenses for legal services are allocated to Business Y and $5x are allocated to Business Z.

(c) *Allocating interest expense and interest income that is properly allocable to a trade or business.*— (1) *General rule.*—(i) *In general.*—Except as otherwise provided in this section, the amount of a taxpayer's interest expense and interest income that is properly allocable to a trade or business is allocated to the taxpayer's excepted or non-excepted trades or businesses for purposes of section 163(j) based upon the relative amounts of the taxpayer's adjusted basis in the assets, as determined under paragraph (c)(5) of this section, used in its excepted or non-excepted trades or businesses. The taxpayer must determine the adjusted basis in its assets as of the close of each determination date, as defined in paragraph (c)(6) of this section, in the taxable year and average those amounts to determine the relative amounts of asset basis for its excepted and non-excepted trades or businesses for that year. It is not necessary to allocate interest expense or interest income under this paragraph (c) for purposes of determining a taxpayer's business interest expense and business interest income if

all of the taxpayer's interest income and expense is allocable to excepted trades or businesses (in which case the taxpayer is not subject to the section 163(j) limitation) or if all of the taxpayer's interest income and expense is allocable to non-excepted trades or businesses.

(ii) *De minimis exception.*—If 90 percent or more of the taxpayer's basis in its assets for the taxable year is allocable to either excepted or non-excepted trades or businesses pursuant to this paragraph (c), then all of the taxpayer's interest expense and interest income for that year that is properly allocable to a trade or business is treated as allocable to either excepted or non-excepted trades or businesses, respectively.

(2) *Example.*—The following example illustrates the principles of paragraph (c)(1) of this section: T is a calendar-year C corporation engaged in an electing real property trade or business, the business of selling wine, and the business of selling hand-carved wooden furniture. In Year 1, T has $100x of interest expense that is deductible except for the potential application of section 163(j). Based upon determinations made on the determination dates of March 31, June 30, September 30, and December 31, T's average adjusted basis in the assets used in the electing real property trade or business (an excepted trade or business) in Year 1 is $800x, and T's total average adjusted basis in the assets used in the other two businesses in Year 1 is $200x. Thus, $80x (($800x / ($800x + $200x)) x $100x) of T's interest expense for Year 1 is allocable to T's electing real property trade or business and is not business interest expense subject to limitation under section 163(j). The remaining $20x of T's interest expense is business interest expense for Year 1 that is subject to limitation under section 163(j).

(3) *Asset used in more than one trade or business.*—(i) *General rule.*—If an asset is used in more than one trade or business during a determination period, as defined in paragraph (c)(6) of this section, the taxpayer's adjusted basis in the asset is allocated to each trade or business using the permissible methodology under this paragraph (c)(3) that most reasonably reflects the use of the asset in each trade or business during that determination period. An allocation methodology most reasonably reflects the use of the asset in each trade or business if it most properly reflects the proportionate benefit derived from the use of the asset in each trade or business. If none of the permissible methodologies set forth in paragraph (c)(3)(ii) of this section reasonably reflects the use of the asset in each trade or business, the taxpayer's basis in the asset is not taken into account for purposes of this paragraph (c).

(ii) *Permissible methodologies for allocating asset basis between or among two or more trades or businesses.*—Subject to the special rules in paragraphs (c)(3)(iii) and (c)(5) of this section, a taxpayer's basis in an asset used in two or more trades or businesses during a determination period may be allocated to those trades or businesses based upon—

(A) The relative amounts of gross income that an asset generates, has generated, or may reasonably be expected to generate, within the meaning of § 1.861-9T(g)(3), with respect to the trades or businesses;

(B) If the asset is land or an inherently permanent structure, the relative amounts of physical space used by the trades or businesses; or

(C) If the trades or businesses generate the same unit of output, the relative amounts of output of those trades or businesses (for example, if an asset is used in two trades or businesses, one of which is an excepted regulated utility trade or business, and the other of which is a non-excepted regulated utility trade or business, the taxpayer may allocate basis in the asset based upon the relative amounts of kilowatt-hours generated by each trade or business).

(iii) *Special rules.—(A) Consistent allocation methodologies.—(1) In general.*—Except as otherwise provided in paragraph (c)(3)(iii)(A)(2) of this section, a taxpayer may not vary its allocation methodology from one determination period to the next within a taxable year or from one taxable year to the next.

(2) *Consent to change allocation methodology.*—If a taxpayer determines that a different allocation methodology properly reflects the proportionate benefit derived from the use of assets in its trades or businesses, the taxpayer may change its method of allocation under paragraphs (c)(3)(i) and (ii) of this section with the consent of the Commissioner. To obtain consent, a taxpayer must submit a request for a letter ruling under the applicable administrative procedures, and consent only will be granted in extraordinary circumstances.

(B) *De minimis exceptions.—(1) De minimis amount of gross income from trades or businesses.*—If at least 90 percent of gross income that an asset generates, has generated, or may reasonably be expected to generate, within the meaning of § 1.861-9T(g)(3), during a determination period is with respect to either excepted trades or businesses or non-excepted trades or businesses, the taxpayer's entire basis in the asset for the determination period must be allocated to either excepted or non-excepted trades or businesses, respectively.

(2) *De minimis amount of asset basis allocable to a trade or business.*—If 90 percent or more of the taxpayer's basis in an asset would be allocated to either excepted trades or businesses or non-excepted trades or businesses during a determination period pursuant to this paragraph (c)(3), the taxpayer's entire basis in the asset for the determination period must be allocated to either excepted or non-excepted trades or businesses, respectively.

(C) *Allocations of excepted regulated utility trades or businesses.—(1) In general.*—Except as provided in the de minimis rule in paragraph (c)(3)(iii)(C)(3) of this section, if a taxpayer is engaged in the trade or business of the furnishing or sale of items described in § 1.163(j)-1(b)(13)(i)(A), the taxpayer is engaged in an excepted regulated utility trade or business only to the extent the rates for the items furnished and sold are described in § 1.163(j)-1(b)(13)(i)(B). Thus, for example, electricity sold at market rates rather than on a cost of service and rate of return basis must be treated as electricity sold by a non-excepted regulated utility trade or business. The taxpayer must allocate under this paragraph (c) the basis of assets used in the utility trade or business between its excepted and non-excepted trades or businesses.

(2) *Permissible method for allocating asset basis for utility trades or businesses.*—In the case of a utility trade or business described in paragraph (c)(3)(iii)(C)(1) of this section, and except as provided in the de minimis rule in paragraph (c)(3)(iii)(C)(3) of this section, the method described in paragraph (c)(3)(ii)(C) of this section is the only permissible method for allocating the taxpayer's basis in assets used in the trade or business between the taxpayer's excepted and non-excepted trades or businesses of selling or furnishing the items described in § 1.163(j)-1(b)(13)(i)(A).

(3) *De minimis rule for excepted utility trades or businesses.*—If a taxpayer is engaged in a utility trade or business described in paragraph (c)(3)(iii)(C)(1) of this section, and if more than 90 percent of the items described in § 1.163(j)-1(b)(13)(i)(A) are furnished or sold at rates determined in the manner described in § 1.163(j)-1(b)(13)(i)(B), the taxpayer's entire trade or business is an excepted regulated utility trade or business, and paragraph (c)(3)(iii)(C)(2) of this section does not apply.

(4) *Example.*—The following example illustrates the principles of this paragraph (c)(3)(iii)(C):

(i) *Facts.* X, a C corporation, is engaged in the trade or business of generating electrical energy. During each determination period in the taxable year, 80 percent of the kilowatts generated in the electricity generation trade or business is sold at rates established by a public utility commission on a rate of return basis. The remaining 20 percent of the kilowatts is sold on the wholesale markets at rates not established on a rate of return basis or by the governing or ratemaking body of an electric cooperative. None of the assets used in X's utility generation trade or business are used in any other trade or business.

**Prop. Reg. § 1.163(j)-10(c)(3)(iii)(C)(4)**

*(ii) Analysis.* For purposes of section 163(j), under paragraph (c)(3)(iii)(C)(*1*) of this section, 80 percent of X's electricity generation business is an excepted regulated utility trade or business, and the remaining 20 percent of X's business is a non-excepted utility trade or business. Under paragraph (c)(3)(iii)(C)(*2*) of this section, X must allocate 80 percent of the basis of the assets used in its utility business to excepted trades or business and the remaining 20 percent of the basis in its assets to non-excepted trades or businesses.

*(4) Disallowed business interest expense carryforwards; floor plan financing interest expense.*—Disallowed business interest expense carryforwards (which were treated as allocable to a non-excepted trade or business in a prior taxable year) are not re-allocated between non-excepted and excepted trades or businesses in a succeeding taxable year. Instead, the carryforwards continue to be treated as allocable to a non-excepted trade or business. Floor plan financing interest expense also is not subject to allocation between excepted and non-excepted trades or businesses (see § 1.163(j)-1(b)(17)) and is always treated as allocable to non-excepted trades or businesses.

*(5) Additional rules relating to basis.*—(i) *Calculation of adjusted basis.*—(A) *Non-depreciable property other than land.*—Except as otherwise provided in paragraph (c)(5)(i)(E) of this section, for purposes of this section, the adjusted basis of an asset other than land with respect to which no deduction is allowable under section 167, section 168 of the Internal Revenue Code of 1954 (former section 168), or section 197, as applicable, is the adjusted basis of the asset for determining gain or loss from the sale or other disposition of that asset as provided in § 1.1011-1. Self-created intangible assets are not taken into account for purposes of this paragraph (c).

(B) *Depreciable property other than inherently permanent structures.*—For purposes of this section, the adjusted basis of any tangible asset with respect to which a deduction is allowable under section 167, other than inherently permanent structures, is determined by using the alternative depreciation system under section 168(g) before any application of the additional first-year depreciation deduction (for example, under section 168(k) or (m)), and the adjusted basis of any tangible asset with respect to which a deduction is allowable under former section 168, other than inherently permanent structures, is determined by using the taxpayer's method of computing depreciation for the asset under former section 168. The depreciation deduction with respect to the property described in this paragraph (c)(5)(i)(B) is allocated ratably to each day during the period in the taxable year to which the depreciation relates.

(C) *Special rule for land and inherently permanent structures.*—Except as otherwise pro-

vided in paragraph (c)(5)(i)(E) of this section, for purposes of this section, the adjusted basis of any asset that is land, including nondepreciable improvements to land, or an inherently permanent structure is its unadjusted basis.

(D) *Depreciable or amortizable intangible property and depreciable income forecast method property.*—For purposes of this section, the adjusted basis of any intangible asset with respect to which a deduction is allowable under section 167 or 197, as applicable, is determined in accordance with section 167 or 197, as applicable, and the adjusted basis of any asset described in section 167(g)(6) for which the deduction allowable under section 167 is determined by the taxpayer under section 167(g), is determined in accordance with section 167(g). The depreciation or amortization deduction with respect to the property described in this paragraph (c)(5)(i)(D) is allocated ratably to each day during the period in the taxable year to which the depreciation or amortization relates.

(E) *Assets not yet used in a trade or business.*—Assets that have been acquired or that are under development but that are not yet used in a trade or business are not taken into account for purposes of this paragraph (c). For example, construction works in progress (such as buildings, airplanes, or ships) are not taken into account for purposes of this paragraph (c). Similarly, land acquired by a taxpayer for construction of a building by the taxpayer to be used in a trade or business is not taken into account for purposes of this paragraph (c) until the building is placed in service. This rule does not apply to interests in a partnership or stock in a corporation.

(F) *Trusts established to fund specific liabilities.*—Trusts required by law to fund specific liabilities (for example, pension trusts and plant decommissioning trusts) are not taken into account for purposes of this paragraph (c).

(G) *Inherently permanent structure.*—For purposes of this section, the term *inherently permanent structure* has the meaning provided in § 1.856-10(d)(2).

(ii) *Partnership interests; stock in non-consolidated domestic corporations.*—(A) *Partnership interests.*—(*1*) *Calculation of asset basis.*—For purposes of this section, a partner's interest in a partnership is treated as an asset of the partner. For these purposes, the partner's adjusted basis in a partnership interest is reduced, but not below zero, by the partner's share of partnership liabilities, as determined under section 752, and is further reduced as provided in paragraph (c)(5)(ii)(A)(*2*)(*iii*) of this section.

(*2*) *Allocation of asset basis.*—(*i*) *In general.*—For purposes of determining the extent to which a partner's adjusted basis in its partnership interest is allocable to an excepted or non-excepted trade or business, the partner may look through to such partner's share of the partnership's basis in the partnership's assets, taking into account any adjustments under sections 734(b) and 743(b), and adjusted to the extent required under paragraph (d)(4) of this section, except as otherwise provided in paragraph (c)(5)(ii)(D) of this section. For purposes of the preceding sentence, such partner's share of partnership assets is determined using a reasonable method taking into account special allocations under section 704(b). Notwithstanding paragraph (c)(7) of this section, if a partner's direct and indirect interest in a partnership is greater than or equal to 80 percent of the partnership's capital or profits, the partner must apply the rules in this paragraph (c)(5)(ii)(A) to look through to the partnership's basis in the partnership's assets.

(*ii*) *De minimis rule.*—If, after applying paragraph (c)(5)(ii)(A)(2)(*iii*) of this section, at least 90 percent of a partner's share of a partnership's basis in its assets (including adjustments under sections 734(b) and 743(b)) is allocable to either excepted trades or businesses or non-excepted trades or businesses, without regard to assets not properly allocable to a trade or business, the partner's entire basis in its partnership interest is treated as allocable to either excepted or non-excepted trades or businesses, respectively. For purposes of the preceding sentence, such partner's share of partnership assets is determined using a reasonable method taking into account special allocations under section 704(b).

(*iii*) *Partnership assets not properly allocable to a trade or business.*—For purposes of applying paragraphs (c)(5)(ii)(A)(2)(*i*) and (*ii*) of this section with respect to a partner that is a C corporation or tax-exempt corporation, such partner's share of a partnership's assets that are not properly allocable to a trade or business is treated as properly allocable to an excepted or non-excepted trade or business with respect to such partner in the same manner that such assets would be treated if held directly by such partner. With respect to a partner other than a C corporation or tax-exempt corporation, a partnership's assets that are not properly allocable to a trade or business are treated as neither excepted nor non-excepted trade or business assets, and such partner's adjusted basis in its partnership interest is reduced by that partner's share of the partnership's asset basis with respect to those assets. For purposes of this paragraph (c)(5)(ii)(A)(2)(*iii*), such partner's share of a partnership's assets is determined under a reasonable method taking into account special allocations under section 704(b).

(*iv*) *Inapplicability of partnership look-through rule.*—If a partner, other than a C corporation or a tax-exempt corporation, chooses not to look through to the partnership's basis in the partnership's assets under paragraph (c)(5)(ii)(A)(2)(*i*) of this section or is precluded by paragraph (c)(5)(ii)(D) of this section from apply-

ing such partnership look-through rule, the partner generally will treat its basis in the partnership interest as either an asset held for investment or a non-excepted trade or business asset as determined under section 163(d). If a partner that is a C corporation or a tax-exempt corporation chooses not to look through to the partnership's basis in the partnership's assets under paragraph (c)(5)(ii)(A)(2)(*i*) of this section or is precluded by paragraph (c)(5)(ii)(D) of this section from applying such partnership look-through rule, the taxpayer must treat its entire basis in the partnership interest as allocable to a non-excepted trade or business.

(B) *Stock in non-consolidated domestic corporations.*—(*1*) *In general.*—For purposes of this section, if a taxpayer owns stock in a domestic C corporation that is not a member of the taxpayer's consolidated group, or if the taxpayer owns stock in an S corporation, the stock is treated as an asset of the taxpayer.

(*2*) *Domestic non-consolidated C corporations.*—(*i*) *Allocation of asset basis.*—If a shareholder satisfies the minimum ownership threshold in paragraph (c)(7) of this section, then, for purposes of determining the extent to which the shareholder's basis in its stock in the domestic non-consolidated C corporation is allocable to an excepted or non-excepted trade or business, the shareholder must look through to the corporation's basis in the corporation's assets, adjusted to the extent required under paragraph (d)(4) of this section, except as otherwise provided in paragraph (c)(5)(ii)(D) of this section.

(*ii*) *De minimis rule.*—If at least 90 percent of the domestic non-consolidated C corporation's basis in the corporation's assets is allocable to either excepted trades or businesses or non-excepted trades or businesses, the shareholder's entire interest in the corporation's stock is treated as allocable to either excepted or non-excepted trades or businesses, respectively.

(*iii*) *Inapplicability of corporate look-through rule.*—If a shareholder other than a C corporation or a tax-exempt corporation does not satisfy the minimum ownership threshold in paragraph (c)(7) of this section or is precluded by paragraph (c)(5)(ii)(D) of this section from applying the corporation look-through rule of paragraph (c)(5)(ii)(B)(2)(*i*) of this section, the shareholder generally will treat its entire basis in the corporation's stock as an asset held for investment. If a shareholder that is a C corporation or a tax-exempt corporation does not satisfy the minimum ownership threshold in paragraph (c)(7) of this section or is precluded by paragraph (c)(5)(ii)(D) of this section from applying the corporation look-through rule of paragraph (c)(5)(ii)(B)(2)(*i*) of this section, the shareholder must treat its entire basis in the corporation's stock as allocable to a non-excepted trade or business.

**Prop. Reg. §1.163(j)-10(c)(5)(ii)(B)(2)(iii)**

*(3) S corporations.—(i) Calculation of asset basis.*—For purposes of this section, a shareholder's share of stock in an S corporation is treated as an asset of the shareholder. Additionally, for these purposes, the shareholder's adjusted basis in a share of S corporation stock is adjusted to take into account the modifications in paragraph (c)(5)(i)(A) of this section with respect to the assets of the S corporation (for example, a shareholder's adjusted basis in its S corporation stock is increased by the shareholder's share of depreciation with respect to an inherently permanent structure owned by the S corporation).

*(ii) Allocation of asset basis.*—For purposes of determining the extent to which a shareholder's basis in its stock of an S corporation is allocable to an excepted or non-excepted trade or business, the shareholder may look through to such shareholder's share of the S corporation's basis in the S corporation's assets, allocated on a pro rata basis, adjusted to the extent required under paragraph (d)(4) of this section, except as otherwise provided in paragraph (c)(5)(ii)(D) of this section. Notwithstanding paragraph (c)(7) of this section, if a shareholder's direct and indirect interest in an S corporation is greater than or equal to 80 percent of the S corporation's stock by vote and value, the shareholder must apply the rules in this paragraph (c)(5)(ii)(B)(3) to look through to the S corporation's basis in the S corporation's assets.

*(iii) De minimis rule.*—If at least 90 percent of a shareholder's share of an S corporation's basis in its assets is allocable to either excepted trades or businesses or non-excepted trades or businesses, the shareholder's entire basis in its S corporation stock is treated as allocable to either excepted or non-excepted trades or businesses, respectively.

*(iv) Inapplicability of S corporation look-through rule.*—If a shareholder chooses not to look through to the S corporation's basis in the S corporation's assets under paragraph (c)(5)(ii)(B)(3)(*ii*) of this section or is precluded by paragraph (c)(5)(ii)(D) of this section from applying such S corporation look-through rule, the shareholder generally will treat its basis in the S corporation stock as either an asset held for investment or a non-excepted trade or business asset as determined under section 163(d).

*(C) Stock in CFCs.*—The rules applicable to domestic non-consolidated C corporations in paragraph (c)(5)(ii)(B) of this section also apply to CFCs.

*(D) Inapplicability of look-through rule to partnerships or non-consolidated corporations to which the small business exemption applies.*—A taxpayer may not apply the look-through rules in paragraphs (b)(3) and (c)(5)(ii)(A), (B), and (C) of this section to a partnership, S corporation, or non-consolidated corporation that is eligible for the small business exemption under section 163(j)(3) and § 1.163(j)-2(d)(1).

*(E) Tiered entities.*—If a taxpayer applies the look-through rules of this paragraph (c)(5)(ii), the taxpayer must do so for all lower-tier entities with respect to which the taxpayer satisfies, directly or indirectly, the minimum ownership threshold in paragraph (c)(7) of this section, subject to the limitation in paragraph (c)(5)(ii)(D) of this section, beginning with the lowest-tier entity.

*(iii) Cash and cash equivalents and customer receivables.*—Except as otherwise provided in paragraph (d)(2) of this section, a taxpayer's basis in its cash and cash equivalents and customer receivables is not taken into account for purposes of this paragraph (c). This rule also applies to a lower-tier entity if a taxpayer looks through to the assets of that entity under paragraph (c)(5)(ii) of this section. For purposes of this paragraph (c)(5)(iii), the term *cash and cash equivalents* includes cash, foreign currency, commercial paper, any interest in an investment company registered under the Investment Company Act of 1940 (1940 Act) and regulated as a money market fund under 17 CFR 270.2a-7 (Rule 2a-7 under the 1940 Act), any obligation of a government, and any derivative that is substantially secured by an obligation of a government, or any similar asset. For purposes of this paragraph (c)(5)(iii), a *derivative* is a derivative described in section 59A(h)(4)(A), without regard to section 59A(h)(4)(C). For purposes of this paragraph (c)(5)(iii), the term *government* means the United States or any agency or instrumentality of the United States; a State or any political subdivision thereof, including the District of Columbia and any possession or territory of the United States, within the meaning of section 103 and § 1.103-1; or any foreign government, any political subdivision of a foreign government, or any wholly owned agency or instrumentality of any one of the foregoing within the meaning of § 1.1471-6(b).

*(iv) Deemed asset sale.*—Solely for purposes of determining the amount of basis allocable to excepted and non-excepted trades or businesses under this section, an election under section 336, 338, or 754, as applicable, is deemed to have been made for any acquisition of corporate stock or partnership interests with respect to which the taxpayer demonstrates to the satisfaction of the Commissioner, in the information statement required by paragraph (c)(6)(iii)(B) of this section, that the taxpayer was eligible to make an election but was actually or effectively precluded from doing so by a regulatory agency with respect to an excepted regulated utility trade or business. Any additional basis taken into account under this rule is reduced ratably over a 15-year period beginning with the month of the acquisition and is not subject to the anti-abuse rule in paragraph (c)(8) of this section.

**Prop. Reg. § 1.163(j)-10(c)(5)(ii)(B)(3)(i)**

*(v) Other adjustments.*—The Commissioner may make appropriate adjustments to prevent a taxpayer from intentionally and artificially increasing its basis in assets attributable to an excepted trade or business.

*(6) Determination dates; determination periods; reporting requirements.*—(i) *Definitions.*—For purposes of this section, the term *determination date* means the last day of each quarter of the taxpayer's taxable year (and the last day of the taxpayer's taxable year, if the taxpayer has a short taxable year), and the term *determination period* means the period beginning the day after one determination date and ending on the next determination date.

*(ii) Application of look-through rules.*—If a taxpayer that applies the look-through rules of paragraph (c)(5)(ii) of this section has a different taxable year than the partnership or non-consolidated corporation to which the taxpayer is applying those rules, then, for purposes of this paragraph (c)(6), the taxpayer must use the most recent quarterly figures from the partnership or non-consolidated corporation. For example, assume that PS1 is a partnership with a May 31 taxable year, and that C (a calendar-year C corporation) is a partner whose ownership interest satisfies the ownership threshold in paragraph (c)(7) of this section. PS1's determination dates are February 28, May 31, August 31, and November 30. In turn, C's determination dates are March 31, June 30, September 30, and December 31. If C looks through to PS1's basis in its assets under paragraph (c)(5)(ii) of this section, then, for purposes of determining the amount of C's asset basis that is attributable to its excepted and non-excepted businesses on March 31, C must use PS1's asset basis calculations for February 28.

*(iii) Reporting requirements.*—(A) *Books and records.*—A taxpayer must maintain books of account and other records and data as necessary to substantiate the taxpayer's use of an asset in an excepted trade or business and to substantiate the adjustments to asset basis for purposes of applying paragraph (c) of this section. One indication demonstrating that a particular asset is used in a particular trade or business is if the taxpayer maintains separate books and records for all of its excepted and non-excepted trades or businesses, and can show the asset in the books and records of a particular excepted or non-excepted trade or business. For rules governing record retention, see § 1.6001-1.

*(B) Information statement.*—Except as otherwise provided in publications, forms, instructions, or other guidance, each taxpayer that is making an allocation under this paragraph (c) must prepare a statement containing the information described in this paragraph (c)(6)(iii) and must attach the statement to its timely filed Federal income tax return for the taxable year. The statement, which must be titled "Section 163(j) Asset Basis Calculations," must include the following information:

*(1)* The taxpayer's adjusted basis in the assets used in its excepted and non-excepted businesses, determined on a quarterly basis as set forth in this section, including detailed information for the different groups of assets identified in paragraphs (c)(5)(i), (c)(5)(ii), and (d) of this section;

*(2)* The determination dates on which asset basis was measured during the taxable year;

*(3)* The names and taxpayer identification numbers (TINs) of all entities for which basis information is being provided, including partnerships and corporations if the taxpayer that owns an interest in a partnership or corporation looks through to the partnership's or corporation's basis in the partnership's or corporation's assets under paragraph (c)(5)(ii) of this section. If the taxpayer is a member of a consolidated group, the name and TIN of the agent for the group, as defined in § 1.1502-77, must be provided, but the taxpayer need not provide the names and TINs of all other consolidated group members;

*(4)* Asset basis information for corporations or partnerships if the taxpayer looks through to the corporation's or partnership's basis in the corporation's or partnership's assets under paragraph (c)(5)(ii) of this section; and

*(5)* A summary of the method or methods used to determine asset basis in property used in both excepted and non-excepted businesses, as well as information regarding any deemed sale under paragraph (c)(5)(iv) of this section.

*(iv) Failure to file statement.*—If a taxpayer fails to file the statement described in paragraph (c)(6)(iii) of this section or files a statement that does not comply with the requirements of paragraph (c)(6)(iii) of this section, the Commissioner may treat the taxpayer as if all of its interest expense is properly allocable to a non-excepted trade or business, unless the taxpayer shows that there was reasonable cause for failing to comply with, and the taxpayer acted in good faith with respect to, the requirements of paragraph (c)(6)(iii) of this section, taking into account all pertinent facts and circumstances.

*(7) Ownership threshold for look-through rules.*—(i) *Corporations.*—(A) *Asset basis.*—A shareholder must look through to the assets of a non-consolidated domestic C corporation or a CFC under paragraph (c)(5)(ii) of this section for purposes of allocating the shareholder's basis in its stock in the corporation between excepted and non-excepted trades or businesses if the shareholder's direct and indirect interest in the corporation satisfies the ownership requirements of section 1504(a)(2). A shareholder may look through to the assets of an S corporation under paragraph (c)(5)(ii) of this section for purposes of allocating the shareholder's basis in its stock in the S corporation between excepted and non-excepted trades or businesses regardless of the

shareholder's direct and indirect interest in the S corporation.

(B) *Dividends.*—A shareholder must look through to the activities of a non-consolidated domestic C corporation or a CFC under paragraph (b)(3) of this section if the shareholder's direct and indirect interest in the corporation satisfies the ownership requirements of section 1504(a)(2). A shareholder may look through to the activities of an S corporation under paragraph (b)(3) of this section regardless of the shareholder's direct and indirect interest in the S corporation.

(ii) *Partnerships.*—A partner may look through to the assets of a partnership under paragraph (c)(5)(ii) of this section for purposes of allocating the partner's basis in its partnership interest between excepted and non-excepted trades or businesses regardless of the partner's direct and indirect interest in the partnership.

(iii) *Inapplicability of look-through rule.*— For circumstances in which a taxpayer that satisfies the ownership threshold in this paragraph (c)(7) may not apply the look-through rules in paragraphs (b)(3) and (c)(5)(ii) of this section, see paragraph (c)(5)(ii)(D) of this section.

(8) *Anti-abuse rule.*—If a principal purpose for the acquisition, disposition, or change in use of an asset was to artificially shift the amount of basis allocable to excepted or non-excepted trades or businesses on a determination date, the additional basis or change in use will not be taken into account for purposes of this section. For example, if an asset is used in a non-excepted trade or business for most of the taxable year, and if the taxpayer begins using the asset in an excepted trade or business towards the end of the year with a principal purpose of shifting the amount of basis in the asset that is allocable to the excepted trade or business, the change in use is disregarded for purposes of this section. A purpose may be a principal purpose even though it is outweighed by other purposes (taken together or separately). In determining whether a taxpayer has a principal purpose described in this paragraph (c)(8), factors to be considered include, for example, the following: the business purpose for the acquisition, disposition, or change in use; the length of time the asset was used in a trade or business; whether the asset was acquired from a related person; and whether the taxpayer's aggregate basis in its assets increased or decreased temporarily on or around a determination date. A principal purpose is presumed to be present in any case in which the acquisition, disposition, or change in use lacks a substantial business purpose and increases the taxpayer's basis in its assets used in its excepted trades or businesses by more than 10 percent during the taxable year.

(d) *Direct allocations.*—(1) *In general.*—For purposes of this section, a taxpayer with qualified nonrecourse indebtedness, within the meaning of §1.861-10T(b), must directly allocate interest expense from the indebtedness to the taxpayer's assets in the manner and to the extent provided in §1.861-10T(b).

(2) *Financial services entities.*—For purposes of this section, a taxpayer that is engaged in the trade or business of banking, within the meaning of section 581, insurance, financing, or a similar business that derives active financing income as described in §1.904-4(e)(2) (an active financing business) must directly allocate interest expense and interest income from that business to the taxpayer's assets used in that business. The special rule for cash and cash equivalents in paragraph (c)(5)(iii) of this section does not apply to an entity that qualifies as a financial services entity as described in §1.904-4(e)(3).

(3) *Assets used in more than one trade or business.*—If an asset is used in more than one trade or business, the taxpayer must apply the rules in paragraph (c)(3) of this section to determine the extent to which interest that is directly allocated under this paragraph (d) is allocable to excepted or non-excepted trades or businesses.

(4) *Adjustments to basis of assets to account for direct allocations.*—In determining the amount of a taxpayer's basis in the assets used in its excepted and non-excepted trades or businesses for purposes of paragraph (c) of this section, adjustments must be made to reflect direct allocations under this paragraph (d). These adjustments consist of reductions in the amount of the taxpayer's basis in its assets for purposes of paragraph (c) of this section to reflect assets to which interest expense is directly allocated under this paragraph (d). These adjustments must be made before the taxpayer averages the adjusted basis in its assets as determined on each determination date during the taxable year.

(5) *Example: Direct allocation of interest expense.*—(i) *Facts.* T conducts an electing real property trade or business (Business X) and operates a retail store that is a non-excepted trade or business (Business Y). In Year 1, T issues Note A to a third party in exchange for $1,000x for the purpose of acquiring Building B. Note A is qualified nonrecourse indebtedness (within the meaning of §1.861-10T(b)) secured by Building B. T then uses those funds to acquire Building B for $1,200x, and T uses Building B in Business X. During Year 1, T pays $500x of interest, of which $100x is interest payments on Note A. For Year 1, T's basis in its assets used in Business X (as determined under paragraph (c) of this section) is $3,600x (excluding cash and cash equivalents), and T's basis in its assets used in Business Y (as determined under paragraph (c) of this section) is $800x (excluding cash and cash equivalents). Each of Business X and Business Y also has $100x of cash and cash equivalents.

(ii) *Analysis.* Because Note A is qualified nonrecourse indebtedness that is secured by Building B, in allocating interest expense between Businesses X and Y, T first must directly allocate the $100x of interest expense it paid with respect to Note A to Business X in accordance with paragraph (d)(1) of this section. Thereafter, T must allocate the remaining $400x of interest expense between Businesses X and Y under paragraph (c) of this section. After excluding T's $1,200x cost basis in Building B (see paragraph (d)(4) of this section), and without regard to T's $200x of cash and cash equivalents (see paragraph (c)(5)(iv) of this section), T's basis in assets used in Businesses X and Y is $2,400x and $800x (75 percent and 25 percent), respectively. Thus, $300x of the remaining $400x of interest expense would be allocated to Business X, and $100x would be allocated to Business Y.

(e) *Examples.*—The examples in this paragraph (e) illustrate the principles of this section. For purposes of these examples, assume that no taxpayer is eligible for the small business exemption under section 163(j)(3) and § 1.163(j)-2(d), no taxpayer has floor plan financing interest expense, and no taxpayer has qualified nonrecourse indebtedness within the meaning of § 1.861-10T(b).

(1) *Example 1: Interest allocation within a consolidated group*—(i) *Facts.* S is a member of a consolidated group of which P is the common parent. P conducts an electing real property trade or business (Business X), and S conducts a non-excepted trade or business (Business Y). In Year 1, P pays or accrues (without regard to section 163(j)) $35x of interest expense and receives $10x of interest income, and S pays or accrues (without regard to section 163(j)) $115x of interest expense and receives $5x of interest income (for a total of $150x of interest expense and $15x of interest income). For purposes of this example, assume that, pursuant to paragraph (c) of this section, $30x of the P group's interest expense and $3x of the P group's interest income is allocable to Business X, and the remaining $120x of interest expense and $12x of interest income is allocable to Business Y.

(ii) *Analysis.* Under paragraph (a)(4) of this section, 20 percent of the P group's Year 1 interest expense ($30x / $150x) and interest income ($3x / $15x) is allocable to an excepted trade or business. Thus, $7x ($35x x 20 percent) of P's interest expense and $2x ($10x x 20 percent) of P's interest income is allocable to an excepted trade or business. The remaining $28x of P's interest expense is business interest expense subject to limitation under section 163(j), and the remaining $8x of P's interest income is business interest income that increases the group's section 163(j) limitation. In turn, $23x ($115x x 20 percent) of S's interest expense and $1x ($5x x 20 percent) of S's interest income is allocable to an excepted trade or business. The remaining $92x of S's interest expense is business interest expense subject to limitation under section 163(j), and the remaining $4x of S's interest income is business interest income that increases the group's section 163(j) limitation.

(2) *Example 2: Interest allocation within a consolidated group with assets used in more than one trade or business*—(i) *Facts.* S is a member of a consolidated group of which P is the common parent. P conducts an electing real property trade or business (Business X), and S conducts a non-excepted trade or business (Business Y). In Year 1, P pays or accrues (without regard to section 163(j)) $50x of interest expense, and S pays or accrues $100x of interest expense (without regard to section 163(j)). P leases 40 percent of space in Building V (which P owns) to S for use in Business Y, and P leases the remaining 60 percent of space in Building V to third parties. For purposes of allocating interest expense under paragraph (c) of this section, the P group's basis in its assets (excluding Building V) used in Businesses X and Y is $180x and $620x, respectively. The P group's basis in Building V for purposes of allocating interest expense under paragraph (c) of this section is $200x.

(ii) *Analysis.* Under paragraph (c)(3)(ii) of this section, the P group's basis in Building V ($200x) is allocated to excepted and non-excepted trades or businesses in accordance with the use of space by Business Y (40 percent) and Business X (the remainder, or 60 percent). Accordingly, $120x of the basis in Building V is allocated to excepted trades or businesses (60 percent x $200x), and $80x is allocated to non-excepted trades or businesses (40 percent x $200x). After allocating the basis in Building V, the P group's total basis in the assets used in excepted and non-excepted trades or businesses is $300x and $700x, respectively. Under paragraphs (a)(4) and (c) of this section, 30 percent ($300x / $1000x) of the P group's Year 1 interest expense is properly allocable to an excepted trade or business. Thus, $15x ($50x x 30 percent) of P's interest expense is properly allocable to an excepted trade or business, and the remaining $35x of P's interest expense is business interest expense subject to limitation under section 163(j). In turn, $30x ($100x x 30 percent) of S's interest expense is properly allocable to an excepted trade or business, and the remaining $70x of S's interest expense is business interest expense subject to limitation under section 163(j).

(3) *Example 3: Application of look-through rules*—(i) *Facts.* (A) A and B are unrelated individual taxpayers. A owns 100 percent of the stock of Corp 1, a calendar-year domestic C corporation. The basis of A's stock in Corp 1 is $500x. Corp 1 owns 10 percent of the interests in PS1 (a domestic partnership), and B owns the remaining 90 percent. Corp 1's basis in its PS1 interests is $25x, and B's basis in its PS1 interests is $225x. PS1 owns 100 percent of the stock of Corp 2, a calendar-year domestic C corporation. PS1 has a basis of $1000x in its Corp 2 stock.

(B) In 2020, Corp 1 was engaged solely in a non-excepted trade or business. That same year, PS1's only activity was holding Corp 2 stock. In turn, Corp 2 was engaged in both an electing farming business and a non-excepted trade or business. Under the allocation rules in paragraph (c) of this section, 50 percent of Corp 2's asset basis in 2020 was allocable to the electing farming business. The remaining 50 percent was allocable to the non-excepted trade or business.

(C) Individuals A and B each paid or accrued (without regard to section 163(j)) $150x of interest expense allocable to a trade or business under § 1.163-8T (along with personal interest and investment interest). A's trade or business was an excepted trade or business, and B's trade or business was a non-excepted trade or business. A's basis in the assets used in its trade or business was $100x, and B's basis in the assets used in its trade or business was $112.5x.

(ii) *Analysis.* (A) As provided in paragraph (c)(5)(ii)(E) of this section, if a taxpayer applies the look-through rules of paragraph (c)(5)(ii) of this section, the taxpayer must begin with the lowest-tier entity to which it is eligible to apply the look-through rules. A directly owns 100 percent of the stock of Corp 1; thus, A satisfies the 80 percent minimum ownership threshold with respect to Corp 1. A also owns 10 percent of the interests in PS1. There is no minimum ownership threshold for partnerships; thus, A may apply the look-through rules to PS1. However, A does not directly or indirectly own at least 80 percent of the stock of Corp 2; thus, A may not look through its indirect interest in Corp 2. In turn, B directly owns 90 percent of the interests in PS1, and B indirectly owns at least 80 percent of the stock of Corp 2. Thus, B may apply the look-through rules to both PS1 and Corp 2.

(B) From A's perspective, PS1 is not engaged in a trade or business for purposes of section 163(j); instead, PS1 is merely holding its Corp 2 stock as an investment. Under paragraph (c)(5)(ii)(A)(2) of this section, if a partnership is not engaged in a trade or business, then its C corporation partner must treat its entire basis in the partnership interest as allocable to a non-excepted trade or business. Thus, for purposes of A's application of the look-through rules, Corp 1's entire basis in its PS1 interest ($25x) is allocable to a non-excepted trade or business. Corp 1's basis in its other assets also is allocable to a non-excepted trade or business (the only trade or business in which Corp 1 is engaged). Thus, under paragraph (c) of this section, A's $500x basis in its Corp 1 stock is allocable entirely to a non-excepted trade or business. A's $100x basis in its other business assets is allocable to an excepted trade or business. Thus, 5/6 (or $125x) of A's $150x of interest expense is properly allocable to a non-excepted trade or business and is business interest expense subject to limitation under section 163(j), and the remaining $25x of A's $150x of interest expense is allocable to an excepted trade or business and is not subject to limitation under section 163(j).

(C) From B's perspective, PS1 must look through its stock in Corp 2 to determine the extent to which PS1's basis in the stock is allocable to an excepted or non-excepted trade or business. Half of Corp 2's basis in its assets is

allocable to an excepted trade or business, and the other half is allocable to a non-excepted trade or business. Thus, from B's perspective, $500x of PS1's basis in its Corp 2 stock (PS1's only asset) is allocable to an excepted trade or business, and the other half is allocable to a non-excepted trade or business. B's basis in its PS1 interests is $225x. Applying the look-through rules to B's PS1 interests, $112.5x of B's basis in its PS1 interests is allocable to an excepted trade or business, and $112.5x of B's basis in its PS1 interests is allocable to a non-excepted trade or business. Since B's basis in the assets used in its non-excepted trade or business also was $112.5x, two-thirds of B's interest expense ($100x) is properly allocable to a non-excepted trade or business and is business interest expense subject to limitation under section 163(j), and one-third of B's interest expense ($50x) is allocable to an excepted trade or business and is not subject to limitation under section 163(j).

(4) *Example 4: Excepted and non-excepted trades or businesses in a consolidated group*—(i) *Facts.* P is the common parent of a consolidated group of which A and B are the only other members. A conducts an electing real property trade or business (Business X), and B conducts a non-excepted trade or business (Business Y). In Year 1, A pays or accrues (without regard to section 163(j)) $50x of interest expense and earns $70x of gross income in the conduct of Business X, and B pays or accrues (without regard to section 163(j)) $100x of interest expense and earns $150x of gross income in the conduct of Business Y. B owns Building V, which it uses in Business Y. For purposes of allocating the P group's Year 1 business interest expense between excepted and non-excepted trades or businesses under paragraph (c) of this section, the P group's basis in its assets (other than Building V) used in Businesses X and Y is $180x and $620x, respectively, and the P group's basis in Building V is $200x. At the end of Year 1, B sells Building V to a third party and realizes a gain of $60x in addition to the $150x of gross income B earned that year from the conduct of Business Y.

(ii) *Analysis.* (A) Under paragraphs (a)(4) and (c) of this section, the P group's basis in its assets used in its trades or businesses is allocated between the P group's excepted trade or business (Business X) and its non-excepted trade or business (Business Y) as though these trades or businesses were conducted by a single corporation. Under paragraph (c) of this section, the P group's basis in its assets used in Businesses X and Y is $180x and $820x, respectively. Accordingly, 18 percent ($180x / $1,000x) of the P group's total interest expense ($150x) is properly allocable to an excepted trade or business ($27x), and the remaining 82 percent of the P group's total interest expense is business interest expense properly allocable to a non-excepted trade or business ($123x).

(B) To determine the P group's section 163(j) limitation, paragraph (a) of this section requires that certain items of income and deduction be allocated to the excepted and non-excepted trades or businesses of the P group as though these trades or businesses were conducted by a single corporation. In Year 1, the P group's excepted trade or business (Business X) has gross income of $70x, and the P group's non-excepted trade or business (Business Y) has gross income of $150x. Because Building V was used exclusively in Business Y, the $60x of gain from the sale of Building V in Year 1 is attributed to Business Y under paragraph (b)(2) of this section. The P group's section 163(j) limitation is $63x (30 percent x $210x), which allows the P group to deduct $63x of the $123x of business interest expense allocated to the P group's non-excepted trades or businesses. The group's $27x of interest expense that is allocable to excepted trades or businesses may be deducted without limitation under section 163(j).

(iii) *Intercompany transaction.* The facts are the same as in *Example 4* in paragraph (e)(4)(i) of this section, except that A owns Building V and leases it to B in Year 1 for $20x for use in Business Y, and A sells Building V to a third party for a $60 gain at the end of Year 1. Under paragraphs (a)(4) and (c) of this section, all members of the P group are treated as a single corporation. As a result, the P group's basis in its assets used in its trades or businesses is allocated between the P group's excepted trade or business (Business X) and its non-excepted trade or business (Business Y) as though these trades or businesses were conducted by a single corporation. A lease between two divisions of a single corporation would produce no rental income or expense. Thus, the $20x of rent paid by B to A does not affect the P group's ATI. Moreover, under paragraph (c) of this section, Building V is an asset used in the P group's non-excepted trade or business (Business Y). Accordingly, although A owns Building V, the basis in Building V is added to the P group's basis in assets used in Business Y for purposes of allocating interest expense under paragraph (c) of this section. In the same vein, when A sells Building V to a third party at a gain of $60x, the gain is included in the P group's ATI because Building V was used in a non-excepted trade or business of the P group (Business Y) prior to its sale.

(5) *Example 5: Captive activities*—(i) *Facts.* S and T are members of a consolidated group of which P is the common parent. P conducts an electing real property trade or business (Business X), S conducts a non-excepted trade or business (Business Y), and T provides transportation services to Businesses X and Y but does not have any customers outside of the P group. For Year 1, T provides transportation services using a single bus with a basis of $120x.

(ii) *Analysis.* Under paragraph (a)(4) of this section, activities conducted by a consolidated group are treated as though those activities were conducted by a single corporation. Because the activities of T are limited to providing intercompany transportation services, T does not conduct a trade or business for purposes of section 163(j).

Under paragraph (c)(3) of this section, business interest expense is allocated to excepted and non-excepted trades or businesses based on the relative basis of the assets used in those businesses. The basis in T's only asset, a bus, is therefore allocated between Business X and Business Y according to the use of T's bus by these businesses. Business X uses one-third of T's services, and Business Y uses two-thirds of T's services. Thus, $40x of the basis of T's bus is allocated to Business X, and $80x of the basis of T's bus is allocated to Business Y.

(f) *Applicability date.*—This section applies to taxable years ending after the date the Treasury decision adopting these regulations as final regulations is published in the **Federal Register**. However, taxpayers and their related parties, within the meaning of sections 267(b) and 707(b)(1), may apply the rules of this section to a taxable year beginning after December 31, 2017, so long as the taxpayers and their related parties consistently apply the rules of the section 163(j) regulations, and if applicable, §§1.263A-9, 1.381(c)(20)-1, 1.382-6, 1.383-1, 1.469-9, 1.882-5, 1.1502-13, 1.1502-21, 1.1502-36, 1.1502-79, 1.1502-91 through 1.1502-99 (to the extent they effectuate the rules of §§1.382-6 and 1.383-1), and 1.1504-4 to those taxable years. [Reg. §1.163(j)-10.]

[Proposed 12-28-2018.]

### [Prop. Reg. §1.163(j)-11]

**§1.163(j)-11. Transition rules.**—(a) *Application of section 163(j) limitation if a corporation joins a consolidated group with a taxable year beginning before January 1, 2018.*—(1) *In general.*—If a corporation (S) joins a consolidated group whose taxable year began before January 1, 2018, and if S is subject to the section 163(j) limitation at the time of its change in status, then section 163(j) will apply to S's short taxable year that ends on the day of S's change in status, but section 163(j) will not apply to S's short taxable year that begins the next day (when S is a member of the acquiring consolidated group). Any business interest expense paid or accrued (without regard to section 163(j)) by S in its short taxable year ending on the day of S's change in status for which a deduction is disallowed under section 163(j) will be carried forward to the acquiring group's first taxable year beginning after December 31, 2017. Those disallowed business interest expense carryforwards may be subject to limitation under other provisions of these regulations (see, for example, §1.163(j)-5(c), (d), (e), and (f)).

(2) *Example.*—Acquiring Group is a consolidated group with a fiscal year end of November 30; Target is a stand-alone calendar-year C corporation. On May 31, 2018, Acquiring Group acquires Target in a transaction that is not an ownership change for purposes of section 382. Acquiring Group is not subject to the section 163(j) limitation during its taxable year begin-

ning December 1, 2017. As a result of the acquisition, Target has a short taxable year beginning January 1, 2018 and ending May 31, 2018. Target is subject to the section 163(j) limitation during this short taxable year. However, Target (as a member of Acquiring Group) is not subject to the section 163(j) limitation during Acquiring Group's taxable year ending November 30, 2018. Any disallowed business interest expense carryforwards from Target's taxable year ending May 31, 2018, will not be available for use in Acquiring Group's taxable year ending November 30, 2018. However, that disallowed business interest expense is carried forward to Acquiring Group's taxable year beginning December 1, 2018, and can be deducted by the group, subject to the separate return limitation year (SRLY) limitation. See § 1.163(j)-5(d).

(b) *Treatment of disallowed disqualified interest.*— (1) *In general.*—Disallowed disqualified interest is carried forward to the taxpayer's first taxable year beginning after December 31, 2017, and is subject to disallowance as a disallowed business interest expense carryforward under section 163(j) and § 1.163(j)-2, except to the extent the interest is properly allocable to an excepted trade or business under § 1.163(j)-10. See § 1.163(j)-10(a)(6).

(2) *Earnings and profits.*—A taxpayer may not reduce its earnings and profits in a taxable year beginning after December 31, 2017, to reflect any disallowed disqualified interest carryforwards to the extent the payment or accrual of the disallowed disqualified interest reduced the earnings and profits of the taxpayer in a prior taxable year.

(3) *Disallowed disqualified interest of members of an affiliated group.*—(i) *Scope.*—This paragraph (b)(3)(i) applies to corporations that were treated as a single taxpayer under old section 163(j)(6)(C) and that had disallowed disqualified interest.

(ii) *Allocation of disallowed disqualified interest to members of the affiliated group.*—(A) *In general.*—Each member of the affiliated group is allocated its allocable share of the affiliated group's disallowed disqualified interest as provided in paragraph (b)(3)(ii)(B) of this section.

(B) *Definitions.*—The following definitions apply for purposes of paragraph (b)(3)(ii) of this section.

(1) *Allocable share of the affiliated group's disallowed disqualified interest.*—The term *allocable share of the affiliated group's disallowed disqualified interest* means, with respect to any member of an affiliated group for the member's last taxable year beginning before January 1, 2018, the product of the total amount of the disallowed disqualified interest of all members of the affiliated group under old section 163(j)(6)(C) and the member's disallowed disqualified interest ratio.

(2) *Disallowed disqualified interest ratio.*—The term *disallowed disqualified interest ratio* means, with respect to any member of an affiliated group for the member's last taxable year beginning before January 1, 2018, the ratio of the exempt related person interest expense of the member for the last taxable year beginning before January 1, 2018, to the sum of the amounts of exempt related person interest expense for all members of the affiliated group.

(3) *Exempt related person interest expense.*—The term *exempt related person interest expense* means interest expense that is, or is treated as, paid or accrued by a domestic C corporation, or by a foreign corporation with income, gain, or loss that is effectively connected, or treated as effectively connected, with the conduct of a trade or business in the United States, to—

(i) Any person related to the taxpayer, within the meaning of sections 267(b) or 707(b)(1), applying the constructive ownership and attribution rules of section 267(c), if no U.S. tax is imposed with respect to the interest under subtitle A of the Internal Revenue Code, determined without regard to net operating losses or net operating loss carryovers, and taking into account any applicable treaty obligation of the United States. For this purpose, interest that is subject to a reduced rate of tax under any treaty obligation of the United States applicable to the recipient is treated as in part subject to the statutory tax rate under sections 871 or 881 and in part not subject to tax, based on the proportion that the rate of tax under the treaty bears to the statutory tax rate. Thus, for purposes of section 163(j), if the statutory tax rate is 30 percent, and pursuant to a treaty U.S. tax is instead limited to a rate of 10 percent, two-thirds of the interest is considered interest not subject to U.S. tax under subtitle A of the Internal Revenue Code;

(ii) A person that is not related to the taxpayer, within the meaning of sections 267(b) or 707(b)(1), applying the constructive ownership and attribution rules of section 267(c), with respect to indebtedness on which there is a disqualified guarantee, within the meaning of paragraph (6)(D) of old section 163(j), of such indebtedness, and no gross basis U.S. tax is imposed with respect to the interest. For purposes of this paragraph (b)(3)(ii)(B)(3)(ii), a *gross basis U.S. tax* means any tax imposed by this subtitle A of the Internal Revenue Code that is determined by reference to the gross amount of any item of income without any reduction for any deduction allowed by subtitle A of the Internal Revenue Code. Interest that is subject to a gross basis U.S. tax that is eligible for a reduced rate of tax under any treaty obligation of the United States applicable to the recipient is treated as, in part, subject to the statutory tax rate under sections 871 or 881 and, in part, not subject to a gross basis U.S. tax, based on the proportion that the rate of tax under the treaty bears to the statutory tax rate. Thus, for purposes of section 163(j), if the statutory tax rate is 30 percent, and

**Prop. Reg. § 1.163(j)-11(b)**

pursuant to a treaty U.S. tax is instead limited to a rate of 10 percent, two-thirds of the interest is considered interest not subject to a gross basis U.S. tax under subtitle A of the Internal Revenue Code; or

 *(iii)* A REIT, directly or indirectly, to the extent that the domestic C corporation, or a foreign corporation with income, gain, or loss that is effectively connected, or treated as effectively connected, with the conduct of a trade or business in the United States, is a taxable REIT subsidiary, as defined in section 856(l), with respect to the REIT.

 (iii) *Treatment of carryforwards.*—The amount of disallowed disqualified interest allocated to a taxpayer pursuant to paragraph (b)(3)(ii) of this section is treated in the same manner as described in paragraph (b)(1) of this section.

 (4) *Application of section 382.*—(i) *Ownership change occurring before the date the Treasury decision adopting these regulations as final regulations is published in the* **Federal Register.**—(A) *Pre-change loss.*—For purposes of section 382(d)(3), unless the rules of § 1.382-2(a)(7) apply, disallowed disqualified interest is not a pre-change loss under § 1.382-2(a) subject to a section 382 limitation with regard to an ownership change on a change date occurring before the date the Treasury decision adopting these regulations as final regulations is published in the **Federal Register.** But see section 382(h)(6)(B) (regarding built-in deduction items).

 (B) *Loss corporation.*—For purposes of section 382(k)(1), unless the rules of § 1.382-2(a)(7) apply, disallowed disqualified interest is not a carryforward of disallowed disqualified interest described in section 381(c)(20) with regard to an ownership change on a change date occurring before the date the Treasury decision adopting these regulations as final regulations is published in the **Federal Register.** But see section 382(h)(6) (regarding built-in deductions).

 (ii) *Ownership change occurring on or after the date the Treasury decision adopting these regulations as final regulations is published in the* **Federal Register.**—(A) *Pre-change loss.*—For rules governing the treatment of disallowed disqualified interest as a pre-change loss for purposes of section 382 with regard to an ownership change on a change date occurring on or after the date the Treasury decision adopting these regulations as final regulations is published in the **Federal Register,** see §§ 1.382-2(a)(2) and 1.382-6(c)(3).

 (B) *Loss corporation.*—For rules governing when disallowed disqualified interest causes a corporation to be a loss corporation with regard to an ownership change occurring on or after the date the Treasury decision adopting these regulations as final regulations is published in the **Federal Register,** see § 1.382-2(a)(1)(i)(A).

 (iii) *Definitions.*—For purposes of this paragraph (b)(4), the terms *ownership change* and *change date* have the meanings provided in section 382 and the regulations thereunder.

 (5) [Reserved]

 (6) *Treatment of excess limitation from taxable years beginning before January 1, 2018.*—No amount of excess limitation under old section 163(j)(2)(B) may be carried forward to taxable years beginning after December 31, 2017.

 (7) *Example: Members of an affiliated group.*—(i) *Facts.* A, B, and C are calendar-year domestic C corporations that are members of an affiliated group (within the meaning of section 1504(a)) that was treated as a single taxpayer under old section 163(j)(6)(C) and the proposed regulations thereunder (see formerly proposed § 1.163(j)-5). For the taxable year ending December 31, 2017, the separately determined amounts of exempt related person interest expense of A, B, and C were $0, $600x, and $150x, respectively (for a total of $750x). The affiliated group has $200x of disallowed disqualified interest in that year.

 (ii) *Analysis.* The affiliated group's disallowed disqualified interest expense for the 2017 taxable year ($200x) is allocated among A, B, and C based on the ratio of each member's exempt related person interest expense to the group's exempt related person interest expense. Because A has no exempt related person interest expense, no disallowed disqualified interest is allocated to A. Disallowed disqualified interest of $160x is allocated to B (($600x / $750x) x $200x), and disallowed disqualified interest of $40x is allocated to C (($150x / $750x) x $200x). Thus, B and C have $160x and $40x, respectively, of disallowed disqualified interest that is carried forward to the first taxable year beginning after December 31, 2017. No excess limitation that was allocated to A, B, or C under old section 163(j) will carry forward to the first taxable year beginning after December 31, 2017.

 (iii) *Carryforward of disallowed disqualified interest to 2018 taxable year.* The facts are the same as in the *Example* in paragraph (b)(7)(i) of this section, except that, for the taxable year ending December 31, 2018, A, B, and C are members of a consolidated group that has a section 163(j) limitation of $140x, current-year business interest expense (as defined in § 1.163(j)-5(a)(2)(i)) of $80x, and no excepted trade or business. Under paragraph (b)(1) of this section, disallowed disqualified interest is carried to the taxpayer's first taxable year beginning after December 31, 2017, and is subject to disallowance under section 163(j) and § 1.163(j)-2. Under § 1.163(j)-5(b)(3)(ii)(D)(*1*), a consolidated group that has section 163(j) limitation remaining for the current year after deducting all current-year business interest expense deducts each member's disallowed disqualified interest carryforwards from prior taxable years, starting with the earliest taxable year, on a pro rata basis (subject to certain limitations). In accordance with paragraph (b)(1) of this section, the rule in § 1.163(j)-5(b)(3)(ii)(D)(*1*) applies to disallowed disqualified interest carried forward to the taxpayer's first taxable year beginning after December 31, 2017. Accordingly, after deducting $80x of current-year business interest expense in 2018, the group may deduct $60x of its $200x disallowed disqualified interest carryforwards. Under paragraph (b)(3) of this section, B has $160x of disallowed disqualified interest carryforwards, and C has $40x of disallowed disqualified interest carryforwards. Thus, $48x (($160x / $200x) x $60x) of B's disallowed disqualified interest carryforwards, and $12x (($40x / $200x) x $60x) of C's disallowed disqualified interest carryforwards, are deducted by the consolidated group in the 2018 taxable year.

(c) *Applicability date.*—This section applies to taxable years ending after the date the Treasury decision adopting these regulations as final regulations is published in the **Federal Register**. However, taxpayers and their related parties, within the meaning of sections 267(b) and 707(b)(1), may apply the rules of this section to a taxable year beginning after December 31, 2017, so long as the taxpayers and their related parties consistently apply the rules of the section 163(j) regulations, and if applicable, § § 1.263A-9, 1.381(c)(20)-1, 1.382-6, 1.383-1, 1.469-9, 1.882-5, 1.1502-13, 1.1502-21, 1.1502-36, 1.1502-79, 1.1502-91 through 1.1502-99 (to the extent they effectuate the rules of § § 1.382-6 and 1.383-1), and 1.1504-4 to those taxable years. [Reg. § 1.163(j)-11.]

[Proposed 12-28-2018.]

[Prop. Reg. § 1.167(a)-14]

**§ 1.167(a)-14. Treatment of certain intangible property excluded from section 197.**

* * *

(e) * * *

(3) * * * The language "or § 1.168(k)-2, as applicable," in the third sentence in paragraph (b)(1) of this section applies to computer software that is qualified property under section 168(k)(2) and placed in service by a taxpayer during or after the taxpayer's taxable year that includes the date of publication of a Treasury decision adopting these rules as final regulations in the **Federal Register**. However, a taxpayer may rely on the language "or § 1.168(k)-2, as applicable," in the third sentence in paragraph (b)(1) of this section in these proposed regulations for computer software that is qualified property under section 168(k)(2) and acquired and placed in service after September 27, 2017, by the taxpayer during taxable years ending on or after September 28, 2017, and ending before the taxpayer's taxable year that includes the date of publication of a Treasury decision adopting these rules as final regulations in the **Federal Register**.

[Proposed 8-8-2018.]

[Prop. Reg. § 1.168(b)-1]

**§ 1.168(b)-1. Definitions.**—(a) * * *

(5) *Qualified improvement property.*—(i) Is any improvement that is section 1250 property to an interior portion of a building, as defined in § 1.48-1(e)(1), that is nonresidential real property, as defined in section 168(e)(2)(B), if the improvement is placed in service by the taxpayer after the date the building was first placed in service by any person and if—

(A) For purposes of section 168(e)(6), the improvement is placed in service by the taxpayer after December 31, 2017;

(B) For purposes of section 168(k)(3) as in effect on the day before amendment by section 13204(a)(4)(B) of the Tax Cuts and Jobs Act, Public Law 115-97 (131 Stat. 2054 (December 22, 2017)) ("Act"), the improvement is acquired by the taxpayer before September 28, 2017, the improvement is placed in service by the taxpayer before January 1, 2018, and the improvement meets the original use requirement in section 168(k)(2)(A)(ii) as in effect on the day before amendment by section 13201(c)(1) of the Act; or

(C) For purposes of section 168(k)(3) as in effect on the day before amendment by section 13204(a)(4)(B) of the Act, the improvement is acquired by the taxpayer after September 27, 2017; the improvement is placed in service by the taxpayer after September 27, 2017, and before January 1, 2018; and the improvement meets the requirements in section 168(k)(2)(A)(ii) as amended by section 13201(c)(1) of the Act; and

(ii) Does not include any qualified improvement for which an expenditure is attributable to—

(A) The enlargement, as defined in § 1.48-12(c)(10), of the building;

(B) Any elevator or escalator, as defined in § 1.48-1(m)(2); or

(C) The internal structural framework, as defined in § 1.48-12(b)(3)(iii), of the building.

(b) *Effective date.*—(1) *In general.*—Except as provided in paragraph (b)(2) of this section, this section is applicable on or after February 27, 2004.

(2) *Application of paragraph (a)(5) of this section.*—(i) *In general.*—Except as provided in paragraph (b)(2)(ii) of this section, paragraph (a)(5) of this section is applicable on or after the date of publication of a Treasury decision adopting these rules as final regulations in the **Federal Register**.

(ii) *Early application of paragraph (a)(5) of this section.*—A taxpayer may rely on the provisions of paragraph (a)(5) of this section in these proposed regulations for the taxpayer's taxable years ending on or after September 28, 2017, and ending before the taxpayer's taxable year that includes the date of publication of a Treasury decision adopting these rules as final regulations in the **Federal Register**.

[Proposed 8-8-2018.]

### [Prop. Reg. §1.168(d)-1]

**§1.168(d)-1. Applicable conventions—half-year and mid-quarter conventions.**

\* \* \*

(b) \* \* \*

(3) \* \* \*

(ii) \* \* \* Further, see §1.168(k)-2(f)(1) for rules relating to qualified property under section 168(k), as amended by the Tax Cuts and Jobs Act, Public Law 115-97 (131 Stat. 2054 (December 22, 2017)), that is placed in service by the taxpayer in the same taxable year in which either a partnership is terminated as a result of a technical termination under section 708(b)(1)(B) or the property is transferred in a transaction described in section 168(i)(7).

\* \* \*

(7) \* \* \*

(ii) \* \* \* However, see §1.168(k)-2(f)(1)(iii) for a special rule regarding the allocation of the additional first year depreciation deduction in the case of certain contributions of property to a partnership under section 721.

\* \* \*

(d) \* \* \*

(2) \* \* \* The last sentences in paragraphs (b)(3)(ii) and (b)(7)(ii) of this section apply to qualified property under section 168(k)(2) placed in service by a taxpayer during or after the taxpayer's taxable year that includes the date of publication of a Treasury decision adopting these rules as final regulations in the **Federal Register**. However, a taxpayer may rely on the last sentences in paragraphs (b)(3)(ii) and (b)(7)(ii) of this section in these proposed regulations for qualified property under section 168(k)(2) acquired and placed in service after September 27, 2017, by the taxpayer during taxable years ending on or after September 28, 2017, and ending before the taxpayer's taxable year that includes the date of publication of a Treasury decision adopting these rules as final regulations in the **Federal Register**.

\* \* \*

[Proposed 8-8-2018.]

### [Prop. Reg. §1.168(i)-4]

**§1.168(i)-4. Changes in use.**

\* \* \*

(g) \* \* \*

(1) \* \* \* Except as provided in paragraph (g)(2) of this section, this section applies to any change in the use of MACRS property in a taxable year ending on or after June 17, 2004. \* \* \*

(2) *Qualified property under section 168(k) acquired and placed in service after September 27, 2017.*—The language "or §1.168(k)-2(f)(6)(iii), as applicable" in paragraph (b)(1) of this section, the language "or §1.168(k)-2(f)(6)(ii), as applica-

ble" in paragraph (c) of this section, and the language "or §1.168(k)-2(f)(6)(iv), as applicable" in paragraphs (d)(3)(i)(C) and (d)(4)(i) of this section applies to any change in use of MACRS property, which is qualified property under section 168(k)(2), by a taxpayer during or after the taxpayer's taxable year that includes the date of publication of a Treasury decision adopting these rules as final regulations in the **Federal Register**. However, a taxpayer may rely on the language "or §1.168(k)-2(f)(6)(iii), as applicable" in paragraph (b)(1) of this section, the language "or §1.168(k)-2(f)(6)(ii), as applicable" in paragraph (c) of this section, and the language "or §1.168(k)-2(f)(6)(iv), as applicable" in paragraphs (d)(3)(i)(C) and (d)(4)(i) of this section in these proposed regulations for any change in use of MACRS property, which is qualified property under section 168(k)(2) and acquired and placed in service after September 27, 2017, by the taxpayer during taxable years ending on or after September 28, 2017, and ending before the taxpayer's taxable year that includes the date of publication of a Treasury decision adopting these rules as final regulations in the **Federal Register**.

\* \* \*

[Proposed 8-8-2018.]

### [Prop. Reg. §1.168(i)-6]

**§1.168(i)-6. Like-kind exchanges and involuntary conversions.**

\* \* \*

(d) \* \* \*

(4) \* \* \* Further, see §1.168(k)-2(f)(5)(iv) for replacement MACRS property that is qualified property under section 168(k), as amended by the Tax Cuts and Jobs Act, Public Law 115-97 (131 Stat. 2054 (December 22, 2017)).

\* \* \*

(h) \* \* \* Further, see §1.168(k)-2(f)(5) for qualified property under section 168(k), as amended by the Tax Cuts and Jobs Act, Public Law 115-97 (131 Stat. 2054 (December 22, 2017)).

\* \* \*

(k) \* \* \*

(4) *Qualified property under section 168(k) acquired and placed in service after September 27, 2017.*—The language "1.168(k)-2(f)(5)," in paragraphs (d)(3)(ii)(B) and (E) of this section and the last sentences in paragraphs (d)(4) and (h) of this section apply to a like-kind exchange or an involuntary conversion of MACRS property, which is qualified property under section 168(k)(2), for which the time of replacement occurs on or after the date of publication of a Treasury decision adopting these rules as final regulations in the **Federal Register**. However, a taxpayer may rely on the language "1.168(k)-2(f)(5)," in paragraphs (d)(3)(ii)(B) and (E) of this section and the last sentences in paragraphs (d)(4) and (h) of this section in these proposed regulations for a like-kind exchange or an involuntary conversion of MACRS property,

which is qualified property under section 168(k)(2), for which the time of replacement occurs on or after September 28, 2017, and occurs before the date of publication of a Treasury decision adopting these rules as final regulations in the **Federal Register**.

[Proposed 8-8-2018.]

### [Prop. Reg. § 1.168(k)-2]

**§ 1.168(k)-2. Additional first year depreciation deduction for property acquired and placed in service after September 27, 2017.**—(a) *Scope and definitions.*—(1) *Scope.*—This section provides rules for determining the additional first year depreciation deduction allowable under section 168(k) for qualified property acquired and placed in service after September 27, 2017.

(2) *Definitions.*—For purposes of this section—

(i) *Act* is the Tax Cuts and Jobs Act, Public Law 115-97 (131 Stat. 2054 (December 22, 2017)); and

(ii) *Applicable percentage* is the percentage provided in section 168(k)(6).

(b) *Qualified property.*—(1) *In general.*—Qualified property is depreciable property, as defined in § 1.168(b)-1(a)(1), that meets all the following requirements in the first taxable year in which the property is subject to depreciation by the taxpayer whether or not depreciation deductions for the property are allowable:

(i) The requirements in § 1.168(k)-2(b)(2) (description of qualified property);

(ii) The requirements in § 1.168(k)-2(b)(3) (original use or used property acquisition requirements);

(iii) The requirements in § 1.168(k)-2(b)(4) (placed-in-service date); and

(iv) The requirements in § 1.168(k)-2(b)(5) (acquisition of property).

(2) *Description of qualified property.*—(i) *In general.*—Depreciable property will meet the requirements of this paragraph (b)(2) if the property is—

(A) MACRS property, as defined in § 1.168(b)-1(a)(2), that has a recovery period of 20 years or less. For purposes of this paragraph (b)(2)(i)(A) and section 168(k)(2)(A)(i)(I), the recovery period is determined in accordance with section 168(c) regardless of any election made by the taxpayer under section 168(g)(7). This paragraph (b)(2)(i)(A) includes the following MACRS property that is acquired by the taxpayer after September 27, 2017, and placed in service by the taxpayer after September 27, 2017, and before January 1, 2018:

(1) Qualified leasehold improvement property as defined in section 168(e)(6) as in effect on the day before amendment by section 13204(a)(1) of the Act;

(2) Qualified restaurant property, as defined in section 168(e)(7) as in effect on the day before amendment by section 13204(a)(1) of

the Act, that is qualified improvement property as defined in § 1.168(b)-1(a)(5)(i)(C) and (a)(5)(ii); and

(3) Qualified retail improvement property as defined in section 168(e)(8) as in effect on the day before amendment by section 13204(a)(1) of the Act;

(B) Computer software as defined in, and depreciated under, section 167(f)(1) and the regulations under section 167(f)(1);

(C) Water utility property as defined in section 168(e)(5) and depreciated under section 168;

(D) Qualified improvement property as defined in § 1.168(b)-1(a)(5)(i)(C) and (a)(5)(ii) and depreciated under section 168;

(E) Qualified film or television production, as defined in section 181(d) and § 1.181-3, for which a deduction would have been allowable under section 181 without regard to section 181(a)(2) and (g), or section 168(k);

(F) Qualified live theatrical production, as defined in section 181(e), for which a deduction would have been allowable under section 181 without regard to section 181(a)(2) and (g), or section 168(k); or

(G) A specified plant, as defined in section 168(k)(5)(B), for which the taxpayer has properly made an election to apply section 168(k)(5) for the taxable year in which the specified plant is planted, or grafted to a plant that has already been planted, by the taxpayer in the ordinary course of the taxpayer's farming business, as defined in section 263A(e)(4) (for further guidance, see paragraph (e) of this section).

(ii) *Property not eligible for additional first year depreciation deduction.*—Depreciable property will not meet the requirements of this paragraph (b)(2) if the property is—

(A) Described in section 168(f) (for example, automobiles for which the taxpayer uses the optional business standard mileage rate);

(B) Required to be depreciated under the alternative depreciation system of section 168(g) pursuant to section 168(g)(1)(A), (B), (C), (D), (F), or (G), or other provisions of the Internal Revenue Code (for example, property described in section 263A(e)(2)(A) if the taxpayer or any related person, as defined in section 263A(e)(2)(B), has made an election under section 263A(d)(3), or property described in section 280F(b)(1));

(C) Included in any class of property for which the taxpayer elects not to deduct the additional first year depreciation (for further guidance, see paragraph (e) of this section);

(D) A specified plant that is placed in service by the taxpayer during the taxable year and for which the taxpayer made an election to apply section 168(k)(5) for a prior taxable year;

(E) Included in any class of property for which the taxpayer elects to apply section 168(k)(4). This paragraph (b)(2)(ii)(E) applies to property placed in service in any taxable year beginning before January 1, 2018;

(F) Described in section 168(k)(9)(A) and placed in service in any taxable year beginning after December 31, 2017; or

(G) Described in section 168(k)(9)(B) and placed in service in any taxable year beginning after December 31, 2017.

(3) *Original use or used property acquisition requirements.*—(i) *In general.*—Depreciable property will meet the requirements of this paragraph (b)(3) if the property meets the original use requirements in paragraph (b)(3)(ii) of this section or if the property meets the used property acquisition requirements in paragraph (b)(3)(iii) of this section.

(ii) *Original use.*—(A) *In general.*—Depreciable property will meet the requirements of this paragraph (b)(3)(ii) if the original use of the property commences with the taxpayer. Except as provided in paragraphs (b)(3)(ii)(B) and (C) of this section, original use means the first use to which the property is put, whether or not that use corresponds to the use of the property by the taxpayer. Additional capital expenditures incurred by a taxpayer to recondition or rebuild property acquired or owned by the taxpayer satisfy the original use requirement. However, the cost of reconditioned or rebuilt property does not satisfy the original use requirement (but may satisfy the used property acquisition requirements in paragraph (b)(3)(iii) of this section). The question of whether property is reconditioned or rebuilt property is a question of fact. For purposes of this paragraph (b)(3)(ii)(A), property that contains used parts will not be treated as reconditioned or rebuilt if the cost of the used parts is not more than 20 percent of the total cost of the property, whether acquired or self-constructed.

(B) *Conversion to business or income-producing use.*—(1) *Personal use to business or income-producing use.*—If a taxpayer initially acquires new property for personal use and subsequently uses the property in the taxpayer's trade or business or for the taxpayer's production of income, the taxpayer is considered the original user of the property. If a person initially acquires new property for personal use and a taxpayer subsequently acquires the property from the person for use in the taxpayer's trade or business or for the taxpayer's production of income, the taxpayer is not considered the original user of the property.

(2) *Inventory to business or income-producing use.*—If a taxpayer initially acquires new property and holds the property primarily for sale to customers in the ordinary course of the taxpayer's business and subsequently withdraws the property from inventory and uses the property primarily in the taxpayer's trade or business or primarily for the taxpayer's production of income, the taxpayer is considered the original user of the property. If a person initially acquires new property and holds the property primarily for sale to customers in the ordinary course of

the person's business and a taxpayer subsequently acquires the property from the person for use primarily in the taxpayer's trade or business or primarily for the taxpayer's production of income, the taxpayer is considered the original user of the property. For purposes of this paragraph (b)(3)(ii)(B)(2), the original use of the property by the taxpayer commences on the date on which the taxpayer uses the property primarily in the taxpayer's trade or business or primarily for the taxpayer's production of income.

(C) *Fractional interests in property.*—If, in the ordinary course of its business, a taxpayer sells fractional interests in new property to third parties unrelated to the taxpayer, each first fractional owner of the property is considered as the original user of its proportionate share of the property. Furthermore, if the taxpayer uses the property before all of the fractional interests of the property are sold but the property continues to be held primarily for sale by the taxpayer, the original use of any fractional interest sold to a third party unrelated to the taxpayer subsequent to the taxpayer's use of the property begins with the first purchaser of that fractional interest. For purposes of this paragraph (b)(3)(ii)(C), persons are not related if they do not have a relationship described in section 267(b) or 707(b) and the regulations under section 267(b) or 707(b).

(iii) *Used property acquisition requirements.*—(A) *In general.*—Depreciable property will meet the requirements of this paragraph (b)(3)(iii) if the acquisition of the used property meets the following requirements:

(1) Such property was not used by the taxpayer or a predecessor at any time prior to such acquisition;

(2) The acquisition of such property meets the requirements of section 179(d)(2)(A), (B), and (C), and § 1.179-4(c)(1)(ii), (iii), and (iv), or 1.179-4(c)(2) (property is acquired by purchase); and

(3) The acquisition of such property meets the requirements of section 179(d)(3) and § 1.179-4(d) (cost of property) (for further guidance regarding like-kind exchanges and involuntary conversions, see paragraph (f)(5) of this section).

(B) *Property was not used by the taxpayer at any time prior to acquisition.*—(1) *In general.*—Solely for purposes of paragraph (b)(3)(iii)(A)(1) of this section, the property is treated as used by the taxpayer or a predecessor at any time prior to acquisition by the taxpayer or predecessor if the taxpayer or the predecessor had a depreciable interest in the property at any time prior to such acquisition, whether or not the taxpayer or the predecessor claimed depreciation deductions for the property. If a lessee has a depreciable interest in the improvements made to leased property and subsequently the lessee acquires the leased property of which the improvements are a part, the unadjusted depreciable basis, as defined in § 1.168(b)-1(a)(3), of the acquired property that is

Prop. Reg. § 1.168(k)-2(b)(3)(iii)(B)(1)

eligible for the additional first year depreciation deduction, assuming all other requirements are met, must not include the unadjusted depreciable basis attributable to the improvements.

(2) *Taxpayer has a depreciable interest in a portion of the property.*—If a taxpayer initially acquires a depreciable interest in a portion of the property and subsequently acquires a depreciable interest in an additional portion of the same property, such additional depreciable interest is not treated as used by the taxpayer at any time prior to its acquisition by the taxpayer. This paragraph (b)(3)(iii)(B)(2) does not apply if the taxpayer or a predecessor previously had a depreciable interest in the subsequently acquired additional portion. For purposes of this paragraph (b)(3)(iii)(B)(2), a portion of the property is considered to be the percentage interest in the property. If a taxpayer holds a depreciable interest in a portion of the property, sells that portion or a part of that portion, and subsequently acquires a depreciable interest in another portion of the same property, the taxpayer will be treated as previously having a depreciable interest in the property up to the amount of the portion for which the taxpayer held a depreciable interest in the property before the sale.

(3) *Application to members of a consolidated group.*—(i) *Same consolidated group.*—Solely for purposes of applying paragraph (b)(3)(iii)(A)(1) of this section, if a member of a consolidated group, as defined in § 1.1502-1(h), acquires depreciable property in which the consolidated group had a depreciable interest at any time prior to the member's acquisition of the property, the member will be treated as having a depreciable interest in the property prior to the acquisition. For purposes of this paragraph (b)(3)(iii)(B)(3)(i), a consolidated group will be treated as having a depreciable interest in property during the time any current or previous member of the group had a depreciable interest in the property while a member of the group.

(ii) *Certain acquisitions pursuant to a series of related transactions.*—Solely for purposes of applying paragraph (b)(3)(iii)(A)(1) of this section, if a series of related transactions includes one or more transactions in which property is acquired by a member of a consolidated group and one or more transactions in which a corporation that had a depreciable interest in the property becomes a member of the group, the member that acquires the property will be treated as having a depreciable interest in the property prior to the time of its acquisition.

(iii) *Time for testing membership.*—Solely for purposes of applying paragraph (b)(3)(iii)(B)(3)(i) and (ii) of this section, if a series of related transactions includes one or more transactions in which property is acquired by a member of a consolidated group and one or more transactions in which the transferee of the property ceases to be a member of a consolidated group, whether the taxpayer is a member of a consolidated group is tested immediately after the last transaction in the series.

(C) *Special rules for a series of related transactions.*—Solely for purposes of section 168(k)(2)(E)(ii) and paragraph (b)(3)(iii)(A) of this section, in the case of a series of related transactions (for example, a series of related transactions including the transfer of a partnership interest, the transfer of partnership assets, or the disposition of property and the disposition, directly or indirectly, of the transferor or transferee of the property)—

(1) The property is treated as directly transferred from the original transferor to the ultimate transferee; and

(2) The relation between the original transferor and the ultimate transferee is tested immediately after the last transaction in the series.

(iv) *Application to partnerships.*— (A) *Section 704(c) remedial allocations.*—Remedial allocations under section 704(c) do not satisfy the requirements of paragraph (b)(3) of this section. See § 1.704-3(d)(2).

(B) *Basis determined under section 732.*— Any basis of distributed property determined under section 732 does not satisfy the requirements of paragraph (b)(3) of this section.

(C) *Section 734(b) adjustments.*—Any increase in basis of depreciable property under section 734(b) does not satisfy the requirements of paragraph (b)(3) of this section.

(D) *Section 743(b) adjustments.*—(1) *In general.*—For purposes of determining whether the transfer of a partnership interest meets the requirements of paragraph (b)(3)(iii)(A) of this section, each partner is treated as having a depreciable interest in the partner's proportionate share of partnership property. Any increase in basis of depreciable property under section 743(b) satisfies the requirements of paragraph (b)(3)(iii)(A) of this section if—

(i) At any time prior to the transfer of the partnership interest that gave rise to such basis increase, neither the transferee partner nor a predecessor of the transferee partner had any depreciable interest in the portion of the property deemed acquired to which the section 743(b) adjustment is allocated under section 755 and the regulations under section 755; and

(ii) The transfer of the partnership interest that gave rise to such basis increase satisfies the requirements of paragraphs (b)(3)(iii)(A)(2) and (3) of this section.

(2) *Relatedness tested at partner level.*— Solely for purposes of paragraph (b)(3)(iv)(D)(1)(ii) of this section, whether the parties are related or unrelated is determined by comparing the transferor and the transferee of the transferred partnership interest.

(v) *Syndication transaction.*—If a lessor has a depreciable interest in the property and the lessor and any predecessor did not previously have a depreciable interest in the property, and the property is sold by the lessor or any subsequent purchaser within three months after the date the property was originally placed in service by the lessor (or, in the case of multiple units of property subject to the same lease, within three months after the date the final unit is placed in service, so long as the period between the time the first unit is placed in service and the time the last unit is placed in service does not exceed 12 months), and the user of the property after the last sale during the three-month period remains the same as when the property was originally placed in service by the lessor, the purchaser of the property in the last sale during the three-month period is considered the taxpayer that acquired the property for purposes of applying paragraphs (b)(3)(ii) and (iii) of this section.

(vi) *Examples.*—The application of this paragraph (b)(3) is illustrated by the following examples. Unless the facts specifically indicate otherwise, assume that the parties are not related within the meaning of section 179(d)(2)(A) or (B) and §1.179-4(c), no corporation is a member of a consolidated or controlled group, and the parties do not have predecessors:

*Example 1.* (i) On August 1, 2018, A buys a new machine for $35,000 from an unrelated party for use in A's trade or business. On July 1, 2020, B buys that machine from A for $20,000 for use in B's trade or business. On October 1, 2020, B makes a $5,000 capital expenditure to recondition the machine. B did not have any depreciable interest in the machine before B acquired it on July 1, 2020.

(ii) A's purchase price of $35,000 satisfies the original use requirement of paragraph (b)(3)(ii) of this section and, assuming all other requirements are met, qualifies for the additional first year depreciation deduction.

(iii) B's purchase price of $20,000 does not satisfy the original use requirement of paragraph (b)(3)(ii) of this section, but it does satisfy the used property acquisition requirements of paragraph (b)(3)(iii) of this section. Assuming all other requirements are met, the $20,000 purchase price qualifies for the additional first year depreciation deduction. Further, B's $5,000 expenditure satisfies the original use requirement of paragraph (b)(3)(ii) of this section and, assuming all other requirements are met, qualifies for the additional first year depreciation deduction, regardless of whether the $5,000 is added to the basis of the machine or is capitalized as a separate asset.

*Example 2.* C, an automobile dealer, uses some of its automobiles as demonstrators in order to show them to prospective customers. The automobiles that are used as demonstrators by C are held by C primarily for sale to customers in the ordinary course of its business. On November 1, 2017, D buys from C an automobile that was previously used as a demonstrator by C. D will use the automobile solely for business purposes. The use of the automobile by C as a demonstrator does not constitute a "use" for purposes of the original use requirement and, therefore, D will be considered the original user of the automobile for purposes of paragraph (b)(3)(ii) of this section. Assuming all other requirements are met, D's purchase price of the automobile qualifies for the additional first year depreciation deduction for D, subject to any limitation under section 280F.

*Example 3.* On April 1, 2015, E acquires a horse to be used in E's thoroughbred racing business. On October 1, 2018, F buys the horse from E and will use the horse in F's horse breeding business. F did not have any depreciable interest in the horse before F acquired it on October 1, 2018. The use of the horse by E in its racing business prevents F from satisfying the original use requirement of paragraph (b)(3)(ii) of this section. However, F's acquisition of the horse satisfies the used property acquisition requirements of paragraph (b)(3)(iii) of this section. Assuming all other requirements are met, F's purchase price of the horse qualifies for the additional first year depreciation deduction for F.

*Example 4.* In the ordinary course of its business, G sells fractional interests in its aircraft to unrelated parties. G holds out for sale eight equal fractional interests in an aircraft. On October 1, 2017, G sells five of the eight fractional interests in the aircraft to H and H begins to use its proportionate share of the aircraft immediately upon purchase. On February 1, 2018, G sells to I the remaining unsold $3/8$ fractional interests in the aircraft. H is considered the original user as to its $5/8$ fractional interest in the aircraft and I is considered the original user as to its $3/8$ fractional interest in the aircraft. Thus, assuming all other requirements are met, H's purchase price for its $5/8$ fractional interest in the aircraft qualifies for the additional first year depreciation deduction and I's purchase price for its $3/8$ fractional interest in the aircraft qualifies for the additional first year depreciation deduction.

*Example 5.* On September 1, 2017, J, an equipment dealer, buys new tractors that are held by J primarily for sale to customers in the ordinary course of its business. On October 15, 2017, J withdraws the tractors from inventory and begins to use the tractors primarily for producing rental income. The holding of the tractors by J as inventory does not constitute a "use" for purposes of the original use requirement and, therefore, the original use of the tractors commences with J on October 15, 2017, for purposes of paragraph (b)(3)(ii) of this section. However, the tractors are not eligible for the 100-percent additional first year depreciation deduction because J acquired the tractors before September 28, 2017.

*Example 6.* K is in the trade or business of leasing equipment to others. During 2016, K buys a new machine (Machine #1) and then leases it to L for use in L's trade or business. The lease between K and L for Machine #1 is a true lease for federal income tax purposes. During 2018, L enters into a written binding contract with K to buy Machine #1 at its fair market value on May 15, 2018. L did not have any depreciable interest in Machine #1 before L acquired it on May 15, 2018. As a result, L's acquisition of Machine #1 satisfies the used property acquisition requirements of paragraph (b)(3)(iii) of this section. Assuming all other requirements are met, L's purchase price of Machine #1 qualifies for the additional first year depreciation deduction for L.

*Example 7.* The facts are the same as in *Example 6* of this paragraph (b)(3)(vi), except that K and L are related parties within the meaning of section 179(d)(2)(A) or (B) and §1.179-4(c). As a result, L's acquisition of Machine #1 does not satisfy the used property acquisition requirements of paragraph (b)(3)(iii) of this section. Thus, Machine #1 is not eligible for the additional first year depreciation deduction for L.

*Example 8.* The facts are the same as in *Example 6* of this paragraph (b)(3)(vi), except L incurred capital expenditures of $5,000 to improve Machine #1 on September 5, 2017, and has a depreciable interest in such improvements. L's purchase price of $5,000 for the improvements to Machine #1 satisfies the original use requirement of §1.168(k)-1(b)(3)(i) and, assuming all other requirements are met, qualifies for the 50-percent additional first year depreciation deduction. Because L had a depreciable interest only in the improvements to Machine #1, L's acquisition of Machine #1, excluding L's improvements to such machine, satisfies the used property acquisition requirements of paragraph (b)(3)(iii) of this section. Assuming all other requirements are met, L's unadjusted depreciable basis of Machine #1, excluding the amount of such unadjusted depreciable basis attributable to L's improvements to Machine #1, qualifies for the 100-percent additional first year depreciation deduction.

*Example 9.* During 2016, M and N purchased used equipment for use in their trades or businesses and each own a 50 percent interest in such equipment. Prior to this acquisition, M and N did not have any depreciable interest in the equipment. Assume this ownership arrangement is not a partnership. During 2018, N enters into a written binding contract with M to buy M's interest in the equipment. Pursuant to paragraph (b)(3)(iii)(B)(2) of this section, N is not treated as using M's interest in the equipment prior to N's acquisition of M's interest. As a result, N s acquisition of M's interest in the equipment satisfies the used property acquisition requirements of paragraph (b)(3)(iii) of this section. Assuming all other requirements are met, N's purchase price of M's interest in the equipment qualifies for the additional first year depreciation deduction for N.

*Example 10.* The facts are the same as in *Example 9* of this paragraph (b)(3)(vi), except N

had a 100 percent depreciable interest in the equipment prior to 2016 and M purchased from N a 50 percent interest in the equipment during 2016. As a result, N's acquisition of M's interest in the equipment during 2018 does not satisfy the used property acquisition requirements of paragraphs (b)(3)(iii)(A)(1) and (b)(3)(iii)(B)(1) of this section. Paragraph (b)(3)(iii)(B)(2) of this section does not apply because N initially acquired a 100 percent depreciable interest in the equipment. Accordingly, N's purchase price of M's interest in the equipment during 2018 does not qualify for the additional first year depreciation deduction for N.

*Example 11.* The facts are the same as in *Example 9* of this paragraph (b)(3)(vi), except during 2018, M also enters into a written binding contract with N to buy N's interest in the equipment. Pursuant to paragraph (b)(3)(iii)(B)(2) of this section, both M and N are treated as previously having a depreciable interest in a 50-percent portion of the equipment. Accordingly, the acquisition by M of N's 50-percent interest and the acquisition by N of M's 50-percent interest in the equipment during 2018 do not qualify for the additional first year depreciation deduction.

*Example 12.* O and P form an equal partnership, OP, in 2018. O contributes cash to OP, and P contributes equipment to OP. OP's basis in the equipment contributed by P is determined under section 723. Because OP's basis in such equipment is determined in whole or in part by reference to P's adjusted basis in such equipment, OP's acquisition of such equipment does not satisfy section 179(d)(2)(C) and §1.179-4(c)(1)(iv) and, thus, does not satisfy the used property acquisition requirements of paragraph (b)(3)(iii) of this section. Accordingly, OP's acquisition of such equipment is not eligible for the additional first year depreciation deduction.

*Example 13.* Q, R, and S form an equal partnership, QRS, in 2019. Each partner contributes $100, which QRS uses to purchase a retail motor fuels outlet for $300. Assume this retail motor fuels outlet is QRS' only property and is qualified property under section 168(k)(2)(A)(i). QRS makes an election not to deduct the additional first year depreciation for all qualified property placed in service during 2019. QRS has a section 754 election in effect. QRS claimed depreciation of $15 for the retail motor fuels outlet for 2019. During 2020, when the retail motor fuels outlet's fair market value is $600, Q sells all of his partnership interest to T in a fully taxable transaction for $200. T never previously had a depreciable interest in the retail motor fuels outlet. T takes an outside basis of $200 in the partnership interest previously owned by Q. T's share of the partnership's previously taxed capital is $95. Accordingly, T's section 743(b) adjustment is $105 and is allocated entirely to the retail motor fuels outlet under section 755. Assuming all other requirements are met, T's section 743(b) adjustment qualifies for the additional first year depreciation deduction.

*Example 14.* The facts are the same as in *Example 13* of this paragraph (b)(3)(vi), except that Q sells his partnership interest to U, a related person within the meaning of section 179(d)(2)(A) or (B) or §1.179-4(c). U's section 743(b) adjustment does not qualify for the additional first year depreciation deduction.

*Example 15.* The facts are the same as in *Example 13* of this paragraph (b)(3)(vi), except that Q dies and his partnership interest is transferred to V. V takes a basis in Q's partnership interest under section 1014. As a result, section 179(d)(2)(C)(ii) and §1.179-4(c)(1)(iv) are not satisfied, and V's section 743(b) adjustment does not qualify for the additional first year depreciation deduction.

*Example 16.* The facts are the same as in *Example 13* of this paragraph (b)(3)(vi), except that QRS purchased the retail motor fuels outlet from T prior to T purchasing Q's partnership interest in QRS. T had a depreciable interest in such retail motor fuels outlet. Because T had a depreciable interest in the retail motor fuels outlet before T acquired its interest in QRS, T's section 743(b) adjustment does not qualify for the additional first year depreciation deduction.

*Example 17.* In November 2017, AA Corporation purchases a used drill press costing $10,000 and is granted a trade-in allowance of $2,000 on its old drill press. The used drill press is qualified property under section 168(k)(2)(A)(i). The old drill press had a basis of $1,200. Under sections 1012 and 1031(d), the basis of the used drill press is $9,200 ($1,200 basis of old drill press plus cash expended of $8,000). Only $8,000 of the basis of the used drill press satisfies the requirements of section 179(d)(3) and §1.179-4(d) and, thus, satisfies the used property acquisition requirement of paragraph (b)(3)(iii) of this section. The remaining $1,200 of the basis of the used drill press does not satisfy the requirements of section 179(d)(3) and §1.179-4(d) because it is determined by reference to the old drill press. Accordingly, assuming all other requirements are met, only $8,000 of the basis of the used drill press is eligible for the additional first year depreciation deduction.

*Example 18.* In a series of related transactions, a father sells a machine to an unrelated party who sells the machine to the father's daughter for use in the daughter's trade or business. Pursuant to paragraph (b)(3)(iii)(C) of this section, the transfers of the machine are treated as a direct transfer from the father to his daughter and the time to test whether the parties are related is immediately after the last transaction in the series. Because the father and the daughter are related parties within the meaning of section 179(d)(2)(A) and §1.179-4(c)(ii), the daughter's acquisition of the machine does not satisfy the used property acquisition requirements of paragraph (b)(3)(iii) of this section. Further, because the transfers of the machine are treated as a direct transfer from the father to his daughter, the unrelated party's acquisition of the machine

is not eligible for the additional first year depreciation deduction.

*Example 19.* Parent owns all of the stock of B Corporation and C Corporation. Parent, B Corporation, and C Corporation are all members of the Parent consolidated group. C Corporation has a depreciable interest in Equipment #1. During 2018, C Corporation sells Equipment #1 to B Corporation. Prior to this acquisition, B Corporation never had a depreciable interest in Equipment #1. B Corporation's acquisition of Equipment #1 does not satisfy the used property acquisition requirements of paragraph (b)(3)(iii) of this section for two reasons. First, B Corporation and C Corporation are related parties within the meaning of section 179(d)(2)(B) and §1.179-4(c)(2)(iii). Second, pursuant to paragraph (b)(3)(iii)(B)(3)(i) of this section, B Corporation is treated as previously having a depreciable interest in Equipment #1 because B Corporation is a member of the Parent consolidated group and C Corporation, while a member of the Parent consolidated group, had a depreciable interest in Equipment #1. Accordingly, B Corporation's acquisition of Equipment #1 is not eligible for the additional first year depreciation deduction.

*Example 20.* (i) Parent owns all of the stock of D Corporation and E Corporation. Parent, D Corporation, and E Corporation are all members of the Parent consolidated group. D Corporation has a depreciable interest in Equipment #2. No other members of the Parent consolidated group ever had a depreciable interest in Equipment #2. During 2018, D Corporation sells Equipment #2 to BA, a person not related, within the meaning of section 179(d)(2)(A) or (B) and §1.179-4(c), to any member of the Parent consolidated group. In an unrelated transaction during 2019, E Corporation acquires Equipment #2 from BA or another person not related to any member of the Parent consolidated group within the meaning of section 179(d)(2)(A) or (B) and §1.179-4(c).

(ii) Pursuant to paragraph (b)(3)(iii)(B)(3)(i) of this section, E Corporation is treated as previously having a depreciable interest in Equipment #2 because E Corporation is a member of the Parent consolidated group, and D Corporation, while a member of the Parent consolidated group, had a depreciable interest in Equipment #2. As a result, E Corporation's acquisition of Equipment #2 does not satisfy the used property acquisition requirements of paragraph (b)(3)(iii) of this section. Thus, E Corporation's acquisition of Equipment #2 is not eligible for the additional first year depreciation deduction. The results would be the same if D Corporation had ceased to be a member of the Parent consolidated group prior to E Corporation's acquisition of Equipment #2.

*Example 21.* (i) Parent owns all of the stock of F Corporation and G Corporation. Parent, F Corporation, and G Corporation are all members of the Parent consolidated group. G Corporation has a depreciable interest in Equipment #3. No

**Prop. Reg. §1.168(k)-2(b)(3)(vi)**

other members of the Parent consolidated group ever had a depreciable interest in Equipment #3. X Corporation is the common parent of a consolidated group and is not related, within the meaning of section 179(d)(2)(A) or (B) and § 1.179-4(c), to any member of the Parent consolidated group. No member of the X consolidated group ever had a depreciable interest in Equipment #3. In a series of related transactions, G Corporation sells Equipment #3 to F Corporation, and Parent sells all of the stock of F Corporation to X Corporation.

(ii) F Corporation was a member of the Parent consolidated group at the time it acquired Equipment #3 from G Corporation, another member of the group. Paragraph (b)(3)(iii)(B)(3)(*i*) of this section generally treats each member of a consolidated group as having a depreciable interest in property during the time any member of the group had a depreciable interest in such property while a member of the group. Nevertheless, because there is a series of related transactions that includes the acquisition of Equipment #3 and a transaction in which F Corporation, the transferee of the property, leaves the Parent consolidated group and joins the X consolidated group, the time to test whether F Corporation is a member of the Parent consolidated group for purposes of paragraph (b)(3)(iii)(B)(3)(*i*) of this section is met is immediately after the last transaction in the series, that is, the sale of the F Corporation stock to X Corporation. See paragraph (b)(3)(iii)(B)(3)(*iii*) of this section. Accordingly, because F Corporation is not a member of the Parent consolidated group after the last transaction of the series, F Corporation is not treated as previously having a depreciable interest in Equipment #3 by virtue of G Corporation's depreciable interest in Equipment #3 under paragraph (b)(3)(iii)(B)(3)(*i*) of this section.

(iii) After the sale of the F Corporation stock to X Corporation, F Corporation is a member of the X consolidated group. Because no member of the X consolidated group previously had a depreciable interest in Equipment #3, F Corporation is not treated as previously having a depreciable interest in Equipment #3 under paragraph (b)(3)(iii)(B)(3)(*i*) of this section.

(iv) Because relatedness is tested after F Corporation leaves the Parent consolidated group, F Corporation and G Corporation are not related within the meaning of section 179(d)(2)(A) or (B) and § 1.179-4(c). Accordingly, F Corporation's acquisition of Equipment #3 satisfies the used property acquisition requirements of paragraph (b)(3)(iii)(A)(*1*) of this section and, assuming all other requirements are met, F Corporation's acquisition of Equipment #3 is eligible for the additional first year depreciation deduction.

*Example 22.* (i) H Corporation, which is not a member of a consolidated group, has a depreciable interest in Equipment #4. Parent owns all the stock of I Corporation, and Parent and I Corporation are members of the Parent consolidated group. No member of the Parent consolidated group ever had a depreciable interest in Equipment #4. Neither Parent nor I Corporation is related to H Corporation within the meaning of section 179(d)(2)(A) or (B) and § 1.179-4(c). During 2018, H Corporation sells Equipment #4 to a person not related to H Corporation, Parent, or I Corporation within the meaning of section 179(d)(2)(A) or (B) and § 1.179-4(c). In a series of related transactions, during 2019, Parent acquires all of the stock of H Corporation, and I Corporation purchases Equipment #4 from an unrelated person.

(ii) In a series of related transactions, H Corporation became a member of the Parent consolidated group, and I Corporation, also a member of the Parent consolidated group, acquired Equipment #4. Because H Corporation previously had a depreciable interest in Equipment #4, pursuant to paragraph (b)(3)(iii)(B)(3)(*ii*) of this section, I Corporation is treated as having a depreciable interest in Equipment #4. As a result, I Corporation's acquisition of Equipment #4 does not satisfy the used property acquisition requirements of paragraph (b)(3)(iii) of this section. Accordingly, I Corporation's acquisition of Equipment #4 is not eligible for the additional first year depreciation deduction.

*Example 23.* (i) J Corporation, K Corporation, and L Corporation are unrelated parties within the meaning of section 179(d)(2)(A) or (B) and § 1.179-4(c). None of J Corporation, K Corporation, and L Corporation is a member of a consolidated group. J Corporation has a depreciable interest in Equipment #5. During 2018, J Corporation sells Equipment #5 to K Corporation. During 2020, J Corporation merges into L Corporation in a transaction described in section 368(a)(1)(A). In 2021, L Corporation acquires Equipment #5 from K Corporation.

(ii) Because J Corporation is the predecessor of L Corporation and J Corporation previously had a depreciable interest in Equipment #5, L Corporation's acquisition of Equipment #5 does not satisfy paragraphs (b)(3)(iii)(A)(*1*) and (b)(3)(iii)(B)(*1*) of this section and, thus, does not satisfy the used property acquisition requirements of paragraph (b)(3)(iii) of this section. Accordingly, L Corporation's acquisition of Equipment #5 is not eligible for the additional first year depreciation deduction.

*Example 24.* (i) M Corporation acquires and places in service a used airplane on March 26, 2018. Prior to this acquisition, M Corporation never had a depreciable interest in this airplane. On March 26, 2018, M Corporation also leases the used airplane to N Corporation, an airline company. On May 27, 2018, M Corporation sells to O Corporation the used airplane subject to the lease with N Corporation. M Corporation and O Corporation are related parties within the meaning of section 179(d)(2)(A) or (B) and § 1.179-4(c). As of May 27, 2018, N Corporation is still the lessee of the used airplane. Prior to this acquisition, O Corporation never had a depreciable interest in the used airplane. O Corporation is a calendar-year taxpayer.

(ii) The sale transaction of May 27, 2018, satisfies the requirements of paragraph (b)(3)(v) of this section. As a result, O Corporation is considered the taxpayer that acquired the used airplane for purposes of applying the used property acquisition requirements in paragraph (b)(3)(iii) of this section. In applying these rules, the fact that M Corporation and O Corporation are related parties is not taken into account because O Corporation, not M Corporation, is treated as acquiring the used airplane. Further, pursuant to paragraph (b)(4)(iv) of this section, the used airplane is treated as originally placed in service by O Corporation on May 27, 2018. Because O Corporation never had a depreciable interest in the used airplane and assuming all other requirements are met, O Corporation's purchase price of the used airplane qualifies for the 100-percent additional first year depreciation deduction for O Corporation.

*Example 25.* (i) The facts are the same as in *Example 24* of this paragraph (b)(3)(vi). Additionally, on September 5, 2018, O Corporation sells to P Corporation the used airplane subject to the lease with N Corporation. Prior to this acquisition, P Corporation never had a depreciable interest in the used airplane.

(ii) Because O Corporation, a calendar-year taxpayer, placed in service and disposed of the used airplane during 2018, the used airplane is not eligible for the additional first year depreciation deduction for O Corporation pursuant to paragraph (f)(1)(i) of this section.

(iii) Because P Corporation never had a depreciable interest in the used airplane and assuming all other requirements are met, P Corporation's purchase price of the used airplane qualifies for the 100-percent additional first year depreciation deduction for P Corporation.

(4) *Placed-in-service date.*—(i) *In general.*— Depreciable property will meet the requirements of this paragraph (b)(4) if the property is placed in service by the taxpayer for use in its trade or business or for production of income after September 27, 2017; and, except as provided in paragraphs (b)(2)(i)(A) and (D) of this section, before January 1, 2027, or, in the case of property described in section 168(k)(2)(B) or (C), before January 1, 2028.

(ii) *Specified plant.*—If the taxpayer has properly made an election to apply section 168(k)(5) for a specified plant, the requirements of this paragraph (b)(4) are satisfied only if the specified plant is planted before January 1, 2027, or is grafted before January 1, 2027, to a plant that has already been planted, by the taxpayer in the ordinary course of the taxpayer's farming business, as defined in section 263A(e)(4).

(iii) *Qualified film, television, or live theatrical production.*—(A) For purposes of this paragraph (b)(4), a qualified film or television production is treated as placed in service at the time of initial release or broadcast as defined under § 1.181-1(a)(7).

(B) For purposes of this paragraph (b)(4), a qualified live theatrical production is treated as placed in service at the time of the initial live staged performance. Solely for purposes of this paragraph, the term *initial live staged performance* means the first commercial exhibition of a production to an audience. However, the term *initial live staged performance* does not include limited exhibition, prior to commercial exhibition to general audiences, if the limited exhibition is primarily for purposes of publicity, determining the need for further production activity, or raising funds for the completion of production. For example, an initial live staged performance does not include a preview of the production if the preview is primarily to determine the need for further production activity.

(iv) *Syndication transaction.*—If a lessor has a depreciable interest in the property and the lessor and any predecessor did not previously have a depreciable interest in the property, and the property is sold by the lessor or any subsequent purchaser within three months after the date the property was originally placed in service by the lessor (or, in the case of multiple units of property subject to the same lease, within three months after the date the final unit is placed in service, so long as the period between the time the first unit is placed in service and the time the last unit is placed in service does not exceed 12 months), and the user of the property after the last sale during this three-month period remains the same as when the property was originally placed in service by the lessor, the property is treated as originally placed in service by the purchaser of the property in the last sale during the three-month period but not earlier than the date of the last sale.

(v) *Technical termination of a partnership.*— For purposes of this paragraph (b)(4), in the case of a technical termination of a partnership under section 708(b)(1)(B) occurring in a taxable year beginning before January 1, 2018, qualified property placed in service by the terminated partnership during the taxable year of termination is treated as originally placed in service by the new partnership on the date the qualified property is contributed by the terminated partnership to the new partnership.

(vi) *Section 168(i)(7) transactions.*—For purposes of this paragraph (b)(4), if qualified property is transferred in a transaction described in section 168(i)(7) in the same taxable year that the qualified property is placed in service by the transferor, the transferred property is treated as originally placed in service on the date the transferor placed in service the qualified property. In the case of multiple transfers of qualified property in multiple transactions described in section 168(i)(7) in the same taxable year, the placed-in-service date of the transferred property is

**Prop. Reg. § 1.168(k)-2(b)(4)(vi)**

deemed to be the date on which the first transferor placed in service the qualified property.

(5) *Acquisition of property.*—(i) *In general.*—This paragraph (b)(5) provides rules for the acquisition requirements in section 13201(h) of the Act. These rules apply to all property, including self-constructed property or property described in section 168(k)(2)(B) or (C).

(ii) *Acquisition date.*—Except as provided in paragraph (b)(5)(vi) of this section, depreciable property will meet the requirements of this paragraph (b)(5) if the property is acquired by the taxpayer after September 27, 2017, or is acquired by the taxpayer pursuant to a written binding contract entered into by the taxpayer after September 27, 2017. Property that is manufactured, constructed, or produced for the taxpayer by another person under a written binding contract that is entered into prior to the manufacture, construction, or production of the property for use by the taxpayer in its trade or business or for its production of income is acquired pursuant to a written binding contract. If a taxpayer acquired the property pursuant to a written binding contract and such contract states the date on which the contract was entered into and a closing date, delivery date, or other similar date, the date on which the contract was entered into is the date the taxpayer acquired the property. See paragraph (b)(5)(v) of this section for when a qualified film, television, or live theatrical production is treated as acquired for purposes of this paragraph (b)(5).

(iii) *Definition of binding contract.*—(A) *In general.*—A contract is binding only if it is enforceable under State law against the taxpayer or a predecessor, and does not limit damages to a specified amount (for example, by use of a liquidated damages provision). For this purpose, a contractual provision that limits damages to an amount equal to at least 5 percent of the total contract price will not be treated as limiting damages to a specified amount. In determining whether a contract limits damages, the fact that there may be little or no damages because the contract price does not significantly differ from fair market value will not be taken into account. For example, if a taxpayer entered into an irrevocable written contract to purchase an asset for $100 and the contract did not contain a provision for liquidated damages, the contract is considered binding notwithstanding the fact that the asset had a fair market value of $99 and under local law the seller would only recover the difference in the event the purchaser failed to perform. If the contract provided for a full refund of the purchase price in lieu of any damages allowable by law in the event of breach or cancellation, the contract is not considered binding.

(B) *Conditions.*—A contract is binding even if subject to a condition, as long as the condition is not within the control of either party or a predecessor. A contract will continue to be binding if the parties make insubstantial changes in its terms and conditions or if any term is to be determined by a standard beyond the control of either party. A contract that imposes significant obligations on the taxpayer or a predecessor will be treated as binding notwithstanding the fact that certain terms remain to be negotiated by the parties to the contract.

(C) *Options.*—An option to either acquire or sell property is not a binding contract.

(D) *Letter of intent.*—A letter of intent for an acquisition is not a binding contract.

(E) *Supply agreements.*—A binding contract does not include a supply or similar agreement if the amount and design specifications of the property to be purchased have not been specified. The contract will not be a binding contract for the property to be purchased until both the amount and the design specifications are specified. For example, if the provisions of a supply or similar agreement state the design specifications of the property to be purchased, a purchase order under the agreement for a specific number of assets is treated as a binding contract.

(F) *Components.*—A binding contract to acquire one or more components of a larger property will not be treated as a binding contract to acquire the larger property. If a binding contract to acquire the component does not satisfy the requirements of this paragraph (b)(5), the component does not qualify for the additional first year depreciation deduction.

(iv) *Self-constructed property.*—(A) *In general.*—If a taxpayer manufactures, constructs, or produces property for use by the taxpayer in its trade or business or for its production of income, the acquisition rules in paragraph (b)(5)(ii) of this section are treated as met for the property if the taxpayer begins manufacturing, constructing, or producing the property after September 27, 2017. This paragraph (b)(5)(iv) does not apply to property that is manufactured, constructed, or produced for the taxpayer by another person under a written binding contract that is entered into prior to the manufacture, construction, or production of the property for use by the taxpayer in its trade or business or for its production of income (for further guidance, see paragraphs (b)(5)(ii) and (iii) of this section).

(B) *When does manufacture, construction, or production begin.*—(1) *In general.*—For purposes of paragraph (b)(5)(iv)(A) of this section, manufacture, construction, or production of property begins when physical work of a significant nature begins. Physical work does not include preliminary activities such as planning or designing, securing financing, exploring, or researching. The determination of when physical work of a significant nature begins depends on the facts and circumstances. For example, if the taxpayer constructs a retail motor fuels outlet on-site for use by the taxpayer in its trade or business, construction begins when physical work of a significant nature commences at the site by the taxpayer; that is, when work begins on the excavation for footings, pouring the pads for the outlet, or the driving of foundation pilings into the ground. Preliminary work, such as clearing a site, test drilling to determine soil condition, or excavation to change the contour of the land (as distinguished from excavation for footings) does not constitute the beginning of construction. However, if the taxpayer assembles a retail motor fuels outlet on-site from modular units manufactured off-site by the taxpayer and delivered to the site where the outlet will be used, manufacturing begins when physical work of a significant nature commences at the off-site location by the taxpayer.

(2) *Safe harbor.*—For purposes of paragraph (b)(5)(iv)(B)(1) of this section, a taxpayer may choose to determine when physical work of a significant nature begins in accordance with this paragraph (b)(5)(iv)(B)(2). Physical work of a significant nature will be considered to begin at the time the taxpayer incurs (in the case of an accrual basis taxpayer) or pays (in the case of a cash basis taxpayer) more than 10 percent of the total cost of the property (excluding the cost of any land and preliminary activities such as planning or designing, securing financing, exploring, or researching). A taxpayer chooses to apply this paragraph (b)(5)(iv)(B)(2) by filing a federal income tax return for the placed-in-service year of the property that determines when physical work of a significant nature begins consistent with this paragraph (b)(5)(iv)(B)(2).

(C) *Components of self-constructed property.*—(1) *Acquired components.*—If a binding contract, as defined in paragraph (b)(5)(iii) of this section, to acquire a component does not satisfy the requirements of paragraph (b)(5)(ii) of this section, the component does not qualify for the additional first year depreciation deduction. A binding contract described in the preceding sentence to acquire one or more components of a larger self-constructed property will not preclude the larger self-constructed property from satisfying the acquisition rules in paragraph (b)(5)(iv)(A) of this section. Accordingly, the unadjusted depreciable basis of the larger self-constructed property that is eligible for the additional first year depreciation deduction, assuming all other requirements are met, must not include the unadjusted depreciable basis of any component that does not satisfy the requirements of paragraph (b)(5)(ii) of this section. If the manufacture, construction, or production of the larger self-constructed property begins before September 28, 2017, the larger self-constructed property and any acquired components related to the larger self-constructed property do not qualify for the additional first year depreciation deduction under this section.

(2) *Self-constructed components.*—If the manufacture, construction, or production of a component by the taxpayer does not satisfy the requirements of this paragraph (b)(5)(iv), the component does not qualify for the additional first year depreciation deduction. However, if the manufacture, construction, or production of a component does not satisfy the requirements of this paragraph (b)(5)(iv), but the manufacture, construction, or production of the larger self-constructed property satisfies the requirements of this paragraph (b)(5)(iv), the larger self-constructed property qualifies for the additional first year depreciation deduction, assuming all other requirements are met, even though the component does not qualify for the additional first year depreciation deduction. Accordingly, the unadjusted depreciable basis of the larger self-constructed property that is eligible for the additional first year depreciation deduction, assuming all other requirements are met, must not include the unadjusted depreciable basis of any component that does not qualify for the additional first year depreciation deduction. If the manufacture, construction, or production of the larger self-constructed property began before September 28, 2017, the larger self-constructed property and any self-constructed components related to the larger self-constructed property do not qualify for the additional first year depreciation deduction under this section.

(v) *Qualified film, television, or live theatrical production.*—(A) For purposes of section 13201(h)(1)(A) of the Act, a qualified film or television production is treated as acquired on the date principal photography commences.

(B) For purposes of section 13201(h)(1)(A) of the Act, a qualified live theatrical production is treated as acquired on the date when all of the necessary elements for producing the live theatrical production are secured. These elements may include a script, financing, actors, set, scenic and costume designs, advertising agents, music, and lighting.

(vi) *Specified plant.*—If the taxpayer has properly made an election to apply section 168(k)(5) for a specified plant, the requirements of this paragraph (b)(5) are satisfied if the specified plant is planted after September 27, 2017, or is grafted after September 27, 2017, to a plant that has already been planted, by the taxpayer in the ordinary course of the taxpayer's farming business, as defined in section 263A(e)(4).

(vii) *Examples.*—The application of this paragraph (b)(5) is illustrated by the following examples. Unless the facts specifically indicate otherwise, assume that the parties are not related within the meaning of section 179(d)(2)(A) or (B) and § 1.179-4(c), and the parties do not have predecessors:

*Example 1.* On September 1, 2017, *BB*, a corporation, entered into a written agreement with *CC*, a manufacturer, to purchase 20 new lamps for $100 each within the next two years. Although the agreement specifies the number of lamps to be purchased, the agreement does not

**Prop. Reg. § 1.168(k)-2(b)(5)(vii)**

specify the design of the lamps to be purchased. Accordingly, the agreement is not a binding contract pursuant to paragraph (b)(5)(iii)(E) of this section.

*Example 2.* The facts are the same as in *Example 1* of this paragraph (b)(5)(vii). On December 1, 2017, *BB* placed a purchase order with *CC* to purchase 20 new model XPC5 lamps for $100 each for a total amount of $2,000. Because the agreement specifies the number of lamps to be purchased and the purchase order specifies the design of the lamps to be purchased, the purchase order placed by *BB* with *CC* on December 1, 2017, is a binding contract pursuant to paragraph (b)(5)(iii)(E) of this section. Accordingly, assuming all other requirements are met, the cost of the 20 lamps qualifies for the 100-percent additional first year depreciation deduction.

*Example 3.* The facts are the same as in *Example 1* of this paragraph (b)(5)(vii), except that the written agreement between *BB* and *CC* is to purchase 100 model XPC5 lamps for $100 each within the next two years. Because this agreement specifies the amount and design of the lamps to be purchased, the agreement is a binding contract pursuant to paragraph (b)(5)(iii)(E) of this section. However, because the agreement was entered into before September 28, 2017, no lamp acquired by *BB* under this contract qualifies for the 100-percent additional first year depreciation deduction.

*Example 4.* On September 1, 2017, *DD* began constructing a retail motor fuels outlet for its own use. On November 1, 2018, *DD* ceases construction of the retail motor fuels outlet prior to its completion. Between September 1, 2017, and November 1, 2018, *DD* incurred $3,000,000 of expenditures for the construction of the retail motor fuels outlet. On May 1, 2019, *DD* resumed construction of the retail motor fuels outlet and completed its construction on August 31, 2019. Between May 1, 2019, and August 31, 2019, *DD* incurred another $1,600,000 of expenditures to complete the construction of the retail motor fuels outlet and, on September 1, 2019, *DD* placed the retail motor fuels outlet in service. None of *DD*'s total expenditures of $4,600,000 qualify for the 100-percent additional first year depreciation deduction because, pursuant to paragraph (b)(5)(iv)(A) of this section, *DD* began constructing the retail motor fuels outlet before September 28, 2017.

*Example 5.* The facts are the same as in *Example 4* of this paragraph (b)(5)(vii) except that *DD* began constructing the retail motor fuels outlet for its own use on October 1, 2017, and *DD* incurred the $3,000,000 between October 1, 2017, and November 1, 2018. *DD*'s total expenditures of $4,600,000 qualify for the 100-percent additional first year depreciation deduction because, pursuant to paragraph (b)(5)(iv)(A) of this section, *DD* began constructing the retail motor fuels outlet after September 27, 2017, and *DD* placed the retail motor fuels outlet in service on September 1, 2019. Accordingly, assuming all other requirements are met, the additional first

year depreciation deduction for the retail motor fuels outlet will be $4,600,000, computed as $4,600,000 multiplied by 100 percent.

*Example 6.* On August 15, 2017, *EE* entered into a written binding contract with *FF* to manufacture an aircraft described in section 168(k)(2)(C) for use in *EE*'s trade or business. *FF* begins to manufacture the aircraft on October 1, 2017. *EE* places the aircraft in service on March 1, 2018. Pursuant to paragraph (b)(5)(ii) of this section, the aircraft is acquired by *EE* pursuant to a written binding contract. Because *EE* entered into such contract before September 28, 2017, the aircraft does not qualify for the 100-percent additional first year depreciation deduction.

*Example 7.* On June 1, 2017, *HH* entered into a written binding contract to acquire a new component part of property that is being constructed by *HH* for its own use in its trade or business. *HH* commenced construction of the property in November 2017, and placed the property in service in November 2018. Because *HH* entered into a written binding contract to acquire a component part prior to September 28, 2017, pursuant to paragraphs (b)(5)(ii) and (b)(5)(iv)(C)(1) of this section, the component part does not qualify for the 100-percent additional first year depreciation deduction. However, pursuant to paragraphs (b)(5)(iv)(A) and (b)(5)(iv)(C)(1) of this section, the property constructed by *HH* will qualify for the 100-percent additional first year depreciation deduction, because construction of the property began after September 27, 2017, assuming all other requirements are met. Accordingly, the unadjusted depreciable basis of the property that is eligible for the 100-percent additional first year depreciation deduction must not include the unadjusted depreciable basis of the component part.

*Example 8.* The facts are the same as in *Example 7* of this paragraph (b)(5)(vii) except that *HH* entered into the written binding contract to acquire the new component part on September 30, 2017, and *HH* commenced construction of the property on August 1, 2017. Pursuant to paragraphs (b)(5)(iv)(A) and (C) of this section, neither the property constructed by *HH* nor the component part will qualify for the 100-percent additional first year depreciation deduction, because *HH* began construction of the property prior to September 28, 2017.

*Example 9.* On September 1, 2017, *II* acquired and placed in service equipment. On October 15, 2017, *II* sells the equipment to *JJ* and leases the property back from *JJ* in a sale-leaseback transaction. Pursuant to paragraph (b)(5)(ii) of this section, *II*'s cost of the equipment does not qualify for the 100-percent additional first year depreciation deduction because *II* acquired the equipment prior to September 28, 2017. However, *JJ* acquired used equipment from an unrelated party after September 27, 2017, and, assuming all other requirements are met, *JJ*'s cost of the used equipment does qualify for the 100-percent additional first year depreciation deduction for *JJ*.

*Example 10.* On July 1, 2017, *KK* began constructing property for its own use in its trade or business. *KK* placed this property in service on September 15, 2017. On October 15, 2017, *KK* sells the property to *LL* and leases the property back from *LL* in a sale-leaseback transaction. Pursuant to paragraph (b)(5)(iv) of this section, *KK's* cost of the property does not qualify for the 100-percent additional first year depreciation deduction because construction began prior to September 28, 2017. However, *LL* acquired used property from an unrelated party after September 27, 2017, and, assuming all other requirements are met, *LL's* cost of the used property does qualify for the 100-percent additional first year depreciation deduction for *LL*.

(c) *Property described in section 168(k)(2)(B) or (C).*—(1) *In general.*—Property described in section 168(k)(2)(B) or (C) will meet the acquisition requirements of section 168(k)(2)(B)(i)(III) or (k)(2)(C)(i) if the property is acquired by the taxpayer before January 1, 2027, or acquired by the taxpayer pursuant to a written binding contract that is entered into before January 1, 2027. Property described in section 168(k)(2)(B) or (C) also must meet the acquisition requirement in section 13201(h)(1)(A) of the Act (for further guidance, see paragraph (b)(5) of this section).

(2) *Definition of binding contract.*—For purposes of this paragraph (c), the rules in paragraph (b)(5)(iii) of this section for a binding contract apply.

(3) *Self-constructed property.*—(i) *In general.*—If a taxpayer manufactures, constructs, or produces property for use by the taxpayer in its trade or business or for its production of income, the acquisition rules in paragraph (c)(1) of this section are treated as met for the property if the taxpayer begins manufacturing, constructing, or producing the property before January 1, 2027. Property that is manufactured, constructed, or produced for the taxpayer by another person under a written binding contract, as defined in paragraph (b)(5)(iii) of this section, that is entered into prior to the manufacture, construction, or production of the property for use by the taxpayer in its trade or business or for its production of income is considered to be manufactured, constructed, or produced by the taxpayer. If a taxpayer enters into a written binding contract, as defined in paragraph (b)(5)(iii) of this section, before January 1, 2027, with another person to manufacture, construct, or produce property described in section 168(k)(2)(B) or (C) and the manufacture, construction, or production of this property begins after December 31, 2026, the acquisition rule in paragraph (c)(1) of this section is met.

(ii) *When does manufacture, construction, or production begin.*—(A) *In general.*—For purposes of this paragraph (c)(3), manufacture, construction, or production of property begins when physical work of a significant nature begins. Physical work does not include preliminary activities such as planning or designing, securing financing, exploring, or researching. The determination of when physical work of a significant nature begins depends on the facts and circumstances. For example, if a retail motor fuels outlet is to be constructed on-site, construction begins when physical work of a significant nature commences at the site; that is, when work begins on the excavation for footings, pouring the pads for the outlet, or the driving of foundation pilings into the ground. Preliminary work, such as clearing a site, test drilling to determine soil condition, or excavation to change the contour of the land (as distinguished from excavation for footings) does not constitute the beginning of construction. However, if a retail motor fuels outlet is to be assembled on-site from modular units manufactured off-site and delivered to the site where the outlet will be used, manufacturing begins when physical work of a significant nature commences at the off-site location.

(B) *Safe harbor.*—For purposes of paragraph (c)(3)(ii)(A) of this section, a taxpayer may choose to determine when physical work of a significant nature begins in accordance with this paragraph (c)(3)(ii)(B). Physical work of a significant nature will be considered to begin at the time the taxpayer incurs (in the case of an accrual basis taxpayer) or pays (in the case of a cash basis taxpayer) more than 10 percent of the total cost of the property (excluding the cost of any land and preliminary activities such as planning or designing, securing financing, exploring, or researching). When property is manufactured, constructed, or produced for the taxpayer by another person, this safe harbor test must be satisfied by the taxpayer. For example, if a retail motor fuels outlet is to be constructed for an accrual basis taxpayer by another person for the total cost of $200,000 (excluding the cost of any land and preliminary activities such as planning or designing, securing financing, exploring, or researching), construction is deemed to begin for purposes of this paragraph (c)(3)(ii)(B) when the taxpayer has incurred more than 10 percent (more than $20,000) of the total cost of the property. A taxpayer chooses to apply this paragraph (c)(3)(ii)(B) by filing a federal income tax return for the placed-in-service year of the property that determines when physical work of a significant nature begins consistent with this paragraph (c)(3)(ii)(B).

(iii) *Components of self-constructed property.*—(A) *Acquired components.*—If a binding contract, as defined in paragraph (b)(5)(iii) of this section, to acquire a component does not satisfy the requirements of paragraph (c)(1) of this section, the component does not qualify for the additional first year depreciation deduction. A binding contract described in the preceding sentence to acquire one or more components of a larger self-constructed property will not preclude the larger self-constructed property from satisfying the acquisition rules in paragraph (c)(3)(i) of this section. Accordingly, the unad-

**Prop. Reg. § 1.168(k)-2(c)(3)(iii)(A)**

justed depreciable basis of the larger self-constructed property that is eligible for the additional first year depreciation deduction, assuming all other requirements are met, must not include the unadjusted depreciable basis of any component that does not satisfy the requirements of paragraph (c)(1) of this section. If a binding contract to acquire the component is entered into before January 1, 2027, but the manufacture, construction, or production of the larger self-constructed property does not begin before January 1, 2027, the component qualifies for the additional first year depreciation deduction, assuming all other requirements are met, but the larger self-constructed property does not.

(B) *Self-constructed components.*—If the manufacture, construction, or production of a component by the taxpayer does not satisfy the requirements of paragraph (c)(3)(i) of this section, the component does not qualify for the additional first year depreciation deduction. However, if the manufacture, construction, or production of a component does not satisfy the requirements of paragraph (c)(3)(i) of this section, but the manufacture, construction, or production of the larger self-constructed property satisfies the requirements of paragraph (c)(3)(i) of this section, the larger self-constructed property qualifies for the additional first year depreciation deduction, assuming all other requirements are met, even though the component does not qualify for the additional first year depreciation deduction. Accordingly, the unadjusted depreciable basis of the larger self-constructed property that is eligible for the additional first year depreciation deduction, assuming all other requirements are met, must not include the unadjusted depreciable basis of any component that does not qualify for the additional first year depreciation deduction. If the manufacture, construction, or production of a component begins before January 1, 2027, but the manufacture, construction, or production of the larger self-constructed property does not begin before January 1, 2027, the component qualifies for the additional first year depreciation deduction, assuming all other requirements are met, but the larger self-constructed property does not.

(iv) *Examples.*—The application of this paragraph (c) is illustrated by the following examples:

*Example 1.* On June 1, 2017, *MM* decided to construct property described in section 168(k)(2)(B) for its own use. However, one of the component parts of the property had to be manufactured by another person for *MM*. On August 15, 2017, *MM* entered into a written binding contract with *NN* to acquire this component part of the property for $100,000. The manufacture of the component part commenced on September 1, 2018, and *MM* received the completed component part on February 1, 2020. The cost of this component part is 9 percent of the total cost of the property to be constructed by *MM*. *MM* began constructing the property described in sec-

tion 168(k)(2)(B) on January 15, 2020, and placed this property, including all component parts, in service on November 1, 2021. Pursuant to paragraphs (b)(5)(iv)(C)(*1*) and (c)(1) of this section, the component part of $100,000 manufactured by *NN* for *MM* is not eligible for the 100-percent additional first year depreciation deduction because the written binding contract to acquire such component part was entered into before September 28, 2017. However, pursuant to paragraph (c)(3)(i) of this section, the cost of the property described in section 168(k)(2)(B), excluding the cost of the component part of $100,000 manufactured by *NN* for *MM*, is eligible for the 100-percent additional first year depreciation deduction, assuming all other requirements are met, because construction of the property began after September 27, 2017, and before January 1, 2027, and the property described in section 168(k)(2)(B) was placed in service by *MM* before January 1, 2028.

*Example 2.* On June 1, 2026, *OO* decided to construct property described in section 168(k)(2)(B) for its own use. However, one of the component parts of the property had to be manufactured by another person for *OO*. On August 15, 2026, *OO* entered into a written binding contract with *PP* to acquire this component part of the property for $100,000. The manufacture of the component part commenced on September 1, 2026, and *OO* received the completed component part on February 1, 2027. The cost of this component part is 9 percent of the total cost of the property to be constructed by *OO*. *OO* began constructing the property described in section 168(k)(2)(B) on January 15, 2027, and placed this property, including all component parts, in service on November 1, 2027. Pursuant to paragraph (c)(3)(iii)(B) of this section, the self-constructed component part of $100,000 manufactured by *PP* for *OO* is eligible for the additional first year depreciation deduction, assuming all other requirements are met, because the manufacturing of the component part began before January 1, 2027, and the property described in section 168(k)(2)(B), the larger self-constructed property, was placed in service by *OO* before January 1, 2028. However, pursuant to paragraph (c)(3)(i) of this section, the cost of the property described in section 168(k)(2)(B), excluding the cost of the self-constructed component part of $100,000 manufactured by *PP* for *OO*, is not eligible for the additional first year depreciation deduction because construction of the property began after December 31, 2026.

*Example 3.* On December 1, 2026, *QQ* entered into a written binding contract, as defined in paragraph (b)(5)(iii) of this section, with *RR* to manufacture an aircraft described in section 168(k)(2)(C) for use in *QQ*'s trade or business. *RR* begins to manufacture the aircraft on February 1, 2027. *QQ* places the aircraft in service on August 1, 2027. Pursuant to paragraph (c)(3)(i) of this section, the aircraft meets the requirements of paragraph (c)(1) of this section because the aircraft was acquired by *QQ* pursuant to a written binding contract entered into before January 1, 2027. Further, the aircraft was placed in service by *QQ* before January 1, 2028. Thus, assuming all other requirements are met, *QQ*'s cost of the aircraft is eligible for the additional first year depreciation deduction.

(d) *Computation of depreciation deduction for qualified property.*—(1) *Additional first year depreciation deduction.*—(i) *Allowable taxable year.*—The additional first year depreciation deduction is allowable—

(A) Except as provided in paragraph (d)(1)(i)(B) or (f) of this section, in the taxable year in which the qualified property is placed in service by the taxpayer for use in its trade or business or for the production of income; or

(B) In the taxable year in which the specified plant is planted, or grafted to a plant that has already been planted, by the taxpayer in the ordinary course of the taxpayer's farming business, as defined in section 263A(e)(4), if the taxpayer properly made the election to apply section 168(k)(5) (for further guidance, see paragraph (e) of this section).

(ii) *Computation.*—Except as provided in paragraph (f)(5) of this section, the allowable additional first year depreciation deduction for qualified property is determined by multiplying the unadjusted depreciable basis, as defined in §1.168(b)-1(a)(3), of the qualified property by the applicable percentage. Except as provided in paragraph (f)(1) of this section, the additional first year depreciation deduction is not affected by a taxable year of less than 12 months. See paragraph (f)(1) of this section for qualified property placed in service or planted or grafted, as applicable, and disposed of during the same taxable year. See paragraph (f)(5) of this section for qualified property acquired in a like-kind exchange or as a result of an involuntary conversion.

(iii) *Property described in section 168(k)(2)(B).*—For purposes of paragraph (d)(1)(ii) of this section, the unadjusted depreciable basis, as defined in §1.168(b)-1(a)(3), of qualified property described in section 168(k)(2)(B) is limited to the property's unadjusted depreciable basis attributable to the property's manufacture, construction, or production before January 1, 2027.

(iv) *Alternative minimum tax.*—(A) *In general.*—The additional first year depreciation deduction is allowable for alternative minimum tax purposes—

(1) Except as provided in paragraph (d)(1)(iv)(A)(2) of this section, in the taxable year in which the qualified property is placed in service by the taxpayer; or

(2) In the taxable year in which a specified plant is planted by the taxpayer, or grafted by the taxpayer to a plant that was previously planted, if the taxpayer properly made the

election to apply section 168(k)(5) (for further guidance, see paragraph (e) of this section).

(B) *Special rules.*—In general, the additional first year depreciation deduction for alternative minimum tax purposes is based on the unadjusted depreciable basis of the property for alternative minimum tax purposes. However, see paragraph (f)(5)(iii)(E) of this section for qualified property acquired in a like-kind exchange or as a result of an involuntary conversion.

(2) *Otherwise allowable depreciation deduction.*—(i) *In general.*—Before determining the amount otherwise allowable as a depreciation deduction for the qualified property for the placed-in-service year and any subsequent taxable year, the taxpayer must determine the remaining adjusted depreciable basis of the qualified property. This remaining adjusted depreciable basis is equal to the unadjusted depreciable basis, as defined in §1.168(b)-1(a)(3), of the qualified property reduced by the amount of the additional first year depreciation allowed or allowable, whichever is greater. The remaining adjusted depreciable basis of the qualified property is then depreciated using the applicable depreciation provisions under the Internal Revenue Code for the qualified property. The remaining adjusted depreciable basis of the qualified property that is MACRS property is also the basis to which the annual depreciation rates in the optional depreciation tables apply (for further guidance, see section 8 of Rev. Proc. 87-57 (1987-2 C.B. 687) and §601.601(d)(2)(ii)(*b*) of this chapter). The depreciation deduction allowable for the remaining adjusted depreciable basis of the qualified property is affected by a taxable year of less than 12 months.

(ii) *Alternative minimum tax.*—For alternative minimum tax purposes, the depreciation deduction allowable for the remaining adjusted depreciable basis of the qualified property is based on the remaining adjusted depreciable basis for alternative minimum tax purposes. The remaining adjusted depreciable basis of the qualified property for alternative minimum tax purposes is depreciated using the same depreciation method, recovery period (or useful life in the case of computer software), and convention that apply to the qualified property for regular tax purposes.

(3) *Examples.*—This paragraph (d) is illustrated by the following examples:

*Example 1.* On March 1, 2023, *SS*, a calendar-year taxpayer, purchased and placed in service qualified property that costs $1 million and is 5-year property under section 168(e). *SS* depreciates its 5-year property placed in service in 2023 using the optional depreciation table that corresponds with the general depreciation system, the 200-percent declining balance method, a 5-year recovery period, and the half-year convention.

For 2023, *SS* is allowed an 80-percent additional first year depreciation deduction of $800,000 (the unadjusted depreciable basis of $1 million multiplied by 0.80). Next, *SS* must reduce the unadjusted depreciable basis of $1 million by the additional first year depreciation deduction of $800,000 to determine the remaining adjusted depreciable basis of $200,000. Then, *SS'* depreciation deduction allowable in 2023 for the remaining adjusted depreciable basis of $200,000 is $40,000 (the remaining adjusted depreciable basis of $200,000 multiplied by the annual depreciation rate of 0.20 for recovery year 1).

*Example 2.* On June 1, 2023, *TT*, a calendar-year taxpayer, purchased and placed in service qualified property that costs $1,500,000. The property qualifies for the expensing election under section 179 and is 5-year property under section 168(e). *TT* did not purchase any other section 179 property in 2023. *TT* makes the election under section 179 for the property and depreciates its 5-year property placed in service in 2023 using the optional depreciation table that corresponds with the general depreciation system, the 200-percent declining balance method, a 5-year recovery period, and the half-year convention. Assume the maximum section 179 deduction for 2023 is $1,000,000. For 2023, *TT* is first allowed a $1,000,000 deduction under section 179. Next, *TT* must reduce the cost of $1,500,000 by the section 179 deduction of $1,000,000 to determine the unadjusted depreciable basis of $500,000. Then, for 2023, *TT* is allowed an 80-percent additional first year depreciation deduction of $400,000 (the unadjusted depreciable basis of $500,000 multiplied by 0.80). Next, *TT* must reduce the unadjusted depreciable basis of $500,000 by the additional first year depreciation deduction of $400,000 to determine the remaining adjusted depreciable basis of $100,000. Then, *TT*'s depreciation deduction allowable in 2023 for the remaining adjusted depreciable basis of $100,000 is $20,000 (the remaining adjusted depreciable basis of $100,000 multiplied by the annual depreciation rate of 0.20 for recovery year 1).

(e) *Elections under section 168(k).*—(1) *Election not to deduct additional first year depreciation.*—(i) *In general.*—A taxpayer may make an election not to deduct the additional first year depreciation for any class of property that is qualified property placed in service during the taxable year. If this election is made, the election applies to all qualified property that is in the same class of property and placed in service in the same taxable year, and no additional first year depreciation deduction is allowable for the property placed in service during the taxable year in the class of property, except as provided in § 1.743-1(j)(4)(i)(B)(*1*).

(ii) *Definition of class of property.*—For purposes of this paragraph (e)(1), the term *class of property* means:

(A) Except for the property described in paragraphs (e)(1)(ii)(B) and (D), and (e)(2) of this section, each class of property described in section 168(e) (for example, 5-year property);

(B) Water utility property as defined in section 168(e)(5) and depreciated under section 168;

(C) Computer software as defined in, and depreciated under, section 167(f)(1) and the regulations under section 167(f)(1);

(D) Qualified improvement property as defined in § 1.168(b)-1(a)(5)(i)(C) and (a)(5)(ii), and depreciated under section 168;

(E) Each separate production, as defined in § 1.181-3(b), of a qualified film or television production;

(F) Each separate production, as defined in section 181(e)(2), of a qualified live theatrical production; or

(G) A partner's basis adjustment in partnership assets under section 743(b) for each class of property described in paragraphs (e)(1)(ii)(A) through (F), and (e)(2) of this section (for further guidance, see § 1.743-1(j)(4)(i)(B)(*1*)).

(iii) *Time and manner for making election.*—(A) *Time for making election.*—Any election specified in paragraph (e)(1)(i) of this section must be made by the due date, including extensions, of the Federal tax return for the taxable year in which the qualified property is placed in service by the taxpayer.

(B) *Manner of making election.*—Any election specified in paragraph (e)(1)(i) of this section must be made in the manner prescribed on Form 4562, "Depreciation and Amortization," and its instructions. The election is made separately by each person owning qualified property (for example, for each member of a consolidated group by the common parent of the group, by the partnership (including basis adjustments in the partnership assets under section 743(b)), or by the S corporation). If Form 4562 is revised or renumbered, any reference in this section to that form shall be treated as a reference to the revised or renumbered form.

(iv) *Failure to make election.*—If a taxpayer does not make the election specified in paragraph (e)(1)(i) of this section within the time and in the manner prescribed in paragraph (e)(1)(iii) of this section, the amount of depreciation allowable for that property under section 167(f)(1) or 168, as applicable, must be determined for the placed-in-service year and for all subsequent taxable years by taking into account the additional first year depreciation deduction. Thus, any election specified in paragraph (e)(1)(i) of this section shall not be made by the taxpayer in any other manner (for example, the election cannot be made through a request under section 446(e) to change the taxpayer's method of accounting).

(2) *Election to apply section 168(k)(5) for specified plants.*—(i) *In general.*—A taxpayer may make an election to apply section 168(k)(5) to one or more specified plants that are planted, or grafted to a plant that has already been planted,

by the taxpayer in the ordinary course of the taxpayer's farming business, as defined in section 263A(e)(4). If this election is made for a specified plant, such plant is not treated as qualified property under section 168(k) and this section in its placed-in-service year.

(ii) *Time and manner for making election.*— (A) *Time for making election.*—Any election specified in paragraph (e)(2)(i) of this section must be made by the due date, including extensions, of the Federal tax return for the taxable year in which the taxpayer planted or grafted the specified plant to which the election applies.

(B) *Manner of making election.*—Any election specified in paragraph (e)(2)(i) of this section must be made in the manner prescribed on Form 4562, "Depreciation and Amortization," and its instructions. The election is made separately by each person owning specified plants (for example, for each member of a consolidated group by the common parent of the group, by the partnership, or by the S corporation). If Form 4562 is revised or renumbered, any reference in this section to that form shall be treated as a reference to the revised or renumbered form.

(iii) *Failure to make election.*—If a taxpayer does not make the election specified in paragraph (e)(2)(i) of this section for a specified plant within the time and in the manner prescribed in paragraph (e)(2)(ii) of this section, the specified plant is treated as qualified property under section 168(k), assuming all requirements are met, in the taxable year in which such plant is placed in service by the taxpayer. Thus, any election specified in paragraph (e)(2)(i) of this section shall not be made by the taxpayer in any other manner (for example, the election cannot be made through a request under section 446(e) to change the taxpayer's method of accounting).

(3) *Election for qualified property placed in service during the 2017 taxable year.*—(i) *In general.*— A taxpayer may make an election to deduct 50 percent, instead of 100 percent, additional first year depreciation for all qualified property acquired after September 27, 2017, by the taxpayer and placed in service by the taxpayer during its taxable year that includes September 28, 2017. If a taxpayer makes an election to apply section 168(k)(5) for its taxable year that includes September 28, 2017, the taxpayer also may make an election to deduct 50 percent, instead of 100 percent, additional first year depreciation for all specified plants that are planted, or grafted to a plant that has already been planted, after September 27, 2017, by the taxpayer in the ordinary course of the taxpayer's farming business during such taxable year.

(ii) *Time and manner for making election.*— (A) *Time for making election.*—Any election specified in paragraph (e)(3)(i) of this section must be made by the due date, including extensions, of the Federal tax return for the taxpayer's taxable year that includes September 28, 2017.

(B) *Manner of making election.*—Any election specified in paragraph (e)(3)(i) of this section must be made in the manner prescribed on the 2017 Form 4562, "Depreciation and Amortization," and its instructions. The election is made separately by each person owning qualified property (for example, for each member of a consolidated group by the common parent of the group, by the partnership, or by the S corporation).

(iii) *Failure to make election.*—If a taxpayer does not make the election specified in paragraph (e)(3)(i) of this section within the time and in the manner prescribed in paragraph (e)(3)(ii) of this section, the amount of depreciation allowable for qualified property under section 167(f)(1) or 168, as applicable, acquired and placed in service, or planted or grafted, as applicable, by the taxpayer after September 27, 2017, must be determined for the taxable year that includes September 28, 2017, and for all subsequent taxable years by taking into account the 100-percent additional first year depreciation deduction, unless the taxpayer makes the election specified in paragraph (e)(1)(i) of this section within the time and in the manner prescribed in paragraph (e)(1)(iii) of this section for the class of property in which the qualified property is included. Thus, any election specified in paragraph (e)(3)(i) of this section shall not be made by the taxpayer in any other manner (for example, the election cannot be made through a request under section 446(e) to change the taxpayer's method of accounting).

(4) *Alternative minimum tax.*—If a taxpayer makes an election specified in paragraph (e)(1) of this section for a class of property or in paragraph (e)(2) of this section for a specified plant, the depreciation adjustments under section 56 and the regulations under section 56 do not apply to the property or specified plant, as applicable, to which that election applies for purposes of computing the taxpayer's alternative minimum taxable income. If a taxpayer makes an election specified in paragraph (e)(3) of this section for all qualified property, see paragraphs (d)(1)(iv) and (d)(2)(ii) of this section.

(5) *Revocation of election.*—(i) *In general.*— Except as provided in paragraph (e)(5)(ii) of this section, an election specified in this paragraph (e), once made, may be revoked only by filing a request for a private letter ruling and obtaining the Commissioner of Internal Revenue's written consent to revoke the election. The Commissioner may grant a request to revoke the election if the taxpayer acted reasonably and in good faith, and the revocation will not prejudice the interests of the Government. See generally §301.9100-3 of this chapter. An election specified in this paragraph (e)may not be revoked through a request under section 446(e) to change the taxpayer's method of accounting.

**Prop. Reg. §1.168(k)-2(e)(5)(i)**

(ii) *Automatic 6-month extension.*—If a taxpayer made an election specified in this paragraph (e), an automatic extension of 6 months from the due date of the taxpayer's Federal tax return, excluding extensions, for the placed-in-service year or the taxable year in which the specified plant is planted or grafted, as applicable, is granted to revoke that election, provided the taxpayer timely filed the taxpayer's Federal tax return for the placed-in-service year or the taxable year in which the specified plant is planted or grafted, as applicable, and, within this 6-month extension period, the taxpayer, and all taxpayers whose tax liability would be affected by the election, file an amended Federal tax return for the placed-in-service year or the taxable year in which the specified plant is planted or grafted, as applicable, in a manner that is consistent with the revocation of the election.

(f) *Special rules.*—(1) *Property placed in service and disposed of in the same taxable year.*—(i) *In general.*—Except as provided in paragraphs (f)(1)(ii) and (iii) of this section, the additional first year depreciation deduction is not allowed for qualified property placed in service or planted or grafted, as applicable, and disposed of during the same taxable year. Also if qualified property is placed in service and disposed of during the same taxable year and then reacquired and again placed in service in a subsequent taxable year, the additional first year depreciation deduction is not allowable for the property in the subsequent taxable year.

(ii) *Technical termination of a partnership.*—In the case of a technical termination of a partnership under section 708(b)(1)(B) in a taxable year beginning before January 1, 2018, the additional first year depreciation deduction is allowable for any qualified property placed in service or planted or grafted, as applicable, by the terminated partnership during the taxable year of termination and contributed by the terminated partnership to the new partnership. The allowable additional first year depreciation deduction for the qualified property shall not be claimed by the terminated partnership but instead shall be claimed by the new partnership for the new partnership's taxable year in which the qualified property was contributed by the terminated partnership to the new partnership. However, if qualified property is both placed in service or planted or grafted, as applicable, and contributed to a new partnership in a transaction described in section 708(b)(1)(B) by the terminated partnership during the taxable year of termination, and if such property is disposed of by the new partnership in the same taxable year the new partnership received such property from the terminated partnership, then no additional first year depreciation deduction is allowable to either partnership.

(iii) *Section 168(i)(7) transactions.*—If any qualified property is transferred in a transaction described in section 168(i)(7) in the same taxable year that the qualified property is placed in service or planted or grafted, as applicable, by the transferor, the additional first year depreciation deduction is allowable for the qualified property. The allowable additional first year depreciation deduction for the qualified property for the transferor's taxable year in which the property is placed in service or planted or grafted, as applicable, is allocated between the transferor and the transferee on a monthly basis. This allocation shall be made in accordance with the rules in § 1.168(d)-1(b)(7)(ii) for allocating the depreciation deduction between the transferor and the transferee. However, solely for purposes of this section, if the qualified property is transferred in a section 721(a) transaction to a partnership that has as a partner a person, other than the transferor, who previously had a depreciable interest in the qualified property, in the same taxable year that the qualified property is placed in service or planted or grafted, as applicable, by the transferor, the allowable additional first year depreciation deduction is allocated entirely to the transferor, and not to the partnership. Additionally, if qualified property is both placed in service or planted or grafted, as applicable, and transferred in a transaction described in section 168(i)(7) by the transferor during the same taxable year, and if such property is disposed of by the transferee, other than by a transaction described in section 168(i)(7), during the same taxable year the transferee received such property from the transferor, then no additional first year depreciation deduction is allowable to either party.

(iv) *Examples.*—The application of this paragraph (f)(1) is illustrated by the following examples:

*Example 1. UU* and *VV* are equal partners in *Partnership JL*, a general partnership. *Partnership JL* is a calendar-year taxpayer. On October 1, 2017, *Partnership JL* purchased and placed in service qualified property at a cost of $30,000. On November 1, 2017, *UU* sells its entire 50 percent interest to *WW* in a transfer that terminates the partnership under section 708(b)(1)(B). As a result, terminated *Partnership JL* is deemed to have contributed the qualified property to new *Partnership JL*. Pursuant to paragraph (f)(1)(ii) of this section, new *Partnership JL*, not terminated *Partnership JL*, is eligible to claim the 100-percent additional first year depreciation deduction allowable for the qualified property for the taxable year 2017, assuming all other requirements are met.

*Example 2.* On January 5, 2018, *XX* purchased and placed in service qualified property for a total amount of $9,000. On August 20, 2018, *XX* transferred this qualified property to *Partnership BC* in a transaction described in section 721(a). No other partner of *Partnership BC* has ever had a depreciable interest in the qualified property. *XX* and *Partnership BC* are calendar-year taxpayers. Because the transaction between *XX* and *Partnership BC* is a transaction described in section 168(i)(7), pursuant to paragraph (f)(1)(iii) of this section, the 100-percent additional first year depreciation deduction allowable for the qualified property is allocated between *XX* and *Partnership BC* in accordance with the rules in § 1.168(d)-1(b)(7)(ii) for allocating the depreciation deduction between the transferor and the transferee. Accordingly, the 100-percent additional first year depreciation deduction allowable of $9,000 for the qualified property for 2018 is allocated between *XX* and *Partnership BC* based on the number of months that *XX* and *Partnership BC* held the qualified property in service during 2018. Thus, because the qualified property was held in service by *XX* for 7 of 12 months, which includes the month in which *XX* placed the qualified property in service but does not include the month in which the qualified property was transferred, *XX* is allocated $5,250 ($^7/_{12}$ × $9,000 additional first year depreciation deduction). *Partnership BC* is allocated $3,750, the remaining $^5/_{12}$ of the $9,000 additional first year depreciation deduction allowable for the qualified property.

(2) *Redetermination of basis.*—If the unadjusted depreciable basis, as defined in § 1.168(b)-1(a)(3), of qualified property is redetermined (for example, due to contingent purchase price or discharge of indebtedness) before January 1, 2027, or in the case of property described in section 168(k)(2)(B) or (C), is redetermined before January 1, 2028, the additional first year depreciation deduction allowable for the qualified property is redetermined as follows:

(i) *Increase in basis.*—For the taxable year in which an increase in basis of qualified property occurs, the taxpayer shall claim an additional first year depreciation deduction for qualified property by multiplying the amount of the increase in basis for this property by the applicable percentage for the taxable year in which the underlying property was placed in service by the taxpayer. For purposes of this paragraph (f)(2)(i), the additional first year depreciation deduction applies to the increase in basis only if the underlying property is qualified property. To determine the amount otherwise allowable as a depreciation deduction for the increase in basis of qualified property, the amount of the increase in basis of the qualified property must be reduced by the additional first year depreciation deduction allowed or allowable, whichever is greater, for the increase in basis and the remaining increase in basis of—

(A) Qualified property, except for computer software described in paragraph (b)(2)(i)(B) of this section, is depreciated over the recovery period of the qualified property remaining as of the beginning of the taxable year in which the increase in basis occurs, and using the same depreciation method and convention applicable to the qualified property that applies for the taxable year in which the increase in basis occurs; and

(B) Computer software, as defined in paragraph (b)(2)(i)(B) of this section, that is qualified property is depreciated ratably over the remainder of the 36-month period, the useful life under section 167(f)(1), as of the beginning of the first day of the month in which the increase in basis occurs.

(ii) *Decrease in basis.*—For the taxable year in which a decrease in basis of qualified property occurs, the taxpayer shall reduce the total amount otherwise allowable as a depreciation deduction for all of the taxpayer's depreciable property by the excess additional first year depreciation deduction previously claimed for the qualified property. If, for such taxable year, the excess additional first year depreciation deduction exceeds the total amount otherwise allowable as a depreciation deduction for all of the taxpayer's depreciable property, the taxpayer shall take into account a negative depreciation deduction in computing taxable income. The excess additional first year depreciation deduction for qualified property is determined by multiplying the amount of the decrease in basis for this property by the applicable percentage for the taxable year in which the underlying property was placed in service by the taxpayer. For purposes of this paragraph (f)(2)(ii), the additional first year depreciation deduction applies to the decrease in basis only if the underlying property is qualified property. Also, if the taxpayer establishes by adequate records or other sufficient evidence that the taxpayer claimed less than the additional first year depreciation deduction allowable for the qualified property before the decrease in basis, or if the taxpayer claimed more than the additional first year depreciation deduction allowable for the qualified property before the decrease in basis, the excess additional first year depreciation deduction is determined by multiplying the amount of the decrease in basis by the additional first year depreciation deduction percentage actually claimed by the taxpayer for the qualified property before the decrease in basis. To determine the amount to reduce the total amount otherwise allowable as a depreciation deduction for all of the taxpayer's depreciable property for the excess depreciation previously claimed, other than the additional first year depreciation deduction, resulting from the decrease in basis of the qualified property, the amount of the decrease in basis of the qualified property must be adjusted by the excess additional first year depreciation deduction that reduced the total amount otherwise allowable as a depreciation deduction, as determined under this paragraph (f)(2)(ii), and the remaining decrease in basis of—

(A) Qualified property, except for computer software described in paragraph (b)(2)(i)(B) of this section, reduces the amount otherwise allowable as a depreciation deduction over the recovery period of the qualified property remaining as of the beginning of the taxable year in which the decrease in basis occurs, and using the same depreciation method and convention of the qualified property that applies in the taxable year in which the decrease in basis occurs. If, for any taxable year, the reduction to the amount otherwise allowable as a depreciation deduction, as determined under this paragraph (f)(2)(ii)(A), exceeds the total amount otherwise allowable as a depreciation deduction for all of the taxpayer's depreciable property, the taxpayer shall take into account a negative depreciation deduction in computing taxable income; and

(B) Computer software, as defined in paragraph (b)(2)(i)(B) of this section, that is qualified property reduces the amount otherwise allowable as a depreciation deduction over the remainder of the 36-month period, the useful life under section 167(f)(1), as of the beginning of the first day of the month in which the decrease in basis occurs. If, for any taxable year, the reduction to the amount otherwise allowable as a depreciation deduction, as determined under this paragraph (f)(2)(ii)(B), exceeds the total amount otherwise allowable as a depreciation deduction for all of the taxpayer's depreciable property, the taxpayer shall take into account a negative depreciation deduction in computing taxable income.

(iii) *Definitions.*—Except as otherwise expressly provided by the Internal Revenue Code (for example, section 1017(a)), the regulations under the Internal Revenue Code, or other guidance published in the Internal Revenue Bulletin for purposes of this paragraph (f)(2)—

(A) An increase in basis occurs in the taxable year an amount is taken into account under section 461; and

(B) A decrease in basis occurs in the taxable year an amount would be taken into account under section 451.

(iv) *Examples.*—The application of this paragraph (f)(2) is illustrated by the following examples:

*Example 1.* (i) On May 15, 2023, YY, a cash-basis taxpayer, purchased and placed in service qualified property that is 5-year property at a cost of $200,000. In addition to the $200,000, YY agrees to pay the seller 25 percent of the gross profits from the operation of the property in 2023. On May 15, 2024, YY paid to the seller an additional $10,000. YY depreciates the 5-year property placed in service in 2023 using the optional depreciation table that corresponds with the general depreciation system, the 200-percent declining balance method, a 5-year recovery period, and the half-year convention.

(ii) For 2023, YY is allowed an 80-percent additional first year depreciation deduction of $160,000 (the unadjusted depreciable basis of $200,000 multiplied by 0.80). In addition, YY's depreciation deduction for 2023 for the remaining adjusted depreciable basis of $40,000 (the unadjusted depreciable basis of $200,000 reduced by the additional first year depreciation deduc-

tion of $160,000) is $8,000 (the remaining adjusted depreciable basis of $40,000 multiplied by the annual depreciation rate of 0.20 for recovery year 1).

(iii) For 2024, YY's depreciation deduction for the remaining adjusted depreciable basis of $40,000 is $12,800 (the remaining adjusted depreciable basis of $40,000 multiplied by the annual depreciation rate of 0.32 for recovery year 2). In addition, pursuant to paragraph (f)(2)(i) of this section, YY is allowed an additional first year depreciation deduction for 2024 for the $10,000 increase in basis of the qualified property. Consequently, YY is allowed an additional first year depreciation deduction of $8,000 (the increase in basis of $10,000 multiplied by 0.80, the applicable percentage for 2023). Also, YY is allowed a depreciation deduction for 2024 attributable to the remaining increase in basis of $2,000 (the increase in basis of $10,000 reduced by the additional first year depreciation deduction of $8,000). The depreciation deduction allowable for 2024 attributable to the remaining increase in basis of $2,000 is $889 (the remaining increase in basis of $2,000 multiplied by 0.4444, which is equal to 1/remaining recovery period of 4.5 years at January 1, 2024, multiplied by 2). Accordingly, for 2024, YY's total depreciation deduction allowable for the qualified property is $21,689 ($12,800 plus $8,000 plus $889).

*Example 2.* (i) On May 15, 2023, ZZ, a calendar-year taxpayer, purchased and placed in service qualified property that is 5-year property at a cost of $400,000. To purchase the property, ZZ borrowed $250,000 from Bank1. On May 15, 2024, Bank1 forgives $50,000 of the indebtedness. ZZ makes the election provided in section 108(b)(5) to apply any portion of the reduction under section 1017 to the basis of the depreciable property of the taxpayer. ZZ depreciates the 5-year property placed in service in 2023 using the optional depreciation table that corresponds with the general depreciation system, the 200-percent declining balance method, a 5-year recovery period, and the half-year convention.

(ii) For 2023, ZZ is allowed an 80-percent additional first year depreciation deduction of $320,000 (the unadjusted depreciable basis of $400,000 multiplied by 0.80). In addition, ZZ's depreciation deduction allowable for 2023 for the remaining adjusted depreciable basis of $80,000 (the unadjusted depreciable basis of $400,000 reduced by the additional first year depreciation deduction of $320,000) is $16,000 (the remaining adjusted depreciable basis of $80,000 multiplied by the annual depreciation rate of 0.20 for recovery year 1).

(iii) For 2024, ZZ's deduction for the remaining adjusted depreciable basis of $80,000 is $25,600 (the remaining adjusted depreciable basis of $80,000 multiplied by the annual depreciation rate 0.32 for recovery year 2). Although Bank1 forgave the indebtedness in 2024, the basis of the property is reduced on January 1, 2025, pursuant to sections 108(b)(5) and 1017(a) under which basis is reduced at the beginning of the

IRS Proposed Regulations **829**

taxable year following the taxable year in which the discharge of indebtedness occurs.

(iv) For 2025, ZZ's deduction for the remaining adjusted depreciable basis of $80,000 is $15,360 (the remaining adjusted depreciable basis of $80,000 multiplied by the annual depreciation rate 0.192 for recovery year 3). However, pursuant to paragraph (f)(2)(ii) of this section, ZZ must reduce the amount otherwise allowable as a depreciation deduction for 2025 by the excess depreciation previously claimed for the $50,000 decrease in basis of the qualified property. Consequently, ZZ must reduce the amount of depreciation otherwise allowable for 2025 by the excess additional first year depreciation of $40,000 (the decrease in basis of $50,000 multiplied by 0.80, the applicable percentage for 2023). Also, ZZ must reduce the amount of depreciation otherwise allowable for 2025 by the excess depreciation attributable to the remaining decrease in basis of $10,000 (the decrease in basis of $50,000 reduced by the excess additional first year depreciation of $40,000). The reduction in the amount of depreciation otherwise allowable for 2025 for the remaining decrease in basis of $10,000 is $5,714 (the remaining decrease in basis of $10,000 multiplied by 0.5714, which is equal to (1/remaining recovery period of 3.5 years at January 1, 2025) multiplied by 2). Accordingly, assuming the qualified property is the only depreciable property owned by ZZ, for 2025, ZZ has a negative depreciation deduction for the qualified property of $30,354 ($15,360 minus $40,000 minus $5,714).

(3) *Sections 1245 and 1250 depreciation recapture.*—For purposes of section 1245 and the regulations under section 1245, the additional first year depreciation deduction is an amount allowed or allowable for depreciation. Further, for purposes of section 1250(b) and the regulations under section 1250(b), the additional first year depreciation deduction is not a straight line method.

(4) *Coordination with section 169.*—The additional first year depreciation deduction is allowable in the placed-in-service year of a certified pollution control facility, as defined in § 1.169-2(a), that is qualified property even if the taxpayer makes the election to amortize the certified pollution control facility under section 169 and the regulations under section 169 in the certified pollution control facility's placed-in-service year.

(5) *Like-kind exchanges and involuntary conversions.*—(i) *Scope.*—The rules of this paragraph (f)(5) apply to replacement MACRS property or replacement computer software that is qualified property at the time of replacement provided the time of replacement is after September 27, 2017, and before January 1, 2027; or, in the case of replacement MACRS property or replacement computer software that is qualified property described in section 168(k)(2)(B) or (C), the time of

replacement is after September 27, 2017, and before January 1, 2028.

(ii) *Definitions.*—For purposes of this paragraph (f)(5), the following definitions apply:

(A) *Replacement MACRS property* has the same meaning as that term is defined in § 1.168(i)-6(b)(1).

(B) *Relinquished MACRS property* has the same meaning as that term is defined in § 1.168(i)-6(b)(2).

(C) *Replacement computer software* is computer software, as defined in paragraph (b)(2)(i)(B) of this section, in the hands of the acquiring taxpayer that is acquired for other computer software in a like-kind exchange or in an involuntary conversion.

(D) *Relinquished computer software* is computer software that is transferred by the taxpayer in a like-kind exchange or in an involuntary conversion.

(E) *Time of disposition* has the same meaning as that term is defined in § 1.168(i)-6(b)(3) for relinquished MACRS property. For relinquished computer software, *time of disposition* is when the disposition of the relinquished computer software takes place under the convention determined under § 1.167(a)-14(b).

(F) Except as provided in paragraph (f)(5)(iv) of this section, the *time of replacement* has the same meaning as that term is defined in § 1.168(i)-6(b)(4) for replacement MACRS property. For replacement computer software, the *time of replacement* is, except as provided in paragraph (f)(5)(iv) of this section, the later of—

(1) When the replacement computer software is placed in service under the convention determined under § 1.167(a)-14(b); or

(2) The time of disposition of the relinquished property.

(G) *Exchanged basis* has the same meaning as that term is defined in § 1.168(i)-6(b)(7) for MACRS property, as defined in § 1.168(b)-1(a)(2). For computer software, the *exchanged basis* is determined after the amortization deductions for the year of disposition are determined under § 1.167(a)-14(b) and is the lesser of—

(1) The basis in the replacement computer software, as determined under section 1031(d) and the regulations under section 1031(d), or section 1033(b) and the regulations under section 1033(b); or

(2) The adjusted depreciable basis of the relinquished computer software.

(H) *Excess basis* has the same meaning as that term is defined in § 1.168(i)-6(b)(8) for replacement MACRS property. For replacement computer software, the *excess basis* is any excess of the basis in the replacement computer software, as determined under section 1031(d) and the regulations under section 1031(d), or section 1033(b) and the regulations under section

**Prop. Reg. § 1.168(k)-2(f)(5)(ii)(H)**

1033(b), over the exchanged basis as determined under paragraph (f)(5)(ii)(G) of this section.

(I) *Remaining exchanged basis* is the exchanged basis as determined under paragraph (f)(5)(ii)(G) of this section reduced by—

(1) The percentage of such basis attributable to the taxpayer's use of property for the taxable year other than in the taxpayer's trade or business or for the production of income; and

(2) Any adjustments to basis provided by other provisions of the Code and the regulations under the Code (including section 1016(a)(2) and (3)) for periods prior to the disposition of the relinquished property.

(J) *Remaining excess basis* is the excess basis as determined under paragraph (f)(5)(ii)(H) of this section reduced by—

(1) The percentage of such basis attributable to the taxpayer's use of property for the taxable year other than in the taxpayer's trade or business or for the production of income;

(2) Any portion of the basis the taxpayer properly elects to treat as an expense under section 179 or 179C; and

(3) Any adjustments to basis provided by other provisions of the Code and the regulations under the Code.

(K) *Year of disposition* has the same meaning as that term is defined in §1.168(i)-6(b)(5).

(L) *Year of replacement* has the same meaning as that term is defined in §1.168(i)-6(b)(6).

(M) *Like-kind exchange* has the same meaning as that term is defined in §1.168(i)-6(b)(11).

(N) *Involuntary conversion* has the same meaning as that term is defined in §1.168(i)-6(b)(12).

(iii) *Computation.*—(A) *In general.*—If the replacement MACRS property or the replacement computer software, as applicable, meets the original use requirement in paragraph (b)(3)(ii) of this section and all other requirements of section 168(k) and this section, the remaining exchanged basis for the year of replacement and the remaining excess basis, if any, for the year of replacement for the replacement MACRS property or the replacement computer software, as applicable, are eligible for the additional first year depreciation deduction. If the replacement MACRS property or the replacement computer software, as applicable, meets the used property acquisition requirements in paragraph (b)(3)(iii) of this section and all other requirements of section 168(k) and this section, only the remaining excess basis for the year of replacement for the replacement MACRS property or the replacement computer software, as applicable, is eligible for the additional first year depreciation deduction. See paragraph (b)(3)(iii)(A)(3) of this section. The additional first year depreciation deduction applies to the remaining exchanged basis and any remaining excess basis, as applicable, of the replacement MACRS property or the replacement computer software, as applicable, if the time of replacement is after September 27, 2017, and before January 1, 2027; or, in the case of replacement MACRS property or replacement computer software, as applicable, described in section 168(k)(2)(B) or (C), the time of replacement is after September 27, 2017, and before January 1, 2028. The additional first year depreciation deduction is computed separately for the remaining exchanged basis and any remaining excess basis, as applicable.

(B) *Year of disposition and year of replacement.*—The additional first year depreciation deduction is allowable for the replacement MACRS property or replacement computer software in the year of replacement. However, the additional first year depreciation deduction is not allowable for the relinquished MACRS property or the relinquished computer software, as applicable, if the relinquished MACRS property or the relinquished computer software, as applicable, is placed in service and disposed of in a like-kind exchange or in an involuntary conversion in the same taxable year.

(C) *Property described in section 168(k)(2)(B).*—For purposes of paragraph (f)(5)(iii)(A) of this section, the total of the remaining exchanged basis and the remaining excess basis, if any, of the replacement MACRS property that is qualified property described in section 168(k)(2)(B) and meets the original use requirement in paragraph (b)(3)(ii) of this section is limited to the total of the property's remaining exchanged basis and remaining excess basis, if any, attributable to the property's manufacture, construction, or production after September 27, 2017, and before January 1, 2027. For purposes of paragraph (f)(5)(iii)(A) of this section, the remaining excess basis, if any, of the replacement MACRS property that is qualified property described in section 168(k)(2)(B) and meets the used property acquisition requirements in paragraph (b)(3)(iii) of this section is limited to the property's remaining excess basis, if any, attributable to the property's manufacture, construction, or production after September 27, 2017, and before January 1, 2027.

(D) *Effect of §1.168(i)-6(i)(1) election.*—If a taxpayer properly makes the election under §1.168(i)-6(i)(1) not to apply §1.168(i)-6 for any MACRS property, as defined in §1.168(b)-1(a)(2), involved in a like-kind exchange or involuntary conversion and either of the following:

(1) The replacement MACRS property meets the original use requirement in paragraph (b)(3)(ii) of this section and all other requirements of section 168(k) and this section, the total of the exchanged basis, as defined in §1.168(i)-6(b)(7), and the excess basis, as defined in §1.168(i)-6(b)(8), if any, in the replacement

MACRS property is eligible for the additional first year depreciation deduction; or

(2) The replacement MACRS property meets the used property acquisition requirements in paragraph (b)(3)(iii) of this section and all other requirements of section 168(k) and this section, only the excess basis, as defined in § 1.168(i)-6(b)(8), if any, in the replacement MACRS property is eligible for the additional first year depreciation deduction.

(E) *Alternative minimum tax.*—The additional first year depreciation deduction is allowed for alternative minimum tax purposes for the year of replacement of replacement MACRS property or replacement computer software, as applicable, that is qualified property. If the replacement MACRS property or the replacement computer software, as applicable, meets the original use requirement in paragraph (b)(3)(ii) of this section and all other requirements of section 168(k) and this section, the additional first year depreciation deduction for alternative minimum tax purposes is based on the remaining exchanged basis and the remaining excess basis, if any, of the replacement MACRS property or the replacement computer software, as applicable, for alternative minimum tax purposes. If the replacement MACRS property or the replacement computer software, as applicable, meets the used property acquisition requirements in paragraph (b)(3)(iii) of this section and all other requirements of section 168(k) and this section, the additional first year depreciation deduction for alternative minimum tax purposes is based on the remaining excess basis, if any, of the replacement MACRS property or the replacement computer software, as applicable, for alternative minimum tax purposes.

(iv) *Replacement MACRS property or replacement computer software that is acquired and placed in service before disposition of relinquished MACRS property or relinquished computer software.*—If, in an involuntary conversion, a taxpayer acquires and places in service the replacement MACRS property or the replacement computer software, as applicable, before the time of disposition of the involuntarily converted MACRS property or the involuntarily converted computer software, as applicable; and the time of disposition of the involuntarily converted MACRS property or the involuntarily converted computer software, as applicable, is after December 31, 2026, or, in the case of property described in service 168(k)(2)(B) or (C), after December 31, 2027, then—

(A) The time of replacement for purposes of this paragraph (f)(5) is when the replacement MACRS property or replacement computer software, as applicable, is placed in service by the taxpayer, provided the threat or imminence of requisition or condemnation of the involuntarily converted MACRS property or involuntarily converted computer software, as applicable, existed before January 1, 2027, or, in the

case of property described in section 168(k)(2)(B) or (C), existed before January 1, 2028; and

(B) The taxpayer depreciates the replacement MACRS property or replacement computer software, as applicable, in accordance with paragraph (d) of this section. However, at the time of disposition of the involuntarily converted MACRS property, the taxpayer determines the exchanged basis, as defined in § 1.168(i)-6(b)(7), and the excess basis, as defined in § 1.168(i)-6(b)(8), of the replacement MACRS property and begins to depreciate the depreciable exchanged basis, as defined in § 1.168(i)-6(b)(9), of the replacement MACRS property in accordance with § 1.168(i)-6(c). The depreciable excess basis, as defined in § 1.168(i)-6(b)(10), of the replacement MACRS property continues to be depreciated by the taxpayer in accordance with the first sentence of this paragraph (f)(5)(iv)(B). Further, in the year of disposition of the involuntarily converted MACRS property, the taxpayer must include in taxable income the excess of the depreciation deductions allowable, including the additional first year depreciation deduction allowable, on the unadjusted depreciable basis of the replacement MACRS property over the additional first year depreciation deduction that would have been allowable to the taxpayer on the remaining exchanged basis of the replacement MACRS property at the time of replacement, as defined in paragraph (f)(5)(v)(A) of this section, plus the depreciation deductions that would have been allowable, including the additional first year depreciation deduction allowable, to the taxpayer on the depreciable excess basis of the replacement MACRS property from the date the replacement MACRS property was placed in service by the taxpayer, taking into account the applicable convention, to the time of disposition of the involuntarily converted MACRS property. Similar rules apply to replacement computer software.

(v) *Examples.*—The application of this paragraph (f)(5) is illustrated by the following examples:

*Example 1.* (i) In April 2016, *CSK*, a calendar-year corporation, acquired for $200,000 and placed in service Canopy V1, a gas station canopy. Canopy V1 is qualified property under section 168(k)(2), as in effect on the day before amendment by the Act, and is 5-year property under section 168(e). *CSK* depreciated Canopy V1 under the general depreciation system of section 168(a) by using the 200-percent declining balance method of depreciation, a 5-year recovery period, and the half-year convention. *CSK* elected to use the optional depreciation tables to compute the depreciation allowance for Canopy V1. In November 2017, Canopy V1 was destroyed in a fire and was no longer usable in *CSK*'s business. In December 2017, in an involuntary conversion, *CSK* acquired and placed in service Canopy W1 with all of the $160,000 of insurance proceeds *CSK* received due to the loss of Canopy V1. Canopy W1 is qualified property under section 168(k)(2) and this section, and is 5-year property under section 168(e). Canopy W1 also meets the original use requirement in paragraph (b)(3)(ii) of this section. *CSK* did not make the election under § 1.168(i)-6(i)(1).

(ii) For 2016, *CSK* is allowed a 50-percent additional first year depreciation deduction of $100,000 for Canopy V1 (the unadjusted depreciable basis of $200,000 multiplied by 0.50), and a regular MACRS depreciation deduction of $20,000 for Canopy V1 (the remaining adjusted depreciable basis of $100,000 multiplied by the annual depreciation rate of 0.20 for recovery year 1).

(iii) For 2017, *CSK* is allowed a regular MACRS depreciation deduction of $16,000 for Canopy V1 (the remaining adjusted depreciable basis of $100,000 multiplied by the annual depreciation rate of 0.32 for recovery year 2 ×½ year).

(iv) Pursuant to paragraph (f)(5)(iii)(A) of this section, the additional first year depreciation deduction allowable for Canopy W1 for 2017 equals $64,000 (100 percent of Canopy W1's remaining exchanged basis at the time of replacement of $64,000 (Canopy V1's remaining adjusted depreciable basis of $100,000 minus 2016 regular MACRS depreciation deduction of $20,000 minus 2017 regular MACRS depreciation deduction of $16,000)).

*Example 2.* (i) The facts are the same as in *Example 1* of this paragraph (f)(5)(v), except *CSK* elected not to deduct the additional first year depreciation for 5-year property placed in service in 2016. *CSK* deducted the additional first year depreciation for 5-year property placed in service in 2017.

(ii) For 2016, *CSK* is allowed a regular MACRS depreciation deduction of $40,000 for Canopy V1 (the unadjusted depreciable basis of $200,000 multiplied by the annual depreciation rate of 0.20 for recovery year 1).

(iii) For 2017, *CSK* is allowed a regular MACRS depreciation deduction of $32,000 for Canopy V1 (the unadjusted depreciable basis of $200,000 multiplied by the annual depreciation rate of 0.32 for recovery year 2 ×½ year).

(iv) Pursuant to paragraph (f)(5)(iii)(A) of this section, the additional first year depreciation deduction allowable for Canopy W1 for 2017 equals $128,000 (100 percent of Canopy W1's remaining exchanged basis at the time of replacement of $128,000 (Canopy V1's unadjusted depreciable basis of $200,000 minus 2016 regular MACRS depreciation deduction of $40,000 minus 2017 regular MACRS depreciation deduction of $32,000)).

*Example 3.* The facts are the same as in *Example 1* of this paragraph (f)(5)(v), except Canopy W1 meets the used property acquisition requirements in paragraph (b)(3)(iii) of this section. Because the remaining excess basis of Canopy W1 is zero, *CSK* is not allowed any additional first year depreciation for Canopy W1

pursuant to paragraph (f)(5)(iii)(A) of this section.

*Example 4.* (i) In December 2016, *AB*, a calendar-year corporation, acquired for $10,000 and placed in service Computer X2. Computer X2 is qualified property under section 168(k)(2), as in effect on the day before amendment by the Act, and is 5-year property under section 168(e). *AB* depreciated Computer X2 under the general depreciation system of section 168(a) by using the 200-percent declining balance method of depreciation, a 5-year recovery period, and the half-year convention. *AB* elected to use the optional depreciation tables to compute the depreciation allowance for Computer X2. In November 2017, *AB* acquired Computer Y2 by exchanging Computer X2 and $1,000 cash in a like-kind exchange. Computer Y2 is qualified property under section 168(k)(2) and this section, and is 5-year property under section 168(e). Computer Y2 also meets the original use requirement in paragraph (b)(3)(ii) of this section. *AB* did not make the election under § 1.168(i)-6(i)(1).

(ii) For 2016, *AB* is allowed a 50-percent additional first year depreciation deduction of $5,000 for Computer X2 (unadjusted basis of $10,000 multiplied by 0.50), and a regular MACRS depreciation deduction of $1,000 for Computer X2 (the remaining adjusted depreciable basis of $5,000 multiplied by the annual depreciation rate of 0.20 for recovery year 1).

(iii) For 2017, *AB* is allowed a regular MACRS depreciation deduction of $800 for Computer X2 (the remaining adjusted depreciable basis of $5,000 multiplied by the annual depreciation rate of 0.32 for recovery year 2 ×½ year).

(iv) Pursuant to paragraph (f)(5)(iii)(A) of this section, the 100-percent additional first year depreciation deduction for Computer Y2 for 2017 is allowable for the remaining exchanged basis at the time of replacement of $3,200 (Computer X2's unadjusted depreciable basis of $10,000 minus additional first year depreciation deduction allowable of $5,000 minus the 2016 regular MACRS depreciation deduction of $1,000 minus the 2017 regular MACRS depreciation deduction of $800) and for the remaining excess basis at the time of replacement of $1,000 (cash paid for Computer Y2). Thus, the 100-percent additional first year depreciation deduction allowable for Computer Y2 totals $4,200 for 2017.

*Example 5.* (i) In July 2017, *BC*, a calendar-year corporation, acquired for $20,000 and placed in service Equipment X3. Equipment X3 is qualified property under section 168(k)(2), as in effect on the day before amendment by the Act, and is 5-year property under section 168(e). *BC* depreciated Equipment X3 under the general depreciation system of section 168(a) by using the 200-percent declining balance method of depreciation, a 5-year recovery period, and the half-year convention. *BC* elected to use the optional depreciation tables to compute the depreciation allowance for Equipment X3. In

December 2017, *BC* acquired Equipment Y3 by exchanging Equipment X3 and $5,000 cash in a like-kind exchange. Equipment Y3 is qualified property under section 168(k)(2) and this section, and is 5-year property under section 168(e). Equipment Y3 also meets the used property acquisition requirements in paragraph (b)(3)(iii) of this section. *BC* did not make the election under § 1.168(i)-6(i)(1).

(ii) Pursuant to § 1.168(k)-1(f)(5)(iii)(B), no additional first year depreciation deduction is allowable for Equipment X3 and, pursuant to § 1.168(d)-1(b)(3)(ii), no regular depreciation deduction is allowable for Equipment X3, for 2017.

(iii) Pursuant to paragraph (f)(5)(iii)(A) of this section, no additional first year depreciation deduction is allowable for Equipment Y3's remaining exchanged basis at the time of replacement of $20,000 (Equipment X3's unadjusted depreciable basis of $20,000). However, pursuant to paragraph (f)(5)(iii)(A) of this section, the 100-percent additional first year depreciation deduction is allowable for Equipment Y3's remaining excess basis at the time of replacement of $5,000 (cash paid for Equipment Y3). Thus, the 100-percent additional first year depreciation deduction allowable for Equipment Y3 is $5,000 for 2017.

*Example 6.* (i) The facts are the same as in *Example 5* of this paragraph (f)(5)(v), except *BC* properly makes the election under § 1.168(i)-6(i)(1) not to apply § 1.168(i)-6 to Equipment X3 and Equipment Y3.

(ii) Pursuant to § 1.168(k)-1(f)(5)(iii)(B), no additional first year depreciation deduction is allowable for Equipment X3 and, pursuant to § 1.168(d)-1(b)(3)(ii), no regular depreciation deduction is allowable for Equipment X3, for 2017.

(iii) Pursuant to § 1.168(i)-6(i)(1), *BC* is treated as placing Equipment Y3 in service in December 2017 with a basis of $25,000 (the total of the exchanged basis of $20,000 and the excess basis of $5,000). However, pursuant to paragraph (f)(5)(iii)(D)(2) of this section, the 100-percent additional first year depreciation deduction is allowable only for Equipment Y3's excess basis at the time of replacement of $5,000 (cash paid for Equipment Y3). Thus, the 100-percent additional first year depreciation deduction allowable for Equipment Y3 is $5,000 for 2017.

(6) *Change in use.*—(i) *Change in use of depreciable property.*—The determination of whether the use of depreciable property changes is made in accordance with section 168(i)(5) and § 1.168(i)-4.

(ii) *Conversion to personal use.*—If qualified property is converted from business or income-producing use to personal use in the same taxable year in which the property is placed in service by a taxpayer, the additional first year depreciation deduction is not allowable for the property.

(iii) *Conversion to business or income-producing use.*—(A) *During the same taxable year.*—If,

during the same taxable year, property is acquired by a taxpayer for personal use and is converted by the taxpayer from personal use to business or income-producing use, the additional first year depreciation deduction is allowable for the property in the taxable year the property is converted to business or income-producing use, assuming all of the requirements in paragraph (b) of this section are met. See paragraph (b)(3)(ii) of this section relating to the original use rules for a conversion of property to business or income-producing use.

(B) *Subsequent to the acquisition year.*—If property is acquired by a taxpayer for personal use and, during a subsequent taxable year, is converted by the taxpayer from personal use to business or income-producing use, the additional first year depreciation deduction is allowable for the property in the taxable year the property is converted to business or income-producing use, assuming all of the requirements in paragraph (b) of this section are met. For purposes of paragraphs (b)(4) and (5) of this section, the property must be acquired by the taxpayer for personal use after September 27, 2017, and converted by the taxpayer from personal use to business or income-producing use by January 1, 2027. See paragraph (b)(3)(ii) of this section relating to the original use rules for a conversion of property to business or income-producing use.

(iv) *Depreciable property changes use subsequent to the placed-in-service year.*—(A) If the use of qualified property changes in the hands of the same taxpayer subsequent to the taxable year the qualified property is placed in service and, as a result of the change in use, the property is no longer qualified property, the additional first year depreciation deduction allowable for the qualified property is not redetermined.

(B) If depreciable property is not qualified property in the taxable year the property is placed in service by the taxpayer, the additional first year depreciation deduction is not allowable for the property even if a change in the use of the property subsequent to the taxable year the property is placed in service results in the property being qualified property in the taxable year of the change in use.

(v) *Examples.*—The application of this paragraph (f)(6) is illustrated by the following examples:

*Example 1.* (i) On January 1, 2019, *FFF*, a calendar year corporation, purchased and placed in service several new computers at a total cost of $100,000. *FFF* used these computers within the United States for 3 months in 2019 and then moved and used the computers outside the United States for the remainder of 2019. On January 1, 2020, *FFF* permanently returns the computers to the United States for use in its business.

(ii) For 2019, the computers are considered as used predominantly outside the United States in 2019 pursuant to § 1.48-1(g)(1)(i). As a result, the computers are required to be depreciated under the alternative depreciation system of section 168(g). Pursuant to paragraph (b)(2)(ii)(B) of this section, the computers are not qualified property in 2019, the placed-in-service year. Thus, pursuant to paragraph (f)(6)(iv)(B) of this section, no additional first year depreciation deduction is allowed for these computers, regardless of the fact that the computers are permanently returned to the United States in 2020.

*Example 2.* (i) On February 8, 2023, GGG, a calendar year corporation, purchased and placed in service new equipment at a cost of $1,000,000 for use in its California plant. The equipment is 5-year property under section 168(e) and is qualified property under section 168(k). GGG depreciates its 5-year property placed in service in 2023 using the optional depreciation table that corresponds with the general depreciation system, the 200-percent declining balance method, a 5-year recovery period, and the half-year convention. On June 4, 2024, due to changes in GGG's business circumstances, GGG permanently moves the equipment to its plant in Mexico.

(ii) For 2023, GGG is allowed an 80-percent additional first year depreciation deduction of $800,000 (the adjusted depreciable basis of $1,000,000 multiplied by 0.80). In addition, GGG's depreciation deduction allowable in 2023 for the remaining adjusted depreciable basis of $200,000 (the unadjusted depreciable basis of $1,000,000 reduced by the additional first year depreciation deduction of $800,000) is $40,000 (the remaining adjusted depreciable basis of $200,000 multiplied by the annual depreciation rate of 0.20 for recovery year 1).

(iii) For 2024, the equipment is considered as used predominantly outside the United States pursuant to §1.48-1(g)(1)(i). As a result of this change in use, the adjusted depreciable basis of $160,000 for the equipment is required to be depreciated under the alternative depreciation system of section 168(g) beginning in 2024. However, the additional first year depreciation deduction of $800,000 allowed for the equipment in 2023 is not redetermined.

(7) *Earnings and profits.*—The additional first year depreciation deduction is not allowable for purposes of computing earnings and profits.

(8) *Limitation of amount of depreciation for certain passenger automobiles.*—For a passenger automobile as defined in section 280F(d)(5), the limitation under section 280F(a)(1)(A)(i) is increased by $8,000 for qualified property acquired and placed in service by a taxpayer after September 27, 2017.

(9) *Coordination with section 47.*—(i) *In general.*—If qualified rehabilitation expenditures, as defined in section 47(c)(2) and §1.48-12(c), incurred by a taxpayer with respect to a qualified rehabilitated building, as defined in section 47(c)(1) and §1.48-12(b), are qualified property, the taxpayer may claim the rehabilitation credit

provided by section 47(a), provided the requirements of section 47 are met—

(A) With respect to the portion of the basis of the qualified rehabilitated building that is attributable to the qualified rehabilitation expenditures if the taxpayer makes the applicable election under paragraph (e)(1)(i) of this section not to deduct any additional first year depreciation for the class of property that includes the qualified rehabilitation expenditures; or

(B) With respect to the portion of the remaining rehabilitated basis of the qualified rehabilitated building that is attributable to the qualified rehabilitation expenditures if the taxpayer claims the additional first year depreciation deduction on the unadjusted depreciable basis, as defined in §1.168(b)-1(a)(3) but before the reduction in basis for the amount of the rehabilitation credit, of the qualified rehabilitation expenditures; and the taxpayer depreciates the remaining adjusted depreciable basis, as defined in paragraph (d)(2)(i) of this section, of such expenditures using straight line cost recovery in accordance with section 47(c)(2)(B)(i) and §1.48-12(c)(7)(i). For purposes of this paragraph (f)(9)(i)(B), the remaining rehabilitated basis is equal to the unadjusted depreciable basis, as defined in §1.168(b)-1(a)(3) but before the reduction in basis for the amount of the rehabilitation credit, of the qualified rehabilitation expenditures that are qualified property reduced by the additional first year depreciation allowed or allowable, whichever is greater.

(ii) *Example.*—The application of this paragraph (f)(9) is illustrated by the following example:

*Example.* (i) Between February 8, 2023, and June 4, 2023, JM, a calendar-year taxpayer, incurred qualified rehabilitation expenditures of $200,000 with respect to a qualified rehabilitated building that is nonresidential real property under section 168(e). These qualified rehabilitation expenditures are qualified property and qualify for the 20-percent rehabilitation credit under section 47(a)(1). JM's basis in the qualified rehabilitated building is zero before incurring the qualified rehabilitation expenditures and JM placed the qualified rehabilitated building in service in July 2023. JM depreciates its nonresidential real property placed in service in 2023 under the general depreciation system of section 168(a) by using the straight line method of depreciation, a 39-year recovery period, and the mid-month convention. JM elected to use the optional depreciation tables to compute the depreciation allowance for its depreciable property placed in service in 2023. Further, for 2023, JM did not make any election under paragraph (e) of this section.

(ii) Because JM did not make any election under paragraph (e) of this section, JM is allowed an 80-percent additional first year depreciation deduction of $160,000 for the qualified rehabilitation expenditures for 2023 (the unadjusted depreciable basis of $200,000 (before reduction in basis for the rehabilitation credit) multiplied by 0.80). JM also is allowed to claim a rehabilitation credit of $8,000 for the remaining rehabilitated basis of $40,000 (the unadjusted depreciable basis (before reduction in basis for the rehabilitation credit) of $200,000 less the additional first year depreciation deduction of $160,000, multiplied by 0.20 to calculate the rehabilitation credit). For 2023, the ratable share of the rehabilitation credit of $8,000 is $1,600. Further, JM's depreciation deduction for 2023 for the remaining adjusted depreciable basis of $32,000 (the unadjusted depreciable basis (before reduction in basis for the rehabilitation credit) of $200,000 less the additional first year depreciation deduction of $160,000 less the rehabilitation credit of $8,000) is $376.64 (the remaining adjusted depreciable basis of $32,000 multiplied by the depreciation rate of 0.01177 for recovery year 1, placed in service in month 7).

(10) *Coordination with section 514(a)(3).*—The additional first year depreciation deduction is not allowable for purposes of section 514(a)(3).

(g) *Applicability dates.*—(1) *In general.*—Except as provided in paragraph (g)(2) of this section, the rules of this section apply to—

(i) Qualified property under section 168(k)(2) that is placed in service by the taxpayer during or after the taxpayer's taxable year that includes the date of publication of a Treasury decision adopting these rules as final regulations in the **Federal Register**; and

(ii) A specified plant for which the taxpayer properly made an election to apply section 168(k)(5) and that is planted, or grafted to a plant that was previously planted, by the taxpayer during or after the taxpayer's taxable year that includes the date of publication of a Treasury decision adopting these rules as final regulations in the **Federal Register**.

(2) *Early application.*—A taxpayer may rely on the provisions of this section in these proposed regulations for—

(i) Qualified property under section 168(k)(2) acquired and placed in service after September 27, 2017, by the taxpayer during taxable years ending on or after September 28, 2017, and ending before the taxpayer's taxable year that includes the date of publication of a Treasury decision adopting these rules as final regulations in the **Federal Register**; and

(ii) A specified plant for which the taxpayer properly made an election to apply section 168(k)(5) and that is planted, or grafted to a plant that was previously planted, after September 27, 2017, by the taxpayer during taxable years ending on or after September 28, 2017, and ending before the taxpayer's taxable year that includes the date of publication of a Treasury decision adopting these rules as final regulations in the **Federal Register**. [Reg. § 1.168(k)-2.]

[Proposed 8-8-2018.]

**[Prop. Reg. § 1.169-3]**

**§ 1.169-3. Amortizable basis.**—(a) * * * Further, before computing the amortization deduction allowable under section 169, the adjusted basis for purposes of determining gain for a facility that is acquired and placed in service after September 27, 2017, and that is qualified property under section 168(k), as amended by the Tax Cuts and Jobs Act, Public Law 115-97 (131 Stat. 2054 (December 22, 2017)) (the "Act"), or § 1.168(k)-2, must be reduced by the amount of the additional first year depreciation deduction allowed or allowable, whichever is greater, under section 168(k), as amended by the Act.

* * *

(g) * * * The last sentence of paragraph (a) of this section applies to a certified pollution control facility that is qualified property under section 168(k)(2) and placed in service by a taxpayer during or after the taxpayer's taxable year that includes the date of publication of a Treasury decision adopting these rules as final regulations in the **Federal Register**. However, a taxpayer may rely on the last sentence in paragraph (a) of this section in these proposed regulations for a certified pollution control facility that is qualified property under section 168(k)(2) and acquired and placed in service after September 27, 2017, by the taxpayer during taxable years ending on or after September 28, 2017, and ending before the taxpayer's taxable year that includes the date of publication of a Treasury decision adopting these rules as final regulations in the **Federal Register**.

[Proposed 8-8-2018.]

**[Prop. Reg. § 1.170A-1]**

**§ 1.170A-1. Charitable, etc., contributions and gifts; allowance of deduction.**

* * *

(h) * * *

(3) *Payments resulting in state or local tax benefits.*—(i) *State or local tax credits.*—Except as provided in paragraph (h)(3)(v) of this section, if a taxpayer makes a payment or transfers property to or for the use of an entity listed in section 170(c), the amount of the taxpayer's charitable contribution deduction under section 170(a) is reduced by the amount of any state or local tax credit that the taxpayer receives or expects to receive in consideration for the taxpayer's payment or transfer.

(ii) *State or local tax deductions.*—(A) *In general.*—If a taxpayer makes a payment or transfers property to or for the use of an entity listed in section 170(c), and the taxpayer receives or expects to receive a state or local tax deduction that does not exceed the amount of the taxpayer's payment or the fair market value of the property transferred by the taxpayer to such entity, the taxpayer is not required to reduce its charitable contribution deduction under section 170(a) on account of such state or local tax deduction.

(B) *Excess state or local tax deductions.*—If the taxpayer receives or expects to receive a state or local tax deduction that exceeds the amount of the taxpayer's payment or the fair market value of the property transferred, the taxpayer's charitable contribution deduction under section 170 is reduced.

(iii) *In consideration for.*—For purposes of paragraph (h)(3)(i) of this section, the term *in consideration for* shall have the meaning set forth in §1.170A-13(f)(6), except that the state or local tax credit need not be provided by the donee organization.

(iv) *Amount of reduction.*—For purposes of paragraph (h)(3)(i) of this section, the amount of any state or local tax credit is the maximum credit allowable that corresponds to the amount of the taxpayer's payment or transfer to the entity listed in section 170(c).

(v) *State or local tax.*—For purposes of paragraph (h)(3) of this section, the term *state or local tax* means a tax imposed by a State, a possession of the United States, or by a political subdivision of any of the foregoing, or by the District of Columbia.

(vi) *Exception.*—Paragraph (h)(3)(i) of this section shall not apply to any payment or transfer of property if the amount of the state or local tax credit received or expected to be received by the taxpayer does not exceed 15 percent of the taxpayer's payment, or 15 percent of the fair market value of the property transferred by the taxpayer.

(vii) *Examples.*—The following examples illustrate the provisions of this paragraph (h)(3). The examples in paragraph (h)(6) of this section are not illustrative for purposes of this paragraph (h)(3).

*Example 1.* A, an individual, makes a payment of $1,000 to X, an entity listed in section 170(c). In exchange for the payment, A receives or expects to receive a state tax credit of 70% of the amount of A's payment to X. Under paragraph (h)(3)(i) of this section, A's charitable contribution deduction is reduced by $700 (70% x $1,000). This reduction occurs regardless of whether A is able to claim the state tax credit in that year. Thus, A's charitable contribution deduction for the $1,000 payment to X may not exceed $300.

*Example 2.* B, an individual, transfers a painting to Y, an entity listed in section 170(c). At the time of the transfer, the painting has a fair market value of $100,000. In exchange for the painting, B receives or expects to receive a state tax credit equal to 10% of the fair market value of the painting. Under paragraph (h)(3)(vi) of this section, B is not required to apply the general rule of paragraph (h)(3)(i) of this section

because the amount of the tax credit received or expected to be received by B does not exceed 15% of the fair market value of the property transferred to Y. Accordingly, the amount of B's charitable contribution deduction for the transfer of the painting is not reduced under paragraph (h)(3)(i) of this section.

*Example 3.* C, an individual, makes a payment of $1,000 to Z, an entity listed in section 170(c). In exchange for the payment, under state M law, C is entitled to receive a state tax deduction equal to the amount paid by C to Z. Under paragraph (h)(3)(ii)(A) of this section, C is not required to reduce its charitable contribution deduction under section 170(a) on account of the state tax deduction.

(viii) *Effective/applicability date.*—This paragraph (h)(3) applies to amounts paid or property transferred by a taxpayer after August 27, 2018.

* * *

[Proposed 8-27-2018.]

**[Prop. Reg. §1.179-4]**

**§1.179-4. Definitions.**

* * *

(c) * * *

(2) Property deemed to have been acquired by a new target corporation as a result of a section 338 election (relating to certain stock purchases treated as asset acquisitions) or a section 336(e) election (relating to certain stock dispositions treated as asset transfers) will be considered acquired by purchase.

* * *

[Proposed 8-8-2018.]

**[Prop. Reg. §1.179-6]**

**§1.179-6. Effective/applicability dates.**—(a) * * * Except as provided in paragraphs (b), (c), (d), and (e) of this section, the provisions of §§1.179-1 through 1.179-5 apply for property placed in service by the taxpayer in taxable years ending after January 25, 1993. * * *

* * *

(e) *Application of §1.179-4(c)(2).*—(1) *In general.*—Except as provided in paragraph (e)(2) of this section, the provisions of §1.179-4(c)(2) relating to section 336(e) are applicable on or after the date of publication of a Treasury decision adopting these rules as final regulations in the **Federal Register**.

(2) *Early application.*—A taxpayer may rely on the provisions of §1.179-4(c)(2) relating to section 336(e) in these proposed regulations for the taxpayer's taxable years ending on or after September 28, 2017, and ending before the date of publication of a Treasury decision adopting these rules as final regulations in the **Federal Register**.

[Proposed 8-8-2018.]

**[Prop. Reg. §1.199A-3]**

**§1.199A-3. Qualified business income, qualified REIT dividends, and qualified PTP income.—**

\* \* \*

(b) \*\*\*

(1) \* \* \*

(iv) *Previously disallowed losses.*—(A) *In general.*—Previously disallowed losses or deductions (including losses disallowed under sections 465, 469, 704(d), and 1366(d)) allowed in the taxable year generally are taken into account for purposes of computing QBI to the extent the disallowed loss or deduction is otherwise allowed by section 199A and this section. These losses shall be used, for purposes of section 199A and these regulations, in order from the oldest to the most recent on a first-in, first-out (FIFO) basis and shall be treated as losses from a separate trade or business. To the extent such losses relate to a PTP, they must be treated as a loss from a separate PTP in the taxable year the losses are taken into account. However, losses or deductions that were disallowed, suspended, limited, or carried over from taxable years ending before January 1, 2018 (including under sections 465, 469, 704(d), and 1366(d)), are not taken into account in a later taxable year for purposes of computing QBI.

(B) *Attributes of disallowed loss determined in year loss is incurred.*—Whether a disallowed loss or deduction is attributable to a trade or business, and otherwise meets the requirements of this section is determined in the year the loss is incurred. Whether a disallowed loss or deduction is attributable to a specified service trade or business (including whether an individual has taxable income under the threshold amount, within the phase-in range, or in excess of the phase-in range) also is determined in the year the loss is incurred. To the extent a loss is partially disallowed, QBI in the year of disallowance must be reduced proportionately.

\* \* \*

(d) *Section 199A dividends paid by a regulated investment company.*—(1) *In general.*—If section 852(b) applies to a regulated investment company (RIC) for a taxable year, the RIC may pay section 199A dividends, as defined in this paragraph (d).

(2) *Definition of section 199A dividend.*—(i) *In general.*—Except as provided in paragraph (d)(2)(ii) of this section, a section 199A dividend is any dividend or part of such a dividend that a RIC pays to its shareholders and reports as a section 199A dividend in written statements furnished to its shareholders.

(ii) *Reduction in the case of excess reported amounts.*—If the aggregate reported amount with respect to the RIC for any taxable year exceeds the RIC's qualified REIT dividend income for the taxable year, then a section 199A dividend is equal to—

(A) The reported section 199A dividend amount, reduced by;

(B) The excess reported amount that is allocable to that reported section 199A dividend amount.

(iii) *Allocation of excess reported amount.*—(A) *In general.*—Except as provided in paragraph (d)(2)(iii)(B) of this section, the excess reported amount (if any) that is allocable to the reported section 199A dividend amount is that portion of the excess reported amount that bears the same ratio to the excess reported amount as the reported section 199A dividend amount bears to the aggregate reported amount.

(B) *Special rule for noncalendar-year RICs.*—In the case of any taxable year that does not begin and end in the same calendar year, if the post-December reported amount equals or exceeds the excess reported amount for that taxable year, paragraph (d)(2)(iii)(A) of this section is applied by substituting "post-December reported amount" for "aggregate reported amount," and no excess reported amount is allocated to any dividend paid on or before December 31 of that taxable year.

(3) *Definitions.*—For purposes of paragraph (d) of this section—

(i) *Reported section 199A dividend amount.*—The term *reported section 199A dividend amount* means the amount of a dividend distribution reported to the RIC's shareholders under paragraph (d)(2)(i) of this section as a section 199A dividend.

(ii) *Excess reported amount.*—The term *excess reported amount* means the excess of the aggregate reported amount over the RIC's qualified REIT dividend income for the taxable year.

(iii) *Aggregate reported amount.*—The term *aggregate reported amount* means the aggregate amount of dividends reported by the RIC under paragraph (d)(2)(i) of this section as section 199A dividends for the taxable year (including section 199A dividends paid after the close of the taxable year and described in section 855).

(iv) *Post-December reported amount.*—The term *post-December reported amount* means the aggregate reported amount determined by taking into account only dividends paid after December 31 of the taxable year.

(v) *Qualified REIT dividend income.*—The term *qualified REIT dividend income* means, with respect to a taxable year of a RIC, the excess of the amount of qualified REIT dividends, as defined in §1.199A-3(c)(2), includible in the RIC's taxable income for the taxable year over the

**Prop. Reg. §1.199A-3(d)(3)(v)**

amount of the RIC's deductions that are properly allocable to such income.

(4) *Treatment of section 199A dividends by shareholders.*—(i) *In general.*—For purposes of section 199A and the regulations under section 199A, a section 199A dividend is treated by a taxpayer that receives the section 199A dividend as a qualified REIT dividend.

(ii) *Holding period.*—Paragraph (d)(4)(i) does not apply to any dividend received with respect to a share of RIC stock—

(A) That is held by the shareholder for 45 days or less (taking into account the principles of section 246(c)(3) and (4)) during the 91-day period beginning on the date which is 45 days before the date on which the share becomes ex-dividend with respect to such dividend; or

(B) To the extent that the shareholder is under an obligation (whether pursuant to a short sale or otherwise) to make related payments with respect to positions in substantially similar or related property.

(5) *Example.*—The following example illustrates the provisions of this paragraph (d).

(i) *Example.* (A) X is a corporation that has elected to be a RIC. For its taxable year ending March 31, 2019, X has $25,000x of net long-term capital gain, $60,000x of qualified dividend income, $25,000x of taxable interest income, $15,000x of net short-term capital gain, and $25,000x of qualified REIT dividends. X has $15,000x of deductible expenses, of which $3,000x is allocable to the qualified REIT dividends. On December 31, 2018, X pays a single dividend of $100,000x on December 31, and reports $20,000x of the dividend as a section 199A dividend in written statements to its shareholders. On March 31, 2019, X pays a dividend of $35,000x, and reports $5,000x of the dividend as a section 199A dividend in written statements to its shareholders.

(B) X's qualified REIT dividend income under paragraph (d)(3)(v) of this section is $22,000x, which is the excess of X's $25,000x of qualified REIT dividends over $3,000x in allocable expenses. The reported section 199A dividend amounts for the December 31, 2018, and March 31, 2019, distributions are $20,000x and $5,000x, respectively. For the taxable year ending March 31, 2019, the aggregate reported amount of section 199A dividends is $25,000x, and the excess reported amount under paragraph (d)(3)(ii) of this section is $3,000x. Because X is a noncalendar-year RIC and the post-December reported amount of $5,000x exceeds the excess reported amount of $3,000x, the entire excess reported amount is allocated under paragraphs (d)(2)(iii)(A) and (B) of this section to the reported section 199A dividend amount for the March 31, 2019, distribution. No portion of the excess reported amount is allocated to the reported section 199A dividend amount for the December 31, 2018, distribution. Thus, the section 199A dividend on March 31, 2019, is

$2,000x, which is the reported section 199A dividend amount of $5,000x reduced by the $3,000x of allocable excess reported amount. The section 199A dividend on December 31, 2018, is the $20,000x that X reports as a section 199A dividend.

(C) Shareholder A, a United States person, receives a dividend from X of $100x on December 31, 2018, of which $20x is reported as a section 199A dividend. If A meets the holding period requirements in paragraph (d)(4)(ii) of this section with respect to the stock of X, A treats $20x of the dividend from X as a qualified REIT dividend for purposes of section 199A for A's 2018 taxable year.

(D) A receives a dividend from X of $35x on March 31, 2019, of which $5x is reported as a section 199A dividend. If A meets the holding period requirements in paragraph (d)(4)(ii) of this section with respect to the stock of X, A may only treat $2x of the dividend from X as a section 199A dividend for A's 2019 taxable year.

(6) *Applicability date.*—The provisions of paragraph (d) of this section apply to taxable years ending after the date the Treasury decision adopting these regulations as final regulations is published in the Federal Register. However, taxpayers may rely on the rules of this section until the date the Treasury decision adopting these regulations as final regulations is published in the Federal Register.

\* \* \*

[Proposed 2-8-2019.]

### [Prop. Reg. § 1.199A-6]

**§ 1.199A-6. Relevant passthrough entities (RPEs), publicly traded partnerships (PTPs), trusts, and estates..—**

\* \* \*

(d) \*\*\*

(3) \*\*\*

(iii) *Separate shares.*—In the case of a trust described in section 663(c) with substantially separate and independent shares for multiple beneficiaries, such trust will be treated as a single trust for purposes of determining whether the taxable income of the trust exceeds the threshold amount.

\* \* \*

(v) *Charitable remainder trusts.*—A charitable remainder trust described in section 664 is not entitled to and does not calculate a section 199A deduction and the threshold amount described in section 199A(e)(2) does not apply to the trust. However, any taxable recipient of a unitrust or annuity amount from the trust must determine and apply the recipient's own threshold amount for purposes of section 199A taking into account any annuity or unitrust amounts received from the trust. A recipient of a unitrust or annuity amount from a trust may take into account QBI, qualified REIT dividends, or qualified PTP income for purposes of determining the recipient's section 199A deduction for the taxable year to the extent that the unitrust or annuity amount distributed to such recipient consists of such section 199A items under §1.664-1(d). For example, if a charitable remainder trust has investment income of $500, qualified dividend income of $200, and qualified REIT dividends of $1,000, and distributes $1,000 to the recipient, the trust would be treated as having income in two classes within the category of income described in §1.664-1(d)(1)(i)(*a*)(*1*), for purposes of §1.664-1(d)(1)(ii)(*b*). Because the annuity amount first carries out income in the class subject to the highest income tax rate, the entire annuity payment comes from the class with the investment income and qualified REIT dividends. Thus, the charitable remainder trust would be treated as distributing a proportionate amount of the investment income ($500/(1,000+500)*1,000 = $333) and qualified REIT dividends ($1000/(1,000+500)*1000 = $667) because the investment income and qualified REIT dividends are taxed at the same rate and within the same class, which is higher than the rate of tax for the qualified dividend income which is in a separate class. The charitable remainder trust in this example would not be treated as distributing any of the qualified dividend income until it distributed all of the investment income and qualified REIT dividends (more than $1,500 in total) to the recipient. To the extent that a trust is treated as distributing QBI, qualified REIT dividends, or qualified PTP income to more than one unitrust or annuity recipient in the taxable year, the distribution of such income will be treated as made to the recipients proportionately, based on their respective shares of the total of QBI, qualified REIT dividends, or qualified PTP income distributed for that year. The trust allocates and reports any W-2 wages or UBIA of qualified property to the taxable recipient of the annuity or unitrust interest based on each recipient's share of the trust's total QBI (whether or not distributed) for that taxable year. Accordingly, if 10 percent of the QBI of a charitable remainder trust is distributed to the recipient and 90 percent of the QBI is retained by the trust, 10 percent of the W-2 wages and UBIA of qualified property is allocated and reported to the recipient and 90 percent of the W-2 wages and UBIA of qualified property is treated as retained by the trust. However, any W-2 wages retained by the trust do not carry over to subsequent taxable years for section 199A purposes. Any QBI, qualified REIT dividends, or qualified PTP income of the trust that is unrelated business taxable income is subject to excise tax and that tax must be allocated to the corpus of the trust under §1.664-1(c).

\* \* \*

[Proposed 2-8-2019.]

### [Prop. Reg. §1.245A(e)-1]

**§1.245A(e)-1. Special rules for hybrid dividends.**—(a) *Overview.*—This section provides rules for hybrid dividends. Paragraph (b) of this section disallows the deduction under section 245A(a) for a hybrid dividend received by a United States shareholder from a CFC. Paragraph (c) of this section provides a rule for hybrid dividends of tiered corporations. Paragraph (d) of this section sets forth rules regarding a hybrid deduction account. Paragraph (e) of this section provides an anti-avoidance rule. Paragraph (f) of this section provides definitions. Paragraph (g) of this section illustrates the application of the rules of this section through examples. Paragraph (h) of this section provides the applicability date.

(b) *Hybrid dividends received by United States shareholders.*—(1) *In general.*—If a United States shareholder receives a hybrid dividend, then—

(i) The United States shareholder is not allowed a deduction under section 245A(a) for the hybrid dividend; and

(ii) The rules of section 245A(d) (disallowance of foreign tax credits and deductions) apply to the hybrid dividend.

(2) *Definition of hybrid dividend.*—The term *hybrid dividend* means an amount received by a United States shareholder from a CFC for which but for section 245A(e) and this section the United States shareholder would be allowed a deduction under section 245A(a), to the extent of the sum of the United States shareholder's hybrid deduction accounts (as described in paragraph (d) of this section) with respect to each share of stock of the CFC, determined at the close of the CFC's taxable year (or in accordance with paragraph (d)(5) of this section, as applicable). No other amount received by a United States shareholder from a CFC is a hybrid dividend for purposes of section 245A.

(3) *Special rule for certain dividends attributable to earnings of lower-tier foreign corporations.*—This paragraph (b)(3) applies if a domestic corporation sells or exchanges stock of a foreign corporation and, pursuant to section 1248, the gain recognized on the sale or exchange is included in gross income as a dividend. In such a case, for purposes of this section—

(i) To the extent that earnings and profits of a lower-tier CFC gave rise to the dividend under section 1248(c)(2), those earnings and profits are treated as distributed as a dividend by the lower-tier CFC directly to the domestic corporation under the principles of §1.1248-1(d); and

(ii) To the extent the domestic corporation indirectly owns (within the meaning of section 958(a)(2)) shares of stock of the lower-tier CFC, the hybrid deduction accounts with respect to those shares are treated as hybrid deduction accounts of the domestic corporation. Thus, for example, if a domestic corporation sells or exchanges all the stock of an upper-tier CFC and under this paragraph (b)(3) there is considered to be a dividend paid directly by the lower-tier CFC to the domestic corporation, then the dividend is generally a hybrid dividend to the extent of the sum of the upper-tier CFC's hybrid deduction accounts with respect to stock of the lower-tier CFC.

(4) *Ordering rule.*—Amounts received by a United States shareholder from a CFC are subject to the rules of section 245A(e) and this section based on the order in which they are received. Thus, for example, if on different days during a CFC's taxable year a United States shareholder receives dividends from the CFC, then the rules of section 245A(e) and this section apply first to the dividend received on the earliest date (based on the sum of the United States shareholder's hybrid deduction accounts with respect to each share of stock of the CFC), and then to the dividend received on the next earliest date (based on the remaining sum).

(c) *Hybrid dividends of tiered corporations.*—(1) *In general.*—If a CFC (the *receiving* CFC) receives a tiered hybrid dividend from another CFC, and a domestic corporation is a United States shareholder with respect to both CFCs, then, notwithstanding any other provision of the Code—

(i) The tiered hybrid dividend is treated for purposes of section 951(a)(1)(A) as subpart F income of the receiving CFC for the taxable year of the CFC in which the tiered hybrid dividend is received;

(ii) The United States shareholder must include in gross income an amount equal to its pro rata share (determined in the same manner as under section 951(a)(2)) of the subpart F income described in paragraph (c)(1)(i) of this section; and

(iii) The rules of section 245A(d) (disallowance of foreign tax credit, including for taxes that would have been deemed paid under section 960(a) or (b), and deductions) apply to the amount included under paragraph (c)(1)(ii) of this section in the United States shareholder's gross income.

(2) *Definition of tiered hybrid dividend.*—The term *tiered hybrid dividend* means an amount received by a receiving CFC from another CFC to the extent that the amount would be a hybrid dividend under paragraph (b)(2) of this section if, for purposes of section 245A and the regulations under section 245A as contained in 26 CFR part 1 (except for section 245A(e)(2) and this paragraph (c)), the receiving CFC were a domestic corporation. A tiered hybrid dividend does not include an amount described in section 959(b). No other amount received by a receiving CFC from another CFC is a tiered hybrid dividend for purposes of section 245A.

(3) *Special rule for certain dividends attributable to earnings of lower-tier foreign corporations.*—This paragraph (c)(3) applies if a CFC sells or exchanges stock of a foreign corporation and pursuant to section 964(e)(1) the gain recognized on the sale or exchange is included in gross income as a dividend. In such a case, rules similar to the rules of paragraph (b)(3) of this section apply.

(4) *Interaction with rules under section 964(e).*—To the extent a dividend described in section 964(e)(1) (gain on certain stock sales by CFCs treated as dividends) is a tiered hybrid dividend, the rules of section 964(e)(4) do not apply and, therefore, the United States shareholder is not allowed a deduction under section 245A(a) for the amount included in gross income under paragraph (c)(1)(ii) of this section.

(d) *Hybrid deduction accounts.*—(1) *In general.*—A specified owner of a share of CFC stock must maintain a hybrid deduction account with respect to the share. The hybrid deduction account with respect to the share must reflect the amount of hybrid deductions of the CFC allocated to the share (as determined under paragraphs (d)(2) and (3) of this section), and must be maintained in accordance with the rules of paragraphs (d)(4) through (6) of this section.

(2) *Hybrid deductions.*—(i) *In general.*—The term *hybrid deduction* of a CFC means a deduction or other tax benefit (such as an exemption, exclusion, or credit, to the extent equivalent to a deduction) for which the requirements of paragraphs (d)(2)(i)(A) and (B) of this section are both satisfied.

(A) The deduction or other tax benefit is allowed to the CFC (or a person related to the CFC) under a relevant foreign tax law.

(B) The deduction or other tax benefit relates to or results from an amount paid, accrued, or distributed with respect to an instrument issued by the CFC and treated as stock for U.S. tax purposes. Examples of such a deduction or other tax benefit include an interest deduction, a dividends paid deduction, and a deduction with respect to equity (such as a notional interest deduction). *See* paragraph (g)(1) of this section. However, a deduction or other tax benefit relating to or resulting from a distribution by the CFC with respect to an instrument treated as stock for purposes of the relevant foreign tax law is considered a hybrid deduction only to the extent it has the effect of causing the earnings that funded the distribution to not be included in income (determined under the principles of § 1.267A-3(a)) or otherwise subject to tax under the CFC's tax law. Thus, for example, a refund to a shareholder of a CFC (including through a credit), upon a distribution by the CFC to the shareholder, of taxes paid by the CFC on the earnings that funded the distribution results in a hybrid deduction of the CFC, but only to the extent that the shareholder, if a tax resident of the CFC's country, does not include the distribution in income under the CFC's tax law or, if not a tax resident of the CFC's country, is not subject to withholding tax (as defined in section 901(k)(1)(B)) on the distribution under the CFC's tax law. *See* paragraph (g)(2) of this section.

(ii) *Application limited to items allowed in taxable years beginning after December 31, 2017.*—A deduction or other tax benefit allowed to a CFC (or a person related to the CFC) under a relevant foreign tax law is taken into account for purposes of this section only if it was allowed with respect to a taxable year under the relevant foreign tax law beginning after December 31, 2017.

(3) *Allocating hybrid deductions to shares.*—A hybrid deduction is allocated to a share of stock of a CFC to the extent that the hybrid deduction (or amount equivalent to a deduction) relates to an amount paid, accrued, or distributed by the CFC with respect to the share. However, in the case of a hybrid deduction that is a deduction with respect to equity (such as a notional interest deduction), the deduction is allocated to a share of stock of a CFC based on the product of—

(i) The amount of the deduction allowed for all of the equity of the CFC; and

(ii) A fraction, the numerator of which is the value of the share and the denominator of which is the value of all of the stock of the CFC.

(4) *Maintenance of hybrid deduction accounts.*—(i) *In general.*—A specified owner's hybrid deduction account with respect to a share of stock of a CFC is, as of the close of the taxable year of the CFC, adjusted pursuant to the following rules.

(A) First, the account is increased by the amount of hybrid deductions of the CFC allocable to the share for the taxable year.

(B) Second, the account is decreased by the amount of hybrid deductions in the account that gave rise to a hybrid dividend or tiered hybrid dividend during the taxable year. If a specified owner has more than one hybrid deduction account with respect to its stock of the CFC, then a pro rata amount in each hybrid deduction account is considered to have given rise to the hybrid dividend or tiered hybrid dividend, based on the amounts in the accounts before applying this paragraph (d)(4)(i)(B).

(ii) *Acquisition of account.*—(A) *In general.*—The following rules apply when a person (the *acquirer*) acquires a share of stock of a CFC from another person (the *transferor*).

(1) In the case of an acquirer that is a specified owner of the share immediately after the acquisition, the transferor's hybrid deduction account, if any, with respect to the share becomes the hybrid deduction account of the acquirer.

(2) In the case of an acquirer that is not a specified owner of the share immediately after the acquisition, the transferor's hybrid deduction account, if any, is eliminated and accordingly is not thereafter taken into account by any person.

(B) *Additional rules.*—The following rules apply in addition to the rules of paragraph (d)(4)(ii)(A) of this section.

(1) *Certain section 354 or 356 exchanges.*—The following rules apply when a shareholder of a CFC (the CFC, the *target CFC;* the shareholder, the *exchanging shareholder*) exchanges stock of the target CFC for stock of another CFC (the *acquiring CFC*) pursuant to an exchange described in section 354 or 356 that occurs in connection with a transaction described in section 381(a)(2) in which the target CFC is the transferor corporation.

(i) In the case of an exchanging shareholder that is a specified owner of one or more shares of stock of the acquiring CFC immediately after the exchange, the exchanging shareholder's hybrid deduction accounts with respect to the shares of stock of the target CFC that it exchanges are attributed to the shares of stock of the acquiring CFC that it receives in the exchange.

(ii) In the case of an exchanging shareholder that is not a specified owner of one or more shares of stock of the acquiring CFC immediately after the exchange, the exchanging shareholder's hybrid deduction accounts with respect to its shares of stock of the target CFC are eliminated and accordingly are not thereafter taken into account by any person.

(2) *Section 332 liquidations.*—If a CFC is a distributor corporation in a transaction described in section 381(a)(1) (the *distributing CFC*) in which a controlled foreign corporation is the acquiring corporation (the *distributee CFC*), then each hybrid account with respect to a share of stock of the distributee CFC is increased pro rata by the sum of the hybrid accounts with respect to shares of stock of the distributing CFC.

(3) *Recapitalizations.*—If a shareholder of a CFC exchanges stock of the CFC pursuant to a reorganization described in section 368(a)(1)(E) or a transaction to which section 1036 applies, then the shareholder's hybrid deduction accounts with respect to the stock of the CFC that it exchanges are attributed to the shares of stock of the CFC that it receives in the exchange.

(5) *Determinations and adjustments made on transfer date in certain cases.*—This paragraph (d)(5) applies if on a date other than the date that is the last day of the CFC's taxable year a United States shareholder of the CFC or an upper-tier CFC with respect to the CFC directly or indirectly transfers a share of stock of the CFC, and, during the taxable year, but on or before the transfer date, the United States shareholder or upper-tier CFC receives an amount from the CFC that is subject to the rules of section 245A(e) and this section. In such a case, as to the United States shareholder or upper-tier CFC and the United States shareholder's or upper-tier CFC's hybrid deduction accounts with respect to each share of stock of the CFC (regardless of whether such share is transferred), the determinations and adjustments under this section that would

otherwise be made at the close of the CFC's taxable year are made at the close of the date of the transfer. Thus, for example, if a United States shareholder of a CFC exchanges stock of the CFC in an exchange described in § 1.367(b)-4(b)(1)(i) and is required to include in income as a deemed dividend the section 1248 amount attributable to the stock exchanged, the sum of the United States shareholder's hybrid deduction accounts with respect to each share of stock of the CFC is determined, and the accounts are adjusted, as of the close of the date of the exchange. For this purpose, the principles of § 1.1502-76(b)(2)(ii) apply to determine amounts in hybrid deduction accounts at the close of the date of the transfer.

(6) *Effects of CFC functional currency.*— (i) *Maintenance of the hybrid deduction account.*—A hybrid deduction account with respect to a share of CFC stock must be maintained in the functional currency (within the meaning of section 985) of the CFC. Thus, for example, the amount of a hybrid deduction and the adjustments described in paragraphs (d)(4)(i)(A) and (B) of this section are determined based on the functional currency of the CFC. In addition, for purposes of this section, the amount of a deduction or other tax benefit allowed to a CFC (or a person related to the CFC) is determined taking into account foreign currency gain or loss recognized with respect to such deduction or other tax benefit under a provision of foreign tax law comparable to section 988 (treatment of certain foreign currency transactions).

(ii) *Determination of amount of hybrid dividend.*—This paragraph (d)(6)(ii) applies if a CFC's functional currency is other than the functional currency of a United States shareholder or upper-tier CFC that receives an amount from the CFC that is subject to the rules of section 245A(e) and this section. In such a case, the sum of the United States shareholder's or upper-tier CFC's hybrid deduction accounts with respect to each share of stock of the CFC is, for purposes of determining the extent that a dividend is a hybrid dividend or tiered hybrid dividend, translated into the functional currency of the United States shareholder or upper-tier CFC based on the spot rate (within the meaning of § 1.988-1(d)) as of the date of the dividend.

(e) *Anti-avoidance rule.*—Appropriate adjustments are made pursuant to this section, including adjustments that would disregard the transaction or arrangement, if a transaction or arrangement is undertaken with a principal purpose of avoiding the purposes of this section. For example, if a specified owner of a share of CFC stock transfers the share to another person, and a principal purpose of the transfer is to shift the hybrid deduction account with respect to the share to the other person or to cause the hybrid deduction account to be eliminated, then for purposes of this section the shifting or elimination of the hybrid deduction account is disregarded as to the transferor. As another example, if a trans-

action or arrangement is undertaken to affirmatively fail to satisfy the holding period requirement under section 246(c)(5) with a principal purpose of avoiding the tiered hybrid dividend rules described in paragraph (c) of this section, the transaction or arrangement is disregarded for purposes of this section.

(f) *Definitions.*—The following definitions apply for purposes of this section.

(1) The term *controlled foreign corporation* (or *CFC*) has the meaning provided in section 957.

(2) The term *person* has the meaning provided in section 7701(a)(1).

(3) The term *related* has the meaning provided in this paragraph (f)(3). A person is related to a CFC if the person is a related person within the meaning of section 954(d)(3).

(4) The term *relevant foreign tax law* means, with respect to a CFC, any regime of any foreign country or possession of the United States that imposes an income, war profits, or excess profits tax with respect to income of the CFC, other than a foreign anti-deferral regime under which a person that owns an interest in the CFC is liable to tax. Thus, the term includes any regime of a foreign country or possession of the United States that imposes income, war profits, or excess profits tax under which—

(i) The CFC is liable to tax as a resident;

(ii) The CFC has a branch that gives rise to a taxable presence in the foreign country or possession of the United States; or

(iii) A person related to the CFC is liable to tax as a resident, provided that under such person's tax law the person is allowed a deduction for amounts paid or accrued by the CFC (because, for example, the CFC is fiscally transparent under the person's tax law).

(5) The term *specified owner* means, with respect to a share of stock of a CFC, a person for which the requirements of paragraphs (f)(5)(i) and (ii) of this section are satisfied.

(i) The person is a domestic corporation that is a United States shareholder of the CFC, or is an upper-tier CFC that would be a United States shareholder of the CFC were the upper-tier CFC a domestic corporation.

(ii) The person owns the share directly or indirectly through a partnership, trust, or estate. Thus, for example, if a domestic corporation directly owns all the shares of stock of an upper-tier CFC and the upper-tier CFC directly owns all the shares of stock of another CFC, the domestic corporation is the specified owner with respect to each share of stock of the upper-tier CFC and the upper-tier CFC is the specified owner with respect to each share of stock of the other CFC.

(6) The term *United States shareholder* has the meaning provided in section 951(b).

(g) *Examples.*—This paragraph (g) provides examples that illustrate the application of this section. For purposes of the examples in this paragraph (g), unless otherwise indicated, the following facts are presumed. US1 is a domestic corporation. FX and FZ are CFCs formed at the beginning of year 1. FX is a tax resident of Country X and FZ is a tax resident of Country Z. US1 is a United States shareholder with respect to FX and FZ. No distributed amounts are attributable to amounts which are, or have been, included in the gross income of a United States shareholder under section 951(a). All instruments are treated as stock for U.S. tax purposes.

(1) *Example 1. Hybrid dividend resulting from hybrid instrument*—(i) *Facts.* US1 holds both shares of stock of FX, which have an equal value. One share is treated as indebtedness for Country X tax purposes ("Share A"), and the other is treated as equity for Country X tax purposes ("Share B"). During year 1, under Country X tax law, FX accrues $80x of interest to US1 with respect to Share A and is allowed a deduction for the amount (the "Hybrid Instrument Deduction"). During year 2, FX distributes $30x to US1 with respect to each of Share A and Share B. For U.S. tax purposes, each of the $30x distributions is treated as a dividend for which, but for section 245A(e) and this section, US1 would be allowed a deduction under section 245A(a). For Country X tax purposes, the $30x distribution with respect to Share A represents a payment of interest for which a deduction was already allowed (and thus FX is not allowed an additional deduction for the amount), and the $30x distribution with respect to Share B is treated as a dividend (for which no deduction is allowed).

(ii) *Analysis.* The entire $30x of each dividend received by US1 from FX during year 2 is a hybrid dividend, because the sum of US1's hybrid deduction accounts with respect to each of its shares of FX stock at the end of year 2 ($80x) is at least equal to the amount of the dividends ($60x). *See* paragraph (b)(2) of this section. This is the case for the $30x dividend with respect to Share B even though there are no hybrid deductions allocated to Share B. *See id.* As a result, US1 is not allowed a deduction under section 245A(a) for the entire $60x of hybrid dividends and the rules of section 245A(d) (disallowance of foreign tax credits and deductions) apply. *See* paragraph (b)(1) of this section. Paragraphs (g)(1)(ii)(A) through (D) of this section describe the determinations under this section.

(A) At the end of year 1, US1's hybrid deduction accounts with respect to Share A and Share B are $80x and $0, respectively, calculated as follows.

(1) The $80x Hybrid Instrument Deduction allowed to FX under Country X tax law (a relevant foreign tax law) is a hybrid deduction of FX, because the deduction is allowed to FX and relates to or results from an amount accrued with respect to an instrument issued by FX and treated as stock for U.S. tax purposes. *See* paragraph (d)(2)(i) of this section. Thus, FX's hybrid deductions for year 1 are $80x.

(2) The entire $80x Hybrid Instrument Deduction is allocated to Share A, because the de-

duction was accrued with respect to Share A. *See* paragraph (d)(3) of this section. As there are no additional hybrid deductions of FX for year 1, there are no additional hybrid deductions to allocate to either Share A or Share B. Thus, there are no hybrid deductions allocated to Share B.

(3) At the end of year 1, US1's hybrid deduction account with respect to Share A is increased by $80x (the amount of hybrid deductions allocated to Share A). *See* paragraph (d)(4)(i)(A) of this section. Because FX did not pay any dividends with respect to either Share A or Share B during year 1 (and therefore did not pay any hybrid dividends or tiered hybrid dividends), no further adjustments are made. *See* paragraph (d)(4)(i)(B) of this section. Therefore, at the end of year 1, US1's hybrid deduction accounts with respect to Share A and Share B are $80x and $0, respectively.

(B) At the end of year 2, and before the adjustments described in paragraph (d)(4)(i)(B) of this section, US1's hybrid deduction accounts with respect to Share A and Share B remain $80x and $0, respectively. This is because there are no hybrid deductions of FX for year 2. *See* paragraph (d)(4)(i)(A) of this section.

(C) Because at the end of year 2 (and before the adjustments described in paragraph (d)(4)(i)(B) of this section) the sum of US1's hybrid deduction accounts with respect to Share A and Share B ($80x, calculated as $80x plus $0) is at least equal to the aggregate $60x of year 2 dividends, the entire $60x dividend is a hybrid dividend. *See* paragraph (b)(2) of this section.

(D) At the end of year 2, US1's hybrid deduction account with respect to Share A is decreased by $60x, the amount of the hybrid deductions in the account that gave rise to a hybrid dividend or tiered hybrid dividend during year 2. *See* paragraph (d)(4)(i)(B) of this section. Because there are no hybrid deductions in the hybrid deduction account with respect to Share B, no adjustments with respect to that account are made under paragraph (d)(4)(i)(B) of this section. Therefore, at the end of year 2 and taking into account the adjustments under paragraph (d)(4)(i)(B) of this section, US1's hybrid deduction account with respect to Share A is $20x ($80x less $60x) and with respect to Share B is $0.

(iii) *Alternative facts – notional interest deductions.* The facts are the same as in paragraph (g)(1)(i) of this section, except that for each of year 1 and year 2 FX is allowed $10x of notional interest deductions with respect to its equity, Share B, under Country X tax law (the "NIDs"). In addition, during year 2, FX distributes $47.5x (rather than $30x) to US1 with respect to each of Share A and Share B. For U.S. tax purposes, each of the $47.5x distributions is treated as a dividend for which, but for section 245A(e) and this section, US1 would be allowed a deduction under section 245A(a). For Country X tax purposes, the $47.5x distribution with respect to Share A represents a payment of interest for which a deduction was already allowed (and thus FX is not allowed an additional deduction for the amount), and the $47.5x distribution with respect to Share B is treated as a dividend (for which no deduction is allowed). The entire $47.5x of each dividend received by US1 from FX during year 2 is a hybrid dividend, because the sum of US1's hybrid deduction accounts with respect to each of its shares of FX stock at the end of year 2 ($80x plus $20x, or $100x) is at least equal to the amount of the dividends ($95x). See paragraph (b)(2) of this section. As a result, US1 is not allowed a deduction under section 245A(a) for the $95x hybrid dividend and the rules of section 245A(d) (disallowance of foreign tax credits and deductions) apply. See paragraph (b)(1) of this section. Paragraphs (g)(1)(iii)(A) through (D) of this section describe the determinations under this section.

(A) The $10x of NIDs allowed to FX under Country X tax law in year 1 are hybrid deductions of FX for year 1. See paragraph (d)(2)(i) of this section. The $10x of NIDs is allocated equally to each of Share A and Share B, because the hybrid deduction is with respect to equity and the shares have an equal value. See paragraph (d)(3) of this section. Thus, $5x of the NIDs is allocated to each of Share A and Share B for year 1. For the reasons described in paragraph (g)(1)(ii)(A) of this section, the entire $80x Hybrid Instrument Deduction is allocated to Share A. Therefore, at the end of year 1, US1's hybrid deduction accounts with respect to Share A and Share B are $85x and $5x, respectively.

(B) Similarly, the $10x of NIDs allowed to FX under Country X tax law in year 2 are hybrid deductions of FX for year 2, and $5x of the NIDs is allocated to each of Share A and Share B for year 2. See paragraphs (d)(2)(i) and (d)(3) of this section. Thus, at the end of year 2 (and before the adjustments described in paragraph (d)(4)(i)(B) of this section), US1's hybrid deduction account with respect to Share A is $90x ($85x plus $5x) and with respect to Share B is $10x ($5x plus $5x). See paragraph (d)(4)(i) of this section.

(C) Because at the end of year 2 (and before the adjustments described in paragraph (d)(4)(i)(B) of this section) the sum of US1's hybrid deduction accounts with respect to Share A and Share B ($100x, calculated as $90x plus $10x) is at least equal to the aggregate $95x of year 2 dividends, the entire $95x of dividends are hybrid dividends. See paragraph (b)(2) of this section.

(D) At the end of year 2, US1's hybrid deduction accounts with respect to Share A and Share B are decreased by the amount of hybrid deductions in the accounts that gave rise to a hybrid dividend or tiered hybrid dividend during year 2. See paragraph (d)(4)(i)(B) of this section. A total of $95x of hybrid deductions in the accounts gave rise to a hybrid dividend during year 2. For the hybrid deduction account with respect to Share A, $85.5x in the account is considered to have given rise to a hybrid deduction (calculated as $95x multiplied by $90x/$100x). See id. For the hybrid deduction account with

respect to Share B, $9.5x in the account is considered to have given rise to a hybrid deduction (calculated as $95x multiplied by $10x/$100x). See id. Thus, following these adjustments, at the end of year 2, US1's hybrid deduction account with respect to Share A is $4.5x ($90x less $85.5x) and with respect to Share B is $0.5x ($10x less $9.5x).

(iv) Alternative facts – deduction in branch country—(A) Facts. The facts are the same as in paragraph (g)(1)(i) of this section, except that for Country X tax purposes Share A is treated as equity (and thus the Hybrid Instrument Deduction does not exist and under Country X tax law FX is not allowed a deduction for the $30x distributed in year 2 with respect to Share A). However, FX has a branch in Country Z that gives rise to a taxable presence under Country Z tax law, and for Country Z tax purposes Share A is treated as indebtedness and Share B is treated as equity. Also, during year 1, for Country Z tax purposes, FX accrues $80x of interest to US1 with respect to Share A and is allowed an $80x interest deduction with respect to its Country Z branch income. Moreover, for Country Z tax purposes, the $30x distribution with respect to Share A in year 2 represents a payment of interest for which a deduction was already allowed (and thus FX is not allowed an additional deduction for the amount), and the $30x distribution with respect to Share B in year 2 is treated as a dividend (for which no deduction is allowed).

(B) Analysis. The $80x interest deduction allowed to FX under Country Z tax law (a relevant foreign tax law) with respect to its Country Z branch income is a hybrid deduction of FX for year 1. See paragraphs (d)(2)(i) and (f)(4) of this section. For reasons similar to those discussed in paragraph (g)(1)(ii) of this section, at the end of year 2 (and before the adjustments described in paragraph (d)(4)(i)(B) of this section), US1's hybrid deduction accounts with respect to Share A and Share B are $80x and $0, respectively, and the sum of the accounts is $80x. Accordingly, the entire $60x of the year 2 dividend is a hybrid dividend. See paragraph (b)(2) of this section. Further, for the reasons described in paragraph (g)(1)(ii)(D) of this section, at the end of year 2 and taking into account the adjustments under paragraph (d)(4)(i)(B) of this section, US1's hybrid deduction account with respect to Share A is $20x ($80x less $60x) and with respect to Share B is $0.

(2) Example 2. Tiered hybrid dividend rule; tax benefit equivalent to a deduction—(i) Facts. US1 holds all the stock of FX, and FX holds all 100 shares of stock of FZ (the "FZ shares"), which have an equal value. The FZ shares are treated as equity for Country Z tax purposes. During year 2, FZ distributes $10x to FX with respect to each of the FZ shares, for a total of $1,000x. The $1,000x is treated as a dividend for U.S. and Country Z tax purposes, and is not deductible for Country Z tax purposes. If FX were a domestic corporation, then, but for section 245A(e) and this section, FX would be allowed a deduction

under section 245A(a) for the $1,000x. Under Country Z tax law, 75% of the corporate income tax paid by a Country Z corporation with respect to a dividend distribution is refunded to the corporation's shareholders (regardless of where such shareholders are tax residents) upon a dividend distribution by the corporation. The corporate tax rate in Country Z is 20%. With respect to FZ's distributions, FX is allowed a refundable tax credit of $187.5x. The $187.5x refundable tax credit is calculated as $1,250x (the amount of pre-tax earnings that funded the distribution, determined as $1,000x (the amount of the distribution) divided by 0.8 (the percentage of pre-tax earnings that a Country Z corporation retains after paying Country Z corporate tax)) multiplied by 0.2 (the Country Z corporate tax rate) multiplied by 0.75 (the percentage of the Country Z tax credit). Under Country Z tax law, FX is not subject to Country Z withholding tax (or any other tax) with respect to the $1,000x dividend distribution.

(ii) *Analysis.* $937.5x of the $1,000x of dividends received by FX from FZ during year 2 is a tiered hybrid dividend, because the sum of FX's hybrid deduction accounts with respect to each of its shares of FZ stock at the end of year 2 is $937.5x. *See* paragraphs (b)(2) and (c)(2) of this section. As a result, the $937.5x tiered hybrid dividend is treated for purposes of section 951(a)(1)(A) as subpart F income of FX and US1 must include in gross income its pro rata share of such subpart F income, which is $937.5x. *See* paragraph (c)(1) of this section. In addition, the rules of section 245A(d) (disallowance of foreign tax credits and deductions) apply with respect to US1's inclusion. *Id.* Paragraphs (g)(2)(ii)(A) through (C) of this section describe the determinations under this section. The characterization of the FZ stock for Country X tax purposes (or for purposes of any other foreign tax law) does not affect this analysis.

(A) The $187.5x refundable tax credit allowed to FX under Country Z tax law (a relevant foreign tax law) is equivalent to a $937.5x deduction, calculated as $187.5x (the amount of the credit) divided by 0.2 (the Country Z corporate tax rate). The $937.5x is a hybrid deduction of FZ because it is allowed to FX (a person related to FZ), it relates to or results from amounts distributed with respect to instruments issued by FZ and treated as stock for U.S. tax purposes, and it has the effect of causing the earnings that funded the distributions to not be included in income under Country Z tax law. *See* paragraph (d)(2)(i) of this section. $9.375x of the hybrid deduction is allocated to each of the FZ shares, calculated as $937.5x (the amount of the hybrid deduction) multiplied by 1/100 (the value of each FZ share relative to the value of all the FZ shares). *See* paragraph (d)(3) of this section. The result would be the same if FX were instead a tax resident of Country Z (and not Country X) and under Country Z tax law FX were to not include the $1,000x in income (because, for example, Country Z tax law provides Country Z resident corporations a

100% exclusion or dividends received deduction with respect to dividends received from a resident corporation). *See* paragraph (d)(2)(i) of this section.

(B) Thus, at the end of year 2, and before the adjustments described in paragraph (d)(4)(i)(B) of this section, the sum of FX's hybrid deduction accounts with respect to each of its shares of FZ stock is $937.5x, calculated as $9.375x (the amount in each account) multiplied by 100 (the number of accounts). *See* paragraph (d)(4)(i) of this section. Accordingly, $937.5x of the $1,000x dividend received by FX from FZ during year 2 is a tiered hybrid dividend. *See* paragraphs (b)(2) and (c)(2) of this section.

(C) Lastly, at the end of year 2, each of FX's hybrid deduction accounts with respect to its shares of FZ is decreased by the $9.375x in the account that gave rise to a hybrid dividend or tiered hybrid dividend during year 2. *See* paragraph (d)(4)(i)(B) of this section. Thus, following these adjustments, at the end of year 2, each of FX's hybrid deduction accounts with respect to its shares of FZ stock is $0, calculated as $9.375x (the amount in the account before the adjustments described in paragraph (d)(4)(i)(B) of this section) less $9.375x (the adjustment described in paragraph (d)(4)(i)(B) of this section with respect to the account).

(iii) *Alternative facts – imputation system that taxes shareholders.* The facts are the same as in paragraph (g)(2)(i) of this section, except that under Country Z tax law the $1,000 dividend to FX is subject to a 30% gross basis withholding tax, or $300x, and the $187.5x refundable tax credit is applied against and reduces the withholding tax to $112.5x. The $187.5x refundable tax credit provided to FX is not a hybrid deduction because FX was subject to Country Z withholding tax of $300x on the $1,000x dividend (such withholding tax being greater than the $187.5x credit). *See* paragraph (d)(2)(i) of this section.

(h) *Applicability date.*—This section applies to distributions made after December 31, 2017. [Reg. § 1.245A(e)-1.]

[Proposed 12-28-2018.]

**[Prop. Reg. §1.263A-9]**

**§1.263A-9. The avoided cost method.**

\* \* \*

(g) \* \* \*

(1) \* \* \*

(i) Interest must be capitalized under section 263A(f) before the application of section 163(d) (regarding the investment interest limitation), section 163(j) (regarding the limitation on business interest expense), section 266 (regarding the election to capitalize carrying charges), section 469 (regarding the limitation on passive losses), and section 861 (regarding the allocation of interest to United States sources). \* \* \* However, in applying section 263A(f) with respect to the excess expenditure amount, the taxpayer must capitalize all interest that is neither investment interest under section 163(d), business interest expense under section 163(j), nor passive interest under section 469 before capitalizing any interest that is either investment interest, business interest expense, or passive interest. * * *

* * *

[Proposed 12-28-2018.]

**[Prop. Reg. §1.267A-1]**

**§1.267A-1. Disallowance of certain interest and royalty deductions.**—(a) *Scope.*—This section and §§1.267A-2 through 1.267A-5 provide rules regarding when a deduction for any interest or royalty paid or accrued is disallowed under section 267A. Section 1.267A-2 describes hybrid and branch arrangements. Section 1.267A-3 provides rules for determining income inclusions and provides that certain amounts are not amounts for which a deduction is disallowed. Section 1.267A-4 provides an imported mismatch rule. Section 1.267A-5 sets forth definitions and special rules that apply for purposes of section 267A. Section 1.267A-6 illustrates the application of section 267A through examples. Section 1.267A-7 provides applicability dates.

(b) *Disallowance of deduction.*—This paragraph (b) sets forth the exclusive circumstances in which a deduction is disallowed under section 267A. Except as provided in paragraph (c) of this section, a specified party's deduction for any interest or royalty paid or accrued (the amount paid or accrued with respect to the specified party, a *specified payment*) is disallowed under section 267A to the extent that the specified payment is described in this paragraph (b). *See also* §1.267A-5(b)(5) (treating structured payments as specified payments). A specified payment is described in this paragraph (b) to the extent that it is—

(1) A disqualified hybrid amount, as described in §1.267A-2 (hybrid and branch arrangements);

(2) A disqualified imported mismatch amount, as described in §1.267A-4 (payments offset by a hybrid deduction); or

(3) A specified payment for which the requirements of the anti-avoidance rule of §1.267A-5(b)(6) are satisfied.

(c) *De minimis exception.*—Paragraph (b) of this section does not apply to a specified party for a taxable year in which the sum of the specified party's interest and royalty deductions (determined without regard to this section) is less than $50,000. For purposes of this paragraph (c), specified parties that are related (within the meaning of §1.267A-5(a)(14)) are treated as a single specified party. [Reg. §1.267A-1.]

[Proposed 12-28-2018.]

**[Prop. Reg. §1.267A-2]**

**§1.267A-2. Hybrid and branch arrangements.**—(a) *Payments pursuant to hybrid transactions.*—(1) *In general.*—If a specified payment is made pursuant to a hybrid transaction, then, subject to §1.267A-3(b) (amounts included or includible in income), the payment is a disqualified hybrid amount to the extent that—

(i) A specified recipient of the payment does not include the payment in income, as determined under §1.267A-3(a) (to such extent, a *no-inclusion*); and

(ii) The specified recipient's no-inclusion is a result of the payment being made pursuant to the hybrid transaction. For this purpose, the specified recipient's no-inclusion is a result of the specified payment being made pursuant to the hybrid transaction to the extent that the no-inclusion would not occur were the specified recipient's tax law to treat the payment as interest or a royalty, as applicable. *See* §1.267A-6(c)(1) and (2).

(2) *Definition of hybrid transaction.*—The term *hybrid transaction* means any transaction, series of transactions, agreement, or instrument one or more payments with respect to which are treated as interest or royalties for U.S. tax purposes but are not so treated for purposes of the tax law of a specified recipient of the payment. Examples of a hybrid transaction include an instrument a payment with respect to which is treated as interest for U.S. tax purposes but, for purposes of a specified recipient's tax law, is treated as a distribution with respect to equity or a return of principal. In addition, a specified payment is deemed to be made pursuant to a hybrid transaction if the taxable year in which a specified recipient recognizes the payment under its tax law ends more than 36 months after the end of the taxable year in which the specified party would be allowed a deduction for the payment under U.S. tax law. *See also* §1.267A-6(c)(8). Further, a specified payment is not considered made pursuant to a hybrid transaction if the payment is a disregarded payment, as described in paragraph (b)(2) of this section.

(3) *Payments pursuant to securities lending transactions, sale-repurchase transactions, or similar transactions.*—This paragraph (a)(3) applies if a specified payment is made pursuant to a repo transaction and is not regarded under a foreign tax law but another amount connected to the payment (the *connected amount*) is regarded under such foreign tax law. For this purpose, a *repo transaction* means a transaction one or more payments with respect to which are treated as interest (as defined in §1.267A-5(a)(12)) or a structured payment (as defined in §1.267A-5(b)(5)(ii)) for U.S. tax purposes and that is a securities lending transaction or sale-repurchase transaction (including as described in §1.861-2(a)(7)), or other similar transaction or series of related transactions in which legal title to property is transferred and the property (or similar property, such as securities of the same class and issue) is reacquired or expected to be reacquired. For example, this paragraph (a)(3) applies if a specified payment arising from characterizing a repo transaction of stock in accor-

dance with its substance (that is, characterizing the specified payment as interest) is not regarded as such under a foreign tax law but an amount consistent with the form of the transaction (such as a dividend) is regarded under such foreign tax law. When this paragraph (a)(3) applies, the determination of the identity of a specified recipient of the specified payment under the foreign tax law is made with respect to the connected amount. In addition, if the specified recipient includes the connected amount in income (as determined under § 1.267A-3(a), by treating the connected amount as the specified payment), then the amount of the specified recipient's no-inclusion with respect to the specified payment is correspondingly reduced. See § 1.267A-6(c)(2). Further, the principles of this paragraph (a)(3) apply to cases similar to repo transactions in which a foreign tax law does not characterize the transaction in accordance with its substance.

(b) *Disregarded payments.*—(1) *In general.*— Subject to § 1.267A-3(b) (amounts included or includible in income), the excess (if any) of the sum of a specified party's disregarded payments for a taxable year over its dual inclusion income for the taxable year is a disqualified hybrid amount. See § 1.267A-6(c)(3) and (4).

(2) *Definition of disregarded payment.*—The term *disregarded payment* means a specified payment to the extent that, under the tax law of a tax resident or taxable branch to which the payment is made, the payment is not regarded (for example, because under such tax law it is a disregarded transaction involving a single taxpayer or between group members) and, were the payment to be regarded (and treated as interest or a royalty, as applicable) under such tax law, the tax resident or taxable branch would include the payment in income, as determined under § 1.267A-3(a). In addition, a disregarded payment includes a specified payment that, under the tax law of a tax resident or taxable branch to which the payment is made, is a payment that gives rise to a deduction or similar offset allowed to the tax resident or taxable branch (or group of entities that include the tax resident or taxable branch) under a foreign consolidation, fiscal unity, group relief, loss sharing, or any similar regime. Moreover, a disregarded payment does not include a deemed branch payment, or a specified payment pursuant to a repo transaction or similar transaction described in paragraph (a)(3) of this section.

(3) *Definition of dual inclusion income.*—With respect to a specified party, the term *dual inclusion income* means the excess, if any, of—

(i) The sum of the specified party's items of income or gain for U.S. tax purposes, to the extent the items of income or gain are included in the income of the tax resident or taxable branch to which the disregarded payments are made, as determined under § 1.267A-3(a) (by treating the items of income or gain as the specified payment); over

(ii) The sum of the specified party's items of deduction or loss for U.S. tax purposes (other than deductions for disregarded payments), to the extent the items of deduction or loss are allowable (or have been or will be allowable during a taxable year that ends no more than 36 months after the end of the specified party's taxable year) under the tax law of the tax resident or taxable branch to which the disregarded payments are made.

(4) *Payments made indirectly to a tax resident or taxable branch.*—A specified payment made to an entity an interest of which is directly or indirectly (determined under the rules of section 958(a) without regard to whether an intermediate entity is foreign or domestic) owned by a tax resident or taxable branch is considered made to the tax resident or taxable branch to the extent that, under the tax law of the tax resident or taxable branch, the entity to which the payment is made is fiscally transparent (and all intermediate entities, if any, are also fiscally transparent).

(c) *Deemed branch payments.*—(1) *In general.*— If a specified payment is a deemed branch payment, then the payment is a disqualified hybrid amount if the tax law of the home office provides an exclusion or exemption for income attributable to the branch. See § 1.267A-6(c)(4).

(2) *Definition of deemed branch payment.*—The term *deemed branch payment* means, with respect to a U.S. taxable branch that is a U.S. permanent establishment of a treaty resident eligible for benefits under an income tax treaty between the United States and the treaty country, any amount of interest or royalties allowable as a deduction in computing the business profits of the U.S. permanent establishment, to the extent the amount is deemed paid to the home office (or other branch of the home office) and is not regarded (or otherwise taken into account) under the home office's tax law (or the other branch's tax law). A deemed branch payment may be otherwise taken into account for this purpose if, for example, under the home office's tax law a corresponding amount of interest or royalties is allocated and attributable to the U.S. permanent establishment and is therefore not deductible.

(d) *Payments to reverse hybrids.*—(1) *In general.*—If a specified payment is made to a reverse hybrid, then, subject to § 1.267A-3(b) (amounts included or includible in income), the payment is a disqualified hybrid amount to the extent that—

(i) An investor of the reverse hybrid does not include the payment in income, as determined under § 1.267A-3(a) (to such extent, a *no-inclusion*); and

(ii) The investor's no-inclusion is a result of the payment being made to the reverse hybrid. For this purpose, the investor's no-inclusion is a result of the specified payment being made to the reverse hybrid to the extent that the no-inclusion would not occur were the investor's tax law to treat the reverse hybrid as fiscally transparent (and treat the payment as interest or a royalty, as applicable). *See* § 1.267A-6(c)(5).

(2) *Definition of reverse hybrid.*—The term *reverse hybrid* means an entity (regardless of whether domestic or foreign) that is fiscally transparent under the tax law of the country in which it is created, organized, or otherwise established but not fiscally transparent under the tax law of an investor of the entity.

(3) *Payments made indirectly to a reverse hybrid.*—A specified payment made to an entity an interest of which is directly or indirectly (determined under the rules of section 958(a) without regard to whether an intermediate entity is foreign or domestic) owned by a reverse hybrid is considered made to the reverse hybrid to the extent that, under the tax law of an investor of the reverse hybrid, the entity to which the payment is made is fiscally transparent (and all intermediate entities, if any, are also fiscally transparent).

(e) *Branch mismatch payments.*—(1) *In general.*—If a specified payment is a branch mismatch payment, then, subject to § 1.267A-3(b) (amounts included or includible in income), the payment is a disqualified hybrid amount to the extent that—

(i) A home office, the tax law of which treats the payment as income attributable to a branch of the home office, does not include the payment in income, as determined under § 1.267A-3(a) (to such extent, a *no-inclusion*); and

(ii) The home office's no-inclusion is a result of the payment being a branch mismatch payment. For this purpose, the home office's no-inclusion is a result of the specified payment being a branch mismatch payment to the extent that the no-inclusion would not occur were the home office's tax law to treat the payment as income that is not attributable a branch of the home office (and treat the payment as interest or a royalty, as applicable). *See* § 1.267A-6(c)(6).

(2) *Definition of branch mismatch payment.*—The term *branch mismatch payment* means a specified payment for which the following requirements are satisfied:

(i) Under a home office's tax law, the payment is treated as income attributable to a branch of the home office; and

(ii) Either—

(A) The branch is not a taxable branch; or

(B) Under the branch's tax law, the payment is not treated as income attributable to the branch.

(f) *Relatedness or structured arrangement limitation.*—A specified recipient, a tax resident or taxable branch to which a specified payment is made, an investor, or a home office is taken into account for purposes of paragraphs (a), (b), (d), and (e) of this section, respectively, only if the specified recipient, the tax resident or taxable branch, the investor, or the home office, as applicable, is related (as defined in § 1.267A-5(a)(14)) to the specified party or is a party to a structured arrangement (as defined in § 1.267A-5(a)(20)) pursuant to which the specified payment is made. [Reg. § 1.267A-2.]

[Proposed 12-28-2018.]

### [Prop. Reg. § 1.267A-3]

**§ 1.267A-3. Income inclusions and amounts not treated as disqualified hybrid amounts.—** (a) *Income inclusions.*—(1) *General rule.*—For purposes of section 267A, a tax resident or taxable branch includes in income a specified payment to the extent that, under the tax law of the tax resident or taxable branch—

(i) It includes (or it will include during a taxable year that ends no more than 36 months after the end of the specified party's taxable year) the payment in its income or tax base at the full marginal rate imposed on ordinary income; and

(ii) The payment is not reduced or offset by an exemption, exclusion, deduction, credit (other than for withholding tax imposed on the payment), or other similar relief particular to such type of payment. Examples of such reductions or offsets include a participation exemption, a dividends received deduction, a deduction or exclusion with respect to a particular category of income (such as income attributable to a branch, or royalties under a patent box regime), and a credit for underlying taxes paid by a corporation from which a dividend is received. A specified payment is not considered reduced or offset by a deduction or other similar relief particular to the type of payment if it is offset by a generally applicable deduction or other tax attribute, such as a deduction for depreciation or a net operating loss. For this purpose, a deduction may be treated as being generally applicable even if it is arises from a transaction related to the specified payment (for example, if the deduction and payment are in connection with a back-to-back financing arrangement).

(2) *Coordination with foreign hybrid mismatch rules.*—Whether a tax resident or taxable branch includes in income a specified payment is determined without regard to any defensive or secondary rule contained in hybrid mismatch rules, if any, under the tax law of the tax resident or taxable branch. For this purpose, a defensive or secondary rule means a provision of hybrid mismatch rules that requires a tax resident or taxable branch to include an amount in income if a deduction for the amount is not disallowed under applicable tax law.

(3) *Inclusions with respect to reverse hybrids.*—With respect to a tax resident or taxable branch that is an investor of a reverse hybrid, whether the investor includes in income a specified payment made to the reverse hybrid is determined

without regard to a distribution from the reverse hybrid (or right to a distribution from the reverse hybrid triggered by the payment).

(4) *De minimis inclusions and deemed full inclusions.*—A preferential rate, exemption, exclusion, deduction, credit, or similar relief particular to a type of payment that reduces or offsets 90 percent or more of the payment is considered to reduce or offset 100 percent of the payment. In addition, a preferential rate, exemption, exclusion, deduction, credit, or similar relief particular to a type of payment that reduces or offsets 10 percent or less of the payment is considered to reduce or offset none of the payment.

(b) *Certain amounts not treated as disqualified hybrid amounts to extent included or includible in income.*—(1) *In general.*—A specified payment, to the extent that but for this paragraph (b) it would be a disqualified hybrid amount (such amount, a *tentative disqualified hybrid amount*), is reduced under the rules of paragraphs (b)(2) through (4) of this section, as applicable. The tentative disqualified hybrid amount, as reduced under such rules, is the disqualified hybrid amount. *See* § 1.267A-6(c)(3) and (7).

(2) *Included in income of United States tax resident or U.S. taxable branch.*—A tentative disqualified hybrid amount is reduced to the extent that a specified recipient that is a tax resident of the United States or a U.S. taxable branch takes the tentative disqualified hybrid amount into account in its gross income.

(3) *Includible in income under section 951(a)(1).*—A tentative disqualified hybrid amount is reduced to the extent that the tentative disqualified hybrid amount is received by a CFC and includible under section 951(a)(1) (determined without regard to properly allocable deductions of the CFC and qualified deficits under section 952(c)(1)(B)) in the gross income of a United States shareholder of the CFC. However, the tentative disqualified hybrid amount is reduced only if the United States shareholder is a tax resident of the United States or, if the United States shareholder is not a tax resident of the United States, then only to the extent that a tax resident of the United States would take into account the amount includible under section 951(a)(1) in the gross income of the United States shareholder.

(4) *Includible in income under section 951A(a).*—A tentative disqualified hybrid amount is reduced to the extent that the tentative disqualified hybrid amount increases a United States shareholder's pro rata share of tested income (within the meaning of section 951A(c)(2)(A)) with respect to a CFC, reduces the shareholder's pro rata share of tested loss (within the meaning of section 951A(c)(2)(B)) of the CFC, or both. However, the tentative disqualified hybrid amount is reduced only if the United States shareholder is a tax resident of the United States or, if the United States shareholder is not a tax resident of the United States, then only to the extent that a tax resident of the

United States would take into account the amount that increases the United States shareholder's pro rata share of tested income with respect to the CFC, reduces the shareholder's pro rata share of tested loss of the CFC, or both. [Reg. § 1.267A-3.]

[Proposed 12-28-2018.]

### [Prop. Reg. § 1.267A-4]

§ 1.267A-4. Disqualified imported mismatch amounts.—(a) *Disqualified imported mismatch amounts.*—A specified payment (to the extent not a disqualified hybrid amount, as described in § 1.267A-2) is a disqualified imported mismatch amount to the extent that, under the set-off rules of paragraph (c) of this section, the income attributable to the payment is directly or indirectly offset by a hybrid deduction incurred by a tax resident or taxable branch that is related to the specified party (or that is a party to a structured arrangement pursuant to which the payment is made). For purposes of this section, any specified payment (to the extent not a disqualified hybrid amount) is referred to as an *imported mismatch payment*; the specified party is referred to as an *imported mismatch payer*; and a tax resident or taxable branch that includes the imported mismatch payment in income (or a tax resident or taxable branch the tax law of which otherwise prevents the imported mismatch payment from being a disqualified hybrid amount, for example, because under such tax law the tax resident's no-inclusion is not a result of hybridity) is referred to as the *imported mismatch payee*. *See* § 1.267A-6(c)(8), (9), and (10).

(b) *Hybrid deduction.*—A hybrid deduction means, with respect to a tax resident or taxable branch that is not a specified party, a deduction allowed to the tax resident or taxable branch under its tax law for an amount paid or accrued that is interest (including an amount that would be a structured payment under the principles of § 1.267A-5(b)(5)(ii)) or royalty under such tax law (regardless of whether or how such amounts would be recognized under U.S. law), to the extent that a deduction for the amount would be disallowed if such tax law contained rules substantially similar to those under §§ 1.267A-1 through 1.267A-3 and 1.267A-5. In addition, with respect to a tax resident that is not a specified party, a hybrid deduction includes a deduction allowed to the tax resident with respect to equity, such as a notional interest deduction. Further, a hybrid deduction for a particular accounting period includes a loss carryover from another accounting period, to the extent that a hybrid deduction incurred in an accounting period beginning on or after December 20, 2018 comprises the loss carryover.

(c) *Set-off rules.*—(1) *In general.*—In the order described in paragraph (c)(2) of this section, a hybrid deduction directly or indirectly offsets the income attributable to an imported mismatch payment to the extent that, under paragraph (c)(3) of this section, the payment directly or indirectly funds the hybrid deduction.

(2) *Ordering rules.*—The following ordering rules apply for purposes of determining the extent that a hybrid deduction directly or indirectly offsets income attributable to imported mismatch payments.

(i) First, the hybrid deduction offsets income attributable to a factually-related imported mismatch payment that directly or indirectly funds the hybrid deduction. For this purpose, a *factually-related imported mismatch payment* means an imported mismatch payment that is made pursuant to a transaction, agreement, or instrument entered into pursuant to the same plan or series of related transactions that includes the transaction, agreement, or instrument pursuant to which the hybrid deduction is incurred.

(ii) Second, to the extent remaining, the hybrid deduction offsets income attributable to an imported mismatch payment (other than a factually-related imported mismatch payment) that directly funds the hybrid deduction.

(iii) Third, to the extent remaining, the hybrid deduction offsets income attributable to an imported mismatch payment (other than a factually-related imported mismatch payment) that indirectly funds the hybrid deduction.

(3) *Funding rules.*—The following funding rules apply for purposes of determining the extent that an imported mismatch payment directly or indirectly funds a hybrid deduction.

(i) The imported mismatch payment directly funds a hybrid deduction to the extent that the imported mismatch payee incurs the deduction.

(ii) The imported mismatch payment indirectly funds a hybrid deduction to the extent that the imported mismatch payee is allocated the deduction.

(iii) The imported mismatch payee is allocated a hybrid deduction to the extent that the imported mismatch payee directly or indirectly makes a funded taxable payment to the tax resident or taxable branch that incurs the hybrid deduction.

(iv) An imported mismatch payee indirectly makes a funded taxable payment to the tax resident or taxable branch that incurs a hybrid deduction to the extent that a chain of funded taxable payments exists connecting the imported mismatch payee, each intermediary tax resident or taxable branch, and the tax resident or taxable branch that incurs the hybrid deduction.

(v) The term *funded taxable payment* means, with respect to a tax resident or taxable branch that is not a specified party, a deductible amount paid or accrued by the tax resident or taxable branch under its tax law, other than an amount that gives rise to a hybrid deduction. However, a funded taxable payment does not include an amount deemed to be an imported mismatch payment pursuant to paragraph (f) of this section.

(vi) If, with respect to a tax resident or taxable branch that is not a specified party, a deduction or loss that is not incurred by the tax resident or taxable branch is directly or indirectly made available to offset income of the tax resident or taxable branch under its tax law, then, for purposes of this paragraph (c), the tax resident or taxable branch to which the deduction or loss is made available and the tax resident or branch that incurs the deduction or loss are treated as a single tax resident or taxable branch. For example, if a deduction or loss of one tax resident is made available to offset income of another tax resident under a tax consolidation, fiscal unity, group relief, loss sharing, or any similar regime, then the tax residents are treated as a single tax resident for purposes of paragraph (c) of this section.

(d) *Calculations based on aggregate amounts during accounting period.*—For purposes of this section, amounts are determined on an accounting period basis. Thus, for example, the amount of imported mismatch payments made by an imported mismatch payer to a particular imported mismatch payee is equal to the aggregate amount of all such payments made by the payer during the accounting period.

(e) *Pro rata adjustments.*—Amounts are allocated on a pro rata basis if there would otherwise be more than one permissible manner in which to allocate the amounts. Thus, for example, if multiple imported mismatch payers make an imported mismatch payment to a particular imported mismatch payee, the amount of such payments exceeds the hybrid deduction incurred by the payee, and the payments are not factually-related imported mismatch payments, then a pro rata portion of each payer's payment is considered to directly fund the hybrid deduction. *See* § 1.267A-6(c)(9).

(f) *Certain amounts deemed to be imported mismatch payments for certain purposes.*—For purposes of determining the extent that income attributable to an imported mismatch payment is directly or indirectly offset by a hybrid deduction, an amount paid or accrued by a tax resident or taxable branch that is not a specified party is deemed to be an imported mismatch payment (and such tax resident or taxable branch and a specified recipient of the amount, determined under § 1.267A-5(a)(19), by treating the amount as the specified payment, are deemed to be an imported mismatch payer and an imported mismatch payee, respectively) to the extent that—

(1) The tax law of such tax resident or taxable branch contains hybrid mismatch rules; and

(2) Under a provision of the hybrid mismatch rules substantially similar to this section, the tax resident or taxable branch is denied a deduction for all or a portion of the amount. *See* § 1.267A-6(c)(10). [Reg. § 1.267A-4.]

[Proposed 12-28-2018.]

**[Prop. Reg. §1.267A-5]**

**§1.267A-5. Definitions and special rules.—**
(a) *Definitions.*—For purposes of §§1.267A-1
through 1.267A-7 the following definitions
apply.

(1) The term *accounting period* means a taxable year, or a period of similar length over
which, under a provision of hybrid mismatch
rules substantially similar to §1.267A-4, computations similar to those under that section are
made under a foreign tax law.

(2) The term *branch* means a taxable presence of a tax resident in a country other than its
country of residence under either the tax resident's tax law or such other country's tax law.

(3) The term *branch mismatch payment* has
the meaning provided in §1.267A-2(e)(2).

(4) The term *controlled foreign corporation* (or
*CFC*) has the meaning provided in section 957.

(5) The term *deemed branch payment* has the
meaning provided in §1.267A-2(c)(2).

(6) The term *disregarded payment* has the
meaning provided in §1.267A-2(b)(2).

(7) The term *entity* means any person (as
described in section 7701(a)(1), including an entity that under §§301.7701-1 through 301.7701-3
of this chapter is disregarded as an entity separate from its owner) other than an individual.

(8) The term *fiscally transparent* means, with
respect to an entity, fiscally transparent with respect to an item of income as determined under
the principles of §1.894-1(d)(3)(ii) and (iii), without regard to whether a tax resident (either the
entity or interest holder in the entity) that derives the item of income is a resident of a country
that has an income tax treaty with the United
States.

(9) The term *home office* means a tax resident
that has a branch.

(10) The term *hybrid mismatch rules* means
rules, regulations, or other tax guidance substantially similar to section 267A, and includes rules
the purpose of which is to neutralize the deduc-
tion/no-inclusion outcome of hybrid and branch
mismatch arrangements. Examples of such rules
would include rules based on, or substantially
similar to, the recommendations contained in
OECD/G-20, *Neutralising the Effects of Hybrid
Mismatch Arrangements, Action 2: 2015 Final Report* (October 2015), and OECD/G-20, *Neutralising the Effects of Branch Mismatch Arrangements,
Action 2: Inclusive Framework on BEPS* (July 2017).

(11) The term *hybrid transaction* has the
meaning provided in §1.267A-2(a)(2).

(12) The term *interest* means any amount
described in paragraph (a)(12)(i) or (ii) of this
section (as adjusted by amounts described in
paragraph (a)(12)(iii) of this section) that is paid
or accrued, or treated as paid or accrued, for the
taxable year or that is otherwise designated as
interest expense in paragraph (a)(12)(i) or (ii) of
this section (as adjusted by amounts described in
paragraph (a)(12)(iii) of this section).

(i) *In general.*—Interest is an amount paid,
received, or accrued as compensation for the use
or forbearance of money under the terms of an
instrument or contractual arrangement, including a series of transactions, that is treated as a
debt instrument for purposes of section 1275(a)
and §1.1275-1(d), and not treated as stock under
§1.385-3, or an amount that is treated as interest
under other provisions of the Internal Revenue
Code (Code) or the regulations under 26 CFR
part 1. Thus, for example, interest includes—

(A) Original issue discount (OID);

(B) Qualified stated interest, as adjusted by the issuer for any bond issuance
premium;

(C) OID on a synthetic debt instrument
arising from an integrated transaction under
§1.1275-6;

(D) Repurchase premium to the extent
deductible by the issuer under §1.163-7(c);

(E) Deferred payments treated as interest under section 483;

(F) Amounts treated as interest under a
section 467 rental agreement;

(G) Forgone interest under section
7872;

(H) De minimis OID taken into account
by the issuer;

(I) Amounts paid or received in connection with a sale-repurchase agreement treated
as indebtedness under Federal tax principles; in
the case of a sale-repurchase agreement relating
to tax-exempt bonds, however, the amount is not
tax-exempt interest;

(J) Redeemable ground rent treated as
interest under section 163(c); and

(K) Amounts treated as interest under
section 636.

(ii) *Swaps with significant nonperiodic payments.*—(A) *Non-cleared swaps.*—A swap that is
not a cleared swap and that has significant
nonperiodic payments is treated as two separate
transactions consisting of an on-market, level
payment swap and a loan. The loan must be
accounted for by the parties to the contract independently of the swap. The time value component associated with the loan, determined in
accordance with §1.446-3(f)(2)(iii)(A), is recognized as interest expense to the payor.

(B) [Reserved]

(C) *Definition of cleared swap.*—The term
*cleared swap* means a swap that is cleared by a
derivatives clearing organization, as such term is
defined in section 1a of the Commodity Exchange Act (7 U.S.C. 1a), or by a clearing agency,
as such term is defined in section 3 of the Securities Exchange Act of 1934 (15 U.S.C. 78c), that is
registered as a derivatives clearing organization
under the Commodity Exchange Act or as a
clearing agency under the Securities Exchange
Act of 1934, respectively, if the derivatives clearing organization or clearing agency requires the
parties to the swap to post and collect margin or
collateral.

**Prop. Reg. §1.267A-5(a)(12)(ii)(C)**

(iii) *Amounts affecting the effective cost of borrowing that adjust the amount of interest expense.*—Income, deduction, gain, or loss from a derivative, as defined in section 59A(h)(4)(A), that alters a person's effective cost of borrowing with respect to a liability of the person is treated as an adjustment to interest expense of the person. For example, a person that is obligated to pay interest at a floating rate on a note and enters into an interest rate swap that entitles the person to receive an amount that is equal to or that closely approximates the interest rate on the note in exchange for a fixed amount is, in effect, paying interest expense at a fixed rate by entering into the interest rate swap. Income, deduction, gain, or loss from the swap is treated as an adjustment to interest expense. Similarly, any gain or loss resulting from a termination or other disposition of the swap is an adjustment to interest expense, with the timing of gain or loss subject to the rules of § 1.446-4.

(13) The term *investor* means, with respect to an entity, any tax resident or taxable branch that directly or indirectly (determined under the rules of section 958(a) without regard to whether an intermediate entity is foreign or domestic) owns an interest in the entity.

(14) The term *related* has the meaning provided in this paragraph (a)(14). A tax resident or taxable branch is related to a specified party if the tax resident or taxable branch is a related person within the meaning of section 954(d)(3), determined by treating the specified party as the "controlled foreign corporation" referred to in that section and the tax resident or taxable branch as the "person" referred to in that section. In addition, for these purposes, a tax resident that under §§ 301.7701-1 through 301.7701-3 of this chapter is disregarded as an entity separate from its owner for U.S. tax purposes, as well as a taxable branch, is treated as a corporation. Further, for these purposes neither section 318(a)(3), nor § 1.958-2(d) or the principles thereof, applies to attribute stock or other interests to a tax resident, taxable branch, or specified party.

(15) The term *reverse hybrid* has the meaning provided in § 1.267A-2(d)(2).

(16) The term *royalty* includes amounts paid or accrued as consideration for the use of, or the right to use—

(i) Any copyright, including any copyright of any literary, artistic, scientific or other work (including cinematographic films and software);

(ii) Any patent, trademark, design or model, plan, secret formula or process, or other similar property (including goodwill); or

(iii) Any information concerning industrial, commercial or scientific experience, but does not include—

(A) Amounts paid or accrued for after-sales services;

(B) Amounts paid or accrued for services rendered by a seller to the purchaser under a warranty;

(C) Amounts paid or accrued for pure technical assistance; or

(D) Amounts paid or accrued for an opinion given by an engineer, lawyer or accountant.

(17) The term *specified party* means a tax resident of the United States, a CFC (other than a CFC with respect to which there is not a United States shareholder that owns (within the meaning of section 958(a)) at least ten percent (by vote or value) of the stock of the CFC), and a U.S. taxable branch. Thus, an entity that is fiscally transparent for U.S. tax purposes is not a specified party, though an owner of the entity may be a specified party. For example, in the case of a payment by a partnership, a domestic corporation or a CFC that is a partner of the partnership is a specified party whose deduction for its allocable share of the payment is subject to disallowance under section 267A.

(18) The term *specified payment* has the meaning provided in § 1.267A-1(b).

(19) The term *specified recipient* means, with respect to a specified payment, any tax resident that derives the payment under its tax law or any taxable branch to which the payment is attributable under its tax law. The principles of § 1.894-1(d)(1) apply for purposes of determining whether a tax resident derives a specified payment under its tax law, without regard to whether the tax resident is a resident of a country that has an income tax treaty with the United States. There may be more than one specified recipient with respect to a specified payment.

(20) The term *structured arrangement* means an arrangement with respect to which one or more specified payments would be a disqualified hybrid amount (or a disqualified imported mismatch amount) if the specified payment were analyzed without regard to the relatedness limitation in § 1.267A-2(f) (or without regard to the language "that is related to the specified party" in § 1.267A-4(a)) (either such outcome, a *hybrid mismatch*), provided that either paragraph (a)(20)(i) or (ii) of this section is satisfied. A *party to a structured arrangement* means a tax resident or taxable branch that participates in the structured arrangement. For this purpose, an entity's participation in a structured arrangement is imputed to its investors.

(i) The hybrid mismatch is priced into the terms of the arrangement.

(ii) Based on all the facts and circumstances, the hybrid mismatch is a principal purpose of the arrangement. Facts and circumstances that indicate the hybrid mismatch is a principal purpose of the arrangement include—

(A) Marketing the arrangement as tax-advantaged where some or all of the tax advantage derives from the hybrid mismatch;

(B) Primarily marketing the arrangement to tax residents of a country the tax law of which enables the hybrid mismatch;

(C) Features that alter the terms of the arrangement, including the return, in the event the hybrid mismatch is no longer available; or

(D) A below-market return absent the tax effects or benefits resulting from the hybrid mismatch.

(21) The term *tax law* of a country includes statutes, regulations, administrative or judicial rulings, and treaties of the country. When used with respect to a tax resident or branch, tax law refers to—

(i) In the case of a tax resident, the tax law of the country or countries where the tax resident is resident; and

(ii) In the case of a branch, the tax law of the country where the branch is located.

(22) The term *taxable branch* means a branch that has a taxable presence under its tax law.

(23) The term *tax resident* means either of the following:

(i) A body corporate or other entity or body of persons liable to tax under the tax law of a country as a resident. For this purpose, a body corporate or other entity or body of persons may be considered liable to tax under the tax law of a country as a resident even though such tax law does not impose a corporate income tax. A body corporate or other entity or body of persons may be a tax resident of more than one country.

(ii) An individual liable to tax under the tax law of a country as a resident. An individual may be a tax resident of more than one country.

(24) The term *United States shareholder* has the meaning provided in section 951(b).

(25) The term *U.S. taxable branch* means a trade or business carried on in the United States by a tax resident of another country, except that if an income tax treaty applies, the term means a permanent establishment of a tax treaty resident eligible for benefits under an income tax treaty between the United States and the treaty country. Thus, for example, a U.S. taxable branch includes a U.S. trade or business of a foreign corporation taxable under section 882(a) or a U.S. permanent establishment of a tax treaty resident.

(b) *Special rules.*—For purposes of §§1.267A-1 through 1.267A-7, the following special rules apply.

(1) *Coordination with other provisions.*—Except as otherwise provided in the Code or in regulations under 26 CFR part 1, section 267A applies to a specified payment after the application of any other applicable provisions of the Code and regulations under 26 CFR part 1. Thus, the determination of whether a deduction for a specified payment is disallowed under section 267A is made with respect to the taxable year for which a deduction for the payment would otherwise be allowed for U.S. tax purposes. See, for example, sections 163(e)(3) and 267(a)(3) for rules that may defer the taxable year for which a deduction is allowed. *See also* §1.882-5(a)(5) (providing that provisions that disallow interest ex-

pense apply after the application of §1.882-5). In addition, provisions that characterize amounts paid or accrued as something other than interest or royalty, such as §1.894-1(d)(2), govern the treatment of such amounts and therefore such amounts would not be treated as specified payments.

(2) *Foreign currency gain or loss.*—Except as set forth in this paragraph (b)(2), section 988 gain or loss is not taken into account under section 267A. Foreign currency gain or loss recognized with respect to a specified payment is taken into account under section 267A to the extent that a deduction for the specified payment is disallowed under section 267A, provided that the foreign currency gain or loss is described in §1.988-2(b)(4) (relating to exchange gain or loss recognized by the issuer of a debt instrument with respect to accrued interest) or §1.988-2(c) (relating to items of expense or gross income or receipts which are to be paid after the date accrued). If a deduction for a specified payment is disallowed under section 267A, then a proportionate amount of foreign currency loss under section 988 with respect to the specified payment is also disallowed, and a proportionate amount of foreign currency gain under section 988 with respect to the specified payment reduces the amount of the disallowance. For this purpose, the proportionate amount is the amount of the foreign currency gain or loss under section 988 with respect to the specified payment multiplied by the amount of the specified payment for which a deduction is disallowed under section 267A.

(3) *U.S. taxable branch payments.*—(i) *Amounts considered paid or accrued by a U.S. taxable branch.*—For purposes of section 267A, a U.S. taxable branch is considered to pay or accrue an amount of interest or royalty equal to—

(A) The amount of interest or royalty allocable to effectively connected income of the U.S. taxable branch under section 873(a) or 882(c)(1), as applicable; or

(B) In the case of a U.S. taxable branch that is a U.S. permanent establishment of a treaty resident eligible for benefits under an income tax treaty between the United States and the treaty country, the amount of interest or royalty deductible in computing the business profits attributable to the U.S. permanent establishment, if such amounts differ from the amounts allocable under paragraph (b)(3)(i)(A) of this section.

(ii) *Treatment of U.S. taxable branch payments.*—(A) *Interest.*—Interest considered paid or accrued by a U.S. taxable branch of a foreign corporation under paragraph (b)(3)(i) of this section is treated as a payment directly to the person to which the interest is payable, to the extent it is paid or accrued with respect to a liability described in §1.882-5(a)(1)(ii)(A) (resulting in directly allocable interest) or with respect to a U.S. booked liability, as defined in §1.882-5(d)(2). If the amount of interest allocable to the U.S. taxable branch exceeds the interest paid or accrued on its U.S. booked liabilities, the excess amount is treated as paid or accrued by the U.S. taxable branch on a pro-rata basis to the same persons and pursuant to the same terms that the home office paid or accrued interest for purposes of the calculations described in paragraph (b)(3)(i) of this section, excluding any interest treated as already paid directly by the branch.

(B) *Royalties.*—Royalties considered paid or accrued by a U.S. taxable branch under paragraph (b)(3)(i) of this section are treated solely for purposes of section 267A as paid or accrued on a pro-rata basis by the U.S. taxable branch to the same persons and pursuant to the same terms that the home office paid or accrued such royalties.

(C) *Permanent establishments and inter-branch payments.*—If a U.S. taxable branch is a permanent establishment in the United States, rules analogous to the rules in paragraphs (b)(3)(ii)(A) and (B) of this section apply with respect to interest and royalties allowed in computing the business profits of a treaty resident eligible for treaty benefits. This paragraph (b)(3)(ii)(C) does not apply to interbranch interest or royalty payments allowed as deduction under certain U.S. income tax treaties (as described in § 1.267A-2(c)(2)).

(4) *Effect on earnings and profits.*—The disallowance of a deduction under section 267A does not affect whether or when the amount paid or accrued that gave rise to the deduction reduces earnings and profits of a corporation.

(5) *Application to structured payments.*—(i) *In general.*—For purposes of section 267A and the regulations under section 267A as contained in 26 CFR part 1, a structured payment (as defined in paragraph (b)(5)(ii) of this section) is treated as a specified payment.

(ii) *Structured payment.*—A structured payment means any amount described in paragraphs (b)(5)(ii)(A) or (B) of this section (as adjusted by amounts described in paragraph (b)(5)(ii)(C) of this section).

(A) *Certain payments related to the time value of money (structured interest amounts).*—(1) *Substitute interest payments.*—A substitute interest payment described in § 1.861-2(a)(7).

(2) *Certain amounts labeled as fees.*—(i) *Commitment fees.*—Any fees in respect of a lender commitment to provide financing if any portion of such financing is actually provided.

(ii) [Reserved]

(3) *Debt issuance costs.*—Any debt issuance costs subject to § 1.446-5.

(4) *Guaranteed payments.*—Any guaranteed payments for the use of capital under section 707(c).

(B) *Amounts predominately associated with the time value of money.*—Any expense or loss, to the extent deductible, incurred by a person in a transaction or series of integrated or related transactions in which the person secures the use of funds for a period of time, if such expense or loss is predominately incurred in consideration of the time value of money.

(C) *Adjustment for amounts affecting the effective cost of funds.*—Income, deduction, gain, or loss from a derivative, as defined in section 59A(h)(4)(A), that alters a person's effective cost of funds with respect to a structured payment described in paragraph (b)(5)(ii)(A) or (B) of this section is treated as an adjustment to the structured payment of the person.

(6) *Anti-avoidance rule.*—A specified party's deduction for a specified payment is disallowed to the extent that both of the following requirements are satisfied:

(i) The payment (or income attributable to the payment) is not included in the income of a tax resident or taxable branch, as determined under § 1.267A-3(a) (but without regard to the de minimis and full inclusion rules in § 1.267A-3(a)(3)).

(ii) A principal purpose of the plan or arrangement is to avoid the purposes of the regulations under section 267A. [Reg. § 1.267A-5.]

[Proposed 12-28-2018.]

**[Prop. Reg. § 1.267A-6]**

**§ 1.267A-6. Examples.**—(a) *Scope.*—This section provides examples that illustrate the application of § § 1.267A-1 through 1.267A-5.

(b) *Presumed facts.*—For purposes of the examples in this section, unless otherwise indicated, the following facts are presumed:

(1) US1, US2, and US3 are domestic corporations that are tax residents solely of the United States.

(2) FW, FX, and FZ are bodies corporate established in, and tax residents of, Country W, Country X, and Country Z, respectively. They are not fiscally transparent under the tax law of any country.

(3) Under the tax law of each country, interest and royalty payments are deductible.

(4) The tax law of each country provides a 100 percent participation exemption for dividends received from non-resident corporations.

(5) The tax law of each country, other than the United States, provides an exemption for income attributable to a branch.

(6) Except as provided in paragraphs (b)(4) and (5) of this section, all amounts derived (determined under the principles of § 1.894-1(d)(1)) by a tax resident, or attributable to a taxable branch, are included in income, as determined under § 1.267A-3(a).

(7) Only the tax law of the United States contains hybrid mismatch rules.

(c) *Examples.*—(1) *Example 1. Payment pursuant to a hybrid financial instrument*—(i) *Facts.* FX holds all the interests of US1. FX holds an instrument issued by US1 that is treated as equity for Country X tax purposes and indebtedness for U.S. tax purposes (the FX-US1 instrument). On date 1, US1 pays $50x to FX pursuant to the instrument. The amount is treated as an excludible dividend for Country X tax purposes (by reason of the Country X participation exemption) and as interest for U.S. tax purposes.

(ii) *Analysis.* US1 is a specified party and thus a deduction for its $50x specified payment is subject to disallowance under section 267A. As described in paragraphs (c)(1)(ii)(A) through (C) of this section, the entire $50x payment is a disqualified hybrid amount under the hybrid transaction rule of §1.267A-2(a) and, as a result, a deduction for the payment is disallowed under §1.267A-1(b)(1).

(A) US1's payment is made pursuant to a hybrid transaction because a payment with respect to the FX-US1 instrument is treated as interest for U.S. tax purposes but not for purposes of Country X tax law (the tax law of FX, a specified recipient that is related to US1). *See* §1.267A-2(a)(2) and (f). Therefore, §1.267A-2(a) applies to the payment.

(B) For US1's payment to be a disqualified hybrid amount under §1.267A-2(a), a no-inclusion must occur with respect to FX. *See* §1.267A-2(a)(1)(i). As a consequence of the Country X participation exemption, FX includes $0 of the payment in income and therefore a $50x no-inclusion occurs with respect to FX. *See* §1.267A-3(a)(1). The result is the same regardless of whether, under the Country X participation exemption, the $50x payment is simply excluded from FX's taxable income or, instead, is reduced or offset by other means, such as a $50x dividends received deduction. *See id.*

(C) Pursuant to §1.267A-2(a)(1)(ii), FX's $50x no-inclusion gives rise to a disqualified hybrid amount to the extent that it is a result of US1's payment being made pursuant to the hybrid transaction. FX's $50x no-inclusion is a result of the payment being made pursuant to the hybrid transaction because, were the payment to be treated as interest for Country X tax purposes, FX would include $50x in income and, consequently, the no-inclusion would not occur.

(iii) *Alternative facts – multiple specified recipients.* The facts are the same as in paragraph (c)(1)(i) of this section, except that FX holds all the interests of FZ, which is fiscally transparent for Country X tax purposes, and FZ holds all of the interests of US1. Moreover, the FX-US1 instrument is held by FZ (rather than by FX) and US1 makes its $50x payment to FZ (rather than to FX); the payment is derived by FZ under its tax law and by FX under its tax law and, accordingly, both FZ and FX are specified recipients of the payment. Further, the payment is treated as

interest for Country Z tax purposes and FZ includes it in income. For the reasons described in paragraph (c)(1)(ii) of this section, FX's no-inclusion causes the payment to be a disqualified hybrid amount. FZ's inclusion in income (regardless of whether Country Z has a low or high tax rate) does not affect the result, because the hybrid transaction rule of §1.267A-2(a) applies if any no-inclusion occurs with respect to a specified recipient of the payment as a result of the payment being made pursuant to the hybrid transaction.

(iv) *Alternative facts – preferential rate.* The facts are the same as in paragraph (c)(1)(i) of this section, except that for Country X tax purposes US1's payment is treated as a dividend subject to a 4% tax rate, whereas the marginal rate imposed on ordinary income is 20%. FX includes $10x of the payment in income, calculated as $50x multiplied by 0.2 (.04, the rate at which the particular type of payment (a dividend for Country X tax purposes) is subject to tax in Country X, divided by 0.2, the marginal tax rate imposed on ordinary income). *See* §1.267A-3(a)(1). Thus, a $40x no-inclusion occurs with respect to FX ($50x less $10x). The $40x no-inclusion is a result of the payment being made pursuant to the hybrid transaction because, were the payment to be treated as interest for Country X tax purposes, FX would include the entire $50x in income at the full marginal rate imposed on ordinary income (20%) and, consequently, the no-inclusion would not occur. Accordingly, $40x of US1's payment is a disqualified hybrid amount.

(v) *Alternative facts – no-inclusion not the result of hybridity.* The facts are the same as in paragraph (c)(1)(i) of this section, except that Country X has a pure territorial regime (that is, Country X only taxes income with a domestic source). Although US1's payment is pursuant to a hybrid transaction and a $50x no-inclusion occurs with respect to FX, FX's no-inclusion is not a result of the payment being made pursuant to the hybrid transaction. This is because if Country X tax law were to treat the payment as interest, FX would include $0 in income and, consequently, the $50x no-inclusion would still occur. Accordingly, US1's payment is not a disqualified hybrid amount. *See* §1.267A-2(a)(1)(ii). The result would be the same if Country X instead did not impose a corporate income tax.

(2) *Example 2. Payment pursuant to a repo transaction*—(i) *Facts.* FX holds all the interests of US1, and US1 holds all the interests of US2. On date 1, US1 and FX enter into a sale and repurchase transaction. Pursuant to the transaction, US1 transfers shares of preferred stock of US2 to FX in return for $1,000x paid from FX to US1, subject to a binding commitment of US1 to reacquire those shares on date 3 for an agreed price, which represents a repayment of the $1,000x plus a financing or time value of money return reduced by the amount of any distributions paid with respect to the preferred stock between dates 1 and 3 that are retained by FX. On date 2, US2

pays a $100x dividend on its preferred stock to FX. For Country X tax purposes, FX is treated as owning the US2 preferred stock and therefore is the beneficial owner of the dividend. For U.S. tax purposes, the transaction is treated as a loan from FX to US1 that is secured by the US2 preferred stock. Thus, for U.S. tax purposes, US1 is treated as owning the US2 preferred stock and is the beneficial owner of the dividend. In addition, for U.S. tax purposes, US1 is treated as paying $100x of interest to FX (an amount corresponding to the $100x dividend paid by US2 to FX). Further, the marginal tax rate imposed on ordinary income under Country X tax law is 25%. Moreover, instead of a participation exemption, Country X tax law provides its tax residents a credit for underlying foreign taxes paid by a non-resident corporation from which a dividend is received; with respect to the $100x dividend received by FX from US2, the credit is $10x.

(ii) *Analysis.* US1 is a specified party and thus a deduction for its $100x specified payment is subject to disallowance under section 267A. As described in paragraphs (c)(2)(ii)(A) through (D) of this section, $40x of the payment is a disqualified hybrid amount under the hybrid transaction rule of § 1.267A-2(a) and, as a result, $40x of the deduction is disallowed under § 1.267A-1(b)(1).

(A) Although US1's $100x interest payment is not regarded under Country X tax law, a connected amount (US2's dividend payment) is regarded and derived by FX under such tax law. Thus, FX is considered a specified recipient with respect to US1's interest payment. *See* § 1.267A-2(a)(3).

(B) US1's payment is made pursuant to a hybrid transaction because a payment with respect to the sale and repurchase transaction is treated as interest for U.S. tax purposes but not for purposes of Country X tax law (the tax law of FX, a specified recipient that is related to US1), which does not regard the payment. *See* § 1.267A-2(a)(2) and (f). Therefore, § 1.267A-2(a) applies to the payment.

(C) For US1's payment to be a disqualified hybrid amount under § 1.267A-2(a), a no-inclusion must occur with respect to FX. *See* § 1.267A-2(a)(1)(i). As a consequence of Country X tax law not regarding US1's payment, FX includes $0 of the payment in income and therefore a $100x no-inclusion occurs with respect to FX. *See* § 1.267A-3(a). However, FX includes $60x of a connected amount (US2's dividend payment) in income, calculated as $100x (the amount of the dividend) less $40x (the portion of the connected amount that is not included in Country X due to the foreign tax credit, determined by dividing the amount of the credit, $10x, by 0.25, the tax rate in Country X). *See id.* Pursuant to § 1.267A-2(a)(3), FX's inclusion in income with respect to the connected amount correspondingly reduces the amount of its no-inclusion with respect to US1's payment. Therefore, for purposes of § 1.267A-2(a), FX's no-inclusion with respect to US1's payment is considered to be $40x ($100x less $60x). *See* § 1.267A-2(a)(3).

(D) Pursuant to § 1.267A-2(a)(1)(ii), FX's $40x no-inclusion gives rise to a disqualified hybrid amount to the extent that FX's no-inclusion is a result of US1's payment being made pursuant to the hybrid transaction. FX's $40x no-inclusion is a result of US1's payment being made pursuant to the hybrid transaction because, were the sale and repurchase transaction to be treated as a loan from FX to US1 for Country X tax purposes, FX would include US1's $100x interest payment in income (because it would not be entitled to a foreign tax credit) and, consequently, the no-inclusion would not occur.

(iii) *Alternative facts – structured arrangement.* The facts are the same as in paragraph (c)(2)(i) of this section, except that FX is a bank that is unrelated to US1. In addition, the sale and repurchase transaction is a structured arrangement and FX is a party to the structured arrangement. The result is the same as in paragraph (c)(2)(ii) of this section. That is, even though FX is not related to US1, it is taken into account with respect to the determinations under § 1.267A-2(a) because it is a party to a structured arrangement pursuant to which the payment is made. *See* § 1.267A-2(f).

(3) *Example 3. Disregarded payment*—(i) *Facts.* FX holds all the interests of US1. For Country X tax purposes, US1 is a disregarded entity of FX. During taxable year 1, US1 pays $100x to FX pursuant to a debt instrument. The amount is treated as interest for U.S. tax purposes but is disregarded for Country X tax purposes as a transaction involving a single taxpayer. During taxable year 1, US1's only other items of income, gain, deduction, or loss are $125x of gross income and a $60x item of deductible expense. The $125x item of gross income is included in FX's income, and the $60x item of deductible expense is allowable for Country X tax purposes.

(ii) *Analysis.* US1 is a specified party and thus a deduction for its $100x specified payment is subject to disallowance under section 267A. As described in paragraphs (c)(3)(ii)(A) and (B) of this section, $35x of the payment is a disqualified hybrid amount under the disregarded payment rule of § 1.267A-2(b) and, as a result, $35x of the deduction is disallowed under § 1.267A-1(b)(1).

(A) US1's $100x payment is not regarded under the tax law of Country X (the tax law of FX, a related tax resident to which the payment is made) because under such tax law the payment is a disregarded transaction involving a single taxpayer. *See* § 1.267A-2(b)(2) and (f). In addition, were the tax law of Country X to regard the payment (and treat it as interest), FX would include it in income. Therefore, the payment is a disregarded payment to which § 1.267A-2(b) applies. *See* § 1.267A-2(b)(2).

(B) Under § 1.267A-2(b)(1), the excess (if any) of US1's disregarded payments for taxable year 1 ($100x) over its dual inclusion income for the taxable year is a disqualified hybrid amount. US1's dual inclusion income for taxable year 1 is $65x, calculated as $125x (the amount of US1's gross income that is included in FX's income) less $60x (the amount of US1's deductible expenses, other than deductions for disregarded payments, that are allowable for Country X tax purposes). See § 1.267A-2(b)(3). Therefore, $35x is a disqualified hybrid amount ($100x less $65x). See § 1.267A-2(b)(1).

(iii) *Alternative facts – non-dual inclusion income arising from hybrid transaction.* The facts are the same as in paragraph (c)(3)(i) of this section, except that US1 holds all the interests of FZ (a CFC) and US1's only item of income, gain, deduction, or loss during taxable year 1 (other than the $100x payment to FX) is $80x paid to US1 by FZ pursuant to an instrument treated as indebtedness for U.S. tax purposes and equity for Country X tax purposes (the US1-FZ instrument). In addition, the $80x is treated as interest for U.S. tax purposes and an excludible dividend for Country X tax purposes (by reason of the Country X participation exemption). Paragraphs (c)(3)(iii)(A) and (B) of this section describe the extent to which the specified payments by FZ and US1, each of which is a specified party, are disqualified hybrid amounts.

(A) The hybrid transaction rule of § 1.267A-2(a) applies to FZ's payment because such payment is made pursuant to a hybrid transaction, as a payment with respect to the US1-FZ instrument is treated as interest for U.S. tax purposes but not for purposes of Country X's tax law (the tax law of FX, a specified recipient that is related to FZ). As a consequence of the Country X participation exemption, an $80x no-inclusion occurs with respect to FX, and such no-inclusion is a result of the payment being made pursuant to the hybrid transaction. Thus, but for § 1.267A-3(b), the entire $80x of FZ's payment would be a disqualified hybrid amount. However, because US1 (a tax resident of the United States that is also a specified recipient of the payment) takes the entire $80x payment into account in its gross income, no portion of the payment is a disqualified hybrid amount. See § 1.267A-3(b)(2).

(B) The disregarded payment rule of § 1.267A-2(b) applies to US1's $100x payment to FX, for the reasons described in paragraph (c)(3)(ii)(A) of this section. In addition, US1's dual inclusion income for taxable year 1 is $0 because, as a result of the Country X participation exemption, no portion of FZ's $80x payment to US1 (which is derived by FX under its tax law) is included in FX's income. See § § 1.267A-2(b)(3) and 1.267A-3(a). Therefore, the entire $100x payment from US1 to FX is a disqualified hybrid amount, calculated as $100x (the amount of the payment) less $0 (the amount of dual inclusion income). See § 1.267A-2(b)(1).

(4) *Example 4. Payment allocable to a U.S. taxable branch*—(i) *Facts.* FX1 and FX2 are foreign corporations that are bodies corporate established in and tax residents of Country X. FX1 holds all the interests of FX2, and FX1 and FX2 file a consolidated return under Country X tax law. FX2 has a U.S. taxable branch ("USB"). During taxable year

1, FX2 pays $50x to FX1 pursuant to an instrument (the "FX1-FX2 instrument"). The amount paid pursuant to the instrument is treated as interest for U.S. tax purposes but, as a consequence of the Country X consolidation regime, is treated as a disregarded transaction between group members for Country X tax purposes. Also during taxable year 1, FX2 pays $100x of interest to an unrelated bank that is not a party to a structured arrangement (the instrument pursuant to which the payment is made, the "bank-FX2 instrument"). FX2's only other item of income, gain, deduction, or loss for taxable year 1 is $200x of gross income. Under Country X tax law, the $200x of gross income is attributable to USB, but is not included in FX's income because Country X tax law exempts income attributable to a branch. Under U.S. tax law, the $200x of gross income is effectively connected income of USB. Further, under section 882, $75x of interest is, for taxable year 1, allocable to USB's effectively connected income. USB has neither liabilities that are directly allocable to it, as described in § 1.882-5(a)(1)(ii)(A), nor booked liabilities, as defined in § 1.882-5(d)(2).

(ii) *Analysis.* USB is a specified party and thus any interest or royalty allowable as a deduction in determining its effectively connected income is subject to disallowance under section 267A. Pursuant to § 1.267A-5(b)(3)(i)(A), USB is treated as paying $75x of interest, and such interest is thus a specified payment. Of that $75x, $25x is treated as paid to FX1, calculated as $75x (the interest allocable to USB under section 882) multiplied by 1/3 ($50x, FX2's payment to FX1, divided by $150x, the total interest paid by FX2). See § 1.267A-5(b)(3)(ii)(A). As described in paragraphs (c)(4)(ii)(A) and (B) of this section, the $25x of the specified payment treated as paid by USB to FX1 is a disqualified hybrid amount under the disregarded payment rule of § 1.267A-2(b) and, as a result, a deduction for that amount is disallowed under § 1.267A-1(b)(1).

(A) USB's $25x payment to FX1 is not regarded under the tax law of Country X (the tax law of FX1, a related tax resident to which the payment is made) because under such tax law the payment is a disregarded transaction between group members. See § 1.267A-2(b)(2) and (f). In addition, were the tax law of Country X to regard the payment (and treat it as interest), FX1 would include it in income. Therefore, the payment is a disregarded payment to which § 1.267A-2(b) applies. See § 1.267A-2(b)(2).

(B) Under § 1.267A-2(b)(1), the excess (if any) of USB's disregarded payments for taxable year 1 ($25x) over its dual inclusion income for the taxable year is a disqualified hybrid amount. USB's dual inclusion income for taxable year 1 is $0. This is because, as a result of the Country X exemption for income attributable to a branch, no portion of USB's $200x item of gross income is included in FX2's income. See § 1.267A-2(b)(3). Therefore, the entire $25x of the specified payment treated as paid by USB to FX1 is a disqualified hybrid amount, calculated as $25x (the amount of the payment) less $0 (the amount of dual inclusion income). *See* § 1.267A-2(b)(1).

(iii) *Alternative facts – deemed branch payment.* The facts are the same as in paragraph (c)(4)(i) of this section, except that FX2 does not pay any amounts during taxable year 1 (thus, it does not pay the $50x to FX1 or the $100x to the bank). However, under an income tax treaty between the United States and Country X, USB is a U.S. permanent establishment and, for taxable year 1, $25x of royalties is allowable as a deduction in computing the business profits of USB and is deemed paid to FX2. Under Country X tax law, the $25x is not regarded. Accordingly, the $25x is a specified payment that is a deemed branch payment. *See* § § 1.267A-2(c)(2) and 1.267A-5(b)(3)(i)(B). The entire $25x is a disqualified hybrid amount for which a deduction is disallowed because the tax law of Country X provides an exclusion or exemption for income attributable to a branch. *See* § 1.267A-2(c)(1).

(5) *Example 5. Payment to a reverse hybrid*—(i) *Facts.* FX holds all the interests of US1 and FY, and FY holds all the interests of FV. FY is an entity established in Country Y, and FV is an entity established in Country V. FY is fiscally transparent for Country Y tax purposes but is not fiscally transparent for Country X tax purposes. FV is fiscally transparent for Country X tax purposes. On date 1, US1 pays $100x to FY. The amount is treated as interest for U.S. tax purposes and Country X tax purposes.

(ii) *Analysis.* US1 is a specified party and thus a deduction for its $100x specified payment is subject to disallowance under section 267A. As described in paragraphs (c)(5)(ii)(A) through (C) of this section, the entire $100x payment is a disqualified hybrid amount under the reverse hybrid rule of § 1.267A-2(d) and, as a result, a deduction for the payment is disallowed under § 1.267A-1(b)(1).

(A) US1's payment is made to a reverse hybrid because FY is fiscally transparent under the tax law of Country Y (the tax law of the country in which it is established) but is not fiscally transparent under the tax law of Country X (the tax law of FX, an investor that is related to US1). *See* § 1.267A-2(d)(2) and (f). Therefore, § 1.267A-2(d) applies to the payment. The result would be the same if the payment were instead made to FV. *See* § 1.267A-2(d)(3).

(B) For US1's payment to be a disqualified hybrid amount under § 1.267A-2(d), a no-inclusion must occur with respect to FX. *See* § 1.267A-2(d)(1)(i). Because FX does not derive the $100x payment under Country X tax law (as FY is not fiscally transparent under such tax law), FX includes $0 of the payment in income and therefore a $100x no-inclusion occurs with respect to FX. *See* § 1.267A-3(a).

(C) Pursuant to § 1.267A-2(d)(1)(ii), FX's $100x no-inclusion gives rise to a disqualified hybrid amount to the extent that it is a result of US1's payment being made to the reverse hybrid. FX's $100x no-inclusion is a result of the payment

being made to the reverse hybrid because, were FY to be treated as fiscally transparent for Country X tax purposes, FX would include $100x in income and, consequently, the no-inclusion would not occur. The result would be the same if Country X tax law instead viewed US1's payment as a dividend, rather than interest. *See* § 1.267A-2(d)(1)(ii).

(iii) *Alternative facts – inclusion under anti-deferral regime.* The facts are the same as in paragraph (c)(5)(i) of this section, except that, under a Country X anti-deferral regime, FX includes in its income $100x attributable to the $100x payment received by FY. If under the rules of § 1.267A-3(a) FX includes the entire attributed amount in income (that is, if FX includes the amount in its income at the full marginal rate imposed on ordinary income and the amount is not reduced or offset by certain relief particular to the amount), then a no-inclusion does not occur with respect to FX. As a result, in such a case, no portion of US1's payment would be a disqualified hybrid amount under § 1.267A-2(d).

(iv) *Alternative facts – multiple investors.* The facts are the same as in paragraph (c)(5)(i) of this section, except that FX holds all the interests of FZ, which is fiscally transparent for Country X tax purposes; FZ holds all the interests of FY, which is fiscally transparent for Country Z tax purposes; and FZ includes the $100x payment in income. Thus, each of FZ and FX is an investor of FY, as each directly or indirectly holds an interest of FY. *See* § 1.267A-5(a)(13). A no-inclusion does not occur with respect to FZ, but a $100x no-inclusion occurs with respect to FX. FX's no-inclusion is a result of the payment being made to the reverse hybrid because, were FY to be treated as fiscally transparent for Country X tax purposes, then FX would include $100x in income (as FZ is fiscally transparent for Country X tax purposes). Accordingly, FX's no-inclusion is a result of US1's payment being made to the reverse hybrid and, consequently, the entire $100x payment is a disqualified hybrid amount.

(v) *Alternative facts – portion of no-inclusion not the result of hybridity.* The facts are the same as in paragraph (c)(5)(i) of this section, except that the $100x is viewed as a royalty for U.S. tax purposes and Country X tax purposes, and Country X tax law contains a patent box regime that provides an 80% deduction with respect to certain royalty income. If the payment would qualify for the Country X patent box deduction were FY to be treated as fiscally transparent for Country X tax purposes, then only $20x of FX's $100x no-inclusion would be the result of the payment being paid to a reverse hybrid, calculated as $100x (the no-inclusion with respect to FX that actually occurs) less $80x (the no-inclusion with respect to FX that would occur if FY were to be treated as fiscally transparent for Country X tax purposes). *See* § 1.267A-3(a). Accordingly, in such a case, only $20x of US1's payment would be a disqualified hybrid amount.

(6) *Example 6. Branch mismatch payment*—(i) *Facts.* FX holds all the interests of US1 and FZ.

FZ owns BB, a Country B branch that gives rise to a taxable presence in Country B under Country Z tax law but not under Country B tax law. On date 1, US1 pays $50x to FZ. The amount is treated as a royalty for U.S. tax purposes and Country Z tax purposes. Under Country Z tax law, the amount is treated as income attributable to BB and, as a consequence of County Z tax law exempting income attributable to a branch, is excluded from FZ's income.

(ii) *Analysis.* US1 is a specified party and thus a deduction for its $50x specified payment is subject to disallowance under section 267A. As described in paragraphs (c)(6)(ii)(A) through (C) of this section, the entire $50x payment is a disqualified hybrid amount under the branch mismatch rule of § 1.267A-2(e) and, as a result, a deduction for the payment is disallowed under § 1.267A-1(b)(1).

(A) US1's payment is a branch mismatch payment because under Country Z tax law (the tax law of FZ, a home office that is related to US1) the payment is treated as income attributable to BB, and BB is not a taxable branch (that is, under Country B tax law, BB does not give rise to a taxable presence). *See* § 1.267A-2(e)(2) and (f). Therefore, § 1.267A-2(e) applies to the payment. The result would be the same if instead BB were a taxable branch and, under Country B tax law, US1's payment were treated as income attributable to FZ and not BB. *See* § 1.267A-2(e)(2).

(B) For US1's payment to be a disqualified hybrid amount under § 1.267A-2(e), a no-inclusion must occur with respect to FZ. See § 1.267A-2(e)(1)(i). As a consequence of the Country Z branch exemption, FZ includes $0 of the payment in income and therefore a $50x no-inclusion occurs with respect to FZ. *See* § 1.267A-3(a).

(C) Pursuant to § 1.267A-2(e)(1)(ii), FZ's $50x no-inclusion gives rise to a disqualified hybrid amount to the extent that it is a result of US1's payment being a branch mismatch payment. FZ's $50x no-inclusion is a result of the payment being a branch mismatch payment because, were the payment to not be treated as income attributable to BB for Country Z tax purposes, FZ would include $50x in income and, consequently, the no-inclusion would not occur.

(7) *Example 7. Reduction of disqualified hybrid amount for certain amounts includible in income*—(i) *Facts.* US1 and FW hold 60% and 40%, respectively, of the interests of FX, and FX holds all the interests of FZ. Each of FX and FZ is a CFC. FX holds an instrument issued by FZ that it is treated as equity for Country X tax purposes and as indebtedness for U.S. tax purposes (the FX-FZ instrument). On date 1, FZ pays $100x to FX pursuant to the FX-FZ instrument. The amount is treated as a dividend for Country X tax purposes and as interest for U.S. tax purposes. In addition, pursuant to section 954(c)(6), the amount is not foreign personal holding company income of FX. Further, under section 951A, the payment is included in FX's tested income. Lastly, Country X tax law provides an 80% par-

ticipation exemption for dividends received from nonresident corporations and, as a result of such participation exemption, FX includes $20x of FZ's payment in income.

(ii) *Analysis.* FZ, a CFC, is a specified party and thus a deduction for its $100x specified payment is subject to disallowance under section 267A. But for § 1.267A-3(b), $80x of FZ's payment would be a disqualified hybrid amount (such amount, a "tentative disqualified hybrid amount"). *See* §§ 1.267A-2(a) and 1.267A-3(b)(1). Pursuant to § 1.267A-3(b), the tentative disqualified hybrid amount is reduced by $48x. *See* § 1.267A-3(b)(4). The $48x is the tentative disqualified hybrid amount to the extent that it increases US1's pro rata share of tested income with respect to FX under section 951A (calculated as $80x multiplied by 60%). *See id.* Accordingly, $32x of FZ's payment ($80x less $48x) is a disqualified hybrid amount under § 1.267A-2(a) and, as a result, $32x of the deduction is disallowed under § 1.267A-1(b)(1).

(iii) *Alternative facts – United States shareholder not a tax resident of the United States.* The facts are the same as in paragraph (c)(7)(i) of this section, except that US1 is a domestic partnership, 90% of the interests of which are held by US2 and the remaining 10% of which are held by a foreign individual that is a nonresident alien (as defined in section 7701(b)(1)(B)). As is the case in paragraph (c)(7)(ii) of this section, $48x of the $80x tentative disqualified hybrid amount increases US1's pro rata share of the tested income of FX. However, US1 is not a tax resident of the United States. Thus, the $48x reduces the tentative disqualified hybrid amount only to the extent that the $48x would be taken into account by a tax resident of the United States. *See* § 1.267A-3(b)(4). US2 (a tax resident of the United States) would take into account $43.2x of such amount (calculated as $48x multiplied by 90%). Thus, $36.8x of FZ's payment ($80x less $43.2x) is a disqualified hybrid amount under § 1.267A-2(a). *See id.*

(8) *Example 8. Imported mismatch rule – direct offset*—(i) *Facts.* FX holds all the interests of FW, and FW holds all the interests of US1. FX holds an instrument issued by FW that is treated as equity for Country X tax purposes and indebtedness for Country W tax purposes (the FX-FW instrument). FW holds an instrument issued by US1 that is treated as indebtedness for Country W and U.S. tax purposes (the FW-US1 instrument). In accounting period 1, FW pays $100x to FX pursuant to the FX-FW instrument. The amount is treated as an excludible dividend for Country X tax purposes (by reason of the Country X participation exemption) and as interest for Country W tax purposes. Also in accounting period 1, US1 pays $100x to FW pursuant to the FW-US1 instrument. The amount is treated as interest for Country W and U.S. tax purposes and is included in FW's income. The FX-FW instrument was not entered into pursuant to the same plan or series of related transactions pursuant to which the FW-US1 instrument was entered into.

(ii) *Analysis.* US1 is a specified party and thus a deduction for its $100x specified payment is subject to disallowance under section 267A. The $100x payment is not a disqualified hybrid amount. In addition, FW's $100x deduction is a hybrid deduction because it is a deduction allowed to FW that results from an amount paid that is interest under Country W tax law, and were Country X law to have rules substantially similar to those under §§ 1.267A-1 through 1.267A-3 and 1.267A-5, a deduction for the payment would be disallowed (because under such rules the payment would be pursuant to a hybrid transaction and FX's no-inclusion would be a result of the hybrid transaction). *See* §§ 1.267A-2(a) and 1.267A-4(b). Under § 1.267A-4(a), US1's payment is an imported mismatch payment, US1 is an imported mismatch payer, and FW (the tax resident that includes the imported mismatch payment in income) is an imported mismatch payee. The imported mismatch payment is a disqualified imported mismatch amount to the extent that the income attributable to the payment is directly or indirectly offset by the hybrid deduction incurred by FX (a tax resident that is related to US1). *See* § 1.267A-4(a). Under § 1.267A-4(c)(1), the $100x hybrid deduction directly or indirectly offsets the income attributable to US1's imported mismatch payment to the extent that the payment directly or indirectly funds the hybrid deduction. The entire $100x of US1's payment directly funds the hybrid deduction because FW (the imported mismatch payee) incurs at least that amount of the hybrid deduction. *See* § 1.267A-4(c)(3)(i). Accordingly, the entire $100x payment is a disqualified imported mismatch amount under § 1.267A-4(a) and, as a result, a deduction for the payment is disallowed under § 1.267A-1(b)(2).

(iii) *Alternative facts – long-term deferral.* The facts are the same as in paragraph (c)(8)(i) of this section, except that the FX-FW instrument is treated as indebtedness for Country X and Country W tax purposes, and FW does not pay any amounts pursuant to the instrument during accounting period 1. In addition, under Country W tax law, FW is allowed to deduct interest under the FX-FW instrument as it accrues, whereas under Country X tax law FX does not recognize income under the FX-FW instrument until interest is paid. Further, FW accrues $100x of interest during accounting period 1, and FW will not pay such amount to FX for more than 36 months after the end of the accounting period. The results are the same as in paragraph (c)(8)(ii) of this section. That is, FW's $100x deduction is a hybrid deduction, *see* §§ 1.267A-2(a), 1.267A-3(a), and 1.267A-4(b), and the income attributable to US1's $100x imported mismatch payment is offset by the hybrid deduction for the reasons described in paragraph (c)(8)(ii) of this section. As a result, a deduction for the payment is disallowed under § 1.267A-1(b)(2).

(iv) *Alternative facts – notional interest deduction.* The facts are the same as in paragraph (c)(8)(i) of this section, except that the FX-FW instrument

does not exist and thus FW does not pay any amounts to FX during accounting period 1. However, during accounting period 1, FW is allowed a $100x notional interest deduction with respect to its equity under Country W tax law. Pursuant to § 1.267A-4(b), FW's notional interest deduction is a hybrid deduction. The results are the same as in paragraph (c)(8)(ii) of this section. That is, the income attributable to US1's $100x imported mismatch payment is offset by FW's hybrid deduction for the reasons described in paragraph (c)(8)(ii) of this section. As a result, a deduction for the payment is disallowed under § 1.267A-1(b)(2).

(v) *Alternative facts – foreign hybrid mismatch rules prevent hybrid deduction.* The facts are the same as in paragraph (c)(8)(i) of this section, except that the tax law of Country W contains hybrid mismatch rules and under such rules FW is not allowed a deduction for the $100x that it pays to FX on the FX-FW instrument. The $100x paid by FW therefore does not give rise to a hybrid deduction. *See* § 1.267A-4(b). Accordingly, because the income attributable to US1's payment is not directly or indirectly offset by a hybrid deduction, the payment is not a disqualified imported mismatch amount. Therefore, a deduction for the payment is not disallowed under § 1.267A-2(b)(2).

(9) *Example 9. Imported mismatch rule – indirect offsets and pro rata allocations—*(i) *Facts.* FX holds all the interests of FZ, and FZ holds all the interests of US1 and US2. FX has a Country B branch that, for Country X and Country B tax purposes, gives rise to a taxable presence in Country B and is therefore a taxable branch ("BB"). Under the Country B-Country X income tax treaty, BB is a permanent establishment entitled to deduct expenses properly attributable to BB for purposes of computing its business profits under the treaty. BB is deemed to pay a royalty to FX for the right to use intangibles developed by FX equal to cost plus y%. The deemed royalty is a deductible expense properly attributable to BB under the Country B-Country X income tax treaty. For Country X tax purposes, any transactions between BB and X are disregarded. The deemed royalty amount is equal to $80x during accounting period 1. In addition, an instrument issued by FZ to FX is properly reflected as an asset on the books and records of BB (the FX-FZ instrument). The FX-FZ instrument is treated as indebtedness for Country X, Country Z, and Country B tax purposes. In accounting period 1, FZ pays $80x pursuant to the FX-FZ instrument; the amount is treated as interest for Country X, Country Z, and Country B tax purposes, and is treated as income attributable to BB for Country X and Country B tax purposes (but, for Country X tax purposes, is excluded from FX's income as a consequence of the Country X exemption for income attributable to a branch). Further, in accounting period 1, US1 and US2 pay $60x and $40x, respectively, to FZ pursuant to instruments that are treated as indebtedness for Country Z and U.S. tax purposes; the amounts are treated

as interest for Country Z and U.S. tax purposes and are included in FZ's income for Country Z tax purposes. Lastly, neither the instrument pursuant to which US1 pays the $60x nor the instrument pursuant to which US2 pays the $40x was entered into pursuant to a plan or series of related transactions that includes the transaction or agreement giving rise to BB's deduction for the deemed royalty.

(ii) *Analysis.* US1 and US2 are specified parties and thus deductions for their specified payments are subject to disallowance under section 267A. Neither of the payments is a disqualified hybrid amount. In addition, BB's $80x deduction for the deemed royalty is a hybrid deduction because it is a deduction allowed to BB that results from an amount paid that is treated as a royalty under Country B tax law (regardless of whether a royalty deduction would be allowed under U.S. law), and were Country B tax law to have rules substantially similar to those under §§ 1.267A-1 through 1.267A-3 and 1.267A-5, a deduction for the payment would be disallowed because under such rules the payment would be a deemed branch payment and Country X has an exclusion for income attributable to a branch. *See* §§ 1.267A-2(c) and 1.267A-4(b). Under § 1.267A-4(a), each of US1's and US2's payments is an imported mismatch payment, US1 and US2 are imported mismatch payers, and FZ (the tax resident that includes the imported mismatch payments in income) is an imported mismatch payee. The imported mismatch payments are disqualified imported mismatch amounts to the extent that the income attributable to the payments is directly or indirectly offset by the hybrid deduction incurred by BB (a taxable branch that is related to US1 and US2). *See* § 1.267A-4(a). Under § 1.267A-4(c)(1), the $80x hybrid deduction directly or indirectly offsets the income attributable to the imported mismatch payments to the extent that the payments directly or indirectly fund the hybrid deduction. Paragraphs (c)(9)(ii)(A) and (B) of this section describe the extent to which the imported mismatch payments directly or indirectly fund the hybrid deduction.

(A) Neither US1's nor US2's payment directly funds the hybrid deduction because FZ (the imported mismatch payee) did not incur the hybrid deduction. *See* § 1.267A-4(c)(3)(i). To determine the extent to which the payments indirectly fund the hybrid deduction, the amount of the hybrid deduction that is allocated to FZ must be determined. *See* § 1.267A-4(c)(3)(ii). FZ is allocated the hybrid deduction to the extent that it directly or indirectly makes a funded taxable payment to BB (the taxable branch that incurs the hybrid deduction). *See* § 1.267A-4(c)(3)(iii). The $80x that FZ pays pursuant to the FX-FZ instrument is a funded taxable payment of FZ to BB. *See* § 1.267A-4(c)(3)(v). Therefore, because FZ makes a funded taxable payment to BB that is at least equal to the amount of the hybrid deduction, FZ is allocated the entire amount of the hybrid deduction. *See* § 1.267A-4(c)(3)(iii).

(B) But for US2's imported mismatch payment, the entire $60x of US1's imported mismatch payment would indirectly fund the hybrid deduction because FZ is allocated at least that amount of the hybrid deduction. *See* § 1.267A-4(c)(3)(ii). Similarly, but for US1's imported mismatch payment, the entire $40x of US2's imported mismatch payment would indirectly fund the hybrid deduction because FZ is allocated at least that amount of the hybrid deduction. *See id.* However, because the sum of US1's and US2's imported mismatch payments to FZ ($100x) exceeds the hybrid deduction allocated to FZ ($80x), pro rata adjustments must be made. *See* § 1.267A-4(e). Thus, $48x of US1's imported mismatch payment is considered to indirectly fund the hybrid deduction, calculated as $80x (the amount of the hybrid deduction) multiplied by 60% ($60x, the amount of US1's imported mismatch payment to FZ, divided by $100x, the sum of the imported mismatch payments that US1 and US2 make to FZ). Similarly, $32x of US2's imported mismatch payment is considered to indirectly fund the hybrid deduction, calculated as $80x (the amount of the hybrid deduction) multiplied by 40% ($40x, the amount of US2's imported mismatch payment to FZ, divided by $100x, the sum of the imported mismatch payments that US1 and US2 make to FZ). Accordingly, $48x of US1's imported mismatch payment, and $32x of US2's imported mismatch payment, is a disqualified imported mismatch amount under § 1.267A-4(a) and, as a result, a deduction for such amounts is disallowed under § 1.267A-1(b)(2).

(iii) *Alternative facts – loss made available through foreign group relief regime.* The facts are the same as in paragraph (c)(9)(i) of this section, except that FZ holds all the interests in FZ2, a body corporate that is a tax resident of Country Z, FZ2 (rather than FZ) holds all the interests of US1 and US2, and US1 and US2 make their respective $60x and $40x payments to FZ2 (rather than to FZ). Further, in accounting period 1, a $10x loss of FZ is made available to offset income of FZ2 through a Country Z foreign group relief regime. Pursuant to § 1.267A-4(c)(3)(vi), FZ and FZ2 are treated as a single tax resident for purposes of § 1.267A-4(c) because a loss that is not incurred by FZ2 (FZ's $10x loss) is made available to offset income of FZ2 under the Country Z group relief regime. Accordingly, the results are the same as in paragraph (c)(9)(ii) of this section. That is, by treating FZ and FZ2 as a single tax resident for purposes of § 1.267A-4(c), BB's hybrid deduction offsets the income attributable to US1's and US2's imported mismatch payments to the same extent as described in paragraph (c)(9)(ii) of this section.

(10) *Example 10. Imported mismatch rule – ordering rules and rule deeming certain payments to be imported mismatch payments*—(i) *Facts.* FX holds all the interests of FW, and FW holds all the interests of US1, US2, and FZ. FZ holds all the interests of US3. FX advances money to FW pursuant to an instrument that is treated as equity

for Country X tax purposes and indebtedness for Country W tax purposes (the FX-FW instrument). In a transaction that is pursuant to the same plan pursuant to which the FX-FW instrument is entered into, FW advances money to US1 pursuant to an instrument that is treated as indebtedness for Country W and U.S. tax purposes (the FW-US1 instrument). In accounting period 1, FW pays $125x to FX pursuant to the FX-FW instrument; the amount is treated as an excludible dividend for Country X tax purposes (by reason of the Country X participation exemption regime) and as deductible interest for Country W tax purposes. Also in accounting period 1, US1 pays $50x to FW pursuant to the FW-US1 instrument; US2 pays $50x to FW pursuant to an instrument treated as indebtedness for Country W and U.S. tax purposes (the FW-US2 instrument); US3 pays $50x to FZ pursuant to an instrument treated as indebtedness for Country Z and U.S. tax purposes (the FZ-US3 instrument); and FZ pays $50x to FW pursuant to an instrument treated as indebtedness for Country W and Country Z tax purposes (FW-FZ instrument). The amounts paid by US1, US2, US3, and FZ are treated as interest for purposes of the relevant tax laws and are included in the respective specified recipient's income. Lastly, neither the FW-US2 instrument, the FW-FZ instrument, nor the FZ-US3 instrument was entered into pursuant to a plan or series of related transactions that includes the transaction pursuant to which the FX-FW instrument was entered into.

(ii) *Analysis.* US1, US2, and US3 are specified parties (but FZ is not a specified party, see § 1.267A-5(a)(17)) and thus deductions for US1's, US2's, and US3's specified payments are subject to disallowance under section 267A. None of the specified payments is a disqualified hybrid amount. Under § 1.267A-4(a), each of the payments is thus an imported mismatch payment, US1, US2, and US3 are imported mismatch payers, and FW and FZ (the tax residents that include the imported mismatch payments in income) are imported mismatch payees. The imported mismatch payments are disqualified imported mismatch amounts to the extent that the income attributable to the payments is directly or indirectly offset by FW's $125x hybrid deduction. See § 1.267A-4(a) and (b). Under § 1.267A-4(c)(1), the $125x hybrid deduction directly or indirectly offsets the income attributable to the imported mismatch payments to the extent that the payments directly or indirectly fund the hybrid deduction. Paragraphs (c)(10)(ii)(A) through (C) of this section describe the extent to which the imported mismatch payments directly or indirectly fund the hybrid deduction and are therefore disqualified hybrid amounts for which a deduction is disallowed under § 1.267A-1(b)(2).

(A) First, the $125x hybrid deduction offsets the income attributable to US1's imported mismatch payment, a factually-related imported mismatch payment that directly funds the hybrid deduction. See § 1.267A-4(c)(2)(i). The entire $50x of US1's payment directly funds the hybrid deduction because FW (the imported mismatch payee) incurs at least that amount of the hybrid deduction. See § 1.267A-4(c)(3)(i). Accordingly, the entire $50x of the payment is a disqualified imported mismatch amount under § 1.267A-4(a).

(B) Second, the remaining $75x hybrid deduction offsets the income attributable to US2's imported mismatch payment, a factually-unrelated imported mismatch payment that directly funds the remaining hybrid deduction. § 1.267A-4(c)(2)(ii). The entire $50x of US2's payment directly funds the remaining hybrid deduction because FW (the imported mismatch payee) incurs at least that amount of the remaining hybrid deduction. See § 1.267A-4(c)(3)(i). Accordingly, the entire $50x of the payment is a disqualified imported mismatch amount under § 1.267A-4(a).

(C) Third, the $25x remaining hybrid deduction offsets the income attributable to US3's imported mismatch payment, a factually-unrelated imported mismatch payment that indirectly funds the remaining hybrid deduction. See § 1.267A-4(c)(2)(iii). The imported mismatch payment indirectly funds the remaining hybrid deduction to the extent that FZ (the imported mismatch payee) is allocated the remaining hybrid deduction. § 1.267A-4(c)(3)(ii). FZ is allocated the remaining hybrid deduction to the extent that it directly or indirectly makes a funded taxable payment to FW (the tax resident that incurs the hybrid deduction). § 1.267A-4(c)(3)(iii). The $50x that FZ pays to FW pursuant to the FW-FZ instrument is a funded taxable payment of FZ to FW. § 1.267A-4(c)(3)(v). Therefore, because FZ makes a funded taxable payment to FW that is at least equal to the amount of the remaining hybrid deduction, FZ is allocated the remaining hybrid deduction. § 1.267A-4(c)(3)(iii). Accordingly, $25x of US3's payment indirectly funds the $25x remaining hybrid deduction and, consequently, $25x of US3's payment is a disqualified imported mismatch amount under § 1.267A-4(a).

(iii) *Alternative facts – amount deemed to be an imported mismatch payment.* The facts are the same as in paragraph (c)(10)(i) of this section, except that US1 is not a domestic corporation but instead is a body corporate that is only a tax resident of Country E (hereinafter, "FE") (thus, for purposes of this paragraph (c)(10)(iii), the FW-US1 instrument is instead issued by FE and is the "FW-FE instrument"). In addition, the tax law of Country E contains hybrid mismatch rules and, under a provision of such rules substantially similar to § 1.267A-4, FE is denied a deduction for the $50x it pays to FW under the FW-FE instrument. Pursuant to § 1.267A-4(f), the $50x that FE pays to FW pursuant to the FW-FE instrument is deemed to be an imported mismatch payment for purposes of determining the extent to which the income attributable to US2's and US3's imported mismatch payments is offset by FW's hybrid deduction. The results are the same as in paragraphs (c)(10)(ii)(B) and (C) of this section. That is, by treating the $50x that FE pays to FW as an imported mismatch payment, FW's hybrid deduction offsets the income attributable to US2's and US3's imported mismatch payments to the same extent as described in paragraphs (c)(10)(ii)(B) and (C) of this section.

(iv) *Alternative facts – amount deemed to be an imported mismatch payment not treated as a funded taxable payment.* The facts are the same as in paragraph (c)(10)(i) of this section, except that FZ holds its interests of US3 indirectly through FE, a body corporate that is only a tax resident of Country E (hereinafter, "FE"), and US3 makes its $50x payment to FE (rather than to FZ); US3's $50x payment is treated as interest for Country E tax purposes and FE includes the payment in income. In addition, during accounting period 1, FE pays $50x of interest to FZ pursuant to an instrument and such amount is included in FZ's income. Further, the tax law of Country E contains hybrid mismatch rules and, under a provision of such rules substantially similar to § 1.267A-4, FE is denied a deduction for $25x of the $50x it pays to FZ, because under such provision $25x of the income attributable to FE's payment is considered offset against $25x of FW's hybrid deduction. With respect to US1 and US2, the results are the same as described in paragraphs (c)(10)(ii)(A) and (B) of this section. However, no portion of US3's payment is a disqualified imported mismatch amount. This is because the $50x that FE pays to FZ is not considered to be a funded taxable payment, because under a provision of Country E's hybrid mismatch rules that is substantially similar to § 1.267A-4, FE is denied a deduction for a portion of the $50x. See § 1.267A-4(c)(3)(v) and (f). Therefore, there is no chain of funded taxable payments connecting US3 (the imported mismatch payer) and FW (the tax resident that incurs the hybrid deduction); as a result, US3's payment does not indirectly fund the hybrid deduction. See § 1.267A-4(c)(3)(ii) through (iv). [Reg. § 1.267A-6.]

[Proposed 12-28-2018.]

#### [Prop. Reg. § 1.267A-7]

**§ 1.267A-7. Applicability dates.**—(a) *General rule.*—Except as provided in paragraph (b) of this section, §§ 1.267A-1 through 1.267A-6 apply to taxable years beginning after December 31, 2017.

(b) *Special rules.*—Sections 1.267A-2(b), (c), (e), 1.267A-4, and 1.267A-5(b)(5) apply to taxable years beginning on or after December 20, 2018. In addition, § 1.267A-5(a)(20) (defining structured arrangement), as well as the portions of §§ 1.267A-1 through 1.267A-3 that relate to structured arrangements and that are not otherwise described in this paragraph (b), apply to taxable years beginning on or after December 20, 2018. [Reg. § 1.267A-7.]

[Proposed 12-28-2018.]

#### [Prop. Reg. § 1.381(c)(20)-1]

**§ 1.381(c)(20)-1. Carryforward of disallowed business interest.**—(a) *Carryover requirement.*—Section 381(c)(20) provides that the acquiring corporation in a transaction described in section 381(a) will succeed to and take into account the carryover of disallowed business interest described in section 163(j)(2) to taxable years ending after the date of distribution or transfer.

(b) *Carryover of disallowed business interest described in section 163(j)(2).*—For purposes of section 381(c)(20) and this section, the term *carryover of disallowed business interest described in section 163(j)(2)* means the disallowed business interest expense carryforward (within the meaning of § 1.163(j)-1(b)(9)), including any disallowed disqualified interest (within the meaning of § 1.163(j)-1(b)(10)), and including the distributor or transferor corporation's disallowed business interest expense from the taxable year that ends on the date of distribution or transfer. For the application of section 382 to disallowed business interest expense described in section 163(j)(2), see the regulations under section 382, including but not limited to § 1.382-2.

(c) *Limitation on use of disallowed business interest expense carryforwards in the acquiring corporation's first taxable year ending after the date of distribution or transfer.*—(1) *In general.*—In determining the extent to which the acquiring corporation may use disallowed business interest expense carryforwards in its first taxable year ending after the date of distribution or transfer, the principles of §§ 1.381(c)(1)-1 and 1.381(c)(1)-2 apply with appropriate adjustments, including but not limited to the adjustments described in paragraphs (c)(2) and (3) of this section.

(2) *One date of distribution or transfer within the acquiring corporation's taxable year.*—If the acquiring corporation succeeds to the disallowed business interest expense carryforwards of one or more distributor or transferor corporations on a single date of distribution or transfer within one taxable year of the acquiring corporation, then, for the acquiring corporation's first taxable year ending after the date of distribution or transfer, that part of the acquiring corporation's business interest expense deduction (if any) that is attributable to the disallowed business interest expense carryforwards of the distributor or transferor corporation is limited under this paragraph (c) to an amount equal to the post-acquisition portion of the acquiring corporation's section 163(j) limitation, as defined in paragraph (c)(4) of this section.

(3) *Two or more dates of distribution or transfer in the taxable year.*—If the acquiring corporation succeeds to the disallowed business interest expense carryforwards of two or more distributor or transferor corporations on two or more dates of distribution or transfer within one taxable

year of the acquiring corporation, the limitation to be applied under this paragraph (c) is determined by applying the principles of § 1.381(c)(1)-2(b) to the post-acquisition portion of the acquiring corporation's section 163(j) limitation, as defined in paragraph (c)(4) of this section.

(4) *Definition.*—For purposes of this paragraph (c), the term *post-acquisition portion of the acquiring corporation's section 163(j) limitation* means the amount that bears the same ratio to the acquiring corporation's section 163(j) limitation (within the meaning of § 1.163(j)-1(b)(31)) (or, if the acquiring corporation is a member of a consolidated group, the consolidated group's section 163(j) limitation) for the first taxable year ending after the date of distribution or transfer (taking into account items to which the acquiring corporation succeeds under section 381, other than disallowed business interest expense carryforwards) as the number of days in that year after the date of distribution or transfer bears to the total number of days in that year.

(5) *Examples.*—For purposes of this paragraph (c)(5), unless otherwise stated, X, Y, and Z are taxable domestic C corporations that were incorporated on January 1, 2018 and that file their tax returns on a calendar-year basis; none of X, Y, or Z is a member of a consolidated group; the small business exemption in § 1.163(j)-2(d) does not apply; interest expense is deductible except to the extent of the potential application of section 163(j); and the facts set forth the only corporate activity. The principles of this paragraph (c) are illustrated by the following examples.

(i) *Example 1: Transfer before last day of acquiring corporation's taxable year*—(A) *Facts.* On October 31, 2019, X transferred all of its assets to Y in a statutory merger to which section 361 applies. For the 2018 taxable year, X had $400x of disallowed business interest expense, and Y had $0 of disallowed business interest expense. For the taxable year ending October 31, 2019, X had an additional $350x of disallowed business interest expense (X did not deduct any of its 2018 carryforwards in its 2019 taxable year). For the taxable year ending December 31, 2019, Y had business interest expense of $100x, business interest income of $200x, and adjusted taxable income (ATI) of $1,000x. Y's section 163(j) limitation for the 2019 taxable year was $500x ($200x + (30 percent x $1,000x) = $500x).

(B) *Analysis.* Pursuant to § 1.163(j)-5(b)(2), Y deducts its $100x of current-year business interest expense (as defined in § 1.163(j)-5(a)(2)(i)) before any disallowed business interest expense carryforwards (including X's carryforwards) from a prior taxable year are deducted. The aggregate disallowed business interest expense of X carried forward under section 381(c)(20) to Y's taxable year ending December 31, 2019, is $750x. However, pursuant to paragraph (c)(2) of this section, for Y's first taxable year ending after the date of distribution or transfer, the maximum

amount of X's disallowed business interest expense carryforwards that Y can deduct is equal to the post-acquisition portion of Y's section 163(j) limitation. Pursuant to paragraph (c)(4) of this section, the post-acquisition portion of Y's section 163(j) limitation means Y's section 163(j) limitation times the ratio of the number of days in the taxable year after the date of distribution or transfer to the total number of days in that year. Therefore, only $84x of the aggregate amount ($500x x (61/365) = $84x) may be deducted by Y in that year, and the remaining $666x ($750x - $84x = $666x) is carried forward to the succeeding taxable year.

(C) *Transfer on last day of acquiring corporation's taxable year.* The facts are the same as in *Example 1* in paragraph (c)(5)(i)(A) of this section, except that X's transfer of its assets to Y occurred on December 31, 2019. For the taxable year ending December 31, 2019, X had an additional $350x of disallowed business interest expense (X did not deduct any of its 2018 carryforwards in its 2019 taxable year). For the taxable year ending December 31, 2020, Y had business interest expense of $100x, business interest income of $200x, and ATI of $1,000x. Y's section 163(j) limitation for the 2020 taxable year was $500x ($200x + (30 percent x $1,000x) = $500x). The aggregate disallowed business interest expense of X carried under section 381(c)(20) to Y's taxable year ending December 31, 2020, is $750x. Paragraph (c)(2) of this section does not limit the amount of X's disallowed business interest expense carryforwards that may be deducted by Y in the 2020 taxable year. Since the amount of Y's section 163(j) limit for the 2020 taxable year was $500x, Y may deduct the full amount ($100x) of its own business interest expense for the 2020 taxable year, along with $400x of X's disallowed business interest expense carryforwards.

(ii) *Example 2: Multiple transferors on same date*—(A) *Facts.* On October 31, 2019, X and Y transferred all of their assets to Z in statutory mergers to which section 361 applies. For the 2018 taxable year, X had $300x of disallowed business interest expense, Y had $200x, and Z had $0. For the taxable year ending October 31, 2019, each of X and Y had an additional $125x of disallowed business interest expense (neither X nor Y deducted any of its 2018 carryforwards in 2019). For the taxable year ending December 31, 2019, Z had business interest expense of $100x, business interest income of $200x, and ATI of $1,000x. Z's section 163(j) limitation for the 2019 taxable year was $500x ($200x + (30 percent x $1,000x) = $500x).

(B) *Analysis.* The aggregate disallowed business interest expense of X and Y carried under section 381(c)(20) to Z's taxable year ending December 31, 2019, is $750x. However, pursuant to paragraph (c)(2) of this section, only $84x of the aggregate amount ($500x x (61/365) = $84x) may be deducted by Z in that year. Moreover, under paragraph (b)(2) of this section, this amount only may be deducted by Z in that year after Z has deducted its $100 of current-year business interest expense (as defined in § 1.163(j)-5(a)(2)(i)).

(d) *Applicability date.*—This section applies to taxable years ending after the date the Treasury decision adopting these regulations as final regulations is published in the **Federal Register**. However, taxpayers and their related parties, within the meaning of sections 267(b) and 707(b)(1), may apply the rules of this section to a taxable year beginning after December 31, 2017, so long as the taxpayers and their related parties consistently apply the rules of this section, the section 163(j) regulations (within the meaning of § 1.163(j)-1(b)(32)), and if applicable, § § 1.263A-9, 1.381(c)(20)-1, 1.382-6, 1.383-1, 1.469-9, 1.882-5, 1.1502-13, 1.1502-21, 1.1502-36, 1.1502-79, 1.1502-91 through 1.1502-99 (to the extent they effectuate the rules of § § 1.382-6 and 1.383-1), and 1.1504-4 to those taxable years. [Reg. § 1.381(c)(20)-1.]

[Proposed 12-28-2018.]

### [Prop. Reg. § 1.382-2]

**§ 1.382-2. General rules for ownership change.**—(a) * * *

(1) * * *

(i) * * *

(A) Is entitled to use a net operating loss carryforward, a capital loss carryover, a carryover of excess foreign taxes under section 904(c), a carryforward of a general business credit under section 39, a carryover of a minimum tax credit under section 53, or a section 382 disallowed business interest carryforward described in paragraph (a)(7) of this section;

* * *

(ii) *Distributor or transferor loss corporation in a transaction under section 381.*—Notwithstanding that a loss corporation ceases to exist under state law, if its disallowed business interest expense carryforwards, net operating loss carryforwards, excess foreign taxes, or other items described in section 381(c) are succeeded to and taken into account by an acquiring corporation in a transaction described in section 381(a), such loss corporation shall be treated as continuing in existence until—

(A) Any pre-change losses (excluding pre-change credits described in § 1.383-1(c)(3)), determined as if the date of such transaction were the change date, are fully utilized or expire under section 163(j), 172, or 1212;

* * *

(2) * * *

(vi) Any section 382 disallowed business interest carryforward.

* * *

(7) *Section 382 disallowed business interest carryforward.*—The term *section 382 disallowed business interest carryforward* includes the following items:

(i) The loss corporation's disallowed business interest expense carryforwards, as defined in § 1.163(j)-1(b)(9), including disallowed disqualified interest, within the meaning of § 1.163(j)-1(b)(10), as of the ownership change.

(ii) The carryforward of the loss corporation's disallowed business interest expense (within the meaning of § 1.163(j)-1(b)(8)) paid or accrued (without regard to section 163(j)) in the pre-change period (within the meaning of § 1.382-6(g)(2)) in the year of the testing date, determined by allocating an equal portion of the disallowed business interest expense paid or accrued (without regard to section 163(j)) in the year of the testing date to each day in that year, regardless of whether the loss corporation has made a closing-of-the-books election under § 1.382-6(b)(2).

(8) *Testing period.*—Notwithstanding the temporal limitations provided in § 1.382-2T(d)(3)(i), the testing period for a loss corporation can begin as early as the first day of the first taxable year from which there is a section 382 disallowed business interest carryforward to the first taxable year ending after the testing date.

(b) * * *

(3) *Rules provided in paragraphs (a)(1)(i)(A), (a)(1)(ii), (iv), and (v), (a)(2)(iv) through (vi), (a)(3)(i), and (a)(4) through (8) of this section.*—The rules provided in paragraphs (a)(1)(i)(A), (a)(1)(ii), (iv), and (v), (a)(2)(iv) through (vi), (a)(3)(i), and (a)(4) through (8) of this section apply to testing dates occurring on or after the date the Treasury decision adopting these regulations as final regulations is published in the **Federal Register**. For loss corporations that have testing dates occurring before the date the Treasury decision adopting these regulations as final regulations is published in the **Federal Register**, see § 1.382-2 as contained in 26 CFR part 1, revised April 1, 2018. However, taxpayers and their related parties, within the meaning of sections 267(b) and 707(b)(1), may apply the rules of this section to testing dates occurring during a taxable year beginning after December 31, 2017, so long as the taxpayers and their related parties consistently apply the rules of this section, the section 163(j) regulations (within the meaning of § 1.163(j)-1(b)(32)), § § 1.382-5, 1.382-6, and 1.383-1, and if applicable, § § 1.263A-9, 1.381(c)(20)-1, 1.469-9, 1.882-5, 1.1502-13, 1.1502-21, 1.1502-36, 1.1502-79, 1.1502-91 through 1.1502-99 (to the extent they effectuate the rules of § § 1.382-2, 1.382-5, 1.382-6, and 1.383-1), and 1.1504-4 to taxable years beginning after December 31, 2017.

[Proposed 12-28-2018.]

### [Prop. Reg. § 1.382-5]

**§ 1.382-5. Section 382 limitation.**

* * *

(d) * * *

(1) * * * If a loss corporation has two (or more) ownership changes, any losses or section 382 disallowed business interest carryforwards

(within the meaning of § 1.382-2(a)(7)) attributable to the period preceding the earlier ownership change are treated as pre-change losses with respect to both ownership changes. Thus, the later ownership change may result in a lesser (but never in a greater) section 382 limitation with respect to such pre-change losses. * * *

* * *

(f) * * * Paragraph (d)(1) of this section applies with respect to an ownership change occurring on or after the date the Treasury decision adopting these regulations as final regulations is published in the **Federal Register**. For loss corporations that have undergone an ownership change before or after the date the Treasury decision adopting these regulations as final regulations is published in the **Federal Register**, see § 1.382-5 as contained in 26 CFR part 1, revised April 1, 2018. However, taxpayers and their related parties, within the meaning of sections 267(b) and 707(b)(1), may apply the rules of this section to testing dates occurring during a taxable year beginning after December 31, 2017, so long as the taxpayers and their related parties consistently apply the rules of this section, the section 163(j) regulations (within the meaning of § 1.163(j)-1(b)(32)), § § 1.382-2, 1.382-6, and 1.383-1, and if applicable, § § 1.263A-9, 1.381(c)(20)-1, 1.469-9, 1.882-5, 1.1502-13, 1.1502-21, 1.1502-36, 1.1502-79, 1.1502-91 through 1.1502-99 (to the extent they effectuate the rules of § § 1.382-2, 1.382-5, 1.382-6, and 1.383-1), and 1.1504-4 to taxable years beginning after December 31, 2017.

[Proposed 12-28-2018.]

### [Prop. Reg. § 1.382-6]

**§ 1.382-6.  Allocation of income and loss to periods before and after the change date for purposes of section 382.**

* * *

(b) * * *

(4) *Allocation of business interest expense.*— (i) *In general.*—Regardless of whether a loss corporation has made a closing-of-the-books election pursuant to paragraph (b) of this section, for purposes of calculating the taxable income of a loss corporation attributable to the pre-change period, the amount of the loss corporation's deduction for current-year business interest expense, within the meaning of § 1.163(j)-5(a)(2)(i), is calculated based on a single tax year and is allocated between the pre-change period and the post-change period by ratably allocating an equal portion to each day in the year.

(ii) *Example.*—(A) *Facts.* X is a calendar-year C corporation that is not a member of a consolidated group. On May 26, 2019, X is acquired by Z (an unrelated third-party) in a transaction that qualifies as an ownership change under section 382(g). For calendar year 2019, X has paid or accrued $100x of current-year business interest expense (within the meaning of § 1.163(j)-5(a)(2)(i)) and has an $81x section 163(j)

limitation (within the meaning of § 1.163(j)-1(b)(31)).

(B) *Analysis.* Pursuant to paragraph (b)(4)(i) of this section, regardless of whether X has made a closing-of-the-books election pursuant to paragraph (b) of this section, X's business interest expense deduction is ratably allocated between the pre-change and post-change periods. For calendar year 2019, X may deduct $81x of business interest expense (see § 1.163(j)-2(b)), of which $32.4x ($81x x (146 days/365 days) = $32.4x) is allocable to the pre-change period. The remaining $19x of interest that was paid or accrued in calendar year 2019 is disallowed business interest expense, of which $7.6x ($19x x (146 days/365 days) = $7.6x) is allocable to the pre-change period. The $7.6x of disallowed business interest expense is treated as a section 382 disallowed business interest carryforward (see § 1.382-2(a)(7)), and thus is a pre-change loss within the meaning of § 1.382-2(a)(2).

* * *

(h) *Applicability date.*—(1) *In general.*—This section applies to ownership changes occurring on or after June 22, 1994.

(2) *Paragraphs (b)(1) and (4) of this section.*— Paragraphs (b)(1) and (4) of this section apply with respect to an ownership change occurring during a taxable year ending after the date the Treasury decision adopting these regulations as final regulations is published in the **Federal Register**. For ownership changes occurring during a taxable year ending before the date the Treasury decision adopting these regulations is published in the **Federal Register**, see § 1.382-6 as contained in 26 CFR part 1, revised April 1, 2018. However, taxpayers and their related parties, within the meaning of sections 267(b) and 707(b)(1), may apply the rules of this section to testing dates occurring during a taxable year beginning after December 31, 2017, so long as the taxpayers and their related parties consistently apply the rules of this section, and the section 163(j) regulations (within the meaning of § 1.163(j)-1(b)(32)) and § 1.383-1, and if applicable, § § 1.263A-9, 1.381(c)(20)-1, 1.469-9, 1.882-5, 1.1502-13, 1.1502-21, 1.1502-36, 1.1502-79, 1.1502-91 through 1.1502-99 (to the extent they effectuate the rules of § § 1.382-6 and 1.383-1), and 1.1504-4 to taxable years beginning after December 31, 2017.

[Proposed 12-28-2018.]

### [Prop. Reg. § 1.382-7]

**§ 1.382-7.  Built in gains and losses.**—(a) * * * Examples to which this paragraph (a) will apply include, but are not limited to, income received prior to the change date that is deferred under section 455 or Rev. Proc. 2004-34 (2004-1 CB 991 (June 1, 2004)) (or any successor revenue procedure) (see § 601.601(d)(2)(ii)(*b*)).

* * *

[Proposed 10-15-2018.]

**[Prop. Reg. §1.383-0]**

**1.383-0. Effective date.**—(a) The regulations under section 383 (other than the regulations described in paragraph (b) of this section) reflect the amendments made to sections 382 and 383 by the Tax Reform Act of 1986 and the amendments made to section 382 by the Tax Cuts and Jobs Act of 2017. See §1.383-1(j) for effective date rules.

\* \* \*

[Proposed 12-28-2018.]

**[Prop. Reg. §1.383-1]**

**1.383-1. Special limitations on certain capital losses and excess credits.**—(a) \* \* \*

\* \* \*

(d) \* \* \*
  (1) \* \* \*
    (i) In general.
    (ii) Ordering rule for losses or credits from same taxable year.

\* \* \*

(e) \* \* \*
  (3) [Reserved]

\* \* \*

(j) Applicability date.
  (1) In general.
  (2) Interaction with section 163(j).

\* \* \*

(c) \* \* \*
  (6) \* \* \*

  (ii) *Example.*—L, a new loss corporation, is a calendar-year taxpayer. L has an ownership change on December 31, 2019. For 2020, L has taxable income (prior to the use of any pre-change losses) of $100,000. In addition, L has a section 382 limitation of $25,000, a pre-change net operating loss carryover of $12,000, a pre-change general business credit carryforward under section 39 of $50,000, and no items described in §1.383-1(d)(2)(i) through (iv). L's section 383 credit limitation for 2020 is the excess of its regular tax liability computed after allowing a $12,000 net operating loss deduction (taxable income of $88,000; regular tax liability of $18,480), over its regular tax liability computed after allowing an additional deduction in the amount of L's section 382 limitation remaining after the application of paragraphs (d)(2)(i) through (v) of this section, or $13,000 (taxable income of $75,000; regular tax liability of $15,750). L's section 383 credit limitation is therefore $2,730 ($18,480 minus $15,750).

(d) \* \* \*

  (1) *In general.*—(i) *In general.*—The amount of taxable income of a new loss corporation for any post-change year that may be offset by pre-change losses shall not exceed the amount of the section 382 limitation for the post-change year. The amount of the regular tax liability of a new loss corporation for any post-change year that may be offset by pre-change credits shall not

exceed the amount of the section 383 credit limitation for the post-change year.

  (ii) *Ordering rule for losses or credits from same taxable year.*—A loss corporation's taxable income is offset first by losses subject to a section 382 limitation, to the extent the section 382 limitation for that taxable year has not yet been absorbed, before being offset by losses of the same type from the same taxable year that are not subject to a section 382 limitation. For example, assume that Corporation X has an ownership change in Year 1 and carries over disallowed business interest expense within the meaning of §1.163(j)-1(b)(8), some of which constitutes a section 382 disallowed business interest carryforward, from Year 1 to Year 2. To the extent of its section 163(j) limitation, within the meaning of §1.163(j)-1(b)(31), and its remaining section 382 limitation, Corporation X offsets its Year 2 income with the section 382 disallowed business interest carryforward before using any of the disallowed business interest expense that is not a section 382 disallowed business interest carryforward. Similar principles apply to the use of tax credits.

  (2) \* \* \*

    (iii) Pre-change losses that are described in §1.382-2(a)(2)(iii), other than losses that are pre-change capital losses, that are recognized and are subject to the section 382 limitation in such post-change year;

    (iv)(A) With respect to an ownership change date occurring prior to the date the Treasury decision adopting these regulations as final regulations is published in the **Federal Register**, but during the taxable year which includes the date the Treasury decision adopting these regulations as final regulations is published in the **Federal Register**, the pre-change loss described in section 382(d)(3);

    (B) With respect to an ownership change date occurring on or after the date the Treasury decision adopting these regulations as final regulations is published in the **Federal Register**, section 382 disallowed business interest carryforwards (within the meaning of §1.382-2(a)(7));

    (v) Pre-change losses not described in paragraphs (d)(2)(i) through (iv) of this section;

\* \* \*

  (3) \* \* \*

  (ii) *Example.*—L, a calendar-year taxpayer, has an ownership change on December 31, 2019. For 2020, L has taxable income of $300,000 and a regular tax liability of $63,000. L has no pre-change losses, but it has a business credit carryforward from 2018 of $25,000. L has a section 382 limitation for 2020 of $50,000. L's section 383 credit limitation is $10,500, an amount equal to the excess of L's regular tax liability ($63,000) over its regular tax liability calculated by allowing an additional deduction of $50,000 ($52,500). Pursuant to the limitation contained in section 38(c), however, L is entitled to use only $9,500 (($63,000 - $25,000) x 25 percent) of its business credit carryforward in 2020. The unabsorbed portion of L's section 382 limitation (computed pursuant to paragraph (e) of this section) is carried forward under section 382(b)(2). The unused portion of L's business credit carryforward, $1,000, is carried forward to the extent provided in section 39.

* * *

(f) * * *

(2) *Example 2*—(i) *Facts*. L, a calendar-year taxpayer, has an ownership change on December 31, 2019. For 2020, L has $750,000 of ordinary taxable income (before the application of carryovers) and a section 382 limitation of $1,500,000. L's only carryovers are from pre-2019 taxable years and consist of a $500,000 net operating loss (NOL) carryover, and a $200,000 foreign tax credit carryover (all of which may be used under the section 904 limitation). The NOL carryover is a pre-change loss, and the foreign tax credit carryover is a pre-change credit. L has no other pre-change losses or credits that can be used in 2020.

(ii) *Analysis*. The following computation illustrates the application of this section for 2020:

| | |
|---|---:|
| 1. Taxable income before carryovers | $750,000 |
| 2. Pre-change NOL carryover | $500,000 |
| 3. Section 382 limitation | $1,500,000 |
| 4. Amount of pre-change NOL carryover that can be used (least of line 1, 2, or 3) | $500,000 |
| 5. Taxable income (line 1 minus line 4) | $250,000 |
| 6. Section 382 limitation remaining (line 3 minus line 4) | $1,000,000 |
| 7. Pre-change credit carryover | $200,000 |
| 8. Regular tax liability (line 5 x section 11 rates) | $52,500 |
| 9. Modified tax liability (line 5 minus line 6 (but not less than zero) x section 11 rates) | $0 |
| 10. Section 383 credit limitation (line 8 minus line 9) | $52,500 |
| 11. Amount of pre-change credits that can be used in 2020 (lesser of line 7 or line 10) | $52,500 |
| 12. Amount of pre-change credits to be carried over to 2021 under section 904(c) (line 7 minus line 11) | $147,500 |
| 13. Section 383 credit reduction amount: $52,500/0.21 | $250,000 |
| 14. Section 382 limitation to be carried to 2021 under section 382(b)(2) (line 6 minus line 13) | $750,000 |

(3) *Example 3*—(i) *Facts*. L, a calendar-year taxpayer, has an ownership change on December 31, 2019. L has $80,000 of ordinary taxable income (before the application of carryovers) and a section 382 limitation of $25,000 for 2020, a post-change year. L's only carryover is from a pre-2019 taxable year and is a general business credit carryforward under section 39 in the amount of $10,000 (no portion of which is attributable to the investment tax credit under section 46). The general business credit carryforward is a pre-change credit. L has no other credits which can be used in 2020.

(ii) *Analysis*. The following computation illustrates the application of this section:

| | |
|---|---:|
| 1. Taxable income before carryovers | $80,000 |
| 2. Section 382 limitation | $25,000 |
| 3. Pre-change credit carryover | $10,000 |
| 4. Regular tax liability (line 1 x section 11 rates) | $16,800 |
| 5. Modified tax liability ((line 1 minus line 2) x section 11 rates) | $11,550 |
| 6. Section 383 credit limitation (line 4 minus line 5) | $5,250 |
| 7. Amount of pre-change credits that can be used (lesser of line 3 or line 6) | $5,250 |
| 8. Amount of pre-change credits to be carried over to 2021 under sections 39 and 382(l)(2) (line 3 minus line 7) | $4,750 |
| 9. Regular tax payable (line 4 minus line 7) | $11,550 |
| 10. Section 383 credit reduction amount: $5,250/0.21 | $25,000 |
| 11. Section 382 limitation to be carried to 2021 under section 382(b)(2) (line 2 minus line 10) | $0 |

* * *

(j) Applicability date.—(1) *In general.*—* * *

(2) *Interaction with section 163(j).*— Paragraphs (c)(6)(i)(B) and (c)(6)(ii), (d)(1),

(d)(2)(iii) through (viii), (d)(3)(ii), (e)(1) through (3), (f), and (g) of this section apply with respect to ownership changes occurring during a taxable year ending after the Treasury decision adopting these regulations as final regulations is published in the **Federal Register**. For loss corporations that have undergone an ownership change during a taxable year ending before the date the Treasury decision adopting these regulations as final regulations is published in the **Federal Register**, see § 1.383-1 as contained in 26 CFR part 1, revised April 1, 2018. However, taxpayers and their related parties, within the meaning of sections 267(b) and 707(b)(1), may apply the rules of this section to an ownership change occurring during a taxable year beginning after December 31, 2017, so long as the taxpayers and their related parties consistently apply either the rules of this section, except paragraph (d)(2)(iv)(B) of this section, the section 163(j) regulations, within the meaning of § 1.163(j)-1(b)(32), and § 1.382-6, and if applicable, § § 1.263A-9, 1.381(c)(20)-1, 1.469-9, 1.882-5, 1.1502-13, 1.1502-21, 1.1502-36, 1.1502-79, 1.1502-91 through 1.1502-99 (to the extent they effectuate the rules of § § 1.382-6 and 1.383-1), and 1.1504-4; or the rules of this section (except paragraph (d)(2)(iv)(A) of this section), the section 163(j) regulations, within the meaning of § 1.163(j)-1(b)(32), and § § 1.382-2, 1.382-5, 1.382-6, and 1.383-1, and if applicable, § § 1.263A-9, 1.381(c)(20)-1, 1.469-9, 1.882-5, 1.1502-13, 1.1502-21, 1.1502-36, 1.1502-79, 1.1502-91 through 1.1502-99 (to the extent they effectuate the rules of § § 1.382-2, 1.382-5, 1.382-6, and 1.383-1), and 1.1504-4, to those ownership changes.

[Proposed 12-28-2018.]

### [Prop. Reg. § 1.383-1]

**§ 1.383-1. Special limitations on certain capital losses and excess credits.**

* * *

(d) * * *

(3) * * *

(i) * * * The application of section 59A is not a limitation contained in subtitle A for purposes of this paragraph (d)(3)(i). Therefore, the treatment of pre-change losses and pre-change credits in the computation of the base erosion minimum tax amount will not affect whether such losses or credits result in absorption of the section 382 limitation and the section 383 credit limitation.

* * *

[Proposed 12-21-2018.]

### [Prop. Reg. § 1.446-3]

**§ 1.446-3. Notional principal contracts.**

* * *

(g) * * *

(4) *Swaps with significant nonperiodic payments.*—For swaps with significant nonperiodic payments, see § 1.163(j)-1(b)(20)(ii).

* * *

(j) * * *

(2) The rules provided in paragraph (g)(4) of this section apply to notional principal contracts entered into on or after the date of publication of a Treasury decision adopting these rules as final regulations in the **Federal Register**. Taxpayers may apply the rules provided in paragraph (g)(4) of this section to notional principal contracts entered into before the date of publication of a Treasury decision adopting these rules as final regulations in the **Federal Register**.

[Proposed 12-28-2018.]

### [Prop. Reg. § 1.469-9]

**§ 1.469-9. Rules for certain rental real estate activities.**

* * *

(b) * * *

(2) *Real property trade or business.*—The following terms have the following meanings in determining whether a trade or business is a real property trade or business for purposes of section 469(c)(7)(C) and this section.

(i) *Real property.*—(A) *In general.*—The term *real property* includes land, buildings, and other inherently permanent structures that are permanently affixed to land. Any interest in real property, including fee ownership, co-ownership, a leasehold, an option, or a similar interest is real property under this section. Tenant improvements to land, buildings, or other structures that are inherently permanent or otherwise classified as real property within the meaning of this section are real property for purposes of section 469(c)(7)(C). However, property produced for sale that is not real property in the hands of the producing taxpayer or a related person, but that may be incorporated into real property by an unrelated person, is not treated as real property of the producing taxpayer for purposes of section 469(c)(7)(C) and this section (for example, bricks, nails, paint, and windowpanes).

(B) *Land.*—The term *land* includes water and air space superjacent to land and natural products and deposits that are unsevered from the land. Natural products and deposits, such as plants, crops, trees, water, ores, and minerals, cease to be real property when they are harvested, severed, extracted, or removed from the land. Accordingly, any trade or business that involves the cultivation and harvesting of plants, crops, or trees, or severing, extracting, or removing natural products or deposits from land is not a real property trade or business for purposes of section 469(c)(7)(C) and this section. The storage or maintenance of severed or extracted natural products or deposits, such as plants, crops, trees, water, ores, and minerals, in or upon real property does not cause the stored property to be recharacterized as real property, and any trade or business relating to or involving such storage or maintenance of severed or extracted natural products or deposits is not a real property trade or business, even though such storage or maintenance otherwise may occur upon or within real property.

(C) *Inherently permanent structure.*—The term *inherently permanent structure* means any permanently affixed building or other permanently affixed structure. If the affixation is reasonably expected to last indefinitely, based on all the facts and circumstances, the affixation is considered permanent. However, an asset that serves an active function, such as an item of machinery or equipment (for example, HVAC system, elevator or escalator), is not a building or other inherently permanent structure, and therefore is not real property for purposes of section 469(c)(7)(C) and this section, even if such item of machinery or equipment is permanently affixed to or becomes incorporated within a building or other inherently permanent structure. Accordingly, a trade or business that involves the manufacture, installation, operation, maintenance, or repair of any asset that serves an active function will not be a real property trade or business, or a unit or component of another real property trade or business, for purposes of section 469(c)(7)(C) and this section.

(D) *Building.*—*(1) In general.*—A *building* encloses a space within its walls and is generally covered by a roof or other external upper covering that protects the walls and inner space from the elements.

(2) *Types of buildings.*—Buildings include the following assets if permanently affixed to land: houses; townhouses; apartments; condominiums; hotels; motels; stadiums; arenas; shopping malls; factory and office buildings; warehouses; barns; enclosed garages; enclosed transportation stations and terminals; and stores.

(E) *Other inherently permanent structures.*—*(1) In general.*—Other inherently permanent structures include the following assets if permanently affixed to land: parking facilities; bridges; tunnels; roadbeds; railroad tracks; pipelines; storage structures such as silos and oil and gas storage tanks; and stationary wharves and docks.

(2) *Facts and circumstances determination.*—The determination of whether an asset is an inherently permanent structure is based on all the facts and circumstances. In particular, the following factors must be taken into account:

(i) The manner in which the asset is affixed to land and whether such manner of affixation allows the asset to be easily removed from the land;

(ii) Whether the asset is designed to be removed or to remain in place indefinitely on the land;

(iii) The damage that removal of the asset would cause to the asset itself or to the land to which it is affixed;

(iv) Any circumstances that suggest the expected period of affixation is not indefinite (for example, a lease that requires or permits removal of the asset from the land upon the expiration of the lease); and

(v) The time and expense required to move the asset from the land.

(ii) *Other definitions.*—(A) through (G) [Reserved]

(H) *Real property operation.*—The term *real property operation* means handling, by a direct or indirect owner of the real property, the day-to-day operations of a trade or business, within the meaning of paragraph (b)(1) of this section, relating to the maintenance and occupancy of the real property that affect the availability and functionality of that real property used, or held out for use, by customers where payments received from customers are principally for the customers' use of the real property. The principal purpose of such business operations must be the provision of the use of the real property, or physical space accorded by or within the real property, to one or more customers, and not the provision of other significant or extraordinary personal services, within the meaning of § 1.469-1T(e)(3)(iv) and (v), to customers in conjunction with the customers' incidental use of real property or physical space. If the real property or physical space is provided to a customer to be used to carry on the customer's trade or business, the principal purpose of the business operations must be to provide the customer with exclusive use of the real property or physical space in furtherance of the customer's trade or business, and not to provide other significant or extraordinary personal services to the customer in addition to or in conjunction with the use of the real property or physical space, regardless of whether the customer pays for the services separately. However, other incidental personal services may be provided to the customer in conjunction with the use of real property or physical space, as long as such services are insubstantial in relation to the customer's use of the real property or physical space and the receipt of such services is not a significant factor in the customer's decision to use the real property or physical space.

(I) *Real property management.*—The term *real property management* means handling, by a professional manager, the day-to-day operations of a trade or business, within the meaning of paragraph (b)(1) of this section, relating to the maintenance and occupancy of real property that affect the availability and functionality of that property used, or held out for use, by customers where payments received from customers are principally for the customers' use of the real property. The principal purpose of such business operations must be the provision of the use of the real property, or physical space accorded by or within the real property, to one or more customers, and not the provision of other significant or extraordinary personal services, within the meaning of §1.469-1T(e)(3)(iv) and (v), to customers in conjunction with the customers' incidental use of the real property or physical space. If the real property or physical space is provided to a customer to be used to carry on the customer's trade or business, the principal purpose of the business operations must be to provide the customer with exclusive use of the real property or physical space in furtherance of the customer's trade or business, and not to provide other significant or extraordinary personal services to the customer in addition to or in conjunction with the use of the real property or physical space, regardless of whether the customer pays for the services separately. However, other incidental personal services may be provided to the customer in conjunction with the use of real property or physical space, as long as such services are insubstantial in relation to the customer's use of the real property or physical space and the receipt of such services is not a significant factor in the customer's decision to use the real property or physical space. A professional manager is a person responsible, on a full-time basis, for the overall management and oversight of the real property or properties and who is not a direct or indirect owner of the real property or properties.

(J) and (K) [Reserved]

(iii) *Examples.*—The following examples illustrate the operation of this paragraph (b)(2):

(A) *Example 1.* A owns farmland and uses the land in A's farming business to grow and harvest crops of various kinds. As part of this farming business, A utilizes a greenhouse that is an inherently permanent structure to grow certain crops during the winter months. Under the rules of this section, any trade or business that involves the cultivation and harvesting of plants, crops, or trees is not a real property trade or business for purposes of section 469(c)(7)(C) and this section, even though the cultivation and harvesting of crops occurs upon or within real property. Accordingly, under these facts, A is not engaged in a real property trade or business for purposes of section 469(c)(7)(C) and this section.

(B) *Example 2.* B is a retired farmer and owns farmland that B rents exclusively to C to operate a farm. The arrangement between B and C is a trade or business (within the meaning of paragraph (b)(1) of this section) where payments by C are principally for C's use of B's real property. B also provides certain farm equipment for C's use. However, C is solely responsible for the maintenance and repair of the farm equipment along with any costs associated with operating the equipment. B also occasionally provides oral advice to C regarding various aspects of the farm operation, based on B's prior experience as a farmer. Other than the provision of this occasional advice, B does not provide any significant or extraordinary personal services to C in connection with the rental of the farmland to C.

Under these facts, B is engaged in a real property trade or business (which does not include the use or deemed rental of any farm equipment) for purposes of section 469(c)(7)(C) and this section, and B's oral advice is an incidental personal service that B provides in conjunction with C's use of the real property. Nevertheless, under these facts, C is not engaged in a real property trade or business for purposes of section 469(c)(7)(C) and this section because C is engaged in the business of farming.

(C) *Example 3.* D owns a building in which D operates a restaurant and bar. Even though D provides customers with use of the physical space inside the building, D is not engaged in a trade or business where payments by customers are principally for the use of real property or physical space. Instead, the payments by D's customers are principally for the receipt of significant or extraordinary personal services (within the meaning of §1.469-1T(e)(3)(iv) and (v)), mainly food and beverage preparation and presentation services, and the use of the physical space by customers is incidental to the receipt of these personal services. Under the rules of this section, any trade or business that involves the provision of significant or extraordinary personal services to customers in conjunction with the customers' incidental use of real property or physical space is not a real property trade or business, even though the business operations occur upon or within real property. Accordingly, under these facts, D is not engaged in a real property trade or business for purposes of section 469(c)(7)(C) and this section.

(D) *Example 4.* E owns a majority interest in an S corporation, X, that is engaged in the trade or business of manufacturing industrial cooling systems for installation in commercial buildings and for other uses. E also owns a majority interest in an S corporation, Y, that purchases the industrial cooling systems from X and that installs, maintains, and repairs those systems in both existing commercial buildings and commercial buildings under construction. Under the rules of this section, any trade or business that involves the manufacture, installation, operation, maintenance, or repair of any machinery or equipment that serves an active function will not be a real property trade or business (or a unit or component of another real property trade or business) for purposes of section 469(c)(7)(C) and this section, even though the machinery or equipment will be permanently affixed to real property once it is installed. In this case, the industrial cooling systems are machinery or equipment that serves an active function. Accordingly, under these facts, E, X and Y will not be treated as engaged in one or more real property trades or businesses for purposes of section 469(c)(7)(C) and this section.

(E) *Example 5.* (1) F owns an interest in P, a limited partnership. P owns and operates a luxury hotel. In addition to providing rooms and suites for use by customers, the hotel offers many additional amenities such as in-room food and beverage service, maid and linen service, parking valet service, concierge service, front desk and bellhop service, dry cleaning and laundry service, and in-room barber and hairdresser service. P contracted with M to provide maid and janitorial services to P's hotel. M is an S corporation principally engaged in the trade or business of providing maid and janitorial services to various types of businesses, including hotels. G is a professional manager employed by M who handles the day-to-day business operations relating to M's provision of maid and janitorial services to M's various customers, including P.

(2) Even though the personal services that P provides to the customers of its hotel are significant personal services within the meaning of § 1.469-1T(e)(3)(iv), the principal purpose of P's hotel business operations is the provision of use of the hotel's rooms and suites to customers, and not the provision of the significant personal services to P's customers in conjunction with the customers' incidental use of those rooms or suites. The provision of these significant personal services by P to P's customers is incidental to the customers' use of the hotel's real property. Accordingly, under these facts, F and P are treated as engaged in a real property trade or business for purposes of section 469(c)(7)(C) and this section.

(3) With respect to the maid and janitorial services provided by M, M's operations affect the availability and functionality of real property used, or held out for use, by customers in a trade or business where payments by customers are principally for the use of real property (in this case, P's hotel). However, M does not operate or manage real property. Instead, M is engaged in a trade or business of providing maid and janitorial services to customers, such as P, that are engaged in real property trades or businesses. Thus, M's business operations are merely ancillary to real property trades or businesses. Therefore, M is not engaged in real property operations or management as defined in this section. Accordingly, under these facts, M is not engaged in a real property trade or business within the meaning of section 469(c)(7)(C) and this section.

(4) With respect to the day-to-day business operations that G handles as a professional manager of M, the business operations that G manages is not the provision of use of P's hotel rooms and suites to customers. G does not operate or manage real property. Instead, G manages the provision of maid and janitorial services to customers, including P's hotel. Therefore, G is not engaged in real property management as defined in this section. Accordingly, under these facts, G is not engaged in a real property trade or business within the meaning of section 469(c)(7)(C) and this section.

* * *

[Proposed 12-28-2018.]

**[Prop. Reg. § 1.469-11]**

**§ 1.469-11. Effective date and transition rules.**—(a) * * *

(3) The rules contained in § 1.469-9, other than paragraph (a)(4) of this section, apply for taxable years beginning on or after January 1, 1995, and to elections made under § 1.469-9(g) with returns filed on or after January 1, 1995, and the rules contained in § 1.469-11(a)(4) apply for taxable years beginning on or after the date of the Treasury decision adopting these regulations as final regulations is published in the **Federal Register**;

(4) The rules contained in § 1.469-9(b)(2) apply to taxable years beginning after December 31, 2018. Paragraph (b) of this section applies to loss corporations that have undergone an ownership change during a taxable year ending after the date of the Treasury decision adopting these regulations as final regulations is published in the **Federal Register**. However, taxpayers and their related parties, within the meaning of sections 267(b) and 707(b)(1), may rely on the rules of this section if applied consistently by the taxpayers and their related parties, until the date the Treasury decision adopting these regulations as final regulations is published in the **Federal Register**;

* * *

[Proposed 12-28-2018.]

**[Prop. Reg. § 1.642(c)-3]**

**§ 1.642(c)-3. Adjustments and other special rules for determining unlimited charitable contributions deduction.**

* * *

(g) *Payments resulting in state or local tax benefits.*—(1) *In general.*—If the trust or decedent's estate makes a payment of gross income for a purpose specified in section 170(c), and the trust or decedent's estate receives or expects to receive a state or local tax benefit in consideration for such payment, § 1.170A-1(h)(3) applies in determining the charitable contribution deduction under section 642(c).

(2) *Effective/applicability date.*—Paragraph (g)(1) of this section applies to payments of gross income after August 27, 2018.

[Proposed 8-27-2018.]

**[Prop. Reg. § 1.704-1]**

**§ 1.704-1. Partner's distributive share.**

* * *

(b) * * *

(1) * * *

(ii) * * *

(a) * * * The last sentence of paragraph (b)(2)(iv)(g)(3) of this section is applicable for partnership taxable years ending on or after the date of publication of a Treasury decision adopting these rules as final regulations in the **Federal**

**Register**. However, a partnership may rely on the last sentence in paragraph (b)(2)(iv)(*g*)(3) of this section in these proposed regulations for the partnership's taxable years ending on or after September 28, 2017, and ending before the partnership's taxable year that includes the date of publication of a Treasury decision adopting these rules as final regulations in the **Federal Register**.

\* \* \*

(2) \* \* \*

(iv) \* \* \*

(*g*) \* \* \*

(3) \* \* \* For purposes of the preceding sentence, additional first year depreciation deduction under section 168(k) is not a reasonable method.

\* \* \*

[Proposed 8-8-2018.]

### [Prop. Reg. § 1.704-3]

**§ 1.704-3. Election of limitation of tax for individuals.**

\* \* \*

(d) \* \* \*

(2) \* \* \* However, the additional first year depreciation deduction under section 168(k) is not a permissible method for purposes of the preceding sentence and, if a partnership has acquired property in a taxable year for which the additional first year depreciation deduction under section 168(k) has been used of the same type as the contributed property, the portion of the contributed property's book basis that exceeds its adjusted tax basis must be recovered under a reasonable method. See § 1.168(k)-2(b)(3)(iv)(B).

\* \* \*

(f) \* \* \* With the exception of paragraphs (a)(1), (a)(8)(ii) and (iii), and (a)(10) and (11) of this section, and of the last sentence in paragraph (d)(2) of this section, this section applies to properties contributed to a partnership and to restatements pursuant to § 1.704-1(b)(2)(iv)(*f*) on or after December 21, 1993. \* \* \* The last sentence of paragraph (d)(2) of this section applies to property contributed to a partnership on or after the date of publication of a Treasury decision adopting these rules as final regulations in the **Federal Register**. However, a taxpayer may rely on the last sentence in paragraph (d)(2) of this section in these proposed regulations for property contributed to a partnership on or after September 28, 2017, and ending before the date of publication of a Treasury decision adopting these rules as final regulations in the **Federal Register**.

\* \* \*

[Proposed 8-8-2018.]

### [Prop. Reg. § 1.743-1]

**§ 1.743-1. Optional adjustment to basis of partnership property.**

\* \* \*

(j) \* \* \*

(4) \* \* \*

(i) \* \* \*

(B) \* \* \*

(*1*) \* \* \* Notwithstanding the above, the partnership is allowed to deduct the additional first year depreciation under section 168(k) and § 1.168(k)-2 for an increase in the basis of qualified property, as defined in section 168(k) and § 1.168(k)-2, under section 743(b) in a class of property, as defined in § 1.168(k)-2(e)(1)(ii)(A) through (F), even if the partnership made the election under section 168(k)(7) and § 1.168(k)-2(e)(1) not to deduct the additional first year depreciation for all other qualified property of the partnership in the same class of property, as defined in § 1.168(k)-2(e)(1)(ii)(A) through (F), and placed in service in the same taxable year, provided the section 743(b) basis adjustment meets all requirements of section 168(k) and § 1.168(k)-2. Further, the partnership may make an election under section 168(k)(7) and § 1.168(k)-2(e)(1) not to deduct the additional first year depreciation for an increase in the basis of qualified property, as defined in section 168(k) and § 1.168(k)-2, under section 743(b) in a class of property, as defined in § 1.168(k)-2(e)(1)(ii)(A) through (F), and placed in service in the same taxable year, even if the partnership does not make that election for all other qualified property of the partnership in the same class of property, as defined in § 1.168(k)-2(e)(1)(ii)(A) through (F), and placed in service in the same taxable year. In this case, the section 743(b) basis adjustment must be recovered under a reasonable method.

\* \* \*

(l) \* \* \* The last three sentences of paragraph (j)(4)(i)(B)(*1*) of this section apply to transfers of partnership interests that occur on or after the date of publication of a Treasury decision adopting these rules as final regulations in the **Federal Register**. However, a partnership may rely on the last three sentences in paragraph (j)(4)(i)(B)(*1*) of this section in these proposed regulations for transfers of partnership interests that occur on or after September 28, 2017, and ending before the date of publication of a Treasury decision adopting these rules as final regulations in the **Federal Register**.

[Proposed 8-8-2018.]

### [Prop. Reg. § 1.860C-2]

**§ 1.860C-2. Determination of REMIC taxable income or net loss.**

\* \* \*

(b) \* \* \*

(2) *Deduction allowable under section 163.*— (i) A REMIC is allowed a deduction, determined without regard to section 163(d), for any interest expense accrued during the taxable year.

(ii) For taxable years beginning after December 31, 2017, a REMIC is allowed a deduction, determined without regard to section 163(j), for any interest expense accrued during the taxable year.

\* \* \*

[Proposed 12-28-2018.]

**[Prop. Reg. § 1.861-8]**

**§ 1.861-8. Computation of taxable income from sources within the United States and from other sources and activities.**

\* \* \*

(c) \* \* \*

(2) *Apportionment based on assets.*—Certain taxpayers are required by paragraph (e)(2) of this section and § 1.861-9T to apportion interest expense on the basis of assets. A taxpayer may apportion other deductions based on the comparative value of assets that generate income within each grouping, provided that this method reflects the factual relationship between the deduction and the groupings of income and is applied in accordance with the rules of § 1.861-9T(g). In general, such apportionments must be made either on the basis of the tax book value of those assets or, except in the case of interest expense, on the basis of their fair market value. *See* § 1.861-9(h). Taxpayers using the fair market value method for their last taxable year beginning before January 1, 2018, must change to the tax book value method (or the alternative tax book value method) for purposes of apportioning interest expense for their first taxable year beginning after December 31, 2017. The Commissioner's approval is not required for this change. In the case of any corporate taxpayer that—

(i) Uses tax book value or alternative tax book value, and

(ii) Owns directly or indirectly (within the meaning of § 1.861-12T(c)(2)(ii)(B)) 10 percent or more of the total combined voting power of all classes of stock entitled to vote in any other corporation (domestic or foreign) that is not a member of the affiliated group (as defined in section 864(e)(5)), the taxpayer must adjust its basis in that stock in the manner described in § 1.861-12(c)(2).

\* \* \*

(d) \* \* \*

(2) *Allocation and apportionment to exempt, excluded, or eliminated income.*—(i) *In general.*—[Reserved]. For further guidance, see § 1.861-8T(d)(2)(i).

(ii) *Exempt income and exempt asset defined.*—(A) *In general.*—For purposes of this section, the term *exempt income* means any gross income to the extent that it is exempt, excluded, or eliminated for Federal income tax purposes. The term *exempt asset* means any asset to the extent income from the asset is (or is treated as under paragraph (d)(2)(ii)(B) or (C) of this section) exempt, excluded, or eliminated for Federal income tax purposes.

(B) [Reserved]. For further guidance, see § 1.861-8T(d)(2)(ii)(B).

(C) *Foreign-derived intangible income and inclusions under section 951A(a).*—(1) *Exempt income.*—The term "exempt income" includes an amount of a domestic corporation's gross income included in foreign-derived intangible income (as defined in section 250(b)(1)), and also includes an amount of a domestic corporation's gross income from an inclusion under section 951A(a) and the gross up under section 78 attributable to such an inclusion, in each case equal to the amount of the deduction allowed under section 250(a) for such gross income (taking into account the reduction under section 250(a)(2)(B), if any). Therefore, for purposes of apportioning deductions using a gross income method, gross income does not include gross income included in foreign-derived intangible income, an inclusion under section 951A(a), or the gross up under section 78 attributable to an inclusion under section 951A(a), in an amount equal to the amount of the deduction allowed under section 250(a)(1)(A), (B)(i), or (B)(ii), respectively (taking into account the reduction under section 250(a)(2)(B), if any).

(2) *Exempt assets.*—(i) *Assets that produce foreign-derived intangible income.*—The term "exempt asset" includes the portion of a domestic corporation's assets that produce gross income included in foreign-derived intangible income equal to the amount of such assets multiplied by the fraction that equals the amount of the domestic corporation's deduction allowed under section 250(a)(1)(A) (taking into account the reduction under section 250(a)(2)(B)(i), if any) divided by its foreign-derived intangible income. No portion of the value of stock in a foreign corporation is treated as an exempt asset by reason of this paragraph (d)(2)(ii)(C)(2)(i), including by reason of a transfer of intangible property to a foreign corporation subject to section 367(d) that gives rise to income eligible for a deduction under section 250(a)(1)(A).

(ii) *Controlled foreign corporation stock that gives rise to inclusions under section 951A(a).*—The term "exempt asset" includes a portion of the value of a United States shareholder's stock in a controlled foreign corporation if the United States shareholder is a domestic corporation that is eligible for a deduction under section 250(a) with respect to income described in section 250(a)(1)(B)(i) and all or a portion of the domestic corporation's stock in the controlled foreign corporation is characterized as GILTI inclusion stock. The portion of foreign corporation stock that is treated as an exempt asset for a taxable year equals the portion of the value of such foreign corporation stock (determined in accordance with §§ 1.861-9(g), 1.861-12, and 1.861-13) that is characterized as GILTI inclusion stock multiplied by a fraction that equals the amount of the domestic corporation's deduction allowed under section 250(a)(1)(B)(i) (taking into account the reduction under section 250(a)(2)(B)(ii), if any) divided by its GILTI inclusion amount (as defined in § 1.951A-1(c)(1) or, in the case of a member of a consolidated group, § 1.1502-51(b)) for such taxable year. The portion of controlled foreign corporation stock treated as an exempt asset under this paragraph (d)(2)(ii)(C)(2)(ii) is treated as attributable to the relevant categories of GILTI inclusion stock described in each of paragraphs (d)(2)(ii)(C)(3)(i) through (v) of this section based on the relative value of the portion of the stock in each such category.

(3) *GILTI inclusion stock.*—For purposes of paragraph (d)(2)(ii)(C)(2)(ii) of this section, the term *GILTI inclusion stock* means the aggregate of the portions of the value of controlled foreign corporation stock that are—

(i) Assigned to the section 951A category under § 1.861-13(a)(2);

(ii) Assigned to a particular treaty category under § 1.861-13(a)(3)(i) (relating to resourced gross tested income stock);

(iii) Assigned under § 1.861-13(a)(1) to the gross tested income statutory grouping within the foreign source passive category less the amount described in § 1.861-13(a)(5)(iii)(A);

(iv) Assigned under § 1.861-13(a)(1) to the gross tested income statutory grouping within the U.S. source general category less the amount described in § 1.861-13(a)(5)(iv)(A); and

(v) Assigned under § 1.861-13(a)(1) to the gross tested income statutory grouping within the U.S. source passive category less the amount described in § 1.861-13(a)(5)(iv)(B).

(4) *Non-applicability to section 250(b)(3).*—This paragraph (d)(2)(ii)(C) does not apply when apportioning deductions for purposes of determining deduction eligible income under the operative section of section 250(b)(3).

(5) *Example.*—The following example illustrates the application of this paragraph (d)(2)(ii)(C).

(i) *Facts.* USP, a domestic corporation, directly owns all of the stock of CFC1 and CFC2, both of which are controlled foreign corporations. The tax book value of CFC1 and CFC2's stock is $10,000 and $9,000, respectively. Pursuant to § 1.861-13(a), $6,100 of the stock of CFC1 is assigned to the section 951A category under § 1.861-13(a)(2) ("section 951A category stock") and the remaining $3,900 of the stock of CFC1 is assigned to the general category ("general category stock"). Additionally, $4,880 of the stock of CFC2 is section 951A category stock and the remaining $4,120 of the stock of CFC2 is general category stock. Under section 951A and the section 951A regulations (as defined in § 1.951A-1(a)(1)), USP's GILTI inclusion amount is $610. The portion of USP's deduction under section 250 described in section 250(a)(1)(B)(i) is

$305. No portion of USP's deduction is reduced by reason of section 250(a)(2)(B)(ii).

(ii) *Analysis.* Under paragraph (d)(2)(ii)(C)(1) of this section, $305 of USP's gross income attributable to its GILTI inclusion amount is exempt income for purposes of apportioning deductions for purposes of section 904. Under paragraph (d)(2)(ii)(C)(3) of this section, the GILTI inclusion stock of CFC1 is the $6,100 of stock that is section 951A category stock and the GILTI inclusion stock of CFC2 is the $4,880 of stock that is section 951A category stock. Under paragraph (d)(2)(ii)(C)(2) of this section, the portion of the value of the stock of CFC1 and CFC2 that is treated as an exempt asset equals the portion of the value of the stock of CFC1 and CFC2 that is GILTI inclusion stock multiplied by 50% ($305/$610). Accordingly, the exempt portion of the stock of CFC1 is $3,050 (50% x $6,100) and the exempt portion of CFC2's stock is $2,440 (50% x $4,880). Therefore, the stock of CFC1 taken into account for purposes of apportioning deductions is $3,050 of non-exempt section 951A category stock and $3,900 of general category stock. The stock of CFC2 taken into account for purposes of apportioning deductions is $2,440 of non-exempt section 951A category stock and $4,120 of general category stock.

(d)(2)(iii) through (d)(2)(iii)(B) [Reserved]. For further guidance, see § 1.861-8T(d)(2)(iii) through § 1.861-8T(d)(2)(iii)(B).

(C) Dividends for which a deduction is allowed under section 245A;

(D) Foreign earned income as defined in section 911 and the regulations thereunder (however, the rules of § 1.911-6 do not require the allocation and apportionment of certain deductions, including home mortgage interest, to foreign earned income for purposes of determining the deductions disallowed under section 911(d)(6)); and

(E) Inclusions for which a deduction is allowed under section 965(c). *See* § 1.965-6(d).

(iv) *Value of stock attributable to previously taxed earnings and profits.*—No portion of the value of stock in a controlled foreign corporation is treated as an exempt asset by reason of the adjustment under § 1.861-12(c)(2) in respect of previously taxed earnings and profits described in section 959(c)(1) or (c)(2) (including earnings and profits described in section 959(c)(2) by reason of section 951A(f)(1) and § 1.951A-6(b)(1)). *See also* § 1.965-6(d).

(e) * * *

(1) * * * Paragraphs (e)(13) and (14) of this section contain rules with respect to the allocation and apportionment of the deduction allowed under section 250(a). Paragraph (e)(15) of this section contains rules with respect to the allocation and apportionment of a taxpayer's distributive share of a partnership's deductions. * * *

* * *

(6) * * *

(i) *In general.*—The deduction for foreign income, war profits and excess profits taxes (*foreign income taxes*) allowed by section 164 is allocated and apportioned among the applicable statutory and residual groupings under the principles of § 1.904-6(a)(1)(i), (ii), and (iv). The deduction for state and local taxes (*state income taxes*) allowed by section 164 is considered definitely related and allocable to the gross income with respect to which such state income taxes are imposed. * * *

* * *

(13) *Foreign-derived intangible income.*—The portion of the deduction that is allowed for foreign-derived intangible income under section 250(a)(1)(A) (taking into account the reduction under section 250(a)(2)(B)(i), if any) is considered definitely related and allocable to the class of gross income included in the taxpayer's foreign-derived deduction eligible income (as defined in section 250(b)(4)). If necessary, the portion of the deduction is apportioned within the class ratably between the statutory grouping (or among the statutory groupings) of gross income and the residual grouping of gross income based on the relative amounts of foreign-derived deduction eligible income in each grouping.

(14) *Global intangible low-taxed income and related section 78 gross up.*—The portion of the deduction that is allowed for the global intangible low-taxed income amount described in section 250(a)(1)(B)(i) (taking into account the reduction under section 250(a)(2)(B)(ii), if any) is considered definitely related and allocable to the class of gross income included under section 951A(a). If necessary (for example, because a portion of the inclusion under section 951A(a) is passive category income or U.S. source income), the portion of the deduction is apportioned within the class ratably between the statutory grouping (or among the statutory groupings) of gross income and the residual grouping of gross income based on the relative amounts of gross income in each grouping. Similar rules apply to allocate and apportion the portion of the deduction that is allowed for the section 78 gross up under section 250(a)(1)(B)(ii).

(15) *Distributive share of partnership deductions.*—In general, if deductions are incurred by a partnership in which the taxpayer is a partner, the taxpayer's deductions that are allocated and apportioned include the taxpayer's distributive share of the partnership's deductions. See §§ 1.861-9(e), 1.861-17(f), and 1.904-4(n)(1)(ii) for special rules for apportioning a partner's distributive share of deductions of a partnership.

(f) * * *

(1) * * *

(i) *Separate foreign tax credit limitations.*— Section 904(d)(1) and other sections described in § 1.904-4(m) require that a separate foreign tax credit limitation be determined with respect to

each separate category of income specified in those sections. Accordingly, the foreign source income within each separate category described in § 1.904-5(a)(4)(v) constitutes a separate statutory grouping of income. U.S. source income is treated as income in the residual category for purposes of determining the limitation on the foreign tax credit.

* * *

(h) *Applicability date.*—This section applies to taxable years that both begin after December 31, 2017, and end on or after December 4, 2018.

[Proposed 12-7-2018.]

**[Prop. Reg. § 1.861-9]**

**§ 1.861-9. Allocation and apportionment of interest expense and rules for asset-based apportionment.**—(a) through (c)(4) [Reserved]. For further guidance, see § 1.861-9T(a) through (c)(4).

(5) *Section 163(j).*—If a taxpayer is subject to section 163(j), the taxpayer's deduction for business interest expense is limited to the sum of the taxpayer's business interest income, 30 percent of the taxpayer's adjusted taxable income for the taxable year, and the taxpayer's floor plan financing interest expense. In the taxable year that any deduction is permitted for business interest expense with respect to a disallowed business interest carryforward, that business interest expense is apportioned for purposes of this section under rules set forth in paragraphs (d), (e), or (f) of this section (as applicable) as though it were incurred in the taxable year in which the expense is deducted.

(d) through (e)(1) [Reserved]. For further guidance, see § 1.861-9T(d) through (e)(1).

* * *

(4) *Entity rule for less than 10 percent limited partners and less than 10 percent corporate general partners.*—(i) *Partnership interest expense.*—A limited partner (whether individual or corporate) or corporate general partner whose ownership, together with ownership by persons that bear a relationship to the partner described in section 267(b) or section 707, of the capital and profits interests of the partnership is less than 10 percent directly allocates its distributive share of partnership interest expense to its distributive share of partnership gross income. Under § 1.904-4(n)(1)(ii), such a partner's distributive share of foreign source income of the partnership is treated as passive income (subject to the high-taxed income exception of section 904(d)(2)(B)(iii)(II)), except in the case of income from a partnership interest held in the ordinary course of the partner's active trade or business, as defined in § 1.904-4(n)(1)(ii)(B). A partner's distributive share of partnership interest expense (other than partnership interest expense that is directly allocated to identified property under § 1.861-10T) is apportioned in accordance with the partner's relative distributive share of gross foreign source income in each separate category

and of gross domestic source income from the partnership. To the extent that partnership interest expense is directly allocated under § 1.861-10T, a comparable portion of the income to which such interest expense is allocated is disregarded in determining the partner's relative distributive share of gross foreign source income in each separate category and domestic source income. The partner's distributive share of the interest expense of the partnership that is directly allocable under § 1.861-10T is allocated according to the treatment, after application of § 1.904-4(n)(1), of the partner's distributive share of the income to which the expense is allocated.

(e)(4)(ii) through (e)(7) [Reserved]. For further guidance, see § 1.861-9T(e)(4)(ii) through (e)(7).

(8) *Special rule for specified partnership loans.*—(i) *In general.*—For purposes of apportioning interest expense that is not directly allocable under paragraph (e)(4) of this section or § 1.861-10T, the disregarded portion of a specified partnership loan is not considered an asset of a SPL lender. The disregarded portion of a specified partnership loan is the portion of the value of the loan (as determined under paragraph (h)(4)(i) of this section) that bears the same proportion to the total value of the loan as the matching income amount that is included by the SPL lender for a taxable year with respect to the loan bears to the total amount of SPL interest income that is included directly or indirectly in gross income by the SPL lender with respect to the loan during that taxable year.

(ii) *Treatment of interest expense and interest income attributable to a specified partnership loan.*— If a SPL lender (or any other person in the same affiliated group as the SPL lender) takes into account a distributive share of SPL interest expense, the SPL lender includes the matching income amount for the taxable year that is attributable to the same loan in gross income in the same statutory and residual groupings as the statutory and residual groupings of gross income from which the SPL interest expense is deducted by the SPL lender (or any other person in the same affiliated group as the SPL lender).

(iii) *Anti-avoidance rule for third party back-to-back loans.* If, with a principal purpose of avoiding the rules in this paragraph (e)(8), a person makes a loan to a person that is not related (within the meaning of section 267(b) or 707) to the lender, the unrelated person makes a loan to a partnership, and the first loan would constitute a specified partnership loan if made directly to the partnership, then the rules of this paragraph (e)(8) apply as if the first loan was made directly to the partnership. Such a series of loans will be subject to this recharacterization rule without regard to whether there was a principal purpose of avoiding the rules in this paragraph (e)(8) if the loan to the unrelated person would not have been made or maintained on substantially the same terms irrespective of the loan of funds by the unrelated person to the partnership. The principles of this paragraph (e)(8)(iii) also apply to similar transactions that involve more than two loans and regardless of the order in which the loans are made.

(iv) *Anti-avoidance rule for loans held by CFCs.*—A loan receivable held by a controlled foreign corporation with respect to a loan to a partnership in which a United States shareholder (as defined in § 1.904-5(a)(4)(vi)) of the controlled foreign corporation owns an interest, directly or indirectly through one or more other partnerships or other pass-through entities (as defined in § 1.904-5(a)(4)(iv)), is recharacterized as a loan receivable held directly by the United States shareholder with respect to the loan to such partnership for purposes of this paragraph (e)(8) if the loan was made or transferred with a principal purpose of avoiding the rules in this paragraph (e)(8).

(v) *Interest equivalents.*—The principles of this paragraph (e)(8) apply in the case of a partner, or any person in the same affiliated group as the partner, that takes into account a distributive share of an expense or loss (to the extent deductible) that is allocated and apportioned in the same manner as interest expense under § 1.861-9T(b) and has a matching income amount with respect to the transaction that gives rise to that expense or loss.

(vi) *Definitions.*—For purposes of this paragraph (e)(8), the following definitions apply.

(A) *Affiliated group.*—The term *affiliated group* has the meaning provided in § 1.861-11(d)(1).

(B) *Matching income amount.*—The term *matching income amount* means the lesser of the total amount of the SPL interest income included directly or indirectly in gross income by the SPL lender for the taxable year with respect to a specified partnership loan or the total amount of the distributive shares of the SPL interest expense of the SPL lender (or any other person in the same affiliated group as the SPL lender) with respect to the loan.

(C) *Specified partnership loan.*—The term *specified partnership loan* means a loan to a partnership for which the loan receivable is held, directly or indirectly through one or more other partnerships, either by a person that owns an interest, directly or indirectly through one or more other partnerships, in the partnership, or by any person in the same affiliated group as that person.

(D) *SPL interest expense.*—The term *SPL interest expense* means an item of interest expense paid or accrued with respect to a specified partnership loan, without regard to whether the expense was currently deductible (for example, by reason of section 163(j)).

**Prop. Reg. § 1.861-9(e)(8)(vi)(D)**

(E) *SPL interest income.*—The term *SPL interest income* means an item of gross interest income received or accrued with respect to a specified partnership loan.

(F) *SPL lender.*—The term *SPL lender* means the person that holds the receivable with respect to a specified partnership loan. If a partnership holds the receivable, then any partner in the partnership (other than a partner described in paragraph (e)(4)(i) of this section) is also considered a SPL lender.

(9) *Characterizing certain partnership assets as foreign branch category assets.*—For purposes of applying this paragraph (e) to section 904 as the operative section, a partner that is a United States person that has a distributive share of partnership income that is treated as foreign branch category income under § 1.904-4(f)(1)(i)(B) characterizes its pro rata share of the partnership assets that give rise to such income as assets in the foreign branch category.

(f) through (f)(1) [Reserved]. For further guidance, see § 1.861-9T(f) through (f)(1).

(2) *Section 987 QBUs of domestic corporations.*—(i) *In general.*—In the application of the asset method described in paragraph (g) of this section, a domestic corporation—

(A) Takes into account the assets of any section 987 QBU (as defined in § 1.987-1(b)(2)), translated according to the rules set forth in paragraph (g) of this section, and

(B) Combines with its own interest expense any deductible interest expense incurred by a section 987 QBU, translated according to the rules of section 987 and the regulations under that section.

(ii) *Coordination with section 987(3).*—For purposes of computing foreign currency gain or loss under section 987(3) (including section 987 gain or loss recognized under § 1.987-5), the rules of this paragraph (f)(2) do not apply. *See* § 1.987-4.

(iii) *Example.*—The following example illustrates the application of this paragraph (f)(2).

(A) *Facts.* X is a domestic corporation that operates B, a branch doing business in a foreign country. B is a section 987 QBU (as defined in § 1.987-1(b)(2)) as well as a foreign branch (as defined in § 1.904-4(f)(3)(iii)). In 2020, without regard to B, X has gross domestic source income of $1,000 and gross foreign source general category income of $500 and incurs $200 of interest expense. Using the tax book value method of apportionment, X, without regard to B, determines the value of its assets that generate domestic source income to be $6,000 and the value of its assets that generate foreign source general category income to be $1,000. Applying the translation rules of section 987, X (through B) earned $500 of gross foreign source foreign branch category income and incurred $100 of interest expense. B incurred no other expenses.

For 2020, the average functional currency book value of B's assets that generate foreign source foreign branch category income translated at the year-end rate for 2020 is $3,000.

(B) *Analysis.* The combined assets of X and B for 2020 (averaged under § 1.861-9T(g)(3)) consist 60% ($6,000/$10,000) of assets generating domestic source income, 30% ($3,000/$10,000) of assets generating foreign source foreign branch category income, and 10% ($1,000/$10,000) of assets generating foreign source general category income. The combined interest expense of X and B is $300. Thus, $180 ($300 x 60%) of the combined interest expense is apportioned to domestic source income, $90 ($300 x 30%) is apportioned to foreign source foreign branch category income, and $30 ($300 x 10%) is apportioned to foreign source general category income, yielding net U.S. source income of $820 ($1,000 – $180), net foreign source foreign branch category income of $410 ($500 – $90), and net foreign source general category income of $470 ($500 – $30).

(3) *Controlled foreign corporations.*—(i) *In general.*—For purposes of computing subpart F income and tested income and computing earnings and profits for all Federal income tax purposes, the interest expense of a controlled foreign corporation may be apportioned using either the asset method described in paragraph (g) of this section or the modified gross income method described in paragraph (j) of this section, subject to the rules of paragraph (f)(3)(ii) and (iii) of this section.

\* \* \*

(4) *Noncontrolled 10-percent owned foreign corporations.*—\* \* \*

(iii) *Stock characterization.*—The stock of a noncontrolled 10-percent owned foreign corporation is characterized under the rules in § 1.861-12(c)(4).

(5) [Reserved]. For further guidance, see § 1.861-9T(f)(5).

(g) through (g)(1)(i) [Reserved]. For further guidance, see § 1.861-9T(g) through (g)(1)(i).

(ii) A taxpayer may elect to determine the value of its assets on the basis of either the tax book value or the fair market value of its assets. However, for taxable years beginning after December 31, 2017, the fair market value method is not allowed with respect to allocations and apportionments of interest expense. *See* section 864(e)(2). For rules concerning the application of an alternative method of valuing assets for purposes of the tax book value method, see paragraph (i) of this section. For rules concerning the application of the fair market value method, see paragraph (h) of this section.

(iii) [Reserved]

(iv) For rules relating to earnings and profits adjustments by taxpayers using the tax book value method for the stock in certain 10 percent owned corporations, see § 1.861-12(c)(2).

**Prop. Reg. § 1.861-9(e)(8)(vi)(E)**

(v) [Reserved]

(2) *Asset values.*—(i) *General rule.*—(A) *Average of values.*—For purposes of determining the value of assets under this section, an average of values (book or market) within each statutory grouping and the residual grouping is computed for the year on the basis of values of assets at the beginning and end of the year. For the first taxable year beginning after December 31, 2017 (*post-2017 year*), a taxpayer that determined the value of its assets on the basis of the fair market value method for purposes of apportioning interest expense in its prior taxable year may choose to determine asset values under the tax book value method (or the alternative tax book value method) by treating the value of its assets as of the beginning of the post-2017 year as equal to the value of its assets at the end of the first quarter of the post-2017 year, provided that each member of the affiliated group (as defined in § 1.861-11T(d)) determines its asset values on the same basis. Where a substantial distortion of asset values would result from averaging beginning-of-year and end-of-year values, as might be the case in the event of a major corporate acquisition or disposition, the taxpayer must use a different method of asset valuation that more clearly reflects the average value of assets weighted to reflect the time such assets are held by the taxpayer during the taxable year.

(B) *Tax book value method.*—Under the tax book value method, the value of an asset is determined based on the adjusted basis of the asset. For purposes of determining the value of stock in a 10 percent owned corporation at the beginning and end of the year under the tax book value method, the tax book value is determined without regard to any adjustments under section 961(a) or 1293(d), see § 1.861-12(c)(2)(i)(B)(*1*), and before the adjustment required by § 1.861-12(c)(2)(i)(A) to the basis of stock in the 10 percent owned corporation. The average of the tax book value of the stock at the beginning and end of the year is then adjusted with respect to earnings and profits as described in § 1.861-12(c)(2)(i).

(g)(2)(ii) through (g)(2)(ii)(A)(*1*) [Reserved]. For further guidance, see § 1.861-9T(g)(2)(ii) through (g)(2)(ii)(A)(*1*).

(2) *United States dollar approximate separate transactions method.*—In the case of a branch to which the United States dollar approximate separate transactions method of accounting described in § 1.985-3 applies, the beginning-of-year dollar amount of the assets is determined by reference to the end-of-year balance sheet of the branch for the immediately preceding taxable year, adjusted for United States generally accepted accounting principles and United States tax accounting principles, and translated into U.S. dollars as provided in § 1.985-3(c). The end-of-year dollar amount of the assets of the branch is determined in the same manner by reference to the end-of-year balance sheet for the current

taxable year. The beginning-of-year and end-of-year dollar tax book value of assets, as so determined, within each grouping is then averaged as provided in paragraph (g)(2)(i) of this section.

(g)(2)(ii)(B) through (g)(3) [Reserved]. For further guidance, see § 1.861-9T(g)(2)(ii)(B) through (g)(3).

(h) *Fair market value method.*—An affiliated group (as defined in section 1.861-11T(d)) or other taxpayer (the *taxpayer*) that elects to use the fair market value method of apportionment values its assets according to the methodology described in this paragraph (h). Effective for taxable years beginning after December 31, 2017, the fair market value method is not allowed for purposes of apportioning interest expense. *See* section 864(e)(2). However, a taxpayer may continue to apportion deductions other than interest expense that are properly apportioned based on fair market value according to the methodology described in this paragraph (h). *See* § 1.861-8(c)(2).

(h)(1) through (h)(3) [Reserved]. For further guidance, see § 1.861-9T(h)(1) through (h)(3).

\* \* \*

(5) *Characterizing stock in related persons.*—Stock in a related person held by the taxpayer or by another related person shall be characterized on the basis of the fair market value of the taxpayer's pro rata share of assets held by the related person attributed to each statutory grouping and the residual grouping under the stock characterization rules of § 1.861-12T(c)(3)(ii), except that the portion of the value of intangible assets of the taxpayer and related persons that is apportioned to the related person under § 1.861-9T(h)(2) shall be characterized on the basis of the net income before interest expense of the related person within each statutory grouping or residual grouping (excluding income that is passive under § 1.904-4(b)).

\* \* \*

(i) \* \* \*

(2) \* \* \*

(i) Except as provided in this paragraph (i)(2)(i), a taxpayer may elect to use the alternative tax book value method. For the taxpayer's first taxable year beginning after December 31, 2017, the Commissioner's approval is not required to switch from the fair market value method to the alternative tax book value method for purposes of apportioning interest expense. \* \* \*

\* \* \*

(j) through (j)(2)(i) [Reserved]. For further guidance, see § 1.861-9T(j) through (j)(2)(i).

(ii) *Step 2.*—Moving to the next higher-tier controlled foreign corporation, combine the gross income of such corporation within each grouping with its pro rata share (as determined under principles similar to section 951(a)(2)) of the gross income net of interest expense of all lower-tier controlled foreign corporations held by such higher-tier corporation within the same grouping adjusted as follows:

(A) Exclude from the gross income of the higher-tier corporation any dividends or other payments received from the lower-tier corporation other than interest income received from the lower-tier corporation;

(B) Exclude from the gross income net of interest expense of any lower-tier corporation any gross subpart F income, net of interest expense apportioned to such income;

(C) Exclude from the gross income net of interest expense of any lower-tier corporation any gross tested income as defined in §1.951A-2(c)(1), net of interest expense apportioned to such income;

(D) Then apportion the interest expense of the higher-tier controlled foreign corporation based on the adjusted combined gross income amounts; and

(E) Repeat paragraphs (j)(2)(ii)(A) through (D) of this section for each next higher-tier controlled foreign corporation in the chain.

(k) *Applicability date.*—This section applies to taxable years that both begin after December 31, 2017, and end on or after December 4, 2018.

[Proposed 12-7-2018.]

### [Prop. Reg. §1.861-10]

**§1.861-10. Special allocations of interest expense.**

\* \* \*

(e) \* \* \*

(8) \* \* \*

(vi) *Classification of hybrid stock.*—In determining the amount of its related group indebtedness for any taxable year, a U.S. shareholder must not treat stock in a related controlled foreign corporation as related group indebtedness, regardless of whether the related controlled foreign corporation claims a deduction for interest under foreign law for distributions on such stock. For purposes of determining the foreign base period ratio under paragraph (e)(2)(iv) of this section for a taxable year that ends on or after December 4, 2018, the rules of this paragraph (e)(8)(vi) apply to determine the related group debt-to-asset ratio in each taxable year included in the foreign base period, including in taxable years that end before December 4, 2018.

\* \* \*

(10) [Reserved]

\* \* \*

(f) *Applicability date.*—This section applies to taxable years that end on or after December 4, 2018.

[Proposed 12-7-2018.]

### [Prop. Reg. §1.861-11]

**§1.861-11. Special rules for allocating and apportioning interest expense of an affiliated group of corporations.**—(a) [Reserved]. For further guidance, see §1.861-11T(a).

(b) *Scope of application.*—(1) *Application of section 864(e)(1) and (5) (concerning the definition and treatment of affiliated groups).*—Section 864(e)(1) and (5) and the portions of this section implementing section 864(e)(1) and (5) apply to the computation of foreign source taxable income for purposes of section 904 (relating to various limitations on the foreign tax credit). Section 864(e)(1) and (5) and the portions of this section implementing section 864(e)(1) and (5) also apply in connection with section 907 to determine reductions in the amount allowed as a foreign tax credit under section 901. Section 864(e)(1) and (5) and the portions of this section implementing section 864(e)(1) and (5) also apply to the computation of the combined taxable income of the related supplier and a foreign sales corporation (FSC) (under sections 921 through 927) as well as the combined taxable income of the related supplier and a domestic international sales corporation (DISC) (under sections 991 through 997).

(b)(2) through (c) [Reserved]. For further guidance, see §1.861-11T(b)(2) through (c).

(d) \* \* \*

(2) [Reserved]

\* \* \*

(h) *Applicability dates.*—This section applies to taxable years that both begin after December 31, 2017, and end on or after December 4, 2018.

[Proposed 12-7-2018.]

### [Prop. Reg. §1.861-12]

**§1.861-12. Characterization rules and adjustments for certain assets.**—(a) *In general.*—The rules in this section are applicable to taxpayers in apportioning expenses under an asset method to income in the various separate categories described in §1.904-5(a)(4)(v), and supplement other rules provided in §§1.861-9 through 1.861-11T. The principles of the rules in this section are also applicable in apportioning expenses among statutory and residual groupings for any other operative section. See also §1.861-8(f)(2)(i) for a rule requiring conformity of allocation methods and apportionment principles for all operative sections. Paragraph (b) of this section describes the treatment of inventories. Paragraph (c)(1) of this section concerns the treatment of various stock assets. Paragraph (c)(2) of this section describes a basis adjustment for stock in 10 percent owned corporations. Paragraph (c)(3) of this section sets forth rules for characterizing the stock in controlled foreign corporations. Paragraph (c)(4) of this section describes the treatment of stock of noncontrolled 10-percent owned foreign corporations. Paragraph (d)(1) of this section concerns the treatment of notes. Paragraph (d)(2) of this section concerns the treatment of notes of controlled foreign corporations. Paragraph (e) of this section describes the treatment of certain portfolio securities that constitute inventory or generate income primarily in the form of gains. Paragraph (f) of this section describes the treatment of assets that are subject to the capitalization rules of section 263A. Paragraph (g) of this section concerns the treatment of FSC stock and of assets of the related supplier generating foreign trade income. Paragraph (h) of this section concerns the treatment of DISC stock and of assets of the related supplier generating qualified export receipts. Paragraph (i) of this section is reserved. Paragraph (j) of this section sets forth an example illustrating the rules of this section, as well as the rules of § 1.861-9(g).

(b) through (c)(1) [Reserved]. For further guidance, see § 1.861-12T(b) through (c)(1).

(2) *Basis adjustment for stock in 10 percent owned corporations.*—(i) * * *

(B) *Computational rules.*—(1) *Adjustments to basis.*—(i) *Application of section 961 or 1293(d).*—For purposes of this section, a taxpayer's adjusted basis in the stock of a foreign corporation does not include any amount included in basis under section 961 or 1293(d) of the Code.

(ii) *Application of section 965(b).*—If a taxpayer owned the stock of a specified foreign corporation (as defined in § 1.965-1(f)(45)) as of the close of the last taxable year of the specified foreign corporation that began before January 1, 2018, the taxpayer's adjusted basis in the stock of the specified foreign corporation for that taxable year and any subsequent taxable year is determined as if the taxpayer made the election described in § 1.965-2(f)(2)(i) (regardless of whether the election was actually made) but does not include the amount included (or that would be included if the election were made) in basis under § 1.965-2(f)(2)(ii)(A) (without regard to whether any portion of the amount is netted against the amounts of any other basis adjustments under § 1.965-2(h)(2)).

(2) *Amount of earnings and profits.*— For purposes of this paragraph (c)(2), earnings and profits (or deficits) are computed under the rules of section 312 and, in the case of a foreign corporation, sections 964(a) and 986 for taxable years of the 10 percent owned corporation ending on or before the close of the taxable year of the taxpayer. Accordingly, the earnings and profits of a controlled foreign corporation includes all earnings and profits described in section 959(c). The amount of the earnings and profits with respect to stock of a foreign corporation held by the taxpayer is determined according to the attribution principles of section 1248 and the regulations under section 1248. The attribution principles of section 1248 apply without regard to the requirements of section 1248 that are not relevant to the determination of a shareholder's pro rata portion of earnings and profits, such as whether earnings and profits (or deficits) were derived (or incurred) during taxable years beginning before or after December 31, 1962.

(3) *Annual noncumulative adjustment.*—The adjustment required by paragraph (c)(2)(i)(A) of this section is made annually and is noncumulative. Thus, the adjusted basis of the stock (determined without regard to prior years' adjustments under paragraph (c)(2)(i)(A) of this section) is adjusted annually by the amount of accumulated earnings and profits (or deficits) attributable to the stock as of the end of each year.

(4) *Translation of non-dollar functional currency earnings and profits.*—Earnings and profits (or deficits) of a qualified business unit that has a functional currency other than the dollar must be computed under this paragraph (c)(2) in functional currency and translated into dollars using the exchange rate at the end of the taxpayer's current taxable year (and not the exchange rates for the years in which the earnings and profits or deficits were derived or incurred).

(C) *Examples.*—The following examples illustrate the application of paragraph (c)(2)(i)(B) of this section.

(1) *Example 1: No election described in § 1.965-2(f)(2)(i)*—(i) *Facts.* USP, a domestic corporation, owns all of the stock of CFC1 and CFC2, both controlled foreign corporations. USP, CFC1, and CFC2 all use the calendar year as their U.S. taxable year. USP owned CFC1 and CFC2 as of December 31, 2017, and CFC1 and CFC2 were specified foreign corporations with respect to USP. USP did not make the election described in § 1.965-2(f)(2)(i), but if USP had made the election, USP's basis in the stock of CFC1 would have been increased by $75 under § 1.965-2(f)(2)(ii)(A) and USP's basis in the stock of CFC2 would have been decreased by $75 under § 1.965-2(f)(2)(ii)(B). For purposes of determining the value of the stock of CFC1 and CFC2 at the beginning of the 2019 taxable year, without regard to amounts included in basis under section 961 or 1293(d), USP's adjusted basis in the stock of CFC1 is $100 and its adjusted basis in the stock of CFC2 is $350 (before the application of this paragraph (c)(2)(i)(B)).

(ii) *Analysis.* Under paragraph (c)(2)(i)(B)(1) of this section, USP's adjusted basis in CFC1 and CFC2 is determined as if USP had made the election described in § 1.965-2(f)(2)(i), and therefore USP's adjusted basis in CFC2 includes the $75 reduction USP would have made to its basis in that stock under § 1.965-2(f)(2)(ii)(B). However, USP's adjusted basis in the stock of CFC1 does not include the $75 that USP would have included in its basis in that stock under § 1.965-2(f)(2)(ii)(A). Accordingly, for purposes of determining the value of stock of CFC1 and CFC2 at the beginning of the 2019 taxable year, USP's adjusted basis in the stock of CFC1 is $100 and USP's adjusted basis in the stock of CFC2 is $275 ($350 – $75).

(2) *Example 2: Election described in § 1.965-2(f)(2)(i)*—(i) *Facts.* USP, a domestic corporation, owns all of the stock of CFC1, which

owns all of the stock of CFC2, both foreign corporations. USP, CFC1, and CFC2 all use the calendar year as their U.S. taxable year. USP owned CFC1, and CFC1 owned CFC2 as of December 31, 2017, and CFC1 and CFC2 were specified foreign corporations with respect to USP. USP made the election described in § 1.965-2(f)(2)(i). As a result of the election, USP was required to increase its basis in CFC1 by $90 under § 1.965-2(f)(2)(ii)(A), and to decrease its basis in CFC1 by $90 under § 1.965-2(f)(2)(ii)(B). Pursuant to § 1.965-2(h)(2), USP netted the increase of $90 against the decrease of $90 and made no net adjustment to the basis of the stock of CFC1. For purposes of determining the value of the stock of CFC1 at the beginning of the 2019 taxable year, without regard to amounts included in basis under section 961 or 1293(d), USP's adjusted basis in the stock of CFC1 is $600 (before the application of this paragraph (c)(2)(i)(B)).

(ii) *Analysis.* Under paragraph (c)(2)(i)(B)(1) of this section, USP's adjusted basis in CFC1 is determined as if USP had made the election described in § 1.965-2(f)(2)(i), and therefore USP's adjusted basis in CFC1 includes the $90 reduction USP would have made to its basis in that stock, without regard to the netting rule described in § 1.965-2(h)(2). However, USP's adjusted basis in the stock of CFC1 does not include the amount that would have been included in basis under § 1.965-2(f)(2)(ii)(A) without regard to the netting rule described in § 1.965-2(h)(2). Accordingly, for purposes of determining the value of stock of CFC1 at the beginning of the 2019 taxable year, USP's adjusted basis in the stock of CFC1 is $510 ($600 – $90).

(c)(2)(ii) through (c)(2)(vi) [Reserved]. For further guidance, see § 1.861-12T(c)(2)(ii) through (c)(2)(vi).

(3) *Characterization of stock of controlled foreign corporations.*—(i) *Operative sections.*—(A) *Operative sections other than section 904.*—For purposes of applying this section to an operative section other than section 904, stock in a controlled foreign corporation (as defined in section 957) is characterized as an asset in the relevant groupings on the basis of the asset method described in paragraph (c)(3)(ii) of this section, or the modified gross income method described in paragraph (c)(3)(iii) of this section. Stock in a controlled foreign corporation whose interest expense is apportioned on the basis of assets is characterized in the hands of its United States shareholders under the asset method described in paragraph (c)(3)(ii) of this section. Stock in a controlled foreign corporation whose interest expense is apportioned on the basis of modified gross income is characterized in the hands of its United States shareholders under the modified gross income method described in paragraph (c)(3)(iii) of this section.

(B) *Section 904 as operative section.*—For purposes of applying this section to section 904 as the operative section, § 1.861-13 applies to

characterize the stock of a controlled foreign corporation as an asset producing foreign source income in the separate categories described in § 1.904-5(a)(4)(v), or as an asset producing U.S. source income in the residual grouping, in the hands of the United States shareholder, and to determine the portion of the stock that gives rise to an inclusion under section 951A(a) that is treated as an exempt asset under § 1.861-8(d)(2)(ii)(C). Section 1.861-13 also provides rules for subdividing the stock in the various separate categories and the residual grouping into a section 245A subgroup and a non-section 245A subgroup in order to determine the amount of the adjustments required by section 904(b)(4) and § 1.904(b)-3(c) with respect to the section 245A subgroup, and provides rules for determining the portion of the stock that gives rise to a dividend eligible for a deduction under section 245(a)(5) that is treated as an exempt asset under § 1.861-8(d)(2)(ii)(B).

(ii) [Reserved]. For further guidance, see § 1.861-12T(c)(3)(ii).

(iii) *Modified gross income method.*—Under the modified gross income method, the taxpayer characterizes the tax book value of the stock of the first-tier controlled foreign corporation based on the gross income, net of interest expense, of the controlled foreign corporation (as computed under § 1.861-9T(j) to include certain gross income, net of interest expense, of lower-tier controlled foreign corporations) within each relevant category for the taxable year of the controlled foreign corporation ending with or within the taxable year of the taxpayer. For this purpose, however, the gross income, net of interest expense, of the first-tier controlled foreign corporation includes the total amount of gross subpart F income, net of interest expense, of any lower-tier controlled foreign corporation that was excluded under the rules of § 1.861-9(j)(2)(ii)(B). The gross income, net of interest expense, of the first-tier controlled foreign corporation also includes the total amount of gross tested income, net of interest expense, of any lower-tier controlled foreign corporation that was excluded under the rules of § 1.861-9(j)(2)(ii)(C).

(4) *Characterization of stock of noncontrolled 10-percent owned foreign corporations.*—(i) *In general.*—Except in the case of a nonqualifying shareholder described in paragraph (c)(4)(ii) of this section, the principles of § 1.861-12(c)(3), including the relevant rules of § 1.861-13 when section 904 is the operative section, apply to characterize stock in a noncontrolled 10-percent owned foreign corporation (as defined in section 904(d)(2)(E)). Accordingly, stock in a noncontrolled 10-percent owned foreign corporation is characterized as an asset in the various separate categories on the basis of either the asset method described in § 1.861-12T(c)(3)(ii) or the modified gross income method described in § 1.861-12(c)(3)(iii). Stock in a noncontrolled 10-percent owned foreign corporation the interest expense of which is apportioned on the basis

of assets is characterized in the hands of its shareholders under the asset method described in § 1.861-12T(c)(3)(ii). Stock in a noncontrolled 10-percent owned foreign corporation the interest expense of which is apportioned on the basis of gross income is characterized in the hands of its shareholders under the modified gross income method described in § 1.861-12(c)(3)(iii).

(ii) *Nonqualifying shareholders.*—Stock in a noncontrolled 10-percent owned foreign corporation is characterized as a passive category asset in the hands of a shareholder that either is not a domestic corporation or is not a United States shareholder with respect to the noncontrolled 10-percent owned foreign corporation for the taxable year. Stock in a noncontrolled 10-percent owned foreign corporation is characterized as in the separate category described in section 904(d)(4)(C)(ii) in the hands of any shareholder with respect to whom look-through treatment is not substantiated. *See also* § 1.904-5(c)(4)(iii)(B). In the case of a noncontrolled 10-percent owned foreign corporation that is a passive foreign investment company with respect to a shareholder, stock in the noncontrolled 10-percent owned foreign corporation is characterized as a passive category asset in the hands of the shareholder if such shareholder does not meet the ownership requirements described in section 904(d)(2)(E)(i)(II).

(d) *Treatment of notes.*—(1) *General rule.*—[Reserved]. For further guidance, see § 1.861-12T(d)(1).

(2) *Characterization of related controlled foreign corporation notes.*—The debt of a controlled foreign corporation is characterized in the same manner as the interest income derived from that debt obligation. See §§ 1.904-4 and 1.904-5(c)(2) for rules treating interest income as income in a separate category.

(e) through (j) [Reserved]. For further guidance, see § 1.861-12T(e) through (j).

(k) *Applicability date.*—This section applies to taxable years that both begin after December 31, 2017, and end on or after December 4, 2018. Section 1.861-12(c)(2)(i)(B)(1)(ii) also applies to the last taxable year of a foreign corporation that begins before January 1, 2018, and with respect to a United States person, the taxable year in which or with which such taxable year of the foreign corporation ends.

[Proposed 12-7-2018.]

**[Prop. Reg. § 1.861-13]**

**§ 1.861-13. Payment and returns of tax withheld by the acquiring agency.**—
(a) *Methodology.*—For purposes of allocating and apportioning deductions for purposes of section 904 as the operative section, stock in a controlled foreign corporation owned directly or indirectly through a partnership or other pass-through entity by a United States shareholder is characterized by the United States shareholder under the rules described in this section. In general, paragraphs (a)(1) through (5) of this section characterize the stock of the controlled foreign corporation as an asset in the various statutory groupings and residual grouping based on the type of income that the stock of the controlled foreign corporation generates, has generated, or may reasonably be expected to generate when the income is included by the United States shareholder.

(1) *Step 1: Characterize stock as generating income in statutory groupings under the asset or modified gross income method.*—(i) *Asset method.*— United States shareholders using the asset method to characterize stock of a controlled foreign corporation must apply the asset method described in § 1.861-12T(c)(3)(ii) to assign the assets of the controlled foreign corporation to the statutory groupings described in paragraphs (a)(1)(i)(A)(1) through (10) and (a)(1)(i)(B) of this section. If the controlled foreign corporation owns stock in a lower-tier noncontrolled 10-percent owned foreign corporation, the assets of the lower-tier noncontrolled 10-percent owned foreign corporation are assigned to a gross subpart F income grouping to the extent such assets generate income that, if distributed to the controlled foreign corporation, would be gross subpart F income of the controlled foreign corporation. *See also* § 1.861-12(c)(4).

(A) *General and passive categories.*— Within each of the controlled foreign corporation's general category and passive category, each of the following subgroups within each category is a separate statutory grouping—

(1) Foreign source gross tested income;

(2) For each applicable treaty, U.S. source gross tested income that, when taken into account by a United States shareholder under section 951A, is resourced in the hands of the United States shareholder (*resourced gross tested income*);

(3) U.S. source gross tested income not described in paragraph (a)(1)(i)(A)(2) of this section;

(4) Foreign source gross subpart F income;

(5) For each applicable treaty, U.S. source gross subpart F income that, when included by a United States shareholder under section 951(a)(1), is resourced in the hands of the United States shareholder (*resourced gross subpart F income*);

(6) U.S. source gross subpart F income not described in paragraph (a)(1)(i)(A)(5) of this section;

(7) Foreign source gross section 245(a)(5) income;

(8) U.S. source gross section 245(a)(5) income;

(9) Any other foreign source gross income (*specified foreign source general category in-*

come or *specified foreign source passive category income*, as the case may be); and

(10) Any other U.S. source gross income (*specified U.S. source general category gross income* or *specified U.S. source passive category gross income*, as the case may be).

(B) *Section 901(j) income.*—For each country described in section 901(j), all gross income from sources in that country.

(ii) *Modified gross income method.*—United States shareholders using the modified gross income method to characterize stock in a controlled foreign corporation must apply the modified gross income method under § 1.861-12(c)(3)(iii) to assign the modified gross income of the controlled foreign corporation to the statutory groupings described in paragraphs (a)(1)(i)(A)(1) through (10) and (a)(1)(i)(B) of this section. For this purpose, the rules described in §§ 1.861-12(c)(3)(iii) and 1.861-9T(j)(2) apply to combine gross income in a statutory grouping that is earned by the controlled foreign corporation with gross income of lower-tier controlled foreign corporations that is in the same statutory grouping. For example, foreign source general category gross tested income (net of interest expense) earned by the controlled foreign corporation is combined with its pro rata share of the foreign source general category gross tested income (net of interest expense) of lower-tier controlled foreign corporations. If the controlled foreign corporation owns stock in a lower-tier noncontrolled 10-percent owned foreign corporation, gross income of the lower-tier noncontrolled 10-percent owned foreign corporation is assigned to a gross subpart F income grouping to the extent that the income, if distributed to the upper-tier controlled foreign corporation, would be gross subpart F income of the upper-tier controlled foreign corporation. *See also* § 1.861-12(c)(4).

(2) *Step 2: Assign stock to the section 951A category.*—A controlled foreign corporation is not treated as earning section 951A category income. The portion of the value of the stock of the controlled foreign corporation that is assigned to the section 951A category equals the value of the portion of the stock of the controlled foreign corporation that is assigned to the foreign source gross tested income statutory groupings within the general category (*general category gross tested income stock*) multiplied by the United States shareholder's inclusion percentage. Under § 1.861-8(d)(2)(ii)(C)(2)(*ii*), a portion of the value of stock assigned to the section 951A category may be treated as an exempt asset. The portion of the general category gross tested income stock that is not characterized as a section 951A category asset remains a general category asset and may result in expenses being disregarded under section 904(b)(4). See paragraph (a)(5)(ii) of this section and § 1.904(b)-3. No portion of the passive category gross tested income stock or U.S.

source gross tested income stock is assigned to the section 951A category.

(3) *Step 3: Assign stock to a treaty category.*—(i) *Inclusions under section 951A(a).*—The portion of the value of the stock of the controlled foreign corporation that is assigned to a particular treaty category due to an inclusion of U.S. source income under section 951A(a) that was resourced under a particular treaty equals the value of the portion of the stock of the controlled foreign corporation that is assigned to the resourced gross tested income statutory grouping within each of the controlled foreign corporation's general or passive categories (*resourced gross tested income stock*) multiplied by the United States shareholder's inclusion percentage. Under § 1.861-8(d)(2)(ii)(C)(2)(*ii*), a portion of the value of stock assigned to a particular treaty category by reason of this paragraph (a)(3)(i) may be treated as an exempt asset. The portion of the resourced gross tested income stock that is not characterized as a treaty category asset remains a U.S. source general and passive category asset, as the case may be, that is in the residual grouping and may result in expenses being disregarded under section 904(b)(4) for purposes of determining entire taxable income under section 904(a). *See* paragraph (a)(5)(iv) of this section and § 1.904(b)-3.

(ii) *Inclusions under section 951(a)(1).*—The portion of the value of the stock of the controlled foreign corporation that is assigned to a particular treaty category due to an inclusion of U.S. source income under section 951(a)(1) that was resourced under a treaty equals the value of the portion of the stock of the controlled foreign corporation that is assigned to the resourced gross subpart F income statutory grouping within each of the controlled foreign corporation's general category or passive category.

(4) *Step 4: Aggregate stock within each separate category and assign stock to the residual grouping.*—The portions of the value of stock of the controlled foreign corporation assigned to foreign source statutory groupings that were not specifically assigned to the section 951A category under paragraph (a)(2) of this section (Step 2) are aggregated within the general category and the passive category to characterize the stock as general category stock and passive category stock, respectively. The portions of the value of stock of the controlled foreign corporation assigned to U.S. source statutory groupings that were not specifically assigned to a particular treaty category under paragraph (a)(3) of this section (Step 3) are aggregated to characterize the stock as U.S. source category stock, which is in the residual grouping. Stock assigned to the separate category for income described in section 901(j)(1) remains in that category.

(5) *Step 5: Determine section 245A and non-section 245A subgroups for each separate category*

*and U.S. source category.*—(i) *In general.*—In the case of stock of a controlled foreign corporation that is held directly or indirectly through a partnership or other pass-through entity by a United States shareholder that is a domestic corporation, stock of the controlled foreign corporation that is general category stock, passive category stock, and U.S. source category stock is subdivided between a section 245A subgroup and a non-section 245A subgroup under paragraphs (a)(5)(ii) through (v) of this section for purposes of applying section 904(b)(4) and §1.904(b)-3(c). Each subgroup is treated as a statutory grouping under §1.861-8(a)(4) for purposes of allocating and apportioning deductions under §§1.861-8 through 1.861-14T and 1.861-17 in applying section 904 as the operative section. Deductions apportioned to each section 245A subgroup are disregarded under section 904(b)(4). *See* §1.904(b)-3. Deductions apportioned to the statutory groupings for gross section 245(a)(5) income are not disregarded under section 904(b)(4); however, a portion of the stock assigned to those groupings is treated as exempt under §1.861-8T(d)(2)(ii)(B).

(ii) *Section 245A subgroup of general category stock.*—The portion of the general category stock of the controlled foreign corporation that is assigned to the section 245A subgroup of the general category equals the value of the general category gross tested income stock of the controlled foreign corporation that is not assigned to the section 951A category under paragraph (a)(2) of this section (Step 2), plus the value of the portion of the stock of the controlled foreign corporation that is assigned to the specified foreign source general category income statutory grouping.

(iii) *Section 245A subgroup of passive category stock.*—The portion of passive category stock of the controlled foreign corporation that is assigned to the section 245A subcategory of the passive category equals the sum of—

(A) The value of the portion of the stock of the controlled foreign corporation that is assigned to the gross tested income statutory grouping within foreign source passive category income multiplied by a percentage equal to 100 percent minus the United States shareholder's inclusion percentage for passive category gross tested income; and

(B) The value of the portion of the stock of the controlled foreign corporation that was assigned to the specified foreign source passive category income statutory grouping.

(iv) *Section 245A subgroup of U.S. source category stock.*—The portion of U.S. source category stock of the controlled foreign corporation that is assigned to the section 245A subgroup of the U.S. source category equals the sum of—

(A) The value of the portion of the stock of the controlled foreign corporation that is assigned to the U.S. source general category gross tested income statutory grouping multi-

plied by a percentage equal to 100 percent minus the United States shareholder's inclusion percentage for the general category;

(B) The value of the portion of the stock of the controlled foreign corporation that is assigned to the U.S. source passive category gross tested income statutory grouping multiplied by a percentage equal to 100 percent minus the United States shareholder's inclusion percentage for the passive category;

(C) The value of the resourced gross tested income stock of the controlled foreign corporation that is not assigned to a particular treaty category under paragraph (a)(3)(i) of this section (Step 3);

(D) The value of the portion of the stock of the controlled foreign corporation that is assigned to the specified U.S. source general category gross income statutory grouping; and

(E) The value of the portion of the stock of the controlled foreign corporation that is assigned to the specified U.S. source passive category gross income statutory grouping.

(v) *Non-section 245A subgroup.*—The value of stock of a controlled foreign corporation that is not assigned to the section 245A subgroup within the general or passive category or the residual grouping is assigned to the non-section 245A subgroup within such category or grouping. The value of stock of a controlled foreign corporation that is assigned to the section 951A category, the separate category for income described in section 901(j)(1), or a particular treaty category is always assigned to a non-section 245A subgroup.

(b) *Definitions.*—This paragraph (b) provides definitions that apply for purposes of this section.

(1) *Gross section 245(a)(5) income.*—The term *gross section 245(a)(5) income* means all items of gross income described in section 245(a)(5)(A) and (B).

(2) *Gross subpart F income.*—The term *gross subpart F income* means all items of gross income that are taken into account by a controlled foreign corporation in determining its subpart F income under section 952, except for items of gross income described in section 952(a)(5).

(3) *Gross tested income.*—The term *gross tested income* has the meaning provided in §1.951A-1(c)(1).

(4) *Inclusion percentage.*—The term *inclusion percentage* has the meaning provided in §1.960-2(c)(2).

(5) *Separate category.*—The term *separate category* has the meaning provided in §1.904-5(a)(4)(v).

(6) *Treaty category.*—The term *treaty category* means a category of income earned by a controlled foreign corporation for which section

**Prop. Reg. §1.861-13(b)(6)**

904(a), (b), and (c) are applied separately as a result of income being resourced under a treaty. See, for example, section 245(a)(10), 865(h), or 904(h)(10). A United States shareholder may have multiple treaty categories for amounts of income resourced by the United States shareholder under a treaty. *See* § 1.904-5(m)(7).

(7) *U.S. source category.*—The term *U.S. source category* means the aggregate of U.S. source income in each separate category listed in section 904(d)(1).

(c) *Examples.*—The following examples illustrate the application of the rules in this section.

(1) *Example 1: Asset method*—(i) *Facts*—(A) USP, a domestic corporation, directly owns all of the stock of a controlled foreign corporation, CFC1. The tax book value of CFC1's stock is $20,000. USP uses the asset method described in § 1.861-12T(c)(3)(ii) to characterize the stock of CFC1. USP's inclusion percentage is 70%.

(B) CFC1 owns the following assets with the following values as determined under §§ 1.861-9(g)(2) and 1.861-9T(g)(3): assets that generate income described in the foreign source gross tested income statutory grouping within the general category ($4,000), assets that generate income described in the foreign source gross subpart F income statutory grouping within the general category ($1,000), assets that generate specified foreign source general category income ($3,000), and assets that generate income described in the foreign source gross subpart F income statutory grouping within the passive category ($2,000).

(C) CFC1 also owns all of the stock of CFC2, a controlled foreign corporation. The tax book value of CFC1's stock in CFC2 is $5,000. CFC2 owns the following assets with the following values as determined under §§ 1.861-9(g)(2) and 1.861-9T(g)(3): assets that generate income described in the foreign source gross subpart F income statutory grouping within the general category ($2,250) and assets that generate specified foreign source general category income ($750).

(ii) *Analysis*—(A) *Step 1*—(1) *Characterization of CFC2 stock.* CFC2 has total assets of $3,000, $2,250 of which are in the foreign source gross subpart F income statutory grouping within the general category and $750 of which are in the specified foreign source general category income statutory grouping. Accordingly, CFC2's stock is characterized as $3,750 ($2,250/$3,000 x $5,000) in the foreign source gross subpart F income statutory grouping within the general category and $1,250 ($750/$3,000 x $5,000) in the specified foreign source general category income statutory grouping.

(2) *Characterization of CFC1 stock.* CFC1 has total assets of $15,000, $4,000 of which are in the foreign source gross tested income statutory grouping within the general category, $4,750 of which are in the foreign source gross subpart F income statutory grouping within the general category (including the portion of CFC2 stock

assigned to that statutory grouping), $4,250 of which are in the specified foreign source general category income statutory grouping (including the portion of CFC2 stock assigned to that statutory grouping), and $2,000 of which are in the foreign source gross subpart F income statutory grouping within the passive category. Accordingly, CFC1's stock is characterized as $5,333 ($4,000/$15,000 x $20,000) in the foreign source gross tested income statutory grouping within the general category, $6,333 ($4,750/$15,000 x $20,000) in the foreign source gross subpart F income statutory grouping within the general category, $5,667 ($4,250/$15,000 x $20,000) in the specified foreign source general category income statutory grouping, and $2,667 ($2,000/$15,000 x $20,000) in the foreign source gross subpart F income statutory grouping within the passive category.

(B) *Step 2.* The portion of the value of the stock of CFC1 that is general category gross tested income stock is $5,333. USP's inclusion percentage is 70%. Accordingly, under paragraph (a)(2) of this section, $3,733 of the stock of CFC1 is assigned to the section 951A category and a portion thereof may be treated as an exempt asset under § 1.861-8(d)(2)(ii)(C)(2)(*ii*). The remainder, $1,600, remains a general category asset.

(C) *Step 3.* No portion of the stock of CFC1 is resourced gross tested income stock or assigned to the resourced gross subpart F income statutory grouping in any treaty category. Accordingly, no portion of the stock of CFC1 is assigned to a treaty category under paragraph (a)(3) of this section.

(D) *Step 4*—(1) *General category stock.* The total portion of the value of the stock of CFC1 that is general category stock is $13,600, which is equal to $1,600 (the portion of the value of the general category stock of CFC1 that was not assigned to the section 951A category in Step 2) plus $5,667 (the value of the portion of the stock of CFC1 assigned to the specified foreign source income statutory grouping within the general category) plus $6,333 (the value of the portion of the stock of CFC1 assigned to the foreign source gross subpart F income statutory grouping within the general category).

(2) *Passive category stock.* The total portion of the value of the stock of CFC1 that is passive category stock is $2,667.

(3) *U.S source category stock.* No portion of the value of the stock of CFC1 is U.S. source category stock.

(E) *Step 5*—(1) *General category stock.* Under paragraph (a)(5)(ii) of this section, the value of the stock of CFC1 assigned to the section 245A subgroup of general category stock is $7,267, which is equal to $1,600 (the portion of the value of the general category stock of CFC1 that was not assigned to the section 951A category in Step 2) plus $5,667 (the value of the portion of the stock of CFC1 assigned to the specified foreign source general category income statutory grouping). Under paragraph (a)(5)(v) of this section, the remainder of the general category stock of

CFC1, $6,333, is assigned to the non-section 245A subgroup of general category stock.

(2) *Passive category stock.* No portion of the passive category stock of CFC1 is in the foreign source gross tested income statutory grouping or the specified foreign source passive category income statutory grouping. Accordingly, under paragraph (a)(5)(iii) of this section, no portion of the value of the stock of CFC1 is assigned to the section 245A subgroup of passive category stock. Under paragraph (a)(5)(v) of this section, the passive category stock of CFC1, $2,667 is assigned to the non-section 245A subgroup of passive category stock.

(3) *Section 951A category stock.* Under paragraph (a)(5)(v) of this section, all of the section 951A category stock, $3,733, is assigned to the non-section 245A subgroup of section 951A category stock.

(F) *Summary.* For purpose of the allocation and apportionment of expenses, $13,600 of the stock of CFC1 is characterized as general category stock, $7,267 of which is in the section 245A subgroup and $6,333 of which is in the non-section 245A subgroup; $2,667 of the stock of CFC1 is characterized as passive category stock, all of which is in the non-section 245A subgroup; and $3,733 of the stock of CFC1 is characterized as section 951A category stock, all of which is in the non-section 245A subgroup.

(2) *Example 2: Asset method with noncontrolled 10-percent owned foreign corporation*—(i) *Facts.* The facts are the same as in paragraph (c)(1)(i) of this section, except that CFC1 does not own CFC2 and instead owns 20% of the stock of FC2, a foreign corporation that is a noncontrolled 10-percent owned foreign corporation. The tax book value of CFC1's stock in FC2 is $5,000. FC2 owns assets with the following values as determined under §§ 1.861-9(g)(2) and 1.861-9T(g)(3): assets that generate specified foreign source general category income ($3,000). All of the assets of FC2 generate income that, if distributed to CFC1 as a dividend, would be foreign source gross subpart F income in the general category to CFC1.

(ii) *Analysis*—(A) *Step 1*—(1) *Characterization of FC2 stock.* All of the assets of FC2 generate income that, if distributed to CFC1, would be foreign source gross subpart F income in the general category to CFC1. Accordingly, under paragraph (a)(1)(i) of this section, all of CFC1's stock in FC2 ($5,000) is characterized as in the foreign source gross subpart F income statutory grouping within the general category.

(2) *Characterization of CFC1 stock.* CFC1 has total assets of $15,000, $4,000 of which are in the foreign source gross tested income statutory grouping within the general category, $6,000 of which are in the foreign source gross subpart F income statutory grouping within the general category (including the FC2 stock assigned to that statutory grouping), $3,000 of which are in the specified foreign source general category income statutory grouping, and $2,000 of which are in the foreign source gross subpart F income

statutory grouping within the passive category. Accordingly, CFC1's stock is characterized as $5,333 ($4,000/$15,000 x $20,000) in the foreign source gross tested income statutory grouping within the general category, $8,000 ($6,000/$15,000 x $20,000) in the foreign source gross subpart F income statutory grouping within the general category, $4,000 ($3,000/$15,000 x $20,000) in the specified foreign source general category income statutory grouping, and $2,667 ($2,000/$15,000 x $20,000) in the foreign source gross subpart F income statutory grouping within the passive category.

(B) *Step 2.* The analysis is the same as in paragraph (c)(1)(ii)(B) of this section.

(C) *Step 3.* The analysis is the same as in paragraph (c)(1)(ii)(C) of this section.

(D) *Step 4*—(1) *General category stock.* The total portion of the value of the stock of CFC1 that is general category stock is $13,600, which is equal to $1,600 (the portion of the value of the general category stock of CFC1 that was not assigned to the section 951A category in Step 2) plus $4,000 (the value of the portion of the stock of CFC1 assigned to the specified foreign source income statutory grouping within the general category general category) plus $8,000 (the value of the portion of the stock of CFC1 assigned to the foreign source gross subpart F income statutory grouping within the general category).

(2) *Passive category stock.* The analysis is the same as in paragraph (c)(1)(ii)(D)(2) of this section.

(E) *Step 5*—(1) *General category stock.* Under paragraph (a)(5)(ii) of this section, the value of the stock of CFC1 assigned to the section 245A subgroup of general category stock is $5,600, which is equal to $1,600 (the portion of the value of the general category stock of CFC1 that was not assigned to the section 951A category in Step 2) plus $4,000 (the value of the portion of the stock of CFC1 assigned to the specified foreign source general category income statutory grouping). Under paragraph (a)(5)(v) of this section, the remainder of the general category stock of CFC1, $8,000, is assigned to the non-section 245A subgroup of general category stock.

(2) *Passive category stock.* The analysis is the same as in paragraph (c)(1)(ii)(E)(2) of this section.

(3) *Section 951A category stock.* The analysis is the same as in paragraph (c)(1)(ii)(E)(3) of this section.

(F) *Summary.* For purpose of the allocation and apportionment of expenses, $13,600 of the stock of CFC1 is characterized as general category stock, $5,600 of which is in the section 245A subgroup and $8,000 of which is in the non-section 245A subgroup; $2,667 of the stock of CFC1 is characterized as passive category stock, all of which is in the non-section 245A subgroup; and $3,733 of the stock of CFC1 is characterized as section 951A category stock, all of which is in the non-section 245A subgroup.

**Prop. Reg. § 1.861-13(c)**

(3) *Example 3: Modified gross income method*—(i) *Facts*—(A) USP, a domestic corporation, directly owns all of the stock of a controlled foreign corporation, CFC1. The tax book value of CFC1's stock is $100,000. CFC1 owns all of the stock of CFC2, a controlled foreign corporation. USP uses the modified gross income method described in § 1.861-12(c)(3)(iii) to characterize the stock in CFC1. USP's inclusion percentage is 100%.

(B) CFC1 earns $1,500 of foreign source gross tested income within the general category and $500 of foreign source gross subpart F income within the passive category. CFC1 incurs $200 of interest expense.

(C) CFC2 earns $3,000 of foreign source gross tested income within the general category, $2,000 of foreign source gross subpart F income within the general category, and $1,000 of specified foreign source general category income. CFC2 incurs $3,000 of interest expense.

(ii) *Analysis*—(A) *Step 1*—(1) *Determination of CFC2 gross income (net of interest expense)*. CFC2 has total gross income of $6,000. CFC2's $3,000 of interest expense is apportioned among the statutory groupings of gross income based on the gross income of CFC2 to determine the gross income (net of interest expense) of CFC2 in each statutory grouping. As a result, $1,500 ($3,000/$6,000 x $3,000) of interest expense is apportioned to foreign source gross tested income within the general category, $1,000 ($2,000/$6,000 x $3,000) of interest expense is apportioned to foreign source gross subpart F income within the general category, and $500 ($1,000/$6,000 x $3,000) of interest expense is apportioned to specified foreign source general category income. Accordingly, CFC2 has the following amounts of gross income (net of interest expense): $1,500 ($3,000 − $1,500) of foreign source gross tested income within the general category, $1,000 ($2,000 − $1,000) of foreign source gross subpart F income within the general category, and $500 ($1,000 − $500) of specified foreign source general category income.

(2) *Determination of CFC1 gross income (net of interest expense)*. Before including the gross income consisting of subpart F income and tested income (net of interest expense) of CFC2, CFC1 has total gross income of $2,500, including $500 of CFC2's specified foreign source general category income which is combined with CFC1's items of gross income under § 1.861-9(j)(2)(ii). CFC1's $200 of interest expense is apportioned among the statutory groupings of gross income of CFC1 to determine the gross income (net of interest expense) of CFC1 in each statutory grouping. As a result, $120 ($1,500/$2,500 x $200) of interest expense is apportioned to foreign source gross tested income within the general category, $40 ($500/$2,500 x $200) to foreign source gross subpart F income within the passive category, and $40 ($500/$2,500 x $200) to specified foreign source general category income. Accordingly, CFC1 has the following amounts of gross income (net of interest expense) before including the gross income (net of interest expense) of CFC2: $1,380 ($1,500 − $120) of foreign source gross tested income within the general category, $460 ($500 − $40) of foreign source gross subpart F income within the passive category, and $460 ($500 − $40) of specified foreign source general category income. After including the gross income consisting of subpart F income and tested income (net of interest expense) of CFC2, CFC1 has the following amounts of gross income (net of interest expense): $2,880 ($1,380 + $1,500) of foreign source gross tested income within the general category, $1,000 of foreign source gross subpart F income within the general category, $460 of specified foreign source general category income, and $460 of foreign source gross subpart F income within the passive category.

(3) *Characterization of CFC1 stock*. CFC1 is considered to have a total of $4,800 of gross income (net of interest expense) for purposes of characterizing the stock of CFC1. Accordingly, CFC1's stock is characterized as $60,000 ($2,880/$4,800 x $100,000) in the foreign source gross tested income statutory grouping within the general category, $20,834 ($1,000/$4,800 x $100,000) in the foreign source gross subpart F income statutory grouping within the general category, $9,583 ($460/$4,800 x $100,000) in the specified foreign source general category income statutory grouping, and $9,583 ($460/$4,800 x $100,000) in the foreign source gross subpart F income statutory grouping within the passive category.

(B) *Step 2*. The portion of the value of the stock of CFC1 that is general category gross tested income stock is $60,000. USP's inclusion percentage is 100%. Accordingly, under paragraph (a)(2) of this section, all of the $60,000 of the stock of CFC1 is assigned to the section 951A category.

(C) *Step 3*. No portion of the stock of CFC1 is resourced gross tested income or assigned to the resourced gross subpart F income statutory group in any treaty category. Accordingly, no portion of the stock of CFC1 is assigned to a treaty category under paragraph (a)(3) of this section.

(D) *Step 4*—(1) *General category stock*. The total portion of the value of the stock of CFC1 that is general category stock is $30,417, which is equal to $20,834 (the value of the portion of the stock of CFC1 assigned to the subpart F income statutory grouping within the general category income statutory grouping) plus $9,583 (the value of the portion of the stock of CFC1 assigned to the specified foreign source general category income statutory grouping).

(2) *Passive category stock*. The total portion of the value of the stock of CFC1 that is passive category stock is $9,583.

(3) *U.S. source category stock*. No portion of the value of the stock of CFC1 is U.S. source category stock.

(E) *Step 5*—(1) *General category stock*. All of the value of the general category gross tested income stock of CFC1 was assigned to the section 951A category in Step 2. Accordingly, under paragraph (a)(5)(ii) of this section, the value of the stock of CFC1 assigned to the section 245A subgroup of general category stock is $9,583, which is equal to the value of the portion assigned to the specified foreign source general category income statutory grouping. Under paragraph (a)(5)(v) of this section, the remainder of the general category stock of CFC1, $20,834, is assigned to the non-section 245A subgroup of general category stock.

(2) *Passive category stock.* No portion of the passive category stock of CFC1 is in the foreign source gross tested income statutory grouping or the specified foreign source passive category income statutory grouping. Accordingly, under paragraph (a)(5)(iii) of this section, no portion of the value of the stock of CFC1 is assigned to the section 245A subgroup. Under paragraph (a)(5)(v) of this section, the passive category stock of CFC1, $9,534, is assigned to the non-section 245A subgroup of passive category stock.

(3) *Section 951A category stock.* Under paragraph (a)(5)(v) of this section, all of the section 951A category stock, $60,000, is assigned to the non-section 245A subgroup of section 951A category stock.

(F) *Summary.* For purposes of the allocation and apportionment of expenses, $60,000 of the stock of CFC1 is characterized as section 951A category stock, all of which is in the non-section 245A subgroup; $30,417 of the stock of CFC1 is characterized as general category stock, $9,583 of which is in the section 245A subgroup and $20,834 of which is in the non-section 245A subgroup; and $9,583 of the stock of CFC1 is characterized as passive category stock, all of which is in the non-section 245A subgroup.

(d) *Applicability dates.*—This section applies for taxable years that both begin after December 31, 2017, and end on or after December 4, 2018. [Reg. § 1.861-13.]

[Proposed 12-7-2018.]

### [Prop. Reg. § 1.861-17]

**§ 1.861-17. Allocation and apportionment of research and experimental expenditures.**

\* \* \*

(e) \* \* \*

(3) *Change of method for first taxable year beginning after December 31, 2017.*—A taxpayer otherwise subject to the binding election described in paragraph (e)(1) of this section may change its method once for its first taxable year beginning after December 31, 2017, without the prior consent of the Commissioner. The taxpayer's use of a new method constitutes a binding election to use the new method for its return filed for the first year for which the taxpayer uses the new method and for four taxable years thereafter.

\* \* \*

(g) [Reserved]

\* \* \*

(i) *Applicability date.*—This section applies to taxable years that both begin after December 31, 2017, and end on or after December 4, 2018.

[Proposed 12-7-2018.]

### [Prop. Reg. § 1.864(c)(8)-1]

**§ 1.864(c)(8)-1. Gain or loss by foreign persons on the disposition of certain partnership interests.**—(a) *Overview.*—This section provides rules and definitions under section 864(c)(8). Paragraph (b) of this section provides the general rule treating gain or loss recognized by a nonresident alien individual or foreign corporation from the sale or exchange of a partnership interest as effectively connected gain or effectively connected loss. Paragraph (c) of this section provides rules for determining the limitation on the amount of effectively connected gain or effectively connected loss under section 864(c)(8) and paragraph (b) of this section. Paragraph (d) of this section provides rules regarding coordination with section 897. Paragraph (e) of this section provides rules regarding certain tiered partnerships. Paragraph (f) of this section provides rules regarding U.S. income tax treaties. Paragraph (g) of this section provides definitions. Paragraph (h) of this section provides a rule regarding certain contributions of property to a partnership. Paragraph (i) of this section contains examples illustrating the rules set forth in this section. Paragraph (j) of this section provides the applicability date.

(b) *Gain or loss treated as effectively connected gain or loss.*—(1) *In general.*—Notwithstanding any other provision of subtitle A of the Internal Revenue Code, if a foreign transferor owns, directly or indirectly, an interest in a partnership that is engaged in the conduct of a trade or business within the United States, outside capital gain, outside capital loss, outside ordinary gain, or outside ordinary loss (each as defined in paragraph (b)(2) of this section) recognized by the foreign transferor on the transfer of all (or any portion) of the interest is treated as effectively connected gain or effectively connected loss, subject to the limit described in paragraph (b)(3) of this section. Except as provided in paragraph (d) of this section, this section does not apply to prevent any portion of the gain or loss that is otherwise treated as effectively connected gain or effectively connected loss under provisions of the Internal Revenue Code other than section 864(c)(8) from being so treated.

(2) *Determination of outside gain and loss.*—(i) *In general.*—The amount of gain or loss recognized by the foreign transferor in connection with the transfer of its partnership interest is determined under all relevant provisions of the Internal Revenue Code and the regulations thereunder. See, e.g., §§ 1.741-1(a) and 1.751-1(a)(2). For purposes of this section, the amount of gain or loss that is treated as capital gain or capital loss under sections 741 and 751 is

referred to as *outside capital gain* or *outside capital loss*, respectively. The amount of gain or loss that is treated as ordinary gain or ordinary loss under sections 741 and 751 is referred to as *outside ordinary gain* or *outside ordinary loss*, respectively.

(ii) *Nonrecognition provisions.*—A foreign transferor's gain or loss recognized in connection with the transfer of its partnership interest does not include gain or loss to the extent that the gain or loss is not recognized by reason of one or more nonrecognition provisions of the Internal Revenue Code.

(3) *Limitations.*—This paragraph (b)(3) limits the amount of gain or loss recognized by a foreign transferor that may be treated as effectively connected gain or effectively connected loss.

(i) *Capital gain limitation.*—Outside capital gain recognized by a foreign transferor is treated as effectively connected gain to the extent it does not exceed aggregate deemed sale EC capital gain determined under paragraph (c)(3)(ii)(B) of this section.

(ii) *Capital loss limitation.*—Outside capital loss recognized by a foreign transferor is treated as effectively connected loss to the extent it does not exceed aggregate deemed sale EC capital loss determined under paragraph (c)(3)(ii)(B) of this section.

(iii) *Ordinary gain limitation.*—Outside ordinary gain recognized by a foreign transferor is treated as effectively connected gain to the extent it does not exceed aggregate deemed sale EC ordinary gain determined under paragraph (c)(3)(ii)(A) of this section.

(iv) *Ordinary loss limitation.*—Outside ordinary loss recognized by a foreign transferor is treated as effectively connected loss to the extent it does not exceed aggregate deemed sale EC ordinary loss determined under paragraph (c)(3)(ii)(A) of this section.

(c) *Amount treated as effectively connected with the conduct of a trade or business within the United States.*—This paragraph (c) describes the steps to be followed in computing the limitations described in paragraph (b)(3) of this section.

(1) *Step 1: Determine deemed sale gain and loss.*—Determine the amount of gain or loss that the partnership would recognize with respect to each of its assets (other than interests in partnerships described in paragraph (e) of this section) upon a deemed sale of all of the partnership's assets on the date of the transfer of the partnership interest described in paragraph (b)(1) of this section (deemed sale). For this purpose, a deemed sale is a hypothetical sale by the partnership to an unrelated person of each of its assets (tangible and intangible) in a fully taxable transaction for cash in an amount equal to the fair market value of each asset (taking into account section 7701(g)) immediately before the

partner's transfer of the interest in the partnership. For rules concerning the deemed sale of certain partnership interests, see paragraph (e) of this section.

(2) *Step 2: Determine deemed sale EC gain and loss.*—(i) *In general.*—With respect to each asset deemed sold in paragraph (c)(1) of this section, determine the amount of gain or loss from the deemed sale that would be treated as effectively connected gain or effectively connected loss (including by reason of section 897, taking into account any exceptions thereto, such as section 897(k) or section 897(l)). Gain described in this paragraph (c)(2) is referred to as *deemed sale EC gain*, and loss described in this paragraph (c)(2) is referred to as *deemed sale EC loss*. Section 864 and the regulations thereunder apply for purposes of determining whether gain or loss that would arise in a deemed asset sale would be treated as effectively connected gain or loss. For purposes of this paragraph (c)(2)(i), gain or loss from the deemed sale of an asset is treated as attributable to an office or other fixed place of business maintained by the partnership in the United States, and is not treated as sold for use, disposition, or consumption outside the United States in a sale in which an office or other fixed place of business maintained by the partnership in a foreign country materially participated in the sale.

(ii) *Exception.*—Gain or loss from the deemed sale of an asset described in paragraph (c)(2)(i) of this section (other than a United States real property interest) is not treated as deemed sale EC gain or deemed sale EC loss if—

(A) No income or gain produced by the asset was taxable as income that was effectively connected with the conduct of a trade or business within the United States by the partnership (or a predecessor of the partnership) during the ten-year period ending on the date of the transfer; and

(B) The asset has not been used, or held for use, in the conduct of a trade or business within the United States by the partnership (or a predecessor of the partnership) during the ten-year period ending on the date of the transfer.

(3) *Step 3: Determine the foreign transferor's distributive share of deemed sale EC gain or deemed sale EC loss.*—(i) *In general.*—Determine the foreign transferor's distributive share of deemed sale EC gain and deemed sale EC loss. A foreign transferor's distributive share of deemed sale EC gain or deemed sale EC loss with respect to each asset is the amount of the deemed sale EC gain and deemed sale EC loss determined under paragraph (c)(2) of this section that would have been allocated to the foreign transferor by the partnership under all applicable Code sections (including section 704) upon the deemed sale described in paragraph (c)(1) of this section, taking into account allocations of tax items applying the principles of section 704(c), including any remedial allocations under §1.704-3(d), and any

section 743 basis adjustment pursuant to § 1.743-1(j)(3)).

(ii) *Aggregate deemed sale EC items.*—
(A) *Ordinary gain or loss.*—A foreign transferor's *aggregate deemed sale EC ordinary gain* (if the aggregate results in a gain) or *aggregate deemed sale EC ordinary loss* (if the aggregate results in a loss) is the sum of—

(1) The portion of the foreign transferor's distributive share of deemed sale EC gain and deemed sale EC loss that is attributable to the deemed sale of the partnership's assets that are section 751(a) property; and

(2) Deemed sale EC gain and deemed sale EC loss from the sale of assets that are section 751(a) property that would be allocated to the foreign transferor with respect to interests in partnerships that are engaged in the conduct of a trade or business within the United States under paragraph (e)(1)(ii) of this section upon the deemed asset sales described in paragraph (e)(1)(i) of this section.

(B) *Capital gain or loss.*—A foreign transferor's *aggregate deemed sale EC capital gain* (if the aggregate of the foreign transferor's distributive share of the deemed sale EC capital gain and loss results in a gain) or *aggregate deemed sale EC capital loss* (if the aggregate of the foreign transferor's distributive share of the deemed sale EC capital gain and loss results in a loss) is the sum of—

(1) The portion of the foreign transferor's distributive share of deemed sale EC gain and deemed sale EC loss that is attributable to the deemed sale of assets that are not section 751(a) property; and

(2) Deemed sale EC gain and deemed sale EC loss from the sale of assets that are not section 751(a) property and that would be allocated to the foreign transferor with respect to all interests in partnerships that are engaged in the conduct of a trade or business within the United States under paragraph (e)(1)(ii) of this section upon the deemed asset sales described in paragraph (e)(1)(i) of this section.

(iii) *Partial transfers.*—If a foreign transferor transfers less than all of its interest in a partnership, then for purposes of paragraph (c)(3)(i) of this section, the foreign transferor's distributive share of deemed sale EC gain and deemed sale EC loss is determined by reference to the amount of deemed sale EC gain or deemed sale EC loss determined under paragraph (c)(3)(i) of this section that is attributable to the portion of the foreign transferor's partnership interest that was transferred.

(d) *Coordination with section 897.*—If a foreign transferor transfers an interest in a partnership in a transfer that is subject to section 864(c)(8), and the partnership owns one or more United States real property interests (as defined in section 897(c)), then the foreign transferor determines its effectively connected gain and effectively con-

nected loss under this section, and not pursuant to section 897(g). Accordingly, with respect to a transfer described in the preceding sentence, section 864(c)(8)(C) does not reduce the amount of gain or loss treated as effectively connected gain or loss under this section. For rules regarding a transfer not subject to section 864(c)(8) of an interest in a partnership that owns one or more United States real property interests, see section 897(g) and the regulations thereunder.

(e) *Tiered partnerships.*—(1) *Transfers of upper-tier partnerships.*—Assets sold in a deemed sale described in paragraph (c)(1) of this section do not include interests in partnerships that are engaged in the conduct of a trade or business within the United States or interests in partnerships that hold, directly or indirectly, partnerships that are engaged in the conduct of a trade or business within the United States. Rather, if a foreign transferor transfers an interest in a partnership (upper-tier partnership) that owns, directly or indirectly, an interest in one or more partnerships that are engaged in the conduct of a trade or business within the United States, then—

(i) Beginning with the lowest-tier partnership that is engaged in the conduct of a trade or business within the United States in a chain of partnerships and going up the chain, each partnership that is engaged in the conduct of a trade or business within the United States is treated as selling its assets in a deemed sale in accordance with the principles of paragraph (c)(1) of this section; and

(ii) Each partnership must determine its deemed sale EC gain and deemed sale EC loss in accordance with the principles of paragraph (c)(2) of this section, and determine the distributive share of deemed sale EC gain and deemed sale EC loss for each partner that is either a partnership (in which the foreign transferor is a direct or indirect partner) or a foreign transferor, in accordance with the principles of paragraph (c)(3)(i) of this section.

(2) *Transfers by upper-tier partnerships.*—If a foreign transferor is a direct or indirect partner in an upper-tier partnership and the upper-tier partnership transfers an interest in a partnership that is engaged in the conduct of a trade or business within the United States (including a partnership held indirectly through one or more partnerships), then the principles of this section (including paragraph (e)(1) of this section) apply with respect to the gain or loss on the transfer that is allocated to the foreign transferor by the upper-tier partnership.

(3) *Coordination with section 897.*—For purposes of this paragraph (e), a lower-tier partnership that holds one or more United States real property interests is treated as engaged in the conduct of a trade or business within the United States.

**Prop. Reg. § 1.864(c)(8)-1(e)(3)**

(f) *Income tax treaties.*—(1) *In general.*—This paragraph (f) describes how the provisions of a U.S. income tax treaty apply to the transfer by a foreign transferor that is eligible for benefits under the treaty of an interest in a partnership that is engaged in the conduct of a trade or business within the United States.

(2) *Application of gains article.*—Treaty provisions applicable to gains from the alienation of property forming part of a permanent establishment, including gains from the alienation of a permanent establishment in the United States, apply to the transfer by a foreign transferor of an interest in a partnership with a permanent establishment in the United States.

(3) *Coordination rule.*—For purposes of applying paragraph (c) of this section to gains described in paragraph (f)(2) of this section, a foreign transferor's distributive share of deemed sale EC gain and deemed sale EC loss are determined with respect to the assets of the partnership that form part of the partnership's permanent establishment in the United States and that are not otherwise exempt from U.S. taxation under the treaty.

(g) *Definitions.*—The following definitions apply for purposes of this section.

(1) *Effectively connected gain.*—The term *effectively connected gain* means gain that is treated as effectively connected with the conduct of a trade or business within the United States.

(2) *Effectively connected loss.*—The term *effectively connected loss* means loss treated as effectively connected with the conduct of a trade or business within the United States.

(3) *Foreign transferor.*—The term *foreign transferor* means a nonresident alien individual or foreign corporation.

(4) *Section 751(a) property.*—The term *section 751(a) property* means unrealized receivables described in section 751(c) and inventory items described in section 751(d).

(5) *Transfer.*—The term *transfer* means a sale, exchange, or other disposition, and includes a distribution from a partnership to a partner to the extent that gain or loss is recognized on the distribution, as well as a transfer treated as a sale or exchange under section 707(a)(2)(B).

(h) *Anti-stuffing rule.*—If a foreign transferor (or a person that is related to a foreign transferor within the meaning of section 267(b) or 707(b)) transfers property (including another partnership interest) to a partnership in a transaction with a principal purpose of reducing the amount of gain treated as effectively connected gain, or increasing the amount of loss treated as effectively connected loss, under section 864(c)(8) or section 897, the transfer is disregarded for purposes of section 864(c)(8) or section 897, as appropriate, or otherwise recharacterized in accordance with its substance.

(i) *Examples.*—This paragraph provides examples that illustrate the rules of this section. For purposes of this paragraph, unless otherwise provided, the following facts are presumed. FP is a foreign corporation. USP is a domestic corporation. PRS is a partnership that was formed on January 1, 2018, when FP and USP each contributed $100x in cash. PRS has made no distributions and received no contributions other than those described in paragraph (i)(1)(iii) of this section. FP's adjusted basis in its interest in PRS is $100x. X is a foreign corporation that is unrelated to FP, USP, or PRS. Upon the formation of PRS, FP and USP entered into an agreement providing that all income, gain, loss, and deduction of PRS will be allocated equally between FP and USP. PRS is engaged in the conduct of a trade or business within the United States (the U.S. Business) and an unrelated business in Country A (the Country A Business). In a deemed sale described in paragraph (c)(1) of this section, gain or loss on assets of the U.S. Business would be treated as effectively connected gain or effectively connected loss, and gain or loss on assets of the Country A Business would not be so treated (including by reason of paragraph (c)(2)(ii) of this section). PRS has no liabilities. FP does not qualify for the benefits of an income tax treaty between the United States and another country.

(1) *Example 1. Deemed sale limitation*—(i) *Facts.* On January 1, 2019, FP sells its entire interest in PRS to X for $105x. Immediately before the sale, PRS's balance sheet appears as follows:

|  | Adjusted Basis | Fair Market Value |
| --- | --- | --- |
| U.S. Business capital asset | $100x | $104x |
| Country A Business capital asset | 100x | 106x |
| Total | $200x | $210x |

(ii) *Analysis*—(A) *Outside gain or loss.* FP is a foreign transferor (within the meaning of paragraph (g)(3) of this section) and transfers (within the meaning of paragraph (g)(5) of this section) its interest in PRS to X. FP recognizes a $5x capital gain under section 741, which is an outside capital gain within the meaning of paragraph (b)(2)(i) of this section. Under paragraph (b)(1) of this section, FP's $5x capital gain is treated as effectively connected gain to the extent that it does not exceed the limitation described in paragraph (b)(3)(i) of this section, which is FP's aggregate deemed sale EC capital gain.

(B) *Deemed sale.* FP's aggregate deemed sale EC capital gain is determined according to the three-step process set forth in paragraph (c) of this section. First, the amount of gain or loss that PRS would recognize with respect to each of its assets upon a deemed sale described in paragraph (c)(1) of this section is a $4x gain with respect to the U.S. Business capital asset and a $6x gain with respect to the Country A Business capital asset. Second, under paragraph (c)(2) of this section, PRS's deemed sale EC gain is $4x. PRS recognizes no deemed sale EC gain or loss with respect to the Country A Business capital asset under section 864 and paragraph (c)(2)(ii) of this section. Third, under paragraph (c)(3)(ii)(B) of this section, FP's aggregate deemed sale EC capital gain is $2x (that is, the aggregate of its distributive share of deemed sale EC gain attributable

to the deemed sale of assets that are not section 751(a) property, which is 50% of $4x).

(C) *Limitation.* Under paragraph (b)(3)(i) of this section, the $5x outside capital gain recognized by FP is treated as effectively connected gain to the extent that it does not exceed FP's $2x aggregate deemed sale EC capital gain. Accordingly, FP recognizes $2x of capital gain that is treated as effectively connected gain.

(2) *Example 2. Outside gain limitation*—(i) *Facts.* On January 1, 2019, FP sells its entire interest in PRS to X for $110x. Immediately before the sale, PRS's balance sheet appears as follows:

|  | Adjusted Basis | Fair Market Value |
|---|---|---|
| U.S. Business capital asset | $100x | $150x |
| Country A Business capital asset | 100x | 70x |
| Total | $200x | $220x |

(ii) *Analysis*—(A) *Outside gain or loss.* FP is a foreign transferor (within the meaning of paragraph (g)(3) of this section) and transfers (within the meaning of paragraph (g)(5) of this section) its interest in PRS to X. FP recognizes a $10x capital gain under section 741, which is an outside capital gain within the meaning of paragraph (b)(2)(i) of this section. Under paragraph (b)(1) of this section, FP's $10x capital gain is treated as effectively connected gain to the extent that it does not exceed the limitation described in paragraph (b)(3)(i) of this section, which is FP's aggregate deemed sale EC capital gain.

(B) *Deemed sale.* FP's aggregate deemed sale EC capital gain is determined according to the three-step process set forth in paragraph (c) of this section. First, the amount of gain or loss that PRS would recognize with respect to each of its assets upon a deemed sale described in paragraph (c)(1) of this section is a $50x gain with respect to the U.S. Business capital asset and a $30x loss with respect to the Country A Business capital asset. Second, under paragraph (c)(2) of this section, PRS's deemed sale EC gain is $50x. PRS

recognizes no deemed sale EC gain or loss with respect to the Country A Business capital asset under section 864 and paragraph (c)(2)(ii) of this section. Third, under paragraph (c)(3) of this section, FP's aggregate deemed sale EC capital gain is $25x (that is, the aggregate of its distributive share of deemed sale EC gain attributable to the deemed sale of assets that are not section 751(a) property, which is 50% of $50x).

(C) *Limitation.* Under paragraph (b)(3)(i) of this section, the $10x outside capital gain recognized by FP is treated as effectively connected gain to the extent that it does not exceed FP's $25x aggregate deemed sale EC capital gain. Accordingly, FP recognizes $10x of capital gain that is treated as effectively connected gain.

(3) *Example 3. Interaction with section 751(a)*—(i) *Facts.* On January 1, 2019, FP sells its entire interest in PRS to X for $95x. Through both its U.S. Business and its Country A Business, PRS holds inventory items that are section 751 property (as defined in § 1.751-1(a)). Immediately before the sale, PRS's balance sheet appears as follows:

|  | Adjusted Basis | Fair Market Value |
|---|---|---|
| U.S. Business capital asset | $20x | $50x |
| U.S. Business inventory | 30x | 50x |
| Country A Business capital asset | 100x | 80x |
| Country A Business inventory | 50x | 10x |
| Total | $200x | $190x |

(ii) *Analysis*—(A) *Outside gain or loss.* FP is a foreign transferor (within the meaning of paragraph (g)(3) of this section) and transfers (within the meaning of paragraph (g)(5) of this section) its interest in PRS to X. Under sections 741 and 751, FP recognizes a $10x ordinary loss and a $5x capital gain. See § 1.751-1(a). Under paragraph (b)(2)(i) of this section, FP has outside ordinary loss equal to $10x and outside capital gain equal to $5x. Under paragraph (b)(1) of this section, FP's outside ordinary loss and outside capital gain are treated as effectively connected loss and effectively connected gain to the extent that each does not exceed the applicable limitation de-

scribed in paragraph (b)(3) of this section. In the case of FP's outside ordinary loss, the applicable limitation is FP's aggregate deemed sale EC ordinary loss. In the case of FP's outside capital gain, the applicable limitation is FP's aggregate deemed sale EC capital gain.

(B) *Deemed sale.* FP's aggregate deemed sale EC ordinary loss and aggregate deemed sale EC capital gain are determined according to the three-step process set forth in paragraph (c) of this section.

(1) *Step 1.* The amount of gain or loss that PRS would recognize with respect to each of its assets

**Prop. Reg. §1.864(c)(8)-1(i)**

upon a deemed sale described in paragraph (c)(1) of this section is as follows:

| Asset | Gain/(Loss) |
| --- | --- |
| U.S. Business capital asset | $30x |
| U.S. Business inventory | 20x |
| Country A Business capital asset | (20x) |
| Country A Business inventory | (40x) |

(2) *Step 2.* Under paragraph (c)(2) of this section, PRS's deemed sale EC gain and deemed sale EC loss must be determined with respect to each asset. The amounts determined under paragraph (c)(2) of this section are as follows:

| Asset | Deemed Sale EC Gain/(Loss) |
| --- | --- |
| U.S. Business capital asset | $30x |
| U.S. Business inventory | 20x |
| Country A Business capital asset | 0 |
| Country A Business inventory | 0 |

(3) *Step 3.* Under paragraph (c)(3) of this section, FP's aggregate deemed sale EC capital gain is $15x (that is, the aggregate of its distributive share of deemed sale EC gain that is attributable to the deemed sale of assets that are not section 751(a) property, which is 50% of $30x) and FP's aggregate deemed sale EC ordinary loss is $0 (that is, the aggregate of its distributive share of deemed sale EC loss that is attributable to the deemed sale of assets that are section 751(a) property).

(C) *Limitation*—(i) *Capital gain.* Under paragraph (b)(3)(i) of this section, the $5x outside capital gain recognized by FP is treated as effectively connected gain to the extent that it does not exceed FP's $15x aggregate deemed sale EC capital gain. Accordingly, the amount of FP's capital gain that is treated as effectively connected gain is $5x.

(ii) *Ordinary loss.* Under paragraph (b)(3)(iv) of this section, the $10x outside ordinary loss recognized by FP is treated as effectively connected loss to the extent that it does not exceed FP's $0 aggregate deemed sale EC ordinary loss. Accordingly, the amount of FP's ordinary loss that is treated as effectively connected loss is $0.

(j) *Applicability date.*—This section applies to transfers occurring on or after November 27, 2017. [Reg. § 1.864(c)(8)-1.]

[Proposed 12-27-2018.]

### [Prop. Reg. § 1.882-5]

**§ 1.882-5. Determination of interest deduction.**—(a) * * *

(5) * * * For rules regarding the coordination of this section and section 163(j), see § 1.163(j)-8(e).

* * *

[Proposed 12-28-2018.]

### [Prop. Reg. § 1.901(j)-1]

**§ 1.901(j)-1. Payment and returns of tax withheld by the acquiring agency.**—(a) *Sourcing rule for related party payments and inclusions.*—Any income paid or accrued through one or more entities is treated as income from sources within a country described in section 901(j)(2) if the income was, without regard to such entities, from sources within that country.

(b) *Applicability date.*—This section applies to taxable years that end on or after December 4, 2018. [Reg. § 1.901(j)-1.]

[Proposed 12-7-2018.]

### [Prop. Reg. § 1.904-1]

**§ 1.904-1. Limitation on credit for foreign taxes.**—(a) *In general.*—For each separate category described in § 1.904-5(a)(4)(v), the total credit for taxes paid or accrued (including those deemed to have been paid or accrued other than by reason of section 904(c)) shall not exceed that proportion of the tax against which such credit is taken which the taxpayer's taxable income from foreign sources (but not in excess of the taxpayer's entire taxable income) in such separate category bears to his entire taxable income for the same taxable year.

(b) *Special computation of taxable income.*—For purposes of computing the limitation under paragraph (a) of this section, the taxable income in the case of an individual, estate, or trust is computed without any deduction for personal exemptions under section 151 or 642(b).

(c) *Joint return.*—In the case of spouses making a joint return, the applicable limitation prescribed by section 904(a) on the credit for taxes paid or accrued to foreign countries and possessions of the United States is applied with respect to the aggregate taxable income in each separate category from sources without the United States, and the aggregate taxable income from all sources, of the spouses.

(d) *Consolidated group.*—For rules relating to the computation of the foreign tax credit limitation for a consolidated group, see § 1.1502-4.

(e) *Applicability dates.*—This section applies to taxable years that both begin after December 31, 2017, and end on or after December 4, 2018.

[Proposed 12-7-2018.]

### [Prop. Reg. §1.904-2]

**§1.904-2. Carryback and carryover of unused foreign tax.**—(a) *Credit for foreign tax carryback or carryover.*—A taxpayer who chooses to claim a credit under section 901 for a taxable year is allowed a credit under that section not only for taxes otherwise allowable as a credit but also for taxes deemed paid or accrued in that year as a result of a carryback or carryover of an unused foreign tax under section 904(c). However, the taxes so deemed paid or accrued are not allowed as a deduction under section 164(a). Foreign tax paid or accrued with respect to section 951A category income, including section 951A category income that is reassigned to a separate category for income resourced under a treaty, may not be carried back or carried forward or deemed paid or accrued under section 904(c). For special rules regarding these computations in case of taxes paid, accrued, or deemed paid with respect to foreign oil and gas extraction income or foreign oil related income, see section 907(f) and the regulations under that section.

(b) *Years to which foreign taxes are carried.*—If the taxpayer chooses the benefits of section 901 for a taxable year, any unused foreign tax paid or accrued in that year is carried first to the immediately preceding taxable year and then, as applicable, to each of the ten succeeding taxable years, in chronological order, but only to the extent not absorbed as taxes deemed paid or accrued under paragraph (d) of this section in a prior taxable year.

(c) *Definitions.*—This paragraph (c) provides definitions that apply for purposes of this section.

(1) *Unused foreign tax.*—The term *unused foreign tax* means, with respect to each separate category for any taxable year, the excess of the amount of creditable foreign tax paid or accrued, or deemed paid under section 902 (as in effect on December 21, 2017) or section 960, in such year, over the applicable foreign tax credit limitation under section 904 for the separate category in such year. Unused foreign tax does not include any amount for which a credit is disallowed, including foreign income taxes for which a credit is disallowed or reduced when the tax is paid, accrued, or deemed paid.

(2) *Separate category.*—The term *separate category* has the same meaning as provided in §1.904-5(a)(4)(v).

(3) *Excess limitation.*—(i) *In general.*—The term *excess limitation* means, with respect to a separate category for any taxable year (the *excess limitation year*) and an unused foreign tax carried from another taxable year (the *excess credit year*), the amount (if any) by which the limitation for

that separate category with respect to that excess limitation year exceeds the sum of—

(A) The creditable foreign tax actually paid or accrued or deemed paid under section 902 (as in effect on December 21, 2017) or section 960 with respect to the separate category in the excess limitation year, and

(B) The portion of any unused foreign tax for a taxable year preceding the excess credit year that is absorbed as taxes deemed paid or accrued in the excess limitation year under paragraph (a) of this section.

(ii) *Deduction years.*—Excess limitation for a taxable year absorbs unused foreign tax, regardless of whether the taxpayer chooses to claim a credit under section 901 for the year. In such case, the amount of the excess limitation, if any, for the year is determined in the same manner as though the taxpayer had chosen to claim a credit under section 901 for that year. For purposes of this determination, if the taxpayer has an overall foreign loss account, the excess limitation in a deduction year is determined based on the amount of the overall foreign loss the taxpayer would have recaptured if the taxpayer had chosen to claim a credit under section 901 for that year and had not made an election under §1.904(f)-2(c)(2) to recapture more of the overall foreign loss account than is required under §1.904(f)-2(c)(1).

(d) *Taxes deemed paid or accrued.*—(1) *Amount deemed paid or accrued.*—The amount of unused foreign tax with respect to a separate category that is deemed paid or accrued in any taxable year to which such unused foreign tax may be carried under paragraph (b) of this section is equal to the smaller of—

(i) The portion of the unused foreign tax that may be carried to the taxable year under paragraph (b) of this section, or

(ii) The amount, if any, of the excess limitation for such taxable year with respect to such unused foreign tax.

(2) *Carryback or carryover tax deemed paid or accrued in the same separate category.*—Any unused foreign tax, which is deemed to be paid or accrued under section 904(c) in the year to which it is carried, is deemed to be paid or accrued with respect to the same separate category as the category to which it was assigned in the year in which it was actually paid or accrued. However, see paragraphs (h) through (j) of this section for transition rules in the case of certain carrybacks and carryovers.

(3) *No duplicate disallowance of creditable foreign tax.*—Foreign income taxes for which a credit is partially disallowed, including when the tax is paid, accrued, or deemed paid, are not reduced again by reason of the unused foreign tax being deemed to be paid or accrued in the year to which it is carried under section 904(c).

\* \* \*

(g) [Reserved]

(h) *Transition rules for carryovers of pre-2003 unused foreign tax and carrybacks of post-2002 unused foreign tax paid or accrued with respect to dividends from noncontrolled section 902 corporations.*—For transition rules for carryovers of pre-2003 unused foreign tax, and carrybacks of post-2002 unused foreign tax, paid or accrued with respect to dividends from noncontrolled section 902 corporations, see 26 CFR § 1.904-2(h) (revised as of April 1, 2018).

(i) *Transition rules for carryovers of pre-2007 unused foreign tax and carrybacks of post-2006 unused foreign tax.*—For transition rules for carryovers of pre-2007 unused foreign tax, and carrybacks of post-2006 unused foreign tax, see 26 CFR § 1.904-2(i) (revised as of April 1, 2018).

(j) *Transition rules for carryovers and carrybacks of pre-2018 and post-2017 unused foreign tax.*— (1) *Carryover of unused foreign tax.*—(i) *In general.*—For purposes of this paragraph (j), the terms *post-2017 separate category, pre-2018 separate category*, and *specified separate category* have the meanings set forth in § 1.904(f)-12(j)(1). The rules of this paragraph (j)(1) apply to reallocate to the taxpayer's post-2017 separate categories for foreign branch category income, general category income, passive category income, and specified separate categories of income, any unused foreign taxes (as defined in paragraph (c)(1) of this section) that were paid or accrued or deemed paid under sections 902 and 960 with respect to income in a pre-2018 separate category.

(ii) *Allocation to the same separate category.*—Except as provided in paragraph (j)(1)(iii) of this section, to the extent any unused foreign taxes paid or accrued or deemed paid with respect to a separate category of income are carried forward to a taxable year beginning after December 31, 2017, such taxes are allocated to the same post-2017 separate category as the pre-2018 separate category from which the unused foreign taxes are carried.

(iii) *Exception for certain general category unused foreign taxes.*—(A) *In general.*—To the extent any unused foreign taxes paid or accrued (but not taxes deemed paid) with respect to general category income are carried forward to a taxable year beginning after December 31, 2017, a taxpayer may choose to allocate those taxes to the taxpayer's post-2017 separate category for foreign branch category income to the extent those taxes would have been allocated to the taxpayer's post-2017 separate category for foreign branch category income if the taxes were paid or accrued in a taxable year beginning after December 31, 2017. Any remaining unused foreign taxes paid or accrued or deemed paid with respect to general category income carried forward to a taxable year beginning after December 31, 2017, are allocated to the taxpayer's post-2017 separate category for general category income.

(B) *Rules regarding the exception.*—A taxpayer applying the exception described in paragraph (j)(1)(iii)(A) of this section (the *branch carryover exception*) must apply the exception to all of its unused foreign taxes paid or accrued with respect to general category income that are carried forward to all taxable years beginning after December 31, 2017. A taxpayer may choose to apply the branch carryover exception on a timely filed original return (including extensions) or an amended return. A taxpayer that applies the exception on an amended return must make appropriate adjustments to eliminate any double benefit arising from application of the exception to years that are not open for assessment.

(2) *Carryback of unused foreign tax.*—(i) *In general.*—The rules of this paragraph (j)(2) apply to any unused foreign taxes that were paid or accrued, or deemed paid under section 960, with respect to income in a post-2017 separate category.

(ii) *Passive category income and specified separate categories of income described in § 1.904-4(m).*—Any unused foreign taxes paid or accrued or deemed paid with respect to passive category income or a specified separate category of income in a taxable year beginning after December 31, 2017, that are carried back to a taxable year beginning before January 1, 2018, are allocated to the same pre-2018 separate category as the post-2017 separate category from which the unused foreign taxes are carried.

(iii) *General category income and foreign branch category income.*—Any unused foreign taxes paid or accrued or deemed paid with respect to general category income or foreign branch category income in a taxable year beginning after December 31, 2017, that are carried back to a taxable year beginning before January 1, 2018, are allocated to the taxpayer's pre-2018 separate category for general category income.

(k) *Applicability date.*—Paragraphs (a) through (i) of this section apply to taxable years that both begin after December 31, 2017, and end on or after December 4, 2018. Paragraph (j) of this section applies to taxable years beginning after December 31, 2017. Paragraph (j)(2) of this section also applies to the last taxable year beginning before January 1, 2018.

[Proposed 12-7-2018.]

### [Prop. Reg. § 1.904-3]

**§ 1.904-3. Carryback and carryover of unused foreign tax by spouses making a joint return.**— (a) * * * The rules in this section apply separately with respect to each separate category as defined in § 1.904-5(a)(4)(v).

\* \* \*

(e) *Amounts carried from or through a joint return year to or through a separate return year.*— (1) *In general.*—It is necessary to allocate to each spouse the spouse's share of an unused foreign tax or excess limitation for any taxable year for which the spouses filed a joint return if—

(i) The spouses file separate returns for the current taxable year and an unused foreign tax is carried thereto from a taxable year for which they filed a joint return;

(ii) The spouses file separate returns for the current taxable year and an unused foreign tax is carried to such taxable year from a year for which they filed separate returns but is first carried through a year for which they filed a joint return; or

(iii) The spouses file a joint return for the current taxable year and an unused foreign tax is carried from a taxable year for which they filed joint returns but is first carried through a year for which they filed separate returns.

(2) *Computation and adjustments.*—In the cases described in paragraph (e)(1) of this section, the separate carryback or carryover of each spouse to the current taxable year shall be computed in the manner described in § 1.904-2 but with the modifications set forth in paragraph (f) of this section. Where applicable, appropriate adjustments are made to take into account the fact that, for any taxable year involved in the computation of the carryback or the carryover, either spouse has combined foreign oil and gas income described in section 907(b) with respect to which the limitation in section 907(a) applies.

(f) * * *

(1) *Separate category limitation.*—The limitation in a separate category of a particular spouse for a taxable year for which a joint return is made shall be the portion of the limitation on the joint return which bears the same ratio to such limitation as such spouse's foreign source taxable income (with gross income and deductions taken into account to the same extent as taken into account on the joint return) in such separate category (but not in excess of the joint foreign source taxable income) bears to the joint foreign source taxable income in such separate category.

(2) *Unused foreign tax.*—For purposes of this section, the term *unused foreign tax* means, with respect to a particular spouse and separate category for a taxable year for which a joint return is made, the excess of the foreign tax paid or accrued by that spouse with respect to that separate category over that spouse's separate category limitation.

(3) *Excess limitation.*—For purposes of this section, the term *excess limitation* means, with respect to a particular spouse and separate category for a taxable year for which a joint return is made, the excess of that spouse's separate category limitation over the foreign taxes paid or accrued by such spouse with respect to that separate category for such taxable year.

* * *

(g) [Reserved]

(h) *Applicability date.*—This section is applicable for taxable years that both begin after December 31, 2017, and end on or after December 4, 2018.

[Proposed 12-7-2018.]

### [Prop. Reg. § 1.904-4]

**§ 1.904-4. Separate application of section 904 with respect to certain categories of income.**— (a) *In general.*—A taxpayer is required to compute a separate foreign tax credit limitation for income received or accrued in a taxable year that is described in section 904(d)(1)(A) (section 951A category income), 904(d)(1)(B) (foreign branch category income), 904(d)(1)(C) (passive category income), 904(d)(1)(D) (general category income), or paragraph (m) of this section (specified separate categories). For purposes of this section, the definitions in § 1.904-5(a)(4) apply.

(b) * * *

(2) * * *

(i) * * *

(C) Distributive shares of partnership income treated as passive category income under paragraph (n)(1) of this section, and income from the sale of a partnership interest treated as passive category income under paragraph (n)(2) of this section; or

(D) Income treated as passive category income under the look-through rules in § 1.904-5.

(ii) *Exceptions.*—Passive income does not include any export financing interest (as defined in paragraph (h) of this section), any high-taxed income (as defined in paragraph (c) of this section), financial services income (as defined in paragraph (e)(1)(ii) of this section), or any active rents and royalties (as defined in paragraph (b)(2)(iii) of this section). In addition, passive income does not include any income that would otherwise be passive but is excluded from passive category income under § 1.904-5(b)(1).* * *

* * *

(c) * * *

(1) * * * Income is considered to be high-taxed income if, after allocating expenses, losses, and other deductions of the United States person to that income under paragraph (c)(2) of this section, the sum of the foreign income taxes paid or accrued, and deemed paid under section 960, by the United States person with respect to such income (reduced by any portion of such taxes for which a credit is not allowed) exceeds the highest rate of tax specified in section 1 or 11, whichever applies (and with reference to section 15 if applicable), multiplied by the amount of such income (including the amount treated as a dividend under section 78). If, after application of this paragraph (c), income that would otherwise be passive income is determined to be high-taxed income, the income is treated as general category income, foreign branch category income, section 951A category income, or income

in a specified separate category, as determined under the rules of this section, and any taxes imposed on that income are considered related to the same separate category of income under § 1.904-6. If, after application of this paragraph (c), passive income is zero or less than zero, any taxes imposed on the passive income are considered related to the same separate category of income to which the passive income (if not reduced to zero or less than zero) would have been assigned had the income been treated as high-taxed income (general category, foreign branch category, section 951A category, or a specified separate category). * * *

\* \* \*

(3) * * * Paragraph (c)(4) of this section provides additional rules for inclusions under section 951(a)(1) or 951A(a) that are passive income, dividends from a controlled foreign corporation or noncontrolled 10-percent owned foreign corporation that are passive income, and income that is received or accrued by a United States person through a foreign QBU that is passive income. For purposes of this paragraph (c), a foreign QBU is a qualified business unit (as defined in section 989(a)), other than a controlled foreign corporation or noncontrolled 10-percent owned foreign corporation, that has its principal place of business outside the United States. These rules apply whether the income is received from a controlled foreign corporation of which the United States person is a United States shareholder, from a noncontrolled 10-percent owned foreign corporation of which the United States person is a United States shareholder that is a domestic corporation, or from any other person. In applying these rules, passive income is not treated as subject to a withholding tax or other foreign tax for which a credit is disallowed in full, for example, under section 901(k). * * *

(4) *Dividends and inclusions from controlled foreign corporations, dividends from noncontrolled 10-percent owned foreign corporations, and income attributable to foreign QBUs.*—Except as provided in paragraph (c)(5) of this section, the rules of this paragraph (c)(4) apply to all dividends and all amounts included in gross income of a United States shareholder under section 951(a)(1) or 951A(a) with respect to the foreign corporation that (after application of the look-through rules of section 904(d)(3) and § 1.904-5) are attributable to passive income received or accrued by a controlled foreign corporation, all dividends from a noncontrolled 10-percent owned foreign corporation that are received or accrued by a United States shareholder that (after application of the look-through rules of section 904(d)(4) and § 1.904-5) are treated as passive income, and all amounts of passive income received or accrued by a United States person through a foreign QBU. The grouping rules of paragraph (c)(3)(i) through (iv) of this section apply separately to dividends, to inclusions under section 951(a)(1) and to inclusions under section 951A(a) with respect to each controlled foreign corporation of

which the taxpayer is a United States shareholder, and to dividends with respect to each noncontrolled 10-percent owned foreign corporation of which the taxpayer is a United States shareholder that is a domestic corporation. The grouping rules of paragraph (c)(3)(i) through (iv) of this section also apply separately to income attributable to each foreign QBU of a controlled foreign corporation, noncontrolled 10-percent owned foreign corporation, any other look-through entity as defined in § 1.904-5(i), or any United States person.

(5) * * *

(ii) *Treatment of partnership income.*—A partner's distributive share of income from a foreign or United States partnership that is treated as passive income under paragraph (n)(1)(ii) of this section (generally providing that a less than 10 percent partner's distributive share of partnership income is passive income) is treated as a single item of income and is not grouped with other amounts. A distributive share of income from a partnership that is treated as passive income under paragraph (n)(1)(i) of this section is grouped according to the rules in paragraph (c)(3) of this section, except that the portion, if any, of the distributive share of income attributable to income earned by a United States partnership through a foreign QBU is separately grouped under the rules of paragraph (c)(4) of this section.

\* \* \*

(6) * * *

(i) * * * The determination of whether an amount included in gross income under section 951(a)(1) or 951A(a) is high-taxed income is made in the taxable year the income is included in the gross income of the United States shareholder under section 951(a) or 951A(a) (for purposes of this paragraph (c), the *year of inclusion*). * * *

\* \* \*

(iii) * * * If an item of income is considered high-taxed income in the year of inclusion and paragraph (c)(6)(i) of this section applies, then any increase in foreign income taxes imposed with respect to that item are considered to be related to the same separate category to which the income was assigned in the taxable year of inclusion. * * * The taxpayer shall treat any taxes paid or accrued, or deemed paid, on the distribution in excess of this amount as taxes related to the same category of income to which such inclusion would have been assigned had the income been treated as high-taxed income in the year of inclusion (general category income, section 951A category income, or income in a specified separate category). If these additional taxes are not creditable in the year of distribution, the carryover rules of section 904(c) apply (see section 904(c) and § 1.904-2(a) for rules disallowing carryovers in the section 951A category). For purposes of this paragraph (c)(6), the foreign tax on an inclusion under section 951(a)(1) or

951A(a) is considered increased on distribution of the earnings and profits associated with that inclusion if the total of taxes paid and deemed paid on the inclusion and the distribution (taking into account any reductions in tax and any withholding taxes) exceeds the total taxes deemed paid in the year of inclusion. * * *

(iv) *Increase in taxes paid by successors.*—If passive earnings and profits previously included in income of a United States shareholder are distributed to a person that was not a United States shareholder of the distributing corporation in the year the earnings were included, any increase in foreign taxes paid or accrued, or deemed paid, on that distribution is treated as tax related to general category income (or income in a specified separate category, if applicable) in the case of earnings and profits previously included under section 951(a)(1), and is treated as tax related to section 951A category income (or income in a specified separate category, if applicable) in the case of earnings and profits previously included under section 951A(a), regardless of whether the previously-taxed income was considered high-taxed income under section 904(d)(2)(F) in the year of inclusion.

(7) * * *

(i) * * * If the inclusion is considered to be high-taxed income, then the taxpayer shall treat the inclusion as general category income, section 951A category income or income in a specified separate category as provided in paragraph (c)(1) of this section. * * * For this purpose, the foreign tax on an inclusion under section 951(a)(1) or 951A(a) shall be considered reduced on distribution of the earnings and profits associated with the inclusion if the total taxes paid and deemed paid on the inclusion and the distribution (taking into account any reductions in tax and any withholding taxes) is less than the total taxes deemed paid in the year of inclusion. * * *

* * *

(d) *General category income.*—The term *general category income* means all income other than passive category income, foreign branch category income, section 951A category income, and income in a specified separate category. Any item that is excluded from the passive category under section 904(d)(2)(B)(iii) or § 1.904-5(b)(1) is included in general category income only to the extent that such item does not meet the definition of another separate category. General category income also includes income treated as general category income under the look-through rules referenced in § 1.904-5(a)(2).

(e) * * *

(1) *In general.*—(i) *Treatment of financial services income.*—Financial services income that meets the definition of foreign branch category income is treated as income in that category. Financial services income of a controlled foreign corporation that is included in gross income of a United States shareholder under section 951A(a)

is treated as section 951A category income in the hands of the United States shareholder. Financial services income that is neither treated as foreign branch category income nor treated as section 951A category income is treated as general category income.

(ii) *Definition of financial services income.*—The term *financial services income* means income derived by a financial services entity, as defined in paragraph (e)(3) of this section, that is:

(A) Income derived in the active conduct of a banking, insurance, financing, or similar business (active financing income as defined in paragraph (e)(2) of this section);

(B) Passive income as defined in section 904(d)(2)(B) and paragraph (b) of this section as determined before the application of the exception for high-taxed income but after the application of the exception for export financing interest; or

(C) Incidental income as defined in paragraph (e)(4) of this section.

(2) * * *

(i) * * *

(W) [Reserved]

* * *

(f) *Foreign branch category income.*—(1) *Foreign branch category income.*—(i) *In general.*—Except as provided in paragraph (f)(1)(ii) of this section, the term *foreign branch category income* means income of a United States person, other than a pass-through entity, that is—

(A) Income attributable to foreign branches of the United States person held directly or indirectly through disregarded entities;

(B) A distributive share of partnership income that is attributable to foreign branches held by the partnership directly or indirectly through disregarded entities, or held indirectly by the partnership through another partnership or other pass-through entity that holds the foreign branch directly or indirectly through disregarded entities; and

(C) Income from other pass-through entities determined under principles similar to those described in paragraph (f)(1)(i)(B) of this section.

(ii) *Passive category income excluded from foreign branch category income.*—Income assigned to the passive category under paragraph (b) of this section is not foreign branch category income, regardless of whether the income is described in paragraph (f)(1)(i) of this section. Income that is treated as passive category income under the look-through rules in § 1.904-5 is also excluded from foreign branch category income, regardless of whether the income is attributable to a foreign branch. However, income that would be passive category income but for the application of section 904(d)(2)(B)(iii) (export financing interest and high-taxed income) or 904(d)(2)(C) (financial services income) and the regulations under those sections and also meets

**Prop. Reg. § 1.904-4(f)(1)(ii)**

the definition of foreign branch category income is foreign branch category income.

(2) *Gross income attributable to a foreign branch.*—(i) *In general.*—Except as provided in this paragraph (f)(2), gross income is attributable to a foreign branch to the extent the gross income (as adjusted to conform to Federal income tax principles) is reflected on the separate set of books and records (as defined in § 1.989(a)-1(d)(1) and (2)) of the foreign branch. Gross income that is not attributable to the foreign branch and is therefore attributable to the foreign branch owner is treated as income in a separate category (other than the foreign branch category) under the other rules of this section.

(ii) *Income attributable to U.S. activities.*— Gross income attributable to a foreign branch does not include items arising from activities carried out in the United States, regardless of whether the items are reflected on the foreign branch's separate books and records.

(iii) *Income arising from stock.*—(A) *In general.*—Except as provided in paragraph (f)(2)(iii)(B) of this section, gross income attributable to a foreign branch does not include items of income arising from stock of a corporation (whether foreign or domestic), including gain from the disposition of such stock or any inclusion under sections 951(a), 951A(a), or 1293(a).

(B) *Exception for dealer property.*—Paragraph (f)(2)(iii)(A) of this section does not apply to gain recognized from dispositions of stock in a corporation, if the stock would be dealer property (as defined in § 1.954-2(a)(4)(v)) if the foreign branch were a controlled foreign corporation.

(iv) *Disposition of interests in certain entities.*—(A) *In general.*—Except as provided in paragraph (f)(2)(iv)(B) of this section, gross income attributable to a foreign branch does not include gain from the disposition of an interest in a partnership or other pass-through entity or an interest in a disregarded entity. See also paragraph (n)(2) of this section for general rules relating to the sale of a partnership interest.

(B) *Exception for sales by a foreign branch in the ordinary course of business.*—The rule in paragraph (f)(2)(iv)(A) of this section does not apply to gain from the sale or exchange of an interest in a partnership or other pass-through entity or an interest in a disregarded entity if the gain is reflected on the books and records of a foreign branch and the interest is held by the foreign branch in the ordinary course of its active trade or business. An interest is considered to be held in the ordinary course of the foreign branch's active trade or business if the foreign branch engages in the same or a related trade or business as the partnership or other pass-through entity (other than through a less than 10 percent interest) or disregarded entity.

(v) *Adjustments to items of gross income reflected on the books and records.*—If a principal purpose of recording or failing to record an item of gross income on the books and records of a foreign branch, or of making a disregarded payment described in paragraph (f)(2)(vi) of this section, is the avoidance of Federal income tax, the purposes of section 904, or the purposes of section 250 (in connection with section 250(b)(3)(A)(i)(VI)), the item must be attributed to one or more foreign branches or the foreign branch owner in a manner that reflects the substance of the transaction. For purposes of this paragraph (f)(2)(v), interest received by a foreign branch from a related person is presumed to be attributable to the foreign branch owner (and not to the foreign branch) unless the interest income meets the definition of financial services income under paragraph (e)(1)(ii) of this section. For purposes of this paragraph (f)(2)(v), a related person is any person that bears a relationship to the foreign branch owner described in section 267(b) or 707.

(vi) *Attribution of gross income to which disregarded payments are allocable.*—(A) *In general.*— If a foreign branch makes a disregarded payment to its foreign branch owner and the disregarded payment is allocable to non-passive category gross income of the foreign branch reflected on the foreign branch's separate set of books and records under paragraph (f)(2)(i) of this section, the gross income attributable to the foreign branch is adjusted downward to reflect the allocable amount of the disregarded payment, and the general category gross income attributable to the foreign branch owner is adjusted upward by the same amount, translated (if necessary) from the foreign branch's functional currency to U.S. dollars at the spot rate, as defined in § 1.988-1(d), on the date of the disregarded payment. Similarly, if a foreign branch owner makes a disregarded payment to its foreign branch and the disregarded payment is allocable to general category gross income of the foreign branch owner that was not reflected on the separate set of books and records of any foreign branch of the foreign branch owner, the gross income attributable to the foreign branch owner is adjusted downward to reflect the allocable amount of the disregarded payment, and the gross income attributable to the foreign branch is adjusted upward by the same amount, translated (if necessary) from U.S. dollars to the foreign branch's functional currency at the spot rate, as defined in § 1.988-1(d), on the date of the disregarded payment. An adjustment to the attribution of gross income under this paragraph (f)(2)(vi) does not change the total amount, character, or source of the United States person's gross income. Similar rules apply in the case of disregarded payments between a foreign branch and another foreign branch with the same foreign branch owner.

(B) *Allocation of disregarded payments.*—
(1) *In general.*—Whether a disregarded payment
is allocable to gross income of a foreign branch
or its foreign branch owner, and the source and
separate category of the gross income to which
the disregarded payment is allocable, is determined under the following rules:

(i) Disregarded payments from a
foreign branch owner to its foreign branch are
allocable to gross income attributable to the foreign branch owner to the extent a deduction for
that payment, if regarded, would be allocated
and apportioned to general category gross income of the foreign branch owner under the
principles of §§1.861-8 through 1.861-14T and
1.861-17 by treating foreign source general category gross income and U.S. source general category gross income each as a statutory grouping;
and

(ii) Disregarded payments from a
foreign branch to its foreign branch owner are
allocable to gross income attributable to the foreign branch to the extent a deduction for that
payment, if regarded, would be allocated and
apportioned to gross income of the foreign
branch under the principles of §§1.861-8
through 1.861-14T and 1.861-17 by treating foreign source gross income in the foreign branch
category and U.S. source gross income in the
foreign branch category each as a statutory
grouping.

(2) *Disregarded sales of property.*—The
principles of paragraph (f)(2)(vi)(B)(1)(i) and (ii)
of this section apply in the case of disregarded
payments in consideration for the transfer of
property between a foreign branch and its foreign branch owner to the extent the disregarded
payment, if regarded, would, for purposes of
determining gross income, be subtracted from
gross receipts that are regarded for Federal income tax purposes.

(3) *Conditions and timing of reallocation.*—The gross income attributable to the foreign branch is adjusted only in the taxable year,
and only to the extent, that a disregarded payment, if regarded, would be allowed as a deduction or otherwise would be taken into account
(for example, as an increase to cost of goods
sold).

(C) *Exclusion of certain disregarded payments.*—Paragraph (f)(2)(vi)(A) of this section
does not apply to the following payments, accruals, or other transfers between a foreign branch
and its foreign branch owner that are disregarded for Federal income tax purposes:

(1) Interest and interest equivalents
that, if regarded, would be described in
§1.861-9T(b);

(2) Remittances from the foreign
branch to its foreign branch owner, except as
provided in paragraph (f)(2)(vi)(D) of this section; or

(3) Contributions of money, securi-
ties, and other property from the foreign branch

owner to its foreign branch, except as set forth in
paragraph (f)(2)(vi)(D) of this section.

(D) *Certain transfers of intangible property.*—For purposes of applying this paragraph
(f)(2)(vi), the amount of gross income attributable to a foreign branch (and the amount of gross
income attributable to its foreign branch owner)
that is not passive category income must be adjusted under the principles of paragraph
(f)(2)(vi)(B) of this section to reflect all transactions that are disregarded for Federal income tax
purposes in which property described in section
367(d)(4) is transferred to or from a foreign
branch, whether or not a disregarded payment is
made in connection with the transfer. In determining the amount of gross income that is attributable to a foreign branch that must be adjusted
by reason of this paragraph (f)(2)(vi)(D), the
principles of sections 367(d) and 482 apply. For
example, if a foreign branch owner transfers
property described in section 367(d)(4), the principles of section 367(d) are applied by treating
the foreign branch as a separate corporation to
which the property is transferred in exchange for
stock of the corporation in a transaction described in section 351.

(E) *Amount of disregarded payments.*—
The amount of each disregarded payment used
to make an adjustment under this paragraph
(f)(2)(vi) (or the absence of any adjustment) must
be determined in a manner that results in the
attribution of the proper amount of gross income
to each of a foreign branch and its foreign branch
owner under the principles of section 482, applied as if the foreign branch were a corporation.

(F) *Ordering rules.*—For purposes of applying this paragraph (f)(2)(vi), adjustments related to disregarded payments from a foreign
branch to its foreign branch owner are computed
first, followed by adjustments related to disregarded payments from a foreign branch owner
to its foreign branch.

(3) *Definitions.*—The following definitions
apply for purposes of this paragraph (f).

(i) *Disregarded entity.*—The term *disregarded entity* means an entity described in
§301.7701-2(c)(2) of this chapter that is disregarded as an entity separate from its owner for
Federal income tax purposes.

(ii) *Disregarded payment.*—The term *disregarded payment* means any amount described in
paragraph (f)(3)(ii)(A) or (B) of this section.

(A) *Payments to or from a disregarded entity.*—An amount described in this paragraph
(f)(3)(ii)(A) is an amount that is paid to or by a
disregarded entity in connection with a transaction that is disregarded for Federal income tax
purposes and that is reflected on the separate set
of books and records of a foreign branch.

(B) *Other disregarded amounts.*—An
amount described in this paragraph (f)(3)(ii)(B)

**Prop. Reg. §1.904-4(f)(3)(ii)(B)**

is any amount reflected on the separate set of books and records of a foreign branch that would constitute an item of income, gain, deduction, or loss (other than an amount described in paragraph (f)(3)(ii)(A) of this section) if the transaction to which the amount is attributable were regarded for Federal income tax purposes.

(iii) *Foreign branch.*—(A) *In general.*—The term *foreign branch* means a qualified business unit (QBU), as defined in § 1.989(a)-1(b)(2)(ii) and (b)(3), that conducts a trade or business outside the United States. For an illustration of the principles of this paragraph (f)(3)(iii), see paragraph (f)(4)(i) *Example 1* of this section.

(B) *Trade or business outside the United States.*—Activities carried out in the United States, whether or not such activities are described in § 1.989(a)-1(b)(3), do not constitute the conduct of a trade or business outside the United States. Activities carried out outside the United States that constitute a permanent establishment under the terms of an income tax treaty between the United States and the country in which the activities are carried out are presumed to constitute a trade or business conducted outside the United States for purposes of this paragraph (f)(3)(iii)(B). In determining whether activities constitute a trade or business under § 1.989(a)-1(c), disregarded payments are taken into account and may give rise to a trade or business, provided that the activities (together with any other activities of the QBU) would otherwise satisfy the rule in § 1.989(a)-1(c).

(C) *Activities of a partnership, estate, or trust.*—(1) *Treatment as a foreign branch.*—For purposes of this paragraph (f)(3)(iii), the activities of a partnership, estate, or trust that conducts a trade or business that satisfies the requirements of § 1.989(a)-1(b)(2)(ii)(A) (as modified by paragraph (f)(3)(iii)(B) of this section) are—

(i) Deemed to satisfy the requirements of § 1.989(a)-1(b)(2)(ii)(B); and

(ii) Comprise a foreign branch.

(2) *Separate set of books and records.*—A foreign branch described in this paragraph (f)(3)(iii)(C) is treated as maintaining a separate set of books and records with respect to the activities described in paragraph (f)(3)(iii)(C)(1) of this section, and must determine, as the context requires, the items of gross income, disregarded payments, and any other items that would be reflected on those books and records in applying this paragraph (f) with respect to the foreign branch.

(iv) *Foreign branch owner.*—The term *foreign branch owner* means, with respect to a foreign branch, the person (including a foreign or domestic partnership or other pass-through entity) that owns the foreign branch, either directly or indirectly through one or more disregarded entities. For this purpose, the foreign branch owner does not include the foreign branch or

another foreign branch of the person that owns the foreign branch.

(v) *Remittance.*—The term *remittance* means a transfer of property (within the meaning of section 317(a)) by a foreign branch that would be treated as a distribution if the foreign branch were treated as a separate corporation.

(4) *Examples.*—The following examples illustrate the application of this paragraph (f).

(i) *Example 1: Determination of foreign branches and foreign branch owner*—(A) *Facts*—(1) P, a domestic corporation, is a partner in PRS. All other partners in PRS are unrelated to P. PRS conducts activities solely in Country A (the Country A Business), and those activities constitute a trade or business outside the United States within the meaning of paragraph (f)(3)(iii)(B) of this section. PRS reflects items of income, gain, loss, and expense of the Country A Business on the books and records of PRS's home office. PRS's functional currency is the U.S. dollar. PRS is in the business of manufacturing bicycles.

(2) PRS owns FDE1, a disregarded entity organized in Country B. FDE1 conducts activities in Country B (the Country B Business), and those activities constitute a trade or business outside the United States within the meaning of paragraph (f)(3)(iii)(B) of this section. FDE1 maintains a set of books and records that are separate from those of PRS, and the separate set of books and records reflects items of income, gain, loss, and expense with respect to the Country B Business. Country B Business's functional currency is the U.S. dollar. FDE1 is in the business of selling bicycles manufactured by PRS.

(3) FDE1 owns FDE2, a disregarded entity organized in Country C. FDE2 conducts activities in Country C (the Country C Business), and those activities constitute a trade or business outside the United States within the meaning of paragraph (f)(3)(iii)(B) of this section. FDE2 maintains a set of books and records that are separate from those of PRS and FDE1, and the separate set of books and records reflects items of income, gain, loss, and expense with respect to the Country C Business. Country C Business's functional currency is the U.S. dollar. FDE2 sells paper. FDE2's paper business is not related to FDE1's bicycle sales business, and FDE1 does not hold its interest in FDE2 in the ordinary course of its trade or business.

(B) *Analysis*—(1) Country A Business's activities comprise a trade or business conducted outside the United States within the meaning of § 1.989(a)-1(b)(2)(ii)(A) and (b)(3) (in each case, as modified by paragraph (f)(3)(iii) of this section). PRS does not maintain a separate set of books and records with respect to the Country A Business. However, under paragraph (f)(3)(iii)(C) of this section, the Country A Business's activities are deemed to satisfy the requirement of § 1.989(a)-1(b)(2)(ii)(B) that a QBU maintain a separate set of books and records

**Prop. Reg. § 1.904-4(f)(3)(iii)(A)**

with respect to the relevant activities. Thus, for purposes of this paragraph (f), the activities of the Country A Business constitute a QBU as defined in § 1.989-1(b)(2)(ii) and (b)(3), as modified by paragraph (f)(3)(iii) of this section, that conducts a trade or business outside the United States. Accordingly, the activities of the Country A Business constitute a foreign branch within the meaning of paragraph (f)(3)(iii) of this section. PRS, the person that owns the Country A Business, is the foreign branch owner, within the meaning of paragraph (f)(3)(iv) of this section, with respect to the Country A Business.

(2) Country B Business's activities comprise a trade or business outside the United States within the meaning of § 1.989(a)-1(b)(2)(ii)(A) and (b)(3) (in each case, as modified by paragraph (f)(3)(iii) of this section). PRS maintains a separate set of books and records with respect to the Country B Business, as described in § 1.989(a)-1(b)(2)(ii)(B). Thus, for purposes of this section, the activities of the Country B Business constitute a QBU as defined in § 1.989-1(b)(2)(ii) and (b)(3), as modified by paragraph (f)(3)(iii) of this section, that conducts a trade or business outside the United States. Accordingly, the activities of the Country B Business constitute a foreign branch within the meaning of paragraph (f)(3)(iii) of this section. Under paragraph (f)(3)(iv) of this section, PRS, the person that owns the Country B Business indirectly through FDE1 (a disregarded entity), but not including the activities of PRS that constitute the Country A business, is the foreign branch owner with respect to the Country B Business.

(3) The same analysis that applies to the Country B Business applies to the Country C Business. Accordingly, the activities of the Country C Business constitute a foreign branch within the meaning of paragraph (f)(3)(iii) of this section. PRS, the person that owns the Country C Business indirectly through FDE1 and FDE2 (disregarded entities), but not including the activities of PRS that constitute the Country A Business, is the foreign branch owner with respect to the Country C Business.

(ii) *Example 2: Sale of foreign branch*—(A) *Facts*. The facts are the same as in paragraph (f)(4)(i)(A) of this section, except that in 2019, FDE1 sold FDE2 to an unrelated person, recording gain from the sale on its books and records. In 2020, PRS sells FDE1 to another unrelated person, recording gain from the sale on its books and records. In each year, PRS allocates a portion of the gain to P.

(B) *Analysis*—(1) *Sale of FDE2*. Under paragraph (f)(1)(i)(B) of this section, P's distributive share of gain recognized by PRS in connection with the sales of FDE1 and FDE2 constitutes foreign branch category income if it is attributable to a foreign branch held by PRS directly or indirectly through one or more disregarded entities. PRS's gross income from the 2019 sale of FDE2 is reflected on the separate set of books and records maintained with respect to the Country B Business (a foreign branch) operated

by FDE1. Therefore, absent an exception, under paragraph (f)(2)(i) of this section PRS's gross income from the sale of FDE2 would be attributable to the Country B Business, and would constitute foreign branch category income. However, under paragraph (f)(2)(iv) of this section, gross income attributable to the Country B Business does not include gain from the sale or exchange of an interest in FDE2, a disregarded entity, unless the interest in FDE2 is held by the Country B Business in the ordinary course of its active trade or business (within the meaning of paragraph (f)(2)(iv)(B) of this section). In this case, the Country B Business does not hold FDE2 in the ordinary course of its active trade or business within the meaning of paragraph (f)(2)(iv)(B) of this section. As a result, P's distributive share of gain from the sale of FDE2 is not attributable to a foreign branch, and is not foreign branch category income.

(2) *Sale of FDE1*. The analysis of PRS's sale of FDE1 in 2020 is the same as the analysis for the sale of FDE2, except that PRS, through its Country A Business, holds FDE1 in the ordinary course of its active trade or business within the meaning of paragraph (f)(2)(iv)(B) of this section because the Country A Business engages in a trade or business that is related to the trade or business of FDE1. Therefore, P's distributive share of gain from the sale of FDE1 is attributable to a foreign branch, and is foreign branch category income.

(iii) *Example 3: Disregarded payment for services*—(A) *Facts*. P, a domestic corporation, owns FDE, a disregarded entity that is a foreign branch within the meaning of paragraph (f)(3)(iii) of this section. FDE's functional currency is the U.S. dollar. In 2019, P accrued and recorded on its books and records (and not FDE's books and records) $1,000 of gross income from the performance of services to unrelated parties that was not passive category income, $400 of which was foreign source income in respect of services performed outside the United States by employees of FDE and $600 of which was United States source income in respect of services performed in the United States. Absent the application of paragraph (f)(2)(vi) of this section, the $1,000 of gross income earned by P would be general category income that would not be attributable to FDE. FDE provided services in support of P's gross income from services. P compensated FDE for its services with an arm's length payment of $400, which was disregarded for Federal income tax purposes. The deduction for the payment of $400 from P to FDE would be allocated and apportioned to the $400 of P's foreign source services income if the payment were regarded for Federal income tax purposes.

(B) *Analysis*. The disregarded payment from P, a United States person, to FDE, its foreign branch, is not recorded on FDE's separate books and records (as adjusted to conform to Federal income tax principles) within the meaning of paragraph (f)(2)(i) of this section because it is disregarded for United States tax purposes.

**Prop. Reg. § 1.904-4(f)(4)**

However, the disregarded payment is allocable to gross income attributable to P because a deduction for the payment, if it were regarded, would be allocated to P's $1,000 of gross services income and apportioned between U.S. and foreign source income under § 1.861-8. Under paragraph (f)(2)(vi)(A) of this section, the amount of gross income attributable to the FDE foreign branch (and the gross income attributable to P) is adjusted to take the disregarded payment into account. As such, all of P's $400 of foreign source gross income from the performance of services is attributable to the FDE foreign branch for purposes of this section. Therefore, $400 of the foreign source gross income that P earned with respect to its services in 2019 constitutes gross income that is assigned to the foreign branch category.

(g) *Section 951A category income.*—(1) *In general.*—Except as provided in paragraph (g)(2) of this section, the term *section 951A category income* means amounts included (directly or indirectly through a pass-through entity) in gross income of a United States person under section 951A(a).

(2) *Exceptions for passive category income.*—Section 951A category income does not include any amounts included under section 951A(a) that are allocable to passive category income under § 1.904-5(c)(6). Section 951A category income also does not include any amounts treated as passive category income under paragraph (n)(2) of this section.

(h) * * *

(2) *Treatment of export financing interest.*—Except as provided in paragraph (h)(3) of this section, if a taxpayer (including a financial services entity) receives or accrues export financing interest from an unrelated person, then that interest is not treated as passive category income. Instead, the interest income is treated as foreign branch category income, section 951A category income, general category income, or income in a specified separate category under the rules of this section.

* * *

(5) * * *

(i) *Income other than interest.*—If any foreign person receives or accrues income that is described in section 864(d)(7) (income on a trade or service receivable acquired from a related person in the same foreign country as the recipient) and such income would also meet the definition of export financing interest if section 864(d)(1) applied to such income (income on a trade or service receivable acquired from a related person treated as interest), then the income is considered to be export financing interest and is not treated as passive category income. The income is treated as foreign branch category income, section 951A category income, general category income, or income in a specified separate category under the rules of this section.

(ii) *Interest income.*—If export financing interest is received or accrued by any foreign person and that income would otherwise be treated as related person factoring income of a controlled foreign corporation under section 864(d)(6) if section 864(d)(7) did not apply, section 904(d)(2)(B)(iii)(I) applies and the interest is not treated as passive category income. The income is treated as general category income in the hands of the controlled foreign corporation.

* * *

(k) *Separate category under section 904(d)(6) for items resourced under treaties.*—(1) *In general.*—Except as provided in paragraph (k)(4)(i) of this section, sections 904(a), (b), (c), (d), (f), and (g), and sections 907 and 960 are applied separately to any item of income that, without regard to a treaty obligation of the United States, would be treated as derived from sources within the United States, but under a treaty obligation of the United States such item of income would be treated as arising from sources outside the United States, and the taxpayer chooses the benefits of such treaty obligation.

(2) *Aggregation of items of income in each other separate category.*—For purposes of applying the general rule of paragraph (k)(1) of this section, items of income in each other separate category of income that are resourced under each applicable treaty are aggregated in a single separate category for income in that separate category that is resourced under that treaty. For example, all items of general category income that would otherwise be treated as derived from sources within the United States but which the taxpayer chooses to treat as arising from sources outside the United States pursuant to a provision of a bilateral U.S. income tax treaty are treated as income in a separate category for general category income resourced under the particular treaty. Resourced items are not combined with other income that is foreign source income under the Code, even if the other income arises from sources within the treaty country and is included in the same separate category to which the resourced income would be assigned without regard to section 904(d)(6).

(3) *Related taxes.*—Foreign taxes are allocated to each separate category described in paragraph (k)(2) of this section in accordance with § 1.904-6.

(4) *Coordination with certain income tax treaty provisions—.*—(i) *Exception for special relief from double taxation for individual residents of treaty countries.*—Section 904(d)(6)(A) and paragraph (k)(1) of this section do not apply to any item of income deemed to be from foreign sources by reason of the relief from double taxation rules in any U.S. income tax treaty that is solely applicable to United States citizens who are residents of the other Contracting State.

(ii) *U.S. competent authority assistance.*—For purposes of applying paragraph (k)(1) of this section, if, under the mutual agreement procedure provisions of an applicable income tax treaty, the U.S. competent authority agrees to allow a taxpayer to treat an item of income as foreign source income, where such item of income would otherwise be treated as derived from sources within the United States, then the taxpayer is considered to have chosen the benefits of such treaty obligation to treat the item as foreign source income.

(5) *Coordination with other Code provisions.*—Section 904(d)(6)(A) and paragraph (k)(1) of this section do not apply to any item of income to which any of sections 245(a)(10), 865(h), or 904(h)(10) applies. *See* paragraph (l) of this section.

(l) *Priority rule.*—Income that meets the definitions of a specified separate category and another category of income described in section 904(d)(1) is subject to the separate limitation described in paragraph (m) of this section and is not treated as general category income, foreign branch category income, passive category income, or section 951A category income.

(m) *Income treated as allocable to a specified separate category.*—If section 904(a), (b), and (c) are applied separately to any category of income under the Internal Revenue Code and regulations (for example, under section 245(a)(10), 865(h), 901(j), 904(d)(6), or 904(h)(10), and the regulations under those sections), that category of income is treated for all purposes of the Internal Revenue Code and regulations as if it were a separate category listed in section 904(d)(1). For purposes of this section, a separate category that is treated as if it were listed in section 904(d)(1) by reason of the first sentence in this paragraph (m) is referred to as a *specified separate category.*

(n) *Income from partnerships and other pass-through entities.*—(1) *Distributive shares of partnership income.*—(i) *In general.*—Except as provided in paragraph (n)(1)(ii) of this section, a partner's distributive share of partnership income is characterized as passive category income to the extent that the distributive share is a share of income earned or accrued by the partnership in the passive category. A partner's distributive share of partnership income that is not described in the first sentence of this paragraph is treated as foreign branch category income, section 951A category income, general category income, or income in a specified separate category under the rules of this section. Similar principles apply for a person's share of income from any other pass-through entity.

(ii) *Less than 10 percent partners partnership interests.*—(A) *In general.*—Except as provided in paragraph (n)(1)(ii)(B) of this section, if any limited partner or corporate general partner owns less than 10 percent of the value in a partnership, the partner's distributive share of partnership income from the partnership is passive income to the partner (subject to the high-taxed income exception of section 904(d)(2)(B)(iii)(II)), and the partner's distributive share of partnership deductions from the partnership is allocated and apportioned under the principles of section 1.861-8 only to the partner's passive income from that partnership. See also § 1.861-9(e)(4) for rules for apportioning partnership interest expense.

(B) *Exception for partnership interest held in the ordinary course of business.*—If a partnership interest described in paragraph (n)(1)(ii)(A) of this section is held in the ordinary course of a partner's active trade or business, the rules of paragraph (n)(1)(i) of this section apply for purposes of characterizing the partner's distributive share of the partnership income. A partnership interest is considered to be held in the ordinary course of a partner's active trade or business if the partner (or a member of the partner's affiliated group of corporations (within the meaning of section 1504(a) and without regard to section 1504(b)(3))) engages (other than through a less than 10 percent interest in a partnership) in the same or a related trade or business as the partnership.

(2) *Income from the sale of a partnership interest.*—(i) *In general.*—To the extent a partner recognizes gain on the sale of a partnership interest, that income shall be treated as passive category income to the partner, unless the income is considered to be high-taxed under section 904(d)(2)(B)(iii)(II) and paragraph (c) of this section.

(ii) *Exception for sale by 25-percent owner.*—Except as provided in paragraph (f)(2)(iv) of this section, in the case of a sale of an interest in a partnership by a partner that is a 25-percent owner of the partnership, determined by applying section 954(c)(4)(B) and substituting "partner" for "controlled foreign corporation" every place it appears, for purposes of determining the separate category to which the income recognized on the sale of the partnership interest is assigned such partner is treated as selling the proportionate share of the assets of the partnership attributable to such interest.

(3) *Value of a partnership interest.*—For purposes of paragraphs (n)(1) and (2) of this section, a partner will be considered as owning 10 percent of the value of a partnership for a particular year if the partner, together with any person that bears a relationship to the partner described in section 267(b) or 707, owns 10 percent of the capital and profits interest of the partnership. For this purpose, value will be determined at the end of the partnership's taxable year.

(o) *Separate category of section 78 gross up.*—The amount included in income under section 78 by reason of taxes deemed paid under section 960 is assigned to the separate category to which the taxes are allocated under § 1.904-6(b).

**Prop. Reg. § 1.904-4(o)**

(p) *Separate category of foreign currency gain or loss.*—Foreign currency gain or loss recognized under section 986(c) with respect to a distribution of previously taxed earnings and profits (as described in section 959 or 1293(c)) is assigned to the separate category or categories of the previously taxed earnings and profits from which the distribution is made. See § 1.987-6(b) for rules on assigning section 987 gain or loss on a remittance from a section 987 QBU to a separate category or categories.

(q) *Applicability dates.*—This section applies for taxable years that both begin after December 31, 2017, and end on or after December 4, 2018.

[Proposed 12-7-2018.]

**[Prop. Reg. § 1.904-5]**

**§ 1.904-5. Look-through rules as applied to controlled foreign corporations and other entities.**—(a) *Scope and definitions.*—(1) *Look-through rules under section 904(d)(3) to passive category income.*—Paragraph (c) of this section provides rules for determining the extent to which dividends, interest, rents, and royalties received or accrued by certain eligible persons, and inclusions under sections 951(a)(1) and 951A(a), are treated as passive category income. Paragraph (g) of this section provides rules applying the principles of paragraph (c) of this section to foreign source interest, rents, and royalties paid by a United States corporation to a related corporation. Paragraph (h) of this section provides rules for assigning a partnership payment to a partner described in section 707 to the passive category. Paragraph (i) of this section provides rules applying the principles of this section to assign distributions and payments from certain related entities to the passive category or to treat the distributions and payments as not in the passive category.

(2) *Other look-through rules under section 904(d).*—Under section 904(d)(4) and paragraph (c)(4)(iii) of this section, certain dividends from noncontrolled 10-percent owned foreign corporations are treated as income in a separate category. Under section 904(d)(3)(H) and paragraph (j) of this section, certain inclusions under section 1293 are treated as income in a separate category. Paragraph (i) of this section provides rules applying the principles of this section to assign distributions from certain related entities to separate categories.

(3) *Other rules provided in this section.*—Paragraph (b) of this section provides operative rules for this section. Paragraph (d) of this section provides rules addressing exceptions to passive category income for certain purposes in the case of controlled foreign corporations that meet the requirements of section 954(b)(3)(A) (de minimis rule) or section 954(b)(4) (high-tax exception). Paragraph (e) of this section provides rules for characterizing a controlled foreign corporation's foreign base company income and gross insurance income when section 954(b)(3)(B) (full in-

clusion rule) applies. Paragraph (f) of this section modifies the look-through rules for certain types of income. Paragraph (k) of this section provides ordering rules for applying the look-through rules. Paragraph (l) of this section provides examples illustrating the application of certain rules in this section. Paragraphs (m) and (n) of this section provide rules related to the resourcing rules described in section 904(h).

(4) *Definitions.*—For purposes of this section, the following definitions apply:

(i) The term *controlled foreign corporation* has the meaning given such term by section 957 (taking into account the special rule for certain captive insurance companies contained in section 953(c)).

(ii) The term *look-through rules* means the rules described in this section that assign income to a separate category based on the separate category of the income to which it is allocable.

(iii) The term *noncontrolled 10-percent owned foreign corporation* has the meaning provided in section 904(d)(2)(E)(i).

(iv) The term *pass-through entity* means a partnership, S corporation, or any other person (whether domestic or foreign) other than a corporation to the extent that the income or deductions of the person are included in the income of one or more direct or indirect owners or beneficiaries of the person. For example, if a domestic trust is subject to Federal income tax on a portion of its income and its owners are subject to tax on the remaining portion, the domestic trust is treated as a domestic pass-through entity with respect to such remaining portion.

(v) The term *separate category* means, as the context requires, any category of income described in 904(d)(1)(A), (B), (C), or (D), any specified separate category of income as defined in § 1.904-4(m), or any category of earnings and profits to which income described in such provisions is attributable.

(vi) The term *United States shareholder* has the meaning given such term by section 951(b) (taking into account the special rule for certain captive insurance companies contained in section 953(c)), except that for purposes of this section, a United States shareholder includes any member of the controlled group of the United States shareholder. For this purpose the controlled group is any member of the affiliated group within the meaning of section 1504(a)(1) except that "more than 50 percent" is substituted for "at least 80 percent" wherever it appears in section 1504(a)(2). When used in reference to a noncontrolled 10-percent owned foreign corporation described in section 904(d)(2)(E)(i)(II), the term *United States shareholder* also means a taxpayer that meets the stock ownership requirements described in section 904(d)(2)(E)(i)(II).

(b) *Operative rules.*—(1) *Assignment of income not assigned under the look-through rules.*—Except as provided by the look-through rules, dividends, interest, rents, and royalties received or accrued by a taxpayer from a controlled foreign corporation in which the taxpayer is a United States shareholder are excluded from passive category income. Income excluded from the passive category under this paragraph (b)(1) is assigned to another separate category (other than the passive category) under the rules in § 1.904-4.

(2) *Priority and ordering of look-through rules.*—Except as provided in § 1.904-4(l), to the extent the look-through rules assign income to a separate category, the income is assigned to that separate category rather than the separate category to which the income would have been assigned under § 1.904-4 (not taking into account § 1.904-4(l)). See paragraph (k) of this section for ordering rules for applying the look-through rules.

(c) * * *

(1) *Scope.*—Subject to the exceptions in paragraph (f) of this section, paragraphs (c)(2) through (c)(6) (other than paragraph (c)(4)(iii)) of this section provide look-through rules with respect to interest, rents, royalties, dividends, and inclusions under section 951(a)(1) and 951A(a) that are received or accrued from a controlled foreign corporation in which the taxpayer is a United States shareholder. Paragraph (c)(4)(iii) of this section provides a look-through rule for dividends received from a noncontrolled 10-percent owned foreign corporation by a domestic corporation that is a United States shareholder in the foreign corporation.

(2) * * *

(i) * * * Related person interest is treated as passive category income to the extent it is allocable to passive category income of the controlled foreign corporation. If related person interest is received or accrued from a controlled foreign corporation by two or more persons, the amount of interest received or accrued by each person that is allocable to passive category income is determined by multiplying the amount of related person interest allocable to passive category income by a fraction. * * *

* * *

(3) *Rents and royalties.*—Any rents or royalties received or accrued from a controlled foreign corporation in which the taxpayer is a United States shareholder are treated as passive category income to the extent they are allocable to passive category income of the controlled foreign corporation under the principles of §§ 1.861-8 through 1.861-14T.

(4) * * *

(i) * * * Except as provided in paragraph (d)(2) of this section, any dividend paid or accrued out of the earnings and profits of any controlled foreign corporation is treated as passive category income in proportion to the ratio of the portion of earnings and profits attributable to passive category income to the total amount of earnings and profits of the controlled foreign corporation. * * *

* * *

(iii) *Look-through rule for dividends from noncontrolled 10-percent owned foreign corporations.*—(A) *In general.*—Except as provided in paragraph (c)(4)(iii)(B) of this section, any dividend that is distributed by a noncontrolled 10-percent owned foreign corporation and received or accrued by a domestic corporation that is a United States shareholder of such foreign corporation is treated as income in a separate category in proportion to the ratio of the portion of earnings and profits attributable to income in such category to the total amount of earnings and profits of the noncontrolled 10-percent owned foreign corporation.

(B) *Inadequate substantiation.*—A dividend distributed by a noncontrolled 10-percent owned foreign corporation is treated as income in the separate category described in section 904(d)(4)(C)(ii) if the Commissioner determines that the look-through characterization of the dividend cannot reasonably be determined based on the available information.

* * *

(5) *Inclusions under section 951(a)(1)(A).*—(i) Any amount included in gross income under section 951(a)(1)(A) is treated as passive category income to the extent the amount included is attributable to income received or accrued by the controlled foreign corporation that is passive category income. All other amounts included in gross income under section 951(a)(1)(A) are treated as general category income or income in a specified separate category under the rules in § 1.904-4. For rules concerning a distributive share of partnership income, see § 1.904-4(n). For rules concerning the gross up under section 78, see § 1.904-4(o). For rules concerning inclusions under section 951(a)(1)(B), see paragraph (c)(4)(i) of this section.

(ii) [Reserved]

(6) *Inclusions under section 951A(a).*—Any amount included in gross income under section 951A(a) is treated as passive category income to the extent the amount included is attributable to income received or accrued by the controlled foreign corporation that is passive category income. All other amounts included in gross income under section 951A(a) are treated as section 951A category income or income in a specified separate category under the rules in § 1.904-4. For rules concerning a distributive share of partnership income, see § 1.904-4(n). For rules concerning the gross up under section 78, see § 1.904-4(o).

(d) * * *

(1) *De minimis amount of subpart F income.*—If the sum of a controlled foreign corporation's gross foreign base company income (determined under section 954(a) without regard to section 954(b)(5)) and gross insurance income (deter-

mined under section 953(a)) for the taxable year is less than the lesser of 5 percent of gross income or $1,000,000, then none of that income is treated as passive category income. In addition, if the test in the first sentence of this paragraph is satisfied, for purposes of paragraphs (c)(2)(ii)(D) and (E) of this section (apportionment of interest expense to passive income using the asset method), any passive category assets are not treated as passive category assets but are treated as assets in the general category or a specified separate category. The determination in the first sentence is made before the application of the exception for certain income subject to a high rate of foreign tax described in paragraph (d)(2) of this section.

(2) *Exception for certain income subject to high foreign tax.*—Except as provided in § 1.904-4(c)(7)(iii) (relating to reductions in tax upon distribution), for purposes of the dividend look-through rule of paragraph (c)(4)(i) of this section, an item of net income that would otherwise be passive income (after application of the priority rules of § 1.904-4(l)) and that is received or accrued by a controlled foreign corporation is not treated as passive category income, and the earnings and profits attributable to such income is not treated as passive category earnings and profits, if the taxpayer establishes to the satisfaction of the Secretary under section 954(b)(4) that the income was subject to an effective rate of income tax imposed by a foreign country greater than 90 percent of the maximum rate of tax specified in section 11 (with reference to section 15, if applicable). Such income is treated as general category income or income in a specified separate category under the rules in § 1.904-4. The first sentence of this paragraph has no effect on amounts (other than dividends) paid or accrued by a controlled foreign corporation to a United States shareholder of such controlled foreign corporation to the extent those amounts are allocable to passive category income of the controlled foreign corporation.

\* \* \*

(f) \* \* \*

(1) [Reserved]

\* \* \*

(h) *Application of look-through rules to payments from a partnership or other pass-through entity.*— Payments to a partner described in section 707 (e.g., payments to a partner not acting in capacity as a partner) are characterized as passive category income to the extent that the payment is attributable under the principles of § 1.861-8 and this section to passive category income of the partnership, if the payments are interest, rents, or royalties that would be characterized under the controlled foreign corporation look-through rules of paragraph (c) of this section if the partnership were a foreign corporation, and the partner who receives the payment owns 10 percent or more of the value of the partnership (as determined under § 1.904-4(n)(3)). A pay-

ment by a partnership to a member of the controlled group (as defined in paragraph (a)(4)(vi) of this section) of the partner is characterized under the look-through rules of this paragraph (h) if the payment would be a section 707 payment entitled to look-through treatment if it were made to the partner. Similar principles apply for a payment from any other pass-through entity. The rules in this paragraph (h) do not apply with respect to interest to the extent the interest income is assigned to a separate category under the specified partnership loan rules described in § 1.861-9(e)(8).

(i) \* \* \*

(1) \* \* \* For purposes of this paragraph (i)(1), indirect ownership of stock is determined under section 318 and the regulations under that section. In the case of a partnership or other pass-through entity, indirect ownership and value is determined under the rules in paragraph (i)(2) of this section.

(2) *Indirect ownership and value of a partnership interest.*—A person is considered as owning, directly or indirectly, more than 50 percent of the value of a partnership if the person, together with other any person that bears a relationship to the first person that is described in section 267(b) or 707, owns more than 50 percent of the capital and profits interests of the partnership. For this purpose, value will be determined at the end of the partnership's taxable year. Similar principles apply for a person that owns a pass-through entity other than a partnership.

(3) *Special rule for dividends between certain foreign corporations.*—Solely for purposes of dividend payments between controlled foreign corporations, noncontrolled 10-percent owned foreign corporations, or a controlled foreign corporation and a noncontrolled 10-percent owned foreign corporation, the two foreign corporations are considered related look-through entities if the same person is a United States shareholder of both foreign corporations.

(4) [Reserved]

\* \* \*

(k) \* \* \*

(2) \* \* \*

(iii) Inclusions under sections 951(a)(1)(A) and 951A(a) and distributive shares of partnership income;

\* \* \*

(m) \* \* \*

(2) \* \* \*

(ii) *Interest payments from noncontrolled 10-percent owned foreign corporations.*—If interest is received or accrued by a shareholder from a noncontrolled 10-percent owned foreign corporation (where the shareholder is a domestic corporation that is a United States shareholder of such noncontrolled 10-percent owned foreign corporation), the rules of paragraph (m)(2)(i) of this section apply in determining the portion of the interest payment that is from sources within the United States, except that the related party interest rules of paragraph (c)(2)(ii)(C) of this section do not apply.

\* \* \*

(4) \* \* \*

(i) *Rule.*—Any dividend or distribution treated as a dividend under this paragraph (m) (including an amount included in gross income under section 951(a)(1)(B)) that is received or accrued by a United States shareholder from a controlled foreign corporation, or any dividend that is received or accrued by a domestic corporation from a noncontrolled 10-percent owned foreign corporation with respect to which the shareholder is a United States shareholder, are treated as income in a separate category derived from sources within the United States in proportion to the ratio of the portion of the earnings and profits of the controlled foreign corporation or noncontrolled 10-percent owned foreign corporation in the corresponding separate category from United States sources to the total amount of earnings and profits of the controlled foreign corporation or noncontrolled 10-percent owned foreign corporation in that separate category.

\* \* \*

(5) \* \* \*

(i) \* \* \* Any amount included in the gross income of a United States shareholder of a controlled foreign corporation under section 951(a)(1)(A), 951A, or in the gross income of a domestic corporation that is a United States shareholder of a noncontrolled 10-percent owned foreign corporation described in section 904(d)(2)(E)(i)(II) that is a qualified electing fund under section 1293 is treated as income subject to a separate category that is derived from sources within the United States to the extent the amount is attributable to income of the controlled foreign corporation or qualified electing fund, respectively, in the corresponding category of income from sources within the United States. \* \* \*

\* \* \*

(n) \* \* \* Section 904(d)(3), (d)(4), and (h), and this section are then applied for purposes of characterizing and sourcing income received, accrued, or included by a United States shareholder of the foreign corporation that is attributable or allocable to income or earnings and profits of the foreign corporation.

(o) *Applicability dates.*—This section is applicable for taxable years that both begin after December 31, 2017, and end on or after December 4, 2018.

[Proposed 12-7-2018.]

### [Prop. Reg. § 1.904-6]

**§ 1.904-6. Allocation and apportionment of taxes.**—(a) \* \* \*

(1) \* \* \*

(i) \* \* \* The amount of foreign taxes paid or accrued with respect to a separate category (as defined in § 1.904-5(a)(4)(v)) of income (including United States source income within the separate category) includes only those taxes that are related to income in that separate category. \* \* \* Income included in the foreign tax base is calculated under foreign law, but characterized as income in a separate category under United States tax principles. For example, a foreign tax imposed on an amount realized on the disposition of controlled foreign corporation stock that is characterized as a capital gain under foreign law but as a dividend under section 1248 is generally assigned to the general category, not the passive category. \* \* \*

\* \* \*

(iv) *Base and timing differences.*—If, under the law of a foreign country or possession of the United States, a tax is imposed on a type of item that does not constitute income under Federal income tax principles (a *base difference*), such as gifts or life insurance proceeds, that tax is treated as imposed with respect to income in the separate category described in section 904(d)(2)(H)(i). If, under the law of a foreign country or possession of the United States, a tax is imposed on an item of income that constitutes income under Federal income tax principles but is not recognized for Federal income tax purposes in the current year (a *timing difference*), that tax is allocated and apportioned to the appropriate separate category or categories to which the tax would be allocated and apportioned if the income were recognized under Federal income tax principles in the year in which the tax was imposed. If the amount of an item of income as computed for foreign tax purposes is positive but is greater than the amount of income that is currently recognized for Federal income tax purposes, for example, due to a difference in depreciation conventions or the timing of recognition of gross income, or because of a permanent difference between U.S. and foreign tax law in the amount of deductions that are allowed to reduce gross income, the tax is allocated or apportioned to the separate category to which the income is assigned, and no portion of the tax is attributable to a base difference. In addition, a tax imposed on a distribution that is excluded from gross income under section 959(a) or section 959(b) is treated as attributable to a timing difference (and not a base difference) and is treated as tax imposed on the earnings and profits from which the distribution was paid.

(2) *Special rules for foreign branches.*—(i) *In general.*—Except as provided in this paragraph (a)(2), any foreign tax reflected on the books and records of a foreign branch under the principles of § 1.987-2(b) is allocated and apportioned under the rules of paragraph (a)(1) of this section.

(ii) *Disregarded reallocation transactions.*— (A) *Foreign branch to foreign branch owner.*—In the case of a disregarded payment from a foreign branch to a foreign branch owner that is treated as a disregarded reallocation transaction that results in foreign branch category income being reallocated to the general category, any foreign tax imposed solely by reason of that payment, such as a withholding tax imposed on the disregarded payment, is allocated and apportioned to the general category.

(B) *Foreign branch owner to foreign branch.*—In the case of a disregarded payment from a foreign branch owner to a foreign branch that is treated as a disregarded reallocation transaction that results in general category income being reallocated to the foreign branch category, any foreign tax imposed solely by reason of that transaction is allocated and apportioned to the foreign branch category.

(iii) *Other disregarded payments.*—(A) *Foreign branch to foreign branch owner.*—In the case of a disregarded payment from a foreign branch to a foreign branch owner that is not a disregarded reallocation transaction, foreign tax imposed solely by reason of that disregarded payment is allocated and apportioned to a separate category under the principles of paragraph (a)(1) of this section based on the nature of the item (determined under Federal income tax principles) that is included in the foreign tax base. For example, if a remittance of an appreciated asset results in gain recognition under foreign law, the tax imposed on that gain is treated as attributable to a timing difference with respect to recognition of the gain, and is allocated and apportioned to the separate category to which gain on a sale of that asset would have been assigned if it were recognized for Federal income tax purposes. However, a gross basis withholding tax on a remittance is attributable to a timing difference in taxation of the income out of which the remittance is made, and is allocated and apportioned to the separate category or categories to which a section 987 gain or loss would be assigned under § 1.987-6(b).

(B) *Foreign branch owner to foreign branch.*—In the case of a disregarded payment from a foreign branch owner to a foreign branch that is not a disregarded reallocation transaction, any foreign tax imposed solely by reason of that disregarded payment is allocated and apportioned to the foreign branch category.

(iv) *Definitions.*—The following definitions apply for purposes of this paragraph (a)(2):

(A) *Disregarded reallocation transaction.*—The term *disregarded reallocation transaction* means a disregarded payment or a transfer described in § 1.904-4(f)(2)(vi)(D) that results in an adjustment to the gross income attributable to the foreign branch under § 1.904-4(f)(2)(vi)(A).

(B) The terms *disregarded payment, foreign branch, foreign branch owner*, and *remittance* have the same meaning given to those terms in § 1.904-4(f)(3).

(3) *Taxes imposed on high-taxed income.*—For rules on the treatment of taxes imposed on high-taxed income, see § 1.904-4(c).

(b) *Allocation and apportionment of deemed paid taxes and certain creditable foreign tax expenditures.*—(1) *Taxes deemed paid under section 960(a) or (d).*—If a domestic corporation that is a United States shareholder includes any amount in gross income under sections 951(a)(1)(A) or 951A(a), any foreign tax deemed paid with respect to such amount under section 960(a) or (d) is allocated to the separate category to which the inclusion is assigned.

(2) *Taxes deemed paid under section 960(b)(1).*—If a domestic corporation that is a United States shareholder receives a distribution of previously taxed earnings and profits from a first-tier corporation that is excluded from the domestic corporation's income under section 959(a) and § 1.959-1, any foreign tax deemed paid under section 960(b)(1) with respect to such distribution is allocated to the same separate category as the annual PTEP account and PTEP group (as defined in § 1.960-3(c)) from which the distribution is made.

(3) *Taxes deemed paid under section 960(b)(2).*—If a controlled foreign corporation receives a distribution of previously taxed earnings and profits from an immediately lower-tier corporation that is excluded from such controlled foreign corporation's gross income under section 959(b) and § 1.959-2, any foreign tax deemed paid under section 960(b)(2) with respect to such distribution is allocated to the same separate category as the annual PTEP account and PTEP group (as defined in § 1.960-3(c)) from which the distribution is made. *See also* § 1.960-3(c)(2).

(4) *Creditable foreign tax expenditures.*—(i) *In general.*—Except as provided in paragraph (b)(4)(ii) of this section, creditable foreign tax expenditures (CFTEs) allocated to a partner under § 1.704-1(b)(4)(viii)(*a*) are allocated for purposes of this section to the same separate category as the separate category to which the taxes were allocated in the hands of the partnership under the rules of paragraph (a) of this section.

(ii) *Foreign branch category.*—CFTEs allocated to a partner in a partnership under § 1.704-1(b)(4)(viii)(*a*) are allocated and apportioned to the foreign branch category of the partner to the extent that:

(A) The CFTEs are allocated and apportioned by the partnership under the rules of paragraph (a) of this section to the general category;

(B) In the hands of the partnership, the CFTEs are related to general category income attributable to a foreign branch (as described in

§1.904-4(f)(2)) under the principles of paragraph (a) of this section; and

(C) The partner's distributive share of the income described in paragraph (b)(4)(ii)(B) of this section is foreign branch category income of the partner under §1.904-4(f)(1)(i)(B).

* * *

(d) *Applicability dates.*—This section is applicable for taxable years that both begin after December 31, 2017, and end on or after December 4, 2018.

[Proposed 12-7-2018.]

### [Prop. Reg. §1.904(b)-3]

**§1.904(b)-3. Disregard of certain dividends and deductions under section 904(b)(4).—** (a) *Disregard of certain dividends and deductions.*— (1) *In general.*—For purposes of section 904(a), in the case of a domestic corporation which is a United States shareholder with respect to a specified 10-percent owned foreign corporation (as defined in section 245A(b)), the domestic corporation's foreign source taxable income in a separate category and entire taxable income is determined without regard to the following items:

(i) Any dividend for which a deduction is allowed under section 245A;

(ii) Deductions properly allocable or apportioned to gross income in the section 245A subgroup as determined under paragraphs (b) and (c)(1) of this section; and

(iii) Deductions properly allocable or apportioned to stock of specified 10-percent owned foreign corporations in the section 245A subgroup as determined under paragraphs (b) and (c) of this section.

(2) *Deductions properly allocable or apportioned to the residual grouping.*—Deductions that are properly allocable or apportioned to gross income or stock in the section 245A subgroup of the residual grouping (consisting of U.S. source income) are disregarded solely for purposes of determining entire taxable income under section 904(a).

(b) *Determining properly allocable or apportioned deductions.*—The amount of deductions properly allocable or apportioned to gross income or stock described in paragraphs (a)(1)(ii) and (iii) of this section is determined by subdividing the United States shareholder's gross income and assets in each separate category described in §1.904-5(a)(4)(v) into a section 245A subgroup and a non-section 245A subgroup. Gross income and assets in the residual grouping for U.S. source income are also subdivided into a section 245A subgroup and a non-section 245A subgroup. Each section 245A subgroup is treated as a statutory grouping under §1.861-8(a)(4). Deductions properly allocable or apportioned to dividends or stock described in paragraphs (a)(1)(ii) and (iii) of this section only include those deductions that are allocated and appor-

tioned under §§1.861-8 through 1.861-14T and 1.861-17 to the section 245A subgroups. The deduction allowed under section 245A(a) for dividends is allocated and apportioned solely among the section 245A subgroups on the basis of the relative amounts of gross income from such dividends in each section 245A subgroup.

(c) *Income and assets in the 245A subgroups.*— (1) *In general.*—For purposes of applying the allocation and apportionment rules under §§1.861-8 through 1.861-14T and 1.861-17 to the deductions of a United States shareholder, the only gross income included in a section 245A subgroup is dividend income for which a deduction is allowed under section 245A. The only asset included in a section 245A subgroup is the portion of the value of stock of each specified 10-percent owned foreign corporation that is assigned to the section 245A subgroup determined under paragraph (c)(2) of this section.

(2) *Assigning stock to a subgroup.*—The value of stock of a specified 10-percent owned foreign corporation is characterized as an asset in a separate category described in §1.904-5(a)(4)(v) or the residual grouping for U.S. source income under the rules of §1.861-12(c). If the specified 10-percent owned foreign corporation is not a controlled foreign corporation, all of the value of its stock (other than the portion of stock assigned to the statutory groupings for gross section 245(a)(5) income under §§1.861-12(c)(4) and 1.861-13) in each separate category and in the residual grouping for U.S. source income is assigned to the section 245A subgroup in such separate category or residual grouping. If the specified 10-percent owned foreign corporation is a controlled foreign corporation, a portion of the value of stock in each separate category and in the residual grouping for U.S. source income is subdivided between a section 245A and non-section 245A subgroup under §1.861-13(a)(5).

(d) *Coordination with OFL and ODL rules.*—Section 904(b)(4) and this section apply before the operation of the overall foreign loss rules in section 904(f) and the overall domestic loss rules in section 904(g).

(e) *Example.*—The following example illustrates the application of this section.

(1) *Facts* (i) *Income and assets of USP.* USP is a domestic corporation. USP owns a factory in the United States with a tax book value of $21,000. USP also directly owns all of the stock of each of the following three controlled foreign corporations: CFC1, CFC2, and CFC3. USP's tax book value in each of CFC1, CFC2, and CFC3 is $10,000. USP incurs $1,500 of interest expense and earns $1,600 of U.S. source gross income. Under section 951A and the section 951A regulations (as defined in §1.951A-1(a)(1)), USP's GILTI inclusion amount is $2,200. USP's deduction under section 250 is $1,100 ("section 250 deduction"), all of which is by reason of section 250(a)(1)(B)(i). No portion of USP's section 250

deduction is reduced by reason of section 250(a)(2)(B). None of the CFCs makes any distributions.

(ii) *Characterization of CFC stock.* After application of § 1.861-13(a), USP determined that $7,300 of the stock of each of CFC1, CFC2, and CFC3 is assigned to the section 951A category ("section 951A category stock") in the non-section 245A subgroup and the remaining $2,700 of the stock of each of CFC1, CFC2, and CFC3 is assigned to the general category ("general category stock") in the section 245A subgroup. Additionally, under § 1.861-8(d)(2)(ii)(C)(2), $3,650 of the stock of each of CFC1, CFC2, and CFC3 that is section 951A category stock is an exempt asset. Accordingly, with respect to the stock of its controlled foreign corporations in the aggregate, USP has $10,950 of section 951A category stock in a non-section 245A subgroup; $8,100 of general category stock in a section 245A subgroup; and $10,950 of stock that is an exempt asset.

(iii) *Apportioning of expenses.* Taking into account USP's factory and its stock in CFC1, CFC2, and CFC3, the tax book value of USP's assets for purposes of apportioning expenses is $40,050 (excluding the $10,950 of exempt assets). Under § 1.861-9T(g), USP's $1,500 of interest expense is apportioned as follows: $410 ($1,500 x $10,950/$40,050) to section 951A category income, $303 ($1,500 x $8,100/$40,050) to general category income, and the remaining $787 ($1,500 x $21,000/$40,050) to the residual U.S. source grouping. Under § 1.861-8(e)(14), all of USP's section 250 deduction is allocated and apportioned to section 951A category income.

(2) *Analysis*—(i) *USP's pre-credit U.S. tax.* USP's worldwide taxable income is $1,200, which equals its GILTI inclusion amount of $2,200 plus its U.S. source gross income of $1,600, less its deduction under section 250 of $1,100 and its interest expense of $1,500. For purposes of applying section 904(a), before taking into account any foreign tax credit under section 901, USP's federal income tax liability is 21% of $1,200, or $252.

(ii) *Application of section 904(b)(4).* Under section 904(d)(1), USP applies section 904(a) separately to each separate category of income.

(A) *General category income.* Before application of section 904(b)(4) and the rules in this section, USP's foreign source taxable income in the general category is a loss of $303, which equals $0 (USP's foreign source general category income) less $303 (interest expense apportioned to general category income), and USP's worldwide taxable income is $1,200. Under paragraph (d) of this section, the rules in section 904(f) and (g) apply after section 904(b)(4) and the rules in this section. Under paragraphs (b) and (c)(1) of this section, USP has no deductions properly allocable or apportioned to gross income in the section 245A subgroup because USP has no dividend income in the general category for which a deduction is allowed under section 245A. Under paragraphs (b) and (c) of this section, USP has

$303 of deductions for interest expense that are properly allocable or apportioned to stock of specified 10-percent owned foreign corporations in the section 245A subgroup because USP's only general category assets are the general category stock of CFC1, CFC2, and CFC3, all of which are in the section 245A subgroup. Therefore, under paragraph (a) of this section, USP's foreign source taxable income in the general category and its worldwide taxable income are determined without regard to the $303 of deductions for interest expense. Accordingly, USP's foreign source taxable income in the general category is $0 and its worldwide taxable income is $1,503, and therefore, there is no separate limitation loss for purposes of section 904(f). Under section 904(a) and (d)(1) USP's foreign tax credit limitation for the general category is $0.

(B) *Section 951A category income.* Before application of section 904(b)(4) and the rules in this section, USP's foreign source taxable income in the section 951A category is $690, which equals $2,200 (USP's GILTI inclusion amount) less $1,100 (USP's section 250 deduction) less $410 (interest apportioned to section 951A category income). Under paragraphs (b) and (c)(1) of this section, USP has no deductions properly allocable and apportioned to gross income in a section 245A subgroup of the section 951A category. Under paragraphs (b) and (c) of this section, USP has no deductions properly allocable and apportioned to stock of specified 10-percent owned foreign corporations in a section 245A subgroup of section 951A category stock because no portion of section 951A category stock is assigned to a section 245A subgroup. *See* § 1.861-13(a)(5)(v). Therefore, under paragraph (a) of this section no adjustment is made to USP's foreign source taxable income in the section 951A category. However, the adjustments to USP's worldwide taxable income described in paragraph (e)(2)(ii)(A) of this section apply for purposes of calculating USP's foreign tax credit limitation for the section 951A category. Accordingly, USP's foreign source taxable income in the section 951A category is $690 and its worldwide taxable income is $1,503. Under section 904(a) and (d)(1), USP's foreign tax credit limitation for the section 951A category is $116 ($252 x $690/$1,503).

(f) *Applicability date.*—Except as provided in this paragraph (f), this section applies to taxable years beginning after December 31, 2017. For a taxable year that both begins before January 1, 2018, and ends after December 31, 2017, this section applies without regard to the rules relating to inclusions arising under section 951A. [Reg. § 1.904(b)-3.]

[Proposed 12-7-2018.]

**[Prop. Reg. § 1.904(f)-12]**

**§ 1.904(f)-12. Payment and returns of tax withheld by the acquiring agency.**

\* \* \*

(i) [Reserved]

(j) *Recapture in years beginning after December 31, 2017, of separate limitation losses, overall foreign losses, and overall domestic losses incurred in years beginning before January 1, 2018.*—(1) *Definitions.*—(i) The term *pre-2018 separate categories* means the separate categories of income described in section 904(d) and any specified separate categories of income, as applicable to taxable years beginning before January 1, 2018.

(ii) The term *post-2017 separate categories* means the separate categories of income described in section 904(d) and any specified separate categories of income, as applicable to taxable years beginning after December 31, 2018.

(iii) The term *specified separate category* has the meaning set forth in § 1.904-4(m)).

(2) *Losses related to pre-2018 passive category income or a specified separate category of income.*—(i) *Allocation of separate limitation loss or overall foreign loss account incurred in a pre-2018 separate category for passive category income or a specified separate category of income.*—To the extent that a taxpayer has a balance in any separate limitation loss or overall foreign loss account in a pre-2018 separate category for passive category income or a specified separate category of income at the end of the taxpayer's last taxable year beginning before January 1, 2018, the amount of such balance is allocated on the first day of the taxpayer's next taxable year to the same post-2017 separate category as the pre-2018 separate category of the separate limitation loss or overall foreign loss account.

(ii) *Recapture of separate limitation loss or overall domestic loss that reduced pre-2018 passive category income or a specified separate category of income.*—To the extent that at the end of the taxpayer's last taxable year beginning before January 1, 2018, a taxpayer has a balance in any separate limitation loss or overall domestic loss account which offset pre-2018 separate category income that was passive category income or income in a specified separate category, such loss is recaptured in subsequent taxable years as income in the same post-2017 separate category as the pre-2018 separate category of income that was offset by the loss.

(3) *Losses related to pre-2018 general category income.*—(i) *Allocation of separate limitation loss or overall foreign loss account incurred in a pre-2018 separate category for general category income.*—To the extent that a taxpayer has a balance in any separate limitation loss or overall foreign loss account in a pre-2018 separate category for general category income at the end of the taxpayer's last taxable year beginning before January 1, 2018, the amount of such balance is allocated on the first day of the taxpayer's next taxable year to the taxpayer's post-2017 separate category for general category income, or, if the taxpayer applies the exception described in § 1.904-2(j)(1)(iii), on a pro rata basis to the tax-

payer's post-2017 separate categories for general category and foreign branch category income, based on the proportion in which any unused foreign taxes in the same pre-2018 separate category for general category income are allocated under § 1.904-2(j)(1)(iii)(A). If the taxpayer has no unused foreign taxes in the pre-2018 separate category for general category income, then any loss account balance in that category is allocated to the post-2017 separate category for general category income.

(ii) *Recapture of separate limitation loss or overall domestic loss that reduced pre-2018 general category income.*—To the extent that a taxpayer's separate limitation loss or overall domestic loss offset pre-2018 separate category income that was general category income, the balance in the loss account at the end of the taxpayer's last taxable year beginning before January 1, 2018, is recaptured in subsequent taxable years as income in the post-2017 separate category for general category income, or, if the taxpayer applies the exception described in § 1.904-2(j)(1)(iii), on a pro rata basis as income in the post-2017 separate categories for general category and foreign branch category income, based on the proportion in which any unused foreign taxes in the pre-2018 separate category for general category income are allocated under § 1.904-2(j)(1)(iii)(A). If the taxpayer has no unused foreign taxes in the pre-2018 separate category for general category income, then the loss account balance shall be recaptured in subsequent taxable years solely as income in the post-2017 separate category for general category income.

(4) *Treatment of foreign losses that are part of net operating losses incurred in pre-2018 taxable years which are carried forward to post-2017 taxable years.*—A foreign loss that is part of a net operating loss incurred in a taxable year beginning before January 1, 2018, which is carried forward, pursuant to section 172, to a taxable year beginning after December 31, 2017, will be carried forward under the rules of § 1.904(g)-3(b)(2). For purposes of applying those rules, the portion of a net operating loss carryforward that is attributable to a foreign loss from the pre-2018 separate category for passive category income or a specified separate category of income will be treated as a loss in the same post-2017 separate category as the pre-2018 separate category. The portion of a net operating loss carryforward that is attributable to a foreign loss from the pre-2018 separate category for general category income must be treated as a loss in the post-2017 separate category for general or branch category income under the allocation principles of paragraph (j)(3)(i) of this section.

(5) *Applicability date.*—This paragraph (j) applies to taxable years beginning after December 31, 2017.

[Proposed 12-7-2018.]

**Prop. Reg. § 1.904(f)-12(j)(5)**

**[Prop. Reg. § 1.951-1]**

**§ 1.951-1. Amounts included in gross income of United States shareholders.**—(a) *In general.*— If a foreign corporation is a controlled foreign corporation (within the meaning of section 957) at any time during any taxable year of such corporation, every person—

\* \* \*

(e) *Pro rata share of subpart F income defined.*—(1) *In general.*—(i) *Hypothetical distribution.*—For purposes of paragraph (b) of this section, a United States shareholder's pro rata share of a controlled foreign corporation's subpart F income for a taxable year is the amount that bears the same ratio to the corporation's subpart F income for the taxable year as the amount of the corporation's current earnings and profits that would be distributed with respect to the stock of the corporation which the United States shareholder owns (within the meaning of section 958(a)) for the taxable year bears to the total amount of the corporation's current earnings and profits that would be distributed with respect to the stock owned by all the shareholders of the corporation if all the current earnings and profits of the corporation for the taxable year (not reduced by actual distributions during the year) were distributed (*hypothetical distribution*) on the last day of the corporation's taxable year on which such corporation is a controlled foreign corporation (*hypothetical distribution date*).

(ii) *Determination of current earnings and profits.*—For purposes of this paragraph (e), the amount of current earnings and profits of a controlled foreign corporation for a taxable year is treated as the greater of the following two amounts:

(A) The earnings and profits of the corporation for the taxable year determined under section 964; or

(B) The sum of the subpart F income (as determined under section 952 and increased as provided under section 951A(c)(2)(B)(ii) and § 1.951A-6(d)) of the corporation for the taxable year and the tested income (as defined in section 951A(c)(2)(A) and § 1.951A-2(b)(1)) of the corporation for the taxable year.

(2) *One class of stock.*—If a controlled foreign corporation for a taxable year has only one class of stock outstanding, the amount of the corporation's current earnings and profits distributed in the hypothetical distribution with respect to each share in the class of stock is determined as if the hypothetical distribution were made pro rata with respect to each share in the class of stock.

(3) *More than one class of stock.*—If a controlled foreign corporation for a taxable year has more than one class of stock outstanding, the amount of the corporation's current earnings and profits distributed in the hypothetical distribution with respect to each class of stock is determined under this paragraph (e)(3) based on the distribution rights of each class of stock on the hypothetical distribution date, and then further distributed pro rata with respect to each share in the class of stock. Subject to paragraphs (e)(4) through (6) of this section, the distribution rights of a class of stock are determined taking into account all facts and circumstances related to the economic rights and interest in the current earnings and profits of the corporation of each class, including the terms of the class of stock, any agreement among the shareholders and, where appropriate, the relative fair market value of shares of stock.

(4) *Special rules.*—(i) *Redemptions, liquidations, and returns of capital.*—Notwithstanding the terms of any class of stock of the controlled foreign corporation or any agreement or arrangement with respect thereto, no amount of current earnings and profits is distributed in the hypothetical distribution with respect to a particular class of stock to the extent that a distribution of such amount would constitute a distribution in redemption of stock (even if such redemption would be treated as a distribution of property to which section 301 applies pursuant to section 302(d)), a distribution in liquidation, or a return of capital.

(ii) *Certain cumulative preferred stock.*—If a controlled foreign corporation has outstanding a class of redeemable preferred stock with cumulative dividend rights and dividend arrearages that do not compound at least annually at a rate that equals or exceeds the applicable Federal rate (as defined in section 1274(d)(1)) (*AFR*), the amount of the corporation's current earnings and profits distributed in the hypothetical distribution with respect to the class of stock may not exceed the amount of dividends actually paid during the taxable year with respect to the class of stock plus the present value of the unpaid current dividends with respect to the class determined using the AFR that applies on the date the stock is issued for the term from such issue date to the mandatory redemption date and assuming the dividends will be paid at the mandatory redemption date. For purposes of this paragraph (e)(4)(ii), if the class of preferred stock does not have a mandatory redemption date, the mandatory redemption date is the date that the class of preferred stock is expected to be redeemed based on all facts and circumstances.

(iii) *Dividend arrearages.*—If there is an arrearage in dividends for prior taxable years with respect to a class of preferred stock of a controlled foreign corporation, an amount of the corporation's current earnings and profits is distributed in the hypothetical distribution to the class of preferred stock by reason of the arrearage only to the extent the arrearage exceeds the accumulated earnings and profits of the controlled foreign corporation remaining from prior taxable years beginning after December 31, 1962, as of the beginning of the taxable year, or the date on which such stock was issued, whichever is later. If there is an arrearage in dividends for prior taxable years with respect to more than one class of preferred stock, the previous sentence is applied to each class in order of priority, except that the accumulated earnings and profits remaining after the applicable date are reduced by the earnings and profits necessary to satisfy arrearages with respect to classes of stock with a higher priority. For purposes of this paragraph (e)(4)(iii), the amount of any arrearage is determined by taking into account the time value of money principles in paragraph (e)(4)(ii) of this section.

(5) *Restrictions or other limitations on distributions.*—(i) *In general.*—A restriction or other limitation on distributions of an amount of earnings and profits by a controlled foreign corporation is not taken into account in determining the amount of the corporation's current earnings and profits distributed in a hypothetical distribution to a class of stock of the controlled foreign corporation.

(ii) *Definition.*—For purposes of paragraph (e)(5)(i) of this section, a restriction or other limitation on distributions includes any limitation that has the effect of limiting the distribution of an amount of earnings and profits by a controlled foreign corporation with respect to a class of stock of the corporation, other than currency or other restrictions or limitations imposed under the laws of any foreign country as provided in section 964(b).

(iii) *Exception for certain preferred distributions.*—For purposes of paragraph (e)(5)(i) of this section, the right to receive periodically a fixed amount (whether determined by a percentage of par value, a reference to a floating coupon rate, a stated return expressed in terms of a certain amount of U.S. dollars or foreign currency, or otherwise) with respect to a class of stock the distribution of which is a condition precedent to a further distribution of earnings and profits that year with respect to any class of stock (not including a distribution in partial or complete liquidation) is not a restriction or other limitation on the distribution of earnings and profits by a controlled foreign corporation.

(iv) *Illustrative list of restrictions and limitations.* Except as provided in paragraph (e)(5)(iii) of this section, restrictions or other limitations on distributions include, but are not limited to—

(A) An arrangement that restricts the ability of a controlled foreign corporation to pay dividends on a class of stock of the corporation until a condition or conditions are satisfied (for example, until another class of stock is redeemed);

(B) A loan agreement entered into by a controlled foreign corporation that restricts or otherwise affects the ability to make distributions on its stock until certain requirements are satisfied; or

(C) An arrangement that conditions the ability of a controlled foreign corporation to pay dividends to its shareholders on the financial condition of the corporation.

(6) *Transactions and arrangements with a principal purpose of reducing pro rata shares.*—For purposes of this paragraph (e), any transaction or arrangement that is part of a plan a principal purpose of which is the avoidance of Federal income taxation, including, but not limited to, a transaction or arrangement to reduce a United States shareholder's pro rata share of the subpart F income of a controlled foreign corporation, which transaction or arrangement would avoid Federal income taxation without regard to this paragraph (e)(6), is disregarded in determining such United States shareholder's pro rata share of the subpart F income of the corporation. This paragraph (e)(6) also applies for purposes of the pro rata share rules described in § 1.951A-1(d) that reference this paragraph (e), including the rules in § 1.951A-1(d)(3) that determine the pro rata share of qualified business asset investment based on the pro rata share of tested income.

(7) *Examples.*—The application of this section is illustrated by the examples in this paragraph (e)(7).

(i) Common facts for examples in paragraph (e)(7). Except as otherwise stated, the following facts are assumed for purposes of the examples.

(A) FC1 is a controlled foreign corporation.

(B) USP1, USP2, and USP3 are domestic corporations and United States shareholders of FC1.

(C) Individual A is a foreign individual, and FC2 is a foreign corporation.

(D) All persons use the calendar year as their taxable year.

(E) Any ownership of FC1 by any shareholder is for all of Year 1.

(F) The common shareholders of FC1 are entitled to dividends when declared by FC1's board of directors.

(G) There are no accrued but unpaid dividends with respect to preferred shares, and common shares have positive liquidation value.

(H) FC1 makes no distributions during Year 1.

(I) There are no other facts and circumstances related to the economic rights and interest of any class of stock in the current earnings and profits of a foreign corporation, and no transaction or arrangement was entered into as part of a plan a principal purpose of which is the avoidance of Federal income taxation.

(J) FC1 does not have tested income within the meaning of section 951A(c)(2)(A) and § 1.951A-2(b)(1) or tested loss within the meaning of section 951A(c)(2)(B) and § 1.951A-2(b)(2).

**Prop. Reg. § 1.951-1(e)(7)(J)**

(ii) *Example 1: single class of stock*—(A) *Facts.* FC1 has outstanding 100 shares of one class of stock. USP1 owns 60 shares of FC1. USP2 owns 40 shares of FC1. For Year 1, FC1 has $1,000x of earnings and profits and $100x of subpart F income within the meaning of section 952.

(B) *Analysis.* FC1 has one class of stock. Therefore, under paragraph (e)(2) of this section, FC1's current earnings and profits of $1,000x are distributed in the hypothetical distribution pro rata to each share of stock. Accordingly, under paragraph (e)(1) of this section, for Year 1, USP1's pro rata share of FC1's subpart F income is $60x ($100x x $600x/$1,000x) and USP2's pro rata share of FC1's subpart F income is $40x ($100x x $400x/$1,000x).

(iii) *Example 2: common and preferred stock*— (A) *Facts.* FC1 has outstanding 70 shares of common stock and 30 shares of 4% nonparticipating, voting preferred stock with a par value of $10x per share. USP1 owns all of the common shares. Individual A owns all of the preferred shares. For Year 1, FC1 has $100x of earnings and profits and $50x of subpart F income within the meaning of section 952. In Year 1, FC1 distributes as a dividend $12x to Individual A with respect to Individual A's preferred shares.

(B) *Analysis.* The distribution rights of the preferred shares are not a restriction or other limitation within the meaning of paragraph (e)(5) of this section. Under paragraph (e)(3) of this section, the amount of FC1's current earnings and profits distributed in the hypothetical distribution with respect to Individual A's preferred shares is $12x and with respect to USP1's common shares is $88x. Accordingly, under paragraph (e)(1) of this section, USP1's pro rata share of FC1's subpart F income is $44x ($50x x $88x/$100x) for Year 1.

(iv) *Example 3: restriction based on cumulative income*—(A) *Facts.* FC1 has outstanding 10 shares of common stock and 400 shares of 2% nonparticipating, voting preferred stock with a par value of $1x per share. USP1 owns all of the common shares. FC2 owns all of the preferred shares. USP1 and FC2 cause the governing documents of FC1 to provide that no dividends may be paid to the common shareholders until FC1 cumulatively earns $100,000x of income. For Year 1, FC1 has $50x of earnings and profits and $50x of subpart F income within the meaning of section 952. In Year 1, FC1 distributes as a dividend $8x to FC2 with respect to FC2's preferred shares.

(B) *Analysis.* The agreement restricting FC1's ability to pay dividends to common shareholders until FC1 cumulatively earns $100,000x of income is a restriction or other limitation within the meaning of paragraph (e)(5) of this section. Therefore, the restriction is disregarded for purposes of determining the amount of FC1's current earnings and profits distributed in the hypothetical distribution to a class of stock. The distribution rights of the preferred shares are not a restriction or other limitation within the meaning of paragraph (e)(5) of this section. Under

paragraph (e)(3) of this section, the amount of FC1's current earnings and profits distributed in the hypothetical distribution with respect to FC2's preferred shares is $8x and with respect to USP1's common shares is $42x. Accordingly, under paragraph (e)(1) of this section, USP1's pro rata share of FC1's subpart F income is $42x for Year 1.

(v) *Example 4: redemption rights*—(A) *Facts.* FC1 has outstanding 40 shares of common stock and 10 shares of 4% nonparticipating, voting preferred stock with a par value of $50x per share. Pursuant to the terms of the preferred stock, FC1 has the right to redeem at any time, in whole or in part, the preferred stock. FC2 owns all of the preferred shares. USP1, wholly owned by FC2, owns all of the common shares. For Year 1, FC1 has $100x of earnings and profits and $100x of subpart F income within the meaning of section 952. In Year 1, FC1 distributes as a dividend $20x to FC2 with respect to FC2's preferred shares.

(B) *Analysis.* If FC1 were treated as having redeemed any preferred shares, the redemption would be treated as a distribution to which section 301 applies under section 302(d) due to FC2's constructive ownership of the common shares. However, under paragraph (e)(4)(i) of this section, no amount of earnings and profits is distributed in the hypothetical distribution to the preferred shareholders on the hypothetical distribution date as a result of FC1's right to redeem, in whole or in part, the preferred shares. FC1's redemption rights with respect to the preferred shares cannot affect the distribution of current earnings and profits in the hypothetical distribution to FC1's shareholders. As a result, the amount of FC1's current earnings and profits distributed in the hypothetical distribution with respect to FC2's preferred shares is $20x and with respect to USP1's common shares is $80x. Accordingly, under paragraph (e)(1) of this section, USP1's pro rata share of FC1's subpart F income is $80x for Year 1.

(vi) *Example 5: shareholder owns common and preferred stock*—(A) *Facts.* FC1 has outstanding 40 shares of common stock and 60 shares of 6% nonparticipating, nonvoting preferred stock with a par value of $100x per share. USP1 owns 30 shares of the common stock and 15 shares of the preferred stock during Year 1. The remaining 10 shares of common stock and 45 shares of preferred stock of FC1 are owned by Individual A. For Year 1, FC1 has $1,000x of earnings and profits and $500x of subpart F income within the meaning of section 952.

(B) *Analysis.* Under paragraph (e)(5)(iii) of this section, the right of the holder of the preferred stock to receive 6% of par value is not a restriction or other limitation within the meaning of paragraph (e)(5) of this section. The amount of FC1's current earnings and profits distributed in the hypothetical distribution with respect to FC1's preferred shares is $360x (0.06 x $100x x 60) and with respect to its common shares is $640x ($1,000x - $360x). As a result, the amount of FC1's current earnings and profits distributed in the hypothetical distribution to USP1 is $570x, the sum of $90x ($360x x 15/60) with respect to its preferred shares and $480x ($640x x 30/40) with respect to its common shares. Accordingly, under paragraph (e)(1) of this section, USP1's pro rata share of the subpart F income of FC1 is $285x ($500x x $570x/$1,000x).

(vii) *Example 6: subpart F income and tested income*—(A) *Facts.* FC1 has outstanding 700 shares of common stock and 300 shares of 4% nonparticipating, voting preferred stock with a par value of $100x per share. USP1 owns all of the common shares. USP2 owns all of the preferred shares. For Year 1, FC1 has $10,000x of earnings and profits, $2,000x of subpart F income within the meaning of section 952, and $9,000x of tested income within the meaning of section 951A(c)(2)(A) and § 1.951A-2(b)(1).

(B) *Analysis*—(1) *Pro rata share of subpart F income.* The current earnings and profits of FC1 determined under paragraph (e)(1)(ii) of this section are $11,000x, the greater of FC1's earnings and profits as determined under section 964 ($10,000x) or the sum of FC1's subpart F income and tested income ($2,000x + $9,000x). The amount of FC1's current earnings and profits distributed in the hypothetical distribution with respect to USP2's preferred shares is $1,200x (.04 x $100x x 300) and with respect to USP1's common shares is $9,800x ($11,000x - $1,200x). Accordingly, under paragraph (e)(1) of this section, USP1's pro rata share of FC1's subpart F income is $1,782x ($2,000x x $9,800x/$11,000x), and USP2's pro rata share of FC1's subpart F income is $218x ($2,000x x $1,200x/$11,000x).

(2) *Pro rata share of tested income.* The same analysis applies for the hypothetical distribution with respect to the tested income as under paragraph (ii)(A) of this *Example 6* with respect to the subpart F income. Accordingly, under § 1.951A-1(d)(2), USP1's pro rata share of FC1's tested income is $8,018x ($9,000x x $9,800x/ $11,000x), and USP2's pro rata share of FC1's tested income is $982x ($9,000x x $1,200x/ $11,000x) for Year 1.

(viii) *Example 7: subpart F income and tested loss*—(A) *Facts.* The facts are the same as in paragraph (A) of *Example 6*, except that for Year 1, FC1 has $8,000x of earnings and profits, $10,000x of subpart F income within the meaning of section 952 (but without regard to the limitation in section 952(c)), and $2,000x of tested loss within the meaning of section 951A(c)(2)(B) and § 1.951A-2(b)(2). Under section 951A(c)(2)(B)(ii) and § 1.951A-6(d), the earnings and profits of FC1 are increased for purposes of section 952 by the amount of FC1's tested loss. Accordingly, taking into account section 951A(c)(2)(B)(ii) and § 1.951A-6(d), the subpart F income of FC1 is $10,000x.

(B) *Analysis*—(1) *Pro rata share of subpart F income.* The current earnings and profits determined under paragraph (e)(1)(ii) of this section are $10,000x, the greater of the earnings and profits of FC1 determined under section 964

($8,000x) or the sum of FC1's subpart F income and tested income ($10,000x + $0). The amount of FC1's current earnings and profits distributed in the hypothetical distribution with respect to USP2's preferred shares is $1,200x (.04 x $100x x 300) and with respect to Corp A's common shares is $8,800x ($10,000x - $1,200x). Accordingly, under paragraph (e)(1) of this section, for Year 1, USP1's pro rata share of FC1's subpart F income is $8,800x and USP2's pro rata share of FC1's subpart F income is $1,200x.

(2) *Pro rata share of tested loss.* The current earnings and profits determined under § 1.951A-1(d)(4)(i)(B) are $2,000x, the amount of FC1's tested loss. Under § 1.951A-1(d)(4)(i)(C), the entire $2,000x tested loss is distributed in the hypothetical distribution with respect to USP1's common shares. Accordingly, USP1's pro rata share of the tested loss is $2,000x.

\* \* \*

(g) \* \* \*

(1) *In general.*—For purposes of sections 951 through 964, the term "United States shareholder" means, with respect to a foreign corporation, a United States person (as defined in section 957(c)) who owns within the meaning of section 958(a), or is considered as owning by applying the rules of ownership of section 958(b), 10 percent or more of the total combined voting power of all classes of stock entitled to vote of such foreign corporation, or 10 percent or more of the total value of shares of all classes of stock of such foreign corporation.

\* \* \*

(h) *Special rule for partnership blocker structures.*—(1) *In general.*—For purposes of sections 951 through 964, a controlled domestic partnership is treated as a foreign partnership in determining the stock of a controlled foreign corporation owned (within the meaning of section 958(a)) by a United States person if the following conditions are satisfied—

(i) Without regard to this paragraph (h), the controlled domestic partnership owns (within the meaning of section 958(a)) stock of a controlled foreign corporation; and

(ii) If the controlled domestic partnership (and all other controlled domestic partnerships in the chain of ownership of the controlled foreign corporation) were treated as foreign—

(A) The controlled foreign corporation would continue to be a controlled foreign corporation; and

(B) At least one United States shareholder of the controlled foreign corporation would be treated as owning (within the meaning of section 958(a)) stock of the controlled foreign corporation through another foreign corporation that is a direct or indirect partner in the controlled domestic partnership.

(2) *Definition of a controlled domestic partnership.*—For purposes of paragraph (h)(1) of this section, the term *controlled domestic partnership*

means, with respect to a United States shareholder described in paragraph (h)(1)(ii)(B) of this section, a domestic partnership that is controlled by the United States shareholder and persons related to the United States shareholder. For purposes of this paragraph (h)(2), control generally is determined based on all the facts and circumstances, except that a partnership will be deemed to be controlled by a United States shareholder and related persons in any case in which those persons, in the aggregate, own (directly or indirectly through one or more partnerships) more than 50 percent of the interests in the partnership capital or profits. For purposes of this paragraph (h)(2), a related person is, with respect to a United States shareholder, a person that is related to the United States shareholder within the meaning of section 267(b) or 707(b)(1).

(3) *Example.*—(i) *Facts.*—USP, a domestic corporation, owns all of the stock of CFC1 and CFC2. CFC1 and CFC2 own 60% and 40%, respectively, of the interests in the capital and profits of DPS, a domestic partnership. DPS owns all of the stock of CFC3. Each of CFC1, CFC2, and CFC3 is a controlled foreign corporation. USP, DPS, CFC1, CFC2, and CFC3 all use the calendar year as their taxable year. For Year 1, CFC3 has $100x of subpart F income (as defined under section 952) and $100x of earnings and profits.

(ii) *Analysis.*—DPS is a controlled domestic partnership with respect to USP within the meaning of paragraph (h)(2) of this section because more than 50% of the interests in its capital or profits are owned by persons related to USP within the meaning of section 267(b) (that is, CFC1 and CFC2), and thus DPS is controlled by USP and related persons. Without regard to paragraph (h) of this section, DPS is a United States shareholder that owns (within the meaning of section 958(a)) stock of CFC3, a controlled foreign corporation. If DPS were treated as foreign, CFC3 would continue to be a controlled foreign corporation, and USP would be treated as owning (within the meaning of section 958(a)) stock in CFC3 through CFC1 and CFC2, which are both partners in DPS. Thus, under paragraph (h)(1) of this section, DPS is treated as a foreign partnership for purposes of determining the stock of CFC3 owned (within the meaning of section 958(a)) by USP. Accordingly, USP's pro rata share of CFC3's subpart F income for Year 1 is $100x, and USP includes in its gross income $100x under section 951(a)(1)(A). DPS is not a United States shareholder of CFC3 for purposes of sections 951 through 964.

(i) *Applicability dates.*—Paragraphs (a), (e)(1)(ii)(B), and (g)(1) of this section apply to taxable years of foreign corporations beginning after December 31, 2017, and to taxable years of United States shareholders with or within which such taxable years of foreign corporations end. Except for paragraph (e)(1)(ii)(B), paragraph (e) of this section applies to taxable years of United States shareholders ending on or after October 3, 2018. Paragraph (h) of this section applies to taxable years of domestic partnerships ending on or after May 14, 2010.

\* \* \*

[Proposed 10-10-2018.]

### [Prop. Reg. § 1.951A-1]

**§ 1.951A-1. General provisions.**—(a) *Overview.*—(1) *In general.*—This section and §§ 1.951A-2 through 1.951A-7 (collectively, the *section 951A regulations*) provide rules to determine a United States shareholder's income inclusion under section 951A and certain definitions for purposes of section 951A and the section 951A regulations. This section provides general rules for determining a United States shareholder's inclusion of global intangible low-taxed income. Section 1.951A-2 provides rules for determining a controlled foreign corporation's tested income or tested loss. Section 1.951A-3 provides rules for determining a controlled foreign corporation's qualified business asset investment. Section 1.951A-4 provides rules for determining a controlled foreign corporation's tested interest expense and tested interest income. Section 1.951A-5 provides rules relating to the application of section 951A and the section 951A regulations to domestic partnerships and their partners. Section 1.951A-6 provides rules relating to the treatment of the inclusion of global intangible low-taxed income for certain purposes and adjustments to earnings and profits and basis of a controlled foreign corporation related to a tested loss. Section 1.951A-7 provides dates of applicability.

(2) *Scope.*—Paragraph (b) of this section provides the general rule requiring a United States shareholder to include in gross income its global intangible low-taxed income for a U.S. shareholder inclusion year. Paragraph (c) of this section provides rules for determining the amount of a United States shareholder's global intangible low-taxed income for the U.S. shareholder inclusion year, including a rule for the application of section 951A and the section 951A regulations to consolidated groups. Paragraph (d) of this section provides rules for determining a United States shareholder's pro rata share of certain items for purposes of determining the United States shareholder's global intangible low-taxed income. Paragraph (e) of this section provides additional general definitions for purposes of this section and the section 951A regulations.

(b) *Inclusion of global intangible low-taxed income.*—Each person who is a United States shareholder (as defined in section 951(b)) of any controlled foreign corporation (as defined in section 957) and owns section 958(a) stock (as defined in paragraph (e)(3) of this section) in any such controlled foreign corporation includes in gross income in the U.S. shareholder inclusion year (as defined in paragraph (e)(4) of this section) the shareholder's GILTI inclusion amount (as defined in paragraph (c) of this section), if any, for the U.S. shareholder inclusion year.

(c) *Determination of GILTI inclusion amount.*— (1) *In general.*—Except as provided in paragraph (c)(4) of this section, the term *GILTI inclusion amount* means, with respect to a United States shareholder and a U.S. shareholder inclusion year, the excess (if any) of—

(i) The shareholder's net CFC tested income (as defined in paragraph (c)(2) of this section) for the year, over

(ii) The shareholder's net deemed tangible income return (as defined in paragraph (c)(3) of this section) for the year.

(2) *Definition of net CFC tested income.*—The term *net CFC tested income* means, with respect to a United States shareholder and a U.S. shareholder inclusion year, the excess (if any) of—

(i) The aggregate of the shareholder's pro rata share of the tested income of each tested income CFC (as defined in § 1.951A-2(b)(1)) for the year, over

(ii) The aggregate of the shareholder's pro rata share of the tested loss of each tested loss CFC (as defined in § 1.951A-2(b)(2)) for the year.

(3) *Definition of net deemed tangible income return.*—(i) *In general.*—The term *net deemed tangible income return* means, with respect to a United States shareholder and a U.S. shareholder inclusion year, the excess (if any) of—

(A) The shareholder's deemed tangible income return (as defined in paragraph (c)(3)(ii) of this section) for the year, over

(B) The shareholder's specified interest expense (as defined in paragraph (c)(3)(iii) of this section) for the year.

(ii) *Definition of deemed tangible income return.*—The term *deemed tangible income return* means, with respect to a United States shareholder and a U.S. shareholder inclusion year, 10 percent of the aggregate of the shareholder's pro rata share of the qualified business asset investment (as defined in § 1.951A-3(b)) of each tested income CFC for the year.

(iii) *Definition of specified interest expense.*— The term *specified interest expense* means, with respect to a United States shareholder and a U.S. shareholder inclusion year, the excess (if any) of—

(A) The aggregate of the shareholder's pro rata share of the tested interest expense (as defined in § 1.951A-4(b)(1)) of each controlled foreign corporation for the year, over

(B) The aggregate of the shareholder's pro rata share of the tested interest income (as defined in § 1.951A-4(b)(2)) of each controlled foreign corporation for the year.

(4) *Determination of GILTI inclusion amount for consolidated groups.*—For purposes of section 951A and the section 951A regulations, a mem-

ber of a consolidated group (as defined in § 1.1502-1(h)) determines its GILTI inclusion amount under the rules provided in § 1.1502-51.

(d) *Determination of pro rata share.*—(1) *In general.*—For purposes of paragraph (c) of this section, each United States shareholder that owns section 958(a) stock in a controlled foreign corporation as of a CFC inclusion date (as defined in paragraph (e)(1) of this section) determines for a U.S. shareholder inclusion year that includes such CFC inclusion date its pro rata share (if any) of the controlled foreign corporation's tested income, tested loss, qualified business asset investment, tested interest expense, and tested interest income (each a *CFC tested item*), as applicable, for the CFC inclusion year (as defined in paragraph (e)(2) of this section). Except as otherwise provided in this paragraph (d), a United States shareholder's pro rata share of each CFC tested item is determined independently of its pro rata share of any other CFC tested item. Except as modified in this paragraph (d), a United States shareholder's pro rata share of any CFC tested item is determined under the rules of section 951(a)(2) and § 1.951-1(b) and (e) in the same manner as those provisions apply to subpart F income. Under section 951(a)(2) and § 1.951-1(b) and (e), as modified by this paragraph (d), a United States shareholder's pro rata share of any CFC tested item for a U.S. shareholder inclusion year is determined with respect to the section 958(a) stock of the controlled foreign corporation owned by the United States shareholder on the CFC inclusion date. A United States shareholder's pro rata share of any CFC tested item is translated into United States dollars using the average exchange rate for the CFC inclusion year of the controlled foreign corporation. Paragraphs (d)(2) through (5) of this section provide rules for determining a United States shareholder's pro rata share of each CFC tested item of a controlled foreign corporation.

(2) *Tested income.*—(i) *In general.*—Except as provided in paragraph (d)(2)(ii) of this section, a United States shareholder's pro rata share of the tested income of each tested income CFC for a U.S. shareholder inclusion year is determined under section 951(a)(2) and § 1.951-1(b) and (e), substituting "tested income" for "subpart F income" each place it appears, other than in § 1.951-1(c)(1)(ii)(B).

(ii) *Special rule for prior allocation of tested loss.*—In any case in which tested loss has been allocated to any class of stock in a prior CFC inclusion year under paragraph (d)(4)(iii) of this section, tested income is first allocated to each such class of stock in the order of its liquidation priority to the extent of the excess (if any) of the sum of the tested loss allocated to each such class of stock for each prior CFC inclusion year under paragraph (d)(4)(iii) of this section, over the sum of the tested income allocated to each such class of stock for each prior CFC inclusion year under this paragraph (d)(2)(ii). Paragraph (d)(2)(i) of this section applies for purposes of determining a United States shareholder's pro rata share of the remainder of the tested income, except that, for purposes of the hypothetical distribution of section 951(a)(2)(A) and § 1.951-1(b) and (e), the amount of current earnings and profits of the tested income CFC is reduced by the amount of tested income allocated under the first sentence of this paragraph (d)(2)(ii). For an example of the application of this paragraph (d)(2), see *Example 2* of paragraph (d)(4)(iv) of this section.

(3) *Qualified business asset investment.*—(i) *In general.*—Except as provided in paragraph (d)(3)(ii) of this section, a United States shareholder's pro rata share of the qualified business asset investment of a tested income CFC for a U.S. shareholder inclusion year bears the same ratio to the total qualified business asset investment of the tested income CFC for the CFC inclusion year as the United States shareholder's pro rata share of the tested income of the tested income CFC for the U.S. shareholder inclusion year bears to the total tested income of the tested income CFC for the CFC inclusion year.

(ii) *Special rule for preferred stock in case of excess QBAI.*—If a tested income CFC's qualified business asset investment for a CFC inclusion year exceeds 10 times its tested income for the CFC inclusion year (such excess, *excess QBAI*), a United States shareholder's pro rata share of the tested income CFC's qualified business asset investment is the sum of its pro rata share determined under paragraph (d)(3)(i) of this section without regard to the excess QBAI, plus its pro rata share determined under paragraph (d)(3)(i) of this section solely with respect to the excess QBAI and without regard to tested income allocated to any share of preferred stock of the tested income CFC under paragraph (d)(2) of this section.

(iii) *Examples.*—The following examples illustrate the application of paragraphs (d)(2) and (3) of this section. See also § 1.951-1(e)(7), *Example 6* (illustrating a United States shareholder's pro rata share of tested income).

(A) *Example 1*—(1) *Facts.* FS, a controlled foreign corporation, has outstanding 70 shares of common stock and 30 shares of 4% nonparticipating, cumulative preferred stock with a par value of $10x per share. P Corp, a domestic corporation and a United States shareholder of FS, owns all of the common shares. Individual A, a United States shareholder, owns all of the preferred shares. Both FS and P Corp use the calendar year as their taxable year. Individual A and P Corp are shareholders of FS for all of Year 4. At the beginning of Year 4, FS had no dividend arrearages with respect to its preferred stock. For Year 4, FS has $100x of earnings and profits, $120x of tested income, and no subpart F income within the meaning of section 952. FS also has $750x of qualified business asset investment for Year 4.

(2) *Analysis*—(i) *Determination of pro rata share of tested income.* For purposes of determining P Corp's pro rata share of FS's tested income under paragraph (d)(2) of this section, the amount of FS's current earnings and profits for purposes of the hypothetical distribution described in § 1.951-1(e)(1)(i) is $120x, the greater of its earnings and profits as determined under section 964 ($100x) or the sum of its subpart F income and tested income ($0 + $120x). Under paragraph (d)(2) of this section and § 1.951-1(e)(3), the amount of FS's current earnings and profits distributed in the hypothetical distribution is $12x (.04 x $10x x 30) with respect to Individual A's preferred shares and $108x ($120x - $12x) with respect to P Corp's common shares. Accordingly, under paragraph (d)(2) of this section and § 1.951-1(e)(1), Individual A's pro rata share of FS's tested income is $12x, and P Corp's pro rata share of FS's tested income is $108x for Year 4.

(ii) *Determination of pro rata share of qualified business asset investment.* The special rule of paragraph (d)(3)(ii) of this section does not apply because FS's qualified business asset investment of $750x does not exceed $1,200x, which is 10 times FS's tested income of $120x. Accordingly, under the general rule of paragraph (d)(3)(i) of this section, Individual A's and P Corp's pro rata share of FS's qualified business asset investment bears the same ratio to FS's total qualified business asset investment as Individual A's and P Corp's pro rata share, respectively, of FS's tested income bears to FS's total tested income. Thus, Individual A's pro rata share of FS's qualified business asset investment is $75x ($750x x $12x/$120x), and P Corp's pro rata share of FS's qualified business asset investment is $675x ($750x x $108x/$120x).

(B) *Example 2*—(1) *Facts.* The facts are the same as in paragraph (i) of *Example 1*, except that FS has $1,500x of qualified business asset investment for Year 4.

(2) *Analysis.* (i) *Determination of pro rata share of tested income.* The analysis and the result are the same as in paragraph (ii)(A) of *Example 1*.

(ii) *Determination of pro rata share of qualified business asset investment.* The special rule of paragraph (d)(3)(ii) of this section applies because FS's qualified business asset investment of $1,500x exceeds $1,200x, which is 10 times FS's tested income of $120x. Under paragraph (d)(3)(ii) of this section, Individual A's and P Corp's pro rata share of FS's qualified business asset investment is the sum of their pro rata share determined under paragraph (d)(3)(i) of this section without regard to the excess QBAI plus their pro rata share with respect to the excess QBAI but without regard to tested income allocated to preferred stock under paragraph (d)(2) of this section. Without regard to the excess QBAI of $300x, Individual A's pro rata share of FS's qualified business asset investment is $120x ($1,200x x $12x/$120x), and P Corp's pro rata share of FS's qualified business asset investment is $1,080x ($1,200x x $108x/$120x). Solely with respect to the excess QBAI and without regard to tested income allocated to the preferred stock under paragraph (d)(2) of this section, Individual A's pro rata share of FS's qualified business asset investment is $0 ($300x x $0/$108x), and P Corp's pro rata share of FS's qualified business asset investment is $300x ($300x x $108x/$108x). Thus, Individual A's pro rata share of FS's qualified business asset investment is $120x ($120x + $0), and P Corp's pro rata share of FS's qualified business asset investment is $1,380x ($1,080x + $300x).

(4) *Tested loss.*—(i) *In general.*—A United States shareholder's pro rata share of the tested loss of each tested loss CFC for a U.S. shareholder inclusion year is determined under section 951(a)(2) and §1.951-1(b) and (e) with the following modifications—

(A) "Tested loss" is substituted for "subpart F income" each place it appears;

(B) For purposes of the hypothetical distribution described in section 951(a)(2)(A) and §1.951-1(e)(1)(i), the amount of current earnings and profits of a controlled foreign corporation for a CFC inclusion year is treated as being equal to the tested loss of the tested loss CFC for the CFC inclusion year;

(C) Except as provided in paragraphs (d)(4)(ii) and (iii) of this section, the hypothetical distribution described in section 951(a)(2)(A) and §1.951-1(e)(1)(i) is treated as made solely with respect to the common stock of the tested loss CFC; and

(D) The amount of the dividend received by any other person for purposes of section 951(a)(2)(B) and §1.951-1(b)(1)(ii) is treated as being equal to the amount of the tested loss of the tested loss CFC for the CFC inclusion year (regardless of whether, or the extent to which, the other person actually receives a dividend).

(ii) *Special rule in case of accrued but unpaid dividends.*—If a tested loss CFC's earnings and profits that have accumulated since the issuance of preferred shares are reduced below the amount necessary to satisfy any accrued but unpaid dividends with respect to such preferred shares, then the amount by which the tested loss reduces the earnings below the amount necessary to satisfy the accrued but unpaid dividends is distributed in the hypothetical distribution described in section 951(a)(2)(A) and §1.951-1(e)(1)(i) with respect to the preferred stock of the tested loss CFC and the remainder of the tested loss is distributed with respect to the common stock of the tested loss CFC.

(iii) *Special rule for stock with no liquidation value.*—If a tested loss CFC's common stock has a liquidation value of zero and there is at least one other class of equity with a liquidation preference relative to the common stock, then the tested loss is distributed in the hypothetical distribution described in section 951(a)(2)(A) and §1.951-1(e)(1)(i) with respect to the most junior

class of equity with a positive liquidation value to the extent of such liquidation value. Thereafter, tested loss is distributed with respect to the next most junior class of equity to the extent of its liquidation value and so on. All determinations of liquidation value are to be made as of the beginning of the CFC inclusion year of the tested loss CFC.

(iv) *Examples.*—The following examples illustrate the application of this paragraph (d)(4). See also §1.951-1(e)(7), *Example 7* (illustrating a United States shareholder's pro rata share of subpart F income and tested loss).

(A) *Example 1*—(1) *Facts.* FS, a controlled foreign corporation, has outstanding 70 shares of common stock and 30 shares of 4% nonparticipating, cumulative preferred stock with a par value of $10x per share. P Corp, a domestic corporation and a United States shareholder of FS, owns all of the common shares. Individual A, a United States citizen and a United States shareholder, owns all of the preferred shares. FS, Individual A, and P Corp all use the calendar year as their taxable year. Individual A and P Corp are shareholders of FS for all of Year 5. At the beginning of Year 5, FS had earnings and profits of $120x, which accumulated after the issuance of the preferred stock. At the end of Year 5, the accrued but unpaid dividends with respect to the preferred stock are $36x. For Year 5, FS has a $100x tested loss, and no other items of income, gain, deduction or loss. At the end of Year 5, FS has earnings and profits of $20x.

(2) *Analysis.* FS is a tested loss CFC for Year 5. Before taking into account the tested loss in Year 5, FS had sufficient earnings and profits to satisfy the accrued but unpaid dividends of $36x. The amount of the reduction in earnings below the amount necessary to satisfy the accrued but unpaid dividends attributable to the tested loss is $16x ($36x - ($120x - $100x)). Accordingly, under paragraph (d)(4)(ii) of this section, Individual A's pro rata share of the Year 5 tested loss is $16x, and P Corp's pro rata share of the tested loss is $84x ($100x - $16x).

(B) *Example 2*—(1) *Facts.* FS, a controlled foreign corporation, has outstanding 100 shares of common stock and 50 shares of 4% nonparticipating, cumulative preferred stock with a par value of $100x per share. P Corp, a domestic corporation and a United States shareholder of FS, owns all of the common shares. Individual A, a United States citizen and a United States shareholder, owns all of the preferred shares. FS, Individual A, and P Corp all use the calendar year as their taxable year. Individual A and P Corp are shareholders of FS for all of Year 1 and Year 2. At the beginning of Year 1, the common stock had no liquidation value and the preferred stock had a liquidation value of $5,000x and no accrued but unpaid dividends. In Year 1, FS has a tested loss of $1,000x and no other items of income, gain, deduction, or loss. In Year 2, FS has tested income of $3,000x and no other items of income, gain, deduction, or loss and paid no dividends.

**Prop. Reg. §1.951A-1(d)(4)(iv)**

FS has earnings and profits of $3,000x for Year 2. At the end of Year 2, FS has accrued but unpaid dividends of $400x with respect to the preferred stock ($5000x x 0.04 for Year 1 and $5000x x 0.04 for Year 2).

(2) *Analysis*—(i) *Year 1.* FS is a tested loss CFC in Year 1. The common stock of FS has liquidation value of zero and the preferred stock has a liquidation preference relative to the common stock. The tested loss ($1,000x) does not exceed the liquidation value of the preferred stock ($5,000x). Accordingly, under paragraph (d)(4)(iii) of this section, the tested loss is distributed with respect to the preferred stock in the hypothetical distribution described in section 951(a)(2)(A) and § 1.951-1(e). Individual A's pro rata share of the tested loss is $1,000x, and P Corp's pro rata share of the tested loss is $0.

(ii) *Year 2.* FS is a tested income CFC in Year 2. Because $1,000x of tested loss was allocated to the preferred stock in Year 1 under paragraph (d)(4)(iii) of this section, the first $1,000x of tested income in Year 2 is allocated to the preferred stock under paragraph (d)(2)(ii) of this section. P Corp's and Individual A's pro rata shares of the remaining $2,000x of tested income are determined under the general rule of paragraph (d)(2)(i) of this section, except that for purposes of the hypothetical distribution the amount of FS's current earnings and profits is reduced by the tested income allocated under paragraph (d)(2)(ii) of this section to $2,000x ($3,000x - $1,000x). Accordingly, under paragraph (d)(2)(i) of this section, the amount of FS's current earnings and profits distributed in the hypothetical distribution with respect to Individual A's preferred stock is $400x ($400x of accrued but unpaid dividends) and with respect to P Corp's common stock is $1,600x ($2,000x - $400x). Individual A's pro rata share of the tested income is $1,400x ($1,000x + $400x), and P Corp's pro rata share of the tested income is $1,600x.

(5) *Tested interest expense.*—A United States shareholder's pro rata share of tested interest expense of a controlled foreign corporation for a U.S. shareholder inclusion year is equal to the amount by which the tested interest expense reduces the shareholder's pro rata share of tested income of the controlled foreign corporation for the U.S. shareholder inclusion year, increases the shareholder's pro rata share of tested loss of the controlled foreign corporation for the U.S. shareholder inclusion year, or both.

(6) *Tested interest income.*—A United States shareholder's pro rata share of tested interest income of a controlled foreign corporation for a U.S. shareholder inclusion year is equal to the amount by which the tested interest income increases the shareholder's pro rata share of tested income of the controlled foreign corporation for the U.S. shareholder inclusion year, reduces the shareholder's pro rata share of tested loss of the controlled foreign corporation for the U.S. shareholder inclusion year, or both.

(e) *Definitions.*—This paragraph (e) provides additional definitions that apply for purposes of the section 951A regulations. Other definitions relevant to the section 951A regulations are included in § § 1.951A-2 through 1.951A-6.

(1) *CFC inclusion date.*—The term *CFC inclusion date* means the last day of a CFC inclusion year on which a foreign corporation is a controlled foreign corporation.

(2) *CFC inclusion year.*—The term *CFC inclusion year* means any taxable year of a foreign corporation beginning after December 31, 2017, at any time during which the corporation is a controlled foreign corporation.

(3) *Section 958(a) stock.*—The term *section 958(a) stock* means stock of a controlled foreign corporation owned (directly or indirectly) by a United States shareholder within the meaning of section 958(a).

(4) *U.S. shareholder inclusion year.*—The term *U.S. shareholder inclusion year* means a taxable year of a United States shareholder that includes a CFC inclusion date of a controlled foreign corporation of the United States shareholder. [Reg. § 1.951A-1.]

[Proposed 10-10-2018.]

### [Prop. Reg. § 1.951A-2]

**§ 1.951A-2. Tested income and tested loss.**— (a) *Scope.*—This section provides general rules for determining the tested income or tested loss of a controlled foreign corporation for purposes of determining a United States shareholder's net CFC tested income under § 1.951A-1(c)(2). Paragraph (b) of this section provides definitions related to tested income and tested loss. Paragraph (c) of this section provides rules for determining the gross tested income of a controlled foreign corporation and the deductions that are properly allocable to gross tested income.

(b) *Definitions related to tested income and tested loss.*—(1) *Tested income and tested income CFC.*— The term *tested income* means the excess (if any) of a controlled foreign corporation's gross tested income for a CFC inclusion year, over the allowable deductions (including taxes) properly allocable to the gross tested income for the CFC inclusion year (a controlled foreign corporation with tested income for a CFC inclusion year, a *tested income CFC*).

(2) *Tested loss and tested loss CFC.*—The term *tested loss* means the excess (if any) of a controlled foreign corporation's allowable deductions (including taxes) properly allocable to gross tested income (or that would be allocable to gross tested income if there were gross tested income) for a CFC inclusion year, over the gross tested income of the controlled foreign corporation for the CFC inclusion year (a controlled foreign corporation without tested income for a CFC inclusion year, a *tested loss CFC*).

(c) *Rules relating to the determination of tested income and tested loss.*—(1) *Definition of gross tested income.*—The term *gross tested income* means the gross income of a controlled foreign corporation for a CFC inclusion year determined without regard to—

(i) Items of income described in section 952(b),

(ii) Gross income taken into account in determining the subpart F income of the corporation,

(iii) Gross income excluded from the foreign base company income (as defined in section 954) or the insurance income (as defined in section 953) of the corporation solely by reason of an election made under section 954(b)(4) and § 1.954-1(d)(5),

(iv) Dividends received by the corporation from related persons (as defined in section 954(d)(3)), and

(v) Foreign oil and gas extraction income (as defined in section 907(c)(1)) of the corporation.

(2) *Determination of gross income and allowable deductions.*—For purposes of determining tested income and tested loss, the gross income and allowable deductions of a controlled foreign corporation for a CFC inclusion year are determined under the rules of § 1.952-2 for determining the subpart F income of a controlled foreign corporation.

(3) *Allocation of deductions to gross tested income.*—Any deductions of a controlled foreign corporation allowable under paragraph (c)(2) of this section are allocated and apportioned to gross tested income under the principles of section 954(b)(5) and § 1.954-1(c), by treating gross tested income that falls within a single separate category (as defined in § 1.904-5(a)(1)) as a single item of gross income, in addition to the items set forth in § 1.954-1(c)(1)(iii).

(4) *Nonapplication of section 952(c).*—(i) *In general.*—The gross tested income and allowable deductions properly allocable to gross tested income of a controlled foreign corporation for a CFC inclusion year are determined without regard to the application of section 952(c).

(ii) *Example.*—The following example illustrates the application of this paragraph (c)(4).

(A) *Example*—(1) *Facts.* A Corp, a domestic corporation, owns 100% of the single class of stock of FS, a controlled foreign corporation. Both A Corp and FS use the calendar year as their taxable year. In Year 1, FS has foreign base company income of $100x, a loss in foreign oil and gas extraction income of $100x, and earnings and profits of $0. FS has no other income. In Year 2, FS has gross income of $100x and earnings and profits of $100x. Without regard to section 952(c)(2), in Year 2 FS has no income described in any of the categories of income excluded from gross tested income in paragraphs (c)(1)(i) through (v) of this section. FS has no allowable

deductions properly allocable to gross tested income for Year 2.

(2) *Analysis.* As a result of the earnings and profits limitation of section 952(c)(1), FS has no subpart F income in Year 1, and A Corp has no inclusion with respect to FS under section 951(a)(1)(A). Under paragraph (c)(4)(i) of this section, the gross tested income of FS is determined without regard to section 952(c)(1). Therefore, in determining the gross tested income of FS in Year 1, the $100x foreign base company income of FS in Year 1 is excluded under paragraph (c)(1)(ii) of this section, and FS has no gross tested income in Year 1. In Year 2, under section 952(c)(2), FS's earnings and profits ($100x) in excess of its subpart F income ($0) are treated as subpart F income. Therefore, FS has subpart F income of $100x in Year 2, and A Corp has an inclusion of $100x with respect to FS under section 951(a)(1)(A). Under paragraph (c)(4)(i) of this section, the gross tested income of FS is determined without regard to section 952(c)(2). Accordingly, FS's income in Year 2 is not subpart F income described in paragraph (c)(1)(ii) of this section, and FS has $100x of gross tested income in Year 2.

(5) *Disregard of basis in property related to certain transfers during the disqualified period.*—(i) *In general.*—Any deduction or loss attributable to disqualified basis of any specified property allocated and apportioned to gross tested income under paragraph (c)(3) of this section is disregarded for purposes of determining tested income or tested loss of a controlled foreign corporation. For purposes of this paragraph (c)(5), in the case that a deduction or loss arises with respect to specified property with disqualified basis and adjusted basis other than disqualified basis, the deduction or loss is treated as attributable to the disqualified basis in the same proportion that the disqualified basis bears to the total adjusted basis of the property.

(ii) *Definition of specified property.*—The term *specified property* means property that is of a type with respect to which a deduction is allowable under section 167 or 197.

(iii) *Definition of disqualified basis.*—Solely for purposes of paragraph (c)(5)(i) of this section, the term *disqualified basis* has the meaning set forth in § 1.951A-3(h)(2)(ii) (including with respect to property owned by a partnership by reason of § 1.951A-3(g)(3)), except that, in applying the provisions of § 1.951A-3(h)(2) to determine the disqualified basis, the term "specified property" is substituted for "specified tangible property" and the term "controlled foreign corporation" is substituted for "tested income CFC" each place they appear.

(iv) *Example.*—(A) *Facts.* USP, a domestic corporation, owns all of the stock of CFC1 and CFC2, each a controlled foreign corporation. Both USP and CFC1 use the calendar year as their taxable year. CFC2 uses a taxable year ending November 30. On November 1, 2018, before the start of its first CFC inclusion year, CFC2 sells intangible property to CFC1 that is amortizable under section 197 in exchange for $100x of cash. The intangible property has a basis of $20x in the hands of CFC2, and CFC2 recognizes $80x of gain as a result of the sale ($100x - $20x). CFC2's gain is not subject to U.S. tax or taken into account in determining USP's inclusion under section 951(a)(1)(A).

(B) *Analysis.* The sale by CFC1 is a disqualified transfer (within the meaning of §1.951A-3(h)(2)(ii)(C), as modified by paragraph (c)(5)(iii) of this section) because it is a transfer of specified property, CFC2 and CFC1 are related persons, and the transfer occurs during the disqualified period (within the meaning of §1.951A-3(h)(2)(ii)(D)). The disqualified basis is $80x, the excess of CFC1's adjusted basis in the property immediately after the disqualified transfer ($100x), over the sum of CFC2's basis in the property immediately before the transfer ($20x) and the qualified gain amount (as defined in §1.951A-3(h)(2)(ii)(B)) ($0). Accordingly, under paragraph (c)(5)(i) of this section, any deduction or loss attributable to the disqualified basis is disregarded for purposes of determining the tested income or tested loss of any CFC for any CFC inclusion year. [Reg. §1.951A-2.]

[Proposed 10-10-2018.]

### [Prop. Reg. §1.951A-3]

**§1.951A-3. Qualified business asset investment.**—(a) *Scope.*—This section provides general rules for determining the qualified business asset investment of a controlled foreign corporation for purposes of determining a United States shareholder's deemed tangible income return under §1.951A-1(c)(3)(ii). Paragraph (b) of this section defines qualified business asset investment. Paragraph (c) of this section defines tangible property and specified tangible property. Paragraph (d) of this section provides rules and examples for determining the portion of property that is specified tangible property when the property is used in the production of both gross tested income and gross income that is not gross tested income. Paragraph (e) of this section provides rules for determining the adjusted basis of specified tangible property. Paragraph (f) of this section provides rules for determining qualified business asset investment of a tested income CFC with a short taxable year. Paragraph (g) of this section provides rules and examples for increasing the qualified business asset investment of a tested income CFC by reason of property owned through a partnership. Paragraph (h) of this section provides anti-abuse rules that disregard the basis of specified tangible property transferred in certain transactions when determining the qualified business asset investment of a tested income CFC.

(b) *Definition of qualified business asset investment.*—The term *qualified business asset investment* means the average of a tested income CFC's

aggregate adjusted bases as of the close of each quarter of a CFC inclusion year in specified tangible property that is used in a trade or business of the tested income CFC and is of a type with respect to which a deduction is allowable under section 167. A tested loss CFC has no qualified business asset investment. See paragraph (f) of this section for rules relating to the qualified business asset investment of a tested income CFC with a short taxable year.

(c) *Specified tangible property.*—(1) *In general.*—The term *specified tangible property* means, subject to paragraph (d) of this section, tangible property used in the production of gross tested income. None of the tangible property of a tested loss CFC is specified tangible property.

(2) *Tangible property.*—The term *tangible property* means property for which the depreciation deduction provided by section 167(a) is eligible to be determined under section 168 without regard to section 168(f)(1), (2), or (5) and the date placed in service.

(d) *Dual use property.*—(1) *In general.*—In the case of tangible property of a tested income CFC that is used in both the production of gross tested income and the production of gross income that is not gross tested income in a CFC inclusion year, the portion of the adjusted basis in the property treated as adjusted basis in specified tangible property for the CFC inclusion year is determined by multiplying the average of the tested income CFC's adjusted basis in the property by the dual use ratio with respect to the property for the CFC inclusion year.

(2) *Dual use ratio.*—The term *dual use ratio* means, with respect to specified tangible property:

(i) In the case of specified tangible property that produces directly identifiable income for a CFC inclusion year, the ratio of the gross tested income produced by the property for the CFC inclusion year to the total amount of gross income produced by the property for the CFC inclusion year.

(ii) In the case of specified tangible property that does not produce directly identifiable income for a CFC inclusion year, the ratio of the gross tested income of the tested income CFC for the CFC inclusion year to the total amount of gross income of the tested income CFC for the CFC inclusion year.

(3) *Example.*—The following example illustrates the application of this paragraph (d).

(i) *Example*—(A) *Facts.* FS is a tested income CFC. FS owns a machine that only packages Product A. In Year 1, FS sells Product A to related and unrelated resellers and earns $1,000x of gross income. For Year 1, sales of Product A produce gross tested income of $750x and foreign base company sales income (as defined in section 954(d)) of $250x. The average adjusted basis of the machine for Year 1 in the hands of FS is $4,000x. FS also owns an office building for its administrative functions with an average adjusted basis for Year 1 of $10,000x. The office building does not produce directly identifiable income. FS has no other specified tangible property. For year 1, FS also earns $1,250x of gross tested income and $2,750x of foreign base company sales income from sales of Product B. Neither the machine nor the office building is used in the production of income related to Product B. For Year 1, FS's gross tested income is $2,000x and its total gross income is $5,000x.

(B) *Analysis.* The machine and office building are both property for which the depreciation deduction provided by section 167(a) is eligible to be determined under section 168. Therefore, under paragraph (c)(2) of this section, the machine and office building are tangible property. Under paragraph (d)(1) of this section, the portion of the basis in the machine treated as basis in specified tangible property is equal to FS's average basis in the machine for the year ($4,000x), multiplied by the dual use ratio under paragraph (d)(2)(i) of this section (75%), which is the proportion that the gross tested income produced by the property ($750x) bears to the total gross income produced by the property ($1,000x). Accordingly, $3,000x ($4,000x x 75%) of FS's adjusted basis in the machine is taken into account in determining the average of FS's aggregate adjusted bases described in paragraph (b) of this section. Under paragraph (d)(1) of this section, the portion of the basis in the office building treated as basis in specified tangible property is equal to FS's average basis in the office building for the year ($10,000x), multiplied by the dual use ratio under paragraph (d)(2)(ii) of this section (40%), which is the ratio of FS's gross tested income for Year 1 ($2,000x) to FS's total gross income for Year 1 ($5,000x). Accordingly, $4,000x ($10,000x x 40%) of FS's adjusted basis in the office building is taken into account in determining the average of FS's aggregate adjusted bases described in paragraph (b) of this section.

(e) *Determination of adjusted basis of specified tangible property.*—(1) *In general.*—The adjusted basis in specified tangible property is determined by using the alternative depreciation system under section 168(g), and by allocating the depreciation deduction with respect to such property for the CFC inclusion year ratably to each day during the period in the taxable year to which such depreciation relates.

(2) *Effect of change in law.*—The determination of adjusted basis for purposes of paragraph (b) of this section is made without regard to any provision of law enacted after December 22, 2017, unless such later enacted law specifically and directly amends the definition of qualified business asset investment under section 951A.

(3) *Specified tangible property placed in service before enactment of section 951A.*—The adjusted basis in property placed in service before December

ber 22, 2017, is determined using the alternative depreciation system under section 168(g), as if this system had applied from the date that the property was placed in service.

(f) *Special rules for short taxable years.*—(1) *In general.*—In the case of a tested income CFC that has a CFC inclusion year that is less than twelve months (a *short taxable year*), the rules for determining the qualified business asset investment of the tested income CFC under this section are modified as provided in paragraphs (f)(2) and (3) of this section with respect to the CFC inclusion year.

(2) *Determination of quarter closes.*—For purposes of determining quarter closes, in determining the qualified business asset investment of a tested income CFC for a short taxable year, the quarters of the tested income CFC for purposes of this section are the full quarters beginning and ending within the short taxable year (if any), determining quarter length as if the tested income CFC did not have a short taxable year, plus one or more short quarters (if any).

(3) *Reduction of qualified business asset investment.*—The qualified business asset investment of a tested income CFC for a short taxable year is the sum of—

(i) The sum of the tested income CFC's aggregate adjusted bases in specified tangible property as of the close of each full quarter (if any) in the CFC inclusion year divided by four, plus

(ii) The tested income CFC's aggregate adjusted bases in specified tangible property as of the close of each short quarter (if any) in the CFC inclusion year multiplied by the sum of the number of days in each short quarter divided by 365.

(4) *Example.*—The following example illustrates the application of this paragraph (f).

(i) *Example*—(A) *Facts.* USP1, a domestic corporation, owns all of the stock of FS, a controlled foreign corporation. USP1 owns FS from the beginning of Year 1. On July 15, Year 1, USP1 sells FS to USP2, an unrelated person. USP2 makes a section 338(g) election with respect to the purchase of FS, as a result of which FS's taxable year is treated as ending on July 15. USP1, USP2, and FS all use the calendar year as their taxable year. FS's aggregate adjusted bases in specified tangible property are $250x as of March 31, $300x as of June 30, $275x as of July 15, $500x as of September 30, and $450x as of December 31.

(B) *Analysis*—(1) *Determination of short taxable years and quarters.* FS has two short taxable years in Year 1. The first short taxable year is from January 1 to July 15, with two full quarters (January 1-March 31 and April 1-June 30) and one short quarter (July 1-July 15). The second taxable year is from July 16 to December 31, with one short quarter (July 16-September 30) and one full quarter (October 1-December 31).

**Prop. Reg. §1.951A-3(f)(4)**

(2) *Calculation of qualified business asset investment for the first short taxable year.* Under paragraph (f)(2) of this section, for the first short taxable year in Year 1, FS has three quarter closes (March 31, June 30, and July 15). Under paragraph (f)(3) of this section, the qualified business asset investment of FS for the first short taxable year is $148.80x, the sum of $137.50x (($250x + $300x)/4) attributable to the two full quarters and $11.30x ($275x x 15/365) attributable to the short quarter.

(3) *Calculation of qualified business asset investment for the second short taxable year.* Under paragraph (f)(2) of this section, for the second short taxable year in Year 1, FS has two quarter closes (September 30 and December 31). Under paragraph (f)(3) of this section, the qualified business asset investment of FS for the second short taxable year is $217.98x, the sum of $112.50x ($450x/4) attributable to the one full quarter and $105.48x ($500x x 77/365) attributable to the short quarter.

(g) *Partnership property.*—(1) *In general.*—For purposes of paragraph (b) of this section, if a tested income CFC holds an interest in one or more partnerships as of the close of the CFC inclusion year, the qualified business asset investment of the tested income CFC for the CFC inclusion year is increased by the sum of the tested income CFC's partnership QBAI with respect to each partnership for the CFC inclusion year. A tested loss CFC has no partnership QBAI for a CFC inclusion year.

(2) *Definitions related to partnership QBAI.*—(i) *In general.*—The term *partnership QBAI* means the sum of the tested income CFC's share of the partnership's adjusted basis in partnership specified tangible property as of the close of a partnership taxable year that ends with or within a CFC inclusion year. A tested income CFC's share of the partnership's adjusted basis in partnership specified tangible property is determined separately with respect to each partnership specified tangible property of the partnership by multiplying the partnership's adjusted basis in the property by the partnership QBAI ratio with respect to the property. If the partnership's taxable year is less than twelve months, the principles of paragraph (f) of this section apply in determining a tested income CFC's partnership QBAI with respect to the partnership.

(ii) *Partnership QBAI ratio.*—The term *partnership QBAI ratio* means, with respect to partnership specified tangible property:

(A) In the case of partnership specified tangible property that produces directly identifiable income for a partnership taxable year, the ratio of the tested income CFC's distributive share of the gross income produced by the property for the partnership taxable year that is included in the gross tested income of the tested income CFC for the CFC inclusion year to the total gross income produced by the property for the partnership taxable year.

(B) In the case of partnership specified tangible property that does not produce directly identifiable income for a partnership taxable year, the ratio of the tested income CFC's distributive share of the gross income of the partnership for the partnership taxable year that is included in the gross tested income of the tested income CFC for the CFC inclusion year to the total amount of gross income of the partnership for the partnership taxable year.

(iii) *Partnership specified tangible property.*—The term *partnership specified tangible property* means tangible property (as defined in paragraph (c)(2) of this section) of a partnership that is—

(A) Used in the trade or business of the partnership,

(B) Of a type with respect to which a deduction is allowable under section 167, and

(C) Used in the production of tested income.

(3) *Determination of adjusted basis.*—For purposes of this paragraph (g), a partnership's adjusted basis in partnership specified tangible property is determined based on the average of the partnership's adjusted basis in the property as of the close of each quarter in the partnership taxable year. The principles of paragraphs (e) and (h) of this section apply for purposes of determining a partnership's adjusted basis in partnership specified tangible property and the portion of such adjusted basis taken into account in determining a tested income CFC's partnership QBAI.

(4) *Examples.*—The following examples illustrate the rules of this paragraph (g).

(i) *Example 1*—(A) *Facts.* FC, a tested income CFC, is a partner in PRS. Both FC and PRS use the calendar year as their taxable year. PRS owns two assets, Asset A and Asset B, both of which are tangible property used in PRS's trade or business that it depreciates under section 168. The average of PRS's adjusted basis as of the close of each quarter of PRS's taxable year in Asset A is $100x and the average of PRS's adjusted basis as of the end of each quarter of PRS's taxable year in Asset B is $50x. Asset A produces $10x of directly identifiable gross income in Year 1, and Asset B produces $50x of directly identifiable gross income in Year 1. FC's distributive share of the gross income from Asset A is $8x and its distributive share of the gross income from Asset B is $10x. FC's entire distributive share of income from Asset A and Asset B is included in FC's gross tested income for Year 1. PRS partners' distributive shares satisfy the requirements of section 704.

(B) *Analysis.* Each of Asset A and Asset B is partnership specified tangible property because each is tangible property, of a type with respect to which a deduction is allowable under section 167, used in PRS's trade or business, and used in the production of tested income. FC's partnership QBAI ratio for Asset A is 80%, the ratio of FC's distributive share of the gross income from Asset A for Year 1 that is included in FC's gross tested income ($8x) to the total gross income produced by Asset A for Year 1 ($10x). FC's partnership QBAI ratio for Asset B is 20%, the ratio of FC's distributive share of the gross income from Asset B for Year 1 that is included in FC's gross tested income ($10x) to the total gross income produced by Asset B for Year 1 ($50x). FC's share of the average of PRS's adjusted basis of Asset A is $80x, PRS's adjusted basis in Asset A of $100x multiplied by FC's partnership QBAI ratio for Asset A of 80%. FC's share of the average of PRS's adjusted basis of Asset B is $10x, PRS's adjusted basis in Asset B of $50x multiplied by FC's partnership QBAI ratio for Asset B of 20%. Therefore, FC's partnership QBAI with respect to PRS is $90x ($80x + $10x). Accordingly, under paragraph (g)(1) of this section, FC increases its qualified business asset investment for Year 1 by $90x.

(ii) *Example 2*—(A) *Facts.* FC, a tested income CFC, owns a 50% interest in PRS. PRS owns Asset A, which is specified tangible property. The average of PRS's adjusted basis as of the close of each quarter of PRS's taxable year in Asset A is $100x. FC has the same taxable year as PRS. Asset A produces $20x of directly identifiable gross income in Year 1, and PRS has $22x of expenses in Year 1 that are properly allocable to such income. Therefore, FC's allocation of net income or loss from PRS is $1x loss, which is comprised of FC's distributive share of the gross income from Asset A of $10x, all of which is included in FC's gross tested income for Year 1, and FC's distributive share of the expenses related to Asset A of $11x, all of which is taken into account in determining its tested income under § 1.951-2(c). PRS has no other income or loss in Year 1. FC also has $8x of gross tested income from other sources in Year 1, and no deductions properly allocable to such income. PRS partners' distributive shares satisfy the requirements of section 704.

(B) *Analysis.* FC's partnership QBAI ratio for Asset A is 50%, the ratio of FC's distributive share of the gross income from Asset A for Year 1 that is included in FC's gross tested income ($10x) to the total gross income produced by Asset A for Year 1 ($20x). FC's share of the average of PRS's adjusted basis in Asset A is $50x, PRS's adjusted basis in Asset A of $100x multiplied by FC's partnership QBAI ratio for Asset A of 50%. FC increases its qualified business asset investment by $50x, notwithstanding that FC would not be a tested income CFC but for its $8x of gross tested income from other sources.

(h) *Anti-abuse rules for certain transfers of property.*—(1) *Disregard of basis in specified tangible property held temporarily.*—If a tested income CFC (*acquiring CFC*) acquires specified tangible property (as defined in paragraph (c)(1) of this section) with a principal purpose of reducing the GILTI inclusion amount of a United States share-

holder for any U.S. shareholder inclusion year, and the tested income CFC holds the property temporarily but over at least the close of one quarter, the specified tangible property is disregarded in determining the acquiring CFC's average adjusted basis in specified tangible property for purposes of determining the acquiring CFC's qualified business asset investment for any CFC inclusion year during which the tested income CFC held the property. For purposes of this paragraph (h)(1), specified tangible property held by the tested income CFC for less than a twelve month period that includes at least the close of one quarter during the taxable year of a tested income CFC is treated as temporarily held and acquired with a principal purpose of reducing the GILTI inclusion amount of a United States shareholder for a U.S. shareholder inclusion year if such acquisition would, but for this paragraph (h)(1), reduce the GILTI inclusion amount of a United States shareholder for a U.S. shareholder inclusion year.

(2) *Disregard of basis in specified tangible property related to transfers during the disqualified period.*—(i) *In general.*—For purposes of determining the qualified business asset investment of a tested income CFC for a CFC inclusion year, in applying the alternative depreciation system under section 168(g) to determine the tested income CFC's adjusted basis in specified tangible property, any disqualified basis with respect to the specified tangible property is not taken into account.

(ii) *Determination of disqualified basis.*—(A) *In general.*—The term *disqualified basis* means, with respect to specified tangible property, the excess (if any) of the property's adjusted basis immediately after a disqualified transfer, over the sum of the property's adjusted basis immediately before the disqualified transfer and the qualified gain amount with respect to the disqualified transfer. Disqualified basis may be reduced or eliminated through depreciation, amortization, sales or exchanges, section 362(e), and other methods. In such circumstances, in the case of specified tangible property with disqualified basis and adjusted basis other than disqualified basis, the disqualified basis is reduced or eliminated in the same proportion that the disqualified basis bears to the total adjusted basis of the property.

(B) *Definition of qualified gain amount.*—The term *qualified gain amount* means, with respect to a disqualified transfer, the sum of the following amounts:

(1) The amount of gain recognized by a controlled foreign corporation (*transferor CFC*) on the disqualified transfer of the specified tangible property that is subject to U.S. federal income tax under section 882 (except to the extent the gain is subject to a reduced rate of tax, or is exempt from tax, pursuant to an applicable treaty obligation of the United States); and

**Prop. Reg. §1.951A-3(h)(2)(ii)(B)(1)**

*(2)* Any United States shareholder's pro rata share of the gain recognized by the transferor CFC on the disqualified transfer of the specified tangible property (determined without regard to properly allocable deductions) taken into account in determining the United States shareholder's inclusion under section 951(a)(1)(A), excluding any amount that is described in paragraph (h)(2)(ii)(B)(*1*) of this section.

*(C) Definition of disqualified transfer.*— The term *disqualified transfer* means a transfer of specified tangible property during a transferor CFC's disqualified period by the transferor CFC to a related person in which gain was recognized, in whole or in part, by the transferor CFC, regardless of whether the property was specified tangible property in the hands of the transferor CFC. For purposes of the preceding sentence, a transfer includes any disposition, sale or exchange, contribution, or distribution of the specified tangible property, and includes an indirect transfer (for example, a transfer of an interest in a partnership is treated as a transfer of the assets of the partnership and transfer by or to a partnership is treated as a transfer by or to its partners).

*(D) Definition of disqualified period.*—The term *disqualified period* means, with respect to a transferor CFC, the period beginning on January 1, 2018, and ending as of the close of the transferor CFC's last taxable year that is not a CFC inclusion year. A transferor CFC that has a CFC inclusion year beginning January 1, 2018, has no disqualified period.

*(E) Related person.*—For purposes of this paragraph (h)(2), a person is related to a controlled foreign corporation if the person bears a relationship to the controlled foreign corporation described in section 267(b) or 707(b) immediately before or immediately after the transfer.

*(iii) Examples.*—The following examples illustrate the application of this paragraph (h)(2).

*(A) Example 1*—(1) *Facts.* USP, a domestic corporation, owns all of the stock of CFC1 and CFC2, each a controlled foreign corporation. Both USP and CFC1 use the calendar year as their taxable year. CFC2 uses a taxable year ending November 30. On November 1, 2018, before the start of its first CFC inclusion year, CFC2 sells specified tangible property that has a basis of $10x in the hands of CFC2 to CFC1 in exchange for $100x of cash. CFC2 recognizes $90x of gain as a result of the sale ($100x - $10x), $30x of which is foreign base company income (within the meaning of section 954). USP includes in gross income under section 951(a)(1)(A) its pro rata share of the subpart F income of $30x. CFC2's gain is not otherwise subject to U.S. tax or taken into account in determining USP's inclusion under section 951(a)(1)(A).

*(2) Analysis.* The transfer is a disqualified transfer because it is a transfer of specified tangi-

ble property; CFC1 and CFC2 are related persons; and the transfer occurs during the disqualified period, the period that begins on January 1, 2018, and ends the last day before the first CFC inclusion year of CFC2 (November 30, 2018). The disqualified basis is $60x, the excess of CFC1's adjusted basis in the property immediately after the disqualified transfer ($100x), over the sum of CFC2's basis in the property immediately before the transfer ($10x) and USP's pro rata share of the gain recognized by CFC1 on the transfer of the property taken into account by USP under section 951(a)(1)(A) ($30x). Accordingly, under paragraph (h)(2)(i) of this section, for purposes of determining the qualified business asset investment of any tested income CFC for any CFC inclusion year, in applying section 168(g) to determine the CFC's basis in the specified tangible property, the $60x disqualified basis of the property is not taken into account.

*(B) Example 2*—(1) *Facts.* The facts are the same as in paragraph (i) of *Example 1*, except that CFC2 uses the calendar year as its taxable year.

*(2) Analysis.* Because CFC2 has a taxable year beginning January 1, 2018, CFC2 has no disqualified period. Accordingly, the property was not transferred during a disqualified period of CFC2, and there is no disqualified basis with respect to the property. [Reg. § 1.951A-3.]

[Proposed 10-10-2018.]

### [Prop. Reg. § 1.951A-4]

**§ 1.951A-4. Tested interest expense and tested interest income.**—(a) *Scope.*—This section provides general rules for determining the tested interest expense and tested interest income of a controlled foreign corporation for purposes of determining a United States shareholder's specified interest expense under § 1.951A-1(c)(3)(iii). Paragraph (b) of this section provides the definitions related to tested interest expense and tested interest income. Paragraph (c) of this section provides examples illustrating these definitions and the application of § 1.951A-1(c)(3)(iii). The amount of specified interest expense determined under § 1.951A-1(c)(3)(iii) and this section is the amount of interest expense described in section 951A(b)(2)(B).

(b) *Definitions related to specified interest expense.*—(1) *Tested interest expense.*—(i) *In general.*—The term *tested interest expense* means interest expense paid or accrued by a controlled foreign corporation taken into account in determining the tested income or tested loss of the controlled foreign corporation for the CFC inclusion year under § 1.951A-2(c), reduced by the qualified interest expense of the controlled foreign corporation.

(ii) *Interest expense.*—The term *interest expense* means any expense or loss that is treated as interest expense by reason of the Internal Revenue Code or the regulations thereunder, and any other expense or loss incurred in a transaction or series of integrated or related transactions in which the use of funds is secured for a period of time if such expense or loss is predominately incurred in consideration of the time value of money.

(iii) *Qualified interest expense.*—The term *qualified interest expense* means, with respect to a qualified CFC, the interest expense paid or accrued by the qualified CFC taken into account in determining the tested income or tested loss of the qualified CFC for the CFC inclusion year, multiplied by the fraction (not to exceed one) described in paragraph (b)(1)(iii)(A) of this section, and then reduced (but not to less than zero) by the amount described in paragraph (b)(1)(iii)(B) of this section.

(A) The numerator of the fraction described in this paragraph (b)(1)(iii)(A) is the average of the aggregate adjusted bases as of the close of each quarter of obligations or financial instruments held by the qualified CFC that give rise to income excluded from foreign personal holding company income (as defined in section 954(c)(1)) by reason of section 954(h) or (i), and the denominator is the average of the aggregate adjusted bases as of the close of each quarter of all assets held by the qualified CFC. For purposes of this paragraph (b)(1)(iii)(A), the basis of the stock of another qualified CFC held by a qualified CFC is treated as basis of an obligation or financial instrument giving rise to income excluded from foreign personal holding company income by reason of section 954(h) or (i) in an amount equal to the basis of the stock multiplied by the fraction described in this paragraph (b)(1)(iii)(A) determined with respect to the assets of such other qualified CFC.

(B) The amount described in this paragraph (b)(1)(iii)(B) is the amount of interest income of the qualified CFC for the CFC inclusion year that is excluded from foreign personal holding company income (as defined in section 954(c)(1)) by reason of section 954(c)(3) or (6).

(iv) *Qualified CFC.*—The term *qualified CFC* means an eligible controlled foreign corporation (within the meaning of section 954(h)(2)) or a qualifying insurance company (within the meaning of section 953(e)(3)).

(2) *Tested interest income.*—(i) *In general.*— The term *tested interest income* means interest income included in the gross tested income of a controlled foreign corporation for the CFC inclusion year, reduced by qualified interest income of the controlled foreign corporation.

(ii) *Interest income.*—The term *interest income* means any income or gain that is treated as interest income by reason of the Internal Revenue Code or the regulations thereunder, and any other income or gain recognized in a transaction or series of integrated or related transactions in which the forbearance of funds is secured for a period of time if such income or gain is predominately derived from consideration of the time value of money.

(iii) *Qualified interest income.*—The term *qualified interest income* means, with respect to a qualified CFC, interest income of the qualified CFC included in the gross tested income of the qualified CFC for the CFC inclusion year that is excluded from foreign personal holding company income (as defined in section 954(c)(1)) by reason of section 954(h) or (i).

(c) *Examples.*—The following examples illustrate the application of this section.

(1) *Example 1: wholly-owned CFCs*—(i) *Facts.* A Corp, a domestic corporation, owns 100% of the single class of stock of each of FS1 and FS2, each a controlled foreign corporation. A Corp, FS1, and FS2 all use the calendar year as their taxable year. In Year 1, FS1 pays $100x of interest to FS2. Also, in Year 1, FS2 pays $100x of interest to a bank that is not related to A Corp, FS1, or FS2. The interest paid by each of FS1 and FS2 is taken into account in determining the tested income and tested loss of FS1 and FS2 under §1.951A-2(c), and the interest received by FS2 is not foreign personal holding company income (as defined in section 954(c)(1)) by reason of section 954(c)(6) and thus is included in gross tested income. For Year 1, taking into account interest income and expense, FS1 has $500x of tested income and FS2 has $400x of tested loss. Neither FS1 nor FS2 is a qualified CFC.

(ii) *Analysis*—(A) *CFC-level determination; tested interest expense and tested interest income.* FS1 has $100x of tested interest expense for Year 1. FS2 has $100x of tested interest expense and $100x of tested interest income for Year 1.

(B) *United States shareholder-level determination; pro rata share and specified interest expense.* Under §1.951A-1(d)(5) and (6), A Corp's pro rata share of FS1's tested interest expense is $100x, its pro rata share of FS2's tested interest expense is $100x, and its pro rata share of FS2's tested interest income is $100x. For Year 1, A Corp's aggregate pro rata share of tested interest expense is $200x and its aggregate pro rata share of tested interest income is $100x. Accordingly, under §1.951A-1(c)(3)(iii), A Corp's specified interest expense is $100x ($200x - $100x) for Year 1.

(2) *Example 2: less than wholly-owned CFCs*—(i) *Facts.* The facts are the same as in paragraph (i) of *Example 1*, except that A Corp owns 50% of the single class of stock of FS1 and 80% of the single class of stock of FS2.

(ii) *Analysis.* (A) *CFC-level determination; tested interest expense and tested interest income.* The analysis is the same as in paragraph (ii)(A) of *Example 1*.

(B) *United States shareholder-level determination; pro rata share and specified interest expense.* Under §1.951A-1(d)(5) and (6), A Corp's pro rata share of FS1's tested interest expense is $50x ($100x x 0.50), its pro rata share of FS2's tested interest expense is $80x ($100x x 0.80), and its pro rata share of FS2's tested interest income is $80x ($100x x 0.80). For Year 1, A Corp's aggregate pro rata share of the tested interest expense is $130x

**Prop. Reg. §1.951A-4(c)**

and its aggregate pro rata share of the tested interest income is $80x. Accordingly, under §1.951A-1(c)(3)(iii), A Corp's specified interest expense is $50x ($130x - $80x) for Year 1.

(3) *Example 3: qualified CFC*—(i) *Facts.* B Corp, a domestic corporation, owns 100% of the single class of stock of each of FS1 and FS2, a controlled foreign corporation. B Corp, FS1, and FS2 all use the calendar year as their taxable year. FS2 is an eligible controlled foreign corporation within the meaning of section 954(h)(2). In Year 1, FS1 pays $100x of interest to FS2, which interest income is excluded from the foreign personal holding company income (as defined in section 954(c)(1)) of FS2 by reason of section 954(c)(6). Also, in Year 1, FS2 pays $250x of interest to a bank, and receives an additional $300x of interest from customers that are not related to FS2, which interest income is excluded from foreign personal holding company income by reason of section 954(h). The interest paid by each of FS1 and FS2 is taken into account in determining the tested income and tested loss of FS1 and FS2, and the interest received by FS2 is included in gross tested income. FS1 is not a qualified CFC. FS2 does not own stock in any qualified CFC. FS2's average adjusted bases in obligations or financial instruments that give rise to income excluded from foreign personal holding company income by reason of section 954(h) is $8,000x, and FS2's average adjusted bases in all its assets is $10,000x.

(ii) *Analysis*—(A) *CFC-level determination; tested interest expense and tested interest income.* FS1 has $100x of tested interest expense for Year 1. FS2 is a qualified CFC because it is an eligible controlled foreign corporation within the meaning of section 954(h)(2). As a result, in determining the tested interest income and tested interest expense of FS2, the qualified interest income and qualified interest expense of FS2 are excluded. FS2 has qualified interest income of $300x, the amount of FS2's interest income that is excluded from foreign personal holding company income by reason of section 954(h). In addition, FS2 has qualified interest expense of $100x, the amount of FS2's interest expense taken into account in determining FS2's tested income or tested loss under §1.951A-2(c) ($250x), multiplied by a fraction, the numerator of which is FS2's average adjusted bases in obligations or financial instruments that give rise to income excluded from foreign personal holding company income by reason of section 954(h) ($8,000x), and the denominator of which is F2's average adjusted bases in all its assets ($10,000x), and then reduced by the amount of the interest income received from FS1 excluded from foreign personal holding company income by reason of section 954(c)(6) ($100x). Therefore, for Year 1, FS2 has tested interest income of $100x ($400x - $300x) and tested interest expense of $150x ($250x - $100x).

(B) *United States shareholder-level determination; pro rata share and specified interest expense.* Under §1.951A-1(d)(5) and (6), B Corp's pro rata share

of FS1's tested interest expense is $100x, its pro rata share of FS2's tested interest expense is $150x, and its pro rata share of FS2's tested interest income is $100x. For Year 1, B Corp's aggregate pro rata share of tested interest expense is $250x ($100x + $150x) and its aggregate pro rata share of tested interest income is $100x ($0 + $100x). Accordingly, under §1.951A-1(c)(3)(iii), B Corp's specified interest expense is $150x ($250x - $100x) for Year 1. [Reg. §1.951A-4.]

[Proposed 10-10-2018.]

### [Prop. Reg. §1.951A-5]

**§1.951A-5. Domestic partnerships and their partners.**—(a) *Scope.*—This section provides rules regarding the application of section 951A and the section 951A regulations to domestic partnerships that own (within the meaning of section 958(a)) stock in one or more controlled foreign corporations and to partners of such domestic partnerships, including United States persons (within the meaning of section 957(c)). Paragraph (b) of this section provides rules for the determination of the GILTI inclusion amount of a domestic partnership and the distributive share of such amount of a partner that is not a United States shareholder with respect to one or more controlled foreign corporations owned by the domestic partnership. Paragraph (c) of this section provides rules for the determination of the GILTI inclusion amount of a partner that is a United States shareholder with respect to one or more controlled foreign corporations owned by a domestic partnership. Paragraph (d) of this section provides rules for tiered domestic partnerships. Paragraph (e) of this section provides the definitions of CFC tested item, partnership CFC, U.S. shareholder partner, and U.S. shareholder partnership. Paragraph (f) of this section requires a domestic partnership to provide certain information to each partner necessary for the partner to determine its GILTI inclusion amount or its distributive share of the partnership's GILTI inclusion amount. Paragraph (g) of this section provides examples illustrating the rules of this section. For rules regarding the treatment of certain controlled domestic partnerships owned through one or more foreign corporations as foreign partnerships for purposes of sections 951 through 964, including section 951A and the section 951A regulations, see §1.951-1(h).

(b) *In general.*—(1) *Determination of GILTI inclusion amount of a U.S. shareholder partnership.*— A U.S. shareholder partnership determines its GILTI inclusion amount for its U.S. shareholder inclusion year under the general rules applicable to United States shareholders in section 951A and the section 951A regulations.

(2) *Determination of distributive share of U.S. shareholder partnership's GILTI inclusion amount of a partner other than a U.S. shareholder partner.*— Each partner of a U.S. shareholder partnership that is not a U.S. shareholder partner takes into account its distributive share of the U.S. share-

holder partnership's GILTI inclusion amount (if any) for the U.S. shareholder inclusion year in accordance with section 702 and § 1.702-1(a)(8)(ii).

(c) *Determination of GILTI inclusion amount of a U.S. shareholder partner.*—For purposes of section 951A and the section 951A regulations, section 958(a) stock of a partnership CFC owned by a U.S. shareholder partnership is treated as section 958(a) stock owned proportionately by each U.S. shareholder partner that is a United States shareholder of the partnership CFC in the same manner as if the U.S. shareholder partnership were a foreign partnership under section 958(a)(2) and § 1.958-1(b). Accordingly, for purposes of determining a U.S. shareholder partner's GILTI inclusion amount, the U.S. shareholder partner determines its pro rata share of any CFC tested item of a partnership CFC based on the section 958(a) stock owned by the U.S. shareholder partner by reason of this paragraph (c). In addition, a U.S. shareholder partner's distributive share of the GILTI inclusion amount of a U.S. shareholder partnership is determined without regard to the partnership's pro rata share of any CFC tested item of a partnership CFC with respect to which the U.S. shareholder partner is a United States shareholder.

(d) *Tiered U.S. shareholder partnerships.*—In the case of tiered U.S. shareholder partnerships, section 958(a) stock of a partnership CFC treated as owned under paragraph (c) of this section by a U.S. shareholder partner that is also a U.S. shareholder partnership is treated as section 958(a) stock owned by the U.S. shareholder partnership for purposes of applying paragraph (c) of this section to a U.S. shareholder partner of such U.S. shareholder partnership.

(e) *Definitions.*—The following definitions apply for purposes of this section:

(1) *CFC tested item.*—The term *CFC tested item* has the meaning set forth in § 1.951A-1(d)(1).

(2) *Partnership CFC.*—The term *partnership CFC* means, with respect to a U.S. shareholder partnership, a controlled foreign corporation stock of which is owned (within the meaning of section 958(a)) by the U.S. shareholder partnership.

(3) *U.S. shareholder partner.*—The term *U.S. shareholder partner* means, with respect to a U.S. shareholder partnership and a partnership CFC of the U.S. shareholder partnership, a United States person that is a partner in the U.S. shareholder partnership and that is also a United States shareholder (as defined in section 951(b)) of the partnership CFC.

(4) *U.S. shareholder partnership.*—The term *U.S. shareholder partnership* means a domestic partnership (within the meaning of section 7701(a)(4)) that is a United States shareholder of one or more controlled foreign corporations.

(f) *Reporting requirement.*—A U.S. shareholder partnership must furnish to each partner on or with such partner's Schedule K-1 (Form 1065 or successor form) for each U.S. shareholder inclusion year of the partnership the partner's distributive share of the partnership's GILTI inclusion amount (if any) and, with respect to a U.S. shareholder partner, the partner's proportionate share of the partnership's pro rata share (if any) of each CFC tested item of each partnership CFC of the partnership and any other information required in the form or instructions. See section 6031(b).

(g) *Examples.*—The following examples illustrate the rules of this section. None of the persons in the following examples own an interest in any controlled foreign corporation other than as described.

(1) *Example 1: domestic partnership with partners that are not United States shareholders.* (i) *Facts.* Eleven U.S. citizens ("individuals") each own a 9% interest of PRS, a domestic partnership. The remaining 1% interest of PRS is owned by X Corp, a domestic corporation. None of the individuals or X Corp are related. PRS owns 100% of the single class of stock of FC, a controlled foreign corporation. The individuals, X Corp, PRS, and FC all use the calendar year as their taxable year. In Year 1, FC has $130x of tested income and $50x of qualified business asset investment.

(ii) *Analysis*—(A) *Partnership-level calculation.* PRS is a U.S. shareholder partnership with respect to FC. Under paragraph (b)(1) of this section, PRS determines its GILTI inclusion amount for Year 1. PRS's pro rata share of FC's tested income is $130x. PRS's pro rata share of FC's qualified business asset investment is $50x. PRS's net CFC tested income is $130x. PRS's net deemed tangible income return is $5x ($50x x 0.10). PRS's GILTI inclusion amount for Year 1 is $125x ($130x - $5x).

(B) *Partner-level calculation.* Neither X Corp nor the individuals are U.S. shareholder partners with respect to FC. Accordingly, under paragraph (b)(2) of this section, each of the individuals and X Corp includes its distributive share of PRS's GILTI inclusion amount ($11.25x each for the individuals and $1.25x for X Corp) in gross income for Year 1.

(2) *Example 2: domestic partnership with partners that are United States shareholders; multiple partnership CFCs.* (i) *Facts.* X Corp and Y Corp are domestic corporations that own 40% and 60%, respectively, of PRS, a domestic partnership. PRS owns 100% of the single class of stock of FC1 and of FC2, each a controlled foreign corporation. X Corp, Y Corp, PRS, FC1, and FC2 all use the calendar year as their taxable year. In Year 1, FC1 has $130x of tested income and $50x of qualified business asset investment, and FC2 has $30x of tested loss.

(ii) *Analysis*—(A) *Partnership-level calculation.* PRS is a U.S. shareholder partnership with respect to each of FC1 and FC2. Under paragraph (b)(1) of this section, PRS determines its GILTI

**Prop. Reg. §1.951A-5(g)**

inclusion amount for Year 1. PRS's pro rata share of FC1's tested income is $130x and of FC2's tested loss is $30x. PRS's pro rata share of FC1's qualified business asset investment is $50x. PRS's net CFC tested income is $100x ($130x − $30x). PRS's net deemed tangible income return is $5x ($50x x 0.10). PRS's GILTI inclusion amount for Year 1 is $95x ($100x - $5x).

(B) *Partner-level calculation.* X Corp and Y Corp are U.S. shareholder partners with respect to FC1 and FC2. Accordingly, under paragraph (c) of this section, X Corp and Y Corp are treated as owning section 958(a) stock of FC1 and FC2 proportionately as if PRS were a foreign partnership. Thus, X Corp's pro rata share of FC1's tested income is $52x ($130x x 0.40), and its pro rata share of FC2's tested loss is $12x ($30x x 0.40). X Corp's pro rata share of FC1's qualified business asset investment is $20x ($50x x 0.40). Accordingly, X Corp's net CFC tested income is $40x ($52x - $12x), and its net deemed tangible income return is $2x ($20x x 0.10). X Corp's GILTI inclusion amount for Year 1 is $38x ($40x - $2x). Y Corp's pro rata share of FC1's tested income is $78x ($130x x 0.60), and its pro rata share of FC2's tested loss is $18x ($30x x 0.60). Y Corp's pro rata share of FC1's qualified business asset investment is $30x ($50x x 0.60). Accordingly, Y Corp's net CFC tested income is $60x ($78x - $18x), and its net deemed tangible income return is $3x ($30x x 0.10). Y Corp's GILTI inclusion amount for Year 1 is $57x ($60x - $3x). Because X Corp and Y Corp are both U.S. shareholder partners with respect to FC1 and FC2, the only partnership CFCs of PRS, X Corp and Y Corp each includes its proportionate share of PRS's share of each CFC tested item of FC1 and FC2 under paragraph (c) of this section rather than including a distributive share of the GILTI inclusion amount of PRS.

(3) *Example 3: domestic partnership with partners that are United States shareholders with respect to some, but not all, of the controlled foreign corporations owned by the domestic partnership.* (i) *Facts.* X Corp and Y Corp are domestic corporations that own 40% and 60%, respectively, of PRS, a domestic partnership. PRS owns 20% of the single class of stock of FC1 and 10% of the single class of stock of FC2. In addition, Y Corp owns 100% of the single class of stock of FC3. FC1, FC2, and FC3 are controlled foreign corporations. X Corp, Y Corp, PRS, FC1, FC2, and FC3 all use the calendar year as their taxable year. In Year 1, FC1 has $100x of tested income, FC2 has $80x of tested income, and FC3 has $10x of tested loss.

(ii) *Analysis.* (A) *Partnership-level calculation.* PRS is a U.S. shareholder partnership with respect to each of FC1 and FC2. Under paragraph (b)(1) of this section, PRS determines its GILTI inclusion amount for Year 1. PRS's pro rata share of FC1's tested income is $20x ($100x x 0.20) and of FC2's tested income is $8x ($80x x 0.10). PRS's net CFC tested income is $28x ($20x + $8x). PRS has no net deemed tangible income return. PRS's GILTI inclusion amount for Year 1 is $28x.

(B) *Partner-level calculation*—(1) X Corp. X Corp is not a U.S. shareholder partner with respect to either FC1 or FC2 because X Corp owns (within the meaning of section 958) less than 10% of each of FC1 (40% x 20% = 8%) and FC2 (40% x 10% = 4%). Accordingly, under paragraph (b)(2) of this section, X Corp includes in income its distributive share, or $11.20x ($28x x 0.40), of PRS's GILTI inclusion amount in Year 1.

(2) *Y Corp.* Y Corp is a United States shareholder of FC3. Y Corp is also a U.S. shareholder partner with respect to FC1, because it owns (within the meaning of section 958) at least 10% (60% x 20% = 12%) of the stock of FC1, but not with respect to FC2, because Y Corp owns (within the meaning of section 958) less than 10% of the stock of FC2 (60% x 10% = 6%). Accordingly, under paragraph (c) of this section, Y Corp is treated as owning section 958(a) stock of FC1 proportionately as if PRS were a foreign partnership. Thus, Y Corp's pro rata share of FC1's tested income is $12x ($20x x 0.60). Y Corp's pro rata share of FC3's tested loss is $10x ($10x x 1). Accordingly, Y Corp's net CFC tested income is $2x ($12x - $10x) and Y Corp has no net deemed tangible income return. Y Corp's GILTI inclusion amount for Year 1 is $2x. In addition, under paragraph (c) of this section, for purposes of determining Y Corp's distributive share of PRS's GILTI inclusion amount, Y Corp's distributive share of PRS's GILTI inclusion amount is determined without regard to PRS's pro rata share of any item of FC1. PRS's GILTI inclusion amount computed solely with respect to FC2 is $8x ($80x x 0.10). Y Corp's distributive share of PRS's GILTI inclusion amount is $4.80x ($8x x 0.60) in Year 1.

(4) *Example 4: tiered domestic partnerships*—(i) *Facts.* X Corp and Y Corp are domestic corporations that own, respectively, a 20% interest and an 80% interest in PRS1, an upper-tier domestic partnership. PRS1 owns a 40% interest in PRS2, a lower-tier domestic partnership. The remaining 60% of PRS2 is owned by Z Corp, a controlled foreign corporation. PRS2 is not a controlled domestic partnership within the meaning of § 1.951-1(h)(2) (because no United States shareholder of Z Corp (or related persons) controls PRS2). PRS2 owns 80% of the single class of stock of FC, a controlled foreign corporation. X Corp, Y Corp, Z Corp, PRS1, PRS2, and FC all use the calendar year as their taxable year. In Year 1, FC has $100x of tested income and $50x of qualified business asset investment.

(ii) *Analysis.* (A) *Lower-tier partnership-level calculation.* PRS2 is a U.S. shareholder partnership with respect to FC, because PRS2 directly owns 80% of the single class of stock of FC. Under paragraph (b)(1) of this section, PRS2 determines its GILTI inclusion amount for its taxable year. PRS2's pro rata share of FC's tested income is $80x ($100x x 0.80). PRS2's pro rata share of FC's qualified business asset investment is $40x ($50x x 0.80). PRS2's net CFC tested income is $80x, and its net deemed tangible income return is $4x

($40x x 0.10). PRS2's GILTI inclusion amount for Year 1 is $76x ($80x - $4x).

(B) *Non-U.S. shareholder partner calculation.* Z Corp is not a U.S. shareholder partner of FC. Therefore, under paragraph (b)(2) of this section, in Year 1, Z Corp includes in income Z Corp's distributive share of PRS2's GILTI inclusion amount, or $45.60x ($76x x 0.60). Z Corp's gross tested income in Year 1 includes this amount.

(C) *Upper-tier partnership-level calculation.* PRS1 is a U.S. shareholder partner with respect to FC because it owns (within the meaning of section 958) more than 10% of the stock of FC (40% x 100% (by reason of the application of section 958(b)(2)) = 40%). Accordingly, under paragraph (c) of this section, PRS1 is treated as owning section 958(a) stock of FC proportionately as if PRS2 were a foreign partnership. Thus, PRS1's pro rata share of FC's tested income is $32x ($100x x 0.80 x 0.40), and its pro rata share of FC's qualified business asset investment is $16x ($50x x 0.80 x 0.40). PRS1's net CFC tested income is $32x, and its net deemed tangible income return is $1.60x ($16x x 0.10). PRS1's GILTI inclusion amount for Year 1 is $30.40x ($32x - $1.60x).

(D) *Upper-tier partnership partner-level calculation*—(1) *Treatment of upper-tier partnership.* For purposes of applying paragraph (c) of this section to determine X Corp and Y Corp's GILTI inclusion amount, PRS1 is treated as owning section 958(a) stock of FC.

(2) *X Corp.* X Corp is not a U.S. shareholder partner with respect to FC because it owns (within the meaning of section 958) less than 10% (20% x 40% x 100% (by reason of the application of section 958(b)(2)) = 8%) of the stock of FC. Accordingly, under paragraph (b)(2) of this section, X Corp includes its distributive share of PRS1's GILTI inclusion amount in Year 1, which is $6.08x ($30.40x x 0.20).

(3) *Y Corp.* Y Corp is a U.S. shareholder partner with respect to FC because it owns (within the meaning of section 958) more than 10% (80% x 40% x 100% (by reason of the application of section 958(b)(2)) = 32%) of the stock of FC. Accordingly, under paragraphs (c) and (d) of this section, Y Corp is treated as owning section 958(a) stock of FC proportionately as if PRS1 and PRS2 were foreign partnerships. Thus, Y Corp's pro rata share of FC's tested income is $25.60x ($100x x 0.80 x 0.40 x 0.80), and its pro rata share of FC's qualified business asset investment is $12.80x ($50x x 0.80 x 0.40 x 0.80). Y Corp's net CFC tested income is $25.60x, its net deemed tangible income return is $1.28x ($12.80x x 0.10), and its GILTI inclusion amount is $24.32x ($25.60x - $1.28x). Because Y Corp is a U.S. shareholder partner with respect to FC, the only partnership CFC of PRS1, Y Corp has no distributive share of the GILTI inclusion amount of PRS1 under paragraph (c) of this section.

(5) *Example 5: S corporation and its shareholders*—(i) *Facts.* Individual A, a U.S. citizen, and Grantor Trust, a trust all of which is treated under sections 671 through 679 as owned by

Individual B, a U.S. citizen, respectively own 5% and 95% of the single class of stock of Corporation X, an S corporation. Corporation X owns 100% of the single class of stock of FC, a controlled foreign corporation. Individual A, Grantor Trust, Individual B, Corporation X, and FC all use the calendar year as their taxable year. In Year 1, FC has $200x of tested income and $100x of qualified business asset investment.

(ii) *Analysis*—(A) *S corporation-level calculation.* An S corporation is treated as a partnership for purposes of sections 951 through 965 under section 1373. Corporation X is a U.S. shareholder partnership with respect to FC, a partnership CFC. Accordingly, under paragraph (b)(1) of this section, Corporation X determines its GILTI inclusion amount for Year 1. Corporation X's pro rata share of FC's tested income is $200x, and its pro rata share of FC's qualified business asset investment is $100x. Corporation X's net CFC tested income is $200x, and its net deemed tangible income return is $10x ($100x x 0.10). Corporation X's GILTI inclusion amount for Year 1 is $190x ($200x - $10x).

(B) *S corporation shareholder-level calculation*-(1) *Individual A.* Individual A is not a U.S. shareholder partner with respect to FC because it owns (within the meaning of section 958) less than 10% (5% x 100% = 5%) of the FC stock. Accordingly, under paragraph (b)(2) of this section, Individual A includes in gross income its proportionate share of Corporation X's GILTI inclusion amount, which is $9.50x ($190x x 0.05).

(2) *Grantor Trust.* Because Individual B is treated as owning all of Grantor Trust under sections 671 through 679, Individual B is treated as if it directly owns the shares of stock in Corporation X owned by Grantor Trust. As a result, Individual B is treated as a U.S. shareholder partner with respect to FC because it owns (within the meaning of section 958) more than 10% (95% x 100% = 95%) of the FC stock. Accordingly, under paragraph (c) of this section, Individual B is treated as owning section 958(a) stock of FC proportionately as if Corporation X were a foreign partnership. Thus, Individual B's pro rata share of FC's tested income is $190x ($200x x 0.95) and its pro rata share of FC's qualified business asset investment is $95x ($100x x 0.95). Individual B's net CFC tested income is $190x, and its net deemed tangible income return is $9.50x ($95x x 0.10). Individual B's GILTI inclusion amount for Year 1 is $180.5x ($190x - $9.50x). Because Individual B is a U.S. shareholder partner with respect to FC, the only partnership CFC of Corporation X, Individual B has no distributive share of the GILTI inclusion amount of Corporation X under paragraph (c) of this section.

(6) *Example 6: domestic partnership with no GILTI inclusion amount*—(i) *Facts.* X Corp is a domestic corporation that owns a 90% interest in PRS, a domestic partnership. The remaining 10% of PRS is owned by Y, a foreign individual. PRS owns 100% of the single class of stock of FC1, a controlled foreign corporation, and 100% of the sin-

gle class of stock of FC2, a controlled foreign corporation. X Corp owns 100% of the single class of stock of FC3, a controlled foreign corporation. X Corp, PRS, FC1, FC2, and FC3 all use the calendar year as their taxable year. In Year 1, FC1 has $100x of tested loss and $80x of tested interest expense, FC2 has $50x of tested income, and FC3 has $150x of tested income and $500x of qualified business asset investment in Year 1.

(ii) *Analysis*—(A) *Partnership-level calculation.* PRS is a U.S. shareholder partnership with respect to FC1 and FC2. Under paragraph (b)(1) of this section, PRS determines its GILTI inclusion amount for Year 1. PRS's pro rata share of FC1's tested loss is $100x, and PRS's pro rata share of FC2's tested income is $50x. PRS's net CFC tested income is $0 ($50x - 100x), and therefore PRS has no GILTI inclusion amount for Year 1.

(B) *Partner-level calculation.* X Corp is a U.S. shareholder partner with respect to FC1 and FC2 because X Corp owns (within the meaning of section 958) at least 10% of each (90% × 100% = 90%). Accordingly, under paragraph (c) of this section, X Corp is treated as owning section 958(a) stock of FC1 and FC2 proportionately as if PRS were a foreign partnership. X Corp's pro rata share of FC1's tested loss is $90x ($100x × 0.90), and X Corp's pro rata share of FC1's tested interest expense is $72x ($80 × 0.90). X Corp's pro rata share of FC2's tested income is $45x ($50x × 0.90). X Corp's pro rata share of FC3's tested income is $150x, and its pro rata share of FC3's qualified business asset investment is $500x. X Corp's net CFC tested income is $105x ($45x + $150x - $90x). X Corp's deemed tangible income return is $50x ($500x × 0.10), but its net deemed tangible income return is $0 ($50x - $72x). X Corp has a GILTI inclusion amount of $105x ($105x - $0) for Year 1. [Reg. § 1.951A-5.]

[Proposed 10-10-2018.]

## [Prop. Reg. § 1.951A-6]

**§1.951A-6. Treatment of GILTI inclusion amount and adjustments to earnings and profits and basis related to tested loss CFCs.—** (a) *Scope.*—This section provides rules relating to the treatment of GILTI inclusion amounts and adjustments to earnings and profits and basis to account for tested losses. Paragraph (b) of this section provides that a GILTI inclusion amount is treated in the same manner as an amount included under section 951(a)(1)(A) for purposes of applying certain sections of the Code. Paragraph (c) of this section provides rules for the treatment of amounts taken into account in determining the net CFC tested income when applying sections 163(e)(3)(B)(i) and 267(a)(3)(B). Paragraph (d) of this section provides rules that increase the earnings and profits of a tested loss CFC for purposes of section 952(c)(1)(A). Paragraph (e) of this section provides rules for certain basis adjustments to the stock of a controlled foreign corporation by reason of tested losses used to reduce a domestic corporation's net CFC tested income upon the disposition of the stock of the controlled foreign corporation.

(b) *Treatment as subpart F income for certain purposes.*—(1) *In general.*—A GILTI inclusion amount is treated in the same manner as an amount included under section 951(a)(1)(A) for purposes of applying sections 168(h)(2)(B), 535(b)(10), 851(b), 904(h)(1), 959, 961, 962, 993(a)(1)(E), 996(f)(1), 1248(b)(1), 1248(d)(1), 1411, 6501(e)(1)(C), 6654(d)(2)(D), and 6655(e)(4), and with respect to other sections of the Internal Revenue Code as provided in other guidance published in the Internal Revenue Bulletin.

(2) *Allocation of GILTI inclusion amount to tested income CFCs.*—(i) *In general.*—For purposes of the sections referred to in paragraph (b)(1) of this section, the portion of the GILTI inclusion amount of a United States shareholder treated as being with respect to each controlled foreign corporation of the United States shareholder for the U.S. shareholder inclusion year is—

(A) In the case of a tested loss CFC, zero, and

(B) In the case of a tested income CFC, the portion of the GILTI inclusion amount of the United States shareholder which bears the same ratio to such inclusion amount as the United States shareholder's pro rata share of the tested income of the tested income CFC for the U.S. shareholder inclusion year bears to the aggregate amount of the United States shareholder's pro rata share of the tested income of each tested income CFC for the U.S. shareholder inclusion year.

(ii) *Example.*—(A) *Facts.* USP, a domestic corporation, owns all of the stock of three controlled foreign corporations, CFC1, CFC2, and CFC3. USP, CFC1, CFC2, and CFC3 all use the calendar year as their taxable year. In Year 1, CFC1 has tested income of $100x, CFC2 has tested income of $300x, and CFC3 has tested loss of $50x. Neither CFC1 nor CFC2 has qualified business asset investment.

(B) *Analysis.* In Year 1, USP has a GILTI inclusion amount of $350x ($100x + $300x - $50x). The aggregate amount of USP's pro rata share of tested income from CFC1 and CFC2 is $400x ($100x + $300x). The portion of USP's GILTI inclusion amount treated as being with respect to CFC1 is $87.50x ($350x × $100x/ $400x). The portion of USP's GILTI inclusion amount treated as being with respect to CFC2 is $262.50x ($350x × $300x/$400x). The portion of USP's GILTI inclusion amount treated as being with respect to CFC3 is $0 because CFC3 is a tested loss CFC.

(iii) *Translation of portion of GILTI inclusion amount allocated to tested income CFC.*—The portion of the GILTI inclusion amount of a United States shareholder allocated to a tested income CFC under section 951A(f)(2) and paragraph (b)(2)(i) of this section is translated into the functional currency of the tested income CFC using the average exchange rate for the CFC inclusion year of the tested income CFC.

(c) *Treatment as an amount includible in the gross income of a United States person.*—(1) *In general.*— For purposes of sections 163(e)(3)(B)(i) and 267(a)(3)(B), an item (including original issue discount) is treated as includible in the gross income of a United States person to the extent that such item increases a United States shareholder's pro rata share of tested income of a controlled foreign corporation for a U.S. shareholder inclusion year, reduces the shareholder's pro rata share of tested loss of a controlled foreign corporation for the U.S. shareholder inclusion year, or both.

(2) *Special rule for a United States shareholder that is a domestic partnership.*—In the case of a United States shareholder that is a domestic partnership (within the meaning of section 7701(a)(4)), an item is described in paragraph (c)(1) of this section only to the extent one or more United States persons (other than domestic partnerships) that are direct or indirect partners of the domestic partnership include in gross income their distributive share of the GILTI inclusion amount (if any) of the domestic partnership for the U.S. shareholder inclusion year of the domestic partnership in which such item accrues or such item is taken into account under paragraph (c)(1) of this section by a U.S. shareholder partner (within the meaning of §1.951A-5(e)(3)) of the domestic partnership by reason of §1.951A-5(c).

(d) *Increase of earnings and profits of tested loss CFC for purposes of section 952(c)(1)(A).*—For purposes of section 952(c)(1)(A) with respect to a CFC inclusion year, the earnings and profits of a tested loss CFC are increased by an amount equal to the tested loss of the tested loss CFC for the CFC inclusion year.

(e) *Adjustments to basis related to net used tested loss.*—(1) *In general.*—(i) *Disposition of stock of a controlled foreign corporation.*—In the case of a disposition of section 958(a) stock of a controlled foreign corporation owned (directly or indirectly) by a domestic corporation (*specified stock*), the adjusted basis of the specified stock is reduced immediately before the disposition by the domestic corporation's net used tested loss amount with respect to the controlled foreign corporation (if any) attributable to the specified stock. If the reduction described in the preceding sentence exceeds the adjusted basis in the specified stock immediately before the disposition, such excess is treated as gain from the sale or exchange of the stock for the taxable year in which the disposition occurs.

(ii) *Disposition of stock of an upper-tier controlled foreign corporation.*—In the case of a disposition of specified stock of a controlled foreign corporation (*upper-tier CFC*) by reason of which a domestic corporation owns, or has owned, section 958(a) stock of any other controlled foreign corporation (*lower-tier CFC*), for purposes of determining the reduction under paragraph (e)(1)(i) of this section, the domestic corpora-

tion's net used tested loss amount (if any) with respect to the upper-tier CFC attributable to the specified stock is—

(A) Increased by the sum of the domestic corporation's net used tested loss amounts with respect to each lower-tier CFC attributable to the specified stock; and

(B) Reduced (but not below zero) by the sum of the domestic corporation's net offset tested income amounts with respect to the upper-tier CFC and each lower-tier CFC attributable to the specified stock.

(iii) *Disposition of an interest in a foreign entity other than a controlled foreign corporation.*— In the case of a disposition of an interest in a foreign entity other than a controlled foreign corporation through which entity a domestic corporation owns section 958(a) stock of a controlled foreign corporation, for purposes of paragraph (e)(1)(i) and (ii) of this section, the controlled foreign corporation is treated as a lower-tier CFC, the interest in the entity is treated as specified stock of a controlled foreign corporation, and the entity is treated as an upper-tier CFC with respect to which the domestic corporation has neither a net used tested loss amount nor a net offset tested income amount.

(iv) *Order of application of basis reductions.*—In the event of an indirect disposition described in paragraph (e)(6)(ii)(B) of this section, the basis reduction described in paragraph (e)(1)(i) of this section is deemed to occur at the lowest-tier CFC first and, thereafter, up the chain of ownership until adjustments are made to the specified stock directly owned by the person making the disposition described in paragraph (e)(6)(ii)(A) of this section.

(v) *No duplicative adjustments.*—No item is taken into account under this paragraph (e)(1) to adjust the basis of specified stock of a controlled foreign corporation to the extent that such amount has previously been taken into account with respect to a prior basis adjustment with respect to such stock under this paragraph (e)(1). Moreover, the basis of specified stock is not reduced to the extent a taxpayer can demonstrate to the satisfaction of the Secretary that such adjustments would duplicate prior reductions to the basis of such stock under section 362(e)(2).

(2) *Net used tested loss amount.*—(i) *In general.*—The term *net used tested loss amount* means, with respect to a domestic corporation and a controlled foreign corporation, the excess (if any) of—

(A) The aggregate of the domestic corporation's used tested loss amount with respect to the controlled foreign corporation for each U.S. shareholder inclusion year, over

(B) The aggregate of the domestic corporation's offset tested income amount with respect to the controlled foreign corporation for each U.S. shareholder inclusion year.

**Prop. Reg. §1.951A-6(e)(2)(i)(B)**

(ii) *Used tested loss amount.*—The term *used tested loss amount* means, with respect to a domestic corporation and a tested loss CFC for a U.S. shareholder inclusion year—

(A) In the case of a domestic corporation that has net CFC tested income for the U.S. shareholder inclusion year, the domestic corporation's pro rata share of the tested loss of the tested loss CFC for the U.S. shareholder inclusion year, or

(B) In the case of a domestic corporation without net CFC tested income for the U.S. shareholder inclusion year, the amount that bears the same ratio to the domestic corporation's pro rata share of the tested loss of the tested loss CFC for the U.S. shareholder inclusion year as the aggregate of the domestic corporation's pro rata share of the tested income of each tested income CFC for the U.S. shareholder inclusion year bears to the aggregate of the domestic corporation's pro rata share of the tested loss of each tested loss CFC for the U.S. shareholder inclusion year.

(3) *Net offset tested income amount.*—(i) *In general.*—The term *net offset tested income amount* means, with respect to a domestic corporation and a controlled foreign corporation, the excess (if any) of the amount described in paragraph (e)(2)(i)(B) of this section over the amount described in paragraph (e)(2)(i)(A) of this section.

(ii) *Offset tested income amount.*—The term *offset tested income amount* means, with respect to a domestic corporation and a tested income CFC for a U.S. shareholder inclusion year—

(A) In the case of a domestic corporation that has net CFC tested income for the U.S. shareholder inclusion year, the amount that bears the same ratio to the domestic corporation's pro rata share of the tested income of the tested income CFC for the U.S. shareholder inclusion year as the aggregate of the domestic corporation's pro rata share of the tested loss of each tested loss CFC for the U.S. shareholder inclusion year bears to the aggregate of the domestic corporation's pro rata share of the tested income of each tested income CFC for the U.S. shareholder inclusion year, or

(B) In the case of a domestic corporation without net CFC tested income for the U.S. shareholder inclusion year, the domestic corporation's pro rata share of the tested income of the tested income CFC for the U.S. shareholder inclusion year.

(4) *Attribution to stock.*—(i) *In general.*—The portion of a domestic corporation's net used tested loss amount or net offset tested income amount with respect to a controlled foreign corporation (including a lower-tier CFC) attributable to specified stock for purposes of paragraph (e)(1) of this section is determined based on the domestic corporation's pro rata share of the tested loss and tested income, as applicable, of the controlled foreign corporation for each U.S. shareholder inclusion year with respect to such

specified stock. See §1.951A-1(d)(1), (2), and (4) for rules regarding the determination of pro rata share amounts of tested income and tested loss.

(ii) *Nonrecognition transactions.*—In the case of specified stock acquired by a domestic corporation in a nonrecognition transaction (as defined in section 7701(a)(45)), the principles of §1.1248-8 apply to determine the domestic corporation's net used tested loss amount or net offset tested income amount with respect to a controlled foreign corporation attributable to specified stock. For purposes of applying the principles of §1.1248-8, tested income is treated as earnings and profits and tested loss is treated as a deficit in earnings and profits.

(5) *Section 381 transactions.*—If a controlled foreign corporation with respect to which a United States shareholder has a net used tested loss amount or net offset tested income amount is a distributor or transferor corporation in a transaction described in section 381(a) (*acquired CFC*) in which a controlled foreign corporation is the acquiring corporation (*acquiring CFC*), the domestic corporation's net used tested loss amount or net offset tested income amount with respect to the acquiring CFC is increased by the amount of the net used tested loss amount or net offset tested income amount of the acquired CFC. This paragraph (e)(5) does not apply to the extent that the acquiring CFC is an upper-tier CFC and such amounts would be taken into account under paragraph (e)(1)(ii) of this paragraph if the stock of the acquiring CFC were disposed of.

(6) *Other definitions.*—The following additional definitions apply for purposes of this paragraph (e):

(i) *Domestic corporation.*—The term *domestic corporation* means a domestic corporation other than a real estate investment trust (as defined in section 856) or a regulated investment company (as defined in section 851).

(ii) *Disposition.*—The term *disposition* means—

(A) Any transfer of specified stock that is taxable, in whole or in part, including a sale or exchange, contribution, or distribution of the stock, including a deemed sale or exchange by reason of the specified stock becoming worthless within the meaning of section 165(g), or

(B) Any indirect disposition of specified stock of a lower-tier CFC as a result of a disposition described in paragraph (e)(6)(ii)(A) of this section of specified stock of an upper-tier CFC.

(7) *Special rule for disposition by controlled foreign corporation less than 100 percent owned by a single domestic corporation.*—In the case of a disposition by a controlled foreign corporation that is not 100 percent owned, within the meaning of section 958(a), by a single domestic corporation, if a reduction to basis described in paragraph

(e)(1) of this section by reason of a domestic corporation's net used tested loss amount results in an increase to the controlled foreign corporation's foreign personal holding company income (as defined in section 954(c)(1)), the domestic corporation's pro rata share of the subpart F income of the controlled foreign corporation, as otherwise determined under section 951(a)(2) and § 1.951-1(b) and (e), is increased by the amount of such increase, and no other shareholder takes such subpart F income into account under section 951(a)(1)(A).

(8) *Special rules for members of a consolidated group.*—For purposes of the section 951A regulations, a member determines its net used tested loss amount and the adjustments made as a result of the amount under the rules provided in § 1.1502-51(c).

(9) *Examples.*—The following examples illustrate the application of the rules in this paragraph (e).

(i) *Example 1*—(A) *Facts.* USP, a domestic corporation, owns 100% of the single class of stock of CFC1 and CFC2. USP1, CFC1, and CFC2 all use the calendar year as their taxable year. In Year 1, CFC2 has $90x of tested loss and CFC1 has $100x of tested income. At the beginning of Year 2, USP sells all of the stock of CFC2 to an unrelated buyer for cash. USP has no used tested loss amount or offset tested income amount with respect to CFC2 in any year prior to Year 1. USP has not owned stock in any other CFC by reason of owning stock of CFC1 and CFC2.

(B) *Analysis.* At the time of the disposition, USP has a net used tested loss amount of $90x with respect to CFC2 attributable to the CFC2 stock, which is the specified stock. Because USP does not own (and has not owned), within the meaning of section 958(a)(2), stock in any lower-tier CFCs by reason of the CFC2 stock, there is no adjustment to the net used tested loss amount of $90x pursuant to paragraph (e)(1)(ii) of this section. Accordingly, immediately before the disposition of the CFC2 stock, the basis of the CFC2 stock is reduced by $90x under paragraph (e)(1)(i) of this section.

(ii) *Example 2*—(A) *Facts.* The facts are the same as in paragraph (A) of *Example 1*, except that USP sells only 90% of the shares of CFC2.

(B) *Analysis.* The analysis is the same as in paragraph (B) of *Example 1*, except that USP's net used tested loss amount attributable to the CFC2 stock that was disposed of is only $81x (90% x $90x) under paragraph (e)(4)(i) of this section. Accordingly, immediately before the disposition of such stock, the basis in the CFC2 stock disposed of is reduced by $81x under paragraph (e)(1)(i) of this section.

(iii) *Example 3*—(A) *Facts.* The facts are the same as in paragraph (A) of *Example 1*, except that USP sells the CFC2 stock at the beginning of Year 3 and during Year 2 CFC1 has $10x of tested loss that offsets Year 2 tested income of CFC2.

(B) *Analysis.* USP has a net used tested loss amount of $80x with respect to CFC2 attributable to the CFC2 stock, the amount of USP's used tested loss amount with respect to the CFC2 attributable to the CFC2 stock in Year 1 of $90x reduced by USP's offset tested income amount with respect to CFC2 attributable to the CFC2 stock in Year 2 of $10x. Accordingly, immediately before the disposition of the CFC2 stock, the basis of the CFC2 stock is reduced by $80x under paragraph (e)(1)(i) of this section.

(iv) *Example 4*—(A) *Facts.* USP, a domestic corporation, owns 100% of the single class of stock of CFC1, and CFC1 owns 100% of the single class of stock of CFC2. USP1, CFC1, and CFC2 all use the calendar year as their taxable year. In Year 1, CFC1 has $100x of tested loss that offsets CFC2's $100x of tested income. USP sells the stock of CFC1 at the beginning of Year 2. USP has no used tested loss amount or offset tested income amount with respect to CFC1 of CFC2 in any year prior to Year 1. USP has not owned stock in any other CFC by reason of owning stock of CFC1 and CFC2.

(B) *Analysis.* (1) *Direct disposition.* At the time of the disposition, USP has a net used tested loss amount of $100x with respect to CFC1 attributable to the CFC1 stock. However, because USP owns, within the meaning of section 958(a)(2), CFC2 stock by reason of the CFC1 stock, USP's $100x net used tested loss amount with respect to CFC1 attributable to the CFC1 stock is reduced by USP's $100x net offset tested income amount with respect to CFC2 attributable to the CFC1 stock. Accordingly, there is no adjustment to the basis of the CFC1 stock under paragraph (e)(1)(i) of this section.

(2) *Indirect disposition.* Under paragraph (e)(6)(ii)(B) of this section, USP's disposition of the CFC1 stock also constitutes an indirect disposition of the CFC2 stock because CFC1 is an upper-tier CFC and CFC2 is a lower-tier CFC within the meaning of paragraph (e)(1)(ii) of this section. However, USP has no net used tested loss amount with respect to CFC2 attributable to the CFC2 stock. Accordingly, there is no adjustment to the basis of the CFC2 stock under paragraph (e)(1) of this section.

(v) *Example 5*—(A) *Facts.* The facts are the same as in paragraph (A) of *Example 4*, except that in Year 1 CFC2 has $100x of tested loss that offsets CFC1's $100x of tested income. CFC1 sells the stock of CFC2 at the beginning of Year 2.

(B) *Analysis.* USP, a domestic corporation, owns within the meaning of section 958(a) stock of CFC2. Accordingly, immediately before the disposition, CFC1's basis in the CFC2 stock is reduced by USP's net used tested loss amount with respect to CFC2 attributable to the CFC2 stock of $100x under paragraph (e)(1)(i) of this section.

(vi) *Example 6*—(A) *Facts.* The facts are the same as in paragraph (A) of *Example 5*, except that instead of CFC1 selling the stock of CFC2, USP sells the stock of CFC1.

(B) *Analysis*—(1) *Direct disposition*. USP has no net used tested loss amount with respect to CFC1 attributable to the stock of CFC1. However, because USP owns, within the meaning of section 958(a)(2), stock of CFC2 by reason of owning stock of CFC1, under paragraph (e)(1)(ii) of this section, USP's net used tested loss amount attributable to the stock of CFC1 ($0) is increased by USP's net used tested loss amount with respect to CFC2 attributable to the CFC1 stock ($100x), and reduced by USP's net offset tested income amount with respect to CFC1 attributable to the CFC1 stock ($100x). Accordingly, there is no adjustment to the basis of the CFC1 stock under paragraph (e)(1) of this section.

(2) *Indirect disposition*. Under paragraph (e)(6)(ii)(B) of this section, USP's disposition of CFC1 stock also constitutes an indirect disposition of the CFC2 stock because CFC1 is an upper-tier CFC and CFC2 is a lower-tier CFC within the meaning of paragraph (e)(1)(ii) of this section. Accordingly, immediately before the disposition, CFC1's basis in the CFC2 stock is reduced by USP's net used tested loss amount with respect to CFC2 attributable to the CFC2 stock of $100x under paragraph (e)(1)(i) of this section. Under paragraph (e)(1)(iv) of this section, the basis reduction to CFC2's shares is deemed to occur immediately before any reductions occur with respect to the stock of CFC1, of which there are none.

(vii) *Example 7*—(A) *Facts*. USP1, a domestic corporation, owns 90% of the single class of stock of CFC1, and CFC1 owns 100% of the single class of stock of CFC2. USP1 also owns 100% of the single class of stock of CFC3. The remaining 10% of the stock of CFC1 is owned by USP2, a person unrelated to USP1. USP2 owns no other CFCs. USP1, USP2, CFC1, CFC2, and CFC3 all use the calendar year as their taxable year. In Year 1, CFC1 has no tested income or tested loss, CFC2 has tested loss of $100x, and CFC3 has tested income of $100x. CFC1 has no other earnings or income in Year 1. At the beginning of Year 2, CFC1 sells CFC2. Without regard to this paragraph (e), CFC1 would recognize no gain or loss with respect to the CFC2 stock. USP1 has not owned stock in any other controlled foreign corporation by reason of owning stock of CFC1, CFC2, and CFC3.

(B) *Analysis*. At the time of the disposition, USP2 has no net used tested loss amount with respect to CFC2. At the time of the disposition, USP1 has a net used tested loss amount of $90x with respect to CFC2 attributable to the CFC2 stock, which is the specified stock. Because USP1 does not own (and has not owned), within the meaning of section 958(a)(2), stock in any lower-tier CFCs by reason of the CFC2 stock, there is no adjustment to the net used tested loss amount of $90x pursuant to paragraph (e)(1)(ii) of this section. Accordingly, immediately before the disposition of the CFC2 stock, the basis of the CFC2 stock is reduced by $90x under paragraph

(e)(1)(i) of this section. As a result, CFC1 recognizes gain of $90x on the disposition of the CFC2 stock, which results in $90x of foreign personal holding company income and $90x of earnings and profits. Under paragraph (e)(7) of this section, USP1's pro rata share of the subpart F income of CFC1 is increased by $90x, and USP2 does not take such subpart F income into account under section 951(a)(1)(A).

(viii) *Example 8*—(A) *Facts*. USP, a domestic corporation, owns 100% of the single class of stock of CFC1 and CFC2, and CFC1 owns 100% of the single class of stock of CFC3 and CFC4. USP, CFC1, CFC2, CFC3, and CFC4 all use the calendar year as their taxable year. In Year 1, CFC1 has no tested income or tested loss, CFC2 has $200x of tested income, and CFC3 and CFC4 each have tested loss of $100x. During Year 2, CFC3 liquidates into CFC1 in a nontaxable transaction described under section 332, and CFC1 sells the stock of CFC4 to an unrelated third party for cash. During Year 2, none of CFC1, CFC2, CFC3, or CFC4 earn tested income or tested loss. At the beginning of Year 3, USP sells the stock of CFC1 to an unrelated third party for cash. USP has not owned stock in any other CFC by reason of owning stock in CFC1, CFC2, CFC3, or CFC4.

(B) *Analysis*. (1) CFC3's liquidation into CFC1 is not a disposition within the meaning of paragraph (e)(6)(ii)(A) of this section because CFC1 does not recognize gain or loss in whole or in part with respect to the stock of CFC3 under section 332. Furthermore, CFC1 does not inherit CFC3's net used tested loss amount under paragraph (e)(5) of this section because CFC1 is an upper-tier CFC with respect to CFC3 and would take such amounts into account under paragraph (e)(1)(ii) of this section at the time of a future disposition. That is, the CFC3 stock is section 958(a) stock that USP has owned by reason of its ownership of CFC1 within the meaning of paragraph (e)(1)(ii) of this section.

(2) At the time of CFC1's sale of the stock of CFC4, USP has a $100x net used tested loss amount with respect to CFC4 attributable to the CFC4 stock, which is the specified stock. Because USP has not owned, within the meaning of section 958(a)(2), stock in any lower-tier CFCs by reason of the CFC4 stock, there is no adjustment to the net used tested loss amount of $100x pursuant to paragraph (e)(1)(ii) of this section. Accordingly, immediately before the disposition of the CFC4 stock, the basis of the CFC4 stock is reduced by $100x under paragraph (e)(1)(i) of this section.

(3) At the time of USP's sale of CFC1, USP has no net used tested loss amount with respect to CFC1 attributable to the CFC1 stock. However, USP has owned, within the meaning of section 958(a)(2), stock of lower-tier CFCs (CFC3 and CFC4) by reason of its ownership of CFC1. Thus, USP's net used tested loss amount attributable to the stock of CFC1 ($0) is increased by USP's net used tested loss amounts with respect to CFC3 and CFC4 attributable to the CFC1 stock

($200x). Accordingly, immediately before the disposition of the CFC1 stock, the basis of the CFC1 stock is reduced by $200x under paragraph (e)(1)(i) of this section. The rule prohibiting duplicative adjustments under paragraph (e)(1)(v) of this section does not prevent this basis reduction because the net used tested loss amounts with respect to the CFC3 and CFC4 stock were not previously taken into account to reduce the basis of CFC1 stock. [Reg. § 1.951A-6.]

[Proposed 10-10-2018.]

### [Prop. Reg. §1.951A-7]

**§1.951A-7. Applicability dates.**—Sections 1.951A-1 through 1.951A-6 apply to taxable years of foreign corporations beginning after December 31, 2017, and to taxable years of United States shareholders in which or with which such taxable years of foreign corporations end. [Reg. § 1.951A-7.]

[Proposed 10-10-2018.]

### [Prop. Reg. §1.954-1]

**§1.954-1. Foreign base company income.**

\* \* \*

(d) \* \* \*

(3) \* \* \*

(i) \* \* \* Except as provided in the next sentence, the amount of foreign income taxes paid or accrued with respect to a net item of income, determined in the manner provided in this paragraph (d), is not affected by a subsequent reduction in foreign income taxes attributable to a distribution to shareholders of all or part of such income. To the extent the foreign income taxes paid or accrued by the controlled foreign corporation are reasonably certain to be returned by the foreign jurisdiction imposing such taxes to a shareholder, directly or indirectly, through any means (including, but not limited to, a refund, credit, payment, discharge of an obligation, or any other method) on a subsequent distribution to such shareholder, the foreign income taxes are not treated as paid or accrued for purposes of this paragraph (d)(3)(i).

(ii) \* \* \* However, notwithstanding the rules in § 1.904-4(c)(7), to the extent the foreign income taxes paid or accrued by the controlled foreign corporation are reasonably certain to be returned by the foreign jurisdiction imposing such taxes to a shareholder, directly or indirectly, through any means (including, but not limited to, a refund, credit, payment, discharge of an obligation, or any other method) on a subsequent distribution to such shareholder, the foreign income taxes are not treated as paid or accrued for purposes of this paragraph (d)(3)(ii).

\* \* \*

(h) *Applicability dates.*—(1) *Paragraphs (d)(3)(i) and (ii).*—Paragraphs (d)(3)(i) and (ii) of this section apply to taxable years of a controlled foreign corporation ending on or after December 4, 2018.

(2) *Paragraph (g).*—Paragraph (g) of this section applies to taxable years of a controlled foreign corporation beginning on or after July 23, 2002.

[Proposed 12-7-2018.]

### [Prop. Reg. §1.960-1]

**§1.960-1. Overview, definitions, and computational rules for determining foreign income taxes deemed paid under section 960(a), (b), and (d).**—(a) *Overview.*—(1) *Scope of §§1.960-1 through 1.960-3.*—This section and §§1.960-2 and 1.960-3 provide rules to associate foreign income taxes of a controlled foreign corporation with the income that a domestic corporation that is a United States shareholder of the controlled foreign corporation takes into account in determining a subpart F inclusion or GILTI inclusion amount of the domestic corporation, as well as to associate foreign income taxes of a controlled foreign corporation with distributions of previously taxed earnings and profits. These regulations provide the exclusive rules for determining the foreign income taxes deemed paid by a domestic corporation. Therefore, only foreign income taxes of a controlled foreign corporation that are associated under these rules with a subpart F inclusion or GILTI inclusion amount of a domestic corporation that is a United States shareholder of the controlled foreign corporation, or with previously taxed earnings and profits, are eligible to be deemed paid. This section provides definitions and computational rules for determining foreign income taxes deemed paid under section 960(a), (b), and (d). Section 1.960-2 provides rules for computing the amount of foreign income taxes deemed paid by a domestic corporation that is a United States shareholder of a controlled foreign corporation under section 960(a) and (d). Section 1.960-3 provides rules for computing the amount of foreign income taxes deemed paid by a domestic corporation that is a United States shareholder of a controlled foreign corporation, or by a controlled foreign corporation, under section 960(b).

(2) *Scope of this section.*—Paragraph (b) of this section provides definitions for purposes of this section and §§1.960-2 and 1.960-3. Paragraph (c) of this section provides computational rules to coordinate the various calculations under this section and §§1.960-2 and 1.960-3. Paragraph (d) of this section provides rules for computing the income in an income group within a section 904 category, and for associating foreign income taxes with an income group. Paragraph (e) of this section provides a rule for the creditability of taxes associated with the residual income group. Paragraph (f) of this section provides an example illustrating the application of this section.

**(b)** *Definitions.*—The following definitions apply for purposes of this section and §§ 1.960-2 and 1.960-3.

**(1)** *Annual PTEP account.*—The term *annual PTEP account* has the meaning set forth in § 1.960-3(c)(1).

**(2)** *Controlled foreign corporation.*—The term *controlled foreign corporation* means a foreign corporation described in section 957(a).

**(3)** *Current taxable year.*—The term *current taxable year* means the U.S. taxable year of a controlled foreign corporation that is an inclusion year, or during which the controlled foreign corporation receives a section 959(b) distribution or makes a section 959(a) distribution or a section 959(b) distribution.

**(4)** *Current year taxes.*—The term *current year taxes* means foreign income taxes paid or accrued by a controlled foreign corporation in a current taxable year. Foreign income taxes accrue when all the events have occurred that establish the fact of the liability and the amount of the liability can be determined with reasonable accuracy. *See* §§ 1.446-1(c)(1)(ii)(A) and 1.461-4(g)(6)(iii)(B) (economic performance exception for certain foreign taxes). Withholding taxes described in section 901(k)(1)(B) that are withheld from a payment accrue when the payment is made. Foreign income taxes calculated on the basis of net income recognized in a foreign taxable year accrue on the last day of the foreign taxable year. Accordingly, current year taxes include foreign withholding taxes that are withheld from payments made to the controlled foreign corporation during the current taxable year, and foreign income taxes that accrue in the controlled foreign corporation's current taxable year in which or with which its foreign taxable year ends. Additional payments of foreign income taxes resulting from a redetermination of foreign tax liability, including contested taxes that accrue when the contest is resolved, "relate back" and are considered to accrue as of the end of the foreign taxable year to which the taxes relate.

**(5)** *Foreign income taxes.*—The term *foreign income taxes* means income, war profits, and excess profits taxes as defined in § 1.901-2(a), and taxes included in the term income, war profits, and excess profits taxes by reason of section 903 and § 1.903-1(a), that are imposed by a foreign country or a possession of the United States, including any such taxes that are deemed paid by a controlled foreign corporation under section 960(b). Income, war profits, and excess profits taxes do not include amounts excluded from the definition of those taxes pursuant to section 901 and the regulations under that section. See, for example, section 901(f), (g), and (i). Foreign income taxes also do not include taxes paid by a controlled foreign corporation for which a credit is disallowed at the level of the controlled foreign corporation. See, for example, sections

245A(e)(3), 901(k)(1), (l), and (m), 909, and 6038(c)(1)(B). Foreign income taxes, however, include taxes that may be deemed paid but for which a credit is reduced or disallowed at the level of the United States shareholder. See, for example, sections 901(e), 901(j), 901(k)(2), 908, 965(g) and 6038(c)(1)(A).

**(6)** *Foreign taxable year.*—The term *foreign taxable year* has the meaning set forth in section 7701(a)(23), applied by substituting "under foreign law" for the phrase "under subtitle A."

**(7)** *GILTI inclusion amount.*—The term *GILTI inclusion amount* has the meaning set forth in § 1.951A-1(c)(1) (or, in the case of a member of a consolidated group, § 1.1502-51(b)).

**(8)** *Gross tested income.*—The term *gross tested income* has the meaning set forth in § 1.951A-2(c)(1).

**(9)** *Inclusion percentage.*—The term *inclusion percentage* has the meaning set forth in § 1.960-2(c)(2).

**(10)** *Inclusion year.*—The term *inclusion year* means the U.S. taxable year of a controlled foreign corporation which ends during or with the taxable year of a United States shareholder of the controlled foreign corporation in which the United States shareholder includes an amount in income under section 951(a)(1) or 951A(a) with respect to the controlled foreign corporation.

**(11)** *Income group.*—The term *income group* means a group of income described in paragraph (d)(2)(ii) of this section.

**(12)** *Partnership CFC.*—The term *partnership CFC* has the meaning set forth in § 1.951A-5(e)(2).

**(13)** *Passive category.*—The term *passive category* means the separate category of income described in section 904(d)(1)(C) and § 1.904-4(b).

**(14)** *Previously taxed earnings and profits.*—The term *previously taxed earnings and profits* means earnings and profits described in section 959(c)(1) or (2), including earnings and profits described in section 959(c)(2) by reason of section 951A(f)(1) and § 1.951A-6(b)(1).

**(15)** *PTEP group.*—The term *PTEP group* has the meaning set forth in § 1.960-3(c)(2).

**(16)** *PTEP group taxes.*—The term *PTEP group taxes* has the meaning set forth in § 1.960-3(d)(1).

**(17)** *Recipient controlled foreign corporation.*—The term *recipient controlled foreign corporation* has the meaning set forth in § 1.960-3(b)(2).

**(18)** *Reclassified previously taxed earnings and profits.*—The term *reclassified previously taxed earnings and profits* has the meaning set forth in § 1.960-3(c)(4).

(19) *Reclassified PTEP group.*—The term *reclassified PTEP group* has the meaning set forth in §1.960-3(c)(4).

(20) *Residual income group.*—The term *residual income group* has the meaning set forth in paragraph (d)(2)(ii)(D) of this section.

(21) *Section 904 category.*—The term *section 904 category* means a separate category of income described in §1.904-5(a)(4)(v).

(22) *Section 951A category.*—The term *section 951A category* means the separate category of income described in section 904(d)(1)(A) and §1.904-4(g).

(23) *Section 959 distribution.*—The term *section 959 distribution* means a section 959(a) distribution or a section 959(b) distribution.

(24) *Section 959(a) distribution.*—The term *section 959(a) distribution* means a distribution excluded from the gross income of a United States shareholder under section 959(a).

(25) *Section 959(b) distribution.*—The term *section 959(b) distribution* means a distribution excluded from the gross income of a controlled foreign corporation for purposes of section 951(a) under section 959(b).

(26) *Section 959(c)(2) PTEP group.*—The term *section 959(c)(2) PTEP group* has the meaning set forth in §1.960-3(c)(4).

(27) *Subpart F inclusion.*—The term *subpart F inclusion* has the meaning set forth in §1.960-2(b)(1).

(28) *Subpart F income.*—The term *subpart F income* has the meaning set forth in section 952 and §1.952-1(a).

(29) *Subpart F income group.*—The term *subpart F income group* has the meaning set forth in paragraph (d)(2)(ii)(B)(*1*) of this section.

(30) *Tested foreign income taxes.*—The term *tested foreign income taxes* has the meaning set forth in §1.960-2(c)(3).

(31) *Tested income.*—The term *tested income* means the amount with respect to a controlled foreign corporation that is described in section 951A(c)(2)(A) and §1.951A-2(b)(1).

(32) *Tested income group.*—The term *tested income group* has the meaning set forth in paragraph (d)(2)(ii)(C) of this section.

(33) *United States shareholder.*—The term *United States shareholder* has the meaning set forth in section 951(b).

(34) *U.S. shareholder partner.*—The term *U.S. shareholder partner* has the meaning set forth in §1.951A-5(e)(3).

(35) *U.S. shareholder partnership.*—The term *U.S. shareholder partnership* has the meaning set forth in §1.951A-5(e)(4).

(36) *U.S. taxable year.*—The term *U.S. taxable year* has the same meaning as that of the term *taxable year* set forth in section 7701(a)(23).

(c) *Computational rules.*—(1) *In general.*—For purposes of computing foreign income taxes deemed paid by either a domestic corporation that is a United States shareholder with respect to a controlled foreign corporation under §1.960-2 or 1.960-3 or by a controlled foreign corporation under §1.960-3 for the current taxable year, the following rules apply in the following order, beginning with the lowest-tier controlled foreign corporation in a chain with respect to which the domestic corporation is a United States shareholder:

(i) First, items of gross income of the controlled foreign corporation for the current taxable year other than a section 959(b) distribution are assigned to section 904 categories and included in income groups within those section 904 categories under the rules in paragraph (d)(2) of this section. The receipt of a section 959(b) distribution by the controlled foreign corporation is accounted for under §1.960-3(c)(3).

(ii) Second, deductions (other than for current year taxes) of the controlled foreign corporation for the current taxable year are allocated and apportioned to reduce gross income in the section 904 categories and the income groups within a section 904 category. See paragraph (d)(3)(i) of this section. Additionally, the functional currency amounts of current year taxes of the controlled foreign corporation for the current taxable year are allocated and apportioned to reduce gross income in the section 904 categories and the income groups within a section 904 category, and to reduce earnings and profits in any PTEP groups that were increased as provided in paragraph (c)(1)(i) of this section. See paragraph (d)(3)(ii) of this section. For purposes of computing foreign taxes deemed paid, current year taxes allocated and apportioned to income groups and PTEP groups in the section 904 categories are translated into U.S. dollars in accordance with section 986(a). See paragraph (c)(3) of this section.

(iii) Third, current year taxes deemed paid under section 960(a) and (d) by the domestic corporation with respect to income of the controlled foreign corporation are computed under the rules of §1.960-2. In addition, foreign income taxes deemed paid under section 960(b)(2) with respect to the receipt of a section 959(b) distribution by the controlled foreign corporation are computed under the rules of §1.960-3(b).

(iv) Fourth, any previously taxed earnings and profits of the controlled foreign corporation resulting from subpart F inclusions and GILTI inclusion amounts with respect to the controlled foreign corporation's current taxable year are separated from other earnings and profits of the controlled foreign corporation and added to an annual PTEP account, and a PTEP group within the PTEP account, under the rules of §1.960-3(c).

(v) Fifth, paragraphs (c)(1)(i) through (iv) of this section are repeated for each next higher-tier controlled foreign corporation in the chain.

(vi) Sixth, with respect to the highest-tier controlled foreign corporation in a chain that is owned directly (or indirectly through a partnership) by the domestic corporation, foreign income taxes that are deemed paid under section 960(b)(1) in connection with the receipt of a section 959(a) distribution by the domestic corporation are computed under the rules of §1.960-3(b).

(2) *Inclusion of current year items.*—For a current taxable year, the items of income and deductions (including for taxes), and the U.S. dollar amounts of current year taxes, that are included in the computations described in this section and assigned to income groups and PTEP groups for the taxable year are the items that the controlled foreign corporation accrues and takes into account during the current taxable year.

(3) *Functional currency and translation.*—The computations described in this paragraph (c) that relate to income and earnings and profits are made in the functional currency of the controlled foreign corporation (as determined under section 985), and references to taxes deemed paid are to U.S. dollar amounts (translated in accordance with section 986(a)).

(d) *Computing income in a section 904 category and an income group within a section 904 category.*—(1) *Scope.*—This paragraph (d) provides rules for assigning gross income (including gains) of a controlled foreign corporation for the current taxable year to a section 904 category and income group within a section 904 category, and for allocating and apportioning deductions (including losses and current year taxes) and the U.S. dollar amount of current year taxes of the controlled foreign corporation for the current taxable year among the section 904 categories, income groups within a section 904 category, and PTEP groups. For rules regarding maintenance of previously taxed earnings and profits in an annual PTEP account, and assignment of those previously taxed earnings and profits to PTEP groups, see §1.960-3.

(2) *Assignment of gross income to section 904 categories and income groups within a category.*—(i) *Assigning items of gross income to section 904 categories.*—Items of gross income of the controlled foreign corporation for the current taxable year are first assigned to a section 904 category of the controlled foreign corporation under §§1.904-4 and 1.904-5, and under §1.960-3(c)(1) in the case of gross income relating to a section 959(b) distribution received by the controlled foreign corporation. Income of a controlled foreign corporation, other than gross income relating to a section 959(b) distribution, cannot be assigned to the section 951A category or the foreign branch category. See §1.904-4(f) and (g).

(ii) *Grouping gross income within a section 904 category.*—(A) *In general.*—Gross income within a section 904 category is assigned to an income group under the rules of this paragraph (d)(2)(ii), or to a PTEP group under the rules of §1.960-3(c)(3). Gross income other than a section 959(b) distribution is assigned to a subpart F income group, tested income group, or residual income group.

(B) *Subpart F income groups.*—(1) *In general.*—The term *subpart F income group* means an income group within a section 904 category that consists of income that is described in paragraph (d)(2)(ii)(B)(2) of this section. Gross income that is treated as a single item of income under §1.954-1(c)(1)(iii) is in a separate subpart F income group under paragraph (d)(2)(ii)(B)(2)(*i*) of this section. Items of gross income that give rise to income described in paragraph (d)(2)(ii)(B)(2)(*ii*) of this section are aggregated and treated as gross income in a separate subpart F income group. Similarly, items of gross income that give rise to income described in each one of paragraphs (d)(2)(ii)(B)(2)(*iii*) through (*v*) of this section are aggregated and treated as gross income in a separate subpart F income group.

(2) *Income in subpart F income groups.*—The income included in subpart F income groups is:

(*i*) Items of foreign base company income treated as a single item of income under §1.954-1(c)(1)(iii);

(*ii*) Insurance income described in section 952(a)(1);

(*iii*) Income subject to the international boycott factor described in section 952(a)(3);

(*iv*) Income from certain bribes, kickbacks and other payments described in section 952(a)(4); and

(*v*) Income subject to section 901(j) described in section 952(a)(5).

(C) *Tested income groups.*—The term *tested income group* means an income group that consists of tested income within a section 904 category. Items of gross tested income in each section 904 category are aggregated and treated as gross income in a separate tested income group.

(D) *Residual income group.*—The term *residual income group* means the income group within a section 904 category that consists of income not described in paragraph (d)(2)(ii)(B) or (C) of this section.

(E) *Examples.*—The following examples illustrate the application of this paragraph (d)(2)(ii).

(1) *Example 1: Subpart F income groups*—(i) *Facts.* CFC, a controlled foreign corporation, is incorporated in Country X. CFC uses the "u" as its functional currency. At all relevant times, 1u=$1. CFC earns from sources outside of Coun-

try X portfolio dividend income of 100,000u, portfolio interest income of 1,500,000u, and 70,000u of royalty income that is not derived from the active conduct of a trade or business. CFC also earns 50,000u from the sale of personal property to a related person for use outside of Country X that gives rise to foreign base company sales income under section 954(d). Finally, CFC earns 45,000u for performing consulting services outside of Country X for related persons that gives rise to foreign base company services income under section 954(e). None of the income is taxed by Country X. The dividend income is subject to a 15 percent third-country withholding tax after application of the applicable income tax treaty. The interest income and the royalty income are subject to no third-country withholding tax. CFC incurs no expenses.

(ii) *Analysis.* Under paragraph (d)(2)(i) of this section and § 1.904-4, the interest income, dividend income, and royalty income are passive category income and the sales and consulting income are general category income. Under paragraph (d)(2)(ii)(B) of this section, CFC has a separate subpart F income group within the passive category with respect to the 100,000u of dividend income, which is foreign personal holding company income described in § 1.954-1(c)(1)(iii)(A)(*1*)(*i*) (dividends, interest, rents, royalties and annuities) that falls within a single group of income under § 1.904-4(c)(3)(i) for passive income that is subject to withholding tax of fifteen percent or greater. CFC also has a separate subpart F income group within the passive category with respect to the 1,500,000u of interest income and the 70,000u of royalty income (in total 1,570,000u) that together are foreign personal holding company income described in § 1.954-1(c)(1)(iii)(A)(*1*)(*i*) (dividends, interest, rents, royalties and annuities) that falls within a single group of income under § 1.904-4(c)(3)(iii) for passive income that is subject to no withholding tax or other foreign tax. With respect to its 50,000u of sales income, CFC has a separate subpart F income group with respect to foreign base company sales income described in § 1.954-1(c)(1)(iii)(A)(2)(*i*) within the general category. With respect to its 45,000u of services income, CFC has a separate subpart F income group with respect to foreign base company services income described in § 1.954-1(c)(1)(iii)(A)(2)(*ii*) within the general category.

(2) *Example 2: Tested income groups*—(i) *Facts.* CFC, a controlled foreign corporation, is incorporated in Country X. CFC uses the "u" as its functional currency. At all relevant times, 1u=$1. CFC earns 500u from the sale of goods to unrelated parties. CFC also earns 75u for performing consulting services for unrelated parties. All of its income is gross tested income. CFC incurs no deductions.

(ii) *Analysis.* Under paragraph (d)(2)(i) of this section and section 904 and § 1.904-4, the sales income and services income are both general category income. Under paragraph

(d)(2)(ii)(C) of this section, with respect to the 500u of sales income and 75u services income (in total 575u), CFC has one tested income group within the general category.

(3) *Allocation and apportionment of deductions among section 904 categories, income groups within a section 904 category, and certain PTEP groups.*— (i) *In general.*—Gross income of the controlled foreign corporation in each income group within each section 904 category is reduced by deductions (including losses) of the controlled foreign corporation for the current taxable year under the following rules.

(A) First, the rules of sections 861 through 865 and 904(d) and the regulations under those sections (taking into account the rules of section 954(b)(5) and § 1.954-1(c), and section 951A(c)(2)(A)(ii) and § 1.951A-2(c)(3), as appropriate) apply to allocate and apportion to reduce gross income (or create a loss) in each section 904 category and income group within a section 904 category any deductions of the controlled foreign corporation that are definitely related to less than all of the controlled foreign corporation's gross income as a class. See paragraph (d)(3)(ii) of this section for special rules for allocating and apportioning current year taxes to section 904 categories, income groups, and PTEP groups.

(B) Second, related person interest expense is allocated to and apportioned among the subpart F income groups within the passive category under the principles of § 1.904-5(c)(2) and § 1.954-1(c)(1)(i).

(C) Third, any remaining deductions are allocated and apportioned to reduce gross income (or create a loss) in the section 904 categories and income groups within each section 904 category under the rules referenced in paragraph (d)(3)(i)(A) of this section. No deductions of the controlled foreign corporation for the current taxable year other than a deduction for current year taxes imposed solely by reason of the receipt of a section 959(b) distribution are allocated or apportioned to reduce earnings and profits in a PTEP group.

(ii) *Allocation and apportionment of current year taxes.*—(A) *In general.*—Current year taxes are allocated and apportioned among the section 904 categories under the rules of § 1.904-6(a)(1)(i) and (ii) on the basis of the amount of taxable income computed under foreign law in each section 904 category that is included in the foreign tax base. Current year taxes in a section 904 category are then allocated and apportioned among the income groups within a section 904 category under the principles of § 1.904-6(a)(1)(i) and (ii). If the amount of previously taxed earnings and profits in a PTEP group is increased in the current taxable year of the controlled foreign corporation under § 1.960-3(c)(3) by reason of the receipt of a section 959(b) distribution, then for purposes of allocating and apportioning current year taxes that are imposed solely by reason of

**Prop. Reg. § 1.960-1(d)(3)(ii)(A)**

the receipt of the section 959(b) distribution under this paragraph (d)(3)(ii)(A), the PTEP group is treated as an income group within the section 904 category. In applying §1.904-6(a)(1)(i) and (ii) for purposes of this paragraph (d)(3)(ii)(A), the gross items of income and deduction calculated under foreign law that are included in a section 904 category, income group, or PTEP group that is treated as an income group are the items that are included in taxable income under foreign law for the foreign taxable year of the controlled foreign corporation that ends with or within the controlled foreign corporation's current taxable year. For purposes of determining foreign income taxes deemed paid under the rules in §§1.960-2 and 1.960-3, the U.S. dollar amounts of current year taxes are assigned to the section 904 categories, income groups, and PTEP groups, if any, to which the current year taxes are allocated and apportioned.

(B) *Base and timing differences.—(1) In general.*—Current year taxes that are attributable to a base difference described in §1.904-6(a)(1)(iv) are not allocated and apportioned to any subpart F income group, tested income group or PTEP group, but are treated as related to income in the residual income group. Except as provided in paragraph (d)(3)(ii)(B)(2) of this section, current year taxes that are attributable to a timing difference described in §1.904-6(a)(1)(iv) are treated as related to the appropriate section 904 category and income group within a section 904 category to which the particular tax would be assigned if the income on which the tax is imposed were recognized under Federal income tax principles in the year in which the tax was imposed.

(2) *Tax on previously taxed earnings and profits.*—Current year taxes imposed solely by reason of the controlled foreign corporation's receipt of a section 959(b) distribution are not allocated and apportioned under the general rule for timing differences but are allocated or apportioned to a PTEP group. Current year taxes imposed with respect to previously taxed earnings and profits by reason of any other timing difference are allocated or apportioned, under the general rule described in paragraph (d)(3)(ii)(B)(1) of this section, to the income group to which the income that gave rise to the previously taxed earnings and profits was assigned in the inclusion year. For example, a net basis tax imposed on a controlled foreign corporation's receipt of a section 959(b) distribution by the corporation's country of residence is allocated or apportioned to a PTEP group. Similarly, a withholding tax imposed with respect to a controlled foreign corporation's receipt of a section 959(b) distribution is allocated and apportioned to a PTEP group. In contrast, a withholding tax imposed on a disregarded payment from a disregarded entity to its controlled foreign corporation owner is treated as a timing difference and is never treated as related to a PTEP group, even if all of the controlled foreign corporation's earnings are previ-

ously taxed earnings and profits, because the tax is not imposed solely by reason of a section 959(b) distribution. Such a withholding tax, however, may be treated as related to a subpart F income group or tested income group under the general rule for timing differences.

(e) *No deemed paid credit for current year taxes related to residual income group.*—Current year taxes paid or accrued by a controlled foreign corporation that are allocated and apportioned under paragraph (d)(3)(ii) of this section to a residual income group cannot be deemed paid under section 960 for any taxable year.

(f) *Example.*—The following example illustrates the application of this section and §1.960-3.

(1) *Facts*—(i) *Income of CFC1 and CFC2.* CFC1, a controlled foreign corporation, conducts business in Country X. CFC1 uses the "u" as its functional currency. At all relevant times, 1u=$1. CFC1 owns all of the stock of CFC2, a controlled foreign corporation. CFC1 and CFC2 both use the calendar year as their U.S. and foreign taxable years. In 2019, CFC1 earns 2,000,000u of gross income that is foreign oil and gas extraction income, within the meaning of section 907(c)(1), and 2,000,000u of interest income from unrelated persons, for both U.S. and Country X tax law purposes. Country X exempts interest income from tax. In 2019, CFC1 also receives a section 959(b) distribution from CFC2 of 4,000,000u of previously taxed earnings and profits attributable to an inclusion under section 965(a) for CFC2's 2017 U.S. taxable year. The inclusion under section 965(a) was income in the general category. There are no PTEP group taxes associated with the previously taxed earnings and profits distributed by CFC2 at the level of CFC2. The section 959(b) distribution is treated as a dividend taxable to CFC1 under Country X law. In 2019, CFC2 earns no gross income and receives no distributions.

(ii) *Pre-tax deductions of CFC1 and CFC2.* For both U.S. and Country X tax purposes, in 2019, CFC1 incurs 1,500,000u of deductible expenses other than current year taxes that are allocable to all gross income. For U.S. tax purposes, under §§1.861-8 through 1.861-14T, 750,000u of such deductions are apportioned to each of CFC1's foreign oil and gas extraction income and interest income. Under Country X law, 1,000,000u of deductions are allocated and apportioned to the 4,000,000u treated as a dividend, and 500,000u of deductions are allocated and apportioned to the 2,000,000u of foreign oil and gas extraction income. Under Country X law, no deductions are allocable to the interest income. Country X imposes tax of 900,000u on a base of 4,500,000u (6,000,000u gross income – 1,500,000u deductions) consisting of 3,000,000u (4,000,000u – 1,000,000u) attributable to CFC1's section 959(b) distribution and 1,500,000u (2,000,000u – 500,000u) attributable to CFC1's foreign oil and gas extraction income. In 2019, CFC2 has no expenses (including current year taxes).

(iii) *United States shareholders of CFC1.* All of the stock of CFC1 is owned (within the meaning of section 958(a)) by corporate United States shareholders that use the calendar year as their U.S. taxable year. In 2019, the United States shareholders of CFC1 include in gross income subpart F inclusions in the passive category totaling $1,250,000 with respect to 1,250,000u of subpart F income of CFC1.

(2) *Analysis*—(i) *CFC2.* Under paragraph (c)(1) of this section, the computational rules of paragraph (c)(1) of this section are applied beginning with CFC2. However, CFC2 has no gross income or expenses in 2019 (the "current taxable year"). Accordingly, the computational rules described in paragraph (c)(1)(i) through (iv) of this section are not relevant with respect to CFC2. Under paragraph (c)(1)(v) of this section, the rules in paragraph (c)(1)(i) through (iv) of this section are then applied to CFC1.

(ii) *CFC1.* (A) *Step 1.* Under paragraph (c)(1)(i) of this section, CFC1's items of gross income for the current taxable year are assigned to section 904 categories and included in income groups within those section 904 categories. In addition, CFC1's receipt of a section 959(b) distribution is assigned to a PTEP group. Under paragraph (d)(2)(i) of this section and § 1.904-4, the interest income is passive category income and the foreign oil and gas extraction income is general category income. Under paragraph (d)(2)(ii) of this section, the 2,000,000u of interest income is assigned to a subpart F income group (the "subpart F income group") within the passive category because it is foreign personal holding company income described in § 1.954-1(c)(1)(iii)(A)(1)(i) that falls within a single group of income under § 1.904-4(c)(3)(iii) for passive income that is subject to no withholding tax or other foreign tax. The 2,000,000u of foreign oil and gas extraction income is assigned to the residual income group within the general category. Under § 1.960-3(c), the 4,000,000u section 959(b) distribution is assigned to the PTEP group described in § 1.960-3(c)(2)(vii) within the 2017 annual PTEP account (the "PTEP group") within the general category.

(B) *Step 2*—(1) *Allocation and apportionment of deductions for expenses other than taxes.* Under paragraph (c)(1)(ii) of this section, CFC1's deductions for the current taxable year are allocated and apportioned among the section 904 categories, income groups within a section 904 category, and any PTEP groups that were increased as provided in paragraph (c)(1)(i) of this section. Under paragraph (d)(3)(i) of this section and § 1.861-8 through 1.861-14T, 750,000u of deductions are allocated and apportioned to the residual income group within the general category, and 750,000u of deductions are allocated and apportioned to the subpart F income group within the passive category. Therefore, CFC1 has 1,250,000u (2,000,000u – 750,000u) of pre-tax income attributable to the residual income group

within the general category and 1,250,000u (2,000,000u – 750,000u) of pre-tax income attributable to the subpart F income group within the passive category. For U.S. tax purposes, no deductions other than current year taxes are allocated and apportioned to the 4,000,000u in CFC1's PTEP group.

(2) *Allocation and apportionment of current year taxes.* Under paragraph (c)(1)(ii) of this section, CFC1's current year taxes are allocated and apportioned among the section 904 categories, income groups within a section 904 category, and any PTEP groups that were increased as provided in paragraph (c)(1)(i) of this section. Under paragraphs (d)(3)(i) and (ii) of this section, for purposes of allocating and apportioning taxes to reduce the income in a section 904 category, an income group, or PTEP group, § 1.904-6(a)(1) and (ii) are applied to determine the amount of taxable income computed under Country X law in each section 904 category, income group, and PTEP group that is included in the Country X tax base. For Country X purposes, 1,000,000u of deductions are apportioned to CFC1's PTEP group within the general category, 500,000u of deductions are apportioned to the residual income group within the general category, and no deductions are apportioned to the subpart F income group in the passive category. Therefore, for Country X purposes, CFC1 has 3,000,000u of income attributable to the PTEP group within the general category, 1,500,000u of income attributable to the residual income group within the general category, and no income attributable to the subpart F income group within the passive category. Under paragraph (d)(3)(ii) of this section, 600,000u (3,000,000u/4,500,000u x 900,000u) of the 900,000u current year taxes paid by CFC1 are related to the PTEP group within the general category, and 300,000u (1,500,000u/4,500,000u x 900,000u) are related to the residual income group within the general category. No current year taxes are allocated or apportioned to the subpart F income group within the passive category because the interest expense is exempt from Country X tax. Thus, for U.S. tax purposes, CFC1 has 3,400,000u of previously taxed earnings and profits (4,000,000u – 600,000u) in the PTEP group within the general category, 1,250,000u of income in the subpart F income group within the passive category, and 950,000u of income (1,250,000u – 300,000u) in the residual income group within the general category. For purposes of determining foreign taxes deemed paid under section 960, CFC1 has $600,000 of foreign income taxes in the PTEP group within the general category and $300,000 of current year taxes in the residual income group within the general category. Under paragraph (e) of this section, the United States shareholders of CFC1 cannot claim a credit with respect to the $300,000 of taxes on CFC1's income in the residual income group.

(C) *Step 3.* Under paragraph (c)(1)(iii) of this section, the United States shareholders of CFC1 compute current year taxes deemed paid under section 960(a) and (d) and the rules of § 1.960-2.

**Prop. Reg. § 1.960-1(f)**

None of the Country X tax is allocated to CFC1's subpart F income group. Therefore, there are no current year taxes deemed paid by CFC1's United States shareholders with respect to their passive category subpart F inclusions. See §1.960-2(b)(5) and (c)(7) for examples of the application of section 960(a) and (d) and the rules in §1.960-2. Additionally, under paragraph (c)(1)(iii) of this section, foreign income taxes deemed paid under section 960(b)(2) by CFC1 are determined with respect to the section 959(b) distribution from CFC2 under the rules of §1.960-3. There are no PTEP group taxes associated with the previously taxed earnings and profits distributed by CFC2 in the hands of CFC2. Therefore, there are no foreign income taxes deemed paid by CFC1 under section 960(b)(2) with respect to the section 959(b) distribution from CFC2. See §1.960-3(e) for examples of the application of section 960(b) and the rules in §1.960-3.

(D) *Step 4.* Under paragraph (c)(1)(iv) of this section, previously taxed earnings and profits resulting from subpart F inclusions and GILTI inclusion amounts with respect to CFC1's current taxable year are separated from CFC1's other earnings and profits and added to an annual PTEP account and PTEP group within the PTEP account, under the rules of §1.960-3(c). The United States shareholders of CFC1 include in gross income subpart F inclusions totaling $1,250,000 with respect to 1,250,000u of subpart F income of CFC1, and the subpart F inclusions are passive category income. Therefore, under §1.960-3(c)(2), 1,250,000u of previously taxed earnings and profits resulting from the subpart F inclusions is added to CFC1's PTEP group described in §1.960-3(c)(2)(x) within the 2019 annual PTEP account within the passive category.

(E) *Step 5.* Paragraph (c)(1)(v) of this section does not apply because CFC1 is the highest-tier controlled foreign corporation in the chain.

(F) *Step 6.* Paragraph (c)(1)(vi) of this section does not apply because CFC1 did not make a section 959(a) distribution.

[Proposed 12-7-2018.]

**[Prop. Reg. §1.960-2]**

**§1.960-2. Foreign income taxes deemed paid under sections 960(a) and (d).**—(a) *Scope.*—Paragraph (b) of this section provides rules for computing the amount of foreign income taxes deemed paid by a domestic corporation that is a United States shareholder of a controlled foreign corporation under section 960(a). Paragraph (c) of this section provides rules for computing the amount of foreign income taxes deemed paid by a domestic corporation that is a United States shareholder of a controlled foreign corporation under section 960(d).

(b) *Foreign income taxes deemed paid under section 960(a).*—(1) *In general.*—If a domestic corporation that is a United States shareholder of a controlled foreign corporation includes in gross income under section 951(a)(1)(A) its pro rata share of the subpart F income of the controlled foreign corporation (a *subpart F inclusion*), the domestic corporation is deemed to have paid the amount of the controlled foreign corporation's foreign income taxes that are properly attributable to the items of income in a subpart F income group of the controlled foreign corporation that give rise to the subpart F inclusion of the domestic corporation that is attributable to the subpart F income group. For each section 904 category, the domestic corporation is deemed to have paid foreign income taxes equal to the sum of the controlled foreign corporation's foreign income taxes that are properly attributable to the items of income in the subpart F income groups to which the subpart F inclusion is attributable. See §1.904-6(b)(1) for rules on assigning the foreign income tax to a section 904 category. No foreign income taxes are deemed paid under section 960(a) with respect to an inclusion under section 951(a)(1)(B).

(2) *Properly attributable.*—The amount of the controlled foreign corporation's foreign income taxes that are properly attributable to the items of income in the subpart F income group of the controlled foreign corporation to which a subpart F inclusion is attributable equals the domestic corporation's proportionate share of the current year taxes of the controlled foreign corporation that are allocated and apportioned under §1.960-1(d)(3)(ii) to the subpart F income group. No other foreign income taxes are considered properly attributable to an item of income of the controlled foreign corporation.

(3) *Proportionate share.*—(i) *In general.*—A domestic corporation's proportionate share of the current year taxes of a controlled foreign corporation that are allocated and apportioned under §1.960-1(d)(3)(ii) to a subpart F income group within a section 904 category of the controlled foreign corporation is equal to the total U.S. dollar amount of current year taxes that are allocated and apportioned under §1.960-1(d)(3)(ii) to the subpart F income group multiplied by a fraction (not to exceed one), the numerator of which is the portion of the domestic corporation's subpart F inclusion that is attributable to the subpart F income group and the denominator of which is the total net income in the subpart F income group, both determined in the functional currency of the controlled foreign corporation. If the numerator or denominator of the fraction is zero or less than zero, then the proportionate share of the current year taxes that are allocated and apportioned under §1.960-1(d)(3)(ii) to the subpart F income group is zero.

(ii) *Effect of qualified deficits.*—Neither an accumulated deficit nor any prior year deficit in the earnings and profits of a controlled foreign corporation reduces its net income in a subpart F income group. Accordingly, any such deficit does not affect the denominator of the fraction described in paragraph (b)(3)(i) of this section.

However, the first sentence of this paragraph (b)(3)(ii) does not affect the application of section 952(c)(1)(B) for purposes of determining the domestic corporation's subpart F inclusion. Any reduction to the domestic corporation's subpart F inclusion under section 952(c)(1)(B) is reflected in the numerator of the fraction described in paragraph (b)(3)(i) of this section.

(iii) *Effect of current year E&P limitation or chain deficit.*—To the extent that an amount of income in a subpart F income group is excluded from the subpart F income of the controlled foreign corporation under section 952(c)(1)(A) or (C), the net income in the subpart F income group that is the denominator of the fraction described in paragraph (b)(3)(i) of this section is reduced (but not below zero) by the amount excluded. The domestic corporation's subpart F inclusion that is the numerator of the fraction described in paragraph (b)(3)(i) of this section is based on the controlled foreign corporation's subpart F income computed with the application of section 952(c)(1)(A) and (C).

(4) *Domestic partnerships.*—For purposes of applying this paragraph (b), in the case of a domestic partnership that is a U.S. shareholder partnership with respect to a partnership CFC, the distributive share of a U.S. shareholder partner of the U.S. shareholder partnership's subpart F inclusion with respect to the partnership CFC is treated as a subpart F inclusion of the U.S. shareholder partner with respect to the partnership CFC.

(5) *Example.*—The following example illustrates the application of this paragraph (b).

(i) *Facts.* USP, a domestic corporation, owns 80% of the stock of CFC, a controlled foreign corporation. The remaining portion of the stock of CFC is owned by an unrelated person. USP and CFC both use the calendar year as their U.S. taxable year, and CFC also uses the calendar year as its foreign taxable year. CFC uses the "u" as its functional currency. At all relevant times, 1u=$1. For its U.S. taxable year ending December 31, 2018, after the application of the rules in § 1.960-1(d) the income of CFC after foreign taxes is assigned to the following income groups: 1,000,000u of dividend income in a subpart F income group within the passive category ("subpart F income group 1"); 2,400,000u of gain from commodities transactions in a subpart F income group within the passive category ("subpart F income group 2"); and 1,800,000u of foreign base company services income in a subpart F income group within the general category ("subpart F income group 3"). CFC has current year taxes, translated into U.S. dollars, of $740,000 that are allocated and apportioned as follows: $50,000 to subpart F income group 1; $240,000 to subpart F income group 2; and $450,000 to subpart F income group 3. USP has a subpart F inclusion with respect to CFC of 4,160,000u = $4,160,000, of which 800,000u is attributable to subpart F income group 1, 1,920,000u to subpart F income

group 2, and 1,440,000u to subpart F income group 3.

(ii) *Analysis*—(A) *Passive category.* Under paragraphs (b)(2) and (3) of this section, the amount of CFC's current year taxes that are properly attributable to items of income in subpart F income group 1 to which a subpart F inclusion is attributable equals USP's proportionate share of the current year taxes that are allocated and apportioned under § 1.960-1(d)(3)(ii) to subpart F income group 1, which is $40,000 ($50,000 x 800,000u/1,000,000u). Under paragraphs (b)(2) and (3) of this section, the amount of CFC's current year taxes that are properly attributable to items of income in subpart F income group 2 to which a subpart F inclusion is attributable equals USP's proportionate share of the current year taxes that are allocated and apportioned under § 1.960-1(d)(3)(ii) to subpart F income group 2, which is $192,000 ($240,000 x 1,920,000u/2,400,000u). Accordingly, under paragraph (b)(1), USP is deemed to have paid $232,000 ($40,000 + $192,000) of passive category foreign income taxes of CFC with respect to its $2,720,000 subpart F inclusion in the passive category.

(B) *General category.* Under paragraphs (b)(2) and (3) of this section, the amount of CFC's current year taxes that are properly attributable items of income in subpart F income group 3 to which a subpart F inclusion is attributable equals USP's proportionate share of the foreign income taxes that are allocated and apportioned under § 1.960-1(d)(3)(ii) to subpart F income group 3, which is $360,000 ($450,000 x 1,440,000u/1,800,000u). CFC has no other subpart F income groups within the general category. Accordingly, under paragraph (b)(1) of this section, USP is deemed to have paid $360,000 of general category foreign income taxes of CFC with respect to its $1,440,000 subpart F inclusion in the general category.

(c) *Foreign income taxes deemed paid under section 960(d).*—(1) *In general.*—If a domestic corporation that is a United States shareholder of one or more controlled foreign corporations includes an amount in gross income under section 951A(a) and § 1.951A-1(b), the domestic corporation is deemed to have paid an amount of foreign income taxes equal to 80 percent of the product of its inclusion percentage multiplied by the sum of all tested foreign income taxes in the tested income group within each section 904 category of the controlled foreign corporation or corporations.

(2) *Inclusion percentage.*—The term *inclusion percentage* means, with respect to a domestic corporation that is a United States shareholder of one or more controlled foreign corporations, the domestic corporation's GILTI inclusion amount divided by the aggregate amount described in section 951A(c)(1)(A) and § 1.951A-1(c)(2)(i) with respect to the United States shareholder.

**Prop. Reg. § 1.960-2(c)(2)**

(3) *Tested foreign income taxes.*—The term *tested foreign income taxes* means, with respect to a domestic corporation that is a United States shareholder of a controlled foreign corporation, the amount of the controlled foreign corporation's foreign income taxes that are properly attributable to tested income taken into account by the domestic corporation under section 951A and § 1.951A-1.

(4) *Properly attributable.*—The amount of the controlled foreign corporation's foreign income taxes that are properly attributable to tested income taken into account by the domestic corporation under section 951A(a) and § 1.951A-1(b) equals the domestic corporation's proportionate share of the current year taxes of the controlled foreign corporation that are allocated and apportioned under § 1.960-1(d)(3)(ii) to the tested income group within each section 904 category of the controlled foreign corporation. No other foreign income taxes are considered properly attributable to tested income.

(5) *Proportionate share.*—A domestic corporation's proportionate share of current year taxes of a controlled foreign corporation that are allocated and apportioned under § 1.960-1(d)(3)(ii) to a tested income group within a section 904 category of the controlled foreign corporation is the U.S. dollar amount of current year taxes that are allocated and apportioned under § 1.960-1(d)(3)(ii) to a tested income group within a section 904 category of the controlled foreign corporation multiplied by a fraction (not to exceed one), the numerator of which is the portion of the tested income of the controlled foreign corporation in the tested income group within the section 904 category that is included in computing the domestic corporation's aggregate amount described in section 951A(c)(1)(A) and § 1.951A-1(c)(2)(i), and the denominator of which is the income in the tested income group within the section 904 category, both determined in the functional currency of the controlled foreign corporation. If the numerator or denominator of the fraction is zero or less than zero, the domestic corporation's proportionate share of the current year taxes allocated and apportioned under § 1.960-1(d)(3)(ii) to the tested income group is zero.

(6) *Domestic partnerships.*—See § 1.951A-5 for rules regarding the determination of the GILTI inclusion amount of a U.S. shareholder partner.

(7) *Examples.*—The following examples illustrate the application of this paragraph (c).

(i) *Example 1: Directly owned controlled foreign corporation*—(A) *Facts.* USP, a domestic corporation, owns 100% of the stock of a number of controlled foreign corporations, including CFC1. USP and CFC1 each use the calendar year as their U.S. taxable year. CFC1 uses the "u" as its functional currency. At all relevant times, 1u=$1. For its U.S. taxable year ending December 31, 2018, after application of the rules in § 1.960-1(d),

the income of CFC1 is assigned to a single income group: 2,000u of income from the sale of goods in a tested income group within the general category ("tested income group"). CFC1 has current year taxes, translated into U.S. dollars, of $400 that are all allocated and apportioned to the tested income group. For its U.S. taxable year ending December 31, 2018, USP has a GILTI inclusion amount determined by reference to all of its controlled foreign corporations, including CFC1, of $6,000, and an aggregate amount described in section 951A(c)(1)(A) and § 1.951A-1(c)(2)(i) of $10,000. All of the income in CFC1's tested income group is included in computing USP's aggregate amount described in section 951A(c)(1)(A) and § 1.951A-1(c)(2)(i).

(B) *Analysis.* Under paragraph (c)(5) of this section, USP's proportionate share of the current year taxes that are allocated and apportioned under § 1.960-1(d)(3)(ii) to CFC1's tested income group is $400 ($400 x 2,000u/2,000u). Therefore, under paragraph (c)(4) of this section, the amount of current year taxes properly attributable to tested income taken into account by USP under section 951A(a) and § 1.951A-1(b) is $400. Under paragraph (c)(3) of this section, USP's tested foreign income taxes with respect to CFC1 are $400. Under paragraph (c)(2) of this section, USP's inclusion percentage is 60% ($6,000/$10,000). Accordingly, under paragraph (c)(1) of this section, USP is deemed to have paid $192 of the foreign income taxes of CFC1 (80% x 60% x $400).

(ii) *Example 2: Controlled foreign corporation owned through domestic partnership*—(A) *Facts*—(1) US1, a domestic corporation, owns 95% of PRS, a domestic partnership. The remaining 5% of PRS is owned by US2, a domestic corporation that is unrelated to US1. PRS owns all of the stock of CFC1, a controlled foreign corporation. In addition, US1 owns all of the stock of CFC2, a controlled foreign corporation. US1, US2, PRS, CFC1, and CFC2 all use the calendar year as their taxable year. CFC1 and CFC2 both use the "u" as their functional currency. At all relevant times, 1u=$1. For its U.S. taxable year ending December 31, 2018, after application of the rules in § 1.960-1(d), the income of CFC1 is assigned to a single income group: 300u of income from the sale of goods in a tested income group within the general category ("CFC1's tested income group"). CFC1 has current year taxes, translated into U.S. dollars, of $100 that are all allocated and apportioned to CFC1's tested income group. The income of CFC2 is also assigned to a single income group: 200u of income from the sale of goods in a tested income group within the general category ("CFC2's tested income group"). CFC2 has current year taxes, translated into U.S. dollars, of $20 that are allocated and apportioned to CFC2's tested income group.

(2) In the same year, US1 is a U.S. shareholder partner with respect to CFC1, a partnership CFC, and accordingly, determines its GILTI inclusion amount under § 1.951A-5(c), as if US1 owned (within the meaning of section 958(a))

95% of the stock of CFC1. Taking into account both CFC1 and CFC2, US1 has a GILTI inclusion amount in the general category of $485, and an aggregate amount described in section 951A(c)(1)(A) and §1.951A-1(c)(2)(i) within the general category of $485. 285u (95% x 300u) of the income in CFC1's tested income group and 200u of the income in CFC2's tested income group is included in computing US1's aggregate amount described in section 951A(c)(1)(A) and §1.951A-1(c)(2)(i) within the general category. Because US2 is not a U.S. shareholder partner with respect to CFC1, US2 does not take into account CFC1's tested income in determining its GILTI inclusion amount. However, under §1.951A-5(b)(2), US2 includes in income $15, its distributive share of PRS's GILTI inclusion amount.

(B) *Analysis*—(1) *US1*—(i) *CFC1.* Under paragraph (c)(5) and (6) of this section, US1's proportionate share of the current year taxes that are allocated and apportioned under §1.960-1(d)(3)(ii) to CFC1's tested income group is $95 ($100 x 285u/300u). Therefore, under paragraph (c)(4) of this section, the amount of the current year taxes properly attributable to tested income taken into account by US1 under section 951A(a) and §1.951A-1(b) is $95. Under paragraph (c)(3) of this section, US1's tested foreign income taxes with respect to CFC1 are $95. Under paragraph (c)(2) of this section, US1's inclusion percentage is 100% ($485/$485). Accordingly, under paragraph (c)(1) of this section, US1 is deemed to have paid $76 of the foreign income taxes of CFC1 (80% x 100% x $95).

(ii) *CFC2.* Under paragraph (c)(5) of this section, US1's proportionate share of the foreign income taxes that are allocated and apportioned under §1.960-1(d)(3)(ii) to CFC2's tested income group is $20 ($20 x 200u/200u). Therefore, under paragraph (c)(4) of this section, the amount of foreign income taxes properly attributable to tested income taken into account by US1 under section 951A(a) and §1.951A-1(b) is $20. Under paragraph (c)(3) of this section, US1's tested foreign income taxes with respect to CFC2 are $20. Under paragraph (c)(2) of this section, US1's inclusion percentage is 100% ($485/$485). Accordingly, under paragraph (c)(1) of this section, US1 is deemed to have paid $16 of the foreign income taxes of CFC2 (80% x 100% x $20).

(2) *US2.* US2 is not a United States shareholder of CFC1 or CFC2. Accordingly, under paragraph (c)(1) of this section, US2 is not deemed to have paid any of the foreign income taxes of CFC1 or CFC2.

[Proposed 12-7-2018.]

### [Prop. Reg. §1.960-3]

**§1.960-3. Foreign income taxes deemed paid under section 960(b).**—(a) *Scope.*—Paragraph (b) of this section provides rules for computing the amount of foreign income taxes deemed paid by a domestic corporation that is a United States shareholder of a controlled foreign corporation, or by a controlled foreign corporation, under

section 960(b). Paragraph (c) of this section provides rules for the establishment and maintenance of PTEP groups within an annual PTEP account. Paragraph (d) of this section defines the term PTEP group taxes. Paragraph (e) of this section provides examples illustrating the application of this section.

(b) *Foreign income taxes deemed paid under section 960(b).*—(1) *Foreign income taxes deemed paid by a domestic corporation with respect to a section 959(a) distribution.*—If a controlled foreign corporation makes a distribution to a domestic corporation that is a United States shareholder with respect to the controlled foreign corporation and that distribution is, in whole or in part, a section 959(a) distribution with respect to a PTEP group within a section 904 category, the domestic corporation is deemed to have paid the amount of the foreign corporation's foreign income taxes that are properly attributable to the section 959(a) distribution with respect to the PTEP group and that have not been deemed to have been paid by a domestic corporation under section 960 for the current taxable year or any prior taxable year. See §1.965-5(c)(1)(iii) for rules disallowing credits in relation to a distribution of certain previously taxed earnings and profits resulting from the application of section 965. For each section 904 category, the domestic corporation is deemed to have paid foreign income taxes equal to the sum of the controlled foreign corporation's foreign income taxes that are properly attributable to section 959(a) distributions with respect to all PTEP groups within the section 904 category. See §1.904-6(b)(2) for rules on assigning the foreign income tax to a section 904 category.

(2) *Foreign income taxes deemed paid by a controlled foreign corporation with respect to a section 959(b) distribution.*—If a controlled foreign corporation (*distributing controlled foreign corporation*) makes a distribution to another controlled foreign corporation (*recipient controlled foreign corporation*) and the distribution is, in whole or in part, a section 959(b) distribution from a PTEP group within a section 904 category, the recipient controlled foreign corporation is deemed to have paid the amount of the distributing controlled foreign corporation's foreign income taxes that are properly attributable to the section 959(b) distribution from the PTEP group and that have not been deemed to have been paid by a domestic corporation under section 960 for the current taxable year or any prior taxable year. See §1.904-6(b)(3) for rules on assigning the foreign income tax to a section 904 category.

(3) *Properly attributable.*—The amount of foreign income taxes that are properly attributable to a section 959 distribution from a PTEP group within a section 904 category equals the domestic corporation's or recipient controlled foreign corporation's proportionate share of the PTEP group taxes with respect to the PTEP group within the section 904 category. No other foreign

income taxes are considered properly attributable to a section 959 distribution.

(4) *Proportionate share.*—A domestic corporation's or recipient controlled foreign corporation's proportionate share of the PTEP group taxes with respect to a PTEP group within a section 904 category is equal to the total amount of the PTEP group taxes with respect to the PTEP group multiplied by a fraction (not to exceed one), the numerator of which is the amount of the section 959 distribution from the PTEP group, and the denominator of which is the total amount of previously taxed earnings and profits in the PTEP group, both determined in the functional currency of the controlled foreign corporation. If the numerator or denominator of the fraction is zero or less than zero, then the proportionate share of the PTEP group taxes with respect to the PTEP group is zero.

(5) *Domestic partnerships.*—For purposes of applying this paragraph (b), in the case of a domestic partnership that is a U.S. shareholder partnership with respect to a partnership CFC, the distributive share of a U.S. shareholder partner of a U.S. shareholder partnership's section 959(a) distribution from the partnership CFC is treated as a section 959(a) distribution received by the U.S. shareholder partner from the partnership CFC.

(c) *Accounting for previously taxed earnings and profits.*—(1) *Establishment of annual PTEP account.*—A separate, annual account (*annual PTEP account*) must be established for the previously taxed earnings and profits of the controlled foreign corporation to which inclusions under section 951(a) and GILTI inclusion amounts of United States shareholders of the CFC are attributable. Each account must correspond to the inclusion year of the previously taxed earnings and profits and to the section 904 category to which the inclusions under section 951(a) or GILTI inclusion amounts were assigned at the level of the United States shareholders. Accordingly, a controlled foreign corporation may have an annual PTEP account in the section 951A category or a treaty category (as defined in § 1.861-13(b)(6)), even though income of the controlled foreign corporation that gave rise to the previously taxed earnings and profits cannot initially be assigned to the section 951A category or a treaty category.

(2) *PTEP groups within an annual PTEP account.*—The amount in an annual PTEP account is further assigned to one or more of the following groups of previously taxed earnings and profits (each, a *PTEP group*) within the account:

(i) Earnings and profits described in section 959(c)(1)(A) by reason of section 951(a)(1)(B) and not by reason of the application of section 959(a)(2);

(ii) Earnings and profits described in section 959(c)(1)(A) that were initially described in section 959(c)(2) by reason of section 965(a);

(iii) Earnings and profits described in section 959(c)(1)(A) that were initially described in section 959(c)(2) by reason of section 965(b)(4)(A);

(iv) Earnings and profits described in section 959(c)(1)(A) that were initially described in section 959(c)(2) by reason of section 951A;

(v) Earnings and profits described in section 959(c)(1)(A) that were initially described in section 959(c)(2) by reason of section 951(a)(1)(A) (other than as a result of the application of section 965);

(vi) Earnings and profits described in section 959(c)(1)(B);

(vii) Earnings and profits described in section 959(c)(2) by reason of section 965(a);

(viii) Earnings and profits described in section 959(c)(2) by reason of section 965(b)(4)(A);

(ix) Earnings and profits described in section 959(c)(2) by reason of section 951A;

(x) Earnings and profits described in section 959(c)(2) by reason of section 951(a)(1)(A) (other than as a result of the application of section 965).

(3) *Accounting for distributions of previously taxed earnings and profits.*—With respect to a recipient controlled foreign corporation that receives a section 959(b) distribution, such distribution amount is added to the annual PTEP account, and PTEP group within the annual PTEP account, that corresponds to the inclusion year and section 904 category of the annual PTEP account, and PTEP group within the annual PTEP account, from which the distributing controlled foreign corporation is treated as making the distribution under section 959 and the regulations under that section. Similarly, with respect to a controlled foreign corporation that makes a section 959 distribution, such distribution amount reduces the annual PTEP account, and PTEP group within the annual PTEP account, that corresponds to the inclusion year and section 904 category of the annual PTEP account, and PTEP group within the annual PTEP account, from which the controlled foreign corporation is treated as making the distribution under section 959 and the regulations under that section. Earnings and profits in a PTEP group are reduced by the amount of current year taxes that are allocated and apportioned to the PTEP group under § 1.960-1(d)(3)(ii), and the U.S. dollar amount of the taxes are added to an account of PTEP group taxes under the rules in paragraph (d)(1) of this section.

(4) *Accounting for reclassifications of earnings and profits described in section 959(c)(2) to earnings and profits described in section 959(c)(1).*—If an amount of previously taxed earnings and profits that is in a PTEP group described in paragraphs (c)(2)(vii) through (x) of this section (each, a *section 959(c)(2) PTEP group*) is reclassified as previously taxed earnings and profits described in

section 959(c)(1) (*reclassified previously taxed earnings and profits*), the section 959(c)(2) PTEP group is reduced by the functional currency amount of the reclassified previously taxed earnings and profits. This amount is added to the corresponding PTEP group described in paragraphs (c)(2)(ii) through (v) of this section (each, a *reclassified PTEP group*) in the same section 904 category and same annual PTEP account as the reduced section 959(c)(2) PTEP group.

(d) *PTEP group taxes.*—(1) *In general.*—The term *PTEP group taxes* means the U.S. dollar amount of foreign income taxes (translated in accordance with section 986(a)) that are paid, accrued, or deemed paid with respect to an amount in each PTEP group within an annual PTEP account. The foreign income taxes that are paid, accrued, or deemed paid with respect to a PTEP group within an annual PTEP account of a controlled foreign corporation are—

(i) The sum of—

(A) The current year taxes paid or accrued by the controlled foreign corporation that are allocated and apportioned to the PTEP group under § 1.960-1(d)(3)(ii);

(B) Foreign income taxes that are deemed paid under section 960(b)(2) and paragraph (b)(2) of this section by the controlled foreign corporation with respect to a section 959(b) distribution received by the controlled foreign corporation, the amount of which is added to the PTEP group under paragraph (c)(3) of this section; and

(C) In the case of a reclassified PTEP group of the controlled foreign corporation, reclassified PTEP group taxes that are attributable to the section 959(c)(2) PTEP group that corresponds to the reclassified PTEP group;

(ii) Reduced by—

(A) Foreign income taxes that were deemed paid under section 960(b)(2) and paragraph (b)(2) of this section by another controlled foreign corporation that received a section 959(b) distribution from the controlled foreign corporation, the amount of which is subtracted from the controlled foreign corporation's PTEP group under paragraph (c)(3) of this section;

(B) Foreign income taxes that were deemed paid under section 960(b)(1) and paragraph (b)(1) of this section by a domestic corporation that is a United States shareholder of the controlled foreign corporation that received a section 959(a) distribution from the controlled foreign corporation, the amount of which is subtracted from the controlled foreign corporation's PTEP group under paragraph (c)(3) of this section; and

(C) In the case of a section 959(c)(2) PTEP group of the controlled foreign corporation, reclassified PTEP group taxes.

(2) *Reclassified PTEP group taxes.*—Reclassified PTEP group taxes are foreign income taxes that are initially included in PTEP group taxes with respect to a section 959(c)(2) PTEP group

under paragraph (d)(1)(i)(A) or (B) of this section multiplied by a fraction, the numerator of which is the portion of the previously taxed earnings and profits in the section 959(c)(2) PTEP group that become reclassified previously taxed earnings and profits, and the denominator of which is the total previously taxed earnings and profits in the section 959(c)(2) PTEP group.

(3) *Foreign income taxes deemed paid with respect to PTEP groups established for pre-2018 inclusion years.*—Foreign income taxes paid or accrued with respect to an annual PTEP account, and a PTEP group within such account, that was established for an inclusion year that begins before January 1, 2018, are treated as PTEP group taxes of a controlled foreign corporation for purposes of this section only if those foreign income taxes were—

(i) Paid or accrued in a taxable year of the controlled foreign corporation that began before January 1, 2018;

(ii) Not included in a controlled foreign corporation's post-1986 foreign income taxes (as defined in section 902(c)(2) as in effect on December 21, 2017) used to compute foreign taxes deemed paid under section 902 (as in effect on December 21, 2017) in any taxable year that began before January 1, 2018; and

(iii) Not treated as deemed paid under section 960(a)(3) (as in effect on December 21, 2017) by a domestic corporation that was a United States shareholder of the controlled foreign corporation.

(e) *Examples.*—The following examples illustrate the application of this section.

(1) *Example 1: Establishment of PTEP groups and PTEP accounts*—(i) *Facts.* USP, a domestic corporation, owns all of the stock of CFC1, a controlled foreign corporation. CFC1 owns all of the stock of CFC2, a controlled foreign corporation. USP, CFC1, and CFC2 each use the calendar year as their U.S. taxable year. CFC1 and CFC2 use the "u" as their functional currency. At all relevant times, 1u = $1. With respect to CFC2, USP includes in gross income a subpart F inclusion of 1,000,000u = $1,000,000 for the taxable year ending December 31, 2018. The inclusion is with respect to passive category income. In its U.S. taxable year ending December 31, 2019, CFC2 distributes 1,000,000u to CFC1. CFC2 has no earnings and profits except for the 1,000,000u of previously taxed earnings and profits resulting from USP's 2018 taxable year subpart F inclusion. CFC2's country of organization, Country X, imposes a withholding tax on CFC2's distribution to CFC1. Under § 1.960-1(d)(3)(ii), CFC1's 300,000u of current year taxes are allocated and apportioned to the PTEP group within the annual PTEP account within the section 904 category to which the 1,000,000u of previously taxed earnings and profits are assigned.

(ii) *Analysis*—(A) Under paragraph (c)(1) of this section, a separate annual PTEP account in the passive category for the 2018 taxable year is established for CFC2 as a result of USP's subpart F inclusion. Under paragraph (c)(2) of this section, this account contains one PTEP group, which is described in paragraph (c)(2)(x) of this section.

(B) Under paragraph (c)(3) of this section, in the 2019 taxable year, the 1,000,000u related to the section 959(b) distribution from CFC2 is added to CFC1's annual PTEP account for the 2018 taxable year in the passive category and to the PTEP group within such account described in paragraph (c)(2)(x) of this section. Similarly, CFC2's 2018 taxable year annual PTEP account within the passive category, and the PTEP group within such account described in paragraph (c)(2)(x) of this section, is reduced by the amount of the 1,000,000u section 959(b) distribution to CFC1. Additionally, CFC1's annual PTEP account for the 2018 taxable year in the passive category, and the PTEP group within such account described in paragraph (c)(2)(x) of this section, is reduced by the 300,000u of withholding taxes imposed on CFC1 by Country X. Therefore, CFC1's annual PTEP account for the 2018 taxable year within the passive category and the PTEP group within such account described in paragraph (c)(2)(x) of this section is 700,000u.

(C) Under paragraph (d)(1) of this section, the 300,000u of withholding tax is translated into U.S. dollars and $300,000 is added to the PTEP group taxes with respect to CFC1's PTEP group described in paragraph (c)(2)(x) of this section within the annual PTEP account for the 2018 taxable year within the passive category.

(2) *Example 2: Foreign income taxes deemed paid under section 960(b)*—(i) *Facts.* USP, a domestic corporation, owns 100% of the stock of CFC1, which in turn owns 60% of the stock of CFC2, which in turn owns 100% of the stock of CFC3. USP, CFC1, CFC2, and CFC3 all use the calendar year as their U.S. taxable year. CFC1, CFC2, and CFC3 all use the "u" as their functional currency. At all relevant times, 1u=$1. On July 1, 2020, CFC2 distributes 600u to CFC1 and the entire distribution is a section 959(b) distribution ("distribution 1"). On October 1, 2020, CFC1 distributes 800u to USP and the entire distribution is a section 959(a) distribution ("distribution 2"). CFC1 and CFC2 make no other distributions in the year ending December 31, 2020, earn no other income, and incur no taxes on distribution 1 or distribution 2. Before taking into account distribution 1, CFC2 has 1,000u in a PTEP group described in paragraph (c)(2)(x) of this section within an annual PTEP account for the 2016 taxable year within the general category. The previously taxed earnings and profits in CFC2's PTEP group relate to subpart F income of CFC3 that was included by USP in 2016. CFC3 distributed the earnings and profits to CFC2 before the 2020 taxable year and, solely as a result of the distribution of the previously taxed earnings and profits, CFC2 incurred withholding and net basis tax, resulting in $150 of PTEP group taxes with respect to the PTEP group. Before taking into

account distribution 1 and distribution 2, CFC1 has 200u in a PTEP group described in paragraph (c)(2)(ix) of this section within an annual PTEP account for the 2018 taxable year within the section 951A category. The previously taxed earnings and profits in CFC1's PTEP group relate to the portion of a GILTI inclusion amount that was included by USP in 2018 and allocated to CFC2 under section 951A(f)(2) and § 1.951A-6(b)(2). CFC2 distributed the earnings and profits to CFC1 before the 2020 taxable year and, solely as a result of the distribution of the previously taxed earnings and profits, CFC1 incurred withholding and net basis tax, resulting in $25 of PTEP group taxes with respect to the PTEP group.

(ii) *Analysis*—(A) *Foreign income taxes deemed paid by CFC1.* With respect to distribution 1 from CFC2 to CFC1, under paragraph (b)(4) of this section CFC1's proportionate share of PTEP group taxes with respect to CFC2's PTEP group described in paragraph (c)(2)(x) of this section within an annual PTEP account for the 2016 taxable year within the general category is $90 ($150 x 600u/1,000u). Under paragraph (b)(3) of this section, the amount of foreign income taxes that are properly attributable to distribution 1 is $90. Accordingly, under paragraph (b)(2) of this section, CFC1 is deemed to have paid $90 of general category foreign income taxes of CFC2 with respect to its 600u section 959(b) distribution in the general category.

(B) *Adjustments to PTEP accounts of CFC1 and CFC2.* Under paragraph (c)(3) of this section, the 600u related to distribution 1 is added to CFC1's PTEP group described in paragraph (c)(2)(x) of this section within an annual PTEP account for the 2016 taxable year within the general category. Similarly, CFC2's PTEP group described in paragraph (c)(2)(x) of this section within an annual PTEP account for the 2016 taxable year within the general category is reduced by 600u, the amount of the section 959(b) distribution to CFC1. Additionally, under paragraph (d) of this section, CFC1's PTEP group taxes with respect to its PTEP group described in paragraph (c)(2)(x) of this section within an annual PTEP account for the 2016 taxable year within the general category are increased by $90 and CFC2's PTEP group described in paragraph (c)(2)(x) of this section within an annual PTEP account for the 2016 taxable year within the general category are reduced by $90.

(C) *Foreign income taxes deemed paid by USP.* With respect to distribution 2 from CFC1 to USP, because CFC1 has PTEP groups in more than one section 904 category, this section is applied separately to each section 904 category (that is, distribution 2 of 800u is applied separately to the 200u of CFC1's PTEP group described in paragraph (c)(2)(ix) of this section and 600u of CFC1's PTEP group described in paragraph (c)(2)(x) of this section).

(*1*) *Section 951A category.* Under paragraph (b)(4) of this section, USP's proportionate share of PTEP group taxes with respect to CFC1's PTEP group described in paragraph (c)(2)(ix) of this section within an annual PTEP account for the 2018 taxable year within the section 951A category is $25 ($25 x 200u/200u). Under paragraph (b)(3) of this section, the amount of foreign income taxes within the section 951A category that are properly attributable to distribution 2 is $25. Accordingly, under paragraph (b)(1) of this section USP is deemed to have paid $25 of section 951A category foreign income taxes of CFC1 with respect to its 200u section 959(a) distribution in the section 951A category.

(2) *General category.* Under paragraph (b)(4) of this section, USP's proportionate share of PTEP group taxes with respect to CFC1's PTEP group described in paragraph (c)(2)(x) of this section within an annual PTEP account for the 2016 taxable year within the general category is $90 ($90 x 600u/600u). Under paragraph (b)(3) of this section, the amount of foreign income taxes that are properly attributable to distribution 2 is $90. Accordingly, under paragraph (b)(1), USP is deemed to have paid $90 of general category foreign income taxes of CFC1 with respect to its 600u section 959(a) distribution in the general category.

[Proposed 12-7-2018.]

### [Prop. Reg. §1.960-4]

**§1.960-4. Additional foreign tax credit in year of receipt of previously taxed earnings and profits.**—(a) * * *

(1) * * * For purposes of this section, an amount included in gross income under section 951A(a) is treated as an amount included in gross income under section 951(a). The amount of the increase in the foreign tax credit limitation allowed by this section is determined with regard to each separate category of income described in § 1.904-5(a)(4)(v).

* * *

(d) * * * For purposes of this paragraph (d), the term "foreign income taxes" includes foreign income taxes paid or accrued, foreign income taxes deemed paid or accrued under section 904(c), and foreign income taxes deemed paid under section 960, for the taxable year of inclusion.

* * *

[Proposed 12-7-2018.]

### [Prop. Reg. §1.960-7]

**§1.960-7. Applicability dates.**—*Applicability dates.* Sections 1.960-1 through 1.960-6 apply to a taxable year of a foreign corporation beginning after December 31, 2017, and a taxable year of a domestic corporation that is a United States shareholder of the foreign corporation in which or with which such taxable year of such foreign corporation ends.

[Proposed 12-7-2018.]

### [Prop. Reg. §1.965-5]

**§1.965-5. Allowance of a credit or deduction for foreign income taxes.**

* * *

(c) * * *

(1) * * *

(iii) *Foreign income taxes deemed paid under section 960(b) (as applicable to taxable years of controlled foreign corporations beginning after December 31, 2017, and to taxable years of United States persons in which or with which such taxable years of foreign corporations end).*—No credit is allowed for the applicable percentage of foreign income taxes deemed paid under section 960(b) (as in effect for a taxable year of a controlled foreign corporation beginning after December 31, 2017, and a taxable year of a United States person in which or with which such controlled foreign corporation's taxable year ends) and § 1.960-3(b)(1) with respect to distributions to the domestic corporation of section 965(a) previously taxed earnings and profits or section 965(b) previously taxed earnings and profits. The foreign income taxes deemed paid under § 1.960-3(b)(1) with respect to a distribution to the domestic corporation of section 965(a) previously taxed earnings and profits or section 965(b) previously taxed earnings and profits is equal to the foreign income taxes properly attributable to a distribution from the distributing controlled foreign corporation's individual PTEP groups described in § 1.960-3(c)(2)(ii), (iii), (vii), or (viii). For purposes of this paragraph (c)(1)(iii), the terms "properly attributable" and "PTEP group" have the meanings set forth in § 1.960-3(b)(3) and (c)(2) respectively. In addition, foreign income taxes that would have been deemed paid under section 960(a)(1) (as in effect on December 21, 2017) with respect to the portion of a section 965(a) earnings amount that was reduced under § 1.965-1(b)(2) or § 1.965-8(b) are not eligible to be deemed paid under section 960(b) and § 1.960-3(b)(1) or any other section of the Code.

* * *

[Proposed 12-7-2018.]

### [Prop. Reg. §1.965-7]

**§1.965-7. Elections, payment, and other special rules.**

* * *

(e) * * *

(1) * * *

(i) * * * If the section 965(n) election creates or increases a net operating loss under section 172 for the taxable year, then the taxable income of the person for the taxable year cannot be less than the amount described in paragraph (e)(1)(ii) of this section. The amount of deductions equal to the amount by which a net operating loss is created or increased for the taxable year by reason of the section 965(n) election (the "deferred amount") is not taken into account in computing taxable income or the separate foreign tax credit limitations under section 904 for that year. The source and separate category (as defined in § 1.904-5(a)(4)(v)) components of the deferred amount are determined in accordance with paragraph (e)(1)(iv) of this section.

\* \* \*

(iv) *Effect of section 965(n) election.*—(A) *In general.*—The section 965(n) election for a taxable year applies solely for purposes of determining the amount of net operating loss under section 172 for the taxable year and determining the amount of taxable income for the taxable year (computed without regard to the deduction allowable under section 172) that may be reduced by net operating loss carryovers or carrybacks to such taxable year under section 172. Paragraph (e)(1)(iv)(B) of this section provides a rule for coordinating the section 965(n) election's effect on section 172 with the computation of the separate foreign tax credit limitations under section 904.

(B) *Ordering rule for allocation and apportionment of deductions for purposes of the section 904 limitation.*—The effect of a section 965(n) election with respect to a taxable year on the computation of the separate foreign tax credit limitations under section 904 is computed as follows and in the following order.

(1) Deductions that would have been allowed for the taxable year but for the section 965(n) election, other than the amount of any net operating loss carryover or carryback to that year that is not allowed by reason of the section 965(n) election, are allocated and apportioned under §§ 1.861-8 through 1.861-17 to the relevant statutory and residual groupings, taking into account the amount described in paragraph (e)(1)(ii) of this section. The source and separate category of the net operating loss carryover or carryback to the taxable year, if any, is determined under the rules of § 1.904(g)-3(b), taking into account the amount described in paragraph (e)(1)(ii) of this section. If the amount of the net operating loss carryover or carryback to the taxable year is reduced by reason of the section 965(n) election to an amount less than the U.S. source loss component of the net operating loss, the potential carryovers (or carrybacks) of the separate limitation losses that are part of the net operating loss are proportionally reduced as provided in § 1.904(g)-3(b)(3)(ii).

(2) If a net operating loss is created or increased for the taxable year by reason of the section 965(n) election, the deferred amount (as defined in paragraph (e)(1)(i) of this section) is not allowed as a deduction for the taxable year. See paragraph (e)(1)(i) of this section. The deferred amount (which is the corresponding addition to the net operating loss for the taxable year) comprises a ratable portion of the deductions (other than the deduction allowed under section 965(c)) allocated and apportioned to each statu-

tory and residual grouping under paragraph (e)(1)(iv)(B)(1) of this section. Such ratable portion equals the deferred amount multiplied by a fraction, the numerator of which is the deductions allocated and apportioned to the statutory or residual grouping under paragraph (e)(1)(iv)(B)(1) of this section (other than the section 965(c) deduction) and the denominator of which is the total deductions (other than the section 965(c) deduction) described in paragraph (e)(1)(iv)(B)(1) of this section. Accordingly, the fraction described in the previous sentence takes into account the deferred amount.

(3) Taxable income and the separate foreign tax credit limitations under section 904 for the taxable year are computed without taking into account any deferred amount. Deductions allocated and apportioned to the statutory and residual groupings under paragraph (e)(1)(iv)(B)(1)) of this section, to the extent deducted in the taxable year rather than deferred to create or increase a net operating loss, are combined with income in the statutory and residual groupings to which those deductions are assigned in order to compute the amount of separate limitation income or loss in each separate category and U.S. source income or loss for the taxable year. Section 904(b), (f), and (g) are then applied to determine the applicable foreign tax credit limitations for the taxable year.

\* \* \*

[Proposed 12-7-2018.]

**[Prop. Reg. § 1.1400Z-2(a)-1]**

**§ 1.1400Z-2(a)-1. Deferring tax on capital gains by investing in opportunity zones.**— (a) *In general.*—Under section 1400Z-2(a) of the Internal Revenue Code (Code) and this section, an eligible taxpayer may elect to defer recognition of some or all of its eligible gains to the extent that the taxpayer timely invests (as provided for by section 1400Z-2(a)(1)(A)) in eligible interests of a qualified opportunity fund (QOF), as defined in section 1400Z-2(d)(1). Paragraph (b) of this section defines eligible taxpayers, eligible gains, and eligible interests and contains related operational rules. Paragraph (c) of this section provides rules for applying section 1400Z-2 to a partnership, S corporation, trust, or estate that recognizes an eligible gain or would recognize such a gain if it did not elect to defer the gain under section 1400Z-2(a).

(b) *Definitions and related operating rules.*—The following definitions and rules apply for purposes of section 1400Z-2 and the regulations thereunder:

(1) *Eligible taxpayer.*—An *eligible taxpayer* is a person that may recognize gains for purposes of Federal income tax accounting. Thus, eligible taxpayers include individuals; C corporations, including regulated investment companies (RICs) and real estate investment trusts (REITs); partnerships; S corporations; trusts and estates. An eligible taxpayer may elect to defer recogni-

tion of one or more eligible gains in accordance with the requirements of section 1400Z-2.

(2) *Eligible gain.*—(i) *In general.*—An amount of gain is an *eligible gain*, and thus is eligible for deferral under section 1400Z-2(a), if the gain—

(A) Is treated as a capital gain for Federal income tax purposes;

(B) Would be recognized for Federal income tax purposes before January 1, 2027, if section 1400Z-2(a)(1) did not apply to defer recognition of the gain; and

(C) Does not arise from a sale or exchange with a person that, within the meaning of section 1400Z-2(e)(2), is related to the taxpayer that recognizes the gain or that would recognize the gain if section 1400Z-2(a)(1) did not apply to defer recognition of the gain.

(ii) *Gain not already subject to an election.*— In the case of a taxpayer who has made an election under section 1400Z-2(a) with respect to some but not all of an eligible gain, the term "eligible gain" includes the portion of that eligible gain with respect to which no election has yet been made.

(iii) *Gains under section 1256 contracts.*— (A) *General rule.*—The only gain arising from section 1256 contracts that is eligible for deferral under section 1400Z-2(a)(1) is capital gain net income for a taxable year. This net amount is determined by taking into account the capital gains and losses for a taxable year on all of a taxpayer's section 1256 contracts, including all amounts determined under section 1256(a), both those determined on the last business day of a taxable year and those that section 1256(c) requires to be determined under section 1256(a) because of the termination or transfer during the taxable year of the taxpayer's position with respect to a contract. The 180-day period with respect to any capital gain net income from section 1256 contracts for a taxable year begins on the last day of the taxable year, and the character of that gain when it is later included under section 1400Z-2(a)(1)(B) and (b) is determined under the general rule in paragraph (b)(5) of this section. See paragraph (b)(2)(iii)(B) of this section for limitations on the capital gains eligible for deferral under this paragraph (b)(2)(iii)(A).

(B) *Limitation on deferral for gain from 1256 contracts.*—If, at any time during the taxable year, any of the taxpayer's section 1256 contracts was part of an offsetting positions transaction (as defined in paragraph (b)(2)(iv) of this section) and any other position in that transaction was not a section 1256 contract, then no gain from any section 1256 contract is an eligible gain with respect to that taxpayer in that taxable year.

(iv) *No deferral for gain from a position that is or has been part of an offsetting-positions transaction.*—If a capital gain is from a position that is or has been part of an offsetting-positions transaction, the gain is not eligible for deferral under

section 1400Z-2(a)(1). For purposes of this paragraph (b)(2)(iv), an offsetting-positions transaction is a transaction in which a taxpayer has substantially diminished the taxpayer's risk of loss from holding one position with respect to personal property by holding one or more other positions with respect to personal property (whether or not of the same kind). It does not matter whether either of the positions is with respect to actively traded personal property. An offsetting-positions transaction includes a straddle as defined in section 1092 and the regulations thereunder, including section 1092(d)(4), which provides rules for positions held by related persons and certain flow-through entities (for example, a partnership). An offsetting-positions transaction also includes a transaction that would be a straddle (taking into account the principles referred to in the preceding sentence) if the straddle definition did not contain the active trading requirement in section 1092(d)(1). For example, an offsetting-positions transaction includes positions in closely held stock or other non-traded personal property and substantially offsetting derivatives.

(3) *Eligible interest.*—(i) *In general.*—For purposes of section 1400Z-2, an *eligible interest* in a QOF is an equity interest issued by the QOF, including preferred stock or a partnership interest with special allocations. Thus, the term eligible interest excludes any debt instrument within the meaning of section 1275(a)(1) and § 1.1275-1(d).

(ii) *Use as collateral permitted.*—Provided that the eligible taxpayer is the owner of the equity interest for Federal income tax purposes, status as an eligible interest is not impaired by using the interest as collateral for a loan, whether as part of a purchase-money borrowing or otherwise.

(iii) *Deemed contributions not constituting investment.*—See § 1.1400Z-2(e)-1(a)(2) for rules regarding deemed contributions of money to a partnership pursuant to section 752(a).

(4) *180-day period.*—(i) *In general.*—Except as otherwise provided elsewhere in this section, the 180-day period referred to in section 1400Z-2(a)(1)(A) with respect to any eligible gain (180-day period) begins on the day on which the gain would be recognized for Federal income tax purposes if the taxpayer did not elect under section 1400Z-2 to defer recognition of that gain.

(ii) *Examples.*—The following examples illustrate the principles of paragraph (b)(4)(i) of this section.

*Example 1. Regular-way trades of stock.* If stock is sold at a gain in a regular-way trade on an exchange, the 180-day period with respect to the gain on the stock begins on the trade date.

*Example 2. Capital gain dividends received by RIC and REIT shareholders.* If an individual RIC or REIT shareholder receives a capital gain dividend (as described in section 852(b)(3) or section

857(b)(3)), the shareholder's 180-day period with respect to that gain begins on the day on which the dividend is paid.

*Example 3. Undistributed capital gains received by RIC and REIT shareholders.* If section 852(b)(3)(D) or section 857(b)(3)(D) (concerning undistributed capital gains) requires the holder of shares in a RIC or REIT to include an amount in the shareholder's long-term capital gains, the shareholder's 180-day period with respect to that gain begins on the last day of the RIC or REIT's taxable year.

*Example 4. Additional deferral of previously deferred gains*—(i) *Facts.* Taxpayer A invested in a QOF and properly elected to defer realized gain. During 2025, taxpayer A disposes of its entire investment in the QOF in a transaction that, under section 1400Z-2(a)(1)(B) and (b), triggers an inclusion of gain in A's gross income. Section 1400Z-2(b) determines the date and amount of the gain included in A's income. That date is the date on which A disposed of its entire interest in the QOF. A wants to elect under section 1400Z-2 to defer the amount that is required to be included in income.

(ii) *Analysis.*—Under paragraph (b)(4)(i) of this section, the 180-day period for making another investment in a QOF begins on the day on which section 1400Z-2(b) requires the prior gain to be included. As prescribed by section 1400Z-2(b)(1)(A), that is the date of the inclusion-triggering disposition. Thus, in order to make a deferral election under section 1400Z-2, A must invest the amount of the inclusion in the original QOF or in another QOF during the 180-day period beginning on the date when A disposed of its entire investment in the QOF.

(5) *Attributes of gains that section 1400Z-2(a)(1)(B) includes in income.*—If section 1400Z-2(a)(1)(B) and (b) require a taxpayer to include in income some or all of a previously deferred gain, the gain so included has the same attributes in the taxable year of inclusion that it would have had if tax on the gain had not been deferred. These attributes include those taken into account by sections 1(h), 1222, 1256, and any other applicable provisions of the Code.

(6) *First-In, First-Out (FIFO) method to identify which interest in a QOF has been disposed of.*— (i) *FIFO requirement.*—If a taxpayer holds investment interests with identical rights (fungible interests) in a QOF that were acquired on different days and if, on a single day, the taxpayer disposes of less than all of these interests, then the first-in-first-out (FIFO) method must be used to identify which interests were disposed of. Fungible interests may be equivalent shares of stock in a corporation or partnership interests with identical rights.

(ii) *Consequences of identification.*—The FIFO method determines—

(A) Whether an investment is described in section 1400Z-2(e)(1)(A)(i)(an invest-

ment to which a gain deferral election under section 1400Z-2(a) applies) or section 1400Z-2(e)(1)(A)(ii) (an investment which was not part of a gain deferral election under section 1400Z-2(a));

(B) In the case of investments described in section 1400Z-2(e)(1)(A)(i), the attributes of the gain subject to a deferral election under section 1400Z-2(a), at the time the gain is included in income (the attributes addressed in paragraph (b)(5) of this section); and

(C) The extent, if any, of an increase under section 1400Z-2(b)(2)(B) in the basis of an investment interest that is disposed of.

(7) *Pro-rata method.*—If, after application of the FIFO method, a taxpayer is treated as having disposed of less than all of the investment interests that the taxpayer acquired on one day and if the interests acquired on that day vary with respect to the characteristics described in paragraph (b)(6)(ii) of this section, then a proportionate allocation must be made to determine which interests were disposed of (pro-rata method).

(8) *Examples.*—The following examples illustrate the rules of paragraph (b)(5) through (7) of this section.

*Example 1. Short-term gain.* For 2018, taxpayer B properly made an election under section 1400Z-2 to defer $100 of gain that, if not deferred, would have been recognized as short-term capital gain, as defined in section 1222(1). In 2022, section 1400Z-2(a)(1)(B) and (b) requires taxpayer B to include the gain in gross income. Under paragraph (b)(5) of this section, the gain included is short-term capital gain.

*Example 2. Collectibles gain.* For 2018, taxpayer C properly made an election under section 1400Z-2 to defer a gain that, if not deferred, would have been collectibles gain as defined in IRC section 1(h)(5). In a later taxable year, section 1400Z-2(a)(1)(B) and (b) requires some or all of that deferred gain to be included in gross income. The gain included is collectibles gain.

*Example 3. Net gains from section 1256 contracts.* For 2019, taxpayer D had $100 of capital gain net income from section 1256 contracts. D timely invested $100 in a QOF and properly made an election under section 1400Z-2 to defer that $100 of gain. In 2023, section 1400Z-2(a)(1)(B) and (b) requires taxpayer D to include that deferred gain in gross income. Under paragraph (b)(5) of this section, the character of the inclusion is governed by section 1256(a)(3) (which requires a 40:60 split between short-term and long-term capital gain). Accordingly, $40 of the inclusion is short-term capital gain and $60 of the inclusion is long-term capital gain.

*Example 4. FIFO method.* For 2018, taxpayer E properly made an election under section 1400Z-2 to defer $300 of short-term capital gain. For 2020, E properly made a second election under section 1400Z-2 to defer $200 of long-term capital gain.

**Prop. Reg. §1.1400Z-2(a)-1(b)(5)**

In both cases, E properly invested in QOF Q the amount of the gain to be deferred. The two investments are fungible interests and the price of the interests was the same at the time of the two investments. E did not purchase any additional interest in QOF Q or sell any of its interest in QOF Q until 2024, when E sold for a gain 60 percent of its interest in QOF Q. Under paragraph (b)(6)(i) of this section, E must apply the FIFO method to identify which investments in QOF Q that E disposed of. As determined by this identification, E sold the entire 2018 initial investment in QOF Q. Under section 1400Z-2(a)(1)(B) and (b), the sale triggered an inclusion of deferred gain. Because the inclusion has the same character as the gain that had been deferred, the inclusion is short-term capital gain.

*Example 5. FIFO method.* In 2018, before Corporation R became a QOF, Taxpayer F invested $100 cash to R in exchange for 100 R common shares. Later in 2018, after R was a QOF, F invested $500 cash to R in exchange for 400 R common shares and properly elected under section 1400Z-2 to defer $500 of independently realized short-term capital gain. Even later in 2018, on different days, F realized $300 of short-term capital gain and $700 of long-term capital gain. On a single day that fell during the 180-day period for both of those gains, F invested $1,000 cash in R in exchange for 800 R common shares and properly elected under section 1400Z-2 to defer the two gains. In 2020, F sold 100 R common shares. Under paragraph (b)(6)(i) of this section, F must apply the FIFO method to identify which investments in R F disposed of. As determined by that identification, F sold the initially acquired 100 R common shares, which were not part of a deferral election under section 1400Z-2. R must recognize gain or loss on the sale of its R shares under the generally applicable Federal income tax rules, but the sale does not trigger an inclusion of any deferred gain.

*Example 6. FIFO method.* The facts are the same as example 5, except that, in addition, during 2021 F sold an additional 400 R common shares. Under paragraph (b)(6)(i) of this section, F must apply the FIFO method to identify which investments in R were disposed of. As determined by this identification, F sold the 400 common shares which were associated with the deferral of $500 of short-term capital gain. Thus, the deferred gain that must be included upon sale of the 400 R common shares is short-term capital gain.

*Example 7. Pro-rata method.* The facts are the same as in examples 5 and 6, except that, in addition, during 2022 F sold an additional 400 R common shares. Under paragraph (b)(6)(i) of this section, F must apply the FIFO method to identify which investments in R were disposed of. In 2022, F is treated as holding only the 800 R common shares purchased on a single day, and the section 1400Z-2 deferral election associated with these shares applies to gain with different characteristics (described in paragraph (b)(6)(ii) of this section). Under paragraph (b)(7) of this section, therefore, R must use the pro-rata method to determine which of the characteristics pertain to the deferred gain required to be included as a result of the sale of the 400 R common shares. Under the pro-rata method, $150 of the inclusion is short-term capital gain ($300 × 400/800) and $350 is long-term capital gain ($700 × 400/800).

(c) *Special rules for pass-through entities.*— (1) *Eligible gains that a partnership elects to defer.*— A partnership is an eligible taxpayer under paragraph (b)(1) of this section and may elect to defer recognition of some or all of its eligible gains under section 1400Z-2(a)(2).

(i) *Partnership election.*—If a partnership properly makes an election under section 1400Z-2(a)(2), then—

(A) The partnership defers recognition of the gain under the rules of section 1400Z-2 (that is, the partnership does not recognize gain at the time it otherwise would have in the absence of the election to defer gain recognition);

(B) The deferred gain is not included in the distributive shares of the partners under section 702 and is not subject to section 705(a)(1); and

(ii) *Subsequent recognition.*—Absent any additional deferral under section 1400Z-2(a)(1)(A), any amount of deferred gain that an electing partnership subsequently must include in income under sections 1400Z-2(a)(1)(B) and (b) is recognized by the electing partnership at the time of inclusion and is subject to sections 702 and 705(a)(1) in a manner consistent with recognition at that time.

(2) *Eligible gains that the partnership does not defer.*—(i) *Tax treatment of the partnership.*—If a partnership does not elect to defer some, or all, of the gains for which it could make a deferral election under section 1400Z-2, the partnership's treatment of any such amounts is unaffected by the fact that the eligible gain could have been deferred under section 1400Z-2.

(ii) *Tax treatment by the partners.*—If a partnership does not elect to defer some, or all, of the gains for which it could make a deferral election under section 1400Z-2—

(A) The gains for which a deferral election are not made are included in the partners' distributive shares under section 702 and are subject to section 705(a)(1);

(B) If a partner's distributive share includes one or more gains that are eligible gains with respect to the partner, the partner may elect under section 1400Z-2(a)(1)(A) to defer some or all of its eligible gains; and

(C) A gain in a partner's distributive share is an eligible gain with respect to the partner only if it is an eligible gain with respect to the partnership and it did not arise from a sale or exchange with a person that, within the meaning of section 1400Z-2(e)(2), is related to the partner.

(iii) *180-day period for a partner electing deferral.*—(A) *General rule.*—If a partner's distributive share includes a gain that is described in paragraph (c)(2)(ii)(C) of this section (gains that are eligible gains with respect to the partner), the 180-day period with respect to the partner's eligible gains in the partner's distributive share generally begins on the last day of the partnership taxable year in which the partner's allocable share of the partnership's eligible gain is taken into account under section 706(a).

(B) *Elective rule.*—Notwithstanding the general rule in paragraph (c)(2)(iii)(A) of this section, if a partnership does not elect to defer all of its eligible gain, the partner may elect to treat the partner's own 180-day period with respect to the partner's distributive share of that gain as being the same as the partnership's 180-day period.

(C) The following example illustrates the principles of this paragraph (c)(2)(iii).

*Example.* Five individuals have identical interests in partnership P, there are no other partners, and P's taxable year is the calendar year. On January 17, 2019, P realizes a capital gain of $1000x that it decides not to elect to defer. Two of the partners, however, want to defer their allocable portions of that gain. One of these two partners invests $200x in a QOF during February 2020. Under the general rule in paragraph (c)(2)(iii)(A) of this section, this investment is within the 180-day period for that partner (which begins on December 31, 2019). The fifth partner, on the other hand, decides to make the election provided in paragraph (c)(2)(iii)(B) of this section and invests $200x in a QOF during February 2019. Under that elective rule, this investment is within the 180-day period for that partner (which begins on January 17, 2019).

(3) *Pass-through entities other than partnerships.*—If an S corporation; a trust; or a decedent's estate recognizes an eligible gain, or would recognize an eligible gain if it did not elect to defer recognition of the gain under section 1400Z-2(a), then rules analogous to the rules of paragraph (c)(1) and (2) of this section apply to that entity and to its shareholders or beneficiaries, as the case may be.

(d) *Elections.*—The Commissioner may prescribe in guidance published in the Internal Revenue Bulletin or in forms and instructions (*see* §§601.601(d)(2) and 601.602 of this chapter), both the time, form, and manner in which an eligible taxpayer may elect to defer eligible gains under section 1400Z-2(a) and also the time, form, and manner in which a partner may elect to apply the elective 180-day period provided in paragraph (c)(2)(iii)(B) of this section.

(e) *Applicability date.*—This section applies to eligible gains that would be recognized in the absence of deferral on or after the date of publication in the **Federal Register** of a Treasury decision adopting these proposed rules as final

regulations. An eligible taxpayer, however, may rely on the proposed rules in this section with respect to eligible gains that would be recognized before that date, but only if the taxpayer applies the rules in their entirety and in a consistent manner. [Reg. § 1.1400Z-2(a)-1.]

[Proposed 10-29-2018.]

### [Prop. Reg. §1.1400Z-2(c)-1]

**§1.1400Z-2(c)-1. Investments held for at least 10 years.**—(a) *Limitation on the 10-year rule.*—As required by section 1400Z-2(e)(1)(B) (treatment of investments with mixed funds), section 1400Z-2(c) (special rule for investments held for at least 10 years) applies only to the portion of an investment in a QOF with respect to which a proper election to defer gain under section 1400Z-2(a)(1) is in effect.

(b) *Extension of availability of the election described in section 1400Z-2(c).*—The ability to make an election under section 1400Z-2(c) for investments held for at least 10 years is not impaired solely because, under section 1400Z-1(f), the designation of one or more qualified opportunity zones ceases to be in effect. The preceding sentence does not apply to elections under section 1400Z-2(c) that are related to dispositions occurring after December 31, 2047.

(c) *Examples.*—The following examples illustrate the principles of paragraphs (a) and (b) of this section.

*Example 1.* (i) *Facts.* In 2020, taxpayer G invests $100 in QOF S in exchange for 100 common shares of QOF S and properly makes an election under section 1400Z-2(a) to defer $100 of gain. G also acquires 200 additional common shares in QOF in exchange for $z. G does not make a section 1400Z-2(a) deferral election with respect to any of the $z investments. At the end of 2028, the qualified opportunity zone designation expires for the population census tract in which QOF S primarily conducts its trade or business. In 2031, G sells all of its 300 QOF S shares, realizes gain, and makes an election to increase the qualifying basis in G's QOF S shares to fair market value. But for the expiration of the designated zones in section 1400Z-1(f), QOF S and G's conduct is consistent with continued eligibility to make the election under section 1400Z-2(c).

(ii) *Analysis.* Under paragraph (b) of this section, although the designation expired on December 31, 2028, the expiration of the zone's designation does not, without more, invalidate G's ability to make an election under section 1400Z-2(c). Accordingly, pursuant to that election, G's basis is increased in the one-third portion of G's investment in QOF S with respect to which G made a proper deferral election under section 1400Z-2(a)(2) (100 common shares / 300 common shares). Under section 1400Z-2(e)(1) and paragraph (a) of this section, however, the election under section 1400Z-2(c) is unavailable for the remaining two-thirds portion of G's investment in QOF S because G did not make a deferral election under section 1400Z-2(a)(2) for this portion of its investment in QOF S (200 common shares / 300 common shares).

(d) *Applicability date.*—This section applies to an election under section 1400Z-2(c) related to dispositions made after the date of publication in the **Federal Register** of a Treasury decision adopting these proposed rules as final regulations. A taxpayer, however, may rely on the proposed rules in this section with respect to dispositions of investment interests in QOFs in situations where the investment was made in connection with an election under section 1400Z-2(a) that relates to the deferral of a gain such that the first day of 180-day period for the gain was before the date of applicability of that section. The preceding sentence applies only if the taxpayer applies the rules of this section in their entirety and in a consistent manner. [Reg. § 1.1400Z-2(c)-1.]

[Proposed 10-29-2018.]

#### [Prop. Reg. § 1.1400Z-2(d)-1]

**§ 1.1400Z-2(d)-1. Qualified Opportunity Funds.**—(a) *Becoming a QOF.*—(1) *Self-certification.*—Except as provided in paragraph (e)(1) of this section, if a taxpayer that is classified as a corporation or partnership for Federal tax purposes is eligible to be a QOF, the taxpayer may self-certify that it is QOF. This section refers to such a taxpayer as an *eligible entity*. The following rules apply to the self-certification:

(i) *Time, form, and manner.*—The self-certification must be effected at such time and in such form and manner as may be prescribed by the Commissioner in IRS forms or instructions or in publications or guidance published in the Internal Revenue Bulletin (*see* §§ 601.601(d)(2) and 601.602 of this chapter).

(ii) *First taxable year.*—The self-certification must identify the first taxable year that the eligible entity wants to be a QOF.

(iii) *First month.*—The self-certification may identify the first month (in that initial taxable year) in which the eligible entity wants to be a QOF.

(A) *Failure to specify first month.*—If the self-certification fails to specify the month in the initial taxable year that the eligible entity first wants to be a QOF, then the first month of the eligible entity's initial taxable year as a QOF is the first month that the eligible entity is a QOF.

(B) *Investments before first month not eligible for deferral.*—If an investment in eligible interests of an eligible entity occurs prior to the eligible entity's first month as a QOF, any election under section 1400Z-2(a)(1) made for that investment is invalid.

(2) *Becoming a QOF in a month that is not the first month of the taxable year.*—If an eligible entity's self-certification as a QOF is first effective for a month that is not the first month of that entity's taxable year—

(i) For purposes of section 1400Z-2(d)(1)(A) and (B) in the first year of the QOF's existence, the phrase *first 6-month period of the taxable year of the fund* means the first 6 months each of which is in the taxable year and in each of which the entity is a QOF. Thus, if an eligible entity becomes a QOF in the seventh or later month of a 12-month taxable year, the 90-percent test in section 1400Z-2(d)(1) takes into account only the QOF's assets on the last day of the taxable year.

(ii) The computation of any penalty under section 1400Z-2(f)(1) does not take into account any months before the first month in which an eligible entity is a QOF.

(3) *Pre-existing entities.*—There is no legal barrier to a pre-existing eligible entity becoming a QOF, but the eligible entity must satisfy all of the requirements of section 1400Z-2 and the regulations thereunder, including the requirements regarding qualified opportunity zone property, as defined in section 1400Z-2(d)(2). In particular, that property must be acquired after December 31, 2017.

(b) *Valuation of assets for purposes of the 90-percent asset test.*—(1) *In general.*—For a taxable year, if a QOF has an applicable financial statement within the meaning of § 1.475(a)-4(h), then the value of each asset of the QOF for purposes of the 90-percent asset test in section 1400Z-2(d)(1) is the value of that asset as reported on the QOF's applicable financial statement for the relevant reporting period.

(2) *QOF without an applicable financial statement.*—If paragraph (b)(1) of this section does not apply to a QOF, then the value of each asset of the QOF for purposes of the 90-percent asset test in section 1400Z-2(d)(1) is the QOF's cost of the asset.

(c) *Qualified opportunity zone property.*—(1) *In general.*—Pursuant to section 1400Z-2(d)(2)(A), the following property is *qualified opportunity zone property:*

(i) Qualified opportunity zone stock as defined in paragraph (c)(2) of this section,

(ii) Qualified opportunity zone partnership interest as defined in paragraph (c)(3) of this section, and

(iii) Qualified opportunity zone business property as defined in paragraph (c)(4) of this section.

(2) *Qualified opportunity zone stock.*—(i) *In general.*—Except as provided in paragraphs (c)(2)(ii) and (e)(2) of this section, if an entity is classified as a corporation for Federal tax purposes (corporation), then an equity interest (stock) in the entity is *qualified opportunity zone stock* if—

(A) The stock is acquired by a QOF after December 31, 2017, at its original issue (directly or through an underwriter) from the corporation solely in exchange for cash,

(B) As of the time the stock was issued, the corporation was a qualified opportunity zone business as defined in section 1400Z-2(d)(3) and paragraph (d) of this section (or, in the case of a new corporation, the corporation was being organized for purposes of being such a qualified opportunity zone business), and

(C) During substantially all of the QOF's holding period for the stock, the corporation qualified as a qualified opportunity zone business as defined in section 1400Z-2(d)(3) and paragraph (d) of this section.

(ii) *Redemptions of stock.*—Pursuant to section 1400Z-2(d)(2)(B)(ii), rules similar to the rules of section 1202(c)(3) apply for purposes of determining whether stock in a corporation qualifies as qualified opportunity zone stock.

(A) *Redemptions from taxpayer or related person.*—Stock acquired by a QOF is not treated as qualified opportunity zone stock if, at any time during the 4-year period beginning on the date 2 years before the issuance of the stock, the corporation issuing the stock purchased (directly or indirectly) any of its stock from the QOF or from a person related (within the meaning of section 267(b) or 707(b)) to the QOF. Even if the purchase occurs after the issuance, the stock was never qualified opportunity zone stock.

(B) *Significant redemptions.*—Stock issued by a corporation is not treated as qualified opportunity zone stock if, at any time during the 2-year period beginning on the date 1 year before the issuance of the stock, the corporation made 1 or more purchases of its stock with an aggregate value (as of the time of the respective purchases) exceeding 5 percent of the aggregate value of all of its stock as of the beginning of the 2-year period. Even if one or more of the disqualifying purchases occurs after the issuance, the stock was never qualified opportunity zone stock.

(C) *Treatment of certain transactions.*—If any transaction is treated under section 304(a) as a distribution in redemption of the stock of any corporation, for purposes of paragraphs (c)(2)(ii)(A) and (B) of this section, that corporation is treated as purchasing an amount of its stock equal to the amount that is treated as such a distribution under section 304(a).

(3) *Qualified opportunity zone partnership interest.*—Except as provided in paragraph (e)(2) of this section, if an entity is classified as a partnership for Federal tax purposes (partnership), any capital or profits interest (partnership interest) in the entity is a *qualified opportunity zone partnership interest* if—

(i) The partnership interest is acquired by a QOF after December 31, 2017, from the partnership solely in exchange for cash,

(ii) As of the time the partnership interest was acquired, the partnership was a qualified

opportunity zone business as defined in section 1400Z-2(d)(3) and paragraph (d) of this section (or, in the case of a new partnership, the partnership was being organized for purposes of being a qualified opportunity zone business), and

(iii) During substantially all of the QOF's holding period for the partnership interest, the partnership qualified as a qualified opportunity zone business as defined in section 1400Z-2(d)(3) and paragraph (d) of this section.

(4) *Qualified opportunity zone business property of a QOF.*—Tangible property used in a trade or business of a QOF is qualified opportunity zone business property for purposes of paragraph (c)(1)(iii) of this section if—

(i) The tangible property satisfies section 1400Z-2(d)(2)(D)(i)(I);

(ii) The original use of the tangible property in the qualified opportunity zone, within the meaning of paragraph (c)(7) of this section, commences with the QOF, or the QOF substantially improves the tangible property within the meaning of paragraph (c)(8) of this section (which defines substantial improvement in this context); and

(iii) During substantially all of the QOF's holding period for the tangible property, substantially all of the use of the tangible property was in a qualified opportunity zone.

(5) *Substantially all of a QOF's holding period for property described in paragraphs (c)(2), (c)(3), and (c)(4) of this section.*—[Reserved].

(6) *Substantially all of the usage of tangible property by a QOF in a qualified opportunity zone.*—[Reserved].

(7) *Original use of tangible property.*—[Reserved].

(8) *Substantial improvement of tangible property.*—(i) *In general.*—Except as provided in paragraph (c)(8)(ii) of this section, for purposes of paragraph (c)(4)(ii) of this section, tangible property is treated as substantially improved by a QOF only if, during any 30-month period beginning after the date of acquisition of the property, additions to the basis of the property in the hands of the QOF exceed an amount equal to the adjusted basis of the property at the beginning of the 30-month period in the hands of the QOF.

(ii) *Special rules for land and improvements on land.*—(A) *Buildings located in the zone.*—If a QOF purchases a building located on land wholly within a QOZ, under section 1400Z-2(d)(2)(D)(ii) a substantial improvement to the purchased tangible property is measured by the QOF's additions to the adjusted basis of the building. Under section 1400Z-2(d), measuring a substantial improvement to the building by additions to the QOF's adjusted basis of the building does not require the QOF to separately substantially improve the land upon which the building is located.

(B) [*Reserved*].

(d) *Qualified opportunity zone business.*—(1) *In general.*—A trade or business is a *qualified opportunity zone business* if—

(i) Substantially all of the tangible property owned or leased by the trade or business is qualified opportunity zone business property as defined in paragraph (d)(2) of this section,

(ii) Pursuant to section 1400Z-2(d)(3)(A)(iii), the trade or business satisfies the requirements of section 1397C(b)(2), (4), and (8) as defined in paragraph (d)(5) of this section, and

(iii) Pursuant to section 1400Z-2(d)(3)(A)(iii), the trade or business is not described in section 144(c)(6)(B) as defined in paragraph (d)(6) of this section.

(2) *Qualified opportunity zone business property of the qualified opportunity zone business for purposes of paragraph (d)(1)(i) of this section.*—(i) *In general.*—The tangible property used in a trade or business of an entity is qualified opportunity zone business property for purposes of paragraph (d)(1)(i) of this section if—

(A) The tangible property satisfies section 1400Z-2(d)(2)(D)(i)(l);

(B) The original use of the tangible property in the qualified opportunity zone commences with the entity or the entity substantially improves the tangible property within the meaning of paragraph (d)(4) of this section (which defines substantial improvement in this context); and

(C) During substantially all of the entity's holding period for the tangible property, substantially all of the use of the tangible property was in a qualified opportunity zone.

(ii) *Substantially all of a qualified opportunity zone business's holding period for property described in paragraph (d)(2)(i)(C) of this section.*—[Reserved].

(iii) *Substantially all of the usage of tangible property by a qualified opportunity zone business in a qualified opportunity zone.*—[Reserved].

(3) *Substantially all requirement of paragraph (d)(1)(i) of this section.*—(i) *In general.*—A trade or business of an entity is treated as satisfying the *substantially all* requirement of paragraph (d)(1)(i) of this section if at least 70 percent of the tangible property owned or leased by the trade or business is qualified opportunity zone business property as defined in paragraph (d)(2) of this section.

(ii) *Calculating percent of tangible property owned or leased in a trade or business.*—(A) *In general.*—If an entity has an applicable financial statement within the meaning of § 1.475(a)-4(h), then the value of each asset of the entity as reported on the entity's applicable financial statement for the relevant reporting period is used for determining whether a trade or business of the entity satisfies the first sentence of paragraph (d)(3)(i) of this section (concerning

whether the trade or business is a qualified opportunity zone business).

(B) *Entity without an applicable financial statement.*—If paragraph (d)(3)(ii)(A) of this section does not apply to an entity and a taxpayer both holds an equity interest in the entity and has self-certified as a QOF, then that taxpayer may value the entity's assets using the same methodology under paragraph (b) of this section that the taxpayer uses for determining its own compliance with the 90-percent asset requirement of section 1400Z-2(d)(1) (Compliance Methodology), provided that no other equity holder in the entity is a Five-Percent Zone Taxpayer. If paragraph (d)(3)(ii)(A) of this section does not apply to an entity and if two or more taxpayers that have self-certified as QOFs hold equity interests in the entity and at least one of them is a Five-Percent Zone Taxpayer, then the values of the entity's assets may be calculated using the Compliance Methodology that both is used by a Five-Percent Zone Taxpayer and that produces the highest percentage of qualified opportunity zone business property for the entity.

(C) *Five Percent Zone Taxpayer.*—A *Five-Percent Zone Taxpayer* is a taxpayer that has self-certified as a QOF and that holds stock in the entity (if it is a corporation) representing at least 5 percent in voting rights and value or holds an interest of at least 5 percent in the profits and capital of the entity (if it is a partnership).

(iii) *Example.*—The following example illustrates the principles of paragraph (d)(3)(ii) of this section.

*Example.* Entity ZS is a corporation that has issued only one class of stock and that conducts a trade or business. Taxpayer X holds 94% of the ZS stock, and Taxpayer Y holds the remaining 6% of that stock. (Thus, both X and Y are Five Percent Zone Taxpayers within the meaning of paragraph (d)(3)(ii)(C) of this section.) ZS does not have an applicable financial statement, and, for that reason, a determination of whether ZS is conducting a qualified opportunity zone business may employ the Compliance Methodology of X or Y. X and Y use different Compliance Methodologies permitted under paragraph (d)(3)(ii) (B) of this section for purposes of satisfying the 90-percent asset test of section 1400Z-2(d)(1). Under X's Compliance Methodology (which is based on X's applicable financial statement), 65% of the tangible property owned or leased by ZS's trade or business is qualified opportunity zone business property. Under Y's Compliance Methodology (which is based on Y's cost), 73% of the tangible property owned or leased by ZS's trade or business is qualified opportunity zone business property. Because Y's Compliance Methodology would produce the higher percentage of qualified opportunity zone business property for ZS (73%), both X and Y may use Y's Compliance Methodology to value ZS's owned or leased tangible property. If ZS's trade or business satisfies all additional requirements in section 1400Z-2(d)(3), the trade or business is a qualified opportunity zone business. Thus, if all of the additional requirements in section 1400Z-2(d)(2)(B) are satisfied, stock in ZS is qualified opportunity zone stock in the hands of a taxpayer that has self-certified as a QOF.

(4) *Substantial improvement of tangible property for purposes of paragraph (d)(2)(i)(B) of this section.*—(i) *In general.*—Except as provided in paragraph (d)(4)(ii) of this section, for purposes of paragraph (d)(2)(i)(B) of this section, tangible property is treated as substantially improved by a qualified opportunity zone business only if, during any 30-month period beginning after the date of acquisition of such tangible property, additions to the basis of such tangible property in the hands of the qualified opportunity zone business exceed an amount equal to the adjusted basis of such tangible property at the beginning of such 30-month period in the hands of the qualified opportunity zone business.

(ii) *Special rules for land and improvements on land.*—(A) *Buildings located in the zone.*—If a QOF purchases a building located on land wholly within a QOZ, under section 1400Z-2(d)(2)(D)(ii) a substantial improvement to the purchased tangible property is measured by the QOF's additions to the adjusted basis of the building. Under section 1400Z-2(d), measuring a substantial improvement to the building by additions to the QOF's adjusted basis of the building does not require the QOF to separately substantially improve the land upon which the building is located.

(B) [*Reserved*].

(5) *Operation of section 1397C requirements incorporated by reference.*—(i) *Gross income requirement.*—Section 1400Z-2(d)(3)(A)(iii) incorporates section 1397C(b)(2), requiring that for each taxable year at least 50 percent of the gross income of a qualified opportunity zone business is derived from the active conduct of a trade or business in the qualified opportunity zone.

(ii) *Use of intangible property requirement.*—(A) *In general.*—Section 1400Z-2(d)(3) incorporates section 1397C(b)(4), requiring that, with respect to any taxable year, a substantial portion of the intangible property of an opportunity zone business is used in the active conduct of a trade or business in the qualified opportunity zone.

(B) *Active conduct of a trade or business.*—[Reserved].

(iii) *Nonqualified financial property limitation.*—Section 1400Z-2(d)(3) incorporates section 1397C(b)(8), limiting in each taxable year the average of the aggregate unadjusted bases of the property of a qualified opportunity zone business that may be attributable to nonqualified financial property. Section 1397C(e)(1), which defines the term *nonqualified financial property* for

purposes of section 1397C(b)(8), excludes from that term reasonable amounts of working capital held in cash, cash equivalents, or debt instruments with a term of 18 months or less (working capital assets).

(iv) *Safe harbor for reasonable amount of working capital.*—Solely for purposes of applying section 1397C(e)(1) to the definition of a qualified opportunity zone business under section 1400Z-2(d)(3), working capital assets are treated as reasonable in amount for purposes of sections 1397C(b)(2) and 1400Z-2(d)(3)(A)(ii), if all of the following three requirements are satisfied:

(A) *Designated in writing.*—These amounts are designated in writing for the acquisition, construction, and/or substantial improvement of tangible property in a qualified opportunity zone, as defined in section 1400Z-1(a).

(B) *Reasonable written schedule.*—There is a written schedule consistent with the ordinary start-up of a trade or business for the expenditure of the working capital assets. Under the schedule, the working capital assets must be spent within 31 months of the receipt by the business of the assets.

(C) *Property consumption consistent.*—The working capital assets are actually used in a manner that is substantially consistent with paragraph (d)(5)(iv)(A) and (B) of this section.

(v) *Safe harbor for gross income derived from the active conduct of business.*—Solely for purposes of applying the 50-percent test in section 1397C(b)(2) to the definition of a qualified opportunity zone business in section 1400Z-2(d)(3), if any gross income is derived from property that paragraph (d)(5)(iv) of this section treats as a reasonable amount of working capital, then that gross income is counted toward satisfaction of the 50-percent test.

(vi) *Safe harbor for use of intangible property.*—Solely for purposes of applying the use requirement in section 1397C(b)(4) to the definition of a qualified opportunity zone business under section 1400Z-2(d)(3), the use requirement is treated as being satisfied during any period in which the business is proceeding in a manner that is substantially consistent with paragraphs (d)(5)(iv)(A) through (C) of this section.

(vii) *Safe harbor for property on which working capital is being expended.*—If paragraph (d)(5)(iv) of this section treats some financial property as being a reasonable amount of working capital because of compliance with the three requirements of paragraph (d)(5)(iv)(A)-(C) and if the tangible property referred to in paragraph (d)(5)(iv)(A) is expected to satisfy the requirements of section 1400Z-2(d)(2)(D)(1) as a result of the planned expenditure of those working capital assets, then that tangible property is not treated as failing to satisfy those requirements solely because the scheduled consumption of the working capital is not yet complete.

(viii) *Example.*—The following example illustrates the rules of this paragraph (d)(5):

(i) *Facts.* In 2019, Taxpayer H realized $w million of capital gains and within the 180-day period invested $w million in QOF T, a qualified opportunity fund. QOF T immediately acquired from partnership P a partnership interest in P, solely in exchange for $w million of cash. P immediately placed the $w million in working capital assets, which remained in working capital assets until used. P had written plans to acquire land in a qualified opportunity zone on which it planned to construct a commercial building. Of the $w million, $x million was dedicated to the land purchase, $y million to the construction of the building, and $z million to ancillary but necessary expenditures for the project. The written plans provided for purchase of the land within a month of receipt of the cash from QOF T and for the remaining $y and $z million to be spent within the next 30 months on construction of the building and on the ancillary expenditures. All expenditures were made on schedule, consuming the $w million. During the taxable years that overlap with the first 31-month period, P had no gross income other than that derived from the amounts held in those working capital assets. Prior to completion of the building, P's only assets were the land it purchased, the unspent amounts in the working capital assets, and P's work in process as the building was constructed.

(ii) *Analysis of construction*—(A) P met the three requirements of the safe harbor provided in paragraph (d)(5)(iv) of this section. P had a written plan to spend the $w received from QOF T for the acquisition, construction, and/or substantial improvement of tangible property in a qualified opportunity zone, as defined in section 1400Z-1(a). P had a written schedule consistent with the ordinary start-up for a business for the expenditure of the working capital assets. And, finally, P's working capital assets were actually used in a manner that was substantially consistent with its written plan and the ordinary start-up of a business. Therefore, the $x million, the $y million, and the $z million are treated as reasonable in amount for purposes of sections 1397C(b)(2) and 1400Z-2(d)(3)(A)(ii).

(B) Because P had no other gross income during the 31 months at issue, 100 percent of P's gross income during that time is treated as derived from an active trade or business in the qualified opportunity zone for purposes of satisfying the 50-percent test of section 1397C(b)(2).

(C) For purposes of satisfying the requirement of section 1397C(b)(4), during the period of land acquisition and building construction a substantial portion of P's intangible property is treated as being used in the active conduct of a trade or business in the qualified opportunity zone.

(D) All of the facts described are consistent with QOF T's interest in P being a qualified opportunity zone partnership interest for purposes of satisfying the 90-percent test in section 1400Z-2(d)(1).

(iii) *Analysis of substantial improvement.* The above conclusions would also apply if P's plans had been to buy and substantially improve a pre-existing commercial building. In addition, the fact that P's basis in the building has not yet doubled does not cause the building to fail to satisfy section 1400Z-2(d)(2)(D)1)(III).

(6) *Trade or businesses described in section 144(c)(6)(B) not eligible.*—Pursuant to section 1400Z-2(d)(3)(A)(iii), the following trades or businesses described in section 144(c)(6)(B) cannot qualify as a qualified opportunity zone business:

(i) Any private or commercial golf course,

(ii) Country club,

(iii) Massage parlor,

(iv) Hot tub facility,

(v) Suntan facility,

(vi) Racetrack or other facility used for gambling, or

(vii) Any store the principal business of which is the sale of alcoholic beverages for consumption off premises.

(e) *Exceptions based on where an entity is created, formed, or organized.*—(1) *QOFs.*—If a partnership or corporation (an entity) is not organized in one of the 50 states, the District of Columbia, or the U.S. possessions, it is ineligible to be a QOF. If an entity is organized in a U.S. possession but not in one of the 50 States or the District of Columbia, it may be a QOF only if it is organized for the purpose of investing in qualified opportunity zone property that relates to a trade or business operated in the U.S. possession in which the entity is organized.

(2) *Entities that can issue qualified opportunity zone stock or qualified opportunity zone partnership interests.*—If an entity is not organized in one of the 50 states, the District of Columbia, or the U.S. possessions, an equity interest in the entity is neither qualified opportunity zone stock nor a qualified opportunity zone partnership interest. If an entity is organized in a U.S. possession but not in one of the 50 States or the District of Columbia, an equity interest in the entity may be qualified opportunity zone stock or a qualified opportunity zone partnership interest, as the case may be, only if the entity conducts a qualified opportunity zone business in the U.S. possession in which the entity is organized. An entity described in the preceding sentence is treated as satisfying the "domestic" requirement in section 1400Z-2(d)(2)(B)(i) or section 1400Z-2(C)(i).

(3) *U.S. possession defined.*—For purposes of this paragraph (e), a U.S. possession means any

jurisdiction other than the 50 States and the District of Columbia where a designated qualified opportunity zone exists under section 1400Z-1.

(f) *Applicability date.*—This section applies for QOF taxable years that begin on or after the date of publication in the **Federal Register** of a Treasury decision adopting these proposed rules as final regulations. A QOF, however, may rely on the proposed rules in this section with respect to taxable years that begin before the date of applicability of this section, but only if the QOF applies the rules in their entirety and in a consistent manner. [Reg. 1.1400Z-2(d)-1.]

[Proposed 10-29-2018.]

### [Prop. Reg. § 1.1400Z-2(e)-1]

**§ 1.1400Z-2(e)-1. Applicable rules.**— (a) *Treatment of investments with mixed funds.*— (1) *Investments to which no election under section 1400Z-2(a) applies.*—If a taxpayer invests money in a QOF and does not make an election under section 1400Z-2(a) with respect to that investment, the investment is one described in section 1400Z-2(e)(1)(A)(ii)(a separate investment to which section 1400Z-2(a), (b), and (c) do not apply).

(2) *Treatment of deemed contributions of money under 752(a).*—In the case of a QOF classified as a partnership for Federal income tax purposes, the deemed contribution of money described in section 752(a) does not create or increase an investment in the fund described in section 1400Z-2(e)(1)(A)(ii). Thus, any basis increase resulting from a deemed section 752(a) contribution is not taken into account in determining the portion of a partner's investment subject to section 1400Z-2(e)(1)(A)(i) or (ii).

(3) *Example.*—The following example illustrates the rules of this paragraph (a):

(i) Taxpayer A owns a 50 percent capital interest in Partnership P. Under section 1400Z-2(e)(1), 90 percent of A's investment is described in section 1400Z-2(e)(1)(A)(i) (an investment that only includes amounts to which the election under section 1400Z-2(a) applies), and 10 percent is described in section 1400Z-2(e)(1)(A)(ii) (a separate investment consisting of other amounts). Partnership P borrows $8 million. Under section 752 and the regulations thereunder, taking into account the terms of the partnership agreement, $4 million of the $8 million liability is allocated to A. Under section 752(a), A is treated as contributing $4 million to Partnership P. Under paragraph (2) of this section, A's deemed $4 million contribution to Partnership P is ignored for purposes of determining the percentage of A's investment in Partnership P subject to the deferral election under section 1400Z-2(a) or the portion not subject to such the deferral election under section 1400Z-2(a). As a result, after A's section 752(a) deemed contribution, 90 percent of A's investment in Partnership P is described in section 1400Z-2(e)(1)(A)(i) and

10 percent is described in section 1400Z-2(e)(1)(A)(ii).

(ii) [Reserved]

(b) [*Reserved*].

(c) *Applicability date.*—This section applies to investments in, and deemed contributions of money to, a QOF that occur on or after the date of publication in the **Federal Register** of a Treasury decision adopting these proposed rules as final regulations. An eligible taxpayer, however, may rely on the proposed rules in this section with respect to investments, and deemed contributions, before the date of applicability of this section, but only if the taxpayer applies the rules in their entirety and in a consistent manner. [Reg. § 1.1400Z-2(e)-1.]

[Proposed 10-29-2018.]

### [Prop. Reg. § 1.1473-1]

**§ 1.1473-1. Section 1473 definitions.**— (a) *Definition of withholdable payment.*—(1) *In general.*—Except as otherwise provided in this paragraph (a) and § 1.1471-2(b) (regarding grandfathered obligations), the term *withholdable payment* means any payment of U.S. source FDAP income (as defined in paragraph (a)(2) of this section).

\* \* \*

(3) [Reserved]

(4) \* \* \*

(iii) *Excluded nonfinancial payments.*—Payments for the following: services (including wages and other forms of employee compensation (such as stock options)), the use of property, office and equipment leases, software licenses, transportation, freight, gambling winnings, awards, prizes, scholarships, interest on outstanding accounts payable arising from the acquisition of goods or services, and premiums for insurance contracts that do not have cash value (as defined in § 1.1471-5(b)(3)(vii)(B)). Notwithstanding the preceding sentence, excluded nonfinancial payments do not include the following: payments in connection with a lending transaction (including loans of securities), a forward, futures, option, or notional principal contract, or a similar financial instrument; premiums for cash value insurance contracts or annuity contracts; amounts paid under cash value insurance or annuity contracts; dividends; interest (including substitute interest described in § 1.861-2(a)(7)) other than interest described in the preceding sentence; investment advisory fees; custodial fees; and bank or brokerage fees.

\* \* \*

[Proposed 12-18-2018.]

### [Prop. Reg. § 1.1502-2]

**§ 1.1502-2. Computation of tax liability.**— (a) *Taxes imposed.*—The tax liability of a group for a consolidated return year is determined by adding together—

(1) The tax imposed by section 11(a) in the amount described in section 11(b) on the consolidated taxable income for the year (reduced by the taxable income of a member described in paragraphs (a)(5) through (8) of this section);

(2) The tax imposed by section 541 on the consolidated undistributed personal holding company income;

(3) If paragraph (a)(2) of this section does not apply, the aggregate of the taxes imposed by section 541 on the separate undistributed personal holding company income of the members which are personal holding companies;

(4) If neither paragraph (a)(2) nor (3) of this section apply, the tax imposed by section 531 on the consolidated accumulated taxable income (see § 1.1502–43);

(5) The tax imposed by section 594(a) in lieu of the taxes imposed by section 11 on the taxable income of a life insurance department of the common parent of a group which is a mutual savings bank;

(6) The tax imposed by section 801 on consolidated life insurance company taxable income;

(7) The tax imposed by section 831(a) on consolidated insurance company taxable income of the members which are subject to such tax;

(8) Any increase in tax described in section 1351(d)(1) (relating to recoveries of foreign expropriation losses); and

(9) The tax imposed by section 59A on base erosion payments of taxpayers with substantial gross receipts.

(b) *Credits.*—A group is allowed as a credit against the taxes described in paragraph (a) (except for paragraph (a)(9) of this section) of this section: the general business credit under section 38 (see § 1.1502-3), the foreign tax credit under section 27 (see § 1.1502-4), and any other applicable credits provided under the Internal Revenue Code. Any increase in tax due to the recapture of a tax credit will be taken into account. See section 59A and the regulations thereunder for credits allowed against the tax described in paragraph (a)(9) of this section.

(c) *Allocation of dollar amounts.*—For purposes of this section, if a member or members of the consolidated group are also members of a controlled group that includes corporations that are not members of the consolidated group, any dollar amount described in any section of the Internal Revenue Code is apportioned among all members of the controlled group in accordance with the provisions of the applicable section and the regulations thereunder.

(d) *Applicability date.*—(1) Except as provided in paragraph (d)(2) of this section, this section applies to any consolidated return year for which the due date of the income tax return (without regard to extensions) is on or after the date of publication of the Treasury Decision adopting these rules as final regulations in the **Federal Register**.

(2) Paragraph (a)(9) of this section applies to consolidated return years beginning after December 31, 2017.
[Proposed 12-21-2018.]

**[Prop. Reg. § 1.1502-4]**

**§ 1.1502-4. Consolidated foreign tax credit.**

\* \* \*

(d) \* \* \*

(3) *Computation of tax against which credit is taken.*—The tax against which the limiting fraction under section 904(a) is applied will be the consolidated tax liability of the group determined under § 1.1502-2, but without regard to paragraphs (a)(2), (3), (4), (8), and (9) of that section, and without regard to any credit against such liability.

\* \* \*

[Proposed 12-21-2018.]

**[Prop. Reg. § 1.1502-12]**

**§ 1.1502-12. Separate taxable income.**

\* \* \*

(s) See § 1.1502-51 for rules relating to the computation of a member's GILTI inclusion amount under section 951A and related basis adjustments.
[Proposed 10-10-2018.]

**[Prop. Reg. § 1.1502-13]**

**§ 1.1502-13. Intercompany transactions.**

\* \* \*

(f) \* \* \*

(7) \* \* \*

*Example 4.* \* \* \*

(c) *Application of § 1.1502-51(c)(5) to all cash intercompany reorganization under section 368(a)(1)(D).*—The facts are the same as in paragraph (a) of this *Example 4*, except that S's sole asset is stock of a controlled foreign corporation, within the meaning of section 957, with respect to which S has a net used tested loss amount (within the meaning of § 1.1502-51(e)(15)) of $15. As in paragraph (b) of this *Example 4*, S is treated as receiving additional B stock with a fair market value of $100 (in lieu of the $100) and, under section 358, a basis of $25 which S distributes to M in liquidation. Immediately after the sale, pursuant to § 1.1502-51(c)(5), the basis in the B stock received by M is reduced by $15 (the amount of the net used tested loss amount with respect to the controlled foreign corporation) to $10. Following the basis reduction pursuant to § 1.1502-51(c)(5), the B stock (with the exception of the nominal share which is still held by M) received by M is treated as redeemed for $100, and the redemption is treated under section 302(d) as a distribution to which section 301 applies. M's basis of $10 in the B stock is reduced under § 1.1502-32(b)(3)(v), resulting in an excess loss account of $90 in the nominal share. (See § 1.302-2(c).) M's deemed distribution of the nominal share of B stock to P under §1.368-2(l) will result in M generating an intercompany gain under section 311(b) of $90, to be subsequently taken into account under the matching and acceleration rules.

* * *

[Proposed 10-10-2018.]

### [Prop. Reg. §1.1502-13]

**§1.1502-13. Intercompany transactions.—** (a) * * *

(6) * * *

(ii) * * *

*Matching rule. (§1.1502-13(c)(7)(ii))*

* * *

(R) Example 18. Transfer of partnership interests in an intercompany sale.

(S) Example 19. Intercompany transfer of partnership interests in a non-recognition transaction.

* * *

*Anti-avoidance rules. (§1.1502-13(h)(2))*

* * *

(vi) Example 6. Section 163 interest limitation.

* * *

(c) * * *

(7) * * *

(ii) * * *

(R) *Example 18: Transfer of partnership interests in an intercompany sale—(1) Facts.* P wholly owns S and B, both of which are members of the consolidated group of which P is the common parent. S and A (an unrelated third party) are equal partners in PS1, which was formed in Year 1. At the end of Year 1, the fair market value of PS1 is $200x, and S's adjusted basis in its partnership interest is $100x. During Year 2, PS1 borrows money, pays $100x of business interest expense, and repays the debt. PS1's section 163(j) limitation is $0; thus, the $100x of Year 2 business interest expense is disallowed as a deduction to PS1, is characterized as excess business interest expense, and is allocated proportionally to PS1's partners. S reduces its basis in its PS1 interest under §1.163(j)-6(h) to reflect the $50x of excess business interest expense allocated to S, but the reduction is not treated as a noncapital, nondeductible expense (see §1.163(j)-4(d)(4)(ii)). On the last day of Year 2, S sells its PS1 partnership interest to B for $50x. S has not used any of the excess business interest expense allocated from PS1; thus, immediately before the sale, S's basis in its PS1 interest is increased by $50x (to $100x) under §1.163(j)-6(h). This basis increase is not treated as tax-exempt income (see §1.163(j)-4(d)(4)(ii)). During Year 3, PS1 earns $50x of income, all of which is reported to the partners as excess taxable income, and $25x of which is allocated to B. B's basis in its PS1 interest is increased accordingly. Additionally, during Year 3, B earns $25x of business interest income and has no business interest expense other than its allocation of business interest ex-

pense from PS1. At the close of business on the last day of Year 4, B sells its PS1 partnership interest to Z (an unrelated third party) for $85x. At the time of the sale, B's basis in its PS1 interest is $75x.

*(2) Definitions.* Under paragraph (b)(1) of this section, S's sale of its PS1 interest to B in Year 2 is an intercompany transaction, with S as the selling member and B as the buying member. S's $50x capital loss on the sale is an intercompany item within the meaning of paragraph (b)(2)(i) of this section. B's $25 of ordinary income in Year 3 and its $10x gain on the sale of the PS1 interest to Z in Year 4 are both corresponding items within the meaning of paragraph (b)(3)(i) of this section.

*(3) Timing and attributes.* S takes its $50x loss into account to reflect the difference in each consolidated return year between B's corresponding items taken into account for the year and the recomputed corresponding item for the year. If S and B were divisions of a single corporation and the intercompany sale were a transfer between divisions, the single entity would have had zero income inclusion in Year 3, as the $25x of excess taxable income attributable to the single entity's interest in PS1 would have allowed the single entity to use $25x of the excess business interest expense allocation from PS1 in Year 2. However, on a separate entity basis, B's corresponding item for Year 3 is $25x of ordinary income (the excess taxable income from PS1). As a result, under §1.1502-13(c)(ii), S takes into account $25x of its loss in Year 3, the difference between the recomputed corresponding item and B's corresponding item in Year 3 ($0 - $25x = - $25x). Under paragraphs (c)(1)(i) and (c)(4)(i)(A) of this section, the $25x is redetermined to be ordinary. The remaining $25x of S's loss continues to be deferred. The recomputed corresponding item in Year 4 is a $15x capital loss ($85x of sales proceeds minus $100x basis (the original $100x basis, minus a $50 reduction in basis under §1.163(j)-6(h), plus a $25x increase for its allocable share of PS1's income, plus a $25x increase under §1.163(j)-6(h)). B's corresponding item is a $10x capital gain ($85x sales proceeds minus $75x basis). Accordingly, the remaining $25x of S's $50x Year 2 capital loss is taken into account in Year 4.

(S) *Example 19: Intercompany transfer of partnership interests in a nonrecognition transaction—(1) Facts.* P wholly owns B, which is a member of the consolidated group of which P is the common parent. P and A (an unrelated third party) are equal partners in PS1, which was formed in Year 1. At the end of Year 1, the fair market value of PS1 is $200x, and P's adjusted basis in its partnership interest is $100x. At the beginning of Year 2, PS1 borrows money and purchases inventory. During Year 2, PS1 pays $100x of business interest expense, sells inventory for $100x (net of cost of goods sold), and repays the debt in full. PS1's section 163(j) limitation for Year 2 is $30x (30 percent x $100x). Thus, $70x of PS1's Year 2 business interest expense is disallowed as a deduction to PS1, is characterized as excess business interest, and is allocated proportionally to PS1's partners. P reduces its basis in its PS1 interest under § 1.163(j)-6(h) to reflect the $35x of excess business interest allocated to P. P's basis in its PS1 interest also is increased to reflect the $35x of income allocated to P, leaving P with a basis in its PS1 interest of $100x at the end of Year 2. On the first day of Year 3, P contributes its PS1 partnership interest to B in exchange for B stock in a non-recognition exchange under section 351. At the time, P had not used any of the excess business interest expense allocated from PS1. During Year 4, B sells its PS1 partnership interest to Z (an unrelated third party) for $200x.

(2) *Analysis.* P's transfer of its interest in PS1 to B is an intercompany transaction. The transfer also is a disposition for purposes of § 1.163(j)-6(h). Therefore, immediately before the transfer, P increases its $100x basis in its PS1 interest by $35x (the amount of P's unused excess business interest expense). Under section 362, B receives a carryover basis of $135x in the PS1 interest. P has no intercompany item, but B's $65x of capital gain from its sale of the PS1 interest to Z is a corresponding item because the PS1 interest was acquired in an intercompany transaction. B takes the $65x of capital gain into account in Year 4.

\* \* \*

(h) \* \* \*

(2) \* \* \*

(vi) *Example 6: Section163(j) interest limitation*—(A) *Facts.* S1 and S2 are members of a consolidated group of which P is the common parent. S1 is engaged in an excepted trade or business, and S2 is engaged in a non-excepted trade or business. If S1 were to lend funds directly to S2 in an intercompany transaction, under § 1.163(j)-10(a)(4)(i), the intercompany obligation of S2 would not be considered an asset of S1 for purposes of § 1.163(j)-10 (concerning allocations of interest and other taxable items between excepted and non-excepted trades or businesses for purposes of section 163(j)). With a principal purpose of avoiding treatment of a lending transaction between S1 and S2 as an intercompany transaction (and increasing the P group's basis in its assets allocable to excepted trades or businesses), S1 lends funds to X (an unrelated third party). X then on-lends funds to S2 on substantially similar terms.

(B) *Analysis.* A principal purpose of the steps undertaken was to avoid treatment of a lending transaction between S1 and S2 as an intercompany transaction. Therefore, under paragraph (h)(1) of this section, appropriate adjustments are made, and the X obligation in the hands of S1 is not treated as an asset of S1 for purposes of § 1.163(j)-10, to the extent of the loan from X to S2.

\* \* \*

[Proposed 12-28-2018.]

**[Prop. Reg. § 1.1502-21]**

**§ 1.1502-21.  Net operating losses.**

\* \* \*

(d) *Cross-reference.*—For rules governing the application of a SRLY limitation to business interest expense for which a deduction is disallowed under section 163(j), see § 1.163(j)-5(d) and (f).

\* \* \*

[Proposed 12-28-2018.]

**[Prop. Reg. § 1.1502-32]**

**§ 1.1502-32.  Investment adjustments.**

\* \* \*

(b) \* \* \*

(3) \* \* \*

(ii) \* \* \*

(E) *Adjustment for the offset tested income amount of a controlled foreign corporation in relation to section 951A.*—S's tax-exempt income for a taxable year includes the aggregate of S's offset tested income amounts (within the meaning of § 1.1502-51(c)(3)) with respect to a controlled foreign corporation (within the meaning of section 957) for all of its U.S. shareholder inclusion years (within the meaning of § 1.951A-1(e)(4)), to the extent such aggregate does not exceed the excess (if any) of—

(1) The aggregate of S's used tested loss amounts (within the meaning of § 1.1502-51(c)(2)) with respect to the controlled foreign corporation for all of its U.S. shareholder inclusion years, over

(2) The aggregate of S's offset tested income amounts with respect to the controlled foreign corporation for all of its U.S. shareholder inclusion years previously treated as tax-exempt income pursuant to this paragraph.

(F) *Adjustment for the net offset tested income amount of a controlled foreign corporation in relation to section 951A.*—S will be treated as having tax-exempt income immediately prior to a transaction (*recognition event*) in which another member of the group recognizes income, gain, deduction, or loss with respect to a share of S's stock to the extent provided in this paragraph (b)(3)(ii)(F). S's tax-exempt income is equal to the portion of the allocable amount that would have been characterized as a dividend to which section 245A, but not section 1059, would have applied if the allocable amount had been distributed by a controlled foreign corporation to the owner of the transferred shares immediately before the recognition event. For purposes of this paragraph—

(1) The term *transferred shares* means the shares of a[Proposed 12-28-2018.] controlled foreign corporation that S owns within the meaning of section 958(a) or is considered to own by applying the rules of ownership of sec-

tion 958(b) and that are indirectly transferred as part of the recognition event; and

(2) The term *allocable amount* means the net offset tested income amount (within the meaning of §1.1502-51(e)(14)) allocable to the transferred shares.

(iii) * * *

(C) *Adjustment for the used tested loss amount of a controlled foreign corporation in relation to section 951A.*—S's noncapital, nondeductible expense includes its amount of used tested loss amount (within the meaning of §1.1502-51(c)(2)) with respect to a controlled foreign corporation (within the meaning of section 957) for a U.S. shareholder inclusion year (within the meaning of §1.951A-1(e)(4)).

* * *

(j) *Applicability date.*—(1) *In general.*—Paragraph (b)(4)(iv) of this section applies to any original consolidated Federal income tax return due (without extensions) after June 14, 2007. For original consolidated Federal income tax returns due (without extensions) after May 30, 2006, and on or before June 14, 2007, see §1.1502-32T as contained in 26 CFR part 1 in effect on April 1, 2007. For original consolidated Federal income tax returns due (without extensions) on or before May 30, 2006, see §1.1502-32 as contained in 26 CFR part 1 in effect on April 1, 2006.

(2) *Adjustment for the offset tested income amount, net offset tested income amount, and used tested loss amount of a controlled foreign corporation.*—Paragraphs (b)(3)(ii)(E), (b)(3)(ii)(F), and (b)(3)(iii)(C) of this section apply to any consolidated Federal income tax return for a taxable year in which or with which the taxable year of a controlled foreign corporation beginning after December 31, 2017, ends.

* * *

[Proposed 10-10-2018.]

### [Prop. Reg. §1.1502-36]

### §1.1502-36. Unified loss rule.

* * *

(f) * * *

(2) * * * Such provisions include, for example, sections 163(j), 267(f), and 469, and §1.1502-13. * * *

* * *

(h) *Applicability date.*—(1) *In general.*—* * *

(2) *Definition in paragraph (f)(2) of this section.*—Paragraph (f)(2) of this section applies to taxable years ending after the date of the Treasury decision adopting these regulations as final regulations is published in the **Federal Register**. For taxable years ending before the date of the Treasury decision adopting these regulations as final regulations is published in the **Federal Register**, see §1.1502-36 as contained in 26 CFR part 1, revised April 1, 2018. However, taxpayers and their related parties, within the meaning of sec-

tions 267(b) and 707(b)(1), may apply the rules of this section to a taxable year beginning after December 31, 2017, so long as the taxpayers and their related parties consistently apply the rules of this section, the section 163(j) regulations (within the meaning of §1.163(j)-1(b)(32)), and if applicable, §§1.263A-9, 1.381(c)(20)-1, 1.469-9, 1.882-5, 1.1502-13, 1.1502-21, 1.1502-79, 1.1502-91 through 1.1502-99 (to the extent they effectuate the rules of §§1.382-6 and 1.383-1), and 1.1504-4 to those taxable years.

[Proposed 12-28-2018.]

### [Prop. Reg. §1.1502-43]

### §1.1502-43. Consolidated accumulated earnings tax.

* * *

(b) * * *

(2) * * *

(i) * * *

(A) The consolidated liability for tax determined without §1.1502-2(a)(2) through (a)(4), and without the foreign tax credit provided by section 27, over

* * *

[Proposed 12-21-2018.]

### [Prop. Reg. §1.1502-47]

### §1.1502-47. Consolidated returns by life-nonlife groups.

* * *

(f) * * *

(7) * * *

(iii) Any taxes described in §1.1502-2 (other than by paragraphs (a)(1) and (d)(6) of that section).

* * *

[Proposed 12-21-2018.]

### [Prop. Reg. §1.1502-51]

### §1.1502-51. Consolidated section 951A.—
(a) *In general.*—This section provides rules for applying section 951A and §§1.951A-1 through 1.951A-7 (the *section 951A regulations*) to each member of a consolidated group (each, a *member*) that is a United States shareholder of any controlled foreign corporation. Paragraph (b) describes the inclusion of the GILTI inclusion amount by a member of a consolidated group. Paragraph (c) modifies the rules provided in §1.951A-6(e) for adjustments to basis related to used tested loss amount. Paragraph (d) provides rules governing basis adjustments to member stock resulting from the application of §1.951A-6(e) and paragraph (c) of this section. Paragraph (e) provides definitions for purposes of this section. Paragraph (f) provides examples illustrating the rules of this section. Paragraph (g) provides an applicability date.

(b) *Calculation of the GILTI inclusion amount for a member of a consolidated group.*—Each member who is a United States shareholder of any controlled foreign corporation includes in gross income in the U.S. shareholder inclusion year the member's GILTI inclusion amount, if any, for the U.S. shareholder inclusion year. See section 951A(a) and § 1.951A-1(b). The GILTI inclusion amount of a member for a U.S. shareholder inclusion year is the excess (if any) of the member's net CFC tested income for the U.S. shareholder inclusion year, over the member's net deemed tangible income return for the U.S. shareholder inclusion year, determined using the definitions provided in paragraph (e) of this section.

(c) *Adjustments to basis related to used tested loss amount.*—(1) *In general.*—The adjusted basis of the section 958(a) stock of a controlled foreign corporation that is owned (directly or indirectly) by a member (*specified stock*) or an interest in a foreign entity other than a controlled foreign corporation by reason of which a domestic corporation owns (within the meaning of section 958(a)(2)) stock of a controlled foreign corporation is adjusted immediately before its disposition pursuant to § 1.951A-6(e). The amount of the adjustment is determined using the rules provided in paragraphs (c)(2), (3), and (4) of this section.

(2) *Determination of used tested loss amount.*— For purposes of the section 951A regulations and this section, the term *used tested loss amount* means, with respect to a member and a tested loss CFC for a U.S. shareholder inclusion year—

(i) In the case of the consolidated group tested income equaling or exceeding the consolidated group tested loss for a U.S. shareholder inclusion year, the member's pro rata share (determined under § 1.951A-1(d)(4)) of the tested loss of the tested loss CFC for the U.S. shareholder inclusion year.

(ii) In the case of the consolidated group tested income being less than the consolidated group tested loss for a U.S. shareholder inclusion year, the amount that bears the same ratio to the member's pro rata share (determined under § 1.951A-1(d)(4)) of the tested loss of the tested loss CFC for the U.S. shareholder inclusion year as the consolidated group tested income for the U.S. shareholder inclusion year bears to the consolidated group tested loss for the U.S. shareholder inclusion year.

(3) *Determination of offset tested income amount.*—For purposes of the section 951A regulations and this section, the term *offset tested income amount* means, with respect to a member and a tested income CFC for a U.S. shareholder inclusion year—

(i) In the case of the consolidated group tested income exceeding the consolidated group tested loss for a U.S. shareholder inclusion year, the amount that bears the same ratio to the member's pro rata share (determined under § 1.951A-1(d)(2)) of the tested income of the tested income CFC for the U.S. shareholder inclusion year as the consolidated group tested

loss for the U.S. shareholder inclusion year bears to the consolidated group tested income for the U.S. shareholder inclusion year.

(ii) In the case of the consolidated group tested income equaling or being less than the consolidated group tested loss for a U.S. shareholder inclusion year, the member's pro rata share (determined under § 1.951A-1(d)(2)) of the tested income of the tested income CFC for the U.S. shareholder inclusion year.

(4) *Special rule for disposition by a controlled foreign corporation less than 100 percent owned by a single domestic corporation.*—For purposes of determining the application of § 1.951A-6(e)(7), the amount of stock in the controlled foreign corporation a member owns, within the meaning of section 958(a), includes any stock that the member is considered as owning by applying the rules of ownership of section 958(b).

(5) *Special rule for intercompany nonrecognition transactions.*—If a member engages in a nonrecognition transaction (within the meaning of section 7701(a)(45)), with another member in which stock of a controlled foreign corporation that has a net used tested loss amount is directly transferred, the adjusted basis of the nonrecognition property (within the meaning of section 358) received in the nonrecognition transaction is immediately reduced by the amount of the net used tested loss amount. In cases of intercompany transactions that are governed by § 1.368-2(l), the reduction in basis pursuant to this paragraph (c)(5) is made prior to the application of § 1.1502-13(f)(3). See § 1.1502-13(f)(7), Example 4(c).

(d) *Adjustments to the basis of a member.*—For adjustments to the basis of a member related to paragraph (c) of this section, see § 1.1502-32(b)(3)(ii)(E), (b)(3)(ii)(F), and (b)(3)(iii)(C).

(e) *Definitions.*—The following definitions apply for purposes of the section—

(1) *Aggregate tested income.*—With respect to a member, the term *aggregate tested income* means the aggregate of the member's pro rata share (determined under § 1.951A-1(d)(2)) of the tested income of each tested income CFC for a U.S. shareholder inclusion year.

(2) *Aggregate tested loss.*—With respect to a member, the term *aggregate tested loss* means the aggregate of the member's pro rata share (determined under § 1.951A-1(d)(4)) of the tested loss of each tested loss CFC for a U.S. shareholder inclusion year.

(3) *Allocable share.*—The term *allocable share* means, with respect to a member that is a United States shareholder and a U.S. shareholder inclusion year—

(i) With respect to consolidated group QBAI, the product of the consolidated group

QBAI of the member's consolidated group and the member's GILTI allocation ratio.

(ii) With respect to consolidated group specified interest expense, the product of the consolidated group specified interest expense of the member's consolidated group and the member's GILTI allocation ratio.

(iii) With respect to consolidated group tested loss, the product of the consolidated group tested loss of the member's consolidated group and the member's GILTI allocation ratio.

(4) *Consolidated group QBAI.*—With respect to a consolidated group, the term *consolidated group QBAI* means the sum of each member's pro rata share (determined under §1.951A-1(d)(3)) of the qualified business asset investment of each tested income CFC for a U.S. shareholder inclusion year.

(5) *Consolidated group specified interest expense.*—With respect to a consolidated group, the term *consolidated group specified interest expense* means the excess (if any) of—

(i) The sum of each member's pro rata share (determined under §1.951A-1(d)(5)) of the tested interest expense of each controlled foreign corporation for the U.S. shareholder inclusion year, over

(ii) The sum of each member's pro rata share (determined under §1.951A-1(d)(6)) of the tested interest income of each controlled foreign corporation for the U.S. shareholder inclusion year.

(6) *Consolidated group tested income.*—With respect to a consolidated group, the term *consolidated group tested income* means the sum of each member's aggregate tested income for a U.S. shareholder inclusion year.

(7) *Consolidated group tested loss.*—With respect to a consolidated group, the term *consolidated group tested loss* means the sum of each member's aggregate tested loss for a U.S. shareholder inclusion year.

(8) *Controlled foreign corporation.*—The term *controlled foreign corporation* means a controlled foreign corporation as defined in section 957.

(9) *Deemed tangible income return.*—With respect to a member, the term *deemed tangible income return* means 10 percent of the member's allocable share of the consolidated group QBAI.

(10) *GILTI allocation ratio.*—With respect to a member, the term *GILTI allocation ratio* means the ratio of—

(i) The aggregate tested income of the member for a U.S. shareholder inclusion year, to

(ii) The consolidated group tested income of the consolidated group of which the member is a member for the U.S. shareholder inclusion year.

(11) *GILTI inclusion amount.*—With respect to a member, the term *GILTI inclusion amount* has

the meaning provided in paragraph (b) of this section.

(12) *Net CFC tested income.*—With respect to a member, the term *net CFC tested income* means the excess (if any) of—

(i) The member's aggregate tested income, over

(ii) The member's allocable share of the consolidated group tested loss.

(13) *Net deemed tangible income return.*—With respect to a member, the term *net deemed tangible income return* means the excess (if any) of the member's deemed tangible income return over the member's allocable share of the consolidated group specified interest expense.

(14) *Net offset tested income amount.*—The term *net offset tested income amount* means, with respect to a member and a controlled foreign corporation, the excess (if any) of the amount described in paragraph (e)(15)(ii) of this section over the amount described in paragraph (e)(15)(i) of this section.

(15) *Net used tested loss amount.*—The term *net used tested loss amount* means, with respect to a member and a controlled foreign corporation, the excess (if any) of —

(i) The aggregate of the member's pro rata share of each used tested loss amount of the controlled foreign corporation for each U.S. shareholder inclusion year over

(ii) The aggregate of the member's pro rata share of each offset tested income amount of the controlled foreign corporation for each U.S. shareholder inclusion year.

(16) *Offset tested income amount.*—The term *offset tested income amount* has the meaning provided in paragraph (c)(3) of this section.

(17) *Qualified business asset investment.*—The term *qualified business asset investment* has the meaning provided in §1.951A-3(b).

(18) *Tested income.*—The term *tested income* has the meaning provided in §1.951A-2(b)(1).

(19) *Tested income CFC.*—The term *tested income CFC* has the meaning provided in §1.951A-2(b)(1).

(20) *Tested interest expense.*—The term *tested interest expense* has the meaning provided in §1.951A-4(b)(1).

(21) *Tested interest income.*—The term *tested interest income* has the meaning provided in §1.951A-4(b)(2).

(22) *Tested loss.*—The term *tested loss* has the meaning provided in §1.951A-2(b)(2).

(23) *Tested loss CFC.*—The term *tested loss CFC* has the meaning provided in §1.951A-2(b)(2).

(24) *United States shareholder.*—The term *United States shareholder* has the meaning provided in § 1.951-1(g)(1).

(25) *U.S. shareholder inclusion year.*—The term *U.S. shareholder inclusion year* has the meaning provided in § 1.951A-1(e)(4).

(26) *Used tested loss amount.*—The term *used tested loss amount* has the meaning provided in paragraph (c)(2) of this section.

(f) *Examples.*—The following examples illustrate the rules of this section. For purposes of the examples in this section, unless otherwise stated: P is the common parent of the P consolidated group; P owns all of the single class of stock of subsidiaries USS1, USS2, and USS3, all of whom are members of the P consolidated group; CFC1, CFC2, CFC3, and CFC4 are all controlled foreign corporations (within the meaning of paragraph (e)(8) of this section); and the taxable year of all persons is the calendar year.

(1) *Example 1: calculation of net CFC tested income within a consolidated group when all CFCs are wholly owned by a member*—(i) *Facts.* USS1 owns all of the single class of stock of CFC1. USS2 owns all of the single class of stock of each of CFC2 and CFC3. USS3 owns all of the single class of stock of CFC4. In Year 1, CFC1 has tested loss of $100, CFC2 has tested income of $200x, CFC3 has tested loss of $200x, and CFC4 has tested income of $600x. Neither CFC2 nor CFC4 has qualified business asset investment in Year 1.

(ii) *Analysis*—(A) *Consolidated group tested income and GILTI allocation ratio.* USS1 has no aggregate tested income; USS2's aggregate tested income is $200x, its pro rata share (within the meaning of § 1.951A-1(d)(2)) of CFC2's tested income; and USS3's aggregate tested income is $600x, its pro rata share (within the meaning of § 1.951A-1(d)(2)) of CFC4's tested income. Therefore, under paragraph (e)(6) of this section, the P consolidated group's consolidated group tested income is $800x ($200x + $600x). As a result, the GILTI allocation ratios of USS1, USS2, and USS3 are 0 ($0/$800x), 0.25 ($200x/$800x), and 0.75 ($600x/$800x), respectively.

(B) *Consolidated group tested loss.* Under paragraph (e)(7) of this section, the P consolidated group's consolidated group tested loss is $300x ($100x + $200x), the aggregate of USS1's aggregate tested loss, which is equal to its pro rata share (within the meaning of § 1.951A-1(d)(4)) of CFC1's tested loss ($100x), and USS2's aggregate tested loss, which is equal to its pro rata share (within the meaning of § 1.951A-1(d)(4)) of CFC3's tested loss ($200x). Under paragraph (e)(3)(iii) of this section, a member's allocable share of the consolidated group tested loss is the product of the consolidated group tested loss of the member's consolidated group and the member's GILTI allocation ratio. Therefore, the allocable shares of the consolidated group tested loss of USS1, USS2, and USS3 are $0 (0 x $300x), $75x (0.25 x $300x), and $225x (0.75 x $300x), respectively.

(C) *Calculation of net CFC tested income.* Under paragraph (e)(12) of this section, a member's net CFC tested income is the excess (if any) of the member's aggregate tested income over the member's allocable share of the consolidated group tested loss. As a result, USS1's, USS2's, and USS3's net CFC tested income amounts are $0 ($0 - $0), $125x ($200x - $75x), and $375x ($600x - $225x), respectively.

(2) *Example 2: calculation of net CFC tested income within a consolidated group when ownership of a tested loss CFC is split between members*—(i) *Facts.* The facts are the same as in paragraph (i) of *Example 1*, except that USS2 and USS3 each own 50% of the single class of stock of CFC3.

(ii) *Analysis.* As in paragraph (ii) of *Example 1*, USS1 has no aggregate tested income and a GILTI allocation ratio of 0, USS2 has $200x of aggregate tested income and a GILTI allocation ratio of 0.25, and USS3 has $600x of aggregate tested income and a GILTI allocation ratio of 0.75. Additionally, the P consolidated group's consolidated group tested loss is $300x (the aggregate of USS1's aggregate tested loss, which is equal to its pro rata share (within the meaning of § 1.951A-1(d)(4)) of CFC1's tested loss ($100x); USS2's aggregate tested loss, which is equal to its pro rata share (within the meaning of § 1.951A-1(d)(4)) of CFC3's tested loss ($100x); and USS3's aggregate tested loss, which is equal to its pro rata share (within the meaning of § 1.951A-1(d)(4)) of CFC3's tested loss ($100x)). As a result, under paragraph (e)(12) of this section, as in paragraph (ii)(C) of *Example 1*, USS1's, USS2's, and USS3's net CFC tested income amounts are $0 ($0 - $0), $125x ($200x - $75x), and $375x ($600x - $225x), respectively.

(3) *Example 3: calculation of GILTI inclusion amount*—(i) *Facts.* The facts are the same as in paragraph (i) of *Example 1*, except that CFC2 and CFC4 have qualified business asset investment of $500x and $2000x, respectively, for Year 1. In Year 1, CFC1 and CFC4 each have tested interest expense (within the meaning of § 1.951A-4(b)(1)) of $25x, and CFC1, CFC2, CFC3, and CFC4 have $0 of tested interest income (within the meaning of § 1.951A-4(b)(2)). CFC1's tested loss of $100x and CFC4's tested income of $600x take into account the interest paid.

(ii) *Analysis*—(A) *GILTI allocation ratio.* As in paragraph (ii) of *Example 1*, the GILTI allocation ratios of USS1, USS2, and USS3 are 0 ($0/$800x), 0.25 ($200x/$800x), and 0.75 ($600x/$800x), respectively.

(B) *Consolidated group QBAI.* Under paragraph (e)(4) of this section, the P consolidated group's consolidated group QBAI is $2,500x ($500x + $2,000x), the aggregate of USS2's pro rata share (determined under § 1.951A-1(d)(3)) of the qualified business asset investment of CFC2 and USS3's pro rata share (determined under § 1.951A-1(d)(3)) of the qualified business asset investment of CFC4. Under paragraph (e)(3)(i) of this section, a member's allocable share of consolidated group QBAI is the product of the consolidated group QBAI of the member's consolidated group and the member's GILTI allocation ratio. Therefore, the allocable shares of the consolidated group QBAI of each of USS1, USS2, and USS3 are $0 (0 x $2,500x), $625x (0.25 x $2,500x), and $1,875x (0.75 x $2,500x), respectively.

(C) *Consolidated group specified interest expense—(1) Pro rata share of tested interest expense.* USS1's pro rata share of the tested interest expense of CFC1 is $25x, the amount by which the tested interest expense increases USS1's pro rata share of CFC1's tested loss (from $75x to $100x) for Year 1. USS3's pro rata share of the tested interest expense of CFC4 is also $25x, the amount by which the tested interest expense decreases USS1's pro rata share of CFC4's tested income (from $625x to $600x). See § 1.951A-1(d)(5).

(2) *Consolidated group specified interest expense.* Under paragraph (e)(5) of this section, the P consolidated group's consolidated group specified interest expense is $50x, the excess of the sum of each member's pro rata share of the tested interest expense of each controlled foreign corporation ($50x, $25x from USS1 + $25x from USS3), over the sum of each member's pro rata share of tested interest income ($0). Under paragraph (e)(3)(ii) of this section, a member's allocable share of consolidated group specified interest expense is the product of the consolidated group specified interest expense of the member's consolidated group and the member's GILTI allocation ratio. Therefore, the allocable shares of consolidated group specified interest expense of USS1, USS2, and USS3 are $0 (0 x $50x), $12.50x (0.25 x $50x), and $37.50x (0.75 x $50x), respectively.

(D) *Calculation of deemed tangible income return.* Under paragraph (e)(9) of this section, a member's deemed tangible income return means 10 percent of the member's allocable share of the consolidated group QBAI. As a result, USS1's, USS2's, and USS3's deemed tangible income returns are $0 (0.1 x $0), $62.50x (0.1 x $625x), and $187.50x (0.1 x $1,875x), respectively.

(E) *Calculation of net deemed tangible income return.* Under paragraph (e)(13) of this section, a member's net deemed tangible income return means the excess (if any) of a member's deemed tangible income return over the member's allocable share of the consolidated group specified interest. As a result, USS1's, USS2's, and USS3's net deemed tangible income returns are $0 ($0 - $0), $50x ($62.50x - $12.50x), and $150x ($187.50x - $37.50x), respectively.

(F) *Calculation of GILTI inclusion amount.* Under paragraph (b) of this section, a member's GILTI inclusion amount for a U.S. shareholder inclusion year is the excess (if any) of the member's net CFC tested income for the U.S. shareholder inclusion year, over the shareholder's net deemed tangible income return for the U.S. shareholder inclusion year. As described in paragraph (ii)(C) of *Example 1*, the amounts of USS1's, USS2's, and USS3's net CFC tested in-

come are $0, $125x, and $375x, respectively. As described in paragraph (ii)(E) of this *Example 3*, the amounts of USS1's, USS2's, and USS3's net deemed tangible income return are $0, $50x, and $150x, respectively. As a result, under paragraph (b) of this section, USS1's, USS2's, and USS3's GILTI inclusion amounts are $0 ($0 - $0), $75x ($125x - $50x), and $225x ($375x - $150x), respectively.

(G) *Calculation of used tested loss amount and offset tested income amount.* As described in paragraph (ii)(A) of *Example 1*, P consolidated group's consolidated group tested income is $800x. As described in paragraph (ii)(B) of *Example 1*, P consolidated group's consolidated group tested loss is $300x. Therefore, the P consolidated group's consolidated group tested income exceeds its consolidated group tested loss. As a result, USS1 has a $100x used tested loss amount with respect to CFC1 and USS2 has a $200x used tested loss amount with respect to CFC3. Additionally, USS2 has a $75x offset tested income amount with respect to CFC2 ($200x x $300x/$800x) and USS3 has a $225x offset tested income amount with respect to CFC3 ($600x x $300x/$800x). See paragraph (c) of this section. P will adjust its basis in USS1 and USS2 pursuant to the rule in § 1.1502-32(b)(3)(iii)(C).

(g) *Applicability date.*—This section applies to taxable years of foreign corporations beginning after December 31, 2017, and to taxable years of United States shareholders in which or with which such taxable years of foreign corporations end. [Reg. § 1.1502-51.]

[Proposed 10-10-2018.]

### [Prop. Reg. § 1.1502-59A]

**§ 1.1502-59A. Payment and returns of tax withheld by the acquiring agency.**— (a) *Scope.*—This section provides rules for the application of section 59A and the regulations thereunder (the *section 59A regulations*, see §§ 1.59A-1 through 1.59A-10) to consolidated groups and their members (as defined in § 1.1502-1(h) and (b), respectively). Rules in the section 59A regulations apply to consolidated groups except as modified in this section. Paragraph (b) of this section provides rules treating a consolidated group (rather than each member of the group) as a single taxpayer, and a single applicable taxpayer, as relevant, for certain purposes. Paragraph (c) of this section coordinates the application of the business interest stacking rule under § 1.59A-3(c)(4) to consolidated groups. Paragraph (d) of this section addresses how the base erosion minimum tax amount is allocated among members of the consolidated group. Paragraph (e) of this section sets forth definitions. Paragraph (f) of this section provides examples. Paragraph (g) of this section provides the applicability date and a transition rule.

(b) *Consolidated group as the applicable taxpayer.*—(1) *In general.*—For purposes of determining whether the consolidated group is an applicable taxpayer (within the meaning of §1.59A-2(b)) and the amount of tax due pursuant to section 59A(a), all members of a consolidated group are treated as a single taxpayer. Thus, for example, members' deductions are aggregated in making the required computations under section 59A. In addition, items resulting from intercompany transactions (as defined in §1.1502-13(b)(1)(i)) are disregarded for purposes of making the required computations. For example, additional depreciation deductions resulting from intercompany asset sales are not taken into account for purposes of applying the base erosion percentage test under §1.59A-2(e).

(2) *Consolidated group as member of the aggregate group.*—The consolidated group is treated as a single member of an aggregate group for purposes of §1.59A-2(c).

(3) *Related party determination.*—For purposes of section 59A and the section 59A regulations, if a person is a related party with respect to any member of a consolidated group, that person is a related party of the group and of each of its members.

(c) *Coordination of section 59A(c)(3) and section 163(j) in a consolidated group.*—(1) *Overview.*— This paragraph (c) provides rules regarding the application of §1.59A-3(c)(4) to a consolidated group's section 163(j) interest deduction. The classification rule in paragraph (c)(3) of this section addresses how to determine if, and to what extent, the group's section 163(j) interest deduction is a base erosion tax benefit. These regulations contain a single-entity classification rule with regard to the deduction of the consolidated group's aggregate current year business interest expense ("BIE"), but a separate-entity classification rule for the deduction of the consolidated group's disallowed BIE carryforwards. Paragraph (c)(3) of this section classifies the group's aggregate current year BIE deduction, in conformity with §1.59A-3(c)(4), as constituting domestic related current year BIE deduction, foreign related current year BIE deduction, or unrelated current year BIE deduction. The allocation rules in paragraph (c)(4) of this section then allocate to specific members of the group the domestic related current year BIE deduction, foreign related current year BIE deduction, and unrelated current year BIE deduction taken in the taxable year. Any member's current year BIE that is carried forward to the succeeding taxable year as a disallowed BIE carryforward is allocated a status as domestic related BIE carryforward, foreign related BIE carryforward, or unrelated BIE carryforward under paragraph (c)(5) of this section. The status of any disallowed BIE carryforward deducted by a member in a later year is classified on a separate-entity basis by the deducting member under paragraph (c)(3) of this section, based on the status allocated to the member's disallowed BIE carryforward under paragraph (c)(5) of this section. This paragraph (c) also provides rules regarding the

consequences of the deconsolidation of a corporation that has been allocated a domestic related BIE carryforward status, a foreign related BIE carryforward status, or an unrelated BIE carryforward status; and the consolidation of a corporation with a disallowed BIE carryforward classified as from payments to a domestic related party, foreign related party, or unrelated party.

(2) *Absorption rule for the group's business interest expense.*—To determine the amount of the group's section 163(j) interest deduction, and to determine the year in which the member's business interest expense giving rise to the deduction was incurred or accrued, see §§1.163(j)-4(d) and 1.163(j)-5(b)(3).

(3) *Classification of the group's section 163(j) interest deduction.*—(i) *In general.*—Consistent with §1.59A-3(c)(4)(i) and paragraph (b) of this section, the classification rule of this paragraph (c)(3) determines whether the consolidated group's section 163(j) interest deduction is a base erosion tax benefit. To the extent the consolidated group's business interest expense is permitted as a deduction under section 163(j)(1) in a taxable year, the deduction is classified first as from business interest expense paid or accrued to a foreign related party and business interest expense paid or accrued to a domestic related party (on a pro-rata basis); any remaining deduction is treated as from business interest expense paid or accrued to an unrelated party.

(ii) *Year-by-year application of the classification rule.*—If the consolidated group's section 163(j) interest deduction in any taxable year is attributable to business interest expense paid or accrued in more than one taxable year (for example, the group deducts the group's aggregate current year BIE, the group's disallowed BIE carryforward from year 1, and the group's disallowed BIE carryforward from year 2), the classification rule in paragraph (c)(3)(i) of this section applies separately to each of those years, pursuant to paragraphs (c)(3)(iii) and (iv) of this section.

(iii) *Classification of current year BIE deductions.*—Current year BIE deductions are classified under the section 59A regulations and this paragraph (c) as if the consolidated group were a single taxpayer that had paid or accrued the group's aggregate current year BIE to domestic related parties, foreign related parties, and unrelated parties. The rules of paragraph (c)(4) of this section apply for allocating current year BIE deductions among members of the consolidated group. To the extent the consolidated group's aggregate current year BIE exceeds its section 163(j) limitation, the rules of paragraph (c)(5) of this section apply.

(iv) *Classification of deductions of disallowed BIE carryforwards.*—Each member of the group applies the classification rule in this paragraph (c)(3) to its deduction of any part of a disallowed

BIE carryforward from a year, after the group applies paragraph (c)(5) of this section to the consolidated group's disallowed BIE carryforward from that year. Therefore, disallowed BIE carryforward that is actually deducted by a member is classified based on the status of the components of that carryforward, assigned pursuant to paragraph (c)(5) of this section.

(4) *Allocation of domestic related current year BIE deduction status and foreign related current year BIE deduction status among members of the consolidated group.*—(i) *In general.*—This paragraph (c)(4) applies if the group has domestic related current year BIE deductions, foreign related current year BIE deductions, or both, as a result of the application of the classification rule in paragraph (c)(3) of this section. Under this paragraph (c)(4), the domestic related current year BIE, foreign related current year BIE, or both, that is treated as deducted in the current year are deemed to have been incurred pro-rata by all members that have current year BIE deduction in that year, regardless of which member or members actually incurred the current year BIE to a domestic related party or a foreign related party.

(ii) *Domestic related current year BIE deduction.*—(A) *Amount of domestic related current year BIE deduction status allocable to a member.*—The amount of domestic related current year BIE deduction status that is allocated to a member is determined by multiplying the group's domestic related current year BIE deduction (determined pursuant to paragraph (c)(3) of this section) by the percentage of current year BIE deduction allocable to such member in that year.

(B) *Percentage of current year BIE deduction allocable to a member.*—The percentage of current year BIE deduction allocable to a member is equal to the amount of the member's current year BIE deduction divided by the amount of the group's aggregate current year BIE deduction.

(iii) *Amount of foreign related current year BIE deduction status allocable to a member.*—The amount of foreign related current year BIE deduction status that is allocated to a member is determined by multiplying the group's foreign related current year BIE deduction (determined pursuant to paragraph (c)(3) of this section) by the percentage of current year BIE deduction allocable to such member (defined in paragraph (c)(4)(ii)(B) of this section).

(iv) *Treatment of amounts as having unrelated current year BIE deduction status.*—To the extent the amount of a member's current year BIE that is absorbed under paragraph (c)(2) of this section exceeds the domestic related current year BIE deduction status and foreign related current year BIE deduction status allocated to the member under paragraph (c)(4)(ii) and (iii) of this section, such excess amount is treated as from payments or accruals to an unrelated party.

(5) *Allocation of domestic related BIE carryforward status and foreign related BIE carryforward status to members of the group.*—(i) *In general.*—This paragraph (c)(5) applies in any year the consolidated group's aggregate current year BIE exceeds its section 163(j) limitation. After the application of paragraph (c)(4) of this section, any remaining domestic related current year BIE, foreign related current year BIE, and unrelated current year BIE is deemed to have been incurred pro-rata by members of the group pursuant to the rules in paragraph (c)(5)(ii), (iii), and (iv) of this section, regardless of which member or members actually incurred the business interest expense to a domestic related party, foreign related party, or unrelated party.

(ii) *Domestic related BIE carryforward.*—(A) *Amount of domestic related BIE carryforward status allocable to a member.*—The amount of domestic related BIE carryforward status that is allocated to a member equals the group's domestic related BIE carryforward from that year multiplied by the percentage of disallowed BIE carryforward allocable to the member.

(B) *Percentage of disallowed BIE carryforward allocable to a member.*—The percentage of disallowed BIE carryforward allocable to a member for a taxable year equals the member's disallowed BIE carryforward from that year divided by the consolidated group's disallowed BIE carryforwards from that year.

(iii) *Amount of foreign related BIE carryforward status allocable to a member.*—The amount of foreign related BIE carryforward status that is allocated to a member equals the group's foreign related BIE carryforward from that year multiplied by the percentage of disallowed BIE carryforward allocable to the member (as defined in paragraph (c)(5)(ii)(B) of this section).

(iv) *Treatment of amounts as having unrelated BIE carryforward status.*—If a member's disallowed BIE carryforward for a year exceeds the amount of domestic related BIE carryforward status and foreign related BIE carryforward status that is allocated to the member pursuant to paragraphs (c)(5)(ii) and (iii) of this section, respectively, the excess carryforward amount is treated as from payments or accruals to an unrelated party.

(v) *Coordination with section 381.*—If a disallowed BIE carryforward is allocated a status as a domestic related BIE carryforward, foreign related BIE carryforward, or unrelated BIE carryforward under the allocation rule of paragraph (c)(5) of this section, the acquiring corporation in a transaction described in section 381(a) will succeed to and take into account the allocated status of the carryforward for purposes of section 59A. See § 1.381(c)(20)-1.

(6) *Member deconsolidates from a consolidated group.*—When a member deconsolidates from a

group (the original group), the member's disallowed BIE carryforwards retain their allocated status, pursuant to paragraph (c)(5) of this section, as a domestic related BIE carryforward, foreign related BIE carryforward, or unrelated BIE carryforward (as applicable). Following the member's deconsolidation, no other member of the original group is treated as possessing the domestic related BIE carryforward status, foreign related BIE carryforward status, or unrelated BIE carryforward status that is carried forward by the departing member.

(7) *Corporation joins a consolidated group.*—If a corporation joins a consolidated group (the acquiring group), and that corporation was allocated a domestic related BIE carryforward status, foreign related BIE carryforward status, or unrelated BIE carryforward status pursuant to paragraph (c)(5) of this section from another consolidated group (the original group), or separately has a disallowed BIE carryforward that is classified as from payments or accruals to a domestic related party, foreign related party, or unrelated party, the status of the carryforward is taken into account in determining the acquiring group's base erosion tax benefit when the corporation's disallowed BIE carryforward is absorbed.

(d) *Allocation of the base erosion minimum tax amount to members of the consolidated group.*—For rules regarding the allocation of the base erosion minimum tax amount, see section 1552. Allocations under section 1552 take into account the classification and allocation provisions of paragraphs (c)(3) through (5) of this section.

(e) *Definitions.*—The following definitions apply for purposes of this section –

(1) *Aggregate current year BIE.*—The consolidated group's *aggregate current year BIE* is the aggregate of all members' current year BIE.

(2) *Aggregate current year BIE deduction.*— The consolidated group's *aggregate current year BIE deduction* is the aggregate of all members' current year BIE deductions.

(3) *Applicable taxpayer.*—The term *applicable taxpayer* has the meaning provided in § 1.59A-2(h).

(4) *Base erosion minimum tax amount.*—The consolidated group's *base erosion minimum tax amount* is the tax imposed under section 59A.

(5) *Base erosion tax benefit.*—The term *base erosion tax benefit* has the meaning provided in § 1.59A-3(c)(1).

(6) *Business interest expense.*—The term *business interest expense*, with respect to a member and a taxable year, has the meaning provided in § 1.163(j)-1(b)(2), and with respect to a consolidated group and a taxable year, has the meaning provided in § 1.163(j)-4(d)(2)(iii).

(7) *Consolidated group's disallowed BIE carryforwards.*—The term *consolidated group's disallowed BIE carryforwards* has the meaning provided in § 1.163(j)-5(b)(3)(i).

(8) *Current year BIE.*—A member's *current year BIE* is the member's business interest expense that would be deductible in the current taxable year without regard to section 163(j) and that is not a disallowed business interest expense carryforward from a prior taxable year.

(9) *Current year BIE deduction.*—A member's *current year BIE deduction* is the member's current year BIE that is permitted as a deduction in the taxable year.

(10) *Domestic related BIE carryforward.*—The consolidated group's *domestic related BIE carryforward* for any taxable year is the excess of the group's domestic related current year BIE over the group's domestic related current year BIE deduction (if any).

(11) *Domestic related current year BIE.*—The consolidated group's *domestic related current year BIE* for any taxable year is the consolidated group's aggregate current year BIE paid or accrued to a domestic related party.

(12) *Domestic related current year BIE deduction.*—The consolidated group's *domestic related current year BIE deduction* for any taxable year is the portion of the group's aggregate current year BIE deduction classified as from interest paid or accrued to a domestic related party under paragraph (c)(3) of this section.

(13) *Domestic related party.*—A *domestic related party* is a related party that is not a foreign related party and is not a member of the same consolidated group.

(14) *Disallowed BIE carryforward.*—The term *disallowed BIE carryforward* has the meaning provided in § 1.163(j)-1(b)(9).

(15) *Foreign related BIE carryforward.*—The consolidated group's *foreign related BIE carryforward* for any taxable year, is the excess of the group's foreign related current year BIE over the group's foreign related current year BIE deduction (if any).

(16) *Foreign related current year BIE.*—The consolidated group's *foreign related current year BIE* for any taxable year is the consolidated group's aggregate current year BIE paid or accrued to a foreign related party.

(17) *Foreign related current year BIE deduction.*—The consolidated group's *foreign related current year BIE deduction* for any taxable year is the portion of the consolidated group's aggregate current year BIE deduction classified as from interest paid or accrued to a foreign related party under paragraph (c)(3) of this section.

**Prop. Reg. § 1.1502-59A(e)(17)**

(18) *Foreign related party.*—A *foreign related party* has the meaning provided in §1.59A-1(b)(12).

(19) *Related party.*—The term *related party* has the meaning provided in §1.59A-1(b)(17), but excludes members of the same consolidated group.

(20) *Section 163(j) interest deduction.*—The term *section 163(j) interest deduction* means, with respect to a taxable year, the amount of the consolidated group's business interest expense permitted as a deduction pursuant to §1.163(j)-5(b)(3) in the taxable year.

(21) *Section 163(j) limitation.*—The term *section 163(j) limitation* has the meaning provided in §1.163(j)-1(b)(31).

(22) *Unrelated BIE carryforward.*—The consolidated group's *unrelated BIE carryforward* for any taxable year is the excess of the group's unrelated current year BIE over the group's unrelated current year BIE deduction.

(23) *Unrelated current year BIE.*—The consolidated group's *unrelated current year BIE* for any taxable year is the consolidated group's aggregate current year BIE paid or accrued to an unrelated party.

(24) *Unrelated current year BIE deduction.*—The consolidated group's *unrelated current year BIE deduction* for any taxable year is the portion of the group's aggregate current year BIE deduction classified as from interest paid or accrued to an unrelated party under paragraph (c)(3) of this section.

(25) *Unrelated party.*—An *unrelated party* is a party that is not a related party.

(f) *Examples.*—The following examples illustrate the general application of this section. For purposes of the examples, a foreign corporation (FP) wholly owns domestic corporation (P), which in turn wholly owns S1 and S2. P, S1, and S2 are members of a consolidated group. The consolidated group is a calendar year taxpayer.

(1) *Example 1: Computation of the consolidated group's base erosion minimum tax amount.* (i) *The consolidated group is the applicable taxpayer.* (A) *Facts.* The members have never engaged in intercompany transactions. For the 2019 taxable year, P, S1, and S2 were permitted the following amounts of deductions (within the meaning of section 59A(c)(4)), $2,400x, $1,000x, and $2,600x; those deductions include base erosion tax benefits of $180x, $370x, and $230x. The group's consolidated taxable income for the year is $150x. In addition, the group satisfies the gross receipts test in §1.59A-2(d).

(B) *Analysis.* Pursuant to paragraph (b) of this section, the receipts and deductions of P, S1, and S2 are aggregated for purposes of making the computations under section 59A. The group's base erosion percentage is 13% (($180x + $370x + $230x)/($2,400x + $1,000x + $2,600x)). The con-

solidated group is an applicable taxpayer under §1.59A-2(b) because the group satisfies the gross receipts test and the group's base erosion percentage (13%) is higher than 3%. The consolidated group's modified taxable income is computed by adding back the members' base erosion tax benefits (and, when the consolidated group has consolidated net operating loss available for deduction, the consolidated net operating loss allowed times base erosion percentage) to the consolidated taxable income, $930x ($150x + $180x + $370x + $230x). The group's base erosion minimum tax amount is then computed as 10 percent of the modified taxable income less the regular tax liability, $61.5x ($930x × 10% - $150x × 21%).

(ii) *The consolidated group engages in intercompany transactions.* (A) *Facts.* The facts are the same as in paragraph (f)(1)(i)(A) of this section (the facts in *Example 1*(i)), except that S1 sold various inventory items to S2 during 2019. Such items are depreciable in the hands of S2 (but would not have been depreciable in the hands of S1) and continued to be owned by S2 during 2019.

(B) *Analysis.* The result is the same as paragraph (f)(1)(i)(A) of this section (the facts in *Example 1*(i)),. Pursuant to paragraph (b)(2) of this section, items resulting from the intercompany sale (for example, gross receipts, depreciation deductions) are not taken into account in computing the group's gross receipts under §1.59A-2(d) and base erosion percentage under §1.59A-2(e)(3).

(2) *Example 2: Business interest expense subject to section 163(j) and the group's domestic related current year BIE and foreign related current year BIE for the year equals its section 163(j) limitation.* (i) *Facts.* During the current year (Year 1), P incurred $150x of business interest expense to domestic related parties; S1 incurred $150x of business interest expense to foreign related parties; and S2 incurred $150x of business interest expense to unrelated parties. The group's section 163(j) limitation for the year is $300x. After applying the rules in §1.163(j)-5(b)(3), the group deducts $150x of P's Year 1 business interest expense, and $75x each of S1 and S2's Year 1 business interest expense. Assume the group is an applicable taxpayer for purposes of section 59A.

(ii) *Analysis*—(A) *Application of the absorption rule in paragraph (c)(2) of this section.* Following the rules in section 163(j), the group's section 163(j) interest deduction for Year 1 is $300x, and the entire amount is from members' Year 1 business interest expense.

(B) *Application of the classification rule in paragraph (c)(3) of this section.* Under paragraph (c)(3) of this section, the group's aggregate current year BIE deduction of $300x is first classified as payments or accruals to related parties (pro-rata among domestic related parties and foreign related parties), and second as payments or accruals to unrelated parties. For Year 1, the group has $150x of domestic related current year BIE and $150x of foreign related current year BIE, and the group's aggregate current year BIE deduction will be classified equally among the related party expenses. Therefore, $150x of the group's deduction is classified as domestic related current year BIE deduction and $150x is classified as a foreign related current year BIE deduction.

(C) *Application of the allocation rule in paragraph (c)(4) of this section.* After the application of the classification rule in paragraph (c)(3) of this section, the group has $150x each of domestic related current year BIE deduction and foreign related current year BIE deduction from the group's aggregate current year BIE in Year 1. The domestic related current year BIE deduction and foreign related current year BIE deduction will be allocated to P, S1, and S2 based on each member's deduction of its Year 1 business interest expense.

(1) *Allocations to P.* The percentage of current year BIE deduction attributable to P is 50% (P's deduction of its Year 1 current year BIE, $150x, divided by the group's aggregate current year BIE deduction for Year 1, $300x). Thus, the amount of domestic related current year BIE deduction status allocated to P is $75x (the group's domestic related current year BIE deduction, $150x, multiplied by the percentage of current year BIE deduction allocable to P, 50%); and the amount of foreign related current year BIE deduction status allocated to P is $75x (the group's foreign related current year BIE deduction, $150x, multiplied by the percentage of current year BIE deduction allocable to P, 50%).

(2) *Allocations to S1 and S2.* The percentage of current year BIE deduction attributable to S1 is 25% (S1's deduction of its Year 1 current year BIE, $75x, divided by the group's aggregate current year BIE deduction for Year 1, $300x). Thus, the amount of domestic related current year BIE deduction status allocated to S1 is $37.5x (the group's domestic related current year BIE deduction, $150x, multiplied by the percentage of current year BIE deduction allocable to S1, 25%); and the amount of foreign related current year BIE deduction status allocated to S1 is $37.5x (the group's foreign related current year BIE deduction, $150x, multiplied by the percentage of current year BIE deduction allocable to S1, 25%). Because S2 also deducted $75 of its Year 1 current year BIE, S2's deductions are allocated the same pro-rata status as those of S1 under this paragraph (f)(2)(ii)(C)(2).

(D) *Application of the allocation rule in paragraph (c)(5) of this section.* Although the group will have disallowed BIE carryforwards after Year 1 (the group's aggregate current year BIE of $450x ($150x + $150x + $150x) exceeds the section 163(j) limitation of $300x), all of the domestic related current year BIE and foreign related current year BIE in Year 1 has been taken into account pursuant to the classification rule in paragraph (c)(3) of this section. Thus, under paragraph (c)(5)(iv) of this section, each member's disallowed BIE carryforward is treated as from payments or accruals to unrelated parties.

(3) *Example 3: Business interest expense subject to section 163(j).* (i) *The group's domestic related current year BIE and foreign related current year BIE for the year exceeds its section 163(j) limitation.* (A) *Facts.* During the current year (Year 1), P incurred $60x of business interest expense to domestic related parties; S1 incurred $40x of business interest expense to foreign related parties; and S2 incurred $80x of business interest expense to unrelated parties. The group's section 163(j) limitation for the year is $60x. After applying the rules in § 1.163(j)-5(b)(3), the group deducts $20x each of P, S1, and S2's current year business interest expense. Assume the group is an applicable taxpayer for purposes of section 59A.

(B) *Analysis*—(1) *Application of the absorption rule in paragraph (c)(2) of this section.* Following the rules in section 163(j), the group's section 163(j) interest deduction is $60x, and the entire amount is from members' Year 1 business interest expense.

(2) *Application of the classification rule in paragraph (c)(3) of this section.* Under paragraph (c)(3) of this section, the group's $60x of aggregate current year BIE deduction is first classified as payments or accruals to related parties (pro-rata among domestic related parties and foreign related parties), and second as payments or accruals from unrelated parties. The group's total related party interest expense in Year 1, $100x (sum of the group's Year 1 domestic related current year BIE, $60x, and the group's Year 1 foreign related current year BIE, $40x), exceeds the group's aggregate current year BIE deduction of $60x. Thus, the group's aggregate current year BIE deduction will be classified, pro-rata, as from payments or accruals to domestic related parties and foreign related parties. Of the group's aggregate current year BIE deduction in Year 1, $36x is classified as a domestic related current year BIE deduction (the group's aggregate current year BIE deduction, $60x, multiplied by the ratio of domestic related current year BIE over the group's total Year 1 related party interest expense ($60x / ($60x+$40x))); and $24x of the group's aggregate current year BIE deduction is classified as a foreign related current year BIE deduction (the group's section 163(j) interest deduction, $60x, multiplied by the ratio of foreign related current year BIE over the group's total Year 1 related party interest expense ($40x / ($60x+$40x))).

(3) *Application of the allocation rule in paragraph (c)(4) of this section.* After the application of the classification rule in paragraph (c)(3) of this section, the group has $36x of domestic related current year BIE deduction and $24x of foreign related current year BIE deduction from the group's aggregate current year BIE in Year 1. The domestic related current year BIE deduction and foreign related current year BIE deduction will be allocated to P, S1, and S2 based on each member's current year BIE deduction in Year 1.

**Prop. Reg. § 1.1502-59A(f)**

(i) *Allocation of the group's domestic related current year BIE deduction status.* Because each member is deducting $20x of its Year 1 business interest expense, all three members have the same percentage of current year BIE deduction attributable to them. The percentage of current year BIE deduction attributable to each of P, S1, and S2 is 33.33% (each member's current year BIE deduction in Year 1, $20x, divided by the group's aggregate current year BIE deduction for Year 1, $60x). Thus, the amount of domestic related current year BIE deduction status allocable to each member is $12x (the group's domestic related current year BIE deduction, $36x, multiplied by the percentage of current year BIE deduction allocable to each member, 33.33%).

(ii) *Allocations of the group's foreign related current year BIE deduction status.* The amount of foreign related current year BIE deduction status allocable to each member is $8x (the group's foreign related current year BIE deduction, $24x, multiplied by the percentage of current year BIE deduction allocable to each member, 33.33%, as computed earlier in paragraph (f)(3) of this section (*Example 3*).

(4) *Application of the allocation rule in paragraph (c)(5) of this section.* In Year 1 the group has $60x of domestic related current year BIE, of which $36x is deducted in the year (by operation of the classification rule). Therefore, the group has $24x of domestic related BIE carryforward. Similarly, the group has $40x of foreign related current year BIE in Year 1, of which $24x is deducted in the year. Therefore, the group has $16x of foreign related BIE carryforward. The $24x domestic related BIE carryforward status and $16x foreign related BIE carryforward status will be allocated to P, S1, and S2 in proportion to the amount of each member's disallowed BIE carryforward.

(i) *Allocation to P.* The percentage of disallowed BIE carryforward allocable to P is 33.33% (P's Year 1 disallowed BIE carryforward, $40x ($60x-$20x), divided by the group's Year 1 disallowed BIE carryforward, $120x ($60x + $40x + 80x - $60x)). Thus, the amount of domestic related BIE carryforward status allocated to P is $8x (the group's domestic related BIE carryforward, $24x, multiplied by the percentage of disallowed BIE carryforward allocable to P, 33.33%); and the amount of foreign related BIE carryforward status allocated to P is $5.33x (the group's foreign related BIE carryforward, $16x, multiplied by the percentage of disallowed BIE carryforward allocable to P, 33.33%). Under paragraph (c)(5)(iv) of this section, P's disallowed BIE carryforward that has not been allocated a status as either a domestic related BIE carryforward or a foreign related BIE carryforward will be treated as interest paid or accrued to an unrelated party. Therefore, $26.67x ($40x P's disallowed BIE carryforward - $8x domestic related BIE carryforward status allocated to P - $5.33x foreign related BIE carryforward status allocated to P) is treated as interest paid or accrued to an unrelated party.

(ii) *Allocation to S1.* The percentage of disallowed BIE carryforward allocable to S1 is 16.67% (S1's Year 1 disallowed BIE carryforward, $20x ($40x - $20x), divided by the group's Year 1 disallowed BIE carryforward, $120x ($60x + $40x + 80x - $60x). Thus, the amount of domestic related BIE carryforward status allocated to S1 is $4x (the group's domestic related BIE carryforward, $24x, multiplied by the percentage of disallowed BIE carryforward allocable to S1, 16.67%); and the amount of foreign related BIE carryforward status allocated to S1 is $2.67x (the group's foreign related BIE carryforward, $16x, multiplied by the percentage of disallowed BIE carryforward allocable to S1, 16.67%). Under paragraph (c)(5)(iv) of this section, S1's disallowed BIE that has not been allocated a status as either a domestic related BIE carryforward or a foreign related BIE carryforward will be treated as interest paid or accrued to an unrelated party. Therefore, $13.33x ($20x S1's disallowed BIE carryforward - $4x domestic related BIE carryforward status allocated to S1 - $2.67x foreign related BIE carryforward status allocated to S1) is treated as interest paid or accrued to an unrelated party.

(iii) *Allocation to S2.* The percentage of disallowed BIE carryforward allocable to S2 is 50% (S2's Year 1 disallowed BIE carryforward, $60x ($80x-$20x), divided by the group's Year 1 disallowed BIE carryforward, $120x ($60x+$40x+80x-$60x). Thus, the amount of domestic related BIE carryforward status allocated to S2 is $12x (the group's domestic related BIE carryforward, $24x, multiplied by the percentage of disallowed BIE carryforward allocable to S2, 50%); and the amount of foreign related BIE carryforward status allocated to S2 is $8x (the group's foreign related BIE carryforward, $16x, multiplied by the percentage of disallowed BIE carryforward allocable to S2, 50%). Under paragraph (c)(5)(iv) of this section, S2's disallowed BIE that has not been allocated a status as either a domestic related BIE carryforward or a foreign related BIE carryforward will be treated as interest paid or accrued to an unrelated party. Therefore, $40x ($60x S2's disallowed BIE carryforward - $12x domestic related BIE carryforward status allocated to S2 - $8x foreign related BIE carryforward status allocated to S2) is treated as interest paid or accrued to an unrelated party.

(ii) *The group deducting its disallowed BIE carryforwards.* (A) *Facts.* The facts are the same as in paragraph (f)(3)(i)(A) of this section (the facts in *Example 3*(i)), and in addition, none of the members incurs any business interest expense in Year 2. The group's section 163(j) limitation for Year 2 is $30x.

(B) *Analysis*—(1) *Application of the absorption rule in paragraph (c)(2) of this section.* Following the rules in section 163(j), each member of the group is deducting $10x of its disallowed BIE carryforward from Year 1. Therefore, the group's section 163(j) deduction for Year 2 is $30x.

(2) *Application of the classification rule in paragraph (c)(3) of this section.* Under paragraph (c)(3)(iv) of this section, to the extent members are deducting their Year 1 disallowed BIE carryforward in Year 2, the classification rule will apply to the disallowed BIE carryforward in Year 2 after the allocation rule in paragraph (c)(5) of this section has allocated the related and unrelated party status to the member's disallowed BIE carryforward in Year 1. The allocation required under paragraph (c)(5) of this section is described in paragraph (f)(3)(i)(B)(4) of this section.

(i) *Use of P's allocated domestic related BIE carryforward status and foreign related BIE carryforward status.* P has $40x of Year 1 disallowed BIE carryforward, and P was allocated $8x of domestic related BIE carryforward status and $5.33x of foreign related BIE carryforward status. In Year 2, P deducts $10x of its Year 1 disallowed BIE carryforward. Under the classification rule of paragraph (c)(3) of this section, P is treated as deducting pro-rata from its allocated status of domestic related BIE carryforward and foreign related BIE carryforward. Therefore, P is treated as deducting $6x of its allocated domestic related BIE carryforward ($10x × $8x / ($8x + $5.33x)), and $4x of its allocated foreign related BIE carryforward ($10x × $5.33x / $8x + $5.33x)). After Year 2, P has remaining $30x of Year 1 disallowed BIE carryforward, of which $2x has a status of domestic related BIE carryforward, $1.33x has the status of foreign related BIE carryforward, and $26.67x of interest treated as paid or accrued to unrelated parties.

(ii) *Use of S1's allocated domestic related BIE carryforward status and foreign related BIE carryforward status.* S1 has $20x of Year 1 disallowed BIE carryforward, and S1 was allocated $4x of domestic related BIE carryforward status and $2.67x of foreign related BIE carryforward status. In Year 2, S2 deducts $10x of its Year 1 disallowed BIE carryforward. Because S2's deduction of its Year 1 disallowed BIE carryforward, $10x, exceeds its allocated domestic related BIE carryforward status ($4x) and foreign related BIE carryforward status ($2.67x), all of the allocated related party status are used up. After Year 2, all of S1's Year 1 disallowed BIE carryforward, $10x, is treated as interest paid or accrued to an unrelated party.

(iii) *Use of S2's allocated domestic related BIE carryforward status and foreign related BIE carryforward status.* S2 has $60x of Year 1 disallowed BIE carryforward, and S2 was allocated $12x of domestic related BIE carryforward status and $8x of foreign related BIE carryforward status. In Year 2, S2 deducts $10x of its Year 1 disallowed BIE carryforward. Under the classification rule of paragraph (c)(3) of this section, S2 is treated as deducting $6x of its allocated domestic related BIE carryforward ($10x × $12x / ($12x + $8x)), and $4x of its allocated foreign related BIE carryforward ($10x × $8x / $8x + $12x)). After Year 2, P has remaining $50x of Year 1 disallowed BIE carryforward, of which $6x has a status of domestic related BIE carryforward, $4x has the sta-

tus of foreign related BIE carryforward, and $40x of interest treated as paid or accrued to unrelated parties.

(g) *Applicability date.*—(1) *In general.*—Except as provided in this paragraph (g), this section applies to taxable years beginning after December 31, 2017.

(2) *Application of section 59A if S joins a consolidated group with a taxable year beginning before January 1, 2018.*—If during calendar year 2018 a corporation (S) joins a consolidated group during a consolidated return year beginning before January 1, 2018, then section 59A will not apply to S's short taxable year that is included in the group's consolidated return year, even though S's short taxable year begins after December 31, 2017. [Reg. § 1.1502-59A.]

[Proposed 12-21-2018.]

### [Prop. Reg. § 1.1502-79]

### § 1.1502-79. Separate return years.
\* \* \*

(f) *Disallowed business interest expense carryforwards.*—For the treatment of disallowed business interest expense carryforwards (within the meaning of § 1.163(j)-1) of a member arising in a separate return limitation year, see § 1.163(j)-5(d) and (f).

[Proposed 12-28-2018.]

### [Prop. Reg. § 1.1502-91]

### § 1.1502-91. Application of section 382 with respect to a consolidated group.
\* \* \*

(e) \* \* \*

(2) *Example*—(i) *Facts.* The L group has a consolidated net operating loss arising in Year 1 that is carried over to Year 2. The L loss group has an ownership change at the beginning of Year 2.

(ii) *Analysis.* The net operating loss carryover of the L loss group from Year 1 is a pre-change consolidated attribute because the L group was entitled to use the loss in Year 2 and therefore the loss was described in paragraph (c)(1)(i) of this section. Under paragraph (a)(2)(i) of this section, the amount of consolidated taxable income of the L group for Year 2 that may be offset by this loss carryover may not exceed the consolidated section 382 limitation of the L group for that year. See § 1.1502-93 for rules relating to the computation of the consolidated section 382 limitation.

(iii) *Business interest expense.* The facts are the same as in the *Example* in paragraph (e)(2)(i) of this section, except that, rather than a consolidated net operating loss, a member of the L group pays or accrues a business interest expense in Year 1 for which a deduction is disallowed in that year under section 163(j) and § 1.163(j)-2(b). The disallowed business interest expense is carried over to Year 2 under section 163(j)(2) and § 1.163(j)-2(c). Thus, the disallowed business interest expense carryforward is a pre-change loss. Under section 163(j), the L loss group is entitled to deduct the carryforward in Year 2; however, the amount of consolidated taxable income of the L group for Year 2 that may be offset by this carryforward may not exceed the consolidated section 382 limitation of the L group for that year. See § 1.1502-98(b) (providing that §§ 1.1502-91 through 1.1502-96 apply section 382 to business interest expense, with appropriate adjustments).

\* \* \*

[Proposed 12-28-2018.]

### [Prop. Reg. § 1.1502-95]

### § 1.1502-95.   Rules on ceasing to be a member of a consolidated group (or loss subgroup).

\* \* \*

(b) \* \* \*

  (4) \* \* \*

    (ii) \* \* \*

      (B) \* \* \* The analysis would be similar if the L loss group had an ownership change under § 1.1502-92 in Year 2 with respect to disallowed business interest expense paid or accrued by L2 in Year 1 and carried forward under section 163(j)(2) to Year 2 and Year 3. See § 1.1502-98(b) (providing that §§ 1.1502-91 through 1.1502-96 apply section 382 to business interest expense, with appropriate adjustments).

\* \* \*

[Proposed 12-28-2018.]

### [Prop. Reg. § 1.1502-98]

### § 1.1502-98.   Coordination with sections 383 and 163(j).—(a) *Coordination with section 383.*—\* \* \*

(b) *Application to section 163(j).*—(1) *In general.*—The regulations under sections 163(j), 382, and 383 contain rules governing the application of section 382 to interest expense governed by section 163(j) and the regulations thereunder. See, for example, §§ 1.163(j)-11(b), 1.382-2, 1.382-6, and 1.383-1. The rules contained in §§ 1.1502-91 through 1.1502-96 apply these rules to members of a consolidated group, or corporations that join or leave a consolidated group, with appropriate adjustments. For example, for purposes of §§ 1.1502-91 through 1.1502-96, the term *loss group* includes a consolidated group in which any member is entitled to use a disallowed business interest expense carryforward, within the meaning of § 1.163(j)-1(b)(9), that did not arise, and is not treated as arising, in a SRLY with regard to that group. Additionally, a reference to net operating loss carryovers in §§ 1.1502-91 through 1.1502-96 generally includes a reference to disallowed business interest expense carryforwards. References to a loss or losses in §§ 1.1502-91 through 1.1502-96 include references to disallowed business interest expense carryforwards or section 382 disallowed business interest carryforwards, within the meaning of § 1.382-2(a)(7), as appropriate.

(2) *Appropriate adjustments.*—For purposes of applying the rules in §§ 1.1502-91 through 1.1502-96 to current-year business interest expense (within the meaning of § 1.163(j)-5(a)(2)(i)), disallowed business interest expense carryforwards, and section 382 disallowed business interest carryforwards, appropriate adjustments are required.

[Proposed 12-28-2018.]

### [Prop. Reg. § 1.1502-99]

### § 1.1502-99.   Effective/applicability dates.

\* \* \*

(d) *Application to section 163(j).*—(1) *Sections 1.382-2 and 1.382-5.*—To the extent the rules of §§ 1.1502-91 through 1.1502-99 effectuate the rules of §§ 1.382-2 and 1.382-5, the provisions apply with respect to ownership changes occurring on or after the date the Treasury decision adopting these regulations as final regulations is published in the **Federal Register**. For loss corporations that have ownership changes occurring before the date the Treasury decision adopting these regulations as final regulations is published in the **Federal Register**, see §§ 1.1502-91 through 1.1502-99 as contained in 26 CFR part 1, revised April 1, 2018. However, taxpayers and their related parties, within the meaning of sections 267(b) and 707(b)(1), may apply the rules of §§ 1.1502-91 through 1.1502-99 to the extent they apply the rules of §§ 1.382-2 and 1.382-5, to ownership changes occurring during a taxable year beginning after December 31, 2017, as well as consistently applying the rules of the §§ 1.1502-91 through 1.1502-99 to the extent they effectuate the rules of §§ 1.382-2, 1.382-5, 1.382-6, and 1.383-1, the section 163(j) regulations (within the meaning of § 1.163(j)-1(b)(32)), and if applicable, §§ 1.263A-9, 1.381(c)(20)-1, 1.469-9, 1.882-5, 1.1502-13, 1.1502-21, 1.1502-36, 1.1502-79, and 1.1504-4 to taxable years beginning after December 31, 2017.

(2) *Sections 1.382-6 and 1.383-1.*—To the extent the rules of §§ 1.1502-91 through 1.1502-98 effectuate the rules of §§ 1.382-6 and 1.383-1, the provisions apply with respect to ownership changes occurring during a taxable year ending after the date the Treasury decision adopting these regulations as final regulations is published in the **Federal Register**. For the application of these rules to an ownership change with respect to an ownership change occurring during a taxable year ending before the date the Treasury decision adopting these regulations as final regulations is published in the **Federal Register**, see §§ 1.1502-91 through 1.1502-99 as contained in 26 CFR part 1, revised April 1, 2018. However, taxpayers and their related parties, within the meaning of sections 267(b) and 707(b)(1), may apply the rules of §§ 1.1502-91 through 1.1502-99 (to the extent that those rules effectuate the rules of §§ 1.382-6 and 1.383-1), to ownership changes occurring during a taxable year beginning after December 31, 2017, so long

as the taxpayers and their related parties consistently apply the rules of the section 163(j) regulations (within the meaning of §1.163(j)-1(b)(32)), and if applicable, §§1.263A-9, 1.381(c)(20)-1, 1.469-9, 1.882-5, 1.1502-13, 1.1502-21, 1.1502-36, 1.1502-79, and 1.1504-4 to taxable years beginning after December 31, 2017.

[Proposed 12-28-2018.]

### [Prop. Reg. §1.1502-100]

#### §1.1502-100. Corporations exempt from tax.
\* \* \*

(b) The tax liability for a consolidated return year of an exempt group is the tax imposed by section 511(a) on the consolidated unrelated taxable income for the year (determined under paragraph (c) of this section), and by allowing the credits provided in §1.1502-2(b).

\* \* \*

[Proposed 12-21-2018.]

### [Prop. Reg. §1.1503(d)-1]

#### §1.1503(d)-1. Definitions and special rules for filings under section 1503(d).

\* \* \*

(b) \* \* \*
  (2) \* \* \*

    (iii) A domestic consenting corporation (as defined in §301.7701-3(c)(3)(i) of this chapter), as provided in paragraph (c)(1) of this section. *See* §1.1503(d)-7(c)(41).

\* \* \*

(c) *Treatment of domestic consenting corporation as a dual resident corporation.*—(1) *Rule.*—A domestic consenting corporation is treated as a dual resident corporation under paragraph (b)(2)(iii) of this section for a taxable year if, on any day during the taxable year, the following requirements are satisfied:

    (i) Under the tax law of a foreign country where a specified foreign tax resident is tax resident, the specified foreign tax resident derives or incurs (or would derive or incur) items of income, gain, deduction, or loss of the domestic consenting corporation (because, for example, the domestic consenting corporation is fiscally transparent under such tax law).

    (ii) The specified foreign tax resident bears a relationship to the domestic consenting corporation that is described in section 267(b) or 707(b). *See* §1.1503(d)-7(c)(41).

  (2) *Definitions.*—The following definitions apply for purposes of this paragraph (c).

    (i) The term *fiscally transparent* means, with respect to a domestic consenting corporation or an intermediate entity, fiscally transparent as determined under the principles of §1.894-1(d)(3)(ii) and (iii), without regard to whether a specified foreign tax resident is a resident of a country that has an income tax treaty with the United States.

    (ii) The term *specified foreign tax resident* means a body corporate or other entity or body of persons liable to tax under the tax law of a foreign country as a resident.

\* \* \*

[Proposed 12-28-2018.]

### [Prop. Reg. §1.1503(d)-3]

#### §1.1503(d)-3. Foreign use.
\* \* \*

(e) \* \* \*

  (3) *Exception for domestic consenting corporations.*—Paragraph (e)(1) of this section will not apply so as to deem a foreign use of a dual consolidated loss incurred by a domestic consenting corporation that is a dual resident corporation under §1.1503(d)-1(b)(2)(iii).

[Proposed 12-28-2018.]

### [Prop. Reg. §1.1503(d)-7]

#### §1.1503(d)-7. Examples.
\* \* \*

(c) \* \* \*

  (41) *Example 41. Domestic consenting corporation—treated as dual resident corporation—*(i) *Facts.* FSZ1, a Country Z entity that is subject to Country Z tax on its worldwide income or on a residence basis and is classified as a foreign corporation for U.S. tax purposes, owns all the interests in DCC, a domestic eligible entity that has filed an election to be classified as an association. Under Country Z tax law, DCC is fiscally transparent. For taxable year 1, DCC's only item of income, gain, deduction, or loss is a $100x deduction and such deduction comprises a $100x net operating loss of DCC. For Country Z tax purposes, FSZ1's only item of income, gain, deduction, or loss, other than the $100x loss attributable to DCC, is $60x of operating income.

    (ii) *Result.* DCC is a domestic consenting corporation because by electing to be classified as an association, it consents to be treated as a dual resident corporation for purposes of section 1503(d). *See* §301.7701-3(c)(3) of this chapter. For taxable year 1, DCC is treated as a dual resident corporation under §1.1503(d)-1(b)(2)(iii) because FSZ1 (a specified foreign tax resident that bears a relationship to DCC that is described in section 267(b) or 707(b)) derives or incurs items of income, gain, deduction, or loss of DCC. *See* §1.1503(d)-1(c). FSZ1 derives or incurs items of income, gain, deduction, or loss of DCC because, under Country Z tax law, DCC is fiscally transparent. Thus, DCC has a $100x dual consolidated loss for taxable year 1. *See* §1.1503(d)-1(b)(5). Because the loss is available to, and in fact does, offset income of FSZ1 under Country Z tax law, there is a foreign use of the dual consolidated loss in year 1. Accordingly, the dual consolidated loss is subject to the domestic use limitation rule of §1.1503(d)-4(b). The result would be the same if FSZ1 were to indirectly own its DCC stock through an intermediate entity that is fiscally transparent under Country Z tax law, or if an individual were to wholly own FSZ1 and FSZ1 were a disregarded entity. In addition, the result would be the same if FSZ1 had no items of income, gain, deduction, or loss, other than the $100x loss attributable to DCC.

(iii) *Alternative facts – DCC not treated as a dual resident corporation.* The facts are the same as in paragraph (c)(41)(i) of this section, except that DCC is not fiscally transparent under Country Z tax law and thus under Country Z tax law FSZ1 does not derive or incur items of income, gain, deduction, or loss of DCC. Accordingly, DCC is not treated as a dual resident corporation under § 1.1503(d)-1(b)(2)(iii) for year 1 and, consequently, its $100x net operating loss in that year is not a dual consolidated loss.

(iv) *Alternative facts – mirror legislation.* The facts are the same as in paragraph (c)(41)(i) of this section, except that, under provisions of Country Z tax law that constitute mirror legislation under § 1.1503(d)-3(e)(1) and that are substantially similar to the recommendations in Chapter 6 of OECD/G-20, *Neutralising the Effects of Hybrid Mismatch Arrangements, Action 2: 2015 Final Report* (October 2015), Country Z tax law prohibits the $100x loss attributable to DCC from offsetting FSZ1's income that is not also subject to U.S. tax. As is the case in paragraph (c)(41)(ii) of this section, DCC is treated as a dual resident corporation under § 1.1503(d)-1(b)(2)(iii) for year 1 and its $100x net operating loss is a dual consolidated loss. Pursuant to § 1.1503(d)-3(e)(3), however, the dual consolidated loss is not deemed to be put to a foreign use by virtue of the Country Z mirror legislation. Therefore, DCC is eligible to make a domestic use election for the dual consolidated loss.

[Proposed 12-28-2018.]

**[Prop. Reg. § 1.1503(d)-8]**

**§ 1.1503(d)-8.  Effective dates.**

* * *

(b) * * *

(6) *Rules regarding domestic consenting corporations.*—Section 1.1503(d)-1(b)(2)(iii), (c), and (d), as well § 1.1503(d)-3(e)(1) and (e)(3), apply to determinations under § § 1.1503(d)-1 through 1.1503(d)-7 relating to taxable years ending on or after December 20, 2018. For taxable years ending before December 20, 2018, see § § 1.1503(d)-1(c) (previous version of § 1.1503(d)-1(d)) and 1.1503(d)-3(e)(1) (previous version of § 1.1503(d)-3(e)(1)) as contained in 26 CFR part 1 revised as of April 1, 2018.

(7) *Compulsory transfer triggering event exception.*—Sections 1.1503(d)-6(f)(5)(i) through (iii) apply to transfers that occur on or after December 20, 2018. For transfers occurring before December 20, 2018, see § 1.1503(d)-6(f)(5)(i) through (iii) as contained in 26 CFR part 1 revised as of April 1, 2018. However, taxpayers may consistently apply § 1.1503(d)-6(f)(5)(i) through (iii) to transfers occurring before December 20, 2018.

[Proposed 12-28-2018.]

**[Prop. Reg. § 1.1504-4]**

**§ 1.1504-4.  Treatment of warrants, options, convertible obligations, and other similar interests.**

* * *

(i) * * * Paragraph (a)(2) of this section applies with respect to taxable years ending after the date the Treasury decision adopting these regulations as final regulations is published in the **Federal Register**. However, taxpayers and their related parties, within the meaning of sections 267(b) and 707(b)(1), may apply the rules of this section to a taxable year beginning after December 31, 2017, so long as the taxpayers and their related parties consistently apply the rules of this section, the section 163(j) regulations (within the meaning of § 1.163(j)-1(b)(32)), and if applicable, § § 1.263A-9, 1.381(c)(20)-1, 1.382-6, 1.383-1, 1.469-9, 1.882-5, 1.1502-13, 1.1502-21, 1.1502-36, 1.1502-79, and 1.1502-91 through 1.1502-99 (to the extent they effectuate the rules of § § 1.382-6, and 1.383-1), to those taxable years.

[Proposed 12-28-2018.]

**[Prop. Reg. § 20.2010-1]**

**§ 20.2010-1.  Unified credit against estate tax; in general.**

* * *

(c) *Special rule in the case of a difference between the basic exclusion amount applicable to gifts and that applicable at the donor's date of death.*—(1) *Rule.*—Changes in the basic exclusion amount that occur between the date of a donor's gift and the date of the donor's death may cause the basic exclusion amount allowable on the date of a gift to exceed that allowable on the date of death. If the total of the amounts allowable as a credit in computing the gift tax payable on the decedent's post-1976 gifts, within the meaning of section 2001(b)(2), to the extent such credits are based solely on the basic exclusion amount as defined and adjusted in section 2010(c)(3), exceeds the credit allowable within the meaning of section 2010(a) in computing the estate tax, again only to the extent such credit is based solely on such basic exclusion amount, in each case by applying the tax rates in effect at the decedent's death, then the portion of the credit allowable in computing the estate tax on the decedent's taxable estate that is attributable to the basic exclusion amount is the sum of the amounts attributable to the basic exclusion amount allowable as a credit in computing the gift tax payable on the decedent's post-1976 gifts. The amount allowable as a credit in computing gift tax payable for any year may not exceed the tentative tax on the gifts made during that year, and the amount allowable as a credit in computing the estate tax may not exceed the net tentative tax on the taxable estate. Sections 2505(c) and 2010(d).

(2) *Example.*—Individual A (never married) made cumulative post-1976 taxable gifts of $9

million, all of which were sheltered from gift tax by the cumulative total of $10 million in basic exclusion amount allowable on the dates of the gifts. A dies after 2025 and the basic exclusion amount on A's date of death is $5 million. A was not eligible for any restored exclusion amount pursuant to Notice 2017-15. Because the total of the amounts allowable as a credit in computing the gift tax payable on A's post-1976 gifts (based on the $9 million basic exclusion amount used to determine those credits) exceeds the credit based on the $5 million basic exclusion amount applicable on the decedent's date of death, under paragraph (c)(1) of this section, the credit to be applied for purposes of computing the estate tax is based on a basic exclusion amount of $9 million, the amount used to determine the credits allowable in computing the gift tax payable on the post-1976 gifts made by A.

\* \* \*

(e) \* \* \*

(3) *Basic exclusion amount.*—Except to the extent provided in paragraph (e)(3)(iii) of this section, the basic exclusion amount is the sum of the amounts described in paragraphs (e)(3)(i) and (ii) of this section.

(i) For any decedent dying in calendar year 2011 or thereafter, $5,000,000; and

(ii) For any decedent dying after calendar year 2011, $5,000,000 multiplied by the cost-of-living adjustment determined under section 1(f)(3) for the calendar year of decedent's death by substituting "calendar year 2010" for "calendar year 2016" in section 1(f)(3)(A)(ii) and rounded to the nearest multiple of $10,000.

(iii) In the case of the estates of decedents dying after December 31, 2017, and before January 1, 2026, paragraphs (e)(3)(i) and (ii) of this section will be applied by substituting "$10,000,000" for "$5,000,000."

(f) *Applicability dates.*—(1) *In general.*—Except as provided in paragraph (f)(2) of this section, this section applies to the estates of decedents dying after June 11, 2015. For the rules applicable to estates of decedents dying after December 31, 2010, and before June 12, 2015, see § 20.2010-1T, as contained in 26 CFR part 20, revised as of April 1, 2015.

(2) *Exceptions.*—Paragraph (c) of this section applies to estates of decedents dying on and after the date of publication of a Treasury decision adopting these rules as final regulations. Paragraph (e)(3) of this section applies to the estates of decedents dying after December 31, 2017.

[Proposed 11-23-2018.]

**[Prop. Reg. § 1.6038-2]**

**§ 1.6038-2. Information returns required of United States persons with respect to annual**

accounting periods of certain foreign corporations.—(a) *Requirement of return.*—Every U.S. person shall make a separate annual information return with respect to each annual accounting period (described in paragraph (e) of this section) of each foreign corporation which that person controls (as defined in paragraph (b) of this section) at any time during such annual accounting period. \* \* \*

\* \* \*

(m) *Applicability dates.*—This section applies to taxable years of foreign corporations beginning on or after October 3, 2018. See 26 CFR 1.6038-2 (revised as of April 1, 2018) for rules applicable to taxable years of foreign corporations beginning before such date.

[Proposed 10-10-2018.]

**[Prop. Reg. § 1.6038-2]**

**§ 1.6038-2. Information returns required of United States persons with respect to annual accounting periods of certain foreign corporations beginning after December 31, 1962.**

\* \* \*

(f) \* \* \*

(13) *Amounts involving hybrid transactions or hybrid entities under section 267A.*—If for the annual accounting period, the corporation pays or accrues interest or royalties for which a deduction is disallowed under section 267A and the regulations under section 267A as contained in 26 CFR part 1, then Form 5471 (or successor form) must contain such information about the disallowance in the form and manner and to the extent prescribed by the form, instruction, publication, or other guidance published in the Internal Revenue Bulletin.

(14) *Hybrid dividends under section 245A.*—If for the annual accounting period, the corporation pays or receives a hybrid dividend or a tiered hybrid dividend under section 245A and the regulations under section 245A as contained in 26 CFR part 1, then Form 5471 (or successor form) must contain such information about the hybrid dividend or tiered hybrid dividend in the form and manner and to the extent prescribed by the form, instruction, publication, or other guidance published in the Internal Revenue Bulletin.

\* \* \*

(m) *Applicability dates.*—\* \* \* Paragraphs (f)(13) and (14) of this section apply with respect to information for annual accounting periods beginning on or after December 20, 2018.

[Proposed 12-28-2018.]

### §1.6038-3. Information returns required of certain United States persons with respect to controlled foreign partnerships (CFPs).

\* \* \*

(g) \* \* \*

(3) *Amounts involving hybrid transactions or hybrid entities under section 267A.*—In addition to the information required pursuant to paragraphs (g)(1) and (2) of this section, if, during the partnership's taxable year for which the Form 8865 is being filed, the partnership paid or accrued interest or royalties for which a deduction is disallowed under section 267A and the regulations under section 267A as contained in 26 CFR part 1, the controlling fifty-percent partners must provide information about the disallowance in the form and manner and to the extent prescribed by Form 8865 (or successor form), instruction, publication, or other guidance published in the Internal Revenue Bulletin.

\* \* \*

(l) *Applicability dates.*—\* \* \* Paragraph (g)(3) of this section applies for taxable years of a foreign partnership beginning on or after December 20, 2018.

[Proposed 12-28-2018.]

### §1.6038-5. Information returns required of certain United States persons to report amounts determined with respect to certain foreign corporations for global intangible low-taxed income (GILTI) purposes.

—(a) *Requirement of return.*—Except as provided in paragraph (d) of this section, each United States person who is a United States shareholder (as defined in section 951(b)) of any controlled foreign corporation must make an annual return on Form 8992, "U.S. Shareholder Calculation of Global Intangible Low-Taxed Income (GILTI)," (or successor form) for each U.S. shareholder inclusion year (as defined in §1.951A-1(e)(4)) setting forth the information with respect to each such controlled foreign corporation, in such form and manner, as Form 8992 (or successor form) prescribes.

(b) *Time and manner for filing.*—Returns on Form 8992 (or successor form) required under paragraph (a) of this section for a taxable year must be filed with the United States person's income tax return on or before the due date (taking into account extensions) for filing that person's income tax return.

(c) *Failure to furnish information.*—(1) *Penalties.*—If any person required to file Form 8992 (or successor form) under section 6038 and this section fails to furnish the information prescribed on Form 8992 within the time prescribed by paragraph (b) of this section, the penalties imposed by section 6038(b) and (c) may apply.

(2) *Increase in penalty.*—If a failure described in paragraph (c)(1) of this section continues for more than 90 days after the date on which the Director of Field Operations, Area Director, or Director of Compliance Campus Operations mails notice of such failure to the person required to file Form 8992, such person shall pay a penalty of $10,000, in addition to the penalty imposed by section 6038(b)(1), for each 30-day period (or a fraction of) during which such failure continues after such 90-day period has expired. The additional penalty imposed by section 6038(b)(2) and this paragraph (c)(2) shall be limited to a maximum of $50,000 for each failure.

(3) *Reasonable cause.*—(i) For purposes of section 6038(b) and (c) and this section, the time prescribed for furnishing information under paragraph (b) of this section, and the beginning of the 90-day period after mailing of notice by the director under paragraph (c)(2) of this section, shall be treated as being not earlier than the last day on which reasonable cause existed for failure to furnish the information.

(ii) To show that reasonable cause existed for failure to furnish information as required by section 6038 and this section, the person required to report such information must make an affirmative showing of all facts alleged as reasonable cause for such failure in a written statement containing a declaration that it is made under the penalties of perjury. The statement must be filed with the director where the return is required to be filed. The director shall determine whether the failure to furnish information was due to reasonable cause, and if so, the period of time for which such reasonable cause existed. In the case of a return that has been filed as required by this section except for an omission of, or error with respect to, some of the information required, if the person who filed the return establishes to the satisfaction of the director that the person has substantially complied with this section, then the omission or error shall not constitute a failure under this section.

(d) *Exception from filing requirement.*—Any United States person that does not own, within the meaning of section 958(a), stock of a controlled foreign corporation in which the United States person is a United States shareholder for a taxable year is not required to file Form 8992. For this purpose, a U.S. shareholder partner (as defined in §1.951A-5(e)(3)) with respect to a partnership CFC (as defined in §1.951A-5(e)(2)) is treated as owning, within the meaning of section 958(a), stock of the partnership CFC.

(e) *Applicability date.*—This section applies to taxable years of controlled foreign corporations beginning on or after October 3, 2018. [Reg. §1.6038-5.]

[Proposed 10-10-2018.]

## [Prop. Reg. § 1.6038A-1]

### § 1.6038A-1. General requirements and definitions.

\* \* \*

(n) \* \* \*

(2) \* \* \* Section 1.6038A-2(a)(3), (b)(6), and (b)(7) apply for taxable years beginning after December 31, 2017.

(3) \* \* \* For taxable years ending on or before December 31, 2017, see § 1.6038A-4 as contained in 26 CFR part 1 revised as of April 1, 2018.

\* \* \*

[Proposed 12-21-2018.]

### [Prop. Reg. § 1.6038A-2]

### § 1.6038A-2. Requirement of return.—
(a) *Forms required.*—(1) *Form 5472.*—\* \* \*

(2) *Reportable transaction.*—A reportable transaction is any transaction of the types listed in paragraphs (b)(3) and (4) of this section, and, in the case of a reporting corporation that is an applicable taxpayer, as defined under § 1.59A-2(b), any other arrangement that, to prevent avoidance of the purposes of section 59A, is identified on Form 5472 as a reportable transaction. However, except as the Secretary may prescribe otherwise for an applicable taxpayer, the transaction is not a reportable transaction if neither party to the transaction is a United States person as defined in section 7701(a)(30) (which, for purposes of section 6038A, includes an entity that is a reporting corporation as a result of being treated as a corporation under § 301.7701-2(c)(2)(vi) of this chapter) and the transaction—

(i) Will not generate in any taxable year gross income from sources within the United States or income effectively connected, or treated as effectively connected, with the conduct of a trade or business within the United States, and

(ii) Will not generate in any taxable year any expense, loss, or other deduction that is allocable or apportionable to such income.

(3) *Form 8991.*—Each reporting corporation that is an applicable taxpayer, as defined under § 1.59A-2(b), must make an annual information return on Form 8991. The obligation of an applicable taxpayer to report on Form 8991 does not depend on applicability of tax under section 59A or obligation to file Form 5472.

(b) \* \* \*

(1) \* \* \*

(ii) The name, address, and U.S. taxpayer identification number, if applicable, of all its direct and indirect foreign shareholders (for an indirect 25-percent foreign shareholder, explain the attribution of ownership); whether any 25-percent foreign shareholder is a surrogate foreign corporation under section 7874(a)(2)(B) or a member of an expanded affiliated group as defined in section 7874(c)(1); each country in which each 25-percent foreign shareholder files an income tax return as a resident under the tax laws of that country; the places where each 25-percent shareholder conducts its business; and the country or countries of organization, citizenship, and incorporation of each 25-percent foreign shareholder.

\* \* \*

(2) \* \* \*

(iv) The relationship of the reporting corporation to the related party (including, to the extent the form may prescribe, any intermediate relationships).

(3) \* \* \* The total amount of such transactions, as well as the separate amounts for each type of transaction described below, and, to the extent the form may prescribe, any further description, categorization, or listing of transactions within these types, must be reported on Form 5472, in the manner the form prescribes. \* \* \*

\* \* \*

(6) *Compilation of reportable transactions across multiple related parties.*—A reporting corporation must, to the extent and in the manner Form 5472 may prescribe, include a schedule tabulating information with respect to related parties for which the reporting corporation is required to file Forms 5472. The schedule will not require information (beyond totaling) that is not required for the individual Forms 5472. The schedule may include the following:

(i) The identity and status of the related parties;

(ii) The reporting corporation's relationship to the related parties;

(iii) The reporting corporation's reportable transactions with the related parties; and

(iv) Other items required to be reported on Form 5472.

(7) *Information on Form 5472 and Form 8991 regarding base erosion payments.*—If any reporting corporation is an applicable taxpayer, as defined under § 1.59A-2(b), it must report the information required by Form 8991 and by any Form 5472 it is required to file, regarding:

(i) Determination of whether a taxpayer is an applicable taxpayer;

(ii) Computation of base erosion minimum tax amount, including computation of regular tax liability as adjusted for purposes of computing base erosion minimum tax amount;

(iii) Computation of modified taxable income;

(iv) Base erosion tax benefits;

(v) Base erosion percentage calculation;

(vi) Base erosion payments;

(vii) Amounts with respect to services as described in § 1.59A-3(b)(3)(i), including a breakdown of the amount of the total services cost and any mark-up component;

(viii) Arrangements or transactions described in § 1.59A-9;

**Prop. Reg. § 1.6038A-2(b)(7)(viii)**

(ix) Any qualified derivative payment, including:

(A) The aggregate amount of qualified derivative payments for the taxable year, including as determined by type of derivative contract;

(B) The identity of each counterparty and the aggregate amount of qualified derivative payments made to that counterparty; and

(C) A representation that all payments satisfy the requirements of § 1.59A-6(b)(2), and

(x) Any other information necessary to carry out section 59A.

\* \* \*

(c) *Method of reporting.*—All statements required on or with the Form 5472 or Form 8991 under this section and § 1.6038A-5 must be in the English language. All amounts required to be reported under paragraph (b) of this section must be expressed in United States currency, with a statement of the exchange rates used, and, to the extent the forms may require, must indicate the method by which the amount of a reportable transaction or item was determined.

(d) \* \* \* A Form 5472 and Form 8991 required under this section must be filed with the reporting corporation's income tax return for the taxable year by the due date (including extensions) of that return. \* \* \*

\* \* \*

(g) \* \* \* Paragraph (b)(7)(ix) of this section applies to taxable years beginning one year after final regulations are published in the **Federal Register**. Before these regulations are applicable, a taxpayer will be treated as satisfying the reporting requirement described in § 1.59A-6(b)(2) only to the extent that it reports the aggregate amount of qualified derivative payments on Form 8991.

[Proposed 12-21-2018.]

### [Prop. Reg. § 1.6038A-2]

### § 1.6038A-2. Requirement of return.

\* \* \*

(b) \* \* \*

(5) \* \* \*

(iii) If, for the taxable year, a reporting corporation pays or accrues interest or royalties for which a deduction is disallowed under section 267A and the regulations under section 267A as contained in 26 CFR part 1, then the reporting corporation must provide such information about the disallowance in the form and manner and to the extent prescribed by Form 5472 (or successor form), instruction, publication, or other guidance published in the Internal Revenue Bulletin.

\* \* \*

**Prop. Reg. § 1.6038A-2(b)(7)(ix)**

(g) \* \* \* Paragraph (b)(5)(iii) of this section applies with respect to information for annual accounting periods beginning on or after December 20, 2018.

[Proposed 12-28-2018.]

### [Prop. Reg. § 301.7701-3]

### § 301.7701-3. Classification of certain business entities.—(a) *In general.*—\* \* \* Paragraph (c) of this section provides rules for making express elections, including a rule under which a domestic eligible entity that elects to be classified as an association consents to be subject to the dual consolidated loss rules of section 1503(d).

\* \* \*

(c) \* \* \*

(3) *Consent to be subject to section 1503(d).*— (i) *Rule.*—A domestic eligible entity that elects to be classified as an association consents to be treated as a dual resident corporation for purposes of section 1503(d) (such an entity, a *domestic consenting corporation*), for any taxable year for which it is classified as an association and the condition set forth in § 1.1503(d)-1(c)(1) of this chapter is satisfied.

(ii) *Transition rule — deemed consent.*—If, as a result of the applicability date relating to paragraph (c)(3)(i) of this section, a domestic eligible entity that is classified as an association has not consented to be treated as a domestic consenting corporation pursuant to paragraph (c)(3)(i) of this section, then the domestic eligible entity is deemed to consent to be so treated as of its first taxable year beginning on or after December 20, 2019. The first sentence of this paragraph (c)(3)(ii) does not apply if the domestic eligible entity elects, on or after December 20, 2018 and effective before its first taxable year beginning on or after December 20, 2019, to be classified as a partnership or disregarded entity such that it ceases to be a domestic eligible entity that is classified as an association. For purposes of the election described in the second sentence of this paragraph (c)(3)(ii), the sixty month limitation under paragraph (c)(1)(iv) of this section is waived.

(iii) *Applicability date.*—The sixth sentence of paragraph (a) of this section and paragraph (c)(3)(i) of this section apply to a domestic eligible entity that on or after December 20, 2018 files an election to be classified as an association (regardless of whether the election is effective before December 20, 2018). Paragraph (c)(3)(ii) of this section applies as of December 20, 2018.

\* \* \*

[Proposed 12-28-2018.]

# Topical Index

*References are to paragraph (¶) numbers*

7

## A

**Accounting methods**
. accrual method
. . advance payments, recognition deferral . . . 580
. . financial accounting treatment, income
    recognition . . . 580
. cash method
. . small business gross receipts test . . . 570

**Accrual method of accounting**
. advance payments, recognition deferral . . . 580
. financial accounting treatment, income
    recognition . . . 580

**Achieving a Better Life Experience (ABLE) accounts**
. contribution amount increased . . . 645
. rollovers from qualified tuition plans . . . 645

**Advance payments**
. recognition deferral, accrual method . . . 580

**Agricultural or horticultural cooperatives**
. qualified business income, new deduction . . . 330

**Alaska Native Settlement Trusts**
. payments and transfers . . . 325

**Alimony**
. deduction and exclusion . . . 255

**Alternative minimum tax**
. corporations, repeal . . . 310
. individuals, exemption and phaseout threshold
    amounts increased . . . 110
. prior year minimum credit
. . accelerated credits in lieu of bonus depreciation,
    election stricken . . . 410
. . refundability . . . 310

**Automobiles**
. bonus depreciation
. . coordination with passenger automobile
    depreciation caps . . . 410; 415
. luxury car depreciation caps, increased limits . . . 415
. sport utility vehicles, Sec. 179 deduction . . . 405

## B

**Banks and financial institutions**
. FDIC premiums, deduction limitation . . . 565

**Base erosion**
. U.S. source income, minimum tax amount . . . 750

**Bicycle commuting**
. reimbursement exclusion, suspension . . . 615

**Bonds**
. state and local bonds
. . advance refunding bonds, exclusion eliminated . . .
    870
. tax credit bonds
. . repeal, post-2017 issuances . . . 875

**Bonus depreciation**
. increased allowance . . . 410
. prior year minimum credit
. . accelerated credits in lieu of deduction, election
    stricken . . . 410

**Bonus depreciation**—continued
. qualifying property . . . 410

**Business expenses**
. banks and financial institutions
. . FDIC premiums, deduction limitation . . . 565
. Congressional members
. . living expenses, deduction stricken . . . 560
. employee achievement awards
. . nontangible personal property, deduction
    prohibited . . . 537
. employee compensation
. . excessive compensation, limitations expanded . . .
    540
. entertainment, meals, and commuting expenses
. . deductions eliminated . . . 535
. fines and penalties
. . prohibition of deduction, modification . . . 545
. local lobbying expenses
. . deduction repealed . . . 555
. research and experimental expenses
. . five-year amortization period . . . 525
. settlement payments subject to nondisclosure
    agreement
. . deduction prohibited . . . 550

## C

**Capital gains and losses**
. opportunity zone reinvestment, deferral of gain . . .
    145
. partnerships
. . carried interest, holding period extended . . . 335
. rollover of securities gain from SSBICs . . . 270
. self-created property, disposition . . . 130

**Cash method of accounting**
. small businesses, gross receipts test . . . 570

**Casualty and theft losses**
. citrus plant replanting costs, deductibility . . . 440
. deduction limited to disaster areas . . . 235

**Charitable contributions**
. electing small business trusts . . . 365
. percentage limit increased . . . 230
. substantiation exception repealed . . . 230

**Child tax credit**
. credit amount and phaseout threshold increased . . .
    280
. qualifying relative . . . 280

**Collection of tax**
. wrongful levies
. . time limits for civil suits and return of property
    increased . . . 880

**Combat zone**
. Sinai Peninsula . . . 135

**Computers**
. depreciation
. . listed property designation removed . . . 420

**Congressional members**
. living expenses, DC official business
. . deduction stricken . . . 560

2

**CON**

*References are to paragraph (¶) numbers*

*References are to paragraph (¶) numbers*

*References are to paragraph (¶) numbers*